UNIVERSITY CASEBOOK SERIES

CONTRACT LAW AND LEGAL METHODS

by

DANIEL MARKOVITS
Guido Calabresi Professor of Law
Yale Law School

FOUNDATION PRESS
2012

THOMSON REUTERS

© 2012 By THOMSON REUTERS/FOUNDATION PRESS

     1 New York Plaza, 34th Floor

     New York, NY 10004

     Phone Toll Free 1–877–888–1330

     Fax 646–424–5201

     foundation–press.com

Printed in the United States of America

ISBN 978–1–59941–445–4

Mat #40696162

for Guido Calabresi

A NOTE ON THE CASES

Like conventional casebooks, *Contract Law and Legal Methods* employs reproductions of reported opinions to introduce and illustrate many of the ideas that it elaborates. Unlike conventional casebooks, this text includes only main cases and no note cases. Every opinion that the text reproduces plays a substantial and distinctive role in the overall argument; no opinion merely illustrates a familiar point in a new or peculiar context. Almost all the opinions reproduced in the text have been ruthlessly edited. To preserve ease of reading, the edited opinions do not indicate where text has been excised.

ACKNOWLEDGEMENTS

Many of the ideas reported in *Contract Law and Legal Methods* were developed by others, and footnotes placed throughout the text acknowledge these debts. Some other ideas, and some of the language used to express them, borrow from my own prior work. Rather than weigh down the text with particular references, it seems better to acknowledge these sources all together and at once. They are: *Contract and Collaboration*, 113 YALE LAW JOURNAL 1417 (2004); *The No Retraction Principle and the Morality of Negotiations*, 152 UNIVERSITY OF PENNSYLVANIA LAW REVIEW 1903 (2004); *Making and Keeping Contracts*, 92 VIRGINIA L. REV. 1325 (2006) (symposium on political philosophy and private law); A MODERN LEGAL ETHICS: ADVERSARY ADVOCACY IN A DEMOCRATIC AGE (2008); *Promise as an Arm's Length Relation*, in H. SCHEINMAN, ed., PROMISES AND AGREEMENTS: PHILOSOPHICAL ESSAYS (2010); *Arbitration's Arbitrage: Social Solidarity at the Nexus of Adjudication and Contract*, 59 DEPAUL L. REV. 431 (2010); *The Myth of Efficient Breach: New Defenses of the Expectation Interest*, 97 VIRGINIA LAW REVIEW 1939 (2011) (with Alan Schwartz); *The Expectation Remedy and the Promissory Basis of Contract*, SUFFOLK LAW REVIEW (forthcoming 2012) (symposium in honor of the 30th anniversary of the publication of *Contract as Promise*) (with Alan Schwartz); *Market Solidarity Part 1: Price as Commensuration, Contract as Integration* (working paper); *Market Solidarity Part II: Solidarity in an Age of Mass Contracts* (working paper); *Promise Made Pure* (working paper).

In addition, any number of people have helped to produce the text. Colleagues at Yale Law School and elsewhere have influenced me immeasurably concerning law and legal methods generally. Any adequate list would be so long that inclusion would cease meaningfully to signal appreciation even as inevitable errors of omission would continue to insult. With respect to contract law in particular, two debts stand out: Robert Gordon taught me the subject as my first-term contracts professor; and Alan Schwartz taught it to me as my colleague. My own students have also contributed mightily to a text that began, after all, as teaching materials. My first term contracts classes at Yale and the Coker Fellows who helped to teach them made many differences—small and large—to the ideas that the text develops and the manner of their expression. I could not have compiled and digested the materials included in the book—and the many others left on the cutting room floor—without the hard work of skilled research assistants, including: Jane Cooper, Lindsey Counts, Jeff Lingwall, Jonathan Manes, and Emily Stolzenberg. A casebook like this one could not be conceived without the imaginative support of a publisher, and John Bloomquist and Tessa Boury at Foundation Press have been exemplary editors. The text would not exist without the unflagging assistance of Yale Law School's Patty Milardo. The physical book was expertly made by Roxanne Birkel.

Many thanks to you all.

DSM

PREFACE

The greatest contracts casebook ever published was also the first. As it happens, Christopher Columbus Langdell's 1871 *Selection of Cases on the Law of Contracts* was the first casebook published in any subject. Langdell's casebook inaugurated a revolution in law teaching; and today's law schools still live in its shadow. It is time, however, to make another beginning.

Langdell's greatness consisted in matching the generic style of the law school teaching text to the substance of the subject then taught. As Louis Brandeis, writing while still a young lawyer, observed, "[b]elieving that law is a science, and recognizing that the source of our law is the adjudicated cases, Professor Langdell declared that, like other sciences, the law was to be learned only by going to the original sources."[1]

This made perfect sense. Nineteenth century American lawyers thought of the common law as a largely free-standing set of principles, which developed autonomously in appellate courts, and which were organized according to their own, internal logics. Given this view of what law is, the best teaching tools consisted in the appellate opinions that simultaneously reported and constituted the development of the law. Langdell's casebook allowed law school classes to "eviscerate" these opinions, as Brandeis also said, and reveal their inner workings. In this way law students might come both to know the principles and to internalize as a "habit of mind" the scientific structure of legal doctrine and thus also the methods by which future legal developments might be divined.[2] Langdell himself summarized this approach to law and law teaching in the preface to his casebook:

> Law, considered as a science, consists of certain principles or doctrines. . . . Each of these doctrines has arrived at its present state by slow degrees; in other words, it is a growth, extending in many cases through centuries. This growth is to be traced in the main through a series of cases; and much the shortest and best, if not the only way of mastering the doctrine effectually is by studying the cases in which it is embodied.[3]

Once again, given the assumption that law is a science and that appellate opinions contain the law immanently and completely within them, no better teaching tool than the Langdellian casebook is imaginable.

Lawyers today, however, emphatically reject the Langdellian view of what law is. Many radical legal realists—whose moral and political commitments range from critical legal studies on the left to law and economics on

---

1. Louis D. Brandeis, *The Harvard Law School*, 1 Green Bag 10, 19 1889.
2. *Id.* at 20.
3. Christopher Columbus Langdell, Select Cases on the Law of Contracts, (October, 1871).

the right—doubt that legal doctrine materially influences case outcomes at all. According to these views, outcomes are fixed by interests and values that precede the law. Doctrine is epiphenomenal. Moreover, no contemporary lawyers or law professors believe that doctrine develops, or can be applied, entirely free from the considerations involving power, politics, economics, morals, and culture that otherwise inform the lived conflicts that legal doctrine aspires to regulate. Law, as it is conceived of today, is not a science. Certainly it is not independent or self-contained.

Thoughts like these led the legal realists to add so-called "materials"—statutes, descriptions of actual practice, and even excerpts of scholarly commentary—to their casebooks. Such thoughts also led later authors to infuse a skeptical sensibility—which aimed to lay bare the extra-legal concerns that the doctrinal arguments in opinions disguise—into chapter and verse of the casebooks that they produced. But these substantive changes were grafted onto an enduring form. The generic character of the casebook remains unchanged since Langdell's time. Casebooks today continue to be dominated by appellate opinions; and they devote only secondary attention to commentary that places the cases in broader context. Most importantly, today's casebooks still make virtually no explicit effort to construct an over-arching theory of the body of law that they report—no systematic and explicit effort to organize doctrine into the broader context established by the moral, political, economic, and social world out of which the law arises and in which it intervenes.

The traditional casebook is as ill-suited to teaching law conceived on the realist model as it was well-suited to teaching law as Langdell conceived it. The generic structure that today's casebooks retain thus burdens teaching and learning. Several burdens matter especially.

First, contemporary legal education slights doctrine. Although considerations from outside law remain at the margins of even contemporary casebooks, they come quickly to dominate classroom discussion. But the study of legal doctrine is demanding; legal rules are difficult to understand, both individually and in their inter-connections, and difficult to adjust subtly to recalcitrant facts. The case method was for Langdell and remains today a powerful way to teach doctrine; but it is labor intensive. To succeed, case-based doctrinal instruction must be law school's main event; but today it is increasingly a side-show. And so doctrine is slighted in modern legal education, even as modern teaching texts continue to valorize it. For example, virtually no contemporary contracts classes systematically explain the structural distinction that doctrine erects between contract and tort. But it is impossible to understand contract doctrine at any depth without internalizing this distinction as second nature.[4]

---

4. The distinction may be simply stated in the following way, although it will take much of this text to unpack it: Tort law, and in particular the law establishing tort liability for misrepresentation, insists that a party asserting misrepresentation must have relied (reasonably, no less) *directly on the truth of the representation at issue*; and it expressly rejects that

Second, contemporary legal education slights the allied fields—economics, philosophy, politics, and sociology—that modern lawyers believe inform law and legal decision-making. Ideas from these fields are constantly brought to bear on cases in class discussions (and sometimes even in notes included in the "materials" sections of casebooks). But the ideas are applied to cases—often in complex and challenging ways—without ever being explained on their own terms. For example, most contracts casebooks and courses regularly refer to economic efficiency or freedom of contract. But virtually none elaborates theories of efficiency and freedom or explains why these are valuable.[5]

Third, the mis-match between the older Langdellian generic style of contemporary casebooks and the newer realist substance of the legal ideas that they are called upon to teach distorts the intellectual tenor of legal education. Conventional casebooks tempt teachers to present doctrinal reasoning as disguising the real interests and values that determine legal outcomes behind a façade of formal rules, so that doctrine becomes reduced to an exercise in misdirection. Sometimes doctrine disguises interests in this fashion, to be sure. But the reflexive instinct to see such bad faith teaches bad intellectual habits. Law teaching can adopt a knowing style—in which the class assumes a superiority over the texts being discussed—that belittles both the difficulty of doctrinal analysis and the integrity that legal doctrine can have (even in a realist world, in which it also responds to extra-legal concerns). Law school can also belittle the complexity and difficulty of the values that influence judicial decision from without legal doctrine: efficiency and freedom are famously complex and difficult ideals, after all, both in general and as they apply to particular cases, so that realist legal analysis is never simple or easy. The best law school teaching insistently emphasizes that law is a deep and difficult discipline; conventional casebooks disguise this.

Contract Law and Legal Methods aims to avoid the intellectual and pedagogic sins that conventional casebooks invite. It purses this ambition by embracing Langdell's great insight—that the generic structure of a teaching text should fit the conceptual structure of the subject taught—in the shadow of modern ideas about the nature of law. *Contract Law and Legal Methods* aspires to match the modern vision of law as neatly as Langdell's *Selection of Cases on the Law of Contracts* fit law as he conceived it. The text attempts both to present an integrated doctrinal account of what contract law is—of what makes contract a distinctive form of private

---

the prospect of subsequent legal enforcement through a tort claim might satisfy the reliance requirement. By contrast, such bootstrapping is the essence of contract.

5. Efficiency, as this text will explain, is a property of allocations of resources; and its value (at least in connection with contract) is closely connected to the fact that contracting parties will tend to prefer contracts that establish efficient allocations over those that do not. Freedom of contract, for its part, is an immensely complex ideal, less related to flat freedom (the simple absence of external constraint) than to the affirmative capacity to project one's intentions effectively into the future, through the specific mechanism of chosen legal obligation. One of the aims of this text is to unpack these cryptic formulations.

legal obligation—and to embed its treatment of contract law in the broader constellations of ideas and values (from without the law) that influence contractual practice.

The text's doctrinal engagement reflects the fact that, even as they embrace the influence of extra-legal ideals on legal processes and indeed insist on the porousness of doctrine, the best contemporary theories of law also reject the crassly realist claim that doctrine has no effect on courts or outcomes. *Contract Law and Legal Methods* thus takes doctrine seriously— more seriously than other contemporary casebooks. Seriousness shows itself in two ways. First, the argument throughout the text returns again and again to questions concerning the deep doctrinal structure of contract law. In particular the text repeatedly asks whether contract constitutes a distinctive form of legal obligation or, instead, simply elaborates a special case of the tort duty not to harm, applied to harms committed through misrepresentations of current intentions or future conduct. And second, the text, in its central Part, systematically examines the various styles in which legal doctrine might be made, both to assess their strengths and weaknesses and to show the ways in which choices made at one point in the law's doctrinal development require complementary choices elsewhere.

Contract Law and Legal Methods also aspires seriously to teach about extra-legal values that prominently influence contract law. Two constellations of value matter especially: economic efficiency and freedom. Part One of the text thus develops an economic analysis of contract remedies. The argument begins by setting out—in a conceptually sophisticated but nontechnical fashion—what economic efficiency is and how efficiency analysis works. The text then asks to what degree the positive law of contract remedies—the doctrines through which courts administer remedies—might be understood as a long and complex working out of economic efficiency in this area of law and life. Part Three of the text presents an analogous elaboration of the ideal of freedom of contract, once again both in theory and in doctrine. The argument begins by investigating what freedom of contract—as opposed to freedom generally or flat freedom—involves. This leads the argument to explain the idea that contract is a form of voluntary obligation—that is, obligation arising directly out of the intentions of the persons to whom it applies. The argument then uses this idea to elaborate the central doctrines through which the law fixes the metes and bounds of freedom of contract.

A final prefatory remark is worth making, at the risk of seeming to emanate from a stuffed shirt, only because contract law is taught in the first term of law school.

Learning law is difficult. Both doctrine itself and the values that doctrine answers to can be intricate and occasionally profound. The nature of modern law schools adds to the difficulty in a distinctive way. Law professors are increasingly scholars, devoted to academic values and often trained in disciplines besides law. Law students, by contrast, continue overwhelmingly to intend to become practicing lawyers: they do not, nor should they, aspire to become their teachers, or to internalize their teachers' perspectives.

Law school owes much of its appeal to this contrast. Law students learn to understand law's context and its deeper structure in ways that will improve their performance as technicians in their first jobs and as policy makers in their last ones. And law professors remain connected to the world, and legal scholarship resists the worship of technique and descent into fantasy that increasingly blights the social and human sciences.

The tension between professors' and students' interests in the law can be frustrating also. There are many ways to characterize the frustration, but the following is as good as any: legal scholars incline to get to the bottom of legal problems, whereas practicing lawyers incline to paper the problems over, to make them go away; and this difference causes scholarly pre-occupations to seem indulgent to the more practically inclined. The students' perspective on this tension is reasonable, but it is only a partial perspective nevertheless. Most importantly, practicing lawyers who understand doctrine's context and deep structure will do much better at durably papering over problems, to provide lasting resolutions for their clients, than those who do not. It takes deep understanding of legal problems to construct successful shallow solutions. That is why law professors are valued as consultants and why the best practical lawyers—especially in private law—possess an excellent academic knowledge of their fields.

You will therefore be better practicing lawyers—you will serve your clients more effectively and achieve greater professional success for yourselves—if you give yourselves over to your teachers *for a time*, and at least for a term. If you find some parts of what you are taught uncongenial, remember that you need not embrace your teachers' perspective to profit from it. But you do need to understand it; and understanding takes devotion.

SUMMARY OF CONTENTS

TABLE OF CONTENTS

xix

TABLE OF CASES

Principal cases are in bold type. Non-principal cases are in roman type. References are to Pages.

CONTRACT LAW AND LEGAL METHODS

PART ONE

REMEDIES (HEREIN OF LAW AND ECONOMICS)

CHAPTER 1

INTRODUCTION

When a contractual promisor fails to do as she has promised, her promisee may go to law to seek a remedy for the breach. A contractual remedy is the mechanism through which the law vindicates a contractual right.

Beginning the study of contracts with the law of contract remedies may seem backwards therefore. Certainly it begins the *study* of contracts at the endgame of the actual *experience* of contracting. But reversing the path of experience is helpful for gaining understanding. When it comes time, later on, to study contract formation and interpretation, for example, or to compare contract to other forms of obligation, or even to assess the moral or political limits that the law places on the types of contracts that it will recognize and enforce, it will be invaluable to know, already, what is at stake in deciding whether a contract has been created and what it means, or whether the law should disapprove of some or other class of contracts on moral or political grounds. Contrariwise, arguments about these (seemingly antecedent) topics that are not grounded in an understanding of contract remedies will be inevitably erratic and capricious because they will lack any solid sense of what is, finally, at stake. How can one possibly say, for example, whether the law should make it easy or difficult to create contracts—how the law should balance the costs of imposing contractual obligations on those who did not choose them against the costs of failing to recognize contractual obligations that persons did choose—without knowing just how the obligations and entitlements that arise under a valid contract differ from the obligations and entitlements that exist among bargainers, or even complete strangers, in any case?

And so it makes sense to begin with contract remedies.

The purpose of this brief introduction is to identify the basic doctrinal and conceptual distinctions at play in contract remedies. The most basic of these is the distinction between the total size of a remedy or the *quantum of damages*, on the one hand, and the specific *interests* or the *categories of loss* that the remedy is designed to vindicate, on the other. It is impossible to understand contract remedies without beginning from the realization that contract law does not simply award disappointed promisees an amount of money that seems—intuitively and overall—fair and reasonable. Instead, the law of contract remedies involves a much greater and more refined conceptual and doctrinal structure. First, the law distinguishes, one might say purely abstractly, among several conceptually very different promisee interests. Then, it adopts general rules that say which of these interests it will vindicate and so which categories of a promisee's loss it will require breaching promisors to recompense. Next, the law identifies, for particular cases, which of a promisee's claims fall into the protected categories of loss. And only then does the law place money values on these claims, to come up with a final quantum of damages to award to the promisee.

This quantum of damages is of course what matters most to the litigants—it is their bottom line, so to speak. But it cannot be predicted or calculated without a mastery of conceptual distinctions, concerning categories of loss, that inform legal doctrine. The quantum of damages is thus generally more like a brute fact than like a legal principle. Indeed, dollar amounts generally figure only incidentally in the distinctively legal arguments concerning contract remedies that follow, and then only as stand-ins for the categories of loss that they are designed to recompense.

The materials below introduce the doctrinal and conceptual framework that governs contract remedies. The section from the Restatement identifies several contractual interests that the law might vindicate, and so several categories of loss that the law might recompense. The case illustrates how one might reason using these categories and, as it happens, how such reasoning might go awry.

Restatement 2d of Contracts

§ 344   Purposes of Remedies

Judicial remedies under the rules stated in this Restatement serve to protect one or more of the following interests of a promisee:

(a) his "expectation interest," which is his interest in having the benefit of his bargain by being put in as good a position as he would have been in had the contract been performed,

(b) his "reliance interest," which is his interest in being reimbursed for loss caused by reliance on the contract by being put in as good a position as he would have been in had the contract not been made, or

(c) his "restitution interest," which is his interest in having restored to him any benefit that he has conferred on the other party.

Comments & Illustrations:

Comment a. Three interests. The law of contract remedies implements the policy in favor of allowing individuals to order their own affairs by making legally enforceable promises. Ordinarily, when a court concludes that there has been a breach of contract, it enforces the broken promise by protecting the expectation that the injured party had when he made the contract. It does this by attempting to put him in as good a position as he would have been in had the contract been performed, that is, had there been no breach. The interest protected in this way is called the "expectation interest." It is sometimes said to give the injured party the "benefit of the bargain." This is not, however, the only interest that may be protected.

The promisee may have changed his position in reliance on the contract by, for example, incurring expenses in preparing to perform, in performing, or in foregoing opportunities to make other contracts. In that case, the court may recognize a claim based on his reliance rather than on his expectation. It does this by attempting to put him back in the position in which he would have been had the contract not been made. The interest protected in this way is called "reliance interest." Although it may be equal to the expectation interest, it is ordinarily smaller because it does not include the injured party's lost profit.

In some situations a court will recognize yet a third interest and grant relief to prevent unjust enrichment. This may be done if a party has not only changed his own position in reliance on the contract but has also conferred a benefit on the other party by, for example, making a part payment or furnishing services under the contract. The court may then require the other party to disgorge the benefit that he has received by returning it to the party who conferred it. The interest of the claimant protected in this way is called the "restitution interest." Although it may be equal to the expectation or reliance interest, it is ordinarily smaller because it includes neither the injured party's lost profit nor that part of his expenditures in reliance that resulted in no benefit to the other party.

The interests described in this Section are not inflexible limits on relief and in situations in which a court grants such relief as justice requires, the relief may not correspond precisely to any of these interests. See §§ 15, 87, 89, 90, 139, 158 and 272.

Illustrations:

1. A contracts to building for B on B's land for $100,000. B repudiates the contract before either party has done anything in reliance on it. It would have cost A $90,000 to build the building. A has an expectation interest of $10,000, the difference between the $100,000 price and his savings of $90,000 in not having to do the work. Since A has done nothing in reliance, A's reliance interest is zero. Since A has conferred no benefit on B, A's restitution interest is zero.

2. The facts being otherwise as stated in Illustration 1, B does not repudiate until A has spent $60,000 of the $90,000. A has been paid nothing and can salvage nothing from the $60,000 that he has spent. A now has an expectation interest of $70,000, the difference between the $100,000 price and his saving of $30,000 in not having to do the work. A also has a reliance interest of $60,000, the amount that he has spent. If the benefit to B of the partly finished building is $40,000, A has a restitution interest of $40,000.

Comment b. Expectation interest. In principle, at least, a party's expectation interest represents the actual worth of the contract to him rather than to some reasonable third person. Damages based on the expectation interest therefore take account of any special circumstances that are peculiar to the situation of the injured party, including his personal values and even his idiosyncrasies, as well as his own needs and opportunities. See Illustration 3. In practice, however, the injured party is often held to a more objective valuation of his expectation interest because he may be barred from recovering for loss resulting from such special circumstances on the ground that it was not foreseeable or cannot be shown with sufficient certainty. See §§ 351 and 352. Furthermore, since he cannot recover for loss that he could have avoided by arranging a substitute transaction on the market (§ 350), his recovery is often limited by the objective standard of market price. See Illustration 4. The expectation interest is not based on the injured party's hopes when he made the contract but on the actual value that the contract would have had to him had it been performed. See Illustration 5. It is therefore based on the circumstances at the time for performance and not those at the time of the making of the contract.

Illustrations:

3. A, who is about to produce a play, makes a contract with B, an actor, under which B is to play the lead in the play at a stated salary for the season. A breaks the contract and has the part played by another actor. B's expectation interest includes the extent to which B's reputation would have been enhanced if he had been allowed to play the lead in A's play, as well as B's loss in salary, both subject to the limitations stated in Topic 2.

4. A contracts to construct a monument in B's yard for $10,000 but abandons the work after the foundation has been laid. It will cost B $6,000 to have another contractor complete the work. The monument planned is so ugly that it would decrease the market price of the house. Nevertheless, B's expectation interest is the value of the monument to him, which, under the rule stated in § 348(2)(b), would be measured by the cost of completion, $6,000.

5. A makes a contract with B under which A is to pay B for drilling an oil well on B's land, adjacent to that of A, for development and exploration purposes. Both A and B believe that the well will be productive and will substantially enhance the value of A's land in an amount that they estimate to be $1,000,000. Before A has paid anything, B breaks the contract by refusing to drill the well. Other exploration then proves that there is no oil in the region. A's expectation interest is zero.

Comment c. Reliance interest. If it is reliance that is the basis for the enforcement of a promise, a court may enforce the promise but limit the promisee to recovery of his reliance interest. See §§ 87, 89, 90, 139. There are also situations in which a court may grant recovery based on the reliance interest even though it is consideration that is the basis for the enforcement of the promise. These situations are dealt with in §§ 349 and 353.

Comment d. Restitution interest. Since restitution is the subject of a separate Restatement, this Chapter is concerned with problems of restitution only to the extent that they arise in connection with contracts. Such problems arise when a party, instead of seeking to enforce an agreement, claims relief on the ground that the other party has been unjustly enriched as a result of some benefit conferred under the agreement. In some cases a party's choice of the restitution interest is dictated by the fact that the agreement is not enforceable, perhaps because of his own breach (§ 374), as a result of impracticability of performance or frustration of purpose (§ 377(1)), under the Statute of Frauds (§ 375), or in consequence of the other party's avoidance for some reason as misrepresentation, duress, mistake or incapacity (§ 376). Occasionally a party chooses the restitution interest even though the contract is enforceable because it will give a larger recovery than will enforcement based on either the expectation or reliance interest. These rare instances are dealt with in § 373. Sometimes the restitution interest can be protected by requiring restoration of the specific thing, such as goods or land, that has resulted in the benefit. See § 372. Where restitution in kind is not appropriate, however, a sum of money will generally be allowed based on the restitution interest. See § 371.

Sullivan v. O'Connor

Supreme Judicial Court of Massachusetts, 1973.
296 N.E.2d 183.

■ KAPLAN, J. The plaintiff patient secured a jury verdict of $13,500 against the defendant surgeon for breach of contract in respect to an operation upon the plaintiff's nose. The substituted consolidated bill of exceptions presents questions about the correctness of the judge's instructions on the issue of damages.

The declaration was in two counts. In the first count, the plaintiff alleged that she, as patient, entered into a contract with the defendant, a surgeon, wherein the defendant promised to perform plastic surgery on her nose and thereby to enhance her beauty and improve her appearance; that he performed the surgery but failed to achieve the promised result; rather the result of the surgery was to disfigure and deform her nose, to cause her pain in body and mind, and to subject her to other damage and expense. The second count, based on the same transaction, was in the conventional form for malpractice, charging that the defendant had been guilty of negligence in performing the surgery. Answering, the defendant entered a general denial.

On the plaintiff's demand, the case was tried by jury. At the close of the evidence, the judge put to the jury, as special questions, the issues of liability under the two counts, and instructed them accordingly. The jury returned a verdict for the plaintiff on the contract count, and for the defendant on the negligence count. The judge then instructed the jury on the issue of damages.

As background to the instructions and the parties' exceptions, we mention certain facts as the jury could find them. The plaintiff was a professional entertainer, and this was known to the defendant. The agreement was as alleged in the declaration. More particularly, judging from exhibits, the plaintiff's nose had been straight, but long and prominent; the defendant undertook by two operations to reduce its prominence and somewhat to shorten it, thus making it more pleasing in relation to the plaintiff's other features. Actually the plaintiff was obliged to undergo three operations, and her appearance was worsened. Her nose now had a concave line to about the midpoint, at which it became bulbous; viewed frontally, the nose from bridge to midpoint was flattened and broadened, and the two sides of the tip had lost symmetry. This configuration evidently could not be improved by further surgery. The plaintiff did not demonstrate, however, that her change of appearance had resulted in loss of employment. Payments by the plaintiff covering the defendant's fee and hospital expenses were stipulated at $622.65.

The judge instructed the jury, first, that the plaintiff was entitled to recover her out-of-pocket expenses incident to the operations. Second, she could recover the damages flowing directly, naturally, proximately, and foreseeably from the defendant's breach of promise. These would comprehend damages for any disfigurement of the plaintiff's nose—that is, any change of appearance for the worse—including the effects of the consciousness of such disfigurement on the plaintiff's mind, and in this connection the jury should consider the nature of the plaintiff's profession. Also consequent upon the defendant's breach, and compensable, were the pain and suffering involved in the third operation, but not in the first two. As there was no proof that any loss of earnings by the plaintiff resulted from the breach, that element should not enter into the calculation of damages.

By his exceptions the defendant contends that the judge erred in allowing the jury to take into account anything but the plaintiff's out-of-pocket expenses (presumably at the stipulated amount). The defendant excepted to the judge's refusal of his request for a general charge to that effect, and, more specifically, to the judge's refusal of a charge that the plaintiff could not recover for pain and suffering connected with the third operation or for impairment of the plaintiff's appearance and associated mental distress.[1]

The plaintiff on her part excepted to the judge's refusal of a request to charge that the plaintiff could recover the difference in value between the nose as promised and the nose as it appeared after the operations. However, the plaintiff in her brief expressly waives this exception and others made by her in case this court overrules the defendant's exceptions; thus she would be content to hold the jury's verdict in her favor.

We conclude that the defendant's exceptions should be overruled.

---

1. The defendant also excepted to the judge's refusal to direct a verdict in his favor, but this exception is not pressed and could not be sustained.

It has been suggested on occasion that agreements between patients and physicians by which the physician undertakes to effect a cure or to bring about a given result should be declared unenforceable on grounds of public policy. See *Guilmet v. Campbell*, 188 N.W.2d 601, 610 (Mich. 1971) (dissenting opinion). But there are many decisions recognizing and enforcing such contracts, see annotation, 43 A.L.R. 3d 1221, 1225, 1229–1233, and the law of Massachusetts has treated them as valid, although we have had no decision meeting head on the contention that they should be denied legal sanction.... These causes of action are, however, considered a little suspect, and thus we find courts straining sometimes to read the pleadings as sounding only in tort for negligence, and not in contract for breach of promise, despite sedulous efforts by the pleaders to pursue the latter theory.

It is not hard to see why the courts should be unenthusiastic or skeptical about the contract theory. Considering the uncertainties of medical science and the variations in the physical and psychological conditions of individual patients, doctors can seldom in good faith promise specific results. Therefore it is unlikely that physicians of even average integrity will in fact make such promises. Statements of opinion by the physician with some optimistic coloring are a different thing, and may indeed have therapeutic value. But patients may transform such statements into firm promises in their own minds, especially when they have been disappointed in the event, and testify in that sense to sympathetic juries.[2] If actions for breach of promise can be readily maintained, doctors, so it is said, will be frightened into practicing "defensive medicine." On the other hand, if these actions were outlawed, leaving only the possibility of suits for malpractice, there is fear that the public might be exposed to the enticements of charlatans, and confidence in the profession might ultimately be shaken. The law has taken the middle of the road position of allowing actions based on alleged contract, but insisting on clear proof. Instructions to the jury may well stress this requirement and point to tests of truth, such as the complexity or difficulty of an operation as bearing on the probability that a given result was promised. See annotation, 43 A.L.R. 3d 1225, 1225–1227.

If an action on the basis of contract is allowed, we have next the question of the measure of damages to be applied where liability is found. Some cases have taken the simple view that the promise by the physician is to be treated like an ordinary commercial promise, and accordingly that the successful plaintiff is entitled to a standard measure of recovery for breach of contract—"compensatory" ("expectancy") damages, an amount intended to put the plaintiff in the position he would be in if the contract had been performed, or, presumably, at the plaintiff's election, "restitution" damages, an amount corresponding to any benefit conferred by the plaintiff

---

2. Judicial skepticism about whether a promise was in fact made derives also from the possibility that the truth has been tortured to give the plaintiff the advantage of the longer period of limitations sometimes available for actions on contract as distinguished from those in tort or for malpractice. See Lillich, The Malpractice Statute of Limitations in New York and Other Jurisdictions, 47 Cornell L. Q. 339; annotation, 80 A. L. R. 2d 368.

upon the defendant in the performance of the contract disrupted by the defendant's breach. Thus in *Hawkins v. McGee*, 146 A. 641 (N.H. 1929), the defendant doctor was taken to have promised the plaintiff to convert his damaged hand by means of an operation into a good or perfect hand, but the doctor so operated as to damage the hand still further. The court, following the usual expectancy formula, would have asked the jury to estimate and award to the plaintiff the difference between the value of a good or perfect hand, as promised, and the value of the hand after the operation. (The same formula would apply, although the dollar result would be less, if the operation had neither worsened nor improved the condition of the hand.) If the plaintiff had not yet paid the doctor his fee, that amount would be deducted from the recovery. There could be no recovery for the pain and suffering of the operation, since that detriment would have been incurred even if the operation had been successful; one can say that this detriment was not "caused" by the breach. But where the plaintiff by reason of the operation was put to more pain than he would have had to endure, had the doctor performed as promised, he should be compensated for that difference as a proper part of his expectancy recovery. It may be noted that on an alternative count for malpractice the plaintiff in the *Hawkins* case had been nonsuited; but on ordinary principles this could not affect the contract claim, for it is hardly a defense to a breach of contract that the promisor acted innocently and without negligence.

Other cases, including a number in New York, without distinctly repudiating the *Hawkins* type of analysis, have indicated that a different and generally more lenient measure of damages is to be applied in patient-physician actions based on breach of alleged special agreements to effect a cure, attain a stated result, or employ a given medical method. This measure is expressed in somewhat variant ways, but the substance is that the plaintiff is to recover any expenditures made by him and for other detriment (usually not specifically described in the opinions) following proximately and foreseeably upon the defendant's failure to carry out his promise. This, be it noted, is not a "restitution" measure, for it is not limited to restoration of the benefit conferred on the defendant (the fee paid) but includes other expenditures, for example, amounts paid for medicine and nurses; so also it would seem according to its logic to take in damages for any worsening of the plaintiff's condition due to the breach. Nor is it an "expectancy" measure, for it does not appear to contemplate recovery of the whole difference in value between the condition as promised and the condition actually resulting from the treatment. Rather the tendency of the formulation is to put the plaintiff back in the position he occupied just before the parties entered upon the agreement, to compensate him for the detriments he suffered in reliance upon the agreement. This kind of intermediate pattern of recovery for breach of contract is discussed in the suggestive article by Fuller and Perdue, The Reliance Interest in Contract Damages, 46 Yale L. J. 52, 373, where the authors show that, although not attaining the currency of the standard measures, a "reliance" measure has for special reasons been applied by the courts in a variety of settings, including noncommercial settings. See 46 Yale L. J. at 396–401.[4]

For breach of the patient-physician agreements under consideration, a recovery limited to restitution seems plainly too meager, if the agreements are to be enforced at all. On the other hand, an expectancy recovery may well be excessive. The factors, already mentioned, which have made the cause of action somewhat suspect, also suggest moderation as to the breadth of the recovery that should be permitted. Where, as in the case at bar and in a number of the reported cases, the doctor has been absolved of negligence by the trier, an expectancy measure may be thought harsh. We should recall here that the fee paid by the patient to the doctor for the alleged promise would usually be quite disproportionate to the putative expectancy recovery. To attempt, moreover, to put a value on the condition that would or might have resulted, had the treatment succeeded as promised, may sometimes put an exceptional strain on the imagination of the fact finder. As a general consideration, Fuller and Perdue argue that the reasons for granting damages for broken promises to the extent of the expectancy are at their strongest when the promises are made in a business context, when they have to do with the production or distribution of goods or the allocation of functions in the market place; they become weaker as the context shifts from a commercial to a noncommercial field. 46 Yale L. J. at 60–63.

There is much to be said, then, for applying a reliance measure to the present facts, and we have only to add that our cases are not unreceptive to the use of that formula in special situations. We have, however, had no previous occasion to apply it to patient-physician cases.

The question of recovery on a reliance basis for pain and suffering or mental distress requires further attention. We find expressions in the decisions that pain and suffering (or the like) are simply not compensable in actions for breach of contract. The defendant seemingly espouses this proposition in the present case. True, if the buyer under a contract for the purchase of a lot of merchandise, in suing for the seller's breach, should claim damages for mental anguish caused by his disappointment in the transaction, he would not succeed; he would be told, perhaps, that the asserted psychological injury was not fairly foreseeable by the defendant as a probable consequence of the breach of such a business contract. But there is no general rule barring such items of damage in actions for breach of contract. It is all a question of the subject matter and background of the contract, and when the contract calls for an operation on the person of the plaintiff, psychological as well as physical injury may be expected to figure somewhere in the recovery, depending on the particular circumstances. Again, it is said in a few of the New York cases, concerned with the classification of actions for statute of limitations purposes, that the absence

---

4. Some of the exceptional situations mentioned where reliance may be preferred to expectancy are those in which the latter measure would be hard to apply or would impose too great a burden; performance was interfered with by external circumstances; the contract was indefinite. See 46 Yale L. J. at 373–386; 394–396.

of allegations demanding recovery for pain and suffering is characteristic of a contract claim by a patient against a physician, that such allegations rather belong in a claim for malpractice. These remarks seem unduly sweeping. Suffering or distress resulting from the breach going beyond that which was envisaged by the treatment as agreed, should be compensable on the same ground as the worsening of the patient's conditions because of the breach. Indeed it can be argued that the very suffering or distress "contracted for"—that which would have been incurred if the treatment achieved the promised result—should also be compensable on the theory underlying the New York cases. For that suffering is "wasted" if the treatment fails. Otherwise stated, compensation for this waste is arguably required in order to complete the restoration of the status quo ante.[6]

In the light of the foregoing discussion, all the defendant's exceptions fail: the plaintiff was not confined to the recovery of her out-of-pocket expenditures; she was entitled to recover also for the worsening of her condition,[7] and for the pain and suffering and mental distress involved in the third operation. These items were compensable on either an expectancy or a reliance view. We might have been required to elect between the two views if the pain and suffering connected with the first two operations contemplated by the agreement, or the whole difference in value between the present and the promised conditions, were being claimed as elements of damage. But the plaintiff waives her possible claim to the former element, and to so much of the latter as represents the difference in value between the promised condition and the condition before the operations.

Plaintiff's exceptions waived.

Defendant's exceptions overruled.

* * *

Much of the *Sullivan* opinion considers matters that lie far from center stage here—including most notably whether or not the law should enforce the class of contracts at issue in the case, that is, whether or not doctors should be able to give warranties. The crucial question, for present purposes, is much narrower, namely what remedy the law should award on the assumption that the warranty was valid and that it was breached.

---

6. Recovery on a reliance basis for breach of the physician's promise tends to equate with the usual recovery for malpractice, since the latter also looks in general to restoration of the condition before the injury. But this is not paradoxical, especially when it is noted that the origins of contract lie in tort. A few cases have considered possible recovery for breach by a physician of a promise to sterilize a patient, resulting in birth of a child to the patient and spouse. If such an action is held maintainable, the reliance and expectancy measures would, we think, tend to equate, because the promised condition was preservation of the family status quo.

It would, however, be a mistake to think in terms of strict "formulas." For example, a jurisdiction which would apply a reliance measure to the present facts might impose a more severe damage sanction for the wilful use by the physician of a method of operation that he undertook not to employ.

7. That condition involves a mental element and appraisal of it properly called for consideration of the fact that the plaintiff was an entertainer. Cf. *McQuaid v. Michou*, 157 A. 881 (N.H. 1932) (discussion of continuing condition resulting from physician's breach).

The court begins addressing this question by asking which interest in a warranty the law should vindicate—restitution, reliance, or expectation. The court, without much argument, rejects restitution as too little. It then observes that the case at hand does not require a choice between the reliance and the expectation measures, since the plaintiff, who had won a reliance award below, waived her cross appeal in case the defendant's appeal was rejected. This might (and perhaps should) have been the end of the opinion. Nevertheless, the court proceeds, in dicta, to argue against applying the law's general preference for the expectation remedy in the circumstances at issue and in favor, instead, of the legal rule that doctors' warranties should be enforceable by what the court calls a reliance remedy.

The arguments that the court offers for this conclusion are not especially impressive. In some moments, the opinion seems to propound what one might call the "Goldilocks" theory of adjudication—restitution damages are too little, expectation damages are too much, and reliance is just right. Presumably, the idea that the court had in mind is that a reliance remedy strikes the optimal balance between the policy concerns—defensive medicine if doctors can be held to promises of success versus unscrupulous promises if they cannot be—that the court discussed in deciding, initially, whether doctors' warranties should be legally enforceable at all. But the court offers no serious evidence that a restitution rule would tilt the balance unduly in favor of unscrupulous doctors, or that an expectation rule would engender unduly defensive medicine in honorable doctors, or that the reliance rule that the court prefers strikes the right balance. Nor, indeed, is it clear how a court could gather and process the evidence needed to reach any such conclusion. Common law courts, and especially appellate courts, lack the staff, the expertise, and (since the development of the facts is generally left to the parties and confined to the initial trial) even the control over their own proceedings necessary for making such judgments reliably.

Moreover, when this court argues in a style more suited to its institutional character, its arguments are, on their own terms, bad. First, the court mentions that it is a strike against the expectation rule that the plaintiffs' expectations in a case like this one—involving her future earnings as a night-club singer—are so difficult to measure. But are they really more difficult to measure (and to monetize) than the pain and suffering that figures so prominently in the reliance award that the court prefers? Surely problems concerning measurement, if they are taken as dispositive, counsel preferring restitution and not reliance.

Second, the court proposes that the price the plaintiff paid for the surgery and the promise of success was too low to support treating the promise as a warranty in the ordinary way, backed by an expectation remedy. This argument, which is essentially an exercise in contract interpretation, has substantial formal appeal. Indeed it is a form of argument that will reappear in the pages to come. It sets out from the proposition, which will be important and should be non-obvious, that the parties may choose (at least within limits) with what remedies to back up their contractual promises. It then interprets the low price as evidence that the parties did not choose the standard expectation remedy, because that remedy would cost the doctor too much, given the fee.

But although the form of argument is appealing, the court misapplies this form to the facts of the case. The intuitions that the fee is too small and that the expectation remedy would be too expensive are under-theorized. There are few grounds for interpreting the contract to guarantee the doctor a substantial profit. In a competitive market, after all, contract prices are competed down until the entire surplus goes to consumers. And although the medical profession (like the legal profession) maintains a cartel in order to secure super-competitive profits, there is no reason to think that this cartelization will always work or that these profits will always be substantial. The court has nothing near the empirical basis it would need to make a sound inference from the price to the nature of the remedy. Certainly it cannot support its conclusion that the price term reveals that reliance, as opposed to some remedy in between expectation and reliance, was chosen by the parties. Finally, the interpretive argument gives no basis for styling the remedy in terms of reliance at all. The pressures of the interpretive argument can be equally satisfied by retaining the standard commitment to the expectation form, but simply re-interpreting the warranty to make a more modest (and therefore less costly) guarantee—no longer of a perfect nose, say, but merely of a reasonable improvement.

But all of this is, for present purposes, still really a sideshow. The same reasons for which the court was ill-suited to settle the basic question what remedy is appropriate make a law school class ill-suited also. There is simply no way, in either forum, to gather and process the information needed to make a responsible judgment about the balance of benefits and burdens of the several possible remedy rules.

The main event, for present purposes, involves the application of the reliance principle to the facts of the case. This application presents a case study in the conceptual and doctrinal mechanics of contract remedies, with an emphasis on the analytic structure of the several interests and categories of loss that contract law identifies. It also, as it happens, illustrates how easily even sophisticated lawyers (and the Supreme Judicial Court of Massachusetts is a sophisticated court) can get these analytics at least partly wrong.

To see this, begin by following the table below and identifying the categories of loss that are included in each of the three interests.

| Expectation | Put plaintiff in the same position as performance would have done | (Value of nose as promised)— (Value of nose as is)

Pain and suffering of 3rd surgery but not first 2 |

		Additional nursing costs, etc., due to 3rd surgery
Reliance	Return plaintiff to the position she would have occupied had there been no contract	Return of fee

(Value of nose as was)—
(Value of nose as is)

Pain and suffering of all 3 surgeries

All nursing costs, etc. |
| Restitution | Restore what plaintiff paid to defendant | Return of fee |

Table 1.1

**The Expectation, Reliance, and Restitution
Interests in *Sullivan v. O'Connor***

Now compare these measures to what the plaintiff actually received under the trial verdict that the appellate court left in place. Specifically, notice that the plaintiff did not recover compensation for the pain and suffering associated with the first two operations, as the reliance measure, properly understood, requires. Accordingly, although the court purports to be making a legal rule that reliance damages will be awarded for breaches of medical warranties, it in fact awards some other measure of damages in the case before it.

Why is this? The opinion answers that the plaintiff waived her claim to greater damages than the trial court ordered in case the appellate court rejected the defendant's appeal seeking to reduce the trial court's award.[1] A choice between expectation and reliance would have been required only if the plaintiff had insisted on recovering either damages for the pain and suffering caused by the first two operations (included in reliance but not in expectation) or damages for the difference between the nose as promised and the nose as it was before the operations (included in expectation but not reliance). As the higher court observes, the damages that the lower court actually awarded were recoverable on either a reliance or an expec-

---

1. It is not clear that this is right. Earlier in the opinion, the appellate court characterizes both the plaintiff's appeal and her waiver exclusively in terms of a claim to the difference between the nose as promised and the nose as it turned out. It seems plausible, then, that the plaintiff neither laid claim to compensation for the pain and suffering associated with the first two operations nor waived this element of her appeal, should the verdict below be affirmed. In light of the general confusion surrounding the reliance remedy in the opinion, it is not surprising that this point in particular gets lost. But is an important point nevertheless. In fact, both the expectation and the reliance remedies, understood as contract doctrine traditionally does, would award the plaintiff greater damages than the trial court did.

Finally, although these details are important, they should not obscure a large, and striking point, namely that the court defers to the plaintiff's waiver of her claim. That entails that the parties can (to a significant degree) control the legal questions that the court reaches. This turns out to be a deep feature of our legal system. Is it a good one?

tancy view, so that the higher court was not forced finally to choose between them. Nor, one might add, was the higher court forced to become clear about the true structure of the reliance measure—and in particular the fact that it includes recovery for losses (the pain and suffering associated with the first two operations) that the expectation measure excludes.

This feature of the reliance measure is important to the case, and in a way that the opinion, at least on its face, fails to recognize. Thus the higher court asserts, in a footnote, that "[r]ecovery on a reliance basis for breach of the physician's promise tends to equate with the usual recovery for malpractice, since the latter also looks in general to restoration of the condition before the injury." The general association between reliance damages in contract and a tort-like approach to contractual obligation is correct, as later arguments will explain in greater detail. But the specific connection that the opinion draws between reliance damages for breach of medical warranty and tort-damages for medical malpractice is mistaken. This is because the "injury" in each case is different, and the *status quos ante* to which the contract and tort reliance damages look are commensurately distinct.

In contract, the reliance remedy returns the plaintiff to the position that she would have enjoyed had there been no agreement. In this case, that is the pre-surgery position. In tort, the contract remedy returns the plaintiff to the position that she would have enjoyed had there been no wrongdoing. In this case, the relevant wrongdoing is the alleged malpractice by the doctor, and so the tort remedy puts the plaintiff in the position that she would have enjoyed had the doctor performed the surgery competently. The principal difference between the two is that under the contract remedy, the plaintiff recovers for the pain and suffering associated with all three operations, whereas under the tort remedy, she recovers for the pain and suffering associated with only the third.[2] This is because the doctor had (we may assume, reasonably) anticipated that the plaintiff would undergo two surgeries in any event, no matter how skillfully they were performed, so that any negligence caused only the third surgery, and not the first two.

These observations reveal that the damages that the plaintiff recovers are lower than what she would be entitled to under either the expectation or the reliance remedies, as these are understood in contract law. They include neither compensation for the gap between the nose as promised and the nose as it was (included in expectation but not reliance) nor compensation for the pain and suffering associated with the first two operations (included in reliance but not in expectation). So although the appellate

---

2. A second difference is that under the contract remedy, the plaintiff recovers only for the difference between the nose as it has turned out and the nose as it initially was, whereas under the tort remedy, the plaintiff recovers the larger difference between the nose as it has turned out and the nose as it would have been had the doctor performed reasonably. Whether or not this difference is substantial depends on the extent to which reasonable medical skill will securely produce an improvement. In some cases, this may be substantial. In the case of plastic surgery, it seems plausible that improvements are hard to come by and subjective, so that the most reasonable skill can secure is that there is no worsening. If that is true, then the second difference between the contract and tort remedies disappears, at least in the case at hand.

court proceeded under the banner of an argument in favor of reliance damages as they are understood in contract, the court in fact awards damages that look much more like the tort version of a reliance award. And that seems, simply, a confusion.

But was the court really confused? There is an alternative way to read the opinion, as involving a subterfuge. It may seem incredible, at least to a non-doctor reader of the facts reported in the appellate opinion, that the plaintiff lost at trial on her malpractice claim. Certainly it seems incredible to this reader, and the justices of the Supreme Judicial Court of Massachusetts may have had a similar response. Suspicion of the tort verdict below will only be increased, moreover, by the knowledge (which the Massachusetts justices surely had) that at the time of the dispute, plaintiffs in medical malpractice cases had a notoriously difficult time finding doctors willing to break ranks with their profession and testify that a colleague had performed negligently.

Someone who held such suspicions would like, naturally, to revisit the tort element of the plaintiff's case, but the procedural posture of the case makes it difficult to do so. The malpractice claim turns on whether the doctor employed reasonable medical skill and care, which is, at least in the general run of things, a question of fact. And appellate courts are severely constrained in their capacity to reverse fact-finding at trial. (Moreover, although no formal distinction is made between judge and jury fact-finding, appellate courts feel the constraints to be particularly binding when, as in this case, they are reviewing jury verdicts.) The justices may have felt that they could not openly reject the jury's findings. But they could (with the assistance of the plaintiff's waiver) reverse the tort verdict below surreptitiously, by affirming a damage award that was, properly speaking, appropriate for the malpractice claim that the plaintiff lost, but not for the contract claim that the plaintiff won. And perhaps this is just what they did.[3]

Finally, the appellate court might have been able to reach the ultimate outcome that it preferred, and grant the plaintiff a tort-like remedy, even without the subterfuge (and without overturning the jury's verdict concerning malpractice). In many states, the standard of skill and care that the law of negligence requires a professional to display varies according to the level of specialized training and expertise that the professional holds herself out as having.[4] Accordingly, a doctor who claimed to specialize in plastic

---

3. Note that in doing so, the justices were not necessarily flouting the jury's deeper intentions. The jury, after all, gave a tort-like remedy that was inconsistent with both its stated rejection of the malpractice claim and it stated approval of the contract claim. The jury perhaps felt some of the same frustrations as the justices, and so treated the doctor as negligent even in the face of testimony that could not support an overt finding to this effect.

4. In Massachusetts, for example, at the time when *Sullivan* was decided:

"The proper standard [of care, in a medical malpractice case] is whether the physician, if a general practitioner, has exercised the degree of care and skill of the average qualified practitioner, taking into account the advances in the profession. One holding himself out as a specialist should be held to the standard of care and skill of the average member of the profession practising the specialty, taking into account the advances in the profession. And, as in the case of the general practitioner, it is permissible to consider the medical resources available to him."

surgery would be held to higher standards of skill in performing a nose-reshaping surgery than a general surgeon who performed the same procedure. (An analogous regime applies, incidentally to professional malpractice for lawyers: lawyers who claim to be specialists in an area are similarly required to display greater skill concerning work in that area than generalist lawyers doing the same work.) This doctrinal fact opens up the way to a new interpretation of the doctor's guarantee of a perfect nose. In addition to, or even instead of, treating this claim as creating a warranty, the law might treat this and analogous claims as assertions of special medical training and expertise, of a type that raise the standard of skill that doctors who make such claims are required, by the law of professional malpractice, to display.

Had the appellate court adopted this route, it might have been able to revive the plaintiff's malpractice claim openly and without reversing any of the jury's fact-finding. Instead of concluding that the jury was unreasonable in finding that the defendant's conduct conformed to the standard of skill and care required of medical professionals, the appellate court might have held that the jury reached this finding by applying the legally incorrect standard of care—that whereas the jury was applying the standard of care associated with ordinary doctors, the promise of a perfect nose raised the standard of care mandated in this case to the level associated with specialist plastic surgeons. This holding would not have allowed the appellate court to affirm the verdict below, however. Instead, it would have had to order a new trial of the plaintiff's tort claim, governed by the correct standard of skill. And there would, of course, have been the ever-present risk that, even under the higher legal standard, the plaintiff would again lose on the facts.

This discussion has addressed only a small and, from the point of view of the development of contract law in general, secondary part of an already short opinion. The purpose of subjecting *Sullivan v. O'Connor* to such close analysis is not to provide instruction in the positive law governing contract remedies, either in general or in connection with breaches of medical warranties. As Restatement § 344 states, and as *Sullivan* recognizes (although it does not follow), the standard remedy for breach of contract is not reliance but rather expectation. Moreover, *Sullivan* may well reach an idiosyncratic resolution of the warranty question even within the narrow confines of promises of medical success. Finally, such promises are anyway a far too specialized area of law to be studied profitably in an introduction to contract law writ large.

Rather, the discussion has sought to combat any intuitive sense that contract remedies may be fixed by asking what quantum of damages will produce, in a holistic sense, a fair outcome. Instead, the correct application of the law of contract remedies requires paying careful attention to the interests that contract law protects and the categories of loss that plaintiffs have endured. This approach requires a kind of close conceptual argument that doctrinal legal analysis demands quite generally. Mastering such

---

Brune v. Belinkoff, 354 Mass. 102, 109 (1968).

argument is a formal and all-purpose legal skill rather than a piece of substantive legal knowledge connected to a specific area of the law. This introduction therefore serves to introduce not just the law of contract remedies, but all of contract law, and indeed doctrinal legal reasoning quite generally. Certainly the conceptual demands of doctrinal legal argument will remain an ever-present subtext throughout the rest of these materials.

The next chapters build on this introduction, therefore, but they add two further themes. First, they begin a systematic study of a specific area of substantive law, namely the status of expectation damages as the preferred remedy for breach of contract. They identify and explain the legal doctrines that implement this preference, describing how a plaintiff's contractual expectations are calculated and the doctrinal limits that exist on a plaintiff's capacity to recover his full expectations. Second, they present one of the core extra-doctrinal arguments in favor of the law's preference for expectation damages—the argument that the expectation remedy, both abstractly and as it is administered in the law, is economically efficient.

After this detailed survey of the legal preference for expectation damages is complete, the first part of the book will conclude by reconsidering alternatives to the expectation remedy. This conclusion will once again emphasize conceptual analysis, and it will ask whether the standard, expectation-centric account of contract remedies that the coming chapters develop is in fact the most accurate one.

CHAPTER 2

ECONOMIC EFFICIENCY

The discussion of *Sullivan v. O'Connor* emphasized that there is an *internal logic* to the administration of contract remedies, which answers to the conceptual and doctrinal structure of the several interests that contract remedies might protect. But the *Sullivan* opinion also illustrates that there is *judgment* involved in deciding which interest—expectation, reliance, restitution, or, for that matter, something else entirely—contract remedies should protect to begin with. The treatment of contract remedies below will emphasize this question of judgment (although it will also recur regularly to the internal logic of remedial doctrine), developing, as a case study, an extended argument about which remedy contract law should provide. That argument will come down in favor of the expectation remedy, suitably elaborated and modified. This is (as Restatement § 344 makes plain) the remedy that the law in fact prefers.

The argument will have an economic character—it will claim that the expectation remedy is economically efficient. The importance of this conclusion should not be overstated, of course. As the discussion in this chapter will reveal, economic efficiency should play only a limited role in policy-making or indeed in practical deliberations generally. For one thing, efficiency (in each of its several conceptions) is only an imperfect proxy for the ideal of overall welfare from which it derives its appeal. Moreover, even overall welfare is at best one value among many, and even efficient legal rules should be rejected if they offend too badly against justice, for example, or against other moral values. The economic focus of the treatment of contract remedies that follows should therefore not be taken as an endorsement of a single-mindedly economic approach to law—not even for the special case of contract law and certainly not for law in general.

Instead, it should be approached as a case study, designed to illustrate one among several methods of legal analysis, which sometimes converge and sometimes compete, and whose relative influence is always a contentious matter. The economic analysis of contract remedies provides an example of how a simple basic idea can organize and explain (albeit highly imperfectly) a wide, varied, and complex body of legal rules. This example is worth studying as an object lesson in law and economics. It also provides a useful introduction to interdisciplinary legal methods more generally, by illustrating what a successful interdisciplinary approach to law looks like.

In later pages, some of the alternatives to law and economics will themselves be illustrated through application to other parts of contract law. Occasionally, several methods will be applied to the same set of facts and doctrines, although generally direct confrontations between alternative approaches to law will be avoided. This is because the purpose of this introduction to contract law and legal method is not to argue in favor of one approach or against another, but rather to teach how each works, on its own terms.

2.1   WHY EFFICIENCY?

Later parts of these materials will propose that law establishes an intrinsically valuable form of joint life among the persons subject to it. According to this idea, law creates a public point of view in which citizens can share on free and equal terms. Contracts can be understood as establishing a similar shared perspective, and a similar form of respectful recognition, only now specifically among the parties who enter into them. The role of contract is a private analog to the public value of the rule of law.

But a more conventional thought holds that law is best understood as a tool or technique to be employed in producing human flourishing, understood in law-independent terms. According to this approach, law is best when those who live subject to it flourish most. Rather than being an end in itself, law (including the relation among persons of being governed by law) is just a means to other ends.

This is, once again, a conventional way to understand law. But it butts up, almost at once, against substantial problems in application. Perhaps the greatest of these problems, at least with respect to the instrumental study of law in open, pluralist societies, concerns how to adjudicate among the several conceptions of human flourishing adopted by those who live under a legal order. It is one thing for law to be used as a tool for promoting a single, dominant, religious or ethical creed, as in a totalitarian legal system. It is quite another for law to be used to promote the aggregate of the many competing values and ideals of the several citizens of a cosmopolitan state. In the first case, the measure of success could hardly be clearer, in the second, it could hardly be muddier.

This problem naturally led those interested in social engineering in pluralist societies to try to develop a metric for aggregating the flourishing of the subjects in such societies without having to resolve their ideological disputes about in what such flourishing consists. One prominent approach to this task has been to take a subjective attitude towards flourishing— replacing the question what ends persons ought to pursue in order to live well with the question how successfully persons are pursuing the ends that they have set themselves, whatever these are. Put crassly, flourishing consists, on this view, not in achieving the right thing but in getting what one wants.[1]

---

1. This formulation masks many difficulties, of course, and some objective elements must surely creep back into the argument. To pick just one familiar example, it is difficult to accept that a thirsty person who believes a glass of bleach to be of water promotes her flourishing by drinking it. As soon as this is accepted, it becomes inevitable that conditions

The turn away from substantive ideals and towards preference satisfaction promises to avoid the quagmire of resolving moral pluralism on the merits. Whether it actually achieves this promise is another matter. Persons in the grip of substantive moral ideals will tend to think that they prefer certain outcomes because the outcomes are valuable and not, as the preference-satisfaction view suggests, that the outcomes are valuable because preferred. Indeed, they will often consider the very suggestion that their preferences might underwrite the value of their values a direct affront against those values. Sidestepping moral disagreement is not so easy, as the substantive disputes tend doggedly to reassert themselves.

The turn towards preference satisfaction suffers another difficulty besides this one. Even if preference-satisfaction can in principle sustain an accommodation among competing moral creeds without resolving the disputes among them, it remains difficult to *combine* persons' many individual satisfactions and frustrations into an overall measure of aggregate satisfaction, for a society taken as a whole. Persons ascribe different degrees of importance to their different preferences. And certain preferences (for sweet food, for example) are easier to satisfy than others (say, for artistic creation). The former fact makes it difficult to come up with an a single metric of overall preference satisfaction even within a person, and the latter makes it virtually impossible to come up with a metric that can compare overall preference satisfaction across persons. Any successful measure of aggregate social satisfaction must, of course, do both things.

The conceptions of economic efficiency presented below might be understood, among other ways, as efforts to come up with a measure of overall social preference-satisfaction, or at least of comparing the aggregate satisfaction in different states of the world, that avoids the difficulties described above. The economic analysis of law aspires, in this way, to measure a law's instrumental success in a pluralist world and thus to compare the overall appeal of various legal rules that might possibly be adopted.

Economic efficiency achieves this result by sidestepping many of the deeper questions of value that moral pluralism raises. Some of the criticisms of the efficiency analysis of law that will be presented below involve the reassertion of these questions against the economic program of avoidance. Just how far the avoidance can succeed even in the face of the recalcitrance of normative complexity remains an open question. But whatever that question's ultimate answer, it is quite clear that economics succeeds sufficiently, at least in the minds of many, to make the economic analysis of law worth studying.[2]

---

will be imposed on the rationality of preferences before their satisfaction will be taken to constitute flourishing. It turns out to be difficult to elaborate these conditions without turning to substantive ideas about in what flourishing consists—about what outcomes it is rational for a person to want. And this re-introduces an objective component into even the most insistently subjective account of flourishing as preference-satisfaction.

2.   For more on economic efficiency, see MATTHEW ADLER, WELL-BEING AND FAIR DISTRIBUTION (2012); RICHARD MARKOVITS, TRUTH OR ECONOMICS (2008).

2.2   PARETO EFFICIENCY

It is important to begin the economic analysis of contract law (and indeed of law generally) with a clear account of what economic efficiency is. Understanding this will also be important, of course, to balancing economic efficiency against other values that the law might promote, in order to decide how important economic efficiency is for the law, all-things-considered.

Formally speaking, efficiency is a property of allocations of resources. Such allocations are efficient if, in the relevant respect, they cannot be improved. Often, claims are made for the efficiency not of allocations of resources but rather of legal rules. Such claims should be understood to say that the adoption of the efficient legal rules will usher in efficient allocations of resources.

There exist several conceptions of economic efficiency. The simplest and least controversial is *Pareto efficiency*. An allocation of resources is said to be Pareto efficient if it is such that no person could be made better off without also making someone else worse off. An allocation is not Pareto efficient if someone could be made better off without making anyone else worse off, or, as is sometimes said, if a Pareto improvement is possible. To fix ideas, imagine distributing one dollar across two people. An allocation in which one person gets 40 cents and the other gets 60 cents is Pareto efficient; an allocation in which one person gets 20 cents and the other gets 70 cents (with 10 cents thrown away) is not.

Pareto efficiency is for two reasons more or less uncontroversially desirable. First, a Pareto improvement harms no one (at least when harm is measured against the base-line of the Pareto-inefficient state). Generally, no one will object to improvements towards Pareto efficiency. Second, Pareto efficiency can be applied (assessments of Pareto efficiency can be made) without making any interpersonal comparisons of human flourishing or even welfare. Only within-person comparisons are required to identify Pareto efficient allocations or to see how to improve on Pareto inefficient allocations. This makes Pareto efficiency attractive to people who are skeptical about interpersonal comparisons, either because they believe that people's flourishing or welfare cannot be measured sufficiently reliably to make interpersonal comparisons or because they believe that interpersonal comparisons of flourishing or welfare are, strictly speaking, impossible or even incoherent.

But the spareness of the Paretian conception of efficiency suffers an important drawback also. It establishes only a partial ordering among allocations, which makes Pareto efficiency too indeterminate to be of much use in legal analysis.

Thus there will generally exist many possible Pareto efficient allocations, and the Pareto criterion supports no way of choosing among them. The earlier example, involving dividing a dollar between two people, illustrates this point. Figure 2.1 below presents a graphical depiction of the example.

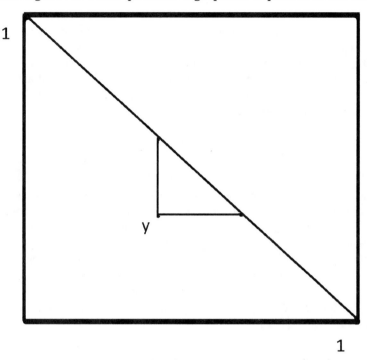

Figure 2.1

Pareto Efficient Allocations of a Dollar Between Two People

All allocations that pay out the entire dollar are Pareto superior over all allocations that leave some money undistributed. But these allocations—the 40–60 allocation contemplated earlier, a 60–40 allocation, a 50–50 allocation, and indeed an allocation in which either person gets the entire dollar and the other gets nothing—are all equally Pareto efficient. No matter how equal or unequal the allocations, as long as the entire dollar is distributed, no person can be made better off (by giving her more money) without making the other worse off (by taking money away). Only allocations that leave money on the table—for example, the allocation represented by point y in the figure—allow for Pareto improvements. These are the allocations that lie above and to the right of the inefficient allocation, as illustrated by the triangle in the figure. Opportunities for Pareto improvement end at the Pareto frontier.

The distributive properties of these allocations—which all belong to the set often called the Pareto frontier—are very different. Some are egalitarian, for example, whereas others are radically inegalitarian, and in opposite directions.

Moreover, most choices among legal rules—including choices among legal rules that all achieve the Pareto frontier—have distributive implications very like those in the example. A simple example—more realistic than the divide-the-dollar game—illustrates the point.

Imagine that a person lives next door to a factory, which must make substantial noise in order to produce its output. Suppose that the noise disturbs the homeowner, imposing a cost on him. Say that the cost is $100, in the sense that the homeowner would pay up to $100 to silence the noise, but no more. (To keep matters simple, suppose that the noise does not disturb anyone associated with the factory, say because it is projected out of the factory building and so cannot be heard by the employees.) Now imagine that a noise damper is invented, which eliminates the noise at a cost of $50. Employing the damper thus generates a gain of $50—the difference between the most that the homeowner will pay to eliminate the noise and the cost of using the damper to do so.

The gain entails that the damper creates the possibility of a Pareto improvement, or (put the other way around) that leaving the damper unused is not Pareto efficient. To make the Pareto improvement, the homeowner must pay the factory anywhere between $50.01 and $99.99 to install the damper. Any payment in this range leaves both parties better off. It leaves the homeowner better off because he receives silence worth $100 to him for less than $100. And it leaves the factory—really its owner—better off because she receives more than $50 to install a damper that costs her only $50.

But the Pareto criterion cannot select among the various payments between $50.01 and $99.99. How much (within this range) the homeowner pays the factory in effect determines how the surplus created by the installation of the damper is distributed. And, as in the case of splitting the dollar, all the divisions of this surplus—representing all payments between $50.01 and $99.99—are Pareto incomparable.

Finally, most legal rules or government policies are quite different from both the divide-the-dollar problem and the installation of the damper, in that they make some people better off and others worse off. The problem of the homeowner, the factory, and the damper illustrates this also.

The problem has been presented in a posture in which the factory's entitlement to make noise is unquestioned, so that factory may simply refuse to install the damper. This ensures that the invention of the damper cannot make the factory worse off. In order to get the damper installed, the homeowner must pay, and must pay enough so that the factory benefits (or at least is made whole) net of installation costs. Of course, the homeowner will not pay more than the silence is worth to him, so he also cannot be made worse off by the invention of the damper.

But suppose, plausibly, that the homeowner wants silence without paying for it, or at least without paying for it extraordinarily and directly. Suppose that the homeowner takes the view that as long as the costs of silence are reasonable (we will return presently to what this might mean), they should not all fall on him, just because he happens to live next to the factory. Rather, these costs should be distributed more broadly, perhaps across all of the factory's owners, employees, and customers. Finally, suppose that the law agrees and gives the homeowner a right to insist (without paying) that the factory take reasonable measures to silence the noise produced by its operations.

Given the costs and benefits of the damper in this story, it seems plausible to say that the damper is a reasonable means of noise-reduction. Accordingly, the factory would, under the legal order just described, be required to install it. But the installation would now no longer involve a Pareto improvement. The homeowner would be made better off, and the factory worse off. If one is inclined to favor installing the damper (and indeed to favor the law requiring installation) nevertheless, then this may be because—in some for the moment rough and intuitive sense—the benefits that the damper gives the homeowner exceed the burdens that it imposes on the factory.

One might even say, in light of this balance of benefit and burden, that requiring the damper is efficient. But this remains for the moment a purely intuitive and far from rigorous idea. It is therefore natural—both in theory and in connection with more practical legal applications—to want a conception of efficiency that yields more determinate results than the Pareto criterion can do.

2.3 MONETIZED CONCEPTIONS OF EFFICIENCY

Because of the drawbacks of the Pareto conception—both in general and as they become more pronounced in connection with specifically legal analysis—most economic analyses of law employ very different conceptions of economic efficiency. These conceptions abandon the effort to do without interpersonal comparisons of flourishing or well-being and instead elaborate efficiency in a way that constructs a total ordering of allocations, based on monetized assessments of the flourishing that these allocations produce. According to these conceptions, a redistribution increases the efficiency of an allocation if the dollar value of the gains conferred on those whom the redistribution benefits exceeds the dollar value of the losses that the redistribution imposes on those whom it burdens.

Implementing this intuitive idea in a systematic and rigorous way turns out to be surprisingly difficult. The traditional approach to making this monetized conception of efficiency operational employs something called the *Kaldor–Hicks* test. According to this test, a shift from one allocation to another (or a legal rule that engenders this shift) improves efficiency if those who benefit from the shift would be able, hypothetically, to buy out those who suffer under it. Stated a little more precisely, a legal rule is efficient under the Kaldor–Hicks test if the maximum amount that the beneficiaries of the rule could pay to acquire the benefits that the rule extends them (and still be better off all-told) exceeds the minimum that the victims of the rule would have to be paid in order to accept the losses that the rule imposes on them (and not be worse off all-told).[3]

The example involving the homeowner and factory illustrates the test in operation. Recall that in its last iteration, the possibility arose of a rule requiring the factory to install the noise damper, where reasonable, even without receiving any payment from the homeowner. Such a requirement would leave the factory worse off even as it left the homeowner better off, and so could not possibly create a Pareto improvement. But it seemed, intuitively, that the requirement would nevertheless be efficient, roughly speaking because the burden that the damper imposed on the factory ($50) was smaller than the benefit that it conferred on the homeowner ($100). The Kaldor–Hicks test renders this intuition articulate and precise. The maximum that the beneficiary of the legal rule—the homeowner—is willing to pay to receive the rule's benefits (namely $100) exceeds the minimum that the rule's victim—the factory—would have to be paid to accept it (namely $50). The rule is thus efficient, *never mind that the payments are never actually made*. Indeed, the noise-reduction rule in the example might be interpreted in a way that ensures its efficiency. Recall that the statement of the rule referred to *reasonable* means of procuring silence, where the meaning of reasonable was left unclear. If reasonable is taken to mean efficient—that is, Kaldor–Hicks improving—then the legal rule, by construction, secures efficient noise-reduction.

The Kaldor–Hicks test imposes a more complete ordering on allocations, which makes it possible to say that every shift from one allocation to another either improves or decreases efficiency.[4] Moreover, the Kaldor–Hicks test makes it relatively straightforward to say when efficiency is increased or decreased, simply by asking the persons who are affected by the shift. This makes the Kaldor–Hicks test well-suited for practical applications, including legal analysis.

In spite of these advantages, the Kaldor–Hicks test, and indeed every such monetized conception of efficiency, suffers two important principled drawbacks. These drawbacks make Kaldor–Hicks efficiency an at best unreliable guide to all-things-considered judgments of the desirability of legal rules.

First, although the monetized conception of efficiency carries more distributive content than the Pareto conception of efficiency, the concep-

---

3. The Kaldor–Hicks test is often stated in terms of willingness to pay for rules and willingness to accept them. This is fine, so long as it is understood that holdouts and other strategic demands for payment must be ignored in assessing willingness.

4. This is not quite true. One source of incompleteness will be explored more closely below in connection with something called the Scitovsky paradox.

A second, although not especially important, source of incompleteness may be mentioned now. It is always possible that the beneficiaries and victims of a reallocation place identical, although opposite, values on the shift, in which case it will neither increase nor decrease Kaldor–Hicks efficiency. But this is nothing like as great a drawback as the prospect of Pareto-incomparability imposes on the Pareto conception. It will almost never happen that two distributions are equivalently Kaldor–Hicks in this way, whereas it very commonly happens that two distributions are Pareto incomparable.

tion's treatment of distributive concerns will remain unsatisfactory to many friends of equality. Most narrowly, the test does not contemplate that the imagined buyouts or transfers are actually taken from the beneficiaries and given to the victims of a redistribution. Instead, these amounts are notional only, so that improvements in efficiency can (and generally do) generate significant winners and losers—significant departures from the distributive status quo.[5] More generally, the monetized conception of efficiency incorporates a relatively weak conception of equality, which philosophers sometimes call *marginalist*. Thus, the monetized conception of efficiency treats all people equally in that it counts all of their valuations equally as contributions, on the margin, to the aggregate of gains and losses that determines what efficiency requires.[6] By contrast many people are attracted to what philosophers sometimes call *prioritarian* conceptions of equality, according to which those persons who bear the greatest burdens, or who are worst off absolutely, receive the greatest consideration. A simple example illustrates this difference (and the counterintuitive implications of the monetized approach to efficiency): a legal rule that imposes burdens valued at $100 each by 10 people who are already poor in order to grant benefits valued at $1 each by 1001 people who are already rich is Kaldor–Hicks efficient. But it hardly seems equal, fair, or indeed desirable.

Second, a dependence on money valuations of benefits and burdens—which are based, moreover, on winners' and losers' individual preferences—causes the monetized conception of efficiency to depart from the idea of utility-maximization, which gives it its most natural moral foundation. Not all people are equally effective converters of money into flourishing—so the fact that one person is willing to pay more for a benefit than another does not guarantee that the benefit will contribute more to the success (or even to the well-being) of the first than the second. Accordingly, a conception of efficiency that—like the orthodox Kaldor–Hicks test—maximizes money-valuation will not necessarily maximize aggregate flourishing, as utilitarianism (say) recommends.

Moreover, the departures from utilitarianism on which Kaldor–Hicks efficiency embarks will likely have disturbing distributive (and not just aggregate) implications. Differences in people's money-valuations of benefits and burdens will generally track their wealth, so that at every level of benefit the rich will generally be willing to pay more for policies than the

---

5. The fact that the victims of a redistribution are not actually paid compensation highlights that although the Kaldor–Hicks test is often couched in terms of willingness to accept, redistributions that are deemed efficient may be (and indeed often are) *imposed* on people. When this occurs, it may require a re-valuation of a policy's benefits and burdens. The amount that a person would have to be paid in order voluntarily to accept a burden may be different from the amount that she would have to be paid to make her whole after the burden is imposed on her, without her consent. Often (although perhaps not always) the second amount will be greater than the first.

6. Even this is an improvement over the Pareto criterion, whose sole egalitarian commitment is to treating each person's flourishing as a good in the overall calculus of efficiency rather than as neutral or even as a bad. Pareto efficiency has no conception of treating different people's flourishing as equally good, because it makes no interpersonal comparisons of flourishing at all.

poor, simply because they have more to pay. Monetized tests of efficiency therefore tend to favor the rich and to have less concern for the poor in ways that would be rejected not just by prioritarian conceptions of equality but also by the utilitarian conception of equality with which efficiency shares its marginalist structure.

In spite of these shortcomings, the economic analysis of contract remedies that follows will implicitly adopt Kaldor–Hicks of efficiency. The deepest objection to pursuing a monetized conception of efficiency—the objection based on prioritarian intuitions about equality—invokes a moral ideal that represents one side of one of the central disputes in contemporary moral philosophy. It is not reasonable to require adjacent fields to settle every philosophical dispute that they bring into play before proceeding to address their own concerns. To do so would be, in effect, to demand that every thinker become, first, a philosopher. Moreover, many of the distributive objections that may be raised (at every level) against pursuing a monetized conception of economic efficiency have only limited relevance in the special circumstances of contract law.[7] Contractual obligations, after all, are voluntarily assumed (at least in the core cases), and their substantive content varies according to the will of the parties who assume them. This bolsters the case for rendering contract *law* efficient, because the parties to particular contracts can always adjust the distributive effects of legal rules by varying the substance—most obviously, the price term—of the contractual obligations that they assume. An efficient contract law simply maximizes the surplus that is available for the parties to a contract to divide, leaving the distribution of the surplus up to the parties. Indeed, as the analysis of the unconscionability doctrine in Chapter 24 will explain, it is often (although not always) the case that introducing distributive considerations directly into contract doctrine harms the very people who are the source of the distributive concern. Finally, insofar as the parties to contracts are organizations (and in particular economic firms with highly diversified shareholders), distributive considerations become anyway less compelling, because the organizations are not in themselves appropriate objects for distributive concern, and the shareholders, being highly diversified, will tend to be equally benefited and burdened by any attempted redistribution.

None of this, of course, is to deny that a person might reasonably find economic efficiency (especially in its monetized conception) a singularly uncompelling value. The economic approach to law, including to contract law, will not appeal to all tastes, nor should it. But this does not distinguish the economic approach from the other approaches that will figure, at various places, in these pages. Once again, the purpose of the investigation of legal methods that these pages pursue is not to judge the methods on display— and certainly not to judge them against one another—but rather to display their internal workings, in order to open multiple pathways into the complex and various practice that constitutes the law.

---

7. Here a helpful contrast is to the application—through the practice of cost-benefit analysis—of a monetized conception of efficiency to administrative law. In this context, the distributive objections take center stage.

CHAPTER 3

THE EFFICIENCY OF EXPECTATION DAMAGES—THE CORE ARGUMENT

The central idea in the economic case for the expectation remedy is that this remedy uniquely gives the parties to contracts incentives to act efficiently throughout the creation and administration of their contractual obligations: as they choose with whom to contract, fix the terms of their contracts, perform according to these terms, and respond to breaches. The materials that follow will illustrate the economic argument by explaining how the expectation remedy, suitably developed, provides efficient incentives in each of these contexts. The argument will, of course, be an illustration only. It will make no effort to be either extensively or intensively exhaustive: that is, it will make no effort to address every facet of contractual practice or even to consider every complication that informs even the limited aspects of contract that it does address. Nevertheless, the argument will consider enough elements of contracting and contract law to show how a spare economic principle—the principle of efficiency—may be applied to organize and explain a rich and various body of legal rules.

This project will begin by considering the efficiency implications of contract remedies for the promisor's decision whether to perform her contract or to breach it, elaborating the theory of efficient breach that is economic analysis's most famous contribution to contract law. Throughout the discussion of efficient breach, as indeed throughout all of this chapter, promisors will be sellers and will be referred to by the female pronouns (she, her), while promisees will be buyers, referred to by the male pronouns (he, his). This is, of course, an expository technique only, which serves to render otherwise confusing and boring recitations of fact patterns clearer and less repetitive.

3.1 THE PERFORM–OR–BREACH DECISION (WITH A DIGRESSION CONCERNING THE COASE THEOREM)

The first result that the economic analysis of contract remedies establishes is that only perfectly compensatory expectation damages provide sellers with an incentive to breach their contracts when and only when it is efficient for them to do so. This is the famous theory of efficient breach.

The idea of efficient breach, and its distinctive connection to the expectation remedy, may be illustrated and explained by reference to an example. Imagine that a seller, S, has sold her car to a buyer, B_1, for $9,000 dollars. Suppose that B_1 values the car at \$10,500, in the sense that he would find it worthwhile to pay up to \$10,500 for the car, but not a penny more. Now imagine that a second buyer, B_2, appears to the seller but remains unknown to B_1 (more on this factor in a moment). Suppose that in some cases B_2 values the car at \$10,000, and in other cases B_2 values the car at \$11,000.

Efficiency requires that the car be possessed by B_1 rather than B_2 when B_2's valuation is only \$10,000 and that the car be possessed by B_2 rather than B_1 when B_2's valuation is \$11,000. That is, efficiency requires that the car be possessed, in each case, by the person who values it most highly. This is a direct application of the monetized conception of efficiency: for any redistribution of the car from a lower to a higher valuer, the maximum that the person receiving the car would pay to get it exceeds the minimum that the person losing the car would have to be paid to give it up. The remedy rule imposed by contract law will influence efficiency, in this case, because it fixes what will happen to S should she choose to breach her contract and deliver the car to B_2 rather than to B_1.

Now if what economists call *ex post transactions costs*[1]—the costs associated with re-transferring the car between B_1 and B_2 once S has delivered it to whomever she chooses—are low enough (and especially if they are zero), then the efficient result will be achieved no matter what remedy rule contract law adopts. B_2 and B_1 will arrange for the car to end up in the hands of the higher valuer no matter where S initially delivers it. If S performs, delivering the car to B_1, even though B_2 values the car at \$11,000, then B_1 and B_2 will arrange for a subsequent resale at a price somewhere between \$10,500 and \$11,000, because this sale will leave them both better off. And if S breaches, delivering the car to B_2, even though B_2 values the car at only \$10,000, B_2 and B_1 will again arrange for a subsequent resale, this time at a price somewhere between \$10,000 and \$10,500, which will again leave both better off.

Moreover, if *ex ante transactions costs*[2]—the costs associated with replacing whatever remedy rules the law selects as a general matter with an alternative rule that the parties prefer—are low enough (and again, especially if they are zero), then the efficient result will again be achieved no matter what remedy rule the law adopts, as long only as the law's remedy rule remains a mere default, which the parties may change by agreement, rather than a mandatory rule that the parties may not alter.[3]

---

1. These are called *ex post* because they arise after the initial contract was made. In this case, they prominently include the costs—search costs, inspection costs, sales taxes—associated with contracting and performing a second sale between the two buyers.

2. These are called *ex ante* because they arise before the initial contract was made, typically in the conceiving of and completing the contract. In this case they prominently include the costs—especially of identifying and agreeing on the appropriate rule to replace the default remedy—associated with negotiating and drafting the contract.

3. One might (from the narrow perspective of efficiency) think of a mandatory legal rule as nothing more than a species of transactions cost whose size is fixed by the cost of evading the rule.

This is because any inefficient default remedy will be replaced, by the parties, with the efficient alternative.

This style of reasoning was first adopted by Ronald Coase, who famously argued that when transactions costs are zero (and certain other ideal conditions regarding the rationality and knowledge of the parties are satisfied[4]), then the eventual allocation of resources will be efficient no matter what legal rule is adopted as a default. The general idea behind this result—called the Coase Theorem—is illustrated in the example. When transactions costs are zero, people will bargain in the shadow of and even around legal rules until resources fall into the hands of the person who values them most highly (so that an efficient allocation has been reached). There will always be benefits to such bargains, and because they are costless (transactions costs being zero) they will always be struck and performed. One might say, speaking colloquially, that resources have a natural tendency to float upwards, to their highest valuers, and that as long as there are no transactions costs to keep them down, they will float all the way to the surface—that is, to an efficient allocation.

It is important to be careful and clear about exactly what the Coase Theorem does and does not entail. Two confusions in particular must be avoided. First, the Coase Theorem addresses efficiency only and not distribution. Even when transactions costs are zero, legal rules will continue to have distributional effects. This is illustrated, in fact, by the example involving the car. Even when *ex post* transactions costs are zero, so that subsequent transfers between B_1 and B_2 will ensure an efficient allocation of the car no matter where S delivers it, remedy rules will have distributional implications as between S and B_1. In particular, a rule establishing the expectation remedy will allow S, if confronted by a B_2 who values the car more highly than B_1, to capture some of the surplus that this higher valuation represents. By contrast, a remedy rule that requires S to deliver the car to B_1 regardless of how much B_2 offers—a rule, as lawyers say, that requires specific performance of the initial sales contract—will allow B_1 to capture some of the surplus associated with a higher-valuing B_2. This result will be demonstrated presently (and some complications will be considered). For now, a simple intuition is enough. A higher valuing B_2 represents an offer to buy at a price that exceeds B_1's valuation: the expectation remedy allows S to accept this offer and pay B_1 damages that reflect only his lower valuation; a rule requiring specific performance requires S to forsake this gain and allows B_1 to realize it instead.

The second confusion regarding the Coase Theorem involves the distinction between the efficiency of an allocation and the actual, physical deployment of resources that the allocation represents. Although the Coase Theorem entails that (when there are no transactions costs, etc.) the

---

4. These other conditions may of course themselves be conceived of in terms of there being zero transactions costs—perfect rationality, for example, may be thought of as referring to a state of mind in which perfectly accurate judgments are formed without any effort or investment. This is just to say that what is understood as a transactions cost and what counts as a departure from some other ideal condition is in general simply a matter of convention.

allocation of resources will be efficient no matter what the legal rule, it does *not* entail that the physical deployment resources will be *the same* no matter what the legal rule. If the distributional effects of a legal rule are large, then these may give rise to wealth effects (changes in willingness to pay brought on by changes in wealth, like those that arose in connection with the discussion of efficiency and the Kaldor–Hicks test) that change what physical deployment of resources is efficient (even as they do not prevent the efficient allocation, whatever it turns out to be, from being reached). This feature of the Coase Theorem, and the distinction between the physical deployment of resources in an allocation and the allocation's economic efficiency that underlies it, is not easy to grasp. It is best approached through an example, and the simplest examples involve not contract but tort.

Therefore, imagine once again, that a factory and a house stand side-by-side. The operation of the factory makes noise, which disturbs the homeowner. Tort law must decide whether or not the disturbance makes the noise a nuisance.

Now consider again two possible legal rules—two nuisance doctrines—that might govern the relationship between the factory and homeowner: under the first rule, the noise is not a nuisance and the factory has the right to operate and make the noise; under the second, the noise does constitute a nuisance and the homeowner has the right to quiet, and so to prevent the factory from operating. The Coase Theorem says that if transactions costs are zero, etc., then the tradeoff between factory production and quiet will be made efficiently no matter which legal rule is adopted. If the production is worth more to the factory than the quiet is worth to the homeowner, then the factory will buy out the homeowner in case she has the right to quiet. And so the efficient result will be reached notwithstanding an (initially inefficient) entitlement in the homeowner. Alternatively, if quiet is worth more to the homeowner than production is worth to the factory, then the homeowner will buy out the factory in case it has the right to operate. And so the efficient result will again be reached notwithstanding an (initially inefficient) entitlement in the factory.

So far, so good—the example simply illustrates (again) that when transactions costs are zero, the parties will bargain around inefficient legal rules to reach an efficient ultimate allocation of resources. But now focus on the distributional consequences of the choice of legal rule in this case. More specifically, note that the homeowner will be richer if she has the right to quiet than she will be if the factory has the right to operate and make noise: in the former case, she will have the choice between enjoying quiet for free and being paid to endure noise; in the second case, she will have to pay to enjoy quiet or endure noise without compensation.

Suppose, then, that the factory works in two shifts—day and night. Imagine further (and plausibly) that if the factory has the right to operate and make noise, then the homeowner cares enough about her sleep to pay the factory to abandon the night-shift. This payment leaves the homeowner in need of money—so much so that she spends little time at home (she works all the time) and must lead a spare material existence even when she is home. Accordingly, it is not worthwhile for her, given her depleted wealth and its effects on her lifestyle, to pay the factory to remain silent during the day. The result of the legal rule that the factory may operate in spite of making noise, therefore, is that the factory operates in the day but not at night. This result is efficient.

But now suppose that the opposite legal rule is in place—that the homeowner has a right to quiet. In this case, the homeowner may silence the factory at night for free and the factory (suppose) does not value production highly enough to buy her off. Moreover, even when she insists on quiet at night (and so receives no payments from the factory) the homeowner possesses more money than she did under the rule giving the factory the right to operate (she still saves what she had to pay for nighttime quiet under that other rule). She therefore works a little less and furnishes her home more extravagantly, perhaps buying a fancy stereo. But now she spends more time at home and, moreover, values quiet when she is home more highly (she likes hearing her stereo). If fact, she may now enjoy her days listening to music so much that the factory cannot profitably buy her off even during the day. Accordingly, the result of the legal rule giving the homeowner a right to quiet is that the factory will never operate and make noise, neither at night nor in the day. Once again, this result is efficient.

The example therefore illustrates that the Coase Theorem entails only that (when transactions costs are zero, etc.) the eventual allocation of resources will be efficient no matter what legal rule is adopted, and not that it will always be the same. The example also illustrates the reason for this: because legal rules can have distributive effects, they can influence the values that people place on various resources, and therefore the bargains that they strike on the route to achieving an efficient allocation, and finally the physical deployment of resources that this efficient allocation involves.[5]

Now return specifically to contracts and to the expectation remedy and the example involving the sale of the car. Recall that S has contracted to sell the car to B_1 for $9,000, and that B_1 values the car at $10,500. Finally, recall that B_2 appears (to S but not to B_1) and values the car at either $10,000 or $11,000. The Coase Theorem entails that when transactions

---

5. A further structural limit of Kaldor–Hicks efficiency is vividly illustrated by the example in the main text. It is impossible—in the sense of incoherent or not strictly meaningful—to compare the efficiency of the following two states: (1) the factory has the right to make noise and so the homeowner and factory bargain for the factory to operate in the day but not at night; and (2) the homeowner has the right to quiet and so the homeowner and factory bargain for the factory to remain closed both night and day. These two states cannot be compared because, by allocating the entitlement with respect to noise differently, they fix the wealth of the parties' differently and hence establish different (and incompatible) baselines against which the parties' preferences are set. So the states (1) and (2) are quite literally Kaldor–Hicks incompatible.

But it remains natural to ask which is better or preferable. Indeed that is in a sense the central policy question raised by the example (at least once Coasean bargains have all settled out). Utilitarianism could give an answer, if it were confident of interpersonal comparisons of utility. Any number of other value frameworks can give an answer also. But economic efficiency, at least on the Kaldor–Hicks model, cannot.

costs are zero, the efficient result (delivery of the car to B_2 if he values it at $11,000 but not if he values it at $10,000) will be achieved regardless of the remedy rule that governs S's contract with B_1.

But suppose that transactions costs are not low enough. Specifically, suppose that the transactions costs that arise *ex post*, in conjunction with transferring the car between B_1 and B_2, after S has delivered the car to whichever buyer she chooses, exceed $500. (One way to capture this is by saying that B_2 appears to S but not to B_1, which is in effect to say that transactions costs between B_1 and B_2 are infinite.) In these circumstances, a high-valuing B_2 will not be able profitably to buy the car from B_1 should S deliver it to him, and B_1 will not be able profitably to buy the car from a low valuing B_2, should S deliver it to him. In each case, the transactions costs generated by the resale exceed the difference in value attributed to the car by the parties to the potential resale.

Accordingly, when *ex post* (buyer-buyer) transactions costs are high enough, a remedy rule that determines whether S performs her contract and delivers the car to B_1 or, instead, breaches and delivers the car to B_2 will have consequences for efficiency. The several potential buyers cannot, given the transactions costs that they face, afford to correct any inefficient allocation that the remedy rule encourages S to make.

Efficiency in a transactions costly world therefore requires a remedy rule that induces sellers to breach their contracts and desert promisees in favor of alternative buyers when and only when the alternative buyers value the contractual performance more highly than the original promisees. The first result in the economic argument in favor of the expectation remedy is that only expectation damages generate precisely these efficient incentives.

This is easy to illustrate by further pursuing the example involving the seller of the car and the two prospective buyers.

Consider first a remedy rule that requires breaching sellers to pay disappointed promisees damages that exceed their contractual expectations—say, that equal twice these expectations. B_1's expectation under the contract with S is the difference between his private valuation of the car and the price that the contract set him to pay for it—that is ($10,500—$9,000), which equals $1,500. Twice B_1's expectation is therefore $3,000, which is what S would have to pay B_1 in case she breached. Given this remedial obligation, S will breach in response only to an offer that exceeds the contract price by more than $3,000—an offer, that is, of $12,000 or more. (Accepting any lower offer would leave S worse off, after paying the $3,000 in damages to B_1, than she would be if she simply transferred the car to B_1 as promised.) But alternative buyers who value the car more highly than B_1 but at less than $12,000 (including the high valuing B_2 in the example) will be unable profitably to make offers above $12,000, and therefore will fail to acquire the car. They will be unable to buy the car, moreover, even though efficiency clearly recommends that they should possess the car in preference over B_1. Remedies in excess of expectation damages—super-compensatory remedies, as lawyers sometimes call them—therefore create incentives for sellers to inefficiently fail to breach.

Second, consider a remedial rule that requires breaching sellers to pay disappointed promisees damages that fall below their contractual expectations—say, that equal half these expectations. Since B_1's expectation is, once again, $1,500, this remedy rule would require a breaching S to pay only $750 in damages. Given this remedial obligation, S will breach in response to any offer that exceeds the contract price by $750 or more—any offer, that is, greater than $9,750. Now alternative buyers who value the car less highly than B_1 but at greater than $9,750 (including the low valuing B_2 in the example) will be able profitably to make offers large enough to acquire the car. They will be able to buy the car, moreover, although efficiency clearly recommends that B_1 should possess the car in their stead. Remedies below expectation damages—sub-compensatory remedies—therefore create incentives for sellers inefficiently to breach.

These two cases, of course, serve merely to illustrate a point: they do not constitute a formal proof. But the illustration makes it intuitively clear that when *ex post* transactions costs are high, expectation damages are distinctive in that they both induce all efficient breaches and eliminate all inefficient breaches. Accordingly, the only remedy rule that will encourage breach when and only when breaching is efficient is the expectation remedy. Under this rule, a seller will profit from breaching when and only when her new buyer values performance sufficiently highly to be able to pay a price that exceeds her original buyer's valuation.

Finally, this argument may be recharacterized in a way that intuitively tracks the real-world circumstances in which sellers are tempted to breach in response to offers made by alternative buyers (by B_2s). Super-compensatory remedies, it was observed earlier (and the example reveals), have the effect of transferring some of the gain from an efficient breach from sellers to buyers. Of course, this transfer will not come free to the buyer; instead, sellers will respond by charging a higher price up front. This result will soon be illustrated through a concrete example, but it may be rendered intuitive even without the example. In effect, a super-compensatory remedy imposes on the contract a trade between the seller and buyer in which the seller relinquishes a larger but uncertain gain (the full benefit generated by a possible efficient breach) and receives a smaller but certain gain (the rise in the contract price) and the buyer makes the opposite exchange.

A super-compensatory remedy therefore shifts risk from the seller to the buyer. Furthermore, since it is much more likely that the prospect for an efficient breach will arise in response to the seller's business activities than in response to any activity by the buyer, the risk that is transferred is in effect a business risk of the seller. This insight makes it possible to characterize the super-compensatory remedy in a new way, by revealing that it effectively ties to the buyer's purchase of the good an investment, by the buyer, in the seller's business. And while a general shifting of risk from the seller to the buyer may be efficient if the buyer has a greater tolerance for risk than the seller, there is no reason to think it efficient for the risk transfer to take the form of this coupling of purchasing and investing. It will surely be more efficient to decouple the two transactions and to allow the seller to sell her stock apart from her product and the buyer to buy as much of each as he wishes, given prices. This is what the expectation remedy achieves. Moreover, by achieving the decoupling, and giving sellers complete ownership of the business risk associated with drumming up possibilities for efficient breach, expectation damages give sellers the incentive to devote an efficient level of resources into discovering such opportunities.

And so the first claim in the economic analysis of contract remedies is established. When transactions costs (and in particular *ex post* transactions costs) are high enough, expectations damages are the uniquely efficient remedy with respect to promisors' perform-or-breach decisions.

3.2   THE SELECTION AND PRECAUTION DECISIONS

The Coase Theorem entails, once again, that if *ex ante* transactions costs are zero, then any default remedy rule will be efficient, in effect because parties for whom a particular rule is inefficient will be able (costlessly) to bargain around the rule, replacing it with an efficient alternative. (Such parties will, moreover, always have an incentive to make the replacement, because the efficient alternative will increase the total surplus associated with their transaction—that is just what efficiency means—and therefore increase both parties' shares of the surplus, whatever these shares are.) Of course, *ex ante* transactions costs are effectively never zero, and indeed are only rarely small. *Ex ante* transactions costs include the costs of identifying and understanding the infinitely many contingencies that can arise over the life of a contract and then negotiating how each of these contingencies will be managed and drafting contract language that gives effect to the outcomes of these negotiations. Such complete contracting is prohibitively costly even for sophisticated parties who contract over large sums, must less for unsophisticated parties whose contracts involve only relatively little money. Accordingly, many legal rules are sticky, or (to change metaphors) display inertia, even though they are styled merely as defaults. This is a reason for favoring efficient default rules.

The argument for the distinctive efficiency of the expectation remedy in connection with the perform-or-breach decision had to contend with a second possibility, however, namely that zero (or sufficiently low) *ex post* transactions costs might again allow parties to contract around (or, more specifically, to renegotiate) inefficient remedy rules—not during the making of the contracts but only much later, at the time of performance. In the example employed above—involving the sale, and potential resale, of a car—it seemed more than plausible that *ex post* transactions costs were sufficiently greater than zero to render renegotiation impracticable. (Indeed, the high costs of buying a used car—of inspecting it, registering it, and paying the sales tax—figure prominently in the narratives of everyday life.) But *ex post* transactions costs will not always be so high, and there is certainly no *ex post* counterpart to the general argument that *ex ante* transactions costs are too high to rely on the Coase Theorem to secure efficiency regardless of the rules that the law establishes as defaults. Renegotiations, after all, need not contemplate the myriad contingencies whose multiplicity bedevils *ex ante* negotiations, but can instead focus narrowly on such contingencies as actually arise and become relevant. (The discussion of mass-produced form contacts in Chapter 20 will revisit this phenomenon to give it a non-economic interpretation.) Accordingly, an argument for the distinctive efficiency of the expectation remedy that relies (as the argument concerning the perform-or-breach decision relied) on high *ex post* transactions costs will be, inevitably, insecure.

A broader case for the distinctive efficiency of the expectation remedy can be made, however, without relying on the assumption that *ex post* transactions costs are high. This is because the expectation remedy is distinctively efficient with respect to any number of decisions besides the perform-or-breach decision, which, unlike that decision, must be made before performance comes due—that is, *ex ante* rather than *ex post*. This point may be illustrated by considering the effects of remedy rules on two such decisions in particular—the selection decision and the precaution decision. Once again, expectation damages establish distinctively efficient incentives with respect to these decisions.[6] These observations, and others like them, are sufficient to secure the economic case for the expectation remedy as long only as *ex ante* transactions costs remain high.

The argument for the efficiency of the expectation remedy with respect to the perform-or-breach decision treated breaches of contract as voluntary, in the sense that sellers choose whether or not to breach (by balancing the costs and benefits of doing so) at the moment at which they must make their perform-or-breach decisions. But in reality, many breaches are not voluntary in this strict sense. Instead, by the time the breach occurs, the seller no longer has any real choice in the matter: she will breach even if, at the time of performance, she makes her best efforts to perform. The seller's supplier may fail to deliver necessary inputs, for example, or her production facility may break down or suffer disruptions, or she may, in spite of trying to avoid it, manufacture a defective good.

Nevertheless, the fact that the perform-or-breach decision is involuntary at the moment of performance does not mean that it is entirely out of the seller's control whether she will perform or breach. Sellers can take steps in advance of performance in order to reduce the chance that they will be unable to perform when the time comes. They can acquire back-up supply channels, vigilantly maintain their factories, and deploy elaborate testing mechanisms to identify defective products and remove them from their inventories. Sellers, in short, can take *precautions* against involuntary breach.

---

6. The discussion of the selection and precaution decisions below loosely follows Richard Craswell, *Contract Remedies, Renegotiation, and the Theory of Efficient Breach*, 61 S. CAL. L. REV. 629 (1988).

Similarly, a seller will generally face many possible buyers, and contracts with these buyers will involve different risks of breach for the seller and different costs of breach to the buyers. Sellers can reduce the risk of breaching by choosing buyers for whom they will find it easier to perform and avoiding buyers for whom performance will be more difficult. And sellers can reduce the harms associated with even a constant risk of breaching by choosing buyers on whom breaches will impose relatively low costs and avoiding buyers for whom breaches will be costly. Sellers, in other words, can *select* buyers while bearing the expected harm caused by breaching in mind.

When sellers know their risks of breaching (both in general and as these vary with respect to various buyers) and also the harms that their breaches will cause, then the expectation remedy is again distinctively efficient, because it again distinctively induces sellers to take efficient levels of precaution against involuntary breaches and to make an efficient selection of buyers. Thus, the efficiency-based argument for the expectation remedy endures even when *ex post* transactions costs (the costs of renegotiation at the moment of the perform-or-breach decision) are low.

The efficiency of the expectation remedy with respect to the precaution decision arises because the precautions that sellers can take to reduce the chance of involuntary breaches are themselves costly. Thus it is a question, both from the point of view of a seller and from the point of view of efficiency, what costs sellers should bear in the name of precaution. Remedy rules will affect the precautionary costs sellers are willing to bear, by affecting the costs imposed on sellers as a result of the involuntary breaches that the precautions prevent: specifically, sellers will spend a dollar on precaution as long as this expenditure saves at least a dollar in cost-of-breach. This way of putting the point makes it plain that expectation damages will lead the seller to bear herself (or, as economists say, to internalize) precisely the costs the buyer suffers on the seller's breach. And this will lead the seller to take an efficient level of precaution against breaching. Higher than expectation damages will lead the seller to take inefficiently many precautions, by contrast; and lower than expectation damages will lead the seller to take inefficiently few precautions.

The distinctive efficiency of the expectation remedy with respect to the selection decision arises because efficiency requires that sellers and buyers are matched up in such a way that pairings involving a greater expected harm from breach—a great risk of breach or a greater harm should there actually be a breach—arise only when they generate a surplus commensurate to this greater expected harm, and that pairings that generate a sufficiently large expected surplus from performance occur even though they involve a greater expected cost from breach. Sub-compensatory damages upwardly distort the attractiveness of contracts involving riskier sellers and buyers (sellers whose chance of breach is higher and buyers whose damages from breach are higher) and hence will cause sellers to pursue some contracts in spite of the fact that the surplus they generate is insufficiently large to warrant the risk of loss they involve. Super-compensatory damages downwardly distort the attractiveness of contracts involving riskier sellers and buyers and hence will cause sellers to avoid some contracts in spite of the fact that the surplus they generate is sufficiently large to warrant the risk of loss they involve.[7]

---

7. Buyers will of course face opposite incentives. The main text focuses on sellers on account of the fact that sellers (especially in a retail context) are commonly more sophisticated than buyers and hence more responsive to economic incentives.

CHAPTER 4

A COMPLICATION: LIMITING EXPECTATION BY CERTAINTY AND FORESEEABILITY

The discussion up to this point has considered what might be called *perfect* expectation damages—that is, damages that put disappointed promisees in a position that is exactly as valuable to them as performance would have been. This is expressly reflected in the definition of the expectation remedy that appears in § 344 of the Restatement. And it is, moreover, the implicit assumption underlying the economic argument for the expectation remedy's efficiency. When all of contract law's remedial doctrines are taken together, however, they do not, in fact, fulfill this promise to secure disappointed promisees' complete expectations. Instead, the remedies that the law finally offers are, in any number of ways, less valuable to promisees than performance would have been.

Two doctrines contribute particularly importantly to this result. First, the law allows plaintiffs to recover damages in respect only of those elements of their contractual expectations that they can establish and quantify with sufficient confidence and precision. Damages for disappointed expectations that are unquantifiable, or only uncertainly quantifiable, are not recoverable, even if it is overwhelmingly likely that the value of these contractual expectations to the promisees exceeds zero. And second, damages that arise in light of contractual expectations that promisors could not reasonably have foreseen are also not recoverable.

By imposing these two requirements—of *certainty* and *foreseeability*—on promisees' claims concerning their contractual expectations, the law departs significantly, and sometimes even dramatically, from its initial promise of putting disappointed promisees in positions that they regard as just as good as performance would have been. Both doctrines may be defended, including on economic terms—and the argument for the efficiency of the foreseeability requirement is particularly elegant (and also revealing about the deeper economic structure of contract remedies). The economic analysis of contract remedies therefore need not settle for explaining only the most general commitments of contract law, but may instead be carried inward into some of the law's doctrinal interstices.

4.1   THE CERTAINTY REQUIREMENT

Contract law allows disappointed promisees to recover damages only in virtue of contractual expectations that they prove up with a sufficient degree of certainty. Certainty is, unsurprisingly in this context, a term of art. The following cases begin to illuminate what it means.

Rombola v. Cosindas

Supreme Judicial Court of Massachusetts, 1966.
220 N.E.2d 919.

■ KIRK, J. The sole question presented by the bill of exceptions of the plaintiff (Rombola) in this action of contract is whether the judge committed error in directing a verdict for the defendant (Cosindas) on the plaintiff's opening statement to the jury.

We state the substance of the plaintiff's case, as outlined in the opening statement. By the terms of a written contract with Cosindas, Rombola agreed to train, maintain and race Cosindas's horses, Margy Sampson and Margy Star, for the period November 8, 1962, to December 1, 1963. The present action relates only to the horse Margy Sampson. Rombola was to assume all expenses and to receive seventy-five per cent of all gross purses; Cosindas was to receive the remaining twenty-five per cent. Rombola took possession of Margy Sampson and, because there was no winter racing in the area, maintained and trained her at his stable throughout the winter. In the spring and summer of 1963, Rombola entered the horse in a total of twenty-five races, run at four racing meets which were held at three different racetracks. In the fall, Rombola entered Margy Sampson in six stake races in a thirty-three day meet to be held at Suffolk Downs. The expiration date of Rombola's contract coincided with the closing date of the meet. Margy Sampson had already raced against several of the horses who were entered in the six stake races scheduled for the Suffolk Downs meet. On October 25, 1963, before the meet started, Cosindas, without Rombola's knowledge or consent, took possession of the horse at Suffolk Downs and thereby deprived Rombola of his right to race the horse. The horse did not race between October 25 and December 1, 1963.

On the issue of damages Rombola would show that generally, in a stake race, there are eight or nine starters and that the purse is shared by the first five finishers at diminishing percentages. The purse is determined before the race and is not affected by the amount of money wagered by patrons at the track. In the year preceding the contract, Margy Sampson as a three-year old had won a total of approximately $400–$450 in four races. In the year of the contract, of the twenty-five races in which the horse was entered by Rombola, she had won ten and shared in the purse money in a total of twenty races, earning, in all, purses approximating $12,000. In the year following the expiration of Rombola's contract with Cosindas, the horse raced twenty-nine times and won money in an amount almost completely consistent percentagewise with the money won during the period of the contract. A person who is in the business of racing horses is able, on the basis of a horse's past earnings record, to approximate its future earnings. Rombola, who has trained, raced and owned trotting horses as a means of livelihood for eight years, is an expert in this field and had an opinion as to how much the horse would have won in the six stake races.

Treating, as we must, all of the statements in the opening as facts, and construing them, as we must, in the light most favorable to the plaintiff, it is clear that the essentials of an action of contract have been set out. The opening statement reveals that (1) there was a written agreement supported by valid consideration, (2) the plaintiff was ready, willing and able to perform, and (3) the defendant's breach has prevented the plaintiff from performing. The breach, once established, entitled the plaintiff to at least nominal damages in an action at law, regardless of his ability to prove substantial damages. It was error, therefore, to direct a verdict for the defendant.

We think further that Rombola would be entitled to show substantial damages on the theory of loss of prospective profits. The right to recover prospective damages must in each case be decided on its own facts, and a comparatively insignificant factor, in combination with others, may lead to a conclusion in one decision apparently at variance with that reached in others. In determining the amount of damages to be awarded, mathematical accuracy of proof is not required. The likelihood of prospective profits may be proved by an established earnings record. Expert opinion may be introduced to substantiate the amount of prospective profits.

We apply these principles to the present case. It appears that Margy Sampson had already been accepted as a participant in the stake races and transported to the site of the meet. She had already proved her ability both prior to and while under Rombola's management and training, over an extended period of time, against many competitors and under varying track conditions. Her consistent performance in the year subsequent to the breach negates any basis for an inference of a diminution in ability or in earning capacity at the time of the Suffolk Downs meet. While it is possible that no profits would have been realized if Margy Sampson had participated in the scheduled stake races, that possibility is inherent in any business venture. It is not sufficient to foreclose Rombola's right to prove prospective profits. Her earnings record, while not conclusive, is admissible as evidence of the extent of damages caused by the breach. Rombola's opinion would also be admissible as evidence of the extent of damages if his qualifications as an expert witness are accepted by the trial judge.

Rombola was entitled to proceed to a trial of the issues.

Exceptions sustained

Freund v. Washington Square Press, Inc.

Court of Appeals of New York, 1974.
314 N.E.2d 419.

■ RABIN, J. In this action for breach of a publishing contract, we must decide what damages are recoverable for defendant's failure to publish plaintiff's manuscript. In 1965, plaintiff, an author and a college teacher, and defendant, Washington Square Press, Inc., entered into a written agreement which, in relevant part, provided as follows. Plaintiff ("author") granted defendant ("publisher") exclusive rights to publish and sell in book form plaintiff's work on modern drama. Upon plaintiff's delivery of the manuscript, defendant agreed to complete payment of a nonreturnable $2,000 "advance." Thereafter, if defendant deemed the manuscript not "suitable for publication," it had the right to terminate the agreement by written notice within 60 days of delivery. Unless so terminated, defendant agreed to publish the work in hardbound edition within 18 months and afterwards in paperbound edition. The contract further provided that defendant would pay royalties to plaintiff, based upon specified percentages of sales. (For example, plaintiff was to receive 10% of the retail price of the first 10,000 copies sold in the continental United States.) If defendant failed to publish within 18 months, the contract provided that "this agreement shall terminate and the rights herein granted to the Publisher shall revert to the Author. In such event all payments theretofore made to the Author shall belong to the Author without prejudice to any other remedies which the Author may have." The contract also provided that controversies were to be determined pursuant to the New York simplified procedure for court determination of disputes.

Plaintiff performed by delivering his manuscript to defendant and was paid his $2,000 advance. Defendant thereafter merged with another publisher and ceased publishing in hardbound. Although defendant did not exercise its 60–day right to terminate, it has refused to publish the manuscript in any form.

Plaintiff commenced the instant action pursuant to the simplified procedure practice and initially sought specific performance of the contract. The Trial Term Justice denied specific performance but, finding a valid contract and a breach by defendant, set the matter down for trial on the issue of monetary damages, if any, sustained by the plaintiff. At trial, plaintiff sought to prove: (1) delay of his academic promotion; (2) loss of royalties which would have been earned; and (3) the cost of publication if plaintiff had made his own arrangements to publish. The trial court found that plaintiff had been promoted despite defendant's failure to publish, and that there was no evidence that the breach had caused any delay. Recovery of lost royalties was denied without discussion. The court found, however, that the cost of hardcover publication to plaintiff was the natural and probable consequence of the breach and, based upon expert testimony, awarded $10,000 to cover this cost. It denied recovery of the expenses of paperbound publication on the ground that plaintiff's proof was conjectural.

The Appellate Division, (3 to 2) affirmed, finding that the cost of publication was the proper measure of damages. In support of its conclusion, the majority analogized to the construction contract situation where the cost of completion may be the proper measure of damages for a builder's failure to complete a house or for use of wrong materials. The dissent concluded that the cost of publication is not an appropriate measure of damages and consequently, that plaintiff may recover nominal damages only. We agree with the dissent. In so concluding, we look to the basic purpose of damage recovery and the nature and effect of the parties' contract.

It is axiomatic that, except where punitive damages are allowable, the law awards damages for breach of contract to compensate for injury caused by the breach—injury which was foreseeable, i.e., reasonably within the contemplation of the parties, at the time the contract was entered into. Money damages are substitutional relief designed in theory "to put the injured party in as good a position as he would have been put by full performance of the contract, at the least cost to the defendant and without charging him with harms that he had no sufficient reason to foresee when he made the contract." (5 Corbin, Contracts, § 1002, pp. 31–32; 11 Williston, Contracts [3d ed.], § 1338, p. 198.) In other words, so far as possible, the law attempts to secure to the injured party the benefit of his bargain, subject to the limitations that the injury—whether it be losses suffered or gains prevented—was foreseeable, and that the amount of damages claimed be measurable with a reasonable degree of certainty and, of course, adequately proven. But it is equally fundamental that the injured party should not recover more from the breach than he would have gained had the contract been fully performed.

Measurement of damages in this case according to the cost of publication to the plaintiff would confer greater advantage than performance of the contract would have entailed to plaintiff and would place him in a far better position than he would have occupied had the defendant fully performed. Such measurement bears no relation to compensation for plaintiff's actual loss or anticipated profit. Far beyond compensating plaintiff for the interests he had in the defendant's performance of the contract—whether restitution, reliance or expectation (see Fuller & Perdue, Reliance Interest in Contract Damages, 46 Yale L.J. 52, 53–56) an award of the cost of publication would enrich plaintiff at defendant's expense.

Pursuant to the contract, plaintiff delivered his manuscript to the defendant. In doing so, he conferred a value on the defendant which, upon defendant's breach, was required to be restored to him. Special Term, in addition to ordering a trial on the issue of damages, ordered defendant to return the manuscript to plaintiff and plaintiff's restitution interest in the contract was thereby protected.

At the trial on the issue of damages, plaintiff alleged no reliance losses suffered in performing the contract or in making necessary preparations to perform. Had such losses, if foreseeable and ascertainable, been incurred, plaintiff would have been entitled to compensation for them.

As for plaintiff's expectation interest in the contract, it was basically two-fold—the "advance" and the royalties. (To be sure, plaintiff may have expected to enjoy whatever notoriety, prestige or other benefits that might have attended publication, but even if these expectations were compensable, plaintiff did not attempt at trial to place a monetary value on them.) There is no dispute that plaintiff's expectancy in the "advance" was fulfilled—he has received his $2,000. His expectancy interest in the royalties—the profit he stood to gain from sale of the published book—while theoretically compensable, was speculative. Although this work is not plaintiff's first, at trial he provided no stable foundation for a reasonable estimate of royalties he would have earned had defendant not breached its promise to publish. In these circumstances, his claim for royalties falls for uncertainty.

Since the damages which would have compensated plaintiff for anticipated royalties were not proved with the required certainty, we agree with the dissent in the Appellate Division that nominal damages alone are recoverable. Though these are damages in name only and not at all compensatory, they are nevertheless awarded as a formal vindication of plaintiff's legal right to compensation which has not been given a sufficiently certain monetary valuation.

In our view, the analogy by the majority in the Appellate Division to the construction contract situation was inapposite. In the typical construction contract, the owner agrees to pay money or other consideration to a builder and expects, under the contract, to receive a completed building in return. The value of the promised performance to the owner is the properly constructed building. In this case, unlike the typical construction contract, the value to plaintiff of the promised performance—publication—was a percentage of sales of the books published and not the books themselves. Had the plaintiff contracted for the printing, binding and delivery of a number of hardbound copies of his manuscript, to be sold or disposed of as he wished, then perhaps the construction analogy, and measurement of damages by the cost of replacement or completion, would have some application.

Here, however, the specific value to plaintiff of the promised publication was the royalties he stood to receive from defendant's sales of the published book. Essentially, publication represented what it would have cost the defendant to confer that value upon the plaintiff, and, by its breach, defendant saved that cost. The error by the courts below was in measuring damages not by the value to plaintiff of the promised performance but by the cost of that performance to defendant. Damages are not measured, however, by what the defaulting party saved by the breach, but by the natural and probable consequences of the breach *to the plaintiff*. In this case, the consequence to plaintiff of defendant's failure to publish is that he is prevented from realizing the gains promised by the contract—the royalties. But, as we have stated, the amount of royalties plaintiff would have realized was not ascertained with adequate certainty and, as a consequence, plaintiff may recover nominal damages only.

Accordingly, the order of the Appellate Division should be modified to the extent of reducing the damage award of $10,000 for the cost of publication to six cents, but with costs and disbursements to the plaintiff.

Order modified, with costs and disbursements to plaintiff-respondent, in accordance with opinion herein and, as so modified, affirmed.

* * *

Rombola and *Freund* together provide an excellent introduction to the law's requirement that plaintiffs must prove up their contractual expectations with reasonable certainty in order to recover damages when these expectations are disappointed (or, to put the point the other way around, that unduly speculative damages claims will not succeed). If one understands why the plaintiff in *Rombola* wins while the plaintiff in *Freund* loses, one understands the basic idea behind the certainty requirement.

But before taking up this difference between *Rombola* and *Freund*, it will be useful briefly to review *Freund* with another purpose in mind, namely to reprise the accounting of expectation damages. Mr. Freund claimed damages in light of three distinct ways in which Washington Square Press's breach left him worse off than performance would have—his delay in receiving tenure, his lost royalties, and the costs associated with self-publication of the book. The first two losses invoke the certainty requirement, but the third does not, and although the appellate court reversed a trial court judgment awarding Mr. Freund the costs of self-publication, the certainty requirement did not figure among the grounds for the reversal. Instead, the trial court committed a simple accounting error. Washington Square's performance would indeed have resulted in the publication of the book, but it would not have given Mr. Freund ownership of the actual, published volumes. Instead, Washington Square's performance would have left Mr. Freund with a right merely to royalties based on the monies received for any books sold—which is only a fraction of the value of a portion of the volumes. Even if the cost of making the books were a good estimate of the value of the made books—something that there is reason to doubt, since Washington Square's breach suggests that it did not think the books worth their costs of production—this remedy would give Mr. Freund the whole of something of which the contract gave him only a part.[1] One must be careful, in accounting for contractual expectations, to focus not generally on what performance would have brought, but rather, and more specifically, on what it would have brought the promisee.

Return now to the main topic—the certainty requirement—and ask what separates the outcomes in *Rombola* and *Freund*? Why are Mr. Rombola's lost shares of the race-purses recoverable, whereas Mr. Freund's lost royalties, lost prestige, and delayed tenure are unrecoverably uncer-

---

1. Note that a remedy based on the cost of self-publication may have appealed to the trial court for another reason also, namely that it approximates the expenses that Washington Square saved by breaching. But this intuition makes another conceptual mistake. A plaintiff's expectation damages are measured by his losses and not by the defendant's gains. Indeed, that is the central insight of the theory of efficient breach (and Washington Square's breach was likely an example of an efficient breach).

tain? The answer lies in a conceptual distinction between simple *risk* on the one hand and *uncertainty* proper on the other. Risk arises when the underlying probability distribution of possible outcomes is known and only the particular outcome that will eventuate from out of this distribution remains unknown. (Here think of asking what number will come up on rolling a fair, six-sided die, whose faces are labeled 1 to 6.) Uncertainty, by contrast, arises when even the underlying distribution of possible outcomes remains unknown. (Here think of asking what number will come up on rolling a die where one does not know how the die is weighted, how many sides it has, or indeed how the sides are labeled.)

Valuing risks is relatively straightforward. At least for someone who is risk-neutral, the value of a risk is simply the expected value of the distribution from which the risk is drawn. Thus, the value of a promise to pay a number of dollars equal to the result of a single throw of a fair six-sided die labeled 1 to 6 is $3.50. Of course, people in practice depart from risk neutrality in varying ways: risk averse people prefer guaranteed receipt of the expected value of a distribution over the chance of receiving whatever value out of this distribution eventuates; and risk seeking people have the opposite preference. (Indeed, a single person may have different preferences for different classes of risks—as when a person simultaneously buys home insurance and plays the lottery.) But once a person's risk preferences (whatever they are) become known, the value that she accords a risk can be calculated precisely, and she can make reasonable decisions about how to act in the face of risk. Indeed, this possibility is borne out by actual experience, in the myriad markets for risk—insurance markets, for example, and investment markets—in which people participate throughout their economic and even personal lives.

Uncertainty, by contrast, is effectively impossible to value. Insofar as someone operates in conditions of genuine uncertainty, she has quite literally no reason for attributing any particular value to the eventual outcome of her circumstances. Thus, there is simply nothing that can be said about the value of a promise to pay a number of dollars equal to the result of a throw of a die whose weighting, number of sides, and markings are unknown: are all sides even possible outcomes; how many different outcomes are there; and what range of numbers might appear (for example, are all the numbers positive or are some, or even all, of them negative)? As uncertainty grows, the opportunity for reasonable conduct in its face decreases. This is once again borne out by experience: even as there are many markets for risk, there are literally *no* markets for uncertainty? How could there possibly be, given that the value of uncertainty is rationally indeterminate?[2]

Rombola and *Freund* fall at nearly opposite poles of the distinction between risk and uncertainty. The disappointed expectation in *Rombola* involves nearly pure risk. The probability distribution of the outcomes of horse races is well-known: there exist experts who set initial odds on all the

---

2. There are, by contrast, many markets for *reducing* uncertainty. Indeed, this is one of the principal functions of research and expertise.

entrants in races; and there exist well-developed betting markets through which betters influence the odds until a quasi-equilibrium is reached. The expected value of Paul Rombola's lost expectation may therefore be quite precisely calculated. Moreover, the opportunities for betting on horses are effectively inexhaustible, so that this expected value may be easily converted into a new risk distribution that mimics the one of which Mr. Rombola was deprived by the breach, which would put Mr. Rombola in the same position as performance would have, regardless of Rombola's risk preferences. The remedy in *Rombola* therefore reliably secures the plaintiff's contractual expectations. Only a contract involving a promise to buy lottery tickets or to gamble at some other game of pure chance would present a clearer, cleaner case of risky contractual expectations.

Freund, by contrast, involves nearly pure uncertainty. The pacing of tenure cases, and even their eventual outcomes, are famously unpredictable; the paths to academic notoriety, much less fame, are notoriously irregular; and everyone in publishing knows that betting on a book's sales is taking a shot in the dark. Moreover, each academic career is entirely idiosyncratic, so that once derailed, it cannot be put back on track by a money award: even if the expected path of Freund's career on publication could be known, its value to Freund could not be, and so he could not reliably be returned to the position that he would have enjoyed had Washington Square not breached.[3] Any remedy in *Freund* would therefore be almost entirely speculative. Only a contract involving a promise of idiosyncratically contingent personal fulfillment would present a clearer, cleaner case of uncertain contractual expectations.

The lesson of *Rombola* and *Freund*, therefore, is that the law will remedy risky losses but not uncertain ones. This lesson, moreover, suggests that there is an important place for good lawyers in the quest to recover compensation for contractual expectations—namely, that skillful lawyering transforms uncertainty into risk. The next two cases illustrate this possibility. In the first, the transformation succeeds, and the plaintiff recovers. The second pushes up against the limits of transforming uncertainty into risk, and the plaintiff's damages claim fails.

Fera v. Village Plaza, Inc.

Supreme Court of Michigan, 1976.
242 N.W.2d 372.

■ KAVANAGH, J. Plaintiffs received a jury award of $200,000 for loss of anticipated profits in their proposed new business as a result of defendants'

---

3. Is the loss that the breach caused Freund rendered even more uncertain by the fact that, had it not breached, Washington Square could have avoided publishing the book even while honoring the contract, by availing themselves of an opt-out provision that allowed the company to terminate the contract if the delivered manuscript was not "suitable for publication?" When may a defendant avoid compensating a plaintiff for a wrongful injury by arguing that, had he not acted wrongfully, he would have produced the same result without violating her rights. For a direct analysis of this question (although in a tort context) see *Bigelow v. RKO Radio Pictures*, 327 U.S. 251 (1946) (Frankfurter, J. dissenting).

breach of a lease. The Court of Appeals reversed. We reverse and reinstate the jury's award.

Facts

On August 20, 1965 plaintiffs and agents of Fairborn–Village Plaza executed a ten-year lease for a "book and bottle" shop in defendants' proposed shopping center. This lease provided for occupancy of a specific location at a rental of $1,000 minimum monthly rent plus 5% of annual receipts in excess of $240,000. A $1,000 deposit was paid by plaintiffs.

When the space was finally ready for occupancy, plaintiffs were refused the space for which they had contracted because the lease had been misplaced, and the space rented to other tenants. Alternative space was offered but refused by plaintiffs as unsuitable for their planned business venture.

Plaintiffs initiated suit in Wayne Circuit Court, alleging *inter alia* a claim for anticipated lost profits. The jury returned a verdict for plaintiffs against all defendants for $200,000.

The Court of Appeals reversed and remanded for new trial on the issue of damages only, holding that the trial court "erroneously permitted lost profits as the measure of damages for breach of the lease."

In *Jarrait v Peters*, 108 N.W. 432 (Mich. 1906), plaintiff was prevented from taking possession of the leased premises. The jury gave plaintiff a judgment which included damages for lost profits. This Court reversed:

> "It is well settled upon authority that the measure of damages when a lessor fails to give possession of the leased premises is the difference between the actual rental value and the rent reserved. 1 Sedgwick on Damages (8th ed), § 185. Mr. Sedgwick says:
>
> 'If the business were a new one, since there could be no basis on which to estimate profits, the plaintiff must be content to recover according to the general rule.'
>
> The rule is different where the business of the lessee has been interrupted.
>
> The evidence admitted tending to show the prospective profits plaintiff might have made for the ensuing two years should therefore have been excluded under the objections made by defendant, and the jury should have been instructed that the plaintiff's damages, if any, would be the difference between the actual rental value of the premises and the rent reserved in the lease."

Six years later, in *Isbell v Anderson Carriage Co*, 136 N.W. 457 (Mich. 1912), the Court wrote:

> "It has sometimes been stated as a rule of law that prospective profits are so speculative and uncertain that they cannot be recognized in the measure of damages. This is not because they are profits, but because they are so often not susceptible of proof to a reasonable degree of certainty. Where the proof is available,

prospective profits may be recovered, when proven, as other damages. But the jury cannot be asked to guess. They are to try the case upon evidence, not upon conjecture."

These cases and others since should not be read as stating a rule of law which prevents *every* new business from recovering anticipated lost profits for breach of contract. The rule is merely an application of the doctrine that "[i]n order to be entitled to a verdict, or a judgment, for damages for breach of contract, the plaintiff must lay a basis for a reasonable estimate of the extent of his harm, measured in money." 5 Corbin on Contracts, § 1020, p 124. The issue becomes one of sufficiency of proof. "The jury should not [be] allowed to speculate or guess upon this question of the amount of loss of profits." *Kezeli v River Rouge Lodge IOOF*, 161 N.W. 838 (Mich. 1917).

"Assuming, therefore, that profits prevented may be considered in measuring the damages, are profits to be divided into classes and kinds? Does the term 'speculative profits' express one of these classes, differing in nature from nonspeculative profits? Do 'uncertain' profits differ in kind from 'certain' profits? The answer is assuredly, No. There is little that can be regarded as 'certain,' especially with respect to what would have happened if the march of events had been other than it in fact has been. Neither court nor jury is required to attain 'certainty' in awarding damages; and this is just as true with respect to 'value' as with respect to 'profits'. Therefore, the term 'speculative and uncertain profits' is not really a classification of profits, but is instead a characterization of the evidence that is introduced to prove that they would have been made if the defendant had not committed a breach of contract. The law requires that this evidence shall not be so meager or uncertain as to afford no reasonable basis for inference, leaving the damages to be determined by sympathy and feelings alone. The amount of evidence required and the degree of its strength as a basis of inference varies with circumstances." 5 Corbin on Contracts, § 1022, pp 139–140.

The rule was succinctly stated in *Shropshire v Adams*, 89 S.W. 448, 450 (Tex. 1905):

> "Future profits as an element of damage are in no case excluded merely because they are profits but because they are uncertain. In any case when by reason of the nature of the situation they may be established with reasonable certainty they are allowed."

It is from these principles that the "new business"/"interrupted business" distinction has arisen.

"If a business is one that has already been established a reasonable prediction can often be made as to its future on the basis of its past history. If the business has not had such a history as to make it possible to prove with reasonable accuracy what its profits have been in fact, the profits prevented are often but not necessarily too uncertain for recovery." 5 Corbin on Contracts, § 1023, pp 147, 150–151.

The Court of Appeals based its opinion reversing the jury's award on two grounds: First, that a new business cannot recover damages for lost profits for breach of a lease. We have expressed our disapproval of that rule. Secondly, the Court of Appeals held plaintiffs barred from recovery because the proof of lost profits was entirely speculative. We disagree.

The trial judge in a thorough opinion made the following observations upon completion of the trial:

"On the issue of lost profits, there were days and days of testimony. The defendants called experts from the Michigan Liquor Control Commission and from Cunningham Drug Stores, who have a store in the area, and a man who ran many other stores. The plaintiffs called experts and they, themselves, had experience in the liquor sales business, in the book sales business and had been representatives of liquor distribution firms in the area.

The issue of the speculative, conjectural nature of future profits was probably the most completely tried issue in the whole case. Both sides covered this point for days on direct and cross-examination. The proofs ranged from no lost profits to two hundred and seventy thousand dollars over a ten-year period as the highest in the testimony. A witness for the defendants, an expert from Cunningham Drug Company, testified the plaintiffs probably would lose money. Mr. Fera, an expert in his own right, testified the profits would probably be two hundred and seventy thousand dollars. The jury found two hundred thousand dollars. This is well within the limits of the high and the low testimony presented by both sides, and a judgment was granted by the jury.

The court must decide whether or not the jury had enough testimony to take this fact from the speculative-conjecture category and find enough facts to be able to make a legal finding of fact. This issue [damages for lost profits] was the most completely tried issue in the whole case. Both sides put in testimony that took up days and encompassed experts on both sides. This fact was adequately taken from the category of speculation and conjecture by the testimony and placed in the position of those cases that hold that even though loss of profits is hard to prove, if proven they should be awarded by the jury. In this case, the jury had ample testimony to make this decision from both sides.

The jury award was approximately seventy thousand dollars less than the plaintiffs asked and their proofs showed they were entitled to. The award of the jury was well within the range of the proofs and the court cannot legally alter it, as determination of damages is a jury function and their finding is justified by the law in light of the evidence in this case.

The loss of profits are often speculative and conjectural on the part of witnesses. When this is true, the court should deny loss of profits because of the speculative nature of the testimony and the proofs. However, the law is also clear that where lost profits are shown, and there is ample proof on this point, they should not be denied merely because they are hard to prove. In this case, both parties presented testimony on this issue for days. This testimony took the lost profits issue out of the category of speculation and conjecture. The jury was given an instruction on loss of profits and what the proofs must show, and the nature of the proofs, and if they found them to be speculative they could not award damages therefor. The jury, having found damages to exist, and awarded the same in this case in accord with the proper instructions, the court cannot, now, overrule the jury's finding."

As Judge Wickens observed, the jury was instructed on the law concerning speculative damages. The case was thoroughly tried by all the parties. Apparently, the jury believed the plaintiffs. That is its prerogative.

The testimony presented during the trial was conflicting. The weaknesses of plaintiffs' specially prepared budget were thoroughly explored on cross-examination. Defendants' witnesses testified concerning the likelihood that plaintiffs would not have made profits if the contract had been performed. There was conflicting testimony concerning the availability of a liquor license. All this was spread before the jury. The jury weighed the conflicting testimony and determined that plaintiffs were entitled to damages of $200,000.

As we stated in *Anderson v Conterio*, 5 N.W.2d 572 (Mich. 1942):

> "The testimony is in direct conflict, and that of plaintiff was impeached to some extent. However, it cannot be said as a matter of law that the testimony thus impeached was deprived of all probative value or that the jury could not believe it. The credibility of witnesses is for the jury, and it is not for us to determine who is to be believed."

The trial judge, who also listened to all of the conflicting testimony, denied defendants' motion for a new trial, finding that the verdict was justified by the evidence. We find no abuse of discretion in that decision. "The trial court has a large amount of discretion in determining whether to submit the question of profits to the jury; and when it is so submitted, the jury will also have a large amount of discretion in determining the amount of its verdict." 5 Corbin on Contracts, § 1022, pp 145–146.

"[W]here injury to some degree is found, we do not preclude recovery for lack of precise proof. We do the best we can with what we have. We do not, 'in the assessment of damages, require a mathematical precision in situations of injury where, from the very nature of the circumstances precision is unattainable.' Particularly is this true where it is defendant's own act or neglect that has caused the imprecision." *Godwin v Ace Iron & Metal Co*, 137 N.W.2d 151 (Mich. 1965).

While we might have found plaintiffs' proofs lacking had we been members of the jury, that is not the standard of review we employ. "As a reviewing court we will not invade the fact-finding of the jury or remand for entry of judgment unless the factual record is so clear that reasonable minds may not disagree." *Hall v Detroit*, 177 N.W.2d 161 (Mich. 1970). This is not the situation here.

The Court of Appeals is reversed and the trial court's judgment on the verdict is reinstated.

Costs to plaintiffs.

COLEMAN, J., concurring in part, dissenting in part. Although anticipated profits from a new business may be determined with a reasonable degree of certainty such was not the situation regarding loss of profits from liquor sales as proposed by plaintiffs.

First, plaintiffs had no license and a Liquor Control Commission regional supervisor and a former commissioner testified that the described book and bottle store could not obtain a license. Further, the proofs of possible profits from possible liquor sales—if a license could have been obtained—were too speculative. The speculation of possible licensing plus the speculation of profits in this case combine to cause my opinion that profits from liquor sales should not have been submitted to the jury.

Freidus v. Eisenberg

Supreme Court of New York, Appellate Division, Second Department, 1986.
510 N.Y.S.2d 139.

[The full history of the dispute in this case is complex and involved. As a result of this history, the party that was naturally the plaintiff in the contract dispute became the defendant in the lawsuit as it was actually framed. The brief account of the facts that follows is sufficient for present purposes. It re-labels the plaintiff and defendant so that the labels reflect the natural and intuitive positions of the parties.

On June 10, 1969, the plaintiff, Todem Homes, entered into a contract for the defendant to purchase a 20–acre parcel of land. The contract gave Todem Homes the right to repurchase 17 of the unimproved acres within a period of 30 months, for $40,000. When Todem Homes exercised its option, the defendant refused to reconvey the land and Todem Homes sought specific performance of the option contract (reconveyance of the land and damages for the 15–year delay caused by the resulting litigation). The trial court ordered the land returned to Todem Homes, and awarded $408,000 in damages for the use and occupancy of the land during the period of the delay, and another $65,096 for increased costs of road construction suffered as a result of defendant's failure to reconvey. The main issue in the case is whether this damage award was proper.]

■ LAZER, J. The case is illustrative of the susceptibility of our legal system to dilatory tactics designed to avoid a result. In any event, the defendant's liability was finally established on March 23, 1982, by the Court of Appeals affirmance of our order granting specific performance to Todem Homes on its counterclaim in this action (see, *Freidus v Todem Homes*, 80 A.D.2d 575, aff'd 56 N.Y.2d 526).

The principal question is whether the judgment in the total amount of $478,514.15 has a sufficient basis to permit it to stand. The defendant challenges the two principal components of that award: $408,000 for the use and occupancy of the property during the period of the delay, and $65,096 for the increase in road construction costs resulting from the plaintiff's failure to convey. The remainder of the judgment amount consisted of the costs and disbursements of the action and the stipulated liability of the defendant for commitment and bond fees and interest. The defendant argues that the damages sought by the plaintiff are not cognizable under law; that the plaintiff failed to prove that the damages she sought were within the contemplation of the parties; that the plaintiff's proof of damages for loss of use of the property was uncertain, contingent and speculative; that the plaintiff failed to mitigate damages; that the period for which damages were calculated should have ended in 1981, since Todem Homes could have sought a closing at that time; that the defendant was entitled to an offset in the judgment for interest on the unpaid purchase money; and that the rulings and conduct of the court were prejudicial to the defendant. The defendant also claims that the award for increased road construction costs was not based on admissible evidence. We conclude that the judgment must be reversed to the extent it awards damages for use and occupancy of the property and increased road construction costs, since the plaintiff failed to establish either.

At the outset of our analysis, it is important to note that the underlying action is in equity for specific performance of a contract to convey real property, and the issue at the jury trial was the amount of damages flowing from the delay in complying with the contract. The action is not one at law to recover damages for breach of contract. In a breach of contract action, the purchaser is compensated for loss of bargain by recovering the difference between the value of the property and the contract price, together with such incidental damages as flow from the breach. Here, with specific performance granted, the contract is being performed, and the purchaser has not lost the value of the bargain. Although legal damages are therefore inappropriate, equity "will, so far as possible, place the parties in the same situation as they would have been in if the contract had been performed according to its terms" *(Worrall v Munn*, 38 N.Y. 137, 142 [1869]). To achieve that end, the court will award to the purchaser, in addition to specific performance of the contract, such items of damage as naturally flow from the breach, are within the contemplation of the parties, and can be proven to a reasonable degree of certainty. Here, the plaintiff claims compensation under this rule for the two items at issue on this appeal, the value of the use and occupancy of the property and the increase in road construction costs resulting from the delay in performing.

Since the defendant remained in possession of the property throughout the period of her wrongful failure to convey, the plaintiff is entitled to the value of the use and occupancy of the property, i.e., its rental value, for that period. The measure of the value of the use and occupancy is the rental value of the property, and not any profits which might be derived from its development (see, *Worrall v Munn*, 38 N.Y. 137, *supra).* In

Worrall, the value of the property was predicated primarily, if not solely, upon its clay deposits, which the purchaser intended to use to make bricks for a profit. Despite this prospective value, the Court of Appeals denied the purchaser damages for such lost profits and limited his recovery to the value of using the land as it was, which was minimal. Similarly here, while the primary value of the land in question may be for development, the profits which might be derived from such a future use do not constitute the present measure of damages. The question is the value of the rent that could have been obtained during the period of delay. The evidence submitted by the plaintiff, however, did not establish that rental value.

Rather than relying upon values derived from the rental of comparable parcels or for that matter on any other cognizable method of arriving at what a tenant or other occupant would have paid to rent the 17 acres of hills and ravine, the plaintiff's appraiser arrived at his figure for the value of the use and occupancy by calculating the fair market value of the land separately for each year of delay and applying to that amount the interest rate payable on treasury bonds for that year. On this basis—the creation of fictional annual leases—the expert concluded that the rental value of the property was $37,000 for 1977, the first year of the damages period, $43,000 for 1978, with the annual amount increasing each year until it reached the sum of $98,000 for 1984. While this approach might establish what a fair return on the cash value of the property might have been had it been sold each successive year in question—a conversion theory—it was not evidence at all of the reasonable rent that a tenant or occupant of the property might pay. The prospect that any person would pay even $37,000, much less $98,000, for a one-year rental of a vacant, 17–acre property consisting of hills and ravine zoned residential, in Lloyd Harbor makes the testimony seem ludicrous. The plaintiff's expert thus did not establish the value of the defendant's use and occupancy of the property.

The defendant's position was that the parcel had no rental value at all. On direct examination, the defendant's expert stated that because this property was vacant land which could be used for residential purposes only, it had no rental value. Although on cross-examination this expert seemed to agree that the interest rate on government securities might be a way to arrive at rental value under some circumstances, his testimony was in response to questions which bore little relevance to the issue being tried.

The defendant's position throughout the trial was that there was no rental value to the property. Since the damages awarded by the jury for use and occupancy were obviously based upon the plaintiff's erroneous theory and the only proof of rental value in the record is that the parcel has no rental value, the award for the value of use and occupancy cannot stand. Although value is a question of fact, an erroneous theory of valuation is an error of law. Since an erroneous theory formed the basis for the jury's verdict on use and occupancy, the amount of the judgment must be reduced accordingly.

Our dissenting colleagues agree that the proper measure of damages is the rental value of the property, but argue that because this plaintiff has been wronged, she should be permitted to recover a fair return on the value of the land each year, even though she cannot establish that the property had any rental value at all and there is no proof that the figure arrived at bears any relation to the rental value of the property. The authorities, however, do not support such a conclusion. Under *Worrall v. Munn* (38 N.Y. 137, *supra*), the purchaser is entitled to rental value only, even where the land's potential value is far greater. This rather conservative approach is predicated essentially upon the view that the seller has contracted merely to sell the property, not to guarantee the purchaser a profit. Having wrongfully retained possession of the land, the seller must compensate the purchaser in the form of rental value, but since the seller did not contract to provide the purchaser with the return he would have had on treasury bonds or any other return based on reinvestment of the fair market value of the property, that cannot be the measure of compensation. To put the matter in a practical context, the rule which our dissenting colleagues would have us adopt would overturn prevailing concepts and permit proof of the rental value of any property by calculating a return on its fair market value. In a case such as this, the purchaser would thus be receiving a guaranteed annual return on the fair market value (as altered each year) of unrentable and unproductive property and would receive as well the appreciation on the value of the property.

Here, the testimony as to rental value was wholly unconnected to economic damage. Since the property had no rental value, to affirm the judgment would be to affirm a punitive award that lacks connection with economic reality and which would become a precedent in all specific performance damage cases.

The award of the increase in road construction costs during the period of the delay must also be excluded from the judgment because the plaintiff failed in its proof on this issue. The evidence of the cost of building a road across the property in 1976 was mere hearsay—a letter from an engineering firm to the chairman of the Village Planning Board consisting of its cost estimate for the purpose of setting a performance bond. There were no minutes to show that the Planning Board had approved the letter and no testimony that it had been written in the ordinary course of business. Although Todem's principal, Anthony DeMarco, testified that the Village Planning Board had approved the letter estimate, there was no competent evidence of that fact. DeMarco's additional testimony, that at a closing scheduled for October 12, 1976, the defendant and her attorneys accepted the letter with respect to the amount of the performance bond was conclusory and insufficient to competently establish the 1976 cost of the road that Todem was required to build in connection with the subdivision of the property.

THOMPSON, J., concurring in part and dissenting in part. While I concur in the majority's reduction of the jury award to the extent that it excluded the amount representing increased road construction costs because of a failure of proof on that issue, I do not share their view that the jury's verdict as to use and occupancy of the property in issue must be vacated. In this protracted legal war, the major casualty has been Todem Homes, which had the right under an option contract to repurchase 17 acres of the 20–acre parcel in issue. During the pendency of this litigation—a period which exceeds 14 years—the defendant, Ella Freidus, has unreasonably and without apparent justification refused to perform in accordance with the terms of the option contract. The vacatur of the damages as to use and occupancy, as directed by the majority, flies in the face of the familiar maxim that equity will not suffer a wrong to be without a remedy. Equity will also not allow a wrongdoer to profit by her own misconduct. The majority's decision with respect to the measure of compensation for the defendant's delay in performance would work a manifest injustice by permitting the defendant to reap a substantial benefit simply because of the considerable difficulty involved in fairly evaluating the full extent of the harm Todem Homes suffered in this case and in making an accurate calculation of damages. I believe that the exercise of sound judicial discretion in granting the remedy of specific performance also permits this court to exercise a measure of flexibility in fashioning a remedy which will provide reasonably adequate compensation to the injured party. Accordingly, because I find that the evidence adduced at the trial was sufficient to support the theory of valuation advanced by Todem Homes, I dissent and vote to sustain the $408,000 awarded by the jury for the use and occupancy of the subject 17–acre parcel.

It is well settled that as an incident to a judgment of specific performance to a purchaser of property, a trial court may award damages for any direct and consequential loss suffered as a result of the seller's delay in conveying the land in accordance with the terms of the contract of sale. Such an award does not arise as legal damages from the breach of the contract; rather, it is more in the nature of an equitable accounting between the parties in affirmance of the contract. Thus, in determining the standard for recovery of losses in such cases, courts will largely analogize to general principles relating to legal damages, although exercising a range of discretion not recognized in actions at law. In this regard, the courts have a duty when granting specific performance to place the parties, insofar as possible, in the same position they would have been in had the contract been performed according to its terms.

Pursuant to these principles, the majority correctly notes that because of the defendant's delay in conveying the property, the plaintiff is clearly entitled to an award for the value of the use and occupancy of the land, i.e., damages equal to the rental value of the real property. With respect to the subject premises, however, the plaintiff was faced with obvious difficulties, in the unusual circumstances of this case, in establishing the fair rental value of the property. The parcel in question was heavily wooded, hilly and ravine-like. Thus, the ordinary measure of damages using actual rental values of comparable parcels is not an accurate measure of the damages suffered by the plaintiff in being kept out of possession for these many years. However, in my considered opinion, the inappropriateness of this measure of damages does not preclude recovery by the plaintiff. Todem Homes was entitled to pursue other measures because our damage law is flexible enough to develop means to compensate those who have suffered an injury. The plaintiff attempted to demonstrate the dollar amount of damages for use and occupancy through its appraiser's testimony that a fair rental value could be calculated by ascertaining the fair market value for each year that the defendant was in possession and applying to that amount the interest rate payable on governmental securities for that year. Thus, for the period from October 1976, when specific performance of the option contract was first ordered, until April 1985, when the trial on damages was held, the rental value was calculated at a total of $594,000. Furthermore, although my colleagues in the majority read the testimony of the defendant's expert differently, the defendant's expert essentially conceded that a fair rental value of the property could be determined by estimating the value of the land and taking a percentage of the value from various sources such as capitalization and interest rates.

Drawing on this expert testimony and recognizing equity's interest in making an injured party whole, I can find no occasion to disturb the portion of the jury verdict awarding the plaintiff $408,000 for the defendant's use and occupancy of the land over an 8 1/2–year period. The verdict was fairly based on evidence presented to the jury and has support in the expert testimony. More importantly, it fairly gives redress according to the circumstances of this particular case (see, *Worrall v. Munn*, 38 N.Y. 137, 142, supra).

Vacatur of the award rewards the defendant for her prolonged wrongful occupancy and unreasonable conduct in depriving the defendant of all use and enjoyment of the premises. During the 8 1/2–year period of the defendant's delay in conveying the property, the value of her three-acre parcel was greatly enhanced because she was thereby provided with a 17–acre zone of privacy. The majority's rigid adherence to an inflexible valuation approach permits the defendant to use a traditional approach developed in the law of damages as a sword for injustice rather than as a shield from improper or speculative valuation.

Although the decisional law of this State provides no direct authority for the theory of valuation evident at bar, we may draw support from the decision of the Court of Appeals in the case of *Matter of Merrick Holding Corp. v. Board of Assessors* (45 N.Y.2d 538 [1978]) which, in the context of a tax certiorari proceeding, emphasized the importance of flexibility in valuation determinations and advised that a rigid, inflexible valuation approach would not be tolerated to benefit an individual taxpayer at the expense of the community of taxpayers. Similarly, in the context of a condemnation case it has been held that "[there] is no fixed formula for computing the rental value of condemned lands any more than such a standard exists to point out the value of the fee of condemned property" (*Matter of City of New York [Rego Park Houses]*, 201 Misc. 126, 127 [holding that for the city's temporary interest in the condemned lands the only competent evidence was that the condemned lands would have returned 4% of the value of the land].

In sum, the discretion of the court permits flexibility in calculating damages sufficient to adequately compensate an injured party and to prevent a wrongdoer from profiting from his wrongful conduct. The use and occupancy award at issue should be upheld as reasonably calculated to redress the harm wrought by this interminable litigation. We will also thereby advance the interest of justice in discouraging practices like those evident in the record before us. Accordingly, for the reasons above stated, I concur in the majority opinion except as to the vacatur of the jury verdict awarding damages for use and occupancy of the subject parcel.

* * *

The contract in *Fera* is interesting entirely apart from the eventual dispute that it engendered, because it illustrates the types of problems that can beleaguer efforts to reach a mutually beneficial agreement and the ways in which skillful contracting can overcome them (never mind that a dispute eventually arose nevertheless). The contract created a long-term gross lease—that is, a lease that gave the tenant a long period of occupancy, at a rent that would vary (substantially) with the tenant's gross receipts. It is interesting to ask why the parties would settle on these terms, which seem (both in the length of the lease and in the formula for the rental price) very different from the terms of residential leases (which commonly have short terms and fixed rents).

A plausible answer is that the long-term gross lease elegantly solves a series of problems involving hold-ups and misrepresentations in ways that do without the expensive enforcement mechanisms of formal adjudication. To begin with, the tenant—a retail business—wants at least the option of a long-term lease. This is because a short-term lease would leave a successful tenant hostage to its landlord on renewal. If the tenant's business takes off, then it will have amassed a substantial customer base that has adjusted its buying habits to the tenant's location. This is an example of what is known as site-specific firm capital—that is, an (in this case, intangible) asset that makes the tenant's business worth more in its current location than in another one. If the tenant has only a short-term lease, then the landlord will be able to expropriate some of the value of this site-specific capital by raising the rent on renewal to above what the market in general would bear, leaving the tenant with no options other than to pay the premium or lose her site-specific business. The tenant will naturally wish to avoid being put in this position. Moreover, although the landlord will benefit if an unwitting tenant allows herself to become trapped in this way, the prospect of the trap will reduce the tenant's incentives to invest in her business and therefore also the rent that the premises can command from a savvy tenant, and so it will harm the landlord as well.

The solution, of course, is for the tenant to sign a long-term lease, but this carries costs of its own. In particular, it exposes the tenant to substantial risk if its business fails, especially if the failure occurs in a period of falling rents. In these circumstances, a long term lease at a fixed rent leaves the tenant who wishes to quit the premises obligated to pay the landlord potentially substantial damages for breach of contract. (The expectation remedy would give the landlord the difference between the rental income she could generate from the tenant's lease and the rental income that she could, given the falling rental market, generate from other sources should the tenant breach.) These damages, moreover, would be owed by the tenant just when, his business having failed, he was least able to pay them. Especially if the landlord owns many rental properties and the tenant owns only one business (a common pattern), the landlord is a better bearer of at least a portion of these risks than the tenant, because she can pool the risk of business failure across tenants.

This insight explains why the rent should vary with the tenant's business success. This variation protects the tenant against the business risk mentioned in the preceding paragraph, because it entails that if the tenant's business fails, his rent will likely fall to such low levels so that he will owe no contract damages on breaking the lease. So the variable rent shifts a part of the tenant's risk of failure to the landlord, who can pool such risks across his several tenants, and in this way reduce them. The landlord will, or course, expect to be paid for assuming the risk, but the payment must not undo the risk-transfer. Making the rent depend on the tenant's business success achieves this result also, because it gives the landlord the payment only if the tenant's business does well. Finally, the measure of business success is gross receipts, rather than the perhaps more intuitive net profits, because net profits may be easily manipulated by the tenant (for example, by paying himself or his family members an unreasonably high wage), whereas gross receipts are straightforwardly verifiable and calculable.

Interesting as this all is—and it is included because it vividly illustrates the skill and even wisdom that can be involved in doing even a relatively simple deal—it remains peripheral to the main concern at present—namely, the certainty doctrine. *Fera* is important from this perspective not because of the facts behind the lease but rather because the legal discussion in the opinion presents a primer on how the law invites plaintiffs to transform uncertainty into risk and how lawyers might successfully accept this invitation. The decision that the new business rule imposes merely an evidentiary requirement rather than a *per se* ban on new business' recovery of lost profits amounts to a clear adoption of the doctrinal distinction between risk and uncertainty earlier teased out of *Rombola* and *Freund*. Since no business profits can ever be a sure thing, the most that the evidence at issue could possibly do would be to establish the probability distribution out of which these profits might eventuate—that is, to replace uncertainty about the new business's prospects with a quantified account of the risk that the business faced. Finally, the opinion identifies several ways in which a party, through her lawyers, might achieve this quantification of business risk—through evidence of the profitability of similar business, for example, or by expert testimony involving business models and projections.

Friedus pursues this strategy of transforming uncertainty into risk to its extreme outer edge and even, the court finally concluded, beyond. The problem, in *Friedus*, was that no direct evidence existed that might shed light on the distribution of business prospects that Todem Homes lost as a result of the defendant's failure to reconvey the land. The land, being undeveloped, had no appreciable rental value. Moreover, the tract, especially given its size, was too idiosyncratic for comparable parcels elsewhere to establish the distribution from which Todem Homes's business outcomes would be realized. The techniques for converting uncertainty into risk mentioned in *Fera* were simply unavailable in *Friedus*.

Todem Homes's lawyers therefore sought to convert the uncertainty in its lost profits claim into risk through the use of generic evidence. Their client, they claimed, was not in business to lose money, or indeed to do worse than the opportunity costs of investing in her business rather than elsewhere. Accordingly, whatever her expectation as a developer, and whatever distribution of outcomes this expectation reflected, it must have exceeded the safe return on the capital that she invested in the land. Assuming only that Todem Homes was a professionally and reasonably run business, the safe return to capital presents a floor for the distribution of profits that Todem Homes faced. Todem Homes proposed to calculate the floor by appraising the market value of the land for each year in which it was wrongly deprived of possession and applying to that value the interest rate on U.S. Treasury Bonds. Although nothing else might be known about the distribution of Todem Homes's profits, it is certain that her expected profits were at least as great as what she would have earned from this investment strategy. And so an award of lost profits calculated in this way would exclude all the speculative components of Todem Homes's contractual expectations.

In spite of this logic, Todem Homes lost the case. It is not clear that there is any good principled reason why. The result in *Friedus* illustrates not just that the law sets uncertain damages presumptively at zero (a choice for which there is, by hypothesis, no justification) but also that plaintiffs can avoid this bias only by developing narrowly fact specific evidence about their expectations, given their circumstances. Evidence that invokes only general ideas about rational business behavior is not enough to reduce uncertainty to risk and allow plaintiffs to recover for lost profits. One might say, if one were inclined to give a lawyerly account of this pattern, that the opposite rule—the rule that would have allowed Todem Homes to recover lost profits damages—in effect shifts the burden of proof from the plaintiff to the defendant. After all, every business—at least, every professional business—can claim without offering any evidence concerning its particular business plan that it reasonably anticipated an expected return at least equal to its opportunity costs, which are at least the safe return on invested capital. And so every business plaintiff, no matter how uncertain its particular prospects, could always recover lost profits up to at least this amount; at least unless defendants produced specific evidence that the distribution of profits plaintiffs faced was less appealing than this. This may not be an ultimately very satisfying answer, since the decision to allocate the burden of proof to plaintiffs itself requires a justification, and the lawyerly attitude that this allocation belongs to the uninspected bedrock of legal practice is not the right kind of justification at all. But it is perhaps the best answer that may be given. And it will have to be given again, later in the discussion of remedies, when the *Friedus* fact pattern is refracted through the prism of doctrines that arise around the reliance remedy, to reveal a doctrinal impasse that has no satisfactory resolution, even for those who prefer not to dig beneath doctrinal bedrock.

4.2   THE FORESEEABILITY REQUIREMENT

Just as the law allows disappointed promisees to recover their contractual expectations only insofar as they are certain, so it also allows promisees to recover their expectations only insofar as they are *foreseeable*. Foreseeability is, of course, once again a term of art. Calling a harm a foreseeable consequence of a wrong might mean any one of three things in ordinary language:

  (a) that the harm is an imaginable or conceivable consequence of the wrong;

  (b) that the harm is not extraordinary in light of the wrong, so that the wrong made the chances of the harm more than marginal or insignificant; and

  (c) that the harm is a probable or usual consequence of the wrong.[4]

Tort law, which also includes a foreseeability rule, adopts something like the second meaning of foreseeable. Thus, the general rule in tort is that a plaintiff may recover damages for a tortious harm so long only as the harm was not, as Restatement (Second) of Torts § 435 says, "highly extraordinary." (However, as the discussion of *Evra* below illustrates, this rule is not always followed with respect to torts that arise in a contract-like setting.[5])

Contract law, by contrast, adopts the third meaning of foreseeable, and, moreover, makes the point at which foreseeability is assessed not the moment of breach (in tort, it is the moment of the wrong) but rather the moment at which the contract is made. This account of foreseeability is reflected in Restatement (Second) of Contracts § 351, which limits a plaintiff's recovery to damages that the defendant had, at the time the

---

4. This distinction follows Melvin Eisenberg, *The Principle of* Hadley v. Baxendale, 80 CALIF. L. REV. 563, 568 (1992).

5. Another context in which the usual, more plaintiff-friendly tort standard of foreseeability is not followed involves claims for compensation for certain harms—including most notably lost profits—caused by defects in goods that a plaintiff has bought. (These are, in effect, breach of warranty claims, which, as later materials will make plain, have one foot in contract and one in tort.) As *Victoria Laundry* illustrates, the *Hadley* rule functions to limit the damages that a plaintiff who styles his claim to sound in contract may recover. But it may be open to a plaintiff to style his claim to sound in tort instead (in particular, in products liability), and a plaintiff may do so in the hope of exploiting the more generous foreseeability standards of tort law. Will he succeed? In general, no. See *Seely v. White Motor Co.*, 403 P.2d 145 (Cal. 1965), *East River S.S. Corp. v. Transamerica Delaval*, 476 U.S. 858 (1986).

contract was made, reason to foresee as a *probable* result of the breach. The full section of the Restatement elaborates on what reasonable promisors will foresee. The cases that follow it present the historical origins of the foreseeability rule, illustrate its modern elaboration, and identify one rationale in its favor.

Restatement 2d of Contracts

§ 351   Unforeseeability and Related Limitations on Damages

(1) Damages are not recoverable for loss that the party in breach did not have reason to foresee as a probable result of the breach when the contract was made.

(2) Loss may be foreseeable as a probable result of a breach because it follows from the breach

> (a) in the ordinary course of events, or

> (b) as a result of special circumstances, beyond the ordinary course of events, that the party in breach had reason to know.

(3) A court may limit damages for foreseeable loss by excluding recovery for loss of profits, by allowing recovery only for loss incurred in reliance, or otherwise if it concludes that in the circumstances justice so requires in order to avoid disproportionate compensation.

Comments & Illustrations:

Comment a. Requirement of foreseeability. A contracting party is generally expected to take account of those risks that are foreseeable at the time he makes the contract. He is not, however, liable in the event of breach for loss that he did not at the time of contracting have reason to foresee as a probable result of such a breach. The mere circumstance that some loss was foreseeable, or even that some loss of the same general kind was foreseeable, will not suffice if the loss that actually occurred was not foreseeable. It is enough, however, that the loss was foreseeable as a probable, as distinguished from a necessary, result of his breach. Furthermore, the party in breach need not have made a "tacit agreement" to be liable for the loss. Nor must he have had the loss in mind when making the contract, for the test is an objective one based on what he had reason to foresee. There is no requirement of foreseeability with respect to the injured party. In spite of these qualifications, the requirement of foreseeability is a more severe limitation of liability than is the requirement of substantial or "proximate" cause in the case of an action in tort or for breach of warranty. Compare *Restatement, Second, Torts § 431*; Uniform Commercial Code § 2–715(2)(b). Although the recovery that is precluded by the limitation of foreseeability is usually based on the expectation interest and takes the form of lost profits (see Illustration 1), the limitation may also preclude recovery based on the reliance interest (see Illustration 2).

Illustrations:

1. A, a carrier, contracts with B, a miller, to carry B's broken crankshaft to its manufacturer for repair. B tells A when they make the contract that the crankshaft is part of B's milling machine and that it must be sent at once, but not that the mill is stopped because B has no replacement. Because A delays in carrying the crankshaft, B loses profit during an additional period while the mill is stopped because of the delay. A is not liable for B's loss of profit. That loss was not foreseeable by A as a probable result of the breach at the time the contract was made because A did not know that the broken crankshaft was necessary for the operation of the mill.

2. A contracts to sell land to B and to give B possession on a stated date. Because A delays a short time in giving B possession, B incurs unusual expenses in providing for cattle that he had already purchased to stock the land as a ranch. A had no reason to know when they made the contract that B had planned to purchase cattle for this purpose. A is not liable for B's expenses in providing for the cattle because that loss was not foreseeable by A as a probable result of the breach at the time the contract was made.

Comment b. "General" and "special" damages. Loss that results from a breach in the ordinary course of events is foreseeable as the probable result of the breach. See Uniform Commercial Code § 2–714(1). Such loss is sometimes said to be the "natural" result of the breach, in the sense that its occurrence accords with the common experience of ordinary persons. For example, a seller of a commodity to a wholesaler usually has reason to foresee that his failure to deliver the commodity as agreed will probably cause the wholesaler to lose a reasonable profit on it. See Illustrations 3 and 4. Similarly, a seller of a machine to a manufacturer usually has reason to foresee that his delay in delivering the machine as agreed will probably cause the manufacturer to lose a reasonable profit from its use, although courts have been somewhat more cautious in allowing the manufacturer recovery for loss of such profits than in allowing a middleman recovery for loss of profits on an intended resale. See Illustration 5. The damages recoverable for such loss that results in the ordinary course of events are sometimes called "general" damages.

If loss results other than in the ordinary course of events, there can be no recovery for it unless it was foreseeable by the party in breach because of special circumstances that he had reason to know when he made the contract. See Uniform Commercial Code § 2–715(2)(a). For example, a seller who fails to deliver a commodity to a wholesaler is not liable for the wholesaler's loss of profit to the extent that it is extraordinary nor for his loss due to unusual terms in his resale contracts unless the seller had reason to know of these special circumstances. See Illustration 6. Similarly, a seller who delays in delivering a machine to a manufacturer is not liable for the manufacturer's loss of profit to the extent that it results from an intended use that was abnormal unless the seller had reason to know of this special circumstance. See Illustration 7. In the case of a written agreement, foreseeability is sometimes established by the use of recitals in the agreement itself. The parol evidence rule (§ 213) does not, however, preclude the use of negotiations prior to the making of the contract to show for this purpose circumstances that were then known to a party. The damages recoverable for loss that results other than in the ordinary course of events are sometimes called "special" or "consequential" damages. These terms are often misleading, however, and it is not necessary to distinguish between "general" and "special" or "consequential" damages for the purpose of the rule stated in this Section.

Illustrations:

3.   A and B make a written contract under which A is to recondition by a stated date a used machine owned by B so that it will be suitable for sale by B to C. A knows when they make the contract that B has contracted to sell the machine to C but knows nothing of the terms of B's contract with C. Because A delays in returning the machine to B, B is unable to sell it to C and loses the profit that he would have made on that sale. B's loss of reasonable profit was foreseeable by A as a probable result of the breach at the time the contract was made.

4.   A, a manufacturer of machines, contracts to make B his exclusive selling agent in a specified area for the period of a year. Because A fails to deliver any machines, B loses the profit on contracts that he would have made for their resale. B's loss of reasonable profit was foreseeable by A as a probable result of the breach at the time the contract was made.

5.   A and B make a contract under which A is to recondition by a stated date a used machine owned by B so that it will be suitable for use in B's canning factory. A knows that the machine must be reconditioned by that date if B's factory is to operate at full capacity during the canning season, but nothing is said of this in the written contract. Because A delays in returning the machine to B, B loses its use for the entire canning season and loses the profit that he would have made had his factory operated at full capacity. B's loss of reasonable profit was foreseeable by A as a probable result of the breach at the time the contract was made.

6.   The facts being otherwise as stated in Illustration 3, the profit that B would have made under his contract with A was extraordinarily large because C promised to pay an exceptionally high price as a result of a special need for the machine of which A was unaware. A is not liable for B's loss of profit to the extent that it exceeds what would ordinarily result from such a contract. To that extent the loss was not foreseeable by A as a probable result of the breach at the time the contract was made.

7. The facts being otherwise as stated in Illustration 5, the profit that B would have made from the use of the machine was unusually large because of an abnormal use to which he planned to put it of which A was unaware. A is not liable for B's loss of profit to the extent that it exceeds what would ordinarily result from the use of such a machine. To that extent the loss was not foreseeable by A at the time the contract was made as a probable result of the breach.

Comment c. Litigation or settlement caused by breach. Sometimes a breach of contract results in claims by third persons against the injured party. The party in breach is liable for the amount of any judgment against the injured party together with his reasonable expenditures in the litigation, if the party in breach had reason to foresee such expenditures as the probable result of his breach at the time he made the contract. See Illustrations 8, 10, 11 and 12. This is so even if the judgment in the litigation is based on a liquidated damage clause in the injured party's contract with the third party. See Illustration 8. A failure to notify the party in breach in advance of the litigation may prevent the result of the litigation from being conclusive as to him. But to the extent that the injured party's loss resulting from litigation is reasonable, the fact that the party in breach was not notified does not prevent the inclusion of that loss in the damages assessed against him. In furtherance of the policy favoring private settlement of disputes, the injured party is also allowed to recover the reasonable amount of any settlement made to avoid litigation, together with the costs of settlement. See Illustration 9.

Illustrations:

8. The facts being otherwise as stated in Illustration 3, B not only loses the profit that he would have made on sale of the machine to C, but is held liable for damages in an action brought by C for breach of contract. The damages paid to C and B's reasonable expenses in defending the action were also foreseeable by A as a probable result of the breach at the time he made the contract with B. The result is the same even though they were based on a liquidated damage clause in the contract between B and C if A knew of the clause or if the use of such a clause in the contract between B and C was foreseeable by A at the time he made the contract with B.

9. The facts being otherwise as stated in Illustration 3, B not only loses the profit that he would have made on sale of the machine to C, but settles with C by paying C a reasonable sum of money to avoid litigation. The amount of the settlement paid to C and B's reasonable expenses in settling were also foreseeable by A at the time he made the contract with B as a probable result of the breach.

10. A contracts to supply B with machinery for unloading cargo. A, in breach of contract, furnishes defective machinery, and C, an employee of B, is injured. C sues B and gets a judgment,

which B pays. The amount of the judgment and B's reasonable expenditures in defending the action were foreseeable by A at the time the contract was made as a probable result of the breach.

11.   A contracts to procure a right of way for B, for a railroad. Because A, in breach of contract, fails to do this, B has to acquire the right of way by condemnation proceedings. B's reasonable expenditures in those proceedings were foreseeable by A at the time the contract was made as a probable result of the breach.

12.   A leases land to B with a covenant for quiet enjoyment. C brings an action of ejectment against B and gets judgment. B's reasonable expenditures in defending the action were foreseeable by A as the probable result of the breach at the time the contract was made.

Comment d. Unavailability of substitute. If several circumstances have contributed to cause a loss, the party in breach is not liable for it unless he had reason to foresee all of them. Sometimes a loss would not have occurred if the injured party had been able to make substitute arrangements after breach, as, for example, by "cover" through purchase of substitute goods in the case of a buyer of goods (see Uniform Commercial Code § 2–712). If the inability of the injured party to make such arrangements was foreseeable by the party in breach at the time he made the contract, the resulting loss was foreseeable. See Illustration 13. On the impact of this principle on contracts to lend money, see Comment *e.*

Illustration:

13.   A contracts with B, a farmer, to lease B a machine to be used harvesting B's crop, delivery to be made on July 30. A knows when he makes the contract that B's crop will be ready on that date and that B cannot obtain another machine elsewhere. Because A delays delivery until August 10, B's crop is damaged and he loses profit. B's loss of profit was foreseeable by A at the time the contract was made as a probable result of the breach.

Comment e. Breach of contract to lend money. The limitation of foreseeability is often applied in actions for damages for breach of contracts to lend money. Because credit is so widely available, a lender often has no reason to foresee at the time the contract is made that the borrower will be unable to make substitute arrangements in the event of breach. See Comment *d.* In most cases, then, the lender's liability will be limited to the relatively small additional amount that it would ordinarily cost to get a similar loan from another lender. However, in the less common situation in which the lender has reason to foresee that the borrower will be unable to borrow elsewhere or will be delayed in borrowing elsewhere, the lender may be liable for much heavier damages based on the borrower's inability to take advantage of a specific opportunity (see Illustration 14), his having to postpone or abandon a profitable project (see Illustration 15), or his forfeiture of security for failure to make prompt payment (see Illustration 16).

Illustrations:

14.   A contracts to lend B $100,000 for one year at eight percent interest for the stated purpose of buying a specific lot of goods for resale. B can resell the goods at a $20,000 profit. A delays in making the loan, and although B can borrow money on the market at ten percent interest, he is unable to do so in time and loses the opportunity to buy the goods. Unless A had reason to foresee at the time that he made the contract that such a delay in making the loan would probably cause B to lose the opportunity, B can only recover damages based on two percent of the amount of the loan.

15.   A contracts to lend $1,000,000 to B for the stated purpose of enabling B to build a building and takes property of B as security. After construction is begun, A refuses to make the loan or release the security. Because B lacks further security, he is unable to complete the building, which becomes a total loss. B's loss incurred in partial construction of the building was foreseeable by A at the time of the contract as a probable result of the breach.

16.   A, who holds B's land as security for a loan, contracts to lend B a sum of money sufficient to pay off other liens on the land at the current rate of interest. A repudiates and informs B in time to obtain money elsewhere on the market, but B is unable to do so. The liens are foreclosed and the land sold at a loss. Unless A knew when he made the contract that B would probably be unable to borrow the money elsewhere, B's loss on the foreclosure sale was not foreseeable as a probable result of A's breach.

Comment f. Other limitations on damages. It is not always in the interest of justice to require the party in breach to pay damages for all of the foreseeable loss that he has caused. There are unusual instances in which it appears from the circumstances either that the parties assumed that one of them would not bear the risk of a particular loss or that, although there was no such assumption, it would be unjust to put the risk on that party. One such circumstance is an extreme disproportion between the loss and the price charged by the party whose liability for that loss is in question. The fact that the price is relatively small suggests that it was not intended to cover the risk of such liability. Another such circumstance is an informality of dealing, including the absence of a detailed written contract, which indicates that there was no careful attempt to allocate all of the risks. The fact that the parties did not attempt to delineate with precision all of the risks justifies a court in attempting to allocate them fairly. The limitations dealt with in this Section are more likely to be imposed in connection with contracts that do not arise in a commercial setting. Typical examples of limitations imposed on damages under this discretionary power involve the denial of recovery for loss of profits and the restriction of damages to loss incurred in reliance on the contract. Sometimes these limits are covertly imposed, by means of an especially demanding requirement of foreseeability or of certainty. The rule stated in this Section recognizes that what is done in such cases is the imposition of a limitation in the interests of justice.

Illustrations:

17. A, a private trucker, contracts with B to deliver to B's factory a machine that has just been repaired and without which B's factory, as A knows, cannot reopen. Delivery is delayed because A's truck breaks down. In an action by B against A for breach of contract the court may, after taking into consideration such factors as the absence of an elaborate written contract and the extreme disproportion between B's loss of profits during the delay and the price of the trucker's services, exclude recovery for loss of profits.

18. A, a retail hardware dealer, contracts to sell B an inexpensive lighting attachment, which, as A knows, B needs in order to use his tractor at night on his farm. A is delayed in obtaining the attachment and, since no substitute is available, B is unable to use the tractor at night during the delay. In an action by B against A for breach of contract, the court may, after taking into consideration such factors as the absence of an elaborate written contract and the extreme disproportion between B's loss of profits during the delay and the price of the attachment, exclude recovery for loss of profits.

19. A, a plastic surgeon, makes a contract with B, a professional entertainer, to perform plastic surgery on her face in order to improve her appearance. The result of the surgery is, however, to disfigure her face and to require a second operation. In an action by B against A for breach of contract, the court may limit damages by allowing recovery only for loss incurred by B in reliance on the contract, including the fees paid by B and expenses for hospitalization, nursing care and medicine for both operations, together with any damages for the worsening of B's appearance if these can be proved with reasonable certainty, but not including any loss resulting from the failure to improve her appearance.

Hadley v. Baxendale

Court of Exchequer, 1854.
156 Eng. Rep. 145.

At the trial before Crompton, J., at the last Gloucester Assizes, it appeared that the plaintiffs carried on an extensive business as millers at Gloucester; and that, on the 11th of May, their mill was stopped by a breakage of the crank shaft by which the mill was worked. The steam-engine was manufactured by Messrs. Joyce & Co., the engineers, at Greenwich, and it became necessary to send the shaft as a pattern for a new one to Greenwich. The fracture was discovered on the 12th, and on the 13th the plaintiffs sent one of their servants to the office of the defendants, who are the well-known carriers trading under the name of Pickford & Co., for the purpose of having the shaft carried to Greenwich. The plaintiffs' servant told the clerk that the mill was stopped, and that the shaft must be sent immediately; and in answer to the inquiry when the shaft would be taken, the answer was, that if it was sent up by twelve o'clock an day, it would be delivered at Greenwich on the following day. On the following day the shaft was taken by the defendants, before noon, for the purpose of being conveyed to Greenwich, and the sum of £ 2, 4s. was paid for its carriage for the whole distance; at the same time the defendants' clerk was told that a special entry, if required, should be made to hasten its delivery. The delivery of the shaft at Greenwich was delayed by some neglect; and the consequence was, that the plaintiffs did not receive the new shaft for several days after they would otherwise have done, and the working of their mill was thereby delayed, and they thereby lost the profits they would otherwise have received.

On the part of the defendants, it was objected that these damages were too remote, and that the defendants were not liable with respect to them. The learned Judge left the case generally to the jury, who found a verdict with £ 25 damages beyond the amount paid into Court.

The judgment of the Court was now delivered by

■ ALDERSON, B. We think that there ought to be a new trial in this case; but, in so doing, we deem it to be expedient and necessary to state explicitly the rule which the Judge, at the next trial, ought, in our opinion, to direct the jury to be governed by when they estimate the damages.

It is, indeed, of the last importance that we should do this; for, if the jury are left without any definite rule to guide them, it will, in such cases as these, manifestly lead to the greatest injustice.

"There are certain establishing rules," this Court says, in Alder v. Keighley (15 M. & W. 117), "according to which the jury ought to find." And the Court, in that case, adds: "and here there is a clear rule, that the amount which would have been received if the contract had been kept, is the measure of damages if the contract is broken."

Now we think the proper rule is such as the present is this: Where two parties have made a contract which one of them has broken, the damages which the other party ought to receive in respect of such breach of contract should be such as may fairly and reasonably be considered either arising naturally, i.e., according to the usual course of things, from such breach of contract itself, or such as may reasonably be supposed to have been in the contemplation of both parties, at the time they made the contract, as the probable result of the breach of it. Now, if the special circumstances under which the contract was actually made where communicated by the plaintiffs to the defendants, and thus known to both parties, the damages resulting from the breach of such a contract, which they would reasonably contemplate, would be the amount of injury which would ordinarily follow from a breach of contract under these special circumstances so known and communicated. But, on the other hand, if these special circumstances were wholly unknown to the party breaking the contract, he, at the most, could only be supposed to have had in his contemplation the amount of injury which would arise generally, and in the great multitude of cases not affected by any special circumstances, from such a breach of contract. For such loss would neither have flowed naturally from the breach of this contract in the great multitude of such cases occurring under ordinary circumstances, nor were the special circumstances, which, perhaps, would have made it a reasonable and natural consequence of such breach of contract, communicated to or known by the defendants. The Judge ought, therefore, to have told the jury, that, upon the facts then before them, they ought not to take the loss of profits into consideration at all in estimating the damages. There must therefore be a new trial in this case.

Rule absolute.

Victoria Laundry (Windsor) Ltd. v. Newman Indus. Ltd.

Court of Appeal, 1949.
2 K.B. 528.

■ ASQUITH, LJ. This is an appeal by the plaintiffs against a judgment of Streatfeild J. in so far as that judgment limited the damages to £110 in respect of an alleged breach of contract by the defendants, which is now uncontested. The breach of contract consisted in the delivery of a boiler sold by the defendants to the plaintiffs some twenty odd weeks after the time fixed by the contract for delivery. The short point is whether, in addition to the £110 awarded, the plaintiffs were entitled to claim in respect of loss of profits which they say they would have made if the boiler had been delivered punctually. Seeing that the issue is as to the measure of recoverable damage and the application of the rules in *Hadley v. Baxendale*, it is important to inquire what information the defendants possessed at the time when the contract was made, as to such matters as the time at which, and the purpose for which, the plaintiffs required the boiler. The defendants knew before, and at the time of the contract, that the plaintiffs were laundrymen and dyers, and required the boiler for purposes of their business as such. They also knew that the plaintiffs wanted the boiler for immediate use. On the latter point the correspondence is important. The contract was concluded by, and is contained in, a series of letters. In the earliest phases of the correspondence—that is, in letters of January 31 and February 1, 1946—(which letters, as appears from their terms, followed a telephone call on the earlier date)—the defendants undertook to make the earliest possible arrangements for the dismantling and removal of the boiler. The natural inference from this is that in the telephone conversation referred to the plaintiffs had conveyed to the defendants that they required the boiler urgently. Again, on February 7 the plaintiffs write to the defendants: 'We should appreciate your letting us know how quickly your people can dismantle it'; and finally, on April 26, in the concluding letter of the series by which the contract was made: 'We are most anxious that this' (that is, the boiler) 'should be put into use in the shortest possible space of time.' Hence, up to and at the very moment when a concluded contract emerged, the plaintiffs were pressing upon the defendants the need for expedition; and the last letter was a plain intimation that the boiler was wanted for immediate use. The defendants did not know at the material time the precise role for which the boiler was cast in the plaintiffs' economy, e.g. whether (as the fact was) it was to function in substitution for an existing boiler of inferior capacity, or in replacement of an existing boiler of equal capacity, or as an extra unit to be operated side by side with and in addition to any existing boiler. It has indeed been argued strenuously that, for all they knew, it might have been wanted as a 'spare' or 'standby,' provided in advance to replace an existing boiler when, perhaps some time hence, the latter should wear out; but such an intention to reserve it for future use seems quite inconsistent with the intention expressed in the letter of April 26, to 'put it into use in the shortest possible space of time.'

On June 5 the plaintiffs, having heard that the boiler was ready, sent a lorry to Harpenden to take delivery. Mr. Lennard, a director of the plaintiff company, preceded the lorry in a car. He discovered on arrival that four days earlier the contractors employed by the defendants to dismantle the boiler had allowed it to fall on its side, sustaining injuries. Mr. Lennard declined to take delivery of the damaged boiler in its existing condition and insisted that the damage must be made good. He was, we think, justified in this attitude, since no similar article could be bought in the market. After a long wrangle, the defendants agreed to perform the necessary repairs and, after further delay through the difficulty of finding a contractor who was free and able to perform them, completed the repairs by October 28. Delivery was taken by the plaintiffs on November 8 and the boiler was erected and working by early December. The plaintiffs claim, as part—the disputed part—of the damages, loss of the profits they would have earned if the machine had been delivered in early June instead of November. Evidence was led for the plaintiffs with the object of establishing that if the boiler had been punctually delivered, then, during the twenty odd weeks between then and the time of actual delivery, (1) they could have taken on a very large number of new customers in the course of their laundry business, the demand for laundry services at that time being insatiable—they did in fact take on extra staff in the expectation of its delivery—and (2) that they could and would have accepted a number of highly lucrative dyeing contracts for the Ministry of Supply. In the statement of claim, the loss of profits under the first of these heads was quantified at £ 16 a week and under the second at £ 262 a week.

The evidence, however, which promised to be voluminous, had not gone very far when Mr. Paull, for the defendants, submitted that in law no loss of profits was recoverable at all, and that to continue to hear evidence as to its quantum was merely waste of time. He suggested that the question of remoteness of damage under this head should be decided on the existing materials, including the admissions to which we have referred. The learned judge accepted Mr. Paull's submission, and on that basis awarded £110 damages under certain minor heads, but nothing in respect of loss of profits, which he held to be too remote. It is from that decision that the plaintiffs now appeal.

The ground of the learned judge's decision, which we consider more fully later, may be summarized as follows: He took the view that the loss of profit claimed was due to special circumstances and therefore recoverable, if at all, only under the second rule in *Hadley v. Baxendale* and not recoverable in this case because such special circumstances were not at the time of the contract communicated to the defendants. He also attached much significance to the fact that the object supplied was not a self-sufficient profit-making article, but part of a larger profit-making whole.

What propositions applicable to the present case emerge from the authorities as a whole? We think they include the following:

(1) It is well settled that the governing purpose of damages is to put the party whose rights have been violated in the same position, so far as money can do so, as if his rights had been observed: This purpose, if relentlessly pursued, would provide him with a complete indemnity for all loss de facto resulting from a particular breach, however improbable, however unpredictable. This, in contract at least, is recognized as too harsh a rule. Hence,

(2) In cases of breach of contract the aggrieved party is only entitled to recover such part of the loss actually resulting as was at the time of the contract reasonably forseeable as liable to result from the breach.

(3) What was at that time reasonably so foreseeable depends on the knowledge then possessed by the parties or, at all events, by the party who later commits the breach.

(4) For this purpose, knowledge 'possessed' is of two kinds; one imputed, the other actual. Everyone, as a reasonable person, is taken to know the 'ordinary course of things' and consequently what loss is liable to result from a breach of contract in that ordinary course. This is the subject matter of the 'first rule' in *Hadley v. Baxendale*. But to this knowledge, which a contract-breaker is assumed to possess whether he actually possesses it or not, there may have to be added in a particular case knowledge which he actually possesses, of special circumstances outside the 'ordinary course of things,' of such a kind that a breach in those special circumstances would be liable to cause more loss. Such a case attracts the operation of the 'second rule' so as to make additional loss also recoverable.

(5) In order to make the contract-breaker liable under either rule it is not necessary that he should actually have asked himself what loss is liable to result from a breach. As has often been pointed out, parties at the time of contracting contemplate not the breach of the contract, but its performance. It suffices that, if he

had considered the question, he would as a reasonable man have concluded that the loss in question was liable to result.

(6) Nor, finally, to make a particular loss recoverable, need it be proved that upon a given state of knowledge the defendant could, as a reasonable man, foresee that a breach must necessarily result in that loss. It is enough if he could foresee it was likely so to result. It is indeed enough, to borrow from the language of Lord du Parcq in the same case, at page 158, if the loss (or some factor without which it would not have occurred) is a 'serious possibility' or a 'real danger.' For short, we have used the word 'liable' to result. Possibly the colloquialism 'on the cards' indicates the shade of meaning with some approach to accuracy.

If these, indeed, are the principles applicable, what is the effect of their application to the facts of this case? We have, at the beginning of this judgment, summarized the main relevant facts. The defendants were an engineering company supplying a boiler to a laundry. We reject the submission for the defendants that an engineering company knows no more than the plain man about boilers or the purposes to which they are commonly put by different classes of purchasers, including laundries. The defendant company were not, it is true, manufacturers of this boiler or dealers in boilers, but they gave a highly technical and comprehensive description of this boiler to the plaintiffs by letter of January 19, 1946, and offered both to dismantle the boiler at Harpenden and to re-erect it on the plaintiffs' premises. Of the uses or purposes to which boilers are put, they would clearly know more than the uninstructed layman. Again, they knew they were supplying the boiler to a company carrying on the business of laundrymen and dyers, for use in that business. The obvious use of a boiler, in such a business, is surely to boil water for the purpose of washing or dyeing. A laundry might conceivably buy a boiler for some other purpose; for instance, to work radiators or warm bath water for the comfort of its employees or directors, or to use for research, or to exhibit in a museum. All these purposes are possible, but the first is the obvious purpose which, in the case of a laundry, leaps to the average eye. If the purpose then be to wash or dye, why does the company want to wash or dye, unless for purposes of business advantage, in which term we, for the purposes of the rest of this judgment, include maintenance or increase of profit, or reduction of loss? (We shall speak henceforward not of loss of profit, but of 'loss of business.') No commercial concern commonly purchases for the purposes of its business a very large and expensive structure like this—a boiler 19 feet high and costing over £ 2,000—with any other motive, and no supplier, let alone an engineering company, which has promised delivery of such an article by a particular date, with knowledge that it was to be put into use immediately on delivery, can reasonably contend that it could not foresee that loss of business (in the sense indicated above) would be liable to result to the purchaser from a long delay in the delivery thereof. The suggestion that, for all the supplier knew, the boiler might have been needed simply as a 'standby,' to be used in a possibly distant future, is gratuitous and was plainly negatived by the terms of the letter of April 26, 1946.

Since we are differing from a carefully reasoned judgment, we think it due to the learned judge to indicate the grounds of our dissent. In that judgment, after stressing the fact that the defendants were not manufacturers of this boiler or of any boilers (a fact which is indisputable), nor (what is disputable) people possessing any special knowledge not common to the general public of boilers or laundries as possible users thereof, he goes on to say: 'That is the general principle and I think that the principle running through the cases is this—and to this extent I agree with Mr. Beney—that if there is nothing unusual, if it is a normal user of the plant, then it may well be that the parties must be taken to contemplate that the loss of profits may result from non-delivery, or the delay in delivery, of the particular article. On the other hand, if there are, as I think there are here, special circumstances, I do not think that the defendants are liable for loss of profits unless these special circumstances were drawn to their notice. In looking at the cases, I think there is a distinction as Mr. Paull has pointed out and insists upon, between the supply of the part of the profit-making machine, as against the profit-making machine itself.' Then, after referring to *Portman v. Middleton*, he continues: 'It is to be observed that not only must the circumstances be known to the supplier, but they must be such that the object must be taken to have been within the contemplation of both parties. I do not think that on the facts of the case as I have heard them, and upon the admissions, it can be said that it was within the contemplation of the supplier, namely, the defendants, that any delay in the delivery of this boiler was going to lead necessarily to loss of profits. There was nothing that I know of in the evidence to indicate how it was to be used or whether delivery of it by a particular day would necessarily be vital to the earning of these profits. I agree with the propositions of Mr. Paull that it was no part of the contract, and it cannot be taken to have been the basis of the contract, that the laundry would be unable to work if there was a delay in the delivery of the boiler, or that the laundry was extending its business, or that it had any special contracts which they could fulfil only by getting delivery of this boiler. In my view, therefore, this case falls within the second rule of *Hadley v. Baxendale* under which they are not liable for the payment of damages for loss of profits unless there is evidence before the court—which there is not—that the special object of this boiler was drawn to their attention and that they contracted upon the basis that delay in the delivery of the boiler would make them liable to payment of loss of profits.'

The answer to this reasoning has largely been anticipated in what has been said above, but we would wish to add: First, that the learned judge appears to infer that because certain 'special circumstances' were, in his view, not 'drawn to the notice of' the defendants and therefore, in his view, the operation of the 'second rule' was excluded, ergo nothing in respect of loss of business can be recovered under the 'first rule.' This inference is, in our view, no more justified in the present case than it was in the case of *Cory v. Thames Ironworks Company*. Secondly, that while it is not wholly clear what were the 'special circumstances' on the non-communication of which the learned judge relied, it would seem that they were, or included, the following: (a) the 'circumstance' that delay in delivering the boiler was going to lead 'necessarily' to loss of profits. But the true criterion is surely not what was bound 'necessarily' to result, but what was likely or liable to do so, and we think that it was amply conveyed to the defendants by what was communicated to them (plus what was patent without express communication) that delay in delivery was likely to lead to 'loss of business'; (b) the 'circumstance' that the plaintiffs needed the boiler 'to extend their business.' It was surely not necessary for the defendants to be specifically informed of this, as a precondition of being liable for loss of business. Reasonable, persons in the shoes of the defendants must be taken to foresee without any express intimation, that a laundry which, at a time when there was a famine of laundry facilities, was paying £ 2,000 odd for plant and intended at such a time to put such plant 'into use' immediately, would be likely to suffer in pocket from five months' delay in delivery of the plant in question, whether they intended by means of it to extend their business, or merely to maintain it, or to reduce a loss; (c) the 'circumstance' that the plaintiffs had the assured expectation of special contracts, which they could only fulfill by securing punctual delivery of the boiler. Here, no doubt, the learned judge had in mind the particularly lucrative dyeing contracts to which the plaintiffs looked forward and which they mention in para. 10 of the statement of claim. We agree that in order that the plaintiffs should recover specifically and as such the profits expected on these contracts, the defendants would have had to know, at the time of their agreement with the plaintiffs, of the prospect and terms of such contracts. We also agree that they did not in fact know these things. It does not, however, follow that the plaintiffs are precluded from recovering some general (and perhaps conjectural) sum for loss of business in respect of dyeing contracts to be reasonably expected, any more than in respect of laundering contracts to be reasonably expected.

Thirdly, the other point on which Streatfeild J. largely based his judgment was that there is a critical difference between the measure of damages applicable when the defendant defaults in supplying a self-contained profit-earning whole and when he defaults in supplying a part of that whole. In our view, there is no intrinsic magic, in this connexion, in the whole as against a part. The fact that a part only is involved is only significant in so far as it bears on the capacity of the supplier to foresee the consequences of non-delivery. If it is clear from the nature of the part (or the supplier of it is informed) that its non-delivery will have the same effect as non-delivery of the whole, his liability will be the same as if he had defaulted in delivering the whole. The cases of *Hadley v. Baxendale, British Columbia Sawmills v. Nettleship* and *Portman v. Middleton*, which were so strongly relied on for the defence and by the learned judge, were all cases in which, through want of a part, catastrophic results ensued, in that a whole concern was paralysed or sterilized; a mill stopped, a complex of machinery unable to be assembled, a threshing machine unable to be delivered in time for the harvest and therefore useless. In all three cases the defendants were absolved from liability to compensate the plaintiffs for the resulting loss of business, not because what they had failed to deliver was a part, but because there had been nothing to convey to them that want of that part would stultify the whole business of the person for whose benefit the part was contracted for. There is no resemblance between these cases and the present, in which, while there was no question of a total stoppage resulting from non-delivery, yet there was ample means of knowledge on the part of the defendants that business loss of some sort would be likely to result to the plaintiffs from the defendants' default in performing their contract.

We are therefore of opinion that the appeal should be allowed and the issue referred to an official referee as to what damage, if any, is recoverable in addition to the £ 110 awarded by the learned trial judge. The official referee would assess those damages in consonance with the findings in this judgment as to what the defendants knew or must be taken to have known at the material time, either party to be at liberty to call evidence as to the quantum of the damage in dispute.

Evra Corp. v. Swiss Bank Corp.

United States Court of Appeals for the Seventh Circuit, 1982.
673 F.2d 951.

■ POSNER, J. The question—one of first impression—in this diversity case is the extent of a bank's liability for failure to make a transfer of funds when requested by wire to do so. The essential facts are undisputed. In 1972 Hyman–Michaels Company, a large Chicago dealer in scrap metal, entered into a two-year contract to supply steel scrap to a Brazilian corporation. Hyman–Michaels chartered a ship, the Pandora, to carry the scrap to Brazil. The charter was for one year, with an option to extend the charter for a second year; specified a fixed daily rate of pay for the hire of the ship during both the initial and the option period, payable semi-monthly "in advance"; and provided that if payment was not made on time the Pandora's owner could cancel the charter. Payment was to be made by deposit to the owner's account in the Banque de Paris et des Pays–Bas (Suisse) in Geneva, Switzerland.

The usual method by which Hyman–Michaels, in Chicago, got the payments to the Banque de Paris in Geneva was to request the Continental Illinois National Bank and Trust Company of Chicago, where it had an account, to make a wire transfer of funds. Continental would debit Hyman–Michaels' account by the amount of the payment and then send a telex to its London office for retransmission to its correspondent bank in Geneva–Swiss Bank Corporation-asking Swiss Bank to deposit this amount in the Banque de Paris account of the Pandora's owner. The transaction was completed by the crediting of Swiss Bank's account at Continental by the same amount.

When Hyman–Michaels chartered the Pandora in June 1972, market charter rates were very low, and it was these rates that were fixed in the charter for its entire term-two years if Hyman–Michaels exercised its option. Shortly after the agreement was signed, however, charter rates began to climb and by October 1972 they were much higher than they had been in June. The Pandora's owners were eager to get out of the charter if they could.

At the end of October they thought they had found a way, for the payment that was due in the Banque de Paris on October 26 had not arrived by October 30, and on that day the Pandora's owner notified Hyman–Michaels that it was canceling the charter because of the breach of the payment term. Hyman–Michaels had mailed a check for the October 26 installment to the Banque de Paris rather than use the wire-transfer method of payment. It had done this in order to have the use of its money for the period that it would take the check to clear, about two weeks. But the check had not been mailed in Chicago until October 25 and of course did not reach Geneva on the twenty-sixth.

When Hyman–Michaels received notification that the charter was being canceled it immediately wired payment to the Banque de Paris, but the Pandora's owner refused to accept it and insisted that the charter was indeed canceled. The matter was referred to arbitration in accordance with the charter. On December 5, 1972, the arbitration panel ruled in favor of Hyman–Michaels. The panel noted that previous arbitration panels had "shown varying degrees of latitude to Charterers"; "In all cases, a pattern of obligation on Owners' part to protest, complain, or warn of intended withdrawal was expressed as an essential prerequisite to withdrawal, in spite of the clear wording of the operative clause. No such advance notice was given by Owners of M/V Pandora." One of the three members of the panel dissented; he thought the Pandora's owner was entitled to cancel.

Hyman–Michaels went back to making the charter payments by wire transfer. On the morning of April 25, 1973, it telephoned Continental Bank and requested it to transfer $27,000 to the Banque de Paris account of the Pandora's owner in payment for the charter hire period from April 27 to May 11, 1973. Since the charter provided for payment "in advance," this payment arguably was due by the close of business on April 26. The requested telex went out to Continental's London office on the afternoon of April 25, which was nighttime in England. Early the next morning a telex operator in Continental's London office dialed, as Continental's Chicago office had instructed him to do, Swiss Bank's general telex number, which rings in the bank's cable department. But that number was busy, and after trying unsuccessfully for an hour to engage it the Continental telex operator dialed another number, that of a machine in Swiss Bank's foreign exchange department which he had used in the past when the general number was engaged. We know this machine received the telexed message because it signaled the sending machine at both the beginning and end of the transmission that the telex was being received. Yet Swiss Bank failed to comply with the payment order, and no transfer of funds was made to the account of the Pandora's owner in the Banque de Paris.

No one knows exactly what went wrong. One possibility is that the receiving telex machine had simply run out of paper, in which event it would not print the message although it had received it. Another is that whoever took the message out of the machine after it was printed failed to deliver it to the banking department. Unlike the machine in the cable department that the Continental telex operator had originally tried to reach, the machines in the foreign exchange department were operated by junior foreign exchange dealers rather than by professional telex operators, although Swiss Bank knew that messages intended for other departments were sometimes diverted to the telex machines in the foreign exchange department.

At 8:30 a.m. the next day, April 27, Hyman–Michaels in Chicago received a telex from the Pandora's owner stating that the charter was canceled because payment for the April 27–May 11 charter period had not been made. Hyman–Michaels called over to Continental and told them to keep trying to effect payment through Swiss Bank even if the Pandora's owner rejected it. This instruction was confirmed in a letter to Continental dated April 28, in which Hyman–Michaels stated: "please instruct your London branch to advise their correspondents to persist in attempting to make this payment. This should be done even in the face of a rejection on the part of Banque de Paris to receive this payment. It is paramount that in order to strengthen our position in an arbitration that these funds continue to be readily available." Hyman–Michaels did not attempt to wire the money directly to the Banque de Paris as it had done on the occasion of its previous default. Days passed while the missing telex message was hunted unsuccessfully. Finally Swiss Bank suggested to Continental that it retransmit the telex message to the machine in the cable department and this was done on May 1. The next day Swiss Bank attempted to deposit the $27,000 in the account of the Pandora's owner at the Banque de Paris but the payment was refused.

Again the arbitrators were convened and rendered a decision. In it they ruled that Hyman–Michaels had been "blameless" up until the morning of April 27, when it first learned that the Banque de Paris had not received payment on April 26, but that "being faced with this situation," Hyman–Michaels had "failed to do everything in (its) power to remedy it. The action taken was immediate but did not prove to be adequate, in that (Continental) Bank and its correspondent required some 5/6 days to trace and effect the lost instruction to remit. (Hyman–Michaels) could have ordered an immediate duplicate payment-or even sent a Banker's check by hand or special messengers, so that the funds could have reached owner's Bank, not later than April 28th." By failing to do any of these things Hyman–Michaels had "created the opening" that the Pandora's owner was seeking in order to be able to cancel the charter. It had "acted imprudently." The arbitration panel concluded, reluctantly but unanimously, that this time the Pandora's owner was entitled to cancel the agreement. The arbitration decision was confirmed by a federal district court in New York.

Hyman–Michaels then brought this diversity action against Swiss Bank, seeking to recover its expenses in the second arbitration proceeding plus the profits that it lost because of the cancellation of the charter. The contract by which Hyman–Michaels had agreed to ship scrap steel to Brazil had been terminated by the buyer in March 1973 and Hyman–Michaels had promptly subchartered the Pandora at market rates, which by April 1973 were double the rates fixed in the charter. Its lost profits are based on the difference between the charter and subcharter rates.

The case was tried to a district judge without a jury. In his decision, 522 F. Supp. 820 (N.D.Ill. 1981), he first ruled that the substantive law applicable to Hyman–Michaels' claim against Swiss Bank was that of Illinois, rather than Switzerland as urged by Swiss Bank, and that Swiss Bank had been negligent and under Illinois law was liable to Hyman–Michaels for $2.1 million in damages. This figure was made up of about $16,000 in arbitration expenses and the rest in lost profits on the subcharter of the Pandora. The case comes to us on Swiss Bank's appeal from the judgment in favor of Hyman–Michaels.

When a bank fails to make a requested transfer of funds, this can cause two kinds of loss. First, the funds themselves or interest on them may be lost, and of course the fee paid for the transfer, having bought nothing, becomes a loss item. These are "direct" (sometimes called "general") damages. Hyman–Michaels is not seeking any direct damages in this case and apparently sustained none. It did not lose any part of the $27,000; although its account with Continental Bank was debited by this amount prematurely, it was not an interest-bearing account so Hyman–Michaels lost no interest; and Hyman–Michaels paid no fee either to Continental or to Swiss Bank for the aborted transfer. A second type of loss, which either the payor or the payee may suffer, is a dislocation in one's business triggered by the failure to pay. Swiss Bank's failure to transfer funds to the Banque de Paris when requested to do so by Continental Bank set off a chain reaction which resulted in an arbitration proceeding that was costly to Hyman–Michaels and in the cancellation of a highly profitable contract. It is those costs and lost profits-"consequential" or, as they are sometimes called, "special" damages-that Hyman–Michaels seeks in this lawsuit, and recovered below. It is conceded that if Hyman–Michaels was entitled to consequential damages, the district court measured them correctly. The only issue is whether it was entitled to consequential damages.

If a bank loses a check, its liability is governed by Article 4 of the Uniform Commercial Code, which precludes consequential damages unless the bank is acting in bad faith. If Article 4 applies to this transaction, Hyman–Michaels cannot recover the damages that it seeks, because Swiss Bank was not acting in bad faith. Maybe the language of Article 4 could be stretched to include electronic fund transfers, see section 4–102(2), but they were not in the contemplation of the draftsmen. For purposes of this case we shall assume that Article 4 is inapplicable, and apply common law principles instead.

Hadley v. Baxendale, 9 Ex. 341, 156 Eng.Rep. 145 (1854), is the leading common law case on liability for consequential damages caused by failure or delay in carrying out a commercial undertaking. The engine shaft in plaintiffs' corn mill had broken and they hired the defendants, a common carrier, to transport the shaft to the manufacturer, who was to make a new one using the broken shaft as a model. The carrier failed to deliver the shaft within the time promised. With the engine shaft out of service the mill was shut down. The plaintiffs sued the defendants for the lost profits of the mill during the additional period that it was shut down because of the defendants' breach of their promise. The court held that the lost profits were not a proper item of damages, because "in the great multitude of cases of millers sending off broken shafts to third persons by a carrier under ordinary circumstances, such consequences (the stoppage of the mill and resulting loss of profits) would not, in all probability, have occurred; and these special circumstances were here never communicated by the plaintiffs to the defendants." 156 Eng.Rep. at 151.

The rule of *Hadley v. Baxendale*—that consequential damages will not be awarded unless the defendant was put on notice of the special circumstances giving rise to them-has been applied in many Illinois cases, and *Hadley* cited approvingly. In Siegel, the plaintiff had delivered $200 to Western Union with instructions to transmit it to a friend of the plaintiff's. The money was to be bet (legally) on a horse, but this was not disclosed in the instructions. Western Union misdirected the money order and it did not reach the friend until several hours after the race had taken place. The horse that the plaintiff had intended to bet on won and would have paid $1650 on the plaintiff's $200 bet if the bet had been placed. He sued Western Union for his $1450 lost profit, but the court held that under the rule of *Hadley v. Baxendale* Western Union was not liable, because it "had no notice or knowledge of the purpose for which the money was being transmitted." 37 N.E.2d at 871.

The present case is similar, though Swiss Bank knew more than Western Union knew in Siegel; it knew or should have known, from Continental Bank's previous telexes, that Hyman–Michaels was paying the Pandora Shipping Company for the hire of a motor vessel named Pandora. But it did not know when payment was due, what the terms of the charter were, or that they had turned out to be extremely favorable to Hyman–Michaels. And it did not know that Hyman–Michaels knew the Pandora's owner would try to cancel the charter, and probably would succeed, if Hyman–Michaels was ever again late in making payment, or that despite this peril Hyman–Michaels would not try to pay until the last possible moment and in the event of a delay in transmission would not do everything in its power to minimize the consequences of the delay. Electronic funds transfers are not so unusual as to automatically place a bank on notice of extraordinary consequences if such a transfer goes awry. Swiss Bank did not have enough information to infer that if it lost a $27,000 payment order it would face a liability in excess of $2 million.

It is true that in both *Hadley* and *Siegel* there was a contract between the parties and here there was none. We cannot be certain that the Illinois courts would apply the principles of those cases outside of the contract area. As so often in diversity cases, there is an irreducible amount of speculation involved in attempting to predict the reaction of a state's courts to a new issue. The best we can do is to assume that the Illinois courts would look to the policies underlying cases such as *Hadley* and *Siegel* and, to the extent they found them pertinent, would apply those cases here. We must therefore ask what difference it should make whether the parties are or are not bound to each other by a contract. On the one hand, it seems odd that the absence of a contract would enlarge rather than limit the extent of liability. After all, under Swiss law the absence of a contract would be devastating to Hyman–Michaels' claim. Privity is not a wholly artificial concept. It is one thing to imply a duty to one with whom one has a contract and another to imply it to the entire world.

On the other hand, contract liability is strict. A breach of contract does not connote wrongdoing; it may have been caused by circumstances beyond the promisor's control—a strike, a fire, the failure of a supplier to deliver an essential input. And while such contract doctrines as impossibility, impracticability, and frustration relieve promisors from liability for some failures to perform that are beyond their control, many other such failures are actionable although they could not have been prevented by the exercise of due care. The district judge found that Swiss Bank had been negligent in losing Continental Bank's telex message and it can be argued that Swiss Bank should therefore be liable for a broader set of consequences than if it had only broken a contract. But Siegel implicitly rejects this distinction. Western Union had not merely broken its contract to deliver the plaintiff's money order; it had "negligently misdirected" the money order. "The company's negligence is conceded." 37 N.E.2d at 869, 871. Yet it was not liable for the consequences.

Siegel, we conclude, is authority for holding that Swiss Bank is not liable for the consequences of negligently failing to transfer Hyman–Michaels' funds to Banque de Paris; reason for such a holding is found in the animating principle of *Hadley v. Baxendale*, which is that the costs of the untoward consequence of a course of dealings should be borne by that party who was able to avert the consequence at least cost and failed to do so. In Hadley the untoward consequence was the shutting down of the mill. The carrier could have avoided it by delivering the engine shaft on time. But the mill owners, as the court noted, could have avoided it simply by having a spare shaft. 156 Eng.Rep. at 151. Prudence required that they have a spare shaft anyway, since a replacement could not be obtained at once even if there was no undue delay in carting the broken shaft to and the replacement shaft from the manufacturer. The court refused to imply a duty on the part of the carrier to guarantee the mill owners against the consequences of their own lack of prudence, though of course if the parties had stipulated for such a guarantee the court would have enforced it. The notice requirement of *Hadley v. Baxendale* is designed to assure that such an improbable guarantee really is intended.

This case is much the same, though it arises in a tort rather than a contract setting. Hyman–Michaels showed a lack of prudence throughout. It was imprudent for it to mail in Chicago a letter that unless received the next day in Geneva would put Hyman–Michaels in breach of a contract that was very profitable to it and that the other party to the contract had every interest in canceling. It was imprudent thereafter for Hyman–Michaels, having narrowly avoided cancellation and having (in the words of its appeal brief in this court) been "put on notice that the payment provision of the Charter would be strictly enforced thereafter," to wait till arguably the last day before payment was due to instruct its bank to transfer the necessary funds overseas. And it was imprudent in the last degree for Hyman–Michaels, when it received notice of cancellation on the last possible day payment was due, to fail to pull out all the stops to get payment to the Banque de Paris on that day, and instead to dither while Continental and Swiss Bank wasted five days looking for the lost telex message. Judging from the obvious reluctance with which the arbitration panel finally decided to allow the Pandora's owner to cancel the charter, it might have made all the difference if Hyman–Michaels had gotten payment to the Banque de Paris by April 27 or even by Monday, April 30, rather than allowed things to slide until May 2.

This is not to condone the sloppy handling of incoming telex messages in Swiss Bank's foreign department. But Hyman–Michaels is a sophisticated business enterprise. It knew or should have known that even the Swiss are not infallible; that messages sometimes get lost or delayed in transit among three banks, two of them located 5000 miles apart, even when all the banks are using reasonable care; and that therefore it should take its own precautions against the consequences-best known to itself-of a mishap that might not be due to anyone's negligence.

We are not the first to remark the affinity between the rule of *Hadley v. Baxendale* and the doctrine, which is one of tort as well as contract law and is a settled part of the common law of Illinois, of avoidable consequences. If you are hurt in an automobile accident and unreasonably fail to seek medical treatment, the injurer, even if negligent, will not be held liable for the aggravation of the injury due to your own unreasonable behavior after the accident. If in addition you failed to fasten your seat belt, you may be barred from collecting the tort damages that would have been prevented if you had done so. Hyman–Michaels' behavior in steering close to the wind prior to April 27 was like not fastening one's seat belt; its failure on April 27 to wire a duplicate payment immediately after disaster struck was like refusing to seek medical attention after a serious accident. The seat-belt cases show that the doctrine of avoidable consequences applies whether the tort victim acts imprudently before or after the tort is committed. See Prosser, *Handbook of the Law of Torts* 424 (4th ed. 1971). Hyman–Michaels did both.

The rule of *Hadley v. Baxendale* links up with tort concepts in another way. The rule is sometimes stated in the form that only foreseeable damages are recoverable in a breach of contract action. E.g., *Restatement (Second) of Contracts § 351* (1979). So expressed, it corresponds to the tort principle that limits liability to the foreseeable consequence of the defendant's carelessness. See, e.g., *Neering v. Illinois Cent. R.R. Co.*, 50 N.E.2d 497, 503 (1943). The amount of care that a person ought to take is a function of the probability and magnitude of the harm that may occur if he does not take care. If he does not know what that probability and magnitude are, he cannot determine how much care to take. That would be Swiss Bank's dilemma if it were liable for consequential damages from failing to carry out payment orders in timely fashion. To estimate the extent of its probable liability in order to know how many and how elaborate fail-safe features to install in its telex rooms or how much insurance to buy against the inevitable failures, Swiss Bank would have to collect reams of information about firms that are not even its regular customers. It had no banking relationship with Hyman–Michaels. It did not know or have reason to know how at once precious and fragile Hyman–Michaels' contract with the Pandora's owner was. These were circumstances too remote from Swiss Bank's practical range of knowledge to have affected its decisions as to who should man the telex machines in the foreign department or whether it should have more intelligent machines or should install more machines in the cable department, any more than the falling of a platform scale because a conductor jostled a passenger who was carrying fireworks was a prospect that could have influenced the amount of care taken by the Long Island Railroad.

In short, Swiss Bank was not required in the absence of a contractual undertaking to take precautions or insure against a harm that it could not measure but that was known with precision to Hyman–Michaels, which could by the exercise of common prudence have averted it completely. As Chief Judge Cardozo (the author of [*Palsgraf* v. Long Island Railroad Co., 162 N.E. 99 (N.Y. 1928)]) remarked in discussing the application of *Hadley v. Baxendale* to the liability of telegraph companies for errors in transmission, "The sender can protect himself by insurance in one form or another if the risk of nondelivery or error appears to be too great. The company, if it takes out insurance for itself, can do no more than guess at the loss to be avoided." *Kerr S.S. Co. v. Radio Corp. of America*, 157 N.E. 140, 142 (1927).

But Kerr is a case from New York, not Illinois, and Hyman–Michaels argues that two early Illinois telegraph cases compel us to rule in its favor against Swiss Bank. *Postal Tel. Cable Co. v. Lathrop*, 23 N.E. 583 (1890), involved the garbled transmission of two telegrams from a coffee dealer-who as the telegraph company knew was engaged in buying and selling futures contracts-to his broker. The first telegram (there is no need to discuss the second) directed the broker to buy 1000 bags of August coffee for the dealer's account. This got changed in transmission to 2000 bags, and because the price fell the dealer sustained an extra loss for which he sued the telegraph company. The court held that the company had had notice enough to make it liable for consequential damages under the rule of *Hadley v. Baxendale*. It knew it was transmitting buy and sell orders in a fluctuating market and that a garbled transmission could result in large losses. There was no suggestion that the dealer should have taken his own precautions against such mistakes. In *Providence–Washington Ins. Co. v. Western Union Tel. Co.*, 93 N.E. 134 (1910), a telegram from an insurance company canceling a policy was misdirected, and before it turned up there was a fire and the insurance company was liable on the policy. This was the precise risk created by delay, it was obvious on the face of the telegram, and the telegraph company was therefore liable for the insurance company's loss on the policy. Again there was no suggestion that the plaintiff had neglected any precaution. Both cases are distinguishable from the present case: the defendants had more information and the plaintiffs were not imprudent.

The legal principles that we have said are applicable to this case were not applied below. Although the district judge's opinion is not entirely clear, he apparently thought the rule of *Hadley v. Baxendale* inapplicable and the imprudence of Hyman–Michaels irrelevant. See 522 F. Supp. at 833. He did state that the damages to Hyman–Michaels were foreseeable because "a major international bank" should know that a failure to act promptly on a telexed request to transfer funds could cause substantial damage; but Siegel—and for that matter Lathrop and Providence–Washington-make clear that that kind of general foreseeability, which is present in virtually every case, does not justify an award of consequential damages.

We could remand for new findings based on the proper legal standard, but it is unnecessary to do so. The undisputed facts, recited in this opinion, show as a matter of law that Hyman–Michaels is not entitled to recover consequential damages from Swiss Bank.

The judgment in favor of Hyman–Michaels against Swiss Bank is reversed with directions to enter judgment for Swiss Bank.

SO ORDERED.

* * *

The Restatement section, *Hadley*, and *Victoria Laundry* are reasonably self-explanatory. It is important, in reading *Hadley*, to understand that although the recitation of the facts suggests that the miller's servant informed the carrier that his mill was stopped and would remain so until the new crankshaft was received, the judges' opinions make plain that they reached the opposite conclusion. This confusion is an artifact of the method of compiling the reports of cases in English courts at the time. In any event, the Restatement section codifies the *Hadley* standard of foreseeability (*Hadley* is so famous that the foreseeability rule, to this day, retains its name), although it organizes the various possibilities involving actual and imputed knowledge somewhat differently from the statement of the rule in *Hadley* itself. Finally, *Victoria Laundry* illustrates the rule in action, specifically with respect to the questions what knowledge of probable consequences of breach will be imputed to which types of promisors.

Evra is much more complicated. The first line of reasoning in the opinion suggests an economic rationale for the *Hadley* rule that is adapted from the law and economics of torts. (*Evra* is, after all, technically a tort case, since the defendant bank was not the plaintiff's own, but merely a corresponding bank, so that no contract between plaintiff and defendant existed.) This argument proposes that allowing disappointed promisees to recover even unforeseeable damages is inefficient, because these damages might be more cheaply avoided by the promisees themselves than by the breaching promisors. The miller in *Hadley* might have kept a spare crankshaft on hand, and the charteree in *Evra* might have paid more promptly or wired replacement payment directly to the ship-owner as soon as he learned of the delay. Each of these avoidance moves is much cheaper than requiring all carriers to make extravagant efforts that ensure on-time delivery or all banks to install triplicate backup systems that ensure that all telex instructions are implemented immediately upon receipt. In each case, then, allowing the plaintiffs to recover damages for their losses would allocate the obligation of loss-avoidance to a party on whom it was unnecessarily burdensome, with inefficient results: insofar as the avoidance was made, this would be costlier than efficient; insofar as the avoidance was not made, there would be inefficiently many losses; and the contemplation of both these possibilities would lead to an inefficiently low level of profitable but risk-of-loss-imposing activity.[6]

This argument plausibly explains why the plaintiffs in *Evra*, and also in *Hadley*, should lose. But it does not do very well at explaining why the doctrinal mechanism for producing this outcome should be *Hadley*'s foreseeability rule, with all of the broader implications that this rule has for the many other cases that it covers. In particular, it is not at all clear—and the argument just rehearsed does not make it clear—why the identity of the cheaper cost avoider in cases like *Hadley* and *Evra* should track whether or not the defendant is able to foresee the plaintiff's eventual loss, on the specific understanding of foreseeability introduced by *Hadley* and adopted in the Restatement. Certainly the balance of costs between maintaining a supply of spare crankshafts and ensuring speedy carriage, or between making early and backup payments and ensuring that telex instructions are promptly implemented, bears no immediate or obvious connection to the questions concerning the defendant's knowledge of the plaintiff's vulnerabilities that form the centerpiece of the *Hadley* doctrine. An adequate economic explanation of the foreseeability rule must therefore look elsewhere, or at least to an argument that develops the general idea of the cheaper cost avoider for the special context of the defendant's knowledge.

Something like this argument is indeed hinted at in the second rationale that the *Evra* opinion provides for the case's outcome, namely the suggestion that the plaintiff could (and indeed should) have expressly asked the defendant to guarantee his profits in case of a delay in implementing his telexed money transfer. This suggestion is worth investigating more closely, in order to understand its connection to economic efficiency and its implications for the recovery of unforeseeable contract damages.

To develop the argument, consider a stylization of the general context—involving a firm, call it a shipper, that transports goods (*Hadley*), or money (*Evra*), or even just information) for many customers.[7] To simplify

---

6. This of course assumes that transactions costs prevent prospective plaintiffs and prospective defendants from changing the legal rule to make it efficient. The Coase Theorem, after all, applies in torts as well as in contracts.

7. This development of the argument follows Gwyn Quillen, *Contract Damages and Cross-Subsidization*, 61 S. CAL. L. REV. 1125 (1988).

matters (but without loss of generality) suppose that there are only two types of customers who employ the shipper, and that since the customers' shipments look the same from the outside, the shipper cannot afford to distinguish between them. More specifically, suppose that:

> 1/2 of the shippers are cheap-breach customers, who send packages worth $10.

> 1/2 of the shippers are expensive-breach customers, who send packages worth $100.

Suppose also (again, without loss of generality) that the only way in which the shipper ever breaches is by irretrievably losing a shipment, and that the chance of such a breach is 1 in 100. Finally, and again just to fix ideas, suppose that the seller's marginal cost—the cost of processing and transporting one additional shipment—is $0.50.

Efficiency requires the seller to charge all buyers a price that reflects her marginal cost of providing the shipping plus the damages for which she will be liable in case she breaches. On the facts just stated, this amounts to $0.50 (marginal cost) for all customers plus $0.10 (expected damages) for cheap-breach customers and $1.00 (expected damages) for expensive breach customers. Accordingly, the efficient pricing policy for the seller would be to charge

> $0.60 to each cheap-breach customer, and

> $1.50 to each expensive-breach customer.

But the seller cannot charge different prices to the two classes of buyer (recall the assumption that she cannot profitably distinguish between cheap and expensive packages, because they look the same from the outside and are prohibitively costly to open and reseal). Accordingly, the seller must charge buyers of both types the same price. In particular, she will charge a single price equal to marginal cost plus average expected damages. This price is

> $0.50 + 1/2 ($0.10 + $1.00) = $1.05.

Compared to the efficient pricing policy, this price overcharges the cheap-breach customers and undercharges the expensive-breach customers. In this way, the single price generates a *cross subsidization* from the former to the latter. The cheap-breach customers must pay for a portion of the cost of servicing the expensive-breach customers—specifically, for 45 cents of this cost.

This is an unattractive result. Certainly, it is inefficient. On the one hand, the cheap-breach customers are being charged more than the true cost of servicing them (the additional charge is being used to subsidize the expensive-breach customers). Thus the cheap-breach customers will under-consume the shipping service. In particular, those cheap-breach customers who value the shipping service at more than the true cost of providing it to them but less than the price they are charged—that is at more that $0.60 but less than $1.05—will not engage it when they should. On the other hand, the expensive-breach customers are being charged less than the true cost of servicing them (they are receiving a subsidy from the cheap-breach customers). Thus the expensive-breach customers will over-consume the shipping service. Those expensive-breach customers who value the shipping service at less than the true cost of providing it to them but more than the price they are charged—that is, at less than $1.50 but more than $1.05—will engage it when they should not.

Such cross-subsidization may also be unfair (although it will not always be). It fails fully to reward the cheap-breach customers, whoever they are, for imposing lower costs on society. And the cheap-breach customers may well be special objects of concern under broader principles of distributive justice—it may be, for example, that the fact that they send less valuable packages is explained by their being poorer quite generally.

The source of these difficulties is the interaction between the shipper's inability to distinguish among her customers and the full expectation remedy. When the seller cannot price differently in dealings with cheap-breach and expensive-breach buyers, then granting full expectation damages to both classes of buyers—damages that place each class of buyer in the position that performance would have done—causes the cheap-breach buyers to subsidize the expensive-breach buyers, with the result that the wrong buyers purchase the seller's goods or services.

This makes it natural to ask how the law might avoid such cross-subsidization and the inefficiency and unfairness that it generates. The answer is to step back from the full expectation remedy, to limit damages to those needed to secure the contractual expectations that are common to all buyers. Under this remedy rule, the shipper in the example would be liable for only $0.10 in damages to all customers—both cheap-breach and expensive-breach—and would charge all customers a base price $0.60. Customers who wished to recover greater damages in case their shipments are lost could always do so, but only by informing the seller of the greater value of their shipments, and paying a premium commensurate to the greater risks that shipping their more valuable goods imposes on the shipper. Now there will be no cross-subsidization, and all and only those customers who value the shipper's services at more than their true economic costs will engage the shipper.

And this, no doubt by now unsurprisingly, is precisely the result secured by the rule of *Hadley v. Baxendale*, which acts under the heading of foreseeability, to limit damages, unless there is special notification, to the normal losses sustained in the ordinary course of events, i.e., to the losses common to all buyers, including cheap-breach buyers.[8]

---

8. The *Hadley* rule may not be strictly necessary for achieving this result, because it may always be possible for sellers to achieve the limitations of liability that the rule contemplates by adopting such limits in the express language of their contracts. But although sellers might be able to achieve the *Hadley* result by express contract terms (subject to limitations on form-contracting discussed below), doing so will cost them something—in drafting and, especially for naive sellers, in identifying and thinking through the problem. By shifting the default from liability for full expectations (to be limited by express contract) to liability for foreseeable expectations (to be expanded by express contract) the *Hadley* rule lowers contracting costs.

Moreover, this analysis may be connected back to the argument about the cheaper cost avoider presented in *Evra*. That argument imagined that the avoidance mechanisms were physical—maintaining a spare crank shaft, or sending a replacement payment. But the cheapest avoidance mechanism, in many such cases, is simply to tell the shipper of one's special vulnerability to loss—perhaps, as in the *Evra* opinion's suggestion, by asking the shipper to guarantee one's losses. *Hadley* is, in the final analysis, an information-forcing rule, which is designed to induce the exposure of economically valuable information by the party who can produce and communicate it most cheaply. This way of putting the point reveals the limits of the economic argument in favor of the *Hadley* rule. If the buyer is not the cheapest producer of information about her risk of harm—perhaps, to return to the example, because the harm is caused by damaging rather than losing the shipment, and the shipper has greater expertise about the nature of this type or risk—then the *Hadley* rule will no longer be efficient. Indeed, a similar difficulty will arise if sellers have varying chances of losing packages in their care, which they know but which buyers cannot affordably discover.

Finally, it is worth briefly mentioning now one specific consequence of the foreseeability doctrine, which will be important to later materials. This doctrine is commonly employed to exclude damages for emotional distress from plaintiffs' recoveries for breach of contract, on the grounds that it is not foreseeable that breaches will cause such distress. Contract damages are, in this respect, substantially less generous than tort damages (although tort law also includes a range of doctrines that limit, at least in some circumstances, tortfeasors' liability for causing their victims emotional distress).

Two exceptions to this rule against emotional distress damages for breach of contract contemplate (a) cases in which the emotional distress accompanies a bodily injury, as in *Sullivan v. O'Connor*,[9] and (b) cases in which the breached contract is of a kind such that serious emotional disturbance is a particularly likely result of a breach. This second exception is, however, more narrowly construed than a literal interpretation (or indeed the interpretation given to the analogous words in the *Hadley* rule more generally) would suggest. Thus although emotional distress damages are commonly allowed in connection with breaches of contracts to prepare wedding dresses or to preserve bodies for burial,[10] for example, they may be denied in circumstances in which emotional distress damages are equally likely to result from breach but the distress is less sympathetically synchro-

---

9. Note that the contract breaches in such cases almost always involve an accompanying tort, although *Sullivan* illustrates that this is not necessarily so.

10. *See Lewis v. Holmes*, 34 So. 66 (La. 1903) (allowing a bride to recover for "deprivation of intellectual enjoyment and for mental suffering" that resulted from tailor's delivery of an ill-fitting wedding dress); *Flores v. Baca*, 871 P.2d 962 (N.M. 1994) (holding a funeral home director liable for a family's emotional distress when the director failed to honor his agreement to embalm a body, and noting that emotional distress damages are "especially [appropriate] in those cases in which the purpose of the contract would be frustrated unless damages for mental anguish were awarded for breach.")

nized with prevailing cultural preconceptions or political ideology. A particularly dramatic, although not necessarily practically important, example of such a case is *Keltner v. Washington County*, 800 P. 2d 752 (Or. 1990), in which emotional distress damages were denied for breach of a contract in which state police broke their oral promise to a child witness to protect her identity. (The child had learned the name of an alleged murderer from an acquaintance, but felt reluctant to pass along the information without assurances that authorities would protect her. State police promised to keep her statements anonymous, but they revealed her name to prosecutors who passed it on to the suspect's defense attorney.)

Other examples of the law's reluctance to award emotional distress damages are less dramatic but much more important. Foremost among these is the rule that emotional distress damages are virtually never recoverable for wrongful terminations—that is, breaches of employment contracts—in spite of the fact that such distress is surely an expected consequence of being fired. This special case will be taken up in greater detail later on, in conjunction with the materials on employment at will.

CHAPTER 5

EFFICIENCY AND BUYER DECISIONS

Up until now, the argument has expressly focused exclusively on sellers' decisions. But the discussion of foreseeability introduced, albeit in the background, the possibility that buyers—by their nature, and perhaps also by their decisions—can influence both the likelihood of breach and the size of the harm that a breach produces. Indeed, as the discussion below will elaborate in some detail, buyers can in any number of ways have substantial effects on the expected costs associated with the possibility of a seller's breach. This makes it important to consider the effects of contract law's remedy rules on buyers' decisions.

5.1 DOUBLE RESPONSIBILITY AT THE MARGIN

Breach of contract is not special in this respect.[1] Instead, breach of contract merely presents one of many circumstances, cutting across social and economic practices and doctrinal legal categories, in which the activities of two (or more) parties are jointly necessary causes of a loss. When a car strikes a pedestrian, for example, and breaks her legs, the occurrence of the loss depends on the activities of both the driver and the person on foot: if either had been elsewhere at the moment of impact, there would have been no accident. (This remains the case, moreover, even when the pedestrian is standing entirely innocently on a sidewalk that the driver recklessly drives over.) Similarly, when a seller fails to deliver goods that a buyer has purchased (or delivers defective goods) and the buyer suffers disappointed expectations or even a reliance loss, the occurrence of this loss again depends on the activities of both the seller and buyer: there would have been no loss if the seller had not breached, of course; but there would equally have been no loss if the buyer had not formed any contractual expectations, including by developing her business plan in reliance on the seller's performance. (This remains true, once again, even when the buyer acts responsibly and the seller's breach is reckless or even in bad faith.)

In such circumstances, economic efficiency draws no fundamental distinction between the parties—pedestrian and driver; or buyer and seller. There may, to be sure, be moral differences as between the parties, and these moral differences may make it natural to call the driver a tortfeasor and the seller a breacher and to call the pedestrian and buyer victims. But these concerns, insofar as they survive reflection, must be based on

---

1. The discussion below follows Robert Cooter, *Unity in Tort, Contract, and Property*, 73 CAL. L. REV. 1 (1985).

considerations other than economic efficiency. As long as the loss may be avoided by altering either party's conduct, economic efficiency requires that each party be given incentives to avoid insofar as it can avoid more cheaply.

This idea may be stated more precisely in another way. Assume that the expected size of a loss is determined by the conduct of two parties (who can each influence either the chance that the loss will occur or its severity in case it does occur), whom we will call, by stipulation, the injurer and the victim or the seller and the buyer. In such a case, efficiency requires each party fully to bear the costs and benefits of all her behaviors that affect the occurrence and size of the loss, including the changes in the expected loss that these behaviors engender—to bear these costs herself, rather than passing them on to the other party. As an economist would say, efficiency requires each party to *internalize* these costs and benefits of her conduct. In particular, when both parties can take precautions against the loss, efficiency requires that both bear, at the margin, the full cost of the loss— that both parties are held, at the margin, to be fully responsible for any loss that they could have prevented, but did not.

The rationale behind this "double responsibility" principle is not hard to see: if a party can affect the expected size of a loss, then efficiency requires that that party take the loss appropriately into account when considering whether or not to engage in the loss-affecting conduct. Any liability rule that relieves that party of all or some of the cost of the loss insulates the party from the consequences of its actions—in particular, such a rule shields a party that fails to take measures to avoid the loss from the costs, in the form of a greater expected loss, that this failure imposes. Such rules are therefore inefficient, because they leave parties with inadequate incentives to take efficient precautions to avoid inefficient losses. (Of course this assumes, recall the Coase Theorem, that transactions costs are high enough so that those left to bear the losses cannot buy an efficient level of the party's precautionary conduct.)

But now the argument has run up against a paradox of sorts. And although it is a shallow paradox only, which may be fairly easily resolved, the paradox must be stated before its resolution can be properly understood.

> First, efficiency requires that tortfeasors and promisors whose conduct affects the losses suffered from accidents and breaches bear the full costs of this conduct—by paying damages equal to the full harm that they have caused.

> Second, efficiency requires that victims whose conduct affects the losses suffered from accidents and breaches bear the full costs of this conduct—by receiving no compensation for their injuries from an accident or breach.

These requirement may easily be met, for example by leaving victims to bear the full burdens of whatever losses they have suffered and, at the same time, requiring tortfeasors and promisors to pay fines (remitted to the state or to some other third party) that also equal the full burdens of the losses. But private law generally does without such fines, paid to third parties, and this establishes the final leg on which the paradox of compensation stands.

Third, in private law, the damages paid by an injurer equal the compensation received by a victim.

This is a paradox because the three principles cannot all be implemented at once. Insofar as damages paid by injurers are received as compensation by victims, imposing responsibility on injurers *relieves* victims of responsibility, and allowing responsibility to remain with victims *relieves* injurers of responsibility.

Thus in torts, if both the tortfeasor and the victim must take precautions to reduce the loss to an optimal level, strict liability with damages set at any fraction of the harm is inefficient. If the rule of law is zero liability then the injurer has no incentive to take any precautions, no matter how cheap and effective. If the rule of law is strict liability with 100% compensation then the victim has no incentive to take precautions, no matter how cheap and effective. And if the rule creates strict liability with compensation set at some fraction of the loss then both the tortfeasor and the victim will have inadequate incentives to take precautions.

Similarly in contract, if the rule of law requires promisors to compensate none of the burdens that their breaches impose, then promisors have no incentive to perform. If the rule of law requires promisors to compensate 100% of the burdens that their breaches cause, then promisees have no incentive to take precautions that reduce the expected burdens from breach. And if the rule requires promisors to pay a fixed fraction of the burdens breaches cause, then promisors have insufficient incentive to perform and promisees have insufficient incentive to take precautions.

In private law, it seems, both parties cannot be responsible at once—and so efficiency cannot be achieved.

The way out of the paradox is actually not difficult to implement, but it can be hard to see. The crucial insight is that incentives influence behavior *on the margin*. Thus punishments, for example, deter the full range of criminal conduct only insofar they are applied additively to each incrementally more criminal act. And efficient penal orders must match each addition in criminality with an increase in sanction sufficient to deter it. (Thus it is famously inefficient to impose too great sanctions on petty crimes, because once these sanctions have been imposed insufficient additional sanctions are available to deter persons who have committed these petty crimes, and incurred the sanctions, from moving on to more serious crimes, for which no adequate new sanctions can be imposed.) Similarly, the rules of private law encourage precautions only insofar as each increment of carelessness engenders an appropriate increment of liability. Accordingly, efficient remedies in private law require the internalization not of total costs but rather of *marginal* costs, because the tradeoffs that affect decision-making always occur on the margin.

This is important because it is possible, even in private law (where injurers or breachers pay remedies to victims) for both parties involved in a loss to bear 100% of the cost of the loss *on the margin*. The implementation of this way out is easiest to see in tort, where an efficient result can be achieved by liability rules that assign liability according to the fault of the parties, as in a simple negligence regime. If the substantive standard of negligence is set to correspond to the efficient level of injurer precaution, then the result is double responsibility at the margin: the tortfeasor bears the loss if he takes any less than the efficient level of precaution, but he can escape liability by demonstrating this level of care; and, once the tortfeasor demonstrates the appropriate level of care, any losses that nevertheless occur lie where they fall, that is, with the victim. Consequently, an efficient legal standard of care will cause the tortfeasor to behave efficiently. And given this efficient behavior by the tortfeasor, the victim will be left bearing the entire residual loss and so will also take efficient precautions (at least in equilibrium). Finally, as long as the substantive standard of care is set at the efficient level, then efficient levels of precaution can be achieved consistent with a wide range of distributional outcomes—negligence, negligence with contributory negligence, and comparative negligence can all be efficient.

So much for torts, which serve, here, merely as a convenient illustration of the general point. The real focus, at present, is on contracts, and the application of double responsibility on the margin to this area will be developed in greater detail. The starting-point for this development is the thought, explained earlier, that unqualified expectation damages—which put the buyer whatever position performance would have done, regardless of her own conduct—cause a breaching promisor-seller to internalize the *whole* of the promisee-buyer's loss and therefore to act efficiently with respect to the decision whether to perform or breach. But now suppose, as is often that case, that the buyer can affect the value he attributes to performance or the losses he suffers on breach. In particular, buyers can have such effects at (at least) three points in the contract process: prior to performance, buyers can make investments in *reliance* on their sellers' performance that increase their contractual expectations but also increase their losses on breach; following breach, buyers can *mitigate* the losses that the breach imposes on them, by securing substitute performance, for example, or avoiding consequential losses; and following a remedy award, buyers can *cure* the losses that they have suffered, for example by deploying the remedy to replace performance. Unqualified expectation damages—damages that impose on breaching sellers an absolute duty to secure their buyers' contractual expectations, whatever they are—relieve buyers of any incentive to manage their expectations and the various processes of making them whole following breach. Accordingly, efficiency requires modifying the simple version of the expectation remedy introduced earlier to impose double responsibility on the margin and give buyers incentives to behave efficiently with respect to reliance, mitigation, and cure.

As it happens, the law of contract remedies includes doctrines qualifying the expectation remedy that may be interpreted to do just this.

5.2 THE RELIANCE DECISION

A buyer can increase the returns to a contract by taking action in reliance on his seller's performance before the seller has in fact performed—the buyer, in effect, invests in the seller's performance. Up to a point, such buyer reliance is efficient—it increases the value of performance to the buyer by more than its expected costs. Indeed, a core purpose of contractual obligation is to encourage such reliance by enabling sellers to credibly commit to their promises—a credible commitment to perform is worth more than a bare intention precisely because of the opportunities for reliance that the commitment supports but the intention cannot. At the same time, however, the reliance that contractual promises invite also increases the losses that follow a breach by the seller: the investment may be specific to the promised performance, in which cases its costs may be unrecoverable on breach; and the investment may even tie the buyer's existing resources more closely to the specific seller on whom she relies, thereby rendering the buyer less nimble following a breach than she would have been had the contract never been made to begin with.

Both the gains and the losses associated with relying on a contract may be illustrated by a simple example. Imagine that a seller and her buyer contract for her to sell him flour for his bakery with delivery set for some future date. Prior to taking delivery of the flour, the buyer must choose the skill level of the bakers he hires to bake the bread. The more skilled the bakers that the buyer hires, the more he can charge for the bread and the higher will be his profits in case his seller performs. But, at the same time, the more skilled the bakers that the buyer hires, the higher their wages, and the larger the buyer's loss in case the seller breaches. The buyer's reliance decision in such a case functions as the inverse of a potential tort victim's precaution decision—whereas a potential tort victim who takes precautions incurs a small certain cost in order to avoid a large uncertain cost (associated with the accident that the precautions avoid), a promisee who relies incurs a small certain cost as an invitation to a large but less than certain gain (associated with the increase value of the performance that the reliance anticipates).

This makes it clear that efficiency requires the buyer to hire bakers of a particular level of skill—to display a particular level of reliance (and neither less, nor more). Efficiency requires that the buyer adjust—downwardly—his reliance in light of the probability that his seller will breach and the reliance will simply be a wasted cost.[2] In the example, efficiency requires the buyer (assuming that he is risk-neutral) to increase the skill level of his bakers until the increase in profit from a marginal rise in the skill level discounted by the chance that his seller will perform just equals

---

2. For simplicity, assume here that buyer cannot, either in general or in particular through his reliance decision, affect the probability that the seller will breach.

the increased costs of carrying the more skilled bakers' higher wages, discounted by the chance that the seller will breach.

Moreover, this observation straightforwardly entails that the expectation remedy *simpliciter* leads buyers to make inefficient reliance decisions. Because unqualified expectation damages put buyers in the same position as performance would have done, taking the buyers' reliance (whatever it is) as given, they leave buyers—at every level of reliance—indifferent between their sellers' performing and breaching. The unqualified expectation remedy therefore causes breaching sellers (and not buyers) to bear the entire cost of buyers' reliance, at every level of reliance. In this way, expectation damages induce buyers to neglect the possibility of breach and its associated costs in making their reliance decisions and therefore inefficiently to over-rely.

The solution to this problem is to implement the paradigm of double responsibility at the margin, and indeed to proceed in direct analogy to the solution that the negligence regime established for the parallel problem in torts. To secure efficient reliance, the law should award buyers damages that do not vary with the level of their reliance. In this case, buyers will internalize the costs of their marginal reliance, and (subject to the problem of sellers' incentives) the law will once again secure double responsibility at the margin.

Any such reliance-invariant damages rule will secure efficient reliance by buyers. But as noted a moment ago, the problem of sellers' incentives remains, and the need to secure efficient seller decisions must not be ignored. And as the earlier analysis of seller decisions indicates, remedies that depart from the general expectation formula inefficiently distort any number of seller decisions—from the perform-or-breach decision on back. In order to secure efficient seller decisions, the law must fix the buyer's expectation damages not just at any level, but rather at precisely the contractual expectations that the buyer would have enjoyed if he had made an optimal reliance decision. Stipulatively fixing a buyer's expectation remedy so that it puts him in the position that would have ensued following both optimal reliance and performance secures efficient buyer reliance by leaving the buyer to bear the full costs of his actual reliance, and (since buyers facing this rule will rely efficiently, at least in equilibrium) it secures efficient seller behavior by leaving sellers to bear the full costs of their decisions, too.

Several prominent legal doctrines may be understood as contributing to achieving double-responsibility at the margin, and hence economic efficiency, in this way. That is, they qualify the expectation remedy, *simpliciter*, to reduce or to eliminate the sensitivity that buyers' damages display to their reliance, and instead to fix buyers' contractual expectations according to what would follow from efficient reliance. Some of these doctrines will be introduced only later in this chapter: one example is the law's willingness to enforce liquidated damages clauses, in which parties specify fixed damages for breach in the terms of their contracts (and, insofar as they are rational and seek to maximize their contractual surplus, set these damages at the levels that would ensue given efficient reliance); another is the rule, which applies especially in contracts for the sale of goods, that damages should equal the difference between contract and market prices.

Another such doctrine is already familiar. The rule that denies buyers recovery for unforeseeable contractual expectations may be applied to achieve double responsibility at the margin simply by characterizing expectations that arise only in light of inefficient over-reliance as unforeseeable. *Hadley* itself may be interpreted in just this light: the miller's decision to free up the resources needed to maintain a spare crank shaft and to redirect these resources into projects that would yield returns only on the carrier's performance might be thought a case of inefficient over-reliance. And this fact—that no reasonable miller would do without a spare crank-shaft—may explain the court's conclusion that the miller's urgent need was unforeseeable to the carrier.

5.3 THE MITIGATION DECISION

Another decision that a buyer can make that affects the costs of his seller's breach occurs after the breach and involves the buyer's response to the losses that the breach threatens to impose. Often, a buyer can take action to reduce these losses, while other actions would leave the losses undiminished, or even increase them. In example above, the baker who learns that his seller will not deliver the flour as contracted must choose between leaving her bakery idle and seeking an alternative seller—even one who supplies only an inferior or more expensive product—from whom to buy replacement flour in an effort to salvage at least some of her contractual expectations. A disappointed buyer, lawyers say, can *mitigate* her losses.

Unqualified expectation damages are once again inefficient because, by imposing an absolute requirement that breaching sellers restore buyers to the position that performance would have achieved, they relieve buyers of all responsibility for reducing the burdens of breach and so leave buyers with insufficient incentives to mitigate damages for themselves. Double responsibility at the margin again requires a very different regime, in which both buyers and sellers bear, on the margin, the costs of the decisions they take in connection with the sellers' breaches. Such a regime is not difficult to achieve. All that is needed is to subject buyers to an appropriate duty to mitigate the damages that follow from their sellers' breaches. Sellers' should be required to pay damages equal to the losses that buyers would have sustained had they mitigated appropriately, and buyers should be left bearing any additional losses that they suffer in light of their actual mitigation decisions. Finally, the standard of appropriate mitigation should be set to require buyers to mitigate their losses on breach just in case the mitigation reduces these losses (and hence reduces the damages that sellers' owe) by more than it costs buyers to achieve. This arrangement gives buyers efficient incentives to mitigate, since it causes them to internalize 100% of the costs and benefits of their mitigation. The arrangement also subjects sellers to efficient incentives surrounding their breach decision: since buyers face efficient incentives to mitigate, sellers' decisions to perform-or-breach will (at least in equilibrium) occur in a context in which the remedies that the law imposes for breaches will reflect the breaches' true social costs.

Finally, the law does indeed subject buyers to a duty to mitigate damages from breach. The doctrine of avoidable consequences denies a victim of a contract breach recovery for any losses he unreasonably failed to avoid. Whether or not this doctrine achieves efficiency turns on whether or not the law identifies as unreasonable precisely those failures to mitigate in which mitigation would have cost the buyer less than it saved the seller. Some lawyer-economists have proposed that the positive law be interpreted in this light.[3] The cases below suggest that this reconstruction of the law is only partly accurate. Although some part of the mitigation doctrine is surely motivated by the prospect of avoiding inefficiently (and even self-indulgently) passive promisees, non-economic considerations—including moral and even cultural ideals of a type that will be highlighted in later chapters that emphasize alternative approaches to contract law—also seem to influence both doctrines and outcomes in this area.

Rockingham County v. Luten Bridge Co.

United States Court of Appeals for the Fourth Circuit, 1929.
35 F.2d 301.

■ Parker, Circuit Judge. This was an action at law instituted in the court below by the Luten Bridge Company, as plaintiff, to recover of Rockingham county, North Carolina, an amount alleged to be due under a contract for the construction of a bridge. The county admits the execution and breach of the contract, but contends that notice of cancellation was given the bridge company before the erection of the bridge was commenced, and that it is liable only for the damages which the company would have sustained, if it had abandoned construction at that time. The judge below instructed a verdict for plaintiff for the full amount of its claim. From the judgment on this verdict the county has appealed.

The facts out of which the case arises, as shown by the affidavits and offers of proof appearing in the record, are as follows: On January 7, 1924, the board of commissioners of Rockingham county voted to award to plaintiff a contract for the construction of the bridge in controversy. Three of the five commissioners favored the awarding of the contract and two opposed it.

At [a later] meeting, a regularly advertised called meeting held on February 21st, a resolution was unanimously adopted declaring that the contract for the building of the bridge was not legal and valid, and directing the clerk of the board to notify plaintiff that it refused to recognize same as

---

3. The most prominent example is Charles Goetz & Robert Scott, *The Mitigation Principle: Toward a General Theory of Contractual Obligation*, 69 Va. L. Rev. 967 (1983).

a valid contract, and that plaintiff should proceed no further thereunder. This resolution also rescinded action of the board theretofore taken looking to the construction of a hard-surfaced road, in which the bridge was to be a mere connecting link. The clerk duly sent a certified copy of this resolution to plaintiff.

At the regular monthly meeting of the board on March 3d, a resolution was passed directing that plaintiff be notified that any work done on the bridge would be done by it at its own risk and hazard, that the board was of the opinion that the contract for the construction of the bridge was not valid and legal, and that, even if the board were mistaken as to this, it did not desire to construct the bridge, and would contest payment for same if constructed. A copy of this resolution was also sent to plaintiff. At the regular monthly meeting on April 7th, a resolution was passed, reciting that the board had been informed that one of its members was privately insisting that the bridge be constructed. It repudiated this action on the part of the member and gave notice that it would not be recognized. At the September meeting, a resolution was passed to the effect that the board would pay no bills presented by plaintiff or any one connected with the bridge. At the time of the passage of the first resolution, very little work toward the construction of the bridge had been done, it being estimated that the total cost of labor done and material on the ground was around $1,900; but, notwithstanding the repudiation of the contract by the county, the bridge company continued with the work of construction.

On November 24, 1924, plaintiff instituted this action against Rockingham county, and against Pruitt, Pratt, McCollum, Martin, and Barber, as constituting its board of commissioners. Complaint was filed, setting forth the execution of the contract and the doing of work by plaintiff thereunder, and alleging that for work done up until November 3, 1924, the county was indebted in the sum of $18,301.07.

As the county now admits the execution and validity of the contract, and the breach on its part, the ultimate question in the case is one as to the measure of plaintiff's recovery, and the exceptions must be considered with this in mind. The principal question [arising] for our consideration [is] whether plaintiff can recover under the contract for work done after [the notices] were received, or is limited to the recovery of damages for breach of contract as of that date.

[W]e do not think that, after the county had given notice, while the contract was still executory, that it did not desire the bridge built and would not pay for it, plaintiff could proceed to build it and recover the contract price. It is true that the county had no right to rescind the contract, and the notice given plaintiff amounted to a breach on its part; but, after plaintiff had received notice of the breach, it was its duty to do nothing to increase the damages flowing therefrom. If A enters into a binding contract to build a house for B, B, of course, has no right to rescind the contract without A's consent. But if, before the house is built, he decides that he does not want it, and notifies A to that effect, A has no right to proceed with the building and thus pile up damages. His remedy is to treat the contract as broken when he receives the notice, and sue for the recovery of such damages, as he may have sustained from the breach, including any profit which he would have realized upon performance, as well as any other losses which may have resulted to him. In the case at bar, the county decided not to build the road of which the bridge was to be a part, and did not build it. The bridge, built in the midst of the forest, is of no value to the county because of this change of circumstances. When, therefore, the county gave notice to the plaintiff that it would not proceed with the project, plaintiff should have desisted from further work. It had no right thus to pile up damages by proceeding with the erection of a useless bridge.

The contrary view was expressed by Lord Cockburn in *Frost v. Knight*, L. R. 7 Ex. 111, but, as pointed out by Prof. Williston (Williston on Contracts, vol. 3, p. 2347), it is not in harmony with the decisions in this country. The American rule and the reasons supporting it are well stated by Prof. Williston as follows:

> "There is a line of cases running back to 1845 which holds that, after an absolute repudiation or refusal to perform by one party to a contract, the other party cannot continue to perform and recover damages based on full performance. This rule is only a particular application of the general rule of damages that a plaintiff cannot hold a defendant liable for damages which need not have been incurred; or, as it is often stated, the plaintiff must, so far as he can without loss to himself, mitigate the damages caused by the defendant's wrongful act. The application of this rule to the matter in question is obvious. If a man engages to have work done, and afterwards repudiates his contract before the work has been begun or when it had been only partially done, it is inflicting damage on the defendant without benefit to the plaintiff to allow the latter to insist on proceeding with the contract. The work may be useless to the defendant, and yet he would be forced to pay the full contract price. On the other hand, the plaintiff is interested only in the profit he will make out of the contract. If he receives this it is equally advantageous for him to use his time otherwise."

The judgment below will accordingly be reversed, and the case remanded for a new trial.

Reversed.

Canadian Industrial Alcohol Co. v. Dunbar Molasses Co.

Court of Appeals of New York, 1932.
179 N.E. 383.

■ CARDOZO, J. A buyer sues a seller for breach of an executory contract of purchase and sale.

The subject-matter of the contract was "approximately 1,500,000 wine gallons Refined Blackstrap [molasses] of the usual run from the National Sugar Refinery, Yonkers, N. Y., to test around 60% sugars."

The order was given and accepted December 27, 1927, but shipments of the molasses were to begin after April 1, 1928, and were to be spread out during the warm weather.

After April 1, 1928, the defendant made delivery from time to time of 344,083 gallons. Upon its failure to deliver more, the plaintiff brought this action for the recovery of damages.

The plaintiff kept the contract alive till October 25, 1928, when it gave notice that it would go out into the open market, buy what molasses it required, and charge the defendant with the difference.

On June 27, 1928, while the defendant was still holding out the hope that deliveries might be made, it offered to supply the plaintiff with other molasses (400,000 gallons), the output of a different refinery, at six and one-half cents per gallon, about a cent less than the average market price in June. The offer was coupled with a notice that it would be deemed to be revoked unless the plaintiff's order for the molasses so offered was received by the defendant not later than July 2.

The price quoted in this offer was less than the market price in June, but substantially more than the price (four and three-quarters cents per gallon) at which the plaintiff had agreed to buy.

We see no merit in the claim that plaintiff, while still keeping the contract open, was chargeable with a duty to accept the substitute for performance tendered by the delinquent seller (*Havemeyer* v. *Cunningham*, 35 Barb. 515).

The defendant, in making the tender, did not suggest that the plaintiff was under a duty to accept it. The tender was made "not as a matter of obligation," but for accommodation solely. The plaintiff might accept or reject as it preferred.

Another tender of substituted performance was made by the defendant on October 26, 1928, upon receipt of notice from the plaintiff that there would be a purchase in the market. Again in a spirit of "accommodation" the defendant made a tender, not of molasses, but of another contract for molasses. "We are willing to let you have 400,000 to 850,000 gallons of molasses, at our option, 7-1/4 cent per gallon, f. o. b., New York or Philadelphia," the offer to be deemed revoked if not accepted by return mail. The market price at that time was about one-half a cent higher.

The plaintiff replied in substance that it had no longer any faith in the defendant's readiness or ability to live up to its engagements, and did not wish to add another contract to the one already broken.

The law did not charge it with a duty to make such an experiment again.

Parker v. Twentieth Century–Fox Film Corp.

Supreme Court of California, 1970.
474 P.2d 689.

■ BURKE, J. Defendant Twentieth Century–Fox Film Corporation appeals from a summary judgment granting to plaintiff the recovery of agreed compensation under a written contract for her services as an actress in a motion picture. As will appear, we have concluded that the trial court correctly ruled in plaintiff's favor and that the judgment should be affirmed.

Plaintiff is well known as an actress, and in the contract between plaintiff and defendant is sometimes referred to as the "Artist." Under the contract, dated August 6, 1965, plaintiff was to play the female lead in defendant's contemplated production of a motion picture entitled "Bloomer Girl." The contract provided that defendant would pay plaintiff a minimum "guaranteed compensation" of $53,571.42 per week for 14 weeks commencing May 23, 1966, for a total of $750,000. Prior to May 1966 defendant decided not to produce the picture and by a letter dated April 4, 1966, it notified plaintiff of that decision and that it would not "comply with our obligations to you under" the written contract.

By the same letter and with the professed purpose "to avoid any damage to you," defendant instead offered to employ plaintiff as the leading actress in another film tentatively entitled "Big Country, Big Man" (hereinafter, "Big Country"). The compensation offered was identical, as were 31 of the 34 numbered provisions or articles of the original contract.[1] Unlike "Bloomer Girl," however, which was to have been a musical production, "Big Country" was a dramatic "western type" movie. "Bloomer Girl" was to have been filmed in California; "Big Country" was to be produced in Australia. Also, certain terms in the proffered contract varied from those of the original.[2] Plaintiff was given one week within which to

---

1. Among the identical provisions was the following found in the last paragraph of Article 2 of the original contract: "We [defendant] shall not be obligated to utilize your [plaintiff's] services in or in connection with the Photoplay hereunder, our sole obligation, subject to the terms and conditions of this Agreement, being to pay you the guaranteed compensation herein provided for."

2. Article 29 of the original contract specified that plaintiff approved the director already chosen for "Bloomer Girl" and that in case he failed to act as director plaintiff was to have approval rights of any substitute director. Article 31 provided that plaintiff was to have the right of approval of the "Bloomer Girl" dance director, and Article 32 gave her the right of approval of the screenplay.

Defendant's letter of April 4 to plaintiff, which contained both defendant's notice of breach of the "Bloomer Girl" contract and offer of the lead in "Big Country," eliminated or impaired each of those rights. It read in part as follows:

"The terms and conditions of our offer of employment are identical to those set forth in the 'Bloomer Girl' Agreement, Articles 1 through 34 and Exhibit A to the Agreement, except as follows:

1. Article 31 of said Agreement will not be included in any contract of employment regarding 'Big Country, Big Man' as it is not a musical and it thus will not need a dance director.

2. In the 'Bloomer Girl' agreement, in Articles 29 and 32, you were given certain director and screenplay approvals and you had preapproved certain matters.

accept; she did not and the offer lapsed. Plaintiff then commenced this action seeking recovery of the agreed guaranteed compensation.

The complaint sets forth two causes of action. The first is for money due under the contract; the second, based upon the same allegations as the first, is for damages resulting from defendant's breach of contract. Defendant in its answer admits the existence and validity of the contract, that plaintiff complied with all the conditions, covenants and promises and stood ready to complete the performance, and that defendant breached and "anticipatorily repudiated" the contract. It denies, however, that any money is due to plaintiff either under the contract or as a result of its breach, and pleads as an affirmative defense to both causes of action plaintiff's allegedly deliberate failure to mitigate damages, asserting that she unreasonably refused to accept its offer of the leading role in "Big Country."

Plaintiff moved for summary judgment under *Code of Civil Procedure section 437c*, the motion was granted, and summary judgment for $750,000 plus interest was entered in plaintiff's favor. This appeal by defendant followed.

As stated, defendant's sole defense to this action which resulted from its deliberate breach of contract is that in rejecting defendant's substitute offer of employment plaintiff unreasonably refused to mitigate damages.

The general rule is that the measure of recovery by a wrongfully discharged employee is the amount of salary agreed upon for the period of service, less the amount which the employer affirmatively proves the employee has earned or with reasonable effort might have earned from other employment. However, before projected earnings from other employment opportunities not sought or accepted by the discharged employee can be applied in mitigation, the employer must show that the other employment was comparable, or substantially similar, to that of which the employee has been deprived; the employee's rejection of or failure to seek other available employment of a different or inferior kind may not be resorted to in order to mitigate damages.

In the present case defendant has raised no issue of *reasonableness of efforts* by plaintiffs to obtain other employment; the sole issue is whether plaintiff's refusal of defendant's substitute offer of "Big Country" may be used in mitigation. Nor, if the "Big Country" offer was of employment different or inferior when compared with the original "Bloomer Girl" employment, is there an issue as to whether or not plaintiff acted reason-

---

Since there simply is insufficient time to negotiate with you regarding your choice of director and regarding the screenplay and since you already expressed an interest in performing the role in 'Big Country, Big Man,' we must exclude from our offer of employment in 'Big Country, Big Man' any approval rights as are contained in said Articles 29 and 32; however, we shall consult with you respecting the director to be selected to direct the photoplay and will further consult with you with respect to the screenplay and any revisions or changes therein, provided, however, that if we fail to agree the decision of [defendant] with respect to the selection of a director and to revisions and changes in the said screenplay shall be binding upon the parties to said agreement."

ably in refusing the substitute offer. Despite defendant's arguments to the contrary, no case cited or which our research has discovered holds or suggests that reasonableness is an element of a wrongfully discharged employee's option to reject, or fail to seek, different or inferior employment lest the possible earnings therefrom be charged against him in mitigation of damages.[5]

Applying the foregoing rules to the record in the present case, with all intendments in favor of the party opposing the summary judgment motion—here, defendant—it is clear that the trial court correctly ruled that plaintiff's failure to accept defendant's tendered substitute employment could not be applied in mitigation of damages because the offer of the "Big Country" lead was of employment both different and inferior, and that no factual dispute was presented on that issue. The mere circumstance that "Bloomer Girl" was to be a musical revue calling upon plaintiff's talents as a dancer as well as an actress, and was to be produced in the City of Los Angeles, whereas "Big Country" was a straight dramatic role in a "Western Type" story taking place in an opal mine in Australia, demonstrates the difference in kind between the two employments; the female lead as a dramatic actress in a western style motion picture can by no stretch of imagination be considered the equivalent of or substantially similar to the lead in a song-and-dance production.

Additionally, the substitute "Big Country" offer proposed to eliminate or impair the director and screenplay approvals accorded to plaintiff under the original "Bloomer Girl" contract (see fn. 2, *ante*), and thus constituted an offer of inferior employment. No expertise or judicial notice is required in order to hold that the deprivation or infringement of an employee's rights held under an original employment contract converts the available "other employment" relied upon by the employer to mitigate damages, into inferior employment which the employee need not seek or accept. (See *Gonzales v. Internat. Assn. of Machinists,* 213 Cal.App.2d 817, 823–824 [1963]; and fn. 5, *post.*)

In view of the determination that defendant failed to present any facts showing the existence of a factual issue with respect to its sole defense—plaintiff's rejection of its substitute employment offer in mitigation of damages—we need not consider plaintiff's further contention that for various reasons, including the provisions of the original contract set forth in footnote 1, *ante*, plaintiff was excused from attempting to mitigate damages.

The judgment is affirmed.

■ SULLIVAN, ACTING C.J., dissenting. The basic question in this case is whether or not plaintiff acted reasonably in rejecting defendant's offer of alternate employment. The answer depends upon whether that offer (starring in "Big Country, Big Man") was an offer of work that was substantial-

---

5. Instead, in each case the reasonableness referred to was that of the *efforts* of the employee to obtain other employment that was not different or inferior; his right to reject the latter was declared as an unqualified rule of law.

ly similar to her former employment (starring in "Bloomer Girl") or of work that was of a different or inferior kind. To my mind this is a factual issue which the trial court should not have determined on a motion for summary judgment. The majority have not only repeated this error but have compounded it by applying the rules governing mitigation of damages in the employer-employee context in a misleading fashion. Accordingly, I respectfully dissent.

The familiar rule requiring a plaintiff in a tort or contract action to mitigate damages embodies notions of fairness and socially responsible behavior which are fundamental to our jurisprudence. Most broadly stated, it precludes the recovery of damages which, through the exercise of due diligence, could have been avoided. Thus, in essence, it is a rule requiring reasonable conduct in commercial affairs. This general principle governs the obligations of an employee after his employer has wrongfully repudiated or terminated the employment contract. Rather than permitting the employee simply to remain idle during the balance of the contract period, the law requires him to make a reasonable effort to secure other employment.[1] He is not obliged, however, to seek or accept any and all types of work which may be available. Only work which is in the same field and which is of the same quality need be accepted.[2]

Over the years the courts have employed various phrases to define the type of employment which the employee, upon his wrongful discharge, is under an obligation to accept. Thus in California alone it has been held that he must accept employment which is "substantially similar"; employment "in the same general line of the first employment"; "employment in a similar capacity"; employment which is "not of a different or inferior kind."

For reasons which are unexplained, the majority cite several of these cases yet select from among the various judicial formulations which they contain one particular phrase, "Not of a different or inferior kind," with which to analyze this case. I have discovered no historical or theoretical reason to adopt this phrase, which is simply a negative restatement of the affirmative standards set out in the above cases, as the exclusive standard. Indeed, its emergence is an example of the dubious phenomenon of the law responding not to rational judicial choice or changing social conditions, but to unrecognized changes in the language of opinions or legal treatises.

---

1. The issue is generally discussed in terms of a duty on the part of the employee to minimize loss. The practice is long-established and there is little reason to change despite Judge Cardozo's observation of its subtle inaccuracy. "The servant is free to accept employment or reject it according to his uncensored pleasure. What is meant by the supposed duty is merely this, that if he unreasonably reject, he will not be heard to say that the loss of wages from then on shall be deemed the jural consequence of the earlier discharge. He has broken the chain of causation, and loss resulting to him thereafter is suffered through his own act." (*McClelland v. Climax Hosiery Mills*, 169 N.E. 605, 609 (1930), concurring opinion.)

2. This qualification of the rule seems to reflect the simple and humane attitude that it is too severe to demand of a person that he attempt to find and perform work for which he has no training or experience. Many of the older cases hold that one need not accept work in an inferior rank or position nor work which is more menial or arduous. This suggests that the rule may have had its origin in the bourgeois fear of resubmergence in lower economic classes.

However, the phrase is a serviceable one and my concern is not with its use as the standard but rather with what I consider its distortion.

The relevant language excuses acceptance only of employment which is of a *different kind*. It has never been the law that the mere existence of *differences between two jobs in the same field* is sufficient, as a matter of law, to excuse an employee wrongfully discharged from one from accepting the other in order to mitigate damages. Such an approach would effectively eliminate any obligation of an employee to attempt to minimize damage arising from a wrongful discharge. The only alternative job offer an employee would be required to accept would be an offer of his former job by his former employer.

Although the majority appear to hold that there was a difference "in kind" between the employment offered plaintiff in "Bloomer Girl" and that offered in "Big Country" (*ante,* at p. 183), an examination of the opinion makes crystal clear that the majority merely point out differences between the two *films* (an obvious circumstance) and then apodically assert that these constitute a difference in the *kind* of *employment.* The entire rationale of the majority boils down to this: that the *"mere circumstances"* that "Bloomer Girl" was to be a musical revue while "Big Country" was a straight drama "demonstrates the difference in kind" since a female lead in a western is not "the equivalent of or substantially similar to" a lead in a musical. This is merely attempting to prove the proposition by repeating it. It shows that the vehicles for the display of the star's talents are different but it does not prove that her employment as a star in such vehicles is of necessity different *in kind* and either inferior or superior.

I believe that the approach taken by the majority (a superficial listing of differences with no attempt to assess their significance) may subvert a valuable legal doctrine.[5] The inquiry in cases such as this should not be whether differences between the two jobs exist (there will always be differences) but whether the differences which are present are substantial enough to constitute differences in the *kind* of employment or, alternatively, whether they render the substitute work employment of an *inferior kind*.

It seems to me that *this* inquiry involves, in the instant case at least, factual determinations which are improper on a motion for summary judgment. Resolving whether or not one job is substantially similar to another or whether, on the other hand, it is of a different or inferior kind, will often (as here) require a critical appraisal of the similarities and differences between them in light of the importance of these differences to the employee. This necessitates a weighing of the evidence, and it is precisely this undertaking which is forbidden on summary judgment.

---

5. The values of the doctrine of mitigation of damages in this context are that it minimizes the unnecessary personal and social (e.g., nonproductive use of labor, litigation) costs of contractual failure. If a wrongfully discharged employee can, through his own action and without suffering financial or psychological loss in the process, reduce the damages accruing from the breach of contract, the most sensible policy is to require him to do so. I fear the majority opinion will encourage precisely opposite conduct.

This is not to say that summary judgment would never be available in an action by an employee in which the employer raises the defense of failure to mitigate damages. No case has come to my attention, however, in which summary judgment has been granted on the issue of whether an employee was obliged to accept available alternate employment. Nevertheless, there may well be cases in which the substitute employment is so manifestly of a dissimilar or inferior sort, the declarations of the plaintiff so complete and those of the defendant so conclusionary and inadequate that no factual issues exist for which a trial is required. This, however, is not such a case.

It is not intuitively obvious, to me at least, that the leading female role in a dramatic motion picture is a radically different endeavor from the leading female role in a musical comedy film. Nor is it plain to me that the rather qualified rights of director and screenplay approval contained in the first contract are highly significant matters either in the entertainment industry in general or to this plaintiff in particular. Certainly, none of the declarations introduced by plaintiff in support of her motion shed any light on these issues. Nor do they attempt to explain why she declined the offer of starring in "Big Country, Big Man." Nevertheless, the trial court granted the motion, declaring that these approval rights were "critical" and that their elimination altered "the essential nature of the employment."

I cannot accept the proposition that an offer which eliminates *any* contract right, regardless of its significance, is, as a matter of law, an offer of employment of an inferior kind. Such an absolute rule seems no more sensible than the majority's earlier suggestion that the mere existence of differences between two jobs is sufficient to render them employment of different kinds. Application of such per se rules will severely undermine the principle of mitigation of damages in the employer-employee context.

I remain convinced that the relevant question in such cases is whether or not a particular contract provision is so significant that its omission creates employment of an inferior kind. This question is, of course, intimately bound up in what I consider the ultimate issue: whether or not the employee acted reasonably. This will generally involve a factual inquiry to ascertain the importance of the particular contract term and a process of weighing the absence of that term against the countervailing advantages of the alternate employment. In the typical case, this will mean that summary judgment must be withheld.

In the instant case, there was nothing properly before the trial court by which the importance of the approval rights could be ascertained, much less evaluated. Thus, in order to grant the motion for summary judgment, the trial court misused judicial notice. In upholding the summary judgment, the majority here rely upon per se rules which distort the process of determining whether or not an employee is obliged to accept particular employment in mitigation of damages.

I believe that the judgment should be reversed so that the issue of whether or not the offer of the lead role in "Big Country, Big Man" was of employment comparable to that of the lead role in "Bloomer Girl" may be determined at trial.

Bomberger v. McKelvey

Supreme Court of California, 1950.
220 P.2d 729.

■ Gibson, J. Plaintiffs brought this action against D. P. McKelvey to recover a sum of money promised for the demolition and removal of a building which stood on real property purchased by McKelvey from plaintiffs. Further, plaintiffs, as assignees of Mr. and Mrs. Fred L. Hill, sought to recover a sum of money which McKelvey promised to pay to the Hills in return for the latters' surrender of a lease of the premises. A counterclaim and cross-complaint was filed against plaintiffs and the Hills seeking damages for trespass and waste. R. G. McKelvey, who had become a co-owner of the property, joined in this pleading, and as a result thereof the trial court ordered that he be made a party defendant with D. P. McKelvey and that the Hills be made parties cross-defendant. Defendants have appealed from a judgment granting the relief requested in the complaint.

Early in 1946 defendants purchased 12 lots in the city of Modesto for the purpose of constructing a building and adjoining parking facilities for rental to a chain grocery store. Four of these lots, including Lots 15 and 16, were acquired from plaintiffs for $60,000. At this time Lots 15 and 16 were improved by a business structure occupied by the Hills under a lease, which plaintiffs assigned to defendants on March 16, 1946.

During negotiations for the sale of the lots the Hills agreed to surrender their lease upon payment of $4,000 by defendants, less $300 per month rent after March 1, 1946, and to vacate the premises "immediately upon the completion" of a new building to be built for the Hills by plaintiffs elsewhere in Modesto. A written agreement or "Deposit Receipt" entered into by plaintiffs and defendants on February 28, 1946, provided that the sale of the real property to defendants should be subject to the temporary occupancy of the old building on Lots 15 and 16 by the Hills at a rental of $300 per month and that "The seller warrants such occupancy shall terminate and the improvements shall be removed not later than 20 days prior to the completion" of the contemplated chain store building. The instrument provided for payment of $70 for each day the old building remained standing after the agreed date unless the delay was caused by certain specified events, such as strikes, which prevented completion of the new building for the Hills. The deposit receipt also provided that plaintiffs "retained" certain dwellings on the remainder of the property and agreed to remove them within 60 days, but no such reservation of title was made with respect to the building on Lots 15 and 16.

It was orally agreed that defendants would pay plaintiffs $3,500 upon the demolition and removal of the old building on Lots 15 and 16. During the various conversations relating to the transaction defendants stated that they did not want the old building or any part of it, and it appears that

Lots 15 and 16 were to be used as a parking lot by the chain store. Plaintiffs informed defendants that they intended to use whatever material they could from the old building in constructing the new one for the Hills.

The oral agreement was confirmed by a letter from defendants to plaintiffs on March 11, 1946, wherein defendants recited that plaintiffs were to "remove the existing improvements therefrom" and that in consideration for this defendants would pay them $3,500. The letter further stated that if plaintiffs were prevented by strikes, government regulations, or the like, from completing the new building, the Hills could continue to occupy the old building and the time for its "removal" should be "extended to coincide with the completion of said new building." In reliance upon this letter and the agreement to tear down the old building, plaintiffs changed the plans for the new building "to fit the possible use of salvage" from the old building, namely, plate glass and skylights, and for this reason did not order those items, which were then scarce and could be obtained only after a delay of at least 90 to 120 days. In addition sheet metal for skylights was under priority by reason of governmental restrictions. There is testimony that the new building could not be completed without the glass and skylights from the old one.

Plaintiffs commenced construction of the new store for occupancy by the Hills, but due to governmental restrictions defendants were unable to get materials for the contemplated chain store and parking lot. Because of this delay defendants on August 2, 1946, notified plaintiffs that construction of the chain store building was not contemplated in the immediate future, that until further written notice plaintiffs were not to proceed with the demolition, and that notice would be given in ample time for plaintiffs to have the improvements "dismantled and removed." Plaintiffs answered by letter that they intended to proceed since the plate glass and skylights in the old building were needed for use in the construction of the new store. On September 10 defendants wrote to plaintiffs that they were not to dismantle the improvements on Lots 15 and 16 nor to enter the premises except as customers of the Hills until such time as written permission was given by defendants, and that "for any known violations of these instructions redress at law will be had."

Toward the end of October plaintiffs removed the plate glass and skylights from the old building and completed the new building for the Hills. About October 30 the Hills abandoned the old building, and plaintiffs thereupon entered defendants' premises and demolished and removed the building. On November 1 the Hills moved to the new store constructed for them by plaintiffs. In December the court sustained, with leave to amend, a demurrer to an amended complaint for declaratory relief, and no further action was taken in that proceeding.

Defendants refused to pay either the agreed price of $3,500 due upon demolition of the old building or the unpaid balance of $2,500 due to the Hills for surrender of the lease. The Hills assigned their claim to plaintiffs, who brought the present action to recover both amounts.

The trial court found and concluded that defendants had agreed to pay $3,500 upon removal of the building and the salvage, that the agreement had not been renounced by defendants, that they were estopped from changing their position or maintaining an action against the cross-defendants or repudiating the contract, that plaintiffs had the legal right to demolish the building and to take the salvage, and that they had fully performed the agreement on their part. The court also concluded that the sum promised by defendants to the Hills became due and payable when the Hills moved into the new building constructed for them by plaintiffs. Judgment was entered for plaintiffs in the sum of $6,000, which was the total amount sought in the complaint.

The deposit receipt did not fix a definite date for demolition of the old building or specify how the salvaged materials were to be disposed of but provided only that the building was to be "removed not later than twenty days prior to the completion" of the chain store building, subject to payment of $70 per day in the event of failure to perform on time. It is undisputed, however, that the building was to be left standing for occupancy by the Hills until a new building was constructed elsewhere for them. Further, there is testimony that defendants stated during the negotiations that they did not want any part of the old building and that plaintiffs were to get it off just as soon as possible, and plaintiffs told defendants that they were going to use whatever material they could from the old building in constructing the new one for the Hills. From this evidence the trial court could reasonably infer that the parties had agreed that plaintiffs were to wreck the old building as soon as practicable after construction of the new store for the Hills and that plaintiffs should be entitled to the salvaged material after it had been removed.

Under the contract as thus construed, there was an implied covenant that plaintiffs would be given possession of the premises for the agreed purpose at a reasonable time to be chosen by them. Defendants' conduct in forbidding plaintiffs to enter, therefore, was sufficient not only to excuse their performance but also to constitute a breach or anticipatory breach of the contract. The principal question for our determination, however, is whether plaintiffs could ignore the express notification from defendants not to enter the land and could proceed to demolish the building.

It is the general rule in California and in practically all other jurisdictions that either party to an executory contract has the power to stop performance of the contract by giving notice or direction to that effect, subjecting himself to liability for damages, and upon receipt of such notice the other party cannot continue to perform and recover damages based on full performance. This is an application of the principle that a plaintiff must mitigate damages so far as he can without loss to himself.

The reason for this rule is twofold: Ordinarily a plaintiff is interested only in the profit he will make from his contract, and if he receives this he obtains the full benefit of his bargain; on the other hand, performance by the plaintiff might be useless to the defendant, although he would have to pay the entire contract price if the plaintiff were permitted to perform, and this would inflict damage on the defendant without benefit to the plaintiff. If these reasons are not present, the rule is not applied. For example, where the plaintiff is not interested solely in profit from the agreement but must proceed with the work in order to fulfill contract obligations to others, or where refraining from performance might involve closing a factory, damages may be inadequate and the plaintiff may have a right to continue performance

The general rule is also subject to the jurisdiction of equity to order specific performance of the contract, and, apparently in recognition of this principle, it has been held that in cases where damages will not afford adequate compensation and where specific performance will lie, the plaintiff may continue to perform, in spite of a notice to stop, and thereafter recover on the basis of his continued performance.

In the present case the trial court granted relief similar to that which has been allowed under this exception to the general rule. The court determined that plaintiffs acted properly in performing the contract on their part and that, having performed, they were entitled to the full amount of $6,000 due under the agreement. In the light of the foregoing, we must consider whether the facts bring this case within the reasons underlying the general rule or the reasons for the exception, and we must determine whether there is sufficient evidence to show that plaintiffs would have been entitled to specific performance and that damages would have been inadequate.

Unlike the situations presented in *Richardson v. Davis*, 116 Cal.App. 388, (2 P.2d 860), and *Crawford v. Pioneer Box & Lumber Co.*, 105 Cal.App. 760 (288 P. 694), relied upon by defendants, the agreement involved here did not provide simply for the payment of money in return for the performance of services. As we have seen, it was contemplated that plaintiffs were to keep all salvaged material. During the negotiations for the agreement they informed defendants that they planned to use as much of this material as they could in constructing the new building for the Hills, and, in reliance on the contract, they altered the plans for the new building to permit use of the glass and skylights from the old one. These materials were then scarce, and sheet metal for the skylights was under priority. There was testimony that it would take from 90 to 120 days to obtain new glass and skylights, and some other glass required for the new building did not arrive until about five months after it was ordered. Except for the glass and skylights the new building was completed sometime in October, and the lack of these materials left it exposed to the weather and apparently unsuitable for occupation by the Hills. Thus it is obvious that an essential element of the rule giving one party the power to stop performance by giving notice not to perform is lacking here since plaintiffs were not interested solely in the profit to be derived from tearing down the old building and selling the salvage, but they had an additional interest in obtaining actual performance of the agreement so that they could secure scarce materials and complete the new building.

The fact that the agreement involved property which was scarce and under priority is of particular importance in the present case. There are analogous decisions in other jurisdictions holding that a purchaser does not have an adequate remedy at law and may obtain specific performance of a contract to sell materials if he needs them in his business and cannot obtain them or their equivalent within the local marketing area.

Under these circumstances the trial court could properly conclude that inability to obtain the salvage from the old building would seriously interfere with completion of the new building, that equivalent materials could not then be secured by plaintiffs and that in an action for breach of contract damages would be difficult to ascertain and would be inadequate.

Defendants argue that plaintiffs were not entitled to proceed with performance because they could have covered up the holes in the new building with boards to protect it from the weather until new glass and skylights could be obtained and, further, that the glass and skylights from the old building, even if required, could have been removed without tearing down the entire structure. Boarding up the new building, however, would have rendered it unusable for an indefinite period. Also, removal of part of the old building without demolition of the remainder was not authorized by the agreement, and there is nothing in the record to indicate that defendants had suggested or would have consented to such a step, even though they knew that the need for the glass and skylights was the principal reason for plaintiffs' insistence upon full performance of the contract. All of these factors were, of course, to be considered by the trial court in passing upon the propriety of plaintiffs' conduct, and we cannot say as a matter of law that plaintiffs were required to adopt one of the solutions now mentioned by defendants.

Defendants introduced testimony that the value of the old building, if allowed to remain on the property for continued use, was $26,250, and they contend that demolition of such a valuable structure was not justified by plaintiffs' need for the salvage, which, it is asserted, could have been replaced for $540. Regardless of the weight to be given this testimony, however, the trial court could properly consider the facts that defendants had purchased the property for construction of a chain grocery store, that they had made a lease to the chain store operators by which they agreed to deliver possession of Lots 15 and 16 for use as a parking lot with all improvements removed, and that for this reason the building had little if any value for continued use on the property. On the other hand the value of the salvage to plaintiffs was enhanced by their need of materials for the new building.

In view of the foregoing we conclude that the facts found by the trial court, supported by the evidence, are sufficient to justify the determination that plaintiffs acted within their rights in fully performing the agreement, that they did not commit trespass, and that they were not liable for damages for destruction of the old building. Defendants, on the other hand, became liable to pay plaintiffs the sum due under the contract upon completion of the demolition.

The judgment is affirmed.

* * *

Before taking up the question whether the law—at least as it is recorded in this set of cases—establishes the efficient mitigation principle proposed by economic analysis, consider briefly a curiosity concerning the facts of the first case, *Luten Bridge Co.*. This will serve, first, as another opportunity to practice the calculus of contractual expectations—always a useful pedagogical exercise. It will also illustrate the importance of facts in the proper adjudication of disputes and the ways in which judicial opinions can skew facts to support the results that they impose (and also the ways in which casebook editors, including this one, can further skew facts to serve their own illustrative purposes). This exercise should promote a healthy skepticism about claims that cases capture a precise doctrinal idea, and indeed about all claims to doctrinal purity in the law.

The central factual mystery in *Luten Bridge Co.* is why Luten Bridge completed construction after being ordered to stop. To see why this is mysterious, imagine that Luten Bridge's total costs of complete construction were $20,000, and that the contract price—the total fee Luten Bridge was to receive for building the completed bridge—was $25,000. Now suppose that Luten Bridge was ordered to stop work after having expended $2,000 in construction costs. Luten Bridge's two options, and their consequences, may be summarized in the table below:

Complete bridge and sue later	
Costs expended—	$20,000
Contract price—	$25,000
Expected gain from performance—	$5,000
Remedy recovered to vindicate expectation interest—	$25,000
Net gain to Luten Bridge—$25,000 − $20,000 =	$5,000

Stop work and sue at once	
Expected gain from performance (as above)—	$5,000
Costs expended—	$2,000
Remedy recovered to vindicate expectation interest—	$7,000
Net gain to Luten Bridge—$7,000 − $2,000 =	$5,000

Table 5.1

Choices and Their Consequences in *Luten Bridge*

Completing construction, this stylized tabulation of the fact makes plain, simply had the effect of increasing Luten Bridge's costs by precisely the same amount by which it increased its recovery—leaving Luten Bridge no better off than it would have been had it stopped and sued at once. So why on earth did Luten Bridge decide to complete?

One possible answer, which exerts the least revisionary pressure on the account of contract remedies developed so far, is that Luten Bridge worried it would be unable to establish its costs of completion with the precision demanded by the certainty doctrine. Perhaps Luten Bridge worried that if it stopped and sued, it would be prevented, by that doctrine, from recovering its full contractual expectations. This answer is not absurd—as *Friedus* illustrates, the certainty requirement surely can leave even sophisticated plaintiffs unable to vindicate their contractual expectations—but it is also less than fully persuasive. Luten Bridge was an established firm, operating in a well-developed construction market, and so the obstacles to proving its costs of completion, although not trivial, would have been far from insurmountable. Moreover, the risk of tripping over the certainty doctrine on stopping and suing had to be balanced against the risk of tripping over the mitigation requirement on continuing work (a risk that, the opinion makes plain, eventuated). It seems unlikely that the balance of risks favored pressing on.

Two other explanations for Luten Bridge's behavior have potentially broader-ranging effects for the tidy economic reconstruction of the law of contract remedies developed here. To begin with, Rockingham County's instructions to stop were not as clear as the edited version of the opinion printed above suggests. As even the opinion acknowledges, the Rockingham County Commissioners, who made such decisions on behalf of the County, were divided about where to place the road that the bridge was to serve and issued Luten Bridge with inconsistent instructions: one group wished to move the road, so that the bridge would be isolated and useless (as the opinion describes); another group wished to build the road as originally planned, in which case the bridge would be essential to the road's usefulness. Matters were further complicated by a tangle of resignations, withdrawals of the resignations, and appointments of substitutes that rendered the composition of the Board of Commissioners, and hence the relative strengths of the two groups, uncertain. Luten Bridge had to decide which group spoke for the County, and therefore whether or not the contract had been repudiated at all. This, at least as much as the duty to mitigate, was one of the central issues in the case, and Luten Bridge got it wrong. And as long as Luten Bridge was reasonable to think that that commissioners who wished to proceed with the road as planned were the County's true decision-makers, then its choice to continue building was also perfectly reasonable—since a decision to stop may have placed *it* in breach of contract. But this suggests that the economic analysis of contract remedies cannot proceed in isolation from any number of other doctrines in contract law, including doctrines that concern contract formation and interpretation. And although it may be that economic analysis can persuasively address these questions also, that remains to be seen.

Finally, Luten Bridge's decision to complete the bridge is not necessarily mysterious even on the assumption that Rockingham County's instructions to cease work were authoritative and unequivocal. The analysis so far has treated Luten Bridge's costs of completion as pure expenses—that is, as conferring no benefit on Luten Bridge itself. But is this necessarily accurate? Some of the monies to be expended in completing the bridge no doubt reflected payments for materials to be bought from strangers and not yet ordered. But others of these expenditures were almost certainly to be made to parties in whom Luten Bridge had a greater interest. Some were likely payments for materials already ordered from suppliers with whom Luten Bridge had an ongoing relationship. Others were likely wages to be paid to Luten Bridge's employees, perhaps to employees of long-standing. It is even possible (and indeed quite plausible) that some of Luten Bridge's owners also worked for the firm—that is, were self-employed—and therefore stood to benefit from the contract with Rockingham County both by sharing in the company's profits and by receiving as wages what were to the company expenses. For all these reasons, the value of the completed bridge to Luten Bridge likely exceeded the company's formal contractual expectations. And this excess value could be recovered by completing construction.

To be sure, some of these sources of value might also have been recovered as damages in an earlier lawsuit. Insofar as Luten Bridge would itself have breached contracts by stopping work, and hence owed damages to its promisees, these damages could have been included in remedial claims against the County (although they would have been subjected to the rigors of the certainty and foreseeability doctrines). But other of Luten Bridge's interests in completion almost certainly could not have been vindicated by this formal route. Damage to Luten Bridge's reputation from breaching contracts with its suppliers (and surely from breaking off negotiations with suppliers that had a developed a firm psychological and business foundation but had not yet ripened into formal legal obligation), even if legally cognizable in principle, would almost certainly have been too unforeseeable or too speculative to provide a basis for recovery at law. Moreover, other of Luten Bridge's interests in completion would not have received legal recognition, even in principle. Thus Luten Bridge's employees were (as a later chapter will explain in greater detail) almost surely employees at will, who could be fired without cause and therefore had no claim against Luten Bridge for their lost wages. Moreover, Luten Bridge's employees also could not recover their lost wages by making claims directly against the County, since they enjoyed no contractual relations with the County and did not fall within the narrow class of third party beneficiaries that the law recognizes as enjoying contractual rights at one remove. Thus Luten Bridge's contract remedy could not vindicate these derivative interests in its contract with Rockingham County (and certainly could not vindicate the further interests of persons at two removes from the contract, for example, the interests of Luten Bridge's employees' landlords). But these interests were no less real for being unrecoverable. And insofar as Luten Bridge cared about them, it could vindicate them only by performing, and not by suing.

This raises a fundamental challenge to the economic analysis of law, because it suggests that efficiency cannot be assessed locally (in partial equilibrium) but only globally (in general equilibrium), taking into account all the effects of a decision as the ripples that it produces propagate throughout the economy. To take all of these effects into account, economic analysis must determine whether each of the persons whom a decision touches, at however many removes, will herself be influenced, by these effects to behave more or less efficiently. And this burden of this calculation—the burden, for example, of deciding whether it is an efficiency gain or loss for Luten Bridge's employees to drive cheaper, and hence less polluting cars as a result of losing their jobs following Rockingham County's breach—may be simply too great for economic analysis to bear.

Such complications and concerns are important, to be sure, and they may in the end defeat the project of the economic analysis of law. But however that may be, the complexities do not render the economic analysis of law no longer worth understanding, because economic theory, like any other theory, is entitled to its stylizations and simplifications, and to defend these only after showing that (if they are accepted) they usefully organize otherwise unruly phenomena. And so it is sensible to return, once again, to the interior of the economic analysis of law, to ask whether (accepting its simplifications) the efficiency-based understanding of the mitigation requirement is reflected, and perhaps even adopted, in legal doctrine.

Even here the economic interpretation of the positive law remains on shaky ground. *Luten Bridge* does, to be sure, assert the doctrine that a disappointed promisee must take reasonable steps to mitigate her losses following a breach. And one of the intuitive grounds for finding that Luten Bridge in particular failed reasonably to mitigate (and a ground that no doubt figured prominently in the mind of the court that decided the case) is surely that it is wildly inefficient to expend resources building a bridge that is not connected to any road. But the economic interpretation of the mitigation doctrine asserts more than this: it makes the specific claim that the legal principle requiring reasonable mitigation can and should be interpreted to identify as reasonable any loss-reducing actions that cost a disappointed promisee less than they save his breaching promisor. And the cases that follow *Luten Bridge Co.* above suggest that when the law speaks of reasonable mitigation it has something very different in mind.

Canadian Industrial Alcohol presents a conceptually precise, if very narrow, counterexample to the economic interpretation of reasonable mitigation. The below-market price of the replacement contract offered by Dunbar Molasses necessarily made accepting this contract the cheapest way for Canadian Industrial Alcohol to redeem its contractual expectation, so that when Canadian Industrial purchased substitute performance on the market instead (and at the higher price) it straightforwardly failed reasonably to mitigate in the economic sense. Nevertheless, the law unambiguously treated Canadian Industrial's conduct as reasonable. As Cardozo wrote, the plaintiff "did not wish to add another contract to the one already broken [and] [t]he law did not charge it with a duty to make such an experiment again." *Canadian Industrial Alcohol*, then, announces a departure from the economic interpretation of reasonable mitigation.

But perhaps this departure may be limited to the special facts of the case. There is something intuitively wrong about a promisee's being forced to return to a promisor who has disappointed him (as the saying goes, "fool me once, shame on you; fool me twice, shame on me"). Moreover, a mitigation rule that required promisees to accept a breaching promisor's offer of a repeat engagement would allow promisors to delay making their promisees whole, including (potentially) in circumstances (for example, involving the possibility a promisor's insolvency) in which a remedy delayed becomes a remedy denied. And it is not hard to see why that might itself be inefficient.

Accordingly, although *Canadian Industrial Alcohol* raises doubts about whether the law adopts the economic interpretation of reasonable mitigation, the opinion may be thought to be more a special exception to the economic approach than a general rejection of it. Moreover, although *Parker* also seems clearly to reject the economic account of reasonable mitigation, the holding there may also be treated as involving a special case, and on similar ground.[4]

To be sure, it is difficult to square *Parker's* finding that Shirley Maclaine's refusal to accept a role in *Big Country, Big Man* as a substitute for the role she that had been promised in *Bloomer Girl* with the idea that failures to engage in joint-cost-minimizing mitigation are unreasonable. This is especially difficult given that the *Parker* court (over a dissenter's express objections) reached this conclusion on *summary judgment*—that is, accepting all of Twentieth Century Fox's factual assertions about the two movie roles as true. That amounted to giving actresses in Shirley Maclaine's position absolute discretion to judge whether acknowledged differences in the genres, direction, or settings of two films have the evaluative consequence of making a role in one different from or inferior to a role in the other.[5] The *Parker* court's refusal even to investigate the burdens to Shirley Maclaine of accepting the replacement role can only be understood as an implicit rejection of the idea that Maclaine's reasonableness turns on the relative size (surely a question of fact) of these burdens and the burdens that turning down the replacement role imposed on Twentieth Century Fox. And *Parker* therefore necessarily abandons the suggestion that the reasonableness of mitigation depends on the balance of costs, as the idea of efficient mitigation proposes.

But although *Parker* rejects the economic interpretation of the mitigation requirement for the case of a movie star's employment contract, this

---

4. Note that one might have thought that the rule of *Canadian Industrial Alcohol* straightforwardly decides *Parker*, since offer of the new role that she rejected was, in effect, an offer to mitigate damages by a repeat engagement with the same promisor (exactly what *Canadian Industrial Alcohol* holds promisees are not required to accept). The cases were decided in different jurisdictions, however. Moreover, it would probably anyway be too strong to read *Canadian Industrial Alcohol* as never requiring a promisee to enter into a new contract with his breaching promisor. The holding might not extent to circumstances in which there is no suggestion that the promisor's breach was opportunistic and no reason to believe that the initial breach indicated that the promisor's chances of a future breaches were unusually high.

5. Note that "different from or inferior to" is here used as a term of art to mark just those roles that Maclaine might reasonably reject, and whose rejection therefore does not violate the law's requirement that she mitigate damages. The majority in *Parker* writes confusingly on this point, as when it inexplicably says that that the mitigation doctrine does not require an employee to be reasonable in rejecting "different or inferior" employment. This is confusing because reasonableness is already built into the definition of "different or inferior," which specifically identifies the class of alternative employment that an employee may reject without violating her duty reasonably to mitigate her losses.

rejection should not be read too generally or expansively. Many things about Shirley Maclaine and her circumstances combine to make hers a special case. The contract at issue in the case is for employment and therefore has an ineliminably personal component. This personal element of the arrangement is increased by the fact that the contemplated employment involved mental and not just physical labor, and indeed that the work—acting—was artistic and so had an emotional as well as a rational component. Finally, Shirley Maclaine was not just any actress but a movie actress (that is, an actress in a high-status medium) and a star at that. All of these reasons combined to engage a set of cultural values concerning work, art, status, and dignity, which together gave Maclaine a measure of discretionary control over her work and working conditions that more ordinary promisees, in more banal contractual settings, do not enjoy. Indeed, as the dissenter pointed out (although not necessarily out of friendliness to the economic view of mitigation), more ordinary employees,[6] doing more ordinary jobs, would enjoy considerably less discretion and would be considerably more likely, under the guise of the mitigation requirement, to be required to accept alternative employment that saved their employers money. So although *Parker* pretty clearly rejects the joint-cost-minimizing interpretation of the mitigation doctrine proposed by the economic approach to contract, this rejection may plausibly be limited, if not to the precise circumstances of the *Parker* case (as in *Canadian Industrial Alcohol*), then to a sufficiently narrow class of cases so that the best interpretation of the mitigation requirement, in general, remains an open question.

Bomberger, by contrast, is much more difficult to explain away or even to cabin in this fashion.[7] Instead, the *Bomberger* holding seems to abandon the economic interpretation of reasonable mitigation quite generally, including even for impersonal contracts. The *Bomberger* court acknowledges that a mitigation doctrine exists in the law, and that the purpose of this requirement is to prevent wasteful promisee behavior following a breach. But the court expressly adopts a must laxer standard of wastefulness than the demanding joint-cost-minimizing standard needed to secure economic efficiency. Moreover, the facts of the Bomberger case—which involved the destruction of a $26,250 building to salvage skylights worth $540 and avoid a 6 month delay in the occupation of premises whose monthly rent was in the region of $300—drive home just how inefficient promisee behavior may be and still be held reasonable and thus consistent with the duty to

---

6. Note, finally, that under American law most employees subjected to a firing like Maclaine's would have no contractual cause of action at all, so that the question of mitigation would never arise. As Chapter 22 will explain in greater detail, most American workers are employees at will, who may be fired at any time, for no reason, and certainly for the reason that a change in their employer's business prospects makes their continued employment no longer profitable for her.

7. *Bomberger* appears here as a result of Mark Gergen's work, see, e.g., Mark Gergen, *Transcript of Panel Discussion—Transactional Economics: Victor Goldberg's Framing Contract Law*, 49 S. Tex. L. Rev. 469 (2007), which has also greatly influenced the discussion of mitigation more generally. Gergen considers the result in *Bomberger* more typical than the result in *Luten Bridge*.

mitigate. Indeed, in some respects, the extent of inefficiency seems not to have concerned the *Bomberger* court at all: *Bomberger* expressly identifies a broad class of circumstances in which a plaintiff may take steps that fail to minimize the joint costs of breach without being held to have failed reasonably to mitigate, that is, whenever plaintiff's actions reflect not just an "interest[] solely in profit" but also a desire to "fulfill contract obligations to others."[8]

Outcomes like this one led an English judge to observe that identifying the limits of the law's mitigation requirement can "involve drawing a line between conduct which is merely unreasonable and conduct which is wholly unreasonable."[9] The words in themselves are of course conclusory, without more, but the sentiment behind them, and its direct rejection of the economic interpretation of the mitigation requirement, is impossible to mistake. All in all, then, although economic analysis explains the need for a mitigation doctrine and identifies precisely which mitigation rule would be efficient, the fit between economic prescription and legal doctrine seems less exact in this connection than at any other point considered so far.

5.4   THE CURE DECISION

The efficiency of contract remedies depends on establishing double responsibility at the margin at another, final, point in the contracting process also. This arises when a disappointed promisee calculates what quantum of damages is necessary to vindicate his contractual expectations—that is, to put him in a position as good as the one that he would have enjoyed on performance. In particular, efficiency requires that a disappointed promisee use his remedy to vindicate his expectation interest in the cheapest possible way, rather than proceeding wastefully. A promisee who may waste his remedy—claiming a quantum of damages that reflects an unnecessarily expensive route to vindicating his contractual expectations—loses the incentive to cure efficiently. And this inefficiency propagates backwards throughout the entire contracting process—driving up his promisor's costs of breach and with them the expected costs of the promise

---

8. *Bomberger v. McKelvey*, 220 P.2d 729, 733 (Cal. 1950). Admittedly, this principle cannot plausibly be given the fullest scope of its application. The plaintiff in *Luten Bridge Co.*, after all, almost certainly continued work at least in part to honor contractual obligations that it had undertaken in contemplation of the bridge project. At the very least, continuing the work surely had the effect that these contracts were honored.

Note that *Bomberger* also identifies a second class of cases in which a promisee plausibly should not be required to mitigate at all, namely when the law entitles her not just to expectation damages but to specific performance of her promisor's contractual undertakings— that is, to having her promisor actually do as she promised. Specific performance—both its economic appeal and its prominence in the law—will be discussed later in these materials. For now, just note that this is another place at which the conceptual structure of legal doctrine matters, in the sense of having entailments that determine the outcomes of cases. If the plaintiff is entitled to specific performance, then she cannot possibly be required to mitigate, at least insofar as mitigation involves accepting substitute performance or payment of money damages. Such a requirement would undermine her right to specific performance.

9. *See generally White & Carter Ltd. v. McGregor*, 2 W.L.R. 17 (1962).

and, finally, the price that the promisor charges for making it—reducing the size of the contractual surplus in which the promisee and his promisor may share. On the other hand, a remedial regime that fixes damages according to the cheapest route to vindicating promisee expectations secures double responsibility at the margin and therefore promotes efficient contracting. The promisor remains responsible for 100% of any contractual expectations that she disappoints; and the promisee becomes 100% responsible for how he uses his remedy to vindicate his expectation interests.

The difficulty of inefficient cure may seem like a non-problem, however, or at most a theoretical possibility without any practical application. It may seem that this difficulty can be avoided simply by determining the promisee's true dollar valuation of performance and fixing damages at this quantity. But this solution is too quick, because awarding money damages equal to the dollar value that a promisee places on performance may, and indeed typically will, overcompensate the promisee. Insofar as performance is worth more to a promisee than its market price, vindicating the promisee's expectation interest does not require paying his private value of performance: it is enough, instead, to go to the market and buy him substitute performance or even to give him the (smaller) amount of money necessary for him to buy substitute performance himself.

An example will help to illustrate this possibility and also to fix ideas. Imagine that a theater-lover pays a booking agent $20 to buy a ticket to see a play. Now suppose that the theatergoer's private valuation of the ticket— the smallest sum that he would accept in order to forego seeing the play—is $100. (Postpone, although only for a brief moment, the question why ticket price may nevertheless be only $20.) His expectation interest in the contract in this case is $100 (a return of the $20 purchase price plus the $80 gain that the contract represents for him). But vindicating this interest in case the agent fails to deliver the ticket does not require paying him the $100, because the booking agent's breach does not actually make it impossible for the theatergoer to see the play, or its equivalent. Instead, the booking agent may put her promisee in a position that he values as highly as performance by paying a money remedy sufficient to allow the theatergoer to go to the market (perhaps a secondary market for scalped tickets) and buy a substitute ticket, quite likely for less than $100. Indeed, even if no other ticket for the particular play is available, the booking agent might make the theatergoer whole by providing an alternative ticket to another play (perhaps for a slightly better seat to a performance that the theatergoer finds slightly less appealing), again at a cost that is less than $100. In either case, the cheapest way of curing the theatergoer's loss costs less than the theatergoer's private valuation of performance, and a theatergoer who pursued a path to vindicating his expectations that cost his entire private valuation—perhaps eating a $100 meal at a posh restaurant that he found as appealing as seeing the play—would act inefficiently.

It is, in fact, quite common—indeed it is the norm—for promisees to attach private valuations to their contractual rights that exceed the price those rights can command on the market. This is a straightforward consequence of the operation of market mechanisms. Insofar as sellers must charge the same price to all their buyers—insofar as sellers are unable to price discriminate—competition will drive prices, for all buyers, down to the price needed to secure the custom of the marginal buyer, that is, the lowest-valuing buyer who is nevertheless willing to pay more for a good than its cost to the seller. Any seller who charges more than this will lose all her buyers, including buyers who would find it profitable to pay more, to a competitor who priced at cost. Inframarginal buyers—buyers who would be willing to pay more for the good if required to—will reap the benefits of competition for the marginal buyer. They will—as did the theatergoer in the example—be able to purchase goods for (far) less than the values that they privately ascribe to the goods. They will enjoy what economists call buyers' (or owners') surplus.[10] And this surplus opens up the possibility of inefficient cure that an efficient regime of contract remedies must avoid.

Nevertheless, the gap between a promisee's private valuation of performance and the market price of this performance will pose no practical difficulties for remedies law as long as the market for the performance in question is functioning suitably smoothly. As long as there exists a well-functioning market, contract remedies can ignore promisees' private valuations of performance (making no direct inquiry into what they are) and nevertheless vindicate their full contractual expectations. The law can simply fix damages at the amount needed for the promisee to go to the market and secure a true substitute for performance—that is, a substitute that puts him in a position that is not just as good (for the him) as performance would have been but that is, in effect, *the same* as performance. To return to the earlier example, as long as there exists a secondary market for scalped theater tickets (for the particular play that the promised ticket named), the law can fix the theatergoer's remedy at the price of buying a ticket on that market, from a scalper. This remedy will not undercompensate the theatergoer, because the replacement ticket is identical to the one he would have received on performance. Importantly, the remedy also will not overcompensate the theatergoer, because regardless of his buyers' surplus (even if he is a marginal or nearly marginal ticket-buyer), his expectation interest is bounded below by the value that the ticket acquired on the secondary market, since he could always sell the ticket on that market if the new price came to exceed his own valuation of attending the play.

This tidy solution falls apart, however, when markets for substitute performance break down, or fail to exist entirely—for example because

---

10. Buyers' surplus is not the only reason for which a promisee's private valuation of contractual performance may exceed its market value. Various psychological mechanisms—for example, the endowment effect, according to which people who are indifferent between acquiring two goods and come to possess one subsequently value the good that they possess more highly, simply for possessing it already—may also explain this difference. It is increasingly fashionable to turn to such psychological mechanisms, or *behavioral* effects (as they are often called) in explaining economic phenomena. But although behavioral effects often do improve explanations, it is not always necessary to turn to them. The case at hand serves as an illustration.

(temporary) dislocations in supply prevent a market from clearing at the existing price (and no new higher price has formed); because legal prohibitions (such as an effectively enforced anti-scalping law) or informational asymmetries (such as those that arise around the reliability of used cars) prevent the market price from reflecting the performance's true value; or even because the performance is so unusual that the market for it attracts too few sellers and buyers for an equilibrium price to form, or indeed for replacement performance to be available at all. In such cases, a promisee's expectation interest cannot be vindicated by giving a remedy that enables him to secure replacement performance from the market—because no market for replacement performance exists. Instead, vindicating the promisee's expectation requires discerning, directly, the valuation that the promisee privately places on the contemplated performance (the amount that the promisee would have to spend on alternative, and possibly totally different, goods and services, that do not in any straightforward way replace the contract's performance but instead present a new way of making the promisee as well off as performance would have done).

It is exceedingly difficult to identify this private valuation in the absence of market mechanisms. The root of the difficulty is that the promisee has a strong incentive to over-report how highly he values performance—to exaggerate the quantum of damages needed to make him whole. This has, unsurprisingly, led the law to seek a way of valuing a promisee's expectation without relying on the promisee's self-reporting even where there is no market for replacement performance to turn to for help. One possible such measure is the cost of providing the promisee not replacement performance, for which no market exists, but rather the exact performance that the contract contemplated—the cost of completing the contract following the breach. This *cost of completion* certainly establishes a ceiling over the promisee's true private valuation of performance, for the same reason for which the market price of replacement performance would, if a market existed. But unlike the market measure, the cost of completion may exceed the promisee's private valuation, because (given that no replacement market exists) the promisee cannot convert the completed performance back into its cost. Indeed, the fact of the breach is often itself an indicator that, whatever the promisee's private valuation, there is no market that values completing the contract at the cost of doing so (or indeed at anywhere near this cost).

When a promisee does not value the contractual performance at the cost of completing it, awarding the cost of completion represents an inefficient means of cure—a greater expenditure than is necessary to leave the promisee as well-off as performance would have done. The inefficiency endures, moreover, even when a promisee who has been awarded cost-of-completion damages does not actually waste the remedy on completing the contract, but instead pockets a windfall. As argued earlier, the inefficiency inherent in the excess remedy propagates backward through the contract process, increasing the promisor's expected costs and the price that promisees generally must pay for the contract, and therefore decreasing the contractual surplus available for the promisor and promisee to divide.

The following cases illustrate the law's flirtation with the cost of completion approach to measuring a promisee's private valuation of a contractual performance for which no replacement market exists. In each case, the failure of the replacement market arises because the performance is tied to a particular, individual good—in one case to a specific house and in two others to specific plots of land.

Jacob & Youngs, Inc. v. Kent

Court of Appeals of New York, 1921.
129 N.E. 889.

■ CARDOZO, J. The plaintiff built a country residence for the defendant at a cost of upwards of $77,000, and now sues to recover a balance of $3,483.46, remaining unpaid. The work of construction ceased in June, 1914, and the defendant then began to occupy the dwelling. There was no complaint of defective performance until March, 1915. One of the specifications for the plumbing work provides that "all wrought iron pipe must be well galvanized, lap welded pipe of the grade known as 'standard pipe' of Reading manufacture." The defendant learned in March, 1915, that some of the pipe, instead of being made in Reading, was the product of other factories. The plaintiff was accordingly directed by the architect to do the work anew. The plumbing was then encased within the walls except in a few places where it had to be exposed. Obedience to the order meant more than the substitution of other pipe. It meant the demolition at great expense of substantial parts of the completed structure. The plaintiff left the work untouched, and asked for a certificate that the final payment was due. Refusal of the certificate was followed by this suit.

The evidence sustains a finding that the omission of the prescribed brand of pipe was neither fraudulent nor willful. It was the result of the oversight and inattention of the plaintiff's subcontractor. Reading pipe is distinguished from Cohoes pipe and other brands only by the name of the manufacturer stamped upon it at intervals of between six and seven feet. Even the defendant's architect, though he inspected the pipe upon arrival, failed to notice the discrepancy. The plaintiff tried to show that the brands installed, though made by other manufacturers, were the same in quality, in appearance, in market value and in cost as the brand stated in the contract—that they were, indeed, the same thing, though manufactured in another place. The evidence was excluded, and a verdict directed for the defendant. The Appellate Division reversed, and granted a new trial.

We think the evidence, if admitted, would have supplied some basis for the inference that the defect was insignificant in its relation to the project. The courts never say that one who makes a contract fills the measure of his duty by less than full performance. They do say, however, that an omission, both trivial and innocent, will sometimes be atoned for by allowance of the resulting damage, and will not always be the breach of a condition to be followed by a forfeiture. The distinction is akin to that between dependent and independent promises, or between promises and conditions (Anson on

Contracts [Corbin's ed.], sec. 367; 2 Williston on Contracts, sec. 842). Some promises are so plainly independent that they can never by fair construction be conditions of one another. Others are so plainly dependent that they must always be conditions. Others, though dependent and thus conditions when there is departure in point of substance, will be viewed as independent and collateral when the departure is insignificant. Considerations partly of justice and partly of presumable intention are to tell us whether this or that promise shall be placed in one class or in another. The simple and the uniform will call for different remedies from the multifarious and the intricate. The margin of departure within the range of normal expectation upon a sale of common chattels will vary from the margin to be expected upon a contract for the construction of a mansion or a "skyscraper." There will be harshness sometimes and oppression in the implication of a condition when the thing upon which labor has been expended is incapable of surrender because united to the land, and equity and reason in the implication of a like condition when the subject-matter, if defective, is in shape to be returned. From the conclusion that promises may not be treated as dependent to the extent of their uttermost minutiae without a sacrifice of justice, the progress is a short one to the conclusion that they may not be so treated without a perversion of intention. Intention not otherwise revealed may be presumed to hold in contemplation the reasonable and probable. If something else is in view, it must not be left to implication. There will be no assumption of a purpose to visit venial faults with oppressive retribution.

Those who think more of symmetry and logic in the development of legal rules than of practical adaptation to the attainment of a just result will be troubled by a classification where the lines of division are so wavering and blurred. Something, doubtless, may be said on the score of consistency and certainty in favor of a stricter standard. The courts have balanced such considerations against those of equity and fairness, and found the latter to be the weightier. The decisions in this state commit us to the liberal view, which is making its way, nowadays, in jurisdictions slow to welcome it (*Dakin & Co.* v. *Lee*, 1 K. B. 566, 579 [1916]). Where the line is to be drawn between the important and the trivial cannot be settled by a formula. "In the nature of the case precise boundaries are impossible" (2 Williston on Contracts, sec. 841). The same omission may take on one aspect or another according to its setting. Substitution of equivalents may not have the same significance in fields of art on the one side and in those of mere utility on the other. Nowhere will change be tolerated, however, if it is so dominant or pervasive as in any real or substantial measure to frustrate the purpose of the contract. There is no general license to install whatever, in the builder's judgment, may be regarded as "just as good". The question is one of degree, to be answered, if there is doubt, by the triers of the facts, and, if the inferences are certain, by the judges of the law. We must weigh the purpose to be served, the desire to be gratified, the excuse for deviation from the letter, the cruelty of enforced adherence. Then only can we tell whether literal fulfillment is to be implied by law as a condition. This is not to say that the parties are not free by apt and certain words to effectuate a purpose that performance of every term shall be a condition of recovery. That question is not here. This is merely to say that the law will be slow to impute the purpose, in the silence of the parties, where the significance of the default is grievously out of proportion to the oppression of the forfeiture. The willful transgressor must accept the penalty of his transgression. For him there is no occasion to mitigate the rigor of implied conditions. The transgressor whose default is unintentional and trivial may hope for mercy if he will offer atonement for his wrong.

In the circumstances of this case, we think the measure of the allowance is not the cost of replacement, which would be great, but the difference in value, which would be either nominal or nothing. Some of the exposed sections might perhaps have been replaced at moderate expense. The defendant did not limit his demand to them, but treated the plumbing as a unit to be corrected from cellar to roof. In point of fact, the plaintiff never reached the stage at which evidence of the extent of the allowance became necessary. The trial court had excluded evidence that the defect was unsubstantial, and in view of that ruling there was no occasion for the plaintiff to go farther with an offer of proof. We think, however, that the offer, if it had been made, would not of necessity have been defective because directed to difference in value. It is true that in most cases the cost of replacement is the measure. The owner is entitled to the money which will permit him to complete, unless the cost of completion is grossly and unfairly out of proportion to the good to be attained. When that is true, the measure is the difference in value. Specifications call, let us say, for a foundation built of granite quarried in Vermont. On the completion of the building, the owner learns that through the blunder of a subcontractor part of the foundation has been built of granite of the same quality quarried in New Hampshire. The measure of allowance is not the cost of reconstruction. "There may be omissions of that which could not afterwards be supplied exactly as called for by the contract without taking down the building to its foundations, and at the same time the omission may not affect the value of the building for use or otherwise, except so slightly as to be hardly appreciable". The rule that gives a remedy in cases of substantial performance with compensation for defects of trivial or inappreciable importance, has been developed by the courts as an instrument of justice. The measure of the allowance must be shaped to the same end.

The order should be affirmed, and judgment absolute directed in favor of the plaintiff upon the stipulation, with costs in all courts.

■ McLAUGHLIN, J., dissenting. I dissent. The plaintiff did not perform its contract. Its failure to do so was either intentional or due to gross neglect which, under the uncontradicted facts, amounted to the same thing, nor did it make any proof of the cost of compliance, where compliance was possible.

Under its contract it obligated itself to use in the plumbing only pipe (between 2,000 and 2,500 feet) made by the Reading Manufacturing Company. The first pipe delivered was about 1,000 feet and the plaintiff's superintendent then called the attention of the foreman of the subcontractor, who was doing the plumbing, to the fact that the specifications annexed to the contract required all pipe used in the plumbing to be of the Reading Manufacturing Company. They then examined it for the purpose of ascertaining whether this delivery was of that manufacture and found it was. Thereafter, as pipe was required in the progress of the work, the foreman of the subcontractor would leave word at its shop that he wanted a specified number of feet of pipe, without in any way indicating of what manufacture. Pipe would thereafter be delivered and installed in the building, without any examination whatever. Indeed, no examination, so far as appears, was made by the plaintiff, the subcontractor, defendant's architect, or any one else, of any of the pipe except the first delivery, until after the building had been completed. Plaintiff's architect then refused to give the certificate of completion, upon which the final payment depended, because all of the pipe used in the plumbing was not of the kind called for by the contract. After such refusal, the subcontractor removed the covering or insulation from about 900 feet of pipe which was exposed in the basement, cellar and attic, and all but 70 feet was found to have been manufactured, not by the Reading Company, but by other manufacturers, some by the Cohoes Rolling Mill Company, some by the National Steel Works, some by the South Chester Tubing Company, and some which bore no manufacturer's mark at all. The balance of the pipe had been so installed in the building that an inspection of it could not be had without demolishing, in part at least, the building itself.

I am of the opinion the trial court was right in directing a verdict for the defendant. The plaintiff agreed that all the pipe used should be of the Reading Manufacturing Company. Only about two-fifths of it, so far as appears, was of that kind. If more were used, then the burden of proving that fact was upon the plaintiff, which it could easily have done, since it knew where the pipe was obtained. The question of substantial performance of a contract of the character of the one under consideration depends in no small degree upon the good faith of the contractor. If the plaintiff had intended to, and had complied with the terms of the contract except as to minor omissions, due to inadvertence, then he might be allowed to recover the contract price, less the amount necessary to fully compensate the defendant for damages caused by such omissions. But that is not this case. It installed between 2,000 and 2,500 feet of pipe, of which only 1,000 feet at most complied with the contract. No explanation was given why pipe called for by the contract was not used, nor was any effort made to show what it would cost to remove the pipe of other manufacturers and install that of the Reading Manufacturing Company. The defendant had a right to contract for what he wanted. He had a right before making payment to get what the contract called for. It is no answer to this suggestion to say that the pipe put in was just as good as that made by the Reading Manufacturing Company, or that the difference in value between such pipe and the pipe made by the Reading Manufacturing Company would be either "nominal or nothing." Defendant contracted for pipe made by the Reading Manufacturing Company. What his reason was for requiring this kind of pipe is of no importance. He wanted that and was entitled to it. It may have been a mere whim on his part, but even so, he had a right to this kind of pipe, regardless of whether some other kind, according to the opinion of the contractor or experts, would have been "just as good, better, or done just as well." He agreed to pay only upon condition that the pipe installed were made by that company and he ought not to be compelled to pay unless that condition be performed. The rule, therefore, of substantial performance, with damages for unsubstantial omissions, has no application.

I am of the opinion the trial court did not err in ruling on the admission of evidence or in directing a verdict for the defendant.

For the foregoing reasons I think the judgment of the Appellate Division should be reversed and the judgment of the Trial Term affirmed.

Peevyhouse v. Garland Coal & Mining Co.

Supreme Court of Oklahoma, 1962.
382 P.2d 109.

■ JACKSON, J. In the trial court, plaintiffs Willie and Lucille Peevyhouse sued the defendant, Garland Coal and Mining Company, for damages for breach of contract. Judgment was for plaintiffs in an amount considerably less than was sued for. Plaintiffs appeal and defendants cross-appeal.

In the briefs on appeal, the parties present their argument and contentions under several propositions; however, they all stem from the basic question of whether the trial court properly instructed the jury on the measure of damages.

Briefly stated, the facts are as follows: plaintiffs owned a farm containing coal deposits, and in November, 1954, leased the premises to defendant for a period of five years for coal mining purposes. A 'strip-mining' operation was contemplated in which the coal would be taken from pits on the surface of the ground, instead of from underground mine shafts. In addition to the usual covenants found in a coal mining lease, defendant specifically agreed to perform certain restorative and remedial work at the end of the lease period. It is unnecessary to set out the details of the work to be done, other than to say that it would involve the moving of many thousands of cubic yards of dirt, at a cost estimated by expert witnesses at about $29,000.00. However, plaintiffs sued for only $25,000.00.

During the trial, it was stipulated that all covenants and agreements in the lease contract had been fully carried out by both parties, except the remedial work mentioned above; defendant conceded that this work had not been done.

Plaintiffs introduced expert testimony as to the amount and nature of the work to be done, and its estimated cost. Over plaintiffs' objections, defendant thereafter introduced expert testimony as to the 'diminution in value' of plaintiffs' farm resulting from the failure of defendant to render performance as agreed in the contract—that is, the difference between the present value of the farm, and what its value would have been if defendant had done what it agreed to do.

At the conclusion of the trial, the court instructed the jury that it must return a verdict for plaintiffs, and left the amount of damages for jury determination. On the measure of damages, the court instructed the jury that it might consider the cost of performance of the work defendant agreed to do, 'together with all of the evidence offered on behalf of either party.'

It thus appears that the jury was at liberty to consider the 'diminution in value' of plaintiffs' farm as well as the cost of 'repair work' in determining the amount of damages.

It returned a verdict for plaintiffs for $5000—only a fraction of the 'cost of performance,' *but more than the total value of the farm even after the remedial work is done.*

On appeal, the issue is sharply drawn. Plaintiffs contend that the true measure of damages in this case is what it will cost plaintiffs to obtain performance of the work that was not done because of defendant's default. Defendant argues that the measure of damages is the cost of performance 'limited, however, to the total difference in the market value before and after the work was performed.'

It appears that this precise question has not heretofore been presented to this court.

Plaintiffs rely on *Groves v. John Wunder Co.*, 286 N.W. 235 (Minn. 1939). In that case, the Minnesota court, in a substantially similar situation, adopted the 'cost of performance' rule as opposed to the 'value' rule. The result was to authorize a jury to give plaintiff damages in the amount of $60,000, where the real estate concerned would have been worth only $12,160, even if the work contracted for had been done.

It may be observed that *Groves v. John Wunder Co.*, *supra*, is the only case which has come to our attention in which the cost of performance rule has been followed under circumstances where the cost of performance greatly exceeded the diminution in value resulting from the breach of contract. Incidentally, it appears that this case was decided by a plurality rather than a majority of the members of the court.

Defendant relies principally upon *Sandy Valley & E. R. Co. v. Hughes*, 194 S.W. 344 (Ky. 1917); *Bigham v. Wabash–Pittsburg Terminal Ry. Co.*, 72 A. 318 (Pa. 1909); and *Sweeney v. Lewis Const. Co.*, 119 P. 1108 (Wash. 1912). These were all cases in which, under similar circumstances, the appellate courts followed the 'value' rule instead of the 'cost of performance' rule. Plaintiff points out that in the earliest of these cases (*Bigham*) the court cites as authority on the measure of damages an earlier Pennsylvania *tort* case, and that the other two cases follow the first, with no explanation as to why a measure of damages ordinarily followed in cases sounding in tort should be used in contract cases. Nevertheless, it is of some significance that three out of four appellate courts have followed the diminution in value rule under circumstances where, as here, the cost of performance greatly exceeds the diminution in value.

The explanation may be found in the fact that the situations presented are artificial ones. It is highly unlikely that the ordinary property owner would agree to pay $29,000 (or its equivalent) for the construction of 'improvements' upon his property that would increase its value only about ($300) three hundred dollars. The result is that we are called upon to apply principles of law theoretically based upon reason and reality to a situation which is basically unreasonable and unrealistic.

In *Groves v. John Wunder Co., supra*, in arriving at its conclusions, the Minnesota court apparently considered the contract involved to be analogous to a building and construction contract, and cited authority for the proposition that the cost of performance or completion of the building as contracted is ordinarily the measure of damages in actions for damages for the breach of such a contract.

In an annotation following the Minnesota case, the annotator places the three cases relied on by defendant (*Sandy Valley*, *Bigham* and *Sweeney*) under the classification of cases involving 'grading and excavation contracts.'

We do not think either analogy is strictly applicable to the case now before us. The primary purpose of the lease contract between plaintiffs and defendant was neither 'building and construction' nor 'grading and excavation.' It was merely to accomplish the economical recovery and marketing of coal from the premises, to the profit of all parties. The special provisions of the lease contract pertaining to remedial work were incidental to the main object involved.

Even in the case of contracts that are unquestionably building and construction contracts, the authorities are not in agreement as to the factors to be considered in determining whether the cost of performance rule or the value rule should be applied. The American Law Institute's Restatement of the Law, Contracts, Volume 1, Sections 346(1)(a)(i) and (ii) submits the proposition that the cost of performance is the proper measure of damages 'if this is possible and does not involve *unreasonable economic waste*'; and that the diminution in value caused by the breach is the proper measure 'if construction and completion in accordance with the contract would involve *unreasonable economic waste*.' (Emphasis supplied.) In an explanatory comment immediately following the text, the Restatement makes it clear that the 'economic waste' referred to consists of the destruction of a substantially completed building or other structure. Of course no such destruction is involved in the case now before us.

On the other hand, in McCormick, Damages, Section 168, it is said with regard to building and construction contracts that 'in cases where the defect is one that can be repaired or cured without *undue expense*' the cost of performance is the proper measure of damages, but where 'the defect in material or construction is one that cannot be remedied without *an expenditure for reconstruction disproportionate to the end to be attained*' (emphasis supplied) the value rule should be followed. The same idea was expressed in *Jacob & Youngs, Inc. v. Kent*, 129 N.E. 889, as follows:

'The owner is entitled to the money which will permit him to complete, unless the cost of completion is grossly and unfairly out of proportion to the good to be attained. When that is true, the measure is the difference in value.'

It thus appears that the prime consideration in the Restatement was 'economic waste'; and that the prime consideration in McCormick, Damages, and in *Jacob & Youngs, Inc. v. Kent, supra*, was the relationship between the expense involved and the 'end to be attained'—in other words, the 'relative economic benefit.'

In view of the unrealistic fact situation in the instant case, and certain Oklahoma statutes to be hereinafter noted, we are of the opinion that the 'relative economic benefit' is a proper consideration here.

23 O.S.1961 §§ 96 and *97* provide as follows:

'§ 96. Notwithstanding the provisions of this chapter, no person can recover a greater amount in damages for the breach of an obligation, than he would have gained by the full performance thereof on both sides.

§ 97. Damages must, in all cases, be reasonable, and where an obligation of any kind appears to create a right to unconscionable and grossly oppressive damages, contrary to substantial justice no more than reasonable damages can be recovered.'

Although it is true that the above sections of the statute are applied most often in tort cases, they are by their own terms, and the decisions of this court, also applicable in actions for damages for breach of contract. It would seem that they are peculiarly applicable here where, under the 'cost of performance' rule, plaintiffs might recover an amount about nine times the total value of their farm. Such would seem to be 'unconscionable and grossly oppressive damages, contrary to substantial justice' within the meaning of the statute. Also, it can hardly be denied that if plaintiffs here are permitted to recover under the 'cost of performance' rule, they will receive a greater benefit from the breach than could be gained from full performance, contrary to the provisions of *Sec. 96*.

An analogy may be drawn between the cited sections, and the provisions of *15 O.S.1961 §§ 214* and *215*. These sections tend to render void any provisions of a contract which attempt to fix the amount of stipulated damages to be paid in case of a breach, except where it is impracticable or extremely difficult to determine the actual damages. This results in spite of the agreement of the parties, and the obvious and well known rationale is that insofar as they exceed the actual damages suffered, the stipulated damages amount to a penalty or forfeiture which the law does not favor.

23 O.S.1961 §§ 96 and *97* have the same effect in the case now before us. *In spite of the agreement of the parties*, these sections limit the damages recoverable to a reasonable amount not 'contrary to substantial justice'; they prevent plaintiffs from recovering a 'greater amount in damages for the breach of an obligation' than they would have 'gained by the full performance thereof.'

We therefore hold that where, in a coal mining lease, lessee agrees to perform certain remedial work on the premises concerned at the end of the lease period, and thereafter the contract is fully performed by both parties except that the remedial work is not done, the measure of damages in an action by lessor against lessee for damages for breach of contract is ordinarily the reasonable cost of performance of the work; however, where the contract provision breached was merely incidental to the main purpose in view, and where the economic benefit which would result to lessor by full performance of the work is grossly disproportionate to the cost of performance, the damages which lessor may recover are limited to the diminution in value resulting to the premises because of the non-performance.

We believe the above holding is in conformity with the intention of the Legislature as expressed in the statutes mentioned, and in harmony with the better-reasoned cases from the other jurisdictions where analogous fact situations have been considered. It should be noted that the rule as stated does not interfere with the property owner's right to 'do what he will with his own' (*Chamberlain v. Parker*, 45 N.Y. 569), or his right, if he chooses, to contract for 'improvements' which will actually have the effect of reducing his property's value. Where such result is in fact contemplated by the parties, and is a main or principal purpose of those contracting, it would seem that the measure of damages for breach would ordinarily be the cost of performance.

The above holding disposes of all of the arguments raised by the parties on appeal.

Under the most liberal view of the evidence herein, the diminution in value resulting to the premises because of non-performance of the remedial work was $300.00. After a careful search of the record, we have found no evidence of a higher figure, and plaintiffs do not argue in their briefs that a greater diminution in value was sustained. It thus appears that the judgment was clearly excessive, and that the amount for which judgment should have been rendered is definitely and satisfactorily shown by the record.

We are of the opinion that the judgment of the trial court for plaintiffs should be, and it is hereby, modified and reduced to the sum of $300.00, and as so modified it is affirmed.

■ IRWIN, J., dissenting. By the specific provisions in the coal mining lease under consideration, the defendant agreed as follows:

> '7b Lessee agrees to make fills in the pits dug on said premises on the property line in such manner that fences can be placed thereon and access had to opposite sides of the pits.

> 7c Lessee agrees to smooth off the top of the spoil banks on the above premises.

> 7d Lessee agrees to leave the creek crossing the above premises in such a condition that it will not interfere with the crossings to be made in pits as set out in 7b.

> 7f Lessee further agrees to leave no shale or dirt on the high wall of said pits.'

Following the expiration of the lease, plaintiffs made demand upon defendant that it carry out the provisions of the contract and to perform those covenants contained therein.

Defendant admits that it failed to perform its obligations that it agreed and contracted to perform under the lease contract and there is nothing in the record which indicates that defendant could not perform its obligations. Therefore, in my opinion defendant's breach of the contract was willful and not in good faith.

Although the contract speaks for itself, there were several negotiations between the plaintiffs and defendant before the contract was executed. Defendant admitted in the trial of the action, that plaintiffs insisted that the above provisions be included in the contract and that they would not agree to the coal mining lease unless the above provisions were included.

In consideration for the lease contract, plaintiffs were to receive a certain amount as royalty for the coal produced and marketed and in addition thereto their land was to be restored as provided in the contract.

Defendant received as consideration for the contract, its proportionate share of the coal produced and marketed and in addition thereto, the *right to use* plaintiffs' land in the furtherance of its mining operations.

The cost for performing the contract in question could have been reasonably approximated when the contract was negotiated and executed and there are no conditions now existing which could not have been reasonably anticipated by the parties. Therefore, defendant had knowledge, when it prevailed upon the plaintiffs to execute the lease, that the cost of performance might be disproportionate to the value or benefits received by plaintiff for the performance.

Defendant has received its benefits under the contract and now urges, in substance, that plaintiffs' measure of damages for its failure to perform should be the economic value of performance to the plaintiffs and not the cost of performance.

If a peculiar set of facts should exist where the above rule should be applied as the proper measure of damages, (and in my judgment those facts do not exist in the instant case) before such rule should be applied, consideration should be given to the benefits received or contracted for by the party who asserts the application of the rule.

Defendant did not have the right to mine plaintiffs' coal or to use plaintiffs' property for its mining operations without the consent of plaintiffs. Defendant had knowledge of the benefits that it would receive under the contract and the approximate cost of performing the contract. With this knowledge, it must be presumed that defendant thought that it would be to its economic advantage to enter into the contract with plaintiffs and that it would reap benefits from the contract, or it would have not entered into the contract.

Therefore, if the value of the performance of a contract should be considered in determining the measure of damages for breach of a contract, the value of the benefits received under the contract by a party who breaches a contract should also be considered. However, in my judgment, to give consideration to either in the instant action, completely rescinds and holds for naught the solemnity of the contract before us and makes an entirely new contract for the parties.

In my judgment, we should follow the case of *Groves v. John Wunder Company*, 286 N.W. 235 (Minn. 1939), which defendant agrees 'that the fact situation is apparently similar to the one in the case at bar', and where the Supreme Court of Minnesota held:

'The owner's or employer's damages for such a breach (i. e. breach hypothesized in 2d syllabus) are to be measured, not in respect to the value of the land to be improved, but by the reasonable cost of doing that which the contractor promised to do and which he left undone.'

The hypothesized breach referred to states that where the contractor's breach of a contract is willful, that is, in bad faith, he is not entitled to any benefit of the equitable doctrine of substantial performance.

In the instant action defendant has made no attempt to even substantially perform. The contract in question is not immoral, is not tainted with fraud, and was not entered into through mistake or accident and is not contrary to public policy. It is clear and unambiguous and the parties understood the terms thereof, and the approximate cost of fulfilling the obligations could have been approximately ascertained. There are no conditions existing now which could not have been reasonably anticipated when the contract was negotiated and executed. The defendant could have performed the contract if it desired. It has accepted and reaped the benefits of its contract and now urges that plaintiffs' benefits under the contract be denied. If plaintiffs' benefits are denied, such benefits would inure to the direct benefit of the defendant.

Therefore, in my opinion, the plaintiffs were entitled to specific performance of the contract and since defendant has failed to perform, the proper measure of damages should be the cost of performance. Any other measure of damage would be holding for naught the express provisions of the contract; would be taking from the plaintiffs the benefits of the contract and placing those benefits in defendant which has failed to perform its obligations; would be granting benefits to defendant without a resulting obligation; and would be completely rescinding the solemn obligation of the contract for the benefit of the defendant to the detriment of the plaintiffs by making an entirely new contract for the parties.

I therefore respectfully dissent to the opinion promulgated by a majority of my associates.

Groves v. John Wunder Co.

Supreme Court of Minnesota, 1939.
286 N.W. 235.

■ STONE, J. Action for breach of contract. Plaintiff got judgment for a little over $15,000. Sorely disappointed by that sum, he appeals.

In August, 1927, S. J. Groves & Sons Company, a corporation (hereinafter mentioned simply as Groves), owned a tract of 24 acres of Minneapolis suburban real estate. It was served or easily could be reached by railroad trackage. It is zoned as heavy industrial property. But for lack of development of the neighborhood its principal value thus far may have been in the deposit of sand and gravel which it carried. The Groves company had a plant on the premises for excavating and screening the gravel. Near by defendant owned and was operating a similar plant.

In August, 1927, Groves and defendant made the involved contract. For the most part it was a lease from Groves, as lessor, to defendant, as lessee; its term seven years. Defendant agreed to remove the sand and gravel and to leave the property "at a uniform grade, substantially the same as the grade now existing at the roadway on said premises, and that in stripping the overburden it will use said overburden for the purpose of maintaining and establishing said grade."

Under the contract defendant got the Groves screening plant. The transfer thereof and the right to remove the sand and gravel made the consideration moving from Groves to defendant, except that defendant incidentally got rid of Groves as a competitor. On defendant's part it paid Groves $105,000. So that from the outset, on Groves' part the contract was executed except for defendant's right to continue using the property for the stated term. (Defendant had a right to renewal which it did not exercise.)

Defendant breached the contract deliberately. It removed from the premises only "the richest and best of the gravel" and wholly failed, according to the findings, "to perform and comply with the terms, conditions, and provisions of said lease with respect to the condition in which the surface of the demised premises was required to be left." Defendant surrendered the premises, not substantially at the grade required by the contract "nor at any uniform grade." Instead, the ground was "broken, rugged, and uneven."

As the contract was construed below, the finding is that to complete its performance 288,495 cubic yards of overburden would need to be excavated, taken from the premises, and deposited elsewhere. The reasonable cost of doing that was found to be upwards of $60,000. But, if defendant had left the premises at the uniform grade required by the lease, the reasonable value of the property on the determinative date would have been only $12,160. The judgment was for that sum, including interest, thereby nullifying plaintiff's claim that cost of completing the contract rather than difference in value of the land was the measure of damages. The gauge of damage adopted by the decision was the difference between the market value of plaintiff's land in the condition it was when the contract was made and what it would have been if defendant had performed. The one question for us arises upon plaintiff's assertion that he was entitled, not to that difference in value, but to the reasonable cost to him of doing the work called for by the contract which defendant left undone.

Defendant's breach of contract was willful. There was nothing of good faith about it. Hence, that the decision below handsomely rewards bad faith and deliberate breach of contract is obvious. That is not allowable. Here the rule is well settled, and has been since *Elliott v. Caldwell*, 45 N.W. 845 (Minn. 1890), that where the contractor willfully and fraudulently varies from the terms of a construction contract he cannot sue thereon and have the benefit of the equitable doctrine of substantial performance. That is the rule generally.

Jacob & Youngs, Inc. v. Kent, 129 N.E. 889, 891 (N.Y. Ct. of App. 1921), is typical. It was a case of substantial performance of a building contract. (This case is distinctly the opposite.) Mr. Justice Cardozo, in the course of his opinion, stressed the distinguishing features. "Nowhere," he said, "will change be tolerated, however, if it is so dominant or pervasive as in any real or substantial measure to frustrate the purpose of the contract." Again, "the willful transgressor must accept the penalty of his transgression."

Never before, so far as our decisions show, has it even been suggested that lack of value in the land furnished to the contractor who had bound himself to improve it any escape from the ordinary consequences of a breach of the contract.

Value of the land (as distinguished from the value of the intended product of the contract, which ordinarily will be equivalent to its reasonable cost) is no proper part of any measure of damages for willful breach of a building contract. The reason is plain.

The summit from which to reckon damages from trespass to real estate is its actual value at the moment. The owner's only right is to be compensated for the deterioration in value caused by the tort. That is all he has lost. But not so if a contract to improve the same land has been breached by the contractor who refuses to do the work, especially where, as here, he has been paid in advance. The summit from which to reckon damages for that wrong is the hypothetical peak of accomplishment (not value) which would have been reached had the work been done as demanded by the contract.

The owner's right to improve his property is not trammeled by its small value. It is his right to erect thereon structures which will reduce its value. If that be the result, it can be of no aid to any contractor who declines performance. As said long ago in *Chamberlain v. Parker*, 45 N.Y. 569, 572:

> "A man may do what he will with his own, and if he chooses to erect a monument to his caprice or folly on his premises, and employs and pays another to do it, it does not lie with a defendant who has been so employed and paid for building it, to say that his own performance would not be beneficial to the plaintiff."

To diminish damages recoverable against him in proportion as there is presently small value in the land would favor the faithless contractor. It would also ignore and so defeat plaintiff's right to contract and build for the future. To justify such a course would require more of the prophetic vision than judges possess. This factor is important when the subject matter is trackage property in the margin of such an area of population and industry as that of the Twin Cities.

It is suggested that because of little or no value in his land the owner may be unconscionably enriched by such a reckoning. The answer is that there can be no unconscionable enrichment, no advantage upon which the law will frown, when the result is but to give one party to a contract only what the other has promised; particularly where, as here, the delinquent has had full payment for the promised performance.

It follows that there must be a new trial. The initial question will be as to the proper construction of the contract. Thus far the case has been considered from the standpoint of the construction adopted by plaintiff and acquiesced in, very likely for strategic reasons, by defendants. The question has not been argued here, so we intimate no opinion concerning it, but we put the question whether the contract required removal from the premises of any overburden. The requirement in that respect was that the overburden should be used for the purpose of "establishing and maintaining" the grade. A uniform slope and grade were doubtless required. But whether, if it could not be accomplished without removal and deposit elsewhere of large amounts of overburden, the contract required as a *condition* that the grade everywhere should be as low as the one recited as "now existing at the roadway" is a question for initial consideration below.

■ OLSON, J., dissenting. The involved lease provides that the granted premises were to be used by defendant "for the purpose of removing the sand and gravel therefrom." The cash consideration was $105,000, plus defendant's covenant to level and grade the premises to a specified base. There was no segregation or allocation of the cash consideration made applicable to any of the various items going into the deal, and the instrument does not suggest any sum as being representative of the cost of performance by defendant of the leveling and grading process. Nor is there any finding that the contractor "willfully and fraudulently" violated the terms of its contract. All that can be said is that defendant did nothing except to mine the sand and gravel purchased by it and deemed best suited to its own interest and advantage. No question of partial or substantial performance of its covenant is involved since it did nothing in that behalf. The sole question here is whether the rule adopted by the court respecting recoverable damages is wrong. The essential facts, not questioned, are that—

> "The fair and reasonable value as of the end of the term of said lease, May 1, 1934, of performing the said work necessary to put the premises in the condition in which they were required by the terms of said lease to be left, is the sum of $60,893.28," and that if defendant "had left said premises at a uniform grade as required by said lease, the fair and reasonable value of said premises on May 1, 1934, would have been the sum of $12,160."

In that sum, plus interest from May 1, 1934, plaintiff was awarded judgment, $15,053.58. His sole contention before the trial court and here is that upon these findings the court, as a matter of law, should have allowed him the cost of performance, $60,893.28, plus interest since date of the breach, May 1, 1934, amounting to more than $76,000.

Since there is no issue of fact, we should limit our inquiry to the single legal problem presented: What amount in money will adequately compensate plaintiff for his loss caused by defendant's failure to render performance?

When the parties entered into this contract each had a right to rely upon the promise of full and complete performance on the part of the other. And by "performance" is meant "such a thorough fulfillment of a duty as puts an end to obligations by leaving nothing more to be done." *McGuire v. J. Neils Lbr. Co.*, 107 N.W. 130, 132 (Minn. 1906).

But the "obligation of the contract does not inhere or subsist in the agreement itself *proprio vigore,* but in the law applicable to the agreement, that is, in the act of the law in binding the promisor to perform his promise. When it is said that one who enters upon an undertaking assumes the legal duties relating to it, what is really meant is that the law imposes the duties on him. A contract is not a law, nor does it make law. It is the agreement plus the law that makes the ordinary contract an enforceable obligation." 12 Am. Jur., Contracts, § 2.

Another principle, of universal application, is that a party is entitled to have that for which he contracted, or its equivalent. What that equivalent is depends upon the circumstances of each case. If the effect of performance is such that the defective part "may be remedied without the destruction of any substantial part of the benefit which the owner's property has received by reason of the contractor's work, the equivalent to which the owner is entitled is the cost of making the work conform to the contract." 9 Am. Jur., Building and Construction Contracts, § 152. Here, however, defendant did nothing. As such plaintiff "is entitled to be placed, in so far as this can be done by money, in the same position he would have occupied if the contract had been performed." But "his recovery is limited to the loss he has actually suffered by reason of the breach; he is not entitled to be placed in a better position than he would have been in if the contract had not been broken." 15 Am. Jur., Damages, § 43. The measure of damages "is not affected by the financial condition of the one entitled to the damages"; nor may there be included in the assessment of damages "the motive of the defendant in breaking" his contract, compensatory damages alone being involved. In such a case the measure is "the same whatever the cause of the breach, regardless of whether it was due to mistake, accident, or inability to perform or was willful and malicious." *Id.* § 48. Liability in damages has for its basis the value of the promised performance to the promisee, not what it would cost the promisor in completing performance. Plaintiff as the injured party is entitled to have compensation for all injuries sustained by him due to defendant's default. But he is only entitled to recover "actual pecuniary compensation," and this is true "whether the action is on contract or in tort," there being here no circumstances warranting allowance of exemplary damages. 8 R.C.L. § 8, pp. 431, 432, and cases cited under notes 16, 17, and 18.

"Since one who has been injured by the breach of a contract or the commission of a tort is entitled to a just and adequate compensation for such injury and no more, it follows that his recovery must be limited to a fair compensation and indemnity for his injury and loss. And so in no case should the injured party be placed in a better position than he would be in had the wrong not been done, or the contract not been broken. The defendant may therefore show that, notwithstanding his default, the plaintiff has suffered no damages. And if any circumstances exist which mitigate the injury, they must be considered and taken into account." 8 R.C.L. § 9, pp. 434–435, and cases under notes 9, 10, 11, and 12.

We have here then a situation where, concededly, if the contract had been performed, plaintiff would have had property worth, in round numbers, no more than $12,000. If he is to be awarded damages in an amount exceeding $60,000 he will be receiving at least 500 per cent more than his property, properly leveled to grade by actual performance, was intrinsically worth when the breach occurred. To so conclude is to give him something far beyond what the parties had in mind or contracted for. There is no showing made, nor any finding suggested, that this property was unique, specially desirable for a particular or personal use, or of special value as to location or future use different from that of other property surrounding it. Under the circumstances here appearing, it seems clear that what the parties contracted for was to put the property in shape for general sale. And the lease contemplates just that, for by the terms thereof defendant agreed "from time to time, as the sand and gravel are removed from the various lots leased, it will surrender said lots to the lessor" if of no further use to defendant "in connection with the purposes for which this lease is made."

The theory upon which plaintiff relies for application of the cost of performance rule must have for its basis cases where the property or the improvement to be made is unique or personal instead of being of the kind ordinarily governed by market values. His action is one at law for damages, not for specific performance. As there was no affirmative showing of any peculiar fitness of this property to a unique or personal use, the rule to be applied is, I think, the one applied by the court. The cases bearing directly upon this phase so hold. Briefly, the rule here applicable is this: Damages recoverable for breach of a contract to construct is the difference between the market value of the property in the condition it was when delivered to and received by plaintiff and what its market value would have been if defendant had fully complied with its terms. It is interesting to note that in the Kentucky case the court reversed its former opinion found in 172 Ky. 65, 188 S.W. 894. Its reason for changing its mind is thus stated (175 Ky. 320–321):

"In our original opinion we fixed as the measure of damages the reasonable cost of reducing the land from which the earth and stone were taken to the level of the railroad grade and in condition for building purposes. Upon a reconsideration of the question, we conclude that this measure of damages is incorrect. From plaintiffs' avowal on the first trial it appears that it would cost at least $15,000.00 to do the work required by the contract, and from other testimony in the record it is by no means improbable that the cost would be far in excess of that sum. If this be true, the cost would far exceed the market value of the entire farm. If the contract had been performed, plaintiff would have had a farm with the place from which the earth and stone were taken reduced to the level of the railroad grade and in condition for building purposes. As the case stands, this provision of the contract has not been complied with. What, then, was plaintiff's damage? *Manifestly, not what it would cost to do the work, for, if the work had been done, plaintiff would not have received the cost of the work, but would have been benefited only to the extent that the work increased the market value of his land.* We, therefore, conclude that the measure of damages is the difference between the market value of the farm in its present condition and what its market value would have been if the land from which the earth and stone were removed had been reduced to the level of the railroad grade and left in condition for building purposes." (Italics supplied.)

In *Karst v. St. P.S. & T.F.R. Co.*, 22 Minn. 118, 123, this court said:

"For unlawful excavation and removal of his soil, a party is entitled to recover, not the cost of refilling, but the amount of the diminution of the value of the property by the excavation and removal, that being the amount of the injury directly resulting from the acts complained of."

And is not that the most feasible measure in such a situation? It accomplishes the object to which damage law is directed, *i.e.,* toward full recompense to an injured plaintiff for his loss. If, then, the landowner received full compensation by this measure, why is he not also fully compensated by receiving the same amount in the case before us? Once it has been held that the market value wholly restores the landowner when his property is permanently damaged, it must be held that he is also entirely repaid by the same measure in our present situation. So it would seem that whether plaintiff's damages are to be measured by the rule applicable to the theory of breach of contract cases or that of tortious conduct the extent of his recovery can be no greater than his actual loss. In either case he may not be heard to complain that because the equivalent to defendant's performance will cost a larger amount than that, therefore he should receive such greater amount rather than his real loss.

No one doubts that a party may contract for the doing of anything he may choose to have done (assuming what is to be done is not unlawful) "although the thing to be produced had no marketable value." (45 N.Y. 572.) In Restatement, Contracts, § 346, pp. 576, 577, Illustrations of Subsection (1), par. 4, the same thought is thus stated:

"A contracts to construct a monumental fountain in B's yard for $5,000, but abandons the work after the foundation has been laid and $2,800 has been paid by B. The contemplated fountain is so ugly that it would decrease the number of possible buyers of the place. The cost of completing the fountain would be $4,000. B can get judgment for $1,800, the cost of completion less the part of price unpaid.''

But that is not what plaintiff's predecessor in interest contracted for. Such a provision might well have been made, but the parties did not. They could undoubtedly have provided for liquidated damages for nonperformance (2 Dunnell, Minn. Dig. [2 ed. & Supps.] §§ 2536, 2537), or they might have determined in money what the value of performance was considered to be and thereby have contractually provided a measure for failure of performance.

I think the judgment should be affirmed.

* * *

Because the plaintiffs in each case assert a special interest in the particular performance that their contracts contemplated—Kent in his particular house and the Peevyhouses and the Groves company in their particular plots of land—no markets for replacement performance exist. The cost of replacement performance therefore cannot discipline the plaintiffs' valuations of their contractual expectations. Instead, each plaintiff can reliably be made whole only by completing the actual performance of the contract or providing damages sufficient to allow him to achieve his private valuation of that performance through entirely distinct avenues of consumption. And although the cost of completion places a ceiling over each plaintiff's private valuation of performance, the private valuation may in fact be much, much lower than the cost of completion. Certainly others do not value performance at anywhere near the cost of completion in any of the cases—hence the gap between the cost of completion on the one hand, and, on the other, the diminution that the breaches caused in the market values of the house and the two plots of land. Indeed, the plaintiffs' claimed valuations seem not just out of step with those of others but idiosyncratic and perhaps even outlandish, although the peculiarity of the plaintiffs' claims varies across the cases (with Kent's being the most peculiar and the Peevyhouse's being the least). Nevertheless, if the plaintiffs truly do ascribe an idiosyncratic value to the contractual performance that exceeds the cost of completion, then efficiency requires awarding the cost of completion as a remedy, and an award of the diminution in value attributable to the breach is inefficiently under compensatory. Thus the central question in all three cases: are the plaintiffs' assertions of idiosyncratic value genuine?

It seems plausible that all three opinions get the answer wrong—that each decision mistakes whether or not the promisee's idiosyncratic valuation of performance is genuine and approaches the cost to the promisor of completing the contract, or at least exceeds the diminution in value associated with the promisor's breach.

Two features of the facts in *Jacob and Youngs* render the decision dubious. To begin with, the language of the contract contained not only a specific instruction to use name-brand Reading Pipe but also a separate clause stating that the remedy for a failure to use specifically this pipe would be to tear down the house as necessary to install the Reading Pipe. While it is plausible that the clause naming Reading pipe was intended simply as a shorthand for pipe of a certain quality (much as *Xerox* or *Kleenex* often function to identify a process or product rather than a specific brand), the addition of the tear down clause places great pressure on this reading of the contract. The tear down clause seems a direct way of insisting on a preference specifically for Reading brand pipe. Indeed, it is hard to know how the contract could have been clearer, and it seems that no amount of verbiage insisting specifically (and obdurately, etc.) on Reading pipe could overcome the opinion's logic.[11] Thus, given the presence of the tear down clause, the holding leaves it unclear how a homeowner could ever successfully insist on a particular brand of building material, for which he had an idiosyncratic preference.

Moreover, the refusal of the architect to sign off on the construction project signals that he, at least, accepted the promisee's account of the valuation. Architects in such construction contracts function as neutral third parties—almost as arbitrators—who resolve contractual disputes. Given his intimate involvement with the building project (from its beginnings), the architect was better placed than the court to determine the parties' true intent in drafting the Reading pipe and tear-down clauses.

The language of the contract in *Peevyhouse* similarly supports the plaintiffs' contention that their private valuation of performance exceeds the cost of completion, so that ordering completion of the contract is the appropriate way to vindicate their contractual expectations. Like *Jacob and Youngs*, *Peevyhouse* involved a contract that contains an express provision requiring the remedy that the promisee sought to insist on. In fact, the Peevyhouses expressly negotiated for the inclusion of a contract provision requiring Garland Coal to regrade their land following the completion of mining (which replaced a standard provision requiring the payment of damages for surface harm). Although the majority asserts that the regrading provision was merely incidental to the purposes of the contract (presumably, the extraction of the coal) this is simply an implausible account of the contract language, both on its face and in light of the negotiations that led up to it. As in *Jacob and Youngs*, if the steps taken by the Peevyhouses to protect their idiosyncratic valuation of their land fail, then it is not clear what measures (no matter how direct or how explicit) might reliably allow *any* landowner with similar concerns to succeed.

---

11. The point is not that the opinion commits a straightforward interpretive error. Once *Reading pipe* is read in its generic sense, as a shorthand for a quality rather than as a brand name, then the tear down clause no longer applies to the case, because the primary duty for whose breach it prescribes a remedy has not been breached. But although this reading makes perfect sense of the contract, it threatens to undermine contractual freedom more generally, by making it almost impossible to craft a form of words that will reliably have the effect of insisting on a brand named pipe. It will always be open to a promisor to argue that the promisee's use of the brand name was intended simply to identify a certain generally recognized level of quality, and that the promisee's (express, repeated, etc.) insistence on the brand should be understood only to emphasize the importance of this level of quality. And, always, a court might (especially if the promisee's special attachment to the brand is sufficiently idiosyncratic or outlandish) agree.

Moreover, the negotiations surrounding the regrading clause in *Peevyhouse* could provide at least some evidence concerning the size of the Peevyhouse's private valuation of the regrading. After all, the Peevyhouses presumably paid for the right to insist on regrading, in the form of lower royalties on the extracted coal. And, entirely regardless of the diminution in the market value of the Peevyhouse's land caused by Garland's refusal to regrade—the size of this payment at least places a floor on the Peevyhouse's private valuation of the regrading (since it was sacrificed in order to secure the regrading).[12] So at the very least, the Peevyhouses should have been entitled to damages equal to the royalties that they gave up in exchange for the regrading clause.[13] Of course, these forsaken royalties may be less than the actual costs of regrading—because they reflect only Garland Coal's expected costs of regrading, and not the costs that arose in light of the mining operation as it developed. (Note that one factor reducing these expected costs might have been Garland Coal's belief that it could win a lawsuit to avoid regrading in spite of the clause.) Moreover, note again that even the actual costs of regrading do not place a ceiling on the Peevyhouse's private valuation of the regarded land, but only on the cheapest way to secure this valuation.

In contrast to both *Jacob and Youngs* and *Peevyhouse*, and probably also the bulk of precedent, the plaintiff in *Groves* won a remedy based on the cost of completion (in this case, once again, regrading). But although this might have been an appealing remedy in those other cases, it seems likely that the court once again reached the wrong result in *Groves*. The period of the lease in *Groves* included an enormous, exogenous, economic shock, which could not have been predicted when the lease was signed—namely, the Great Depression. This dramatically reduced the value of the plaintiff's land, especially in its regarded state, and it is plausible that this reduction in value accounts for the fact that costs of regrading came to exceed the amount by which the damage associated with the strip-mining reduced the land's market value.

If this is indeed what occurred, then one way in which to understand the case is as a dispute about whether the landowner or the tenant mining-company bears the economic risk of a drop in land prices. A decision awarding the plaintiff merely the diminution in value places this risk on the landowner, since it caps the plaintiff's remedy according to the new

---

12. This suggestion is explored in Alan Schwartz and Robert Scott, *Market Damages, Efficient Contracting, and the Economic Waste Fallacy*, 108 Colum. L. Rev. 1610 (2008).

13. Note that the amount of these forsaken royalties will not always be easy to identify, because the final royalty terms reflect not just the expected cost to Garland Coal of completing the contract but also the relative bargaining power of the parties. One landowner may receive greater royalties than another even though the costs of mining his land are greater simply because he is a better bargainer, and so recovers a sufficiently greater share of the contractual surplus to outweigh the fact that the surplus he recovers a share of is smaller. There is reason to believe that something like this actually occurred in the Peevyhouse's case. In spite of negotiating for a regrading clause that cost Garland Coal more than the standard remedial regime that it replaced, the Peevyhouses received a royalty rate of twenty cents per ton of mined coal where the standard rate in a Garland contract was fifteen cents per ton. *See* Judith Maute, Peevyhouse v. Garland Coal & Mining Co. *Revisited: The Ballad of Willie and Lucille*, 89 Nw. U. L. Rev. 1341, 1364 (1995)

market value of the land. The actual decision in *Groves*, by contrast, insulates the plaintiff landowner from the economic risk of a drop in land prices, at least up to the costs of regrading. It in effect couples the mining contract with an insurance contract, in which the mining-company insures the value of the plaintiff-owner's land, up to the cost of regrading. This account of the regrading clause casts its continued operation in the face of a massive drop in the value of the plaintiff's land as unexpected, and indeed even unfair. Certainly most people would expect the general economic risk associated with fluctuating property values to stay with a landowner rather than being passed over to a tenant. On this view, *Groves* is wrongly decided.

But something may perhaps be said in the decision's favor nevertheless. One exception to the general rule that the risks of fluctuating property values belong to the owner rather than the tenant is that a tenant who breaches by abandoning rather than damaging the premises must pay his landlord damages based on the rental prices stated in the contract, even when actual rents have fallen much lower, in connection with a drop in property values. So a tenant does insure the market value of his owner's property up to the amount of the rent. Accordingly, a final assessment of the *Groves* decision depends on whether or not the regrading clause may be read as in effect fixing a higher rent over the period of the mining lease. It is certainly possible to read the clause in this way, but the reading must confront the troubling question why, if the parties meant the regrading provision to provide the plaintiff-owner with land-value insurance, they did not adopt a higher rent instead, which would certainly have had this effect. The most natural reading of the regrading provision—the one that most likely tracks the parties' intentions—treats it as distinct from the rental term, with respect precisely to its interaction with a drop in the value of the plaintiff-owner's land.

So much for the majority opinions in the three cases. But two of the cases also registered dissents, and it is worth pausing for a moment to consider these as well. The *Groves* dissent is important for a deep observation that it reports on the way to reaching its conclusion that that diminution in values would have been the right remedy. Thus the dissenter (quoting a legal encyclopedia) says that:

> "[T]he obligation of the contract does not inhere or subsist in the agreement itself *proprio vigore*, but in the law applicable to the agreement, that is, in the act of the law in binding the promisor to perform his promise. When it is said that one who enters upon an undertaking assumes the legal duties relating to it, what is really meant is that the law imposes duties on him. A contract is not a law, nor does it make law. It is the agreement plus the law that makes the ordinary contract an enforceable obligation."

The point of this somewhat cryptic remark is that it is the law and not the contract that fixes the plaintiff's expectation (or indeed any other category) as the category of value that contract remedies protect. Although it is sometimes said (as this chapter will consider in a moment) that contract remedies may be varied by the agreement of the parties, any agreement merely fills in what this category of value contains—what the plaintiff's contractual expectations are. In particular, the regrading clause merely causes the plaintiff's expectations to include, in appropriate circumstances, having a level piece of land at the end of the strip-mining operation—that is, the clause makes level land part of the conditions that the plaintiff would, in appropriate circumstances, enjoy on the contract's performance. By contrast, the regrading clause does not, because it could not possibly, entitle the promisee to do better following breach and remedy than following performance.

Accordingly, the appropriate remedy depends entirely on the relationship among the diminution in the land's value due to the strip-mining, the plaintiff's private valuation of the regarded land, and the cost of regrading. Again, the regrading clause cannot change this, and certainly cannot entitle the plaintiff to a remedy that makes him better off following a breach than he would have been following performance. And because there is no evidence in the record that the plaintiff placed an idiosyncratic value on his land, any remedy greater than the diminution in value is, under this standard, excessive.

The *Peevyhouse* dissent is important for a very different reason, involving the consequences of dissenting and the balance between a judge's—especially an appellate judge's—obligations to the parties before her and to the law. The majority opinion claims to adopt a rule that makes the ordinary measure of damages in cases like *Peevyhouse* the cost of completion rather than the diminution in market value, but requires the smaller diminution in value remedy in *Peevyhouse* itself on account of the special facts of that case, in particular because the disproportion between the two remedies was too great and the regrading provision at issue was merely incidental to the main purpose of the contract. The dissenter points out that this is nonsense, or at least wildly implausible: that the plaintiffs insisted on the regrading provision (indeed, in a fashion that make the idiosyncratic value they accorded their land abundantly clear), and that the defendants were unusually well-placed to price this provision into the overall contract. In this way, the dissent vindicates the plaintiffs' position, although (given that its arguments lost) only rhetorically. The dissenter therefore discharges his duty to the plaintiffs—to adjudicate their specific claim on its legal merits, as he sees them.

But in doing so, the dissent has the effect of expanding the scope of the majority opinion, specifically by pointing out that the limitations that the majority wrote into the legal rule it announced—concerning the incidental character of the regrading provision—must have (at least in the mind of the majority) an almost vanishingly narrow application. The facts of the Peevyhouse case, the dissenter points out, all suggest that the regrading provision was very important to the plaintiffs, and indeed a necessary condition for their agreeing to the mining contract at all. And if the majority was willing to interpret these facts as making the regrading provision incidental, then it is difficult to see what facts would support finding such a clause not incidental. As the dissenter says, if the Peevy-houses could not get a cost of completion remedy, then no plaintiff can. It would therefore have been far better—from the point of view of limiting the damage that the majority opinion did to the law (at least as the dissenter saw it)—for the dissenter to have remained silent, or even to have written a concurrence (or even to co-opt the majority opinion) emphasizing that Peevyhouse was a special case in light of the incidental nature of the regrading clause, and that the majority's rule expressly adopts a cost-of-completion remedy in the run of cases in which the breached provision is not so clearly incidental. Of course, either path would deny the Peevyhous-es such vindication as the dissenter's true views afforded.

Finally it is worth noting that although all three opinions proceed as if the only two possible remedies in the circumstances that they address are diminution in value and cost of completion, in fact there are also many other possibilities, some of which may well be more appealing than either of these core cases. The jury in *Peevyhouse* seems to have taken one such alternative route, simply naming as damages a sum ($5,000) that lay between the two extremes. This approach is, however, bedeviled by *ad hocery*, and its appeal therefore relies heavily on the jury's (dubious) claim to be able to look into the mind of the plaintiff and identify his true private valuation of contractual performance.

But there are also other approaches that avoid this pitfall, by trying to induce the plaintiff himself accurately to reveal his true valuation, roughly speaking by removing his incentive to exaggerate. Perhaps the simplest such remedy is to award the plaintiff the cost of completion, but give the defendant the right to insist on actually completing the performance (by replacing the pipe or regrading the land) instead of paying this cost. This right will induce a plaintiff whose true valuation of performance lies below the cost of completion to bargain in order to avoid the defendant's actually completing, specifically by agreeing to accept cash damages below the cost of completion (but above his true valuation) in lieu of the full cost.

Such a remedy likely represents an improvement over a simple award of either diminution in value or cost of completion, but it remains highly imperfect. To begin with, the result of the negotiations that the remedy invites will still likely overcompensate some plaintiffs, since plaintiffs whose private valuations lie below the cost of completion will still be able to recover a windfall equal to the share of the excess that the their bargaining position allows them to negotiate. Moreover, the negotiation that the remedy invites has the form of a bilateral monopoly, in which each side can deal only with the other, and without potential competitors to discipline each side's bargaining (by making it obvious that many demands are simply non-starters), and it is therefore likely that the negotiation will be extreme-ly transactions costly.

Considerations such as these suggest searching for other, more sophis-ticated, revelatory mechanisms. Some (still fairly straightforward) possibili-ties include:

Giving defendants the ability to require any injunction to complete awarded to plaintiffs to be inalienable—i.e., allowing defendants to choose to forego their power to buy their way out of the injunction.

Allowing promisors to act—prior to their promisees' committing to injunctive relief—to increase the level of money damages that promisees could recover instead of any injunction to above market-based levels.

There is of course much more that might be said along these lines.[14]

---

14. Here see Ian Ayres and Kristin Madison, *Threatening Inefficient Performance of Injunctions and Contracts*, 148 U. PA. L. REV. 45 (1999), from which the brief discussion in these pages is derived.

CHAPTER 6

SALES OF GOODS AND THE UNIFORM COMMERCIAL CODE

The law presented up to this point has all been common law—that is, judge-made law, developed by the slow accretion of precedents generated by the need to resolve disputes that have arisen under a prior state of the law. This section presents a source of contract law of a very different character—the Uniform Commercial Code, or UCC—which governs, among other things, contracts for the sale of goods.

The UCC is a statute, that is, a systematic effort to state a set of principles self-consciously designed not just to decide a pre-existing dispute, which serves as the necessary occasion for the development of the rule that decides it, but rather prospectively to decide a wide range of disputes. It is, as will become clear, a statute written in a common law style—that is, in a style inviting relatively free-wheeling interpretation and the accretion of case-driven interpretive precedents. This distinguishes the UCC from more mechanical statutes such as the Internal Revenue Code (although even in that case, implementing the statute requires a surprising degree of common law interpretation, which the statute in some measure invites). Nevertheless, the legal skills needed to navigate the UCC are quite different from the skills introduced in the previous sections. In particular, they include a greater attentiveness to the requirements of technical language and a capacity to follow such language through multiple cross references, in order accurately to apply several interconnected statutory provisions together.

The importance of such skills to modern legal practice, which is rent through with statutory law, is one reason for including an introduction to the UCC in these materials. Another is the prominence of the UCC in contemporary contract law writ large, both because of the broad range of cases expressly governed by the UCC and because of the influence of UCC-style reasoning in areas that are only adjacent to the statute's express subject-matter. Other reasons for including the UCC relate to its several excellences, which will (hopefully) become apparent over the course of this chapter, and which introduce an aspirational quality into the engagement with the statute.

The full UCC comprises 9 Articles, whose subjects are:

Art. 1:   General Provisions
Art. 2:   Sales
Art. 2A: Leases
Art. 3:   Negotiable Instruments

Art. 4:   Bank Deposit
Art. 5:   Letters of Credit
Art. 6:   Bulk Transfers and Bulk Sales
Art. 7:   Warehouse Receipts, Bills of Lading and Other Documents of
            Title
Art. 8:   Investment Securities
Art. 9:   Secured Transactions

The treatment of the UCC that follows will expressly limit itself to Article 2, on contracts for the sale of goods.

Precisely what counts as a contract for the sale of goods will be left to intuition rather than expressly addressed, principally because the question raises relatively few points of broader legal or pedagogic interest. Suffice it to say that borderline or hybrid cases must be resolved one way or the other and that the resolution will turn generally on the nature of the preponderance of the contractual arrangements.

The stated purpose of the UCC was to unify the commercial law of the several states in order to ease interstate commercial transactions. When jurisdictions have different commercial law, contracting becomes more complicated and expensive, both in connection with contractual negotiations and when it comes time to resolve the contractual disputes that will inevitably arise. Negotiation costs go up because parties, and their lawyers, must inform themselves about multiple legal regimes.[1] Dispute resolution costs go up both because courts, like lawyers, must inform themselves of multiple legal regimes and because, insofar as these regimes differ in significant ways, each contract dispute becomes potentially also a secondary dispute about which contract law governs the primary dispute. Indeed, an entire field of law—variously called Conflict of Laws or Choice of Law—makes answering this secondary question its central subject.[2] Moreover, although the UCC clearly was intended to serve this coordination and simplification function, its various drafters also, unsurprisingly, had further purposes in drafting the code, which reflected their views about what contract law was best. These views, as the materials that follow will make plain, had both substantive components—concerning the proper content of particular legal rules—and formal components—concerning the legal style in which rules should be drafted. Both types of preferences turned out, at various times, to be controversial.

Being a statute, the UCC is formally enacted by state legislatures. (In fact, the opinions that your read below will generally refer to UCC

---

1. Note that legal differences across jurisdictions generate employment prospects for local lawyers. It is therefore perhaps not a surprise that the rise of uniform state laws has (loosely) coincided with the increasing standardization of legal education across states and the rising integration and prominence of a national bar.

2. Various approaches to choice of law in contract disputes have risen and fallen in prominence over the years, ranging from a formal rule that the contracts are governed by the law of the place of contracting to a more open-ended inquiry that makes the law governing a contract depend on the balance of various jurisdictions' interests in the contract in question. Each approach must, moreover, contend with efforts by the parties to influence which law will govern a contract, both by including choice of law clauses when a contract is made and by litigation stratagems, including most notably forum-shopping, after disputes arise.

provisions by their numbers in the relevant state's statute books, although these statute books will generally be organized to retain the basic labels of the un-adopted UCC.) But the uniformity of the UCC is secured by its being drafted centrally rather than by the several legislatures that enact it. The institutional authors of the UCC are the National Conference of Commissioners on Uniform State Laws (the "Conference")—an expert body that is funded, and whose members are appointed, by state legislatures and governors—and the American Law Institute (the "ALI")—a body of elite lawyers, judges, and legal academics. Moreover, although these collective bodies play important roles in developing the UCC—and in particular dominate the ongoing process of revising various of the UCC's provision—the code owes its basic structure and much of its general gestalt to a single person—a law professor named Karl Llewellyn.[3]

Llewellyn was one of the greatest contracts scholars of the twentieth century—and indeed one of the century's greatest legal thinkers quite generally.[4] In 1940, in "Five weeks' work by the clock and uninterrupted," Llewellyn drafted an 88 page uniform sales act.[5] The draft was revised and adopted by the Conference and the ALI by 1944, and in 1945 the comprehensive UCC project began. By 1949, a draft of the 9 Article Code existed and, even before it had been formally enacted by any State's legislature, was being cited by courts in much the same way in which they cited the Restatements. Nevertheless, the UCC's early intellectual influence was concentrated in certain segments of the legal profession. The UCC was in various ways a radical document, and opposition from other parts of the profession delayed the Code's political acceptance and enactment as actual, binding law. By 1957, only Pennsylvania had adopted the UCC. Only sixteen states had adopted the Code by 1962, and it was 1967 before all States save one, Louisiana, had adopted the UCC. Finally, in 1974, Louisiana adopted all of the UCC save articles 2 and 6. Indeed, the opposition to the UCC may have softened in the late 1950's and 1960's only because certain courts had, by then, anyway adopted important of the UCC's radical themes and indeed extended these themes beyond the UCC's initial con-

---

3. The most recent systematic offer to revise Article 2 of the U.C.C. culminated in textual revisions proposed in 2003. The 2003 revisions at once generated controversy, which did not subside. They were withdrawn in 2011. Accordingly these pages will generally report pre-2003 versions of U.C.C. sections that they discuss. On a few occasions, the text will also report the 2003 revised text, insofar as the revisions serve to illustrate a point or drive home a lesson.

4. In addition to his principal work in commercial law, Llewellyn wrote two minor classics (minor only because their arguments proceed at a skew angle to the subsequent developments of the fields to which they most naturally belong.) *The Bramble Bush*, initially delivered as a lecture to law students at Columbia University, takes up—more perceptively than almost all of subsequent legal ethics—the broad question how a lawyer's professional activities and commitments may be integrated into a life worth living. And *The Cheyenne Way*—which is ostensibly a detailed empirical study of dispute resolution in one Native American tribe—sketches out a striking and powerful theory of the role of lawyers, and lawyerly skills in sustaining social cohesion in societies quite generally.

5. The quotation is reported in Grant Gilmore, THE DEATH OF CONTRACT (1974). The account of the history of the UCC that follows owes a great deal to Gilmore.

templation. So although the statue was radical as drafted, it became (in a way) conservative as enacted.

The radicalism of the UCC proceeded along two dimensions. First and most obviously, although not most importantly, the substantive law of the UCC includes some roughly speaking egalitarian distributional commitments. Thus the UCC as enacted, and Llewellyn's initial draft even more so, systematically distinguishes between the legal standards that apply to merchants and to non-merchants, in ways that generally favor non-merchants. For example, where a seller is a merchant, the risk that goods sold are lost or destroyed generally shifts to the buyer only on the buyer's receipt, whereas for a non-merchant seller, the risk of loss shifts as soon as she tenders the goods, which is to say, roughly, makes them available to the buyer.[6]

The real radicalism of the UCC, which is less obvious but more important, proceeds along another dimension, however, and has to do with the style of law that the UCC pursued. Moreover, it is here, perhaps more than anywhere else, that Llewellyn placed his individual stamp on the Code. Llewellyn believed that between roughly 1800 and 1850 American common law judges had engaged in what he called a "grand style" of legal reasoning. This was a creative and flexible approach in which judges consulted precedent but not mechanically, and so rendered decisions based not just on backward-looking fidelity to what had been done before but also on a forward-looking concern for the consequences of what they decided. Llewellyn admired this style of law-making, but thought that it had been lost over the second half of the nineteenth century, so that by the start of the twentieth century this grand tradition had been replaced by what he called, derisively, a "formal style" of legal reasoning.[7] This was a rigid approach to judging that was finicky about precedent and aspired to proceed in isolation from the ongoing social, economic, and political affairs that generated the disputes that judges were called on to resolve. Indeed, Llewellyn believed, where the formal style could not entirely divorce itself from the actual life of the disputes that it addressed—because no system of adjudication can do this—it retreated to subterfuge, disguising its concern for consequences and concealing any changes in the law that this concern engendered. (This theme will be pursued further in Part Two below.) Llewellyn distrusted and even despised this formal approach to law: he rejected the formal style's ambition to divorce itself from the world it governed as wrongheaded and impossible, and he descried the subterfuges to which courts wedded to this style inevitably had to turn. "Covert tools," he was fond of saying, "are never good tools."

---

6. UNIF. COM. CODE § 2–509(3)

7. It is not clear that Llewellyn's description of late nineteenth century lawyering and judging was accurate. More recent historical scholarship suggests that even the high formalists were much more, and much more openly, concerned with consequences than Llewellyn credited them with being. The conceptual and historical character of formalism will be taken up more systematically in the second Part of these materials. For now, note that Llewellyn described the style of legal reasoning that Langdell had in mind when he invented the casebook.

Llewellyn believed that the lawyers and judges of his day were re-newedly receptive to the grand style of legal reasoning, and he intended the UCC to help them to recapture this style. The Code's aim was thus to shake up commercial law without insisting (or indeed even encouraging) that it resettle in any particular pattern: put a little crassly, the Code's aim was to destroy the past without determining the future. In order to achieve this aim, Llewellyn sought to convert commercial law from a free-standing and prescriptive legal order into an enabler of the underlying economic, business, and even social practices of the entities whose transactions it sought to govern. Thus, the UCC piggy-backs, pervasively and often ex-pressly, on pre-existing commercial practice. Its provisions are full of open-ended terms, such as *reasonable*, and it advocates interpreting these terms according to the exigencies of the commercial context in which they arise. Moreover, even where the UCC makes it own substantive law, it is default rule oriented, permitting, and even encouraging, interested parties to replace its provisions with their own preferred ones.

This style of lawmaking rather than any substantive egalitarian lean-ings accounted for the bulk of the opposition that the UCC faced, which was professional (in the sense of growing out of lawyers' sensibilities as specialists or experts) rather than political (in the ordinary sense of growing out of a faction's material interests or moral beliefs). This is illustrated by a leading casebook's warning, issued as recently as the late 1990's, that UCC style legal reasoning might face opposition from judges, such as a Madison, Wisconsin trial judge who repeatedly called Article 2 of the UCC unconstitutional on grounds of its vagueness. The UCC's rocky and frustrating path to enactment, because it highlights the power of lawyers' professional ideology, serves as an object lesson in the existence of such ideological professional self-understandings to begin with (which is itself a good reason for studying the UCC).

Whatever one thinks of the merits of the UCC's style of law-making, one should not mistake the grandeur of the UCC's ambition or the skill with which the Code pursues it. Both are easily missed, especially insofar as there is a tendency to regard commercial life as a realm of the ordinary, and indeed as banal. (This tendency is shared by many who engage professionally in commerce and most who do not, the difference between the two groups being whether ordinariness and banality are terms of praise or disdain.) But even the briefest effort to mimic the UCC's project immediately reveals the Code's suppleness and depth. Just imagine trying to write down a set of principles to regulate some collective project that you belong to—a club, for example, or a housing cooperative (including even just a group of roommates), or sports team—not just in general, as a constitution might do, but in all its particulars, including in connection with disputes that arise as the project is pursued. Now try abstracting from the principles that govern a particular collective project to produce a set of principles that might govern all such projects—all clubs or all housing cooperatives or all sports teams. Finally, try abstracting again, to generate a single set of principles that can govern all these various endeavors—

clubs, and housing cooperatives, and sports teams. Something like is this is what the UCC aspired to do and, roughly, achieved.

Article 2 alone governs—by a small number of relatively brief provisions—an absolutely vast array of commercial arrangements: sales among merchants and between merchants and consumers; sales embedded in ongoing commercial relations and sales that arise as a one-off between total strangers; sales that occur against the backdrop of thick markets involving many competitors, and sales that arise in relative isolation from ordinary competitive pressures. Moreover, unlike the common law, whose achievements are the product of a slow accretion of the wisdom of many minds, aided by the discipline and creativity that an engagement with individual cases engenders, the UCC was the product of only a few minds—in a sense, really, of a single mind—generated in the abstract out of its internal resources only.

The materials that follow take up only a small part of Article 2, which is itself only a small part of the UCC. They focus on the UCC's approach to contract remedies. This approach owes much to the common law, but also adds much of its own. As you work through the materials that follow, pause occasionally to consider how impressive the statue is.

6.1 SELLERS' REMEDIES UNDER THE UCC

The basic framework for sellers' remedies under the UCC is set out in UCC § 2–703.

Uniform Commercial Code

§ 2–703 Seller's Remedies in General

Where the buyer wrongfully rejects or revokes acceptance of goods or fails to make a payment due on or before delivery or repudiates with respect to a part or the whole, then with respect to any goods directly affected and, if the breach is of the whole contract (Section 2–612), then also with respect to the whole undelivered balance, the aggrieved seller may

(a) withhold delivery of such goods;

(b) stop delivery by any bailee as hereafter provided (Section 2–705);

(c) proceed under the next section respecting goods still unidentified to the contract;

(d) resell and recover damages as hereafter provided (Section 2–706);

(e) recover damages for non-acceptance (Section 2–708) or in a proper case the price (Section 2–709);

(f) cancel.

Official Comment

Prior Uniform Statutory Provision: No comparable index section. See Section 53, Uniform Sales Act.

Purposes:

1.   This section is an index section which gathers together in one convenient place all of the various remedies open to a seller for any breach by the buyer. This Article rejects any doctrine of election of remedy as a fundamental policy and thus the remedies are essentially cumulative in nature and include all of the available remedies for breach. Whether the pursuit of one remedy bars another depends entirely on the facts of the individual case.

2.   The buyer's breach which occasions the use of the remedies under this section may involve only one lot or delivery of goods, or may involve all of the goods which are the subject matter of the particular contract. The right of the seller to pursue a remedy as to all the goods when the breach is as to only one or more lots is covered by the section on breach in installment contracts. The present section deals only with the remedies available after the goods involved in the breach have been determined by that section.

3.   In addition to the typical case of refusal to pay or default in payment, the language in the preamble, "fails to make a payment due," is intended to cover the dishonor of a check on due presentment, or the non-acceptance of a draft, and the failure to furnish an agreed letter of credit.

4.   It should also be noted that this Act requires its remedies to be liberally administered and provides that any right or obligation which it declares is enforceable by action unless a different effect is specifically prescribed (Section 1–106).

* * *

Several of the provisions of this section focus on sellers' self-help remedies—withholding delivery, for example, or reselling or salvaging. Such remedies are in practice extremely important, especially given the expense (and also uncertainty) associated with efforts to secure court-ordered remedies, through litigation. But set them aside here and focus, instead, on the provisions that address court-ordered remedies. These identify three very different such remedies and direct readers to the sections that govern each. Under UCC § 2–706, a seller who resells the goods may in addition recover damages, based on the difference between the contract price and the resale price. Under UCC § 2–708, a seller may recover damages based on the difference between the contract price of the goods and their market price. And under UCC § 2–709, a seller may recover the contract price of the goods to be sold. The materials that follow consider each of these three options, beginning with the seller's action for the price.

6.1.A THE SELLER'S ACTION FOR THE PRICE

Uniform Commercial Code

§ 2–709 Action for the Price

(1) When the buyer fails to pay the price as it becomes due the seller may recover, together with any incidental damages under the next section, the price

(a) of goods accepted or of conforming goods lost or damaged within a commercially reasonable time after risk of their loss has passed to the buyer; and

(b) of goods identified to the contract if the seller is unable after reasonable effort to resell them at a reasonable price or the circumstances reasonably indicate that such effort will be unavailing.

(2) Where the seller sues for the price he must hold for the buyer any goods which have been identified to the contract and are still in his control except that if resale becomes possible he may resell them at any time prior to the collection of the judgment. The net proceeds of any such resale must be credited to the buyer and payment of the judgment entitles him to any goods not resold.

(3) After the buyer has wrongfully rejected or revoked acceptance of the goods or has failed to make a payment due or has repudiated (Section 2–610), a seller who is held not entitled to the price under this section shall nevertheless be awarded damages for non-acceptance under the preceding section.

Official Comment

Prior Uniform Statutory Provision: Section 63, Uniform Sales Act. Changes: Rewritten, important commercially needed changes being incorporated.

Purposes of Changes: To make it clear that:

1. Neither the passing of title to the goods nor the appointment of a day certain for payment is now material to a price action.

2. The action for the price is now generally limited to those cases where resale of the goods is impracticable except where the buyer has accepted the goods or where they have been destroyed after risk of loss has passed to the buyer.

3. This section substitutes an objective test by action for the former "not readily resalable" standard. An action for the price under subsection (1)(b) can be sustained only after a "reasonable effort to resell" the goods "at reasonable price" has actually been made or where the circumstances "reasonably indicate" that such an effort will be unavailing.

4. If a buyer is in default not with respect to the price, but on an obligation to make an advance, the seller should recover not under this section for the price as such, but for the default in the collateral (though coincident) obligation to finance the seller. If the agreement between the parties contemplates that the buyer will acquire, on making the advance, a security interest in the goods, the buyer on making the advance has such an interest as soon as the seller has rights in the agreed collateral. See Section 9–204.

5. "Goods accepted" by the buyer under subsection (1)(a) include only goods as to which there has been no justified revocation of acceptance, for such a revocation means that there has been a default by the seller which bars his rights under this section. "Goods lost or damaged" are covered by the section on risk of loss. "Goods identified to the contract" under subsection (1)(b) are covered by the section on identification and the section on identification notwithstanding breach.

6. This section is intended to be exhaustive in its enumeration of cases where an action for the price lies.

7. If the action for the price fails, the seller may nonetheless have proved a case entitling him to damages for non-acceptance. In such a situation, subsection (3) permits recovery of those damages in the same action.

Uniform Commercial Code

2–606.   What Constitutes Acceptance of Goods.

(1) Acceptance of goods occurs when the buyer

(a) after a reasonable opportunity to inspect the goods signifies to the seller that the goods are conforming or that he will take or retain them in spite of their non-conformity; or

(b) fails to make an effective rejection (subsection (1) of Section 2–602), but such acceptance does not occur until the buyer has had a reasonable opportunity to inspect them; or

(c) does any act inconsistent with the seller's ownership; but if such act is wrongful as against the seller it is an acceptance only if ratified by him.

(2) Acceptance of a part of any commercial unit is acceptance of that entire unit.

Official Comment

Prior Uniform Statutory Provision: Section 48, Uniform Sales Act.

Changes: Rewritten, the qualification in paragraph (c) and subsection (2) being new; otherwise the general policy of the prior legislation is continued.

Purposes of Changes and New Matter: To make it clear that:

1.   Under this Article "acceptance" as applied to goods means that the buyer, pursuant to the contract, takes particular goods which have been appropriated to the contract as his own, whether or not he is obligated to do so, and whether he does so by words, action, or silence when it is time to speak. If the goods conform to the contract, acceptance amounts only to the performance by the buyer of one part of his legal obligation.

2.   Under this Article acceptance of goods is always acceptance of identified goods which have been appropriated to the contract or are appropriated by the contract. There is no provision for "acceptance of title" apart from acceptance in general, since acceptance of title is not material under this Article to the detailed rights and duties of the parties. (See Section 2–401). The refinements of the older law between acceptance of goods and of title become unnecessary in view of the provisions of the sections on effect and revocation of acceptance, on effects of identification and on risk of loss, and those sections which free the seller's and buyer's remedies from the complications and confusions caused by the question of whether title has or has not passed to the buyer before breach.

3.   Under paragraph (a), payment made after tender is always one circumstance tending to signify acceptance of the goods but in itself it can never be more than one circumstance and is not conclusive. Also, a conditional communication of acceptance always remains subject to its expressed conditions.

4.   Under paragraph (c), any action taken by the buyer, which is inconsistent with his claim that he has rejected the goods, constitutes an acceptance. However, the provisions of paragraph (c) are subject to the sections dealing with rejection by the buyer which permit the buyer to take certain actions with respect to the goods pursuant to his options and duties imposed by those sections, without effecting an acceptance of the goods. The second clause of paragraph (c) modifies some of the prior case law and makes it clear that "acceptance" in law based on the wrongful act of the acceptor is acceptance only as against the wrongdoer and then only at the option of the party wronged.

In the same manner in which a buyer can bind himself, despite his insistence that he is rejecting or has rejected the goods, by an act inconsistent with the seller's ownership under paragraph (c), he can obligate himself by a communication of acceptance despite a prior rejection under paragraph (a). However, the sections on buyer's rights on improper delivery and on the effect of rightful rejection, make it clear that after he once rejects a tender, paragraph (a) does not operate in favor of the buyer unless the seller has re-tendered the goods or has taken affirmative action indicating that he is holding the tender open. See also Comment 2 to Section 2–601.

5.   Subsection (2) supplements the policy of the section on buyer's rights on improper delivery, recognizing the validity of a partial acceptance

but insisting that the buyer exercise this right only as to whole commercial units.

Uniform Commercial Code

2–602.   Manner and Effect of Rightful Rejection.

(1) Rejection of goods must be within a reasonable time after their delivery or tender. It is ineffective unless the buyer seasonably notifies the seller.

(2) Subject to the provisions of the two following sections on rejected goods (Sections 2–603 and 2–604),

(a) after rejection any exercise of ownership by the buyer with respect to any commercial unit is wrongful as against the seller; and

(b) if the buyer has before rejection taken physical possession of goods in which he does not have a security interest under the provisions of this Article (subsection (3) of Section 2–711), he is under a duty after rejection to hold them with reasonable care at the seller's disposition for a time sufficient to permit the seller to remove them; but

(c) the buyer has no further obligations with regard to goods rightfully rejected.

(3) The seller's rights with respect to goods wrongfully rejected are governed by the provisions of this Article on Seller's remedies in general (Section 2–703).

Official Comment

Prior Uniform Statutory Provision: Section 50, Uniform Sales Act.

Changes: Rewritten.

Purposes of Changes: To make it clear that:

1.   A tender or delivery of goods made pursuant to a contract of sale, even though wholly non-conforming, requires affirmative action by the buyer to avoid acceptance. Under subsection (1), therefore, the buyer is given a reasonable time to notify the seller of his rejection, but without such seasonable notification his rejection is ineffective. The sections of this Article dealing with inspection of goods must be read in connection with the buyer's reasonable time for action under this subsection. Contract provisions limiting the time for rejection fall within the rule of the section on "Time" and are effective if the time set gives the buyer a reasonable time for discovery of defects. What constitutes a due "notifying" of rejection by the buyer to the seller is defined in Section 1–201.

2.   Subsection (2) lays down the normal duties of the buyer upon rejection, which flow from the relationship of the parties. Beyond his duty

to hold the goods with reasonable care for the buyer's [seller's] disposition, this section continues the policy of prior uniform legislation in generally relieving the buyer from any duties with respect to them, except when the circumstances impose the limited obligation of salvage upon him under the next section.

3.   The present section applies only to rightful rejection by the buyer. If the seller has made a tender which in all respects conforms to the contract, the buyer has a positive duty to accept and his failure to do so constitutes a "wrongful rejection" which gives the seller immediate remedies for breach. Subsection (3) is included here to emphasize the sharp distinction between the rejection of an improper tender and the non-acceptance which is a breach by the buyer.

4.   The provisions of this section are to be appropriately limited or modified when a negotiation is in process.

Uniform Commercial Code

2–503.   Manner of Seller's Tender of Delivery.

(1) Tender of delivery requires that the seller put and hold conforming goods at the buyer's disposition and give the buyer any notification reasonably necessary to enable him to take delivery. The manner, time and place for tender are determined by the agreement and this Article, and in particular

> (a) tender must be at a reasonable hour, and if it is of goods they must be kept available for the period reasonably necessary to enable the buyer to take possession; but

> (b) unless otherwise agreed the buyer must furnish facilities reasonably suited to the receipt of the goods.

(2) Where the case is within the next section respecting shipment tender requires that the seller comply with its provisions.

(3) Where the seller is required to deliver at a particular destination tender requires that he comply with subsection (1) and also in any appropriate case tender documents as described in subsections (4) and (5) of this section.

(4) Where goods are in the possession of a bailee and are to be delivered without being moved

> (a) tender requires that the seller either tender a negotiable document of title covering such goods or procure acknowledgment by the bailee of the buyer's right to possession of the goods; but

> (b) tender to the buyer of a non-negotiable document of title or of a written direction to the bailee to deliver is sufficient tender unless the buyer seasonably objects, and receipt by the bailee of notification of the buyer's rights fixes those rights as against the

bailee and all third persons; but risk of loss of the goods and of any failure by the bailee to honor the non-negotiable document of title or to obey the direction remains on the seller until the buyer has had a reasonable time to present the document or direction, and a refusal by the bailee to honor the document or to obey the direction defeats the tender.

(5) Where the contract requires the seller to deliver documents

(a) he must tender all such documents in correct form, except as provided in this Article with respect to bills of lading in a set (subsection (2) of Section 2–323); and

(b) tender through customary banking channels is sufficient and dishonor of a draft accompanying the documents constitutes non-acceptance or rejection.

Official Comment

Prior Uniform Statutory Provision: See Sections 11, 19, 20, 43 (3) and (4), 46 and 51, Uniform Sales Act.

Changes: The general policy of the above sections is continued and supplemented but subsection (3) changes the rule of prior section 19(5) as to what constitutes a "destination" contract and subsection (4) incorporates a minor correction as to tender of delivery of goods in the possession of a bailee.

Purposes of Changes:

1. The major general rules governing the manner of proper or due tender of delivery are gathered in this section. The term "tender" is used in this Article in two different senses. In one sense it refers to "due tender" which contemplates an offer coupled with a present ability to fulfill all the conditions resting on the tendering party and must be followed by actual performance if the other party shows himself ready to proceed. Unless the context unmistakably indicates otherwise this is the meaning of "tender" in this Article and the occasional addition of the word "due" is only for clarity and emphasis. At other times it is used to refer to an offer of goods or documents under a contract as if in fulfillment of its conditions even though there is a defect when measured against the contract obligation. Used in either sense, however, "tender" connotes such performance by the tendering party as puts the other party in default if he fails to proceed in some manner.

2. The seller's general duty to tender and deliver is laid down in Section 2–301 and more particularly in Section 2–507. The seller's right to a receipt if he demands one and receipts are customary is governed by Section 1–205. Subsection (1) of the present section proceeds to set forth two primary requirements of tender: first, that the seller "put and hold conforming goods at the buyer's disposition" and, second, that he "give the buyer any notice reasonably necessary to enable him to take delivery."

In cases in which payment is due and demanded upon delivery the "buyer's disposition" is qualified by the seller's right to retain control of the goods until payment by the provision of this Article on delivery on condition. However, where the seller is demanding payment on delivery he must first allow the buyer to inspect the goods in order to avoid impairing his tender unless the contract for sale is on C.I.F., C.O.D., cash against documents or similar terms negating the privilege of inspection before payment.

In the case of contracts involving documents the seller can "put and hold conforming goods at the buyer's disposition" under subsection (1) by tendering documents which give the buyer complete control of the goods under the provisions of Article 7 on due negotiation.

3.   Under paragraph (a) of subsection (1) usage of the trade and the circumstances of the particular case determine what is a reasonable hour for tender and what constitutes a reasonable period of holding the goods available.

4.   The buyer must furnish reasonable facilities for the receipt of the goods tendered by the seller under subsection (1), paragraph (b). This obligation of the buyer is no part of the seller's tender.

5.   For the purposes of subsections (2) and (3) there is omitted from this Article the rule under prior uniform legislation that a term requiring the seller to pay the freight or cost of transportation to the buyer is equivalent to an agreement by the seller to deliver to the buyer or at an agreed destination. This omission is with the specific intention of negating the rule, for under this Article the "shipment" contract is regarded as the normal one and the "destination" contract as the variant type. The seller is not obligated to deliver at a named destination and bear the concurrent risk of loss until arrival, unless he has specifically agreed so to deliver or the commercial understanding of the terms used by the parties contemplates such delivery.

6.   Paragraph (a) of subsection (4) continues the rule of the prior uniform legislation as to acknowledgment by the bailee. Paragraph (b) of subsection (4) adopts the rule that between the buyer and the seller the risk of loss remains on the seller during a period reasonable for securing acknowledgment of the transfer from the bailee, while as against all other parties the buyer's rights are fixed as of the time the bailee receives notice of the transfer.

7.   Under subsection (5) documents are never "required" except where there is an express contract term or it is plainly implicit in the peculiar circumstances of the case or in a usage of trade. Documents may, of course, be "authorized" although not required, but such cases are not within the scope of this subsection. When documents are required, there are three main requirements of this subsection: (1) "All": each required document is essential to a proper tender; (2) "Such": the documents must be the ones actually required by the contract in terms of source and substance; (3) "Correct form": All documents must be in correct form.

When a prescribed document cannot be procured, a question of fact arises under the provision of this Article on substituted performance as to whether the agreed manner of delivery is actually commercially impracticable and whether the substitute is commercially reasonable.

Uniform Commercial Code

2–319.   F.O.B. and F.A.S. Terms.

(1) Unless otherwise agreed the term F.O.B. (which means "free on board" at a named place, even though used only in connection with the stated price, is a delivery term under which

(a) when the term is F.O.B. the place of shipment, the seller must at that place ship the goods in the manner provided in this Article (Section 2–504) and bear the expense and risk of putting them into the possession of the carrier; or

(b) when the term is F.O.B. the place of destination, the seller must at his own expense and risk transport the goods to that place and there tender delivery of them in the manner provided in this Article (Section 2–503);

(c) when under either (a) or (b) the term is also F.O.B. vessel, car or other vehicle, the seller must in addition at his own expense and risk load the goods on board. If the term is F.O.B. vessel the buyer must name the vessel and in an appropriate case the seller must comply with the provisions of this Article on the form of bill of lading (Section 2–323).

(2) Unless otherwise agreed the term F.A.S. vessel (which means "free alongside" at a named port, even though used only in connection with the stated price, is a delivery term under which the seller must

(a) at his own expense and risk deliver the goods alongside the vessel in the manner usual in that port or on a dock designated and provided by the buyer; and

(b) obtain and tender a receipt for the goods in exchange for which the carrier is under a duty to issue a bill of lading.

(3) Unless otherwise agreed in any case falling within subsection (1)(a) or (c) or subsection (2) the buyer must seasonably give any needed instructions for making delivery, including when the term is F.A.S. or F.O.B. the loading berth of the vessel and in an appropriate case its name and sailing date. The seller may treat the failure of needed instructions as a failure of cooperation under this Article (Section 2–311). He may also at his option move the goods in any reasonable manner preparatory to delivery or shipment.

(4) Under the term F.O.B. vessel or F.A.S. unless otherwise agreed the buyer must make payment against tender of the required documents and

the seller may not tender nor the buyer demand delivery of the goods in substitution for the documents.

Official Comment

Prior Uniform Statutory Provision: None.

Purposes:

1. This section is intended to negate the uncommercial line of decision which treats an "F.O.B." term as "merely a price term." The distinctions taken in subsection (1) handle most of the issues which have on occasion led to the unfortunate judicial language just referred to. Other matters which have led to sound results being based on unhappy language in regard to F.O.B. clauses are dealt with in this Act by Section 2–311(2) (seller's option re arrangements relating to shipment) and Sections 2–614 and 615 (substituted performance and seller's excuse).

2. Subsection (1)(c) not only specifies the duties of a seller who engages to deliver "F.O.B. vessel," or the like, but ought to make clear that no agreement is soundly drawn when it looks to reshipment from San Francisco or New York, but speaks merely of "F.O.B." the place.

3. The buyer's obligations stated in subsection (1)(c) and subsection (3) are, as shown in the text, obligations of cooperation. The last sentence of subsection (3) expressly, though perhaps unnecessarily, authorizes the seller, pending instructions, to go ahead with such preparatory moves as shipment from the interior to the named point of delivery. The sentence presupposes the usual case in which instructions "fail"; a prior repudiation by the buyer, giving notice that breach was intended, would remove the reason for the sentence, and would normally bring into play, instead, the second sentence of Section 2–704, which duly calls for lessening damages.

4. The treatment of "F.O.B. vessel" in conjunction with F.A.S. fits, in regard to the need for payment against documents, with standard practice and caselaw; but "F.O.B. vessel" is a term which by its very language makes express the need for an "on board" document. In this respect, that term is stricter than the ordinary overseas "shipment" contract (C.I.F., etc., Section 2–320).

Unlaub v. Sexton

United States Court of Appeals for the Eighth Circuit, 1977.
568 F.2d 72.

■ VAN OOSTERHOUT, SENIOR CIRCUIT JUDGE. This is a diversity action brought by the Unlaub Company, Inc. (Unlaub), an Oklahoma corporation with principal place of business in Oklahoma, against Sam Sexton, Jr., a citizen and resident of Arkansas, to recover an alleged $54,177.00 balance due, with interest from July 22, 1975, on the price of certain coal screen units which are the subject of a contract of sale between Unlaub as seller and Paul Rees Coal Company (the coal company) as buyer. Sexton is president of, and in writing personally guaranteed performance of the contract by, the coal company. The district court granted summary judgment for Unlaub in the amount claimed. We affirm.

The contract in question, dated May 7, 1975, specified a total price for the coal screen units of $67,721.00 and required a down payment in the amount of $13,544.00, which the parties agree was paid by the coal company. Under the contract the coal screen units were to be manufactured by Simplicity Engineering Company (Simplicity) at Durand, Michigan, and were to be picked up there by the coal company upon receipt of notice from Unlaub that the goods were available. The contract was contained in the following letter, which we reproduce in full:

Paul Reese [sic] Coal Company

Fort Smith, Arkansas 72901

Gentlemen:

This letter is to confirm in writing our agreement regarding your purchase from us of Simplicity screen units, as set forth in Proposal JM 041175–1, dated April 11, 1975, from Simplicity Engineering Company, which is incorporated herein.

This Proposal shall become your purchase order to us with a result that the total purchase price, F.O.B. Durand, Michigan, shall be $67,721.00 plus applicable sales or use taxes, of which your cashier's or certified check for 20% or $13,544.00 shall accompany your acceptance of this letter and the remaining $54,177.00, plus applicable sales or use taxes, shall either (i) be placed in escrow with a Fort Smith bank to be mutually selected by us on or before May 1, 1975, or (ii) Sam Sexton, Jr. and Robert Lane, the owners of all of the outstanding capital stock of Paul Reese Coal Company, shall personally guaranty full performance and payment of all obligations of Paul Reese Coal Company pursuant thereto. The balance of $54,177.00, plus applicable sales or use taxes, shall be paid to The Unlaub Company upon receipt by you of notice that the Simplicity screen units are available to be picked up by you at Durand, Michigan. Title and risk of loss shall pass to you at such time.

If this is satisfactory to you, please accept this agreement in the space below and return it to us with your check for $13,544.00 payable to The Unlaub Company and provide us with either an escrow agreement for our approval or the signatures of the Guarantors in the spaces provided below.

Very truly yours, THE UNLAUB COMPANY

By /s/ B.J. Coulter

The foregoing is approved and accepted on 5/7/75.

PAUL REESE [sic] COAL COMPANY

By /s/ Sam Sexton, Jr.

Sam Sexton, Jr., President and duly authorized representative

/s/ Sam Sexton, Jr.

Sam Sexton, Jr., as Guarantor

/s/ Robert Lane

Robert Lane, as Guarantor

Sexton admits that his signatures to this contract were authorized by him.

On July 22, 1975, Unlaub allegedly sent, by registered mail, the following notification to Sexton that the goods were available to be picked up in Durand, Michigan:

MR. SAM SEXTON, JR.

515 GARRISON ST. FORT SMITH, ARKANSAS 72901

DEAR MR. SEXTON,

THIS WILL CONFIRM THE SEVERAL TELEPHONE CALLS BY OUR MR. JENNINGS, NOTIFYING YOU THAT THE FOUR SIMPLICITY SCREENS COVERED BY THE PURCHASE CONTRACT DATED MAY 7, 1975, ARE READY FOR YOU TO HAVE PICKED UP AT THE SIMPLICITY FACTORY AT DURAND, MICHIGAN.

AS PROVIDED IN THE CONTRACT, UPON THIS NOTIFICATION YOU ARE TO PAY US THE BALANCE OF THE PURCHASE PRICE, FIFTY FOUR THOUSAND ONE HUNDRED SEVENTY SEVEN DOLLARS ($54177.00), PLUS ANY SALES OR USE TAXES WHICH MAY BE DUE. SINCE WE HAVE NOT RECEIVED ANY SALES TAX EXEMPTION CERTIFICATION FROM YOU, THE PROPER ARKANSAS OR OKLAHOMA TAXES MUST BE ADDED TO THIS CONTRACT BALANCE.

WE WILL ASK THAT YOU ACT PROMPTLY ON THIS MATTER, AS SIMPLICITY IS PRESSING US FOR THE PAYMENT DUE THEM, AS WELL AS FOR DISPOSITION OF THE EQUIPMENT.

CORDIALLY YOURS,

THE UNLAUB COMPANY, INC.

/s/ C. G. Unlaub

Copies of this letter and of the registry and return receipts therefor, the latter dated July 23, 1975, are attached to Unlaub's complaint and to supporting affidavits filed by Unlaub.

[W]e agree with the district court that, on the basis of facts not genuinely disputed, Unlaub is entitled as a matter of law to recover from Sexton the unpaid balance of the price of the coal screen units. This result follows necessarily from unambiguous provisions of Article II of the Uniform Commercial Code as adopted in Arkansas, Ark. Stat. Ann. §§ 85–2–101 *et seq.* (Add. 1961), and from the most basic principles of guarantor liability.

Uniform Commercial Code subsection 2–709(1) provides in pertinent part: "When the buyer fails to pay the price as it becomes due the seller may recover the price (a) of goods accepted."[3] Under subsection 2–606(1), "Acceptance of goods occurs when the buyer (b) fails to make an effective rejection (subsection (1) of *Section 2–602*), but such acceptance does not occur until the buyer has had a reasonable opportunity to inspect them." Subsection 2–602(1) in turn provides: "Rejection of goods must be within a reasonable time after their delivery or tender. It is ineffective unless the buyer seasonably notifies the seller." Finally, under subsection 2–503(1):

> Tender of delivery requires that the seller put and hold conforming goods at the buyer's disposition and give the buyer any notification reasonably necessary to enable him to take delivery. The manner, time and place for tender are determined by the agreement and this Article, and in particular
>
> (a) tender must be at a reasonable hour, and if it is of goods they must be kept available for the period reasonably necessary to enable the buyer to take possession.

When these provisions are read in conjunction with facts in this case not genuinely disputed, Unlaub's right to recover the unpaid balance of the contract price is established as a matter of law.

Under the terms of the May 7 contract, tender would occur "upon receipt by [the coal company] of notice that the Simplicity screen units are available to be picked up by [the coal company] at Durand, Michigan."[4] Tender was made in accordance with this contractual provision by letter dated July 22. As previously noted, Sexton does not genuinely dispute that the letter was sent and received. There is similarly no genuine issue raised as to the reasonableness of the tender or the conformity of the goods to the contract. The tender was accordingly a proper one under the contract and subsection 2–503(1).

---

3. Subsection 2–709(1) also provides that an unpaid seller may recover the price "(b) of goods identified to the contract if the seller is unable after reasonable effort to resell them at a reasonable price or the circumstances reasonably indicate that such effort will be unavailing." The district court concluded Unlaub was entitled to relief under this provision. *427 F. Supp. at 1368.* While there is substantial support in the record for that conclusion, we cannot say the record reveals no genuine dispute of material fact with respect thereto. We accordingly do not affirm on that basis.

Section 2–709 on its face makes clear in the context of this case that a seller is under no obligation to attempt a resale of accepted goods.

4. The contract also contained the delivery term "F.O.B. Durand, Michigan."Uniform Commercial Code subsection 2–319(1) in part provides (emphasis supplied):

Unless otherwise agreed the term F.O.B. (which means "free on board") at a named place, even though used only in connection with the stated price, is a delivery term under which

(a) when the term is F.O.B. the place of shipment, the seller must at that place ship the goods in the manner provided in this Article (*Section 2–504*) and bear the expense and risk of putting them into the possession of the carrier.

The parties, in contracting that title and risk of loss would pass to the buyer at the time of payment, which was to occur upon receipt of notice that the goods were available to be picked up by the buyer at Durand, Michigan, plainly agreed otherwise.

Sexton has similarly failed to support any contention that either he or the coal company rejected, or even attempted to reject, the tender. By affidavit Jim Jennings on behalf of Unlaub recited: "Prior to [the July 22 letter] I had, on several occasions, telephoned Mr. Sexton or his representatives to advise that the screens were ready for delivery upon performance of the purchase agreement of May 7, 1975. In each of these conversations I was told the screens would be picked up within a few days." Although Sexton did file an affidavit, he did not therein or otherwise controvert this recitation. The record is devoid of any indication that either Sexton or the coal company complied with subsection 2–602(1), as there is no indication that notice, either seasonable or unseasonable, was given to Unlaub that the goods would not be accepted. Nor does the record reveal any basis upon which the tender could properly have been rejected. Once again we necessarily reach the conclusion that no rejection occurred.

Because it is equally clear that an opportunity to inspect the goods has been provided, it follows immediately that the goods were accepted under subsection 2–606(1)(b) and that Unlaub is accordingly entitled to recover the unpaid balance of the contract price under subsection 2–709(1)(a).

The judgment appealed from is affirmed.

* * *

When it applies, UCC § 2–709 in effect allows a seller to replace the general principle that a contract remedy should put her in as good a position as her buyer's performance would have done with a remedy that puts her in exactly the same position as performance would have done. It thus presents a special case of what the law calls "specific performance." (Its special-ness consists not least in the fact that specific performance under the special circumstances addressed by § 2–709 consists in the payment of money damages.) There will be more on the broader class specific performance latter. For now, focus on the mechanics of § 2–709 and also on the statute's broader purposes and the interpretive questions that it raises.

First focus on the mechanics of § 2–709, and note that these are indeed literally mechanical. Applying the statute requires figuring out exactly which of its provisions apply and the following these provisions' instructions as they lead through the rest of the UCC.

The trail begins with § 2–709 itself, which allows sellers to recover the contract price from their breaching buyers only in certain circumstances. The one that is relevant in *Unlaub* is that a seller may recover the price from a breaching buyer who has accepted the goods (§ 2–709(1)(a)).[8] So the central issue in the case is whether or not the buyer accepted.

---

8. Note that this is not the only circumstance in which a seller may recover the contract price. In addition, where the goods have not been accepted by a buyer or where they have been destroyed after risk of loss has passed to a buyer, then a seller can maintain an action for the price as long as resale is not reasonable. (To take advantage of this provision, a seller must show that resale has failed in spite of its reasonable efforts or that circumstances reasonably indicate that such efforts will be unavailing.) Unif. Com. Code § 2–709(1).

The answer to this question begins with § 2–606(1), which says that a buyer accepts goods when (after having a reasonable chance to inspect the goods) he fails to make an effective *rejection* under § 2–602. Now read that provision, and especially § 2–602(1), which says, among other things, that a buyer must reject within a reasonable time after *tender* or delivery. So look for the meaning that the UCC attributes to tender, which appears in § 2–503(1). That section says that tender occurs when a seller puts the goods at the disposition of her buyer, in a reasonable manner and with reasonable notification, and adds that the particulars of manner, time, and place of tender are to be determined by the UCC defaults or the agreement of the parties. So from this we know that if the seller tendered (§ 2–503) the goods to her buyer at Durand, then the buyer accepted (§ 2–601) by failing to reject (§ 2–602), and so the seller can recover the price (§ 2–709). Note how mechanical the reasoning up to this point is—that it requires carefully following the definitions and cross-references of the statute, wherever they lead.

But this mechanical reasoning does not resolve the case—it just reframes (narrows) the issue to be whether or not the seller tendered the goods at Durand. So did the seller tender the goods? Well, the contract in *Unlaub* specified:

(1) that the price was for the goods F.O.B. (free on board) Durand, and

(2) that payment was due when the buyer was notified that the goods were available for its collection at Durand.

One must thus ask how these terms determine what counts as tender. The answer once again requires mechanically charting a path through the various provisions of the UCC. But now mechanical application of the code, although it remains necessary, is no longer sufficient for analyzing the case.

Under U.C.C. § 2–319(1), an "F.O.B. place of shipment" term creates a default obligation in the seller to ship the goods by a means approved in § 2–504 and to bear the risk and expense of putting them into possession of the carrier. So under the default meaning that the UCC accords to the part of the contract reprised in (1), the seller did not tender the goods, because she never placed them into the hands of an approved carrier, but merely notified the buyer that the goods were available. But this is a default interpretation only, and § 2–319 expressly takes this approach to tender only as long as the parties do not otherwise agree. And in *Unlaub*, the parties (as the part of the contract reprised in (2) suggests) expressly agreed that the buyer was to collect the goods at Durand, and that the S did not have to deliver them to a carrier. Therefore, at least under a mechanical reading of the UCC, the seller did tender the goods at Durand,

---

This makes it natural to ask why sellers must make only reasonable resales. Why not require sellers to resell at any price, even an unreasonable one, and then to proceed under § 2–706 to collect damages based on the differential between the contract and resale prices? Does this suggest that one should read § 2–709(1)(b) as focusing principally on cases in which resale is strictly impossible, because there is no market at all for the goods?

so that buyer accepted the goods (by not rejecting them), so that the seller may recover the price. And this is what the court decided.

But it is not at all clear that this result best implements the broader purposes of the remedy regime that the UCC establishes. In particular, § 2–709 seems designed to allow sellers to recover the contract price in specifically those classes of cases in which they are not the most efficient resellers of the goods following a breach: when the goods cannot reasonably be resold; when they are lost or damaged (after the risk of loss has passed to the buyer); and (as in *Unlaub*) when buyers have already accepted. This suggests that the standard of "acceptance" that best integrates § 2–709(1)(a) into the whole of § 2–709—that best connects the acceptance provision to the theme that unifies the section—should connect whether or not the buyer has accepted to whether or not he has replaced the seller as the most efficient reseller of the goods. And in *Unlaub*, it surely seems that the plaintiff, and not her buyer, was the most efficient reseller of bulky coal screens that remained in her delegated manufacturer's city of business, far from her buyer's location, and not yet in the hands of a carrier.

This reasoning, moreover, may be carried over into the textual argument over whether or not the buyer in *Unlaub* actually did accept. The basic idea is that whether or not a buyer has accepted should not be determined by a formalism but rather by the practical economic realities of the situation, and in particular by who retains (or can most cheaply exercise) possession and control over the goods. The UCC's default approach to contracts whose tender terms specify "F.O.B. place of shipment" tracks this reasoning. It treats such terms as making it a condition of tender that sellers place the goods into the hands of a carrier, and this act does seem to establish the boundary-between the seller's and the buyer's natural dominion and control. So if the default interpretation of the contract's language had governed, the outcome in *Unlaub* would have been reversed, so that the seller's action for the price would have failed. This outcome, moreover, would have been consistent with the general policy underlying the UCC's limited grant to sellers of the right to bring an action for the price. It does seem likely that the seller in *Unlaub* in fact remained the most efficient reseller.

This result was not reached in *Unlaub* because the court treated the parties, through the express language of their contract, as abandoning the default in favor of a different rule, according to which tender turned not on the realities of possession and control but on the more formal notification of the buyer. But it is not clear that the court was required to read the contract in this way, and an alternative interpretation of the contract would have produced the opposite, and probably preferable, result.

In particular, nothing required the court to read the contract clause stating that the buyer should collect the screens on receiving notice that the seller had made them available at Durand as an interpretive gloss on the clause stating that the price was for the goods F.O.B., Durand. That approach completely *eliminated* the default meaning of the F.O.B. clause from the case—that tender required the seller to place the screens in the hands of a carrier at Durand—because that meaning of the F.O.B. clause was *replaced* by clause saying that tender required only that the seller's notify the buyer that the screens were available for collection at Durand. The default meaning of the F.O.B. clause need not, however, have been eliminated in this way. Instead, the court might have allowed the F.O.B. clause to retain this meaning and treated the second clause—concerning notification by the seller and collection by the buyer—not as interpreting the F.O.B. clause but as introducing a second, and inconsistent, approach to tender into the contract. The court would then have had to decide which approach to tender to follow—which most accurately reflected the parties' true intentions in their agreement. It is not clear how that question might have been answered, but the fact that the default meaning of the F.O.B. clause would place the duty to resell on the presumptively most efficient reseller (thus increasing the contractual surplus available *ex ante* for the parties to divide) is surely an argument in favor of making it interpretively dominant.

Finally, note a slight artificiality in § 2–709, which is related to the question how closely the seller's right to recover the contract price should depend on her no longer being the most efficient reseller. § 2–709 applies when a buyer has accepted the goods and therefore also when a buyer, following an acceptance, wrongfully (and hence ineffectively) revokes that acceptance. But § 2–709 does not apply when a buyer has never accepted the goods, including even when the buyer's rejection (although technically effective) was wrongful. This makes sense as long as the distinction between cases in which a buyer has accepted, including cases in which he has wrongfully revoked, and cases in which the buyer has rejected, including wrongfully, tracks effective possession of and control ever the goods. But it makes less sense in circumstances in which the difference between a buyer's acceptance and wrongful revocation and her wrongful rejection is merely verbal, and has nothing to do with effective possession and control. This observation only increases the pressure—already observed in the criticism of *Unlaub* presented a moment ago—that § 2–709 places on the UCC's regime governing tender, acceptance, and rejection. That regime was designed to replace an older set of rules that emphasized legal formalities regarding whether title to goods had passed to the buyer with an approach that emphasized the commercial realities of effective dominion and control. Once again, in order for § 2–709 to succeed in implementing its ambitions, this regime concerning tender, acceptance, and rejection must succeed in implementing its ambitions.

6.1.B DAMAGES BASED ON CONTRACT-RESALE AND CONTRACT-MARKET PRICE DIFFERENCES

Now turn to the other two UCC provisions fixing sellers' damages—§§ 2–706 and 2–708. § 2–706 applies where there has been an appropriate resale by a seller and fixes the seller's damages according to the contract-resale price differential. § 2–708 applies when there has been no resale sanctioned under § 2–706 and bases the sellers' damages on the contract-market price differential. § 2–723 governs the proof of market price, and hence the administration of the market based damages formula.

Uniform Commercial Code

§ 2–706   Seller's Resale Including Contract for Resale

(1) Under the conditions stated in Section 2–703 on seller's remedies, the seller may resell the goods concerned or the undelivered balance thereof. Where the resale is made in good faith and in a commercially reasonable manner the seller may recover the difference between the resale price and the contract price together with any incidental damages allowed under the provisions of this Article (Section 2–710), but less expenses saved in consequence of the buyer's breach.

(2) Except as otherwise provided in subsection (3) or unless otherwise agreed resale may be at public or private sale including sale by way of one or more contracts to sell or of identification to an existing contract of the seller. Sale may be as a unit or in parcels and at any time and place and on any terms but every aspect of the sale including the method, manner, time, place and terms must be commercially reasonable. The resale must be reasonably identified as referring to the broken contract, but it is not necessary that the goods be in existence or that any or all of them have been identified to the contract before the breach.

(3) Where the resale is at private sale the seller must give the buyer reasonable notification of his intention to resell.

(4) Where the resale is at public sale

(a) only identified goods can be sold except where there is a recognized market for a public sale of futures in goods of the kind; and

(b) it must be made at a usual place or market for public sale if one is reasonably available and except in the case of goods which are perishable or threaten to decline in value speedily the seller must give the buyer reasonable notice of the time and place of the resale; and

(c) if the goods are not to be within the view of those attending the sale the notification of sale must state the place where the goods are located and provide for their reasonable inspection by prospective bidders; and

(d) the seller may buy.

(5) A purchaser who buys in good faith at a resale takes the goods free of any rights of the original buyer even though the seller fails to comply with one or more of the requirements of this section.

(6) The seller is not accountable to the buyer for any profit made on any resale. A person in the position of a seller (Section 2–707) or a buyer

who has rightfully rejected or justifiably revoked acceptance must account for any excess over the amount of his security interest, as hereinafter defined (subsection (3) of Section 2–711).

Official Comment

Prior Uniform Statutory Provision: Section 60, Uniform Sales Act. Changes: Rewritten.

Purposes of Changes: To simplify the prior statutory provision and to make it clear that:

1. The only condition precedent to the seller's right of resale under subsection (1) is a breach by the buyer within the section on the seller's remedies in general or insolvency. Other meticulous conditions and restrictions of the prior uniform statutory provision are disapproved by this Article and are replaced by standards of commercial reasonableness. Under this section the seller may resell the goods after any breach by the buyer. Thus, an anticipatory repudiation by the buyer gives rise to any of the seller's remedies for breach, and to the right of resale. This principle is supplemented by subsection (2) which authorizes a resale of goods which are not in existence or were not identified to the contract before the breach.

2. In order to recover the damages prescribed in subsection (1) the seller must act "in good faith and in a commercially reasonable manner" in making the resale. This standard is intended to be more comprehensive than that of "reasonable care and judgment" established by the prior uniform statutory provision. Failure to act properly under this section deprives the seller of the measure of damages here provided and relegates him to that provided in Section 2–708.

Under this Article the seller resells by authority of law, in his own behalf, for his own benefit and for the purpose of fixing his damages. The theory of a seller's agency is thus rejected.

3. If the seller complies with the prescribed standard of duty in making the resale, he may recover from the buyer the damages provided for in subsection (1). Evidence of market or current prices at any particular time or place is relevant only on the question of whether the seller acted in a commercially reasonable manner in making the resale.

The distinction drawn by some courts between cases where the title had not passed to the buyer and the seller had resold as owner, and cases where the title had passed and the seller had resold by virtue of his lien on the goods, is rejected.

4. Subsection (2) frees the remedy of resale from legalistic restrictions and enables the seller to resell in accordance with reasonable commercial practices so as to realize as high a price as possible in the circumstances. By "public" sale is meant a sale by auction. A "private" sale may be effected by solicitation and negotiation conducted either directly or through a broker. In choosing between a public and private sale the character of the goods must be considered and relevant trade practices and usages must be observed.

5. Subsection (2) merely clarifies the common law rule that the time for resale is a reasonable time after the buyer's breach, by using the language "commercially reasonable." What is such a reasonable time depends upon the nature of the goods, the condition of the market and the other circumstances of the case; its length cannot be measured by any legal yardstick or divided into degrees. Where a seller contemplating resale receives a demand from the buyer for inspection under the section of preserving evidence of goods in dispute, the time for resale may be appropriately lengthened.

On the question of the place for resale, subsection (2) goes to the ultimate test, the commercial reasonableness of the seller's choice as to the place for an advantageous resale. This Article rejects the theory that the seller is required to resell at the agreed place for delivery and that a resale elsewhere can be permitted only in exceptional cases.

6. The purpose of subsection (2) being to enable the seller to dispose of the goods to the best advantage, he is permitted in making the resale to depart from the terms and conditions of the original contract for sale to any extent "commercially reasonable" in the circumstances.

7. The provision of subsection (2) that the goods need not be in existence to be resold applies when the buyer is guilty of anticipatory repudiation of a contract for future goods, before the goods or some of them have come into existence. In such a case the seller may exercise the right of resale and fix his damages by "one or more contracts to sell" the quantity of conforming future goods affected by the repudiation. The companion provision of subsection (2) that resale may be made although the goods were not identified to the contract prior to the buyer's breach, likewise contemplates an anticipatory repudiation by the buyer but occurring after the goods are in existence. If the goods so identified conform to the contract, their resale will fix the seller's damages quite as satisfactorily as if they had been identified before the breach.

8. Where the resale is to be by private sale, subsection (3) requires that reasonable notification of the seller's intention to resell must be given to the buyer. The length of notification of a private sale depends upon the urgency of the matter. Notification of the time and place of this type of sale is not required.

Subsection (4)(b) requires that the seller give the buyer reasonable notice of the time and place of a public resale so that he may have an opportunity to bid or to secure the attendance of other bidders. An exception is made in the case of goods "which are perishable or threaten to decline speedily in value."

9. Since there would be no reasonable prospect of competitive bidding elsewhere, subsection (4) requires that a public resale "must be made at a usual place or market for public sale if one is reasonably available;" i.e., a place or market which prospective bidders may reasonably be expected to attend. Such a market may still be "reasonably available" under this subsection, though at a considerable distance from the place where the

goods are located. In such a case the expense of transporting the goods for resale is recoverable from the buyer as part of the seller's incidental damages under subsection (1). However, the question of availability is one of commercial reasonableness in the circumstances and if such "usual" place or market is not reasonably available, a duly advertised public resale may be held at another place if it is one which prospective bidders may reasonably be expected to attend, as distinguished from a place where there is no demand whatsoever for goods of the kind.

Paragraph (a) of subsection (4) qualifies the last sentence of subsection (2) with respect to resales of unidentified and future goods at public sale. If conforming goods are in existence the seller may identify them to the contract after the buyer's breach and then resell them at public sale. If the goods have not been identified, however, he may resell them at public sale only as "future" goods and only where there is a recognized market for public sale of futures in goods of the kind.

The provisions of paragraph (c) of subsection (4) are intended to permit intelligent bidding.

The provision of paragraph (d) of subsection (4) permitting the seller to bid and, of course, to become the purchaser, benefits the original buyer by tending to increase the resale price and thus decreasing the damages he will have to pay.

10. This Article departs in subsection (5) from the prior uniform statutory provision in permitting a good faith purchaser at resale to take a good title as against the buyer even though the seller fails to comply with the requirements of this section.

11. Under subsection (6), the seller retains profit, if any, without distinction based on whether or not he had a lien since this Article divorces the question of passage of title to the buyer from the seller's right of resale or the consequences of its exercise. On the other hand, where "a person in the position of a seller" or a buyer acting under the section on buyer's remedies, exercises his right of resale under the present section he does so only for the limited purpose of obtaining cash for his "security interest" in the goods. Once that purpose has been accomplished any excess in the resale price belongs to the seller to whom an accounting must be made as provided in the last sentence of subsection (6).

Uniform Commercial Code

§ 2–708 Seller's Damages for Non-acceptance or Repudiation.

(1) Subject to subsection (2) and to the provisions of this Article with respect to proof of market price (Section 2–723), the measure of damages for non-acceptance or repudiation by the buyer is the difference between the market price at the time and place for tender and the unpaid contract price together with any incidental damages provided in this Article (Section 2–710), but less expenses saved in consequence of the buyer's breach.

(2) If the measure of damages provided in subsection (1) is inadequate to put the seller in as good a position as performance would have done then the measure of damages is the profit (including reasonable overhead) which the seller would have made from full performance by the buyer, together with any incidental damages provided in this Article (Section 2–710), due allowance for costs reasonably incurred and due credit for payments or proceeds of resale.

Official Comment

Prior Uniform Statutory Provision: Section 64, Uniform Sales Act. Changes: Rewritten.

Purposes of Changes: To make it clear that:

1. The prior uniform statutory provision is followed generally in setting the current market price at the time and place for tender as the standard by which damages for non-acceptance are to be determined. The time and place of tender is determined by reference to the section on manner of tender of delivery, and to the sections on the effect of such terms as FOB, FAS, CIF, C & F, Ex Ship and No Arrival, No Sale.

In the event that there is no evidence available of the current market price at the time and place of tender, proof of a substitute market may be made under the section on determination and proof of market price. Furthermore, the section on the admissibility of market quotations is intended to ease materially the problem of providing competent evidence.

2. The provision of this section permitting recovery of expected profit including reasonable overhead where the standard measure of damages is inadequate, together with the new requirement that price actions may be sustained only where resale is impractical, are designed to eliminate the unfair and economically wasteful results arising under the older law when fixed price articles were involved. This section permits the recovery of lost profits in all appropriate cases, which would include all standard priced goods. The normal measure there would be list price less cost to the dealer or list price less manufacturing cost to the manufacturer. It is not necessary to a recovery of "profit" to show a history of earnings, especially of a new venture is involved.

3. In all cases the seller may recover incidental damages.

Uniform Commerical Code

2–723 Proof of Market Price: Time and Place

(1) If an action based on anticipatory repudiation comes to trial before the time for performance with respect to some or all of the goods, any damages based on market price (Section 2–708 or Section 2–713) shall be determined according to the price of such goods prevailing at the time when the aggrieved party learned of the repudiation.

(2) If evidence of a price prevailing at the times or places described in this Article is not readily available the price prevailing within any reasonable time before or after the time described or at any other place which in commercial judgment or under usage of trade would serve as a reasonable substitute for the one described may be used, making any proper allowance for the cost of transporting the goods to or from such other place.

(3) Evidence of a relevant price prevailing at a time or place other than the one described in this Article offered by one party is not admissible unless and until he has given the other party such notice as the court finds sufficient to prevent unfair surprise.

Official Comment

Prior Uniform Statutory Provision: None.

Purposes of Changes: To eliminate the most obvious difficulties arising in connection with the determination of market price, when that is stipulated as a measure of damages by some provision of this Article. Where the appropriate market price is not readily available the court is here granted reasonable leeway in receiving evidence of prices current in other comparable markets or at other times comparable to the one in question. In accordance with the general principle of this Article against surprise, however, a party intending to offer evidence of such a substitute price must give suitable notice to the other party.

This section is not intended to exclude the use of any other reasonable method of determining market price or of measuring damages if the circumstances of the case make this necessary.

Uniform Commerical Code

§ 2–723 Proof of Market: Time and Place (2003 proposed amendments)

(1) If evidence of a price prevailing at the times or places described in this Article is not readily available, the price prevailing within any reasonable time before or after the time described or at any other place that in commercial judgment or under usage of trade would serve as a reasonable substitute for the one described may be used, making any proper allowance for the cost of transporting the goods to or from the other place.

(2) Evidence of a relevant price prevailing at a time or place other than the one described in this Article offered by one party is not admissible unless and until the party has given the other party such notice as the court finds sufficient to prevent unfair surprise.

Official Comment

Prior Uniform Statutory Provision: None.

Purposes: To eliminate the most obvious difficulties arising in connection with the determination of market price, when that is stipulated as a measure of damages by some provision of this Article. Where the appropriate market price is not readily available the court is here granted reasonable leeway in receiving evidence of prices current in other comparable markets or at other times comparable to the one in question. In accordance with the general principle of this Article against surprise, however, a party intending to offer evidence of such a substitute price must give suitable notice to the other party.

1.   This section is not intended to exclude the use of any other reasonable method of determining market price or of measuring damages if the circumstances of the case make this necessary.

2.   In the case of repudiation Sections 2–708(1)(b) and 2–713(1)(b) provide the rule for the proper measure of damages.

* * *

These provisions unsurprisingly raise many questions, not all of which will be dealt with here. Perhaps most obviously, although § 2–706 invites a discussion of the precise meaning of the requirements that it imposes on valid resales, these will not be elaborated in any detail. Among other reasons, these conditions are best addressed against the backdrop of the conditions that the UCC imposes on sales of security interests by creditors seeking to recover defaulted loans, a topic that properly belongs to a course in secured transactions. Instead, the discussion below will focus on two questions: first, the interplay between the two sections, and in particular the relation between the rules by which the UCC allocates sellers' damages based on resale or market prices and fixes market prices on the one hand, and the sellers' preferences concerning these matters on the other; and, second, the special problem of the lost volume seller, as this arises in the context of § 2–708(2). This second question is quite specialized—no less specialized, really, than the question of the requirements on valid resales that is set aside. The problem of the lost volume seller merits discussion nevertheless because (apart from its intrinsic interest) it serves as an object lesson in the complexity of the economic analysis needed to decide even seemingly simple questions in contract law, and it therefore strikes an important cautionary note in a presentation of the law and economics of contract that might otherwise seem straightforward.

The principal attraction for sellers of the resales contemplated under § 2–706 is that they allow sellers to fix damages in a relatively mechanical way, which relieves sellers of the burdens of subjecting the precise quantum of their damages to the independent judgment of a court.[9] All that a seller need do to recover under § 2–706 is to make a qualifying resale, and the standards for what qualifies (with their emphasis on reasonableness) are relatively simply satisfied. Recovering market-based damages under

---

9.   Notice that § 2–706 has an analog, in this respect, on the buyer's side. § 2–712, to be studied below, grants buyers whose sellers have breached the right to fix their damages by "covering," that is, purchasing substitute performance on the market.

§ 2–708, by contrast, is a much more burdensome affair. § 2–708, in conjunction with § 2–723, allocates to sellers the burden of proving up market price, at the appropriate time and place, to a court's satisfaction. Giving sellers this burden makes sense insofar as determining market prices expends not just the sellers' resources but also the court's. Moreover, sellers generally prefer to proceed under § 2–706 rather than § 2–708. The case that follows illustrates this preference, and also illustrates one way in which a dispute may nevertheless end up being adjudicated under § 2–708. The discussion following the case raises the further possibility that sellers might, in some circumstances, actually prefer § 2–708 and asks whether the law should allow such sellers to secure this preference.

Dehahn v. Innes

Supreme Judicial Court of Maine, 1976.
356 A.2d 711.

■ DUFRESNE, C.J. The defendant, Richard A. Innes, appeals from a judgment in favor of the plaintiff, Everett D. Dehahn, in the amount of $8,800.00 arising out of a civil complaint for breach of contract. The case was heard by a single Justice of the Superior Court (Kennebec County) jury-waived. We sustain the appeal on the issue of damages only.

The facts giving rise to the complaint may be summarized as follows:

Until March, 1972 Mr. Dehahn was road commissioner for the Town of Wayne. In his work for the town he used, for the most part, his own heavy equipment and was compensated for his services at an hourly rate. Failing reelection at the annual town meeting in 1972, the plaintiff sought to interest the defendant and one King to purchase his business, including incidental goodwill, for the price of $60,000.00.

After Mr. King withdrew from the negotiations, the plaintiff and the defendant further explored the possibilities of reaching an agreement of purchase and sale, which they did at the end of April. By oral contract, so the presiding Justice found, Dehahn agreed to sell and Innes agreed to buy for the price of $35,000.00 the plaintiff's 52 acre gravel pit, a back hoe, a bulldozer, a loader, a dump truck with plow, another truck with plow and a home-made low bed trailer. The Justice found that the parties had receded from the original intent to sell and buy the business as such.

The plaintiff had agreed to deliver the equipment in a "ready-to-go condition." In compliance with this part of the agreement the plaintiff sent his employee Riggs to do the job which needed to be done such as the removal of the plows from the trucks, plus such other maintenance work as was necessary. Most of the plaintiff's equipment, with the defendant's consent, had already been moved by the plaintiff to the defendant's field across from the driveway to his home, with the keys to the equipment left in the machines. It is conceded that Mr. Riggs did work on the equipment, with the assistance of the defendant Innes, for somewhat less than a full day.

There was evidence that Innes did use the bulldozer on a job prior to his rescission of the agreement. Whether this use was at the request and for the benefit of the plaintiff or as part of the defendant's new business undertaking was a matter for the presiding Justice to settle as a question of fact on disputed testimony.

After numerous complaints about the plaintiff's failure to put the equipment in a "ready-to-go condition," the defendant informed the plaintiff that he was cancelling the agreement and no payments were ever made pursuant to the contract.

The issues raised for our consideration concern 1) the applicability of the statute of frauds to the oral transaction, 2) whether the defendant's conduct amounted to a breach of the agreement and 3) the propriety of the amount of damages awarded by the presiding Justice.

I.   Statute of Frauds

The contract between the parties was not in writing. The defendant contends it is unenforceable for that reason. [The court goes on to "conclude that the verbal agreement between the parties was enforceable" under the Statute of Frauds.]

II.   Tender of Delivery

On the issue of tender of delivery the evidence was conflicting. The plaintiff asserts that the removal of the equipment, with the keys in the machines, to the defendant's field near the defendant's home was a tender of delivery within the meaning of *Section 2-507* of the Code,[2] while the defendant characterizes the removal as a mere accommodation for the benefit of the plaintiff who had to quit town property where the equipment was kept when the plaintiff held the office of road commissioner.

While no explicit finding was made on this issue by the presiding Justice, he did state in his decision that "[partial] steps toward the implementation of the contract were taken." We believe that implicit in this statement is the Justice's conclusion that the removal of the equipment to the defendant's field was found by him to be such a surrender of possession by the plaintiff to the defendant as to constitute a tender of delivery. We believe that there is substantial evidence in the record to support this conclusion.

The defendant admitted that his attorney would be drafting the documents necessary to implement the sale. A fortiori, when in mid-May, 1972 the plaintiff was advised that the sale was off, tender of a deed of the gravel pit was then excused as a useless gesture and failure to make tender is no bar to recovery for breach of this "entire" mixed contract involving "goods" and nongoods. The rejection of the whole contract by the defen-

---

2.   *11 M.R.S.A., § 2-507* provides as follows:

"(1) Tender of delivery is a condition to the buyer's duty to accept the goods and, unless otherwise agreed, to his duty to pay for them. Tender entitles the seller to acceptance of the goods and to payment according to the contract."

dant rendered unnecessary any requirement, or necessity, by the plaintiff to proceed further with the agreement and tender a deed of the realty to the defendant. The purpose of a tender is to put the other party in violation. When the other party has already repudiated the agreement, a tender would be a futile act and is not required by law. It is a well established rule of law that a tender is excused where such tender would be a useless and idle ceremony.

III. Acceptance of the Goods

True, the tendered "goods: were not in full conformity with the terms of the verbal contract since the parties had agreed that the "goods" would be in a "ready-to-go" condition. Nevertheless, the presiding Justice found that the "[defendant's] claim of rescission because of a breach on the part of Plaintiff represents an unsubstantiated position." In order so to decide, the Justice below had to conclude, as an underlying fact, that the defendant, notwithstanding his protests of defective operational condition of the equipment, had not rejected the contract outright, but had accepted the goods with reasonable expectation that the defects would be corrected. In this, the record supports him. There was evidence to the effect that the defendant himself did work on the equipment to put it in proper condition and that he used some of the machinery for his own purposes.

The Uniform Commercial Code (*11 M.R.S.A., § 2–606*) provides:

"(1) Acceptance of goods occurs when the buyer

(c) Does any act inconsistent with the seller's ownership;"

Whether there is an acceptance of goods by reason of acts of the buyer inconsistent with the seller's ownership within the provision of *11 M.R.S.A., § 2–606(1)(c)* is a question of fact for the trier of facts to be determined from the evidence in each particular case.

In resolving this issue in favor of the plaintiff, we cannot say that the single Justice was clearly wrong.

IV. Revocation of Acceptance

An acceptance of nonconforming goods upon the reasonable expectation that their nonconformity will be corrected may be rightfully revoked under certain circumstances. An indispensable requirement of revocability under the Code for nonconformity is that the nonconformity of the goods substantially impairs their value to the accepting party.[3]

The underlying reason for requiring a substantial impairment of value to legitimize a revocation of acceptance under 11 M.R.S.A., § 2–608(1)(a) is to bar revocation for trivial defects or defects which may be easily corrected. *Rozmus v. Thompson's Lincoln–Mercury Co., 1966, 209 Pa. Super. 120.*

---

3. *11 M.R.S.A., § 2–608* provides:

"(1) The buyer may revoke his acceptance of a lot or commercial unit whose nonconformity *substantially* impairs its value to him if he has accepted it

(a) On the reasonable assumption that its nonconformity would be cured and it has not been seasonably cured."

The presiding Justice found that the nonconformity of the goods delivered and accepted could be easily remedied at the cost of no more than two hundred ($200.00) dollars, which he considered as a "de minimis" expense and an insufficient basis for revocation of acceptance by the defendant. In so deciding, the Justice impliedly found no substantial impairment of value. On this aspect of the case, we cannot say that he was clearly wrong.

V. Damages

The presiding Justice adjudged the plaintiff's damages for the defendant's breach of contract in the amount of eight thousand eight hundred ($8,800.00) dollars. He reached this ultimate monetary award after finding as a fact that the total price of the equipment and land to which the parties had agreed was thirty-five thousand ($35,000.00) dollars from which he subtracted the sum of twenty-six thousand two hundred ($26,200.00) dollars, the aggregate values he ascribed respectively to 1) the equipment which the plaintiff resold following the defendant's revocation of acceptance ($25,500.00 resale price), 2) the home-made low bed trailer retained by the plaintiff ($500.00) and 3) the cost of services to cure nonconformity ($200.00).

In doing so, we believe the single Justice used the proper measure of damages by applying the generally accepted rule that, when the buyer unjustifiably revokes his acceptance of the goods which he contracted to buy, as well as when he fails to receive and pay for the goods, the seller may recover the difference between the contract price and the fair market value of the goods at the time of the breach.

The Code is declaratory of the former Maine law in this respect. Under *11 M.R.S.A., § 2–709(3)*, it is provided:

"(3) After the buyer has wrongfully rejected or revoked acceptance of the goods, a seller who is held not entitled to the price under this section shall nevertheless be awarded damages for nonacceptance under *section 2–708*."

Section 2–708(1) in turn states:

"(1) Subject to the measure of damages for nonacceptance or repudiation by the buyer is the difference between the market price at the time and place for tender and the unpaid contract price together with any incidental damages provided in this Article (section 2–710), but less expenses saved in consequence of the buyer's breach."

Similarly, unless otherwise stipulated in the contract itself, the same general rule applies to contracts involving real estate, the proper measure of damages being the difference between the contract price and the market value of the property at the time of breach of the contract.

The defendant, however, claims that in the instant case the plaintiff could not recover at all, because he failed to give the defendant reasonable notification of his intention to resell at private sale as provided in *11*

M.R.S.A., § 2–706.[4] The situation is not comparable to that in *Camden National Bank v. St. Clair, 1973, Me., 309 A.2d 329*, where this Court held that compliance with the requirements of the Uniform Commercial Code for notification as to disposition of collateral in a foreclosure-type procedure was a condition precedent to a secured creditor's right to recover the deficiency remaining due on the secured instrument.

The Court, in *Camden National Bank*, carried over into the Uniform Commercial Code the public policy doctrine espoused in *C.I.T. Corporation v. Haynes, 1965, 161 Me. 353*, to the effect that a debtor's right to redeem his collateral in a secured transaction cannot be foreclosed except in strict compliance with the mandatory requirements of the statute.

Furthermore, in *Camden National Bank*, we pointed out that a right of action established by one section of the Code, absent clear expression to the contrary, "must be held cumulative in the context of remedies previously, or otherwise, afforded." Such construction implements the mandate of *11 M.R.S.A., § 1–106* which says in part that "[the] remedies provided by this Title shall be liberally administered to the end that the aggrieved party may be put in as good a position as if the other party had fully performed." *Id. 332.*

We hold that *Section 2–703* which enumerates the seller's remedies, where the buyer wrongfully rejects or revokes acceptance of goods, are cumulative as between the right to

"(4) Resell and recover damages as hereafter provided (*section 2–706*); and

(5) Recover damages for nonacceptance (*section 2–708*) or in a proper case the price (*section 2–709*)."

Such was the conclusion of the drafters of the Code. See Maine Code Comment, Vol. 4 of the Maine Revised Statutes Annotated, page 307 under subsection (3) of *section 2–706* of the Code.

The record is silent concerning the type of resale involved in the instant case. But, assuming that the plaintiff did resell at private sale as contended by the defendant, we would find no difficulty in sustaining the presiding Justice in his use of the resale price as evidence of market values of the property resold.

Although the plaintiff testified only in terms of the selling prices he received for the several articles of equipment and the land he resold, it is evident that the Justice below equated the plaintiff's testimony as an

---

4. *11 M.R.S.A., § 2–706* provides in pertinent part:

"(1) Under the conditions stated in *section 2–703* on seller's remedies, the seller may resell the goods concerned or the undelivered balance thereof. Where the resale is made in good faith and in a commercially reasonable manner, the seller may recover the difference between the resale price and the contract price together with any incidental damages allowed under the provisions of this Article (section 2–710), but less expenses saved in consequence of the buyer's breach.

(3) Where the resale is at private sale the seller must give the buyer reasonable notification of his intention to resell."

expression of opinion by the owner respecting the value of his properties, since he did testify, in relation to the home-made low bed trailer kept by him, that it was worth about $500.00.

Maine stands with the weight of authority in holding an owner of goods or of real estate, by reason of his owner-relationship alone, competent to express his opinion of their value. *Simmons v. State, 1967, Me., 234 A.2d 330.*

Furthermore, the resale price of goods or real estate is competent relevant evidence of probative evidentiary force to establish values.

In *Norton*, our Court said:

"It is a common thing to allow competent witnesses to give their opinions as to what property is worth and how much it would probably sell for. *A fortiori*, is it proper to prove how much the property has in fact sold for. It is sometimes competent to show how much similar property has sold for, in order to arrive at the value of property in question. And it would be strange if it were improper to show the price at which the same property was sold for."

Assuming, however, that the evidence could have been excluded upon objection because of the form in which it was introduced, nevertheless it was received without any objection whatsoever, and was "consent evidence" to be considered by the factfinder and given its natural and logical probative effect. *Goldthwaite v. Sheraton Restaurant, 1958, 154 Me. 214.*

It is apparent from the record that the Justice below accepted the resale prices to which the plaintiff testified as the values of the properties involved at the time of the breach of contract. The defendant's revocation of acceptance was placed at the latest in mid-May 1972. The trial took place on January 8, 1974. There is no evidence as to when the resale of each piece of equipment or of the land took place within that period of time. The Justice in response to a request for additional findings by the defendant had this to say:

"There was no evidence or indication that the plaintiff received less than the value of the components when he sold them. This value is determined to be what he received for them."

Notwithstanding its status as consent evidence, the weight thereof, absent any other explanatory circumstances, depended as to its strength or weakness upon the closeness in time the resales were to the time of the breach. If the resale time is different or later than the time of the breach, then evidence should be adduced as to the difference, if any, in the market value between the two dates.

While the sale price of property subsequent to the time when the contract was breached may be considered as some indication of the market value at the time of breach, it is not conclusive and the actual market value at the time of breach should be properly established and not left to speculation.

In using the resale price of the equipment and land to determine the difference between the market value at the time of the breach and the unpaid contract price in measurement of the plaintiff's loss by reason of the defendant's unjustified revocation of acceptance of the goods and land, it was the ultimate burden of the plaintiff, in an action for the recovery of damages based on *Section 2–708*, not only to show the nonlikelihood of a change in market value of the property involved between the date of the breach and that of the resale, but also that the resale was fair and made in good faith, i.e. in the exercise of reasonable care and judgment.

The record is silent as to the time of the resales and the circumstances surrounding them. In this respect, the plaintiff failed to sustain his burden of proof as to the extent of the damages to which he is entitled.

The entry will be:

Appeal denied as to the issue of liability.

Appeal sustained as to the issue of damages.

Remanded to the Superior Court for further proceedings.

* * *

Dehann v. Innes illustrates the general run of cases involving the interplay between § 2–706 and § 2–708. In these cases, sellers prefer to resell and proceed under § 2–706 because this saves them the expense and risk of proving up market prices under § 2–708 (and § 2–723). In *Dehann* itself, the seller failed, most likely because of carelessness, to make a qualifying resale. Moreover, although a resale might provide evidence of the market price for purposes of recovering under § 2–708, the resale in question was made in the wrong market, so that any evidence it could provide was attenuated, at best.

But although sellers in most circumstances prefer to recover under § 2–706 over § 2–708, something like the reverse state of affairs can also arise. It can happen that a seller prefers to prove up market price under § 2–723 and to claim market-based damages under § 2–708. Indeed, even sellers who have actually resold (including in sales that qualify for resale-based damages under § 2–706) may prefer nevertheless to proceed under § 2–708. It is natural to ask, in such cases, whether they should be allowed to do so.

To answer this question, begin by considering a stylized example of the circumstances in which the question arises.[10] Suppose that a seller and her buyer contract for the seller to sell the buyer a widget "F.O.B. the seller's city." Further, suppose that the seller puts the widget into the hands of a carrier in her city, who delivers the widget to the buyer's city. Finally, suppose that the buyer then wrongfully rejects the widget, whereupon the seller resells the widget (in the buyer's city) and sues for damages.

Now imagine that the prices for the widget are as follows

---

10. The example and the discussion that follows it are based on Robert Scott, *The Case for Market Damages: Revisiting the Lost Profits Puzzle*, 57 U. Chi. L. Rev. 1155 (1990).

Contract Price	Market Price at Seller's City	Market Price at Buyer's City
10	7	9

The seller's resale (which occurs, recall, in the buyer's city) therefore fetches her $9, which entitles her to recover damages of $1, if she proceeds under § 2–706.[11] But the seller might achieve a greater recovery if she sought market-based damages under § 2–708. Under §§ 2–708 and 2–723, market-based damages are calculated using the market price at the time and place for tender. And as *Unlaub* illustrated, under § 2–319(1), the contract term "F.O.B. seller's city" makes this place the seller's local market. Moreover, this market price is only $7, so that the seller, by abandoning the § 2–706 claim based on her resale and instead proceeding under § 2–708, can recover market based damages of $(10 − 7) = $3. Finally, it appears that the seller can do this even though she has resold at $9. If the seller recovers these damages, she will end up with a total revenue from the sale of $(9 + 3) = $12, which is $2 more than the contract price. This $2 appears to represent a windfall to the seller.

May and ought the seller be permitted both to resell at $9 in her buyer's city and to claim the $3 in market-based damages based on the market price in her city? (Suppose, for example, that she simply ignores her resale in her lawsuit or even tries to foreclose the application of § 2–706 by reselling in a manner that violates the conditions specified in that section.) What does the UCC allow in such a case, and what should it allow?

Part of the difficulty in identifying the positive law here is textual and involves an asymmetry between the treatment of sellers' remedies and buyers' remedies in the UCC. § 2–713, which will be addressed below, establishes market-based buyers' remedies that serve as the analog to the sellers' remedies of § 2–708. Comment 5 to that section expressly states that "The present section provides a remedy which is completely alternative to cover under the preceding section [the section that serves as the buyers' analog to § 2–706] and applies only when and to the extent that the buyer has not covered."

So § 2–713 appears expressly to contemplate this type of windfall problem from the buyers' side and to deny buyers the windfall recovery. § 2–708, however, contains no analogous comment on the sellers' side. This leaves the interpretation of that section unsettled. On the one hand, the comment in § 2–713 might plausibly be taken to identify a general UCC principle against windfalls (and merely to apply this principle to the special case of buyer's remedies), in which case the same principle might also be applied, even without any analogous comment, to sellers, to prohibit a seller from reselling at a one price and recovering market-based damages at a lower price. On the other hand, the existence of the comment to § 2–713 may be thought to cut in favor of allowing the windfall recovery for sellers, since it shows that the UCC drafters were aware of the problem and knew

---

11. Note that here, as indeed throughout the analysis of UCC remedies, incidental damages (associated, for example, with the transactions costs of resale) will be ignored.

how to rule out the windfall when they wished to. One might plausibly infer from this that, in the sellers' context, they did not wish to deny it.[12]

So the best textual approach to the UCC is in this respect contestable. But beyond these textual quibbles, it remains to decide whether the seller *should* be able to recover based on the lower market price when she has resold at a higher price. Given what has been said already about the efficiency of the expectation remedy and the inefficiencies associated with supercompensatory damages, it seems clear that sellers should not be allowed to resell and still recover market damages based on lower-than-resale market prices if doing so leaves them better off than performance would have done. But is the extra recovery in such cases really a windfall? There are two reasons to think that it might not be, although neither is conclusive.

First, suppose that the prices were reversed, so that the price in the buyer's city were lower than in the seller's city and that the seller had had to make a resale in the buyer's city that did not conform to § 2–706. Adapting the prior example, imagine:

Contract Price	Market Price at Seller's City	Market Price at Buyer's City
10	9	7

In this case, such a seller would be *forced* into § 2–708 (because of the non-qualifying resale), and she would be stuck with damages, based once again on the price at her city, of $1. This would happen, moreover, even though she had resold only at $7, so that she would, in this case, suffer a *shortfall* of $2. (This is the exact counterpart to the windfall in the prior case.) Of course, the seller might avoid this fate by conforming her resale to the

---

12. This argument relies on there being a close general analogy between §§ 2–708 and 2–713, since the existence of this analogy is needed in order sensibly to interpret the silence in connection with § 2–708 as an implicit rejection of what is said in connection with § 2–713. There is at least one reason to question the broader analogy, and hence also the inference that the silence in connection § 2–708 represents an implicit endorsement of the seller's windfall. This has to do with § 2–708(2), which expressly addresses cases in which resale is not an adequate remedy. This section, which has no analog in § 2–713, entails that the remedies provided for by § 2–708 simply cannot, as a generally matter, be completely alternative to the remedies provided for by § 2–706: in other words, § 2–708(2) contemplates precisely a case in which resale is not an adequate measure of damages but must be supplemented by additional market-based damages, so that remedies associated with both sections must be provided together. This does not make it impossible to write a § 2–708 analog to the comment denying a windfall in § 2–713, but the task becomes more difficult, or at the very least different, so that inferences from silence to rejection aren't as straightforward as they otherwise might be.

Indeed, this difficulty is illustrated by a comment introduced in connection with the 2003 proposed revisions to UCC § 2–708. The comment says (borrowing from the comments to § 2–713) that an aggrieved party's resale should in some cases prevent market-based recovery under § 2–708. But the comment makes plain (as it must do in light of § 2–708(2)'s express mention of cases in which resale leaves a buyer undercompensated) that breaching buyers can take advantage of this rule only when they can both prove the resale and show that the effects of the resale were to limit the plaintiff-seller's loss to less than the contract-market price difference. And as the discussion of § 2–708(2) and the lost volume problem reveals, showing this can be *very* difficult.

The discussion in this note follows J. WHITE AND R. SUMMERS, 1 THE UNIFORM COMMERCIAL CODE 307–313 (3d ed. 1988).

requirements of § 2–706. But although these are not terribly demanding, they are not entirely trivial either, and even an innocent seller may fall foul of them, in which case a legal rule that denies the windfall but imposes the shortfall becomes, from the ex ante point of view, undercompensatory.[13]

Moreover, it may be that, at least in some circumstances, sellers in cases like these should be freed entirely from the pressure to make their resales conform to § 2–706. Over time, the market prices in the two cities should equalize through arbitrage (always assuming, of course, that there is no structural reason for the price difference—that widgets are not perishable, are cheap to transport, can be equally cheaply built in either city, etc.). And at least some sellers (in at least some circumstances) will be unable, on average, to outguess the market and will therefore be unable to game the interplay between §§ 2–706 and 2–708 in order to reap the windfall and avoid the shortfall. Insofar as these sellers should, on whatever grounds, be encouraged to resell quickly (without bothering about the formalities of § 2–706) and make market-based damages under § 2–708 into their principal remedial avenue, this is possible only if they are allowed to recover the excess when their resales occur at higher prices than those on which the § 2–708 remedy is based to make up for suffering the shortfalls that they suffer when their resales occur at lower prices.

Second, suppose that the prices in the buyer's city are indeed higher than in his seller's city. How is a court to know that, but for the buyer's breach, the seller would not have sold to this buyer and also (acting as an arbitrageur) shipped another, additional widget to the buyer's city for another sale at the higher price? How, in other words, is a court to know that the seller would not have made two sales in the buyer's city but for the breach instead of the one resale that she made following the breach. If the seller would have made two sales in the buyer's city—if the buyer's breach in effect cost her one arbitrage sale—then the two scenarios (non-breach and breach) would play out for her as follows:

Non-breach:	• Seller sells one widget to buyer for $10,
	• Seller makes a second arbitrage sale in buyer's city for a gain of $2.
Breach & resale:	• Seller makes one sale in buyer's city for $9.

In this case, the seller's loss as a result of the buyer's breach—the amount that the seller must receive in order to be made as well off as his performance would have left her—is $3: $1 on the lost contract sale because a sale at $10 to the buyer has been replaced by a resale at $9, and $2 on the lost arbitrage sale. Allowing the seller to resell in the buyer's city and still recover $3 based on the market price in her city (as § 2–708

---

13. The argument of this paragraph obviously does not apply to cases in which a seller opportunistically makes resales that fail to qualify under § 2–706 when and only when doing so allows her to exploit the difference in market prices between her city and her buyer's. (But note that although it may seem many sellers would do this, there are much easier ways to make gains as an arbitrageur than playing such a game with contract remedies.)

specifies) allows her precisely to vindicate her contractual expectations. On reflection, the elective recovery under § 2–708 does not, in this case, produce a windfall at all. Instead, it contains, as one of its components, the gain from the arbitrage sale that the seller has lost as a result of the breach.[14]

Of course, the question now naturally arises: Precisely when would the seller have made two sales but for the breach and when is the resale merely a substitute for the contract (that is, a sale made possible only by the buyer's breach)? That is the question at the core of the lost profits puzzle, to which the argument now turns.

6.1.C THE LOST PROFITS PUZZLE

The previous discussion concluded by suggesting that, at least in some circumstances, resale-based remedies might be inadequate to vindicating a disappointed seller's contractual expectations. But that discussion turned on a factual anomaly, namely the possibility of arbitrage between the seller's and the buyer's cities. This circumstance is intuitively unstable, because the arbitrage that it involves is self-limiting: as arbitrageurs exploit it, the market prices in the two cities will converge, until the arbitrage opportunity disappears and takes with it the under-compensatory nature of the resale-based remedy.

But if the geographic account of the price gap is replaced with an account based on economic specialization and the division of labor, the possibility of a sustained opportunity to make gains by buying cheap and selling dear becomes less counterintuitive. That, after all, is precisely the business model of retail sales—which involves buying at wholesale, selling at retail, and taking the difference (minus selling costs) as profit. It will turn out, though, that some of the difficulties that haunted the analysis above—difficulties involving whether or not the disappointed seller would actually have made the additional arbitrage-sale on which her claim to damages in excess of the contract-resale formula rests—will reappear, now front and center, in this context also.

Imagine that a retailer contracts to sell an item out of her stock to a consumer and that the consumer breaches. Imagine further that the

---

14. The key here is that the resale in the buyer's city would have happened regardless of the breach so that it should not be treated as offset against the seller's expectations on the sale to the buyer. Once this is made clear, the result in the main text follows. That result might, moreover, be characterized in another way also, which is formally different from but substantively equivalent to the account in the text. The account in the main text treats the remedy as fundamentally resale-price based. The seller recovers damages of $1 for the resale of the widget that would have been sold to the breaching buyer (plus a further $2 for the lost arbitrage sale). An alternative (and equivalent) account treats the remedy as fundamentally market-price based. On this account, vindicating the seller's expectations requires awarding damages equal to the difference between the contract and market prices in the seller's city, namely $(10-7) = \$3$, which is precisely what allowing the seller to claim under § 2–708 achieves. The two accounts produce the same outcome because, as the main text notes, the § 2–708 remedy contains as part of the difference between the contract price and market price in the seller's city the gain from the arbitrage sale that the seller has lost as a result of the breach.

retailer subsequently resells the item in question to another consumer, at the exact same price as specified in the contract with the original consumer. (Unless the item has been damaged in some way, this is precisely what one would expect the retailer, who charges fixed prices after all, to do.) In such a case, both the contract-resale price difference based remedy associated with § 2–706 and the contract-market price difference based remedy associated with § 2–708(1) are zero: the resale price and the market price both exactly equal the contract price.

Nevertheless, the retail seller may claim, with a certain intuitive plausibility, that these remedies undercompensate her: she may claim that she would have made the resale in any event, so that if the buyer had performed she would have made two sales rather than just one; and she may claim, therefore, that vindicating her contractual expectations requires awarding her damages equal to one lost profit—the profit on the additional sale that the buyer's breach has cost her. (This lost profit is the analog of the lost arbitrage gain claimed by the seller in the prior example.)

The question, as before, is whether this intuitively plausible claim can survive sustained and rigorous scrutiny. When it is the case that a breach by one of her buyers costs a retail seller one lost sale, and when is it the case that the retailer's resale is a substitute for the original contract, in the sense that it would not have been made had her buyer performed? The analysis that follows will not get to the bottom of this question, or indeed get anywhere near to a dispositive answer. The problem turns out to be highly technical, and there is no scholarly consensus about its right answer, or indeed even about how best to approach the problem or to structure efforts to analyze it. This is an area in which serious people remain deeply, and self-consciously, uncertain.

This uncertainty will make the argument that follows necessarily modest. There will be no pretense of identifying necessary and sufficient conditions for the correctness of a retail seller's lost volume claim. Instead, it will be enough to explain why the issue is so difficult, to show why the most obvious answers (including the intuitively plausible claim that most retailers facing buyer-breaches are lost volume sellers) fail, and to connect the logics of economic analyses of the lost volume problem to the doctrinal categories of the law.

The uncertainty should perhaps generate a second, and much more general, kind of humility also. If it turns out that there is no consensus about how to answer a question about contractual expectations that seems as intuitively straightforward as the one raised in the lost volume problem, then this should perhaps raise doubts about the capacity of economics to generate determinate answers to real cases more generally. Even if the economic case for the expectation remedy is rock-solid in the abstract, what practical good is it if it turns out to be almost impossible to calculate actual promisors' expectations with sufficient certainty and precision to implement the remedy in the fact of particular contractual disputes?

With this introduction in place, turn to a pair of famous cases. After a brief doctrinal interlude, the argument will take up the economic plausibility of the retail sellers' underlying lost-volume claim.

Lenobel v. Senif

Supreme Court of New York, Appellate Division, Second Department, 1937.
252 A.D. 533.

■ CARSWELL, JJ. Plaintiff is the official Plymouth car dealer for Long Island City. On May 27, 1936, the defendant Senif, under a written contract, bought from plaintiff a Plymouth car for $781.50, making a $50 down payment. The buyer, Senif, on June 1, 1936, in writing, assumed to cancel the contract, but the dealer refused to concede his right so to do. The dealer then resold the same car for $781.50. It then brought this action against the buyer for claimed loss of gross profits of $226.50, as damages arising from the breach by the buyer of the contract of sale. The buyer counterclaimed for the return of the deposit.

The trial court dismissed the complaint and granted the defendant buyer judgment on the counterclaim. The judgment on the counterclaim was reversed by the Appellate Term and a new trial ordered. The dismissal of the complaint, however, was affirmed, on the ground that no damages were shown.

The trial court excluded evidence of overhead of the dealer. The proffered evidence thus excluded related to the employment of salesmen, advertising expenses, the furnishing of cars and gasoline, and the payment of men to seek and interview prospective buyers and to demonstrate cars. It was proffered on the theory that these items of overhead were "special circumstances" entitling plaintiff to a recovery of the amount of gross profits. These rulings have been held to be correct.

An appeal has been allowed to review but one question—the proper measure of damages applicable herein.

The vendor appellant claims that the proof excluded was relevant under subdivision 3 of section 145 of the Personal Property Law. That section is headed "Action for damages for nonacceptance of the goods." It concerns actions by vendors against vendees. Subdivisions 2 and 3 of section 145 read:

> "2.   The measure of damages is the estimated loss directly and naturally resulting, in the ordinary course of events, from the buyer's breach of contract.
>
> 3.   Where there is an available market for the goods in question, the measure of damage is, *in the absence of special circumstances, showing proximate damage of a greater amount*, the difference between the contract price and the market or current price at the time or times when the goods ought to have been accepted, or, if no time was fixed for acceptance, then at the time of the refusal to accept."

The foregoing subdivision 3 has a counterpart in subdivision 3 of section 148 of the Personal Property Law, which relates to converse situations—actions by vendees against vendors.

The provision in respect of "special circumstances" was considered in a case that involved section 148, in an action by a vendee against a vendor. (*Czarnikow–Rionda Co. v. Federal S. R. Co., 255 N. Y. 33 (1930).*) There the defendant contracted to sell to the plaintiff in stated installments an amount of sugar. The defendant vendor breached its contract. It was held that special loss or damage, growing out of resale contracts made by the vendee, as a "special circumstance," could be visited upon the vendor only if it " 'knew that other goods of the kind contracted for could not be obtained by the buyer' " for delivery on the resale. Otherwise, only general damages could be had.

In the case at bar there is no proffered proof that the vendee had any knowledge of the elements of the vendor's overhead. It may not be said, therefore, that the defendant vendee contracted with the plaintiff vendor in contemplation of such matters as "special circumstances" upon which might be predicated a claim for damages of an amount greater than obtains on the breach of an ordinary contract of purchase and sale of a commodity; *i. e.*, the difference between the contract price and the market value at the time and place of delivery

The "special circumstances" invoked by the dealer seem to be that (a) it may sell in a limited area only; (b) its sales price is fixed by its manufacturer and this becomes the retail market value; and (c) it has certain overhead that must be met out of gross profits from its sales quota. As a consequence of all this, it says that this retail market value has an unnatural element, unlike the market value of an ordinary commodity. No matter how the market value is arrived at—it is the market value, whether it be fixed by a restriction of a manufacturer or the unrestricted actions of buyers and sellers in a free market. This is so whether the commodity sold be a ton of coal, a fur coat, or an automobile. The same elements of overhead are common to the sellers of innumerable commodities who are not affected by manufacturers' restrictions; hence, in the absence of special agreement, these elements cannot fairly be said to be "special circumstances," unless the vendors and vendees of practically every commodity are deemed to be similarly affected by "special circumstances," so as to entitle vendors to the amount of gross profits as damages for the breach of a contract of sale.

The plaintiff says such a view leaves it remediless; that on the resale to replace the defendant it depleted its number of prospects to the extent of one, and, therefore, its overhead, as a consequence of defendant's breach of contract, receives no contribution from the gross profits on at least one sale. This contention is specious. If the buyer had in effect assigned his contract of purchase by taking a delivery and immediately selling to another in the same area, and had thus abandoned his purpose to get a new car for himself, a depletion of prospects to the same degree would have occurred and but one commission would have inured to the plaintiff. But plaintiff had other remedies. It could have exacted a larger down payment in cash or notes to protect itself against a breach of contract by the vendee. In place of the contrary provision as to title now set out in the contract, it could have provided in its contract that title was to pass to the buyer when the sale was made (Pers. Prop. Law, §§ 99, 100), and have the common-law rule (*Agar v. Orda, 264 N. Y. 248 (1934)*) prevail by agreement. It could then have held the car and sued for the entire purchase price (Pers. Prop. Law, § 144) and thus have avoided depleting immediately the number of its prospects. It could have inserted in its contract a provision that its relations with its manufacturers and the effect thereof in reference to its overhead should be deemed "special circumstances" within subdivision 3 of section 145 of the Personal Property Law, entitling it, in the event of a breach by the vendee, to recover, as damages, the amount of gross profits on the sale. This would have brought home knowledge to the vendee and he would have been deemed to have contracted in contemplation of this element of damages beyond the general rule ordinarily applicable to the sale of a commodity. Adopting plaintiff's contention would result in an awkward and cumbersome inquiry into elements of overhead respecting which the buyer ordinarily has no knowledge and has no means of meeting or refuting the claims of the vendor, in whole or part.

This view in respect of a contract of sale of an automobile by a dealer and the consequence of a breach thereof by a buyer is not novel. Here the sale was one of goods *in esse*; it was not a contract for the sale of an article to be manufactured, for breach of which loss of profits may be had. (*Belle of Bourbon Co. v. Leffler, 87 App. Div. 302.*) (N.Y. 1903) The article had market value and was not subject to the rule applicable where there is no market value or where the commodity is of a perishable nature.

It is urged that the measure of damages in any event, in a situation such as this, should be the difference between the contract price to the vendee and the dealer's market price or value; that is, the cost to the dealer. This would be contrary to long-settled doctrine. The market value against which a contract price is to be considered is the fairly comparable market value. If the contract price is fixed in a retail sale, the fairly comparable market value is the retail market value. Likewise, if the contract price is fixed on a wholesale or trade sale, the fairly comparable market value is the trade or wholesale market value.

The chief reliance of the plaintiff is *Stewart v. Hansen (62 Utah, 281 (1923))*, where recovery for loss of profits was permitted. That case in turn is based on *Torkomian v. Russell (90 Conn. 481 (1916))*. The authority of the latter is weakened by *Sabas v. Gregory (91 Conn. 26 (1916))*. The reasoning of these cases does not commend itself. It imports into the contracts of the parties something that is not there and incorrectly assumes that if this be not done the vendor is without remedy.

These views leave untouched the opportunity to a vendor to proffer proof that he was put to a special or added expense on a particular resale which would possibly constitute a "special circumstance" that would be a further element of damage, but this item would not be evidenced by mere proof of the amount of gross profits on the original sale, or mere proof of general elements of overhead.

The order of the Appellate Term should be affirmed, with costs.

Neri v. Retail Marine Corporation

Court of Appeals of New York, 1972.
285 N.E.2d 311.

■ GIBSON, J. The appeal concerns the right of a retail dealer to recover loss of profits and incidental damages upon the buyer's repudiation of a contract governed by the Uniform Commercial Code. This is, indeed, the correct measure of damage in an appropriate case and to this extent the code (§ 2–708[(2)]) effected a substantial change from prior law, whereby damages were ordinarily limited to "the difference between the contract price and the market or current price".[1] Upon the record before us, the courts below erred in declining to give effect to the new statute and so the order appealed from must be reversed.

The plaintiffs contracted to purchase from defendant a new boat of a specified model for the price of $12,587.40, against which they made a deposit of $40. They shortly increased the deposit to $4,250 in consideration of the defendant dealer's agreement to arrange with the manufacturer for immediate delivery on the basis of "a firm sale", instead of the delivery within approximately four to six weeks originally specified. Some six days after the date of the contract plaintiffs' lawyer sent to defendant a letter rescinding the sales contract for the reason that plaintiff Neri was about to undergo hospitalization and surgery, in consequence of which, according to the letter, it would be "impossible for Mr. Neri to make any payments". The boat had already been ordered from the manufacturer and was delivered to defendant at or before the time the attorney's letter was received. Defendant declined to refund plaintiffs' deposit and this action to recover it was commenced. Defendant counterclaimed, alleging plaintiffs' breach of the contract and defendant's resultant damage in the amount of $4,250, for which sum defendant demanded judgment. Upon motion, defendant had summary judgment on the issue of liability tendered by its counterclaim; and Special Term directed an assessment of damages, upon which it would be determined whether plaintiffs were entitled to the return of any portion of their down payment.

Upon the trial so directed, it was shown that the boat ordered and received by defendant in accordance with plaintiffs' contract of purchase was sold some four months later to another buyer for the same price as that negotiated with plaintiffs. From this proof the plaintiffs argue that defendant's loss on its contract was recouped, while defendant argues that but for plaintiffs' default, it would have sold two boats and have earned two profits instead of one. Defendant proved, without contradiction, that its

---

1. Personal Property Law, § 145, repealed by Uniform Commercial Code, § 10–102 (L. 1962, ch. 553, eff. Sept. 27, 1964); *Lenobel, Inc. v. Senif, 252 App. Div. 533.*

profit on the sale under the contract in suit would have been $2,579 and that during the period the boat remained unsold incidental expenses aggregating $674 for storage, upkeep, finance charges and insurance were incurred. Additionally, defendant proved and sought to recover attorneys' fees of $1,250.

The trial court found "untenable" defendant's claim for loss of profit, inasmuch as the boat was later sold for the same price that plaintiffs had contracted to pay; found, too, that defendant had failed to prove any incidental damages; further found "that the terms of *section 2–718, sub section 2(b), of the Uniform Commercial Code* are applicable and same make adequate and fair provision to place the sellers in as good a position as performance would have done" and, in accordance with paragraph (b) of subsection (2) thus relied upon, awarded defendant $500 upon its counter-claim and directed that plaintiffs recover the balance of their deposit, amounting to $3,750. The ensuing judgment was affirmed, without opinion, at the Appellate Division and defendant's appeal to this court was taken by our leave.

The issue is governed in the first instance by *section 2–718 of the Uniform Commercial Code* which provides, among other things, that the buyer, despite his breach, may have restitution of the amount by which his payment exceeds: (a) reasonable liquidated damages stipulated by the contract or (b) absent such stipulation, 20% of the value of the buyer's total performance or $500, whichever is smaller (*§ 2–718[(2)(a)–(b)]*). As above noted, the trial court awarded defendant an offset in the amount of $500 under paragraph (b) and directed restitution to plaintiffs of the balance. *Section 2–718*, however, establishes, in paragraph (a) of subsection (3), an alternative right of offset in favor of the seller, as follows: "(3) The buyer's right to restitution under subsection (2) is subject to offset to the extent that the seller establishes (a) a right to recover damages under the provisions of this Article other than subsection (1)".

Among "the provisions of this Article other than subsection (1)" are those to be found in *section 2–708*, which the courts below did not apply. Subsection (1) of that section provides that "the measure of damages for non-acceptance or repudiation by the buyer is the difference between the market price at the time and place for tender and the unpaid contract price together with any incidental damages provided in this Article (*Section 2–710*), but less expenses saved in consequence of the buyer's breach." However, this provision is made expressly subject to subsection (2), provid-ing: "(2) If the measure of damages provided in subsection (1) is inadequate to put the seller in as good a position as performance would have done then the measure of damages is the profit (including reasonable overhead) which the seller would have made from full performance by the buyer, together with any incidental damages provided in this Article (*Section 2–710*), due allowance for costs reasonably incurred and due credit for payments or proceeds of resale."

The provision of the code upon which the decision at Trial Term rested (*§ 2–718[(2)(b)]*) does not differ greatly from the corresponding provisions of the prior statute (Personal Property Law, § 145–a[(1)(b)]) except as the new act includes the alternative remedy of a lump sum award of $500. Neither does the present reference (in *§ 2–718[(3)(a)]*) to the recovery of damages pursuant to other provisions of the article differ from a like reference in the prior statute to an alternative measure of damages under section 145 of that act; but section 145 made no provision for recovery of lost profits as does *section 2–708[(2)]* of the code. The new statute is thus innovative and significant and its analysis is necessary to the determination of the issues here presented.

Prior to the code, the New York cases "applied the 'profit' test, contract price less cost of manufacture, only in cases where the seller [was] a manufacturer or an agent for a manufacturer" (1955 Report of N. Y. Law Rev. Comm., vol. 1, p. 693). [Under the Uniform Commercial Code, and] as the parties concede, the only question before us is that as to the proper measure of damage to be applied. The conclusion is clear from the record—indeed with mathematical certainty—that "the measure of damages provided in subsection (1) is inadequate to put the seller in as good a position as performance would have done" (*Uniform Commercial Code, § 2–708[(2)]*) and hence—again under subsection (2)—that the seller is entitled to its "profit (including reasonable overhead) together with any incidental damages, due allowance for costs reasonably incurred and due credit for payments or proceeds of resale."

It is evident, first, that this retail seller is entitled to its profit and, second, that the last sentence of subsection (2), as hereinbefore quoted, referring to "due credit for payments or proceeds of resale" is inapplicable to this retail sales contract.

The record which in this case establishes defendant's entitlement to damages in the amount of its prospective profit, at the same time confirms defendant's cognate right to "any incidental damages provided in this Article (*Section 2–710)*"[3] (*Uniform Commercial Code, § 2–708[(2)]*). From the language employed it is too clear to require discussion that the seller's right to recover loss of profits is not exclusive and that he may recoup his "incidental" expenses as well (*Procter & Gamble Distr. Co. v. Lawrence Amer. Field Warehousing Corp., 16 N Y 2d 344, 354 (1965)*). Although the trial court's denial of incidental damages in the uncontroverted amount of $674 was made in the context of its erroneous conclusion that paragraph (b) of subsection (2) of *section 2–718* was applicable and was "adequate to place the sellers in as good a position as performance would have done", the denial seems not to have rested entirely on the court's mistaken application of the law, as there was an explicit finding "that defendant completely failed to show that it suffered any incidental damages." We find no basis for the court's conclusion with respect to a deficiency of proof inasmuch as the proper items of the $674 expenses (being for storage,

---

3. "Incidental damages to an aggrieved seller include any commercially reasonable charges, expenses or commissions incurred in stopping delivery, in the transportation, care and custody of goods after the buyer's breach, in connection with return or resale of the goods or otherwise resulting from the breach" (*Uniform Commercial Code, § 2–710*).

upkeep, finance charges and insurance for the period between the date performance was due and the time of the resale) were proven without objection and were in no way controverted, impeached or otherwise challenged, at the trial or on appeal. Thus the court's finding of a failure of proof cannot be supported upon the record and, therefore, and contrary to plaintiffs' contention, the affirmance at the Appellate Division was ineffective to save it.

The trial court correctly denied defendant's claim for recovery of attorney's fees incurred by it in this action.

It follows that plaintiffs are entitled to restitution of the sum of $4,250 paid by them on account of the contract price less an offset to defendant in the amount of $3,253 on account of its lost profit of $2,579 and its incidental damages of $674.

The order of the Appellate Division should be modified, with costs in all courts, in accordance with this opinion, and, as so modified, affirmed.

Ordered accordingly.

* * *

Now, *Lenobel* was decided before the enactment of the UCC and *Neri* was decided afterwards. And so it may seem that the difference in the cases' outcomes is due specifically and narrowly to UCC § 2–708(2), which does indeed figure prominently in the reasoning of the *Neri* court. But it is important to understanding the cases, and also the broader character of the UCC and its impact on contract law, to see that the differences between the two opinions are deeper and broader than the references specifically to § 2–708(2).

On the one hand, begin by noting that the economic argument made by the *Lenobel* court—that the seller's lost volume claim is implausible because the buyer would have deprived her of the extra sale even had he performed, only now by entering the market as her competitor and reselling himself—would, if it were taken seriously, leave the case's outcome unchanged even under § 2–708(2). (After all, if the buyer would generally have resold in a way that deprived the seller of the additional sale in any event, then the contract-market price based remedy, although zero, would not be "inadequate to put the seller in as good a position as performance would have done," and § 2–708(2) would not be triggered.) If the economic argument in *Lenobel* is a good one, then it remains doctrinally determinative even under the UCC. Accordingly, a clarifying account of *Lenobel* and *Neri*, one that explains the divergence between the two cases, must rely on something other than the economic effects of the buyer's potential resale.

On the other hand, the economic argument as stated in *Lenobel* is patently not a good one, and it should not have disposed of the case even under pre-UCC law. Whatever the ultimate merits of the seller's lost volume claim, the suggestion that the claim fails because a car-buyer can resell a now used car in a manner that effectively competes with his seller is manifestly implausible.[15] Accordingly, a sympathetic interpretation of the *Lenobel* opinion, one that aims to make that opinion's outcome sustained by its argument, must look to something other than the factual claim that the breach did not in fact cost the retail seller any sales volume.

Moreover, the materials for such a clarifying and sympathetic interpretation of *Lenobel* are present in the opinion. In particular, the *Lenobel* court noted that if the seller had wanted to retain her lost profits in the event of her buyer's breach, she had an easy way of doing so. All that she would have had to do is include a contractual provision making title to the car pass to the buyer on the sale of the car rather than (as in the actual contract at issue) only on delivery. Had the seller included such a provision, she could have sued the buyer for the purchase price, thereby recovering her lost profit—although also inviting (indeed forcing) him into competition with her, with the attendant risk of depriving herself of some other sale and its associated profit. And the fact that the seller did not include such an obvious provision strongly suggests that the contract did not contemplate that she would be entitled to claim lost profits in the event of the buyer's breach. The result in *Lenobel* is thus at least partly, and probably substantially, justified not by an economic argument that a lost profit remedy would be over-compensatory but rather by an interpretive argument that the seller, in agreeing that title to the car would pass to the buyer only on delivery, was in effect forswearing precisely this remedy, directly contradicting her subsequent claims to deserve it.

Finally, this method of recovering lost profits is no longer available under the UCC, or at least not so easily adopted. Recall the earlier discussion of UCC § 2–709, which governs a seller's action for the price, and in particular the idea that this section (together with its comments and the sections that it cross-references) expressly rejects the highly formal style of legal reasoning that the *Lenobel* court's suggestion employed. For the UCC, the seller's entitlement to recover the contract price turns not on the formalities of title, or indeed on any other formalism, but rather (as the analysis of *Unlaub* emphasized again and again) on the economic and practical realities of possession and control. The UCC therefore denies the parties the ability to establish a seller's lost profits remedy by the simple stipulation that the *Lenobel* court contemplated, or indeed by any stipulation.[16] And in doing so, the UCC places the question of retail sellers' actual

---

15. Recall the *ex post* transactions costs that prevented the resale of the car in the initial account of the distinctive efficiency of the expectation remedy. Indeed, the difficulties faced by private sellers of cars are famous among economists. *See* George Ackerloff, *The Market for Lemons: Quality Uncertainty and the Market Mechanism*, 34 QUARTERLY J. OF ECON. 488 (1970).

16. This remark should be read as anticipating a broader discussion of efforts by contracting parties to replace the law's default remedies with remedies of their own making. In particular, there is a general doctrine that says that agreements to overcompensate promisors in the face of breaches—agreements establishing what the law variously calls *overliquidated damages* or *penalties*—are unenforceable. This rule is not new to the UCC, but also existed when *Lenobel* was decided. That explains why the *Lenobel* court suggested that the parties might secure a lost profits remedy by the pretense of making title pass at sale rather than more directly, by agreeing that a breaching buyer would pay a penalty (or perhaps

expectations—the question of the actual merits of their lost volume claims—unavoidably at the center of disputes of this kind. In a way, UCC § 2–708(2) is a reaction to this rather than an instigator. It simply instructs courts to take seriously the possibility that lost volume claims may have merit. And it therefore makes it essential to ask whether they do have merit.

Begin considering this question by once more restating the sellers' basic lost volume claim and the basic economic problem that it raises—just to foreclose confusion and to fix ideas. Although the sellers in *Lenobel* and *Neri* both ultimately resold the specific item that had been earmarked for their breaching buyers (and resold at the same price as contemplated in the original contracts), the sellers in each case claim that had their buyers not breached they would have made two sales rather than just the one that they ended up making. Accordingly, the sellers claim, they would, but for the breach, have made two profits rather than just one. The sellers seek to recover the one lost profit.

Perhaps the simplest way to begin to assess the sellers' lost profits claim is to notice that the assertion that the buyers' breaches cost the sellers lost sales volume is correct only if the resale that they make following the breach is *independent* of the first sale contemplated in the contract. The lost volume claim is correct only if the first sale would not have precluded the second and the second would have been made even if the first buyer had not breached. In other words, the sellers' lost volume claims are correct only if it would have been *possible* for the sellers to make both sales, and not if the two sales were replacements for each other.

So to decide the sellers' lost volume claims, one must get a grip on the question when, that is, under what conditions, the two sales are indeed independent—when, in other words, both are possible. It is easiest to begin with examples that give *independent* and *possible* intuitive, almost physical meanings. But these words in fact capture economic ideas. And so the core of the argument will try to explain how to think about the independence of the contract sale and the resale, and the possibility of both sales, in economic terms. Once the outlines of the economic issues have been explained, the argument will take up the subsidiary question how the relevant economic ideas may be given a doctrinal expression in terms of § 2–708. This will suggest that the two remedies at issue in cases like *Lenobel* and *Neri*—market- or resale-price based damages and lost-profits damages—are perhaps not really so fundamentally different from each other as the might initially seem.

Begin the argument with the simplest case, to illustrate the most intuitive sense in which a contract-sale and a resale may or may not be independent of each other. Imagine that a seller owns a one-of-a-kind chattel—say, FDR's cigarette holder—and receives, out of the blue, several offers to buy it for $100,000. (Notice that she has received the offers out of

---

a non-refundable deposit) equal to the seller's profit. That provision would likely have been held an unenforceable penalty clause.

the blue and has not had to incur any costs in generating them. This will matter to the doctrinal argument that comes later.) She accepts one offer, from Bernard, but he breaches and, on hearing this, Benito contacts her to renew his offer. She sells to Benito for precisely the price that she would have received from Bernard. The seller in this case cannot possibly be a lost volume seller. The sales to Bernard and Benito were clearly mutually exclusive, simply in virtue of the uniqueness of the good sold. Benito's purchase therefore replaced Bernard's, and the correct measure of the seller's damage, given by both the contract-resale and the contract-market formulas, is $0.

Now imagine a contrasting case, in which a seller has an infinite (or practically infinite) supply of some other chattel—say, Groucho Marx's cigar stubs—and she receives, again out of the blue (that is, without incurring any costs), several offers to buy one of the stubs for $10. (Unsurprisingly, this seller possesses many more stubs than she will ever receive offers for—which is what makes her supply "practically infinite.") Suppose that she accepts Bernard's offer, and Benito's and every other offer that she receives, and that Bernard once again breaches. Eventually, the seller receives a new offer (from Bill), and she resells the stub that had been earmarked for Bernard for the precisely the price that she would have received from Bernard had he not breached. Once again, both the contract-resale and the contract-market price difference measures of the seller's remedy yield damages of $0. But as long as Bernard can't resell his cigar stub to any of the seller's actual or potential buyers, the seller in this case clearly is a lost volume seller. No buyer replaced Bernard, and but for Bernard's breach, the seller would have made one additional sale. Hence, assuming that the seller's cost in the cigar stubs is $0, the correct measure of her damages is $10.

These clear cases illustrate how replacement figures in the calculation of sellers' remedies, at least in principle. They reveal that when replacement occurs, market-or resale-based damages are clearly accurate and that when replacement is inconceivable, market or resale-based damages are clearly inadequate.

But the mechanisms that govern whether or not the sellers in the examples suffer lost volume are highly stylized—so stylized, in fact, as to be almost completely unrealistic. To begin to get a sense for the plausibility of actual lost volume claims, it is necessary to abandon the formal conceits of the examples in favor of more realistic mechanisms governing sellers' resale prospects. These more realistic mechanisms are also necessarily much more complex. Accordingly, whereas both the failure and the success of the sellers' lost volume claims in the examples is clear-cut, the correctness of lost volume claims in more realistic cases will be necessarily uncertain.[17]

---

17. The analysis in the next several paragraphs owes much to Robert Scott, *The Case for Market Damages: Revisiting the Lost Profits Puzzle*, 57 U. CHI. L. REV. 1155 (1990) and *Charles Goetz & Robert Scott, Measuring Sellers' Damages: The Lost Profits Puzzle*, 31 STAN. L. REV. 323 (1979).

A volume seller sells many items to many buyers, but not an infinite number of items to an infinite number of buyers. The constraint that governs the number of sales that she finally makes will, moreover, in general be economic rather than (as in the earlier example) physical: she will not literally run out of supply or exhaust the demand that she faces but will instead have a greater potential supply of goods and face a greater demand than she can serve consistent with maximizing her profits. The reason for this is that the seller's marginal costs of selling her goods will (over the relevant range) be increasing in the number of goods that she sells. In other words, in the range surrounding her actual profit-maximizing sales numbers, each additional sale will cost her more to handle than the one before. The seller will continue to sell more and more goods until the marginal cost incurred in making an additional sale just equals the marginal revenue received from the sale. At this point, the seller will stop selling.

For sellers who operate in a competitive market—that is, who face sufficient competition that they can have no influence over the total number of buyers served by all sellers or the price as which sales are made—this analysis of the seller's position straightforwardly entails that her lost volume claim should fail. If such a seller loses a sale (due to a buyer's breach) and then makes another sale, then she could not have made both sales consistent with maximizing her profits. This is because of the seller's increasing marginal costs. The resale was profitable for her only because the initial buyer's breach pushed her back down her marginal cost curve, opening up (as it were) space for one more profitable sale. The breach is therefore essential to the profitability of the sale to the new customer. The fact that her initial volume was optimal entails that if the seller tried to make both sales, her increasing marginal costs would make her lose money on the second. Even if she could physically make both sales (in the sense of there existing adequate physical quantities of the good), she could not make them both profitably.

Notice that this argument makes no mention of the effects of the breach, etc. on the price at which the seller sells generally and also makes no mention of the possibility that the buyer might have resold the good, in competition with the seller, had he performed. There is no need to consider either question because of the assumption that the market in which the seller operates is competitive. This entails that neither her decisions to seek a replacement buyer, nor her initial buyer's decision to resell, will have any impact on the price at which she sells. In a perfectly competitive market, the seller's profit-maximizing volume is determined entirely by her internal cost structure, rather than by incremental changes in the demand that she faces. This makes the argument rejecting the perfectly competitive seller's lost volume claim so straightforward.

The argument becomes more complicated if the seller is a monopolist or operates in an imperfectly competitive market. But there is still some reason to doubt the seller's lost volume claim, or at least to suspect that even if the buyer's breach costs the seller something, it does not cost her a full profit. An imperfectly competitive seller will sell at price and quantity levels so as to maximize the rents she can extract from her buyers. *Very* roughly, if a buyer breaches, this will, as in the competitive case, tend to allow her to service a new buyer whom she could not before have serviced consistently with maximizing her profits. This does not fully eliminate the imperfectly competitive seller's lost profits claim, however. The imperfectly competitive seller has influenced the price at which she sells, and as long as she faces a downward sloping demand curve, she will have to lower her price to attract this new buyer and hence will lose some profit. But now the question of the buyer's performing and re-selling also comes into play. Unlike one of many competitive sellers, an imperfectly competitive seller will gain profits when demand shifts upwards and lose profits when demand shifts downwards, roughly because such shifts will increase and decrease (respectively) the size of the surplus from which she can extract monopoly rents. For this reason, a potential re-sale by a monopolist's buyer (at least insofar as the buyer does not face obstacles to reselling[18]) might cost her profits in any case by depressing the demand that she faces. Accordingly, the remedy to which an imperfectly competitive volume seller is entitled depends on the balance of these two profit-lowering effects. And it turns out, under plausible conditions, that the monopolist is made no worse of by the buyer's breaching that she would have been made by the buyer's performing, so that the buyer's breach once again causes her no lost profits. But while these conditions are plausible, they do not necessarily or certainly obtain. So the monopolist's lost volume claim is dubious, but possible.[19]

This argument suggests that volume sellers' lost profits claims should be approached with skepticism. Because the sales that a seller can profitably make will almost always be *rationed*, then whenever a seller adjusts to a breach by procuring a resale, then the sale and resale will never be independent of each other and the resale will always be a replacement sale. In this case, market damages get the seller's remedy right and lost profits damages get the remedy wrong.

But note that the argument (in both its perfect-competition and imperfect-competition variants) rests on an important assumption, namely that sellers cannot differentiate among their buyers by charging prices that vary with the buyers' valuations of the goods sold. Relaxing this assumption may change the outcome of the economic argument, to suggest that the lost profits measure is in the end an appropriate way of safeguarding seller expectations, at least with respect to sellers who possess market power.[20]

---

18.   Recall the obstacles that a car-buyer faces in reselling a new car as used.

19.   Another possibility is that a sophisticated monopolist, who knows that some of her buyers will breach, will change her price in response to the law's remedy rule. If lost profits are denied, prices will be higher; and buyers will pay the higher prices on account of being relieved of lost profits damages should they breach. Now breaking buyers should not be required to pay lost profit damages, as no profits are lost (being paid as a cross-subsidy) by non-breaching buyers.

20.   The discussion in subsequent paragraphs follows Alan Schwartz, *Price Discrimination with Contract Terms: The Lost Volume Problem*, 12 AM. L. ECON. REV. 394 (2010). Schwartz

This approach to the lost volume problem begins by recharacterizing the scenarios in which the problem arises. These scenarios—including the circumstances that generated both *Lenobel* and *Neri*—generally involves sales that proceed in two stages. In the first, the seller and buyer contract for the sale and the buyer pays a deposit. And in the second, the seller delivers and the buyer pays the balance of the purchase price. When seen in this light, the dispute between the lost profit and market-based (or resale-based) measures of damages becomes, in effect, a dispute about whether the seller may impose on the buyer a non-refundable deposit: lost-profits damages fix non-refundable deposits at the size of the seller's profits, whereas market-based damages set the maximum non-refundable deposit effectively at zero (more precisely, at the seller's incidental damages).[21]

A non-refundable deposit in effect raises the total price the buyer must pay for the good, by causing the buyer to have to pay some money to the seller even when she does not take delivery. But the extent by which it raises the total price is not constant across buyers, because the expected additional payment that the non-refundable deposit involves depends on the likelihood that the buyer will seek to pull out. For buyers who are certain to complete their purchases, the increase in the expected price is zero; for buyers who are certain to breach, the increase is the full non-refundable deposit; and for buyers who have an intermediate chance of breaching, the increase lies somewhere in between.

Now as compared to the lower market-price based remedy, the lost profits remedy will therefore shift the seller's supply curve for the good out and to the right (since the seller will now receive greater expected value from the contract at each price for completion). Similarly, it will shift the demand curve in and to the left (since the buyer will have to pay more in expectation at every price). As long as sellers and buyers have identical attitudes towards the risk of breach and identical predictions of this risk (and also as long as the chance of breach does not vary with the remedial rule)—then the two shifts will be of precisely equal magnitude, so that the quantity sold under both regimes will be identical, and the price will vary (to be lower when lost profits are available) by precisely the expected per-contract cost of breach. In this case, the non-refundable deposit will simply couple the sale of the good to a gamble between buyers and sellers who value it identically, at its actuarial worth.[22]

But now suppose that not all buyers have equal chances of breaching and that buyers know their chances while sellers do not. Buyers for whom breach is probable dislike high down payments, which they will likely

---

concerns himself not just with whether a seller's lost volume claim is plausible, but also with whether it is socially optimal—economically efficient—for the law to enable volume sellers to contract to secure private returns through methods that enable them to retain lost volume profits on breach. Schwartz concludes that allowing recovery of lost volume profits is efficient, but for second-order reasons.

21. Here recall, from an earlier note, that this entire argument proceeds against the background of a doctrine holding agreements to impose remedies that exceed a disappointed promisee's expectations unenforceable penalty clauses.

22. This discussion reprises a variation on the observation in note 18 above.

forfeit. Buyers with a low probability of breach will prefer high down payments coupled with commensurately lower overall prices for completed transactions. Now a lost profits remedy of the sort awarded in *Neri* effectively imposes a non-refundable deposit equal to the seller's profit; and a remedy of zero of the sort awarded in *Lenobel* effectively makes every deposit fully refundable. The lost profit remedy thus inefficiently discourages purchases from buyers who are unlikely to complete, by making them cross-subsidize high-probability-of-completion buyers. The zero remedy, by contract, inefficiently discourages (completed) purchases from even high-probability-of-completion buyers, by raising the total price of completed purchases and making them cross-subsidize lower-probability-of-completion buyers. Enforcing contracts that set non-refundable deposits at levels between zero and a full lost profit produces distortions of each type, but more modestly. Which remedy is most efficient thus depends on the preponderance of high- and low-chance-of-completion buyers and their relative sensitivities to the forms of cross-subsidization just described. A full lost profits remedy can be optimal if enough low-chance-of-completion buyers contract in spite of its costs to them; a zero remedy can be optimal if enough high-chance-of-completion buyers contract in spite the costs that the associated high completion price imposes on them; an intermediate party-specified non-refundable deposit is optimal otherwise. Finally, there is no general reason for believing that either mandatory rule is more efficient than allowing the parties to fix the non-refundable deposit and treating such deposits as caps on sellers' damages.

Finally, consider whether there exists a doctrinal argument that casts the choice between lost profits damages on the one hand and contract-market (or contract-resale) price based damages on the other in a softer light. Lost profits damages, remember, grant a seller the difference between the contract price and her costs *minus* expenses saved due to the breach. By contrast, market-based (or resale-based) damages grant the seller the difference between the contract price and the market price *plus* incidental damages in the form of additional selling expenses attributable to the breach. If one focuses on only the first component of each damage measure—contract price minus costs on the one hand and contract price minus market price on the other—then the choice between these damages measures appears conceptually clean and stark. Lost profits damages will result in an often substantial award and market-based damages will often (generally) result in an award of zero. But things change if one takes the second component of each measure into consideration as well. The expenses saved as a result of breach that must be *subtracted* from a lost profits award (the variable expenses associated with completing a sale) can be substantial. And the incidental damages that must be *added* to a market-based award might also be substantial. If sellers incur sunk costs in anticipation of selling (because they possess monopoly power and expect to recoup these costs) then a buyer's breach might be said to shift that sale's share of the seller's sunk costs to other sales, and these shifted costs might be styled incidental damages imposed on the rest of the seller's business.

(This is a doctrinal re-interpretation of the cross-subsidization in the model just described.[23]) So although the lost profits award will tend to exceed the market-based award, these two remedies may be less dramatically and starkly different in the final analysis than they appear at first blush.

This profusion of approaches to the lost profits puzzle may seem confusing—and the account of it here is designed to produce this effect.[24] Again, it is just difficult to identify a set of necessary and sufficient conditions for the soundness of a seller's lost profits claim. This should generate uncertainty about what the law should do in this case. But it should perhaps also have a broader effect. The problem at the heart of the uncertainty here is that economic analysis cannot settle on how properly to apply the general principle that efficiency requires remedies that precisely vindicate disappointed promisors' contractual expectations—neither more, nor less—to particular cases, because it cannot identify precisely how far promisors' contractual expectations have been disappointed.

That should, perhaps, generate some modesty about the larger economic project. This problem—of precisely calculating contractual expectations or the extent to which they are harmed by breaches—has not previously been addressed with such particularity in these materials. And perhaps confusion in connection with such efforts to decide cases is the rule rather than the exception. Insofar as this is the case, the striking capacity of law and economics to account for contract law's general doctrinal outlines becomes an illusion only, because it applies only at a level of doctrinal abstraction greater than that at which legal doctrines operate when they when they perform their core function, which is actually to decide particular cases.

6.2   BUYERS' REMEDIES UNDER THE UCC

The general framework for buyers' remedies under the UCC is established by § 2–711, which functions as a close analog to § 2–703 on the sellers' side.

---

23. An article by Victor Goldberg pursues a version of this argument, but in connection with an economic model that assumes competitive sellers and hence cannot explain sunk investments in selling to begin with. See Victor Goldberg, *An Economic Analysis of the Lost Volume Seller*, 57 S.CAL. LAW REV. 283 (1984).

24. Might the best response to the uncertainty described in the main text be to change the subject of analysis, away from asking which rule of law is best to asking which rule, fixed as a default, will most likely be changed by parties who know it to be unsuited to their particular circumstances. This style of argument is appealing, and it will appear prominently later in this chapter. In its most basic form, it recommends picking defaults that disfavor those who are most likely to have the knowledge and expertise needed to discover and depart from them (in the current case this argues for default rules that disfavor generally more sophisticated retail sellers and favor generally less sophisticated consumer-buyers). But it is far from clear that this form of argument can help much here, because the question what remedy maximizes contractual surplus by accurately tracking seller's expectations is so complicated that even sophisticated sellers are unlikely to know the answer and hence unlikely to act efficiently in varying whatever default the law adopts.

Uniform Commercial Code

§ 2-711   Buyer's Remedies in General; Buyer's Security Interest in Rejected Goods.

(1) Where the seller fails to make delivery or repudiates or the buyer rightfully rejects or justifiably revokes acceptance then with respect to any goods involved, and with respect to the whole if the breach goes to the whole contract (Section 2–612), the buyer may cancel and whether or not he has done so may in addition to recovering so much of the price as has been paid

(a) "cover" and have damages under the next section as to all the goods affected whether or not they have been identified to the contract; or

(b) recover damages for non-delivery as provided in this Article (Section 2–713).

(2) Where the seller fails to deliver or repudiates the buyer may also

(a) if the goods have been identified recover them as provided in this Article (Section 2–502); or

(b) in a proper case obtain specific performance or replevy the goods as provided in this Article (Section 2–716).

(3) On rightful rejection or justifiable revocation of acceptance a buyer has a security interest in goods in his possession or control for any payments made on their price and any expenses reasonably incurred in their inspection, receipt, transportation, care and custody and may hold such goods and resell them in like manner as an aggrieved seller (Section 2–706).

Official Comment

Prior Uniform Statutory Provision: No comparable index section; Subsection (3)-Section 69(5), Uniform Sales Act. Changes: The prior uniform statutory provision is generally continued and expanded in Subsection (3).

Purposes of Changes and New Matter:

1. To index in this section the buyer's remedies, subsection (1) covering those remedies permitting the recovery of money damages, and subsection (2) covering those which permit reaching the goods themselves. The remedies listed here are those available to a buyer who has not accepted the goods or who has justifiably revoked his acceptance. The remedies available to a buyer with regard to goods finally accepted appear in the section dealing with breach in regard to accepted goods. The buyer's right to proceed as to all goods when the breach is as to only some of the goods is determined by the section on breach in installment contracts and by the section on partial acceptance.

Despite the seller's breach, proper retender of delivery under the section on cure of improper tender or replacement can effectively preclude the buyer's remedies under this section, except for any delay involved.

2. To make it clear in subsection (3) that the buyer may hold and resell rejected goods if he has paid a part of the price or incurred expenses of the type specified. "Paid" as used here includes acceptance of a draft or other time negotiable instrument or the signing of a negotiable note. His freedom of resale is coextensive with that of a seller under this Article except that the buyer may not keep any profit resulting from the resale and is limited to retaining only the amount of the price paid and the costs involved in the inspection and handling of the goods. The buyer's security interest in the goods is intended to be limited to the items listed in subsection (3), and the buyer is not permitted to retain such funds as he might believe adequate for his damages. The buyer's right to cover, or to have damages for non-delivery, is not impaired by his exercise of his right of resale.

3. It should also be noted that this Act requires its remedies to be liberally administered and provides that any right or obligation which it declares is enforceable by action unless a different effect is specifically prescribed (Section 1–106).

* * *

As on the seller's side, this key to buyers' remedies under the UCC includes some buyers' self-help remedies—which in essence allow buyers who are in possession of goods that turn out to be defective to exploit these goods in their efforts to recover any monies that they have already paid their breaching sellers. Once again, self-help remedies are in practice important for buyers, but they will again be set aside in favor of discussing the range of court-ordered remedies that the UCC grants buyers. As on the seller's side, so § 2–711 directs buyers to three basic remedies. § 2–712 allows buyers to "cover" their contracts, by making reasonable replacement purchases on the market and claiming damages equal to the difference between the cover price and the contract price. (This cover provision is the buyer's analog of the seller's right to resell under § 2–706.) § 2–713 allows buyers who do not cover to receive money damages equal to the difference between the market price at an appropriate place and time (more on this later) and the contract price, subject to the provisions in § 2–723 governing proof of market price. (This is the buyer's analog to the seller's right to receive market based damages under § 2–708.) Finally, § 2–716 allows buyers, in appropriate circumstances, to compel sellers specifically to perform their contracts—that is, not to provide money damages calculated to compensate buyers' disappointed expectations but rather to satisfy these expectations directly, by delivering the promised goods themselves. (This is the buyer's analog to the seller's action for the contract price, although notice that the fact that the specific performance for buyers involves in-kind rather than in-cash remedies makes this remedy distinctive and perhaps complicates it.) As happened for sellers, the materials that follow consider each of these buyers' remedies.

6.2.A   DAMAGES BASED ON CONTRACT-COVER AND CONTRACT-MARKET PRICE DIFFERENCES

Begin by taking up the relationship between the right of a buyer whose seller has breached to procure substitute performance, that is, "cover," and claim damages based on the contract-cover price difference and a buyer's right to abandon his purchase entirely and claim damages based on the difference between the contract and market prices. As happened in the case of sellers' remedies, cover-based damages are generally better for buyers than market-based damages, because covering relieves buyers of the burdens of proving up market price under § 2–723. The case that follows illustrates the disadvantage of market damages and serves also to reprise ideas that have been introduced in the some of the previous discussions.

Uniform Commercial Code

§ 2–712   "Cover"; Buyer's Procurement of Substitute Goods

(1) After a breach within the preceding section the buyer may "cover" by making in good faith and without unreasonable delay any reasonable purchase of or contract to purchase goods in substitution for those due from the seller.

(2) The buyer may recover from the seller as damages the difference between the cost of cover and the contract price together with any incidental or consequential damages as hereinafter defined (Section 2–715), but less expenses saved in consequence of the seller's breach.

(3) Failure of the buyer to effect cover within this section does not bar him from any other remedy.

Official Comment

Prior Uniform Statutory Provision: None.

Purposes:

1. This section provides the buyer with a remedy aimed at enabling him to obtain the goods he needs thus meeting his essential need. This remedy is the buyer's equivalent of the seller's right to resell.

2. The definition of "cover" under subsection (1) envisages a series of contracts or sales, as well as a single contract or sale; goods not identical with those involved but commercially usable as reasonable substitutes under the circumstances of the particular case; and contracts on credit or delivery terms differing from the contract in breach, but again reasonable under the circumstances. The test of proper cover is whether at the time and place the buyer acted in good faith and in a reasonable manner, and it is immaterial that hindsight may later prove that the method of cover used was not the cheapest or most effective.

The requirement that the buyer must cover "without unreasonable delay" is not intended to limit the time necessary for him to look around and decide as to how he may best effect cover. The test here is similar to that generally used in this Article as to reasonable time and seasonable action.

3.   Subsection (3) expresses the policy that cover is not a mandatory remedy for the buyer. The buyer is always free to choose between cover and damages for non-delivery under the next section.

However, this subsection must be read in conjunction with the section which limits the recovery of consequential damages to such as could not have been obviated by cover. Moreover, the operation of the section on specific performance of contracts for "unique" goods must be considered in this connection for availability of the goods to the particular buyer for his particular needs is the test for that remedy and inability to cover is made an express condition to the right of the buyer to replevy the goods.

4.   This section does not limit cover to merchants, in the first instance. It is the vital and important remedy for the consumer buyer as well. Both are free to use cover: the domestic or non-merchant consumer is required only to act in normal good faith while the merchant buyer must also observe all reasonable commercial standards of fair dealing in the trade, since this falls within the definition of good faith on his part.

Uniform Commercial Code

§ 2–713   Buyer Damages for Non-delivery or Repudiation

(1) Subject to the provisions of this Article with respect to proof of market price (Section 2–723), the measure of damages for non-delivery or repudiation by the seller is the difference between the market price at the time when the buyer learned of the breach and the contract price together with any incidental and consequential damages provided in this Article (Section 2–715), but less expenses saved in consequence of the seller's breach.

(2) Market price is to be determined as of the place for tender or, in cases of rejection after arrival or revocation of acceptance, as of the place of arrival.

Official Comment

Prior Uniform Statutory Provision: Section 67(3), Uniform Sales Act

Changes: Rewritten

Purposes of Changes: To clarify the former rule so that:

1.   The general baseline adopted in this section uses as a yardstick the market in which the buyer would have obtained cover had he sought that relief. So the place for measuring damages is the place of tender (or the

place of arrival if the goods are rejected or their acceptance is revoked after reaching their destination) and the crucial time is the time at which the buyer learns of the breach.

2. The market or current price to be used in comparison with the contract price under this section is the price for goods of the same kind and in the same branch of trade.

3. When the market price under this section is difficult to prove the section on determination and proof of market price is available to permit a showing of a comparable market price, or, where no market price is available, evidence of spot sale prices is proper. Where the unavailability of a market price is caused by a scarcity of goods of the type involved, a good case is normally made for specific performance under this Article. Such scarcity conditions, moreover, indicate that the price has risen and under the section providing for liberal administration of remedies, opinion evidence as to the value of goods would be admissible in the absence of a market price and a liberal construction of allowable consequential damages should also result.

4. This section carries forward the standard rule that the buyer must deduct from his damages any expenses saved as a result of the breach.

5. The present section provides a remedy which is completely alternative to cover under the preceding section and applies only when and to the extent that the buyer has not covered.

Uniform Commercial Code

§ 2–713 Buyer's Damages for Nondelivery or Repudiation (2003 proposed amendments)

(1) Subject to Section 2–723, if the seller wrongfully fails to deliver or repudiates or the buyer rightfully rejects or justifiably revokes acceptance:

(a) the measure of damages in the case of wrongful failure to deliver by the seller or rightful rejection or justifiable revocation of acceptance by the buyer is the difference between the market price at the time for tender under the contract and the contract price together with any incidental or consequential damages under Section 2–715, but less expenses saved in consequence of the seller's breach; and

(b) the measure of damages for repudiation by the seller is the difference between the market price at the expiration of a commercially reasonable time after the buyer learned of the repudiation, but no later than the time stated in paragraph (a), and the contract price together with any incidental or consequential damages provided in this Article (Section 2–715), less expenses saved in consequence of the seller's breach.

(2) Market price is to be determined as of the place for tender or, in cases of rejection after arrival or revocation of acceptance, as of the place of arrival.

In this Section, the original Official Comment has been substantially revised or replaced by the following 2003 Official Comment. However, the original Official Comment may remain appropriate legislative history. For that reason, the original Official Comment may be found [below] for the convenience of those who may wish to study it.

Official Comment

1.   This section provides a rule for anticipatory repudiation cases. This is consistent with the new rule for sellers in Section 2–708(1)(b). In a case not involving repudiation, the buyer's damages will be based on the market price at the time for tender under the agreement. This changes the former rule where the time for measuring damages was at the time the buyer learned of the breach.

2.   This section provides for a buyer's expectancy damages when the seller wrongfully fails to deliver the goods or repudiates the contract or the buyer rightfully rejects or justifiably revokes acceptance. This section provides an alternative measure of damages to the cover remedy provided for in Section 2–712.

3.   Under subsection (1)(a), the measure of damages for a wrongful failure to deliver the goods by the seller or a rightful rejection or justifiable revocation of acceptance by the buyer is the difference between the market price at the time for tender under the agreement and the contract price.

4.   Under subsection (1)(b), in the case of an anticipatory repudiation by the seller the market price should be measured at the place where the buyer would have covered at a commercially reasonable time after the buyer learned of the repudiation, but no later than the time of tender under the agreement. This time approximates the market price at the time the buyer would have covered even though the buyer has not done so under Section 2–712. This subsection is designed to put the buyer in the position the buyer would have been in if the seller had performed by approximating the harm the buyer has suffered without allowing the buyer an unreasonable time to speculate on the market at the seller's expense.

5.   The market price to be used in comparison with the contract price under this section is the price for goods of the same kind and in the same branch of trade.

When the market price under this section is difficult to prove, Section 2–723 on the determination and proof of market price is available to permit a showing of a comparable market price. When no market price is available, evidence of spot sale prices may be used to determine damages under this section. When the unavailability of a market price is caused by a scarcity of goods of the type involved, a good case may be made for specific performance under Section 2–716. *See* the Official Comment to that Section.

6. In addition to the damages provides in this section, the buyer is entitled to incidental and consequential damages under Section 2–715.

7. A buyer that has covered under Section 2–712 may not recover the contract price market price difference under this section, but instead must base the damages on those provided in Section 2–712. To award an additional amount because the buyer could show the market price was higher than the contract price would put the buyer in a better position than performance would have. Of course, the seller would bear the burden of proving that cover had the economic effect of limiting the buyer's actual loss to an amount less than the contract price-market price difference.

An apparent cover, which does not in fact replace the goods contracted for, should not foreclose the use of the contract price-market price measure of damages. If the breaching seller cannot prove that the new purchase is in fact a replacement for the one not delivered under the contract, the "cover" purchase should not foreclose the buyer's recovery under 2–713 of the market contract difference.

Maxwell v. Norwood Marine, Inc.

Massachusetts District Court, Appellate Division, Northern District, 1976.
19 UCC Rep. Sev. 829.

Appeal from the First District Court of Southern Middlesex (Framingham).

■ FLYNN, J. This is the unusual case where the plaintiff appellant was the prevailing party at the trial court level. Nominal damages were awarded and the plaintiff appellate claims to be aggrieved upon the question of damages.

This is an action of contact in which the plaintiff seeks to recover damages for the defendant's breach of contract to sell the plaintiff a boat.

The answer is a general denial and eight affirmative defenses: (1) payment, (2) genuineness of the signature on the bill of sale, (3) compromise and settlement, (4) accord and satisfaction, (5) novation, (6) statute of frauds, (7) excuse from performance, (8) lack of consideration.

At the trial, there was evidence tending to show:

The plaintiff and defendant entered into a contract on December 31, 1973 under which the plaintiff agreed to purchase a 1973 25–foot Chris Craft from the defendant for $4,200.00, plus a trade-in of the plaintiff's 1973 18–foot Glastron for delivery approximately April 15, 1974.

The defendant on March 23, 1974 sold for $9,000.00 the 1973 25–foot Chris Craft it had previously agreed and then refused to sell the plaintiff.

The plaintiff bought a 1974 22–foot Sea Ray on April 9, 1974, and was credited $3,000.00 on the trade-in of his 1973 18–foot Glastron.

The court found the following facts:

"The plaintiff and defendant entered into an oral agreement on December 31, 1973 whereby the defendant agreed to sell and the plaintiff to purchase a 1973 25–foot Chris Craft boat for the sum of $4,200.00, plus a trade-in on the plaintiff's 1973 18–foot Glastron boat.

"The defendant breached said contract in that it refused to consummate the sale.

"The plaintiff purchased a 1974 22–foot Sea Ray boat as a replacement for the boat he had originally contracted to purchase from the defendant, which 22–foot Sea Ray boat was not a boat comparable and in like kind to the boat the plaintiff had agreed to purchase from the defendant.

"The plaintiff was not damaged by the defendant's breach of contract."

Both parties submitted requests for ruling of law. The trial judge denied all of the defendant's requests and treated all the plaintiff's requests as having been waived. The plaintiff claims to be aggrieved by such action and by, in effect, the denial of his requests #6 through #9.

The requests in question are as follows:

#6. If the plaintiff is not entitled to damages under GL c 106, § 2–712 (which section of the Uniform Commercial Code pertains to the buyer's "cover" in the event of a breach by the seller), then he is entitled to damages in the amount of the difference between the market price of the 1973 Chris Craft and the contract price. GL c 106, §§ 2–711 (1), 2–713.

#7. The price at which the defendant sold the 1973 25–foot Chris Craft three months after it contracted to sell the boat to the plaintiff and prior to the approximate delivery date to the plaintiff is the value of the 1973 25–foot Chris Craft.

#8. The market value of the 18–foot Glastron on trade was $3,000.00, the amount given to the plaintiff in trade when he purchased the 1974 Sea Ray.

#9. If the plaintiff is not entitled to damages based on the cost of cover, he is entitled to the damages as follows:

Market value of the 1973 25–foot Chris Craft	$9,000.00
Less contract price (including value of 18–foot Glastron)	$7,200.00
	$1,800.00

Requests #6 and #7 should be denied as incorrect statement of law.

GL c 106, § 2–713, which is part of the Uniform Commercial Code provides that "the measure of damages for non-delivery of repudiation by the seller is the difference between the market price *when the buyer learned of the breach* and the contract price" (emphasis supplied).

Neither the summary of the evidence in the report not the judge's findings disclose the exact date the plaintiff learned of the defendant's breach other than it was previous to March 23, 1974 when the defendant the Sea Ray [sic] boat to another. No where has the plaintiff introduced evidence as to the market value of the boat on that crucial date and such proof would be necessary for a proper application of the statute.

Request #8 is clearly directed to a finding of fact and not a ruling of law and should be denied.

Request #9 also should be denied as being inconsistent with the judge's special findings, as well as being premised on the incorrect assumption that the market value to be used in application of the statute is the later selling price and not the market price when the plaintiff learned of the breach.

The judge specifically found as a fact that the plaintiff was not damaged by the defendant's breach. The finding must stand unless the making of it amounts to an abuse of discretion on the part of the trial judge. "An abuse of discretion consists of judicial action that no conscientious judge, acting intelligently, could honestly have taken." *Bartley v. Phillips*, 317 Mass 35, 43 (1944).

We find no such abuse of discretion and rule that the trial judge's finding that the plaintiff was not damaged was warranted by the evidence as contained in the report. In view of the result we have reached, we rule that the trial judge's treatment of the plaintiff's requests #6 through #9 was at most a harmless error.

Report dismissed.

* * *

To understand the issue raised by *Maxwell*, begin by reviewing a highly stylized version of the facts of the case, which developed in three stages. First, the buyer and his seller agreed for the buyer to purchase a boat of type A, paying $4,200 cash plus the trade-in of the buyer's old boat. Second, the seller breached, selling the type A boat to a third party for $9,000 and delivering nothing to the buyer. And third, the buyer bought a boat of a different type, B, elsewhere, receiving $3,000 as a trade-in value for his old boat. The buyer subsequently sued, seeking damages equal to the difference between the market value of the type A boat he had contracted to receive and the contract price. The buyer proposed that the market price of the type A boat was $9,000 (as evidenced by the seller's resale) and that the contract price was $7,200, namely the sum of the $4,200 cash and the $3,000 trade-in value of his old boat (as evidence by the trade-in allowance he received on buying the type B boat). The buyer therefore sought $1,800 in damages.

The buyer lost, becoming trapped in between the demands of §§ 2–712 and 2–713. To begin with, the buyer was held not to have covered under § 2–712, because the type B boat he ended up buying was found not comparable to the type A boat named in the contract. In addition, the buyer was held not to have made an adequate proof of market price under §§ 2–713 and 2–723. The relevant market under the statute is the one existing at the time that the buyer learns of the breach. But the buyer learned that the seller had breached before the seller resold the type A boat. And this made the resale price inadequate to proving up market price for purposes of recovering under § 2–713. Accordingly as did the seller in *Dehann*, so the buyer in *Maxwell* stumbled over the demands of proving market price, and ended up unable to vindicate his contractual expectations.

The slightly peculiar nature of the buyer's remedial calculation means that, in addition to illustrating the basic idea that market-based damage claims require disappointed promisees to assume a potentially onerous burden of proving market prices, *Maxwell* also illustrates a number of other issues that arise in and around buyers' remedies under the UCC.

First, and most obviously, *Maxwell* illustrates a tension that arises in connection with the provisions governing cover. On the one hand, the cover provision is designed to allow buyers to fix their damages, by direct analogy to the resale provision for sellers. And in order to serve this purpose, the cover that the buyer purchases must replace the contracted-for performance not just for the buyer but also from the perspective of the market. The buyer's cover in Maxwell—because it involved a different type of boat from that named in the original contract—failed this purpose. Because the replacement boat may have been either a less or a more expensive model than the original, simply looking at its price gives no firm information about the extent of the buyer's loss due to the breach.

But on the other hand, cover for buyers serves another purpose also, namely that it encourages buyers to get the goods that they need in order to limit their consequential damages. (The fungibility of money and the availability of capital markets make this purpose largely fall away on the sellers' side, because sellers can relatively easily avoid consequential damages simply by borrowing if they need to, perhaps even against their remedy entitlements.) In order to serve this purpose, the new good need be equivalent to the old in only the buyer's eyes, and market valuations are irrelevant. The type B boat seems to have functioned in this way for the buyer in *Maxwell*, and so the holding that buying it did not constitute adequate cover reduced the cover provision's effectiveness at promoting buyer mitigation.[25]

Second, the *Maxwell* buyer's damages calculation raises the host of complications just discussed in connection with *Neri*. The buyer in *Maxwell* claimed that he had bought a boat with a market value of $9000 for a contract price equivalent to $7200, and therefore that the breach cost him a "good deal" worth $1800. The buyer suggested that he suffered these

---

25. Notice that the buyer in *Maxwell*, who seems to have wanted to use the boat for pleasure rather than commercial purposes, almost certainly suffered no substantial consequential damages from delay in acquiring it. So on the facts of *Maxwell*, the remedy-fixing purpose of the cover provision probably dominated the mitigation-encouraging function. Might the outcome have been different if the buyer had been a business, in desperate need of a boat (any boat) in order to secure its stream of revenues?

damages because he failed to get a below-market price on the boat he purchased instead when the seller breached. But might the buyer have suffered the $1800 lost expectation even if he had found an equivalently good deal on his replacement boat? After all, the value of his good deal was in effect a profit for the buyer on the transaction.[26] And this suggests that the buyer might have had a good claim even if he had found a good deal on his replacement boat—that he is, in effect, a lost volume buyer, who but for the breach would have made two good deals rather than one. To see this, just imagine that the buyer wanted the boat not for his own use but to resell it—that he was acting as a boat broker, who seeks used boats at good prices to sell to consumer-buyers who cannot (for whatever reason) search for themselves. Of course, the question whether the buyer is really a lost volume buyer—whether he could profitably have exploited both good deals—raises all the difficulties just discussed on the seller's side.

Third, what does the buyer's difficulty concerning cover entail for the proper administration of the market-priced based remedy under § 2–713? The relatively high burden of proof established for market price by the combination of §§ 2–713 and 2–723 makes sense in order to encourage cover. But *Maxwell* illustrates that cover—at least legally adequate cover—may not always be possible, and indeed may be less possible for buyers than resale is for sellers (since goods can be idiosyncratic in a way in which money-payments are not). This is especially true insofar as (under the first heading above) courts administer the cover provision solely with an eye to fixing damages and give little or no leeway to buyers who have found non-market-equivalent replacements for performance in an effort to reduce consequential damages. And it seems a mistake to subject buyers to the conventional, and demanding, burden of proving market prices even when the alternative route that this burden is designed to encourage is not practically available to them. (At the very least, the observation that it is more likely that legally adequate cover will be impossible for buyers than that legally adequate resale will be impossible for sellers suggests that it is a mistake to subject buyers to the same burden of proving market price as sellers face.)

The fourth point about *Maxwell* is specific to that case's peculiar facts, but perhaps no less interesting for this. Might the buyer have avoided at least some of the problems that plagued him in *Maxwell*—specifically, the problem that his effort to sidestep the burdens of proving market price by proceeding under § 2–712 was doomed from the start because his cover involved a non-market-equivalent boat—by taking his somewhat idiosyncratic remedial accounting to its logical conclusion and proceeding not as a buyer but rather as a *seller*? The buyer, after all, explained his remedial demand through a calculation that used the trade-in he subsequently received on his old boat in order to fix the contract price and hence also the extent of his good deal. Might the buyer instead have characterized the contract as a sale, by him, of his old boat to the seller, for a purchase price equal to the value of the type A boat that he was to receive under the

---

26.   Insofar as the good deal is attributed to an excessive trade-in allowance it is literally a profit on the sale of his old boat, a point that will be taken up in a moment.

contract minus his cash payment to the seller? If the type A boat was indeed worth $9,000, then he in effect contracted to sell his trade-in boat to the seller for $4,800 (which sum the seller then added to his $4,200 cash payment to make up the $9,000 value of the type A boat that the buyer was to receive). And when he traded his boat in for $3,000 in conjunction with his subsequent purchase of the type B boat, this was a resale under § 2–706. As long as the resale met the conditions established by that section, the Maxwell plaintiff (now proceeding as a seller) could recover damages based on the contract-resale price difference. And (critically) the question whether the type B and type A boats are reasonable substitutes—the question that tripped up the buyer's § 2–713 claim almost from the get-go—never even arises under § 2–706.[27]

6.2.B ANTICIPATORY REPUDIATION

A special problem involving buyers' remedies arises when a seller announces that she intends not to perform her promise before the time at which the contractual performance is due—when, as the law says, a seller anticipatorily repudiates her contract. This conduct raises two main questions: first, may a buyer whose seller repudiates treat the contract as breached from the moment of the repudiation, or must he wait until the time for performance arrives and the seller actually fails to perform; and, second, if a buyer may treat the contract as breached when it is repudiated, with respect to what time should the buyer's market-based remedies be determined? (Although the analysis that follows focuses on buyers, both questions might arise symmetrically for sellers whose buyers anticipatorily repudiate. Indeed, the earlier example involving the choice of market for sellers' remedies when inter-city price differences exist presents a structural analog of the some of what will follow here, with place standing in for time.)

Begin with the first question. May a buyer whose seller anticipatorily repudiates treat the contract as breached from the moment of the repudiation? This question was for a time uncertain, but the answer is today clear.

Hochster v. De La Tour

Queen's Bench, 1853.
2 E. & B. 678.

■ LORD CAMPBELL, C.J. [I]t cannot be laid down as a universal rule that, where by agreement an act is to be done on a future day, no action can be

---

27. Of course, even on this theory the buyer would still have to prove that the type A boat had a market value of $9,000, since without this he could not establish that the "sales price" on his trade-in boat was $4,800. This remains a burden for the buyer, to be sure, but it is not clear that it would be quite so large a burden as proving up the market price of the type A boat under §§ 2–713 and 2–723. In particular, although a court might import those sections' finicky and hence burdensome standards for market price into this new context, is need not do so. And it might be that a buyer who successfully styled his purchase of the replacement boat as an effort to mitigate damages might persuade a court to relieve him of some part of this burden, since there would be no statutory language directly on point, and the effect of the burden would be to catch him in the trap in which the *Maxwell* buyer was, in fact, caught.

brought for a breach of the agreement till the day for doing the act has arrived. If a man promises to marry a woman on a future day, and before that day marries another woman, he is instantly liable to an action for breach of promise of marriage; *Short v Stone* (8 Q.B. 358). If a man contracts to execute a lease on and from a future day for a certain term, and, before that day, executes a lease to another for the same term, he may be immediately sued for breaking the contract; *Ford v Tiley* (6 B. & C. 325). So, if a man contracts to sell and deliver specific goods on a future day, and before the day he sells and delivers them to another, he is immediately liable to an action at the suit of the person with whom he first contracted to sell and deliver them; *Bowdell v Parsons* (10 East, 359).

If the plaintiff has no remedy for breach of the contract unless he treats the contract as in force, and acts upon it down to the 1st June 1852, it follows that, till then, he must enter into no employment which will interfere with his promise 'to start with the defendant on such travels on the day and year,' and that he must then be properly equipped in all respects, as a courier for a three months tour on the continent of Europe. But it is surely much more rational, and more for the benefit of both parties, that, after the renunciation of the agreement by the defendant, the plaintiff should be at liberty to consider himself absolved from any future performance of it, retaining his right to sue for any damage he has suffered from the breach of it. Thus, instead of remaining idle and laying out money in preparations which must be useless, he is at liberty to seek service under another employer, which would go in mitigation of the damages to which he would otherwise be entitled for a breach of the contract.

The man who wrongfully renounces a contract into which he has deliberately entered cannot justly complain if he is immediately sued for a compensation in damages by the man whom he has injured; and it seems reasonable to allow an option to the injured party, either to sue immediately, or to wait till the time when the act was to be done. An argument against the action before the 1st of June is urged from the difficulty of calculating the damages: but this argument is equally strong against an action before the 1st of September, when the three months would expire. In either case, the jury in assessing the damages would be justified in looking to all that had happened, or was likely to happen, to increase or mitigate the loss of the plaintiff down to the day of trial. We do not find any decision contrary to the view we are taking of this case.

[W]e must give judgment for the plaintiff.

Uniform Commercial Code

2–610 Anticipatory Repudiation

When either party repudiates the contract with respect to a performance not yet due the loss of which will substantially impair the value of the contract to the other, the aggrieved party may

(a) for a commercially reasonable time await performance by the repudiating party; or

(b) resort to any remedy for breach (Section 2–703 or Section 2–711), even though he has notified the repudiating party that he would await the latter's performance and has urged retraction; and

(c) in either case suspend his own performance or proceed in accordance with the provisions of this Article on the seller's right to identify goods to the contract notwithstanding breach or to salvage unfinished goods (Section 2–704).

Official Comment

Prior Uniform Statutory Provision: See Sections 63(2) and 65, Uniform Sales Act.

Purposes: To make it clear that:

1. With the problem of insecurity taken care of by the preceding section and with provision being made in this Article as to the effect of a defective delivery under an installment contract, anticipatory repudiation centers upon an overt communication of intention or an action which renders performance impossible or demonstrates a clear determination not to continue with performance.

Under the present section when such a repudiation substantially impairs the value of the contract, the aggrieved party may at any time resort to his remedies for breach, or he may suspend his own performance while he negotiates with, or awaits performance by, the other party. But if he awaits performance beyond a commercially reasonable time he cannot recover resulting damages which he should have avoided.

2. It is not necessary for repudiation that performance be made literally and utterly impossible. Repudiation can result from action which reasonably indicates a rejection of the continuing obligation. And, a repudiation automatically results under the preceding section on insecurity when a party fails to provide adequate assurance of due future performance within thirty days after a justifiable demand therefor has been made. Under the language of this section, a demand by one or both parties for more than the contract calls for in the way of counter-performance is not in itself a repudiation nor does it invalidate a plain expression of desire for future performance. However, when under a fair reading it amounts to a statement of intention not to perform except on conditions which go beyond the contract, it becomes a repudiation.

3. The test chosen to justify an aggrieved party's action under this section is the same as that in the section on breach in installment contracts-namely the substantial value of the contract. The most useful test of substantial value is to determine whether material inconvenience or injustice will result if the aggrieved party is forced to wait and receive an ultimate tender minus the part or aspect repudiated.

4. After repudiation, the aggrieved party may immediately resort to any remedy he chooses provided he moves in good faith (see Section 1–203). Inaction and silence by the aggrieved party may leave the matter open but it cannot be regarded as misleading the repudiating party. Therefore the aggrieved party is left free to proceed at any time with his options under this section, unless he has taken some positive action which in good faith requires notification to the other party before the remedy is pursued.

Uniform Commercial Code

§ 2–610   Anticipatory Repudiation (2003 proposed amendments)

(1) If either party repudiates the contract with respect to a performance not yet due the loss of which will substantially impair the value of the contract to the other, the aggrieved party may:

>   (a) for a commercially reasonable time await performance by the repudiating party; or

>   (b) resort to any remedy for breach (Section 2–703 or Section 2–711), even if the aggrieved party has notified the repudiating party that it would await the latter's performance and has urged retraction; and

>   (c) in either case suspend performance or proceed in accordance with the provisions of this Article on the seller's right to identify goods to the contract notwithstanding breach or to salvage unfinished goods (Section 2–704).

(2) Repudiation includes language that a reasonable person would interpret to mean that the other party will not or cannot make a performance still due under the contract or voluntary, affirmative conduct that would appear to a reasonable person to make a future performance by the other party impossible.

Comment 5 added in 2003. The original official comment has not been amended to reflect the change from "writing" to "record."

Official Comment

Prior Uniform Statutory Provision: See Sections 63(2) and 65, Uniform Sales Act.

Purposes: To make it clear that:

1. With the problem of insecurity taken care of by the preceding section and with provision being made in this Article as to the effect of a defective delivery under an installment contract, anticipatory repudiation centers upon an overt communication of intention or an action which renders performance impossible or demonstrates a clear determination not to continue with performance.

Under the present section when such a repudiation substantially impairs the value of the contract, the aggrieved party may at any time resort to his remedies for breach, or he may suspend his own performance while he negotiates with, or awaits performance by, the other party. But if he awaits performance beyond a commercially reasonable time he cannot recover resulting damages which he should have avoided.

2. It is not necessary for repudiation that performance be made literally and utterly impossible. Repudiation can result from action which reasonably indicates a rejection of the continuing obligation. And, a repudiation automatically results under the preceding section on insecurity when a party fails to provide adequate assurance of due future performance within thirty days after a justifiable demand therefor has been made. Under the language of this section, a demand by one or both parties for more than the contract calls for in the way of counter-performance is not in itself a repudiation nor does it invalidate a plain expression of desire for future performance. However, when under a fair reading it amounts to a statement of intention not to perform except on conditions which go beyond the contract, it becomes a repudiation.

3. The test chosen to justify an aggrieved party's action under this section is the same as that in the section on breach in installment contracts—namely the substantial value of the contract. The most useful test of substantial value is to determine whether material inconvenience or injustice will result if the aggrieved party is forced to wait and receive an ultimate tender minus the part or aspect repudiated.

4. After repudiation, the aggrieved party may immediately resort to any remedy he chooses provided he moves in good faith (see Section 1–203). Inaction and silence by the aggrieved party may leave the matter open but it cannot be regarded as misleading the repudiating party. Therefore the aggrieved party is left free to proceed at any time with his options under this section, unless he has taken some positive action which in good faith requires notification to the other party before the remedy is pursued.

5. Subsection (2) provides guidance on when a party can be considered to have repudiated a performance obligation based upon the Restatement (Second) of Contracts § 250 and does not purport to be an exclusive statement of when a repudiation has occurred. Repudiation centers upon an overt communication of intention, actions which render performance impossible, or a demonstration of a clear determination not to perform. Failure to provide adequate assurance of due performance under Section 2–609 also operates as a repudiation.

* * *

So modern law holds that in cases of anticipatory repudiation, an aggrieved party may choose between (a) encouraging, for a commercially reasonable time, the breaching party to retract its repudiation and perform and (b) treating the contract as breached and seeking its ordinary remedies therefore. This means that when, as in the case that follows, the repudiating party is the seller, a buyer may seek to recover market-based remedies under UCC §§ 2–713 and 2–723. This raises the second question mentioned earlier—with respect to market conditions at what time should such a buyer's market-based remedies be determined? The materials below address this question, first with respect to the answer enshrined in the positive law, and then by asking what answer economic theory recommends.

Cargill v. Stafford

United States Court of Appeals for the 10th Circuit, 1977.
553 F.2d 1222.

■ BREITENSTEIN, CIRCUIT JUDGE. This diversity jurisdiction case relates to two transactions for the sale of wheat by defendant Stafford to plaintiff Cargill. The court denied recovery on the first and allowed recovery on the second. Both parties have appealed. We affirm except as to the amount of damages recoverable from the second transaction.

Cargill is a cash merchandiser of agricultural commodities. Stafford owns and operates a country grain elevator under the name "Stafford Elevator" in Campo, Colorado. Stafford and his wife run the elevator business. Stafford's brother and son-in-law operate a completely separate grain elevator under the name "Stafford Brothers Elevator" located 35–40 miles from Campo in Keyes, Oklahoma.

On July 23, 1973, Julsonnet, an agent of Cargill, telephoned Stafford about buying some wheat. Stafford said that he had 40,000 bushels of wheat which "I might let you have." Stafford testified that he told Julsonnet to send a confirmation "and if it looks all right, I will sign it and send it back." Julsonnet prepared and mailed a confirmation but addressed it to "Stafford Brothers Elevator, El Campo, Colorado." Mrs. Stafford received the letter and noted the addressee. She knew that Cargill had done business with Stafford Brothers. Without opening the letter, she forwarded it to Stafford Brothers who returned the letter to Stafford Elevator on August 17.

On July 31 Stafford telephoned Julsonnet and said that a protein premium should be included in the confirmation. Julsonnet agreed and promised to send a written confirmation of the contract change. During the same telephone conversation Stafford agreed to sell, and Cargill to buy, an additional 26,000 bushels of wheat. The confirmation of the second sale was correctly made to Stafford Elevator. The confirmation of the contract change on the first transaction was again incorrectly sent to Stafford Brothers Elevator.

On August 21 Stafford wrote Cargill objecting to the provision of the confirmations giving Cargill an option to cancel and saying: "Thus contract void." An agent of Cargill called Stafford on August 27 and urged him to perform. Stafford insisted that the confirmations were void because of the optional cancellation provisions. Cargill continued to urge performance. After Stafford told Cargill on September 6 that he would not perform,

Cargill told Stafford that the contracts were cancelled and that Stafford owed Cargill the difference between the contract prices and the September 6 price. The price of wheat rose from the end of July, reaching a high point on August 21. Stafford refused to pay and Cargill brought suit for breach of the contracts.

The parties agree that Colorado law controls. We first consider the July 23 transaction. The trial court held that recovery was foreclosed because of the statute-of-fraud provisions of the Uniform Commercial Code as adopted in Colorado. The applicable provision is *C.R.S. § 4–2–201* which requires something in writing except in specified situations. One of these relates to merchants. Both Stafford and Cargill are merchants within the statutory definition of that term. See § 4–2–104(1). *Section 4–2–201(2)* says that a writing is sufficient:

"Between merchants, if *within a reasonable time* a writing in confirmation of the contract and sufficient against the sender is received and the party receiving it has reason to know its contents, it satisfies the requirements of subsection (1) of this section against such party *unless written notice of objection to its contents is given within ten days after it is received.*" (Emphasis supplied.)

The trial court, after reviewing the evidence relating to the Cargill confirmation of the July 23 transaction, the misdirection of the confirmation to Stafford Brothers, and the return of the letter to Stafford Elevator on August 17, said:

"The Court finds the delay in delivery [of the confirmation] was the result of erroneous addressing on the part of the plaintiff [Cargill] and that the confirmation was not received by defendant [Stafford] within 'a reasonable time' within the meaning of Section 2 [§ 4–2–201(2)] of the foregoing statute."

The court also found that the August 21 objection of Stafford to the confirmation because of the cancellation clause was within the ten-day period provided in *§ 4–2–201(2)*.

Cargill objects to the court's findings as unsupported by the record. Our review of the evidence convinces us that the findings are supported by substantial evidence and are not clearly erroneous.

Cargill urges that Stafford admitted a valid contract covering the July 23 transaction. See *§ 4–2–201(b)*. We do not agree. When Cargill's agent called Stafford on July 23, Stafford said that he might make the sale; that he would check over the written confirmation; and "if it looks all right, I will sign it and send it back." Stafford did not sign the confirmation or return it to Cargill. He never admitted the existence of a valid contract.

Next, Cargill relies on unjust enrichment as support for recovery on the July 23 transaction. The elements of unjust enrichment are: (1) a benefit conferred on the defendant by the plaintiff; (2) acceptance of the benefit by the defendant; and (3) circumstances which make it inequitable for the defendant to retain the benefit. See *Dass v. Epplen, 162 Colo. 60 (1967)*. Cargill did not perform any services for, convey any rights to, or confer any benefit on Stafford. Because of the unenforceability of the July 23 contract, Stafford was under no legal obligation to Cargill. There was no benefit for him to accept. If unjust enrichment can be used to gain benefits from executory oral contracts barred enforcement by a statute of frauds, that statute is rendered meaningless. We agree with the trial court that the July 23 transaction does not entitle Cargill to any recovery from Stafford.

We turn to the July 31 transaction. The parties made on the telephone an oral contract for the sale by Stafford of 26,000 bushels of wheat to Cargill. A written confirmation was received by Stafford on August 7. The confirmation was thus received within the "reasonable time" requirement of § 4-2-201(2). Stafford's rejection of the confirmation occurred on August 21, and was not within the ten-day requirement of the statute. Ibid.

[The court determines, in agreement with the trial court, that the July 31 transaction resulted in a valid and enforceable contract that Stafford breached.]

The remaining question is the damages to which Cargill is entitled. The trial court awarded damages in the amount of $27,300 plus interest which was the difference in the price of wheat on September 6 over that on July 31. September 6 is the day on which Cargill acted upon Stafford's statement that he would not perform. The court gave no reason for its selection of the September 6 date. The final day for performance was September 30.

Stafford repudiated the contract by an August 21 letter which was received by Cargill on August 24. Cargill argues alternatively that, (1) it should recover the difference between the price of wheat on August 24 and on July 31, and (2) the difference between the price on September 30 when performance was due and the price on July 31.

Section 4-2-711 provides that when a seller repudiates the buyer may (1) cover (buy substitute goods) and recover the difference in price, (2) recover damages for non-delivery under § 4-2-713, or sue for specific performance under § 4-2-716. Cargill has not attempted to obtain specific performance. The record contains scant, if any, evidence that Cargill covered the wheat. *Section 4-2-713* relates to non-delivery and provides:

> "Subject to the provisions of this article with respect to proof of market price (section 4-2-723), the measure of damages for nondelivery or repudiation by the seller is the difference between the market price *at the time when the buyer learned of the breach* and the contract price together with any incidental and consequential damages provided in this article (section 4-2-715), but less expenses saved in consequence of the seller's breach." (Emphasis supplied.)

The basic question is whether "time when buyer learned of the breach" means "time when buyer learned of the repudiation" or means "time of performance" in anticipatory repudiation cases. See discussion in J. White and R. Summers, Uniform Commercial Code, 197–202 (1972). The authors conclude, Ibid. at 201, that the soundest arguments support the interpretation of "learned of the breach" to mean "time of performance" in the anticipatory repudiation case. We agree for two reasons.

First, before the adoption of the Code in Colorado and other states, damages were measured from the time when performance was due and not from the time when the buyer learned of repudiation. See Colo.Rev.Stat. (1953) § 121–1–67(3), and A. Corbin, 5 Corbin on Contracts, § 1053 at 309 (1964). A clear deviation from past law would not ordinarily be accomplished by Code ambiguities.

Second, Code § 4–2–723(1) discusses when to measure damages in a suit for anticipatory repudiation which comes to trial before the time for performance. That section says:

> "Any damages based on market price (section 4–2–708 or *section 4–2–713*) shall be determined according to the price of such goods prevailing at the time when the aggrieved party *learned of the repudiation*." (Emphasis supplied.)

Thus, when the Code drafters intended to base damages on the date a party "learned of the repudiation," they did so by explicit language. We conclude that under *§ 4–2–713* damages normally should be measured from the time when performance is due and not from the time when the buyer learns of repudiation.

To support its contention that the time when it learned of the repudiation controls Cargill cites two cases. *Sawyer Farmers Coop. Ass'n v. Linke, N.D., 231 N.W.2d 791 (1975)* is not helpful because the date for determination of the market price was controlled by a contract provision and not by § 2–713. *Oloffson v. Coomer, 11 Ill. App. 3d 918 (1973),* is more nearly in point. There the buyer contracted in 1969 with the seller-farmer for delivery of corn in 1970. In June 1970 the seller notified the buyer that he was not planting corn because of weather conditions and would not deliver in September. The buyer refused to cover and urged performance even though he knew there would be none. The court refused to award damages based on the September price but based its award on the price of corn on the June date when the seller notified the buyer that he would not deliver. In so doing the court pointed out that there was an easily accessible market for purchase of the grain, Ibid. at 874, and that the words "for a commercially reasonable time" appearing in Code § 2–610(a) [Colorado § 4–2–610(a)], relating to anticipatory repudiation "must be read relatively to the obligation of good faith that is defined in Section 2–103(1)(b) [Colorado § 4–2–103(1)(b)] and imposed expressly in Section 1–203 [Colorado § 4–1–203]." Ibid. at 875.

This brings us to § 4–2–712 which provides that the buyer may "cover" by the reasonable purchase of substitute goods. A buyer is allowed to buy substitute goods so long as he does not delay unreasonably. *Section 4–2–713* relates to a buyer's damages for non-delivery or repudiation. The official comment to that section says:

"The general baseline adopted in this section uses as a yardstick the market in which the buyer would have obtained cover had he sought that relief."

We conclude that under *§ 4–2–713* a buyer may urge continued performance for a reasonable time. At the end of a reasonable period he should cover if substitute goods are readily available. If substitution is readily available and buyer does not cover within a reasonable time, damages should be based on the price at the end of that reasonable time rather than on the price when performance is due. If a valid reason exists for failure or refusal to cover, damages may be calculated from the time when performance is due.

Specifically, this means that Cargill had a reasonable time after the August 24 anticipatory repudiation to cover. This reasonable time expired on September 6 when Cargill cancelled the contract. The record does not show that Cargill covered or attempted to cover. Nothing in the record shows the continued availability or non-availability of substitute wheat. On remand the court must determine whether Cargill had a valid reason for failure or refusal to cover. If Cargill did not have a valid reason, the court's award based on the September 6 price should be reinstated. If Cargill had a valid reason for not covering, damages should be awarded on the difference between the price on September 30, the last day for performance, and the July 31 contract price.

The judgment is affirmed except for the award of damages to Cargill under the July 31 transaction. The case is remanded for determination, in the light of this opinion, of the damages recoverable by Cargill.

Each party shall bear his own costs.

* * *

There are three possible times with respect to which a buyer's market damages might be measured when his seller anticipatorily repudiates: first, when the buyer learns of the repudiation; second, a commercially reasonable time after the buyer learns of the repudiation; and third, when the contractual performance becomes due and the seller finally fails to make it. The UCC was traditionally less than ideally clear about which of these alternatives it enshrined as law. Thus § 2–713 said that the relevant market price, for purposes of determining a buyer's market-based damages, is the price "at the time when the buyer learned of the breach," subject to the provisions for proving market price that appear in § 2–723. But that later section then used quite different language to describe the relevant time, stating that when an action for anticipatory repudiation comes to trial before the time for performance has passed, then market damages shall be based on market prices prevailing "at the time when the aggrieved party learned of the repudiation." This raises interpretive uncertainty concerning the meaning of "when the buyer learned of the breach" in § 2–713. Does a buyer "learn of a breach" as soon as a seller repudiates or only later, when the time for performance arrives and the seller fails to perform?

Cargill, through a complex effort to read the relevant sections in the context of both the UCC as a whole (including its comments) and the common law rules that existed before the UCC and that the UCC sought to replace, produces a mixed answer to this question.[28] Under *Cargill*, a buyer whose seller anticipatorily repudiates may urge performance for a commercially reasonable time but, when this time expires, should cover if it is reasonable for him to do so. If cover is reasonably available and the buyer does not cover, then market damages should be based on the market price at the end of the reasonable time. So in this case, *Cargill* interprets "the time the buyer learns of the breach" to be the time that the buyer reasonably should have covered. On the other hand, if it is reasonable for the buyer not to cover, then, *Cargill* says, market damages should be based on the market price at the time that the performance was due. *Cargill* has proved quite influential. For example, the proposed 2003 amendments to the UCC (see in particular revised § 2–713(1)(b)) seemed to adopt something like the "commercially reasonable time" view.

All of this discussion of the positive law is in a way beside the point, however. The more interesting question—especially in a chapter devoted to illustrating the economic analysis of contract law—is what rule the law should adopt, what rule would be economically efficient.[29] Indeed, the "commercially reasonable time" standard itself invites this analysis, since reasonableness may plausibly be fixed according to what efficiency recommends.

Cargill's facts illustrate the general context in which economically interesting cases of anticipatory repudiation arise. The pattern is this. A

---

28.   Three considerations dominate this interpretive argument.

First, *Cargill* notes that the old common law rule measured damages from the time when performance was due (and not from the time when the buyer learned of the repudiation). It is a cannon of statutory construction that statutes in derogation of the common law shall be narrowly construed—that is, that a departure from the common law will not be accomplished by an ambiguous statute.

Second, *Cargill* observes that § 2–723 says that if an anticipatory repudiation suit comes to trial *prior* to the time when performance was due, then market-based damages will be assessed with respect to the market price "at the time when the aggrieved party learned of the repudiation." This suggests that the code knows how to select a rule other than the traditional time of performance rule when it wants to. Again, this reasoning suggests that for lawsuits that are brought to trial *after* the time of performance has passed, market-based damages should be measured using the market price at the time when performance was due.

But third, *Cargill* emphasizes that a buyer in an anticipatory repudiation case may also cover and seek cover-based rather than market-based damages. In such a case, the buyer will get cover-based damages as long as he covers within a reasonable time. Furthermore, the comments to § 2–713 on market-based damages say that the general baseline is to measure such damages with respect to the market in which the buyer would have covered had he sought that relief. And, additionally, § 2–610 allows a buyer facing an anticipatory repudiation to await performance for a commercially reasonable time only. This all suggests that if a buyer should reasonably have covered prior to the time at which the seller's performance finally became due, but did not so cover, then his market-based damages should be assessed not under the common law rule but at the time at which he should reasonably have covered.

Together, these considerations support the hybrid conclusion reported in the main text.

29.   The discussion of economic efficiency below follows Thomas Jackson, *"Anticipatory Repudiation" and the Temporal Element of Contract Law: An Economic Inquiry into Contract Damages in Cases of Prospective Non–Performance.* 31 Stanford Law Review 69 (1978).

buyer and seller agree at the present time, T1, for the buyer to purchase a widget from the seller at a set price, say $400, for delivery at some future time, T3. Such a contract, it is important to realize, involves two components: a purchase and sale of the widget, and a pair of opposite bets as to how the price of widgets (for T3 delivery) will change between T1 and T3. Specifically the seller is betting that the price of widgets will go down between T1 and T3, and the buyer is betting that the price will go up. Indeed, the seller may not have the widgets at T1, but may intend instead to acquire them on the "spot-market" at T3, and then deliver them to the buyer. Anticipatory repudiation of such contracts most commonly occurs when—at some time, T2, after T1 but before T3—the price of widgets has risen sufficiently, say to $500, that the seller wants out of her bet, i.e., wants no longer to bear the risk of a further increase in the price of widgets. The seller therefore repudiates the contract. The question at issue is whether, in such cases, the buyer's damages should be measured by the difference between the contract price and the market price (of widgets for T3 delivery) measured at T2 (the time of the repudiation) or the difference between the contract price and the market price at T3 (when the time for performance comes due and the seller fails to perform). These simple, stylized facts are set out in the table below.

Time	Market Price of Widgets for Delivery at T3
T1—Time of contracting	$400
T2—Time of repudiation	$500
T3—Time of delivery	$???

Table 6.2

A Stylized Pattern for Anticipatory Repudiation

One thing is plain from the outset. The law cannot allow the buyer to wait until T3 and then choose between basing damages on the T2 and T3 prices. Under this rule, the seller's repudiation would make damages based on the T2 price (in this case, $100) into a floor on the buyer's recovery while simultaneously allowing the buyer greater recovery following further price increases between T2 and T3: if the T3 price were smaller than $500, the buyer would chose to base damages on the T2 price; and if the T3 price were greater than $500, the buyer would choose to base damages on the T3 price. Thus under this rule, the seller's anticipatory repudiation could only increase, and never decrease, the damages she had to pay. Accordingly, no seller would ever anticipatorily repudiate under this rule. Instead, sellers would simply decide for themselves that they would breach, and not inform the buyers until they did breach. And since anticipatory repudiation by a seller serves the important purpose of putting the buyer on notice that he should prepare to cover (and perhaps cease to incur further reliance costs), the prospect of such behavior by the seller renders the rule allowing the buyer to chose his damages measure unattractive.

Therefore, the two plausible legal rules are to base the buyers' damages on the T2 market price, on the one hand, and the T3 market price, on the other. So which is the better (that is, more efficient) rule? There follow two arguments in favor of T2–based damages. Both arguments emphasize that anticipatory repudiation characteristically arises in connection with contracts that involve opposing bets on the future price of some good and ask what remedy rule best supports the efficient administration of these bets.

The first argument in favor of T2–based damages investigates what effect each damage rule has on the bets involved in contract for future delivery and asks which rule allows the parties the greatest flexibility to administer their bets as they wish. Under a T2–based damages rule, a seller's anticipatory repudiation locks in her loss on the contract and also her buyer's gain and therefore ends both parties' gambles on widget prices as of T2. By contrast, under a T3–based damages rule a seller's anticipatory repudiation causes both the seller and the buyer to retain their gambles, which will not be resolved until T3, as their initial contract specified. Neither outcome is unavoidable, however. If a buyer facing anticipatory repudiation under a T2–based remedy regime wants to re-acquire his gamble, he can do so simply by using the damages he receives from the seller at T2 to buy—also at T2 and hence at the T2 price—a new futures contract for delivery of widgets at T3 (leaving him with exactly the same gamble that his initial contract created).[30] Similarly, a seller contemplating anticipatory repudiation under a T3–based damages regime can sill get out of her gamble, in spite of the remedy rule, simply by herself buying (at T2 and hence at the T2 price) a widget for delivery at T3. (This will enable the seller to perform on her contract with the buyer at T3 at no extra cost, no matter what the T3 spot price, by delivering to the buyer the widget the seller will herself receive at T3 under the second contract.)[31]

Under either rule, therefore, both the seller and the buyer can stay in or get out of their gamble by making further contracts at T2. The choice of remedy rules thus turns at least partly on which set of further arrangements will more cheaply (and hence efficiently) allow the seller and the buyer to circumvent the consequences of the rule should they want to. In the case of the seller's anticipatory repudiation in a rising market, this criterion will likely select the rule that bases damages on the T2 price. Under this rule, this the seller can get out of the gamble simply by repudiating, and although the seller's repudiation initially forces the buyer out of the gamble also, the buyer can get back in the gamble simply by buying. Under the T3 rule, by contrast, the seller cannot get out of the

---

30. A seller who wishes to retain her gamble under a T2–based damages rule can of course do so simply by not repudiating.

31. A buyer who wishes to get out of his gamble at T2 (in order, in the typical case, to lock in his gains) can of course do so even under the T3 remedy rule, simply by selling, at T2 and hence at the T2 price, a widget for delivery at T3. If the seller has anticipatorily repudiated under a T3–based remedy regime, the buyer can use his T3 price based damages to buy the widget he needs to satisfy this contract on the T3 spot market. Of course, if the seller does not breach, the buyer can satisfy this contract using the widget that the seller delivers.

gamble save by buying her own futures contract. And there is at least some reason to believe that it will generally be transactions-costs-cheaper for the buyer to buy than for the seller to buy (since buyers are by their nature quite generally better and more experienced buyers than are sellers).

The second argument in favor of basing damages for anticipatory repudiation on the T2 price emphasizes that the alternative T3–based rule is open to exploitive manipulation by savvy buyers. Calculating market based damages using the market price at T2 charges sellers with the harm that their repudiation causes the buyer at the time it occurs. By contrast, calculating market based damages using the market price at T3 threatens to allow buyers to continue to gamble on the market at their sellers' expense.

To see this, notice that even though the T2 futures price is above the contract price, it is still possible that by T3 the spot price for the widget will have fallen below the contract price. All that the T2 price indicates, after all, is that the seller's bet has gone badly (and the buyer's has gone well) *as of T2*, and markets being what they are, the parties' fortunes may of course be reversed by T3. To illustrate this possibility and the difficulty it poses for the T3 rule, imagine that although the price of a widget for T3 delivery has risen over the life of the contract from $400 at T1 to $500 at T2, the spot market price at T3 will with probability 1/2 be $300 and with probability 1/2 be $700. (Note that this produces the T2 futures price of $500, at least in a world of risk neutral buyers and sellers.)

This circumstance creates a critical strategic asymmetry, which a savvy buyer might exploit. In particular, a buyer whose seller anticipatorily repudiates under a T3–based damages rule might not sue at T2 but instead wait to observe the spot price that actually arises at T3. If the spot price at T3 turns out to be $700, then the buyer will sue for breach of contract, citing the seller's anticipatory repudiation, and recover $300 in damages. But if the spot price at T3 turns out to be only $300, then the buyer may attempt simply to renounce the contract based on the seller's anticipatory repudiation. In this case, the buyer will of course receive no damages. But the seller will also have difficulty obtaining the $100 damages to which she would ordinarily, given the buyer's renunciation, be entitled. Having repudiated in advance, the seller will not find it easy to reclaim the benefits of her contract when, in spite of the early bad turn, she turns out to have won her bet. If the buyer can successfully exploit this asymmetry to gamble on his seller's account, it turns out that although his damages at the time of the seller's repudiation—T2—are only 100 (namely the $500 T2 market price minus the $400 contract price), the T3–based damages rule is worth $150 to the buyer (1/2 * $(700 − 400) + 1/2 * $0).

Insofar as T3–based damages allow buyers to engage in such strategic manipulation, they are inefficient. This is easy to see by imagining that at T2 the spot price for the widget is $510. In such a case, there exist people in the market who value the widget at T2 more highly than the buyer values the right at T2 to acquire it at T3. Accordingly, the efficient result is for the seller to breach (anticipatorily to repudiate) and to deliver the widget to some third party for $510 and then to pay the buyer damages of $100, enabling the buyer to acquire a new futures contract for delivery of a widget at T3. This is an efficient breach—it places the widget in the hands of the highest valuer. But the $510 spot price will support a damages payment of no more than $110, whereas (at least if can employ the trick described above) the T3 damages rule is worth $150 to the buyer, so that the seller will be made unable afford to breach, even though efficiency recommends it.[32]

Of course, adopting the T3–based damages rule does not *require* allowing buyers to manipulate their sellers in this way. The law might instead demand that buyers assert their claims for anticipatory repudiation at T2, when the repudiation occurs (even if damages aren't fixed until later), or abandon these claims and, with them, the possibility of renouncing the contract (free from liability for breach) at T3. Indeed, something like the language of UCC § 2–610, which allows buyers facing anticipatory repudiation to encourage performance for only a commercially reasonable time might accomplish this result, because it is surely not commercially reasonable for a buyer to delay seeking damages for repudiation only in order to exploit a strategic opportunity to gamble at his repudiating seller's expense. But this is far from a bright-line rule, and even if such an approach can reduce buyers' abilities to manipulate a T3–based damages regime, it probably cannot eliminate such opportunities, or the associated inefficiency, entirely.

Accordingly, a T3–based remedies regime will tend to deter sellers in contracts for future delivery from getting out of losing bets when it would be efficient for them to do so: it makes anticipatory repudiation ineffective as a means for sellers to get out of their bets, and it exposes sellers who do repudiate to excessive remedial obligations, which discourage them from abandoning their bets even when abandonment would be efficient. A T2 rule, by contrast, makes it easy for sellers to abandon their bad bets and gives them efficient incentives to make the abandonment decision. This is the core of the case in favor of the T2–based damages rule for anticipatory repudiation.

The argument is persuasive, but it rests on an assumption that bears brief further reflection. The argument assumes that the true size of a buyer's loss from anticipatory repudiation, at T2 (the moment of the repudiation), is the T2 contract—market differential. More precisely, the case for T2–based damages assumes that the T2 contract-market differential accurately reports the buyer's expected loss—that the futures price at T2 accurately reflects the best estimate of the actual T3 spot price, and in particular that sellers cannot outguess the market at T2. If this assumption is false, so that sellers of futures in rising markets can know when futures

---

32. Of course, even under the T3 damages rule, the seller could always sell to the third party on the spot market and then itself buy a new contract for delivery of the widget to the buyer at T3 on the T2 futures market. But the seller will be able to do this only if her transactions costs in buying the new futures contract are small enough (in the example, less than $10). And as the last argument suggested the costs of buying born by those who usually sell will often be quite high.

prices do not yet reflect the full rise in widget prices that will have happened by T3, then the T2–based damages rule will be undercompensatory. In this case, sellers will breach only when the T2–futures price underreports the damages that buyers will have suffered by T3, and they will perform otherwise. In other words, if sellers know, by T2, how their buyers' gambles will have turned out at T3, then the T2 rule allows them costlessly to deny their buyers the benefits of the second half of the buyers' winning gambles.[33] This scenario, insofar as it actually materializes, makes the T3–based damages rule more appealing again. But it is important to note that the scenario is improbable—it imagines not just that sellers can beat the market (which people can rarely do) but also that they become able to beat the market between T1 and T2.

---

33.   Here it is important that, for reasons that are explained below, buyers will generally be unable to force anticipatorily repudiating sellers specifically to perform their contracts. The goods at issue, which are generally traded on thick markets, are the opposite of unique.

CHAPTER 7

REMEDIES SPECIFIED BY THE PARTIES

The law's preference for the expectation remedy, it is commonly said, is only a default rule: The parties to contracts may, if they wish it, agree to substitute an alternative remedy that they prefer, and such agreements will (within certain limits) be enforced to govern the legal treatment of future breaches. The most prominent among such agreements establish liquidated damages clauses, so-called because they liquidate promisors' general obligations to secure their promisees' contractual expectations in favor of a specific obligation to pay a specified sum.

There is much in this view, to be sure: sophisticated parties certainly do commonly specify what remedies they will owe one another in case they breach their contracts, and liquidated damages clauses are often enforced. Moreover, there are many reasons for parties to adopt such clauses. Because liquidated damages are easier to calculate than the default expectation remedy, liquidated damages clauses can dramatically reduce the transactions costs that the parties must bear in resolving disputes following a breach by one of them. Moreover, because liquidated damages are not just cheaper to implement than the expectation remedy but more predictable as well, liquidated damages also increase the predictability of contracting (which is appealing to parties, who are generally risk averse). These reductions in the expected costs of administering an agreement increase the contractual surplus that is available for the parties to divide, so that liquidated damages clauses are often in both parties' interests, *ex ante*,[1] including even in cases in which, after a breach, one party or the other would prefer a contest over the size of the expectation remedy over a mechanical award of liquidated damages. Finally, liquidated damages clauses can also be efficient risk shifting devices, as Section 7.2.B below will illustrate.

Accordingly, a sound general case for enforcing liquidated damages provisions can be made, and the law appears to promote (or at least to

---

1. Of course, the parties must set the costs of drafting a liquidated damages clause—the cost of identifying the appropriate level of liquidated damages, coming to agreement on this level, and crafting language to implement this agreement—against these benefits. These costs perhaps explain why liquidated damages clauses are not ubiquitous, especially among unsophisticated parties, for whom the drafting costs are likely greatest. Moreover, whereas the parties must bear all the costs of drafting liquidated damages clauses themselves, some of the dispute-resolution costs that liquidated damages clauses offset would, because of the public subsidization of courts, be externalized to others. This suggests that, all else equal, liquidated damages clauses are inefficiently undersupplied by contracting parties.

respect) efforts by contracting parties to draft such clauses by rendering them (at least generically) enforceable. Certainly this is the dominant view of liquidated damages in modern contract law. But this standard view should not be accepted too readily. A variety of doctrines nip at the edges of the basic principle that liquidated damages provisions are enforceable, and these doctrines together impose significant limits on enforceability. Moreover, these limits suggest that, at least as a conceptual matter, it is a mistake to interpret the law's respect for such liquidated damages clauses as it does enforce as revealing that the expectation remedy is a default rule only. At least as a conceptual matter, a case for the mandatory character of the expectation remedy can still be made.

7.1 ENFORCING LIQUIDATED DAMAGE CLAUSES

Restatement 2d of Contracts

§ 356 Liquidated Damages and Penalties

(1) Damages for breach by either party may be liquidated in the agreement but only at an amount that is reasonable in the light of the anticipated or actual loss caused by the breach and the difficulties of proof of loss. A term fixing unreasonably large liquidated damages is unenforceable on grounds of public policy as a penalty.

(2) A term in a bond providing for an amount of money as a penalty for non-occurrence of the condition of the bond is unenforceable on grounds of public policy to the extent that the amount exceeds the loss caused by such non-occurrence.

Comments & Illustrations

Comment a. Liquidated damages or penalty. The parties to a contract may effectively provide in advance the damages that are to be payable in the event of breach as long as the provision does not disregard the principle of compensation. The enforcement of such provisions for liquidated damages saves the time of courts, juries, parties and witnesses and reduces the expense of litigation. This is especially important if the amount in controversy is small. However, the parties to a contract are not free to provide a penalty for its breach. The central objective behind the system of contract remedies is compensatory, not punitive. Punishment of a promisor for having broken his promise has no justification on either economic or other grounds and a term providing such a penalty is unenforceable on grounds of public policy. See Chapter 8. The rest of the agreement remains enforceable, however, under the rule stated in § 184(1), and the remedies for breach are determined by the rules stated in this Chapter. See Illustration 1. A term that fixes an unreasonably small amount as damages may be unenforceable as unconscionable. See § 208. As to the liquidation of damages and modification or limitation of remedies in contracts of sale, see Uniform Commercial Code §§ 2–718, 2–719.

Comment b. Test of penalty. Under the test stated in Subsection (1), two factors combine in determining whether an amount of money fixed as damages is so unreasonably large as to be a penalty. The first factor is the anticipated or actual loss caused by the breach. The amount fixed is reasonable to the extent that it approximates the actual loss that has resulted from the particular breach, even though it may not approximate the loss that might have been anticipated under other possible breaches. See Illustration 2. Furthermore, the amount fixed is reasonable to the extent that it approximates the loss anticipated at the time of the making of the contract, even though it may not approximate the actual loss. See Illustration 3. The second factor is the difficulty of proof of loss. The greater the difficulty either of proving that loss has occurred or of establishing its amount with the requisite certainty (see § 351), the easier it is to show that the amount fixed is reasonable. To the extent that there is uncertainty as to the harm, the estimate of the court or jury may not accord with the principle of compensation any more than does the advance estimate of the parties. A determination whether the amount fixed is a penalty turns on a combination of these two factors. If the difficulty of proof of loss is great, considerable latitude is allowed in the approximation of anticipated or actual harm. If, on the other hand, the difficulty of proof of loss is slight, less latitude is allowed in that approximation. If, to take an extreme case, it is clear that no loss at all has occurred, a provision fixing a substantial sum as damages is unenforceable. See Illustration 4.

Illustrations:

1.   A and B sign a written contract under which A is to act in a play produced by B for a ten week season for $4,000. A term provides that "if either party shall fail to perform as agreed in any respect he will pay $10,000 as liquidated damages and not as a penalty." A leaves the play before the last week to take another job. The play is sold out for that week and A is replaced by a suitable understudy. The amount fixed is unreasonable in the light of both the anticipated and the actual loss and, in spite of the use of the words "liquidated damages," the term provides for a penalty and is unenforceable on grounds of public policy. The rest of the agreement is enforceable (§ 184(1)), and B's remedies for A's breach are governed by the rules stated in this Chapter.

2.   A, B and C form a partnership to practice veterinary medicine in a town for ten years. In the partnership agreement, each promises that if, on the termination of the partnership, the practice is continued by the other two members, he will not practice veterinary medicine in the same town during its continuance up to a maximum of three years. A term provides that for breach of this duty "he shall forfeit $50,000 to be collected by the others as damages." A leaves the partnership, and the practice is continued by B and C. A immediately begins to practice veterinary

medicine in the same town. The loss actually caused to B and C is difficult of proof and $50,000 is not an unreasonable estimate of it. Even though $50,000 may be unreasonable in relation to the loss that might have resulted in other circumstances, it is not unreasonable in relation to the actual loss. Therefore, the term does not provide for a penalty and its enforcement is not precluded on grounds of public policy. See Illustration 14 to § 188.

3. A contracts to build a grandstand for B's race track for $1,000,000 by a specified date and to pay $1,000 a day for every day's delay in completing it. A delays completion for ten days. If $1,000 is not unreasonable in the light of the anticipated loss and the actual loss to B is difficult to prove, A's promise is not a term providing for a penalty and its enforcement is not precluded on grounds of public policy.

4. The facts being otherwise as stated in Illustration 3, B is delayed for a month in obtaining permission to operate his race track so that it is certain that A's delay of ten days caused him no loss at all. Since the actual loss to B is not difficult to prove, A's promise is a term providing for a penalty and is unenforceable on grounds of public policy.

Comment c. Disguised penalties. Under the rule stated in this Section, the validity of a term providing for damages depends on the effect of that term as interpreted according to the rules stated in Chapter 9. Neither the parties' actual intention as to its validity nor their characterization of the term as one for liquidated damages or a penalty is significant in determining whether the term is valid. Sometimes parties attempt to disguise a provision for a penalty by using language that purports to make payment of the amount an alternative performance under the contract, that purports to offer a discount for prompt performance, or that purports to place a valuation on property to be delivered. Although the parties may in good faith contract for alternative performances and fix discounts or valuations, a court will look to the substance of the agreement to determine whether this is the case or whether the parties have attempted to disguise a provision for a penalty that is unenforceable under this Section. In determining whether a contract is one for alternative performances, the relative value of the alternatives may be decisive.

Illustration:

5. A contracts to build a house for B for $50,000 by a specified date or in the alternative to pay B $1,000 a week during any period of delay. A delays completion for ten days. If $1,000 a week is unreasonable in the light of both the anticipated and actual loss, A's promise to pay $1,000 a week is, in spite of its form, a term providing for a penalty and is unenforceable on grounds of public policy.

Comment d. Related types of provisions. This Section does not purport to cover the wide variety of provisions used by parties to control the remedies available to them for breach of contract. A term that fixes as damages an amount that is unreasonably small does not come within the rule stated in this Section, but a court may refuse to enforce it as unconscionable under the rule stated in § 208. A mere recital of the harm that may occur as a result of a breach of contract does not come within the rule stated in this Section, but may increase damages by making that harm foreseeable under the rule stated § 351. As to the effect of a contract provision on the right to equitable relief, see Comment a to § 359. As to the effect of a term requiring the occurrence of a condition where forfeiture would result, see § 229. Although attorneys' fees are not generally awarded to the winning party, if the parties provide for the award of such fees the court will award a sum that it considers to be reasonable. If, however, the parties specify the amount of such fees, the provision is subject to the test stated in this Section.

Comment e. Penalties in bonds. Bonds often fix a flat sum as a penalty for non-occurrence of the condition of the bond. A term providing for a penalty is not unenforceable in its entirety but only to the extent that it exceeds the loss caused by the non-occurrence of the condition.

Illustration:

6. A executes a bond obligating himself to pay B $10,000, on condition that the bond shall be void, however, if C, who is B's cashier, shall properly account for all money entrusted to him. C defaults to the extent of $500. A's promise is unenforceable on grounds of public policy to the extent that it exceeds the actual loss, $500.

Uniform Commercial Code

§ 2–718 Liquidation or Limitation of Damages; Deposits

(1) Damages for breach by either party may be liquidated in the agreement but only at an amount which is reasonable in the light of the anticipated or actual harm caused by the breach, the difficulties of proof of loss, and the inconvenience or nonfeasibility of otherwise obtaining an adequate remedy. A term fixing unreasonably large liquidated damages is void as a penalty.

(2) Where the seller justifiably withholds delivery of goods because of the buyer's breach, the buyer is entitled to restitution of any amount by which the sum of his payments exceeds

(a) the amount to which the seller is entitled by virtue of terms liquidating the seller's damages in accordance with subsection (1), or

(b) in the absence of such terms, twenty per cent of the value of the total performance for which the buyer is obligated under the contract or $500, whichever is smaller.

(3) The buyer's right to restitution under subsection (2) is subject to offset to the extent that the seller establishes

(a) a right to recover damages under the provisions of this Article other than subsection (1), and

(b) the amount or value of any benefits received by the buyer directly or indirectly by reason of the contract.

(4) Where a seller has received payment in goods their reasonable value or the proceeds of their resale shall be treated as payments for the purposes of subsection (2); but if the seller has notice of the buyer's breach before reselling goods received in part performance, his resale is subject to the conditions laid down in this Article on resale by an aggrieved seller (Section 2–706).

Official Comment

Prior Uniform Statutory Provision: None.

Purposes:

1.   Under subsection (1) liquidated damage clauses are allowed where the amount involved is reasonable in the light of the circumstances of the case. The subsection sets forth explicitly the elements to be considered in determining the reasonableness of a liquidated damage clause. A term fixing unreasonably large liquidated damages is expressly made void as a penalty. An unreasonably small amount would be subject to similar criticism and might be stricken under the section on unconscionable contracts or clauses.

2.   Subsection (2) refuses to recognize a forfeiture unless the amount of the payment so forfeited represents a reasonable liquidation of damages as determined under subsection (1). A special exception is made in the case of small amounts (20% of the price or $500, whichever is smaller) deposited as security. No distinction is made between cases in which the payment is to be applied on the price and those in which it is intended as security for performance. Subsection (2) is applicable to any deposit or down or part payment. In the case of a deposit or turn in of goods resold before the breach, the amount actually received on the resale is to be viewed as the deposit rather than the amount allowed the buyer for the trade in. However, if the seller knows of the breach prior to the resale of the goods turned in, he must make reasonable efforts to realize their true value, and this is assured by requiring him to comply with the conditions laid down in the section on resale by an aggrieved seller.

Vines v. Orchard Hills

Supreme Court of Connecticut, 1980.
435 A.2d 1022.

This case concerns the right of purchasers of real property, after their own default, to recover moneys paid at the time of execution of a valid contract of sale. The plaintiffs, Euel D. Vines and his wife Etta Vines, contracted, on July 11, 1973, to buy Unit No. 10, Orchard Hills Condominium, New Canaan, from the defendant Orchard Hills, Inc. for $78,800. On or before that date, they had paid the defendant $7880 as a down payment toward the purchase. Alleging that the sale of the property was never consummated, the plaintiffs sought to recover their down payment. The trial court, *I. Levine, J.,* overruled the defendant's demurrer to the plaintiffs' amended complaint; subsequently, after a hearing, the trial court, *Novack, J.,* rendered judgment for the plaintiffs for $7880 plus interest. The defendant's appeal maintains that its demurrer should have been sustained, that its liquidated damages clause should have been enforced, and that evidence of the value of the property at the time of the trial should have been excluded.

The facts underlying this litigation are straightforward and undisputed. When the purchasers contracted to buy their condominium in July, 1973, they paid $7880, a sum which the contract of sale designated as liquidated damages.[1] The purchasers decided not to take title to the condominium because Euel D. Vines was transferred by his employer to New Jersey; the Vines so informed the seller by a letter dated January 4, 1974. There has never been any claim that the seller has failed, in any respect, to conform to his obligations under the contract, nor does the complaint allege that the purchasers are legally excused from their performance under the contract. In short, it is the purchasers and not the seller whose breach precipitated the present cause of action.

In the proceedings below, the purchasers established that the value of the condominium that they had agreed to buy for $78,800 in 1973 had, by the time of the trial in 1979, a fair market value of $160,000. The trial court relied on this figure to conclude that, because the seller had gained what it characterized as a windfall of approximately $80,000, the purchasers were entitled to recover their down payment of $7880. Neither the purchasers nor the seller proffered any evidence at the trial to show the market value of the condominium at the time of the purchasers' breach of their contract or the damages sustained by the seller as a result of that breach.

The seller's principal argument on this appeal is that the trial court improperly disregarded the parties' valid liquidated damages clause. That claim is pursued both by a renewal of the seller's position that the purchasers' complaint was demurrable and by an argument on the merits of the evidence presented at the trial. As to the demurrer, now denominated a motion to strike by Practice Book, 1978, § 152, we find no error. Whether a party may recover payments made despite its own default and despite its agreement to a liquidated damages clause is a question that presents issues of fact which transcend the legal sufficiency of the com-

---

1. Paragraph 9 of the contract of sale provided: "DEFAULT: In the event Purchaser fails to perform any of the obligations herein imposed on the Purchaser, the Seller performing all obligations herein imposed on the Seller, the Seller shall retain all sums of money paid under this Contract, as liquidated damages, and all rights and liabilities of the parties hereto shall be at an end."

plaint, as the trial itself demonstrated. The trial court was, however, in error in its conclusion that the evidence before it was sufficient to sustain a judgment in favor of the purchasers.

The ultimate issue on this appeal is the enforceability of a liquidated damages clause as a defense to a claim of restitution by purchasers in default on a land sale contract. Although the parties, both in the trial court and here, have focused on the liquidated damages clause per se, we must first consider when, if ever, purchasers who are themselves in breach of a valid contract of sale may affirmatively invoke the assistance of judicial process to recover back moneys paid to, and withheld by, their seller.

I

The right of a contracting party, despite his default, to seek restitution for benefits conferred and allegedly unjustly retained has been much disputed in the legal literature and in the case law. Although earlier cases often refused to permit a party to bring an action that could be said to be based on his own breach[,] many of the more recent cases support restitution in order to prevent unjust enrichment and to avoid forfeiture.

In this state, at the turn of the century, in *Pierce v. Staub, 78 Conn. 459, 466 (1906)*, this court acknowledged the equitable claim of a purchaser in breach to recover moneys paid under a contract to purchase real property. *Pierce* v. *Staub* is distinguishable from the case before us, because the court there found (p. 465) that the parties had, after the buyer's breach, rescinded the contracts in question. Apart from *Pierce* v. *Staub*, we have never directly decided whether a purchaser of real estate may, despite his breach, recover payments made to his seller. But *Pierce* v. *Staub* is an impressive, and an impressively early, guidepost toward permitting such a cause of action. The court's narrow reliance on the possibly artificial conclusion of mutual rescission should not obscure the breadth of its language deploring forfeiture. *Pierce* v. *Staub, supra, 466*. We therefore conclude that a purchaser whose breach is not willful has a restitutionary claim to recover moneys paid that unjustly enrich his seller. In this case, no one has alleged that the purchasers' breach, arising out of a transfer to a more distant place of employment, should be deemed to have been willful. The trial court was therefore not in error in initially overruling the seller's demurrer and entertaining the purchasers' cause of action.

II

The purchaser's right to recover in restitution requires the purchaser to establish that the seller has been unjustly enriched. The purchaser must show more than that the contract has come to an end and that the seller retains moneys paid pursuant to the contract. To prove unjust enrichment, in the ordinary case, the purchaser, because he is the party in breach, must prove that the damages suffered by his seller are less than the moneys received from the purchaser. It may not be easy for the purchaser to prove the extent of the seller's damages, it may even be strategically advantageous for the seller to come forward with relevant evidence of the losses he has incurred and may expect to incur on account of the buyer's breach. Nonetheless, only if the breaching party satisfies his burden of proof that the innocent party has sustained a net gain may a claim for unjust enrichment be sustained. Dobbs, Remedies § 12.14 (1973); 1 Palmer, Restitution § 5.4 (1978).

In the case before us, the parties themselves stipulated in the contract of sale that the purchasers' down payment of 10 percent of the purchase price represents the damages that would be likely to flow from the purchasers' breach. The question then becomes whether the purchasers have demonstrated the seller's unjust enrichment in the face of the liquidated damages clause to which they agreed.

This is not a suitable occasion for detailed review of the checkered history of liquidated damages clauses. Despite the judicial resistance that such clauses have encountered in the past[,] this court has recognized the principle that there are circumstances that justify private agreements to supplant judicially determined remedies for breach of contract. This court has however refused to enforce an otherwise valid liquidated damages clause upon a finding that no damages whatsoever ensued from the particular breach of contract that actually occurred. *Norwalk Door Closer Co. v. Eagle Lock & Screw Co., 153 Conn. 681, 689 (1966).*

Most of the litigation concerning liquidated damages clauses arises in the context of an affirmative action by the party injured by breach to enforce the clause in order to recover the amount therein stipulated. In such cases, the burden of persuasion about the enforceability of the clause naturally rests with its proponent. See, e.g., *Norwalk Door Closer Co. v. Eagle Lock & Screw Co., supra, 688.* In the case before us, by contrast, where the plaintiffs are themselves in default, the plaintiffs bear the burden of showing that the clause is invalid and unenforceable. It is not unreasonable in these circumstances to presume that a liquidated damages clause that is appropriately limited in amount bears a reasonable relationship to the damages that the seller has actually suffered. See Restatement (Second), Contracts § 388, esp. subsection (2) (Tent. Draft No. 14, 1979).[2] The seller's damages, as Professor Palmer points out, include not only his expectation damages suffered through loss of his bargain, and his incidental damages such as broker's commissions, but also less quantifiable costs arising out of retention of real property beyond the time of the originally contemplated sale. 1 Palmer, Restitution §§ 5.4, 5.8 (1978). See also Goetz & Scott, supra, 577. A liquidated damages clause allowing the seller to

---

2. Section 388 of the Restatement (Second) of Contracts (Tent. Draft No. 14, 1979) provides: "RESTITUTION IN FAVOR OF PARTY IN BREACH.

(1) Subject to the rule stated in Subsection (2), if a party justifiably refuses to perform on the ground that his remaining duties of performance have been discharged by the other party's breach, the party in breach is entitled to restitution for any benefit that he has conferred on the injured party by way of part performance or reliance.

(2) To the extent that, under the manifested assent of the parties, a party's performance is to be retained in the case of breach, that party is not entitled to restitution if the value of the performance as liquidated damages is reasonable in the light of the anticipated or actual loss caused by the breach and the difficulties of proof of loss."

retain 10 percent of the contract price as earnest money is presumptively a reasonable allocation of the risks associated with default.

The presumption of validity that attaches to a clause liquidating the seller's damages at 10 percent of the contract price in the event of the purchaser's unexcused nonperformance is, like most other presumptions, rebuttable. The purchaser, despite his default, is free to prove that the contract, or any part thereof, was the product of fraud or mistake or unconscionability. Cf. *Hamm v. Taylor, 180 Conn. 491, 495–96(1980).* In the alternative, the purchaser is free to offer evidence that his breach in fact caused the seller no damages or damages substantially less than the amount stipulated as liquidated damages. See *Norwalk Door Closer Co. v. Eagle Lock & Screw Co., supra, 689.*

The trial court concluded that the plaintiff purchasers had successfully invoked the principle of *Norwalk Door Closer Co.* v. *Eagle Lock & Screw Co.* by presenting evidence of increase in the value of the real property between the date of the contract of sale and the date of the trial. That conclusion was in error. The relevant time at which to measure the seller's damages is the time of breach. Benefits to the seller that are attributable to a rising market subsequent to breach rightfully accrue to the seller. There was no evidence before the court to demonstrate that the seller was not injured at the time of the purchasers' breach by their failure then to consummate the contract. Neither the seller's status as a developer of a condominium project nor the absence of willfulness on the part of the purchasers furnishes a justification for disregarding the liquidated damages clause, although these factors may play some role in the ultimate determination of whether the seller was in fact unjustly enriched by the down payment he retained.

Because the availability of, and the limits on, restitutionary claims by a plaintiff in default have not previously been clearly spelled out in our cases, it is appropriate to afford to the purchasers herein another opportunity to proffer evidence to substantiate their claim. What showing the purchasers must make cannot be spelled out with specificity in view of the sparsity of the present record. The purchasers may be able to demonstrate that the condominium could, at the time of their breach, have been resold at a price sufficiently higher than their contract price to obviate any loss of profits and to compensate the seller for any incidental and consequential damages. Alternatively, the purchasers may be able to present evidence of unconscionability or of excuse, to avoid the applicability of the liquidated damages clause altogether. The plaintiffs' burden of proof is not an easy one to sustain, but they are entitled to their day in court.

There is error, the judgment is set aside, and the case is remanded for further proceedings in conformity with this opinion.

In this opinion the other judges concurred.

* * *

As these materials clearly reveal, the law is willing to enforce liquidated damages clauses—at least as long as the damages that they contemplate constitute a fair estimate of contractual expectations that are difficult to value with precision following a breach. Liquidated damages clauses, in other words, are an approved method for reducing the transactions costs associated with calculating a disappointed promisee's actual expectation remedy. Finally, *Vines* illustrates the operation of liquidated damages clauses in the core case, but with a twist. At least in Connecticut, when a promisee wishes to assert a liquidated damages clause against his breaching promisor, he bears the burden of proving the clause's validity; but when a breaching promisor wishes to avoid a liquidated damages clause this burden shifts, and she must prove it invalid.

7.2   LIMITS ON ENFORCEABILITY

Although liquidated damages clauses are as a general matter enforceable, there are two exceptions to this general rule. The first, which is doctrinally clearer and in practice more prominent, is that over-liquidated damages clauses—which function to impose a penalty for breach—are invalid. The second, which is doctrinally less clear and also in practice less prominent, is that certain under-liquidated damages clauses—those that function not just to limit a promisee's contractual remedies but also to leave the promisee with no effective contractual remedy at all—are also invalid.

7.2.A   OVER-LIQUIDATED DAMAGES AND PENALTY CLAUSES

The first and clearest case in which party-selected remedies are unenforceable is when they serve not to identify the value that a promisee places on performance—not to help calculate a promisee's contractual expectations—but rather, by increasing the burdens a breach imposes on a promisor, to compel performance. Such liquidated damages, which overcompensate a disappointed promisee, making him better off than performance would have done, are disapproved by the law. They are labeled penalty clauses, and held unenforceable.

Lake River Corp. v. Carborundum Co.

United States Court of Appeals for the Seventh Circuit, 1985.
769 F.2d 1284.

■ POSNER, CIRCUIT JUDGE. This diversity suit between Lake River Corporation and Carborundum Company requires us to consider questions of Illinois commercial law, and in particular to explore the fuzzy line between penalty clauses and liquidated-damages clauses.

Carborundum manufactures "Ferro Carbo," an abrasive powder used in making steel. To serve its Midwestern customers better, Carborundum made a contract with Lake River by which the latter agreed to provide distribution services in its warehouse in Illinois. Lake River would receive Ferro Carbo in bulk from Carborundum, "bag" it, and ship the bagged product to Carborundum's customers. The Ferro Carbo would remain Carborundum's property until delivered to the customers.

Carborundum insisted that Lake River install a new bagging system to handle the contract. In order to be sure of being able to recover the cost of the new system ($89,000) and make a profit of 20 percent of the contract price, Lake River insisted on the following minimum-quantity guarantee:

> In consideration of the special equipment [i.e., the new bagging system] to be acquired and furnished by LAKE–RIVER for handling the product, CARBORUNDUM shall, during the initial three-year term of this Agreement, ship to LAKE–RIVER for bagging a minimum quantity of [22,500 tons]. If, at the end of the three-year term, this minimum quantity shall not have been shipped, LAKE–RIVER shall invoice CARBORUNDUM at the then prevailing rates for the difference between the quantity bagged and the minimum guaranteed.

If Carborundum had shipped the full minimum quantity that it guaranteed, it would have owed Lake River roughly $533,000 under the contract.

After the contract was signed in 1979, the demand for domestic steel, and with it the demand for Ferro Carbo, plummeted, and Carborundum failed to ship the guaranteed amount. When the contract expired late in 1982, Carborundum had shipped only 12,000 of the 22,500 tons it had guaranteed. Lake River had bagged the 12,000 tons and had billed Carborundum for this bagging, and Carborundum had paid, but by virtue of the formula in the minimum-guarantee clause Carborundum still owed Lake River $241,000—the contract price of $533,000 if the full amount of Ferro Carbo had been shipped, minus what Carborundum had paid for the bagging of the quantity it had shipped.

When Lake River demanded payment of this amount, Carborundum refused, on the ground that the formula imposed a penalty. At the time, Lake River had in its warehouse 500 tons of bagged Ferro Carbo, having a market value of $269,000, which it refused to release unless Carborundum paid the $241,000 due under the formula. Lake River did offer to sell the bagged product and place the proceeds in escrow until its dispute with Carborundum over the enforceability of the formula was resolved, but Carborundum rejected the offer and trucked in bagged Ferro Carbo from the East to serve its customers in Illinois, at an additional cost of $31,000.

Lake River brought this suit for $241,000, which it claims as liquidated damages. Carborundum counterclaimed for the value of the bagged Ferro Carbo when Lake River impounded it and the additional cost of serving the customers affected by the impounding. The theory of the counterclaim is that the impounding was a conversion, and not as Lake River contends the assertion of a lien. The district judge, after a bench trial, gave judgment for both parties. Carborundum ended up roughly $42,000 to the good: $269,000 + $31,000 – $24100 – $17,000, the last figure representing prejudgment interest on Lake River's damages. (We have rounded off all dollar figures to the nearest thousand.) Both parties have appealed.

The only issue that is not one of damages is whether Lake River had a valid lien on the bagged Ferro Carbo that it refused to ship to Carborundum's customers—that, indeed, it holds in its warehouse to this day. Although Ferro Carbo does not deteriorate with age, the domestic steel industry remains in the doldrums and the product is worth less than it was in 1982 when Lake River first withheld it. If Lake River did not have a valid lien on the product, then it converted it, and must pay Carborundum the $269,000 that the Ferro Carbo was worth back then.

It might seem that if the minimum-guarantee clause was a penalty clause and hence unenforceable, the lien could not be valid, and therefore that we should discuss the penalty issue first. But this is not correct. If the contractual specification of damages is invalid, Lake River still is entitled to any actual damages caused by Carborundum's breach of contract in failing to deliver the minimum amount of Ferro Carbo called for by the contract. The issue is whether an entitlement to damages, large or small, entitles the victim of the breach to assert a lien on goods that are in its possession though they belong to the other party.

Lake River has not been very specific about the type of lien it asserts. We think it best described as a form of artisan's lien, the "lien of the bailee, who does work upon or adds materials to chattels." *Restatement of Security § 61, comment on* clause (a), at p. 165 (1941). Lake River was the bailee of the Ferro Carbo that Carborundum delivered to it, and it did work on the Ferro Carbo—bagging it, and also storing it (storage is a service, too). If Carborundum had refused to pay for the services that Lake River performed on the Ferro Carbo delivered to it, then Lake River would have had a lien on the Ferro Carbo in its possession, to coerce payment. Cf. *National Bank of Joliet v. Bergeron Cadillac, Inc., 66 Ill. 2d 140, 143–44 (1977).* But in fact, when Lake River impounded the bagged Ferro Carbo, Carborundum had paid in full for all bagging and storage services that Lake River had performed on Ferro Carbo shipped to it by Carborundum. The purpose of impounding was to put pressure on Carborundum to pay for services not performed, Carborundum having failed to ship the Ferro Carbo on which those services would have been performed.

Unlike a contractor who, having done the work contracted for without having been paid, may find himself in a box, owing his employees or suppliers money he does not have—money he was counting on from his customer—Lake River was the victim of a breach of a portion of the contract that remained entirely unexecuted on either side. Carborundum had not shipped the other 10,500 tons, as promised; but on the other hand Lake River had not had to bag those 10,500 tons, as it had promised. It is not as if Lake River had bagged those tons, incurring heavy costs that it expected to recoup from Carborundum, and then Carborundum had said, "Sorry, we won't pay you; go ahead and sue us."

A lien is strong medicine; it clogs up markets, as the facts of this case show. Its purpose is to provide an effective self-help remedy for one who has done work in expectation of payment and then is not paid. The vulnerable position of such a person gives rise to "the artisan's privilege of holding the balance for *work done in the past." United States v. Toys of the World Club, Inc., 288 F.2d 89, 94 (2d Cir. 1961)* (Friendly, J.) (emphasis added). A lien is thus a device for preventing unjust enrichment—not for forcing the other party to accede to your view of a contract dispute. "The right to retain possession of the property to enforce a possessory lien continues until such time as the charges for such materials, labor and services are paid." *Bull v. Mitchell, 114 Ill. App. 3d 177, 181 (1983)*; cf. Ill. Rev. Stat. ch. 82, § 40. Since here the charges were paid before the lien was asserted, the lien was no good.

Lake River tries to compare its position to that of a conventional lien creditor by pointing out that it made itself particularly vulnerable to a breach of contract by buying specialized equipment at Carborundum's insistence, to the tune of $89,000, before performance under the contract began. It says it insisted on the minimum guarantee in order to be sure of being able to amortize this equipment over a large enough output of bagging services to make the investment worthwhile. But the equipment was not completely useless for other contracts—Lake River having in fact used it for another contract; it was not the major cost of fulfilling the contract; and Lake River received almost $300,000 during the term of the contract, thus enabling it to amortize much of the cost of the special equipment. Although Lake River may have lost money on the contract (but as yet there is no proof it did), it was not in the necessitous position of a contractor who completes his performance without receiving a dime and then is told by his customer to sue for the price. The recognition of a lien in such a case is based on policies akin to those behind the rule that a contract modification procured by duress will not be enforced. See, e.g., *Selmer Co. v. Blakeslee–Midwest Co., 704 F.2d 924 (7th Cir. 1983)*. When as a practical matter the legal remedy may be inadequate because it operates too slowly, self-help is allowed. But we can find no case recognizing a lien on facts like these, no ground for thinking that the Illinois Supreme Court would be the first court to recognize such a lien if this case were presented to it, and no reason to believe that the recognition of such a lien would be a good thing. It would impede the marketability of goods without responding to any urgent need of creditors.

Conrow v. Little, 115 N.Y. 387, 393 (1889), on which Lake River relies heavily because the lien allowed in that case extended to "money expended in the preparation of instrumentalities," is not in point. The plaintiffs, dealers in paper, had made extensive deliveries to the defendants for which they had received no payment. See *id. at 390–91, 22 N.E. at 346*. If Lake River had bagged several thousand tons of Ferro Carbo without being paid anything, it would have had a lien on the Ferro Carbo; and maybe—if *Conrow* is good law in Illinois, a question we need not try to answer—the lien would have included not only the contract price for the Ferro Carbo that Lake River had bagged but also the unreimbursed, unsalvageable cost of the special bagging system that Lake River had installed. But that is not this case. Carborundum was fully paid up and Lake River has made no effort to show how much if any money it stood to lose because the bagging system was not fully amortized. The only purpose of the lien was to collect damages which would have been unrelated to—and certainly exceeded—the investment in the bagging system.

It is no answer that the bagging system should be presumed to have been amortized equally over the life of the contract, and therefore to have been only half amortized when Carborundum broke the contract. Amortization is an accounting device; it need not reflect cash flows. There is no evidence that when the contract was broken, Lake River was out of pocket a cent in respect of the bagging system, especially when we consider that the bagging system was still usable, and was used to fulfill another contract.

The hardest issue in the case is whether the formula in the minimum-guarantee clause imposes a penalty for breach of contract or is merely an effort to liquidate damages. Deep as the hostility to penalty clauses runs in the common law, see Loyd, *Penalties and Forfeitures*, 29 Harv. L. Rev. 117 (1915), we still might be inclined to question, if we thought ourselves free to do so, whether a modern court should refuse to enforce a penalty clause where the signator is a substantial corporation, well able to avoid improvident commitments. Penalty clauses provide an earnest of performance. The clause here enhanced Carborundum's credibility in promising to ship the minimum amount guaranteed by showing that it was willing to pay the full contract price even if it failed to ship anything. On the other side it can be pointed out that by raising the cost of a breach of contract to the contract breaker, a penalty clause increases the risk to his other creditors; increases (what is the same thing and more, because bankruptcy imposes "dead-weight" social costs) the risk of bankruptcy; and could amplify the business cycle by increasing the number of bankruptcies in bad times, which is when contracts are most likely to be broken. But since little effort is made to prevent businessmen from assuming risks, these reasons are no better than makeweights.

A better argument is that a penalty clause may discourage efficient as well as inefficient breaches of contract. Suppose a breach would cost the promisee $12,000 in actual damages but would yield the promisor $20,000 in additional profits. Then there would be a net social gain from breach. After being fully compensated for his loss the promisor would be no worse off than if the contract had been performed, while the promisor would be better off by $8,000. But now suppose the contract contains a penalty clause under which the promisor if he breaks his promise must pay the promisee $25,000. The promisor will be discouraged from breaking the contract, since $25,000, the penalty, is greater than $20,000, the profits of the breach; and a transaction that would have increased value will be forgone.

On this view, since compensatory damages should be sufficient to deter inefficient breaches (that is, breaches that cost the victim more than the gain to the contract breaker), penal damages could have no effect other than to deter some efficient breaches. But this overlooks the earlier point that the willingness to agree to a penalty clause is a way of making the promisor and his promise credible and may therefore be essential to inducing some value-maximizing contracts to be made. It also overlooks the more important point that the parties (always assuming they are fully competent) will, in deciding whether to include a penalty clause in their contract, weigh the gains against the costs—costs that include the possibility of discouraging an efficient breach somewhere down the road—and will include the clause only if the benefits exceed those costs as well as all other costs.

On this view the refusal to enforce penalty clauses is (at best) paternalistic—and it seems odd that courts should display parental solicitude for large corporations. But however this may be, we must be on guard to avoid importing our own ideas of sound public policy into an area where our proper judicial role is more than usually deferential. The responsibility for making innovations in the common law of Illinois rests with the courts of Illinois, and not with the federal courts in Illinois. And like every other state, Illinois, untroubled by academic skepticism of the wisdom of refusing to enforce penalty clauses against sophisticated promisors, see, e.g., Goetz & Scott, *Liquidated Damages, Penalties and the Just Compensation Principle*, 77 Colum. L. Rev. 554 (1977), continues steadfastly to insist on the distinction between penalties and liquidated damages. To be valid under Illinois law a liquidation of damages must be a reasonable estimate at the time of contracting of the likely damages from breach, and the need for estimation at that time must be shown by reference to the likely difficulty of measuring the actual damages from a breach of contract after the breach occurs. If damages would be easy to determine then, or if the estimate greatly exceeds a reasonable upper estimate of what the damages are likely to be, it is a penalty. See, e.g., *M.I.G. Investments, Inc. v. Marsala, 92 Ill. App. 3d 400, 405–06 (1981)*.

The distinction between a penalty and liquidated damages is not an easy one to draw in practice but we are required to draw it and can give only limited weight to the district court's determination. Whether a provision for damages is a penalty clause or a liquidated-damages clause is a question of law rather than fact, and unlike some courts of appeals we do not treat a determination by a federal district judge of an issue of state law as if it were a finding of fact, and reverse only if persuaded that clear error has occurred, though we give his determination respectful consideration.

Mindful that Illinois courts resolve doubtful cases in favor of classification as a penalty, we conclude that the damage formula in this case is a penalty and not a liquidation of damages, because it is designed always to assure Lake River more than its actual damages. The formula—full contract price minus the amount already invoiced to Carborundum—is invariant to the gravity of the breach. When a contract specifies a single sum in damages for any and all breaches even though it is apparent that all are not of the same gravity, the specification is not a reasonable effort to estimate damages; and when in addition the fixed sum greatly exceeds the actual damages likely to be inflicted by a minor breach, its character as a penalty becomes unmistakable. This case is within the gravitational field of these principles even though the minimum-guarantee clause does not fix a single sum as damages.

Suppose to begin with that the breach occurs the day after Lake River buys its new bagging system for $89,000 and before Carborundum ships any Ferro Carbo. Carborundum would owe Lake River $533,000. Since Lake River would have incurred at that point a total cost of only $89,000, its net gain from the breach would be $444,000. This is more than four times the profit of $107,000 (20 percent of the contract price of $533,000) that Lake River expected to make from the contract if it had been performed: a huge windfall.

Next suppose (as actually happened here) that breach occurs when 55 percent of the Ferro Carbo has been shipped. Lake River would already have received $293,000 from Carborundum. To see what its costs then would have been (as estimated at the time of contracting), first subtract Lake River's anticipated profit on the contract of $107,000 from the total contract price of $533,000. The difference—Lake River's total cost of performance—is $426,000. Of this, $89,000 is the cost of the new bagging system, a fixed cost. The rest ($426,000 − $89,000 = $337,000) presumably consists of variable costs that are roughly proportional to the amount of Ferro Carbo bagged; there is no indication of any other fixed costs. Assume, therefore, that if Lake River bagged 55 percent of the contractually agreed quantity, it incurred in doing so 55 percent of its variable costs, or $185,000. When this is added to the cost of the new bagging system, assumed for the moment to be worthless except in connection with the contract, the total cost of performance to Lake River is $274,000. Hence a breach that occurred after 55 percent of contractual performance was complete would be expected to yield Lake River a modest profit of $19,000 ($293,000 − $274,000). But now add the "liquidated damages" of $241,000 that Lake River claims, and the result is a total gain from the breach of $260,000, which is almost two and a half times the profit that Lake River expected to gain if there was no breach. And this ignores any use value or salvage value of the new bagging system, which is the property of Lake River—though admittedly it also ignores the time value of money; Lake River paid $89,000 for that system before receiving any revenue from the contract.

To complete the picture, assume that the breach had not occurred till performance was 90 percent complete. Then the "liquidated damages" clause would not be so one-sided, but it would be one-sided. Carborundum would have paid $480,000 for bagging. Against this, Lake River would have incurred its fixed cost of $89,000 plus 90 percent of its variable costs of $337,000, or $303,000. Its total costs would thus be $392,000, and its net profit $88,000. But on top of this it would be entitled to "liquidated damages" of $53,000, for a total profit of $141,000—more than 30 percent more than its expected profit of $107,000 if there was no breach.

The reason for these results is that most of the costs to Lake River of performing the contract are saved if the contract is broken, and this saving is not reflected in the damage formula. As a result, at whatever point in the life of the contract a breach occurs, the damage formula gives Lake River more than its lost profits from the breach—dramatically more if the breach occurs at the beginning of the contract; tapering off at the end, it is true. Still, over the interval between the beginning of Lake River's performance and nearly the end, the clause could be expected to generate profits ranging from 400 percent of the expected contract profits to 130 percent of those profits. And this is on the assumption that the bagging system has no value apart from the contract. If it were worth only $20,000 to Lake River, the range would be 434 percent to 150 percent.

Lake River argues that it would never get as much as the formula suggests, because it would be required to mitigate its damages. This is a dubious argument on several grounds. First, mitigation of damages is a doctrine of the law of court-assessed damages, while the point of a liquidated-damages clause is to substitute party assessment; and that point is blunted, and the certainty that liquidated-damages clauses are designed to give the process of assessing damages impaired, if a defendant can force the plaintiff to take less than the damages specified in the clause, on the ground that the plaintiff could have avoided some of them. It would seem therefore that the clause in this case should be read to eliminate any duty of mitigation, that what Lake River is doing is attempting to rewrite the clause to make it more reasonable, and that since actually the clause is designed to give Lake River the full damages it would incur from breach (and more) even if it made no effort to find a substitute use for the equipment that it bought to perform the contract, this is just one more piece of evidence that it is a penalty clause rather than a liquidated-damages clause. See *Northwest Collectors, Inc. v. Enders, 74 Wash. 2d 585, 594 (1968)*.

But in any event mitigation would not mitigate the penal character of this clause. If Carborundum did not ship the guaranteed minimum quantity, the reason was likely to be—the reason was—that the steel industry had fallen on hard times and the demand for Ferro Carbo was therefore down. In these circumstances Lake River would have little prospect of finding a substitute contract that would yield it significant profits to set off against the full contract price, which is the method by which it proposes to take account of mitigation. At argument Lake River suggested that it might at least have been able to sell the new bagging equipment to someone for something, and the figure $40,000 was proposed. If the breach occurred on the first day when performance under the contract was due and Lake River promptly sold the bagging equipment for $40,000, its liquidated damages would fall to $493,000. But by the same token its costs would fall to $49,000. Its profit would still be $444,000, which as we said was more than 400 percent of its expected profit on the contract. The penal component would be unaffected.

With the penalty clause in this case compare the liquidated-damages clause in *Arduini v. Board of Education, supra*, which is representative of such clauses upheld in Illinois. The plaintiff was a public school teacher whose contract provided that if he resigned before the end of the school year he would be docked 4 percent of his salary. This was a modest fraction of the contract price. And the cost to the school of an untimely resignation would be difficult to measure. Since that cost would be greater the more senior and experienced the teacher was, the fact that the liquidated damages would be greater the higher the teacher's salary did not make the clause arbitrary. Even the fact that the liquidated damages were the same whether the teacher resigned at the beginning, the middle, or the end of the school year was not arbitrary, for it was unclear how the amount of actual damages would vary with the time of resignation. Although one might think that the earlier the teacher resigned the greater the damage to the school would be, the school might find it easier to hire a replacement for the whole year or a great part of it than to bring in a replacement at the last minute to grade the exams left behind by the resigning teacher. Here, in contrast, it is apparent from the face of the contract that the damages provided for by the "liquidated damages" clause are grossly disproportionate to any probable loss and penalize some breaches much more heavily than others regardless of relative cost.

We do not mean by this discussion to cast a cloud of doubt over the "take or pay" clauses that are a common feature of contracts between natural gas pipeline companies and their customers. Such clauses require the customer, in consideration of the pipeline's extending its line to his premises, to take a certain amount of gas at a specified price—and if he fails to take it to pay the full price anyway. The resemblance to the minimum-guarantee clause in the present case is obvious, but perhaps quite superficial. Neither party has mentioned take-or-pay clauses, and we can find no case where such a clause was even challenged as a penalty clause—though in one case it was argued that such a clause made the damages unreasonably *low*. See *National Fuel Gas Distribution Corp. v. Pennsylvania Public Utility Comm'n, 76 Pa. Commw. 102, 126–27 n.8 (1983)*. If, as appears not to be the case here but would often be the case in supplying natural gas, a supplier's fixed costs were a very large fraction of his total costs, a take-or-pay clause might well be a reasonable liquidation of damages. In the limit, if *all* the supplier's costs were incurred before he began supplying the customer, the contract revenues would be an excellent measure of the damages from breach. But in this case, the supplier (Lake River, viewed as a supplier of bagging services to Carborundum) incurred only a fraction of its costs before performance began, and the interruption of performance generated a considerable cost saving that is not reflected in the damage formula.

The fact that the damage formula is invalid does not deprive Lake River of a remedy. The parties did not contract explicitly with reference to the measure of damages if the agreed-on damage formula was invalidated, but all this means is that the victim of the breach is entitled to his common law damages. See, e.g., *Restatement, Second, Contracts § 356, comment a (1981)*. In this case that would be the unpaid contract price of $241,000 minus the costs that Lake River saved by not having to complete the contract (the variable costs on the other 45 percent of the Ferro Carbo that it never had to bag). The case must be remanded to the district judge to fix these damages.

Two damage issues remain. The first concerns Carborundum's expenses of delivering bagged Ferro Carbo to its customers to replace that impounded by Lake River. The district judge gave Carborundum the full market value of the bagged Ferro Carbo. Lake River argues that it should not have to pay for Carborundum's expense of selling additional Ferro Carbo—additional in the sense that Carborundum is being given credit for the full retail value of the product that Lake River withheld. To explain, suppose that Carborundum had an order for $1,000 worth of bagged Ferro Carbo, which Lake River was supposed to deliver; and because it refused, Carborundum incurred a transportation cost of $100 to make a substitute shipment of bagged Ferro Carbo to the customer. Carborundum would still get $1,000 from the customer, and if that price covered the transportation cost it would still make a profit. In what sense, therefore, is that cost a separate item of damage, of loss? On all Ferro Carbo (related to this case) sold by Carborundum in the Midwest, Carborundum received the full market price, either from its customers in the case of Ferro Carbo actually delivered to them, or from Lake River in the case of the Ferro Carbo that Lake River refused to deliver. Having received a price designed to cover all expenses of sale, a seller cannot also get an additional damage award for any of those expenses.

If, however, the additional Ferro Carbo that Carborundum delivered to its Midwestern customers in substitution for Ferro Carbo previously delivered to, and impounded by, Lake River would have been sold in the East at the same price but lower cost, Carborundum would have had an additional loss, in the form of reduced profits, for which it could recover additional damages. But it made no effort to prove such a loss. Maybe it had no unsatisfied eastern customers, and expanded rather than shifted output to fulfill its Midwestern customers' demand. The damages on the counter-claim must be refigured also.

The judgment of the district court is affirmed in part and reversed in part, and the case is returned to that court to redetermine both parties' damages in accordance with the principles in this opinion. The parties may present additional evidence on remand, and shall bear their own costs in this court.

Affirmed in part, reversed in part, and remanded.

* * *

The legal rule announced in these materials—that efforts by contracting parties to establish super-compensatory remedies by agreeing to over-liquidated damages constitute invalid penalty clauses—is fairly straightforward, especially in its core application, as in *Lake River*. As Judge Posner notes, the liquidated damages clause at issue in *Lake River* (because it calculated the plaintiff's damages based on lost revenues with no correction for variable costs saved) would have over-compensated the plaintiff in *every* future state of the world—no matter when the defendant breached. The over-compensatory, or penal, nature of the liquidated damages clause was therefore apparent both *ex ante*, at the moment that it was drafted, and *ex post*, when the breach occurred and the specified remedy was sought. *Lake River* is therefore in a sense an easy case (at least once the overcompensation built into the method of calculating damages has been explained), and the most interesting issues in the opinion arise not at its core holding, but on it margins.

To begin with, it is worth briefly noting the discussion that rejects Lake River's claim to hold an artisan's lien (sometimes also called a mechanic's lien) on the unbagged ferro-carbo that it had impounded, not least because (astoundingly enough) an analogous issue can arise in the context of disputes between lawyers and their clients. It is an old common law rule that people who have (pursuant to a contract) worked on materials, but have not been paid what they are owed for their work, may assert liens against their work product, as a kind of self-help remedy to secure payment. These are called artisan's liens because the image that the law has in mind is of an artisan—say a cartwright—who repairs a customer's property—fixing a wagon-wheel—but is not paid for his work and asserts a lien against the repaired property to secure payment. Similar liens are also available to lawyers, who may in certain circumstances (although subject constraints imposed by the law governing lawyers) also retain their work product—a drafted contract, for example—in order to exert pressure on reluctant clients to pay for their services. But as Posner's opinion makes clear, such liens are valid only within the strict limits imposed by the law that creates them—and in particular apply only to recover payment for work already done and not to efforts to extract payment (even if this payment is contractually required) for work not yet done. Because Lake River impounded unbagged ferro-carbo it did the latter, and had no valid lien. Hence it committed conversion, which is the tort analog of the crime theft.

Moreover, it is also worth considering Posner's efforts to distinguish *Lake River* from other cases, in which liquidated damages clauses should be held valid in spite of having a structure that is formally equivalent to the invalidated clause in *Lake River*. The most important such cases involve take or pay clauses in natural gas (or, for that matter, other utility) contracts, in which a customer agrees, as a condition of being extended service, to pay for a minimum quantity of gas, whether he uses it or not.[2] The payment term in such contracts establishes a liquidated damages

---

2. Posner's other example—involving a contract in which a teacher agrees to forfeit 4% of his pay if he resigns before the end of a school year—does not in fact present an analogy to *Lake River* at all. This formula, which imposes the same damages for late as for early resignations, may appear to overcompensate schools when teachers resign late, and hence to subject such teachers to unenforceable penalties. But as Posner himself recognizes, this appearance is an illusion: to begin with, the formula does adjust damages in proportion to the quitting teacher's salary (and thus plausibly also to his value to the school); and furthermore, the fact that fewer class-sessions remain untaught does not relieve a school whose teacher breaches late from the burden of finding a replacement, and the special difficulties associated with finding later replacements may counterbalance there being less at stake, overall, if they prove worse teachers than those whom they replace.

regime that formally mirrors the regime in *Lake River*, under which a customer who uses less but must pay for the agreed amount anyway overcompensates the utility, in light of there being no offset for the utility's variable cost savings due to not having to provide the unused gas. But this resemblance is formal only. Whereas the fixed-cost bagging system in *Lake River* represented less than a quarter of Lake River's total costs of performance, the fixed-costs of extending service to a new customer (of laying pipes or wires, and perhaps even of expanding capacity) represent a very large portion of the total costs of supplying gas. Accordingly, the overcompensation associated with a take-or-pay provision in a gas contract (even when applied to a very early breach) is modest compared to the overall losses the breach imposes on the gas-provider. The take-or-pay clause therefore imposes a penalty in a technical sense only, and insisting on treating such a provision as an invalid penalty-clause involves misplaced rigorism—misplaced, not least, because liquidated damages clauses will never *precisely* track contractual expectations even in the core cases of their operation, in which (after all) they present easy-to-calculate approximations (and possibly over-estimates) of much-more-difficult to assess lost expectations. Of course, just where to draw the line between these two formally analogous cases remains a difficult question and Posner offers little guidance in exercising the necessary judgment.

Next, it is worth asking whether the parties in *Lake River* might have drafted around the legal rule invalidating penalty clauses, to achieve the same effect as the clause that was struck down without triggering the law's scrutiny. Suppose that instead of terming the payments owed by Carborundum (in the event it shipped too little ferro-carbo) "damages", the parties had instead incorporated these payments into the price paid for bagging such ferro-carbo as Carborundum did ship. More precisely, suppose that the parties had agreed to a variable price structure—involving high prices for the first tons bagged, medium prices for the middle tons, and low prices, well below Lake River's per-ton marginal cost of bagging, for the last tons (up to 22,500 tons). Such a price structure would produce a pattern of payments much like the penalty clause that Posner invalidated: in which early breaches by Carborundum would leave Lake River (much) better off than full performance, because they would allow Lake River to forgo bagging the last tons of Carborundum's order, at below its costs.[3] Would a court see through this formal manipulation? Especially if the penalties imposed by the price structure were reasonably modest, it might well not do. This arrangement would also have the advantage, from Lake River's perspective, of changing the procedural posture of any dispute about the "penalty" arrangement. Whereas in the case as litigated, Lake River had to try to extract the liquidated damages payment from Carborundum (a need

---

3. The pattern might not be quite so dramatic as under the liquidated damages clause, because the price of the first bag could not plausibly be made high enough so that, on its own, it produced the massive windfall on early breach associated with the liquidated damages clause. But this difference might have no practical importance at all. If the parties were sure that Carborundum would bag at least a significant portion of the quantity named in the contract, then they could establish a price structure to mimic the liquidated damages clause, from this portion onwards.

that tempted it to assert its disastrously misjudged artisan's lien), the alternative arrangement, involving a variable price structure, would leave Carborundum to recover amounts already paid to Lake River, on the ground that they represented an overpayment that amounted to a penalty imposed on its breach. (Here note the potential application of the burden-shifting rule of *Vines*.)

Furthermore, one should ask about other cases, whose facts render them considerably more difficult and doctrinally uncertain than *Lake River*. As noted earlier, the liquidated damages clause in Lake River was over-compensatory both *ex ante* and *ex post*—both in expectation and in application. This makes it the clearest case of an invalid penalty. But what does the law say about other cases, in which *ex ante* and *ex post* evaluations of a liquidated damages clause come apart?

One the one hand, what is the legal rule in cases in which a liquidated damages clause that makes an *ex ante* reasonable estimate of a plaintiff's damages on balance turns out, *ex post* and in the peculiar circumstances at issue, to overcompensate the plaintiff? The doctrinal logic of the rule that penalty clauses are invalid seems to require a clear result in such cases. To see what this is, ask what it means for a liquidated damages clause to be *ex ante* reasonable in spite of, at least in one set of circumstances, being over-compensatory *ex post*. Surely this is inconsistent with its being the case that the circumstances in which the clause became over-compensatory were anticipated in advance, since that would be inconsistent with the assumption that the liquidated damages established by the clause were a reasonable estimate of actual damages, *ex ante*. So when a liquidated damages clause that was judged reasonable *ex ante* turns out, given how events have transpired, to be over-compensatory *ex post*, it must be that the events that have made the clause over-compensatory *ex post* were not anticipated *ex ante*, that is, when the clause was agreed to. (It must be, in other words, that the possibility of these events did not figure in the analysis that declared the clause *ex ante* reasonable.) If this is so, then even if the liquidated damages clause is held valid, it should also be held not to cover the facts at hand, so that damages awarded on these facts should reflect the plaintiff's true expectations and not the formula contained in the clause.

So logic suggests that when a liquidated damages clause that appears reasonable *ex ante* turns out to be unreasonable *ex post*, then either the appearance of reasonableness *ex ante* is deceptive, and the clause is in fact an unenforceable penalty; or, if the clause is in fact reasonable *ex ante*, then the clause by its own terms does not apply to the facts in which it its over-compensatory, and so should be set aside. Either way, it seems, the *ex post* over-compensatory nature of a liquidated damages clause should be suffi-cient to render the clause's remedy rule ineffective in the circumstances in which it is over-compensatory, regardless of how the clause appeared *ex ante*.[4] It is not, however, clear that all courts have followed this logic, and jurisdictions seem to split on how to respond to cases of this nature.

---

4. For a structurally analogous argument developed in the context of under-liquidated damages clauses, see the discussion below of *Northern Illinois Gas Co. v. Energy Cooperative*, 461 N.E.2d 1049 (Ill. App. 1984).

On the other hand, it is worth noting the possibility that even a liquidated damages clause that is unreasonable *ex ante* may turn out to present a reasonable estimate of a plaintiff's lost expectations as circumstances have developed *ex post*. To illustrate this possibility, image a contract in which a seller agrees to deliver, by a fixed date, a good without which her buyer cannot conduct his business and that the contract specifies liquidated damages for every delay set at a reasonable expectation of one year's worth of her buyer's profits. This liquidated damages provision is in general an invalid penalty, since for breaches involving delays of (dramatically) less than a year, it is (dramatically) over-compensatory. But now suppose that the seller delivers the good exactly a year late, so that her buyer has lost exactly a year's profits. Now the liquidated damages are no longer over-compensatory, and the buyer may wish to enforce the clause, in order to avoid the expense of proving up his lost profits and the risk that a court will not find his proof sufficiently certain. Can he do it?

The doctrinal route to reaching this result is to separate the liquidated damages clause into two—an unenforceable penalty clause contemplating delays of less than a year, and an enforceable, because *ex ante* reasonable, clause contemplating delays of a year. If this seems altogether too neat and formal a trick, consider that the plaintiff might be able to introduce contextual evidence suggesting that the clause was drafted with a one-year delay in mind (and perhaps even that the parties had implicitly agreed to use the sum specified by the clause as a base-line against which to compute, by pro-rating, the damages owed for shorter delays). If the plaintiff can succeed in this maneuver—his chances depend partly on doctrinal considerations concerning contract interpretation that will be discussed in detail below—then he may be able to render the liquidated damages clause enforceable, after all.

Finally, step back from the details of the positive law to ask more generally what the law's attitude towards over-liquidated damages clauses should be, and, in keeping with the general methodological approach of this chapter, whether the law's hostility to penalty clauses serves efficiency. In his opinion in *Lake River*, Posner suggests that although it may be appropriate for the law to invalidate penalty clauses involving unsophisticated parties, in order to protect such parties from inefficient (and unfair!) exploitation, penalty clauses ought, on balance, to be enforceable against sophisticated parties who have agreed to them. Both parts of his analysis proceed too quickly, however.

First, as regards unsophisticated parties, it remains to explain why the law should adopt a categorical rule against the specific form of exploitation associated with penalty clauses, when the law's general attitude towards exploitation is much more relaxed and less protective. As later chapters will explain in greater detail, even the unsophisticated are in general held to the terms of their bargains, including their bad ones. Moreover, such protections as the law does afford the unwary tend to be procedural—involving grace-periods for backing out of agreements, information-forcing rules that require the sophisticated to explain what agreements involve, and (in limited cases) outright bans on certain means of inducing agreement—rather than substantive. Certainly there is no general principle of contract law that protects the unsophisticated against substantively unfair, or even exploitative contract terms by rendering these terms invalid. (As later materials will explain, the one rule that might function in this way, the unconscionability doctrine, has not been interpreted and applied to have this effect.[5]) So a defense of the rule invalidating penalty clauses, even in the limited context involving their application against unsophisticated parties, requires an argument explaining why such clauses raise special problems of exploitation, which justify departing from the law's general treatment of these matters. Posner's opinion does not provide one.

Second, and more importantly, Posner's argument in favor of changing current doctrine to enforce penalty clauses against sophisticated parties is also unpersuasive. Posner presents two principal reasons in favor of enforcement: that penalty clauses, by providing an earnest of performance, increase the credibility of promises and thus enhance efficiency by making otherwise impossible exchanges possible; and that the fact that sophisticated parties, who weigh the costs and benefits of the contract provisions that they adopt, agree to them suggests that penalty clauses must be efficient. Neither argument is correct, however.

The mistake in the first argument should be plain from what has been said earlier in this chapter. If the argument for the efficiency of the expectation remedy is correct, as it is, then this remedy provides precisely the efficient earnest of performance. By contrast, greater remedies, including the remedies introduced by penalty clauses, inefficiently over-deter breach, as well as introducing any number of other inefficiencies into the contracting process.

The mistake in the second argument is more subtle. Rational and sophisticated parties might employ penalty clauses in spite of their being inefficient because the cost of such clauses is disproportionately borne by third parties. For example, when a monopolist seller faces a potential competitor, the monopolist and her buyer may wish to write a contract in which the buyer accepts a penalty for non-performance in exchange for a lower price. By accepting the penalty clause, the buyer credibly commits to not dealing with the competitor (since abandoning her seller in favor of the competitor's better offer would subject her to the penalty). In exchange, she receives a price below the oligopoly price that would arise if the competitor entered the market. This is good for the buyer because he pays less. It is good for the monopolist because, although she receives less profit per sale, given the lower price, she makes more sales, since the potential competitor makes none. In effect, the monopolist and her buyer are splitting the rent that accrues to keeping the competitor out of the market. This result is

---

5. The difference between the per se rule invalidating penalty clauses and the much weaker scrutiny that the law gives exploitative contractual provisions more generally is rendered especially vivid by the contrasts that the UCC draws between the treatment of penalty clauses and their near-neighbors, under-liquidated damages clauses. As comment [1] to § 2–718(1) expressly observes, over-liquidated damages clauses are always invalid, whereas under-liquidated damages clauses are invalid only if unconscionable under UCC § 2–302.

inefficient, however, since this rent is less than the gain from the competitor's entering—as increased competition quite generally increases efficiency.

Accordingly, contrary to Posner's suggestions in *Lake River*, there are good general grounds for doubting the efficiency of penalty clauses, and there are good grounds for doubting that the fact that parties resort to such causes suggests that they are efficient, even in the cases in question. Nevertheless, it is far from clear that these observations justify the blanket rule invalidating penalty clauses that the law adopts. There do, as it turns out, exist good reasons for which sophisticated parties might adopt penalty clauses in their contracts—there exist scenarios in which penalty clauses might increase the efficiency of contract. Thus penalty clauses might function to induce efficient relation-specific investment, to name just one example.[6] But it is uncertain, to say the least, whether courts can accurately distinguish between the efficient and the inefficient use of such clauses, or if courts cannot accurately distinguish, what the efficiency effects of penalty clauses are, on balance. And the question of what general treatment the law should give to such clauses therefore admits of no easy answer.

7.2.B   Under-Liquidated Damages and the Requirement of a Truly Contractual Remedy

The most common class of liquidated damages clauses—certainly commoner than penalty clauses and probably commoner even than clauses designed simply to track actual contractual expectations with an easily computable formula—set damages for breach at less (often significantly less) than a promisee's disappointed contractual expectations. Whereas it is not clear whether over-liquidated damages clauses serve or disserve efficiency—even in particular circumstances, much less on balance—the efficiency case for enforcing such under-liquidated damages clauses is easy to make.

Insofar as a promisee can influence the chance of breach (in unverifiable ways) full expectation damages leave promisees with insufficient incentives to keep this probability low, and a liquidated damages clause limiting their remedies can help to rectify this inefficiency. (This is just a special case of the rule, noted earlier, that liquidated damages, by making a promisee's remedy independent of her conduct, help to secure double responsibility at the margin.) Moreover, where a promisee's contractual expectations are principally comprised of his profits, so that the disappointment of these expectations following a breach is effectively a business risk of the promisee, the promisee may be sufficiently better placed to evaluate and to bear this risk as to make it efficient to exclude these profits from his

---

6. This suggestion is developed in Aaron S. Edlin, *Cadillac Contracts and Up-front Payments: Efficient Investment Under Expectation Damages*, 12 J.L. Econ. & Org. 98, 104–11 (1996); Aaron S. Edlin & Alan Schwartz, Optimal *Penalties in Contracts*, 78 Chi.-Kent. L. Rev. 33, 44–52 (2003); see also Steven Shavell, *Damage Measures for Breach of Contract*, 11 Bell J. Econ. 466, 472 (1980).

remedies on breach. A typical example of such a case arises in contracts for the sale of parts for large and complicated profit-generating machines. These contracts typically include clauses limiting buyers' remedies for defective parts to the costs of replacing the parts or repairing the machines and exclude any lost profits that the promisees suffer when a defective part shuts the machines down. Such exclusions may, to be sure, sometimes leave promisors with an inefficient under-incentive to perform. But this inefficiency may be outweighed by the inefficiency that would arise if promisors had to identify and calculate all their promisees' potential lost profits in order to know how to chose their contracting partners and set their prices (and by the inefficient cross-subsidization that would arise if promisors could not discriminate among promisees in this way). And promisees may anyway be best placed to secure themselves against the losses in question, for example by testing parts' interactions specifically with their machines before installing them, or by keeping backup parts on hand.[7]

Accordingly, the principal doctrinal questions raised by under-liquidated damages clauses involve not whether the clauses are enforceable—they generally are—but rather whether they apply to the facts of particular disputes, or as the law says, whether they are exclusive. At the same time, the question whether an under-liquidated damages clause is valid does sometimes arise; and although it arises rarely enough to have little practical importance, it remains theoretically important to understanding the conceptual structure of contract law.

Northern Illinois Gas Co. v. Energy Cooperative, Inc.

Appellate Court of Illinois, Third District, 1984.
461 N.E.2d 1049.

■ HEIPLE, J. An action was brought in the circuit court of Grundy County by Northern Illinois Gas Company (hereinafter NI–Gas), seeking a declaratory judgment that it had properly ceased performance under a long-term supply contract with Energy Cooperative, Inc. (hereinafter ECI). ECI counterclaimed for breach of contract and the jury returned a verdict for $305.5 million on ECI's counterclaim. The facts are as follows.

NI–Gas is a public utility which distributes natural gas to customers throughout the northern third of Illinois (excluding Chicago). As a public utility, NI–Gas is subject to regulation by the Illinois Commerce Commission (hereinafter ICC) under the Public Utilities Act (Ill. Rev. Stat. 1981, ch. 111 2/3, pars. 1 through 95).

In order to deal with a natural gas shortage in the early to mid–1970's NI–Gas received permission from the ICC to construct a supplemental natural gas (SNG) plant. The plant began operation in 1974 using various types of feedstock which were converted into natural gas. One type of

---

7. These arguments of course reprise the economic analysis of the foreseeability rule of *Hadley v. Baxendale*. This should come as no surprise, since that rule would likely come into play to exclude remedies for some (but not all) lost profits in such cases even in the absence of contractual provisions providing for the exclusion.

feedstock was naphtha, which was supplied by Atlantic Richfield Company (ARCO), pursuant to a contract entered into with NI–Gas in 1973. The ARCO contract was assigned to ECI in 1976.

The contract was to remain in force for 10 years or until 56 million barrels of naphtha had been delivered to NI–Gas. By late 1979 and early 1980 it became apparent to NI–Gas that the demand for natural gas was decreasing while the price of naphtha was steadily increasing. These changes were caused essentially by Federal decontrol of natural gas supplies in 1978 and increases in the price of crude oil which determined the price ECI charged for naphtha.

Between 1974 and 1978 NI—Gas had been holding large amounts of gas in storage facilities. In 1980, the ICC denied NI–Gas' request for a rate increase partly because NI–Gas was holding, in ICC's opinion, an unreasonably large amount of gas in storage. Since NI–Gas was not permitted to raise its rates, it decided to reduce the inventory by cutting back on SNG production, which was its most expensive source of gas.

NI–Gas successfully negotiated reductions in SNG feedstock shipments with two of its suppliers. At the time of the ICC rate order, ECI had been voluntarily delivering reduced quantities of naphtha. Rather than seek further reductions, NI–Gas attempted to negotiate an end to the contract with ECI. When negotiations failed, NI–Gas terminated its performance as of March 31, 1980.

On March 17, 1980, NI–Gas filed suit seeking a declaratory judgment that it had no further obligations under the contract and that ECI's damages, if any, were limited to the amount specified by the liquidated damages clause of the contract. ECI counterclaimed for $230 million in damages (the alleged difference between the contract and market prices of naphtha on February 29, 1980, when ECI asserted it learned of NI–Gas' termination of the contract), and unspecified additional damages.

NI–Gas' reply to the counterclaim alleged [] affirmative defenses.

The second amended complaint also added the allegations that ECI had deliberately overcharged NI–Gas for naphtha during the first three months of 1980, that ECI had not complied with its obligation of good faith in the performance of the contract and therefore had breached the contract, and, in addition, that NI–Gas had been damaged in an amount in excess of $3,000,000.

On June 10, 1982, the circuit court (1) denied NI–Gas' motion for summary judgment on the *force majeure* [meaning, that the circumstances were beyond its control] and liquidated damages defenses; (2) granted ECI's motion to strike NI–Gas' liquidated damages defense; and (3) granted summary judgment for ECI on NI–Gas' *force majeure*, frustration of purpose, and public utility defenses. Later, the trial court granted summary judgment for ECI on NI–Gas' allegations of fraud and breach of contract by ECI because of its alleged overcharges to NI–Gas during the first quarter of 1982.

Liquidated Damages

NI–Gas argues that the trial court erred in denying its motion for summary judgment on the liquidated damages clause and in striking the liquidated damages defense. The court held that the liquidated damages clause of the contract (section 13) gave the nonbreaching party the choice of recovering either actual or liquidated damages. ECI chose to pursue actual damages resulting in a jury award of $305.5 million.

NI–Gas contends that the liquidated damages clause is clear and unambiguous and provides the exclusive measure of damages in the event of default:

"XIII. *Liquidated Damages*:

If, prior to the delivery to PURCHASER of the total number of Barrels of Feedstock specified in Section III hereof, this Agreement is terminated by reason of either party's default, prior to the expiration of the term set forth in Section II above, then, upon demand of the party not in default, the defaulting party shall pay to the other as liquidated damages, a sum in cash determined by multiplying one cent ($0.01) by the difference between the total gallons specified in Section III, and the gallons actually delivered to PURCHASER pursuant to this Agreement.

It is further agreed that nothing herein contained shall prejudice the rights of either party to terminate this Agreement as hereinafter provided for and in the event the foregoing provision for liquidated damages is determined to be unenforceable for any reason, the party not in default shall not be precluded from exercising any other rights or remedies to which the party may be entitled under the terms of this Agreement or otherwise at law or equity."

According to NI–Gas' calculations, this section would limit ECI's recovery to a maximum of $13,576,002.30.

ECI responds that section 13 contains two conditions which must be satisfied before the liquidated damages clause may be invoked. ECI also argues that section 13 is presumed to be nonexclusive under section 2—719 of the Uniform Commercial Code (Ill. Rev. Stat. 1981, ch. 26, par. 2—719).

ECI interprets section 13 as being contingent upon a demand for liquidated damages and termination pursuant to section 14 of the contract:

"XIV. *Default and Termination*

In the event either party is in default of any of its obligations hereunder, in addition to any other rights or remedies available at law or equity, the party not in default may cancel this Agreement by giving not less than thirty (30) Days prior written notice to the party in default; provided that such notice of default shall not be effective if the party claimed to be in default shall cure such default within thirty (30) Days after having received such notice. Any such termination shall be an additional remedy and shall not prejudice the rights of the party not in default to recover any amounts due it hereunder for any damage or loss suffered by it by virtue of such default, and shall not constitute a waiver of any other remedy to which the party not in default may be entitled for breach of this Agreement. Waiver of any defaults shall not be deemed a continuing waiver or a waiver of any subsequent default whether of the same or a different provision of this Agreement.''

ECI argues that liquidated damages are not available because ECI (the nonbreaching party) did not terminate under section 14 and did not demand liquidated damages. We find that sections 13 and 14 do not have to be read together, nor may the nonbreaching party avoid the liquidated measure of damages simply by failing to make a demand.

Section 13 clearly provides that liquidated damages are available when the contract is terminated by default. It does not say that the contract must be terminated pursuant to section 14, which simply provides the non-breaching party with a means of formally ending the contract while reserving the right to recover damages for the unperformed portion. An additional distinction between the two sections is found in the language of section 14 which states that ''any such termination shall be an additional remedy and shall not prejudice the rights of the party not in default to recover any amounts due hereunder.'' This provision is inconsistent with any construction making termination pursuant to section 14 a prerequisite to recovery of liquidated damages. Section 14 is clearly an additional means of relief. This conclusion is also supported by similar language in section 13 stating that ''nothing herein shall prejudice the rights of either party to terminate this agreement as hereinafter provided.'' Inclusion of this language in both section 13 and 14 convinces us that the parties did not intend that the availability of relief under one section be conditioned on the operation of the other section.

ECI also contends that it has not made a demand for liquidated damages and, therefore, it has the option of seeking actual damages. Failure to demand a contractual right does not create rights greater than those bargained for. A liquidated damages clause is the agreement of the parties as to the amount of damages which must be paid in the event of default. (5 Corbin on Contracts sec. 1062, at 355–56 (1964).) Proof of liability is all that is required to entitle the injured party to recover the liquidated amount. (*Weiss v. United States Fidelity & Guaranty Co. (1921), 300 Ill. 11.*) If the nondefaulting party does not wish to demand this amount, he will not be forced to do so. But this does not create the right to seek a greater measure of damages than the amount bargained for.

Next, ECI relies on section 2—719(1)(b) of the Uniform Commercial Code, in arguing that the liquidated damages clause does not provide the exclusive measure of damages unless it is expressly agreed to be exclusive and labeled as such.

''Sec. 2—719. Contractual Modification or Limitation of Remedy.
(1) Subject to the provisions of subsections (2) and (3) of this

Section and of the preceding section on liquidation and limitation of damages,

(a) the agreement may provide for remedies in addition to or in substitution for those provided in this Article and may limit or alter the measure of damages recoverable under this Article, as by limiting the buyer's remedies to return of the goods and repayment of the price or to repair and replacement of nonconforming goods or parts; and

(b) resort to a remedy as provided is optional unless the remedy is expressly agreed to be exclusive, in which case it is the sole remedy." Ill. Rev. Stat. 1981, ch. 26, par. 2—719.

There are no Illinois cases which address the question of whether section 2—719(1)(b) applies to a liquidated damages clause. Other authorities are split on the issue.

NI–Gas takes the position that section 2—719(b) applies only to contract provisions which limit a remedy. A liquidated damages clause does not limit a remedy but instead provides an agreed upon measure of damages. Therefore, section 2—719(b) does not govern the liquidated damages clause in the contract with ECI.

The only reported decision which addresses this precise issue is a North Dakota Supreme Court case. *Ray Farmers Union Elevator Co. v. Weyrauch (N.D. 1975), 238 N.W.2d 47*, involved the anticipatory breach of three grain supply contracts which contained liquidated damage clauses. The plaintiffs claimed to have the option of seeking actual damages since the liquidated damage clauses were not declared to be exclusive as allegedly required by section 2—719(a)(b). The court rejected this argument holding that a liquidated damages clause is not a remedy within the portent of section 2—719. In accord with this decision is the commentary found in C. Bunn, H. Snead & R. Speidel, An Introduction to the Uniform Commercial Code 192 (1964), which characterizes section 2—719 as "primarily concerned with *what* remedies are available rather than the monetary amount of damage." (Emphasis in original.)

ECI makes no distinction between a remedy and a measure of damages in arguing that a liquidated damages clause is subject to section 2—719(1)(b). ECI relies on *Commonwealth Edison Co. v. Atlantic Richfield Co.* (No. 76L3951, N.D. Ill., filed June 15, 1978), where, in a memorandum opinion, the Federal District Court held that the liquidated damages clause of the contract did not limit the plaintiff's damages to the liquidated amount. The court found that the parties had inserted a provision into the contract which stated that liquidated damages were in addition to any other rights or remedies. Therefore, liquidated damages were optional. Although the court referred to 2—719(1)(b) in reaching its decision, its holding was based primarily on the express terms of the contract which made liquidated damages optional. We do not regard this as a definitive statement requiring liquidated damage clauses to comply with 2—719(1)(b) in order to be exclusive. We also note that this is an unpublished Federal trial court decision, which has no *stare decisis* effect in this court.

ECI also cites 6 D Willier & Hart, U.C.C. Reporter Digest sec. 2—719, at 2—666.58 (1983), which is critical of the majority opinion in *Weyrauch*. In this commentary, the authors point to section 1—201(34) of the code which defines "remedy" as "any remedial right to which an aggrieved party is entitled with or without resort to a tribunal." The authors contend that this definition is broad enough to encompass a liquidated damages clause. This is the same position taken by one dissenting justice in *Weyrauch*. For reasons which follow, we prefer the position taken by NI–Gas.

A liquidated damages clause which provides an agreed upon formula for calculating the amount of money damages owed in the event of nonperformance is not a limitation on a remedy. Liquidation or limitation of damages is governed by section 2—718; limitation of remedies falls under 2—719. The concepts are separate and distinct. The only cross reference between the two sections is found in 2—719 which states that it is "subject to" 2—718. If, instead, 2—718 were made subject to 2—719, then the restrictions of 2—719(1)(b) would arguably apply to a liquidated damages clause. But the fact that 2—719 is subject to 2—718 indicates that any restriction on the right to liquidate damages by agreement is contained in 2—718 and nowhere else. We see no reason to impose the additional restraints of 2—719(1)(b).

The trial court erred in finding that the liquidated damages clause did not prevent ECI from seeking an alternate measure of damages. The parties agreed to a liquidated sum a their damages in the event of default. This is often done in order to avoid the difficulty and uncertainty of proving damages by using market value, resale value or otherwise. Such an agreement is binding. Therefore, we reverse the court's order striking the liquidated damages defense. Because of our decision on this issue, it is not necessary for us to review NI–Gas' contention that the jury was improperly instructed on how to calculate ECI's damages.

[The court's discussion of the affirmative defenses offered by NI–Gas and trial court's evidentiary rulings have been omitted.]

To summarize our decision, we reverse the judgment of the circuit court of Grundy County granting ECI's motion to strike the defense based on the liquidated damages clause of the contract. The jury's award of damages in the amount of $305.5 million is vacated and the cause is remanded for determination of ECI's damages according to the formula contained in the liquidated damages clause. In all other respects, the judgment is affirmed.

Affirmed in part; reversed in part; remanded with directions.

Uniform Commercial Code

§ 2–719   Contractual Modification or Limitation of Remedy

(1) Subject to the provisions of subsections (2) and (3) of this section and of the preceding section on liquidation and limitation of damages,

(a) the agreement may provide for remedies in addition to or in substitution for those provided in this Article and may limit or alter the measure of damages recoverable under this Article, as by limiting the buyer's remedies to return of the goods and repayment of the price or to repair and replacement of non-conforming goods or parts; and

(b) resort to a remedy as provided is optional unless the remedy is expressly agreed to be exclusive, in which case it is the sole remedy.

(2) Where circumstances cause an exclusive or limited remedy to fail of its essential purpose, remedy may be had as provided in this Act.

(3) Consequential damages may be limited or excluded unless the limitation or exclusion is unconscionable. Limitation of consequential damages for injury to the person in the case of consumer goods is prima facie unconscionable but limitation of damages where the loss is commercial is not.

Official Comment

Prior Uniform Statutory Provision: None.

Purposes:

1.   Under this section parties are left free to shape their remedies to their particular requirements and reasonable agreements limiting or modifying remedies are to be given effect.

However, it is of the very essence of a sales contract that at least minimum adequate remedies be available. If the parties intend to conclude a contract for sale within this Article they must accept the legal consequence that there be at least a fair quantum of remedy for breach of the obligations or duties outlined in the contract. Thus any clause purporting to modify or limit the remedial provisions of this Article in an unconscionable manner is subject to deletion and in that event the remedies made available by this Article are applicable as if the stricken clause had never existed. Similarly, under subsection (2), where an apparently fair and reasonable clause because of circumstances fails in its purpose or operates to deprive either party of the substantial value of the bargain, it must give way to the general remedy provisions of this Article.

2.   Subsection (1)(b) creates a presumption that clauses prescribing remedies are cumulative rather than exclusive. If the parties intend the term to describe the sole remedy under the contract, this must be clearly expressed.

3.   Subsection (3) recognizes the validity of clauses limiting or excluding consequential damages but makes it clear that they may not operate in an unconscionable manner. Actually such terms are merely an allocation of unknown or undeterminable risks. The seller in all cases is free to disclaim warranties in the manner provided in Section 2–316.

Kearney & Trecker Corp. v. Master Engraving Co.

Supreme Court of New Jersey, 1987.
527 A.2d 429.

■ STEIN, J. The critical issue posed by this appeal is whether the Uniform Commercial Code, *N.J.S.A. 12A:1–101* to 10–106 (U.C.C. or Code), permits the enforcement of a contractual exclusion of consequential damages where the buyer's limited remedy authorized in the contract of sale has failed to achieve its essential purpose. Despite a specific exclusion of consequential damages in the contract between these parties, the trial court instructed the jury that it could award consequential damages if the seller, acting under its repair and replacement warranty, did not "make the machine as warranted." The Appellate Division affirmed the judgment entered on the jury verdict assessing damages against the seller, concluding that "the allocation of risk through exclusion of consequential damages was inextricably tied to the limitation of remedies." *Kearney & Trecker Corp. v. Master Engraving Co., 211 N.J. Super. 376, 381 (1986).* Our analysis of the U.C.C. persuades us, however, that the enforceability of an exclusion of consequential damages does not necessarily depend on the effectiveness of the limited remedies afforded by the contract of sale, and that in this case the exclusion should have been enforced, even though the jury may have determined that the repair and replacement warranty failed of its essential purpose. Accordingly, we reverse the judgment below and remand the matter to the Law Division for a new trial.

I

Kearney & Trecker Corporation (K & T) is the manufacturer of the Milwaukee–Matic 180 (MM–180), a computer-controlled machine tool capable of performing automatically a series of machining operations on metal parts. At the time of trial K & T had sold approximately 700 of these machines throughout the world. Master Engraving Company, Inc. (Master) is engaged in the manufacture and engraving of component parts for industrial application. Organized in 1955, Master operated 22 machines at the time of trial, six of which were computer controlled.

In the fall of 1978, the parties began discussions about Master's purchase of an MM–180. K & T furnished Master with a sales brochure describing the MM–180: "The new Milwaukee–Matic 180 combines simplicity with efficiency. It was designed using fewer parts. It is this simplicity of design that does much to explain the MM 180's amazing low maintenance requirements."

In response to a proposal from K & T, Master issued its purchase order for the MM–180 in December 1978, and the order was promptly acknowledged and accepted by K & T. The purchase price was $167,000. The written proposal included the following provision:

> WARRANTY, DISCLAIMER, LIMITATION OF LIABILITY AND REMEDY: Seller warrants the products furnished hereunder to be free from defects in material and workmanship for the shorter of

(i) twelve (12) months from the date of delivery or (ii) four thousand (4,000) operating hours.

THE WARRANTY EXPRESSED HEREIN IS IN LIEU OF ANY OTHER WARRANTIES EXPRESS OR IMPLIED INCLUDING, WITHOUT LIMITATION, ANY IMPLIED WARRANTY OF MERCHANTABILITY OR FITNESS FOR A PARTICULAR PURPOSE AND IS IN LIEU OF ANY AND ALL OTHER OBLIGATIONS OR LIABILITY ON SELLER'S PART. UNDER NO CIRCUMSTANCES WILL SELLER BE LIABLE FOR ANY INCIDENTAL OR CONSEQUENTIAL DAMAGES, OR FOR ANY OTHER LOSS, DAMAGE OR EXPENSE OF ANY KIND, INCLUDING LOSS OF PROFITS ARISING IN CONNECTION WITH THIS CONTRACT OR WITH THE USE OF OR INABILITY TO USE SELLER'S PRODUCTS FURNISHED UNDER THIS CONTRACT. SELLER'S MAXIMUM LIABILITY SHALL NOT EXCEED AND BUYER'S REMEDY IS LIMITED TO EITHER (i) REPAIR OR REPLACEMENT OF THE DEFECTIVE PART OF PRODUCT, OR AT SELLER'S OPTION, (ii) RETURN OF THE PRODUCT AND REFUND OF THE PURCHASE PRICE, AND SUCH REMEDY SHALL BE BUYER'S ENTIRE AND EXCLUSIVE REMEDY.

The MM–180 was delivered in March 1980. According to Master's witnesses, the machine malfunctioned frequently during the first year of operation, and was inoperable from 25% to 50% of the time available for its use, substantially more than the industry average of five percent "downtime" for comparable machines. No specific defect was predominant, according to Master's witnesses. Problems with tool changing, control, alignment and spindles were among Master's complaints. Over K & T's objection, testimony was introduced estimating lost profits on customer orders allegedly unfilled because of the inoperability of the machine. It was conceded that the machine's performance improved after the first year and that the machine was still in use at the time of trial, in September and October 1984. Master did not attempt to return the machine to K & T and obtain a refund of the purchase price.

K & T's witnesses disputed Master's account of the machine's first year of operation. Although conceding a substantial number of service calls, K & T's area service manager testified that only four or five of thirteen service calls were "valid." K & T's service personnel contended that Master had programmed the machine improperly and that the programs were extensively edited, thereby impairing the efficiency of the MM–180. K & T's witnesses testified that Master did not have adequate testing equipment or spare parts for the machine, and that Master's employees lacked the ability to "troubleshoot" and perform regular maintenance. The testimony about "downtime" during the first year was also disputed; the K & T witnesses testified that the MM–180 was not inoperative on most occasions that K & T service personnel visited the Master's plant. K & T's manager of technical services testified that no service calls were requested from May

1981 to March 1982, and that during the second year of operation the MM–180 was operable approximately 98% of the time available for its use.

Suit was instituted by K & T in July 1981 to recover the cost of two service calls made after the one-year warranty had expired; Master counterclaimed, seeking the damages that are the subject of this appeal.

At the conclusion of the trial, the trial court instructed the jury that it could award consequential damages notwithstanding the contractual exclusion if it found that K & T failed "to make the machine as warranted." The jury was not instructed concerning the proof necessary to demonstrate that the repair or replacement warranty had failed of its essential purpose.

The critical portion of the jury charge follows:

> You may find that there was an agreement between the parties to limit the remedy in the event that the machine was not as described in the plaintiff's warranties. You may also find that the plaintiff's contract contained a provision which limited the plaintiff's responsibilities in the event the machine was not as warranted to the repair or replacement of defective parts and that that limitation was limiting his liability to the repair or replacement of defective parts. *However, if you find that the plaintiff's actions in repairing and replacing the defective parts did not make the machine as warranted, that is, free from the defects in material and workmanship, then you may find that the defendant is entitled to all of its consequential economic losses and damages despite the language of the contract.* A manufacturer and buyer may agree that only certain warranties shall apply and all others be excluded. Any implied warranty may be excluded if at the time of the sale the manufacturer-seller specifically makes known to the buyer that such warranties are excluded. Any warranties of the machine center involved in this case was [*sic*] based upon the assumption that it would be used in a reasonable manner appropriate to the purpose for which it was intended. (Emphasis added.)

The jury returned a verdict in favor of Master for $57,000. In answer to written questions on the verdict sheet, the jury found that although K & T had not sold a defectively-designed product, it had nevertheless breached its contract with Master. In affirming, the Appellate Division interpreted the jury verdict to mean that the limited remedy of repair and replacement had failed of its essential purpose. *N.J.S.A. 12A:2–719(2).* The Appellate Division concluded that under the circumstance of this case "the failure adequately to repair the machine rendered ineffective the exclusion of consequential damages." *211 N.J. Super. at 381.*

II

An understanding of the appropriate relationship between the U.C.C. provisions authorizing the exclusion of consequential damages, *N.J.S.A. 12A:2–719(3)*, and the relief available to a buyer when a limited remedy fails of its essential purpose, *id.* at 12A:2–719(2), is enhanced by reference to the purpose and policies of the Code. These are:

(a) to simplify, clarify and modernize the law governing commercial transactions;

(b) to permit the continued expansion of commercial practices through custom, usage and agreement of the parties;

(c) to make uniform the law among the various jurisdictions. [*Id.* at 12A:1–102(2).]

The Code instructs that it "shall be liberally construed to promote [these] purposes and policies," *id.* at 12A:1–102(1), and that the effect of its provisions "may be varied by agreement," *id.* at 12A:1–102(3). The Official Comments to the Code emphasize that it is to be interpreted in a commercially reasonable manner, and that parties are free to vary its terms through custom, usage or express agreement:

This Act is drawn to provide flexibility so that, since it is intended to be a semi-permanent piece of legislation, it will provide its own machinery for expansion of commercial practices. It is intended to make it possible for the law embodied in this Act to be developed by the courts in the light of unforeseen and new circumstances and practices. [Comment 1, *N.J.S.A. 12A:1–102.*]

Subsection (3) states affirmatively at the outset that freedom of contract is a principle of the Code: "the effect" of its provisions may be varied by "agreement." The meaning of the statute itself must be found in its text, including its definitions, and in appropriate extrinsic aids; it cannot be varied by agreement. But an agreement can change the legal consequences which would otherwise flow from the provisions of the Act. "Agreement" here includes the effect given to course of dealing, usage of trade and course of performance. [Comment 2, *N.J.S.A. 12A:1–102.*]

See also Spring Motors Distribs., Inc. v. Ford Motor Co., 98 N.J. 555, 571 (1985) ("Underlying the U.C.C. policy is the principle that parties should be free to make contracts of their choice.").

Under the Code, consequential losses constitute a recoverable item of damages in the event of a breach by the seller. *N.J.S.A. 12A:2–714(3).* However, the potential significance of liability for consequential damages in commercial transactions undoubtedly prompted the Code's drafters, consistent with the Code's endorsement of the principle of freedom of contract, to make express provision for the limitation or exclusion of such damages. *N.J.S.A. 12A:2–719.*[3] For certain sellers, exposure to liability for consequential damages could drastically affect the conduct of their business, causing them to increase their prices or limit their markets. As one commentator has observed:

---

3. *N.J.S.A. 12A:2–719(3) provides:*

Consequential damages may be limited or excluded unless the limitation or exclusion is unconscionable. Limitation of consequential damages for injury to the person in the case of consumer goods is prima facie unconscionable but limitation of damages where the loss is commercial is not.

As a general matter, consequential damages exclusions are hands down the most significant limitation of liability in a contract for the sale of goods. Potential liability for consequential damages in commercial contexts, usually in the form of the buyer's lost profits from the use or resale of the goods in its business, is enormous in comparison to the contract price of the goods. On the other hand, the general or direct damages that a buyer may suffer upon a seller's breach are finite and can be gauged at a maximum amount either in terms of the contract price or market price of the goods to be sold. Potential consequential losses are a much different proposition. They can exceed, and most likely will exceed, the value of the goods by an unknown quantum, depending not so much on the actions and machinations of the seller as on the individual operating structure of the buyer and on the buyer's contracts and relationships with third parties. [Anderson, "Failure of Essential Purpose and Essential Failure on Purpose: A Look at Section 2–719 of the Uniform Commercial Code," 32 *Sw.L.J.* 759, 774 (1977) (hereinafter Anderson).]

In a commercial setting, the seller's right to exclusion of consequential damages is recognized as a beneficial risk-allocation device that reduces the seller's exposure in the event of breach.

An equally fundamental principle of the Code, comparable in importance to the right of parties to limit or exclude consequential damages, is the Code's insistence that for a party aggrieved by breach of a sales contract, "at least minimum adequate remedies be available." Comment 1, *N.J.S.A. 12A:2–719.* To this end, the Code provides that

> [w]here circumstances cause an exclusive or limited remedy to fail of its essential purpose, remedy may be had as provided in this Act. [*N.J.S.A. 12A:2–719(2).*]

The Code comment explains the purpose of this provision:

> [I]t is of the very essence of a sales contract that at least minimum adequate remedies be available. If the parties intend to conclude a contract for sale within this Article they must accept the legal consequence that there be at least a fair quantum of remedy for breach of the obligations or duties outlined in the contract. Thus any clause purporting to modify or limit the remedial provisions of this Article in an unconscionable manner is subject to deletion and in that event the remedies made available by this Article are applicable as if the stricken clause had never existed. Similarly, under subsection (2), where an apparently fair and reasonable clause because of circumstances fails in its purpose or operates to deprive either party of the substantial value of the bargain, it must give way to the general remedy provisions of this Article. [Comment 1, *N.J.S.A. 12A:2–719.*]

These competing policies—freedom of contract, including the right to exclude liability for consequential damages, and the insistence upon minimum adequate remedies to redress a breach of contract—frame the issue before us. If a limitation or exclusion of consequential damages is not unconscionable when the contract is made, must it be held unenforceable if the limited remedies provided in the contract do not achieve their intended purpose?

To the extent that the U.C.C. addresses this issue, its response is inconclusive. The Code provides merely that when a limited remedy fails of its essential purpose, "remedy may be had as provided in this Act." *N.J.S.A. 12A:2–719(2)*. As noted, consequential damages is a buyer's remedy "provided in this Act," *N.J.S.A. 12A:2–714(3)*, but the Code is silent as to whether that remedy survives if the sales contract excludes it.

A related question concerns the extent of the remedies other than consequential damages that are available to a buyer relegated to a limited remedy that has failed to achieve its essential purpose. Typically, the limited remedy most often offered by sellers is the repair and replacement warranty found in the sales contract in this case. *See* Eddy, "On the 'Essential' Purposes of Limited Remedies: The Metaphysics of UCC Section 2–719(2), 65 *Cal.L.Rev.* 28, 61 (1977) (hereinafter Eddy). When a repair and replacement warranty is combined, as here, with an exclusion of consequential damages, the commercial objectives of the contracting parties are reasonably evident. As summarized in *Beal v. General Motors Corp., supra, 354 F.Supp. at 426*:

> The purpose of an exclusive remedy of replacement or repair of defective parts, whose presence constitute a breach of an express warranty, is to give the seller an opportunity to make the goods conforming while limiting the risks to which he is subject by excluding direct and consequential damages that might otherwise arise. From the point of view of the buyer the purpose of the exclusive remedy is to give him goods that conform to the contract within a reasonable time after a defective part is discovered. When the warrantor fails to correct the defect as promised within a reasonable time he is liable for a breach of that warranty.

The commonly-applied formula to compute a buyer's damages for breach of any warranty, including the repair or replacement warranty, is the difference "between the value of the goods accepted and the value they would have had if they had been as warranted." *N.J.S.A. 12A:2–714(2)*; *see Chatlos Sys. v. National Cash Register Corp.*, 635 F.2d 1081, 1087 (3d Cir.1980); White & Summers, *supra* § 10–2, at 376. Concededly, in many cases the fair market value of defective goods will be difficult to prove. As White and Summers explain:

> When repair or replacement is not possible, determining the value of defective goods *as accepted* may be more difficult than ascertaining the value as warranted. Several courts have used the price received on a prompt resale as the appropriate measure. Others have accepted the appraisal testimony of expert witnesses as evidence of actual market value at the time of acceptance. In a few cases, courts have found (or allowed the jury to find) that the value

of accepted goods was zero and permitted the buyer to recover the purchase price. [White & Summers, *supra* § 10–2, at 281 (footnotes omitted).]

The Code also affords to the buyer the right to recover incidental damages, *N.J.S.A. 12A:2–714(3)*, as well as the right to revoke acceptance of the goods within a reasonable time after discovery of a nonconformity that substantially impairs the value of the goods to the buyer, *N.J.S.A. 12A:2–608*; *see* Eddy, *supra*, 65 *Cal.L.Rev.* at 84. A buyer who revokes his acceptance of goods may also seek damages for the seller's breach. New Jersey Study Comment 2, *N.J.S.A. 12A:2–608*; *N.J.S.A. 12A:2–711(1)*.

Courts that have considered the validity of an exclusion of consequential damages in the context of a repair or replacement warranty that has not fulfilled its purpose have reached significantly different results. A substantial number of courts seem to have adopted the view that there is an integral relationship between the exclusion of consequential damages and the limited remedy of repair or replacement, so that the failure of the limited remedy necessarily causes the invalidation of the exclusion of consequential damages. Characteristic of the rationale employed by these courts is this excerpt from the opinion in the *Birdsboro* case:

> It is the specific breach of the warranty to repair that plaintiff alleges caused the bulk of its damages. This Court would be in an untenable position if it allowed the defendant to shelter itself behind one segment of the warranty when it has allegedly repudiated and ignored its very limited obligations under another segment of the same warranty, which alleged repudiation has caused the very need for relief which the defendant is attempting to avoid. [*Jones & McKnight Corp. v. Birdsboro Corp., supra, 320 F.Supp. at 43–44.*]

In sharp contrast, a number of other courts have concluded that an exclusion of consequential damages is to be viewed independently of a limited warranty of repair or replacement, so that if the warranty fails to fulfill its purpose, the validity of the consequential damages exclusion depends upon the specific circumstances and the probable intention of the parties.

The Third Circuit's opinion in *Chatlos* is typical of the reasoning articulated in these cases. In *Chatlos*, a manufacturer of telecommunications equipment purchased a computer system from National Cash Register (NCR) to perform a number of bookkeeping and accounting functions. The sales agreement warranted that the system would be free from defects for twelve months, excluded liability for consequential damages, and limited NCR's responsibilities to the correction of any errors or defects within sixty days. *Chatlos Sys., Inc. v. National Cash Register Corp., supra, 635 F.2d at 1084, 1085.* When the computer system's defects could not satisfactorily be corrected by NCR's technicians, Chatlos instituted suit. *Id. at 1084.* The trial court, applying New Jersey law, awarded damages for breach of warranty, *N.J.S.A. 12A:2–714(2)*, and also awarded consequential damages for lost profits since it concluded that the contractual exclusion was unenforceable. *Ibid.*

The Third Circuit agreed that the limited repair remedy had failed of its essential purpose, *id. at 1086*, but reversed the trial court's award of consequential damages, concluding that the contractual exclusion of consequential damages should be enforced:

> It appears to us that the better reasoned approach is to treat the consequential damage disclaimer as an independent provision, valid unless unconscionable. This poses no logical difficulties. A contract may well contain no limitation on breach of warranty damages but specifically exclude consequential damages. Conversely, it is quite conceivable that some limitation might be placed on a breach of warranty award, but consequential damages would expressly be permitted.

The limited remedy of repair and a consequential damages exclusion are two discrete ways of attempting to limit recovery for breach of warranty. *See id. § 12A:2–719(1)(a)*; *Beal v. General Motors Corp., supra*. The Code, moreover, tests each by a different standard. The former survives unless it fails of its essential purpose, while the latter is valid unless it is unconscionable. We therefore see no reason to hold, as a general proposition, that the failure of the limited remedy provided in the contract without more, invalidates a wholly distinct term in the agreement excluding consequential damages. The two are not mutually exclusive.

Whether the preclusion of consequential damages should be effective in this case depends upon the circumstances involved. The repair remedy's failure of essential purpose, while a discrete question, is not completely irrelevant to the issue of the conscionability of enforcing the consequential damages exclusion. The latter term is "merely an allocation of unknown or undeterminable risks." U.C.C. § 2–719, Official Comment 3, *N.J.Stat.Ann. § 12A:2–719*, at 537 (West 1962). Recognizing this, the question here narrows to the unconscionability of the buyer retaining the risk of consequential damages upon the failure of the essential purpose of the exclusive repair remedy.

It is also important that the claim is for commercial loss and the adversaries are substantial business concerns. We find no great disparity in the parties' bargaining power or sophistication. Apparently, Chatlos, a manufacturer of complex electronic equipment, had some appreciation of the problems that might be encountered with a computer system. Nor is there a "surprise" element present here. The limitation was clearly expressed in a short, easily understandable sales contract. This is not an instance of an ordinary consumer being misled by a disclaimer hidden in a "linguistic maze." *Cf. Gladden v. Cadillac Motor Car Division, 83 N.J. 320 (1980)*.

Thus, at the time the contract was signed there was no reason to conclude that the parties could not competently agree upon the allocation of risk involved in the installation of the computer system.

From the perspective of the later events, it appears that the type of damage claimed here came within the realm of expectable losses. Some disruption of normal business routines, expenditure of employee time, and impairment of efficiency cannot be considered highly unusual or unforeseeable in a faulty computer installation. Moreover, although not determinative, it is worth mentioning that even though unsuccessful in correcting the problems within an appropriate time, NCR continued in its efforts. Indeed, on the date of termination NCR was still actively working on the system at the Chatlos plant. In fact, the trial court thought that Chatlos should have cooperated further by accepting the installation of the programs. This is not a case where the seller acted unreasonably or in bad faith.

In short, there is nothing in the formation of the contract or the circumstances resulting in failure of performance that makes it unconscionable to enforce the parties' allocation of risk. We conclude, therefore, that the provision of the agreement excluding consequential damages should be enforced, and the district court erred in making an award for such losses. [*635 F.2d at 1086–87* (footnotes omitted).]

We adopt as the better reasoned analysis the approach of the Third Circuit in *Chatlos*. It is consistent with the view articulated by Justice Pollock, writing for the Court in *Spring Motors Distribs., Inc. v. Ford Motor Co., supra*:

> As between commercial parties, then, the allocation of risks in accordance with their agreement better serves the public interest than an allocation achieved as a matter of policy without reference to that agreement. [*98 N.J. at 577.*]

We are also persuaded that many routine business transactions would be dislocated by a rule requiring the invalidation of a consequential damage exclusion whenever the prescribed contractual remedy fails to operate as intended. Concededly, well-counseled businesses could avoid the problem posed by better draftsmanship of their sales contracts. *See* White & Summers, *supra* § 12–11, at 470–71. But the commercial reality is that for many sellers, immunity from liability for their customers' consequential damages may be indispensable to their pricing structure and, in extreme cases, to their solvency.

Nor do we find that enforcement of a consequential damages limitation when a limited remedy has failed of its essential purpose is necessarily inequitable to the buyer. As noted earlier, the Code affords remedies other than consequential damages when a warranty is breached. *See supra* at *596–598*. Ordinarily, the availability of such remedies will assure the buyer of "a fair quantum of remedy for breach of the obligations or duties outlined in the contract." Comment 1, *N.J.S.A. 12A:2–719.*

Accordingly, we conclude that *N.J.S.A. 12A:2–719* does not require the invalidation of an exclusion of consequential damages when limited contractual remedies fail of their essential purpose. It is only when the circumstances of the transaction, including the seller's breach, cause the consequential damage exclusion to be inconsistent with the intent and reasonable commercial expectations of the parties that invalidation of the exclusionary clause would be appropriate under the Code. For example, although a buyer may agree to the exclusion of consequential damages, a seller's wrongful repudiation of a repair warranty may expose a buyer to consequential damages not contemplated by the contract, and other Code remedies may be inadequate. In such circumstances, a court might appropriately decline to enforce the exclusion. *See* Anderson, *supra*, 31 *Sw.L.J.* at 791–92; *cf.* Eddy, *supra*, 65 *Cal.L.Rev.* at 92–93 (courts should analyze circumstances of each case in deciding whether to enforce consequential damages exclusion).

III

In this case, a sophisticated buyer purchased for $167,000 a complex, computer-controlled machine tool. The sales agreement allocated to Master the risk of consequential damages. K & T's responsibility was to repair or replace the machine or any defective parts in order that the machine would be "free from defects in material and workmanship" for the shorter of twelve months or four thousand operating hours. The testimony at trial demonstrated that the MM–180 was a complex piece of equipment and that its normal operation could be adversely affected by a wide variety of factors, including deficiencies in maintenance or in computer-programming for which Master's employees were responsible. The machine possessed characteristics analogous to the machine described in *American Electric Power Co. v. Westinghouse Electric Corp., supra*, where an exclusion of consequential damages was upheld despite the failure of a limited remedy:

> [T]he rule that the agreed-upon allocation of commercial risk should not be disturbed is particularly appropriate where, as here, the warranted item is a highly complex, sophisticated, and in some ways experimental piece of equipment. Moreover, compliance with a warranty to repair or replace must depend on the type of machinery in issue. In the case of a multi-million dollar turbine-generator, we are not dealing with a piece of equipment that either works or does not, or is fully repaired or not at all. On the contrary, the normal operation of a turbine-generator spans too large a spectrum for such simple characterizations. [*American Elec. Power Co. v. Westinghouse Electric Corp., 418 F.Supp. 435, 458 (S.D.N.Y 1976)*.]

Furthermore, although the sales contract provided for the alternative remedy of return of the machine and refund of the purchase price with K & T's consent, there was no evidence indicating that Master ever attempted to invoke this relief. To the contrary, the evidence indicated that the machine's performance continued to improve and that it was in use at the time of trial, four-and-one-half years after delivery.

Nor was there any contention by Master that K & T did not make service calls when requested. The evidence at trial verified that K & T made at least thirteen service calls during the first twelve months of operation, at times sending several service personnel to work on the

Master's machine. What was sharply disputed was Master's claim that the machine was defective during the first year, since K & T's witnesses testified that most of the problems encountered during this period were the fault of Master's employees.

Under these factual circumstances, the trial court's instruction to the jury was inappropriate. The jury was charged that it could award consequential damages "despite the language of the contract" if it found that K & T failed "to make the machine as warranted."[6] In our view, the facts in this record do not justify invalidation of the consequential damage exclusion, a risk allocation agreed to by both parties. We do not agree with the Appellate Division's conclusion that "the allocation of risk through exclusion of consequential damages was inextricably tied to the limitation of remedies."

Master could have offered evidence, although it did not, that the value of the MM–180 was less than the contract price because of the erratic performance during the first year. In such event Master would have been entitled to a jury instruction as to the measure of damages for breach of the repair and replacement warranty. *N.J.S.A. 12A:2–714(2)*; *ante* at 596–597. We are fully satisfied that the availability of damages for breach of the repair and replacement warranty under *N.J.S.A. 12A:2–714(2)*, combined with the return and refund provision in the contract of sale not invoked by Master, adequately fulfills the U.C.C.'s mandate that "at least minimum adequate remedies be available" when a limited remedy fails to achieve its purpose.

For the reasons stated, the judgment of the Appellate Division is reversed and the matter is remanded to the Law Division for a new trial.

* * *

Northern Illinois Gas illustrates the first set of questions—concerning the exclusivity of agreements to limit contractual remedies. The contract at issue in that case called for Energy Cooperative to sell Northern 56 million barrels of naphtha over an extended period, which Northern planned to convert into natural gas. The contract contained a liquidated damages clause providing that if one party defaulted before the full quantity of naphtha had been bought and sold, the other could, on demand, recover damages of one cent for every gallon not delivered. During the period of the contract, the United States government eased price restrictions on natural gas, making it cheaper for Northern to buy the gas directly and dispense with the conversion; Northern breached its contract and did just this. At the time of breach, applying the liquidated damages clause would have entitled Energy Cooperative to $13.5 million in damages. However, the regulatory change had, unsurprisingly, changed the value of naphtha not

---

6. We would also observe that the jury should have been more thoroughly instructed as to the standards to use in determining whether the limited warranty had failed of its essential purpose. In view of the sharply conflicting testimony as to the cause of the machine's erratic operation during the first year and the extent of its "downtime," a more comprehensive instruction in the context of the evidence adduced would have enhanced the reliability of the jury's verdict.

just for Northern but also on the market generally, so that the naphtha price specified in the contract had come far to exceed the market price that Energy Cooperative could expect to receive on resale. Accordingly, Energy Cooperative's actual disappointed expectations, calculated according to contract-market price differentials, came to $305.5 million. Unsurprisingly, Energy Cooperative sought to recover the larger amount, and Northern sought to limit recovery to the smaller amount, arguing that the liquidated damages clause established Energy Cooperative's exclusive remedy.

The trial court ruled in favor of Energy Cooperative, and Northern appealed. The appellate court considered two arguments in favor of Energy Cooperative's claim to its actual lost expectations. Neither side of the first argument—which turns on the legal effect of Energy Cooperative's decision not to claim its rights under the liquidated damages clause—is intelligibly presented in the edited opinion, and so the entire argument is best set aside here.

The opinion turns, instead, on a statutory argument, involving the interaction between UCC §§ 2–718 and 2–719. § 2–718, as comment [1] explains, renders even under-liquidated damages clauses enforceable as long as they are not unconscionable. The clause at issue in *Northern Illinois Gas* is therefore legally enforceable, and the live issue in the case is not its enforceability but rather its scope. This issue is addressed by UCC § 2–719, which says that subject to the commands of § 2–718, the parties to a contract may agree to a specified remedy to alter or limit the remedies otherwise available under the Code, and that—according to § 2–719(1)(b)—"resort to a remedy specified by a contract is optional unless the remedy is expressly agreed to be exclusive, in which case it becomes the sole remedy." The central question in the case, at least as presented by the appellate opinion, is what effect this provision has on the liquidated damages clause in the contract. Energy Cooperative argued that because the liquidated damages clause in the contract did not expressly claim to be exclusive, the provision, straightforwardly applied, permitted it to seek recovery for its actual damages. Northern Illinois countered by drawing a distinction between provisions that "limit a remedy," to which § 2–719(1)(b)'s requirement of express exclusivity applies, and provisions that fix an agreed upon measure of damages, to which § 2–719(1)(b) does not apply, and which may be exclusive even though not expressly claiming to be so.

The court accepted Northern Illinois' highly formal approach to the case and so ruled that Energy Cooperative could recover no more than the $13.5 million specified by the liquidated damages clause. It sought to draw a distinction between a *remedy*—which picks out a category of loss (for example, consequential damages)—and a *measure of damages*—which merely identifies the size of a loss within a fixed category. The court held that a liquidated damages clause, which provides an agreed upon formula for calculating the amount of money damages owed, is a measure of damages and not a limitation of remedies. The clause at issue therefore did not limit a remedy within the meaning of § 2–719(1)(b), and therefore might be exclusive even though not expressly so. In reaching this conclusion, the court relied substantially on what it viewed as the structure of the UCC, specifically the fact that the Code separates the treatment of liquidated damages clauses (§ 2–718) and clauses establishing limitations of remedies (§ 2–719), and, moreover, conditions its treatment of the latter on its treatment of the former, and not the other way around. This led the court to limit scope of § 2–719(1)(b)'s requirement that exclusivity be express to apply only to clauses that limit remedies and not to liquidated damages clauses, such as the one at issue in *Northern Illinois Gas*.

Northern Illinois Gas illustrates the basic doctrinal difference between the treatment of over- and under-liquidated damages clauses: in the over-compensatory case, the question is whether the clause is valid; in the under-compensatory case the principal question is whether the clause is exclusive. It is far from clear, however, whether the *Northern Illinois Gas* opinion does a good job of addressing the question that it (properly) posed. The distinction that the opinion develops—in essence between a category of loss and a quantum of damages—should be familiar by now, and is surely worth making. But whether § 719(b)(1) means to pick out this distinction, and *a fortiori* whether a particular liquidated damages clause means to engage the distinction, are of course different questions entirely.

Moreover, there are good reasons not to apply this formalism rigidly to the facts of *Northern Illinois Gas*. After all, only one class of remedy—based on the lost sales revenues suffered by Energy Cooperative—was ever really at play in the case (as will be true whenever a victim of breach has a clear duty to resell or to cover, so that only damages based on contract-market or contract-resale/cover price differentials will ever be recoverable). Accordingly, questions concerning categories of loss could never sensibly have arisen on the facts at hand—the only live question being the one that involved the quantum of contract-market damages, or their equivalent. Insofar as the idea behind § 2–791(1)(b)'s principle that exclusive remedies must be expressly exclusive is that promisees who accept one way of vindicating their promissory entitlements should not be held to abandon alternatives unless they have done so explicitly, then this idea surely suggests applying the rule that exclusivity must be express to Energy Cooperative's circumstances also.

These considerations are only made more persuasive by the fact that the liquidated damages clause at issue in *Northern Illinois Gas*, when treated as exclusive, deprived Energy Cooperative of roughly 95% of its claim, which is in effect depriving it of compensation for a whole category of loss. Finally, the court's argument becomes weaker still in light of the fact that § 2–719(1)(b)'s insistence that exclusivity be express would clearly have applied had Energy Cooperative sought specific performance rather than money damages, since as to this claim the liquidated damages clause clearly functions as a limitation of remedy. Moreover, Energy Cooperative's specific performance claim would, on the facts of the case, have been simply an action for the price (recall UCC § 2–709), that is, a claim for precisely the same money damages that its market-price based damages claim sought. The court's approach therefore seems to entail that the damages

Energy Cooperative can recover will vary, by a factor of 20, depending on a purely formal change in the way in which Energy Cooperative styles its claim. But this seems madness—surely the formalism is, in the present circumstances, simply too artificial to bear so great a weight. Even the narrow sense in which the distinction between a claim for contract-market damages and an action for the price is not purely formal—the fact that an action for the price is not always possible but is instead available only to sellers who meet the conditions (involving, roughly, acceptance by the buyer or the impossibility of resale) set out in § 2–709—emphasizes the deep oddity of the court's approach. Why should the exclusivity of a liquidated damages clause depend on these surely wholly orthogonal facts?

But although the *Northern Illinois Gas* court's reasoning (and hence also the legal rule that the case establishes) is highly dubious, the outcome the opinion reached may perhaps be defended, on other grounds. The real issue in the case is not the formal question whether the liquidated damages clause announces a limitation of remedy or merely a measure of damages but rather the substantive question—in effect a question of contract interpretation—what scope the parties intended to give the liquidated damages clause when they agreed to it. As mentioned earlier, some liquidated damages clauses are intended simply as transactions-costs minimizing devices, which establish an easily computable formula that tracks, more or less accurately, actual contractual expectations. Other liquidated damages clauses, by contrast, involve an allocation of risks, for example of the risk of price fluctuations, and these may be under-compensatory. Such an under-compensatory liquidated damages clause allocates the risk of price increases to the buyer by allowing the seller to breach and capture the increase without reimbursing the buyer for her now higher cover costs. And it allocates the risk of price-decreases to the seller, by allowing the buyer to breach, as Northern did breach, and capture the value of the price decrease without reimbursing the seller for her now lower resale revenues.

This distinction becomes problematic in the face of unusual price fluctuations. Although it is always possible for a liquidated damages clause to anticipate and allocate the risk of even the most outlandish price changes, unusual price fluctuations are unlikely to have been anticipated. Moreover, unanticipated price changes will render even liquidated damages clauses that were intended to be transactions-costs saving compensatory devices under-compensatory in application. Thus it becomes necessary to ask, when applying a liquidated damages clause in the context of an extraordinary price fluctuation, whether the clause was intended to cover the circumstances that have arisen and, if it was not, which party should bear the residual risk that the circumstances present.[8] This is, of course, just the exclusivity question now reformulated, in substantive rather than formal terms, as a question about the best reconstruction of a contract's risk-allocation provisions.

---

8. This argument is analogous to the argument developed above that liquidated damages clauses that turn out to be over-compensatory should not be enforced even if they appeared, *ex ante*, to be reasonable.

This way of posing the question suggests that the *Northern Illinois Gas* court—in limiting Energy Cooperative's recovery to the smaller damages contemplated by the liquidated damages clause—might have reached the right outcome. The dramatic downward shift in the price of naphtha that triggered the dispute—being caused not by ordinary market fluctuations in supply and demand but rather by an exogenous regulatory change—was plausibly not anticipated when the liquidated damages clause at issue in the case was drafted. If this was so, then it seems reasonable that such an unanticipated risk should be born by a seller, Energy Cooperative, whose business was naphtha, rather than a buyer, Northern, who merely used naphtha as one substitutable input. And that is precisely the result that the court's admittedly strained formal reasoning in the end imposed. To be sure, if it turned out that Energy Cooperative merely produced naphtha as a byproduct of some other business activity and that Northern was a naphtha dealer, then these considerations might cut the other way. The opinion, unsurprisingly, does not clearly develop the relevant facts (although these might have been in the record), since its formal approach does not recognize their relevance.

Although the questions concerning exclusivity that dominate *Northern Illinois Gas* are by far the most prominent questions that arise in connection with under-liquidated damages clauses, questions concerning the *validity* of under-liquidated damages clauses also occasionally come up. And although these questions matter only on the margins of contractual practice, they may figure more prominently in the theoretical reconstruction of contract law. This makes them worth taking seriously.

To begin with, comment [1] to UCC § 2–718 observes that an under-liquidated damages clause may be invalid because is unconscionable (under UCC § 2–302).[9] Moreover, UCC § 2–719 identifies an additional and more-precise circumstance in which even under-liquidated damages that pass the unconscionability test might nevertheless be invalid. Specifically, § 2–719(2) states that when a limited remedy, such as one established by a liquidated damages clause taken as exclusive, "fails of its essential purpose," then becomes invalid, and the law's default remedies become renewedly available to disappointed promisees, or, as the UCC puts it, "remedy may be had as provided under this Act."

The issues raised by this provision are revealed in *Kearney & Trecker Corp.* Kearney agreed to sell Master Engraving a complicated, computer-controlled machine that performed machining operations on metal parts. The sales contract warranted that the machine would be free from defects and would require relatively little maintenance.[10] The contract also contained two further provisions: one that expressly exempted Kearney from

---

9. Note that UCC § 2–719(3) expands on § 2–302 to identify a specific class of under-liquidated damages clauses that are, in effect, inherently unconscionable: "Limitation of consequential damages for injury to the person in the case of consumer goods is prima facie unconscionable but limitation of damages where the loss is commercial is not."

10. These warranties were established by the contract's language and also, in some measure, by Kearney's advertising. Warranties will be discussed more extensively below.

liability for any incidental or consequential damages (including lost profits) arising out of a breach of the contract; and another stating that Kearney's liability in case of defects in the machine would not exceed either the costs of repairing the defects or replacing the machine, or the costs of accepting return of the defective machine and granting a refund and adding that these would be Master Engraving's exclusive remedies under the contract. As it turned out, the machine that Kearney delivered malfunctioned and, in spite of Kearney's efforts to repair it, remained inoperable between 25% and 50% of the time. Master Engraving sued and sought to include lost profits in its damages, in spite of the two clauses limiting its remedies to exclude lost profits.

The lower courts allowed Master Engraving's lost profits claim to go to the jury notwithstanding the two contract clauses purporting to limits its remedies, and the jury returned a substantial verdict in its favor. Kearney appealed to the New Jersey Supreme Court, which issued a careful opinion addressing the limits of the validity of under liquidated damages clauses.

The opinion begins by observing that although consequential damages (including for lost profits) are ordinarily recoverable under the UCC, the parties may by agreement limit or exclude recovery for such damages. However, the UCC also makes clear that although agreements excluding recovery of consequential damages for injury to the person in the case of consumer goods are prima facie unconscionable, agreements excluding recovery for consequential damages associated with commercial losses are not. These principles reflect the UCC's general commitment to freedom of contract, coupled with a more particular recognition that a seller's ability to exclude consequential damages can be a beneficial risk-allocation device, especially when the consequential damages arise in light of lost profits, which may exceed by many times the sales price of the good in question and are in any case effectively business risks of the buyer. Moreover, although unconscionable limitations of remedy will be struck down as invalid (as will be all unconscionable contract terms), limitations of remedy in the commercial context, including those that prevent recovery of substantial commercial losses, are not generally unconscionable. This conclusion reflects the general tendency of the UCC (and indeed of contract law more broadly) to reserve the unconscionability doctrine for exceptional cases, typically involving the exploitation of unsophisticated or otherwise vulnerable parties, and almost never to apply the doctrine for the benefit of sophisticated commercial entities.[11]

However, the UCC also contains § 2–719(2), which provides that when a limited remedy fails of its essential purpose, then "remedy may be had as provided under this Act." These remedies—the default remedies established by the UCC in the absence of any special agreement by the parties—allow recovery for consequential losses, including in particular for lost profits. The provision reflects the UCC's policy that "it is of the very essence of a sales contract that at least minimum adequate remedies be

---

11. This point will be developed in greater detail in the materials directly devoted to unconscionability in a subsequent chapter.

available" so that "if the parties intend to conclude a contract for sale within this Article they must accept the legal consequence that there be at least a fair quantum of remedy for breach of the obligation or duties outlined in the contract."[12] The UCC thus opens up the possibility that a limitation of remedies clause that is not unconscionable when adopted may nevertheless be unenforceable where the limited remedies that it specifies do not achieve their essential purpose. As the comment to § 2–719 explains, "where an apparently fair and reasonable clause because of the circumstances fails in its purpose or operates to deprive either party of the substantial value of the bargain, it must give way to the general remedy provisions of this Article"[13]—that is, to the general remedies, including consequential damages, that are available under the UCC.

The typical case applying UCC § 2–719(2) arises when, as in *Kearney & Trecker Corp.*, a contract contains a clause limiting a seller's remedy to repairing or replacing a defective machine or part, but the seller proves unable or unwilling to repair or replace within a reasonable time. In light of this failure, the repair or replacement remedy fails of its essential purpose—so that treating this as the only available remedy will, in effect, leave the buyer with no remedy at all—and the code therefore suggests that the exclusions of other remedies contemplated by the repair or replace clause should be struck down, and the default remedies of the UCC, including consequential damages for lost profits, should be reinstated.

This much is uncontroversial,[14] but *Kearney & Trecker Corp.*, like many cases arising under § 2–917(2), presents a further twist. The contract at issue includes not one limitation of remedy clause but two: in addition to the clause stating that Kearney's liability in case of defects would not exceed the cost of repair or replacement, the contract contained another, separate clause that expressly exempted Kearney from liability for any incidental or consequential damages (including lost profits). *Kearney & Trecker Corp.* therefore raises the further question whether the failure of the repair and replace remedy to operate as intended or fulfill its purpose should invalidate not just the general exclusion of all other remedies incorporated in the contract clause establishing the repair or replace remedy but also the additional exclusion of consequential damages announced by a separate clause in the contract.

Jurisdictions are split on this issue. Some courts treat the failure of the limited repair and replace remedy to invalidate all limitations of remedy in the contract, all exclusions of consequential damages, on the grounds that all of these remedy clauses (regardless of where they appear on the page) should be read together as establishing a unified whole. A seller who

---

12. UCC § 2–719 comment [1].

13. UCC § 2–719 comment [1].

14. As one commentator has observed, "[t]here is now broad consensus among the courts that a seller's failure to effect a timely and satisfactory cure indicates that an exclusive repair or replacement limitation has failed of its essential purpose." John A. Sebert, Jr., *Rejection, Revocation, and Cure Under Article 2 of the Uniform Commercial Code: Some Modest Proposals*, 84 Nw. U. L. REV. 375, 396 (1990).

repudiates her agreement to repair and replace cannot then shelter herself behind a limitation of remedy clause that, wherever it is located in the contractual text, in effect belongs to (or is at least intertwined with) this agreement. Other courts, including the New Jersey Supreme Court in *Kearney & Trecker Corp.*, have taken the opposite view, treating the two remedy clauses as separate and independent. On this approach, the mere fact that a repair or replace warranty fails of its essential purpose is not in itself sufficient to invalidate an additional accompanying limitation of liability to exclude consequential damages. Thus the New Jersey Court held that such an exclusionary clause is invalid only when it is separately unconscionable or when the circumstances of the case cause the operation of the exclusionary clause to be inconsistent with the intent of the parties.

This last suggestion, concerning the intent of the parties, emphasizes that (like many cases concerning liquidated damages clauses) *Kearney & Trecker Corp.* in the end raises a question of contractual interpretation. This may seem to undermine the entire preceding analysis, because it replaces the focus on the UCC's policies that drove this analysis with a very different focus on the parties' intents. But statutory and policy-based considerations do not recede nearly so quickly or completely in this context. The meaning of the contractual text (including as informed by inferences about the parties' intents) will often remain obscure in these cases, and so interpretive presumptions based on statutory and policy considerations will be difficult to shift. This is, in effect what guided the result in *Kearney & Trecker Corp.* itself: the New Jersey Court was impressed with the utility of limiting remedies to repair and replacement, especially in cases in which a contract involves a complex machine whose buyer will have substantial and unobservable control over the conditions of its operation and whose lost profits figure centrally in any consequential damages claim.[15] The Court was therefore unwilling to invalidate a plausible effort to achieve this limitation, save in extraordinary circumstances.[16]

Kearney & Trecker Corp., raises one final doctrinal puzzle, involving UCC § 2–316, which governs disclaimers of warranties by sellers. Warranties will be considered more systematically in later materials, but it is obvious even without more that such disclaimers have an effect that substantially overlaps with the effect of limitations of remedies of the sort governed by § 2–719. If a seller sells a good to a buyer and successfully

---

15. For many machines, including likely the one at issue in *Kearney & Trecker Corp.*, a certain percentage of malfunctions is inevitable, and consequential losses following these malfunctions are inevitable. If such loses are recoverable, then there will be expensive litigation about how to compute them. The expected costs of such litigation reduce the contractual surplus—the amount available for the buyer and seller to divide on whatever terms their negotiations conclude. Accordingly, it is better for both parties to rule out recovery for such hard to compute losses up front and split the benefits of lower transactions costs by doing the deal at a lower price. Buyers who wish it may then take out separate insurance (if it is available) against some consequential losses.

16. An example of such circumstances, mentioned by the Court, arises when a seller's wrongful repudiation of a repair or replacement warranty exposes the buyer to consequential damages *not* contemplated in making the contract. (In *Kearney & Trecker Corp.*, by contrast, the lost profits clearly were contemplated and indeed were precisely what the parties had in mind in drafting the limitations.)

disclaims all warranties, then the buyer cannot recover consequential damages it suffers due to defects in the good, cannot recover contract-cover price differentials, and cannot even recover repair costs. Furthermore, § 2–316 places no substantive limits on the seller's power to disclaim warranties (other than the general limits imposed by § 2–302's doctrine of unconscionability). This makes it natural to ask why sellers do not achieve through § 2–316 what they cannot achieve through § 2–719? One possibility is that disclaimers of warranty are less popular with buyers than are limitations of remedies. This possibility is made especially salient, moreover, by the fact that § 2–316 does impose on sellers seeking to disclaim a warranty the requirement that the disclaimer must be conspicuous. There is no analogous procedural requirement in § 2–719.

7.3 LIQUIDATED DAMAGES *REDUX*

In the core case, liquidated damages clauses function purely as transactions-cost reducing devices—as formulas to facilitate the calculation of otherwise difficult to quantify contractual expectations. One might say that these liquidated damages clauses are merely actuarial. In other cases, however, and in particular when they function as limitations of remedies, liquidated damages clauses serve not just to quantify but rather to alter contractual expectations: they do not so much calculate the value to the promisee of the primary performance that the contract contemplates as establish what might be viewed, formally, as an alternative, secondary, set of contractual expectations, which the promisor is entitled, in appropriate circumstances, to vindicate in substitution for her primary performance. For example, a clause limiting a promisee's remedy to the repair or replacement of a machine provided by the promisor in effect changes the promisee's contractual expectations from the value of a working machine to the value of the promisors' reasonably effective efforts to provide a working machine.

The announced rule favoring the enforcement of liquidated damages provisions is generally applied with respect to core-case, actuarial liquidated damages clauses. But as the discussions of the prior subsections reveal, things are much more complicated with respect to over- and under-liquidated damages clauses. Agreements to establish penalties for breach are quite generally invalid. And agreements (including ones that are not unconscionable) to limit contractual remedies to less than the promisees' ordinary contractual expectations—to less than the value that the promisee would have enjoyed on full performance—are valid only as long as they leave the promisee in possession of what the comment to the UCC calls "a fair quantum of remedy for breach of the obligation or duties outlined in the contract."[17]

These rules leave contracting parties a fair amount of substantive free-play to allocate contractual risks as they wish, to be sure. Contracts that

---

17. UCC § 2–719 comment [1].

contemplate reasonable recovery for broad and speculative consequential damages are enforceable, as are contracts that effectively eliminate recovery for consequential damages. But this wide substantive range disguises the constraints that the rules limiting enforceability of liquidated damages clauses impose on contracts. Moreover, as the analyses of the previous subsections demonstrate, the constraints that the law imposes on party-selected remedies cannot naturally be explained in terms of economic efficiency. Penalty clauses are generally invalid even though they may sometimes be efficient. And the UCC's willingness to invalidate clauses limiting contractual remedies also departs from economic efficiency—as is revealed (in a backhanded way) by the New Jersey Supreme Court's effort to restrict the application of the statute in the name of efficiency.

Contrary to the common claim that the enforcement of party-chosen remedies renders the expectation remedy a default rule only, these surveys suggest that the expectation remedy, properly understood, is a mandatory rule. Specifically, it is essential to contract law that a promisee retain a remedy that may be cast, conceptually, as vindicating his contractual expectations. Moreover, the ground of the law's insistence that party-chosen contract remedies retain the formal properties of expectation regime is best explained not in instrumental terms—including terms that focus on the efficiency of contract remedies—but in formal terms. At least as a descriptive matter, the economic approach to law seems unable to accommodate doctrinal practice on this front.

This formal idea—that expectation remedy, conceptually understood, functions as a mandatory part of contract law—can explain the law's refusal to enforce penalty clauses. Unlike traditional contract damages, contractual penalties are not an alternative means of vindicating the contractual expectations of disappointed promisees. The penalties established by over-liquidated damages clauses are not intended ever to be paid. Indeed, they are intended not to be paid—never to be paid. Penalty clauses are, as the cases sometimes say, designed not to remedy a breach but rather to compel performance—not to vindicate a promisee's disappointed expectations but rather to ensure that his expectations will never be disappointed in the first place. Contractual penalties therefore present no problem as long as the deterrence that they impose is effective—as long as no breach occurs. But if, in spite of the penalty, a breach does occur, then the penalty becomes otiose: it has failed of its purpose, which was to prevent rather than to compensate breach, and it has thus become unnecessary to the law's ongoing purpose of vindicating contractual rights, now by compensating the breach. By invalidating penalty clauses, the law declares its continuing commitment to vindicating contractual expectations. Contracting parties are free to expand on their expectations, including by choosing non-standard remedies to vindicate these expectations if they are disappointed. But the parties cannot step outside contract law's expectation-based conceptual framework. They cannot enforceably adopt remedies that abandon this framework in favor of another.

The law governing under-liquidated damages clauses is amenable to an analogous analysis, this time focusing on the lower bound of the conceptual category "contractual expectations." Many limitations on damages can, of course, straightforwardly be recast simply as altering promisee expectations (at least in certain contingencies). Clauses that exclude consequential damages from a promisee's remedies present a typical and prominent example. Viewed conceptually, these clauses do not retreat from the principle of vindicating promisee expectations but instead simply alter the *content* of a promisee's expectations: whereas a contract without the limitation of remedy clause underwrites promisee expectations to enjoy the full value of performance in every state of the world, a contract that includes the expressly limited remedy underwrites promisee expectations to enjoy the full value of performance only in some cases, and the less valuable limited remedy in others. Thus, when the law, enforcing the limitation of remedy clause, still requires the promisor to provide the limited remedy that the clause identifies, it vindicates the promisee's expectations.

But not every limitation of damages can be understood as consistent with the conceptual structure of the expectation remedy in this way. Certainly an agreement that there should be no remedy in the event of breach is inconsistent with the basic concept of vindicating contractual expectations. A "contract" containing a clause freeing a breaching promisor from every obligation to provide any remedy does not underwrite contractual expectations at all; indeed it does not involve a promise at all. Moreover, other, less extreme limitations of remedy are similarly inconsistent with the conceptual structure of the expectation remedy. Perhaps most important among these are agreements that a disappointed promisee's damages shall be limited to his reliance. A contract term that limits a promisee's remedy to reliance damages also undermines any contractual expectations that the promisee might otherwise entertain. Such a term expressly rejects any *forward-looking* commitments that the contract containing it might otherwise encompass and replaces these contractual expectations with a purely backward-looking regime. Under this regime, a breach does not so much disappoint the promisee by depriving him of what he was to receive as harm him by depriving him of something he already enjoyed.

This is not to say that persons who exchange assurances but limit their liability to reliance enter into no legal relation at all. By giving notice that their representations may be relied upon, such persons may opt into the legal framework governing the tort of misrepresentation (expanding this framework beyond its usual narrow bounds). Indeed, as a later chapter will discuss at greater length, much of what is called contract law may be reinterpreted as an extensive expansion and elaboration of this tort. But they have not undertaken any forward-looking project or any obligations to respect one another's expectations in such a project of the type that lie at contract's conceptual core. Critically, they have not undertaken to vindicate the success of any joint undertaking, even in the purely formal sense associated with the conceptual account of the expectation remedy. If contract is to remain a distinctive form of obligation, it must retain this forward-looking component, and it must therefore insist that contracting parties form and honor genuinely forward-looking contractual expectations.

The language of the UCC and its official comment—the emphasis that even the most reasonable, most conscionable limited contract remedy must not in its application fail of the essential purpose of contract law and that this purpose makes it the "the very essence of a sales contract that at least minimum adequate remedies be available," which must include "at least a fair quantum of remedy for breach of the obligation or duties outlined in the contract"[18]—may plausibly be read to track this understanding of the conceptual structure of the expectation remedy. These provisions may be read to require, in other words, that promisees retain some distinctively promissory remedy, some remnant of the value of the bargain, something that may be cast as a contractual expectation. To be sure, the cases interpreting and applying the statute do not cleanly support this interpretation. This is perhaps because the logic of the conceptual argument leaves open an alternative to the UCC's treatment of limitations of remedy that leave no distinctive contractual remedies in place. Instead of, as the UCC proposes, striking down the limitations and imposing, in their stead, the full range of expectation-based damages contemplated by the background law, one might read the failed remedies as destroying the contractual nature of the parties relationship *tout court*, leaving the plaintiff with, at most, a tort-like claim based on the defendant's misrepresentation.[19]

These observations suggest that whatever the substantive free-play that the law accords contracting parties in setting the nature and bounds of their contractual expectations, including through the use of party-drafted remedy clauses, the law insists that, as a formal matter, the parties retain a commitment to vindicating one another's contractual expectations. Liquidated damages clauses that depart from this commitment are generally rendered invalid by contract law. And accordingly, although the conventional content of the expectation remedy—that it includes both direct and consequential damages, for example, and that consequential damages extend to include lost profits—is a default rule only, contract law's commitment to the *conceptual* structure of the expectation remedy is expressed in a *mandatory* rule. All of this, finally, is just long-winded and explicit way of making the point that the dissenters in *Groves* made more briefly and cryptically:

> "[T]he obligation of the contract does not inhere or subsist in the agreement itself ... but in ... the act of the law in binding the promisor to perform his promise. A contract is not a law, nor does it make law. It is the agreement plus the law that makes the ordinary contract an enforceable obligation."

And the law—even as it allows parties to vary their contractual expectations more or less freely—insists that promisees retain remedies that vindicate what remain expectations, properly so called.

---

18.   UCC § 2–719 comment [1].

19.   Certainly courts applying § 2–719(2) sometimes limit a buyer's remedy to some form of returning the goods and receiving a refund of their purchase price, which is in effect the reliance remedy that, although insufficient to underwrite a contractual relationship, is natural under the tort-based approach.

CHAPTER 8

PUNITIVE DAMAGES

The legal rule invalidating party-generated penalty clauses has a direct analog in the doctrine that punitive damages are not available for simple breach of contract.

Uniform Commercial Code

§ 1–305   Remedies to be Liberally Administered

(a) The remedies provided by [the Uniform Commercial Code] must be liberally administered to the end that the aggrieved party may be put in as good a position as if the other party had fully performed but neither consequential or special damages nor penal damages may be had except as specifically provided in [the Uniform Commercial Code] or by other rule of law.

(b) Any right or obligation declared by [the Uniform Commercial Code] is enforceable by action unless the provision declaring it specifies a different and limited effect.

Official Comment

2004 Main Volume. Source: Former Section 1–106. Changes from former law: Other than changes in the form of reference to the Uniform Commercial Code, this section is identical to former Section 1–106.

1.   Subsection (a) is intended to effect three propositions. The first is to negate the possibility of unduly narrow or technical interpretation of remedial provisions by providing that the remedies in the Uniform Commercial Code are to be liberally administered to the end stated in this section. The second is to make it clear that compensatory damages are limited to compensation. They do not include consequential or special damages, or penal damages; and the Uniform Commercial Code elsewhere makes it clear that damages must be minimized. Cf. Sections 1–304, 2–706(1), and 2–712(2). The third purpose of subsection (a) is to reject any doctrine that damages must be calculable with mathematical accuracy. Compensatory damages are often at best approximate: they have to be proved with whatever definiteness and accuracy the facts permit, but no more. Cf. Section 2–204(3).

2.   Under subsection (b), any right or obligation described in the Uniform Commercial Code is enforceable by action, even though no remedy

may be expressly provided, unless a particular provision specifies a different and limited effect. Whether specific performance or other equitable relief is available is determined not by this section but by specific provisions and by supplementary principles. Cf. Sections 1–103, 2–716.

3. "Consequential" or "special" damages and "penal" damages are not defined in the Uniform Commercial Code; rather, these terms are used in the sense in which they are used outside the Uniform Commercial Code.

Restatement 2d of Contracts

§ 355 Punitive Damages

Punitive damages are not recoverable for a breach of contract unless the conduct constituting the breach is also a tort for which punitive damages are recoverable.

Comments & Illustrations

Comment a. Compensation not punishment. The purposes of awarding contract damages is to compensate the injured party. See Introductory Note to this Chapter. For this reason, courts in contract cases do not award damages to punish the party in breach or to serve as an example to others unless the conduct constituting the breach is also a tort for which punitive damages are recoverable. Courts are sometimes urged to award punitive damages when, after a particularly aggravated breach, the injured party has difficulty in proving all of the loss that he has suffered. In such cases the willfulness of the breach may be taken into account in applying the requirement that damages be proved with reasonable certainty (Comment *a* to § 352); but the purpose of awarding damages is still compensation and not punishment, and punitive damages are not appropriate. In exceptional instances, departures have been made from this general policy. A number of states have enacted statutes that vary the rule stated in this Section, notably in situations involving consumer transactions or arising under insurance policies.

Illustrations:

1. A is employed as a school teacher by B. In breach of contract and without notice B discharges A by excluding him from the school building and by stating in the presence of the pupils that he is discharged. Regardless of B's motive in discharging A, A cannot recover punitive damages from B. A can recover compensatory damages under the rule stated in § 347, including any damages for emotional disturbance that are allowable under the rule stated in § 353.

2. A and B, who are neighbors, make a contract under which A promises to supply water to B from A's well for ten years in return for B's promise to make monthly payments and share the cost of repairs. After several years, the relationship between A and B deteriorates and A, in breach of contract and to spite B, shuts off

the water periodically. B cannot recover punitive damages from A. B can recover compensation damages under the rule stated in § 347 if he can prove them with reasonable certainty (§ 352), and the court may take into account the willfulness of A's breach in applying that requirement. See Comment *a* to § 352.

Comment b. Exception for tort. In some instances the breach of contract is also a tort, as may be the case for a breach of duty by a public utility. Under modern rules of procedure, the complaint may not show whether the plaintiff intends his case to be regarded as one in contract or one in tort. The rule stated in this Section does not preclude an award of punitive damages in such a case if such an award would be proper under the law of torts. See *Restatement, Second, Torts § 908.* The term "tort" in the rule stated in this Section is elastic, and the effect of the general expansion of tort liability to protect additional interests is to make punitive damages somewhat more widely available for breach of contract as well. Some courts have gone rather far in this direction.

Illustrations:

3. A, a telephone company, contracts with B to render uninterrupted service. A, tortiously as well as in breach of contract, fails to maintain service at night and B is unable to telephone a doctor for his sick child. B's right to recover punitive damages is governed by *Restatement, Second, Torts § 908.*

4. A borrows money from B, pledging jewelry as security for the loan. B, tortiously as well as in breach of contract, sells the jewelry to a good faith purchaser for value. A's right to recover punitive damages is governed by *Restatement, Second, Torts § 908.*

* * *

The unequivocal rule set out in these materials, it might be thought, leaves nothing left to discuss concerning contract and punitive damages. But the simple statement of the rule is deceptive, and the role of punitive damages in contract law is both conceptually interesting and practically important. The rejection of punitive damages is conceptually interesting because the reasons for which punitive damages are never available for simple breaches of contract open a window into the deeper moral structure of contractual obligation. Contract doctrine concerning punitive damages is practically important because although punitive damages are never available in an action for simple breach of contract, punitive damages are available in connection with a wide range of conduct that arises in and around breach of contract. As even the Restatement accepts, punitive damages clearly become available when a breach of contract is accompanied by an independent tort, of a type for which punitive damages are allowed. Most commonly, a breach of contract may be accompanied by fraud, (gross) negligence, conversion, or even tortuous interference with contractual relations. Moreover, there have been suggestions (although tentative and halting) in the case-law, that there may exist a separate tort of bad faith breach of contract, which can also sustain awards of punitive damages. This is just a summary, of course, and it is an intricate matter to identify the precise relationship between a breach of contract and a concomitant tort that is required in order for the tort to be able to sustain a punitive damages award in conjunction with the breach of contract. Answers to the question how much more than simple breach is required before punitive damages become available turn out to have substantial impact on contractual practice, and the question is therefore highly contested.

This chapter takes up contract law's attitude towards punitive damages: the justification for the basic rule that punitive damages are not available for simple breach of contract, without more; and the elaborations that have arisen around this basic rule to explain just what more is required for punitive damages to become available. Addressing these questions will require a brief comparison between contract and tort. It will also require paying careful attention to what might be called, perhaps a little pompously, the distinction between ontology and epistemology: it is one thing to characterize conduct concerning breach of contract that can, in principle, justify an award of punitive damages against the breacher; it is quite another to fashion doctrines that will allow courts as they actually are—given their imperfections and in particular the many obstacles that exist to reliable judicial fact-finding—accurately to identify when punitive damages are justified, or even to manage punitive damages in a way so that the threat of their being awarded does not damage, or indeed undermine, commercial practice.

One final point is worth making by way of introduction. The discussion that follows will focus single-mindedly on the question when punitive damages are appropriate at all, to the exclusion of a second question, concerning the appropriate size of punitive damages awards (even when they are justified). This question—and in particular the question of the outer bound of the legitimate ratio between punitive and compensatory damages—has been much discussed by courts in recent years. Indeed, this has probably been the dominant issue concerning punitive damages in American law.[1] If it is not addressed here, that is only because of substantive divisions among doctrinal areas of law. The question of the appropriateness of punitive damages, *tout court*, involves basic questions concerning the doctrinal structure of contract. Questions concerning the proper limits on the size of punitive damage awards do not, but instead involve questions at the intersection between civil procedure and constitutional law, and in particular concerning the demands of due process.

8.1 JUSTIFYING PUNITIVE DAMAGES

Punitive damages, as is often observed, arise at the intersection of public and private law. They are public-law-like in that, like criminal

---

1. The leading cases include: *TXO Production Corp. v. Alliance Resources, Corp.*, 509 U.S. 443 (1993); *BMW v. Gore*, 517 U.S. 559 (1996); *State Farm Mutual Auto Insurance Co. v. Campbell*, 538 U.S. 408 (2003).

punishment, they look beyond the vindication of the private right of plaintiffs (which is secured by adequate compensatory damages) to the public condemnation of defendants' conduct, announced by the punitive character of the damage awards. At the same time, punitive damages are private-law-like in that, their non-compensatory character to the contrary notwithstanding, they are remitted not to the public fisc (as criminal fines are) but to individual plaintiffs. Punitive damages thus raise questions concerning both the justification for extracting super-compensatory remedies from defendants and the justification for remitting these remedies to plaintiffs. The materials below nevertheless focus principally (and indeed almost exclusively) on the first question. This is the question that raises the more basic matters of principle. On the one hand, if extracting punitive damages from defendants cannot be justified, then the practice falls down, even if there would be nothing wrong with allowing plaintiffs to be overcompensated. On the other hand, if super-compensatory judgments against defendants can be justified, then it seems surely within the discretion of the state (perhaps on a loose analogy to prosecutorial discretion) to dispose of the excess damages as it sees fit, including by disbursing them to plaintiffs (although when and whether it is wise to do so, and when the better course is to contribute the excess awards to some public fund or other, of course remains an open question).

Two very different families of arguments may be brought to bear in answering the question when it is justified to impose punitive damages on defendants: economic arguments concerning the efficient deterrence of the conduct that gives rise to punitive damage awards; and moral arguments concerning retribution against defendants whose wrongful conduct deserves punishment.

The main outlines of the economic case for punitive damages are straightforward and proceed along analogous lines in contract and tort. Insofar as so-called compensatory damages are in fact under-compensatory, so that deserving plaintiffs are not, on average, actually made whole, compensatory damages under-deter the behavior that harms these plaintiffs and others who are similarly situated. Moreover, there are good reasons for suspecting that compensatory damages do not in fact fully restore plaintiffs to the positions that they would have enjoyed but for being wronged. Some of the sources of under-compensation in contract law should by now be familiar: the certainty requirement, for example, in effect sets speculative damages at zero, even when it is clear that some damages have in fact been sustained; and the foreseeability requirement (especially when coupled with transactions costs that prevent promisees from notifying their promisors of their vulnerability to the types of unusual damages that this requirement excludes) similarly threatens to leave plaintiffs undercompensated. Nor are these the only sources of under-compensation in private law. One especially important effect—which applies not just in contract but also (and perhaps even more) in tort—is that many deserving plaintiffs simply make no effort to vindicate their rights, because they do not wish to bear the costs of doing so, do not know how to do it, or perhaps do not even know that their rights have been violated.[2]

This pattern of under-compensation from so-called compensatory remedies entails that efficient deterrence requires giving some plaintiffs remedies that are, as to them, super-compensatory. In the simplest case—in which the only source of under-compensation is that some deserving plaintiffs do not sue or sue and do not win—efficient deterrence requires awarding punitive damages to successful plaintiffs in quantities such that these plaintiffs' total recoveries equal their actual losses multiplied by the inverse of the probability of a similarly situated plaintiff's successfully vindicating her rights. Of course, elaborating this idea to accommodate the many imperfections in the actual compensatory regimes provided by private law is an immensely difficult and complex exercise.[3] But the basic idea remains straightforward.

The economic argument is also plainly insufficient to make the case for punitive damages, all-things-considered. Insofar as punitive damages genuinely impose punishments on the defendants against whom they are awarded, the fact that it would be efficient to award them cannot sustain their justification by itself. Punishment, after all, should be reserved for the wicked, which means that it must be *deserved*—and specifically deserved by the person who is punished. Thus it is plain beyond peradventure that, in an ordinary criminal context, punishing the innocent cannot be justified by the fact that doing so achieves optimal deterrence. And the mere fact that punitive damages are quasi-private whereas criminal law is purely public presents no good reason for abandoning this requirement of desert. (Indeed, it may even serve to increase the need for desert. The authority of the private citizen who initiates an action for punitive damages is surely less than the authority of the executive officer who initiates a criminal prosecution. And the institutional checks in place to prevent the private citizen from abusing his position are surely less effective than the institutional checks to prevent prosecutorial abuses.) Even if it were possible to develop a moral argument showing that desert is not required for the justification of punitive damages (perhaps proceeding by analogy to the moral arguments marshaled in favor of strict liability regimes for compensatory damages), then the basic case for punitive damages would be made by this moral argument and not by economic considerations involving efficiency.

In any event, the positive law clearly accepts the idea that, no matter what efficiency requires, punitive damages may be awarded only where they are deserved. It is an essential problem in the law of remedies—

---

2. To be sure, it also sometimes happens that undeserving plaintiffs successfully extract damages to which they are not entitled. But empirical research demonstrates quite conclusively that the extent of under-claiming far exceeds the extent of over-claiming. *See* William Felstiner, Richard Abel & Austin Sarat, *The Emergence and Transformation of Disputes: Naming, Blaming, Claiming*, 15 LAW & SOC'Y REV. 631, 632 (1980); Tom Baker, *Blood Money, New Money, and the Moral Economy of Tort Law in Action*, 35 LAW & SOC'Y REV. 275 (2001).

3. For some sample efforts see, e.g., STEVEN SHAVELL, ECONOMIC ANALYSIS OF ACCIDENT LAW 162 (1987); Robert Cooter, *Punitive Damages for Deterrence: When and How Much*, 40 ALA. L. REV. 1143, 1146–48 (1989).

spanning both contract and tort—to identify the class of conduct for which private-law punishment is deserved. And this problem—the problem of characterizing the wrongs that can support punitive damage awards—will be the focus of the presentation of the doctrinal materials below. In particular, the materials below will make a systematic approach at answering the question, precisely when is conduct arising in and around a breach of contract sufficiently wicked to merit extracting punitive damages from the breacher?

Of course, once this question has been answered—once the classes of conduct that can justify punitive damages have been identified and characterized—concerns for efficiency may come back into play. Desert, after all, is a necessary but not a sufficient condition for punitive damages being all-things-considered desirable, and it may be unwise or imprudent to punish even those who could not legitimately object to being punished. This suggestion, as it turns out, appears prominently in arguments against awarding punitive damages, in the context both of tort and of contract.

Given that the under-compensation of supposedly compensatory damages is so well-documented and that the theoretical argument that the efficient response to such under-compensation is not to reject but rather to *embrace* punitive damages is so well-established, it may seem surprising that self-styled "efficiency-based" objections to punitive damages abound. Nevertheless, opponents of punitive damages are often heard to suggest that the juries that typically award punitive damages are irrational, capricious, and even biased against (especially corporate) defendants. They then add that the threat of enormous and wholly unjustified punitive damage awards introduces such uncertainty into the affairs of potential defendants (again, especially corporations) so as inefficiently to over-deter beneficial conduct, no matter what may be true concerning the under-compensatory nature of private law remedies, on average.[4]

But while it may be possible, in theory, for the uncertainty associated with the threat of unwarranted punitive damages to generate over-deterrence of beneficial conduct that outweighs the under-deterrence of wrongful conduct associated with the under-compensatory nature of ordinary private law damages, it is quite implausible that the actual threat of punitive damages is anywhere near large enough to produce this effect. Even in tort, where punitive damages are in principle available, there is overwhelming evidence that juries only very rarely award them—that punitives are awarded in only 2–4% of plaintiffs' victories. Moreover, punitive damages are not just rare but also relatively small, in the sense that they constitute an insignificant portion of the overall damages that are awarded. Thus, in a large-scale study of jury verdicts, punitive damages constituted only 5% of total tort liability. And even in areas in which the threat of punitives is much trumpeted, these damages constituted only a relatively small proportion of total damage awards: 27% in toxic torts, 0.6%

---

4. A typical example is W. Kip Viscusi, *The Social Costs of Punitive Damages Against Corporations in Environmental and Safety Torts*, 87 GEO. L.J. 285 (1998).

in medical malpractice, and 0.05% in products liability.[5] These numbers suggest that punitive damages are not the main (or even a substantial) liability-based deterrent to corporate activity. Again, it is hard to see how they could possibly overbalance the under-deterrence associated with the fact that Americans fail even to file claims in about 90% of accidents.[6]

The data from tort therefore suggests that, at least in this area of law, prudence does not counsel against imposing punitive damages where they are deserved. There is, of course, no analogous data available for contract, since the law disfavors punitive damages in this area. And the speculative argument that punitive damages are imprudent may well be stronger in contract than it is in tort, as the materials below will suggest. Nevertheless, it remains clear from what has been said that punitive damages are nowhere so clearly imprudent as to render irrelevant the question when they are deserved. Accordingly, the materials below begin by taking up this question in greater doctrinal detail—first, and by way of illustration, in tort, and then in contract.

8.2   PUNITIVE DAMAGES IN TORT

An early and famous tort case illustrates the main issues as well, and perhaps even better, than any other.

Grimshaw v. Ford Motor Co.

Court of Appeals of California, Fourth District, 1981.
119 Cal.App.3d 757.

■ TAMURA, J. A 1972 Ford Pinto hatchback automobile unexpectedly stalled on a freeway, erupting into flames when it was rear ended by a car proceeding in the same direction. Mrs. Lilly Gray, the driver of the Pinto, suffered fatal burns and 13–year–old Richard Grimshaw, a passenger in the Pinto, suffered severe and permanently disfiguring burns on his face and entire body. Grimshaw and the heirs of Mrs. Gray (Grays) sued Ford Motor Company and others. Following a six-month jury trial, verdicts were returned in favor of plaintiffs against Ford Motor Company. Grimshaw was awarded $2,516,000 compensatory damages and $125 million punitive damages; the Grays were awarded $559,680 in compensatory damages. On Ford's motion for a new trial, Grimshaw was required to remit all but $3 1/2 million of the punitive award as a condition of denial of the motion.

Ford appeals from the judgment and from an order denying its motion for a judgment notwithstanding the verdict as to punitive damages. Grim-

---

5. *See* David Luban, *A Flawed Case Against Punitive Damages*, 87 GEO. L.J. 359 (1998). For other useful discussions, *see* Galanter & Luban, *Poetic Justice: Punitive Damages and Legal Pluralism*, 42 AM. U. L. REV. 1393 (1993); Dorsey D. Ellis, *Fairness and Efficiency in the Law of Punitive Damages*, 56 S. CAL. L. REV. 1 (1982); *and* Daniel & Martin, *Myth and Reality in Punitive Damages*, 75 MINN. L. REV. 1 (1990).

6. Luban, *supra* note 5 at 90.

shaw appeals from the order granting the conditional new trial and from the amended judgment entered pursuant to the order. The Grays have cross-appealed from the judgment and from an order denying leave to amend their complaint to seek punitive damages.

Ford assails the judgment as a whole, assigning a multitude of errors and irregularities, including misconduct of counsel, but the primary thrust of its appeal is directed against the punitive damage award. Ford contends that the punitive award was statutorily unauthorized and constitutionally invalid. In addition, it maintains that the evidence was insufficient to support a finding of malice or corporate responsibility for malice. Grimshaw's cross-appeal challenges the validity of the new trial order and the conditional reduction of the punitive damage award. The Grays' cross-appeal goes to the validity of an order denying them leave to amend their wrongful death complaint to seek punitive damages.

Facts

Since sufficiency of the evidence is in issue only regarding the punitive damage award, we make no attempt to review the evidence bearing on all of the litigated issues. Subject to amplification when we deal with specific issues, we shall set out the basic facts pertinent to these appeals in accordance with established principles of appellate review: We will view the evidence in the light most favorable to the parties prevailing below, resolving all conflicts in their favor, and indulging all reasonable inferences favorable to them.

The Accident

On May 28, 1972, Mrs. Gray, accompanied by 13–year–old Richard Grimshaw, set out in the Pinto from Anaheim for Barstow to meet Mr. Gray. The Pinto was then 6 months old and had been driven approximately 3,000 miles. Mrs. Gray stopped in San Bernardino for gasoline, got back onto the freeway (Interstate 15) and proceeded toward her destination at 60–65 miles per hour. As she approached the Route 30 off-ramp where traffic was congested, she moved from the outer fast lane to the middle lane of the freeway. Shortly after this lane change, the Pinto suddenly stalled and coasted to a halt in the middle lane. It was later established that the carburetor float had become so saturated with gasoline that it suddenly sank, opening the float chamber and causing the engine to flood and stall. A car traveling immediately behind the Pinto was able to swerve and pass it but the driver of a 1962 Ford Galaxie was unable to avoid colliding with the Pinto. The Galaxie had been traveling from 50 to 55 miles per hour but before the impact had been braked to a speed of from 28 to 37 miles per hour.

At the moment of impact, the Pinto caught fire and its interior was engulfed in flames. According to plaintiffs' expert, the impact of the Galaxie had driven the Pinto's gas tank forward and caused it to be punctured by the flange or one of the bolts on the differential housing so that fuel sprayed from the punctured tank and entered the passenger compartment through gaps resulting from the separation of the rear wheel well sections from the floor pan. By the time the Pinto came to rest after the collision, both occupants had sustained serious burns. When they emerged from the vehicle, their clothing was almost completely burned off. Mrs. Gray died a few days later of congestive heart failure as a result of the burns. Grimshaw managed to survive but only through heroic medical measures. He has undergone numerous and extensive surgeries and skin grafts and must undergo additional surgeries over the next 10 years. He lost portions of several fingers on his left hand and portions of his left ear, while his face required many skin grafts from various portions of his body. Because Ford does not contest the amount of compensatory damages awarded to Grimshaw and the Grays, no purpose would be served by further description of the injuries suffered by Grimshaw or the damages sustained by the Grays.

Design of the Pinto Fuel System

In 1968, Ford began designing a new subcompact automobile which ultimately became the Pinto. Mr. Iacocca, then a Ford vice president, conceived the project and was its moving force. Ford's objective was to build a car at or below 2,000 pounds to sell for no more than $2,000.

Ordinarily marketing surveys and preliminary engineering studies precede the styling of a new automobile line. Pinto, however, was a rush project, so that styling preceded engineering and dictated engineering design to a greater degree than usual. Among the engineering decisions dictated by styling was the placement of the fuel tank. It was then the preferred practice in Europe and Japan to locate the gas tank over the rear axle in subcompacts because a small vehicle has less "crush space" between the rear axle and the bumper than larger cars. The Pinto's styling, however, required the tank to be placed behind the rear axle leaving only 9 or 10 inches of "crush space"—far less than in any other American automobile or Ford overseas subcompact. In addition, the Pinto was designed so that its bumper was little more than a chrome strip, less substantial than the bumper of any other American car produced then or later. The Pinto's rear structure also lacked reinforcing members known as "hat sections" (two longitudinal side members) and horizontal cross-members running between them such as were found in cars of larger unitized construction and in all automobiles produced by Ford's overseas operations. The absence of the reinforcing members rendered the Pinto less crush resistant than other vehicles. Finally, the differential housing selected for the Pinto had an exposed flange and a line of exposed bolt heads. These protrusions were sufficient to puncture a gas tank driven forward against the differential upon rear impact.

Crash Tests

During the development of the Pinto, prototypes were built and tested. Some were "mechanical prototypes" which duplicated mechanical features of the design but not its appearance while others, referred to as "engineering prototypes," were true duplicates of the design car. These prototypes as well as two production Pintos were crash tested by Ford to determine, among other things, the integrity of the fuel system in rear-end accidents. Ford also conducted the tests to see if the Pinto as designed would meet a proposed federal regulation requiring all automobiles manufactured in 1972 to be able to withstand a 20–mile–per–hour fixed barrier impact without significant fuel spillage and all automobiles manufactured after January 1, 1973, to withstand a 30–mile–per–hour fixed barrier impact without significant fuel spillage.

The crash tests revealed that the Pinto's fuel system as designed could not meet the 20–mile–per–hour proposed standard. Mechanical prototypes struck from the rear with a moving barrier at 21 miles per hour caused the fuel tank to be driven forward and to be punctured, causing fuel leakage in excess of the standard prescribed by the proposed regulation. A production Pinto crash tested at 21 miles per hour into a fixed barrier caused the fuel neck to be torn from the gas tank and the tank to be punctured by a bolt head on the differential housing. In at least one test, spilled fuel entered the driver's compartment through gaps resulting from the separation of the seams joining the rear wheel wells to the floor pan. The seam separation was occasioned by the lack of reinforcement in the rear structure and insufficient welds of the wheel wells to the floor pan.

Tests conducted by Ford on other vehicles, including modified or reinforced mechanical Pinto prototypes, proved safe at speeds at which the Pinto failed. Where rubber bladders had been installed in the tank, crash tests into fixed barriers at 21 miles per hour withstood leakage from punctures in the gas tank. Vehicles with fuel tanks installed above rather than behind the rear axle passed the fuel system integrity test at 31–miles–per–hour fixed barrier. A Pinto with two longitudinal hat sections added to firm up the rear structure passed a 20–mile–per–hour rear impact fixed barrier test with no fuel leakage.

The Cost to Remedy Design Deficiencies

When a prototype failed the fuel system integrity test, the standard of care for engineers in the industry was to redesign and retest it. The vulnerability of the production Pinto's fuel tank at speeds of 20 and 30–miles–per–hour fixed barrier tests could have been remedied by inexpensive "fixes," but Ford produced and sold the Pinto to the public without doing anything to remedy the defects. Design changes that would have enhanced the integrity of the fuel tank system at relatively little cost per car included the following: Longitudinal side members and cross members at $2.40 and $1.80, respectively; a single shock absorbent "flak suit" to protect the tank at $4; a tank within a tank and placement of the tank over the axle at $5.08 to $5.79; a nylon bladder within the tank at $5.25 to $8; placement of the tank over the axle surrounded with a protective barrier at a cost of $9.95 per car; substitution of a rear axle with a smooth differential housing at a cost of $2.10; imposition of a protective shield between the differential housing and the tank at $2.35; improvement and reinforcement of the bumper at $2.60; addition of eight inches of crush space a cost of $6.40. Equipping the car with a reinforced rear structure, smooth axle, improved bumper and additional crush space at a total cost of $15.30 would have made the fuel tank safe in a 34 to 38–mile–per–hour rear-end collision by a vehicle the size of the Ford Galaxie. If, in addition to the foregoing, a bladder or tank within a tank were used or if the tank were protected with a shield, it would have been safe in a 40 to 45–mile–per–hour rear impact. If the tank had been located over the rear axle, it would have been safe in a rear impact at 50 miles per hour or more.

Management's Decision to Go Forward With Knowledge of Defects

Harley Copp, a former Ford engineer and executive in charge of the crash testing program, testified that the highest level of Ford's management made the decision to go forward with the production of the Pinto, knowing that the gas tank was vulnerable to puncture and rupture at low rear impact speeds creating a significant risk of death or injury from fire and knowing that "fixes" were feasible at nominal cost. He testified that management's decision was based on the cost savings which would inure from omitting or delaying the "fixes."

Mr. Copp's testimony concerning management's awareness of the crash tests results and the vulnerability of the Pinto fuel system was corroborated by other evidence.

The fact that two of the crash tests were run at the request of the Ford chassis and vehicle engineering department for the specific purpose of demonstrating the advisability of moving the fuel tank over the axle as a possible "fix" further corroborated Mr. Copp's testimony that management knew the results of the crash tests. Mr. Kennedy, who succeeded Mr. Copp as the engineer in charge of Ford's crash testing program, admitted that the test results had been forwarded up the chain of command to his superiors.

Finally, Mr. Copp testified to conversations in late 1968 or early 1969 with the chief assistant research engineer in charge of cost-weight evaluation of the Pinto, and to a later conversation with the chief chassis engineer who was then in charge of crash testing the early prototype. In these conversations, both men expressed concern about the integrity of the Pinto's fuel system and complained about management's unwillingness to deviate from the design if the change would cost money.

The Action

Grimshaw (by his guardian ad litem) and the Grays sued Ford and others. Grimshaw was permitted to amend his complaint to seek punitive damages but the Grays' motion to amend their complaint for a like purpose was denied. The cases were thereafter consolidated for trial. Grimshaw's case was submitted to the jury on theories of negligence and strict liability; the Grays' case went to the jury only on the strict liability theory.

Ford's Appeal

On the issue of punitive damages, Ford contends that its motion for judgment notwithstanding the verdict should have been granted because the punitive award was statutorily unauthorized and constitutionally invalid and on the further ground that the evidence was insufficient to support a finding of malice or corporate responsibility for malice. Ford also seeks reversal of the punitive award for claimed instructional errors on malice and proof of malice as well as on the numerous grounds addressed to the judgment as a whole. Finally, Ford maintains that even if punitive damages were appropriate in this case, the amount of the award was so excessive as to require a new trial or further remittitur of the award.

In the ensuing analysis (ad nauseam) of Ford's wide-ranging assault on the judgment, we have concluded that Ford has failed to demonstrate that any errors or irregularities occurred during the trial which resulted in a miscarriage of justice requiring reversal.

Punitive Damages

Ford contends that it was entitled to a judgment notwithstanding the verdict on the issue of punitive damages on two grounds: First, punitive damages are statutorily and constitutionally impermissible in a design defect case; second, there was no evidentiary support for a finding of malice or of corporate responsibility for malice. In any event, Ford maintains that the punitive damage award must be reversed because of erroneous instructions and excessiveness of the award.

(1) *"Malice" Under Civil Code Section 3294*:

The concept of punitive damages is rooted in the English common law and is a settled principle of the common law of this country. The doctrine was a part of the common law of this state long before the Civil Code was adopted. When our laws were codified in 1872, the doctrine was incorporated in *Civil Code section 3294*, which at the time of trial read: "In an action for the breach of an obligation not arising from contract, where the defendant has been guilty of oppression, fraud, or malice, express or implied, the plaintiff, in addition to the actual damages, may recover damages for the sake of example and by way of punishing the defendant."[11]

---

11. *Section 3294* was amended in 1980 (Stats. 1980, ch. 1242, § 1, p. 4217, eff. Jan. 1, 1981) to read: "(a) In an action for the breach of an obligation not arising from contract, where the defendant has been guilty of oppression, fraud, or malice, the plaintiff, in addition to the actual damages, may recover damages for the sake of example and by way of punishing the defendant.

(b) An employer shall not be liable for damages pursuant to subdivision (a), based upon acts of an employee of the employer, unless the employer had advance knowledge of the unfitness of the employee and employed him or her with a conscious disregard of the rights or safety of others or authorized or ratified the wrongful conduct for which the damages are awarded or was personally guilty of oppression, fraud, or malice. With respect to a corporate employer, the advance knowledge, ratification, or act of oppression, fraud, or malice must be on the part of an officer, director, or managing agent of the corporation.

(c) As used in this section, the following definitions shall apply:

(1) 'Malice' means conduct which is intended by the defendant to cause injury to the plaintiff or conduct which is carried on by the defendant with a conscious disregard of the rights or safety of others.

(2) 'Oppression' means subjecting a person to cruel and unjust hardship in conscious disregard of that person's rights.

(3) 'Fraud' means an intentional misrepresentation, deceit, or concealment of a material fact known to the defendant with the intention on the part of the defendant of thereby depriving a person of property or legal rights or otherwise causing injury."

Ford argues that "malice" as used in *section 3294* and as interpreted by our Supreme Court in *Davis v. Hearst (1911) 160 Cal. 143*, requires *animus malus* or evil motive—an intention to injure the person harmed—and that the term is therefore conceptually incompatible with an unintentional tort such as the manufacture and marketing of a defectively designed product. This contention runs counter to our decisional law. As this court recently noted, numerous California cases after *Davis v. Hearst, supra*, have interpreted the term "malice" as used in *section 3294* to include, not only a malicious intention to injure the specific person harmed, but conduct evincing "a conscious disregard of the probability that the actor's conduct will result in injury to others."

In *Taylor v. Superior Court, supra, 24 Cal.3d 890*, our high court's most recent pronouncement on the subject of punitive damages, the court observed that the availability of punitive damages has not been limited to cases in which there is an actual intent to harm plaintiff or others. (*Id., at p. 895.*) The court concurred with the *Searle (G.D. Searle & Co. v. Superior Court, (1975) 49 Cal.App.3d 22)* court's suggestion that conscious disregard of the safety of others is an appropriate description of the *animus malus* required by *Civil Code section 3294*, adding: "In order to justify an award of punitive damages on this basis, the plaintiff must establish that the defendant was aware of the probable dangerous consequences of his conduct, and that he willfully and deliberately failed to avoid those consequences." (*Id., at pp. 895–896.*)

Ford attempts to minimize the precedential force of the foregoing decisions on the ground they failed to address the position now advanced by Ford that intent to harm a particular person or persons is required because that was what the lawmakers had in mind in 1872 when they adopted *Civil Code section 3294*. Ford argues that the Legislature was thinking in terms of traditional intentional torts, such as, libel, slander, assault and battery, malicious prosecution, trespass, etc., and could not have intended the statute to be applied to a products liability case arising out of a design defect in a mass produced automobile because neither strict products liability nor mass produced automobiles were known in 1872.

A like argument was rejected in *Li v. Yellow Cab Co. (1975) 13 Cal.3d 804*, where the court held that in enacting section 1714 as part of the 1872 Civil Code, the Legislature did not intend to prevent judicial development of the common law concepts of negligence and contributory negligence. As the court noted, the code itself provides that insofar as its provisions are substantially the same as the common law, they should be construed as continuations thereof and not as new enactments (*Civ. Code, §§ 4, 5*), and thus the code has been imbued "with admirable flexibility from the standpoint of adaptation to changing circumstances and conditions." (*Id., at p. 816.*) In light of the common law heritage of the principle embodied in *Civil Code section 3294*, it must be construed as a "continuation" of the common law and liberally applied "with a view to effect its objects and to promote justice." (*Civ. Code, §§ 4, 5.*) To paraphrase *Li v. Yellow Cab Co., supra, 13 Cal.3d 804*, the applicable rules of construction "permit if not require that *section [3294]* be interpreted so as to give dynamic expression to the fundamental precepts which it summarizes." (*Id., at p. 822.*)

The interpretation of the word "malice" as used in *section 3294* to encompass conduct evincing callous and conscious disregard of public safety by those who manufacture and market mass produced articles is consonant with and furthers the objectives of punitive damages. The primary purposes of punitive damages are punishment and deterrence of like conduct by the wrongdoer and others. (*Civ. Code, § 3294*; Owen, *supra*, pp. 1277, 1279–1287; Mallor & Roberts, *supra*, pp. 648–650.) In the traditional noncommercial intentional tort, compensatory damages alone may serve as an effective deterrent against future wrongful conduct but in commerce-related torts, the manufacturer may find it more profitable to treat compensatory damages as a part of the cost of doing business rather than to remedy the defect. (Owen, *supra*, p. 1291; Note, *Mass Liability and Punitive Damages Overkill* (1979) 30 Hastings L.J. 1797, 1802.) Deterrence of such "objectionable corporate policies" serves one of the principal purposes of *Civil Code section 3294*. Governmental safety standards and the criminal law have failed to provide adequate consumer protection against the manufacture and distribution of defective products. Punitive damages thus remain as the most effective remedy for consumer protection against defectively designed mass produced articles. They provide a motive for private individuals to enforce rules of law and enable them to recoup the expenses of doing so which can be considerable and not otherwise recoverable.

We find no statutory impediments to the application of *Civil Code section 3294* to a strict products liability case based on design defect.

(3) *Sufficiency of the Evidence to Support the Finding of Malice and Corporate Responsibility*

Ford contends that its motion for judgment notwithstanding the verdict should have been granted because the evidence was insufficient to support a finding of malice or corporate responsibility for such malice. The record fails to support the contention.

The rules circumscribing the power of a trial judge to grant a motion for judgment notwithstanding the verdict are well established. The power to grant such a motion is identical to the power to grant a directed verdict; the judge cannot weigh the evidence or assess the credibility of witnesses; if the evidence is conflicting or if several reasonable inferences may be drawn, the motion should be denied; the motion may be granted "only if it appears from the evidence, viewed in the light most favorable to the party securing the verdict, that there is no substantial evidence to support the verdict." (*Castro v. State of California* (1981) 114 Cal.App.3d 503, 512.) There was ample evidence to support a finding of malice and Ford's responsibility for malice.

Through the results of the crash tests Ford knew that the Pinto's fuel tank and rear structure would expose consumers to serious injury or death in a 20– to 30–mile–per–hour collision. There was evidence that Ford could have corrected the hazardous design defects at minimal cost but decided to defer correction of the shortcomings by engaging in a cost-benefit analysis balancing human lives and limbs against corporate profits. Ford's institutional mentality was shown to be one of callous indifference to public safety. There was substantial evidence that Ford's conduct constituted "conscious disregard" of the probability of injury to members of the consuming public.

Ford's argument that there can be no liability for punitive damages because there was no evidence of corporate ratification of malicious misconduct is equally without merit. California follows the Restatement rule that punitive damages can be awarded against a principal because of an action of an agent if, but only if, " '(a) the principal authorized the doing and the manner of the act, or (b) the agent was unfit and the principal was reckless in employing him, or (c) the agent was employed in a managerial capacity and was acting in the scope of employment, or (d) the principal or a managerial agent of the principal ratified or approved the act.' (Rest.2d Torts (Tent. Draft No. 19, 1973) § 909.)" The present case comes within one or both of the categories described in subdivisions (c) and (d).

There is substantial evidence that management was aware of the crash tests showing the vulnerability of the Pinto's fuel tank to rupture at low speed rear impacts with consequent significant risk of injury or death of the occupants by fire. There was testimony from several sources that the test results were forwarded up the chain of command; vice president Robert Alexander admitted to Mr. Copp that he was aware of the test results; vice president Harold MacDonald, who chaired the product review meetings, was present at one of those meetings at which a report on the crash tests was considered and a decision was made to defer corrective action; and it may be inferred that Mr. Alexander, a regular attender of the product review meetings, was also present at that meeting. McDonald and Alexander were manifestly managerial employees possessing the discretion to make "decisions that will ultimately determine corporate policy." (*Egan v. Mutual of Omaha Ins. Co., supra,* 24 Cal.3d 809, 823.) There was also evidence that Harold Johnson, an assistant chief engineer of research, and Mr. Max Jurosek, chief chassis engineer, were aware of the results of the crash tests and the defects in the Pinto's fuel tank system. Ford contends those two individuals did not occupy managerial positions because Mr. Copp testified that they admitted awareness of the defects but told him they were powerless to change the rear-end design of the Pinto. It may be inferred from the testimony, however, that the two engineers had approached management about redesigning the Pinto or that, being aware of management's attitude, they decided to do nothing. In either case the decision not to take corrective action was made by persons exercising managerial authority. Whether an employee acts in a "managerial capacity" does not necessarily depend on his "level" in the corporate hierarchy. (*Id., at p. 822.*) As the *Egan* court said: " 'Defendant should not be allowed to insulate itself from liability by giving an employee a nonmanagerial title and relegating to him crucial policy decisions.' " (*Id., at p. 823.*)

While much of the evidence was necessarily circumstantial, there was substantial evidence from which the jury could reasonably find that Ford's management decided to proceed with the production of the Pinto with knowledge of test results revealing design defects which rendered the fuel tank extremely vulnerable on rear impact at low speeds and endangered the safety and lives of the occupants. Such conduct constitutes corporate malice. (See *Toole v. Richardson–Merrell, Inc., supra,* 251 Cal.App.2d 689, 713.)

Disposition

In *Grimshaw* v. *Ford Motor Co.*, the judgment, the conditional new trial order, and the order denying Ford's motion for judgment notwithstanding the verdict on the issue of punitive damages are affirmed.

* * *

The plaintiffs in *Grimshaw* were rear-ended while driving their Ford Pinto. The car's fuel system leaked and the car caught fire, killing one plaintiff and severely disfiguring another. The fire was caused because of a design defect in the Pinto, which offered less protection against rear-end crashes and less rear crumple-space than virtually any other car made at the time, in either the United States or Europe. This left the Pinto's gas tank unusually exposed to puncture in rear-end collisions, of just the kind that occurred in *Grimshaw*. Ford knew that Pinto prototypes had failed fuel spillage tests in rear end crashes at even 20 mph—a speed that represented a proposed federal standard to go into effect on cars manufactured in the near future.[7] Furthermore, Ford engineers determined that a range of changes in the Pinto's design costing between $1.80 and $15.30 per car could have made the car much, much safer in rear-end collisions. The *Grimshaw* plaintiffs recovered $3 million in compensatory damages and, following a remittitur, $3.5 million in punitives. Ford appealed, and a central issue in the appeal was whether Ford's conduct was sufficiently bad for it to deserve being subjected to punitive damages.[8]

The legal standard of desert adopted in *Grimshaw* is relatively simply stated: An award of punitive damages requires that a defendant act intentionally with the purpose of injuring another person or at least with a conscious disregard for injuries that the action will probably cause.[9] But

---

7. Note that *Grimshaw* therefore illustrates a common issue in products liability cases—namely whether existing statutory or administrative safety regulations establish a safe-harbor, in the sense that conforming to them grants immunity from common law tort liability, or merely a regulatory floor.

8. A subsidiary issue was whether Ford bore corporate responsibility as to punitive damages for the acts of its employees. The court stated that simple *respondeat superior* liability will not create corporate liability for *punitive* damages. Instead, such corporate liability requires that (a) the principal authorized the agent's act, (b) the agent was unfit and the principal was reckless in employing him, (c) the agent was employed in a managerial capacity and was acting inside the scope of employment, or (d) the principal or a managerial agent of the principal ratified or approved the act. The court found that in *Grimshaw* sufficiently many sufficiently high up Ford employees were involved in the design question so that (c) and (d) were satisfied.

9. The jury instructions in *Grimshaw* articulated this standard less clearly than they might have done. Specifically, the instruction referred to "a motive to and willingness to injure

understanding just what class of conduct this standard identifies is not simple at all. Courts, including the *Grimshaw* court, sometimes speak in terms of *malice*, but this is not, strictly speaking, a necessary condition at all. As the commonly used phrase *conscious disregard* indicates, actual intent specifically to harm is not required: it is enough for a person to pay no heed to harms that are sufficiently plainly foreseeable. Moreover, the case-law fairly clearly indicates that extreme recklessness (when it is sufficiently extreme) can support punitive damages awards even when the reckless person never bothered to identify the harms his conduct threatened, and so never even consciously disregarded them. The various statements of the legal standard for deserving punitive damages therefore cannot be understood, in any straightforward way, to pick out and characterize a precise mental state.

Instead, it seems that these statements of the standard amount, in the end, to a general suggestion that punitive damages are available only for grossly tortious conduct and not for ordinary negligence. The more particular forms of words—malice, conscious disregard, and so forth—through which this suggestion is made serve less to elaborate a workable theory of gross tortiousness than to establish a screening device to allow judges, when they wish it, to decide that punitive damages are not available as a matter of law (because there has been no malice, or conscious disregard, for instance), thus keeping the question of punitive damages from juries. Of course, a technique for jury control cannot help judges, in their own minds, make the decision how to exercise the powers of control that they have reserved. It remains necessary to answer the basic question of principle: how grossly tortious must conduct be before punitive damages become deserved. *Grimshaw* is such an illustrative case because some of its background facts provide a way in to a systematic argument addressing this question of principle.

It turns out that Ford, in addition to being aware that a relatively cheap fix would substantially reduce the risk of the injuries suffered in *Grimshaw*, chose not to adopt the fix through a decision-process that involved a particularly ruthless calculation. Specifically, Ford conducted a cost-benefit analysis that concluded that if retro-fitting the fuel tanks cost $11 per car, the total costs of the cure were nearly three times greater than the benefits, which Ford calculated by valuing a life at $200,000 and lesser injuries on a commensurate scale.[10] Suppose that these numbers reflected the costs and benefits of the retro-fit *to Ford*: that is, that values that the cost-benefit analysis accorded life and limb reflected the average tort liability that Ford could expect to suffer for each life lost as a result of

---

another person [which may be shown by] showing that the defendant's conduct was willful, intentional, and done in conscious disregard of its possible result." The defendant argued the jury should have been instructed in terms of probable or highly probable results, and the court agreed that this instruction would have been preferable. But the court concluded that the instruction as a whole clearly conveyed the required willingness to harm, so that any error in its precise wording was harmless.

10. Gary T. Schwartz, *The Myth of the Ford Pinto Case*, 43 RUTGERS L. REV. 1013, 1020 (1991). Ford denied relying on this analysis in reaching its decision. *Id.*

failing to fix the Pinto's fuel tanks. This undervalued the injuries caused by the Pinto's defects in at least two ways: first, it discounted injuries by the chance that an injured party would fail to sue Ford or, if it did sue, would not prevail; and second, it valued the injuries purely from Ford's point of view, wholly neglecting the points of view of the victims who were harmed.[11]

The ordinarily tortious character of Ford's conduct was established by the fact that the actual social value of the injuries that retro-fitting the Pinto would have prevented was higher than the aggregate cost of the retro-fit: Ford was negligent because it failed to take a precaution whose benefits exceeded its costs. But taken together, both the fact and the narrow focus of Ford's cost-benefit analysis reveal that Ford committed a still greater wrong. First, having employed its narrow-minded cost-benefit analysis to cast the retro-fit as inefficient, Ford surely would have realized that a cost-benefit analysis made from society's point of view (in which injuries were valued more highly and not discounted by the chance that persons harmed would never recover compensation) would yield the opposite conclusion, namely that the retro-fit's social benefits exceeded its social costs. Ford was therefore not just negligent but proceeded in the knowledge that it was being negligent. And second, the numbers at play in Ford's cost-benefit analysis suggest that Ford's conduct was dramatically socially inefficient—that the social benefits of the retro-fit that Ford abandoned substantially exceeded its social costs.

Conduct that harms others is tortious in the ordinary sense—associated with simple negligence or nuisance—when its social costs exceed its social benefits. Such conduct could be justified only on the premise that those whom it benefits are more valuable than those whom it harms, and the imposition of tort liability for compensatory damages reflects society's

---

11. This is not, of course, to say that the appropriate social valuation of the harms at issue should proceed exclusively from the victims' perspectives—and certainly not from the perspectives of the actual, known victims. Since the value that a known victim attributes to his life or health is virtually all he has, focusing exclusively on the victim's perspective in valuing harms would render nearly every risky activity impermissible. Thus, although it is not easy to give the appropriate point of view for valuing the costs and benefits of any activity a precise formulation, it is clear that this point of view should take into account the perspectives both of those whom the activity benefits and those whom it burdens.

For some activities, for example for driving a car, all people are (more or less equally) potentially benefited and burdened: all people are both potential drivers and accident-victims. In these cases, the benefits and burdens of the activity may be valued and balanced *ex ante*, behind a kind of veil of ignorance, by persons who know what these benefits and burdens will be, and the probabilities that they will befall any particular person, but do not yet know whether they personally will be benefited or burdened. Tort law, in such a case, seeks to identify the standard for negligence that establishes an optimal combination of the right to compensation for being harmed by a negligent actor and the right to do the activity non-negligently, including even when this harms others. This idea is developed more extensively in Jennifer Arlen, *An Economic Analysis of Tort Damages for Wrongful Death*, 60 N.Y.U. L. REV. 1113 (1995).

Other activities are not amenable to this approach. Medical malpractice presents one example, since doctors are much more likely than average to be tortfeasors, and probably less likely than average to be tort victims. The conduct at issue in *Grimshaw* presents another example, because Ford (including its managers and owners) is more likely than average to cause injury through its cars and less likely than average to a victim of such injury.

egalitarian rejection of that premise. Grossly tortious conduct—conduct that deserves punitive damages—occurs when a tortfeasor not only acts in ways whose justification would require asserting that he is more valuable than his victims but actually adopts this reasoning as the ground for his actions. Such action deserves punitive damages because the gross tortfeasor not only *violates* the equality of all persons but *rejects* it. Such a rejection may be inferred, moreover, from either the self-consciousness of a tortfeasor's tortiousness, or the extent of his tortiousness (the amount by which his conduct's social costs exceed its social benefits), or both. The doctrinal language of malice and extreme recklessness picks out these two possibilities, respectively. Ford's conduct in *Grimshaw* illustrates them both.

8.3   PUNITIVE DAMAGES IN CONTRACT

These principles concerning when punitive damages are deserved in tort may be applied to contract, both to explain the basic doctrine that punitive damages are not available for breach of contract without more and to explain the various exceptions to this basic rule that arise at the boundaries of contract law.

Most straightforwardly, the conduct involved in a simple breach of contract does not meet the standard of wrongfulness necessary for sustaining an award of punitive damages. This is obvious when the breach is efficient. Because an efficient breach generates gains that exceed its losses, it may be justified on grounds that accept the equal worth of both the promisor who breaches and the promisee who is harmed, something that contract law recognizes, after all, when it encourages efficient breaches on precisely such grounds. Indeed, as long as she pays compensatory damages that secure her promisee's contractual expectations (either off her own motion or in response to a court order), a promisor who breaches (efficiently) does not (in the end) even disappoint her promisee. Instead, she vindicates his contractual expectations, simply not in the primary way that was intended when the contract was made.

Cases involving inefficient breaches—in which a promisor's actions reduce the total contractual surplus and benefit the promisor only by redistributing the remaining surplus disproportionately to her benefit—present a more complex problem. Some commentators—Richard Posner, for example[12]—have thought that the distinction between efficient and inefficient breaches, which they have called *willful* breaches, might justify awarding punitive damages for willful breaches.

But the distinction is insufficiently fine-grained to play the role that the argument asks of it. Certainly the term *willful*, insofar as it carries a connotation of moral blameworthiness, is misleading and cannot sustain the conclusion that the breaches that it describes deserve to be punished.

---

12.   RICHARD A. POSNER, THE ECONOMIC ANALYSIS OF LAW 119 (7th ed. 2007). *See also* Richard Craswell, *When is a Willful Breach 'Willful'? The Link Between Definitions and Damages*, 107 MICH. L. REV. 1015 (2009).

After all, efficient breaches may be (and, at least from the point of view of contract theory typically are) intentional and indeed calculated—they arise when a promisor responds to a better offer—so that willful breaches do not in any obvious way involve a distinctively blameworthy or even responsible mental state. Moreover, the mere fact that so-called willful breaches are inefficient merely makes such breaches like simple negligence or nuisance. Just as negligence arises when the cheaper cost avoider fails to avoid an accident and nuisance arises when a person carries on an activity that costs his neighbor more than it would cost him to stop, so willful breaches arise when a promisor fails to perform even though this failure benefits her less than it harms her promisee. This just shows that willful, or inefficient, breaches demonstrate the degree of culpability needed to support ordinary tort liability: inefficient breach could be justified only on the ground that the breaching promisor's interests are more important than her disappointed promisee's. A breach's inefficiency does not, without more, entail that the breach involves the heightened culpability, associated with gross tortiousness, needed to justify punitive damages. Even inefficient breachers do not necessarily adopt, as the grounds for their breaches, the principle that their interests are more valuable than the interests of their promisees. Although inefficient breachers necessarily do violate the principle of the equality of all persons, they do not necessarily reject it.

None of this is to say that breaching promisors never reject the equality of persons, or that their breaches can never in themselves rise to the level of gross tortiousness. To the contrary, breachers may of course take their superiority as the grounds of their actions, and (just as occurred in tort) their doing so may be inferred either from the size of a breach's inefficiency, or from the self-consciousness with which a promisor approaches her inefficient breach, or both. Contract law has, at some times and in some jurisdictions (although always and everywhere only haltingly) recognized this possibility, principally through the doctrinal category *bad faith* breach of contract, and a legal rule that punitive damages may be awarded in cases of such bad faith. The materials below will elaborate this doctrinal development, and the considerable uncertainties and that it has involved.

8.3.A PUNITIVE DAMAGES WHERE THERE HAS BEEN AN INDEPENDENT TORT

Before taking up this most difficult case of punitive damages awarded in and around contract, the materials will rehearse some easier cases. These involve circumstances in which the culpability that justifies punitive damages may be identified and characterized from within tort-law, as it is ordinarily understood, and thus without resorting to any distinctively contractual ideas. They are cases, put simply, in which a breach of contract also involves a common law tort, and the punitive damages are deserved for the tort, on its own, without finding any additional culpability for the breach.

In some such cases the tort is conceptually free-standing—that is, wholly independent of the breach—so that it is only an accident that it arises in or around a contract. In the course of breaching her contract a promisor may assault her promisee (for example, when a seller's delivery of defective goods is accompanied by a threat of physical harm in case the buyer refuses to pay for them regardless of the defects), or convert her promisee's property (for example, when a buyer removes goods from her seller's possession without paying for them), or commit any number of other torts. And these tortious acts may—based purely on free-standing principles of tort law—deserve punitive damages. Although this list of independent torts is of course incomplete, the structure of the cases on the list is completely straightforward and requires no further elaboration here. A representative example of such a case follows.

Excel Handbag Co. v. Edison Bros. Stores Inc.

United States Court of Appeals for the Fifth Circuit, 1980.
630 F.2d 379.

■ FAY, CIRCUIT JUDGE. In an action for breach of contract, arising out of appellee's alleged failure to pay for certain goods, appellant received a jury award of $110,810.56, as compensatory damages. Appellant appeals the trial court's directed verdict for appellee on the question of punitive damages. We reverse and remand on the issue of punitive damages.

The Facts

Plaintiff-appellant, Excel Handbag Co., Inc. (Excel), manufactures women's handbags. Defendant-appellee, Edison Brothers Stores, Inc. (Edison), purchases handbags from Excel, as well as other manufacturers, and resells them through its chain of retail stores. Excel and Edison enjoyed harmonious business relations for twenty-five years, until this litigation arose.

The central character in this story is Joseph Fingerhut (Fingerhut), a former employee of Edison. Fingerhut was responsible, with one other individual, for purchasing all of Edison's handbag requirements. He was accountable for his purchases only to Bert Talcoff, an Edison vice-president and the director of Edison's merchandise division.

In the spring of 1976, Edison undertook an investigation into certain allegations that Fingerhut had accepted bribes from some or all of the vendors from whom he purchased handbags. The investigation was conducted primarily by Herbert Robinson (Robinson), an attorney having considerable expertise in such matters. The investigation resulted in an indication that many of the manufacturers from whom Edison purchased goods were paying Fingerhut kickbacks, based on either a percentage of the total sale or a fixed price per dozen handbags. The only evidence uncovered with respect to Excel was (1) that its president, Marvin Fink (Fink), who allegedly was known as a "kickback artist," had thrown a number of $100 bills into the air during a meeting with an unknown party and said, "I'm going to St. Louis," and (2) that Fingerhut allegedly admitted receiving five-hundred dollars from Fink "occasionally" "around Christmastime."

The alleged statement that Fink gave Fingerhut five-hundred dollars occasionally around Christmastime came at a meeting between Fingerhut, Robinson, and Julian Edison on May 10, 1976. At that time, Excel was in the process of filling an order for Edison having a total sales price of approximately $110,000.[4] Excel also had shipped $43,831.50 worth of goods to Edison's warehouse, where it was kept in storage.[5]

Upon discovery of what it thought to be widespread bribery between Fingerhut and a number of its suppliers, Edison took the position that it would not continue doing business with any of them until they had cleared themselves of all allegations. In Excel's case, this meant that Edison would place no more orders and would not pay for the Count I goods, until Excel cleared itself. As the existence of this action indicates, Excel was unable to clear itself to Edison's satisfaction. Fink had a number of conversations with Robinson and other Edison officials involved in the investigation, in which he denied that he or his company ever gave bribes, money, or gifts to any Edison employee. He offered to sign an affidavit so stating. Fink was not willing, however, to comply with Robinson's request that he submit to a polygraph examination. Robinson, in turn, refused to give Excel clearance until Fink would agree to take the test.

The facts surrounding the Count III goods are quite different.[7] They were ordered on May 7, 1976, and were to be invoiced on July 5, 1976. Sometime around July 5, 1976, Robinson called Bernard Mandler (Mandler), counsel for Excel, and indicated Edison's intention to take legal possession of the Count III goods on the date that they originally were to have been invoiced. Mandler responded that Excel would not relinquish title to those goods unless Edison agreed to pay for the Count I goods as well as the Count III goods. Robinson testified that he responded, "I told Mandler that Edison would pay for the goods...." Robinson then called Eric Newman (Newman), an executive vice-president and the secretary of Edison, and explained Excel's position that the Count III goods were not to be taken down[10] until the Count I goods were paid for. Robinson advised Newman to pay for the Count III goods, and Newman agreed. The Count I

---

4. These are the goods on which Count I of Excel's complaint is based (Count I goods).

5. These are the goods on which Count III of Excel's complaint, for conversion, is based (Count III goods). By contract the parties had agreed that Edison would store the goods in its warehouse, but that Excel would retain title to the goods until Edison received an invoice. Under normal circumstances, the invoice was received on the date Edison wanted to take possession of the goods. Payment for the goods was due thirty days after receiving the invoice. This procedure was employed primarily for accounting purposes.

As will be discussed, infra, it was Edison's failure to adhere to this procedure that gave rise to Excel's claim for punitive damages.

7. On appeal, Edison does not contend that it was error to grant Excel's motion for a directed verdict with respect to the Count III claim for conversion. The Count III goods bear on this appeal only to the extent Excel contends that Edison's conduct with respect thereto indicates willful and wanton acts sufficient to sustain their claim for punitive damages. Therefore, the only facts pertaining to the Count III goods included herein are those going to the question of punitive damages.

10. "Taken down" is an expression meaning that title to the goods shifts from the vendor to the vendee, and the vendee is moving them from inventory into its chain of distribution.

goods were not paid for, and Excel did not relinquish title to the Count III goods by invoicing them. Nonetheless, on July 6, 1976 the Count III goods were taken down by Edison. The next day, Robinson called Mandler to inform him that the Count III goods had been taken down and that Edison intended to pay for them. Payment was not forthcoming, however, and when Robinson received a copy of the complaint in this case, on July 28, 1976, he telephoned Newman and told him payment needed to be made.[11] Newman telephoned Miller Walton (Walton), Edison's attorney in Florida, and informed him that Edison was forwarding a check to him in an amount equal that due Excel for the Count III goods. Newman further testified that he instructed Walton to tender the check to Excel. Walton received the check, dated August 17, 1967, some three weeks after that conversation. Walton tendered the check to Mandler, on the condition that payment would not be made unless Excel agreed to dismiss its claim for punitive damages in the present action.[12] Mandler rejected the tender so conditioned. As of the time of trial, in September of 1977, none of the goods had been paid for.

Punitive Damages

Excel's only contention on appeal is that the trial court erred in granting Edison's motion for a directed verdict on Excel's claim for punitive damages. Excel asserts that sufficient evidence was introduced to create a question of fact for the jury concerning the willful, wanton, and malicious character of Edison's conduct with respect to the Count III goods. For the reasons indicated below, we agree that the issue was one for the jury.

The initial issue is whether a federal District Judge deciding if there is sufficient evidence to create a jury question should use the sufficiency of evidence test of the state in which the court is located or the federal test. We start with the proposition that in diversity actions, such as this, federal courts are required to apply the substantive law of the jurisdiction in which the district court hearing the case is located. *Erie Railroad Co. v. Tompkins, 304 U.S. 64 (1938).* This Court uniformly has held, however, that the federal rather than the state test should be applied to determine if there is sufficient evidence to create a jury question because the issue is one of procedural rather than substantive law. *Kicklighter v. Nails by Jannee, Inc., 616 F.2d 734, 738 (5th Cir. 1980)* (en banc).

The test in this Circuit for deciding the appropriateness of a directed verdict is that it should not be granted if a reasonably minded jury could

---

11. Newman explained at that time, as Edison has continued to assert, that payment was not made because, pursuant to the contract between the parties, payment was not due. Under that contract, Edison was required to make payment within thirty days of receiving an invoice for the goods. As we indicated earlier, however, Excel did not invoice the Count III goods because it did not want Edison to take title without paying for the Count I goods.

12. Edison denies that such a condition was attached to its tender. For the purpose of deciding whether the trial court erred in directing a verdict against Excel on its punitive damages claim, we must view the evidence in a light most favorable to Excel. Because there was some evidence that such a condition existed, we assume it to be a fact for the limited purpose hereof. It, of course, will be up to the jury to decide that fact conclusively when the issue is retried.

arrive at a verdict other than that sought by the party requesting the directed verdict. Id.; *Cora Pub, Inc. v. Continental Gas Co., 619 F.2d 482, 484 (5th Cir. 1980)*. In making that determination, the evidence must be considered as a whole and viewed in a light most favorable to the party opposing the directed verdict. Id. A directed verdict is not limited to those situations in which there is a complete absence of probative facts to support a jury verdict. It is also warranted when there is no conflict in substantial evidence. *Broad v. Rockwell International Corp., 614 F.2d 418, 425 (5th Cir. 1980)*. Applying this standard to the present action, the trial court concluded that Excel had failed to establish sufficient evidence of willful, wanton, or malicious conduct to create a jury question as to punitive damages, and, accordingly, directed a verdict for Edison on that count.

Our first step in reviewing the trial court's conclusion is to determine what is required under Florida law to justify the award of punitive damages. Recent decisions of the Florida Supreme Court and other Florida courts clearly state that punitive damages are not to be awarded in an action for breach of contract unless the breach also constitutes an independent tort. An independent tort must be specifically pled. *Roger Lee, Inc. v. Trend Mills, Inc., 410 F.2d 928, 929 (5th Cir. 1969)*. Moreover, the party seeking punitive damages must establish that the tort was committed willfully, wantonly, maliciously, or with conscious disregard for the legal rights of the injured party. *American International Land Corp., supra*; *Griffith, supra*.

There is no doubt that an independent tort was both pled and established in the present action. The trial court directed a verdict for Excel on its Count III for conversion, and Edison does not appeal that ruling. The next question is whether there was sufficient evidence from which a reasonably minded jury possibly could conclude that Edison's conduct was willful, wanton, malicious, or in conscious disregard of Excel's legal rights. We hold that there was sufficient evidence from which a jury could so conclude.

Recent decisions of this Court interpreting Florida law, as well as decisions of various state courts of Florida, have held that the essential elements of willful and wanton misconduct are "(1) the actor must have knowledge, actual or constructive, of the likelihood that his conduct will cause injury to other persons or property; and (2) the conduct must indicate a reckless indifference to the rights of others, that is, conduct which may be termed equivalent to an intentional violation of those rights." *Boyce v. Pi Kappa Alpha Holding Corp., 476 F.2d 447, 452 (5th Cir. 1978)*; *Glaab v. Caudill, 236 So.2d 180, 184 n. 13 (Fla.D.C.A. 2, 1970)*.

In *Jonat Properties v. Gateman, 226 So.2d 703 (Fla.D.C.A. 3)*, cert. denied, *234 So.2d 123 (Fla.1969)* the Florida Court of Appeals was called upon to decide whether the trial court erred in allowing the question of punitive damages to go to the jury. In that case, appellee received in a divorce settlement her husband's one-half interest in a promissory note executed by appellant. Prior to its maturity, appellant executed an agreement with the holder of the other one-half interest extending the maturity date of the note. This was done without the knowledge of the appellee.

Appellant refused to make payment on the note on the date it was originally to come due, asserting the written extension as a defense. Appellee brought an action for tortious interference with her contract rights. The court held that appellant's failure to make payment when due was sufficient evidence of willful and wanton conduct to properly raise a jury question as to punitive damages.

The present action is similar to *Jonat Properties, Inc., supra,* to the extent that both required the court to consider whether tortious acts involving failure to pay a debt owed could be evidence of willful and wanton conduct. We conclude that Edison's course of conduct with regard to the Count III goods, that is taking them down after being told they could do so only if they intended to pay for all the goods and then failing to pay for any goods during the fifteen month period it took for this case to come to trial, could be construed as willful and wanton. Though the trial court was correct that this evidence could be construed as indicating good faith efforts between counsel to resolve the conflict, it could also be interpreted as a conscious decision by Edison to wrongfully take the goods and to withhold payment therefore for the purpose of forcing Excel to relinquish some of its legal rights. We, of course, do not suggest which of these possible interpretations is more plausible. That is a question for a jury to decide. Accordingly, the case must be remanded for a retrial on the issue of punitive damages.

Summary

Though we believe the trial court correctly identified the test in Florida for the imposition of punitive damages, we conclude that there was some evidence from which a reasonable jury could conclude that the elements of the test were established. Accordingly, we must reverse the trial court's ruling in this regard and remand the case for a retrial on the question of punitive damages.

Affirmed in part, reversed and remanded in part.

* * *

One doctrinal difficulty can arise to complicate the case for punitive damages even where the damages claim is based on the commission of an independent common-law tort. Specifically, there is precedent to support the rule that punitive damages will be available in such a case only where there has also been an award of compensatory damages in conjunction with the independent tort and not where all the compensation has been given in conjunction with the contract claim.

Formosa Plastics Corp. v. Presidio Engineers & Contractors, Inc.

Supreme Court of Texas, 1998.
960 S.W.2d 41.

■ ABBOT, J. We overrule Respondent's motion for rehearing and motion for voluntary remittitur. We withdraw our opinion of July 9, 1997, and substitute the following in its place.

In *Southwestern Bell Telephone Co. v. DeLanney, 809 S.W.2d 493, 494–95 (Tex. 1991)*, this Court held that a cause of action for negligence could not be based on an allegation that a party had negligently failed to perform a contract because such a claim sounded in contract, not in tort. Today we are requested to apply a similar analysis to preclude a recovery in tort for a fraudulent inducement of contract claim. We decline to do so, holding instead that our *DeLanney* analysis is not applicable to such a claim. However, because there is no probative evidence to support the entire amount of damages awarded by the trial court, we reverse the judgment of the court of appeals and remand the case to the trial court for a new trial.

In 1989, Formosa Plastics Corporation began a large construction "expansion project" at its facility in Point Comfort, Texas. Presidio Engineers and Contractors, Inc. received an "Invitation to Bid" from Formosa on that part of the project requiring the construction of 300 concrete foundations. The invitation was accompanied by a bid package containing technical drawings, specifications, general information, and a sample contract. The bid package also contained certain representations about the foundation job. These representations included that (1) Presidio would arrange and be responsible for the scheduling, ordering, and delivery of all materials, including those paid for by Formosa; (2) work was to progress continually from commencement to completion; and (3) the job was scheduled to commence on July 16, 1990, and be completed 90 days later, on October 15, 1990.

Presidio's president, Bob Burnette, testified that he relied on these representations in preparing Presidio's bid. Because the bid package provided that the contractor would be responsible for all weather and other unknown delays, he added another 30 days to his estimate of the job's scheduled completion date. He submitted a bid on behalf of Presidio in the amount of $600,000. Because Presidio submitted the lowest bid, Formosa awarded Presidio the contract.

The job was not completed in 120 days. Rather, the job took over eight months to complete, more than twice Burnette's estimate and almost three times the scheduled time provided in the bid package. The delays caused Presidio to incur substantial additional costs that were not anticipated when Presidio submitted its bid.

Presidio asserted a claim under paragraph 17 of the parties' contract, which provided that Formosa was liable for all delay damages within the "control of the owner." Formosa countered that, while it may have been liable for some of the delays, it was not responsible for all of the delays and losses asserted by Presidio. Because the parties were not able to resolve their dispute, Presidio sued Formosa for breach of contract and breach of a duty of good faith and fair dealing. Presidio also brought fraudulent inducement of contract and fraudulent performance of contract claims based on representations made by Formosa that Presidio discovered were false after commencing performance of the contract. Formosa counterclaimed for breach of contract, urging that Presidio had not properly completed some of its work.

Presidio presented evidence to the jury that Formosa had an intentional, premeditated scheme to defraud the contractors working on its expansion project. Under this scheme, Formosa enticed contractors to make low bids by making misrepresentations in the bid package regarding scheduling, delivery of materials, and responsibility for delay damages. Jack Lin, the director of Formosa's civil department, admitted that Formosa acted deceptively by representing in the bid package that the contractors would have the ability to schedule the delivery of concrete when in truth Formosa had secretly decided to set up its own delivery schedule in order to save money. Formosa also scheduled multiple contractors, doing mutually exclusive work, to be in the same area at the same time. For instance, Formosa scheduled another contractor to install underground pipe in Presidio's work area at the same time that Presidio was supposed to be pouring foundations. Thomas Pena, Formosa's inspector, admitted that Formosa knew that contractors would be working right on top of each other, but this information was not passed on to the contractors. Of course, once the contractors were on the job, they would realize that, due to such unexpected delays caused by Formosa, their bids were inadequate. But when the contractors requested delay damages under the contract, Formosa would rely on its superior economic position and offer the contractors far less than the full and fair value of the delay damages. In fact, Ron Robichaux, head of Formosa's contract administration division, testified that Formosa, in an effort to lower costs, would utilize its economic superiority to string contractors along and force them to settle. Robichaux added that "if [a contractor] continued to complain then [Formosa] would take the contract from him and make sure he loses his money." Under this scheme, Formosa allegedly stood to save millions of dollars on its $1.5 billion expansion project.

The jury found that Formosa defrauded Presidio and awarded Presidio $1.5 million. The jury also found that Formosa breached a duty of good faith and fair dealing and awarded Presidio $1.5 million as a result. Based on its findings that Formosa's fraud and breach of a duty of good faith and fair dealing were done willfully, wantonly, intentionally, or with conscious indifference to the rights of Presidio, the jury further awarded Presidio $10 million as exemplary damages. Additionally, the jury found that Formosa breached its contract with Presidio, causing $1.267 million in damages. On the other hand, the jury also concluded that Presidio did not fully comply with the contract, causing Formosa $107,000 in damages.

The trial court suggested a remittitur reducing the tort damages to $700,000 and the contract damages to $467,000, which Presidio accepted. Based on Presidio's election to recover tort rather than contract damages, the trial court rendered a judgment in favor of Presidio for $700,000 in actual damages, $10 million in punitive damages, prejudgment interest, attorney's fees, and costs. The damages caused by Presidio's breach of contract were offset against the judgment.

Formosa appealed the judgment to the court of appeals, which affirmed the judgment of the trial court. *941 S.W.2d 138*. We granted Formosa's application for writ of error to consider, among other things, whether Presidio has a viable fraud claim when it suffered only economic losses related to the performance and subject matter of the parties' contract, whether there was legally sufficient evidence of fraud, and whether there was legally sufficient evidence to support the entire amount of damages awarded. We conclude that, while Presidio has a viable fraud claim, it failed to present legally sufficient evidence to support the entire amount of damages awarded. Accordingly, we reverse the judgment of the court of appeals and remand the cause for a new trial.

II

Formosa asserts that Presidio's fraud claim cannot be maintained because "Presidio's losses were purely economic losses related to performance and the subject matter of the contract." Formosa contends that our decision in *Southwestern Bell Telephone Co. v. DeLanney, 809 S.W.2d 493 (Tex. 1991)*, compels us to examine the substance of Presidio's tort claim to determine whether the claim is, in reality, a re-packaged breach of contract claim. Formosa urges that, in making this determination, we should analyze the nature of the alleged injury, the source of the breached duty, and whether the loss or risk of loss is contractually contemplated by the parties. Presidio counters that a *DeLanney-type* analysis does not apply to fraud claims. For the reasons discussed below, we agree with Presidio.

A

Over the last fifty years, this Court has analyzed the distinction between torts and contracts from two different perspectives. At first, we merely analyzed the source of the duty in determining whether an action sounded in tort or contract. For instance, in *International Printing Pressmen & Assistants' Union v. Smith, 145 Tex. 399, 409 (Tex. 1946)*, this Court held that " 'an action in contract is for the breach of a duty arising out of a contract either express or implied, while an action in tort is for a breach of duty imposed by law.' " *Id.* (quoting 1 C.J.S. *Actions* § 44).

Later, we overlaid an analysis of the nature of the remedy sought by the plaintiff. In *Jim Walter Homes, Inc. v. Reed, 711 S.W.2d 617 (Tex. 1986)*, we recognized that, while the contractual relationship of the parties could create duties under both contract law and tort law, the "nature of the injury most often determines which duty or duties are breached. When the injury is only the economic loss to the subject of a contract itself, the action sounds in contract alone." *Id. at 618.* Because a mere breach of contract cannot support recovery of exemplary damages, and because the plaintiffs did not "prove a distinct tortious injury with actual damages," we rendered judgment that the plaintiffs take nothing on their exemplary damages claim. *Id.*

We analyzed both the source of the duty and the nature of the remedy in *DeLanney*. DeLanney asserted that Bell was negligent in failing to publish his Yellow Pages advertisement as promised. The trial court rendered judgment for DeLanney, and the court of appeals affirmed. This Court, however, held that the claim sounded in contract, not negligence, and accordingly rendered judgment in favor of Bell. We provided the following guidelines on distinguishing contract and tort causes of action:

> If the defendant's conduct—such as negligently burning down a house—would give rise to liability independent of the fact that a contract exists between the parties, the plaintiff's claim may also sound in tort. Conversely, if the defendant's conduct—such as failing to publish an advertisement—would give rise to liability only because it breaches the parties' agreement, the plaintiff's claim ordinarily sounds only in contract. In determining whether the plaintiff may recover on a tort theory, it is also instructive to examine the nature of the plaintiff's loss. When the only loss or damage is to the subject matter of the contract, the plaintiff's action is ordinarily on the contract.

DeLanney, 809 S.W.2d at 494. In applying these guidelines, we first determined that Bell's duty to publish DeLanney's advertisement arose solely from the contract. We then concluded that DeLanney's damages, lost profits, were only for the economic loss caused by Bell's failure to perform the contract. Thus, while DeLanney pleaded his action as one in negligence, he clearly sought to recover the benefit of his bargain with Bell such that Bell's failure to publish the advertisement was not a tort. *Id. at 495.*

B

Several appellate courts have considered the application of our decisions in *DeLanney* and *Reed* to fraudulent inducement claims. Some of these courts have concluded that these decisions mandate that tort damages are not recoverable for a fraudulent inducement claim unless the plaintiff suffers an injury that is distinct, separate, and independent from the economic losses recoverable under a breach of contract claim. The United States Court of Appeals for the Fifth Circuit has also adopted this view of Texas law. Other Texas appellate decisions, however, have rejected the application of *DeLanney* and *Reed* to preclude the recovery of tort damages for fraudulent inducement claims.

We too reject the application of *DeLanney* to preclude tort damages in fraud cases. Texas law has long imposed a duty to abstain from inducing another to enter into a contract through the use of fraudulent misrepresentations. As a rule, a party is not bound by a contract procured by fraud. Moreover, it is well established that the legal duty not to fraudulently procure a contract is separate and independent from the duties established by the contract itself. *See Dallas Farm Mach., 307 S.W.2d at 239* (" 'The law long ago abandoned the position that a contract must be held sacred regardless of the fraud of one of the parties in procuring it.' ") (quoting *Bates v. Southgate, 308 Mass. 170, 31 N.E.2d 551, 558 (Mass. 1941)).*

This Court has also repeatedly recognized that a fraud claim can be based on a promise made with no intention of performing, irrespective of whether the promise is later subsumed within a contract. For example, in *Crim Truck & Tractor Co. v. Navistar Int'l Transp. Corp., 823 S.W.2d 591, 597 (Tex. 1992),* we noted: "As a general rule, the failure to perform the terms of a contract is a breach of contract, not a tort. However, when one party enters into a contract with no intention of performing, that misrepresentation may give rise to an action in fraud." Similarly, in *Spoljaric v. Percival Tours, Inc., 708 S.W.2d 432, 434 (Tex. 1986)*, we held that a fraud claim could be maintained, under the particular facts of that case, for the breach of an oral agreement to pay a bonus because a "promise to do an act in the future is actionable fraud when made with the intention, design and purpose of deceiving, and with no intention of performing the act."

Our prior decisions also clearly establish that tort damages are not precluded simply because a fraudulent representation causes only an economic loss. Almost 150 years ago, this Court held in *Graham v. Roder, 5 Tex. 141, 149 (1849)*, that tort damages were recoverable based on the plaintiff's claim that he was fraudulently induced to exchange a promissory note for a tract of land. Although the damages sustained by the plaintiff were purely economic, we held that tort damages, including exemplary damages, were recoverable. Since *Graham*, this Court has continued to recognize the propriety of fraud claims sounding in tort despite the fact that the aggrieved party's losses were only economic losses. Moreover, we have held in a similar context that tort damages were not precluded for a tortious interference with contract claim, notwithstanding the fact that the damages for the tort claim compensated for the same economic losses that were recoverable under a breach of contract claim. *American Nat'l Petroleum Co. v. Transcontinental Gas Pipe Line Corp., 798 S.W.2d 274, 278 (Tex. 1990)*.

Accordingly, tort damages are recoverable for a fraudulent inducement claim irrespective of whether the fraudulent representations are later subsumed in a contract or whether the plaintiff only suffers an economic loss related to the subject matter of the contract. Allowing the recovery of fraud damages sounding in tort only when a plaintiff suffers an injury that is distinct from the economic losses recoverable under a breach of contract claim is inconsistent with this well-established law, and also ignores the fact that an independent legal duty, separate from the existence of the contract itself, precludes the use of fraud to induce a binding agreement. We therefore disapprove of the following appellate court opinions to the extent that they hold that tort damages cannot be recovered for a fraudulent inducement claim absent an injury that is distinct from any permissible contractual damages: *Grace Petroleum Corp. v. Williamson, 906 S.W.2d 66, 68–69 (Tex. App.—Tyler 1995, no writ); Parker v. Parker, 897 S.W.2d 918, 924 (Tex. App—Fort Worth 1995, writ denied); Barbouti v. Munden, 866 S.W.2d 288, 293–94 (Tex. App.—Houston [14th Dist.] 1993, writ denied); River Consulting, Inc. v. Sullivan, 848 S.W.2d 165, 170 (Tex. App.—Houston [1st Dist.] 1992, writ denied); C & C Partners v. Sun Exploration & Prod Co., 783 S.W.2d 707, 719–20 (Tex. App.—Dallas 1989, writ denied); Hebisen v. Nassau Dev. Co., 754 S.W.2d 345, 348 (Tex. App.—Houston [14th Dist.] 1988, writ denied); Allen v. Allen, 751 S.W.2d 567, 574–75 (Tex. App.—Houston [14th Dist.] 1988, writ denied)*. We instead conclude that, if a plaintiff presents legally sufficient evidence on each of the elements of a fraudulent inducement claim, any damages suffered as a result of the fraud sound in tort.

We thus conclude that Presidio has a viable fraud claim that it can assert against Formosa. However, this conclusion does not end our inquiry. We must also determine whether legally sufficient evidence supports the jury's fraud and damage findings.

III

A fraud cause of action requires "a material misrepresentation, which was false, and which was either known to be false when made or was asserted without knowledge of its truth, which was intended to be acted upon, which was relied upon, and which caused injury." *Sears, Roebuck & Co. v. Meadows, 877 S.W.2d 281, 282 (Tex. 1994); DeSantis v. Wackenhut Corp., 793 S.W.2d 670, 688 (Tex. 1990), cert. denied, 498 U.S. 1048, 112 L. Ed. 2d 775, 111 S. Ct. 755 (1991); see also Stone v. Lawyers Title Ins. Corp., 554 S.W.2d 183, 185 (Tex. 1977).* A promise of future performance constitutes an actionable misrepresentation if the promise was made with no intention of performing at the time it was made. *Schindler v. Austwell Farmers Coop., 841 S.W.2d 853, 854 (Tex. 1992).* However, the mere failure to perform a contract is not evidence of fraud. *See id.* Rather, Presidio had to present evidence that Formosa made representations with the intent to deceive and with no intention of performing as represented. Moreover, the evidence presented must be relevant to Formosa's intent at the time the representation was made. *Spoljaric, 708 S.W.2d at 434.*

Presidio alleges that Formosa made three representations that it never intended to keep in order to induce Presidio to enter into the contract. First, the bid package and contract represented that Presidio would "arrange the delivery schedule of [Formosa]-supplied material and be responsible for the delivery of all materials (this includes material supplied by [Formosa])." Second, the bid package and the contract provided the job was scheduled to begin on July 16, 1990, and be completed on October 15, 1990, 90 days later. Third, paragraph 17 of the contract represented that Formosa would be responsible for the payment of any delay damages within its control.

The jury agreed with Presidio and found that Formosa committed fraud. In our review of this finding, all of the record evidence must be considered in a light most favorable to the party in whose favor the verdict has been rendered, and every reasonable inference deducible from the evidence is to be indulged in that party's favor. *Harbin v. Seale, 461 S.W.2d 591, 592 (Tex. 1970).* Anything more than a scintilla of evidence is legally sufficient to support the finding.

We conclude that Presidio presented legally sufficient evidence that Formosa made representations with no intention of performing as represented in order to induce Presidio to enter into this contract at a low bid price. In the bid package and the contract, Formosa represented that Presidio would have control of the delivery of the concrete necessary for the project. While Formosa argues that other more general provisions contained in the contract refute this representation, the contract and the bid package specifically and unequivocally provide that Presidio would "arrange the delivery schedule of [Formosa]-supplied material and be responsible for the delivery of all materials." Further, even Formosa's own witnesses admitted that, under the plain language of the contract, Presidio had control over the scheduling and delivery of concrete. Accordingly, there is clearly sufficient evidence that this representation was in fact made by Formosa.

In contravention of this representation, Formosa decided, two weeks before the contract was signed, to take over the delivery of the concrete without informing Presidio. Jack Lin, Formosa's civil department director, testified that Formosa, in an effort to save money, decided to take over the concrete delivery and set up its own delivery schedule. However, Presidio was not informed of this change until after the contract was signed. Lin admitted that Formosa acted deceptively by taking over the concrete delivery and scheduling when the bid package expressly provided that the contractor would have control. He further admitted that Formosa knew that Presidio would rely on this representation in preparing its bid.

Presidio's president, Bob Burnette, testified that Presidio did in fact rely on this representation in preparing its bid. Burnette further testified that every concrete pour was delayed one-to-two days while Presidio waited for Formosa to obtain the requested concrete. Because Burnette did not calculate such delays into his bid, the actual cost of the project exceeded the contract price.

This testimony provides more than a scintilla of evidence supporting Presidio's contention that Formosa intentionally made representations that it never intended to keep in order to induce Presidio to enter into the contract at a low bid price and that Presidio relied on these misrepresentations to its detriment. Thus, legally sufficient evidence supports the jury's fraud finding. We need not consider whether any other representations Formosa allegedly made were fraudulent.

Formosa contends, however, that the award of $700,000 in fraud damages to Presidio is excessive as a matter of law. Presidio counters that the damage award is supported by Burnette's testimony that, if he had been told the truth about the project, he "would have bid in the neighborhood of $1,300,000" to perform the contract, and that that amount was a reasonable and necessary cost for doing the work. Presidio maintains that, by subtracting the amount they were paid on the contract, $600,000, from the $1,300,000 reasonable and necessary cost for doing the work, there is legally sufficient evidence to support the damage award of $700,000. But Formosa objected at trial to this testimony on the basis that it was both speculative and an improper measure of damages. Formosa argued again in its motion for new trial that the damages awarded were excessive because Burnette's testimony was speculative and based on an improper measure of damages. Formosa re-urges these complaints to this Court.

Texas recognizes two measures of direct damages for common-law fraud: the out-of-pocket measure and the benefit-of-the-bargain measure.

The out-of-pocket measure computes the difference between the value paid and the value received, while the benefit-of-the-bargain measure computes the difference between the value as represented and the value received.

The out-of-pocket measure allows the injured party "to recover the *actual injury* suffered measured by 'the difference between the value of that which he has *parted with,* and the value of that which he has received.'" *Leyendecker, 683 S.W.2d at 373* (because out-of-pocket fraud damages are intended to provide actual compensation for the injury rather than profit, the proper measure of damages is the difference between the value of what was parted with and what was received). Burnette's testimony regarding what he would have bid if he had known the truth is not the proper measure of out-of-pocket damages. Burnette computed his $1.3 million bid by taking the total amount Presidio spent on the labor, materials, supplies, and equipment used on the job, $831,000, divided by the original expected cost of the job, $370,000, multiplied by his actual bid of $600,000. He also performed an alternative calculation that reached a similar result by dividing the 264 days the job actually took by the 134 days the job should have taken multiplied by his actual bid of $600,000. Basically, both of these methods multiplied the actual bid price of $600,000, which included a profit margin on the job, by a ratio comparing what actually occurred to what was anticipated. Thus, both of these calculations incorporated expected lost profits on a bargain that was never made. But the out-of-pocket measure only compensates for actual injuries a party sustains through parting with something, not loss of profits on a bid not made, and a profit never realized, in a hypothetical bargain never struck. Thus, the $1.3 million hypothetical bid less the $600,000 actually received is not probative of Presidio's out-of-pocket loss. The proper out-of-pocket calculation of damages, based on Burnette's testimony, was $831,000 less the amount he actually received, $600,000, for damages of $231,000.

Burnette's testimony regarding the $1.3 million hypothetical bid is also not probative evidence of benefit-of-the-bargain damages. Under the benefit-of-the bargain measure, lost profits on the bargain may be recovered if such damages are proved with reasonable certainty. *See RESTATEMENT (SECOND) OF TORTS § 549(2) (1977)* ("The recipient of a fraudulent misrepresentation in a business transaction is also entitled to recover additional damages sufficient to give him the benefit of his contract with the maker, if these damages are proved with reasonable certainty."). But, while a benefit-of-the-bargain measure can include lost profits, it only compensates for the profits that would have been made if the bargain had been performed as promised. Accordingly, the proper calculation of benefit-of-the-bargain damages is Presidio's anticipated profit on the $600,000 bid plus the actual cost of the job less the amount actually paid by Formosa. Based on Burnette's testimony, Presidio's benefit-of-the-bargain damages are not $700,000, but rather $461,000 (bid price of $600,000 less original expected cost of $370,000 for profit of $230,000, plus $831,000 actual cost less $600,000 actually paid).

Burnette calculated his hypothetical $1.3 million bid by multiplying his $600,000 bid, including his anticipated profit, by a factor of about 2.2. However, this doubling of Presidio's bid is entirely speculative because there is no evidence that Presidio would have been awarded the project if it had made a $1.3 million bid. In fact, if any inference could be drawn, it would lead to the opposite conclusion because two of the three other bids Formosa received were lower than $1.3 million. Burnette's testimony as to what he would have bid had he known the truth simply does not establish the benefit of any bargain made with Formosa. It is not based on the expenses incurred and profits lost on this contract because of Formosa's representations, but rather is based on an entirely hypothetical, speculative bargain that was never struck and would not have been consummated. This testimony is therefore not legally sufficient evidence supporting an award of $700,000 in damages.

We accordingly hold that there is no probative evidence supporting the entire amount of damages awarded by the judgment. There is, however, clearly legally sufficient evidence that Presidio suffered some damages as a result of Formosa's fraud; in fact, Burnette's testimony, while it does not support a damage award of $700,000, does support an out-of-pocket damage award of $231,000 or a benefit-of-the-bargain damage award of $461,000. But, because the issue of damages was contested by Formosa, we cannot render judgment in favor of Presidio for a lesser dollar amount. Instead, because there is no legally sufficient evidence to support the entire amount of damages, but there is some evidence of the correct measure of damages, we reverse the judgment of the court of appeals and remand the cause for a new trial. *See Texarkana Mem'l Hosp. v. Murdock, 946 S.W.2d 836, 841 (Tex. 1997).*

IV

In conclusion, we hold that, when a party fraudulently procures a contract by making a promise without any intent of keeping the promise in order to induce another into executing the contract, a tort cause of action for that fraud exists. Accordingly, Presidio has a viable fraud claim against Formosa even though it only seeks damages for economic losses related to the subject matter and performance of the contract between the parties. We cannot affirm the court of appeals' judgment, however, because there is no evidence to support the entire damage award. We therefore reverse the judgment of the court of appeals and remand this case for a new trial.

* * *

Formosa Plastics illustrates the artificiality of the doctrine that punitive damages require not just the commission of an independent tort but also that this tort sustains a distinctly tort-like compensatory award. The case also demonstrates this doctrine's tenuous hold over the courts. The defendant in *Formosa Plastics* served as its own general contractor on a large construction project expanding its plant, and hired the plaintiff as one of the subcontractors to do part of the work—specifically to build a series of concrete foundations. During the bidding process, the defendant had represented that it would accept responsibility for any delays that the plaintiff incurred as a result of delays in the larger construction project's overall work schedule. Although the plaintiff had expected the job to take 120 days (and had bid accordingly) the foundations ended up taking 8 months to complete. This delay occurred because the defendant (contrary to its own representations) had set up its own materials delivery schedule in order to save money and also scheduled multiple contractors doing mutually exclusive tasks to work in the same place at the same time. When the plaintiff requested damages for the delay, the defendant relied on its superior economic position to offer far less than the full extent of these damages. The defendant had had these plans to take over materials delivery, double book, and not pay delay damages even at the time it had solicited the plaintiff's bid. The plaintiff sued the defendant for breach of contract and, in tort, for fraudulent inducement and fraudulent performance of contract.

The plaintiff claimed that its projected costs on the contract were $370,000, which, given the $600,000 contract price, would have given it a profit of $230,000. It also claimed that the defendant's delaying conduct caused its costs to rise to $831,000, and that it would have made a bid of $1.3 million had it known of these costs. In light of these numbers, the plaintiff's contract damages (its lost contractual expectations[13]) were $461,000: this was the difference between the $230,000 ($600,000 contract price minus $370,000 costs of performance) profit that it would have realized on performance and the $231,000 ($600,000 contract price minus $831,000 costs) loss that it actually suffered given the breach. The plaintiff's tort damages (the losses that it suffered in reliance on the defendant's fraud[14] were $700,000: this was the difference between the $231,000 loss that the plaintiff suffered and the $469,000 ($1.3 million contract price minus $831,000 cost) gain that it would have enjoyed but for the fraud.

The trial court (modifying a jury verdict) made findings with respect to both the contract and tort-based compensatory claims. It awarded $467,000 in contract damages (aiming, it seems, at $461,000 but getting the sums wrong) and $700,000 in tort damages, and allowed the plaintiff to choose which award to receive. The appellate court took a different view, holding that even if the plaintiff's claim sounded in tort (in the defendant's fraudulent misrepresentations) its compensatory damages were limited to the lost expectation of the contract.[15] The appellate court therefore rejected the tort-based damage award (over two vigorous dissents) and left the plaintiff to recover contract-based compensatory damages only.

This holding—that whatever the merits of the plaintiff's tort claim, the only harm in need of compensation came from the lost contractual expectancy—made the punitive damages part of the case harder. Although the

---

13. This, recall, is the difference between the position that it would have occupied had the defendant performed and its position given the breach.

14. This is the difference between the position that the plaintiff actually occupied given the defendant's fraud and the position that it would have occupied had it made the contract it would have made but for the fraud.

15. It is not at all clear why. One plausible argument is that the plaintiff's compensatory tort claim was too speculative—how could a court know that plaintiff would have bid $1.3 million but for defendant's fraud. But this argument is surely not watertight.

plaintiff won $10 million in punitive damages at trial, this award was vulnerable on appeal, because it fell under the shadow of the doctrine (to be considered in detail below) that punitive damages cannot be awarded for breach of contract, *simpliciter*, but only where, in addition to breaching a contract, a defendant has committed an independent tort. *Formosa Plastics* tests the practical scope of this rule. Specifically, the rule has three possible interpretations.

First, the rule might look to the source of the duty whose breach causes the harm that needs compensation: if this duty arises out of the agreement of the parties, then there is only a contract claim and so no punitive damages may be awarded; if the duty is imposed independently by law, then there is an independent tort for which punitives may be awarded. Second, the rule might look to the nature of the compensatory remedy sought: if this remedy is compensation for merely economic loss to the subject matter of the contract, then there is only a contract claim and punitive damages are again forbidden; if the compensatory remedy is compensation for actual harm to interests independent of the contractual expectation, then there is an independent tort and punitives are permitted. On both these interpretations, the plaintiff in *Formosa Plastics* loses on its claim for punitive damages. The duty whose breach harmed the plaintiff was the defendant's duty under the contract to secure the conditions for the plaintiff's timely completion. This duty arose out of agreement by the parties. The *Formosa Plastics* court did *not* focus, for purposes of the compensation claim, on the duty not to misrepresent the contract as it was being made, as was evidenced by the court's rejection of the plaintiff's claim for tort-based compensatory damages. Moreover, the harm for which compensation was sought was the purely economic loss of contractual expectation. This was made explicit in the opinion, once again through the decision to award only $461,000 in contractual expectation damages rather than $700,000 in tort damages.

Formosa Plastics, however, adopted the third interpretation of the doctrine that punitive damages are available in conjunction with breach of contract only where there has been an independent tort. Specifically, the *Formosa Plastics* Court allowed for the separation of the duty whose violation causes the harm that serves as the basis for compensation and the duty whose violation may constitute an independent tort that underwrites punitive damages. In *Formosa Plastics*, the duty whose breach required compensation was the duty to perform under the contract (hence the compensation was to the contractual expectation, and amounted to $461,000). The duty whose breach constituted the independent tort and gave rise to the claim for punitive damages was the defendant's duty not to promise a delivery and work schedule that it never intended to provide. Thus, the plaintiff could sustain punitive damages on its tort claim even though its only compensable harm sounded purely in contract.

8.3.B   SUBJECT-MATTER SPECIFIC PUNITIVE DAMAGES

In some cases, the torts on which punitive damages awards are based are less common, or at least less familiar. Even though these torts may also be explained without reference to any distinctively contractual ideas—and certainly without reference to contractual bad faith—they depend on the specific subject matters of the contracts in connection with whose breach they arise. It will therefore be worthwhile briefly to consider their structure. Among other things, these cases will illuminate the distinctive normative structure of contract and hence also shed light on the distinctive wrong associated with contractual bad faith.

The cases that follow award punitive damages for grossly negligent or even malicious breaches of certain types of contracts, identified by their subject matters. The theme in each class of cases is the same: the contracts at issue involve subjects with respect to which freedom of contract has been severely curtailed, by operation of background law; breaches of these contracts, in appropriate circumstances, violate the legal obligations that this background law announces; violations of these legal obligations are, in essence, torts, and when the violations are gross enough, tort-based punitive damages may be imposed.

Ft. Smith & W. R. Co. v. Ford

Supreme Court of Oklahoma, 1912.
126 P. 745.

■ SHARP, J. Defendant in error, plaintiff below, recovered judgment in the county court of Le Flore county against the plaintiff in error, defendant below, for damages occasioned by the negligence of defendant in carrying the plaintiff, who was a passenger on one of its trains, through a station to which he had purchased a ticket on defendant company's line of railroad. The verdict was for $75. Nine specifications of error are assigned by the plaintiff in error, but two of which are discussed in the brief. The first is that, the action being one for a breach of contract, there was no proof that plaintiff sustained any damages; the second, that the verdict of the jury was excessive. The petition in part charges that on the 7th day of February, 1910, plaintiff was a passenger on one of defendant's regular passenger trains, having purchased a ticket and paid for transportation from Spiro to Skullyville, and that while on said train the employees of defendant company took up plaintiff's ticket; and further charged that it was the duty of said company to stop its train at the said station of Skullyville, to permit the plaintiff to alight there from, but that, disregarding its duty in that respect, defendant company failed and refused to stop its train at said station, and willfully and wrongfully carried plaintiff by and past his said destination.

Section 1379, Comp. Laws 1909, provides that, in case of a neglect or refusal of a railroad company to discharge or deliver passengers at the regularly appointed place, the offending company shall pay the party aggrieved all damages which shall be sustained thereby, with costs of action. This is but declaratory of the duty of carriers of passengers that existed at common law. It is clear that, upon a failure to discharge its duty by affording an opportunity for the passenger to alight at his destination, there was such a violation of duty as would entitle plaintiff to recover at least nominal damages. Plaintiff in error admits its liability for nominal damages, but upon the ground of a breach of contract to transport defendant in error to his destination. If the action, therefore, is one predicated upon contract, the only damages recoverable would be such as would afford full compensation for the injury, if any, sustained by plaintiff, and, there being no testimony tending to show that plaintiff sustained any actual damages, the verdict of the jury would therefore be without evidence to support it. It is therefore necessary to consider whether the action is one arising *ex contractu* or *ex delicto*.

In our system of pleading the formal distinction between actions is abolished, and the petition should state facts constituting the cause of action, plainly and distinctly. In determining the character of the action, we look to the substance of the entire pleading, and not to the mere formal language in which it is expressed. We have regard to the facts constituting the cause of complaint, and afford the plaintiff the most ample redress which the facts will justify, consistent with the rights of the defendant. It is the policy of our system to trammel the rights of the parties as lightly as possible by technicalities of mere form, but so to shape pleadings as to bring before the court or jury the matter in issue between the parties. Hence, when the facts are plainly and distinctly stated, the action will be regarded as either in tort or contract, having regard, first, to the character of the remedy such facts indicate; and, second, to the most complete and ample redress which upon the facts stated the law affords. The character of the action is to be determined by the nature of the grievance rather than the form of the petition, and in cases of the character at hand, courts are inclined to consider it is as founded in tort, unless a special contract very clearly appears to have been made the gravamen and object of the complaint in the petition. The case before us presents, under these views, the inquiry whether the petition seeks to recover for a breach of the contract stated therein, or whether the wrong and injury complained of was that the plaintiff, after acquiring by contract the right to travel on defendant's train to a certain station, and to there be afforded a reasonable opportunity to alight from said train at the station at his point of destination, was wrongfully carried by said station by the negligence of the railroad company, and in violation of its public duty.

The contract is stated as an inducement to the action, as the foundation of plaintiff's right to be on the train, to show that plaintiff was lawfully there. It next charges that without the consent of plaintiff the railroad company willfully and wrongfully, and with disregard of its duty to plaintiff, failed and refused to stop its train at Skullyville station, and carried plaintiff beyond his destination to a point about one mile distant therefrom. There is testimony to show that plaintiff requested the employees in charge of said train to back it to the station, but that they refused so to do. Here is not only a breach of contract and a violation of public duty by the plaintiff in error as a common carrier, but a willful, deliberate, conscious wrong.

The question here presented is ably discussed in *Canaday v. United Rys. Co. of St. Louis, 134 Mo. App. 282, 114 S.W. 88*, where many authorities are collected. It was there said:

In view of the fact that the relation of passenger and carrier can arise only through contract, express or implied, it would indeed be difficult to state a cause of action without some reference to the contract out of which the relation arose. And so it is, when the action sounds in tort, the allegation of the contract of carriage is regarded as mere inducement to the action to show the plaintiff's right to sue as a passenger. Therefore, in cases of this class, where the plaintiff alleges the payment of his fare, the promise of the company to carry him, and then proceeds to state the tort, and his claim is for damages arising on account thereof, the action is declared to be one in tort. This for the reason the gravamen or gist of the action proceeds *ex delicto* on the breach of the duty owing to the public imposed by law.

It is patent that the action was one based, not upon the breach of a contract of carriage, but, as charged in the petition, upon a disregard of duty arising out of the relations of the parties, and was therefore one sounding in tort. As a general rule in such cases, it may be said that exemplary, punitive, or vindictive damages will not be awarded unless there is proof going to show a wrongful purpose or reckless indifference to consequences, oppression, insult, rudeness, caprice, willfulness, or other causes of aggravation in the act or omission causing the injury, or because the circumstances showed a reckless indifference to duty.

What evidence, therefore, was there tending to bring the case within this rule? That the train on which the plaintiff was a passenger did not stop at Skullyville stands admitted. There were three other passengers on the train who had tickets to Skullyville. The conductor had taken up the plaintiff's ticket before reaching Skullyville, hence knew of his presence on the train. No excuse why the train failed to stop at Skullyville was given. The train slowed down and let off three of the passengers near a mile past the station, and, upon discovery that plaintiff was still aboard, the train slowed down a second time. There was a sharp conflict in the testimony as to whether the train stopped on these two occasions; several witnesses testifying that it did not, while defendant's witnesses testified that it did. Plaintiff testified that he jumped off the train while in motion, and fell on his hands and knees, though he was not injured; that it was near ten o'clock at night, in the month of February, and was raining at the time. Plaintiff's testimony in part is as follows:

I asked him to move me back up to the station, and he said, 'He had been there once and was not going anymore.' He says, 'Do you want off,' and I says, 'Yes; I have business to attend to tomorrow, I am not well, and I want off.' We slowed up again. We had kept going on until we got to Rain Prairie. It is a very rough place. I was acquainted with the place, so I went down on the step and he went along with me. He says, 'Get off,' and it had slowed up reasonably slow. I am getting old. I am 52 years old, not a real old man, but I have lost my eyesight. It was dark and rainy.

The plaintiff then attempted to follow an old cow trail, but missed it, and then followed a wire fence for a guide a distance of a half mile to a neighbor's, when he again followed another wire fence until he reached home. It appears that the conductor's time was occupied largely with taking up fares and counting tickets. He was civil in his treatment of the plaintiff, more than can be said of the brakeman, who appears to have had active charge in assisting the various Skullyville passengers to alight. The conductor explained that, even though he had been requested, he could not have backed the train up to the station, on account of the fact that he was being followed by a Kansas City Southern train, using the same track. Witnesses for plaintiff, however, testified that the train had preceded the train of defendant company out of Spiro. The train had but two coaches, and no sufficient reason was shown or attempted why it did not stop at Skullyville. The brakeman testified that there was something wrong with the signal cord, and that the engineer did not get the signal to stop, but it further appears that he had no trouble in stopping the train (as claimed by him) twice after it had passed the station to let off different passengers. The conductor testified that it was the brakeman's duty to assist passengers in getting off in safety. The witness Casey testified that the brakeman told him, "I don't know where in hell he is" (referring to plaintiff), and, when asked why he did not put back to this station, he replied, "To hell with the station. I've passed it, fall off!" This conversation was had with other passengers alike affected, a few moments before the train slowed up the first time.

The neglect and indifference of the conductor and the contempt and disdain exhibited by the brakeman on the occasion tended to show a reckless disregard of duty and indifference to consequences. Where negligence is accompanied with contempt of the plaintiff's rights and conveniences, exemplary damages may be awarded. There is a difference between an injury which is the mere result of such negligence as amounts to little more than an accident, and an injury, willful and negligent, which is accompanied by an expression of insolence. *Memphis & C. R. Co. v. Whitfield, 44 Miss. 466,* and authorities cited. While the testimony does not show the case to be one of a particularly aggravated nature, and while it does not appear that any lasting injury or loss was sustained, yet the high duty imposed by law upon the defendant, taken in connection with the seemingly willful disregard of plaintiff's rights, in view of the facts established, makes it clear that the verdict of the jury was warranted. In such cases it is the province of the jury to award exemplary or punitive damages.

The testimony considered, the verdict is not excessive, but, on the contrary, is exceedingly reasonable.

The judgment of the trial court should be affirmed.

Hutchinson v. Southern Railway Co.

Supreme Court of North Carolina, 1905.
52 S.E. 263.

■ CLARK, C.J. The *feme* plaintiff, a widow, bought a ticket from Hickory, North Carolina, to Liberty, South Carolina. The agent at Hickory told her she would make connection with the 1 p.m. train at Charlotte. On arriving at Charlotte, where she had to change cars, her train missed connection and she took the next train which left there at 10:20 p.m. This was a train which did not stop at all stations, Liberty being one of those at which, by the defendant's printed schedule, it did not stop, but the plaintiff testified that she was not aware of that fact and no one so informed her; on the contrary, the conductor on the train, before getting to Charlotte, told her she would miss connection, but said this 10:20 train from Charlotte would take her to Liberty that night; that in the 18 months previous she had twice traveled on that same 10:20 train and each time had been put off at Liberty; that soon after leaving Charlotte, the conductor on taking up her ticket exclaimed in a loud, imperative and commanding tone, "What are you doing in here? You have no business in here. Who told you to get on here?" that he kept repeating this, rebuking her, and she was deeply humiliated. She says she asked him to give her back her ticket and put her off at the first station (Gastonia); that if he had done this she would have spent the night there, and have gone on in the day time next morning to Liberty, but instead of this he kept the ticket and later came back again, rebuking her in a loud voice, heard distinctly all over the coach, telling her she had no business in there and saying, "I want to know who told you to get on"—adding that she knew the train did not stop at Liberty; that he spoke in a very ill-natured tone and loud voice; that she tried to reason with him and again asked him to put her off at the first stop; that he came back the third time with the same loud, boisterous charges; that when she did not reply, being very nervous and humiliated, he "looked at her very furiously and said, 'What if he didn't put me off there.'" To this she says she replied finally that she had paid her fare and did not deserve such indignities and that he would hear from her; that at Gastonia he did not return her ticket as requested, so she could not stop; that he did not stop at Liberty, where her people were on the platform as she passed, she having telegraphed her daughter from Charlotte that having missed connection she would be on that train, but she was carried past to Seneca, about 25 miles further on, where she was put out at 2:30 at night, and had to sit on the platform alone till 4:30, when she took the train back, reaching Liberty before daylight in a shattered nervous condition, and walked in the dark up to her son-in-law's house alone, a half mile away, and was so exhausted by the nervous strain and exposure to the night air, that she was ill, called in a physician and was confined to her bed several days.

The conductor in his testimony denied any discourtesy or rudeness, but says that he was polite and carried her on to Seneca because he suggested to her that she would get to Liberty six hours earlier by taking the northbound train back than if she stopped at a station this side and waited for a southbound train to Liberty, and that she consented to this.

In this conflict of evidence the jury found upon the issues submitted to them:

1. Did the defendant wrongfully refuse to stop its train at Liberty and permit the plaintiff to depart there from? Yes.

2. Did the defendant maliciously or willfully, wantonly and rudely mistreat and humiliate the plaintiff while a passenger on its train? Yes.

The latter was a pure issue of fact and the finding of the jury is conclusive, the judge having refused to set the verdict aside. As to the first issue, it is a reasonable regulation of the defendant that certain trains shall not stop at all stations, provided there are enough to serve the purposes of local travel, and it does not appear that there was not. If the plaintiff had been aware that this train did not stop at Liberty, she could not complain if she had been put off at Gastonia, the first stop, with her ticket endorsed with leave to pursue her journey by the next train stopping at Liberty. But she testifies that she had no such information, on the contrary, that she had twice in 18 months previously been on the same train which stopped and put her off at Liberty. The notice on the printed schedule of the company was not brought home to her and there was no evidence that she had any actual notice. There was nothing on the face of her ticket to show that it was not good on that train. It was the duty of the defendant to have had an agent at the gate (as is usual) to examine the tickets and allow no one to get upon a train which does not stop at his destination. Not having done this, but having received the plaintiff into this train, without objection, with a ticket calling for Liberty, a regular station, as her destination, and she not knowing that this train did not stop there, it was the duty of the defendant to stop the train at that point for her. On the question of damages His Honor correctly instructed the jury that if the conductor maliciously or with wanton recklessness carried her by her station, or if he maliciously or wantonly mistreated and humiliated her, the jury could assess punitive damages.

The authorities are plenary that the passenger is entitled to recover punitive damages for insult or mistreatment on the part of any employee of the common carrier.

It is equally true that The Code, section 1963, provides that passengers shall be put off at the destination to which they have paid, and that the carrier "shall be liable to the party aggrieved in an action for damages for any neglect or refusal in the premises;" and that when the refusal to take on or discharge a passenger, where he is entitled to be received or discharged, is reckless and wanton, punitive damages may be recovered. Certainly the plaintiff, an unprotected female, was entitled to recover if recklessly and willfully carried against her protest 25 miles beyond her station, was put out at 2:30 at night at a strange station, where she sat at dead of night two hours alone on the platform, and at last reached her destination before day to be met by no one, and had to walk to her daughter's house alone and with shattered nerves had to take her bed and call in a physician.

The authorities are uniform, here and elsewhere, that if the passenger is carried by his station he is entitled to damages, and if it is done recklessly or willfully, as the jury here find, he is entitled to punitive damages. The only decision we can find in the books to the contrary is *Smith v. Railroad, 130 N.C. 304*, which holds that if there is no bodily harm or actual damages a recovery cannot be had. That decision was by a divided court and is in conflict with the statute (Code, section 1963,) above quoted, and unsupported by precedent, and we take this first opportunity to correct and overrule it.

Upon examination of all the exceptions and without discussing them *seriatim,* we find No Error.

* * *

Ford and *Hutchinson* are both about mishaps of the sort that give children nightmares when they are eight or nine and start traveling alone on mass-transit: a public conveyance refuses to allow them to alight at their usual stops, and instead takes them to strange and threatening places, where they are left without any obvious way home. In both cases the plaintiffs are vulnerable—*Ford* involves a partly blind old man and *Hutchinson* a widowed woman—and the defendants negligently abandon their announced routes[16] and callously deposit the plaintiffs at unsuitable spots (a rough field, a deserted station after midnight), all the while insulting and abusing them.

Although the plaintiffs' claims in both cases nominally sound in contract—specifically in the defendants' breaches of the contracts associated with the tickets that they sold—their real centers of gravity lie in tort. Both defendants were common carriers, that is public conveyances operating under a legal duty to serve the general public which included, at the very least, a duty to provide all who were able to pay with the services announced by their published timetables (subject, of course, to the constraints of availability). Ordinary contractual promisors may contract, and refuse to contract, with whomever they please (subject only to constraints, for example, involving anti-discrimination law or the law of competition, that operate at the margins of their choices). Indeed, this is of the very essence of freedom of contract. By contrast, the defendants in *Ford* and *Hutchinson* were under a legal obligation to contract with their plaintiffs. Accordingly, when they breached their contracts, they also violated this legal obligation, and the harms that the breaches imposed on the plaintiffs were, in effect, tortious. As the *Ford* opinion observed, the defendant railroad committed a "breach of contract" but also "a violation of public duty by the plaintiff in error as a common carrier." And insofar as the breach of this duty was sufficiently gross—insofar as it imposed harms sufficiently in excess of its benefits, or insofar as it was sufficiently premeditated—it involved the kind of culpability that can justified punitive damages.

Comunale v. Traders & General Ins. Co.

California Supreme Court, 1958.
328 P.2d 198.

■ GIBSON, J. Mr. and Mrs. Comunale were struck in a marked pedestrian crosswalk by a truck driven by Percy Sloan. Mr. Comunale was seriously

---

16. In *Ford*, a train fails to make a scheduled stop, and in *Hutchinson*, a conductor mistakenly reports that a train will make a stop at a station that the published timetables accurately say will be skipped.

injured, and his wife suffered minor injuries. Sloan was insured by defendant Traders and General Insurance Company under a policy that contained limits of liability in the sum of $10,000 for each person injured and $20,000 for each accident. He notified Traders of the accident and was told that the policy did not provide coverage because he was driving a truck that did not belong to him. When the Comunales filed suit against Sloan, Traders refused to defend the action, and Sloan employed competent counsel to represent him. On the second day of the trial Sloan informed Traders that the Comunales would compromise the case for $4,000, that he did not have enough money to effect the settlement, and that it was highly probable the jury would return a verdict in excess of the policy limits. Traders was obligated to defend any personal injury suit covered by the policy, but it was given the right to make such settlement as it might deem expedient. Sloan demanded that Traders assume the defense and settlement of the case. Traders refused, and the trial proceeded to judgment in favor of Mr. Comunale for $25,000 and Mrs. Comunale for $1,250.

Sloan did not pay the judgment, and the Comunales sued Traders under a provision in the policy that permitted an injured party to maintain an action after obtaining judgment against the insured. (See *Ins. Code, § 11580, subd. (b)(2)*.) In that suit judgment was rendered in favor of Mr. Comunale for $10,000 and in favor of Mrs. Comunale for $1,250. This judgment was satisfied by Traders after it was affirmed in *Comunale v. Traders & General Ins. Co., 116 Cal.App.2d 198*.

Comunale obtained an assignment of all of Sloan's rights against Traders and then commenced the present action to recover from Traders the portion of his judgment against Sloan which was in excess of the policy limits. The jury returned a verdict in Comunale's favor, but the trial court entered a judgment for Traders notwithstanding the verdict.

The following questions are presented on Comunale's appeal from the judgment: (1) Did Sloan have a cause of action against Traders for the amount of the judgment in excess of the policy limits? (2) Was Sloan's cause of action against Traders assignable?

Liability in Excess of the Policy Limits

In determining whether Traders is liable for the portion of the judgment against Sloan in excess of the policy limits, we must take into consideration the fact that Traders not only wrongfully refused to defend the action against Sloan but also refused to accept an offer of settlement within the policy limits. It is not claimed the settlement offer was unreasonable in view of the extent of the injuries and the probability that Sloan would be found liable, and Traders' only reason for refusing to settle was its claim that the accident was not covered by the policy. Because of its wrongful denial of coverage, Traders failed to consider Sloan's interest in having the suit against him compromised by a settlement within the policy limits.

(1) There is an implied covenant of good faith and fair dealing in every contract that neither party will do anything which will injure the right of

the other to receive the benefits of the agreement. (*Brown v. Superior Court, 34 Cal.2d 559, 564.*) This principle is applicable to policies of insurance. (*Hilker v. Western Automobile Ins. Co., 204 Wis. 1* (aff'd on rehg., *204 Wis.*) In the Hilker case it is pointed out that the rights of the insured "go deeper than the mere surface of the contract written for him by defendant" and that implied obligations are imposed "based upon those principles of fair dealing which enter into every contract." (*231 N.W. at p. 258.*) (2) It is common knowledge that a large percentage of the claims covered by insurance are settled without litigation and that this is one of the usual methods by which the insured receives protection. (See *Douglas v. United States Fidelity & Guaranty Co., 81 N.H. 371 [127 A. 708, 712]*; *Hilker v. Western Automobile Ins. Co., supra.*) (3) Under these circumstances the implied obligation of good faith and fair dealing requires the insurer to settle in an appropriate case although the express terms of the policy do not impose such a duty.

(4) The insurer, in deciding whether a claim should be compromised, must take into account the interest of the insured and give it at least as much consideration as it does to its own interest. (See *Ivy v. Pacific Automobile Ins. Co., 156 Cal.App.2d 652, 659 [320 P.2d 140].*) (5) When there is great risk of a recovery beyond the policy limits so that the most reasonable manner of disposing of the claim is a settlement which can be made within those limits, a consideration in good faith of the insured's interest requires the insurer to settle the claim. Its unwarranted refusal to do so constitutes a breach of the implied covenant of good faith and fair dealing.

(6) There is an important difference between the liability of an insurer who performs its obligations and that of an insurer who breaches its contract. The policy limits restrict only the amount the insurer may have to pay in the performance of the contract as compensation to a third person for personal injuries caused by the insured; they do not restrict the damages recoverable by the insured for a breach of contract by the insurer.

(7) The decisive factor in fixing the extent of Traders' liability is not the refusal to defend; it is the refusal to accept an offer of settlement within the policy limits. (8) Where there is no opportunity to compromise the claim and the only wrongful act of the insurer is the refusal to defend, the liability of the insurer is ordinarily limited to the amount of the policy plus attorneys' fees and costs. (*Mannheimer Bros. v. Kansas Casualty & Surety Co., 149 Minn. 482*) In such a case it is reasoned that, if the insured has employed competent counsel to represent him, there is no ground for concluding that the judgment would have been for a lesser sum had the defense been conducted by insurer's counsel, and therefore it cannot be said that the detriment suffered by the insured as the result of a judgment in excess of the policy limits was proximately caused by the insurer's refusal to defend. (*Cf. Lane v. Storke, 10 Cal.App. 347, 350.*) This reasoning, however, does not apply where the insurer wrongfully refuses to accept a reasonable settlement within the policy limits.

Most of the cases dealing with the insurer's failure to settle involve an insurer who had assumed the defense of the action against the insured. (9) It is generally held that since the insurer has reserved control over the litigation and settlement it is liable for the entire amount of a judgment against the insured, including any portion in excess of the policy limits, if in the exercise of such control it is guilty of bad faith in refusing a settlement. Those cases are, of course, factually distinguishable from the present one since Traders never assumed control over the defense. (10) However, the reason Traders was not in control of the litigation is that it wrongfully refused to defend Sloan, and the breach of its express obligation to defend did not release it from its implied duty to consider Sloan's interest in the settlement.

(11) We do not agree with the cases that hold there is no liability in excess of the policy limits where the insurer, believing there is no coverage, wrongfully refuses to defend and without justification refuses to settle the claim. (See *State Farm Mut. Auto. Ins. Co. v. Skaggs, 251 F.2d 356, 359*, and *Fidelity & Casualty Co. of New York v. Gault, 196 F.2d 329, 330*.) (12) An insurer who denies coverage does so at its own risk, and, although its position may not have been entirely groundless, if the denial is found to be wrongful it is liable for the full amount which will compensate the insured for all the detriment caused by the insurer's breach of the express and implied obligations of the contract. Certainly an insurer who not only rejected a reasonable offer of settlement but also wrongfully refused to defend should be in no better position than if it had assumed the defense and then declined to settle. The insurer should not be permitted to profit by its own wrong.

(13) A breach which prevents the making of an advantageous settlement when there is a great risk of liability in excess of the policy limits will, in the ordinary course of things, result in a judgment against the insured in excess of those limits. *Section 3300 of the Civil Code* provides that the measure of damages for a breach of contract is the amount which will compensate the party aggrieved for all the detriment proximately caused by the breach, or which, in the ordinary course of things, would be likely to result from it.

It is clear that *section 3300 of the Civil Code* authorizes a recovery in excess of the policy limits, and in our opinion there is no merit in Traders' contention that *section 3358 of the Civil Code* so qualifies *section 3300* as to prevent such a recovery. *Section 3358* provides that a person cannot recover a greater amount in damages for the breach of an obligation than he could have gained by full performance. The question is what would Sloan have gained from the full performance of the policy contract with Traders. (*Cf. Henderson v. Oakes–Waterman, Builders, 44 Cal.App.2d 615, 618*.) If Traders had performed its contract, it would have settled the action against Sloan, thereby protecting him from all liability. The allowance of a recovery in excess of the policy limits will not give the insured any additional advantage but merely place him in the same position as if the contract had been performed.

(14) It follows from what we have said that an insurer, who wrongfully declines to defend and who refuses to accept a reasonable settlement within the policy limits in violation of its duty to consider in good faith the interest of the insured in the settlement, is liable for the entire judgment against the insured even if it exceeds the policy limits.

Assignability of the Cause of Action

(15) An action for damages in excess of the policy limits based on an insurer's wrongful failure to settle is assignable whether the action is considered as sounding in tort or in contract. (See *Civ. Code, § 954*; *Brown v. Guarantee Ins. Co., 155 Cal.App.2d 679, 693–695.*) (16) Traders relies on a clause in the policy which provides that an assignment of an interest under the policy shall be binding only if Traders consents thereto. However, it is well settled that such a provision does not preclude the transfer of a cause of action for damages for breach of a contract. (*Trubowitch v. Riverbank Canning Co., 30 Cal.2d 335, 339–340.*) This rule has been applied to provisions against assignability in insurance policies similar to the provision involved here. Accordingly, Sloan could assign his cause of action to Comunale.

The judgment is reversed with directions to the superior court to enter judgment on the verdict.

Crisci v. Security Ins. Co. of New Haven

Supreme Court of California, 1967.
426 P.2d 173.

■ PETERS, J. In an action against The Security Insurance Company of New Haven, Connecticut, the trial court awarded Rosina Crisci $91,000 (plus interest) because she suffered a judgment in a personal injury action after Security, her insurer, refused to settle the claim. Mrs. Crisci was also awarded $25,000 for mental suffering. Security has appealed.

June DiMare and her husband were tenants in an apartment building owned by Rosina Crisci. Mrs. DiMare was descending the apartment's outside wooden staircase when a tread gave way. She fell through the resulting opening up to her waist and was left hanging 15 feet above the ground. Mrs. DiMare suffered physical injuries and developed a very severe psychosis. In a suit brought against Mrs. Crisci, the DiMares alleged that the step broke because Mrs. Crisci was negligent in inspecting and maintaining the stairs. They contended that Mrs. DiMare's mental condition was caused by the accident, and they asked for $400,000 as compensation for physical and mental injuries and medical expenses.

Mrs. Crisci had $10,000 of insurance coverage under a general liability policy issued by Security. The policy obligated Security to defend the suit against Mrs. Crisci and authorized the company to make any settlement it deemed expedient. Security hired an experienced lawyer, Mr. Healy, to handle the case. Both he and defendant's claims manager believed that unless evidence was discovered showing that Mrs. DiMare had a prior mental illness, a jury would probably find that the accident precipitated Mrs. DiMare's psychosis. And both men believed that if the jury felt that the fall triggered the psychosis, a verdict of not less than $100,000 would be returned.

An extensive search turned up no evidence that Mrs. DiMare had any prior mental abnormality. As a teenager Mrs. DiMare had been in a Washington mental hospital, but only to have an abortion. Both Mrs. DiMare and Mrs. Crisci found psychiatrists who would testify that the accident caused Mrs. DiMare's illness, and the insurance company knew of this testimony. Among those who felt the psychosis was not related to the accident were the doctors at the state mental hospital where Mrs. DiMare had been committed following the accident. All the psychiatrists agreed, however, that a psychosis could be triggered by a sudden fear of falling to one's death.

The exact chronology of settlement offers is not established by the record. However, by the time the DiMares' attorney reduced his settlement demands to $10,000, Security had doctors prepared to support its position and was only willing to pay $3,000 for Mrs. DiMare's physical injuries. Security was unwilling to pay one cent for the possibility of a plaintiff's verdict on the mental illness issue. This conclusion was based on the assumption that the jury would believe all of the defendant's psychiatric evidence and none of the plaintiff's. Security also rejected a $9,000 settlement demand at a time when Mrs. Crisci offered to pay $2,500 of the settlement.

A jury awarded Mrs. DiMare $100,000 and her husband $1,000. After an appeal (*DiMare v. Cresci, 58 Cal.2d 292*) the insurance company paid $10,000 of this amount, the amount of its policy. The DiMares then sought to collect the balance from Mrs. Crisci. A settlement was arranged by which the DiMares received $22,000, a 40 percent interest in Mrs. Crisci's claim to a particular piece of property, and an assignment of Mrs. Crisci's cause of action against Security. Mrs. Crisci, an immigrant widow of 70, became indigent. She worked as a babysitter, and her grandchildren paid her rent. The change in her financial condition was accompanied by a decline in physical health, hysteria, and suicide attempts. Mrs. Crisci then brought this action.

The liability of an insurer in excess of its policy limits for failure to accept a settlement offer within those limits was considered by this court in *Comunale v. Traders & General Ins. Co., 50 Cal.2d 654*. It was there reasoned that in every contract, including policies of insurance, there is an implied covenant of good faith and fair dealing that neither party will do anything which will injure the right of the other to receive the benefits of the agreement; that it is common knowledge that one of the usual methods by which an insured receives protection under a liability insurance policy is by settlement of claims without litigation; that the implied obligation of good faith and fair dealing requires the insurer to settle in an appropriate case although the express terms of the policy do not impose the duty; that in determining whether to settle the insurer must give the interests of the insured at least as much consideration as it gives to its own interests; and that when "there is great risk of a recovery beyond the policy limits so that the most reasonable manner of disposing of the claim is a settlement which can be made within those limits, a consideration in good faith of the insured's interest requires the insurer to settle the claim." (*50 Cal.2d at p. 659.*)

(1) In determining whether an insurer has given consideration to the interests of the insured, the test is whether a prudent insurer without policy limits would have accepted the settlement offer.

Several cases, in considering the liability of the insurer, contain language to the effect that bad faith is the equivalent of dishonesty, fraud, and concealment. (2) Obviously a showing that the insurer has been guilty of actual dishonesty, fraud, or concealment is relevant to the determination whether it has given consideration to the insured's interest in considering a settlement offer within the policy limits. The language used in the cases, however, should not be understood as meaning that in the absence of evidence establishing actual dishonesty, fraud, or concealment no recovery may be had for a judgment in excess of the policy limits. *Comunale v. Traders & General Ins. Co., supra, 50 Cal.2d 654, 658–659*, makes it clear that liability based on an implied covenant exists whenever the insurer refuses to settle in an appropriate case and that liability may exist when the insurer unwarrantedly refuses an offered settlement where the most reasonable manner of disposing of the claim is by accepting the settlement. (3) Liability is imposed not for a bad faith breach of the contract but for failure to meet the duty to accept reasonable settlements, a duty included within the implied covenant of good faith and fair dealing. Moreover, examination of the balance of the *Palmer, Critz*, and *Davy* opinions makes it abundantly clear that recovery may be based on unwarranted rejection of a reasonable settlement offer and that the absence of evidence, circumstantial or direct, showing actual dishonesty, fraud, or concealment is not fatal to the cause of action.

Amicus curiae argues that, whenever an insurer receives an offer to settle within the policy limits and rejects it, the insurer should be liable in every case for the amount of any final judgment whether or not within the policy limits. As we have seen, the duty of the insurer to consider the insured's interest in settlement offers within the policy limits arises from an implied covenant in the contract, and ordinarily contract duties are strictly enforced and not subject to a standard of reasonableness. Obviously, it will always be in the insured's interest to settle within the policy limits when there is any danger, however slight, of a judgment in excess of those limits. Accordingly the rejection of a settlement within the limits where there is any danger of a judgment in excess of the limits can be justified, if at all, only on the basis of interests of the insurer, and, in light of the common knowledge that settlement is one of the usual methods by which an insured receives protection under a liability policy, it may not be unreasonable for an insured who purchases a policy with limits to believe that a sum of money equal to the limits is available and will be used so as to avoid liability on his part with regard to any covered accident. In view of such expectation an insurer should not be permitted to further its own interests by rejecting opportunities to settle within the policy limits unless it is also willing to absorb losses which may result from its failure to settle.

The proposed rule is a simple one to apply and avoids the burdens of a determination whether a settlement offer within the policy limits was reasonable. The proposed rule would also eliminate the danger than an insurer, faced with a settlement offer at or near the policy limits, will reject it and gamble with the insured's money to further its own interests. Moreover, it is not entirely clear that the proposed rule would place a burden on insurers substantially greater than that which is present under existing law. (4) The size of the judgment recovered in the personal injury action when it exceeds the policy limits, although not conclusive, furnishes an inference that the value of the claim is the equivalent of the amount of the judgment and that acceptance of an offer within those limits was the most reasonable method of dealing with the claim.

Finally, and most importantly, there is more than a small amount of elementary justice in a rule that would require that, in this situation where the insurer's and insured's interests necessarily conflict, the insurer, which may reap the benefits of its determination not to settle, should also suffer the detriments of its decision. On the basis of these and other considerations, a number of commentators have urged that the insurer should be liable for any resulting judgment where it refuses to settle within the policy limits.

(5) We need not, however, here determine whether there might be some countervailing considerations precluding adoption of the proposed rule because, under *Comunale v. Traders & General Ins. Co., supra, 50 Cal.2d 654*, and the cases following it, the evidence is clearly sufficient to support the determination that Security breached its duty to consider the interests of Mrs. Crisci in proposed settlements. Both Security's attorney and its claims manager agreed that if Mrs. DiMare won an award for her psychosis, that award would be at least $100,000. Security attempts to justify its rejection of a settlement by contending that it believed Mrs. DiMare had no chance of winning on the mental suffering issue. That belief in the circumstances present could be found to be unreasonable. Security was putting blind faith in the power of its psychiatrists to convince the jury when it knew that the accident could have caused the psychosis, that its agents had told it that without evidence of prior mental defects a jury was likely to believe the fall precipitated the psychosis, and that Mrs. DiMare had reputable psychiatrists on her side. Further, the company had been told by a psychiatrist that in a group of 24 psychiatrists, 12 could be found to support each side.

(6) The trial court found that defendant "knew that there was a considerable risk of substantial recovery beyond said policy limits" and that "the defendant did not give as much consideration to the financial interests of its said insured as it gave to its own interests." That is all that was required. The award of $91,000 must therefore be affirmed.

Restatement 2d of Contracts

§ 205   Duty of Good Faith and Fair Dealing

Every contract imposes upon each party a duty of good faith and fair dealing in its performance and its enforcement.

Comments & Illustrations

Comment a. Meanings of "good faith." Good faith is defined in Uniform Commercial Code § 1–201(19) as "honesty in fact in the conduct or transaction concerned." "In the case of a merchant" Uniform Commercial Code § 2–103(1)(b) provides that good faith means "honesty in fact and the observance of reasonable commercial standards of fair dealing in the trade." The phrase "good faith" is used in a variety of contexts, and its meaning varies somewhat with the context. Good faith performance or enforcement of a contract emphasizes faithfulness to an agreed common purpose and consistency with the justified expectations of the other party; it excludes a variety of types of conduct characterized as involving "bad faith" because they violate community standards of decency, fairness or reasonableness. The appropriate remedy for a breach of the duty of good faith also varies with the circumstances.

Comment b. Good faith purchase. In many situations a good faith purchaser of property for value can acquire better rights in the property than his transferor had. See, e.g., § 342. In this context "good faith" focuses on the honesty of the purchaser, as distinguished from his care or negligence. Particularly in the law of negotiable instruments inquiry may be limited to "good faith" under what has been called "the rule of the pure heart and the empty head." When diligence or inquiry is a condition of the purchaser's right, it is said that good faith is not enough. This focus on honesty is appropriate to cases of good faith purchase; it is less so in cases of good faith performance.

Comment c. Good faith in negotiation. This Section, like Uniform Commercial Code § 1–203, does not deal with good faith in the formation of a contract. Bad faith in negotiation, although not within the scope of this Section, may be subject to sanctions. Particular forms of bad faith in bargaining are the subjects of rules as to capacity to contract, mutual assent and consideration and of rules as to invalidating causes such as fraud and duress. See, for example, §§ 90 and 208. Moreover, remedies for bad faith in the absence of agreement are found in the law of torts or restitution. For examples of a statutory duty to bargain in good faith, see, e.g., National Labor Relations Act § 8(d) and the federal Truth in Lending Act. In cases of negotiation for modification of an existing contractual relationship, the rule stated in this Section may overlap with more specific rules requiring negotiation in good faith. See §§ 73, 89; Uniform Commercial Code § 2–209 and Comment.

Comment d. Good faith performance. Subterfuges and evasions violate the obligation of good faith in performance even though the actor believes his conduct to be justified. But the obligation goes further: bad faith may be overt, or may consist of inaction, and fair dealing may require more than honesty. A complete catalogue of types of bad faith is impossible, but the following types are among those which have been recognized in judicial decisions: evasion of the spirit of the bargain, lack of diligence and slacking off, willful rendering of imperfect performance, abuse of a power to specify terms, and interference with or failure to cooperate in the other party's performance.

Illustrations:

1. A, an oil dealer, borrows $100,000 from B, a supplier, and agrees to buy all his requirements of certain oil products from B on stated terms until the debt is repaid. Before the debt is repaid, A makes a new arrangement with C, a competitor of B. Under the new arrangement A's business is conducted by a corporation formed and owned by A and C and managed by A, and the corporation buys all its oil products from C. The new arrangement may be found to be a subterfuge or evasion and a breach of contract by A.

2. A, owner of a shopping center, leases part of it to B, giving B the exclusive right to conduct a supermarket, the rent to be a percentage of B's gross receipts. During the term of the lease A acquires adjoining land, expands the shopping center, and leases part of the adjoining land to C for a competing supermarket. Unless such action was contemplated or is otherwise justified, there is a breach of contract by A.

3. A Insurance Company insures B against legal liability for certain bodily injuries to third persons, with a limit of liability of $10,000 for an accident to any one person. The policy provides that A will defend any suit covered by it but may settle. C sues B on a claim covered by the policy and offers to settle for $9,500. A refuses to settle on the ground that the amount is excessive, and judgment is rendered against B for $20,000 after a trial defended by A. A then refuses to appeal, and offers to pay $10,000 only if B satisfies the judgment, impairing B's opportunity to negotiate for settlement. B prosecutes an appeal, reasonably expending $7,500, and obtains dismissal of the claim. A has failed to deal fairly and in good faith with B and is liable for B's appeal expense.

4. A and B contract that A will perform certain demolition work for B and pay B a specified sum for materials salvaged, the contract not to "become effective until" certain insurance policies "are in full force and effect." A makes a good faith effort to obtain the insurance, but financial difficulty arising from injury to an employee of A on another job prevents A from obtaining them. A's duty to perform is discharged.

5. B submits and A accepts a bid to supply approximately 4000 tons of trap rock for an airport at a unit price. The parties

execute a standard form of "Invitation, Bid, and Acceptance (Short Form Contract)" supplied by A, including typed terms "to be delivered to project as required," "delivery to start immediately," "cancellation by A may be effected at any time." Good faith requires that A order and accept the rock within a reasonable time unless A has given B notice of intent to cancel.

6. A contracts to perform services for B for such compensation "as you, in your sole judgment, may decide is reasonable." After A has performed the services, B refuses to make any determination of the value of the services. A is entitled to their value as determined by a court.

7. A suffers a loss of property covered by an insurance policy issued by B, and submits to B notice and proof of loss. The notice and proof fail to comply with requirements of the policy as to form and detail. B does not point out the defects, but remains silent and evasive, telling A broadly to perfect his claim. The defects do not bar recovery on the policy.

Comment e. Good faith in enforcement. The obligation of good faith and fair dealing extends to the assertion, settlement and litigation of contract claims and defenses. See, e.g., §§ 73, 89. The obligation is violated by dishonest conduct such as conjuring up a pretended dispute, asserting an interpretation contrary to one's own understanding, or falsification of facts. It also extends to dealing which is candid but unfair, such as taking advantage of the necessitous circumstances of the other party to extort a modification of a contract for the sale of goods without legitimate commercial reason. See Uniform Commercial Code § 2–209, Comment 2. Other types of violation have been recognized in judicial decisions: harassing demands for assurances of performance, rejection of performance for unstated reasons, willful failure to mitigate damages, and abuse of a power to determine compliance or to terminate the contract. For a statutory duty of good faith in termination, see the federal Automobile Dealer's Day in Court Act, *15 U.S.C. §§ 1221*–25 (1976).

Illustrations:

8. A contracts to sell and ship goods to B on credit. The contract provides that, if B's credit or financial responsibility becomes impaired or unsatisfactory to A, A may demand cash or security before making shipment and may cancel if the demand is not met. A may properly demand cash or security only if he honestly believes, with reason, that the prospect of payment is impaired.

9. A contracts to sell and ship goods to B. On arrival B rejects the goods on the erroneous ground that delivery was late. B is thereafter precluded from asserting other unstated grounds then known to him which A could have cured if stated seasonably.

Uniform Commercial Code

§ 1–304   Obligation of Good Faith

Every contract or duty within [the Uniform Commercial Code] imposes an obligation of good faith in its performance and enforcement.

Official Comments

Source: Former Section 1–203. Changes from former law: Except for changing the form of reference to the Uniform Commercial Code, this section is identical to former Section 1–203.

1. This section sets forth a basic principle running throughout the Uniform Commercial Code. The principle is that in commercial transactions good faith is required in the performance and enforcement of all agreements or duties. While this duty is explicitly stated in some provisions of the Uniform Commercial Code, the applicability of the duty is broader than merely these situations and applies generally, as stated in this section, to the performance or enforcement of every contract or duty within this Act. It is further implemented by Section 1–303 on course of dealing, course of performance, and usage of trade. This section does not support an independent cause of action for failure to perform or enforce in good faith. Rather, this section means that a failure to perform or enforce, in good faith, a specific duty or obligation under the contract, constitutes a breach of that contract or makes unavailable, under the particular circumstances, are medial right or power. This distinction makes it clear that the doctrine of good faith merely directs a court towards interpreting contracts within the commercial context in which they are created, performed, and enforced, and does not create a separate duty of fairness and reasonableness which can be independently breached.

2. "Performance and enforcement" of contracts and duties within the Uniform Commercial Code include the exercise of rights created by the Uniform Commercial Code.

* * *

Although *Comunale* and *Crisci* do not directly involve punitive damages (as will be discussed in greater detail in a moment), these cases illustrate another context in which tort-like duties arise in and around contract, so that a breach of contract may also constitute a tort, and thus may (if appropriately gross) underwrite an award of punitive damages. The insurance cases are, moreover, in a way more revealing than the earlier cases concerning common carriers. Whereas in the common carrier cases the tort arose in light of a background legal norm that is a purely contingent historical artifact, in the insurance cases, the tort arises in light of certain structural features of the contract relations at issue. This opens up the possibility, which the next section will investigate in earnest, that breaching a contract may in appropriate circumstances (that is, where the breach is sufficiently grossly in bad faith) constitute a tort.

Begin considering the insurance cases by adopting a highly abbreviat-ed, highly stylized statement of the facts in *Comunale*. The Comunales were struck by a truck driven by a man named Sloan, who was insured by Traders under a policy announcing coverage limits of $10,000 per person and $20,000 per accident. When the Comunales sued Sloan, Traders denied coverage and refused to aid in Sloan's defense, on the grounds that he was not driving his own truck and so was not covered by the policy. The Comunales offered to settle for $4000, and Sloan informed Traders, ex-plaining that this was a good offer but that he did not have the cash to accept it, and again asking Traders to assume his defense and accept the settlement. Traders again refused on both counts, and the Comunales eventually won their lawsuit, recovering $26,250. Sloan did not pay the verdict (most likely because he could not), and the Comunales sued Trad-ers, after obtaining an assignment of all Sloan's rights against Traders

Now assume that Traders wrongfully refused to defend Sloan *and* also wrongfully refused to accept an offer of settlement within the policy limits. This raises the question whether, having taken these actions, Traders became liable (to Sloan or, on assignment, to the Comunales) for the verdict in excess of the limits on the policy. The court concluded that Traders was liable for the excess. The reasons it adduced to support the conclusion go a long way towards establishing a tort of bad faith breach of contract.

The court began its analysis by observing that there exists an implied in law covenant of good faith in every contract. This covenant, the court observed, requires insurers to settle claims in appropriate cases, even when insurance policies do not expressly require such settlements. Moreover, the court took a broad view of what counts as an appropriate case for settle-ment. Thus, the court observed that an insurer's downside risk on refusing to settle is capped by the limits on the policy whereas the insured's downside risk is not so capped, so that as a settlement offer approaches these policy limits, the insurer has much less reason to accept it than the insured. The court responded to this conflict by announcing the rule that in deciding whether or not to accept a settlement offer, good faith requires an insurer to give at least as much consideration to the insured's interest as to its own. The court concluded that (quite apart from any refusal to defend) Traders refusal to accept the Comunales' $4,000 settlement offer breached good faith understood in this way. Finally, and critically, the court conclud-ed that the Traders' liability for this breach was not capped by the policy limits announced in Sloan's policy. Such policy limits, the court explained, just state the maximum amount that the insurer must pay if it performs its obligation. When the insurer breaches by improperly refusing to settle, it becomes liable for whatever verdict issues.

Now it is not immediately obvious why *Comunale* should be included in a discussion of punitive damages. It may seem that the case is not about punitive damages at all, but rather about consequential damages: specifical-ly, about whether the policy limits function (in effect as a limitation of remedy clause) to prevent an insured person from recovering for losses exceeding these limits that she suffers as a result of her insurer's breach of its duty to defend and settle. *Crisci*, however, makes the reason for including *Comunale* here plain. The argument in *Crisci* reveals that *Comunale* is interesting, in the context of a discussion of punitive damages for breach of contract, not in light of the remedy that it ordered,[17] but rather in light of the theory that it inaugurated concerning the duty whose breach occasioned the remedy.

The crucial passage in *Crisci*—the paragraph that identifies the tort-like logic immanent in *Comunale's* account of good faith—appears at the midpoint of the opinion, and discusses an argument made in an amicus brief. That argument began from *Comunale's* observation that an insurer's incentives to accept a settlement diminish as the settlement offer approaches the insured's policy limits. It added the further observation that *whenever* a settlement offer within an insured's policy limits is accompanied by a chance of a verdict in excess of these limits, it will always be in the interest of the insured to settle.[18] In other words, the *only* interest *ever* served by refusing such a settlement offer is the insurer's, so that *every* such refusal is necessarily in bad faith. Accordingly, the loose requirement, announced in *Comunale*, that good faith requires an insurer deciding whether or not to accept a settlement offer fairly to balance its own interests against the insured's in fact resolves itself into a strict rule that good faith requires the insurer to accept every offer of settlement within the policy limits.[19] This logic is, moreover, further reinforced by the roughly sociological observation that given the common practice of settling claims, it is reasonable for an insured to think that his policy limits state the amount that will be available to protect him from liability by any means necessary, including by settling. Indeed, any other regime leaves the insured subject to some remaining risk, which is exactly what he bought the insurance to avoid. Finally, and really as an afterthought, an insurer who does not accept an offer of settlement within the policy limits thereby assumes liability for the entirety of any verdict, no matter how far in excess of the policy limits, that follows the refusal to settle.

Comunale and *Crisci* therefore establish the logical pre-requisites for treating bad faith breach of contract as, in itself, constituting an identifiable and actionable tort. The duty of good faith, being implied in law, is mandatory for every contract. It is thus outside the realm of the parties' discretion—outside the realm of their freedom of contract—and, like the duties imposed on the common carriers in *Ford* and *Hutchinson*, tort-like rather than contractual. Ordinarily, however, the duty of good faith is too vague to have bite: indeed, it is generally left to the parties to specify its content, as the comments to the Restatement and the UCC both make

---

17. The fact that this remedy, which exceeded the policy limits, might appear in a way super-compensatory is really just a red herring.

18. Settling guarantees the insured no residual liability, whereas fighting might yield a verdict in excess of the policy limit.

19. Note that this argument was not formally adopted in *Crisci* because the court concluded that *Crisci* should win even under weaker *Comunale* balancing test.

plain.[20] But *Crisci's* account of *Comunale* reveals that, at least in the insurance context, the implied in law duty of good faith is not just a vague standard but a very precise rule, with identifiable entailments, which may be unequivocally breached. And once the duty of good faith is understood in this way, then punitive damages for its gross breach become available as they would for any other gross tort. Should there be any doubt concerning this, one more case (on which no comment is required) makes the point plain.

State Farm Mutual Auto Ins. Co. v. Campbell

United States Supreme Court, 2003.
538 U.S. 408.

■ JUSTICE KENNEDY delivered the opinion of the Court.

We address once again the measure of punishment, by means of punitive damages, a State may impose upon a defendant in a civil case. The question is whether, in the circumstances we shall recount, an award of $145 million in punitive damages, where full compensatory damages are $1 million, is excessive and in violation of the Due Process Clause of the *Fourteenth Amendment to the Constitution* of the United States.

I

In 1981, Curtis Campbell (Campbell) was driving with his wife, Inez Preece Campbell, in Cache County, Utah. He decided to pass six vans traveling ahead of them on a two-lane highway. Todd Ospital was driving a small car approaching from the opposite direction. To avoid a head-on collision with Campbell, who by then was driving on the wrong side of the highway and toward oncoming traffic, Ospital swerved onto the shoulder, lost control of his automobile, and collided with a vehicle driven by Robert G. Slusher. Ospital was killed, and Slusher was rendered permanently disabled. The Campbells escaped unscathed.

In the ensuing wrongful death and tort action, Campbell insisted he was not at fault. Early investigations did support differing conclusions as to who caused the accident, but "a consensus was reached early on by the investigators and witnesses that Mr. Campbell's unsafe pass had indeed caused the crash." Campbell's insurance company, petitioner State Farm Mutual Automobile Insurance Company (State Farm), nonetheless decided to contest liability and declined offers by Slusher and Ospital's estate (Ospital) to settle the claims for the policy limit of $50,000 ($25,000 per claimant). State Farm also ignored the advice of one of its own investigators and took the case to trial, assuring the Campbells that "their assets were safe, that they had no liability for the accident, that [State Farm] would represent their interests, and that they did not need to procure separate counsel." To the contrary, a jury determined that Campbell was

---

20. *See* RESTATEMENT (SECOND) CONTRACTS § 205 cmt. a (1981); U.C.C. § 1–304 cmt. n.1 (1977).

100 percent at fault, and a judgment was returned for $185,849, far more than the amount offered in settlement.

At first State Farm refused to cover the $135,849 in excess liability. Its counsel made this clear to the Campbells: " 'You may want to put for sale signs on your property to get things moving.' " Nor was State Farm willing to post a supersedeas bond to allow Campbell to appeal the judgment against him. Campbell obtained his own counsel to appeal the verdict. During the pendency of the appeal, in late 1984, Slusher, Ospital, and the Campbells reached an agreement whereby Slusher and Ospital agreed not to seek satisfaction of their claims against the Campbells. In exchange the Campbells agreed to pursue a bad faith action against State Farm and to be represented by Slusher's and Ospital's attorneys. The Campbells also agreed that Slusher and Ospital would have a right to play a part in all major decisions concerning the bad faith action. No settlement could be concluded without Slusher's and Ospital's approval, and Slusher and Ospital would receive 90 percent of any verdict against State Farm.

In 1989, the Utah Supreme Court denied Campbell's appeal in the wrongful death and tort actions. *Slusher v. Ospital, 777 P.2d 437.* State Farm then paid the entire judgment, including the amounts in excess of the policy limits. The Campbells nonetheless filed a complaint against State Farm alleging bad faith, fraud, and intentional infliction of emotional distress. The trial court initially granted State Farm's motion for summary judgment because State Farm had paid the excess verdict, but that ruling was reversed on appeal. *840 P.2d 130 (Utah App. 1992).* On remand State Farm moved *in limine* to exclude evidence of alleged conduct that occurred in unrelated cases outside of Utah, but the trial court denied the motion. At State Farm's request the trial court bifurcated the trial into two phases conducted before different juries. In the first phase the jury determined that State Farm's decision not to settle was unreasonable because there was a substantial likelihood of an excess verdict.

Before the second phase of the action against State Farm we decided *BMW of North America, Inc. v. Gore, 517 U.S. 559 (1996),* and refused to sustain a $2 million punitive damages award which accompanied a verdict of only $4,000 in compensatory damages. Based on that decision, State Farm again moved for the exclusion of evidence of dissimilar out-of-state conduct. App. to Pet. for Cert. 168a–172a. The trial court denied State Farm's motion. *Id., at 189*a.

The second phase addressed State Farm's liability for fraud and intentional infliction of emotional distress, as well as compensatory and punitive damages. The Utah Supreme Court aptly characterized this phase of the trial:

> State Farm argued during phase II that its decision to take the case to trial was an 'honest mistake' that did not warrant punitive damages. In contrast, the Campbells introduced evidence that State Farm's decision to take the case to trial was a result of a national scheme to meet corporate fiscal goals by capping payouts on claims company wide. This scheme was referred to as State

Farm's 'Performance, Planning and Review,' or PP & R, policy. To prove the existence of this scheme, the trial court allowed the Campbells to introduce extensive expert testimony regarding fraudulent practices by State Farm in its nation-wide operations. Although State Farm moved prior to phase II of the trial for the exclusion of such evidence and continued to object to it at trial, the trial court ruled that such evidence was admissible to determine whether State Farm's conduct in the Campbell case was indeed intentional and sufficiently egregious to warrant punitive damages.

Evidence pertaining to the PP & R policy concerned State Farm's business practices for over 20 years in numerous States. Most of these practices bore no relation to third-party automobile insurance claims, the type of claim underlying the Campbells' complaint against the company. The jury awarded the Campbells $2.6 million in compensatory damages and $145 million in punitive damages, which the trial court reduced to $1 million and $25 million respectively. Both parties appealed.

The Utah Supreme Court sought to apply the three guideposts we identified in *Gore, supra, at 574–575*, and it reinstated the $145 million punitive damages award. Relying in large part on the extensive evidence concerning the PP & R policy, the court concluded State Farm's conduct was reprehensible. The court also relied upon State Farm's "massive wealth" and on testimony indicating that "State Farm's actions, because of their clandestine nature, will be punished at most in one out of every 50,000 cases as a matter of statistical probability," and concluded that the ratio between punitive and compensatory damages was not unwarranted. Finally, the court noted that the punitive damages award was not excessive when compared to various civil and criminal penalties State Farm could have faced, including $10,000 for each act of fraud, the suspension of its license to conduct business in Utah, the disgorgement of profits, and imprisonment. We granted certiorari. *535 U.S. 1111 (2002).*

II

We recognized in *Cooper Industries, Inc. v. Leatherman Tool Group, Inc., 532 U.S. 424 (2001)*, that in our judicial system compensatory and punitive damages, although usually awarded at the same time by the same decisionmaker, serve different purposes. *Id., at 432.* Compensatory damages "are intended to redress the concrete loss that the plaintiff has suffered by reason of the defendant's wrongful conduct." *Ibid.* By contrast, punitive damages serve a broader function; they are aimed at deterrence and retribution

While States possess discretion over the imposition of punitive damages, it is well established that there are procedural and substantive constitutional limitations on these awards. The Due Process Clause of the *Fourteenth Amendment* prohibits the imposition of grossly excessive or arbitrary punishments on a tortfeasor. The reason is that "elementary notions of fairness enshrined in our constitutional jurisprudence dictate that a person receive fair notice not only of the conduct that will subject him to punishment, but also of the severity of the penalty that a State may impose." *Id., at 574.* To the extent an award is grossly excessive, it furthers no legitimate purpose and constitutes an arbitrary deprivation of property. *Haslip, supra, at 42.*

Although these awards serve the same purposes as criminal penalties, defendants subjected to punitive damages in civil cases have not been accorded the protections applicable in a criminal proceeding. This increases our concerns over the imprecise manner in which punitive damages systems are administered. We have admonished that "punitive damages pose an acute danger of arbitrary deprivation of property. Jury instructions typically leave the jury with wide discretion in choosing amounts, and the presentation of evidence of a defendant's net worth creates the potential that juries will use their verdicts to express biases against big businesses, particularly those without strong local presences." *Honda Motor, supra, at 432.* Our concerns are heightened when the decisionmaker is presented, as we shall discuss, with evidence that has little bearing as to the amount of punitive damages that should be awarded. Vague instructions, or those that merely inform the jury to avoid "passion or prejudice," App. to Pet. for Cert. 108a–109a, do little to aid the decisionmaker in its task of assigning appropriate weight to evidence that is relevant and evidence that is tangential or only inflammatory.

In light of these concerns, in *Gore supra, 517 U.S. 559,* we instructed courts reviewing punitive damages to consider three guideposts: (1) the degree of reprehensibility of the defendant's misconduct; (2) the disparity between the actual or potential harm suffered by the plaintiff and the punitive damages award; and (3) the difference between the punitive damages awarded by the jury and the civil penalties authorized or imposed in comparable cases. *Id., at 575.* We reiterated the importance of these three guideposts in *Cooper Industries* and mandated appellate courts to conduct *de novo* review of a trial court's application of them to the jury's award. *532 U.S., at 424.* Exacting appellate review ensures that an award of punitive damages is based upon an " 'application of law, rather than a decisionmaker's caprice.' " *Id., at 436.*

III

Under the principles outlined in *BMW of North America, Inc. v. Gore,* this case is neither close nor difficult. It was error to reinstate the jury's $145 million punitive damages award. We address each guidepost of *Gore* in some detail.

[The analysis of the case under the principles set out in *BMW v. Gore* is omitted.]

IV

An application of the *Gore* guideposts to the facts of this case, especially in light of the substantial compensatory damages awarded (a portion of which contained a punitive element), likely would justify a punitive damages award at or near the amount of compensatory damages. The punitive award of $145 million, therefore, was neither reasonable nor proportionate to the wrong committed, and it was an irrational and arbitrary deprivation of the property of the defendant. The proper calculation of punitive damages under the principles we have discussed should be resolved, in the first instance, by the Utah courts.

The judgment of the Utah Supreme Court is reversed, and the case is remanded for proceedings not inconsistent with this opinion.

It is so ordered.

* * *

This makes it critical to ask how far the logic of bad faith breach of contract—identified in the insurance context—sweeps. Can the doctrinal logic that treats bad faith as a tort, and hence treats gross bad faith as grounds for punitive damages, be extended beyond the context of insurance (or other similar contexts[21]), to underwrite a case for punitive damages in connection with gross breaches of contracts in a general business setting? Alternatively, is bad faith legally tractable only in the context of special relationships whose strategic structure makes it possible to give bad faith a precise meaning?

8.3.C PUNITIVE DAMAGES FOR BREACH OF CONTRACT IN GENERAL COMMERCIAL SETTINGS

Efficient breaches of contract (including, characteristically, when they are intentional and even calculated) are consistent with the equality of persons and are (properly) encouraged by the law. Even inefficient breaches are, without more, analogous merely to ordinary torts—such as negligence and nuisance—and therefore cannot justify punitive damage awards against the promisors who commit them. But nothing rules out that a breach of contract may be morally analogous to a gross tort. Breachers may take their superiority as the grounds of their actions, and either the size of a breach's inefficiency or the self-consciousness with which a promisor approaches her inefficient breach may reveal that this is what they have done. Moreover, the cases concerning insurance contracts demonstrate that the predicates of bad faith may, at least in certain strategic contexts, be given sufficiently precise elaborations to make the bad faith readily justiciable. There is not in principle any difficulty in treating bad faith breach of contract as, in effect, a free-standing tort and awarding punitive damages for sufficiently gross cases of the tort.

All the difficulty arises in practical application: can the law fashion a standard for gross bad faith that allows courts, imperfect as they are, reliably to identify cases in which punitive damages are appropriate? The cases below illustrate one jurisdiction's (California's) recent experiments in this direction—an initial foray into adopting a doctrine allowing punitive damages for bad faith breach of contract followed by a retreat from this doctrine, amounting more or less to a reversal. This experience is not

---

21. Contracts concerning employment spring especially to mind here. For more on the employment contract, see Chapter 22 below.

unique—doctrinal developments in other jurisdictions show a similar pattern of advance and retreat.[22] The pattern suggests (although of course not dispositively) that whatever may be true in principle, courts cannot in practice successfully administer punitive damages for breach of contract.

Seaman's Direct Buying Service, Inc. v. Standard Oil Co.

Supreme Court of California, 1984.
686 P.2d 1158.

OPINION BY THE COURT. This case, which arises out of a complex factual setting, presents three issues for decision. (1) Was the letter agreement signed by Seaman's Direct Buying Service, Inc. and Standard Oil of California, Inc. sufficient to satisfy the statute of frauds? (2) Is "intent" an element of a cause of action for intentional interference with contractual relations? (3) May a plaintiff recover in tort for breach of an implied covenant of good faith and fair dealing in a noninsurance, commercial contract?

I.

Plaintiff, Seaman's Direct Buying Service, Inc. (Seaman's), is a close corporation composed of three shareholders. During the late 1960's and early 1970's, Seaman's operated as a ship chandler, i.e., a dealer in ship supplies and equipment, in the City of Eureka (City). By 1970, Seaman's business encompassed a number of activities including acting as a "general contractor" for incoming vessels, i.e., refurbishing their supplies, selling tax-free goods for offshore use, and managing a small marine fueling station as the consignee of Mobil Oil Company (Mobil).

Around this time, the City decided to condemn the decrepit waterfront area where Seaman's was located for development into a modern marina. To this end, it sought funds from the federal Economic Development Agency (EDA). Seaman's saw the redevelopment as a way to expand and modernize its operations. Accordingly, the company approached the City with a plan to lease a large portion of the new marina. Seaman's planned to use some of the area for its own operations and to profitably sublet the remainder.

---

22. Indiana presents one example: *Vernon Fire & Casualty Insurance Co. v. Sharp*, N.E. 2d 173 (Ind. 1976), created a free-standing tort of bad faith breach of contract, capable of supporting punitive damage awards, when a breach of contract involves a tort-like wrong that does not fit into the doctrinal torts that are recognized and when the public interest will be served by the deterrent effect that punitive damages will have on the wrongdoer; soon thereafter *Miller Brewing Co. v. Best Beers of Bloomington, Inc.*, 608 N.E.2d 975 (Ind. 1993), abandoned the tort and restored the rule that punitive damages are available in connection with a breach of contract suit only where the conduct of the breaching party independently establishes the elements of a common law tort of a type for which punitive damages are allowed.

Hawai'i presents another example: *Dold v. Outrigger Hotel*, 501 P.2d 368 (Haw. 1972) and *Chung v. Kaonohi Ctr. Co.*, 618 P.2d 283 (Haw. 1980) established bad-faith breach of contract as a free-standing tort capable of sustaining punitive damages; *Francis v. Lee Enterprises Inc.*, 971 P.2d 707 (Haw. 1999) reversed this rule.

In early 1971, Seaman's and the City signed an initial lease for a relatively small area, with the understanding that the lease could be renegotiated to include the larger area that Seaman's wanted. The renegotiation was conditioned on Seaman's providing evidence of financial responsibility to both the EDA and the City's bonding consultants.

A major element of Seaman's planned expansion, and the key to approval of the larger lease, was Seaman's operation of a marine fuel dealership with modernized fueling equipment. To secure such a dealership, Seaman's opened negotiations with several oil companies, but soon narrowed the field to Mobil and the defendant here, Standard Oil of California (Standard).

While negotiations with both companies were progressing, the City began pressuring Seaman's for a final decision on the marina lease. The City's bonding consultants demanded written evidence of a binding agreement with an oil supplier before they would approve leasing the larger area to Seaman's.

Upon reaching a tentative agreement with Standard, Seaman's requested evidence of that agreement—"something that would be binding on both parties"—to show to the City. In response, Standard sent a "letter of intent" setting forth the terms of negotiation. However, the letter explicitly provided that the terms were not binding. Since Seaman's needed a binding commitment, it continued to negotiate with Mobil.

Finally, Seaman's and Standard reached an agreement on all major points. Upon Seaman's repeated requests for an instrument evidencing a binding commitment, Standard, on October 11, 1972, wrote a letter setting forth the terms of the agreement. In the letter, Standard proposed (1) to sign a Chevron Marine Dealer agreement with Seaman's for an initial term of 10 years; (2) to advance Seaman's the cost of the new fueling facilities, or up to $75,000, which sum was to be amortized over the life of the agreement at the rate of one cent per gallon of oil; (3) to provide a 4.5 cent discount per gallon off the posted price of fuel; and (4) to sign an agreement providing for Standard's right to cure in case of default by Seaman's.

The letter concluded "this offer is subject to our mutual agreement on the specific wording of contracts to be drawn, endorsement and/or approval by governmental offices involved, and continued approval of Seaman's credit status at the time the agreements are to go into effect. If this approach and proposal meets with your approval, *we would appreciate your acknowledgement and acceptance of these terms by signing and returning two copies of this letter*. We can then proceed further with the drafting of the final agreements." (Italics added.) The letter was signed by an agent of Standard and—under the legend, *"we accept and agree to the terms and conditions stated herein"*—by an agent of Seaman's. (Italics added.)

According to Seaman's, the signing of this letter was a momentous occasion. One of those present suggested, "Well, shouldn't we have souvenir pens here and I will exchange pens," as "when the President signs a bill into law." Standard's representative exclaimed that it was "going to be great doing business with [Seaman's]" and that the agreement was a "feather in his cap." One of the parties declared, "We finally have a contact" and "we're on our way."

Seaman's immediately presented the letter to the City and shortly thereafter signed a 40–year lease for the entire area it sought in the marina. Seaman's also ended negotiations with Mobil after informing them that a contract had been signed with Standard.

Conditions in the oil industry soon changed, however. By the end of 1972, what had been a "buyer's market" had become a "seller's market." As a result, in January of 1973, Standard adopted a "no new business" policy. During 1973, Standard and Seaman's signed a temporary marine dealership agreement designed to supply Seaman's with the fuel it needed while the new marina was under construction. The marine dealership agreement contemplated in the October 11, 1972, letter, however, was never signed.

In November of 1973, a federal program mandating the allocation of petroleum products among existing customers went into effect. By letter dated November 20, 1973, Standard told Seaman's that the new federal "regulations require suppliers to supply those purchasers to whom they sold during [the base period of 1972]. Our records disclose that we did not supply diesel fuel to you at any time during 1972. [para.] Under the circumstances, we will not be able to go forward with the financing we [have] been discussing. In the event the mandatory program is withdrawn and our supply situation improves, we would, of course, be pleased to again discuss supplying your needs."

In telephone calls and personal meetings with Seaman's, Standard indicated that the new federal regulations were the *only* barrier to the contract "[If] it wasn't for the [federal agency], [Standard] would be willing to go ahead with the contract." "If [Seaman's could] get the federal government to change that order so that Standard could supply [Seaman's] with fuel [Standard] would be very happy." Standard even supplied Seaman's with the forms necessary to seek a supply authorization from the federal agency and helped fill them out.

As a result of these efforts, a supply order was issued on February 4, 1974. Standard responded by changing its position. The company contended now that no binding agreement with Seaman's had ever been reached. Therefore, Standard decided to appeal the order "[because] [it] did not want to take on any new business." When Seaman's learned of the appeal, it twice wrote to Standard requesting an explanation. None was forthcoming. Standard's federal appeal was successful. Internal memoranda reveal Standard's reaction to this result: "[great]!!" We are recommending to other [divisions] that they follow your example."

Seaman's then appealed and this decision was, in turn, reversed. The new decision provided that an order "[directing] [Standard] to fulfill supply obligations to Seaman's" would be issued upon the filing of a copy of a court decree that a valid contract existed between the parties under state law.

Seaman's asked Standard to stipulate to the existence of a contract, explaining that it could not continue in operation throughout the time that a trial would take. In reply, Standard's representative laughed and said, "See you in court." Seaman's testified that if Standard had cooperated, Seaman's would have borrowed funds to remain in business until 1976 when the new marina opened.

Seaman's discontinued operations in early 1975. Soon thereafter, the company filed suit against Standard, charging Standard with breach of contract, fraud, breach of the implied covenant of good faith and fair dealing, and interference with Seaman's contractual relationship with the City. The case was tried before a jury which returned a verdict for Seaman's on all but the fraud cause of action. For breach of contract, the jury awarded compensatory damages of $397,050. For tortious breach of the implied covenant of good faith and fair dealing, they awarded $397,050 in compensatory damages and $11,058,810 in punitive damages. Finally, for intentional interference with an advantageous business relationship, the jury set compensatory damages at $1,588,200 and punitive damages at $11,058,810.

Standard moved for a new trial, charging, inter alia, that the damages were excessive as a matter of law. The trial court conditionally granted the motion unless Seaman's consented to a reduction of punitive damages on the interference count to $6 million and on the good faith count to $1 million. Seaman's consented to the reduction, and judgment was entered accordingly. Standard appeals from the judgment. Seaman's has filed a cross-appeal.

IV.

The principal issue raised by this appeal is whether, and under what circumstances, a breach of the implied covenant of good faith and fair dealing in a commercial contract may give rise to an action in tort. Standard contends that a tort action for breach of the implied covenant has always been, and should continue to be, limited to cases where the underlying contract is one of insurance. Seaman's, pointing to several recent cases decided by this court and the Courts of Appeal, challenges this contention. A brief review of the development of the tort is in order.

It is well settled that, in California, the law implies in *every* contract a covenant of good faith and fair dealing. Broadly stated, that covenant requires that neither party do anything which will deprive the other of the benefits of the agreement. (1 Witkin, *op. cit. supra, at p. 493.*)

California courts have recognized the existence of this covenant, and enforced it, in cases involving a wide variety of contracts. Courts have provided contract remedies for breach of the covenant in such diverse contracts as agreements to make mutual wills, agreements to sell real property, employee incentive contracts, leases, and contracts to provide utility services.

In the seminal cases of *Comunale v. Traders & General Ins. Co., supra, 50 Cal.2d 654,* and *Crisci v. Security Ins. Co., supra, 66 Cal.2d 425,* this court held that a breach of the covenant of good faith and fair dealing by an insurance carrier may give rise to a cause of action in tort as well as in contract. (*Crisci, supra, at p. 432.*)

While the proposition that the law implies a covenant of good faith and fair dealing in all contracts is well established, the proposition advanced by Seaman's—that breach of the covenant always gives rise to an action in tort—is not so clear. In holding that a tort action is available for breach of the covenant in an insurance contract, we have emphasized the "special relationship" between insurer and insured, characterized by elements of public interest, adhesion, and fiduciary responsibility. (*Egan v. Mutual of Omaha Ins. Co., supra, 24 Cal.3d at p. 820.*) No doubt there are other relationships with similar characteristics and deserving of similar legal treatment.

When we move from such special relationships to consideration of the tort remedy in the context of the ordinary commercial contract, we move into largely uncharted and potentially dangerous waters. Here, parties of roughly equal bargaining power are free to shape the contours of their agreement and to include provisions for attorney fees and liquidated damages in the event of breach. They may not be permitted to disclaim the covenant of good faith but they are free, within reasonable limits at least, to agree upon the standards by which application of the covenant is to be measured.[7] In such contracts, it may be difficult to distinguish between breach of the covenant and breach of contract, and there is the risk that interjecting tort remedies will intrude upon the expectations of the parties. This is not to say that tort remedies have no place in such a commercial context, but that it is wise to proceed with caution in determining their scope and application.

For the purposes of this case it is unnecessary to decide the broad question which Seaman's poses. Indeed, it is not even necessary to predicate liability on a breach of the implied covenant. It is sufficient to recognize that a party to a contract may incur tort remedies when, in addition to breaching the contract, it seeks to shield itself from liability by denying, in bad faith and without probable cause, that the contract exists.

It has been held that a party to a contract may be subject to tort liability, including punitive damages, if he coerces the other party to pay more than is due under the contract terms through the threat of a lawsuit, made " 'without probable cause and with no belief in the existence of the cause of action.' " (*Adams v. Crater Well Drilling, Inc. (1976) 276 Ore. 789.*) There is little difference, in principle, between a contracting party obtaining excess payment in such manner, and a contracting party seeking to avoid all liability on a meritorious contract claim by adopting a "stonewall"

---

7. California's *Commercial Code section 1102* prohibits disclaimer of the good faith obligation, as well as the obligations of diligence, reasonableness, and care, but provides that "the parties may by agreement determine the standards by which the performance of such obligations is to be measured if such standards are not manifestly unreasonable."

position ("see you in court") without probable cause and with no belief in the existence of a defense. Such conduct goes beyond the mere breach of contract. It offends accepted notions of business ethics. (See *Jones v. Abriani (1976) 169 Ind.App. 556 [350 N.E.2d 635].*) Acceptance of tort remedies in such a situation is not likely to intrude upon the bargaining relationship or upset reasonable expectations of the contracting parties.

Turning to the facts of this case, the jury was instructed that "where a binding contract [has] been agreed upon, the law implies a covenant that neither party will deny the existence of a contract, since doing so violates the legal prohibition against doing anything to prevent realization of the promises of the performance of the contract."

According to Standard, this instruction erroneously allowed the jury to hold Standard liable if it found that Standard denied the existence of a valid contract, regardless of whether that denial was in good or bad faith.

Of course, "it is not a tort for a contractual obligor to dispute his liability under [a] contract" (*Sawyer v. Bank of America (1978) 83 Cal. App.3d 135*) if the dispute is honest and undertaken in good faith. Similarly, it is not a tort for one party to deny, in good faith, the existence of a binding contract.

Since Standard's denial of the existence of a binding contract would not have been tortious if made in good faith, the trial court erred in failing to so instruct the jury. It is then necessary to decide whether this error requires that the judgment be reversed.

[The Court determined that the error was indeed reversible.]

"Where it seems probable that the jury's verdict may have been based on the erroneous instruction prejudice appears and this court 'should not speculate upon the basis of the verdict.' " (*Robinson v. Cable, supra,* 55 Cal.2d at p. 428; *Henderson v. Harnischfeger Corp., supra,* 12 Cal.3d at p. 670.) (23b) Here, it seems probable that the jury may have imposed liability on Standard as a result of the trial court's failure to instruct as to the bad faith requirement. Accordingly, the judgment in favor of Seaman's for breach of the duty of good faith and fair dealing must be reversed.

V.

The judgment in favor of Seaman's for breach of contract is affirmed. The judgment for intentional interference with contractual relations and for breach of the duty of good faith and fair dealing is reversed with directions to conduct further proceedings consistent with this opinion.

BIRD, C.J., concurring in part, dissenting in part. I concur in sections I, II and III of the court's opinion. However, I dissent in part from section IV. A contracting party should not be able to deny the existence of a valid contract in order to shield itself from liability for breach of that contract. Today, the court holds that an action will lie in tort against such conduct. However, it refuses to acknowledge that its holding is compelled by this court's past decisions analyzing the scope of the implied covenant of good faith and fair dealing. This court should not continue to retreat from its own decisional authority in this area.

I also write separately because I believe that this court should forthrightly recognize the principle that, under certain circumstances, a breach of contract may support a tort cause of action for breach of implied covenant.

I.

Over 25 years ago, this court held that a breach of the implied covenant of good faith and fair dealing may give rise to a tort cause of action. Since that time, a substantial body of law has developed defining the scope of that duty with criteria for the award and measurement of compensatory and punitive tort damages.

California has not been alone in recognizing that a breach of the implied covenant may give rise to a cause of action in tort. The courts of many other states have allowed a tort recovery for the breach of this covenant. (See Kornblum, *Recent Cases Interpreting the Implied Covenant of Good Faith and Fair Dealing* (1981) 30 Def.L.J. 411, 431–432, fn. 50 [collecting cases].)

This development has taken place primarily in the context of insurance contracts. However, this court has never expressly or impliedly limited the tort action to insurance cases.

Moreover, California courts have expressly recognized the availability of a tort recovery for breach of the covenant in other contexts. (See generally, Louderback & Jurika, *Standards for Limiting the Tort of Bad Faith Breach of Contract* (1982) 16 U.S.F. L.Rev. 187.) For example, in *Tameny v. Atlantic Richfield Co. (1980) 27 Cal.3d 167*, the late Justice Mathew O. Tobriner writing for a near unanimous court acknowledged the possibility that a tort action for the breach of the implied covenant was applicable in the area of employment contracts.

The *Tameny* court noted that "past California cases have held that a breach of this implied-at-law covenant *sounds in tort as well as in contract*." (*Id., at p. 179, fn. 12*, italics added.) Following the *Tameny* cue, two recent cases in the Court of Appeal have recognized that a tort cause of action for the breach of the duty of good faith and fair dealing will lie outside the insurance context. This case raises this issue and it should be resolved.

When determining what conduct constitutes a tortious breach of the duty of good faith and fair dealing, courts first consider the parties' "reasonable expectations" concerning the nature of their agreement and their rights and responsibilities thereunder. (*Jarchow v. Transamerica Title Ins. Co., supra, 48 Cal.App.3d at p. 941.*) " 'Good faith performance or enforcement of a contract emphasizes faithfulness to an agreed common purpose and consistency with the justified expectations of the other party.' " (*Neal v. Farmers Ins. Exchange, supra, 21 Cal.3d at p. 922, fn. 5.*) Once those "justified expectations" are established, "good faith" requires the parties to act "reasonably" in light of those expectations.

Past cases which have recognized a tort cause of action for breach of the covenant emphasize "reasonableness." In *Egan v. Mutual of Omaha Ins. Co., supra, 24 Cal.3d at p. 819*, for example, the court first examined both the motivation and expectations of the insured in obtaining a policy of insurance. In light of those expectations, the court held that the implied covenant imposed a duty on the insurer to thoroughly investigate the foundation of an insured's claim before it could "*reasonably* and in *good faith* deny payments to its insured." (*Ibid.*, italics added.) Breach of that duty was a tort. (*Ibid.*)

Similarly, in *Crisci v. Security Ins. Co., supra, 66 Cal.2d at page 429*, the court noted that "one of the usual methods by which an insured receives protection under a liability insurance policy is by settlement of claims without litigation." Therefore, an insurer breaches the duty of good faith and fair dealing, the court concluded, when it "unwarrantedly refuses an offered settlement where the most *reasonable* manner of disposing of the claim is by accepting the settlement." (*Id., at p. 430*, italics added.) And, in *Gruenberg v. Aetna Ins. Co., supra, 9 Cal.3d at page 573*, the duty to act fairly and in good faith was held to include "a duty not to withhold *unreasonably* payments due under a policy." (Italics added; see also *Neal v. Farmers Ins. Exchange, supra, 21 Cal.3d at p. 920*; *Silberg v. California Life Ins. Co., supra, 11 Cal.3d at pp. 460–461* [tort liability where "the insurer *unreasonably* and in bad faith withholds payment of the claim of the insured," italics added].) The standard of good faith conduct that emerges from these decisions is that both contracting parties must act reasonably in light of the justified expectations of the other. (See generally the discussion in *Austero v. National Cas. Co. (1978) 84 Cal.App.3d 1, 27–32 [148 Cal.Rptr. 653]*.)

The precise nature and extent of the duty imposed by the implied promise of good faith and fair dealing in any *particular* contract, therefore, depends upon the expectations of the parties and the purposes of the contract. While the extent of the duty varies from contract to contract, the duty itself inheres in *every* contract.

Insurance contracts have several characteristics not shared by ordinary commercial contracts entered into by corporations. For example, consumers purchase such contracts not to obtain a commercial advantage, but to protect themselves against calamity. (See *Egan v. Mutual of Omaha, supra, 24 Cal.3d at p. 819*.) Thus, insurance contracts may create a "special relationship" between insurer and insured. (*Id., at p. 820*.) These characteristics undoubtedly help shape the justified expectations of the contracting parties, and, therefore, help determine the nature and extent of the duty of good faith between them. (See *id., at p. 819*.)

In commercial contracts which lack those characteristics, the expectations and purposes of the parties necessarily differ from those of insurer and insured. Thus, the requirements of good faith in a commercial contract are different than the requirements imposed on an insurer. While those requirements are probably less stringent in a commercial context, *they definitely exist.*

Certain expectations derive from assumptions so basic to the very notion of a contract that they are shared by virtually all contracting parties. Foremost among these is the expectation that a breaching party will compensate the other party for losses caused by the breaching party's failure to perform. The availability of contract damages, in turn, supports the equally fundamental assumption that breach is a foreseeable and, in most situations, acceptable possibility.

Indeed, the assumption that parties may breach at will, risking only contract damages, is one of the cornerstones of contract law. "[It] is not the policy of the law to compel adherence to contracts, but only to require each party to choose between performing in accordance with the contract and compensating the other party for injury resulting from a failure to perform. This view contains an important economic insight. In many cases it is uneconomical to induce the completion of the contract after it has been breached." (Posner, Economic Analysis of Law (1972) p. 55.) In most commercial contracts, recognition of this economic reality leads the parties to accept the possibility of breach, particularly since their right to recover contract damages provides adequate protection.

For example, one party to a contract may decide to breach if it concludes that the market will bring a higher price for its product than that set forth in the contract. In commercial contracts, the risk of such a breach is widely recognized and generally accepted. "[Intentional], willful, selfishly induced [breaches] of contract [are] often an anticipated, expected and encouraged reality of commercial life." (Diamond, *The Tort of Bad Faith Breach of Contract: When, If At All, Should It Be Extended Beyond Insurance Transactions?* (1981) 64 Marq.L.Rev. 425, 438.)

When the breaching party acts in bad faith to shield itself entirely from liability for contract damages, however, the duty of good faith and fair dealing is violated. (See Diamond, *The Tort of Bad Faith Breach of Contract: When, If At All, Should It Be Extended Beyond Insurance Transactions?, supra,* 64 Marq.L.Rev. at p. 447; see also Keeton, *Liability Insurance and Responsibility for Settlement* (1954) 67 Harv.L.Rev. 1136, 1139, fn. 6 [bad faith is frequently defined as "the intentional disregard of the financial interests of the (other contracting party) in the hope of escaping full responsibility."])

This type of conduct violates the nonbreaching party's justified expectation that it will be able to recover damages for its losses in the event of a breach. That expectation must be protected. Otherwise, the acceptance of the possibility of breach by the contracting parties and by society as a whole may be seriously undermined.

There is no danger that permitting tort recovery for bad faith denial of the existence of a valid commercial contract will make every breach of contract a tort. First, the vast majority of contract breaches in the commercial context do *not* involve this type of bad faith conduct.

Second, "it [is] well established in this state that if the cause of action arises from a breach of a promise set forth in the contract, the action is ex contractu, *but if it arises from a breach of duty growing out of the contract it is ex delicto.'* " (Italics added.) [Citations.] (*Tameny v. Atlantic Richfield Co., supra, 27 Cal.3d at p. 175.*) Thus, tort "[liability] is imposed *not* for a bad faith breach of the contract, but for failure to meet the duty included within the implied covenant of good faith and fair dealing." (*Crisci v. Security Ins. Co., supra, 66 Cal.2d at p. 430*, italics added.) There are many situations in which a defendant's actions may sound both in tort and contract. The fact that overlapping remedies may exist in some situations does not make every breach of contract a tort.

Similarly, an attempt to avoid any liability for contract damages may involve a discrete course of conduct or it may be indistinguishable from the breach of contract itself. "Breach of the covenant provides the injured party with a tort action for 'bad faith,' notwithstanding that the acts complained of may also constitute a breach of contract.

It is a well-established principle of law that the parties' reasonable expectations should govern the determination of what conduct constitutes a tortious breach of the implied covenant of good faith and fair dealing. Application of that principle is fully warranted here. The duty of good faith and fair dealing was violated because a party attempted to avoid all liability for a contract breach by denying, in bad faith, the very existence of the contract. Such conduct violates the nearly universal expectation that the injured party will be compensated for losses caused by the breaching party's failure to perform. This tort remedy was recognized by this court in its earlier decisions involving the implied covenant of good faith and fair dealing. Those decisions should be the basis for the holding here.

II.

A breach of contract may also constitute a tortious breach of the covenant of good faith and fair dealing in a situation where the possibility that the contract will be breached is not accepted or reasonably expected by the parties.

This could happen, for example, if at the time of contracting, the parties expressly indicate their understanding that a breach would be impermissible. Or, it could happen if it were clear from the inception of the contract that contract damages would be unavailable or would be inadequate compensation for a breach. Under these circumstances, a breach of the contract could well constitute a tortious breach of the duty of good faith and fair dealing.

Insurance and employment contracts are good examples of the latter situation. Both the insurer and the insured know that, once an injury has occurred, the insured or the insured's beneficiary will suffer great hardship if benefits are not paid promptly. Thus, a breach of contract by the insurer will almost certainly cause a type of harm for which contract damages would be inadequate. Insureds, therefore, are justified in expecting that their insurance contract will *not* be breached. Similarly, breach of an employment contract by the employer can, in some situations, cause severe harm to an employee's reputation and ability to find new employment. The harm caused cannot be undone by an award of back pay. Thus, employees may be entitled to expect that their contracts will not be breached for frivolous or improper reasons.

These are just a few examples. If a plaintiff can show that, under the circumstances or characteristics of his contract, he was justified in expecting that the other party would not breach, then a voluntary breach by that party could well constitute a violation of the duty to deal fairly and in good faith.

On this record, there is ample evidence to support the conclusion that the parties' reasonable expectations did not include the possibility of breach. Standard was repeatedly informed that Seaman's needed a "binding commitment." Throughout the negotiations, there was an emphasis on the need for such a commitment and for a stable relationship between Seaman's and its supplier. Standard knew that Seaman's lease, and, to some extent, the entire marina development depended on these factors. Under these circumstances, it would be reasonable to conclude that the parties' justified expectations did not include the possibility of breach.

Under this cause of action, no independent showing of bad faith should be required. Where the possibility of breach was not reasonably expected at the inception of the contract, the voluntary breach of an acknowledged contract is in itself a violation of the duty to deal fairly and in good faith.

Standard's breach did not take the form of a refusal to perform under the terms of an acknowledged contract. Instead, Standard denied the existence of the contract to the federal agency and subsequently refused to stipulate to its existence. This action was tantamount to a denial. Those denials constituted anticipatory breaches of the contract. (*Taylor v. Johnston (1975) 15 Cal.3d 130, 137.*)

In this setting, the simple fact that a breach occurred will not support tort recovery without a showing of bad faith. Just as a denial of the existence of a binding contract provides the basis for tort liability only upon a finding of bad faith (majority opn., *ante*, at pp. 769–770), a contract breach predicated upon such a denial will support tort recovery on the theory of unexpected and unacceptable breach only if the denial is found to have been made in bad faith.

III.

The trial court failed to include a bad faith requirement in its instruction on the duty to refrain from denying the existence of a binding contract. This failure constituted error. Recovery will lie in tort if the denial was made in bad faith.

The undisputed evidence at trial showed that Standard did not deny that a contract existed until *after* it was ordered by the federal government to supply fuel to Seaman's. Until that time, Standard continually assured Seaman's that, but for the federal regulations, the contract would be honored. Standard fostered this idea by helping Seaman's to obtain and complete the forms necessary to secure relief from the federal regulations.

These actions on the part of Standard constitute strong evidence that it recognized that a binding contract existed. Standard also knew that an open repudiation of its obligation to perform would constitute a breach of contract for which it would be liable in damages. It would appear that Standard believed that a decision not to repudiate the contract and to rely on the regulations to justify nonperformance would effectively shield it from *all* liability. Clearly, using the federal regulations as a shield, Standard hoped to avoid *both* performance *and* liability for nonperformance of the contract, whose existence it could not deny.

An examination of the relationship between the defense of supervening legal impossibility and the duty of good faith and fair dealing is instructive. A contractual duty is discharged, and performance is excused, when performance is rendered impossible by a change in statute, ordinance, or administrative regulation after the contract is formed. However, the covenant of good faith and fair dealing imposes certain duties on a contracting party if that party seeks to justify its nonperformance on this basis.

First, the party's obligation to perform will be excused only if it has diligently attempted to contest the application of the new law.

Further, the duty of good faith and fair dealing imposes an obligation on a contracting party to refrain from initiating or facilitating the enforcement of an order or regulation that would render performance illegal. This negative duty is a corollary to the affirmative duty to seek an exemption from the application of such a law where the circumstances permit it.

In this case, federal fuel allocation regulations were promulgated after the contract between the parties had been formed. The regulations appeared to prohibit Standard from performing its contractual duty to supply fuel to Seaman's. Standard responded initially by assuring Seaman's that it would be willing to go ahead with the contract if the federal government could be persuaded to change the supply order. Standard provided Seaman's with the forms necessary to secure relief from the regulations and helped Seaman's fill them out.

By assisting Seaman's in this way, Standard complied with its duty to take whatever reasonable steps were necessary to make the performance of its contractual obligations legal. The joint effort of the parties was successful and resulted in the issuance by the federal agency of a supply order that authorized Standard to supply fuel to Seaman's.

In response, Standard abruptly reversed its position. It did not reaffirm its previously expressed willingness to go forward with the contract if the barrier posed by the regulations could be removed. Instead, Standard appealed the supply order it had helped Seaman's to obtain. By appealing the order, Standard breached its duty to refrain from actively seeking the application of regulations that would excuse performance of its contractual obligations. (*Webster v. Southern Cal. First Nat. Bank, supra,* 68 Cal. App.3d at p. 416.)

Standard's appeal was successful, and the order authorizing it to supply Seaman's was rescinded. Standard was delighted, apparently believing that the decision shielded it from any contractual liability to Seaman's. As the preceding discussion of the applicable legal principles demonstrates, however, Standard's contractual duties would not have been discharged if the chain of appeals and reversals regarding the supply order had ended there.

The decision rescinding the supply order was the direct result of Standard's appeal. By taking the appeal, Standard breached its duty to refrain from actions that would make its performance legally impossible. Accordingly, the renewed application of the regulations to prohibit Standard from supplying Seaman's with fuel would not have discharged Standard's contractual duty. Seaman's would have been entitled to recover contract damages resulting from Standard's breach of that duty, even though Standard's only alternative to breach at that point would have required it to violate the federal regulations.

The chain of appeals and reversals did not stop with the decision rescinding the supply order, however. Seaman's appealed again, this time relying on the existence of its supply contract with Standard as the basis for an exception to the regulations. Standard opposed the granting of an exception. For the first time in its dealings with the federal agency regarding the supply order, Standard now contended that no contract existed between the parties.

Despite the objections raised by Standard, Seaman's obtained a favorable decision. Under the terms of the decision, Standard would be ordered to fulfill its supply obligations to Seaman's, provided that the federal agency received a copy of a court decree establishing the existence of a valid contract between the parties. Seaman's asked Standard to stipulate as to the existence of a contract. Standard refused.

Standard's denial of the existence of the contract to the federal agency and the subsequent refusal to stipulate were anticipatory breaches of the contract. (*Taylor* v. *Johnston, supra*, 15 Cal.3d at p. 137.) Neither the breach nor the underlying resistance to an assertion of contract liability is a tort if undertaken in good faith. In this case, however, Standard did not deny that a contract existed until it had been ordered by the federal government to supply fuel to Seaman's. Moreover, Standard did not make its denials forthrightly as a defense to an action for breach of contract. It used them as a trump card in its final attempt to avoid all liability for nonperformance. The timing and the intended effect of both denials tend strongly to establish that they were made in bad faith.

I would affirm the judgment for Seaman's for breach of contract and breach of the duty of good faith and fair dealing.

Freeman & Mills, Inc. v. Belcher Oil Co.

Supreme Court of California, 1995.
900 P.2d 669.

■ LUCAS, C.J. We granted review in this case to resolve some of the widespread confusion that has arisen regarding the application of our opinion in *Seaman's Direct Buying Service, Inc. v. Standard Oil Co. (1984) 36 Cal. 3d 752 (Seaman's)*. We held in that case that a tort cause of action might lie "when, in addition to breaching the contract, [defendant] seeks to shield itself from liability by denying, in bad faith and without probable cause, that the contract exists." (*Id. at p. 769.*)

In the present case, the Court of Appeal reversed judgment for plaintiff and remanded the case for a limited retrial, but also suggested that "it is time for the Supreme Court to reexamine the tort of 'bad faith denial of contract.'" We agree, and proceed to do so here. As our order granting review stated, "the issue to be argued before this court is limited to whether, and under what circumstances, a party to a contract may recover in tort for another party's bad faith denial of the contract's existence."

In light of certain developments occurring subsequent to *Seaman's* that call into question its continued validity, we find it appropriate to reexamine that decision. As will appear, we have concluded that the *Seaman's* court incorrectly recognized a tort cause of action based on the defendant's bad faith denial of the existence of a contract between the parties. That holding has been widely criticized by legal scholars, has caused considerable confusion among lower courts, and has been rejected by the courts of several other jurisdictions. These critics convincingly argue that the *Seaman's* decision is confusing and ambiguous, analytically flawed, and promotes questionable policy. After careful review of all the foregoing considerations, we conclude that our *Seaman's* holding should be overruled.

I. FACTS

We first review the underlying facts, taken largely from the Court of Appeal opinion herein. In June 1987, defendant Belcher Oil Company (Belcher Oil) retained the law firm of Morgan, Lewis & Bockius (Morgan) to defend it in a Florida lawsuit. Pursuant to a letter of understanding signed by Belcher Oil's general counsel (William Dunker) and a Morgan partner (Donald Smaltz), Belcher Oil was to pay for costs incurred on its behalf, including fees for accountants. In February 1988, after first obtaining Dunker's express authorization, Smaltz hired plaintiff, the accounting firm of Freeman & Mills, Incorporated (Freeman and Mills), to provide a financial analysis and litigation support for Belcher Oil in the Florida lawsuit.

In March, an engagement letter was signed by both Morgan and Freeman & Mills. At about this time, William Dunker left Belcher Oil and was replaced by Neil Bowman. In April 1988, Bowman became dissatisfied with Morgan's efforts and the lawyers were discharged. Bowman asked Morgan for a summary of the work performed by Freeman & Mills and, at the same time, directed Smaltz to have Freeman & Mills stop their work for Belcher Oil. Smaltz did as he was asked. Freeman & Mills's final statement was for $70,042.50 in fees, plus $7,495.63 for costs, a total of $77,538.13.

Freeman & Mills billed Morgan, but no payment was forthcoming. Freeman & Mills then billed Belcher Oil directly and, for about a year, sent monthly statements and regularly called Bowman about the bill, but no payment was forthcoming. In August 1989, Smaltz finally told Freeman & Mills that Belcher Oil refused to pay their bill. Freeman & Mills then wrote to Bowman asking that the matter be resolved. In September 1989, Bowman responded, complaining that Belcher Oil had not been consulted about the extent of Freeman & Mills's services and suggesting Freeman & Mills should look to Morgan for payment of whatever amounts were claimed due.

Ultimately, Freeman & Mills filed this action against Belcher Oil, alleging (in its second amended complaint) causes of action for breach of contract, "bad faith denial of contract," and quantum meruit. Belcher Oil answered and the case was presented to a jury in a bifurcated trial, with punitive damages reserved for the second phase. According to the evidence presented during the first phase, the amount owed to Freeman & Mills (as indicated on their statements) was $77,538.13.

The jury returned its first phase verdict. On Freeman & Mills's breach of contract claim, the jury found that Belcher Oil had authorized Morgan to retain Freeman & Mills on Belcher Oil's behalf, that Freeman & Mills had performed its obligations under the contract, that Belcher Oil had breached the contract, and that the amount of damages suffered by Freeman & Mills was $25,000. The jury also answered affirmatively the questions about whether Belcher Oil had denied the existence of the contract and had acted with oppression, fraud, or malice. Thereafter, the jury returned its verdict awarding $477,538.13 in punitive damages and judgment was entered consistent with the jury's verdicts.

In three post-trial motions, Freeman & Mills asked for orders (1) "correcting" the jury's verdicts and the court's judgment to reflect compensatory damages of $77,538.13 and punitive damages of $425,000 (on the ground that the jury's questions showed this was its true intent); (2) awarding attorney fees as sanctions for the litigation tactics of Belcher Oil's attorneys; and (3) awarding prejudgment interest on the compensatory damage award. Over Belcher Oil's opposition, all three motions were granted—but with some changes in the course of correcting the judgment— by giving Freeman & Mills $131,614.93 in compensatory damages (the $25,000 actually awarded by the jury, plus the $77,538.13 included in the punitive damage award, plus $29,076.80 for prejudgment interest), and $400,000 (not $425,000 as requested) in punitive damages.

Belcher Oil appealed from the "corrected" judgment. Freeman & Mills cross-appealed from a mid-trial order denying its request to amend its complaint to add a cause of action for fraud, an issue not presently before us. The Court of Appeal majority, finding no "special relationship" between the parties to justify a tort theory of recovery under *Seaman's*, reversed the judgment and remanded the case to the trial court for a retrial limited to the issue of damages under plaintiff's breach of contract cause of action. (The Court of Appeal dissenting justice would have sustained the tort cause of action and remanded for retrial of the damage issue as to both causes of action.) As will appear, we affirm the judgment of the Court of Appeal, concluding that a tort recovery is unavailable in this case.

II. THE SEAMAN'S DECISION

The tort of bad faith "denial of contract" was established in a per curiam opinion in *Seaman's, supra, 36 Cal. 3d 752.*

III. STARE DECISIS

As we explain below, developments occurring subsequent to the *Seaman's* decision convince us that it was incorrectly decided, that it has generated unnecessary confusion, costly litigation, and inequitable results, and that it will continue to produce such effects unless and until we overrule it.

IV. SUBSEQUENT DEVELOPMENTS

A. *California Supreme Court Decisions*—Subsequent opinions of this court indicate a continuing reluctance, originally reflected in *Seaman's* itself, to authorize tort recovery for noninsurance contract breaches.

In *Foley v. Interactive Data Corp. (1988) 47 Cal. 3d 654 (Foley),* we considered the availability of tort damages for the wrongful termination of a discharged employee. Declining to rely on dictum in *Seaman's* (see *id.* at p. 769 & fn. 6) regarding the possible availability of tort remedies for breach of the implied covenant of good faith and fair dealing (hereafter the implied covenant) in the employment context, we refused to afford such remedies for the essentially contractual claim of breach of the implied covenant arising in that context. (See *Foley, supra, 47 Cal. 3d at pp. 683–693.*)

In reaching our conclusion in *Foley,* we relied in part on certain basic principles relevant to contract law, including the need for "predictability about the cost of contractual relationships," and the purpose of contract damages to compensate the injured party rather than punish the breaching party. (*47 Cal. 3d at p. 683.*) Focusing on the implied covenant, we observed that, with the exception of insurance contracts, "[b]ecause the covenant is a contract term, compensation for its breach has almost always been limited to contract rather than tort remedies." (*Id.* at p. 684.)

We acknowledged in *Foley* that "[t]he insurance cases were a major departure from traditional principles of contract law," and we stressed that the courts should take "great care" before extending "the exceptional approach taken in those cases" to "another contract setting." (*47 Cal. 3d at p. 690.*) We concluded that "the employment relationship is not sufficiently similar to that of insurer and insured to warrant judicial extension of the proposed additional tort remedies."(*Id.* at p. 693.)

Thereafter, in *Hunter v. Up–Right, Inc. (1993) 6 Cal. 4th 1174, 1180–1182 (Hunter),* we held that *Foley's* analysis would preclude recovery of tort damages for employer misrepresentations made to induce termination of employment. In the course of our analysis, and without mentioning *Seaman's,* we nonetheless confirmed that, with the exception of insurance contracts, remedies for breach of the implied covenant "have almost always been limited to contract damages." (*6 Cal. 4th at p. 1180.*)

We reasoned in *Hunter* that the defendant's misrepresentations were "merely the means to the end desired by the employer, i.e., termination of employment. They cannot serve as a predicate for tort damages." (*Hunter, supra, 6 Cal. 4th at p. 1185.*) Similar analysis would apply to a defendant's denial of the existence of the underlying contract. Although such "stonewalling" conduct may have been intended to terminate the contractual relationship, there is no logical reason why it should serve as a predicate for tort damages.

Most recently, in *Applied Equipment Corp. v. Litton Saudi Arabia Ltd. (1994) 7 Cal. 4th 503 (Applied Equipment)*, we held that a contracting party may not be held liable in tort for conspiring with another to interfere with his own contract. We reiterated the important differences between contract and tort theories of recovery, stating that "[c]onduct amounting to a breach of contract becomes tortious only when it also violates an independent duty arising from principles of tort law" (*7 Cal. 4th at p. 515*), and that "the law generally does not distinguish between good and bad motives for breaching a contract" (*7 Cal. 4th at p. 516*). We noted that limiting contract breach damages to those within the reasonably foreseeable contemplation of the parties when the contract was formed "serves to encourage contractual relations and commercial activity by enabling parties to estimate in advance the financial risks of their enterprise." (*7 Cal. 4th at p. 515.*)

Our decisions in *Foley*, *Hunter*, and *Applied Equipment* each contains language that strongly suggests courts should limit tort recovery in contract breach situations to the insurance area, at least in the absence of violation of an independent duty arising from principles of tort law other than denial of the existence of, or liability under, the breached contract.

B. *Court of Appeal Decisions*—Subsequent decisions of the Courts of Appeal have encountered considerable difficulty in applying our *Seaman's* decision. As one recent commentary stated, "The *Seaman's* tort has generated confusion among California courts. Consequently, in recent decisions, almost every court offers a different interpretation of the tort." (Comment, *California's Detortification of Contract Law: Is the Seaman's Tort Dead?* (1992) 26 Loyola L.A. L.Rev. 213, 223 (hereafter Detortification Comment).)

Without analyzing the particular facts of each case, it is sufficient to observe that our *Seaman's* holding has presented the lower courts with a number of unanswered questions, and that these courts have reached varying, and often inconsistent, conclusions in response.

Several of the foregoing cases criticize our *Seaman's* holding, raise doubts as to its continued viability, or urge our reconsideration of that decision.

As these cases indicate, much confusion and conflict has arisen regarding the scope and application of our *Seaman's* holding. For example, does the *Seaman's* tort derive from breach of the implied covenant or from some other independent tort duty?

The foregoing "special relationship" conflict extends to the present case, for as previously noted, the Court of Appeal herein concluded that the *Seaman's* tort requires a showing of a special relationship between the parties. As the Court of Appeal stated, "Whatever need there may be to provide special remedies to cover special relationships, there is no similar need in routine business cases. For this reason, we believe our colleagues in Division Two were correct when they interpreted *Seaman's* narrowly, limiting the tort of bad faith denial of contract to the situations where, in addition to whatever other elements may be required (which depends on which case is cited), there is (1) a special relationship and (2) conduct extraneous to the contract (as there was in *Seaman's*). (*Okun v. Morton, supra, 203 Cal. App. 3d at pp. 823–826*) We also think it is time for the Supreme Court to grant review and resolve the conflict created by *Okun* on the one hand and the *Quigley* line of cases on the other."

Confusion and conflict alone might not justify a decision to abrogate *Seaman's*, for we could attempt to resolve all the uncertainties engendered by that decision. But there are additional considerations that convince us to forgo that predictably Herculean effort. Many of the pertinent Court of Appeal decisions recognize compelling *policy* reasons supporting the preclusion of tort remedies for contractual breaches outside the insurance context.

For example, in *DuBarry, supra, 231 Cal. App. 3d at page 569*, the court refused to extend the *Seaman's* tort to bad faith *defenses* to contract claims. The court explained: "If the rule were otherwise, then any party attempting to defend a disputed contract claim would risk, at the very least, exposure to the imposition of tort damages and an expensive and time-consuming expansion of the litigation into an inquiry as to the motives and state of mind of the breaching party. The distinction between tort and contract actions, and their purposefully different measures of damages, would be blurred if not erased. The insult to commercial predictability and certainty would only be exceeded by the increased burden on the already overworked judicial system." (*Ibid.*) Many of these considerations are equally applicable to the *Seaman's* tort itself.

Similarly, in *Harris, supra, 14 Cal. App. 4th 70*, the Court of Appeal denied a tort recovery for bad faith contract breach in violation of public policy. The court elaborated on the applicable policy considerations as follows: "The traditional goal of contract remedies is compensation of the promisee for the loss resulting from the breach, not compulsion of the promisor to perform his promises. Therefore, 'willful' breaches have not been distinguished from other breaches. [Citation.] The restrictions on contract remedies serve purposes not found in tort law. They protect the parties' freedom to bargain over special risks and they promote contract formation by limiting liability to the value of the promise. This encourages efficient breaches, resulting in increased production of goods and services at lower cost to society. [Citation.] Because of these overriding policy considerations, the California Supreme Court has proceeded with caution in carving out exceptions to the traditional contract remedy restrictions. [Citations.]'' (*14 Cal. App. 4th at p. 77.*)

The *Harris* court set forth as reasons for denying tort recovery in contract breach cases (1) the different objectives underlying the remedies for tort and contract breach, (2) the importance of predictability in assuring commercial stability in contractual dealings, (3) the potential for converting every contract breach into a tort, with accompanying punitive damage recovery, and (4) the preference for legislative action in affording appropriate remedies. (*Harris, supra,* 14 Cal. App. 4th at pp. 81–82; see also *Foley, supra,* 47 Cal. 3d at pp. 683, 694, fn. 31, 696.)

As we shall see (pt. V., *post,* pp. 102–103), the foregoing policy considerations fully support our decision to overrule *Seaman's* rather than attempt to clarify its uncertain boundaries.

C.   *Criticism by Courts of Other Jurisdictions*

We decided *Seaman's* in 1984. Since then, courts of other jurisdictions have either criticized or declined to follow our *Seaman's* analysis. Of all the states, only Montana has recognized the tort of bad faith in typical arm's length commercial contracts, and recently even that state has qualified the tort by requiring a showing of a special relationship between the contracting parties.

Ninth Circuit Judge Kozinski expressed his candid criticism of *Seaman's* in a concurring opinion in *Oki America, Inc. v. Microtech Intern., Inc.* (9th Cir.1989) 872 F.2d 312, 314–317 (*Oki America*). Among other criticism, Judge Kozinski found the *Seaman's* holding unduly imprecise and confusing. As he stated, "It is impossible to draw a principled distinction between a tortious denial of a contract's existence and a permissible denial of liability under the terms of the contract. The test . . . seems to be whether the conduct 'offends accepted notions of business ethics.' [Citation.] This gives judges license to rely on their gut feelings in distinguishing between a squabble and a tort. As a result, both the commercial world and the courts are needlessly burdened." (*Oki America, supra,* 872 F.2d at p. 315.)

Judge Kozinski also mentioned the substantial costs associated with *Seaman's* litigation, and the resulting interference with contractual relationships. "Perhaps most troubling, the willingness of courts to subordinate voluntary contractual arrangements to their own sense of public policy and proper business decorum deprives individuals of an important measure of freedom. The right to enter into contracts—to adjust one's legal relationships by mutual agreement [] is too easily smothered by government officers eager to tell us what's best for us." (*872 F.2d at p. 316.*) Judge Kozinski concluded by observing that "*Seaman's* is a prime candidate for reconsideration." (*Id. at p. 317.*)

Similarly, in *Air–Sea Forwarders, Inc. v. Air Asia Co., Ltd., supra,* 880 F.2d at pages 184–185, Judge Hall observed that *Seaman's* "ambiguous" holding had caused widespread confusion among the lower courts. As Judge

Hall stated, "Indeed, the *Seaman's* court's failure to explain *why* it was not necessary to predicate its holding on the implied covenant of good faith and fair dealing, or to *justify* the dramatically greater liability for the bad faith denial of the existence of a contract as compared to the bad faith dispute of a contract's terms, undoubtedly spawned the confusion in the appellate division cases discussed *infra*." (*Id. at p. 184, fn. 11*.)

Other federal courts have found similar difficulty interpreting and applying *Seaman's*. Thus, in *Elxsi v. Kukje America Corp. (N.D.Cal. 1987) 672 F. Supp. 1294, 1296*, Judge Aguilar observed: "The major difficulty confronting jurists and commentators trying to understand and apply *Seaman's* is the faithful interpretation of the passage [condemning "stonewalling" "without probable cause and with no belief in the existence of a defense"]. The initial sentence states that the new tort is denial of the existence *of a contract*, while the subsequent passage describes denial of the *existence of liability*. Ultimately, the dilemma involves determining whether the subsequent passage is definitional or descriptive."

As we stated in *Moradi–Shalal, supra, 46 Cal. 3d 287, 298*, in which we were faced with a similar tide of critical or contrary authority from other jurisdictions regarding one of our prior decisions, "[A]lthough holdings from other states are not controlling, and we remain free to steer a contrary course, nonetheless the near unanimity of agreement indicates we should question the advisability of continued allegiance to our minority approach."

D. *Scholarly Criticism*

Scholarly commentary on *Seaman's* also has been generally critical of our *Seaman's* holding and underlying analysis.

Many of the foregoing articles and commentaries observe that the *Seaman* decision, being unclear and subject to multiple interpretations, has resulted in widespread confusion among the lower courts.

Additionally, several of these commentaries emphasize the extreme difficulty courts experience in distinguishing between tortious denial of a contract's existence and permissible denial of *liability* under the terms of the contract. Further confusion concerns the quantum of proof required to establish a denial of the existence of the contract and, as previously discussed, whether or not proof is required of a "special relationship" between the contracting parties.

The foregoing commentaries raise a wide variety of additional criticisms that support reconsideration of the *Seaman's* decision, including widespread confusion among judges and juries in applying its holding, inappropriately excessive damage awards, overcrowded court dockets and speculative litigation, delay and complication of ordinary contract breach claims, deterrence of contract formation, and restraint on zealous advocacy. As one article observes, *Seaman's* created "intolerable uncertainty" and constitutes a "dangerous misstep" that this court should "promptly correct." (Putz & Klippen, *supra*, 21 U.S.F. L.Rev. at p. 499.)

As we stated in *Moradi–Shalal, supra, 46 Cal. 3d at page 299,* "the breadth of the criticism is disturbing and, like the flood of contrary decisions of other state courts, is pertinent to our determination whether or not to reconsider that decision. [Citation.]"

V.   SEAMAN'S SHOULD BE OVERRULED

As previously indicated, the *Seaman's* decision has generated uniform confusion and uncertainty regarding its scope and application, and widespread doubt about the necessity or desirability of its holding. These doubts and criticisms, express or implied, in decisions from this state and from other state and federal courts, echoed by the generally adverse scholarly comment cited above, convince us that *Seaman's* should be overruled in favor of a general rule precluding tort recovery for noninsurance contract breach, at least in the absence of violation of "an independent duty arising from principles of tort law" (*Applied Equipment, supra, 7 Cal. 4th at p. 515*) other than the bad faith denial of the existence of, or liability under, the breached contract.

As set forth above, the critics stress, among other factors favoring *Seaman's* abrogation, the confusion and uncertainty accompanying the decision, the need for stability and predictability in commercial affairs, the potential for excessive tort damages, and the preference for legislative rather than judicial action in this area.

Even if we were unimpressed by the nearly unanimous criticism leveled at *Seaman's*, on reconsideration the analytical defects in the opinion have become apparent. It seems anomalous to characterize as "tortious" the bad faith denial of the existence of a contract, while treating as "contractual" the bad faith denial of liability or responsibility under an acknowledged contract. In both cases, the breaching party has acted in bad faith and, accordingly, has presumably committed acts offensive to "accepted notions of business ethics." (*Seaman's, supra, 36 Cal. 3d at p. 770.*) Yet to include bad faith denials of liability within *Seaman's* scope could potentially convert every contract breach into a tort. Nor would limiting *Seaman's* tort to incidents involving "stonewalling" adequately narrow its potential scope. Such conduct by the breaching party, essentially telling the promisee, "See you in court," could incidentally accompany *every* breach of contract.

For all the foregoing reasons, we conclude that *Seaman's* should be overruled. We emphasize that nothing in this opinion should be read as affecting the existing precedent governing enforcement of the implied covenant in insurance cases. Further, nothing we say here would prevent the Legislature from creating additional civil remedies for noninsurance contract breach, including such measures as providing litigation costs and attorney fees in certain aggravated cases, or assessing increased compensatory damages covering lost profits and other losses attributable to the breach, as well as restoration of the *Seaman's* holding if the Legislature deems that course appropriate. Thus far, however, the Legislature has not manifested an intent either to expand contract breach recovery or to provide tort damages for ordinary contract breach.

VII.   CONCLUSION

The judgment of the Court of Appeal, reversing the trial court's judgment in plaintiff's favor and remanding the case for a retrial limited to the issue of damages under plaintiff's breach of contract cause of action, and for judgment in favor of defendant on plaintiff's bad faith denial of contract cause of action, is affirmed.

■ Mosk, J., concurring and dissenting. I concur in the judgment. I disagree, however, with the majority's conclusion that *Seaman's* was wrongly decided. Although in retrospect I believe its holding was too broad, our task, both for the sake of sound public policy and stare decisis, is to clarify rather than repudiate that holding.

The majority would displace *Seaman's* with "a general rule precluding tort recovery for noninsurance contract breach,[1] at least in the absence of violation of 'an independent duty arising from principles of tort law' [citation] other than the bad faith denial of the existence of, or liability under, the breached contract." (Maj. opn., *ante*, at p. 102.) I agree that the bad faith denial of the existence of a contract or contractual liability, *alone*, cannot give rise to tort liability. I agree as well with the tautological proposition that a breach of contract is made tortious only when some "independent duty arising from tort law" is violated.

In my view, however, this "independent duty arising from tort law" can originate from torts other than those traditionally recognized at common law. There are some types of intentionally tortious behavior unique to the contractual setting that do not fit into conventional tort categories. Allowing for the possibility of tort causes of action outside conventional categories is consistent with the malleable and continuously evolving nature of tort law. " 'The law of torts is anything but static, and the limits of its development are never set. When it becomes clear that the plaintiff's interests are entitled to legal protection against the conduct of the defendant, the mere fact that the claim is novel will not of itself operate as a bar to the remedy.' " (*Soldano v. O'Daniels (1983) 141 Cal. App. 3d 443, 454–455.*

Seaman's should be viewed within the context of this common law tradition of innovation. When *Seaman's* is understood in light of its facts, it stands for the proposition, in my view, that a contract action may also sound in tort when the breach of contract is intentional and in bad faith,

---

1.   The majority's holding, precluding tort recovery for "noninsurance contract breach" should not be misinterpreted. We have found that the breach of the covenant of good faith and fair dealing by an insurer against an insured will sound in tort, due to the "special relationship" between the two parties. *See* Egan v. Mutual of Omaha Ins. Co., 24 Cal. 3d 809, 820 (1979). In *Foley v. Interactive Data Corp.*, 47 Cal. 3d 654, (1988) (Foley), while this court declined to find a similar "special relationship" in the employment context, it also explicitly did not decide the question whether such a relationship could be found elsewhere. (*Id. at pp. 687–688.*) As the majority recognize, the present case does not concern parties involved in an allegedly special relationship; Freeman & Mills, Inc., admits that no such special relationship existed. Therefore, the majority's holding should not be taken as deciding a question not before this court, and left open by *Foley*, whether there are relationships between contracting parties outside the insurance field which may give rise to tort remedies for breach of the covenant of good faith and fair dealing.

and is aggravated by certain particularly egregious forms of intentionally injurious activity. Because, as will be explained, there is no such tortious activity in the present case, I concur in the majority's disposition.

I will discuss below the various circumstances under which courts have found or may find a breach of contract to be tortious—circumstances broader than may be suggested by the majority's holding. As I will explain, a tortious breach of contract outside the insurance context may be found when (1) the breach is accompanied by a traditional common law tort, such as fraud or conversion; (2) the means used to breach the contract are tortious, involving deceit or undue coercion or; (3) one party intentionally breaches the contract intending or knowing that such a breach will cause severe, unmitigatable harm in the form of mental anguish, personal hardship, or substantial consequential damages. I will then explain why in my view *Seaman's* was correctly decided. Finally, I will explain why *Seaman's* is distinguishable from the present case.

I.

The notion that a breach of contract might be tortious causes conceptual difficulty because of the fundamental difference between the objectives of contract and tort law. " ' "[Whereas] [c]ontract actions are created to protect the interest in having promises performed," "[t]ort actions are created to protect the interest in freedom from various kinds of harm. The duties of conduct which give rise to them are imposed by law, and are based primarily on social policy, not necessarily based upon the will or intention of the parties." ' " (*Applied Equipment Corp.*, 515, quoting *Tameny v. Atlantic Richfield Co.* (1980) 27 Cal. 3d 167, 176.)

This difference in purpose has its greatest practical significance in the differing types of damages available under the two bodies of law. "Contract damages are generally limited to those within the contemplation of the parties when the contract was entered into or at least reasonably foreseeable by them at that time; consequential damages beyond the expectations of the parties are not recoverable." (*Applied Equipment Corp., supra,* 7 Cal. 4th at p. 515.) Damages for emotional distress and mental suffering, as well as punitive damages, are also generally not recoverable. (*Id. at p. 516.*) "This limitation on available damages serves to encourage contractual relations and commercial activity by enabling parties to estimate in advance the financial risks of their enterprise." (*Id. at p. 515.*) "In contrast, tort damages are awarded to compensate the victim for injury suffered. [Citation.] 'For the breach of an obligation not arising from contract, the measure of damages is the amount which will compensate for all the detriment proximately caused thereby, whether it could have been anticipated or not.' (*Civ. Code, § 3333.*)" (*Applied Equipment Corp., supra,* 7 Cal. 4th at p. 516.) Both emotional distress damages and punitive damages are, under the proper circumstances, available to the tort victim.

Tort and contract law also differ in the moral significance that each places on intentional injury. Whereas an intentional tort is seen as reprehensible—the deliberate or reckless harming of another—the intentional breach of contract has come to be viewed as a morally neutral act, as exemplified in Justice Holmes's remark that "[t]he duty to keep a contract at common law means a prediction that you must pay damages if you do not keep it—and nothing else." (Holmes, *The Path of the Law* (1897) 10 Harv. L.Rev. 457, 462.) This amoral view is supported by the economic insight that an intentional breach of contract may create a net benefit to society. The efficient breach of contract occurs when the gain to the breaching party exceeds the loss to the party suffering the breach, allowing the movement of resources to their more optimal use. (See Posner, Economic Analysis of Law (1986) pp. 107–108.) Contract law must be careful "not to exceed compensatory damages if it doesn't want to deter efficient breaches." (*Id. at p. 108.*)

But while the purposes behind contract and tort law are distinct, the boundary line between the two areas of the law is neither clear nor fixed. As Justice Holmes also observed, "the distinction between tort and breaches of contract, and especially between the remedies for the two, is not found ready made." (Holmes, The Common Law (1881) p. 13.) Courts have long permitted a party to a contract to seek tort remedies if behavior constituting a contract breach also violates some recognized tort duty. The courts "have extended the tort liability for misfeasance to virtually every type of contract where defective performance may injure the promisee. An attorney or an abstractor examining a title, a physician treating a patient, a surveyor, an agent collecting a note or lending money or settling a claim, or a liability insurer defending a suit, all have been held liable in tort for their negligence. . . . The principle which seems to have emerged from the decisions in the United States is that there will be liability in tort for misperformance of a contract whenever there would be liability for gratuitous performance without the contract—which is to say, whenever such misperformance involves a foreseeable, unreasonable risk of harm to the interests of the plaintiff." (Prosser & Keeton on Torts (5th ed. 1984) Tort and Contract, pp. 660–661, fns. omitted.) Stated another way, " '[c]onduct which merely is a breach of contract is not a tort, but the contract may establish a relationship demanding the exercise of proper care and acts and omissions in performance may give rise to tort liability.' " (*Groseth Intern., Inc. v. Tenneco, Inc. (S.D. 1989) 440 N.W.2d 276, 279.*)

Nor are the rules that determine whether the action will sound in tort or contract, or both, clear-cut. When the breach of contract also involves physical injury to the promisee, or the destruction of tangible property, as opposed to damage to purely economic interests, then the action will generally sound in tort. Thus, a manufacturer that sells defective automobiles may be liable to an automobile dealer in contract for delivery of nonconforming goods, but will be liable in tort if one of the nonconforming automobiles leads to an accident resulting in physical injury. But society also imposes tort duties to protect purely economic interests between contracting parties—such as the duty of care imposed on accountants for malpractice (see *Lindner v. Barlow, Davis & Wood (1962) 210 Cal. App. 2d 660, 665*), or on banks for wrongfully dishonoring checks (see *Weaver v. Bank of America (1953) 59 Cal. 2d 428, 431*)—as well as the recognition of intentional torts such as promissory fraud. The complete failure to perform a contractual obligation generally sounds in contract, but once a contractual obligation has begun, a failure to perform which injures the promisee may sometimes sound in tort. (Prosser & Keeton on Torts, *supra*, pp. 661–662.) Perhaps the most reliable manner to differentiate between actions that are purely contract breaches and those that are also tort violations is the following abstract rule: courts will generally enforce the breach of a contractual promise through contract law, except when the actions that constitute the breach violate a social policy that merits the imposition of tort remedies.

It is also true that public policy does not always favor a limitation on damages for *intentional* breaches of contract. The notion that society gains from an efficient breach must be qualified by the recognition that many intentional breaches are not efficient. As Judge Posner explained in *Patton v. Mid–Continent Systems, Inc., (7th Cir. 1988) 841 F.2d 742, 751*: "Not all breaches of contract are involuntary or otherwise efficient. Some are opportunistic; the promisor wants the benefit of the bargain without bearing the agreed-upon costs, and exploits the inadequacies of purely compensatory remedies (the major inadequacies being that pre-and post-judgment interest rates are frequently below market levels when the risk of nonpayment is taken into account and that the winning party cannot recover ... attorney's fees." Commentators have also pointed to other "inadequacies of purely compensatory remedies" that encourage inefficient breaches (i.e. breaches that result in greater losses to the promisee than gains for the promisor): the lack of emotional distress damages, even when such damages are the probable result of the breach, and the restriction of consequential damages to those in the contemplation of the parties at the time the contract was formed.

In addition to fully compensating contract plaintiffs and discouraging inefficient breaches, the imposition of tort remedies for certain intentional breaches of contract serves to punish and deter business practices that constitute distinct social wrongs independent of the breach. For example, we permit the plaintiff to recover exemplary damages in cases in which the breached contract was induced through promissory fraud, even though the plaintiff has incurred the same loss whether the contract was fraudulently induced or not. (See *Walker v. Signal Companies, Inc. (1978) 84 Cal. App. 3d 982, 995–998*.) Our determination to allow the plaintiff to sue for fraud and to potentially recover exemplary damages is not justified by the plaintiff's greater loss, but by the fact that the breach of a fraudulently induced contract is a significantly greater wrong, from society's standpoint, than an ordinary breach. "We are aware of the danger of grafting tort liability on what ordinarily should be a breach of contract action. However, no public policy is served by permitting a party who never intended to fulfill his obligations to fraudulently induce another to enter into an agreement." (*Las Palmas Associates v. Las Palmas Center Associates (1991) 235 Cal. App. 3d 1220.*)

As the above illustrate, the rationale for limiting actions for intentional breaches of contract to contract remedies—that such limitation promotes commercial stability and predictability and hence advances commerce—is not invariably a compelling one. Breaches accompanied by deception or infliction of intentional harm may be so disruptive of commerce and so reprehensible in themselves that the value of deterring such actions through the tort system outweighs the marginal loss in the predictability of damages that may result. But in imposing tort duties to deter intentionally harmful acts among contracting parties, courts must be cautious not to fashion remedies which overdeter the illegitimate and as a result chill legitimate activities. (See Posner, Economic Analysis of Law, *supra*, at p. 108.) Thus, courts should be careful to apply tort remedies only when the conduct in question is so clear in its deviation from socially useful business practices that the effect of enforcing such tort duties will be, as in the case of fraud, to aid rather than discourage commerce.

As observed above, not all tortious breaches of contract arise from conventional torts. Numerous courts have recognized types of intentionally tortious activity that occur exclusively or distinctively within the context of a contractual relationship. The most familiar type of tortious breach of contract in this state is that of the insurer, whose unreasonable failure to settle or resolve a claim has been held to violate the covenant of good faith and fair dealing. (*Egan v. Mutual of Omaha Ins. Co., supra, 24 Cal. 3d 809.*) Tort liability is imposed primarily because of the distinctive characteristics of the insurance contract: the fiduciary nature of the relationship, the fact that the insurer offers a type of quasi-public service that provides financial security and peace of mind, and the fact that the insurance contract is generally one of adhesion. (*Id. at pp. 820–821.*) In these cases, the special relationship between insurer and insured supports the elevation of the covenant of good faith and fair dealing, a covenant implied by law in every contract and generally used as an aid to contract interpretation (*Foley, supra, 47 Cal. 3d at p. 684*), into a tort duty.

Because the good faith covenant is so broad and all-pervasive, this court and others have been reluctant to expand recognition of the action for tortious breach of the covenant beyond the insurance context. (See *Foley, supra, 47 Cal. 3d at p. 692* [no special relationship in the employment context]; but see *id. at pp. 701, 715, 723* (separate conc. and dis. opns. of Broussard, J., Kaufman, J., and Mosk, J.).) Unfortunately, the preoccupation of California courts with limiting the potentially enormous scope of this tort has diverted attention away from the useful task of identifying *specific practices* employed by contracting parties that merit the imposition of tort remedies. Other jurisdictions not so preoccupied have made greater progress in developing a common law of tortious breach of contract. While the cases are not easily amenable to classification, they appear to fit into two broad categories.

The first category focuses on tortious *means* used by one contracting party to coerce or deceive another party into foregoing its contractual rights. For example, in *Advanced Medical v. Arden Medical Systems (3d Cir. 1992) 955 F.2d 188*, Advanced Medical, Inc. (Advanced), a distributor of medical products, entered into an agreement with a manufacturer of a high-technology blood analysis device, whereby the former was designated as the latter's exclusive distributor for the mid-Atlantic region. The manufacturing company was eventually acquired by Johnson & Johnson, which disapproved of the exclusive distributorship. Instead of merely breaching the agreement, Johnson & Johnson used a variety of questionable tactics to "drive Advanced out of the contract," including marketing competing products not made available to Advanced, and withholding its support services. (*Id.* at pp. 190–191.) The court, applying Pennsylvania law, held that in addition to a breach of contract, there was sufficient evidence to submit the question of punitive damages to a jury on a theory of Johnson & Johnson's "tortious interference" with its own contract. (*Id.* at pp. 201–202.) One commentator provides another example of this kind of tortious breach derived from a case that was originally a companion to *Seaman's*: a major motion picture studio threatens to blacklist an actor appearing in one of its productions if he does not forfeit his contractual right to a prominent billing. (Ashley, Bad Faith Actions: Liability and Damages (1994) § 11.04, p. 6.)

The use of tortious means to breach a contract can also entail the use of deception by one of the contracting parties for the purpose of causing the other party to forego its contractual rights. In *Motley, Green & Co. v. Detroit Steel & Spring Co. (C.C.S.D.N.Y. 1908) 161 F. 389*, for example, the plaintiff was an exclusive sales agent within a given territory for the defendant, an automobile parts company. The defendant allegedly made a sham sale to another company for the sole purpose of extricating itself from the contract with the plaintiff. The court concluded that it was tortious for the defendant, in addition to breaching the contract, "to invite a third party to unite with him and aid him in breaking the contract in such a way as possibly to escape liability in an action for nonperformance." (*Id.* at p. 397.) The court compared the case to one cited in a tort treatise of a plaintiff who was an " 'actor, ... engaged to perform in the character of Hamlet, and that the defendants and others maliciously conspired together to prevent the plaintiff from so performing, and from exercising his profession in the theater, and in pursuance of the conspiracy hired and procured divers persons to go to the theater and hoot the plaintiff, and the persons so hired, did.' " (*Ibid.*)

A second type of tortious intentional breach has been found when the *consequences* of the breach are especially injurious to the party suffering the breach, and the breaching party intentionally or knowingly inflicts such injury. Cases of this type have generally occurred outside the commercial context, involving manifestly unequal contracting parties and contracts concerning matters of vital personal significance, in which great mental anguish or personal hardship are the probable result of the breach. In these cases, courts have permitted substantial awards of emotional distress damages and/or punitive damages, both as a means of providing extra sanctions for a defendant engaging in intentionally injurious activities against vulnerable parties, and as a way of fully compensating plaintiffs for types of injury that are neither readily amendable to mitigation nor generally recoverable as contract damages. For example, in *K Mart Corp. v.*

Ponsock (1987) 103 Nev. 39, disapproved on other grounds by *Ingersoll–Rand Co. v. McClendon (1990) 498 U.S. 133, 137*, the Nevada Supreme Court allowed a $50,000 award of punitive damages to stand when an employer discharged a long-term employee on a fabricated charge for the purpose of defeating the latter's contractual entitlement to retirement benefits. (See also *Ainsworth v. Franklin Cty. Cheese Corp. (1991) 156 Vt. 325 [592 A.2d 871, 871, 874–875]* [punitive damages permitted when a defendant/employer discharged on pretext of good cause the plaintiff/employee in order to extricate itself from the obligation to pay severance benefits].)

In other cases of this type, an intentional breach of a warranty of habitability by a landlord or building contractor has given rise to substantial emotional distress or punitive damages awards. For example, Missouri courts recognize that a wrongful eviction will sound in tort as well as contract. (*Ladeas v. Carter (Mo.App.1992) 845 S.W.2d 45, 52*; see also *Emden v. Vitz (1948) 88 Cal. App. 2d 313, 318–319 [198 P.2d 696]* [wrongful eviction accompanied by verbal abuse sounds in tort]; *Hilder v. St. Peter (1984) 144 Vt. 150 [478 A.2d 202, 210]* [punitive damages permitted against a landlord who, "after receiving notice of a defect, fails to repair the facility that is essential to the health and safety of his or her tenant"]; *B & M Homes, Inc. v. Hogan (Ala. 1979) 376 So. 2d 667, 671–672 [7 A.L.R.4th 1162]* [substantial emotional distress damages award against contractor who refused to repair construction defects leading to great personal discomfort]; *Ducote v. Arnold (La.Ct.App. 1982) 416 So. 2d 180, 183–185* [damages for mental anguish permitted for breach of home remodeling contract].) The New Mexico Supreme Court, in *Romero v. Mervyn's (1989) 109 N.M. 249*, citing *Seaman's* with approval, upheld a punitive damage award against a department store, which had entered into an oral agreement to pay the medical expenses of a customer accidentally injured on its premises, and then reneged on its agreement.

The principle that certain contractual interests of vulnerable parties deserve greater protection than ordinary contract damages would otherwise provide has led our Legislature to authorize special sanctions for various types of intentional breaches. For example, one who is the victim of an intentional breach of warranty of consumer goods may recover twice the amount of actual damages (*Civ. Code, § 1794, subd. (c)*) and treble damages may be awarded to a retail seller who is injured by "willful or repeated" warranty violations (*id.*, § 1794.1, subd. (a)). *Labor Code section 206* provides for treble damages for the willful failure to pay wages after the Labor Commissioner determines the wages are owing. But the fact that the Legislature has acted in some instances to afford these special protections does not mean that it has preempted the courts from exercising their traditional role of fashioning appropriate tort remedies for various kinds of intentionally injurious conduct.

In sum, the above cited cases show that an intentional breach of contract may be found to be tortious when the breaching party exhibits an extreme disregard for the contractual rights of the other party, either knowingly harming the vital interests of a promisee so as to create substantial mental distress or personal hardship, or else employing coercion or dishonesty to cause the promisee to forego its contractual rights. These cases illustrate the recognition by a number of jurisdictions that an intentional breach of contract outside the insurance context, and not accompanied by any conventional tortious behavior such as promissory fraud, may nonetheless be deemed tortious when accompanied by these kinds of aggravating circumstances.

With this in mind, I next reconsider the *Seaman's* case.

II.

Seaman's was correct, in my view, in refusing to rely on the general breach of the covenant of good faith and fair dealing as a justification for imposing tort remedies, and instead seeking to identify specific practices used by Standard that violated "accepted notions of business ethics." *Seaman's* wisely recognized that courts do not have to choose between the wholesale transformation of a breach of the implied good faith covenant into a tort and the complete refusal to recognize a cause of action for tortious breach of contract. In retrospect, however, *Seaman's* holding appears to be both overly broad and overly narrow. It was overly narrow because, as numerous authorities cited by the majority point out, there is no logical reason to distinguish between the tort of "bad faith denial of the existence of a contract" and "bad faith denial of liability under a contract." The former is but a subspecies of the latter. Both forms of bad faith are equally reprehensible on the defendant's part and equally injurious to plaintiff.

Seaman's was overly broad because, for a number of reasons, it appears to have been unwise to impose tort liability for *all* breaches that involve bad faith denial of a contract or liability under the contract. Although the bad faith denial of contractual liability may be ethically inexcusable, we should hesitate to categorically impose tort liability on such activity for fear it may overly deter legitimate activities that we wish to permit or encourage. Specifically, the bad faith denial of the existence of a contract consists of two actions on the defendant's part that do not, taken individually, give rise to tort liability: First, the defendant intentionally breaches its contract. As discussed above, because of our notions of efficient breach and the freedom of the marketplace, we have generally not considered an intentional breach tortious.

Second, the defendant asserts a bad faith defense to liability under the contract—or, more precisely, *threatens* to assert such a defense We have consistently refused to recognize a tort of "malicious defense" that would be equivalent to that of malicious prosecution. The refusal to recognize such a tort "protect[s] the right of a defendant, involuntarily haled into court, to conduct a vigorous defense." (*Bertero v. National General Corp. (1974) 13 Cal. 3d 43,*.) Instead, the Legislature has fashioned a more limited punishment to fit the "crime" OF BAD FAITH DEFENSE TO A CIVIL ACTION: the awarding of attorney fees and other reasonable expenses incurred by a party to litigation as the result of another's bad faith actions "that are frivolous or solely intended to cause unnecessary delay." (*Code Civ. Proc., § 128.5, subd. (a).*) So too, the proper remedy to deter intentional breaches that are combined with bad faith denials of liability is to consistently award attorney fees to the plaintiffs as a sanction. (See Putz & Klippen, *supra*, 21 U.S.F. L.Rev. at pp. 493–495). But if a bad faith defense is not a tortious act, then the threat of such defense, as occurred in *Seaman's*, also cannot be considered tortious.

Seaman's was nonetheless correctly decided, in my view, on narrower grounds than bad faith denial of the contract's existence. As discussed above, a number of cases allow tort damages for an intentional breach which the breaching party knows will probably result in significant emotional distress or personal hardship. In the commercial sphere, we do not as a rule permit such recovery for personal distress—the frustrations that attend breached contracts, unreliable suppliers, and the like are part of the realities of commerce. Society expects the business enterprise to go to the marketplace to seek substitutes to mitigate its losses, and to seek contract damages for those losses that cannot be mitigated. But there are some commercial cases in which the harm intentionally inflicted on an enterprise cannot be mitigated, and in which ordinary contract damages are insufficient compensation. *Seaman's* is such a case. In *Seaman's*, because of the unusual combination of market forces and government regulation set in motion by the 1973 oil embargo, Standard's conduct had a significance beyond the ordinary breach: its practical effect was to shut *Seaman's* out of the oil market entirely, forcing it out of business. In other words, Standard intentionally breached its contract with Seaman's with the knowledge that the breach would result in Seaman's demise. Having thus breached its contract with blithe disregard for the severe and, under these rare circumstances, unmitigatable injury it caused Seaman's, Standard was justly subject to tort damages.

In sum, I would permit an action for tortious breach of contract in a commercial setting when a party intentionally breaches a contractual obligation with neither probable cause nor belief that the obligation does *not* exist, *and* when the party intends or knows that the breach will result in severe consequential damages to the other party that are not readily subject to mitigation, and such harm in fact occurs. This rule is a variant of the more general rule of tort law that, as Holmes said, "the intentional infliction of temporal damage is a cause of action, which, as a matter of substantive law, requires a justification if the defendant is to escape." (*Aikens v. Wisconsin (1904) 195 U.S. 194,.*) A breach should not be considered tortious if the court determines that it was justified by avoidance of some substantial, unforeseen cost on the part of the breaching party, even if such cost does not excuse that party's nonperformance. (See 3A Corbin on Contracts (1994 Supp.) § 654E, p. 109.) Nor should a tortious breach under these circumstances be recognized if it is clear that the party suffering the harm voluntarily accepted that risk under the contract. But the intentional or knowing infliction of severe consequential damages on a business enterprise through the unjustified, bad faith breach of a contract is reprehensible and costly both for the party suffering the breach and for society as a whole, and is therefore appropriately sanctioned through the tort system.

III.

The present case, on the other hand, is essentially a billing dispute between two commercial entities. Belcher Oil Company claimed, apparently in bad faith and without probable cause, that it had no contractual agreement with Freeman & Mills. That is, Belcher Oil not only intentionally breached its contract, but then asserted a bad faith defense to its liability. As explained above, the solution which the Legislature has devised for this kind of transgression is the awarding of the other party's attorney fees, and this is precisely what occurred—Freeman & Mills was awarded $212,891 in attorney fees pursuant to *Code of Civil Procedure sections 128.5* and *2033, subdivision (c)*. To permit the award of punitive damages in addition to this sum would upset the legislative balance established in the litigation sanctions statutes and make tortious actions—intentional breach of contract and the assertion of a bad faith defense—which we have consistently held not to be tortious.

On this basis, I concur in the majority's disposition in favor of Belcher Oil on the bad faith denial of contract cause of action.

* * *

The plaintiff in *Seaman's* sought to open a marine fuel dealership in a new city marina and was required by the city to acquire a fuel supply contract before being permitted to lease marina space. The plaintiff therefore entered into a contract with the defendant under which (among other things) the defendant was to supply plaintiff's fuel requirements for a ten-year period. On making its contract with the defendant, the plaintiff signed a lease for its marina space. Shortly thereafter, the 1973 oil embargo occurred and changed market conditions in the fuel supply business. Among other things, a federal fuel allocation program came into effect. The defendant claimed that the program prohibited it from supplying the plaintiff under the contract but offered to help the plaintiff to acquire a variance. In fact, however, when the plaintiff acquired its variance, the defendant appealed to have the variance reversed. The defendant's appeal was initially successful, but the plaintiff eventually had its variance reinstated and acquired an order requiring the defendant to supply its fuel under the contract, upon the plaintiff's filing a copy of a court decree stating that it had a valid fuel supply contract with defendant. When the plaintiff asked the defendant to stipulate to the existence of the contract, the defendant answered "I'll see you in court." The plaintiff's inability to get supplied with fuel drove it out of business, and the plaintiff sued, bringing (among other claims) a contract claim for breach of the obligation to supply fuel and a tort claim for violation of the implied in law covenant of good faith and fair dealing. On this tort claim, the plaintiff recovered $400,000 in compensatory damages $11 million in punitive damages, which were reduced to $1 million on remittitur. The defendant appealed.

Seaman's involved complicated facts and raised many legal issues, but the central issue for present purposes is "whether, and under what circumstances, a breach of the implied covenant of good faith and fair dealing in a commercial contract may give rise to an action in tort," with the concomitant possibility of punitive damages. The defendant sought to limit tort remedies for breaches of good faith to the insurance context addressed in *Comunale* and *Crisci*, and the plaintiff sought to expand this tort to cover commercial contracts quite generally.

The majority opinion begins by observing that the law implies the covenant of good faith and fair dealing in every contract and that in the insurance context (as under *Comunale* and *Crisci*) breaches of this covenant give rise to an action in tort as well as in contract. The opinion acknowledges, however, that the decisions reaching this result for insurance contracts have emphasized the special relationship between insurers and insureds, which involves adhesion (in the insured) and public trust and fiduciary duty (in the insurer). (Here one might add, parroting the argument emphasized in the earlier discussion of *Crisci*, that the strategic structure of disputes in the insurance context makes it possible to give the self-serving nature of bad faith a precise elaboration.) The opinion worries, therefore, that it will not be easy to extend the treatment of bad faith developed in connection with insurance contracts to a more general commercial setting.

Although the court does not quite put the point this way, the problem with expanding the idea that bad faith breach of contract can be a free-standing tort involves a tension between this tort and underlying principles of freedom of contract. When the parties to a contract have roughly equal information and bargaining power, then they should (under the autonomy respecting principles of contract law) be able to specify the content and terms of their bargain—that is, in the absence of the kinds of imbalances that are involved in, say, insurance contracts (and perhaps also in other kinds of highly unequal contractual relations) the parties should govern their own relations rather than having obligations forced upon them. Included within this general rule is the principle that although the parties may not abrogate the implied in law covenant of good faith and fair dealing entirely (this is what it means for the covenant to be implied in law), they may specify the standards by which the covenant shall be applied.

This has a very important consequence: Where freedom of contract reigns broadly (and can even set the operational boundaries of good faith and fair dealing), it will be very, very difficult to distinguish breaches of the covenant of good faith and fair dealing from simple breaches of only the contract itself. (This problem is not nearly so difficult in the insurance context, where the regulated character of the business entails that much less of the arrangement between the parties belongs to the contract and much more to the implied in law covenant, and where the strategic structure of the interaction makes conduct that constitutes bad faith on any terms easily identifiable.) Because only breaches of bad faith can give rise to tort remedies, including to punitive damages, the possibility of confusion requires courts that step into this area to tread very carefully indeed.

Accordingly, any rule allowing punitive damages for breach of the implied covenant of good faith and fair dealing in the general commercial context must be narrowly drawn to pick out *only* breaches of this covenant and *never* simple breaches of the contract. The *Seaman's* opinion seeks to achieve this goal through a rigid but clear formalism, which the facts of that case themselves suggest. The holding in *Seaman's* announced the rule that when a party, in addition to breaching a contract, acts in bad faith and without probable cause to *deny that the contract exists (at all)*, then there is also a breach of the implied covenant of good faith and fair dealing, which constitutes a tort for which punitive damages may be available. The opinion observes that this rule comports with "accepted notions of business ethics," since denying, in bad faith, the very existence of a contract "offends against" these notions.[23] But this observation, although much cited, is not strictly necessary to the rule, which reflects an epistemic judgment and not an ontological one: it states a way of knowing (securely) when the covenant of good faith and fair dealing has been breached but does not present an account of the exclusive circumstances that constitute a breach. In any event, the defendant in *Seaman's* did deny, in bad faith, the very existence of its contract with plaintiff, and the tort award against it, including the punitive damages, was therefore affirmed.[24]

One Justice—Rose Bird[25]—would have gone further still. Although Bird accepted that breach of contract (and especially efficient breach) is an ordinary and proper feature of commercial life, and that mere breach of contract should not be a tort and should not give rise to punitives, she was still less impressed than the majority with the difficulty of drawing reliable distinctions between merely contractual breaches of an agreement's contin-

---

23. The opinion also observes that there exists a close analogy between the bad faith denial of the existence of a contract and another tort, namely malicious prosecution, which can be committed by bringing a lawsuit based on the bad faith assertion of a contract. Note that the same reasons that have led courts narrowly to cabin the tort bad faith breach of contract also support narrow limitations on the tort malicious prosecution. Thus the traditional common law tort malicious prosecution applies only to legal proceedings that, in addition to being wrongful have a "quasi-criminal" character, substantially interfere with a person's liberty or damage her reputation, or interfere with property interests (such as in attachment or involuntary bankruptcy proceedings). *See* W. Prosser, Handbook of the Law of Torts 851–52 (4th ed. 1971), and also Restatement (Second) of Torts § 674 (1977) Although a growing majority of jurisdictions recognize malicious prosecution without the requirement of special injury, a substantial minority of jurisdictions continue to follow the "English rule," which denies actions for malicious prosecution based groundless civil suits in the absence of special harms of the type just described. *See, e.g.,* Bickel v. Mackie, 447 F. Supp. 1376, 1380 (N.D. Iowa 1978); Garcia v. Wall & Ochs, Inc., 389 A.2d 607, 608, 610 (Pa.Super. 1978); Prosser, *supra* at 850–53.

24. *Seaman's* presented one further complication in this connection. The trial court had instructed the jury that the defendant's denial, *simplicter*, of the contract's existence could constitute a violation of good faith and fair dealing and support punitive damages. This was error, since only a *bad faith* denial is a tort. Moreover, the Supreme Court found this error not harmless, so that although existence of a tort of breaching the implied covenant of good faith and fair dealing was affirmed, the verdict for the plaintiff was on this count reversed.

25. Justice Bird's views, and the political context in which she acted, will be considered again (and more carefully) in later materials concerning employment at will.

gent terms and tortious breaches of the mandatory covenant of good faith and fair dealing. Accordingly, Bird would have held that any breach of contract in which the "breaching party acts in bad faith to shield itself entirely from liability for contract damages" involves a breach of the duty of good faith and fair dealing and is a tort. Moreover, although she agreed that the reasonable expectations of the parties should govern what counts as a tortious breach of good faith and fair dealing, Bird insisted that in some circumstances a simple breach of contract might count as a tort under this test: she imagined that the parties might expressly indicate in their contract that any breach (or at least any voluntary breach) is impermissible; or even, where (as, for example, in insurance contracts, and perhaps also in employment contracts) the structure of the contract relation clearly entails that ordinary contract damages will be inadequate remedies for breach, that the rule that all (voluntary) breaches constitute bad faith might be implied.

In spite of losing on the question of the scope of the new tort, Bird might have had reason to be optimistic in light of the *Seaman's* decision. After all, the *Seaman's* majority had adopted her view of the tort on many of the key points. The majority opinion makes plain that although bad faith breach of contract is a new and free-standing tort, there is nothing mysterious—and indeed nothing fundamentally contractual—in the tort. It is just the recovery mechanism for infringements of the mandatory, non-discretionary, and therefore non-contractual right to be treated in good faith in the administration of one's contracts. The new tort was, in a sense, a creature of tort law all the way down, in the same way in which assault is a creature of tort law all the way down (the only novelty being the identification of a new interest whose deprivation underwrites a tort claim). Again, the difference between the majority's views and Bird's was merely epistemic, and Bird had good reason to expect that as courts became more familiar with the new tort, their epistemic confidence would grow, and the circumstances in which the tort might be found would expand in her direction.

Things did not, however, turn out that way at all, and instead of flourishing, the new tort was cut down, constricted, and, in *Freeman & Mills,* eventually rooted out entirely. The defendant in that case hired a law firm—Morgan, Lewis & Brockius—to defend it in a Florida lawsuit, agreeing to pay the costs associated with the Florida litigation, including certain fees to be paid to accountants. The plaintiffs were hired by Morgan, Lewis to serve as accountants in connection with the Florida case. Eventually, the defendant fired Morgan, Lewis as its lawyers and directed Morgan, Lewis to instruct the plaintiff to stop doing its work, also. The plaintiff stopped, but billed first Morgan, Lewis and then the defendant for such work as it had already done. When the defendant answered that it had not been consulted about the extent of the plaintiff's work and that the plaintiff should look to Morgan, Lewis for payment, the plaintiff sued the defendant alleging, among other things, bad faith denial of a contract. This, of course, was just the specific form of the general tort of bad faith denial of the covenant of good faith and fair dealing identified by *Seaman's*. A jury found that the defendant had authorized Morgan, Lewis to retain the plaintiff on its behalf and that, in denying its obligations to the plaintiff, the defendant acted with oppression, fraud, or malice. The jury then awarded roughly $100,000 in compensatory damages and $400,000 in punitives.[26] The defendant appealed.

The case eventually reached the California Supreme Court. After describing *Seaman's* and its holding, the Court's opinion reprises some of Bird's observations about that holding, but applies them to the opposite effect from what Bird had intended. Thus, the *Freeman & Mills* opinion agrees that no meaningful distinction can be drawn between a bad faith denial of the *existence* of a contract, which underwrites a tort under *Seamen's*, and bad faith denial of *liability* under a contract, which does not. Accordingly, the opinion concludes, it makes no sense for a court to grant punitives in the former case but not the latter. The *Freeman & Mills* Court finds this very troubling, principally because it fears precisely the development that Bird had invited: this is that *Seaman's* cannot in practice be contained, so that it will in the end render tort damages (including punitives) at least colorably available in every contract dispute. This result, the *Freeman & Mills* majority worries, would undermine the predictability of commercial litigation, thereby undoing all the efficiency gains generated by expectation damages and the encouraging of efficient breaches and, moreover, burdening the judicial system. *Seaman's* was therefore overruled, and there is no longer in California tort liability for bad faith denial of the existence of a contract in the general commercial setting. (Note, however, that *Freeman & Mills* left *Comunale* and *Crisci* in place, so that in the insurance context, breach of the implied covenant of good faith and fair dealing continues to give rise to potential tort liability, including for punitive damages.)

Justice Mosk's partial dissent agreed that the facts of *Freeman & Mills* were distinguishable from *Seaman's*, and that no tort liability should arise on these facts. But Mosk insisted that the door to tort liability for bad faith breach of general commercial contracts should not be shut entirely. Specifically, Mosk would have allowed an action for tortious breach of contract in a commercial setting when a party (a) intentionally breaches a contractual obligation with neither probable cause nor the belief that the obligation does not exist, *and* (b) intends or knows that the breach will result in severe consequential damages to the other party that are not readily subject to mitigation, and such harm actually occurs. Such conduct, Mosk thought, is just undeniably tortious, and he was surely right. But identifying a clear case of the tort of bad faith breach of contract cannot answer the majority's argument in *Freeman & Mills*, which was, again, epistemic rather than ontological.

---

26. The jury's actual verdict was different, but seems to have involved a mechanical mistake (something which is surprisingly common). Thus the jury awarded $25,000 in compensatories and $477,000 in punitives, which the trial court "corrected" to become $102,000 (= $25,000 + $77,000) in compensatories and $400,000 in punitives.

To answer this argument, it would be necessary to show that allowing the Seaman's tort to stand will not chill efficient business practices (including intentional efficient breaches), either because the tort can be effectively cabined or because even though it cannot be, the damages actually awarded in connection with the tort are too insubstantial to have much practical significance. That is precisely the style of answer that, earlier materials observed, has been given to rebut claims that punitive damages in connection with ordinary torts (medical malpractice, products liability, industrial pollution) deter innovation and other desirable economic activity.

The experience of tort liability for bad faith breach of contract (both in California and in other jurisdictions) is not as substantial as it is in these other contexts, and so empirical arguments are less easy to make. There are, however, some intuitive grounds for thinking, with the *Freeman & Mills* majority, that punitive damages pose special problems of over-deterrence in connection with bad faith breach of contract. Every contract dispute (or almost every contract dispute) involves one party's keeping property the other party claims a right to, and, moreover, denying the existence or validity of one or another contractual undertaking. Without doing so, it becomes almost impossible to contest a contract. In other words, every contract dispute involves one party's acting in a manner that closely resembles the actions that proponents of tort liability for bad faith breach of contract identify as the core cases of the tort. And if contesting a contract in these ways exposed a party to punitive damages, the assertion of uncertain contractual rights would become enormously hazardous.

Whatever its merits, this style of argument seems to be winning the day in practice. Although many states experimented with tort liability for bad faith breach of contract in the 1970s and 1980s, a 1999 survey reported that by then 39 American jurisdictions did not allow punitive damages in contract claims unless the plaintiff established an ordinary and independent tort, and that only 12 jurisdictions allowed punitive damages in limited circumstances for tortious breach of contract.[27]

---

27. William S. Dodge, *The Case for Punitive Damages in Contract*, 48 Duke L.J. 629 (1999). These jurisdictions are Alabama, Alaska, Arkansas, California, Colorado, Connecticut, Delaware, the District of Columbia, Florida, Georgia, Illinois, Indiana, Iowa, Kansas, Kentucky, Louisiana, Maine, Maryland, Massachusetts, Michigan, Minnesota, Missouri, Nebraska, New York, New Hampshire, New Jersey, North Carolina, North Dakota, Ohio, Oklahoma, Oregon, Pennsylvania, South Dakota, Texas, Utah, Virginia, Washington, West Virginia, and Wisconsin. *Id.* at n. 87 and n. 88.

CHAPTER 9

Specific Performance

The discussion so far has focused on remedies through which breaching promisors *compensate* their promisees, by paying *money damages* that place the promisees in a position that is *equivalently attractive* to the position that they would have occupied had their promisors performed as promised. It might be thought, however, that contractual entitlements might be more straightforwardly vindicated by a very different remedy, which at one stroke avoids all the difficulties of calculating adequate compensation that have dominated the discussion, namely an order that the promisor simply *do what she has promised*. And indeed, contract law does contemplate that this remedy—which the law calls specific performance—may be ordered, although the official self-understanding of the law is that specific performance is an exceptional remedy, to be applied in limited circumstances only.

This chapter takes up specific performance, proceeding in three stages. The first reports the law's official position concerning specific performance, through some illustrative cases. The second, pursuing the economic theme that has dominated these pages so far, considers the efficiency argument for expanding specific performance beyond the narrow classes of cases in which the law's official self-understanding makes the remedy available. And the third, shifting styles (as something of a preview into the approach that will dominate the second part of these materials), asks whether there is a sense in which the law in fact already makes specific performance, properly understood, the core remedy for breach of contract.

9.1 The Official Account of Specific Performance

For much of the history of English law, and for the early history of American law, there existed a doctrinal (and in many cases institutional) distinction between two legal orders, which co-existed (often, although not always, complementarily) side-by-side. The first was called *law* and the second was called *equity*, although these words must be understood as terms of art, and equity was just as legal as law, in the ordinary sense of the word. Law was administered in England by the Crown's common law courts, and in the United States by American courts exercising their common law jurisdiction. The contract doctrines considered so far in these pages were, in this technical sense, doctrines of law. Equity was administered by in England by a second, and largely parallel, system of courts, called courts of equity, and in the United States by American courts exercising their equitable jurisdiction. Specific performance, by contrast, was an equitable remedy, to be administered by these courts.

The distinction between law and equity has been largely, but not completely, eliminated in both English and American legal practice.[1] In England, this was done by the Judicature Acts, and in the United States, at least for the Federal Courts, by the Federal Rules of Civil Procedure, which emphatically rejected the notion that there should exist several, parallel systems of dispute resolution in favor of the position that "There shall be one form of action to be known as 'civil action.'"[2] Even before this, the distinction could be obscure, to say the least. Whatever had been true in the past, by the nineteenth century the distinction between law and equity had become a historical and institutional matter rather than a conceptual one. Thus the great English legal historian Maitland once answered the question "What is equity?" by writing that equity is "[t]hat body of rules administered by our English courts of justice which, were it not for the operation of the Judicature Acts, would be administered only by those courts which would be known as Courts of Equity."[3]

All of this is relevant here because specific performance, being a species of injunction (in which a court enjoins a defendant to do as she has promised), is an equitable remedy. Specific performance was therefore traditionally governed by something called the Irreparable Injury Rule—which states that equity will not act where there is an adequate remedy at law. Hence the standard doctrinal line on specific performance: namely, that specific performance is available to a disappointed promisee only where the promisee can show that, because the contractual performance is in some way or other *unique*, money damages will not allow her to *replace* the contractual performance using another source and, moreover, cannot adequately *compensate* her for being deprived of it.

Of course, as with so much else in this area, this simple-sounding rule is not so straightforward in practice, where courts make judgments concerning uniqueness and irreparability in heterodox and hence unpredictable ways. The following materials serve to illustrate some of the complexities.

Uniform Commercial Code

2–716 Buyer Right to Specific Performance or Replevin

(1) Specific performance may be decreed where the goods are unique or in other proper circumstances.

---

1. The distinction between law and equity has not been entirely eliminated, however. In most jurisdictions, for example, a defendant has a right to trial by jury when the plaintiff's claim sounds in law but not when it sounds in equity. *See* 50A C.J.S. *Juries* § 24 (2009).

2. FED. R. CIV. P. 2. Law and equity have also been merged in most state court systems. One notable exception is Delaware, which retains its Court of Chancery (the leading court for Corporate law in America).

3. Frederic William Maitland, Equity: A Course of Lectures 1 (1909).

(2) The decree for specific performance may include such terms and conditions as to payment of the price, damages, or other relief as the court may deem just.

(3) The buyer has a right of replevin for goods identified to the contract if after reasonable effort he is unable to effect cover for such goods or the circumstances reasonably indicate that such effort will be unavailing or if the goods have been shipped under reservation and satisfaction of the security interest in them has been made or tendered. In the case of goods bought for personal, family, or household purposes, the buyer's right of replevin vests upon acquisition of a special property, even if the seller had not then repudiated or failed to deliver.

Official Comment

Prior Uniform Statutory Provision: Section 68, Uniform Sales Act.

Changes: Rephrased.

Purposes of Changes: To make it clear that:

1.   The present section continues in general prior policy as to specific performance and injunction against breach. However, without intending to impair in any way the exercise of the court's sound discretion in the matter, this Article seeks to further a more liberal attitude than some courts have shown in connection with the specific performance of contracts of sale.

2.   In view of this Article's emphasis on the commercial feasibility of replacement, a new concept of what are "unique" goods is introduced under this section. Specific performance is no longer limited to goods which are already specific or ascertained at the time of contracting. The test of uniqueness under this section must be made in terms of the total situation which characterizes the contract. Output and requirements contracts involving a particular or peculiarly available source or market present today the typical commercial specific performance situation, as contrasted with contracts for the sale of heirlooms or priceless works of art which were usually involved in the older cases. However, uniqueness is not the sole basis of the remedy under this section for the relief may also be granted "in other proper circumstances" and inability to cover is strong evidence of "other proper circumstances".

3.   The legal remedy of replevin is given to the buyer in cases in which cover is reasonably unavailable and goods have been identified to the contract. This is in addition to the buyer's right to recover identified goods under Section 2–502. For consumer goods, the buyer's right to replevin vests upon the buyer's acquisition of a special property, which occurs upon identification of the goods to the contract. See Section 2–501. Inasmuch as a secured party normally acquires no greater rights in its collateral that its debtor had or had power to convey, see Section 2–403(1) (first sentence), a buyer who acquires a right of replevin under subsection (3) will take free of a security interest created by the seller if it attaches to the goods after the goods have been identified to the contract. The buyer will take free, even if

the buyer does not buy in ordinary course and even if the security interest is perfected. Of course, to the extent that the buyer pays the price after the security interest attaches, the payments will constitute proceeds of the security interest.

4. This section is intended to give the buyer rights to the goods comparable to the seller's rights to the price.

5. If a negotiable document of title is outstanding, the buyer's right of replevin relates of course to the document not directly to the goods. See Article 7, especially Section 7–602.

Sedmak v. Charlie's Chevrolet, Inc.

Court of Appeals of Missouri, 1981.
622 S.W.2d 694.

This is an appeal from a decree of specific performance. We affirm.

■ MEHAN, J. In their petition, plaintiffs, Dr. and Mrs. Sedmak (Sedmaks), alleged they entered into a contract with defendant, Charlie's Chevrolet, Inc. (Charlie's), to purchase a Corvette automobile for approximately $15,000.00. The Corvette was one of a limited number manufactured to commemorate the selection of the Corvette as the Pace Car for the Indianapolis 500. Charlie's breached the contract, the Sedmaks alleged, when, after the automobile was delivered, an agent for Charlie's told the Sedmaks they could not purchase the automobile for $15,000.00 but would have to bid on it.

The trial court found the parties entered into an oral contract and also found the contract was excepted from the Statute of Frauds. The court then ordered Charlie's to make the automobile "available for delivery" to the Sedmaks.

Charlie's raises three points on appeal: (1) the existence of an oral contract is not supported by the credible evidence; (2) if an oral contract exists, it is unenforceable because of the Statute of Frauds; and (3) specific performance is an improper remedy because the Sedmaks did not show their legal remedies were inadequate.

[T]he record reflects the Sedmaks to be automobile enthusiasts, who, at the time of trial, owned six Corvettes. In July, 1977, "Vette Vues," a Corvette fancier's magazine to which Dr. Sedmak subscribed, published an article announcing Chevrolet's tentative plans to manufacture a limited edition of the Corvette. The limited edition of approximately 6,000 automobiles was to commemorate the selection of the Corvette as the Indianapolis 500 Pace Car. The Sedmaks were interested in acquiring one of these Pace Cars to add to their Corvette collection. In November, 1977, the Sedmaks asked Tom Kells, sales manager at Charlie's Chevrolet, about the availability of the Pace Car. Mr. Kells said he did not have any information on the car but would find out about it. Kells also said if Charlie's were to receive a Pace Car, the Sedmaks could purchase it.

On January 9, 1978, Dr. Sedmak telephoned Kells to ask him if a Pace Car could be ordered. Kells indicated that he would require a deposit on the car, so Mrs. Sedmak went to Charlie's and gave Kells a check for $500.00. She was given a receipt for that amount bearing the names of Kells and Charlie's Chevrolet, Inc. At that time, Kells had a pre-order form listing both standard equipment and options available on the Pace Car. Prior to tendering the deposit, Mrs. Sedmak asked Kells if she and Dr. Sedmak were "definitely going to be the owners." Kells replied, "Yes." After the deposit had been paid, Mrs. Sedmak stated if the car was going to be theirs, her husband wanted some changes made to the stock model. She asked Kells to order the car equipped with an L82 engine, four speed standard transmission and AM/FM radio with tape deck. Kells said that he would try to arrange with the manufacturer for these changes. Kells was able to make the changes, and, when the car arrived, it was equipped as the Sedmaks had requested.

Kells informed Mrs. Sedmak that the price of the Pace Car would be the manufacturer's retail price, approximately $15,000.00. The dollar figure could not be quoted more precisely because Kells was not sure what the ordered changes would cost, nor was he sure what the "appearance package"—decals, a special paint job—would cost. Kells also told Mrs. Sedmak that, after the changes had been made, a "contract"—a retail dealer's order form—would be mailed to them. However, no form or written contract was mailed to the Sedmaks by Charlie's.

On January 25, 1978, the Sedmaks visited Charlie's to take delivery on another Corvette. At that time, the Sedmaks asked Kells whether he knew anything further about the arrival date of the Pace Car. Kells replied he had no further information but he would let the Sedmaks know when the car arrived. Kells also requested that Charlie's be allowed to keep the car in their showroom for promotional purposes until after the Indianapolis 500 Race. The Sedmaks agreed to this arrangement.

On April 3, 1978, the Sedmaks were notified by Kells that the Pace Car had arrived. Kells told the Sedmaks they could not purchase the car for the manufacturer's retail price because demand for the car had inflated its value beyond the suggested price. Kells also told the Sedmaks they could bid on the car. The Sedmaks did not submit a bid. They filed this suit for specific performance.

Charlie's also appears to argue there was no contract because the parties did not agree to a price.

[T]here was evidence to support the trial court's conclusion that the parties agreed the selling price would be the price suggested by the manufacturer. Whether this price accurately reflects the market demands on any given day is immaterial. The manufacturer's suggested retail price is ascertainable and, thus, if the parties choose, sufficiently definite to meet the price requirements of an enforceable contract. Failure to specify the selling price in dollars and cents did not render the contract void or voidable. *See, e.g., Klaber v. Lahar, 63 S.W.2d 103, 106–107 (Mo. 1933); see also, § 400.2–305 RSMo 1978.* As long as the parties agreed to a method by which the price was to be determined and as long as the price could be ascertained at the time of performance, the price requirement for a valid and enforceable contract was satisfied. This point is without merit.

Charlie's next complains that if there were an oral contract, it is unenforceable under the Statute of Frauds. [The court finds that the contract was removed from the Statute of Frauds.]

Finally, Charlie's contends the Sedmaks failed to show they were entitled to specific performance of the contract. We disagree. Although it has been stated that the determination whether to order specific performance lies within the discretion of the trial court, *Landau v. St. Louis Public Service Co., 364 Mo. 1134 (1954)*, this discretion is, in fact, quite narrow. When the relevant equitable principles have been met and the contract is fair and plain, " 'specific performance goes as a matter of right.' " *Miller v. Coffeen, 365 Mo. 204 (1955)*. Here, the trial court ordered specific performance because it concluded the Sedmaks "have no adequate remedy at law for the reason that they cannot go upon the open market and purchase an automobile of this kind with the same mileage, condition, ownership and appearance as the automobile involved in this case, except, if at all, with considerable expense, trouble, loss, great delay and inconvenience." Contrary to defendant's complaint, this is a correct expression of the relevant law and it is supported by the evidence.

Under the Code, the court may decree specific performance as a buyer's remedy for breach of contract to sell goods "where the goods are unique or in other proper circumstances." *§ 400.2–716(1) RSMo 1978*. The general term "in other proper circumstances" expresses the drafters' intent to "further a more liberal attitude than some courts have shown in connection with the specific performance of contracts of sale." *§ 400.2–716*, U.C.C., Comment 1. This Comment was not directed to the courts of this state, for long before the Code, we, in Missouri, took a practical approach in determining whether specific performance would lie for the breach of contract for the sale of goods and did not limit this relief only to the sale of "unique" goods. *Boeving v. Vandover, 240 Mo. App. 117 (1945)*. In *Boeving*, plaintiff contracted to buy a car from defendant. When the car arrived, defendant refused to sell. The car was not unique in the traditional legal sense but, at that time, all cars were difficult to obtain because of war-time shortages. The court held specific performance was the proper remedy for plaintiff because a new car "could not be obtained elsewhere except at considerable expense, trouble or loss, which cannot be estimated in advance and under such circumstances [plaintiff] did not have an adequate remedy at law." *Id. at 177–178*. Thus, *Boeving*, presaged the broad and liberalized language of *§ 400.2–716(1)* and exemplifies one of the "other proper circumstances" contemplated by this subsection for ordering specific performance. § 400.2–716, Missouri Code Comment 1. The present facts track those in *Boeving*.

The Pace Car, like the car in *Boeving*, was not unique in the traditional legal sense. It was not an heirloom or, arguably, not one of a kind. However, its "mileage, condition, ownership and appearance" did make it difficult, if not impossible, to obtain its replication without considerable expense, delay and inconvenience. Admittedly, 6,000 Pace Cars were produced by Chevrolet. However, as the record reflects, this is limited production. In addition, only one of these cars was available to each dealer, and only a limited number of these were equipped with the specific options ordered by plaintiffs. Charlie's had not received a car like the Pace Car in the previous two years. The sticker price for the car was $14,284.21. Yet Charlie's received offers from individuals in Hawaii and Florida to buy the Pace Car for $24,000.00 and $28,000.00 respectively. As sensibly inferred by the trial court, the location and size of these offers demonstrated this limited edition was in short supply and great demand. We agree, with the trial court. This case was a "proper circumstance" for ordering specific performance.

Judgment affirmed.

All concur.

Klein v. PepsiCo, Inc.

United States Court of Appeals for the Fourth Circuit, 1988.
845 F.2d 76.

■ ERVIN, CIRCUIT JUDGE. This case turns on whether a contract was formed between Universal Jet Sales, Inc. ("UJS") and PepsiCo, Inc., ("PepsiCo") for the sale of a Gulfstream G–II corporate jet to UJS for resale to one Eugene V. Klein. If a contract was formed, the question remains whether the district court acted within his discretion by ordering specific performance of the contract. We believe the district court properly found that a contract was formed; however, we conclude that the remedy of specific performance is inappropriate. Accordingly, we affirm in part, reverse and remand in part.

I.

In March 1986, Klein began looking for a used corporate jet; specifically, he wanted a G–II. He contacted Patrick Janas, President of UJS, who provided information to Klein about several aircraft including the PepsiCo aircraft. Klein's pilot and mechanic, Mr. Sherman and Mr. Quaid, inspected the PepsiCo jet in New York. Mr. James Welsch served as the jet broker for PepsiCo.

Klein asked that the jet be flown to Arkansas for his personal inspection. On March 29, 1986, he inspected the jet. Mr. Rashid, PepsiCo Vice President for Asset Management and Corporate Service, accompanied the jet to Arkansas and met Mr. Klein. Janas also went to Arkansas. Klein gave Janas $200,000 as a deposit on the jet, and told Janas to offer $4.4 million for the aircraft.

On March 31, 1986, Janas telexed the $4.4 million offer to Welsch. The telex said the offer was subject to a factory inspection satisfactory to the purchaser, and a definitive contract. On April 1, PepsiCo counteroffered with a $4.7 million asking price. After some dickering, Welsch offered the jet for $4.6 million. Janas accepted the offer by telex on April 3. Janas then planned to sell the aircraft to Klein for $4.75 million. Judge Williams declared that a contract had been formed at this point.

Judge Williams ruled that a contract was evidenced by Janas' confirming telex which "accepted" PepsiCo's offer to sell the jet, and noted that a $100,000 down payment would be wired. The telex also asked for the proper name of the company selling the aircraft.

On April 3, Janas sent out copies of the Klein/UJS agreement and the UJS–PepsiCo agreement to the respective parties. Janas also sent a bill of sale to PepsiCo (to Rashid). PepsiCo sent the bill of sale to the escrow agent handling the deal on April 8. Mr. Rochoff, PepsiCo's corporate counsel, spoke with Janas about the standard contract sent by Janas to PepsiCo. He noted only that the delivery date should be changed.

On Monday, April 7, the aircraft was flown to Savannah, Georgia for the pre-purchase inspection. Quaid was present at the inspection for Klein. Archie Walker, PepsiCo's chief of maintenance, was present for the seller. Walker and Quaid discussed a list of repairs to be made to the jet. Most of the problems were cured during the inspection. However, one cosmetic problem was to be corrected in New York, and there were cracks in the engine blades of the right engine.

On April 8, a boroscopic examination conducted by Aviall revealed eight to eleven cracks on the turbine blades. Walker told Rashid that the cost of repairing the blades would be between $25,000 to $28,000. Judge Williams found that PepsiCo, through Walker and Rashid, agreed to pay for the repair to the engine.

On April 9, the plane was returned to New York. Rashid wanted the plane grounded; however, it was sent to retrieve the stranded PepsiCo Chairman of the Board from Dulles airport that same evening. Donald Kendall, the Chairman, on April 10, called Rashid and asked that the jet be withdrawn from the market. Rashid called Welsch who effected the withdrawal. On the 11th Janas told Klein that PepsiCo refused to tender the aircraft. The deal was supposed to close on Friday, April 11.

On April 14, Klein telexed UJS demanding delivery of the aircraft. That same day, UJS telexed PepsiCo demanding delivery and expressing satisfaction with the pre-purchase inspection. On April 15, PepsiCo responded with a telex to UJS saying that it refused to negotiate further because discussions had not reached the point of agreement; in particular, Klein was not prepared to go forward with the deal.

Judge Williams' decision to grant specific performance is reviewed only for an abuse of discretion. Keeping these standards in mind, we now turn to whether the district court clearly erred in finding that a contract arose between PepsiCo and UJS.

II.

[A] contract exists between PepsiCo and UJS for the sale of one G–II Gulfstream aircraft. Because PepsiCo failed to deliver the aircraft, the district court ordered relief in the form of specific performance. We now consider the appropriateness of the relief ordered.

III.

The *Virginia Code § 8.2–716* permits a jilted buyer of goods to seek specific performance of the contract if the goods sought are unique, or in other proper circumstances. Judge Williams ruled that: 1) the G–II aircraft involved in this case is unique and 2) Klein's inability to cover with a comparable aircraft is strong evidence of "other proper circumstances." These conclusions are not supported in the record.

We note first that Virginia's adoption of the Uniform Commercial Code does not abrogate the maxim that specific performance is inappropriate where damages are recoverable and adequate. *Griscom v. Childress, 183 Va. 42 (1944).* In this case Judge Williams repeatedly stated that money damages would make Klein whole. Klein argued that he wanted the plane to resell it for a profit. Finally, an increase in the cost of a replacement does not merit the remedy of specific performance. *Hilmor Sales Co. v. Helen Neuschalfer Division of Supronics Corp., 6 U.C.C. Rep. Serv. 325 (N.Y. Sup. Ct. 1969).* There is no room in this case for the equitable remedy of specific performance.

Turning now to the specific rulings of the court below, Judge Williams explained that the aircraft was unique because only three comparable aircraft existed on the market. Therefore, Klein would have to go through considerable expense to find a replacement. Klein's expert testified that there were twenty-one other G–II's on the market, three of which were roughly comparable. Klein's chief pilot said that other G–II's could be purchased. Finally, we should note that UJS bought two G–II's which they offered to Klein after this deal fell through, and Klein made bids on two other G–II's after PepsiCo withdrew its aircraft from the market. Given these facts, we find it very difficult to support a ruling that the aircraft was so unique as to merit an order of specific performance.

Judge Williams ruled further that Klein's inability to cover his loss is an "other proper circumstance" favoring specific performance. Klein testified himself that he didn't purchase another G–II because prices had started to rise. Because of the price increase, he decided to purchase a G–III aircraft. As noted earlier, price increases alone are no reason to order specific performance. Because money damages would clearly be adequate in this case, and because the aircraft is not unique within the meaning of the Virginia Commercial Code, we reverse the grant of specific performance and remand the case to the district court for a trial on damages.

Affirmed in part, reversed and remanded in part.

Van Wagner Advertising Corp. v. S & M Enterprises

Court of Appeals of New York, 1986.
492 N.E.2d 756.

Opinion of the Court. Specific performance of a contract to lease "unique" billboard space is properly denied when damages are an adequate remedy to compensate the tenant and equitable relief would impose a disproportionate burden on the defaulting landlord. However, owing to an error in the assessment of damages, the order of the Appellate Division should be modified so as to remit the matter to Supreme Court, New York County, for further proceedings with respect to damages.

By agreement dated December 16, 1981, Barbara Michaels leased to plaintiff, Van Wagner Advertising, for an initial period of three years plus option periods totaling seven additional years space on the eastern exterior wall of a building on East 36th Street in Manhattan. Van Wagner was in the business of erecting and leasing billboards, and the parties anticipated that Van Wagner would erect a sign on the leased space, which faced an exit ramp of the Midtown Tunnel and was therefore visible to vehicles entering Manhattan from that tunnel.

In early 1982 Van Wagner erected an illuminated sign and leased it to Asch Advertising, Inc. for a three-year period commencing March 1, 1982. However, by agreement dated January 22, 1982, Michaels sold the building to defendant S & M Enterprises. Michaels informed Van Wagner of the sale in early August 1982, and on August 19, 1982 S & M sent Van Wagner a letter purporting to cancel the lease as of October 18 pursuant to section 1.05, which provided:

> Notwithstanding anything contained in the foregoing provisions to the contrary, Lessor (or its successor) may terminate and cancel this lease on not less than 60 days prior written notice in the event and only in the event of:
>
> a) a bona fide sale of the building to a third party unrelated to Lessor.

Van Wagner abandoned the space under protest and in November 1982 commenced this action for declarations that the purported cancellation was ineffective and the lease still in existence, and for specific performance and damages.

In the litigation the parties differed sharply on the meaning of section 1.05 of the lease. Van Wagner contended that the lease granted a right to cancel only to the owner as it was about to sell the building—not to the new purchaser—so that the building could be conveyed without the encumbrance of the lease. S & M, in contrast, contended that the provision clearly gave it, as Michaels' successor by virtue of a bona fide sale, the right to cancel the lease on 60 days' notice. Special Term denied Van Wagner's motion for a preliminary injunction, concluding that the lease by its terms gave S & M the authority to cancel and that Van Wagner was therefore not likely to succeed on the merits.

At a nonjury trial, both parties introduced parol evidence, in the form of testimony about negotiations, to explain the meaning of section 1.05. Additionally, one of S & M's two partners testified without contradiction that, having already acquired other real estate on the block, S & M purchased the subject building in 1982 for the ultimate purpose of demolishing existing buildings and constructing a mixed residential-commercial development. The project is to begin upon expiration of a lease of the subject building in 1987, if not sooner.

Trial Term concluded that Van Wagner's position on the issue of contract interpretation was correct, either because the lease provision unambiguously so provided or, if the provision were ambiguous, because the parol evidence showed that the "parties to the lease intended that only an owner making a bona fide sale could terminate the lease. They did not intend that once a sale had been made that any future purchaser could terminate the lease at will." Trial Term declared the lease "valid and subsisting" and found that the "demised space is unique as to location for the particular advertising purpose intended by Van Wagner and Michaels, the original parties to the Lease." However, the court declined to order specific performance in light of its finding that Van Wagner "has an adequate remedy at law for damages". Moreover, the court noted that specific performance "would be inequitable in that its effect would be disproportionate in its harm to the defendant and its assistance to plaintiff." Concluding that "[the] value of the unique qualities of the demised space has been fixed by the contract Van Wagner has with its advertising client, Asch for the period of the contract", the court awarded Van Wagner the lost revenues on the Asch sublease for the period through trial, without prejudice to a new action by Van Wagner for subsequent damages if S & M did not permit Van Wagner to reoccupy the space. On Van Wagner's motion to resettle the judgment to provide for specific performance, the court adhered to its judgment.

On cross appeals the Appellate Division affirmed, without opinion. We granted both parties leave to appeal.

Whether or not a contract provision is ambiguous is a question of law to be resolved by a court *(Sutton v East Riv. Sav. Bank, 55 NY2d 550, 554 (1982)).* In our view, section 1.05 is ambiguous. Reasonable minds could differ as to whether the lease granted a purchaser of the property a right to cancel the lease, or limited that right to successive sellers of the property *(see, Chimart Assoc. v Paul, 66 NY2d 570, 573 (1986)).* However, Trial Term's alternate finding—that the parol evidence supported Van Wagner's interpretation of the provision—was one of fact. That finding, having been affirmed by the Appellate Division and having support in the record, is beyond the scope of our review *(see, Huntley v State of New York, 62 NY2d 134, 137 (1984)).* Thus, S & M's cancellation of Van Wagner's lease constituted a breach of contract.

Given defendant's unexcused failure to perform its contract, we next turn to a consideration of remedy for the breach: Van Wagner seeks specific performance of the contract, S & M urges that money damages are adequate but that the amount of the award was improper.[2]

---

2. We note that the parties' contentions regarding the remedy of specific performance in general, mirror a scholarly debate that has persisted throughout our judicial history, reflecting fundamentally divergent views about the quality of a bargained-for promise. While the usual remedy in Anglo–American law has been damages, rather than compensation "in kind" *(see* Holmes, *The Path of the Law,* 10 HARV. L. REV. 457, 462 [1897]; HOLMES, THE COMMON LAW, 299–

Whether or not to award specific performance is a decision that rests in the sound discretion of the trial court, and here that discretion was not abused. Considering first the nature of the transaction, specific performance has been imposed as the remedy for breach of contracts for the sale of real property, but the contract here is to lease rather than sell an interest in real property. While specific performance is available, in appropriate circumstances, for breach of a commercial or residential lease, specific performance of real property leases is not in this State awarded as a matter of course *(see, Gardens Nursery School v Columbia Univ., 94 Misc 2d 376, 378 (N.Y. 1978))*.

Van Wagner argues that specific performance must be granted in light of the trial court's finding that the "demised space is unique as to location for the particular advertising purpose intended". The word "uniqueness" is not, however, a magic door to specific performance. A distinction must be drawn between physical difference and economic interchangeability. The trial court found that the leased property is physically unique, but so is every parcel of real property and so are many consumer goods. Putting aside contracts for the sale of real property, where specific performance has traditionally been the remedy for breach, uniqueness in the sense of physical difference does not itself dictate the propriety of equitable relief.

By the same token, at some level all property may be interchangeable with money. Economic theory is concerned with the degree to which consumers are willing to substitute the use of one good for another *(see,* Kronman, *Specific Performance,* 45 U Chi L Rev 351, 359)*, the underlying assumption being that "every good has substitutes, even if only very poor ones", and that "all goods are ultimately commensurable" *(id.)*. Such a view, however, could strip all meaning from uniqueness, for if all goods are ultimately exchangeable for a price, then all goods may be valued. Even a rare manuscript has an economic substitute in that there is a price for which any purchaser would likely agree to give up a right to buy it, but a court would in all probability order specific performance of such a contract on the ground that the subject matter of the contract is unique.

The point at which breach of a contract will be re-addressable by specific performance thus must lie not in any inherent physical uniqueness of the property but instead in the uncertainty of valuing it: "What matters, in measuring money damages, is the volume, refinement, and reliability of the available information about substitutes for the subject matter of the breached contract. When the relevant information is thin and unreliable, there is a substantial risk that an award of money damages will either exceed or fall short of the promisee's actual loss. Of course this risk can always be reduced—but only at great cost when reliable information is

301 [1881]; and GILMORE, THE DEATH OF CONTRACT, 14–15), the current trend among commentators appears to favor the remedy of specific performance *(see* Farnsworth, *Legal Remedies for Breach of Contract,* 70 COLUM. L. REV. 1145, 1156 [1970]; Linzer, *On the Amorality of Contract Remedies—Efficiency, Equity, and the Second Restatement,* 81 COLUM. L. REV. 111 [1981]; and Schwartz, *The Case for Specific Performance,* 89 YALE L.J. 271 [1979]), but the view is not unanimous *(see* POSNER, ECONOMIC ANALYSIS OF LAW, § 4.9 at 89–90 [2d ed. 1977]; Yorio, *In Defense of Money Damages for Breach of Contract,* 82 COLUM. L. REV. 1365 [1982]).

difficult to obtain. Conversely, when there is a great deal of consumer behavior generating abundant and highly dependable information about substitutes, the risk of error in measuring the promisee's loss may be reduced at much smaller cost. In asserting that the subject matter of a particular contract is unique and has no established market value, a court is really saying that it cannot obtain, at reasonable cost, enough information about substitutes to permit it to calculate an award of money damages without imposing an unacceptably high risk of under-compensation on the injured promisee. Conceived in this way, the uniqueness test seems economically sound." (45 U Chi L Rev, at 362.) This principle is reflected in the case law, and is essentially the position of the Restatement (Second) of Contracts, which lists "the difficulty of proving damages with reasonable certainty" as the first factor affecting adequacy of damages (Restatement [Second] of Contracts § 360 [a]).

Thus, the fact that the subject of the contract may be "unique as to location for the particular advertising purpose intended" by the parties does not entitle a plaintiff to the remedy of specific performance.

Here, the trial court correctly concluded that the value of the "unique qualities" of the demised space could be fixed with reasonable certainty and without imposing an unacceptably high risk of under compensating the injured tenant. Both parties complain: Van Wagner asserts that while lost revenues on the Asch contract may be adequate compensation, that contract expired February 28, 1985, its lease with S & M continues until 1992, and the value of the demised space cannot reasonably be fixed for the balance of the term. S & M urges that future rents and continuing damages are necessarily conjectural, both during and after the Asch contract, and that Van Wagner's damages must be limited to 60 days—the period during which Van Wagner could cancel Asch's contract without consequence in the event Van Wagner lost the demised space. S & M points out that Van Wagner's lease could remain in effect for the full 10–year term, or it could legitimately be extinguished immediately, either in conjunction with a bona fide sale of the property by S & M, or by a reletting of the building if the new tenant required use of the billboard space for its own purposes. Both parties' contentions were properly rejected.

First, it is hardly novel in the law for damages to be projected into the future. Particularly where the value of commercial billboard space can be readily determined by comparisons with similar uses—Van Wagner itself has more than 400 leases—the value of this property between 1985 and 1992 cannot be regarded as speculative. Second, S & M having successfully resisted specific performance on the ground that there is an adequate remedy at law, cannot at the same time be heard to contend that damages beyond 60 days must be denied because they are conjectural. If damages for breach of this lease are indeed conjectural, and cannot be calculated with reasonable certainty, then S & M should be compelled to perform its contractual obligation by restoring Van Wagner to the premises. Moreover, the contingencies to which S & M points do not, as a practical matter, render the calculation of damages speculative. While S & M could terminate the Van Wagner lease in the event of a sale of the building, this building has been sold only once in 40 years; S & M paid several million dollars, and purchased the building in connection with its plan for major development of the block. The theoretical termination right of a future tenant of the existing building also must be viewed in light of these circumstances. If any uncertainty is generated by the two contingencies, then the benefit of that doubt must go to Van Wagner and not the contract violator. Neither contingency allegedly affecting Van Wagner's continued contractual right to the space for the balance of the lease term is within its own control; on the contrary, both are in the interest of S & M *(see,* by analogy, *Amerman v Deane, 132 NY 355 (1892))*. Thus, neither the need to project into the future nor the contingencies allegedly affecting the length of Van Wagner's term render inadequate the remedy of damages for S & M's breach of its lease with Van Wagner.

The trial court, additionally, correctly concluded that specific performance should be denied on the ground that such relief "would be inequitable in that its effect would be disproportionate in its harm to defendant and its assistance to plaintiff" *(see, Matter of Burke v Bowen, 40 NY2d 264, 267 (1976); Cox v City of New York, 265 NY 411 (1934)*; Restatement [Second] of Contracts § 364 [1] [b])*. It is well settled that the imposition of an equitable remedy must not itself work an inequity, and that specific performance should not be an undue hardship *(see,* Pomeroy and Mann, Specific Performance of Contracts § 185 [3d ed 1926])*. This conclusion is "not within the absolute discretion of the Supreme Court" *(McClure v Leaycraft, 183 NY 36, 42 (1905)*; *see, Trustees of Columbia Col. v Thacher, 87 NY 311*; *cf. Forstmann v Joray Holding Co., 244 NY 22)*. Here, however, there was no abuse of discretion; the finding that specific performance would disproportionately harm S & M and benefit Van Wagner has been affirmed by the Appellate Division and has support in the proof regarding S & M's projected development of the property.

While specific performance was properly denied, the court erred in its assessment of damages. Our attention is drawn to two alleged errors.

First, both parties are dissatisfied with the award of lost profits on the Asch contract: Van Wagner contends that the award was too low because it failed to take into account incidental damages such as sign construction, and S & M asserts that it was too high because it failed to take into account offsets against alleged lost profits such as painting costs. Both arguments are precluded. Although the trial was not bifurcated or limited to the issue of liability, the Asch contract was placed in evidence and neither party chose to submit additional proof of incidental damages or other expenses for that period. Nor—as is evident from the judgment—did the trial court understand that any separate presentations would be made as to damages for that period. Based on the Asch contract indicating revenues, and the lease indicating expenses, the trial court properly calculated Van Wagner's lost profits. Having found that the value of the space was fixed by the Asch contract for the entire period of that contract, however, the court erred in awarding the lost revenues only through November 23, 1983. Damages should have been awarded for the duration of the Asch contract.

Second, the court fashioned relief for S & M's breach of contract only to the time of trial, and expressly contemplated that "[if] defendant continues to exclude plaintiff from the leased space action for continuing damages may be brought." In requiring Van Wagner to bring a multiplicity of suits to recover its damages the court erred. Damages should have been awarded through the expiration of Van Wagner's lease.

Accordingly, the order of the Appellate Division should be modified, with costs to plaintiff, and the case remitted to Supreme Court, New York County, for further proceedings in accordance with this opinion and, as so modified, affirmed.

* * *

UCC § 2–716, which is the buyer-side analog to the seller's action for the price under UCC § 2–709, addresses the question of specific performance in statutory form. It is widely understood to liberalize the availability of specific performance. Most obviously, the Code makes specific performance available not just when goods are unique but also "in other proper circumstances."[4] For example, sellers in output contracts (in which a buyer agrees to purchase a seller's entire product) or buyers in requirements contracts (in which a seller agrees to supply a buyer's entire demand) may receive specific performance even when the goods at issue are not themselves unique, or even distinctive, by showing that their contracting partners are distinctively reliable sources of demand or supply. Moreover, the UCC is also widely taken to relax the standard of uniqueness itself, so that uniqueness does not require that a good be literally one-of-a-kind—for example, a family portrait or a distinctive antique—but only that finding a substitute is not economical.

Sedmak is perhaps typical of cases under this doctrinal strand of the UCC. The plaintiff and defendant entered into an oral contract for the purchase and sale of a specially equipped limited edition (one of 6000 made) Chevrolet Corvette at a price of $15,000. The car became a hot item, and the defendants, on receiving offers from other buyers for almost $30,000, declared that they would not honor their agreement with the plaintiffs, who would have to bid anew for the car against these other potential buyers. The plaintiffs sued, seeking specific performance. The court observed the UCC's intent to liberalize the standard for specific performance. It concluded that under this standard, the difficulty that the plaintiffs would face in obtaining a substitute limited edition Corvette (a difficulty

---

4. Note that UCC § 2–716 also addresses the buyer's use of specific performance as a self-help remedy. Here, the UCC identifies the conditions under which he may exercise his right of replevin; that is, his right to take possession of the disputed goods even prior to a judicial determination of his claim. Note that this section of the UCC functions, at least when conditions set out in § 2–716(3) are met, to create a specific performance remedy that the courts have no discretion to refuse.

illustrated by the aggressive efforts of other buyers to acquire the car at issue in the case) was sufficient to justify granting the remedy.[5]

Nevertheless, plaintiffs do not always win specific performance, even under the UCC, as *Klein* illustrates. And although the result in *Klein* is probably less typical than the result in *Sedmak*, it certainly should not be ignored. The plaintiff in *Klein* contracted to buy a Gulfstream GII airplane from the defendant, and when the defendant pulled out of the deal, the plaintiff sued, seeking specific performance. Although the trial court awarded specific performance, the appeals court reversed (and indeed reversed even though, being an equitable remedy, an order of specific performance is reviewed for abuse of discretion only). Specifically, although the trial court found the GII unique, the appeals court observed that 21 other GII's were on the market, three of which were comparable, and that the plaintiff had in fact bid on two of these. This, the appeals court thought, was sufficient to reject the airplane's uniqueness. Moreover, the appeals court also concluded that the case did not present the "other proper circumstances" for specific performance referred to by the UCC. The plaintiff claimed that a sharp rise in the market price of GII's constituted a circumstance justifying specific performance, but the appeals court disagreed, observing that both cover- and market-based damages might make the plaintiff whole in spite of the rise.

Taken together, *Sedmak* and *Klein* illustrate the uncertainty that exists concerning specific performance. The outcomes in the two cases, at least when viewed in combination, seem counterintuitive: was the Corvette in *Sedmak*—one of 6000—really more unique than the airplane in *Klein*— one of only 21 (or even of only 3)? *Sedmak* is, in this respect, probably truer to the UCC, and more representative of the run of cases, than *Klein*. The official comment to UCC § 2–716 observes that "inability to cover is strong evidence of 'other proper circumstances' " rendering an award of specific performance appropriate. Moreover, it makes sense to read inability to cover generously, to encompass cases like *Klein*. After all, the *Klein* holding seems to have the unpalatable consequence for buyers in rising markets: either they must cover and bear the risk that their cover will be deemed unreasonable (perhaps because given the rising prices, they should have bought a substitute good, such as the GIII in *Klein*, instead); or they must seek market-based damages and bear the expense and risk of proving up an appropriate market price (and indeed of being told that they should reasonably have covered). These difficulties render the expectation remedy significantly under-compensatory, at least in circumstances like those in *Klein*. Specific performance is a way of avoiding such under-compensation.

Regardless of whether *Sedmak* or *Klein* reaches the better outcome, the reasoning in both opinions remains unsatisfying. The discussions of

---

5. The other issue in the case was whether the contract (being based on an oral agreement) satisfied the UCC's requirement that contracts for the sale of goods for over $500 be in writing. The court (based on careful interpretation of the statute) concluded that the requirement was satisfied by the buyer's payment of a deposit. The validity of oral contracts and the requirement of writings in certain circumstances will be taken up later in the materials, in connection with the Statute of Frauds.

uniqueness in the two opinions are, without more, conclusory. Almost no good is literally unique, in the sense of being the only one of kind that admits of no proxies. Instead, there are always substitutes for every good, so that the question inevitably becomes just how imperfect or inadequate the substitutes must be for a good to count as unique. Accordingly, when the opinions announce that a good is unique or not, this gives little insight into their reasoning but instead appears simply to report their conclusions about whether or not specific performance will be ordered. What is needed, to make sense of the law, is an account that reduced the attribution of uniqueness to more primitive terms.

Van Wagner tries to be a little more systematic—to elaborate a positive theory of what, as general rule, constitutes uniqueness. The plaintiff in Van Wagner entered into a three-year lease of billboard space on an exterior wall of a building facing an exit ramp out of the Midtown tunnel into Manhattan. When the defendants bought the building and cancelled the lease, the plaintiff sued, seeking specific performance. The trial court denied the plaintiff's request, and the Court of Appeals affirmed (finding no abuse of discretion). In doing so, the high court presented a theory of uniqueness to serve as a solid foundation to support the otherwise impressionistic and indeed conclusory judgments that seem to dominate cases such as *Sedmak* and *Klein*.

The argument of the *Van Wagner* opinion proceeds in two stages. The first is to recognize that (at least in commercial contracts) uniqueness is an economic and not a physical property. Even a literally one-of-a-kind good is not unique if it has ready and fully satisfactory economic substitutes; and even a good that has many replicas may be unique if neither these (nor any substitutes) are available to a plaintiff who has been deprived of it. The second stage in the *Van Wagner* argument is to recognize that economic substitutability must be given an interpretation suitable to the imperfect actual world and not the perfect world of ideal economic theory. Even if every good is substitutable in principle, in the sense that there exists a sum of money that will leave a plaintiff indifferent between receiving it and the good in question, reliably divining this sum is not always possible in practice, and certainly not with acceptable accuracy and at an acceptable cost. Whether or not a good is unique in the sense meant by the doctrinal test for specific performance depends, therefore, on whether the money damages needed to provide an adequate substitute may be reasonably calculated.[6] In *Van Wagner* itself, the court concluded, the existence of a mature and well-functioning market for billboard space meant that, although the location of the lease at issue was physically unique, the economic value of the least could reasonably be measured, so that the lease was not economically unique, and specific performance should not be awarded.

Sedmak, *Klein*, and *Van Wagner* together illustrate the range of positions, and the styles of reasoning, that courts adopt in addressing

---

6. In reasoning in this way, the court followed Anthony Kronman, *Specific Performance*, 45 U. CHI. L. REV. 351 (1978).

specific performance in ordinary commercial settings. Douglas Laycock, who has likely read more cases on this question than anyone else in the world, summarizes the state of play as follows.[7] At one extreme, specific performance is always granted when cover is simply impossible, because the goods are literally one-of-a-kind, and it is granted without asking whether money damages could adequately compensate the plaintiff for being conclusively deprived of the actual contractual performance. At the other extreme, specific performance is never an issue, because it is never sought, when cover is trivially possible, since a disappointed promisee can simply take his money damages and acquire a perfect substitute for the promised contractual performance. All the uncertainty, Laycock proposes, arises in intermediate cases, in which cover is not literally impossible but is genuinely difficult and costly. Here, as *Sedmak* and *Klein* illustrate, courts go both ways.

Laycock concludes from this that specific performance is a much more prominent remedy for breach of contract than the law acknowledges, and indeed that there is a sense in which specific performance is the central remedy that the law offers: money damages, Laycock says, are awarded in preference over specific performance only when they allow a disappointed promisee to buy the precise performance that he was deprived of by the breach, only that is, when they serve to secure *replacement* performance and not when they merely *compensate* for an enduring deprivation of the thing that was actually promised.

This conclusion is perhaps somewhat overstated. Most narrowly, it is not hard to find counter-examples to Laycock's summary of the law: *Van Wagner* itself seems to present one, since specific performance was denied even though the leased space could not be replaced by money damages, which did merely compensate. Moreover, Laycock's view underestimates the prominence of the intermediate cases, in which plaintiffs facing difficult but not impossible cover are left (at least by some courts) to recoup only money damages and (given the burdens of covering) abandon the quest for replacement performance, preferring instead to keep these damages as compensation for use in some venture entirely different from that contemplated in the breach contract. Next, and probably more importantly, Laycock underestimates the extent to which contract law and the commercial practices that arise through it have expanded the class of things that count as replacement performance, to include many remedies that might but for this legal ordering be thought of as merely compensatory: money damages awarded to a buyer for breach of a fuel contract, and used to acquire an alternative source of energy, count for Laycock as supplying replacement performance, even though the new energy source is chemically and physically different from the promised fuel, so that the money damages might ordinarily be understood more along the lines of compensation. Finally, Laycock's conclusion ignores the conceptual possibility, explored at greater length below, that many contracts should be interpreted to count

---

7. Laycock develops these conclusions in DOUGLAS LAYCOCK, THE DEATH OF THE IRREPARABLE INJURY RULE (1991).

paying money damages (even when these damages cannot be used to replace the primary performance) as a secondary form of performance. In this case, specific performance becomes the principal contractual remedy, but in a formal rather than a substantive sense.

In any event, it is surely right that the law's official position that specific performance is an extraordinary remedy is significantly, and increasingly, overstated, at least in connection with ordinary commercial contracts. These are not the only kinds of contracts, however, and as the next case illustrates, the question of specific performance becomes more fraught when contracts address subjects besides the sale of goods, for example when they govern ongoing relations among the parties, and especially when they address the provision of personal services.

American Broadcasting Companies, Inc. v. Wolf

Court of Appeals of New York, 1981.
420 N.E.2d 363.

OPINION OF THE COURT. This case provides an interesting insight into the fierce competition in the television industry for popular performers and favorable ratings. It requires legal resolution of a rather novel employment imbroglio.

The issue is whether plaintiff American Broadcasting Companies, Incorporated (ABC), is entitled to equitable relief against defendant Warner Wolf, a New York City sportscaster, because of Wolf's breach of a good faith negotiation provision of a now expired broadcasting contract with ABC. In the present circumstances, it is concluded that the equitable relief sought by plaintiff—which would have the effect of forcing Wolf off the air—may not be granted.

I.

Warner Wolf, a sportscaster who has developed a rather colorful and unique on-the-air personality, had been employed by ABC since 1976. In February, 1978, ABC and Wolf entered into an employment agreement which, following exercise of a renewal option, was to terminate on March 5, 1980. The contract contained a clause, known as a good faith negotiation and first-refusal provision, that is at the crux of this litigation: "You agree, if we so elect, during the last ninety (90) days prior to the expiration of the extended term of this agreement, to enter into good faith negotiations with us for the extension of this agreement on mutually agreeable terms. You further agree that for the first forty-five (45) days of this renegotiation period, you will not negotiate for your services with any other person or company other than WABC–TV or ABC. In the event we are unable to reach an agreement for an extension by the expiration of the extended term hereof, you agree that you will not accept, in any market for a period of three (3) months following expiration of the extended term of this agreement, any offer of employment as a sportscaster, sports news reporter, commentator, program host, or analyst in broadcasting (including television, cable television, pay television and radio) without first giving us, in writing, an opportunity to employ you on substantially similar terms and you agree to enter into an agreement with us on such terms." Under this provision, Wolf was bound to negotiate in good faith with ABC for the 90–day period from December 6, 1979 through March 4, 1980. For the first 45 days, December 6 through January 19, the negotiation with ABC was to be exclusive. Following expiration of the 90–day negotiating period and the contract on March 5, 1980, Wolf was required, before *accepting* any other offer, to afford ABC a right of first refusal; he could comply with this provision either by refraining from accepting another offer or by first tendering the offer to ABC. The first-refusal period expired on June 3, 1980 and on June 4 Wolf was free to accept any job opportunity, without obligation to ABC.

Wolf first met with ABC executives in September, 1979 to discuss the terms of a renewal contract. Counterproposals were exchanged, and the parties agreed to finalize the matter by October 15. Meanwhile, unbeknownst to ABC, Wolf met with representatives of CBS in early October. Wolf related his employment requirements and also discussed the first refusal-good faith negotiation clause of his ABC contract. Wolf furnished CBS a copy of that portion of the ABC agreement. On October 12, ABC officials and Wolf met, but were unable to reach agreement on a renewal contract. A few days later, on October 16 Wolf again discussed employment possibilities with CBS.

Not until January 2, 1980 did ABC again contact Wolf. At that time, ABC expressed its willingness to meet substantially all of his demands. Wolf rejected the offer, however, citing ABC's delay in communicating with him and his desire to explore his options in light of the impending expiration of the 45–day exclusive negotiation period.

On February 1, 1980, after termination of that exclusive period, Wolf and CBS orally agreed on the terms of Wolf's employment as sportscaster for WCBS–TV, a CBS-owned affiliate in New York. During the next two days, CBS informed Wolf that it had prepared two agreements and divided his annual compensation between the two: one covered his services as an on-the-air sportscaster, and the other was an off-the-air production agreement for sports specials Wolf was to produce. The production agreement contained an exclusivity clause which barred Wolf from performing "services of any nature for" or permitting the use of his "name, likeness, voice or endorsement by, any person, firm or corporation" during the term of the agreement, unless CBS consented. The contract had an effective date of March 6, 1980.

Wolf signed the CBS production agreement on February 4, 1980. At the same time, CBS agreed in writing, in consideration of $100 received from Wolf, to hold open an offer of employment to Wolf as sportscaster until June 4, 1980, the date on which Wolf became free from ABC's right of first refusal. The next day, February 5, Wolf submitted a letter of resignation to ABC.

Representatives of ABC met with Wolf on February 6 and made various offers and promises that Wolf rejected. Wolf informed ABC that they had delayed negotiations with him and downgraded his worth. He stated he had no future with the company. He told the officials he had made a "gentlemen's agreement" and would leave ABC on March 5. Later in February, Wolf and ABC agreed that Wolf would continue to appear on the air during a portion of the first-refusal period, from March 6 until May 28.[1]

ABC commenced this action on May 6, 1980, by which time Wolf's move to CBS had become public knowledge. The complaint alleged that Wolf, induced by CBS, breached both the good-faith negotiation and first-refusal provisions of his contract with ABC. ABC sought specific enforcement of its right of first refusal and an injunction against Wolf's employment as a sportscaster with CBS.

After a trial, Supreme Court found no breach of the contract, and went on to note that, in any event, equitable relief would be inappropriate. A divided Appellate Division, while concluding that Wolf had breached both the good-faith negotiation and first-refusal provisions, nonetheless affirmed on the ground that equitable intervention was unwarranted. There should be an affirmance.

II.

Initially, we agree with the Appellate Division that defendant Wolf breached his obligation to negotiate in good faith with ABC from December, 1979 through March, 1980. When Wolf signed the production agreement with CBS on February 4, 1980, he obligated himself not to render services "of any nature" to any person, firm or corporation on and after March 6, 1980. Quite simply, then, beginning on February 4 Wolf was unable to extend his contract with ABC; his contract with CBS precluded him from legally serving ABC in any capacity after March 5. Given Wolf's existing obligation to CBS, any negotiations he engaged in with ABC, without the consent of CBS, after February 4 were meaningless and could not have been in good faith.

At the same time, there is no basis in the record for the Appellate Division's conclusion that Wolf violated the first-refusal provision by entering into an oral sports casting contract with CBS on February 4. The first-refusal provision required Wolf, for a period of 90 days after termination of the ABC agreement, either to refrain from accepting an offer of employment or to first submit the offer to ABC for its consideration. By its own terms, the right of first refusal did not apply to offers accepted by Wolf prior to the March 5 termination of the ABC employment contract. It is apparent, therefore, that Wolf could not have breached the right of first refusal by accepting an offer during the term of his employment with ABC.[2]

---

1. The agreement also provided that on or after June 4, 1980 Wolf was free to "accept an offer of employment with anyone of [his] choosing and immediately begin performing on-air services." The parties agreed that their rights and obligations under the original employment contract were in no way affected by the extension of employment.

2. In any event, the carefully tailored written agreement between Wolf and CBS consisted only of an option prior to June 4, 1979. Acceptance of CBS's offer of employment as

Rather, his conduct violates only the good-faith negotiation clause of the contract. The question is whether this breach entitled ABC to injunctive relief that would bar Wolf from continued employment at CBS.[3] To resolve this issue, it is necessary to trace the principles of specific performance applicable to personal service contracts.

III.

-A-

Courts of equity historically have refused to order an individual to perform a contract for personal services. Originally this rule evolved because of the inherent difficulties courts would encounter in supervising the performance of uniquely personal efforts.[4] During the Civil War era, there emerged a more compelling reason for not directing the performance of personal services: the Thirteenth Amendment's prohibition of involuntary servitude. It has been strongly suggested that judicial compulsion of services would violate the express command of that amendment.[5] For practical, policy and constitutional reasons, therefore, courts continue to decline to affirmatively enforce employment contracts.

Over the years, however, in certain narrowly tailored situations, the law fashioned other remedies for failure to perform an employment agreement. Thus, where an employee refuses to render services to an employer in violation of an existing contract, and the services are unique or extraordinary, an injunction may issue to prevent the employee from furnishing those services to another person for the duration of the contract (see, e.g., *Shubert Theatrical Co. v Gallagher, 206 App Div 514 (1923)*). Such "negative enforcement" was initially available only when the employee had

---

a sportscaster did not occur until after the expiration of the first-refusal period on June 4, 1979.

3. In its complaint, ABC originally sought specific enforcement of the right of first refusal. ABC now suggests that Wolf be enjoined from performing services for CBS for a two-year period. Alternatively, ABC requests this court to "turn the clock back to February 1, 1980" by: (1) setting aside Wolf's agreement with CBS and enjoining CBS from enforcing the agreement; (2) ordering Wolf to enter into good-faith negotiations with ABC for at least the period remaining under the negotiation clause when Wolf breached it; (3) ordering Wolf to honor the 90–day first-refusal period should the parties fail to reach agreement; and (4) enjoining CBS from negotiating with Wolf "for a period sufficient to render meaningful the above-described relief."

4. The New York Court of Chancery in *De Rivafinoli v. Corsetti* (4 Paige Chs. 264, 270) eloquently articulated the traditional rationale for refusing affirmative enforcement of personal service contracts: "I am not aware that any officer of this court has that perfect knowledge of the Italian language, or possesses that exquisite sensibility in the auricular nerve which is necessary to understand, and to enjoy with a proper zest, the peculiar beauties of the Italian opera, so fascinating to the fashionable world. There might be some difficulty, therefore, even if the defendant was compelled to sing under the direction and in the presence of a master in chancery, in ascertaining whether he performed his engagement according to its spirit and intent. It would also be very difficult for the master to determine what effect coercion might produce upon the defendant's singing, especially in the livelier airs; although the fear of imprisonment would unquestionably deepen his seriousness in the graver parts of the drama. But one thing at least is certain; his songs will be neither comic, or even semi-serious, while he remains confined in that dismal cage, the debtor's prison of New York."

5. It is well established that legislative enactments may not coerce performance of services by penalizing nonperformance. *See, e.g.,* People v. Lavender, 398 N.E. 2d 530, 531–533 (1979).

expressly stipulated not to compete with the employer for the term of the engagement Later cases permitted injunctive relief where the circumstances justified implication of a negative covenant. In these situations, an injunction is warranted because the employee either expressly or by clear implication agreed not to work elsewhere for the period of his contract. And, since the services must be unique before negative enforcement will be granted, irreparable harm will befall the employer should the employee be permitted to labor for a competitor (see 5A Corbin, Contracts, § 1206, at p 412).

-B-

After a personal service contract terminates, the availability of equitable relief against the former employee diminishes appreciably. Since the period of service has expired, it is impossible to decree affirmative or negative specific performance. Only if the employee has expressly agreed not to compete with the employer following the term of the contract, or is threatening to disclose trade secrets or commit another tortious act, is injunctive relief generally available at the behest of the employer. Even where there is an express anticompetitive covenant, however, it will be rigorously examined and specifically enforced only if it satisfies certain established requirements.

Indeed, a court normally will not decree specific enforcement of an employee's anticompetitive covenant unless necessary to protect the trade secrets, customer lists or good will of the employer's business, or perhaps when the employer is exposed to special harm because of the unique nature of the employee's services.[6] And, an otherwise valid covenant will not be enforced if it is unreasonable in time, space or scope or would operate in a harsh or oppressive manner. There is, in short, general judicial disfavor of anticompetitive covenants contained in employment contracts (e.g., *Reed, Roberts Assoc. v Strauman, supra, at p 307 (1976)*).

Underlying the strict approach to enforcement of these covenants is the notion that, once the term of an employment agreement has expired, the general public policy favoring robust and uninhibited competition should not give way merely because a particular employer wishes to insulate himself from competition. Important, too, are the "powerful considerations of public policy which militate against sanctioning the loss of a man's livelihood" *(Purchasing Assoc. v Weitz, 13 NY2d, at p 272, supra)*. At the same time, the employer is entitled to protection from unfair or illegal conduct that causes economic injury. The rules governing enforcement of anticompetitive covenants and the availability of equitable relief after termination of employment are designed to foster these interests of the employer without impairing the employee's ability to earn a living or the general competitive mold of society.

---

6. Although an employee's anticompetitive covenant may be enforceable where the employee's services were special or unique, *Reed, Roberts Assoc., Inc. v. Strauman,* 40 N.Y. 2d 303, 308 (1976); *Purchasing Assoc., Inc. v. Weitz*, 13 N.Y. 2d 267, 272–273 (1963), no New York case has been found where enforcement has been granted, following termination of the employment contract, solely on the basis of the uniqueness of the services.

-C-

Specific enforcement of personal service contracts thus turns initially upon whether the term of employment has expired. If the employee refuses to perform during the period of employment, was furnishing unique services, has expressly or by clear implication agreed not to compete for the duration of the contract and the employer is exposed to irreparable injury, it may be appropriate to restrain the employee from competing until the agreement expires. Once the employment contract has terminated, by contrast, equitable relief is potentially available only to prevent injury from unfair competition or similar tortious behavior or to enforce an express and valid anticompetitive covenant. In the absence of such circumstances, the general policy of unfettered competition should prevail.

IV.

Applying these principles, it is apparent that ABC's request for injunctive relief must fail. There is no existing employment agreement between the parties; the original contract terminated in March, 1980. Thus, the negative enforcement that might be appropriate during the term of employment is unwarranted here. Nor is there an express anticompetitive covenant that defendant Wolf is violating, or any claim of special injury from tortious conduct such as exploitation of trade secrets. In short, ABC seeks to premise equitable relief after termination of the employment upon a simple, albeit serious, breach of a general contract negotiation clause.[7] To grant an injunction in that situation would be to unduly interfere with an individual's livelihood and to inhibit free competition where there is no corresponding injury to the employer other than the loss of a competitive edge. Indeed, if relief were granted here, any breach of an employment contract provision relating to renewal negotiations logically would serve as the basis for an open-ended restraint upon the employee's ability to earn a living should he ultimately choose not to extend his employment.[8] Our public policy, which favors the free exchange of goods and services through established market mechanisms, dictates otherwise.

Equally unavailing is ABC's request that the court create a noncompetitive covenant by implication. Although in a proper case an implied-in-fact covenant not to compete for the term of employment may be found to exist,

---

7. Even if Wolf had breached the first-refusal provision, it does not necessarily follow that injunctive relief would be available. Outside the personal service area, the usual equitable remedy for breach of a first-refusal clause is to order the breaching party to perform the contract with the person possessing the first-refusal right (e.g., 5A Corbin, Contracts, § 1197, at pp 377–378). When personal services are involved, this would result in an affirmative injunction ordering the employee to perform services for plaintiff. Such relief, as discussed, cannot be granted.

8. Interestingly, the negative enforcement ABC seeks—an injunction barring Wolf from broadcasting for CBS—is for a two-year period. ABC's request is premised upon the fact that Wolf and CBS entered into a two-year agreement. Had the agreement been for 10 years, presumably ABC would have requested a 10–year restraint. In short, since it lacks an express anticompetitive clause to enforce, plaintiff seeks to measure its relief in a manner unrelated to the breach or the injury. This well illustrates one of the reasons why the law requires an express anticompetitive clause before it will restrain an employee from competing after termination of the employment.

anticompetitive covenants covering the postemployment period will not be implied.[9] Indeed, even an express covenant will be scrutinized and enforced only in accordance with established principles.

This is not to say that ABC has not been damaged in some fashion or that Wolf should escape responsibility for the breach of his good-faith negotiation obligation.[10] Rather, we merely conclude that ABC is not entitled to equitable relief. Because of the unique circumstances presented, however, this decision is without prejudice to ABC's right to pursue relief in the form of monetary damages, if it be so advised.

Accordingly, the order of the Appellate Division should be affirmed.

■ FUCHSBERG, J., dissenting. I agree with all the members of this court, as had all the Justices at the Appellate Division, that the defendant Wolf breached his undisputed obligation to negotiate in good faith for renewal of his contract with ABC. Where we part company is in the majority's unwillingness to mold an equitable decree, even one more limited than the harsh one the plaintiff proposed, to right the wrong.

Central to the disposition of this case is the first-refusal provision. Its terms are worth recounting. They plainly provide that, in the 90–day period immediately succeeding the termination of his ABC contract, before Wolf could accept a position as sportscaster with another company, he first had to afford ABC the opportunity to engage him on like terms. True, he was not required to entertain offers, whether from ABC or anyone else, during that period. In that event he, of course, would be off the air for that 90 days, during which ABC could attempt to orient its listeners from Wolf to his successor. On the other hand, if Wolf wished to continue to broadcast actively during the 90 days, ABC's right of first refusal put it in a position to make sure that Wolf was not doing so for a competitor. One way or the other, however labeled, the total effect of the first refusal agreement was that of an express conditional covenant under which Wolf could be restricted from appearing on the air other than for ABC for the 90–day post termination period.

One need not be in the broadcasting business to understand that the restriction ABC bargained for, and Wolf granted, when they entered into

---

9. Of course, as discussed, tortious interference with the employer's business by a former employee may sometimes be enjoined absent a noncompetitive covenant.

10. It should be noted that the dissenter would ground relief upon the first-refusal clause, a provision of the contract that defendant did not breach. The dissenting opinion fails to specify why the first-refusal clause—or for that matter any other provision of the contract that defendant did not breach—is relevant in determining the availability of equitable relief. And, while the dissent correctly noted the flexibility of equitable remedies, this does not mean that courts of equity totally dispense with governing rules. Our analysis of the relevant principles, guided by important underlying policy considerations, reveals that this case falls well beyond the realm where equitable intervention would be permissible.

The dissenting opinion would now create a new agreement for the parties, and apply the first-refusal clause backwards into the period of the ABC employment, under the guise of equitable interpretation. Although the reach of equity may be broad, so far as we are aware equitable principles have never sanctioned the creation of a new and different contract between sophisticated parties merely to condemn conduct which was permissible under an actual written agreement.

the original employment contract was not inconsequential. The earnings of broadcasting companies are directly related to the "ratings" they receive. This, in turn, is at least in part dependent on the popularity of personalities like Wolf. It therefore was to ABC's advantage, once Wolf came into its employ, especially since he was new to the New York market, that it enhance his popularity by featuring, advertising and otherwise promoting him. This meant that the loyalty of at least part of the station's listening audience would become identified with Wolf, thus enhancing his potential value to competitors, as witness the fact that, in place of the $250,000 he was receiving during his last year with ABC, he was able to command $400,000 to $450,000 per annum in his CBS "deal". A reasonable opportunity during which ABC could cope with such an assault on its good will had to be behind the clause in question.

Moreover, it is undisputed that, when in late February Wolf executed the contract for an extension of employment during the 90–day hiatus for which the parties had bargained, ABC had every right to expect that Wolf had not already committed himself to an exclusivity provision in a producer's contract with CBS in violation of the good-faith negotiation clause (see majority opn at pp 397–398). Surely, had ABC been aware of this gross breach, had it not been duped into giving an uninformed consent, it would not have agreed to serve as a self-destructive vehicle for the further enhancement of Wolf's potential for taking his ABC-earned following with him.

In the face of these considerations, the majority rationalizes its position of powerlessness to grant equitable relief by choosing to interpret the contract as though there were no restrictive covenant, express or implied. However, as demonstrated, there is, in fact, an express three-month negative covenant which, because of Wolf's misconduct, ABC was effectively denied the opportunity to exercise. Enforcement of this covenant, by enjoining Wolf from broadcasting for a three-month period, would depart from no entrenched legal precedent. Rather, it would accord with equity's boasted flexibility.

That said, a few words are in order regarding the majority's insistence that Wolf did not breach the first-refusal clause. It is remarkable that, to this end, it has to ignore its own crediting of the Appellate Division's express finding that, as far back as February 1, 1980, fully a month before the ABC contract was to terminate, "Wolf and CBS orally agreed on the terms of Wolf's employment as sportscaster for WCBS–TV" (majority opn, at p 399; see *American Broadcasting Cos. v Wolf, 76 AD2d 162, 166, 170–171 (1980)*. It follows that the overt written CBS–Wolf option contract, which permitted Wolf to formally accept the CBS sports casting offer at the end of the first-refusal period, was nothing but a charade.

Further, on this score, the majority's premise that Wolf could not have breached the first-refusal clause when he accepted the producer's agreement, exclusivity provision and all, *during* the term of his ABC contract, does not withstand analysis. So precious a reading of the arrangement with ABC frustrates the very purpose for which it had to have been made. Such a classical exaltation of form over substance is hardly to be countenanced by equity (see *Washer v Seager, 272 App Div 297 (1947)*, affd *297 NY 918 (1948)*).

For all these reasons, in my view, literal as well as proverbial justice should have brought a modification of the order of the Appellate Division to include a 90–day injunction—no more and no less than the relatively short and certainly not unreasonable transitional period for which ABC and Wolf struck their bargain.

* * *

In *Wolf*, the plaintiff, a television network, and the defendant, a sports presenter, entered into a complicated contract to govern their negotiations concerning the possible renewal of the defendant's contract to present a popular sports show broadcast on the plaintiff's station. This contract imposed on the defendant various obligations to negotiate with the plaintiff in good faith for one period of time and exclusively for another, and to offer the plaintiff a right of first refusal before accepting an offer to work as a broadcaster for another station. In spite of this, the defendant contracted to work for another station, first in production and then as a sportscaster. The plaintiff sued, and a court concluded that the defendant had breached the agreement to negotiate in good faith, although it also concluded (over a dissent) that he had not breached the first-refusal provision. The main issue in the case concerned the appropriate remedy.

It was effectively conceded by the parties that the defendant's services, at least as an on-air sports personality, were unique, indeed in the literal sense of being one-of-a-kind. Nevertheless, an injunction ordering the defendant to go back to work for the plaintiff as a sportscaster was never even considered, for two reasons. First, such an order would have involved the court in supervising complex ongoing relations between the parties—to determine whether the defendant continued to perform to his traditional standards, for example—and this is a burden that courts only reluctantly, and therefore rarely, accept. Second, it is a holdover from specific performance's equitable origins that the remedy will not be ordered when it would impose an undue hardship on a defendant. This general principle underwrites the more particular rule that contracts for the provision of personal services are never specifically enforced, since to do so would unduly burden those compelled to provide the personal services.[8]

---

8. Two observations are worth making in the margin. First, specifically enforcing a personal services contract is plausibly Unconstitutional, because it would violate the Thirteenth Amendment's prohibition on slavery. The contract doctrine against specifically enforcing personal services contracts does not, however, depend on this Constitutional argument. And second, neither the Constitutional principle nor the rule of contract law applies to contracts for the provision of services that are *not* personal. *These* doctrines (at least) would not prevent a contract between ABC and Wolf, Inc., for Wolf, Inc. to provide one of its (many) employees to work as a broadcaster for ABC, from being specifically enforceable against Wolf, Inc., although objections to specific performance based on courts' reluctance to supervise complex, ongoing relations would continue unabated. (The principles would, of course, prevent Wolf, Inc. from specifically enforcing its contracts with its employees.)

The question of specific performance did, however, arise in the case, albeit in another form. The plaintiff sought an injunction preventing the defendant from working for competitor stations. The injunction was denied, but only after a more intricate argument. Specifically, such an injunction against a past employer may be granted where a unique employee has expressly or by clear implication covenanted not to compete, although subject to certain limits. (Such injunctions are sometimes called, unhappily, orders of "negative specific performance." What they really are, of course, is orders specifically enforcing a negative covenant.) First, where the unique employee breaches his employment contract and seeks to serve another employer during the period of the employment contract, then an injunction against working for competitors can be granted if the employee covenanted not to compete either expressly or by clear implication. And second, where the unique employee seeks to serve a competitor only after his employment contract has terminated, the injunction may be granted only if the employee has expressly agreed not to compete with his employer following the termination of the contract or if the employee is threatening to disclose trade secrets or commit another tortious act. Moreover, even where an express covenant not to compete following termination of employment exists, it will be vigorously examined and specifically enforced only if it is not unreasonable in its extent and does not operated in a harsh or oppressive manner. (Note that this formulation really just elaborates the general idea that specific performance will not be granted where it would impose undue hardship on the defendant, as this idea applies in the context of covenants not to compete.)

The court applied these rules to the plaintiff's request that the defendant be enjoined from working for its competitor. The court concluded that the defendant's employment contract with the plaintiff had expired before he began the employment with the competitor that the plaintiff sought to enjoin. Furthermore, the court—recurring to its earlier interpretations of the first-refusal provision and its earlier conclusion that the defendant had not breached that provision—concluded that the defendant had not expressly covenanted not to compete with the plaintiff after the end of his period of employment for the plaintiff. And as courts will not (under the second of the two rules stated above) create such covenants by implication, the court concluded that the plaintiff's request for the injunction should be denied.[9]

9.2 THE CASE FOR SPECIFIC PERFORMANCE

Specific performance is an example of what is known as a *property rule* protection. That is, an order of specific performance does not require a promisor contemplating a breach to compensate her promisee for a harm

---

9. The dissenter, who interpreted the first-refusal provision more expansively than the majority and concluded that the defendant had breached it, would have applied the same legal regime to enjoin the defendant from working for the competitor for the 90 day period contemplated by the first-refusal provision.

that she is free to cause (as long as she pays compensation) but rather instructs the promisor not to cause the harm (not to breach), period. The expectation remedy, which allows the breach but requires compensation, is an example of a *liability rule* protection. It is worth pausing for a moment to observe that this pair of ways of protecting entitlements—via property rules and via liability rules—when combined with the possibility of two ways of allocating entitlements—to promisors and to promisees—creates four possible legal regimes to govern a contract relation:[10]

> First, the promisee may be entitled to have his contractual expectations vindicated, and this entitlement may be protected by a liability rule. This regime is established in law by the expectation remedy.

> Second, the promisee may be entitled to have his contractual expectations vindicated, and this entitlement may be protected by a property rule. This is regime exists where the law offers promisees specific performance.

> Third, the promisor may be entitled to abandon her undertakings, and this entitlement may be protected by a liability rule. In this case, the promisor could abandon her undertakings unless the promisee (on requiring the promisor to do as she had promised) paid her damages equal to the costs to her of performing. This regime has no common or prominent legal instantiation.

> Finally, the promisor may be entitled to abandon her undertakings, and this entitlement may be protected by a property rule. This case is again familiar in the law—it is just the case in which no contract is recognized.

This categorization is important because making it emphasizes that the question how to protect an entitlement is often just as important as the question to whom an entitlement should be allocated. A long and highly intricate series of articles has addressed this question, discussing when and why property rules and liability rules (and various more complex derivatives of these rules) are the most efficient legal regimes.

That literature is much too complex and difficult even to summarize here, but it should come as no surprise to hear that one of its central themes is that transactions costs—and in particular the costs of measuring damages as needed to implement liability rules and the costs of negotiating around property rules—matter in this context. If transactions costs are zero (or insignificantly low) then the choice between liability rules and property rules straightforwardly has no efficiency implications. In a zero transactions costs world, courts administering liability rules will costlessly set damages at precisely the efficient levels, and parties will costlessly anticipate damages set at these levels, with the result that the liability rules establish efficient incentives for all. Similarly, in a zero transactions

---

10. This way of organizing legal regimes was initiated by Guido Calabresi and A. Douglas Melamed in Guido Calabresi & A. Douglas Melamed, *Property Rules, Liability Rules, and Inalienability: One View of the Cathedral*, 85 HARV. L. REV. 1089 (1972).

costs world, parties will costly negotiate around any injunctions imposed under a property rule regime whenever it is efficient for them to do so. Most notably, promisors subject to orders of specific performance will costless buy out their promisees when and only when their gains of breaching exceed the costs that the breaches impose on the promisees. Again, property rule protections will support efficient behavior by all.

Of course, in the real world, transactions costs are never zero and are often highly significant. And in this world, liability rules face the difficulty that accurately measuring the damages that these rules call on courts to impose is costly for both courts and disputants, with the consequence that adjudication (in order to reduce these costs to manageable levels) must almost always make do with inaccurate damage awards. Liability rules therefore involve some inefficient distortions in the real world, especially when these inaccuracies are not symmetrical, so that damages tend systematically to be either under- or over-compensatory. Similarly, property rules applied to the real world face the difficulty that it is costly to negotiate around the injunctions that they involve. This is both because negotiation is always costly and because, as should be familiar from the earlier discussion of *Peeveyhouse* and *Groves*, injunctions that bind two parties into an exclusive negotiating relationship generate further, and distinctive, negotiation costs. That is because such injunctions place the parties into a relation of bilateral monopoly, in which each can deal only with the other, so that there are no third-party offers or market forces to discipline each side's demands (narrowing the range of disagreement by making it obvious that some demands are simply non-starters). Thus, although efficiency requires that a promisor who is prevented from making an efficient breach by an order of specific performance should buy out her promisee whenever her gains from breach exceed his losses, the negotiation over the terms of the buy-out may be so costly as to swallow up most or even all of the excess (and, in the latter case, prevent her efficient breach altogether).

The core case for the expectation remedy—developed earlier in these pages—emphasized the transactions costs associated with renegotiation following an order of specific performance but downplayed the transactions costs associated with measuring contractual expectations as needed to fix contract damages at efficient levels. However, many of the elaborations of the expectation regime that followed this core argument—including the materials concerning the certainty and foreseeability requirements, and some parts of the materials concerning lost profits and liquidated damages—may be read, in light of the current discussion, as admissions that this pattern of emphasis involved a mistake. In fact, it might be said, the transactions costs associated with calculating expectation damages are very large—so large that a substantial portion of the law of contract remedies is devoted to establishing legal presumptions that cut off certain damage calculations in order to reduce these costs. Moreover, these presumptions operate almost uniformly to reduce the size of the expectation damages that are actually awarded—eliminating speculative damages, for example, including especially damages that arise in respect of lost profits, or striking down over-liquidated damages clauses as penalties.[11] Accordingly, whatever may be true in theory, the expectation remedy as it operates in practice is likely substantially under-compensatory. And although perfect expectation damages may indeed be efficient, actual expectation damages therefore will not be.

The case for making specific performance more readily available for breach of contract has therefore got off the ground,[12] because specific performance must compete not with the highly efficient ideal perfectly compensatory expectation remedy but with the almost certainly under-compensatory, and therefore much less efficient, expectation remedy as actually administered.[13] Moreover, the transactions costs associated with specific performance—the costs of negotiating around an order specifically to perform a contract when efficiency requires that the contract not actually be performed—were likely exaggerated by the earlier argument in favor of expectation damages. To be sure, an order of specific performance may place a promisor and her promisee—a seller and her buyer—in a transactions costly bilateral monopoly. But it need not do. In particular, if a seller who receives a better offer for her goods and thus is tempted to make an efficient breach can herself cheaply cover—that is, purchase a second contractual performance from the market—then she will simply do so, serving her original promisee even as she garners the efficiency gains that tempted her to breach to begin with.

The bilateral monopoly generated by orders of specific performance, and the associated inefficiency, therefore arises only to the extent that sellers cannot cheaply cover. (Once again, when a seller who wishes efficiently to breach but faces an order of specific performance can cover sufficiently cheaply, she will simply take up the offer that triggered her desire to breach and, at the same time, serve her initial buyer, using replacement goods acquired in covering.) And this suggests that, at least as a first cut, the law should not generally reject specific performance (or indeed generally embrace it) but should instead tailor contract remedies according to whether sellers or buyers can more cheaply cover. When sellers can cover more cheaply, then specific performance is appropriate;

---

11. The doctrine that when limited remedies fail of their essential purposes the limitations are struck down and replaced with the full array of default remedies available under the UCC is a possible exception.

12. The development of this case in the coming pages follows Alan Schwartz, *The Case for Specific Performance*, 89 YALE L.J. 271 (1979).

13. It is worth noting, at this point, that the case for specific performance developed here does not answer—nor does it seek to address—the many piecemeal arguments that cut against specific performance in connection with special classes of contracts. Thus it remains true that specific performance of personal services contracts is perhaps Unconstitutional and certainly immoral, and that the ongoing supervision needed to administer specific performance of contracts that involve long term and discretionary relations would involve the courts in a quagmire. But although these objections to specific performance in certain cases are not answered by the argument in the main test, it is important to remember their piecemeal character. They may explain why specific performance should not be given in particular cases, but they cannot explain why specific performance should be generally disfavored by the law. That position relies heavily on the efficiency argument developed earlier in these materials, an argument that the current case for specific performance addresses head-on.

when buyers can cover more cheaply, then the expectation remedy is preferable.

These reflections suggest that the proper scope of the specific performance remedy depends on empirical questions concerning buyers' and sellers' relative cover costs. One view asserts that buyers can generally cover more cheaply, since they are practiced at buying and hence already possess the skills needed to find and acquire cover. As against this, it has been suggested that, at least in well-development markets, covering is so simple that there is no reason to think sellers are unable to cover as well as buyers. Both suggestions are plausible, although their truth depends on certain underlying facts about the natures of sellers, buyers, and the markets in which they operate. The case for specific performance seems now to turn on an empirical question.

The argument therefore seems to have reached an impasse, because there is little hope of resolving the empirical question whether buyers or sellers can cover more cheaply, certainly not for all cases and probably not even at a level of generality that can usefully inform doctrine. But there may be a way out of the impasse, reached by changing the terms of the argument. Even though the law may not be able to craft general rules concerning when buyers and sellers can cover more cheaply, the parties to specific contracts may be able to answer this question for their peculiar circumstances, one case at a time. And the law may be able to piggy-back on this knowledge by asking not which party can cover more cheaply and thus should have to cover but rather *which party is more likely to make the right choice about which party should have to cover.*

If specific performance is commonly available, then a buyer who is faced with a breaching seller can dictate who must cover: he can cover himself and seek money damages; or he can force his seller to cover simply by demanding (and getting) specific performance. Contrariwise, if specific performance is not routinely available, then a seller who confronts a better offer and so desires to breach can dictate who must cover: she can force the buyer to cover by breaching, or she can cover herself and service her original buyer even as she accepts the better offer also. So the choice between a legal regime that prefers specific performance and a legal regime (such as the current law) that prefers expectation damages turns on whether buyers or sellers are more likely to make efficient choices about who should cover. Which is it?

Proponents of specific performance have argued that buyers are more likely to make the right (that is, efficient) choice. They observe that because future dealings with a seller who is present only because of a court order will unlikely be smooth, pleasant, or profitable, buyers have little incentive to demand specific performance and every incentive not to. Accordingly, buyers will prefer to take money damages (as under the expectation remedy) unless these damages are in fact radically under-compensatory—that is, unless buyers are in fact extremely poorly placed to cover. And so, even when they are entitled to it, buyers will rarely demand specific performance, and then only when expectation damages are highly inefficient. Sellers, by contrast, may simply ignore the buyers whom their breaches have forced to cover, and so face no similar disciplinary mechanism.

Opponents of specific performance are not so sure that the incentives align in quite this way. To begin with, the reputational costs of breaching may dissuade sellers from doing so, even under an expectation damages regime, unless performing is radically inefficient, and this may exert a discipline over sellers much like the discipline of antagonistic contractual relations imposes on buyers. Moreover, sellers are subject to a second discipline for which there is no analog on the buyers' side: when a seller breaches and forces her buyer to cover, the damages assessed against her include (as incidental damages) the buyer's cover costs; by contrast, when a buyer demands specific performance and forces her seller to cover, he does not bear her cover costs (because she, after all, is in breach). Sellers, one might say, internalize their buyers' cover costs whereas buyers do not internalize their sellers' cover costs. And this gives sellers an additional reason to make the choice who should cover efficiently—a reason that buyers do not have. Ingenious as it is, the case for specific performance therefore remains less than fully persuasive.

One final wrinkle in the argument is worth mentioning here, not least because it grows naturally out of the observation that sellers internalize the cover costs that they impose on buyers under the expectation remedy whereas buyers do not internalize the cover costs that they impose on sellers under specific performance. It has recently been argued that the problem with specific performance, as traditionally construed, is not that it departs too radically from the expectation remedy but rather that it does not depart radically enough.[14]

Specific performance, as traditionally understood, gives promisees the choice between receiving the value to them of the promised performance as damages and actually having their promisors do what they promised. A moment ago, the argument observed that this choice does not require promisees to internalize the cover costs that their demands of specific performance impose on promisors, who are left able to exploit opportunities for efficient breach only by providing two performances. By contrast, the expectation remedy does require promisors who are considering potentially efficient breaches to internalize all of the costs that these breaches impose on their promisees, including in particular the promisees' costs of covering.

This observation stymied the argument in favor of specific performance because it was difficult to imagine requiring promisees who insist on specific performance to bear their breaching promisors' cover costs: the promisees, after all, are the wronged parties in this context, making it unnatural further to burden them with bearing the costs of undoing the wrong. But this way of thinking disguises another, more radical, possibility, which may be revealed by observing that cover costs do not just measure a

---

14. The discussion below follows Richard R.W. Brooks, *The Efficient Performance Hypothesis*, 116 YALE. L.J. 568 (2006) and *Who Choose and Who Gets What: Efficient Breach and Efficient Performance Hypotheses*, 116 YALE L.J. POCKET PART 414 (2007).

burden, but may instead measure a benefit. A promisor facing an order of specific performance will cover, after all, and serve both her promisee and the third party whose offer tempted her to breach, as long as her cover costs remain smaller than the gains that she will enjoy on dealing with the third party. In other words, the maximum cover costs that the promisor is willing to bear measure the efficiency gains from her breach.

It is now possible, against the background of this recognition, to see how to restructure the specific performance remedy so that it forces promisees who demand specific performance to internalize their promisors' cover costs, without this being a burden on them. Instead of giving promisees the traditional choice between receiving specific performance and expectation damages, an efficient specific performance remedy would give promisees the choice between receiving specific performance and disgorgement of the promisors' gains from breaching (which, it is now apparent, equals the maximum cover costs that the promisor would be willing to bear on specifically performing).

Unlike traditional specific performance, this remedy is the precise mirror image of the expectation remedy. Traditional expectation damages allow the promisor to choose to breach, subject to incentives that require her to weigh the benefits that breaching provides her (her gains from dealing with a third party) against the burdens that it imposes on her promisee (his disappointed contractual expectations). Similarly, the revised specific performance remedy allows the promisee to require the promisor to perform, subject to incentives that require him to weigh the benefits that performance provides him (his contractual expectations) against the burdens that performing imposes on his promisor (her lost opportunity to gain from dealing with a third party). And since the two remedies—the expectation remedy on the one hand and the new version of specific performance (which gives promisees the choice between performance and disgorgement) on the other—are entirely symmetrical, they are both, equally, efficient.

Even this does not end the argument concerning the relative merits of expectation damages and specific performance, however, because the fact that they two remedies are equivalently efficient in the abstract does not entail that they will perform equally efficiently as applied, in the real world. The efficiency of each regime requires that the party charged with making the perform or breach decision (and, of course, other contractual decisions also) possess accurate information concerning the costs and benefits of each choice. Most pressingly, the efficiency of the expectation remedy requires that promisors possess an accurate view of the costs associated with their breaching, that is, of the size of their promisees' contractual expectations;[15] and the efficiency of specific performance (as modified) requires promisees to possess an accurate view of the costs associated with their demanding performance, that is, of the size of the

---

15. Promisors will naturally possess accurate information concerning the benefits against which they must weigh these costs, which are just the gains whose possibility has induced them to consider breaching.

gains from breach that their promisors will be required to disgorge.[16] There are, moreover, good reasons to expect that each will face substantial obstacles in acquiring the necessary information. Promisors will be stymied by their promisees' reluctance, in negotiating the original contract, to reveal their true valuation of performance, for fear that such a revelation will weaken their bargaining position. And promisees will be stymied by their promisors' reluctance to reveal their true gains from breach, for fear that such a revelation will weaken their bargaining position.

Perhaps this impasse may be broken by considering the dynamic character of contractual practice—its responsiveness to the legal regimes that govern contract disputes. The expectation remedy allows promisors to retain the gains associated with efficient breaches, whereas specific performance allocates the gains to promisees. Insofar as opportunities for efficient breach result from promisors' business activities (imagine a seller whose advertising increases her chance of receiving higher offers for a good that she has already sold), the expectation remedy provides promisors with efficient incentives to pursue these opportunities, whereas specific performance does not. Nevertheless, this consideration may also have its counter—after all, promisees could pay promisors to pursue opportunities for efficient breaches (with the payments funded by the disgorgement that these opportunities generate). But then what of the costs of monitoring this commitment? And so the back and for continues.

It may well be that the argument concerning the relative efficiency of expectation damages and specific performance (in whatever version its proponents prefer) has no end, at least in the real world, so that the debate, although heated, addresses a phantom, or, as a prominent commentator once said, weaves "circles in the sky."[17] That would itself be a useful lesson in the current context, where the focus on comparative legal methods renders the limitations of law and economics just as interesting as its successes.

9.3   A RE-CONCEPTUALIZATION

The economic debate about the relative efficiency of expectation damages and specific performance has a thoroughgoingly instrumental character. Law and economics evaluates legal doctrines based on their extra-legal effects and prefers those doctrines whose effects it judges better. Another type of legal argument (which has not received much attention here but will figure more prominently in some of the materials to come) evaluates legal doctrines not according to their consequences but rather by their conceptual character—according to the relations that they constitute

---

16. Promisees will naturally possess accurate information concerning the benefits against which they must weigh these costs, which are just the value to them of the contractual performance.

17. *See* Ian R. MacNeil, *Efficient Breach of Contract: Circles in the Sky*, 68 VA. L. REV. 947 (1982).

among the persons that they govern. The choice between the expectation remedy and specific performance may also be assessed in this more formal way, and the results of such an assessment are revealing. In particular, if the instrumental argument concludes at an impasse—forced into admitting that neither remedy can be said to be generally more efficient than the other—the formal argument will conclude by revealing that the suggestion that a deep distinction exists between expectation damages and specific performance involves a conceptual confusion. The two remedial schemes are not, properly understood, competitors, but rather alternative expressions of the same idea, and the notion of efficient breach, which is meant to separate them, is a nonsense.

This conceptual insight does not undermine the economic analysis of efficient breach entirely—many of the arguments developed by the economic approach retain their importance, although they must be reframed. But the conceptual argument enables important insights that the economic approach ignores, and indeed in some ways disguises. Perhaps the most important is to it refute suggestions, commonly made by proponents of specific performance and reinforced (although perhaps unintentionally) by the way in which the economic approach frames its arguments, that specific performance better respects the idea of an obligation to keep contracts than the expectation remedy and therefore better accords with moral intuition.

Even when the economic approach to contract recommends the expectation remedy as efficient, this in a sense is a coincidence only. As one commentator has observed: the formal category *expectation damages*, the agreement-based idea of securing the benefit of a promisee's bargain, "will not have played any role in the analysis leading up to that conclusion."[18] This contingent attitude towards the expectation remedy is vividly revealed in the economic analysis of the choice between expectation damages and specific performance, including even in the way in which economic analysis frames this dispute—specifically in the suggestion (which the argument below will reveal is misleading, or at least unhelpful) that the expectation remedy is distinguished from specific performance by the fact that it promotes efficient *breaches* of contract whereas specific performance does not.

This way of speaking encourages the thought that the expectation regime establishes a purely remedial rule—which fixes the quantum of damages available to promisees whose promisors divert an expected performance to third parties who value it more highly—but does not alter the promisors' primary obligations to perform or the promisees' legitimate disappointment at the diversion. But as the earlier discussion of liquidated

---

18. Richard Craswell, *Against Fuller and Perdue*, 67 U. Chi. L. Rev. 99, 107 (2000). This is really just a special case of the economic approach's broader disregard for doctrinal categories. As Jody Kraus has observed, the economic analysis of law "rejects the significance of traditional distinctions between apparently different bodies of law," such as contract and tort, and, moreover, "does not take the doctrinal invocations and restatements as legal data to be explained," but instead focuses its attention on explaining case outcomes. *See* Jody Kraus, *Philosophy of Contract Law, in* The Oxford Handbook of Jurisprudence and Philosophy of Law 699 (first quotation), 692 (second quotation) (Jules L. Coleman & Scott Shapiro, eds., 2002).

damages revealed, this attitude mischaracterizes the law. The law's attachment to the expectation remedy treats the remedy not just as a quantum of damages (say, the quantum associated with contract-market price differentials) but precisely as a *formal category of value.* The law insists that contractual remedies vindicate some forward-looking, genuinely promissory, interest. Moreover, once the formal nature of the law's attachment to the expectation remedy is revealed—once it is understood that this remedy is, at its core, a way of vindicating a promisee's interest in the benefits of his bargain, the dispute between expectation damages (now understood as a mere quantum of damages, say, the quantum associated with contract-market price differentials) and specific performance may be recast, as a dispute about what, precisely, the benefit of a promisee's bargain includes. This will reveal, finally, that a better way to understand both the expectation remedy and specific performance is not solely in terms of the contingently calculated quanta of damages that each rule imposes but rather as establishing conflicting interpretive presumptions concerning the contents of promisors' primary obligations to perform.

This idea requires some illustration and unpacking. As has been repeatedly said, it is always possible that, between the time of contracting and the time of performance, the value of a contractually promised performance in the hands of the promisor might grow and indeed come to exceed the value that the specific performance in question confers on the promisee. In the familiar case of a simple contract for the sale of a widget, say, a third party offering an above-market price for the widget, or (more likely) proposing a more profitable use of the productive resources needed to manufacture the widget, may appear to the promisor but remain unavailable to the promisee. The so-called "efficient breaches" that traditionally serve to distinguish expectation damages from specific performance occur precisely in such circumstances. In particular, they occur when a promisor accepts such a third party offer, and diverts the widget from her promisee to the third party. What is meant by saying that the expectation remedy encourages such "breaches" is that it permits the promisor to deal with the third party and pocket any gains left over after compensating her promisee. Specific performance, by contrast, precludes the promisor from diverting the widget without first buying out her promisee (presumably by paying him some of the gains that the expectation remedy would have allowed her to keep). Where the promisor has dealt with the third party anyway, specific performance requires her to disgorge her gains from this deal to her promisee.

Insofar as the arrival of the higher-valuing third party merely represents one of the potential benefits associated with a contract, the promisor and promisee may allocate this benefit by means of the contract, just as they may allocate any other. For example, the contract may cap the promisee's entitlements at the value she herself can extract from the promised performance, in which case promisors would be permitted to profit from dealing with third parties. Alternatively, the contract might specify that the promisee's entitlements include the full value that the promisor could extract from the performance through such dealings with third parties, even when the third parties remain unavailable to the promisee, in which case promisors who "breached efficiently" could not keep any gains for themselves. In this latter case, one might say, adopting a short-hand manner of speech, that promisors' "efficient breaches" are forbidden and that promisors are required "specifically to perform" their contracts. Similarly, one might say that promisors who nevertheless deal with third parties must make "restitution" to their promisees, by disgorging their illicit gains.

But although such language—concerning "efficient breach," "specific performance," and "restitution"—may be helpful as a short-hand, it can also be misleading if taken too literally. The precise contents of promisors' rights concerning their dealings with third parties are, in the final analysis, fixed not by a rule of law but are instead artifacts of the contractual agreement—depending specifically on whether this agreement allocates gains from such dealings to promisors or promisees. Where a contract allocates these gains to promisees, the gains become a part of the promisee's benefit of the bargain; and they are therefore protected not just by specific performance but also by the expectation remedy, properly understood.[19] Specific performance and the expectation remedy are therefore not competitor remedies but rather alternative ways of allocating potential gains. And the law's generally encouraging stance towards so-called "efficient breaches" should be read not as enshrining expectation damages in preference over specific performance on a conceptual level, but rather as establishing a principle of contract interpretation.

According to this interpretive presumption, contracts that are silent are construed to exclude promisors' possible gains from dealing with third parties from a promisees' entitlements, as in Holmes's famous suggestion that a contract just *is* a promise to perform or pay (expectation) damages. And on this understanding, a promisor who diverts her performance and pays expectation damages does not breach the contract at all but rather *keeps* it through paying the damages, which is just an alternate way of specifically honoring her promise, or, as might be equivalently said, of vindicating her promisee's expectations, understood as a formal category of value.[20] On this view, then, the choice between the expectation remedy and

---

19.   This is perhaps obscured somewhat by a common way of speaking, adopted for example in the Restatement, that characterizes a promisee's expectations in terms of "attempting to put him in as good a position as he would have been in had the contract been performed, that is, had there been no breach." RESTATEMENT (SECOND) CONTRACTS § 344 cmt. a (1981). This formulation encourages the thought that specific performance and restitution must be conceptually distinct from expectation because these remedies seem to leave the promisee better off than he would have been "had the contract been performed."

But this characterization—of leaving promisees better off than performance—reflects a confusion, and, indeed, the same confusion that lies behind the view that specific performance and expectation are formally distinct. When a contract allocates the gains from dealings with third parties to a promisee, then a breaching promisor's failure to transfer these gains to the promisee itself represents a breach. And the promisee will receive the benefit of his bargain only if he is put in as good a position as if *this* breach had not occurred—as if the contract had been performed in this respect—which requires, once again, that the promisor disgorge her gains from the efficient breach.

20.   It is sometimes argued that this denial that "efficient breaches" are truly breaches at all itself commits a conceptual confusion: specifically, that it conflates the promisor's *power*

specific performance is simply not about the constitutive question whether contract law allows promisors to break their promises when better opportunities arise or requires them to keep the promises unless released by their promisees. It is rather about the purely interpretive question what content (at least as a default rule) the law takes promises to have: the expectation remedy gives promisors a contractual entitlement to the potential gains from dealing with third parties, whereas specific performance allocates this entitlement to promisees; the expectation remedy treats contracts as contemplating the payment of expectation damages as an alternative form of performance whereas specific performance does not. The "expectation remedy" is therefore best understood not as providing substitutionary relief for a breach of a promise simply to trade goods or services for a price, but rather as providing direct enforcement of a promise in the alternative, to trade *or* to transfer a sum equal to the promisee's value of trade.

This would all be obvious if the law were to require, as a condition of there being a valid contract, that the parties expressly specify the amount of money that promisors must pay their promisees in case they do not do the more particular acts that the contract identifies. If such specifications identified cash amounts whose payment relieved promisors of any further contractual obligations, then they might still be called liquidated damages clauses—as they are in current law—but it would be conceptually plain that the underlying legal order required specific performance of all contracts and that the clauses merely identified alternative means of specifically performing. Alternatively, if such specifications stated that promisors could discharge their contractual obligations only by doing the particular

---

to breach (which the law clearly acknowledges when it refuses to order specific performance) with something very different, namely an *entitlement* to breach. Moreover, it is said, this is a dangerous confusion, because it obscures the fact that a breaching promisor, even though he surely acts within the range of his legal freedom, nevertheless commits a *wrong* and that the expectation remedy is a form of *redress* for this wrong. Finally, it is said that failing to acknowledge the wrongfulness of breach amounts to abandoning contract law's core idea, namely that the existence of the contract changes the normative circumstances of the promisor and her promisee, by giving him the normative powers associated with his entitlement to her performance.

In fact, however, the view that paying expectation damages is merely an alternative form of contractual performance does not have any of these consequences. Treating so-called "efficient breaches" as non-breaches is perfectly consistent with recognizing that contracts change the normative situation of the parties and that true breaches are wrongful. The view in the main text insists only that the promisee's entitlement is to receive primary performance *or* damages (as alternative performance), and that the promisee's normative power is to require the promisor to provide one or the other. A promisor can still act wrongfully, including in the context of an "efficient breach," namely by diverting her primary performance to a third party *and* declining to make good her promisee's expectations. And when the expectation remedy is ordered by a court (as opposed to being volunteered by the promisor), then it is indeed a form of redress for this wrong (which, again, is now the promisor's refusal *both* to render primary performance and voluntarily to offer money satisfaction of her promisee's expectations). Indeed, as the earlier discussion of punitive damages made plain, a promisor who, having diverted her primary performance, also makes a bad faith refusal to pay up her promisee's expectations can act not just wrongfully but sufficiently wrongfully to qualify for punitive damages, at least in principle.

Treating monetary payments to vindicate promisee expectations as an alternative performance is therefore fully consistent with the formal normative structure of contractual obligation. Once again, all that this view does is change the substantive content of the obligations that arise following this form.

acts identified by the contracts, in the example, only by transferring the actual widget to the promisee, then it might be said, using the language adopted by current law, that the promisors were required to provide specific performance. But it would again be conceptually plain that the underlying legal order insisted on vindicating contractual expectations and that the contract clauses merely identified these expectations specifically with the actual transfer of the widget.

Moreover, the same conceptual point clearly applies also to the law as it is. On the one hand, the legal principles that make "expectation damages" the default remedy for breach of contract are just principles of contract interpretation, which (where they apply) treat contracts that are silent on the matter as specifying the payment of appropriate damages as an alternative form of performance. They may therefore be interpreted, at least as a conceptual matter, to make contract law's core remedy specific performance and to establish a presumption that paying appropriate money damages counts as an alternative form of performance. And on the other hand, and analogously, the legal principles that sometimes entitle promisees to what the law calls "specific performance" are similarly just interpretive principles, which (where they apply) treat the absence of an express contractual provision for liquidated damages as identifying promisees' contractual expectations with the particular acts that the contracts contemplate promisors will perform. They may therefore be interpreted, at least as a conceptual matter, as accepting that contract law's core remedy is the expectation remedy and establishing a presumption that promisees' contractual expectations are narrowly focused on the particular performance that the contracts name and contemplate no alternatives.

Both possibilities may be illustrated using examples that are familiar in the law, moreover.

On the one hand, a closer examination of contractual language reveals that many contracts do in fact expressly specify the payment of money equal to the promisee's contractual expectations as an alternative form of performance, although they do not do so self-consciously or indeed at the places in the text at which one might first look for such language. Instead, contracts typically use their price terms to announce that money payments equal to promisees' expectation interests shall be an alternative form of performance. This idea—that a price term may be interpreted to reveal something about the content of a promisor's contractual obligations—is familiar from the very first case discussed in these materials, *Sullivan v. O'Conner*. The *Sullivan* court purported to interpret a low price term to reveal that a plastic surgeon had not assumed the risk that his intervention would fail fully to perfect a patient's nose. There, the inference failed for substantive reasons—the low price was not in fact inconsistent with the doctor's bearing the risk of non-success—but the form of argument remains a good one. And it may be applied to show that, in a wide range of cases in which it is efficient for them to do so, contracts' price terms should be interpreted to say that promisors may substitute cash payments for delivery of goods, as an alternative form of performance.

A simple example will render this point vivid. Imagine that a seller and her buyer, call him B_1, contract for the sale of a widget. Suppose that the seller's cost in the widget is $5 and that B_1's valuation of the widget is $10. Suppose furthermore that a second buyer, B_2, may appear to the seller but not to B_1 (to fix ideas, imagine that B_2 is discovered through the seller's business activities, say, her advertisements) and that B_2's valuation of the widget is $15, so that B_2's appearance presents an opportunity for an efficiency gain, associated with diverting the widget from B_1 (the lower valuer) to B_2 (the higher valuer). Suppose also that the seller can effectively exploit this opportunity only unilaterally—that the transactions costs associated with securing B_1's consent preclude the seller from doing this, so that if the law requires B_1's consent before the seller can proceed to deal with B_2, she will simply ignore B_2 and deal with B_1 in every case. Suppose, finally, that B_2 appears 50% of the time.

Now imagine that contract law imposes on the parties a remedy rule that requires sellers to do just as they have promised and prohibits the payment of money damages as an alternative means of satisfying the contractual expectations of disappointed promisees (this is the remedy typically, but as the argument suggests misleadingly, called "specific performance"). Under this remedial regime, the surplus associated with the contract equals:

1/2 * [the surplus in case B_2 does not appear] + 1/2 * [the surplus in case B_2 appears] =

1/2 * [$5] + 1/2 * [$5] =

$5.

This is gain from trade available for the parties to divide between them, however (following bargaining) they choose. If the parties have equal bargaining power, so that they split the contractual surplus, then their bargaining will settle on a contract price of $7.50 (which allocates $2.50 of surplus to each party).

Next imagine, alternatively, that the law allows promisors confronted with better offers to accept these offers, even when this entails diverting the goods from their intended buyers, as long as they pay the money damages needed to vindicate their initial buyers' contractual expectations (this is typically, although again in a way misleadingly, called the "expectation remedy"). Under this remedial regime, the surplus associated with the contract equals:

1/2 * [the surplus in case B_2 does not appear] + 1/2 * [the surplus in case B_2 appears] =

1/2 * [$5] + 1/2 * [$10] =

$7.50.

This net gain from trade can again be divided between the two parties, according to their bargaining powers. If the parties have equal bargaining power, so that each gets half the surplus, then the parties' bargaining will reach a contract price of $6.25 (which allocates a surplus of $3.75 to each party).[21]

The example therefore illustrates that the price term can function, interpretively, as a liquidated damages clause. A price of $7.50 expresses an implicit agreement that the seller must deliver the widget to B_1 no matter what, or at least no matter that B_2 has come to her with a better offer; by contrast a price of $6.25 expresses the opposite agreement, namely that the seller may deal with B_2 in case he appears, as long only as she makes good B_1's private valuation of the widget. Insofar as the lower price can be interpreted as a liquidated damages clause along these lines, the earlier argument applies to recast paying these damages as an alternative form of performance, so that when the seller deals with B_2 and pays B_1 the money necessary to vindicate his contractual expectations, she has not in fact breached. And what is conventionally called the expectation remedy is recast, in this light, as being merely a special case of specific performance: B_1, after all, is receiving precisely what he had agreed to (or at least one version of it).[22]

---

21. This price straightforwardly leaves the buyer with a surplus of $3.75, since that is precisely the difference between her private valuation and this contract price ($10.00 − $6.25 = $3.75). Seeing that this price leaves the seller enjoying a surplus of $3.75 is a little more complicated. The seller's surplus equals:

1/2 * [her surplus in case B_2 does not appear] + 1/2 * [her surplus in case B_2 appears] =

1/2 * [$6.25 − $5] + 1/2 * [(the price she charges B_2)—(her costs of dealing with B_2)] =

1/2 * [$6.25 − $5] + 1/2 * [(the price she charges B_2)—(her costs in the widget) + (the damages that she must pay B_1 on dealing with B_2)] =

1/2 * [$6.25 − $5] + 1/2 * [(the price she charges B_2)—($5 + $3.75)] =

1/2 * [the price she charges B_2 − $7.50].

When the seller charges B_2 $15.00—that is, his full private valuation (presumably minus a penny, in order to induce B_2 to deal)—then her surplus becomes:

1/2 [$15.00 − $7.50] =

$3.75.

And that is just what the assumption of equal bargaining power requires.

22. One complication is worth noting in the margin. In the example, B_1 is better off under the legal regime that allows his seller to deal with B_2 than under the legal regime that prohibits this: the price that he pays is lower and his contractual surplus is larger. (The reason for this is that the example is set up so that B_1 cannot exploit the efficiency gains represented by B_2's appearance on his own but can do so only by allowing his seller to divert her sale to B_2, and that the equal bargaining power of the parties entails that the seller and B_1 in fact split these gains equally.) A rational seller and B_1 would therefore bargain to give the seller the right to diver the widget to B_2, and a price of $6.25 is very good evidence that the seller and B_1 did in fact so bargain.

Nevertheless, the evidence is not perfect, and the inference from the price term to B_1's subjective understanding of his contract may be flawed. To see this, suppose that buyers in general believe that contract law entitles them to specific performance, on the traditional model. Suppose also that sellers, who are repeat players and more sophisticated than buyers, know that the law in fact allows them to accept better offers and pay (expectation) damages. Finally, suppose that sellers compete only in price (and not in contract terms), so that competition among sellers drives the price of widgets down to $6.25, a price at which sellers can profitably contract only if they may retain the full *ex post* gains from dealing with B_2, should the opportunity arise. This is not an implausible assumption: the transactions costs of explaining the alternative contracts to buyers may exceed the gains available from trade, so that sellers cannot afford to educate their buyers.

And on the other hand, a symmetrical interpretation may be given to cases in which the best interpretation of silent contracts treats them as requiring promisors to do just what they have promised and does not treat paying money damages as an alternative form of performance. Just as the so-called "efficient breaches" that the law *allows* are *not* actually breaches at all (but rather alternative forms of specific performance), so also does the law—regardless of the efficiency gains involved—*forbid* promisors from diverting goods to third parties who make better offers in the rare cases in which the best interpretation of a contract rules out paying (expectation) damages as an alternative form of performance, so that such conduct *truly* involves a breach. As soon as efficient breaches become genuine breaches, they become no longer permitted, as the next case illustrates.

Gassner v. Lockett

Supreme Court of Florida, 1958.
101 So.2d 33.

■ DREW, J. R. W. Baughman, during his lifetime, agreed to convey certain property to Ida J. Lockett. Many months later he agreed to convey the same property to Cameron L. Dowling. The first agreement was not acknowledged and therefore not recorded, while the latter was acknowledged and recorded.

The litigation resulting from Ida Lockett's suit for specific performance brought against Baughman's estate after his death, in which Dowling was a party, resulted in a decree of the lower court directing Baughman's executrix to convey the land to Dowling and awarding a judgment of $1,800 to Ida Lockett as the current market value of the property in question. In its decree the court made the following finding: "Although from the testimony it does not show that R. W. Baughman committed an intentional fraud, it is the judgment of this court that the warranty deed to Ida J. Lockett should be cancelled and set aside, and that in lieu of the property described above, Ida J. Lockett should be paid the sum of eighteen hundred dollars ($1800.00) as the current market value of said lots."

We construe the finding of the learned circuit judge that R.B. Baughman did not commit an intentional fraud as synonymous with the holding that he had not been guilty of bad faith in the transaction, and we think this conclusion is clearly justified from the record in this case. The record shows that Baughman, old, senile and extremely forgetful, dealt extensively in tax deed lands and kept few if any accurate records of his numerous

---

Buyers in such a case are getting a fair deal by the expectation remedy—they are receiving a fair share of the available contractual surplus—but it is not the deal that they think they are getting. This may breed resentment in individual buyers, at least when they discover, *ex post*, that their sellers may keep the full gains from dealing with B_2, in case B_2 appears. At the very least, the legal regime that allows sellers to keep these gains, although it benefits buyers as well as sellers, treats buyers paternalistically. Such paternalism may be justified, however, and is perhaps even mandatory. Buyers, after all, would be made worse off both by adopting the alternative remedy rule and (given transactions costs) by being given the understanding needed in order freely to choose the rule that is in fact better for them.

transactions. The record wholly fails, in our judgment—and, obviously, in the judgment of the chancellor, to show any bad faith in the transactions. In view of this conclusion, it was erroneous to award as damages the current value of the property.

In the first cited case this Court said:

The law is well settled that in an action brought by the vendee against the vendor upon a valid contract for the sale of land when the vendor has breached such contract, the general rule as to the measure of damages is that the vendee is entitled to *such purchase money as he paid, together with interest and expenses of investigating title.* This rule, however, does not apply where there is want of good faith in the vendor, which may be shown by any acts inconsistent with the utmost good faith. In such cases, or in cases where the vendor had no title but acting on the supposition that he might acquire title, he is liable for the value of the land at the time of the breach with interest from that date. (Emphasis supplied.)

In the foregoing case, this Court quoted extensively from Sutherland on Damages, 4th Edition by Berryman, reciting the circumstances under which it was proper to allow, in addition to compensatory damages, damages for the loss of the bargain.

The italicized language in *Key v. Alexander, 91 Fla. 975 (1926),* while applicable to the facts in that case and proper there for the admeasurement of the allowable damages, is not necessarily applicable in all instances. The reason for the rule seems to be that where a vendor acts in good faith he should not be liable for more than the actual loss which might be suffered by the vendee. On the other hand, there is no reason why the vendor should be allowed to benefit from such mistake even though it was made in good faith. Every rule of logic and justice would seem to indicate that where a vendor is unable to perform a prior contract for the sale of lands because of a subsequent sale of the same land, he should be held, to the extent of any profit in the subsequent sale, to be a trustee for the prior vendee and accountable to such vendee for any profit.

The decree appealed from, insofar as it affects the transaction between the deceased Baughman and the original plaintiff Ida J. Lockett, is reversed with directions that a decree be entered in said cause in favor of the said Ida J. Lockett for the purchase money which she has paid, legal interest on each payment thereof from the time made to the date of payment to her, the expenses of investigating the title, and any profit which may have accrued to Baughman or his estate by virtue of the subsequent sale to Dowling.

Reversed and remanded.

* * *

The defendant in *Gassner* conveyed a parcel of real property to the plaintiff (who did not record the sale) and later reconveyed the same parcel to a third party (who did record the sale) for a higher price.[23] The plaintiff sued, seeking specific performance of the original conveyance, which was unavailable in light of the third party's good title to the land. Nevertheless, the court treated the defendant as a trustee for the plaintiff in respect of the land and awarded the plaintiff damages that were not limited by the plaintiff's private valuation of the land but instead included any profit that might have accrued to the defendant by virtue of the resale. The court, moreover, reached this conclusion in spite of an express recognition that the defendant (an old man) had displayed no bad faith in making the second sale but was merely forgetful of the first.[24]

Gassner thus illustrates that when the law, for some independent reason, insists that promisees may expect what is ordinarily called specific performance—so that contracts must be interpreted as identifying promisees' expectations precisely with the contemplated performance and denying that money damages might be an alternative way of satisfying such expectations—then it forbids efficient breaches, which are now truly breaches, regardless of their efficiency. The law prevents the breaches directly where it can, and where it cannot (as in *Gassner*) then it secures promisees' full expectations, the full benefits of their bargains, by requiring promisors to disgorge any gains that they have received from the efficient breaches (which are now truly breaches) that render actual performance somehow impossible.[25]

Together, these arguments establish the conceptual equivalence of the remedies that the law conventionally distinguishes by calling one "expectation damages" and the other "specific performance." These remedies do not identify different formal categories of value, but instead merely establish different interpretive rules concerning what is included in a promisee's benefit of his bargain or, equivalently, what conduct counts as doing what the promisor promised. The formal analysis of the dispute between expectation damages and specific performance therefore clarifies what the economic dispute is about: it is not about the nature of contractual obligation in general but rather about the content that particular contractual obligations should be said to have. This insight does not deprive the economic arguments of their significance, because it remains important to know when contractual surplus is maximized by interpreting contracts to allocate the potential gains from dealing with third parties to promisors and when it is maximized by interpreting contracts to allocate these gains to promisees. But the conceptual clarifications achieved by the formal analysis of contract remedies do not leave *everything* the same, and some of the ideas that arise in and around the standard economic approach to contract remedies must be abandoned in light of this new-found clarity.

---

23.   *Gassner* appears in these materials as a result of conversations with Alan Rau.

24.   For the importance of this fact, see the discussion of *Olwell v. Nye & Nissen Co.*, 173 P.2d 652, in the section on restitution below.

25.   Note that this rule is not uniformly followed. *See Bander v. Grossman*, 611 N.Y.S. 2d 985 (N.Y. Sup. 1994).

The most prominent among these is the idea that, because it encourages efficient *breaches*, the expectation remedy comports badly with the ordinary morality of promising, which treats breaking promises as, simply, wrong. This moralistic preference for specific performance over expectation damages arises out of a literal understanding of the idea of efficient breach: Expectation damages, it is said, allow promisors unfairly to profit from something that is no longer theirs. As is familiar, when a seller and her buyer contract for the sale of some good and an alternative buyer who values the good more highly than the initial buyer appears and presents the possibility of a further gain, expectation damages allocate this gain to the seller, who may satisfy the first buyer's original expectations and resell the good to the second buyer at a price that includes as much of the second buyer's additional valuation as the seller's bargaining power allows her to capture. The seller may proceed in this way, moreover, in spite of the fact that she has contracted to deliver the goods to the first buyer. That has seemed unfair to many, who insist that principles of fidelity or faithfulness require promisors to do what they say they will do and therefore support making specific performance (a cognate of restitution) the remedy for breach of contract. This idea has been repeatedly promoted by a broad range of commentators, including economists who doubt the moral foundations of their methods,[26] moralists who have accepted that the economic characterization of efficient breaches correctly captures the positive law,[27] doctrinalists who emphasize that the expectation remedy renders contract law less solicitous of promisees than tort law is of owners (certainly there is no general tort doctrine of efficient conversion analogous to the contract doctrine of efficient breach), and a small but perhaps growing number of courts who have suggested that breaching promisors should be required to disgorge their gains from efficient breaches under the "principle of the law of restitution that one should not gain by one's own wrong."[28]

It should by now be plain, however, that moral qualms about the expectation remedy, at least insofar as they arise on the grounds just mentioned, are simply mistaken. The claim that the proceeds from an efficient breach should be returned to promisees in "restitution" of wrongful gains is not an independent *argument* for this remedy but just a way of expressing a *conclusion* about the content of the promisees' expectations. The examples just rehearsed illustrate that the idea that promisors should be true to their words (and do wrong to break them) does not yet say what the content of their promises consists in—principles of fidelity are plainly not principles of interpretation. Insofar as contracts, properly interpreted, do not commit promisors to performing in every event but only to performing *or paying damages*, efficient breaches are not truly breaches, and

---

26. See Richard R.W. Brooks, *Who Choose and Who Gets What: Efficient Breach and Efficient Performance Hypotheses*, 116 YALE L.J. POCKET PART 414 (2007).

27. *See, e.g.*, Seana Shiffin, *Could Bread of Contract be Immoral*, 107 MICH. L. REV. 1551 (2009); DOUGLAS LAYCOCK, THE DEATH OF THE IRREPARABLE INJURY RULE 245–64 (1991); Daniel Friedmann, *The Efficient Breach Fallacy*, 18 J. LEGAL STUD. 1,2 (1989).

28. *EarthInfo, Inc. v. Hydrosphere Resource Consultants, Inc.*, 900 P.2d 113, 117–21 (Colo. 1995) (citation omitted).

promisors who profit from them do not profit from wrongs. And insofar as contracts, properly understood, rule out substituting money damages as an alternative performance, the law does not permit promisors to keep their gains from what now are truly breaches. The intuition that expectation damages unfairly favor efficiently breaching promisors, and that fairness requires restitution, thus does not present a moral challenge to the expectation remedy: Once certain conceptual confusions are cleared away, all plausible claims to restitution, understood in this narrow sense, are revealed merely to present special cases of the expectation remedy.

CHAPTER 10

RESTITUTION AND RESCISSION

Restitution is an enormous topic in its own right. Indeed, it is often said, with justification, that restitution constitutes a distinctive third fount of private law obligation, which stands aside contract and tort as a free-standing, and equally fundamental, legal ideal. In some legal systems—including most notably in English law[1]—restitution is not just the theoretical but also the practical peer of contract and tort: a great many cases are decided based on restitutionary principles, which therefore receive enormous attention from both courts and commentators.[2] Restitution is less prominent in American jurisdictions, and so will not receive a systematic treatment here. But (as *Gassner* illustrated) restitutionary claims can arise in and around contracts, and so restitution remains important enough that it should not be ignored entirely.

The central feature of restitution is that liability is based on, and recovery is measured by, the benefit that the defendant received from her wrong actions rather than the harm that these actions imposed on the plaintiff. That is what makes restitution a wholly distinct "third-source" of civil liability—separate from both contract and tort—although restitution is of course available as a remedial measure, in proper cases, in association with both contract and tort. Restitution rises to remove improper gains from persons when it will "give offense to equity and good conscience if [one who has a benefit is] permitted to retain it."[3] Just when this standard is met is one of the central issues in the law of restitution. And although these pages do not attempt a general treatment of the question, it is worth noting that the basic standard immediately entails, as a limiting principle of unjust enrichment, that no restitution is available if the party that has conferred a benefit is a "mere volunteer" or an "officious intermeddler."

Restitution is most commonly claimed in cases in which a promisee seeks to recover something he has transferred to a promisor in connection with a contract that the promisor then breached. In a typical example, a promisee who has rendered part payment for a performance that is never provided seeks to recover his payment in restitution. In such typical cases,

---

1. One reason for restitution's prominence in English law is that the English attitudes towards precedent, which is taken very, very seriously, caused important parts of the law of contract remedies to become frozen, in the nineteenth century, into forms that no longer suit modern commercial practice. In England, restitution has stepped in to occupy legal terrain previously inhabited by a doctrinal structure whose dynamism had become unequal to the regulatory task that it was set.

2. One excellent study is HANOCH DAGAN, THE LAW AND ETHICS OF RESTITUTION (2004).

3. *Atlantic Coast Line Railroad Co. v. Florida*, 295 U.S. 301, 309 (1935) (Cardozo, J).

a promisee's restitution damages will be smaller than his expectation and indeed even than his reliance damages, as the *Restatement* observes: "Although it may be equal to the expectation or reliance interest, [the restitution interest] is ordinarily smaller because it includes neither the injured party's lost profit nor that part of his expenditures in reliance that resulted in no benefit to the other party."[4] Restitution displays this humble character in ordinary cases because the restitution remedy does not focus directly on the injured promisee but rather seeks "to put the party *in breach* back in the position that party would have been in if the contract had not been made."[5]

A promisee will typically seek restitution, therefore, only when there is some special reason to do so. Such reasons exist, and make restitution attractive to plaintiffs in contract-cases, in three basic circumstances. The first arises when, generally because plaintiffs are themselves in breach of contract, the plaintiffs have recourse to no other cause of action to vindicate their claims. Examples of this circumstance include *Neri v. Retail Marine* and *Vines v. Orchard Hills*, both discussed earlier. The plaintiffs in both cases sought recovery—of deposits paid in conjunction with sales contracts—in spite of the fact that they had refused, in breach of their contracts, to complete their purchases. This raises the question (discussed more explicitly in the *Vines* opinion than in *Neri*) whether plaintiffs-in-breach might win restitution—a natural concern given that restitutionary claims depend on defendants' *unjust* enrichment, and it might be thought that where the enrichment is caused by the *plaintiffs'* breach, it is not unjust. Both decisions conclude that a plaintiff's breach does not as a general matter rule out recovery in restitution—although it obviously remains to say whether or not restitution is appropriate in particular cases. This, as the earlier discussions of punitive damages and specific performance reveal, is the right answer: a breach does not wrong a promisee as long as his contractual expectations are vindicated, and promisees therefore may not retain monies received from breaching promisors in excess of the sums needed to secure these expectations. Any excess monies represent unjust enrichment (notwithstanding the promisors' breaches), which promisors may recover, as plaintiffs-in-breach, in restitution.

The second circumstance in which restitution is attractive to plaintiffs in and around contract disputes arises when a plaintiff wishes to recover a particular piece of property that she has given the defendant. This may happen because the plaintiff places a special, intrinsic value on the property in question: for example, an artist or artisan who has sold her work to a buyer partly selected because he appeared sympathetic, might, in case the buyer fails to pay, prefer to recover her work rather than extract its price from a now clearly unsympathetic buyer. Also, and perhaps more commonly, a plaintiff may seek restitution of a specific piece of property rather than proceeding in contract for more instrumental reasons: for example, a seller who has sold an item to a defendant who has become insolvent before

---

4. RESTATEMENT § 344 cmt. a. (1981).

5. E. ALLAN FARNSWORTH, CONTRACTS § 12.19 (3d ed. 1999).

paying the full purchase price may seek restitution of the item in question because (unlike a claim in contract for expectation damages) the restitutionary claim grants her a preference over other creditors with respect to the specific piece of property that used to be hers.

Finally, restitution will be attractive to contracts plaintiffs in circumstances in which the gains that defendants have accumulated from their breaches exceed the losses (including disappointed expectations) that the breaches have imposed on the plaintiffs. Although this will of course happen in all cases of efficient breach—that is, cases in which defendants divert contractual performance to higher-valuing third parties—plaintiffs cannot generally succeed in restitution on these facts alone, without more. To do so would undermine contract law's commitment to the expectation remedy.[6] Also, as the last section explained, it would violate the basic ideals that underlie restitution: since the expectation remedy, properly understood, represents a contractual allocation of the gains from possible "efficient breaches" to promisors (who are now seen to be not in fact breaching at all), promisors who appropriate such gains are not unjustly enriched. Nevertheless, as *Gassner* illustrates, contracts may sometimes (including by operation of background law) allocate gains from efficient deals with third parties to promisees, in which case disappointed promisees may recover restitutionary damages on breach.

Moreover, there exists one other circumstance in which breaching defendants benefit more than they harm plaintiffs, and plaintiffs may successfully capture this benefit by proceeding in restitution rather than contract. Sometimes, defendants breach contracts whose terms are excessively favorable to them and unfavorable to their promisees. These are the unusual cases in which promisors breach contracts that have a negative expectation for their promisees: a contractor may abandon building a house even though the price that she is charging exceeds the market value that the completed house will have; or, as in *Oliver v. Campbell* below, a client may replace her lawyer even though she is underpaying him. In such cases, expectation damages leave promisees with little or no recovery, since their promisors' breaches have, in effect, relieved them of net burdens. But if they have conferred significant value on their promisors prior to the breaches—prior to being fired or replaced—then they may try to recover these benefits by proceeding in restitution.

The restitutionary claims in these various classes of cases vary in substance, but they all share a common basic form. In all of them, the plaintiff alleges that he performed his side of a contract—handing over money, goods, or services to the defendant, and that the defendant failed to render return performance. The plaintiff therefore rescinds the contract, on grounds of the defendant's breach. Once the contract has been rescinded, it

---

6. As Farnsworth observes, courts have refused to allow recovery in restitution "when the injured party seeks to require the party in breach to disgorge gain that has resulted not from the injured party's performance but rather from the other party's breach[,] as where a seller breaks a contract and sells the goods to a third person for more than the contract price." E. ALLAN FARNSWORTH, FARNSWORTH ON CONTRACTS § 12.20 (3d ed. 2003) (emphasis omitted).

is gone, as it were, so that the defendant now possesses property belonging to the plaintiff and to which she is not entitled. In order to prevent the defendant from being unjustly enriched by this possession, the law offers the plaintiff restitutionary remedies fashioned for wrongful takings of property. Where appropriate, the plaintiff can get return of the specific goods he has given to the defendant. In other circumstances, he can recover money damages in an amount calculated (although by sometimes uncertain formulae) to undo the defendant's unjust enrichment.

The following materials present a brief illustration of these ideas in operation.

Restatement 2d of Contracts

§ 371   Measure of Restitution Interest

If a sum of money is awarded to protect a party's restitution interest, it may as justice requires be measured by either

(a) the reasonable value to the other party of what he received in terms of what it would have cost him to obtain it from a person in the claimant's position, or

(b) the extent to which the other party's property has been increased in value or his other interests advanced.

Comments & Illustrations

Comment a. Measurement of benefit. Under the rules stated in §§ 344 and 370, a party who is liable in restitution for a sum of money must pay an amount equal to the benefit that has been conferred upon him. If the benefit consists simply of a sum of money received by the party from whom restitution is sought, there is no difficulty in determining this amount. If the benefit consists of something else, however, such as services or property, its measurement in terms of money may pose serious problems.

Restitution in money is available in a wide variety of contexts, and the resolution of these problems varies greatly depending on the circumstances. If, for example, the party seeking restitution has himself committed a material breach (§ 374), uncertainties as to the amount of the benefit may properly be resolved against him.

A particularly significant circumstance is whether the benefit has been conferred by way of performance or by way of reliance in some other way. See Comment *a* to § 370. Recovery is ordinarily more generous for a benefit that has been conferred by performance. To the extent that the benefit may reasonably be measured in different ways, the choice is within the discretion of the court. Thus a court may take into account the value of opportunities for benefit even if they have not been fully realized in the particular case.

An especially important choice is that between the reasonable value to a party of what he received in terms of what it would have cost him to obtain it from a person in the claimant's position and the addition to the wealth of that party as measured by the extent to which his property has been increased in value or his other interests advanced. In practice, the first measure is usually based on the market price of such a substitute. Under the rule stated in this Section, the court has considerable discretion in making the choice between these two measures of benefit. Under either choice, the court may properly consider the purposes of the recipient of the benefit when he made the contract, even if those purposes were later frustrated or abandoned.

Comment b. Choice of measure. The reasonable value to the party against whom restitution is sought (Paragraph (a)) is ordinarily less than the cost to the party seeking restitution, since his expenditures are excluded to the extent that they conferred no benefit. See Comment *a* to § 344. Nor can the party against whom restitution is sought reduce the amount for which he may himself be liable by subtracting such expenditures from the amount of the benefit that he has received. See Illustration 5 to § 377. The reasonable value to the party from whom restitution is sought (Paragraph (a)), is, however, usually greater than the addition to his wealth (Paragraph (b)). If this is so, a party seeking restitution for part performance is commonly allowed the more generous measure of reasonable value, unless that measure is unduly difficult to apply, except when he is in breach (§ 374). See Illustration 1. In the case of services rendered in an emergency or to save life, however, restitution based on addition to wealth will greatly exceed that based on expense saved and recovery is invariably limited to the smaller amount. See Illustration 2. In the case of services rendered to a third party as the intended beneficiary of a gift promise, restitution from the promisee based on his enrichment is generally not susceptible of measurement and recovery based on reasonable value is appropriate. See Illustration 3.

Illustrations:

1. A, a carpenter, contracts to repair B's roof for $3,000. A does part of the work at a cost of $2,000, increasing the market price of B's house by $1,200. The market price to have a similar carpenter do the work done by A is $1,800. A's restitution interest is equal to the benefit conferred on B. That benefit may be measured either by the addition to B's wealth from A's services in terms of the $1,200 increase in the market price of B's house or the reasonable value to B of A's services in terms of the $1,800 that it would have cost B to engage a similar carpenter to do the same work. If the work was not completed because of a breach by A and restitution is based on the rule stated in § 374, $1,200 is appropriate. If the work was not completed because of a breach by B and restitution is based on the rule stated in § 373, $1,800 is appropriate.

2.   A, a surgeon, contracts to perform a series of emergency operations on B for $3,000. A does the first operation, saving B's life, which can be valued in view of B's life expectancy at $1,000,000. The market price to have an equally competent surgeon do the first operation is $1,800. A's restitution interest is equal to the benefit conferred on B. That benefit is measured by the reasonable value to B of A's services in terms of the $1,800 that it would have cost B to engage a similar surgeon to do the operation regardless of the rule on which restitution is based.

3.   A, a social worker, promises B to render personal services to C in return for B's promise to educate A's children. A renders only part of the services and B then refuses to educate A's children. The market price to have a similar social worker do the services rendered by A is $1,800. If A recovers in restitution under the rule stated in § 373, an appropriate measure of the benefit conferred on B is the reasonable value to B of A's services in terms of the $1,800 that it would have cost B to engage a similar social worker to do the same work.

Restatement 2d of Contracts

§ 372   Specific Restitution

(1) Specific restitution will be granted to a party who is entitled to restitution, except that:

(a) specific restitution based on a breach by the other party under the rule stated in § 373 may be refused in the discretion of the court if it would unduly interfere with the certainty of title to land or otherwise cause injustice, and

(b) specific restitution in favor of the party in breach under the rule stated in § 374 will not be granted.

(2) A decree of specific restitution may be made conditional on return of or compensation for anything that the party claiming restitution has received.

(3) If specific restitution, with or without a sum of money, will be substantially as effective as restitution in money in putting the party claiming restitution in the position he was in before rendering any performance, the other party can discharge his duty by tendering such restitution before suit is brought and keeping his tender good.

Comments & Illustrations

Comment a. Specific restitution on avoidance or in similar circumstances. A party who has a right to restitution under the rule stated in § 376 because he has avoided the contract, generally has a choice of either claiming a sum of money in restitution or seeking specific restitution if the benefit is something that can be returned to him. The same is true of a party who has a right to restitution under the rule stated in § 377 on one of the grounds there stated, even though this rule does not, strictly speaking, result in avoidance of the contract. The right to specific restitution may, however, be subject to rights of third parties. Their rights are not dealt with in this Restatement. For special rules governing the right of a seller under a contract for the sale of goods, see Uniform Commercial Code §§ 2–507, 2–702.

Illustration:

1. A is induced by B's misrepresentation to sell a tract of land to B for $100,000. On discovery of the misrepresentation, A tenders back the $100,000 and sues B for specific restitution of the land. Specific restitution will be granted.

Comment b. Specific restitution on other grounds. A party whose right to restitution is based on the other party's breach also has a right to specific restitution, subject to the limitation stated in Paragraph (a). In the case of a contract for the sale of goods, the Uniform Commercial Code limits much more severely the seller's right to specific restitution, although the seller can protect himself by taking a security interest in the goods. See Uniform Commercial Code § 2–703. The most important problems of specific restitution that remain usually arise in connection with contracts to transfer land. If the buyer of land fails or refuses to pay the price after the transfer of the land to him, the seller is limited to his claim for the price, which may be secured by a vendor's lien as a matter of law or by a security interest that he has reserved. The question of his right to specific restitution does not arise in that situation (§ 373(2)). Specific restitution may, however, be appropriate where there is a right to restitution because the return promise is to do something other than pay money. See Illustrations 2 and 3. In that case, however, a court may refuse specific restitution if it would unduly interfere with the certainty of title to the land. In resolving that question, a court will take into account all the circumstances, including the inadequacy of other relief. A court may also refuse specific restitution if it would otherwise cause injustice as where, for example, it would result in a preference over other creditors in bankruptcy. Specific restitution under the rule stated in this Section is available to the injured party even though enforcement of the contract is barred by the Statute of Frauds. See § 375. Under the exception stated in Paragraph (b), however, it is never available to a party who is himself in breach. See § 374.

Illustrations:

2. A contracts to transfer a tract of land to B in return for B's promise to transfer a tract of land to A at the same time. After A has transferred his tract to B and received a deed from B, A learns that B does not have title to the other tract. A sues B for specific restitution. Specific restitution will be granted, together with compensation to A for the value to B of the use of the land, because the right to specific restitution will not unduly interfere with the certainty of title to land. If B's promise is to transfer his

tract to A ten years after A's transfer of his tract, specific restitution will be denied because a right to specific restitution would unduly interfere with the certainty of title to land during the ten years.

3.   A contracts to transfer a tract of land to B in return for B's promise to support A for life. B repudiates the contract after he has supported A for a time and A has transferred the land to him, and A sues B for specific restitution. Specific restitution will be granted, conditional on compensation by A for any support that he has received less the value to B of the use of the land, because the right to specific restitution will not unduly interfere with the certainty of title to land given the inadequacy of A's right to damages because of the difficulty of proving damages with sufficient certainty (§ 352).

4.   A contracts to transfer a tract of land to B in return for B's promise to transfer a tract of land to A at a later date. After A has transferred his tract of land to B, B sells both tracts to C, a good faith purchaser for value, taking a mortgage to secure the balance of the price on the tract transferred by A. A sues B and C for specific restitution. Specific restitution will be denied but A can get a decree subrogating him to B's right to the balance of the price and to his rights under the purchase money mortgage that secures it.

5.   A contracts to transfer to B half of his 20,000 shares of stock in the X Corporation in return for B's promise to pay $100,000, to organize a holding company to control X Corporation and to protect A's remaining interest as a shareholder. After A has transferred the stock and B has paid the $100,000, B refuses to organize the holding company. A sues B for specific restitution. Specific restitution may properly be granted conditional on repayment by A of the $100,000.

Comment c. Tender of specific restitution. In some circumstances, a party who is liable for restitution can discharge his duty by tendering specific restitution and keeping his tender good. The tender has this result only if specific restitution will be substantially as effective as restitution in money in putting the party claiming restitution in the position he was in before rendering any performance. If tender of a sum of money in addition to specific restitution will do this, such a tender discharges the other party's duty. See Illustration 6. The tender must, however, be made before suit has been brought.

Illustration:

6.   A makes an oral contract with B under which A transfers 1,000 shares of stock to B in return for B's promise to convey a tract of land to A. B repudiates the contract before he has conveyed the land and tenders back the stock and the dividends received from it and keeps his tender good. A rejects the tender

and sues B for restitution of the value to B of the stock. A cannot recover the value of the stock.

Restatement 2d of Contracts

§ 373   Restitution When Other Party is in Breach

(1) Subject to the rule stated in Subsection (2), on a breach by non-performance that gives rise to a claim for damages for total breach or on a repudiation, the injured party is entitled to restitution for any benefit that he has conferred on the other party by way of part performance or reliance.

(2) The injured party has no right to restitution if he has performed all of his duties under the contract and no performance by the other party remains due other than payment of a definite sum of money for that performance.

Comments & Illustrations

Comment a. Restitution as alternative remedy for breach. An injured party usually seeks, through protection of either his expectation or his reliance interest, to enforce the other party's broken promise. See § 344(1). However, he may, as an alternative, seek, through protection of his restitution interest, to prevent the unjust enrichment of the other party. See § 344(2). This alternative is available to the injured party as a remedy for breach under the rule stated in this Section. It is available regardless of whether the breach is by non-performance or by repudiation. If, however, the breach is by non-performance, restitution is available only if the breach gives rise to a claim for damages for total breach and not merely to a claim for damages for partial breach. Compare Illustration 1 with Illustration 2. A party who has lost the right to claim damages for total breach by, for example, acceptance or retention of performance with knowledge of defects (§ 246), has also lost the right to restitution. Restitution is available on repudiation by the other party, even in those exceptional situations in which no claim for damages for total breach arises as a result of repudiation alone. See Comment *d* to § 253. See Illustration 3. The rule stated in this Section applies to all enforceable promises, including those that are enforceable because of reliance. See Illustration 4. An injured party's right to restitution may be barred by election under the rules stated in §§ 378 and 379.

Illustrations:

1.   A contracts to sell a tract of land to B for $100,000. After B has made a part payment of $20,000, A wrongfully refuses to transfer title. B can recover the $20,000 in restitution. The result is the same even if the market price of the land is only $70,000, so that performance would have been disadvantageous to B.

2.   A contracts to build a house for B for $100,000, progress payments to be made monthly. After having been paid $40,000 for

two months, A commits a breach that is not material by inadvertently using the wrong brand of sewer pipe. B has a claim for damages for partial breach but cannot recover the $40,000 that he has paid A.

3. On February 1, A and B make a contract under which, as consideration for B's immediate payment of $50,000, A promises to convey to B a parcel of land on May 1. On March 1, A repudiates by selling the parcel to C. On April 1, B commences an action against C. Although under the rule stated in § 253(1), B has no claim against A for damages for breach of contract until performance is due on May 1, B can recover $50,000 from A in restitution. See Illustration 4 to § 253.

4. A, who holds a mortgage on B's land, promises B that he will not foreclose the mortgage for another year, even if B makes no payments. In reliance on A's promise, B makes valuable improvements. A forecloses in breach of his promise and buys the land at a judicial sale for the amount of the mortgage debt. B can recover in restitution for the value of the improvements. Compare Illustration 1 to § 370; see also Illustration 12 to § 90.

Comment b. When contract price is a limit. The rule stated in Subsection (1) is subject to an important exception. If, after one party has fully performed his part of the contract, the other party then refuses to pay a definite sum of money that has been fixed as the price for that performance, the injured party is barred from recovery of a greater sum as restitution under the rule stated in Subsection (2). Since he is entitled to recover the price in full together with interest, he has a remedy that protects his expectation interest by giving him the very thing that he was promised. Even if he asserts that the benefit he conferred on the other party exceeds the price fixed by the contract, justice does not require that he have the right to recover this larger sum in restitution. To give him that right would impose on the court the burden of measuring the benefit in terms of money in spite of the fact that this has already been done by the parties themselves when they made their contract. See Illustration 5. If, however, the performance to be rendered by the party in breach is something other than the payment of a definite sum in money, this burden is less of an imposition on the court since, even if damages were sought by the injured party, the court would have to measure the value to him of the performance due from the party in breach. The clearest case occurs where the injured party has paid the full price in money for the performance that the party in breach has subsequently failed to render. To allow restitution of the sum paid in that case imposes no burden of measurement on the court and relieves it of the burden that it would have if damages were awarded of measuring the value to the injured party of the performance due from the party in breach. See Illustration 6. For this reason, the rule stated in Subsection (2) is limited to the situation where the only remaining performance due from the party in breach is the payment of a definite sum of money. See Illustrations 6 and 7. If the performance promised by the party in breach consists in part of money and in part of something else, full performance by the injured party does not bar him from restitution unless the party in breach has rendered all of his performance except a money payment.

Illustrations:

5. A contracts to work for B for one month for $10,000. After A has fully performed, B repudiates the contract and refuses to pay the $10,000. A can get damages against B for $10,000, together with interest, but cannot recover more than that sum even if he can show that the benefit to B from the services was greater than $10,000.

6. A contracts to sell a tract of land to B for $100,000. After B has paid the full $100,000, A repudiates and refuses to transfer title. B has a right to $100,000 in restitution.

7. A contracts to build a building for B in return for B's promise to transfer a tract of land to A and to pay $10,000. After A has built the building, B refuses to transfer title or to pay the $10,000. A has a right to the reasonable value of his work and materials.

Comment c. Effect of "divisibility." Sometimes a contract is "divisible" in the sense that parts of the performances to be exchanged on each side are properly regarded as a pair of agreed equivalents. See § 240. The rule stated in Subsection (2) applies by analogy to such contracts. If one party has fully performed his side of such a pair and all that remains on the other side is for the other party to pay a definite sum of money, recovery for the performance rendered is limited to that sum. Restitution is not available as an alternative even if there has been a breach as to other parts of the contract. See Illustration 8. If both parties have fully performed, so that nothing with respect to the pair of agreed equivalents remains to be done on either side, no recovery can be had as to that pair.

Illustrations:

8. A contracts to work as a consultant for B for a fee of $50,000, payable at the end of the year, together with a payment of $200 a month for A's use of his own car and reimbursement of A's expenses. B wrongfully discharges A at the end of six months. A cannot recover in restitution for the use of his car or for his expenses, but can recover for these items as provided in the contract. As to his recovery for his services, see Illustration 12.

9. A contracts to build a house for B for $50,000, progress payments to be made monthly in an amount equal to 85% of the price of the work performed during the preceding month, the balance to be paid on the architect's certificate of satisfactory completion of the house. B makes the first three payments and then repudiates the contract and has another builder finish the house. A can recover in restitution for the reasonable value of his work, labor and materials, less the amount of the three payments.

The performance during each month and the corresponding progress payments are not agreed equivalents under the rule stated in § 240. See Illustration 7 to § 240.

Comment d. Losing contracts. An injured party who has performed in part will usually prefer to seek damages based on his expectation interest (§ 347) instead of a sum of money based on his restitution interest because such damages include his net profit and will give him a larger recovery. Even if he cannot prove what his net profit would have been, he will ordinarily seek damages based on his reliance interest (§ 348), since this will compensate him for all of his expenditures, regardless of whether they resulted in a benefit to the party in breach. See Comment *a* to § 344. In the case of a contract on which he would have sustained a loss instead of having made a profit, however, his restitution interest may give him a larger recovery than would damages on either basis. The right of the injured party under a losing contract to a greater amount in restitution than he could have recovered in damages has engendered much controversy. The rules stated in this Section give him that right. He is entitled to such recovery even if the contract price is stated in terms of a rate per unit of work and the recovery exceeds that rate. There are, however, two important limitations. The first limitation is one that is applicable to any claim for restitution: the party in breach is liable only to the extent that he has benefited from the injured party's performance. If he has, for example, taken advantage of the injured party's part performance by having the rest of the work completed after his breach, the extent of his benefit is easy to measure in terms of the reasonable value of the injured party's performance. See Illustration 10. If, however, he has abandoned the project and not completed the work, that measurement will be more difficult. See Illustration 11. In that situation, the court may exercise its sound discretion in choosing between the two measures stated in § 371. In doing so it will take account of all the circumstances including the observance by the parties of standards of good faith and fair dealing during any negotiations leading up to the rupture of contractual relations (§ 208). See Introductory Note to Chapter 10. Since a contract that is a losing one for the injured party is often an advantageous one for the party in breach, the possibility should not be overlooked that the breach was provoked by the injured party in order to avoid having to perform. The second limitation is that stated in Subsection (2). If the injured party has completed performance and nothing remains for the party in breach to do but to pay him the price, his recovery is limited to the price. See Comment *b*.

Illustrations:

   10.   A, a plumbing subcontractor, contracts with B, a general contractor, to install the plumbing in a factory being built by B for C. B promises to pay A $100,000. After A has spent $40,000, B repudiates the contract and has the plumbing finished by another subcontractor at a cost of $80,000. The market price to have a similar plumbing subcontractor do the work done by A is $40,000. A can recover the $40,000 from B in restitution.

11.   A contracts to build a house for B for $100,000. After A has spent $40,000, B discovers that he does not have good title to the land on which the house is to be built. B repudiates the contract and abandons the project. A's work results in no actual benefit to B. A cannot recover in restitution from B, but under the rule stated in § 349 he can recover as damages the $40,000 that he has spent unless B proves with reasonable certainty that A would have sustained a net loss if the contract had been performed. See Illustration 4 to § 349.

12.   A contracts to work as a consultant for B for a fee of $50,000, payable at the end of the year. B wrongfully discharges A at the end of eleven months. A can recover in restitution based on the reasonable value of his services. The terms of the contract are evidence of this value but are not conclusive.

Comment e. Avoidability as a limit on restitution. The rule that precludes restitution for a benefit that has been conferred officiously (*Restatement of Restitution § 2*), applies to preclude recovery for performances that a party has rendered following a repudiation by the other party. Compare the rule stated in § 350.

Illustration:

13.   A contracts to build a bridge for B for $100,000. B repudiates the contract shortly after A has begun work on the bridge, telling A that he no longer has need for it. A nevertheless spends an additional $10,000 in continuing to perform. A's restitution interest under the rule stated in § 370 does not include the benefit conferred on B by the $10,000. See Illustration 1 to § 350.

Restatement 2d of Contracts

§ 374   Restitution in Favor of Party in Breach

(1) Subject to the rule stated in Subsection (2), if a party justifiably refuses to perform on the ground that his remaining duties of performance have been discharged by the other party's breach, the party in breach is entitled to restitution for any benefit that he has conferred by way of part performance or reliance in excess of the loss that he has caused by his own breach.

(2) To the extent that, under the manifested assent of the parties, a party's performance is to be retained in the case of breach, that party is not entitled to restitution if the value of the performance as liquidated damages is reasonable in the light of the anticipated or actual loss caused by the breach and the difficulties of proof of loss.

Comments & Illustrations

Comment a. Restitution in spite of breach. The rule stated in this Section applies where a party, after having rendered part performance, commits a breach by either non-performance or repudiation that justifies the other party in refusing further performance. It is often unjust to allow the injured party to retain the entire benefit of the part performance rendered by the party in breach without paying anything in return. The party in breach is, in any case, liable for the loss caused by his breach. If the benefit received by the injured party does not exceed that loss, he owes nothing to the party in breach. If the benefit received exceeds that loss, the rule stated in this Section generally gives the party in breach the right to recover the excess in restitution. If the injured party has a right to specific performance and remains willing and able to perform, he may keep what he has received and sue for specific performance of the balance.

The rule stated in this Section is of particular importance in connection with breach by the buyer under a land sale contract (see Illustration 1) and breach by the builder under a construction contract (see Illustrations 2, 3 and 4). It is less important in the case of the defaulting employee, who has the protection afforded by statutes that require salary payments at relatively short intervals. The case of defaulting buyer of goods is governed by Uniform Commercial Code § 2–718(2), which generally allows restitution of all but an amount fixed by that section. Furthermore, to the extent that the contract is "divisible" so that pairs of part performances on each side are agreed equivalents (§ 240), the party in breach can recover under the terms of the contract and does not need restitution to obtain relief.

Comment b. Measurement of benefit. If the party in breach seeks restitution of money that he has paid, no problem arises in measuring the benefit to the other party. See Illustration 1. If, however, he seeks to recover a sum of money that represents the benefit of services rendered to the other party, measurement of the benefit is more difficult. Since the party seeking restitution is responsible for posing the problem of measurement of benefit, doubts will be resolved against him and his recovery will not exceed the less generous of the two measures stated in § 370, that of the other party's increase in wealth. See Illustration 3. If no value can be put on this, he cannot recover. See Illustration 5. Although the contract price is evidence of the benefit, it is not conclusive. However, in no case will the party in breach be allowed to recover more than a ratable portion of the total contract price where such a portion can be determined.

A party who intentionally furnishes services or builds a building that is materially different from what he promised is properly regarded as having acted officiously and not in part performance of his promise and will be denied recovery on that ground even if his performance was of some benefit to the other party. This is not the case, however, if the other party has accepted or agreed to accept the substitute performance. See §§ 278, 279.

Illustrations:

1. A contracts to sell land to B for $100,000, which B promises to pay in $10,000 installments before transfer of title. After B has paid $30,000 he fails to pay the remaining installments and A sells the land to another buyer for $95,000. B can recover $30,000 from A in restitution less $5,000 damages for B's breach of

contract, or $25,000. If A does not sell the land to another buyer and obtains a decree of specific performance against B, B has no right to restitution.

2.   A contracts to make repairs to B's building in return for B's promise to pay $10,000 on completion of the work. After spending $8,000 on the job, A fails to complete it because of insolvency. B has the work completed by another builder for $4,000, increasing the value of the building to him by a total of $9,000, but he loses $500 in rent because of the delay. A can recover $5,000 from B in restitution less $500 in damages for the loss caused by the breach, or $4,500.

3.   A contracts to make repairs to B's building in return for B's promise to pay $10,000 on completion of the work. A makes repairs costing him $8,000 but inadvertently fails to follow the specifications in such material respects that there is no substantial performance. See Comment *d* to § 237. The defects cannot be corrected without the destruction of large parts of the building, but the work confers a benefit on B by increasing the value of the building to him by $4,000. A can recover $4,000 from B in restitution.

4.   The facts being otherwise as stated in Illustration 3, the defects do not require destruction of large parts of the building and can be corrected for $4,000, which will confer a benefit on B by increasing the value of the building to him by a total of $9,000. A can recover $5,000 from B in restitution.

5.   A contracts to tutor B's son for six months in preparation for an examination, in return for which B promises to pay A $2,000 at the end of that time. After A has worked for three months, he leaves to take another job and B is unable to find a suitable replacement. In the absence of any reliable basis for measuring the benefit to B from A's part performance, restitution will be denied.

Comment c. Exception for money paid. Instead of promising to pay a fixed sum as liquidated damages in case of breach, a promisor may actually pay a sum of money that the parties understand is to be retained by the promisee if the promise is not performed. If the sum is a reasonable one that would be sustained as liquidated damages under the rule stated in § 356, the promisee is entitled to retain it. If it is not, the promisor is entitled to restitution under the rule stated in Subsection (1). The test of reasonableness is the same as that applicable to a provision for liquidated damages. See Comment *b* to § 356. The understanding of the parties may be shown by the terms of their agreement, by description of the sum as "earnest money" or by usage. The sum may or may not be part of the price to be paid by the promisor. The same principle applies if what is to be retained by the promisee is property other than money.

Illustrations:

6. The facts being otherwise as stated in Illustration 1, the contract provides that on default by B, A has the right to retain the first $10,000 installment paid by B. If $10,000 is a reasonable amount, B can recover only $20,000 from A in restitution.

7. The facts being otherwise as stated in Illustration 1, the contract provides that on default by B, A has the right to retain any installments paid by B. The provision is not valid, and B can still recover $30,000 from A in restitution less $5,000 damages for B's breach of contract, or $25,000.

Oliver v. Campbell

Supreme Court of California, 1954.
273 P.2d 15.

■ CARTER, J. Plaintiff appeals from a judgment for defendant, administratrix of the estate of Roy Campbell, deceased, in an action for attorney's fees.

Plaintiff's cause of action was stated in a common count alleging that Roy Campbell became indebted to him in the sum of $10,000, the reasonable value of services rendered as attorney for Campbell; that no part had been paid except $450. Campbell died after the services were rendered by plaintiff. Plaintiff filed a claim against his estate for the fees which defendant rejected. Defendant in her answer denied the allegations made and as a "further" defense alleged that plaintiff and Campbell entered into an "express written contract" employing plaintiff as attorney for a stated fee of $750, and all work alleged to have been performed by plaintiff was performed under that contract.

According to the findings of the trial court the claim against the estate was founded on the alleged reasonable value of legal services rendered by plaintiff for Campbell in an action for separate maintenance by defendant, Campbell's wife, against Campbell and in which the latter cross-complained for a divorce. Plaintiff was not counsel when the pleadings in that action were filed. He came into the case on December 16, 1949, before trial of the action. He and Campbell entered into a written contract on that date for plaintiff's representation of Campbell in the action, the contract stating that plaintiff agrees to represent Campbell in the separate maintenance and divorce action which has been set for trial in the superior court for a "total fee" of $750 plus court costs and other incidentals in the sum of $100 making a total of $850. The fees were to be paid after trial. Plaintiff represented Campbell at the trial consuming 29 days and lasting until May, 1950. (Defendant's complaint for separate maintenance was changed to one for divorce.) After the trial ended the court indicated its intention to give Mrs. Campbell a divorce. But while her proposed findings were under consideration by plaintiff and the court, defendant Campbell substituted himself instead of plaintiff and thereby the representation by plaintiff of

Campbell was "terminated." The findings in the divorce action were filed in May, 1951. Plaintiff's services were furnished pursuant to the contract. The reasonable value of the services was $5,000. Campbell paid $450 to plaintiff and the $100 costs.

The court concluded that plaintiff should take nothing because neither his claim against the estate nor his action was on the contract but were in *quantum meruit* and no recovery could be had for the reasonable value of the services because the compensation for those services was covered by the express contract.

According to plaintiff's undisputed testimony Campbell told him after defendant had offered proposed findings in the divorce action that he was dissatisfied with plaintiff as his counsel and would discharge him and asked him if he would sign a substitution of attorneys under which Campbell would represent himself. Plaintiff replied that he recognized Campbell had a right to discharge him but that he was prepared to carry the case to conclusion; that he expected to be paid the reasonable value of his services which would be as much as defendant's counsel in the divorce action received, $9,000, to which Campbell replied he was not going to pay "a cent more." (At that time Campbell had paid $450.) Thereupon the substitution (dated January 25, 1951) was signed and Campbell took plaintiff's file in the divorce case with him.

It seems that the contract of employment contemplated that plaintiff was to continue his services and representation at least until and including final judgment in the divorce action. See *Neblett v. Getty*, 20 Cal.App.2d 65 (1937). It might thus appear that plaintiff was discharged before he had fully completed his services under the contract and the discharge prevented him from completing his performance. (That question is later discussed.)

One alleged rule of law applied by the trial court and that urged by defendant is that where there is a contract of employment for a definite term which fixes the compensation, there cannot be any recovery for the reasonable value of the services even though the employer discharges the employee—repudiates the contract before the end of the term; that the only remedy of the employee is an action on the contract for the fixed compensation or damages for the breach of the contract. The trial court accepted that theory and rendered judgment for defendant because plaintiff did not state a cause of action on the contract nor for damages for its breach; it was for the reasonable value of the services performed before plaintiff's discharge. Accordingly there is no express finding on whether the discharge was wrongful or whether there was a rescission of the contract by plaintiff because of Campbell's breach of it, or whether plaintiff had substantially performed at the time of this discharge.

The rule applied is not in accord with the general contract law, the law applicable to employment contracts or employment of an attorney by a client. The general rule is stated: "that one who has been injured by a breach of contract has an election to pursue any of three remedies, to wit: 'He may treat the contract as rescinded and may recover upon a quantum meruit so far as he has performed; or he may keep the contract alive, for the benefit of both parties, being at all times ready and able to perform; or, third, he may treat the repudiation as putting an end to the contract for all purposes of performance, and sue for the profits he would have realized if he had not been prevented from performing.' " (*Alder v. Drudis*, 30 Cal.2d 372, 381 (1947); see 12 Cal.Jur.2d, Contracts, § 253; Rest. Contracts, § 347.) It is the same in agency or contract for services cases.

"If the principal, in violation of the contract of employment, terminates or repudiates the employment, or the agent properly terminates it because of breach of contract by the principal, the agent is entitled at his election to receive either:

"(a) the amount of the net losses caused and gains prevented by the principal's breach or, if there are no such losses or gains, a small sum as nominal damages; or

"(b) the reasonable value of the services previously rendered the principal, not limited by the contract price, except that for services for which a price is apportioned by the terms of the contract he is entitled to receive the contract price and no more.

"*Comment*:

"*a*. In no event is the agent entitled to compensation for services unperformed. If, however, the principal terminates the relationship in breach of contract, or if the agent chooses to terminate it because of a total breach by the principal, the agent is entitled, at his option, to affirm or disaffirm the contract. If he affirms the contract, he can maintain an action for its breach and recover damages in accordance with the rule stated in Clause (a). For a complete statement as to the amount of damages recoverable, if he chooses this alternative, see the Restatement of Contracts, §§ 326–346. The rule stated in Clause (b) is based upon the disaffirmance of the contract by the agent, and damages are given him by way of restitution. The Restatement of Contracts, § 347, states the consequences of disaffirmance and the non-availability of restitution as a remedy where part performance has been completed, for which compensation has been apportioned." (Rest. Agency, § 455.) "If the performance rendered consists of services, there cannot ordinarily, from the nature of legal remedies, be actual restitution, but it is possible to give the equivalent in value under a common count. Since money paid may be thus recovered and similarly in the United States in many instances, land, logic would require such a remedy; and it is allowed in part, but only in part. If the plaintiff has fully performed the contract, or a severable part thereof, and 'if the only part of the agreed exchange for such performance that has not been rendered by the defendant is a sum of money constituting a liquidated sum,' the only redress he has for breach of contract by the other side is damages for the breach. It is true that if the performance to which he is entitled in return is a liquidated sum of money, he may sue in *indebitatus assumpsit* and not on the special contract, but the measure of damages is what he ought to have received—not the value of what he has given. If, however, the plaintiff has only partly performed and has been excused from further performance by prevention or by the repudiation or abandonment of the contract by the defendant, he may recover, either in England or America, the value of the services rendered, though such a remedy is no more necessary than where he has fully performed, since in both cases alike the plaintiff has an effectual remedy in an action on the contract for damages. In some jurisdictions, if a price or rate of compensation is fixed by the contract, that is made the conclusive test of the value of the services rendered. More frequently, however, the plaintiff is allowed to recover the real value of the services though in excess of the contract price. The latter rule seems more in accordance with the theory on which the right of action must be based—that the contract is treated as rescinded, and the plaintiff restored to his original position as nearly as possible." (Williston on Contracts (rev. ed.), § 1459.)

And in entire contracts employing an attorney for a fixed fee it has been said that when the client wrongfully discharges the attorney before he has completed the contract, the attorney may recover the reasonable value of the services performed to the time of discharge. Inasmuch as the contract has been repudiated by the employer before its term is up and after the employee has partly performed and the employee may treat the contract as "rescinded," there is no longer any contract upon which the employer can rely as fixing conclusively the limit of the compensation—the reasonable value of services recoverable by the employee for his part performance.

Hence it is stated in *Lessing v. Gibbons*, 6 Cal.App.2d 598, 607 (1935), that: "It is well settled that one who is wrongfully discharged and prevented from further performance of his contract may elect as a general rule to treat the contract as rescinded, may sue upon a *quantum meruit* as if the special contract of employment had never been made and may recover the reasonable value of the services performed even though such reasonable value exceeds the contract price." That statement is quoted with approval in *Neblett v. Getty, supra*, 20 Cal.App.2d 65, 70 (1937) (dictum). The same is said in *Laiblin v. San Joaquin Agr. Corp.*, 60 Cal.App. 516 (1923), quoting with approval from sections 1459, *supra*, and 1485 of Williston on Contracts.

Of course the contract price is competent evidence bearing on the reasonable value of the services.

It is true that in the Lessing case, *supra* (6 Cal.App.2d 598), the trial court found against an express contract of employment of the attorney fixing his compensation, but in affirming the judgment for reasonable value of the services the District Court of Appeal as one of its grounds, and in making the above quoted statement, assumed that there was an express contract fixing the fees. In *Elconin v. Yalen*, 208 Cal. 546 (1929), there was involved a case where the fees were not stated in the contract of employment and the court's statement that if there had been such a fixing it would have "measured" the amount of recovery, was dictum. It is not clear whether it was meant that such a contract would be only evidence of the amount or the conclusive measure. Moreover it cited for its dictum *Kirk v. Culley*, 202 Cal. 501 (1927), and *Webb v. Trescony*, 76 Cal. 621 (1888), which merely held that where an attorney is wrongfully discharged under a partially performed contract he may sue for damages for the breach and in a proper case the full contract price may be the measure of damages. The same is true of *Denio v. City of Huntington Beach, 22 Cal.2d 580 (1943)*, and *Zurich G. A. & L. Ins. Co., Ltd. v. Kinsler, 12 Cal.2d 98 (1938)*.

Inherent in the right to plead by common count in *quantum meruit* where the employee has partly performed but has been prevented from full performance by the employer's repudiation of the contract, is the principle that he need not plead the contract or its repudiation and his rescission of it. There are cases indicating that those special facts should be pleaded but the well established rule is that a common count declaration is sufficient under the circumstances above mentioned.

A common count may be used where the only thing that remains to be done is the payment of money. In the instant case all that remained to be done by defendant was the payment of the amount still due on the contract as it became due by its terms after the trial of the divorce action.

It should further be noted that under the only evidence on the subject, above mentioned, plaintiff in effect promptly notified Campbell of the rescission of the contract when he advised him that he would execute the substitution of attorneys when he was discharged by Campbell but told Campbell he would hold him for the reasonable value of the services.

On the issue of the necessity of restoration or offer to restore the part payment for the services which Campbell had made, the rule applies that such restoration is not necessary where plaintiff would be entitled to it in any event. It is clear that plaintiff was entitled to receive the $450 paid to him either under the contract or for the reasonable value of his services.

The question remains, however, of the application of the foregoing rules to the instant case. Plaintiff had performed practically all of the services he was employed to perform when he was discharged. The trial was at an end. The court had indicated its intention to give judgment against Campbell and all that remained was the signing of findings and judgment. The full sum called for in the contract was payable because the trial had ended.

Under these circumstances it would appear that in effect, plaintiff had completed the performance of his services and the rule would apply that: "The remedy of restitution in money is not available to one who has fully performed his part of a contract, if the only part of the agreed exchange for such performance that has not been rendered by the defendant is a sum of money constituting a liquidated debt; but full performance does not make restitution unavailable if any part of the consideration due from the defendant in return is something other than a liquidated debt." (Rest. Contracts, § 350.) In such cases he recovers the full contract price and no more. As we have seen, as far as pleading is concerned, however, the action may be stated as a common count other than a declaration on the special contract. Here plaintiff alleged an indebtedness on defendant's part for services performed by plaintiff of a reasonable value of $10,000 of which only $450 had been paid.

While it may have been more appropriate for him to have alleged that the price of such services was the contract figure, any deficiency of the pleading is eliminated by defendant's answer setting forth that factor. Plaintiff's action can thus be said to be common count *indebitatus assumpsit*, and there being no dispute as to the amount called for in the contract, the services having been in effect fully performed, the court should have rendered judgment for the balance due on the contract which is conceded to be $300.

The judgment is therefore reversed and the trial court is directed to render judgment in favor of plaintiff for the sum of $300.

■ SCHAUER, J., dissenting. I dissent. I agree with a great deal of the discussion in the majority opinion, and even to a larger extent with the authorities therein cited, relative to the rules of law which should govern this case but I think this court misapplies the very rules it cites.

Specifically, I think this court errs when it says "there being no dispute as to the amount called for in the contract, the services having been in effect fully performed, the court should have rendered judgment for the balance due on the contract which is conceded to be $300." The foregoing statement is neither supported factually by the record nor legally by the authorities cited.

Upon the record and the authorities the judgment should be reversed and the cause remanded either (a) with directions to the trial court to enter judgment for the plaintiff for $5,000 or (b) for a retrial upon all issues. I would prefer to end the litigation by adopting alternative (a) and in my view the record fully justifies that disposition of the cause. Directed to that conclusion is the succinctly stated opinion prepared by Justice Vallee when the cause was before the District Court of Appeal (reported at (Cal.App.) pp. 932–933, 265 P.2d) and I adopt it as a most worthy presentation of the views which I think should prevail:

> I am of the opinion that the judgment should be reversed with directions to the superior court to render judgment for plaintiff for $5,000. The court found that the reasonable value of the services performed by plaintiff is $5,000. Plaintiff was the only witness who testified concerning his discharge by Dr. Campbell. The opinion of this court fails to state all of the testimony of plaintiff with respect to his discharge. I think no reasonable conclusion can be drawn from the evidence other than that the discharge amounts to a clear repudiation and abrogation of the contract in its entirety, in which case plaintiff is entitled to recover the reasonable value of the service performed. *The contract plaintiff made with Dr. Campbell did not limit his services to the trial of the case.* Under the contract he agreed to represent the doctor until final judgment, and he told the doctor that he 'thought the case would be reversed on appeal.' Manifestly, the evidence will be no different on a retrial. Dr.

Campbell is dead. Plaintiff is the only witness who can testify to the conversation. There is nothing in plaintiff's testimony to impugn his integrity. He did all any lawyer of the highest professional standards could have done under the conditions. Defendant waived plaintiff's disqualification under the dead man's statute. (*Deacon v. Bryans*, 212 Cal. 87, 90–93 (1931).) Defendant will be unable to make any showing to the contrary of the testimony of plaintiff. Under these circumstances, the judgment should be reversed with directions as I have indicated. (*Conner v. Grosso*, 41 Cal.2d 229, 232 (1953).)

Olwell v. Nye & Nissen Co.

Supreme Court of Washington, 1946.
173 P.2d 652.

■ MALLERY, J. On May 6, 1940, plaintiff, E. L. Olwell, sold and transferred to the defendant corporation his one-half interest in Puget Sound Egg Packers, a Washington corporation having its principal place of business in Tacoma. By the terms of the agreement, the plaintiff was to retain full ownership in an "Eggsact" egg-washing machine, formerly used by Puget Sound Egg Packers. The defendant promised to make it available for delivery to the plaintiff on or before June 15, 1940.

It appears that the plaintiff arranged for and had the machine stored in a space adjacent to the premises occupied by the defendant but not covered by its lease. Due to the scarcity of labor immediately after the outbreak of the war, defendant's treasurer, without the knowledge or consent of the plaintiff, ordered the egg washer taken out of storage. The machine was put into operation by defendant on May 31, 1941, and thereafter, for a period of three years, was used approximately one day a week in the regular course of the defendant's business.

Plaintiff first discovered this use in January or February of 1945, when he happened to be at the plant on business and heard the machine operating. Thereupon, plaintiff offered to sell the machine to defendant for six hundred dollars or half of its original cost in 1929. A counteroffer of fifty dollars was refused, and, approximately one month later, this action was commenced to recover the reasonable value of defendant's use of the machine, and praying for twenty-five dollars per month from the commencement of the unauthorized use until the time of trial. A second cause of action was alleged, but was not pressed and hence is not here involved. The court entered judgment for plaintiff in the amount of ten dollars per week for the period of 156 weeks covered by the statute of limitations, or $1,560, and gave the plaintiff his costs.

Defendant has appealed to this court, assigning error upon the judgment, upon the trial of the cause on the theory of unjust enrichment, upon the amount of damages, and upon the court's refusal to make a finding as to the value of the machine, and in refusing to consider such value in measuring damages.

The theory of the respondent was that the tort of conversion could be "waived" and suit brought in quasi contract, upon a contract implied in law, to recover, as restitution, the profits which inured to appellant as a result of its wrongful use of the machine. With this the trial court agreed and, in its findings of facts, found that the use of the machine

> "resulted in a benefit to the users, in that said use saves the users approximately $1.43 per hour of use as against the expense which would be incurred were eggs to be washed by hand; that said machine was used by Puget Sound Egg Packers and defendant, on an average of one day per week from May of 1941, until February of 1945 at an average saving of $10.00 per each day of use."

In substance, the argument presented by the assignments of error is that the principle of unjust enrichment, or quasi contract, is not of universal application but is imposed only in exceptional cases because of special facts and circumstances and in favor of particular persons; that respondent had an adequate remedy in an action at law for replevin or claim and delivery; that any damages awarded to the plaintiff should be based upon the use or rental value of the machine and should bear some reasonable relation to its market value. Appellant therefore contends that the amount of the judgment is excessive.

It is uniformly held that in cases where the defendant *tort feasor* has benefited by his wrong, the plaintiff may elect to "waive the tort" and bring an action *in assumpsit* for restitution. Such an action arises out of a duty imposed by law devolving upon the defendant to repay an unjust and unmerited enrichment.

It is clear that the saving in labor cost which appellant derived from its use of respondent's machine constituted a benefit.

According to the *Restatement of Restitution 12, § 1 (b),*

> A person confers a benefit upon another if he gives to the other possession of or some other interest in money, land, chattels, or choses in action, performs services beneficial to or at the request of the other, satisfies a debt or a duty of the other, or in any way adds to the other's security or advantage. *He confers a benefit not only where he adds to the property of another, but also where he* saves the other from expense or loss. The word 'benefit,' therefore, denotes any form of advantage. (Italics ours.)

It is also necessary to show that, while appellant benefited from its use of the egg-washing machine, respondent thereby incurred a loss. It is argued by appellant that, since the machine was put into storage by respondent, who had no present use for it, and for a period of almost three years did not know that appellant was operating it, and since it was not injured by its operation and the appellant never adversely claimed any title to it, nor contested respondent's right of repossession upon the latter's discovery of the wrongful operation, that the respondent was not damaged, because he is as well off as if the machine had not been used by appellant.

The very essence of the nature of property is the right to its exclusive use. Without it, no beneficial right remains. However plausible, the appellant cannot be heard to say that its wrongful invasion of the respondent's property right to exclusive use is not a loss compensable in law. To hold otherwise would be subversive of all property rights, since its use was admittedly wrongful and without claim of right. The theory of unjust enrichment is applicable in such a case.

We agree with appellant that respondent could have elected a "common garden variety of action," as he calls it, for the recovery of damages. It is also true that, except where provided for by statute, punitive damages are not allowed, the basic measure for the recovery of damages in this state being compensation. If, then, respondent had been *limited* to redress *in tort* for damages, as appellant contends, the court below would be in error in refusing to make a finding as to the value of the machine. In such case, the award of damages must bear a reasonable relation to the value of the property. *Hoff v. Lester*, 25 Wn. (2d) 86 (1946).

But respondent here had an election. He chose rather to waive his right of action *in tort* and to sue *in assumpsit* on the implied contract. Having so elected, he is entitled to the measure of restoration which accompanies the remedy.

> Actions for restitution have for their primary purpose taking from the defendant and restoring to the plaintiff something to which the plaintiff is entitled, or if this is not done, causing the defendant to pay the plaintiff an amount which will restore the plaintiff to the position in which he was before the defendant received the benefit. If the value of what was received and what was lost were always equal, there would be no substantial problem as to the amount of recovery, since actions of restitution are not punitive. In fact, however, the plaintiff frequently has lost more than the defendant has gained, and sometimes the defendant has gained more than the plaintiff has lost.

> In such cases the measure of restitution is determined with reference to the tortiousness of the defendant's conduct or the negligence or other fault of one or both of the parties in creating the situation giving rise to the right to restitution. If the defendant was tortious in his acquisition of the benefit he is required to pay for what the other has lost although that is more than the recipient benefited. *If he was consciously tortious in acquiring the benefit, he is also deprived of any profit derived from his subsequent dealing with it*. If he was no more at fault than the claimant, he is not required to pay for losses in excess of benefit received by him and he is permitted to retain gains which result from his dealing with the property." (Italics ours.) Restatement of Restitution 595–6.

Respondent may recover the profit derived by the appellant from the use of the machine.

* * *

The plaintiff in *Oliver* was a lawyer hired by a man to defend against his wife's claim for a separate maintenance and to cross-claim for divorce. The representation contract provided that the plaintiff would be paid $750 in fees and $100 in costs. After the plaintiff had done substantial work in the representation, indeed after the trial had ended (unsuccessfully), the client expressed dissatisfaction with his services and said that he wanted to begin representing himself. At this point, the plaintiff had been paid $450 in fees and $100 in costs. The plaintiff answered that his client had a right to dismiss him but that he was prepared to carry the case to a conclusion. He also said that he expected to be paid not the contract price but rather the reasonable value of his services, which he claimed was the same as the fee that the lawyer on the other side had received, namely $9000. Sometime in the course of the now extended legal proceedings the client died and his wife, now acting as administratrix of his estate, abandoned her claim for divorce. The plaintiff sued the wife-cum-widow, seeking restitution, to the tune of $10,000, for the fair value of the services that he had rendered.

Oliver makes plain that a party who has been injured by a breach of contract may abandon his contractual rights (to keep the contract alive, when it is reasonable, and pursue performance, or to seek contract damages for the breach) and instead treat the contract as rescinded and seek to recover in restitution—in this context sometimes also called *quantum meruit*—for the performance that he has rendered. Where a plaintiff chooses to proceed in *quantum meruit*, moreover, he may recover the real value of his services, even though they exceed the contract price. However, the court says, this restitutionary option is not available to a promisee who has fully performed his side of a contract, when the only performance that the breaching promisor has failed to render is the payment of a liquidated sum. And, the court concludes, *Oliver* is such a case: the trial had been completed before the plaintiff was fired, and he had no services left to perform under the contract. All that remained in order to complete the contract entirely was for the defendant to pay him the remaining $300 of his fee, which represents the only remedy to which he is entitled.

A dissenter doubted whether the legal principles that the majority announced actually supported the outcome in the case. The contract, the dissenter believed, did not limit the representation to the initial trial, and the lawyer and client had expressly contemplated an appeal. Accordingly, completing the contract required more than just the payment of a liquidated sum, and so the plaintiff's *quantum meruit* claim should have succeeded. This fact-specific argument has little general interest, but the dissenter also doubted the wisdom of the legal rule that the majority announced, seeing no reason why restitutionary recovery should be precluded simply because a promisee has completed his performance and a breaching promisor needs only to pay a fixed sum to complete hers. The dissenter did not explain why he thought this way, but it is not hard to think of good reasons. For one thing, the majority's rule seems to punish promisees for their diligence in performing. For another, the rule creates a sharp discontinuity in the remedy to which a promisee is entitled, depicted graphically in the figure below.

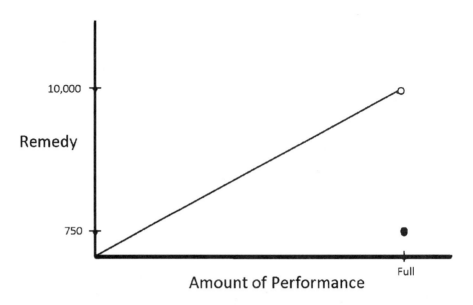

Figure 10.1

The Disappearing Remedy in *Oliver v. Campbell*

Such discontinuities generally produce inefficient incentives at the points where they arise—because they eliminate the capacity to fine-tune costs and benefits on which efficient incentives depend—and the rule in *Oliver* is no exception. In particular, that rule gives promisees who suspect that their promisors might breach a strong incentive to delay completing their own contractual performance, especially in cases (and *Oliver*, see below, surely presents such a circumstance) in which such delays are difficult or impossible for promisors to identify or to verify before courts. Even the prospect of such delaying tactics, moreover, will undermine the confidence of wavering promisors, and so encourage contractual coordination to unravel.

One other feature of *Oliver* is worth noting here, which suggests that although the case may have been decided on the basis of the reasons reported in the text of the opinions, the real foundations for the decision may, instead, lie in the context in which the dispute arose. The plaintiff was a lawyer and was, in effect, suing his client to recover fees in excess of those he had announced upon commencing the representation. Contracts between lawyers and their clients are special, and indeed special in a way that renders them unrepresentative of contracts more generally (in a fashion that resembles the specialness noted earlier concerning contracts that involve common carriers or insurance companies).

Lawyers claim to be not just ordinary service providers but rather *professionals*. This claim carries a range of social and class implications, which though interesting are not directly relevant here. But the claim to professional status also has more direct legal implications: specifically, the bar asserts, under the heading of its professionalism, a right to regulate itself, free from the controls ordinarily exerted by both the ordinary legislative process and the market. The justifications offered for this claim are not worth pursuing here, but its entailments do matter. Specifically, it is part of lawyers' professionalism to claim that they, rather than their clients, are the best judges of the quantity and quality of the legal services that the clients require (this view is intertwined with the legal profession's claim to stand apart from market forces). This claim may seem dubious, and it is nowadays coming under threat from a variety of forces, but insofar as it succeeds it entails that lawyers may not fix and adjust their fees through arms-length negotiations, pursuant to the principles of freedom of contract, and subject only to whatever discipline market competition imposes. Instead, lawyers' contractual freedom is constrained by obligations to deal fairly and above all openly with their clients, enshrined, for example, in rules of professional conduct that require lawyers to charge only reasonable fees and encourage (if they do not always require) lawyers to explain the legal fees that a representation will involve, in writing, before commencing work.[7] The plaintiff in *Oliver* violated at least the spirit of these rules, and this, rather than any contract principles, may explain the somewhat artificial ground on which he eventually lost.

Now although *Oliver* vividly illustrates that a plaintiff's restitutionary interest can dramatically exceed his expectation interest, there is no problem in that case in assessing the size of this interest—that is, in measuring the value of the performance given. In other circumstances, however, this measurement question can raise deep doctrinal puzzles. The origin of the problem is that there are three ways to measure the "value of performance given" for purposes of a restitutionary remedy. This value may equal:

(a) the cost that the recipient would have had to pay to obtain the performance from a third party (or the price that a third party would be willing to pay for performance that was rendered) on the open market;

(b) the cost to performer of rendering the performance (this is really a reliance measure); or

(c) the value of this performance in hands of the recipient (i.e., the amount by which performance has increased the recipient's net worth)

The Restatement says that one should choose between (a) and (c) as justice requires.[8]

It may seem that this is, quite literally, a trivial choice. After all, when a person unjustly uses a resource to which he is not entitled, the amount by which this use increases his net worth (the restitutionary remedy announced in (c)) is surely bounded above by the cost to him of actually paying for the resource on the market and bounded below by the return he

---

7. MODEL RULES OF PROFESSIONAL CONDUCT R. 1.5 (2009).

8. RESTATEMENT (SECOND) OF CONTRACT § 371 (1981).

could achieve by selling the resources on the market (the restitutionary remedy announced in (a)). So the two remedies appear to be equivalent. But while this will be true whenever there exist well-functioning markets for the resource in question, it will not be true when such markets do not exist or have broken down. In that case, it may be that although a notional market price for the resource exists, it is impossible actually to acquire the resource at that price. And in this case, the amount of the unjust enrichment brought on by using the resource is not the saved costs of having had to pay for it otherwise, since it could not actually have been bought, but rather the (potentially much greater) revenues generated through its use. When markets break down, (a) and (c) come apart. Moreover, problems of unjust enrichment tend to arise precisely when markets have broken down, since this is the circumstance in which people most commonly find themselves wishing to use resources that they cannot acquire by paying for them.

When (a) and (c) come apart, the choice between them is not always so easy to make, and making it can implicate the core remedial form and purposes of contract law. The text of the Restatement, moreover, offers little guidance on how to choose. But the conceptual structure of contract law can offer substantial guidance.

Both the difficulties and also the legal resources for dealing with them are revealed by comparing the reasoning in *Olwell* with the earlier discussion of *Gassner*. In *Olwell*, the plaintiff sold the defendant an egg-packing business but retained exclusive ownership of an egg-washing machine that had been used by the concern. Sometime after the sale, the Second World War broke out, causing an acute labor shortage, and the defendant began, without permission, to use the egg-washing machine. When the plaintiff discovered this, he offered to sell the machine to the defendant for $600 (half of its price when new). The defendant declined, and offered to pay only $50, whereupon the plaintiff sued, seeking recovery of the reasonable value of the defendant's use of the machine.

The trial court found that, given the cost of the labor, the machine had saved the defendant $10 per week for 156 weeks and therefore awarded the plaintiff $1560 in damages. The defendant appealed, arguing that the plaintiff's damages should be limited to his traditional tort damages, namely the loss to him of having been deprived of the machine (measured, perhaps, by the rental value of the machine). Note, moreover, that although the case is styled as a contest between restitutionary and tort-based recovery, it equally raises, purely within restitution, the question how to measure the extent of the defendant's unjust enrichment. The trial court chose to apply standard (c) above—and equated the extent by which the defendant's wrongful use of the machine had increased his net worth with his labor costs saved. This made sense in light of the on-going war, which likely entailed that had the defendant forgone use of the plaintiff's machine, he would not have been able simply to rent another machine. The defendant's enrichment was therefore not limited by the rental fees that his unjust appropriation of the plaintiff's machine saved his having to pay.

The defendant nevertheless sought to apply a market-value standard to the plaintiff's recovery, by invoking rule (a) above to limit the damages he owed to the (now notional) rental value of the machine over the period of time for which he used it.

The *Olwell* court announced a seemingly straightforward rule for choosing between (a) and (c) in cases like the one that it confronted. First, when a defendant's conduct is not intentionally tortious but merely negligent, the court said, then a plaintiff may recover only his losses (as measured by the market value of the resource he was deprived of) and not the defendant's greater gains from using the resources (not even when the breakdown of markets entailed that, had the defendant not appropriated the resource, he could not have bought an equivalent on the market and so would have forsaken all of whatever gains the resource generated).[9] And second, if the defendant's conduct is consciously tortious, then the plaintiff may recover the defendant's full gains even though they exceed the plaintiff's losses and thus also the market price of acquiring the resource in question non-tortiously. Applying these rules, the appellate court affirmed the judgment at trial awarding the plaintiff $1560.

The contrast between the rule announced in *Olwell* and the holding in *Gassner* should not be overlooked. The plaintiff in *Gassner* received a restitutionary recovery equal to the full amount by which the defendant was enriched on resale, as under rule (b), notwithstanding that the breach was expressly recognized to be innocent, or at most negligent, so that a literal reading of *Olwell* would recommend applying rule (a), to generate a smaller recovery, which did not include disgorgement of whatever portion of the proceeds on resale reflected an above-market price.

The result in *Gassner* is the right one, however. It is right doctrinally because of the conceptual point that the *Gassner* plaintiff's restitutionary claim wins because it is also, and more fundamentally, a claim for expectation damages, and this claim proceeds under a theory of strict liability rather than negligence. Whereas the defendants in the tort cases have a duty only to avoid unreasonably damaging the plaintiffs' property, the defendants in contracts cases have an absolute duty not to disappoint their promisees' contractual expectations. Accordingly, even an innocent (much less a negligent) breach of contract is wrongful, so that when this is truly a breach (that is, when the contract does not allow paying money damages as an alternative form of performance), then restitution of wrongfully acquired gains is required, including even when these gains exceed the (notional) market value of the improperly denied performance.

Finally, note that the formal structure of a plaintiff's restitutionary claim requires that the plaintiff first rescind the breached contract before

---

9. A related principle appeals in *Vincent v. Lake Erie Transp. Co.*, 124 N.W. 221 (Minn. 1910), in which the defendant damaged the plaintiff's dock while trespassing to save his boat in a storm, and the plaintiff recovered only the cost of repairs to the dock and not larger value of defendant's saved boat. Note that *Vincent* also involved a breakdown of markets—the storm meant that although it would ordinarily be cheaper for the defendant to contract to rent a dock than to lose his boat, he could not have acquired use of the dock contractually when he needed it.

proceeding. Rescission can be appealing, and may be declared, in circumstances beyond restitution. In general, rescission is available in cases of fraud, substantial breach of contract (that is, breach that defeats the purpose of the contract), mutual mistake of fact concerning the contract's basic assumptions and defeating the contract's purpose, unilateral mistake of fact known to the other party, and duress. A broader discussion of mistake and duress must abide later materials. The following case, which requires no further explanation, illustrates some of the other issues that can arise concerning rescission.

Mutual Benefit Life Ins. Co. v. JMR Electronics Corp.

United States Court of Appeals for the Second Circuit, 1988.
848 F.2d 30.

■ PER CURIAM. JMR Electronics Corporation ("JMR") appeals from a judgment of the District Court for the Southern District of New York (Robert W. Sweet, Judge) ordering rescission of a life insurance policy issued by plaintiff-appellant The Mutual Benefit Life Insurance Company ("Mutual") and dismissing JMR's counterclaim for the policy's proceeds. Judge Sweet ruled that a misrepresentation made in the policy application concerning the insured's history of cigarette smoking was material as a matter of law. Appellant contends that the misrepresentation was not material because Mutual would have provided insurance—albeit at a higher premium rate—even if the insured's smoking history had been disclosed. We agree with the District Court that summary judgment was appropriate and therefore affirm.

The basic facts are not in dispute. On June 24, 1985, JMR submitted an application to Mutual for a $250,000 "key man" life insurance policy on the life of its president, Joseph Gaon, at the non-smoker's discounted premium rate. Mutual's 1985 Ratebook provides: "The Non–Smoker rates are available when the proposed insured is at least 20 years old and has not smoked a cigarette for at least twelve months prior to the date of the application." Question 13 of the application inquired about the proposed insured's smoking history. Question 13(a) asked, "Do you smoke cigarettes? How many a day?" Gaon answered this question, "No." Question 13(b) asked, "Did you ever smoke cigarettes?" Gaon again answered, "No." Based on these representations, Mutual issued a policy on Gaon's life at the non-smoker premium rate.

Gaon died on June 22, 1986, within the period of contestability contained in the policy, see N.Y. Ins. Law § 3203 (a)(3) (McKinney 1985). Upon routine investigation of JMR's claim for proceeds under the policy, Mutual discovered that the representations made in the insurance application concerning Gaon's smoking history were untrue. JMR has stipulated that, at the time the application was submitted, Gaon in fact "had been smoking one-half of a pack of cigarettes per day for a continuous period of not less than 10 years." Mutual brought this action seeking a declaration that the policy is void. Judge Sweet granted Mutual's motion for summary judgment, dismissed JMR's counterclaim for the proceeds of the policy, and ordered rescission of the insurance policy and return of JMR's premium payments, with interest.

Under New York law, which governs this diversity suit, "it is the rule that even an innocent misrepresentation as to [the applicant's medical history], if material, is sufficient to allow the insurer to avoid the contract of insurance or defeat recovery thereunder." *Process Plants Corp. v. Beneficial National Life Insurance Co.,385 N.Y.S.2d 308, 310 (1st Dep't 1976), aff'd mem., 42 N.Y.2d 928 (1977).* A "misrepresentation" is defined by statute as a false "statement as to past or present fact, made to the insurer at or before the making of the insurance contract as an inducement to the making thereof." *N.Y. Ins. Law § 3105(a)* (McKinney 1985). A misrepresentation is "material" if "knowledge by the insurer of the facts misrepresented would have led to a refusal by the insurer to make such contract." *Id. § 3105(b).* Case law has somewhat broadened the materiality inquiry: "The question is not whether the company *might have issued* the policy even if the information had been furnished; the question in each case is whether the company has been induced to accept an application which it *might otherwise have refused." Geer v. Union Mutual Life Insurance Co., 273 N.Y. 261, 269 (1937)* (emphasis in original). The materiality determination normally presents an issue of fact for the jury, but "where the evidence concerning the materiality is clear and substantially uncontradicted, the matter is one of law for the court to determine." *Process Plants Corp. v. Beneficial National Life Insurance Company, supra, 385 N.Y.S.2d at 310–11; see also Friedman v. Prudential Life Insurance Co. of America, 589 F. Supp. 1017, 1026 (S.D.N.Y. 1984)* (citing New York cases).

In the present case JMR has stipulated that Gaon's smoking history was misrepresented in the insurance application. However, JMR disputes that this misrepresentation is material as a matter of law. JMR argues that under New York law a misrepresentation is not material unless the insurer can demonstrate that, had the applicant provided complete and accurate information, coverage either would have been refused or at the very least withheld pending a more detailed underwriting examination. In JMR's view summary judgment was inappropriate on the facts of this case because a jury could reasonably have found that even "had appellee been aware of Gaon's smoking history, a policy at the smoker's premium rate would have been issued," Appellant's Br. at 4 (emphasis omitted). JMR takes the position that the appropriate remedy in this situation is to permit recovery under the policy in the amount that the premium actually paid would have purchased for a smoker.

We agree with Judge Sweet that this novel theory is without basis in New York law. The plain language of the statutory definition of "materiality," found in section 3105(b), permits avoidance of liability under the policy where "knowledge by the insurer of the facts misrepresented would have led to a refusal by the insurer to make *such contract.*" (Emphasis added). Moreover, numerous courts have observed that the materiality inquiry under New York law is made with respect to the particular policy issued in reliance upon the misrepresentation. In *Barrett v. State Mutual Life Assurance Co.*, 396 N.Y.S.2d 848 (1st Dep't 1977), *aff'd*, 44 N.Y.2d 872 (1978), *cert. denied*, 440 U.S. 912 (1979), for example, the Court found that misrepresentations concerning the insured's medical history contained in his application for life insurance were material as a matter of law, notwithstanding a jury's verdict granting recovery under the policy. The evidence conclusively demonstrated, said the Court, that "had [the insurer] known the truth, the policy in evidence, *whatever may have been done about a possible higher premium rate*, would not have issued in the form found here." *Id.* at 323, (emphasis added). Our conclusion is supported as well in case law from other jurisdictions and by the commentators.

There is no doubt that Mutual was induced to issue the non-smoker, discounted-premium policy to JMR precisely as a result of the misrepresentations made by Gaon concerning his smoking history. That Mutual might not have refused the risk on *any* terms had it known the undisclosed facts is irrelevant. Most risks are insurable at some price. The purpose of the materiality inquiry is not to permit the jury to rewrite the terms of the insurance agreement to conform to the newly disclosed facts but to make certain that the risk insured was the risk covered by the policy agreed upon. If a fact is material to the risk, the insurer may avoid liability under a policy if that fact was misrepresented in an application for that policy whether or not the parties might have agreed to some other contractual arrangement had the critical fact been disclosed. As observed by Judge Sweet, a contrary result would reward the practice of misrepresenting facts critical to the underwriter's task because the unscrupulous (or merely negligent) applicant "would have everything to gain and nothing to lose" from making material misrepresentations in his application for insurance. Such a claimant could rest assured not only that he may demand full coverage should he survive the contestability period, N.Y. Ins. Law § 3203 (a)(3), but that even in the event of a contested claim, he would be entitled to the coverage that he might have contracted for had the necessary information been accurately disclosed at the outset. New York law does not permit this anomalous result. The judgment of the District Court is affirmed.

CHAPTER 11

RELIANCE

The final issue concerning contract remedies, and perhaps also the structurally deepest issue of all, involves the reliance remedy. This remedy, remember, abandons the forward-looking effort—characteristic of the expectation-damages/specific-performance nexus—to put disappointed promisees in a position that is equivalent to the position that they would have enjoyed on performance. Reliance instead seeks, in a purely backward-looking mode, to restore the *status quo ante*, returning plaintiffs to the positions that they would have occupied had there been no contract at all. The reliance remedy therefore abandons, as has been observed in passing, the very features of contract that render it a distinctive form of legal obligation and instead merges contract into the family of loss-based obligations that find legal expression in tort, specifically into the branch of that family concerning obligations that arise in connection with loss-causing misrepresentations.

The reliance remedy is no mere intellectual curiosity, which appears only at contract's outer edge. The law's official presentation of reliance damages treats these as a secondary alternative, made available so that promisees whose expectation-based claims fail for one technical reason or another are not left wholly without redress. But it is in fact possible to recharacterize much of the expectation remedy as in fact merely elaborating an expansive, but in no way conceptually distinctive or novel, interpretation of backward-looking reliance. Moreover, in the rare cases in which the expectation remedy cannot be recharacterized in terms of reliance in this way, the law's commitment to vindicating contractual expectations wavers. This renders it uncertain whether the law's self-presentation should be taken at face value: whether the law is actually committed to vindicating the forward-looking entitlements that belong distinctively to expectation damages and specific performance at all.

11.1 RELIANCE AS EXPECTATION

The first step in tracing out this doctrinal and theoretical development is to understand how the reliance remedy functions and why it will in many cases produce the same damages as the expectation remedy. This equivalence raises the question how far the reliance remedy may be employed as a means of circumventing some of the limits on expectation damages investigated earlier—including, most notably, the certainty requirement. The following materials illustrate the issues.

463

Security Stove & Mfg. Co. v. American Railway Express Co.

Court of Appeals of Missouri, 1932.
51 S.W.2d 572.

■ Bland, J. This is an action for damages for the failure of defendant to transport, from Kansas City to Atlantic City, New Jersey, within a reasonable time, a furnace equipped with a combination oil and gas burner. The cause was tried before the court without the aid of a jury, resulting in a judgment in favor of plaintiff in the sum of $801.50 and interest, or in a total sum of $1000. Defendant has appealed.

The facts show that plaintiff manufactured a furnace equipped with a special combination oil and gas burner it desired to exhibit at the American Gas Association Convention held in Atlantic City in October, 1926. The president of plaintiff testified that plaintiff engaged space for the exhibit for the reason "that the Henry L. Dougherty Company was very much interested in putting out a combination oil and gas burner; we had just developed one, after we got through, better than anything on the market and we thought this show would be the psychological time to get in contact with the Dougherty Company;" that "the thing wasn't sent there for sale but primarily to show;" that at the time the space was engaged it was too late to ship the furnace by freight so plaintiff decided to ship it by express, and, on September 18, 1926, wrote the office of the defendant in Kansas City, stating that it had engaged a booth for exhibition purposes at Atlantic City, New Jersey, from the American Gas Association, for the week beginning October 11th; that its exhibition consisted of an oil burning furnace, together with two oil burners which weighed at least 1500 pounds; that, "In order to get this exhibit in place on time it should be in Atlantic City not later than October the 8th. What we want you to do is to tell us how much time you will require to assure the delivery of the exhibit on time."

Mr. Bangs, chief clerk in charge of the local office of the defendant, upon receipt of the letter, sent Mr. Johnson, a commercial representative of the defendant, to see plaintiff. Johnson called upon plaintiff taking its letter with him. Johnson made a notation on the bottom of the letter giving October 4th, as the day that defendant was required to have the exhibit in order for it to reach Atlantic City on October 8th.

On October 1st, plaintiff wrote the defendant at Kansas City, referring to its letter of September 18th, concerning the fact that the furnace must be in Atlantic City not later than October 8th, and stating what Johnson had told it, saying: "Now, Mr. Banks, we want to make doubly sure that this shipment is in Atlantic City not later than October 8th and the purpose of this letter is to tell you that you can *have your truck call for the shipment between 12 and 1 o'clock on Saturday, October 2nd for this.*" (Italics plaintiff's.) On October 2nd, plaintiff called the office of the express company in Kansas City and told it that the shipment was ready. Defendant came for the shipment on the last mentioned day, received it and delivered the express receipt to plaintiff. The shipment contained twenty-one packages. Each package was marked with stickers backed with glue and covered with silica of soda, to prevent the stickers being torn off in shipping. Each package was given a number. They ran from one to twenty-one.

Plaintiff's president made arrangements to go to Atlantic City to attend the convention and install the exhibit, arriving there about October 11th. When he reached Atlantic City he found the shipment had been placed in the booth that had been assigned to plaintiff. The exhibit was set up, but it was found that one of the packages shipped was not there. This missing package contained the gas manifold, or that part of the oil and gas burner that controlled the flow of gas in the burner. This was the most important part of the exhibit and a like burner could not be obtained in Atlantic City.

Wires were sent and it was found that the stray package was at the "over and short bureau" of defendant in St. Louis. Defendant reported that the package would be forwarded to Atlantic City and would be there by Wednesday, the 13th. Plaintiff's president waited until Thursday, the day the convention closed, but the package had not arrived at the time, so he closed up the exhibit and left. About a week after he arrived in Kansas City, the package was returned by the defendant.

Banks testified that the reasonable time for a shipment of this kind to reach Atlantic City from Kansas City would be four days; that if the shipment was received on October 4th, it would reach Atlantic City by October 8th; that plaintiff did not ask defendant for any special rate; that the rate charged was the regular one; that plaintiff asked no special advantage in the shipment; that all defendant, under its agreement with plaintiff was required to do was to deliver the shipment at Atlantic City in the ordinary course of events; that the shipment was found in St. Louis about Monday afternoon or Tuesday morning; that it was delivered at Atlantic City at the Ritz Carlton Hotel, on the 16th of the month. There was evidence on plaintiff's part that the reasonable time for a shipment of this character to reach Atlantic City from Kansas City was not more than three or four days.

The petition upon which the case was tried alleges that plaintiff, on October 2, 1926, delivered the shipment to the defendant; that defendant agreed, in consideration of the express charges received from plaintiff, to carry the shipment from Kansas City to Atlantic City, and "to deliver the same to plaintiff at Atlantic City, New Jersey, on or before October 8, 1926, *the same being the reasonable and proper time necessary to transport said shipment to Atlantic City*, in as good condition as when received of defendant (plaintiff) at Kansas City, Missouri; that previous to the delivery of said goods to defendant at Kansas City, Missouri, this plaintiff apprised defendant of the kind and nature of the goods and told defendant of the necessity of having the goods at Atlantic City by October 8, 1926, and the reason therefor; that defendant knew that the goods were intended for an exhibit at the place and that they would have to be at Atlantic City by that date to be of any service to the defendant (plaintiff)." (Italics ours.)

Plaintiff asked damages, which the court in its judgment allowed as follows: $147 express charges (on the exhibit); $45.12 freight on the exhibit from Atlantic City to Kansas City; $101.39 railroad and pullman fares to and from Atlantic City, expended by plaintiff's president and a workman taken by him to Atlantic City; $48 hotel room for the two; $150 for the time of the president; $40 for wages of plaintiff's other employee and $270 for rental of the booth, making a total of $801.51.

Defendant contends that the court erred in allowing plaintiff's expenses as damages; that the only damages, if any, that can be recovered in cases of this kind, are for loss of profits and that plaintiff's evidence is not sufficient to base any recovery on this ground.

Boiled down to its last analysis, the agreement was nothing more than that the shipment would be transported within the ordinary time. Plaintiff sought no special advantage, was asking nothing that would be denied any other shipper, was asking no particular route, no particular train, nor for any expedited service. It was simply seeking the same rights any other shipper could have enjoyed on the same terms. No special instructions were given or involved in the case.

We think, under the circumstances in this case, that it was proper to allow plaintiff's expenses as its damages. Ordinarily the measure of damages where the carrier fails to deliver a shipment at destination within a reasonable time is the difference between the market value of the goods at the time of the delivery and the time when they should have been delivered. But where the carrier has notice of peculiar circumstances under which the shipment is made, which will result in an unusual loss by the shipper in case of delay in delivery, the carrier is responsible for the real damage sustained from such delay if the notice given is of such character, and goes to such extent, in informing the carrier of the shipper's situation, that the carrier will be presumed to have contracted with reference thereto. *Central Trust Co. v. Savannah & W. R. Co.*, 69 F. 683, 685 (N.D. Ga. 1895).

In the case at bar defendant was advised of the necessity of prompt delivery of the shipment. Plaintiff explained to Johnson the "importance of getting the exhibit there on time." Defendant knew the purpose of the exhibit and ought to respond for its negligence in failing to get it there. As we view the record this negligence is practically conceded. The undisputed testimony shows that the shipment was sent to the over and short department of the defendant in St. Louis. As the packages were plainly numbered this, prima facie, shows mistake or negligence on the part of the defendant. No effort was made by it to show that it was not negligent in sending it there, or not negligence in not forwarding it within a reasonable time after it was found.

There is no evidence or claim in this case that plaintiff suffered any loss of profits by reason of the delay in the shipment. In fact defendant states in its brief:

> The plaintiff introduced not one whit of evidence showing or tending to show that he would have made any sales as a result of

his exhibit but for the negligence of the defendant. On the contrary Blakesley testified that the main purpose of the exhibit was to try to interest the Henry L. Dougherty Company in plaintiff's combination oil and gas burner, yet that was all the evidence that there was as to the benefit plaintiff expected to get from the exhibit.

As a matter of evidence, it is clear that the plaintiff would not have derived a great deal of benefit from the exhibit by any stretch of the imagination.

Nowhere does plaintiff introduce evidence showing that the Henry L. Doherty Company in all probability would have become interested in the combination oil and gas burner and made a profitable contract with the plaintiff.

There is evidence that the exhibit was not sent to make a sale.

Defendant contends that plaintiff "is endeavoring to achieve a return of the *status quo* in a suit bases on a breach of contract. Instead of seeking to recover what he would have had, had the contract not been broken, plaintiff is trying to recover what he would have had, had there never been any contract of shipment;" that the expenses sued for would have been incurred in any event. It is no doubt, the general rule that where there is a breach of contract the party suffering the loss can recover only that which he would have had, had the contract not been broken, and this is all the cases decided upon which defendant relies, including *C. M. & St. P. Ry. v. McCaull–Dinsmore Co.*, 253 U.S. 97 (1920). But this is merely a general statement of the rule and is not inconsistent with the holdings that, in some instances, the injured party may recover expenses incurred in relying upon the contract, although such expenses would have been incurred had the contract not been breached.

In *Sperry et al. v. O'Neill–Adams Co.*, 185 F. 231 (2nd Cir., 1911), the court held that the advantages resulting from the use of trading stamps as a means of increasing trade are so contingent that they cannot form a basis on which to rest a recovery for a breach of contract to supply them. In lieu of compensation based thereon the court directed a recovery in the sum expended in preparation for carrying on business in connection with the use of the stamps. The court said, 185 F. 231, 239:

> Plaintiff in its complaint had made a claim for lost profits, but, finding it impossible to marshal any evidence which would support a finding of exact figures, abandoned that claim. Any attempt to reach a precise sum would be mere blind guesswork. Nevertheless a contract, which both sides conceded would prove a valuable one, had been broken and the party who broke it was responsible for resultant damage. In order to carry out this contract, the plaintiff made expenditures which otherwise it would not have made. The trial judge held, as we think rightly, that plaintiff was entitled at least to recover these expenses to which it had been put in order to secure the benefits of a contract of which defendant's conduct deprived it.

The case at bar was to recover damages for loss of profits by reason of the failure of the defendant to transport the shipment within a reasonable time, so that it would arrive in Atlantic City for the exhibit. There were no profits contemplated. The furnace was to be shown and shipped back to Kansas City. There was no money loss, except the expenses, that was of such a nature as any court would allow as being sufficiently definite or lacking in pure speculation. Therefore, unless plaintiff is permitted to recover the expenses that it went to, which were a total loss to it by reason of its inability to exhibit the furnace and equipment, it will be deprived of any substantial compensation for its loss. The law does not contemplate any such injustice. It ought to allow plaintiff, as damages, the loss in the way of expenses that it sustained, and which it would not have been put to if it had not been for its reliance upon the defendant to perform its contract. There is no contention that the exhibit would have been entirely valueless and whatever it might have accomplished defendant knew of the circumstances and ought to respond for whatever damages plaintiff suffered. In cases of this kind the method of estimating the damages should be adopted which is the most definite and certain and which best achieves the fundamental purpose of compensation. Had the exhibit been shipped in order to realize a profit on sales and such profits could have been realized, or to be entered in competition for a prize, and plaintiff failed to show loss of profits with sufficient definiteness, or that he would have won the prize, defendant's cases might be in point. But as before stated, no such situation exists here.

While, it is true that plaintiff already had incurred some of these expenses, in that it had rented space at the exhibit before entering into the contract with defendant for the shipment of the exhibit and this part of plaintiff's damages, in a sense, arose out of a circumstance which transpired before the contract was even entered into, yet, plaintiff arranged for the exhibit knowing that it could call upon defendant to perform its common-law duty to accept and transport the shipment with reasonable dispatch. The whole damage, therefore, was suffered in contemplation of defendant performing its contract, which it failed to do, and would not have been sustained except for the reliance by plaintiff upon defendant to perform it. It can, therefore, be fairly said that the damages or loss suffered by plaintiff grew out of the breach of the contract, for had the shipment arrived on time, plaintiff would have had the benefit of the contract, which was contemplated by all parties, defendant being advised of the purpose of the shipment.

The judgment is affirmed. All concur.

L. Albert & Son v. Armstrong Rubber Co.

United States Court of Appeals for the Second Circuit, 1949.
178 F.2d 182.

■ HAND, CIRCUIT JUDGE. Both sides appeal from the judgment in an action brought by the Albert Company, in which we shall speak of as the Seller, against the Armstrong Company, which we shall call the Buyer. The action was to recover the agreed price of four 'Refiners,' machines designed to recondition old rubber; the contract of sale was by an exchange of letters in December, 1942, and the Seller delivered two of the four 'Refiners' in August, 1943, and the other two on either August 31st or September 8th, 1945. Because of the delay in delivery of the second two, the Buyer refused to accept all four in October, 1945—the exact day not being fixed—and it counterclaimed for the Seller's breach. The judge dismissed both the complaint and the counterclaim; but he gave judgment to the Seller for the value without interest on a part of the equipment delivered—a 300 horse-power motor and accessories—which the Buyer put into use on February 20th, 1946. On the appeal the Seller's position is that its delay was not too long; that in any event the Buyer accepted delivery of the four 'Refiners'; and that they were in accordance with the specifications. As an alternative it insists that the Buyer is liable, not only for the value of the motor, but for interest upon it; and, as to the counterclaim, that the Buyer proved no damages, assuming that there was a breach. The judge found that all four 'Refiners' conformed to the specifications, or could have been made to do so with slight trouble and expense; that the contract was inseparable and called for four not two and two; that the delivery of the second two was too late; and that, as the Buyer rejected all four, it was not liable on the contract at all. On the other hand, as we have said, he found that the Buyer's use for its own purposes of the motor, although not an acceptance of the 'Refiners,' made it liable for the value of the motor in quasi contract, but without interest. He dismissed the Buyer's counterclaim because it had failed to prove any damages.

The first issue is whether the Seller's delivery of the second two 'Refiners' was too late, and justified the Buyer's rejection of all four in October of that year. We agree that the delivery was too late.

[The court holds that the contract was indivisible, and because "the buyer 'had no right to accept one part and to reject the rest[,]' the Buyer's use of the motor in the case at bar constituted a retraction of its rejection." In terms of damages, the court holds that the "Seller should have been awarded interest on the value of the motor and its accessories from the date of the Buyer's appropriation—February 20th, 1946."]

Coming next to the Buyer's appeal, it does not claim any loss of profit, but it does claim the expenses which it incurred in reliance upon the Seller's promise. These were of three kinds: its whole investment in its 'reclaim department,' $118,478; the cost of its 'rubber scrap,' $27,555.63; the cost of the foundation which it laid for the 'Refiners,' $3,000. The judge in his opinion held that the Buyer had not proved that 'the lack of production' of the reclaim department 'was caused by the delay in delivery of plaintiffs' refiners'; but that that was 'only one of several possible causes. Such a possibility is not sufficient proof of causation to impose liability on the plaintiffs for the cost of all machinery and supplies for the reclaim department.' The record certainly would not warrant our holding that this holding was 'clearly erroneous'; indeed, the evidence preponderates in its favor. The Buyer disposed of all its 'scrap rubber' in April and May, 1945; and, so far as appears, until it filed its counterclaim in May, 1947, it never suggested that the failure to deliver two of the four 'Refiners' was the cause of the collapse of its 'reclaim department.' The counterclaim for these items has every appearance of being an afterthought, which can scarcely have been put forward with any hope of success.

The claim for the cost of the foundation which the Buyer built for the 'Refiners,' stands upon a different footing. Normally a promisee's damages for breach of contract are the value of the promised performance, less his outlay, which includes, not only what he must pay to the promisor, but any expenses necessary to prepare for the performance; and in the case at bar the cost of the foundation was such an expense. The sum which would restore the Buyer to the position it would have been in, had the Seller performed, would therefore be the prospective net earnings of the 'Refiners' while they were used (together with any value they might have as scrap after they were discarded), less their price—$25,500—together with $3,000, the cost of installing them. The Buyer did not indeed prove the net earnings of the 'Refiners' or their scrap value; but it asserts that it is nonetheless entitled to recover the cost of the foundation upon the theory that what it expended in reliance upon the Seller's performance was a recoverable loss. In cases where the venture would have proved profitable to the promisee, there is no reason why he should not recover his expenses. On the other hand, on those occasions in which the performance would not have covered the promisee's outlay, such a result imposes the risk of the promisee's contract upon the promisor. We cannot agree that the promisor's default in performance should under this guise make him an insurer of the promisee's venture; yet it does not follow that the breach should not throw upon him the duty of showing that the value of the performance would in fact have been less than the promisee's outlay. It is often very hard to learn what the value of the performance would have been; and it is a common expedient, and a just one, in such situations to put the peril of the answer upon that party who by his wrong has made the issue relevant to the rights of the other. *Story Parchment Co. v. Paterson Parchment Paper Co.*, 282 U.S. 555, 563 (1931). On principle therefore the proper solution would seem to be that the promisee may recover his outlay in preparation for the performance, subject to the privilege of the promisor to reduce it by as much as he can show that the promisee would have lost, if the contract had been performed.

The decisions leave much to be desired. There is language in *United States v. Behan*, 110 U.S. 338, 345, 346 (1884), which, read literally, would allow the promisee to recover his outlay in all cases: the promisor is said to be 'estopped' to deny that the value of the performance would not equal it. We doubt whether the Supreme Court would today accept the explanation, although the result was right under the rule which we propose. Moreover, in spite of the authority properly accorded to any decision of that court, we are here concerned only with Connecticut law; and the decisions in that state do not seem to be in entire accord. In the early case of *Bush v. Canfield*, 2 Conn. 485 (1818), the buyer sued to recover a payment of

$5,000 made in advance for the purchase of 2,000 barrels of flour at $7.00 a barrel. Although at the time set for delivery the value of the flour had fallen to $5.50, the seller for some undisclosed reason failed to perform. The action was on the case for the bench, not in indebitatus assumpsit, and the court, Hosmer, J., dissenting, allowed the buyer to recover the full amount of his payment over the seller's objection that recovery should be reduced by the buyer's loss. The chief justice gave the following reason for his decision which we take to be that of the court, *2 Conn. page 488*: 'The defendant has violated his contract; and it is not for him to say that if he had fulfilled it, the plaintiffs would have sustained a great loss, and that this ought to be deducted from the money advanced.' If there is no difference between the recovery of money received by a promisor who later defaults, and a promisee's outlay preparatory to performance, this decision is in the Buyer's favor. However, when the promisor has received any benefit, the promisee's recovery always depends upon whether the promisor has been 'unjustly enriched'; and, judged by that nebulous standard, there may be a distinction between imposing the promisee's loss on the promisor by compelling him to disgorge what he has received and compelling him to pay what he never has received. It is quite true that the only difference is between allowing the promisee to recover what he has paid to the promisor and what he has paid to others; but many persons would probably think that difference vital.

In any event, unless this be a valid distinction, it appears to us that *Santoro v. Mack*, 108 Conn. 683, 145 A. 273 (1929), must be read as taking the opposite view. The plaintiff, the vendee under a contract for the sale of land, had paid an electrician and an architect whom he had employed in reliance upon the promised conveyance. These payments he sought to recover, and was unsuccessful on the ground that they had not benefited the vendor, and that they had been incurred without the vendor's knowledge or consent. Yet it would seem that such expenses were as much in reasonable preparation for the use of the land, as the cost of the foundation was for the use of the 'Refiners.' The point now before us was apparently not raised, but the decision, as it stands, seems to deny any recovery whatever. Three other Connecticut decisions—the only ones which at all approach the question—do not throw any light upon the point. *Edward De V. Tompkins, Inc. v. City of Bridgeport*, 94 Conn. 659, 110 A. 183, 191 (1920); *Kastner v. Beacon Oil Co.*, 114 Conn. 190, 158 A. 214, 81 A.L.R. 97 (1932); *Jordan v. Patterson*, 67 Conn. 473, 35 A. 521 (1896).

The result is equally inconclusive if we consider the few decisions in other jurisdictions. The New Jersey Court of Errors and Appeals in *Holt v. United Security Life Insurance & Trust Co.*, 76 N.J.L. 585, 72 A. 301, 21 L.R.A.,N.S., 691 (1909), recognized as the proper rule that, although the promisor had the burden of proving that the value of the performance was less than the promisee's outlay, if he succeeded in doing so, the recovery would be correspondingly limited. In *Bernstein v. Meech*, 130 N.Y. 354, 360, 29 N.E. 255, 257 (1891), the promisee recovered his full outlay, and no limitation upon it appears to have been recognized, as may be inferred from the following sentence: 'It cannot be assumed that any part of this loss would have been sustained by the plaintiff if he had been permitted to perform his contract.' In *Reynolds v. Levi*, 122 Mich. 115, 80 N.W. 999 (1899), the promisee was a well digger, who had made three unsuccessful efforts to reach water, and the promisor—a farmer-stopped him before he had completed his fourth. The court limited the recovery to the amount earned on the fourth attempt, but for reasons that are not apparent. It appears to us therefore that the reported decisions leave it open to us to adopt the rule we have stated. Moreover, there is support for this result in the writings of scholars. The Restatement of Contracts, § 333(d), allows recovery of the promisee's outlay 'in necessary preparation' for the performance, subject to several limitations, of which one is that the promisor may deduct whatever he can prove the promisee would have lost, if the contract had been fully performed. Professor McCormick thinks, MCCOR-MICK ON DAMAGES §§ 142, 584, that 'the jury should be instructed not to go beyond the probable yield' of the performance to the promisee, but he does not consider the burden of proof. Much the fullest discussion of the whole subject is Professor Fuller's in the Yale Law Journal. 46 YALE L.J. 752, pp. 75–80. The situation at bar was among those which he calls cases of 'essential reliance,' and for which he favors the rule we are adopting. It is one instance of his 'very simple formula: We will not in a suit for reimbursement of losses incurred in reliance on a contract knowingly put the plaintiff in a better position than he would have occupied, had the contract been fully performed.'

The judgment will therefore be affirmed with the following modification. To the allowance for the motor and accessories will be added interest from February 20th, 1946. The Buyer will be allowed to set off $3,000 against the Seller's recovery with interest from October, 1945, subject to the Seller's privilege to deduct from that amount any sum which upon a further hearing it can prove would have been the Buyer's loss upon the contract, had the 'Refiners' been delivered on or before May 1st, 1945.

Judgment modified as above, and affirmed as so modified.

* * *

Security Stove displays the basic doctrine at work, although it also raises some of the more difficult conceptual question that the basic statement of the doctrine disguises. This reveals that the structural entailments of the reliance remedy are never far away in even the most seemingly straightforward cases. They are no mere theoretical possibilities but instead may impinge, inevitably and almost at every turn, on the actual application of the law.

The plaintiff in *Security Stove* had booked a booth at a trade fair, hoping to display its new stove in an effort to attract custom. The plaintiff contracted with the defendant for the carriage of the stove to the fair's location, repeatedly and expressly informing the defendant that the stove must arrive at the fair on time and that a delay would cost it the opportunity to impress an important potential customer. The stove was packed into many boxes, most of which arrived without incident, but (in a striking bit of bad luck) the box containing the manifold, which represented the stove's central innovation, did not reach the fair on time. The plaintiff sued, seeking reliance damages in an amount equal to the sum of the charges it had paid for the shipping service, the travel and lodging expenses of its representatives at the fair and also the value of their time, and the cost that the plaintiff had incurred in renting the booth at the fair.

The opinion begins with a long discussion concerning whether the shipping contract contemplated delivery by a specified date or, instead, only ordinarily speedy delivery (under circumstances in which such delivery would get the stove to the fair by the required date). The court opts for the latter—that this was just an ordinary shipping contract, which matters to the outcome because a delivery date-certain might have rendered the whole shipping contract unenforceable under the Interstate Commerce Act. The details of this regulatory regime do not matter for present purposes, although its existence does: it emphasizes that, as has occurred in earlier materials concerning common carriers, the agreement at issue was subject to a regulatory regime that limited the parties' freedom of contract. This will matter in a moment.

Once the court concluded that plaintiff had had a valid contract which defendant had breached, the question of remedy came to the fore. The defendant argued that the plaintiff's contract damages equaled her expectation interest, and that the plaintiff had not proved any lost expectations because it had not proved that an on-time delivery would have produced a profitable deal with the customer whom it had sought to impress. The defendant thus asserted a version of the certainty requirement: it argued that the expectations the plaintiff sought to vindicate were speculative only, too speculative to support a remedy. The court accepted this argument, as far as it went, observing that the plaintiff had not gone to the fair intending to make a sale but only to drum up interest. But, the court added, a contract that was valuable to the plaintiff was nevertheless broken, and the plaintiff should not be left wholly without a remedy.

The court reasoned, in effect, that the plaintiff was a money-making enterprise, which would not have gone to the expense of attending the fair unless the attendance would, somewhere down the line, generate gains to recoup its costs.[1] Accordingly, the court said, even though the plaintiff could not prove up its contractual expectations with the certainty required to support the expectation remedy, it might nevertheless recover as damages "the loss in the way of expenses that it sustained, and which it would not have been put to if it had not been for its reliance upon the defendant

---

1. Note in passing that the court said something that made absolutely no sense about the fact that the plaintiff was not seeking any profit as a result of the shipping contract. The court said that if the exhibit had been shipped "in order to realize a profit on sales and such profits could have been realized" and the plaintiff had failed to show lost profits with sufficient determinateness, then the defendant might have been in a stronger position. But how can this be? On the actual facts of the case, the plaintiff was clearly seeking to profit from the shipping and the fair, only the profit was very remote. How can it possibly be that the plaintiff can successfully claim reliance damages in this case but not in a case in which his prospective profit, although so remote as to be unrecoverable as expectation, is less remote than in the case as it arose?

to perform its contract." In other words, a plaintiff who cannot prove up his expectations may (at least if he is a profit-making business) at his option seek to recover reliance damages instead.

All of this is fairly straightforward. The real interest in *Security Stove* lies in the damages that the plaintiff was permitted to recover under the heading reliance. That the court should have allowed recovery for the cost of shipping and the travel, lodging, and time costs of attending the fair is straightforward. The plaintiff incurred these expenses after it had made its contract with the defendant, so that these were literally losses sustained in reliance on that contract. But the court's reliance award contemplated recovery for another expense also, namely the plaintiff's costs in renting the booth at the fair. And this loss cannot, in any easily literal way, be said to have been sustained in reliance on the contract with the defendant. The booth was rented, after all, and the rental-costs incurred, *before* the plaintiff's shipping contract with the defendant had ever been made.

The court suggested that the defendant's status as a common carrier might step in to fill the gap in the plaintiff's argument for recovering his booth rental as a reliance loss. As a common carrier, the defendant was legally obligated to accept shipments according to its published rates, and so the plaintiff, even though it could not have relied on its contract with the defendant when it rented the booth, may have relied on the defendant's doing its legal duty and accepting the shipment when the plaintiff proffered it. Including the booth rental in the plaintiff's recovery seems natural on this approach, and it also seems natural to style the plaintiff's broader claim in terms of reliance. After all, the defendant's duty has now become independent of the contract—it is the mandatory duty of all common carriers—and the defendant's breach, being a failure to fulfill a mandatory duty, has taken on a tort-like quality. The *Security Stove* opinion certainly contains notes that sound in this register, as when it refers to the defendant's *negligence* in handling the shipment. Negligence is irrelevant to the plaintiff's contract claim, since contractual liability is strict. But if plaintiff is really making a tort claim (as the inclusion of the booth rental in plaintiff's damages suggests) then negligence becomes essential to his success.

The inclusion of the booth rental fee in the plaintiff's reliance recovery in *Security Stove* expands the reliance remedy beyond a simple-minded and literal reading that limits reliance to costs whose specific connection to the contract figures in a plaintiff's mind when they are incurred to encompass not just these costs but also costs whose connection to the contract is purely abstract and counterfactual. Moreover, although the facts of *Security Stove* apply this expansion to include a cost, the booth rental, whose connection to the contract was particularly intimate—both because the defendant's common carrier status made the plaintiff's entitlement to rely uncontroversial and because the contract's subject matter was physically to fill the booth—the logic of the expanded reliance argument is not tethered to either of these limiting conditions.

First, if market realities mean that manufacturers are certain to be able to find many shippers who will send samples to trade fairs at competitive prices, then the formal legal rules requiring common carriers to accept all shipments become functionally irrelevant. While such market conditions may not make it reasonable to rely on a particular shipper to accept every shipment, they surely do make it reasonable to rely on the fact that some shipper will accept every shipment, and indeed will accept it at the market rates charged by all shippers. In this case just as in the common carrier case, the defendant's failure to deliver the manifold on time will have had the effect of depriving the plaintiff of a service whose benefits, as a practical matter, he might reasonably rely on enjoying. And so the booth rental might once again be included in the plaintiff's reliance recovery, even without the crutch of the defendant's common carrier status.

And second, once the booth rental is included in the plaintiff's reliance damages, there is no principled reason for stopping there. Instead, it seems that every cost that the plaintiff incurred in expectation of successfully shipping the manifold to the trade fair might be included in his reliance, including (but not limited to) the costs of advertising the manifold to potential customers in order to encourage them to view it in person at the fair, the costs of completing a proto-type in time for displaying it at the fair, and any portion of the entire costs of developing the manifold that was incurred in light of the sales opportunity represented at the fair. This class of costs is highly abstract, of course, and not amenable to easy or direct calculation, but as long as the plaintiff was making and selling stoves in a competitive market, the total of these costs would approach her entire contractual expectations, as traditionally understood. Indeed, a much simpler and conceptually more powerful argument yields the same result more directly. As long as the defendant shipper was operating in a competitive market, then one of the costs that the plaintiff incurred in reliance on dealing with her was the opportunity cost of forsaking a practically equivalent shipping contract with one of the defendant's competitors. And the value of this opportunity, once again, equals the plaintiff's entire contractual expectation, as traditionally understood.

Once reliance is understood in its logical, counterfactual sense, and once lost opportunities are included within reliance costs, then a plaintiff's reliance begins to approach her expectation interest. And at least where the parties operate in competitive markets, a plaintiff's reliance interest comes to *equal* her expectation interest. This observation has long been familiar to contract lawyers—it was first made by Lon Fuller and William Perdue in a famous pair of articles in the 1930s.[2]

Moreover, as has also been familiar since Fuller and Perdue wrote, the observation threatens a conceptual upheaval in contract law. Perhaps—the law's explicit self-characterizations to the contrary notwithstanding—the core contract remedy is not expectation but reliance. Perhaps the expectation remedy is awarded only insofar as it is—in light of the earlier

---

2. L.L. Fuller & William R. Perdue, Jr., *The Reliance Interest in Contract Damages (pts. 1–2)*, 46 YALE L.J. 52, 373 (1936–37).

argument about lost opportunity costs—a quick and accurate way of quantifying the reliance. Certainly the central cases in which expectation damages are awarded in practice have this feature. Expectation awards based on contract-market or contract-cover differentials are just quick and easy ways of valuing the lost opportunities that disappointed promisees have given up by dealing with their breaching promisors and of enabling them to recover these lost opportunities to exploit them even in spite of the promisors' breaches. Moreover, in other cases—in which the absence of market prices or easily comparable forms of covering renders the opportunity costs of a promisor's breach difficult to quantify—a series of familiar doctrines (involving foreseeability, certainty, etc.) step in to limit a plaintiff's expectation remedy to levels that are easily reinterpreted as reliance losses in more direct ways. Although it surely contravenes the law's official self-presentation, treating reliance as the core remedy in contract thus seems, in the end, far from outlandish.

Whatever their broader interest, these general speculations leave one important issue in *Security Stove* unaddressed, however. The defendant, recall, suggested that the plaintiff should be unable to recover anything because he had not proved that his fair display would have succeeded had the manifold been delivered on time and therefore had not established his contractual expectations with the certainty required by law. This argument, moreover, remains a good one even under the general approach to reliance just described: if the plaintiff would not have enjoyed better results from the fair had the manifold arrived, then although it would remain true that the defendant's breach cost him the opportunity to get the manifold to the fair on time by other means, that opportunity would not have had any value. And so whatever *Security Stove's* theoretical appeal, it does seem that the court in that case did not deal entirely satisfactorily with the defendant before it.

L. Albert attempts to fill the breach. The buyer in that case bought four rubber refiners from the seller for use in a rubber recycling business. The seller delivered two machines on time and two late. Over the course of the defendant's delay, the Second World War ended, causing the bottom to drop out of the recycled rubber market. The buyer refused to accept all four machines but did accept a 300 horsepower motor that the seller had also delivered. Thereupon, the seller sued the buyer for breaching its contract by refusing to accept the machines and also sought recovery for the value of the motor that the buyer did accept. The buyer counterclaimed seeking recovery for the cost of foundations that it had built to house the machines, rubber scrap that it had acquired to reprocess using the machines, and its entire investment in its rubber "Reclamation Department," which it claimed the seller's late delivery rendered unprofitable and in need of dissolution.

The dispute raised several issues which are not relevant to reliance damages: Did the seller's lateness constitute a breach of the entire contract, which was for four machines, or just of one of two independent contracts for two machines each? (The lateness was treated as a breach of one contract for all four machines.) Might the seller recover in restitution for the value of the accepted motor? (The seller was awarded restitution.) The case is most famous, however, for taking up the question left over by *Security Stove*: namely, what effect did the possibility that the end of the war left the buyer with a negative contractual expectation (that the buyer would have lost money even if the seller had performed) have on the buyer's damages request, styled as a reliance claim?

The opinion decided this question in application to the buyer's claim for $3000 in reliance damages for the costs of building the foundations that were to support the machines.[3] The court began by observing that the ordinary remedy for breach of contract is an award of expectation damages. Nevertheless, the court admitted, where a contract would have proved profitable for the victim of its breach, the victim may opt instead to recover its reliance expenses. But this rule, the court observed, has bad consequences in cases in which the promisee would have had a losing contract, but for his promisor's breach. Allowing recovery of reliance damages even on a losing contract would convert the breaching promisor into the insurer of the promisee's venture, and the promisor's default, the court held, should not throw him into this position. As the court said, "we will not in a suit for re-imbursement of losses incurred in reliance on a contract knowingly put the plaintiff in a better position than he would have occupied, had the contract been fully performed."

Nevertheless, the court reasoned, although a breaching promisor should not be liable for reliance damages insofar as the promisee would have made a loss even on performance, it is fair and reasonable to shift the burden concerning this question away from its ordinary allocation. Whereas the certainty requirement ordinarily operates so that a disappointed promisee must prove up his contractual expectations in order to recover his expectation remedy, when a promisee seeks recovery merely for reliance, this burden shifts. Now the promisor can limit her promisee's reliance recovery only by proving that he would have had a losing contract even had she performed. The case thus held that a disappointed promisee may recover, as reliance, his outlay in preparation for performance, subject to the privilege of the promisor to reduce this recovery by as much as he can show that the promisee would have lost even if the contract had been

---

3. The opinion rejected the buyer's two larger reliance claims—concerning the costs of the leftover scrap rubber and indeed of the rubber reclamation department writ large—on purportedly more straightforward grounds, although the opinion's arguments in this connection turn out to be quite dubious. On the one hand, the opinion sometimes suggests that the buyer's reliance claim for the scrap rubber and Reclamation Department must fail because the buyer did not establish that he had incurred these costs in reliance specifically on his contract with the seller, not least because most of these costs were incurred before that contract was completed. This approach, however, simply ignores the broader, conceptual account of reliance that figured (rightly, it seems) in *Security Stove*. On the other hand, the opinion suggests that these elements of the buyer's reliance claim should be rejected because the buyer failed entirely to show that these losses were caused by the seller's breach, as the scrap might have been worthless and the Reclamation Department might have failed even but for the breach. This argument is not much more satisfactory than the one just rehearsed, since it seems to require, at least if it is read literally, reprising the burden-shifting approach that the court expressly adopted with respect to the third element of the buyer's reliance claim, as is discussed in the main text.

performed.[4] In other words, although a promisee may elect to recover reliance rather than expectation damages, his expectation interest (as it is proved up by his promisor) limits the reliance damages that he may receive.[5]

L. Albert therefore goes some way towards answering the defendant's complaint in security stove. But it does not go all the way, or indeed even far enough. This may be seen by reconsidering the facts in *Friedus v. Eisenberg*. In that case, remember, a plaintiff who had been improperly denied title to a parcel of land sought damages for her lost expectations concerning the land's development. She failed because she could not prove up her expectations with the certainty that the law requires; and she failed even though she offered to apply a risk-free rate of return—the return on a United States Treasury Bond—to the principal value of the land in each year for which she was deprived of title, and in this way to establish (with substantial certainty) a floor for her actual expected profits.

Now imagine that the plaintiff, instead of stopping there, had been one step cleverer. Suppose that she had acknowledged that she simply could not satisfy the certainty requirement for proving contractual expectations and had proposed, therefore, to pursue a reliance-based recovery instead. Finally, suppose that she had calculated her reliance by identifying the minimum return that she would have enjoyed had she invested the value that was tied up in the land she had been deprived of in safe way, that is, in precisely the same Treasury Bond she had sought to use to establish a floor under her expectation claim. Under *L. Albert*, the only obstacle to the plaintiff's recovery on this theory would be the defendant's privilege of reducing her recovery in respect of any negative expectations that he could prove her actual development plans would have subjected her to. But just as the plaintiff could not satisfy the certainty requirements with respect to her positive expectations from developing the land, so the defendant would

---

4. Note that the *L. Albert* opinion is careful to distinguish between the case in which a plaintiff's reliance costs are paid to a third party (as in that case) and the case in which they are paid to the defendant. In the latter case, a plaintiff can claim in restitution and not just in reliance, and a defendant has no right to limit damages by proving the plaintiff's negative expectation. It is not, however, so clear that this is the right rule. In particular, it seems at odds with the law's generally permissive attitude towards efficient breach and also with the principle, announced as a foundation of the *L. Albert* rule, that a breaching promisor should not be made insurer of the promisee's venture. If promisors are to be encouraged to abandon a contractual performance as soon as this becomes efficient, why should they be made insurers of their promisees' ventures simply because these ventures involve paying them rather than others?

One simple reason for the special treatment of restitution may just involve moral hazard—without the different rule for restitution, a promisor who can prove that his promisee is on a losing contract can encourage further reliance (in the form of payments to the promisor) and then breach and just keep them.

5. Note that the rule is not that the promisee's expectation *damages* limit the reliance damages he may receive. This natural mistake may be illustrated by using the following example: Suppose that a disappointed promisee proves $5000 in reliance costs on a contract. Suppose further that the breaching promisor can prove that even if she had performed, the promisee would have suffered a $1000 loss (that is, that her contractual expectation was $–1000). In this case, the cap on the promisee's reliance damages is $4000. These damages would put the promisee in the same position as if his expectations had been honored, namely suffering a loss of $1000.

also be unable to establish her negative expectations with sufficient certainty. And so—at least if *Security Stove* and *L. Albert* are read literally—the certainty requirement would allow the plaintiff to recover in reliance precisely the remedy that it had denied her in expectation.

That result cannot be right. Opportunity costs can always be included in lost reliance, and the value of lost opportunities often approaches (or even equals) a plaintiff's expectation interest. Accordingly, allowing plaintiffs to shift the burden of proof with respect to their contractual expectations (as in the modified version of *Friedus*) would allow plaintiffs quite generally to circumvent the burden of proving up their contractual damages—more precisely, to shift this burden to defendants—by employing a simple formalism. There is no chance that courts would allow this gambit. The certainty requirement, which is really just a special case of the general principle that the burden of proof lies with plaintiffs, is too central to contract law to allow it. Just how courts confronted with the argument rehearsed above would achieve this result is not so clear, however. They would simply find a way.

11.2 EXPECTATION WITHOUT RELIANCE

Expectation damages may, in almost all cases, be recast in terms of lost reliance, sufficiently abstractly understood. Certainly this will be true in all the core cases—involving market-based damages—in which the law vindicates promisees' full contractual expectations: as long as contracts arise in competitive markets, promisees' opportunity costs necessarily include passing up identically appealing alternative contracts, so that their reliance interests necessarily include their full contractual expectations. This alternative account of contract remedies in their commonest applications, it has been suggested, casts doubts on whether the expectation remedy is in fact as structurally central for contract law as the law's official statements suggest. And that doubt, once sown, calls into question whether contract is an independent form of legal obligation at all, or whether it is rather just a special case of the loss-based obligation which is generally compensated by the reliance damages implemented through tort law.

Such doubts are only increased, moreover, by contemplating the rare cases in which a promisee's contractual expectations cannot be recast in terms of lost reliance. Certainly promisees' claims to recover their expectations seem intuitively to be unusually brittle or even feeble in such cases. Expectation damages give buyers in such cases the full benefits of their bargains, and it may seem that such purely executory promises, unconnected to any detrimental reliance, are simply too insubstantial to support this result—that buyers in such cases are getting more than they deserve. As one prominent commentary put it: When it enforces the expectation remedy apart from reliance losses, "[t]he law no longer seeks merely to heal a disturbed status quo, but to bring into being a new situation. It ceases to act defensively or restoratively, and assumes a more active role. With the transition, the justification for legal relief loses its self-evident quality."[6] Expectation damages, in such cases, seem unreasonably to give promisees something for nothing.[7]

Finally, the positive law (perhaps responding to similar doubts) displays an uncertain and indeed uncommitted attitude towards promisees' efforts to vindicate their contractual expectations insofar as these are indeed unsupported by contractual reliance. Although plaintiffs seeking to recover expectation damages in such circumstances sometimes succeed, they also sometimes fail. The following cases illustrate both outcomes.

Uniform Commercial Code

§ 2–313   Express Warranties by Affirmation, Promise, Description, Sample

(1) Express warranties by the seller are created as follows:

(a) Any affirmation of fact or promise made by the seller to the buyer which relates to the goods and becomes part of the basis of the bargain creates an express warranty that the goods shall conform to the affirmation or promise.

(b) Any description of the goods which is made part of the basis of the bargain creates an express warranty that the goods shall conform to the description.

(c) Any sample or model which is made part of the basis of the bargain creates an express warranty that the whole of the goods shall conform to the sample or model.

(2) It is not necessary to the creation of an express warranty that the seller use formal words such as "warrant" or "guarantee" or that he have a specific intention to make a warranty, but an affirmation merely of the value of the goods or a statement purporting to be merely the seller's opinion or commendation of the goods does not create a warranty.

Official Comment

Prior Uniform Statutory Provision: Sections 12, 14 and 16, Uniform Sales Act. Changes: Rewritten.

Purposes of Changes: To consolidate and systematize basic principles with the result that:

---

6. Lon Fuller & William Perdue, *The Reliance Interest in Contract Damages: 1*, 46 Yale L.J. 52, 56–57 (1936).

7. Notice that the point does not necessarily depend on the buyer's having incurred absolutely *no* reliance costs but may perhaps extend naturally to every case in which expectation damages exceed reliance—in which the expectation remedy places a buyer in a better position than she occupied in the status quo ante. One might say that, in all such cases, expectation damages give buyers more than they deserve, precisely to the extent that they exceed reliance damages.

1.   "Express" warranties rest on "dickered" aspects of the individual bargain, and go so clearly to the essence of that bargain that words of disclaimer in a form are repugnant to the basic dickered terms. "Implied" warranties rest so clearly on a common factual situation or set of conditions that no particular language or action is necessary to evidence them and they will arise in such a situation unless unmistakably negated.

This section reverts to the older case law insofar as the warranties of description and sample are designated "express" rather than "implied".

2.   Although this section is limited in its scope and direct purpose to warranties made by the seller to the buyer as part of a contract for sale, the warranty sections of this Article are not designed in any way to disturb those lines of case law growth which have recognized that warranties need not be confined either to sales contracts or to the direct parties to such a contract. They may arise in other appropriate circumstances such as in the case of bailments for hire, whether such bailment is itself the main contract or is merely a supplying of containers under a contract for the sale of their contents. The provisions of Section 2–318 on third party beneficiaries expressly recognize this case law development within one particular area. Beyond that, the matter is left to the case law with the intention that the policies of this Act may offer useful guidance in dealing with further cases as they arise.

3.   The present section deals with affirmations of fact by the seller, descriptions of the goods or exhibitions of samples, exactly as any other part of a negotiation which ends in a contract is dealt with. No specific intention to make a warranty is necessary if any of these factors is made part of the basis of the bargain. In actual practice affirmations of fact made by the seller about the goods during a bargain are regarded as part of the description of those goods; hence no particular reliance on such statements need be shown in order to weave them into the fabric of the agreement. Rather, any fact which is to take such affirmations, once made, out of the agreement requires clear affirmative proof. The issue normally is one of fact.

4.   In view of the principle that the whole purpose of the law of warranty is to determine what it is that the seller has in essence agreed to sell, the policy is adopted of those cases which refuse except in unusual circumstances to recognize a material deletion of the seller's obligation. Thus, a contract is normally a contract for a sale of something describable and described. A clause generally disclaiming "all warranties, express or implied" cannot reduce the seller's obligation with respect to such description and therefore cannot be given literal effect under Section 2–316.

This is not intended to mean that the parties, if they consciously desire, cannot make their own bargain as they wish. But in determining what they have agreed upon good faith is a factor and consideration should be given to the fact that the probability is small that a real price is intended to be exchanged for a pseudo-obligation.

5. Paragraph (1)(b) makes specific some of the principles set forth above when a description of the goods is given by the seller.

A description need not be by words. Technical specifications, blueprints and the like can afford more exact description than mere language and if made part of the basis of the bargain goods must conform with them. Past deliveries may set the description of quality, either expressly or impliedly by course of dealing. Of course, all descriptions by merchants must be read against the applicable trade usages with the general rules as to merchantability resolving any doubts.

6. The basic situation as to statements affecting the true essence of the bargain is no different when a sample or model is involved in the transaction. This section includes both a "sample" actually drawn from the bulk of goods which is the subject matter of the sale, and a "model" which is offered for inspection when the subject matter is not at hand and which has not been drawn from the bulk of the goods.

Although the underlying principles are unchanged, the facts are often ambiguous when something is shown as illustrative, rather than as a straight sample. In general, the presumption is that any sample or model just as any affirmation of fact is intended to become a basis of the bargain. But there is no escape from the question of fact. When the seller exhibits a sample purporting to be drawn from an existing bulk, good faith of course requires that the sample be fairly drawn. But in mercantile experience the mere exhibition of a "sample" does not of itself show whether it is merely intended to "suggest" or to "be" the character of the subject-matter of the contract. The question is whether the seller has so acted with reference to the sample as to make him responsible that the whole shall have at least the values shown by it. The circumstances aid in answering this question. If the sample has been drawn from an existing bulk, it must be regarded as describing values of the goods contracted for unless it is accompanied by an unmistakable denial of such responsibility. If, on the other hand, a model of merchandise not on hand is offered, the mercantile presumption that it has become a literal description of the subject matter is not so strong, and particularly so if modification on the buyer's initiative impairs any feature of the model.

7. The precise time when words of description or affirmation are made or samples are shown is not material. The sole question is whether the language or samples or models are fairly to be regarded as part of the contract. If language is used after the closing of the deal (as when the buyer when taking delivery asks and receives an additional assurance), the warranty becomes a modification, and need not be supported by consideration if it is otherwise reasonable and in order (Section 2–209).

8. Concerning affirmations of value or a seller's opinion or commendation under subsection (2), the basic question remains the same: What statements of the seller have in the circumstances and in objective judgment become part of the basis of the bargain? As indicated above, all of the statements of the seller do so unless good reason is shown to the contrary. The provisions of subsection (2) are included, however, since common

experience discloses that some statements or predictions cannot fairly be viewed as entering into the bargain. Even as to false statements of value, however, the possibility is left open that a remedy may be provided by the law relating to fraud or misrepresentation.

Overstreet v. Norden Laboratories, Inc.

United States Court of Appeals for the Sixth Circuit, 1982.
669 F.2d 1286.

■ KEITH, CIRCUIT JUDGE. This is a direct appeal of a judgment involving a breach of expressed and implied warranty under Ky.Rev.Stat. §§ 355.2–313, 2–314, brought pursuant to the district court's diversity jurisdiction *28 U.S.C. § 1332.*

Defendant-appellant Norden Laboratories, Inc. ("Norden") appeals from a judgment of $40,500.00, awarded in favor of plaintiff-appellee Dr. Luel P. Overstreet, a Kentucky veterinarian and horse owner.

On appeal Norden alleges that the failure to instruct the jury on the requirement that the plaintiff must have relied on the express warranty was error. We agree. Reliance is an element of a cause of action for express warranty under Ky.Rev.Stat. § 355.2–313(1)(a). We therefore vacate the judgment entered below and remand for proceedings consistent with this opinion.

Facts

Dr. Overstreet is a practicing veterinarian and operator of a standard bred horse farm in Henderson County, Kentucky. Equine rhinopneumonitis is a virus which causes horses to exhibit symptoms which generally resemble a common cold. In pregnant mares, however, the virus will cause abortions. Norden Laboratories, Inc., a Nebraska corporation, manufactures and markets various drugs to veterinarians. Rhinomune, one of the drugs manufactured by Norden, is a vaccine designed to inoculate horses against equine rhinopneumonitis.

Rhinomune was first marketed by Norden in the spring of 1973. Norden's marketing program for the new, unique drug utilized magazine advertisements, brochures and sales persons. In the spring of 1973, about the time Norden began marketing Rhinomune, two mares on Dr. Overstreet's farm aborted their foals. Dr. Overstreet became concerned about a possible outbreak of equine rhinopneumonitis virus among his breeding horses. It was later determined that an equine rhinopneumonitis virus caused the abortions.

A Norden sales representative called on Dr. Overstreet's office and spoke with an associate of the doctor's concerning rhinomune. Dr. Overstreet became interested in the drug and allegedly read rhinomune promotional literature. Dr. Overstreet asserts that he then ordered a quantity of rhinomune, because of the representations contained in Norden's advertisements.

The rhinomune vaccine was administered to a number of Dr. Overstreet's horses during the three months prior to November, 1973. Six of the inoculated mares on Dr. Overstreet's farm aborted their foals during the spring of 1974.

Dr. Overstreet instituted this breach of warranty action under Ky.Rev. Stat. §§ 355.2–313, 2–314 against Norden to recover losses resulting from the aborted foals. At trial, Dr. Overstreet alleged that Norden breached expressed and implied warranties which Norden made concerning its rhinomune vaccine. A jury returned a verdict of $40,500.00 in favor of Dr. Overstreet.

Norden made motions for judgment n.o.v. and, in the alternative, for a new trial. Both motions were denied. Defendant Norden perfected this appeal. Norden assigns as error jury instructions on the issue of its liability under Ky.Rev.Stat. §§ 355.2–313, 2–314. Norden argues that the trial court should have instructed the jury that in order to recover, plaintiff must establish that he relied on any warranty which Norden made. Appellant's challenge is well founded, but imprecise. As Norden contends, reliance is an element of a breach of an expressed warranty action under Kentucky law, and the jury should have been instructed accordingly. However, the implied warranty of merchantability Ky.Rev.Stat. § 355.2–314 is a duty imposed by Kentucky law and plaintiff's reliance thereon is not a requisite to defendant's liability for breach.

The verdict form allowed the jury to award a judgment against Norden without stating which warranty was breached, consequently we cannot determine under which theory appellant's liability was imposed. We find these jury instructions were erroneous. Because the instructions were erroneous and, for the reasons set forth below, we reverse the trial court's judgment and remand for proceedings consistent with this opinion.

A.   Implied Warranty of Merchantability

The implied warranty of merchantability as set forth in the Ky.Rev. Stat. § 355.2–314 provides in pertinent part:

> (1) Unless excluded or modified (KRS 355.2–316), a warranty that the goods shall be merchantable is implied in a contract for their sale if the seller is a merchant with respect to goods of that kind. . . .

To be merchantable, goods must, inter alia, "be fit for the ordinary purposes for which such goods are used." Ky.Rev.Stat. § 355.2–314(2)(c).

The implied warranty of merchantability arises by operation of law. As such, it does not require reliance as an element of a purchaser's recovery. Consequently, Norden's reliance argument, so far as it relates to the implied warranty of merchantability, is without merit. We find that Judge Gordon properly instructed the jury on the implied warranty theory. However, we hold that there is insufficient evidence on this record to sustain a finding that Norden breached its implied warrant of merchantability.

B. Express Warranty

Appellant contends that the jury instructions and verdict form[2] were improper, because neither required a finding of reliance as an element of recovery under the express warranty. We agree.

We appreciate the formidable task which confronts a trial judge in charging a jury. We must nevertheless remain loyal to the mandate of *Erie Railroad Co. v. Tompkins*, 304 U.S. 64 (1938), which requires a federal court sitting in diversity to apply the substantive law of the state in which it sits. In the instant case, however, no Kentucky court has construed Ky.Rev.Stat. § 355.2–313.[3] Thus, it is the duty of the federal court to decide such unsettled issues of state law[4] as a Kentucky state court would. "(A) federal court without benefit of guidance from the forum state's highest court or its state legislature should analyze the indications and determine the path that state would follow." *Delduca v. U.S. Fidelity and Guaranty Co.*, 357 F.2d 204, 207 (5th Cir. 1966).

Appellant noted above that the jury instructions did not include a charge that Dr. Overstreet must have relied on the express warranty. Moreover, the record before us does not reflect that the trial court properly ascertained whether reliance was an element of appellee's recovery. Accordingly, we hold that these instructions were erroneous. We must now decide,

---

2. Verdict of Jury on Issue of Liability:

Questions:

1. Did Dr. Overstreet violate any duties owed by him as a buyer to the seller Norden in his use of the drug Rhinomune?

Yes No x

If your answer to the above question is "yes", you will not answer question 2, but will return to the courtroom. If your answer to question 1 above is "no", then answer question 2.

2. Did Norden violate any of its warranties of its product Rhinomune to Dr. Overstreet?

Yes x No See App. 28.

3. Ky.Rev.Stat. § 355.2–313 provides:

Express Warranties By Affirmation, Promise, Description, Sample.

(1) Express warranties by the seller are created as follows:

(a) Any affirmation of fact or promise made by the seller to the buyer which relates to the goods and becomes part of the basis of the bargain creates an express warranty that the goods shall conform to the affirmation or promise.

(b) Any description of the goods which is made part of the basis of the bargain creates an express warranty that the goods shall conform to the description.

(c) Any sample or model which is made part of the basis of the bargain creates an express warranty that the whole of the goods shall conform to the sample or model. (1958 c 77, § 2–313. Eff. 7–1–60).

(2) It is not necessary to the creation of an express warranty that the seller use formal words such as "warrant" or "guarantee" or that he have a specific intention to make a warranty, but an affirmation merely of the value of the goods or a statement purporting to be merely the seller's opinion or commendation of the goods does not create a warranty (1958 c 77, § 2–313. Eff. 7–1–60).

4. Where a federal court's jurisdiction is based solely on diversity of citizenship, the difficulty of ascertaining what the state courts may thereafter determine the state law to be does not in itself afford a sufficient ground for declining to exercise its jurisdiction. *Meredith v. Winter Haven*, 320 U.S. 228 (1943).

as we think a Kentucky court would decide, the elements of an express warranty action.

An express warranty may be created by any affirmation of fact or promise made by a seller which relates to the goods. Ky.Rev.Stat.Ann. § 355.2–313(1)(a) (Baldwin). The language creating an express warranty need not contain special phrases or formal words such as guarantee or warranty. Ky.Rev.Stat. § 355.2–313(2). In fact, a seller need not have intended that the language create an express warranty. Ky.Rev.Stat.Ann. § 355.2–313(2) (Baldwin). Every statement made by a seller, however, does not create an express warranty. A seller may puff his wares and state his opinion on their value without creating an express warranty. Ky.Rev.Stat. Ann. § 355.2–313(2) (Baldwin).

The existence of an express warranty depends upon the particular circumstances in which the language is used and read. A catalog description or advertisement may create an express warranty in appropriate circumstances. The trier of fact must determine whether the circumstances necessary to create an express warranty are present in a given case. The test is "whether the seller assumes to assert a fact of which the buyer is ignorant, or whether he merely states an opinion or expresses a judgment about a thing as to which they may each be expected to have an opinion and exercise a judgment."

The mere existence of a warranty is insufficient to sustain an action for breach of an express warranty. The warranty must be "part of the basis of the bargain" between the parties. Ky.Rev.Stat.Ann. § 355.2–313(1)(a) (Baldwin). A warranty is the basis of the bargain if it has been relied upon as one of the inducements for purchasing the product. See Ky.Rev.Stat. Ann. § 355.2–313(1) (a), Comment 1(C) (Baldwin).[5]

A buyer is not under a duty to investigate the seller's representations; he may accept them at face value. However, a buyer may not rely blindly on a statement or affirmation that he knows is incorrect. A buyer does not disregard any special knowledge he possesses or his accumulated experience with a product in determining whether to enter the bargain. Consequently, a statement known to be incorrect cannot be an inducement to enter a bargain. An incorrect representation by the seller which is qualified in any manner may become the basis of a bargain to the extent it is believed and relied upon. For example, a seller represents in its advertising that its product is capable of lifting 100 pounds. The buyer is aware that the product cannot lift the weight claimed in its advertising. Nevertheless, he relies on his subjective belief that the product could lift 75 pounds and purchases the product. The product fails to lift 75 pounds. In an action for breach of express warranty against the seller, the buyer will prevail. The

---

5.   Comment 1(c) states in full:

Materiality of Affirmation, Promise, Description, Sample. Under the Code, the qualification that affirmations, etc. create a warranty if made "as the basis of" the bargain, appears to be substantially the same as the "reliance" qualification in § 12 of the Uniform Sales Act, former *KRS 361.120. Van Deren Hardware Co. v. Preston*, 224 Ky. 170, 5 S.W.2d 1052 (1928).

seller cannot complain because his product failed to perform at a level of proficiency lower than that originally claimed in its advertising.

We do not reach the issue of whether an expert may rely on the representations of another expert in his area of specialty. At a minimum, however, an expert may rely on the representations of a seller of a newly marketed, unique product. *Butcher v. Garrett–Enumclaw Co.*, 20 Wash.App. 361 (Ct.App.1978). In Butcher, the court held that an expert with many years of experience as a conventional saw mill operator and consultant could rely on the representations of the seller of a newly developed portable small log sawmill. Where the capabilities and properties of a unique, newly developed product are known only to the seller, the expert is in no better position to evaluate the representations of the seller than a layperson. Therefore, he is entitled to reply on representations concerning such a novel product. See *Grinnell v. Charles Pfizer & Company*, 274 Cal.App.2d 424 (Ct.App.1969) (Physician could rely upon representations of drug manufacturer where manufacturer possessed superior knowledge concerning the properties of the drug.)

C. Damages

Norden contends that the trial court improperly instructed the jury (1) on the issue of causation, and (2) as to the proper measure of damages. Although both Judges Engel and Kennedy agree, I remain unpersuaded.

Causation

I cannot agree with my colleagues that causation was not established as a matter of law. Although the trial court did not issue model instructions, they were adequate on the issue of causation as an element of Norden's liability.[6] The instructions permit recovery only for those damages directly resulting from the seller's breach. The problem is that the

---

6. The trial court instructed the jury as follows:

(N)ow, in this case Dr. Overstreet claims that the defendant breached its seller's warranty of the drug Rhinomune in that said drug was not fit for the use for which it was sold and failed to perform as set forth in the advertised data furnished to persons practicing veterinary medicine by the defendant Norden in that when administered to the healthy animals as directed by the seller Norden, the drug failed to effectively immunize his mares from the disease of equine rhinopneumonitis, all to his damage.

It is further the law that if the seller makes any additional printed or oral statements in such form as imports special warranties of performance of the product then the product must perform generally to the extent so promised by the seller, provided it is used by the buyer in the manner prescribed by the seller for its effective use.

Thus, we see that if special warranties (express) are given by the seller, and if the buyer administers and uses the product to the extent and manner as required by the seller for the use of the product and the product fails to substantially perform as warranted and the buyer suffers damage directly resulting therefrom, then in those circumstances, under the law, the buyer would be entitled to be compensated for any damage suffered.

The question here for your decision is not whether the drug so caused the abortion, as Dr. Overstreet does not make that contention. The question is whether or not when administered under the required recommendations of healthy animals, the product substantially met the standard of the warranties given, that is, to prevent the contracting of the disease and the resulting abortions. (emphasis supplied) Trial transcript at 85–86.

causation language was not repeated on the issue of damages. The trial was not bifurcated. However, the jury was asked first to decide whether there was a breach of warranty. The jury returned a verdict holding Norden liable. The jury was then instructed on the issue of damages.

> Since you have established liability in this case on the part of Norden Industries, you are not called upon to award such damages as you may believe from the evidence will fairly and reasonably compensate Dr. Overstreet for the loss of the aborted fetuses of his six mares in 1974 at the time of the abortions.
>
> In arriving at the damages, if any, you will fix the damage as to each mare by what you find to be the difference between the fair market value of said mare with her foal and the fair market value of said mare after the loss of her foal at the point in time 1974 of the abortion, but in no event shall you award a total award in excess of $119,500, the amount claimed by Dr. Overstreet in his testimony. As I instructed you in the case of liability, the burden remains with Dr. Overstreet to prove his damage by a preponderance of the evidence. That is, the greater weight of the credible evidence. Trial Transcript at 144–145.

This instruction did not permit the jury to determine which of appellee's losses were caused by appellant's breach. In effect, it held as a matter of law that the measure of damages was the value of the aborted foals, leaving for the jury only the issue of what that value was. The instructions should have included causation language equivalent to that used to establish the breach.

Measure of Damages

The trial court relied on *Schleicher v. Gentry*, 554 S.W.2d 884 (Ky.App. 1977), and instructed the jury that the proper measure of damages was "the difference between the fair and reasonable market value of each of the mares with foal and the fair and reasonable market without foal." Trial transcript at 144.

Norden argues that plaintiff's recovery is limited under Ky.Rev.Stat. § 355.3–714(2) to the cost of the vaccine. Norden reasons as follows. Norden's vaccine did not cause the equine rhinopneumonitis in the mares, and plaintiff would not have used any other preventative. Therefore, the cost of the vaccine is the only loss plaintiff has suffered.

Norden relies heavily upon its contention that Dr. Overstreet made conflicting statements concerning whether he would have used another product. However, the resolution of factual disputes lies clearly within the province of the jury.

Norden argues that to recover consequential damages plaintiff must establish that the vaccine or the breach caused the injury. The specific facts necessary to sustain an action for breach of warranty vary with each warranty made. Therefore, a determination of what exactly the defendant warranted is essential. A warrantor, by words or acts, establishes the conditions and circumstances which may give rise to his liability. *Brown v. Globe Laboratories, Inc.*, 165 Neb. 138 (1957).

Alternative Product Rule

Judges Kennedy and Engel reason that Dr. Overstreet must establish that an equally effective alternative product was available and would have been used by Dr. Overstreet before he can recover consequential damages for breach of Norden's express warranty. I disagree. The alternative product rule announced today is not supported by the law or public policy.

First, the proposed rule would require plaintiff to prove that at the time the warranted product was purchased, he was aware that an available alternative product existed. Second, the proposed rule minimizes the purpose and effect of reliance on a product warranty. It is unreasonable to assume that consumers are able to determine the relative effectiveness of a given product. The available alternative product rule, therefore, will penalize consumers because they lack meaningful independent information about the products they purchase. Moreover, warranty actions generally arise where there is a disparity in the relevant information possessed by the consumer and warrantor.

At the second trial of this case, a jury may find: 1) that Norden warranted that the vaccine Rhinomune would prevent equine rhinopneumonitis, a disease which almost invariably induces abortions in mares; and 2) that Norden breached its warranty when six of Dr. Overstreet's horses, properly inoculated with Rhinomune, contracted the disease and aborted. The essence of Norden's warranty would be the representation that mares inoculated with Rhinomune would not contract equine rhinopneumonitis and abort. It therefore would be foreseeable that if the vaccine failed to perform as warranted, a purchaser would probably sustain losses due to aborted foals. In my view these losses are precisely the type of losses contemplated under Ky.Rev.Stat. § 355.2–714(3).[9]

Norden's liability arose because its product failed to prevent the disease as warranted, not because plaintiff's mares aborted foals. Accordingly, I would allow plaintiff to recover without considering the alternate product rule.

Conclusion

We have analyzed the Kentucky cases involving express warranties which were decided prior to the enactment of Ky.Rev.Stat. 2–313(1)(a).

---

9. Ky.Rev.Stat. § 355.2–715(2)(a) provides:

(2) Consequential damages resulting from the seller's breach include:

(a) any loss resulting from general or particular requirements and needs of which the seller at the time of contracting had reason to know and which could not reasonably be prevented by cover or otherwise; and

(b) injury to person or property proximately resulting from any breach of warranty.

However, we note with interest that the official comment (1) to Ky.Rev.Stat. § 355.2–715.2(2) construes subsection (2)(a) as imposing on a buyer a requirement "to attempt to minimize damages by cover or otherwise" under appropriate circumstances. It does not, however, operate as a defense to an otherwise actionable breach.

Further, we sought guidance from other Erie indicators of state law, including the sparse legislative and scholarly commentary. These Erie-indicators support our conclusion that reliance is an element in an action for express warranty under Kentucky law. Further, my colleagues hold that the trial court improperly instructed the jury on the measure of damages.

For these reasons, and those noted above, we reverse and remand for proceedings consistent with this opinion. It is so ordered.

■ ENGEL AND KENNEDY, CIRCUIT JUDGES, concurring specially. We agree with Judge Keith that the evidence is insufficient to sustain a finding that appellant breached any implied warranty. We also agree that while there was sufficient evidence for the jury to find that appellant expressly warranted that Rhinomune prevents equine rhinopneumonitis, the trial court's instructions on express warranty erroneously failed to include appellee's reliance on the warranty as a necessary element of the claim. However, we do not agree with Judge Keith that the District Court correctly instructed the jury on the measure of damages.

The District Court's instruction on damages required the jury to award appellee, after it found a breach of warranty, the difference in value between the mares with foal and the same mares without foal. In directing the jury to award this amount the District Court was holding that the value of the foals was the correct measure of damages in all circumstances which the jury could find. This was error.

The measure of damages for breach of warranty in Kentucky is set out in Ky.Rev.Stat. §§ 355.2–714 and 355.2–715. Section 355.2–714(2) provides for the recovery of "the difference at the time and place of acceptance between the value of the goods accepted and the value they would have had if they had been as warranted," Thus, if appellee persuades the jury on remand that appellant breached an express warranty, he is entitled to the difference in value between Rhinomune as he received it and the value Rhinomune would have enjoyed if it had worked as promised. Section 355.2–714(3) permits recovery as well for damages incidental to and a consequence of the breach. Section 355.2–715(1) defines incidental damages. This section entitles appellee to recover costs incurred in handling and administering the Rhinomune and any other expenses of this type. The District Court failed to instruct the jury on these elements of damages.

The only item of consequential damages appellee claimed here was the value of the aborted foals. Appellee might have established a causal link between the loss of the foals and the breach in any of several ways. He might have claimed that the abortions were directly due to some effect of the vaccine, or that this batch of Rhinomune was ineffective and a good batch of Rhinomune would better have prevented the abortions. He might have claimed that the warranty induced him to forego some other, effective means of preventing the abortions, or that he acted to his detriment in some other way in reliance on the warranty. Of these possible claims, there is evidence in the present record to support the claims that appellee would have used another abortion preventive but for the Rhinomune warranty or possibly that appellee's lot of Rhinomune was ineffective as compared to other Rhinomune. The evidence on these theories is conflicting. Thus, causation was not established as a matter of law. If neither Rhinomune nor any other product or device would have been effective or could have been used by appellee to prevent the abortions, then any breach of warranty did not cause the abortions. The fact that the abortions were foreseeable if the Rhinomune did not work does not mean the breach of warranty was the cause of the abortions. There was simply a failure to prevent an occurrence that nothing would have prevented, and appellee may not recover the value of the foals.

Judge Keith correctly notes that appellant established the conditions of liability when it warranted that Rhinomune would prevent equine rhinopneumonitis. However, the warranty did not further establish, by itself, appellant's liability for particular items of consequential damage in the event of a breach. Ky.Rev.Stat. § 355.2–715(2) clearly requires that the additional element of causation be proved to establish liability for consequential damages. The concern that Judge Engel and I share is that the jury was not permitted to decide whether appellant's promises caused any damage to result from the breach where the evidence on this issue was in dispute.

The result we reach does not insulate manufacturers from liability for consequential damages or lead to absurd results, as Judge Keith fears. Liability for truly consequential damages, including damages flowing from reliance on the warrantor's promise, should be a sufficient deterrent to unsupportable claims of performance. If not, a suit alleging fraud might be appropriate, and there are many state and federal agencies that police false advertising. It is not also necessary to award damages where no damage has been caused, in effect imposing absolute liability for a breach of warranty, as Judge Keith would do. This would render the consequential damages provision of Kentucky's statute meaningless. It is not a windfall to the warrantor to be liable only for losses that it causes, nor is it a hardship to the warrantee only to recover for losses caused by the breach.

Chatlos Systems, Inc. v. National Cash Register Corp.

United States Court of Appeals for the Third Circuit, 1982.
670 F.2d 1304.

OPINION OF THE COURT. This appeal from a district court's award of damages for breach of warranty in a diversity case tried under New Jersey law presents two questions: whether the district court's computation of damages under N.J.Stat.Ann. § 12A:2–714(2) was clearly erroneous, and whether the district court abused its discretion in supplementing the damage award with pre-judgment interest. We answer both questions in the negative and, therefore, we will affirm.

Plaintiff-appellee Chatlos Systems, Inc., initiated this action in the Superior Court of New Jersey, alleging, inter alia, breach of warranty regarding an NCR 399/656 computer system it had acquired from defendant National Cash Register Corp. The case was removed under 28 U.S.C.

§ 1441(a) to the United States District Court for the District of New Jersey. Following a non-jury trial, the district court determined that defendant was liable for breach of warranty and awarded $57,152.76 damages for breach of warranty and consequential damages in the amount of $63,558.16. Defendant appealed and this court affirmed the district court's findings of liability, set aside the award of consequential damages, and remanded for a recalculation of damages for breach of warranty. On remand, applying the "benefit of the bargain" formula of *N.J.Stat.Ann. § 12A:2–714(2) (Uniform Commercial Code § 2–714(2))*,[1] the district court determined the damages to be $201,826.50,[2] to which it added an award of prejudgment interest. Defendant now appeals from these damage determinations, contending that the district court erred in failing to recognize the $46,020 contract price of the delivered NCR computer system as the fair market value of the goods as warranted, and that the award of damages is without support in the evidence presented. Appellant also contests the award of prejudgment interest.

Waiving the opportunity to submit additional evidence as to value on the remand which we directed, appellant chose to rely on the record of the original trial and submitted no expert testimony on the market value of a computer which would have performed the functions NCR had warranted. Notwithstanding our previous holding that contract price was not necessarily the same as market value, appellant faults the district judge for rejecting its contention that the contract price for the NCR 399/656 was the only competent record evidence of the value of the system as warranted. The district court relied instead on the testimony of plaintiff-appellee's expert, Dick Brandon, who, without estimating the value of an NCR model 399/656, presented his estimate of the value of a computer system that would perform all of the functions that the NCR 399/656 had been warranted to perform. Brandon did not limit his estimate to equipment of any one manufacturer; he testified regarding manufacturers who could have made systems that would perform the functions that appellant had warranted the NCR 399/656 could perform. He acknowledged that the systems about which he testified were not in the same price range as the NCR 399/656. Appellant likens this testimony to substituting a Rolls Royce for a Ford, and concludes that the district court's recomputed damage award was therefore clearly contrary to the evidence of fair market value-which in NCR's view is the contract price itself.

Appellee did not order, nor was it promised, merely a specific NCR computer model, but an NCR computer system with specified capabilities. The correct measure of damages, under N.J.Stat.Ann. § 12A:2–714(2), is

---

1. Section 12A:2–714(2) states:

The measure of damages for breach of warranty is the difference at the time and place of acceptance between the value of the goods accepted and the value they would have had if they had been as warranted, unless special circumstances show proximate damages of a different amount.

2. The district court found the fair market value of the system as warranted to be $207,826.50; from this it subtracted its determination of the value of the goods delivered, $6,000.

the difference between the fair market value of the goods accepted and the value they would have had if they had been as warranted. Award of that sum is not confined to instances where there has been an increase in value between date of ordering and date of delivery. It may also include the benefit of a contract price which, for whatever reason quoted, was particularly favorable for the customer. Evidence of the contract price may be relevant to the issue of fair market value, but it is not controlling. *Mulvaney v. Tri State Truck & Auto Body, Inc.*, 70 Wis.2d 760, 767 (1975). Appellant limited its fair market value analysis to the contract price of the computer model it actually delivered. Appellee developed evidence of the worth of a computer with the capabilities promised by NCR, and the trial court properly credited the evidence.

Appellee was aided, moreover, by the testimony of Frank Hicks, NCR's programmer, who said that he told his company's officials that the "current software was not sufficient in order to deliver the program that the customer (Chatlos) required. They would have to be rewritten or a different system would have to be given to the customer." Hicks recommended that Chatlos be given an NCR 8200 but was told, "that will not be done." Gerald Greenstein, another NCR witness, admitted that the 8200 series was two levels above the 399 in sophistication and price. This testimony supported Brandon's statement that the price of the hardware needed to perform Chatlos' requirements would be in the $100,000 to $150,000 range.

Essentially, then, the trial judge was confronted with the conflicting value estimates submitted by the parties. Chatlos' expert's estimates were corroborated to some extent by NCR's supporters. NCR, on the other hand, chose to rely on contract price. Credibility determinations had to be made by the district judge. Although we might have come to a different conclusion on the value of the equipment as warranted had we been sitting as trial judges, we are not free to make our own credibility and factual findings. We may reverse the district court only if its factual determinations were clearly erroneous. *Krasnov v. Dinan*, 465 F.2d 1298 (3d Cir. 1972).[5]

Upon reviewing the evidence of record, therefore, we conclude that the computation of damages for breach of warranty was not clearly erroneous. We hold also that the district court acted within its discretion in awarding pre-judgment interest.

The judgment of the district court will be affirmed.

■ Rosen, Circuit Judge, dissenting. The primary question in this appeal involves the application of Article 2 of the Uniform Commercial Code as adopted by New Jersey in N.J.S.A. 12A:2–101 et seq. (1962) to the measure of damages for breach of warranty in the sale of a computer system. I respectfully dissent because I believe there is no probative evidence to support the district court's award of damages for the breach of warranty in

---

5. The dissent essentially is based on disagreement with the estimates provided by Chatlos' expert, Brandon. The record reveals that he was well qualified; the weight to be given his testimony is the responsibility of the fact-finder, not an appellate court.

a sum amounting to almost five times the purchase price of the goods. The measure of damages also has been misapplied and this could have a significant effect in the marketplace, especially for the unique and burgeoning computer industry.[1]

In July 1974, National Cash Register Corporation (NCR) sold Chatlos Systems, Inc. (Chatlos), a NCR 399/656 disc computer system (NCR 399) for $46,020 (exclusive of 5 percent sales tax of $1,987.50). The price and system included:

The computer (hardware)	$40,165.00
Software (consisting of 6 computer programs)[2]	5,855.00
	46,020.00

NCR delivered the disc computer to Chatlos in December 1974 and in March 1975 the payroll program became operational. By March of the following year, however, NCR was still unsuccessful in installing an operational order entry program and inventory deletion program. Moreover, on August 31, 1976, Chatlos experienced problems with the payroll program. On that same day and the day following NCR installed an operational state income tax program, but on September 1, 1976, Chatlos demanded termination of the lease and removal of the computer.

When this case was previously before us, we upheld the district court's liability decision but remanded for a reassessment of damages, instructing the court that under the purchase contract and the law consequential damages could not be awarded. Consequential damages, therefore, are no longer an issue here.

On remand, the district court, on the basis of the previous record made in the case, fixed the fair market value of the NCR 399 as warranted at the time of its acceptance in August 1975 at $207,826.50. It reached that figure by valuing the hardware at $131,250.00 and the software at $76,575.50, for a total of $207,826.50. The court then determined that the present value of the computer hardware, which Chatlos retained, was $6,000. Putting no value on the accepted payroll program, the court deducted the $6,000 and arrived at an award of $201,826.50 plus pre-judgment interest at the rate of 8 percent per annum from August 1975.

Chatlos contends before this court, as it had before the district court on remand, that under its benefit of the bargain theory the fair market value of the goods as warranted was several times the purchase price of $46,020. As the purchaser, Chatlos had the burden of proving the extent of the loss. *Council Brothers, Inc. v. Ray Burner Co.*, 473 F.2d 400, 408 (5th

---

1. Plaintiff's expert, Brandon, testified that generally 40 percent of all computer installations result in failures. He further testified that successful installations of computer systems require not only the computer companies' attention but also the attention of the customers' top management.

2. The six basic computer programs were: (1) accounts receivable, (2) payroll, (3) order entry, (4) inventory deletion, (5) state income tax, and (6) cash receipts. The contract price also included installation.

Cir. 1973). In remanding to the district court for a reassessment of the damages, we did not reject the contract price for the goods sold as the proper valuation of the computer as warranted. We merely corrected the district court's misconception that the language of the New Jersey statute precluded consideration of fair market value. We held that "value" in section 2–714(2) must mean fair market value at the time and place of acceptance. We pointed out:

It may be assumed that in many cases fair market value and contract price are the same, and therefore, if a party wishes to show a difference between the two he should produce evidence to that effect.

Chatlos Systems, Inc. v. National Cash Register Corp., 635 F.2d 1081, 1088 (3d Cir. 1980) (emphasis added) on remand, No. 77–2548 (D.N.J., filed Mar. 12, 1981). Thus, the sole issue before us now is whether the district court erred in fixing the fair market value of the computer system as warranted at the time of the acceptance in August 1975 at $207,826.50.

II.

A.

I believe that the district court committed legal error. The majority conclude that the standard of review of the district court's determination of the fair market value of the goods for the purpose of awarding damages is whether the trial judge's determination of market value is clearly erroneous. I disagree. Had the court merely miscalculated the amount of damages, I might agree with the majority's standard, for then our concern would be with basic facts. Here, however, no evidence was introduced as to the market value of the specific goods purchased and accepted had the system conformed to the warranty. Thus, the matter before us is one of legal error, and our standard of review is plenary. But even under the standard applied by the majority, the district court should be reversed because its determination of market value is not supported by probative evidence.

There are a number of major flaws in the plaintiff's attempt to prove damages in excess of the contract price. I commence with an analysis of plaintiff's basic theory. Chatlos presented its case under a theory that although, as a sophisticated purchaser, it bargained for several months before arriving at a decision on the computer system it required and the price of $46,020, it is entitled, because of the breach of warranty, to damages predicated on a considerably more expensive system. Stated another way, even if it bargained for a cheap system, i.e., one whose low cost reflects its inferior quality, because that system did not perform as bargained for, it is now entitled to damages measured by the value of a system which, although capable of performing the identical functions as the NCR 399, is of far superior quality and accordingly more expensive.

The statutory measure of damages for breach of warranty specifically provides that the measure is the difference at the time and place of acceptance between the value "of the goods accepted" and the "value they would have had if they had been as warranted." The focus of the statute is upon "the goods accepted"-not other hypothetical goods which may perform equivalent functions. "Moreover, the value to be considered is the reasonable market value of the goods delivered, not the value of the goods to a particular purchaser or for a particular purpose." *KLPR–TV, Inc. v. Visual Electronics Corp.*, 465 F.2d 1382, 1387 (8th Cir. 1972) (emphasis added). The court, however, arrived at value on the basis of a hypothetical construction of a system as of December 1978 by the plaintiff's expert, Brandon. The court reached its value by working backward from Brandon's figures, adjusting for inflation.

In presenting its case Chatlos developed its expert testimony as though it were seeking "cover" damages—the cost for the replacement of the computer system under section 2–712 of the statute. First, "cover" damages are obviously inappropriate here because both the district court and this court in its earlier decision held that the measure of damages is governed by section 2–714(2). Furthermore, Chatlos did not "cover" in this case and, although there was testimony that it would use an IBM Series 1 mini-computer to perform the NCR 399 functions, the president of Chatlos personally testified that the IBM "wasn't purchased with intent to replace the 399 system at the time of purchase." Second, Chatlos gave no evidence as to the cost of the IBM Series 1 computer system. However, under the applicable section of the statute, 2–714, the measure of damages is specifically confined to "the difference between the value of the goods accepted and the value they would have had if they had been as warranted" and does not include "the difference between the cost of cover and the contract price" as provided by section 2–712.

Although NCR warranted performance, the failure of its equipment to perform, absent any evidence of the value of any NCR 399 system on which to base fair market value, does not permit a market value based on systems wholly unrelated to the goods sold. Yet, instead of addressing the fair market value of the NCR 399 had it been as warranted, Brandon addressed the fair market value of another system that he concocted by drawing on elements from other major computer systems manufactured by companies such as IBM, Burroughs, and Honeywell, which he considered would perform "functions identical to those contracted for" by Chatlos. He conceded that the systems were "perhaps not within the same range of dollars that the bargain was involved with" and he did not identify specific packages of software. Brandon had no difficulty in arriving at the fair market value of the inoperable NCR equipment but instead of fixing a value on the system had it been operable attempted to fashion a hypothetical system on which he placed a value. The district court, in turn, erroneously adopted that value as the fair market value for an operable NCR 399 system. NCR rightly contends that the "comparable" systems on which Brandon drew were substitute goods of greater technological power and capability and not acceptable in determining damages for breach of warranty under section 2–714. Furthermore, Brandon's hypothetical system did not exist and its valuation was largely speculation.

B.

A review of Brandon's testimony reveals its legal inadequacy for establishing the market value of the system Chatlos purchased from NCR.

Brandon never testified to the fair market value which the NCR 399 system would have had had it met the warranty at the time of acceptance. He was not even asked the question. His estimate of the cost of the hardware in 1976 was "in the range of $100,000 to $150,000."

Not only did Brandon not testify in terms of the value of the NCR 399, but he spoke vaguely of "a general estimate as to what the cost might be of, let's say, developing a payroll or purchasing a payroll package today and installing it at Chatlos." He explained that what he would do, without identifying specific packages, would be to obtain price lists "from the foremost organizations selling packages in our field, in that area," organizations such as Management Science of America in Atlanta, and take their prices for specific packages. When asked what packages he would use for this system, he replied, "I would shop around, frankly." Speculating, he testified, "I think that I would go to two or three alternatives in terms of obtaining packages." When asked to address himself to the packages that he would provide for this system, he acknowledged that the programs he had in mind were only available "(for) certain types of machines." For example, he conceded that these programs would not be available for the Series 1 IBM mini-computer, "with the possible exception of payroll."

Thus, the shortcomings in Brandon's testimony defy common sense and the realities of the marketplace. First, ordinarily, the best evidence of fair market value is what a willing purchaser would pay in cash to a willing seller. In the instant case we have clearly "not an unsophisticated consumer," who for a considerable period of time negotiated and bargained with an experienced designer and vendor of computer systems. The price they agreed upon for an operable system would ordinarily be the best evidence of its value. Based on [Brandon's] testimony, Chatlos asserts in effect that a multi-national sophisticated vendor of computer equipment, despite months of negotiation, incredibly agreed to sell an operable computer system for $46,020 when, in fact, it had a fair market value of $207,000.

Second, expert opinion may, of course, be utilized to prove market value but it must be reasonably grounded. Brandon did not testify to the fair market value "of the goods accepted" had they met the warranty. Instead, he testified about a hypothetical system that he mentally fashioned. He ignored the realistic cost advantage in purchasing a unified system as contrasted with the "cost of acquiring seven separate application components" from various vendors.

Third, in arriving at his figure of $102,000 for the software, Brandon improperly included the time and cost of training the customer's personnel associated with the installation of the system.

Fourth, the record contains testimony which appears undisputed that computer equipment falls into one of several tiers, depending upon the degree of sophistication. The more sophisticated equipment has the capability of performing the functions of the least sophisticated equipment, but the less sophisticated equipment cannot perform all of the functions of those in higher levels. The price of the more technologically advanced equipment is obviously greater.

Fifth, when it came to the valuation of the hardware, Brandon did not offer an opinion as to the market value of the hypothetical system he was proposing. Instead, he offered a wide ranging estimate of $100,000 to $150,000 for a hypothetical computer that would meet Chatlos' programming requirements. The range in itself suggests the speculation in which he indulged.

III.

The purpose of the N.J.S.A. 12A:2–714 is to put the buyer in the same position he would have been in if there had been no breach. See Uniform Commercial Code 1–106(1). The remedies for a breach of warranty were intended to compensate the buyer for his loss; they were not intended to give the purchaser a windfall or treasure trove. The buyer may not receive more than it bargained for; it may not obtain the value of a superior computer system which it did not purchase even though such a system can perform all of the functions the inferior system was designed to serve. Thus, in *Meyers v. Antone*, 227 A.2d 56 (D.C.App.1967), the court held that where the buyers contracted for a properly functioning used oil heating system which proved defective, they were free to substitute a gas system (which they did), change over to forced air heating, or even experiment with a solar heating plant. "They could not, however, recover the cost of such systems. They contracted for a used oil system that would function properly, and can neither receive more than they bargained for nor be put in a better position than they would have been had the contract been fully performed. *Id. at 59* (citations omitted).

This court, in directing consideration of fair market value as the starting point in deciding damages noted Chatlos' contention that exclusive use of contract price deprives the dissatisfied buyer of the "benefit of his bargain." We accepted the concept of "benefit of the bargain" and explicated our understanding of the concept as follows:

If the value of the goods rises between the time the contract is executed and the time of acceptance, the buyer should not lose the advantage of a favorable contract price because of the seller's breach of warranty.

Conversely, if the value drops, the seller is entitled to the resulting lower computation.

Chatlos, supra, 635 F.2d at 1088. Ironically, this example of benefit of the bargain is actually based on contract price. If on the date of acceptance the fair market value of the goods has risen or declined from the contract price, that variation must be taken into account in awarding damages. But here plaintiff's market value figures, accepted by the district court on remand, have no connection whatsoever with the contract price.

Because Brandon's testimony does not support Chatlos' grossly extravagant claim of the fair market value of the NCR 399 at the time of its acceptance, the only evidence of the market value at the time is the price negotiated by the parties for the NCR computer system as warranted.

There are many cases in which the goods will be irreparable or not replaceable and therefore the costs of repair or replacement cannot serve as a yardstick of the buyer's damages. When fair market value cannot be easily determined the purchase price may turn out to be strong evidence of the value of the goods as warranted.

Thus, where there is no proof that market value of the goods differs from the contract price, the contract price will govern, and in this case that amounts to $46,020. Chatlos has retained the system hardware and the district court fixed its present value in the open market at $6,000. The court properly deducted this sum from the damages awarded.

IV.

Chatlos purchased the NCR payroll program and acknowledged at trial that the program operated fully and satisfactorily beginning February or March 1975 until October 1978 when it discontinued its use. The district court assigned no value to it because there was no evidence of fair market value. However, the law is clear that without evidence of a value other than contract price, that price should be accepted as the fair market value of the payroll program. The parties agreed on a contract price of $1,000 and that sum should be deducted from the measure of damages.

V.

[The dissent's discussion and conclusion that Chatlos is not entitled to prejudgment interest is omitted.]

VI.

On this record, therefore, the damages to which plaintiff is entitled are $46,020 less $6,000, the fair market value at time of trial of the retained hardware, and less $1,000, the fair market value of the payroll program, or the net sum of $39,020.

Accordingly, I would reverse the judgment of the district court and direct it to enter judgment for the plaintiff in the sum of $39,020 with interest from the date of entry of the initial judgment at the rate allowed by state law.

Texaco, Inc. v. Pennzoil, Co.

Court of Appeals of Texas, 1987.
729 S.W.2d 768.

■ WARREN, J. This is an appeal from a judgment awarding Pennzoil damages for Texaco's tortious interference with a contract between Pennzoil and the "Getty entities" (Getty Oil Company, the Sarah C. Getty Trust, and the J. Paul Getty Museum).

On December 28, 1983, Pennzoil announced an unsolicited, public tender offer for 16 million shares of Getty Oil at $100 each. [The Getty Oil board insisted that $100/share was too low, and eventually Pennzoil and Getty Oil agreed on a price of $110 per share plus a $5 per share "stub" that would be paid within five years. On January 4, 1984, both parties issued a press release announcing their agreement. However, Getty Oil's investment banker, Geoffrey Boisi, continued to contact other companies, including Texaco, looking for a higher price than what Pennzoil had offered.]

After talking briefly with Boisi, Texaco management called several meetings with its in-house financial planning group, which over the course of the day studied and reported to management on the value of Getty Oil, the Pennzoil offer terms, and a feasible price range at which Getty might be acquired.

The board of Texaco also met on January 5, authorizing its officers to make an offer for 100% of Getty Oil and to take any necessary action in connection therewith. [After Texaco offered $125 per share, the Getty Oil board] voted to withdraw its previous counter-proposal to Pennzoil and unanimously voted to accept Texaco's offer. Texaco immediately issued a press release announcing that Getty Oil and Texaco would merge.

Soon after the Texaco press release appeared, Pennzoil telexed the Getty entities, demanding that they honor their agreement with Pennzoil. Later that day, prompted by the telex, Getty Oil filed a suit in Delaware for declaratory judgment that it was not bound to any contract with Pennzoil.

Damages

Texaco claims that the evidence was legally and factually insufficient to support the jury's compensatory damage award[].

Texaco attacks Pennzoil's use of a replacement cost model to prove its compensatory damages. It urges that: (1) the court should have instructed the jury that the correct measure of Pennzoil's compensatory damages was the difference between the market price and contract price of Getty stock at the time of the breach; (2) the punitive damages award is contrary to New York law and public policy; (3) the punitive and compensatory damages are excessive; (4) and prejudgment interest should not have been allowed.

In a case involving a tortious interference with an existing contract, New York courts allow a plaintiff to recover the full pecuniary loss of the benefits it would have been entitled to under the contract. *Guard–Life Corp. v. S. Parker Hardware Manufacturing Corp.*, 50 N.Y.2d 183 (1980). The plaintiff is not limited to the damages recoverable in a contract action, but instead is entitled to the damages allowable under the more liberal rules recognized in tort actions. *Id.*

Pennzoil relied on two witnesses to prove the amount of its damages: Dr. Thomas Barrow and Dr. Ronald Lewis.

Texaco presented no witnesses to refute the testimony of Dr. Barrow or Dr. Lewis.

By Dr. Barrow's testimony, Pennzoil showed that because of Texaco's interference with its Getty contract, it was deprived of its right to acquire 3/7th's of Getty's proven reserves, amounting to 1.008 billion barrels of oil equivalent (B.O.E.), at a cost of $3.40 a barrel. Pennzoil's evidence further showed that its cost to find equivalent reserves (based on its last five years of exploration costs) was $10.87 per barrel. Therefore, Pennzoil contended that it suffered damages equal to 1.008 billion B.O.E. times $7.47 (the difference between $10.87, the cost of finding equivalent reserves, and $3.40, the cost of acquiring Getty's reserves) or $7.53 billion. The jury agreed.

Texaco first alleges that the trial judge should have instructed the jury that the measure of Pennzoil's damages was the difference between the market value of Getty Oil stock and its contract price at the time of the breach. [This difference was less than $500 million.] We reject this contention. The Getty/Pennzoil agreement contemplated something more than a simple buy-sell stock transaction. Pennzoil's cause of action against Texaco was in tort, not in contract, and Pennzoil's measure of damages was the pecuniary loss of the benefits it would have been entitled to under the contract. *Guard–Life Corporation*, 50 N.Y.2d 183. There was ample evidence that the reason Pennzoil (and later, Texaco) wanted to buy Getty was to acquire control of Getty Oil's reserves, and not for any anticipated profit from the later sale of Getty stock. There was evidence that such fluctuations in market price are primarily of interest to holders of small, minority share positions.

The court correctly instructed the jury that the measure of damages was the amount necessary to put Pennzoil in as good a position as it would have been in if its agreement, if any, with the Getty entities had been performed. If the measure of damages suggested by Texaco was correct, then there would have been no necessity to submit an issue at all, because no issue of fact would have existed, there being no dispute about the market value of the stock or the contract price of the stock at the time of the breach.

Texaco next contends that the replacement cost theory is based on the speculative and remote contention that Pennzoil would have gained direct access to Getty's assets. Texaco strongly urges that Pennzoil had a "good faith" obligation under its alleged contract to attempt to reorganize and restructure Getty Oil rather than to divide its assets. We agree. Under New York law, a duty of fair dealing and good faith is implied in every contract. But a duty of good faith and fair dealing does not require that Pennzoil completely subordinate its financial well-being to the proposition of reorganization or restructuring.

The directors of Pennzoil would have had a duty to the company's shareholders to obtain the greatest benefit from the merger assets, by either restructuring, reorganizing, or taking the assets in kind. If taking the assets in kind would be the most advantageous to Pennzoil, its directors would, in the absence of a great detriment to Getty, have a duty to take in kind. So the acquisition of a pro rata share of Getty Oil's reserves would be more than a mere possibility, unless the restructuring or reorganization of Getty would be just as profitable to Pennzoil as taking the assets in kind.

Next, Texaco urges that the jury's use of the replacement cost model resulted in a gross overstatement of Pennzoil's loss because:

(a) Pennzoil sought to replace Getty's low value reserves with reserves of a much higher value;

(b) Pennzoil based its replacement cost on its costs to find oil only during the period from 1980 to 1984, rather than over a longer period;

(c) Pennzoil improperly included future development costs in its exploration costs;

(d) Pennzoil used pre-tax rather than post-tax figures; and

(e) Pennzoil failed to make a present value adjustment of its claim for future expenses.

Our problem in reviewing the validity of these Texaco claims is that Pennzoil necessarily used expert testimony to prove its losses by using three damages models. In the highly specialized field of oil and gas, expert testimony that is free of conjecture and speculation is proper and necessary to determine and estimate damages. Texaco presented no expert testimony to refute the claims but relied on its cross-examination of Pennzoil's experts to attempt to show that the damages model used by the jury was flawed. Dr. Barrow testified that each of his three models would constitute an accepted method of proving Pennzoil's damages. It is inevitable that there will be some degree of inexactness when an expert is attempting to make an educated estimate of the damages in a case such as this one. Prices and costs vary, depending on the locale, and the type of crude found. The law recognizes that a plaintiff may not be able to prove its damages to a certainty. But this uncertainty is tolerated when the difficulty in calculating damages is attributable to the defendant's conduct. *Whitney v. Citibank, N.A.*, 782 F.2d 1106 (2d Cir. 1986).

In his replacement cost model, Dr. Barrow estimated the cost to replace 1.008 billion barrels of oil equivalent that Pennzoil had lost. Dr. Barrow admitted that some of Getty's reserves consisted of heavy crude, which was less valuable than lighter crude, and that he had made no attempt to determine whether there was an equivalency between the lost Getty barrels and the barrels used to calculate Pennzoil's exploration costs. Dr. Barrow also testified that there was no way to determine what grade of reserves Pennzoil would find in its future exploration; they could be better or worse than the Getty reserves. Finally Dr. Barrow testified that in spite of his not determining the value equivalency, the replacement cost model was an accepted method of figuring Pennzoil's loss. Dr. Lewis testified that with improved refining technology, the difference in value between light and heavy crude was becoming less significant.

Texaco next urges that Pennzoil should have calculated replacement cost by using a longer time period and industry wide figures rather than using only its own exploration costs, over a five year period. Dr. Lewis admitted that it might have been more accurate to use a longer period of time to estimate exploration costs, but he and Dr. Barrow both testified that exploration costs had been consistently rising each year and that the development cost estimates were conservative. Dr. Barrow testified that in his opinion, Pennzoil would, in the future, have to spend a great deal more than $10.87 a barrel to find crude. Dr. Lewis testified that industry wide exploration costs were higher than Pennzoil's, and those figures would result in a higher cost estimate than the $10.87 per barrel used by Pennzoil.

Next, Texaco claims that Pennzoil inflated its exploration costs by $1.86 per barrel by including "future development cost" in its historical exploration costs. Both Dr. Lewis' and Dr. Barrow's testimony refuted that contention. Texaco neither offered evidence to refute their testimony, nor did its cross-examination reveal that this was an unwarranted cost.

Texaco also claims that Pennzoil should have used post-tax rather than pre-tax figures in figuring its loss calculations. First, it contends that there are large tax incentives for exploration and development that are not applicable to acquisition of reserves. Second, it contends that there was a $2 billion tax penalty attached to the Pennzoil/Getty agreement, and Pennzoil's $900 million share of that penalty would have increased its $3.40 pre-tax acquisition cost by nearly a dollar.

Dr. Barrow testified that the fact that Pennzoil included $997 million as recapture tax in its costs of acquiring the Getty reserves, made the pre-tax comparison between the $3.40 per barrel to acquire Getty reserves and the $10.87 per barrel for Pennzoil to find new oil, "apples and apples"; in other words, the $997 million tax adjustment compensated for the tax benefits reaped when discovering, as compared with purchasing, reserves. Further, there was no conclusive proof that the Internal Revenue Service would have assessed a $2 billion penalty to Getty's purchase of the Museum's shares under the Pennzoil/Getty agreement, as alleged by Texaco. Several witnesses, familiar with tax law, testified that it was unlikely that such a tax would be imposed; therefore it was for the jury to decide when assessing damages, whether Pennzoil's pro rata share of the speculative tax penalty should reduce the amount of its damages.

Texaco's contention that Pennzoil's cost replacement model should be discounted to present value ignores the fact that Pennzoil's suit is not for future damages but for those already sustained. Pennzoil would have had an interest in the Getty reserves immediately if the agreement had been consummated, and it did not seek damages for reserves to be recovered in the future. The cases cited by Texaco are inapposite here because all involve damages that the plaintiff would incur in the future, such as lost wages or future yearly payments. Also, Texaco requested no jury instruction on a discount or a discount rate; therefore, any complaint of the court's failure to submit the issue or instruction is waived. See Tex. R. Civ. P. 279. Nor was Texaco entitled to an omitted finding by the court under rule 279, because the omitted discount and discount rate were not issues "necessarily referable" to the damages issue. *Id.*

Texaco's Points of Error [concerning the jury's award compensatory damages] are overruled.

* * *

The most common cases of contractual expectations unbacked by reliance (not even in the form of lost opportunities) involve plaintiffs who sue on exaggerated warranties. These cases typically arise when sellers make commercially unrealistic claims for their products and disappointed buyers sue to enforce promissory expectations based on these claims. Such expectations are unbacked by any reliance (including by any lost opportunities) because the exaggerated character of the sellers' promises render them much more valuable to the buyers than any alternatives that were available. *Overstreet* and *Chatlos* each fit into this category of fact-pattern, although they reach opposite outcomes.

In *Overstreet*, the defendant-seller incorrectly advertised that a vaccine would protect horses from a disease that causes mares to miscarry. The plaintiff-buyer, having read the advertisement, bought the vaccine and administered it to his horses. In spite of this, the horses miscarried, and the plaintiff sued to recover the value of the lost foals, alleging breach of warranty. The disappointed buyer was, over vigorous dissent, denied recovery for the value of horses he had lost to the disease on the grounds that because no other vaccine existed, and nothing else could have been done by the buyer to prevent the disease, the buyer's horses were not lost in reliance on the warranty.

The court's argument towards this conclusion began by distinguishing two warranty claims—both having statutory roots in the UCC—that the buyer in *Overstreet* might assert. The first—for breach of an implied warranty of merchantability—failed even to get going: in the court's mind, there was insufficient evidence to sustain a finding that the seller had breached its implied warrant of merchantability.[8] The second—for breach of an express warranty—had a surer footing in the facts of the case. An express warranty may be created in a variety of ways, including by statements made by a seller. In this case, the court concluded, there was sufficient evidence to allow a jury to find that the defendant—through its advertisements—had expressly warranted the effectiveness of its vaccine. This holding was not, however, sufficient to sustain a victory for the plaintiff. The damages for a breach of warranty (under U.C.C. § 2–714) are the difference between the value of the goods as warranted and the value as sold (§ 2–714(2)) plus any incidental and consequential damages that arise from the breach (§ 2–714(3)). Consequential damages, in cases of breach of warranty, are further governed by § 2–715(2), which allows plaintiffs to recover for only injuries "proximately resulting from" the breach of war-

---

8. Note that had such evidence existed, the outcome of the case might have been different. The implied warranty of merchantability arises by operation of law and therefore, in the court's view, does not require reliance by the purchaser as an element of the purchaser's cause of action for its breach. As the main text observes, the need to show reliance is what ultimately tripped up the plaintiff's efforts to recover damages for the breach of the express warranty that the court recognized did occur.

ranty. The *Overstreet* plaintiff's claim for the value of the lost foals was a claim for consequential damages, and the success of this claim therefore required the plaintiff to show that the loss of the foals proximately resulted from the breach of the warranty. The *Overstreet* majority concluded that the plaintiff could not make the required showing.

Now it is a commonplace that the mere existence of an express warranty is insufficient to sustain an action for breach of an express warranty. Unlike other contractual promises, an express warranty must become a part of the basis of the bargain between the parties in order to be binding—that is, the warranty must have functioned as one of the inducements for purchasing the warranted product.[9] This unambiguously introduces a reliance requirement into warranty claims, but it is a thin one. There is no question that it was satisfied in *Overstreet*, since the plaintiff surely would not have purchased the vaccine unless he had believed that it would work and so clearly did rely on the warranty in making his purchase.

But the *Overstreet* holding—through its discussion of what the majority variously terms "causation" and "reliance"—introduces an additional, and much more demanding, reliance requirement into the law of warranties. Under the *Overstreet* majority's view, damages for breach of an express warranty are available only to the extent that the promisee has actually expended costs in reliance on the warranty, either in the form of direct expenditures or in the form of the opportunity costs of not buying a substitute good in place of the warranted one. Thus the majority would have given the plaintiff recovery if he had forsaken an alternative vaccine in reliance on the warranty, or even if he had just had his mares impregnated or entered into contracts to sell his foals in reliance on their being born healthy. But given that the plaintiff had done none of these things, the majority held, his losses were not caused by the breach of warranty.

This is the feature of *Overstreet* that denies legal vindication for pure contractual expectations, unbacked by actual reliance *losses*. Although the court does not speak in quite these terms, it makes the question against what base-line the proximate consequences of the defendant's breach of warranty should be measured into the central issue of the case. On the one hand, if the appropriate base-line is what would have happened had the warranty been honored, then the only remaining question is whether the foals would have been born live had the mares not suffered from the disease that the medicine was warranted to prevent. This is the view taken by the dissenter, and it leads to a victory for the buyer. On the other hand, if the base-line is what would have happened had the warranty not been made, then the question is whether the plaintiff, who would then not have bought the vaccine at all, would have protected the mares by some other means. If the answer to this is that the plaintiff could not possibly have done (say, because no alternative vaccine was available), then the foals (which would have been miscarried anyway) were not actually lost in reliance on the warranty, so that their deaths were not proximately caused

---

9. *See* U.C.C. § 2–313.

by the breach of warranty, and plaintiff could not recover consequential damages in light of the deaths.[10] This is the view of the majority, and it leaves the buyer facing much more precarious prospects.[11] The majority held that the trial court had erred in failing to instruct the jury concerning this reliance requirement, and hence remanded the case for further findings on that question.[12]

Overstreet therefore takes a hard line against recovery for contractual expectations unbacked by actual reliance losses. *Chatlos* takes a slightly less hard line, although it should not (in spite of initial appearances) be read as providing confident support for plaintiffs seeking to recover pure promissory expectations, unbacked by reliance losses.

The defendant in *Chatlos* agreed to sell the plaintiff a computer system for roughly $50,000, which it had warranted to be capable of performing certain specified tasks. The system could not in fact perform these tasks, and the plaintiff sued for breach of the warranty. Expert testimony established that a system actually capable of doing the tasks in question would cost roughly $250,000, and the plaintiff recovered $200,000 in expectation damages, reflecting the difference between the value of the computer system as warranted and as delivered.

Chatlos may seem, therefore, to take precisely the opposite view from *Overstreet*. The remedy that the *Chatlos* plaintiff received vindicated his purely promissory expectations, unbacked by the actual reliance losses that the *Overstreet* majority insisted on. Because the defendant had sold the warranted system at a dramatically below-market price, the plaintiff had not lost anything—not even the lost opportunity of buying a system from one of the defendant's competitors—in reliance on its contract with the defendant. Analogously, the *Chatlos* remedy measures the buyer's losses against the baseline of what would have happened had the seller satisfied its warranty rather than, as in *Overstreet*, against the baseline of what would have happened had the warranty never been made. It treats the breach of warranty as having caused the buyer's loss even though the promise and breach together clearly did no such thing, since there existed no alternative means to achieving his contractual expectations, which the buyer might have forsaken in reliance on his contract with the seller.

---

10. Once again even on this view the plaintiff could (as the majority notes) recover for costs—for example, costs of sales efforts that he would ordinarily delay until after the foals were born but accelerated in light of the seller's promise that the mares would not miscarry—that he could have avoided even though he could not have protected his mares by other means.

11. Note that the *Overstreet* rule creates an asymmetry between the remedies available to plaintiffs for whom a warranted product is the only possibility and those for whom it is not. Suppose that A and B both suffer gout. A can be cured by x and y; B by y only. Both A and B buy y, which is warranted to work, but does not, and both sue the seller for breach of warranty. On the majority rule, A can recover, B cannot. Is this fair?

12. It is not clear that the majority's view presents the best interpretation of the U.C.C. on this question. The statute refers to injuries proximately resulting from any "*breach* of warranty" and not just "from any *warranty*." See U.C.C. § 2–714 (emphasis added). This suggests that the base-line against which to measure the consequences of a *breach* is what would have happened had there been a warranty that was not breached. And that suggests that the *Overstreet* plaintiff should not have had to show that he could have protected the mares by some other means.

Chatlos therefore in effect gave the plaintiff a windfall, at least as compared to the best that the plaintiff could have hoped to achieve in the absence of the contract. This is precisely the result that the *Overstreet* majority sought to avoid.[13]

The tone of the *Chatlos* opinion suggests, however, that its holding should not be taken at face value, and certainly should not be understood to announce any general rule that the law will vindicate purely promissory expectations, at full face value. To begin with, both the majority and the dissent treat the case as a straightforward factual dispute about identifying the value of the computer system as promised, but that is surely misleading. The real issue is clearly how much liability the defendant should bear for overpromising, in the strict sense of promising qualitatively more than market-value.[14] Moreover, the open subtext of the case involves a dispute between the majority and the dissenter about whether or not the seller in *Chatlos* had knowingly overpromised in order to mislead the buyer into purchasing an inappropriate machine: the majority believed that she did and thus had effectively committed fraud; the dissenter believed that she did not—indeed that she had never really promised the more expensive capabilities—and that a sophisticated buyer was trying to undo its own mistake. The majority's willingness to award damages that gave the buyer a windfall should be read in light of its belief that the seller had not just made a mistake, nor even just a negligent mistake, but instead had acted in bad faith and exploitatively. But although it believed these things, the majority could not, in an appeal, revisit the relevant factual issues. *Chatlos* should therefore be read less as an affirmation of the law's commitment to protecting pure promissory expectations than as an object lesson in the limits of appellate review in a common law system.

The pure promissory expectations created in *Overstreet* and *Chatlos* both involved warranty promises—formally, promises *that* certain facts obtained rather than promises *to* do certain things. This is, of course, a

---

13. One doctrinal difference between *Overstreet* and *Chatlos* should not be ignored, namely that the plaintiff in *Overstreet* sought consequential damages whereas the *Chatlos* plaintiff sought the difference between the value as warranted and the value as delivered. But this purely formal difference cannot plausibly explain the divergence between the outcomes of the cases. It makes no sense to hang the law's willingness to protect purely contractual expectations on whether these expectations are consequential or direct.

14. Note that the dissent's arguments attacking the majority's view of the value of the machine as promised are clear losers. Although the dissent claims that it is inadequate—in effect because it is too speculative—to determine the value of the system as promised by reference to the market value of a hypothetical computer system with the promised capabilities, there was expert testimony in the case establishing the value of the system as promised by reference to actual computer systems then on the market. Moreover, the dissent's argument that damages may reflect only the market value of the machine as warranted and not its value to the plaintiff (that a seller who makes a warranty does not guarantee her buyer's profits from using the warranted good) is simply irrelevant. The remedy that the majority awarded was based on the market value of a machine with the warranted capacities. Finally, the dissent's suggestion that the buyer's remedy should be based on the market value of the make and model machine actually sold and not on the market value of some other machine that could perform the tasks at issue is inconsistent with the breach-of-warranty framework that, the dissenter and the majority agree, governs the case. Basing the remedy on the promised make and model rather than on the promised capabilities amounts, in effect, to denying that the promise that the machine had these capabilities created a warranty at all.

formal distinction only: *Overstreet* and *Chatlos* might equally naturally be read to involve promises *to* provide goods as warranted. The formal structure of the promises is worth noting only because it might explain why purely promissory expectations typically arise in connection with warranties: it is much easier mistakenly to promise that facts obtain which do not than it is to promise to do things on unreasonably good terms. The various disciplinary mechanisms that ordinarily prevent unreasonably generous promises do not quite apply in the same way. Nevertheless, purely promissory expectations can and sometimes even do arise in a second kind of case, involving promises to, in which a promisor-seller and promisee-buyer agree on terms—say, a below-market purchase price—that are exceptionally favorable to the buyer, and that the seller breaches almost at once, or at least before the buyer has incurred any costs in reliance on the contract. (Note that the below market price entails that the buyer has not incurred any opportunity costs, since no equivalently appealing alternative deals existed to forsake).

Texaco v. Pennzoil presents a prominent, and extreme, example of such expectations. It also represents the clearest and most self-confident legal statement that the law will vindicate purely promissory expectations just as surely as other contractual expectations, even in the face of the fact that they are unbacked by any detrimental reliance.

The stylized facts were these: Getty Oil sold itself to Pennzoil for $3.5 billion in spite of holding net assets (in the form of proven oil reserves) worth at least $11 billion (an amount reflecting the exploration costs of identifying equivalent reserves elsewhere).[15] Forty-eight hours later, and in response to an inducement, it breached the contract and resold itself to Texaco for a much higher price. Pennzoil sued claiming its expectation under the contract. (Technically, Pennzoil sued Texaco on a theory of tortious interference with the contract, but this is not relevant in the current context.[16]) The main issue in the case, certainly for present purposes, was not liability but rather, once liability was established, the

---

15. The actual market value of the reserves was greater still—roughly $30 billion. Why Getty Oil's stock should have been so much less valuable than its proven assets is one of the great mysteries of the case. One answer is that most stockholders cannot get at the assets by holding the stock, since their percentage ownership is too small for control of Getty and hence of its oil. Accordingly, insofar as Getty was badly run, its stock price would be deflated relative to the value of its assets, which Getty's management was in effect wasting. On this view, controlling a company yields a premium over just investing in it. Nevertheless, the purchase price here represented an implausibly large control premium. Still large value discrepancies, although not perhaps quite so enormous as in this case, were at least for a time pervasive in natural resource companies.

This explanation for the discrepancy between Getty's stock price and the value of its oil reserves is consistent with basing Pennzoil's recovery on the value of the reserves, since that would be Getty Oil's value in Pennzoil's hands. Other explanations are less consistent with the way in which the remedy was calculated. For example, given the volatility of oil prices, the value of the oil, including in Pennzoil's hands, should perhaps have been risk-adjusted downwards.

16. The measure of damages for a tortious interference with contract claim is the lost expectation on the contract plus consequential damages. Pennzoil presumably styled its suit as a tort claim because Texaco had more money than Getty Oil, so that the only contract defendant was not the defendant that the plaintiff wanted to sue.

appropriate remedy. Pennzoil, of course, had suffered no losses whatsoever as a result of the breach, including, once again, no lost opportunities to make money in some other way. Nevertheless, the court concluded that the proper remedy was the difference between the Getty Oil's purchase price and its value in Pennzoil's hands,[17] and a jury awarded Pennzoil $7.53 billion in expectation damages. The Supreme Court of Texas refused a writ of error, and while a petition for certiorari was pending, the parties settled for $3 billion.

Now, given its magnitude, the case as it was actually argued of course raised many complexities that have been glossed over here—involving, for example, whether Pennzoil would have been legally permitted to break up Getty in order to release the full value of its reserves,[18] the proper methods for calculating and discounting future oil exploration and recovery costs and future oil flows (as necessary in order accurately to assess the present value of Getty's proven reserves),[19] and an offset against damages for tax liabilities that Texaco alleged Pennzoil would have incurred in connection with the purchase.[20] But these are in the end just details. *Texaco v. Pennzoil* represents a clear and confident statement that the law will protect even contractual expectations that cannot be re-conceptualized in

---

17. Texaco had argued that the right measure of damages was in fact the difference between the purchase price that Pennzoil and Getty Oil had agreed and the market price, at the time of purchase, of the Getty shares that Pennzoil had acquired. This difference never exceeded $500 million. The court reject this argument, noting that the parties had clearly contemplated Pennzoil's purchase as a means of getting at Getty Oil's assets and not just as an ordinary stock transaction. The court also suggested, somewhat mysteriously, that because this suit sounded in tort rather than contract, Pennzoil's recovery should be the pecuniary loss of the benefits it would have been entitled to under the contract. But it is hard to see how the same outcome would not be required had the suit proceeded in contract, in which case, the contract-market stock price difference would have been direct damages and the value of the oil would have been clearly foreseeable, clearly non-speculative consequential damages. (Note, however, that the two awards could not have both be given without double counting, since recouping the oil directly would as a consequence deplete the value of the stock.)

18. Pennzoil's deal with Getty required it to try in good faith to keep Getty Oil intact, which might have limited its ability to get at Getty's reserves. The court ruled, however, that Pennzoil's managers would have had a duty to their share-holders to take the oil rather than the stock if this was most valuable, which it quite likely would have been.

19. The court resolved the discounting question by saying that no discounting was necessary since Pennzoil would have had the oil at once and not just in the future.

This is a dubious argument, however. There was so much oil at stake that Pennzoil could not plausibly have cashed out all the oil at once at the prevailing market price, because extracting the oil would have taken substantial periods of time and because even if the oil could have been all sold at once, any effort to do so might have flooded the market and diminished the price. And if the sale of the oil was necessarily delayed, should not the stream of receipts it involved have been discounted to present value?

20. The resolution of the tax argument shows the jury system at its craziest. The court held that there was no conclusive proof concerning the question whether Pennzoil would have been charged with a tax on acquiring the oil, which it was saved by Texaco and which should therefore be credited to Texaco in damages calculation. The court then observed that several people familiar with the tax laws testified, and that the question was therefore one for the jury. (In the circumstance in which the tax question arose in this case, it was a question of fact rather than law, since the question was what in fact would Pennzoil have had to pay.)

This is just insanity on the march—the amount of the tax seems to have been $2 billion. How can a jury reasonably decide this question of tax law without having had the trial directed expressly and exhaustively at the question?

terms of reliance losses (no matter how broadly opportunity costs are understood). Moreover, the case applied this rule in a huge way—to the tune of nearly $8 billion. Although that may seem to many to represent an unjustified windfall to Pennzoil, one court (at least) was willing to take the official presentation of the expectation remedy at its word and award it.

Nevertheless, cases like *Texaco v. Pennzoil* to the contrary notwithstanding, the reliance remedy continues to strike at the very core of contract law's claims to represent a conceptually distinctive and free-standing form of private law obligation, characterized by its commitment to promisees' forward-looking entitlements to have their contractual expectations vindicated and not just their backward-looking entitlements not to be left worse off than they would have been had they avoided their contracts entirely. In almost every case—in all cases in which contractual promises arise against a backdrop of well-functioning markets—the law's professed commitment to vindicating contractual expectations may be recharacterized as a commitment to protecting promisees from reliance losses, now understood to include the lost opportunities of dealing with third parties in place of their promisors. And when contractual expectations cannot be recast in terms of reliance in this way—because promisees expect extraordinary, above-market returns from their contracts—then the law's commitment to vindicating their expectations—which are now characterized as involving *windfalls* that by their nature, give rise to only insecure claims—wavers and sometimes, as in *Overstreet*, fails outright. Regardless of the forward-looking ideal to which contract law turns in its *self-presentation*, it seems that contract remedies, as they are actually *applied*, often implement a backward-looking form of obligation that belongs firmly to tort. Finally, when these interpretive observations are considered in the context of the well-known normative puzzle concerning how purely forward-looking obligations like those involved in contract (and promise) as traditionally understood could ever be justified, even in principle—a puzzle that will be investigated in detail later in these materials—suggestions that the traditional presentation of the expectation remedy mischaracterizes the law gain still greater plausibility.

Together, these reflections suggest that contract is perhaps not a distinctive or free-standing form of legal obligation at all but is instead the elaboration of a special class of torts, namely those having to do with misrepresentations concerning present intentions and future actions. This suggestion concludes the discussion of contract remedies with a question and a call for re-appraisal. It also provides a window through which to view the materials to come. These will take up many themes, of course—too many to unify in any simple or orderly way. But one prominent (if not dominant) theme will be to develop an account of the contract relation, and of the normative foundations on which this relation stands, that can answer the question raised here on terms that sustain contract law's traditional self-presentation as a distinctively forward-looking form of legal obligation. Insofar as the materials live up to that ambition, the puzzle concerning reliance damages introduced here will turn out to be *merely* that and nothing more—a curious observation that the law might achieve much of what it in fact allocates to contract from within tort, rather than the foundation of a fundamental challenge to contract's self-presentation as a distinctive body of law, which elaborates a free-standing form of obligation.

PART TWO

Making Contracts and Making Contractual Meaning (Herein of Formalism, Realism, and the Styles of Legal Doctrine)

CHAPTER 12

INTRODUCTION

Remedies, it is commonly said, play a secondary role in contract law. They come into play only in the shadow of breach, to vindicate the primary rights and enforce the primary obligations that a contract creates. Part I challenged this thought with respect to some parts of remedies law, explaining that certain parts of the law (most notably, the rules governing expectation damages) that are conventionally understood as remedial, in fact help to fix the content of primary contract rights and obligations. This style of argument makes it natural to ask how contracts are created, and how their content is established, more generally.

The discussion in Part I swept these questions under the rug: it assumed that the parties had successfully entered into a contract and, moreover, that the content of their primary contractual obligations was well-understood. Of course, often either or both of these assumptions are unwarranted. In the cases, promisors commonly defend themselves against promisees' remedial claims by arguing either that there was no valid contract (so that they have not incurred any legal obligations at all) or that there was no breach (so that they have done whatever it was that the contract, properly understood, obligated them to do).

This Part of the text takes up the questions implicit in these two possibilities: it asks how the law governs the entry into a contract relation (what is involved in successfully making a contract and establishing the legal obligations that contracts involve); and it asks how the content of contractual obligations is determined (what materials make up a contract and how these materials are understood). This Part takes up what one might think are the first questions concerning contract law, that is, questions concerning the primary obligations that contract law involves. The discussion in Part II, however, will reveal why the text overall is organized as it is: One of the central questions posed here will be how readily the law should recognize contractual obligations (both *tout court*, and in respect of particular claims concerning their substantive content); and as the introduction to Part I observed, these questions can sensibly be addressed only against the backdrop of an understanding of what is actually at stake in their answers—what the law is prepared to deliver, by way of secondary obligations, to enforce whatever primary contractual obligations it recognizes.

Obviously both the topics just mentioned—concerning how contractual obligations arise and how their content is determined—will be elaborated in considerable detail below. But it will nevertheless be helpful, by way of introduction, to say something brief about what these topics include and what they do not.

First, the discussion concerning how contractual obligations arise—what is required for a valid contract to be made—will not take up the scope of contract or of contractual capacity in general but rather what is necessary for establishing particular contracts within that scope. Questions concerning the limits of freedom of contract—for example, whether immoral or illegal promises can generate legally enforceable obligations (and less obviously, but more significantly) whether certain very important transactions and relationships can be managed on the promissory model at all—will be taken up in Part III. Here, the issue is whether a contract of a type that clearly *might* be made has *in fact* been made in a particular instance. Thus, although it is quite clear that an owner of a farm may in principle sell it to a willing buyer, it may (as in *Lucy v. Zehmer* below) be entirely unclear whether a particular exchange of utterances and writings has actually established a contract of sale.

Similarly, the discussion concerning how the law fixes the content of a successfully made contract—concerning what materials are included in the contractual text and how this text should be interpreted—will not take up a contract's mandatory terms but rather the meaning of a contract's discretionary and variable terms. Again, questions concerning legal rules that absolutely forbid sellers from disclaiming liability for bodily injury to consumers, for example,[1] or that impose a mandatory duty of good faith in performance,[2] will be addressed elsewhere. Here, the issue will be whether or not a promise that clearly might or might not be included in a contract has in fact been incorporated by the language, etc., of a particular agreement. Thus, although it is quite clear that a seller and her buyer may reserve for the seller an option to repurchase what he has sold for a specified price at a specified future date, it may (as in *Masterson v. Sine* below) be entirely unclear whether a particular contract of sale actually makes such a reservation.

This Part of the text takes up these questions—broadly speaking, of contract *formation* on the one hand and, on the other, of what the law calls (employing a distinction to which the argument will return) contract *construction* and *interpretation*. It will do so using a new method of legal analysis, which focuses not on the law as an instrument to produce certain outcomes (in the case of law and economics, to promote efficiency) but rather on the formal—or *free-standing* or *autonomous*—structure of legal rules. This new focus is worth explaining before the materials that follow apply the new approach in earnest and in connection with particular legal rules.

Perhaps the best way to explain the *formalist* idea of autonomous legal doctrine is by setting up a contrast with the economic approach that Part I made familiar. The economic analysis of law is one prominent branch of a

---

1.   See, e.g., UCC § 2–719(3); RESTATEMENT (Second) of Contracts § 195.

2.   See, e.g., UCC § 1–304; RESTATEMENT (Second) of Contracts § 205.

general approach to law called legal *realism*.[3] And formalism is, in a rough sense, the opposite of realism.

Legal realism asserts that legal doctrine should be understood as purely and entirely derivative of extra-legal values and that law quite generally is merely a means for promoting the ends that these values announce.

On the plane of fact, realism proposes that doctrine cannot successfully contain or resist the pursuit of such values—that doctrine is sufficiently malleable that it is not a successful constraint on power. Legal rules, on this view, are merely ways in which legal actors (quintessentially courts) rationalize what they have done, where the real reasons for their decisions make no mention of the rules. In the extreme, realists deny doctrine any independent, or formal, existence at all. They are concerned not with the rules that courts (or others) employ to explain their decisions, but rather directly with the *outcomes* that these decisions impose. As Holmes once proposed, the law (legal doctrine) is *nothing* more than a prediction of what courts will do in particular cases.[4] Rules, on this view, are entirely epiphenomenal to the law.

And on the plane of value, realists insist that this is as it should be. They reject the idea that doctrine might legitimately have free-standing value or authority and instead treat the law purely as an instrument that serves extra-legal values, such as efficiency (as elaborated in Part I), or fairness (where fairness is understood in a way that makes no essential reference to following the rules), or perfectionist morality (for example, some account of personal virtue and vice). To be sure, realists accept (because they could not plausibly deny) that legal rules are on their face *normative*, in the sense of identifying "correct" and "incorrect" outcomes and distinguishing between them.[5] But, realists insist, the norms an-

---

3. Other branches of legal realism include the broadly progressive realism associated with Llewellyn (this is more the root of realism, at least in American law, than a branch, in the sense that these progressives founded the expressly instrumental approach to law more generally) and the more politically radical realism associated with the Critical Legal Studies movement of the end of the last century (which sought to unmask the ways in which legal orders sustain economic and political inequalities). All these varieties of realists agree, methodologically, that the law should be understood as a tool that serves pre-legal ends. They disagree about whether the law that we have is desirable, and about what would make a body of law desirable, but they agree that the answers must come from entirely outside the law.

4. See Oliver Wendell Holmes, Jr., *The Path of the Law*, 10 HARV. L. REV. 457 (1897) ("The prophecies of what courts will do in fact, and nothing more pretentious, are what I mean by the law.").

5. Notice how the word "normative" is used in this sentence, because it is generally *mis*-used in legal discourse.

Often, the word "normative" is used to pick out specifically *moral* values, as when "normative legal analysis" is used to refer to arguments concerning what the law *should be*, in contrast to "positive legal analysis," which addresses what the law *is*. But this is a reverse synecdoche, and hence involves a conceptual confusion. Morality is only one part of normativity (and it is an open question in philosophy whether or not it is even a privileged part), so that there exist many norms that are not moral. The norms of arithmetic—which specify the correct relations among numbers—are one obvious example; norms of etiquette are another. Legal doctrine establishes yet another normative system, at least insofar as the law's doctrinal rules identify the "correct" and "incorrect" resolutions of legal questions. Thus, to recur to an

nounced by legal doctrine are thin or (to change metaphors) shallow, perhaps like the norms announced by the rules of a parlor game. They deserve no independent weight in practical deliberations—they should be allowed to have no free-standing impact on the outcomes of cases—but are instead appealing only insofar as they serve other, more fundamental values, just as a game's rules are appealing only insofar as they make the game that they govern fun to play.[6] Rules, on this approach, are fully revisable; their rule-like character does not in itself justify giving them any inertia in the face of external considerations that suggest it would be better to change or abandon them. Put a little differently, this perspective insists that practical deliberations must always and at every moment be made from a perspective that stands outside of rule-governed practices—outside of games and outside of the law—so that rules are always assessed *de novo*, which is to say skeptically.

The shallowness that realists accord legal doctrine was well-illustrated by the economic analysis of contract remedies in Part I. The efficiency of allocations was the only thing that ultimately mattered there, and legal rules or doctrines were useful only insofar as they served, or even tracked, economic efficiency. To be sure, efficiency might require that outcomes of particular disputes be predictable in advance, so that regularity in court decisions might be desirable even for the (economically minded) realist. But the rule-like structure of legal doctrine (that legal doctrine is general, fixed in advance, public, etc.) did not *in itself* play any part the analysis and certainly gave no authority to doctrines that (even taking into account the virtues of predictability) are inefficient, at least once they are recognized to be so.[7]

---

example made familiar in the law of remedies, a court that responded to a breach of contract by awarding the disappointed promisee damages equal only to her out of pocket expenses would be making a mistake, which is to say reaching the doctrinally wrong outcome.

The issue between realists and formalists is not whether legal doctrine is normative in this sense, but rather how important doctrinal normativity is to normative analysis all-things-considered. Realists say not important at all, so that extra legal values do and should simply trump the law's norms whenever the two conflict. Formalists wish to give legal norms greater force than this.

6. Even such shallow rules may be constitutive of the acts done under them—they may, to use language introduced by John Rawls, be practice rules (which create the types of action that they govern) rather than mere rules of thumb (which just summarize considerations that apply quite apart from the rules in the service of avoiding the transactions costs of case-by-case deliberations). See John Rawls, *Two Concepts of Rules*, 64 PHILOSOPHICAL REVIEW 3 (1955). Thus a card-player cannot "knock" except by complying with the rules of Gin Rummy, and a contracting party cannot "offer" terms except in accordance with the rules of contract law.

Realists insist that even when rules are constitutive of practices in this way, obeying the rules (and hence participating in the practices) is justified only insofar as the practices that the rules constitute can themselves be justified by reference to values that arise independent of the rules. Card games must give players pleasure, for example; and contract law must serve efficiency. Moreover, nothing stops the realist from abandoning a practice (by violating its rules) at any moment, as soon as she decides that the practice no longer best serves whatever antecedent values its justification depends on. Again, even as she participates in a practice, its rules exercise no free-standing hold over the realist.

7. Law and economics shares this skepticism of rules with its utilitarian ancestor. Indeed, the classical utilitarians were partly motivated by hostility to what they regarded as the rule worship that characterized the everyday (religious) morality of the Victorian age. For

Formalism rejects this view and instead insists that the rule-like structure of the law—the normativity associated with legal doctrine—is deep and capable of resisting external to law values. In its classical expression, at least on the stylized view of formalism against which the early realists defined themselves, the internal normativity of legal rules establishes the dominant or even exclusive values to which legal analysis should answer.[8] According to this classical formalism, law is a closed and complete system, whose rules fully determine outcomes in particular cases and, moreover, bind simply in virtue of their rule-like form rather than because of their substance or connection to extra-legal values and indeed even when the outcomes that they produce are condemned by these extra-legal values. In the words of Langdell, who was perhaps the most famous and formidable formalist of all, it is simply "irrelevant" that the internal logic of legal rules might produce "absurd and unjust" results.[9] As Grant Gilmore once said, for the formalist "law is doctrine and nothing but doctrine—pure, absolute, abstract, scientific—a logician's dream of heaven."[10] When faced with a legal problem, the formalist wants to know the purely *legal* answer. She never asks whether legal norms look good as judged by extra legal norms. The metaphors through which this position is described immediately reveal it to be the polar opposite of realism: the openness of law is replaced with an insistence that law is closed off from other realms of normativity; and the external perspective is replaced with a practical standpoint that resides entirely inside the law.

The worshipful attitude towards legal rules that formalism displays is sometimes called *doctrinalism*, which is classical formalism's characteristic method of legal analysis, its approach to deciding particular cases. Doctrinalism accepts the law's norms literally without questioning them. It analyses legal problems by the immediate (in the sense of un-mediated) application of legal rules, where (critically) the content of these legal rules, and the connections among them, may be determined simply from the face of the rules (sometimes read singly and sometimes in combination), without looking outside them to whatever extra-legal values they might serve.

The main objections to formalism and doctrinalism are not hard to see, at least for someone with a contemporary cast of mind. Whatever else it may be, law is obviously *also* a tool of policy, and unless it is open to, and indeed aggressively seeks out, the values that determine good policy, law will surely be a very bad tool. When he spoke of the "logician's dream,"

---

a more modern statement of this view, see J.J.C. SMART AND BERNARD WILLIAMS, UTILITARIANISM: FOR AND AGAINST (1973). For more on this feature of law and economics, with special reference to the analysis of contract law, see Jody Kraus, *The Methodological Committments of Contemporary Contract Theory, in* THE OXFORD HANDBOOK OF JURISPRUDENCE AND PHILOSOPHY OF LAW. (John Coleman and Scot Shapiro, eds., 2002).

8. Note that this is likely a caricature of the views that even the classical formalists actually held. See, e.g., Thomas Grey, *Langdell's Orthodoxy*, 45 U. PITT. L. REV. 1 (1983); DAVID RABBAN, REFORMIST EVOLUTIONARY HISTORY, NOT CONSERVATIVE DEDUCTIVE FORMALISM: RETHINKING LATE NINETEENTH-CENTURY AMERICAN LEGAL THOUGHT.

9. C.C. LANGDELL, A SELECTION OF CASES IN THE LAW OF CONTRACTS 995–96 (2d ed. 1897). Langdell was writing about the mailbox rule, of which more below.

10. GRANT GILMORE, THE DEATH OF CONTRACT 98 (1974).

Gilmore was being snide. For himself, he clearly preferred Holmes's aphorism that "the life of the law is not logic but experience."[11] Moreover, these general objections are not hard to make concrete for particular bodies of law and particular cases. In the context of contract law, the fact that formalist legal analysis seeks to make the law insensitive to both extra legal norms and to the particular contexts in which individual contracts arise leads formalism to favor outcomes that are obviously inefficient and unfair and, moreover, do not track what the parties to the contracts at issue had in mind.

Nevertheless, there is something to be said for formalism, at least if it is given a less rigoristic elaboration than the classical version involved.[12]

Even purely instrumental approaches to law—the approaches most closely associated with legal realism in general and with law and economics in particular—have in recent years come to recognize that part of the law's usefulness as a tool depends on its employing rules that are able to resist, at least in some measure, revision based on extra-legal values. Persons are not frictionless or costless deliberators but instead must devote time and resources to discovering and analyzing facts and even values. This means that they will often most successfully promote whatever values they espouse by following rules designed to promote these values in general, without reconsidering these rules in particular cases (including even in particular cases in which the rules do not best promote the values). Moreover, persons are not even frictionless or costless implementers of the conclusions of their deliberations but must instead devote energy to motivating themselves actually to do what they have concluded is best (persons may conclude that they have most reason to lose weight, for example, but never even intend to diet, or they may intend to diet but abandon their intentions on seeing the first bakery). This means that they will often most successfully achieve their ambitions by adopting general habits of action that they do not revisit in particular cases (including even when they might do better by re-directing their motivations). Indeed, both sets of bounds on human rationality re-appear at one greater level of abstraction, so that persons may, given the costs of identifying and conforming to new general rules of conduct, do best by retaining sub-optimal rules. Finally, these bounds on human rationality become only more pressing when the focus shifts from the individual person to collectives of persons, who are differently able to discover and verify various facts and values, whose strategic circumstances may open up any number of possibilities for opportunism, and who therefore will find it to their advantage to establish rules that some must defer to others on particular questions.

In contract law, the parties themselves are often thought to be better able to assess their own interests than are courts, and possibilities for opportunistic revisionism concerning the intentions of the parties or the meanings that they attributed to contractual language abound. Some

---

11. OLIVER WENDELL HOLMES, THE COMMON LAW 5 (Mark DeWolfe Howe ed., 1963) (1881).

12. For general discussions in this area, see Fred Schauer, *Formalism*, 97 YALE L.J. 509 (1988) and also Symposium: *Formalism Revisited*, 66 U. CHI. L. REV. 529–942 (1999).

lawyer-economists have thought that these features of contracting together entail that legal regimes full of formalist rules concerning contract formation and contractual meaning, which give courts deciding whether contracts have successfully been formed or what they mean little opportunity directly to consider extra-legal values such as efficiency or fairness, will better promote these values than a legal regime that instructs courts to pursue them directly, as realists.[13]

A second defense of (appropriately modest) formalism involves a more thoroughgoing rejection of realism, and in particular rejects the instrumental approach to law in favor of an approach that understands law, and in particular the law's rule-like structure, to have intrinsic merit. According to this argument, law is not just a tool for promoting extra legal ends but also in itself a distinctive way in which persons might relate to one another—in which persons might engage one another to form a community. Formal rules, so the argument goes, are necessary for creating what might be called the *point of view of the law*, a public point of view in which all subject to the law can share, and which serves as the substrate in which the community established by the law arises. This community, one might say, can exist only in the medium of the law's rules, which must (in order to provide the required medium) sustain a normative order that cannot be reduced to external social, economic, political, or moral values.

On this view, law is in essence a socially integrative practice, and the law achieves its integrative essence through its rules, which must have a formal existence in order to be integrative. This type of formalism seeks to identify certain values—in particular, values associated with community and respect—that are fundamentally legal, in the sense that they are not so much promoted (instrumentally) by law as immanent in law (in virtue of law's basic character). It then argues that in order to achieve these values, the law must maintain a formal existence: legal rules must be treated—as formalists have wished to do—as establishing a free-standing, or autonomous, normative order. Indeed, to achieve these integrative values, legal rules must be valued for their own sakes. The structure of the argument is a little like the structure of Henry Sidgwick's argument concerning the paradox of pleasure. To take pleasure in many things, one must value the things not just instrumentally but intrinsically: to take pleasure in art, for example, one must value not just pleasure, but art, and art for its own sake.[14]

---

13. See, e.g., Alan Schwartz and Robert Scott, *Contract Theory and the Limits of Contract Law*, 113 Yale L.J. 541 (2003). Other lawyer-economists disagree, and believe that realist contract law best promotes realist values, even given transactions costs. See, e.g., Albert Choi and George Triantis, *Strategic Vagueness in Contract Design: The case of Corporate Acquisitions*, 119 Yale L. J. 848 (2010); Albert Choi and George Triantis, *Completing Contracts in the Shadow of Costly Verification*, 37 J. Legal Stud. 503 (2008).

14. This version of formalism is connected to the natural law tradition, insofar as the values—community, respect—that it invokes have a universal appeal, which does not rest on any particular positive legal order. But the formalism is also connected to positivist jurisprudence, because it proposes that these universal values may be achieved only through positive law, and not directly. Here see Jeremy Waldron, *Kant's Legal Positivism*, 109 Harv. L. Rev. 1535 (1996).

These two arguments in favor of a modest formalism are important in their own rights, of course, and Part III of these materials (on the limits of freedom of contract) will take up the second argument in earnest for the special case of contract law. But for now this brief discussion will have to suffice. If a metaphor will help to fix ideas, here is one: classical formalism approached the law as a closed and shuttered room, and sought to know only what the room looked like from within; realism threw open the shutters, but at the same time insisted that the room be viewed only from the outside, looking in through the newly open windows; and modern formalism suggests that it might be worth revisiting the room from the inside, to see what it looks like from that perspective, now with the shutters wide open.

This Part of the text begins to identify just how far, or in what way, formalism might resist the realist onslaught. This Part also seeks to understand the internal workings of formalism and realism in their doctrinal details, that is, to see how each general view concerning the nature and purposes of law works itself out in a particular style of legal rule-making and legal reasoning. The contrast between formalism and realism is best illustrated by focusing on the classical formalism that, at least according to the standard legal histories, dominated U.S. contract law in last quarter of the 19th and first quarter of the 20th centuries—on the idea, more or less, that contract law could and should function as a set of free-standing legal rules completely divorced from any extra-legal values.

One of the leading themes of the discussion will be to show that successful law-making requires consistency with respect to the choice between formalism and realism—that a classical approach to one area of doctrine requires a classical approach in another, seemingly unrelated area, in order to keep the whole doctrinal tapestry from unraveling. Even a very little overt realism turns out to be toxic—fatally so—to a classical doctrinal order (at least in the case of contract law).

The materials below will explain why realism is toxic in this way and demonstrate the paths along which the realist toxin travels to take effect. More specifically, they will reveal that the classical approach to contract *formation* was necessarily paired with a stylistically related approach to contractual meaning (to contract construction and contract interpretation) which treated language as creating meaning through a closed and formal set of interpretive rules, which might be discerned and applied independent

---

Moreover, this connection to positivism works itself into the interstices of the formalist argument, which displays a homomorphism to one of the core positivist arguments for the authority of law. That argument, associated with Joseph Raz, proposes that the authority of law depends on its being the case that people better conform to the reasons that independently apply to them by following the law's commands than by deliberating about these reasons directly, and suggests that some measure of formalism is necessary for law to provide this deliberative service (because if the law depends on, or in the extreme case, simply restates, extra-legal reasons, then it cannot aid deliberation in the required way). Similarly, formalism proposes that the value of law is connected to its establishing a public point of view in which all who are subject to it can share and suggests that some measure of formalism is necessary for the law to establish this point of view (because if the law depends entirely on extra-legal values, then it will simply reproduce the fractured multiplicity of independent perspectives from which these values are perceived).

from both extra-legal values (such as reasonableness or fairness) and also the particular contexts or practices in which the language is used. This approach to contractual meaning is essential in order to make contract formation, on the classical model, possible at all. It is also an approach that cannot easily survive modern commercial practice, and so that materials that follow provide one kind of explanation for why the classical edifice of contract law was exposed to realist ideas, which inevitably destroyed it, leaving us with the a contract law that is deeply realist in the ways that Part I described.[15]

In this respect, much of the argument that follows will be purely descriptive. The idea is not so much to choose between formalism and realism as it is to understand the character of each and what happens when they interact.

But another theme of the argument will be more (or at least more nearly) evaluative. The materials that follow are also designed to show how, in case after case, classical formalism in fact depends on certain value judgments from without the legal system, without which it cannot decide cases and which its insistent claims to normative autonomy simply hide. In particular, classical formalism in contract law depended on the idea that the greatest value a system of contract law might pursue is freedom *from* contract—that it is essential for the law to protect potential promisors from liabilities that they did not intend to acquire (and, in particular, that it is more important to do this than to protect potential promisees from having contractual expectations disappointed). As Gilmore put it, the classical theory seems "to have been dedicated to the proposition that, ideally, no one should be liable to anyone for anything."[16] Thus the classical view of contract formation makes promisors into the masters of their offers, and the classical approaches to construction and interpretation make promisors the masters of contractual meaning.[17] In the end, the classical view collapsed because this nearly fanatical privileging of freedom from contract over freedom to contract—this focus on avoiding unwanted liability even at the risk of disappointing contractual expectations—proved indefensible. Its distributive effects were unappealing and, perhaps more importantly still, it adopted an *ex post* perspective of the interests of those who might be subject to liability that failed even to serve the parties whom it was designed to protect. If there is single lesson of the economic analysis of contract law pursued in Part I, it is that even promisors wish, *ex ante*, to be

---

15. I say "one kind of explanation" because other, parallel, explanations are of course also possible, involving (for example) the interaction between contract law and economic power, or the charismatic powers of particular important judges and scholars. These explanations are not necessarily competitors. The argument in these pages merely highlights the mechanisms within legal doctrine through which such other forces as these might impose themselves on the law.

16. GRANT GILMORE, THE DEATH OF CONTRACT 14 (1974).

17. Note that here the classical approach came up against its own limits. As the text that follows will explain, classical contract law's textualist approach to interpretation was necessary to prevent its subjective approach to contract formation from literally undoing contractual obligation entirely, rendering every contractual obligation effectively voidable more or less at the will of the promisor.

able to bind themselves, despite the fact that they may sometimes come, *ex post*, to regret what they have done. The power to make commitments greatly expands a potential promisor's range of action and in particular the types of coordination in which she can engage. And so a formalism that too narrowly cabins contractual obligation in the end betrays the very purposes for which contract law exists to begin with.

Of course, this is all very abstract. To really understand any of it, one must get down to details, including essentially to doctrinal details. The following chapters do just that.

CHAPTER 13

OFFER AND ACCEPTANCE

Contracts are traditionally formed when an *offer* is *met* with an *acceptance*. So understanding contract formation—at least for the core cases—requires understanding what constitutes a legally valid offer, what constitutes an acceptance, and how the two must be related in order for them to meet. This chapter takes up offers.

Before taking up these details, however, it is worth pausing for a moment to reflect on how language functions in contract formation.

When most people think, intuitively, about what language does, they focus on language's capacity to describe reality, characteristically by asserting things. The principles that govern how to understand and evaluate assertions turn out to be very complicated. (Some of them will be taken up in greater detail, although not in a philosophically systematic way, in the materials on construction and interpretation.) Nevertheless, a simple example, will serve to fix ideas for present purposes: when a person utters the sentence "Snow is white" she asserts that the thing snow possesses the property whiteness.

Language may also be used in another, very different way. It may be used not to describe reality but to change it. Language that is used in this way—as what is sometimes called a *speech act*—does not assert some independently true proposition about reality but rather makes something the case by saying that it is so.[1] A dignitary who *christens a ship*, for example, says "I name this ship *The U.S.S. Constitution*," and that act quite literally gives the ship its name. Similarly, a head of state who *declares war* causes, through this declaration, a state of war to exist.

Contracts are also formed through speech acts—namely offers and (appropriately related) acceptances. An offer—for example, "I offer to sell you my car for $1000"—does not assert something concerning an independently existing state of affairs but rather by its own operation creates a new state of affairs. In particular, it exposes the offeror to acquiring certain contractual rights and obligations in case the offer is accepted by the offeree, rights and obligations that did not previously exist. An accep-

---

1. This formulation hides many difficulties, which a few simple examples bring to light. Thus, when I say "I exhale," I am making it the case that I exhale by saying that it is so. But this is hardly a speech act. The relation between my saying something and its becoming so must be more than merely causal, although just how turns out to be a very difficult question. Doubts that the question really is difficult may be quickly dispelled by considering how to describe the relationship between a person's testing a microphone by (1) coughing into it, (2) saying "hello" to a person who will be able to hear only amplified speech, and (3) saying "testing, testing, one, two, three."

tance—for example, "I accept your offer to sell the car for $1000"—is similarly a speech act. It again does not describe but rather changes reality. In particular, it converts the potential for contractual rights and obligations created by the offer into actual contractual rights and obligations. To understand contract formation therefore requires understanding how offer and acceptance function as speech acts.

Not all speech acts succeed—speech acts do not always make the case what they say is the case. So it becomes interesting to ask when speech acts do succeed—when, that is, they are performed *felicitously*. Speech acts may fail in at least two ways, each of which will turn out to be relevant for contract law.

First, a speech act may fail to be felicitous because it *misfires*. A speech act may misfire because the speaker lacks the capacity to do the act in question. Thus I (Daniel Markovits, the author of this text) may say to someone "I appoint you Chief Justice of the United States Supreme Court," but the person will not, of course, be so appointed. I lack the authority of appointment, which is to say, the power to change the allocation of this office in this way. Similarly, some speech acts require their addressee to make an appropriate uptake in order for them to succeed. Thus, although I may forgive you (who have wronged me) without your doing anything in reply, I cannot successfully challenge you (to a race or a duel) without your taking up the challenge. In some cases, it is uncertain what uptake demands, or indeed whether uptake is required at all. Can I successfully apologize even if you do not accept the apology? These ways of misfiring will both be relevant to contract law. Certainly the problem of capacity looms large: there are some things that no one has the power to do by speech act, for example, to vindicate a judgment (although demagogues often try); and this makes it natural to ask whether persons generally possess the normative power to create obligations by speech act, a question that will be taken up in earnest in Part III. The problem of uptake is similarly important in connection with the speech acts that establish contracts: offers plainly require some form of acceptance before an obligation arises, but just what acceptance involves, and just how acceptances and offers must be related—how they must engage each other—are thorny questions, which will figure prominently in the next chapter.

A speech act may fail to be felicitous in a second way also, specifically because it is *abused*. After belittling you in a meeting, I may apologize, but the apology will not be effective if I am not sincere. Indeed, an insincere apology may even compound my initial wrong, as evidenced by your justifiably renewed anger on learning of my insincerity. Similarly, even if it is sincere, an apology may fail for being insufficiently targeted, as in the familiar case in which a person, having made a chauvinistic remark in public, says "I did not mean to belittle anyone and apologize for any offense that I have caused." In this case, the apology fails (even if sincere) because the admission that the remark may have caused people in general to be offended mistakes the wrong that requires the apology, namely that the remark was, constitutively, offensive in virtue of the particular class of persons that it belittled.

The cases below take up both these ways in which a remark that resembles an offer may fail on account of abusing the offer form. The first set of cases asks whether offers must be sincere in order to expose offerors to the possibility that acceptances will establish contractual obligations. The second set of cases asks how narrowly targeted offers must be—how specifically they must identify and engage their addressees—in order to be effective.

13.1   SUBJECTIVE VERSUS OBJECTIVE STANDARDS OF INTENT

When an apology fails for being insincere, the person who apologizes typically intends the mismatch between the ordinary meaning of her words and her actual mental state—she intends, as it were, to say something other than what she means. (Whether or not she intends to mislead is of course a separate question, since she may wish it to be common knowledge that her speech act has only the form and not the substance of an apology, as when a child who is forced by her parents to apologize for taking a sibling's toy says a rebellious and angry "sorry.") Offers made during contracting are rarely insincere in this intentional way, however.[2] Instead, the typical cases involve offerors who do not believe that their acts and utterances constitute offers at all, and who are surprised (and dismayed) when offerees accept and insist that contracts have been formed.

The central doctrinal issue raised by such cases is whether, on the one hand, an offer arises only where an offeror has formed the *actual* intent to enter a bargain in case her offeree accepts or, on the other hand, an offer arises whenever a *reasonable observer* would interpret the offeror's acts and utterances as revealing an intent to enter a bargain on acceptance (regardless of what intent the offeror actually had). The law typically characterizes these two alternatives as involving a *subjective* theory of intent on the one hand and an *objective* theory on the other.

---

2.   To be sure, contractual promisors sometimes make promises (and hence also offers) that they do not intend to perform. There is even a doctrinal category for dealing with insincere promises—promissory fraud—which will be discussed later in these materials.

But the promises (and offers) in such cases are not necessarily (and perhaps not even characteristically) insincere in the sense at issue here. Contractual promises involve two intentions: the intent to do what is promised and, separately, the intent to become obligated to do what is promised. Someone who commits promissory fraud certainly promises without intending to perform, but the question whether or not she intends to become obligated is much more complicated. Certainly she *may* so intend (nothing in the structure of promissory fraud prohibits this). Moreover, it is plausible to suppose that most people committing promissory fraud *do* intend to be bound, at least in the weak sense that they intend to invoke a legal order that will obligate them.

The cases at issue here are very different. They involve promisors who do not intend to assume legal obligations, or indeed to establish legal relations, at all, but whose actions and utterances might nevertheless reasonably be interpreted to reflect just this intent.

These terms are fine, as long as they are properly understood. In particular, the distinction between subjective and objective accounts of contractual intent is *not* a distinction between theories that make intent subjective in the sense of being a matter of opinion and those that make intent objective in the sense of being a matter of fact. Instead, both subjective and objective theories of intent make the question of intent a matter of fact; they disagree only in respect of what the fact consists in. On the subjective theory of intent, the relevant fact is the state of mind of the putative offeror at the time of making the alleged offer (a fact about which the offeror can be wrong, of course). On the objective theory of intent, the relevant fact is what a reasonable person in the position of the offeree would have inferred about the offeror's state of mind based on the acts and utterances that allegedly constitute the offer.

The materials that follow illustrate both the subjective and the objective accounts of offer. The subjective theory is the older approach, associated with classical, formalist approaches to contract law quite generally. Modern contract law adopts an objective approach to intent.

Bailey v. West

Supreme Court of Rhode Island, 1969.
249 A.2d 414.

Action to recover reasonable value of services rendered in feeding, care and maintenance of horse. The Superior Court, Providence and Bristol Counties, Perkins, J., entered judgment for plaintiff. The plaintiff appealed and defendant cross appealed. The Supreme Court, Paolino, J., held that where plaintiff knew there was dispute as to ownership of horse when he accepted it, neither defendant nor his trainer had ever had any business transactions with plaintiff or used his farm to board horses, and defendant's trainer told van driver, who took horse to plaintiff, that defendant would not be responsible for boarding horse on any farm, there was no intent to contract for plaintiff's boarding horse and defendant was not liable to plaintiff for cost of maintaining horse on basis of implied contract to do so.

Plaintiff's appeal denied and dismissed, defendant's cross appeal sustained and cause remanded for entry of judgment for defendant.

■ PAOLINO, J. This is a civil action wherein the plaintiff alleges that the defendant is indebted to him for the reasonable value of his services rendered in connection with the feeding, care and maintenance of a certain race horse named "Bascom's Folly" from May 3, 1962 through July 3, 1966. The case was tried before a justice of the superior court sitting without a jury, and resulted in a decision for the plaintiff for his cost of boarding the horse for the five months immediately subsequent to May 3, 1962, and for certain expenses incurred by him in trimming its hoofs. The cause is now before us on the plaintiff's appeal and defendant's cross appeal from the judgment entered pursuant to such decision.

The facts material to a resolution of the precise issues raised herein are as follows. In late April 1962, defendant, accompanied by his horse trainer, went to Belmont Park in New York to buy race horses. On April 27, 1962, defendant purchased "Bascom's Folly" from a Dr. Strauss and arranged to have the horse shipped to Suffolk Downs in East Boston, Massachusetts. Upon its arrival defendant's trainer discovered that the horse was lame, and so notified defendant, who ordered him to reship the horse by van to the seller at Belmont Park. The seller refused to accept delivery at Belmont on May 3, 1962, and thereupon, the van driver, one Kelly, called defendant's trainer and asked for further instructions. Although the trial testimony is in conflict as to what the trainer told him, it is not disputed that on the same day Kelly brought "Bascom's Folly" to plaintiff's farm where the horse remained until July 3, 1966, when it was sold by plaintiff to a third party.

While "Bascom's Folly" was residing at his horse farm, plaintiff sent bills for its feed and board to defendant at regular intervals. According to testimony elicited from defendant at the trial, the first such bill was received by him some two or three months after "Bascom's Folly" was placed on plaintiff's farm. He also stated that he immediately returned the bill to plaintiff with the notation that he was not the owner of the horse nor was it sent to plaintiff's farm at his request. The plaintiff testified that he sent bills monthly to defendant and that the first notice he received from him disclaiming ownership was "maybe after a month or two or so" subsequent to the time when the horse was left in plaintiff's care.

In his decision the trial judge found that defendant's trainer had informed Kelly during their telephone conversation of May 3, 1962, that "he would have to do whatever he wanted to do with the horse, that he wouldn't be on any farm at the defendant's expense." He also found, however, that when "Bascom's Folly" was brought to his farm, plaintiff was not aware of the telephone conversation between Kelly and defendant's trainer, and hence, even though he knew there was a controversy surrounding the ownership of the horse, he was entitled to assume that 'there is an implication here that, "I am to take care of this horse." Continuing his decision, the trial justice stated that in view of the result reached by this court in a recent opinion wherein we held that the instant defendant was liable to the original seller, Dr. Strauss, for the purchase price of this horse, there was a contract "implied in fact" between the plaintiff and defendant to board "Bascom's Folly" and that this contract continued until plaintiff received notification from defendant that he would not be responsible for the horse's board. The trial justice further stated that "I think there was notice given at least at the end of the four months, and I think we must add another month on there for a reasonable disposition of his property."

In view of the conclusion we reach with respect to defendant's first two contentions, we shall confine ourselves solely to a discussion and resolution of the issues necessarily implicit therein, and shall not examine other subsidiary arguments advanced by plaintiff and defendant.

I

The defendant alleges in his brief and oral argument that the trial judge erred in finding a contract "implied in fact" between the parties. We agree.

The following quotation from 17 C.J.S. Contracts s 4 at pp. 557–560, illustrates the elements necessary to the establishment of a contract "implied in fact":

> A "contract implied in fact," or an implied contract in the proper sense, arises where the intention of the parties is not expressed, but an agreement in fact, creating an obligation, is implied or presumed from their acts, or, as it has been otherwise stated, where there are circumstances which, according to the ordinary course of dealing and the common understanding of men, show a mutual intent to contract.
>
> It has been said that a contract implied in fact must contain all the elements of an express contract. So, such a contract is dependent on mutual agreement or consent, and on the intention of the parties: and a meeting of the minds is required. A contract implied in fact is to every intent and purpose an agreement between the parties, and it cannot be found to exist unless a contract status is shown. Such a contract does not arise out of an implied legal duty or obligation, but out of facts from which consent may be inferred; there must be a manifestation of assent arising wholly or in part from acts other than words, and a contract cannot be implied in fact where the facts are inconsistent with its existence.

Therefore, essential elements of contracts 'implied in fact' are mutual agreement, and intent to promise, but the agreement and the promise have not been made in words and are implied from the facts.

In the instant case, plaintiff sued on the theory of a contract "implied in law." There was no evidence introduced by him to support the establishment of a contract "implied in fact," and he cannot now argue solely on the basis of the trial justice's decision for such a result.

The source of the obligation in a contract "implied in fact," as in express contracts, is in the intention of the parties. We hold that there was no mutual agreement and "intent to promise" between the plaintiff and defendant so as to establish a contract 'implied in fact' for defendant to pay plaintiff for the maintenance of this horse. From the time Kelly delivered the horse to him plaintiff knew there was a dispute as to its ownership, and his subsequent actions indicated he did not know with whom, if anyone, he had a contract. After he had accepted the horse, he made inquiries as to its ownership and, initially, and for some time thereafter, sent his bills to both defendant and Dr. Strauss, the original seller.

There is also uncontroverted testimony in the record that prior to the assertion of the claim which is the subject of this suit neither defendant nor his trainer had ever had any business transactions with plaintiff, and had never used his farm to board horses. Additionally, there is uncontradicted evidence that this horse, when found to be lame, was shipped by defendant's trainer not to plaintiff's farm, but back to the seller at Belmont Park. What is most important, the trial justice expressly stated that he believed the testimony of defendant's trainer that he had instructed Kelly that defendant would not be responsible for boarding the horse on any farm.

From our examination of the record we are constrained to conclude that the trial justice overlooked and misconceived material evidence which establishes beyond question that there never existed between the parties an element essential to the formulation of any true contract, namely, an "intent to contract."

II

The defendant's second contention is that, even assuming the trial justice was in essence predicating defendant's liability upon a quasi-contractual theory, his decision is still unsupported by competent evidence and is clearly erroneous.

The following discussion of quasi-contracts appears in 12 Am.Jur., Contracts, s 6 (1938) at pp. 503 to 504:

> A quasi contract has no reference to the intentions or expressions of the parties. The obligation is imposed despite, and frequently in frustration of, their intention. For a quasi contract neither promise nor privity, real or imagined, is necessary. In quasi contracts the obligation arises, not from consent of the parties, as in the case of contracts, express or implied in fact, but from the law of natural immutable justice and equity. The act, or acts, from which the law implies the contract must, however, be voluntary. Where a case shows that it is the duty of the defendant to pay, the law imputes to him a promise to fulfill that obligation. The duty, which thus forms the foundation of a quasicontractual obligation, is frequently based on the doctrine of unjust enrichment.

> The law will not imply a promise against the express declaration of the party to be charged, made at the time of the supposed undertaking, unless such party is under legal obligation paramount to his will to perform some duty, and he is not under such legal obligation unless there is a demand in equity and good conscience that he should perform the duty.

Therefore, the essential elements of a quasi-contract are a benefit conferred upon defendant by plaintiff, appreciation by defendant of such benefit, and acceptance and retention by defendant of such benefit under such circumstances that it would be inequitable to retain the benefit without payment of the value thereof.

The key question raised by this appeal with respect to the establishment of a quasi-contract is whether or not plaintiff was acting as a "volunteer" at the time he accepted the horse for boarding at his farm. There is a long line of authority which has clearly enunciated the general rule that "if a performance is rendered by one person without any request by another, it is very unlikely that this person will be under a legal duty to pay compensation." 1 A Corbin, Contracts s 234.

The Restatement of Restitution, § 2 (1937) provides: "A person who officiously confers a benefit upon another is not entitled to restitution therefor." Comment a in the above-mentioned section states in part as follows:

> Policy ordinarily requires that a person who has conferred a benefit by way of giving another services should not be permitted to require the other to pay therefor, unless the one conferring the benefit had a valid reason for so doing. A person is not required to deal with another unless he so desires and, ordinarily, a person should not be required to become an obligor unless he so desires.

Applying those principles to the facts in the case at bar it is clear that plaintiff cannot recover. The plaintiff's testimony on cross-examination is the only evidence in the record relating to what transpired between Kelly and him at the time the horse was accepted for boarding. The defendant's attorney asked plaintiff if he had any conversation with Kelly at that time, and plaintiff answered in substance that he had noticed that the horse was very lame and that Kelly had told him: "That's why they wouldn't accept him at Belmont Track." The plaintiff also testified that he had inquired of Kelly as to the ownership of "Bascom's Folly," and had been told that "Dr. Strauss made a deal and that's all I know." It further appears from the record that plaintiff acknowledged receipt of the horse by signing a uniform livestock bill of lading, which clearly indicated on its face that the horse in question had been consigned by defendant's trainer not to plaintiff, but to Dr. Strauss's trainer at Belmont Park. Knowing at the time he accepted the horse for boarding that a controversy surrounded its ownership, plaintiff could not reasonably expect remuneration from defendant, nor can it be said that defendant acquiesced in the conferment of a benefit upon him. The undisputed testimony was that defendant, upon receipt of plaintiff's first bill, immediately notified him that he was not the owner of "Bascom's Folly" and would not be responsible for its keep.

It is our judgment that the plaintiff was a mere volunteer who boarded and maintained "Bascom's Folly" at his own risk and with full knowledge that he might not be reimbursed for expenses he incurred incident thereto.

The plaintiff's appeal is denied and dismissed, the defendant's cross appeal is sustained, and the cause is remanded to the superior court for entry of judgment for the defendant.

Plate v. Durst

Supreme Court of Appeals of West Virginia, 1896.
24 S.E. 580.

Where a minor, residing with a near relative, other than her parents, is led to believe, by the kindness, conduct, and conversations, in jest or in earnest, of such relative, that she is to receive compensation for her future services rendered in promotion of his business, in some form, and, in expectation of such compensation, she faithfully performs such services, and he afterwards discharges her without compensating her in the manner in which he led her to believe he would do, and denies all liability to her, she is entitled to recover the actual value of such services, in an action of assumpsit, even though such relative testifies that such promises were made in jest, and he had no expectation or intention of recompensing her for her services, but was only acting towards her in loco parentis.

Error to circuit court, Ohio county.

Assumpsit by Amelia C. Plate against George L. Durst. There was a judgment for plaintiff, and defendant brings error. Affirmed.

■ Dent, J. George L. Durst, defendant, on writ of error to the judgment of the circuit court of Ohio county rendered in favor of Amelia C. Plate on the 26th day of February, 1895, for the sum of $877.40, interest and costs, assigns the following errors, to wit: "(1) The said circuit court erred in admitting certain evidence against your petitioner's objections, on the trial of the cause before the jury. (2) The circuit court erred in excluding from the jury, upon the trial of the cause, certain evidence offered by your petitioner. (3) The circuit court erred in overruling your petitioner's motion, made when the plaintiff rested her case, to exclude the plaintiff's evidence from the jury. (4) The circuit court erred in giving to the jury certain instructions against your petitioner's objections, and in refusing to give certain instructions requested by your petitioner, and in modifying certain other instructions requested by your petitioner. (5) The circuit court erred in overruling your petitioner's motion to set aside the verdict of the jury and grant him a new trial."

The proof is abundant to establish the nature and value of the services rendered, and there is therefore but the naked legal question as to whether the evidence is sufficient to justify any recovery; in other words, whether the services, however valuable, were given gratuitously in excess of voluntary gifts on the one part, and received on the other without any expectancy of recompense or remuneration.

The material facts in the case are as follows, to wit: When the plaintiff was about twelve years of age, in the absence of other home, she went to live with the defendant, her brother-in-law. This was in the year 1885. For the first three or four years she was sent to school, and during the whole period she lived in the family as the defendant's own daughter might have done. She was furnished with a comfortable room, with suitable clothing and other necessaries, was supplied with money for shopping and other purposes, accompanied the defendant's wife on various pleasure trips, went to the World's Fair with money furnished by the defendant, received numerous presents at Christmas and other times, and was treated by the defendant with great kindness and consideration in every way. On her part, the plaintiff rendered services such as might have been required and expected from a daughter; attending to the marketing, and assisting in the care of the young children. In addition to these services the plaintiff assisted the defendant in his store, attending to customers, looking after entertainments the defendant had in charge, and doing whatever else the exigencies of the business, and her own capacities, from time to time suggested. The defendant and his wife had an unfortunate misunderstanding, and in August, 1894, the defendant's wife, with her two young children, went to Oakland, accompanied by the plaintiff and another friend. The misunderstanding had existed for some time, and there had been more or less coolness between the plaintiff and the defendant on account of it. The Oakland party made their preparations without informing the defendant, and started off with no more notice to him, according even to the plaintiff's claim, than a statement, just as they were going out of the door, that they were going to Oakland. The defendant resented this, and when the plaintiff and the others returned he told the plaintiff that she could leave his home. She did so, and soon afterwards instituted this action. During all the time of the plaintiff's stay with the defendant, she had never received or demanded any pay for her services. The money, clothing, and presents which she received she herself says were not regarded as wages. She never brought forward in any way the question of compensation, and, even after the alleged conversation on which the case was made to turn in the court below, no visible change was made in the relations between the parties. According to the plaintiff's testimony, a conversation took place four years before August, 1894, late one evening, in the store of the defendant. This conversation was repeated several times in the plaintiff's testimony, and was given by her as follows: "Mr. Durst asked me if I was tired. I said, 'Yes, sir;' and he said, 'How long have you been with me now?' and I told him, 'Five years;' and he said, 'Well, when you are with me ten years, I will give you one thousand dollars.'" On another occasion, defendant remarked that when she (the plaintiff) should get married he would give her $1,000, and a $500 diamond ring. Defendant does not positively deny either of these conversations, except as to the time of the first, but intimates that he was not in earnest, but jesting. It must be admitted, in any view of the matter, that this was jesting on a very serious subject to this unfortunate and parentless young girl,-still, in the eyes of the law, an infant,-engaged early and late, week days and Sunday, at home and abroad, actively, earnestly, and faithfully endeavoring to promote the worldly interests of the defendant. Jokes are sometimes taken seriously by the young and inexperienced in the deceptive ways of the business world, and if such is the case, and thereby the person deceived is led to give valuable services in the full belief and expectation that the joker is in earnest, the law will also take the joker at his word, and give him good reason to smile. The law discountenances deceit, even practiced under the form of a jest, if the weak, immature, or confiding are thereby imposed on to their injury. Where the law raises a presumption of gratuitous service, because of the relationship of the parties, the person rendering such service must rebut such presumption by either showing an express contract, "or such facts and circumstances as will authorize the jury to find the services were rendered in expectation by one of receiving, and by the other of making, compensation." This is the rule as announced in the case of *Riley v. Riley*, 38 W. Va.

290, and followed in the case of *Cann v. Cann*, 40 W. Va. 138. In this case there is no express contract on which the plaintiff could sue, and hence it must be determined whether, in the absence thereof, the facts and circumstances warranted the finding of the jury. The services were rendered in advancement of the defendant's business. They were valuable and necessary, and he so regarded them. Up until she was 17, nothing was said as to compensation; but she was clothed, fed, furnished spending money, and received some so-called presents from the hands of the defendant. She had then arrived at an age when she had become quite proficient in his business—that of a caterer and confectioner; was very useful to him, and diligent and attentive about his business. It was also quite time for her to begin thinking about her own future. He, as a sensible business man, undoubtedly realized this fact, and also that he was receiving gratuitously services to which he was not wholly entitled, and that, as soon as she became fully informed as to her own worth and rights, she would ask compensation at his hands, or seek other employment. Under such circumstances as this, he, in a sympathetic manner, approached plaintiff, and asked her if she was tired, and she answered. "Yes." He then asked her how long she had been with him, and she replied, "Five years." He said, "When you are with me ten years, I will give you a thousand dollars." And at another time, admitted by the defendant, he told her that when she got married he would give her $1,000 and diamond earrings. For five years she had given unremitting service to his affairs, and he, evidently moved by a righteous obligation to do so, temporarily, inspires her with the hope of future reward. The defendant says he was not in earnest, but only jesting. Admitting such to be the case, these conversations, whether he was in earnest or not, were calculated to mislead her, and leave the impression on her mind that in any event he would deal justly by her, and fully compensate her for her services; and in this manner he retained her in his employ until it suited his convenience to discharge her without compensation, which he did, to say the least, in an unkind and heartless manner, ill becoming a stranger, much less a brother-in-law. And now it devolves upon us to say whether she is entitled to pay for what her services were actually worth, or does the law, from the fact that he was only misleading her, and never intended to pay her, excuse him from doing so? A person is estopped from denying the sincerity of his conduct, to the injury of a person misled thereby. We therefore must conclude that these promises, in spite of the declaration of the defendant to the contrary, were made in sincerity, as an inducement to her future service. As these promises are not here sued on, the question of the statute of frauds does not arise; but, the plaintiff having been prevented by the defendant from performing her part of the undertaking, she is entitled to recover for the services already rendered, in view of the compensation promised. The conversations were therefore proper to go to the jury, not as a complete basis of recovery, within themselves, but as facts and circumstances tending to rebut the presumption that the services were gratuitous, and to show the peculiar means adopted by the defendant to induce the plaintiff to remain quietly in his service, to promote his pecuniary interests, without expecting, on his part, to be called upon to compensate her therefor. The statute of frauds cannot be used as an instrument of fraud. 3 Am. & Eng. Enc. Law, 860.

The plaintiff asked the court to give the jury seven instructions. The court gave two, to both of which the defendant objected. The defendant asked for ten instructions. The court gave two modified, and gave six, and refused to give two. For this court to copy into its opinion, and comment on, all these instructions separately, is an unnecessary and burdensome task not required of it, in the due and orderly administration of justice, but would greatly interfere with the consideration, and occupy the space belonging to other more weighty matters. And when the court finds, on examination of the whole case, that substantial justice has been done, it will not reverse the judgment, simply to gratify litigious dispositions, for any error committed by the circuit court, unless such error, if it had not been committed, would have tended, in some measure, to have produced a different result.

Most of the instructions asked by the defendant, and refused or modified, were based on the theory that the plaintiff was bound to prove a distinct or express contract; and they were modified by the court so as to include a mutual understanding, to be derived from the circumstances and relationship of the parties, and in no event could she recover unless it appeared that the defendant expected to pay her for her services. These instructions were founded on the law as stated in the cases of *Riley v. Riley* and *Cann v. Cann*, before cited. Both those cases were suits against decedents' estates, wherein one of the alleged contracting parties was dead, and therefore the other was held to a strict compliance with the law. In this case both parties are alive, and both testify. If the defendant had been dead, and the plaintiff had just as fully established her case as she has done with him living, her right to recovery would have been unquestionable. *Thompson v. Stevens*, 71 Pa. St. 162. But the defendant being alive, and being permitted to testify that he had no expectation or intention of compensating the plaintiff for her services, but what he said with regard thereto was a mere jest, distinguishes this case from the cases above cited, so as to render the principle established by them to some extent inapplicable to the present case. His having fully established the want of intention or expectation on his part presents the question whether, in the absence of such expectation or intention, the law, against his will and protest, will compel him to pay her what her services were reasonably worth. In section 508, 1 Story, Cont., it is said that, if a contract is understood by the parties thereto as a mere jest, it has no binding force. But it is also held that if one of the parties thereto accepted it in earnest, and acted thereon to his own detriment and loss, to that extent it would be binding and valid. *Armstrong v. McGhee*, Add. 261; 1 Story, Cont. § 12, note 1. In Add. Cont. 24, it is said: "In a third class of cases the law prescribes the rights and liabilities of persons who have not in reality entered into any contract at all with one another, but between whom circumstances have arisen which make it just that one should have a right, and the other should be subject to a liability, similar to the rights and liabilities which exist in certain cases of express contract. Thus, if one man has obtained money from another through the medium of oppression, imposition, deceit, or by the commission of a trespass, such money may be recovered back; for the law implies a promise from the wrongdoer to restore it to the rightful owner, although it is obvious that it is the very opposite of his intention. Implied or constructive contracts of this nature are similar to the constructive trusts of courts of equity, and in fact are not contracts at all.'' When any deceit is practiced, by which a man obtains the labor, money, or other property of another, with the other's consent, in the expectation of recompense, although such deceiver has no intention of paying therefor, but expects the benefit thereof wholly without just recompense, the law implies a quasi or constructive contract; for it never permits a wrongdoer to take advantage of his own wrong, to the detriment or injury of another. The plaintiff was deceived into the belief, by the kindness, conduct, and conversations of the defendant, that he intended to faithfully compensate her for her services, justly and fully, at such time as she might marry, or reach an age when she might feel like undertaking business for herself; and he thereby secured her careful attention, labor, and co-operation in the advancement of his business affairs. But, before the time arrives for his meeting his promised undertaking, he gets rid of her, without fulfillment of such undertaking, and pleads that he was merely jesting, and that, as he never intended or expected to compensate her for her services he is entitled to them gratuitously. She testifies that she accepted his promises in earnest, and expected him to fulfill them. What course she might have pursued, had these promises not been made to her, it is impossible for us to say, except that, presumptively, at least, as soon as her eyes became open to her true worth, she would have asked him to pay her a just wage, or have sought other employment, although, on account of her tender years and female dependency, she may have hesitated to take such a step. However this may be, his jesting promises, taken by her in earnest, were sufficient to justify the court in compelling him to treat her with fairness and honesty. The instructions, therefore, in so far as they required the existence of a distinct contract or a mutual understanding, were erroneous as to the plaintiff; but the jury having properly disregarded them, and found a verdict in her favor, in accordance with the law as it should have been given them, they furnish no grounds for the reversal of the judgment thereon. We therefore conclude that the circuit court did not err in refusing to give any of the defendant's instructions, or in giving any of the plaintiff's, but the errors committed were against the plaintiff, wholly. Numerous exceptions were taken by the defendant as to the admission and refusal to admit evidence, but, if the circuit court erred in all of these (which is in no wise apparent, from our view of this case), such errors could not have possibly changed the just result reached. The judgment is therefore affirmed.

* * *

Bailey and *Plate* illustrate the classical, subjective intent approach to offer and also that approach's implications, some of its drawbacks, and the need for the classical cases to step back from their express commitments in order to avoid absurd and unpalatable outcomes in certain limit cases.[3]

The defendant in *Bailey* purchased a horse, which turned out, on delivery, to be lame. The seller refused to accept the return of the horse, and the driver who tried to effectuate the return brought the horse to the plaintiff's farm for boarding. Although the defendant told the driver that he would not pay to board the horse, the plaintiff never learned of this communication. The plaintiff sent bills for the horse's board to the defendant (and at first also to the seller). Eventually (that is, after the passage of several months) the plaintiff received notification from the defendant that he did not regard the horse as his, but rather considered it returned to the seller, and hence would not pay for the boarding fees. The plaintiff sued the defendant for the price of the boarding services that he had provided.

The plaintiff in *Plate* moved in with the defendant, her brother-in-law, in 1885, while still a young child. She grew up in his household and provided a range of services in support of his business. She was cared for and given room and board, but she was never paid for this work. In 1890 the defendant (so the plaintiff claimed) promised her a payment of one thousand dollars once she had been with him for ten years. (On other occasions, not relevant for present purposes, the defendant promised the plaintiff a thousand dollars and a five hundred dollar diamond ring in case she should marry.) In 1894, a dispute arose between the plaintiff and the defendant, which led the defendant to expel the plaintiff from his house and the plaintiff, eventually, to sue the defendant seeking damages connected with his breach of these promises. The defendant did not deny making the promises, but claimed only that he had made them in jest.

On the subjective theory of contractual intent, *Bailey* and *Plate* are both easy cases, whose only possible outcome is for the defendant. In *Bailey*, it is hard to imagine that the defendant subjectively intended to strike a bargain that involved his paying the plaintiff to board a horse whose ownership he denied. The uncontroverted evidence, after all, shows that he expressly told his driver that he did not wish to enter such a bargain. This led the court to conclude that the evidence "establishe[d] beyond question that there never existed between the parties an element essential to the formulation of any true contract, namely, an 'intent to contract.' " In *Plate*, the analogous conclusion about subjective intent—that the defendant's promise-like remarks were indeed just jests—comes less naturally, at least to this reader; but the court was prepared, for purposes of deciding the lawsuit, to "admit[] such to be the case." And insofar as the

---

3. Other limitations will not become apparent until the argument turns to contract construction and interpretation. It will turn out that in order to prevent promisors from opportunistically avoiding contractual liability—by claiming that they used language idiosyncratically, so that utterances that might ordinarily be offers did not, in their case, reflect a subjective intent to open themselves up to contractual obligation—the classical approach to contract formation must be paired with an implausibly rigid, mechanical, and narrowly textualist approach to contract construction and interpretation. This connection will be elaborated more systematically in Chapter 17 below.

two defendants lacked the intent to be contractually bound, they could not be bound . . . at least in contract.

That might have been the end of the matter in each case. But although the cases are easy as applications of the subjective theory of intent, they are not easy all-things-considered, and neither court thought them so. Thus, each court, even as it thinks that there is obviously no contractual liability on the facts at hand, at once asks whether the defendants might be liable on other legal theories, in particular theories of liability that sound in restitution (also known, variously, as "unjust enrichment" or "quantum meruit").

In *Bailey*, the court answers that there is no liability in restitution. The court reasons, first, that the defendant never actually accepted (indeed, never even took possession of) the benefits produced by boarding the horse and, second, that the plaintiff knew that the ownership of the horse was contested. Accordingly, the court concludes, the plaintiff acted as what the law calls a "mere volunteer" or an "officious intermeddler." There can be liability in restitution only where the defendant is both enriched and unjustly so. In *Bailey*, the court concluded, the defendant was neither: he did not benefit from the plaintiff's boarding of the horse; and, even if he had benefited (say, because the care that the horse received improved the defendant's legal position vis-à-vis the horse's seller), he did not receive the benefit unjustly. The defendant, according to the court, had taken reasonable measures to discourage the plaintiff from providing the benefit, and the plaintiff had not taken reasonable measures to ascertain who had responsibility for the horse's care before he began boarding it.

In *Plate*, the court pursues the same line of inquiry to the opposite conclusion. As the court says, the finding of no contract does not end the question of liability. Instead, the defendant's "having fully established the want of intention or expectation on his part [and hence that there can be no liability in conventional contract] presents the question whether, in the absence of such expectation or intention, the law, against his will and protest, will compel him to pay her what her services were reasonably worth." The court answers this question "yes." It analogizes the defendant's conduct in persuading the plaintiff to work on his behalf to obtaining the services of another by "oppression, imposition, deceit, or by the commission of a trespass," which is to say that (in contradistinction to *Bailey*) the plaintiff in *Plate* was not a volunteer or intermeddler, but rather acted reasonably, given what the defendant had said. And for this reason, the court concluded, the defendant's "jesting promises, taken by her in earnest, were sufficient to justify the court in compelling him to treat her with fairness and honesty." To do so required giving her something approaching the benefit of his (joking) promise. And so the plaintiff in *Plate* wins.

Now the fact that the *Plate* court came down in favor of the plaintiff did not lead it to think, any more than the court in *Bailey* thought, that the defendant's liability sounded in *contract*. Indeed, the *Plate* court insisted, quoting a famous treatise, that "Implied or constructive contracts [like the one on which it based its holding] are similar to the constructive trusts of courts of equity, and in fact are not contracts at all."

But that view of contract law is far from necessary. Indeed, as the next batch of materials reveals, modern contract law adopts a very different approach.

Restatement 2d of Contracts

§ 22   Mode Of Assent: Offer And Acceptance

(1) The manifestation of mutual assent to an exchange ordinarily takes the form of an offer or proposal by one party followed by an acceptance by the other party or parties.

(2) A manifestation of mutual assent may be made even though neither offer nor acceptance can be identified and even though the moment of formation cannot be determined.

Comments & Illustrations

Comment a. The usual practice. Subsection (1) states the usual practice in the making of bargains. One party ordinarily first announces what he will do and what he requires in exchange, and the other then agrees. Where there are more than two parties, the second party to agree may be regarded as accepting the offer made by the first party and as making a similar offer to subsequent parties, and so on. It is theoretically possible for a third person to state a suggested contract to the parties and for them to say simultaneously that they assent. Or two parties may sign separate duplicates of the same agreement, each manifesting assent whether the other signs before or after him. Compare Illustration 5 to § 23.

Comment b. Assent by course of conduct. Problems of offer and acceptance are important primarily in cases where advance commitment serves to shift a risk from one party to the other, as in sales of goods which are subject to rapid price fluctuations, in sales of land, and in insurance contracts. Controversies as to whether and when the commitment is made are less likely to be important even in such cases once performance is well under way. Offer and acceptance become still less important after there have been repeated occasions for performance by one party where the other knows the nature of the performance and has an opportunity for objection to it. See Uniform Commercial Code § 2–208(1); compare Comment *a* to § 19. In such cases it is unnecessary to determine the moment of making of the contract, or which party made the offer and which the acceptance. Thus, Uniform Commercial Code §§ 2–204 and 2–207(3), relating to contracts for the sale of goods, provide that conduct by both parties which recognizes the existence of a contract is sufficient to establish it although the writings of the parties do not otherwise establish a contract. The principle has also been applied in non-sales contexts.

Illustration:

1.   A, a general contractor preparing a bid on a government construction contract, receives a bid by a proposed subcontractor, B, in a given amount. A names B as a subcontractor in A's bid, but after A receives the government contract, A unsuccessfully asks B to reduce its bid, and also unsuccessfully seeks permission from the Government to replace B as a subcontractor.

Pursuant to A's instructions, B proceeds with the work, but refuses to accept a work order from A which recites that A is still seeking permission to replace B. No new work order is issued. A does issue "change orders" using B's bid as the base "contract amount." B completes the job, but A refuses to pay the full amount, contending that B is entitled only to restitutionary damages because there never was a contract. There is an enforceable contract based upon A's assent to B's bid, as manifested by A's conduct, and B is entitled to the amount it bid, as modified by the change orders.

Restatement 2d of Contracts

§ 24   Offer Defined

An offer is the manifestation of willingness to enter into a bargain, so made as to justify another person in understanding that his assent to that bargain is invited and will conclude it.

Comments & Illustrations

Comment a. Offer as promise. An offer may propose an executed sale or barter rather than a contract, or it may propose the exchange of a promise for a performance or an exchange of promises, or it may propose two or more such transactions in combination or in the alternative. In the normal case of an offer of an exchange of promises, or in the case of an offer of a promise for an act, the offer itself is a promise, revocable until accepted. There may also be an offer of a performance, to be exchanged either for a return promise (§ 55) or for a return performance; in such cases the offer is not necessarily a promise, but there are often warranties or other incidental promises.

Illustration:

1.   A says to B, "That book you are holding is yours if you promise to pay me $5 for it." This is an offer empowering B, by making the requested promise, to make himself owner of the book and thus complete A's performance. In that event there is also an implied warranty of title made by A. See Uniform Commercial Code §§ 2–312, 2–401.

Comment b. Proposal of contingent gift. A proposal of a gift is not an offer within the present definition; there must be an element of exchange. Whether or not a proposal is a promise, it is not an offer unless it specifies a promise or performance by the offeree as the price or consideration to be given by him. It is not enough that there is a promise performable on a certain contingency.

Illustration:

2. A promises B $100 if B goes to college. If the circumstances give B reason to know that A is not undertaking to pay B to go to college but is promising a gratuity, there is no offer.

Comment c. Offer as contract. A promise made by the offeror as part of his offer may itself be a contract. Such a contract is commonly called an "option". See § 25.

Leonard v. Pepsico, Inc.

United States District Court, Southern District of New York, 1999.
88 F. Supp. 2d 116.

Television commercial viewer, who submitted 700,000 product "points" or their cash equivalent to soft drink manufacturer, sued to enforce alleged contractual commitment of manufacturer or provide fighter jet aircraft in return. Manufacturer moved for summary judgment. The District Court, Kimba M. Wood, J., held that: (1) commercial was advertisement not constituting any offer; (2) commercial was not akin to "reward," which could result in contract through unilateral action of offeree; (3) there was no offer to which objective offeree could respond, as commercial was made in "jest;" (4) additional discovery would not be allowed; (5) there was no contract satisfying requirements of New York statute of frauds; and (6) viewer did not state claim of fraud under New York law.

Summary judgment for manufacturer.

■ WOOD, District Judge. Plaintiff brought this action seeking, among other things, specific performance of an alleged offer of a Harrier Jet, featured in a television advertisement for defendant's "Pepsi Stuff" promotion. Defendant has moved for summary judgment pursuant to Federal Rule of Civil Procedure 56. For the reasons stated below, defendant's motion is granted.

I. BACKGROUND

This case arises out of a promotional campaign conducted by defendant, the producer and distributor of the soft drinks Pepsi and Diet Pepsi. The promotion, entitled "Pepsi Stuff," encouraged consumers to collect "Pepsi Points" from specially marked packages of Pepsi or Diet Pepsi and redeem these points for merchandise featuring the Pepsi logo. Before introducing the promotion nationally, defendant conducted a test of the promotion in the Pacific Northwest from October 1995 to March 1996. A Pepsi Stuff catalog was distributed to consumers in the test market, including Washington State. Plaintiff is a resident of Seattle, Washington.

While living in Seattle, plaintiff saw the Pepsi Stuff commercial that he contends constituted an offer of a Harrier Jet.

In an Order dated November 24, 1997, in a related case, the Court set forth an initial account of the facts of this case. Because the parties have had additional discovery since that Order and have crafted Local Civil Rule 56.1 Statements and Counterstatements, the recitation of facts herein should be considered definitive.

A. The Alleged Offer

Because whether the television commercial constituted an offer is the central question in this case, the Court will describe the commercial in detail. The commercial opens upon an idyllic, suburban morning, where the chirping of birds in sun-dappled trees welcomes a paperboy on his morning route. As the newspaper hits the stoop of a conventional two-story house, the tattoo of a military drum introduces the subtitle, "MONDAY 7:58 AM." The stirring strains of a martial air mark the appearance of a well-coiffed teenager preparing to leave for school, dressed in a shirt emblazoned with the Pepsi logo, a red-white-and-blue ball. While the teenager confidently preens, the military drum roll again sounds as the subtitle "T–SHIRT 75 PEPSI POINTS" scrolls across the screen. Bursting from his room, the teenager strides down the hallway wearing a leather jacket. The drum roll sounds again, as the subtitle "LEATHER JACKET 1450 PEPSI POINTS" appears. The teenager opens the door of his house and, unfazed by the glare of the early morning sunshine, puts on a pair of sunglasses. The drum roll then accompanies the subtitle "SHADES 175 PEPSI POINTS." A voiceover then intones, "Introducing the new Pepsi Stuff catalog," as the camera focuses on the cover of the catalog.

The scene then shifts to three young boys sitting in front of a high school building. The boy in the middle is intent on his Pepsi Stuff Catalog, while the boys on either side are each drinking Pepsi. The three boys gaze in awe at an object rushing overhead, as the military march builds to a crescendo. The Harrier Jet is not yet visible, but the observer senses the presence of a mighty plane as the extreme winds generated by its flight create a paper maelstrom in a classroom devoted to an otherwise dull physics lesson. Finally, the Harrier Jet swings into view and lands by the side of the school building, next to a bicycle rack. Several students run for cover, and the velocity of the wind strips one hapless faculty member down to his underwear. While the faculty member is being deprived of his dignity, the voiceover announces: "Now the more Pepsi you drink, the more great stuff you're gonna get."

The teenager opens the cockpit of the fighter and can be seen, helmetless, holding a Pepsi. "[L]ooking very pleased with himself," (Pl. Mem. at 3,) the teenager exclaims, "Sure beats the bus," and chortles. The military drum roll sounds a final time, as the following words appear: "HARRIER FIGHTER 7,000,000 PEPSI POINTS." A few seconds later, the following appears in more stylized script: "Drink Pepsi–Get Stuff." With that message, the music and the commercial end with a triumphant flourish.

Inspired by this commercial, plaintiff set out to obtain a Harrier Jet. Plaintiff explains that he is "typical of the 'Pepsi Generation' ... he is young, has an adventurous spirit, and the notion of obtaining a Harrier Jet appealed to him enormously." Plaintiff consulted the Pepsi Stuff Catalog. The Catalog features youths dressed in Pepsi Stuff regalia or enjoying Pepsi Stuff accessories, such as "Blue Shades" ("As if you need another reason to look forward to sunny days."), "Pepsi Tees" ("Live in 'em. Laugh in 'em. Get in 'em."), "Bag of Balls" ("Three balls. One bag. No rules."), and "Pepsi Phone Card" ("Call your mom!"). The Catalog specifies the number of Pepsi Points required to obtain promotional merchandise. The Catalog includes an Order Form which lists, on one side, fifty-three items of Pepsi Stuff merchandise redeemable for Pepsi Points. Conspicuously absent from the Order Form is any entry or description of a Harrier Jet. The amount of Pepsi Points required to obtain the listed merchandise ranges from 15 (for a "Jacket Tattoo" ("Sew 'em on your jacket, not your arm.")) to 3300 (for a "Fila Mountain Bike" ("Rugged. All-terrain. Exclusively for Pepsi.")). It should be noted that plaintiff objects to the implication that because an item was not shown in the Catalog, it was unavailable.

The rear foldout pages of the Catalog contain directions for redeeming Pepsi Points for merchandise. These directions note that merchandise may be ordered "only" with the original Order Form. The Catalog notes that in the event that a consumer lacks enough Pepsi Points to obtain a desired item, additional Pepsi Points may be purchased for ten cents each; however, at least fifteen original Pepsi Points must accompany each order.

Although plaintiff initially set out to collect 7,000,000 Pepsi Points by consuming Pepsi products, it soon became clear to him that he "would not be able to buy (let alone drink) enough Pepsi to collect the necessary Pepsi Points fast enough." Reevaluating his strategy, plaintiff "focused for the first time on the packaging materials in the Pepsi Stuff promotion," and realized that buying Pepsi Points would be a more promising option. Through acquaintances, plaintiff ultimately raised about $700,000.

B.   Plaintiff's Efforts to Redeem the Alleged Offer

On or about March 27, 1996, plaintiff submitted an Order Form, fifteen original Pepsi Points, and a check for $700,008.50. Plaintiff appears to have been represented by counsel at the time he mailed his check; the check is drawn on an account of plaintiff's first set of attorneys. At the bottom of the Order Form, plaintiff wrote in "1 Harrier Jet" in the "Item" column and "7,000,000" in the "Total Points" column. In a letter accompanying his submission, plaintiff stated that the check was to purchase additional Pepsi Points "expressly for obtaining a new Harrier jet as advertised in your Pepsi Stuff commercial.

On or about May 7, 1996, defendant's fulfillment house rejected plaintiff's submission and returned the check, explaining that:

> The item that you have requested is not part of the Pepsi Stuff collection. It is not included in the catalogue or on the order

form, and only catalogue merchandise can be redeemed under this program.

> The Harrier jet in the Pepsi commercial is fanciful and is simply included to create a humorous and entertaining ad. We apologize for any misunderstanding or confusion that you may have experienced and are enclosing some free product coupons for your use.

Plaintiff's previous counsel responded on or about May 14, 1996, as follows:

> Your letter of May 7, 1996 is totally unacceptable. We have reviewed the video tape of the Pepsi Stuff commercial and it clearly offers the new Harrier jet for 7,000,000 Pepsi Points. Our client followed your rules explicitly.

> This is a formal demand that you honor your commitment and make immediate arrangements to transfer the new Harrier jet to our client. If we do not receive transfer instructions within ten (10) business days of the date of this letter you will leave us no choice but to file an appropriate action against Pepsi.

This letter was apparently sent onward to the advertising company responsible for the actual commercial, BBDO New York ("BBDO"). In a letter dated May 30, 1996, BBDO Vice President Raymond E. McGovern, Jr., explained to plaintiff that:

> I find it hard to believe that you are of the opinion that the Pepsi Stuff commercial ("Commercial") really offers a new Harrier Jet. The use of the Jet was clearly a joke that was meant to make the Commercial more humorous and entertaining. In my opinion, no reasonable person would agree with your analysis of the Commercial.

On or about June 17, 1996, plaintiff mailed a similar demand letter to defendant.

On February 22, 1999, the Second Circuit endorsed the parties' stipulations to the dismissal of any appeals taken thus far in this case. Those stipulations noted that Leonard had consented to the jurisdiction of this Court and that PepsiCo agreed not to seek enforcement of the attorneys' fees award. With these issues having been waived, PepsiCo moved for summary judgment pursuant to Federal Rule of Civil Procedure 56. The present motion thus follows three years of jurisdictional and procedural wrangling.

II. Discussion

C. An Objective, Reasonable Person Would Not Have Considered the Commercial an Offer

Plaintiff's understanding of the commercial as an offer must also be rejected because the Court finds that no objective person could reasonably have concluded that the commercial actually offered consumers a Harrier Jet.

1. Objective Reasonable Person Standard

In evaluating the commercial, the Court must not consider defendant's subjective intent in making the commercial, or plaintiff's subjective view of what the commercial offered, but what an objective, reasonable person would have understood the commercial to convey. *See Kay–R Elec. Corp. v. Stone & Webster Constr. Co.,* 23 F.3d 55, 57 (2d Cir.1994) ("[W]e are not concerned with what was going through the heads of the parties at the time [of the alleged contract]. Rather, we are talking about the objective principles of contract law."); *Mesaros,* 845 F.2d at 1581 ("A basic rule of contracts holds that whether an offer has been made depends on the objective reasonableness of the alleged offeree's belief that the advertisement or solicitation was intended as an offer."); Farnsworth, *supra,* § 3.10, at 237; Williston, *supra,* § 4:7 at 296–97.

If it is clear that an offer was not serious, then no offer has been made:

> What kind of act creates a power of acceptance and is therefore an offer? It must be an expression of will or intention. It must be an act that leads the offeree reasonably to conclude that a power to create a contract is conferred. This applies to the content of the power as well as to the fact of its existence. *It is on this ground that we must exclude* invitations to deal or acts of mere preliminary negotiation, and *acts evidently done in jest* or without intent to create legal relations. *Corbin on Contracts,* § 1.11 at 30 (emphasis added).

An obvious joke, of course, would not give rise to a contract. *See, e.g., Graves v. Northern N.Y. Pub. Co.,* 260 A.D. 900, 22 N.Y.S.2d 537 (1940) (dismissing claim to offer of $1000, which appeared in the "joke column" of the newspaper, to any person who could provide a commonly available phone number). On the other hand, if there is no indication that the offer is "evidently in jest," and that an objective, reasonable person would find that the offer was serious, then there may be a valid offer. *See Barnes,* 549 P.2d at 1155 ("[I]f the jest is not apparent and a reasonable hearer would believe that an offer was being made, then the speaker risks the formation of a contract which was not intended."); *see also Lucy v. Zehmer,* 196 Va. 493, 84 S.E.2d 516, 518, 520 (1954) (ordering specific performance of a contract to purchase a farm despite defendant's protestation that the transaction was done in jest as " 'just a bunch of two doggoned drunks bluffing' ").

3. Whether the Commercial Was "Evidently Done In Jest"

Plaintiff's insistence that the commercial appears to be a serious offer requires the Court to explain why the commercial is funny. Explaining why a joke is funny is a daunting task; as the essayist E.B. White has remarked, "Humor can be dissected, as a frog can, but the thing dies in the process."

The commercial is the embodiment of what defendant appropriately characterizes as "zany humor."

First, the commercial suggests, as commercials often do, that use of the advertised product will transform what, for most youth, can be a fairly routine and ordinary experience. The military tattoo and stirring martial music, as well as the use of subtitles in a Courier font that scroll terse messages across the screen, such as "MONDAY 7:58 AM," evoke military and espionage thrillers. The implication of the commercial is that Pepsi Stuff merchandise will inject drama and moment into hitherto unexceptional lives. The commercial in this case thus makes the exaggerated claims similar to those of many television advertisements: that by consuming the featured clothing, car, beer, or potato chips, one will become attractive, stylish, desirable, and admired by all. A reasonable viewer would understand such advertisements as mere puffery, not as statements of fact, *see, e.g., Hubbard v. General Motors Corp.,* 95 Civ. 4362(AGS), 1996 WL 274018, at *6 (S.D.N.Y. May 22, 1996) (advertisement describing automobile as "Like a Rock," was mere puffery, not a warranty of quality); *Lovett,* 207 N.Y.S. at 756; and refrain from interpreting the promises of the commercial as being literally true.

Second, the callow youth featured in the commercial is a highly improbable pilot, one who could barely be trusted with the keys to his parents' car, much less the prize aircraft of the United States Marine Corps. Rather than checking the fuel gauges on his aircraft, the teenager spends his precious preflight minutes preening. The youth's concern for his coiffure appears to extend to his flying without a helmet. Finally, the teenager's comment that flying a Harrier Jet to school "sure beats the bus" evinces an improbably insouciant attitude toward the relative difficulty and danger of piloting a fighter plane in a residential area, as opposed to taking public transportation.

Third, the notion of traveling to school in a Harrier Jet is an exaggerated adolescent fantasy. In this commercial, the fantasy is underscored by how the teenager's schoolmates gape in admiration, ignoring their physics lesson. The force of the wind generated by the Harrier Jet blows off one teacher's clothes, literally defrocking an authority figure. As if to emphasize the fantastic quality of having a Harrier Jet arrive at school, the Jet lands next to a plebeian bike rack. This fantasy is, of course, extremely unrealistic. No school would provide landing space for a student's fighter jet, or condone the disruption the jet's use would cause.

Fourth, the primary mission of a Harrier Jet, according to the United States Marine Corps, is to "attack and destroy surface targets under day and night visual conditions." United States Marine Corps, Factfile: AV–8B Harrier II (last modified Dec. 5, 1995) <http:// www.hqmc.usmc.mil /factfile.nsf>. Manufactured by McDonnell Douglas, the Harrier Jet played a significant role in the air offensive of Operation Desert Storm in 1991. *See id.* The jet is designed to carry a considerable armament load, including Sidewinder and Maverick missiles. *See id.* As one news report has noted, "Fully loaded, the Harrier can float like a butterfly and sting like a bee-albeit a roaring 14–ton butterfly and a bee with 9,200 pounds of bombs and missiles." Jerry Allegood, *Marines Rely on Harrier Jet, Despite Critics,* News & Observer (Raleigh), Nov. 4, 1990, at C1. In light of the Harrier Jet's well-documented function in attacking and destroying surface and air targets, armed reconnaissance and air interdiction, and offensive and defensive anti-aircraft warfare, depiction of such a jet as a way to get to school in the morning is clearly not serious even if, as plaintiff contends, the jet is capable of being acquired "in a form that eliminates [its] potential for military use."

Fifth, the number of Pepsi Points the commercial mentions as required to "purchase" the jet is 7,000,000. To amass that number of points, one would have to drink 7,000,000 Pepsis (or roughly 190 Pepsis a day for the next hundred years-an unlikely possibility), or one would have to purchase approximately $700,000 worth of Pepsi Points. The cost of a Harrier Jet is roughly $23 million dollars, a fact of which plaintiff was aware when he set out to gather the amount he believed necessary to accept the alleged offer. Even if an objective, reasonable person were not aware of this fact, he would conclude that purchasing a fighter plane for $700,000 is a deal too good to be true.

Plaintiff argues that a reasonable, objective person would have understood the commercial to make a serious offer of a Harrier Jet because there was "absolutely no distinction in the manner" in which the items in the commercial were presented. Plaintiff also relies upon a press release highlighting the promotional campaign, issued by defendant, in which "[n]o mention is made by [defendant] of humor, or anything of the sort." These arguments suggest merely that the humor of the promotional campaign was tongue in cheek. Humor is not limited to what Justice Cardozo called "[t]he rough and boisterous joke ... [that] evokes its own guffaws." *Murphy v. Steeplechase Amusement Co.,* 250 N.Y. 479, 483 (1929). In light of the obvious absurdity of the commercial, the Court rejects plaintiff's argument that the commercial was not clearly in jest.

III. CONCLUSION

In sum, there are three reasons why plaintiff's demand cannot prevail as a matter of law. First, the commercial was merely an advertisement, not a unilateral offer. Second, the tongue-in-cheek attitude of the commercial would not cause a reasonable person to conclude that a soft drink company would be giving away fighter planes as part of a promotion. Third, there is no writing between the parties sufficient to satisfy the Statute of Frauds.

For the reasons stated above, the Court grants defendant's motion for summary judgment. The Clerk of Court is instructed to close these cases. Any pending motions are moot.

Lucy v. Zehmer

Supreme Court of Appeals of Virginia, 1954.
84 S.E.2d 516.

Suit to compel specific performance of land purchase contract claimed by defendant vendors to have been entered into as joke. The Circuit Court,

Dinwiddie County, J. G. Jefferson, Jr., J., entered decree denying specific performance and dismissing suit and purchasers appealed. The Supreme Court of Appeals, Buchanan, J., held that evidence showed that contract represented serious business transaction and good faith sale and purchase of farm, that no unusual circumstances existed in its making, and that purchasers were entitled to specific performance.

Reversed and remanded.

■ BUCHANAN, J. This suit was instituted by W. O. Lucy and J. C. Lucy, complainants, against A. H. Zehmer and Ida S. Zehmer, his wife, defendants, to have specific performance of a contract by which it was alleged the Zehmers had sold to W. O. Lucy a tract of land owned by A. H. Zehmer in Dinwiddie county containing 471.6 acres, more or less, known as the Ferguson farm, for $50,000. J. C. Lucy, the other complainant, is a brother of W. O. Lucy, to whom W. O. Lucy transferred a half interest in his alleged purchase.

The instrument sought to be enforced was written by A. H. Zehmer on December 20, 1952, in these words: "We hereby agree to sell to W. O. Lucy the Ferguson Farm complete for $50,000.00, title satisfactory to buyer," and signed by the defendants, A. H. Zehmer and Ida S. Zehmer.

The answer of A. H. Zehmer admitted that at the time mentioned W. O. Lucy offered him $50,000 cash for the farm, but that he, Zehmer, considered that the offer was made in jest; that so thinking, and both he and Lucy having had several drinks, he wrote out "the memorandum" quoted above and induced his wife to sign it; that he did not deliver the memorandum to Lucy, but that Lucy picked it up, read it, put it in his pocket, attempted to offer Zehmer $5 to bind the bargain, which Zehmer refused to accept, and realizing for the first time that Lucy was serious, Zehmer assured him that he had no intention of selling the farm and that the whole matter was a joke. Lucy left the premises insisting that he had purchased the farm.

Depositions were taken and the decree appealed from was entered holding that the complainants had failed to establish their right to specific performance, and dismissing their bill. The assignment of error is to this action of the court.

W. O. Lucy, a lumberman and farmer, thus testified in substance: He had known Zehmer for fifteen or twenty years and had been familiar with the Ferguson farm for ten years. Seven or eight years ago he had offered Zehmer $20,000 for the farm which Zehmer had accepted, but the agreement was verbal and Zehmer backed out. On the night of December 20, 1952, around eight o'clock, he took an employee to McKenney, where Zehmer lived and operated a restaurant, filling station and motor court. While there he decided to see Zehmer and again try to buy the Ferguson farm. He entered the restaurant and talked to Mrs. Zehmer until Zehmer came in. He asked Zehmer if he had sold the Ferguson farm. Zehmer replied that he had not. Lucy said, "I bet you wouldn't take $50,000.00 for that place." Zehmer replied, "Yes, I would too; you wouldn't give fifty."

Lucy said he would and told Zehmer to write up an agreement to that effect. Zehmer took a restaurant check and wrote on the back of it, "I do hereby agree to sell to W. O. Lucy the Ferguson Farm for $50,000 complete." Lucy told him he had better change it to "We" because Mrs. Zehmer would have to sign it too. Zehmer then tore up what he had written, wrote the agreement quoted above and asked Mrs. Zehmer, who was at the other end of the counter ten or twelve feet away, to sign it. Mrs. Zehmer said she would for $50,000 and signed it. Zehmer brought it back and gave it to Lucy, who offered him $5 which Zehmer refused, saying, "You don't need to give me any money, you got the agreement there signed by both of us."

The discussion leading to the signing of the agreement, said Lucy, lasted thirty or forty minutes, during which Zehmer seemed to doubt that Lucy could raise $50,000. Lucy suggested the provision for having the title examined and Zehmer made the suggestion that he would sell it "complete, everything there," and stated that all he had on the farm was three heifers.

Lucy took a partly filled bottle of whiskey into the restaurant with him for the purpose of giving Zehmer a drink if he wanted it. Zehmer did, and he and Lucy had one or two drinks together. Lucy said that while he felt the drinks he took he was not intoxicated, and from the way Zehmer handled the transaction he did not think he was either.

December 20 was on Saturday. Next day Lucy telephoned to J. C. Lucy and arranged with the latter to take a half interest in the purchase and pay half of the consideration. On Monday he engaged an attorney to examine the title. The attorney reported favorably on December 31 and on January 2 Lucy wrote Zehmer stating that the title was satisfactory, that he was ready to pay the purchase price in cash and asking when Zehmer would be ready to close the deal. Zehmer replied by letter, mailed on January 13, asserting that he had never agreed or intended to sell.

Mr. and Mrs. Zehmer were called by the complainants as adverse witnesses. Zehmer testified in substance as follows:

He bought this farm more than ten years ago for $11,000. He had had twenty-five offers, more or less, to buy it, including several from Lucy, who had never offered any specific sum of money. He had given them all the same answer, that he was not interested in selling it. On this Saturday night before Christmas it looked like everybody and his brother came by there to have a drink. He took a good many drinks during the afternoon and had a pint of his own. When he entered the restaurant around eight-thirty Lucy was there and he could see that he was "pretty high." He said to Lucy, "Boy, you got some good liquor, drinking, ain't you?" Lucy then offered him a drink. "I was already high as a Georgia pine, and didn't have any more better sense than to pour another great big slug out and gulp it down, and he took one too."

After they had talked a while Lucy asked whether he still had the Ferguson farm. He replied that he had not sold it and Lucy said, "I bet you wouldn't take $50,000.00 for it." Zehmer asked him if he would give

$50,000 and Lucy said yes. Zehmer replied, "You haven't got $50,000 in cash." Lucy said he did and Zehmer replied that he did not believe it. They argued "pro and con for a long time," mainly about "whether he had $50,000 in cash that he could put up right then and buy that farm."

Finally, said Zehmer, Lucy told him if he didn't believe he had $50,000, "you sign that piece of paper here and say you will take $50,000.00 for the farm." He, Zehmer, "just grabbed the back off of a guest check there" and wrote on the back of it. At that point in his testimony Zehmer asked to see what he had written to "see if I recognize my own handwriting." He examined the paper and exclaimed, "Great balls of fire, I got 'Firgerson' for Ferguson. I have got satisfactory spelled wrong. I don't recognize that writing if I would see it, wouldn't know it was mine."

After Zehmer had, as he described it, "scribbled this thing off," Lucy said, "Get your wife to sign it." Zehmer walked over to where she was and she at first refused to sign but did so after he told her that he "was just needling him [Lucy], and didn't mean a thing in the world, that I was not selling the farm." Zehmer then "took it back over there and I was still looking at the dern thing. I had the drink right there by my hand, and I reached over to get a drink, and he said, 'Let me see it.' He reached and picked it up, and when I looked back again he had it in his pocket and he dropped a five dollar bill over there, and he said, 'Here is five dollars payment on it.' I said, 'Hell no, that is beer and liquor talking. I am not going to sell you the farm. I have told you that too many times before.'"

Mrs. Zehmer testified that when Lucy came into the restaurant he looked as if he had had a drink. When Zehmer came in he took a drink out of a bottle that Lucy handed him. She went back to help the waitress who was getting things ready for next day. Lucy and Zehmer were talking but she did not pay too much attention to what they were saying. She heard Lucy ask Zehmer if he had sold the Ferguson farm, and Zehmer replied that he had not and did not want to sell it. Lucy said, "I bet you wouldn't take $50,000 cash for that farm," and Zehmer replied, "You haven't got $50,000 cash." Lucy said, "I can get it." Zehmer said he might form a company and get it, "but you haven't got $50,000.00 cash to pay me tonight." Lucy asked him if he would put it in writing that he would sell him this farm. Zehmer then wrote on the back of a pad, "I agree to sell the Ferguson Place to W. O. Lucy for $50,000.00 cash." Lucy said, "All right, get your wife to sign it." Zehmer came back to where she was standing and said, "You want to put your name to this?" She said "No," but he said in an undertone, "It is nothing but a joke," and she signed it.

She said that only one paper was written and it said: "I hereby agree to sell," but the "I" had been changed to "We". However, she said she read what she signed and was then asked, "When you read 'We hereby agree to sell to W. O. Lucy,' what did you interpret that to mean, that particular phrase?" She said she thought that was a cash sale that night; but she also said that when she read that part about "title satisfactory to buyer" she understood that if the title was good Lucy would pay $50,000 but if the title was bad he would have a right to reject it, and that that was her understanding at the time she signed her name.

On examination by her own counsel she said that her husband laid this piece of paper down after it was signed; that Lucy said to let him see it, took it, folded it and put it in his wallet, then said to Zehmer, "Let me give you $5.00," but Zehmer said, "No, this is liquor talking. I don't want to sell the farm, I have told you that I want my son to have it. This is all a joke." Lucy then said at least twice, "Zehmer, you have sold your farm," wheeled around and started for the door. He paused at the door and said, "I will bring you $50,000.00 tomorrow. No, tomorrow is Sunday. I will bring it to you Monday." She said you could tell definitely that he was drinking and she said to her husband, "You should have taken him home," but he said, "Well, I am just about as bad off as he is."

The waitress referred to by Mrs. Zehmer testified that when Lucy first came in "he was mouthy." When Zehmer came in they were laughing and joking and she thought they took a drink or two. She was sweeping and cleaning up for next day. She said she heard Lucy tell Zehmer, "I will give you so much for the farm," and Zehmer said, "You haven't got that much." Lucy answered, "Oh, yes, I will give you that much." Then "they jotted down something on paper and Mr. Lucy reached over and took it, said let me see it." He looked at it, put it in his pocket and in about a minute he left. She was asked whether she saw Lucy offer Zehmer any money and replied, "He had five dollars laying up there, they didn't take it." She said Zehmer told Lucy he didn't want his money "because he didn't have enough money to pay for his property, and wasn't going to sell his farm." Both of them appeared to be drinking right much, she said.

She repeated on cross-examination that she was busy and paying no attention to what was going on. She was some distance away and did not see either of them sign the paper. She was asked whether she saw Zehmer put the agreement down on the table in front of Lucy, and her answer was this: "Time he got through writing whatever it was on the paper, Mr. Lucy reached over and said, 'Let's see it.' He took it and put it in his pocket," before showing it to Mrs. Zehmer. Her version was that Lucy kept raising his offer until it got to $50,000.

The defendants insist that the evidence was ample to support their contention that the writing sought to be enforced was prepared as a bluff or dare to force Lucy to admit that he did not have $50,000; that the whole matter was a joke; that the writing was not delivered to Lucy and no binding contract was ever made between the parties.

It is an unusual, if not bizarre, defense. When made to the writing admittedly prepared by one of the defendants and signed by both, clear evidence is required to sustain it.

In his testimony Zehmer claimed that he "was high as a Georgia pine," and that the transaction "was just a bunch of two doggoned drunks bluffing to see who could talk the biggest and say the most." That claim is inconsistent with his attempt to testify in great detail as to what was said and what was done. It is contradicted by other evidence as to the condition of both parties, and rendered of no weight by the testimony of his wife that when Lucy left the restaurant she suggested that Zehmer drive him home. The record is convincing that Zehmer was not intoxicated to the extent of being unable to comprehend the nature and consequences of the instrument he executed, and hence that instrument is not to be invalidated on that ground. It was in fact conceded by defendants' counsel in oral argument that under the evidence Zehmer was not too drunk to make a valid contract.

The evidence is convincing also that Zehmer wrote two agreements, the first one beginning "I hereby agree to sell." Zehmer first said he could not remember about that, then that "I don't think I wrote but one out." Mrs. Zehmer said that what he wrote was "I hereby agree," but that the "I" was changed to "We" after that night. The agreement that was written and signed is in the record and indicates no such change. Neither are the mistakes in spelling that Zehmer sought to point out readily apparent.

The appearance of the contract, the fact that it was under discussion for forty minutes or more before it was signed; Lucy's objection to the first draft because it was written in the singular, and he wanted Mrs. Zehmer to sign it also; the rewriting to meet that objection and the signing by Mrs. Zehmer; the discussion of what was to be included in the sale, the provision for the examination of the title, the completeness of the instrument that was executed, the taking possession of it by Lucy with no request or suggestion by either of the defendants that he give it back, are facts which furnish persuasive evidence that the execution of the contract was a serious business transaction rather than a casual, jesting matter as defendants now contend.

On Sunday, the day after the instrument was signed on Saturday night, there was a social gathering in a home in the town of McKenney at which there were general comments that the sale had been made. Mrs. Zehmer testified that on that occasion as she passed by a group of people, including Lucy, who were talking about the transaction, $50,000 was mentioned, whereupon she stepped up and said, "Well, with the high-price whiskey you were drinking last night you should have paid more. That was cheap." Lucy testified that at that time Zehmer told him that he did not want to "stick" him or hold him to the agreement because he, Lucy, was too tight and didn't know what he was doing, to which Lucy replied that he was not too tight; that he had been stuck before and was going through with it. Zehmer's version was that he said to Lucy: "I am not trying to claim it wasn't a deal on account of the fact the price was too low. If I had wanted to sell $50,000.00 would be a good price, in fact I think you would get stuck at $50,000.00." A disinterested witness testified that what Zehmer said to Lucy was that "he was going to let him up off the deal, because he thought he was too tight, didn't know what he was doing. Lucy said something to the effect that 'I have been stuck before and I will go through with it.' "

If it be assumed, contrary to what we think the evidence shows, that Zehmer was jesting about selling his farm to Lucy and that the transaction was intended by him to be a joke, nevertheless the evidence shows that Lucy did not so understand it but considered it to be a serious business transaction and the contract to be binding on the Zehmers as well as on himself. The very next day he arranged with his brother to put up half the money and take a half interest in the land. The day after that he employed an attorney to examine the title. The next night, Tuesday, he was back at Zehmer's place and there Zehmer told him for the first time, Lucy said, that he wasn't going to sell and he told Zehmer, "You know you sold that place fair and square." After receiving the report from his attorney that the title was good he wrote to Zehmer that he was ready to close the deal.

Not only did Lucy actually believe, but the evidence shows he was warranted in believing, that the contract represented a serious business transaction and a good faith sale and purchase of the farm.

In the field of contracts, as generally elsewhere, "We must look to the outward expression of a person as manifesting his intention rather than to his secret and unexpressed intention. 'The law imputes to a person an intention corresponding to the reasonable meaning of his words and acts.' " *First Nat. Bank v. Roanoke Oil Co.,* 169 Va. 99, 114.

At no time prior to the execution of the contract had Zehmer indicated to Lucy by word or act that he was not in earnest about selling the farm. They had argued about it and discussed its terms, as Zehmer admitted, for a long time. Lucy testified that if there was any jesting it was about paying $50,000 that night. The contract and the evidence show that he was not expected to pay the money that night. Zehmer said that after the writing was signed he laid it down on the counter in front of Lucy. Lucy said Zehmer handed it to him. In any event there had been what appeared to be a good faith offer and a good faith acceptance, followed by the execution and apparent delivery of a written contract. Both said that Lucy put the writing in his pocket and then offered Zehmer $5 to seal the bargain. Not until then, even under the defendants' evidence, was anything said or done to indicate that the matter was a joke. Both of the Zehmers testified that when Zehmer asked his wife to sign he whispered that it was a joke so Lucy wouldn't hear and that it was not intended that he should hear.

The mental assent of the parties is not requisite for the formation of a contract. If the words or other acts of one of the parties have but one reasonable meaning, his undisclosed intention is immaterial except when an unreasonable meaning which he attaches to his manifestations is known to the other party. Restatement of the Law of Contracts, Vol. I, § 71, p. 74.

"The law, therefore, judges of an agreement between two persons exclusively from those expressions of their intentions which are communicated between them." Clark on Contracts, 4 ed., § 3, p. 4.

An agreement or mutual assent is of course essential to a valid contract but the law imputes to a person an intention corresponding to the reasonable meaning of his words and acts. If his words and acts, judged by a reasonable standard, manifest an intention to agree, it is immaterial what may be the real but unexpressed state of his mind. 17 C.J.S., Contracts, § 32, p. 361; 12 Am. Jur., Contracts, § 19, p. 515.

So a person cannot set up that he was merely jesting when his conduct and words would warrant a reasonable person in believing that he intended a real agreement, 17 C.J.S., Contracts, § 47, p. 390; Clark on Contracts, 4 ed., § 27, at p. 54.

Whether the writing signed by the defendants and now sought to be enforced by the complainants was the result of a serious offer by Lucy and a serious acceptance by the defendants, or was a serious offer by Lucy and an acceptance in secret jest by the defendants, in either event it constituted a binding contract of sale between the parties.

Defendants contend further, however, that even though a contract was made, equity should decline to enforce it under the circumstances. These circumstances have been set forth in detail above. They disclose some drinking by the two parties but not to an extent that they were unable to understand fully what they were doing. There was no fraud, no misrepresentation, no sharp practice and no dealing between unequal parties. The farm had been bought for $11,000 and was assessed for taxation at $6,300. The purchase price was $50,000. Zehmer admitted that it was a good price. There is in fact present in this case none of the grounds usually urged against specific performance.

Specific performance, it is true, is not a matter of absolute or arbitrary right, but is addressed to the reasonable and sound discretion of the court. *First Nat. Bank v. Roanoke Oil Co., supra,* 169 Va. at p. 116. But it is likewise true that the discretion which may be exercised is not an arbitrary or capricious one, but one which is controlled by the established doctrines and settled principles of equity; and, generally, where a contract is in its nature and circumstances unobjectionable, it is as much a matter of course for courts of equity to decree a specific performance of it as it is for a court of law to give damages for a breach of it.

The complainants are entitled to have specific performance of the contracts sued on. The decree appealed from is therefore reversed and the cause is remanded for the entry of a proper decree requiring the defendants to perform the contract in accordance with the prayer of the bill.

Reversed and remanded.

* * *

Section 24 of the Restatement sets out the basic standard adopted by the modern law of offer and intent: it is an objective standard, which looks not to the offeror's state of mind but rather to how the offeror's utterances and actions would be interpreted by a reasonable offeree. *Leonard* and *Lucy* apply the objective account of offer to reach opposite conclusions (mirroring the two conclusions reached under the subjective account by *Bailey* and *Plate*).

In *Leonard*, as in *Bailey*, there is no contract. The Pepsi ad at the root of that case announced a "Pepsi Point" program, through which consumers could accumulate credits either by buying Pepsi–Cola or by paying pre-set cash sums directly to Pepsi. The program, as explained in the ad, allowed consumers to exchange points for products. At its end, the ad (interpreted narrowly and literally) suggests that a Hawker–Siddeley Harrier Jump–Jet might be acquired in exchange for seven million Pepsi Points. The plaintiff accumulated seven million points, and tried to get the airplane. The defendant refused to accept the tokens or deliver the jet.

The court sided with Pepsi. The ad, the court observed, adopted a funny tone, and a reasonable viewer (even one who did not know that the Hawker Jump–Jet is very, very expensive) would have recognized the joke. Therefore, Pepsi did not offer to exchange the jet for the points, and no contract arose. This is an easy case but worth reading anyway because of the contrast to *Plate*. In *Plate*, the finding of no-contract required only the conclusion that the purported offeror did not actually intend to strike a bargain. In *Leonard*, the court required more—namely that the offeree could not reasonably have understood the offeror to be proposing a bargain. This style of argument was not absent from *Plate*, of course. It appeared in the discussion of non-contractual liability. Had the *Plate* court concluded that the plaintiff there was unreasonable to believe that the defendant was proposing a bargain, she would have lost, also. So one immediate lesson of reading *Leonard* and *Plate* together is that the objective approach takes matters that the subjective approach considered relevant but non-contractual, and brings them within contract. Had *Plate* been argued before the *Leonard* court and under the modern account of offer, the plaintiff would again have won. Only now, she would have won on contractual grounds.[4]

Lucy illustrates just how such a case might be analyzed. The plaintiff and defendant were drinking, and their high-spirited conversation turned to a farm owned by the defendant and long coveted by the plaintiff. The plaintiff asserted that he would pay $50,000 for the farm, and the defendant answered, in effect, that he was just bragging and in fact hadn't the money. To prove his point, the defendant wrote out a note, which he had his wife sign, saying that he and his wife agreed to sell plaintiff the farm for $50,000. The plaintiff agreed, pocketed the memo, and offered the defendant $5 to bind the bargain,[5] whereupon the defendant, realizing that the plaintiff was serious and appreciating his peril, at once said that he had no intention of selling and that the whole thing was a joke. The plaintiff left the bar insisting that he'd bought the farm, which the defendant denied.

---

4. Similarly, *Bailey* would likely come out in favor of the defendant even under the objective theory of intent. The plaintiff, after all, knew that ownership of the horse was contested, and in particular that the defendant denied ownership. And it seems at least plausible that no reasonable person, possessed of this knowledge, would believe that the defendant intended to pay for the horse's board.

5. It is not clear why the plaintiff thought that the $5 would have any independent legal effect. It might, of course, be evidence about the parties' states of mind, or how others might reasonably interpret their states of mind, in conducting their conversation.

In *Lucy*, as in *Plate*, the court held for the plaintiff. It reached its holding by asking how a reasonable person in the plaintiff's position would have interpreted the defendant's "offer" and concluding that such a person would have thought the defendant serious and the offer real. (The court also disbelieved the defendant's claims that he subjectively thought himself joking, but it made quite clear that the holding of the case does not turn on the conclusion that the defendant did in fact intend to strike a bargain.) In a sense, the argument applying the objective test in *Lucy* once again reprises the argument applying the subjective test in *Plate*, only bringing within contractual analysis considerations that the subjective test addressed without contract. Certainly the outcome in *Plate* would have been the same had the case been decided under the doctrinal principles adopted in *Lucy*.

Of course, *Lucy* is a much harder case than *Plate*. It is far from clear, at least to this reader, that the defendant's conduct in *Lucy* was reasonably understood, given the circumstances, as a serious offer rather than as a snide challenge or boast. The parties interacted in a bar, after all, where they had both been drinking: not enough to become drunk or contractually incapacitated;[6] but plausibly enough to change how a reasonable observer would interpret their words and actions. Certainly the setting was more naturally social than business-like, and although land and buildings do get bought and sold in social settings, competitive talk about income and wealth whose aim is to show off rather than to increase one's holdings is at least as common. The confusion in *Lucy* arose because the showing off there took the form of discussing—and at least play-acting—a possible sale. The court seemed to think such play-acting outlandish (either in general or given the level of detail—the talk of acceptable title and the getting of the wife's signature—that the play-acting involved in this case), and so supposed that the sale must have been real. But this may say more about the limited experience of the court than about the ordinary and reasonable understandings of people who visit bars a little more regularly. For at least some people, the most bizarre feature of the case is surely that the plaintiff didn't get the joke, and took the defendant's taunts as a business proposition.

The most interesting feature of *Lucy*, however, is not connected to the substantive question who should have won. Rather, *Lucy* vividly reveals that although the subjective test of contractual intent necessarily takes up, without contract, some of the very same considerations concerning reasonableness that the objective test takes up within contract, the two tests are not in the end completely or even functionally equivalent. Thus, although *Lucy* is a hard case on the objective test, it would have been an easy victory for the defendant on the subjective test, at least if the court's outlandish factual suggestion that the defendant subjectively intended to strike a bargain is set aside. If the defendant did not subjectively intend to sell his farm, then there could be no liability at all (either within contract or

---

6. These materials will take up questions concerning intoxication and contractual capacity in Part III below.

without it) on the subjective approach. By contrast, as the opinion in *Lucy* makes clear, there might be liability on the objective approach.

This establishes a distinction between *Lucy* and *Plate*, where a court applying the subjective test did find liability (albeit not in contract) even in the face of a finding of no subjective intent to bargain. And this contrast emphasizes that the difference between the subjective and objective approaches is not merely that the subjective approach shifts the objective approach's concern for reasonableness to non-contractual ground. Rather, pushing considerations of reasonableness outside of contract transforms them.

Under the objective test, the reasonableness inquiry focuses on establishing the best understanding of how the parties arranged their affairs by means of contract. And because our legal system embraces freedom of contract, a substantive analysis of the fairness of the parties' arrangements will play only a small role in answering the question whether or not the parties intended to strike a bargain (and will surely not dominate the treatment of this question). Certainly there is no difficulty, on the objective approach, in concluding that a plaintiff was reasonable to treat a defendant's utterances as an offer even where deciding otherwise would expose the plaintiff to no harm. That, after all, is the fact pattern in *Lucy*, where the plaintiffs would have lost nothing had the court concluded that a reasonable person would have interpreted the defendant's talk of selling as just a joke. And there was simply no question of manipulation or exploitation in that case.

Things are quite different under the subjective approach. There, reasonableness comes into play not in connection with establishing the best interpretation of a defendant's utterances but rather in connection with deciding whether a finding of no-liability would unreasonably harm or exploit a plaintiff. Accordingly, whereas a plaintiff whose defendant had no subjective intent to bargain can win under the objective test simply by showing that she reasonably did think a bargain was being offered, such a plaintiff can win on the subjective test only by showing that finding of no liability would unreasonably harm or exploit her. This will be true much more rarely, and so plaintiffs will generally do better under the objective than under the subjective approach to contractual intent.

This difference between the two approaches has its roots deep in the conceptual foundations of contract doctrine. In a way, it is a direct expression of the structural distinction between contract and tort. The objective approach to offer can find contractual liability even where the offeror's lack of subjective intent to strike a bargain does not involve any sort of wrong, and the offeree has not been the victim of any injustice. The subjective approach, by contrast, will find liability in quasi-contract only where a failure of liability would involve a wrong or injustice. And this difference, in turn, is a direct expression of the difference between freedom of contract on the one hand, and the mandatory nature of tort obligations on the other. Many contracts, which apportion gains among the parties in many ways, will be enforced under a regime of freedom of contract; and so a legal order that assimilates offers to contract even without subjective intent to bargain might find liability in connection with an alleged offer not just where the offeror violates a fixed obligation but also where she assumes a variable one. Only certain harms constitute torts, by contrast; and so a legal order that makes subjective intent necessary for contract, and confines liability in the absence of such intent to other doctrinal areas, can find liability only where the alleged offeror violates an obligation fixed independently by these other areas.[7]

Now one question raised at once by this observation about the relatively expansive conception of liability ushered in by introducing an objective

---

7. Both the similarity and the difference between the two approaches receives a vivid doctrinal illustration in *Bailey*, in connection with the fact that the analysis of that case turned on the question whether the defendant's agent had apparent authority to board the horse. Apparent authority is an objective notion, which, moreover, converts tort (concerning giving reasonable notice about the limitations of one's agent's normative powers) into contract (concerning the obligations that these agents can establish where no notice is given).

This makes it natural to ask how subjective theory of intent deals with apparent authority. The answer nicely reveals both that the same practical questions matter to the subjective and objective theories, and that it can matter (including practically) that these questions arise at different points.

Thus apparent authority was recognized even during the heyday of the subjective theory of contractual intent. A 1901 treatise on the law of agency, for example, says that in cases of apparent authority, "the sole legal question then is, had the third party in acting on the representative's statements, reasonable ground for believing that the representative was authorized to make them? In other words, had the agent apparent authority to do what he did? If so, then the employer is *estopped* to deny that which he had to appear to be true is not true, since a third person has acted upon the representation of the principal as to the agent's authority." ERNEST WILSON HUFFCUT, THE LAW OF AGENCY 15 (1901).

On the one hand, this language, in its interstices, commits exactly the sleight-of-hand that subjective theories of contractual intent inevitably require: it reintroduces the objective inquiry, only without contract rather than within it. Certainly, the treatise's explanation cannot render liability in cases of apparent authority on the basis of conventional principles of contract law. Hence the treatise turns, in explaining liability, to notions of reliance (the third person's acting on the principal's representation) and estoppel (which blocks the principal from denying intent that he had invited third parties to infer that he had). But these principles cannot, on their own, explain the conclusion that the principle is liable for the contracts his agents have apparent authority to make. After all, reliance on its own does not underwrite legal liability and certainly not contractual liability (I do not open myself up to legal liability merely by stating my current intentions, even if I know that you will hear me and might adjust to them, because I remain free to change my mind). And estoppel states the conclusion that there is liability rather than an argument in favor of that conclusion. As Grant Gilmore once said, when a court speaks in terms of estoppel, it means merely that, "for reasons which the court does not wish to discuss, there must be judgment for the plaintiff." GRANT GILMORE, THE DEATH OF CONTRACT 64 (1974). Instead, the treatise supports its conclusion that there is liability in cases of apparent authority by observing that in such cases the third party has "reasonable ground for believing that the representative was authorized [that is, actually, subjectively authorized]" to bind his principal. But this is just the inquiry into contractual intent recommended by objective theories of intent. And that, of course, is precisely the lesson of the cases: that subjective theories of intent do not eliminate the reasonableness standard associated with objective theories but instead simply shift the inquiry into reasonable understandings onto non-contractual ground.

On the other hand, this account of reasonable ascriptions of intent, because it changes where in the doctrinal structure these ascriptions are made, also changes the practical effect of inquiries into objective intent on case outcomes. The estoppel argument will be stronger where the plaintiff was not only reasonable in thinking the agent empowered to bind the defendant, but also would be unreasonably harmed (or the defendant unreasonably benefited) if the agent's activities were held not to bind the defendant. Thus, the classical approach to agency limited liability based on apparent authority commensurately more narrowly than the modern doctrine.

account of intent into the law of offer asks just when the law should find offers even where there has been no subjective intent to enter any bargain. By what general principles, embodied in what doctrinal rules, should the law determine when a reasonable observer would understand actions and utterances as genuine offers, which might become binding contracts by being accepted, rather than as just jokes or (more commonly) predictions, statements of intentions, or invitations to negotiate?

One natural way to address this question returns to the style of analysis pursued in Part I and asks what standards for treating utterances as offers (and, in particular, for concluding that offers might arise even in the absence of subjective intent) are efficient. It is not hard to see why *some* move away from a *purely* subjective requirement of intent is efficient. Offers are more valuable than mere predictions (or their analogs): they are more valuable to offerees because they empower offerees unilaterally (that is, simply by accepting) to ripen them into full-fledged legal obligations; and they are more valuable to offerors because offerees, being so empowered, will be more inclined to take the further steps (involving reliance) needed eventually to conclude mutually profitable bargains. Offerors will therefore want credibly to signal that they have made genuine offers, and the objective approach to offer is a natural, indeed likely invaluable, tool enabling them to do so. Of course, a conclusion that an utterance is a genuine offer also imposes costs on offerors, who may now become bound, by their offerees' unilateral actions, even where they do not actually (subjectively) wish to enter any bargain. And the objective approach therefore risks enmeshing offerors in contractual entanglements that they would rather have avoided.

The task for the law, on this approach, is to strike the optimal balance between these two considerations and to render that balance operational through administrable doctrinal principles. Perhaps unsurprisingly, the key to balancing the benefits and costs of an objective standard of offer is to ask who is best-placed to avoid the misunderstandings created by gaps between the reasonable understanding of an offeror's acts and utterances and her subjective intent. One might ask, that is, what legal rule will put incentives for clarity on those who are best placed to respond to them? The rules that have arisen around the objective account of offer, like the foreseeability rule, may be understood as an information management regime. And this is just how a series of functionalist analyses of the modern law of offer approach them.[8]

The functionalist analysis of the law of offer is interesting and important. But it proceeds in the style of the prior Part of these materials, and part of the purpose of this text is to introduce a variety of styles of legal analysis and argument. This Part focuses not on functionalism but on formalism—it engages the law not as a means to an end (in the case of offer, striking the efficient balance between the benefits and costs of opening oneself up to legal liability) but rather for the law's own sake, in

---

8. For a particularly fine example, see Gregory Klass, *Intent to Contract*, 95 Va. L. Rev. 1437 (2009).

an effort to elaborate the immanent normative structure of legal doctrine. And in this connection, the most pressing questions raised by theories of offer are not which legal standard best serves offerors' and offerees' law-independent interests but rather what kind of a thing contractual obligation is: in particular, whether contractual obligation is distinct from the obligation not to harm others that grounds tort law and, if it is distinct, whether contractual obligation is a creature of the parties' intentions, or of the law. The subjective and objective approaches to offer suggest quite different answers to these questions, and the differences between them survive even in the face of whatever convergence on practical outcomes the two approaches display.

The conception of contract immanent in the subjective approach is easy to discern. That approach insists that contractual obligation is structurally distinct from tort and must, moreover, be directly and specifically intended by the parties. This is a purely voluntarist theory of contract, according to which a party possesses absolute control over her contractual entanglements, and the law—of contract, at least—insistently avoids ever subjecting a party to contractual obligations that she did not intentionally acquire. Of course, this approach—commonly called the *classical* account of contract—elaborated a theory of contract only; it did not, because it could not possibly, make any claims about adjacent doctrinal areas, which were (as the theory insisted that they must be) free-standing and entirely independent of contract. Accordingly, other types of legal obligation, including tort-like obligations that could exist apart from the intentions of those to whom they applied, might arise in and around the contractual milieu, including even in cases in which no contract proper was created. And in this way, many (although not, as we have seen, all) of the considerations that the modern law brings within contract might come into play under the classical approach also, only there apart from contract. That is the lesson of *Plate*, and it is a lesson that will be repeated many times, in many variations, throughout the materials to come.

The conception of contract immanent in the modern, objective approach is much less obvious. Properly to understand the theory of contract obligation that is expressed in the objective approach to offer requires taking up one more set of legal materials.

Restatement 2d of Contracts

§ 21   Intention To Be Legally Bound

Neither real nor apparent intention that a promise be legally binding is essential to the formation of a contract, but a manifestation of intention that a promise shall not affect legal relations may prevent the formation of a contract.

Comments & Illustrations

Comment a. Intent to be legally bound. Most persons are now aware of the existence of courts and rules of law and of the fact that some promises are binding. The parties to a transaction often have a reasonably accurate understanding of the applicable law, and an intention to affect legal relations. Such facts may be important in interpreting their manifestations of intention and in determining legal consequences, but they are not essential to the formation of a contract. The parties are often quite mistaken about particular rules of law, but such mistakes do not necessarily deprive their acts of legal effect.

Illustrations:

1. A draws a check for $300 payable to B and delivers it to B in return for an old silver watch worth about $15. Both A and B understand the transaction as a frolic and a banter, but each believes that he would be legally bound if the other dishonestly so asserted. There is no contract.

2. A orally promises to sell B a book in return for B's promise to pay $5. A and B both think such promises are not binding unless in writing. Nevertheless there is a contract, unless one of them intends not to be legally bound and the other knows or has reason to know of that intention.

Comment b. Agreement not to be legally bound. Parties to what would otherwise be a bargain and a contract sometimes agree that their legal relations are not to be affected. In the absence of any invalidating cause, such a term is respected by the law like any other term, but such an agreement may present difficult questions of interpretation: it may mean that no bargain has been reached, or that a particular manifestation of intention is not a promise; it may reserve a power to revoke or terminate a promise under certain circumstances but not others. In a written document prepared by one party it may raise a question of misrepresentation or mistake or overreaching; to avoid such questions it may be read against the party who prepared it.

The parties to such an agreement may intend to deny legal effect to their subsequent acts. But where a bargain has been fully or partly performed on one side, a failure to perform on the other side may result in unjust enrichment, and the term may then be unenforceable as a provision for a penalty or forfeiture. See §§ 185, 229, 356. In other cases the term may be unenforceable as against public policy because it unreasonably limits recourse to the courts or as unconscionably limiting the remedies for breach of contract. See §§ 178–79, 208; Uniform Commercial Code §§ 2–302, 2–719 and Comment 1.

Illustrations:

3. A, an employer, issues to B, an employee, a "certificate of benefit", promising stated sums increasing yearly, payable to a named beneficiary if B dies while still in A's employ. The certificate provides that it "constitutes no contract" and "confers no

legal right." The quoted language may be read as reserving a power of revocation only until B dies.

4. A and B, two business corporations, have a contract by which B is the exclusive distributor in a certain territory of goods made by A. By a detailed written agreement they agree to continue the distributorship for three years. The writing provides that it is not to be a legal agreement or subject to legal jurisdiction in the law courts. The written agreement may be read and given effect to terminate the prior contract and to prevent any legal duty arising from the making of the agreement or from the acceptance of orders under it; but it does not excuse B from paying for goods delivered under it.

Comment c. Social engagements and domestic arrangements. In some situations the normal understanding is that no legal obligation arises, and some unusual manifestation of intention is necessary to create a contract. Traditional examples are social engagements and agreements within a family group. See §§ 189–91. Where the family relation is not close, valuable services rendered in the home may make binding an express or implied promise to pay for the services; but even in such cases it would often be understood that there is no legal obligation while the agreement is entirely executory on both sides. See Comment *a* to § 19, Comment *b* to § 32.

Illustrations:

5. A invites his friend B to dinner in his home, and B accepts. There is no contract. If A promised B a fee for attending and entertaining other guests, and B did so, there would be a contract to pay the fee.

6. A, a husband, is living in harmony with his wife, B. Before A leaves on a trip, A and B assess B's financial needs and agree that A will remit a fixed sum per month to support her. There is no contract.

Persad v. Balram

Supreme Court of Queens County, New York, 2001.
187 Misc.2d 711.

Putative husband brought suit seeking declaration that the parties were never lawfully married, or in the alternative a divorce, and putative wife counterclaimed for divorce. The Supreme Court, Queens County, Darrell L. Gavrin, J., held that parties' formal Hindu wedding ceremony, which was officiated by ordained Hindu priest or "pandit," and during which parties exchanged vows, conformed with all statutory requirements and effected a lawful marriage, even though parties never successfully obtained marriage license.

So ordered.

GAVRIN, J. The plaintiff commenced this action seeking a declaration that the parties were never married or in the alternative for a divorce. The defendant served a verified answer and counterclaim for divorce.

A hearing was commenced before this Court on February 1, 2001 and continued on February 9 to explore and determine the validity of the parties alleged marriage. The relevant facts adduced at the hearing are as follows.

FACTS

On May 22, 1994, the plaintiff and defendant participated in a Hindu marriage or "prayer" ceremony at the home of the defendant's family in Brooklyn, New York. The Hindu prayer ceremony was presided over by Moscan Persad and was attended by 100 to 150 guests. At the time, the plaintiff and defendant were approximately 32 and 28 years old, respectively. During the ceremony, the parties were adorned in traditional Hindu wedding garments, prayers were articulated, the defendant's parent's symbolically gave her to the plaintiff, vows were made and rings and a flower garland were exchanged. The ceremony lasted approximately two hours. At the conclusion of the marriage ceremony, Mr. Persad said a benediction.

Mr. Persad testified that he is an ordained Hindu priest or "pandit" sanctioned since February 21, 1993 to perform wedding ceremonies. Two certificates, issued by USA Pandits' Parishad, Inc., were introduced into evidence certifying Mr. Persad as a "Hindu Priest" and "competent in Kamkand (rituals) and Purohitkarm (priesthood)." Both certificates predate the marriage ceremony in this action.

Immediately following the nuptials, a reception was held for 275 friends and family at Terrace on the Park in Corona, Queens. A photo album was introduced into evidence wherein the plaintiff and defendant are depicted in photographs wearing Hindu marriage garments. In other photos, the plaintiff is wearing a white-on-white tuxedo and the defendant is wearing what appears to be a traditional white wedding gown. At the reception, the parties had a wedding cake and received wedding gifts. After the ceremony and reception the defendant sent the guests "thank you" notes.

It was not disputed that the parties lacked a valid marriage license on May 22, 1994. On three separate occasions, once immediately prior to the ceremony and twice subsequently (January & April 1995), the parties began proceedings to obtain a marriage license, but each time it was not properly secured. Each party blamed the other for the failure to obtain the marriage license. It was also not contested that Moscan Persad was not licensed by the City or State of New York to perform marriage ceremonies.

It was revealed at the hearing that the parties attempted to enter into a pre-marital agreement. Three days prior to the ceremony, the parties met with an attorney, Stephanie Ressler, who drafted a "pre-nuptial" agreement which the defendant refused to sign. Subsequently, in June of 1995, the parties met with Ms. Ressler and defendant again declined to execute the agreement.

Further, the court heard testimony that the parties have filed separate tax returns since the ceremony and that the defendant claimed herself to be single on her returns. Also, it was revealed that the defendant claimed herself as single when she obtained automobile insurance in 1998.

Essentially, the plaintiff contends the marriage is invalid for two reasons: first, the religious ceremony did not comport with the formal legal requirements under the Domestic Relations Law; second, the religious ceremony was merely a custom conducted prior to the parties living together and the parties did not intend to be married until they participated in a civil ceremony.

CONCLUSIONS OF LAW

There is an old cliché that goes "if it walks like a duck and quacks like a duck, and looks like a duck, it's a duck." This familiar maxim appears perfectly suited to the case at the bar, as it conforms with the intent underlying the statutory structure enacted by the Legislature. Essentially, the Domestic Relation Law establishes that where parties participate in a solemn marriage ceremony officiated by a clergyman or magistrate wherein they exchange vows, they are married in the eyes of the law. (*See,* Domestic Relations Law §§ 11, 12, 25; Religious Corporations Law § 2). It is the opinion of the court that this is precisely what occurred in the instant case.

The parties' failure to obtain a marriage license does not render their marriage void. Section 25 of the Domestic Relations Law provides that "[n]othing in [Article 3 of the DRL] shall be construed to render void by reason of a failure to procure a marriage license any marriage solemnized between persons of full age ..." Likewise, Moscan Persad's failure to register with the City of New York pursuant to Domestic Relations Law § 11–b prior to performing the marriage ceremony did not render the parties' marriage void. (*See, Shamsee v. Shamsee,* 381 N.Y.S.2d 127 [2d Dept.1976].) In New York, a marriage may be solemnized by a "[a] clergyman or minister of any religion ..." (DRL § 11[1]). Section 2 of the Religious Corporations Law defines the terms clergyman and minister as:

> includ[ing] a duly authorized pastor, rector priest, rabbi, and a person having authority from, or in accordance with, the rules regulations of the governing ecclesiastical body of the denomination or order, if any, to which the church belongs, or otherwise from the church or synagogue to preside over and direct the spiritual affairs of the church or synagogue.

This statute must be given a broad interpretation so as not to infringe on an individual's constitutional guarantee of religious freedom. (*See, O'Neill v. Hubbard,* 40 N.Y.S.2d 202 [Sup.Ct.Kings Cty.1943].) Subsumed within this constitutional right is the freedom to be married in accordance with the dictates of one's own faith. (*See, Ravenal v. Ravenal,* 338 N.Y.S.2d 324 [Sup.Ct.N.Y.Cty.1972].) Thus, short of finding a religious officiant a charlatan or the religion a mere sham, courts have confirmed the validity of a variety of spiritual faiths and their clergies' authority to solemnize marriages.

At the hearing, neither party contested the validity of the Hindu religion. Also, the testimony adduced from Moscan Persad more than adequately established that on May 22, 1994 he possessed the requisite authority under DRL § 11 to solemnize marriages in the Hindu religion. Indeed, other than establishing that Mr. Persad was not registered with the City of New York under Domestic Relation Law § 11–b, there was no testimony advanced to impugn his authority as a priest empowered to officiate marriages in the Hindu religion.

A further issue exists as to the substance of the ceremony. Section 12 of the Domestic Relations Law provides that a marriage is solemnized when "the parties ... solemnly declare in the presence of a clergyman or magistrate and the attending witness or witnesses that they take each other as husband and wife." (DRL § 12) The statute also states that "[n]o particular form or ceremony is required." (Id.) In the Court's opinion, the testimony conclusively revealed that the parties engaged in an austere ritual pursuant to the Hindu faith. Numerous guests witnessed the nuptials wherein the parties, before a Hindu pandit, exchanged vows and declared their desire to be husband and wife. Accordingly, all the requirements of a lawful marriage under the Domestic Relations Law were fulfilled.

Notwithstanding complete compliance with the statutes, the plaintiff avers a marriage was not consummated because they did not intend to be married by the religious ceremony. Although the plaintiff expresses his objection to the validity of the marriage in terms of the parties' intent, his claim fundamentally is that the parties, either expressly or tacitly, entered into an agreement that the religious ceremony would be one of form not substance and that a subsequent civil ceremony would be held. The defendant claims that the parties' intent is immaterial as it is not expressly delineated as a factor in the Domestic Relations Law.

The plaintiff is correct that an intention to marry is not expressly written in statutes. Nevertheless, "[m]arriage, so far as its validity in the law is concerned, continues to be a civil contract, to which the consent of the parties capable in law of making a contract is essential." (DRL § 10.) Under general contract principles, where parties do not intend to be legally bound by an agreement there is no contract. (*See,* Restatement [Second] of Contracts § 21, comment [a]; Farnsworth, Contracts § 3.7 [2d ed. 1990].) However, while a marriage "is declared a civil contract for certain purposes, ... it is not thereby made synonymous with the word contract employed in the common law or statutes." (*Wade v. Kalbfleisch,* 58 N.Y. 282, 284 [1874].) A marriage, because of its unique status and substance, differs significantly from ordinary contracts. (*See, Cunningham v. Cunningham,* 206 N.Y. 341 [1912].) It is an "institution" about which the state is "deeply concerned" and takes a profound interest in protecting. (*See, Morris v. Morris,* 220 N.Y.S.2d 590 [West.Cty.1961].) As such, a marriage is not a contract protected against impairment of obligations under the U.S. Constitution (*see*, U.S. Const., art. I, § 10, cl. 1; *Fearon v. Treanor*, 272 N.Y. 268 [1936]) and is subject to state regulation and supervision once created. Moreover, a husband and wife are not free to "alter or dissolve" their union by agreement. (*see*, general obligations law § 5–311.)

With these principles in mind, courts confronted with circumstances similar to the one at bar have held marriages valid despite the parties' agreements to the contrary. (*See, Anonymous v. Anonymous,* 49 N.Y.S.2d 314 [Bx.Cty.1944].)

In *Anonymous v. Anonymous,* supra, the husband brought an action for an annulment wherein he advanced the theory that the parties' marriage was invalid because, *inter alia,* a religious ceremony was not performed after the civil ceremony as per the parties' agreement. The court rejected the husband's argument finding that "... the law recognizes no privately imposed condition that would alter the marital status." (Id. at 316.) The court reasoned that marital "status is too much a matter of public concern to allow the parties to tinker with it according to their own notions of what is expedient and proper." (Id.)

This case and the others cited above are not distinguishable because they concern the converse situation from the one at bar (i.e., a religious followed by a civil ceremony as opposed to a civil ceremony followed by a religious one). Since the Domestic Relations Law draws no qualitative distinction between marriages conducted with and without licenses, the salient point in these cases is not that the civil ceremony occurred first, but rather there was a valid marriage the courts were willing to recognize and protect over the parties' agreement.

In this case, there was a religious marriage that conformed with all the statutory requirements. As a result, the State of New York and this court have a vested interest in that union. (*See e.g., Sheils v. Sheils,* supra at 255, 301 N.Y.S.2d 372) Alternatively stated, New York State became a "third party to the marriage." (Id.) and "[a]ny private reservations [the parties] may have made in regard to their respective obligations under the marital status are void and of no effect." (*Gregg v. Gregg,* supra at 111, 231 N.Y.S. 221.)

As a corollary, this court's ruling does not mean parties' intentions can never render a marriage void. This court can imagine a variety of circumstances where a religious union might be considered invalid based on a lack of mutual intent to be wed. For instance, if the ceremony was a prank or the parties were under the influence at the time, a marriage could conceivably be a nullity. This is not the case here. Despite the plaintiff's claim, it is clear to this court the parties' ultimate intention was to be husband and wife. At best, they were laboring under a mistaken belief that their religious ceremony would not have legal effect.

The plaintiff placed great emphasis on post-marriage events averring they confirmed the non-existence of a valid marriage. The defendant's declarations on the tax returns and car insurance that she was single are immaterial in this case. In the court's opinion, these statements reflect some financial or other strategy on behalf of the defendant. In fact, it substantiates the court's belief that the parties were mistaken as to their marital status after the religious ceremony. Furthermore, other more compelling factors, specifically the parties' post-nuptial cohabitation for approximately seven years and the conception of their child, affirms their marital status.

Any claim that the marriage is invalid based on the plaintiff's individual intent not to be married until a civil ceremony was performed is equally unavailing. Since the court has determined the parties mutual intent would not affect their marital status, it would be inapposite to now hold that one party's unilateral intent voided the marriage. This court will not give legal effect to the plaintiff's claim of "crossed fingers" when he solemnly pledged to take the defendant as his wife.

Accordingly, as the plaintiff has failed to overcome the strong presumption favoring the validity of marriages, the marriage is adjudged lawful and the court directs that a declaration be entered to that effect.

* * *

Section 24 of the Restatement, as the previous discussion explains, elaborates the modern rule that offers are identified according to an objective rather than a subjective standard: that is, the whether an offer has been made depends not on whether the offeror actually intends to open herself up to entering a bargain but rather on whether a reasonable person observing the offeror would think that she so intends. Section 21 adds a subtle but immensely important—indeed, structurally essential—gloss to the objective account of intent stated in Section 24. This is that the *content* of the intent that will be evaluated objectively under section 24 is the intent to enter into a bargain and *not* the more particular intent that the bargain be legally recognized or enforceable. Illustration 2 renders this distinction vivid:

> A orally promises to sell B a book in return for B's promise to pay $5. A and B both think such promises are not binding unless in writing. Nevertheless there is a contract, unless one of them intends not to be legally bound and the other knows or has reason to know of that intention.

There is a contract because a reasonable observer would believe that A and B intended to exchange the promise of the book for the promise of the money. It does not matter that the obligations A and B intended to assume were only moral or social and not (given their beliefs about the law) legal. It would not matter, moreover, even if a reasonable observer (indeed, even if A and B themselves) knew that no legal obligation was intended. (This is what the Restatement means when it speaks of "neither real nor *apparent* intention" (emphasis added).) It might matter—the final clause of the illustration suggests—if A and B had appropriately known intentions affirmatively to *avoid* legal obligations, which is a much stronger condition than merely lacking an intention to assume legal obligations. It *might*

matter, but it *need* not. Although the illustration speaks conclusively—
"unless"—the Restatement Section itself says merely that "manifestation
of intention that a promise shall not affect legal relations *may* prevent the
formation of a contract" (emphasis added). In practice, the escape clause
for cases in which parties intend affirmatively to avoid legal obligations
applies principally (indeed, almost exclusively) to circumstances involving
preliminary agreements and ongoing negotiations, in which parties make
moral or social commitments designed to support an ongoing (and costly)
effort to reach a legal agreement. Although such preliminary agreements
may be legally binding, there is good reason for the law to be cautious in
this area: the parties, after all, continue to negotiate precisely because they
are not yet ready to obligate themselves at law, and preliminary agreements designed to support their hopes of eventually striking a contract
should not be mistaken for the contract itself. The escape clause in Section
21 inserts this consideration into the positive law.

The intent specifically that a promise be *legally* binding is rarely
litigated in U.S. law, and where the issue is litigated, courts often confuse
the general question of objective intent with the specific question whether
or not the intent must take legal obligation as its subject. *Persad* is an
exception (although even here, the court gets the law wrong, and thinks
that it must support its results through considerations related specifically
to the law of marriage, whereas the general principles of the Restatement
would have been quite enough to sustain the outcome in the case). The
parties in *Persad* had a religious wedding and threw the party that
conventionally accompanies wedding celebrations, but they never obtained
a secular marriage license. After a series of disputes arose between them,
the plaintiff (the putative husband) sued seeking a declaratory judgment
that no legal marriage had taken place. He argued, among other things,
that "the religious ceremony was merely a custom conducted prior to the
parties living together and the parties did not intend to be married until
they participated in a civil ceremony," which they never did.

The plaintiff thus argued that no marriage contract was ever established, because the parties to that contract never intended to be legally
bound in the manner that marriage involves. (Note that he did *not* argue
that they intended *not* to be legally bound.) The court rejected this
argument, and indeed for the reasons expressed by Restatement Section 21.
Specifically, the court observed that the state, which enforces and supervis-
es marriage agreements, has an interest in protecting the institution and
its obligations. The court observed, in effect, that although *particular*
marriages are chosen by the parties, so that the specific legal obligations
that these marriages involve are voluntary, in the sense of being brought
into existence by the parties' conduct, the *legal form* marriage is not party
chosen but is instead a creature of the state, and in particular of the law.
The law, therefore, is entitled to protect this legal form, including by
finding that it has arisen even in a case in which the parties, although they
freely participated in the conventions that generally establish a legal
marriage, did not as it happens intend to establish one for themselves. The
court thought that, on the facts of *Persad*, protecting the marriage form

required finding a legally valid marriage even though the plaintiff and defendant never intended to make one. The substantive conclusion is of course open to question: is the legal institution marriage ever best served by dragooning people into the law where they wish merely to enter into a religious, moral, or social relation; if the answer to this question is ever "yes," is it "yes" on the facts of *Persad*? The court admits of such doubts when it observes that its "ruling does not mean parties' intentions can never render a marriage void." But the formal point survives all such substantive concerns: the parties' intentions concerning legal obligation cannot, directly, necessarily, and simply in themselves prevent a legal marriage from arising.

To be sure, the court claimed to reach this result on the basis of considerations that lie outside ordinary contract law. Indeed, it claimed that "under general contract principles, where parties do not intend to be legally bound by an agreement there is no contract." But this is, plainly and simply, incorrect as a statement of the law. Indeed, Restatement Section 21, which the court cited in support of its assertion, in fact says precisely the opposite. And the comment to which the court further cites plainly says that "The parties are often quite mistaken about particular rules of law, but such mistakes do not necessarily deprive their acts of legal effect." The fact that the parties to the wedding in *Persad* mistakenly believed that a civil ceremony is necessary to conclude a legally valid marriage therefore does not, under "general principles of contract law," deprive their religious ceremony of legal effect, as long only as the parties possessed (objective) intent to be religiously, morally, or socially bound in matrimony.

Finally, and for present purposes crucially, the court's argument illustrates an immensely important point about the formal structure of contract obligation. This is that there is a deep, and underappreciated, formal distinction between the *agreements of the parties*, on the one hand, and, on the other, the *contract law* that makes these agreements legally binding. The agreements of the parties—the bargain obligations that these agreements involve—are creatures of the parties' intentions. They are, as it were, brought into existence by the parties' actions and mental states. But the rules that govern these obligations are not creatures of the parties' intentions but of the *law*, specifically the law of agreements, which is to say contract law. These reflections reprise—now in greater theoretical and doctrinal detail—the dissenters' observation in *Groves v. John Wunder, Co.*, recited towards the end of Part I:

> "[T]he obligation of the contract does not inhere or subsist in the agreement itself *proprio vigore*, but in the law applicable to the agreement, that is, in the act of the law in binding the promisor to perform his promise. When it is said that one who enters upon an undertaking assumes the legal duties relating to it, what is really meant is that the law imposes duties on him. A contract is not a law, nor does it make law. It is the agreement plus the law that makes the ordinary contract an enforceable obligation."

Contract law cannot—at least insofar as it is to remain distinctively and free-standingly the law of agreements, rather than just being a branch office of the law of harm, which is to say, torts—create a legal obligation in the absence of a bargain, because there would then be nothing—no agreement—for the law to latch on to (although recall, see Section 24, that the bargain may appear in the eye of the reasonable beholder only, and not in the minds of the bargainers themselves). But contract law may make bargains into legal obligations even though the parties do not intend them to become so. Indeed, it may even establish legal obligations where the parties intend that they do *not* arise. (Section 21, recall, says "may" rather than "will" in its escape clause.) The law, when it establishes obligations in such cases, will typically do so for precisely the reasons that the *Persad* court elaborated for what it mistakenly thought is the special case of marriage: because the legal obligations associated with contracts are creatures of law and not just of the parties', the law is, to borrow language from *Persad*, a third party to every contractual bargain. And it will have good reason to intervene to protect itself and to promote its values, including even where the parties do not intend any such intervention.

13.2   REAL OFFERS VERSUS INVITATIONS TO BARGAIN

Not everything that a promisor says in pursuit of a contract constitutes an offer—that is, a speech act that allows a promisee to create a contract simply by accepting. Instead, many of a promisor's remarks, even though they aim at an eventual contract, simply establish the general informational context within which offers, and acceptances, can eventually arise. In particular, the law distinguishes what might be called "real offers," which open offerors up to contractual liability upon acceptance, from mere "invitations to bargain," which merely announce a willingness to consider making or receiving offers (whose content is as yet unspecified) at a later time. An example may help to fix ideas: someone who says "if you promise to pay me $10 in cash by noon tomorrow, I will promise to deliver a hundred pounds of gravel to your residence by then" clearly makes a real offer; someone who says "do you have any interest in buying some gravel from me" clearly merely invites further bargaining. Of course, these clear cases represent the endpoints of a continuum, in between which lie any number of hard cases, where it is unclear whether there has been an offer or merely an invitation to bargain. The materials that follow take up the distinction in connection with such hard cases. They will entertain some functionalist considerations that arise in this area of law, but, in keeping with the general theme of this Part, they will once again conclude with a formalist lesson.

Unlike a mere invitation to bargain, an offer exposes the offeror to immediate liability, at the unilateral option of the offeree. That makes it costly to be in the position of having made a real offer, as circumstances may develop in which the offeror regrets the terms of the offer, and the liability that the offer describes turns out to be unwanted. At the same time, however, people have good reason for making real offers, including real offers to multiple offerees and even to the public at large.

It is never free for a promisee to determine whether he wishes to strike a bargain or not, and it will often be quite expensive for him to do so. A person who is considering whether or not to buy a particular car at a fixed price, for example, will want to make a mechanical inspection of the car prior to making a purchase, and the inspection will cost him both time and money. Similar, a firm contemplating a business deal—a supply contract, for example, or an acquisition of another firm—will have reason to investigate its own commercial prospects, the commercial and technical capacities of the other firms involved in the deal, and even general market conditions. Again, all these types of due diligence are costly to implement.

For this reason, an offeror who makes a real offer—and who thereby creates a power in her offeree to establish a binding legal relationship unilaterally, simply by his acceptance—will be advantaged in acquiring acceptances over someone who utters nothing more than an invitation to bargain. A counterparty who is merely invited to bargain will discount the value of the bargain at issue by the chance that the party issuing the invitation will lose interest and withdraw from the negotiations, even as he has determined that he wishes to proceed. And this will make him less responsive to her invitation than he would have been to a real offer—less willing to make the investment necessary for determining that he does want to proceed.

Certainly a potential buyer will be more willing to inspect a car (and, because passing the inspection is a necessary condition for the purchase, hence more likely to buy the car) if he knows that he possesses the power unilaterally to create a purchase contract in case the car does pass muster. And a firm contemplating an acquisition will be more willing to do the research needed to reveal facts on which the successful completion of the acquisition depends if it possesses the power unilaterally to consummate the acquisition in case its research reveals that these facts obtain. Indeed, an offeree may seek, and be willing to pay for, more protection against his offeror's change of heart than even a real offer provides. A real offer may, after all, be revoked before it is accepted. And the offeree may wish to limit the offeror's power of revocation, either by making an agreement that structures future negotiations with an eye to limiting the circumstances in which the offeror may revoke or even by (for a time) entirely depriving the offeror of the power to revoke, as happens when the offeree acquires an *option*. That offerees are willing to pay for options reveals their value to offerees, and hence the value to offerors of being able to provide them.

Contracts that structure negotiations (and option contracts, representing one extreme form of such structuring) will be taken up later in these materials. For the moment, it is enough to observe that real offers already change the structure of pre-contractual relations, and that this makes them valuable to both offerees and offerors. Once again, they give offerees a unilateral power to create a contract, as mere invitations to bargain do not. And they give offerors the benefit of encouraging reliance among offerees who might, on the basis of this reliance, accept the offers. At the same time, real offers of course subject offerors to the risk of unwanted acceptances, made in circumstances in which a contract on the offer's terms is disadvantageous for the offeror. A legal regime that imposes narrow standards on finding offers and expansive standards concerning invitations to bargain thus jeopardizes potential gains from contracting and protects against potential losses. A legal regime that adopts a broad conception of offer has the opposite effects. The cases that follow, unsurprisingly, try to balance these benefits and costs against each other.

Fairmount Glass Works v. Crunden–Martin Woodenware Co.

Court of Appeals of Kentucky, 1899.
51 S.W. 196.

Action by the Crunden–Martin Woodenware Company against the Fairmount Glass Works to recover damages for breach of contract. Judgment for plaintiff, and defendant appeals. Affirmed.

■ HOBSON, J. On April 20, 1895, appellee wrote appellant the following letter:

> "St. Louis, Mo., April 20, 1895. Gentlemen: Please advise us the lowest price you can make us on our order for ten car loads of Mason green jars, complete, with caps, packed one dozen in a case, either delivered here, or f. o. b. cars your place, as you prefer. State terms and cash discount. Very truly, Crunden–Martin W. W. Co."

To this letter appellant answered as follows:

> "Fairmount, Ind., April 23, 1895. Crunden–Martin Wooden Ware Co., St. Louis, Mo.–Gentlemen: Replying to your favor of April 20, we quote you Mason fruit jars, complete, in one-dozen boxes, delivered in East St. Louis, Ill.: Pints $4.50, quarts $5.00, half gallons $6.50, per gross, for immediate acceptance, and shipment not later than May 15, 1895; sixty days' acceptance, or 2 off, cash in ten days. Yours, truly, Fairmount Glass Works.

> "Please note that we make all quotations and contracts subject to the contingencies of agencies or transportation, delays or accidents beyond our control."

For reply thereto, appellee sent the following telegram on April 24, 1895:

> "Fairmount Glass Works, Fairmount, Ind.: Your letter twenty-third received. Enter order ten car loads as per your quotation. Specifications mailed. Crunden–Martin W. W. Co."

In response to this telegram, appellant sent the following:

"Fairmount, Ind., April 24, 1895. Crunden–Martin W. W. Co., St. Louis, Mo.: Impossible to book your order. Output all sold. See letter. Fairmount Glass Works."

Appellee insists that, by its telegram sent in answer to the letter of April 23d, the contract was closed for the purchase of 10 car loads of Mason fruit jars. Appellant insists that the contract was not closed by this telegram, and that it had the right to decline to fill the order at the time it sent its telegram of April 24. This is the chief question in the case. The court below gave judgment in favor of appellee, and appellant has appealed, earnestly insisting that the judgment is erroneous.

We are referred to a number of authorities holding that a quotation of prices is not an offer to sell, in the sense that a completed contract will arise out of the giving of an order for merchandise in accordance with the proposed terms. There are a number of cases holding that the transaction is not completed until the order so made is accepted. 7 Am. & Eng. Enc. Law (2d Ed.) p. 138; *Smith v. Gowdy*, 8 Allen, 566; *Beaupre v. Telegraph Co.*, 21 Minn. 155. But each case must turn largely upon the language there used. In this case we think there was more than a quotation of prices, although appellant's letter uses the word "quote" in stating the prices given. The true meaning of the correspondence must be determined by reading it as a whole. Appellee's letter of April 20th, which began the transaction, did not ask for a quotation of prices. It reads: "Please advise us the lowest price you can make us on our order for ten car loads of Mason green jars. State terms and cash discount." From this appellant could not fail to understand that appellee wanted to know at what price it would sell it ten car loads of these jars; so when, in answer, it wrote: "We quote you Mason fruit jars pints $4.50, quarts $5.00, half gallons $6.50, per gross, for immediate acceptance; off, cash in ten days,"—it must be deemed as intending to give appellee the information it had asked for. We can hardly understand what was meant by the words "for immediate acceptance," unless the latter was intended as a proposition to sell at these prices if accepted immediately. In construing every contract, the aim of the court is to arrive at the intention of the parties. In none of the cases to which we have been referred on behalf of appellant was there on the face of the correspondence any such expression of intention to make an offer to sell on the terms indicated. In *Fitzhugh v. Jones*, 6 Munf. 83, the use of the expression that the buyer should reply as soon as possible, in case he was disposed to accede to the terms offered, was held sufficient to show that there was a definite proposition, which was closed by the buyer's acceptance. The expression in appellant's letter, "for immediate acceptance," taken in connection with appellee's letter, in effect, at what price it would sell it the goods, is, it seems to us, much stronger evidence of a present offer, which, when accepted immediately, closed the contract. Appellee's letter was plainly an inquiry for the price and terms on which appellant would sell it the goods, and appellant's answer to it was not a quotation of prices, but a definite offer to sell on the terms indicated, and could not be withdrawn after the terms had been accepted. It will be observed that the telegram of acceptance refers to the specifications mailed. These specifications were contained in the following letter: "St. Louis, Mo., April 24, 1895. Fairmount Glass–Works Co., Fairmount, Ind.–Gentlemen: We received your letter of 23rd this morning, and telegraphed you in reply as follows: 'Your letter 23rd received. Enter order ten car loads as per your quotation. Specifications mailed,'—which we now confirm. We have accordingly entered this contract on our books for the ten cars Mason green jars, complete, with caps and rubbers, one dozen in case, delivered to us in East St. Louis at $4.50 per gross for pint, $5.00 for quart, $6.50 for one-half gallon. Terms, 60 days' acceptance, or 2 per cent. for cash in ten days, to be shipped not later than May 15, 1895. The jars and caps to be strictly first-quality goods. You may ship the first car to us here assorted: Five gross pint, fifty-five gross quart, forty gross one-half gallon. Specifications for the remaining 9 cars we will send later. Crunden–Martin W. W. Co." It is insisted for appellant that this was not an acceptance of the offer as made; that the stipulation, "The jars and caps to be strictly first-quality goods," was not in their offer; and that, it not having been accepted as made, appellant is not bound. But it will be observed that appellant declined to furnish the goods before it got this letter, and in the correspondence with appellee it nowhere complained of these words as an addition to the contract. Quite a number of other letters passed, in which the refusal to deliver the goods was placed on other grounds, none of which have been sustained by the evidence. Appellee offers proof tending to show that these words, in the trade in which parties were engaged, conveyed the same meaning as the words used in appellant's letter, and were only a different form of expressing the same idea. Appellant's conduct would seem to confirm this evidence.

Appellant also insists that the contract was indefinite, because the quantity of each size of the jars was not fixed, that 10 car loads is too indefinite a specification of the quantity sold, and that appellee had no right to accept the goods to be delivered on different days. The proof shows that "10 car loads" is an expression used in the trade as equivalent to 1,000 gross, 100 gross being regarded a car load. The offer to sell the different sizes at different prices gave the purchaser the right to name the quantity of each size, and, the offer being to ship not later than May 15th, the buyer had the right to fix the time of delivery at any time before that. The petition, if defective, was cured by the judgment, which is fully sustained by the evidence. Judgment affirmed.

Lefkowitz v. Great Minneapolis Surplus Store, Inc.

Supreme Court of Minnesota, 1957.
86 N.W.2d 689.

Action arising out of alleged refusal of defendant to sell to plaintiff a certain fur piece which it had offered for sale in a newspaper advertisement. From an order of the Municipal Court, Hennepin County, Lindsay G. Arthur, J., denying defendant's motion for amended findings of fact, or, in the alternative, for a new trial, the defendant appealed. The Supreme

Court, Murphy, J., held that newspaper advertisement of a stole 'worth $139.50' for $1.00, first come, first serve, was a clear, definite, and explicit offer of sale by defendant and left nothing open for negotiation, and plaintiff, who was first to appear at defendant's place of business to be served, was entitled to performance on part of defendant.

Affirmed.

Murphy, J. This is an appeal from an order of the Municipal Court of Minneapolis denying the motion of the defendant for amended findings of fact, or, in the alternative, for a new trial. The order for judgment awarded the plaintiff the sum of $138.50 as damages for breach of contract.

This case grows out of the alleged refusal of the defendant to sell to the plaintiff a certain fur piece which it had offered for sale in a newspaper advertisement. It appears from the record that on April 6, 1956, the defendant published the following advertisement in a Minneapolis newspaper:

'Saturday 9 A.M. Sharp 3 Brand New Fur Coats Worth to $100.00

First Come First Served $1 Each'

On April 13, the defendant again published an advertisement in the same newspaper as follows: 'Saturday 9 A.M. 2 Brand New Pastel Mink 3–Skin Scarfs Selling for.$89.50

Out they go Saturday. Each . . . $1.00

1 Black Lapin Stole Beautiful, worth $139.50 . . . $1.00

First Come First Served'

The record supports the findings of the court that on each of the Saturdays following the publication of the above-described ads, the plaintiff was the first to present himself at the appropriate counter in the defendant's store and on each occasion demanded the coat and the stole so advertised and indicated his readiness to pay the sale price of $1. On both occasions, the defendant refused to sell the merchandise to the plaintiff, stating on the first occasion that by a 'house rule' the offer was intended for women only and sales would not be made to men, and on the second visit that plaintiff knew defendant's house rules.

The trial court properly disallowed plaintiff's claim for the value of the fur coats since the value of these articles was speculative and uncertain. The only evidence of value was the advertisement itself to the effect that the coats were 'Worth to $100.00,' how much less being speculative especially in view of the price for which they were offered for sale. With reference to the offer of the defendant on April 13, 1956, to sell the '1 Black Lapin Stole worth $139.50' the trial court held that the value of this article was established and granted judgment in favor of the plaintiff for that amount less the $1 quoted purchase price.

1. The defendant contends that a newspaper advertisement offering items of merchandise for sale at a named price is a 'unilateral offer' which may be withdrawn without notice. He relies upon authorities which hold

that, where an advertiser publishes in a newspaper that he has a certain quantity or quality of goods which he wants to dispose of at certain prices and on certain terms, such advertisements are not offers which become contracts as soon as any person to whose notice they may come signifies his acceptance by notifying the other that he will take a certain quantity of them. Such advertisements have been construed as an invitation for an offer of sale on the terms stated, which offer, when received, may be accepted or rejected and which therefore does not become a contract of sale until accepted by the seller; and until a contract has been so made, the seller may modify or revoke such prices or terms. *Craft v. Elder & Johnson Co.*, 34 Ohio L.A. 603.

The defendant relies principally on Craft v. Elder & Johnston Co. supra. In that case, the court discussed the legal effect of an advertisement offering for sale, as a one-day special, an electric sewing machine at a named price. The view was expressed that the advertisement was (34 Ohio L.A. 605) 'not an offer made to any specific person but was made to the public generally. Thereby it would be properly designated as a unilateral offer and not being supported by any consideration could be withdrawn at will and without notice.' It is true that such an offer may be withdrawn before acceptance. Since all offers are by their nature unilateral because they are necessarily made by one party or on one side in the negotiation of a contract, the distinction made in that decision between a unilateral offer and a unilateral contract is not clear. On the facts before us we are concerned with whether the advertisement constituted an offer, and, if so, whether the plaintiff's conduct constituted an acceptance.

There are numerous authorities which hold that a particular advertisement in a newspaper or circular letter relating to a sale of articles may be construed by the court as constituting an offer, acceptance of which would complete a contract.

The test of whether a binding obligation may originate in advertisements addressed to the general public is 'whether the facts show that some performance was promised in positive terms in return for something requested.' 1 Williston, Contracts (Rev. ed.) s 27.

The authorities above cited emphasize that, where the offer is clear, definite, and explicit, and leaves nothing open for negotiation, it constitutes an offer, acceptance of which will complete the contract. The most recent case on the subject is *Johnson v. Capital City Ford Co.*, La.App., 85 So.2d 75, in which the court pointed out that a newspaper advertisement relating to the purchase and sale of automobiles may constitute an offer, acceptance of which will consummate a contract and create an obligation in the offeror to perform according to the terms of the published offer.

Whether in any individual instance a newspaper advertisement is an offer rather than an invitation to make an offer depends on the legal intention of the parties and the surrounding circumstances. Annotation, 157 A.L.R. 744, 751; 77 C.J.S., Sales, s 25b; 17 C.J.S., Contracts, s 389. We are of the view on the facts before us that the offer by the defendant of the sale of the Lapin fur was clear, definite, and explicit, and left nothing open for negotiation. The plaintiff having successful managed to be the first one to appear at the seller's place of business to be served, as requested by the advertisement, and having offered the stated purchase price of the article, he was entitled to performance on the part of the defendant. We think the trial court was correct in holding that there was in the conduct of the parties a sufficient mutuality of obligation to constitute a contract of sale.

2. The defendant contends that the offer was modified by a 'house rule' to the effect that only women were qualified to receive the bargains advertised. The advertisement contained no such restriction. This objection may be disposed of briefly by stating that, while an advertiser has the right at any time before acceptance to modify his offer, he does not have the right, after acceptance, to impose new or arbitrary conditions not contained in the published offer.

Affirmed.

Restatement 2d of Contracts

§ 26 Preliminary Negotiations

A manifestation of willingness to enter into a bargain is not an offer if the person to whom it is addressed knows or has reason to know that the person making it does not intend to conclude a bargain until he has made a further manifestation of assent.

Comments & Illustrations

Comment a. Interpretation of proposals for exchange. The rule stated in this Section is a special application of the definition in § 24 and of the principles governing the interpretation of manifestations of assent. See § 20 and Chapter 9. Conduct which resembles an offer may not be so intended either because there is an intent not to affect legal relations (see § 18), or because the actor does not intend to engage in the conduct (see § 19), or because the proposal is not addressed to the recipient or is not received by the addressee (see § 23), or because the proposal contemplates a gift rather than a bargain (see Comment *b* to § 24). This Section deals rather with the case where the actor intends to make a bargain in the future, but only if he makes some further manifestation of assent. If the addressee of a proposal has reason to know that no offer is intended, there is no offer even though he understands it to be an offer. "Reason to know" depends not only on the words or other conduct, but also on the circumstances, including previous communications of the parties and the usages of their community or line of business.

Comment b. Advertising. Business enterprises commonly secure general publicity for the goods or services they supply or purchase. Advertisements of goods by display, sign, handbill, newspaper, radio or television are not ordinarily intended or understood as offers to sell. The same is true of catalogues, price lists and circulars, even though the terms of suggested bargains may be stated in some detail. It is of course possible to make an offer by an advertisement directed to the general public (see § 29), but there must ordinarily be some language of commitment or some invitation to take action without further communication.

Illustrations:

1.   A, a clothing merchant, advertises overcoats of a certain kind for sale at $50. This is not an offer, but an invitation to the public to come and purchase. The addition of the words "Out they go Saturday; First Come First Served" might make the advertisement an offer.

2.   A advertises that he will pay $5 for every copy of a certain book that may be sent to him. This is an offer, and A is bound to pay $5 for every copy sent while the offer is unrevoked.

Comment c. Quotation of price. A "quotation" of price is usually a statement of price per unit of quantity; it may omit the quantity to be sold, time and place of delivery, terms of payment, and other terms. It is sometimes associated with a price list or circular, but the word "quote" is commonly understood as inviting an offer rather than as making one, even when directed to a particular customer. But just as the word "offer" does not necessarily mean that an offer is intended, so the word "quote" may be used in an offer. In determining whether an offer is made relevant factors include the terms of any previous inquiry, the completeness of the terms of the suggested bargain, and the number of persons to whom a communication is addressed.

Illustration:

3.   A writes to B, "I can quote you flour at $5 a barrel in carload lots." This is not an offer, in view of the word "quote" and incompleteness of the terms. The same words, in response to an inquiry specifying detailed terms, would probably be an offer; and if A added "for immediate acceptance" the intent to make an offer would be unmistakable.

Comment d. Invitation of bids or other offers. Even though terms are specified in detail, it is common for one party to request the other to make an offer. The words "Make me an offer" would normally indicate that no offer is being made, and other conduct such as the announcement of an auction may have similar effect. See § 28. A request for bids on a construction project is similar, even though the practice may be to accept the lowest bid conforming to specifications and other requirements. And forms used or statements made by a traveling salesman may make it clear that the customer is making an offer to be accepted at the salesman's home office. See § 69.

Illustration:

4.   A writes B, "I am eager to sell my house. I would consider $20,000 for it." B promptly answers, "I will buy your house for

$20,000 cash." There is no contract. A's letter is a request or suggestion that an offer be made to him. B has made an offer.

Comment e. Written contract documents. A standard method of making an offer is to submit to the offeree a written agreement signed by the offeror and to invite the offeree to sign on a line provided for that purpose. See § 27. But the signature even in such a case is not conclusive if the other party has reason to know that no offer is intended. More common is the use of promissory expressions or words of assent in unsigned documents or letters where the document is intended not as an offer but only as a step in the preliminary negotiation of terms, or as a specimen for use in other transactions, or as something to be shown to a third person to influence his action. Reason to know that such is the intention may exist even though the document on its face seems to be clear and unambiguous.

Comment f. Preliminary manifestations as terms of later offer. Even though a communication is not an offer, it may contain promises or representations which are incorporated in a subsequent offer and hence become part of the contract made when the offer is accepted. Indeed, the preliminary communication may thus form part of a written contract, or of a memorandum satisfying the Statute of Frauds, or of an integrated contract. See Comment *c* to § 20, §§ 132, 202.

* * *

These materials illustrate two basic principles concerning offers. First, as the Restatement section makes plain, price quotations, issued to the world at large, are not considered real offers but rather invitations to bargain. Thus, in a typical retail purchase contract—for example, when a shopper buys a pint of milk at a grocery store—the price tag on the shelf is not an offer but merely an invitation to bargain. The offeror in this case is not the store but the consumer, who makes the offer when she takes the milk to the cash register. The store (through its agent, the check-out-clerk) accepts the offer together with the consumer's money, at which point there is a contract. Second, real offers are constituted not by any formality or magic words but rather the substantive information that they convey. In particular, an utterance is more likely to count as a real offer as it includes more details concerning the terms of the bargain that it contemplates, as it more narrowly and precisely identifies the offerees who may accept it, and as it more fully specifies how to accept (that is, what an acceptance consists in). These principles make perfect sense in light of the benefits and costs associated with real offers identified earlier. As an offer becomes more complete along the dimensions described, its value to an offeree will increase, because the resources expended by the offeree to investigate whether the offer is attractive will yield a greater informational return. At the same time, as an offer more narrowly identifies its addressees and the means of acceptance, the costs that it imposes on the offeror will decrease, since the extent of the liability to which the offeror will expose herself if she is understood to have made a real offer becomes narrower and more predictable.

Fairmount Glass and *Lefkowitz* also illustrate these principles in application to closer cases. In *Fairmount Glass*, the plaintiff asked the defendant to quote his best price for ten car loads of mason jars. The defendant answered: "We quote you: Pints $4.50, quarts $5.00, half-gallons $6.50, per gross, for immediate acceptance, and shipment no later than May 15." The plaintiff answered "Enter order 10 car loads as per your quotation" and in the same day sent a second communication specifying sizes. The court, acknowledging the first principle announced above, accepted that mere price quotations generally do not constitute offers. But the parties' choice of terms does not control, the court observed, and in this case even though plaintiff and defendant both spoke in terms of a "quote," plaintiff clearly asked for not just a quote but an offer, and defendant replied specifically to plaintiff, included instructions about how to accept ("for immediate acceptance"), and the exchange included the key specifications needed fully to fix the terms of the bargain (price, maximum quantity, size, and delivery dates). *Fairmount Glass* turns out, then, to be an easy case, even though the parties' communications do not wear their offer-ness expressly on their sleeves.

Lefkowitz is a harder case.

The defendant placed two advertisements in the newspaper, in successive weeks. The first week's advertisement read:

> Saturday 9 a.m.
>
> 3 New Fur Coats.
>
> Worth to $100.
>
> First come, first served.
>
> $1 each.

The second read:

> Saturday 9 a.m.
>
> 1 Black Lapin Stole.
>
> Worth $139.50.
>
> First come, first served.
>
> $1.

The plaintiff, a man, was the first to arrive at the defendant's store on each Saturday and demanded to buy the coats and the stole on the terms set out in the advertisement. The defendant refused to sell, citing a "house rule" that the deals announced in the advertisements were available to women only. The plaintiff sued, seeking damages equal to the total value of the advertised clothing minus its $4 total price. The defendant argued that there could be no contract because its public advertisement did not constitute an offer, but only an invitation to bargain.

On this question, the court sided with the plaintiff. It observed, again, that the law does not require any magic words in order to find that an offer has been made. Instead, the test is functional: did the communication make clear that "some performance was promised in positive terms in return for something requested?" In this case, the court reasoned, the advertisement identified the terms of the offer—fixing price ($1), quality (value less than or equal to $100 and $139.50), and quantity (three coats, one stole)—and said how to accept—by being the first in the store after 9 am on Saturday. Moreover, these details protected the defendant against open-ended liability by limiting how many people might accept and what they might demand. The balance of benefits and costs, in other words, tilted towards treating the advertisement as an offer. The plaintiff accepted the offer by being the first in line, and so a contract was formed, which the defendant breached by refusing to transfer the items. The only remaining question was the remedy. Here the court reasoned that because the first advertisement did not specify the precise value of the coats, the plaintiff could not prove up his damages and should receive nothing. (Is this reasoning persuasive? Did the advertisement assert a minimum value and hence support a minimum remedy?) The second advertisement differed in this respect, and so the court awarded the plaintiff $138.50 for the defendant's breach.

The court's treatment of the first advertisement persuasively illustrates the general principles concerning offers explained above in application to a set of facts that engage all the relevant distinctions together. The treatment of the second advertisement is less persuasive, however, and it raises a set of structural questions that are worth pursuing. By the time the plaintiff read the second advertisement, after all, he had actual notice that the defendant did not consider the advertisement addressed to him. Speaking doctrinally, the fact that the second advertisement was an offer does not yet settle the question what were the offer's terms. In particular, did the offer contain an implied term that limited its addressees to women only, or perhaps to those who had some interest in the store's other merchandise? And had that implied term been made express to the offeree by the second go 'round?

This possibility, moreover, raises some fundamental questions about the structure of the law of offer. There were, in fact, two contracts (or potential contracts) at issue in connection with each of the defendant's advertisements. The first was the contract for the sale and purchase of the advertised items (the coats, the stole). The second was the contract for the sale and purchase of other items that the defendant hoped to sell from its stock. The defendant's purpose, in exposing itself to the first contract, was to increase the chance of consummating the second. The defendant reasoned that it would be costly for potential customers to take the steps necessary for them to decide to become actual customers: paying for transport to the defendant's store, sacrificing other morning activities. It therefore proposed to pay its customers to incur these costs; and it chose, as the method of payment, not a small payment for every customer, but a chance of a large payment (in the form of the advertised bargains) that would be given to only a few. The coats and the stole were loss leaders.

Lefkowitz therefore illustrates a general problem for contract law: namely that the costs of deciding whether a particular contract is worth making may be distributed across potential contracting parties in various ways, including in ways that hinder efficient contract formation. The defendant, in *Lefkowitz*, obviously believed that the value of the additional sales made to customers who would not have visited its store but for the advertisement exceeded the cost to it of honoring the advertisement's terms. The customers (at least insofar as they took an accurate view of their chances of arriving first and getting the advertised bargains) believed that the expected value of the bargains exceeded their costs in visiting the store. The preliminary engagements of the parties therefore constituted a cost-shifting arrangement designed to ensure efficient joint investment in potential consummated contracts. Finally, this efficient investment could not be secured by adjusting the terms of the contracts ultimately consummated because the investment had to be made by a class of parties (potential customers) that differed from the much smaller class of parties (actual customers) for whom the investment revealed a completed contract to be attractive. At the same time, the pre-contractual transfers should be limited to those potential customers for whom the expected surplus associated with their becoming actual customers exceeds the costs of pre-contractual investments that the transfers reallocate. The plaintiff in *Lefkowitz* did not belong to this class, and by the second week this fact was common knowledge between the plaintiff and the defendant.

These observations reveal that the law governing pre-contractual negotiations may assist potential contract partners in structuring their pre-contractual negotiations efficiently. The next two cases illustrate some of the bargaining contexts in which the law must intervene.

Dyno Construction Company v. McWane, Inc.

United States Court of Appeals, Sixth Circuit, 1999.
198 F.3d 567.

Buyer brought suit alleging various breach of contract claims arising out of its purchase of ductile iron pipe that was later found to be defective. The United States District Court for the Northern District of Ohio, John W. Potter, J., rendered judgment on jury verdict for seller, and buyer appealed. The Court of Appeals, Quist, District Judge, sitting by designation, held that: (1) price quotations were not offers; (2) district court's evidentiary rulings were proper; and (3) district court properly refused to give buyer's proposed instruction.

Affirmed.

■ QUIST, DISTRICT JUDGE. Plaintiff, Dyno Construction Company, sued Defendant, McWane, Inc., alleging various breach of contract claims arising out of Dyno's purchase of ductile iron pipe from McWane that was later found to be defective. The district court denied the parties' cross-motions for summary judgment, and a jury returned a general verdict in favor of McWane. The district court denied Dyno's motion for a new trial. Dyno appeals the order denying its motion for summary judgment, the judgment entered after trial, and the order denying Dyno's motion for a new trial. We find no error and affirm.

I.   FACTUAL AND PROCEDURAL BACKGROUND

Dyno is a company engaged in the business of constructing underground utility projects, specifically underground water and sewer lines. Dyno was purchased in the fall of 1995 by Frederick Harrah, Laymond Lewis, and a third party. Prior to purchasing Dyno, Harrah and Lewis were employees of Reynolds, Inc., a large underground pipeline construction company also in the business of installing underground water and sewer lines.

McWane is a manufacturer and seller of ductile iron pipe and fittings for underground utility projects. Harrah and Lewis frequently purchased pipe from McWane during their employment with Reynolds, as McWane was the exclusive supplier of certain types of ductile iron products to Reynolds.

Sometime shortly before November 6, 1995, Dyno submitted a bid to the City of Perrysburg, Ohio, for a multimillion dollar water and sewer system project. In order to prepare the bid, Lewis contacted various suppliers, including McWane, to obtain quotes for necessary materials. On November 6, 1995, Dyno learned that it was the low bidder on the project and would be awarded the contract.

On November 8, 1995, McWane's district sales manager, Kevin Ratcliffe, faxed Dyno a document containing quantities and prices for the materials Dyno requested for the Perrysburg Project. Ratcliffe sent a second fax to Lewis on November 13, 1995, which included handwritten prices and notes next to each item. On the fax cover sheet, Ratcliffe asked Lewis to "[p]lease call."

On or prior to November 22, 1995, Lewis phoned Ratcliffe and told him to order the materials. Lewis testified at his deposition that he thought that there was a "done deal" when he got off the phone with Ratcliffe. However, after the phone call, Ratcliffe prepared and sent a package to Lewis via Federal Express. The Federal Express package included a purchase order, a credit application, and a cover letter in which Ratcliffe asked Lewis to review and sign the purchase order and credit application and return the originals to Ratcliffe. The purchase order and credit application each stated that the sale of the materials was subject to the terms and conditions printed on the reverse sides of those documents. The reverse side of each document contained additional terms and conditions, including a provision which limited McWane's liability for defective materials. The Federal Express invoice kept in McWane's files showed that Dyno received the package on November 24, 1995, at 8:53 a.m.

Lewis called Ratcliffe on December 1, 1995, to inquire about the status of Dyno's order. Lewis testified that Ratcliffe told him that "you have to sign our forms." Lewis indicated both in his deposition and at trial that he was not surprised when Ratcliffe told him that the purchase order and credit application would have to be signed before McWane would ship the materials. Lewis told Ratcliffe that he had not received the forms Ratcliffe sent via Federal Express and could not find the package in his office. At Lewis' request, in order to expedite the transaction, Ratcliffe faxed Lewis copies of the documents that were sent on November 22, 1995. However, Ratcliffe did not fax the back sides of the documents which included, among other things, this provision limiting McWane's liability:

SELLER SHALL NOT BE LIABLE FOR EXEMPLARY, PUNITIVE, SPECIAL, INCIDENTAL, CONSEQUENTIAL DAMAGES OR EXPENSES, INCLUDING BUT NOT LIMITED TO, LOSS PROFIT REVENUES, LOSS OF USE OF THE GOODS, OR ANY ASSOCIATED GOODS OR EQUIPMENT, DAMAGE TO PROPERTY OF BUYER, COST OF CAPITAL, COST OF SUBSTITUTE GOODS, DOWNTIME, LIQUIDATED DAMAGES, OR THE CLAIMS OF BUYER'S CUSTOMERS FOR ANY OF THE AFORESAID DAMAGES, OR FROM ANY OTHER CAUSE RELATING THERETO, AND SELLER'S LIABILITY HEREUNDER IN ANY CASE IS EXPRESSLY LIMITED TO THE REPLACEMENT (IN THE FORM ORIGINALLY SHIPPED) OF GOODS NOT COMPLYING WITH THIS AGREEMENT, OR, AT SELLER'S ELECTION, TO THE REPAYMENT OF, OR CREDITING BUYER WITH, AN AMOUNT EQUAL TO THE PURCHASE PRICE OF SUCH GOODS PRIOR PAID TO AND RECEIVED BY SELLER, WHETHER SUCH CLAIMS ARE FOR BREACH OF WARRANTY OR NEGLIGENCE.

Dyno signed the faxed pages without the quoted damages limitation provision and returned them to Ratcliffe later that day.

Dyno had substantial problems with the pipes it purchased from McWane. Although McWane repaired and reinstalled the pipe to the satisfaction of Dyno, it refused to pay Dyno for consequential damages suffered as a result of the defects in the pipes on the basis of the limitation of damages provision on the back of the purchase order. Dyno filed this suit in an attempt to recover its consequential damages.

Both parties moved for summary judgment with respect to the question of whether the quoted provision limiting McWane's liability for consequential damages was a part of the Dyno/McWane contract. In denying the motions, the district court rejected Dyno's contention that the two written quotations which Ratcliffe sent to Lewis were offers that Dyno accepted when Lewis informed Ratcliffe that Dyno wished to purchase the pipe from McWane because the quotations were part of preliminary negotiations between the parties. Instead, the court concluded that the contract was formed or, alternatively, modified, when Lewis signed the documents he received from Ratcliffe by fax on December 1, 1995. The district court also rejected as a matter of law McWane's arguments that Dyno's acceptance of documents containing the warranty limitation provision established a course of performance and that a course of dealing was established by Lewis' dealings with McWane while Lewis was employed at Reynolds. Instead, the district court found that McWane's argument that Lewis had knowledge of the disputed provision based upon his receipt of the Federal Express package presented a genuine issue of material fact. Thus, the district court framed the issue for the jury with respect to the limitation of damages provision as whether Lewis knew or should have known about McWane's terms and conditions at the time he signed the fax copy.

At trial, during the conference on jury instructions, the district court rejected Dyno's proposed instruction number 7, which would have allowed the jury to find that the contract had been formed on or before November 22, 1995, on the basis of its ruling with respect to the summary judgment motions that the contract was formed on December 1, 1995. At the conclusion of trial, the jury returned a verdict in favor of McWane.

II. ANALYSIS

A. Summary Judgment

Dyno first contends that the district court erred when it found that the contract was formed on December 1, 1995, rather than on November 22, 1995. Although Dyno does not argue that the denial of its motion for summary judgment was erroneous, Dyno asserts that the determination made by the district court in ruling on the motion that the contract was made on December 1, 1995, when Lewis signed the fax documents, was erroneous.

Dyno asserted in its motion for summary judgment, and continues to argue to this Court, that the contract was actually entered into on November 22, 1995, when Lewis told Ratcliffe to go ahead and order the materials that Ratcliffe had listed in his November 8 and November 13 faxes. Dyno claims that the parties agreed to the essential terms of price, quantity, and description, and any other terms to the contract could be supplied by the "gap-filler" provisions of the Uniform Commercial Code, which do not limit the seller's liability for consequential damages.

In order to prove the existence of a contract, a plaintiff is required to demonstrate the essential requirements of an offer, acceptance, and consideration. *See Helle v. Landmark, Inc.,* 15 Ohio App.3d 1, 8 (1984). A valid and binding contract comes into existence when an offer is accepted. *See Realty Dev., Inc. v. Kosydar,* 322 N.E.2d 328, 332 (Ohio Ct.App.1974) (per curiam). Dyno contends that the written price quotations Ratcliffe faxed to Lewis on November 8, 1995, and November 13, 1995, constituted the offer, which Lewis accepted on behalf of Dyno on or about November 22, 1995, when Lewis told Ratcliffe to order the materials listed on the price quote.

"Typically, a price quotation is considered an invitation for an offer, rather than an offer to form a binding contract." *White Consol. Indus., Inc. v. McGill Mfg. Co.,* 165 F.3d 1185, 1190 (8th Cir.1999). Instead, a buyer's purchase agreement submitted in response to a price quotation is usually deemed the offer. *See Master Palletizer Sys., Inc. v. T.S. Ragsdale Co.,* 725 F.Supp. 1525, 1531 (D.Colo.1989). However, a price quotation may suffice for an offer if it is sufficiently detailed and it "reasonably appear[s] from the price quotation that assent to that quotation is all that is needed to ripen the offer into a contract." *Quaker State Mushroom Co. v. Dominick's Finer Foods, Inc., of Illinois,* 635 F.Supp. 1281, 1284 (N.D.Ill.1986). While the inclusion of a description of the product, price, quantity, and terms of payment may indicate that the price quotation is an offer rather than a mere invitation to negotiate, the determination of the issue depends primarily upon the intention of the person communicating the quotation as demonstrated by all of the surrounding facts and circumstances. *See Interstate Indus., Inc. v. Barclay Indus., Inc.,* 540 F.2d 868, 871 (7th Cir.1976). Thus, to constitute an offer, a price quotation must "be made under circumstances evidencing the express or implied intent of the offeror that its acceptance shall constitute a binding contract." *Maurice Elec. Supply,* 632 F.Supp. at 1087.

In *Interstate Industries, Inc. v. Barclay Industries, Inc.,* 540 F.2d 868 (7th Cir.1976), the court determined that a letter sent by the defendant to the plaintiff stating that the defendant would be able to manufacture fiberglass panels for the plaintiff pursuant to specified standards at certain prices did not constitute an offer. Among other things, the court found that the letter's use of the term "price quotation," lack of language indicating that an offer was being made, and absence of terms regarding quantity, time of delivery, or payment terms established that the letter was not intended as an offer. *See id.* at 873. *Thos. J. Sheehan Co. v. Crane Co.,* 418 F.2d 642 (8th Cir.1969), cited by the court in *Interstate Industries,* concluded that a price list for copper tubing which a supplier furnished to a subcontractor in connection with the latter's bid on a job was merely an invitation to engage in future negotiations. The court observed:

> The only evidence of defendant's alleged September 1963 offer is the oral communication to plaintiff that Crane Company could supply copper for the Mansion House Project at a lower price than originally quoted. Reference was made to the new "Chase" price sheet concerning deliveries in minimum quantities of 5000 pounds or 5000 feet, and that prices for copper would be guaranteed for the "duration of the job." At this time nothing was stated by the defendant or plaintiff as to (1) the time in which plaintiff had to accept the "offer," (2) the quantity of copper tubing, fittings, or other supplies to be ordered, (3) the terms of payment or (4) the time when Crane Company promised to perform.

> The "Chase" price sheet was nothing more than a circular sent to distributors by the manufacturer, Wolverine. Without other terms of commitment, we find that the proposal as to "price protection" was related only to the quoted price as a condition upon which the supplier would be willing *in the future* to negotiate a contract of shipment.

> Prices and price factors quoted by suppliers to contractors for the purposes of aiding contractors to make bid estimates, without more specific terms, do not obligate the supplier to comply with any purchase order upon whatever terms and conditions the contractor may choose to offer at some undetermined date in the

future. The fact that the prices quoted are not withdrawn or that a withdrawal of them is not communicated to the contractor is immaterial. No duty exists to revoke terms which without words of commitment merely quote an existing price at which a contract of purchase might be negotiated.

Thos. J. Sheehan, 418 F.2d at 645–46 (italics in original).

Similarly, in *Day v. Amax, Inc.,* 701 F.2d 1258 (8th Cir.1983), the Seventh Circuit affirmed the district court's grant of a directed verdict to the defendant on the issue of whether the defendant's description of mining equipment and a quotation of prices constituted an offer, reasoning that "[a]lthough questions of intent are usually for the jury to decide ... the record discloses no evidence that any of the defendants manifested an intent to enter into a contract with [the plaintiff]." *Id.* at 1263. Thus, the plaintiff's evidence that the defendant had given the plaintiff signed writings containing detailed descriptions of the mining equipment and the terms of sale and had set up an escrow account were insufficient to demonstrate the defendant's intent to enter into a contract. *See id.* at 1264–65; *accord Maurice Elec. Supply,* 632 F.Supp. at 1088 (concluding that the defendant's price quote "was simply a statement of price for three individual high mast poles of varying height" because "[i]t did not specify quality or quantity, time and place of delivery, or terms of payment" and "[t]here was no promise that the quote would remain open for a specified period of time").

In contrast to the cases discussed above, the court in *Bergquist Co. v. Sunroc Corp.,* 777 F.Supp. 1236 (E.D.Pa.1991), found that the question of whether the price quotation at issue constituted an offer was a question of fact for the jury. Some of the factors cited by the court as creating an issue for the jury were: (i) the price quotation was developed by the defendant after the parties had engaged in substantial negotiations; (ii) the quotation included a description of the product, a list of various quantities at various prices, terms of payment, and delivery terms; (iii) the quotation contained the statement "This quotation is offered for your acceptance within 30 days"; and (iv) the price which the purchaser paid was the price listed in the price quotation rather than the price listed in the purchaser's subsequent purchase order. *See id.* at 1249.

In this case, the facts before the district court furnished a sufficient basis for it to conclude as a matter of law that the contract was formed when Lewis signed the fax from Ratcliffe on December 1, 1995, rather than when Lewis told Ratcliffe to order the materials on November 22, 1995. In particular, neither the November 8 nor the November 13 price quotations contained words indicating that Ratcliffe intended to make an offer to Dyno. The word "Estimate" was printed at the top of the document faxed on November 8, and the message "Please call" was printed on the cover sheet for the document faxed on November 13. These words are indicative of an invitation to engage in future negotiations rather than an offer to enter into a contract. Although both price lists set forth descriptions of the materials, prices, and quantities, nothing was stated about the place of delivery, time of performance, or terms of payment. *See Litton Microwave Cooking Prods.,* 15 F.3d at 795 (rejecting the contention that the defendant's price letters and catalogs, which failed to address the place of delivery, quantities, and availability of parts to be purchased were not offers). Finally, the fact that Lewis voluntarily signed the December 1 fax demonstrated that he understood that a binding contract had not been formed as a result of the previous price quotations sent by Ratcliffe. In light of these facts, we agree with the district court that McWane's price quotations did not constitute offers and that the contract was formed on December 1, 1995.

III.   CONCLUSION

For the foregoing reasons, the judgment of the district court is AFFIRMED.

Izadi v. Machado (Gus) Ford, Inc.

District Court of Appeal of Florida, Third District, 1989.
550 So.2d 1135.

Buyer brought action against car dealer, alleging breach of contract, fraud, and statutory violations involving misleading advertising. The Circuit Court, Dade County, George Orr, J., dismissed. Buyer appealed. The District Court of Appeal, Schwartz, C.J., held that: (1) complaint stated cause of action for breach of contract; (2) no cause of action for fraud was properly stated; and (3) complaint properly alleged claims for violations of Deceptive and Unfair Trade Practices Act.

Affirmed in part, reversed in part and remanded.

■ SCHWARTZ, CHIEF JUDGE. This is an appeal from the dismissal with prejudice of a three count complaint for damages arising out of the following advertisement placed by the appellee in the February 21, 1988 edition of the Miami Herald:

The complaint, the allegations of which must at this stage be regarded as true, alleged that the plaintiff Izadi attempted to purchase a 1988 Ford Ranger Pick–Up—the vehicle referred to at the foot of the ad-by tendering Gus Machado Ford $3,595 in cash and an unspecified trade-in.[2] The proposal was made on the basis of his belief that the ad offered $3,000 as a "minimum trade-in allowance" for any vehicle, regardless of its actual value. As is elaborated below, the putative grounds for this understanding were that the $3,000 trade-in figure was prominently referred to at the top of the ad apparently as a portion of the consideration needed to "buy a new Ford" and that it was also designated as the projected deduction from the $7,095 gross cost for the Ranger Pick–Up. Machado, however, in fact refused to recognize this interpretation of its advertisement and turned Izadi down. In doing so, it apparently relied instead on the infinitesimally

---

2. Although the value of the proposed trade-in was not stated, it may be readily assumed that it was substantially less than $3,000.

small print under the $3,000 figure which indicated it applied only toward the purchase of "any New '88 Eddie Bauer Aerostar or Turbo T–Bird in stock"—neither of which was mentioned in the remainder of the ad-and the statements in the individual vehicle portions that the offer was based on a trade-in that was "*worth* $3,000." [e.s.] Izadi then brought the present action based on claims of breach of contract, fraud and statutory violations involving misleading advertising. We hold that the trial judge erroneously held the contract and misleading advertising counts insufficient, but correctly dismissed the claim for fraud.

1. *Breach of Contract.* We first hold, on two somewhat distinct but closely related grounds, that the complaint states a cause of action for breach of an alleged contract which arose when Izadi accepted an offer contained in the advertisement, which was essentially to allow $3,000 toward the purchase of the Ranger for any vehicle the reader-offeree would produce, or, to put the same proposed deal in different words, to sell the Ranger for $3,595, plus any vehicle.

(a) It is of course well settled that a completed contract or, as here, an allegedly binding offer must be viewed as a whole, with due emphasis placed upon each of what may be inconsistent or conflicting provisions. *NLRB v. Federbush Co.*, 121 F.2d 954, 957 (2d Cir.1941) ("Words are not pebbles in alien juxtaposition; they have only a communal existence; and not only does the meaning of each interpenetrate the other, but all in their aggregate take their purport from the setting in which they are used."); *Transport Rental Systems, Inc. v. Hertz Corp.*, 129 So.2d 454, 456 (Fla.3d DCA 1961) ("The real intention, as disclosed by a fair consideration of all parts of a contract, should control the meaning given to mere words or particular provisions when they have reference to the main purpose."). In this case, that process might well involve disregarding both the superfine print and apparent qualification as to the value of the trade-in, as contradictory to the far more prominent thrust of the advertisement to the effect that $3,000 will be allowed for any trade-in on any Ford. *Transport Rental Systems, Inc. v. Hertz Corp.*, 129 So.2d at 456 ("If a contract contains clauses which are apparently repugnant to each other, they must be given such an interpretation as will reconcile them."). We therefore believe that the complaint appropriately alleges that, objectively considered, the advertisement indeed contained just the unqualified $3,000 offer which was accepted by the plaintiff. On the face of the pleadings, the case thus is like many previous ones in which it has been held, contrary to what is perhaps the usual rule, see 1 Williston on Contracts § 27 (W. Jaeger 3d ed. 1957), that an enforceable contract arises from an offer contained in an advertisement.

Of course, if an offer were indeed conveyed by an objective reading of the ad, it does not matter that the car dealer may subjectively have not intended for its chosen language to constitute a binding offer. As Williston states:

[T]he test of the true interpretation of an offer or acceptance is not what the party making it thought it meant or intended it to mean, but what a reasonable person in the position of the parties would have thought it meant.

1 Williston on Contracts § 94, at 339–340. That rule seems directly to apply to this situation.

(b) As a somewhat different, and perhaps more significant basis for upholding the breach of contract claim, we point to the surely permissible conclusion from the carefully chosen language and arrangement of the advertisement itself that Machado-although it did not intend to adhere to the $3,000 trade-in representation-affirmatively, but wrongly sought to make the public believe that it would be honored; that, in other words, the offer was to be used as the "bait" to be followed by a "switch" to another deal when the acceptance of that offer was refused. Indeed, it is difficult to offer any other explanation for the blanket representation of a $3,000 trade-in for *any* vehicle—which is then hedged in sub-microscopic print to apply only to two models which were not otherwise referred to in the ad-or the obvious non-coincidence that the only example of the trade-in for the three vehicles which was set out in the ad was the very same $3,000. This situation invokes the applicability of a line of persuasive authority that a binding offer may be implied from the very fact that deliberately misleading advertising intentionally leads the reader to the conclusion that one exists. See Corbin on Contracts § 64, at 139 (Supp.1989) (where "bait and switch" advertising suspected, public policy "ought to justify a court in holding deceptive advertising to be an offer despite the seller's ... intent not to make any such offer"). In short, the dealer can hardly deny that it did not mean what it purposely misled its customer into believing. This doctrine is expressed in the Restatement (Second) of Contracts which states:

§ 20.   Effect of Misunderstanding

2.   The manifestations of the parties are operative in accordance with the meaning attached to them by one of the parties if

that party does not know of any different meaning attached by the first party[.]

Restatement (Second) of Contracts § 20(2)(a) (1981); Restatement (Second) of Contracts § 20(2)(a) comment d ("[I]f one party knows the other's meaning and manifests assent intending to insist on a different meaning, he may be guilty of misrepresentation. Whether or not there is such misrepresentation as would give the other party the power of avoidance, there is a *contract* under Subsection (2)(a), and the mere negligence of the other party is immaterial." [e.s.]).

In *Johnson v. Capital City Ford Co.*, 85 So.2d 75 (La.App.1955), the court dealt with a case very like this one, in which the issue was whether a newspaper advertisement stating that any purchaser who bought a 1954 automobile before a certain date could exchange it for a newer model without an extra charge constituted a binding offer. The dealership argued that, despite the plain wording of the advertisement, it had no intention of making an offer, but merely sought to lure customers to the sales lot; it claimed also that, because of the small print at the bottom of the contract, any promises by the purchaser to exchange the vehicle for a later model were not binding. The court rejected these contentions on the holding that a contract had been formed even though the dealership "had an erroneous belief as to what the advertisement, as written, meant, or what it would legally convey." *Johnson*, 85 So.2d at 80. As the court said: "There is entirely too much disregard of law and truth in the business, social, and political world of to-day. It is time to hold men to their primary engagements to tell the truth and observe the law of common honesty and fair dealing." *Johnson, 85 So.2d at 82*. We entirely agree.

2.   *Fraud*. Because no cognizable damages arising out of any alleged tortuous misrepresentation were alleged in the complaint, we agree that no cause of action for fraud was stated. See *National Aircraft Servs., Inc. v. Aeroserv Int'l, Inc.*, 544 So.2d 1063 (Fla. 3d DCA 1989). Thus, that count was properly dismissed.

3.   *Statutory Violation*. It follows from what we have said concerning the allegedly misleading nature of the advertisement in making an offer which the advertiser did not intend to keep, that the complaint properly alleged claims for violations of the Florida Deceptive and Unfair Trade Practices Act, sections 501.201–501.213, Florida Statutes (1987), and the statutory prohibition against misleading advertising, section 817.41, Florida Statutes (1987).

* * *

These cases illustrate two important and recurring themes in pre-contractual negotiations. The first is the back-and-forth that occurs as the parties narrow the range of their disagreements and converge on a deal. As they engage in this back-and-forth, the parties typically make sequential investments in determining whether or not a deal will produce surplus to be shared. When the law determines the point at which a contract exists, it allocates the costs and benefits of these investments. But the all-or-nothing character of the law's approach to finding contractual liability—either an utterance is an offer, which creates a contract on acceptance; or it is an invitation to bargain, in which case there is no liability at all—is a blunt instrument for doing the apportioning.

The second theme concerns party efforts to manipulate negotiations in order unfairly or exploitatively to allocate the costs of pre-contractual investment or the gains from contracting. Public advertisements may be efforts to encourage potential buyers to expend costs in considering contracts that are not actually worth considering—whose expected gains are smaller than the expected costs of learning them. Alternatively, where sellers offer payments to buyers as compensation for the cost of considering their offers, the buyers might take the payments but never really consider the offers.

Begin by considering the first theme. *Dyno Construction* exemplifies the back and forth of precontractual negotiations and the bluntness of the law's all-or-nothing approach to liability. In that case the parties engaged in a series of communications that slowly converged on a deal for the sale and purchase of pipe. At first, even the price term was open. That was fixed when the defendant faxed its price list. Then the plaintiff telephoned and the previously provisional quantity became fixed. But even at this stage, the remedy terms of the contract remained open, in particular the terms to govern consequential damages. The defendant wanted to exclude consequential damages from the plaintiff's remedy and sent first a package and then a fax containing a form that included the exclusion. The plaintiff presumably wanted the damages included, but it never expressly said anything concerning the matter. Eventually, the pipes and the purchase money changed hands. The pipes were used by the plaintiff and failed, causing consequential losses.

Depending on when the contract was formed, the defendant's proposed exclusion of consequential damages was either out or in. If the contract was formed on the telephone, then the exclusion was out, as it had not yet been communicated to the plaintiff. If the contract was formed by the later package or fax, then the exclusion was in, and the defendant was protected. (Presumably this is because, although the plaintiff never read the package and the faxed form did not reproduce the side containing the exclusion, the plaintiff was familiar with the defendant's forms and so knew constructively of the exclusion once it knew that the defendant had in this case insisted on its form.) The court held for the defendant, finding that his price quotation was not the offer, so that the plaintiff's telephone call fixing quantity could not be an acceptance. To be sure, a price quotation may become an offer, roughly if it includes sufficient detail so that a buyer's assent is all that's needed to form an operable contract. But in this case, the court concluded, there was so much detail missing from the quotation, and the language of the quotation (which included "estimate" and "please call") so advertised its incompleteness, that the quotation failed to constitute an offer as a matter of law. Accordingly, the offer became the buyer's purchase order, sent after receipt of the seller's form and printed on that form, which included, constructively, at least, the limitation of liability from the seller's form. The seller then accepted, and shipped the goods, subject to the limitation of liability written by the seller but included in the *buyer's* offer.

Now, the first thing to note about this analysis is its high formalism. To begin with, the seller drafted what was treated as the buyer's offer, which the buyer merely signed and sent. While there is no necessary reason why one party can't adopt bargaining language proposed by the other, this does not seem the most natural reconstruction of the social and business realities of the parties' bargaining in this case. Moreover, the law, as set out in *Dyno Construction*, adopts a nothing-or-all approach to contract liability. The only way to create a contract or indeed anything contract-like, on this model, is through offer and acceptance. And offer and acceptance are understood in such a way that only utterances complete enough to elaborate a final contract count as offers and may be accepted. All communications that precede such offers are therefore rendered, by this approach, contractually and legally inert. They do not alter even the potential legal liabilities of the parties at all. Pre-contractual negotiations, on this approach, are utterly immune to contract law.

This legal order departs significantly from the lived experience of negotiations, in which the parties converge by stages on the terms of their final deal. And although the parties do not acquire the full set of obligations described by this bargain until it is struck (until a final offer is accepted), the back-and-forth in which the parties engage on the way to this deal is not—in the social or moral register—obligationally inert. Instead, there exist social and moral norms governing bargaining, which establish increasing obligation along the way to a final deal. As bargaining parties incur greater and greater costs in their negotiations, or sometimes even just as they become increasingly familiar with each other, they come to assume greater solidarity. This solidarity, moreover, underwrites reasons against exploiting or betraying the bargaining relationship. And these reasons can establish liability in at least some circumstances in which the ultimate bargain is never achieved.

Some legal systems acknowledge this directly, for example through the civil law duty of good faith in negotiations. Even the common law, as some of the materials that follow will explain, recognizes that some legal duties can arise out of pre-contractual negotiations: principles of promissory estoppel limit a promisor's freedom to back out of a promise even if it has not created a contract through the ordinary mechanisms of offer and acceptance; and parties may agree, expressly and perhaps even by clear implication, to assume obligations to proceed in a certain way in their pre-contractual bargaining, including even to bargain in good faith. But promissory estoppel is sometimes limited to serving as a corrective for cases in which another conventional requirement of contractual obligation—consideration—fails; and obligations concerning bargaining behavior must generally be expressly assumed, reciprocally, by those who come under them. Thus there exists a tendency, in the common law, to understand such pre-contractual obligations *on the model of the completed contract*—in effect, in terms of a nest of completed contracts, in which the parties make one contract to govern their efforts to make another—rather than to recognize that contractual obligation can arise even in the absence of the ordinary formalities associated with offer and acceptance. There is in this respect a gap between the high formalism of even the modern law and contractual practice on the ground.

Now consider the second theme, which may be helpfully elaborated in terms of the first. That is, it can happen that one party exploits the solidarity associated with pre-contractual bargaining. The defendant in *Lefkowitz* may be understood to argue that the plaintiff did just this, by appropriating a subsidy that the store offered to defray potential customers' pre-contractual investments even though his own obvious lack of interest in buying anything else from the store made clear that he did not belong to the class of potential customers whose investments the store sought to encourage and hence whose costs it intended to defray. Of course, that is not the only possible view of the matter. Thus the plaintiff might have argued, although he seems not to have done, that the breach of bargaining solidarity came from the defendant, whose store's advertisement was designed to lure potential customers into making investments whose costs would not be defrayed, and which would benefit not them but the store.

These possibilities are elaborated in greater detail, and with more realism and more at stake, in *Izadi*. The defendant, in that case, placed an advertisement in a newspaper that promised

The plaintiff tried to buy a new Ford Ranger pickup truck, one of the vehicles referred to in the advertisement, by offering to pay the truck's sticker price, minus $3000, plus his old car. The defendant refused, relying on exceedingly fine print under the $3000 figure saying that the trade in allowance applied to the purchase of certain models only, among which the Ford Ranger was not included, and on statements, made elsewhere in the advertisement, that the $3000 offer was based on trade-ins "worth $3000." The plaintiff sued.

The court held for the plaintiff. It began by trying to reconcile the meaning of the several parts of the advertisement: the prominent text announcing a generally applicable trade-in allowance of $3000 (what might "minimum" mean other than that the allowance, or a greater one, applied to *all* vehicles and *all* trade-ins); and the various less prominent pieces of text restricting the allowance to purchases of certain model cars and to traded-in cars with a certain value. The court observed that the defendant knew and indeed intended customers, including the plaintiff, to focus on the general promise and to neglect the restrictions. That is what the combination of large and small print, and central and marginal layout placement, was designed to accomplish. In such a case, the court argued, in which one party conveys two meanings but knows and indeed intends its counterparty to receive only one of them, the content of the speaking party's utterance is the meaning it intends to be received. This is a direct application of the objective theory of offer. The court is saying, in effect, that a reasonable reader of the advertisement would take the defendant to be announcing a generally applicable $3000 trade-in. The small print, the court thinks, is literally an effort at mis-representation (an effort to render the true content of the advertisement other than what its reasonable reader would think). And in such a case, the court thinks, the advertiser is stuck with the meaning that she knew her audience would take from her utterances.

This may all be right, as far as it goes. (Indeed, it looks forward to principles of contract interpretation that will figure prominently in some of the materials to come.) But the court's argument does not settle the real doctrinal issue in the case, which is not what the advertisement *means*—not the content of the defendant's communication—but rather whether that communication, whatever it means, counts legally as an offer *at all*. The court's only engagement with this question simply *asserts*, without any argument and citing *Lefkowitz*, that the advertisement is an offer and not just (as advertisements usually are) an invitation to bargain.

It is hard to see how the court could be right on this point (certainly, the court is not *obviously* right, and it never bothers to argue for its conclusion). In *Lefkowitz*, the court treated an advertisement as a real offer because the advertisement specified the means of acceptance and, moreover, chose means that automatically limited the number of acceptances that the advertiser might receive, and hence the number of contracts it would be liable for. (Indeed, the advertisements, when they said "first come, first served" set the limit very narrowly, at three and one.) The advertisement in *Lefkowitz* thus protected the defendant store against open-ended contractual liabilities, so that a holding finding it an offer imposed relatively few costs on the defendant, or on advertisers generally.

In *Izadi*, by contrast, the advertisement contained no such analogous limitations. The court's holding therefore exposed the defendant (really, future advertisers who employ language like the defendant's) to open-ended, and potentially very great, contractual liabilities. In principle, there is no ceiling on the number of buyers who might "accept" the defendant's offer, and hence on the number of trade-in allowances that the defendant might have to make. But this shows that, in principle, the advertisement in *Izadi* just is a price quotation—it is structurally equivalent to an advertisement that proposes to sell cars and trucks for roughly $3000 (really, the difference between $3000 and the, likely very small, value of the traded-in vehicles) below their usual prices. And the general rule in consumer purchase transactions makes the merchant's public price quotation merely an invitation to bargain, so that the consumer becomes the offeree when she lays down her money, leaving the merchant free to reject. Accordingly *this* advertisement would surely not constitute an offer. And so it is hard to see why the court concluded, so quickly and confidently, that the advertisement in *Izadi* was an offer.

Such a clear doctrinal error screams out for an explanation. (It is not that a court could *never* fall into so simple a doctrinal confusion; rather, it is that a court is unlikely to fall into such clear confusion without being motivated to do so by some substantial consideration, so that even if the court is genuinely confused, and not just manipulating doctrine to produce results that it likes, the confusion is not simply gratuitous.) The natural explanation, in *Izadi*, is that the court disapproved of the defendant's business and advertising practices. The court believed that the defendant was employing a strategy much like the one that the Great Minneapolis Surplus Store believed Mr. Lefkowitz employed, at least on his second trip to claim the loss-leader: a strategy designed exploitatively to manipulate the allocation of pre-contractual negotiation costs to the advantage of one or the other negotiating party. Thus, where Mr. Lefkowitz sought to exploit a seller subsidy for pre-contractual investigations that was not aimed at subsidizing him, the defendant Ford–Dealer in *Izadi* sought to encourage customers to incur pre-contractual costs by appearing to promise a subsidy that it did not actually intend to provide most (many?) potential customers who incurred the costs. The advertisement was designed, in the court's view, to lure customers to its dealership with false promises in the hope that, once there, they would, having incurred the costs of going to the lot, buy a car even if the advertisement's promises were not kept. This is what the court had in mind when it referred to the defendant's bait-and-switch selling tactics and observed that the plaintiff had properly stated a claim under Florida's Unfair Trade Practices Act.

Accept, at least provisionally (and probably conclusively) that the *Izadi* defendant's business practices were undesirable and even unfair, and indeed unfair in the way that the court had in mind when it reached its result. Accept also that the law should properly be concerned to prevent negotiating parties—both buyers and sellers—from exploitatively manipulating the allocation of the costs incurred in investigating and ultimately reaching a bargain. The question remains, however, what is the proper doctrinal route to this result. The route that the court adopted—finding that the advertisement constituted an offer—is clearly not doctrinally sustainable. The court, one might say, introduced an inconsistency in the law of offer. So the question arises why it did so. What doctrinal alternatives were available to it, and what motivated the decision to proceed in contract law, and the doctrinal error that this way of proceeding involved?

The most immediate alternative route to remedying and preventing the defendant's abuse in *Izadi* involves tort law, and in particular the law of misrepresentation and even fraud. Certainly an ordinary observer considering *Izadi* would think that the defendant had somehow cheated the plaintiff. And fraud is the legal idea that most naturally captures the ordinary concept *cheating*. As it turns out, however, fraud suffers at least two shortcomings as a doctrinal path for dealing with the kind of wrong committed by the *Izadi* defendant. The first has been corrected in the law; the second has not been, and likely cannot be.

To see the first problem with approaching *Izadi* as a case of fraud, recall that fraud is a species of tort and return to the distinction between contract and tort damages elaborated in Part I, indeed, at the very beginning of that Part, in the discussion of *Sullivan v. O'Connor*. Thus, contract damages—specifically through the expectation remedy—seek to bring a plaintiff to the position that she would have occupied had the breaching defendant performed his contract: this is the $138.50 difference between the value of the stole and the $1 Mr. Lefkowitz would have had to pay for it; and the difference between the $3000 promised trade-in and the true value of Mr. Izadi's car. Tort damages, by contrast, emphasize reliance, seeking to place the plaintiff in the position that she would occupy but for the defendant's wrong, generally to return her to the status quo ante, which, for cases involving misrepresentation, is the position the plaintiff would occupy if he had never received, or believed, or acted upon, the defendant's false utterance: Mr. Lefkowitz and Mr. Izadi would receive compensation for the time, expense, and effort that they expended in traveling to Great Minneapolis Surplus Store, or Machado Ford.

These are very different remedies, not just structurally but also, especially in cases like *Lefkowitz* and *Izadi*, quantitatively. Certainly Mr. Izadi's costs in going to the defendant's dealership were nowhere near the value of the promised trade-in allowance. Quite possibly, they were 100 times less. Probably, the reliance remedy is not enough to be worth pursuing for individual plaintiffs, so that a reliance-based remedial regime would not provide defendants with any practical incentive to stop the offending advertisements. Indeed, even if some (stubborn or mad) plaintiffs did pursue the reliance remedy, and succeeded at recovering reliance damages, the payments would still not suffice to deter defendants from the deceptive advertising. Rather, defendants could, and likely would, simply continue their misleading advertisements and simply pay those who chose aggressively to complain. So if the law wants effectively to stop defendants' misconduct in this area, it must employ more than the traditional tort remedy; and the contract remedy seems to fit the bill. It gives plaintiffs the full value of what they reasonably believed defendants had promised, which value is typically large enough to encourage plaintiffs to pursue it and to deter defendants from making their misrepresentations to begin with.

Tort law has recognized this difficulty and departed from its usual remedy scheme for cases of fraud. Chapter 16 will take up the connections between contract and the misrepresentation torts in detail. For now, observe simply that § 549(2) of the Restatement (Second) of Torts gives an innocent victim of fraudulent misrepresentation tort damages as necessary "to give him the benefit of his contract." This produces the incentives described in the prior paragraph. It also cures what might otherwise seem (and what historically did seem) an anomaly. Insofar as a fraudulent promisor does not intend to assume an obligation, the subjective theory of contractual intent would ordinarily have shielded fraudsters from contract liability, indeed, it would have shielded them in virtue of the very nature of their frauds. By contrast, merely negligent misrepresenters might well have subjectively intended to assume their obligations. Accordingly, negligent misrepresenters might have been liable in contract, and hence liable for greater damages than their more culpable intentionally fraudulent counterparts. This, it was thought, could not be right. And the natural solution was to construct an exception to the subjective theory of intent for cases of fraud.[9] Indeed, this solution has already appeared in these materials. It is the driving theme of *Plate v. Durst*. It is also one of the themes of *Izadi*, for example, when the court notes that:

> Of course, if an offer were indeed conveyed by an objective reading of the ad, it does not matter that the car dealer may subjectively have not intended for its chosen language to convey a binding offer [or indeed, the court might have added, that the car dealer may subjectively have intended just the opposite].

This is all very well, as far as it goes. But note that these considerations do not actually address the central doctrinal issue in *Izadi*. In *Plate*, as in the typical instance of fraud, there is no doubt that the defendant's utterances would be understood by a reasonable observer to convey an *attractive offer*. Both italicized words matter: the offer is *attractive*, which is what draws the fraud's victim into it; and the offer is a real *offer*, so that the fraud victim is reasonably justified in thinking that her assent is all that is needed to conclude a bargain. In *Izadi*, by contrast, the defendant's utterances are reasonably understood to convey an attractive *invitation to bargain*, but although they state very attractive terms, they are, and would (according to standard doctrine) reasonably be understood to be, *merely an invitation*.

The *Izadi* court, in effect, elided this distinction between content and form. But the elision is difficult to justify. Because the question, with respect to form, is not whether the plaintiff reasonably thought that the defendant was proposing attractive bargaining terms (he surely did), but rather whether the plaintiff reasonably thought that the defendant was proposing to be bound by these terms just in case the plaintiff accepted the advertisement. And here it seems that the plaintiff probably was *not* reasonable. Most readers of advertisements probably do not believe that the advertisers are opening themselves up to legal obligations, on the advertise-

---

9. Note that the fraudster's precise intent raises complicated questions. Does she intend to assume an obligation (on the model of contract), but not to honor it; or does she not intend even to assume the obligation?

ments' terms, *merely by publishing the advertisements*. Certainly *Lefkowitz* stands for a very different legal rule.

Moreover, this distinction—between intent to mislead concerning the content of a bargaining position and intent to mislead concerning the formal question whether or not an offer has been made—matters not just for contract doctrine but also for tort. Tort law defines fraud narrowly, and in particular in a fashion that makes knowledge of the fraudulent representation's inaccuracy—what the law calls *scienter*—into one of the tort's elements.[10] And it is not at all clear—indeed, it is probably not even *likely*—that the defendant in *Izadi* knew that his advertisement would inaccurately convey to the plaintiff that it was making an offer. Indeed, it may be that the defendant is entitled to rely on the plaintiff's knowledge of the underlying law. Thus, although the defendant may well have knowingly misled the plaintiff, the deception concerned only the defendant's initial suggestion for bargaining. And the remedy for this deception cannot plausibly be to hold the defendant to a bargain that it never actually offered to make. Instead, the most natural remedy is to allow the plaintiff to recover the costs that he incurred in going to the defendant's dealership in reliance on a more favorable negotiation than he actually could expect. But this is precisely the remedy that is inadequate to deterring the defendant's deceptive advertising.

So the result in *Izadi* is at odds with the doctrinal structure of both contract and tort. Nor, finally, is this an accident. Both doctrinal orders seek to strike a balance between the two sets of legal interests described earlier: on the one hand, the interests of those who read advertisements in knowing the bargain that they might make before investing resources in determining whether or not this bargain is attractive; and, on the other, the interests that advertisers have in being able to induce potential buyers to make these investments without exposing themselves open-endedly to legal obligations based on the unilateral actions of buyers. Balancing these interests requires advertisers both to be able to make real offers and to be able to describe their bargaining positions without making real offers. The formal distinctions in contract and tort—the doctrinal details over which *Izadi* runs roughshod—represent the law's effort at balancing. By ignoring these distinctions, *Izadi* chills advertisements by sellers who wish merely to invite bargaining, as these may now be treated as offers. This harms the sellers. It also harms their potential buyers, who will as a result face a less rich information environment in which to make their decisions about which potential bargains to invest in investigating.

An instrumental approach to law, of the type pursued in Part I of these materials, would now seek to establish the optimal balance between these competing considerations. In the current context, however, a different kind

---

10. See Restatement (Second) of Torts § 526. Note that liability for fraud also requires that a plaintiff has justifiably relied on the defendant's fraudulent misrepresentation. This requirement will be taken up in detail in Chapter 16. For now, note only that its complexity appears even in *Izadi*. Did the plaintiff rely (justifiably) on the defendant's advertisement's constituting an offer; a fair and accurate statement of his initial bargaining position?

of question comes to the fore—one that concerns the various styles of striking the balance that a legal order might adopt. The common law—both in contract and in tort—has sought to balance the benefits and costs of treating utterances as real offers through a series of formal distinctions: between offers and mere invitations to bargain in contract; and concerning scienter in tort. What it means for these to be formal is that they are *general in scope*—they employ broadly applicable concepts from philosophy and psychology (intention, knowledge, and indeed offer itself, which is a normative fundamental)—and that they support a *small number of discontinuous legal relationships* (in this case, two each: contract, no contract; and fraud; no fraud). Cases are decided, on this approach, by applying general distinctions in concert to particular sets of facts, to see on which side of the distinctions the facts lie. In this respect, the doctrinal structure of offer is analogous to the doctrinal structure of contract remedies, which also emphasizes the various formal interests (or categories of loss) that the law seeks to vindicate (redress), and makes the quantum of damages into merely an afterthought.

Such formalism may well have advantages—to which the argument will return in Part III—but it also has obvious drawbacks. In particular, the law's formalism is responsible for both the mismatch between the legal and the sociological accounts of bargaining (the fact that the law makes contractual obligation all-or-nothing whereas the sociology of bargaining recognizes an increasing scale of solidaristic engagement) and the mismatch between the legal remedies for deceptive bargaining and the incentives needed optimally to encourage good bargaining behavior (the fact that the law is stuck awarding either de minimis reliance damages or oppressive expectation damages whereas optimal incentives almost certainly require something in between).

Probably the reason why the common law insists on formalism even at the cost of accepting these drawbacks has to do with technical and political limitations on the capacity of courts: technical limitations on courts' ability to identify the optimal balance even in particular cases and certainly in general; and political limitations on courts' legitimate authority to make decisions that obviously reflect contested judgments concerning how best to balance the conflicting interests of various social groups. Thus it is surely no coincidence that, in the case of offer, the legislature has been tempted to step in and make its will felt (even if it has not fully settled matters): the court in *Izadi* refers, after all, to Florida's Unfair Trade Practices Act (even if the Act seems not to have compelled a resolution of the case at hand). The legislature plausibly does have both the technical and political capacity to strike the required balance. Most immediately, it can prohibit specific forms of misleading language (and fix conceptually arbitrary remedies at the level needed optimally to enforce the prohibition) and even mandate clarificatory language. These choices are not bound by the formal matrices offer/invitation to bargain and fraud/no fraud. Instead, they fix the substance of what can be said at whatever point, along the continuum between total and complete accuracy and total freedom to mislead, that the legislature thinks optimal.

Finally, the fact that courts cannot achieve this substantive balance skillfully or openly does not mean that they are immune to the reasons that make the balancing act appealing. Instead, courts inevitably seek, even as they pay lip-service (and sometimes more than lip-service) to the formal categories in which they naturally traffic, to promote or at least to respect the requirements of substantive good sense. They do so, often, by manipulating and even mis-applying their formal categories in the service of what they take to be substantively good outcomes. This is what occurred in *Izadi*, where the court mischaracterized the law of offer, as reflected in *Lefkowitz*, in order to deter a practice that it thought unattractive but that the law, properly characterized, allowed. Of course, each time a court does this, it changes, and probably damages, the formal structure of the law. A precedent like *Izadi* cannot be understood, formally, except as making a claim about offer—a claim that muddies the conceptual structure within which offers, properly understood, necessarily exist.

This has its own costs. Most narrowly, the *Izadi* precedent may now be thought to require, or at least to encourage, holding an advertisement to constitute an offer in subsequent cases in which the equities and good sense cut the other way. More generally, too much muddying of doctrinal waters will eventually mean that doctrine can no longer serve either to structure judicial reasoning and social relations or to check judicial discretion. Thus, Karl Llewellyn perhaps had it right when he said that "covert tools are never good tools."

13.3   ACCEPTANCE

Promises, in our ordinary experience of them, require the active participation not just of promisor but also of promisee. A person's saying "I promise" is not, conventionally, sufficient for establishing a promissory obligation; instead, there must also be some sort of *uptake* by the promisee.

If you are dubious whether promising really requires promisee uptake, consider the following example.[11] A group of people are concerned about overpopulation and therefore want to reduce the number of children that they will have. But each person receives the full benefit of having an additional child and bears only a small portion of the costs. Thus, the persons' several childbearing decisions cause there to be too many children, given the interest in reducing the number of children, overall. To solve the problem, the persons need to limit their childbearing collectively. A law might do the trick, but the persons have no shared government (or no government authorized to legislate in this area). They are, however, moral, or at least they always keep their promises. Accordingly, the persons select a third party and each promise her that they will have only one child.

Do these promises obligate the promisors even if the promisee never takes them up, for example, by accepting them. It seems that they should

---

11. The example comes from CHARLES FRIED, CONTRACT AS PROMISE 41–42 (1982), who borrowed it from Robert Nozick.

not. For if they did, then the third party might be drafted, involuntarily, into the service of a project in which she does not share, and which she might even disapprove (perhaps she thinks that overpopulation is not a worry, or simply that family planning decisions should be made individually and privately). Her status as a person—her capacity to be owed promissory obligations—is being manipulated without her consent. If the promise were validly created, she would, in this sense, be wronged. That is a good reason for making promisee uptake into a necessary condition for the creation of a morally valid promise. And our promissory practice, it is generally agreed, does just this.

To be sure, uptake may in some circumstances involve very little and may be implied: on some views it may be enough for the promisee to learn of the promise (directly from the promisor, or also indirectly) and not reject it. Moreover, when promises are conditional and reciprocal—that is, when promisors condition their assumption of an obligation on their promisees' taking on an obligation in exchange—then the requirements of uptake typically become more demanding. And contract law—as subsequent materials concerning the consideration doctrine will make explicit—recognizes only reciprocal and indeed exchange promises. Accordingly, uptake is a natural and important part of contract law.

The law gives uptake a doctrinal expression through the principle that a contract requires not just offer but also *acceptance*, and through the web of rules governing acceptance. The basic rules are straightforward, and may be elucidated from the materials that follow. The cases also illustrate some of what's at stake in this area of law and some of the complications that arise.

International Telemeter Corp. v. Teleprompter Corp.

United States Court of Appeals, Second Circuit, 1979.
592 F.2d 49.

Appeal was taken from a judgment of the United States District Court for the Southern District of New York, Motley, J., enforcing an agreement settling patent litigation. The Court of Appeals, Lumbard, Circuit Judge, held that: (1) evidence supported district court's conclusion that parties intended to be bound by provisions of settlement agreement prior to signing and delivery of written agreement, and (2) settlement agreement was not unenforceable for reasons of public policy.

Affirmed.

■ LUMBARD, CIRCUIT JUDGE. In this case, originally brought as a suit for patent infringement, defendant Teleprompter Corporation appeals from a judgment of the district court, Motley, J., filed on February 21, 1978 after a bench trial and amended March 7, 1978, insofar as it (1) directs Teleprompter to pay plaintiff International Telemeter Corporation (ITC) $245,000 plus interest and costs for Teleprompter's breach of an agreement settling patent litigation, and (2) dismisses without prejudice Tele-prompter's counterclaim for a declaration of the patent's invalidity.[1]

The parties agree that New York law governs the enforceability of the settlement agreement, which was negotiated, consummated, and to be performed in New York, and which was explicitly made subject to New York law. The issues are (1) whether there was a binding settlement agreement enforceable against Teleprompter, and (2) whether enforcement of the settlement agreement violates the public policy enunciated in *Lear v. Adkins*, 395 U.S. 653 (1969). As Teleprompter has not persuaded us that the district court erred in finding that the parties had consummated a binding settlement agreement or that this agreement violates the policy of Lear, supra, we affirm.

I

The relevant facts are undisputed. The present action arises from a suit for patent infringement commenced by ITC on March 15, 1968 against several defendants in the District Court for the Western District of Washington. On September 1, 1970, Teleprompter intervened as a defendant and counterclaimant in the action, seeking, Inter alia, declarations of patent invalidity and noninfringement. Following the dismissal of several claims and counterclaims, by 1973 the only parties remaining in the litigation were ITC, Teleprompter, and Philip D. Hamlin and Hamlin International Corporation (collectively, the "Hamlin defendants").

In February, 1973, William Bresnan, then President of Teleprompter, wrote to Arthur Groman, a Los Angeles attorney, asking if ITC wished to "discuss a (negotiated) resolution of the patent litigation." On February 9, 1973, Groman responded by sending to Bresnan a draft license agreement proposed by ITC as a basis for settling the litigation. The draft agreement provided for minimum royalties of $75,000 for the first three years and damages for past infringement totaling $240,000. Bresnan turned down the proposed agreement but suggested that a meeting be arranged to discuss possible settlement.

The requested settlement meeting took place in New York City in April, 1973. Present on behalf of Teleprompter were William K. Kerr, Jules P. Kirsch, and Bresnan himself. Present on behalf of ITC were Morton Amster, Thomas Harrison, and Kenneth Merklen. All but Bresnan were acting as lawyers. The first meeting proved inconclusive.

In early July, 1973, after a further settlement proposal of Bresnan made on May 30 was found unacceptable by ITC, the parties met a second time. According to Amster, at this meeting the parties "negotiated the terms of the settlement." The parties assigned to Amster the task of preparing the initial drafts of the agreement, which included the following terms: an aggregate payment by Teleprompter of $245,000 in settlement of all claims against Teleprompter and the Hamlin defendants, the licensing

---

1. The patent at issue is a patent for the design and manufacture of converters used in the transmission of cable television programs.

of Teleprompter and the Hamlin defendants under the disputed patent, the dismissal of the pending litigation, and the issuance of a press release. These basic terms were never altered during the subsequent negotiations.

On July 26, 1973, Amster sent Kerr a copy of the draft agreements together with a proposed schedule for payments totaling $245,000.

There followed a series of minor revisions and exchanges of revised drafts. Amster, as attorney for ITC, and Kirsch, as attorney for Teleprompter, agreed to final changes at a meeting held on August 28 or September 7, 1973. Thereafter, on September 10, 1973, "clean drafts" were forwarded by Amster to Kirsch. On September 26, 1973, Amster sent to Kirsch copies of the Teleprompter and Hamlin license agreements and copies of the stipulation and order of dismissal to be filed in the patent lawsuit pending in the Western District of Washington. In his covering letter, Amster remarked, "Hopefully we have attended to all the minor changes and the documents are in condition for execution. Perhaps upon a review of the papers, you would be willing to advise your local counsel (in the Washington litigation) that the case is settled so that he and (ITC's local counsel) can advise Judge Boldt that the case is settled and that a proposed stipulation and order will be filed shortly."

On October 3, 1973, Kirsch did so advise Teleprompter's Seattle counsel, Richard Williams. That same day, Williams wrote to Judge Boldt that "the final Settlement Agreement has been transmitted to all parties for the purpose of signature we should be in a position to present a Stipulation and Order of Stipulation to the Court for its consideration and entry." Williams further advised the court that the pending trial date "may be vacated." A copy of this letter was sent to Amster. If Williams overstated the parties' proximity to settlement, as Kirsch later claimed at trial, Kirsch failed to correct the allegedly mistaken impression conveyed to the trial court.

Just as the parties were finishing their work on the settlement documents, a dispute arose between Teleprompter and the Hamlin defendants over the Hamlin defendants' obligation to pay amounts claimed by Teleprompter pursuant to its intervention agreement with the Hamlin defendants. Rather than allow the settlement agreement to founder on this last minute disagreement between the defendants, Kirsch acted to secure a separate peace between Teleprompter and ITC. On October 25 and October 26, 1973, he telephoned and wrote to Amster to advise him of the falling out between Teleprompter and the Hamlin defendants and attempted to secure a settlement as to ITC and Teleprompter on precisely the same terms as those already agreed upon. In his October 26 letter, Kirsch wrote as follows to Amster:

> Dear Mort:
>
> As I advised you in our telephone discussions on Thursday and Friday, October 25 and 26, 1973, Mr. Hamlin is unwilling to pay Teleprompter the amounts due Teleprompter pursuant to the August 3, 1970 Intervention Agreement. As a conse-

quence, Teleprompter now wishes to settle the litigation only with respect to Teleprompter on the terms which had been agreed upon with respect to Teleprompter in the Settlement Agreement and the License Agreement which accompanied your September 26, 1973 letter, and I understand that this is agreeable with ITC.

In our telephone conversation on October 26, 1973, you and I agreed that I would revise the Settlement Agreement to limit its terms to Teleprompter only, that Teleprompter will make the payments specified in Schedule 1 to the original Settlement Agreement, that Teleprompter will execute the original ITC–Teleprompter License Agreement, and that I would revise the Stipulation and Order of Dismissal to limit dismissal of the action to Teleprompter only.

Sincerely,

Jules P. Kirsch

(Emphasis added.)

Thus Kirsch's letter committed Teleprompter to a settlement on the terms "which had been agreed upon" and which were already set forth in the draft settlement papers accompanying Amster's September 26, 1973 letter. At trial, Kirsch confirmed that he had Teleprompter's authorization to send this October 26, 1973 letter. In fact, Kirsch sent a copy of this letter to Teleprompter's general counsel, Barry Simon. If this letter inaccurately conveyed Teleprompter's intent to be bound, Simon made no effort to set the matter straight. All that remained to be done before a formal signed agreement could be executed was to eliminate mechanically all reference to the Hamlin defendants in the draft agreement.

Several important events occurred on October 29, 1973. Kirsch duly revised the settlement papers to delete all references to the Hamlin defendants and forwarded the revised documents to Amster on the morning of October 29. These were listed as follows:

1. A revised settlement agreement.

2. An unrevised Schedule 1 to the revised settlement agreement.

3. A revised stipulation and order of dismissal as to Teleprompter only.

4. An unrevised ITC–Teleprompter license agreement.

5. A revised joint announcement of settlement and dismissal of the litigation as to Teleprompter only.

Kirsch also sent a separate letter to Amster asking him to call as soon as he had finished reviewing the settlement papers "so that if there are any changes you wish to have made, we can discuss them. If necessary I can arrange for them to be made before I leave for Los Angeles this afternoon. In that way the final papers can be delivered promptly to Teleprompter for execution and returned to you." No changes were suggested by Amster. All that remained was to obtain the requisite signatures and make delivery. Consequently, that afternoon Kirsch wrote another letter to Amster, enclosing three copies of the stipulation and order of dismissal as to Teleprompter which Kirsch had signed and dated October 29, 1973. Amster also signed the stipulation and order of dismissal that afternoon, as requested by Kirsch. Kirsch also requested that Amster send a ribbon copy of the stipulation and order to ITC's Seattle, Washington counsel and return a signed electrostatic copy to Kirsch. Kirsch advised Amster that he had called Williams, Teleprompter's Seattle counsel, and that Williams would sign the stipulation upon receiving it from ITC's Seattle counsel and would then file it with the court.

That afternoon, October 29, Kirsch sent to Peter A. Gross, the assistant general counsel of Teleprompter, copies of the settlement agreement. Gross was to have these documents executed by Teleprompter and returned to Amster together with a certified check in the amount of $26,250.00 pursuant to Schedule 1 of the settlement agreement. Kirsch advised Gross that Amster would then arrange to have the signed agreements and the check delivered to ITC; duplicate signed copies of the settlement and license agreements would then be returned to Gross. Finally, Kirsch advised Gross that he was arranging to have the stipulation and order of dismissal filed in court by Teleprompter's Seattle counsel.

The following day, October 30, 1973, Teleprompter's president, Bresnan, signed the settlement agreement. Although plaintiff had demanded production of this document before trial, its existence came to light for the first time at trial during the testimony of Bresnan, after Judge Motley had overruled objections to questions concerning communications between Bresnan and Teleprompter's counsel. When the settlement agreement was first brought to him by Gross, Bresnan refused to sign without the approval of Jack Kent Cooke, Chairman of the Board and Chief Executive Officer of Teleprompter. At Gross' insistence, however, Bresnan signed the document "subject to the proviso that it would not be delivered until it had been reviewed with Mr. Cooke and also with Mr. Greene (Teleprompter's treasurer)."

That same day, October 30, Kirsch arrived in California as planned. That afternoon, he received a telephone message at his hotel, which read as follows: "Mr. Gross called. The settlement is O.K. Papers and check will go out tomorrow."

In what was apparently yet another reference to Bresnan's signing of the final agreement, on October 31, 1973, Kirsch wrote to Hamlin, advising him that "Teleprompter has decided to settle with ITC a revised Settlement Agreement as between ITC and Teleprompter only and a revised Stipulation of Dismissal of the Action as to Teleprompter only have been executed." Based on communications with Teleprompter, Kirsch believed these representations to be duly authorized and accurate when made. Indeed, Kirsch sent copies of this letter to Simon and to Gross, Teleprompter's in-house counsel, and to Amster and Harrison, ITC's counsel. If this letter inaccurately conveyed the impression that a settlement had been consummated, Teleprompter did not move to correct that impression.

Thereafter, new management at Teleprompter refused to proceed with the settlement agreement. Accordingly, on November 16, 1973, Kirsch called Amster to tell him that he had been mistaken in his earlier belief that Teleprompter had agreed to the settlement with ITC and had in fact executed the settlement. Kirsch confirmed the telephone conversation in a letter of the same date which reads as follows:

> Dear Mort:
>
> This letter will confirm that in my telephone conversation with you this afternoon I advised you that since I wrote a letter to Mr. Hamlin dated October 31, 1973, a copy of which was sent to you, in which I stated that the revised Settlement Agreement had been executed, I have learned that in fact the revised Settlement Agreement was not executed.
>
> Sincerely,
>
> Jules P. Kirsch

Kirsch's statement in this letter that the settlement agreement had never been executed conflicted not only with his prior statements, but also with Bresnan's later admission at trial that he had in fact signed the agreement. In any event, after sending this letter, Kirsch withdrew as Teleprompter's counsel in this dispute.

On November 28, 1973, Amster wrote to Kirsch stating that he had received Kirsch's November 16 letter but had nevertheless advised ITC that it had a legally enforceable agreement with Teleprompter.

On December 21, 1973, ITC's Seattle counsel, Williams, advised Judge Boldt that the settlement agreement had not been returned to ITC by Teleprompter and that Teleprompter's local counsel had refused to sign the stipulation and order of dismissal. On January 7, 1974, Teleprompter's Seattle counsel advised Judge Boldt that Teleprompter's new management had changed its mind and had decided not to settle.

On December 27, 1973, the district court in Seattle entered a consent decree between ITC and the Hamlin defendants enjoining the Hamlin defendants from further infringing ITC's patent. Thereafter, since both remaining parties, ITC and Teleprompter, were New York corporations, the action was transferred to the Southern District of New York for the convenience of the parties and witnesses pursuant to *28 U.S.C. s 1404(a)*, by order entered March 15, 1974.

By order dated October 3, 1974, the district court approved a stipulation between ITC and Teleprompter, granting ITC leave to file an amended and supplemental complaint containing additional counts seeking to enforce ITC's settlement agreement with Teleprompter.

II

Teleprompter's first claim on appeal is that the district court erred in finding that the parties intended to be bound prior to the actual signing and delivery of the agreement. Teleprompter claims that the parties did not intend to be bound prior to formal delivery and that, since the agreement was never delivered, there was no enforceable contract.

With respect to the standard of review appropriate to passing upon a district court's finding of intent, Teleprompter asserts that the "clearly erroneous" standard is not applicable, but that if it is, the district court's conclusions as to intent are "clearly erroneous." Acceptance of appellant's invitation to exercise more intrusive review than would ordinarily be proper under the "clearly erroneous" standard, however, could not alter our conclusions here. The record amply supports the district court's findings of fact and conclusions of law regardless of the standard of review.

The district court found that the parties had reached a final agreement as to the terms of the settlement and that both had manifested objective indications of their intent to be bound by October 29, 1973. Taken as a whole, the documents themselves suggest on their face an intent to be bound on both sides and a recognition of this intent to be bound. Viewed against the backdrop of the course of the negotiations and the testimony taken at trial, we find nothing in these documents that supports Teleprompter's claim that ITC had reason to know that Teleprompter contemplated that no legal obligation should arise until a formal contract was signed and delivered. Indeed, on several occasions, these documents, along with other communications by Teleprompter to ITC, conveyed the impression of a binding agreement, with physical signing and delivery no more than a formality.

As the district court found, the record strongly suggests that both parties would have signed prior to October 26, 1973 but for the disagreement between Teleprompter and the Hamlin defendants. The October 26 letter clearly indicates that all that remained to be done regarding the written agreement was to eliminate the now superfluous references to the Hamlin defendants. Kirsch's October 26 letter to Amster contains both an unequivocal expression of Teleprompter's intention to settle and a listing by incorporation of all the essential terms of the settlement. Although asked for his comments, Amster had none.

If there remained any doubt as to the nature of the parties' intent as of October 26, that doubt was dispelled by the events of October 29. On that day Kirsch sent to Amster for signing a complete set of settlement papers. All that remained was to have Bresnan sign the settlement agreement, to have local counsel in Seattle sign the stipulation and order of dismissal, and to file the necessary papers in court. Particularly significant, in our view, was the signing and transmittal to opposing counsel of the stipulation and order of dismissal. Teleprompter could have requested that the signed stipulation be held in escrow pending the signing and delivery of the other documents. It did not. Accordingly, Amster acted as any other reasonable person would have when he concluded that there was a binding agreement as of October 29, if not before. As the district court concluded, "these two lawyers would not have signed the stipulation unless they understood that both parties intended to be bound at that juncture and that all that remained to be done was the formalization of what had been agreed."

Subsequent communications by Teleprompter to ITC further support the district court's finding that the parties believed that a binding agreement had been consummated. On October 31, Kirsch stated in a letter to Amster that "Teleprompter had decided to settle with ITC as to Teleprompter only a revised Settlement Agreement and Stipulation of Dismissal have been executed." Teleprompter officials who authorized this communication received copies of this letter and did not disavow its contents.

Teleprompter argues that Kirsch had no authority to bind Teleprompter to a settlement. Kirsch, however, was acting within the ambit of his apparent authority and ITC was entitled to rely upon Kirsch's authority so long as there was no reason to believe that he was exceeding it. Teleprompter knew that ITC believed that Kirsch had the requisite authority and did nothing to correct this impression. In fact, ITC had no reason to think that Kirsch was exceeding his authority and Teleprompter had no reason to correct any misimpression because, as the district court found, Kirsch had full authority to negotiate and consummate a settlement. That a lawyer should have such authority is not rare. In this case, moreover, Kirsch kept Teleprompter apprised at all times of what he was doing. Teleprompter officials were sent copies of all the correspondence which the district court relied upon in finding a binding agreement. Teleprompter officials failed to disavow Kirsch's actions even when Kirsch sent them copies of his October 31 letter announcing that the settlement was executed.

The district court's decision is consistent with New York case law dealing with similar situations.

The cases relied upon by the appellant are distinguishable on their facts from the case at bar. In *Scheck v. Francis*, 26 N.Y.2d 466, (1970) the Court of Appeals found that the parties did not intend to be bound before signing and delivery, and further, that there was no proof that the parties had ever reached an agreement on the terms of the disputed contract. Similarly, in *Schwartz v. Greenberg*, 304 N.Y. 250 (1952), the Court of Appeals held that the refusal to deliver a signed agreement defeated the contract because "the parties did not intend to be bound until a written agreement had been signed and delivered." Whether or not the parties have manifested an intent to be bound must depend in each case on all the circumstances. Here the district court specifically found an intent to be bound prior to signing and delivery of a written agreement.

The settlement agreement entered into by ITC and Teleprompter requires that Teleprompter pay ITC $245,000 in damages for patent infringement through March 31, 1973. The agreement also provides for Teleprompter to receive a royalty-free license for use of the patent from April 1, 1973 through March 31, 1978, and, beginning April 1, 1978, for Teleprompter to pay ITC a royalty of $2.00 for each converter purchased.

Appellant argues that enforcement of this settlement agreement contravenes the public policy against licensee estoppel announced in *Lear v.*

Adkins, 395 U.S. 653 (1969). In Lear, the Supreme Court overruled earlier licensee estoppel cases and held that a patent licensee may assert patent invalidity as a defense to a contract action for nonpayment of royalties. In this way the Court sought to reconcile the policy of the patent law, which requires that all ideas in general circulation be dedicated to the common good unless protected by a valid patent, with the competing policy of contract law forbidding a purchaser from repudiating his promises simply because he later becomes dissatisfied with the bargain he has struck.

Enforcement of the challenged settlement agreement violates neither the letter nor the spirit of Lear. First, enforcement of the settlement agreement does not estop Teleprompter from challenging the validity of ITC's patent when that claim is properly raised. Indeed, Teleprompter has already commenced an action for a declaration of this patent's invalidity in the District Court of Colorado, Teleprompter Corporation v. Athena Cablevision Corporation, Civil Action No. 78–398, filed April 13, 1978. Second, enforcement of this settlement agreement requires that Teleprompter pay damages for past infringement and not royalties. Thus Lear's holding that a licensee can stop paying royalties when he challenges the validity of the underlying patent is not threatened. Lear has not been extended to cover the collection of damages for past infringement. *Ransburg Electro–Coating Corp. v. Spiller & Spiller, Inc.*, 489 F.2d 974 (7th Cir. 1973).

Teleprompter, however, contends that the payments denominated as damages for past infringement are in reality royalties and that requiring Teleprompter to make the payments called for in the settlement agreement therefore violates the spirit if not the letter of the public policy articulated in Lear. The district court found that the language of the settlement agreement was unambiguous in denominating these payments as liquidated damages rather than royalties and held that parol evidence was not admissible to vary the plain meaning of its terms. *Rodolitz v. Neptune Paper Products, Inc.*, 22 N.Y.2d 383 (1968).

Even leaving aside the parol evidence ruling, there is more than enough evidence in the record to support the literal reading of the settlement agreement relied upon by the district court. ITC was originally seeking approximately $240,000 in damages for infringement up to 1973, and royalties thereafter for so long as Teleprompter used ITC's patent. To obtain a settlement, ITC had to give up something. In the offer which formed the basis for the final agreement challenged here, ITC gave up its demand for royalties through 1978, offering a free five-year license as an inducement to settle, while continuing to insist on $240,000 damages. Accordingly, we agree with the trial court that the $240,000 payment is liquidated damages for past infringement and not a royalty payment for future use. Lear does not apply and the settlement agreement is not unenforceable for reasons of public policy.

Judgment affirmed.

■ FRIENDLY, CIRCUIT JUDGE, concurring.

The difficulty in deciding this case comes from the gap between the realities of the formation of complex business agreements and traditional contract formulation. Under a view conforming to the realities of business life, there would be no contract in such cases until the document is signed and delivered; until then either party would be free to bring up new points of form or substance, or even to withdraw altogether. However, I cannot conscientiously assert that the courts of New York or, to the extent they have not spoken, the Restatement of Contracts 2d s 26 and comment C (Tent. Drafts 1–7 Revised and Edited) have gone that far, nor can I find a fair basis for predicting that the New York Court of Appeals is yet prepared to do so.

On the other hand, it does seem to me that the New York cases cited by the majority can be read as holding, or at least as affording a fair basis for predicting a holding, that when the parties have manifested an intention that their relations should be embodied in an elaborate signed contract, clear and convincing proof is required to show that they meant to be bound before the contract is signed and delivered. Such a principle would accord with what I believe to be the intention of most such potential contractors; they view the signed written instrument that is in prospect as "the contract", not as a memorialization of an oral agreement previously reached. Also, from an instrumental standpoint, such a rule would save the courts from a certain amount of vexing litigation. The clear and convincing proof could consist in one party's allowing the other to begin performance, as in *Viacom International, Inc. v. Tandem Productions, Inc.*, 526 F.2d 593 (2d Cir. 1975) and *V'Soske v. Barwick*, 404 F.2d 495 (2 Cir. 1968), Cert. denied, 394 U.S. 921 (1969), or in unequivocal statements by the principals or authorized agents that a complete agreement had been reached and the writing was considered to be of merely evidentiary significance.

The facts forcefully marshaled by Judge Lumbard make a strong case for finding that the latter condition has been satisfied here. What weighs especially with me is Kirsch's letter of October 26, not claimed to have been unauthorized, saying that "Teleprompter now wishes to settle the litigation only with respect to Teleprompter on the terms which had been agreed upon with respect to Teleprompter" in the earlier three-party settlement "and I understand that this is agreeable with ITC". From then on the job of transforming the three-party agreement into a two-party one was largely scrivener's work and Teleprompter manifested no dissatisfaction with Kirsch's performance of this. Upon the understanding that our decision rests on the unique facts here presented and that we are not entering a brave new world where lawyers can commit their clients simply by communicating boldly with each other, I concur in the judgment of affirmance.

Restatement 2d of Contracts

§ 27 Existence of Contract Where Written Memorial is Contemplated

Manifestations of assent that are in themselves sufficient to conclude a contract will not be prevented from so operating by the fact that the parties also manifest an intention to prepare and adopt a written memorial thereof; but the circumstances may show that the agreements are preliminary negotiations.

Comments & Illustrations

Comment a. Parties who plan to make a final written instrument as the expression of their contract necessarily discuss the proposed terms of the contract before they enter into it and often, before the final writing is made, agree upon all the terms which they plan to incorporate therein. This they may do orally or by exchange of several writings. It is possible thus to make a contract the terms of which include an obligation to execute subsequently a final writing which shall contain certain provisions. If parties have definitely agreed that they will do so, and that the final writing shall contain these provisions and no others, they have then concluded the contract.

Comment b. On the other hand, if either party knows or has reason to know that the other party regards the agreement as incomplete and intends that no obligation shall exist until other terms are assented to or until the whole has been reduced to another written form, the preliminary negotiations and agreements do not constitute a contract.

Comment c. Among the circumstances which may be helpful in determining whether a contract has been concluded are the following: the extent to which express agreement has been reached on all the terms to be included, whether the contract is of a type usually put in writing, whether it needs a formal writing for its full expression, whether it has few or many details, whether the amount involved is large or small, whether it is a common or unusual contract, whether a standard form of contract is widely used in similar transactions, and whether either party takes any action in preparation for performance during the negotiations. Such circumstances may be shown by oral testimony or by correspondence or other preliminary or partially complete writings.

Comment d. Even though a binding contract is made before a contemplated written memorial is prepared and adopted, the subsequent written document may make a binding modification of the terms previously agreed to.

Ever–Tite Roofing Corp. v. Green et ux.

Court of Appeal of Louisiana, Second Circuit, 1955.
83 So.2d 449.

Action was brought for damages for breach by defendants of written contract for re-roofing of defendants' residence by plaintiff. The Twenty–Sixth Judicial District Court of the Parish of Webster, James Bolin, J., entered judgment for defendants, and plaintiff appealed. The Court of Appeal, Ayres, J., held that where instrument signed by defendants to obtain services of plaintiff in re-roofing residence of defendants provided that agreement should become binding on written acceptance by plaintiff or on commencement of performance of the work by plaintiff, and plaintiff sent its workmen and two trucks with roofing materials for purpose of performing the contract, and on arrival of the workmen they were notified by defendants that the work had been contracted to third persons, there was actual commencement or performance of the work by plaintiff before receiving notice from defendants of their intention to withdraw from proposed contract, and proposed contract became a completed contract binding on defendants.

Reversed and rendered.

■ AYRES, JUDGE. This is an action for damages allegedly sustained by plaintiff as the result of the breach by the defendants of a written contract for the re-roofing of defendants' residence. Defendants denied that their written proposal or offer was ever accepted by plaintiff in the manner stipulated therein for its acceptance, and hence contended no contract was ever entered into. The trial court sustained defendants' defense and rejected plaintiff's demands and dismissed its suit at its costs. From the judgment thus rendered and signed, plaintiff appealed.

Defendants executed and signed an instrument June 10, 1953, for the purpose of obtaining the services of plaintiff in re-roofing their residence situated in Webster Parish, Louisiana. The document set out in detail the work to be done and the price therefor to be paid in monthly installments. This instrument was likewise signed by plaintiff's sale representative, who, however, was without authority to accept the contract for and on behalf of the plaintiff. This alleged contract contained these provisions:

'This agreement shall become binding only upon written acceptance hereof, by the principal or authorized officer of the Contractor, *or upon commencing performance of the work*. This contract is Not Subject to Cancellation. It is understood and agreed that this contract is payable at office of Ever–Tite Roofing Corporation, 5203 Telephone, Houston, Texas. It is understood and agreed that this Contract provides for attorney's fees and in no case less than ten per cent attorney's fees in the event same is placed in the hands of an attorney for collecting or collected through any court, and further provides for accelerated maturity for failure to pay any installment of principal or interest thereon when due.

'This written agreement is the only and entire contract covering the subject matter hereof and no other representations have been made unto Owner except these herein contained. No guarantee on repair work, partial roof jobs, or paint jobs.' (Emphasis supplied.)

Inasmuch as this work was to be performed entirely on credit, it was necessary for plaintiff to obtain credit reports and approval from the lending institution which was to finance said contract. With this procedure defendants were more or less familiar and knew their credit rating would have to be checked and a report made. On receipt of the proposed contract in plaintiff's office on the day following its execution, plaintiff requested a credit report, which was made after investigation and which was received in due course and submitted by plaintiff to the lending agency. Additional information was requested by this institution, which was likewise in due course transmitted to the institution, which then gave its approval.

The day immediately following this approval, which was either June 18 or 19, 1953, plaintiff engaged its workmen and two trucks, loaded the trucks with the necessary roofing materials and proceeded from Shreveport to defendants' residence for the purpose of doing the work and performing the services allegedly contracted for the defendants. Upon their arrival at defendants' residence, the workmen found others in the performance of the work which plaintiff had contracted to do. Defendants notified plaintiff's workmen that the work had been contracted to other parties two days before and forbade them to do the work.

Formal acceptance of the contract was not made under the signature and approval of an agent of plaintiff. It was, however, the intention of plaintiff to accept the contract by commencing the work, which was one of the ways provided for in the instrument for its acceptance, as will be shown by reference to the extract from the contract quoted hereinabove. Prior to this time, however, defendants had determined on a course of abrogating the agreement and engaged other workmen without notice thereof to plaintiff.

The basis of the judgment appealed was that defendants had timely notified plaintiff before 'commencing performance of work'. The trial court held that notice to plaintiff's workmen upon their arrival with the materials that defendants did not desire them to commence the actual work was sufficient and timely to signify their intention to withdraw from the contract. With this conclusion we find ourselves unable to agree.

Defendants' attempt to justify their delay in thus notifying plaintiff for the reason they did not know where or how to contact plaintiff is without merit. The contract itself, a copy of which was left with them, conspicuously displayed plaintiff's name, address and telephone number. Be that as it may, defendants at no time, from June 10, 1953, until plaintiff's workmen arrived for the purpose of commencing the work, notified or attempted to notify plaintiff of their intention to abrogate, terminate or cancel the contract.

Defendants evidently knew this work was to be processed through plaintiff's Shreveport office. The record discloses no unreasonable delay on plaintiff's part in receiving, processing or accepting the contract or in commencing the work contracted to be done. No time limit was specified in the contract within which it was to be accepted or within which the work was to be begun. It was nevertheless understood between the parties that some delay would ensue before the acceptance of the contract and the commencement of the work, due to the necessity of compliance with the requirements relative to financing the job through a lending agency. The evidence as referred to hereinabove shows that plaintiff proceeded with due diligence.

The general rule of law is that an offer proposed may be withdrawn before its acceptance and that no obligation is incurred thereby. This is, however, not without exceptions. For instance, Restatement of the Law of Contracts stated:

'(1) The power to create a contract by acceptance of an offer terminates at the time specified in the offer, or, if no time is specified, at the end of a reasonable time.

'What is a reasonable time is a question of fact depending on the nature of the contract proposed, the usages of business and other circumstances of the case which the offeree at the time of his acceptance either knows or has reason to know.'

These principles are recognized in the Civil Code. LSA–C.C. Art. 1800 provides that an offer is incomplete as a contract until its acceptance and that before its acceptance the offer may be withdrawn. However, this general rule is modified by the provisions of LSA–C.C. Arts. 1801, 1802, 1804 and 1809, which read as follows:

'Art. 1801. The party proposing shall be presumed to continue in the intention, which his proposal expressed, if, on receiving the unqualified assent of him to whom the proposition is made, he do not signify the change of his intention.

'Art. 1802. He is bound by his proposition, and the signification of his dissent will be of no avail, *if the proposition be made in terms, which evince a design to give the other party the right of concluding the contract by his assent; and if that assent be given within such time as the situation of the parties and the nature of the contract shall prove that it was the intention of the proposer to allow.* * * *

'Art. 1804. The acceptance needs (need) not be made by the same act, or in point of time, immediately after the proposition; *if made at any time before the person who offers or promises has changed his mind, or may reasonably be presumed to have done so, it is sufficient.* * * *

'Art. 1809. The obligation of a contract not being complete, until the acceptance, or in cases where it is implied by law, until the circumstances, which raise such implication, are known to the party proposing; *he may therefore revoke his offer or proposition before such acceptance, but not without allowing such reasonable time as from the terms of his offer he has given, or from the circumstances of the case he may be supposed to have intended to give to the party, to communicate his determination.*' (Emphasis supplied.)

Therefore, since the contract did not specify the time within which it was to be accepted or within which the work was to have been commenced, a reasonable time must be allowed therefor in accordance with the facts and circumstances and the evident intention of the parties. A reasonable time is contemplated where no time is expressed. What is a reasonable time depends more or less upon the circumstances surrounding each particular case. The delays to process defendants' application were not unusual. The contract was accepted by plaintiff by the commencement of the performance of the work contracted to be done. This commencement began with the loading of the trucks with the necessary materials in Shreveport and transporting such materials and the workmen to defendants' residence. Actual commencement or performance of the work therefore began before any notice of dissent by defendants was given plaintiff. The proposition and its acceptance thus became a completed contract.

By their aforesaid acts defendants breached the contract. They employed others to do the work contracted to be done by plaintiff and forbade plaintiff's workmen to engage upon that undertaking. By this breach defendants are legally bound to respond to plaintiff in damages. LSA–C.C. Art. 1930 provides:

> 'The obligations of contract (contracts) extending to whatsoever is incident to such contracts, the party who violates them, is liable, as one of the incidents of his obligations, to the payment of the damages, which the other party has sustained by his default.'

The same authority in Art. 1934 provides the measure of damages for the breach of a contract. This article, in part, states:

> 'Where the object of the contract is anything but the payment of money, the damages due to the creditor for its breach are the amount of the loss he has sustained, and the profit of which he has been deprived'.

Plaintiff expended the sum of $85.37 in loading the trucks in Shreveport with materials and in transporting them to the site of defendants' residence in Webster Parish and in unloading them on their return, and for wages for the workmen for the time consumed. Plaintiff's Shreveport manager testified that the expected profit on this job was $226. None of this evidence is controverted or contradicted in any manner.

True, as plaintiff alleges, the contract provides for attorney's fees where an attorney is employed to collect under the contract, but this is not an action on the contract or to collect under the contract but is an action for damages for a breach of the contract. The contract in that respect is silent with reference to attorney's fees. In the absence of an agreement for the payment of attorney's fees or of some law authorizing the same, such fees are not allowed.

For the reasons assigned, the judgment appealed is annulled, avoided, reversed and set aside and there is now judgment in favor of plaintiff, Ever–Tite Roofing Corporation, against the defendants, G. T. Green and Mrs. Jessie Fay Green, for the full sum of $311.37, with 5 per cent per annum interest thereon from judicial demand until paid, and for all costs.

Reversed and rendered.

Restatement 2d of Contracts

§ 30   Form Of Acceptance Invited

(1) An offer may invite or require acceptance to be made by an affirmative answer in words, or by performing or refraining from perform-

ing a specified act, or may empower the offeree to make a selection of terms in his acceptance.

(2) Unless otherwise indicated by the language or the circumstances, an offer invites acceptance in any manner and by any medium reasonable in the circumstances.

Comments & Illustrations

Comment a. Required form. The offeror is the master of his offer. See Comment *a* to § 29. The form of acceptance is less likely to affect the substance of the bargain than the identity of the offeree, and is often quite immaterial. But the offeror is entitled to insist on a particular mode of manifestation of assent. The terms of the offer may limit acceptance to a particular mode; whether it does so is a matter of interpretation.

Illustration:

1. A sends a letter to B stating the terms of a proposed contract. At the end he writes, "You can accept this offer only by signing on the dotted line below my own signature." A replies by telegram, "I accept your offer." There is no contract.

Comment b. Invited form. Insistence on a particular form of acceptance is unusual. Offers often make no express reference to the form of acceptance; sometimes ambiguous language is used. Language referring to a particular mode of acceptance is often intended and understood as suggestion rather than limitation; the suggested mode is then authorized, but other modes are not precluded. In other cases language which in terms refers to the mode of acceptance is intended and understood as referring to some more important aspect of the transaction, such as the time limit for acceptance. See §§ 60, 63.

Comment c. Term supplied in acceptance. An offer may contain a choice of terms, and may invite or require an acceptance making a selection among the terms stated. Or the offer may indicate a term such as quantity to be filled in by the offeree. An acceptance to be effective must comply with the terms of the offer, and those terms or the circumstances may make it plain that the acceptance must specify terms. Section 60. In such cases the offer does not fail for indefiniteness, but no contract is made by an attempted acceptance which does not supply the term as indicated. See § 33. The offer assents in advance to the term chosen or filled in by the offeree.

Illustration:

2. A offers to deliver to B at any time during the next 30 days any amount of coal, up to 100 tons, for which B will promise to pay $15 a ton. In order to accept this offer B must specify the amount of coal he desires and must promise to pay $15 a ton for it. An order for 50 tons by B concludes a definite agreement.

Comment d. Form not specified. Interpretation of the offer is necessary in order to determine whether there is any limitation on the mode of acceptance. The meaning given the offer by the offeree controls if it is a meaning of which the offeror knew or had reason to know. See §§ 19, 20. Since limitation is not customary, the offeror has reason to know that the offeree may understand that the offer can be accepted in any reasonable manner, and a contrary intention is not operative unless manifested. See Uniform Commercial Code § 2–206(1).

Illustrations:

3.   A orally offers to sell and deliver to B 100 tons of coal at $20 a ton payable 30 days after delivery. B replies, "I accept your offer." B has manifested assent in a sufficient form, even though A neither suggested nor required that form.

4.   A makes a bid at an auction sale. By the usual custom at auctions, the auctioneer may accept by letting the hammer fall, by saying "Sold", or by any words manifesting acceptance.

Comment e. Reasonable manner. As to acceptance by promise or non-promissory performance, see § 32. Cases where the contract leaves terms to be chosen in the course of performance are the subject of § 34. What manner and medium are reasonable is governed by the rules stated in §§ 60 and 65. Sometimes, though not ordinarily, even silent inaction may be effective as a mode of acceptance. See § 69.

Restatement 2d of Contracts

§ 50   Acceptance Of Offer Defined; Acceptance By Performance; Acceptance By Promise

(1) Acceptance of an offer is a manifestation of assent to the terms thereof made by the offeree in a manner invited or required by the offer.

(2) Acceptance by performance requires that at least part of what the offer requests be performed or tendered and includes acceptance by a performance which operates as a return promise.

(3) Acceptance by a promise requires that the offeree complete every act essential to the making of the promise.

Comments & Illustrations

Comment a. Mode of acceptance. The acceptance must manifest assent to the same bargain proposed by the offer, and must also comply with the terms of the offer as to the identity of the offeree and the mode of manifesting acceptance. Offers commonly invite acceptance in any reasonable manner, but a particular mode of acceptance may be required. See § 30. In case of doubt, the offeree may choose to accept either by promising or by rendering the requested performance. See § 32.

Comment b. Acceptance by performance. Where the offer requires acceptance by performance and does not invite a return promise, as in the ordinary case of an offer of a reward, a contract can be created only by the offeree's performance. See Comment *b* to § 32. In such cases the act requested and performed as consideration for the offeror's promise ordinarily also constitutes acceptance; under § 45 the beginning of performance or the tender of part performance of what is requested may both indicate assent and furnish consideration for an option contract. In some other cases the offeree may choose to create a contract either by making a promise or by rendering or tendering performance; in most such cases the beginning of performance or a tender of part performance operates as a promise to render complete performance. See §§ 32, 62. Mere preparation to perform, however, is not acceptance, although in some cases preparation may make the offeror's promise binding under § 87(2).

Illustrations:

1. A, who is about to leave on a month's vacation, tells B that A will pay B $50 if B will paint A's porch while A is away. B says he may not have time, and A says B may decide after A leaves. If B begins the painting, there is an acceptance by performance which operates as a promise to complete the job. See §§ 32, 62.

2. In Illustration 1, B also expresses doubt whether he will be able to finish the job, and it is agreed that B may quit at any time but will be paid only if he finishes the job during A's vacation. If B begins the painting, there is an acceptance by performance creating an option contract. See § 45.

Comment c. Acceptance by promise. The typical contract consists of mutual promises and is formed by an acceptance constituting a return promise by the offeree. A promissory acceptance may be explicitly required by the offer, or may be the only type of acceptance which is reasonable under the circumstances, or the offeree may choose to accept by promise an offer which invites acceptance either by promise or by performance. See §§ 30, 32. The promise may be made in words or other symbols of assent, or it may be implied from conduct, other than acts of performance, provided only that it is in a form invited or required by the offer. An act of performance may also operate as a return promise, but the acceptance in such a case is treated as an acceptance by performance rather than an acceptance by promise; thus the requirement of notification is governed by § 54 rather than by § 56. As appears from § 63, acceptance by promise may be effective when a written promise is started on its way, but the offeree must complete the acts necessary on his part to constitute a promise by him. Similarly, in cases where communication to the offeror is unnecessary under § 69, the acts constituting the promise must be complete.

Illustrations:

3. A sends to B plans for a summer cottage to be built on A's land in a remote wilderness area, and writes, "If you will undertake to build a cottage in accordance with the enclosed plans, I will pay you $5,000." B cannot accept by beginning or completing

performance, since A's letter calls for acceptance by promise. See § 58.

4.   A mails a written order to B, offering to buy on specified terms a machine of a type which B regularly sells from stock. The order provides, "Ship at once." B immediately mails a letter of acceptance. This is an acceptance by promise, even though under § 32 B might have accepted by performance.

5.   A gives an order to B Company's traveling salesman which provides, "This proposal becomes a contract without further notification when approval by an executive officer of B Company is noted hereon at its home office." The notation of approval is an acceptance by promise. See §§ 56, 69 as to the requirement of notification.

* * *

The plaintiff in *International Telemeter* sued several corporations for patent infringement and the eventual defendant in the separate contracts case reported in the opinion intervened as a defendant in that suit. At the defendant's instigation, settlement discussions concerning the patent infringement suit commenced. The basic terms of a settlement as to all the parties in that dispute were worked out, and at the plaintiff's lawyer's prompting, the defendant's outside counsel advised the court that the parties would be in a position to settle the case. Thereafter, another dispute arose between the defendant (in the case reproduced here) and the other defendants in the patent case. This led the defendant's outside counsel to try to preserve the settlement agreement as a separate peace between it and the plaintiff. Accordingly, the defendant's outside counsel wrote to the plaintiff explaining that the defendant wished to settle on the previously-agree-to terms, and that he would modify the settlement agreement so that it applied to the defendant only. The outside counsel sent copies of this letter to defendant's in-house general counsel. Next, defendant's outside counsel signed a copy of the settlement agreement, as did plaintiff's counsel. Once again, defendant's outside counsel sent copies of the agreement to defendant's in-house general counsel. At no point did defendant's in-house counsel raise any doubts or objections concerning the settlement (indeed, defendant's president signed the agreement, although subject to the provision that it not be delivered until it had been reviewed by other members of the defendant's board). The plaintiff's lawyer then received a message saying that the defendant's in-house counsel had approved the settlement and that the defendant would begin performing at once. Finally, defendant's outside counsel notified its co-defendants (in the patent suit) of the settlement, again copying defendant's management, who again did not object to the letter's contents.

The defendant, however, did not perform under the settlement, and (at its instruction) the outside counsel informed the plaintiff that the settlement was not executed. The plaintiff thereupon sued for enforcement of the settlement agreement.[12]

The central issue in the case, of course, is whether or not the defendant accepted the plaintiff's settlement offer. The trial court found that it did, and the appellate court agreed. The acceptance occurred when defendant's outside counsel signed the proposed settlement agreement. Subsequent communications by the defendant, moreover, confirmed its intent to be bound by the contract.

So much is plain from the opinions. But a deeper point lurks in the background of the dispute, and is brought out by Judge Friendly's concurrence. Friendly sought, there, to limit the reach of the holding to the facts of the case, which he regarded as providing clear and convincing evidence that the defendant meant to be bound even before any formal, complete writing was sealed and delivered.

Judge Friendly sought, thereby, to forestall what he thought were two mistakes associated with a broader reading of the majority opinion. The first is less interesting for present purposes, although it may matter a great deal to you in future practice. Friendly worried that the case should not be read to entail that lawyers may commit their clients, especially in settlement negotiations, by communicating badly with each other. He wished, that is, to resist a reading of the case on which the client's silent acquiescence gave the lawyer apparent authority to settle on his behalf. Friendly's wishes, in this respect, reflected some of the deepest doctrinal commitments of the law governing lawyers. Thus Rule 1.2 of the Model Rules of Professional Conduct, which governs the allocation of authority between client and lawyer, allocates the decision whether or not to settle to the client.[13] Indeed, this is a mandatory rather than just a default allocation— contracts between the lawyer and client which attempt to shift the authority over settlements to the lawyer are not enforceable.[14] If the law of agency were construed to allow lawyers to bind their clients to settlements based on apparent authority only, where apparent authority is broadly construed, this would require clients to be vigilant in protecting their control over the settlement decision: they would have to supervise their lawyers closely, in order to ensure that the lawyers did not behave in ways that gave third parties reason to believe that they spoke for the clients. Absent such vigilance, every lawyer's contract of engagement would *in effect* vest some portion of the authority to settle in the lawyer. And that is just what the law considers beyond contract's power to do.

The law has deep reasons for insisting the clients settle directly for themselves, rather than transferring the settlement decision to others.

---

12.   The defendant's outside counsel subsequently withdrew from the representation, probably because of the defendant's misconduct in respect of the settlement and litigation. The defendant, in fact, continued this misconduct in the subsequent contract dispute; the fact that its president had signed the settlement agreement, for example, was not revealed at discovery.

13.   See MODEL RULES OF PROFESSIONAL CONDUCT RULE 1.2(a).

14.   See, e.g., *Jones v. Feiger, Collison & Killmer*, 903 P. 2d 27 (Colo. Ct. App. 1994).

These reasons will figure more prominently in Part III of these materials, which take up some of the sociology of contract and in particular investigate contract's contribution to social solidarity, and compare this contribution to that of other legal orders, including adjudication. For present purposes, it is enough to observe that a lawsuit represents a breach in the social order—a breakdown of solidarity. Adjudication serves to repair that breach, by a method that draws the disputants into an intense engagement with each other and the legal order that governs their disputes. Lawyers serve as the conduits between a technical and often coldly abstract legal order and the informal, personal concerns of the disputants whose conflict this order must authoritatively resolve. To function effectively as conduits, lawyers must bring the disputants—their clients—actively to adjudication; they cannot allow the clients to remain unengaged while they take matters into their own hands.

Contract is like adjudication in that it also underwrites a form of social solidarity—reflected in the authority that contracts possess for the parties to them. Settlement agreements, therefore, also repair the breach in solidarity that engendered the settled lawsuits, but they do so in the modality of contract rather than adjudication. But to achieve the repair, they must (like adjudication) bring the settling disputants into a genuine engagement with each other. When settlement negotiations are devolved to lawyers, and settlements themselves are approved by lawyers acting independently of their clients, then the engagement on which their authority depends is lacking.

These abstract ideas are rendered concrete through the second theme in Judge Friendly's *International Telemeter* concurrence. In addition to worrying that the majority opinion might be read improperly to give lawyers authority to freelance during settlements, Friendly also worried that the opinion might be read to embrace the general principle, expressed in Restatement § 27, that an informal acceptance might be sufficient to conclude a contract even where a writing is expected to follow, and to apply that principle even in the context of settlement negotiations. Friendly wished to resist just this application, which is why he wrote insistently in favor of the principle that where parties manifest intent to be bound by a formal and elaborate writing, only clear and convincing proof can sustain the conclusion that they mean to be bound before the writing is sealed and delivered. A similar thought appears in comment 3 to the Restatement section, which observes that "whether the contract is of a type usually put in writing, whether it needs a formal writing for its full expression, whether it has few or many details, whether the amount involved is large or small, [and] whether it is a common or unusual contract" are all among "the circumstances which may be helpful in determining whether a contract has been concluded." Many contract negotiations are routine and informal and, moreover, conducted in a strategic setting in which both parties have a great deal to gain from reaching an agreement. In these cases, contractual solidarity faces relatively little pressure: even though the two sides wish for different terms, both prefer a wide range of terms over no agreement at all. When litigants are negotiating over settling a lawsuit, the pressure on solidarity is much greater: the grounds of their dispute have been made express, and cast in terms of an alleged wrong; battle lines have been drawn; and the strategic context much more nearly resembles a zero-sum game, in which one side's gain is the other's loss. Indeed, the very fact that a lawsuit has been filed means that agreement-based, contractual modes of solidarity have already failed, so that settlement represents contractual solidarity's second-effort—a kind of hope for redemption. To sustain solidarity in this context, a settlement contract must have some of the ritualistic and participatory properties of the adjudication that it displaces. And the law of offer and acceptance must adjust accordingly, to require or at least to privilege formality and completeness in this context, even if it does not in others. As the formality and seriousness of the circumstances of pre-contractual negotiations rise, the formality and seriousness that an acceptance must display to be effective rise also.

So rather than adopting a one-size-fits-all approach, the law of offer and acceptance adjusts its formal requirements to the circumstances in which contracts are made. Judge Friendly's views in *International Telemeter* represent one extreme on this scale, at which the law requires highly explicit, complete, and written manifestations for acceptance. At the other extreme, an offeree's silence might in some limited circumstances count as accepting an offer that he has received. To be sure, silence does not generally constitute acceptance. Put the other way around, there is no general duty to reply to offers (rejecting them whenever the agreements that they propose are unwanted). But where an offeree silently exercises dominion over the benefits named in an offer, and especially where an offeror additionally relies on a public understanding that silence will constitute acceptance, a silent offeree may find himself legally bound to the terms of the offer.

This last thought suggests another, namely that perhaps the legal standard governing what constitutes acceptance should not be fixed by law (as a mandatory rule) but should instead be determined by the parties (with any substantive legal standard functioning merely as a default). Thus an offeree who establishes or invokes (even just passively?) an expectation that silence coupled with dominion over the offeror's performance constitutes acceptance, might be taken to accept even without any express communication, while an offeree who rejects this principle would not. More broadly, an offeror might be given power to control what will constitute acceptance of her offer, at least in the sense of possessing freedom to specify when she will become bound. The value of this freedom to offerors is connected to the value of offers (distinguished from mere invitations to bargain) *tout court*. By exposing herself to liability simply upon acceptance, and offeror can increase her offeree's incentives to invest in determining whether the proposed deal is appealing to him. These incentives will rise as acceptance itself becomes less independently costly for the offeree: as it becomes more informal, etc. At the same time, the costs for the offeror of making an offer go up as acceptance becomes cheaper, because the risk of an unwanted acceptance increase. Rational offerors will attend to these costs and benefits and adjust the degree of formality in acceptance that they insist upon accordingly.

Ever–Tite illustrates the general point that what counts as acceptance alters the balance of benefit and risk associated with an offer and also the more particular doctrine that an offeror can control what constitutes acceptance (although it illustrates this rule in a slightly unusual, one might even think backwards, setting). Ever–Tite and the Greens were negotiating towards a written contract for Ever–Tite to re-roof the Greens's house. The terms of the writing stated that "This agreement shall become binding only upon written acceptance hereof, [by Ever–Tite], or upon commencing performance of the work."[15] The Greens were to pay for the roof on credit, and so Ever–Tite spent about a week conducting a credit check. The day after the credit check returned information that the Greens's credit was acceptable, Ever–Tite sent a roofing crew over to the Greens's house, only to find that others were already replacing the roof. Ever–Tite sued the Greens for the costs of sending over the crew and for the profits it would have enjoyed on completing the deal.

The trial court held that the Greens's notice to Ever–Tite's workmen that the Greens did not want to proceed with the deal, given when the workmen arrived at the work-site, was sufficient to avoid contractual liability (on the ground, effectively, that it revoked the Greens's earlier offer, inscribed on the Ever–Tite-drafted form, before Ever–Tite had accepted it). The appellate court disagreed. It admitted that an offeror may generally withdraw an offer at any time before acceptance and, moreover, that even an offer that is not withdrawn generally terminates by operation of law following the passage of a "reasonable time." But in this case, the court concluded, Ever–Tite had acted to accept within a reasonable time (one week is a reasonable time for conducting a credit check). And, moreover, Ever–Tite's actions, taken before the Greens attempted revocation, constituted acceptance. An offeror, the court observed, controls her offer, including the method of acceptance. And the Greens's offer specified "commencing performance" as a method of acceptance. Ever–Tite commenced performance when it sent its workers to the job site, and thus accepted the Greens's offer, creating a contract. The Greens were liable under the contract, and so Ever–Tite was entitled to having its contractual expectations vindicated.

Ever–Tite is interesting in part because it illustrates the principles of Restatement § 50 in operation, and so gives some insight into the substantive law of offer: the sense in which an offeror can specify the means of acceptance; and the fact that acceptance need not involve a return promise

---

15. Note that *Ever–Tite* provides a further illustration of the principles discussed in the section on offer. Although the writing in the case was drafted by Ever–Tite, it was issued, as an offer, by the Greens. That is, Ever–Tite issued an invitation to bargain by advertising. The Greens began bargaining by contacting Ever–Tite. Over the course of the bargaining, Ever–Tite prepared a written account of terms that would likely be acceptable to both parties, and provided this account to the Greens. The Greens then issued the account back to Ever–Tite, now as an offer. The question in the case is whether Ever–Tite accepted the offer (that it had drafted, but that the Greens had made).

but may be achieved by performance instead; and the distinction that the law draws between performance and mere preparation. But *Ever–Tite* is more interesting, especially in light of the themes of this Part of the text, because it illustrates the power and limitations of formalism in contract law.

Formalism dominates the analysis through all phases of the *Ever–Tite* opinion. To begin with, observe that it matters to the argument and outcome who the offeror is. The Greens made the offer, and acceptance came from Ever–Tite. That is what made it possible for the contract to be completed based on actions taken by Ever–Tite (sending its workers to the job site) and actually unknown to the Greens (who tried to avoid the contract as soon as they learned of these actions, when the workers appeared at their house). If Ever–Tite had been the offeror, then either its offer would have been accepted by the Greens when they filled in Ever–Tite's initial form, in which case Ever–Tite would have been bound regardless of the results of the credit-check; or its offer would not have been accepted until the Greens allowed its workers onto their house, in which case the Greens's rejection would have been effective, and they would not have been bound. Either of these two outcomes would have been preferable for the Greens over the outcome enshrined in the law. Note, moreover, that the law applied its formalism in spite of the fact that Ever–Tite, rather than the Greens, drafted the text that became the Greens's offer. The lived experience of the situation, almost certainly from the Greens's point of view and probably even from Ever–Tite's (at least until it got its lawyers involved), was that Ever–Tite proposed a plan, with which the Greens indicated that they were happy. One suspects that the Greens never thought about whether or not there was a contract at that point, but were rather waiting to hear about the results of the credit check while still looking around for other roofers. Surely they would have been astounded to know that they had made an offer, conferring on Ever–Tite the unilateral power, by accepting (in a manner that such that the Greens would not learn of it until after-the-fact), to subject them to legal obligations. Even more surprisingly, the rule that an offeror can control the means of acceptance is applied to the Greens, even though not they but their offeree (Ever–Tite) in fact determined what acceptance would involve. Form and substance could hardly be more at odds than they are in this case.

Formalism also dominates the interstices of the court's analysis concerning how to apply the rule regarding acceptance that the contract established. To begin with, the contract in this case is not what the law calls a unilateral contract—a contract in which one party exchanges a promise not for a return promise but instead simply for the other party's *performance*—but rather a bilateral exchange of promises.[16] It is just that in this case, the offer specifies that the mechanism for making the return promise is commencing performance. Next, the court takes up the question what constitutes "commencing performance" and hence accepting the

---

16.   Unilateral contracts will be taken up more systematically in the following section, on revocation.

offer. Here the key distinction (which is elaborated also in Restatement § 50 comment b) is again presented in formal terms: it is the distinction between actually commencing performance on the one hand and "mere preparation" for performance on the other. The court holding turns on its conclusion that although many steps that Ever–Tite took after receiving its own form from the Greens as an offer—the credit check of the Greens, internal scheduling, and perhaps even ordering tools and materials—constituted mere preparation, Ever–Tite commenced performance, and hence accepted, the moment its workers left the shop to drive to the Greens's house.

This proposition is asserted in the opinion, however, more than it is defended; it is conclusory, in the technical sense of reporting the end point of an argument without rehearsing the argument itself. And it turns out that the formal distinction between mere preparation and commencing performance is difficult to elaborate in a way that enables it to be applied to particular cases.

On the one hand, one might think that the court's conclusion was motivated by the fact that loading up workers and materials into a truck and driving to the work site were costly to Ever–Tite and improved the position, including the re-negotiation position—of the Greens. That is, if the Greens were not bound even when Ever–Tite arrived at the site, then they could exploit Ever–Tite's presence. Because the costs of getting to the site were now sunk and hence no longer part of the strategic context, the Greens could extract a better deal from Ever–Tite than they had been able to achieve when these costs were still a cost of the deal, and hence still salient in bargaining over how to divide the deal's surplus. But this argument sweeps too broadly. It applies, after all, to Ever–Tite's costs in conducting the credit check also, and in managing its employees' schedules, and in carrying its overhead during the period between the initial negotiations and setting out for the work site. All of these are costs of the deal, which get paid by one side early and are then sunk, so that the other might re-negotiate a better (and hence exploitative) deal going forward than it could have achieved before the costs were incurred. But on this argument, all preparation counts as commencing performance, and so that formal distinction on which the law on this area turns is dissolved.

On the other hand, considerations such as these might lead one to think that commencing performance requires doing one of the things (the first in a series of such acts) that *motivated* the offeror to seek a contract. In *Ever–Tite*, that would be something like nailing the first new shingle onto the Greens's roof. But this rule makes too much into mere preparation and defers commencing performance until too late in the contractual relationship: in *Ever–Tite*, not just the credit-check, the scheduling, and the travel to the work site but perhaps also removing the old roof would now count as mere preparation (the Greens, after all, were likely motivated exclusively by receiving a completed new roof and probably gave no thought at all to the possibility that this might entail removing what had existed before or even that building the new roof involves multiple steps or stages).

In many cases, the actions on which offerors focus in pursuing their contracts constitute but a small fraction of the offerees' overall costs; they are the tip of the offerees' performance icebergs, as it were. Excluding all such actions from performance would promote exploitation of offerees. It would also, once again, effectively dissolve the formal distinction between mere preparation and commencing performance, this time by treating performance as commenced only when it is completed.

So the formal distinction between mere preparation and commencing performance turns out to suffer an instability: as a purely conceptual matter, each side of the distinction may be made to swallow up the other. That is not to say that the instability is insurmountable. Perhaps another formalism might be brought to bear on the distinction, to shore up the two categories and control the border between them. One natural possibility is to say that performance commences in a case like Ever–Tite when the offeree does the first act that it would be contractually obligated to do under the contract that its acceptance would create. The credit-check of the Greens, or Ever–Tite's internal scheduling would not count as performance in this case, because Ever–Tite might fail to do either of these things and still fulfill its obligations under the contract, as long only as it installed an adequate new roof on the Greens's house. On the other hand, both beginning to install the new roof and removing the old roof would constitute commencing performance, because a failure to do either of these things would constitute a breach: the new roof could not be completed without being begun, and the new roof would not be adequate (merchantable, and compliant with building codes, etc.) if the old roof was not first removed.

But even this gambit probably only appears to save the formalism; it actually just pushes the pressure on the distinction between mere preparation and commencing performance to another part of the argument. In particular, a rule that defines commencing performance in terms of the actions that a finalized contract requires of the offeree places pressure on the meaning of the finalized contract that the contract likely cannot bear, or at least cannot bear on formal accounts of meaning. The offer, and hence the final contract, will inevitably be silent on many matters relating to the obligations of both sides, concerning, for example, the precise work-schedule, the precise composition of Ever–Tite's work-crew, the precise access that the Greens will give to their house, and the precise means and timing of the Greens's payments. Indeed, the contract will typically be silent on just the matter raised by the case: what Ever–Tite's obligations are concerning equipping, scheduling, and dispatching its work crews. Accordingly, it will be impossible to say whether Ever–Tite was contractually obligated to cause its work-crew to appear at the Greens's house just as and when it did, and hence whether failure to do so would have constituted breach, and hence whether, under the new proposed formalism, doing so constituted commencing performance. Finally, it is virtually certain that in order to answer this question, a contract-interpreter would have to consider what means for replacing the roof would appropriately divide the contractual surplus between Ever–Tite and the Greens, and what balance of bargaining power governed their negotiations. Only in this way will it be possible reasonably to fill in their contracts' inevitable gaps. And reasoning such as this cannot be purely formal, but must involve substantive principles, borrowed from outside of the law, and concerning efficiency and fairness.

So *Ever–Tite's* formalism, no matter how it is re-characterized and recast, decays at every turn and depends, for implementation, on substantive principles that come from outside of the law. That this is not surprising may be seen by returning to consider the very first formalism to figure in the court's analysis of the offer that it attributes to the Greens. The court asks whether this offer concerns a bilateral exchange of promises or a unilateral contract, in which the Greens exchanged a promise (to pay) not for a return promise (to re-roof) but rather directly for performance (the actual re-roofing). The court concludes that this is an offer for a bilateral contract, which can be accepted by an action, specifically by not just "mere preparation" but rather "commencing performance." But when the court fills out the details of its analysis—when it actually draws the line between mere preparation and commencing performance, it imposes on the Greens almost the precise treatment that they would have received had they been understood to be proposing a unilateral contract. As the next section will explain in greater detail, modern doctrine has adopted the rule that even though an offeror of a unilateral contract asks not for a promise, nor even for commencing performance, but for completed performance, she will be forbidden from revoking her offer in cases where her offeree has actually commenced performance, at least until the offeree has had a reasonable opportunity to complete the requested performance.[17]

This rule reflects a departure from the general principle that offerors control their offers: although an offeror in a unilateral contract asks for performance, she cannot effectively insist that performance be complete before she becomes bound by her offer. The reason for the departure is straightforward: the law worries that the alternative rule—which would allow offerors to revoke right up to the moment at which performance has been completed—would enable offerors to exploit offerees, by inducing the offerees (often, several of them at once) to commence performance only to revoke their offers just before the performance is done. Insofar as partial performance is valuable to the offerors, this will, ex post, benefit them at their offerees' expense. If offerees are naïve, then offerors might benefit ex ante, in which case the modern rule preventing revocation in such cases serves interests of fairness. Insofar as offerees are sophisticated and understand the problem about revocation, then they will be less willing to respond to offers of unilateral contracts, in which case offerors will be damaged ex ante, too, in which case the modern rule serves the interests of efficiency.

---

17. It is not clear that this approach had taken hold when *Ever–Tite* was decided. The new approach to unilateral contracts was reflected in the Restatement (Second) of Contracts, which was drafted over the decades of the 1960s and 1970s. The Restatement (First) of Contracts, published in 1932, did not include such restrictions on revocation. *Ever–Tite* fell between these texts.

Neither concern, however, plausibly applies in *Ever–Tite*. The sophisticated party, in that case, is not the offeror (the Greens), but rather the offeree (Ever–Tite), who, after all, drafted the offer. *If* the case had been treated as involving a unilateral contract, the standard reasons for preventing the offeror from revoking once performance had been commenced would apply only weakly, if at all. It seems highly implausible that the Greens were trying to exploit Ever–Tite by inducing it to begin performance in response to an offer that the Greens planned opportunistically to revoke later on. The terms of the negotiations, after all, were fixed by Ever–Tite, which would hardly have been the author and planner of its own exploitation. But the same considerations cast doubt on the outcome in *Ever–Tite* as argued, which, after all, in effect imported the rule for unilateral contracts into the bilateral context of that case.

13.4   REVOCATION

The discussion of *Ever–Tite* illustrates that the interplay of offer and acceptance can present problems of coordination and even strategic exploitation. It can be difficult for even good faith offerors and offerees to manage their negotiations, and the reciprocal and costly investments that they must make in order to determine if a mutually beneficial deal is possible, in the optimal way. Moreover, bad faith offerors and offerees can exploit these difficulties, in order to induce their counterparties to make such investments in strategic contexts that prevent the investors from recouping or even crediting the investments' costs in the terms of any deals that are finally struck. This point, of course, is not local to *Ever–Tite*. Similar considerations figured in *Lefkowitz* and *Izadi* also.

The materials in this section take up the problem of revocation a little more systematically. The emphasis, once again, is not on the instrumental aspects of the problem or the question just what solution best promotes efficiency and fairness in contractual life, but rather on the ways in which the law addresses the problem through formalisms, and on the power and limits of formalism as a method of legal analysis.

13.4.A   THE MAILBOX RULE

The mailbox rule belongs among the conventional classics of first-year legal education. It is also neither intrinsically very interesting nor practically particularly relevant in the modern world. On balance, the considerations support presenting the rule, but only in a cursory fashion.

Restatement 2d of Contracts

§ 63   Time When Acceptance Takes Effect

Unless the offer provides otherwise,

(a) an acceptance made in a manner and by a medium invited by an offer is operative and completes the manifestation of mutual assent as soon as put out of the offeree's possession, without regard to whether it ever reaches the offeror; but

(b) an acceptance under an option contract is not operative until received by the offeror.

Comments & Illustrations

Comment a. Rationale. It is often said that an offeror who makes an offer by mail makes the post office his agent to receive the acceptance, or that the mailing of a letter of acceptance puts it irrevocably out of the offeree's control. Under United States postal regulations, however, the sender of a letter has long had the power to stop delivery and reclaim the letter. A better explanation of the rule that the acceptance takes effect on dispatch is that the offeree needs a dependable basis for his decision whether to accept. In many legal systems such a basis is provided by a general rule that an offer is irrevocable unless it provides otherwise. The common law provides such a basis through the rule that a revocation of an offer is ineffective if received after an acceptance has been properly dispatched. See Comment *c* to § 42. Acceptance by telegram is governed in this respect by the same considerations as acceptance by mail.

Illustration:

1. A makes B an offer, inviting acceptance by telegram, and B duly telegraphs an acceptance. A purports to revoke the offer in person or by telephone or telegraph, but the attempted revocation is received by B after the telegram of acceptance is dispatched. There is no effective revocation.

Comment b. Loss or delay in transit. In the interest of simplicity and clarity, the rule has been extended to cases where an acceptance is lost or delayed in the course of transmission. The convenience of the rule is less clear in such cases than in cases of attempted revocation of the offer, however, and the language of the offer is often properly interpreted as making the offeror's duty of performance conditional upon receipt of the acceptance. Indeed, where the receipt of notice is essential to enable the offeror to perform, such a condition is normally implied. See Comment *c* to § 226.

Illustrations:

2. A offers to buy cotton from B, the operator of a cotton gin, B to accept by specifying the number of bales in a telegram sent before 8 p.m. the same day. B duly sends a telegram of acceptance and ships the cotton, but the telegram is not delivered. There is a contract, and A is bound to take and pay for the cotton.

3. A mails to B an offer to lease land, stating, "Telegraph me Yes or No. If I do not hear from you by noon on Friday, I shall conclude No." B duly telegraphs "Yes," but the telegram is not

delivered until after noon on Friday. Any contract formed by the telegraphic acceptance is discharged.

4.   A offers to buy cattle for B, on an understanding that if B telegraphs "Yes" A will notify B of the amount of money needed and B will supply it. B's "Yes" telegram is duly dispatched but does not arrive within a reasonable time. Any contract formed by the dispatch of the telegram is discharged.

Comment c. Revocation of acceptance. The fact that the offeree has power to reclaim his acceptance from the post office or telegraph company does not prevent the acceptance from taking effect on dispatch. Nor, in the absence of additional circumstances, does the actual recapture of the acceptance deprive it of legal effect, though as a practical matter the offeror cannot assert his rights unless he learns of them. An attempt to revoke the acceptance by an overtaking communication is similarly ineffective, even though the revocation is received before the acceptance is received. After mailing an acceptance of a revocable offer, the offeree is not permitted to speculate at the offeror's expense during the time required for the letter to arrive.

A purported revocation of acceptance may, however, affect the rights of the parties. It may amount to an offer to rescind the contract or to a repudiation of it, or it may bar the offeree by estoppel from enforcing it. In some cases it may be justified as an exercise of a right of stoppage in transit or a demand for assurance of performance. Compare Uniform Commercial Code §§ 2–609, 2–702, 2–705. Or the contract may be voidable for mistake or misrepresentation, §§ 151–54, 164. See particularly the provisions of § 153 on unilateral mistake.

Illustrations:

5.   A mails to B a note payable by C with instructions to collect the amount of the note and remit by mailing B's own check. At C's request B mails his own check as instructed. Subsequently, at C's request, B recovers his letter and check from the post office. The recovery does not discharge the contract formed by the mailing of B's check. But if B is a bank, its remittance may be provisional under Uniform Commercial Code § 4–211.

6.   The facts being otherwise as stated in Illustration 5, B recovers his letter and check from the post office because he has learned that C is insolvent and cannot reimburse B. B is entitled to rescind the contract for mistake. See §§ 153–54; compare Uniform Commercial Code § 4–212.

7.   A mails an offer to B to appoint B A's exclusive distributor in a specified area. B duly mails an acceptance. Thereafter B mails a letter which is received by A before the acceptance is received and which rejects the offer and makes a counter-offer. On receiving the rejection and before receiving the acceptance, A executes a contract appointing C as exclusive distributor instead of B. B is estopped to enforce the contract. Compare § 40.

8. The Government mails to A an offer to pay the amount quoted by him for the manufacture of two sets of ship propellers, and A mails an acceptance. A then discovers that by mistake he has quoted the price for a single set, and so informs the Government by a telegram which arrives before the acceptance. A's mailing the acceptance created a contract. The question whether the contract is voidable for mistake is governed by the rules stated in §§ 153–54.

Comment d. Other types of cases. The question when and where an acceptance takes effect may arise in determining the application of tax and regulatory laws, choice of governing law, venue of litigation, and other issues. Such cases often turn on policies beyond the scope of the Restatement of this Subject. To the extent that the issue is referred to the rule governing private contract disputes, the rules stated in this Section are applicable. Where the issue is what obligation is imposed by a contract, whether those rules apply is ordinarily a matter of interpretation.

Illustrations:

9. A mails to B an offer to buy goods, and B mails an acceptance. The application of a new tax statute depends on when title to the goods passes to A, and under Uniform Commercial Code § 2–401(3)(b) title passes at the time of contracting. The time of contracting is the time when B's acceptance is mailed.

10. A offers to insure B's house against fire, the insurance to take effect upon actual payment of the premium, and invites B to reply by mailing his check for a specified amount. B duly mails the check. While B's letter is in transit, the house burns. The loss is within the period of insurance coverage.

Comment e. The offeree's possession. The rule of Subsection (1) gives effect to an acceptance when "put out of the offeree's possession." Its principal application is to the use of mail and telegraph, but it would apply equally to any other similar public service instrumentality, even though the instrumentality may for some purposes be the offeree's agent. See Restatement, Second, Agency § 1. It may also apply to a private messenger service which is independent of the offeree and can be relied on to keep accurate records. But, except where the Government or a telegraph company can make use of its own postal or telegraph facilities, communication by means of the offeree's employee is excluded; the employee's possession is treated as that of the employer.

Illustration:

11. A makes B an offer by mail, or messenger, and B promptly sends an acceptance by his own employee. There is no contract until the acceptance is received by the offeror. As to receipt, see § 68.

Comment f. Option contracts. An option contract provides a dependable basis for decision whether to exercise the option, and removes the primary reason for the rule of Subsection (1). Moreover, there is no objection to speculation at the expense of a party who has irrevocably assumed that risk. Option contracts are commonly subject to a definite time limit, and the usual understanding is that the notification that the option has been exercised must be received by the offeror before that time. Whether or not there is such a time limit, in the absence of a contrary provision in the option contract, the offeree takes the risk of loss or delay in the transmission of the acceptance and remains free to revoke the acceptance until it arrives. Similarly, if there is such a mistake on the part of the offeror as justifies the rescission of his unilateral obligation, the right to rescind is not lost merely because a letter of acceptance is posted. See §§ 151–54.

Illustrations:

12. A, for consideration, gives B an option to buy property, written notice to be given on or before a specified date. Notice dispatched before but not received until after that date is not effective to exercise the option.

13. A submits a bid to supply goods to the Government, which becomes irrevocable when bids are opened. Within a reasonable time the Government mails a notice of award of the contract to A. Until A receives the notice, there is no contract binding on the Government.

Uniform Commercial Code

§ 1–201   General Definitions

(36) "Send" in connection with a writing, record, or notice means:

(A) to deposit in the mail or deliver for transmission by any other usual means of communication with postage or cost of transmission provided for and properly addressed and, in the case of an instrument, to an address specified thereon or otherwise agreed, or if there be none to any address reasonable under the circumstances; or

(B) in any other way to cause to be received any record or notice within the time it would have arrived if properly sent.

Uniform Commercial Code

§ 2–206.   Offer and Acceptance in Formation of Contract.

(1) Unless otherwise unambiguously indicated by the language or circumstances

(a) an offer to make a contract shall be construed as inviting acceptance in any manner and by any medium reasonable in the circumstances;

(b) an order or other offer to buy goods for prompt or current shipment shall be construed as inviting acceptance either by a prompt promise to ship or by the prompt or current shipment of conforming or non-conforming goods, but such a shipment of non-conforming goods does not constitute an acceptance if the seller seasonably notifies the buyer that the shipment is offered only as an accommodation to the buyer.

(2) Where the beginning of a requested performance is a reasonable mode of acceptance an offeror who is not notified of acceptance within a reasonable time may treat the offer as having lapsed before acceptance.

Official Comment

Prior Uniform Statutory Provision: Sections 1 and 3, Uniform Sales Act.

Changes: Completely rewritten in this and other sections of this Article.

Purposes of Changes: To make it clear that:

1.   Any reasonable manner of acceptance is intended to be regarded as available unless the offeror has made quite clear that it will not be acceptable. Former technical rules as to acceptance, such as requiring that telegraphic offers be accepted by telegraphed acceptance, etc., are rejected and a criterion that the acceptance be "in any manner and by any medium reasonable under the circumstances," is substituted. This section is intended to remain flexible and its applicability to be enlarged as new media of communication develop or as the more time-saving present day media come into general use,

2.   Either shipment or a prompt promise to ship is made a proper means of acceptance of an offer looking to current shipment. In accordance with ordinary commercial understanding the section interprets an order looking to current shipment as allowing acceptance either by actual shipment or by a prompt promise to ship and rejects the artificial theory that only a single mode of acceptance is normally envisaged by an offer. This is true even though the language of the offer happens to be "ship at once" or the like. "Shipment" is here used in the same sense as in Section 2-504; it does not include the beginning of delivery by the seller's own truck or by messenger. But loading on the seller's own truck might be a beginning of performance under subsection (2).

3.   The beginning of performance by an offeree can be effective as acceptance so as to bind the offeror only if followed within a reasonable time by notice to the offeror. Such a beginning of performance must unambiguously express the offeree's intention to engage himself. For the protection of both parties it is essential that notice follow in due course to constitute acceptance. Nothing in this section however bars the possibility that under the common law performance begun may have an intermediate effect of temporarily barring revocation of the offer, or at the offeror's option, final effect in constituting acceptance.

4.   Subsection (1)(b) deals with the situation where a shipment made following an order is shown by a notification of shipment to be referable to

that order but has a defect. Such a non-conforming shipment is normally to be understood as intended to close the bargain, even though it proves to have been at the same time a breach. However, the seller by stating that the shipment is nonconforming and is offered only as an accommodation to the buyer keeps the shipment or notification from operating as an acceptance.

United States Domestic Mail Manual (current version)

Chapter 507   Mailer Services

5.0   Package Intercept

5.1   Description of Service

[1–22–12] Package Intercept service provides a method for customers to authorize redirection of any mailable domestic mailpiece to sender. If the mail item is found and redirected, additional postage is charged as provided under 5.2. Package Intercept requests are active for 10 days.

5.1.1   Eligibility

Package Intercept service is available for any Express Mail, Priority Mail, First–Class Mail, First–Class Package Service, Parcel Select, and Package Services, letter, flat, or parcel measuring not more than 108 inches in length and girth combined, with a tracking barcode.

5.1.2   Ineligible

Package Intercept is not available to international and APO/FPO/DPO destinations or on mailpieces requiring a customs label (608.2.4). Package Intercept is also not available for any mailpiece that indicates surface-only transportation such as Label 127, "Surface Mail Only" or bears other hazardous materials markings such as "Consumer Commodity ORM–D".

5.2   Postage and Fees

Customers must pay a nonrefundable per-piece fee to initiate the process of attempting to intercept the mailpiece. All mailpieces that are redirected to the sender may be additionally subject to payment of the applicable postage. Payment of the Package Intercept fee may be made by cash, check, credit card, or debit card. Postage for the redirection to sender will be charged based on how the piece was originally mailed and collected as postage due.

5.3   Adding Extra Services

Extra services cannot be added to mailpieces intercepted and redirected to sender.

5.4   Registered Mail

Package Intercept is available for eligible matter mailed using Registered Mailservice. The maximum declared value for intercepted Registered

Mail is $15,000,000. In addition to 5.2 and 5.5, customers requesting to intercept Registered Mail must write on the receipt "Withdrawn" and sign and surrender the receipt to the Post Office.

5.5   Request for Intercept

Retail and commercial customers may request Package Intercept by submitting PS Form 1509, *Application for Package Intercept*, at the Post Office of mailing along with valid photo identification. Intercepted mail-pieces are only redirected to sender. Only the sender or authorized representative can request Package Intercept.

The Postal Law and Regulations of the United States of America (1879 version)

Sec. 291.   Withdrawal of Letters from Mailing Post-office—

To prevent fraud the postmaster must not permit any letter put into his post-office for transmission by mail to be withdrawn by any person except the writer thereof, or, in case of a minor child, the parent or guardian of the same; and the utmost care must be taken to ascertain that the person applying for such letter is really the writer, parent, or guardian.

Sec. 292.   Proof of Identity of Letter required—

To enable him to know that the person applying for the withdrawal of a letter is the writing, the postmaster may require him, or his messenger, to exhibit to him the same supersecription and seal that are upon the letter. And if the postmaster is satisfied that the handwriting and seal are the same, he will permit the letter to be withdrawn, taking a receipt, and preserving it with the paper containing the superscription, and the order, if one were sent. If the person applying for the letter is the parent or guardian of the minor, the postmaster must require him to identify the particular letter by extrinisic evidence satisfactory to the postmaster.

Sec. 293.   When to refuse Application for Withdrawal—

Postmasters should refuse all applications for the withdrawal of letters in cases where the necessary search would involve the delay of a mail, or retard the regular work of the post-office.

Sec. 294.   Mail-matter beyond Mailing Post-office cannot be Withdrawn—

After a letter, or any other article of mail-matter, has passed from the mailing post-office, the delivery of it cannot be prevented or delayed by any one except upon the order of the Postmaster–General, to whom direct application must be made by the writer.

* * *

The basic principles set out by these rules are easy to fathom. An *acceptance* is effective as soon as it is mailed, although only when the sender has taken such precautions as ordinarily necessary to insure the acceptance's safe transmission. The analogous rule cannot, of course, apply to *revocations*; if it did, acceptances and revocations that crossed in the mail might both be effective, which is impossible. Accordingly, a revocation is effective only when it is received.

Legal rules concerning these matters were practically important, indeed necessary, in a past in which instantaneous communication was difficult or impossible, so that time lags between issuance and receipt of contractual communications—and the associated ambiguities concerning their effectiveness—were inevitable. Moreover, the particular pattern of coordination established by the mailbox rule was sensible in the world that generated the rule. If acceptances were not effective upon mailing, but revocations were, offerors in fluctuating markets might, in effect, gamble on their offerees accounts. An offeror could offer a price and then wait to see what the market did over the time period between her offeree's posting his acceptance, and the acceptance's delivery to her. If the market moved in her favor, so that the price on arrival was more attractive to her than the price when the acceptance was mailed, she could revoke and make a new offer, at the more advantageous price. If the market moved against her, she could abide the arrival of the acceptance, and again receive the better of the two prices. The then-applicable postal technology and practices entailed that senders of letters lost effective control of their communications on posting them (and while regulations permitted recalling letters in principle, they made accommodations to practice that rendered recall often impermissible as well). Accordingly, the offeree had no reliable way to prevent this exploitative strategy.[18]

Something like the opposite result may well apply today. Modern mail tracking technology makes it much cheaper and easier to find and divert

---

18. Senders did sometimes try to recall letters, nevertheless, and they sometimes succeeded:

How to Recall A Letter

Persons Who Change Their Minds After Mailing an Epistle Can Get It Back

A few days ago a young woman visiting in this city mailed letter to some friends at her native place in a distant State. Within ten minutes after dropping her letter into a lamp post mail box she received information which made it extremely desirable that certain statements contained in her letter be suppressed. How to regain possession of the letter at once became a burning question with her. She hastened to the nearest Branch Post Office station, and laid the case before the Superintendent.

The young woman was in doubt whether the rules of the Post Office Department would permit an individual to recall a letter after it had been sent on its way. The Branch Superintendent assured her that the rules of the department were framed to accommodate the people in every way possible, and that her letter would be returned to her. He asked her to give him without delay a facsimile of the envelope used with the address in the same handwriting. This was done and within an hour the desired letter was returned to its writer.

"Persons desiring to recall letters that they have mailed need have but little trouble about it," said the Branch Superintendent, "if they apply at the proper place promptly. The rules of the

mail en route. And the contemporary postal regulation reproduced above allows senders to recall their letters between posting and delivery.[19] Insofar as acceptances can be recalled before they are delivered, the traditional mailbox rule allows accepting offerees to engage in just the manipulation that it prevented offerors from engaging in, under the older regulatory regime. An offeree can send his acceptance, which becomes effective on posting under the mailbox rule. If the market moves in his favor, he simply allows the acceptance to be delivered, secure in the fact that the mailbox rule (which makes revocations effective only upon receipt) entails that his offeror cannot respond to the market's shift by changing the terms of her offer. On the other hand, if the market moves against the offeree, he can nowadays recall his acceptance and replace it with a more advantageous counteroffer. Although this does not in principle prevent it from taking effect, his offeror will never know about the initial acceptance, and will receive the counteroffer only. The offeree will have exploited the market shift.

These observations render concrete the problems posed by time-lags between the sending and receipt of offers, acceptances, and revocations. They also illustrate that no legal rule resolves these problems quite satisfactorily. The real solution is technological—to conduct contractual negotiations using instantaneous communications. This, of course, is what is generally done today.

13.4.B   IRREVOCABLE OFFERS

The problem taken up in *Ever–Tite*—in which an offeree invests in an offer that is subsequently revoked—arises in other contexts also. One

---

department provide that letters which have been deposited in the General Post Office, or at a Branch Post Office station, but have not been dispatched, may be withdrawn if personal application be made within one hour after posting, at the office of the Assistant Postmaster (before 3 P.M.,) or of the Superintendent of the Branch Post Office station. In each instance a facsimile of the envelope used, and of the address in the same handwriting must be submitted as an evidence of good faith, or identity of the applicant. After 3 o'clock P.M. it will be impossible to withdraw a letter from the General Post Office, as the accumulation of mail matter will render it impracticable to divert the employees from their regular duties to make the necessary search."

"There is a way, however, of getting back letters after they have left the General Post Office. Persons wishing to recall such letters must apply, at Room 4, Post Office Building, prepared to give a full description of the outward appearance of the letters, and with facsimile of envelopes and addresses, also with funds to make deposit to cover the cost of telegraphing, & c. Postmasters at offices to which such letters have been sent will not return any letters on the request of senders unless such request is endorsed by the Postmaster at the office of mailing."

The New York Times

Published: January 1, 1898

(c) The New York Times

19.   Indeed, as of April 2012, it will be possible to do so online. See http://about.usps.com/postal-bulletin/2011/pb22326/html/kit.htm.

Moreover, UPS and Federal Express already have online delivery intercept services.

For UPS, see http://www.ups.com/content/us/en/resources/service/delivery/delivery_intercept.html.

For Federal Express, see http://www.fedex.com/us/service-guide/our-services/options/index.html.

particularly important context involves the complex of relations that arise among general contractors, subcontractors, and customers in construction contracts. The cases below take up these relations and the patterns of offer, reliance, and acceptance/revocation that they involve. Once again, formalism figures prominently in the analysis in the opinions. As throughout this part, read the opinions less to decide what outcome or rule is instrumentally optimal—efficient or fair—and more to understand the influence of formalism on legal doctrine and, in particular, the power and limits of legal formalism to determine outcomes in difficult cases.

James Baird Co. v. Gimbel Bros., Inc.

United States Court of Appeals, Second Circuit, 1933.
64 F.2d 344.

Action by the James Baird Company against Gimbel Brothers, Incorporated. From a judgment dismissing the complaint, plaintiff appeals.

Affirmed.

■ HAND, CIRCUIT JUDGE. The plaintiff sued the defendant for breach of a contract to deliver linoleum under a contract of sale; the defendant denied the making of the contract; the parties tried the case to the judge under a written stipulation and he directed judgment for the defendant. The facts as found, bearing on the making of the contract, the only issue necessary to discuss, were as follows: The defendant, a New York merchant, knew that the Department of Highways in Pennsylvania had asked for bids for the construction of a public building. It sent an employee to the office of a contractor in Philadelphia, who had possession of the specifications, and the employee there computed the amount of the linoleum which would be required on the job, underestimating the total yardage by about one-half the proper amount. In ignorance of this mistake, on December twenty-fourth the defendant sent to some twenty or thirty contractors, likely to bid on the job, an offer to supply all the linoleum required by the specifications at two different lump sums, depending upon the quality used. These offers concluded as follows: "If successful in being awarded this contract, it will be absolutely guaranteed, and we are offering these prices for reasonable" (sic), "prompt acceptance after the general contract has been awarded." The plaintiff, a contractor in Washington, got one of these on the twenty-eighth, and on the same day the defendant learned its mistake and telegraphed all the contractors to whom it had sent the offer, that it withdrew it and would substitute a new one at about double the amount of the old. This withdrawal reached the plaintiff at Washington on the afternoon of the same day, but not until after it had put in a bid at Harrisburg at a lump sum, based as to linoleum upon the prices quoted by the defendant. The public authorities accepted the plaintiff's bid on December thirtieth, the defendant having meanwhile written a letter of confirmation of its withdrawal, received on the thirty-first. The plaintiff formally accepted the offer on January second, and, as the defendant persisted in declining to recognize the existence of a contract, sued it for damages on a breach.

Unless there are circumstances to take it out of the ordinary doctrine, since the offer was withdrawn before it was accepted, the acceptance was too late. Restatement of Contracts, § 35. To meet this the plaintiff argues as follows: It was a reasonable implication from the defendant's offer that it should be irrevocable in case the plaintiff acted upon it, that is to say, used the prices quoted in making its bid, thus putting itself in a position from which it could not withdraw without great loss. While it might have withdrawn its bid after receiving the revocation, the time had passed to submit another, and as the item of linoleum was a very trifling part of the cost of the whole building, it would have been an unreasonable hardship to expect it to lose the contract on that account, and probably forfeit its deposit. While it is true that the plaintiff might in advance have secured a contract conditional upon the success of its bid, this was not what the defendant suggested. It understood that the contractors would use its offer in their bids, and would thus in fact commit themselves to supplying the linoleum at the proposed prices. The inevitable implication from all this was that when the contractors acted upon it, they accepted the offer and promised to pay for the linoleum, in case their bid were accepted.

It was of course possible for the parties to make such a contract, and the question is merely as to what they meant; that is, what is to be imputed to the words they used. Whatever plausibility there is in the argument, is in the fact that the defendant must have known the predicament in which the contractors would be put if it withdrew its offer after the bids went in. However, it seems entirely clear that the contractors did not suppose that they accepted the offer merely by putting in their bids. If, for example, the successful one had repudiated the contract with the public authorities after it had been awarded to him, certainly the defendant could not have sued him for a breach. If he had become bankrupt, the defendant could not prove against his estate. It seems plain therefore that there was no contract between them. And if there be any doubt as to this, the language of the offer sets it at rest. The phrase, "if successful in being awarded this contract," is scarcely met by the mere use of the prices in the bids. Surely such a use was not an "award" of the contract to the defendant. Again, the phrase, "we are offering these prices for prompt acceptance after the general contract has been awarded," looks to the usual communication of an acceptance, and precludes the idea that the use of the offer in the bidding shall be the equivalent. It may indeed be argued that this last language contemplated no more than an early notice that the offer had been accepted, the actual acceptance being the bid, but that would wrench its natural meaning too far, especially in the light of the preceding phrase. The contractors had a ready escape from their difficulty by insisting upon a contract before they used the figures; and in commercial transactions it does not in the end promote justice to seek strained interpretations in aid of those who do not protect themselves.

But the plaintiff says that even though no bilateral contract was made, the defendant should be held under the doctrine of "promissory estoppel." This is to be chiefly found in those cases where persons subscribe to a venture, usually charitable, and are held to their promises after it has been completed. It has been applied much more broadly, however, and has now been generalized in section 90, of the Restatement of Contracts. We may arguendo accept it as it there reads, for it does not apply to the case at bar. Offers are ordinarily made in exchange for a consideration, either a counter-promise or some other act which the promisor wishes to secure. In such cases they propose bargains; they presuppose that each promise or performance is an inducement to the other. But a man may make a promise without expecting an equivalent; a donative promise, conditional or absolute. The common law provided for such by sealed instruments, and it is unfortunate that these are no longer generally available. The doctrine of 'promissory estoppel' is to avoid the harsh results of allowing the promisor in such a case to repudiate, when the promisee has acted in reliance upon the promise. But an offer for an exchange is not meant to become a promise until a consideration has been received, either a counter-promise or whatever else is stipulated. To extend it would be to hold the offeror regardless of the stipulated condition of his offer. In the case at bar the defendant offered to deliver the linoleum in exchange for the plaintiff's acceptance, not for its bid, which was a matter of indifference to it. That offer could become a promise to deliver only when the equivalent was received; that is, when the plaintiff promised to take and pay for it. There is no room in such a situation for the doctrine of "promissory estoppel."

Nor can the offer be regarded as of an option, giving the plaintiff the right seasonably to accept the linoleum at the quoted prices if its bid was accepted, but not binding it to take and pay, if it could get a better bargain elsewhere. There is not the least reason to suppose that the defendant meant to subject itself to such one-sided obligation. True, if so construed, the doctrine of 'promissory estoppel' might apply, the plaintiff having acted in reliance upon it, though, so far as we have found, the decisions are otherwise. As to that, however, we need not declare ourselves.

Judgment affirmed.

Restatement 2d of Contracts

§ 35   The Offeree's Power of Acceptance

(1) An offer gives to the offeree a continuing power to complete the manifestation of mutual assent by acceptance of the offer.

(2) A contract cannot be created by acceptance of an offer after the power of acceptance has been terminated in one of the ways listed in § 36.

Comments

Comment a. "Duration of an offer." It is common to speak of the duration "of an offer." But "offer" is defined in § 24 as a manifestation of assent, and the reference here is not to the time occupied by the offeror's conduct but to the duration of its legal operation. Hence this topic speaks of the duration and termination of the offeree's power rather than the duration and termination of the offer.

Comment b. Continuing power. Under Subsection (1) the offeree's power arises when the offeror's manifestation of assent is complete. Since the acceptance must have reference to the offer it is ordinarily necessary that the offeree have knowledge of the offer. See § 23. Once the power arises it continues until terminated. Methods of termination are listed in § 36 and explained in the following sections. There is no requirement that the offer be accompanied by the mental assent of the offeror, or that mental assent which exists at the time of the offer continue until the time of acceptance. See § 19.

Comment c. Creation of contract. Exercise of the power of acceptance concludes an agreement and a bargain, and thus satisfies one of the requirements for formation of an informal contract enforceable as a bargain. See §§ 17, 18. But a contract is not created unless the other requirements are met. Thus there may be no consideration; or impossibility or illegality may prevent any duty of performance from arising.

Restatement 2d of Contracts

§ 36 Methods of Termination of the Power of Acceptance

(1) An offeree's power of acceptance may be terminated by

(a) rejection or counter-offer by the offeree, or

(b) lapse of time, or

(c) revocation by the offeror, or

(d) death or incapacity of the offeror or offeree.

(2) In addition, an offeree's power of acceptance is terminated by the non-occurrence of any condition of acceptance under the terms of the offer.

Comments

Comment a. Scope. This Section merely lists the methods of termination which are possible. The circumstances under which each method operates are stated in §§ 36–49.

Comment b. Conditions of acceptance. Subsection (2) provides for any condition of acceptance arising under the terms of the offer itself. Compare the definition of "condition" in § 224. A condition of acceptance, like a condition, may be express or implied in fact or constructive. See Comment *c* to § 226. Thus by common understanding a reward offer can ordinarily be accepted only once; the first acceptance terminates the power of acceptance of other offerees. See Illustration 1 to § 29. Compare the effect on a bid at an auction when a higher bid is made. See § 28(1)(c).

Comment c. Impossibility and illegality. The power of acceptance may be terminated by the death or destruction of a person or thing essential for performance or by supervening legal prohibition. The extent to which such events have the effect of a failure of a condition of acceptance depends on the terms of the offer and on the circumstances. Such events may also prevent a duty of performance from arising from an acceptance if they occur before the offer is made, or may discharge a duty of performance if they occur after acceptance. The effects of such events are therefore stated in Chapters 6–12, which deal with Mistake (Chapter 6), Misrepresentation, Duress and Undue Influence (Chapter 7), Unenforceability on Grounds of Public Policy (Chapter 8), The Scope of Contractual Obligations (including conditions and similar events) (Chapter 9), Performance and Non-performance (Chapter 10), Impracticability of Performance and Frustration of Purpose (Chapter 11) and Discharge by Assent or Alteration (Chapter 12).

Restatement 2d of Contracts

§ 45   Option Contract by Part Performance or Tender

(1) Where an offer invites an offeree to accept by rendering a performance and does not invite a promissory acceptance, an option contract is created when the offeree tenders or begins the invited performance or tenders a beginning of it.

(2) The offeror's duty of performance under any option contract so created is conditional on completion or tender of the invited performance in accordance with the terms of the offer.

Comments & Illustrations

Comment a. Offer limited to acceptance by performance only. This Section is limited to cases where the offer does not invite a promissory acceptance. Such an offer has often been referred to as an "offer for a unilateral contract." Typical illustrations are found in offers of rewards or prizes and in non-commercial arrangements among relatives and friends. See Comment *b* to § 32. As to analogous cases arising under offers which give the offeree power to accept either by performing or by promising to perform, as he chooses, see §§ 32, 62.

Comment b. Manifestation of contrary intention. The rule of this Section is designed to protect the offeree in justifiable reliance on the offeror's promise, and the rule yields to a manifestation of intention which makes reliance unjustified. A reservation of power to revoke after performance has begun means that as yet there is no promise and no offer. See §§ 2, 24. In particular, if the performance is one which requires the cooperation of both parties, such as the payment of money or the manual delivery of goods, a person who reserves the right to refuse to receive the performance has not made an offer. See § 26.

Illustrations:

1.   B owes A $5000 payable in installments over a five-year period. A proposes that B discharge the debt by paying $4,500 cash within one month, but reserves the right to refuse any such payment. A has not made an offer. A tender by B in accordance with the proposal is an offer by B.

2.   A, an insurance company, issues a bulletin to its agents, entitled "Extra Earnings Agreement," providing for annual bonus payments to the agents varying according to "monthly premiums in force" and "lapse ratio," but reserving the right to change or discontinue the bonus, individually or collectively, with or without notice, at any time before payment. There is no offer or promise.

Comment c. Tender of performance. A proposal to receive a payment of money or a delivery of goods is an offer only if acceptance can be completed without further cooperation by the offeror. If there is an offer, it follows that acceptance must be complete at the latest when performance is tendered. A tender of performance, so bargained for and given in exchange for the offer, ordinarily furnishes consideration and creates a contract. See §§ 17, 71, 72.

This is so whether or not the tender carries with it any incidental promises. See §§ 54, 62. If no commitment is made by the offeree, the contract is an option contract. See § 25.

Illustration:

3.   A promises B to sell him a specified chattel for $5, stating that B is not to be bound until he pays the money. B tenders $5 within a reasonable time, but A refuses to accept the tender. There is a breach of contract.

Comment d. Beginning to perform. If the invited performance takes time, the invitation to perform necessarily includes an invitation to begin performance. In most such cases the beginning of performance carries with it an express or implied promise to complete performance. See § 62. In the less common case where the offer does not contemplate or invite a promise by the offeree, the beginning of performance nevertheless completes the manifestation of mutual assent and furnishes consideration for an option contract. See § 25. If the beginning of performance requires the cooperation of the offeror, tender of part performance has the same effect. Part performance or tender may also create an option contract in a situation where the offeree is invited to take up the option by making a promise, if the offer invites a preliminary performance before the time for the offeree's final commitment.

Illustrations:

4.   A offers a reward for the return of lost property. In response to the offer, B searches for the property and finds it. A then notifies B that the offer is revoked. B makes a tender of the

property to A conditional on payment of the reward, and A refuses. There is a breach of contract by A.

5.   A, a magazine, offers prizes in a subscription contest. At a time when B has submitted the largest number of subscriptions, A cancels the contest. A has broken its contract with B.

6.   A writes to her daughter B, living in another state, an offer to leave A's farm to B if B gives up her home and cares for A during A's life, B remaining free to terminate the arrangement at any time. B gives up her home, moves to A's farm, and begins caring for A. A is bound by an option contract.

7.   A offers to sell a piece of land to B, and promises that if B incurs expense in employing experts to appraise the property the offer will be irrevocable for 30 days. B hires experts and pays for their transportation to the land. A is bound by an option contract.

8.   In January A, an employer, publishes a notice to his employees, promising a stated Christmas bonus to any employee who is continuously in A's employ from January to Christmas. B, an employee hired by the week, reads the notice and continues at work beyond the expiration of the current week. A is bound by an option contract, and if B is continuously in A's employ until Christmas a notice of revocation of the bonus is ineffective.

Comment e. Completion of performance. Where part performance or tender by the offeree creates an option contract, the offeree is not bound to complete performance. The offeror alone is bound, but his duty of performance is conditional on completion of the offeree's performance. If the offeree abandons performance, the offeror's duty to perform never arises. See § 224, defining "condition," and Illustration 4 to that Section. But the condition may be excused, for example, if the offeror prevents performance, waives it, or repudiates. See Comment *b* to § 225 and §§ 239, 278.

Comment f. Preparations for performance. What is begun or tendered must be part of the actual performance invited in order to preclude revocation under this Section. Beginning preparations, though they may be essential to carrying out the contract or to accepting the offer, is not enough. Preparations to perform may, however, constitute justifiable reliance sufficient to make the offeror's promise binding under § 87(2).

In many cases what is invited depends on what is a reasonable mode of acceptance. See § 30. The distinction between preparing for performance and beginning performance in such cases may turn on many factors: the extent to which the offeree's conduct is clearly referable to the offer, the definite and substantial character of that conduct, and the extent to which it is of actual or prospective benefit to the offeror rather than the offeree, as well as the terms of the communications between the parties, their prior course of dealing, and any relevant usages of trade.

Illustration:

9.   A makes a written promise to pay $5000 to B, a hospital, "to aid B in its humanitarian work." Relying upon this and other

like promises, B proceeds in its humanitarian work, expending large sums of money and incurring large liabilities. Performance by B has begun, and A's offer is irrevocable.

Comment g. Agency contracts. This Section frequently applies to agency arrangements, particularly offers made to real estate brokers. Sometimes there is a return promise by the agent, particularly if there is an agreement for exclusive dealing, since such an agreement normally imposes an obligation on the agent to use best efforts. See Uniform Commercial Code § 2–306(2); compare Restatement, Second, Agency § 378. In other cases the agent does not promise to act, but the principal must compensate him if he does act. The rules governing the principal's duty of compensation are stated in detail in Chapter 14 of the Restatement, Second, Agency, particularly §§ 443–57.

Restatement (Second) of Contracts § 90

Promise Reasonably Inducing Action Or Forbearance

(1) A promise which the promisor should reasonably expect to induce action or forbearance on the part of the promisee or a third person and which does induce such action or forbearance is binding if injustice can be avoided only by enforcement of the promise. The remedy granted for breach may be limited as justice requires.

(2) A charitable subscription or a marriage settlement is binding under Subsection (1) without proof that the promise induced action or forbearance.

Comments & Illustrations

Comment a. Relation to other rules. Obligations and remedies based on reliance are not peculiar to the law of contracts. This Section is often referred to in terms of "promissory estoppel," a phrase suggesting an extension of the doctrine of estoppel. Estoppel prevents a person from showing the truth contrary to a representation of fact made by him after another has relied on the representation. See Restatement, Second, Agency § 8B; Restatement, Second, Torts §§ 872, 894. Reliance is also a significant feature of numerous rules in the law of negligence, deceit and restitution. See, e.g., Restatement, Second, Agency §§ 354, 378; Restatement, Second, Torts §§ 323, 537; Restatement of Restitution § 55. In some cases those rules and this Section overlap; in others they provide analogies useful in determining the extent to which enforcement is necessary to avoid injustice.

It is fairly arguable that the enforcement of informal contracts in the action of assumpsit rested historically on justifiable reliance on a promise. Certainly reliance is one of the main bases for enforcement of the half-completed exchange, and the probability of reliance lends support to the enforcement of the executory exchange. See Comments to §§ 72, 75. This

Section thus states a basic principle which often renders inquiry unnecessary as to the precise scope of the policy of enforcing bargains. Sections 87–89 state particular applications of the same principle to promises ancillary to bargains, and it also applies in a wide variety of non-commercial situations. See, e.g., § 94.

Illustration:

1. A, knowing that B is going to college, promises B that A will give him $5,000 on completion of his course. B goes to college, and borrows and spends more than $5,000 for college expenses. When he has nearly completed his course, A notifies him of an intention to revoke the promise. A's promise is binding and B is entitled to payment on completion of the course without regard to whether his performance was "bargained for" under § 71.

Comment b.   Character of reliance protected. The principle of this Section is flexible. The promisor is affected only by reliance which he does or should foresee, and enforcement must be necessary to avoid injustice. Satisfaction of the latter requirement may depend on the reasonableness of the promisee's reliance, on its definite and substantial character in relation to the remedy sought, on the formality with which the promise is made, on the extent to which the evidentiary, cautionary, deterrent and channeling functions of form are met by the commercial setting or otherwise, and on the extent to which such other policies as the enforcement of bargains and the prevention of unjust enrichment are relevant. Compare Comment to § 72. The force of particular factors varies in different types of cases: thus reliance need not be of substantial character in charitable subscription cases, but must in cases of firm offers and guaranties. Compare Subsection (2) with §§ 87, 88.

Illustrations:

2. A promises B not to foreclose, for a specified time, a mortgage which A holds on B's land. B thereafter makes improvements on the land. A's promise is binding and may be enforced by denial of foreclosure before the time has elapsed.

3. A sues B in a municipal court for damages for personal injuries caused by B's negligence. After the one year statute of limitations has run, B requests A to discontinue the action and start again in the superior court where the action can be consolidated with other actions against B arising out of the same accident. A does so. B's implied promise that no harm to A will result bars B from asserting the statute of limitations as a defense.

4. A has been employed by B for 40 years. B promises to pay A a pension of $200 per month when A retires. A retires and forbears to work elsewhere for several years while B pays the pension. B's promise is binding.

Comment c.   Reliance by third persons. If a promise is made to one party for the benefit of another, it is often foreseeable that the beneficiary will rely on the promise. Enforcement of the promise in such cases rests on the same basis and depends on the same factors as in cases of reliance by the promisee. Justifiable reliance by third persons who are not beneficiaries is less likely, but may sometimes reinforce the claim of the promisee or beneficiary.

Illustrations:

5. A holds a mortgage on B's land. To enable B to obtain a loan, A promises B in writing to release part of the land from the mortgage upon payment of a stated sum. As A contemplated, C lends money to B on a second mortgage, relying on A's promise. The promise is binding and may be enforced by C.

6. A executes and delivers a promissory note to B, a bank, to give B a false appearance of assets, deceive the banking authorities, and enable the bank to continue to operate. After several years B fails and is taken over by C, a representative of B's creditors. A's note is enforceable by C.

7. A and B, husband and wife, are tenants by the entirety of a tract of land. They make an oral promise to B's niece C to give her the tract. B, C and C's husband expend money in building a house on the tract and C and her husband take possession and live there for several years until B dies. The expenditures by B and by C's husband are treated like those by C in determining whether justice requires enforcement of the promise against A.

Comment d.   Partial enforcement. A promise binding under this section is a contract, and full-scale enforcement by normal remedies is often appropriate. But the same factors which bear on whether any relief should be granted also bear on the character and extent of the remedy. In particular, relief may sometimes be limited to restitution or to damages or specific relief measured by the extent of the promisee's reliance rather than by the terms of the promise. See §§ 84, 89; compare Restatement, Second, Torts § 549 on damages for fraud. Unless there is unjust enrichment of the promisor, damages should not put the promisee in a better position than performance of the promise would have put him. See §§ 344, 349. In the case of a promise to make a gift it would rarely be proper to award consequential damages which would place a greater burden on the promisor than performance would have imposed.

Illustrations:

8. A applies to B, a distributor of radios manufactured by C, for a "dealer franchise" to sell C's products. Such franchises are revocable at will. B erroneously informs A that C has accepted the application and will soon award the franchise, that A can proceed to employ salesmen and solicit orders, and that A will receive an initial delivery of at least 30 radios. A expends $1,150 in preparing to do business, but does not receive the franchise or any radios. B is liable to A for the $1,150 but not for the lost profit on 30 radios. Compare Restatement, Second, Agency § 329.

9. The facts being otherwise as stated in Illustration 8, B gives A the erroneous information deliberately and with C's approval and requires A to buy the assets of a deceased former dealer and thus discharge C's "moral obligation" to the widow. C is liable to A not only for A's expenses but also for the lost profit on 30 radios.

10.   A, who owns and operates a bakery, desires to go into the grocery business. He approaches B, a franchisor of supermarkets. B states to A that for $18,000 B will establish A in a store. B also advises A to move to another town and buy a small grocery to gain experience. A does so. Later B advises A to sell the grocery, which A does, taking a capital loss and foregoing expected profits from the summer tourist trade. B also advises A to sell his bakery to raise capital for the supermarket franchise, saying "Everything is ready to go. Get your money together and we are set." A sells the bakery taking a capital loss on this sale as well. Still later, B tells A that considerably more than an $18,000 investment will be needed, and the negotiations between the parties collapse. At the point of collapse many details of the proposed agreement between the parties are unresolved. The assurances from B to A are promises on which B reasonably should have expected A to rely, and A is entitled to his actual losses on the sales of the bakery and grocery and for his moving and temporary living expenses. Since the proposed agreement was never made, however, A is not entitled to lost profits from the sale of the grocery or to his expectation interest in the proposed franchise from B.

11.   A is about to buy a house on a hill. Before buying he obtains a promise from B, who owns adjoining land, that B will not build on a particular portion of his lot, where a building would obstruct the view from the house. A then buys the house in reliance on the promise. B's promise is binding, but will be specifically enforced only so long as A and his successors do not permanently terminate the use of the view.

12.   A promises to make a gift of a tract of land to B, his son-in-law. B takes possession and lives on the land for 17 years, making valuable improvements. A then dispossesses B, and specific performance is denied because the proof of the terms of the promise is not sufficiently clear and definite. B is entitled to a lien on the land for the value of the improvements, not exceeding their cost.

Comment e.   Gratuitous promises to procure insurance. This Section is to be applied with caution to promises to procure insurance. The appropriate remedy for breach of such a promise makes the promisor an insurer, and thus may result in a liability which is very large in relation to the value of the promised service. Often the promise is properly to be construed merely as a promise to use reasonable efforts to procure the insurance, and reliance by the promisee may be unjustified or may be justified only for a short time. Or it may be doubtful whether he did in fact rely. Such difficulties may be removed if the proof of the promise and the reliance are clear, or if the promise is made with some formality, or if part performance or a commercial setting or a potential benefit to the promisor provide a substitute for formality.

Illustrations:

13.   A, a bank, lends money to B on the security of a mortgage on B's new home. The mortgage requires B to insure the property. At the closing of the transaction A promises to arrange for the required insurance, and in reliance on the promise B fails to insure. Six months later the property, still uninsured, is destroyed by fire. The promise is binding.

14. A sells an airplane to B, retaining title to secure payment of the price. After the closing A promises to keep the airplane covered by insurance until B can obtain insurance. B could obtain insurance in three days but makes no effort to do so, and the airplane is destroyed after six days. A is not subject to liability by virtue of the promise.

Comment f. Charitable subscriptions, marriage settlements, and other gifts. One of the functions of the doctrine of consideration is to deny enforcement to a promise to make a gift. Such a promise is ordinarily enforced by virtue of the promisee's reliance only if his conduct is foreseeable and reasonable and involves a definite and substantial change of position which would not have occurred if the promise had not been made. In some cases, however, other policies reinforce the promisee's claim. Thus the promisor might be unjustly enriched if he could reclaim the subject of the promised gift after the promisee has improved it.

Subsection (2) identifies two other classes of cases in which the promisee's claim is similarly reinforced. American courts have traditionally favored charitable subscriptions and marriage settlements, and have found consideration in many cases where the element of exchange was doubtful or nonexistent. Where recovery is rested on reliance in such cases, a probability of reliance is enough, and no effort is made to sort out mixed motives or to consider whether partial enforcement would be appropriate.

Illustrations:

15. A promises B $5000, knowing that B desires that sum for the purchase of a parcel of land. Induced thereby, B secures without any payment an option to buy the parcel. A then tells B that he withdraws his promise. A's promise is not binding.

16. A orally promises to give her son B a tract of land to live on. As A intended, B gives up a homestead elsewhere, takes possession of the land, lives there for a year and makes substantial improvements. A's promise is binding.

17. A orally promises to pay B, a university, $100,000 in five annual installments for the purposes of its fund-raising campaign then in progress. The promise is confirmed in writing by A's agent, and two annual installments are paid before A dies. The continuance of the fund-raising campaign by B is sufficient reliance to make the promise binding on A and his estate.

18. A and B are engaged to be married. In anticipation of the marriage A and his father C enter into a formal written agreement by which C promises to leave certain property to A by will. A's subsequent marriage to B is sufficient reliance to make the promise binding on C and his estate.

Uniform Commercial Code

§ 2–205. Firm Offers.

An offer by a merchant to buy or sell goods in a signed writing which by its terms gives assurance that it will be held open is not revocable, for lack of consideration, during the time stated or if no time is stated for a reasonable time, but in no event may such period of irrevocability exceed three months; but any such term of assurance on a form supplied by the offeree must be separately signed by the offeror.

Official Comment

Prior Uniform Statutory Provision: Sections 1 and 3, Uniform Sales Act.

Changes: Completely rewritten by this and other sections of this Article.

Purposes of Changes:

1. This section is intended to modify the former rule which required that "firm offers" be sustained by consideration in order to bind, and to require instead that they must merely be characterized as such and expressed in signed writings.

2. The primary purpose of this section is to give effect to the deliberate intention of a merchant to make a current firm offer binding. The deliberation is shown in the case

of an individualized document by the merchant's signature to the offer, and in the case of an offer included on a form supplied by the other party to the transaction by the separate signing of the particular clause which contains the offer. "Signed" here also includes authentication but the reasonableness of the authentication herein allowed must be determined in the light of the purpose of the section. The circumstances surrounding the signing may justify something less than a formal signature or initialing but typically the kind of authentication involved here would consist of a minimum of initialing of the clause involved. A handwritten memorandum on the writer's letterhead purporting in its terms to "confirm" a firm offer already made would be enough to satisfy this section, although not subscribed, since under the circumstances it could not be considered a memorandum of mere negotiation and it would adequately show its own authenticity. Similarly, an authorized telegram will suffice, and this is true even though the original draft contained only a typewritten signature. However, despite settled courses of dealing or usages of the trade whereby firm offers are made by oral communication and relied upon without more evidence, such offers remain revocable under this Article since authentication by a writing is the essence of this section.

3. This section is intended to apply to current "firm" offers and not to long term options, and an outside time limit of three months during which such offers remain irrevocable has been set. The three month period during which firm offers remain irrevocable under this section need not be stated by days or by date. If the offer states that it is "guaranteed" or "firm" until the happening of a contingency which will occur within the three month period, it will remain irrevocable until that event. A promise made for a longer period will operate under this section to bind the offeror only for the first three months of the period but may of course be renewed.

If supported by consideration it may continue for as long as the parties specify. This section deals only with the offer which is not supported by consideration.

4. Protection is afforded against the inadvertent signing of a firm offer when contained in a form prepared by the offeree by requiring that such a clause be separately authenticated. If the offer clause is called to the offeror's attention and he separately authenticates it, he will be bound; Section 2–302 may operate, however, to prevent an unconscionable result which otherwise would flow from other terms appearing in the form.

5. Safeguards are provided to offer relief in the case of material mistake by virtue of the requirement of good faith and the general law of mistake.

Drennan v. Star Paving Co.

Supreme Court of California, 1958.
333 P.2d 757.

APPEAL from a judgment of the Superior Court of Kern County. William L. Bradshaw, Judge. Affirmed.

Action for damages for refusal to perform certain paving work according to a bid submitted to plaintiff as general contractor. Judgment for plaintiff affirmed.

■ TRAYNOR, J. Defendant appeals from a judgment for plaintiff in an action to recover damages caused by defendant's refusal to perform certain paving work according to a bid it submitted to plaintiff.

On July 28, 1955, plaintiff, a licensed general contractor, was preparing a bid on the "Monte Vista School Job" in the Lancaster school district. Bids had to be submitted before 8 p. m. Plaintiff testified that it was customary in that area for general contractors to receive the bids of subcontractors by telephone on the day set for bidding and to rely on them in computing their own bids. Thus on that day plaintiff's secretary, Mrs. Johnson, received by telephone between 50 and 75 subcontractors' bids for various parts of the school job. As each bid came in, she wrote it on a special form, which she brought into plaintiff's office. He then posted it on a master cost sheet setting forth the names and bids of all subcontractors. His own bid had to include the names of subcontractors who were to perform one-half of one per cent or more of the construction work, and he had also to provide a bidder's bond of 10 per cent of his total bid of $317,385 as a guarantee that he would enter the contract if awarded the work.

Late in the afternoon, Mrs. Johnson had a telephone conversation with Kenneth R. Hoon, an estimator for defendant. He gave his name and telephone number and stated that he was bidding for defendant for the paving work at the Monte Vista School according to plans and specifications and that his bid was $7,131.60. At Mrs. Johnson's request he repeated his bid. Plaintiff listened to the bid over an extension telephone in his office and posted it on the master sheet after receiving the bid form from Mrs. Johnson. Defendant's was the lowest bid for the paving. Plaintiff computed his own bid accordingly and submitted it with the name of defendant as the subcontractor for the paving. When the bids were opened on July 28th, plaintiff's proved to be the lowest, and he was awarded the contract.

On his way to Los Angeles the next morning plaintiff stopped at defendant's office. The first person he met was defendant's construction engineer, Mr. Oppenheimer. Plaintiff testified: "I introduced myself and he immediately told me that they had made a mistake in their bid to me the night before, they couldn't do it for the price they had bid, and I told him I would expect him to carry through with their original bid because I had used it in compiling my bid and the job was being awarded them. And I would have to go and do the job according to my bid and I would expect them to do the same."

Defendant refused to do the paving work for less than $15,000. Plaintiff testified that he "got figures from other people" and after trying for several months to get as low a bid as possible engaged L & H Paving Company, a firm in Lancaster, to do the work for $10,948.60.

The trial court found on substantial evidence that defendant made a definite offer to do the paving on the Monte Vista job according to the plans and specifications for $7,131.60, and that plaintiff relied on defendant's bid in computing his own bid for the school job and naming defendant therein as the subcontractor for the paving work. Accordingly, it entered judgment for plaintiff in the amount of $3,817 (the difference between defendant's bid and the cost of the paving to plaintiff) plus costs.

Defendant contends that there was no enforceable contract between the parties on the ground that it made a revocable offer and revoked it before plaintiff communicated his acceptance to defendant.

There is no evidence that defendant offered to make its bid irrevocable in exchange for plaintiff's use of its figures in computing his bid. Nor is there evidence that would warrant interpreting plaintiff's use of defendant's bid as the acceptance thereof, binding plaintiff, on condition he received the main contract, to award the subcontract to defendant. In sum, there was neither an option supported by consideration nor a bilateral contract binding on both parties.

Plaintiff contends, however, that he relied to his detriment on defendant's offer and that defendant must therefore answer in damages for its refusal to perform. Thus the question is squarely presented: Did plaintiff's reliance make defendant's offer irrevocable?

Section 90 of the Restatement of Contracts states: "A promise which the promisor should reasonably expect to induce action or forbearance of a definite and substantial character on the part of the promisee and which does induce such action or forbearance is binding if injustice can be avoided only by enforcement of the promise." This rule applies in this state.

Defendant's offer constituted a promise to perform on such conditions as were stated expressly or by implication therein or annexed thereto by operation of law. Defendant had reason to expect that if its bid proved the lowest it would be used by plaintiff. It induced "action . . . of a definite and substantial character on the part of the promisee."

Had defendant's bid expressly stated or clearly implied that it was revocable at any time before acceptance we would treat it accordingly. It was silent on revocation, however, and we must therefore determine whether there are conditions to the right of revocation imposed by law or reasonably inferable in fact. In the analogous problem of an offer for a unilateral contract, the theory is now obsolete that the offer is revocable at any time before complete performance. Thus section 45 of the Restatement of Contracts provides: "If an offer for a unilateral contract is made, and part of the consideration requested in the offer is given or tendered by the offeree in response thereto, the offeror is bound by a contract, the duty of immediate performance of which is conditional on the full consideration being given or tendered within the time stated in the offer, or, if no time is stated therein, within a reasonable time." In explanation, comment *b* states that the "main offer includes as a subsidiary promise, necessarily implied, that if part of the requested performance is given, the offeror will not revoke his offer, and that if tender is made it will be accepted. Part performance or tender may thus furnish consideration for the subsidiary promise. Moreover, merely acting in justifiable reliance on an offer may in some cases serve as sufficient reason for making a promise binding (see § 90)."

Whether implied in fact or law, the subsidiary promise serves to preclude the injustice that would result if the offer could be revoked after the offeree had acted in detrimental reliance thereon. Reasonable reliance resulting in a foreseeable prejudicial change in position affords a compelling basis also for implying a subsidiary promise not to revoke an offer for a bilateral contract.

The absence of consideration is not fatal to the enforcement of such a promise. It is true that in the case of unilateral contracts the Restatement finds consideration for the implied subsidiary promise in the part perform- ance of the bargained-for exchange, but its reference to section 90 makes clear that consideration for such a promise is not always necessary. The very purpose of section 90 is to make a promise binding even though there was no consideration "in the sense of something that is bargained for and given in exchange." Reasonable reliance serves to hold the offeror in lieu of the consideration ordinarily required to make the offer binding. In a case involving similar facts the Supreme Court of South Dakota stated that "we believe that reason and justice demand that the doctrine [of section 90] be applied to the present facts. We cannot believe that by accepting this doctrine as controlling in the state of facts before us we will abolish the requirement of a consideration in contract cases, in any different sense than an ordinary estoppel abolishes some legal requirement in its applica- tion. We are of the opinion, therefore, that the defendants in executing the agreement [which was not supported by consideration] made a promise which they should have reasonably expected would induce the plaintiff to submit a bid based thereon to the Government, that such promise did induce this action, and that injustice can be avoided only by enforcement of the promise.''

When plaintiff used defendant's offer in computing his own bid, he bound himself to perform in reliance on defendant's terms. Though defendant did not bargain for this use of its bid neither did defendant make it idly, indifferent to whether it would be used or not. On the contrary it is reasonable to suppose that defendant submitted its bid to obtain the subcontract. It was bound to realize the substantial possibility that its bid would be the lowest, and that it would be included by plaintiff in his bid. It was to its own interest that the contractor be awarded the general contract; the lower the subcontract bid, the lower the general contractor's bid was likely to be and the greater its chance of acceptance and hence the greater defendant's chance of getting the paving subcontract. Defendant had reason not only to expect plaintiff to rely on its bid but to want him to. Clearly defendant had a stake in plaintiff's reliance on its bid. Given this interest and the fact that plaintiff is bound by his own bid, it is only fair that plaintiff should have at least an opportunity to accept defendant's bid after the general contract has been awarded to him.

It bears noting that a general contractor is not free to delay acceptance after he has been awarded the general contract in the hope of getting a better price. Nor can he reopen bargaining with the subcontractor and at the same time claim a continuing right to accept the original offer. In the present case plaintiff promptly informed defendant that plaintiff was being awarded the job and that the subcontract was being awarded to defendant.

Defendant contends, however, that its bid was the result of mistake and that it was therefore entitled to revoke it. It relies on the rescission cases of *M. F. Kemper Const. Co. v. City of Los Angeles,* [235 P.2d 7], and *Brunzell Const. Co. v. G. J. Weisbrod, Inc.,* 134 [285 P.2d 989]. In those cases, however, the bidder's mistake was known or should have been to the offeree, and the offeree could be placed in status quo. Of course, if plaintiff had reason to believe that defendant's bid was in error, he could not justifiably rely on it, and section 90 would afford no basis for enforcing it. (*Robert Gordon, Inc. v. Ingersoll–Rand Co.,* 117 F.2d 654, 660.) Plaintiff, however, had no reason to know that defendant had made a mistake in submitting its bid, since there was usually a variance of 160 per cent between the highest and lowest bids for paving in the desert around Lancaster. He committed himself to performing the main contract in reliance on defendant's figures. Under these circumstances defendant's mistake, far from relieving it of its obligation, constitutes an additional reason for enforcing it, for it misled plaintiff as to the cost of doing the paving. Even had it been clearly understood that defendant's offer was revocable until accepted, it would not necessarily follow that defendant had no duty to exercise reasonable care in preparing its bid. It presented its bid with knowledge of the substantial possibility that it would be used by plaintiff; it could foresee the harm that would ensue from an erroneous underestimate of the cost. Moreover, it was motivated by its own business interest. Whether or not these considerations alone would justify recovery for negligence had the case been tried on that theory, they are persuasive that defendant's mistake should not defeat recovery under the rule of section 90 of the Restatement of Contracts. As between the subcontractor who made the bid and the general contractor who reasonably relied on it, the loss resulting from the mistake should fall on the party who caused it.

The judgment is affirmed.

* * *

Begin to engage these materials by considering the general principles that govern the legal treatment of attempts to revoke offers.

As a general matter, an offer to enter into a bilateral contract may be revoked anytime before it has been accepted (subject, of course, to the mailbox rule that acceptances are effective when sent rather than when received). Moreover, offers lapse even without expressly being revoked after a commercially reasonable period of time. Finally, offers can, in certain circumstances, be made irrevocable (at least for a time) by agreement of the parties. This happens when the parties enter into an option contract, in which one party commits to leaving an offer open (so that the other has the unilateral power to make the offer into a binding contract) during the period of the option. The option, on this model, is created by a formally separate and fully completed contract, which stands apart from the offer that fixes the substantive terms of the option. Thus, in such a conventional case, the offeror, in addition to making the offer, makes a second offer—namely to keep the first offer open for a specified period of time—and the offeree accepts this second offer, creating a completed contract (whose substance concerns the first offer). Critically, the common law required the second, option contract to satisfy all the standard formalities required for creating contractual obligations in general, including offer, acceptance, and in particular the consideration requirement (of which more below). More recently, UCC § 2–205 establishes that an offer for the sale of goods made by a merchant and accompanied by a written promise to keep the offer open is irrevocable for up to 3 months, even if it is not supported by consideration.

A similar development towards recognizing option contracts in the case of unilateral contracts has appeared in the common law. Unilateral contracts, recall from the analysis in *Ever–Tite*, arise when an offeror proposes to exchange a promise not for a return promise but simply for performance. Under the old rule, an offer to enter into a unilateral contract was not accepted until the requested performance had been completely rendered. This rule expressed the formalist principle that an offeror controls the terms of her offer, applied to the fact that the offeror in the unilateral contract, by the formal nature of the contract, makes *completed* perform-ance the means of acceptance. That, after all, is what makes the contract unilateral: if the offeror were willing to treat something less than the completed performance whose prospect motivates her contracting, say merely commenced performance, as acceptance, then she would in effect be asking for a return promise (communicated, as in *Ever–Tite*, by actions rather than words), and the contract would be bilateral.

The modern regime governing unilateral contracts, which is elaborated in Restatement (Second) of Contacts § 45, takes a different approach. Under the new Restatement rule, once an offeree has begun the requested performance, an offer cannot be withdrawn until the offeree has had a reasonable opportunity to complete performance. (Under this rule, the offeror is bound if the offeree completes, but the offeree is not obligated to complete.) The Restatement, in effect, implies an option contract in cases of unilateral offers. That contract, which is itself formally a unilateral contract, involves the offeror's exchanging a promise not to revoke for a reasonable period of time for the offeree's commencing performance. The reason for the change is not hard to see: the courts, and eventually also the Restaters, had become concerned that offerors who made unilateral offers were manipulating offerees, whom they were inducing to take costly steps in commencing performance in circumstances in which they, but not the offerees, knew that the chances that they would revoke their offers before performance was completed were high. For example, offerors were inducing many offerees to commence performance at once, with the intention of comparing them against one another and choosing the one whose performance was most valuable. If the offerees know this and take the risk of losing out into account in calibrating their efforts at performance, competition among them may be benign. (An informative analogy—although only an analogy, as it involves a very different formal structure of offer and acceptance—here is the familiar competition to design a large building, in which several architects develop and submit designs, in the knowledge they may not win the commission.) But if the offerees do not know of one another, or do not know how likely it is that the offeror will revoke her offer before they complete performance, then the old rule governing unilateral contracts generates unfairness and inefficiency. The new rule seeks to cure this problem.

Gimble Bros. and *Drennan* involve an analogous fact pattern, and turn on similar considerations, although now in the formal context of bilateral rather than unilateral contracts. The stylized facts of the two cases are very similar. In each, a general contractor obtained bids from subcontractors as part of preparing its own bid on a construction project. The general asked the subs to make offers (the bids) to complete various parts of the larger project and then used these offers in preparing its own offer, for submission to the client who, ultimately, wished the project to be built. The client, in each case, accepted the general's bid (that is, the general's offer to do the work in the manner and for the price that its bid described), which reflected the sub's bid. After the client accepted the general's bid, so that the general became bound to the client, the sub realized that it had made a mistake in preparing its bid (the mistake in each case was arithmetic or clerical, and resulted in the sub's bid's being too low, which was likely why the general found it attractive in preparing its own bid). Upon realizing its mistake, the sub immediately contacted the general to withdraw its bid, which is to say, to revoke its offer. Although the sub contacted the general before the general communicated its acceptance of the sub's bid to the sub, the general nevertheless claimed that the sub's revocation was ineffective, and that the general's use of the sub's bid in its own, winning bid, was sufficient to obligate the sub to perform according the terms of its bid. The sub refused to honor its bid, and the general sued. In *Gimble Bros.*, Judge Learned Hand (one of the great judges of the last century) held for the sub, finding that the sub had effectively revoked its offer before the general accepted, so that no contract between them was created. In *Drennan*, Judge Roger Traynor (another of the century's great judges) reached precisely the opposite result, finding that the general's foreseeable and indeed intended reliance on the sub's bid rendered the offer reflected in that bid irrevocable, at least in the context in which the sub sought to revoke it.

How should one understand these almost precisely opposed treatments of the same pattern of facts? Answering this question is interesting for three reasons. First, the question when the law makes offers irrevocable is independently practically important. Second, working through the various theories of the cases presents an excellent exercise in applying the formal structures of offer and acceptance in context. And third, coming to grips with the differences between Hand's approach to the case and Traynor's opens a window into the broader conflict between formalism and realism in contract law.

To begin with, it is important to see that *Gimble Bros.* and *Drennan* really do pose a conundrum: although the two cases might be distinguished on their facts, both judges are very careful to make plain that their opinions do not rely on such factual differences between the cases as might support this narrow approach.

First, although the sub in *Gimble Bros.* tried to revoke before the general's bid was accepted, whereas the sub in *Drennan* tried only after its general's bid had been accepted, Hand expressly rejects this as a ground for his decision. As Hand observes, the general was reasonable in not revoking *its* bid in response to the sub's attempted revocation, as that would have cost the general its only chance to bid on the contract. In effect, the general in *Gimble Bros.* was as tied to using the sub's bid as the general in *Drennan*.

Second, although the stylized fact pattern in the cases could easily support the *Drennan* result, including even for Hand, if the sub and general had reached a separate express agreement (ideally involving offer, acceptance, and consideration) that the sub would keep its offer open for a reasonable time after the general's bid was accepted, Traynor clearly rejects any factual suggestion that such an express option contract had been made in *Drennan*.

And third, although the sub's offer in *Gimble Bros.* expressly stated how the general might accept (and did not include "using this offer in its own bid" among the stated methods of acceptance) whereas the sub in *Drennan* did not, this difference in facts also cannot explain the different outcomes in the cases. It is a general principle of contract law that mere reliance on an offer does not count as acceptance of that offer (unless the offer so specifies, and the offer in *Drennan* did not). So the law provides an interpretive regime for offers that fills in the silence in the *Drennan* offer in a fashion that makes it, in the relevant respect, equivalent to the express terms of the offer in *Gimble Bros*.

So the divergence of Hand's treatment and Traynor's cannot be explained by a distinction concerning the facts of the two cases and must instead be explained by a disagreement about the law. The text below will take up this disagreement, and explain it in terms of the difference between formalist and realist doctrinal styles that has been this Part's recurring theme. But first, it is important to see that although the two judges disagree profoundly about many points of contract law, they nevertheless agree on certain others. In particular, Hand's opinion and Traynor's agree in rejecting two possible legal theories of the case.

First, the sub might of course be bound under a conventional bilateral contract whose terms are announced by its offer, which was accepted (in the conventional way, through a reciprocal promise) by the general before the sub withdrew it and supported by the general's return promise to pay the sub's price as consideration. In the cases, however, the general did *not* accept before the sub revoked. Moreover, and in a way more importantly, the general did not even claim to have accepted. The general, after all, wished to retain the freedom to avoid any contract with the sub in case it failed to win the contract from the client. And a bilateral contract established by the sub's offer and the general's acceptance would bind not just the sub but also the *general*.

Second, the sub might be bound under a bilateral contract in which the general accepted the sub's offer by something other than the conventional route of making a return promise to pay the sub's price. For example, the general might have accepted, on the model of *Ever–Tite*, by using the sub's bid in constructing its own bid. Again, Hand and Traynor agree that the facts don't support this theory—for the theory to apply, the sub would have to specify using its bid as a form of acceptance, and, as a factual matter, neither sub so specified. Moreover, this theory suffers the same problem as the last: it would generate the result not just that the sub but also that the general is bound to the terms of the sub's offer. But the general insists that it is not bound to the terms of the sub's offer: certainly the general is not bound if its own offer is unsuccessful.[20]

Now turn to consider the disagreement between Hand and Traynor concerning the legal theories that might sustain the sub's obligation to honor its bid. This disagreement might be cast in two ways, which turn out to be, if not equivalent, at least interdependent.

The first disagreement between Hand and Traynor—the difference that appears most prominently on the face of their opinions—appears not

---

20. It is an open question whether the general is bound if its own offer succeeds. Thus, a general who wins the contract with the client might be tempted to engage in what is called "price-chopping," that is, returning to its subs in search of lower prices now that it has roped in the client. Traynor's opinion asserts (assumes?) that this is impermissible. But it is not clear on what basis Traynor reaches this conclusion.

to concern the orthodox route into contract at all, but rather an alternative account of the grounds of contractual obligation, known as *promissory estoppel*. The orthodox method of making a contract, which these pages have so far been elaborating, involves offer, acceptance, and consideration. The principle of promissory estoppel, now embedded in the law through Restatement (Second) of Contracts § 90, holds that a promise can establish a contract even without offer, acceptance, and consideration as long as it is appropriately connected to appropriate reliance by the promisee. The repeated use of the word "appropriate" signals that the scope and application of this principle is limited and contested, and the principle will be explained in greater detail below (with a special emphasis on just what failures of orthodox contract formation it actually fills in). But it is clear on the face of promissory estoppel that *Gimble Bros.* and *Drennan* do not test the limits of appropriate reliance. The sub's bid, in these cases, predictably resulted in, and indeed invited, reliance by the general, and the general's reliance was in each case reasonable. If estoppel applies, then this reliance is sufficient to obligate the sub to honor the terms of the bid on which the general relied.

Traynor's opinion in *Drennan* seems simply to assert that promissory estoppel applies to bind the sub. Thus Traynor repeats Restatement (Second) § 90, observes that it is law in California, and says that the sub had reason to expect that the general would rely in just the way that the estoppel principle describes and that the general in fact did so rely. That, one might think, settles the case.

But Hand was not innocent of promissory estoppel when he wrote his opinion in *Gimble Bros.*, and although the estoppel principle with which Hand was working differed from the modern principle cited by Traynor, the facial differences between the two principles (which involved the character and extent of reliance) were not germane to the case at hand. Nevertheless, Hand rejected the estoppel argument, and for a seemingly straightforward reason.

Promissory estoppel is a special case of estoppel, which is the general equitable idea that, in certain circumstances, a party's prior conduct can prevent, or estop, it from asserting a claim or defense in a legal dispute. It is not that the prior conduct renders the subsequent claim literally impossible (as when a party, having dissolved a corporation, subsequently seeks to have that corporation act as a legal person). Nor is it that the prior conduct and the subsequent claim are logically incompatible (as when a party, having argued that it never took an action at issue in a tort subsequently claims that it exercised due care in acting). Rather, estoppel applies more broadly, in cases in which the party's prior conduct renders a subsequent claim somehow inequitable or improper. For example, the defendants in *Neri* and *Vines*, from Part One, tried to argue that the plaintiffs were estopped from seeking restitution of their security deposits because they were themselves in breach of contract. Both defendants failed—roughly, because breaching a contract, as the structure of the expectation remedy makes plain, is not a wrong and hence not a basis for estoppel—although the defendant in *Vines* did persuade the court to give it a half victory (shifting the burden of persuasion concerning the validity of the liquidated damages clause). Estoppel is thus a vague—often maddeningly vague—principle, and its vagueness is tied to its equitable roots: to the sense that estoppel aids a court in exercising its discretion to do substantive justice between the parties. Recall Grant Gilmore's observation that estoppel in the end amounts to little more than the brute fact that "for reasons which the court does not wish to discuss, there must be judgment for the plaintiff."[21]

However these general problems concerning estoppel are resolved, a further issue arises in *Gimble Bros*. This is that the general's argument, in that case, concerns not estoppel *simpliciter* but, more narrowly and particularly, *promissory* estoppel. That is the species of estoppel in which the estopping act is a promise. One can see how this might be a plausible version of the general equitable doctrine. Having promised to do something, a party might subsequently be estopped from denying liability under the promise. But, as Hand observes, this version of estoppel doesn't apply to the case at hand: the facts in *Gimble Bros*. do not contain any promise at all by the sub. All that the sub did, in submitting its bid, was to make an *offer*. The offer did not mature into a promise because it was not accepted (or rather, because it was revoked before it could be accepted). And contract law, even if it contains a principle of promissory estoppel, does not contain any principle of *offerory* estoppel. On Hand's view, promissory estoppel is to be literally understood and narrowly cabined. It applies in cases in which there has been offer and acceptance, but some other element of contract formation—most likely, consideration—is lacking. It does not generate a route into contract without acceptance, because without acceptance there can be no promise to which promissory estoppel might apply. And that simple, formal, observation renders *Gimble Bros*., in Hand's mind, an easy case.

Traynor's assertion that promissory estoppel decides the case in favor of the general in *Drennan* seems, when set against this argument, conclusory at best and, at worst, simply wrong. The facts of the case provide Traynor's theory with no promise to latch on to.

Traynor's second departure from Hand's approach to the case becomes relevant at this point. Traynor imagines how the case might be understood on the model not of a bilateral contract—in which the sub invited a return promise from the general, given either conventionally or by taking some act such as using the sub's bid in its own—but of a *unilateral* contract. The analysis of *Ever–Tite* suggests why this is a natural thought: there is little phenomenological difference between a bilateral contract in which an offeror specifies commencing performance as the method of acceptance and a unilateral contract in which the offeror seeks not acceptance but simply performance. In each case, an observer is confronted with an offer, followed by the commencement of performance.

---

21. GRANT GILMORE, THE DEATH OF CONTRACT 64 (1974).

But although the two scenarios are phenomenologically similar, they are formally and legally quite different—and these differences, and in particular the nature of these differences under the legal order in place when Traynor wrote his opinion in *Drennan*, explain why Traynor was able to reach the result that he did.

In Hand's day, an offeror proposing a unilateral contract remained free to revoke even after her offeree had commenced performance and indeed right up to the moment at which the requested performance had been completed.[22] This result was thought a formal entailment of the general rule that an offeror controls her offer: since she asked for performance (which is what makes the proposed contract unilateral, after all), she should not be bound until she has received just what she asked for.

By the time Traynor wrote *Drennan*, however, the law of unilateral contracts had changed. Under Restatement (Second) of Contracts § 45, which is still in effect today, an offeror who issues an offer of a unilateral contract, and whose offeree commences the requested performance, cannot revoke until after the sub has had a reasonable opportunity to complete the requested performance, and in this way bind the offeror to the terms of its offer. This change reflected a realist concern that the law should not elevate its internal formal logic over good—that is, efficient and fair—policy. To be sure, the realist would say, freedom of contract includes not just freedom to make the contracts one wishes but also freedom to avoid contractual entanglements one does not wish. And this entails, as a general matter, that an offeror should be free to fix the terms of her offer, including what actions her offeree must take in order for her to become bound. But, the realist continues, an offeror should not be free to exploit her offeree, including by inducing him to take measures in preparation for performance which are valuable to her and worsen his bargaining position when the time to conclude a completed contract comes around. And an offeree who, facing an offer of a unilateral contract, commences performance sinks some of his costs of performance, and thereby weakens his bargaining position in the negotiations concerning what he will receive in exchange for completing performance. His offeror, having allowed him to expend these costs without compensation, can now apply her bargaining power to the contractual surplus created by completion and hence can capture a greater surplus for herself, and a greater share of the total surplus (calculated including the costs of the steps towards performance that the offeree has already taken), than she could have done had she negotiated for a bilateral contract. And finally, insofar as the offeror knows about the renegotiation that will follow his commencing performance, he

---

22. This reveals that the two cases—on the one hand, concerning an offer of a bilateral contract that makes commenced performance into a means of acceptance and, on the other, of a unilateral contract for the requested performance—had different legal implications in Hand's day also. But neither helped the general: under the bilateral contract, not just the offeror sub but also the accepting general would be bound, which would require the general to pay too high a price, in terms of its own legal obligation, for the revocability it sought; and under the unilateral contract, the sub would remain free to revoke until the general completed the requested performance, which is to say engaged and paid the sub for the work, which is precisely the result Hand reached and the general found unsatisfactory.

will be reluctant to commence, and even the offeree, at least ex ante, will prefer not to possess the extravagant freedom to revoke associated with the formalist approach to unilateral contracts.[23]

The modern doctrine concerning unilateral contracts, applied to the facts of *Drennan*, delivers just the result that Traynor favors. If the sub in *Drennan* had made an offer of a unilateral contract, and using the sub's bid in the general's bid counted as commencing performance, then the sub but not the general would be bound for a reasonable time, which would surely be until the general, having learned the reception of its bid, could take up the construction job. And so the sub could not withdraw after the general had won the client using its bid (at least not unless the general then proceeded, perhaps by bid-chopping, unreasonably to delay engaging the sub to do the bid-for work).

Of course, this doctrinal possibility does not by itself settle the actual dispute in *Drennan*. The sub there did not, as a matter of fact, seek a unilateral contract. And even if the sub's offer had been for a unilateral contract, the performance by the general that the sub's offer described focused exclusively on the manner in which the general would make the work-site available to the sub and the amount and timing of the general's payments, and (even though the sub undoubtedly had an interest in having the general use its bid in preparing her own) did not as a matter of fact include using the sub's bid in preparing her bid to the client. Accordingly, applying something like the distinction from *Ever–Tite*, the general's use of the sub's bid was probably mere preparation, rather than commencing performance. Even the modern approach to unilateral contracts therefore likely could not, at least on the facts of *Drennan*, have sustained the result that the sub was bound as soon as the general used its bid in preparing her own.

But even if the doctrine promulgated by Restatement (Second) § 45 cannot be applied directly to the facts of *Drennan* to sustain the result that Traynor prefers, the realist reasoning that led the Restaters to adopt the new rule might be adapted to the case of a bilateral contract and then applied to *Drennan*. The point of the Restatement was that even though offerors control their offers, they may not use this control to invite reliance in offerees that they then exploit. And this, of course, is just what the sub, at least on Traynor's view, was up to in *Drennan*. Accordingly, just as the Restatement, in the context of a reliance-inviting offer of a unilateral

---

23. This observation makes it natural to ask why one ever observed unilateral contracts under the formalist regime. One reason is that naïve offerees might not know of the exploitation to which they were exposing themselves, and sophisticated offerors might take advantage of this. And even among sophisticated parties, some combination of transactions costs might make this risk of exploitation the lesser of two bads. (Likely these costs include the offeror's inability to assess the quality of the offeree's performance until it has been completed, something that receives its clearest formal expression in the case of competitions, where an offeror literally cannot say which offeree she favors until several have tried to provide her with compete performance.) The realist rule need not deny this possibility categorically. After all, the modern restatement prevents the offeror from revoking only for a "reasonable time" after her offeree has commenced performance, and that time might be very (vanishingly) short.

contract, now implies a secondary offer not to revoke for a reasonable time after the offeree has commenced the requested performance, so, Traynor supposes, the law facing a reliance-inviting offer of a bilateral contract might imply a secondary offer not to revoke this offer for a reasonable time after the reliance has been incurred. In *Drennan*, this logic generates an implied secondary offer, made by the sub, not to revoke its primary offer for a reasonable time if the general uses that offer in generating her own bid. This secondary offer was then accepted by the general, either also by implication or by using the sub's bid. (Note that none of the problems—concerning unwanted liability for the general—that undermined such a bilateral contract approach to primary offer apply when the approach is directed at the secondary offer. That offer does not bind the general to anything other than, at most, using the sub's bid.) And now promissory estoppel has a promise to latch on to—the secondary promise created by sub's accepted offer not to revoke for a reasonable period of time.[24] *That* is the promise that *Drennan* enforces, with the result that the sub is bound but the general is not. And so Traynor's theory of the case is complete, and answers Hand's objections (although not always entirely on their own terms).

With these doctrinal reflections in place, return, finally to more general thoughts concerning the differences between formalist and realist doctrinal orders.

One difference between the two approaches concerns the judges' willingness to work through the policy consequences of their rulings. At each point Hand insists on the total control over his offer by means of its literal terms, regardless of the practical effects of enforcing this control. Hand takes this approach even though, from an ex ante perspective, the offeror might well prefer to be bound. Traynor, the realist, looks to the purposes of the offer and to how it functions in getting the parties to a deal, and he implies whatever is necessary to make the offer function well in this role. In this case, it is necessary to limit the sub's capacity to revoke its offer once the general has used that offer in generating her own bid. It is costly for the general to receive and process the sub's offer in a way that connects this offer to the general's own bid. The sub, moreover, has an interest in having the general incur these costs, since a general who has done so will be more likely to accept the offer that it has investigated. (Indeed, the general might stick with a sub's offer in such a case, even if it receives what appears to be a lower priced offer from another sub, as the price difference might not be worth incurring the additional costs of investigating the new sub's offer for compatibility with the client's requirements and the rest of the general's plans.)

---

24. Note that it is not clear that this approach needs to invoke promissory estoppel at all. Insofar as the sub's secondary promise not to revoke was intended to induce the general to use the sub's primary offer in her own bid, then the general's so using the sub's offer might well constitute consideration for the promise not to revoke, and so the secondary promise might be rendered enforceable along the ordinary path of offer, acceptance, and consideration. But this doesn't in any way undermine the approach to the case Traynor took. On the theory outlined in the main text, § 90 remains a perfectly good foundation for the *Drennan* result.

A second difference concerns the style of rules that the two approaches prefer. The doctrines that Hand formulates state precise rules, which announce that they may be literally and generally applied. The distinction between a promise and a mere offer, for example, may be read off the face of the doctrine and governs all manner of negotiations, regardless of the business or bargaining context in which they occur. Traynor, on the other hand, prefers to develop broader doctrinal standards, which cannot be applied literally but rather derive their content from the several circumstances in which they are applied, and which therefore make the applicable law (in a sense) vary with context.

A third difference combines these two. It is no coincidence that Traynor concluded that the sub was bound whereas Hand concluded that it was not. Formalist contract doctrine emphasized the voluntary nature of contractual obligation and hence that the baseline legal state is the absence of contractual liability. To acquire a liability in contract, on the formalist view, a party had directly to seek it, employing the precise formalisms concerning offer and acceptance that the law described. Realist contract doctrine emphasizes that contractual obligation is a tool that serves the broader plans and intentions of contracting parties. Accordingly, freedom *from* contract plays a less central role in freedom of contract for the realist than for the formalist. In many settings, it is natural and reasonable to suppose that business associates wish to enter a contractual relation, because such a relation is in their joint interest. And in those settings, the realist believes, contract law should not place technical obstacles in the way of the obligation's being formed. To do so would be to burden the parties, and indeed (and here the argument circles back to the idea of contractual intent) to burden them in a fashion that, ex ante, they would not wish.

CHAPTER 14

FAILURES TO ENGAGE

The discussion of offer and acceptance repeatedly returned to the idea that whether or not a contract has been created depends on the terms of the offer—which control what constitutes acceptance. The same idea of course applies to acceptances also: that is, the offeree controls, through the terms of her acceptance, just what it is that she accepts. The same principles that protect the offeror from being bound by an acceptance that is at variance with the terms of his offer also protect the offeree from being bound by an offer that is at variance with the terms of her acceptance.

This is just a longwinded way of saying that for a contract to arise, offer and acceptance must match up, although not perfectly, of course, or in every respect. Moreover, offer and acceptance must not simply agree; they must *engage*—that is, they must agree on a plan of action that might be implemented as a contract.

Failures to engage can occur in at least three, quite different, ways. In the first, offer and acceptance agree, but do not engage. That is to say, terms are left out of whatever agreement is reached, which make it impossible to say what the parties have agreed to, or at least to say this sufficiently comprehensively so that, given the parties' (actual or reasonable) interests and motives, one can say confidently that they have in fact reached an implementable agreement at all. Such cases are governed by the doctrines surrounding incompleteness. In the second, offer and acceptance are each complete, and the parties believe that they match up, even though they in fact do not. Mismatches of this sort are governed by a group of legal doctrines surrounding the notion mistake. In the third case, the parties do not believe that offer and acceptance match up—indeed, offer and acceptance may be not just at odds but expressly so, and may even insist that their mismatch prevents a contract from arising—but the parties nevertheless act as though they have made a contract. Mismatches of this sort are governed by the legal doctrines concerning the battle of the forms.

14.1 INCOMPLETENESS

All contracts—even the most apparently comprehensive—are necessarily to some extent incomplete. Transactions costs preclude addressing every possible contingency (no matter how unlikely) and precisely specifying the duties that the parties will have in each. Just how bad must the weather get before it justifies a delayed delivery in a sales contract, and precisely how long, in every such case, may the delay extend? In what precise order will the provider perform her tasks in a service contract, and how will this order change in light of precisely what actions by the recipient? To answer these and myriad other questions completely, and to address every contingency precisely, would increase the costs of contracting so that they came to swamp whatever surplus the contractual exchange promised to generate. If contracts had to be complete, there would be no contracts at all.

For this reason, both the parties and the law anticipate incompleteness and provide mechanisms for filling in the gaps in incomplete contracts. The parties might specify that delivery will be by some reasonable means, at a reasonable time, and what is reasonable might then be evaluated, ex post, by references to the particular circumstances that have arisen. Alternatively the law might, as in *Unlaub v. Sexton* (from Part I), specify default terms to fill in contractual gaps in general, and in advance. Even though these mechanisms are also not free, the costs that they generate will be incurred only in cases in which the gaps become relevant. This makes it much more efficient to leave gaps ex ante and fill them ex post than it would be to try to draft a fully complete contract from the get-go.

Nothing guarantees, however, that every gap should or indeed can be filled. If contracts become sufficiently incomplete, then the law will, sensibly, refuse to do the parties' negotiating and drafting for them and conclude instead that no contract has been made. If you and I, who are strangers, meet by chance on a train platform, I say "do you want to do a deal?" and you answer "yes," we cannot plausibly claim to have made a contract, and no court will say that we have (much less decide what our "deal" consists in). After all, one of the reasons why total strangers who meet at random do not typically make contracts with each other is precisely that (in expectation, at least) identifying the terms of an efficient trade is much more expensive, given how little the parties know of each other, than whatever surplus the trade might produce. Even though all strangers might profitably trade in a transactions-costless world,[1] the transactions costs that arise everywhere in our actual world swamp these gains from trade for most pairs of strangers. And even in less extreme cases, it may not be efficient for courts to fill in contractual gaps: the costs of gap-filling, at least when done by courts, are not entirely borne by the contracting parties but are partly externalized to the taxpayers who fund the court system; and if parties know that courts will relieve them of these costs, they will (on the margin) make inefficiently gappy contracts, whose internalized costs of contracting are less than the surplus that they generate, even though their total costs of contracting are greater.

Of course, there is a huge difference between the first case just imagined—in which the parties decline to fix the precise consequences for delivery of every kind of bad weather—and the last—in which the parties fail to give their "agreement" any content at all. These are two ends along a continuum, and the interesting cases all fall somewhere in between. As the cases become more interesting, they also (unsurprisingly) become more

---

1. This is just a direct application of the law of comparative advantage.

difficult. Moreover, the outcomes courts reach in difficult cases vary depending on whether the courts follow a formalist approach associated with classical contract law, and employ subjective standards for contractual intent or, instead, follow a realist and functionalist approach, which employs an objective standard. In many respects, the realist approach seems obviously more sensible. At the same time, formalism provides an important insight in this area, and identifies a crucial conceptual distinction, although this distinction turns out to be more helpful for understanding cases than for deciding them.

The cases and materials that follow illustrate how the law—both in its formalist and in its functionalist elaborations—has responded to contractual incompleteness.

Varney v. Ditmars

New York Court of Appeals, 1916.
111 N.E. 822.

Appeal from Supreme Court, Appellate Division, First Department.

Action by George A. Varney against Isaac E. Ditmars. From a judgment of the Appellate Division (144 N.Y. Supp. 1148), affirming a judgment of the trial term dismissing the complaint, plaintiff appeals. Affirmed.

CHASE, J. This is an action brought for an alleged wrongful discharge of an employee. The defendant is an architect employing engineers, draftsmen, and other assistants. The plaintiff is an architect and draftsman. In October, 1910, he applied to the defendant for employment and when asked what wages he wanted, replied that he would start for $40 per week. He was employed at $35 per week. A short time thereafter he informed the defendant that he had another position offered to him, and the defendant said that if he would remain with him and help him through the work in his office he thought he could offer him a better future than anybody else. He continued in the employ of the defendant and became acquainted with a designer in the office, and said designer and the plaintiff from time to time prior to the 1st of February, 1911, talked with the defendant about the work in his office. On that day by arrangement the two remained with the defendant after the regular hours, and the defendant said:

> "I am going to give you $5 more a week; if you boys will go on and continue the way you have been and get me out of this trouble and get these jobs started that were in the office three years, on the 1st of next January I will close my books and give you a fair share of my profits. That was the result of the conversation. That was all of that conversation."

The plaintiff was given charge of the drafting. Thereafter suggestions were made by the plaintiff and said designer about discharging many of the defendant's employees and employing new men, and such suggestions were carried out and the two worked in the defendant's office overtime and many Sundays and holidays. At least one piece of work that the defendant said had been in his office for three years was completed. The plaintiff on his cross-examination told the story of the employment of himself and said designer as follows:

> "And he says at that time, 'I am going to give you $5 more a week starting this week. This was about Thursday. He says, 'You boys go on and continue the work you are doing and the first of January next year I will close my books and give you a fair share of my profits.' Those were his exact words."

Thereafter the plaintiff was paid $40 a week. On November 6, 1911, the night before the general election in this state, the defendant requested that all of his employees that could do so, should work on election day. The plaintiff told the defendant that he wanted to remain at home to attend an election in the village where he lived. About 4 o'clock in the afternoon of election day he was taken ill and remained at his house ill until a time that as nearly as can be stated from the evidence was subsequent to December 1, 1911. On Saturday, November 11th, the defendant caused to be delivered to the plaintiff a letter in which he said:

> "I am sending you herewith your pay for one day's work of seven hours, performed on Monday, the 6th inst. On Monday night, I made it my special duty to inform you that the office would be open all day Election Day and that I expected you and all the men to report for work. Much to my surprise and indignation, on Tuesday you made no appearance and all the men remained away, in obedience of your instructions to them of the previous evening. An act of this kind I consider one of extreme disloyalty and insubordination and I therefore am obliged to dispense with your services."

After the plaintiff had recovered from his illness and was able to do so he went to the defendant's office (the date does not appear) and told him that he was ready, willing, and able to continue his services under the agreement. The defendant denied that he had any agreement with him, and refused to permit him to continue in his service. Thereafter and prior to January 1, 1912, the plaintiff received for special work about $50.

The plaintiff seeks to recover in this action for services from November 7, 1911, to December 31, 1911, inclusive, at $40 per week and for a fair and reasonable percentage of the net profits of the defendant's business from February 1, 1911, to January 1, 1912, and demands judgment for $1,680.

At the trial he was the only witness sworn as to the alleged contract, and at the close of his case the complaint was dismissed. The statement alleged to have been made by the defendant about giving the plaintiff and said designer a fair share of his profits is vague, indefinite, and uncertain, and the amount cannot be computed from anything that was said by the parties or by reference to any document, paper, or other transaction. The minds of the parties never met upon any particular share of the defendant's profits to be given the employee or upon any plan by which such share could be computed or determined. The contract so far as it related to the special promise or inducement was never consummated. It was left subject to the will of the defendant or for further negotiation. It is urged that the defendant by the use of the word "fair," in referring to a share of his profits, was as certain and definite as people are in the purchase and sale of a chattel when the price is not expressly agreed upon, and that if the agreement in question is declared to be too indefinite and uncertain to be enforced, a similar conclusion must be reached in every case where a chattel is sold without expressly fixing the price therefor.

The question whether the words "fair" and "reasonable" have a definite and enforceable meaning when used in business transactions is dependent upon the intention of the parties in the use of such words and upon the subject-matter to which they refer. In cases of merchandising and in the purchase and sale of chattels the parties may use the words "fair and reasonable value" as synonymous with "market value." A promise to pay the fair market value of goods may be inferred from what is expressly agreed by the parties. The fair, reasonable, or market value of goods can be shown by direct testimony of those competent to give such testimony. The competency to speak grows out of experience and knowledge. The testimony of such witnesses does not rest upon conjecture. The opinion of this court in *United Press v. N.Y. Press Co.*, 164 N.Y. 406 was not intended to assert that a contract of sale is unenforceable, unless the price is expressly mentioned and determined.

In the case of a contract for the sale of goods or for hire without a fixed price or consideration being named it will be presumed that a reasonable price or consideration is intended, and the person who enters into such a contract for goods or service is liable therefor as on an implied contract. Such contracts are common, and when there is nothing therein to limit or prevent an implication as to the price they are, so far as the terms of the contract are concerned, binding obligations.

The contract in question, so far as it relates to a share of the defendant's profits, is not only uncertain, but it is necessarily affected by so many other facts that are in themselves indefinite and uncertain that the intention of the parties is pure conjecture. A fair share of the defendant's profits may be any amount from a nominal sum to a material part according to the particular views of the person whose guess is considered. Such an executory contract must rest for performance upon the honor and good faith of the parties making it. The courts cannot aid parties in such a case when they are unable or unwilling to agree upon the terms of their own proposed contract.

It is elementary in the law that, for the validity of a contract, the promise, or the agreement of the parties to it must be certain and explicit, and that their full intention may be ascertained to a reasonable degree of certainty. Their agreement must be neither vague nor indefinite, and, if thus defective, parol proof cannot be resorted to. *United Press v. N.Y. Press Co., supra,* and cases cited; Ruling Case Law, vol. 6, 644.

The courts in this state, in reliance upon and approval of the rule as stated in the United Press Case, have decided many cases involving the same rule. Thus, in *Mackintosh v. Thompson*, 68 N.Y.Supp. 492, and again in *Mackintosh v. Kimball*, 92 N.Y.Supp. 132, the plaintiff sought to recover compensation in addition to a stated salary which he had received and which additional amount rested upon a claim by him that while he was employed by the defendants he informed them that he intended to leave their employ, unless he was given an increase in salary, and that one of the defendants said to him that they would make it worth his while if he would stay on, and would increase his salary, and that his idea was to give him an interest in the profits on certain buildings that they were then erecting. The plaintiff further alleges that he asked what would be the amount of the increase, and was told, "You can depend upon me; I will see that you get a satisfactory amount." The court held that the arrangement was too indefinite to form the basis of any obligation on the part of the defendants.

The rule stated from the United Press Case does not prevent a recovery upon quantum meruit in case one party to an alleged contract has performed in reliance upon the terms thereof, vague, indefinite, and uncertain though they are. In such case the law will presume a promise to pay the reasonable value of the services. Judge Gray, who wrote the opinion in the United Press Case, said therein:

"I entertain no doubt that, where work has been done, or articles have been furnished, a recovery may be based upon quantum meruit, or quantum valebat; but, where a contract is of an executory character and requires performance over a future period of time, as here, and it is silent as to the price which is to be paid to the plaintiff during its term, I do not think that it possesses binding force. As the parties had omitted to make the price a subject of covenant, in the nature of things, it would have to be the subject of future agreement, or stipulation." Page 412 of 164 N.Y., page 529 of 58 N.E. (53 L.R.A. 288).

So in this case, while I do not think that the plaintiff can recover anything as extra work, yet if the work actually performed as stated was worth more than $40 per week he, having performed until November 7, 1910, could, on a proper complaint, recover its value less the amount received.

The plaintiff claims that he at least should have been allowed to go to the jury on the question as to whether he was entitled to recover at the rate of $40 per week from November 7, 1911, to December 31, 1911, inclusive. He did not perform any services for the defendant from November 6th until some time after December 1st, by reason of his illness. He has not shown just when he offered to return. It appears that between the time when he offered to return and January 1st he received $50 for other services.

The amount that the plaintiff could recover, therefore, if any, based upon the agreement to pay $40 per week would be very small, and he did not present to the court facts from which it could be computed. His employment by the defendant was conditional upon his continuing the way he had been working, getting the defendant out of his trouble, and getting certain unenumerated jobs, that were in the office three years, started.

There was nothing in the contract specifying the length of service, except as stated. It was not an unqualified agreement to continue the plaintiff in his service until the 1st of January, and it does not appear whether or not the special conditions upon which the contract was made had been performed. Even apart from the question whether the plaintiff's absence from the defendant's office by reason of his illness would permit the defendant to refuse to take him back into his employ, I do not think that on the testimony as it appears before us it was error to refuse to leave to the jury the question whether the plaintiff was entitled to recover anything at the rate of $40 per week.

The judgment should be affirmed, with costs.

CARDOZO, J., dissenting. I do not think it is true that a promise to pay an employee a fair share of the profits in addition to his salary is always and of necessity too vague to be enforced. The promise must, of course, appear to have been made with contractual intent. *Henderson Bridge Co. v. McGrath*, 134 U.S. 260, 275. But if that intent is present, it cannot be said from the mere form of the promise that the estimate of the reward is inherently impossible. The data essential to measurement may be lacking in the particular instance, and yet they may conceivably be supplied. It is possible, for example, that in some occupations an employee would be able to prove a percentage regulated by custom. The difficulty in this case is not so much in the contract as in the evidence. Even if the data required for computation might conceivably have been supplied, the plaintiff did not supply them. He would not have supplied them if all the evidence which he offered and which the court excluded had been received. He has not failed because the nature of the contract is such that damages are of necessity incapable of proof. He has failed because he did not prove them.

There is nothing inconsistent with this view in *United Press v. N.Y. Press Co.*, 164 N.Y. 406,. The case is often cited as authority for the proposition that an agreement to buy merchandise at a fair and reasonable price is so indefinite that an action may not be maintained for its breach in so far as it is still executory. Nothing of the kind was decided, or with reason could have been. What the court did was to construe a particular agreement, and to hold that the parties intended to reserve the price for future adjustment. If instead of reserving the price for future adjustment, they had manifested an intent on the one hand to pay and on the other to accept a fair price, the case is far from holding that a jury could not determine what such a price would be and assess the damages accordingly. Such an intent, moreover, might be manifested not only through express words, but also through reasonable implication. It was because there was neither an express statement nor a reasonable implication of such an intent that the court held the agreement void to the extent that it had not been executed.

On the ground that the plaintiff failed to supply the data essential to computation, I concur in the conclusion that profits were not to be included as an element of damage. I do not concur, however, in the conclusion that he failed to make out a case of damage to the extent of his loss of salary.

The amount may be small, but none the less it belongs to him. The hiring was not at will. *Watson v. Gugino,* 204 N.Y. 535. The plain implication was that it should continue until the end of the year when the books were to be closed. The evidence would permit the jury to find that the plaintiff was discharged without cause, and he is entitled to damages measured by his salary for the unexpired term.

The judgment should be reversed, and a new trial granted, with costs to abide the event.

* * *

Varney illustrates classical formalism with respect to contractual gap-filling. The plaintiff, an architect and draftsman, took employment with the defendant in October 1910, at an initial salary of $35 per week. After a time, the plaintiff informed the defendant that he'd received a better offer. The defendant was, at that time, badly behind in his work and told the plaintiff that he would give him, in the future, better terms of employment than he would receive anywhere else. On 1 February 1911, the defendant offered to raise the plaintiff's salary to $40 per week and also offered that if plaintiff worked through 1 January 1912, he would receive a fair share of the defendant's profits. The plaintiff remained with the defendant and, over the course of time, helped the defendant to catch up in his work.

An election was held on 7 November 1911, and plaintiff attended an election event in spite of defendant's demand that he work on that day. In addition, plaintiff became ill, which further kept him from work. On 11 November, the defendant fired the plaintiff by letter, and when, in December, the plaintiff tried to return to work, the defendant refused to allow him back. (Plaintiff seems nevertheless to have performed "special services" for defendant in December, for which he was paid about $50.) The plaintiff eventually sued the defendant, seeking wages for the period from 7 November to 31 December at the rate $40 per week plus the fair and reasonable share of defendant's profits that he claimed he'd been promised, which he calculated at $1,680.

The majority found for the defendant, employing classically formalist reasoning. In particular, the majority claimed that the defendant's promise of a fair share of profits was "vague, indefinite and uncertain." Accordingly, the majority observed, "the minds of the parties never met upon any particular share of the defendant's profits to be given the employ[ee] or upon any plan by which such share could be computed or determined." And the majority thus concluded, employing a subjective standard of contractual intent, "the contract so far as it related to the special promise or inducement was never consummated. It was left subject to the will of the defendant or for further negotiation." Finally, the majority admitted that this analysis did not in the end settle the plaintiff's core claim—to a fair share of profits. Thus, the majority admitted that the rule it employed in rejecting the plaintiff's contract claim "does not prevent a recovery upon quantum meruit in case one party to an alleged contract has performed in reliance upon the terms thereof, vague, indefinite, and uncertain though they are. In such case the law will presume a promise to pay the reasonable value of the services."

All the elements of classical formalism introduced in the discussion of *Plate v. Durst* reappear in this analysis. First, the subjective approach to contractual intent—the focus not on what a reasonable person would understand the parties to be doing but rather on the actual states of their minds—functions dramatically to narrow the scope of specifically contractual obligation. Second, this narrowing is applied mechanically, without any inquiry into either what is efficient or what is fair. Thus, at least in its contract-based analysis of the case, the *Varney* majority never suggested (what seems plausible) that the parties would have been better (cheaper, more accurate, more efficient) suppliers of the profit sharing term than the courts; and it never suggested (what is less plausible) that treating the defendant as having promised to share profits would be unfair to him. Third, the mechanically narrowed account of contractual obligation understands freedom *of* contract asymmetrically, to mean freedom *from* contract rather than freedom *to* contract. As elsewhere, so in the context of contractual incompleteness, the formalist, subjective approach to contractual intent is more concerned to promote parties' interests in avoiding contractual entanglements that they have not chosen than to promote parties' interests in the enforcement of contracts that they have chosen. And finally, all these ideas, even as they are insisted upon in connection with contract law proper, are at once abandoned as soon as a plaintiff shifts the formal ground of his claims away from contract and into quantum meruit, no matter that two claims are, in every functionally important respect, substantially identical. Indeed, the internal mechanics of the quantum meruit claim that the *Varney* majority is prepared to embrace are identical to those of the contract claim that it rejects: when the majority observes that, once the plaintiff's claim is styled as sounding in quantum meruit, the law "will presume a promise to pay the reasonable value" of the plaintiff's services, it is instructing a subsequent court, hearing this claim, to perform precisely the inquiry into what would be fair and efficient that it has just refused to perform itself. Talk of "presuming" a promise on these terms even reintroduces—expressly and indeed self-consciously—an objective approach to intent.

Cardozo's dissent points to an alternative, functionalist approach to the case, which adopts an objective standard of contractual intent and emphasizes efficiency and fairness. According to Cardozo, the problem is not in the contract at all. The parties clearly agreed that the plaintiff should receive a fair and reasonable share of the defendant's profits. The problem, rather, is in the proof: how is a fair and reasonable share to be identified, which is to say fixed, with sufficient definiteness? A functionalist analysis would now ask what standard of proof the plaintiff must provide in order to succeed. Should it be the same standard as is imposed by the certainty requirement in remedies law? There is some reason to think that the standard in this context should be more demanding, as the certainty requirement typically appears in contexts in which the parties cannot fix a remedy in advance,[2] whereas the parties in *Varney* clearly could have fixed the plaintiff's share of profits in advance. Accordingly, the law should—all else equal, at least—give the parties an incentive to internalize the costs of bargaining and drafting rather than inefficiently to pass them on to courts and hence taxpayers. A similar result might be achieved, of course, by returning to the *Varney* majority's view of the case, although now articulated on functionalist grounds: a rule that there is no contract, on account of contractual incompleteness, would give the plaintiff (at least) an incentive to pin down his precise share of profits in advance. Of course, it would also give the defendant an incentive to resist pinning down this share, as indefiniteness would favor him. The balance between these considerations is complicated and depends, among other things, on the relative expertise of the parties and their relative capacities, in their negotiations, to exploit whatever legal rule is adopted.

The important task, for a functionalist, is to pursue this line of argument to an implementable conclusion: to say, for various roughly identifiable contexts, how much it is fair and efficient to require the parties specify in their contracts in order for it to be reasonable for a court to provide the rest.[3] But in the context of this Part of the text, it is less important to set about answering the functionalist question than to understand the shift, in the law, away from formalism and towards functionalism. Cardozo was prescient in his dissent. Even the *Varney* majority's formalism was not complete. Although the majority insisted that "the courts cannot aid parties in such a case when they are unable or unwilling to agree upon the terms of their own proposed contract," it also admitted that in contracts for the sale of goods, the courts can and should do just this. Thus, in the sales context, the majority would enforce an agreement on a "fair and reasonable" price fixing the sales price at the market price. And modern courts are much, much more willing to fill the gaps in incomplete contracts, than the *Varney* court was. They will fill in gaps even outside of the sales context, and in the sales context, the gaps that they are willing to fill can be substantial indeed. The following cases and materials illustrate both points.

---

2. But might the parties employ a liquidated damages clause?

3. The central functionalist insight, in this area, is that while the law should sometimes fill in gaps as the parties likely would have wished them to be filled, the law should in other circumstances fill in gaps in a manner that both, or perhaps just one, of the parties would not have wished. The first, majoritarian, kind of gap-filling lowers the costs of contracting and can help to generate efficiencies, insofar as it fills in contingencies that are not worth, in expectation, the parties' time ex ante. The second, penalty, kind of gap-filling provides an incentive for the parties—or for one party, especially where that party is more expert or otherwise better suited to providing the information needed to make a contract more complete—to avoid contractual incompleteness. This kind of rule is especially desirable where contractual incompleteness reflects the fact that one party has strategically withheld information that would increase aggregate contractual surplus in order to increase its share of the surplus by more—where one party has, one might say, employed the gap in order to exploit the other. Penalty defaults may even be sensible in cases in which both parties use incompleteness inefficiently to externalize contracting costs to courts and taxpayers. The rule that certain types of incompleteness cause there to be no contract at all functions as just such a penalty default. The analysis in this note follows Ian Ayra & Robert Gertner, *Filling Gaps in Incomplete Contracts: An Economic Theory of Default Rules*, 99 YALE L.J. 87 (1989).

Corthell v. Summit Thread Co.

Supreme Judicial Court of Maine, 1933.
167 A. 79.

■ STURGIS, J. In this action, the plaintiff declares in special assumpsit for the breach of a written contract, and adds the general money counts with specifications. The plea is the general issue. The case comes forward on report.

The Summit Thread Company, the defendant in this action, and hereinafter referred to as the company, is a cotton yarn finisher with executive offices in Boston, Mass., and a mill and machine shops in East Hampton, Conn. It manufactures spools, bobbins, and other receptacles for winding threads, as also various devices which, to stimulate and retain trade, it loans to its customers for use with its products.

Some time prior to the spring of 1926, Robert N. Corthell, the plaintiff, then employed by the company as a salesman, perfected and patented two bobbin case control adjuncts and a guarding attachment for thread cops, especially adapted for use in stitching machines in shoe shops, and offered to sell them to the company. A thirty-day option, taken but not exercised, led to a conference, which involved, not only the purchase of these inventions, but also future patents which might be taken out by the plaintiff, his remuneration for them and his salary as a salesman. The result was that, on March 31, 1926, the contract in suit was executed. The pre-ambulary provisions of the agreement recite the giving and the reception of the option already referred to, the plaintiff's demand for increased salary, and then read as follows:

> "Whereas, the Summit Thread Company being desirous at all times to be fair and reasonable, now makes the following proposition, which was accepted by the said Corthell, in a rough form at East Hampton, Connecticut, on March 23, 1926.
>
> That beginning on April 1, 1926, the Summit Thread Company agrees to pay R. N. Corthell a salary of $4,000. per annum, for a period of five years, which is $620. additional to Corthell's present salary and that, in event of any distribution of Profits as covered by the Memorandum of Agreement relative to the Distribution of Profits which might be coming to the said Corthell, then the above $620. is to be deducted from whatever the amount coming to him is.
>
> In consideration, of the above, Robert N. Corthell agrees to accept $3,500. from the Summit Thread Company for the three patents mentioned in this agreement, the receipt of which is acknowledged by Corthell's signature to this agreement, and
>
> Furthermore, in consideration of the increased salary to Corthell for five years and the payment of $3500. to Corthell for the three patents, R. N. Corthell agrees that he will turn over to the Summit Thread Company, all future inventions for developments, in which case, reasonable recognition will be made to him by the Summit

Thread Company, the basis and amount of recognition to rest entirely with the Summit Thread Company at all times.

All of the above is to be interpreted in good faith on the basis of what is reasonable and intended and not technically."

The certificate accompanying the report stipulates that the case is to be decided upon so much of the evidence as is legally admissible. The facts already stated are not in controversy. The following summary sets out the findings on other issues:

During the term of the contract, no question was raised by either party to it as to the validity or the binding effect of its several provisions. The plaintiff continued as a salesman for the company, covering the same New England territory and particularly the shoe shop trade. Within five months after the contract was signed, he turned over a new invention for development. The company was marketing thread on a spool or "cop" called the Summit King spool, made up by attaching a smooth frusto-conical wooden base to a tubular fiber core. As an improvement, the plaintiff conceived the idea of grooving the head or base of the spool, making corrugations thereon which would prevent thread convolutions from dropping as they unwound. This invention was brought to the attention of the officers of the company, data and drawings furnished, and, upon application by the general manager and through his assignment, the company, on October 18, 1927, took out letters patent No. 1,646,198.

On April 27, 1927, the plaintiff filed an application on a bobbin controlling adjunct for sewing machine shuttles. This adjunct, composed of an annular sheet metal head provided with a tube or tubular shank to fit the bore of a thread cop, had fixed to its outer surface a thin spring of resilient sheet metal. and was made with the object of taking up the thrust or side play of the thread bobbins used in stitching machines in shoe factories. The plaintiff assigned this patent to the company, and on January 8, 1929, it obtained letters patent No. 1,698,392.

A further invention made by the plaintiff and turned over to the company consists of a celluloid disc with a boss in the center used in Singer I. M. shuttles, so-called, to confine the bobbin ready would with thread in the chamber, the boss acting as a hub for the bobbin to turn on, keeping it steady as the machine runs and the thread is unwound. This was also a device particularly adapted to use in shoe shops, and was patented by the company.

Finally, the plaintiff turned over for development what seems to be termed in the trade as a S. C. B. bobbin with celluloid or paper discs fastened to the tube by four ears pressed down in the center. This was made for use in all sewing machines using ready-wound bobbins. It has never been patented, and its patentability is doubtful.

The plaintiff has never received any compensation for these inventions. He turned them over to the company in accordance with the terms of his contract, and it owns them and the patents which have been issued. Prior to the expiration of the contract, the plaintiff requested "recognition," but received only assurances that he would be fixed up all right, and finally that the matter of his compensation would be taken up when a new contract was made. When, on April 1, 1931, the contract expired, it was not renewed, and, at the end of July, following, the plaintiff's employment was terminated.

No contention is made that the term "reasonable recognition," as used in the contract under consideration, means other than reasonable compensation or payment for such inventions as the plaintiff turned over. The point raised is that coupled with the reservation that the "basis and amount of recognition to rest entirely with" the company "at all times" leaves "reasonable recognition" to the unrestricted judgment and discretion of the company, permitting it to pay, as it here claims the right, nothing at all for the inventions which it has received, accepted, and now owns. It is contended that the vagueness and uncertainty of these provisions relating to the price to be paid renders the contract unenforceable. To this is added the claim that the inventions were worthless and the plaintiff has suffered no damage.

There is no more settled rule of law applicable to actions based on contracts than that an agreement, in order to be binding, must be sufficiently definite to enable the court to determine its exact meaning and fix exactly the legal liability of the parties. Indefiniteness may relate to the time of performance, the price to be paid, work to be done, property to be transferred, or other miscellaneous stipulations of the agreement. If the contract makes no statement as to the price to be paid, the law invokes the standard of reasonableness, and the fair value of the services or property is recoverable. If the terms of the agreement are uncertain as to price, but exclude the supposition that a reasonable price was intended, no contract can arise. And a reservation to either party of an unlimited right to determine the nature and extent of his performance renders his obligation too indefinite for legal enforcement, making it, as it is termed, merely illusory. Williston on Contracts, vol. 1, §§ 37 et seq.

It is accordingly held that a contract is not enforceable in which the price to be paid is indefinitely stated as the cost plus "a nice profit," *Gaines v. Tobacco Co.*, 163 Ky. 716; "a reasonable amount from the profits," *Cauet v. Smith*, 149 N. Y. S. 101, 103; "a sum not exceeding three hundred dollars during each and every week," *United Press v. New York Press Co.* 58 N. E. 527; "a fair share of my profits," *Varney v. Ditmars*, 217 N. Y. 223; and "a due allowance", *In re Vince*, [1819] 2 Q. B. 478.

On the other hand, in *Brennan v. Assurance Corporation*, 213 Mass. 365, the agreement of a contractor to "make it right with" a laborer who had been injured, if he was not able to resume work at the end of six weeks, was held not void for indefiniteness; the words "make it right" meaning fair compensation in money for the injuries received.

In *Silver v. Graves*, 210 Mass. 26, recovery was allowed on the defendant's promise to the plaintiffs that, if they would withdraw their appeal in the matter of the probate of a will, he would "make it right with (them) with a certain sum" and "give (them) a sum of money that would be satisfactory." The terms "right" or "satisfactory" were held there to mean what ought to satisfy a reasonable person or what was fair and just as between the parties.

In *Noble v. Burnett Co.*, 208 Mass. 75, the plaintiff's intestate agreed to produce certain formulas and to permit their use for manufacturing purposes, the contracting firm to manufacture and put upon the market compounds made in accordance with any of these formulas which they believed capable of yielding a profit and to pay the intestate "a fair and equitable share of the net profits." The contract was held to be sufficiently certain as to the price to be paid to be enforced.

In *Henderson Bridge Co. v. McGrath*, 134 U. S. 260, a promise to pay "what was right" was held, if made with a contractual intent, to be a promise to pay a reasonable compensation, and not too indefinite.

The views of Judge Cardozo in the dissenting opinion in *Varney v. Ditmars, supra*, 217 N. Y. 233, are instructive. He seems to be in accord with the cases last cited and to hold the opinion that, if parties manifest, through express words or by reasonable implication, an intent on the one hand to pay and on the other to accept a fair price, a promise to pay a "fair price" is not, as a matter of law, too vague for enforcement, and such damages as can be proved may be recovered.

In the instant case, as in those last cited, the contract of the parties indicates that they both promised with "contractual intent," the one intending to pay and the other to accept a fair price for the inventions turned over. "Reasonable recognition" seems to have meant what was fair and just between the parties; that is, reasonable compensation. The expression is sufficiently analogous to those used in the Massachusetts and concurring cases which have been cited to permit the application of the doctrine, which they lay down, to this case. We accept it as the law of this jurisdiction.

"Reasonable recognition," as used by the parties, was, as already noted, coupled with the reservation that the "basis and amount of recognition (was) to rest entirely with" the company "at all times." Nevertheless, the contract was "to be interpreted in good faith on the basis of what is reasonable and intended, and not technically." In these provisions, we think, the parties continued to exhibit a contractual intent and a contemplation of the payment of reasonable compensation to the plaintiff for his inventions. The company was not free to do exactly as it chose. Its promise was not purely illusory. It was bound in good faith to determine and pay the plaintiff the reasonable value of what it accepted from him. It not appearing that it has performed its promise in this regard, it is liable in this action, and the plaintiff may recover under his count in indebitatus assumpsit. *Bryant v. Flight*, 5 M. & W. 114; Williston on Contracts, § 49.

The evidence indicates that the S. C. B. bobbin disc has no real value. It is doubtful if it is patentable, and its use would expose the company to suits for infringement of other patents. The corrugated spool head, however, effected, indirectly at least, a continuation of the company's monopoly in the Summit King spool, and the bobbin controlling adjunct and the bossed disc patents brought and held profitable customers in the shoe trade. The utility and value of these inventions for the stimulation and retention of trade is apparent, and why production and distribution were discontinued does not satisfactorily appear. The election of the company to abandon their use does not measure their worth. We are of opinion that, at the time these inventions were turned over to the defendant, they had a reasonable value of $5,000, and the plaintiff should recover accordingly. The writ was dated March 5, 1932. Interest from that date must be added. The entry is Judgment for the plaintiff for $5,000 and interest from the date of the writ.

Paloukos v. Intermountain Chevrolet Co.

Supreme Court of Idaho, 1978.
588 P.2d 939.

Buyer brought action against manufacturer, dealer and president of dealer for alleged breach of contract for sale of pickup truck. The Sixth Judicial District Court, Bannock County, Arthur P. Oliver, J., dismissed portion of buyer's complaint seeking specific performance and entered summary judgment in favor of defendants, and buyer appealed. The Supreme Court, Bakes, J., held that: (1) substantial issue of fact precluding summary judgment for dealer existed on issue whether parties intended to enter binding contract; (2) dealer's acceptance of buyer's $120 deposit constituted sufficient part performance of alleged contract for sale of pickup truck to excuse compliance with statute of frauds for sale of goods, and (3) allegations in complaint of buyer did not adequately state claim for specific performance where buyer alleged no facts suggesting anything unique about the pickup truck involved, and buyer did not allege that dealer was in possession of conforming pickup truck which it could sell to him.

Affirmed in part, reversed and remanded in part.

■ BAKES, J. This appeal involves a suit by the plaintiff appellant Gust Paloukos for breach of an alleged contract with defendant respondent Intermountain Chevrolet Co., an Idaho corporation, for the purchase of a 1974 pickup truck. Intermountain does business as Glen's Chevrolet, and defendant respondent Glen Huff is its president. Intermountain is a dealer for vehicles manufactured by defendant respondent General Motors, Inc.

Paloukos brought suit against Intermountain, General Motors and Glen Huff seeking specific performance of the alleged contract and, in the alternative, damages for its breach. The district court dismissed the portion of the complaint seeking specific performance and later entered summary judgments in favor of General Motors, Glen Huff and Intermountain. On appeal, Paloukos does not contest the summary judgment entered in favor of General Motors. We affirm the summary judgment entered in favor of Glen Huff. In general, corporate officers are not individually liable for the contracts of the corporation. Paloukos has alleged nothing which would constitute an exception to that general rule.

We turn now to the principal issues presented in this case, to wit: whether the district court erred in dismissing the portion of Paloukos' complaint seeking specific performance and whether the court erred in granting summary judgment in favor of Intermountain. We consider first the issues concerning the summary judgment, and second those concerning Paloukos' request for specific performance.

The pleadings and affidavits in the record before this Court allege the following facts with respect to the formation of the alleged contract. On November 6, 1973, Paloukos, accompanied by his son Sam Paloukos, visited Intermountain's place of business and spoke with George Rowe, a salesman for Intermountain, concerning the purchase of a 1974 3/4 ton Chevrolet pickup. They agreed to the sale of a pickup and Rowe completed a printed form. The heading on the form contained Intermountain's business name, Glen's Chevrolet Co., its address and phone number and the Chevrolet logo. Beneath the heading and in bold type was printed the caption, "WORK SHEET This is NOT a Purchase Order." On the form Rowe handprinted his name in a space provided for the salesman's name, indicated Paloukos' name and address and described the pickup involved as a new green or yellow 1974 3/4 ton 4–wheel drive vehicle with a radio, V–8 engine and an automotive transmission. The completed form also indicates a purchase price of $3,650.00. Although there is no designated signature line on the form, Paloukos signed at the bottom of the form. The sale and the sales price were approved by Intermountain's sales manager. Intermountain did not have the pickup in stock, however, but Paloukos paid a $120 deposit and was told that the truck would be ordered for him. Five months later, in a letter dated April 11, 1974, Intermountain's sales manager informed Paloukos that "because of a product shortage" the dealership would not be able to deliver the vehicle and returned the deposit.

The first issue which must be addressed is whether there was a contract formed between Paloukos and Intermountain. The trial court granted summary judgment on this issue, concluding that under the facts as submitted to it no contract could have been formed as a matter of law. Recognizing that in a summary judgment proceeding the facts, and all reasonable inferences to be drawn therefrom, should be liberally construed in favor of the party against whom summary judgment is sought, *Straley v. Idaho Nuclear Corp.*, 500 P.2d 218 (Idaho 1972), the question is whether Idaho law compelled the trial court to rule on this record that no contract had been formed between the parties. See *Luke v. Conrad*, 526 P.2d 181 (Idaho 1974).

Chapter 2 of the Idaho version of the Uniform Commercial Code (UCC), which is applicable to this case, I.C. s 28–2–102, states the standard for determining whether a contract has been formed. I.C. s 28–2–204 provides:

> "28–2–204. FORMATION IN GENERAL. (1) A contract for sale of goods may be made in any manner sufficient to show agreement, including conduct by both parties which recognizes the existence of such a contract.
>
> "(3) Even though one or more terms are left open a contract for sale does not fail for indefiniteness if the parties have intended to make a contract and there is a reasonably certain basis for giving an appropriate remedy."

The official comment to this section further explains:

> "If the parties intend to enter into a binding agreement, this subsection recognizes that agreement as valid in law, despite missing terms, if there is any reasonably certain basis for granting a remedy. The test is not certainty as to what the parties were to do nor as to the exact amount of damages due the plaintiff. Nor is the fact that one or more terms are left to be agreed upon enough of itself to defeat an otherwise adequate agreement. Rather, commercial standards on the point of 'indefiniteness' are intended to be applied, this Act making provision elsewhere for missing terms needed for performance, open price, remedies and the like.
>
> "The more terms the parties leave open, the less likely it is that they have intended to conclude a binding agreement, but their actions may be frequently conclusive on the matter despite the omissions." *I.C. s 28–2–204, comment.*

Intermountain argues that the worksheet, the document Paloukos relies upon as a memorial of the agreement, represents only preliminary discussions and is too indefinite to constitute an enforceable contract. In this respect, Intermountain notes that the worksheet fails to specify the specific shade of green or yellow, the specific engine size, the box size and style, and other items concerning the specific kind of truck Paloukos desired. Intermountain's approach, however, is much too narrow. In order to have an enforceable contract, the UCC does not require a document itemizing all the specific terms of the agreement. Rather, the UCC requires a determination whether the circumstances of the case, including the parties' conduct, are "sufficient to show agreement." I.C. s 28–2–204(1). That some terms are undetermined does not defeat the existence of a contract provided the parties "intended to make a contract and there is a reasonably certain basis for giving an appropriate remedy." I.C. s 28–2–204(3). Paloukos has alleged facts which indicate that he and Rowe agreed to the sale of the pickup, that Rowe completed a form which though not entirely complete described the truck Paloukos desired and stated a price, that Paloukos signed the completed form, that the sale was approved by a sales manager, that Paloukos was told the truck would be ordered for him, and that Intermountain accepted and retained for several months a deposit on the truck. In our view these alleged facts could support a conclusion by a trier of fact that under I.C. s 28–2–204 the parties intended to enter into a binding contract, and these facts form a "reasonably certain basis for giving an appropriate remedy." We discuss the remedies appropriate in this case later in this opinion. We do not believe that the paucity of the vehicle description in the worksheet, as a matter of law, precludes the court from concluding that a contract was formed. One inference which could be drawn from the alleged facts is that Intermountain and Paloukos believed the agreement was sufficiently definite to permit Intermountain to order a vehicle acceptable to Paloukos. Moreover, a full development of the facts at a trial may resolve these omitted items with evidence explanative of the notations on the worksheet, evidence of additional terms not included on the worksheet, or evidence of usage of trade. See I.C. s 28-2-202.

The next issue necessary to discuss is whether the alleged contract is nevertheless unenforceable as a matter of law because of the statute of fraud provisions of I.C. s 28-2-201. The statute of frauds defense is an affirmative defense which must be specifically raised by the pleadings. I.R.C.P. 8(c). Intermountain's answer did not assert the defense of statute of frauds. In fact, it appears to be first raised on appeal at oral argument, much too late to be available to support the trial court's judgment on appeal.

However, since on remand the trial court may permit Intermountain to amend its answer to assert that defense, some discussion of the provision of *I.C. s 28-2-201* is appropriate. See I.C. s 1-205; *State v. Ash*, 493 P.2d 701 (Idaho 1971). That section provides:

"28-2-201.   FORMAL   REQUIREMENTS   STATUTE   OF FRAUDS. (1) Except as otherwise provided in this section a contract for the sale of goods for the price of $500 or more is not enforceable by way of action or defense unless there is some writing sufficient to indicate that a contract for sale has been made between the parties and signed by the party against whom enforcement is sought or by his authorized agent or broker. A writing is not insufficient because it omits or incorrectly states a term agreed upon but the contract is not enforceable under this paragraph beyond the quantity of goods shown in such writing."

In our view, the worksheet could suffice as an indication that a contract for sale was made; the only issue is whether it was "signed by the party against whom enforcement is sought." The official comment to I.C. s 28-2-201 defines the term "signed" as "a word which includes any authentication which identifies the party to be charged." I.C. s 28-2-201, comment 1. I.C. s 28-1-201(39) defines "signed" as:

"21-1-201.   GENERAL DEFINITIONS. Subject to additional definitions contained in the subsequent chapters of this act which are applicable to specific chapters or Parts thereof, and unless the context otherwise requires, in this act:

"(39) 'Signed' includes any symbol executed or adopted by a party with present intention to authenticate a writing.

The official comment further explains:

"39.   'Signed.' New. The inclusion of authentication in the definition of 'signed' is to make clear that as the term is used in this Act a complete signature is not necessary. Authentication may be printed, stamped or written; it may be by initials or by thumbprint. It may be on any part of the document and in appropriate cases may be found in a billhead or letterhead. No catalog of possible authentications can be complete and the court must use common sense and commercial experience in passing upon these matters. The question always is whether the symbol was executed or adopted by the party with present intention to authenticate the writing." I.C. s 28–2–201, comment 39.

The worksheet relied upon here contains two symbols, either of which may be an authentication satisfying the signature requirement of I.C. s 28–2–201. First, Intermountain's business name, which is printed in the heading of the form, may satisfy the signature requirement. Indeed, such headings are specifically mentioned in the official comment as examples of satisfactory authentications in appropriate cases. I.C. s 28–1–201, comment 39. Second, Rowe's hand printed signature in the form space for the salesman's name may also suffice as an authentication. Questions whether either symbol was executed with the intention to authenticate the document raise factual issues not properly decided on a motion for summary judgment. In sum, the district court was not entitled to rule in granting summary judgment that the worksheet, as a matter of law, failed to satisfy the writing requirement of I.C. s 28–2–201(1).

Moreover, even if the worksheet did not satisfy the requirements for a writing in I.C. s 28–2–201(1), Paloukos' payment of $120, which was accepted by Intermountain though later returned, constitutes sufficient part performance to excuse compliance with the statute of frauds. I.C. s 28–2–201(3) provides:

> "28–2–201. FORMAL   REQUIREMENTS   STATUTE   OF FRAUDS.

> "(3) A contract which does not satisfy the requirements of subsection (1) but which is valid in other respects is enforceable

> "(c) with respect to goods for which payment has been made and accepted or which have been received and accepted (section 28–2–606)."

The UCC is clear that where the goods are apportionable part payment permits enforcement of the contract only as to the portion of the goods for which payment has been made. See I.C. s 28–2–201, comment 2. However, the UCC is ambiguous with respect to a partial payment in a transaction involving a single, non-divisible item, such as an automobile. We agree with the commentators and the majority of the courts which have considered the issue that part payment for a non-divisible unit, such as an automobile, permits the party under I.C. s 28–2–201(3)(c) to prove and recover in full on the oral contract. The obvious purpose of limiting enforcement of an oral contract to the extent of partial payment is to permit enforcement of that part of the contract verified by the partial performance and to avoid disputes over the quantity. In a case such as this, which involves a single, non-divisible item, there is no dispute over quantity. The partial payment and its acceptance, as is recognized by the UCC, is a sufficiently reliable manifestation of the existence of a contract that the party ought to be afforded the opportunity to prove its existence.

The final issue presented is whether the district court properly dismissed that portion of Paloukos' complaint which sought specific performance of the alleged contract. Under the UCC specific performance is available to a purchaser where "the goods are unique or in other proper circumstances." I.C. s 28–2–716(1). Although the UCC may have liberalized some of the old common law rules, See I.C. s 28–2–716, comment 1, specific performance nevertheless remains an extraordinary remedy generally available only where other remedies are in some way inadequate. In his pleadings Paloukos alleged no facts suggesting anything unique about the pickup involved. The market value of such a vehicle is readily ascertainable and Paloukos' pleadings indicate no reason why damages would not be adequate relief. Moreover, the sole remaining defendant in this case, Intermountain, is a dealer, not a manufacturer, of automobiles. Paloukos does not allege that Intermountain is in possession of a conforming pickup which it could sell him. Indeed, the record suggests quite the contrary. It is well established that the courts will not order the impossible, such as ordering the seller under a sales contract to sell to the buyer that which the seller does not have. We therefore affirm the district court's dismissal of that portion of Paloukos' complaint seeking specific performance.

Paloukos has requested attorney fees for this appeal citing I.C. s 12–120. A prerequisite to an award of attorney fees under that section is that the party prevail. Although Paloukos was successful, in part at least, on this appeal, it nonetheless remains to be determined whether he will ultimately prevail on his cause of action for breach of contract. Should Paloukos ultimately prevail and satisfy the other requirements of I.C. s 12–120 for an award of attorney fees, the district court, in fixing the award, should of course consider the fees incurred in bringing this appeal.

Affirmed in part, reversed and remanded in part.

Uniform Commercial Code

§ 2–204 Formation in General

(1) A contract for sale of goods may be made in any manner sufficient to show agreement, including conduct by both parties which recognizes the existence of such a contract.

(2) An agreement sufficient to constitute a contract for sale may be found even though the moment of its making is undetermined.

(3) Even though one or more terms are left open a contract for sale does not fail for indefiniteness if the parties have intended to make a contract and there is a reasonably certain basis for giving an appropriate remedy.

Official Comment

Prior Uniform Statutory Provision: Sections 1 and 3, Uniform Sales Act.

Changes: Completely rewritten by this and other sections of this Article.

Purposes of Changes:

Subsection (1) continues without change the basic policy of recognizing any manner of expression of agreement, oral, written or otherwise. The legal effect of such an agreement is, of course, qualified by other provisions of this Article.

Under subsection (1) appropriate conduct by the parties may be sufficient to establish an agreement. Subsection (2) is directed primarily to the situation where the interchanged correspondence does not disclose the exact point at which the deal was closed, but the actions of the parties indicate that a binding obligation has been undertaken.

Subsection (3) states the principle as to "open terms" underlying later sections of the Article. If the parties intend to enter into a binding agreement, this subsection recognizes that agreement as valid in law, despite missing terms, if there is any reasonably certain basis for granting a remedy. The test is not certainty as to what the parties were to do nor as to the exact amount of damages due the plaintiff. Nor is the fact that one or more terms are left to be agreed upon enough of itself to defeat an otherwise adequate agreement. Rather, commercial standards on the point of "indefiniteness" are intended to be applied, this Act making provision elsewhere for missing terms needed for performance, open price, remedies and the like.

The more terms the parties leave open, the less likely it is that they have intended to conclude a binding agreement, but their actions may be frequently conclusive on the matter despite the omissions.

Uniform Commercial Code

§ 2–305   Open Price Term

(1) The parties if they so intend can conclude a contract for sale even though the price is not settled. In such a case the price is a reasonable price at the time for delivery if

(a) nothing is said as to price; or

(b) the price is left to be agreed by the parties and they fail to agree; or

(c) the price is to be fixed in terms of some agreed market or other standard as set or recorded by a third person or agency and it is not so set or recorded.

(2) A price to be fixed by the seller or by the buyer means a price for him to fix in good faith.

(3) When a price left to be fixed otherwise than by agreement of the parties fails to be fixed through fault of one party the other may at his option treat the contract as cancelled or himself fix a reasonable price.

(4) Where, however, the parties intend not to be bound unless the price be fixed or agreed and it is not fixed or agreed there is no contract. In such a case the buyer must return any goods already received or if unable so to do must pay their reasonable value at the time of delivery and the seller must return any portion of the price paid on account.

Official Comment

Prior Uniform Statutory Provision: Sections 9 and 10, Uniform Sales Act.

Changes: Completely rewritten.

Purposes of Changes:

1. This section applies when the price term is left open on the making of an agreement which is nevertheless intended by the parties to be a binding agreement. This Article rejects in these instances the formula that "an agreement to agree is unenforceable" if the case falls within subsection (1) of this section, and rejects also defeating such agreements on the ground of "indefiniteness". Instead this Article recognizes the dominant intention of the parties to have the deal continue to be binding upon both. As to future performance, since this Article recognizes remedies such as cover (Section 2–712), resale (Section 2–706) and specific performance (Section 2–716) which go beyond any mere arithmetic as between contract price and market price, there is usually a "reasonably certain basis for granting an appropriate remedy for breach" so that the contract need not fail for indefiniteness.

2. Under some circumstances the postponement of agreement on price will mean that no deal has really been concluded, and this is made express in the preamble of subsection (1) ("The parties if they so intend") and in subsection (4). Whether or not this is so is, in most cases, a question to be determined by the trier of fact.

3. Subsection (2), dealing with the situation where the price is to be fixed by one party rejects the uncommercial idea that an agreement that the seller may fix the price means that he may fix any price he may wish by the express qualification that the price so fixed must be fixed in good faith. Good faith includes observance of reasonable commercial standards of fair dealing in the trade if the party is a merchant. (Section 2–103). But in the normal case a "posted price" or a future seller's or buyer's "given price," "price in effect," "market price," or the like satisfies the good faith requirement.

4. The section recognizes that there may be cases in which a particular person's judgment is not chosen merely as a barometer or index of a fair

price but is an essential condition to the parties' intent to make any contract at all. For example, the case where a known and trusted expert is to "value" a particular painting for which there is no market standard differs sharply from the situation where a named expert is to determine the grade of cotton, and the difference would support a finding that in the one the parties did not intend to make a binding agreement if that expert were unavailable whereas in the other they did so intend. Other circumstances would of course affect the validity of such a finding.

5.   Under subsection (3), wrongful interference by one party with any agreed machinery for price fixing in the contract may be treated by the other party as a repudiation justifying cancellation, or merely as a failure to take cooperative action thus shifting to the aggrieved party the reasonable leeway in fixing the price.

6.   Throughout the entire section, the purpose is to give effect to the agreement which has been made. That effect, however, is always conditioned by the requirement of good faith action which is made an inherent part of all contracts within this Act. (Section 1–203).

* * *

Corthell illustrates the adoption of Cardozo's approach in a context that very closely resembles the fact pattern in *Varney* (indeed, in which the case for finding no contract on grounds of indefiniteness is, if anything, stronger than it was there). The plaintiff in *Corthell* worked as a salesman for the defendant, a yarn and sewing machine accessory business. In addition to his sales work, the plaintiff invented and patented various complements and attachments for sewing machines. The plaintiff and the defendant thereupon entered into a five-year agreement, under which the defendant was to receive the plaintiff's existing patents and the rights to all of the plaintiff's future inventions, and the plaintiff was to receive a substantial raise, a one-time cash payment for his existing patents, and "reasonable recognition" for future inventions, with the precise "basis and amount to rest entirely with [the defendant] at all times." The entire contract, furthermore, was to be "interpreted in good faith and on the basis of what is reasonable and intended and not technically." The plaintiff made several further inventions during the period of the contract (both patentable and not), but the defendant refused to pay the plaintiff any "reasonable recognition." Instead, the defendant first insisted that it would pay plaintiff only on renewal of the contract and then when the time for renewal came, fired the plaintiff. The plaintiff sued.

Under the approach taken in *Varney*, *Corthell* would have been an easy victory (at least in contract) for the defendant. "Reasonable recognition" for inventions is surely if anything more difficult to quantify than profit-sharing in an architectural partnership. (It is much more difficult to know which of a product's features contributed how much to customer demand than to know which architect spent how many hours on which account.[4])

---

4.   The fact that professional partnerships often (generally?) attempt to tie a partner's compensation to his contribution to revenues, whereas technology firms tend to employ engineers on salary, supports this observation.

And the defendant in *Corthell*, unlike the defendant in *Varney*, further reserved for itself the right to fix the "recognition" that the plaintiff would receive.

Nevertheless, the *Corthell* court held for the plaintiff. Although it acknowledged that a promise in which one or the other party reserved the right to determine the extent of its own obligations is illusory and hence not enforceable,[5] the court concluded that the clause requiring the contract to be interpreted reasonably and in good faith sufficiently limited the clause allowing the defendant to fix plaintiff's "recognition" so as to render the defendant's promise real and substantial. Moreover, although the court acknowledged that a contract is enforceable only insofar as it is sufficiently definite for a court to fix its meaning, the court concluded that the contract at issue in *Corthell* was sufficiently definite under this test. After all, there was no dispute that "reasonable recognition," as used in the contract, referred to "reasonable compensation." And, the court thought, it was well within its capacity to identify reasonable compensation for the plaintiff's inventions. Indeed, the court observed, even where a contract is silent concerning the price term, the law imposes a reasonable price. Accordingly, the court found for the plaintiff and fixed his compensation at $5000.

Paloukos applies this approach in a context in which, because the contractual indefiniteness concerns something besides the price term, gap-filling calls for courts to exhibit still greater confidence in their functionalist competence. The plaintiff went to the defendant's car dealership to buy a Chevy truck. Together with the defendant's agent, the plaintiff filled out a form entitled "Work Sheet—This is NOT a Purchase Order," which began to identify the terms of the purchase contract, including fixing the price and the model. The plaintiff thereupon paid the defendant a deposit and the defendant said that the truck would arrive for the plaintiff to collect by a specified date. A "production shortage" of the relevant model induced the defendant to inform the plaintiff that he could not provide the truck and to return the plaintiff's deposit. The plaintiff sued to enforce the sales contract.

The defendant sought summary judgment on the ground that the parties' negotiations, having left so many terms still open, were too incomplete to have established a contract. The court disagreed and denied summary judgment. The court acknowledged that a great many terms—including color, styling, and engine size—remained open. But it applied the UCC's general rule that a contract may be formed in any manner sufficient to show agreement, and that all is required of the agreement is that it reveals the parties' intent to make a contract and gives courts a reasonably certain basis for fashioning a remedy for that contract's breach. In *Paloukos*, the court observed, the parties had reached the stage of fixing a delivery date and making and receiving a down payment. This makes it reasonable to conclude that the parties intended to make a contract. The court was, moreover, unbothered by the open terms. It suspected that

---

5.   Illusory promises are taken up in Chapter 15 below.

evidence at trial might help fill these in, and it was prepared, if the evidence could not, to leave certain terms (for example, the truck's color) to the discretion of the defendant against whom the contract would be enforced. The court was prepared, in other words, to complete the contract in a fashion that produced a fair and reasonable arrangement between the parties, without worrying about whether the parties had ever subjectively (that is to say, in their actual, specific intents) accepted or agreed to the particular arrangement that the court would strike. The key question, for the court, was not the formalist one whether there was a meeting of minds but rather the functionalist one whether there was enough, in the record, to make it reasonable to think that the parties intended to strike a bargain and to allow the court reasonably to fix the bargain's terms. Finally, the court was sufficiently confident, with respect to its gap-filling role, that it was willing to fill in terms (color, style, engine) even where (in contrast to missing prices) the required details could not be read (more or less mechanically) off of market equilibria but instead required the court to exercise free-floating judgment.

Paloukos thus follows the approach taken in *Corthell*, which is to apply functionalist methods to evaluating incomplete contracts. It makes no mention of subjective intent or the meeting of minds and exhibits no preference for freedom *from* contract over freedom *to* contract. *Paloukos* further adopts a confident attitude within the functionalist paradigm. The *Paloukos* court has relatively few doubts about its capacity to fill in a contract on behalf of parties who had not done so.

The core functionalist impulse is both more important, and probably more stably and uniformly accepted, than the additional confidence concerning court capacity reasonably to fill in contractual gaps. Thus modern courts almost uniformly reject all the core formalist ideas that drove opinions such as the one in *Varney*. They employ an objective approach to contractual intent, abandon any special concern for the meeting of minds or freedom from contract, and they pursue the effort to identify reasonable (fair and efficient) specific terms between parties whose general intent was to strike a bargain. Indeed, even where modern courts appear to embrace formalist outcomes—even where they refuse to fill in contractual gaps and hold that incompleteness renders a bargain unenforceable—they do so not on formalist but rather on functionalist grounds. That is, they base their refusals not on any failure of the parties' subjective contractual intentions to engage each other but rather on the functionalist consideration that it would be inefficient or unfair for courts, in such cases, to do the parties' negotiating and drafting for them. So it appears that functionalism has both won the argument and held the day in this area of law.

But in spite of functionalism's impressive successes (both in theory and in practice), there remains a core formalist insight concerning incomplete contracts that functionalism cannot displace, and that retains some practical effect in the positive law, even today. The insight concerns the conceptual nature of a contractual incompleteness or gap, and in particular the formal distinction between the absence of a contract term, on the one hand, and, on the other, the absence of contractual intent, *tout court*. The following materials illustrate this distinction and also the influence on the positive law that formalism retains in its wake.

Restatement 2d of Contracts

§ 26   Preliminary Negotiations
(reprised from Chapter 13)

Joseph Martin, Jr. Delicatessen v. Schumacher

Court of Appeals of New York, 1981.
417 N.E.2d 541.

Tenant brought action to compel landlord to renew lease, and landlord responded by bringing holdover proceeding to regain possession. The Supreme Court, Special Term, Suffolk County, George J. Aspland, J., entered summary judgment in favor of the landlord and dismissed the tenant's complaint, and the Supreme Court entered further order denying tenant's motion for removal and consolidation of landlord's action against it from the district court to the Supreme Court, and the tenant appealed. The Supreme Court, Appellate Division, *419 N.Y.S.2d 558,* reversed. Cross appeals were taken. The Court of Appeals, Fuchsberg, J., held that the agreement to agree on a future rental was unenforceable for uncertainty since it contained no methodology for determining the rent, but, rather, its unrevealing, unamplified language spoke to no more than "annual rentals to be agreed upon" and the words left no room for legal construction or resolution of ambiguity.

Order of Appellate Division reversed.

■ FUCHSBERG, JUDGE. This case raises an issue fundamental to the law of contracts. It calls upon us to review a decision of the Appellate Division, 419 N.Y.S.2d 558 which held that a realty lease's provision that the rent for a renewal period was "to be agreed upon" may be enforceable.

The pertinent factual and procedural contexts in which the case reaches this court are uncomplicated. In 1973, the appellant, as landlord, leased a retail store to the respondent for a five-year term at a rent graduated upwards from $500 per month for the first year to $650 for the fifth. The renewal clause stated that "(t)he Tenant may renew this lease for an additional period of five years at annual rentals to be agreed upon; Tenant shall give Landlord thirty (30) days written notice, to be mailed certified mail, return receipt requested, of the intention to exercise such right". It is not disputed that the tenant gave timely notice of its desire to renew or that, once the landlord made it clear that he would do so only at a rental starting at $900 a month, the tenant engaged an appraiser who opined that a fair market rental value would be $545.41.

The tenant thereupon commenced an action for specific performance in Supreme Court, Suffolk County, to compel the landlord to extend the lease for the additional term at the appraiser's figure or such other sum as the court would decide was reasonable. For his part, the landlord in due course brought a holdover proceeding in the local District Court to evict the tenant. On the landlord's motion for summary judgment, the Supreme Court, holding that a bald agreement to agree on a future rental was unenforceable for uncertainty as a matter of law, dismissed the tenant's complaint. Concordantly, it denied as moot the tenant's motion to remove the District Court case to the Supreme Court and to consolidate the two suits.

It was on appeal by the tenant from these orders that the Appellate Division, expressly overruling an established line of cases in the process, reinstated the tenant's complaint and granted consolidation. In so doing, it reasoned that "a renewal clause in a lease providing for future agreement on the rent to be paid during the renewal term is enforceable if it is established that the parties' intent was not to terminate in the event of a failure to agree". It went on to provide that, if the tenant met that burden, the trial court could proceed to set a "reasonable rent". One of the Justices, concurring, would have eliminated the first step and required the trial court to proceed directly to the fixation of the rent. Each party now appeals by leave of the Appellate Division pursuant to CPLR 5602 (subd. (b), par. 1). The tenant seeks only a modification adopting the concurrer's position. The question formally certified to us by the Appellate Division is simply whether its order was properly made. Since we conclude that the disposition at the Supreme Court was the correct one, our answer must be in the negative.

We begin our analysis with the basic observation that, unless otherwise mandated by law (e. g., residential emergency rent control statutes), a contract is a private "ordering" in which a party binds himself to do, or not to do, a particular thing (*Fletcher v. Peck*, 6 Cranch (10 U.S.) 87, 136.). This liberty is no right at all if it is not accompanied by freedom not to contract. The corollary is that, before one may secure redress in our courts because another has failed to honor a promise, it must appear that the promisee assented to the obligation in question.

It also follows that, before the power of law can be invoked to enforce a promise, it must be sufficiently certain and specific so that what was promised can be ascertained. Otherwise, a court, in intervening, would be imposing its own conception of what the parties should or might have undertaken, rather than confining itself to the implementation of a bargain to which they have mutually committed themselves. Thus, definiteness as to material matters is of the very essence in contract law. Impenetrable vagueness and uncertainty will not do (1 Corbin, Contracts, s 95, p. 394; 6 Encyclopedia of New York Law, Contracts, s 301; *Restatement, Contracts 2d, s 32*, Comment a).

Dictated by these principles, it is rightfully well settled in the common law of contracts in this State that a mere agreement to agree, in which a material term is left for future negotiations, is unenforceable (*Willmott v. Giarraputo*, 184 N.Y.S.2d 97; *Sourwine v. Truscott*, 17 Hun. 432, 434). This is especially true of the amount to be paid for the sale or lease of real property. The rule applies all the more, and not the less, when, as here, the extraordinary remedy of specific performance is sought (11 Williston, Contracts (Jaeger 3d ed.), s 1424; Pomeroy, Equity Jurisprudence, s 1405).

This is not to say that the requirement for definiteness in the case before us now could only have been met by explicit expression of the rent to be paid. The concern is with substance, not form. It certainly would have sufficed, for instance, if a methodology for determining the rent was to be found within the four corners of the lease, for a rent so arrived at would have been the end product of agreement between the parties themselves. Nor would the agreement have failed for indefiniteness because it invited recourse to an objective extrinsic event, condition or standard on which the amount was made to depend. All of these, inter alia, would have come within the embrace of the maxim that what can be made certain is certain (9 Coke, 47a).

But the renewal clause here in fact contains no such ingredients. Its unrevealing, unamplified language speaks to no more than "annual rentals to be agreed upon". Its simple words leave no room for legal construction or resolution of ambiguity. Neither tenant nor landlord is bound to any formula. There is not so much as a hint at a commitment to be bound by the "fair market rental value" which the tenant's expert reported or the "reasonable rent" the Appellate Division would impose, much less any definition of either. Nowhere is there an inkling that either of the parties directly or indirectly assented, upon accepting the clause, to subordinate the figure on which it ultimately would insist, to one fixed judicially, as the Appellate Division decreed be done, or, for that matter, by an arbitrator or other third party.

Finally, in this context, we note that the tenant's reliance on *May Metropolitan Corp. v. May Oil Burner Corp.*, 290 N.Y. 260 is misplaced. There the parties had executed a franchise agreement for the sale of oil burners. The contract provided for annual renewal, at which time each year's sales quota was "to be mutually agreed upon". In holding that the defendant's motion for summary judgment should have been denied, the court indicated that the plaintiff should be given an opportunity to establish that a series of annual renewals had ripened into a course of dealing from which it might be possible to give meaning to an otherwise uncertain term. This decision, in the more fluid sales setting in which it occurred, may be seen as a precursor to the subsequently enacted Uniform Commercial Code's treatment of open terms in contracts for the sale of goods (see Uniform Commercial Code, s 1–205, subd. (1); s 2–204, subd. (3); see, also, Restatement, Contracts 2d, s 249). As the tenant candidly concedes, the code, by its very terms, is limited to the sale of goods. The May case is therefore not applicable to real estate contracts. Stability is a hallmark of the law controlling such transactions (see *Heyert v. Orange & Rockland Utilities*, 17 N.Y.2d 352, 362).

For all these reasons, the order of the Appellate Division should be reversed, with costs, and the orders of the Supreme Court, Suffolk County, reinstated. The certified question, therefore, should be answered in the negative. As to the plaintiff's appeal, since that party was not aggrieved by the order of the Appellate Division, the appeal should be dismissed *(CPLR 5511)*, without costs.

■ MEYER, JUDGE, concurring.

While I concur in the result because the facts of this case do not fit the rule of *May Metropolitan Corp. v. May Oil Burner Corp.*, 290 N.Y. 260, I cannot concur in the majority's rejection of that case as necessarily inapplicable to litigation concerning leases. That the setting of that case was commercial and that its principle is now incorporated in a statute (the Uniform Commercial Code) which by its terms is not applicable to real estate is irrelevant to the question whether the principle can be applied in real estate cases.

As we recognized in *Farrell Lines v. City of New York*, 30 N.Y.2d 76, 82, quoting from *A. Z. A. Realty Corp. v. Harrigan's Cafe*, 185 N.Y.S. 212: "An agreement of lease possesses no peculiar sanctity requiring the application of rules of construction different from those applicable to an ordinary contract." To the extent that the majority opinion can be read as holding that no course of dealing between the parties to a lease could make a clause providing for renewal at a rental "to be agreed upon" enforceable I do not concur.

■ JASEN, JUDGE, dissenting in part.

While I recognize that the traditional rule is that a provision for renewal of a lease must be "certain" in order to render it binding and enforceable, in my view the better rule would be that if the tenant can establish its entitlement to renewal under the lease, the mere presence of a provision calling for renewal at "rentals to be agreed upon" should not prevent judicial intervention to fix rent at a reasonable rate in order to avoid a forfeiture. Therefore, I would affirm the order of the Appellate Division for the reasons stated in the opinion of Justice LEON D. LAZER at the Appellate Division.

Sun Printing & Publishing Ass'n v. Remington Paper & Power Co.

Court of Appeals of New York, 1923.
139 N.E. 470.

Action by the Sun Printing & Publishing Association against the Remington Paper & Power Company, Inc. From an order of the Appellate Division (193 N. Y. Supp. 698), which reversed an order of the Special Term denying plaintiff's motion for judgment on the pleadings, and granted said motion, defendant, by permission, appeals. The following question was certified: 'Does the complaint state facts sufficient to constitute a cause of action?'

Order of Appellate Division reversed, and that of Special Term affirmed, with costs in the Appellate Division, and question answered.

■ CARDOZO, J. Plaintiff agreed to buy and defendant to sell 1,000 tons of paper per month during the months of September, 1919, to December, 1920, inclusive, 16,000 tons in all. Sizes and quality were adequately described. Payment was to be made on the 20th of each month for all paper shipped the previous month. The price for shipments in September, 1919, was to be $3.73 3/4 per 100 pounds, and for shipments in October, November, and December, 1919, $4 per 100 pounds. 'For the balance of the period of this agreement the price of the paper and length of terms for which such price shall apply shall be agreed upon by and between the parties hereto fifteen days prior to the expiration of each period for which the price and length of term thereof have been previously agreed upon, said price in no event to be higher than the contract price for news print charged by the Canadian Export Paper Company to the large consumers, the seller to receive the benefit of any differentials in freight rates.'

Between September, 1919, and December of that year, inclusive, shipments were made and paid for as required by the contract. The time then arrived when there was to be an agreement upon a new price and upon the term of its duration. The defendant in advance of that time gave notice that the contract was imperfect, and disclaimed for the future an obligation to deliver. Upon this the plaintiff took the ground that the price was to be ascertained by resort to an established standard. It made demand that during each month of 1920 the defendant deliver 1,000 tons of paper at the contract price for news print charged by the Canadian Export Paper Company to the large consumers, the defendant to receive the benefit of any differentials in freight rates. The demand was renewed month by month till the expiration of the year. This action has been brought to recover the ensuing damage.

Seller and buyer left two subjects to be settled in the middle of December and at unstated intervals thereafter. One was the price to be paid. The other was the length of time during which such price was to govern. Agreement as to the one was insufficient without agreement as to the other. If price and nothing more had been left open for adjustment, there might be force in the contention that the buyer would be viewed, in the light of later provisions, as the holder of an option. *Cohen & Sons v. Lurie Woolen Co.*, 232 N. Y. 112. This would mean that, in default of an agreement for a lower price, the plaintiff would have the privilege of calling for delivery in accordance with a price established as a maximum. The price to be agreed upon might be less, but could not be more, than 'the contract price for news print charged by the Canadian Export Paper Company to the large consumers.' The difficulty is, however, that ascertainment of this price does not dispense with the necessity for agreement in respect of the term during which the price is to apply. Agreement upon a maximum payable this month or today is not the same as an agreement that it shall continue to be payable next month or tomorrow. Seller and buyer understood that the price to be fixed in December for a term to be agreed upon would not be more than the price then charged by the Canadian Export Paper Company to the large consumers. They did not understand that, if during the term so established the price charged by the Canadian Export Paper Company was changed, the price payable to the seller would fluctuate accordingly. This was conceded by plaintiff's counsel on the argument before us. The seller was to receive no more during the running of the prescribed term, though the Canadian Maximum was raised. The buyer was to pay no less during that term, though the maximum was lowered. In the brief, the standard was to be applied at the beginning of the successive terms, but once applied was to be maintained until the term should have expired. While the term was unknown, the contract was inchoate.

The argument is made that there was no need of an agreement as to time unless the price to be paid was lower than the maximum. We find no evidence of this intention in the language of the contract. The result would then be that the defendant would never know where it stood. The plaintiff was under no duty to accept the Canadian standard. It does not assert that it was. What it asserts is that the contract amounted to the concession of an option. Without an agreement as to time, however, there would be not one option, but a dozen. The Canadian price to-day might be less than the Canadian price to-morrow. Election by the buyer to proceed with performance at the price prevailing in one month would not bind it to proceed at the price prevailing in another. Successive options to be exercised every month would thus be read into the contract. Nothing in the wording discloses the intention of the seller to place itself to that extent at the mercy of the buyer. Even if, however, we were to interpolate the restriction that the option, if exercised at all, must be exercised only once, and for the entire quantity permitted, the difficulty would not be ended. Market prices in 1920 happened to rise. The importance of the time element becomes apparent when we ask ourselves what the seller's position would be if they had happened to fall. Without an agreement as to time, the maximum would be lowered from one shipment to another with every reduction of the standard. With such an agreement, on the other hand, there would be stability and certainty. The parties attempted to guard against the contingency of failing to come together as to price. They did not guard against the contingency of failing to come together as to time. Very likely they thought the latter contingency so remote that it could safely be disregarded. In any event, whether through design or through inadvertence, they left the gap unfilled. The result was nothing more than 'an agreement to agree.' *St. Regis Paper Co. v. Hubbs & Hastings Paper Co.*, 235 N. Y. 30, 36. Defendant 'exercised its legal right' when it insisted that there was need of something more. *St. Regis Paper Co. v. Hubbs & Hastings Paper Co.*, supra; 1 Williston Contracts, § 45. The right is not affected by our appraisal of the motive. *Mayer v. McCreery*, 119 N. Y. 434, 440.

We are told that the defendant was under a duty, in default of an agreement, to accept a term that would be reasonable in view of the nature of the transaction and the practice of the business. To hold it to such a standard is to make the contract over. The defendant reserved the privilege of doing its business in its own way, and did not undertake to conform to the practice and beliefs of others. *United Press v. New York Press Co.*, 164 N. Y. 406, 413, We are told again that there was a duty, in default of other agreement, to act as if the successive terms were to expire every month. The contract says they are to expire at such intervals as the agreement may prescribe. There is need, it is true, of no high degree of ingenuity to show how the parties, with little change of language, could have framed a form of contract to which obligation would attach. The difficulty is that they framed another. We are not at liberty to revise while professing to construe.

We do not ignore the allegation of the complaint that the contract price charged by the Canadian Export Paper Company to the large consumers 'constituted a definite and well-defined standard of price that was readily ascertainable.' The suggestion is made by members of the court that the price so charged may have been known to be one established for the year, so that fluctuation would be impossible. If that was its character, the complaint should so allege. The writing signed by the parties calls for an agreement as to time. The complaint concedes that no such agreement has been made. The result, prima facie, is the failure of the contract. In that situation the pleader has the burden of setting forth the extrinsic circumstances, if there are any, that make agreement unimportant. There is significance, moreover, in the attitude of counsel. No point is made in brief or in argument that the Canadian price, when once established, is constant through the year. On the contrary, there is at least a tacit assumption that it varies with the market. The buyer acted on the same assumption when it renewed the demand from month to month, making tender of performance at the prices then prevailing. If we misconceive the course of dealing, the plaintiff by amendment of its pleading can correct our misconception. The complaint as it comes before us leaves no escape from the conclusion that agreement in respect of time is as essential to a completed contract as agreement in respect of price. The agreement was not reached, and the defendant is not bound.

The question is not here whether the defendant would have failed in the fulfillment of its duty by an arbitrary refusal to reach any agreement as to time after notice from the plaintiff that it might make division of the terms in any way it pleased. No such notice was given, so far as the complaint discloses. The action is not based upon a refusal to treat with the defendant and attempt to arrive at an agreement. Whether any such theory of liability would be tenable we need not now inquire. Even if the plaintiff might have stood upon the defendant's denial of obligation as amounting to such a refusal, it did not elect to do so. Instead, it gave its own construction to the contract, fixed for itself the length of the successive terms, and thereby coupled its demand with a condition which there was no duty to accept. *Rubber Trading Co. v. Manhattan Rubber Mfg. Co.*, 221 N. Y. 120; 3 Williston, Contracts, § 1334. We find no allegation of readiness, and offer to proceed on any other basis. The condition being untenable, the failure to comply with it cannot give a cause of action.

The order of the Appellate Division should be reversed, and that of the Special Term affirmed, with costs in the Appellate Division and in this court, and the question certified answered in the negative.

■ CRANE, J., dissenting. I cannot take the view of this contract that has been adopted by the majority. The parties to this transaction beyond question thought they were making a contract for the purchase and sale of 16,000 tons rolls news print. The contract was upon a form used by the defendant in its business, and we must suppose that it was intended to be what it states to be, and not a trick or device to defraud merchants. It begins by saying that, in consideration of the mutual covenants and agreements herein set forth the Remington Paper & Power Company, Incorporated, of Watertown, state of New York, hereinafter called the seller, agrees to sell and hereby does sell and the Sun Printing & Publishing Association of New York City, state of New York, hereinafter called the purchaser, agrees to buy and pay for and hereby does buy the following paper, 16,000 tons rolls news print. The sizes are then given. Shipment is to be at the rate of 1,000 tons per month to December, 1920, inclusive. There are details under the headings consignee, specifications, price and delivery, terms, miscellaneous, cores, claims, contingencies, cancellations.

Under the head of miscellaneous comes the following:

'The price agreed upon between the parties hereto, for all papers shipped during the month of September, 1919, shall be $3.73 3/4 per hundred pounds gross weight of rolls on board cars at mills.

'The price agreed upon between the parties hereto for all shipments made during the months of October, November and December, 1919, shall be $4.00 per hundred pounds gross weight of rolls on board cars at mills.

'For the balance of the period of this agreement the price of the paper and length of terms for which such price shall apply shall be agreed upon by and between the parties hereto fifteen days prior to the expiration of each period for which the price and length of term thereof has been previously agreed upon, said price in no event to be higher than the contract price for news print charged by the Canadian Export Paper Company to the large consumers, the seller to receive the benefit of any differentials in freight rates.

'It is understood and agreed by the parties hereto that the tonnage specified herein is for use in the printing and publication of the various editions of the Daily and Sunday New York Sun, and any variation from this will be considered a breach of contract.'

After the deliveries for September, October, November, and December, 1919, the defendant refused to fix any price for the deliveries during the subsequent months, and refused to deliver any more paper. It has taken the position that this document was no contract; that it meant nothing; that it was formally executed for the purpose of permitting the defendant to furnish paper or not, as it pleased.

Surely these parties must have had in mind that some binding agreement was made for the sale and delivery of 16,000 tons rolls of paper, and that the instrument contained all the elements necessary to make a binding contract. It is a strain upon reason to imagine the paper house, the Remington Paper & Power Company, Incorporated, and the Sun Printing & Publishing Association, formally executing a contract drawn up upon the defendant's prepared form which was useless and amounted to nothing. We must, at least, start the examination of this agreement by believing that these intelligent parties intended to make a binding contract. If this be so, the court should spell out a binding contract, if it be possible. I not only think it possible, but think the paper itself clearly states a contract recognized under all the rules at law. It is said that the one essential element of price is lacking; that the provision above quoted is an agreement to agree to a price, and that the defendant had the privilege of agreeing or not, as it pleased; that, if it failed to agree to a price, there was no standard by which to measure the amount the plaintiff would have to pay. The contract does state, however, just this very thing. Fifteen days before the 1st of January, 1920, the parties were to agree upon the price of the paper to be delivered thereafter, and the length of the period for which such price should apply. However, the price to be fixed was not 'to be higher than the contract price for news print charged by the Canadian Export Paper Company to large consumers.' Here, surely, was something definite. The 15th day of December arrived. The defendant refused to deliver. At that time there was a price for news print charged by the Canadian Export Paper Company. If the plaintiff offered to pay this price, which was the highest price the defendant could demand, the defendant was bound to deliver. This seems to be very clear.

But, while all agree that the price on the 15th day of December could be fixed, the further objection is made that the period during which that price should continue was not agreed upon. There are many answers to this.

We have reason to believe that the parties supposed they were making a binding contract; that they had fixed the terms by which one was required to take and the other to deliver; that the Canadian Export Paper Company price was to be the highest that could be charged in any event. These things being so, the court should be very reluctant to permit a defendant to avoid its contract. *Wakeman v. Wheeler & Wilson Mfg. Co.*, 101 N. Y. 205.

On the 15th of the fourth month, the time when the price was to be fixed for subsequent deliveries, there was a price charged by the Canadian Export Paper Company to large consumers. As the defendant failed to agree upon a price, made no attempt to agree upon a price, and deliberately broke its contract, it could readily be held to deliver the rest of the paper, 1,000 rolls a month, at this Canadian price. There is nothing in the complaint which indicates that this is a fluctuating price, or that the price of paper as it was on December 15th was not the same for the remaining 12 months. Or we can deal with this contract month by month. The deliveries were to be made 1,000 tons per month. On December 15th 1,000 tons could have been demanded. The price charged by the Canadian Export Paper Company on the 15th of each month on and after December 15, 1919, would be the price for the 1,000–ton delivery for that month. Or, again, the word as used in the miscellaneous provision quoted is not 'price,' but 'contract price'—'in no event to be higher than the contract price.' Contract implies a term or period, and, if the evidence should show that the Canadian contract price was for a certain period of weeks or months, then this period could be applied to the contract in question. Failing any other alternative, the law should do here what it has done in so many other cases-apply the rule of reason and compel parties to contract in the light of fair dealing. It could hold this defendant to deliver its paper as it agreed to do, and take for a price the Canadian Export Paper Company contract price for a period which is reasonable under all the circumstances and conditions as applied in the paper trade.

To let this defendant escape from its formal obligations when any one of these rulings as applied to this contract would given a practical and just result is to give the sanction of law to a deliberate breach.

For these reasons I am for the affirmance of the courts below.

* * *

The Restatement section reminds of the principle, familiar from earlier chapters, that an indication of an interest in making a bargain, or even a willingness to enter one, is not yet sufficient to constitute an offer, much less a contract. Without more, such a willingness constitutes merely an invitation to bargain.

This raises the prospect that both parties to a negotiation may make such invitations reciprocally, and they may even begin to structure their bargain relations, reaching agreement on some points, and narrowing the range of disagreement on others. At the same time, they may not yet form the (reciprocal) intent to contract—indeed, they may expressly intend not to have contracted yet. That is, they may intend *not* to be bound unless they resolve their outstanding disagreements.

This circumstance represents, in effect, precisely the converse of contractual incompleteness. Where there is incompleteness, there is nevertheless contractual intent—that is to say, the parties intend to strike a bargain in general even though certain particular terms have not yet been fixed. In the current case, there is intent not to contract—that is to say, the parties intend to remain free from contractual obligation at least until the terms that remain open, no matter how trivial, are fixed. In the first case, the parties agree to be bound although they do not yet agree on certain details; in the second case, the parties agree on details sufficient for contractual obligation, but they do not agree to enter a contract *tout court*.

Contract law, including today, treats the two cases very differently. Whereas modern contract law is comfortably and confidently functionalist with respect to ordinary incompleteness—and will, once there is intent to be bound, fill in gaps as functionalism recommends—the law remains formalist with respect to threshold questions concerning intent to be bound. Even where preliminary negotiations have produced enough information for courts, employing functionalist reasoning, reasonably to identify a mutually beneficial trade and reasonably to fix its terms, they generally decline to do so. The cases illustrate this, although they also introduce, but do not pursue, a complication, which will be taken up in earnest in a later chapter.

Joseph Martin nicely sets out the formal structure of the law in this area. The tenant in the case leased a storefront from its owner, for a five year period at a series of rents specified in the lease. The lease also contained a renewal clause, which announced that the tenant might renew the lease for another five years, "at annual rentals to be agreed upon," and established a process by which the tenant might notify the owner of its intention to exercise its renewal rights. At the end of the initial five years, the tenant gave the required notice of its intent to renew, whereupon the landlord demanded a rent that far exceeded both the contractually specified rents and the market rent (at least, according to an appraiser engaged by the tenant to determine fair market value). The tenant sued seeking specific performance of the renewal clause at fair market value, and the owner sought to evict.

The dispute traveled through the New York courts, all the way up to the Court of Appeals of New York. That court's opinion is especially useful, in the current context, because it identifies three possible approaches that the law might employ in a case such as this one.

First, the court says, the law might treat this as a case of what might be called primary incompleteness. According to this approach, the parties never intended to complete their contract. Instead, they intended to be bound, period, to the incomplete contract, which is to say that they intended never to fix the price themselves but rather to be bound to whatever price was later fixed. A classically formalist court would of course find that there was no contract in such a case, because there was no meeting of minds on the contract's terms. A functionalist court, however, can fill in the gap that the parties left open, giving the tenant a five year renewal at a reasonable (probably a market) rent.

Second, the law might treat this as a case of what might be called residual incompleteness. On this approach, the parties intended to agree on the rents during the five year renewal. So they intended, eventually, to render their contract complete. At the same time, the parties acknowledged that they might not succeed at filling in the contractual gap concerning the rent, and they intended, in addition, to be bound even if they could not come to the anticipated agreement concerning rents. That is, even as they intended to agree on the rent, they intended not to terminate the lease even in case they turned out to be unable to agree. In this case, also, although a formalist court would find that there is no contract, a functionalist court can fill the unforeseen gap with a reasonable rent (always assuming, of course, that it has previously established the express intent to remain bound even in the face of the failure to agree). This is not surprising. The second approach is really just a special case of the first—it understands the parties to intend to be bound even to the incomplete contract but also to intend to try to complete it themselves.

And third, the law might treat this as a case that concerns not the completeness of contractual intent but rather its existence absolutely. According to this approach, *Joseph Martin* is qualitatively different from the conventional cases concerning incompleteness, because while it is one thing for the parties to a negotiation simply to leave a term out on their way to agreement, it is quite another for them to agree to postpone negotiations concerning a term and to proceed to other facets of their negotiations, subject to subsequent agreement on the postponed matter. In this case, there is no intent to be bound to any third-party-supplied term and, in the extreme case, there may even be an intent not to be bound without reaching agreement on the term that has been set aside. Now, the problem with the contract is not so much that the parties' contractual intent was insufficiently specific as that they had no contractual intent at all, and may even have had (at least for the moment) contract-avoiding intent. Even a functionalist court will not provide the missing term or recognize a contract in this case, because to do so would be not simply to complete the parties' contractual intent as to invent the intent out of whole cloth.

Now the court in *Joseph Martin* was far from a modern, functionalist court. Indeed, the opinion—with its insistence that "before the power of law can be invoked to enforce a promise, it must be sufficiently certain and specific so that what was promised can be ascertained"—reads like an effort to push back functionalist waters that had, by the 1980's mostly engulfed contract law, or at least to dam-off these waters so that they cover only the law of sales. The interesting thing about the opinion is not its outcome but rather the fact that its analysis—and specifically the qualitative distinction between the third approach and the first two—reveals that there are in fact limits to the functionalist approach to incomplete contracts, and hence that there remains a residual truth in the formalist approach to this area of law. Thus, although functionalism properly proposes to fill in any number of gaps in underspecified contractual intentions, it will not conjure a contract in the absence of such intentions, not even where it is very easy to say what content the intentions would have if they were to arise. It may be that the parties to a negotiation have resolved virtually all their differences, and that the way in which they have done so makes it easy to infer how they would resolve any remaining differences. But if, in such a case, the parties nevertheless intend (either expressly, or by implication) not to be bound until they have achieved the (obvious) resolution for themselves, there can be no contract. There can be no contract even though, for all functionalist purposes—concerning the costs and reliability of a court's doing for the parties what they have not done for themselves—it is clear not just that a contract is reasonable but also on what terms.

Even where functionalism enjoys free rein within the province of contractual intent, to fill it in, etc., the formal distinction between cases in which the parties have formed an intent to be bound (*simpliciter*) and those in which they have not remains critical to the creation of contractual duties. This is, finally, necessary to the genetic structure of contract law. If functionalism allowed courts to conjure intent to be bound out of thin air, then persons would, at least in principle, be liable in contract for whatever bargains it would be reasonable for them to make. Contract would then cease to be a form of voluntary obligation at all.

Joseph Martin, as it happens, illustrates precisely this formal distinction. The facts in the case almost certainly render it unreasonable for anyone other than the tenant to occupy the owner's premises. The tenant, after all, was a successful retail business. This means that it had, over the course of its first five-year lease, acquired substantial site-specific firm capital. The shopping habits and travel patterns of its customers made its business much more valuable in its current location than in any other, where it would have to change these habits and patterns or acquire a new customer base. Conversely, the successful business almost certainly gave the owner firm-specific site capital. The developed customer base made the site more valuable when occupied by the existing firm than it would be when occupied by any other. This arrangement left both parties with a great deal to gain from maintaining their relationship. It also left them in a bilateral monopoly: because each valued the other more than any outside option, their negotiations were removed from the disciplining effects of market competition. Finally, insofar as the parties could have anticipated this contingency when they signed their initial lease, they had good reason, then to allow a third party to divide the gains from their co-dependence between them, and hence relieve them of the transactions costs that any negotiated solution would impose on them. Accordingly, *Joseph Martin* constitutes an ideal case for functionalist gap-filling.

But, at least according to the Court of Appeals, the parties had (no doubt foolishly) not followed this logic in their initial negotiations, and had therefore failed to form the intent to be bound in spite of the missing rent term (and perhaps even formed the intent not to be bound unless they could agree on a rent). And while it may be a case of misguided formalism to read the facts in this way; it is formalism of a very different, and entirely proper, kind to conclude that there can be no contract, if these are indeed the facts.

Sun Printing illustrates that even a functionalist must recognize this formalism, in an appropriate case. The plaintiff agreed to buy paper of a specified quantity, size, and quality from the defendant, in 16 monthly shipments. The price was also specified, for the first four months. Thereafter, the contract stated that "the price of the paper and the length of terms for which such price shall apply shall be agreed upon by and between the parties [with the] price in no event to be higher than the contract price charged [in a benchmark sale]." The four shipments whose price had been fixed were made and paid for. Thereafter, the defendant asserted that the contract was "imperfect" and disclaimed any obligations concerning the remaining twelve monthly shipments. Eventually, the plaintiff sued.

Cardozo, who wrote the functionalist dissent in *Varney*, now, writing for the majority, identified the limits of functionalism in this area of law.[6] To begin with, Cardozo observed that the parties had failed to reach complete agreement on two terms concerning transactions to occur after the initial four month period: first, the price; and second, the period during which this price should apply. He insisted that each failure was, independently, sufficient to render the contract incomplete—so that even if a court might reasonably imply a price term into the agreement, the contract remained incomplete overall. Next, Cardozo observed that there existed a *qualitative* difference between the state of the parties' negotiations, when they were broken off, concerning price and concerning period. By fixing a maximum price, Cardozo observed, "the parties attempted to guard against the contingency of failing to come together as to price." By contrast, "They did not guard against the contingency of failing to come together as to time [period]." Employing the distinctions developed in connection with *Joseph Martin*, one might say that the parties intended to be bound, overall, even

---

6. It is perhaps sensible, at this point, to pause briefly to identify another limit of functionalism, not least because it reprises a discussion pursued in Part I and hence helps to unify that part of the text and this one.

It is tempting for functionalists to see every failure by contracting parties to specify a fully complete contract as a gap, and every case in which the law steps in where the parties have remained silent as an instance of gap-filling. Thus, it is common to hear lawyer-economists (who are, after all, the dominant functionalists today) characterize the law's default preference for the expectation remedy as an instance of gap-filling. On this approach, the expectation remedy is simply the default liquated damages clause, employed in cases in which the parties fail to draft a clause of their own.

There is something in this approach, to be sure, and the analysis of liquidated damages clauses in Part I exploited the analogy, at various places. But gap-filling account of the expectation remedy cannot be the last word in explaining remedies law—it does not provide a complete explanation of the relative roles of the party and the law in fixing contract remedies.

This becomes immediately plain as soon as one asks on what basis an express liquidated damages clause is enforced. The answer cannot be that this clause fixes the promisee's contractual expectations, which are then vindicated by application of the expectation remedy—at least, the answer cannot be this if the expectation remedy is understood in the gap-filling way. This kind of explanation is obviously and immediately circular: the liquidated damages clause is enforced by application of the expectation remedy, which is understood as a gap-filling liquidated damages provision, which is enforced why exactly?

This argument reveals that law's provision of a basic contract remedy—which, Part I argued, is in fact properly understood as being specific performance—is not a case of functionalist gap-filling but rather immanent in the very form of contractual obligation. That is, the genetic structure of contractual obligation includes a legally provided remedy (here recall also the discussion, in Part I, of UCC § 2–719(2)'s observation that the existence of a minimally adequate remedy belongs to the essence of a sale's contract). The content of the remedy depends on the content of the obligation that this remedy vindicates, of course. And that content may be fixed by default rules understood as gap fillers. So the expectation remedy may properly be thought of as a gap-filling rule, indeed even as a default liquidated damages clause. But it actually fills in the content of the primary obligation, which is necessarily vindicated through a mandatory (indeed formally required) remedial regime based on specific performance.

Nor is the expectation remedy the only instance in which legal rules that functionalists understand as gap-fillers can more fundamentally be understood as entailments of the formal structure of contractual obligation. Principles of contract interpretation and construction probably have a similar status, for example.

if they could not agree on a price (they intended for the buyer to be able to insist on the price that the contract identified as a maximum); by contrast, the parties did not intend to be bound (and may perhaps have intended not to be bound[7]) even in case they could not agree on period. And, having failed to form the intent to be bound even though they could not agree on this detail, both parties, and in particular the defendant, "reserved the privilege of doing business in its own way, and did not undertake to conform to the practice and beliefs of others."

Although Cardozo writes in terms of the parties' having left a contractual "gap unfilled," that is not, in substance, what he thinks is going on at all. For a functionalist, filling a gap for parties who intend to be bound notwithstanding the gap poses no general problem—the only question is whether the facts and circumstances render it reasonable for a court to fix terms that the parties did and perhaps could not. Cardozo, as his *Varney* dissent reveals, was not shy about his gap-filling capacity (and the dissenter pointed out just how to go about filling any true gap concerning term-length that existed in *Sun Printing*). Rather than involving a simple gap concerning the precise terms on which to be bound, then, *Sun Printing*, at least on Cardozo's view, concerned a failure to form even a general intent to be bound. Thus the problem Cardozo identified in *Sun Printing* was not that the term-length question was too unstructured for reasonable functionalist gap-filling. The problem rather was that, in contrast to the circumstance with respect to price, the seller had not even identified the buyer-concession with respect to time that was sufficient to create a contract. It was not that Cardozo (like the classical formalists) was unwilling to accept an instruction to fill a gap; it was that the instruction had not been given. The absence of this instruction, moreover, constituted a reservation of the right, to refuse to be bound, held by all persons in the absence of a contract. And even the most die-hard functionalist must accept that such a reservation, as a formal matter, *simply cuts off contractual obligation entirely*. It has this effect, moreover, even when a court can (as it surely could have done in *Sun Printing*) confidently identify terms on which the party making the reservation would have agreed to contract, had it formed the requisite intention. To reject this, once again, is to abandon the very idea that contract is a voluntary obligation. This, finally, is the idea that imposes a formalist limit on even the most confident functionalist.

Of course, it is always possible that a party may have formed the intention to be contractually bound even in the event of a failure to agree on precise terms, and then functionalist gap-filling can run wild. Perhaps the defendant in *Sun Printing* formed just this intention, in which case Cardozo got the theory right but the application wrong. This is simply a question of fact.

More interestingly, it is also possible that a party, without forming the intention to be bound in general even when no specific agreement can be reached, might form the intention to limit the grounds on which it might

---

7. Cardozo doubts this, on the facts of the case. As he says, probably the parties regarded a failure to agree as to period as a "contingency so remote that it could safely be disregarded."

refuse to be bound in the future. Indeed, one way in which to understand the negotiations concerning the price term in *Sun Printing* is as reflecting an intention, in the defendant, not to break off dealings with the plaintiff on the specific ground that the plaintiff refused to accept any price above the stated maximum. Cardozo similarly wonders, at the end of his opinion, how the law might treat a promise by the defendant not to break off the relationship "by an arbitrary refusal to reach any agreement." Perhaps more demandingly, a party might agree not to refuse to make a contract on account of receiving a better offer from a third party, or even quite generally to bargain in good faith towards an eventual agreement.

This section so far has considered and distinguished two kinds of cases: (1) cases in which the parties, having left specific terms open, have nevertheless formed the intent to be bound even though they cannot fill in these gaps themselves; and (2) cases in which the parties have not just left specific terms open but have also failed to form the intent to be bound even though they cannot fill them in. Viewed in one way, the possibility just identified represents a middle-ground between these two cases. Even though the parties do not intend to be bound even in the face of ongoing disagreement as to details, they do intend to limit the kinds of reasons for which they may avoid being bound, and hence the kinds of disagreement that might scupper their contract. This characterization leaves it unclear how the law should resolve the case that Cardozo imagines but never seriously analyzes, on which side of the now-familiar distinction this case ultimately falls. Viewed in another way, the parties in this case do intend to be bound, just not to the primary agreement towards which they are negotiating. Instead, the parties have created a second-order agreement, concerning not the subject of these negotiations but the negotiations themselves. They have agreed to carry out these negotiations in a particular fashion. And that agreement, if it is complete, etc., can bind the parties, in the ordinary way, to negotiate in the fashion that it names. Of course, a classical formalist might think that the second-order agreement, because its subject-matter is by nature vague, is necessarily too incomplete to enforce. A functionalist, on the other hand, will see no general problem in this area. Both approaches will be taken up in greater detail later in these materials, under the heading "Pre-Contractual Negotiations."

14.2   MISTAKE

Contracting parties who have false beliefs about the world will find it difficult to plan or to coordinate well. Accordingly, insofar as contract law aims to promote freedom and to support social and economic coordination by enabling parties to implement their intentions and project them forward over time, it is natural for the law to take up the various problems associated with contracting parties' mistakes. Mistakes may happen, of course, at many points in the contracting process, and the law addresses mistakes at different times through different doctrines. Some of these doctrines should already be familiar: the doctrines concerning mitigation, for example, may be understood as regulating (and discouraging) promisee mistakes concerning how best to minimize the costs of breach.

This section takes up mistakes concerning how matters stand at the point of contract formation. Two formally different kinds of mistake can arise at this point: first, mistakes concerning the world, which the law takes up under the name *mistake*; and, second, mistakes concerning the meaning of contract terms, which the law sometimes calls *misunderstandings*. These formal distinctions do not necessarily mark real differences—in the technical sense that each kind of mistake generally may, through a purely formal manipulation, be recharacterized as the other. (This idea— that the formal distinctions the law invokes in this area are inherently unstable—will constitute a continuing theme in this section. It is a special case of a general theme of this Part—that formalism cannot sustain its conclusions save on the backs of extra legal values.)

This should come as no surprise. A purely private language is probably impossible, and in any event, every actual language involves inter subjective conventions of meaning. At the same time, linguistic conventions probably cannot be perfectly fixed, and in any event, every actual language involves substantial imprecision and ambiguity. Consequently, mistakes concerning the world may generally be recharacterized in terms of mistakes concerning the conventional meanings of the contract terms that are being used to describe the world; and mistakes concerning the meanings of contract terms can generally be recharacterized in terms of mistakes concerning the world that these terms aim to describe. Concrete examples of the re-characterizations, developed in the context of actual cases, will help to illustrate the general point, and will be taken up in a moment.

The legal terms of art used in this area—including even the terms *mistake* and *misunderstanding*—are thus unstable. In fact, words are often used in inconsistent ways—so that a single term sometimes refers to one thing and sometimes to quite another. The formal distinctions that the law employs and the doctrines that elaborate them are similarly unstable. Finally, and unsurprisingly in light of these instabilities, the substantive outcomes that courts impose are unpredictable. Accordingly, the discussions below aim less to teach the substantive law than to use this particular area of the law to illustrate certain difficulties to which formalism is more generally susceptible.

Three kinds of incorrect beliefs can arise in and around contract formation.

First, one party may have true beliefs concerning a material fact that is related to the contract and another party may have false beliefs. This pattern is generally called by the name *unilateral mistake. Anderson Bros.*, reproduced below, may be understood as an example of unilateral mistake: the defendant got right that the dredge could cut only a narrow trench while the plaintiff (unilaterally) mistakenly believed that the dredge could cut a wide one.

Second, both parties may have false beliefs about a material fact. This pattern is sometimes called by the name *common mistake* in Commonwealth law and sometimes by the name *mutual mistake* in American jurisdictions. *Sherwood*, again reproduced below, involves this kind of mistake: both parties mistakenly believed that the cow was barren.

And third, each party may make a mistake that interacts with the other party's mistake in such a way that the parties have not, in fact, agreed to anything at all. This pattern—which is the narrowest, most unusual, and least understood of the three kinds of mistake—is sometimes called *mutual mistake* in Commonwealth law and *misunderstanding* in American jurisdictions. The *Peerless* case involves a mistake of this sort, insofar as the parties were referring to different ships and each mistakenly believed that the other was referring to the ship that it had in mind.

Anderson Brothers Corp. v. O'Meara

United States Court of Appeals for the Fifth Circuit, 1962.
306 F.2d 672.

■ JONES, CIRCUIT JUDGE. The appellant, Anderson Brothers Corporation, a Texas corporation engaged in the business of constructing pipelines, sold a barge dredge to the appellee, Robert W. O'Meara, a resident of Illinois who is an oil well driller doing business in several states and Canada. The appellee brought this suit seeking rescission of the sale of, in the alternative, damages. After trial without a jury, the appellee's prayer of rescission was denied, but damages were awarded. The court denied the appellant's counterclaim for the unpaid purchase price of the dredge. Both parties have appealed. Appellant contends that no relief should have been given to the appellee, and the appellee contends that the damages awarded to him were insufficient.

The dredge which the appellant sold to the appellee was specially designed to perform the submarine trenching necessary for burying a pipeline under water. In particular it was designed to cut a relatively narrow trench in areas where submerged rocks, stumps and logs might be encountered. The dredge could be disassembled into its larger component parts, moved over land by truck, and reassembled at the job site. The appellant built the dredge from new and used parts in its own shop. The design was copied from a dredge which appellant had leased and successfully used in laying a pipeline across the Mississippi River. The appellant began fabrication of the dredge in early 1955, intending to use it in performing a contract for laying a pipeline across the Missouri River. A naval architect testified that the appellant was following customary practice in pipeline operations by designing a dredge for a specific use. Dredges so designed can be modified, if necessary, to meet particular situations. For some reason construction of the dredge was not completed in time for its use on the job for which it was intended, and the dredge was never used by the appellant. After it was completed, the dredge was advertised for sale in a magazine. This advertisement came to the appellee's attention in early

December, 1955. The appellee wanted to acquire a dredge capable of digging canals fifty to seventy-five or eighty feet wide and six to twelve feet deep to provide access to off-shore oil well sites in southern Louisiana.

On December 8, 1955, the appellee or someone employed by him contacted the appellant's Houston, Texas, office by telephone and learned that the price of the dredge was $45,000. Terms of sale were discussed, and later that day the appellant sent a telegram to the appellee who was then in Chicago, saying it accepted the appellee's offer of $35,000 for the dredge to be delivered in Houston. The appellee's offer was made subject to an inspection. The next day Kennedy, one of the appellee's employees, went to Houston from New Orleans and inspected the dredge. Kennedy, it appears, knew nothing about dredges but was familiar with engines. After inspecting the engines of the dredge, Kennedy reported his findings to the appellee by telephone and then signed an agreement with the appellant on behalf of the appellee. In the agreement, the appellant acknowledged receipt of $17,500. The agreement made provision for payment of the remaining $17,500 over a period of seventeen months. The dredge was delivered to the appellee at Houston on December 11, 1955, and from there transported by the appellee to his warehouse in southern Louisiana.

The barge was transported by water, and the ladder, that part of the dredge which extends from the barge to the stream bed and to which the cutting devices are attached, was moved by truck. After the dredge arrived at his warehouse the appellee executed a chattel mortgage in favor of the appellant and a promissory note payable to the order of the appellant. A bill of sale dated December 17, 1955, was given the appellee in which the appellant warranted only title and freedom from encumbrances. Both the chattel mortgage and the bill of sale described the dredge and its component parts in detail.

The record contains much testimony concerning the design and capabilities of the dredge including that of a naval architect who, after surveying the dredge, reported 'I found that the subject dredge had been designed for the purpose of dredging a straight trench over a river, lake or other body of water.' The testimony shows that a dredge designed to perform sweep dredging, the term used to describe the dredging of a wide channel, must be different in several respects from one used only for trenching operations. The naval architect's report listed at least five major items to be replaced, modified, or added before the dredge would be suited to the appellee's intended use. It is clear that the appellee bought a dredge which, because of its design, was incapable, without modification, of performing sweep dredging.

On July 10, 1956, about seven months after the sale and after the appellee had made seven monthly payments pursuant to the agreement between the parties, the appellee's counsel wrote the appellant stating in part that 'Mr. O'Meara has not been able to put this dredge in service and it is doubtful that it will ever be usable in its present condition.' After quoting at length from the naval architect's report, which was dated January 28, 1956, the letter suggested that the differences between the parties could be settled amicably by the appellant's contributing $10,000 toward the estimated $12,000 to $15,000 cost of converting the trenching dredge into a sweep dredge. The appellant rejected this offer and on July 23, 1956, the appellee's counsel wrote the appellant tendering return of the dredge and demanding full restitution of the purchase price. This suit followed the appellant's rejection of the tender and demand.

In his complaint the appellee alleged breaches of expressed and implied warranty and fraudulent representations as to the capabilities of the dredge. By an amendment he alleged as an alternative to the fraud count that the parties had been mistaken in their belief as to the operations of which the dredge was capable, and thus there was a mutual mistake which prevented the formation of a contract. The appellee sought damages of over $29,000, representing the total of principal and interest paid the appellant and expenses incurred in attempting to operate the dredge. In the alternative, the appellee asked for rescission and restitution of all money expended by him in reliance on the contract. The appellant answered denying the claims of the appellee and counterclaiming for the unpaid balance.

The district court found that: 'At the time the dredge was sold by the defendant to the plaintiff, the dredge was not capable for performing sweep dredging operations in shallow water, unless it was modified extensively. Defendant had built the dredge and knew the purpose for which it was designed and adapted. None of the defendant's officers or employees knew that plaintiff intended to use the dredge for shallow sweep dredging operations. Gier (an employee of the appellant who talked with the appellee or one of his employees by telephone) mistakenly assumed that O'Meara intended to use the dredge within its designed capabilities.

> 'At the time the plaintiff purchased this dredge he mistakenly believed that the dredge was capable without modification of performing sweep dredging operations in shallow water.'

The court further found that the market value of the dredge on the date of sale was $24,000, and that the unpaid balance on the note given for part of the purchase price was $10,500. Upon its findings the court concluded that:

> 'The mistake that existed on the part of both plaintiff and defendant with respect to the capabilities of the subject dredge is sufficient to and does constitute mutual mistake, and the plaintiff is entitled to recover the damages he has suffered as a result thereof.'

These damages were found to be 'equal to the balance due on the purchase price' plus interest, and were assessed by cancellation of the note and chattel mortgage and vesting title to the barge in the appellee free from any encumbrance in favor of the appellant. The court also concluded that the appellee was 'not entitled to rescission of this contract.' Further findings and conclusions, which are not challenged in this Court, eliminate any considerations of fraud or breach of expressed or implied warranties. The judgment for damages rests entirely upon the conclusion of mutual mistake. The district court's conclusion that the parties were mutually mistaken 'with respect to the capabilities of the subject dredge' is not supported by its findings. 'A mutual mistake is one common to both parties to the contract, each laboring under the same misconception.' *St. Paul Fire & Marine Insurance Co. v. Culwell*, Tex.Com.App., 62 S.W.2d 100. The appellee's mistake in believing that the dredge was capable, without modification, of performing sweep dredging was not a mistake shared by the appellant, who had designed and built the dredge for use in trenching operations and knew its capabilities. The mistake on the part of the appellant's employee in assuming that the appellee intended to use the dredge within its designed capabilities was certainly not one shared by the appellee, who acquired the dredge for use in sweep dredging operations. The appellee alone was mistaken in assuming that the dredge was adapted, without modification, to the use he had in mind.

The appellee insists that even if the findings do not support a conclusion of mutual mistake, he is entitled to relief under the well-established doctrine that knowledge by one party to a contract that the other is laboring under a mistake concerning the subject matter of the contract renders it voidable by the mistaken party. See 3 Corbin, Contracts 692, § 610. As a predicate to this contention, the appellee urges that the trial court erred in finding that 'None of defendant's officers or employees knew that plaintiff intended to use the dredge for shallow sweep dredging operations.' Moreover, the appellee contends that the appellant's knowledge of his intended use of the dredge was conclusively established by the testimony of two of the appellant's employees, because, on the authority of *Griffin v. Superior Insurance Co., 161 Tex. 195*, this testimony constitutes admissions, conclusive against the appellant. In the Griffin case, it was held that a party's testimony must be 'deliberate, clear and unequivocal' before it is conclusive against him. The testimony on which the appellee relies falls short of being 'clear and unequivocal.' It the statement of one witness were taken as conclusive, it would not establish that he knew the appellee intended to use the dredge as a sweep dredge, and the other witness spoke with incertitude. The testimony is not conclusive and is only one factor to be considered by the finder of facts. See 9 Wigmore, Evidence (3d Ed.) 397, 2594a.

There is a conflict in the evidence on the question of the appellant's knowledge of the appellee's intended use, and it cannot be held that the district court's finding is clearly erroneous. Smith v. United States, 5th Cir. 1961, 287 F.2d 299. It is to be noted that the trial court before whom the appellee testified, did not credit his testimony that he had made a telephone call in which, he said, he personally informed an employee of the appellant of his plans for the use of the dredge.

The appellee makes a further contention that when he purchased the dredge he was laboring under a mistake so grave that allowing the sale to stand would be unconscionable. The ground urged is one which has apparently been recognized in some circumstances. *Edwards v. Trinity & B.V.R. Co.*, 54 Tex. Civ.App. 334. However, the Texas courts have held that when unilateral mistake is asserted as a ground for relief, the care which the mistaken complainant exercised or failed to exercise in connection with the transaction sought to be avoided is a factor for consideration. *Wheeler v. Holloway*, Tex.Com.App. 276 S.W. 653; *Ebberts v. Carpenter Production Co.*, Tex.Civ.App., 256 S.W.2d 601; *American Maid Flour Mills v. Lucia*, Tex. Civ.App., 285 S.W. 641; *Cole v. Kjellberg*, Tex.Civ.App., 141 S.W. 120; Edwards v. Trinity & B.V.R. Co., supra; 13 Tex.Jur.2d 482, Contracts § 258. It has been stated that 'though a court of equity will relieve against mistake, it will not assist a man whose condition is attributable to the want of due diligence which may be fairly expected from a reasonable person.' *American Maid Flour Mills v. Lucia, supra.* This is consistent with the general rule of equity that when a person does not avail himself of an opportunity to gain knowledge of the facts, he will not be relieved of the consequences of acting upon supposition. Annot., 1 A.L.R.2d 9, 89; see 30 C.J.S. Equity § 47, p. 376. Whether the mistaken party's negligence will preclude relief depends to a great extent upon the circumstances in each instance. Edwards v. Trinity & B.V.R. Co., supra.

The appellee saw fit to purchase the dredge subject to inspection, yet he sent an employee to inspect it who he knew had no experience with or knowledge of dredging equipment. It was found that someone familiar with such equipment could have seen that the dredge was then incapable of performing channel type dredging. Although, according to his own testimony, the appellee was conscious of his own lack of knowledge concerning dredges, he took no steps, prior to purchase, to learn if the dredge which he saw pictured and described in some detail in the advertisement, was suited to his purpose. Admittedly he did not even inquire as to the use the appellant had made or intended to make of the dredge, and the district court found that he did not disclose to the appellant the use he intended to make of the dredge. The finding is supported by evidence. The appellee did not attempt to obtain any sort of warranty as to the dredge's capabilities. The only conclusion possible is that the appellee exercised no diligence, prior to the purchase, in determining the uses to which the dredge might be put. Had he sent a qualified person, such as the naval architect whom he later employed, to inspect the dredge he would have learned that it was not what he wanted, or had even made inquiry, he would have been informed as to the truth or have had a cause of action for misrepresentation if he had been given misinformation and relied upon it. The appellee chose to act on assumption rather than upon inquiry or information obtained by investigation, and, having learned his assumption was wrong, he asks to be released from the resulting consequences on the ground that, because of his mistaken assumption, it would be unconscionable to allow the sale to stand. The appellee seeks this, although the court has found that the appellant was not guilty of any misrepresentation or fault in connection with the transaction.

The appellant is in the same position as the party seeking relief on the grounds of mistake in *Wheeler v. Holloway, supra*, and the same result must follow. In the Wheeler case it was held that relief should be denied where the mistaken party exercised 'no diligence whatever' in ascertaining the readily accessible facts before he entered into a contract.

The appellee should have taken nothing on his claim; therefore, it is unnecessary to consider the question raised by the cross-appeal. The other questions raised by the appellant need not be considered. The case must be reversed and remanded for further proceeding consistent with what we have here held.

Reversed and remanded.

Sherwood v. Walker

Supreme Court of Michigan, 1887.
33 N.W. 919.

■ MORSE, J. Replevin for a cow. Suit commenced in justice's court. Judgment for plaintiff. Appealed to circuit court of Wayne county, and verdict and judgment for plaintiff in that court. The defendants bring error, and set out 25 assignments of the same.

The main controversy depends upon the construction of a contract for the sale of the cow.

The plaintiff claims that the title passed, and bases his action upon such claim.

The defendants contend that the contract was executory, and by its terms no title to the animal was acquired by plaintiff.

The defendants reside at Detroit, but are in business at Walkerville, Ontario, and have a farm at Greenfield, in Wayne county, upon which were some blooded cattle supposed to be barren as breeders. The Walkers are importers and breeders of polled Angus cattle.

The plaintiff is a banker living at Plymouth, in Wayne county. He called upon the defendants at Walkerville for the purchase of some of their stock, but found none there that suited him. Meeting one of the defendants afterwards, he was informed that they had a few head upon this Greenfield farm. He was asked to go out and look at them, with the statement at the time that they were probably barren, and would not breed.

May 5, 1886, plaintiff went out to Greenfield and saw the cattle. A few days thereafter, he called upon one of the defendants with the view of purchasing a cow, known as "Rose 2d of Aberlone." After considerable talk, it was agreed that defendants would telephone Sherwood at his home in Plymouth in reference to the price. The second morning after this talk he was called up by telephone, and the terms of the sale were finally agreed upon. He was to pay five and one-half cents per pound, live weight, fifty pounds shrinkage. He was asked how he intended to take the cow home, and replied that he might ship her from King's cattle-yard. He requested defendants to confirm the sale in writing, which they did by sending him the following letter:

"Walkerville, May 15, 1886.

"T. C. Sherwood,

> "President, etc.,—
>
> "*Dear Sir*: We confirm sale to you of the cow Rose 2d of Aberlone, lot 56 of our catalogue, at five and a half cents per pound, less fifty pounds shrink. We inclose herewith order on Mr. Graham for the cow. You might leave check with him, or mail to us here, as you prefer.
>
> "Yours truly,
>
> "Hiram Walker & Sons."

The order upon Graham inclosed in the letter read as follows:

> "Walkerville, May 15, 1886.
>
> "*George Graham*: You will please deliver at King's cattle-yard to Mr. T. C. Sherwood, Plymouth, the cow Rose 2d of Aberlone, lot 56 of our catalogue. Send halter with cow, and have her weighed.
>
> "Yours truly,
>
> "Hiram Walker & Sons."

On the twenty-first of the same month the plaintiff went to defendants' farm at Greenfield, and presented the order and letter to Graham, who informed him that the defendants had instructed him not to deliver the cow. Soon after, the plaintiff tendered to Hiram Walker, one of the defendants, $80, and demanded the cow. Walker refused to take the money or deliver the cow. The plaintiff then instituted this suit.

After he had secured possession of the cow under the writ of replevin, the plaintiff caused her to be weighed by the constable who served the writ, at a place other than King's cattle-yard. She weighed 1,420 pounds.

When the plaintiff, upon the trial in the circuit court, had submitted his proofs showing the above transaction, defendants moved to strike out and exclude the testimony from the case, for the reason that it was irrelevant, and did not tend to show that the title to the cow passed, and that it showed that the contract of sale was merely executory. The court refused the motion, and an exception was taken.

The defendants then introduced evidence tending to show that at the time of the alleged sale it was believed by both the plaintiff and themselves that the cow was barren and would not breed; that she cost $850, and if not barren would be worth from $750 to $1,000; that after the date of the letter, and the order to Graham, the defendants were informed by said Graham that in his judgment the cow was with calf, and therefore they instructed him not to deliver her to plaintiff, and on the twentieth of May, 1886, telegraphed to the plaintiff what Graham thought about the cow being with calf, and that consequently they could not sell her. The cow had a calf in the month of October following.

It appears from the record that both parties supposed this cow was barren and would not breed, and she was sold by the pound for an insignificant sum as compared with her real value if a breeder. She was evidently sold and purchased on the relation of her value for beef, unless the plaintiff had learned of her true condition, and concealed such knowledge from the defendants. Before the plaintiff secured possession of the animal, the defendants learned that she was with calf, and therefore of great value, and undertook to rescind the sale by refusing to deliver her. The question arises whether they had a right to do so.

The circuit judge ruled that this fact did not avoid the sale, and it made no difference whether she was barren or not. I am of the opinion that the court erred in this holding. I know that this is a close question, and the dividing line between the adjudicated cases is not easily discerned. But it must be considered as well settled that a party who has given an apparent consent to a contract of sale may refuse to execute it, or he may avoid it after it has been completed, if the assent was founded, or the contract made, upon the mistake of a material fact,—such as the subject-matter of the sale, the price, or some collateral fact materially inducing the agreement; and this can be done when the mistake is mutual.

If there is a difference or misapprehension as to the substance of the thing bargained for, if the thing actually delivered or received is different in substance from the thing bargained for and intended to be sold, then there is no contract; but if it be only a difference in some quality or accident, even though the mistake may have been the actuating motive to the purchaser or seller, or both of them, yet the contract remains binding.

"The difficulty in every case is to determine whether the mistake or misapprehension is as to the substance of the whole contract, going, as it were, to the root of the matter, or only to some point, even though a material point, an error as to which does not affect the substance of the whole consideration." *Kennedy v. Panama, etc., Mail Co.*, L.R. 2 Q.B. 580, 588.

It has been held, in accordance with the principles above stated, that where a horse is bought under the belief that he is sound, and both vendor and vendee honestly believe him to be sound, the purchaser must stand by his bargain, and pay the full price, unless there was a warranty.

It seems to me, however, in the case made by this record, that the mistake or misapprehension of the parties went to the whole substance of the agreement. If the cow was a breeder, she was worth at least $750; if barren, she was worth not over $80. The parties would not have made the contract of sale except upon the understanding and belief that she was incapable of breeding, and of no use as a cow. It is true she is now the identical animal that they thought her to be when the contract was made; there is no mistake as to the identity of the creature. Yet the mistake was not of the mere quality of the animal, but went to the very nature of the thing. A barren cow is substantially a different creature than a breeding one. There is as much difference between them for all purposes of use as there is between an ox and a cow that is capable of breeding and giving milk. If the mutual mistake had simply related to the fact whether she was with calf or not for one season, then it might have been a good sale; but the mistake affected the character of the animal for all time, and for her present and ultimate use. She was not in fact the animal, or the kind of animal, the defendants intended to sell or the plaintiff to buy. She was not a barren cow, and, if this fact had been known, there would have been no contract. The mistake affected the substance of the whole consideration, and it must be considered that there was no contract to sell or sale of the cow as she actually was. The thing sold and bought had in fact no existence. She was sold as a beef creature would be sold; she is in fact a breeding cow, and a valuable one.

The court should have instructed the jury that if they found that the cow was sold, or contracted to be sold, upon the understanding of both parties that she was barren, and useless for the purpose of breeding, and that in fact she was not barren, but capable of breeding, then the defendants had a right to rescind, and to refuse to deliver, and the verdict should be in their favor.

The judgment of the court below must be reversed, and a new trial granted, with costs of this Court to defendants.

■ CAMPBELL, C.J., and CHAMPLIN, J., concurred.

■ SHERWOOD, J., dissenting. I do not concur in the opinion given by my brethren in this case. I think the judgments before the justice and at the circuit were right.

I agree with my Brother Morse that the plaintiff was entitled to a delivery of the property to him when the suit was brought, unless there was a mistake made which would invalidate the contract; and I can find no such mistake.

There is no pretense that there was any fraud or concealment in the case, and an intimation or insinuation that such a thing might have existed on the part of either of the parties would undoubtedly be a greater surprise to them than anything else that has occurred in their dealings or in the case.

As has already been stated by my brethren, the record shows that the plaintiff is a banker, and farmer as well, carrying on a farm, and raising the best breeds of stock, and lived in Plymouth, in the county of Wayne, 23 miles from Detroit; that the defendants lived in Detroit, and were also dealers in stock of the higher grades; that they had a farm at Walkerville, in Canada, and also one in Greenfield, in said county of Wayne, and upon these farms the defendants kept their stock. The Greenfield farm was about 15 miles from the plaintiff's.

In the spring of 1886 the plaintiff, learning that the defendants had some "polled Angus cattle" for sale, was desirous of purchasing some of that breed, and, meeting the defendants, or some of them, at Walkerville, inquired about them, and was informed that they had none at Walkerville, "but had a few head left on their farm in Greenfield, and they asked the plaintiff to go and see them, stating that in all probability they were sterile and would not breed." In accordance with said request, the plaintiff, on the fifth day of May, went out and looked at the defendants' cattle at Greenfield, and found one called "Rose 2d," which he wished to purchase, and the terms were finally agreed upon at five and one-half cents per pound, live weight, 50 pounds to be deducted for shrinkage. The sale was in writing, and the defendants gave an order to the plaintiff directing the man in charge of the Greenfield farm to deliver the cow to plaintiff. This was done on the fifteenth of May. On the twenty-first of May plaintiff went to get his cow, and the defendants refused to let him have her; claiming at the time that the man in charge at the farm thought the cow was with calf, and, if such was the case, they would not sell her for the price agreed upon.

The record further shows that the defendants, when they sold the cow, believed the cow was not with calf, and barren; that from what the plaintiff had been told by defendants (for it does not appear he had any other knowledge or facts from which he could form an opinion) he believed the cow was farrow, but still thought she could be made to breed.

The foregoing shows the entire interview and treaty between the parties as to the sterility and qualities of the cow sold to the plaintiff. The cow had a calf in the month of October.

There is no question but that the defendants sold the cow representing her of the breed and quality they believed the cow to be, and that the purchaser so understood it. And the buyer purchased her believing her to be of the breed represented by the sellers, and possessing all the qualities stated, and even more. He believed she would breed. There is no pretense that the plaintiff bought the cow for beef, and there is nothing in the record indicating that he would have bought her at all only that he thought she might be made to breed. Under the foregoing facts,—and these are all that are contained in the record material to the contract,—it is held that because it turned out that the plaintiff was more correct in his judgment as to one quality of the cow than the defendants, and a quality, too, which could not by any possibility be positively known at the time by either party to exist, the contract may be annulled by the defendants at their pleasure. I know of no law, and have not been referred to any, which will justify and such holding, and I think the circuit judge was right in his construction of the contract between the parties.

It is claimed that a mutual mistake of a material fact was made by the parties when the contract of sale was made. There was no warranty in the case of the quality of the animal. When a mistaken fact is relied upon as ground for rescinding, such fact must not only exist at the time the contract is made, but must have been known to one or both of the parties. Where there is no warranty, there can be no mistake of fact when no such fact exists, or, if in existence, neither party knew of it, or could know of it; and that is precisely this case. If the owner of a Hambletonian horse had speeded him, and was only able to make him go a mile in three minutes, and should sell him to another, believing that was his greatest speed, for $300, when the purchaser believed he could go much faster, and made the purchase for that sum, and a few days thereafter, under more favorable circumstances, the horse was driven a mile in 2 Min. 13 sec., and was found to be worth $20,000, I hardly think it would be held, either at law or in equity, by any one, that the seller in such case could rescind the contract. The same legal principles apply in each case.

In this case neither party knew the actual quality and condition of this cow at the time of the sale. The defendants say, or rather said, to the plaintiff, "they had a few head left on their farm in Greenfield, and asked plaintiff to go and see them, stating to plaintiff that in all probability they were sterile and would not breed." Plaintiff did go as requested, and found there three cows, including the one purchased, with a bull. The cow had been exposed, but neither knew she was with calf or whether she would breed. The defendants thought she would not, but the plaintiff says that he thought she could be made to breed, but believed she was not with calf. The defendants sold the cow for what they believed her to be, and the plaintiff bought her as he believed she was, after the statements made by the defendants. No conditions whatever were attached to the terms of sale by either party. It was in fact as absolute as it could well be made, and I know of no precedent as authority by which this Court can alter the contract thus made by these parties in writing, and interpolate in it a condition by which, if the *defendants should be mistaken in their belief that the cow was barren*, she should be returned to them, and their contract should be annulled.

It is not the duty of courts to destroy contracts when called upon to enforce them, after they have been legally made. There was no mistake of any such material fact by either of the parties in the case as would license the vendors to rescind. There was no difference between the parties, nor misapprehension, as to the substance of the thing bargained for, which was a cow supposed to be barren by one party, and believed not to be by the other. As to the quality of the animal, subsequently developed, both parties were equally ignorant, and as to this each party took his chances. If this were not the law, there would be no safety in purchasing this kind of stock.

I entirely agree with my brethren that the right to rescind occurs whenever "the thing actually delivered or received is different in substance from the thing bargained for, and intended to be sold; but if it be only a difference in some quality or accident, even though the misapprehension may have been the actuating motive" of the parties in making the contract, yet it will remain binding. In this case the cow sold was the one delivered. What might or might not happen to her after the sale formed no element in the contract.

I understand the law to be well settled that "there is no breach of any implied confidence that one party will not profit by his superior knowledge as to facts and circumstances" equally within the knowledge of both, because neither party reposes in any such confidence unless it be specially tendered or required, and that a general sale does not imply warranty of any quality, or the absence of any; and if the seller represents to the purchaser what he himself believes as to the qualities of an animal, and the purchaser buys relying upon his own judgment as to such qualities, there is no warranty in the case, and neither has a cause of action against the other if he finds himself to have been mistaken in judgment.

The only pretense for avoiding this contract by the defendants is that they erred in judgment as to the qualities and value of the animal. I think the principles adopted by Chief Justice Christiancy in *Williams v. Spurr*, 24 Mich. 335, completely cover this case, and should have been allowed to control in its decision. See, also, Story, Sales, §§ 174, 175, 382, and Benj. Sales, § 430.

The judgment should be affirmed.

Raffles v. Wichelhaus

Court of Exchequer, 1864.
2 Hurl. & C. 906.

Declaration.—For that it was agreed between the plaintiff and the defendants, to wit, at Liverpool, that the plaintiff should sell to the defendants, and the defendants buy of the plaintiff, certain goods, to wit, 125 bales of Surat cotton, guarantied middling fair merchant's Dhollorah, to arrive ex "Peerless" from Bombay; and that the cotton should be taken from the quay, and that the defendants would pay the plaintiff for the same at a certain rate, to wit, at the rate of 17¼d. per pound, within a certain time then agreed upon after the arrival of the said goods in England.— Averments; that the said goods did arrive by the said ship from Bombay in England, to wit, Liverpool, and the plaintiff was then and there ready and willing and offered to deliver the said goods to the defendants, & c. Breach: that the defendants refused to accept the said goods or pay the plaintiff for them.

Plea.—That the said ship mentioned in the said agreement was meant and intended by the defendants to be the ship called the "Peerless," which sailed from Bombay, to wit, in October; and that the plaintiff was not ready and willing and did not offer to deliver to the defendants any bales of cotton which arrived by the last-mentioned ship, but instead thereof was only ready and willing and offered to deliver to the defendants 125 bales of Surat cotton which arrived by another and different ship, which was also called the "Peerless," and which sailed from Bombay, to wit, in December.

Demurrer, and joinder therein.

■ MILWARD, in support of the demurrer.—The contract was for the sale of a number of bales of cotton of a particular description, which the plaintiff was ready to deliver. It is immaterial by what ship the cotton was to arrive, so that it was a ship called the "Peerless." The words "to arrive ex 'Peerless,'" only mean that if the vessel is lost on the voyage, the contract is to be at an end. [Pollock C.B.—It would be a question for the jury whether both parties meant the same ship called the "Peerless."] That would be so if the contract was for the sale of a ship called the "Peerless;" but it is for the sale of cotton on board a ship of that name. [Pollock, C.B.— The defendant only bought that cotton which was to arrive by a particular ship. It may as well be said, that if there is a contract for the purchase of certain goods in warehouse A., that is satisfied by the delivery of goods of the same description in warehouse B.] In that case there would be goods in both warehouses; here it does not appear that the plaintiff had any goods on board the other "Peerless." [Martin, B.—It is imposing on the defendant a contract different from that which he entered into. Pollock, C.B.—It is like a contract for the purchase of wine coming from a particular estate in France or Spain, where there are two estates of that name.] The defendant has no right to contradict by parol evidence a written contract good upon the face of it. He does not impute misrepresentation or fraud, but only says that he fancied the ship was a different one. Intention is of no avail, unless stated at the time of the contract. [Pollock, C.B.—One vessel sailed in October and the other in December.] The time of sailing is no part of the contract.

■ MELLISH (COHEN with him), in support of the plea.—There is nothing on the face of the contract to show that any particular ship called the "Peerless" was meant; but the moment it appears that two ships called the "Peerless" were about to sail from Bombay there is a latent ambiguity, and parol evidence may be given for the purpose of showing that the defendant meant one "Peerless" and the plaintiff another. That being so, there was no consensus ad idem [agreement on the same thing], and therefore no binding contract.

Per Curiam. There must be judgment for the defendants.

Judgment for the defendants.

* * *

As the paragraphs preceding these cases say, the three cases illustrate the three distinct patterns of incorrect belief that the law identifies. The outcomes in the cases demonstrate that the law treats these patterns of incorrect belief quite differently. Thus *Anderson Bros.* illustrates the principle that an incorrect factual belief held by one but not the other party to a contract—a unilateral mistake—does not, without more, allow that party to avoid contractual obligation. In general, a party has a duty to learn the facts related to the contracts that it makes and does not have any duty to inform its counter party of such facts (especially where they are equally or nearly equally available to both sides). *Sherwood* illustrates the principle that an incorrect factual belief held by both parties—variously called a common or a mutual mistake—is more likely to allow either party to avoid contractual obligation, at least as long as it is sufficiently material to the exchange. And the *Peerless* case illustrates the principle that incompatible beliefs about the meanings of material contract terms that prevent the parties from reaching agreement at all—variously called a mutual mistake or a misunderstanding—are the most potent of the three patterns at undermining contractual obligation.

This statement of the law is, admittedly, maddeningly vague and relative rather than precise and absolute. Unfortunately, it is not at all clear that anything that is at once true and more clear-cut can be said. The law in this area is a mess, and the outcomes that courts reach on seemingly analogous facts vary widely. The important lesson to draw from these cases is therefore not what the law is—that is, how to get from facts to outcomes. Nor is it even that the law is confused or in some way unsatisfactory. Rather, the insight that the cases yield concerns *why* the law in this area is confused or unsatisfactory. The source of the problem in this area of law is that the doctrine makes outcomes turn on formal distinctions among various patterns of incorrect belief that are unable to support any substantive differences. Almost every pattern of facts can be characterized, almost equally well, in terms of each of the three types of incorrect beliefs.

The three cases vividly illustrate this point: the incorrect beliefs in each may be characterized not just in the formal terms adopted by the courts deciding them, but also according to the two alternative formalisms that the courts reject.

Begin by considering *Anderson Bros*. The appellate court viewed that matter, sensibly, as a case of unilateral mistake—in which, once again, the defendant knew the kind of trench that the dredge could cut whereas the plaintiff did not. But purely as a formal matter, *Anderson Bros*. might also be understood as a case of common or mutual mistake, if one thought that the parties both believed, mistakenly, that the dredge could as a matter of fact dig the trench that the plaintiff required. Note that in this case the parties share a mistake, although they make it for different reasons: the root of the defendant's mistake, on this account of the case, is that it believes that the plaintiff seeks a narrow trench; and the root of the plaintiff's mistake is that it believes that the dredge can cut a wide one. Moreover, *Anderson Bros*. might also be understood, again purely formally, as a case of misunderstanding, if one thought that the defendant believed that the contract was for the sale of the dredge in its possession whereas the plaintiff believed that the contract was for the sale of an unspecified dredge that could cut a wide trench. On this account, the parties in *Anderson Bros*. were referring to different dredges, and each mistakenly believed that the other was referring to the dredge that it had in mind.

Next consider *Sherwood*, which the court viewed as a case of common or mutual mistake. But as a purely formal matter, *Sherwood* might also be understood as a case of unilateral mistake, concerning whether or not the plaintiff could bring the cow being considered to breed: the defendant incorrectly believed that he could not; and the plaintiff correctly believed that he could. (This seems roughly how the dissenter understood the case.) Moreover, *Sherwood* might also be viewed as a case of misunderstanding. On this approach to the case, the defendant believed that the contract was for the sale of a generic barren cow (with the particular cow named serving merely as a place-holder or sample), whereas the plaintiff believed that the contract was for the sale of the particular cow in the defendant's possession. Now the parties are referring to different cows, and each mistakenly believes that the other is referring to the cow that it has in mind.

Finally, consider the *Peerless* case. There the court viewed the matter as involving a misunderstanding—in which the parties were not referring to the same ship. But purely formally, the case might have been characterized as involving a mutual mistake, in which the parties were both referring to the ship named "Peerless" and contracted for "Peerless-delivered" cotton, and made the mutual mistake of believing that the ship, being one of a kind, lived up to its name. Here again, although the parties share a mistake, they make it for different reasons: the plaintiff believes that "Peerless-delivered" cotton will arrive in December; and the defendant believes that "Peerless-delivered" cotton will arrive in October. Finally, the *Peerless* case might also be understood on the model of unilateral mistake, simply by believing that one or the other party correctly identified the conventional meaning of the words "Ship Peerless," and the other got it wrong. This is not so outlandish as one might suppose: it might be, for example, that one ship "Peerless" was an old and trusted deliverer of cotton in the industry in which plaintiff and defendant operated, and the other was new, foreign, or in some other way unknown in that business.

To be sure, the three formal characterizations are not, as a substantive matter, equally plausible in each case. Various factors associated with the parties, the interaction between them, and other considerations render it more or less plausible that the parties actually possessed the beliefs needed to sustain the three formal characterizations and also render these beliefs more or less reasonable, whatever the parties actually believe.

In some cases, these factors are connected to general principles of efficient contracting behavior and the related folk understandings of people in the business of the contracting parties. In *Anderson Bros.*, for example, both the common mistake and the misunderstanding formalizations of the facts require the defendant seller to hold views about the plaintiff buyer's needs which endure even in the face of contrary indications from buyer. That is not how business—at least among parties dealing at arm's length and in free markets—is generally done. Rather, sellers are not required to (and generally do not) form systematic beliefs about their buyers' motivations for contracting or the intentions or purposes with which they seek the contracted-for performance. It would not be efficient for sellers to attend to the details of their buyers businesses in the way that forming such beliefs would require. Accordingly, even if sellers may not misrepresent the goods that they sell, and must in some circumstances disclose facts about these goods to buyers who do not know them, sellers need not in general make any special effort to anticipate their buyers' interests or knowledge. Considerations like these (for example, that the seller did not know and had no duty to learn what the buyer wanted to do with the dredge, and that the buyer failed to exercise reasonable care in discovering the dredge's capacities) figure prominently in the appellate court's reasoning in *Anderson Bros.*

In other cases, the substantive considerations that select among the several formally available characterizations of mistakes in contract-formation are connected to the specific circumstances of the individual contract. Thus in the *Peerless* case, the misunderstanding-based approach that the court took (and also probably an approach that characterized the facts as involving a common mistake that there existed only one ship Peerless) allows the defendant to exploit a timing advantage that arises out of the particular and idiosyncratic pattern of beliefs that the case involves. The defendant-buyers, recall, believed that the contract was for an October delivery, whereas the plaintiff-sellers believed that the contract specified delivery only in December. Accordingly, the buyers became aware of the mistake—however it is formally characterized—before the sellers did: when the October Peerless arrived in harbor, the buyers, but not the sellers, learned that something was amiss. At this point, the buyers might of course inform the sellers of the problem, but they need not. They might instead discover the truth about the two ships Peerless on their own, so that the sellers would remain ignorant of any misunderstanding until the December Peerless arrived, and the time came (in the sellers' minds) for the buyers to receive their cotton and make payment. The holding of the *Peerless* case allows the buyers to exploit this time lag. If the buyers know that the parties' mistake will allow them to avoid the contract, then they can gamble, on their sellers' accounts, on the possibility that the October futures prices for December cotton delivery will differ from the December spot price. If the December spot price is lower, the buyers can respond to the December delivery by saying that they had looked for the cotton in October, hence revealing the mistake and avoiding any obligation under the contract. They can then buy the cotton that the contract specified for less than the contract price, on the December spot market. On the other hand, if the December spot price is higher, the buyers can simply accept delivery, and the sellers will never learn of the misunderstanding or be able to exploit its legal consequences. There is thus at least some reason to think that the outcome in the *Peerless* case is unfair and inefficient, so that the court, from this functionalist perspective, chose the wrong formalism.

These reflections suggest that in addition to being inherently unstable, the formalisms associated with the traditional law of mistake can lead to functionally unappealing outcomes. So perhaps it is better for the law simply to do away with form in this area (or at least to minimize its footprint) and look directly to functionalist questions concerning what it is reasonable for each party to have known and disclosed in making the contract and how legal allocations of the risk of mistake can help to induce efficient or fair knowledge gathering and distribution. There is some reason to suspect that the law is moving in this direction. The formal distinctions are becoming less prominent in the doctrine. They still exist, and they still purport to determine outcomes in some instances. But they are increasingly being embedded in functional ideas that focus on which party is better placed to learn the truth and to act on it. The following sections from the Restatement, which are largely self-explanatory, make this point vivid and plain.

Restatement 2d of Contracts

§ 20   Effect of Misunderstanding

(1) There is no manifestation of mutual assent to an exchange if the parties attach materially different meanings to their manifestations and

(a) neither party knows or has reason to know the meaning attached by the other; or

(b) each party knows or each party has reason to know the meaning attached by the other.

(2) The manifestations of the parties are operative in accordance with the meaning attached to them by one of the parties if

(a) that party does not know of any different meaning attached by the other, and the other knows the meaning attached by the first party; or

(b) that party has no reason to know of any different meaning attached by the other, and the other has reason to know the meaning attached by the first party.

Comments & Illustrations

Comment a. Scope. Subsection (1) states the implications of the rule of *§ 19(2)* as to the meaning of "manifestation of mutual assent" in cases of mistake in the expression of assent. The subject-matter of this Section is more fully treated in Chapter 9 on the scope of contractual obligations. Rules are stated here only for two-party transactions; multi-party transactions are more complex, but are governed by the same principles. As to the meaning of "reason to know," see Comment *b* to *§ 19*.

Comment b. The need for interpretation. The meaning given to words or other conduct depends to a varying extent on the context and on the prior experience of the parties. Almost never are all the connotations of a bargain exactly identical for both parties; it is enough that there is a core of common meaning sufficient to determine their performances with reasonable certainty or to give a reasonably certain basis for an appropriate legal remedy. See *§ 33*. But material differences of meaning are a standard cause of contract disputes, and the decision of such disputes necessarily requires interpretation of the language and other conduct of the parties in the light of the circumstances.

Comment c. Interpretation and agreement. There is a problem of interpretation in determining whether a contract has been made as well as in determining what obligations a contract imposes. Where one party makes a precise and detailed offer and the other accepts it, or where both parties sign the same written agreement, there may be an "integrated" agreement (see *§ 209*) and the problem is then one of interpreting the offer or written agreement. In other cases agreement may be found in a jumble of letters, telegrams, acts and spoken words. In either type of case, the parties may have different understandings, intentions and meanings. Even though the parties manifest mutual assent to the same words of agreement, there may be no contract because of a material difference of understanding as to the terms of the exchange. Where there is no integration, the parties may also differ as to whether there was an offer of any kind, or whether there was an acceptance. Rules of interpretation governing various situations are stated in Chapter 9 on the scope of contractual obligations; those rules are applicable in the determination of what each party "knows or has reason to know."

Comment d. Error in expression. The basic principle governing material misunderstanding is stated in Subsection (1): no contract is formed if neither party is at fault or if both parties are equally at fault. Subsection (2) deals with cases where both parties are not equally at fault. If one party knows the other's meaning and manifests assent intending to insist on a different meaning, he may be guilty of misrepresentation. Whether or not there is such misrepresentation as would give the other party a power of avoidance, there is a contract under Subsection (2)(a), and the mere negligence of the other party is immaterial. See *§ 166* as to reformation of a written contract in such a case. Under Subsection (2)(b) a party may be bound by a merely negligent manifestation of assent, if the other party is not negligent. The question whether such a contract is voidable for mistake is dealt with in *§§ 151–58*.

Illustrations:

1. A offers to sell B goods shipped from Bombay ex steamer "Peerless". B accepts. There are two steamers of the name "Peerless", sailing from Bombay at materially different times. If both parties intend the same Peerless, there is a contract, and it is immaterial whether they know or have reason to know that two ships are named Peerless.

2. The facts being otherwise as stated in Illustration 1, A means Peerless No. 1 and B means Peerless No. 2. If neither A nor B knows or has reason to know that they mean different ships, or if they both know or if they both have reason to know, there is no contract.

3. The facts being otherwise as stated in Illustration 1, A knows that B means Peerless No. 2 and B does not know that there are two ships named Peerless. There is a contract for the sale of the goods from Peerless No. 2, and it is immaterial whether B has reason to know that A means Peerless No. 1. If A makes the contract with the undisclosed intention of not performing it, it is voidable by B for misrepresentation (see *§§ 159–64*). Conversely, if B knows that A means Peerless No. 1 and A does not know that there are two ships named Peerless, there is a contract for the sale of the goods from Peerless No. 1, and it is immaterial whether A has reason to know that B means Peerless No. 2, but the contract may be voidable by A for misrepresentation.

4. The facts being otherwise as stated in Illustration 1, neither party knows that there are two ships Peerless. A has reason to know that B means Peerless No. 2 and B has no reason to know that A means Peerless No. 1. There is a contract for the sale of goods from Peerless No. 2. In the converse case, where B has reason to know and A does not, there is a contract for sale from Peerless No. 1. In either case the question whether the

contract is voidable for mistake is governed by the rules stated in §§ *151–58*.

5.   A says to B, "I offer to sell you my horse for $100." B, knowing that A intends to offer to sell his cow for that price, not his horse, and that the word "horse" is a slip of the tongue, replies, "I accept." The price is a fair one for either the horse or the cow. There is a contract for the sale of the cow and not of the horse. If B makes the contract with the undisclosed intention of not performing it, it is voidable by A for misrepresentation. See §§ *159–64*.

Restatement 2d of Contracts

§ 152   When Mistake of Both Parties Makes a Contract Voidable

(1) Where a mistake of both parties at the time a contract was made as to a basic assumption on which the contract was made has a material effect on the agreed exchange of performances, the contract is voidable by the adversely affected party unless he bears the risk of the mistake under the rule stated in *§ 154*.

(2) In determining whether the mistake has a material effect on the agreed exchange of performances, account is taken of any relief by way of reformation, restitution, or otherwise.

Comments & Illustrations

Comment a. Rationale. Before making a contract, a party ordinarily evaluates the proposed exchange of performances on the basis of a variety of assumptions with respect to existing facts. Many of these assumptions are shared by the other party, in the sense that the other party is aware that they are made. The mere fact that both parties are mistaken with respect to such an assumption does not, of itself, afford a reason for avoidance of the contract by the adversely affected party. Relief is only appropriate in situations where a mistake of both parties has such a material effect on the agreed exchange of performances as to upset the very basis for the contract.

This Section applies to such situations. Under it, the contract is voidable by the adversely affected party if three conditions are met. First, the mistake must relate to a "basic assumption on which the contract was made." Second, the party seeking avoidance must show that the mistake has a material effect on the agreed exchange of performances. Third, the mistake must not be one as to which the party seeking relief bears the risk. The parol evidence rule does not preclude the use of prior or contemporaneous agreements or negotiations to establish that the parties were mistaken. See § 214(d). However, since mistakes are the exception rather than the rule, the trier of the facts should examine the evidence with particular care when a party attempts to avoid liability by proving mistake. See Comment *c* to § 155. The rule stated in this Section is subject to that in § 157 on fault of the party seeking relief. It is also subject to the rules on exercise of the power of avoidance stated in §§ 378–85.

Comment b. Basic assumption. A mistake of both parties does not make the contract voidable unless it is one as to a basic assumption on which both parties made the contract. The term "basic assumption" has the same meaning here as it does in Chapter 11 in connection with impracticability (§§ 261, 266(1)) and frustration (§§ 265, 266(2)). See Uniform Commercial Code § 2–615(a). For example, market conditions and the financial situation of the parties are ordinarily not such assumptions, and, generally, just as shifts in market conditions or financial ability do not effect discharge under the rules governing impracticability, mistakes as to market conditions or financial ability do not justify avoidance under the rules governing mistake. See Comment *b* to § 261. The parties may have had such a "basic assumption," even though they were not conscious of alternatives. See Introductory Note to Chapter 11. Where, for example, a party purchases an annuity on the life of another person, it can be said that it was a basic assumption that the other person was alive at the time, even though the parties never consciously addressed themselves to the possibility that he was dead. See Illustration 6.

Illustrations:

1.   A contracts to sell and B to buy a tract of land, the value of which has depended mainly on the timber on it. Both A and B believe that the timber is still there, but in fact it has been destroyed by fire. The contract is voidable by B.

2.   A contracts to sell and B to buy a tract of land, on the basis of the report of a surveyor whom A has employed to determine the acreage. The price is, however, a lump sum not calculated from the acreage. Because of an error in computation by the surveyor, the tract contains ten per cent more acreage than he reports. The contract is voidable by A. Compare Illustrations 8 and 11 to this Section and Illustration 2 to § 158.

3.   A contracts to sell and B to buy a tract of land. B agrees to pay A $100,000 in cash and to assume a mortgage that C holds on the tract. Both A and B believe that the amount of the mortgage is $50,000, but in fact it is only $10,000. The contract is voidable by A, unless the court supplies a term under which B is entitled to enforce the contract if he agrees to pay an appropriate additional sum, and B does so. See Illustration 2 to § 158.

4.   A contracts to sell and B to buy a debt owed by C to A, and secured by a mortgage. Both A and B believe that there is a building on the mortgaged land so that the value of the mortgaged property exceeds that of the debt, but in fact there is none so that its value is less than half that of the debt. The contract is voidable by B. See § 333.

5.   A contracts to assign to B for $100 a $10,000 debt owed to A by C, who is insolvent. Both A and B believe that the debt is unsecured and is therefore, virtually worthless, but in fact it is secured by stock worth approximately $5,000. The contract is voidable by A.

6.   A pays B, an insurance company, $100,000 for an annuity contract under which B agrees to make quarterly payments to C, who is 50 years old, in a fixed amount for the rest of C's life. A and B believe that C is in good health and has a normal life expectancy, but in fact C is dead. The contract is voidable by A.

Comment c. Material effect on agreed exchange. A party cannot avoid a contract merely because both parties were mistaken as to a basic assumption on which it was made. He must, in addition, show that the mistake has a material effect on the agreed exchange of performances. It is not enough for him to prove that he would not have made the contract had it not been for the mistake. He must show that the resulting imbalance in the agreed exchange is so severe that he cannot fairly be required to carry it out. Ordinarily he will be able to do this by showing that the exchange is not only less desirable to him but is also more advantageous to the other party. Sometimes this is so because the adversely affected party will give, and the other party will receive, something more than they supposed. Sometimes it is so because the other party will give, and the adversely affected party will receive, something less than they supposed. In such cases the materiality of the effect on the agreed exchange will be determined by the overall impact on both parties. In exceptional cases the adversely affected party may be able to show that the effect on the agreed exchange has been material simply on the ground that the exchange has become less desirable for him, even though there has been no effect on the other party. Cases of hardship that result in no advantage to the other party are, however, ordinarily appropriately left to the rules on impracticability and frustration. See Illustration 9 and § 266. The standard of materiality here, as elsewhere in this Restatement (e.g., § 237), is a flexible one to be applied in the light of all the circumstances.

Illustrations:

7.   The facts being as stated in Illustration 3 to § 151, in determining whether the effect on the agreed exchange is material, and the contract therefore voidable by B, the court will consider not only the decrease in its desirability to B but also any advantage to A through his receiving a higher price than the land would have brought on the market had the facts been known. See Illustration 3 to § 151.

8.   A contracts to sell and B to buy a tract of land, which they believe contains 100 acres, at a price of $1,000 an acre. In fact the tract contains 110 acres. The contract is not voidable by either A or B, unless additional facts show that the effect on the agreed exchange of performances is material.

9. A contracts to sell and B to buy a dredge which B tells A he intends to use for a special and unusual purpose, but B does not rely on A's skill and judgment. A and B believe that the dredge is fit for B's purpose, but in fact it is not, although it is merchantable. The contract is not voidable by B because the effect on the agreed exchange of performances is not material. If B's purpose is substantially frustrated, he may have relief under § 266(2). See also Uniform Commercial Code §§ 2–314, 2–315.

Comment d. Significance of other relief. Under the rule stated in Subsection (2), before determining the effect on the agreed exchange, the court will first take account of any relief that may be available to him or granted to the other party under the rules stated in §§ 155 (see Illustration 10) and 158 (see Illustration 11). A party may choose to seek relief by means of reformation even though it makes his own performance more onerous when, absent reformation, the contract would be voidable by the other party. See Introductory Note and Comment *e* to § 155.

Illustrations:

10. A and B agree that A will sell and B will buy a tract of land for $100,000, payable by $50,000 in cash and the assumption of an existing mortgage of $50,000. In reducing the agreement to writing, B's lawyer erroneously omits the provision for assumption of the mortgage, and neither A nor B notices the omission. Under the rule stated in § 155, at the request of either party, the court will decree that the writing be reformed to add the provision for assumption of the mortgage. The contract is, therefore, not voidable by A because, when account is taken of the availability to him of reformation, the effect on the agreed exchange of performances is not material. See Illustration 1 to § 155.

11. A contracts to sell and B to buy a tract of land, described in the contract as containing 100 acres, at a price of $100,000, calculated from the acreage at $1,000 an acre. In fact the tract contains only 90 acres. If B is entitled to a reduction in price of $10,000, under the rule stated in § 158(2), the contract is not voidable by B because when account is taken of the availability to him of a reduction in price, the effect on the agreed exchange of performances is not material. See Illustration 1 to § 158. As to the possibility of an argument based on frustration, see § 266(2).

Comment e. Allocation of risk. A party may be considered to have undertaken to perform in spite of a mistake that has a material effect on the agreed exchange of performances. He then bears the risk of the mistake. Because of the significance of the allocation of risk in the law of mistake, the scope of this exception is spelled out in detail in § 154. (It is assumed in the illustrations to the present Section that the adversely affected party does not bear the risk of the mistake under the rule stated in § 154. See, e.g., Illustration 14.)

Comment f. Releases. Releases of claims have afforded particularly fertile ground for the invocation of the rule stated in this Section. It is, of course, a traditional policy of the law to favor compromises as a means of settling claims without resort to litigation. See Comment *a* to § 74. Nevertheless, a claimant who has executed such a release may later wish to attack it. The situation may arise with respect to any claim, but a particularly common example involves claims for personal injury, where the claimant may have executed the release without full knowledge of the extent or, perhaps, even of the nature of his injuries. Such a claimant has a variety of possible grounds for attacking the release on discovering that his injuries are more serious than he had initially supposed. He may seek to have the release interpreted against the draftsman so as to be inapplicable to the newly discovered injuries (§ 206). He may seek to have the release reformed on the ground that it does not correctly express the prior agreement of the parties (§ 155). He may seek to avoid the release on the ground that it was unfairly obtained through misrepresentation, duress or undue influence (Chapter 7). He may seek to have the release, or at least that part purporting to cover the newly discovered injuries, held unenforceable as unconscionable (§ 208). Or he may seek to avoid the release on the ground that both he and the other party were mistaken as to the nature or extent of his injuries. Assuming that the release is properly interpreted to cover unknown injuries and that it was not unfairly obtained or unconscionable, his case will turn on the application of the rule stated in this Section to his claim of mistake. In dealing with such attacks on releases, a court should be particularly sensitive to obscure or misleading language and especially alert to the possibility of unfairness or unconscionability. However, the same rules relating to mistake apply to such releases as apply to other contracts, and if the results sometimes seem at variance with those rules, the variance can usually be attributed to the presence of one of the alternative grounds listed above.

A claimant's attempt at avoidance based on mistake of both parties, therefore, will frequently turn on a determination, in the light of all the circumstances, of the basic assumptions of the parties at the time of the release. These circumstances may include the fair amount that would be required to compensate the claimant for his known injuries, the probability that the other party would be held liable on that claim, the amount received by the claimant in settlement of his claim, and the relationship between the known injuries and the newly discovered injuries. If, for example, the amount received by the claimant is reasonable in comparison with the fair amount required to compensate him for his known injuries and the probability of the other party being held liable on that claim, this suggests that the parties assumed that his injuries were only those known. Furthermore, even if the parties do not assume that his injuries are only those known, they may assume that any unknown injuries are of the same general nature as the known ones, while differing in extent. Although the parties may fix the assumptions on which the contract is based by an express provision, fairly bargained for, the common recital that the release covers all injuries, known or unknown and of whatever nature or extent, may be disregarded as unconscionable if, in view of the circumstances of the parties, their legal representation, and the setting of the negotiations, it flies in the face of what would otherwise be regarded as a basic assumption of the parties. What has been said here with respect to releases of claims for personal injury is generally true for releases executed in other contexts.

Illustrations:

12.   A has a claim against B for B's admitted negligence, which appears to have caused damage to A's automobile in an amount fairly valued at $600. In consideration of B's payment of $600, A executes a release of "all claims for injury to person or property" that he may have against B. Both A and B believe that A has suffered damage to property only, but A later discovers that he has also suffered personal injuries in the extent of $20,000. The release is voidable by A.

13.   A has a claim against B for B's admitted negligence, which appears to have caused personal injuries to A's back in an amount fairly valued at $10,000, although the parties are aware that A may require further treatment. In consideration of B's payment of $15,000, A executes a release of "all claims for injury to person or property" that he may have against B. A later incurs additional expenses of $20,000 in connection with his back, which was injured more seriously than he had believed. The release is not voidable by A.

Comment g. Relation to breach of warranty. The rule stated in this Section has a close relationship to the rules governing warranties sale by a seller of goods or of other kinds of property. A buyer usually finds it more advantageous to rely on the law of warranty than on the law of mistake. Because of the broad scope of a seller's warranties, a buyer is more often entitled to relief based on a claim of breach of warranty than on a claim based on mistake. Furthermore, because relief for breach of warranty is generally based on the value that the property would have had if it had been as warranted (see Uniform Commercial Code § 2–714(2)), it is ordinarily more extensive than that afforded if he merely seeks to avoid the contract on the ground of mistake. Nevertheless, the warranties are not necessarily exclusive and, even absent a warranty, a buyer may be able to avoid on the ground of mistake if he brings himself within the rule stated in this Section. The effect, on a buyer's claim of mistake, of language purporting to disclaim the seller's responsibility for the goods is governed by the rules on interpretation stated in Chapter 9.

Illustration:

14.   A, a violinist, contracts to sell and B, another violinist, to buy a violin. Both A and B believe that the violin is a Stradivarius, but in fact it is a clever imitation. A makes no express warranty and, because he is not a merchant with respect to violins, makes no implied warranty of merchantability under Uniform Commercial Code § 2–314. The contract is voidable by B.

Comment h. Mistakes as to different assumptions. The rule stated in this Section applies only where both parties are mistaken as to the same basic assumption. Their mistakes need not be, and often they will not be, identical. If, however, the parties are mistaken as to different assumptions, the rule stated in § 153, rather than that stated in this Section, applies.

Restatement 2d of Contracts

§ 153   When Mistake of One Party Makes a Contract Voidable

Where a mistake of one party at the time a contract was made as to a basic assumption on which he made the contract has a material effect on the agreed exchange of performances that is adverse to him, the contract is voidable by him if he does not bear the risk of the mistake under the rule stated in § 154, and

(a) the effect of the mistake is such that enforcement of the contract would be unconscionable, or

(b) the other party had reason to know of the mistake or his fault caused the mistake.

Comments & Illustrations

Comment a. Rationale. Courts have traditionally been reluctant to allow a party to avoid a contract on the ground of mistake, even as to a basic assumption, if the mistake was not shared by the other party. Nevertheless, relief has been granted where the other party actually knew (see §§ 160, 161) or had reason to know of the mistake at the time the contract was made or where his fault caused the mistake. There has, in addition, been a growing willingness to allow avoidance where the consequences of the mistake are so grave that enforcement of the contract would be unconscionable. This Section states a rule that permits avoidance on this latter basis, as well as on the more traditional grounds. The rules stated in this Section also apply to option contracts, under which a party's offer is irrevocable either under a statute, such as one applying to bids for public works, or on other grounds. The parol evidence rule does not preclude the use of prior or contemporaneous agreements or negotiations to establish that a party was mistaken. See § 214(d). Nevertheless, because mistakes are the exception rather than the rule, the trier of the facts should examine the evidence with particular care when a party attempts to avoid liability by proving mistake. See Comment *c* to § 155. The rule stated in this Section is subject to that stated in § 157 on fault of the party seeking relief. It is also subject to the rules on exercise of the power of avoidance stated in §§ 380–85.

Comment b. Similarity to rule where both are mistaken. In order for a party to have the power to avoid a contract for a mistake that he alone made, he must at least meet the same requirements that he would have had to meet had both parties been mistaken (§ 152). The mistake must be one as to a basic assumption on which the contract was made; it must have a material effect on the agreed exchange of performances; and the mistaken party must not bear the risk of the mistake. The most common sorts of such mistakes occur in bids on construction contracts and result from clerical errors in the computation of the price or in the omission of component items. See Illustration 1. The rule stated in this Section is not, however, limited to such cases. It also applies, for example, to a misreading of specifications (see Illustration 4) or such misunderstanding as does not prevent a manifestation of mutual assent (see Illustrations 5 and 6). Where only one party is mistaken, however, he must meet either the additional requirement stated in Subparagraph (a) or one of the additional requirements stated in Subparagraph (b).

Comment c. Additional requirement of unconscionability. Under Subparagraph (a), the mistaken party must in addition show that enforcement of the contract would be unconscionable. The reason for this additional requirement is that, if only one party was mistaken, avoidance of the contract will more clearly disappoint the expectations of the other party than if he too was mistaken. See Introductory Note. Although § 208, Unconscionable Contract or Term, is not itself applicable to such cases since the unconscionability does not appear at the time the contract is made, the standards of unconscionability in such cases are similar to those under § 208 (see Comment *c* to § 208). The mistaken party bears the substantial burden of establishing unconscionability and must ordinarily show not only the position he would have been in had the facts been as he believed them to be but also the position in which he finds himself as a result of his mistake. For example, in the typical case of a mistake as to the price in a bid, the builder must show the profit or loss that will result if he is required to perform, as well as the profit that he would have made had there been no mistake.

Illustrations:

1. In response to B's invitation for bids on the construction of a building according to stated specifications, A submits an offer to do the work for $150,000. A believes that this is the total of a column of figures, but he has made an error by inadvertently omitting a $50,000 item, and in fact the total is $200,000. B, having no reason to know of A's mistake, accepts A's bid. If A performs for $150,000, he will sustain a loss of $20,000 instead of making an expected profit of $30,000. If the court determines that enforcement of the contract would be unconscionable, it is voidable by A.

2. The facts being otherwise as stated in Illustration 1, the item that A inadvertently omits is a $35,000 item which would have made the total $185,000, so that if he does the work for $150,000 he will sustain a loss of $5,000 rather than make a profit of $30,000. The court may reach a result contrary to that in Illustration 1, on the ground that enforcement of the contract would not be unconscionable, and hold that it is not voidable by A.

3. The facts being otherwise as stated in Illustration 1, B has not accepted A's bid before notification of the mistake, but by statute A's bid is an irrevocable option contract because B is a state agency. In addition, A has posted a $10,000 bidder's bond with S as surety. If the court determines that enforcement of the option contract would be unconscionable, it is voidable by A and, on avoidance by A, S is not liable on the bond.

4. The facts being otherwise as stated in Illustration 1, the $50,000 error in A's bid is the result of A's mistake in interpreting B's specifications. If the court determines that enforcement of the contract would be unconscionable, it is voidable by A.

5. A writes B offering to sell for $100,000 a tract of land that A owns known as "201 Lincoln Street." B, who mistakenly believes that this description includes an additional tract of land worth $30,000, accepts A's offer. If the court determines that enforcement of the contract would be unconscionable, it is voidable by B.

6. A offers to sell B goods shipped from Bombay exsteamer "Peerless." B accepts. There are two steamers of the name "Peerless" sailing from Bombay at materially different times. B means Peerless No. 2, and A has reason to know this. A means Peerless No. 1, but B has no reason to know this. Under the rule stated in § 20 there is a contract for the sale of goods from Peerless No. 2, but, under the rule stated in this Section, if the court determines that its enforcement would be unconscionable, it is voidable by A. See Illustration 4 to § 20.

Comment d. Effect of reliance on unconscionability. Reliance by the other party may make enforcement of a contract proper although enforcement would otherwise be unconscionable. If the mistake is discovered and the other party notified before he has relied on the contract, avoidance by the mistaken party deprives the other party only of his expectation, the "benefit of the bargain," (see § 344). If, however, the other party has relied on the contract in some substantial way, avoidance may leave that reliance uncompensated. In such a case, enforcement of the contract would not be unconscionable, even if it otherwise would be. If, however, the court can adequately protect the other party by compensating him for his reliance under the rules stated in § 158, avoidance is not then precluded on this ground.

Illustrations:

7. In response to an invitation from B, a general contractor, for bids from subcontractors, A submits an offer to B to do paving work for $10,000, to be used by B as a partial basis for B's bid on a large building. As A knows, B is required to name his subcontractors in his general bid. Because of the short time in which A has to prepare his bid, A inadvertently totals his bid as $10,000 rather than $15,000. B uses A's bid in arriving at his offer of $100,000,

making A's offer irrevocable as an option contract (§ 87). B's offer is accepted, but A discovers his mistake before B accepts his bid. The option contract is not voidable by A because of B's reliance by using A's offer in making up his own offer. See Illustration 6 to § 87.

8.   The facts being otherwise as stated in Illustration 1, on A's refusal to perform for $150,000, B is no longer able to accept the next lowest bid and has to re-advertise for bids at a cost of $1,000 before getting a bid that he accepts. If the court determines that enforcement of the contract would be unconscionable, the contract is voidable by A in spite of B's reliance, because B can be adequately protected by holding A liable for the $1,000 cost of re-advertising (see § 158(1) and Comment b to that Section).

Comment e. Had reason to know of or caused the mistake. If the other party had reason to know of the mistake, the mistaken party can avoid the contract regardless of whether its enforcement would be unconscionable. (The terminology "reason to know" is used instead of "should know" on the ground explained in Comment b to § 19. The situation in which the other party actually knows of the mistake is covered in § 161. See Comment d to § 161.) Similar results follow where the other party's fault caused the mistake. (If the mistake was the fault of both parties, it was not caused by the other party within the meaning of this Section and the court may exercise its discretion under the rule stated in § 158(2). See Comment c to § 158.) In attempting to unscramble a partially or completely executed transaction, the court may allow the mistaken party recovery under the rules stated in § 158(1).

Illustrations:

9.   The facts being otherwise as stated in Illustration 1, A does not prove what his profit or loss will be if he performs, but B had estimated the expected cost as $180,000 before advertising for bids and the ten other bids were all in the range between $180,000 and $200,000. If it is determined, because of the discrepancy between A's bid on the one hand and B's estimate and the ten other bids on the other, that B had reason to know of A's mistake, the contract is voidable by A.

10.   The facts being otherwise as stated in Illustration 7, if it is determined that B had reason to know of A's mistake, the contract is voidable by A.

Comment f. Allocation of risk. Here, as under § 152, a party may undertake to perform in spite of a mistake that would otherwise allow him to avoid the contract. It is, of course, unusual for a party to bear the risk of a mistake that the other party had reason to know of or that was caused by his fault within Subparagraph (b). Because of the significance of allocation of risk in the law of mistake, the scope of this exception is spelled out in detail in § 154. (It is assumed in the illustrations to the present Section that the adversely affected party does not bear the risk under the rule stated in § 154.)

Comment g. Mistake as to identity. Mistakes as to the identity of a party have sometimes been treated as distinct from other mistakes, but the modern trend is to apply the rules applicable to other mistakes. Cf. Uniform Commercial Code § 2–403(1)(a). Such a mistake is therefore subject generally to the rules stated in this Chapter and, since it is by its nature a mistake of only one of the parties, particularly to the rule stated in this Section. The identity of the other party, as distinguished, for example, from his financial standing (see Comment *b* to § 152), is usually a basic assumption on which a contract is made. If the other party knows that he is not the intended offeree, he cannot accept an offer. That case is governed by § 52. If, however, he accepts without knowing that he is not the intended offeree, a contract may result. See Comment *b* to § 52. Whether that contract is voidable by the offeror on the ground of mistake is governed by the rule stated in this Section. The contract is voidable by the mistaken party, under the rule stated in Subparagraph (b), if the other party has caused a mistake as to his identity or if he had reason to know of the mistake, as long as it has a material effect on the agreed exchange of performances. Otherwise it is not voidable unless enforcement of the contract would be unconscionable, under the rule stated in Subparagraph (a). In some transactions the identity of the other party is of sufficient importance that he will be able to show unconscionability, but often he will not.

The situation in which a party deals with an agent acting secretly for an undisclosed principal is governed by the Restatement, Second, of Agency and not by the Restatement of this Subject. The basic principles there applied are not, however, inconsistent with the rule stated in this Section. The party who deals with such an agent gets that which he expects, the liability of the agent on the contract. See *Restatement, Second, Agency § 322.* Indeed, he gets more, for on disclosure of the agent's principal he can also hold the principal. See *Restatement, Second, Agency § 186.* Although it is also true that he may himself be liable to the principal, as well as to the agent, on the contract, this additional burden has not been regarded by the law of agency as sufficiently important to make enforcement of the contract against him unconscionable, since it does not change the terms of the contract.

Illustrations:

11.   In answer to an inquiry from "J. B. Smith Company," A offers to sell goods for cash on delivery. A mistakenly believes that the offeree is John B. Smith, who has an established business of good repute, but in fact it is a business run by his son, whose business is new and near insolvency. The son accepts, not knowing of A's mistake. If the court concludes that, because payment is to be cash on delivery, enforcement of the contract would not be unconscionable, the contract is not voidable by A.

12.   The facts being otherwise as stated in Illustration 11, A's offer is to sell goods on 90 days credit. If the court determines that, because payment is to be on 90 days credit, enforcement of the contract would be unconscionable, the contract is voidable by A. See §§ 251, 252; Uniform Commercial Code §§ 2–609, 2–702(1).

13.   The facts being otherwise as stated in Illustration 11, A's offer contains references to "your long established business" from which the son had reason to know of A's mistake. The contract is voidable by A.

Restatement 2d of Contracts

§ 154   When a Party Bears the Risk of a Mistake

A party bears the risk of a mistake when

(a) the risk is allocated to him by agreement of the parties, or

(b) he is aware, at the time the contract is made, that he has only limited knowledge with respect to the facts to which the mistake relates but treats his limited knowledge as sufficient, or

(c) the risk is allocated to him by the court on the ground that it is reasonable in the circumstances to do so.

Comments & Illustrations

Comment a. Rationale. Absent provision to the contrary, a contracting party takes the risk of most supervening changes in circumstances, even though they upset basic assumptions and unexpectedly affect the agreed exchange of performances, unless there is such extreme hardship as will justify relief on the ground of impracticability of performance or frustration of purpose. A party also bears the risk of many mistakes as to existing circumstances even though they upset basic assumptions and unexpectedly affect the agreed exchange of performances. For example, it is commonly understood that the seller of farm land generally cannot avoid the contract of sale upon later discovery by both parties that the land contains valuable mineral deposits, even though the price was negotiated on the basic assumption that the land was suitable only for farming and the effect on the agreed exchange of performances is material. In such a case a court will ordinarily allocate the risk of the mistake to the seller, so that he is under a duty to perform regardless of the mistake. The rule stated in this Section determines whether a party bears the risk of a mistake for the purposes of both §§ 152 and 153. Stating these rules in terms of the allocation of risk avoids such artificial and specious distinctions as are sometimes drawn between "intrinsic" and "extrinsic" mistakes or between mistakes that go to the "identity" or "existence" of the subject matter and those that go merely to its "attributes," "quality" or "value." Even though a mistaken party does not bear the risk of a mistake, he may be barred from avoidance if the mistake was the result of his failure to act in good faith and in accordance with reasonable standards of fair dealing. See § 157.

Comment b. Allocation by agreement. The most obvious case of allocation of the risk of a mistake is one in which the parties themselves provide for it by their agreement. Just as a party may agree to perform in spite of impracticability or frustration that would otherwise justify his non-performance, he may also agree, by appropriate language or other manifestations, to perform in spite of mistake that would otherwise justify his avoidance. An insurer, for example, may expressly undertake the risk of loss of property covered as of a date already past. Whether the agreement places the risk on the mistaken party is a question to be answered under the rules generally applicable to the scope of contractual obligations, including those on interpretation, usage and unconscionability. See Chapter 9.

Illustration:

1.   A contracts to sell and B to buy a tract of land. A and B both believe that A has good title, but neither has made a title search. The contract provides that A will convey only such title as he has, and A makes no representation with respect to title. In fact, A's title is defective. The contract is not voidable by B, because the risk of the mistake is allocated to B by agreement of the parties.

Comment c. Conscious ignorance. Even though the mistaken party did not agree to bear the risk, he may have been aware when he made the contract that his knowledge with respect to the facts to which the mistake relates was limited. If he was not only so aware that his knowledge was limited but undertook to perform in the face of that awareness, he bears the risk of the mistake. It is sometimes said in such a situation that, in a sense, there was not mistake but "conscious ignorance."

Illustration:

2.   The facts being otherwise as stated in Illustration 2 to § 152, A proposes to B during the negotiations the inclusion of a provision under which the adversely affected party can cancel the contract in the event of a material error in the surveyor's report, but B refuses to agree to such a provision. The contract is not voidable by A, because A bears the risk of the mistake.

Comment d. Risk allocated by the court. In some instances it is reasonably clear that a party should bear the risk of a mistake for reasons other than those stated in Subparagraphs (a) and (b). In such instances, under the rule stated in Subparagraph (c), the court will allocate the risk to that party on the ground that it is reasonable to do so. A court will generally do this, for example, where the seller of farm land seeks to avoid the contract of sale on the ground that valuable mineral rights have newly been found. See Comment *a.* In dealing with such issues, the court will consider the purposes of the parties and will have recourse to its own general knowledge of human behavior in bargain transactions, as it will in the analogous situation in which it is asked to supply a term under the rule stated in § 204. The rule stated in Subsection (c) is subject to contrary agreement and to usage (§ 221).

Illustrations:

3. The facts being otherwise as stated in Illustration 6 to § 152, C is not dead but is afflicted with an incurable fatal disease and cannot live more than a year. The contract is not voidable by A, because the court will allocate to A the risk of the mistake.

4. A, an owner of land, and B, a builder, make a contract under which B is to take from A's land, at a stated rate per cubic yard, all the gravel and earth necessary for the construction of a bridge, an amount estimated to be 114,000 cubic yards. A and B believe that all of the gravel and earth is above water level and can be removed by ordinary means, but in fact about one quarter of it is below water level, so that removal will require special equipment at an additional cost of about twenty percent. The contract is not voidable by B, because the court will allocate to B the risk of the mistake. Compare Illustration 5 to § 266.

5. A contracts with B to build a house on B's land. A and B believe that subsoil conditions are normal, but in fact some of the land must be drained at an expense that will leave A no profit under the contract. The contract is not voidable by A, because the court will allocate to A the risk of the mistake. Compare Illustration 8 to § 266.

6. The facts being otherwise as stated in Illustration 1 to § 153, the $50,000 error in A's bid is the result of A's mistaken estimate as to the amount of labor required to do the work. A cannot avoid the contract, because the court will allocate to A the risk of the mistake.

14.3 THE BATTLE OF THE FORMS

In spite of the confusions that abound in the law of mistake, all the cases in that area clearly share one thing in common: the incorrect beliefs that they involve are not out in the open among the parties. The materials that follow take up a series of cases in which mismatches between offer and acceptance *are* out in the open. These are cases in which one party openly insists on one set of contract terms and the other openly insists on a different, and even contradictory, set of terms. Indeed, in many of these cases each party to a contract expressly identifies and objects to the other's departure from its terms: each party insists that it will contract *only* on the terms that it has named. And yet, in spite of the mismatch—and in spite of its being open and notorious—the parties proceed as if they have agreed and established a contract.

Now it may not be immediately obvious how this could ever happen— one may suspect that the parties in such a case would simply continue negotiating and refuse to proceed with the conduct that their "contract" contemplates. But the name that the law gives to such cases—*the battle of the forms*—reveals why this suspicion is mistaken. The commonest case of an open and notorious mismatch between offer and acceptance arises among sophisticated contractors, who make sufficiently many contracts for it to be worth their while to create standard forms to use in making and responding to offers. These forms serve various benevolent purposes: they reduce the transactions costs of identifying considerations that affect the shape and value of the bargain and resolving disagreement about such matters; they help to coordinate the several contracts that a party makes so that they are all compatible (as, for example, when a seller employs a standard delivery, service, or warranty term); and they help to control a contracting party's agents (a firm's sales representatives, for example), to prevent them from offering terms that the party does not wish to honor. In addition to serving these and other transactions-costs-reducing functions, forms might seek to increase a party's share of contractual surplus, by inserting favorable terms that the other party is less likely to notice or to resist than if they were individually bargained-over.[8]

In either case, the very reason for employing the forms—namely that individual, case-by-case bargaining is not worth its transactions costs—also explains why the parties who employ the forms might act as if they have reached agreement even as their forms remain, in important respects, at odds. To adjust or correct the forms in light of the facts and circumstances of a particular instance would be to undermine or abandon the purposes that led to using form contracts in the first place. A party can have the benefits of mass-contracting, or the benefits of bespoke bargaining, but not both at once. And one of the disadvantages of mass-contracting is that the forms by which such contracts are produced will not always match up.

The common law's approach to such cases of mismatched forms was highly formalist, and deeply wedded to the notion that an offeror controls the terms of his offer, down to the last detail, and that only this precise offer, and no other, can be accepted. The following materials illustrate this doctrine scheme in application.

Restatement (First) of Contracts

§ 38   Rejection of Offer By Counter–Offer

A counter-offer by the offeree, relating to the same matter as the original offer, is a rejection of the original offer, unless the offeror in his

---

8. This alternative purpose is of course less salutary than the first. It may arise even in contracts between sophisticated parties, who jockey for position in an (inefficient) effort to exploit the transactions costs of bargaining. But the potentially exploitative use of contract forms is particularly prominent, and especially problematic, in the context of contracts between sophisticated repeat players, generally business firms, and unsophisticated one-shot contractors, generally individual consumers. In such cases, there is generally only one form— the firm's—which is presented to the consumer without any real opportunity for bargaining, on a take-it-or-leave-it basis. The issues raised by form contracts of this sort will be taken up later in these materials, under the heading *contracts of adhesion*.

offer, or the offeree in his counter-offer states that in spite of the counter-offer the original offer shall not, be terminated.

Comments & Illustrations

Comment a. A counter-offer amounts in legal effect to a statement by the offeree not only that he is willing to do something different in regard to the matter proposed, but also that he will not agree to the proposal of the offeror. A counter-offer must fulfill the requirements of an original offer. There is none unless there is a manifestation sufficient to create a power of acceptance in the original offeror. This distinguishes a counter-offer from a mere inquiry regarding the possibility of different terms, a request for a better offer, or a comment upon the terms of the offer. Likewise, an offer dealing with an entirely new matter and not proposed as a substitution for the original offer is not a counter-offer.

Comment b. An offeror may state in his offer that it shall continue for a stated time in any event and that in the meanwhile he will be glad to receive counter-offers. Likewise an offeree may state that he is holding the offer under advisement, but that if the offeror desires to close a bargain at once the offeree makes a specific counter-offer. Such an answer will not extend the time that the original offer remains open, but will not cut that time short.

Illustrations:

1. A offers B to sell him Blackacre for $5000, stating that the offer will remain open for thirty days. B replies, "I will pay $4800 for Blackacre," and on A's declining that, B writes, "I accept your offer to sell for $5000." There is no contract, although B's acceptance of these terms was made with in the time limit originally fixed by A in his offer.

2. A makes the same offer to B as that stated in Illustration 1, and B replies, "Won't you take less?" To which A answers, "No." An acceptance thereafter by B, if within the time allowed under A's offer, creates a contract.

3. A makes the same offer to B as that stated in Illustration 1. B replies, "I am keeping your offer under advisement, but if you wish to close the matter at once I will give you $4800." A does not reply, and within the thirty days limited in the original offer B accepts it. There is a contract.

Youngstown Steel Erecting Co. v. MacDonald Engineering Co.

United States District Court, N.D. Ohio, Eastern Division, 1957.
154 F.Supp. 337.

■ WEICK, DISTRICT JUDGE. This action originated in the Common Pleas Court of Cuyahoga County and was removed to this Court on the ground of diversity of citizenship.

The complaint sets forth a cause of action for damages for breach of contract.

The case was tried by the Court without a jury.

The defendant asserted two defenses, viz., (a) that there was no contract and (b) plaintiff suffered no damage.

Defendant was a Delaware corporation engaged in the designing and erecting of various types of structures. It was the general contractor under a contract with Bessemer Limestone & Cement Company for the design and construction of nine cement storage silos at Bessemer, Pennsylvania. The contract provided that defendant was to be paid the actual cost of construction plus a fixed fee.

Plaintiff was an Ohio corporation engaged in steel construction work with its principal place of business in Youngstown, Ohio. It had previous experience in the placing of steel reinforcing rods in concrete.

Plaintiff learned of the Bessemer job from Dodge construction reports to which it was a subscriber. It was interested in bidding on the subcontract for placing reinforcing steel rods in concrete. On or about July 1, 1954, plaintiff's chief officers George Townsend and Albert De Perro called on defendant at the site of the construction work in Bessemer, Pennsylvania. They conferred with James W. MacDonald, President of the defendant company and Binar Bergman, its field superintendent.

After discussing the job and the experience of plaintiff's chief officers, Mr. MacDonald furnished to Messrs. Townsend and De Perro the plans and specifications for their examination so that plaintiff might submit a bid for the placing of the steel reinforcing rods. The work to be performed under the subcontract was principally labor. The material was to be furnished by defendant.

Plaintiff's officers examined the plans and specifications and on July 6, 1955 mailed to defendant a written proposal for a subcontract 'to place all the rods connected with Bessemer Lime Stone Co. (job) including the unloading. For the sum of $55.00 per ton. The Gen. Contractor to furnish all rods, wire, and chairs, also all other accessories.'

Defendant answered the proposal by letter, under date of July 8, 1955, as follows:

'We have your proposal for reinforcing steel on the Bessemer Limestone and Cement Company job covering the reinforcing in the silos. It is understood that we will furnish you the use of our hoist but you will operate it. We will also let you use our crane when available manned with an engineer and oiler but you will furnish all ground crews. In furnishing the rods, wire and chairs it is not contemplated that we will furnish the supports for the foundation slab steel. Whatever you want to support this steel you will furnish. We will furnish all other chairs and supports.

'Please advise us if this is your understanding.'

Plaintiff replied thereto on July 10, 1955 as follows: 'We accept all terms stated in your letter of July 8, 1955, covering the Bessemer Limestone & Cement Co. job. Bessemer, Pa. Thank you for your business.'

This letter was sent by registered mail and was received by defendant.

The above constituted the entire correspondence between the parties.

After receipt of the letter of July 10, 1955, and without notice to plaintiff, defendant proceeded to and did award the subcontract for placing the rods to Bruce Campbell Construction Company of Youngstown.

Plaintiff claims that the writings constituted a binding contract and that defendant breached it by awarding the subcontract to Bruce Campbell Construction Company and that it lost profits as a result thereof for which it claimed damages in the amount of $19,798.33.

It is elementary that in order to constitute a binding contract there must have been a manifestation of assent by the parties thereto. Restatement of the Law of Contracts § 19. There must have been a definite offer and an unequivocal acceptance of it. Restatement of the Law of Contracts § 32, § 58; 1 Williston on Contracts § 37, § 72.

All of the correspondence must be considered in determining whether a contract existed. Also the surrounding facts and circumstances should be taken into account for whatever light they might shed on the intention of the parties.

Plaintiff's proposal of July 6, 1955 did constitute an offer. It was sufficiently definite so that an acceptance would have ripened into a binding contract.

Defendant's letter of July 8, 1955 was not an acceptance of plaintiff's offer, but was a counter offer. Restatement of the Law of Contracts § 38, § 60; 1 Williston on Contracts § 77. It acknowledged receipt of plaintiff's proposal and then stated 'It is understood' that defendant would furnish its hoist, but plaintiff was to operate it. Permission was granted to plaintiff to use defendant's crane together with the engineer and oiler when available, but plaintiff was to furnish all ground crews. Defendant further stipulated that in furnishing rods, wires and chairs it was not contemplated that defendant would furnish the supports for the foundation slab steel and that plaintiff would furnish whatever it wanted to support the steel. Defendant agreed to furnish other chairs and supports.

Surely, defendant would not have enumerated all these items as constituting its understanding of the work which was to be performed if it was not otherwise accepting plaintiff's proposal. While its letter enlarged the work to be performed, no question was raised about the contract price. Since defendant's letter imposed additional terms, it was necessary that the counter offer be accepted before any contract would result. Defendant's letter called for a reply as to whether this was plaintiff's understanding.

Plaintiff promptly accepted the counter offer by its letter of July 10 and thanked defendant for the business.

If these letters did not constitute an agreement, as defendant now contends, defendant had ample opportunity to respond to plaintiff's letter of July 10, and point out plaintiff's alleged error in treating defendant's letter of July 8 as constituting a counter offer. Defendant did not so respond, but remained silent and led plaintiff to believe that it had a contract.

Plaintiff did not learn otherwise until it visited the site of the job in order to find out when to start the work. It finally discovered that defendant had, without notice, awarded the subcontract to Bruce Campbell Construction Co.

Mr. MacDonald testified that the letter of July 10 arrived during his absence and that one of his subordinates put it in the file and he did not see it.

Mr. MacDonald further testified that when he received plaintiff's letter of July 8, he concluded that the proposal was so low that plaintiff did not know what it was doing and he instructed his subordinates to award the subcontract to Bruce Campbell.

It is difficult to understand why defendant wrote the letter of July 8 if it had already determined to award the contract to another person.

Mr. MacDonald also explained that silo design and construction was a specialty with which his company was thoroughly skilled and he thought plaintiff was not sufficiently familiar with this type of operation to properly perform the subcontract.

It must be remembered that plaintiff was not called upon for design of the silo, but merely for labor. Defendant did not call upon Bruce Campbell Construction Company for design, but only for labor which was performed under the supervision of defendant's foremen. Ordinary steelworkers were used, most of whom belonged to and were furnished by the steelworkers' union. If plaintiff had been awarded the subcontract, it would undoubtedly have used some of the same steelworkers.

In other words, the labor which was furnished by Bruce Campbell Construction Company could just as well have been performed by plaintiff.

The fact that defendant customarily used a printed form of subcontract with more detailed provisions has little bearing on the issues here. Plaintiff did not have knowledge of defendant's custom and there is nothing in the correspondence to even suggest a requirement as to a formal written contract.

The parties here entered into a binding contract. Defendant breached the contract by awarding the work to another contractor.

The issue of damages was sharply in dispute.

Plaintiff's testimony was to the effect that it could have performed the work required by the contract at a cost of $21,451.67 and that it lost profits amounting to $19,798.33 because of defendant's breach of contract.

Plaintiff's loss of profits was figured on the basis of 750 tons of reinforcing rods which it had been advised by defendant would be required.

The fact is that only 642 tons of rods were actually used on the job.

Defendant's testimony was to the effect that in figuring the cost of placing the rods for its bid on the general contract, its estimate was $70 a ton or $15 a ton higher than plaintiff's proposal and that actual cost was $71.30 per ton or a total of $45,779.87, and that it had previously performed similar work at comparable labor costs.

Defendant's subcontract with Bruce Campbell Construction Co. was on the basis of cost plus 10%. All Campbell did was to furnish his employees to defendant. Actually some of the workingmen were furnished by the steelworkers' union. The supervisory employees were furnished by defendant.

Campbell's original time records were not produced by defendant, but it did produce Campbell's reports to it.

In view of defendant's original estimate of $70 a ton, it is not understandable why the job was not given to plaintiff for $55 a ton unless defendant was somewhat concerned with the welfare of plaintiff and desired to prevent plaintiff from suffering what it believed would be a substantial loss.

The Court does not believe that plaintiff would have lost money on the labor contract for $55 a ton. Nor is it believed that plaintiff's profits would have been as large as claimed.

Townsend and De Perro are big, husky, skilled steelworkers. They would have worked on the job. These men could have performed much more work than two ordinary steelworkers furnished by the steelworkers' union. It would have been to their interest to do so with a fixed price contract. It is also probable that plaintiff's small organization could have gotten more work out of the men and used less men than were actually used on the cost plus contract. Plaintiff's labor cost would in all probability have been substantially less than the amount charged by Bruce Campbell Construction Co.

The Court finds that the work required under the contract would have cost plaintiff $30,000 to perform and that it would have been entitled to receive $35,310 on the contract and it, therefore, has been damaged in the amount of $5,310.

This memorandum is adopted as findings of fact and conclusions of law. Judgment may be entered in favor of plaintiff for $5,310.

* * *

The basic doctrines that governed the classical approach are announced by Restatement (First) of Contracts § 38. The first is called the *mirror image rule*. This doctrine—which features prominently in *Youngstown Steel Erecting Co.*—holds that unless the terms of an acceptance precisely match the terms of an offer—unless the acceptance accepts the exact arrangements that the offer offers—the acceptance constitutes a counteroffer, which rejects the initial offer and proposes new terms, which the initial offeror now confronts as an offeree.[9]

This rule creates a practical problem: what should the law do if parties who exchange offers and counteroffers in pre-contractual negotiations stop negotiating and begin performing as if they have made a contract even though they have never produced mirror image offer and acceptance? The classical law answered this problem with a second rule, called the *last shot doctrine*. That rule states that where, in spite of non-mirror-image offer and acceptance, the parties commence performance of their "contract," the performance is taken as acceptance of the last counteroffer made, and the parties are bound by the terms of this counteroffer. The last shot doctrine was not required to decide *Youngstown Steel Erecting Co.*, as the plaintiff's 10 July letter (by saying "we accept all terms") constituted a mirror-image acceptance of what was, under the mirror image rule, the defendant's counteroffer. The last shot doctrine would, however, have come into play had the plaintiff not written on 10 July but instead commenced performance. In that case, the contract would have been consummated on the terms of the defendant's letter rather than the plaintiff's, and commencement would, in spite of the plaintiff's initial letter, have been treated as a mirror image acceptance.

The classical regime will strike the modern reader as obviously unsatisfactory. For one thing, it creates inefficient, indeed almost perverse, incentives for the parties to continue sending new forms, with terms that favor them, right up to the moment at which performance begins. Where one party is sophisticated and the other is not, these incentives can produce not just inefficiency but also substantial unfairness. Something like this will be illustrated at the end of this Chapter, by cases that concern the effect of forms in e-commerce.

The classical regime is unsatisfactory for another reason, also, which is perhaps more interesting, at least in the current context, because it reveals something of the internal dynamics, and tensions, of formalist legal doctrine.

The mirror image rule, recall, is deeply connected to the principle that offerors control the terms of their offers and should not be bound save as they consent to be so. In this way, the mirror image rule expresses the classical, formalist, subjective theory of contractual intent. The classical law, when confronted with non-mirror-image offer and acceptance, refuses

---

9. Note that this rule contains two parts, which have a different status from each other.

The first part of the rule holds that a mis-matched acceptance does not create a contract. That is a mandatory rule. Only a mirror-image acceptance can create a contract.

The second part of the traditional rule holds that the mis-matched acceptance counts as a rejection of the original offer and becomes a counteroffer. This is a default rule only. As the Restatement section makes plain, the parties may agree that the original offer will remain open even in the face of a non-mirror image "acceptance," for example as in an option contract. In that case, the question arises what become of the terms in the ineffective acceptance? Do they still constitute an offer? If so, can both the initial offer and the new one be accepted? And if it appears that they are both accepted, which takes precedence?

to ask how reasonable parties employing mis-matched forms would understand their contractual arrangements. Instead, the classical law insists that the offeror's exposure to contractual obligation is limited to his subjective intent in making his offer, which is captured by the meaning of his offer. Where the counteroffer departs from this intent, it fails to accept the offer or to establish a contract.

This is all fine, as far as it goes. But when parties who have made mis-matched offers and acceptances nevertheless proceed to perform as if they have created a contract, the classical law is forced to confront a case in which contract-like activity occurs in spite of, and indeed against, the subjective contractual intentions of those who are engaging in it. Classical contract law was forced to confront this reality of contractual practice, and it did so through the last shot doctrine. That doctrine treats the party that commenced performance as *accepting* its counterparty's last offer, even in the face of the fact that the performing party's own last offer clearly indicates that it did not intend to contract on the terms that the last shot doctrine says constitute the contract. The last shot doctrine, in other words, completely abandons the subjective theory of contractual intent that the mirror image rule insists on. Or, to put the point slightly differently, the last shot doctrine simply presumes that the party that commences performance has an intent that all of that party's prior contractual communications suggest it does not possess.

This illustrates a deep and general shortcoming in formalist contract doctrine. Formalism insists that contract law establishes an internally coherent free-standing set of rules. But the parties to contracts often do not behave as these rules recommend. When contractual life departs from contractual logic, formalism must in some way respond. But formalism's commitment to free-standing legal logic deprives it of the materials on which to base a sensible response, and so it must employ ad hoc and indeed arbitrary presumptions, which allow the world to intrude into the law in precisely the fashion that the formalist ideology most condemns. In the case of the battle of the forms, the formalist insistence on subjective intent deprives formalist doctrine of the materials needed expressly to take up the question how reasonable parties would understand each other's contractual utterances and actions. And so formalism, through the last shot doctrine, must impose on one party notional intentions that are at odds with its subjective intentions in just the way that formalism ordinarily condemns and, furthermore, that are unmoored from any considerations involving reasonableness as well.

The challenge for a realist approach to the battle of the forms, then, is to give doctrinal expression to an open quest for determining what is reasonable when parties whose offer and acceptance do not match up nevertheless perform as if they have made a contract. The materials below illustrate how realist contract law has taken up this challenge and also some problems that have come up along the way.

Restatement 2d of Contracts

§ 39   Counter–Offers

(1) A counter-offer is an offer made by an offeree to his offeror relating to the same matter as the original offer and proposing a substituted bargain differing from that proposed by the original offer.

(2) An offeree's power of acceptance is terminated by his making of a counter-offer, unless the offeror has manifested a contrary intention or unless the counter-offer manifests a contrary intention of the offeree.

Comments & Illustrations:

Comment a. Counter-offer as rejection. It is often said that a counter-offer is a rejection, and it does have the same effect in terminating the offeree's power of acceptance. But in other respects a counter-offer differs from a rejection. A counter-offer must be capable of being accepted; it carries negotiations on rather than breaking them off. The termination of the power of acceptance by a counter-offer merely carries out the usual understanding of bargainers that one proposal is dropped when another is taken under consideration; if alternative proposals are to be under consideration at the same time, warning is expected.

Illustration:

1.   A offers B to sell him a parcel of land for $5,000, stating that the offer will remain open for thirty days. B replies, "I will pay $4,800 for the parcel," and on A's declining that, B writes, within the thirty day period, "I accept your offer to sell for $5,000." There is no contract unless A's offer was itself a contract (see § 37), or unless A's reply to the counter-offer manifested an intention to renew his original offer.

Comment b. Qualified acceptance, inquiry or separate offer. A common type of counter-offer is the qualified or conditional acceptance, which purports to accept the original offer but makes acceptance expressly conditional on assent to additional or different terms. See § 59. Such a counter-offer must be distinguished from an unqualified acceptance which is accompanied by a proposal for modification of the agreement or for a separate agreement. A mere inquiry regarding the possibility of different terms, a request for a better offer, or a comment upon the terms of the offer, is ordinarily not a counter-offer. Such responses to an offer may be too tentative or indefinite to be offers of any kind; or they may deal with new matters rather than a substitution for the original offer; or their language may manifest an intention to keep the original offer under consideration.

Illustration:

2.   A makes the same offer to B as that stated in Illustration 1, and B replies, "Won't you take less?" A answers, "No." An

acceptance thereafter by B within the thirty-day period is effective. B's inquiry was not a counter-offer, and A's original offer stands.

Comment c. Contrary statement of offeror or offeree. An offeror may state in his offer that it shall continue for a stated time in any event and that in the meanwhile he will be glad to receive counter-offers. Likewise an offeree may state that he is holding the offer under advisement, but that if the offeror desires to close a bargain at once the offeree makes a specific counter-offer. Such an answer will not extend the time that the original offer remains open, but will not cut that time short. Compare § 38.

Illustration:

3. A makes the same offer to B as that stated in Illustration 1. B replies, "I am keeping your offer under advisement, but if you wish to close the matter at once I will give you $4,800." A does not reply, and within the thirty-day period B accepts the original offer. B's acceptance is effective.

Restatement 2d of Contracts

§ 59 Purported Acceptance Which Adds Qualifications

A reply to an offer which purports to accept it but is conditional on the offeror's assent to terms additional to or different from those offered is not an acceptance but is a counter-offer.

Comments & Illustrations:

Comment a. Qualified acceptance. A qualified or conditional acceptance proposes an exchange different from that proposed by the original offeror. Such a proposal is a counter-offer and ordinarily terminates the power of acceptance of the original offeree. See § 39. The effect of the qualification or condition is to deprive the purported acceptance of effect. But a definite and seasonable expression of acceptance is operative despite the statement of additional or different terms if the acceptance is not made to depend on assent to the additional or different terms. See § 61; Uniform Commercial Code § 2–207(1). The additional or different terms are then to be construed as proposals for modification of the contract. See Uniform Commercial Code § 2–207(2). Such proposals may sometimes be accepted by the silence of the original offeror. See § 69.

Illustration:

1. A makes an offer to B, and B in terms accepts but adds, "This acceptance is not effective unless prompt acknowledgement is made of receipt of this letter." There is no contract, but a counter-offer.

Comment b. Statement of conditions implied in offer. To accept, the offeree must assent unconditionally to the offer as made, but the fact that the offeree makes a conditional promise is not sufficient to show that his acceptance is conditional. The offer itself may either expressly or by implication propose that the offeree make a conditional promise as his part of the exchange. By assenting to such a proposal the offeree makes a conditional promise, but his acceptance is unconditional. The offeror's promise may also be conditional on the same or a different fact or event.

Illustrations:

2.   A makes a written offer to sell B a patent in exchange for B's promise to pay $10,000 if B's adviser X approves the purchase. B signs the writing in a space labelled "Accepted:" and returns the writing to A. B has made a conditional promise and an unconditional acceptance. There is a contract, but B's duty to pay the price is conditional on X's approval.

3.   A makes a written offer to B to sell him Blackacre. By usage the offer is understood as promising a marketable title. B replies, "I accept your offer if you can convey me a marketable title." There is a contract.

Restatement 2d of Contracts

§ 61   Acceptance Which Requests Change Of Terms

An acceptance which requests a change or addition to the terms of the offer is not thereby invalidated unless the acceptance is made to depend on an assent to the changed or added terms.

Comments & Illustrations:

Comment a. Interpretation of acceptance. An acceptance must be unequivocal. But the mere inclusion of words requesting a modification of the proposed terms does not prevent a purported acceptance from closing the contract unless, if fairly interpreted, the offeree's assent depends on the offeror's further acquiescence in the modification. See Uniform Commercial Code § 2–207(1).

Illustrations:

1.   A offers to sell B 100 tons of steel at a certain price. B replies, "I accept your offer. I hope that if you can arrange to deliver the steel in weekly installments of 25 tons you will do so." There is a contract, but A is not bound to deliver in installments.

2.   A offers to sell specified hardware to B on stated terms. B replies: "I accept your offer; ship in accordance with your statement. Please send me also one No. 5 hand saw at your list price." The request for the saw is a separate offer, not a counter-offer.

Uniform Commercial Code

§ 2–207   Additional Terms in Acceptance or Confirmation

(1) A definite and seasonable expression of acceptance or a written confirmation which is sent within a reasonable time operates as an accep-

tance even though it states terms additional to or different from those offered or agreed upon, unless acceptance is expressly made conditional on assent to the additional or different terms.

(2) The additional terms are to be construed as proposals for addition to the contract. Between merchants such terms become part of the contract unless:

(a) the offer expressly limits acceptance to the terms of the offer;

(b) they materially alter it; or

(c) notification of objection to them has already been given or is given within a reasonable time after notice of them is received.

(3) Conduct by both parties which recognizes the existence of a contract is sufficient to establish a contract for sale although the writings of the parties do not otherwise establish a contract. In such case the terms of the particular contract consist of those terms on which the writings of the parties agree, together with any supplementary terms incorporated under any other provisions of this Act.

Comments

1.   This section is intended to deal with two typical situations. The one is the written confirmation, where an agreement has been reached either orally or by informal correspondence between the parties and is followed by one or both of the parties sending formal memoranda embodying the terms so far as agreed upon and adding terms not discussed. The other situation is offer and acceptance, in which a wire or letter expressed and intended as an acceptance or the closing of an agreement adds further minor suggestions or proposals such as "ship by Tuesday," "rush," "ship draft against bill of lading inspection allowed," or the like. A frequent example of the second situation is the exchange of printed purchase order and acceptance (sometimes called "acknowledgment") forms. Because the forms are oriented to the thinking of the respective drafting parties, the terms contained in them often do not correspond. Often the seller's form contains terms different from or additional to those set forth in the buyer's form. Nevertheless, the parties proceed with the transaction. [Comment 1 was amended in 1966.]

2.   Under this Article a proposed deal which in commercial understanding has in fact been closed is recognized as a contract. Therefore, any additional matter contained in the confirmation or in the acceptance falls within subsection (2) and must be regarded as a proposal for an added term unless the acceptance is made conditional on the acceptance of the additional or different terms. [Comment 2 was amended in 1966.]

3.   Whether or not additional or different terms will become part of the agreement depends upon the provisions of subsection (2). If they are such as materially to alter the original bargain, they will not be included unless expressly agreed to by the other party. If, however, they are terms which would not so change the bargain they will be incorporated unless

notice of objection to them has already been given or is given within a reasonable time.

4. Examples of typical clauses which would normally "materially alter" the contract and so result in surprise or hardship if incorporated without express awareness by the other party are: a clause negating such standard warranties as that of merchantability or fitness for a particular purpose in circumstances in which either warranty normally attaches; a clause requiring a guaranty of 90% or 100% deliveries in a case such as a contract by cannery, where the usage of the trade allows greater quantity leeways; a clause reserving to the seller the power to cancel upon the buyer's failure to meet any invoice when due; a clause requiring that complaints be made in a time materially shorter than customary or reasonable.

5. Examples of clauses which involve no element of unreasonable surprise and which therefore are to be incorporated in the contract unless notice of objection is seasonably given are: a clause setting forth and perhaps enlarging slightly upon the seller's exemption due to supervening causes beyond his control, similar to those covered by the provision of this Article on merchant's excuse by failure of presupposed conditions or a clause fixing in advance any reasonable formula of proration under such circumstances; a clause fixing a reasonable time for complaints within customary limits, or in the case of a purchase for sub-sale, providing for inspection by the sub-purchaser; a clause providing for interest on overdue invoices or fixing the seller's standard credit terms where they are within the range of trade practice and do not limit any credit bargained for; a clause limiting the right of rejection for defects which fall within the customary trade tolerances for acceptance "with adjustment" or otherwise limiting remedy in a reasonable manner (see Sections 2–718 and 2–719).

6. If no answer is received within a reasonable time after additional terms are proposed, it is both fair and commercially sound to assume that their inclusion has been assented to. Where clauses on confirming forms sent by both parties conflict each party must be assumed to object to a clause of the other conflicting with one on the confirmation sent by himself. As a result the requirement that there be notice of objection which is found in subsection (2) is satisfied and the conflicting terms do not become a part of the contract. The contract then consists of the terms originally expressly agreed to, terms on which the confirmations agree, and terms supplied by this Act, including subsection (2). The written confirmation is also subject to Section 2–201. Under that section a failure to respond permits enforcement of a prior oral agreement; under this section a failure to respond permits additional terms to become part of the agreement. [Comment 6 was amended in 1966.]

7. In many cases, as where goods are shipped, accepted and paid for before any dispute arises, there is no question whether a contract has been made. In such cases, where the writings of the parties do not establish a contract, it is not necessary to determine which act or document constituted the offer and which the acceptance. See Section 2–204. The only

question is what terms are included in the contract, and subsection (3) furnishes the governing rule. [Comment 7 was added in 1966.]

Roto–Lith, Ltd. v. F.P. Bartlett & Co.

United States Court of Appeals for the First Circuit, 1962.
297 F.2d 497.

■ ALDRICH, CIRCUIT JUDGE. Plaintiff-appellant Roto–Lith, Ltd., is a New York corporation engaged inter alia in manufacturing, or 'converting,' cellophane bags for packaging vegetables. Defendant-appellee is a Massachusetts corporation which makes emulsion for use as a cellophane adhesive. This is a field of some difficulty, and various emulsions are employed, depending upon the intended purpose of the bags. In May and October 1959 plaintiff purchased emulsion from the defendant. Subsequently bags produced with this emulsion failed to adhere, and this action was instituted in the district court for the District of Massachusetts. At the conclusion of the evidence the court directed a verdict for the defendant. This appeal followed.

Defendant asks us to review the October transaction first because of certain special considerations applicable to the May order. The defense in each instance, however, is primarily the same, namely, defendant contends that the sales contract expressly negatived any warranties. We will deal first with the October order.

On October 23, 1959, plaintiff, in New York, mailed a written order to defendant in Massachusetts for a drum of 'N–132–C' emulsion, stating 'End use: wet pack spinach bags.' Defendant on October 26 prepared simultaneously an acknowledgment and an invoice. The printed forms were exactly the same, except that one was headed 'Acknowledgment' and the other 'Invoice,' and the former contemplated insertion of the proposed, and the latter of the actual, shipment date. Defendant testified that in accordance with its regular practice the acknowledgment was prepared and mailed the same day. The plaintiff's principal liability witness testified that he did not know whether this acknowledgment 'was received, or what happened to it.' On this state of the evidence there is an un-rebutted presumption of receipt. *Johnston v. Cassidy, 1932, 279 Mass. 593*; cf. *Tobin v. Taintor, 1918, 229 Mass. 174.* The goods were shipped to New York on October 27. On the evidence it must be found that the acknowledgment was received at least no later than the goods. The invoice was received presumably a day or two after the goods.

The acknowledgment and the invoice bore in conspicuous type on their face the following legend, 'All goods sold without warranties, express or implied, and subject to the terms on reverse side.' In somewhat smaller, but still conspicuous, type there were printed on the back certain terms of sale, of which the following are relevant:

'1. Due to the variable conditions under which these goods may be transported, stored, handled, or used, Seller hereby expressly excludes any and all warranties, guaranties, or representations whatsoever. Buyer assumes risk for results obtained from use of these goods, whether used alone or in combination with other products. Seller's liability hereunder shall be limited to the replacement of any goods that materially differ from the Seller's sample order on the basis of which the order for such goods was made.

'7.   This acknowledgment contains all of the terms of this purchase and sale. No one except a duly authorized officer of Seller may execute or modify contracts. Payment may be made only at the offices of the Seller. If these terms are not acceptable, Buyer must so notify Seller at once.'(Ital. suppl.)

It is conceded that plaintiff did not protest defendant's attempt so to limit its liability, and in due course paid for the emulsion and used it. It is also conceded that adequate notice was given of breach of warranty, if there were warranties. The only issue which we will consider is whether all warranties were excluded by defendant's acknowledgment.

The first question is what law the Massachusetts court would look to in order to determine the terms of the contract. Under Massachusetts law this is the place where the last material act occurs. *Autographic Register Co. v. Philip Hano Co.*, 1 Cir., 1952, 198 F.2d 208. Under the Uniform Commercial Code, Mass.Gen.Laws Ann. (1958) ch. 106, § 2–206, mailing the acknowledgment would clearly have completed the contract in Massachusetts by acceptance had the acknowledgment not sought to introduce new terms. Section 2–207 provides:

'(1) A definite and seasonable expression of acceptance or a written confirmation which is sent within a reasonable time operates as an acceptance even though it states terms additional to or different from those offered or agreed upon, unless acceptance is expressly made conditional on assent to the additional or different terms.

'(2) The additional terms are to be construed as proposals for addition to the contract. Between merchants such terms become part of the contract unless:

'(a) the offer expressly limits acceptance to the terms of the offer;

'(b) they materially alter it; or

'(c) notification of objection to them has already been given or is given within a reasonable time after notice of them is received.'

Plaintiff exaggerates the freedom which this section affords an offeror to ignore a reply from an offeree that does not in terms coincide with the original offer. According to plaintiff defendant's condition that there should be no warranties constituted a proposal which 'materially altered' the agreement. As to this we concur. See Uniform Commercial Code comment to this section, Mass.Gen.Laws annotation, supra, paragraph 4. Plaintiff goes on to say that by virtue of the statute the acknowledgment effected a completed agreement without this condition, and that as a further proposal the condition never became part of the agreement because plaintiff did not express assent. We agree that section 2–207 changed the existing law, but not to this extent. Its purpose was to modify the strict principle that a response not precisely in accordance with the offer was a rejection and a counteroffer. *Kehlor Flour Mills Co. v. Linden*, 1918, 230 Mass. 119, 123. Now, within stated limits, a response that does not in all respects correspond with the offer constitutes an acceptance of the offer, and a counteroffer only as to the differences. If plaintiff's contention is correct that a reply to an offer stating additional conditions unilaterally burdensome upon the offeror is a binding acceptance of the original offer plus simply a proposal for the additional conditions, the statute would lead to an absurdity. Obviously no offeror will subsequently assent to such conditions.

The statute is not too happily drafted. Perhaps it would be wiser in all cases for an offeree to say in so many words, 'I will not accept your offer until you assent to the following: But businessmen cannot be expected to act by rubric. It would be unrealistic to suppose that when an offeree replies setting out conditions that would be burdensome only to the offeror he intended to make an unconditional acceptance of the original offer, leaving it simply to the offeror's good nature whether he would assume the additional restrictions. To given the statute a practical construction we must hold that a response which states a condition materially altering the obligation solely to the disadvantage of the offeror is an 'acceptance expressly conditional on assent to the additional terms.'

Plaintiff accepted the goods with knowledge of the conditions specified in the acknowledgment. It became bound. Whether the contract was made in Massachusetts or New York, there has been no suggestion that either jurisdiction will not give effect to an appropriate disclaimer of warranties. See Mass., gen.Laws Ann. c. 106, § 2–316. This disposes of the October order.

With respect to the May order a different situation obtains. Here plaintiff ordered a quantity of 'N–136–F,' which was defendant's code number for a drybag emulsion. The order stated as the end use a wet bag. Accordingly, defendant knew, by its own announced standards, that the emulsion ordered was of necessity unfit for the disclosed purpose. In this bald situation plaintiff urges that the defendant cannot be permitted to specify that it made no implied warranty of fitness.

We do not reach this question. In the court below, when plainly asked to state its opposition to the direction of a verdict, plaintiff did not advance the arguments it now makes, and in no way called the court's attention to any distinction between the May and the October orders. An appellant is not normally permitted to have the benefit of a new theory on appeal. It is true that this is not an absolute prohibition. The court in its discretion may relax the rule in exceptional cases in order to prevent a clear miscarriage of justice. *Hormel v. Helvering*, 1941, 312 U.S. 552. Plaintiff's point, however, is by no means clear-cut. Financially the consequences are not large.

Plaintiff was represented by competent counsel, and has had an eight-day trial. We do not think the case one for making an exception to the salutary rule that a party is normally entitled to but one 'day' in court.

No question remains as to the counterclaim.

Judgment will be entered affirming the judgment of the District Court.

Ionics, Inc. v. Elmwood Sensors, Inc.

United States Court of Appeals for the First Circuit, 1997.
110 F.3d 184.

■ TORRUELLA, CHIEF JUDGE. Ionics, Inc. ("Ionics") purchased thermostats from Elmwood Sensors, Inc. ("Elmwood") for installation in water dispensers manufactured by the former. Several of the dispensers subsequently caused fires which allegedly resulted from defects in the sensors. Ionics filed suit against Elmwood in order to recover costs incurred in the wake of the fires. Before trial, the district court denied Elmwood's motion for partial summary judgment. The District Court of Massachusetts subsequently certified to this court "the question whether, in the circumstances of this case, § 2–207 of M.G.L. c. 106 has been properly applied." Order of the district court, November 6, 1995.

I. Standard of Review

We review the grant or denial of summary judgment *de novo*. See *Borschow Hosp. & Medical Supplies v. Cesar Castillo, Inc.*, 96 F.3d 10, 14 (1st Cir. 1996).

II. Background

The facts of the case are not in dispute. Elmwood manufactures and sells thermostats. Ionics makes hot and cold water dispensers, which it leases to its customers. On three separate occasions, Ionics purchased thermostats from Elmwood for use in its water dispensers. Every time Ionics made a purchase of thermostats from Elmwood, it sent the latter a purchase order form which contained, in small type, various "conditions." Of the 20 conditions on the order form, two are of particular relevance:

> 18. REMEDIES—The remedies provided Buyer herein shall be cumulative, and in addition to any other remedies provided by law or equity. A waiver of a breach of any provision hereof shall not constitute a waiver of any other breach. The laws of the state shown in Buyer's address printed on the masthead of this order shall apply in the construction hereof.

> 19. ACCEPTANCE—Acceptance by the Seller of this order shall be upon the terms and conditions set forth in items 1 to 17 inclusive, and elsewhere in this order. Said order can be so accepted only on the exact terms herein and set forth. No terms which are in any manner additional to or different from those herein set forth shall become a part of, alter or in any way control the terms and conditions herein set forth.

Near the time when Ionics placed its first order, it sent Elmwood a letter that it sends to all of its new suppliers. The letter states, in part:

> The information preprinted, written and/or typed on our purchase order is especially important to us. Should you take exception to this information, please clearly express any reservations to us in writing. If you do not, we will assume that you have agreed to the specified terms and that you will fulfill your obligations according to our purchase order. If necessary, we will change your invoice and pay your invoice according to our purchase order.

Following receipt of each order, Elmwood prepared and sent an "Acknowledgment" form containing the following language in small type:

> THIS WILL ACKNOWLEDGE RECEIPT OF BUYER'S ORDER AND STATE SELLER'S WILLINGNESS TO SELL THE GOODS ORDERED BUT ONLY UPON THE TERMS AND CONDITIONS SET FORTH HEREIN AND ON THE REVERSE SIDE HEREOF AS A COUNTEROFFER. BUYER SHALL BE DEEMED TO HAVE ACCEPTED SUCH COUNTEROFFER UNLESS IT IS REJECTED IN WRITING WITHIN TEN (10) DAYS OF THE RECEIPT HEREOF, AND ALL SUBSEQUENT ACTION SHALL BE PURSUANT TO THE TERMS AND CONDITIONS OF THIS COUNTEROFFER ONLY; ANY ADDITIONAL OR DIFFERENT TERMS ARE HEREBY OBJECTED TO AND SHALL NOT BE BINDING UPON THE PARTIES UNLESS SPECIFICALLY AGREED TO IN WRITING BY SELLER.

Although this passage refers to a "counteroffer," we wish to emphasize that this language is not controlling. The form on which the language appears is labelled an "Acknowledgment" and the language comes under a heading that reads "Notice of Receipt of Order." The form, taken as a whole, appears to contemplate an order's confirmation rather than an order's rejection in the form of a counteroffer.

It is undisputed that the Acknowledgment was received prior to the arrival of the shipment of goods. Although the district court, in its ruling on the summary judgment motion, states that "with each shipment of thermostats, Elmwood included an Acknowledgment Form," Order of the District Court, August 23, 1995, this statement cannot reasonably be taken as a finding in support of the claim that the Acknowledgment and the shipment arrived together. First, in its certification order, the court states that "the purchaser, *after* receiving the Acknowledgment, accepted delivery of the goods without objection." Order Pursuant to 28 U.S.C. § 1292(b), Nov. 6, 1995 (emphasis added). This language is clearer and more precise than the previous statement and suggests that the former was simply a poor choice of phrasing. Furthermore, Ionics has not disputed the arrival time of the Acknowledgment. In its Memorandum in Support of Defendant's Motion for Partial Summary Judgment Elmwood stated, under the heading of "Statements of Undisputed Facts," that "for each of the three orders, Ionics received the Acknowledgment prior to receiving the shipment of thermostats." Memorandum in Support of Defendant's Motion for Partial Summary Judgment, at 3. In its own memorandum, Ionics argued that there existed disputed issues of material fact, but did not contradict Elmwood's claim regarding the arrival of the Acknowledgment Form. *See* Plaintiff's Memorandum in Support of its Opposition to Defendant's Motion for Partial Summary Judgment at 4–10. Furthermore, in its appellate brief, Ionics does not argue that the time of arrival of the Acknowledgment Form is in dispute. Ionics repeats language from the district court's summary judgment ruling that "with each shipment of thermostats, Elmwood included an Acknowledgment Form," Appellee's Brief at 7, but does not argue that the issue is in dispute or confront the language in Elmwood's brief which states that "it is undisputed that for each of the three orders, Ionics received the Acknowledgment prior to receiving the shipment of thermostats." Appellant's Brief at 6.

As we have noted, the Acknowledgment Form expressed Elmwood's willingness to sell thermostats on "terms and conditions" that the Form indicated were listed on the reverse side. Among the terms and conditions listed on the back was the following:

9. WARRANTY

All goods manufactured by Elmwood Sensors, Inc. are guaranteed to be free of defects in material and workmanship for a period of ninety (90) days after receipt of such goods by Buyer or eighteen months from the date of manufacturer [sic] (as evidenced by the manufacturer's date code), whichever shall be longer. THERE IS NO IMPLIED WARRANTY OF MERCHANTABILITY AND NO OTHER WARRANTY, EXPRESSED OR IMPLIED, EXCEPT SUCH AS IS EXPRESSLY SET FORTH HEREIN. SELLER WILL NOT BE LIABLE FOR ANY GENERAL, CONSEQUENTIAL OR INCIDENTAL DAMAGES, INCLUDING WITHOUT LIMITATION ANY DAMAGES FROM LOSS OF PROFITS, FROM ANY BREACH OF WARRANTY OR FOR NEGLIGENCE, SELLER'S LIABILITY AND BUYER'S EXCLUSIVE REMEDY BEING EXPRESSLY LIMITED TO THE REPAIR OF DEFECTIVE GOODS F.O.B. THE SHIPPING POINT INDICATED ON THE FACE HEREOF OR THE REPAYMENT OF THE PURCHASE PRICE UPON THE RETURN OF THE GOODS OR THE GRANTING OF A REASONABLE ALLOWANCE ON ACCOUNT OF ANY DEFECTS, AS SELLER MAY ELECT.

Neither party disputes that they entered into a valid contract and neither disputes the quantity of thermostats purchased, the price paid, or the manner and time of delivery. The only issue in dispute is the extent of Elmwood's liability.

In summary, Ionics' order included language stating that the contract would be governed exclusively by the terms included on the purchase order and that all remedies available under state law would be available to Ionics. In a subsequent letter, Ionics added that Elmwood must indicate any objections to these conditions in writing. Elmwood, in turn, sent Ionics an Acknowledgment stating that the contract was governed exclusively by the terms in the Acknowledgment, and Ionics was given ten days to reject this "counteroffer." Among the terms included in the Acknowledgment is a limitation on Elmwood's liability. As the district court stated, "the terms are diametrically opposed to each other on the issue of whether all warranties implied by law were reserved or waived." Order of the District Court, August 23, 1995.

We face, therefore, a battle of the forms. This is purely a question of law. The dispute turns on whether the contract is governed by the language after the comma in § 2–207(1) of the Uniform Commercial Code, according to the rule laid down by this court in *Roto–Lith, Ltd. v. F.P. Bartlett & Co.*, 297 F.2d 497 (1st Cir. 1962), or whether it is governed by subsection (3) of the Code provision, as enacted by both Massachusetts, Mass. Gen. L. ch. 106, § 2–207 (1990 and 1996 Supp.), and Rhode Island, R.I. Gen. Laws § 6A–2–207 (1992). We find the rule of Roto–Lith to be in conflict with the purposes of section 2–207 and, accordingly, we overrule Roto–Lith and find that subsection (3) governs the contract. Analyzing the case under section 2–207, we conclude that Ionics defeats Elmwood's motion for partial summary judgment.

III. Legal Analysis

Our analysis begins with the statute. Section 2–207 reads as follows:

§ 2–207. Additional Terms in Acceptance or Confirmation

(1) A definite and seasonable expression of acceptance or a written confirmation which is sent within a reasonable time operates as an acceptance even though it states terms additional to or different from those offered or agreed upon, unless acceptance is expressly made conditional on assent to the additional or different terms.

(2) The additional or different terms are to be construed as proposals for addition to the contract. Between merchants such terms become part of the contract unless:

> (a) the offer expressly limits acceptance to the terms of the offer;

> (b) they materially alter it; or

> (c) notification of objection to them has already been given or is given within a reasonable time after notice of them is received.

(3) Conduct by both parties which recognizes the existence of a contract is sufficient to establish a contract for sale although the writings of the parties do not otherwise establish a contract. In such case the terms of the particular contract consist of those terms on which the writings of the parties agree, together with any supplementary terms incorporated under any other provisions of this chapter.

Mass. Gen. L. ch. 106, § 2–207 (1990 and 1996 Supp.).

In *Roto–Lith*, Roto–Lith sent a purchase order to Bartlett, who responded with an acknowledgment that included language purporting to limit Bartlett's liability. Roto–Lith did not object. *Roto–Lith*, 297 F.2d at 498–99. This court held that "a response which states a condition materially altering the obligation solely to the disadvantage of the offeror is an 'acceptance expressly conditional on assent to the additional terms.' " *Id*. at 500. This holding took the case outside of section 2–207 by applying the exception after the comma in subsection (1). The court then reverted to common law and concluded that Roto–Lith "accepted the goods with knowledge of the conditions specified in the acknowledgment [and thereby] became bound." *Id*. at 500. In other words, the *Roto–Lith* court concluded that the defendant's acceptance was conditional on assent, by the buyer, to the new terms and, therefore, constituted a counter offer rather than an acceptance. When Roto–Lith accepted the goods with knowledge of Bartlett's conditions, it accepted the counteroffer and Bartlett's terms governed the contract. Elmwood argues that *Roto–Lith* governs the instant appeal, implying that the terms of Elmwood's acknowledgment govern.

Ionics claims that the instant case is distinguishable because in *Roto–Lith* "the seller's language limiting warranties implied at law was proposed as an addition to, but was not in conflict with, the explicit terms of the buyer's form. [In the instant case] the explicit terms of the parties' forms conflict with and reject each other." Appellee's Brief at 21.

We do not believe that Ionics' position sufficiently distinguishes *Roto–Lith*. It would be artificial to enforce language that conflicts with background legal rules while refusing to enforce language that conflicts with the express terms of the contract. Every contract is assumed to incorporate the existing legal norms that are in place. It is not required that every contract explicitly spell out the governing law of the jurisdiction. Allowing later forms to govern with respect to deviations from the background rules but not deviations from the terms in the contract would imply that only the terms in the contract could be relied upon. Aside from being an artificial and arbitrary distinction, such a standard would, no doubt, lead parties to include more of the background rules in their initial forms, making forms longer and more complicated. Longer forms would be more difficult and time consuming to read—implying that even fewer forms would be read than under the existing rules. It is the failure of firms to read their forms that has brought this case before us, and we do not wish to engender more of this type of litigation.

Our inquiry, however, is not complete. Having found that we cannot distinguish this case from *Roto–Lith*, we turn to the Uniform Commercial Code, quoted above. A plain language reading of *section 2–207* suggests that subsection (3) governs the instant case. Ionics sent an initial offer to which Elmwood responded with its "Acknowledgment." Thereafter, the conduct of the parties established the existence of a contract as required by *section 2–207(3)*.

Furthermore, the case before us is squarely addressed in comment 6, which states:

> 6. If no answer is received within a reasonable time after additional terms are proposed, it is both fair and commercially sound

to assume that their inclusion has been assented to. Where clauses on confirming forms sent by both parties conflict[,] each party must be assumed to object to a clause of the other conflicting with one on the confirmation sent by himself. As a result[,] the requirement that there be notice of objection which is found in subsection (2) [of § 2–207] is satisfied and the conflicting terms do not become part of the contract. The contract then consists of the terms originally expressly agreed to, terms on which the confirmations agree, and terms supplied by this Act.

Mass. Gen. L. ch. 106, § 2–207, Uniform Commercial Code, Comment 6. This Comment addresses precisely the facts of the instant case. Any attempt at distinguishing the case before us from section 2–207 strikes us as disingenuous.

We are faced, therefore, with a contradiction between a clear precedent of this court, *Roto–Lith*, which suggests that the language after the comma in subsection (1) governs, and the clear dictates of the Uniform Commercial Code, which indicate that subsection (3) governs. It is our view that the two cannot co-exist and the case at bar offers a graphic illustration of the conflict. We have, therefore, no choice but to overrule our previous decision in *Roto–Lith, Ltd. v. F.P. Bartlett & Co.*, 297 F.2d 497 (1st Cir. 1962). Our decision brings this circuit in line with the majority view on the subject and puts to rest a case that has provoked considerable criticism from courts and commentators and alike.

We hold, consistent with section 2–207 and Official Comment 6, that where the terms in two forms are contradictory, each party is assumed to object to the other party's conflicting clause. As a result, mere acceptance of the goods by the buyer is insufficient to infer consent to the seller's terms under the language of subsection (1). Nor do such terms become part of the contract under subsection (2) because notification of objection has been given by the conflicting forms. *See* § 2–207(2)(c).

The alternative result, advocated by Elmwood and consistent with *Roto–Lith*, would undermine the role of section 2–207. Elmwood suggests that "a seller's expressly conditional acknowledgment constitutes a counteroffer where it materially alters the terms proposed by the buyer, and the seller's terms govern the contract between the parties when the buyer accepts and pays for the goods." Appellant's Brief at 12. Under this view, section 2–207 would no longer apply to cases in which forms have been exchanged and subsequent disputes reveal that the forms are contradictory. That is, the last form would always govern.

The purpose of section 2–207, as stated in *Roto–Lith*, "was to modify the strict principle that a response not precisely in accordance with the offer was a rejection and a counteroffer." *Roto–Lith*, 297 F.2d at 500; *see also Dorton v. Collins & Aikman Corp.*, 453 F.2d 1161, 1165–66 (6th Cir. 1972) (stating that section 2–207 "was intended to alter the 'ribbon-matching' or 'mirror' rule of common law, under which the terms of an acceptance or confirmation were required to be identical to the terms of the offer"). Under the holding advocated by Elmwood, virtually any response that added to or altered the terms of the offer would be a rejection and a counteroffer. We do not think that such a result is consistent with the intent of section 2–207 and we believe it to be expressly contradicted by Comment 6.

Applied to this case, our holding leads to the conclusion that the contract is governed by section 2–207(3). Section 2–207(1) is inapplicable because Elmwood's acknowledgment is conditional on assent to the additional terms. The additional terms do not become a part of the contract under section 2–207(2) because notification of objection to conflicting terms was given on the order form and because the new terms materially alter those in the offer. Finally, the conduct of the parties demonstrates the existence of a contract, as required by section 2–207(3). Thus, section 2–207(3) applies and the terms of the contract are to be determined in accordance with that subsection.

We conclude, therefore, that section 2–207(3) prevails and "the terms of the particular contract consist of those terms on which the writings of the parties agree, together with any supplementary terms incorporated under any other provisions of this chapter." *Mass. Gen. L. ch. 106, § 2–207(3)*.

The reality of modern commercial dealings, as this case demonstrates, is that not all participants read their forms. *See* James J. White & Robert S. Summers, Uniform Commercial Code § 1–3 at 6–7 (4th ed. 1995). To uphold Elmwood's view would not only fly in the face of Official Comment 6 to section 2–207 of the Uniform Commercial Code, and the overall purpose of that section, it would also fly in the face of good sense. The sender of the last form (in the instant case, the seller) could insert virtually any conditions it chooses into the contract, including conditions contrary to those in the initial form. The final form, therefore, would give its sender the power to re-write the contract. Under our holding today, we at least ensure that a party will not be held to terms that are directly contrary to the terms it has included in its own form. Rather than assuming that a failure to object to the offeree's conflicting terms indicates offeror's assent to those terms, we shall make the more reasonable inference that each party continues to object to the other's contradictory terms. We think it too much to grant the second form the power to contradict and override the terms in the first form.

IV. Conclusion

For the reasons stated herein, the district court's order denying Elmwood's motion for partial summary judgment is *affirmed* and the case is *remanded* to the district court for further proceedings.

* * *

UCC § 2–207 appears to contemplate a wholesale rejection of the common law regime. The section is not, however, an ideal of felicitous drafting. It is hard to understand, and hence has (as *Roto–Lith* vividly illustrates) in fact been mis-understood.

Begin with the text of the UCC. Section 2–207(1) contains two clauses. The first clause, variously called "clause 1" and the "clause before the comma," reads: "A definite and seasonable expression of acceptance or a written confirmation which is sent within a reasonable time operates as an acceptance even though it states terms additional to or different from those offered or agreed upon." The second clause, variously called "clause 2" and the "clause after the comma," reads: "unless acceptance is expressly made conditional on assent to the additional or different terms." It is worth taking up each clause separately and then considering the relationship between them.

Section 2–207(1) clause 1 appears to reject the common law approach. It rejects the mirror image rule when it states that an acceptance can be effective—can create a contract—even though it is not a mirror image of the offer that it accepts. And it thus also rejects the last shot doctrine: the offer and its terms remain in place even when they encounter a non-mirror image acceptance followed by performance. Indeed, although there is a need for more rules here, § 2–207(1) clause 1 appears to invite a weak first-shot doctrine: where offer and acceptance do not match up, it suggests, the initial offer will have some say concerning what the terms of the eventual contract are.

So when contracts are formed by mis-matched offer and acceptance under § 2–207(1) clause 1, both the terms of the initial offer and the additional or different terms in the seasonable expression of acceptance remain in play. Section 2–207(2) provides additional rules for resolving the differences between offer and acceptance in such a case. On the one hand, if both parties are merchants (of the goods at issue in the contract), the additional terms become part of the contract *unless* the offer expressly limits acceptance to the terms of the offer, the additional terms materially alter the offer, or the offeror gives reasonable notice of his objection to the additional terms. On the other hand, if one or both parties are *not* merchants then the counter-offer becomes simply a proposal for additions to the contract. Section 2–207(2) therefore establishes a *weak first-shot rule* for contracts that are established by mis-matched offer and acceptance under § 2–207(1) clause 1. The code creates a presumption that the terms of the original offer govern in such cases: for non-merchants, this presumption applies quite generally, and it applies even to merchants insofar as the acceptance makes a material difference or insofar as merchant offerors object to acceptances' departures from their offers either before or after the acceptances arrive.[10]

This is all fairly straightforward. But § 2–207(1) clause 2 immediately appears to complicate the approach of § 2–207(1) clause 1, and indeed to cause real problems. Section 2–207(1) clause 2 states a way of avoiding the regime that clause 1 introduces. Moreover, because it is an open question what legal order governs once clause 1 does not, clause 2 may even create a way to return to the common law approach—including both the mirror

---

10. Note that § 2–207(1) refers to additional or different terms whereas § 2–207(2) refers to only additional terms.

image rule and the last shot doctrine. Finally, § 2–207(1) clause 2 can be triggered simply by "expressly" making an acceptance "conditional" on the terms in respect of which it departs from the offer that it accepts.

So § 2–207(1) clause 2 leaves courts with two important interpretive problems. First, they must say just when a conditional acceptance triggers the clause, and operates as a rejection and counteroffer which begins bargaining anew, as it were. Furthermore, it can of course happen that a conditional acceptance operates in this way—to constitute a counteroffer whose acceptance is expressly conditional on assent to the departures from the initial offer that it contains—but the offeree does *not* assent to these terms, so that her initial offer remains in play. In such a case, § 2–207(1) clause 2 suggests that the offer and counteroffer have not created a contract. Of course, the parties might nevertheless act as if there exists a contract. And now the question inevitably arises, what, in this case, are the terms of the contract that governs their conduct?

Section 2–207(3) appears to govern this case. The section applies when parties exchange non-mirror-image forms (offer and counteroffer) whose terms (roughly, express insistences on the points at which they differ) prevent a contract from being formed under § 2–207(1) and yet nevertheless proceed as if a contract exists between them. In such a case, the common law would apply the last-shot doctrine, and the last form sent before performance commenced—usually, a form that the seller sent with the shipment—would govern. Section 2–207(3) abandons this rule. Instead of making the last form govern, it bases the contract on the terms on which the writings of the two parties agree. It then adds to the contract such supplementary terms—for example, concerning place of delivery (§ 2–308) or implied warranties (§§ 2–314, 2–315)—as are provided as defaults by other provisions of the UCC.

This seems perhaps a little convoluted, but it is in the end clear enough. UCC § 2–207, taken as a whole, makes its theme replacing the common law's mirror image rule and last shot doctrine with a regime in which even non-mirror image offer and acceptance can create a contract (without any need for the parties to begin performing) and, furthermore, the terms of the contract do not favor the last form sent. The convolutions, however, threatened the clarity and hence the effectiveness of the statute, as *Roto–Lith* vividly illustrates.

The buyer in *Roto–Lith* sent the seller-manufacturer a purchase order for emulsion that the buyer wanted to use in gluing together bags that it made. The seller responded with an acknowledgement that included language limiting its liability—language to which the buyer did not object. Next, the seller shipped and the buyer accepted and paid for the goods. *Roto–Lith* thus presents a classic battle of the forms—between a buyer's form that did not include limitations of liability and a seller's form that did. The central issue of the case is whether, in light of the parties' proceeding to performance in spite of this variance between their forms, the seller's limitations of remedy are in or out of the contract.

The *Roto–Lith* court, purporting to apply UCC § 2–207, found for the seller. It observed that the seller's form, by insisting on limited liability, materially altered the buyer's offer solely to the disadvantage of the buyer-offeror. The court thus interpreted the form as making acceptance express-ly conditional on the buyer's assent to its additional terms. Accordingly, the court reasoned, UCC § 2–207 clause 2 applied to the case, and this, the court thought, took the case out of § 2–207 altogether. The court then applied the common law—the mirror image rule and last shot doctrine— and construed the seller's form as a rejection of the buyer's offer and a counteroffer, which the buyer accepted by accepting the goods. Accordingly, the court held, the seller's limitations of liability were in the contract, and the buyer could not recover the damages it sought.

This all seems straightforward enough, but the interpretive approach in *Roto–Lith* effectively eviscerates § 2–207. *Roto–Lith* attacked the spirit of § 2–207 in two respects. First, the *Roto–Lith* approach is ready to interpret almost *any* counteroffers that propose new or different terms as *expressly* conditioning their acceptance of the offers to which they respond on the offerors' assent to these terms. The seller's acknowledgement in *Roto–Lith merely included* the new and different terms limiting liability; it said nothing whatsoever about insisting on these terms or indeed even about their importance to the seller. Yet the *Roto–Lith* court was willing to understand the acknowledgement as expressly conditioning acceptance on these terms based merely on the fact that they advantaged the seller who sent it. In this way, the *Roto–Lith* approach to § 2–207 triggers § 2–207(1) clause 2 quickly and hence often, thereby taking many (most?) cases out of the regime established by §§ 2–207(1) clause 1 and 2–207(2).

And second, the *Roto–Lith* court appears to conclude that where § 2–207(1) clause 2 applies to contract formation, the content of a contract that arises through the parties' performance will be determined not by § 2–207(3), but rather by the common law, and hence by the last shot doctrine.

Together, these features of *Roto–Lith* effectively deprive UCC § 2–207 of any substantial capacity to revise the common law regime: the first feature of the opinion entails that § 2–207(2)'s approach to contractual construction in the battle of the forms will almost never apply; and the second feature of the opinion entails that § 2–207(3)'s approach will almost never apply. On the *Roto–Lith* approach, the UCC leaves little impression on the law in this area.

Ionics takes a very different approach to UCC § 2–207, and gives that section a substantial impact on the law. The seller in *Ionics* sold thermo-stats, some of which the buyer wanted to obtain for use in water coolers that it manufactured. The buyer sent the seller a purchase order, which included, in fine print, clauses that: (1) claimed for the buyer broad remedies generally available in contract law; and (2) required any accep-tance of the purchase order by the seller to be on the terms set forth in that order, including the broad remedy provisions from (1). The buyer also sent the seller a letter separately insisting that if the seller objected to any terms in the buyer's purchase order, it must so inform the buyer; otherwise, the buyer would take the seller to have accepted its terms.

The seller in *Ionics* acknowledged receipt of the buyer's purchase order with its own form, which included, again in fine print, clauses that: (1) limited the seller's liability and the buyer's remedies much more narrowly than the common law; and (2) insisted that any acceptance of the goods by the buyer must be on the terms of the seller's "counteroffer," that the seller objected to any terms at variance with its form (including the limitation of remedy in (1)), and that the buyer must expressly communicate any objections it had to the seller's terms and would, absent such express communication, be taken by the seller to accept its form.

The seller then delivered and the buyer accepted the thermostats. A dispute subsequently arose, in which the extent of the seller's liability mattered. Accordingly, it became important to determine whether the buyer's form, the seller's form, or something else fixed the parties' obligations in this respect.

As in *Roto–Lith* so in *Ionics* the facts present a classic battle of the forms. Moreover, the battle lines in *Ionics* are, if anything, more starkly drawn than they were in *Roto–Lith*. There, the parties' forms merely contradicted each other in substance, and the court *assumed* that the seller's form made its acceptance conditional on the buyer's assent to the new and different terms that the form included. Here, the parties' forms could hardly be more explicit in their insistence that their own terms must govern any eventual contract. Accordingly, whereas in *Roto–Lith* a key question concerned how readily § 2–207(1) clause 2 might be triggered, this clause clearly applies in *Ionics*. The only issue, in *Ionics*, is what § 2–207 directs a court to do with contracts governed by this clause.

Under *Roto–Lith*, the answer would be clear. The second central proposition asserted by the *Roto–Lith* court insists that all cases in which § 2–207(1) clause 2 applies to how a contract is formed are henceforth removed from § 2–207 altogether, so that the content of contracts formed in this way is not determined by § 2–207(3) but rather by the common law, and in particular by the last shot doctrine.

The *Ionics* court, however, refuses to follow this path, and instead announces that *Roto–Lith* is overruled. The *Roto–Lith* approach to UCC § 2–207 renders the statute effectively nugatory, whereas the purpose of the statute is clearly to change the common law, and to reject the last shot doctrine. Moreover, as *Ionics* observes, the plain language of § 2–207, and in particular of § 2–207(3), says that this section applies in the case at issue. The writings of the parties, in this case, did not otherwise establish a contract (because they came under § 2–207(1) clause 2), but the conduct of the parties nevertheless recognized the existence of a contract. Accordingly, under § 2–207(3), the terms concerning which the parties disagree fall out of their contract, and the terms of this contract are those on which the parties agree, supplemented by whatever default terms the UCC supplies to fill in gaps left by the terms that have been struck out. In *Ionics*, these included the UCC's default warranty terms.

Thus, whereas *Roto–Lith* effectively eviscerated UCC § 2–207 in favor of the common law, and in particular the last shot doctrine, *Ionics* asserts § 2–207 against the common law. First, *Ionics* interprets offerors as insisting on their terms even in the face of acceptances that propose different terms, including even when the offerors, on receiving the contradictory acceptances, never expressly re-assert the terms in their offers. In this way, *Ionics* readily finds battles of the forms and so triggers the UCC's mechanisms for fixing the content of contracts created in spite of mis-matched offer and acceptance. And second, *Ionics* carries its tendency to understand parties as insisting on their own terms into the construction of these content-fixing mechanisms. The *Ionics* court places a low threshold on to triggering § 2–207(2)(c), which prevents either side's contradictory terms from getting into the contract, and hence also on triggering § 2–207(3), which strikes down both sides' contradictory terms and replaces them with UCC defaults. In this sense, *Ionics* might be understood as ultimately favoring a neither shot rule.

The conflict between *Roto–Lith* and *Ionics* might be seen, in retrospect, as a natural and perhaps even inevitable consequence of a convoluted and badly drafted statute. The general gestalt of UCC § 2–207 is to reject the common law, and in particular the power that the last shot doctrine gives the party, usually the seller, that sends the final form. But the text of the statute fails clearly to implement this sensibility, and it is a canon of statutory interpretation that statutes in derogation of the common law shall be narrowly construed. The *Roto–Lith* court might be understood simply as protecting the common law. By the time *Ionics* was decided, the tide had turned sufficiently against the common law that a new court was willing to implement the spirit of the UCC. The proposed revision to UCC § 2–207 further extended this spirit, and tried to do so through more artful drafting. The revision is worth reading in spite of having been withdrawn, as it presents an example of how a better-drafted approach to the battle of the forms might go.

Uniform Commercial Code

§ 2–207 Terms of Contract; Effect of Confirmation. (proposed 2003 revision)

Subject to Section 2–202 [concerning parol evidence], if (i) conduct by both parties recognizes the existence of a contract although their records do not otherwise establish a contract, (ii) a contract is formed by an offer and acceptance, or (iii) a contract formed in any manner is confirmed by a record that contains terms additional to or different from those in the contract being confirmed, the terms of the contract are:

(a) terms that appear in the records of both parties;

(b) terms, whether in a record or not, to which both parties agree; and

(c) terms supplied or incorporated under any provision of this Act.

Comments

1. This section applies to all contracts for the sale of goods, and it is not limited only to those contracts where there has been a "battle of the forms."

2. This section applies only when a contract has been created under another section of this Article. The purpose of this section is solely to determine the terms of the contract. When forms are exchanged before or during performance, the result from the application of this section differs from the prior Section 2–207 of this Article and the common law in that this section gives no preference to either the first or the last form; the same test is applied to the terms in each. Terms in a record that insist on all of that record's terms and no other terms as a condition of contract formation have no effect on the operation of this section. When one party insists in that party's record that its own terms are a condition to contract formation, if that party does not subsequently perform or otherwise acknowledge the existence of a contract, if the other party does not agree to those terms, the record's insistence on its own terms will keep a contract from being formed under Sections 2–204 or 2–206, and this section is not applicable. As with original Section 2–207, the courts will have to distinguish between "confirmations" that are addressed in this section and "modifications" that are addressed in Section 2–209.

3. Terms of a contract may be found not only in the consistent terms of records of the parties but also from a straightforward acceptance of an offer, and an expression of acceptance accompanied by one or more additional terms might demonstrate the offeree's agreement to the terms of the offer. If, for example, a buyer sent a purchase order with technical specifications and the seller responded with a record stating "Thank you for your order. We will fill it promptly. Note that we do not make deliveries after 3:00 p.m. on Fridays." it might be reasonable to conclude that both parties agreed to the technical specifications.

Similarly, an offeree's performance is sometimes the acceptance of an offer. If, for example, a buyer sends a purchase order, there is no oral or other agreement, and the seller delivers the goods in response to the purchase order—but the seller does not send the seller's own acknowledgment or acceptance—the seller should normally be treated as having agreed to the terms of the purchase order.

If, however, parties exchange records with conflicting or inconsistent terms, but conduct by both parties recognizes the existence of a contract, subsection (a) provides that the terms of the contract are terms that appear in the records of both parties. But even when both parties send records, there could be nonverbal agreement to additional or different terms that appear in only one of two records. If, for example, both parties' forms called for the sale of 700,000 nuts and bolts but the purchase order or another record of the buyer conditioned the sale on a test of a sample to see if the nuts and bolts would perform properly, the seller's sending a small sample to the buyer might be construed to be an agreement to the buyer's condition. It might also be found that the contract called for arbitration when both forms provided for arbitration but each contained immaterially different arbitration provisions.

In a rare case the terms in the records of both parties might not become part of the contract. This could be the case, for example, when the parties contemplated an agreement to a single negotiated record, and each party submitted to the other party similar proposals and then commenced performance, but the parties never reached a negotiated agreement because of the differences over crucial terms. There is a variety of verbal and nonverbal behavior that may suggest agreement to another's record. This section leaves the interpretation of that behavior to the discretion of the courts.

4.   An "agreement" may include terms derived from a course of performance, a course of dealing, and usage of trade. *See* Sections 1–201(a)(2) and 1–303. If the members of a trade, or if the contracting parties, expect to be bound by a term that appears in the record of only one of the contracting parties, that term is part of the agreement. However, repeated use of a particular term or repeated failure to object to a term on another's record is not normally sufficient in itself to establish a course of performance, a course of dealing or a trade usage.

5.   The section omits any specific treatment of terms attached to the goods, or in or on the container in which the goods are delivered. This article takes no position on whether a court should follow the reasoning in Step–Saver Data Systems, Inc. v. Wyse Technology, 939 F.2d 91 (3d Cir. 1991) and Klocek v. Gateway, Inc. 104 F. Supp. 2d 1332 (D. Kan. 2000) (original 2–207 governs) or the contrary reasoning in Hill v. Gateway 2000, 105 F. 3d 1147 (7th Cir. 1997) (original 2–207 inapplicable).

* * *

The revised version of § 2–207 would have carried forward the basic intuitions that drove the old. It addresses to all contracts, whether or not there has been a battle of the forms. Moreover, the revision no longer purported to determine whether the parties have formed a contract. This was left to UCC § 2–204, which said that "A contract for sale of goods may be made in any manner sufficient to show agreement, including offer and acceptance, conduct by both parties which recognizes the existence of a contract, the interaction of electronic agents, and the interaction of an electronic agent and an individual" and UCC § 2–206, which discussed the various means of acceptance and, among other things, replicated the old UCC § 2–207's statement that "a definite and seasonable expression of acceptance in a record operates as an acceptance even if it contains terms additional to or different from the offer." Finally, § 2–207 no longer distinguished between first and last forms but applied the same standard to each. This standard incorporates into the contract terms on which the parties agree and strikes down terms on which they disagree. It then fills in gaps with UCC defaults.

Comment [5] to the revised § 2–207 expressly excepted an important and controversial class of contracts from the section's scope. These are illustrated by the following cases.

Step–Saver Data Sys. v. Wyse Tech.

United States Court of Appeals for the Third Circuit, 1991.
939 F.2d 91.

■ WISDOM, CIRCUIT JUDGE.

The "Limited Use License Agreement" printed on a package containing a copy of a computer program raises the central issue in this appeal. The trial judge held that the terms of the Limited Use License Agreement governed the purchase of the package, and, therefore, granted the software producer, The Software Link, Inc. ("TSL"), a directed verdict on claims of breach of warranty brought by a disgruntled purchaser, Step–Saver Data Systems, Inc. We disagree with the district court's determination of the legal effect of the license, and reverse and remand the warranty claims for further consideration.

Step–Saver raises several other issues, but we do not find these issues warrant reversal. We, therefore, affirm in all other respects.

I.   FACTUAL AND PROCEDURAL BACKGROUND

The growth in the variety of computer hardware and software has created a strong market for these products. It has also created a difficult choice for consumers, as they must somehow decide which of the many available products will best suit their needs. To assist consumers in this decision process, some companies will evaluate the needs of particular groups of potential computer users, compare those needs with the available technology, and develop a package of hardware and software to satisfy those needs. Beginning in 1981, Step–Saver performed this function as a value added retailer for International Business Machine (IBM) products. It would combine hardware and software to satisfy the word processing, data management, and communications needs for offices of physicians and lawyers. It originally marketed single computer systems, based primarily on the IBM personal computer.

As a result of advances in micro-computer technology, Step–Saver developed and marketed a multi-user system. With a multi-user system, only one computer is required. Terminals are attached, by cable, to the main computer. From these terminals, a user can access the programs available on the main computer.

After evaluating the available technology, Step–Saver selected a program by TSL, entitled Multilink Advanced, as the operating system for the multi-user system. Step–Saver selected WY–60 terminals manufactured by Wyse, and used an IBM AT as the main computer. For applications software, Step–Saver included in the package several off-the-shelf programs, designed to run under Microsoft's Disk Operating System ("MS–

DOS"), as well as several programs written by Step–Saver. Step–Saver began marketing the system in November of 1986, and sold one hundred forty-two systems mostly to law and medical offices before terminating sales of the system in March of 1987. Almost immediately upon installation of the system, Step–Saver began to receive complaints from some of its customers.

Step–Saver, in addition to conducting its own investigation of the problems, referred these complaints to Wyse and TSL, and requested technical assistance in resolving the problems. After several preliminary attempts to address the problems, the three companies were unable to reach a satisfactory solution, and disputes developed among the three concerning responsibility for the problems. As a result, the problems were never solved. At least twelve of Step–Saver's customers filed suit against Step–Saver because of the problems with the multi-user system.

Once it became apparent that the three companies would not be able to resolve their dispute amicably, Step–Saver filed suit for declaratory judgment, seeking indemnity from either Wyse or TSL, or both, for any costs incurred by Step–Saver in defending and resolving the customers' law suits. The district court dismissed this complaint, finding that the issue was not ripe for judicial resolution. We affirmed the dismissal on appeal. Step–Saver then filed a second complaint alleging breach of warranties by both TSL and Wyse and intentional misrepresentations by TSL. The district court's actions during the resolution of this second complaint provide the foundation for this appeal.

On the first day of trial, the district court specifically agreed with the basic contention of TSL that the form language printed on each package containing the Multilink Advanced program ("the box-top license") was the complete and exclusive agreement between Step–Saver and TSL under § 2–202 of the Uniform Commercial Code (UCC). Based on § 2–316 of the UCC, the district court held that the box-top license disclaimed all express and implied warranties otherwise made by TSL. The court therefore granted TSL's motion in limine to exclude all evidence of the earlier oral and written express warranties allegedly made by TSL. After Step–Saver presented its case, the district court granted a directed verdict in favor of TSL on the intentional misrepresentation claim, holding the evidence insufficient as a matter of law to establish two of the five elements of a prima facie case: (1) fraudulent intent on the part of TSL in making the representations; and (2) reasonable reliance by Step–Saver. The trial judge requested briefing on several issues related to Step–Saver's remaining express warranty claim against TSL. While TSL and Step–Saver prepared briefs on these issues, the trial court permitted Wyse to proceed with its defense. On the third day of Wyse's defense, the trial judge, after considering the additional briefing by Step–Saver and TSL, directed a verdict in favor of TSL on Step–Saver's remaining warranty claims, and dismissed TSL from the case.

The trial proceeded on Step–Saver's breach of warranties claims against Wyse. At the conclusion of Wyse's evidence, the district judge denied Step–Saver's request for rebuttal testimony on the issue of the ordinary uses of the WY–60 terminal. The district court instructed the jury on the issues of express warranty and implied warranty of fitness for a particular purpose. Over Step–Saver's objection, the district court found insufficient evidence to support a finding that Wyse had breached its implied warranty of merchantability, and refused to instruct the jury on such warranty. The jury returned a verdict in favor of Wyse on the two warranty issues submitted.

Step–Saver appeals on four points. (1) Step–Saver and TSL did not intend the box-top license to be a complete and final expression of the terms of their agreement. (2) There was sufficient evidence to support each element of Step–Saver's contention that TSL was guilty of intentional misrepresentation. (3) There was sufficient evidence to submit Step–Saver's implied warranty of merchantability claim against Wyse to the jury. (4) The trial court abused its discretion by excluding from the evidence a letter addressed to Step–Saver from Wyse, and by refusing to permit Step–Saver to introduce rebuttal testimony on the ordinary uses of the WY–60 terminal.

II. THE EFFECT OF THE BOX–TOP LICENSE

The relationship between Step–Saver and TSL began in the fall of 1984 when Step–Saver asked TSL for information on an early version of the Multilink program. TSL provided Step–Saver with a copy of the early program, known simply as Multilink, without charge to permit Step–Saver to test the program to see what it could accomplish. Step–Saver performed some tests with the early program, but did not market a system based on it.

In the summer of 1985, Step–Saver noticed some advertisements in Byte magazine for a more powerful version of the Multilink program, known as Multilink Advanced. Step–Saver requested information from TSL concerning this new version of the program, and allegedly was assured by sales representatives that the new version was compatible with ninety percent of the programs available "off-the-shelf" for computers using MS–DOS. The sales representatives allegedly made a number of additional specific representations of fact concerning the capabilities of the Multilink Advanced program.

Based on these representations, Step–Saver obtained several copies of the Multilink Advanced program in the spring of 1986, and conducted tests with the program. After these tests, Step–Saver decided to market a multi-user system which used the Multilink Advanced program. From August of 1986 through March of 1987, Step–Saver purchased and resold 142 copies of the Multilink Advanced program. Step–Saver would typically purchase copies of the program in the following manner. First, Step–Saver would telephone TSL and place an order. (Step–Saver would typically order twenty copies of the program at a time.) TSL would accept the order and promise, while on the telephone, to ship the goods promptly. After the telephone order, Step–Saver would send a purchase order, detailing the items to be purchased, their price, and shipping and payment terms. TSL would ship the order promptly, along with an invoice. The invoice would contain terms essentially identical with those on Step–Saver's purchase order: price, quantity, and shipping and payment terms. No reference was made during the telephone calls, or on either the purchase orders or the invoices with regard to a disclaimer of any warranties.

Printed on the package of each copy of the program, however, would be a copy of the box-top license. The box-top license contains five terms relevant to this action:

(1) The box-top license provides that the customer has not purchased the software itself, but has merely obtained a personal, non-transferable license to use the program.

(2) The box-top license, in detail and at some length, disclaims all express and implied warranties except for a warranty that the disks contained in the box are free from defects.

(3) The box-top license provides that the sole remedy available to a purchaser of the program is to return a defective disk for replacement; the license excludes any liability for damages, direct or consequential, caused by the use of the program.

(4) The box-top license contains an integration clause, which provides that the box-top license is the final and complete expression of the terms of the parties's agreement.

(5) The box-top license states: "Opening this package indicates your acceptance of these terms and conditions. If you do not agree with them, you should promptly return the package unopened to the person from whom you purchased it within fifteen days from date of purchase and your money will be refunded to you by that person."

The district court, without much discussion, held, as a matter of law, that the box-top license was the final and complete expression of the terms of the parties's agreement. Because the district court decided the questions of contract formation and interpretation as issues of law, we review the district court's resolution of these questions *de novo*.

Step–Saver contends that the contract for each copy of the program was formed when TSL agreed, on the telephone, to ship the copy at the agreed price. The box-top license, argues Step–Saver, was a material alteration to the parties's contract which did not become a part of the contract under UCC § 2–207. Alternatively, Step–Saver argues that the undisputed evidence establishes that the parties did not intend the box-top license as a final and complete expression of the terms of their agreement, and, therefore, the parol evidence rule of UCC § 2–202 would not apply.

TSL argues that the contract between TSL and Step–Saver did not come into existence until Step–Saver received the program, saw the terms of the license, and opened the program packaging. TSL contends that too many material terms were omitted from the telephone discussion for that discussion to establish a contract for the software. Second, TSL contends that its acceptance of Step–Saver's telephone offer was conditioned on

Step–Saver's acceptance of the terms of the box-top license. Therefore, TSL argues, it did not accept Step–Saver's telephone offer, but made a counter-offer represented by the terms of the box-top license, which was accepted when Step–Saver opened each package. Third, TSL argues that, however the contract was formed, Step–Saver was aware of the warranty disclaimer, and that Step–Saver, by continuing to order and accept the product with knowledge of the disclaimer, assented to the disclaimer.

In analyzing these competing arguments, we first consider whether the license should be treated as an integrated writing under UCC § 2–202, as a proposed modification under UCC § 2–209, or as a written confirmation under UCC § 2–207. Finding that UCC § 2–207 best governs our resolution of the effect of the box-top license, we then consider whether, under UCC § 2–207, the terms of the box-top license were incorporated into the parties's agreement.

A.   *Does UCC § 2–207 Govern the Analysis?*

As a basic principle, we agree with Step–Saver that UCC § 2–207 governs our analysis. We see no need to parse the parties's various actions to decide exactly when the parties formed a contract. TSL has shipped the product, and Step–Saver has accepted and paid for each copy of the program. The parties's performance demonstrates the existence of a contract. The dispute is, therefore, not over the existence of a contract, but the nature of its terms. When the parties's conduct establishes a contract, but the parties have failed to adopt expressly a particular writing as the terms of their agreement, and the writings exchanged by the parties do not agree, UCC § 2–207 determines the terms of the contract.

As stated by the official comment to § 2–207:

1.   This section is intended to deal with two typical situations. The one is the written confirmation, where an agreement has been reached either orally or by informal correspondence between the parties and is followed by one or more of the parties sending formal memoranda embodying the terms so far as agreed upon and adding terms not discussed....

2.   Under this Article a proposed deal which in commercial understanding has in fact been closed is recognized as a contract. Therefore, any additional matter contained in the confirmation or in the acceptance falls within subsection (2) and must be regarded as a proposal for an added term unless the acceptance is made conditional on the acceptance of the additional or different terms.

Although UCC § 2–202 permits the parties to reduce an oral agreement to writing, and UCC § 2–209 permits the parties to modify an existing contract without additional consideration, a writing will be a final expression of, or a binding modification to, an earlier agreement only if the parties so intend. It is undisputed that Step–Saver never expressly agreed to the terms of the box-top license, either as a final expression of, or a modification to, the parties's agreement. In fact, Barry Greebel, the President of Step–Saver, testified without dispute that he objected to the terms of the box-top license as applied to Step–Saver. In the absence of evidence demonstrating an express intent to adopt a writing as a final expression of, or a modification to, an earlier agreement, we find UCC § 2–207 to provide the appropriate legal rules for determining whether such an intent can be inferred from continuing with the contract after receiving a writing containing additional or different terms.

To understand why the terms of the license should be considered under § 2–207 in this case, we review briefly the reasons behind § 2–207. Under the common law of sales, and to some extent still for contracts outside the UCC, an acceptance that varied any term of the offer operated as a rejection of the offer, and simultaneously made a counteroffer. This common law formality was known as the mirror image rule, because the terms of the acceptance had to mirror the terms of the offer to be effective. If the offeror proceeded with the contract despite the differing terms of the supposed acceptance, he would, by his performance, constructively accept the terms of the "counteroffer", and be bound by its terms. As a result of these rules, the terms of the party who sent the last form, typically the seller, would become the terms of the parties's contract. This result was known as the "last shot rule".

The UCC, in § 2–207, rejected this approach. Instead, it recognized that, while a party may desire the terms detailed in its form if a dispute, in fact, arises, most parties do not expect a dispute to arise when they first enter into a contract. As a result, most parties will proceed with the transaction even if they know that the terms of their form would not be enforced. The insight behind the rejection of the last shot rule is that it would be unfair to bind the buyer of goods to the standard terms of the seller, when neither party cared sufficiently to establish expressly the terms of their agreement, simply because the seller sent the last form. Thus, UCC § 2–207 establishes a legal rule that proceeding with a contract after receiving a writing that purports to define the terms of the parties's contract is not sufficient to establish the party's consent to the terms of the writing to the extent that the terms of the writing either add to, or differ from, the terms detailed in the parties's earlier writings or discussions. In the absence of a party's express assent to the additional or different terms of the writing, section 2–207 provides a default rule that the parties intended, as the terms of their agreement, those terms to which both parties have agreed, along with any terms implied by the provisions of the UCC.

The reasons that led to the rejection of the last shot rule, and the adoption of section 2–207, apply fully in this case. TSL never mentioned during the parties's negotiations leading to the purchase of the programs, nor did it, at any time, obtain Step–Saver's express assent to, the terms of the box-top license. Instead, TSL contented itself with attaching the terms to the packaging of the software, even though those terms differed substantially from those previously discussed by the parties. Thus, the box-top license, in this case, is best seen as one more form in a battle of forms, and the question of whether Step–Saver has agreed to be bound by the terms of the box-top license is best resolved by applying the legal principles detailed in section 2–207.

B. *Application of § 2–207*

TSL advances several reasons why the terms of the box-top license should be incorporated into the parties's agreement under a § 2–207 analysis. First, TSL argues that the parties's contract was not formed until Step–Saver received the package, saw the terms of the box-top license, and opened the package, thereby consenting to the terms of the license. TSL argues that a contract defined without reference to the specific terms provided by the box-top license would necessarily fail for indefiniteness. Second, TSL argues that the box-top license was a conditional acceptance and counter-offer under § 2–207(1). Third, TSL argues that Step–Saver, by continuing to order and use the product with notice of the terms of the box-top license, consented to the terms of the box-top license.

1. Was the contract sufficiently definite?

TSL argues that the parties intended to license the copies of the program, and that several critical terms could only be determined by referring to the box-top license. Pressing the point, TSL argues that it is impossible to tell, without referring to the box-top license, whether the parties intended a sale of a copy of the program or a license to use a copy. TSL cites *Bethlehem Steel Corp. v. Litton Industries*, 488 A.2d 581 (1985), in support of its position that any contract defined without reference to the terms of the box-top license would fail for indefiniteness.

From the evidence, it appears that the following terms, at the least, were discussed and agreed to, apart from the box-top license: (1) the specific goods involved; (2) the quantity; and (3) the price. TSL argues that the following terms were only defined in the box-top license: (1) the nature of the transaction, sale or license; and (2) the warranties, if any, available. TSL argues that these two terms are essential to creating a sufficiently definite contract. We disagree.

Section 2–204(3) of the UCC provides:

> Even though one or more terms are left open a contract for sale does not fail for indefiniteness if the parties have intended to make a contract and there is a reasonably certain basis for giving an appropriate remedy.

Unlike the terms omitted by the parties in *Bethlehem Steel Corp.*, the two terms cited by TSL are not "gaping holes in a multi-million dollar contract that no one but the parties themselves could fill." First, the rights of the respective parties under the federal copyright law if the transaction is characterized as a sale of a copy of the program are nearly identical to the parties's respective rights under the terms of the box-top license. Second, the UCC provides for express and implied warranties if the seller fails to disclaim expressly those warranties. Thus, even though warranties are an important term left blank by the parties, the default rules of the UCC fill in that blank.

We hold that contract was sufficiently definite without the terms provided by the box-top license.

2.   The box-top license as a counter-offer?

TSL advances two reasons why its box-top license should be considered a conditional acceptance under UCC § 2–207(1). First, TSL argues that the express language of the box-top license, including the integration clause and the phrase "opening this product indicates your acceptance of these terms", made TSL's acceptance "expressly conditional on assent to the additional or different terms". Second, TSL argues that the box-top license, by permitting return of the product within fifteen days if the purchaser does not agree to the terms stated in the license (the "refund offer"), establishes that TSL's acceptance was conditioned on Step–Saver's assent to the terms of the box-top license, citing *Monsanto Agricultural Products Co. v. Edenfield*, 426 So.2d 574 (Fla.Dist.Ct.App. 1982). While we are not certain that a conditional acceptance analysis applies when a contract is established by performance, we assume that it does and consider TSL's arguments.

To determine whether a writing constitutes a conditional acceptance, courts have established three tests. Because neither Georgia nor Pennsylvania has expressly adopted a test to determine when a written confirmation constitutes a conditional acceptance, we consider these three tests to determine which test the state courts would most likely apply.

Under the first test, an offeree's response is a conditional acceptance to the extent it states a term "materially altering the contractual obligations solely to the disadvantage of the offeror". Pennsylvania, at least, has implicitly rejected this test. In *Herzog Oil Field Service, Inc.*, 570 A.2d 549 (Pa.Super.Ct. 1990) a Pennsylvania Superior Court analyzed a term in a written confirmation under UCC § 2–207(2), rather than as a conditional acceptance even though the term materially altered the terms of the agreement to the sole disadvantage of the offeror.

Furthermore, we note that adopting this test would conflict with the express provision of UCC § 2–207(2)(b). Under § 2–207(2)(b), additional terms in a written confirmation that "materially alter [the contract]" are construed "as proposals for addition to the contract", not as conditional acceptances.

A second approach considers an acceptance conditional when certain key words or phrases are used, such as a written confirmation stating that the terms of the confirmation are "the only ones upon which we will accept orders". The third approach requires the offeree to demonstrate an unwillingness to proceed with the transaction unless the additional or different terms are included in the contract.

Although we are not certain that these last two approaches would generate differing answers, we adopt the third approach for our analysis because it best reflects the understanding of commercial transactions developed in the UCC. Section 2–207 attempts to distinguish between: (1) those standard terms in a form confirmation, which the party would like a court to incorporate into the contract in the event of a dispute; and (2) the actual terms the parties understand to govern their agreement. The third test properly places the burden on the party asking a court to enforce its form to demonstrate that a particular term is a part of the parties's commercial bargain.

Using this test, it is apparent that the integration clause and the "consent by opening" language is not sufficient to render TSL's acceptance conditional. As other courts have recognized, this type of language provides no real indication that the party is willing to forego the transaction if the additional language is not included in the contract.

The second provision provides a more substantial indication that TSL was willing to forego the contract if the terms of the box-top license were not accepted by Step–Saver. On its face, the box-top license states that TSL will refund the purchase price if the purchaser does not agree to the terms of the license. Even with such a refund term, however, the offeree/counter-offeror may be relying on the purchaser's investment in time and energy in reaching this point in the transaction to prevent the purchaser from returning the item. Because a purchaser has made a decision to buy a particular product and has actually obtained the product, the purchaser may use it despite the refund offer, regardless of the additional terms specified after the contract formed. But we need not decide whether such a refund offer could ever amount to a conditional acceptance; the undisputed evidence in this case demonstrates that the terms of the license were not sufficiently important that TSL would forego its sales to Step–Saver if TSL could not obtain Step–Saver's consent to those terms.

As discussed, Mr. Greebel testified that TSL assured him that the box-top license did not apply to Step–Saver, as Step–Saver was not the end user of the Multilink Advanced program. Supporting this testimony, TSL on two occasions asked Step–Saver to sign agreements that would put in formal terms the relationship between Step–Saver and TSL. Both proposed agreements contained warranty disclaimer and limitation of remedy terms similar to those contained in the box-top license. Step–Saver refused to sign the agreements; nevertheless, TSL continued to sell copies of Multilink Advanced to Step–Saver.

Additionally, TSL asks us to infer, based on the refund offer, that it was willing to forego its sales to Step–Saver unless Step–Saver agreed to the terms of the box-top license. Such an inference is inconsistent with the fact that both parties agree that the terms of the box-top license *did not represent the parties's agreement* with respect to Step–Saver's right to transfer the copies of the Multilink Advanced program. Although the box-top license prohibits the transfer, by Step–Saver, of its copies of the program, both parties agree that Step–Saver was entitled to transfer its copies to the purchasers of the Step–Saver multi-user system. Thus, TSL was willing to proceed with the transaction despite the fact that one of the terms of the box-top license was not included in the contract between TSL and Step–Saver. We see no basis in the terms of the box-top license for inferring that a reasonable offeror would understand from the refund offer that certain terms of the box-top license, such as the warranty disclaimers, were essential to TSL, while others such as the non-transferability provision were not.

Based on these facts, we conclude that TSL did not clearly express its unwillingness to proceed with the transactions unless its additional terms were incorporated into the parties's agreement. The box-top license did not, therefore, constitute a conditional acceptance under UCC § 2–207(1).

3. Did the parties's course of dealing establish that the parties had excluded any express or implied warranties associated with the software program?

TSL argues that because Step–Saver placed its orders for copies of the Multilink Advanced program with notice of the terms of the box-top license, Step–Saver is bound by the terms of the box-top license. Essentially, TSL is arguing that, even if the terms of the box-top license would not become part of the contract if the case involved only a single transaction, the repeated expression of those terms by TSL eventually incorporates them within the contract.

Ordinarily, a "course of dealing" or "course of performance" analysis focuses on the actions of the parties with respect to a particular issue. If, for example, a supplier of asphaltic paving material on two occasions gives a paving contractor price protection, a jury may infer that the parties have incorporated such a term in their agreement by their course of performance. Because this is the parties's first serious dispute, the parties have not previously taken any action with respect to the matters addressed by the warranty disclaimer and limitation of liability terms of the box-top license. Nevertheless, TSL seeks to extend the course of dealing analysis to this case where the only action has been the repeated sending of a particular form by TSL. While one court has concluded that terms repeated in a number of written confirmations eventually become part of the contract even though neither party ever takes any action with respect to the issue addressed by those terms, most courts have rejected such reasoning.

For two reasons, we hold that the repeated sending of a writing which contains certain standard terms, without any action with respect to the issues addressed by those terms, cannot constitute a course of dealing which would incorporate a term of the writing otherwise excluded under § 2–207. First, the repeated exchange of forms by the parties only tells Step–Saver that TSL *desires* certain terms. Given TSL's failure to obtain Step–Saver's express assent to these terms before it will ship the program, Step–Saver can reasonably believe that, while TSL desires certain terms, it has agreed to do business on other terms—those terms expressly agreed upon by the parties. Thus, even though Step–Saver would not be surprised to learn that TSL desires the terms of the box-top license, Step–Saver might well be surprised to learn that the terms of the box-top license have been incorporated into the parties's agreement.

Second, the seller in these multiple transaction cases will typically have the opportunity to negotiate the precise terms of the parties's agreement, as TSL sought to do in this case. The seller's unwillingness or inability to obtain a negotiated agreement reflecting its terms strongly suggests that, while the seller would like a court to incorporate its terms if a dispute were to arise, those terms are not a part of the parties's commercial bargain. For these reasons, we are not convinced that TSL's unilateral act of repeatedly sending copies of the box-top license with its product can establish a course of dealing between TSL and Step–Saver that resulted in the adoption of the terms of the box-top license.

With regard to more specific evidence as to the parties's course of dealing or performance, it appears that the parties have not incorporated the warranty disclaimer into their agreement. First, there is the evidence that TSL tried to obtain Step–Saver's express consent to the disclaimer and limitation of damages provision of the box-top license. Step–Saver refused to sign the proposed agreements. Second, when first notified of the problems with the program, TSL spent considerable time and energy attempting to solve the problems identified by Step–Saver.

Course of conduct is ordinarily a factual issue. But we hold that the actions of TSL in repeatedly sending a writing, whose terms would otherwise be excluded under UCC § 2–207, cannot establish a course of conduct between TSL and Step–Saver that adopted the terms of the writing.

4. Public policy concerns.

TSL has raised a number of public policy arguments focusing on the effect on the software industry of an adverse holding concerning the enforceability of the box-top license. We are not persuaded that requiring software companies to stand behind representations concerning their products will inevitably destroy the software industry. We emphasize, however, that we are following the well-established distinction between conspicuous disclaimers made available before the contract is formed and disclaimers made available only after the contract is formed. When a disclaimer is not expressed until after the contract is formed, UCC § 2–207 governs the interpretation of the contract, and, between merchants, such disclaimers, to the extent they materially alter the parties's agreement, are not incorporated into the parties's agreement.

If TSL wants relief for its business operations from this well-established rule, their arguments are better addressed to a legislature than a court. Indeed, we note that at least two states have enacted statutes that modify the applicable contract rules in this area, but both Georgia and Pennsylvania have retained the contract rules provided by the UCC.

C. *The Terms of the Contract*

Under section 2–207, an additional term detailed in the box-top license will not be incorporated into the parties's contract if the term's addition to the contract would materially alter the parties's agreement. Step–Saver alleges that several representations made by TSL constitute express warranties, and that valid implied warranties were also a part of the parties's agreement. Because the district court considered the box-top license to exclude all of these warranties, the district court did not consider whether other factors may act to exclude these warranties. The existence and nature of the warranties is primarily a factual question that we leave for the district court, but assuming that these warranties were included within the parties's original agreement, we must conclude that adding the disclaimer of warranty and limitation of remedies provisions from the box-top license would, as a matter of law, substantially alter the distribution of risk between Step–Saver and TSL. Therefore, under UCC § 2–207(2)(b), the disclaimer of warranty and limitation of remedies terms of the box-top license did not become a part of the parties's agreement.

Based on these considerations, we reverse the trial court's holding that the parties intended the box-top license to be a final and complete expression of the terms of their agreement. Despite the presence of an integration clause in the box-top license, the box-top license should have been treated as a written confirmation containing additional terms. Because the warranty disclaimer and limitation of remedies terms would materially alter the parties's agreement, these terms did not become a part of the parties's agreement. We remand for further consideration the express and implied warranty claims against TSL.

VI.

We will reverse the holding of the district court that the parties intended to adopt the box-top license as the complete and final expression of the terms of their agreement. We will remand for further consideration of Step–Saver's express and implied warranty claims against TSL. Finding a sufficient basis for the other decisions of the district court, we will affirm in all other respects.

ProCD, Incorporated v. Zeidenberg

United States Court of Appeals for the Seventh Circuit, 1996.
86 F.3d 1447.

■ EASTERBROOK, CIRCUIT JUDGE.

Must buyers of computer software obey the terms of shrinkwrap licenses? The district court held not, for two reasons: first, they are not contracts because the licenses are inside the box rather than printed on the outside; second, federal law forbids enforcement even if the licenses are contracts. 908 F.Supp. 640 (W.D.Wis.1996). The parties and numerous amici curiae have briefed many other issues, but these are the only two that matter—and we disagree with the district judge's conclusion on each. Shrinkwrap licenses are enforceable unless their terms are objectionable on grounds applicable to contracts in general (for example, if they violate a rule of positive law, or if they are unconscionable). Because no one argues that the terms of the license at issue here are troublesome, we remand with instructions to enter judgment for the plaintiff.

I

ProCD, the plaintiff, has compiled information from more than 3,000 telephone directories into a computer database. We may assume that this database cannot be copyrighted, although it is more complex, contains more information (nine-digit zip codes and census industrial codes), is organized differently, and therefore is more original than the single alphabetical directory at issue in *Feist Publications, Inc. v. Rural Telephone Service Co.,* 499 U.S. 340 (1991). See Paul J. Heald, The Vices of Originality, 1991 Sup.Ct. Rev. 143, 160–68. ProCD sells a version of the database, called SelectPhone (trademark), on CD–ROM discs. (CD–ROM means "compact disc-read only memory." The "shrinkwrap license" gets its name from the fact that retail software packages are covered in plastic or cellophane "shrinkwrap," and some vendors, though not ProCD, have written licenses that become effective as soon as the customer tears the wrapping from the package. Vendors prefer "end user license," but we use the more common term.) A proprietary method of compressing the data serves as effective encryption too. Customers decrypt and use the data with the aid of an application program that ProCD has written. This program, which is copyrighted, searches the database in response to users' criteria (such as "find all people named Tatum in Tennessee, plus all firms with 'Door Systems' in the corporate name"). The resulting lists (or, as ProCD prefers, "listings") can be read and manipulated by other software, such as word processing programs.

The database in SelectPhone (trademark) cost more than $10 million to compile and is expensive to keep current. It is much more valuable to some users than to others. The combination of names, addresses, and SIC codes enables manufacturers to compile lists of potential customers. Manufacturers and retailers pay high prices to specialized information intermediaries for such mailing lists; ProCD offers a potentially cheaper alternative. People with nothing to sell could use the database as a substitute for calling long distance information, or as a way to look up old friends who have moved to unknown towns, or just as an electronic substitute for the local phone book. ProCD decided to engage in price discrimination, selling its database to the general public for personal use at a low price (approximately $150 for the set of five discs) while selling information to the trade for a higher price. It has adopted some intermediate strategies too: access to the SelectPhone (trademark) database is available via the America Online service for the price America Online charges to its clients (approximately $3 per hour), but this service has been tailored to be useful only to the general public.

If ProCD had to recover all of its costs and make a profit by charging a single price—that is, if it could not charge more to commercial users than to the general public—it would have to raise the price substantially over $150. The ensuing reduction in sales would harm consumers who value the information at, say, $200. They get consumer surplus of $50 under the current arrangement but would cease to buy if the price rose substantially. If because of high elasticity of demand in the consumer segment of the market the only way to make a profit turned out to be a price attractive to commercial users alone, then all consumers would lose out—and so would the commercial clients, who would have to pay more for the listings because ProCD could not obtain any contribution toward costs from the consumer market.

To make price discrimination work, however, the seller must be able to control arbitrage. An air carrier sells tickets for less to vacationers than to business travelers, using advance purchase and Saturday-night-stay requirements to distinguish the categories. A producer of movies segments the market by time, releasing first to theaters, then to pay-per-view services, next to the videotape and laserdisc market, and finally to cable and commercial tv. Vendors of computer software have a harder task. Anyone can walk into a retail store and buy a box. Customers do not wear tags saying "commercial user" or "consumer user." Anyway, even a commercial-user-detector at the door would not work, because a consumer could buy the software and resell to a commercial user. That arbitrage would break down the price discrimination and drive up the minimum price at which ProCD would sell to anyone.

Instead of tinkering with the product and letting users sort themselves-for example, furnishing current data at a high price that would be attractive only to commercial customers, and two-year-old data at a low price-ProCD turned to the institution of contract. Every box containing its consumer product declares that the software comes with restrictions stated in an enclosed license. This license, which is encoded on the CD–ROM disks as well as printed in the manual, and which appears on a user's screen every time the software runs, limits use of the application program and listings to non-commercial purposes.

Matthew Zeidenberg bought a consumer package of SelectPhone (trademark) in 1994 from a retail outlet in Madison, Wisconsin, but decided to ignore the license. He formed Silken Mountain Web Services, Inc., to resell the information in the SelectPhone (trademark) database. The corporation makes the database available on the Internet to anyone willing to pay its price-which, needless to say, is less than ProCD charges its commercial customers. Zeidenberg has purchased two additional SelectPhone (trademark) packages, each with an updated version of the database, and made the latest information available over the World Wide Web, for a price, through his corporation. ProCD filed this suit seeking an injunction against further dissemination that exceeds the rights specified in the licenses (identical in each of the three packages Zeidenberg purchased). The district court held the licenses ineffectual because their terms do not appear on the outside of the packages. The court added that the second and third licenses stand no different from the first, even though they are identical, because they *might* have been different, and a purchaser does not agree to-and cannot be bound by-terms that were secret at the time of purchase. 908 F.Supp. at 654.

II

Following the district court, we treat the licenses as ordinary contracts accompanying the sale of products, and therefore as governed by the common law of contracts and the Uniform Commercial Code. Whether there are legal differences between "contracts" and "licenses" (which may matter under the copyright doctrine of first sale) is a subject for another day. See *Microsoft Corp. v. Harmony Computers & Electronics, Inc.,* 846 F.Supp. 208 (E.D.N.Y.1994). Zeidenberg does not argue that Silken Mountain Web Services is free of any restrictions that apply to Zeidenberg himself, because any effort to treat the two parties as distinct would put Silken Mountain behind the eight ball on ProCD's argument that copying the application program onto its hard disk violates the copyright laws. Zeidenberg does argue, and the district court held, that placing the package of software on the shelf is an "offer," which the customer "accepts" by paying the asking price and leaving the store with the goods. *Peeters v. State,* 142 N.W. 181 (1913). In Wisconsin, as elsewhere, a contract includes only the terms on which the parties have agreed. One cannot agree to hidden terms, the judge concluded. So far, so good-but one of the terms to which Zeidenberg agreed by purchasing the software is that the transaction was subject to a license. Zeidenberg's position therefore must be that the printed terms on the outside of a box are the parties' contract-except for printed terms that refer to or incorporate other terms. But why would Wisconsin fetter the parties' choice in this way? Vendors can put the entire terms of a contract on the outside of a box only by using microscopic type, removing other information that buyers might find more useful (such as what the software does, and on which computers it works), or both. The "Read Me" file included with most software, describing system requirements and potential incompatibilities, may be equivalent to ten pages of type; warranties and license restrictions take still more space. Notice on the outside, terms on the inside, and a right to return the software for a refund if the terms are unacceptable (a right that the license expressly extends), may be a means of doing business valuable to buyers and sellers alike. See E. Allan Farnsworth, 1 *Farnsworth on Contracts* § 4.26 (1990); *Restatement (2d) of Contracts* § 211 comment a (1981) ("Standardization of agreements serves many of the same functions as standardization of goods and services; both are essential to a system of mass production and distribution. Scarce and costly time and skill can be devoted to a class of transactions rather than the details of individual transactions."). Doubtless a state could forbid the use of standard contracts in the software business, but we do not think that Wisconsin has done so.

Transactions in which the exchange of money precedes the communication of detailed terms are common. Consider the purchase of insurance. The buyer goes to an agent, who explains the essentials (amount of coverage, number of years) and remits the premium to the home office, which sends back a policy. On the district judge's understanding, the terms of the policy are irrelevant because the insured paid before receiving them. Yet the device of payment, often with a "binder" (so that the insurance takes effect immediately even though the home office reserves the right to withdraw coverage later), in advance of the policy, serves buyers' interests by accelerating effectiveness and reducing transactions costs. Or consider the purchase of an airline ticket. The traveler calls the carrier or an agent, is quoted a price, reserves a seat, pays, and gets a ticket, in that order. The ticket contains elaborate terms, which the traveler can reject by canceling the reservation. To use the ticket is to accept the terms, even terms that in retrospect are disadvantageous. See *Carnival Cruise Lines, Inc. v. Shute,* 499 U.S. 585 (1991); see also *Vimar Seguros y Reaseguros, S.A. v. M/V Sky Reefer,* 515 U.S. 528 (1995) (bills of lading). Just so with a ticket to a concert. The back of the ticket states that the patron promises not to record the concert; to attend is to agree. A theater that detects a violation will confiscate the tape and escort the violator to the exit. One *could* arrange things so that every concertgoer signs this promise before forking over the money, but that cumbersome way of doing things not only would lengthen queues and raise prices but also would scotch the sale of tickets by phone or electronic data service.

Consumer goods work the same way. Someone who wants to buy a radio set visits a store, pays, and walks out with a box. Inside the box is a leaflet containing some terms, the most important of which usually is the warranty, read for the first time in the comfort of home. By Zeidenberg's lights, the warranty in the box is irrelevant; every consumer gets the standard warranty implied by the UCC in the event the contract is silent; yet so far as we are aware no state disregards warranties furnished with consumer products. Drugs come with a list of ingredients on the outside and an elaborate package insert on the inside. The package insert describes drug interactions, contraindications, and other vital information—but, if Zeidenberg is right, the purchaser need not read the package insert, because it is not part of the contract.

Next consider the software industry itself. Only a minority of sales take place over the counter, where there are boxes to peruse. A customer may place an order by phone in response to a line item in a catalog or a review in a magazine. Much software is ordered over the Internet by purchasers who have never seen a box. Increasingly software arrives by wire. There is no box; there is only a stream of electrons, a collection of information that includes data, an application program, instructions, many limitations ("MegaPixel 3.14159 cannot be used with BytePusher 2.718"), and the terms of sale. The user purchases a serial number, which activates the software's features. On Zeidenberg's arguments, these unboxed sales are unfettered by terms—so the seller has made a broad warranty and must pay consequential damages for any shortfalls in performance, two "promises" that if taken seriously would drive prices through the ceiling or return transactions to the horse-and-buggy age.

According to the district court, the UCC does not countenance the sequence of money now, terms later. (Wisconsin's version of the UCC does not differ from the Official Version in any material respect, so we use the regular numbering system. Wis. Stat. § 402.201 corresponds to UCC § 2–201, and other citations are easy to derive.) One of the court's reasons—

that by proposing as part of the draft Article 2B a new UCC § 2–2203 that would explicitly validate standard-form user licenses, the American Law Institute and the National Conference of Commissioners on Uniform Laws have conceded the invalidity of shrinkwrap licenses under current law, see 908 F.Supp. at 655–56—depends on a faulty inference. To propose a change in a law's *text* is not necessarily to propose a change in the law's *effect*. New words may be designed to fortify the current rule with a more precise text that curtails uncertainty. To judge by the flux of law review articles discussing shrinkwrap licenses, uncertainty is much in need of reduction—although businesses seem to feel less uncertainty than do scholars, for only three cases (other than ours) touch on the subject, and none directly addresses it. See *Step–Saver Data Systems, Inc. v. Wyse Technology,* 939 F.2d 91 (3d Cir.1991); *Vault Corp. v. Quaid Software Ltd.,* 847 F.2d 255, 268–70 (5th Cir.1988); *Arizona Retail Systems, Inc. v. Software Link, Inc.,* 831 F.Supp. 759 (D.Ariz.1993). As their titles suggest, these are not consumer transactions. Step–Saver is a battle-of-the-forms case, in which the parties exchange incompatible forms and a court must decide which prevails. See *Northrop Corp. v. Litronic Industries,* 29 F.3d 1173 (7th Cir.1994) (Illinois law); Douglas G. Baird & Robert Weisberg, *Rules, Standards, and the Battle of the Forms*: *A Reassessment of* § 2–207, 68 Va. L.Rev. 1217, 1227–31 (1982). Our case has only one form; UCC § 2–207 is irrelevant. *Vault* holds that Louisiana's special shrinkwrap-license statute is preempted by federal law, a question to which we return. And *Arizona Retail Systems* did not reach the question, because the court found that the buyer knew the terms of the license before purchasing the software.

What then does the current version of the UCC have to say? We think that the place to start is § 2–204(1): "A contract for sale of goods may be made in any manner sufficient to show agreement, including conduct by both parties which recognizes the existence of such a contract." A vendor, as master of the offer, may invite acceptance by conduct, and may propose limitations on the kind of conduct that constitutes acceptance. A buyer may accept by performing the acts the vendor proposes to treat as acceptance. And that is what happened. ProCD proposed a contract that a buyer would accept by *using* the software after having an opportunity to read the license at leisure. This Zeidenberg did. He had no choice, because the software splashed the license on the screen and would not let him proceed without indicating acceptance. So although the district judge was right to say that a contract can be, and often is, formed simply by paying the price and walking out of the store, the UCC permits contracts to be formed in other ways. ProCD proposed such a different way, and without protest Zeidenberg agreed. Ours is not a case in which a consumer opens a package to find an insert saying "you owe us an extra $10,000" and the seller files suit to collect. Any buyer finding such a demand can prevent formation of the contract by returning the package, as can any consumer who concludes that the terms of the license make the software worth less than the purchase price. Nothing in the UCC requires a seller to maximize the buyer's net gains.

Section 2–606, which defines "acceptance of goods", reinforces this understanding. A buyer accepts goods under § 2–606(1)(b) when, after an opportunity to inspect, he fails to make an effective rejection under § 2–602(1). ProCD extended an opportunity to reject if a buyer should find the license terms unsatisfactory; Zeidenberg inspected the package, tried out the software, learned of the license, and did not reject the goods. We refer to § 2–606 only to show that the opportunity to return goods can be important; acceptance of an offer differs from acceptance of goods after delivery, see *Gillen v. Atalanta Systems, Inc.,* 997 F.2d 280, 284 n. 1 (7th Cir.1993); but the UCC consistently permits the parties to structure their relations so that the buyer has a chance to make a final decision after a detailed review.

Some portions of the UCC impose additional requirements on the way parties agree on terms. A disclaimer of the implied warranty of merchantability must be "conspicuous." UCC § 2–316(2), incorporating UCC § 1–201(10). Promises to make firm offers, or to negate oral modifications, must be "separately signed." UCC §§ 2–205, 2–209(2). These special provisos reinforce the impression that, so far as the UCC is concerned, other terms may be as inconspicuous as the forum-selection clause on the back of the cruise ship ticket in *Carnival Lines.* Zeidenberg has not located any Wisconsin case—for that matter, any case in any state-holding that under the UCC the ordinary terms found in shrinkwrap licenses require any special prominence, or otherwise are to be undercut rather than enforced. In the end, the terms of the license are conceptually identical to the contents of the package. Just as no court would dream of saying that SelectPhone (trademark) must contain 3,100 phone books rather than 3,000, or must have data no more than 30 days old, or must sell for $100 rather than $150—although any of these changes would be welcomed by the customer, if all other things were held constant—so, we believe, Wisconsin would not let the buyer pick and choose among terms. Terms of use are no less a part of "the product" than are the size of the database and the speed with which the software compiles listings. Competition among vendors, not judicial revision of a package's contents, is how consumers are protected in a market economy. *Digital Equipment Corp. v. Uniq Digital Technologies, Inc.,* 73 F.3d 756 (7th Cir.1996). ProCD has rivals, which may elect to compete by offering superior software, monthly updates, improved terms of use, lower price, or a better compromise among these elements. As we stressed above, adjusting terms in buyers' favor might help Matthew Zeidenberg today (he already has the software) but would lead to a response, such as a higher price, that might make consumers as a whole worse off.

III

The district court held that, even if Wisconsin treats shrinkwrap licenses as contracts, § 301(a) of the Copyright Act, 17 U.S.C. § 301(a), prevents their enforcement. 908 F.Supp. at 656–59. The relevant part of § 301(a) preempts any "legal or equitable rights [under state law] that are equivalent to any of the exclusive rights within the general scope of copyright as specified by section 106 in works of authorship that are fixed in a tangible medium of expression and come within the subject matter of copyright as specified by sections 102 and 103''. ProCD's software and data are "fixed in a tangible medium of expression", and the district judge held that they are "within the subject matter of copyright". The latter conclusion is plainly right for the copyrighted application program, and the judge thought that the data likewise are "within the subject matter of copyright" even if, after Feist, they are not sufficiently original to be copyrighted. 908 F.Supp. at 656–57. *Baltimore Orioles, Inc. v. Major League Baseball Players Ass'n,* 805 F.2d 663, 676 (7th Cir.1986), supports that conclusion, with which commentators agree. E.g., Paul Goldstein, III *Copyright* § 15.2.3 (2d ed.1996); Melville B. Nimmer & David Nimmer, *Nimmer on Copyright* § 101[B] (1995); William F. Patry, II *Copyright Law and Practice* 1108–09 (1994). One function of § 301(a) is to prevent states from giving special protection to works of authorship that Congress has decided should be in the public domain, which it can accomplish only if "subject matter of copyright" includes all works of a *type* covered by sections 102 and 103, even if federal law does not afford protection to them. Cf. *Bonito Boats, Inc. v. Thunder Craft Boats, Inc.,* 489 U.S. 141, 109 S.Ct. 971, 103 L.Ed.2d 118 (1989) (same principle under patent laws).

But are rights created by contract "equivalent to any of the exclusive rights within the general scope of copyright"? Three courts of appeals have answered "no." *National Car Rental System, Inc. v. Computer Associates International, Inc.,* 991 F.2d 426, 433 (8th Cir.1993); *Taquino v. Teledyne Monarch Rubber,* 893 F.2d 1488, 1501 (5th Cir.1990); *Acorn Structures, Inc. v. Swantz,* 846 F.2d 923, 926 (4th Cir.1988). The district court disagreed with these decisions, 908 F.Supp. at 658, but we think them sound. Rights "equivalent to any of the exclusive rights within the general scope of copyright" are rights established *by law*-rights that restrict the options of persons who are strangers to the author. Copyright law forbids duplication, public performance, and so on, unless the person wishing to copy or perform the work gets permission; silence means a ban on copying. A copyright is a right against the world. Contracts, by contrast, generally affect only their parties; strangers may do as they please, so contracts do not create "exclusive rights." Someone who found a copy of SelectPhone (trademark) on the street would not be affected by the shrinkwrap license-though the federal copyright laws of their own force would limit the finder's ability to copy or transmit the application program.

Think for a moment about trade secrets. One common trade secret is a customer list. After *Feist,* a simple alphabetical list of a firm's customers, with address and telephone numbers, could not be protected by copyright. Yet *Kewanee Oil Co. v. Bicron Corp.,* 416 U.S. 470, 94 S.Ct. 1879, 40 L.Ed.2d 315 (1974), holds that contracts about trade secrets may be enforced-precisely because they do not affect strangers' ability to discover and use the information independently. If the amendment of § 301(a) in 1976 overruled *Kewanee* and abolished consensual protection of those trade secrets that cannot be copyrighted, no one has noticed-though abolition is a logical consequence of the district court's approach. Think, too, about everyday transactions in intellectual property. A customer visits a video store and rents a copy of *Night of the Lepus*. The customer's contract with the store limits use of the tape to home viewing and requires its return in two days. May the customer keep the tape, on the ground that § 301(a) makes the promise unenforceable?

A law student uses the LEXIS database, containing public-domain documents, under a contract limiting the results to educational endeavors; may the student resell his access to this database to a law firm from which LEXIS seeks to collect a much higher hourly rate? Suppose ProCD hires a firm to scour the nation for telephone directories, promising to pay $100 for each that ProCD does not already have. The firm locates 100 new directories, which it sends to ProCD with an invoice for $10,000. ProCD incorporates the directories into its database; does it have to pay the bill? Surely yes; *Aronson v. Quick Point Pencil Co.,* 440 U.S. 257, 99 S.Ct. 1096, 59 L.Ed.2d 296 (1979), holds that promises to pay for intellectual property may be enforced even though federal law (in *Aronson,* the patent law) offers no protection against third-party uses of that property. See also *Kennedy v. Wright,* 851 F.2d 963 (7th Cir.1988). But these illustrations are what our case is about. ProCD offers software and data for two prices: one for personal use, a higher price for commercial use. Zeidenberg wants to use the data without paying the seller's price; if the law student and Quick Point Pencil Co. could not do that, neither can Zeidenberg.

Although Congress possesses power to preempt even the enforcement of contracts about intellectual property-or railroads, on which see *Norfolk & Western Ry. v. Train Dispatchers,* 499 U.S. 117 (1991)—courts usually read preemption clauses to leave private contracts unaffected. *American Airlines, Inc. v. Wolens,* 513 U.S. 219 (1995), provides a nice illustration. A federal statute preempts any state "law, rule, regulation, standard, or other provision . . . relating to rates, routes, or services of any air carrier." 49 U.S.C.App. § 1305(a)(1). Does such a law preempt the law of contracts—so that, for example, an air carrier need not honor a quoted price (or a contract to reduce the price by the value of frequent flyer miles)? The Court allowed that it is possible to read the statute that broadly but thought such an interpretation would make little sense. Terms and conditions offered by contract reflect private ordering, essential to the efficient functioning of markets. 513 U.S. at ___–___, 115 S.Ct. at 824–25. Although some principles that carry the name of contract law are designed to defeat rather than implement consensual transactions, *id.* at ___ n. 8, 115 S.Ct. at 826 n. 8, the rules that respect private choice are not preempted by a clause such as § 1305(a)(1). Section 301(a) plays a role similar to § 1301(a)(1): it prevents states from substituting their own regulatory systems for those of the national government. Just as § 301(a) does not itself interfere with private transactions in intellectual property, so it does not prevent states from respecting those transactions. Like the Supreme Court in *Wolens,* we think it prudent to refrain from adopting a rule that anything with the label "contract" is necessarily outside the preemption clause: the variations and possibilities are too numerous to foresee. *National Car Rental* likewise recognizes the possibility that some applications of the law of contract could interfere with the attainment of national objectives and therefore come within the domain of § 301(a). But general enforcement of shrinkwrap licenses of the kind before us does not create such interference.

Aronson emphasized that enforcement of the contract between Aronson and Quick Point Pencil Company would not withdraw any information from the public domain. That is equally true of the contract between ProCD and Zeidenberg. Everyone remains free to copy and disseminate all 3,000 telephone books that have been incorporated into ProCD's database. Anyone can add SIC codes and zip codes. ProCD's rivals have done so. Enforcement of the shrinkwrap license may even make information more readily available, by reducing the price ProCD charges to consumer buyers. To the extent licenses facilitate distribution of object code while concealing the source code (the point of a clause forbidding disassembly), they serve the same procompetitive functions as does the law of trade secrets. *Rockwell Graphic Systems, Inc. v. DEV Industries, Inc.*, 925 F.2d 174, 180 (7th Cir.1991). Licenses may have other benefits for consumers: many licenses permit users to make extra copies, to use the software on multiple computers, even to incorporate the software into the user's products. But whether a particular license is generous or restrictive, a simple two-party contract is not "equivalent to any of the exclusive rights within the general scope of copyright" and therefore may be enforced.

REVERSED AND REMANDED.

I.Lan Sys. v. Netscout Serv. Level Corp.

United States District Court for the District of Massachusetts, 2002.
183 F. Supp. 2d 328.

■ YOUNG, CHIEF JUDGE Has this happened to you? You plunk down a pretty penny for the latest and greatest software, speed back to your computer, tear open the box, shove the CD–ROM into the computer, click on "install" and, after scrolling past a license agreement which would take at least fifteen minutes to read, find yourself staring at the following dialog box: "I agree." Do you click on the box? You probably do not agree in your heart of hearts, but you click anyway, not about to let some pesky legalese delay the moment for which you've been waiting. Is that "clickwrap" license agreement enforceable? Yes, at least in the case described below.

I.   INTRODUCTION

The plaintiff, i.LAN Systems, Inc. ("i.LAN"), helps companies monitor their computer networks. The defendant, NetScout Service Level Corp., formerly known as NextPoint Networks, Inc. ("NextPoint"), sells sophisticated software that monitors networks. In 1998, i.LAN and NextPoint signed a detailed Value Added Reseller ("VAR") agreement whereby i.LAN agreed to resell NextPoint's software to customers. This dispute concerns a transaction that took place in 1999.

i.LAN claims that for $85,231.42 it purchased the unlimited right to use NextPoint's software, replete with perpetual upgrades and support, whereby it effectively could rent, rather than sell, NextPoint's software to customers. In support of its argument, i.LAN points to the purchase order associated with the transaction. NextPoint, in response, points to the 1998 VAR agreement and the clickwrap license agreement contained in the software itself to reach a different conclusion.

The parties continued their relationship for several months without confronting their conflicting interpretations of the 1999 purchase order, but eventually the disagreement erupted into litigation. i.LAN filed a complaint that alleges, among other things, breach of contract and violation of Massachusetts General Laws Chapter 93A. The complaint properly invokes the Court's diversity jurisdiction, 28 U.S.C. § 1332(a)(1).

i.LAN quickly took the offensive and brought a motion for summary judgment. i.LAN argued that it should be awarded specific performance—in particular, perpetual upgrades of NextPoint's software and unlimited support. The Court heard oral argument on i.LAN's motion and took the matter under advisement. Soon after, NextPoint brought a cross-motion for summary judgment, the subject of this memorandum. NextPoint argued that even if i.LAN's allegations were true, the clickwrap license agreement limits NextPoint's liability to the price paid for the software, in this case $85,231.42. The Court heard oral arguments on NextPoint's motion and soon after ruled in favor of NextPoint. This memorandum explains why.

II.   DISCUSSION

Before turning to NextPoint's clickwrap license agreement, the stage must be set. First, the Court will identify the set of rules by which to judge this dispute. Next, the Court will examine what is at stake, in particular i.LAN's claim for specific performance and NextPoint's limitation-of-liability defense. Finally, the Court will address the enforceability of the clickwrap license agreement.

A.   What Law Governs?

1.   Precedence of the 1998, 1999, and Clickwrap Agreements

Three contracts might govern this dispute: the 1998 VAR agreement, the 1999 purchase order, and the clickwrap license agreement to which i.LAN necessarily agreed when it installed the software at issue. The key question for purposes of this memorandum is how the 1998 and 1999 agreements affect the clickwrap license agreement.

The clickwrap license agreement states that it does not affect existing or subsequent written agreements or purchase orders. The language might be read to mean that the clickwrap license agreement is a nullity if a purchase order already exists, but that reading is not the natural one. The natural reading is that to the extent the 1998 VAR agreement and 1999 purchase order are silent, the clickwrap license agreement fills the void.

2.   Common Law vs. UCC

Two bodies of contract law might govern the clickwrap license agreement: Massachusetts common law and the Uniform Commercial Code

("UCC") as adopted by Massachusetts. Article 2 of the UCC applies to "transactions in goods," UCC § 2–102, Mass. Gen. Laws ch. 106, § 2–102, but "unless the context otherwise requires 'contract' and 'agreement' are limited to those relating to the present or future *sale* of goods," *id.* § 2–106(1) (emphasis added). Indeed, the title of Article 2 is "Sales" and the definition of "goods" assumes a sale: "goods" is defined as "all things (including specially manufactured goods) which are movable at the time of identification to the contract for sale...." *Id.* § 2–105(1). The purchase of software might seem like an ordinary contract for the sale of goods, but in fact the purchaser merely obtains a *license* to use the software; never is there a "passing of title from the seller to the buyer for a price," *id.* § 2–106(1). So is the purchase of software a transaction in goods? Despite Article 2's requirement of a *sale*, courts in Massachusetts have assumed, without deciding, that Article 2 governs software *licenses*.

Given [cases to the same effect], i.LAN argues that the UCC should govern the 1999 purchase order and clickwrap license agreement. Next-Point does not disagree with the idea that the UCC might apply to software purchases in general, but under NextPoint's theory of the case, the 1998 VAR agreement is most important to this dispute, and that agreement predominately concerns *services*, rather than the sale of goods. NextPoint, therefore, argues that the UCC should not govern any part of this dispute.

To the extent it matters—and given the facts of this case, it likely does not—the Court will examine the clickwrap license agreement through the lens of the UCC. Admittedly, the UCC technically does not govern software licenses, and very likely does not govern the 1998 VAR agreement, but with respect to the 1999 transaction, the UCC best fulfills the parties' reasonable expectations.

In Massachusetts and across most of the nation, software licenses exist in a legislative void. Legal scholars, among them the Uniform Commissioners on State Laws, have tried to fill that void, but their efforts have not kept pace with the world of business. Lawmakers began to draft a new Article 2B (licenses) for the UCC, which would have been the logical complement to Article 2 (sales) and Article 2A (leases), but after a few years of drafting, those lawmakers decided instead to draft an independent body of law for software licenses, which is now known as the Uniform Computer Information Transactions Act ("UCITA"). So far only Maryland and Virginia have adopted UCITA; Massachusetts has not. Accordingly, the Court will not spend its time considering UCITA. At the same time, the Court will not overlook Article 2 simply because its provisions are imperfect in today's world. Software licenses are entered into every day, and business persons reasonably expect that *some* law will govern them. For the time being, Article 2's familiar provisions—which are the inspiration for UCITA—better fulfill those expectations than would the common law. Article 2 technically does not, and certainly will not in the future, govern software licenses, but for the time being, the Court will assume it does.

B.   What Is at Stake?

1.   Specific Performance

2.   Limitation of Liability

If i.LAN's only remedy is money damages, the limitation of liability found in the clickwrap license agreement becomes very important. The Court holds that i.LAN presents nothing more than a simple breach of contract, so it is not entitled to relief under Chapter 93A, *e.g., Framingham Auto Sales, Inc. v. Workers' Credit Union*, 41 Mass. App. Ct. 416, 418 (1996), but even so, i.LAN's breach of contract claim, if proven, could result in astronomical damages. Recognizing that sellers might want to reduce their exposure to such astronomical damages, the UCC permits waivers of warranties and limitations of liability, *see* UCC § 2–316, Mass. Gen. Laws ch. 106, § 2–316 (exclusion or modification of warranties); *id.* § 2–719 (limitation of remedies), even for Chapter 93A claims. NextPoint properly has tried to avail itself of these provisions of the UCC: the clickwrap license agreement contains a 30–day limited warranty but otherwise disclaims all warranties and limits NextPoint's liability to the fees it received for the license. The key question, then, is whether the clickwrap license agreement is enforceable.

C.   Are Clickwrap License Agreements Enforceable?

The clickwrap license agreement may be analyzed as either (i) forming a contract under UCC section 2–204 or (ii) adding terms to an existing contract under UCC section 2–207, a method of contracting that often results in a "battle of the forms," *e.g., Commerce & Indus. Ins. Co. v. Bayer Corp.*, 433 Mass. 388, 391–96, (2001). The distinction is important.

If the proper analysis is pursuant to UCC section 2–204, the analysis is simple: i.LAN manifested assent to the clickwrap license agreement when it clicked on the box stating "I agree," so the agreement is enforceable. *See Specht v. Netscape Communications Corp.*, 150 F. Supp. 2d 585, 591–96 (S.D.N.Y. 2001).

If the proper analysis is pursuant to UCC section 2–207, the analysis is more complicated. UCC section 2–207 creates two forks in the road for the facts of this case. The first fork is whether or not the clickwrap license agreement is a counteroffer—an acceptance to i.LAN's purchase order "expressly made conditional on assent to the additional or different terms," UCC § 2–207(1), here the additional terms limiting NextPoint's potential liability. The second fork is whether i.LAN accepted the additional terms either explicitly, implicitly, or by default. Clicking on "I agree" could be seen as *explicit* acceptance. Between merchants, if a party never objects to the additional terms, and the additional terms are not "material," then the UCC deems the party to have accepted the additional terms *implicitly*, for lack of a better description. UCC § 2–207(2); *see JOM, Inc. v. Adell Plastics, Inc.*, 193 F.3d 47, 52–59 (1st Cir. 1999) (en banc). The comment to UCC section 2–207 suggests that the test for "materiality" is whether the terms in question would result in unreasonable surprise or hardship to the party if incorporated without the party's express awareness. UCC § 2–207 cmt. 4. Finally, if the additional terms are not accepted either explicitly or implicitly, but the conduct of the parties shows recognition of a contract, then the gap-filler provisions of Article 2 kick in to fill the void with *default* terms. UCC § 2–207(3); *Ionics, Inc. v. Elmwood Sensors, Inc.*, 110 F.3d 184, 188–89 (1st Cir. 1997) (overruling *Roto–Lith, Ltd. v. F.P. Bartlett & Co.*, 297 F.2d 497 (1st Cir. 1962), which held that a response stating a condition materially altering the obligation solely to the disadvantage of the offeror was an acceptance expressly conditioned on assent to the additional terms, which became binding unless specifically rejected).

With respect to the first fork, the clickwrap license agreement is best characterized as a counteroffer, as its language mirrors the language provided after the comma in UCC section 2–207(1): "NEXTPOINT IS WILLING TO LICENSE THE LICENSED PRODUCT TO LICENSEE ONLY ON THE CONDITION THAT LICENSEE ACCEPTS THE TERMS AND CONDITIONS CONTAINED IN THIS AGREEMENT." The first fork only has importance, however, if the parties disagree over the additional terms. In this case, i.LAN's purchase order was silent on the issue of liability, so NextPoint proposed additional terms which, to be extra cautious, NextPoint characterized as a counteroffer. In such a case, if the original offer is silent on the issue of the additional terms, and no objection ever is made to them, then it should not matter whether the additional terms are part of a counteroffer or a proposal. All that should matter in this case, then, is whether i.LAN accepted the additional terms. Article 2 does not limit liability by default, so if i.LAN accepted the clickwrap license agreement it must have done so either explicitly, by clicking on "I agree," or implicitly, as provided in UCC section 2–207(2)

The case to which i.LAN pins its hopes is *Step–Saver Data Systems, Inc. v. Wyse Technology*, 939 F.2d 91 (3d Cir. 1991). *Step–Saver* considered *shrinkwrap* license agreements, where the agreement is printed somewhere on or in the box of software, rather than *clickwrap* license agreements, where the agreement appears on the computer before the software is installed, but otherwise the facts of *Step–Saver* are similar to the facts before this Court: (i) a reseller telephoned a software manufacturer and asked for a shipment of software, which the manufacturer verbally agreed to provide, (ii) the reseller then sent a written purchase order specifying quantity, price, and shipping and payment information, and (iii) the manufacturer then shipped the software along with an invoice matching the purchase order. On the box containing the software, however, was a shrinkwrap license agreement which contained a provision limiting the manufacturer's liability to the price paid for the shipment. The question for the court was whether to enforce the provision of the shrinkwrap license agreement limiting the manufacturer's liability. The court held that the limitation of liability was not enforceable because it was merely a proposed agreement under UCC section 2–207 to which the reseller never agreed; the court refused to imply assent because the limitation of liability was material and UCC section 2–207(2)(b) does not allow *material* terms to be added by implication. *Id.* at 105. This holding was fully adopted in a later case against the same software manufacturer, *Arizona Retail Systems, Inc. v. The Software Link, Inc.*, 831 F. Supp. 759, 766 (D. Ariz. 1993).

Step–Saver once was the leading case on shrinkwrap agreements. Today that distinction goes to a case favoring NextPoint, *ProCD, Inc. v. Zeidenberg*, 86 F.3d 1447 (7th Cir. 1996). The holding of *ProCD* is best summarized as follows: "terms inside a box of software bind consumers who use the software after an opportunity to read the terms and to reject them by returning the product." *Hill v. Gateway 2000, Inc.*, 105 F.3d 1147, 1148 (7th Cir. 1997). *ProCD* did not apply UCC section 2–207: "Our case has only one form; UCC § 2–207 is irrelevant." 86 F.3d at 1452. Instead, *ProCD* applied only UCC section 2–204 and concluded that the absence of a timely rejection was sufficient to show assent.

The analytical difference between *Step–Saver* and *ProCD* is whether "money now, terms later" forms a contract (i) at the time of the purchase order or (ii) when the purchaser receives the box of software, sees the license agreement, and does not return the software. If the purchase order is the contract, UCC section 2–207 applies and material terms cannot be added to the contract without explicit assent. If the contract is not formed until after the purchaser sees the shrinkwrap license agreement, UCC section 2–204 applies and the act of keeping the software implicitly shows assent.

The Court will enforce NextPoint's clickwrap license agreement for two reasons. First and foremost, the Court agrees with those cases embracing the theory of *ProCD*. E.g., *1–A Equipment Co. v. ICode, Inc.*, No. 0057 CV467, 2000 WL 33281687 (Mass. Dist. Nov. 17, 2000) (Winslow, J.). The UCC "shall be liberally construed and applied to promote its underlying purposes and policies," which include "the continued expansion of commercial practices through custom, usage and agreement of the parties." UCC § 1–102, Mass. Gen. Laws ch. 106, § 1–102. "Money now, terms later" is a practical way to form contracts, especially with purchasers of software. If *ProCD* was correct to enforce a shrinkwrap license agreement, where any assent is implicit, then it must also be correct to enforce a clickwrap license agreement, where the assent is explicit. To be sure, shrinkwrap and clickwrap license agreements share the defect of any standardized contract—they are susceptible to the inclusion of terms that border on the unconscionable—but that is not the issue in this case. The only issue before the Court is whether clickwrap license agreements are an appropriate way to form contracts, and the Court holds they are. In short, i.LAN explicitly accepted the clickwrap license agreement when it clicked on the box stating "I agree."

Second, even if the Court were to agree with i.LAN that UCC section 2–207 governs, the Court would hold that i.LAN implicitly accepted the clickwrap license agreement because its additional terms were not material, UCC § 2–207(2)(b). In other words, there can be no unreasonable surprise or hardship to i.LAN from enforcing the limitation of liability. To understand this holding requires a bit of background. When NextPoint and i.LAN first formed their relationship, i.LAN signed the 1998 VAR agreement, which contains warranty disclaimers and limitations of liability nearly identical to those found in the clickwrap license agreement. Furthermore, the 1998 VAR agreement incorporates the clickwrap license agreement by reference and specifically states that NextPoint's liability to end users of the software will be limited by the clickwrap license agreement. Finally, i.LAN had installed the software on many occasions before the transaction in 1999, and each time i.LAN necessarily ran across the clickwrap license agreement. In short, NextPoint consistently included a warranty disclaimer and limitation of liability in every contract it made.

Every contract, that is, except the 1999 purchase order. That contract contains a price, a quantity, and five specific terms, but is silent with respect to warranties and potential liability. Thus, i.LAN argues that NextPoint's "contrived attempt to supersede the [1999 purchase order] with directly contradicting terms or a standardized click license, a license that was neither referenced in the [1999 purchase order] nor even mentioned during negotiations, is absurd." To the contrary, it would be absurd to allow silence to destroy the detailed private ordering created by the 1998 VAR and clickwrap license agreements. Indeed, the clickwrap license agreement specifically was intended to fill any gaps left by the 1999 purchase order. "There is a long tradition in contract law of reading contracts sensibly; contracts—certainly business contracts of the kind involved here—are not parlor games but the means of getting the world's work done." *R.I. Charities Trust v. Engelhard Corp.*, 267 F.3d 3, 7 (1st Cir. 2001). The only sensible interpretation of the 1999 purchase order is that it did not affect the limitations of liability found in the parties' prior and subsequent agreements.

III. CONCLUSION

For the reasons set forth above, NextPoint's cross-motion for partial summary judgment [Docket No. 51] was ALLOWED on September 28, 2001 with respect to i.LAN's claims for specific performance (Count I) and violation of Chapter 93A (Count VII). Furthermore, the Court held that if i.LAN were to prevail on any of its other claims, it would be entitled to recover no more than the amount it paid for the software license at issue, to wit, $85,231.42.

CHAPTER 15

CONSIDERATION

The law requires more than just offer and acceptance to establish a contract.

To begin with, and probably unsurprisingly, the law polices the process of contract formation to require offer and acceptance to be freely and authentically given. Doctrines concerning duress and fraud invalidate contracts obtained by coercion or trickery; and doctrines concerning the limits of contractual capacity invalidate contracts made by parties who, because of youth or mental disability (either temporary or permanent), are deemed not capable of meaningful contractual consent. In addition, and perhaps somewhat more surprisingly, the law also polices the substance of contracts to invalidate certain agreements that it deems unacceptably unfair or immoral. The unconscionability doctrine (although it also has a procedural component) may perhaps be used to avoid contractual obligations, associated, for example, with predatory loans, that are grossly unequal; and a complex of doctrines sounding in public policy invalidate contracts, for example, concerning criminal activity, whose content is deemed immoral or somehow otherwise incompatible with the legal order's basic normative commitments. Each of these topics will be taken up later in these materials, when more philosophical approaches to contract law, and in particular to the limits of freedom of contract, are introduced.

The law also limits the promises that it will enforce in another way, which is much more surprising than these. Contract law distinguishes between what it calls *gratuitous promises*, on the one hand, and, on the other, promises that are supported by what the law calls *consideration*. Only the second class of promises will receive legal recognition and enforcement. Moreover, although the consideration doctrine touches on some of the substantive themes associated with the various more intuitive limits on contract enforcement just catalogued—so that cases, for example *Alaska Packers* (see below), argued under the heading *consideration* may in fact be decided on the basis of ideas concerning duress—the consideration doctrine's imprint on the positive law cannot be reduced to these other broadly substantive ideas. Instead, the consideration doctrine appears to have a purely formal presence in the law. Accordingly, although the doctrine undoubtedly represents one of the great constraints that the contemporary legal order imposes on freedom of contract, it is best presented in the present context, as part of the discussion of the nature and limits of formalism in contract law.

This chapter takes up the consideration doctrine, beginning with its historical and contemporary elaboration and then moving on to its formal structure. As always in this Part of the text, the discussion will emphasize both the possibilities and limitations of giving free-standing importance to legal form. One important theme of the discussion will be the possibility that courts, or the parties themselves, might manufacture consideration and the limits that this possibility imposes on purely formalist legal analysis.

15.1 TWO APPROACHES TO CONSIDERATION

The classical statement of the consideration doctrine, which dominated legal analysis in the nineteenth century, is known as the benefit/detriment test. According to this approach, a contract is supported by consideration only if each of the promises that it involves grants benefits to its promisee or imposes detriments on its promisor (or both, of course). It is easy to see how consideration understood in these terms exists in a conventional sales contract: the seller's promise to transfer the goods confers a benefit on her buyer and imposes a detriment on her; and the buyer's promise to pay confers a benefit on his seller and imposes a detriment on him. In other circumstances, the application of the benefit/detriment theory of consideration is less obvious, as the following case illustrates.

Hamer v. Sidway

Court of Appeals of New York, Second Division, 1891.
27 N.E. 256.

■ PARKER, J. The question which provoked the most discussion by counsel on this appeal, and which lies at the foundation of plaintiff's asserted right of recovery, is whether by virtue of a contract defendant's testator William E. Story became indebted to his nephew William E. Story, 2d, on his twenty-first birthday in the sum of five thousand dollars. The trial court found as a fact that "on the 20th day of March, 1869, William E. Story agreed to and with William E. Story, 2d, that if he would refrain from drinking liquor, using tobacco, swearing, and playing cards or billiards for money until he should become 21 years of age then he, the said William E. Story, would at that time pay him, the said William E. Story, 2d, the sum of $5,000 for such refraining, to which the said William E. Story, 2d, agreed," and that he "in all things fully performed his part of said agreement."

The defendant contends that the contract was without consideration to support it, and, therefore, invalid. He asserts that the promisee by refraining from the use of liquor and tobacco was not harmed but benefited; that that which he did was best for him to do independently of his uncle's promise, and insists that it follows that unless the promisor was benefited, the contract was without consideration. A contention, which if well founded, would seem to leave open for controversy in many cases whether that which the promisee did or omitted to do was, in fact, of such benefit to him as to leave no consideration to support the enforcement of the promisor's agreement. Such a rule could not be tolerated, and is without foundation in the law. The Exchequer Chamber, in 1875, defined consideration as follows: "A valuable consideration in the sense of the law may consist either in some right, interest, profit or benefit accruing to the one party, or some forbearance, detriment, loss or responsibility given, suffered or undertaken by the other." Courts "will not ask whether the thing which forms the consideration does in fact benefit the promisee or a third party, or is of any substantial value to anyone. It is enough that something is promised, done, forborne or suffered by the party to whom the promise is made as consideration for the promise made to him." (Anson's Prin. of Con. 63.)

"In general a waiver of any legal right at the request of another party is a sufficient consideration for a promise." (Parsons on Contracts, 444.)

"Any damage, or suspension, or forbearance of a right will be sufficient to sustain a promise." (Kent, vol. 2, 465, 12th ed.)

Pollock, in his work on contracts, page 166, after citing the definition given by the Exchequer Chamber already quoted, says: "The second branch of this judicial description is really the most important one. Consideration means not so much that one party is profiting as that the other abandons some legal right in the present or limits his legal freedom of action in the future as an inducement for the promise of the first."

Now, applying this rule to the facts before us, the promisee used tobacco, occasionally drank liquor, and he had a legal right to do so. That right he abandoned for a period of years upon the strength of the promise of the testator that for such forbearance he would give him $5,000. We need not speculate on the effort which may have been required to give up the use of those stimulants. It is sufficient that he restricted his lawful freedom of action within certain prescribed limits upon the faith of his uncle's agreement, and now having fully performed the conditions imposed, it is of no moment whether such performance actually proved a benefit to the promisor, and the court will not inquire into it, but were it a proper subject of inquiry, we see nothing in this record that would permit a determination that the uncle was not benefited in a legal sense. Few cases have been found which may be said to be precisely in point, but such as have been support the position we have taken.

The order appealed from should be reversed and the judgment of the Special Term affirmed, with costs payable out of the estate.

* * *

The plaintiff in *Hamer* was promised $5000 by his uncle if he refrained from drinking, using tobacco, swearing, and playing cards or billiards for money until he reached 21 years of age. The plaintiff successfully refrained from these activities for the required years and approached his uncle asking for the money. The uncle agreed but suggested that he keep custody of it until the plaintiff became old enough to manage it, and the plaintiff consented. The uncle then died, and his estate refused to honor the promise, whereupon the nephew sued.

Under the benefit/detriment theory of consideration, the agreement between the uncle and nephew in *Hamer* was enforceable only if each promise conferred a benefit on the promisee or imposed a detriment on the promisor. The uncle's promise posed no problem on this test: it clearly conferred a benefit (the gain of $5000) on the nephew and also imposed a detriment (the loss of $5000) on the uncle. The nephew's promise was much trickier, however.[1] And so the enforceability of the contract depended on whether the nephew's promise constituted good consideration for the uncle's. If not, then the uncle's promise was gratuitous and hence unenforceable.

The uncle, the court was prepared for arguments sake to accept, was *not* benefited by the nephew's forbearance. So in order for consideration to exist under the benefit/detriment test, the nephew's forbearance must have constituted a detriment to him. This raised the possibility that there was no consideration on the nephew's side, as it was in the nephew's interest to forbear from vice as the uncle had requested.

The *Hamer* court found consideration nevertheless. As the court observed, in refraining from drinking, etc., the nephew gave up activities in which he had a legal right to engage. And this counted as a detriment for purposes of the consideration doctrine, thus rendering the uncle's promise not gratuitous and thus also legally enforceable. Indeed, the court *might* have reached the same conclusion even if the activities that the nephew promised to avoid were illegal (drugs and theft, for example). Even if the activities that the contract named had been both harmful to the nephew and illegal, the contract might nevertheless have imposed a detriment on him. Before promising to refrain from these activities, only self-interest and the obligation to obey the law would have blocked the nephew from engaging in them. But after his promise, another bar to these activities might have arisen—namely a bilateral moral obligation specifically to the uncle.[2] Even if the activities that the nephew promised to avoid had been illegal, the promise would have given the uncle a new and additional normative power to demand that the nephew avoid them. And this obligation—by adding another reason to set against the nephew's liberty and desire—might, on the court's logic, have constituted a detriment capable of providing consideration for the uncle's promise.

The benefit/detriment conception of consideration allowed consideration to be found in almost every case. People (almost as a matter of formal

---

1. It is not clear that the nephew made a promise at all, or that the uncle's promise invited one. It may well have been that the uncle sought not the nephew's promise to forebear from vice until aged 21 but rather actual forbearance. In other words, *Hamer* may well present not a bilateral contract, in which there are promises on both sides, but rather a unilateral contract, in which a promisor seeks not a return promise but simply performance.

This does not matter for purposes of the consideration doctrine which now directs its attention not at the return promise but rather at the performance itself. So in *Hamer*, the question becomes whether the nephew's actual forbearance constitutes good consideration. The main text accordingly ignores the question whether *Hamer* involved a unilateral or a bilateral contract.

2. Note that this obligation depends on the contract's being bilateral rather than unilateral. If the uncle had declined to extract any return promise from the nephew, then the nephew, even as he performed, would not have been under any *obligation* to the uncle; and so the additional bar to the nephew's illegal conduct would not have been created. Accordingly, the equivalence observed in the prior footnote depends on the fact that the vices the nephew forbore were ones that he was entitled to engage in.

rationality) make and receive contractual promises only where they have some interest in them, and this interest can almost always be cast in terms of benefit or detriment.[3]

Perhaps for this reason, in response to an effort to limit the scope of contractual obligation, the consideration doctrine underwent a change at roughly the turn of the twentieth century. The benefit/detriment conception of consideration was replaced, in the case law, by what is today called the *bargain theory of consideration*.[4] According to the bargain theory, a contract is supported by consideration only where each party's participation in the contract induces the other's, in the sense that each party makes its contractual promise or performs its contractual obligations with the intention (although, as *St. Peter* below makes plain, not necessarily the motivation) that the other shall make and perform its side of the contractual promise. Consideration, on this approach, requires what Holmes called *reciprocal conventional inducement*.[5]

The bargain theory narrows the scope of agreements that are supported by consideration, as it requires not just that the parties to an agreement have an interest in each other's promises or performance but also that these interests interact in a particular way. This interaction will be central to the effort, in the next section, to understand the formal structure of the consideration doctrine. But first, it is important to see that it can happen that each party possesses the interest in an agreement that the benefit/detriment test required but that these interests do not interact in the formal way associated with bargains. The following case illustrates this possibility.

Kirksey v. Kirksey

Supreme Court of Alabama, 1845.
8 Ala. 131.

ASSUMPSIT by the defendant, against the plaintiff in error. The question is presented in this Court, upon a case agreed, which shows the following facts:

---

3. Does the analysis of *Hamer* suggest that, under the benefit/detriment test, *any* bilateral promise is supported by good consideration? The reciprocal moral duties that such a promise involves reduce the freedom of those who are subject to them, and therefore constitute detriments sufficient for this version of the consideration doctrine.

4. Grant Gilmore observes that the bargain theory of consideration is more restrictive than the older benefits-detriment view and that it became a "tool for narrowing the range of contractual liability." GRANT GILMORE, THE DEATH OF CONTRACT 21 (1974). Gilmore also claims that the bargain theory originated, without precedent, in Holmes's lecture on "The Elements of Contract" and that Holmes was, "quite consciously, proposing revolutionary doctrine." *Id.* at 20. Gilmore's historical characterization of Holmes's engagement with the consideration doctrine has come under criticism. *See, e.g.,* JOHN P. DAWSON, GIFTS AND PROMISES: CONTINENTAL AND AMERICAN LAW COMPARED 199–204 (1980); Richard E. Speidel, *An Essay on the Reported Death and Continued Vitality of Contract*, 27 STAN. L. REV. 1161, 1168–71 (1975).

5. OLIVER WENDELL HOLMES, JR., THE COMMON LAW 293–94 (Dover Publications, Inc. 1991) (1881). Holmes included the word *conventional* to signal that inquiries into consideration should employ an objective standard. The question is not what intentions the parties to a purported contract actually possessed but rather what intentions a reasonable observer would attribute to the parties given their context, actions, and utterances.

The plaintiff was the wife of defendant's brother, but had for some time been a widow, and had several children. In 1840, the plaintiff resided on public land, under a contract of lease, she had held over, and was comfortably settled, and would have attempted to secure the land she lived on. The defendant resided in Talladega county, some sixty or seventy miles off. On the 10th October, 1840, he wrote to her the following letter:

"Dear sister Antillico—Much to my mortification, I heard, that brother Henry was dead, and one of his children. I know that your situation is one of grief, and difficulty. You had a bad chance before, but a great deal worse now. I should like to come and see you, but cannot with convenience at present. * * * I do not know whether you have a preference on the place you live on, or not. If you had, I would advise you to obtain your preference, and sell the land and quit the country, as I understand it is very unhealthy, and I know society is very bad. If you will come down and see me, I will let you have a place to raise your family, and I have more open land than I can tend; and on the account of your situation, and that of your family, I feel like I want you and the children to do well."

Within a month or two after the receipt of this letter, the plaintiff abandoned her possession, without disposing of it, and removed with her family, to the residence of the defendant, who put her in comfortable houses, and gave her land to cultivate for two years, at the end of which time he notified her to remove, and put her in a house, not comfortable, in the woods, which he afterwards required her to leave.

A verdict being found for the plaintiff, for two hundred dollars, the above facts were agreed, and if they will sustain the action, the judgment is to be affirmed, otherwise it is to be reversed.

ORMOND, J. The inclination of my mind, is, that the loss and inconvenience, which the plaintiff sustained in breaking up, and moving to the defendant's, a distance of sixty miles, is a sufficient consideration to support the promise, to furnish her with a house, and land to cultivate, until she could raise her family. My brothers, however think, that the promise on the part of the defendant, was a mere gratuity, and that an action will not lie for its breach. The judgment of the Court below must therefore be reversed, pursuant to the agreement of the parties.

* * *

The plaintiff in Kirksey was married to the defendant's brother, who died, leaving her in financial hardship. The defendant contacted the plaintiff and offered that if she left her home and traveled (some distance) to his, he would let her have a place to stay on his land. The plaintiff moved, and the defendant installed her in a "comfortable house." After two years, the defendant moved her to another house, "not comfortable, in the woods." Finally, the defendant required the plaintiff to quit his land, and she sued him for breach of his promise to let her have a place to stay.

The judge who wrote the opinion would have applied the benefit/detriment test to conclude that the inconvenience and burden that the plaintiff suffered on moving was adequate consideration for the defendant's promise to give her a house. Indeed, although the writing judge did not make the point, the benefit/detriment test would not have required any showing of burden, even. Applying the argument from *Hamer*, it would have been enough to show that the plaintiff was legally free not to move to the defendant's land and therefore, on moving, suffered the "detriment" (even though it served her interests) of taking an action that she was free to refuse.

The writing judge, however, was in the minority on his court. The majority, as he reports, viewed the defendant's promise as a "mere gratuity"—that is, as unsupported by valid consideration and therefore as not enforceable at law. Here one sees the distinction between the benefit/detriment and bargain theories of consideration in action. Although the plaintiff in *Kirksey* did suffer a detriment in moving to the defendant's land— although she moved even though she was free not to—her move was not undertaken *in exchange* for the promise. Rather, her moving was simply a condition of her taking up the gratuitously offered residence—she simply could not live in any of the defendant's houses save by moving to his land.

Matters might have been different had the defendant had an interest in having the plaintiff move near him—so that his intention in making his promise was to get her to move (or, rather, so that a reasonable observer would infer this intention from his promise). The defendant might, for example, have wanted her help in cultivating his lands (which exceeded his capacity to farm) or in running his household; or he might even have simply desired her company. But, the *Kirksey* majority concluded, the defendant's promise was not reasonably understood in any of these lights. It was, rather, a mere gratuity—"you are free to live in one of my houses if you wish"—coupled with an instruction on how to take it up—"to do so, move to where they are located." And as such, it was not legally enforceable.

The bargain theory of consideration therefore turns, in application, on what is surely a nice distinction. Just how finely the lines can be drawn is illustrated by the next case.[6]

---

6. The subtlety of the distinction is also illustrated by the famous case of Williston's tramp, who is told by a benevolent passer-by that if he walks to the clothing shop around the corner he may select an overcoat on his benefactor's credit. *See* 1 WILLISTON AND JAEGER, A TREATIESE ON THE LAW OF CONTRACTS § 112 (3d ed. 1957).

Is this promise supported by good consideration on the bargain theory? The answer depends upon the parties' intentional stances towards the tramp's walk to the clothing store. If the promisor intends the promise to induce the walk, and if the tramp intends the walk to induce the provision of the coat, then there is consideration. (Note that as in other cases, this case involves not a bilateral but a unilateral promise by the passer-by: the consideration that the tramp provides takes the form not of a promise to collect the coat but of the actual coat-collection.) If, on the other hand, the promisor is merely offering to buy the tramp a coat but not to get it for him, and the tramp is merely deciding whether or not to collect on the offer, then there is no consideration. Both possibilities are, incidentally, quite realistic. In the first, the passer-by and the tramp intend to clothe the tramp together (perhaps, the passer-by wishes to assuage her guilt at going to a warm home while the tramp must sleep rough); in the second, the passer-by intends to enable the tramp to cloth himself. A court adjudicating the tramp's contractual claim to the coat may find consideration or not, depending on its view of the facts.

St. Peter v. Pioneer Theatre Corp.

Supreme Court of Iowa, 1940.
291 N.W. 164.

■ MILLER, J. This controversy involves a drawing at a theatre under an arrangement designated as "bank night", not identical with, but substantially similar to the arrangement involved in the controversy heretofore presented to this court by the case of State v. Hundling, 220 Iowa 1369. In that case, we held that the arrangement was not a lottery in violation of the provisions of Section 13218 of the Code, 1931, and that the proprietor of the theatre was not subject to criminal prosecution. In this case, we are confronted with the question whether the arrangement is such that one, to whom the prize is awarded, has a cause of action to enforce the payment thereof.

Plaintiff's petition alleges that the Pioneer Theatre Corporation operates a theatre at Jefferson, Iowa, known as the Iowa Theatre, and that the defendant Parkinson was at all times material herein manager of such theatre. The bank night drawing by defendants was conducted on Wednesday evening, at about 9 p. m. On December 21, 1938, the prize or purse was advertised by defendants in the amount of $275. At about 9 p. m., plaintiff and her husband were outside the theatre when an agent of the defendants announced that plaintiff's name had been called. Plaintiff immediately went into the theatre and made demand upon the manager, who refused to pay her the prize or purse, although plaintiff made demand therefore within the three minutes allowed by defendants. Plaintiff demanded judgment for the $275 and costs.

In count II of the plaintiff's petition, plaintiff alleged that her husband's name was drawn, he presented himself within three minutes, demanded the $275 and payment was refused, if he was not within the allotted time it was due to acts of defendants, her husband assigned his claim to plaintiff and plaintiff demanded judgment as such assignee.

Defendants' answer admitted that the Pioneer Theatre Corporation is operating the Iowa Theatre at Jefferson, Iowa, and that the defendant Parkinson is and has been for more than five years manager of said Iowa Theatre for the corporate defendant. The answer denied all other allegations of both counts of the petition.

The only witnesses to testify at the trial were the plaintiff and her husband. Their testimony is not in conflict. Accordingly, no disputed question of fact is presented, only questions of law.

Williston has his own intuitions about which intentional pattern was more likely. His view of the case was simply that it involved no consideration because "the walk was not requested as the price of the promise, but was merely a condition of a gratuitous promise." *Id.* This approach seems to me to elide the central distinction in the case, namely whether the tramp's walk to the store was a condition of the promisor's intent to provide the coat or a condition of possessing a coat that the promisor unconditionally intended to make available—whether, as it were, the walk functioned as a condition outside or inside the promisor's donative intention. This subtle difference is critical to contract law, because it is the difference between an intention to contract with the tramp and an intention merely to benefit him.

They testified that each had signed the bank night register, plaintiff's number was 6396, her husband's number 212. The husband signed the register at the express invitation and request of Parkinson. Plaintiff signed the register later at the theatre in the presence of an usher. Plaintiff attended every bank night, often accompanied by her husband. Sometimes they attended as patrons of the theatre. Other times they stood on the sidewalk outside. On the occasions when they remained on the sidewalk outside the theatre, one Alice Kafer habitually announced the name that had been drawn inside the theatre. The only other person seen by them to make such announcement was Parkinson.

On the evening of December 21, 1938, plaintiff and her husband were on the sidewalk in front of the theatre. They observed a sign reading "Bank Night $275". About 9 o'clock Alice Kafer came out and said to plaintiff, "Hurry up Mrs. St. Peter, your name is called." Plaintiff entered the theatre and called to Parkinson. He came back and said, "I am sorry, but it was your husband's name that was called, where is your husband?" She said, "He is right behind me," turned around and motioned to him and said, "It's your name that was called." As he started toward them, the lights went out and in the darkness they lost track of Parkinson. They sent an usher to look for him. When Parkinson came out and approached them he said to plaintiff's husband, "You are too late, just one second too late." Mr. St. Peter said, "You have a pretty good watch." Parkinson replied, "One second is just as good as a week." Mr. St. Peter said, "Why don't you call the name outside like you do inside?" Parkinson replied, "I have a lady hired to call the name out." When asked who she was, he said, "It's none of your business." When told that Mr. St. Peter intended to see a lawyer, Parkinson stated, "That is what we want you to do; the law is backing us up on our side." Plaintiff and her husband then left the theatre. Plaintiff's husband testified that he assigned his claim to the plaintiff before the action was commenced.

At the close of plaintiff's evidence, which consisted solely of her testimony, that of her husband, and defendants' bank night register, defendants made a motion for a directed verdict on seven grounds, to wit: (1) there was no adequate or legal consideration for the claimed promise to give the alleged purse, (2) there was no evidence that Alice Kafer was employed by or in any manner authorized by defendants to announce the winner of the drawing, and defendants were not bound by her statements, (3) the most that could be claimed for plaintiff's alleged cause of action was a mere executory agreement to make a gift upon the happening of certain events without legal or adequate consideration, and no recovery could be had, (4) if a verdict were returned for plaintiff under the evidence offered, it would be the duty of the court to set the same aside, (5) there was no evidence that either plaintiff or her husband claimed the purse within the time limit fixed by defendants, (6) there was no relevant, competent or material proof that the name of either plaintiff or her husband was drawn, (7) if there is any legal or sufficient consideration for the promise sought to be enforced, then such consideration would constitute the transaction a lottery and, therefore, an illegal transaction upon which no recovery could be had.

The court sustained the motion generally. A verdict for the defendants was returned accordingly and judgment was entered dismissing the action at plaintiff's costs. Plaintiff appeals, assigning as error the sustaining of the motion and the entry of judgment pursuant thereto.

I.   Since the motion was sustained generally, it is incumbent upon appellant, before she would be entitled to a reversal at our hands, to establish that the motion was not good upon any ground thereof. *People's Trust & Savings Bank v. Smith*, 212 Iowa 124, 126. Realizing such burden, and undertaking to discharge the same, appellant has made seven assignments of error, each attacking a similarly numbered paragraph of the motion for directed verdict.

II.   Appellant's assignments of error Nos. 1, 3 and 7, attacking paragraphs 1, 3 and 7 of the motion for directed verdict, are definitely related to each other, and will be considered together. In such consideration, we are faced at the outset with our decision in the case of *State v. Hundling*, 220 Iowa 1369, heretofore referred to, wherein we held that an arrangement such as is involved herein does not constitute a lottery, and that the proprietor of the theatre is not subject to criminal prosecution on account thereof. In defining a lottery, we state at page 1370 of 220 Iowa, as follows: "The giving away of property or prizes is not unlawful, nor is the gift made unlawful by the fact that the recipient is determined by lot. Our statute provides that the recipient of a public office may be determined by lot in certain cases where there is a tie vote. Section 883, Code 1931. To constitute a lottery there must be a further element, and that is the payment of a valuable consideration for the chance to receive the prize. Thus, it is quite generally recognized that there are three elements necessary to constitute a lottery: First, a prize to be given; second, upon a contingency to be determined by chance; and, third, to a person who has paid some valuable consideration or hazarded something of value for the chance."

In applying such definition to the facts presented in that case, we state at page 1371 of 220 Iowa, as follows:

"The term 'lottery,' as popularly and generally used, refers to a gambling scheme in which chances are sold or disposed of for value and the sums thus paid are hazarded in the hope of winning a much larger sum. That is the predominant characteristic of lotteries which has become known to history and is the source of the evil which attends a lottery, in that it arouses the gambling spirit and leads people to hazard their substance on a mere chance. It is undoubtedly the evil against which our statute is directed. The provisions of the statute making it a crime to have possession of lottery tickets with intent to sell or dispose of them indicates not only what is regarded as characteristic of a lottery, but it indicates the particular incident of a lottery which is regarded as an evil. To have a lottery, therefore, he who has the chance to win the prize must pay, or agree to pay, something of value for that chance.

"In the particular scheme under consideration here, there is no question but what two elements of a lottery are present, first, a prize, and, second, a determination of the recipient by lot. Difficulty arises in the third element, namely, the payment of some valuable consideration for the chance by the holder thereof. The holder of the chance to win the prize in the case at bar was required to do two things in order to be eligible to receive the prize, first, to sign his name in the book, and, second, be in such proximity to the theater as that he could claim the prize within two and one-half minutes after his name was announced. He was not required to purchase a ticket of admission to the theater either as a condition to signing the registration book or claiming the prize when his name was drawn. In other words, paying admission to the theater added nothing to the chance. Where then is the payment by the holder of the chance of a valuable consideration for the chance, which is necessary in order to make the scheme a lottery?"

In holding that there was not such a valuable consideration as would constitute the arrangement a lottery, we state at page 1372 of 220 Iowa, as follows: "It is urged on behalf of the state that the defendant theater manager gained some benefit, or hoped to gain some benefit, from the scheme in the way of increased attendance at his theater, and that this would afford the consideration required. If it be conceded that the attendance at the theater on the particular night that the prize was to be given away was stimulated by reason of the scheme, it is difficult to see how that would make the scheme a lottery. The question is not whether the donor of the prize makes a profit in some remote and indirect way, but, rather, whether those who have a chance at the prize pay anything of value for that chance. Every scheme of advertising, including the giving away of premiums and prizes, naturally has for its object, not purely a philanthropic purpose, but increased business. Profit accruing remotely and indirectly to the person who gives the prize is not a substitute for the requirement that he who has the chance to win the prize must pay a valuable consideration therefor, in order to make the scheme a lottery."

Appellees rely upon the language above quoted to support their contention that the arrangement involved in both cases constitutes merely an offer to make a gift, which is not supported by a valuable consideration and is, therefore, unenforceable.

In 12 American Jurisprudence, pages 564 and 565, in Section 72, it is stated, "It is well settled, however, that ordinarily consideration is an essential element of a simple contract, and want or lack of consideration is an excuse for nonperformance of a promise." It is also stated, "The policy of the courts in requiring a consideration for the maintenance of an action of assumpsit appears to be to prevent the enforcement of gratuitous promises." Such principles have been recognized by this court. In the case of *Farlow v. Farlow*, 154 Iowa 647, we held that a promise to make a gift is without consideration and not enforceable. See, also, *Lanfier v. Lanfier*, Iowa, 288 N.W. 104.

Appellees contend that the foregoing principles, considered with our statements in *State v. Hundling*, supra, show that this action is based upon a promise that cannot be enforced. In the *Hundling* case, we state, "The giving away of property or prizes is not unlawful," and, "profit accruing remotely and indirectly to the person who gives the prize is not a substitute for the requirement that he who has a chance to win the prize must pay a valuable consideration therefor." Appellees contend that these pronouncements commit us to the proposition that the arrangement involved herein constituted nothing more than a promise to make a gift which is not supported by a legal consideration, and, accordingly, is not enforceable. We are unable to agree with the contentions of appellees.

At the outset, it is important to bear in mind that the plaintiff herein seeks to recover on a unilateral contract. A bilateral contract is one in which two promises are made; the promise of each party to the contract is consideration for the promise of the other party. In a unilateral contract, only one party makes a promise. If that promise is made contingent upon the other party doing some act, which he is not under legal obligation to do, or forbearing an action which he has a legal right to take, then such affirmative act or forbearance constitutes the consideration for and acceptance of the promise.

In discussing the difference between bilateral contracts and unilateral contracts, this court, in the case of *Port Huron Mach. Co. v. Wohlers*, 207 Iowa 826, 829, states as follows:

"The law recognizes, as a matter of classification, two kinds of contracts-unilateral and bilateral. In the case at bar a typical example of unilateral contract is found, since it is universally agreed that a 'unilateral contract' is one in which no promisor receives a promise as consideration, whereas, in a 'bilateral contract' there are mutual promises between the two parties to the contract. This matter of definition has recently received careful consideration by the American Law Institute and may be found in the Restatement of the Law of Contracts. Proposed Final Draft No. 1 (April 18, 1928) p. 17, § 12.

"In the instant case the offer of the defendant must be viewed as a promise. It is promissory in terms. The rule is well stated by Prof. Williston: A promise which the promisor should reasonably expect to induce action or forbearance of a definite and substantial character on the part of the promisee, and which does induce such action or forbearance, is binding if injustice can be avoided only by enforcement of the promise. See Williston on Contracts, vol. 1, § 139. Clearly the instant offer signed by the defendant was of this character. Appellant, however, contends that there was no acceptance of the offer. Words are not the only medium of expression of mutual assent. An offer may invite an acceptance to be made by merely an affirmative answer or by performing a specific act. True, if an act other than a promise is requested, no contract exists until what is requested is performed or tendered in whole or in part. We are here dealing with a unilateral contract, and the act requested and performed as consideration for the contract indicates acceptance as well as furnishes the consideration."

The principles applicable to the question of the adequacy of the consideration are clearly and concisely stated by Chief Justice Wright in the early case of *Blake v. Blake*, 7 Iowa 46, 51, as follows: "The essence and requisite of every consideration is, that it should create some benefit to the party promising, or some trouble, prejudice, or inconvenience to the party to whom the promise is made. Whenever, therefore, any injury to the one party, or any benefit to the other, springs from a consideration, it is sufficient to support a contract. Each party to a contract may, ordinarily, exercise his own discretion, as to the adequacy of the consideration; and if the agreement be made bona fide, it matters not how insignificant the benefit may apparently be to the promisor, or how slight the inconvenience or damage appear to be to the promisee, provided it be susceptible of legal estimation. Story on Contracts, section 431. Of course, however, if the inadequacy is so gross as to create a presumption of fraud, the contract founded thereon would not be enforced. But, even then, it is the fraud which is thereby indicated, and not the inadequacy of consideration, which invalidates the contract."

Applying the principles above reviewed, it is readily apparent that, in this action on a unilateral contract, it was necessary for the plaintiff to show that a promise had been made which might be accepted by the doing of an act, which act would constitute consideration for the promise and performance of the contract. There is no basis for any claim of fraud herein. Plaintiff had nothing to do with inducing the defendants' promise. That promise was voluntarily and deliberately made. Defendants exercised their own discretion in determining the adequacy of the consideration for their promise. If the plaintiff did the acts called for by that promise, defendants cannot complain of the adequacy of the consideration.

Of course, it is fundamental that the act which is asserted as the consideration for acceptance and performance of a unilateral contract must be an act which the party sought to be bound bargained for, and the acts must have been induced by the promise made. Appellees contend that the facts are wholly insufficient to meet such requirements, contending as follows: "Although the action of Appellant in writing her name or standing in front of the theater might under some circumstances be such an act as would furnish a consideration for a promise, yet under the facts in the case at bar, no reasonable person could say that the requested acts were actually bargained for in a legal sense so as to give rise to an enforceable promise."

We are unable to concur in the contentions of counsel above quoted. We think that the requested acts were bargained for. We see nothing unreasonable in such holding. If there is anything unreasonable in this phase of the case, it would appear to be the contentions of counsel.

This brings us to the proposition raised by paragraph 7 of the motion for directed verdict, wherein it is asserted that, if there was a legal consideration for the promise sought to be enforced, then such consideration would constitute the transaction a lottery. To sustain such contention would require us to overrule *State v. Hundling*, supra, and to overrule such contention requires a differentiating of that case from this case. We think that the two questions are different and may be logically distinguished.

In the *Hundling* case, we point out that the source of the evil which attends a lottery is that it arouses the gambling spirit and leads people to hazard their substance on a mere chance. Accordingly, it is vitally necessary to constitute a lottery that one who has the chance to win the prize must pay something of value for that chance. The value of the consideration, from a monetary standpoint, is the essence of the crime. However, in a civil action to enforce the promise to pay a prize, the monetary value of the consideration is in no wise controlling. It is only necessary that the act done be that which the promisor specified. The sufficiency of the consideration lies wholly within the discretion of the one who offers to pay the prize. "It matters not how insignificant the benefit may apparently be to the promisor, or how slight the inconvenience or damage appear to be to the promisee, provided it be susceptible of legal estimation." Blake v. Blake, supra. Accordingly, it is entirely possible that the act, specified by the promisor as being sufficient in his discretion to constitute consideration for and acceptance of his promise, might have no monetary value and yet constitute a legal consideration for the promise. Under such circumstances, the arrangement is not a lottery. The promoter of the scheme cannot be prosecuted criminally. But, if the act specified is done, the unilateral contract is supported by a consideration, and, having been performed by the party doing the act, can be enforced against the party making the promise. We hold that such is the situation here. There is no merit in grounds 1, 3 and 7 of the motion for directed verdict.

[Court's discussion of the appellant's second, fourth, fifth, and sixth assignments of error omitted.]

All of appellant's assignments of error are well grounded. No ground of the motion for directed verdict was sufficient to warrant a sustaining of the motion. The court's ruling was erroneous. The judgment entered pursuant thereto must be and it is reversed.

The CHIEF JUSTICE and all the Justices concur.

* * *

The defendants, in *St. Peter*, were a cinema that held bank nights, in which persons could place their names on a list from which one would be drawn, at random, to win a prize—$275, on the night in question in the case. The defendants hoped that those who entered the draw would also become paid ticket-holders at their movie showings, although they could not require this without violating state anti-gambling laws. In modern parlance, the case involved a giveaway to potential customers with "no purchase necessary." The plaintiffs habitually entered their name on the list without becoming ticket-holders, and without any intention or likelihood of ever becoming defendants' paying customers. On the night in question in the case, the plaintiffs' name was drawn from the lottery list, and they claimed their prize. The defendants refused to pay out the money, and the plaintiffs sued.

After clearing away preliminary arguments concerning whether or not the defendants had adequately announced the plaintiffs' name when drawn and whether the plaintiffs claimed their prize within the requisite time-limit,[7] the court took up the main issue in the case—namely whether or not the plaintiffs gave adequate consideration to support (to render enforceable) the defendant's contractual promise to pay them $275 in case their name was drawn. The court found that they had—concluding that "[t]he sufficiency of the consideration lies wholly within the discretion of the one who offers to pay the prize" and thus that any benefit that the plaintiffs conveyed on the defendants, or any detriment that they suffered themselves, might suffice to support enforcing the contract against the defendants. Moreover, and for present purposes critically, the same result would be reached, in *St. Peter*, applying the bargain theory of consideration. Although the court did not make the distinction explicit, the contrast between the facts in *Kirksey* and in *St. Peter* is plain. In *Kirksey*, the action that the defendant's promise required of the plaintiff—moving to the defendant's land—was not required with the intention that the plaintiff should take it. Rather, there was simply no way for the plaintiff to have the defendant's house save by moving there. In *St. Peter*, by contrast, the action that the defendant's promise required of the plaintiffs—appearing at the defendant's place of business and signing the list of entrants—was included in the defendant's promise with the intention that the plaintiff undertake it. The defendant intended for potential customers to come into town and into its theater, on the straightforward ground that doing so increased the likelihood that they would become actual customers. The contract therefore involved a bargain—a promise of inclusion in the bank night exchanged for appearing at the drawing at a time at which the defendants wanted people in or near their theater.[8] No matter that the defendants were *motivated* not by the plaintiffs' mere appearance at the cinema but by the fact that this increased their chance of buying movie tickets. Consideration, under the bargain theory, turns on intent rather than motive.[9]

St. Peter thus illustrates and indeed expressly affirms the modern principle that although consideration requires that a contract involves a

---

7. The court also asked whether the fact that the "no purchase necessary" rule entailed that plaintiffs had provided no "valuable consideration" as defined under the state's anti-gambling laws (and that the bank night therefore did not violate these laws) entailed that there could be no consideration for purposes of contract law, either. The court correctly concluded that no such thing followed. *Consideration* is a term of legal art and might be defined differently in different legal orders. That was the case in *St. Peter*, where the anti-gambling laws defined *consideration* to involve a payment with a cash value whereas contract law defined consideration, much more broadly, to involve any reciprocal, conventional inducement.

8. As the *St. Peter* court noted, this made the contract unilateral rather than bilateral. The plaintiff's performance was both the means of accepting the defendant's offer and the action that the defendant's offer sought to induce.

9. *See* RESTATEMENT (SECOND) OF CONTRACTS § 81.

bargain *in fact*, the consideration doctrine does not police the terms of the bargain and in particular the adequacy of what each side gives and receives. Again, "the sufficiency of the consideration lies wholly within the discretion of the one who offers to pay the prize." Both parts of this rule concerning consideration are simply expressed by Section 71 of the *Restatement (Second) of Contracts* and the comments thereto.

Restatement 2d of Contracts

§ 71 Requirement of Exchange; Types of Exchange

(1) To constitute consideration, a performance or a return promise must be bargained for.

(2) A performance or return promise is bargained for if it is sought by the promisor in exchange for his promise and is given by the promisee in exchange for that promise.

(3) The performance may consist of

(a) an act other than a promise, or

(b) a forbearance, or

(c) the creation, modification, or destruction of a legal relation.

(4) The performance or return promise may be given to the promisor or to some other person. It may be given by the promisee or by some other person.

Comments & Illustrations

Comment a. Other meanings of "consideration." The word "consideration" has often been used with meanings different from that given here. It is often used merely to express the legal conclusion that a promise is enforceable. Historically, its primary meaning may have been that the conditions were met under which an action of assumpsit would lie. It was also used as the equivalent of the quid pro quo required in an action of debt. A seal, it has been said, "imports a consideration," although the law was clear that no element of bargain was necessary to enforcement of a promise under seal. On the other hand, consideration has sometimes been used to refer to almost any reason asserted for enforcing a promise, even though the reason was insufficient. In this sense we find references to promises "in consideration of love and affection," to "illegal consideration," to "past consideration," and to consideration furnished by reliance on a gratuitous promise.

Consideration has also been used to refer to the element of exchange without regard to legal consequences. Consistent with that usage has been the use of the phrase "sufficient consideration" to express the legal conclusion that one requirement for an enforceable bargain is met. Here § 17 states the element of exchange required for a contract enforceable as a bargain as "a consideration." Thus "consideration" refers to an element of exchange which is sufficient to satisfy the legal requirement; the word "sufficient" would be redundant and is not used.

Comment b. "Bargained for." In the typical bargain, the consideration and the promise bear a reciprocal relation of motive or inducement: the consideration induces the making of the promise and the promise induces the furnishing of the consideration. Here, as in the matter of mutual assent, the law is concerned with the external manifestation rather than the undisclosed mental state: it is enough that one party manifests an intention to induce the other's response and to be induced by it and that the other responds in accordance with the inducement. See § 81; compare §§ 19, 20. But it is not enough that the promise induces the conduct of the promisee or that the conduct of the promisee induces the making of the promise; both elements must be present, or there is no bargain. Moreover, a mere pretense of bargain does not suffice, as where there is a false recital of consideration or where the purported consideration is merely nominal. In such cases there is no consideration and the promise is enforced, if at all, as a promise binding without consideration under §§ 82–94. See Comments *b* and *c* to § 87.

Illustrations:

1. A offers to buy a book owned by B and to pay B $10 in exchange therefor. B accepts the offer and delivers the book to A. The transfer and delivery of the book constitute a performance and are consideration for A's promise. See Uniform Commercial Code §§ 2–106, 2–301. This is so even though A at the time he makes the offer secretly intends to pay B $10 whether or not he gets the book, or even though B at the time he accepts secretly intends not to collect the $10.2. A receives a gift from B of a book worth $10. Subsequently A promises to pay B the value of the book. There is no consideration for A's promise. This is so even though B at the time he makes the gift secretly hopes that A will pay him for it. As to the enforcement of such promises, see § 86.3. A promises to make a gift of $10 to B. In reliance on the promise B buys a book from C and promises to pay C $10 for it. There is no consideration for A's promise. As to the enforcement of such promises, see § 90.4. A desires to make a binding promise to give $1000 to his son B. Being advised that a gratuitous promise is not binding, A writes out and signs a false recital that B has sold him a car for $1000 and a promise to pay that amount. There is no consideration for A's promise.5. A desires to make a binding promise to give $1000 to his son B. Being advised that a gratuitous promise is not binding, A offers to buy from B for $1000 a book worth less than $1. B accepts the offer knowing that the purchase of the book is a mere pretense. There is no consideration for A's promise to pay $1000.

Comment c. Mixture of bargain and gift. In most commercial bargains there is a rough equivalence between the value promised and the value received as consideration. But the social functions of bargains include the provision of opportunity for free individual action and exercise of judgment and the fixing of values by private action, either generally or for purposes of the particular transaction. Those functions would be impaired by judicial review of the values so fixed. Ordinarily, therefore, courts do not inquire into the adequacy of consideration, particularly where one or both of the values exchanged are difficult to measure. See § 79. Even where both parties know that a transaction is in part a bargain and in part a gift, the element of bargain may nevertheless furnish consideration for the entire transaction.

On the other hand, a gift is not ordinarily treated as a bargain, and a promise to make a gift is not made a bargain by the promise of the prospective donee to accept the gift, or by his acceptance of part of it. This may be true even though the terms of gift impose a burden on the donee as well as the donor. See Illustration 2 to § 24. In such cases the distinction between bargain and gift may be a fine one, depending on the motives manifested by the parties. In some cases there may be no bargain so long as the agreement is entirely executory, but performance may furnish consideration or the agreement may become fully or partly enforceable by virtue of the reliance of one party or the unjust enrichment of the other. Compare § 90.

Illustration:

6. A offers to buy a book owned by B and to pay B $10 in exchange therefor. B's transfer and delivery of the book are consideration for A's promise even though both parties know that such books regularly sell for $5 and that part of A's motive in making the offer is to make a gift to B. See §§ 79, 81.7. A owns land worth $10,000 which is subject to a mortgage to secure a debt of $5,000. A promises to make a gift of the land to his son B and to pay off the mortgage, and later gives B a deed subject to the mortgage. B's acceptance of the deed is not consideration for A's promise to pay the mortgage debt.8. A and B agree that A will advance $1000 to B as a gratuitous loan. B's promise to accept the loan is not consideration for A's promise to make it. But the loan when made is consideration for B's promise to repay.

Comment d. Types of consideration. Consideration may consist of a performance or of a return promise. Consideration by way of performance may be a specified act of forbearance, or any one of several specified acts or forbearances of which the offeree is given the choice, or such conduct as will produce a specified result. Or either the offeror or the offeree may request as consideration the creation, modification or destruction of a purely intangible legal relation. Not infrequently the consideration bargained for is an act with the added requirement that a certain legal result shall be produced. Consideration by way of return promise requires a promise as defined in § 2. Consideration may consist partly of promise and partly of other acts or forbearances, and the consideration invited may be a performance or a return promise in the alternative. Though a promise is itself an act, it is treated separately from other acts. See § 75.

Illustration:

9.   A promises B, his nephew aged 16, that A will pay B $1000 when B becomes 21 if B does not smoke before then. B's forbearance to smoke is a performance and if bargained for is consideration for A's promise.10. A says to B, the owner of a garage, "I will pay you $100 if you will make my car run properly." The production of this result is consideration for A's promise.11. A has B's horse in his possession. B writes to A, "If you will promise me $100 for the horse, he is yours." A promptly replies making the requested promise. The property in the horse at once passes to A. The change in ownership is consideration for A's promise.12. A promises to pay B $1,000 if B will make an offer to C to sell C certain land for $25,000 and will leave the offer open for 24 hours. B makes the requested offer and forbears to revoke it for 24 hours, but C does not accept. The creation of a power of acceptance in C is consideration for A's promise.13. A mails a written order to B, offering to buy specified machinery on specified terms. The order provides "Ship at once." B's prompt shipment or promise to ship is consideration for A's promise to pay the price. See § 32; Uniform Commercial Code § 2–206(1)(b).

Comment e. Consideration moving from or to a third person. It matters not from whom the consideration moves or to whom it goes. If it is bargained for and given in exchange for the promise, the promise is not gratuitous.

Illustrations:

14.   A promises B to guarantee payment of a bill of goods if B sells the goods to C. Selling the goods to C is consideration for A's promise.15. A makes a promissory note payable to B in return for a payment by B to C. The payment is consideration for the note.16. A, at C's request and in exchange for $1 paid by C, promises B to give him a book. The payment is consideration for A's promise.17. A promises B to pay B $1, in exchange for C's promise to A to give A a book. The promises are consideration for one another.18. A promises to pay $1,000 to B, a bank, in exchange for the delivery of a car by C to A's son D. The delivery of the car is consideration for A's promise.

Restatement (Second) of Contracts

§ 79   Adequacy of Consideration; Mutuality of Obligation

If the requirement of consideration is met, there is no additional requirement of

(a) a gain, advantage, or benefit to the promisor or a loss, disadvantage, or detriment to the promisee; or

(b) equivalence in the values exchanged; or

(c) "mutuality of obligation."

Comments & Illustrations

Comment a. Rationale. In such typical bargains as the ordinary sale of goods each party gives up something of economic value, and the values exchanged are often roughly or exactly equivalent by standards independent of the particular bargain. Quite often promise is exchanged for promise, and the promised performances are sometimes divisible into matching parts. See § 31. Hence it has sometimes been said that consideration must consist of a "benefit to the promisor" or a "detriment to the promisee"; it has frequently been claimed that there was no consideration because the economic value given in exchange was much less than that of the promise or the promised performance; "mutuality of obligation" has been said to be essential to a contract. But experience has shown that these are not essential elements of a bargain or of an enforceable contract, and they are negated as requirements by the rules stated in §§ 71–78. This Section makes that negation explicit.

Comment b. Benefit and detriment. Historically, the common law action of debt was said to require a quid pro quo, and that requirement may have led to statements that consideration must be a benefit to the promisor. But contracts were enforced in the common-law action of assumpsit without any such requirement; in actions of assumpsit the emphasis was rather on the harm to the promisee, and detrimental reliance on a promise may still be the basis of contractual relief. See § 90. But reliance is not essential to the formation of a bargain, and remedies for breach have long been given in cases of exchange of promise for promise where neither party has begun to perform. Today when it is said that consideration must involve a detriment to the promisee, the supposed requirement is often qualified by a statement that a "legal detriment" is sufficient even though there is no economic detriment or other actual loss. It is more realistic to say simply that there is no requirement of detriment.

Illustrations:

1. A contracts to sell property to B. As a favor to B, who is C's friend, and in consideration of A's performance of the contract, C guarantees that B will pay the agreed price. A's performance is consideration for C's promise. See § 73.

2. A has executed a document in the form of a guaranty which imposes no obligation on A and has no value. B's surrender of the document to A, if bargained for, is consideration for a promise by A to pay $10,000. Compare § 74.

Comment c. Exchange of unequal values. To the extent that the apportionment of productive energy and product in the economy are left to private action, the parties to transactions are free to fix their own valuations. The resolution of disputes often requires a determination of value in the more general sense of market value, and such values are commonly fixed as an approximation based on a multitude of private valuations. But in many situations there is no reliable external standard of value, or the general standard is inappropriate to the precise circumstances of the parties. Valuation is left to private action in part because the parties are thought to be better able than others to evaluate the circumstances of particular transactions. In any event, they are not ordinarily bound to follow the valuations of others.

Ordinarily, therefore, courts do not inquire into the adequacy of consideration. This is particularly so when one or both of the values exchanged are uncertain or difficult to measure. But it is also applied even when it is clear that the transaction is a mixture of bargain and gift. See Comment *c* to § 71. Gross inadequacy of consideration may be relevant to issues of capacity, fraud and the like, but the requirement of consideration is not a safeguard against imprudent and improvident contracts except in cases where it appears that there is no bargain in fact.

Illustrations:

3. A borrows $300 from B to enable A to begin litigation to recover a gold mine through litigation, and promises to repay $10,000 when he recovers the mine. The loan is consideration for the promise.

4. A is pregnant with the illegitimate child of B, a wealthy man. A promises to give the child A's surname and B's given name, and B promises to provide for the support and education of the child and to set up a trust of securities to provide the child with a minimum net income of $100 per week until he reaches the age of 21. The naming of the child is consideration for B's promise.

Comment d. Pretended exchange. Disparity in value, with or without other circumstances, sometimes indicates that the purported consideration was not in fact bargained for but was a mere formality or pretense. Such a sham or "nominal" consideration does not satisfy the requirement of § 71. Promises are enforced in such cases, if at all, either as promises binding without consideration under §§ 82–94 or as promises binding by virtue of their formal characteristics under § 6. See, for example, §§ 95–109 on contracts under seal.

Illustrations:

5. In consideration of one cent received, A promises to pay $600 in three yearly installments of $200 each. The one cent is merely nominal and is not consideration for A's promise.

6. A dies leaving no assets and owing $4000 to the B bank. C, A's widow, promises to pay the debt, and B promises to make no claim against A's estate. Without some further showing, B's promise is a mere formality and is not consideration for C's promise.

Comment e. Effects of gross inadequacy. Although the requirement of consideration may be met despite a great difference in the values exchanged, gross inadequacy of consideration may be relevant in the application of other rules. Inadequacy "such as shocks the conscience" is often said to be a "badge of fraud," justifying a denial of specific performance. See § 364(1)(c). Inadequacy may also help to justify rescission or cancellation on the ground of lack of capacity (see §§ 15, 16), mistake, misrepresentation, duress or undue influence (see Chapters 6 and 7). Unequal bargains are also limited by the statutory law of usury, by regulation of the rates of public utilities and some other enterprises, and by special rules developed for the sale of an expectation of inheritance, for contractual penalties and forfeitures (see §§ 229, 356), and for agreements between secured lender and borrower (see Restatement of Security § 55, Uniform Commercial Code § 9–501).

Comment f. Mutuality. The word "mutuality," though often used in connection with the law of Contracts, has no definite meaning. "Mutual assent" as one element of a bargain is the subject of Topic 2 of this Chapter. "Mutuality of remedy" is dealt with in Comment *c* to § 363. Clause (c) of this Section negates any supposed requirement of "mutuality of obligation." Such a requirement has sometimes been asserted in the form, "Both parties must be bound or neither is bound." That statement is obviously erroneous as applied to an exchange of promise for performance; it is equally inapplicable to contracts governed by §§ 82–94 and to contracts enforceable by virtue of their formal characteristics under § 6. Even in the ordinary case of the exchange of promise for promise, § 78 makes it clear that voidable and unenforceable promises may be consideration. The only requirement of "mutuality of obligation" even in cases of mutual promises is that stated in §§ 76–77.

15.2   THE BARGAIN THEORY OF CONSIDERATION AND THE VALUE OF PURE FORM

The application of the consideration doctrine has been anything but straightforward, and the doctrine has generated a host of familiar controversies and puzzles. The root cause of the many difficulties presented by the bargain theory of consideration lies in the fact that its two core features—insistence on the *fact* of a bargain but unconcern for the *adequacy* of the bargain—sit uneasily together.[10]

The tension between these two elements of the doctrine is immediate and indeed appears directly in the comments to the Restatement. Thus comment c explains that "[o]rdinarily, courts do not inquire into the adequacy of consideration" and adds that "[g]ross inadequacy of consideration may be relevant to issues of capacity, fraud, and the like, but the requirement of consideration is not a safeguard against imprudent and improvident contracts except in cases where it appears that there is no

---

10.   This presentation follows CHARLES FRIED, CONTRACT AS PROMISE 29 (1982).

bargain in fact."[11] Comment b of the Restatement, by contrast, at once presses in the opposed direction, in order to prevent the liberality expressed by comment c from rendering the requirement of consideration a nullity: "[D]isparity in value, with or without other circumstances, sometimes indicates that the purported consideration was not in fact bargained for but was a mere formality or pretense. Such a sham or 'nominal' consideration does not satisfy the requirement of [consideration]."[12] In other words, in spite of the earlier comment's disavowal of inquiry into the adequacy of consideration, the "cases where it appears that there is no bargain in fact"[13] are not limited to circumstances involving force or fraud but may instead be identified directly by reference to the inadequacy of consideration.

The cases, predictably, apply these rules in both directions. On the one hand, it is not hard to find venerable opinions that say, for example, "It is the general rule that where there is no fraud, and a party gets all the consideration he contracts for, the contract will be upheld,"[14] and that "a rose, a hawk, or a peppercorn will suffice [for consideration] provided it is what is asked for by the promisor...."[15] And, on the other hand, it is equally easy to find equally venerable opinions that say, for example, "The consideration was not only *unequal*, but *grossly* so ... [and] at best, purely *technical* and *colorable*, and obviously ... wanting in that degree of equitable equality sufficient to support the promise declared upon,"[16] and that "[t]he parties may shout consideration to the house tops, yet, unless consideration is actually present, there is not a legally [enforceable] contract."[17]

Now it is perhaps possible, on a purely formal and doctrinal level, to reconcile these rules and the cases that announce and apply them. One might say that the law does not require enforceable bargains to be fair, or even reasonable, but that it does require them at least to be *real* and to serve, for the parties, some purpose other than the parasitic one of satisfying the demands of the bargain requirement. As Corbin observed, "when the consideration is only a 'peppercorn' or a 'tomtit' or a worthless piece of paper, the requirement of consideration appear[s] ... to be as much of a mere formality as is a seal."[18] A seal standing alone is nowadays generally disfavored as a means of securing the legal enforcement of

---

11. RESTATEMENT (SECOND) OF CONTRACTS § 79 cmt. c.

12. *Id.* § 79 cmt. d.

13. *Id.* § 79 cmt. c.

14. *Wolford v. Powers*, 85 Ind. 294, 296 (1882).

15. *Lucky Calendar Co. v. Cohen*, 117 A.2d 487, 495 (N.J. 1955) (internal quotation marks omitted). The opinion goes on to say that "[t]he law will not inquire as to the adequacy of consideration when the thing to be done is asked to be done, be it ever so small." *Id.* (citing 1 SAMUEL WILLISTON & GEORGE J. THOMPSON, A TREATISE ON THE LAW OF CONTRACTS § 219A (1936))

16. *Shepard v. Rhodes*, 7 R.I. 470, 475 (1863).

17. *In re* Greene, 45 F.2d 428, 430 (S.D.N.Y. 1930).

18. 1 ARTHUR LINTON CORBIN, CORBIN ON CONTRACTS § 127 (2d ed. 1963).

promises.[19] It is natural to read the cases concerning consideration—insofar as they at once refuse to inquire into the adequacy of bargains and yet insist that bargains be real rather than artificial—to develop the doctrine so as to prevent the parties from re-inserting the seal into the law, now in the form of a bare assertion of consideration. This reading is particularly natural in light of the fact that the Restatement (First) of Contracts was much more sympathetic to manufactured consideration and included, in its illustrations, an example in which a buyer's promise to pay $1 is sufficient consideration for a seller's promise to transfer a land worth $5000.[20] The Restatement (Second) expressly reversed course on this question, including two new illustrations in which a manufactured bargain did not include consideration and was not enforceable.

This approach may organize the cases, but it remains difficult to construct a satisfying theoretical defense of the insistence on the fact of a bargain, when coupled with unconcern for the bargain's character; and the reference to the seal merely pushes the problem back one level, since it is difficult to square the doctrine's indifference to the adequacy of consideration with its conclusion that a seal cannot stand in for the very consideration whose adequacy has been declared irrelevant.

Indeed, insofar as the law does adopt the fact-but-not-adequacy approach to consideration, it has been thought puzzling why the law should insist on consideration at all. Charles Fried, for one, attacks the consideration doctrine on precisely this ground. Fried thinks that, by refusing to police the adequacy of consideration, the law "affirms the liberal principle that the free arrangements of rational persons should be respected."[21] But he also thinks that when the law nevertheless insists that enforceable promises involve *some* consideration, when it "limit[s] the class of [enforceable] arrangements to bargains," then the law "holds that individual self-determination is not a sufficient ground of legal obligation."[22] Fried concludes that the consideration doctrine is deeply "internally inconsistent" and therefore indefensible.[23]

Fried's diagnosis of the internal tensions in the consideration doctrine represents the conventional wisdom, although not all those who discuss the doctrine share in his conclusion that it should be abandoned. To some, less concerned than Fried with purity of principle, the internal tensions in the consideration doctrine represent less of a failure. Indeed, beginning with Lon Fuller's classic article *Consideration and Form*,[24] a large literature has

---

19. *See* RESTATEMENT (SECOND) OF CONTRACTS, at Ch. 4 Topic 3 Introductory Note & Statutory Note; U.C.C. § 2–203 (2003); 1A SAMUEL WILLISTON & WALTER H.E. JAEGER, A TREATISE ON THE LAW OF CONTRACTS § 219A (3d ed. 1957); Robert Braucher, *The Status of the Seal Today*, PRAC. LAW., May 1963, at 97. English law, by contrast, continues to recognize the seal. *See* G.H. TREITEL, THE LAW OF CONTRACT 120 (6th ed. 1983).

20. RESTATEMENT (FIRST) OF CONTRACTS § 84 illustration 1 (1932)

21. CHARLES FRIED, CONTRACT AS PROMISE 35 (1982).

22. *Id.* at 35.

23. *Id.* at 35.

24. Lon L. Fuller, *Consideration and Form*, 41 COLUM. L. REV. 799 (1941).

developed increasingly sophisticated, if expansively heterogeneous and una-bashedly pragmatic, arguments roughly in favor of the consideration doc-trine's formal approach to the bargain requirement—its broad willingness to overlook inadequacies in the substance of bargains coupled with its emphatic demand that the bargains in fact exist.

Fuller inaugurated the approach by proposing three broadly instru-mental purposes that the consideration doctrine's formal emphasis on bargains might serve: First, that bargains provide evidence of a contract that aids the legal process of enforcement; second, that bargains caution those who make them of the commitments that they accept and in this way discourage rash and impulsive conduct; and, third, that the preference for bargains channels persons into a legal framework within which they can reliably effectuate their intentions.[25]

Those who follow in Fuller's footsteps have added variations to his basic themes. Some of these variations render the main argument in favor of the law's preference for bargains less certain: Fuller's characterization of gifts as economically "sterile,"[26] for example, must confront the possibility that un-bargained-for promises might serve perfectly ordinarily economic ends related to the fact that a promised performance becomes more valuable to the promisee as it becomes more certain. But other variations reinforce the argument: often gift promises contain implicit excuses for non-performance (for example, a worsening of the promisor's economic position or ingratitude by the promisee) that the law cannot easily adminis-ter;[27] Richard Posner (some of whose opinions you have read, but now writing as a scholar rather than judge) observes that promisees often possess informal social means of enforcing gift promises that render legal enforcement superfluous and indeed undesirable;[28] and others add that legal enforcement of promises outside of the bargain context (and especially in the context of gift promises) will tend inefficiently to depress the supply of such promises.[29]

These and related arguments may, taken together, make a persuasive case for the proposition that not all promises should be enforced through law. But it is plain, even without addressing the several arguments' substantive merits, that such instrumental approaches to the doctrine of consideration cannot possibly account for the law's monotonous, strangely precise, and highly formal focus on reciprocal bargains as the touchstone of enforceability. For if bargains play only an instrumental role in the consideration doctrine, then it is natural to suppose that the doctrine's

---

25. *Id.* at 800–02. Fuller's ideas, and even his language, have achieved canonical status. *See, e.g,* RESTATEMENT (SECOND OF CONTRACTS) § 75 cmt. a ("[T]he fact of bargain tends to satisfy the cautionary and channeling functions of form.").

26. *Id.* at 815.

27. *See* Melvin Eisenberg, *Donative Promises,* 47 U. CHI. L. REV. 1, 13–15 (1979).

28. *See* Richard A. Posner, *Gratuitous Promises in Economics and Law,* 6 J. LEGAL STUD. 411, 417 (1977).

29. *See* Charles Goetz and Robert Scott, *Enforcing Promises: An Examination of the Basis of Contract,* 89 YALE L.J. 1261, 1304 (1980).

effectiveness would be enhanced if at least some other instruments were also admitted to the doctrine and allowed to serve alongside bargains in promoting the doctrine's ends.

Most immediately, the consideration doctrine's formal emphasis on the fact of a bargain cannot be defended on instrumental grounds: Any instrumental function that can be performed by a bargain regardless of its adequacy can surely also be performed by the parties' express insistence (shouted to the house tops) that they have struck a bargain. If the adequacy of a bargain has no role in its instrumental effectiveness, then there is no reason to think that the mere fact of a bargain (however inadequate) is any more instrumentally effective than the express (even if nominal) insistence that this fact obtains. This has led skeptics of functionalism to observe that, "[i]f the fundamental role of consideration is that it fulfills the functions of form, the fact that parties *expressly* treat something as a consideration for the shared reason of giving legal effect to their intentions should be sufficient or at least relevant" for enforceability at law.[30] Indeed, several of those who follow Fuller's justification of the consideration doctrine nevertheless reject the doctrine's refusal to enforce promises that involve expressly asserted but ultimately just nominal consideration, and lament the law's refusal to allow the parties to manufacture enforceability by asserting a bargain's existence or indeed even by means of a seal.[31] The functional theories of consideration can perhaps explain why not every promise should be enforceable at law and even why the bargain context is relevant to the question of enforceability, but they simply cannot (nor, finally, do they purport to) account for the consideration doctrine's formal yet insistent focus on the *fact* of bargains.

Fried found a paradox in the law's concern for the fact but not the adequacy of bargains, and on this basis rejected the doctrine of consideration altogether. The doctrine's instrumental defenders never address this paradox and instead argue that the doctrine, whatever its internal structure, achieves worthwhile external ends. The paradox, however, reasserts itself (as the argument of the previous paragraph reveals), because the law seems to insist on the fact of a bargain even where this fact has no possible instrumental or functional significance. The instrumental mode appears ill-suited to explaining a legal regime that is so narrowly yet insistently formal as the consideration doctrine.

---

30. Peter Benson, *The Unity of Contract Law, in* THE THEORY OF CONTRACT LAW (Peter Benson, ed. 2001) at 118, 167.

31. As Goetz and Scott have observed:

At common law, the formal contract under seal provided a means for promisors to assure enforcement of gratuitous promises. A sham bargain performs a similar function in encouraging deliberation, preserving evidence, and identifying the promisor's intention. Although devices such as seals and sham bargains entail significant administrative costs, the voluntary use of these formal mechanisms suggests that the benefits to both parties of the additional reassurance from legal enforcement outweighs [sic] the transactions costs.

Goetz & Scott supra, note 29, at 1303; *see also* Posner supra, note 28, at 420 (calling the abolition of the seal a "mysterious development" and lamenting the tendency to reject parties' efforts to manufacture nominal consideration).

A more direct explanation of the doctrine's narrow emphasis on the fact of a bargain would therefore surely be preferable. And indeed, the logical space for such an alternative account remains open. The mystery and paradox surrounding the consideration doctrine would dissolve if the bargain form (quite apart from the fairness or adequacy of its substance) could be shown to be *in itself* valuable and, indeed, to display a distinctive connection to the values that underlie the morality of contract more generally.[32] Perhaps, then, the consideration doctrine presents a case study in genuinely free-standing formalism. Perhaps the problems the contract lawyers have had in defending the doctrine (and their consequent inclination to regard the doctrine as not in the end defensible) have been the consequence of insisting that what is, in the end, pure form must serve some independent function.

If this is right, then a theoretically satisfying account of the consideration doctrine, understood along the lines of the bargain theory, might perhaps be found by focusing carefully on the formal structure of bargains. The goal of such an effort would be to describe the bargain form in terms that reveal this form's intrinsic (as opposed to instrumental or functional) value.

This theoretical project requires stepping back for a moment from the special problems associated with consideration to consider contract and indeed promise more generally. Promising involves a form of recognition: to promise to someone is to respect her as a person—to acknowledge her moral personality—in a particular way. Certainly our ordinary practices of promising make clear that only persons can receive promises.[33] We are inclined, when confronted with a promise to a creature other than a person, to attribute the promise to a category error: either to an excessively sentimental anthropomorphizing of the object, as when an owner promises a bone to her dog; or simply to madness. The mechanics of promising give this intuition a practical expression. Promises (recall the discussions in Chapter 13) require offer and acceptance before promissory obligation arises, and only persons possess the power to offer and to accept.[34] Finally,

---

32. It is worth noting here that although the express requirement of consideration is a distinctive feature of the common law of contract, other legal cultures also emphasize bargains and treat them specially, and may even display doctrinal counterparts to consideration. *See, e.g.*, JOHN P. DAWSON, GIFTS AND PROMISES: CONTINENTAL AND AMERICAN LAW COMPARED 199–207 (1980); Arthur T. von Mehren, *Civil Law Analogues to Consideration: An Exercise in Comparative Analysis*, 72 HARV. L. REV. 1009 (1959). Moreover, the recognition of the importance of bargains is no mere surface phenomenon, but is instead connected to the idea, at least as old as Aquinas, that promises establish an order of one person to another. *See* ST. THOMAS AQUINAS, SUMMA THEOLOGICA, II–II, q. 88, a. I Legal Classics Library ed., (1988). Aquinas applied this idea in a broader context than the present one, to argue that all promises must be communicated to be binding rather than to distinguish among subclasses of promises.

33. Insofar as organizations (for example, corporations) can make and accept promises, then this is because they are endowed by law with artificial personality.

34. In philosophy, this connection between promissory capacity and moral personality is rendered most vivid in Nietzsche's remarks that "To breed an animal *that is permitted to promise*—isn't this precisely the paradoxical task nature has set for itself with regard to man? isn't this the real problem *of* man?" and that a person who possesses promissory capacity

contract law—the legal order that has grown up around promise—also follows this line. The connection between legal personality and promise was for a long time expressed in legal rules that deprived human beings whose personality the law did not recognize—slaves and women—of contractual capacity. And even today, the law acknowledges this connection when it denies certain classes of human beings contractual capacity.[35] Indeed, certain human beings, for example minor children[36], may lack contractual capacity but nevertheless sue and be sued in tort, so that having contractual capacity indicates a higher legal status, which reflects a more complete moral personality, than merely enjoying the right not to be harmed. (The doctrines that govern contractual capacity will be taken up in Part III.)

The connection between promises and personhood may be made more precise. When a person makes a promise, she forms intentions in favor of certain ends—the ends associated with the promised performance—that are also available to her promisee. Moreover, the promisee, on whose acceptance the creation of the promissory obligation depends, is not merely drafted into the service of the promisor's pursuit of these ends.[37] Instead, she is engaged by the promise and takes up the promisor's engagement by also forming intentions in favor of the ends associated with the promised performance—generally, the intention to vindicate her promissory rights or at least to administer the promise, as one might say. Moreover, the connection between the promisor's and promisee's intentions is no mere coincidence, and the overlap in their ends is not just incidental. Instead, the promisor, through her promise, intends to entrench her pursuit of the ends announced by the promise and, moreover, to entrench them through the personality of the promisee—she intends to refuse to defect from the promised ends unless the promisee releases her. She intends, in effect, to give the promisee authority over her ends—to pursue, within the sphere of the promise, only ends that the promisee also affirms. She intends, for this authority to be based not on the promisee's special expertise but on his status as a person. She intends to become obligated to the promisee to render the promised performance.[38] And finally, insofar as the promisor

---

holds "his kick in readiness for the frail dogs who promise although they are not permitted to do so." FRIEDRICH NIETZCHE, ON THE GENEOLOGY OF MORALS, Second Essay, Section 2 (1887).

35. *See* RESTATEMENT (SECOND) OF CONTRACTS §§ 12–16, 22.

36. A contract entered into by a minor is voidable at the election of the minor. See RESTATEMENT (SECOND) OF CONTRACTS § 14 ("Unless a statute provides otherwise, a natural person has the capacity to incur only voidable contractual duties until the beginning of the day before the person's eighteenth birthday.") This rule does not apply to contracts for necessities, on the ground that in this case, a rule that allows the minor to avoid her contractual obligations does not on balance serve her interests. Any protection against exploitation that such a rule would provide would be outweighed by the burdens of rendering her unable to procure necessities, because those who might provide them could not reasonably rely on her to perform her side of the bargains to procure them.

37. Recall the discussion of acceptance in Chapter 13.

38. The last two ways of characterizing promissory intentions, which build the idea of obligation (or its cognates) into these intentions, raise the specter that the theory is circular— that the account of recognition out of which the theory derives its defense of promissory obligation builds the very obligation that it is meant to generate into the promissory intentions from which it begins. This is a false worry, however, because the account of

honors the promise—insofar as she refuses to deviate from the promised performance without obtaining a release from the promisee—she carries out the intention not to defect and actually confers this authority over her ends to the promisee.

One might say, then, that the obligations that promises create are not just *in favor of* promisees but are also *owed to* promises and, moreover, are not only owed to promisees but are also, so to speak, *owned by* them: promisors subject themselves to their promisees' authority. Promises and contracts therefore establish special relations among the parties to them. A promisor doesn't just refrain, negatively, from committing force or fraud against her promisee. She also intends, positively, to defer her ends to his will. And through this deference—through placing her ends in his hands—the promisor comes to take the promisee's ends as her own and, moreover, to treat him—his will—as an end.

This account of the promise relation is incomplete, however, because it ignores the possibility that the promisor's deference to her promisee's will, even as it expresses *her* respect for *him*, does not have any entailments concerning *his* respect for *her*. And in this way, promise may have a darker side, and the promise relation may be nothing to celebrate. In particular, a person might recognize others in a manner that involves a retreat from her own humanity, a denial of her own personality. And formally one-sided promises—that is, gratuitous, non-bargain promises—can have precisely this feature.

It can happen, in a gratuitous promise, that the promise's text or subtext includes the thought that while the promisor might obligate herself to the promisee, she lacks the capacity to *receive* promises from him, because she is incapable of the authority over him that receiving such promises would require. In a caste society, for example, the low-born might obligate themselves to the high even as it is regarded as incompatible with high-caste status for the high to owe an obligation—at least, a specifically promissory obligation—to a person of lower caste. Perhaps another example is the practice, adopted by hegemons in various historical periods, to insist that international treaties (a species of promise and contract, after all) bind others but not themselves.[39] The promisors in asymmetrical promises such as these (the low caste, and the non-hegemons) do not just appreciate or

---

recognition can be fully elaborated without any reference specifically to obligation, using simply a promisor's intentions not to defect from her promise unless released by her promisee. Once recognition has been explained in this way, using the language of obligation going forward becomes a harmless concession to expository ease.

39. A more theoretical example of this possibility, familiar from the history of philosophy, is (a highly stylized version of) the Hobbesian social contract—through which the personalities of the subjects are subsumed in a sovereign (think of the image on the frontispiece of the first edition of *Leviathan*) whose absolute authority makes it impossible for him to make binding promises in return. Another illustration is the promise of unconditional obedience made by the slave to his master in Hegel's dialectic and the promise associated with a religious vow made to an omnipotent god. For a final philosophical illustration, consider the suggestion, associated with Feuerbach, that persons who take religious vows project their capacities onto a god as a way of denying that they possesses them themselves. Perhaps this is why, as Jeremy Kessler has pointed out to me, many religions understand such vows on the model not of promise but of love.

respect their promisees, they also deny or disrespect themselves; asymmetrical promisors do not so much express their personalities by promising as retreat from them. And the relations that these promises exemplify involve not just deference or respect but subordination—not just a recognition of the status of the promisee but a denial of the status of the promisor. Indeed, if the bright side of promising involves what moral philosophers sometimes call *recognition*—the phenomenon in which a person comes to appreciate her own moral status by appreciating the status of another, indeed, appreciating him in virtue of his appreciating her (so that she comes to see herself in him)—the dark side of promising can involve *repression*—the phenomenon in which a person denies her status by appreciating the status of another only to submit to it.

This kind of asymmetry—which makes a promisor's recognition of the personality of her promisee into a mechanism for repressing her own personality—cannot arise in reciprocal promises. Reciprocal promises—in which each party is both promissor and promisee, both owing and owed an obligation—guarantee, as it were, that recognition's brighter side will find expression. They guarantee this, moreover, as purely in virtue of such promises' reciprocal *form*: all that is needed for true recognition (for coming to appreciate oneself by observing that one is appreciated by another whom one appreciates) is that each party to a promissory relation respects the moral personality of the other—the other's status as a person, capable of owing and being owed obligations—and that this reciprocal appreciation is out in the open between them. In other words, true recognition—and so the bright side of promising—requires only that the parties to a promise acknowledge each other's *status*—the status of being capable of making and receiving promises. And this necessarily occurs in any promise that is formally reciprocal—in which each party is both promisor and promisee—regardless of its substantive content.

These observations lead naturally back to the bargain theory of consideration, which gives doctrinal expression to *precisely* the formal reciprocity that secures true promissory recognition and with it the morally appealing side of the promise relation. Bargains are bilateral and involve formally symmetric participation by all the parties to them. More precisely, bargains involve a scheme of reciprocally interlocking intentions—in which each party takes the other's intentions as authoritative for her own intentions. Bargains are in their nature wanted by, and invoke the intentions of, all participants. Each party to a bargain expressly intends to give the other authority to require performance, and each party expressly intends to exercise the authority that she enjoys in this connection. Accordingly, the parties to bargains recognize each other's full legal personalities, and the value of this distinctive form of recognition underwrites the case for giving bargains distinctive recognition in the law.[40]

---

40. Note that the forward-looking feature of contractual bargains—the fact that such contracts are commonly what the law calls *executory*, which is to say that they create obligations that at least one party has not yet performed when they are made—is critical to their formal value, on this account. Corbin thus once observed, "mutual, present and fully effective" exchanges "create[] no special right[s] in one party by which to compel a subsequent

When the law insists on the *fact* of a bargain it insists, in effect, that it will enforce only contracts in which each party is both a promisor and a promisee—both owing and owed an obligation. Indeed, the law adopts almost precisely this account of bargains, right down to the language of intention, saying, in the official comments to the Restatement, that the bargain requirement "means that the promisor must manifest an intention to induce the performance or return promise and to be induced by it, and that the promisee must manifest an intention to induce the making of the promise and to be induced by it."[41] Consideration ensures contract relations in which the bargainer-parties engage each other, and subject themselves to each other's authority. The consideration doctrine (on the modern, bargain theory) requires each party to the contract to obligate itself to the other, so contracts necessarily involve authority on both sides.

A related point is also worth making. By requiring not just an exchange of promises but also an exchange in which each promise induces the other,[42] the consideration doctrine selects for promises in which reciprocal authority is not just *granted* but also, because it was sought on each side, actually *exercised*. This introduces an egalitarian element into contract, which is absent from promise *simpliciter*. And, once again, this egalitarian element is secured based purely on the bargain *form*, quite apart from any function that the form serves.

There is thus no need to explain the consideration doctrine along the functionalist lines proposed by Fuller and those who follow him. And the consideration doctrine remains justified even though it is not the only, or indeed even the best, instrument for performing the functions to which it has been linked. The consideration doctrine, at least in its core applications, represents free-standing formalism.

Finally, notice that this formal account of consideration also explains why the law's insistence on the fact of a bargain—on the bargain form—is naturally paired with an indifference to the bargain's adequacy—to its substantive fairness.[43] A contract might allocate virtually all of the contractual surplus to one party or the other and still be supported by adequate consideration,[44] and this is just as it should be. The egalitarianism en-

---

performance by the other;" and this led him to place such exchanges outside of contract. 1 ARTHUR LINTON CORBIN ON CONTRACTS § 4 (2d ed. 1963). This exclusion is naturally explained by the argument pursued here, because such exchanges do not involve any forward-looking intentions in those who make them and certainly do not involve intentions to give others authority over future intentions, and they therefore do not present examples of persons engaging one another or participating in the pattern of reciprocal recognition just described.

41. See RESTATEMENT (SECOND) OF CONTRACTS § 81 cmt. a. The Restatement adopts this account of bargains in express preference over alternative accounts that would require consideration to *motivate* a promisor or to be "the object of the promisor's desire." *Id.*

42. See RESTATEMENT (SECOND) OF CONTRACTS § 71 (1981).

43. See RESTATEMENT (SECOND) OF CONTRACTS § 71 cmt. [c] (1981).

44. A prototypical such case, incidentally, involves contracts of sale in perfectly competitive markets, in which the equilibrium price is competed down until all of the surplus goes to the buyers. Thus although those who worry about unequal surplus sharing in contracts typically imagine cases in which inequality favors sophisticated repeat players at the expense of unsophisticated parties, a large (majority?) share of actual contracts involving grossly

shrined by contract concerns equality of *status*—that is, of the publicly recognized capacity to owe and be owed a certain kind of obligation, a capacity that it closely connected to possessing moral personality. And this formal equality does not require any particular substantive balance of benefit and burden and indeed survives whatever substantive inequalities particular contracts might involve. Bargains, one might say, underwrite recognition among the parties to them simply in virtue of their formal structure, and regardless of their substantive fairness. Indeed, a legal order that imposes requirements concerning substantive equality on contractual relations *threatens* the formal status that contract law, including through the consideration doctrine, seeks to promote: persons who seek to make contracts that such a legal order rejects as unduly unequal are in effect denied contractual capacity; their personalities are denied the recognition that possessing contractual capacity involves. That is one reason why, as the materials in Part III will illustrate, our legal order limits freedom of contract only reluctantly.

The main point of these discussions, at least for present purposes, is not to assess whether or when substantive equality can justify limitations on freedom of contract, all-things-considered. That question will be taken up in Part III of these materials. At the moment, the main point is that freedom of contract requires that the consideration doctrine not be used to police the adequacy of bargains. A secondary point is that the consideration doctrine's insistence on the bargain *form* is not properly understood as a limit on freedom of contract. "Freedom of contract," after all, refers to freedom specifically *to contract* and not freedom to generate obligations generally. And contract, as a moral form, is on its own terms limited by the structural requirements of the moral recognition that gives the contract relation its value, requirements that include the consideration doctrine. This is not just a definitional matter—it is not that contract is defined in terms of consideration—but rather a matter of the moral foundations of contract, which simply do not extend to non-bargain promises.[45]

15.3 IDENTIFYING BARGAINS

The last pages have argued that the consideration doctrine can be explained and defended as an instance of pure form. How does this conclusion sit with the broader theme of this Part, which has been, remember, that formalism cannot generally sustain itself without a hidden reference to substantive, and even functionalist, ideals?

This turns out to be a complicated question. On the one hand, if the account of the consideration doctrine just given is right, then it has gone

---

unequal divisions of surplus favor unsophisticated consumers at the expense of sophisticated retailers.

45. Thus the account of the intrinsic value of the bargain form answers Fried's challenge, from which the discussion of consideration set out, that insisting on the fact of the bargain (even without any separate concern for the bargain's adequacy) offends against freedom of contract. See Fried, *supra* note 21, and accompanying text.

some way towards resuscitating pure formalism, in the sense of showing that legal forms can have a value that cannot be reduced to substantive, and certainly not to functionalist, terms. But on the other hand, the main line of criticism raised against formalism so far remains as forceful as ever—only now with its true nature more clearly revealed. Formalism might succeed as an account of what law, or at least a particular body of law, *is*—that is, formalism may be right to insist that law's value does not depend on, and cannot be reduced to, its function as a tool to promote ends that can be explained without reference to law. But even if formalism is right about this, there remains the question how a court, or indeed any person, might *know*, in an actual case, whether a particular legal form has successfully been established or followed. And even if formalism is right about the nature of law, it may be that this *epistemic* question cannot be answered save by reference to substantive, and perhaps even functionalist, ideas.

This has been the main charge against formalism in these pages so far: *Plate* and *Lucy* illustrated, for example, that the formalisms associated with the subjective theory of intent could not resolve cases without there being an independent inquiry into reasonableness and fairness of the kind that realists champion; *Izadi* illustrated that the formal category *offer* cannot sensibly be understood without reference to a functional analysis of the distribution of costs and benefits in bargaining; *Ever–Tite* illustrated that the formal distinction between mere preparation and commencing performance suffers a fatal, function-drive instability; and so on.

An analogous lesson, it turns out, applies in the context of the consideration doctrine. Even if the bargain form has intrinsic value, which may be explained without making any reference to the functions that bargains might serve, it turns out (once again) to be impossible to tell whether particular cases involve bargains, as a matter of fact, without making reference to the substantive ends that the parties involved in these cases are pursuing, and to the functions that their contracts might serve in promoting these ends.

The following materials illustrate this point in a series of contexts. Once again, they do not undermine the formalist account of what the consideration doctrine *is*. Rather they merely show that, as elsewhere, so in this context also, legal forms cannot be sensibly *identified* without making reference to substantive values. Each sub-section illustrates this point in a particular context. The contexts are presented in order of increasing formalist intransigence in the law: in the first context, the law abandons formalism almost at once; in the last the law, at least historically, developed elaborate formalisms in an effort to disguise the substantive and functionalist judgments that actually decide cases.

15.3.A   SUBJECTIVE VERSUS OBJECTIVE TESTS FOR BARGAINS

Holmes, recall, characterized the bargain theory of consideration in terms of "reciprocal *conventional* inducement." And the Restatement insists that, as in the context of offer and acceptance, so also in connection with consideration, "the law is concerned with the external manifestation rather than the undisclosed mental state"[46] of the contracting parties. As in the context of offer and acceptance, this moves the project of identifying actual bargains—of finding the fact of a bargain—in a functionalist direction. How is a court to say whether or not the pattern of conduct of the parties conventionally involves an exchange save by asking how, reasonably, this conduct is connected to the ends that the parties employ their contracts to pursue?

This is not a new or a deep point. The following materials illustrate the familiar general idea in the current doctrinal circumstances.

Fiege v. Boehm

Court of Appeals of Maryland, 1956.
123 A.2d 316.

Suit by mother against claimed putative father to recover for breach of oral agreement to pay birth expenses and support, upon condition that she would refrain from instituting bastardy proceedings. The Superior Court of Baltimore City, Cornelius P. Mundy, J., entered judgment upon verdict for plaintiff, and defendant appealed. The Court of Appeals, Delaplaine, J., held that if mother of illegitimate child and claimed putative father entered into oral contract, whereby father agreed to pay birth expenses and support upon condition that mother would not institute bastardy proceedings as long as he made such payments, and mother had acted in good faith and belief that man was father, agreement was enforceable as supported by sufficient consideration, though father was acquitted in subsequent bastardy proceedings upon medical proof, in form of blood tests, that he could not have fathered child.

Judgment affirmed.

■ DELAPLAINE, JUDGE. This suit was brought in the Superior Court of Baltimore City by Hilda Louise Boehm against Louis Gail Fiege to recover for breach of a contract to pay the expenses incident to the birth of his bastard child and to provide for its support upon condition that she would refrain from prosecuting him for bastardy.

Plaintiff alleged in her declaration substantially as follows: (1) that early in 1951 defendant had sexual intercourse with her although she was unmarried, and as a result thereof she became pregnant, and defendant acknowledged that he was responsible for her pregnancy; (2) that on September 29, 1951, she gave birth to a female child; that defendant is the father of the child; and that he acknowledged on many occasions that he is its father; (3) that before the child was born, defendant agreed to pay all her medical and miscellaneous expenses and to compensate her for the loss of her salary caused by the child's birth, and also to pay her ten dollars per week for its support until it reached the age of 21, upon condition that she would not institute bastardy proceedings against him as long as he made

---

46. RESTATEMENT (SECOND) OF CONTRACTS § 71 cmt. b.

the payments in accordance with the agreement; (4) that she placed the child for adoption on July 13, 1954, and she claimed the following sums: Union Memorial Hospital, $110; Florence Crittenton Home, $100; Dr. George Merrill, her physician, $50; medicines $70.35; miscellaneous expenses, $20.45; loss of earnings for 26 weeks, $1,105; support of the child, $1,440; total, $2,895.80; and (5) that defendant paid her only $480, and she demanded that he pay her the further sum of $2,415.80, the balance due under the agreement, but he failed and refused to pay the same.

Defendant demurred to the declaration on the ground that it failed to allege that in September, 1953, plaintiff instituted bastardy proceedings against him in the Criminal Court of Baltimore, but since it had been found from blood tests that he could not have been the father of the child, he was acquitted of bastardy. The Court sustained the demurred with leave to amend.

Plaintiff then filed an amended declaration, which contained the additional allegation that, after the breach of the agreement by defendant, she filed a charge with the State's Attorney that defendant was the father of her bastard child; and that on October 8, 1953, the Criminal Court found defendant not guilty solely on a physician's testimony that 'on the basis of certain blood tests made, the defendant can be excluded as the father of the said child, which testimony is not conclusive upon a jury in a trial court.'

Defendant also demurred to the amended declaration, but the Court overruled that demurrer.

Plaintiff, a typist, now over 35 years old, who has been employed by the Government in Washington and Baltimore for over thirteen years, testified in the Court below that she had never been married, but that at about midnight on January 21, 1951, defendant, after taking her to a moving picture theater on York Road and then to a restaurant, had sexual intercourse with her in his automobile. She further testified that he agreed to pay all her medical and hospital expenses, to compensate her for loss of salary caused by the pregnancy and birth, and to pay her ten dollars per week for the support of the child upon condition that she would refrain from instituting bastardy proceedings against him. She further testified that between September 17, 1951, and May, 1953, defendant paid her a total of $480.

Defendant admitted that he had taken plaintiff to restaurants, had danced with her several times, had taken her to Washington, and had brought her home in the country; but he asserted that he had never had sexual intercourse with her. He also claimed that he did not enter into any agreement with her. He admitted, however, that he had paid her a total of $480. His father also testified that he stated 'that he did not want his mother to know, and if it were just kept quiet, kept principally away from his mother and the public and the courts, that he would take care of it.'

Defendant further testified that in May, 1953, he went to see plaintiff's physician to make inquiry about blood tests to show the paternity of the child; and that those tests were made and they indicated that it was not possible that he could have been the child's father. He then stopped making payments. Plaintiff thereupon filed a charge of bastardy with the State's Attorney.

The testimony which was given in the Criminal Court by Dr. Milton Sachs, hematologist at the University Hospital, was read to the jury in the Superior Court. In recent years the blood-grouping test has been employed in criminology, in the selection of donors for blood transfusions, and as evidence in paternity cases. The Landsteiner blood-grouping test is based on the medical theory that the red corpuscles in human blood contain two affirmative agglutinating substances, and that every individual's blood falls into one of the four classes and remains the same throughout life. According to Mendel's law of inheritance, this blood individuality is an hereditary characteristic which passes from parent to child, and no agglutinating substance can appear in the blood of a child which is not present in the blood of one of its parents. The four Landsteiner blood groups, designated as AB, A, B, and O, into which human blood is divided on the basis of the compatibility of the corpuscles and serum with the corpuscles and serum of other persons, are characterized by different combinations of two agglutinogens in the red blood cells and two agglutinins in the serum. Dr. Sachs reported that Fiege's blood group was Type O, Miss Boehm's was Type B, and the infant's was Type A. He further testified that on the basis of these tests, Fiege could not have been the father of the child, as it is impossible for a mating of Type O and Type B to result in a child of Type A.

Although defendant was acquitted by the Criminal Court, the Superior Court overruled his motion for a directed verdict. In the charge to the jury the Court instructed them that defendant's acquittal in the Criminal Court was not binding upon them. The jury found a verdict in favor of plaintiff for $2,415.80, the full amount of her claim.

Defendant filed a motion for judgment n. o. v. or a new trial. The Court overruled that motion also, and entered judgment on the verdict of the jury. Defendant appealed from that judgment.

Defendant contends that, even if he did enter into the contract as alleged, it was not enforceable, because plaintiff's forbearance to prosecute was not based on a valid claim, and hence the contract was without consideration. He, therefore, asserts that the Court erred in overruling (1) his demurrer to the amended declaration, (2) his motion for a directed verdict, and (3) his motion for judgment n. o. v. or a new trial.

It was originally held at common law that a child born out of wedlock is *filius nullius*, and a putative father is not under any legal liability to contribute to the support of his illegitimate child, and his promise to do so is unenforceable because it is based on purely a moral obligation. Some of the courts in this country have held that, in the absence of any statutory obligation on the father to aid in the support of his bastard child, his promise to the child's mother to pay her for its maintenance, resting solely on his natural affection for it and his moral obligation to provide for it, is a promise which the law cannot enforce because of lack of sufficient consideration. *Mercer v. Mercer's Adm'r*, 7 S.W. 401. On the contrary, a few courts have stated that the natural affection of a father for his child and the moral obligation upon him to support it and to aid the woman he has wronged furnish sufficient consideration for his promise to the mother to pay for the support of the child to make the agreement enforceable at law. *Birdsall v. Edgerton*, 25 Wend., N.Y., 619.

However, where statutes are in force to compel the father of a bastard to contribute to its support, the courts have invariably held that a contract by the putative father with the mother of his bastard child to provide for the support of the child upon the agreement of the mother to refrain from invoking the bastardy statute against the father, or to abandon proceedings already commenced, is supported by sufficient consideration. *Jangraw v. Perkins*, 60 A. 385.

In Maryland it is now provided by statute that whenever a person is found guilty of bastardy, the court shall issue an order directing such person (1) to pay for the maintenance and support of the child until it reaches the age of eighteen years, such sum as may be agreed upon, if consent proceedings be had, or in the absence of agreement, such sum as the court may fix, with due regard to the circumstances of the accused person; and (2) to give bond to the State of Maryland in such penalty as the court may fix, with good and sufficient securities, conditioned on making the payments required by the court's order, or any amendments thereof. Failure to give such bond shall be punished by commitment to the jail or the House of Correction until bond is given but not exceeding two years. Code Supp.1955, art. 12, § 8.

Prosecutions for bastardy are treated in Maryland as criminal proceedings, but they are actually civil in purpose. *Kennard v. State*, 10 A.2d 710. While the prime object of the Maryland Bastardy Act is to protect the public from the burden of maintaining illegitimate children, it is so distinctly in the interest of the mother that she becomes the beneficiary of it. Accordingly a contract by the putative father of an illegitimate child to provide for its support upon condition that bastardy proceedings will not be instituted is a compromise of civil injuries resulting from a criminal act, and not a contract to compound a criminal prosecution, and if it is fair and reasonable, it is in accord with the Bastardy Act and the public policy of the State.

Of course, a contract of a putative father to provide for the support of his illegitimate child must be based, like any other contract, upon sufficient consideration. The early English law made no distinction in regard to the sufficiency of a claim which the claimant promised to forbear to prosecute, as the consideration of a promise, other than the broad distinction between good claims and bad claims. No promise to forbear to prosecute an unfounded claim was sufficient consideration. In the early part of the Nineteenth Century, an advance was made from the criterion of the early authorities when it was held that forbearance to prosecute a suit which had already been instituted was sufficient consideration, without inquiring whether the suit would have been successful or not. *Longridge v. Dorville*, 5 B. & Ald. 117.

In 1867 the Maryland Court of Appeals, in the opinion delivered by Judge Bartol in *Hartle v. Stahl*, 27 Md. 157, 172, held: (1) that forbearance to assert a claim before institution of suit, if not in fact a legal claim, is not of itself sufficient consideration to support a promise; but (2) that a compromise of a doubtful claim or a relinquishment of a pending suit is good consideration for a promise; and (3) that in order to support a compromise, it is sufficient that the parties entering into it thought at the time that there was a *bona fide* question between them, although it may eventually be found that there was in fact no such question.

We have thus adopted the rule that the surrender of, or forbearance to assert, an invalid claim by one who has not an honest and reasonable belief in its possible validity is not sufficient consideration for a contract. 1 Restatement, Contracts, sec. 76(b). We combine the subjective requisite that the claim be *bona fide* with the objective requisite that it must have a reasonable basis of support. Accordingly a promise not to prosecute a claim which is not founded in good faith does not of itself give a right of action on an agreement to pay for refraining from so acting, because a release from mere annoyance and unfounded litigation does not furnish valuable consideration.

Professor Williston was not entirely certain whether the test of reasonableness is based upon the intelligence of the claimant himself, who may be an ignorant person with no knowledge of law and little sense as to facts; but he seemed inclined to favor the view that 'the claim forborne must be neither absurd in fact from the standpoint of a reasonable man in the position of the claimant, nor, obviously unfounded in law to one who has an elementary knowledge of legal principles.' 1 Williston on Contracts, Rev. Ed., sec. 135. We agree that while stress is placed upon the honesty and good faith of the claimant, forbearance to prosecute a claim is insufficient consideration if the claim forborne is so lacking in foundation as to make its assertion incompatible with honesty and a reasonable degree of intelligence. Thus, if the mother of a bastard knows that there is no foundation, either in law or fact, for a charge against a certain man that he is the father of the child, but that man promises to pay her in order to prevent bastardy proceedings against him, the forbearance to institute proceedings is not sufficient consideration

On the other hand, forbearance to sue for a lawful claim or demand is sufficient consideration for a promise to pay for the forbearance if the party forbearing had an honest intention to prosecute litigation which is not frivolous, vexatious, or unlawful, and which he believed to be well founded. *Snyder v. Cearfoss*, 187 Md. 635, 643. Thus the promise of a woman who is expecting an illegitimate child that she will not institute bastardy proceedings against a certain man is sufficient consideration for his promise to pay for the child's support, even though it may not be certain whether the man is the father or whether the prosecution would be successful, if she makes the charge in good faith. The fact that a man accused of bastardy is forced to enter into a contract to pay for the support of his bastard child from fear of exposure and the shame that might be case upon him as a result, as well as a sense of justice to render some compensation for the injury he inflicted upon the mother, does not lessen the merit of the contract, but greatly increases it. *Hook v. Pratt*, 78 N.Y. 371.

In the case at bar there was no proof of fraud or unfairness. Assuming that the hematologists were accurate in their laboratory tests and findings, nevertheless plaintiff gave testimony which indicated that she made the charge of bastardy against defendant in good faith. For these reasons the Court acted properly in overruling the demurrer to the amended declaration and the motion for a directed verdict.

Finally, in attacking the action of the Court in overruling the motion for judgment n. o. v. or a new trial, defendant made the additional complaint that there was error in the charge to the jury. As we have said, the Court instructed the jury that defendant's acquittal in the Criminal Court was not binding upon the jury in the case before them. Defendant urged strongly that he had been acquitted by the Criminal Court in consequence of scientific findings from blood tests.

It is immaterial whether defendant was the father of the child or not. In the light of what we have said, we need not make any specific determination on this subject, as defendant took only one exception to the Court's charge, and his only objection was the general one that the charge did not refer to 'a valid binding agreement in law.'

As we have found no reversible error in the rulings and instructions of the trial Court, we will affirm the judgment entered on the verdict of the jury.

Judgment affirmed, with costs.

Restatement 2d of Contracts

§ 74   Settlement of Claims

(1) Forbearance to assert or the surrender of a claim or defense which proves to be invalid is not consideration unless

    (a) the claim or defense is in fact doubtful because of uncertainty as to the facts or the law, or

    (b) the forbearing or surrendering party believes that the claim or defense may be fairly determined to be valid.

(2) The execution of a written instrument surrendering a claim or defense by one who is under no duty to execute it is consideration if the execution of the written instrument is bargained for even though he is not asserting the claim or defense and believes that no valid claim or defense exists.

Comments & Illustrations

Comment a. Relation to legal-duty rule. Subsection (1) elaborates a limitation on the scope of the legal-duty rule stated in § 73. That limitation is based on the traditional policy of favoring compromises of disputed claims in order to reduce the volume of litigation. Surrender of an invalid defense commonly means that a legal duty is performed, but in cases of invalid claims Subsection (1) may go beyond the legal-duty rule, since in many situations any legal duty not to litigate unfounded claims is likely to be unenforceable. In any event, the subject of compromise agreements is of sufficient importance to deserve separate treatment. Subsection (2) is clearly beyond the scope of the legal-duty rule, and merely states for greater clarity an application of § 72.

Comment b. Requirement of good faith. The policy favoring compromise of disputed claims is clearest, perhaps, where a claim is surrendered at a time when it is uncertain whether it is valid or not. Even though the invalidity later becomes clear, the bargain is to be judged as it appeared to the parties at the time; if the claim was then doubtful, no inquiry is necessary as to their good faith. Even though the invalidity should have been clear at the time, the settlement of an honest dispute is upheld. But a mere assertion or denial of liability does not make a claim doubtful, and the fact that invalidity is obvious may indicate that it was known. In such cases Subsection (1)(b) requires a showing of good faith.

Illustrations:

1.   A, a shipowner, has a legal duty to provide maintenance and cure for B, a seaman. B honestly but unreasonably claims that adequate care is not available in a free public hospital and that he is entitled to treatment by a private physician. B's forbearance to press this claim is consideration for A's promise to be responsible for the consequences of any improper treatment in the public hospital.

2.   A, knowing that he has no legal basis for complaint, frequently complains to B, his father, that B has made more gifts to B's other children than to A. B promises that if A will cease complaining, B will forgive a debt owed by A to B. A's forbearance to assert his claim of discrimination is not consideration for B's promise.

3.   A, knowing that B is a married man, cohabits with him for several years. During that time B promises to marry A as soon as he is divorced. After the cohabitation ceases, A surrenders all her claims on account of the promise to marry in consideration of B's promise to pay her $1000 a month during her life. Under applicable state law A has no valid claim. If it is found that A knew there was no valid claim, there is no consideration for B's promise of payment. Compare §§ 189–90.

Comment c. Unliquidated obligations. An undisputed obligation may be unliquidated, that is uncertain or disputed in amount. The settlement of such a claim is governed by the same principles as settlement of a claim the existence of which is doubtful or disputed. The payment of any definite sum of money on account of a single claim which is entirely unliquidated is consideration for a return promise. An admission by the obligor that a minimum amount is due does not liquidate the claim even partially unless he is contractually bound to the admission. But payment of less than is admittedly due may in some circumstances tend to show that a partial defense or offset was not asserted in good faith.

Payment of an obligation which is liquidated and undisputed is not consideration for a promise to surrender an unliquidated claim which is wholly distinct. See § 73. Whether in a particular case there is a single unliquidated claim or a combination of separate claims, some liquidated and some not, depends on the circumstances and the agreements of the parties. If there are no circumstances of unfair pressure or economic coercion and a disputed item is closely related to an undisputed item, the two are treated as making up a single unliquidated claim; and payment of the amount admittedly due can be consideration for a promise to surrender the entire claim.

Illustrations:

4. A, a real estate broker, is entitled to a commission for selling B's land, amounting to five per cent or $1,500. B claims in good faith that he owes only one per cent or $300, and offers to pay that amount in full settlement of the claim for commission. A accepts the offer. The payment is consideration for B's promise to surrender his entire claim.

5. A owes B at least $4,280 on a logging contract. Additional items in the account are unliquidated, and some of them are the subject of honest dispute. A disputes B's right to all above $4,280 on grounds he knows to be untrue, and offers $4,000 in full settlement. A's payment of $4,000 is not consideration for B's promise to surrender his entire claim.

6. A contracts to sell and deliver a lot of goods to B. On delivery B accepts a commercial unit priced at $30 and rejects the rest, priced at $50. See Uniform Commercial Code § 2–601. B claims in good faith but erroneously that the rejected goods are defective. A promises to surrender any claim based on the rejection if B pays the $30. B's payment is consideration for A's promise.

7. A stops payment on a check for $200 drawn on his account in the B bank, but the bank pays the check and charges his account, leaving a balance of $800. There is an honest dispute as to the propriety of the charge, and the bank refuses to pay any part of the $800 until the dispute is settled. To obtain the money, A promises to make no further claim. Payment of the $800 by the bank is not consideration for the promise.

Comment d. Forbearance without surrender. Forbearance to assert a valid claim or a doubtful or honestly-asserted claim may be consideration for a promise, just as surrender of the claim would be. Where the forbearance is temporary and it is contemplated that the claim will be asserted later, there is sometimes a question whether the forbearance is bargained for and given in exchange for the promise. If an offer specifies a return promise to forbear as the requested consideration, forbearance without promise is not an acceptance. Compare § 53. But a promise to forbear may be implied. Compare §§ 32, 62. Whether a promise is consideration depends on the rules stated in §§ 75–78. Forbearance which is not bargained for may in some cases be reliance sufficient to bring § 90 into play.

Illustrations:

8. A owes B $120. Without requesting B to forbear suit, C promises B in April that if A does not pay by October 1 C will pay $100. B's forbearance to sue until October is not consideration for C's promise.

9. A owes B a debt secured by mortgage, and B begins foreclosure proceedings. C requests B to forbear and promises to pay the debt. B's forbearance for a reasonable time is consideration for C's promise.

Comment e. Execution of release or quit-claim deed. Subsection (2) provides for the situation where the party who would be subject to a claim or defense, if one existed, wants assurance of its non-existence. Such assurance may be useful, for example, to enable him to obtain credit or to sell property. Although surrender of a non-existent claim by one who knows he has no claim is not consideration for a promise, the execution of an instrument of surrender may be consideration if there is no improper pressure or deception. See § 79. But there is no consideration if the surrendering party is under a duty to execute the instrument, as under Uniform Commercial Code §§ 3–505(1)(d), 9–208, 9–404.

Illustration:

10. A owns land and desires to mortgage it. He is informed that his title may be defective by reason of a possible interest in B. B says that he has no claim and has previously given a deed to the land to A's grantor. A promises to pay $50 for a new quit-claim deed. B's execution and delivery of such a deed is consideration for A's promise.

* * *

St Peter, from earlier in this Chapter, illustrates the basic application of the idea that bargains are identified by reference to conventional, or reasonable, intentions, rather than by reference to the particular intentions that were actually formed in the minds of the parties—that the bargain theory of consideration is applied objectively rather than subjectively as the law likes to say. The *St. Peter* court did not expressly emphasize the bargain theory of consideration, to be sure. But it did observe that the "bank night" at the center of that case was a form of advertising, and that advertisers "naturally" intend their addressees to change behavior in response to the advertisements that they publish. No inquiry into the defendants' subjective mental state was required to support this conclusion. Rather, the court imparted to the particular defendants before it intentions that persons in the position of the defendants would conventionally (naturally, as the court said) have.

Fiege and the section from the Restatement are a little less straightforward, and may seem, at least on a first reading, to confuse matters. They are included here nevertheless for three reasons. First, and most narrowly, the fact pattern that they raise—in which the claimed consideration consists in some manner of retreat from pressing a legal claim or defense—is quite common and important. Second, and a little more broadly, this fact pattern illustrates the operation of objective or reasonableness-based standards for assessing intentions in a revealing way. And third, the fact pattern presents an opportunity for thinking a little more generally about the relationship between contract and adjudication, and thus for foreshadowing some ideas that will be developed in greater detail when these materials take up arbitration and settlement agreements in Part III below.

The plaintiff in *Fiege* claimed that she had had sexual relations with the defendant and had, as a consequence, borne his child. She further claimed that, prior to the birth of the child, the defendant had agreed to pay the child's expenses in exchange for her promise not to bring bastardy proceedings against him. The defendant refused to pay these expenses, and the plaintiff initiated the bastardy proceedings, in which she lost following a blood test that proved that the defendant was not the child's father. The plaintiff thereupon sued the defendant in contract, claiming that the defendant's refusal to pay for the child's expenses nevertheless violated the agreement that she and he had made. The defendant answered that, because the blood tests had proved that he was not the child's father, the plaintiff's bastardy claim against him was invalid and thus could not constitute consideration for his promise to pay the child's expenses.

The court sided with the plaintiff in the contract dispute and held the defendant's promise enforceable against him. Although parts of the opinion are written in a way that suggests that the court discounted the blood test and refused (in spite of the outcome of the bastardy proceedings) to treat the test as refuting the defendant's paternity and so invalidating the plaintiff's claim, this skepticism about the test is not essential to the holding of the case.[47] Thus the court held, roughly, that forbearance from constituting a claim constitutes good consideration for a reciprocal promise as long as the forbearing party believed in good faith that the claim is valid and the claim has a reasonable basis for support. The Restatement goes even further, holding that forbearance of an ultimately invalid legal claim constitutes good consideration whenever either the claim is reasonable *or* the forbearing party believes in good faith that the claim is valid.

The *or* in the Restatement's rule is the source of the potential confusion. This feature of the rule suggests that forbearance from pressing even an unreasonable claim can constitute good consideration, as long only as the forbearing party subjectively (although unreasonably) believes that the

---

47.   It is common, however, as courts are often reluctant to accept technical or scientific forms of proof, especially when they are new. This reluctance, and the various circumstances in which it arises, constitutes one of the central themes of the law of evidence.

claim is valid. And this sounds a move away from Holmes's account of consideration as reciprocal *conventional* inducement and towards a subjective approach to consideration, in which the existence of consideration turns not on what it is reasonable to attribute to the parties but on their actual mental states.

The Restatement's rule does not, however, have this consequence. To see why not—to see why even the Restatement adopts an objective approach to consideration—one must understand something basic about the nature of adjudication and its purposes in our legal order. In particular, the law refuses to extend generally applicable standards of liability to conduct that involves asserting legal claims or defenses. Thus, a person who harms another by pressing an unreasonable claim or defense is not liable for the harms that she causes simply in virtue of her unreasonableness. This fact will explain why the Restatement rule, which allows forbearance from asserting good faith but unreasonable legal claims to constitute consideration, does not retreat from the general, objective approach of the consideration doctrine. But before it can explain anything, this curious feature of adjudication must be established.

The law protects those who assert mistaken and even unreasonable legal claims (for example, claims that are dismissed or that lose on summary judgment) from liability for the harms that asserting the claims causes, unless these claims are in some way frivolous or malicious.[48] Thus the Federal Rules of Civil Procedure require only that filings are not made for an improper purpose, are nonfrivolous, and have or are likely to have evidentiary support.[49] Indeed, the law governing lawyers even allows lawyers to assist those who seek to press unreasonable, and harmful, legal claims. Model Rule 3.1 of the Model Rules of Professional Conduct, for example, requires only that lawyers have a "basis in law and fact" for the claims they make on behalf of clients "that is not frivolous, which includes a good faith argument for an extension, modification or reversal of existing

---

48. Fee-shifting, which requires losing parties to pay winning parties' fees and costs, imposes some liability on those who assert losing but nonfrivolous legal positions. Fee-shifting has been widely adopted in Great Britain and selectively in the United States. In Britain, see Civ. Proc. R. 44.3(2)(a) (Eng.); see also Michael Zander, *Will the Revolution in the Funding of Civil Litigation in England Eventually Lead to Contingency Fees?*, 52 DePaul L. Rev. 259, 292 n.192 (2002) ("The general rule is that the unsuccessful party will be ordered to pay the costs of the successful party."). In the United States, see 42 U.S.C. § 1988 (2006), which entitles certain successful civil rights plaintiffs to recover their fees and costs, and also Rules 11 and 37 of the Federal Rules of Civil Procedure, which (among other things) require payment of costs (in the narrow sense of court costs) associated with suits that are unreasonable or without substantial justification.

Although fee-shifting arrangements bring the standard of liability for pressing legal claims more nearly into line with the standards applied elsewhere in the law, the liability that they impose is limited to the direct costs of adjudication and does not include the often (as in *Fiege)* much larger (and potentially enormous) indirect costs—for example involving lost opportunities or lost reputations—imposed by the mistaken claims.

49. *See* Fed. R. Civ. P. 11; *see also id.* 26(g) (extending Rule 11 to the discovery process); 28 U.S.C. § 1927 (2006) (making lawyers personally liable for costs and attorney's fees that result when they "multipl[y] the proceedings in any case unreasonably and vexatiously" in federal court).

law."[50] The law, in other words, allows people great leeway to assert their legal rights in adversary proceedings.

The precise limits on the adversary assertiveness that these and other related legal rules allow are of course a subject of substantial dispute. But it is unquestioned that these rules impose a much lower standard of care in pressing legal claims than do the tort standards that govern ordinary conduct that is potentially harmful to others, for example, hunting, lighting fires, or even driving. Certainly, the law does not impose strict liability or even negligence standards on disputants and the lawyers whom they employ. Strict liability would hold disputants liable whenever they asserted claims or defenses that eventually lost. And even negligence would (following a prominent interpretation of reasonableness) hold disputants liable whenever their arguments failed to minimize the total costs—including both error costs of inaccurate dispute resolution and transactions costs of litigation—that they, their opponents, and third parties had jointly to bear. Although the rules prohibiting frivolous litigation sometimes use the word "reasonable," they have never been seriously thought to require disputants and their lawyers to bring only claims that are reasonable in the tort-law-like sense that their expected social benefits exceed their expected social costs. Certainly the prohibitions that they establish are not violated every time a party brings a claim that loses on summary judgment. Indeed, these rules do not require even that the exclusive motive for bringing a dubious claim is the (small) chance that the claim might succeed. Instead, a partially strategic motive for bringing a claim does not render the claim frivolous or unreasonable for purposes of either the law of procedure or the law governing lawyers, not even when the strategic advantages that the claim secures are inefficient and undeserved. Accordingly, regardless of how the interpretive controversies that surround the rules against frivolous litigation are resolved, these rules clearly give disputants and lawyers substantially greater leeway than ordinary standards of liability would allow.[51]

---

50. MODEL RULES OF PROF'L CONDUCT R. 3.1 (2003). Rule 1.2(d) similarly forbids lawyers from counseling clients to do something illegal but allows them to counsel clients to make good faith efforts to determine the "validity, scope, meaning or application of the law." *See id.* R. 1.2(d) (2003).

51. Courts have given this license to exploit procedure practical effect. In a typical case, a lawyer defending a lawsuit brought against his client by the Bank of Israel threatened to countersue, pointing out that the countersuit would embarrass the Bank politically and might slow foreign investment in Israel. Although the countersuit was clearly an effort to exploit a political vulnerability in order to extract a favorable settlement, the Second Circuit refused to sanction the lawyer, observing that "it is both common and proper for lawyers to send demand letters to potential defendants, hoping that the threat will bring a desirable settlement but preparing for litigation if settlement is not possible. The purpose of [the lawyer's] threats and the suit he eventually filed was to put pressure—including the pressure of negative publicity—on his clients' opponents in litigation. There is nothing 'improper' about that, so long as the suit threatened or actually filed is not frivolous." *Sussman v. Bank of Isr.*, 56 F.3d 450 (2d Cir. 1995); *see also* 1 GEOFFREY HAZARD AND W. WILLIAM HODES, THE LAW OF LAWYERING § 3.1:202, at 550 n.1.01 (Supp. 1996). Similarly, courts generally refuse to find that lawyers for unsuccessful tort plaintiffs have violated Model Rule 3.1 (or indeed to find lawyers liable for common law malicious prosecution), even when they bring lawsuits that aim principally at forcing a settlement rather than winning in court. Instead, sanctions are typically applied against lawyers in such cases only when lawyers bring tort claims that are not just unsuccessful but

Moreover, this retreat from ordinary standards of liability for harming others is carried over in the often unnoticed but important fact that tort law also declines to apply the ordinary law of negligence to harms caused when one person asserts legal claims, including losing legal claims, against another. Thus, although there do exist torts of malicious prosecution and abuse of process, they are subject to narrow limits and certainly do not apply generally to impose liability in connection with unreasonable lawsuits or legal arguments that burden others, even when the lawsuits should have been predicted to fail.[52] Once again, the law clearly does not require clients or their lawyers to proceed only with claims that are reasonable (for example, in the sense of joint cost minimizing).

In all these ways, our legal order insulates people from liability for the harms that they impose simply by asserting losing (including predictably losing) legal claims. This is a subtle but enormously important point. The legal system entitles people, with the help of lawyers, aggressively to pursue their legal claims by denying legal recognition to many of the harms that such assertions of legal rights cause others.

Taken together, these observations explain why the Restatement rule making forbearance from pressing a good faith but unreasonable legal claim good consideration does not adopt a subjective approach to the existence of bargains. The good faith test, in the Restatement merely reflects the broader legal order's treatment of liability for the assertion of legal claims. Not just reasonable legal claims like the one in *Fiege*, but even unreasonable claims may be asserted without assuming liability for the harms that their assertion causes. Accordingly, forbearance from asserting the claims is valuable to those against whom they might be asserted, because the "victims" of their assertion cannot recover for these harms. Forbearance from asserting even an unreasonable claim can thus reasonably, and hence conventionally, induce the victim of the claim to provide

---

rather truly outrageous or vexatious. A typical example is *Raine v. Drasin*, 621 S.W.2d 895 (Ky. 1981), in which a lawyer argued that a hospital had broken his client's shoulder when it had in fact attempted to treat a pre-existing break.

In other words, the rules against bringing frivolous or unreasonable claims do not forbid a lawyer from benefiting her client by exploiting an opponent's undeserved strategic vulnerability to nonfrivolous, but ordinarily pointless, claims.

52. The traditional common law tort of malicious prosecution applies only to legal proceedings that, in addition to being wrongful, have a "quasi-criminal" character, substantially interfere with a person's liberty or damage her reputation, or interfere with property interests (such as in attachment or involuntary bankruptcy proceedings). *See* WILLIAM L. PROSSER, HANDBOOK OF THE LAW OF TORTS 851–52 (4th ed. 1971). Although a growing majority of jurisdictions, and also the Restatement (Second) of Torts, recognize malicious prosecution without the requirement of special injury, RESTATEMENT (SECOND) OF TORTS § 674 (1977), a substantial minority of jurisdictions continue to follow the "English rule," which denies actions for malicious-prosecution-based, groundless civil suits in the absence of special harms of the type just described. *See, e.g., Bickel v. Mackie*, 447 F. Supp. 1376, 1380 (N.D. Iowa 1978); *Garcia v. Wall & Ochs*, Inc., 389 A.2d 607, 608, 610 (Pa.Super. 1978); PROSSER, *supra*, at 850–53. Most American jurisdictions also recognize the tort of abuse of process. *See* RESTATEMENT (SECOND) OF TORTS, *supra* § 682; PROSSER, *supra* § 121, at 856–58.

Note that no jurisdiction recognizes the tort of malicious defense. *See* Jonathan K. Van Patten and Robert E. Willar, *The Limits of Advocacy: A Proposal for the Tort of Malicious Defense*, 35 HASTINGS L.J. 891 (1984).

something in exchange. Such a bargain becomes unreasonable only when the person who forebears from asserting the claim does not, in good faith, believe that the claim might succeed, because in this case (roughly), the person against whom the claim was asserted could recover damages for the harms that he suffered as a result of the claim's assertion. And he would not reasonably bargain to avoid harms that he would anyway receive compensation for suffering.[53]

The Restatement's subjective standard concerning belief in the validity of the legal claims whose forbearance constitutes consideration therefore cannot be distributed outside these claims, as it were, to encompass the question whether or not forbearance of the claim is worth bargaining for. That question remains governed by a rigorously objective inquiry, and the doctrine of consideration therefore comports with the broader objective bent in modern contract law.

Finally, this returns the argument to the relationship between form and function. Although the consideration doctrine, properly understood, makes the bargain form, valued for its own sake, essential to legal enforceability, this leaves open the question how a court might know whether the arrangements between the parties have achieved the bargain form. And that question is given a functionalist answer, through an objective approach to bargains that identifies bargains in terms of the reasonable purposes that parties might bring to them.

15.3.B ILLUSORY PROMISES

This functionalist approach to identifying bargains arises in another context also, although here the functionalism is in some instances a little more hidden than in the cases addressed in the previous subsection. In order for a bargain to arise in fact, each side must bring something to the table: in the context of bilateral contracts, this means that each side must make a genuine promise, which is to say incur an obligation to do *something*.[54] It can happen that the language of a contractual promise leaves it an open question whether the promisor has actually, at the end of the day, made any genuine promise. That is, the worry might arise that the

---

53. Even this is not necessarily so, as recovery may be uncertain (because bad faith is hard to prove) and costly (because of lawyers' fees and other costs incurred in the recovery action). The Restatement acknowledges this possibility in subsection (2) of Section 74, which makes a written promise to surrender a legal claim good consideration even if the promisor is neither asserting the claim nor believes in its validity. As comment [e] to the Restatement section emphasizes, assurance that a claim against one will not be asserted can be valuable even when the claim could not reasonably be and is not believed valid. And so protection against being exposed to these costs can, reasonably and hence conventionally, induce a return promise from the party that receives it, and hence can constitute consideration.

Does this analysis suggest that the Restatement would have done better simply to adopt by reference the broader law governing adversary assertiveness and say that forbearance from pressing a claim constitutes good consideration precisely where that claim might be pressed without incurring liability for the harms caused thereby? If so, should the Restatement, as drafted, be interpreted to achieve this result?

54. When a unilateral contract is at issue, one side will typically make no promise and incur no outstanding obligation, but will simply *do* something.

promises one party to a contract makes are merely *illusory*. This is
different from the worry that the promises have so little value, at least
compared to what they are being exchanged for, that the exchange is
unequal or unfair. Remember, the consideration doctrine insists on the fact
of a bargain only, and not on its adequacy. The concern about illusory
promises, thus, is a concern that the promisor has not in fact promised to
do *anything at all*. To answer this concern, one must study the promise, to
see whether it is best interpreted to impose an obligation—any obligation—
on the promisor, or not.

The cases that follow take up this question. In addition, they take up
the question just what the content of the obligation in question might be.
In keeping with the current theme, the discussion will focus on formalism
and its strengths and limits. Although a great deal of a functionalist nature
might be (and in fact has been) said in this area, the materials here will do
no more than identify the main issues.

Wood v. Lucy, Lady Duff–Gordon

Court of Appeals of New York, 1917.
118 N.E. 214.

Appeal from Supreme Court, Appellate Division, First Department.
Action by Otis F. Wood against Lucy, Lady Duff–Gordon. From a judgment
of the Appellate Division (164 N.Y. Supp. 576), which reversed an order
denying defendant's motion for judgment on the pleading, and which
dismissed the complaint, plaintiff appeals. Reversed.

■ CARDOZO, J. The defendant styles herself 'a creator of fashions.' Her favor
helps a sale. Manufacturers of dresses, millinery, and like articles are glad
to pay for a certificate of her approval. The things which she designs,
fabrics, parasols, and what not, have a new value in the public mind when
issued in her name. She employed the plaintiff to help her to turn this
vogue into money. He was to have the exclusive right, subject always to her
approval, to place her indorsements on the designs of others. He was also to
have the exclusive right to place her own designs on sale, or to license
others to market them. In return she was to have one-half of 'all profits
and revenues' derived from any contracts he might make. The exclusive
right was to last at least one year from April 1, 1915, and thereafter from
year to year unless terminated by notice of 90 days. The plaintiff says that
he kept the contract on his part, and that the defendant broke it. She
placed her indorsement on fabrics, dresses, and millinery without his
knowledge, and withheld the profits. He sues her for the damages, and the
case comes here on demurrer.

The agreement of employment is signed by both parties. It has a
wealth of recitals. The defendant insists, however, that it lacks the elements of a contract. She says that the plaintiff does not bind himself to
anything. It is true that he does not promise in so many words that he will
use reasonable efforts to place the defendant's indorsements and market
her designs. We think, however, that such a promise is fairly to be implied.
The law has outgrown its primitive stage of formalism when the precise

word was the sovereign talisman, and every slip was fatal. It takes a broader view today. A promise may be lacking, and yet the whole writing may be 'instinct with an obligation,' imperfectly expressed (Scott, J., in *McCall Co. v. Wright*, 117 N.Y. Supp. 775; *Moran v. Standard Oil Co.*, 211 N.Y. 187, 198) If that is so, there is a contract.

The implication of a promise here finds support in many circumstances. The defendant gave an exclusive privilege. She was to have no right for at least a year to place her own indorsements or market her own designs except through the agency of the plaintiff. The acceptance of the exclusive agency was an assumption of its duties. *Phoenix Hermetic Co. v. Filtrine Mfg. Co..* We are not to suppose that one party was to be placed at the mercy of the other. *Hearn v. Stevens & Bro.*, 97 N. Y. Supp. 566. Many other terms of the agreement point the same way. We are told at the outset by way of recital that:

> 'The said Otis F. Wood possesses a business organization adapted to the placing of such indorsements as the said Lucy, Lady Duff–Gordon, has approved.'

The implication is that the plaintiff's business organization will be used for the purpose for which it is adapted. But the terms of the defendant's compensation are even more significant. Her sole compensation for the grant of an exclusive agency is to be one-half of all the profits resulting from the plaintiff's efforts. Unless he gave his efforts, she could never get anything. Without an implied promise, the transaction cannot have such business 'efficacy, as both parties must have intended that at all events it should have.' Bowen, L. J., in the *Moorcock*, 14 P. D. 64, 68. But the contract does not stop there. The plaintiff goes on to promise that he will account monthly for all moneys received by him, and that he will take out all such patents and copyrights and trade-marks as may in his judgment be necessary to protect the rights and articles affected by the agreement. It is true, of course, as the Appellate Division has said, that if he was under no duty to try to market designs or to place certificates of indorsement, his promise to account for profits or take out copyrights would be valueless. But in determining the intention of the parties the promise has a value. It helps to enforce the conclusion that the plaintiff had some duties. His promise to pay the defendant one-half of the profits and revenues resulting from the exclusive agency and to render accounts monthly was a promise to use reasonable efforts to bring profits and revenues into existence. For this conclusion the authorities are ample.

The judgment of the Appellate Division should be reversed, and the order of the Special Term affirmed, with costs in the Appellate Division and in this court.

Mattei v. Hopper

Supreme Court of California, 1958.
330 P.2d 625.

Purchaser's action for breach of contract by vendor who failed to convey real property in accordance with terms of deposit receipt executed by parties. The Superior Court, Contra Costa County, Wakefield Taylor, J., rendered judgment in favor of vendor, and purchaser appealed. The Supreme Court, Spence, J., held that contract for sale of real estate providing that agreement was subject to purchaser's obtaining leases satisfactory to purchaser was neither illusory nor lacking in mutuality of obligation and was enforceable by purchaser.

Reversed.

■ SPENCE, J. Plaintiff brought this action for damages after defendant allegedly breached a contract by failing to convey her real property in accordance with the terms of a deposit receipt which the parties had executed. After a trial without a jury, the court concluded that the agreement was 'illusory' and lacking in 'mutuality.' From the judgment accordingly entered in favor of defendant, plaintiff appeals.

Plaintiff was a real estate developer. He was planning to construct a shopping center on a tract adjacent to defendant's land. For several months, a real estate agent attempted to negotiate a sale of defendant's property under terms agreeable to both parties. After several of plaintiff's proposals had been rejected by defendant because of the inadequacy of the price offered, defendant submitted an offer. Plaintiff accepted on the same day.

The parties' written agreement was evidenced on a form supplied by the real estate agent, commonly known as a deposit receipt. Under its terms, plaintiff was required to deposit $1,000 of the total purchase price of $57,500 with the real estate agent, and was given 120 days to 'examine the title and consummate the purchase.' At the expiration of that period, the balance of the price was 'due and payable upon tender of a good and sufficient deed of the property sold.' The concluding paragraph of the deposit receipt provided: 'Subject to Coldwell Banker & Company obtaining leases satisfactory to the purchaser.' This clause and the 120–day period were desired by plaintiff as a means for arranging satisfactory leases of the shopping center buildings prior to the time he was finally committed to pay the balance of the purchase price and to take title to defendant's property.

Plaintiff took the first step in complying with the agreement by turning over the $1,000 deposit to the real estate agent. While he was in the process of securing the leases and before the 120 days had elapsed, defendant's attorney notified plaintiff that defendant would not sell her land under the terms contained in the deposit receipt. Thereafter, defendant was informed that satisfactory leases had been obtained and that plaintiff had offered to pay the balance of the purchase price. Defendant failed to tender the deed as provided in the deposit receipt.

Initially, defendant's thesis that the deposit receipt constituted no more than an offer by her, which could only be accepted by plaintiff notifying her that all of the desired leases had been obtained and were satisfactory to him, must be rejected. Nowhere does the agreement mention the necessity of any such notice. Nor does the provision making the agreement 'subject to' plaintiff's securing 'satisfactory' leases necessarily constitute a condition to the existence of a contract. Rather, the whole purchase receipt and this particular clause must be read as merely making plaintiff's performance dependent on the obtaining of 'satisfactory' leases. Thus a contract arose, and plaintiff was given the power and privilege to terminate it in the event he did not obtain such leases. (See 3 Corbin, Contracts (1951), s 647, pp. 581–585.) This accords with the general view that deposit receipts are binding and enforceable contracts. (Cal.Practice Hand Book, Legal Aspects of Real Estate Transactions (1956), p. 63.)

However, the inclusion of this clause, specifying that leases 'satisfactory' to plaintiff must be secured before he would be bound to perform, raises the basic question whether the consideration supporting the contract was thereby vitiated. When the parties attempt, as here, to make a contract where promises are exchanged as the consideration, the promises must be mutual in obligation. In other words, for the contract to bind either party, both must have assumed some legal obligations. Without this mutuality of obligation, the agreement lacks consideration and no enforceable contract has been created. *Shortell v. Evans–Ferguson Corp.*, 98 Cal.App. 650, 660–662; 1 Corbin, Contracts (1950), s 152, pp. 496–502.) Or, if one of the promises leaves a party free to perform or to withdraw from the agreement at his own unrestricted pleasure, the promise is deemed illusory and it provides no consideration. See *J. C. Millett Co. v. Park & Tilford Distillers Corp.*, D.C.N.D.Cal., 123 F.Supp. 484, 493. Whether these problems are couched in terms of mutuality of obligation or the illusory nature of a promise, the underlying issue is the same consideration. Ibid.

While contracts making the duty of performance of one of the parties conditional upon his satisfaction would seem to give him wide latitude in avoiding any obligation and thus present serious consideration problems, such 'satisfaction' clauses have been given effect. They have been divided into two primary categories and have been accorded different treatment on that basis. First, in those contracts where the condition calls for satisfaction as to commercial value or quality, operative fitness, or mechanical utility, dissatisfaction cannot be claimed arbitrarily, unreasonably, or capriciously and the standard of a reasonable person is used in determining whether satisfaction has been received. Of the cited cases, two have expressly rejected the arguments that such clauses either rendered the contracts illusory or deprived the promises of their mutuality of obligation. The remaining cases tacitly assumed the creation of a valid contract. However, it would seem that the factors involved in determining whether a lease is satisfactory to the lessor are too numerous and varied to permit the application of a reasonable man standard as envisioned by this line of cases. Illustrative of some of the factors which would have to be considered in this case are the duration of the leases, their provisions for renewal options, if any, their covenants and restrictions, the amounts of the rentals, the financial responsibility of the lessees, and the character of the lessees' businesses.

This multiplicity of factors which must be considered in evaluating a lease shows that this case more appropriately falls within the second line of authorities dealing with 'satisfaction' clauses, being those involving fancy, taste, or judgment. Where the question is one of judgment, the promisor's determination that he is not satisfied, when made in good faith, has been held to be a defense to an action on the contract. *Tiffany v. Pacific Sewer Pipe Co.*, 180 Cal. 700, 702–705. Although these decisions do not expressly discuss the issues of mutuality of obligation or illusory promises, they necessarily imply that the promisor's duty to exercise his judgment in good faith is an adequate consideration to support the contract. None of these cases voided the contracts on the ground that they were illusory or lacking in mutuality of obligation. Defendant's attempts to distinguish these cases are unavailing, since they are predicated upon the assumption that the deposit receipt was not a contract making plaintiff's performance conditional on his satisfaction. As seen above, this was the precise nature of the agreement. Even though the 'satisfaction' clauses discussed in the above-cited cases dealt with performances to be received as parts of the agreed exchanges, the fact that the leases here which determined plaintiff's satisfaction were not part of the performance to be rendered is not material. The standard of evaluating plaintiff's satisfaction good faith applies with equal vigor to this type of condition and prevents it from nullifying the consideration otherwise present in the promises exchanged.

Moreover, the secondary authorities are in accord with the California cases on the general principles governing 'satisfaction' contracts. 'It has been questioned whether an agreement in which the promise of one party is conditioned on his own or the other party's satisfaction contains the elements of a contract whether the agreement is not illusory in character because conditioned upon the whim or caprice of the party to be satisfied. Since, however, such a promise is generally considered as requiring a performance which shall be satisfactory to him in the exercise of an honest judgment, such contracts have been almost universally upheld.' (3 Williston, Contracts (rev. ed. 1936), s 675A, p. 1943; see also 3 Corbin, Contracts (1951), ss 644, 645, pp. 560–572.) 'A promise conditional upon the promisor's satisfaction is not illusory since it means more than that validity of the performance is to depend on the arbitrary choice of the promisor. His expression of dissatisfaction is not conclusive. That may show only that he has become dissatisfied with the contract; he must be dissatisfied with the performance, as a performance of the contract, and his dissatisfaction must be genuine.' (Restatement, Contracts (1932), s 265, comment a.)

If the foregoing cases and other authorities were the only ones relevant, there would be little doubt that the deposit receipt here should not be deemed illusory or lacking in mutuality of obligation because it contained the 'satisfaction' clause. However, language is two recent cases led the trial court to the contrary conclusion. The first case, *Lawrence Block Co. v. Palston*, 123 Cal.App.2d 300, stated that the following two conditions placed in an offer to buy an apartment building would have made the resulting contract illusory: 'O.P.A. Rent statements to be approved by Buyer' and 'Subject to buyer's inspection and approval of all apartments.' These provisions were said to give the purchaser 'unrestricted discretion' in deciding whether he would be bound to the contract and to provide no 'standard' which could be used in compelling him to perform. 123 Cal. App.2d at pages 308–309. However, this language was not necessary to the decision. The plaintiff in Lawrence Block Co. was a real estate broker seeking a commission, his right to which depended upon the existence of a binding agreement between the buyer and seller. The seller had not accepted the buyer's offer as originally written, but had added other conditions. This change constituted a counter-offer. Since the latter was not accepted by the buyer, no binding contract was created and the broker was not entitled to his commission.

The other case, *Pruitt v. Fontana*, 143 Cal.App.2d 675, presented a similar situation. The court concluded that the written instrument with a provision making the sale of land subject to the covenants and easements being 'approved by the buyers' was illusory. It employed both the reasoning and language of Lawrence Block Co. in deciding that this clause provided no 'objective criterion' preventing the buyers from exercising an 'unrestricted subjective discretion' in deciding whether they would be bound. 143 CalApp.2d at pages 684–685. But again, this language was not necessary to the result reached. The buyers in Pruitt refused to approve all of the easements of record, and the parties entered into a new and different oral agreement. The defendant seller was held to be estopped to assert the statute of frauds against this subsequent contract, and the judgment of dismissal entered after the sustaining of demurrers was reversed.

While the language in these two cases might be dismissed as mere dicta, the fact that the trial court relied thereon requires us to examine the reasoning employed. Both courts were concerned with finding an objective standard by which they could compel performance. This view apparently stems from the statement in Lawrence Block Co. that 'The standard 'as to the satisfaction of a reasonable person' does not apply where the performance involves a matter dependent on judgment.' 123 Cal.App.2d at page 309. By making this assertion without any qualification, the court necessarily implied that there is no other standard available. Of course, this entirely disregards those cases which have upheld 'satisfaction' clauses dependent on the exercise of judgment. In such cases, the criterion becomes one of good faith. Insofar as the language in *Lawrence Block, Co.* and *Pruitt* represented a departure from the established rules governing 'satisfaction' clauses, they are hereby disapproved.

We conclude that the contract here was neither illusory nor lacking in mutuality of obligation because the parties inserted a provision in their contract making plaintiff's performance dependent on his satisfaction with the leases to be obtained by him.

The judgment is reversed.

Eastern Airlines, Inc. v. Gulf Oil Corp.

United States District Court for the Southern District of Florida, 1975.
415 F.Supp. 429.

Airline brought action against oil company, with which it had requirements contract covering aviation fuel at certain airports, seeking to require the oil company to continue to perform under the contract. Following entry of preliminary injunction, the District Court, James Lawrence King, J., held that the requirements contract in question was enforceable; that the airline had not breached the contract through practice of 'fuel freighting;' that conditions created by OPEC boycott, energy crisis and federal controls did not represent failure of presupposed conditions such as would excuse oil company's performance under the contract; that evidence did not demonstrate that performance was commercially impracticable; that the agreed means or manner of payment had not failed because of domestic or foreign governmental regulations; and that airline was entitled to specific performance.

Order accordingly.

■ KING, DISTRICT JUDGE. Eastern Air Lines, Inc., hereafter Eastern, and Gulf Oil Corporation, hereafter Gulf, have enjoyed a mutually advantageous business relationship involving the sale and purchase of aviation fuel for several decades.

This controversy involves the threatened disruption of that historic relationship and the attempt, by Eastern, to enforce the most recent contract between the parties. On March 8, 1974 the correspondence and telex communications between the corporate entities culminated in a demand by Gulf that Eastern must meet its demand for a price increase of Gulf would shut off Eastern's supply of jet fuel within fifteen days.

Eastern responded by filing its complaint with this court, alleging that Gulf had breached its contract and requesting preliminary and permanent mandatory injunctions requiring Gulf to perform the contract in accordance with its terms. By agreement of the parties, a preliminary injunction preserving the status quo was entered on March 20, 1974, requiring Gulf to perform its contract and directing Eastern to pay in accordance with the contract terms, pending final disposition of the case.

Gulf answered Eastern's complaint, alleging that the contract was not a binding requirements contract, was void for want of mutuality, and, furthermore, was 'commercially impracticable' within the meaning of Uniform Commercial Code s 2–615; Fla.Stat. ss 672.614 and 672.615.

The extraordinarily able advocacy by the experienced lawyers for both parties produced testimony at the trial from internationally respected experts who described in depth economic events that have, in recent months, profoundly affected the lives of every American.

THE CONTRACT

On June 27, 1972, an agreement was signed by the parties which, as amended, was to provide the basis upon which Gulf was to furnish jet fuel to Eastern at certain specific cities in the Eastern system. Said agreement supplemented an existing contract between Gulf and Eastern which, on June 27, 1972, had approximately one year remaining prior to its expiration.

The contract is Gulf's standard form aviation fuel contract and is identical in all material particulars with the first contract for jet fuel, dated 1959, between Eastern and Gulf and, indeed, with aviation fuel contracts antedating the jet age. It is similar to contracts in general use in the aviation fuel trade. The contract was drafted by Gulf after substantial arm's length negotiation between the parties. Gulf approached Eastern more than a year before the expiration of the then-existing contracts between Gulf and Eastern, seeking to preserve its historic relationship with Eastern. Following several months of negotiation, the contract, consolidating and extending the terms of several existing contracts, was executed by the parties in June, 1972, to expire January 31, 1977.

The parties agreed that this contract, as its predecessor, should provide a reference to reflect changes in the price of the raw material from which jet fuel is processed, i.e., crude oil, in direct proportion to the cost per gallon of jet fuel.

Both parties regarded the instant agreement as favorable, Eastern, in part, because it offered immediate savings in projected escalations under the existing agreement through reduced base prices at the contract cities; while Gulf found a long term outlet for a capacity of jet fuel coming on stream from a newly completed refinery, as well as a means to relate anticipated increased cost of raw material (crude oil) directly to the price of the refined product sold. The previous Eastern/Gulf contracts contained a price index clause which operated to pass on to Eastern only one-half of any increase in the price of crude oil. Both parties knew at the time of contract negotiations that increases in crude oil prices would be expected, were 'a way of life', and intended that those increases be borne by Eastern in a direct proportional relationship of crude oil cost per barrel to jet fuel cost per gallon.

Accordingly, the parties selected an indicator (West Texas Sour); a crude which is bought and sold in large volume and was thus a reliable indicator of the market value of crude oil. From June 27, 1972 to the fall of 1973, there were in effect various forms of U.S. government imposed price controls which at once controlled the price of crude oil generally, West Texas Sour specifically, and hence the price of jet fuel. As the government authorized increased prices of crude those increases were in turn reflected in the cost of jet fuel. Eastern has paid a per gallon increase under the contract from 11 cents to 15 cents (or some 40%).

The indicator selected by the parties was 'the average of the posted prices for West Texas sour crude, 30.0–30.9 gravity of Gulf Oil Corporation, Shell Oil Company, and Pan American Petroleum Corporation'. The posting of crude prices under the contract 'shall be as listed for these companies in Platts Oilgram Service–Crude Oil Supplement.'

'Posting' has long been a practice in the oil industry. It involves the physical placement at a public location of a price bulletin reflecting the current price at which an oil company will pay for a given barrel of a specific type of crude oil. Those posted price bulletins historically have, in addition to being displayed publicly, been mailed to those persons evincing interest therein, including sellers of crude oil, customers whose price of product may be based thereon, and, among others, Platts Oilgram, publishers of a periodical of interest to those related to the oil industry.

In recent years, the United States has become increasingly dependent upon foreign crude oil, particularly from the 'OPEC' nations most of which are in the Middle East. OPEC was formed in 1970 for the avowed purpose of raising oil prices, and has become an increasingly cohesive and potent organization as its member nations have steadily enhanced their equity positions and their control over their oil production facilities. Nationalization of crude oil resources and shutdowns of production and distribution have become a way of life for oil companies operating in OPEC nations, particularly in the volatile Middle East. The closing of the Suez Canal and the concomitant interruption of the flow of Mid–East oil during the 1967 'Six–Day War', and Libya's nationalization of its oil industry during the same period, are only some of the more dramatic examples of a trend that began years ago. By 1969 'the handwriting was on the wall' in the words of Gulf's foreign oil expert witness, Mr. Blackledge.

During 1970 domestic United States oil production 'peaked'; since then it has declined while the percentage of imported crude oil has been steadily increasing. Unlike domestic crude oil, which has been subject to price control since August 15, 1971, foreign crude oil has never been subject to price control by the United States Government. Foreign crude oil prices, uncontrolled by the Federal Government, were generally lower than domestic crude oil prices in 1971 and 1972; during 1973 foreign prices 'crossed' domestic prices; by late 1973 foreign prices were generally several dollars per barrel higher than controlled domestic prices. It was during late 1973 that the Mid–East exploded in another war, accompanied by an embargo (at least officially) by the Arab oil-producing nations against the United States and certain of its allies. World prices for oil and oil products increased.

Mindful of that situation and for various other reasons concerning the nation's economy, the United States government began a series of controls affecting the oil industry culminating, in the fall of 1973, with the implementation of price controls known as 'two-tier'. In practice 'two-tier' can be described as follows: taking as the bench mark the number of barrels produced from a given well in May of 1972, that number of barrels is deemed 'old' oil. The price of 'old' oil then is frozen by the government at a fixed level. To the extent that the productivity of a given well can be increased over the May, 1972, production, that increased production is deemed 'new' oil. For each barrel of 'new' oil produced, the government authorized the release from price controls of an equivalent number of barrels from those theretofore designated 'old' oil. For example, from a well which in May of 1972, produced 100 barrels of oil; all of the production of that well would, since the imposition of 'two-tier' in August of 1973, be 'old' oil. Increased productivity to 150 barrels would result in 50 barrels of 'new' oil and 50 barrels of 'released' oil; with the result that 100 barrels of the 150 barrels produced from the well would be uncontrolled by the 'two-tier' pricing system, while the 50 remaining barrels of 'old' would remain government price controlled.

The implementation of 'two-tier' was completely without precedent in the history of government price control action. Its impact, however, was nominal, until the imposition of an embargo upon the exportation of crude oil by certain Arab countries in October, 1973. Those countries deemed sympathetic to Israel were embargoed from receiving oil from the Arab oil producing countries. The United States was among the principal countries affected by that embargo, with the result that it experienced an immediate 'energy crises.'

Following closely after the embargo, OPEC (Oil Producing Export Countries) unilaterally increased the price of their crude to the world market some 400% between September, 1973, and January 15, 1974. Since the United States domestic production was at capacity, it was dependent upon foreign crude to meet its requirements. New and released oil (uncontrolled) soon reached parity with the price of foreign crude, moving from approximately $5 to $11 a barrel from September, 1973 to January 15, 1974.

Since imposition of 'two-tier', the price of 'old oil' has remained fixed by government action, with the oil companies resorting to postings reflecting prices they will pay for the new and released oil, and subject to government controls. Those prices, known as 'premiums', are the subject of supplemental bulletins which are likewise posted by the oil companies and furnished to interested parties, including Platts Oilgram.

Platts, since the institution of 'two-tier' has not published the posted prices of any of the premiums offered by the oil companies in the United States, including those of Gulf Oil Corporation, Shell Oil Company and Pan American Petroleum, the companies designated in the agreement. The information which has appeared in Platts since the implementation of 'two-tier' with respect to the price of West Texas Sour crude oil has been the price of 'old' oil subject to government control.

Under the court's restraining order, entered in this cause by agreement of the parties, Eastern has been paying for jet fuel from Gulf on the basis of the price of 'old' West Texas Sour crude oil as fixed by government price control action, i.e., $5 a barrel. Approximately 40 gallons of finished jet fuel product can be refined from a barrel of crude.

Against this factual background we turn to a consideration of the legal issues.

I. THE 'REQUIREMENTS' CONTRACT

Gulf has taken the position in this case that the contract between it and Eastern is not a valid document in that it lacks mutuality of obligation; it is vague and indefinite; and that it renders Gulf subject to Eastern's whims respecting the volume of jet fuel Gulf would be required to deliver to the purchaser Eastern.

The contract talks in terms of fuel 'requirements'. The parties have interpreted this provision to mean that any aviation fuel purchased by Eastern at one of the cities covered by the contract, must be bought from Gulf. Conversely, Gulf must make the necessary arrangements to supply Eastern's reasonable good faith demands at those same locations. This is the construction the parties themselves have placed on the contract and it has governed their conduct over many years and several contracts.

In early cases, requirements contracts were found invalid for want of the requisite definiteness, or on the grounds of lack of mutuality. Many such cases are collected and annotated at 14 A.L.R. 1300.

As reflected in the foregoing annotation, there developed rather quickly in the law the view that a requirements contract could be binding where the purchaser had an operating business. The 'lack of mutuality' and 'indefiniteness' were resolved since the court could determine the volume of goods provided for under the contract by reference to objective evidence of the volume of goods required to operate the specified business. Therefore, well prior to the adoption of the Uniform Commercial Code, case law generally held requirements contracts binding. See 26 A.L.R.2d 1099, 1139.

The Uniform Commercial Code, adopted in Florida in 1965, specifically approves requirements contracts in F.S. 672.306(U.C.C. s 2–306(1)).

'(1) A term which measures the quantity by the output of the seller or the requirements of the buyer means such actual output or requirements as may occur in good faith, except that no quantity unreasonably disproportionate to any stated estimate or in the absence of a stated estimate to any normal or otherwise comparable prior output or requirements may be tendered or demanded.'

The Uniform Commercial Code Official Comment interprets s 2–306(1) as follows:

'2. Under this Article, a contract for output or requirements is not too indefinite since it is held to mean the actual good faith output or requirements of the particular party. Nor does such a contract lack mutuality of obligation since, under this section, the party who will determine quantity is required to operate his plant or conduct his business in good faith and according to commercial standards of fair dealing in the trade so that his output or requirements will approximate a reasonably foreseeable figure. Reasonable elasticity in the requirements is expressly envisaged by this section and good faith variations from prior requirements are permitted even when the variation may be such as to result in discontinuance. A shut-down by a requirements buyer for lack of orders might be permissible when a shut-down merely to curtail losses would not. The essential test is whether the party is acting in good faith. Similarly, a sudden expansion of the plant by which requirements are to be measured would not be included within the scope of the contract as made but normal expansion undertaken in good faith would be within the scope of this section. One of the factors in an expansion situation would be whether the market price has risen greatly in a case in which the requirements contract contained a fixed price. Reasonable variation of an extreme sort is exemplified in *Southwest Natural Gas Co. v. Oklahoma Portland Cement Co.*, 102 F.2d 630 (C.C.A 10, 1939).'

Some of the prior Gulf–Eastern contracts have included the estimated fuel requirements for some cities covered by the contract while others have none. The particular contract contains an estimate for Gainesville, Florida requirement.

The parties have consistently over the years relied upon each other to act in good faith in the purchase and sale of the required quantities of aviation fuel specified in the contract. During the course of the contract, various estimates have been exchanged from time to time, and, since the advent of the petroleum allocations programs, discussions of estimated requirements have been on a monthly (or more frequent) basis.

The court concludes that the document is a binding and enforceable requirements contract.

II. BREACH OF CONTRACT

Gulf suggests that Eastern violated the contract between the parties by manipulating its requirements through a practice known as 'fuel freighting' in the airline industry. Requirements can vary from city to city depending on whether or not it is economically profitable to freight fuel. This fuel freighting practice in accordance with price could affect lifting from Gulf stations by either raising such liftings or lowering them. If the price was higher at a Gulf station, the practice could have reduced liftings there by lifting fuel in excess of its actual operating requirements at a prior station, and thereby not loading fuel at the succeeding high price Gulf station. Similarly where the Gulf station was comparatively cheaper, an aircraft might load more heavily at the Gulf station and not load at other succeeding non-Gulf stations.

The court however, finds that Eastern's performance under the contract does not constitute a breach of its agreement with Gulf and is consistent with good faith and established commercial practices as required by U.C.C. s 2–306.

'Good Faith' means 'honesty in fact in the conduct or transaction concerned' U.C.C. s 1–201(19). Between merchants, 'good faith' means 'honesty in fact and the observance of reasonable commercial standards of fair dealing in the trade'; U.C.C. s 2–103(1)(b) and Official Comment 2 of U.C.C. s 2–306. The relevant commercial practices are 'courses of performance,' 'courses of dealing' and 'usages of trade.'

Throughout the history of commercial aviation, including 30 years of dealing between Gulf and Eastern, airlines' liftings of fuel by nature have been subject to substantial daily, weekly, monthly and seasonal variations, as they are affected by weather, schedule changes, size of aircraft, aircraft load, local airport conditions, ground time, availability of fueling facilities, whether the flight is on time or late, passenger convenience, economy and efficiency of operation, fuel taxes, into-plane fuel service charges, fuel price, and ultimately, the judgment of the flight captain as to how much fuel he wants to take.

All these factors are, and for years have been, known to oil companies, including Gulf, and taken into account by them in their fuel contracts. Gulf's witnesses at trial pointed to certain examples of numerically large 'swings' in monthly liftings by Eastern at various Gulf stations. Gulf never complained of this practice and apparently accepted it as normal procedure. Some of the 'swings' were explained by the fueling of a single aircraft for one flight, or by the addition of one schedule in mid-month. The evidence establishes that Eastern, on one occasion, requested 500,000 additional gallons for one month at one station, without protest from Gulf, and that Eastern increased its requirements at another station more than 50 percent year to year, from less than 2,000,000 to more than 3,000,000 gallons, again, without Gulf objection.

The court concludes that fuel freighting is an established industry practice, inherent in the nature of the business. The evidence clearly demonstrated that the practice has long been part of the established courses of performance and dealing between Eastern and Gulf. As the practice of 'freighting' or 'tankering' has gone on unchanged and unchallenged for many years accepted as a fact of life by Gulf without complaint, the court is reminded of Official Comment 1 to U.C.C. s 2–208:

'The parties themselves know best what they have meant by their words of agreement and their action under that agreement is the best indication of what that meaning was.'

From a practical point of view, 'freighting' opportunities are very few, according to the uncontradicted testimony, as the airline must perform its schedules in consideration of operating realities. There is no suggestion here that Eastern is operating at certain gulf stations but taking no fuel at all. The very reason Eastern initially desired a fuel contract was because the airline planned to take on fuel, and had to have an assured source of supply.

If a customer's demands under a requirements contract become excessive, U.C.C. s 2–306 protects the seller and, in the appropriate case, would allow him to refuse to deliver unreasonable amounts demanded (but without eliminating his basic contract obligation); similarly, in an appropriate case, if a customer repeatedly had no requirements at all, the seller might be excused from performance if the buyer suddenly and without warning should descend upon him and demand his entire inventory, but the court is not called upon to decide those cases here.

Rather, the case here is one where the established courses of performance and dealing between the parties, the established usages of the trade, and the basic contract itself all show that the matters complained of for the first time by Gulf after commencement of this litigation are the fundamental given ingredients of the aviation fuel trade to which the parties have accommodated themselves successfully and without dispute over the years.

'The practical interpretation given to their contracts by the parties to them while they are engaged in their performance, and before any controversy has arisen concerning them, is one of the best indications of their true intent, and courts that adopt and enforce such a construction are not likely to commit serious error.'

Manhattan Life Ins. Co. of New York v. Wright, 126 F. 82, 87 (8th Cir. 1903).

The court concludes that Eastern has not violated the contract.

[Part III, which discusses commercial impracticability, is omitted.]

IV. REMEDY

Having found and concluded that the contract is a valid one, should be enforced, and that no defenses have been established against it, there remains for consideration the proper remedy.

The Uniform Commercial Code provides that in an appropriate case specific performance may be decreed. This case is a particularly appropriate one for specific performance. The parties have been operating for more than a year pursuant to a preliminary injunction requiring specific performance of the contract and Gulf has stipulated that it is able to perform. Gulf presently supplies Eastern with 100,000,000 gallons of fuel annually or 10 percent of Eastern's total requirements. If Gulf ceases to supply this fuel, the result will be chaos and irreparable damage.

Under the U.C.C. a more liberal test in determining entitlement to specific performance has been established than the test one must meet for classic equitable relief. U.C.C. s 2–716(1).

It has previously been found and concluded that Eastern is entitled to Gulf's fuel at the prices agreed upon in the contract. In the circumstances, a decree of specific performance becomes the ordinary and natural relief rather than the extraordinary one. The parties are before the court, the issues are squarely framed, they have been clearly resolved in Eastern's favor, and it would be a vain, useless and potentially harmful exercise to declare that Eastern has a valid contract, but leave the parties to their own devices. Accordingly, the preliminary injunction heretofore entered is made a permanent injunction and the order of this court herein.

CONCLUSIONS

For the foregoing reasons, the court makes the following ultimate findings of fact and conclusions of law:

1. The court has jurisdiction over the parties and the subject matter of this litigation.

2. The contract at issue is a valid requirements contract.

3. The contract was performed by the parties in accordance with its terms up to and including December 31, 1973, and Eastern has continued so to perform since that time.

4.   On December 31, 1973, Gulf breached the contract by declaring it no longer to be in effect.

5.   The contract is not lacking in mutuality nor is it commercially impracticable, and Eastern has performed its obligations thereunder.

6.   Eastern is entitled to enforcement of the contract, and the preliminary injunction heretofore issued, requiring specific performance according to the terms of the contract, be and the same is hereby made permanent.

DONE and ORDERED in chambers at the United States Courthouse for the Southern District of Florida, Miami, Florida this 20th day of October, 1975.

Uniform Commercial Code

§ 2–306.   Output, Requirements and Exclusive Dealings

(1) A term which measures the quantity by the output of the seller or the requirements of the buyer means such actual output or requirements as may occur in good faith, except that no quantity unreasonably disproportionate to any stated estimate or in the absence of a stated estimate to any normal or otherwise comparable prior output or requirements may be tendered or demanded.

(2) A lawful agreement by either the seller or the buyer for exclusive dealing in the kind of goods concerned imposes unless otherwise agreed an obligation by the seller to use best efforts to supply the goods and by the buyer to use best efforts to promote their sale.

Official Comment

Prior Uniform Statutory Provision: None.

Purposes:

1.   Subsection (1) of this section, in regard to output and requirements, applies to this specific problem the general approach of this Act which requires the reading of commercial background and intent into the language of any agreement and demands good faith in the performance of that agreement. It applies to such contracts of nonproducing establishments such as dealers or distributors as well as to manufacturing concerns.

2.   Under this Article, a contract for output or requirements is not too indefinite since it is held to mean the actual good faith output or requirements of the particular party. Nor does such a contract lack mutuality of obligation since, under this section, the party who will determine quantity is required to operate his plant or conduct his business in good faith and according to commercial standards of fair dealing in the trade so that his output or requirements will approximate a reasonably foreseeable figure. Reasonable elasticity in the requirements is expressly envisaged by this section and good faith variations from prior requirements are permitted even when the variation may be such as to result in discontinuance. A

shutdown by a requirements buyer for lack of orders might be permissible when a shutdown merely to curtail losses would not. The essential test is whether the party is acting in good faith. Similarly, a sudden expansion of the plant by which requirements are to be measured would not be included within the scope of the contract as made but normal expansion undertaken in good faith would be within the scope of this section. One of the factors in an expansion situation would be whether the market price had risen greatly in a case in which the requirements contract contained a fixed price. Reasonable variation of an extreme sort is exemplified in Southwest Natural Gas Co. v. Oklahoma Portland Cement Co., 102 F.2d 630 (C.C.A.10, 1939). This Article takes no position as to whether a requirements contract is a provable claim in bankruptcy.

3. If an estimate of output or requirements is included in the agreement, no quantity unreasonably disproportionate to it may be tendered or demanded. Any minimum or maximum set by the agreement shows a clear limit on the intended elasticity. In similar fashion, the agreed estimate is to be regarded as a center around which the parties intend the variation to occur.

4. When an enterprise is sold, the question may arise whether the buyer is bound by an existing output or requirements contract. That question is outside the scope of this Article, and is to be determined on other principles of law. Assuming that the contract continues, the output or requirements in the hands of the new owner continue to be measured by the actual good faith output or requirement., under the normal operation of the enterprise prior to sale. The sale itself is not grounds for sudden expansion or decrease.

5. Subsection (2), on exclusive dealing, makes explicit the commercial rule embodied in this Act under which the parties to such contracts are held to have impliedly, even when not expressly, bound themselves to use reasonable diligence as well as good faith in their performance of the contract. Under such contracts the exclusive agent is required, although no express commitment has been made, to use reasonable effort and due diligence in the expansion of the market or the promotion of the product, as the case may be. The principal is expected under such a contract to refrain from supplying any other dealer or agent within the exclusive territory. An exclusive dealing agreement brings into play all of the good faith aspects of the output and requirement problems of subsection (1). It also raises questions of insecurity and right to adequate assurance under this Article.

* * *

Wood is another great, and famous, early functionalist Cardozo opinion. "The defendant" Cardozo begins, "styles herself a 'Creator of Fashions.' Her favor helps a sale." In fact, Lucy, Lady Duff–Gordon was one of the first modern fashion designers, who pioneered the use of professional mannequins and cat-walk fashion shows. Her imprimatur became valuable independent of the quality of her own designs, and so she sought to realize some of this value by blessing the designs of others with her name. She engaged the plaintiff in the service of this ambition. According to the contract, he was to receive the exclusive right to market fashions under her name, and she was to receive half of the profits that such marketing generated. In spite of having engaged the plaintiff on these terms, the defendant, without informing the plaintiff, endorsed fashions sold through others and withheld the profits. The plaintiff sued.

The defendant sought to avoid liability on the ground that the contract was unenforceable for want of consideration. She argued that although she had promised to give him exclusive rights to market under her name, he had made no promise to do any marketing at all. Because the plaintiff remained free to do nothing, the defendant argued, his promise was illusory. And an illusory promise cannot constitute the consideration that the law demands before enforcing a contract.

Now Cardozo would have none of this argument, and so held for the plaintiff on the ground that he actually had incurred an obligation to market on defendant's behalf. But before reaching Cardozo's argument in this connection, it is worth pausing to note that even if the defendant had been right that the plaintiff remained free to do nothing to market under her name, she should nevertheless have lost the case. For even if the plaintiff was under no obligation to market fashions under the defendant's name, he nevertheless was under an obligation, if he chose to market, to split any profits this generated with her, in equal shares. He was not free, in other words, to seek a greater than half-share. And insofar as the consideration doctrine, ignoring the adequacy of bargains, requires only that there be some genuine exchange, even this (meager) obligation should have been sufficient to constitute consideration.

Cardozo, however, preferred to reject the defendant's argument direct-ly. "The law," he observed "has outgrown its primitive stage of formalism when the precise word was the sovereign talisman, and every slip was fatal." Cardozo insisted, in other words, that contracts need not spell out every obligation with complete precision in order to include obligations on each side. Rather, where the requisite intent to be bound exists, courts will not allow failures specifically to identify the terms on which the parties bind themselves to undo this intent. *Wood*, according to Cardozo, concerned just such a case: The writing was, to be sure "imperfectly expressed," but it was nevertheless "instinct with an obligation." Cardozo thus pursued his gap-filling agenda, familiar from his dissent in *Varney* (see Chapter 14), into the arena of consideration. Just as he opposed the formalist idea that incomplete promises might undermine contractual obligation by preventing there from being a meeting of (subjectively intending) minds, so he opposed this idea's close cousin, namely that an incomplete promise might under-mine contractual obligation by preventing there being consideration on the side that made it. In this case, as in the other, the functionalist remedy is plain: a court should fill in the gap in a reasonable way. Cardozo did just this in *Wood*. He observed that the plaintiff's promise to give the defendant half the profits that he generated would be worthless to the defendant if there were no profits to share, and therefore could not have induced the defendant's promise to give the plaintiff exclusive rights to market under her name. Making sense of the contract, therefore, required reading into it an obligation that the plaintiff use "reasonable efforts to bring [the contemplated] profits and revenues into existence." And once this obligation is revealed, there can no longer be any question that contract memorializes a genuine bargain, supported by good consideration on both sides.

This general approach is surely unobjectionable, at least to lawyers today. But Cardozo's opinion underestimates the degree of difficulty of the exercise in functionalist gap-filling that it involves. *Mattei* presents a way into these difficulties.

The plaintiff, in that case, was a real estate developer who contracted to buy land from the defendant, on which the plaintiff intended to construct a shopping mall. The contract made the plaintiff's obligation to buy "subject to Coldwell Banker's obtaining leases satisfactory" to the plaintiff, from retailers seeking to operate in the contemplated mall. The defendant failed to tender the plaintiff the deed to the land as the contract required, and the plaintiff sued to enforce the contract of sale.

An initial question, in the case, was whether the parties had reached an accepted promise at all. The defendant claimed that her offer to sell could be accepted by plaintiff only by giving notice that he had obtained the satisfactory leases that were contemplated. While the defendant clearly could have structured her offer in this way, the court concluded that she had not done so. Instead, there had been offer and acceptance, but the terms of the agreement gave the plaintiff a right to terminate the (accepted) contract in case he did not receive the satisfactory leases.

The defendant therefore retreated to a second argument, namely that the clause conditioning the plaintiff's obligation to buy on his receiving retail leases "satisfactory" to him rendered his obligations illusory and deprived the contract of consideration. This argument is, of course, formally identical to the one made by the defendant in *Wood*. In each case, a promisor claims that because her promisee's return promise leaves open that the promisee might do nothing, it cannot constitute good consideration, so that there has been no bargain in fact. Now, by the time *Mattei* was decided (in contrast to *Wood*) there was no real possibility that this argument would be accepted. The live issue, for the solidly functionalist court in *Mattei*, was not *whether* the gap in the plaintiff's promise would be filled by a term that limited his discretion to terminate; rather, the live issue was precisely *what* content this discretion-limiting term would have.

The court considered the same solution proposed by Cardozo in *Wood*, namely imposing on the plaintiff a duty to use *reasonable judgment* in determining whether the leases he received were satisfactory. The court concluded that this standard was not administrable—"that the factors involved in determining whether a lease is satisfactory to the lessor are too numerous and varied to permit the application of a reasonable man standard" in this area. The court therefore settled on another solution, which was to impose on the plaintiff the requirement that he might terminate the purchase, based on alleged dissatisfaction with the leases, only if the allegations of dissatisfaction were made in *good faith*. This requirement of good faith, the court concluded, also rendered the plaintiff's promise to buy real rather than illusory, and hence capable of constituting consideration for the defendant's promise to sell.

The court never argued why good faith might be more administrable in this context than reasonableness, nor did it even explain precisely what good faith requires. The nearest that it came was to observe that it would be bad faith for the plaintiff to assert that the leases were unsatisfactory when he in fact found them satisfactory. But this account of good faith is conclusory. Presumably the plaintiff would not assert that the leases were unsatisfactory unless he wished to avoid the obligation to buy the land, at least on the terms to which he'd agreed. And presumably the fact that the plaintiff wishes to avoid this obligation simply entails that the leases are unsatisfactory, at least *in the sense that they are insufficient to render the development of the land appealing to him, compared to his other options.* Indeed, when it is understood in this way, good faith seems not only to be conclusory, but also vacuous: the requirement of good faith seems to involve nothing more than that the plaintiff honestly report whether or not he wants to go through with the sale, all-things-considered, in circumstances in which he has no incentive to be dishonest. But if good faith is understood in this way, then it seems insufficient to answer the defendant's claim that the plaintiff's promise is illusory.

So good faith must in the end mean something else in this context: it must require not only that the plaintiff honestly report his satisfaction or dissatisfaction with the leases, but also that the plaintiff fashion his response to the leases in a particular way. Most narrowly, good faith might require that the plaintiff not become dissatisfied with the leases simply because, given that the defendant has relied on the plaintiff's promise to buy (and has perhaps refused offers from alternative buyers who have now acquired land elsewhere), he could, if he terminated the old agreement, obtain a new agreement to buy the land from the strategically weakened defendant at a better price. Perhaps good faith imposes greater demands than this; and Chapter 19 will take up the nature and meaning of good faith in contract. In any event, even this brief discussion makes clear that good faith is no more readily administrable in this context than reasonableness. Even if it is clear that a functionalist court might in principle fill the gaps in contracts like those in *Wood* and *Mattei* with terms that render the promises therein substantial rather than illusory, the functionalist problem of identifying precisely what these terms are turns out to be more difficult than either Cardozo or the judges in *Mattei* seem to have admitted.

Eastern Airlines, and the section from the UCC, render vivid just how difficult the functionalist problem is. The parties in *Eastern Airlines* contracted for the defendant to supply the plaintiff with its jet fuel requirements over a multi-year period. The contract, in an effort to track market prices in an administrable way, set the price for the fuel by reference to a price indicator called West Texas Sour, published in a periodical called Platts Oilgram. In the middle of the contract period, a global oil crisis arose. As a result of the crisis, fuel prices rose dramatically, and the United States government adopted a series of price controls. The price controls caused—through an intricate chain of connections—the West Texas Sour indicator no longer to reflect market prices generally, as it had done (and had been expected to do) when the contract was signed. The contract thus gave the plaintiff access to jet fuel at a below market price. At the time of contracting, the oil crisis was perhaps unpredictable, the price controls were probably unpredictable, and the interaction between the price controls and the accuracy of the West Texas Sour indicator was almost certainly unpredictable.

The defendant sought to avoid its obligation to supply the plaintiff with its jet fuel requirements, and the plaintiff sought to have the obligation enforced. Following in a by now familiar vein, the defendant tried to argue that the contract was invalid for lack of consideration, on the ground that the plaintiff's promise, because the plaintiff might set its requirements at zero, was illusory. Equally familiarly, the court had no trouble rejecting this argument, on functionalist grounds. The court observed that, at least where a requirements purchaser operated an on-going business, so that a court might manageably identify the actual quantities in which the parties to a requirements contract expected and intended to transact, it had long been the rule that a buyer's promise to buy its requirements imposed real obligations on the buyer, concerning just what requirements it might demand, and so constituted good consideration for the seller's promise to sell. The question, of course, is just what the requirements-buyer's obligations consist in. There, the court looked to the UCC, which, in § 2–306(1) imposes on requirements buyers a duty to set their requirements both in good faith and in such a way that they are not unreasonably disproportionate to either stated estimates or normal or otherwise comparable prior use.

All this is familiar from the other opinions discussed in this section. *Eastern Airlines* is a useful case, nevertheless, because the facts and circumstances surrounding the contract at issue clearly and precisely illustrate the difficulties inherent in reducing general standards such as "good faith" and "not unreasonably disproportionate" to more precise meanings, which make it possible to decide cases. (Notice that the two phrases in scare quotes almost certainly mean different things, and that the UCC does not adequately address the difference.) The contract at issue in *Eastern Airlines* gave the plaintiff access to fuel at substantially below market prices. The question in the case is how much the plaintiff may buy at these prices. Put more precisely, to what extent may the plaintiff increase its requirements in light of the fact that it receives the advantageous price?

It is very difficult to provide a general answer to such questions; indeed, it is difficult to answer them even for specific cases. Chapter 19, which is devoted to good faith, will try and will revisit *Eastern Airlines* in the process. Perhaps *Eastern Airlines*, in particular, might be resolved in a way that sidesteps the hardest problems concerning such line-drawing. The problem, in that case, is entirely an artifact of the choice of the *Platts Oilgram* West Texas Sour indicator as the mechanism for fixing the contract price. That indicator was used (the facts of the case suggest) because the indicator was thought, at the time of contracting, reliably to track market prices. Certainly there was nothing in the record to suggest that the contract was designed to depart from market prices anything like as substantially as it turned out to do. Finally, the reason why the West Texas Sour based price turned out to depart so dramatically from market prices had to do with unanticipated, and almost certainly not reasonably anticipatable, regulatory developments. At the very least, there is nothing in the record to suggest that the parties intended the contract to protect the plaintiff either against an international oil crisis or against the particular regulatory response adopted by the United States. And given all of this, a functionalist court might simply have read the "West Texas Sour" in the contract to mean "market price" or some equivalent. This reading would entirely avoid the difficulty of fixing good faith and reasonableness, as the market price would have aligned the plaintiff's incentives with contractual expectations, so that there would be every reason to think that the plaintiff's actual demand was both in good faith and reasonable. It would turn the case into one concerning styles of contract interpretation, and in particular, the debate between textualist and contractualist approaches to contract language. Chapter 17 takes up this question in earnest.

The point, in this Part, is not to pursue the functionalist analysis any further (probably too much has been said already, at least for narrative grace). Rather, the point is that even if it is possible, in the context of requirements contracts, to verify the fact of a bargain in a purely formal way, this is not enough to decide actual cases, because it is not enough to say what the bargains that have been formally identified consist in. This requires (very difficult) functionalist analysis. And so even where it succeeds on its own terms, formalism cannot succeed, overall, without some sort of functionalist supplement.

15.3.C THE PRE-EXISTING DUTY RULE

A final application of the consideration doctrine is worth considering, not least because it reveals, in vivid and complete detail, that formalist approaches to the doctrine can decide cases only on the back of a hidden functionalist analysis. Indeed, as the following materials illustrate, formalism often hides *the wrong* the functionalist analysis. This section should thus once again be read in the shadow of Llewellyn's remark, quoted before, that "covert tools are never good tools."

In particular, the formalist approach to something called the pre-existing duty rule threatens to invalidate too many contract modifications for wanting consideration. This should not come as any surprise. After all, formalism was designed to limit the scope of contractual obligation. But, as the earlier discussion of formalism and the subjective theory of intent revealed, the design sometimes worked too well. In the context of contractual intent, this led courts, even as they concluded that a lack of intent prevented a contract from being formed, to create equivalent liabilities outside of contract, most commonly in quantum meruit. Quantum meruit was, of course, a functionalist doctrine, and so the formalist analysis in the end reprised functionalist contract law, only on non-contractual ground. The overlap was imperfect, however, because the distinctive values associated with using promises to achieve functionalist ends remained inaccessible to the formalist. The inquiry into reasonableness was, as Chapter 13 argued, transformed by being conducted not within contract but without it. And so in cases—for example, *Lucy v. Zehmer*—in which certain functionalist values could receive adequate expression only within contract, formalism threatened to produce not just bad reasoning, but bad outcomes.

Something similar occurred concerning formalism in the context of the consideration doctrine and the pre-existing duty rule. The formalist approach to consideration, as was just said, threatened quite generally (and therefore much too broadly) to invalidate contract modifications. Some formalist courts, facing this prospect, employed a functionalist analysis that went too far in the other direction, so that they accepted contract modifications more readily than the basic principles of contract law recommend. In the end, the formalist approach to contract modification—because it turned to disguised functionalisms that were ill-suited to addressing the actual problems presented by this area of law—proved simultaneously under- and over-restrictive.

Alaska Packers' Ass'n v. Domenico

United States Court of Appeals for the Ninth Circuit, 1902.
117 Fed. 99.

■ ROSS, CIRCUIT JUDGE. The libel in this case was based upon a contract alleged to have been entered into between the libelants and the appellant corporation on the 22d day of May, 1900, at Pyramid Harbor, Alaska, by which it is claimed the appellant promised to pay each of the libelants, among other things, the sum of $100 for services rendered and to be rendered. In its answer the respondent denied the execution, on its part, of the contract sued upon, averred that it was without consideration, and for a third defense alleged that the work performed by the libelants for it was performed under other and different contracts than that sued on, and that, prior to the filing of the libel, each of the libelants was paid by the respondent the full amount due him thereunder, in consideration of which each of them executed a full release of all his claims and demands against the respondent.

The evidence shows without conflict that on March 26, 1900, at the city and county of San Francisco, the libelants entered into a written contract with the appellants, whereby they agreed to go from San Francisco to Pyramid Harbor, Alaska, and return, on board such vessel as might be designated by the appellant, and to work for the appellant during the fishing season of 1900, at Pyramid Harbor, as sailors and fishermen, agreeing to do 'regular ship's duty, both up and down, discharging and loading; and to do any other work whatsoever when requested to do so by the captain or agent of the Alaska Packers' Association.' By the terms of this agreement, the appellant was to pay each of the libelants $50 for the season, and two cents for each red salmon in the catching of which he took part.

On the 15th day of April, 1900, 21 of the libelants of the libelants signed shipping articles by which they shipped as seamen on the Two Brothers, a vessel chartered by the appellant for the voyage between San Francisco and Pyramid Harbor, and also bound themselves to perform the same work for the appellant provided for by the previous contract of March 26th; the appellant agreeing to pay them therefore the sum of $60 for the season, and two cents each for each red salmon in the catching of which they should respectively take part. Under these contracts, the libelants sailed on board the Two Brothers for Pyramid Harbor, where the appellants had about $150,000 invested in a salmon cannery. The libelants arrived there early in April of the year mentioned, and began to unload the vessel and fit up the cannery. A few days thereafter, to wit, May 19th, they stopped work in a body, and demanded of the company's superintendent there in charge $100 for services in operating the vessel to and from Pyramid Harbor, instead of the sums stipulated for in and by the contracts; stating that unless they were paid this additional wage they would stop work entirely, and return to San Francisco. The evidence showed, and the court below found, that it was impossible for the appellant to get other men to take the places of the libelants, the place being remote, the season short and just opening; so that, after endeavoring for several days without success to induce the libelants to proceed with their work in accordance with their contracts, the company's superintendent, on the 22d day of May, so far yielded to their demands as to instruct his clerk to copy the contracts executed in San Francisco, including the words 'Alaska Packers' Association' at the end, substituting, for the $50 and $60 payments, respectively, of those contracts, the sum of $100, which document, so prepared, was signed by the libelants before a shipping commissioner whom they had requested to be brought from Northeast Point; the superintendent, however, testifying that he at the time told the libelants that he was without authority to enter into any such contract, or to in any way alter the contracts made between them and the company in San Francisco. Upon the return of the libelants to San Francisco at the close of the fishing season, they demanded pay in accordance with the terms of the alleged contract of May 22d, when the company denied its validity, and refused to pay other than as provided for by the contracts of March 26th and April 5th, respectively. Some of the libelants, at least, consulted counsel, and, after receiving his advice, those of them who had signed the shipping articles before the shipping commissioner at San Francisco went before that officer, and received the amount due them thereunder, executing in consideration thereof a release in full, and the others paid at the office of the company, also receipting in full for their demands.

On the trial in the court below, the libelants undertook to show that the fishing nets provided by the respondent were defective, and that it was on that account that they demanded increased wages. On that point, the evidence was substantially conflicting, and the finding of the court was against the libelants the court saying:

> 'The contention of libelants that the nets provided them were rotten and unserviceable is not sustained by the evidence. The defendants' interest required that libelants should be provided with every facility necessary to their success as fishermen, for on such success depended the profits defendant would be able to realize that season from its packing plant, and the large capital invested therein. In view of this self-evident fact, it is highly improbable that the defendant gave libelants rotten and unservice-able nets with which to fish. It follows from this finding that libelants were not justified in refusing performance of their origi-nal contract.' 112 Fed. 554.

The evidence being sharply conflicting in respect to these facts, the conclusions of the court, who heard and saw the witnesses, will not be disturbed.

The real questions in the case as brought here are questions of law, and, in the view that we take of the case, it will be necessary to consider but one of those. Assuming that the appellant's superintendent at Pyramid Harbor was authorized to make the alleged contract of May 22d, and that he executed it on behalf of the appellant, was it supported by a sufficient consideration? From the foregoing statement of the case, it will have been seen that the libelants agreed in writing, for certain stated compensation, to render their services to the appellant in remote waters where the season for conducting fishing operations is extremely short, and in which enter-prise the appellant had a large amount of money invested; and, after having entered upon the discharge of their contract, and at a time when it was impossible for the appellant to secure other men in their places, the libelants, without any valid cause, absolutely refused to continue the services they were under contract to perform unless the appellant would consent to pay them more money. Consent to such a demand, under such circumstances, if given, was, in our opinion, without consideration, for the reason that it was based solely upon the libelants' agreement to render the exact services, and none other, that they were already under contract to render. The case shows that they willfully and arbitrarily broke that obligation. As a matter of course, they were liable to the appellant in damages, and it is quite probable, as suggested by the court below in its opinion, that they may have been unable to respond in damages. But we are unable to agree with the conclusions there drawn, from these facts, in these words:

> 'Under such circumstances, it would be strange, indeed, if the law would not permit the defendant to waive the damages caused by the libelants' breach, and enter into the contract sued upon,—a contract mutually beneficial to all the parties thereto, in that it gave to the libelants reasonable compensation for their labor, and

enabled the defendant to employ to advantage the large capital it had invested in its canning and fishing plant.'

Certainly, it cannot be justly held, upon the record in this case, that there was any voluntary waiver on the part of the appellant of the breach of the original contract. The company itself knew nothing of such breach until the expedition returned to San Francisco, and the testimony is uncontradicted that its superintendent at Pyramid Harbor, who, it is claimed, made on its behalf the contract sued on, distinctly informed the libelants that he had no power to alter the original or to make a new contract, and it would, of course, follow that, if he had no power to change the original, he would have no authority to waive any rights thereunder. The circumstances of the present case bring it, we think, directly within the sound and just observations of the supreme court of Minnesota in the case of *King v. Railway Co.*, 61 Minn. 482:

'No astute reasoning can change the plain fact that the party who refuses to perform, and thereby coerces a promise from the other party to the contract to pay him an increased compensation for doing that which he is legally bound to do, takes an unjustifiable advantage of the necessities of the other party. Surely it would be a travesty on justice to hold that the party so making the promise for extra pay was estopped from asserting that the promise was without consideration. A party cannot lay the foundation of an estoppel by his own wrong, where the promise is simply a repetition of a subsisting legal promise. There can be no consideration for the promise of the other party, and there is no warrant for inferring that the parties have voluntarily rescinded or modified their contract. The promise cannot be legally enforced, although the other party has completed his contract in reliance upon it.'

In *Lingenfelder v. Brewing Co.*, 103 Mo. 578, the court, in holding void a contract by which the owner of a building agreed to pay its architect an additional sum because of his refusal to otherwise proceed with the contract, said:

'It is urged upon us by respondents that this was a new contract. New in what? Jungenfeld was bound by his contract to design and supervise this building. Under the new promise, he was not to do anything more or anything different. What benefit was to accrue to Wainwright? He was to receive the same service from Jungenfeld under the new, that Jungenfeld was bound to tender under the original, contract. What loss, trouble, or inconvenience could result to Jungenfeld that he had not already assumed? No amount of metaphysical reasoning can change the plain fact that Jungenfeld took advantage of Wainwright's necessities, and extorted the promise of five per cent. on the refrigerator plant as the condition of his complying with his contract already entered into. Nor had he even the flimsy pretext that Wainwright had violated any of the conditions of the contract on his part. Jungenfeld himself put it upon the simple proposition that 'if he, as an architect, put up the brewery, and another company put up the refrigerating machinery, it would be a detriment to the Empire Refrigerating Company,' of which Jungenfeld was president. To permit plaintiff to recover under such circumstances would be to offer a premium upon bad faith, and invite men to violate their most sacred contracts that they may profit by their own wrong. That a promise to pay a man for doing that which he is already under contract to do is without consideration is conceded by respondents. The rule has been so long imbedded in the common law and decisions of the highest courts of the various states that nothing but the most cogent reasons ought to shake it. (Citing a long list of authorities.) But it is 'carrying coals to Newcastle' to add authorities on a proposition so universally accepted, and so inherently just and right in itself. The learned counsel for respondents do not controvert the general proposition. They contention is, and the circuit court agreed with them, that, when Jungenfeld declined to go further on his contract, the defendant then had the right to sue for damages, and not having elected to sue Jungenfeld, but having acceded to his demand for the additional compensation defendant cannot now be heard to say his promise is without consideration. While it is true Jungenfeld became liable in damages for the obvious breach of his contract, we do not think it follows that defendant is estopped from showing its promise was made without consideration. It is true that as eminent a jurist as Judge Cooley, in *Goebel v. Linn*, 47 Mich. 489, held that an ice company which had agreed to furnish a brewery with all the ice they might need for their business from November 8, 1879, until January 1, 1881, at $1.75 per ton, and afterwards in May, 1880, declined to deliver any more ice unless the brewery would give it $3 per ton, could recover on a promissory note given for the increased price. Profound as is our respect for the distinguished judge who delivered the opinion, we are still of the opinion that his decision is not in accord with the almost universally accepted doctrine, and is not convincing; and certainly so much of the opinion as holds that the payment, by a debtor, of a part of his debt then due, would constitute a defense to a suit for the remainder, is not the law of this state, nor, do we think, of any other where the common law prevails. What we hold is that, when a party merely does what he has already obligated himself to do, he cannot demand an additional compensation therefor; and although, by taking advantage of the necessities of his adversary, he obtains a promise for more, the law will regard it as nudum pactum, and will not lend its process to aid in the wrong.'

It results from the views above expressed that the judgment must be reversed, and the cause remanded, with directions to the court below to enter judgment for the respondent, with costs. It is so ordered.

* * *

The plaintiffs in *Alaska Packers* were fishermen who had shipped up with the defendant in San Francisco, in order to sail to Alaska to catch salmon. The parties had agreed in San Francisco that, in exchange for their work fishing, the plaintiffs would receive $50 or $60 for the season plus two cents per red salmon caught. The conditions in Alaska were exceptionally harsh. In addition, at least according to the plaintiffs, the fishing nets provided by the defendant were less good than had been promised, making the fishing less productive, and depressing the variable portion of the plaintiffs' pay. In any event, after a short time, the plaintiffs refused to continue working at the previously agreed wages and demanded that they instead be paid $100 for the season. The defendant's foreman (who was unable to procure replacement fishermen in time for the season's catch) agreed to the pay raise. When the plaintiffs returned to San Francisco, the defendant refused to honor the contract modification, and the plaintiffs sued.

The court observed that it was not clear whether the defendant's foreman had the authority (actual or apparent) to bind the defendant contractually. The court concluded, however, that it did not need to reach this question. Instead, it found the contract modification invalid for want of consideration. The plaintiffs, according to the court, gave no promise in exchange for the higher wages save to repeat their earlier promise to work the season. They thus promised to do no more than to perform a duty that they already had (under the unmodified contract). As the court claimed, "consent to [the contract modification] . . . was, in our opinion, without consideration, for the reason that it was based solely upon the libelants' agreement to render the exact services, and none other, that they were already under contract to render." This principle—called the *pre-existing duty rule*—therefore rendered the defendant's return promise to pay a higher wage unenforceable.

Now, there existed several straightforward routes to the other conclusion. The first two involve the plaintiffs' claim that the defendant had provided them with sub-standard fishing nets. First, insofar as this allegation was accurate, the defendant was in breach of the original contract. Accordingly, the plaintiffs' agreement to abandon their legal claims arising out of the breach—something that they were under no duty to do—would have provided perfectly good consideration for the defendant's new wage promise. Second, even insofar as the allegation was not accurate (insofar as the defendant had in fact provided conforming nets), *Fiege* and (today) Restatement § 74 make plain that the plaintiffs' abandonment of their claim could have constituted good consideration as long as the claim was reasonable, or perhaps even just made in good faith.

Third, it is always possible that the plaintiffs agreed to expend greater effort at fishing in exchange for the higher wage, and this additional effort is perfectly good consideration. This suggestion, moreover, is no mere gimmick. The per-fish component of the plaintiffs' pay reveals that the defendant was clearly concerned about the plaintiffs' effort level. Perhaps the defendant felt, once its ship had arrived in Alaska, that this incentive was insufficient. (The state of the nets might, although it need not, figure in this account of the case also, because sub-standard nets may have made fish caught a less reliable indicator of effort than the defendant had supposed.) By paying a higher wage, the defendant increased the cost to each plaintiff of being fired for lack of effort and therefore increased the motivating power of the threat to fire shirkers.[55]

And fourth, even if the plaintiffs had really brought nothing to the new contract other than their willingness to do the work that they were obligated to do under the old, the new contract might nevertheless have been supported by formally unimpeachable consideration, as long as it had been formed in the right way. Thus the plaintiffs and defendant might not simply have modified the old contract to make the new but rather, proceeding in stages, rescinded the old contract and then contracted afresh to make the new one. In the first stage, each party to the old contract would have abandoned its legal rights under that contract in exchange for the other party's abandoning its rights. And each abandonment would unquestionably have constituted good consideration for the other. The two parties would then have stood in *no* contractual relation to each other. And against this blank slate, each party could then have assumed the obligations (to fish on the one hand and to pay on the other) named in the new contract. Once again, each obligation would unquestionably have constituted good consideration for the other. And so the new contract would have been enforceable in just the same way as the one that it had replaced.

The court in *Alaska Packers* held that the contract modification was not supported by good consideration and therefore found for the defendant. It reached this conclusion without clearly identifying or distinguishing these various claims that there did exist consideration, however. Of the four possible paths to consideration, the court clearly addressed only the fourth: it acknowledged that parties seeking to modify a contract can always avoid the pre-existing duty rule by rescinding their old contract and then making a brand new one. But it concluded that this is not what happened in the case before it. The court reached this conclusion more or less without argument—observing only that the defendant needed labor for its capital-intensive fishing operation and that once the ship and the plaintiffs were in Alaska, no alternative source of labor for the defendant existed. The court believed that this demonstrated that there had been no rescission.

The pattern behind this approach is worth identifying precisely. The court's approach, in *Alaska Packers*, implicitly acknowledges that the pre-existing duty rule threatens to render the formalist approach to consider-

---

55. The effect of this would be not just to give the plaintiffs a greater incentive to work but also to reduce the defendant's costs of monitoring the plaintiffs' effort. As the cost to each plaintiff of being fired for shirking goes up, a lower chance of being caught shirking becomes sufficient to encourage work effort (because the expected costs of being caught go up at every probability of being caught). Insofar as monitoring the plaintiffs' effort was costly to the defendant, the higher pay might encourage work more cheaply than increased monitoring. Similar arguments will appear in Part III, in the discussion of employment contracts and what economists call "efficiency wages."

ation too demanding. Applied mechanically, the rule would cause the formalist consideration doctrine to render contracts effectively unmodifiable, or at least to invalidate all one-sided modifications. But contract modifications are often essential to the good functioning of contract relations—which must remain flexible in the face of new contingencies. And often, the required modifications are, or can be made to appear, one-sided. (As when, for example, a contract between a landowner and an excavation firm is modified to increase the firm's fee on account of difficult digging conditions: the increased fee is obvious; the fact that the work turned out to be more onerous than the initial agreement contemplated is must less obvious.) Accordingly, formalist courts had to find a way to allow contract modifications even in the face of the pre-existing duty rule. The idea of reciprocal rescission followed by a new contract creates an exception to the pre-existing duty rule and thus provides the required safety valve. But the exception threatens to swallow the rule—it allows *every* modification to be cast as supported by good consideration. Accordingly, formalist courts had to limit the range of the exception. In *Alaska Packers*, this limitation was achieved by loose talk about the pressure that the plaintiffs exerted against the defendant in Alaska—loose talk, in effect, that the defendant had agreed to the modification only under *duress*.

The court's claims concerning duress are, however, implausible. Indeed, the doubt that *Alaska Packers* really involved duress is emphasized and heightened by the consideration doctrine in whose service duress was raised. The consideration doctrine, recall, insists on only the *fact* and not the *adequacy* of a bargain. Even if the plaintiffs' power, once in Alaska, was very great, and the new bargain correspondingly unfair, this would not yet entail, as the court's opinion supposes, that the bargain was a mere fiction. It would not even make it unreasonable to infer the bargain from the facts, as it is reasonable to suppose that the defendant freely made the best of its bad situation. Instead, in order for the defendant's need of the plaintiffs' labor to undermine consideration, it would have had to be the case that this need was so great that it overpowered the defendant's capacity to form bargain intentions at all, or at least to form them freely. Nothing in the case rules out this possibility, of course. But nothing in the opinion establishes duress, either. And the law of duress, as Part III will explore in greater detail, construes duress very narrowly, so that very few forms of hard bargaining amount to duress. The defendant's vulnerability to the plaintiffs in Alaska could not, by itself, underwrite a claim of duress, as analogous claims of vulnerability made by the plaintiffs in San Francisco (say, that there were many fishermen seeking few jobs and that defendant acted in various ways to maintain this state of affairs) would not have been held to enable them to avoid the initial contract.

Accordingly, *Alaska Packers* is generally thought to be not just badly reasoned but also wrongly decided. The opinion, it is said, illustrates both that the formalist pre-existing duty rule was really about duress and also that this disguise enabled courts to manipulate the law of duress in a fashion that favored capital over labor.

There is, no doubt, something in this interpretation. Certainly the formalist approach to the pre-existing duty rule enabled courts to invalidate a great many contract modifications, and they probably were inclined to invalidate contracts when doing so favored certain economic interests over others.[56] Indeed, this is likely what happened in *Alaska Packers* itself, where the court would almost certainly not have recognized duress had analogous pressure been applied (as it almost certainly was applied) by the defendant fishing company against the plaintiff fishermen.

But there are also important respects in which the standard account of *Alaska Packers* proceeds too quickly. It is, as the materials below will reveal, quite possible, even likely, that the case, although poorly argued, was *rightly* decided, at least in the sense that even an openly functionalist approach to consideration and contract modification would have reached the same conclusion. Moreover, this revision to the conventional wisdom addresses matters that extend well beyond the particulars of the individual case, and concern the broader relationship between functionalism and formalism in contract law.

Certainly, *Alaska Packers*, like all of the other consideration cases, illustrates that even if the importance of the fact of a bargain can be defended on purely formalist grounds, formalism standing alone is not sufficient to distinguish cases in which factual bargains exist from those in which they do not. The fourth route to consideration in that case is *necessarily* available in *every* pre-existing duty case.[58] So the fact that it

---

56. Formalist courts applying the rule were not, however, *only* siding with elites in economic and political disputes. The pre-existing duty rule was also employed to invalidate contracts that had no obvious political component. For example, the rule was employed to invalidate contracts in which a person promised a paying third party a performance that he was already obligated to provide, under an earlier contract, to his original promisee. (A typical case is *McDevitt v. Stokes*, 192 S.W. 681 (Ky. 1917), in which a jockey hired by a horse order to compete in a race made a subsequent contract with a third party who offered a separate payment in case the jockey rode to victory.) Indeed, something like the rule was even employed, by analogy, to hold that reward offers to those who apprehended criminals were not enforceable with respect to either police officers or the victims' private agents, on the ground that these were already obligated to apprehend the perpetrators. (A famous case is *Board of Comm'rs of Montgomery County v. Johnson*, 266 P. 749 (Kan. 1928), which concerned the payment of a reward for the capture of Everett Bible, who had "killed Charles Faurot near Tyro, Kan., and fled the state a fugitive from justice.")

Note that it would not be hard, even for a formalist, to find consideration in each of these cases. Even if the promisees were already—apart from the alleged contracts—obligated to do the *acts* in question, the contracts surely give them additional reasons to do these acts, which made reference to parties not mentioned in the prior obligations. Thus the contracts in *McDevitt* caused the jockey to owe an obligation to try to win not just to the horse's owner but also to the third party; and the contracts in *Johnson* (which were unilateral and hence involved no promissory obligations on the part of the plaintiffs) added the reward incentive to the others that the plaintiffs already possessed. Surely if there might be consideration supporting a bargain in *Hamer*, then there might be consideration in these cases, too.

58. The first three arguments for finding consideration in *Alaska Packers* clearly also cannot be answered save on functionalist grounds (concerning the validity or at least reasonableness of the plaintiffs' claims about the nets and whether it would have been efficient or even sensible for the defendant, given the circumstances, to have paid more for greater effort). But these do not generalize to other cases and so do not necessarily provide any broader insight into the limits of formalism.

cannot be assessed save in a functionalist way renders functionalism essential to the application of the rule.

But even if it is right that here, as elsewhere, formalism cannot stand alone, the standard reading of *Alaska Packers* gives away too much to functionalism. Specifically, the functionalist mechanism that this reading finds behind pre-existing duty cases—the concern for duress—is completely independent of the consideration doctrine, so that these accounts make it seem that nothing of formalism remains (or indeed ever actually influences outcomes) in this line of doctrine. But as the following, unabashedly functionalist materials show, that is not the case.

Ralston Purina Co. v. McNabb

United States District Court for the Western District of Tennessee, 1974.
381 F.Supp. 181.

Grain company brought action against farmer for insufficient delivery of soybeans under contract for sale of soybeans. The District Court, Bailey Brown, Chief Judge, held that defense of impossibility was unavailable to farmer where there was no showing that contract was for sale of the crop from specified lands; that, where farmer objectively accepted extensions of the contract, damages would have to be calculated at final date for delivery under the extensions unless the extensions were offered by buyer in bad faith; that evidence that buyer knew that farmer could not perform fully under the contract and that market price of the soybeans would continue to rise demonstrated that buyer offered the extensions in bad faith and so could collect only the difference between the contract price of the soybeans and their market price on the date of delivery called for in the initial contract.

Judgment for plaintiff.

■ BROWN, CHIEF JUDGE. In this cause plaintiff, Ralston Purina Company, sues defendant, F. R. McNabb, a West Tennessee farmer, for breach of contract, alleging that McNabb failed to deliver 3,771 bushels of the 8,000 bushels of soybeans due under two contracts entered into by Ralston Purina and McNabb in early September, 1972. The case has been tried before a jury which answered interrogatories. Moreover, the parties stipulated numerous facts and further stipulated that the Court should determine any questions of fact that had not been determined either by the jury in its answer or by the parties in their pretrial stipulations of facts.

The stipulations of the parties establish that Ralston Purina and McNabb entered into two contracts (NS–606 and NS–609) for the November delivery of 5,000 bushels of soybeans at $3.33 per bushel and 3,000 bushels of soybeans at $3.29 per bushel. The contracts were executed in writing by McNabb and incorporated by reference the rules of the Grain & Feed Dealers National Association. McNabb made only one delivery (738.23 bushels) to Ralston Purina prior to the November 30th deadline. Ralston Purina sent and McNabb received one month letters of extension for both contracts for the months of December, January and February. McNabb made seven deliveries in December, three deliveries in January, and one delivery in February for a total of 4,228.53 bushels delivered to Ralston Purina, leaving 771.47 bushels undelivered on contract NS–606 and 3,000 bushels undelivered on contract NS–609. On March 17, 1973 Ralston Purina demanded, and McNabb refused to pay, $11,131.32 (using a March 8th market price, the date Ralston Purina contends that it covered by purchase elsewhere, to calculate damages under T.C.A. § 47–2–713) damages resulting from defendant McNabb's failure to deliver on the contracts. The parties stipulated that during the fall and winter of 1972 there was severe weather-in the form of unusually heavy rains and flooding-in the areas where McNabb conducted his farming operations.

Defendant McNabb defends on two grounds: (1) that the severe weather made performance of his contract impossible (T.C.A. § 47–2–615) and (2) in the alternative, any damages (T.C.A. § 47–2–713) that the plaintiff is entitled to should be calculated as of November 30, 1972, the last date for performance under the contracts. The defense of impossibility is unavailable to the defendant since there has been no showing that the contract was to sell a crop from specified land, and therefore no such issue was submitted to the jury.

This leaves only the defendant's assertion that damages should be measured as of November 30, 1972. Despite the receipt of monthly letters of extension, the delivery of soybeans during the extension periods, and the receipt of payment for deliveries in amounts corresponding to the contract price, defendant argues that he did not consent by his conduct to the extension of the contract period. McNabb testified that he regarded the contract as breached on the November 30, 1972 delivery date, that he regarded his later deliveries to Ralston Purina as new sales at the price posted for the day the soybeans were delivered, and that he regarded the checks from Ralston Purina at the old contract price as merely reflecting a method Ralston Purina was using to assure the payment by McNabb of any damages resulting from the November 30, 1972 breach. It should be remembered, however, that the standard for interpreting the actions of parties is the reasonable man standard. Thus 'any course of performance accepted or acquiesced in without objection shall be relevant to determining the meaning of the agreement' and 'such course of performance shall be relevant to show a waiver or modification 'T.C.A. § 47–2–208(1) and (3) (1964); see T.C.A. § 47–2–209 (1964). The code attempts to give effect to 'all necessary and desirable modifications of sales contracts without regard to technicalities' T.C.A. § 47–2–209 Comment 1 (1964). Underlying the code policy favoring preservation of contracts and the allowance of modifications is the strict requirement that all actions of parties must be in good faith, thus in order to have a valid contract modification, especially when that modification may favor a merchant, the modification must be made in demonstrable good faith. T.C.A. § 47–2–209 Comment 2 (1964).

In the instant case, the objective facts all point to valid extensions of the contracts. Each time Ralston Purina offered to extend the contract deadline to the end of the month, McNabb objectively indicated acceptance of the extension by delivering soybeans after the date of the offer and accepted the contract price although the market price was then higher. Thus the final date for delivery was mutually extended and, absent bad faith, damages would have to be calculated at some point after the final delivery date of February 28, 1973. *Balderacchi v. Ruth*, 36 Tenn.App. 421 (1952). McNabb contends, however, that Ralston Purina fails the good faith test-i.e. that Ralston Purina urged defendant to accept an extension so that, in the face of a foreseeably rising market, it could maximize damages. To prove this, defendant offered an exhibit showing the consistent rise in soybean prices from late November until the second week in March-the week in which Ralston Purina chose to cover. Furthermore, defendant offered proof that he attempted to pay damages on November 29, 1972 but his offer was rejected. The stipulated market prices show that in each successive period in which the contract was extended the price of soybeans was significantly higher than the previous month, and at no time did the price show signs of returning to its November 30th level. See Pre–Trial Stipulations of Facts, Exhibit 9, Civil Action 73–391. The uncontradicted testimony of Mr. McNabb that a part of his land had been covered by 10 feet of water in November, 1972, supports the conclusion that a significant portion of the 1972 soybean crop had been destroyed by the wide-spread severe weather as per the parties' stipulation, thus rendering it unlikely that the now reduced supply would satisfy an unchanged demand.

Ralston Purina, however, insists that it sought to modify the contract in good faith. Mr. Joiner, the soybean buying manager for Ralston Purina in Memphis, testified that because of the weather 90% Of its soybean contracts had not been filled by the final delivery date. The company, therefore, extended all the outstanding contracts and eventually 98% Of the contracts were filled. Trial Transcript at 23. Furthermore, Mr. Joiner stated that there 'is no way to know' what soybean prices are going to do, thus it was not possible for Ralston Purina to modify a contract in bad faith to maximize damages, since the price could decline and damages would thus be minimized. Trial Transcript at 42–43.

The two interrogatories answered by the jury go to the question of Ralston Purina's good faith in seeking to modify its contracts. Both answers by the jury favor the defendant McNabb. The jury determined that as early as November 30, 1972 Ralston Purina (1) had knowledge and (2) by the exercise of due diligence should have had knowledge that McNabb would not be able to complete his contract. Possessing such knowledge, Ralston Purina could not, in good faith, modify its contracts with McNabb in a way which would, in view of the past weather conditions and the trend in the market, almost inevitably result in compounding, rather than limiting, any injury to Ralston Purina. See J. White & R. Summers, Uniform Commercial Code (Hornbook) §§ 1–5 at pp. 39–40 (1972). This Court must be controlled by a jury's verdict where, as here, it is supported by substantial evidence. *Werthan Bag Corp. v. Agnew*, 202 F.2d 119 (6th Cir. 1953).

Therefore, damages calculated as of the November 30, 1972 deadline are awarded to the plaintiff. Since McNabb failed to deliver 771.47 bushels of soybeans on contract NS–606 with a contract price of $3.33 per bushel and a market price of $3.69 1/2 per bushel on November 30, 1972, plaintiff's damages on contract NS–606 are $281.59 ($.365 X 771.47 bushels). McNabb failed to deliver all 3,000 bushels on contract NS–609 with a contract price of $3.29 per bushel. The difference between the contract price and the market price of ($3.69 1/2 per bushel) on the date the buyer should have known of the breach is $.40 1/2, thus plaintiff's damages on contract NS–609 are $1,215.00.

The Clerk will therefore enter a judgment for $1,496.59 plus interest from November 30, 1972 for the plaintiff.

Uniform Commercial Code

§ 2–209.   Modification, Rescission, and Waiver

(1) An agreement modifying a contract within this Article needs no consideration to be binding.

(2) A signed agreement which excludes modification or rescission except by a signed writing cannot be otherwise modified or rescinded, but except as between merchants such a requirement on a form supplied by the merchant must be separately signed by the other party.

(3) The requirements of the statute of frauds section of this Article (Section 2–201) must be satisfied if the contract as modified is within its provisions.

(4) Although an attempt at modification or rescission does not satisfy the requirements of subsection (2) or (3) it can operate as a waiver.

(5) A party who has made a waiver affecting an executory portion of the contract may retract the waiver by reasonable notification received by the other party that strict performance will be required of any term waived, unless the retraction would be unjust in view of a material change of position in reliance on the waiver.

Official Comment

Prior Uniform Statutory Provision: Subsection (1)—Compare Section 1, Uniform Written Obligations Act; Subsections (2) to (5)—none.

Purposes of Changes and New Matter:

1.   This section seeks to protect and make effective all necessary and desirable modifications of sales contracts without regard to the technicalities which at present hamper such adjustments.

2.   Subsection (1) provides that an agreement modifying a sales contract needs no consideration to be binding. However, modifications made thereunder must meet the test of good faith imposed by this Act. The

effective use of bad faith to escape performance on the original contract terms is barred, and the extortion of a "modification" without legitimate commercial reason is ineffective as a violation of the duty of good faith. Nor can a mere technical consideration support a modification made in bad faith. The test of "good faith" between merchants or as against merchants includes "observance of reasonable commercial standards of fair dealing in the trade" (Section 2–103), and may in some situations require an objectively demonstrable reason for seeking a modification. But such matters as a market shift which makes performance come to involve a loss may provide such a reason even though there is no such unforeseen difficulty as would make out a legal excuse from performance under Sections 2–615 and 2–616.

3.   Subsections (2) and (3) are intended to protect against false allegations of oral modifications. "Modification or rescission" includes abandonment or other change by mutual consent, contrary to the decision in Green v. Doniger, 300 N.Y. 238, 90 N.E.2d 56 (1949); it does not include unilateral "termination" or "cancellation" as defined in Section 2–106. The Statute of Frauds provisions of this Article are expressly applied to modifications by subsection (3). Under those provisions the "delivery and acceptance" test is limited to the goods which have been accepted, that is, to the past. "Modification" for the future cannot therefore be conjured up by oral testimony if the price involved is $500 or more since such modification must be shown at least by an authenticated memo. And since a memo is limited in its effect to the quantity of goods set forth in it there is safeguard against oral evidence.

Subsection (2) permits the parties in effect to make their own Statute of Frauds as regards any future modification of the contract by giving effect to a clause in a signed agreement which expressly requires any modification to be by signed writing. But note that if a consumer is to be held to such a clause on a form supplied by a merchant it must be separately signed.

4.   Subsection (4) is intended, despite the provisions of subsections (2) and (3), to prevent contractual provisions excluding modification except by a signed writing from limiting in other respects the legal effect of the parties' actual later conduct. The effect of such conduct as a waiver is further regulated in subsection (5).

Restatement 2d of Contracts

§ 89   Modification of Executory Contract

A promise modifying a duty under a contract not fully performed on either side is binding

(a) if the modification is fair and equitable in view of circumstances not anticipated by the parties when the contract was made; or

(b) to the extent provided by statute; or

(c) to the extent that justice requires enforcement in view of material change of position in reliance on the promise.

Comments & Illustrations

Comment a. Rationale. This Section relates primarily to adjustments in on-going transactions. Like offers and guaranties, such adjustments are ancillary to exchanges and have some of the same presumptive utility. See §§ 72, 87, 88. Indeed, paragraph (a) deals with bargains which are without consideration only because of the rule that performance of a legal duty to the promisor is not consideration. See § 73. This Section is also related to § 84 on waiver of conditions: it may apply to cases in which § 84 is inapplicable because a condition is material to the exchange or risk. As in cases governed by § 84, relation to a bargain tends to satisfy the cautionary and channeling functions of legal formalities. See Comment *c* to § 72. The Statute of Frauds may prevent enforcement in the absence of reliance. See §§ 149–50. Otherwise formal requirements are at a minimum.

Comment b. Performance of legal duty. The rule of § 73 finds its modern justification in cases of promises made by mistake or induced by unfair pressure. Its application to cases where those elements are absent has been much criticized and is avoided if paragraph (a) of this Section is applicable. The limitation to a modification which is "fair and equitable" goes beyond absence of coercion and requires an objectively demonstrable reason for seeking a modification. Compare Uniform Commercial Code § 2–209 Comment. The reason for modification must rest in circumstances not "anticipated" as part of the context in which the contract was made, but a frustrating event may be unanticipated for this purpose if it was not adequately covered, even though it was foreseen as a remote possibility. When such a reason is present, the relative financial strength of the parties, the formality with which the modification is made, the extent to which it is performed or relied on and other circumstances may be relevant to show or negate imposition or unfair surprise.

The same result called for by paragraph (a) is sometimes reached on the ground that the original contract was "rescinded" by mutual agreement and that new promises were then made which furnished consideration for each other. That theory is rejected here because it is fictitious when the "rescission" and new agreement are simultaneous, and because if logically carried out it might uphold unfair and inequitable modifications.

Illustrations:

1. By a written contract A agrees to excavate a cellar for B for a stated price. Solid rock is unexpectedly encountered and A so notifies B. A and B then orally agree that A will remove the rock at a unit price which is reasonable but nine times that used in computing the original price, and A completes the job. B is bound to pay the increased amount.

2. A contracts with B to supply for $300 a laundry chute for a building B has contracted to build for the Government for

$150,000. Later A discovers that he made an error as to the type of material to be used and should have bid $1,200. A offers to supply the chute for $1000, eliminating overhead and profit. After ascertaining that other suppliers would charge more, B agrees. The new agreement is binding.

3.   A is employed by B as a designer of coats at $90 a week for a year beginning November 1 under a written contract executed September 1. A is offered $115 a week by another employer and so informs B. A and B then agree that A will be paid $100 a week and in October execute a new written contract to that effect, simultaneously tearing up the prior contract. The new contract is binding.

4.   A contracts to manufacture and sell to B 2,000 steel roofs for corn cribs at $60. Before A begins manufacture a threat of a nationwide steel strike raises the cost of steel about $10 per roof, and A and B agree orally to increase the price to $70 per roof. A thereafter manufactures and delivers 1700 of the roofs, and B pays for 1,500 of them at the increased price without protest, increasing the selling price of the corn cribs by $10. The new agreement is binding.

5.   A contracts to manufacture and sell to B 100,000 castings for lawn mowers at 50 cents each. After partial delivery and after B has contracted to sell a substantial number of lawn mowers at a fixed price, A notifies B that increased metal costs require that the price be increased to 75 cents. Substitute castings are available at 55 cents, but only after several months delay. B protests but is forced to agree to the new price to keep its plant in operation. The modification is not binding.

Comment c. Statutes. Uniform Commercial Code § 2–209 dispenses with the requirement of consideration for an agreement modifying a contract for the sale of goods. Under that section the original contract can provide against oral modification, and the requirements of the Statute of Frauds must be met if the contract as modified is within its provisions; but an ineffective modification can operate as a waiver. The Comment indicates that extortion of a modification without legitimate commercial reason is ineffective as a violation of the duty of good faith imposed by the Code. A similar limitation may be applicable under statutes which give effect to a signed writing as a substitute for the seal, or under statutes which give effect to acceptance by the promisee of the modified performance. In some States statutes or constitutional provisions flatly forbid the payment of extra compensation to Government contractors.

Comment d. Reliance. Paragraph (c) states the application of § 90 to modification of an executory contract in language adapted from Uniform Commercial Code § 2–209. Even though the promise is not binding when made, it may become binding in whole or in part by reason of action or forbearance by the promisee or third persons in reliance on it. In some cases the result can be viewed as based either on estoppel to contradict a representation of fact or on reliance on a promise. Ordinarily reliance by the promisee is reasonably foreseeable and makes the modification binding with respect to performance by the promisee under it and any return performance owed by the promisor. But as under § 84 the original terms can be reinstated for the future by reasonable notification received by the promisee unless reinstatement would be unjust in view of a change of position on his part. Compare Uniform Commercial Code § 2–209(5).

Illustrations:

6.   A defaults in payment of a premium on a life insurance policy issued by B, an insurance company. Pursuant to the terms of the policy, B notifies A of the lapse of the policy and undertakes to continue the insurance until a specified future date, but by mistake specifies a date two months later than the insured would be entitled to under the policy. On inquiry by A two years later, B repeats the mistake, offering A an option to take a cash payment. A fails to do so, and dies one month before the specified date. B is bound to pay the insurance.

7.   A is the lessee of an apartment house under a 99–year lease from B at a rent of $10,000 per year. Because of war conditions many of the apartments become vacant, and in order to enable A to stay in business B agrees to reduce the rent to $5,000. The reduced rent is paid for five years. The war being over, the apartments are then fully rented, and B notifies A that the full rent called for by the lease must be paid. A is bound to pay the full rent only from a reasonable time after the receipt of the notification.

8.   A contracts with B to carry a shipment of fish under refrigeration. During the short first leg of the voyage the refrigeration equipment on the ship breaks down, and A offers either to continue under ventilation or to hold the cargo at the first port for later shipment. B agrees to shipment under ventilation but later changes his mind. A receives notification of the change before he has changed his position. A is bound to ship under refrigeration.

* * *

McNabb involved a contract (really, a pair of contracts) under which the plaintiff was to buy soy-beans from the defendant-grower, once they had been harvested. The defendant suffered severe flooding over the course of the growing season, which rendered him unable to make a timely delivery. The plaintiff sent the defendant several letters extending the delivery deadline, and the defendant made partial late deliveries, receiving the contract price. Eventually, the plaintiff covered, purchasing its soy-beans elsewhere. The plaintiff then sued the defendant for damages in respect of the undelivered portion of the contracts.

The principle dispute between the parties concerned not breach but remedy. The defendant was not the only soy-bean farmer whose crops had been damaged by weather, and so the price of soy-beans had risen steadily between the date that the contract had initially set for delivery and the date on which the defendant eventually covered. The plaintiff therefore took the view that the letters of extension constituted contract modifications, so that its eventual lawsuit proceeded for breach of the last of these. This would have made the date with respect to which damages should be calculated late, and the price on which the calculation should proceed high. The defendant took the view that the letters of extension were not modifications but separate contracts, and that his partial shipments were made under these separate contracts. This would have made the date with respect to which damages (for breach of the original, unmodified contract) should be calculated early, and the price on which the calculation should proceed low.

For a court reasoning in the formalist style of *Alaska Packers* the pre-existing duty rule would apply to make the resolution of *McNabb* turn on whether the letters of extension proceeded in two stages (rescission followed by re-contracting) or just one. If the former, then they would have modified the initial contract, and the plaintiff would win; if the latter, then the letters of extension could not be valid contract modifications (they would lack consideration), and the defendant would win. To answer this question, a court would have to assess whether the circumstances in which the renegotiations occurred so constrained the defendant, who now sought to avoid their effect, as to constitute duress. It would have found, almost certainly, that they did not and therefore that the modification was valid. Accordingly, under *Alaska Packers*, *McNabb* would be decided in favor of the plaintiff.

The *McNabb* court proceeded very differently. It began by observing that section 2–209 of the Uniform Commercial Code replaces the formalisms of the pre-existing duty rule with an unabashedly functionalist approach to contract modifications. Specifically, the UCC gives effect to all necessary and desirable modifications of sales contracts without regard to technicalities—read, consideration—as long, comment [2] insists, as the modifications are made not just without duress but also, and more demandingly, in *good faith*.

While it is clear that there was no duress in *McNabb*, it is far from clear that the plaintiff there exhibited good faith. According to the defendant, the plaintiff, which had rejected an offer to pay damages at the time for delivery set in the initial contract, used the letters in bad faith to delay covering in a rising market. A jury of the trial court agreed, finding that by the initial delivery date, the plaintiff knew or should have known that the defendant, even if given more time, could not possibly complete his performance. The appellate court doubted this finding of fact, but it was unwilling to find clear error on this point. And if the plaintiff did in fact have this knowledge, then in could not in good faith have modified its contract in the manner described in the letters, that is, to grant extensions that would never enable performance but would instead only increase the defendant's ultimate liability. This is a functionalist conclusion—based on the idea that it is neither efficient nor fair for one party to a contract to perform in a manner whose only consequence is to reduce contractual surplus by imposing costs on the other party with no countervailing benefit to it. Accordingly, *McNabb* was decided in favor of the defendant.

So the formalist and functionalist approaches to contract modifications and the pre-existing duty rule produce different outcomes, at least in the circumstances of *McNab*. The difference, however, is not due to the fact that formalism avoids functionalist analysis entirely. The entire analysis of this Part reveals that it could not possibly do that. Rather, formalism and functionalism differ both in respect of their attitudes towards ultimately functionalist analysis—which formalism disguises and functionalism embraces—and the substance of the functionalist analysis that is performed—whether it concerns duress or good faith.

The substantive line taken by the UCC's approach is, moreover, the better one—better even (indeed, especially) when evaluated by the standards embedded in the formalist account of consideration. That account, remember, sought to find and elaborate the value that inheres in all actual bargains, apart from their fairness or adequacy. This value concerns the relationship that inheres in the bargain form in itself. The parties to a bargain respect each other, in the sense of recognizing each other's authority in a formally (although not, of course, substantively) egalitarian way. The consideration doctrine secures this formal equality, by requiring that each party recognize the authority of the other before a contract will be recognized at all. This reveals that there is no inherent reason to worry about contract modifications that proceed without any new consideration. Such modifications are entirely consistent with the ideals of respect and recognition that give the contract relation (purely in virtue of its form) its value. If the initial contract constituted a true bargain, and the modified contract does as well, then the relation that these contracts establish remains reciprocal and formally egalitarian, even if the modification *itself* is not reciprocal.

There is thus no reason to insist on the pre-existing duty rule in general, which is precisely what formalist courts recognized when they observed that even a one-sided contract modification may be supported by good consideration as long as it is achieved by reciprocal rescission followed by reciprocal re-contracting. Accordingly, if the pre-existing duty rule is to have any justification, it must be that the cases it picks out involve some other contractual wrong.

For one party to a bargain to coerce the other to abandon it (only to replace it with a worse bargain) of course violates the respect that bargaining parties owe (and express) to each other. This idea explains why strangers cannot coerce one another into valid contracts to begin with, and the same principle surely applies equally within valid contracts, whose parties are not strangers to each other. The formalist approach is thus right to conclude that contract modifications achieved by duress are unenforceable (even if the *Alaska Packers* court was wrong to find duress on the facts of that case).

But duty to avoid imposing duress, which applies even among strangers, does not exhaust the duties that contract parties—who are, after all, not strangers—owe to each other. In particular, contract parties owe each other an obligation to respect the terms of the bargain that they have struck, even if they did not, before their contract, owe each other any obligation to strike that particular bargain, and even if the bargain is only formally, and not substantively, equal. This obligation arises directly out of the reciprocal respect that constitutes the bargain relation to begin with. To owe someone a contractual obligation is to accept their authority to demand performance of the promise that establishes the obligation, and honoring this authority requires respecting the terms of the promise. Good faith in contract gives substance to this idea by requiring (recall the discussion from Part I's account of bad faith breach of contract) each party to refrain from actions—including contract modifications—that deprive the other of the benefits that the contract was designed to provide.

This returns the argument, finally, to *Alaska Packers*, and offers the court there at least partial vindication. Even if the *Alaska Packers* court did not reason well—even if it was wrong to make duress into the test of the pre-existing duty rule and to find that the defendant had been subjected to duress on the facts of the case—the outcome of the case may well have been correct. The two errors in the reasoning of the *Alaska Packers* court may well have cancelled each other out, as it were: the mistake of looking to duress to determine whether or not the parties had mutually rescinded and recontracted was counteracted by the mistake of finding duress much too readily. Thus, it is easy to imagine that a court *un*willing to find duress on the facts of *Alaska Packers* might nevertheless be willing to find bad faith. And so even the modern, functionalist approach to consideration and the pre-existing duty rule might well have refused to enforce the modification at issue in *Alaska Packers*.

This result, finally, reflects something deep in the structure of the modern approach to consideration and indeed of contractual obligation quite generally. The consideration doctrine, remember, insists on only formal rather than substantive equality. In doing so, it allows formally equal contracts, as long as they are freely entered into, to bind contracting parties even though they are substantively unequal and even though their substantive inequality is related to underserved inequalities in the parties' respective initial bargain powers. Formal contractual equality—the idea that each side to a contract enjoys authority to require the other's performance—is perfectly consistent with the brute fact that the party that can do better without the contract will do better within it. Contractual obligation, therefore, launders injustice: a party who is not entitled to an advantage in bargaining over another becomes entitled, as against the other, to the contractual rights that it is able, in light of its undeserved advantage to secure. This logic precisely plays itself out in *Alaska Packers*. The defendant was not entitled to extract the plaintiffs' promise to fish in exchange for such low wages. Rather, the defendant got the promise on account of exploiting unfair bargaining conditions in the San Francisco labor market. But having given their promises, the plaintiffs could not, consistent with approaching their contractual obligations in good faith, exploit their greater bargaining power in Alaska. And hence the modern, functionalist approach to contract modifications (ironically because it acknowledges the intrinsic value of the bargain form) likely supports the same outcome that the formalist court in *Alaska Packers* achieved by such inadequate reasoning.[59]

---

59. One might even say that formalism, having begun too rigorously—*all* one-sided contract modifications are invalidated by the pre-existing duty rule—is forced (because every such modification may be recast to avoid the rule) to conclude, too laxly, that the rule invalidates only modifications extracted under duress. Functionalism manages to avoid both extremes. It eliminates any particular concern for modifications and pre-existing duties but imposes the general duty of good faith in performance on modifications (as on the rest of the contract relation), to police these more effectively than formalism ever could.

CHAPTER 16

ALTERNATIVE PATHS TO CONTRACT?

According to orthodox contract law, establishing a contract requires offer, acceptance, and consideration. As the previous chapters have displayed in detail, each of these doctrinal categories has been given both formalist and functionalist elaborations over the years. Strikingly, as these chapters have also shown, even the functionalist approach to contract formation, on the orthodox model, has retained all three, discernable elements just mentioned. Even functionalists decline to reduce contract law to a branch line in an undifferentiated program for optimal coordination. Form seems to matter, irreducibly, to contract, at least on the orthodox account.

Functionalist law has retained these elements, moreover, at least partly out of respect for the formalist category *contract*—and in particular for the idea that contract involves *voluntary obligation in the strict sense*. That is, contractual obligation does not just arise in the context of voluntary actions—as, for example, a person's obligation not to be drunk arises in the context of his voluntarily commencing to drive a car. Rather, contractual obligation is directly intended into existence. A promisor (in morality, not law) acquires her promissory obligation by forming and communicating an intention to acquire the obligation in just this way, that is, directly by intending to. The law embellishes this pattern—establishing precisely what counts as offer and acceptance, and imposing the formal equality associated with consideration—but does not, fundamentally, change it. Contractual obligation remains voluntary in the same distinctive way: contracts are creatures of the parties' intentions; they are, literally, *chosen*; or, as one might say, *willed into existence*.

Now, this feature of contract (which it inherits from promise) raises a host of deep philosophical difficulties, which arise in light of the mystery how persons could possibly will an obligation into existence. Obligations are special kinds of reasons, and reasons (because they depend on interests) are things that the mind discovers rather than creates—a person, one might think, could no more will a reason into existence than she could a physical object, like a chair.[1] Unlike, perhaps, gods, persons simply lack the potency,

---

1. She could not, at any rate, simply will the reason (or obligation) into existence, out of whole cloth. She could, of course, reshape her obligations in connection with intentional actions, just as she might reshape previously existing wood into a chair. This is precisely what a person does when, getting behind the wheel of her car, she reshapes her independently

or normative power, to do such a thing. This thought led Hume to think promissory obligation just as mysterious as transubstantiation. Each case involves a transformation of the world of a sort that defies explanation using ordinary tools. These problems will be taken up in greater detail in Part III, which applies moral and social theory to the law concerning the limits of freedom of contract.

For the moment, however, the question is not how contract law, understood on the model of voluntary obligation, is *possible*. Rather the current question is whether voluntary obligation represents, *in fact*, the best model for organizing the positive law. The orthodox doctrines concerning contract formation assert that it is: offer and acceptance represent nothing other than an effort to render the idea of voluntary obligation doctrinally implementable; and if the consideration doctrine slightly narrows the scope of contract to something smaller than promise, it does so in the service of ideals that are themselves connected to the internal structure of voluntary obligation (or, at least, do not attack this structure in any general way).

But, as Part I observed, there is another approach to contract. Contractual obligation arises, on this approach, simply in virtue of the fact that promisors who fail to follow through on their promises harm those who have relied on them. According to this approach, contract is just a species of tort, and in particular an elaboration of the misrepresentation torts. The discussion of reliance damages in Part I demonstrated that this account of contract is at least initially plausible. The argument there showed that once opportunity costs are counted in calculating reliance, it becomes possible (at least in many circumstances) to re-characterize contract law's commitment to vindicating contractual expectations in terms of recouping lost reliance. (Recall that lost reliance includes the value of the alternative contracts that a promisee has forgone in light of the contract that she made, and when markets are functioning well, these alternatives will be only incrementally less valuable to the promisee than the contract that she made, so that reliance will approach expectation.) Moreover, where contractual expectations cannot be recast in terms of reliance, the law's commitment to vindicating expectations turns out to waiver. As soon as expectation damages cannot be simply calculated (using either market, or cover-based damages) by reference to market transactions (which just identify the opportunities that a contractual promisee has lost in reliance on his contract), any number of doctrines—foreseeability, certainty, etc.—prevent contractual expectations from being fully vindicated. Finally, when contractual expectations reflect windfalls, and so cannot possibly be recast in terms of reliance, the law (recall *Overstreet*) is only imperfectly committed to vindicating them at all.

Orthodox contract, these materials have been arguing, elaborates a legally recognized form of promise—of voluntary obligation. But even if orthodox contract announces its promissory structure, it remains an open

---

existing general obligation to take reasonable care not to harm others into a specific obligation not to be drunk.

question how essential, or indeed even central, orthodox contract is to contract law as actually practiced. The considerations from Part I rehearsed above, and others like them, raise the question whether contract law more broadly understood—contract as it is generally practiced—has this promissory, voluntarist character. After all, contract law's commitment to vindicating pure promissory obligation seems shaky. And where contract obligation is less than purely promissory, there might exist other legally recognized forms of obligation that arise in and around what is conventionally called contract but that are not, fundamentally, voluntary or based on promising. That is, it remains possible that offer, acceptance, and consideration—the formal building-blocks of orthodox contract—are not essential to getting the law to recognize contract-like obligations. Indeed, it remains possible that even where the forms of orthodox contract are employed, the best account of the legal recognition of the obligation that ensues does not invoke these forms. Orthodox contract might be, in this way, a narrowly special case, or even just epiphenomenal.

Orthodox contract's promissory self-characterization might, moreover, be not quite innocent. The conventional account of contract formation—through offer, acceptance, and consideration—represents at best a smokescreen and at worst ideology. Perhaps contract law has nothing to do with a distinctive class of speech acts or with normative powers. Perhaps all the conventional talk of these matters merely serves the legal conceit (propagated by, among others, those who have an interest in retaining the current law school curriculum) of the doctrinal distinctness of contract law. Perhaps the conventional story serves the economic interests of those who benefit from an additional route to misleading others without subjecting themselves to liability. Accordingly, an account of contractual practice that abandons the doctrinal niceties of offer and acceptance and instead emphasizes the connection between breach of contract and misrepresentation, on the model of tort, might be not just descriptively more accurate than the orthodox account but also normatively preferable.

The most likely candidates for underwriting a non-promissory reconstruction of contractual practice, as I have been saying, are forms of reliance- or harm-based obligation, where the ground of the obligee's reliance, and hence the source of the harms that he might suffer, is a representation made by the obligor. (Notice that in contrast to the way in which reliance figured in the analysis of Part I, reliance is here not a measure of damages but a ground of obligation.)

Of course, in order to substitute for orthodox contract—to cover the practical ground that orthodox contract claims for its own—this will be a somewhat unconventional reliance-based obligation. In order to account for contractual practice and other doctrines in contract law, the reliance obligation will have to extend to vindicating expectations and not just undoing harms; it will, moreover, have to abandon fault-based standards of obligation and substitute strict liability in their stead. But insofar as such reliance-based obligation is recognized by the law, and recognized sufficiently broadly and generally so that it can account for (much or most of) contractual practice, then it will become tempting (perhaps even compelling) to suppose that this obligation constitutes contract, and constitutes contract as a special case of tort. Contract law, on this understanding, would no longer be the legal recognition of promising, as on the orthodox model. Rather, it would be simply the form of obligation established when generally legally effective ideas concerning reliance are applied to the special case of promises (which are themselves, taken independently, legally inert). This understanding of contract law is appealing to a sensibility that seeks simplification and prefers to avoid two separate doctrinal forms (tort and contract) where just one (tort) will do. It is especially appealing given that the discarded doctrinal form (orthodox contract) is anyway burdened by deep philosophical mysteries concerning its very possibility.

This chapter therefore takes up the possibility that contract might be just a special case of tort, pursuing more systematically the argument begun in the discussions concerning the reliance remedy in Part I. It asks whether contract might be recast as a special case of tort not just in respect of the remedies that the law provides in case of breach but also in respect of the origination of the obligation, that is, in respect of contract formation. According to this tort-based reconstruction, contract obligation is just a special case of the broader obligation incurred by persons who make representations and owed to those who receive (in an appropriate way) the representations that they have made. What contract law calls breach, on this view, is just a case of liability for *mis*-representation.

To succeed, the tort-based reconstruction of contract must demonstrate that when the misrepresentation torts are taken together, they collectively span the legal space conventionally covered by contract. The reconstruction must show, in other words, that every case, or at least most cases, of contract obligation can be recast—in respect of how the obligation arises, in respect of the obligation's content, and in respect of the remedies that the law provides where the obligation is breached—in terms of one or another species of the genus mis-representation, in the family tort.

The argument pursues two quite different ways in which tort might overwhelm contract. The first, and more direct, concerns doctrines that lie openly within tort law and might, taken together, be thought to create obligations that span contract. These are the familiar misrepresentation torts, which may be taken to encroach on contract *from without*. The second way in which tort might overwhelm contract is indirect. Tort might colonize contract *from within*, by implanting inside contract law, and under contract's flag, a doctrine whose structure is harm based and that might be expanded to cover all the ground that contract's promise-based doctrines traditionally covered. This possibility arises in connection with Promissory Estoppel, including especially as it appears in § 90 of the Restatement (Second) of Contracts.

There was a historical time—associated with a trend that reached its apogee in the 1970s—in which contract might plausibly have been thought to be (or at least been thought to be becoming) just a special case of tort. But although the matter remains controversial, more recent doctrinal developments entail that tort-based reconstructions of contract probably fail today. Even though the scope of the misrepresentation torts grew over the course of the twentieth century, and the content of obligations for misrepresentation expanded also, the torts even today remain less expansive than contract. Reliance-based obligation under § 90 similarly remains less expansive than orthodox contract. Perhaps most importantly orthodox contract obligation continues to depart from tort generally and from the misrepresentation torts in particular, and also from obligation that arises under Promissory Estoppel, not just in respect of remedies, or even in respect of the primary interests that these remedies are designed to vindicate, but also in respect of the grounds of liability.

These discussions remain premature, however. At the moment, the question has just been posed: Can the law's approaches to tort sustain efforts to reduce contract to a special case of this broader legal regime? Addressing this question requires approaching the relevant doctrines, and this chapter takes up the task.

A final caveat is in order before commencing the argument in earnest. There is enormous complexity in the law concerning contract's interfaces with its neighbors. Conventional contract, tort, fiduciary law, and restitution all overlap in intricate patterns, and often the same facts will sustain many causes of action under fundamentally different theories. There is commensurate confusion in the courts. So any effort to organize the doctrines and cases must be modest. Indeed, even the most modest effort will be tendentious, in the sense of riding roughshod over at least some opinions that reject the analyses that it proposes. It is best to admit this right up front. At the same time, some order is worth seeking, even if it has to be at least partly imposed from above, based on theoretical distinctions, rather than growing purely up out of induction from the cases.

16.1   THE MISREPRESENTATION TORTS: AN EXTERNAL THREAT TO CONTRACT

A series of legal developments, which together reached a head in the 1970s, plausibly posed an existential threat to contract's survival as a freestanding doctrinal kind. Contract faced being swallowed up by tort.

The threat was widely and prominently acknowledged and much discussed. Patrick Atiyah devoted a large book to chronicling *The Rise and Fall of Freedom of Contract*. Atiyah observed that the law (a) increasingly limited the scope of contract both by imposing mandatory "non-voluntary rights and duties" on transactions,[2] including by (b) imposing a general "decline in the importance attached to consent, promise, or intention,"[3] and, more particularly, by (c) creating "a significant increase in the

---

2. P.S. ATIYAH, THE RISE AND FALL OF FREEDOM OF CONTRACT 716 (1979).

3. *Id.* at 729.

importance of reliance-based, rather than promise-based liability."[4] Grant Gilmore, responding to similar trends, devoted a small book to announcing *The Death of Contract.*

Charles Fried objected to these trends and sought to answer them by re-establishing *Contract as Promise.* Fried acknowledged that the "conception of contractual obligation as essentially self-imposed has been under increasing pressure over the last fifty years,"[5] most particularly through the suggestion (which Fried expressly connected to Atiyah) "that often what is taken as enforcement of a promise is in reality the compensation of an injury sustained by the plaintiff because he relied on the defendant's promise."[6] Unlike Atiyah, and more single-mindedly than Gilmore, Fried lamented this trend. He insisted that "large theoretical and practical matters turn on" whether or not contract is absorbed into tort.[7] Specifically, Fried argued, the "assimilation of contract to tort is the subordination of a quintessentially individualist ground for obligation and form of social control, one that refers to the will of the parties, to a set of standards that are ineluctably collective in origin and thus readily turned to collective ends."[8] Fried devoted *Contract as Promise* to recovering contract's promissory basis, in order to shore up contract law's foundational commitments to the dignity of the individual free will.

The moral foundations of Fried's argument will be revisited in Part III below, in connection with a broader inquiry into the moral basis for contract law and the limits of freedom of contract. Part III will also take up questions concerning the limits on freedom of contract—often grounded in collective ideals concerning justice or efficiency.

This section, by contrast, emphasizes contract law's doctrinal structure rather than its moral foundations; and it sets aside the question what should be the limits on freedom of contract in favor of the question how to characterize the obligations that arise within these limits. The section therefore asks: did the developments that Atiyah and Gilmore emphasized, and that even Fried acknowledged, achieve fruition? Is contract *today* just a special species of tort? Can the obligations that orthodox contract law treats as voluntary—arising through offer, acceptance, and consideration— be equally well characterized as involuntary—arising as special cases of the general tort of misrepresentation?

The simplest way in which tort might overwhelm contract is by announcing and elaborating, within the uncontested province of tort law proper, a series of torts that, together, render every contract obligation also, independently, and indeed primarily or foundationally, a tort obligation. The specific torts through which tort law might accomplish this result are the misrepresentation torts.

---

4. *Id.* at 774.

5. CHARLES FRIED, CONTRACT AS PROMISE 2 (1982).

6. *Id.* at 4.

7. *Id.* at 4.

8. *Id.* at 4–5.

It will take some effort to lay bare the structure of these torts. In the end, that effort will reveal that, regardless of what Atiyah hoped, Gilmore noted, and Fried feared, the law has developed in such a way that the misrepresentation torts do not today displace contract or otherwise render it a merely residual category. Probably this outcome was not contingent, or at least not contingent in a shallow way. Voluntary obligation—obligation that is directly chosen—plays a foundational role in our legal order; a role that even the most expansive account of the mandatory duties associated with tort cannot quite displace. The inquiry into the misrepresentation torts is worth the effort that it will take precisely because of this negative result. Understanding tort, and the ways in which tort cannot quite colonize contract from without, contributes importantly to understanding the deeper structure of contract.

16.1.A   MISREPRESENTATIONS FAR FROM PROMISE

Begin the inquiry into the relation between contract and the misrepresentation torts by observing that the mere fact that misrepresentation is a mechanism through which a tort is committed does not, taken alone, connect that tort to contract *at all*. A brief review of these cases draws a contrast that emphasizes the threat that other misrepresentation torts do pose to contract law.

Tort liability based on misrepresentation poses no real threat to contract as long as the misrepresentations are simply one technique (among many) for accomplishing torts that might also be accomplished by other means, by harming people in the usual way. Plaintiffs may be struck by words just as surely as they may be struck by sticks, and when they are so struck, they may have tort claims. But although the torts may have been committed using words, even brief reflection reveals that they have literally nothing to do with promises. The following materials illustrate this incarnation of tort liability for misrepresentation and why it poses no threat to contract.

Commonwealth v. Stratton

Supreme Judicial Court of Massachusetts, 1873.
114 Mass. 303.

■ WELLS, J. All the judges concur that the evidence introduced at the trial would warrant a conviction of assault and battery, or for a simple assault, which it includes. And in the opinion of a majority of the court, the instructions given required the jury to find all that was essential to constitute the offence of assault and battery.

The jury must have found a physical injury inflicted upon another person by a voluntary act of the defendant, directed towards her, which was without justification and unlawful. Although the defendant was ignorant of the qualities of the drug he administered, and of the effects to be expected from it, and had been assured and believed that it was not deleterious to health, yet he knew it was not ordinary food, that the girl was deceived into taking it, and he intended that she should be induced to take it without her conscious consent, by the deceit which he practiced upon her. It is to be inferred from the statement of the case that he expected it would produce some effect. In the most favorable aspect of the facts for the defendant, he administered to the girl, without her consent and by deceit, a drug or "foreign substance," of the probable effect of which he was ignorant, with the express intent and purpose "to try the effect of it upon" her. This, in itself, was unlawful, and he must be held responsible for whatever effect it produced. Being an unlawful interference with the personal rights of another, calculated to result and in fact resulting in physical injury, the criminal intent is to be inferred from the nature of the act and its actual results. 3 Bl. Com. 120. *Rex v. Long,* 4 C. & P. 398, 407, note. The deceit, by means of which the girl was induced to take the drug, was a fraud upon her will, equivalent to force in overpowering it. *Commonwealth v. Burke,* 105 Mass. 376.

Although force and violence are included in all definitions of assault, or assault and battery, yet, where there is physical injury to another person, it is sufficient that the cause is set in motion by the defendant, or that the person is subjected to its operation by means of any act or control which the defendant exerts. In 3 Chit. Crim. Law, 799, is a count, at common law, for an assault with drugs. For other instances of assault and battery without actual violence directed against the person assaulted, see 1 Gabbett's Crim. Law, 82.

If one should hand an explosive substance to another, and induce him to take it by misrepresenting or concealing its dangerous qualities, and the other ignorant of its character, should receive it and cause it to explode in his pocket or hand, and should be injured by it, the offending party would be guilty of a battery, and that would necessarily include an assault; although he might not be guilty even of an assault, if the substance failed to explode or failed to cause any injury. It would be the same if it exploded in his mouth or stomach. If that which causes the injury is set in motion by the wrongful act of the defendant, it cannot be material whether it acts upon the person injured externally or internally, by mechanical or chemical force.

In *Regina v. Button,* 8 C. & P. 660, one who put Spanish flies into coffee to be drank by another, was convicted of an assault upon the person who took it, although it was done "only for a lark." This decision is said to have been overruled in England. *Regina v. Dilworth,* 2 Mood. & Rob. 531. *The Queen v. Walkden,* 1 Cox C. C. 282. *Regina v. Hanson,* 2 C. & K. 912. In the view of the majority of the court, the last only of these three cases was a direct adjudication, and that entirely upon the authority of mere *dicta* in the other two, and without any satisfactory reasoning or statement of grounds; and the earlier decision in *Regina v. Button* is more consistent with general principles, and the better law.

Exceptions overruled.

Bartolo v. Boardwalk Regency Hotel Casino, Inc.

Superior Court of New Jersey, 1982.
449 A.2d 1339.

■ SKILLMAN, J. S. C. Is it permissible for a casino to detain a patron suspected of being a "card counter" for the purpose of questioning? This issue is presented in the context of a tort action brought by four patrons of a casino who allege that they were falsely imprisoned by its security personnel. Defendants are the Boardwalk Regency Hotel Casino and several of its employees.

The matter is before the court on a motion for summary judgment filed by defendants. Therefore, the court must accept as true for the purpose of the motion the descriptions of the incident provided by plaintiffs in their depositions. *Judson v. Peoples Bank & Trust Co. of Westfield*, 17 N.J. 67, 73–75 (1954).

Plaintiffs are two brothers and two of their friends. All four are occasional social gamblers. They arrived at the Boardwalk Regency on December 26, 1979, played various casino games, including blackjack, and lost money. They returned to the gambling area around 11 a. m. the next morning and began playing blackjack. After playing for about an hour they were approached by two casino security guards dressed in uniforms. Plaintiffs were notified that they had been identified as card counters and were directed to accompany the guards. One plaintiff was grabbed by the back of the collar and pulled away from the blackjack table. The others were grabbed by the arms and led away. This physical removal happened so quickly and so forcefully that some plaintiffs were unable even to remove their chips from the table. All four were led to a nearby area where they were joined by a games manager, who ordered them to produce identification so that they could be registered and prevented from playing blackjack. At first plaintiffs refused to produce identification, protesting that they were not card counters. However, they were threatened with arrest if they refused to cooperate, and they then acceded to the demand. When identifications were produced, the games manager wrote plaintiffs' names on a pad, told them they would not be permitted to play blackjack again at the Boardwalk Regency or any other casino and directed them to leave. During this entire confrontation the two uniformed casino security guards remained on either side of plaintiffs. The three plaintiffs who were deposed all testified that they did not feel free to leave the casino between the time they were pulled away from the blackjack table and when they produced identification.

The [plaintiffs'] complaint sets forth three separate theories of liability arising out of this incident: assault and battery, slander and false imprisonment. However, defendants concede that a contested material issue of fact is presented by the assault and battery claim, and plaintiffs concede that their slander claim must be dismissed due to an inability to show any damage to their business, professional or personal reputations resulting from the incident. Therefore, the sole question at this juncture is whether there is a contested material issue of fact on the false imprisonment claim.

The tort of false imprisonment is established upon showing any "unlawful restraint upon a man's freedom of locomotion." *Earl v. Winne*, 14 N.J. 119, 128 (1953). The unlawful restraint need not be imposed by physical force. Furthermore, the assertion of legal authority to take a person into custody, even where such authority does not in fact exist, may be sufficient to create a reasonable apprehension that a person is under restraint. *Hebrew v. Pulis*, 73 N.J.L. 621 (E. & A. 1906); *see, also*, 1 *Restatement, Torts* 2d, § 41 at 61 (1965).

There can be no serious doubt that the elements of false imprisonment would be established if plaintiffs' version of this incident were believed by a jury. According to plaintiffs, they were accosted by uniformed security guards who physically removed them from the blackjack table. They were then subjected, while surrounded by security guards, to an interrogation by a games manager, who said that they would be arrested unless identification was produced. Under these circumstances, plaintiffs reasonably could have concluded that they would be forcibly restrained if they attempted to leave the site of this interrogation without producing identification and that they were thus under confinement.

[A discussion establishing that the defendants had no legal right to detain the plaintiffs on grounds of card counting is omitted.]

Absent any affirmative statutory authorization to detain suspected card counters, the plaintiffs' version of the incident at the Boardwalk Regency would constitute false imprisonment. Therefore, the defendants' motion for summary judgment, except that part directed at the claim for slander, will be denied.

Restatement (Second) of Torts

§ 310   Conscious Misrepresentation Involving Risk of Physical Harm

An actor who makes a misrepresentation is subject to liability to another for physical harm which results from an act done by the other or a third person in reliance upon the truth of the representation, if the actor

(a) intends his statement to induce or should realize that it is likely to induce action by the other, or a third person, which involves an unreasonable risk of physical harm to the other, and

(b) knows

(i) that the statement is false, or

(ii) that he has not the knowledge which he professes.

Comments & Illustrations

Comment a. If the actor makes a misrepresentation for the purpose of causing, or believing that action in reliance upon it will cause, physical harm, he is liable because he intended the resulting harm. The rule stated in this Section relates to misrepresentations which, though intended to mislead another, are not intended to cause him the physical harm, where, however, the actor should realize that the harm is likely to result from the action which his misrepresentation is likely to induce. His liability is based upon the unreasonable risk of physical harm which is involved in the misrepresentations, and not upon the fact that the misrepresentations are intended to mislead.

Comment b. The representation to which this Section applies may be one of fact, opinion, or law. Where the representation is one of opinion, prediction, or law, the other's reliance upon it may be less reasonable, and so less justified. (Compare §§ 542, 544, and 545.) Where the reliance is justified, however, the rule here stated applies to representations of both opinion and law.

The situation to which the rule stated in this Section is most usually applied is where the misrepresentation is made concerning the physical condition of a thing, either land, structures, or a chattel, and induces the other to believe that the thing is in safe condition for his entry or use, or induces a third person to hold the land or chattel open to the entry or use of the other in the belief that it is safe for the purpose. The rule is, however, equally applicable to misrepresentation of other matters upon which the safety of the person or property of another depends.

Illustrations:

1. A tells B that he has tried the ice on a certain pond and found it thick enough for safe skating. A knows that he has not tried it and knows nothing of the condition of the ice, which in fact is dangerously thin, although it appears to be safe. B, in reliance upon A's statements, attempts to skate upon the pond and falls in, catching a severe cold. A is negligent toward B.

2. A offers B a drink from a bottle of whiskey, telling him that he has himself imported it from Canada, although he knows that he has bought it for a very cheap price from an unidentified bootlegger. B drinks the whiskey, which turns out to be compounded of denatured alcohol, from which the poison has not been completely eliminated. B becomes ill. A is negligent toward B.

3. A police officer comes to A's house to arrest him upon reasonable suspicion of felony. B, A's uncle, who is present, tells A that the officer has no legal authority to arrest him, and advises him to resist arrest. B knows that he has no knowledge of the law as to the arrest, which is in fact valid. A, in reliance upon the representation, resists arrest, and is injured when the officer overpowers him. B is negligent toward A.

Comment c. Liability to third persons. A misrepresentation may be negligent not only toward a person whose conduct it is intended to influence but also toward all others whom the maker should recognize as likely to be imperiled by action taken in reliance upon his misrepresentation. Thus, as stated in § 388, one who, by actively concealing a defect, misrepresents the condition of a chattel which he furnishes to another for use is liable not only (1) to the person to whom he furnishes the chattel and who, in the belief that it is safe, is injured while using it in a way for which it appears safe, but also (2) to such others as the actor permits to use or share in the use of the chattel and, in addition, (3) to others in the vicinity of its expected use who are harmed in person or property by such use. It is immaterial how the actor furnishes the chattel for use. His liability is the same irrespective of whether he sells it, leases it, supplies it for a use in which he has a business interest, or permits its use as a mere gratuity. The same is true of a lessor of land or a possessor of land who invites or permits others to enter the land for his own business purposes, or gratuitously. On the same basis a seller of an automobile who paints over a defective wheel or axle and so conceals its dangerously defective character is liable not only to his immediate buyer who is harmed by the collapse of the wheel or axle, but also to any person to whom the immediate buyer by sale, lease, or license transfers the use of the car, and to other travelers who sustain bodily harm or whose cars are damaged when the defective car gets out of control through the collapse of the wheel or axle.

Comment d. The liability stated in this Section is not confined to those persons whose conduct the misrepresentation is intended to influence, or to harm received in the particular transaction which the misrepresentation was intended to induce. Thus a misrepresentation of the physical condition of a chattel or of land or a structure, whether by express words or concealment, may make a vendor liable not only to his vendee to whom it was addressed and who is thereby induced to purchase it, but also to any person whom the vendee invites or permits to enter or use it. In addition, such a misrepresentation may make the maker liable to travelers on a highway upon which the land or structure abuts, or persons who are likely to be in the neighborhood of the place where the chattel is used, and who are injured by reason of the vendee's failure to repair the defect in the structure because of his ignorance of its existence, or by reason of his use of the chattel in ignorance of its dangerously defective condition.

Haralson v. Jones Truck Line

Supreme Court of Arkansas, 1954.
270 S.W.2d 892.

■ SMITH, J. This is an action for wrongful death, brought by the appellant as administratrix of the estate of Carl Brady Charles. The three defendants are the Jones Truck Line, its employee Jack Fulfer, and Clifton Duvall. At the close of the plaintiff's proof the trial court directed a verdict for the defendants. The question is whether the plaintiff made a case for the jury.

At the trial the plaintiff called the defendants Fulfer and Duvall as witnesses, and she now relies principally upon their testimony. These two men, who appear to have testified with complete candor, are in agreement as to the manner in which Charles met his death.

On the night of April 24, 1953, Fulfer was driving one of his employer's trucks west on Highway 64. For some distance Duvall, in his own truck, had been following Fulfer, awaiting an opportunity to pass him. On a long straight stretch near the town of Blackwell the two trucks met a car coming from the opposite direction. Both men dimmed their headlights. As soon as the approaching car had gone by, Fulfer, with his own headlights still dimmed, flashed his rear clearance lights. Both witnesses testify that this is a signal, well understood among truck drivers, by which the leading driver invites the other to pass.

Duvall, acting upon this signal, entered the lefthand traffic lane and overtook Fulfer's truck; but in doing so he did not switch his headlights to the bright beam. When the vehicles were abreast the two drivers for the first time saw Charles, who was walking west on the left side of the highway, with his back to the oncoming trucks. Both drivers swerved to their right in an effort to avoid an accident, but the extreme left hand side of Duvall's truck hit Charles and killed him. The point of impact was two or three feet from the lefthand edge of the pavement.

The remaining question is whether the proof would have supported a finding of negligence on the part of the truck drivers, or either or them. With respect to Duvall, whose vehicle actually struck Charles, little need be said. His lights were still dimmed when he first saw the decedent, who was then only twenty or twenty-five feet away. The law requires that the bright headlight beam be of sufficient intensity to reveal persons at a distance of at least 350 feet. Ark.Stats.1947, § 75–713. The jury would have been justified in concluding that Duvall was negligent either in failing to brighten his lights or in failing to keep a proper lookout.

Fulfer's truck, on the other hand, did not come in contact with Charles. Hence this defendant and his employer insist that they violated no duty owed to the decedent, since their vehicle remained continuously on its own side of the highway. This argument would be highly persuasive were it not for the fact that Fulfer signaled the trailing vehicle to pass him. We think this fact to be of controlling importance in the case.

Although we all know the signal in question to be widely used by truck drivers, the exact question now presented does not seem to have been considered in any reported decision. In principle, however, it is not difficult. We have defined a negligent act as one 'from which an ordinarily prudent person would foresee such an appreciable risk of harm to others as to cause him not to do the act, or to do it in a more careful manner.' Hill v. Wilson, 216 Ark. 179. It seems perfectly plain that the driver who gives this signal cannot invariably be absolved of all responsibility in the matter. If, for example, the leading driver should reach the crest of a hill and should give the passing signal when he alone could see a car approaching dangerously close from the other side, no one would regard the giver of the signal as wholly blameless if a head-on collision resulted from his action. In that situation an ordinarily prudent person would certainly foresee an appreciable risk of harm to others.

In the case at bar Fulfer testified that he would not have flashed his clearance lights if he had seen a man in the road. Yet he did give that signal without having returned his headlights to the bright position. The proof is that the dim beam is lower that the bright one and is directed to the right, so that the darkest part of the highway is to the left. That is where Charles was walking when he was struck. There was substantial evidence from which the jury might have found that Fulfer's failure to brighten his lights before signaling to Duvall involved a foreseeable risk of injury to others, a risk that an ordinarily prudent man would not have taken.

Nor does it matter that Fulfer was under no legal duty to give any signal at all. As Judge Cardozo observed in the leading case of Glanzer v. Shepard, 233 N.Y. 236: 'It is ancient learning that one who assumes to act, even though gratuitously, may thereby become subject to the duty of acting carefully, if he acts at all.' Even though Fulfer's invitation to Duvall was gratuitous the law required that his conduct be characterized by ordinary care.

Reversed.

Wooderson v. Ortho Pharmaceutical Corp.

Supreme Court of Kansas, 1984.
681 P.2d 1038.

■ MILLER, J.: Plaintiff, Carol Lynn Wooderson, brought this action in the District Court of Sedgwick County for damages for personal injuries which she claims resulted from her ingestion, over a period of years, of the oral contraceptive Ortho–Novum 1/80, manufactured by the defendant, Ortho Pharmaceutical Corporation (Ortho). At the conclusion of a six-week trial, the jury returned a verdict and the court entered judgment for plaintiff and against Ortho for actual damages of $2,000,000 and punitive damages of $2,750,000. Ortho appeals.

[A detailed description of the plaintiff's medical history and injuries is omitted.]

Plaintiff's actual out-of-pocket medical expenses up to the time of trial, plus loss of wages and mileage from her home to and from the hospital, exceeded $215,000. Damages sustained and not covered within that monetary figure include future drug expenses (estimated at $28,800), loss of both kidneys, cataracts in both eyes, increased risk of cancer because of the continued ingestion of steroids, inability to have children, loss of blood flow to part of the large intestine necessitating major abdominal surgery and removal of part of the intestine, risk of further intestinal surgery, and mental anguish, pain and suffering caused by the extended hospitalization, repeated operations, hemodialysis for five and one-half years, loss of her brother's donated kidney, and some fifty-five blood transfusions. Ortho does not argue that the $2,000,000 awarded as compensatory damages is excessive, or that the amount of the award is not supported by the evidence. Instead, Ortho argues that there is no substantial evidence that the oral contraceptives caused plaintiff's kidney failure; that Ortho had no duty to warn of the risk of hemolytic uremic syndrome (HUS); and that even if it did have the duty to warn, its failure to warn bore no causal relationship to Dr. Hermes' decision to prescribe Ortho–Novum 1/80 for the plaintiff. Thus, Ortho's position is not that plaintiff did not sustain the injuries and damages claimed, but that Ortho did not cause them to occur and is therefore not responsible. It challenges causation and responsibility, not injury.

THE PILL AS CAUSATION

[The discussion of causation is omitted.]

We conclude that there is an abundance of substantial, competent evidence to support the jury's finding that Ortho–Novum 1/80 caused the plaintiff's HUS, her acute kidney failure, and her resulting injuries and damages.

DUTY TO WARN

Ortho contends that it had no duty to add to the prescribing instructions for Ortho–Novum 1/80 a statement that there might be an association between the use of that product and HUS, malignant hypertension, or acute renal failure. In support of this contention, it cites Restatement (Second) of Torts § 402A (1965), including the comments thereto, and *Lindquist v. Ayerst Laboratories, Inc.*, 227 Kan. 308, 319 (1980). *Lindquist* was a products liability and medical malpractice case brought against Ayerst Laboratories, Inc., the manufacturer of an anesthetic which had been administered to the decedent, and the two physicians who had administered the anesthetic. Verdict had been entered for the defendants and plaintiff appealed. In the course of the opinion, we said:

> "[T]he jury was properly instructed regarding the doctrine of strict liability expressed in Restatement (Second) of Torts § 402A (1965). The jury was instructed to find Ayerst liable provided they found the drug was in a defective condition and unreasonably dangerous to persons who might be expected to use it, where that defect caused or contributed to the death of Lindquist. The defective condition is the failure of Ayerst to properly warn and instruct the medical profession with respect to the use and possible consequences of the use of Fluothane." 227 Kan. at 319.

Section 402A of the Restatement, together with the applicable portions of Comment *j* thereunder, read as follows:

> "§ 402A. Special Liability of Seller of Product for Physical Harm to User or Consumer

> "(1) One who sells any product in a defective condition unreasonably dangerous to the user or consumer or to his property is subject to liability for physical harm thereby caused to the ultimate user or consumer, or to his property, if

>> (a)the seller is engaged in the business of selling such a product, and

>> (b) it is expected to and does reach the user or consumer without substantial change in the condition in which it is sold.

"(2) The rule stated in Subsection (1) applies although

(a) the seller has exercised all possible care in the preparation and sale of his product, and

(b) the user or consumer has not bought the product from or entered into any contractual relation with the seller.

j. Directions or warning.... Where, however, *the product contains an ingredient to which a substantial number of the population are allergic, and the ingredient is one whose danger is not generally known,* or if known is one which the consumer would reasonably not expect to find in the product, *the seller is required to give warning against it, if he has knowledge, or by the application of reasonable, developed human skill and foresight should have knowledge, of the presence of the ingredient and the danger. Likewise in the case of poisonous drugs, or those unduly dangerous for other reasons, warning as to use may be required.*" (Emphasis supplied.)

Defendant seizes upon that portion of the comment reading "if he has knowledge, or by the application of reasonable, developed human skill and foresight should have knowledge...." Ortho contends, in essence, that an ethical (prescription) drug manufacturer is not bound to provide warnings until the occurrence of side effects is so frequent and the evidence of causation so clear-cut that the drug maker is itself convinced that the drug causes or contributes to such problems. This, we conclude, is not the law.

[A discussion of precedents is omitted.]

We hold that the manufacturer of an ethical drug has a duty to warn the medical profession of dangerous side effects of its products of which it knows, has reason to know, or should know, based upon its position as an expert in the field, upon its research, upon cases reported to it, and upon scientific development, research, and publications in the field. This duty is continuing. We do not need to determine, in this case, what duty, if any, such a manufacturer has to warn the ultimate consumer, the patient. Here, neither was warned by Ortho, but Ortho's failure to warn the physician is sufficient to sustain the finding of negligence or breach of duty against it in this case.

FAILURE TO WARN AS CAUSATION

Ortho next contends that its failure to warn of the association between the use of its product and HUS, malignant hypertension, and acute renal failure was not a cause in fact of plaintiff's injury. To the contrary, we think the evidence was substantial that it was. There was abundant evidence that the early diagnosis of HUS, of malignant hypertension, and of kidney failure is extremely important. In addition, Dr. Hermes testified that he has two of his daughters on a lower dosage of Ortho–Novum 1/50 because of what he has learned as a result of this case. There was evidence indicating that a lower dosage might have prevented HUS, and even if the higher dosage of estrogen contained in Ortho–Novum 1/80 were given, Mrs. Wooderson's attending physicians—if warned of the possibility of HUS-might have made an earlier diagnosis which, according to the expert testimony, might have averted the tragedy. Dr. Hermes testified that he is now alerted to the danger and would look for symptoms. The duty to warn, of course, extends throughout the time that the plaintiff was taking Ortho–Novum 1/80. No warnings were given by Ortho during that period of time, and thus the physicians were not informed to be on the alert for symptoms of HUS, kidney failure, or malignant hypertension. The question of whether this failure to warn was a cause of plaintiff's injury was properly submitted to the jury. With respect to warnings, the *Chapman* court said:

> "... Comment *j* provides a presumption that an adequate warning would be heeded. This operates to the benefits of a manufacturer where adequate warnings in fact are given. Where warnings are inadequate, however, the presumption is in essence a presumption of causation." 180 Ind.App. at 55.

Similarly, the *Seley* court said:

> " 'What the doctor might or might not have done had he been adequately warned is not an element plaintiff must prove as a part of her case.' *Hamilton v. Hardy* [37 Colo.App. 375 (1976)], at page 387. The evidence provided by Dr. Froelich as to his independently acquired knowledge is insufficient to rebut the presumption established by Comment *j*." 67 Ohio St.2d at 201–202.

In this case, the warning was inadequate. On the evidence before it, the jury was entitled to find that this inadequate warning caused Mrs. Wooderson's injuries.

[Discussions of additional unrelated issues are omitted.]

Restatement (Second) of Torts

§ 304   Negligent Misrepresentation Affecting Conduct Of Others

A misrepresentation of fact or law may be negligent conduct.

Comment a. This Section is inserted in order to make complete the catalogue of types of negligent conduct. The rules which determine whether the maker of a misrepresentation of fact or law is subject to liability for harm which he did not intend to bring about are stated in §§ 310 and 311.

Restatement (Second) of Torts

§ 310.   Conscious Misrepresentation Involving Risk Of Physical Harm

An actor who makes a misrepresentation is subject to liability to another for physical harm which results from an act done by the other or a third person in reliance upon the truth of the representation, if the actor

(a) intends his statement to induce or should realize that it is likely to induce action by the other, or a third person, which involves an unreasonable risk of physical harm to the other, and

(b) knows

    (i) that the statement is false, or

    (ii) that he has not the knowledge which he professes.

Comments & Illustrations

Comment a.   If the actor makes a misrepresentation for the purpose of causing, or believing that action in reliance upon it will cause, physical harm, he is liable because he intended the resulting harm. The rule stated in this Section relates to misrepresentations which, though intended to mislead another, are not intended to cause him the physical harm, where, however, the actor should realize that the harm is likely to result from the action which his misrepresentation is likely to induce. His liability is based upon the unreasonable risk of physical harm which is involved in the misrepresentations, and not upon the fact that the misrepresentations are intended to mislead.

Comment b.   The representation to which this Section applies may be one of fact, opinion, or law. Where the representation is one of opinion, prediction, or law, the other's reliance upon it may be less reasonable, and so less justified. (Compare §§ 542, 544, and 545.) Where the reliance is justified, however, the rule here stated applies to representations of both opinion and law.

The situation to which the rule stated in this Section is most usually applied is where the misrepresentation is made concerning the physical condition of a thing, either land, structures, or a chattel, and induces the other to believe that the thing is in safe condition for his entry or use, or induces a third person to hold the land or chattel open to the entry or use of the other in the belief that it is safe for the purpose. The rule is, however, equally applicable to misrepresentation of other matters upon which the safety of the person or property of another depends.

Illustrations:

    1.   A tells B that he has tried the ice on a certain pond and found it thick enough for safe skating. A knows that he has not tried it and knows nothing of the condition of the ice, which in fact is dangerously thin, although it appears to be safe. B, in reliance upon A's statements, attempts to skate upon the pond and falls in, catching a severe cold. A is negligent toward B.

    2.   A offers B a drink from a bottle of whiskey, telling him that he has himself imported it from Canada, although he knows that he has bought it for a very cheap price from an unidentified bootlegger. B drinks the whiskey, which turns out to be compounded of denatured alcohol, from which the poison has not been completely eliminated. B becomes ill. A is negligent toward B.

    3.   A police officer comes to A's house to arrest him upon reasonable suspicion of felony. B, A's uncle, who is present, tells A that the officer has no legal authority to arrest him, and advises him to resist arrest. B knows that he has no knowledge of the law as to the arrest, which is in fact valid. A, in reliance upon the

representation, resists arrest, and is injured when the officer overpowers him. B is negligent toward A.

Comment c. Liability to third persons. A misrepresentation may be negligent not only toward a person whose conduct it is intended to influence but also toward all others whom the maker should recognize as likely to be imperiled by action taken in reliance upon his misrepresentation. Thus, as stated in § 388, one who, by actively concealing a defect, misrepresents the condition of a chattel which he furnishes to another for use is liable not only (1) to the person to whom he furnishes the chattel and who, in the belief that it is safe, is injured while using it in a way for which it appears safe, but also (2) to such others as the actor permits to use or share in the use of the chattel and, in addition, (3) to others in the vicinity of its expected use who are harmed in person or property by such use. It is immaterial how the actor furnishes the chattel for use. His liability is the same irrespective of whether he sells it, leases it, supplies it for a use in which he has a business interest, or permits its use as a mere gratuity. The same is true of a lessor of land or a possessor of land who invites or permits others to enter the land for his own business purposes, or gratuitously. On the same basis a seller of an automobile who paints over a defective wheel or axle and so conceals its dangerously defective character is liable not only to his immediate buyer who is harmed by the collapse of the wheel or axle, but also to any person to whom the immediate buyer by sale, lease, or license transfers the use of the car, and to other travelers who sustain bodily harm or whose cars are damaged when the defective car gets out of control through the collapse of the wheel or axle.

Comment d. The liability stated in this Section is not confined to those persons whose conduct the misrepresentation is intended to influence, or to harm received in the particular transaction which the misrepresentation was intended to induce. Thus a misrepresentation of the physical condition of a chattel or of land or a structure, whether by express words or concealment, may make a vendor liable not only to his vendee to whom it was addressed and who is thereby induced to purchase it, but also to any person whom the vendee invites or permits to enter or use it. In addition, such a misrepresentation may make the maker liable to travelers on a highway upon which the land or structure abuts, or persons who are likely to be in the neighborhood of the place where the chattel is used, and who are injured by reason of the vendee's failure to repair the defect in the structure because of his ignorance of its existence, or by reason of his use of the chattel in ignorance of its dangerously defective condition.

Restatement (Second) of Torts

§ 311 Negligent Misrepresentation Involving Risk Of Physical Harm

(1) One who negligently gives false information to another is subject to liability for physical harm caused by action taken by the other in reasonable reliance upon such information, where such harm results

(a) to the other, or

(b) to such third persons as the actor should expect to be put in peril by the action taken.

(2) Such negligence may consist of failure to exercise reasonable car

(a) in ascertaining the accuracy of the information, or

(b) in the manner in which it is communicated.

Comments & Illustrations

Comment a. The rule stated in this Section represents a somewhat broader liability than the rules stated as to liability for pecuniary loss resulting from negligent misrepresentation, stated in § 552, to which reference should be made for comparison.

Comment b. The rule stated in this Section finds particular application where it is a part of the actor's business or profession to give information upon which the safety of the recipient or a third person depends. Thus it is as much a part of the professional duty of a physician to give correct information as to the character of the disease from which his patient is suffering, where such knowledge is necessary to the safety of the patient or others, as it is to make a correct diagnosis or to prescribe the appropriate medicine. The rule is not, however, limited to information given in a business or professional capacity, or to those engaged in a business or profession. It extends to any person who, in the course of an activity which is in furtherance of his own interests, undertakes to give information to another, and knows or should realize that the safety of the person of others may depend upon the accuracy of the information.

Illustrations

1. A train of the A Railroad is approaching a grade crossing. An employee of the Railroad negligently raises the crossing gates, and so informs approaching automobile drivers that no train is coming. B sees the gates raised, drives onto the crossing, and is struck by the train. A Railroad is subject to liability to B.

2. The A Company is conducting blasting operations near a railroad. B, an employee of the railroad, comes to inquire as to the progress of the work. As he arrives a blast is being set off, and he is advised to take cover. Immediately after the blast the foreman of A Company negligently informs B that all danger is over and he can safely come into the open. A delayed explosion occurs, and B is struck and injured by a rock. A Company is subject to liability to B.

3. A has charge of B, a lunatic of violent tendencies. A advertises for a servant, and C applies for the employment. A informs C that B is insane, but negligently gives C the impression that B is not violent or dangerous. C accepts the employment, and is attacked and injured by B. A is subject to liability to C.

Comment c.   The rule stated in this Section may also apply where the information given is purely gratuitous, and entirely unrelated to any interest of the actor, or any activity from which he derives any benefit. In this respect the rule stated here differs from that stated in § 552, which is concerned only with pecuniary loss suffered as the result of a negligent misrepresentation. Where only such pecuniary loss is sustained, the gratuitous character of the information prevents any liability for negligence in giving it. Where, as under the rule stated in this Section, the harm which results is bodily harm to the person, or physical harm to the property of the one affected, there may be liability for the negligence even though the information is given gratuitously and the actor derives no benefit from giving it.

The fact that the information is gratuitous may, however, affect the reasonableness of the other's reliance upon it in taking action. There may be no reasonable justification for taking the word of a casual bystander, who does not purport to have any special information or any interest in the matter, as to the safety of a bridge or a scaffold, where the plaintiff would be fully justified in accepting the statement of one who purports to have special knowledge of the matter, or special reliability, even though the plaintiff knows that he is receiving gratuitous advice.

Illustrations

4.   A buys a tombstone from B, a dealer in tombstones. A is in doubt as to how to transport it. C, a casual bystander, volunteers the information that the tombstone weighs only 50 pounds, and that A can easily and safely pick it up and carry it to his car. Relying on C's statement, A attempts to do so. In fact the tombstone weighs 150 pounds, and A suffers a hernia as the result of his efforts. C is not liable to A.

5.   The same facts as in Illustration 4, except that the statement is made by B. B is subject to liability to A.

6.   A large trailer truck of the A Company is being driven on a winding highway. B is following it in his automobile, and seeking to pass it, but has not done so because his view is obstructed. At a particular point the driver of the truck signals to B to pass it, thereby representing to B that the highway ahead is clear. In reliance upon the signal B attempts to pass the truck, and is injured by a collision with an approaching car. A Company is subject to liability to B.

7.   The same facts as in Illustration 6, except that the driver calls verbal assurance to B that he can safely pass. The same result.

Comment on Clause (a) of Subsection (2):

Comment d.   Care in ascertaining facts and forming judgment. Where the actor furnishes information upon which he knows or should realize that the security of others depends, he is required to exercise the care of a reasonable man under the circumstances to ascertain the facts, and the judgment of a reasonable man in determining whether, in the light of the discovered facts, the information is accurate. His negligence may consist of failure to make proper inspection or inquiry, or of failure after proper inquiry to recognize that the information given is not accurate.

Illustration

8.   The A Boiler Insurance Company undertakes as part of its services to inspect the boiler of B. It issues a certificate that the boiler is in good condition for use. In reliance upon this certificate, B uses the boiler. The boiler bursts, owing to a defect which a reasonably careful inspection would have disclosed. Explosion of the boiler wrecks the adjacent building of C and causes bodily harm to him. The A Company is subject to liability to C for his bodily harm and the wrecking of his building caused by the explosion of the boiler.

Comment on Clause (b) of Subsection (2):

Comment e.   Care in use of language. The negligence for which the actor is liable under the statement in this Subsection consists in the lack of reasonable care to furnish accurate information. It is, therefore, not enough that the actor has correctly ascertained the facts on which his information is to be based and has exercised reasonable competence in judging the effect of such facts. He must also exercise reasonable care to bring to the understanding of the recipient of the information the knowledge which he has so acquired.

Illustration

9.   The A Boiler Insurance Company undertakes as part of its service to inspect the boiler of B. The A Company makes a careful inspection, and correctly concludes that the boiler is unsafe. Through the negligence of its clerk, it issues a certificate which, while correctly stating all the defects in the boiler, gives the misleading impression that the boiler is nevertheless safe. In reliance on the certificate, B continues to use the boiler, which bursts because of the defects and wrecks the adjacent building of C, causing bodily harm to C. The A Company is subject to liability to C for his bodily harm and the wrecking of his building.

Comment f.   Comments *c* and *d* on § 310 are applicable to this Section.

* * *

Stratton and *Bartolo* represent the simplest fact pattern involving intentional misrepresentation and require no real explanation. In *Stratton*, the defendant, with a bad motive, fed two women figs without telling them that he had laced the food with a "a deleterious and destructive drug" that he believed possessed aphrodisiac properties. The women became ill. Because the defendant did not force-feed the victims, the central wrong concerned deception rather than coercion. Still, the defendant knew that the gift "was not ordinary food, that the girl was deceived into taking it, and he intended that she should be induced to take it without her conscious consent, by the deceit which he practiced upon her." Accordingly, the court reasoned, "[a]lthough force and violence are included in all definitions of assault, or assault and battery, yet, where there is physical injury to another person, it is sufficient that the cause is set in motion by the defendant, or that the person is subjected to its operation by means of any act or control which the defendant exerts." The case was tried as a crime, but the outcome—that the defendant was liable for the plaintiff's loss—and the reasoning—that ground of liability was the defendant's misrepresentation—would have been no different in tort. *Bartolo* analogously holds that a misrepresentation asserting legal authority to detain a person in custody can support a claim for false imprisonment even where the detention involved no actual coercion or force. Nor are these cases, despite their slightly gimmicky facts, just a doctrinalist's parlor trick. Any number of other, really quite ordinary, fact patterns involve torts accomplished by intentional misrepresentation. Common examples include defamation,[9] the intentional infliction of emotional distress,[10] and conversion of chattels accomplished by false claims of ownership.[11] Nor are these the only examples.[12]

Moreover, many other torts, including many of the commonest forms of negligence, involve injuries caused, at bottom, by misrepresentation. Sometimes, the torts are so common and yet so far from contract that the role that misrepresentation plays in them goes almost entirely unnoticed. Traffic accidents caused by negligent use (or non-use) of driving-signals present a case in point. *Haralson* is broadly typical, although the fact pattern includes the atypical (but diagnostically useful) feature that the

---

9. See, e.g., *Fraser v. Park Newspapers of St. Lawrence*, 257 A.D. 2d 961 (N.Y. 1999).

10. See, e.g., 164 *Mulberry St. v. Columbia University*, 4 A.D.3d 49 (N.Y. 2004), in which an unwise Columbia professor, pursuing a foolish research study, sent letters to restaurants falsely accusing them of food poisoning. For the recipients, the letters were "like getting a death warrant from the White House. [Their] Restaurant was turned upside down to try and find out how this could have happened. Much food on hand in [their] kitchen was destroyed, at a cost of thousands of dollars. Vendors were notified and told to check their entire inventory. Staff members were all put on notice that if this were ever traced to a particular person, that individual would not only be fined, but would, probably never work in this field again." The Court concluded that even though the professor "might not have intended harassment, he intended to elicit a response and in doing so may have recklessly disregarded the potential consequences of [his] conduct," which was thus "sufficiently outrageous so as to support" a claim for intentional infliction of emotional distress.

11. See, e.g., *Lomax v. State*, 407 S.E. 2d 462 (Ga. Ct. App. 1991), in which a man sold a car that he did not own to a passerby by pretending to own it.

12. Other examples include: misrepresentations that trick plaintiffs into marriage (*Spellens v. Spellens*, 317 P.2d 613 (Cal. 1957)); misrepresentations that manipulate people into leaving their spouses (see *Work v. Campbell* 164 Cal. 343 (1912) and *Gregg v. Gregg*, 37 Ind. App. 210 (1905), in which a plaintiff successfully sued her mother-in-law for alienating her husband by making false statements); misrepresentations that trick people into employing a child whose true age rendered him legally barred from working, and hence to incur special tort liability following an accident–related injury (see *Stryk v. Mnichowicz*, 167 Wis. 265 (1918) and *American Belt Co. v. Figuereo*, 755 A.2d 77 (Pa. Cmwlth. Ct. 2000); misrepresentations of infertility that cause plaintiffs, having failed to use birth control, to become pregnant and suffer associated medical complications (see *A. v. G.*, 145 Cal. App. 3d 369 (1983)).

defendant's truck struck neither the victim nor anything else. This ensured that misrepresentation was the sole mechanism by which the tort at issue was committed. As the court concluded, a person may be liable in tort for sending a signal that "involves a foreseeable risk of injury to others, a risk that an ordinarily prudent man would not have taken." Even so, the court made no express mention of misrepresentation in its opinion.

Another familiar example of tort liability for misrepresentation in non-contractual settings concerns violations of the duty to warn. Thus, drug-makers are regularly, and uncomplicatedly, held liable for unreasonably failing to notify patients of dangers posed by the drugs that they manufacture. Plaintiffs in these cases seek to be made whole for harms suffered that would have been avoided had they been forewarned of the risks posed by the drugs as manufactured rather than for harms that would have been avoided only had the drugs been re-engineered to avoid the risks entirely. *Wooderson* illustrates the practical application of this distinction. The plaintiff's claim turned, in part, on the proposition that a proper warning would have accelerated her doctor's diagnosis of the drug's side-effects and hence improved his ability to treat them. She argued, in other words, not that the defendant should have made a side-effect free drug, but rather that it should have made adequate representations concerning side-effects whose existence she was (for purposes of this claim) prepared to accept. The distinction has practical consequences: a plaintiff's recovery for inadequate warning is limited to the losses that the warning would have allowed her to avoid, which may be less than the losses that would have been avoided had the drug been risk free.

Stratton, *Bartolo*, *Haralson*, and *Wooderson* involve tort liability for false representations. But they do not threaten to supplant contract's promissory basis with a legal order based in tort; indeed, they do not encroach on contract at all. The reason why not involves the content and context of the representations. The rights invaded in the cases are not creatures of the defendants' representations or of the victims' reactions to them but rather exist entirely apart from any actions by the parties; and the representations neither contain nor imply any promises for tort to encroach on. In *Stratton* the defendant came under an antecedent duty with respect to the wholesomeness and purity of the food that he served the victim, and he therefore was neither called on nor did he make any promise concerning the food's quality. In *Bartolo*, the defendants owed a duty not to infringe on the plaintiff's freedom of movement. In *Haralson*, the defendant owed a general duty of reasonably careful driving with respect to the plaintiff, and his signal to overtake again made no promise concerning the state of the road ahead. And in *Wooderson*, the defendant owed a general duty not to subject the plaintiff to unreasonable risks in connection with drugs that it manufactured and sold. Once again, these cases, and others like them, involve wrongings through false representations. But the false representations function not like promises so much as like cudgels (in *Bartolo*, almost literally like a cudgel). They do not purport to bring any rights into existence in themselves; rather, they are mechanisms by which independently existing rights might be invaded. Sections 304, 310, and 311 of the Restatement, and the cases that they collect, canvass these mechanisms.

The cases are so easy because the mechanisms all share that plaintiffs assert no interest in the truth of representations but seek only to be made whole to the extent that the representation plus their reliance on it has made them worse off. The cases therefore do not encroach on, or indeed even approach, promise.

This, finally, helps to explain why cases such as these often avoid the doctrinal category *misrepresentation* entirely. The Supreme Court observed why that category is avoided when it held that the "misrepresentation exception" to the Federal Tort Claims Act's waiver of sovereign immunity does not bar lawsuits arising from the Coast Guard's negligent failure properly to maintain lighthouses. "Such a claim," the court insisted, "does not 'arise out of misrepresentation,' any more than does one based upon a motor vehicle operator's negligence in giving a misleading turn signal. As Dean Prosser has observed, many familiar forms of negligent conduct may be said to involve an element of 'misrepresentation,' in the generic sense of that word, but '(s)o far as misrepresentation has been treated as giving rise in and of itself to a distinct cause of action in tort, it has been identified with the common law action of deceit,' and has been confined 'very largely to the invasion of interests of a financial or commercial character, in the course of business dealings.' "[13] The reference to financial interests is probably unfortunate—a misplaced synecdoche that treats the financial interests that are commonly at stake in *business* dealings as standing in for the broader category of interests associated with relations that involve commercial exchange. The true gravamen of the observations concerns the emphasis on misrepresentations made in the course of business *dealings*—that is, in the course of exchange relations and the promises that these involve.

The theoretical difference between non-promissory claims for misrepresentation on the model of the materials just reviewed and misrepresentation claims that have a promissory foundation and threaten the autonomy of contract law can be applied to make a practical difference in concrete cases. This is vividly illustrated by one of the very first distinctions drawn in the very first case discussed in these materials, *Sullivan v. O'Conner*. Vindicating the doctor's representations, in that case, required giving the plaintiff the value of their accuracy—that is, the value of a beautiful nose. Compensating the plaintiff for the harms that she suffered in relying on the representations required merely returning the plaintiff to the position that she inhabited before encountering the doctor. It required, that is, undoing the harm that the doctor caused by inducing her to undergo his treatments by misrepresenting their quality. Finally, the qualitative and structural difference between these two claims for compensation may be illustrated by reconsidering a third claim that the case involved—the plaintiff's claim against the doctor for medical malpractice. This claim

---

13. *United States v. Neustadt*, 366 U.S. 696, 711 n. 26 (1961) (citing and quoting Indian Towing Co. v. United States, 350 U.S. 61 (1955)).

sought compensation for the harm that the doctor did the plaintiff not by making false representations that induced her to undergo the surgeries but rather by performing the surgeries unreasonably poorly (that is, without reasonable skill and care). The medical malpractice claim would have produced a different quantum of damages from the misrepresentation claim: in particular, the medical malpractice claim would have included the value of a reasonable improvement in the plaintiff's nose, which the misrepresentation claim excluded; and it would have excluded the pain and suffering that the plaintiff would have undergone even in connection with competent treatment, which the misrepresentation claim included (as the plaintiff would not have undergone treatment at all but for the doctor's representations concerning success). But in spite of their different contents, the two harm-based remedies share a structure, which distinguishes them from the promise based remedy. They each seek to undo something that was done (a misleading remark, a careless cut) rather than to do something that was not done (a promised performance).

The misrepresentation torts properly-so-called, by contrast, focus on misrepresentations made in and around promises. The next sections show that in this guise, the misrepresentation torts do pose a threat to the doctrinal autonomy of contract—they do represent an effort, by tort, to colonize contract from without. The materials also explain, however, that the misrepresentation torts are cabined by a set of doctrines that narrow their range of application and in this way defeat tort's colonizing ambitions. As comments [a] and [c] to § 311 emphasize, liability for true misrepresentation torts, which is governed by § 352 of the Restatement (to be taken up below), is narrower than liability for torts in which misrepresentation functions, cudgel-like, merely as a technique for harming.

16.1.B   MISREPRESENTATIONS NEARER PROMISE

The materials just discussed illustrate that many torts associated with misrepresentations do not even approach promise or contract. But some torts associated with misrepresentation do approach contract. In these torts—the misrepresentation torts properly-so-called—misrepresentation produces harm not on the model of a cudgel, but more nearly on the model of a broken promise.

The misrepresentation torts threaten contract insofar as they allow plaintiffs to recover something that resembles a vindication for expectations that they formed based on representations that they were given, even though (because formalities were not observed) no orthodox contract arose. The idea of *vindicating* expectations is the key. It emphasizes that in true misrepresentation torts (as opposed to torts that merely involve misrepresentation as the technology for producing a more ordinary harm), representations themselves create rights. Plaintiffs pursuing these torts look to defendants' representations not merely as mechanisms for harming antecedent entitlements but as sources of new entitlements. Most directly, the plaintiffs seek to *fulfill* their expectations in the representations at issue. The plaintiffs' demands that their expectations be vindicated indicate that they are pursuing the misrepresentation torts as substitutes for contractual obligation. The following materials illustrate the general approach that such plaintiffs take.

Glanzer v. Shepard

Court of Appeals of New York, 1922.
135 N.E. 275.

■ CARZOZO, J. Plaintiffs bought of Bech, Van Siclen & Co., a corporation, 905 bags of beans. The beans were to be paid for in accordance with weight sheets certified by public weighers. Bech, Van Siclen & Co., the seller, requested the defendants, who are engaged in business as public weighers, to make return of the weight and furnish the buyers with a copy. A letter to the weighers, dated July 20, 1918, informed them that the bags were on the dock, that the beans had been sold to Glanzer Bros., the plaintiffs, who would accept delivery Tuesday, July 23, and that the defendants were to communicate with the plaintiffs, and ascertain whether it would 'be in order' to be on the pier Tuesday morning to weigh the beans before delivery. The defendants did as bidden. They certified the weight of the 905 bags to be 228,380 pounds, and were paid for the service by the seller. Their return recites that it has been made 'by order of' Bech, Van Siclen & Co., 'for G. Bros.' One copy of the return they sent to the seller, and a duplicate to the buyers. Later, 17 bags, containing 4,136 pounds, were withdrawn from the shipment. The others were accepted and paid for on the faith of the certificates. The plaintiffs, upon attempting a resale, found that the actual weight was less by 11,854 pounds than the weight as certified in the return. Upon learning this, they brought suit against the defendants in the City Court of New York for $1,261.26, the amount overpaid. The trial judge, upon motions made by each side for the direction of a verdict, ordered judgment for the plaintiffs. The Appellate Term reversed upon the ground that the plaintiffs had no contract with the defendants, and must seek their remedy against the seller. The Appellate Division reversed the Appellate Term, and reinstated the verdict. The defendants are the appellants here.

We think the law imposes a duty toward buyer as well as seller in the situation here disclosed. The plaintiffs' use of the certificates was not an indirect or collateral consequence of the action of the weighers. It was a consequence which, to the weighers' knowledge, was the end and aim of the transaction. Bech, Van Siclen & Co. ordered, but Glanzer Brothers were to use. The defendants held themselves out to the public as skilled and careful in their calling. They knew that the beans had been sold, and that on the faith of their certificate payment would be made. They sent a copy to the plaintiffs for the very purpose of inducing action. All this they admit. In such circumstances, assumption of the task of weighing was the assumption of a duty to weigh carefully for the benefit of all whose conduct was to be governed. We do not need to state the duty in terms of contract or of privity. Growing out of a contract, it has none the less an origin not exclusively contractual. Given the contract and the relation, the duty is imposed by law (cf. *MacPherson v. Buick Motor Co.*, 217 N. Y. 382, 390).

There is nothing new here in principle. If there is novelty, it is in the instance only. One who follows a common calling may come under a duty to another whom he serves, though a third may give the order or make the payment (1 Street, Foundations of Legal Liability, pp. 187, 188; Bohlen, Affirmative Obligations in the Law of Torts, 44 Am. Law Reg. [N. S.] 209, 218, 293, 294; 3 Holdsworth, History of English Law, p. 332). 'It is the duty of every artificer to exercise his art rightly and truly as he ought' (Fitzherbert Abr., Trespass sue le Case, 94d, quoted by Bohlen, *supra*, p. 293). We must view the act in its setting, which will include the implications and the promptings of usage and fair dealing. The casual response, made in mere friendliness or courtesy (*Fish v. Kelly*, 17 C. B. [N. S.] 194, 205, 207; Bohlen, *supra*, p. 374; Street, *supra*, p. 408) may not stand on the same plane, when we come to consider who is to assume the risk of negligence or error, as the deliberate certificate, indisputably an 'act in the law' (Pollock, Contracts [8th ed.] p. 3), intended to sway conduct. Here the defendants are held, not merely for careless words, (*Le Lievre v. Gould,* 1893, 1 Q. B. D. 491; Pollock, Torts [10th ed.], pp. 301, 302; Jeremiah Smith, Liability for Negligent Language, 14 Harvard Law Review, 184, 195), but for the careless performance of a service—the act of weighing—which happens to have found in the words of a certificate its culmination and its summary (cf. *Corey v. Eastman,* 166 Mass. 279, 287). The line of separation between these diverse liabilities is difficult to draw. It does not lose for that reason its correspondence with realities. Life has relations not capable always of division into inflexible compartments. The moulds expand and shrink.

We state the defendants' obligation, therefore, in terms, not of contract merely, but of duty. Other forms of statement are possible. They involve, at most, a change of emphasis. We may see here, if we please, a phase or an extension of the rule in *Lawrence v. Fox* (20 N. Y. 268) as amplified recently in *Seaver v. Ransom* (224 N. Y. 233). If we fix our gaze upon that aspect, we shall stress the element of contract, and treat the defendants' promise as embracing the rendition of a service, which though ordered and paid for by one, was either wholly or in part for the benefit of another (*DeCicco v. Schweizer,* 221 N. Y. 431; *Rector, etc., St. Mark's Church v. Teed,* 120 N. Y. 583). We may find analogies again in the decisions which treat the sender of a telegram as the agent of the recipient (*Wolfskehl v. W. U. Tel. Co.,* 46 Hun, 542; *Milliken v. W. U. Tel. Co.,* 110 N. Y. 403). These other methods of approach arrive at the same goal, though the paths may seem at times to be artificial or circuitous. We have preferred to reach the goal more simply. The defendants, acting, not casually nor as mere servants, but in the pursuit of an independent calling, weighed and certified at the order of one with the very end and aim of shaping the conduct of another. Diligence was owing, not only to him who ordered, but to him also who relied.

Other points are made by counsel. We have not failed to consider them, but they do not alter our conclusion. Both sides having moved for the direction of a verdict without other request, the ruling of the trial judge stands with the same force as the verdict of a jury (*Adams v. Roscoe Lumber Co.*, 159 N. Y. 176). If the purpose of the parties, the relation that arose between them and the significance of the transaction may be the subject of conflicting inferences, those most favorable to the plaintiffs must be deemed to have been accepted.

The judgment should be affirmed with costs.

* * *

Glanzer concerns a true misrepresentation tort and the threat that an expansive reading of this tort poses to the independence of contract. The seller of a large quantity of beans, pursuant to the terms of its contract with the beans' buyer, made a separate contract with the defendants, "engaged in business as public weighers," to weigh the beans and report the weight to the buyer. The plaintiffs paid for the beans "on the faith of" the defendants' report; but, on attempting a resale, discovered that the actual weight was less than reported, and hence that they had overpaid. The plaintiffs sued the defendants to recover the amount of their overpayment.[14] The defendants answered that the plaintiffs had no claim against them, on account of the fact that their only contract was not with the plaintiffs but with the seller. The defendants argued, in effect, that the plaintiffs could not substitute an action for misrepresentation against them for an action for breach of contract against the seller.

Judge Benjamin Cardozo, writing for the Court of Appeals of New York, disagreed. According to Cardozo, even though the defendants had contracted with the seller only, "the law imposes a duty toward buyer as well as seller in the situation here disclosed." Cardozo observed that even though the plaintiffs were not party to the contract for weighing the beans, their use of the defendant's certificate of weight was not "indirect or collateral" to that contract but rather "within [the defendants'] knowledge" and indeed "the end and aim of [the weighing] transaction." Cardozo thus concluded that "[i]n such circumstances, assumption of the task of weighing was the assumption of a duty to weigh carefully for the benefit of all whose conduct was to be governed. We do not need to state the duty in terms of contract or of privity. Growing out of a contract, it has none the less an origin not exclusively contractual. Given the contract and the relation, the duty is imposed by law."

The scope of the rule set out in *Glanzer* is uncertain. Cardozo devoted substantial attention (both in his direct characterization of the transaction at issue and in the analogies that he drew to other cases) to the fact that although they made no contract with the plaintiffs, the defendants knew

---

14. Note that the plaintiffs seem to have sought recovery only for the losses associated with the original overpayment and not for the lost profits from resale. That is, they calculated their damages by multiplying the weighing error by their per-pound purchase price rather than by their (presumably larger) per-pound resale price. Nothing in Cardozo's opinion requires this modesty. In principle, the plaintiffs might have sought to vindicate their expectation in the defendants' declaration and hence also their profit on the excess of the reported over the actual weight of beans.

and indeed intended the plaintiffs to rely on their representations. As he wrote towards the end of the opinion, the defendants "certified at the order of one with the very end and aim of shaping the conduct of another. Diligence was owing, not only to him who ordered, but to him also who relied." Cardozo also emphasized that the defendants acted "not casually nor as mere servants, but in the pursuit of an independent calling." The defendants' duties thus arose not merely from such agreements as they made but also from the legal order regulating their calling, that is, the business of public weighing. These considerations cabin the holding quite narrowly. But Cardozo also warned against reaching his result by "artificial or circuitous" paths. Indeed, he expressly contemplated that his holding might undermine fixed and rigid doctrinal categories. "The line of separation between these diverse liabilities is difficult to draw," Cardozo wrote. "It does not lose for that reason its correspondence with realities. Life has relations not capable always of division into inflexible compartments. The moulds expand and shrink."

This makes it both natural and essential to ask by how much. What if the weighing error had been discovered (and hence its harms been brought to bear) only later, say by a retailer who sold the beans, already cooked and mixed with other ingredients, to the public? What if the harms had been suffered in respect of a physically entirely distinct commodity—say, because the overpayment had allowed the suddenly more profitable seller to invest in new equipment, driving up the equipment prices faced by others who used similar machines in another sector? Such new plaintiffs unquestionably fall far outside the contemplation of the parties to the initial contract. If they might nevertheless recover damages for its breach (subject only to the general constraints of certainty and foreseeability), then the doctrinal forms of orthodox contract—offer, acceptance, and consideration—will have been effectively abandoned. The new and distant plaintiffs could vindicate contract-like interests in the defendants' representations even though they came nowhere near any actual contract that the defendant made. Moreover, would it not be more natural, in this case, to think of a promisor's liability, *even to her promisee*, as just a special case of the general liability persons have to vindicate their representation?

If so, then the doctrinal forms of orthodox contract will have been *eliminated*. The formalisms of orthodox contract ensure that a contractual promise states that the promisor possesses an intention to obligate herself, to her promisee, to make the promised performance. The promise typically also states or at least implies that the promisor possesses a current intention to perform or even that she is highly likely to perform. But these non-promissory intentions are not sufficient to generate promissory obligation: Only the representation concerning the intention to obligate can make an orthodox contractual promise. The rule set down in *Glanzer*, if expansively applied, abandons this requirement. That rule entails that betraying reliance and disappointing expectations associated with the non-promissory representations produces legally cognizable forms of harm and disappointment to those who are let down. This raises the possibility that non-promissory reliance and expectations, and the harms that occur when these are not met, might explain all or virtually all of the legal obligations conventionally associated with contract. Perhaps even the obligations associated with the promise proper might be understood on the non-promissory model—that is, on terms that deny that there is anything normatively or legally special about intentions to obligate and instead treat these intentions as just one way among many of conveying (reliably) information about the future. Breach of contract, on this view, is simply a species of the genus misrepresentation.

It therefore becomes important to ask: can all, or even just most, of contract be explained on this model? Or do the misrepresentation torts contain structural limitations—gestured towards by Cardozo's opinion in *Glanzer* but not elaborated there—that prevent them from supplanting genuinely voluntary obligation, understood on the model of classical contract?

The answers to these questions turn out to vindicate orthodox contract. Cases like *Glanzer*, subsequent developments emphasize, do turn on the fact that defendants, owing to their peculiar callings, owe generalized duties of skill and care not just to their contractual counterparties but to the broader public. Outside of these special factual circumstances, contractual liability generally requires contractual intentions, made effective by forming contracts in the orthodox way. A person who makes a representation without engaging the formalisms of orthodox contract and without the contractual intent to obligate becomes liable for vindicating that representation only (roughly speaking) where she intends to deceive others into relying on her representations and others are in fact so deceived. This is the teaching of the law of fraud. Liability for non-fraudulent misrepresentations is much more narrowly cabined by doctrines that, roughly: require reliance; limit recovery to reliance losses; and permit recovery at all only where the harms caused by the misrepresentations invade entitlements grounded in rights and duties that precede the representations. This is the teaching of the general law of negligent misrepresentation. Exceptions to these general principles may have modestly increased since Cardozo wrote *Glanzer*, for example in connection with consumer protection laws. But the trend noticed by Atiyah, Gilmore, and Fried never reached the conclusion that drove them to write, and such circumstances remain exceptional.

The next sections elaborate these claims, beginning with fraud, then taking up misrepresentation, and concluding with some materials on consumer protection.

16.1.A.1   Fraud

Fraud is the "knowing misrepresentation of the truth or concealment of a material fact to induce another to act to his or her detriment."[15] The Restatement section on fraud and the comments and cross-references in it unpack the considerable doctrinal density that this simple definition contains. The materials that follow elaborate and comment on the unpacking.

---

15. BLACK'S LAW DICTIONARY.

They also draw out the relationship between tort liability for fraud and contract liability for breach. Both tasks involve some complexity.

Restatement (Second) of Torts

§ 525   Liability For Fraudulent Misrepresentation

One who fraudulently makes a misrepresentation of fact, opinion, intention or law for the purpose of inducing another to act or to refrain from action in reliance upon it, is subject to liability to the other in deceit for pecuniary loss caused to him by his justifiable reliance upon the misrepresentation.

Comments & Illustrations

Comment a.   The rules that determine the fraudulent character of a misrepresentation are stated in §§ 526–530. The rules that deal with the requirement that the representation must be made for the purpose of inducing that conduct of the other from which his harm results are stated in §§ 531–536. The rules that determine whether the recipient of the misrepresentation is justified in relying upon it are stated in §§ 537–545. The measure of damages is stated in § 549.

As to the liability for negligent misrepresentation inducing reliance that causes pecuniary loss, see § 552. As to innocent misrepresentation, see § 552C.

Comment b.   Misrepresentation defined. "Misrepresentation" is used in this Restatement to denote not only words spoken or written but also any other conduct that amounts to an assertion not in accordance with the truth. Thus, words or conduct asserting the existence of a fact constitute a misrepresentation if the fact does not exist.

Illustration

1.   A, a dealer in used automobiles, offers a second-hand car for sale in his showroom. Before doing so he turns the odometer back from 60,000 to 18,000 miles. B, relying on the odometer reading, purchases the car from A. This is a misrepresentation.

Comment c.   A representation of the state of mind of the maker or of a third person is a misrepresentation if the state of mind in question is otherwise than as represented. Thus, a statement that a particular person, whether the maker of the statement or a third person, is of a particular opinion or has a particular intention is a misrepresentation if the person in question does not hold the opinion or have the intention asserted.

Comment d.   Representations of fact, opinion and law. Strictly speaking, "fact" includes not only the existence of a tangible thing or the happening of a particular event or the relationship between particular persons or things, but also the state of mind, such as the entertaining of an intention or the holding of an opinion, of any person, whether the maker of a representation or a third person. Indeed, every assertion of the existence of a thing is a representation of the speaker's state of mind, namely, his belief in its existence. There is sometimes, however, a marked difference between what constitutes justifiable reliance upon statements of the maker's opinion and what constitutes justifiable reliance upon other representations. Therefore, it is convenient to distinguish between misrepresentations of opinion and misrepresentations of all other facts, including intention.

A statement of law may have the effect of a statement of fact or a statement of opinion. It has the effect of a statement of fact if it asserts that a particular statute has been enacted or repealed or that a particular decision has been rendered upon particular facts. It has the effect of a statement of opinion if it expresses only the actor's judgment as to the legal consequence that would be attached to the particular state of facts if the question were litigated. It is therefore convenient to deal separately with misrepresentations of law.

Comment e.   Representation implied from statement of fact. A misrepresentation of fact may concern either an existing or past fact. A statement about the future may imply a representation concerning an existing or past fact. (See Comment *f*). To be actionable, a misrepresentation of fact must be one of a fact that is of importance in determining the recipient's course of action at the time the representation is made. Thus a statement that a horse has recently and consistently trotted a mile in less than two minutes may justifiably be taken as an implied assertion of the capacity of the horse to repeat the performance at the time the statement is made. So, too, a past fact may be one that makes it obligatory or advisable for the recipient to take a particular course of action, as when A falsely tells B that he has caused the arrest of a criminal for whose arrest B has offered a reward, or when in an insurance policy the insured has falsely stated that his father did not die of tuberculosis. A fraudulent misrepresentation of such a fact may be the basis of liability.

Comment f.   Representation implied from statement promissory in form. Similarly a statement that is in form a prediction or promise as to the future course of events may justifiably be interpreted as a statement that the maker knows of nothing which will make the fulfillment of his prediction or promise impossible or improbable. Thus a statement that a second-hand car will run fifteen miles on a gallon of gasoline is an implied assertion that the condition of the car makes it capable of so doing, and is an actionable misrepresentation if the speaker knows that it has never run more than seven miles per gallon of gasoline.

Illustrations

2.   A, in order to induce B to buy a heating device, states that it will give a stated amount of heat while consuming only a stated amount of fuel. B is justified in accepting A's statement as an assurance that the heating device is capable of giving the services that A promises.

3. A, knowing that the X Corporation is hopelessly insolvent, in order to induce B to purchase from him shares of its capital stock assures B that the shares will within five years pay dividends that will amount to the purchase price of the stock. B is justified in accepting these statements as an assurance that A knows of nothing that makes the corporation incapable of making earnings sufficient to pay the dividends.

Comment g.   Representation implied from statement as to past events. On the same basis, a statement that a particular condition has recently existed or that an event has recently occurred or that a particular person has recently by words or acts expressed a particular opinion or intention, may, if reasonable under the circumstances, be understood and accepted as asserting that the situation has not changed since the time when the condition is said to have existed, the event to have occurred or the opinion or intention to have been expressed.

Illustrations

4. A, in order to induce B to buy a horse, falsely states that a veterinary surgeon a week before had examined the horse and had pronounced it sound. Unless B knows of something that might have changed the horse's condition in the interim, B is justified in interpreting A's statement as implying that the horse is sound at the time of the sale.

5. A tells B that C had the day before offered him $2000 for a particular piece of land. In the absence of anything known to him that might indicate the contrary, B is entitled to assume that C's opinion as to the value of the land is unchanged.

Comment h.   Misrepresentation causing physical harm. This Section (and this Chapter) covers pecuniary loss resulting from a fraudulent misrepresentation, and not physical harm resulting from the misrepresentation. As to the latter, see § 557A, which also covers the economic loss deriving from the physical harm. This type of economic loss is not intended to be included in the term, pecuniary loss, as used in this Chapter. See also § 310 (liability in negligence for a conscious misrepresentation involving risk of physical harm) and § 311 (negligent misrepresentation involving risk of physical harm).

* * *

Fraud wrongs those against whom it is committed, and so the Restatement rule establishing liability for fraud should come as no surprise. But although the fact of the wrong is clear, its nature remains complicated and uncertain. Observe that the fraudster in important respects resembles a breaching promisor. She intends not just to make a communication but also that her communication be taken up by its addressees. Moreover, she intends that her communication be taken up in a fashion that raises the moral stakes. Finally, the fraudster, in spite of having raised the stakes, betrays the person whom she defrauds. Considerations such as these bring fraud into close contact with contract; and tort doctrine embraces the connections, including in ways that cast the proximity between fraud and breach in an uncomfortable light. The feature of fraud that is most uncomfortable for contract concerns remedies. The following materials illustrate the problem.

Reno v. Bull

Court of Appeals of New York, 1919.
124 N.E. 144.

■ McLAUGHLIN, J. Action to recover damages for fraud and deceit, by reason of which it is claimed plaintiff was induced to purchase fifty shares, each of the par value of $100, of the capital stock of the American Oriental Company, a Maine corporation. Plaintiff had a verdict for $6,000, and from the judgment entered thereon defendants appealed to the Appellate Division, where the same was unanimously affirmed, and by permission they now appeal to this court.

The unanimous affirmance of the judgment conclusively establishes that the findings of the jury are sustained by evidence. The judgment, therefore, must be affirmed, unless errors, presented by proper exceptions, were committed by the trial court which affect the substantial rights of the defendants.

After a careful consideration of the record, the briefs and argument of respective counsel, I have reached the conclusion that there are at least two errors of this character which are so fundamental that they necessitate the reversal of the judgment. They are instructions given to the jury as to the duty and obligations of the defendants and as to the measure of damages.

As to the duty and obligations of the defendants: At the time the stock was purchased, they were, with others, directors of the corporation. It had a plant, which cost several hundred thousand dollars, for refining crude oil, located on San Francisco bay, in the state of California. The corporation was organized with a capital stock of four million dollars, two million common and two million preferred, and one million of the latter it was desirous of inducing the public to buy. To that end, it made an arrangement with Charles D. Barney & Company, prominent bankers in New York and Philadelphia, to offer the same for sale. Prior to the offering, Barney & Company prepared a circular, or prospectus, signed by them, which consisted of a letter from one Ertz, the president of the corporation, addressed to Barney & Company, which contained statements as to the capacity of the plant, probable earnings of the corporation, crude oil supplied in the state of California, advantages in securing trade in the Orient and large dividends that would be received by holders of the preferred stock. The circular also contained the names of the directors, the advisory committee and other matters unnecessary to state. This circular was adopted and approved by the directors of the corporation. The statements contained in the circular, which the plaintiff claimed were and which the jury have found to be false, were: (a) that the plant was well built, fully completed and had a capacity of refining 2,000 barrels of crude oil per day; (b) that there was an abundance of crude oil in the state of California; and (c) that there was a profitable Oriental market for the sale of the refined products. In connection with these alleged false statements, it was also claimed that the defendants were liable, by reason of a statement made by Ertz, the president of the corporation, to the plaintiff, at or immediately prior to the time he purchased the stock, to the effect that the corporation would begin business with $1,000,000 cash capital.

[The discussion of the obligations of the defendants is omitted.]

The rule as to the measure of damages was not the one to be applied. The court said to the jury that if the plaintiff were entitled to recover, then he should be awarded 'the difference between the value of the stock at the time it was sold to him and the value of the stock as it would have been at that time if the representations were true.' The purpose of an action for deceit is to indemnify the party injured. All elements of profit are excluded. The true measure of damage is indemnity for the actual pecuniary loss sustained as the direct result of the wrong. The plaintiff paid $5,000 for the stock purchased by him. If he were entitled to recover at all, it was the difference between that amount and the value of the stock which he received with interest from that time. He was not entitled to anything else. This is the rule not only in this state, but in the Federal courts (*Sigafus v. Porter,* 179 U. S. 116; *Smith v. Bolles,* 132 U. S. 125), and in many of the states.

My conclusion is that the judgments of the Appellate Division and the Trial Term should be reversed and a new trial ordered, with costs to abide event.

Morse v. Hutchins

Supreme Judicial Court of Massachusetts, 1869.
102 Mass. 439.

TORT for deceit in making false and fraudulent representations to the plaintiff touching the business and profits of a firm of which the defendant was a member, and thereby inducing the plaintiff to buy the interest of the defendant in the stock and good will of the firm. A count in contract for the same cause of action was joined. Answer, a general denial and a plea of a discharge in bankruptcy.

At the trial in the superior court, *Brigham,* C. J., ruled that the discharge in bankruptcy was a defence to the second count, but not to the first count; and the plaintiff relied on the first count only.

The judge instructed the jury that "the measure of damages would be the difference between the actual value of the stock and good will purchased at the time of the purchase and the value of the same had the representation been true."

The jury returned a verdict for the plaintiff, and the defendant alleged exceptions.

■ GRAY, J.

The rule of damages was rightly stated to the jury. It is now well settled that, in actions for deceit or breach of warranty, the measure of damages is the difference between the actual value of the property at the time of the purchase, and its value if the property had been what it was represented or warranted to be. *Stiles v. White,* 11 Met. 356. *Tuttle v. Brown,* 4 Gray, 457. *Whitmore v. South Boston Iron Co.* 2 Allen, 52. *Fisk v. Hicks,* 11 Foster, 535. *Woodward v. Thacher,* 21 Verm. 580. *Muller v. Eno,* 4 Kernan, 597. *Sherwood v. Sutton,* 5 Mason, 1. *Loder v. Kekulé,* 3 C. B. (N. S.) 128. *Dingle v. Hare,* 7 C. B. (N. S.) 145. *Jones v. Just,* Law Rep. 3 Q. B. 197. This is the only rule which will give the purchaser adequate damages for not having the thing which the defendant undertook to sell him. To allow to the plaintiff (as the learned counsel for the defendant argued in this case) only the difference between the real value of the property and the price which he was induced to pay for it would be to make any advantage lawfully secured to the innocent purchaser in the original bargain inure to the benefit of the wrongdoer; and, in proportion as the original price was low, would afford a protection to the party who had broken, at the expense of the party who was ready to abide by, the terms of the contract. The fact that the property sold was of such a character as to make it difficult to ascertain with exactness what its value would have been if it had conformed to the contract affords no reason for exempting the defendant from any part of the direct consequences of his fraud. And the value may be estimated as easily in this action as in an action against him for an entire refusal to perform his contract.

Exceptions overruled.

* * *

The defendants in *Reno* were directors of a corporation, the American Oriental Company, that sought to raise capital by selling its stock. In order to promote the sale, they had prepared and circulated a prospectus that falsely exaggerated the corporation's access to raw materials, its capacity for refining these materials, and the profitability of the market for its refined output. The plaintiff alleged that, induced by these false representations, it purchased 50 shares of the American Oriental's stock, for $5000. The shares did not perform as the plaintiffs had hoped, and the plaintiffs sought to recover damages for fraud and deceit.

One issue in the case concerned the standard of care that the defendants owed the plaintiffs, and in particular whether fraud requires intentional deception or merely negligence. The court observed that the elements of fraud are "representation, falsity, scienter, deception, and injury," and thus insisted that "Misjudgment, however gross, or want of caution, however marked, is not fraud. Intentional fraud, as distinguished from a mere breach of duty or the omission to use due care, is an essential factor in an action for deceit." The materials below will return to the scienter requirement, both to investigate its meaning more closely and to address its implications for the relationship between contract and tort.

For the moment, however, focus on the second issue in the case, which concerned the remedy for fraud. The plaintiff sought to vindicate its interest in the defendants' representation, and the trial court adopted this approach. It thus instructed the jury that, if he could sustain a claim for fraud, the plaintiff should recover damages equal to "the difference between the value of the stock at the time it was sold to him and the value of the stock as it would have been at that time if the representations were true." The Court of Appeals rejected this rule, however, observing that "the purpose of an action for deceit is to indemnify the party injured," so that "the true measure of damage is indemnity for the actual pecuniary loss sustained as the direct result of the wrong." The Court of Appeals insisted, in other words, that fraud's structural foundations lie in tort, and thus that damages for a fraud should reimburse the fraud's victim for the losses incurred in reliance on the defendant's false statements. "All elements of profit," the Court of Appeals insisted, "are excluded" from the fraud remedy. Instead of recovering the difference between the value of the stock as promised and its value in fact, the plaintiff could recover only the difference between the amount that he had paid for the stock ($5000) and its actual value.

The *Reno* rule introduced an incongruity into the law, however, which *Morse* and other cases like it pointed out and sought to correct. Frauds committed in a commercial context commonly arise in the precincts of contracts. *Reno* itself illustrates this—there was, after all, a contract for the sale and purchase of the stock. Often, although not always, the fraudulent representations may be incorporated into the associated contracts, for example as warranties. And where they are so incorporated, plaintiffs will have breach of contract actions that run parallel to their fraud claims, but that (being contract claims) sustain expectation-based remedies. Accordingly, as long as the remedy for fraud remains reliance-based, a defendant in such a case will fare better if found liable for fraud than if found liable for breach of the contract with which the fraud is associated. This result will obtain, moreover, even though the contract liability is strict, whereas liability for fraud requires scienter. *Reno's* insistence on fraud's grounding in tort therefore entails that, in respect of one and the same underlying conduct, the legal claim alleging a greater wrong sustains a lesser remedy. Finally, *Reno's* tort-based remedy is likely too small on its own terms. Recall the discussion of the reliance remedy in Part I, where it was observed that if lost opportunities are included in reliance (as they logically should be), then where markets function well, the reliance remedy, because it includes the lost opportunity of an effectively equivalent contract with another promisor, converges on the expectation remedy. Frauds committed in a commercial context will tend, to at least some extent, to participate in this logic: their victims will lose the value of alternative bargains that they have declined in reliance on the fraud.[16]

---

16. *Reno* has not been reversed, but its effects have been much narrowed, and indeed by applying the logic that treats lost opportunities as reliance losses, and hence recoverable even on the narrow tort model. An example in *Cayuga Harvester, Inc. v. Allis–Chalmers Corp.*, 95 A.D.2d 5 (N.Y. 1983), which distinguished *Reno* and permitted the recovery of crops lost due to

For these reasons, the narrowly tort-based remedy for commercial fraud has been criticized as unfortunate and even absurd. *Morse* illustrates the criticism. The facts in *Morse* closely parallel the facts in *Reno*. The defendant was a member of a firm and made false representations concerning the firm's business and profits, on whose basis the plaintiff bought an equity interest. On discovering the deception, the plaintiff sued, joining claims in contract for breach and in tort for fraud. The Supreme Judicial Court of Massachusetts held that an expectation-based remedy was appropriate: "It is now well settled," the Court said, "that, in actions for deceit or breach of warranty, the measure of damages is the difference between the actual value of the property at the time of the purchase, and its value if the property had been what it was represented or warranted to be." In contexts in which contract and tort overlap, moreover, the same remedy rule must apply to fraud. The rule followed in *Reno*, which would award only "the difference between the real value of the property and the price which [the plaintiff] was induced to pay" must be rejected, because it would "make any advantage lawfully secured to the innocent purchaser in the original bargain inure to the benefit of the wrongdoer." This is nowadays the general consensus, as the Restatement section reproduced below emphasizes.

Restatement (Second) of Torts

§ 549   Measure Of Damages For Fraudulent Misrepresentation

(1) The recipient of a fraudulent misrepresentation is entitled to recover as damages in an action of deceit against the maker the pecuniary loss to him of which the misrepresentation is a legal cause, including

> (a) the difference between the value of what he has received in the transaction and its purchase price or other value given for it; and

> (b) pecuniary loss suffered otherwise as a consequence of the recipient's reliance upon the misrepresentation.

(2) The recipient of a fraudulent misrepresentation in a business transaction is also entitled to recover additional damages sufficient to give him the benefit of his contract with the maker, if these damages are proved with reasonable certainty.

Comment on Subsection (1):

Comment a. Loss may result from a recipient's reliance upon a fraudulent misrepresentation in a business transaction in one of several ways. The most usual is when the falsity of the representation causes the

---

a defective harvesting machine on the ground that the plaintiff, if it had not bought the defendant's machine, would have bought a functional machine and so have kept its crops. See also *Hotaling v. Leach*, 247 N. Y. 84, 159 N. E. 870 (1928); *Continental Cas. Co. v. PricewaterhouseCoopers, LLP*, 933 N.E.2d 738 (N.Y. 2010).

article bought, sold or exchanged to be regarded as of greater or less value than that which it would be regarded as having if the truth were known. The rule applicable in this situation is that stated in Clause (a). The damages so resulting, being those which normally result from a misrepresentation in such transactions, are often called general damages.

Loss that may be suffered in reliance upon a fraudulent misrepresentation otherwise than as stated in Clause (a) includes two types of situations to both of which the rule stated in Clause (b) applies. The first is when the financial position of a third person is misrepresented for the purpose of inducing the recipient to extend credit to him. In this case the loss for which the plaintiff can recover is that suffered because of the third person's inability to meet the credit extended to him. If the third person pays nothing, the loss recoverable is the entire amount of the credit extended. If the third person pays in part, the loss recoverable is the residue remaining unpaid by him. Here again the situation being a usual one, and the loss one that normally results from the recipient's reliance upon the misrepresentation, the damages are often called general. A second situation in which loss may be sustained otherwise than through difference in value as stated in Clause (a) is when a buyer, in reliance upon the misrepresentation, uses the subject matter of the sale in the belief that it is appropriate for a use for which it is harmfully inappropriate or when he has incurred expenses in preparation for a use of the article for which it would have been appropriate if the representation had been true. In these latter situations the loss depends upon the particular use to which the plaintiff puts the article and is not inherent in the nature of the transaction and the damages are often called special or consequential damages.

Comment on Clause (1)(a):

Comment b.   Under the rule stated in Clause (1)(a), the recipient of a fraudulent misrepresentation is entitled to recover from its maker in all cases the actual out-of-pocket loss which, because of its falsity, he sustains through his action or inaction in reliance on it. If, notwithstanding the falsity of the representation, the thing that the plaintiff acquires through the fraudulent transaction is of equal or greater value than the price paid and he has suffered no harm through using it in reliance upon its being as represented, he has suffered no loss and can recover nothing under the rule stated in this Clause. His recovery, if any, must be upon the basis of the rule stated in Subsection (2).

Comment c.   Value, how ascertained. In a sales or exchange transaction the loss for which the recipient of a fraudulent misrepresentation is entitled to recover is usually the difference between the price paid or the value of the thing given in exchange and the value of the thing acquired. The value of the article is normally determined by the price at which it could be resold in an open market or by private sale if its quality or other characteristics that affect its value were known. However, the price that determines the value of the article is not necessarily the price that it would bring at the time the sale is made. In many cases this price is due to the widespread belief of other buyers in misrepresentations similar to that made to the person seeking recovery, as when market price of securities, such as bonds or shares, is the result of widely spread misrepresentations of those who issue or market them. The fact that the market price is inflated or depressed by the misrepresentations is the important factor making the price fictitious; it is, therefore, immaterial that the inflated or depressed price does or does not result from the misrepresentations of the same person who made the misrepresentation on which the person seeking recovery relied. In this case if the recipient of the misrepresentation, in reliance upon it, retains the securities either as a permanent or temporary investment, their value is determined by their market price after the fraud is discovered when the price ceases to be fictitious and represents the consensus of buying and selling opinion of the value of the securities as they actually are. If the plaintiff has resold the securities in the interim, however, his loss is the difference between the price paid and that received.

To this there is one qualification. One who, having acquired securities, retains them in reliance upon another's fraudulent representation is not entitled to recover from him a loss in the value of the securities that is in no way due to the falsity of the representation but is caused by some subsequent event that has no connection with or relation to the matter misrepresented. (See § 548A). Thus, a shareholder in a bank induced to retain his stock by the fraudulent misrepresentation of its president that "wash" sales were bona fide transactions is not entitled to recover for the depreciation of the shares due solely to the subsequent speculations of the cashier of the bank. On the other hand, the mere fact that the subsequent changes in financial or business conditions are factors which, in conjunction with the falsity of the misrepresentation, contribute to diminish or increase the market price of the securities does not prevent the price from fixing the value that determines the loss for which the person defrauded is entitled to recover. Thus, when a promoter induces an investor to subscribe to shares in a corporation by false statements of the amount of capital subscribed and of its assets, the fact that the insolvency of the corporation was in part due to the depressed condition of the industry in question does not prevent the investor from recovering his entire loss from the promoter, since if the corporation had had the capital and assets that it was represented as having, its chance of surviving the depression would have been greatly increased.

In the majority of stock transactions the person seeking recovery discovers the falsity of the misrepresentations at the same time that it becomes known to the investing public and, therefore, at a time when the price of the stock is no longer inflated or depressed by the same or similar misrepresentations. It may be, however, that he discovers the falsity of the representations either earlier or later than the general public. In the first situation his loss is determined by the actual value of the securities in question shown by their market price after the public discovery of the fraud brings the price into accord with the actual value. In the second situation, where the person seeking recovery does not learn of the falsity of the facts represented until sometime after the general public has discovered it, the value of the securities is fixed by the price at which they are selling at the time of his discovery and not that of the public.

Although the market price of securities is more often affected by the wide dissemination of fraudulent misrepresentations than is the market or resale price of other articles, the same considerations are decisive when the price of the articles is thus inflated or depressed. Thus a piece of land may gain a fictitious appearance of value because of widely spread misrepresentations that oil has been found in its close vicinity. In this case a purchaser induced to buy land by the misrepresentation is entitled to the difference between the price he paid and the amount for which land can be sold after the falsity of the representation has become notorious.

Comment on Clause (1)(b):

Comment d. Although the most usual form of financial loss caused by participation in a financial transaction induced by a fraudulent misrepresentation is the lessened value of the subject matter due to its falsity, the loss may result from a purchaser's use of the article for a purpose for which it would be appropriate if the representation were true but for which it is in fact harmfully inappropriate. So, too, it may be the expense to which he has gone in preparation for a use of the article for which it would have been appropriate if the representation had been true.

These "indirect" or "consequential" damages resulting from the misrepresentation are recoverable if the misrepresentation is a legal cause of them, as stated in § 548A. This means that they must be of a kind that might reasonably be expected to result from reliance upon the misrepresentation.

Illustrations

1. A induces B to purchase a bull by showing him a fraudulent pedigree representing it to be of pure Guernsey ancestry. Before discovering the falsity of A's representation, B breeds the bull to his Guernsey cows. B is entitled to recover not only the difference between the price paid and the actual value of the bull but also the loss sustained by the inferiority of the calves got by the bull upon his Guernsey cows.

2. The A Automobile Company puts upon the market cars in part made by itself, in part consisting of parts bought elsewhere and assembled in the cars. B sells to the A Company a quantity of roller bearings by misrepresenting them to be X roller bearings. The X bearings are standard and high class bearings. The bearings sold are in fact inferior and not made by the X Company. After these bearings have been assembled in a number of the cars their true character is discovered and the cars are sold at a lesser price because the bearings are not the X bearings. The A Company is entitled to recover the depreciation in the sales value of its cars because of the inferior bearings.

3. A sells to B, f.o.b. Detroit, a machine that he fraudulently misrepresents to be of great value in the manufacture of B's product. B pays the freight of the machine to his factory and expends money in preparing for its installation. On the arrival of the machine the falsity of the representation is discovered and the machine is found to be useless for the purpose for which it was bought. B is entitled to recover, as special damages, the freight that he has paid and the expense that he has incurred in the installation of the machine as well as for harm done to his raw material by the machine before its uselessness was discovered.

Comment on Subsection (1):

Comment e. Alternative remedies. One who is misled by the fraudulent representations of another may rescind the transaction induced by it. In this case, if the other accepts the subject matter of the transaction and returns the purchase price, the person defrauded can, of course, not recover the difference of the value between the thing received and the price paid for it. If the other on rescission refuses to receive the subject matter of the transaction, the person defrauded may dispose of it and maintain an action for the difference between the amount realized at the sale and the price paid by him. In either event the fact of rescission does not prevent the defrauded person from recovering from the other any loss that he has suffered in consequence of any use which, in reliance upon the misrepresentation, he has made of the article prior to his discovery of the fraud. If the subject matter of the transaction has been accepted by the other and the purchase price refunded the action is for that loss and for it only. If the other has refused to accept the subject matter of the sale and the person defrauded has sold it on his account, the loss resulting from its use is recoverable as part of the damages in addition to the difference between the price paid and the amount realized at the sale.

Comment f. If two persons make fraudulent misrepresentations to the same recipient neither one of which by itself is enough to cause the recipient of them to take the action which results in his loss, but which together are enough to do so, both or either of them is liable at the recipient's election. However, if the recipient by execution or otherwise realizes the amount of a judgment recovered against one of the two, he extinguishes the liability of the other. If only a part of the judgment against one of the two is realized, it operates as an extinguishment pro tanto of the liability of the other.

Comment on Subsection (2):

Comment g. Subsection (1) states the rules normally applicable to determine the measure of damages recoverable for a fraudulent misrepresentation in a tort action of deceit. If the plaintiff is content with these damages, he can always recover them. The rules stated in Subsection (1) are the logical rules for a tort action, since the purpose of a tort action is to compensate for loss sustained and to restore the plaintiff to his former position, and not to give him the benefit of any contract he has made with the defendant. When the plaintiff has not entered into any transaction with the defendant but has suffered his pecuniary loss through reliance upon the misrepresentation in dealing with a third person, these are the rules that must of necessity be applied.

When the plaintiff has made a bargain with the defendant, however, situations arise in which the rules stated in Subsection (1), and particularly that stated in Clause (a) of that Subsection, do not afford compensation that is just and satisfactory. If the value of what the plaintiff has received from the defendant is fully equal to the price he has paid for it or other value he has parted with and he has suffered no consequential damages, he may be unable to recover at all under the rules stated in Subsection (1). He may nevertheless be left with something acquired under the transaction which, because of the matter misrepresented, he does not want and cannot use. He may have lost the opportunity of acquiring a substitute at the same price and because of his commitments made or expenses incurred or for a variety of other reasons he may find rescission of the transaction and recovery of the price paid an unsatisfactory and insufficient remedy. In this case, under the rules stated in Subsection (1), the defrauding party would escape all liability.

The frequency of these situations has led the great majority of the American courts to adopt a broad general rule giving the plaintiff, in an action of deceit, the benefit of his bargain with the defendant in all cases, and making that the normal measure of recovery in actions of deceit.

The rule adopted in Subsection (2) does not take this position. One reason is that in occasional cases the out-of-pocket measure of damages will actually be more profitable and satisfactory from the point of view of the plaintiff than the benefit-of-the-bargain rule. This would be the case, for example, if the owner of valuable property were induced to sell it for less than its value by a representation that it had defects that made it practically worthless. On the basis of the representations, taken to be true, the seller would have sold worthless property for a substantial price and suffered no loss at all. Another and a more important, reason is that there are many cases in which the value that the plaintiff would have received if the bargain made with him had been performed cannot be proved with any satisfactory degree of certainty, because it must necessarily turn upon the estimated value of something non-existent and never in fact received. In this case the benefit-of-the-bargain harm to the plaintiff becomes mere speculation, and ordinary rules of the law of damages preclude the award.

Comment h. This Section therefore follows a compromise position adopted by some jurisdictions, giving the plaintiff the option of either the out-of-pocket or the benefit-of-the-bargain rule in any case in which the latter measure can be established by proof in accordance with the usual rules of certainty in damages. The comments and illustrations that follow deal with the more common situations in which the plaintiff may wish to elect to receive the benefit of his bargain.

Comment i. Value received equal to value paid. When the value of what the plaintiff has received under the transaction with the defendant is fully equal to the value of what he has parted with, he has suffered no out-of-pocket loss, and under the rule stated in Subsection (1), Clause (a), he could recover no damages. This would mean that the defrauding defendant has successfully accomplished his fraud and is still immune from an action in deceit. Even though the plaintiff may rescind the transaction and recover the price paid, the defendant is enabled to speculate on his fraud and still be assured that he can suffer no pecuniary loss. This is not justice between the parties. The admonitory function of the law requires that the defendant not escape liability and justifies allowing the plaintiff the benefit of his bargain.

Illustration

4.   A, seeking to sell land to B, fraudulently tells B that half of the land is covered with good pine timber. B buys the land from A for $5,000. There is no timber on the land but it is still worth $5,000. Competent evidence establishes that if the representation had been true the land, with the timber, would have been worth $9,000. B may recover $4,000 from A.

Comment j.   Thing received useless to plaintiff. Although the thing which the plaintiff has received under the transaction with the defendant may have substantial value and may even be sold to others, it may, because of the matter misrepresented, be entirely useless to the plaintiff for his own purposes. In this case, if the plaintiff is limited to his out-of-pocket loss, he is left with something on his hands that he does not want and cannot use and forced to credit its value to the defendant. To be restored to his original position he must be put to the trouble and expense of seeking a purchaser with all of the risk that he will not realize the value, and he must then begin again to seek the thing that he really wants. This becomes all the more clear when there is no immediate or ready market for the thing in question or when the plaintiff will be delayed and his purpose frustrated before he can obtain the thing which he originally bargained for.

Illustrations

5.   A, seeking to sell B a quantity of textiles, fraudulently tells B that they are of a kind and quality suitable for manufacture in B's mill. B buys the textiles for $10,000. Because of the matters misrepresented, they are in fact worth only $6,000. If they had been as represented they would have been worth $14,000. B is unable to use the textiles in his mill and finding a market for them will involve delay. B is entitled to recover $8,000 from A.

6.   The same facts as in Illustration 5, except that, although the textiles purchased can readily be resold for $6,000, B cannot obtain a supply of suitable textiles without a long delay. The same conclusion.

Comment k.   The preceding Comments and Illustrations are not intended to be exclusive. There may be many other types of situations in which particular circumstances may mean that just compensation cannot be given to the plaintiff under the out-of-pocket rule.

Comment l.   Benefit of the bargain. The damages necessary to give the plaintiff the benefit of the bargain that he has made with the defendant will depend, first of all, upon the nature of the bargain. If the defendant has undertaken to convey property of a certain description to the plaintiff, the plaintiff is entitled to an amount sufficient to give him the value of property of that description. If the defendant has undertaken merely to give the plaintiff accurate information about the property, he is entitled to a sufficient amount to place him in the position he would have occupied if he had had the information. If the defendant has undertaken merely to use care to give accurate information, the plaintiff is entitled only to an amount sufficient to compensate him by placing him in the position he would have occupied if that care had been used.

In order to give the plaintiff the benefit of the bargain, it is not necessary in all cases to give him the value of the thing as represented. He may be fully and fairly compensated if he is given the cost of making it as represented.

Illustrations

7.   A, seeking to sell a farm to B, fraudulently tells B that there is a well on the farm, with an ample supply of water. B buys the farm for $3,000. There is no well but there is water under the land, and a well can easily and quickly be dug for $250. With the well the land would be worth $5,000. B is entitled to recover $250 from A.

8.   A, seeking to acquire students for his dental college, fraudulently tells B that the college gives a good dental education and awards a degree. B takes the dental course, paying A $1,000. The dental education is a good one and worth $1,000, but at the end of the course B finds that the college is not licensed to award a degree, without which B cannot obtain a license to practice dentistry. B is entitled to recover from A the cost of attendance at a licensed dental college for the additional time necessary to obtain a degree.

Comment m.   Situations may arise in which, as a result of the misrepresentation, the plaintiff has been deprived of chattels of fluctuating market exchange value. In these cases the "highest replacement value" rule stated in § 927(1)(b) may be applied.

* * *

The frauds at play in *Reno* and *Morse* and other cases like them arise around contracts. But the fraudulent representations are not yet fully promises. The fraudsters in such cases undoubtedly undertake to do something—to sell shares of stock, for example—and their frauds are relevant to what they undertake to do—to the value of the shares to be sold. But the fraudulent misrepresentations are not themselves undertakings to do anything: if they are promises, then they are promises *that* (the underlying businesses have certain assets, for example, or operate in markets with certain properties) rather than promises *to* of the sort that conventionally constitute contracts. Relatedly, the fraudulent statements are not obviously or most naturally understandable as themselves directly generating obligations. It seems at least odd, for example, to understand the statements made by the defendants in *Reno* as in themselves establishing an obligation, in the defendants, to make them true, presumably by making their firms' assets, access to raw materials, and business prospects conform to the statements descriptions. That would have been impossible, after all; and so treating the representations as creating promissory or orthodox contractual obligation to make things so would violate the bedrock rule that "ought implies can." Perhaps the representations might be reinterpreted to promise the plaintiff not that the defendants' business was as described but rather that the plaintiffs would receive the value of the business as described. Something like this thought presumably animates the *Morse* opinion and also the Restatement. But that approach stumbles over the fact that the defendants' statements, in such cases, as a matter of fact refer to a particular business and not to its generic value. Thoughts like these drive opinions like *Reno*. And while it may be that they produce unappealing and even wrong-headed results, they nevertheless seem accurately to characterize the backdrops against which the cases arise.

The best justification for giving contract remedies in the context of ordinary commercial fraud may thus be purely result-oriented.[17] Little is gained, and more is lost, by attempting to recast the fact patterns so that they fall outside of tort and within contract's core. The Restatement seems to take this view. Subsection 549(2) of the Restatement (Second) of Torts states that "[t]he recipient of a fraudulent misrepresentation in a business transaction is also entitled to recover additional damages sufficient to give him the benefit of his contract with the maker, if these damages are proved with reasonable certainty." As the comments observe, this is an exceptional rule. The rules "normally applicable to determine the measure of damages recoverable for a fraudulent misrepresentation" in a tort action are fixed, by subsection (1) of Section 549, at reliance damages (approximately). Restatement (Second) of Torts § 549 cmt.[g]. This reflects "the logical rules for a tort action, since the purpose of a tort action is to compensate for loss sustained and to restore the plaintiff to his former position, and not to give him the benefit of any contract he has made with the defendant." Restatement (Second) of Torts § 549 cmt.[g]. The special rules of § 549 have been adopted only because the contractual settings of many frauds threaten to leave plaintiffs subject to ordinary tort rules without a meaningful remedy and, indeed, worse off than plaintiffs whose counterparties, in their bargains, have breached innocently rather than fraudulently. Giving contract-like remedies for frauds committed in contract-like settings addresses this injustice. But where frauds do not implicate contract-relations, for example, "[w]hen the plaintiff has not entered into any transaction with the defendant but has suffered his pecuniary loss through reliance upon the misrepresentation in dealing with a third person," then

---

17. Indeed, this solution has already appeared in these materials. It is the driving theme of *Plate v. Durst*. It is also one of the themes of *Izadi*.

the reliance based remedy rules "are the rules that must of necessity be applied." Restatement (Second) of Torts § 549 cmt.[g].

Another set of cases involving commercial fraud is different in this respect and falls more directly and fully within contract's conventional scope. In these cases, which involve what might be called false or lying promises, a breach constitutes the promise (and not extrinsic facts connected to the promise's value) as itself a lie. The falsehoods involved in these frauds concern not just a promise *that* but rather directly reflect the content of a fraudulent promise *to*. As one commentator has observed, "[p]romises are statements, whatever else they may involve," so that "[o]rdinary promises both state an intention of the speaker, and make an assertion about his future action."[18] The promisor necessarily states that he intends to obligate himself to perform. He probably also states that he intends to perform. A false promise—a promise whose breach is anticipated and perhaps even intended—is thus a lie with respect to some subset of these intentions.[19]

The law recognizes this possibility, through the tort *promissory fraud*.[20] An action for promissory fraud, being a species of the broader genus fraud, sounds nominally in tort. But limiting promissory fraud according to the conventional logic of tort, and in particular limiting recovery to tort-like reliance damages, would reproduce the incongruities just observed, only in still starker form. Accordingly, promissory fraud is nowadays treated, by the law, in a fashion that acknowledges and indeed embraces its connection to contract. The following materials make this clear.

Restatement (Second) of Torts

§ 530 Misrepresentation Of Intention

(1) A representation of the maker's own intention to do or not to do a particular thing is fraudulent if he does not have that intention.

(2) A representation of the intention of a third person is fraudulent under the conditions stated in § 526.

Comment on Subsection (1):

Comment a. The state of a man's mind is as much a fact as the state of his digestion. A false representation of the actor's own intention to do or

---

18. Páll S. Árdal, *And That's a Promise*, 18 PHIL. Q. 225, 225–26 (1968).

19. Can a lying promisor lie about his intention to obligate himself (as opposed just about his intentions or capacity to perform)? This is not so clear. For a promisor to lie about his intention to obligate himself he would have to intend not to obligate himself even as he intentionally acts in ways that he knows will create an obligation. He will thus have to intend what he knows to be impossible. It is not clear that such an intention can be formed.

20. For a more elaborate treatment of promissory fraud, see IAN AYERS & GREGORY KLASS, INSINCERE PROMISES: THE LAW OF MISREPRESENTED INTENT (2005).

not to do a particular thing is actionable if the statement is reasonably to be interpreted as expressing a firm intention and not merely as one of those "puffing" statements which are so frequent and so little regarded in negotiations for a business transaction as to make it unjustifiable for the recipient to rely upon them. As to the rules that determine whether the recipient may justifiably rely upon the statement of intention as an inducement to enter into the transaction, see § 544.

Comment b.   To be actionable the statement of the maker's own intention must be fraudulent, which is to say that he must in fact not have the intention stated. If he does not have it, he must of course be taken to know that he does not have it. If the statement is honestly made and the intention in fact exists, one who acts in justifiable reliance upon it cannot maintain an action of deceit if the maker for any reason changes his mind and fails or refuses to carry his expressed intention into effect. If the recipient wishes to have legal assurance that the intention honestly entertained will be carried out, he must see that it is expressed in the form of an enforceable contract, and his action must be on the contract.

Comment c.   Misrepresentation of intention to perform an agreement. The rule stated in this Section finds common application when the maker misrepresents his intention to perform an agreement made with the recipient. The intention to perform the agreement may be expressed but it is normally merely to be implied from the making of the agreement. Since a promise necessarily carries with it the implied assertion of an intention to perform it follows that a promise made without such an intention is fraudulent and actionable in deceit under the rule stated in § 525. This is true whether or not the promise is enforceable as a contract. If it is enforceable, the person misled by the representation has a cause of action in tort as an alternative at least, and perhaps in some instances in addition to his cause of action on the contract. If the agreement is not enforceable as a contract, as when it is without consideration, the recipient still has, as his only remedy, the action in deceit under the rule stated in § 525. The same is true when the agreement is oral and made unenforceable by the statute of frauds, or when it is unprovable and so unenforceable under the parol evidence rule. The tort action may have other advantages, as when it is subject to a longer statute of limitations. In all of these cases, it is immaterial to the tort liability that the damages recoverable are identical with, or substantially the same as, those which could have been recovered in an action of contract if the promise were enforceable.

Comment d.   Proof of intention not to perform agreement. The intention that is necessary to make the rule stated in this Section applicable is the intention of the promisor when the agreement was entered into. The intention of the promisor not to perform an enforceable or unenforceable agreement cannot be established solely by proof of its nonperformance, nor does his failure to perform the agreement throw upon him the burden of showing that his nonperformance was due to reasons which operated after the agreement was entered into. The intention may be shown by any other evidence that sufficiently indicates its existence, as, for example, the certainty that he would not be in funds to carry out his promise.

Comment on Subsection (2):

Comment e. When the intention misrepresented is that of a third person, it stands on the same footing as any other representation of an existing fact. The maker is subject to liability in an action of deceit only if the misrepresentation is fraudulent, as that term is defined in § 526. If it is honestly made there is no liability in deceit, although there may still be liability in an action for negligence under the rule stated in § 552, or strict liability under the rule stated in § 552C. On the other hand, if the statement is made when the maker knows that he does not have the basis for knowledge or belief concerning the intent of the third person that is professed by his assertion, the statement is fraudulent under the rule stated in § 526.

Restatement (Second) of Contracts

§ 171   When Reliance on an Assertion of Intention is Not Justified

(1) To the extent that an assertion is one of intention only, the recipient is not justified in relying on it if in the circumstances a misrepresentation of intention is consistent with reasonable standards of dealing.

(2) If it is reasonable to do so, the promisee may properly interpret a promise as an assertion that the promisor intends to perform the promise.

Comments & Illustrations

Comment a.   Assertions of intention. A statement as to the intention of either the maker or a third person is an assertion of a fact, his state of mind, just as a statement of his opinion is such an assertion. It is therefore a misrepresentation if that state of mind is not as asserted. However, the truth of a statement as to a person's intention depends on his intention at the time that the statement is made and is not affected if he subsequently, for any reason, changes his mind. In order for reliance on an assertion of intention to be justified, the recipient's expectation that the maker's intention will be carried out must be reasonable. If he knows facts that will make it impossible for the maker to carry out his intention, then his reliance cannot be justified. See Illustration 1. As with statements of opinion (§ 169), not all statements of intention are to be taken seriously. In some situations, courts have accorded the maker considerable latitude in misrepresenting his intention, for the reason that such statements are generally regarded as unreliable. A court will take account of all the circumstances, including any usage and the relationship of the parties. A prospective buyer of land may, for example, misrepresent his intended use of the land in order to conceal from the seller some special advantage that the buyer will derive from its purchase, which if known to the seller, would cause him to demand a higher price. The contract is not voidable on this ground if the court concludes that, in all the circumstances, the buyer's misrepresentation is not contrary to reasonable standards of dealing. See Illustration 2. The result will ordinarily be different, however, if the prospective buyer misrepresents his intended use so as to conceal from the seller some harm to the seller's other interests that will be caused if the buyer carries out his actual intention. See Illustration 3.

Illustrations

1. A, the owner of a real estate development, seeking to induce B to make a contract to buy a lot in it, tells B that he intends to construct a golf course in the development. A has no such intention. B is induced by A's statement to make the contract. The contract is voidable by B. If, however, B knows that the terrain is not suitable for a golf course, that there is not enough land for it, and that it could only be constructed by purchase of a large quantity of additional land quite beyond A's means, B's reliance is not justified, and the contract is not voidable by B.

2. A, seeking to induce B to make a contract to sell a tract of land, tells B that he intends to hold the tract as an investment. A intends instead to combine the tract with others as part of a large development but declines to tell B this in order to prevent B from asking a higher price. B is induced by A's statement to make the contract. If the court concludes that, in all the circumstances, A's statement was not contrary to reasonable standards of dealing, the contract is not voidable by B.

3. A, seeking to induce B to make a contract to sell a tract of land, tells B that he intends to use the tract for the construction of a residence. A intends instead to use it for the construction of an industrial building but declines to tell B this because B owns an adjacent tract that will be adversely affected if A carries out his real intention. B is induced by A's non-disclosure to make the contract. The contract is voidable by B.

Comment b. A promise as a statement of intention. It is ordinarily reasonable for the promisee to infer from the making of a promise that the promisor intends to perform it. If, therefore, the promise is made with the intention of not performing it, this implied assertion is false and is a misrepresentation. The promise itself need not be made in words but may be inferred from conduct or even supplied by law. Nor does it need to be a legally enforceable promise. The promisor's intention not to perform his promise cannot be established merely by proof of its non-performance. Nevertheless, the probable inability of a party, at the time the contract is made, to perform it, for instance the insolvency of one who buys land, is evidence bearing on the question of intent not to perform. If the promisor knows or should know that he cannot at least substantially perform his promise, this is strong although not conclusive evidence of an intent not to carry it out. (The effect of a buyer's misrepresentation of solvency or of intent to pay in the case of a contract for the sale of goods is the subject of the special rule of Uniform Commercial Code § 2–702(2).) If a party is entitled to avoid the contract on this ground, he may do so immediately and need not await the time for performance. The application of the rule stated in Subsection (2) does not turn on whether the promisor is the offeror or the offeree. When the parties exchange promises as consideration for each other, each promise is properly regarded as the inducement for the other. Therefore, if the offeree has no intention of performing his promise when he accepts, the contract is voidable by the offeror on the ground that his promise was made in reliance on that of the offeree. See Comment *a* to § 167. As with other assertions, the recipient's reliance must be justified. It is not justified if the promisor has disclosed his intention not to perform or if performance is known not to be within his control.

Illustration

4. A, seeking to induce B to make a contract to have work done on his house, and to make a part payment of $1,000, promises to do the work for a stated price. A does not intend to perform the contract. B is induced by A's promise to make the contract and the part payment. B may interpret A's promise as an assertion of his intention to perform. This assertion is a fraudulent misrepresentation, and the contract is voidable by B.

Hudson v. Insteel Industries, Inc.

United States Court of Appeals for the 6th Circuit, 2001.
5 Fed. Appx. 378.

■ COLE, CIRCUIT JUDGE. Defendants–Appellants Insteel Industries, Inc. ("Insteel"); Insteel Wire Products Company; and H.O. Woltz, III (collectively referred to herein as "Defendants"), appeal the jury verdict for Plaintiff–Appellee John Hudson ("Hudson") in this action for age discrimination in employment and promissory fraud. Defendants assign error to: (1) the district court's refusal to grant Defendants' motion, pursuant to FED. R. CIV. P. 50, for judgment as a matter of law, or, in the alternative, a new trial, with respect to Hudson's age discrimination claim; (2) the district court's refusal to grant Defendants' motion, pursuant to FED. R. CIV. P. 50, for judgment as a matter of law, or, in the alternative, a new trial, with respect to Hudson's promissory fraud claim; and (3) the district court's refusal to grant Defendants' motion, pursuant to FED. R. CIV. P. 59, to amend the judgment, with respect to the jury's $301,500 award to Hudson on his promissory fraud claim, which award Defendants argue was duplicative and excessive. For the reasons that follow, we AFFIRM the order of the district court in its entirety.

I. BACKGROUND

Insteel Industries, Inc. is a manufacturer of various wire products. Its subsidiary, Insteel Wire Products Company, operates two adjacent manufacturing facilities located in Gallatin, Tennessee: the Tennessee Wire Plant and the PC Strand Plant. In 1992, Hudson, then 48 years old, began negotiations with Insteel's president and chief executive officer, H.O.

Woltz, III, to use his business plan for construction of a plant. Some months later, in August 1992, Insteel decided to use Hudson's plan for construction of a PC strand plant in Gallatin, Tennessee.

A.   Pre–Employment Negotiations

Woltz offered Hudson a position with Insteel as general manager, responsible for the development of Insteel's PC strand operation, which Hudson agreed to accept if Insteel provided him with an ownership interest in the venture. By letter dated July 6, 1992, Woltz offered Hudson an "employment arrangement," part of which included an "equity participation" plan. Hudson rejected Insteel's initial proposal for various reasons, principally because Insteel refused to offer him employment for a term of seven years. Hudson believed that a minimum of five years was necessary for the plant to generate significant profits.

By letter dated September 9, 1992, Woltz provided Hudson with information concerning Hudson's potential employment with Insteel. Hudson claims that the letter was merely another proposal with terms to be accepted or rejected by Hudson; Woltz contends that the letter memorialized the terms agreed upon at a September 4, 1992, meeting. Hudson alleges that he accepted Insteel's offer to hire him to implement the PC strand plan in exchange for: (1) a term of seven years' employment, (2) 5% of the profits for seven years, and (3) a position as the general manager of the PC Strand Plant. Insteel denies that any such agreement was ever reached.

B.   Employment Relationship

Hudson began work with Insteel on September 28, 1992. When he requested the written employment contract reflecting the terms upon which he and Insteel had agreed, he was allegedly told that it was not yet ready. Hudson claims that he was not provided the final contract until Woltz called him into his office to sign it. The document, entitled "Supplemental Profit Sharing Plan ('SPSP')," according to Hudson, memorialized the terms to which the parties had agreed prior to Hudson's acceptance of employment with Insteel. Insteel disputes that the SPSP constituted an employment contract-it was precisely what it purported to be, *i.e.,* the terms of the profit-sharing plan agreed upon by the parties—and argues that even if the SPSP were an employment contract, nowhere in it is there a term that provides that Hudson could be terminated only for cause or for serious misconduct. Hudson and Wagner signed the SPSP on October 28, 1992.

Hudson, as general manager, directed the construction of the PC Strand Plant, which was completed and operational by January 1994, and described in Insteel's annual report as "a world class facility" that became "profitable more quickly than any other new venture ever undertaken by Insteel." Woltz, pleased with Hudson's performance in overseeing the construction of the PC Strand Plant, promoted Hudson to General Manager of Tennessee Operations in January 1995, in which capacity, Hudson was responsible for the management of both plants.

In an August 1995 evaluation, Executive Vice President Dale Duensing praised Hudson's management, leadership, and organizational skills, gave Hudson a "superior" rating—the highest rating possible—and recommended a five-percent pay increase for Hudson. Although Insteel alleged that during the latter part of 1995, and throughout 1996, the Tennessee Wire Plant demonstrated a lack of improvement, as indicated by so-called "key performance measurements," Hudson argued that during this period, upper-level management never criticized his performance and in fact was complimentary of his work. Duensing himself testified that he called Hudson on two occasions to congratulate him for the Tennessee Wire Plant's performance. On March 24, 1997, after discussions between Duensing and Woltz about the Tennessee Wire Plant's continued lack of improvement, Woltz terminated Hudson and replaced him with Jim Herman, a man in his thirties. Hudson was 53 years old. Pursuant to the SPSP, Insteel paid Hudson $53,000 in profits.

Hudson brought claims against Defendants alleging age discrimination in violation of the Age Discrimination in Employment Act ("ADEA") and the Tennessee Human Rights Act ("THRA"), breach of contract, and promissory fraud. The matter was tried before a jury. Defendants filed a motion for judgment as a matter of law at the conclusion of Hudson's case, and again at the end of trial; Hudson filed a motion for judgment as a matter of law at the conclusion of Defendants' case. The district court denied both parties' motions and submitted the case to the jury, which returned a verdict in favor of Hudson on the age discrimination and promissory fraud claims, and in favor of Defendants on the breach of contract claim. The jury awarded Hudson $57,575 in back pay and $150,000 in lost profits under the SPSP for his age discrimination claims, and $301,500 in compensatory damages for his promissory fraud claim. Defendants filed the motions that are at issue in the instant appeal, which were denied by the district court.

3.   Promissory Fraud Claim

Actions for promissory fraud, once disfavored under Tennessee Law, are now recognized in cases where a plaintiff can successfully demonstrate: (1) that the defendant made an intentional misrepresentation with respect to a material fact, *see Keith v. Murfreesboro Livestock Mkt., Inc.,* 780 S.W.2d 751 (Tenn.Ct.App.1989); (2) that the representation was made "knowingly" or "without belief in its truth," or "recklessly" without regard to its truth, *Tartera v. Palumbo,* 224 Tenn. 262 (1970), *and* the misrepresentation "embod[ied] a promise of future action without the present intention to carry out the promise," *Keith,* 780 S.W.2d at 754; (3) that the plaintiff reasonably relied on the misrepresentation, *Holt v. American Progressive Life Ins. Co.,* 731 S.W.2d 923, 927 (Tenn.Ct.App.1987); and (4) that the plaintiff suffered damage, *see id.*

a.   Intentional Misrepresentation

Hudson argues that the jury had before it ample evidence to support its finding that Insteel committed promissory fraud. The jury heard testimony that Woltz, on behalf of Insteel, agreed to employ Hudson for a seven-year period and that Insteel agreed to the terms of a seven-year profit-sharing plan. Defendants contend that the jury, as evidenced by its refusal to find for Defendants on the breach of employment claim, apparently rejected Hudson's assertion that Defendants knowingly agreed to such a contract. In the absence of a "meeting of the minds" of the parties, Defendants argue, there necessarily could not have been an intentional misrepresentation that would support a claim of promissory fraud. Hudson argued persuasively—and the district court, in denying Defendants' motion, agreed—that there is no inconsistency in the jury's finding for Hudson on the promissory fraud claim, yet not finding for him on his breach of contract claim. On the basis of the evidence before it, the jury could have reasonably concluded that Defendants misrepresented to Hudson their true intent concerning Hudson's employment and his participation in the SPSP.

b.   Present Intent to Defraud

Intent to defraud is a question of fact. *See Keith,* 780 S.W.2d at 754. A plaintiff must put forward competent and material evidence of an intent to defraud to state successfully a claim for promissory fraud. *See Fowler v. Happy Goodman Family,* 575 S.W.2d 496, 499 (Tenn.1978). In no case may fraud ever be presumed or an inference of fraud made from "circumstances that equally permit reasonable inferences of non-fraudulent conduct." *American Cable Corp. v. ACI Mgmt., Inc.,* No. M1997–00280–COA–R3–CV, 2000 WL 1291265, *4 (Tenn.Ct.App.). A plaintiff must demonstrate that the statement of intention was false when made "by evidence other than subsequent failure to keep the promise or subjective surmise or impression of the promisee." *Farmers & Merchants Bank,* 664 S.W.2d at 80–81.

The jury heard Woltz's deposition testimony that he never intended to enter into an "employment contract" with Hudson. Hudson argues that this evidence, when considered in conjunction with the following, created a factual dispute that the jury could reasonably have resolved in favor of Hudson: (1) the testimony of Hudson and Wagner that Woltz did in fact agree to an employment contract for a term of seven years; (2) Insteel's use of Woltz's father, an attorney, to draft the employment agreement instead of its outside law firm, which ordinarily provided Insteel's legal services; (3) Insteel's removal of the boilerplate language found in other Insteel documents explicitly stating Insteel's policy of not entering into employment contracts; (4) Woltz's statement to Hudson, "We [Insteel] will stand by our word"; (5) Woltz's statement to Hudson, "The deal [is] off if you consult an attorney"; and (6) Insteel's use in the SPSP of the phrases "[t]he term of this [profit-sharing] plan shall be for seven years" and "[t]he benefits ... under this Supplemental Profit Sharing Plan are one hundred percent (100%) vested."

Defendants, in opposition to Hudson's claims, make essentially two arguments: (1) a plaintiff cannot support a claim of promissory fraud by pointing to nothing more than the promisor's subsequent failure to keep that promise, *see Farmers & Merchants Bank,* 664 S.W.2d at 80; and (2) because the jury at trial found that no employment contract existed between the parties, then the employment relationship between Hudson and Insteel was necessarily one at will, which could be terminated by either party at any time, even assuming that one or both parties "promised" to create a relationship for a term of years. Defendants' first argument is merely a challenge to the sufficiency of the evidence underlying Hudson's promissory fraud claim, which we reject in light of the ample evidence proffered by Hudson on this question. Defendants' second argument is disposed of by *Lee v. Hippodrome Oldsmobile, Inc.,* No. 01A01–9705–CV–00202, 1997 WL 629951 (Tenn.Ct.App. Oct.14, 1997), which held that, Tennessee's employment-at-will doctrine notwithstanding, a promissory fraud claim may go forward, in the absence of an employment contract, where "an employer makes an offer of long-term, permanent employment with no present intention of keeping its promises." *Id.* at *2.

Hudson's promissory fraud claim turns on whether he adequately proved at trial that Insteel, at the time it entered into an employment relationship with Hudson, had no intent to perform its promises. In light of the abundant evidence on this point, a jury could have reasonably inferred that Insteel intended to defraud Hudson.

c. Reasonable Reliance

Hudson argues that his reliance on the promises made by Defendants was reasonable in light of the confidentiality agreement signed by the parties in May 1993, whereby Defendants agreed not to reveal the contents of Hudson's PC Strand plan if the joint venture between the parties failed to materialize. Thus, Hudson suggests, he had nothing to lose by relying upon Defendants' representations. A jury could have found that Hudson's reliance on these alleged representations was warranted in light of: (1) the confidentiality agreement; (2) Woltz's statement "We will stand by our word"; and (3) Hudson's pre-employment dealings with Woltz.

d. Damage

Hudson contends that he suffered damage at the hands of Defendants inasmuch as he presented and implemented the plan for construction of the PC Strand Plant and oversaw its production and development into a successful, profitable venture, yet failed to reap any attendant financial benefits. He points to the fact that he was discharged shortly after the plant began to generate substantial revenue and after he began to accrue substantial amounts of money under the SPSP. It is undisputed that if Hudson had continued his employment with Insteel, he would have been entitled to additional profits under the SPSP, and thus, a jury could have reasonably concluded that Insteel's failure to maintain its employment relationship with Hudson caused him harm.

e. Conclusion

In light of the foregoing, we find that judgment as a matter of law on this claim was inappropriate. The district court properly sent this issue to a jury. Accordingly, we AFFIRM the district court's denial of Defendants' Rule 50 motion.

B. Rule 59 Motion

1. Standard of Review

We review a trial court's denial of a motion to alter or amend the judgment, pursuant to FED. R. CIV. P. 59(e), for an abuse of discretion. *See Wilkins v. Baptist Healthcare Sys., Inc.,* 150 F.3d 609, 613 (6th Cir.1998).

2. Analysis

At trial, the district court instructed the jury that if it found for Hudson on his ADEA claim, then it should award Hudson back pay in an amount "equal to the wages and benefits that he would have received from the defendants had he not been discharged from the time that he was discharged until the date of trial," deducting from this sum an amount equal to the total wages earned by plaintiff from other employment during this period. The district court also noted that Hudson was entitled to "other lost compensation," which included both the amount he would have received from the SPSP, and damages for any emotional or physical injuries suffered by Hudson. The jury awarded Hudson $57,575 in back pay, $150,000 in lost compensation under the SPSP, and no damages for emotional or physical injury. Defendants do not challenge this award. With respect to Hudson's promissory fraud claim, the district court instructed the jury that the amount of recovery for Hudson's promissory fraud claim was to be the benefit of the bargain between Hudson and Insteel, which constitutes "the amounts of compensation, benefits, and profit sharing that the plaintiff would have received if he had continued to work for Insteel until the date upon which the plaintiff's employment contract, if any, was due to expire." The jury awarded Hudson $301,500 in compensatory damages for his promissory fraud claim. Defendants challenge this award as duplicative and excessive.

It is well-established that when a party is entitled to recovery of the same damages under separate causes of action, the trial court may allow recovery only once. *See General Tel. Co. v. EEOC,* 446 U.S. 318, 332 (1980) ("[T]he courts can and should preclude double recovery by an individual."). It is undisputed that the damages award for Hudson's ADEA claim included damages for lost pay and lost SPSP earnings, both of which were also compensated by the jury's damages award for Hudson's promissory fraud claim. In fact, the district court specifically instructed the jury that any award for lost profits as compensation for age discrimination was to be calculated from the time that Hudson was terminated (March of 1997) until the date of trial (April of 1999), and any award for lost profits as compensation for promissory fraud was to be calculated for a period of seven years, from October 1, 1992, to September 30, 1999. At a minimum, it appears that Hudson might have received a double recovery for the period beginning March of 1997 and ending April of 1999 for lost pay and lost SPSP earnings, which were apparently compensated both in the jury's award for age discrimination *and* in its award for promissory fraud.

The jury's award, however, did not exceed that which could have reasonably been awarded in the absence of any double recovery. *See Farber v. Massillon Bd. of Educ.*, 917 F.2d 1391, 1395 (6th Cir.1990) (noting that a trial court may in its discretion remit a verdict when, after reviewing all evidence in the light most favorable to the awardee, it determines that the verdict is excessive or the result of passion, bias, or prejudice). The district court instructed the jury that Hudson was entitled to receive only the benefit of the bargain in damages for his promissory fraud claim. The jury found that the benefit of the bargain amounted to $301,500. That amount, coupled with the $207,575 ADEA award ($57,575 in lost pay and $150,000 in lost SPSP earnings), fell well short of the $690,000 that a jury could have reasonably awarded Hudson for lost SPSP earnings alone. We are mindful of the difficult and necessarily speculative task that the jury had before it in determining future profits. Its verdict, however, did not exceed "the maximum damages that the jury reasonably could find to be compensatory for [Hudson's] loss." *Id.* at 1395. Accordingly, we do not find that the district court abused its discretion in denying Defendants' motion.

III.   CONCLUSION

Accordingly, we AFFIRM the district court's denial of Defendants' motion for judgment as a matter of law, or, in the alternative, a new trial as to Hudson's ADEA and THRA claims; we AFFIRM the district court's denial of Defendants' motion for judgment as a matter of law, or, in the alternative, a new trial as to Hudson's promissory fraud claim; and we AFFIRM the district court's denial of Defendants' motion to amend the judgment, with respect to the jury's award.

* * *

Promissory fraud arises when a person makes a promise with the contemporaneous intent not to perform it. It is thus a species of fraud—concerning the actions and intentions to which promissory representations refer—and tort law, as the Restatement makes clear, treats it as such.

In some cases—roughly, where the lying promise was nevertheless successful at establishing a contract by the orthodox path of offer, acceptance, and consideration—a plaintiff alleging promissory fraud might also bring an action for breach of contract. This possibility—that a promissory fraud might also be a breach of contract—puts tort and contract into contact with each other and threatens once again to produce the unpalatable results discussed in connection with fraud more generally. The gap between tort and contract remedies entails that if the fraud remedy were limited to reliance, in the usual way of tort, then many plaintiffs would fare worse, and fraudsters would fare better, where promissory fraud cases are adjudicated as a fraud than where they are adjudicated as ordinary breaches of contract. This result would hold in spite of the fact that fraud involves intentional wrongdoing whereas breach of contract, because it is a strict liability claim, requires no blameworthiness at all. Nor is this merely an academic possibility. In some instances, defendants might be able to avoid contract by successfully arguing fraud. They might, for example, argue that the misrepresentations at the root of their plaintiffs' claims were oral and hence excluded from any contract claim by the requirements of writings imposed by the statute of frauds. Or they might employ the parol evidence rule to argue that the statements, because they contradict a writing, cannot belong to the contract.[21] Plaintiffs, by contrast, might argue that the relevant representations may be divined by properly interpreting a writing that their defendants unquestionably produced in good faith. This way of proceeding—in which plaintiffs argue in effect that defendants are innocent and defendants argue that they are guilty—is patently absurd.

Hudson illustrates both the problem and the way in which contemporary law resolves it. Following several months of complex negotiations, the plaintiff in *Hudson* began working for the defendant, managing a manufacturing plant owned by the defendant and constructed according to a business plan that the plaintiff had provided. Although the plaintiff unquestionably managed the plant, the parties took different views concerning the nature of the legal relation between them. In particular, the plaintiff alleged that he worked pursuant to a seven year employment contract, under which he could be fired only for good cause, while the defendant asserted that the agreement established only a profit-sharing scheme and not an employment relation and, moreover, that even if an employment relation had been established, the plaintiff worked as an employee at will, who might be fired at any time, including without good cause. After roughly five years, during which the plaintiff had received positive performance evaluations, the defendant fired the plaintiff and replaced him with a much younger manager. The plaintiff sued, alleging violations of state and federal statutes prohibiting age discrimination, breach of contract, and promissory fraud. The case was tried to a jury, which found for the plaintiff on the age discrimination and promissory fraud claims but for the defendant on the contract claim.

The case nicely illustrates the intertwining of contract and tort. Although the jury never explained itself, its decision in favor of the defendant on the contract claim presumably reflected a conclusion either that the parties' minds never met sufficiently to establish an employment contract or that the best interpretation of a contract that was agreed gave the defendant the right to fire the plaintiff at will. This conclusion however, did not foreclose the jury's finding for the plaintiff with respect to promissory fraud. As the appellate court noted (although perhaps not in the clearest language), a claim for promissory fraud may survive the failure of a contract claim as long as a plaintiff-employee demonstrates that a defen-

---

21. The parol evidence rule—a rule of contract construction—will be taken up systematically in the next chapter. The possibility that it might figure in the context of promissory fraud is contemplated by the Restatement. See RESTATEMENT (SECOND) OF TORTS § 530 cmt [c].

dant-employer represented an intention to retain the plaintiff on terms (or for a period) even as he in fact intended to do otherwise. The mere fact that the employer's representations failed for technical reasons to establish an employment contract does not foreclose that they might intentionally and materially misrepresent its promissory intentions or that an employee might reasonable and detrimentally rely on them. As the court concluded, "[o]n the basis of the evidence before it, the jury could have reasonably concluded that Defendants misrepresented to Hudson their true intent concerning Hudson's employment and his participation in the [profit-sharing plan]." This possibility should not in the end come as a surprise. A typical promise reports both an intent to obligate and also an intention to perform (and a prediction that performance will follow). Infirmities concerning the intent to obligate—or other technical difficulties—may prevent a contract from arising. But these infirmities do not undo the representations concerning intent to perform and the likelihood of performance. And those representations may thus be fraudulent even though a contract fails.

Once liability for promissory fraud was established, the *Hudson* court considered the appropriate remedy. The court regarded the basic doctrinal issue as uncontroversial: the proper remedy for promissory fraud, the court observed, would give Hudson "the benefit of the bargain between Hudson and Insteel." The only complications concerned the interaction between the fraud remedy and the remedies awarded for the age discrimination claim, and in particular whether an overlap between these remedies entailed that the jury had double-counted the plaintiff's damages.

Promissory fraud is fraud that does not just occur in connection with a contract but takes as its subject the contract itself. It is fraud *about* the fraudster's contractual intentions and actions. So when the modern law of promissory fraud underwrites liability *for promises*, tort law directly acquires at least some of the features of promissory liability and hence of contract proper. In particular, it is forward-looking and operates through the legally ordered vindication of the promise.

Perhaps, then, promissory fraud constitutes the advanced guard of a broader assault on contract generally, by tort generally. Perhaps breach of contract in general might be best explained as a kind of fraud. Certainly people commonly associate promise-breaking with lying. No less than Immanuel Kant, when illustrating the wrong of breach, chose as his example a lying promise and hence a case of promissory fraud. He imagined that a person borrows money that he knows he will be unable to repay, and that he intends not to repay, but nevertheless (in order to procure the loan) gives a firm promise to repay the money within a fixed time.[22] Kant himself never says expressly why his lying promise is a lie in the ordinary sense at all. But he presumably treats it, on the model of promissory fraud just rehearsed, as a lie about the promisor's intention to repay the loan.

This opens up the possibility that contract obligation might be just a special case of the more general obligations associated with fraud—special

---

22. IMMANUEL KANT, GROUNDWORK OF THE METAPHYSIC OF MORALS *422 (1785).

because it is simply fraud obligation applied to the narrow subset of cases in which the fraudulent misrepresentations concern contractual intent.

That possibility is not realized in the law, however. There are at least two respects in which liability for fraud is substantially narrower than contract liability: first, liability for fraud requires that the defendant possessed a specific intent to deceive (sometimes called *scienter*); and second, liability for fraud arises only insofar as the plaintiff in fact relied on the defendant's intentionally false statements. Both restrictions on the tort may be read off the face of a conventional statement of the elements of common law fraud.

16.1.A.1.a   Scienter

Begin by considering the requirement of *scienter*, as elaborated by the following materials.

Restatement (Second) of Torts

§ 526   Conditions Under Which Misrepresentation Is Fraudulent (Scienter)

A misrepresentation is fraudulent if the maker

(a) knows or believes that the matter is not as he represents it to be,

(b) does not have the confidence in the accuracy of his representation that he states or implies, or

(c) knows that he does not have the basis for his representation that he states or implies.

Comment:

Comment a.   The word "fraudulent" is here used as referring solely to the maker's knowledge of the untrue character of his representation. This element of the defendant's conduct frequently is called "scienter" by the courts. Intent and expectation of influencing the other's conduct by the misrepresentation are dealt with in §§ 531–536 as a separate and distinct element necessary to liability under the rule stated in § 525.

Comment b.   This Section states merely the rules that determine whether a misrepresentation is fraudulently made. In order that a misrepresentation even though fraudulently made, may be actionable, it is necessary that the other conditions stated in § 525 exist. The rules that deal with the further conditions necessary to liability under § 525, namely, the maker's purpose to induce the recipient to act in reliance upon the misrepresentation and the recipient's justifiable reliance upon the misrepresentation are stated below, the former in §§ 531–536, the latter in §§ 537–545. The rules that deal with causation of the pecuniary loss are stated in §§ 546–548, and in § 549A.

Comment on Clause (a):

Comment c. If the maker of the representation knows the matter to be otherwise than as represented, the fraudulent character of the misrepresentation is clear. However, knowledge of falsity is not essential; it is enough that he believes the representation to be false.

Comment d. The fact that the misrepresentation is one that a man of ordinary care and intelligence in the maker's situation would have recognized as false is not enough to impose liability upon the maker for a fraudulent misrepresentation under the rule stated in this Section, but it is evidence from which his lack of honest belief may be inferred. So, too, it is a matter to be taken into account in determining the credibility of the defendant if he testifies that he believed his representation to be true. For the rules that determine the liability of the maker of a representation that he believes to be true, but which through his negligence is misleading, see § 552. As to strict liability for innocent misrepresentation, see § 552C.

Comment on Clause (b):

Comment e. In order that a misrepresentation may be fraudulent it is not necessary that the maker know the matter is not as represented. Indeed, it is not necessary that he should even believe this to be so. It is enough that being conscious that he has neither knowledge nor belief in the existence of the matter he chooses to assert it as a fact. Indeed, since knowledge implies a firm conviction, a misrepresentation of a fact so made as to assert that the maker knows it, is fraudulent if he is conscious that he has merely a belief in its existence and recognizes that there is a chance, more or less great, that the fact may not be as it is represented. This is often expressed by saying that fraud is proved if it is shown that a false representation has been made without belief in its truth or recklessly, careless of whether it is true or false.

Comment on Clause (c):

Comment f. A representation of fact may be expressly stated to be based upon the maker's personal knowledge of the fact in question or even upon his personal investigation of the matter. So, too, though not expressly so stated, the representation may be made in a form or under such circumstances as to imply that this is the case. A misrepresentation so made is fraudulent even though the maker is honestly convinced of its truth from hearsay or other sources that he believes to be reliable.

Illustration

1. A states to B that C's financial position justifies B in giving him credit in a particular sales transaction. A knows that B will understand that the statement is based upon A's personal dealings with C. In fact A has had no dealings with C but has heard from what he regards as reliable sources that C's financial position is first rate. C is insolvent and B is unable to collect his debt from him. A is subject to liability to B for the loss that B suffers through relying upon his statement if the circumstances justify his reliance upon A's supposed personal knowledge.

Restatement (Second) of Torts

§ 8A   Intent

The word "intent" is used throughout the Restatement of this Subject to denote that the actor desires to cause consequences of his act, or that he believes that the consequences are substantially certain to result from it.

Comments & Illustrations

Comment a.   "Intent," as it is used throughout the Restatement of Torts, has reference to the consequences of an act rather than the act itself. When an actor fires a gun in the midst of the Mojave Desert, he intends to pull the trigger; but when the bullet hits a person who is present in the desert without the actor's knowledge, he does not intend that result. "Intent" is limited, wherever it is used, to the consequences of the act.

Comment b.   All consequences which the actor desires to bring about are intended, as the word is used in this Restatement. Intent is not, however, limited to consequences which are desired. If the actor knows that the consequences are certain, or substantially certain, to result from his act, and still goes ahead, he is treated by the law as if he had in fact desired to produce the result. As the probability that the consequences will follow decreases, and becomes less than substantial certainty, the actor's conduct loses the character of intent, and becomes mere recklessness, as defined in § 500. As the probability decreases further, and amounts only to a risk that the result will follow, it becomes ordinary negligence, as defined in § 282. All three have their important place in the law of torts, but the liability attached to them will differ.

Illustrations

    1.   A throws a bomb into B's office for the purpose of killing B. A knows that C, B's stenographer, is in the office. A has no desire to injure C, but knows that his act is substantially certain to do so. C is injured by the explosion. A is subject to liability to C for an intentional tort.

    2.   On a curve in a narrow highway A, without any desire to injure B, or belief that he is substantially certain to do so, recklessly drives his automobile in an attempt to pass B's car. As a result of this recklessness, A crashes into B's car, injuring B. A is subject to liability to B for his reckless conduct, but is not liable to B for any intentional tort.

Restatement (Second) of Torts

§ 500   Reckless Disregard Of Safety Defined

The actor's conduct is in reckless disregard of the safety of another if he does an act or intentionally fails to do an act which it is his duty to the other to do, knowing or having reason to know of facts which would lead a reasonable man to realize, not only that his conduct creates an unreasonable risk of physical harm to another, but also that such risk is substantially greater than that which is necessary to make his conduct negligent.

Special Note: The conduct described in this Section is often called "wanton or willful misconduct" both in statutes and judicial opinions. On the other hand, this phrase is sometimes used by courts to refer to conduct intended to cause harm to another.

Comments & Illustrations

Comment a. Types of reckless conduct. Recklessness may consist of either of two different types of conduct. In one the actor knows, or has reason to know, as that term is defined in § 12, of facts which create a high degree of risk of physical harm to another, and deliberately proceeds to act, or to fail to act, in conscious disregard of, or indifference to, that risk. In the other the actor has such knowledge, or reason to know, of the facts, but does not realize or appreciate the high degree of risk involved, although a reasonable man in his position would do so. An objective standard is applied to him, and he is held to the realization of the aggravated risk which a reasonable man in his place would have, although he does not himself have it.

For either type of reckless conduct, the actor must know, or have reason to know, the facts which create the risk. For either, the risk must itself be an unreasonable one under the circumstances. There may be exceptional circumstances which make it reasonable to adopt a course of conduct which involves a high degree of risk of serious harm to others. While under ordinary circumstances it would be reckless to drive through heavy traffic at a high rate of speed, it may not even be negligent to do so if the driver is escaping from a bandit or carrying a desperately wounded man to the hospital for immediately necessary treatment, or if his car has been commandeered by the police for the pursuit of a fleeing felon. So too, there may be occasions in which action which would ordinarily involve so high a degree of danger as to be reckless may be better than no action at all, and therefore both reasonable and permissible. Thus one who finds another in a lonely place, and very seriously hurt, may well be justified in giving him such imperfect surgical aid as a layman can be expected to give, although it would be utterly reckless for him to meddle in the matter if professional assistance were available.

For either type of conduct, to be reckless it must be unreasonable; but to be reckless, it must be something more than negligent. It must not only be unreasonable, but it must involve a risk of harm to others substantially in excess of that necessary to make the conduct negligent. It must involve an easily perceptible danger of death or substantial physical harm, and the probability that it will so result must be substantially greater than is required for ordinary negligence.

Comment b. Perception of risk. Conduct cannot be in reckless disregard of the safety of others unless the act or omission is itself intended, notwithstanding that the actor knows of facts which would lead any reasonable man to realize the extreme risk to which it subjects the safety of others. It is reckless for a driver of an automobile intentionally to cross a through highway in defiance of a stop sign if a stream of vehicles is seen to be closely approaching in both directions, but if his failure to stop is due to the fact that he has permitted his attention to be diverted so that he does not know that he is approaching the crossing, he may be merely negligent and not reckless. So too, if his failure to stop is due to the fact that his brakes fail to act, he may be negligent if the bad condition of the brakes could have been discovered by such an inspection as it is his duty to make, but his conduct is not reckless.

Comment c. Appreciation of extent and gravity of risk. In order that the actor's conduct may be reckless, it is not necessary that he himself recognize it as being extremely dangerous. His inability to realize the danger may be due to his own reckless temperament, or to the abnormally favorable results of previous conduct of the same sort. It is enough that he knows or has reason to know of circumstances which would bring home to the realization of the ordinary, reasonable man the highly dangerous character of his conduct.

Comment d. Knowledge of presence of others within danger zone. If the actor's conduct is such as to involve a high degree of risk that serious harm will result from it to anyone who is within range of its effect, the fact that he knows or has reason to know that others are within such range is conclusive of the recklessness of his conduct toward them. It is not, however, necessary that the actor know that there is anyone within the area made dangerous by his conduct. It is enough that he knows that there is strong probability that others may rightfully come within such zone.

Comment e. Violation of statute. The mere fact that certain precautions are required by a statute rather than the common law does not of itself make the intentional omission of the statutory precaution reckless indifference to the safety of others. In order that the breach of the statute constitute reckless disregard for the safety of those for whose protection it is enacted, the statute must not only be intentionally violated, but the precautions required must be such that their omission will be recognized as involving a high degree of probability that serious harm will result. Thus, the violation of an antiquated speed limit, set by statute at a rate which is today customarily regarded as not particularly dangerous or unsafe, may constitute negligence but cannot amount to reckless misconduct.

Comment f. Intentional misconduct and recklessness contrasted. Reckless misconduct differs from intentional wrongdoing in a very important particular. While an act to be reckless must be intended by the actor, the actor does not intend to cause the harm which results from it. It is enough that he realizes or, from facts which he knows, should realize that there is a strong probability that harm may result, even though he hopes or even expects that his conduct will prove harmless. However, a strong probability is a different thing from the substantial certainty without which he cannot be said to intend the harm in which his act results.

Comment g.   Negligence and recklessness contrasted. Reckless misconduct differs from negligence in several important particulars. It differs from that form of negligence which consists in mere inadvertence, incompetence, unskillfulness, or a failure to take precautions to enable the actor adequately to cope with a possible or probable future emergency, in that reckless misconduct requires a conscious choice of a course of action, either with knowledge of the serious danger to others involved in it or with knowledge of facts which would disclose this danger to any reasonable man. It differs not only from the above-mentioned form of negligence, but also from that negligence which consists in intentionally doing an act with knowledge that it contains a risk of harm to others, in that the actor to be reckless must recognize that his conduct involves a risk substantially greater in amount than that which is necessary to make his conduct negligent. The difference between reckless misconduct and conduct involving only such a quantum of risk as is necessary to make it negligent is a difference in the degree of the risk, but this difference of degree is so marked as to amount substantially to a difference in kind.

Restatement (Second) of Torts

§ 282   Negligence Defined

In the Restatement of this Subject, negligence is conduct which falls below the standard established by law for the protection of others against unreasonable risk of harm. It does not include conduct recklessly disregardful of an interest of others.

Comments

Comment a.   Negligent conduct may consist either of an act (see § 2), or an omission to act when there is a duty to do so (see § 284).

Comment b.   As stated in § 281, negligent conduct subjects the actor to liability only if the conditions stated in Clauses (a), (b), (c), and (d) of that Section exist.

Comment c.   The concept of unreasonable risk includes the existence of a risk and also its unreasonable character. The conditions which determine whether the actor should recognize the existence and extent of the risk involved in his conduct are stated in §§ 289 and 290. The conditions which determine whether the risk is unreasonable are stated in §§ 291–296.

The phrase "conduct involving unreasonable risk" is substantially synonymous with the phrases "unduly dangerous conduct" and "unreasonably dangerous conduct." However, the phrase used in this Section is preferable in that it makes it easier to define the nature and character of the risk.

Comment d.   Negligence contrasted with intended harm. The definition of negligence given in this Section includes only such conduct as creates liability for the reason that it involves a risk and not a certainty of invading the interest of another. It therefore excludes conduct which creates liability because of the actor's intention to invade a legally protected interest of the person injured or of a third person (see 8 A, Comment *b*, which defines "intent" as including knowledge that the conduct will invade the interest, as well as a purpose to invade it). The conditions which create liability for intentional invasions of interests of personality are stated in Chapter 2.

Comment e. Negligence contrasted with recklessness. As defined in this Section, the word "negligence" excludes conduct which the actor does or should realize as involving a risk to others which is not merely in excess of its utility, but which is out of all proportion thereto and is therefore "recklessly disregardful of the interests of others." As the disproportion between risk and utility increases, there enters into the actor's conduct a degree of culpability which approaches and finally becomes indistinguishable from that which is shown by conduct intended to invade similar interests. Therefore, where this disproportion is great, there is a marked tendency to give the conduct a legal effect closely analogous to that given conduct which is intended to cause the resulting harm. The rules which create liability for harm caused by conduct which is recklessly disregardful of the interests of others are stated in §§ 500–503.

Special Note: The word "negligent" is often used to include all conduct which, although not intended to invade any legally protected interest, has the element of social fault. Conduct which is in reckless disregard of a legally protected interest of others is thus constantly spoken of as a form of negligence, the phrases used being "reckless," "wanton," and "willful negligence," as distinguished from "negligence" or "mere negligence." But as stated in §§ 500–503, conduct recklessly disregardful of an interest of another differs from negligence in several important respects:

1. The rule that contributory negligence is no defense to an act intended to invade the plaintiff's interest is applied where the conduct is in reckless disregard of the plaintiff's interest.

2. Greater culpability is recognized by the imposition of punitive damages in many jurisdictions.

3. There is a pronounced tendency to regard reckless conduct as the legal cause of a particular harm, although the actor's conduct if merely negligent would not have been so considered.

4. In some jurisdictions the liability of a landowner to a trespasser or a gratuitous licensee is imposed only when the presence of the trespasser or licensee is known and the risk created by the actor's conduct is out of all proportion to its social utility.

5. In the construction of statutes which specifically refer to gross negligence, that phrase is sometimes construed as equivalent to reckless disregard.

6. In those jurisdictions where the distinction between trespass and trespass on the case is still of importance, reckless disregard is assimilated to intended harm to the extent that an action for trespass will lie.

Notwithstanding the difficulty of drawing the line between negligence and reckless conduct, these differences make it advisable to treat the two subjects separately.

Comment f. Negligence contrasted with liability without fault. The fact that negligence as here defined is conduct which falls below the standard of behavior established by law for the protection of others carries with it the idea of social fault. Therefore it does not include acts which, although done with every precaution which it is practicable to demand, involve an irreducible minimum of danger to others, but which are so far justified by their utility or by traditional usage that even the most perfect system of preventive law would not forbid them. These may for convenience be termed "acts which create a strict liability" and are considered in Volume 3 of the Restatement of this Subject.

Comment g. The word "risk" standing by itself denotes a chance of harm. In so far as risk is of importance in determining the existence of negligence, it is a chance of harm to others which the actor should recognize at the time of his action or inaction.

Comment h. In determining whether the actor should recognize the risks which are involved in his conduct, either of act or omission, only those circumstances which the actor perceives or should perceive at the time of his action or inaction are to be considered. Circumstances which occur after the conduct which is alleged to be negligent are as immaterial as are those circumstances which exist at the time of his action or inaction, but of which the actor neither knows nor should know, although known to third persons. Thus the rule here stated has reference to the reasonable probability that harm will ensue, but not to its extent, so long as the harm itself is unreasonable.

Restatement (Second) of Contracts

§ 162   When a Misrepresentation is Fraudulent or Material

(1) A misrepresentation is fraudulent if the maker intends his assertion to induce a party to manifest his assent and the maker

(a) knows or believes that the assertion is not in accord with the facts, or

(b) does not have the confidence that he states or implies in the truth of the assertion, or

(c) knows that he does not have the basis that he states or implies for the assertion.

(2) A misrepresentation is material if it would be likely to induce a reasonable person to manifest his assent, or if the maker knows that it would be likely to induce the recipient to do so.

Comments & Illustrations

Comment a.   Meaning of "fraudulent." The word "fraudulent" is used in various senses in the law. In order that a misrepresentation be fraudulent within the meaning of this Section, it must not only be consciously false but must also be intended to mislead another. Compare Restatement, Second, Torts § 526. Consequences are intended if a person either acts with the desire to cause them or acts believing that they are substantially certain to result. See Restatement, Second, Torts § 8A. Thus one who believes that another is substantially certain to be misled as a result of a misrepresentation intends to mislead even though he may not desire to do so. See Comment *c* to Restatement, Second, Torts § 531. If the maker knows that his statement is misleading because it is subject to two interpretations, it is fraudulent if he makes it with the intention that it be understood in the false sense. See Restatement, Second, Torts § 527. If the recipient continues to rely on a misrepresentation made in an earlier transaction, the misrepresentation is fraudulent if the maker knows that the recipient is still relying. See Restatement, Second, Torts § 535. Furthermore, the maker need not have a particular person in mind as the recipient at the time the misrepresentation is made. He may merely have reason to expect that it will reach any of a class of persons, of which the recipient is a member, as in the case of the merchant who furnishes information to a credit agency. See Illustration 1. In order that a fraudulent representation have legal effect within this Chapter, it need not be material. Compare §§ 163, 164, 166 with Restatement, Second, Torts §§ 538. It is, however, essential that it actually induce assent. See §§ 163, 164, 166.

Illustration

1.   A makes to B, a credit rating company, a statement of his financial condition that he knows is untrue, intending that its substance be published to B's subscribers. B summarizes the information and transmits the summary to C, a subscriber. C is thereby induced to make a contract to lend money to A. A's statement is a fraudulent misrepresentation and the contract is voidable by C under the rule stated in § 164.

Comment b.   "Scienter." The word "scienter" is often used by courts to refer to the requirement that the maker know of the untrue character of his assertion. Subsection (1) states three ways in which this requirement can be met. First, it is clearly met if the maker knows the fact to be otherwise than as stated. However, knowledge of falsity is not essential, and it is sufficient under the rule stated in Clause (a) if he believes the assertion to be false. It will not suffice merely to show that the misrepresentation is one that a person of ordinary care and intelligence would have recognized as false, although this is evidence from which his belief in its falsity may be inferred. Second, the requirement is met under the rule stated in Clause (b), if the maker, lacking confidence in the truth of his assertion that he states or implies, nevertheless chooses to make it as one of his own knowledge rather than one merely of his opinion. This is so when he is conscious that he has only a belief in its truth and recognizes that there is some chance that it may not be true. This conclusion is often expressed by saying that the misrepresentation has been made without belief in its truth or that it has been made recklessly, without regard to whether it is true or false. Third, the requirement is met under the rule stated in Clause (c), if the maker has said or implied that the assertion is made on some particular basis, such as his personal knowledge or his personal investigation, when it is not so made. This is so even though the maker is honestly convinced of its truth from hearsay or other source that he believes is reliable.

Illustration

2. A, seeking to induce B to make a contract to buy his house, tells B that the plumbing is of pipe of a specified quality. A does not know the quality of the pipe, and it is not of the specified quality. B is induced by A's statement to make the contract. The statement is a fraudulent misrepresentation, both because A does not have the confidence that he implies in its truth, and because he knows that he does not have the basis for it that he implies. The contract is voidable by B under the rule stated in § 164.

Comment c.   Meaning of "material." Although a fraudulent misrepresentation need not be material in order to entitle the recipient to relief under the rule stated in § 164, a non-fraudulent misrepresentation will not entitle him to relief unless it is material. The materiality of a misrepresentation is determined from the viewpoint of the maker, while the justification of reliance is determined from the viewpoint of the recipient. (Contrast also the concept of a "material" failure to perform. See § 241.) The requirement of materiality may be met in either of two ways. First, a misrepresentation is material if it would be likely to induce a reasonable person to manifest his assent. Second, it is material if the maker knows that for some special reason it is likely to induce the particular recipient to manifest his assent. There may be personal considerations that the recipient regards as important even though they would not be expected to affect others in his situation, and if the maker is aware of this the misrepresentation may be material even though it would not be expected to induce a reasonable person to make the proposed contract. One who preys upon another's known idiosyncrasies cannot complain if the contract is held voidable when he succeeds in what he is endeavoring to accomplish. Cf. Restatement, Second, Torts § 538. Although a nonfraudulent misrepresentation that is not material does not make the contract voidable under the rules stated in this Chapter, the recipient may have a claim to relief under other rules, such as those relating to breach of warranty. See Introductory Note to this Topic.

Illustrations

3.   A, while negotiating with B for the sale of A's race horse, tells him that the horse has run a mile in a specified time. A is honestly mistaken, and, unknown to him, the horse has never come close to that time. B is induced by A's assertion to make a contract to buy the horse. A's statement, although not fraudulent, is a material misrepresentation, and the contract is voidable by B under the rule stated in § 164.

4.   A, while negotiating with B for the sale of A's race horse, tells him that the horse was bred in a specified stable. A is honestly mistaken, and, unknown to him, it was bred in another stable of better reputation. The specified stable was, unknown to A, founded by B's grandfather, and B is therefore induced by A's assertion to make a contract to buy the horse. A's misrepresentation is neither fraudulent nor material, and the contract is not voidable by B.

5.   The facts being otherwise as in Illustration 4, A knows that the named stable was founded by B's grandfather and that B would like to own a horse bred there. A's misrepresentation, although not fraudulent, is material, and the contract is voidable by B under the rule stated in § 164.

Derry v. Peek

House of Lords, 1889.
14 App. Cas. 337.

A special Act incorporating a tramway company provided that the carriages might be moved by animal power, and, with the consent of the Board of Trade, by steam power. The directors issued a prospectus containing a statement that by their special Act the company had the right to use steam power instead of horses. The plaintiff took shares on the faith of this statement. The Board of Trade afterwards refused their consent to the use of steam power and the company was wound up. The plaintiff brought an action of deceit against the directors founded upon the false statement.

At the trial before Stirling J. the plaintiff and defendants were called as witnesses

Stirling J. dismissed the action; but that decision was reversed by the Court of Appeal (Cotton L.J., Sir J. Hannen, and Lopes L.J.) who held that the defendants were liable to make good to the plaintiff the loss sustained by his taking the shares, and ordered an inquiry. Against this decision the defendants appealed.

■ Lord Herschell:

My Lords, in the statement of claim in this action the respondent, who is the plaintiff, alleges that the appellants made in a prospectus issued by them certain statements which were untrue, that they well knew that the facts were not as stated in the prospectus, and made the representations fraudulently, and with the view to induce the plaintiff to take shares in the company.

"This action is one which is commonly called an action of deceit, a mere common law action." This is the description of it given by Cotton L.J. in delivering judgment. I think it important that it should be borne in mind that such an action differs essentially from one brought to obtain rescission of a contract on the ground of misrepresentation of a material fact. The principles which govern the two actions differ widely. Where rescission is claimed it is only necessary to prove that there was misrepresentation; then, however honestly it may have been made, however free from blame the person who made it, the contract, having been obtained by misrepresentation, cannot stand. In an action of deceit, on the contrary, it is not enough to establish misrepresentation alone; it is conceded on all hands that something more must be proved to cast liability upon the defendant, though it has been a matter of controversy what additional elements are requisite. I lay stress upon this because observations made by learned judges in actions for rescission have been cited and much relied upon at the bar by counsel for the respondent. Care must obviously be observed in applying the language used in relation to such actions to an action of deceit. Even if the scope of the language used extend beyond the particular action which was being dealt with, it must be remembered that the learned judges were not engaged in determining what is necessary to support an action of deceit, or in discriminating with nicety the elements which enter into it.

There is another class of actions which I must refer to also for the purpose of putting it aside. I mean those cases where a person within whose special province it lay to know a particular fact, has given an erroneous answer to an inquiry made with regard to it by a person desirous of ascertaining the fact for the purpose of determining his course accordingly, and has been held bound to make good the assurance he has given. Burrowes v. Lock may be cited as an example, where a trustee had been asked by an intended lender, upon the security of a trust fund, whether notice of any prior incumbrance upon the fund had been given to him. In cases like this it has been said that the circumstance that the answer was honestly made in the belief that it was true affords no defence to the action. Lord Selborne pointed out in Brownlie v. Campbell that these cases were in an altogether different category from actions to recover damages for false representation, such as we are now dealing with.

In the Court below Cotton L.J. said: "What in my opinion is a correct statement of the law is this, that where a man makes a statement to be acted upon by others which is false, and which is known by him to be false, or is made by him recklessly, or without care whether it is true or false, that is, without any reasonable ground for believing it to be true, he is liable in an action of deceit at the suit of anyone to whom it was addressed or anyone of the class to whom it was addressed and who was materially induced by the misstatement to do an act to his prejudice." About much that is here stated there cannot, I think, be two opinions. But when the learned Lord Justice speaks of a statement made recklessly or without care whether it is true or false, *that is* without any reasonable ground for believing it to be true, I find myself, with all respect, unable to agree that these are convertible expressions. To make a statement careless whether it be true or false, and therefore without any real belief in its truth, appears to me to be an essentially different thing from making, through want of care, a false statement, which is nevertheless honestly believed to be true. And it is surely conceivable that a man may believe that what he states is the fact, though he has been so wanting in care that the Court may think that there were no sufficient grounds to warrant his belief. I shall have to consider hereafter whether the want of reasonable ground for believing the statement made is sufficient to support an action of deceit. I am only concerned for the moment to point out that it does not follow that it is so, because there is authority for saying that a statement made recklessly, without caring whether it be true or false, affords sufficient foundation for such an action.

I think there is here some confusion between that which is evidence of fraud, and that which constitutes it. A consideration of the grounds of belief is no doubt an important aid in ascertaining whether the belief was really entertained. A man's mere assertion that he believed the statement he made to be true is not accepted as conclusive proof that he did so. There may be such an absence of reasonable ground for his belief as, in spite of his assertion, to carry conviction to the mind that he had not really the belief which he alleges. If the learned Lord intended to go further, as apparently he did, and to say that though the belief was really entertained, yet if there were no reasonable grounds for it, the person making the statement was guilty of fraud in the same way as if he had known what he stated to be false, I say, with all respect, that the previous authorities afford no warrant for the view that an action of deceit would lie under such circumstances. A man who forms his belief carelessly, or is unreasonably credulous, may be blameworthy when he makes a representation on which another is to act, but he is not, in my opinion, fraudulent in the sense in which that word was used in all the cases from Pasley v. Freeman down to that with which I am now dealing. Even when the expression "fraud in law" has been employed, there has always been present, and regarded as an essential element, that the deception was willful either because the untrue statement was known to be untrue, or because belief in it was asserted without such belief existing.

I think the authorities establish the following propositions: First, in order to sustain an action of deceit, there must be proof of fraud, and nothing short of that will suffice. Secondly, fraud is proved when it is shewn that a false representation has been made (1) knowingly, or (2) without belief in its truth, or (3) recklessly, careless whether it be true or false. Although I have treated the second and third as distinct cases, I think the third is but an instance of the second, for one who makes a statement under such circumstances can have no real belief in the truth of what he states. To prevent a false statement being fraudulent, there must, I think, always be an honest belief in its truth. And this probably covers the whole ground, for one who knowingly alleges that which is false, has obviously no such honest belief. Thirdly, if fraud be proved, the motive of the person guilty of it is immaterial. It matters not that there was no intention to cheat or injure the person to whom the statement was made.

I have arrived with some reluctance at the conclusion to which I have felt myself compelled, for I think those who put before the public a prospectus to induce them to embark their money in a commercial enterprise ought to be vigilant to see that it contains such representations only as are in strict accordance with fact, and I should be very unwilling to give any countenance to the contrary idea. I think there is much to be said for the view that this moral duty ought to some extent to be converted into a legal obligation, and that the want of reasonable care to see that statements, made under such circumstances, are true, should be made an actionable wrong. But this is not a matter fit for discussion on the present occasion. If it is to be done the legislature must intervene and expressly give a right of action in respect of such a departure from duty. It ought not, I think, to be done by straining the law, and holding that to be fraudulent which the tribunal feels cannot properly be so described. I think mischief is likely to result from blurring the distinction between carelessness and fraud, and equally holding a man fraudulent whether his acts can or cannot be justly so designated.

Adopting the language of Jessel M.R. in Smith v. Chadwich, I conclude by saying that on the whole I have come to the conclusion that the statement, "though in some respects inaccurate and not altogether free from imputation of carelessness, was a fair, honest and bonâ fide statement on the part of the defendants, and by no means exposes them to an action for deceit."

I think the judgment of the Court of Appeal should be reversed.

Ultramares Corp. v. Touche

Court of Appeals of New York, 1931.
174 N.E. 441.

■ CARDOZO, C.J. The action is in tort for damages suffered through the misrepresentations of accountants, the first cause of action being for misrepresentations that were merely negligent and the second for misrepresentations charged to have been fraudulent.

In January, 1924, the defendants, a firm of public accountants, were employed by Fred Stern & Co., Inc., to prepare and certify a balance sheet exhibiting the condition of its business as of December 31, 1923. They had been employed at the end of each of the three years preceding to render a like service. Fred Stern & Co., Inc., which was in substance Stern himself, was engaged in the importation and sale of rubber. To finance its operations, it required extensive credit and borrowed large sums of money from banks and other lenders. All this was known to the defendants. The defendants knew also that in the usual course of business the balance sheet when certified would be exhibited by the Stern company to banks, creditors, stockholders, purchasers or sellers, according to the needs of the occasion, as the basis of financial dealings. Accordingly, when the balance sheet was made up, the defendants supplied the Stern company with thirty-two copies certified with serial numbers as counterpart originals. Nothing was said as to the persons to whom these counterparts would be shown or the extent or number of the transactions in which they would be used. In particular there was no mention of the plaintiff, a corporation doing business chiefly as a factor, which till then had never made advances to the Stern company, though it had sold merchandise in small amounts. The range of the transactions in which a certificate of audit might be expected to play a part was as indefinite and wide as the possibilities of the business that was mirrored in the summary.

By February 26, 1924, the audit was finished and the balance sheet made up. It stated assets in the sum of $2,550,671.88 and liabilities other than capital and surplus in the sum of $1,479,956.62, thus showing a net worth of $1,070,715.26. Attached to the balance sheet was a certificate as follows:

'TOUCHE, NIVEN & CO.

'Public Accountants

'Eighty Maiden Lane

'New York

'*February* 26, 1924.

'Certificate of Auditors

'We have examined the accounts of Fred Stern & Co., Inc., for the year ending December 31, 1923, and hereby certify that the annexed balance sheet is in accordance therewith and with the information and explanations given us. We further certify that, subject to provision for federal taxes on income, the said statement, in our opinion, presents a true and correct view of the financial condition of Fred Stern & Co., Inc., as at December 31, 1923.

'TOUCHE, NIVEN & CO.

'*Public Accountants.*'

Capital and surplus were intact if the balance sheet was accurate. In reality both had been wiped out, and the corporation was insolvent. The books had been falsified by those in charge of the business so as to set forth accounts receivable and other assets which turned out to be fictitious. The plaintiff maintains that the certificate of audit was erroneous in both its branches. The first branch, the asserted correspondence between the accounts and the balance sheet, is one purporting to be made as of the knowledge of the auditors. The second branch, which certifies to a belief that the condition reflected in the balance sheet presents a true and correct picture of the resources of the business, is stated as a matter of opinion. In the view of the plaintiff, both branches of the certificate are either fraudulent or negligent. As to one class of assets, the item of accounts receivable, if not also as to others, there was no real correspondence, we are told, between balance sheet and books, or so the triers of the facts might find. If correspondence, however, be assumed, a closer examination of supporting invoices and records, or a fuller inquiry directed to the persons appearing on the books as creditors or debtors, would have exhibited the truth.

The plaintiff, a corporation engaged in business as a factor, was approached by Stern in March, 1924, with a request for loans of money to finance the sales of rubber. Up to that time the dealings between the two houses were on a cash basis and trifling in amount. As a condition of any loans the plaintiff insisted that it receive a balance sheet certified by public accountants, and in response to that demand it was given one of the certificates signed by the defendants and then in Stern's possession. On the faith of that certificate the plaintiff made a loan which was followed by many others. The course of business was for Stern to deliver to the plaintiff documents described as trust receipts which in effect were executory assignments of the moneys payable by purchasers for goods thereafter to be sold. When the purchase price was due, the plaintiff received the payment, reimbursing itself therefrom for its advances and commissions. Some of these transactions were effected without loss. Nearly a year later, in December, 1924, the house of cards collapsed. In that month, plaintiff made three loans to the Stern company, one of $100,000, a second of $25,000, and a third of $40,000. For some of these loans no security was received. For some of the earlier loans the security was inadequate. On January 2, 1925, the Stern company was declared a bankrupt.

This action, brought against the accountants in November, 1926, to recover the loss suffered by the plaintiff in reliance upon the audit, was in its inception one for negligence. On the trial there was added a second cause of action asserting fraud also. The trial judge dismissed the second cause of action without submitting it to the jury. As to the first cause of action, he reserved his decision on the defendants' motion to dismiss, and took the jury's verdict. They were told that the defendants might be held liable if with knowledge that the results of the audit would be communicated to creditors they did the work negligently, and that negligence was the omission to use reasonable and ordinary care. The verdict was in favor of the plaintiff for $187,576.32. On the coming in of the verdict, the judge granted the reserved motion. The Appellate Division affirmed the dismissal of the cause of action for fraud, but reversed the dismissal of the cause of action for negligence, and reinstated the verdict. The case is here on cross-appeals.

The two causes of action will be considered in succession, first the one for negligence and second that for fraud.

(1) We think the evidence supports a finding that the audit was negligently made, though in so saying we put aside for the moment the question whether negligence, even if it existed, was a wrong to the plaintiff. To explain fully or adequately how the defendants were at fault would

carry this opinion beyond reasonable bounds. A sketch, however, there must be, at least in respect of some features of the audit, for the nature of the fault, when understood, is helpful in defining the ambit of the duty.

We begin with the item of accounts receivable. At the start of the defendant's audit, there had been no posting of the general ledger since April, 1923. Siess, a junior accountant, was assigned by the defendants to the performance of that work. [After he completed posting the general ledger, an employee of the Stern Company added a large entry to the December accounts receivable. Siess supposed] that his task at the moment being merely to post the books, he thought the work of audit or verification might come later, and put it off accordingly. The time sheets, which are in evidence, show very clearly that this was the order of time in which the parts of the work were done. Verification, however, there never was either by Siess or by his superiors, or so the triers of the facts might say. If any had been attempted, or any that was adequate, an examiner would have found [that the large late entry to the December accounts receivable was false].

The December entry of accounts receivable was not the only item that a careful and skillful auditor would have desired to investigate. There was ground for suspicion as to an item of $113,199.60, included in the accounts payable as due from the Baltic Corporation. Both the extent of the discrepancy and its causes might have been found to cast discredit upon the business and the books. There was ground for suspicion again in the record of assigned accounts.

If the defendants owed a duty to the plaintiff to act with the same care that would have been due under a contract of employment, a jury was at liberty to find a verdict of negligence upon a showing of a scrutiny so imperfect and perfunctory. No doubt the extent to which inquiry must be pressed beyond appearances is a question of judgment, as to which opinions will often differ. No doubt the wisdom that is born after the event will engender suspicion and distrust when old acquaintance and good repute may have silenced doubt at the beginning. All this is to be weighed by a jury in applying its standard of behavior, the state of mind and conduct of the reasonable man. Even so, the adverse verdict, when rendered, imports an alignment of the weights in their proper places in the balance and a reckoning thereafter. The reckoning was not wrong upon the evidence before us, if duty be assumed.

We are brought to the question of duty, its origin and measure.

The defendants owed to their employer a duty imposed by law to make their certificate without fraud, and a duty growing out of contract to make it with the care and caution proper to their calling. Fraud includes the pretense of knowledge when knowledge there is none. To creditors and investors to whom the employer exhibited the certificate, the defendants owed a like duty to make it without fraud, since there was notice in the circumstances of its making that the employer did not intend to keep it to himself (*Eaton, Cole & Burnham Co. v. Avery*, 83 N. Y. 31; *Tindle v. Birkett*, 171 N. Y. 520). A different question develops when we ask whether they owed a duty to these to make it without negligence. If liability for negligence exists, a thoughtless slip or blunder, the failure to detect a theft or forgery beneath the cover of deceptive entries, may expose accountants to a liability in an indeterminate amount for an indeterminate time to an indeterminate class. The hazards of a business conducted on these terms are so extreme as to enkindle doubt whether a flaw may not exist in the implication of a duty that exposes to these consequences. We put aside for the moment any statement in the certificate which involves the representation of a fact as true to the knowledge of the auditors. If such a statement was made, whether believed to be true or not, the defendants are liable for deceit in the event that it was false. The plaintiff does not need the invention of novel doctrine to help it out in such conditions. The case was submitted to the jury and the verdict was returned upon the theory that even in the absence of a misstatement of a fact there is a liability also for erroneous opinion. The expression of an opinion is to be subject to a warranty implied by law. What, then, is the warranty, as yet unformulated, to be? Is it merely that the opinion is honestly conceived and that the preliminary inquiry has been honestly pursued, that a halt has not been made without a genuine belief that the search has been reasonably adequate to bring disclosure of the truth? Or does it go farther and involve the assumption of a liability for any blunder or inattention that could fairly be spoken of as negligence if the controversy were one between accountant and employer for breach of a contract to render services for pay?

The assault upon the citadel of privity is proceeding in these days apace. How far the inroads shall extend is now a favorite subject of juridical discussion. In the field of the law of contract there has been a gradual widening of the doctrine of *Lawrence v. Fox* (20 N. Y. 268), until today the beneficiary of a promise, clearly designated as such, is seldom left without a remedy (*Seaver v. Ransom*, 224 N. Y. 233, 238). Even in that field, however, the remedy is narrower where the beneficiaries of the promise are indeterminate or general. Something more must then appear than an intention that the promise shall redound to the benefit of the public or to that of a class of indefinite extension. The promise must be such as to 'bespeak the assumption of a duty to make reparation directly to the individual members of the public if the benefit is lost' (*Moch Co. v. Rensselaer Water Co.*, 247 N. Y. 160, 164; American Law Institute, Restatement of the Law of Contracts, § 145). In the field of the law of torts a manufacturer who is negligent in the manufacture of a chattel in circumstances pointing to an unreasonable risk of serious bodily harm to those using it thereafter may be liable for negligence though privity is lacking between manufacturer and user (*MacPherson v. Buick Motor Co.*, 217 N. Y. 382; American Law Institute. Restatement of the Law of Torts, § 262). A force or instrument of harm having been launched with potentialities of danger manifest to the eye of prudence, the one who launches it is under a duty to keep it within bounds (*Moch Co. v. Rensselaer Water Co.*, *supra*, at p. 168). Even so, the question is still open whether the potentialities of danger that will charge with liability are confined to harm to the person, or include injury to property. In either view, however, what is released or set in motion is a physical force. We are now asked to say that a like liability attaches to the circulation of a thought or a release of the explosive power resident in words.

Three cases in this court are said by the plaintiff to have committed us to the doctrine that words, written or oral, if negligently published with the expectation that the reader or listener will transmit them to another, will lay a basis for liability though privity be lacking. These are *Glanzer v. Shepard* (233 N. Y. 236); *International Products Co. v. Erie R. R. Co.* (244 N. Y. 331), and *Doyle v. Chatham & Phenix Nat. Bank* (253 N. Y. 369).

In *Glanzer v. Shepard* the seller of beans requested the defendants, public weighers, to make return of the weight and furnish the buyer with a copy. This the defendants did. Their return, which was made out in duplicate, one copy to the seller and the other to the buyer, recites that it was made by order of the former for the use of the latter. The buyer paid the seller on the faith of the certificate which turned out to be erroneous. We held that the weighers were liable at the suit of the buyer for the moneys overpaid. Here was something more than the rendition of a service in the expectation that the one who ordered the certificate would use it thereafter in the operations of his business as occasion might require. Here was a case where the transmission of the certificate to another was not merely one possibility among many, but the 'end and aim of the transaction,' as certain and immediate and deliberately willed as if a husband were to order a gown to be delivered to his wife, or a telegraph company, contracting with the sender of a message, were to telegraph it wrongly to the damage of the person expected to receive it. The intimacy of the resulting nexus is attested by the fact that after stating the case in terms of legal duty, we went on to point out that viewing it as a phase or extension of *Lawrence v. Fox (supra)*, or *Seaver v. Ransom (supra)*, we could reach the same result by stating it in terms of contract. The bond was so close as to approach that of privity, if not completely one with it. Not so in the case at hand. No one would be likely to urge that there was a contractual relation, or even one approaching it, at the root of any duty that was owing from the defendants now before us to the indeterminate class of persons who, presently or in the future, might deal with the Stern company in reliance on the audit. In a word, the service rendered by the defendant in *Glanzer v. Shepard* was primarily for the information of a third person, in effect, if not in name, a party to the contract, and only incidentally for that of the formal promisee. In the case at hand, the service was primarily for the benefit of the Stern company, a convenient instrumentality for use in the development of the business, and only incidentally or collaterally for the use of those to whom Stern and his associates might exhibit it thereafter. Foresight of these possibilities may charge with liability for fraud. The conclusion does not follow that it will charge with liability for negligence.

In the next of the three cases *(International Products Co. v. Erie R. R. Co., supra)* the plaintiff, an importer, had an agreement with the defendant, a railroad company, that the latter would act as bailee of goods arriving from abroad. The importer, to protect the goods by suitable insurance, made inquiry of the bailee as to the location of the storage. The warehouse was incorrectly named, and the policy did not attach. Here was a determinate relation, that of bailor and bailee, either present or prospective, with peculiar opportunity for knowledge on the part of the bailee as to the subject-matter of the statement and with a continuing duty to correct it if erroneous. Even the narrowest holdings as to liability for unintentional misstatement concede that a representation in such circumstances may be equivalent to a warranty. There is a class of cases 'where a person within whose special province it lay to know a particular fact, has given an erroneous answer to an inquiry made with regard to it by a person desirous of ascertaining the fact for the purpose of determining his course accordingly, and has been held bound to make good the assurance he has given' (HERSCHELL, L. C., in *Derry v. Peek*, [L. R.] 14 A. C. 337, 360). So in *Burrowes v. Lock* (10 Ves. 470), a trustee was asked by one who expected to make a loan upon the security of a trust fund whether notice of any prior incumbrance upon the fund had been given to him. An action for damages was upheld though the false answer was made honestly in the belief that it was true.

In one respect the decision in *International Products Co. v. Erie R. R. Co.* is in advance of anything decided in *Glanzer v. Shepard*. The latter case suggests that the liability there enforced was not one for the mere utterance of words without due consideration, but for a negligent service, the act of weighing, which happened to find in the words of the certificate its culmination and its summary. This was said in the endeavor to emphasize the character of the certificate as a business transaction, an act in the law, and not a mere casual response to a request for information. The ruling in the case of the *Erie Railroad* shows that the rendition of a service is at most a mere circumstance and not an indispensable condition. The Erie was not held for negligence in the rendition of a service. It was held for words and nothing more. So in the case at hand. If liability for the consequences of a negligent certificate may be enforced by any member of an indeterminate class of creditors, present and prospective, known and unknown, the existence or non-existence of a preliminary act of service will not affect the cause of action. The service may have been rendered as carefully as you please, and its quality will count for nothing if there was negligence thereafter in distributing the summary.

The antidote to these decisions and to the over-use of the doctrine of liability for negligent misstatement may be found in *Jaillet v. Cashman* (235 N. Y. 511) and *Courteen Seed Co. v. Hong Kong & Shanghai Banking Banking Corp.* (245 N. Y. 377). In the first of these cases the defendant supplying ticker service to brokers was held not liable in damages to one of the broker's customers for the consequences of reliance upon a report negligently published on the ticker. If liability had been upheld, the step would have been a short one to the declaration of a like liability on the part of proprietors of newspapers. In the second the principle was clearly stated by POUND, J., that 'negligent words are not actionable unless they are uttered directly, with knowledge or notice that they will be acted on, to one to whom the speaker is bound by some relation of duty, arising out of public calling, contract or otherwise, to act with care if he acts at all.'

From the foregoing analysis the conclusion is, we think, inevitable that nothing in our previous decisions commits us to a holding of liability for negligence in the circumstances of the case at hand, and that such liability, if recognized, will be an extension of the principle of those decisions to different conditions, even if more or less analogous. The question then is whether such an extension shall be made.

The extension, if made, will so expand the field of liability for negligent speech as to make it nearly, if not quite, coterminous with that of liability for fraud. Again and again, in decisions of this court, the bounds of this latter liability have been set up, with futility the fate of every endeavor to dislodge them. Scienter has been declared to be an indispensable element except where the representation has been put forward as true of one's own knowledge (*Hadcock v. Osmer*, 153 N. Y. 604), or in circumstances where the expression of opinion was a dishonorable pretense. Even an opinion, especially an opinion by an expert, may be found to be fraudulent if the grounds supporting it are so flimsy as to lead to the conclusion that there was no genuine belief back of it. Further than that this court has never gone. Directors of corporations have been acquitted of liability for deceit though they have been lax in investigation and negligent in speech (*Reno v. Bull*, 226 N. Y. 546, and cases there cited; *Kountze v. Kennedy*, 147 N. Y. 124). This has not meant, to be sure, that negligence may not be evidence from which a trier of the facts may draw an inference of fraud (*Derry v. Peek*, [L. R.] 14 A. C. 337, 369, 375, 376), but merely that if that inference is rejected, or, in the light of all the circumstances, is found to be unreasonable, negligence alone is not a substitute for fraud. Many also are the cases that have distinguished between the willful or reckless representation essential to the maintenance at law of an action for deceit, and the misrepresentation, negligent or innocent, that will lay a sufficient basis for rescission in equity (*Bloomquist v. Farson*, 222 N. Y. 375; *Seneca Wire & Mfg. Co. v. Leach & Co.*, 247 N. Y. 1). If this action is well conceived, all these principles and distinctions, so nicely wrought and formulated, have been a waste of time and effort. They have even been a snare, entrapping litigants and lawyers into an abandonment of the true remedy lying ready to the call. The suitors thrown out of court because they proved negligence, and nothing else, in an action for deceit, might have ridden to triumphant victory if they had proved the self-same facts, but had given the wrong another label, and all this in a State where forms of action have been abolished. So to hold is near to saying that we have been paltering with justice. A word of caution or suggestion would have set the erring suitor right. Many pages of opinion were written by judges the most eminent, yet the word was never spoken. We may not speak it now. A change so revolutionary, if expedient, must be wrought by legislation (*Landell v. Lybrand*, 264 Penn. St. 406).

We have said that the duty to refrain from negligent representation would become coincident or nearly so with the duty to refrain from fraud if this action could be maintained. A representation even though knowingly false does not constitute ground for an action of deceit unless made with the intent to be communicated to the persons or class of persons who act upon it to their prejudice *(Eaton, Cole & Burnham Co. v. Avery, supra)*. Affirmance of this judgment would require us to hold that all or nearly all the persons so situated would suffer an impairment of an interest legally protected if the representation had been negligent. We speak of all 'or nearly all,' for cases can be imagined where a casual response, made in circumstances insufficient to indicate that care should be expected, would permit recovery for fraud if willfully deceitful. Cases of fraud between persons so circumstanced are, however, too infrequent and exceptional to make the radii greatly different if the fields of liability for negligence and deceit be figured as concentric circles. The like may be said of the possibility that the negligence of the injured party, contributing to the result, may avail to overcome the one remedy, though unavailing to defeat the other.

Neither of these possibilities is noted by the plaintiff in its answer to the suggestion that the two fields would be coincident. Its answer has been merely this, *first*, that the duty to speak with care does not arise unless the words are the culmination of a service, and *second*, that it does not arise unless the service is rendered in the pursuit of an independent calling, characterized as public. As to the first of these suggestions, we have already had occasion to observe that given a relation making diligence a duty, speech as well as conduct must conform to that exacting standard *(International Products Co. v. Erie R. R. Co., supra)*. As to the second of the two suggestions, public accountants are public only in the sense that their services are offered to anyone who chooses to employ them. This is far from saying that those who do not employ them are in the same position as those who do.

Liability for negligence if adjudged in this case will extend to many callings other than an auditor's. Lawyers who certify their opinion as to the validity of municipal or corporate bonds with knowledge that the opinion will be brought to the notice of the public, will become liable to the investors, if they have overlooked a statute or a decision, to the same extent as if the controversy were one between client and adviser. Title companies insuring titles to a tract of land, with knowledge that at an approaching auction the fact that they have insured will be stated to the bidders, will become liable to purchasers who may wish the benefit of a policy without payment of a premium. These illustrations may seem to be extreme, but they go little, if any, farther than we are invited to go now. Negligence, moreover, will have one standard when viewed in relation to the employer, and another and at times a stricter standard when viewed in relation to the public. Explanations that might seem plausible, omissions that might be reasonable, if the duty is confined to the employer, conducting a business that presumably at least is not a fraud upon his creditors, might wear another aspect if an independent duty to be suspicious even of one's principal is owing to investors. 'Everyone making a promise having the quality of a contract will be under a duty to the promisee by virtue of the promise, but under another duty, apart from contract, to an indefinite number of potential beneficiaries when performance has begun. The assumption of one relation will mean the involuntary assumption of a series of new relations, inescapably hooked together' (*Moch Co. v. Rensselaer Water Co., supra*, at p. 168). 'The law does not spread its protection so far' (*Robins Dry Dock & Repair Co. v. Flint, supra*, at p. 309).

Our holding does not emancipate accountants from the consequences of fraud. It does not relieve them if their audit has been so negligent as to justify a finding that they had no genuine belief in its adequacy, for this again is fraud. It does no more than say that if less than this is proved, if there has been neither reckless misstatement nor insincere profession of an opinion, but only honest blunder, the ensuing liability for negligence is one that is bounded by the contract, and is to be enforced between the parties by whom the contract has been made. We doubt whether the average business man receiving a certificate without paying for it and receiving it merely as one among a multitude of possible investors, would look for anything more.

(2) The second cause of action is yet to be considered.

The defendants certified as a fact, true to their own knowledge, that the balance sheet was in accordance with the books of account. If their statement was false, they are not to be exonerated because they believed it to be true. We think the triers of the facts might hold it to be false.

Correspondence between the balance sheet and the books imports something more, or so the triers of the facts might say, than correspondence between the balance sheet and the general ledger, unsupported or even contradicted by every other record. The correspondence to be of any moment may not unreasonably be held to signify a correspondence between the statement and the books of original entry, the books taken as a whole. If that is what the certificate means, a jury could find that the correspondence did not exist and that the defendants signed the certificates without knowing it to exist and even without reasonable grounds for belief in its existence. The fictitious [large entry in the December] accounts receivable, was entered in the ledger after defendant's employee Siess had posted the December sales. He knew of the interpolation, and knew that there was need to verify the entry by reference to books other than the ledger before the books could be found to be in agreement with the balance sheet. The evidence would sustain a finding that this was never done. By concession the interpolated item had no support in the journal, or in any journal voucher, or in the debit memo book, which was a summary of the invoices, or in anything except the invoices themselves. The defendants do not say that they ever looked at the invoices, seventeen in number, representing these accounts. They profess to be unable to recall whether they did so or not. They admit, however, that if they had looked, they would have found omissions and irregularities so many and unusual as to have called for further investigation. When we couple the refusal to say that they did look with the admission that if they had looked, they would or could have seen, the situation is revealed as one in which a jury might reasonably find that in truth they did not look, but certified the correspondence without testing its existence.

In this connection we are to bear in mind the principle already stated in the course of this opinion that negligence or blindness, even when not equivalent to fraud, is none the less evidence to sustain an inference of fraud. At least this is so if the negligence is gross. Not a little confusion has at times resulted from an undiscriminating quotation of statements in *Kountze v. Kennedy (supra)*, statements proper enough in their setting, but capable of misleading when extracted and considered by themselves. 'Misjudgment, however gross,' it was there observed, 'or want of caution, however marked, is not fraud.' This was said in a case where the trier of the facts had held the defendants guiltless. The judgment in this court amounted merely to a holding that a finding of fraud did not follow as an inference of law. There was no holding that the evidence would have required a reversal of the judgment if the finding as to guilt had been the other way. Even *Derry v. Peek*, as we have seen, asserts the probative effect of negligence as an evidentiary fact. We had no thought in *Kountze v. Kennedy* of upholding a doctrine more favorable to wrongdoers, though there was a reservation suggesting the approval of a rule more rigorous. The opinion of this court cites *Derry v. Peek*, and states the holding there made that an action would not lie if the defendant believed the representation made by him to be true, although without reasonable cause for such belief. 'It is not necessary,' we said, 'to go to this extent to uphold the present judgment, for the referee, as has been stated, found that the belief of Kennedy was based upon reasonable grounds.' The setting of the occasion justified the inference that the representations did not involve a profession of knowledge as distinguished from belief (147 N. Y. at p. 133). No such charity of construction exonerates accountants, who by the very nature of their calling profess to speak with knowledge when certifying to an agreement between the audit and the entries.

The defendants attempt to excuse the omission of an inspection of the invoices proved to be fictitious by invoking a practice known as that of testing and sampling. A random choice of accounts is made from the total number on the books, and these, if found to be regular when inspected and investigated, are taken as a fair indication of the quality of the mass. The defendants say that about 200 invoices were examined in accordance with this practice, but they do not assert that any of the seventeen invoices supporting the fictitious sales were among the number so selected. Verification by test and sample was very likely a sufficient audit as to accounts regularly entered upon the books in the usual course of business. It was plainly insufficient, however, as to accounts not entered upon the books where inspection of the invoices was necessary, not as a check upon accounts fair upon their face, but in order to ascertain whether there were any accounts at all. If the only invoices inspected were invoices unrelated to the interpolated entry, the result was to certify a correspondence between the books and the balance sheet without any effort by the auditors, as to [the large December entry] of accounts, to ascertain whether the certified agreement was in accordance with the truth. How far books of account fair upon their face are to be probed by accountants in an effort to ascertain whether the transactions back of them are in accordance with the entries, involves to some extent the exercise of judgment and discretion. Not so, however, the inquiry whether the entries certified as there, are there in very truth, there in the form and in the places where men of business training would expect them to be. The defendants were put on their guard by the circumstances touching the December accounts receivable to scrutinize with special care. A jury might find that with suspicions thus awakened, they closed their eyes to the obvious, and blindly gave assent.

We conclude, to sum up the situation, that in certifying to the correspondence between balance sheet and accounts the defendants made a statement as true to their own knowledge, when they had, as a jury might find, no knowledge on the subject. If that is so, they may also be found to have acted without information leading to a sincere or genuine belief when they certified to an opinion that the balance sheet faithfully reflected the condition of the business.

Whatever wrong was committed by the defendants was not their personal act or omission, but that of their subordinates. This does not relieve them, however, of liability to answer in damages for the consequences of the wrong, if wrong there shall be found to be. It is not a question of constructive notice, as where facts are brought home to the knowledge of subordinates whose interests are adverse to those of the employer (*Henry v. Allen*, 151 N. Y. 1; see, however, American Law Institute, Restatement of the Law of Agency, § 506, subd. 2–a). These subordinates, so far as the record shows, had no interests adverse to the defendants', nor any thought in what they did to be unfaithful to their trust. The question is merely this, whether the defendants, having delegated the performance of this work to agents of their own selection, are responsible for the manner in which the business of the agency was done. As to that the answer is not doubtful.

Upon the defendants' appeal as to the first cause of action, the judgment of the Appellate Division should be reversed, and that of the Trial Term affirmed, with costs in the Appellate Division and in this court.

Upon the plaintiff's appeal as to the second cause of action, the judgment of the Appellate Division and that of the Trial Term should be reversed, and a new trial granted, with costs to abide the event.

Non–Linear Trading Co., Inc. v. Braddis Associates, Inc.

Supreme Court, Appellate Division, First Department, New York, 1998.
243 A.D.2d 107.

■ Rubin, J. On January 12, 1993, plaintiff Non–Linear Trading Company and defendant Braddis Associates entered in to an agreement to form "a joint venture partnership" for the purpose, *inter alia,* of developing a software-based commodities trading system. The agreement recites: "The business of the partnership shall include, but not be limited to, (a) the use of Braddis' existing research by a discretionary commodity interest trader or traders, (b) the development and use of additional research, signals and indicators by a discretionary commodity interest trader or traders, and (3) the development of a mechanically-driven software system or systems for the trading of commodity interests based on the Partnership's proprietary market research, signals and indicators (collectively, the 'Partnership's Products')." These provisions reflect the terms of a letter of intent dated November 24, 1992 drafted by James Park, an attorney and principal of plaintiff Non–Linear Trading Company (although it is referred to in the letter as "the SUMA group").

Paragraph 3 of the partnership agreement provides that plaintiff will make an initial capital contribution of $80,000 and that "the first $400,000 of net operating profits earned by the Partnership (without reduction for the $80,000 expended pursuant to this Paragraph 3) shall be used by the Partnership to fund additional research." With respect to recoupment of plaintiff's investment, paragraph 5 of the agreement provides that "the next $80,000 of net profits shall be allocated to [plaintiff] NLTC". These provisions likewise mirror those contained in Mr. Park's letter of intent with respect to the funding of the joint venture and the return of plaintiff's initial capital contribution. However, paragraph 3 of the partnership agreement adds, in conclusion: "Nothing in this agreement shall be construed as a warranty or representation by Braddis that research and development activities will lead to the actual development of products, or if actually developed, that there will be a commercially usable product."

The agreement grants a license to the partnership, plaintiff, SUMA Capital Corporation and their affiliates to use research and reports assembled by defendant, and provides that any profit derived from their use "shall promptly be paid to the Partnership." With this exception, the agreement is silent with respect to the source of the anticipated $400,000 in operating revenue to be applied to development of the software trading system.

Plaintiff made the initial capital contribution of $80,000 under the agreement early in 1993. By early 1994, it is apparent that plaintiff regarded defendant's efforts to produce the software as unavailing. In a letter dated February 7, 1994 bearing the letterhead of Paradigm Capital Management, Mr. Park makes reference to a conversation in which Ron Brandes, president of defendant Braddis Associates, indicated that the software had not been completed as "promised both in our contract and in continuing conversations over the past year." The letter expresses misgivings at a suggestion by Mr. Brandes that "you and I together attempt to trade the signals that Braddis Associates has been generating." It continues, "Neither of us is a trader (as each of us has proven in the past). Moreover, the whole purpose of the collaboration was for you to create a system of mechanical trading signals that would be valuable (i.e., saleable) to a discretionary trader". Mr. Park goes on to suggest that "it would be best for us to agree that the project has been unsuccessful and move on to other endeavors by retroactively voiding our contract—you would return to us the $80,000, and we would tear up the agreement." He concludes, anomalously, "The obligations that were created under the contract, however, must be satisfied before we can go on. I now believe that the return of the $80,000 is in order."

When the proposed repayment was not forthcoming, plaintiff commenced this action seeking dissolution of the partnership, rescission of the partnership agreement and damages for breach of fiduciary duty. The original complaint dated April 20, 1994 alleges that defendant "failed to perform" its obligation pursuant to the contract, having "failed to develop Partnership Products." It seeks rescission based upon fraudulent inducement (second cause of action) and recovery of expenses based upon breach of fiduciary duty (third cause of action). The complaint seeks recovery of plaintiff's initial capital contribution of $80,000, together with an additional $75,000 in unspecified related expenses.

[Discussions of the plaintiff's claims beside fraud are omitted.]

Finally, plaintiff's claim of fraud in the inducement does no more than restate its action for breach of performance using different terminology. As in *Lanzi v. Brooks* (54 A.D2d 1057), the alleged misrepresentation asserted in the proposed amended pleading relates to future performance. "Absent a present intention to deceive, a statement of future intentions, promises or expectations is not actionable on the grounds of fraud (*Adams v Clark,* 239 NY 403). A complaint based upon a statement of future intention must allege facts to show that the defendant, at the time the promissory representation was made, never intended to honor or act on his statement" (*Lanzi v. Brooks, supra,* at 1058). "A cause of action for breach of contract cannot be converted into one for fraud by merely alleging that defendant did not intend to fulfill the contract" (*Rochelle Assocs. v. Fleet Bank,* 230 A.D.2d 605, 606).

As a general rule, to recover damages for tort in a contract matter, it is necessary that the plaintiff plead and prove "a breach of duty distinct from, or in addition to, the breach of contract" (*North Shore Bottling Co. v. Schmidt & Sons,* 22 N.Y.2d 171, 179). In *Tesoro Petroleum Corp. v. Holborn Oil Co.* (108 A.D.2d 607) the "[p]laintiff asserted that defendants' agent falsely assured plaintiff's employee that defendants would perform under the contract and that the representation was made with the intent to deceive. However, plaintiff did not allege that defendants breached any duty owed to plaintiff separate and apart from the contractual duty when they misrepresented their intent to perform as promised." This Court concluded, "A failure to perform promises of future acts is merely a breach of contract to be enforced by an action on the contract. A cause of action for fraud does not arise when the only fraud charged relates to a breach of contract" (*supra,* citing *Wegman v. Dairylea Coop.,* 50 A.D.2d 108). In a similar case, the Appellate Division, Second Department, noted that the plaintiff's proposed amended pleading alleged, "essentially, that the defendants fraudulently induced them to enter into the contract when the defendants had no intention of abiding by its terms. Accordingly, leave to amend was properly denied '[s]ince the cause of action at issue here does not allege the breach of a duty extraneous to, or distinct from the contract between the parties' " (*Courageous Syndicate v. People–To–People Sports Comm.*, 141 A.D.2d 599, 600; *see also, North Shore Bottling Co. v. Schmidt & Sons, supra*, at 179 [conspiracy to breach contract]).

* * *

The *scienter* requirement is generally said to have entered the common law of fraud through *Derry v. Peek*, 14 App. Cas. 337 (Gr. Brit. 1889). *Derry* concerned an investment prospectus that misleadingly failed to disclose that approval by a local Board of Trade was required before a steam-powered railway might be constructed in its area. The defendants had in good faith but negligently believed that the approval was not required. When it turned out that approval was required, and not readily forthcoming, the plaintiffs, who had subscribed to the investment, were injured and sued, alleging fraud. The court held that "[f]raud is proved when it is shown that a false representation has been made (1) knowingly, or (2) without belief in its truth, or (3) recklessly, careless whether it be true or false." Id. at 374. The defendants' good faith was thus treated as a defense against the fraud action.

The outlines of the legal order set out in *Derry* remain in place U.S. law today. The classical *scienter* requirement insists that, to be liable for fraud a speaker must not just speak intentionally (that is, possess general intent), she must intend (specifically) that her listener is deceived by her misrepresentation. It is thus not hard to find opinions saying things like, "[G]ood faith is an absolute defense to the charge of common law fraud."[23] This rule narrows fraud's scope considerably.

Applying the *scienter* requirement to promissory fraud generates the result that a defendant will be held liable for promissory fraud only where she intended to deceive her promisee about her promissory intentions. A promisor who intends in good faith to perform cannot commit promissory fraud. That is the point of *Non–Linear Trading*. Indeed, there will be no liability for promissory fraud even where a reasonable promisor would anticipate that she would later change her mind or indeed that performance would turn out to be impossible. By contrast, a promisor's protest that she made a good faith effort, indeed her best effort, even, to perform does nothing at all to insulate her from contract's strict liability. Indeed, that is the core case of contractual obligation. The *scienter* requirement, it seems, renders fraud and promissory fraud clearly incapable of colonizing contract.

Things are not quite so straightforward, however. *Ultramares* illustrates the complications. Set aside for a moment the first part of the opinion, concerning the scope of the persons to whom the duties associated with negligent misrepresentation are owed. The materials below will return to this point, but for now, focus on what *Ultramares* says about fraud. Judge Cardozo famously would have permitted recovery for fraud upon a showing that a misrepresentation was made knowingly or willfully, or with

---

23. *C.R. Bard, Inc. v. M3 Systems, Inc.*, 157 F.3d 1340, 1365 (Fed. Cir. 1998).

reckless disregard for its truth or falsity, or without a "genuine belief" in its truth. Further, he suggested, fraud "includes the pretense of knowledge when knowledge there is none." These sorts of ideas substantially expand fraud's (and hence also promissory fraud's) scope. Comment [b] to § 8A elaborates on the expansion. "Intent," it says,

> is not . . . limited to consequences which are desired. If the actor knows that the consequences are certain, or substantially certain, to result from his act, and still goes ahead, he is treated by the law as if he had in fact intended to produce the result. As the probability that the consequences will follow decreases, and becomes less than substantial certainty, the actor's conduct loses the character of intent, and becomes mere recklessness, as defined in § 500. As the probability decreases further, and amounts only to a risk that the result will follow, it becomes ordinary negligence, as defined in § 282.

Comment [e] to § 526 similarly emphasizes that *scienter* might be given an expansive interpretation:

> It is enough [for *scienter*] that being conscious that he has neither knowledge nor belief in the existence of the matter [a speaker] chooses to assert it as a fact. Indeed, since knowledge implies a firm conviction, a misrepresentation of a fact so made as to assert that the maker knows it, is fraudulent if he is conscious that he has merely a belief in its existence and recognizes that there is a chance, more or less great, that the fact may not be as it is represented. This is often expressed by saying that fraud is proved if it is shown that a false representation has been made without belief in its truth or recklessly, careless of whether it is true or false.

Together, these materials suggest that recklessness can establish *scienter*; furthermore, they establish that *scienter*, recklessness, and mere negligence exist together on a sliding scale, so that the differences among them might almost be said to concern degree rather than kind.

Scienter approaches negligence especially closely, and hence casts its net especially broadly, in circumstances in which the context of a transaction entails that promisees will form beliefs not just about the subject matter of their promisors' representations but also about the methods by which the promisors have investigated this subject matter, in order to make their representations. This is easy to see in connection with cases that involve the sale and purchase of investment securities. Sellers of securities commonly make representations concerning the businesses of the issuing firms and hence, by implication, about the economic fundamentals of the securities that they are selling. Buyers form beliefs about these economic fundamentals, but they also form beliefs about the methods by which the sellers have investigated the securities prior to making their representations. Sellers, finally, know that buyers form these beliefs about methods. This pattern entails that even where sellers believe, in good faith, that a security is economically sound, they may be reckless (or even possess straightforward intent to deceive) concerning the basis for their beliefs. And so sellers whose investigations into economic fundamentals employ unreliable or even just unorthodox methods become exposed to liability for fraud. It is as if the law of securities fraud establishes an implied-in-law warranty not with respect to the economic fundamentals of issuing firms but with respect to the quality of the sellers' investigations of these fundamentals. Perhaps the warranty can be disclaimed by revealing unreliable or unorthodox methods. But where buyers' expectations that orthodox methods have been used are strong enough, this is not always so easy to do. And so fraud's scope reaches—at least in areas that have this structure—facts that seem, at first, to involve mere breach of contract.[24]

Nevertheless, in spite of such expansive readings in particular settings, fraud remains ultimately a much narrower form of liability than contract. After a point, *scienter* may be stretched no further, and specific intent reasserts its requirement that falsehood must be known and deception intended.

16.1.A.1.b   Reliance

Another doctrinal limitation, unrelated to the *scienter* requirement, further limits tort liability for fraud and thus also entails that promissory fraud is a narrow, highly specific form of legal liability, which cannot be expanded to colonize contract generally. This concerns the requirement that a plaintiff must have relied on a fraudulent misrepresentation in order to succeed in a fraud action. The following materials state the doctrine and illustrate its application.

Restatement (Second) of Torts

§ 538   Materiality Of Misrepresentation

(1) Reliance upon a fraudulent misrepresentation is not justifiable unless the matter misrepresented is material.

(2) The matter is material if

(a) a reasonable man would attach importance to its existence or nonexistence in determining his choice of action in the transaction in question; or

(b) the maker of the representation knows or has reason to know that its recipient regards or is likely to regard the matter as important in determining his choice of action, although a reasonable man would not so regard it.

---

24. An illustrative case, which concerns securities fraud is *Gebhart v. S.E.C.*, 595 F.3d 1034 (9th Cir. 2010).

Comment:

Comment a.   The rules stated in this Section are concerned only with whether the recipient's reliance upon the misrepresentation is justifiable. The rules that determine the fraudulent character of the misrepresentation are stated in §§ 526 to 530. The rules which determine the persons to whom the maker of the misrepresentation may be liable are stated in §§ 531 to 536. The general rule requiring that the recipient in fact rely on the misrepresentation and that his reliance be justifiable is stated in § 537.

Comment b.   The rule stated in this Section applies not only to misrepresentations of fact but also to those of opinion, intention and law. When the representation is one of opinion or intention, the question of materiality concerns not only the facts about which the opinion is expressed or the proposed action or inaction to which the intention relates, but also the existence of the opinion or intention itself in the particular individual who asserts it. (See §§ 542, 543, and 544).

Comment c.   The rule stated in this Section differs from the rules that determine the right to rescind a contract induced by fraudulent misrepresentation (see Restatement, Second, Contracts § 306) and to obtain restitution for benefits procured by fraudulent misrepresentation. (See Restatement of Restitution, § 9, Comment *b*). In neither of these cases is it required that the misrepresentation, if fraudulent, be as to a matter that is material, materiality being important in them only when the misrepresentation is negligent and not fraudulent.

Comment on Clause (2), (a):

Comment d.   In determining whether a fact is material it is not necessary that it be one that a reasonable man would regard as affecting the pecuniary advantages of the transaction. There are many more-or-less sentimental considerations that the ordinary man regards as important. Thus it is natural that a person should wish to possess portraits of his ancestors even though they have no value as works of art. A fraudulent misrepresentation that a particular picture is a portrait of the purchaser's great-grandfather is a misrepresentation of a material fact.

Comment e.   As in all cases in which the conduct of the reasonable man is the standard, the question of whether a reasonable man would have regarded the fact misrepresented to be important in determining his course of action is a matter for the judgment of the jury subject to the control of the court. The court may withdraw the case from the jury if the fact misrepresented is so obviously unimportant that the jury could not reasonably find that a reasonable man would have been influenced by it. Compare § 285, especially Comments *f* and *g* which state the respective functions of court and jury in negligence cases.

Comment f.   Even though the matter misrepresented is one to which a reasonable man would not attach any importance in determining his course of action in the transaction in hand, it is nevertheless material if the maker knows that the recipient, because of his own peculiarities, is likely to attach importance to it. There are many persons whose judgment, even in important transactions, is likely to be determined by considerations that the normal man would regard as altogether trivial or even ridiculous. One who practices upon another's known idiosyncracies cannot complain if he is held liable when he is successful in what he is endeavoring to accomplish.

Illustrations

1. A, seeking to induce B to buy stock in a corporation, knows that B believes in astrology and governs his conduct according to horoscopes. A fraudulently tells B that the horoscopes of the officers of the corporation all indicate remarkable success for the corporation during the coming year. In reliance upon this statement, B buys the stock from A and as a result suffers pecuniary loss. The misrepresentation is material.

2. A, seeking to induce B to give money to a college about to be founded, fraudulently informs B that it is to be named after X, a deceased friend of B of bad character, whom B has regarded with great affection. A knows that the statement is likely to be regarded by B as an important inducement to make a gift. In reliance upon the statement, B makes the gift. The statement is material.

Restatement (Second) of Torts

§ 544   Statement Of Intention

The recipient of a fraudulent misrepresentation of intention is justified in relying upon it if the existence of the intention is material and the recipient has reason to believe that it will be carried out.

Comments & Illustrations

Comment a.   Existence of intention. The rule stated in this Section applies only when the representation gives its recipient reason to believe that the intention is firmly entertained and, therefore, to expect that it will be carried out. Whether the recipient has reason for this belief depends upon the circumstances under which the statement was made, including the fact that it was made for the purpose of inducing the recipient to act in reliance upon it and the form and manner in which it was expressed.

Comment b.   Materiality of the intention. Under the rule stated in this Section it is not enough that the maker has given the recipient reason to believe that he will carry out his expressed intention; it is also necessary that the existence of the intention be material, in the sense in which that term is defined in § 538(2). In order for this to be true, it is first necessary that the action or inaction to which the intention relates be itself material to the transaction; and it is also necessary that it be material that the particular individual has the intention. Thus a representation by the directors of a corporation that it is their intention to apply the money realized by the sale of bonds to the enlargement of the business when the purpose that they actually have in mind is the payment of a floating indebtedness is a material misrepresentation. This is true because buyers of bonds properly regard the purpose to which the money is to be put as of the utmost importance in determining the advisability of the investment. So, too, the holder of an option is justified in regarding the constantly reiterated statements of a prospective purchaser that he intends to buy the property covered by the option as soon as minor questions are settled as sufficiently material to justify the holder in refraining from offering the option to other possible purchasers until its near expiration has made it impossible for him to dispose of it.

Comment c. Justifiable reliance. In order for reliance upon a statement of intention to be justifiable, the recipient of the statement must be justified in his expectation that the intention will be carried out. If he knows facts that will make it impossible for the maker to do so, he cannot be justified in his reliance.

Illustration

1. A, the owner of a real estate development, seeking to sell a lot in it to B, fraudulently tells B that he intends to construct a golf course in the development. B knows that the terrain is not suitable for a golf course and that there is not enough available land for it, and that it could only be constructed by purchase of a large quantity of additional land beyond A's means. B is not justified in relying on the representation.

Restatement (Second) of Torts

§ 548 Reliance On Action For Misrepresentation

The maker of a fraudulent misrepresentation is not liable to one who does not rely upon its truth but upon the expectation that the maker will be held liable in damages for its falsity.

Comment

In order to justify recovery, the recipient of a misrepresentation must rely upon the truth of the misrepresentation itself, and his reliance upon its truth must be a substantial factor in inducing him to act or to refrain from action. (See § 546). It is not enough that, without belief in its truth, he proceeds to enter into the transaction in the expectation that he will be compensated in an action for damages for its falsity.

Bibb v. Bickford

District Court of Appeal of Florida, First District, 1963.
149 So.2d 592.

■ WIGGINTON, Judge. Plaintiff has appealed a decree dismissing with prejudice his complaint in equity. The sole question presented is whether the complaint states a cause of action.

By his complaint plaintiff alleges that when he was three years of age his mother was declared incompetent and placed in an institution in their home state of New Jersey, where she remained until the time of her death. Thereafter plaintiff, his father and defendant moved to Florida where they lived together as a family unit until the death of his father on February 20, 1951. Plaintiff's father and defendant told him that they had married each other in Mexico. The father left a will in which he devised his entire estate to defendant. During the years of this family relationship plaintiff believed his mother to be dead, and after his father's death he inquired of defendant regarding this matter in response to which he was told that his mother had died quite some time ago. Plaintiff's father's estate was fully administered and closed by order of the County Judge of Escambia County on April 22, 1952. It was not until December, 1960 that plaintiff learned from a relative that his mother had died only three months prior to receiving this information. Investigation revealed that plaintiff's mother had not died many years before the death of his father as told to him by defendant, but as an adjudged incompetent was residing in an institution in New Jersey at the time of the father's death and at all times subsequent thereto until September, 1960. The complaint alleges upon information and belief that defendant was not the legal wife of his father at the time of the latter's death, and that the father's marriage to plaintiff's mother had never been legally dissolved. No guardian or other representative was ever appointed for plaintiff's mother during the period of her incompetency and due to this fact, coupled with plaintiff's ignorance that she was alive at the time of his father's death, no election to take dower in the estate of her deceased husband was made on her behalf. The complaint charges that because of the false and fraudulent misrepresentations made to him by defendant regarding the prior death of his mother he has been injured to the extent of the interest which he would have inherited from his mother had dower in his father's estate been set aside to his mother following the father's death. The complaint prays that plaintiff be awarded an interest in the estate devised to defendant under his father's will in such amount as will represent the dower to which his mother would have been entitled if she had filed an election at the appropriate time to claim dower in the estate following her husband's death.

The statute relating to dower which was in effect at the time plaintiff's father died on February 20, 1951, provides that to entitle a widow to dower, she must so elect by an instrument in writing, signed and acknowledged by her and filed in the office of a county judge in whose court the estate of the deceased husband is being administered within nine months after the first publication of notice to creditors. The right of a widow to make an election to take dower under this statute is a personal right which may be exercised only by her, or on her behalf by a Court of Equity upon the petition of her guardian. Such right is extinguished upon the death of the widow in the event the election is not made by her prior to her demise. Even should it be conceded, a point which we will hereafter discuss, that the complaint sufficiently alleges such facts as would toll the statutory requirement that an election to take dower be filed within nine months after the first publication of the notice to creditors, the death of plaintiff's mother extinguished all right to claim dower in the father's estate. Being a personal right vested only in her, no derivative right thereto vested in plaintiff under the statute in effect at the time of his father's death. We pause here to note that subsequent to the death of plaintiff's father the statute was amended so as to now authorize the guardian of an incompetent widow to file an election on her behalf to take dower in the estate of her deceased husband, with a derivative right vested in any person having a beneficial interest in the estate of a widow to so file an election within the time limited in the event she dies before an election is made.

Reverting to the complaint filed by plaintiff it must be held that it is not sufficient to state a cause of action based upon fraud and deceit. The complaint fails to allege that defendant knew that plaintiff's mother was alive at the time of his father's death, but nevertheless withheld this information from him and fraudulently with intent to deceive, represented to plaintiff that the mother had been dead for many years prior to the death of his father. Furthermore the complaint fails to allege that plaintiff believed and relied to his detriment upon such fraudulent and false misrepresentations. It is well settled in this state that the mere false and fraudulent misrepresentations of one to another is not a sufficient basis for relief in equity unless it is alleged and proved that the person seeking relief believed and relied upon such representations to his detriment.

For the foregoing reasons we conclude and so hold that the complaint fails to state a cause of action and that the chancellor ruled properly in ordering it dismissed.

* * *

In order to sustain a cause of action for fraud, a plaintiff must have reasonably relied on the defendant's false representation. Notice that reliance figures here as an element of the cause of action rather than as a remedy or measure of damages. Thus where a plaintiff has reasonably relied, she may (as we have seen) recover not just her reliance losses but the value to her of the truth of the statement on which she relied. At the same time, a plaintiff who has not relied, or whose reliance was unreasonable, may recover nothing at all. This represents a fundamental departure from contract, which officially refuses to make reliance into a condition of obligation: A contractual promisee may vindicate her expectations even though she has done nothing with respect to the contractual promise other than to accept it.[25]

---

25. Recall, however, that the official story is in a way incomplete. In thick markets, promisees typically will rely, at least in the sense of forgoing equally attractive bargains with alternative promisors. And where markets are not thick, a series of doctrines that limit contract remedies establish roadblocks to plaintiffs' efforts to vindicate expectations that are unbacked by reliance. These are technically remedy rules rather than rules that establish the elements of contractual obligation. But insofar as the remedy rules make recovery depend on reasonable reliance, they effectively condition liability (or at least, liability worth wanting) on reliance as well. Of course, the suggestion that contract remedies are limited to reliance remains controversial; indeed, as Part I showed, it is probably not, all-things-considered, the best reconstruction of the positive law.

The rule of Restatement § 548 prevents a kind of bootstrapping, in which plaintiffs attempt to satisfy reliance requirement by citing the law of fraud, rather than the defendants' representations, as the grounds of reliance. The application of § 548 to promissory fraud is particularly interesting. Promissory fraud, recall, arises when a person misrepresents her promissory intentions—when she represents that she intends to perform a promise while privately intending not to. § 548 operates, in this connection, to ensure that a cause of action for promissory fraud will lie only where a plaintiff has relied directly on the defendant's representations concerning her intentions. The plaintiff may not substitute reliance on the law's stepping in to enforce the false promise. This marks a further, and immensely important, sense in which promissory fraud falls short of true contractual obligation. In contract, promisees regularly rely not just (or not at all) on promisors' spontaneous inclination to honor their promises but rather on legal enforcement of promissory obligation. Indeed, supporting such reliance is one of contract law's central purposes.

Obligation for fraud is thus more narrowly cabined than contractual obligation in at least two respects: fraud requires that the defendant possesses some sort of specific intent to deceive (*scienter*); and fraud requires that the plaintiff reasonably relies on the deceptive statements (materiality). Contract casts its net much more broadly in both respects. Breach of contract and fraud are thus not quite the same wrongs. This should not in the end be too surprising. To begin with, the promisor intends to create an obligation; the fraudster merely intentionally violates one. Moreover, it is quite possible to break a promise without ever being even the slightest bit dishonest. As she is making her promise, a promisor may intend to perform and even have good reason for believing that she will perform. She may have these intentions and beliefs even though she turns out not to perform. And even if her breach is intentional, and indeed free, this does not make *it* in itself a lie. The breach, after all, makes no claims about performance. It just is what it is.

16.1.A.2   Negligent Misrepresentation

Fraud is not the only misrepresentation tort, however. Understanding the relationship between contract and tort therefore requires taking up the other misrepresentation torts also, and in particular the torts (like the tort illustrated already in *Glanzer)* that arise around misrepresentations that are not fraudulent or intentional, but merely negligent.

Restatement § 304, taken up right at the start of this chapter, establishes that the broader tort of negligence may be applied to cases where the mechanism by which negligence produces harm involves representations. The earlier discussion emphasized that this should come as no surprise and, moreover, that in many cases the negligent misrepresentations addressed by this doctrine have no fundamental connection to contract: they harm by means that do not implicate promise at all. But there arise cases in which negligent misrepresentations do enter the precincts of contract. Indeed, they do so in much the same way in which promissory fraud does.

Consider, therefore, an analogy to promissory fraud that has no official legal name but might be called *promissory negligence*. Promissory negligence arises where a speaker makes representations concerning her future conduct (or her current intentions with respect to her future conduct) without taking reasonable care to avoid deceiving others (to their detriment) about what her future conduct will be or about what her intentions with respect to that conduct are. In contrast to promissory fraud, promissory negligence, being a species of negligence, does not require *scienter*. The pattern of conduct associated with promissory negligence should seem familiar, moreover. Earlier materials concerning the objective theories of offer and acceptance emphasized that a subjective intent to be bound is not in fact required to establish contractual obligation. The law holds that it is enough, to establish a contract, that an accepting offeree reasonably concludes that his offeror intends to be bound. But this sounds very much like a rule creating liability for negligently employing offer-like language, that is, for negligent misrepresentation concerning promissory intentions or, as I have called it, promissory negligence.

Identifying promissory negligence as a special case of negligent misrepresentation, and seeing the similarity between promissory negligence and the path by which orthodox contracts (given the objective approach to contractual intent) come into being thus makes it natural to ask whether the orthodox doctrine is surplus to requirements. Perhaps tort law, through the general doctrines that govern negligent misrepresentation and these doctrines' application to promissory negligence in particular, already establishes the forms of liability that orthodox contract law identifies. Perhaps, one might say, orthodox contract law does no more than elaborate a species of misrepresentation tort. Perhaps liability in contract is just the species of tort liability for negligent representation that arises where the content of the misrepresentation concerns intentions in respect of future conduct and in particular the intention to establish an obligation respecting future conduct.

Tempting as it is, this possibility should be rejected, and for deep structural reasons. Even the objective theory of intent continues to make liability turn on the narrow question whether or not contractual representations are reasonably understood to constitute *offers* and *acceptances* (that is, promises) rather than on the broader (tort-like) question whether or not it would be reasonable to rely on these representations. Accordingly, even under the objective theory, offer and acceptance establish obligation (strict liability, no less) even when no reasonable person would (apart from the guarantees provided by the legal enforcement of contracts) rely on what he reasonably identified as a promise. (This is illustrated by the case in which I, who am known never to honor my debts, borrow subject to a promise to repay. As long as a reasonable person would think that I intend to obligate myself, I am bound, including even if no reasonable person, and certainly not my lender, believes that I will actually manage to do as I have promised.) This possibility is foreign to tort-like obligation.

The materials that follow take up this structural difference to elaborate the doctrines through which negligent misrepresentation (and so also promissory negligence) provides a more limited form of legal liability than contract proper.[26] There are again two. First, and most straightforwardly, promissory negligence (in a rough trade for abandoning the requirement of *scienter*) protects a plaintiff's reliance only and not his promissory expectations. The second limit involves a pair of related ideas, which receive interlocking, and not always well-elaborated, doctrinal expression. To begin with, it is said that negligent misrepresentation, including in respect of promissory negligence, generally makes reasonable reliance an element of the tort; reliance is not, by contrast, an element of a cause of action for breach of contract. Furthermore the doctrine states that a speaker will generally be subjected to liability for negligent misrepresentation only where she owes her listener an antecedent duty of care or candor with respect to what she says; contractual obligation, by contrast, may be created between any two persons, regardless of their antecedent relationship and out of whole cloth. The relationship between the two formulations is that reliance is reasonable in the sense of the first only if incurred by one owed an antecedent duty in the sense of the second. The materials that follow take up each of these two doctrines.

16.1.A.2.a   Limiting Remedies to Reliance

Begin with the doctrine that damages for negligent misrepresentation are limited to a plaintiff's reliance losses. This rule, and the contrast between it and the expectation-based remedial rule for fraud, may be straightforwardly read off of the face of the doctrine, which is reproduced below. It requires no further comment.

Restatement (Second) of Torts

§ 552B   Damages For Negligent Misrepresentation

(1) The damages recoverable for a negligent misrepresentation are those necessary to compensate the plaintiff for the pecuniary loss to him of which the misrepresentation is a legal cause, including

(a) the difference between the value of what he has received in the transaction and its purchase price or other value given for it; and

(b) pecuniary loss suffered otherwise as a consequence of the plaintiff's reliance upon the misrepresentation.

---

26. Contract establishes a narrower from of obligation than tort in another respect. The objective theory of intent will not sustain contract obligation in the case in which a reasonable listener would interpret a speaker's words as revealing a sufficient high likelihood of performance to justify reliance but *not* as indicating that the speaker intended, by these words, to open herself up to promissory obligation.

(2) the damages recoverable for a negligent misrepresentation do not include the benefit of the plaintiff's contract with the defendant.

Comment:

Comment a.   The rule stated in this Section applies, as the measure of damages for negligent misrepresentation, the rule of out-of-pocket loss that is stated as to fraudulent misrepresentations in Subsection (1) of § 549. Comments *a* to *f* under § 549 are therefore applicable to this Section, so far as they are pertinent.

Comment b.   This Section rejects, as to negligent misrepresentation, the possibility that, in a proper case, the plaintiff may also recover damages that will give him the benefit of his contract with the defendant, which is stated, as to fraudulent misrepresentations, in Subsection (2) of § 549. This position is consistent with that taken, in § 766C, that there is as a general rule no liability for merely negligent conduct that interferes with or frustrates a contract interest or an expectancy of pecuniary advantage. The considerations of policy that have led the courts to compensate the plaintiff for the loss of his bargain in order to make the deception of a deliberate defrauder unprofitable to him, do not apply when the defendant has had honest intentions but has merely failed to exercise reasonable care in what he says or does.

16.1.A.2.b   Limiting Obligation by Reasonable Reliance and Antecedent Duty

The doctrines concerning reasonable reliance and antecedent duty in connection with negligent misrepresentation are more complex. It will be useful, in discussing them, first to revisit the question of reasonable reliance as it arises in connection with contract proper. The discussions in Part I revealed that although contract law's official self-presentation emphasizes the idea that promisors must perform their promises, the law also contains various doctrines that quietly impose obligations that promisees must meet in order fully to enjoy their contractual entitlements. Promisees, for example, must mitigate damages, which is to say that they may not continue unreasonably to expect performance after it has become clear that performance will not be forthcoming. Similarly, the foreseeability doctrine implicitly requires that, even before the time for performance has arrived, promisees must plan based on reasonable assessments of the likelihood that performance will be forthcoming. Promisees whose plans unreasonably discount obstacles to their promisors' performance cannot vindicate their contractual expectations insofar as these reflect the unreasonable assessments of the promisors' capacities to perform: such expectations are treated, by the law, as unforeseeable and in this way excluded from the expectation remedy. These doctrines entail, in effect, that the scope of a promisor's contractual obligations is limited to vindicating the value that performance would have conferred on her promisee, conditional on the promisee's reasonable (rather than actual) reliance. The promisee's reasonable reliance thus enters contract doctrine not only as a remedial interest but also as a condition for the vindication of his conventional, expectation-based, interest.

This sounds as if a promisee's reasonable reliance is an element of contract obligation, just as it is an element of tort obligation for negligent misrepresentation. But there is a crucial difference between the two cases.

A contractual promisee may adjust his reasonable (and hence foreseeable) contractual expectations—his reasonable efforts to plan in light of her contractual entitlements—not just to the likelihood that his promisor will voluntarily do what she has promised but also in respect of the fact that the law will vindicate his contractual entitlements even if his promisor initially seeks to avoid her obligations. This is revealed most directly in the doctrines that govern anticipatory repudiation, which were also discussed in Part I. These doctrines require promisees whose promisors announce that they will not perform to take reasonable steps to mitigate their losses: concretely, promisees facing anticipatory repudiations may urge performance only for a commercially reasonable time and, when this time expires, must cover if it is reasonable to do so. A promisee who unreasonably insists on his entitlement to performance cannot vindicate expectations associated with plans based on his unreasonable insistence. But at the same time, promisees who face anticipatory repudiation may plan in ways that take their contract remedies into account. A buyer whose seller repudiates, for example, may make purchase substitute performance where his covering is reasonable only conditional on his receiving his remedy for the breached initial contract. That is, the fact that a promisor announces her intention to breach her contract (and to resist efforts to enforce the contract through the law) does not eliminate her promisee's right to rely or to form and vindicate contractual expectations.

Things are quite different with respect to negligent misrepresentation and promissory negligence. Where a promise has failed to create a contract, and a promisee discovers that his promisor will not perform, then he loses the legal right to rely on the performance (even if he previously had that right). And (as in the case of fraud—recall Restatement § 548) he may not bootstrap himself into a right by relying on the enforcement of his misrepresentation claim.

Reliance moreover will support a claim for negligent misrepresentation only insofar as it is *justified*. And unlike in contract proper, where a promisor's promissory representations can in themselves sustain the reasonableness of the promisee's reliance (and indeed of his expectations), reliance on non-promisory representations is justified only insofar as the person making the representations has an appropriate antecedent duty towards the person who relies. Accordingly, although liability for fraud may in principle arise wherever a speaker possesses specific intent to deceive (and fraud's other elements are satisfied), tort liability for merely negligent misrepresentation generally requires that a speaker owes a pre-existing duty—created by law and apart from the intentions of the parties—to her listener. This duty is generally grounded in the relationship between the speaker and her listener. A speaker's liability for negligent misrepresentation may be grounded, for example, in her possession of special expertise with respect to the subject matter of the representation or it may be grounded in her occupying a particular social or economic role. Other similar grounds for liability also exist.

Glanzer illustrates one classic set of circumstances in which a speaker may come under duties that justify reliance. The defendants were public weighers, and that role subjected them to a general duty to weigh carefully. The duty was further enhanced by the circumstance in which the defendants did the weighing, which clearly indicated that a third party would rely (in its business dealings) on the weights that the defendants reported. This at once raises the question how special the circumstances of *Glanzer* are; or; put the other way around, how readily the law will find that a relationship capable of justifying reliance, and hence underwriting a cause of action for negligent misrepresentation, exists in the absence of privity of contract.

Ultramares, in the part of the opinion passed over when that case was first discussed a few pages ago, stated an early and narrow account of the scope of liability for negligent misrepresentation in this respect. Although *Ultramares* recognized what it called the "assault upon the citadel of privity," including expressly in connection with *Glanzer*, it also sought to hold a line concerning the scope of negligent misrepresentation. As Cardozo famously worried, "if liability for negligence exists, a thoughtless slip or blunder, the failure to detect a theft or forgery beneath the cover of deceptive entries, may expose accountants to a liability in an indeterminate amount for an indeterminate time to an inter-determinate class. The hazards of a business conducted on these terms are so extreme as to enkindle doubt whether a flaw may not exist in the implication of a duty that exposes to these consequences." This led Cardozo to insist that "if there has been neither reckless misstatement nor insincere profession of an opinion, but only honest blunder, the ensuing liability for negligence is one that is bounded by the contract."

Liability for negligent misrepresentation, including by accountants, is today much wider than *Ultramares* recognized. New York, for example, modified *Ultramares's* strict privity rule in favor of an approach that allows third parties to recover for accountants' negligent misrepresentations as long as their relationship to a defendant "sufficient[ly] approaches privity," a standard that requires, roughly, that the accountants know the third party will rely on their reports for a particular purpose and are connected to this reliance by conduct that reveals their knowledge.[27] It is even possible to find cases[28] and statutes[29] that subject accountants to potential liability for negligent misrepresentation towards any parties that they know their clients intend their reports to benefit or influence. Moreover, similar principles have been applied to sustain liability for negligent mis-

---

27. See *Credit Alliance Corp. v. Arthur Andersen Co.*, 483 N.E. 2d 110 (N.Y. 1985).

28. See, e.g., *Brumley v. Touche, Ross & Co.*, 487 N.E.2d. 641 (Ill. App. 1985).

29. See, e.g., 225 Illinois Compiled Statute Annotated 450/30.1.

representation towards foreseen users of representations made in other professional settings. These developments in effect expand the subject area scope of the approach taken in *Glanzer*.

The precise metes and bounds of negligent misrepresentation remain in flux. But however these are set, they retain the basic teaching shared by *Glanzer* and *Ultramares*, at least with respect to the structural distinction between negligent misrepresentation and contract proper. In all the cases, liability for negligent misrepresentation arises only where a duty of care exists that *precedes* the false representation at issue. The duty of care that grounds liability for negligent misrepresentation must thus arise independently of the representation, rather than being self-created by it. And as long as this remains so, then changes in the scope of negligent misrepresentation do not alter its fundamentally tort-like structure. The misrepresentation tort remains distinct from the spontaneously arising, chosen obligation associated with contract proper. Language that is reasonably interpreted as a contractual offer can generate contract obligation entirely on its own and in a free-standing fashion, including even among perfect strangers, where the speaker owes her listener no prior duty of care. The Restatement Section reproduced below recognizes and memorializes this structural divide.

Restatement (Second) of Torts

§ 552 Information Negligently Supplied For The Guidance Of Others

(1) One who, in the course of his business, profession or employment, or in any other transaction in which he has a pecuniary interest, supplies false information for the guidance of others in their business transactions, is subject to liability for pecuniary loss caused to them by their justifiable reliance upon the information, if he fails to exercise reasonable care or competence in obtaining or communicating the information.

(2) Except as stated in Subsection (3), the liability stated in Subsection (1) is limited to loss suffered

    (a) by the person or one of a limited group of persons for whose benefit and guidance he intends to supply the information or knows that the recipient intends to supply it; and

    (b) through reliance upon it in a transaction that he intends the information to influence or knows that the recipient so intends or in a substantially similar transaction.

(3) The liability of one who is under a public duty to give the information extends to loss suffered by any of the class of persons for whose benefit the duty is created, in any of the transactions in which it is intended to protect them.

Comments & Illustrations

Comment a. Although liability under the rule stated in this Section is based upon negligence of the actor in failing to exercise reasonable care or competence in supplying correct information, the scope of his liability is not determined by the rules that govern liability for the negligent supplying of chattels that imperil the security of the person, land or chattels of those to whom they are supplied (see §§ 388–402), or other negligent misrepresentation that results in physical harm. (See § 311). When the harm that is caused is only pecuniary loss, the courts have found it necessary to adopt a more restricted rule of liability, because of the extent to which misinformation may be, and may be expected to be, circulated, and the magnitude of the losses which may follow from reliance upon it.

The liability stated in this Section is likewise more restricted than that for fraudulent misrepresentation stated in § 531. When there is no intent to deceive but only good faith coupled with negligence, the fault of the maker of the misrepresentation is sufficiently less to justify a narrower responsibility for its consequences.

The reason a narrower scope of liability is fixed for negligent misrepresentation than for deceit is to be found in the difference between the obligations of honesty and of care, and in the significance of this difference to the reasonable expectations of the users of information that is supplied in connection with commercial transactions. Honesty requires only that the maker of a representation speak in good faith and without consciousness of a lack of any basis for belief in the truth or accuracy of what he says. The standard of honesty is unequivocal and ascertainable without regard to the character of the transaction in which the information will ultimately be relied upon or the situation of the party relying upon it. Any user of commercial information may reasonably expect the observance of this standard by a supplier of information to whom his use is reasonably foreseeable.

On the other hand, it does not follow that every user of commercial information may hold every maker to a duty of care. Unlike the duty of honesty, the duty of care to be observed in supplying information for use in commercial transactions implies an undertaking to observe a relative standard, which may be defined only in terms of the use to which the information will be put, weighed against the magnitude and probability of loss that might attend that use if the information proves to be incorrect. A user of commercial information cannot reasonably expect its maker to have undertaken to satisfy this obligation unless the terms of the obligation were known to him. Rather, one who relies upon information in connection with a commercial transaction may reasonably expect to hold the maker to a duty of care only in circumstances in which the maker was manifestly aware of the use to which the information was to be put and intended to supply it for that purpose.

By limiting the liability for negligence of a supplier of information to be used in commercial transactions to cases in which he manifests an intent to supply the information for the sort of use in which the plaintiff's loss occurs, the law promotes the important social policy of encouraging the flow of commercial information upon which the operation of the economy rests. The limitation applies, however, only in the case of information supplied in good faith, for no interest of society is served by promoting the flow of information not genuinely believed by its maker to be true.

Comment b. The rule stated in this Section applies not only to information given as to the existence of facts but also to an opinion given upon facts equally well known to both the supplier and the recipient. Such an opinion is often given by one whose only knowledge of the facts is derived from the person who asks it. As to the care and competence that the recipient of such an opinion is justified in expecting, see Comment *e*.

Comment on Subsection (1):

Comment c. Pecuniary interest in the transaction. The rule stated in Subsection (1) applies only when the defendant has a pecuniary interest in the transaction in which the information is given. If he has no pecuniary interest and the information is given purely gratuitously, he is under no duty to exercise reasonable care and competence in giving it. The situation is analogous to that of one who gratuitously lends or otherwise supplies a chattel, whose duty is only to disclose any facts he knows that may make it unsafe for use. (See § 405).

Illustrations

1. A, seeking information as to the will of B, asks C Trust Company for a copy of the will. C Trust Company is not in the business of supplying copies of wills, and has no interest in giving this one to A, but gratuitously agrees to supply the copy as a favor to A. By a negligent mistake but in good faith it gives A a copy of the will of another person of the same name as B. In reliance on the copy A incurs pecuniary loss. C Trust Co. is not liable to A.

2. The A Newspaper negligently publishes in one of its columns a statement that a certain proprietary drug is a sure cure for dandruff. B, who is plagued with dandruff, reads the statement and in reliance upon it purchases a quantity of the drug. It proves to be worthless as a dandruff cure and B suffers pecuniary loss. The A Newspaper is not liable to B.

Comment d. The defendant's pecuniary interest in supplying the information will normally lie in a consideration paid to him for it or paid in a transaction in the course of and as a part of which it is supplied. It may, however, be of a more indirect character. Thus the officers of a corporation, although they receive no personal consideration for giving information concerning its affairs, may have a pecuniary interest in its transactions, since they stand to profit indirectly from them, and an agent who expects to receive a commission on a sale may have such an interest in it although he sells nothing.

The fact that the information is given in the course of the defendant's business, profession or employment is a sufficient indication that he has a pecuniary interest in it, even though he receives no consideration for it at the time. It is not, however, conclusive. But when one who is engaged in a business or profession steps entirely outside of it, as when an attorney gives a casual and offhand opinion on a point of law to a friend whom he meets on the street, or what is commonly called a "curbstone opinion," it is not to be regarded as given in the course of his business or profession; and since he has no other interest in it, it is considered purely gratuitous. The recipient of the information is not justified in expecting that his informant will exercise the care and skill that is necessary to insure a correct opinion and is only justified in expecting that the opinion will be an honest one.

Comment e.   Reasonable care and competence. Since the rule of liability stated in Subsection (1) is based upon negligence, the defendant is subject to liability if, but only if, he has failed to exercise the care or competence of a reasonable man in obtaining or communicating the information. (See §§ 283, 288 and 289). What is reasonable is, as in other cases of negligence, dependent upon the circumstances. It is, in general, a matter of the care and competence that the recipient of the information is entitled to expect in the light of the circumstances and this will vary according to a good many factors. The question is one for the jury, unless the facts are so clear as to permit only one conclusion.

The particulars in which the recipient of information supplied by another is entitled to expect the exercise of care and competence depend upon the character of the information that is supplied. When the information concerns a fact not known to the recipient, he is entitled to expect that the supplier will exercise that care and competence in its ascertainment which the supplier's business or profession requires and which, therefore, the supplier professes to have by engaging in it. Thus the recipient is entitled to expect that such investigations as are necessary will be carefully made and that his informant will have normal business or professional competence to form an intelligent judgment upon the data obtained. On the other hand, if the supplier makes no pretense to special competence but agrees for a reward to furnish information that lies outside the field of his business or profession, the recipient is not justified in expecting more than that care and competence that the nonprofessional character of his informant entitles him to expect. When the information consists of an opinion upon facts supplied by the recipient or otherwise known to him, the recipient is entitled to expect a careful consideration of the facts and competence in arriving at an intelligent judgment. In all of these cases the recipient of the information is entitled to expect reasonable conversance with the language employed to communicate the information in question and reasonable care in its use, unless he knows that his informant is ignorant of the language in question or peculiarly careless in its use.

Illustration

3.   XYZ Corporation seeks a credit of $100,000 from F & Co., a factoring concern. Because the latest XYZ financial statements, audited by A & Co., a partnership of certified public accountants, are dated as of the last fiscal year-end of XYZ Corporation which

fell some eight months previously, F & Co., requests that A & Co. be retained to provide unaudited financial statements for the current interim period. A & Co., knowing the statements are being prepared for the consideration of F & Co. in connection with XYZ Corporation's request for the $100,000 credit, prepares financial statements from the books of the corporation without performing any tests of the accuracy of the entries themselves or respecting the transactions represented to underlie them. The statements, furnished under A & Co.'s letterhead, are labeled "unaudited" on each page and accompanied by a written representation that they have not been audited and that, accordingly, A & Co. is not in a position to express an opinion upon them. Nothing comes to the attention of A & Co. in the course of preparing the statements to indicate that they were incorrect, but because the books from which they were prepared were, unknown to A & Co., in error, the financial statements materially misstate the financial position of XYZ Corporation and its results of operations for the period subsequent to the preceding fiscal year-end. F & Co., because it extends the credit in reliance upon the statements, suffers substantial pecuniary loss. A & Co. is not subject to liability to F & Co.

Comment f. The care and competence that the supplier of information for the guidance of others is required under the rule stated in this Section to exercise in order that the information given may be correct, must be exercised in the following particulars. If the matter is one that requires investigation, the supplier of the information must exercise reasonable care and competence to ascertain the facts on which his statement is based. He must exercise the competence reasonably expected of one in his business or professional position in drawing inferences from facts not stated in the information. He must exercise reasonable care and competence in communicating the information so that it may be understood by the recipient, since the proper performance of the other two duties would be of no value if the information accurately obtained was so communicated as to be misleading.

Comment on Subsection (2):

Comment g. Information supplied directly and indirectly. The person for whose guidance the information is supplied is often the person who has employed the supplier to furnish it, in which case, if it is supplied for a consideration paid by that person, he has at his election either a right of action under the rule stated in this Section or a right of action upon the contract under which the information is supplied. In many cases, however, the information is supplied directly to the person who is to act upon it although it is paid for by the other party to the transaction. Thus, when a vendor of beans employs a public weigher to weigh beans, the weigher, who gives to the vendee a certificate which through his carelessness overstates the weight of the beans, is subject to liability to the vendee for the amount that he overpays in reliance upon the certificate. However, direct communication of the information to the person acting in reliance upon it is not necessary. In the situation above the liability of the weigher would not be affected by his giving the certificate to the vendor for communication to the vendee.

Comment h.   Persons for whose guidance the information is supplied. The rule stated in this Section subjects the negligent supplier of misinformation to liability only to those persons for whose benefit and guidance it is supplied. In this particular his liability is somewhat more narrowly restricted than that of the maker of a fraudulent representation (see § 531), which extends to any person whom the maker of the representation has reason to expect to act in reliance upon it.

Under this Section, as in the case of the fraudulent misrepresentation (see § 531), it is not necessary that the maker should have any particular person in mind as the intended, or even the probable, recipient of the information. In other words, it is not required that the person who is to become the plaintiff be identified or known to the defendant as an individual when the information is supplied. It is enough that the maker of the representation intends it to reach and influence either a particular person or persons, known to him, or a group or class of persons, distinct from the much larger class who might reasonably be expected sooner or later to have access to the information and foreseeably to take some action in reliance upon it. It is enough, likewise, that the maker of the representation knows that his recipient intends to transmit the information to a similar person, persons or group. It is sufficient, in other words, insofar as the plaintiff's identity is concerned, that the maker supplies the information for repetition to a certain group or class of persons and that the plaintiff proves to be one of them, even though the maker never had heard of him by name when the information was given. It is not enough that the maker merely knows of the ever-present possibility of repetition to anyone, and the possibility of action in reliance upon it, on the part of anyone to whom it may be repeated.

Even when the maker is informed of the identity of a definite person to whom the recipient intends to transmit the information, the circumstances may justify a finding that the name and identity of that person was regarded by the maker, and by the recipient, as important only because the person in question was one of a group whom the information was intended to reach and for whose guidance it was being supplied. In many situations the identity of the person for whose guidance the information is supplied is of no moment to the person who supplies it, although the number and character of the persons to be reached and influenced, and the nature and extent of the transaction for which guidance is furnished may be vitally important. This is true because the risk of liability to which the supplier subjects himself by undertaking to give the information, while it may not be affected by the identity of the person for whose guidance the information is given, is vitally affected by the number and character of the persons, and particularly the nature and extent of the proposed transaction. On the other hand, the circumstances may frequently show that the identity of the person for whose guidance the information is given is regarded by the person supplying it, and by the recipient, as important and material; and therefore the person giving the information understands that his liability is to be restricted to the named person and to him only. Thus when the information is procured for transmission to a named or otherwise described person, whether the maker is liable to another, to whom in substitution the information is transmitted in order to influence his conduct in an otherwise identical transaction, depends upon whether it is understood between the one giving the information and the one bringing about its transmission, that it is to be given to the named individual and to him only.

Illustrations

4. A, having lots for sale, negligently supplies misinformation concerning the lots to a real estate board, for the purpose of having the information incorporated in the board's multiple listing of available lots, which is distributed by the board to approximately 1,000 prospective purchasers of land each month. The listing is sent by the board to B, and in reliance upon the misinformation B purchases one of A's lots and in consequence suffers pecuniary loss. A is subject to liability to B.

5. A is negotiating with X Bank for a credit of $50,000. The Bank requires an audit by independent public accountants. A employs B & Company, a firm of accountants, to make the audit, telling them that the purpose of the audit is to meet the requirements of X Bank in connection with a credit of $50,000. B & Company agrees to make the audit, with the express understanding that it is for transmission to X Bank only. X Bank fails, and A, without any further communication with B & Company, submits its financial statements accompanied by B & Company's opinion to Y Bank, which in reliance upon it extends a credit of $50,000 to A. The audit is so carelessly made as to result in an unqualified favorable opinion on financial statements that materially misstates the financial position of A, and in consequence Y Bank suffers pecuniary loss through its extension of credit. B & Company is not liable to Y Bank.

6. The same facts as in Illustration 5, except that nothing is said about supplying the information for the guidance of X Bank only, and A merely informs B & Company that he expects to negotiate a bank loan, for $50,000, requires the audit for the purpose of the loan, and has X Bank in mind. B & Company is subject to liability to Y Bank.

7. The same facts as in Illustration 5, except that A informs B & Company that he expects to negotiate a bank loan, but does not mention the name of any bank. B & Company is subject to liability to Y Bank.

8. A, wishing to sell his car to B, writes to C, an expert mechanic, asking him to inspect the car and forward to A a letter

stating its condition, in order that A may give the letter to B, who, as A tells C, is a prospective purchaser. Nothing is said about using the information only for B. C may be found to have supplied the information for the guidance of B only, or for the guidance either of B or of any other purchaser whom A may find.

9.   The City of A is about to ask for bids for work on a sewer tunnel. It hires B Company, a firm of engineers, to make boring tests and provide a report showing the rock and soil conditions to be encountered. It notifies B Company that the report will be made available to bidders as a basis for their bids and that it is expected to be used by the successful bidder in doing the work. Without knowing the identity of any of the contractors bidding on the work, B Company negligently prepares and delivers to the City an inaccurate report, containing false and misleading information. On the basis of the report C makes a successful bid, and also on the basis of the report D, a subcontractor, contracts with C to do a part of the work. By reason of the inaccuracy of the report, C and D suffer pecuniary loss in performing their contracts. B Company is subject to liability to C and to D.

10.   A, an independent public accountant, is retained by B Company to conduct an annual audit of the customary scope for the corporation and to furnish his opinion on the corporation's financial statements. A is not informed of any intended use of the financial statements; but A knows that the financial statements, accompanied by an auditor's opinion, are customarily used in a wide variety of financial transactions by the corporation and that they may be relied upon by lenders, investors, shareholders, creditors, purchasers and the like, in numerous possible kinds of transactions. In fact B Company uses the financial statements and accompanying auditor's opinion to obtain a loan from X Bank. Because of A's negligence, he issues an unqualifiedly favorable opinion upon a balance sheet that materially misstates the financial position of B Company, and through reliance upon it X Bank suffers pecuniary loss. A is not liable to X Bank.

11.   A Bank receives an inquiry from B Bank respecting the credit-worthiness of C Corporation, a customer of A Bank. B Bank informs A Bank that the reason for the inquiry is that D & Co., an advertising agency, has been approached by C Corporation with a request that it manage a $200,000 advertising campaign for C Corporation on the local television station; that under the terms of its customary arrangement with the television station, D & Co. would be guarantor of any amount owing the station, and that D & Co. has requested its bank to ascertain from C Corporation's bank whether C Corporation is sufficiently credit-worthy to incur and satisfy a liability of $200,000. A Bank, without checking C Corporation's account, and without a disclaimer of liability for its answer, replies that it believes C Corporation to be good for such

an obligation. D & Co. arranges for the advertising campaign and shortly thereafter C Corporation enters bankruptcy. A Bank is subject to liability for negligence to D & Co.

12. In 1934, A Company, a firm of surveyors, contracts with B to make a survey and description of B's land. A Company is not informed of any intended use of the survey report but knows that survey reports are customarily used in a wide variety of real estate transactions and that it may be relied upon by purchasers, mortgagees, investors and others. The survey is negligently made and misstates the boundaries and extent of the land. In 1958 C, relying upon the report that B exhibits to him, purchases the land from B, and in consequence suffers pecuniary loss. A Company is not liable to C.

Comment:

Comment i. Comparison with other Sections. When a misrepresentation creates a risk of physical harm to the person, land or chattels of others, the liability of the maker extends, under the rules stated in §§ 310 and 311, to any person to whom he should expect physical harm to result through action taken in reliance upon it. When a misrepresentation is fraudulent and results in pecuniary loss, the liability of the maker extends, under the rule stated in § 531, to any of the class of persons whom he intends or should expect to act in reliance upon it, and to loss suffered by them in any of the general type of transactions in which he intends or should expect their conduct to be influenced.

Under the rule stated in Subsection (2) of this Section, when the misrepresentation is merely negligent and results in pecuniary loss, the scope of the liability is narrower. The maker of the negligent misrepresentation is subject to liability to only those persons for whose guidance he knows the information to be supplied, and to them only for loss incurred in the kind of transaction in which it is expected to influence them, or a transaction of a substantially similar kind. There is an exception, as stated in Subsection (3), when there is a public duty to give the information. (See Comment *k*, below).

Comment j. Transactions for guidance in which the information is supplied. The rule stated in Clause (2)(b) is somewhat more narrowly restricted than in the case of the liability of the maker of a fraudulent representation stated in § 531, Clause (b). The liability of the maker of the fraudulent representation extends to all transactions of the type or kind that the maker intends or has reason to expect. Under this Section, the liability of the maker of a negligent misrepresentation is limited to the transaction that he intends, or knows that the recipient intends, to influence, or to a substantially similar transaction.

Thus independent public accountants who negligently make an audit of books of a corporation, which they are told is to be used only for the purpose of obtaining a particular line of banking credit, are not subject to liability to a wholesale merchant whom the corporation induces to supply it with goods on credit by showing him the financial statements and the accountant's opinion. On the other hand, it is not necessary that the transaction in which the opinion is relied on shall be identical in all of its minute details with the one intended. It is enough that it is substantially the same transaction or one substantially similar. Thus, in the situation above stated, if the corporation, finding that at the moment it does not need the credit to obtain which the audit was procured, uses it a month later to obtain the same credit from the same bank, the accountants will remain subject to liability to the bank for the loss resulting from its extension of credit, unless the financial condition of the corporation has materially changed in the interim or so much time has elapsed that the bank cannot justifiably rely upon the audit.

There may be many minor differences that do not affect the essential character of the transaction. The question may be one of the extent of the departure that the maker of the representation understands is to be expected. If he is told that the information that he supplies is to be used in applying to a particular bank for a loan of $10,000, the fact that the loan is made by that bank for $15,000 will not necessarily mean that the transaction is a different one. But if the loan is for $500,000, the very difference in amount would lead the ordinary borrower or lender to regard it as a different kind of transaction. The ordinary practices and attitudes of the business world are to be taken into account, and the question becomes one of whether the departure from the contemplated transaction is so major and so significant that it cannot be regarded as essentially the same transaction. It is also possible, of course, that more than one kind of transaction may be understood as intended.

Illustrations

13. A negligently furnishes to a title insurance company a letter praising its facilities and operation, for the purpose of aiding it in selling title insurance. The company exhibits the letter to B, who relies on it in taking out title insurance with the company, and is also induced by the letter to purchase stock in the company. The company proves to be insolvent and B suffers pecuniary loss. A is subject to liability to B for his loss on the title insurance but not for his loss on the purchase of the stock.

14. A, an independent public accountant, negligently conducts an audit for B Corporation, and issues an unqualified favorable opinion on its financial statements, although it is in fact insolvent. A knows that B Corporation intends to exhibit the balance sheet to C Corporation, as a basis for applying for credit for the purchase of goods. In reliance upon the balance sheet, C Corporation buys the controlling interest in the stock of B Corporation and as a result suffers pecuniary loss. A is not liable to C Corporation.

15. The same facts as in Illustration 14, except that A is informed that C Corporation will be asked to extend credit for the purchase of washing machines, and credit is extended instead for

the purchase of electric refrigerators. A is subject to liability to C
Corporation.

Comment on Subsection (3):

Comment k. Public duty to give information. When there is a public
duty to supply the information in question, an exception arises to the rule
stated in Subsection (2), and the maker of the negligent misrepresentation
becomes subject to liability to any of the class of persons for whose benefit
the duty is created and for their pecuniary losses suffered in any of the
general type of transactions in which they are intended to be protected.

The usual case in which the exception arises is that of a public officer
who, by his acceptance of his office, has undertaken a duty to the public to
furnish information of a particular kind. Typical is the case of a recording
clerk, whose duty it is to furnish certified copies of the records under his
control. The rule stated is not, however, limited to public officers, and it
may apply to private individuals or corporations who are required by law to
file information for the benefit of the public.

The scope of the defendant's duty to others in these cases will depend
upon the purpose for which the information is required to be furnished.
The purpose may be found to be to protect only a particular and limited
class of persons, as when a statute requiring insurance companies to file
information concerning their finances with a state insurance commissioner
is found to be only for the protection of those buying insurance. In such a
case the liability of the company when it negligently gives false information
extends only to those who take out insurance policies and only to losses
suffered through taking out the policy. On the other hand, the group
protected may be a much broader one and may include any one who may
reasonably be expected to rely on the information and suffer loss as a
result.

Illustrations

16. A, a notary public, in the performance of his official
duties, negligently takes an acknowledgment of a signature on a
deed, and certifies that it is that of B. In fact the person signing is
not B and the signature is a forgery. The deed is recorded, and in
reliance upon the record C purchases the land from D, and as a
result suffers pecuniary loss. A is subject to liability to C.

17. A, a county tax clerk, in the performance of his official
duties, negligently gives B a certificate stating that the taxes on
B's land have been paid. In reliance upon the certificate, C buys
the land from B and as a result suffers pecuniary loss when he is
compelled to pay the taxes. A is subject to liability to C.

18. A, a United States government food inspector, in the
performance of his official duties, negligently stamps a quantity of
B's beef as "Grade A." In fact the beef is of inferior quality. In
reliance upon the stamps, C buys the beef from D, and suffers
pecuniary loss as a result. A is subject to liability to C.

16.1.C   PRODUCTS LIABILITY AND BREACH OF WARRANTY

The previous section documented, again and again, the ways in which the misrepresentation torts fall short of establishing a general colonization of contract by tort. The shortfall is rendered more vivid by contrasting the situation with respect to a general tort on the one hand and, on the other, certain subject-specific circumstances in which liability for negligent misrepresentation does begin to approach contract liability, although within a very, very narrow domain. Where commercial sellers make representations concerning products intended for use by consumers, the gap between contract and tort diminishes dramatically, so that much of contract law merely duplicates rights and duties established involuntarily, by tort. This result obtains because each legal order approaches the other in this area. The misrepresentation torts receive a more assertive elaboration in connection with consumer sales contracts than they generally do. And contract law does not quite retain the self-confidence to insist on its own structural commitments in sales to consumers, but instead remains, to a greater or lesser extent, beholden to tort-like notions. The following materials illustrate the main lines of the doctrine.

16.1.C.1   Reliance and the Benefits of the Bargain

Restatement (Second) of Torts

§ 402B   Misrepresentation By Seller Of Chattels To Consumer

One engaged in the business of selling chattels who, by advertising, labels, or otherwise, makes to the public a misrepresentation of a material fact concerning the character or quality of a chattel sold by him is subject to liability for physical harm to a consumer of the chattel caused by justifiable reliance upon the misrepresentation, even though

(a) it is not made fraudulently or negligently, and

(b) the consumer has not bought the chattel from or entered into any contractual relation with the seller.

Caveat:

The Institute expresses no opinion as to whether the rule stated in this Section may apply

(1) where the representation is not made to the public, but to an individual, or

(2) where physical harm is caused to one who is not a consumer of the chattel.

Comments & Illustrations

Comment a.   The rule stated in this Section is one of strict liability for physical harm to the consumer, resulting from a misrepresentation of the character or quality of the chattel sold, even though the misrepresentation is an innocent one, and not made fraudulently or negligently. Although the Section deals with misrepresentation, it is inserted here in order to complete the rules dealing with the liability of suppliers of chattels for physical harm caused by the chattel. A parallel rule, as to strict liability for pecuniary loss resulting from such a misrepresentation, is stated in § 552D.

Comment b. The rule stated in this Section differs from the rule of strict liability stated in § 402A, which is a special rule applicable only to sellers of products for consumption and does not depend upon misrepresentation. The rule here stated applies to one engaged in the business of selling any type of chattel, and is limited to misrepresentations of their character or quality.

Comment c. History. The early rule was that a seller of chattels incurred no liability for physical harm resulting from the use of the chattel to anyone other than his immediate buyer, unless there was privity of contract between them. (See § 395, Comment *a.*) Beginning with Langridge v. Levy, 150 Eng.Rep. 863 (1837), an exception was developed in cases where the seller made fraudulent misrepresentations to the immediate buyer, concerning the character or quality of the chattel sold, and because of the fact misrepresented harm resulted to a third person who was using the chattel. The remedy lay in an action for deceit, and the rule which resulted is now stated in § 557A.

Shortly after 1930, a number of the American courts began, more or less independently, to work out a further extension of liability for physical harm to the consumer of the chattel, in cases where the seller made misrepresentations to the public concerning its character or quality, and the consumer, as a member of the public, purchased the chattel in reliance upon the misrepresentation and suffered physical harm because of the fact misrepresented. In such cases the seller was held to strict liability for the misrepresentation, even though it was not made fraudulently or negligently. The leading case is *Baxter v. Ford Motor Co.*, 168 Wash. 456 (1932), adhered to on rehearing, 168 Wash. 465, second appeal, 179 Wash. 123 (1934), in which the manufacturer of an automobile advertised to the public that the windshield glass was "shatterproof," and the purchaser was injured when a stone struck the glass and it shattered. In the beginning various theories of liability were suggested, including strict liability in deceit, and a contract resulting from an offer made to the consumer to be bound by the representation, accepted by his purchase.

Comment d. "Warranty." The theory finally adopted by most of the decisions, however, has been that of a non-contractual "express warranty" made to the consumer in the form of the representation to the public upon which he relies. The difficulties attending the use of the word "warranty" are the same as those involved under § 402A, and Comment *m* under that Section is equally applicable here so far as it is pertinent. The liability stated in this Section is liability in tort, and not in contract; and if it is to be called one of "warranty," it is at least a different kind of warranty from that involved in the ordinary sale of goods from the immediate seller to the immediate buyer, and is subject to different rules.

Comment e.   Sellers included. The rule stated in this Section applies to any person engaged in the business of selling any type of chattel. It is not limited to sellers of food or products for intimate bodily use, as was until lately the rule stated in § 402A. It is not limited to manufacturers of the chattel, and it includes wholesalers, retailers, and other distributors who sell it.

The rule stated applies, however, only to those who are engaged in the business of selling such chattels. It has no application to anyone who is not so engaged in business. It does not apply, for example, to a newspaper advertisement published by a private owner of a single automobile who offers it for sale.

Comment f.   Misrepresentation of character or quality. The rule stated applies to any misrepresentation of a material fact concerning the character or quality of the chattel sold which is made to the public by one so engaged in the business of selling such chattels. The fact misrepresented must be a material one, upon which the consumer may be expected to rely in making his purchase, and he must justifiably rely upon it. (See Comment *j.*) If he does so, and suffers physical harm by reason of the fact misrepresented, there is strict liability to him.

Illustration

   1.   A manufactures automobiles. He advertises in newspapers and magazines that the glass in his cars is "shatterproof." B reads this advertising, and in reliance upon it purchases from a retail dealer an automobile manufactured by A. While B is driving the car, a stone thrown up by a passing truck strikes the windshield and shatters it, injuring B. A is subject to strict liability to B.

Comment g.   Material fact. The rule stated in this Section applies only to misrepresentations of material facts concerning the character or quality of the chattel in question. It does not apply to statements of opinion, and in particular it does not apply to the kind of loose general praise of wares sold which, on the part of the seller, is considered to be "sales talk," and is commonly called "puffing"—as, for example, a statement that an automobile is the best on the market for the price. As to such general language of opinion, see § 542, and Comment *d* under that Section, which is applicable here so far as it is pertinent. In addition, the fact misrepresented must be a material one, of importance to the normal purchaser, by which the ultimate buyer may justifiably be expected to be influenced in buying the chattel.

Comment h.   "To the public." The rule stated in this Section is limited to misrepresentations which are made by the seller to the public at large, in order to induce purchase of the chattels sold, or are intended by the seller to, and do, reach the public. The form of the representation is not important. It may be made by public advertising in newspapers or television, by literature distributed to the public through dealers, by labels on the product sold, or leaflets accompanying it, or in any other manner, whether it be oral or written.

Illustrations

2.   A manufactures wire rope. He issues a manual containing statements concerning its strength, which he distributes through dealers to buyers, and to members of the public who may be expected to buy. In reliance upon the statements made in the manual, B buys a quantity of the wire rope from a dealer, and makes use of it to hoist a weight of 1,000 pounds. The strength of the rope is not as great as is represented in the manual, and as a result the rope breaks and the weight falls on B and injures him. A is subject to strict liability to B.

3.   A manufactures a product for use by women at home in giving "permanent waves" to their hair. He places on the bottles labels which state that the product may safely be used in a particular manner, and will not be injurious to the hair. B reads such a label, and in reliance upon it purchases a bottle of the product from a retail dealer. She uses it as directed, and as a result her hair is destroyed. A is subject to strict liability to B.

Comment i.   Consumers. The rule stated in this Section is limited to strict liability for physical harm to consumers of the chattel. The Caveat leaves open the question whether the rule may not also apply to one who is not a consumer, but who suffers physical harm through his justifiable reliance upon the misrepresentation.

"Consumer" is to be understood in the broad sense of one who makes use of the chattel in the manner which a purchaser may be expected to use it. Thus an employee of the ultimate purchaser to whom the chattel is turned over, and who is directed to make use of it in his work, is a consumer, and so is the wife of the purchaser of an automobile who is permitted by him to drive it.

Comment j.   Justifiable reliance. The rule here stated applies only where there is justifiable reliance upon the misrepresentation of the seller, and physical harm results because of such reliance, and because of the fact which is misrepresented. It does not apply where the misrepresentation is not known, or there is indifference to it, and it does not influence the purchase or subsequent conduct. At the same time, however, the misrepresentation need not be the sole inducement to purchase, or to use the chattel, and it is sufficient that it has been a substantial factor in that inducement. (Compare § 546 and Comments.) Since the liability here is for misrepresentation, the rules as to what will constitute justifiable reliance stated in §§ 537–545A are applicable to this Section, so far as they are pertinent.

The reliance need not necessarily be that of the consumer who is injured. It may be that of the ultimate purchaser of the chattel, who because of such reliance passes it on to the consumer who is in fact injured, but is ignorant of the misrepresentation. Thus a husband who buys an automobile in justifiable reliance upon statements concerning its brakes, and permits his wife to drive the car, supplies the element of reliance, even though the wife in fact never learns of the statements.

Illustration

4.   The same facts as in Illustration 2, except that the harm is suffered by C, an employee of B, to whom B turns over the wire rope without informing him of the representations made by A. The same result.

Restatement (Second) of Torts

§ 552C   Misrepresentation In Sale, Rental Or Exchange Transaction

(1) One who, in a sale, rental or exchange transaction with another, makes a misrepresentation of a material fact for the purpose of inducing the other to act or to refrain from acting in reliance upon it, is subject to liability to the other for pecuniary loss caused to him by his justifiable reliance upon the misrepresentation, even though it is not made fraudulently or negligently.

(2) Damages recoverable under the rule stated in this section are limited to the difference between the value of what the other has parted with and the value of what he has received in the transaction.

Caveat:

The Institute expresses no opinion as to whether there may be other types of business transactions, in addition to those of sale, rental and exchange, in which strict liability may be imposed for innocent misrepresentation under the conditions stated in this Section.

Comment on Subsection (1):

Comment a.   History. The rule developed by the English courts, following the leading case of *Derry v. Peek* (1889) 14 A.C. 337, was that there was no liability for a misrepresentation causing only pecuniary loss unless the misrepresentation was fraudulent, as that term is defined in § 526. This rule received wide application in the United States. As to the extent to which it has been modified to permit recovery for misrepresentation that is not fraudulent but merely negligent, see § 552 and Comments. The rule stated in this Section represents a further modification reflected in the decisions of a number of American jurisdictions, some of which, in the case of bargaining transactions, rejected the rule of *Derry v. Peek* or never really accepted the holding of that case despite some judicial language seemingly to the contrary. It is a rule of strict liability for innocent misrepresentation of a material fact, made to another in a sale, rental or exchange transaction.

The courts that apply this rule have expressed it in differing ways. Some have imposed upon a party to a bargaining transaction a "duty" to know. Others have held that an unqualified statement of fact, which is susceptible of personal knowledge and which turns out to be false, is fraudulent insofar as there was no disclaimer of personal knowledge; and this view seems to have been taken without regard to whether the other party was actually deceived by the absence of the disclaimer. Although these courts use the language of scienter, their decisions actually constitute the imposition of liability for innocent misrepresentation.

More significantly, other courts have utilized the rule originating in equity that when a party seeks rescission of a transaction on the ground of a misrepresentation of a material fact by the other party relief will be granted even though the misrepresentation was innocent (just as rescission is also granted for mutual mistake). (See, generally, Restatement of Restitution, §§ 6, 8; Restatement, Second, Contracts §§ 304, 306). This rule of the law of restitution has also been regularly applied in actions at law, at least in situations in which the plaintiff is seeking to recover money paid and has already effected a rescission, so that a decree establishing the rescission is not required. (See Restatement of Restitution, § 28). Under similar circumstances a number of courts have permitted a tort action for damages without regard to the requirement that the transaction be completely rescinded, either by the plaintiff or by the court, and without limiting the action to the restitutionary concept of recovery of money paid.

Comment b.   Relationship to action for restitution or breach of warranty. The remedy provided in this Section is very similar to that afforded under the law of restitution. It differs, however, in a material respect. The plaintiff is permitted to retain what he has received and recover damages, rather than rescind and seek restitution, in which case he must return what he received. The tort action for damages may have a definite advantage to the plaintiff in cases in which he is unable to restore what he received in its original condition; when he has made improvements or for other reasons finds it desirable to keep what he has received rather than return it; when he is barred from rescission by delay or has so far committed himself that he has lost the remedy by an election; or when for some other reason, such as the defendant's change of position, restitution is not available to him. It may even in many cases be a better solution from the point of view of the defendant himself, since it permits the transaction to stand, rather than be upset at a later date.

In view of the many similarities of the rule set forth in this Section to the restitutionary remedy, it is difficult to say with certainty whether this rule should be regarded as one of strict liability in the law of torts, eliminating the requirement of intent or negligence in making the representation, or one of the law of restitution, eliminating the requirement of rescinding and restoring the status quo. Under either classification the rule of this Section retains its usefulness.

It should be added that in cases involving the sale of goods, and probably in other transactions, a somewhat similar remedy has been available in the action for breach of warranty. The latter action, despite its historic relationship to tort, has been subject to important contract defenses, notably among them the parol evidence rule. This is made explicit by the Uniform Commercial Code. (See U.C.C. § 2–202). Further, in cases involving the sale of goods, most of the innocent misrepresentations made actionable by this Section would also be actionable under the Code on the theory of breach of warranty. But it does not necessarily follow that actions for damages founded upon innocent misrepresentation are preempted by the Code. The measure of damages provided by this Section differs from the traditional measure of damages for breach of warranty (now embodied in the Code). Under this Section, damages are solely restitutionary in character. In contrast, the measure of damages for breach of warranty includes compensation for benefit of the bargain and for consequential losses. This difference argues for viewing the tort action under this Section as unburdened by contract (or Code) defenses. However, this issue has gone virtually unnoticed in the jurisdictions that give damages in tort for innocent misrepresentation. In a case in which, as a practical matter, the amount recoverable under this Section is substantially the same as the amount recoverable for breach of warranty, the argument against recognition of defenses traditional to the warranty action loses much of its force.

Comment c.   Sale, rental or exchange. The cases to which the rule of strict liability for innocent misrepresentation stated in this Section has been applied thus far have generally been confined to sale, rental or exchange transactions between the plaintiff and the defendant. This includes any sale, rental or exchange of land, chattels, securities or anything else of value, such as copyrights, patents and other valuable intangible rights. As to possible application of the rule to other types of business transactions, see the Caveat, and Comment *g* below.

Comment d.   Parties. The rule stated is limited to the immediate parties to the sale, rental or exchange transaction itself. It does not apply in favor of a third person who is not a party to the transaction, even though he acts according to expectations in taking action or refraining from it in reliance upon the misrepresentation. The third person may recover only if the misrepresentation is fraudulent or negligent, and thus is within a rule stated in §§ 531 or 552. The same is true of one to whom the misrepresentation is made directly, but who is induced by it to incur loss in a transaction with a third person.

Comment e.   Misrepresentation. In order for the rule stated in this Section to apply there must be a misrepresentation of fact, express or implied. The rule of this Section does not apply to misrepresentations of opinion, intention or law, except as they may imply misrepresentations of fact. (See §§ 542–545). The fact misrepresented must be one that is material to the transaction and of sufficient consequence to justify reliance upon it in entering into the transaction. The representation must be made for the purpose of inducing the plaintiff to rely upon it in acting or refraining from action as a part of the transaction. He must in fact so rely and his reliance must be justifiable under the circumstances. In these respects the rules stated in §§ 531 to 548 are applicable to this Section, so far as they are pertinent.

Comment on Subsection (2):

Comment f. Damages. The damages given under this Section are restitutionary in nature. In the traditional restitution action, the plaintiff returns what he has received in the transaction, and recovers what he has parted with, so that he is in effect restored to the pecuniary position in which he stood before the transaction. A similar and yet different result is achieved by the rule of this Section, in that the plaintiff recovers the difference between the value of what he parted with and the value of what he has received and still retains. Since the defendant's misrepresentation is an innocent one, he is not held liable for other damages; specifically, he is not liable for benefit of the bargain or for consequential damages.

Comment on Caveat:

Comment g.   Under the rule stated in this Section, the strict liability for innocent misrepresentation is limited to sale, rental or exchange transactions between the plaintiff and the defendant. There have, however, been occasional decisions in which the same rule has been applied to other types of business transactions, such as the issuance of an insurance policy or the inducement of an investment or a loan. In a few other instances agents selling for their principals have been held to the strict liability for innocent misrepresentation, when they have received a commission or had some other pecuniary interest in the transaction. The law appears to be still in a process of development, and the ultimate limits of the liability are not yet determined. The Caveat therefore leaves open the question of whether there may be other types of transactions to which the rule stated here may be applied.

Restatement (Third) of Torts: Products Liability

§ 9   Liability of Commercial Product Seller or Distributor for Harm Caused by Misrepresentation

One engaged in the business of selling or otherwise distributing products who, in connection with the sale of a product, makes a fraudulent, negligent, or innocent misrepresentation of material fact concerning the product is subject to liability for harm to persons or property caused by the misrepresentation.

Comment & Illustrations

Comment a. Liability for fraudulent or negligent misrepresentation. The rules in the Restatement, Second, of Torts, governing liability for fraudulent and negligent misrepresentation, are contained in §§ 310 and 311. Case law has followed these Sections. Although these Sections do not explicitly apply to commercial product sellers, they admit of such application. Given the availability to plaintiffs of the rule under § 402B of the Restatement, Second, of Torts, subjecting product sellers to strict liability even in the absence of fraud or negligence, (see Comment *b*), there can be no doubt that product sellers are subject to liability for fraudulent or negligent misrepresentation. By hypothesis, given the rule stated in § 402B, a plaintiff who proves that the misrepresentation that caused harm was made fraudulently or negligently should have a remedy.

Comment b.   Liability for innocent misrepresentation. The rules governing liability for innocent product misrepresentation are stated in the Restatement, Second, of Torts § 402B. Case law has followed that Section. Section 402B contains two caveats. The first caveat leaves open the question whether a seller should be liable under § 402B for an innocent misrepresentation that is made to an individual and not to the public at large. This question remains open. Case law on the subject of liability for innocent misrepresentation has dealt exclusively with public misrepresentations. The second caveat to § 402B leaves open the question whether a seller should be liable for an innocent misrepresentation that causes harm to the person or property of one who is not a consumer of the product. Case law has not resolved the issue of whether an innocent misrepresentation may, in the absence of a product defect, be a basis of liability to a non-consumer who suffers harm as a result of reliance by an intermediary.

Comment c.   The elements of materiality, causation, and contributory fault. It is important to note that § 402B, in Comments *g* and *j*, incorporates by reference §§ 537–548A of the Restatement, Second, of Torts. These Sections define what constitutes a material misrepresentation, see § 538; what is a material fact, see §§ 538–543; the requirement that the misrepresentation be a cause in fact of the harm, see § 546; the requirement that the misrepresentation be a legal cause of the harm, see § 548A; and the role of contributory fault and its relation to justifiable reliance, see § 545A.

Comment d.   No requirement of product defect. This Section does not require the plaintiff to show that the product was defective at the time of sale or distribution within the meaning of other Sections of this Restatement Third of Torts: Products Liability.

Comment e.   Relationship between the rule stated in this Section and express warranty. The rule stated in this Section provides a remedy in tort in many cases in which a remedy for breach of express warranty or implied warranty of fitness for particular purpose is also available to the plaintiff. Breach of these warranties provides an independent basis of liability under the Uniform Commercial Code and may be combined in the same case with a claim for misrepresentation.

Uniform Commercial Code

§ 2–313   Express Warranties by Affirmation, Promise, Description, Sample

(1) Express warranties by the seller are created as follows:

(a) Any affirmation of fact or promise made by the seller to the buyer which relates to the goods and becomes part of the basis of the bargain creates an express warranty that the goods shall conform to the affirmation or promise.

(b) Any description of the goods which is made part of the basis of the bargain creates an express warranty that the goods shall conform to the description.

(c) Any sample or model which is made part of the basis of the bargain creates an express warranty that the whole of the goods shall conform to the sample or model.

(2) It is not necessary to the creation of an express warranty that the seller use formal words such as "warrant" or "guarantee" or that he have a specific intention to make a warranty, but an affirmation merely of the value of the goods or a statement purporting to be merely the seller's opinion or commendation of the goods does not create a warranty.

Official Comment

Prior Uniform Statutory Provision: Sections 12, 14 and 16, Uniform Sales Act.

Changes: Rewritten

Purposes of Changes: To consolidate and systematize basic principles with the result that:

1. "Express" warranties rest on "dickered" aspects of the individual bargain, and go so clearly to the essence of that bargain that words of disclaimer in a form are repugnant to the basic dickered terms. "Implied" warranties rest so clearly on a common factual situation or set of conditions that no particular language or action is necessary to evidence them and they will arise in such a situation unless unmistakably negated.

This section reverts to the older case law insofar as the warranties of description and sample are designated "express" rather than "implied".

2. Although this section is limited in its scope and direct purpose to warranties made by the seller to the buyer as part of a contract for sale, the warranty sections of this Article are not designed in any way to disturb those lines of case law growth which have recognized that warranties need not be confined either to sales contracts or to the direct parties to such a contract. They may arise in other appropriate circumstances such as in the case of bailments for hire, whether such bailment is itself the main contract or is merely a supplying of containers under a contract for the sale of their contents. The provisions of Section 2–318 on third party beneficiaries expressly recognize this case law development within one particular area. Beyond that, the matter is left to the case law with the intention that the policies of this Act may offer useful guidance in dealing with further cases as they arise.

3. The present section deals with affirmations of fact by the seller, descriptions of the goods or exhibitions of samples, exactly as any other

part of a negotiation which ends in a contract is dealt with. No specific intention to make a warranty is necessary if any of these factors is made part of the basis of the bargain. In actual practice affirmations of fact made by the seller about the goods during a bargain are regarded as part of the description of those goods; hence no particular reliance on such statements need be shown in order to weave them into the fabric of the agreement. Rather, any fact which is to take such affirmations, once made, out of the agreement requires clear affirmative proof. The issue normally is one of fact.

4. In view of the principle that the whole purpose of the law of warranty is to determine what it is that the seller has in essence agreed to sell, the policy is adopted of those cases which refuse except in unusual circumstances to recognize a material deletion of the seller's obligation. Thus, a contract is normally a contract for a sale of something describable and described. A clause generally disclaiming "all warranties, express or implied" cannot reduce the seller's obligation with respect to such description and therefore cannot be given literal effect under Section 2–316.

This is not intended to mean that the parties, if they consciously desire, cannot make their own bargain as they wish. But in determining what they have agreed upon good faith is a factor and consideration should be given to the fact that the probability is small that a real price is intended to be exchanged for a pseudo-obligation.

5. Paragraph (1)(b) makes specific some of the principles set forth above when a description of the goods is given by the seller.

A description need not be by words. Technical specifications, blueprints and the like can afford more exact description than mere language and if made part of the basis of the bargain goods must conform with them. Past deliveries may set the description of quality, either expressly or impliedly by course of dealing. Of course, all descriptions by merchants must be read against the applicable trade usages with the general rules as to merchantability resolving any doubts.

6. The basic situation as to statements affecting the true essence of the bargain is no different when a sample or model is involved in the transaction. This section includes both a "sample" actually drawn from the bulk of goods which is the subject matter of the sale, and a "model" which is offered for inspection when the subject matter is not at hand and which has not been drawn from the bulk of the goods.

Although the underlying principles are unchanged, the facts are often ambiguous when something is shown as illustrative, rather than as a straight sample. In general, the presumption is that any sample or model just as any affirmation of fact is intended to become a basis of the bargain. But there is no escape from the question of fact. When the seller exhibits a sample purporting to be drawn from an existing bulk, good faith of course requires that the sample be fairly drawn. But in mercantile experience the mere exhibition of a "sample" does not of itself show whether it is merely intended to "suggest" or to "be" the character of the subject-matter of the contract. The question is whether the seller has so acted with reference to the sample as to make him responsible that the whole shall have at least the values shown by it. The circumstances aid in answering this question. If the sample has been drawn from an existing bulk, it must be regarded as describing values of the goods contracted for unless it is accompanied by an unmistakable denial of such responsibility. If, on the other hand, a model of merchandise not on hand is offered, the mercantile presumption that it has become a literal description of the subject matter is not so strong, and particularly so if modification on the buyer's initiative impairs any feature of the model.

7.   The precise time when words of description or affirmation are made or samples are shown is not material. The sole question is whether the language or samples or models are fairly to be regarded as part of the contract. If language is used after the closing of the deal (as when the buyer when taking delivery asks and receives an additional assurance), the warranty becomes a modification, and need not be supported by consideration if it is otherwise reasonable and in order (Section 2–209).

8.   Concerning affirmations of value or a seller's opinion or commendation under subsection (2), the basic question remains the same: What statements of the seller have in the circumstances and in objective judgment become part of the basis of the bargain? As indicated above, all of the statements of the seller do so unless good reason is shown to the contrary. The provisions of subsection (2) are included, however, since common experience discloses that some statements or predictions cannot fairly be viewed as entering into the bargain. Even as to false statements of value, however, the possibility is left open that a remedy may be provided by the law relating to fraud or misrepresentation.

Uniform Commercial Code

§ 2–314   Implied Warranty: Merchantability; Usage of Trade

(1) Unless excluded or modified (Section 2–316), a warranty that the goods shall be merchantable is implied in a contract for their sale if the seller is a merchant with respect to goods of that kind. Under this section the serving for value of food or drink to be consumed either on the premises or elsewhere is a sale.

(2) Goods to be merchantable must be at least such as

(a) pass without objection in the trade under the contract description; and

(b) in the case of fungible goods, are of fair average quality within the description; and

(c) are fit for the ordinary purposes for which such goods are used; and

(d) run, within the variations permitted by the agreement, of even kind, quality and quantity within each unit and among all units involved; and

(e) are adequately contained, packaged, and labeled as the agreement may require; and

(f) conform to the promise or affirmations of fact made on the container or label if any.

(3) Unless excluded or modified (Section 2–316) other implied warranties may arise from course of dealing or usage of trade.

Official Comment

Prior Uniform Statutory Provision: Section 15(2), Uniform Sales Act.

Changes: Completely rewritten

Purposes of Changes: This section, drawn in view of the steadily developing case law on the subject, is intended to make it clear that:

1. The seller's obligation applies to present sales as well as to contracts to sell subject to the effects of any examination of specific goods. (Subsection (2) of Section 2–316). Also, the warranty of merchantability applies to sales for use as well as to sales for resale.

2. The question when the warranty is imposed turns basically on the meaning of the terms of the agreement as recognized in the trade. Goods delivered under an agreement made by a merchant in a given line of trade must be of a quality comparable to that generally acceptable in that line of trade under the description or other designation of the goods used in the agreement. The responsibility imposed rests on any merchant-seller, and the absence of the words "grower or manufacturer or not" which appeared in Section 15(2) of the Uniform Sales Act does not restrict the applicability of this section.

3. A specific designation of goods by the buyer does not exclude the seller's obligation that they be fit for the general purposes appropriate to such goods. A contract for the sale of second-hand goods, however, involves only such obligation as is appropriate to such goods for that is their contract description. A person making an isolated sale of goods is not a "merchant" within the meaning of the full scope of this section and, thus, no warranty of merchantability would apply. His knowledge of any defects not apparent on inspection would, however, without need for express agreement and in keeping with the underlying reason of the present section and the provisions on good faith, impose an obligation that known material but hidden defects be fully disclosed.

4. Although a seller may not be a "merchant" as to the goods in question, if he states generally that they are "guaranteed" the provisions of this section may furnish a guide to the content of the resulting express warranty. This has particular significance in the case of second-hand sales, and has further significance in limiting the effect of fine-print disclaimer

clauses where their effect would be inconsistent with large-print assertions of "guarantee".

5. The second sentence of subsection (1) covers the warranty with respect to food and drink. Serving food or drink for value is a sale, whether to be consumed on the premises or elsewhere. Cases to the contrary are rejected. The principal warranty is that stated in subsections (1) and (2)(c) of this section.

6. Subsection (2) does not purport to exhaust the meaning of "merchantable" nor to negate any of its attributes not specifically mentioned in the text of the statute, but arising by usage of trade or through case law. The language used is "must be at least such as . . .," and the intention is to leave open other possible attributes of merchantability.

7. Paragraphs (a) and (b) of subsection (2) are to be read together. Both refer, as indicated above, to the standards of that line of the trade which fits the transaction and the seller's business. "Fair average" is a term directly appropriate to agricultural bulk products and means goods centering around the middle belt of quality, not the least or the worst that can be understood in the particular trade by the designation, but such as can pass "without objection." Of course a fair percentage of the least is permissible but the goods are not "fair average" if they are all of the least or worst quality possible under the description. In cases of doubt as to what quality is intended, the price at which a merchant closes a contract is an excellent index of the nature and scope of his obligation under the present section.

8. Fitness for the ordinary purposes for which goods of the type are used is a fundamental concept of the present section and is covered in paragraph (c). As stated above, merchantability is also a part of the obligation owing to the purchaser for use. Correspondingly, protection, under this aspect of the warranty, of the person buying for resale to the ultimate consumer is equally necessary, and merchantable goods must therefore be "honestly" resalable in the normal course of business because they are what they purport to be.

9. Paragraph (d) on evenness of kind, quality and quantity follows case law. But precautionary language has been added as a remainder of the frequent usages of trade which permit substantial variations both with and without an allowance or an obligation to replace the varying units.

10. Paragraph (e) applies only where the nature of the goods and of the transaction require a certain type of container, package or label. Paragraph (f) applies, on the other hand, wherever there is a label or container on which representations are made, even though the original contract, either by express terms or usage of trade, may not have required either the labelling or the representation. This follows from the general obligation of good faith which requires that a buyer should not be placed in the position of reselling or using goods delivered under false representations appearing on the package or container. No problem of extra consideration arises in this connection since, under this Article, an obligation is

imposed by the original contract not to deliver mislabeled articles, and the obligation is imposed where mercantile good faith so requires and without reference to the doctrine of consideration.

11.   Exclusion or modification of the warranty of merchantability, or of any part of it, is dealt with in the section to which the text of the present section makes explicit precautionary references. That section must be read with particular reference to its subsection (4) on limitation of remedies. The warranty of merchantability, wherever it is normal, is so commonly taken for granted that its exclusion from the contract is a matter threatening surprise and therefore requiring special precaution.

12.   Subsection (3) is to make explicit that usage of trade and course of dealing can create warranties and that they are implied rather than express warranties and thus subject to exclusion or modification under Section 2–316. A typical instance would be the obligation to provide pedigree papers to evidence conformity of the animal to the contract in the case of a pedigreed dog or blooded bull.

13.   In an action based on breach of warranty, it is of course necessary to show not only the existence of the warranty but the fact that the warranty was broken and that the breach of the warranty was the proximate cause of the loss sustained. In such an action an affirmative showing by the seller that the loss resulted from some action or event following his own delivery of the goods can operate as a defense. Equally, evidence indicating that the seller exercised care in the manufacture, processing or selection of the goods is relevant to the issue of whether the warranty was in fact broken. Action by the buyer following an examination of the goods which ought to have indicated the defect complained of can be shown as matter bearing on whether the breach itself was the cause of the injury.

Uniform Commercial Code

§ 2–315   Implied Warranty: Fitness for Particular Purpose

Where the seller at the time of contracting has reason to know any particular purpose for which the goods are required and that the buyer is relying on the seller's skill or judgment to select or furnish suitable goods, there is unless excluded or modified under the next section an implied warranty that the goods shall be fit for such purpose.

Official Comment

Prior Uniform Statutory Provision: Section 15(1), (4), (5) Uniform Sales Act.

Changes: Rewritten

Purposes of Changes:

1.   Whether or not this warranty arises in any individual case is basically a question of fact to be determined by the circumstances of the

contracting. Under this section the buyer need not bring home to the seller actual knowledge of the particular purpose for which the goods are intended or of his reliance on the seller's skill and judgment, if the circumstances are such that the seller has reason to realize the purpose intended or that the reliance exists. The buyer, of course, must actually be relying on the seller.

2.   A "particular purpose" differs from the ordinary purpose for which the goods are used in that it envisages a specific use by the buyer which is peculiar to the nature of his business whereas the ordinary purposes for which goods are used are those envisaged in the concept of merchantability and go to uses which are customarily made of the goods in question. For example, shoes are generally used for the purpose of walking upon ordinary ground, but a seller may know that a particular pair was selected to be used for climbing mountains.

A contract may of course include both a warranty of merchantability and one of fitness for a particular purpose.

The provisions of this Article on the cumulation and conflict of express and implied warranties must be considered on the question of inconsistency between or among warranties. In such a case any question of fact as to which warranty was intended by the parties to apply must be resolved in favor of the warranty of fitness for particular purpose as against all other warranties except where the buyer has taken upon himself the responsibility of furnishing the technical specifications.

3.   In connection with the warranty of fitness for a particular purpose the provisions of this Article on the allocation or division of risks are particularly applicable in any transaction in which the purpose for which the goods are to be used combines requirements both as to the quality of the goods themselves and compliance with certain laws or regulations. How the risks are divided is a question of fact to be determined, where not expressly contained in the agreement, from the circumstances of contracting, usage of trade, course of performance and the like, matters which may constitute the "otherwise agreement" of the parties by which they may divide the risk or burden.

4.   The absence from this section of the language used in the Uniform Sales Act in referring to the seller, "whether he be the grower or manufacturer or not," is not intended to impose any requirement that the seller be a grower or manufacturer. Although normally the warranty will arise only where the seller is a merchant with the appropriate "skill or judgment," it can arise as to non-merchants where this is justified by the particular circumstances.

5.   The elimination of the "patent or other trade name" exception constitutes the major extension of the warranty of fitness which has been made by the cases and continued in this Article. Under the present section the existence of a patent or other trade name and the designation of the article by that name, or indeed in any other definite manner, is only one of the facts to be considered on the question of whether the buyer actually

relied on the seller, but it is not of itself decisive of the issue. If the buyer himself is insisting on a particular brand he is not relying on the seller's skill and judgment and so no warranty results. But the mere fact that the article purchased has a particular patent or trade name is not sufficient to indicate nonreliance if the article has been recommended by the seller as adequate for the buyer's purposes.

6.   The specific reference forward in the present section to the following section on exclusion or modification of warranties is to call attention to the possibility of eliminating the warranty in any given case. However it must be noted that under the following section the warranty of fitness for a particular purpose must be excluded or modified by a conspicuous writing.

Uniform Commercial Code

§ 2–316   Exclusion or Modification of Warranties

(1) Words or conduct relevant to the creation of an express warranty and words or conduct tending to negate or limit warranty shall be construed wherever reasonable as consistent with each other; but subject to the provisions of this Article on parol or extrinsic evidence (Section 2–202) negation or limitation is inoperative to the extent that such construction is unreasonable.

(2) Subject to subsection (3), to exclude or modify the implied warranty of merchantability or any part of it the language must mention merchantability and in case of a writing must be conspicuous, and to exclude or modify any implied warranty of fitness the exclusion must be by a writing and conspicuous. Language to exclude all implied warranties of fitness is sufficient if it states, for example, that "There are no warranties which extend beyond the description on the face hereof."

(3) Notwithstanding subsection (2)

(a) unless the circumstances indicate otherwise, all implied warranties are excluded by expressions like "as is", "with all faults" or other language which in common understanding calls the buyer's attention to the exclusion of warranties and makes plain that there is no implied warranty; and

(b) when the buyer before entering into the contract has examined the goods or the sample or model as fully as he desired or has refused to examine the goods there is no implied warranty with regard to defects which an examination ought in the circumstances to have revealed to him; and

(c) an implied warranty can also be excluded or modified by course of dealing or course of performance or usage of trade.

(4) Remedies for breach of warranty can be limited in accordance with the provisions of this Article on liquidation or limitation of damages and on contractual modification of remedy (Sections 2–718 and 2–719).

Official Comment

Prior Uniform Statutory Provision: None. See sections 15 and 71, Uniform Sales Act.

Purposes:

1. This section is designed principally to deal with those frequent clauses in sales contracts which seek to exclude "all warranties, express or implied." It seeks to protect a buyer from unexpected and unbargained language of disclaimer by denying effect to such language when inconsistent with language of express warranty and permitting the exclusion of implied warranties only by conspicuous language or other circumstances which protect the buyer from surprise.

2. The seller is protected under this Article against false allegations of oral warranties by its provisions on parol and extrinsic evidence and against unauthorized representations by the customary "lack of authority" clauses. This Article treats the limitation or avoidance of consequential damages as a matter of limiting remedies for breach, separate from the matter of creation of liability under a warranty. If no warranty exists, there is of course no problem of limiting remedies for breach of warranty. Under subsection (4) the question of limitation of remedy is governed by the sections referred to rather than by this section.

3. Disclaimer of the implied warranty of merchantability is permitted under subsection (2), but with the safeguard that such disclaimers must mention merchantability and in case of a writing must be conspicuous.

4. Unlike the implied warranty of merchantability, implied warranties of fitness for a particular purpose may be excluded by general language, but only if it is in writing and conspicuous.

5. Subsection (2) presupposes that the implied warranty in question exists unless excluded or modified. Whether or not language of disclaimer satisfies the requirements of this section, such language may be relevant under other sections to the question whether the warranty was ever in fact created. Thus, unless the provisions of this Article on parol and extrinsic evidence prevent, oral language of disclaimer may raise issues of fact as to whether reliance by the buyer occurred and whether the seller had "reason to know" under the section on implied warranty of fitness for a particular purpose.

6. The exceptions to the general rule set forth in paragraphs (a), (b) and (c) of subsection (3) are common factual situations in which the circumstances surrounding the transaction are in themselves sufficient to call the buyer's attention to the fact that no implied warranties are made or that a certain implied warranty is being excluded.

7. Paragraph (a) of subsection (3) deals with general terms such as "as is," "as they stand," "with all faults," and the like. Such terms in ordinary commercial usage are understood to mean that the buyer takes the entire risk as to the quality of the goods involved. The terms covered by paragraph (a) are in fact merely a particularization of paragraph (c) which

provides for exclusion or modification of implied warranties by usage of trade.

8. Under paragraph (b) of subsection (3) warranties may be excluded or modified by the circumstances where the buyer examines the goods or a sample or model of them before entering into the contract. "Examination" as used in this paragraph is not synonymous with inspection before acceptance or at any other time after the contract has been made. It goes rather to the nature of the responsibility assumed by the seller at the time of the making of the contract. Of course if the buyer discovers the defect and uses the goods anyway, or if he unreasonably fails to examine the goods before he uses them, resulting injuries may be found to result from his own action rather than proximately from a breach of warranty. See Sections 2–314 and 2–715 and comments thereto.

In order to bring the transaction within the scope of "refused to examine" in paragraph (b), it is not sufficient that the goods are available for inspection. There must in addition be a demand by the seller that the buyer examine the goods fully. The seller by the demand puts the buyer on notice that he is assuming the risk of defects which the examination ought to reveal. The language "refused to examine" in this paragraph is intended to make clear the necessity for such demand.

Application of the doctrine of "caveat emptor" in all cases where the buyer examines the goods regardless of statements made by the seller is, however, rejected by this Article. Thus, if the offer of examination is accompanied by words as to their merchantability or specific attributes and the buyer indicates clearly that he is relying on those words rather than on his examination, they give rise to an "express" warranty. In such cases the question is one of fact as to whether a warranty of merchantability has been expressly incorporated in the agreement. Disclaimer of such an express warranty is governed by subsection (1) of the present section.

The particular buyer's skill and the normal method of examining goods in the circumstances determine what defects are excluded by the examination. A failure to notice defects which are obvious cannot excuse the buyer. However, an examination under circumstances which do not permit chemical or other testing of the goods would not exclude defects which could be ascertained only by such testing. Nor can latent defects be excluded by a simple examination. A professional buyer examining a product in his field will be held to have assumed the risk as to all defects which a professional in the field ought to observe, while a nonprofessional buyer will be held to have assumed the risk only for such defects as a layman might be expected to observe.

9. The situation in which the buyer gives precise and complete specifications to the seller is not explicitly covered in this section, but this is a frequent circumstance by which the implied warranties may be excluded. The warranty of fitness for a particular purpose would not normally arise since in such a situation there is usually no reliance on the seller by the buyer. The warranty of merchantability in such a transaction, however, must be considered in connection with the next section on the cumulation

and conflict of warranties. Under paragraph (c) of that section in case of such an inconsistency the implied warranty of merchantability is displaced by the express warranty that the goods will comply with the specifications. Thus, where the buyer gives detailed specifications as to the goods, neither of the implied warranties as to quality will normally apply to the transaction unless consistent with the specifications.

Uniform Commercial Code

§ 2–318   Third Party Beneficiaries of Warranties Express or Implied

Note: *If this Act is introduced in the Congress of the United States this section should be omitted. (States to select one alternative.)*

Alternative A

A seller's warranty whether express or implied extends to any natural person who is in the family or household of his buyer or who is a guest in his home if it is reasonable to expect that such person may use, consume or be affected by the goods and who is injured in person by breach of the warranty. A seller may not exclude or limit the operation of this section.

Alternative B

A seller's warranty whether express or implied extends to any natural person who may reasonably be expected to use, consume or be affected by the goods and who is injured in person by breach of the warranty. A seller may not exclude or limit the operation of this section.

Alternative C

A seller's warranty whether express or implied extends to any person who may reasonably be expected to use, consume or be affected by the goods and who is injured by breach of the warranty. A seller may not exclude or limit the operation of this section with respect to injury to the person of an individual to whom the warranty extends.

Official Comment

As amended in 1966.

Prior Uniform Statutory Provision: None.

Purposes:

1. The last sentence of this section does not mean that a seller is precluded from excluding or disclaiming a warranty which might otherwise arise in connection with the sale provided such exclusion or modification is permitted by Section 2–316. Nor does that sentence preclude the seller from limiting the remedies of his own buyer and of any beneficiaries, in any manner provided in Sections 2–718 or 2–719. To the extent that the

contract of sale contains provisions under which warranties are excluded or modified, or remedies for breach are limited, such provisions are equally operative against beneficiaries of warranties under this section. What this last sentence forbids is exclusion of liability by the seller to the persons to whom the warranties which he has made to his buyer would extend under this section.

2. The purpose of this section is to give certain beneficiaries the benefit of the same warranty which the buyer received in the contract of sale, thereby freeing any such beneficiaries from any technical rules as to "privity." It seeks to accomplish this purpose without any derogation of any right or remedy resting on negligence. It rests primarily upon the merchant-seller's warranty under this Article that the goods sold are merchantable and fit for the ordinary purposes for which such goods are used rather than the warranty of fitness for a particular purpose. Implicit in the section is that any beneficiary of a warranty may bring a direct action for breach of warranty against the seller whose warranty extends to him [As amended in 1966].

3. The first alternative expressly includes as beneficiaries within its provisions the family, household and guests of the purchaser. Beyond this, the section in this form is neutral and is not intended to enlarge or restrict the developing case law on whether the seller's warranties, given to his buyer who resells, extend to other persons in the distributive chain.

The second alternative is designed for states where the case law has already developed further and for those that desire to expand the class of beneficiaries. The third alternative goes further, following the trend of modern decisions as indicated by Restatement of Torts 2d § 402A (Tentative Draft No. 10, 1965) in extending the rule beyond injuries to the person [As amended in 1966]

Hendricks v. Callahan

United States Court of Appeals for the Eighth Circuit, 1992.
972 F.2d 190.

■ HENLEY, SENIOR CIRCUIT JUDGE.

Appellants, Kenneth A. Hendricks ("Hendricks") and Dealers Supply Holding Company, Inc. ("Dealers Supply"), appeal from the district court's1 order granting summary judgment on one warranty claim and from its order for judgment on the merits of another warranty claim. We affirm.

I.

This case involves a purchase agreement for the sale of stock. In 1985, Dealers Supply, a company whose sole stockholder is Hendricks, agreed to buy the stock of Callahan Steel Supply, Inc. ("Callahan Steel") from appellee, James H. Callahan ("Callahan"), and the Callahan Steel Supply

Profit Sharing Trust. Under this agreement (the "Purchase Agreement"), Callahan made various warranties and promises.

First, Callahan warranted that Callahan Steel's financial statements "fairly reflect the Corporation's assets, liabilities, equity and results of operations as of March 31, 1985" (the "Financial Statement Warranty"). Second, Callahan warranted that Callahan Steel had "good and marketable title to all properties owned by it, as reflected on the balance sheet, free and clear of all title defects, obligations, liabilities, liens, encumbrances, charges and claims of any kind, except for: . . . liens and encumbrances and other matters reflected in the Balance Sheet" (the "Property Warranty"). Third, Callahan promised to "hold the company [Dealers Supply] harmless in and for all liabilities that may inure to the Corporation [Callahan Steel] related to the ABERDEEN DEVELOPMENT CORPORATION, Plaintiff, vs. CALLAHAN STEEL SUPPLY, INC. ET AL, lawsuit now pending in Aberdeen, South Dakota," and promised to "bear all expenses of said litigation" (the "Litigation Indemnity Agreement").

Callahan Steel conducted its business in two locations: Newport, Minnesota and Aberdeen, South Dakota. In Aberdeen, Callahan Steel leased a warehouse from the Aberdeen Development Corp. ("ADC"). In fact, Note 12 of the Financial Statement stated: "The Company [Callahan Steel] leases warehouse and equipment in Aberdeen, South Dakota under an agreement which is cancellable by the Company at any time." When the Purchase Agreement was executed, Callahan Steel was engaged in litigation with ADC, as disclosed in the Litigation Indemnity Agreement, and a mechanic's lien had been placed on the property. It is undisputed that Dealers Supply and Hendricks knew of this lien on the Aberdeen leasehold, even though the lien is not specifically mentioned in the Litigation Indemnity Agreement or the Financial Statement.

In 1987, Hendricks decided to sell Dealers Supply. Certain assets, including the Aberdeen leasehold, were to be sold to A.P.I. Supply Company ("API"). Because the property was still encumbered by the mechanic's lien, and the related litigation was still pending, Dealers Supply was unable to furnish API with clear title. Although Dealers Supply offered to assign the benefit of the Litigation Indemnity Agreement to API, and Callahan was willing to make good on the Litigation Indemnity Agreement, API would not purchase the Aberdeen property without clear title. Callahan refused to settle the litigation or to escrow money to provide clear title, API did not purchase the leasehold, and Dealers Supply did not realize the desired price for the Aberdeen leasehold.

Although Dealers Supply did not sell the Aberdeen leasehold to API, it did sublet the warehouse to API for a time. API eventually left Aberdeen in 1989 and Dealers Supply was unable to relet the property. Because Dealers Supply was no longer actively conducting business, it sought to cancel its Aberdeen lease with ADC. Although Note 12 of the Financial Statement indicated that the Aberdeen lease was "cancellable at any time," the actual lease provisions did not allow Dealers Supply to terminate the lease without liability. Instead, Dealers Supply forfeited a substantial amount of personal property to the lessor in order to cancel and terminate the Aberdeen lease.

Appellants (collectively referred to as "Hendricks") brought this suit against Callahan alleging four counts. The district court ruled in Callahan's favor on all counts, and on appeal Hendricks challenges the district court's rulings on two of those counts. In Count II, Hendricks asserted Callahan breached the Property Warranty and the Litigation Indemnity Agreement by failing to provide clear title to the Aberdeen leasehold. The district court granted Callahan's motion for summary judgment on Count II. In Count III, Hendricks alleged Callahan breached the Financial Statement Warranty because Note 12 of the Financial Statement indicated that the Aberdeen lease was cancellable when, in fact, the lease was not. The district court refused to grant summary judgment on this issue, but after a bench trial ruled that Hendricks had failed to prove his breach of warranty claim.

[The remainder of an intricate fact pattern is omitted. The essential facts are (1) that in connection with the Aberdeen litigation, a mechanic's lien has been placed on a leasehold held by Callahan Steel, and (2) that Dealers Supply and Hendricks knew of this lien, even though it was not specifically mentioned in any of their agreements with Callahan. The lien eventually hindered Hendrick's business activity concerning Dealers Supply, and he brought suit alleging breach of warranty. Hendricks lost in the District Court.]

II.

Hendricks argues the district court erred in finding that Callahan did not breach either the Property Warranty or the Financial Statement Warranty. Essential to the court's rulings is its determination that Minnesota law requires a party alleging a breach of express warranty to have relied on that warranty when making the contract. Before addressing the merits of each warranty claim, we must decide whether Minnesota law requires a purchaser to rely on the warranty to succeed in a breach of warranty claim.

A.   The Requirement of Reliance

As the district court correctly noted, "[w]hether tort-like reliance is a necessary element in a claim for a breach of express warranty is a difficult question, at best." The court determined, however, that "the law of Minnesota appears to require some form of reliance" on the part of the buyer as an element for a breach of express warranty claim. In this diversity case, the elements of a breach of warranty claim are a question of Minnesota law. We review a district court's determination of state law de novo. *Salve Regina College v. Russell*, 499 U.S. 225 (1991).

In concluding that reliance is required, the district court cited only one case, *Midland Loan Finance Co. v. Madsen*, 217 Minn. 267 (1944) ("To enable a party relying upon a breach of express or implied warranty to recover, it must be clear and definite that there was reliance upon the warranties involved."). Hendricks argues that *Midland* no longer reflects the current law in Minnesota and urges us to hold that the buyer's reliance is irrelevant in a breach of warranty claim. We decline to do so.

Hendricks gives several reasons why we should not follow *Midland*. First, he argues that because *Midland* was decided prior to Minnesota's adoption of the Uniform Commercial Code ("UCC"), its discussion of express warranties is no longer valid. In 1966, the UCC became effective in Minnesota. It defines an express warranty as an affirmation "which relates to the goods and becomes the basis of the bargain." Minn.Stat.Ann. § 336.2–313 (1966). This provision replaced § 512.12 of the statutes and omitted the requirement that a buyer "rely" on an express warranty. Hendricks contends the Minnesota legislature has omitted the requirement of reliance in this context and, in effect, overruled *Midland*.

We need not discuss in detail the subtle differences between "reliance" and "basis of the bargain." The transaction in this case (as well as the transaction in *Midland*) was not a "transaction[ ] in goods" and therefore is not covered by the provisions of the UCC. *See* Minn.Stat.Ann. § 336.2–102 (1966). Even if we apply the UCC warranty provisions by analogy, we are not convinced Minnesota has completely abandoned the requirement of reliance. *Compare* Minnesota Code Comment to § 336.2–313, at 280 ("This difference in terminology [between "reliance" and "basis of the bargain"] probably brings about no great change in the results of cases.") *with* Uniform Commercial Code Comment to § 336.2–313, at 282 ("[N]o particular reliance on such statements [*i.e.,* express warranties] need be shown to weave them into the fabric of the agreement."). *See also Wurm v. John Deere Leasing Co.,* 405 N.W.2d 484, 489 (Minn.Ct.App.1987) (applying § 336.2–313, the court stated "[a]ppellant admitted that he *did not rely* on the representations in purchasing [the tractor], therefore, the trial court properly granted partial summary judgment on his claims of misrepresentation and *breach of an express warranty*." (Emphasis added)).

Hendricks also argues that *Midland* has been overruled *sub silentio* by recent Minnesota Supreme Court decisions. He relies on *Peterson v. Bendix Home Systems,* 318 N.W.2d 50 (Minn.1982), for the proposition that the Minnesota Supreme Court no longer requires reliance as an element of a breach of warranty claim. In *Peterson,* the court stated, "To establish a warranty claim the plaintiff must basically prove: [1] the existence of a warranty, [2] a breach, and [3] a causal link between the breach and the alleged harm." 318 N.W.2d at 52–53. That these are the elements of a breach of warranty claim under the UCC in Minnesota is beyond dispute. Hendricks argues that because the requirement of reliance is not an enumerated element in these breach of warranty cases, Minnesota no longer requires reliance.

We are unpersuaded by this argument for two reasons. One, all the cases which recite the three elements of a breach of warranty claim dealt with transactions in goods which are governed by § 336.2–313. Again, neither *Midland* nor the present case involved transactions in goods. Two, although appellants correctly note that none of the elements in *Peterson* requires "reliance," they ignore the fact that the first element-the existence of an express warranty-requires the warranty to be the "basis of the bargain." In each case which recites the three *Peterson* elements, the court found no dispute as to the first element-that an express warranty existed-and therefore never addressed the issue of whether the warranty was the basis of the bargain. In a case decided before *Peterson,* however, the Minnesota Supreme Court briefly discussed whether an express warranty existed and stated that "an express warranty arises when a seller makes an affirmation of fact ... which becomes part of the 'basis of the bargain' between the parties." *Easton Farmers Elevator Co. v. Chromalloy Am.,* 310 Minn. 568 (1976). The court went on to find that the "alleged statements, if credited by the jury, clearly constituted express warranties which were central to the negotiated bargain between the parties." *Id.*

Finally, Hendricks urges us to hold that Minnesota would adopt the "modern view" which provides that the buyer's reliance on the warranty is "wholly irrelevant." This is the position adopted by the New York Court of Appeals in *CBS, Inc. v. Ziff–Davis Publishing Co.,* 75 N.Y.2d 496 (1990) ("This view of 'reliance'—*i.e.,* as requiring no more than reliance on the express warranty as being part of the bargain between the parties-reflects the prevailing perception of an action for breach of express warranty as one that is no longer grounded in tort, but essentially in contract."). We are not persuaded Minnesota would adopt this position; rather we are convinced it would require some sort of reliance.

In sum, because this transaction is not governed by the UCC, because *Peterson* and its progeny are UCC cases, because the Minnesota Supreme Court has affirmed the use of jury instructions which require reliance in a related context, and because the Minnesota Supreme Court has not expressly overruled *Midland,* we are not persuaded that *Midland* no longer reflects the current law in Minnesota. Having determined that appellants must show some form of reliance on the warranty to succeed, we turn to the merits of the two warranty claims in issue.

B. The Property Warranty Claim

Hendricks claims Callahan breached the Property Warranty by failing to provide clear title to the Aberdeen leasehold. In conjunction with this warranty claim, he contends Callahan breached the Litigation Indemnity Agreement by failing to indemnify Dealers Supply from any effect of the lien litigation. The district court granted Callahan's motion for summary judgment on this claim, and we review that decision using the same standard as the district court. We must decide whether there is no genuine issue of material fact and the nonmoving party is entitled to judgment as a matter of law. Fed.R.Civ.P. 56(c). We view the evidence in the light most favorable to the nonmoving party and give the nonmoving party the benefit of all reasonable inferences to be drawn from the evidence. *Moore v. Webster,* 932 F.2d 1229, 1230–31 (8th Cir.1991).

The district court held that "[i]n light of the full disclosure of the litigation in the Purchase Agreement and Cunningham's full knowledge of the lien prior to closing, Callahan's failure to disclose the lien in the

Financial Statements did not breach the Property Warranty in the Purchase Agreement." On appeal, Hendricks concedes that he was aware of the lien and that he did not rely on its non-existence in purchasing the stock of Callahan Steel. Rather, Hendricks claims he relied on Callahan's promises to provide clear title and to indemnify Hendricks from any losses that may result from the existence of the lien.

Essentially, Hendricks argues that Callahan breached the Property Warranty and Litigation Indemnity Agreement by refusing to provide clear title to the Aberdeen leasehold when Hendricks demanded it. Those provisions of the Purchase Agreement, however, do not impose such an obligation upon Callahan. In the Property Warranty, Callahan promised to provide clear title to all its properties, "except for ... liens and encumbrances and other matters reflected in the Balance Sheet." Although the lien on the Aberdeen leasehold was not listed in the balance sheet, Hendricks concedes he was aware of the lien and therefore the lien falls within this exception to the Property Warranty. In the Litigation Indemnity Agreement, Callahan agreed to "hold [Hendricks] harmless in and for all liabilities that may inure to [Callahan Steel] related to the [Aberdeen litigation]." Hendricks argues that the inability to sell the Aberdeen leasehold to API (or more specifically, the fact that API refused to purchase the leasehold subject to the lien) is a "liability related to the [Aberdeen litigation]." We disagree.

When Hendricks purchased the stock of Callahan Steel, he knew there was a lien on the Aberdeen leasehold and agreed to allow Callahan to proceed with the litigation concerning that lien. Callahan promised to hold Hendricks harmless for any liabilities related to the litigation. The Property Warranty did not give Hendricks the right to demand clear title to the Aberdeen leasehold at any time. Hendricks claims that such a construction of the Purchase Agreement is unreasonable because Hendricks must be able to sell the assets he purchased. Under our construction, however, he was free to sell exactly what he purchased-the Aberdeen leasehold, subject to the lien and with Callahan's promise to hold him harmless for any liabilities resulting from the litigation. The fact that API was unwilling to purchase what Hendricks had purchased does not mean that Callahan breached the Property Warranty.

III.

We affirm the district court's entry of summary judgment on the Property Warranty claim and affirm the entry of judgment on the merits of the Financial Statement Warranty claim.

CBS Inc. v. Ziff–Davis Publishing Co.

Court of Appeals of New York, 1990.
553 N.E.2d 997.

■ HANCOCK, JUDGE.

A corporate buyer made a bid to purchase certain businesses based on financial information as to their profitability supplied by the seller. The bid was accepted and the parties entered into a binding bilateral contract for the sale which included, specifically, the seller's express warranties as to the truthfulness of the previously supplied financial information. Thereafter, pursuant to the purchase agreement, the buyer conducted its own investigation which led it to believe that the warranted information was untrue. The seller dismissed as meritless the buyer's expressions of disbelief in the validity of the financial information and insisted that the sale go through as agreed. The closing took place with the mutual understanding that it would not in any way affect the previously asserted position of either party. Did the buyer's manifested lack of belief in and reliance on the truth of the warranted information prior to the closing relieve the seller of its obligations under the warranties? This is the central question presented in the breach of express warranty claim brought by CBS Inc. (CBS) against Ziff–Davis Publishing Co. (Ziff–Davis). The courts below concluded that CBS's lack of reliance on the warranted information was fatal to its breach of warranty claim and, accordingly, dismissed that cause of action on motion under CPLR 3211(a)(7). We granted leave to appeal and, for reasons stated hereinafter, disagree with this conclusion and hold that the warranty claim should be reinstated.

I

The essential facts pleaded-assumed to be true for the purpose of the dismissal motion-are these. In September 1984, Goldman Sachs & Co., acting as Ziff–Davis's investment banker and agent, solicited bids for the sale of the assets and businesses of 12 consumer magazines and 12 business publications. The offering circular, prepared by Goldman Sachs and Ziff–Davis, described Ziff–Davis's financial condition and included operating income statements for the fiscal year ending July 31, 1984 prepared by Ziff–Davis's accountant, Touche Ross & Co. Based on Ziff–Davis's representations in the offering circular, CBS, on November 9, 1984 submitted a bid limited to the purchase of the 12 consumer magazines in the amount of $362,500,000. This was the highest bid.

On November 19, 1984 CBS and Ziff–Davis entered into a binding bilateral purchase agreement for the sale of the consumer magazine businesses for the price of $362,500,000. Under section 3.5 of the purchase agreement, Ziff–Davis warranted that the audited income and expense report of the businesses for the 1984 fiscal year, which had been previously provided to CBS in the offering circular, had "been prepared in accordance with generally accepted accounting principles" (GAAP) and that the report "present[ed] fairly the items set forth". Ziff–Davis agreed to furnish an interim income and expense report (Stub Report) of the businesses covering the period after the end of the 1984 fiscal year, and it warranted under section 3.6 that from July 31, 1984 until the closing, there had "not been any material adverse change in Seller's business of publishing and distributing the Publications, taken as a whole". Section 6.1(a) provided that "all representations and warranties of Seller to Buyer shall be true and correct as of the time of the closing", and in section 8.1, the parties agreed that all "representations and warranties * * * shall survive the closing, notwithstanding any investigation made by or on behalf of the other party." In section 5.1 Ziff–Davis gave CBS permission to "make such investigation" of the magazine businesses being sold "as [it might] desire" and agreed to give CBS and its accountants reasonable access to the books and records pertaining thereto and to furnish such documents and information as might reasonably be requested.

Thereafter, on January 30, 1985 Ziff–Davis delivered the required Stub Report. In the interim, CBS, acting under section 5.1 of the purchase agreement, had performed its own "due diligence" examination of Ziff–Davis's financial condition. Based on this examination and on reports by its accountant, Coopers & Lybrand, CBS discovered information causing it to believe that Ziff–Davis's certified financial statements and other financial reports were not prepared according to GAAP and did not fairly depict Ziff–Davis's financial condition.

In a January 31, 1985 letter, CBS wrote Ziff–Davis that, "[b]ased on the information and analysis provided [to it, CBS was] of the view that there [were] material misrepresentations in the financial statements provided [to CBS] by Touche Ross & Co., Goldman, Sachs & Co. and Ziff–Davis". In response to this letter, Ziff–Davis advised CBS by letter dated February 4, 1985 that it "believe[d] that all conditions to the closing were fulfilled", that "there [was] no merit to the position taken by CBS in its [Jan. 31, 1985] letter" and that the financial statements were properly prepared and fairly presented Ziff–Davis's financial condition. It also warned CBS that, since all conditions to closing were satisfied, closing was required to be held that day, February 4, 1985, and that, if it "should fail to consummate the transactions as provided Ziff–Davis intend[ed] *to pursue all of its rights and remedies as provided by law.*" (Emphasis added.)

CBS responded to Ziff–Davis's February 4, 1985 letter with its own February 4 letter, which Ziff–Davis accepted and agreed to. In its February 4 letter, CBS acknowledged that "a clear dispute" existed between the parties. It stated that it had decided to proceed with the deal because it had "spent considerable time, effort and money in complying with [its] obligations and recogniz[ed] that [Ziff–Davis had] considerably more information available". Accordingly, the parties agreed "to close [that day] on a mutual understanding that the decision to close, and the closing, [would] not *constitute a waiver of any rights or defenses either of us may have*" (emphasis added) under the purchase agreement. The deal was consummated on February 4.

CBS then brought this action claiming in its third cause of action that Ziff–Davis had breached the warranties made as to the magazines' profitability. Based on that breach, CBS alleged that "the price bid and the price paid by CBS were in excess of that which would have been bid and paid by CBS had Ziff–Davis not breached its representation and warranties." Supreme Court granted Ziff–Davis's motion to dismiss the breach of warranty cause of action because CBS alleged "it did not believe that the representations set forth in Paragraphs 3.5 and 3.6 of the contract of sale were true" and thus CBS did not satisfy "the law in New York [which] clearly requires that this reliance be alleged in a breach of warranty action." Supreme Court also dismissed CBS's fourth cause of action relating to an alleged breach of condition. The Appellate Division, First Department, unanimously affirmed for reasons stated by Supreme Court. There should be a modification so as to deny the dismissal motion with respect to the third cause of action for breach of warranties.

II

In addressing the central question whether the failure to plead reliance is fatal to CBS's claim for breach of express warranties, it is necessary to examine the exact nature of the missing element of reliance which Ziff–Davis contends is essential. This critical lack of reliance, according to Ziff–Davis, relates to CBS's disbelief in the truth of the warranted financial information which resulted from its investigation *after* the signing of the agreement and *prior to* the date of closing. The reliance in question, it must be emphasized, does not relate to whether CBS relied on the submitted financial information in making its bid or relied on Ziff–Davis's express warranties as to the validity of this information when CBS committed itself to buy the businesses by signing the purchase agreement containing the warranties.

Under Ziff–Davis's theory, the reliance which is a necessary element for a claim of breach of express warranty is essentially that required for a tort action based on fraud or misrepresentation—i.e., a belief in the truth of the representations made in the express warranty and a change of position in reliance on that belief. Thus, because, prior to the closing of the contract on February 4, 1985, CBS demonstrated its lack of belief in the truth of the warranted financial information, it cannot have closed in reliance on it and its breach of warranty claim must fail. This is so, Ziff–Davis maintains, despite its unequivocal rejection of CBS's expressions of its concern that the submitted financial reports contained errors, despite its insistence that the information it had submitted complied with the warranties and that there was "no merit" to CBS's position, and despite its warnings of legal action if CBS did not go ahead with the closing. Ziff–Davis's primary source for the proposition it urges-that a change of position in reliance on the truth of the warranted information is essential for a cause of action for breach of express warranty-is language found in older New York cases such as *Crocker–Wheeler Elec. Co. v. Johns–Pratt Co.,* 51 N.Y.S. 793.

CBS, on the other hand, maintains that the decisive question is whether it purchased the express warranties as bargained-for contractual terms that were part of the purchase agreement (*see, e.g., Ainger v. Michigan Gen. Corp.,* 476 F.Supp. 1209, 1225 [S.D.N.Y.1979]). It alleges that it did so and that, under these circumstances, the warranty provisions amounted to assurances of the existence of facts upon which CBS relied in committing itself to buy the consumer magazines. Ziff–Davis's assurances of these facts, CBS contends, were the equivalent of promises by Ziff–Davis to indemnify CBS if the assurances proved unfounded. Thus, as continuing promises to indemnify, the express contractual warranties did not lose their operative force when, prior to the closing, CBS formed a belief that the warranted financial information was in error. Indeed, CBS claims that it is precisely because of these warranties that it proceeded with the closing, despite its misgivings.

As authority for its position, CBS cites, *inter alia, Ainger v. Michigan Gen. Corp. (supra)* and Judge Learned Hand's definition of warranty as "an assurance by one party to a contract of the existence of a fact upon which the other party may rely. It is intended precisely to relieve the promisee of any duty to ascertain the fact for himself; *it amounts to a promise to indemnify the promisee for any loss if the fact warranted proves untrue, for obviously the promisor cannot control what is already in the past." (Metropolitan Coal Co. v. Howard,* 155 F.2d 780, 784 [2d Cir.1946] [emphasis added].)

We believe that the analysis of the reliance requirement in actions for breach of express warranties adopted in *Ainger v. Michigan Gen. Corp. (supra)* and urged by CBS here is correct. The critical question is not whether the buyer believed in the truth of the warranted information, as Ziff–Davis would have it, but "whether [it] believed [it] was purchasing the [seller's] promise [as to its truth]." (*Ainger v. Michigan Gen. Corp., supra,* at 1225.) This view of "reliance"—i.e., as requiring no more than reliance on the express warranty as being a part of the bargain between the parties-reflects the prevailing perception of an action for breach of express warranty as one that is no longer grounded in tort, but essentially in contract. (*See, Ainger v. Michigan Gen. Corp., supra,* at 1225.) The express warranty is as much a part of the contract as any other term. Once the express warranty is shown to have been relied on as part of the contract, the right to be indemnified in damages for its breach does not depend on proof that the buyer thereafter believed that the assurances of fact made in the warranty would be fulfilled. The right to indemnification depends only on establishing that the warranty was breached (*see, Glacier Gen. Assur. Co. v. Casualty Indem. Exch.,* 435 F.Supp. 855, 860 [D.Mont.1977] [citing *Metropolitan Coal Co. v. Howard, supra*]; 1 Corbin, Contracts § 14).

If, as is allegedly the case here, the buyer has purchased the seller's promise as to the existence of the warranted facts, the seller should not be relieved of responsibility because the buyer, after agreeing to make the purchase, forms doubts as to the existence of those facts. Stated otherwise, the fact that the buyer has questioned the seller's ability to perform as promised should not relieve the seller of his obligations under the express warranties when he thereafter undertakes to render the promised performance.

The cases which Ziff–Davis cites as authority for the application of its tort-action type of reliance requirement do not support the proposition it urges. None are similar to the case at bar where the warranties sued on are bargained-for terms in a binding bilateral purchase contract. In most, the basis for the decision was a factor other than the buyer's lack of reliance such as, for example, insufficient proof of the existence of the alleged express warranty (*see, e.g., Crocker–Wheeler Elec. Co. v. Johns–Pratt Co.,* 51 N.Y.S. 793).

Ziff–Davis repeatedly cites and the dissent relies upon language contained in the Appellate Division's opinion in *Crocker–Wheeler Elec. Co. v. Johns–Pratt Co. (supra)* which dealt with a claimed breach of an express warranty pertaining to the fitness of insulating material for a certain use. The court held that there was no actionable express warranty claim because the seller *made no warranty with respect to use of the material.* The language which Ziff–Davis quotes as a categorical proposition that should control the case before us-i.e., "[i]t is elementary that, in order to entitle the plaintiff to maintain an action for breach of an express warranty, *it must be established that the warranty was relied on*"(emphasis added)-is contained in dictum (29 App.Div., at 302).

Viewed as a contract action involving the claimed breach of certain bargained-for express warranties contained in the purchase agreement, the case may be summarized this way. CBS contracted to buy the consumer magazine businesses in consideration, among other things, of the reciprocal promises made by Ziff–Davis concerning the magazines' profitability. These reciprocal promises included the express warranties that the audited reports for the year ending July 31, 1984 made by Touche Ross had been prepared according to GAAP and that the items contained therein were fairly presented, that there had been no adverse material change in the business after July 31, 1984, and that all representations and warranties would "be true and correct as of the time of the closing" and would "survive the closing, notwithstanding any investigation" by CBS.

Unquestionably, the financial information pertaining to the income and expenses of the consumer magazines was relied on by CBS in forming its opinion as to the value of the businesses and in arriving at the amount of its bid; the warranties pertaining to the validity of this financial information were express terms of the bargain and part of what CBS contracted to purchase. CBS was not merely buying identified consumer magazine businesses. It was buying businesses which it believed to be of a certain value based on information furnished by the seller which the seller warranted to be true. The determinative question is this: should Ziff–Davis be relieved from any contractual obligation under these warranties, as it contends that it should, because, prior to the closing, CBS and its accountants questioned the accuracy of the financial information and because CBS, when it closed, did so without *believing in* or *relying on* the truth of the information?

We see no reason why Ziff–Davis should be absolved from its warranty obligations under these circumstances. A holding that it should because CBS questioned the truth of the facts warranted would have the effect of depriving the express warranties of their only value to CBS—i.e., as continuing promises by Ziff–Davis to indemnify CBS if the facts warranted proved to be untrue (*see, Metropolitan Coal Co. v. Howard, supra,* at 784).

Ironically, if Ziff–Davis's position were adopted, it would have succeeded in pressing CBS to close despite CBS's misgivings and, at the same time, would have succeeded in *defeating* CBS's breach of warranties action because CBS harbored these *identical misgivings.*

We agree with the lower courts that CBS's fourth cause of action, for breach of section 6.1(f) of the purchase agreement, was properly dismissed inasmuch as section 6.1(f) was a condition to closing, not a representation or warranty, and was waived by CBS.

The order of the Appellate Division should be modified, with costs to the appellant, by denying the motion to dismiss the third cause of action for breach of warranty and the order should be otherwise affirmed.

■ BELLACOSA, JUDGE, dissenting.

The issue is whether a buyer may sue a seller, after consummating a business transaction, for breach of an express warranty on which the buyer chose not to rely. The holding discards reliance as a necessary element to maintain an action for breach of an express warranty. Predictability and reliability with respect to commercial transactions, fostered by 90 years of precedent, are thus sacrificed. I respectfully dissent and would affirm the order of the Appellate Division unanimously affirming Supreme Court's application of the sound and well-settled rule.

Plaintiff CBS contracted to purchase defendant Ziff–Davis's consumer magazine group pursuant to an Asset Purchase Agreement (APA). CBS specifically negotiated *the right to rely* on its own accountant's representations in assessing the validity of the financial information which had been, and would be, provided to CBS by Ziff–Davis (§ 5.1 of the APA). Given the factual and fiscal complexity of this $362,500,000 acquisition, CBS chose to rely on its own investigation. What the CBS inspectors found in the Ziff–Davis books differed significantly from the financial picture the seller had painted. CBS notified Ziff–Davis of the discrepancies by letter on January 31, 1985, four days before the closing date. Despite its protest to the contrary, it had a contractual right under section 6.1(a) of the APA to avert the closing if "all representations and warranties of Seller to Buyer" were not true on the closing date. Clearly then, CBS chose to rely on the results of its own investigation and made a business judgment to consummate the purchase rather than cancel the deal. It took the business risk of a big deal and tried by this subsequent litigation to mitigate whatever risk, if any, inured from that choice; in other words, CBS wanted to have its cake and eat it, too.

Supreme Court determined CBS did not rely on the Ziff–Davis warranties. The Appellate Division made the same determination and the nonreliance is acknowledged by the majority (majority opn., at 998 of 553 N.E.2d). The reliance element is thus unnecessarily excised as a matter of law from the legal proposition governing and defining the cause of action. If I am "missing the point" (majority opn., at 1002, n. 5 of 553 N.E.2d), I believe it is because that is where the appellant's argument and the state of the law have led me.

Part of CBS's argument is that it should prevail because the closing day letter purports to reserve its rights as to the Ziff–Davis warranties and section 8.1 of the APA purports to be a kind of nonmerger survival clause. On a *sui generis* contract basis therefore, without affecting the traditional reliance element of the cause of action, this argument is enticing. Nevertheless, I conclude-and the majority apparently agrees in this respect-that the argument is not dispositive. The warranties given to CBS created a right to rely on the financial data as part of the sales agreement, not a right not to rely on them, then consummate the deal and then sue on them besides. These aspects of the agreement, therefore, merely manifested the parties' intent not to allow the closing to operate as a waiver of CBS's right to rely-a right which was surrendered *before* the closing. If this issue were dispositive, it would render the case and the contract entirely *sui generis* and there would be no need to address or alter the long-standing test with its reliance element. However, the court confronts and decides the broader issue, and on that we see and understand the case all too well in a fundamentally different way.

"It is elementary that, in order to entitle the plaintiff to maintain an action for breach of an express warranty, it must be established that the warranty was relied on." (*Crocker–Wheeler Elec. Co. v. Johns–Pratt Co.*, 51 N.Y.S. 793) This plain language proposition has been recognized by this court and by the Appellate Division. The majority declares the oft-quoted principle of *Crocker–Wheeler* "is not to be followed" (majority opn., at n. 3 of 553 N.E.2d), based in part on a dormant tort/contract categorical bifurcation drawn largely from *Ainger v. Michigan Gen. Corp.*, 476 F.Supp. 1209). Also, part of the justification for this departure from stare decisis in the field of common-law commercial transactions-where the burden for change is very high-is Professor Williston's "criticism" of *Crocker–Wheeler*. Examination of the complete section of the quoted text, however, discloses a significant qualification: "[I]t is generally and rightly held that inspection by the buyer does not excuse the seller from liability for an express warranty, *if the difference between the goods and the description was not detected*"(8 Williston, Contracts § 973, at 501 [3d ed.] [nn omitted; emphasis added]). "The difference" was definitively detected here by CBS pursuant to its express contractual right to personally assess the financial data.

In exchange for the long-standing, well-regarded and well-founded rule, New York law is subordinated to a theory advanced in *Ainger v. Michigan Gen. Corp.*, 476 F.Supp., *supra*, at 1226). Among the problems of this approach, however, is that in affirming *Ainger* the Court of Appeals for the Second Circuit emphasized the limited impact of the District Court's categorical discussion of the precise issue before us. After stating that the District Court Judge's "finding of reliance made a discussion of New York law unnecessary," the Second Circuit said "[b]ecause there was reliance in this case, we will not speculate how the New York courts would decide a case in which there was none." (*Ainger v. Michigan Gen. Corp.*, 632 F.2d 1025, 1026, n. 1.) The reliance on *CPC Intl. v. McKesson Corp.*, 513 N.Y.S.2d 319 also seems misplaced. Again, the trial court in that case extensively discussed the reliance question. However, the appellate courts in an entirely different procedural review significantly minimized the discussion of the pertinent subject matter (*see, CPC Intl. v. McKesson Corp.,* 70 N.Y.2d 268, 285, ["plaintiff, in contracting to purchase (defendant's corporation), relied solely on the warranties"], 507 N.Y.S.2d 984 ["plaintiff relied solely upon the express warranties"]). Lack of reliance, therefore, was not part of the holdings in *Ainger* or *CPC,* even at their trial level citations by the majority. Yet those cases are accorded significant deference on the critical issue and they override superior longer-standing sources.

Finally, while I agree that analogy to the Uniform Commercial Code is "instructive" (majority opn., at 1002, n. 4 of 553 N.E.2d), I believe the directly on-point express warranty section, UCC 2–313, emphasizes the need to stand by our precedents and thus affirm. Official comment 3 of that section indicates that were this a transaction governed by the Uniform Commercial Code, CBS's nonreliance would take the seller's warranties out of the agreement, especially after a buyer consummates the deal with full knowledge and with open disagreement concerning key financial data (UCC 2–313, comment 3; 1 White and Summers, Uniform Commercial Code § 9–5, at 450–451 [Practitioner's 3d ed.]).

Thus, we are presented with no binding or persuasive authorities sufficient to warrant overturning a venerable rule of the kind used especially in the commercial world to reliably order affairs in such a way as to reasonably avoid litigation (*see,* Cardozo, Selected Writings of Benjamin Nathan Cardozo, The Growth of the Law, at 236 ["In this department of activity (commercial law), the current axiology still places stability and certainty in the forefront of the virtues."]). Allowing CBS to consummate the deal, and then sue on warranted financial data it personally investigated and verified as wrong beforehand, unsettles the finality, "stability and certainty" of commercial transactions and business relationships.

CBS chose-for business reasons it knows best-to complete its significant acquisition at the impressively high agreed price with its cyclopean eye wide open. That tips the scales in favor of retaining and applying the traditional rule requiring a reliance element to sue for breach of warranty.

I would affirm the order in its entirety and leave the law where it was and the parties where they put themselves.

Overstreet v. Norden Labs

United States Court of Appeals for the Sixth Circuit, 1982.
669 F.2d 1286.

(Reprised from Chapter 11)

* * *

Warranties—especially where they concern matters that have been fixed in the past or that lie beyond the control of the persons who warrant them—fall uncomfortably between being "statements that" and being "promises to." In the former guise, they are most naturally governed by the tort doctrines concerning misrepresentation. In the latter, they are most naturally governed by contract law. It is therefore unsurprising that both bodies of doctrine weigh in concerning warranties. So begin by briefly considering tort's contributions in this area, including in particular the ways in which tort approaches contract. Then consider contract proper, including in the ways in which it approaches tort.

As the Reporter's note to Restatement (Third) of Products Liability § 9 observes, for much of the history of the common law, claims for breach of warranty sounded expressly in tort rather than in contract, and in particular in the tort of deceit. By the beginning of the nineteenth century, this had changed, and breach of warranty had moved to a new doctrinal home in assumpsit, one of the writs out of which the modern law of contract was eventually to develop. The Restatement documents a modern trend towards expanding the misrepresentation torts so that they once again encompass at least some contract-like claims associated with breach of warranty. This expansion does not undo the developments by which contract came to recognize warranty promises. But it does reduce (although it does not eliminate) the distinctiveness or specialness of the rights that a warranty-recipient might enjoy by giving her legal position a contractual cast.

Among the reasons why the misrepresentation torts fail generally to colonize contract is that they impose liability not strictly (as in contract) but only for intentional or at least negligent conduct. Products liability substantially relaxes this limitation. A person whose business is to sell products may be liable for false representations about the products, made in connection with the sale, even where the misrepresentations are innocently made. She may be liable, moreover, even to parties who did not purchase the products from her, and with whom she has no contractual relationship.[30] All that liability requires is that the injured party reasonably relied on the false representations or, relatedly (but not obviously equivalently) that the misrepresentations were material. Accordingly, this form of tort liability approaches contract liability for breach of warranty, as the comments to the Restatement recognize. (Although the comments also recognize that the tort claim continues to vindicate only lost reliance, whereas the contract claim would give a plaintiff the benefit of his bargain.) Products liability achieves this result, moreover, even where no contract between plaintiff and defendant can be established (for example, because the representations are precluded from becoming part of any contract by the parol evidence rule).

This feature of the products liability misrepresentation torts raises the possibility of a threat to contract's status, or at least its importance, as a free-standing and independent legal form. If liability for misrepresentation

---

30. As the comments emphasize, the outer limits of this form of liability remain unsettled, in particular with respect to whether it attaches to only public representations or also to representations made privately, to a specific person, and also with respect to whether misrepresenting sellers are liable even for losses suffered by persons who are not consumers of the misrepresented products. See cmt. [b].

can arise quite apart from fault and hence in a contract–like way, even without offer and acceptance or any other indicia of contractual privity, perhaps distinctively contractual relations do not ground liability even where they do exist. More specifically, and in respect of a case to which the argument will return in a moment, warranty liability within a contract is perhaps just a species of products liability for misrepresentation. Accordingly, the core ideas of orthodox contract law may, in these areas, at least, be merely epiphenomenal. Contract thus becomes relatively less necessary in this area; tort already achieves much of what contract aspires to do. In this way, the modern trend in products liability shifts the boundary between contract and tort (nonexclusively) back towards tort.

Notwithstanding tort's presence, contract law enters the field. It does so through the doctrines governing warranties. Warranties appear, through a contractual lens, not as "statements that" but rather as "promises to." They cannot plausibly be read as promises directly to establish the states of affairs that they describe, of course. Often, warranties describe past occurrences (as in *Hendricks* and *Ziff–Davis*); sometimes they announce that products have features that they could not possibly have (as in *Overstreet*). Instead, warranties are read as promises to secure for their recipients the *value* of the states of affairs that they describe. As Judge Learned Hand wrote in the middle of the last century, because a promisor "obviously cannot control what is already in the past," a warranty "is intended precisely to relieve the promisee of any duty to ascertain the fact for himself; it amounts to a promise to indemnify the promisee for any loss if the fact warranted proves untrue."[31] Because a promisor who issues a warranty cannot sensibly issue a promise that, her warranty must be interpreted as an implied "promise to."

This approach converts warranties, as a formal matter, into perfectly ordinary contractual promises. In principle, they might therefore be treated, by contract law, in just the manner of every other promise. As it happens, though, contract law does not quite approach warranties in this ordinary way. Perhaps as a result of the historical influence of tort in this area, contract law's treatment of warranties scales back its distinctively contractual ambitions. The formal core of contract, recall, is that contractual obligations are purely creatures of the wills of the contracting parties: contracts arise, as it were, directly at the pleasure of the parties, requiring nothing more than that the parties intend them; and contracts take whatever shape, and include whatever content, the parties wish. The contract doctrines that govern warranties depart from this rule, in two respects.

The first respect in which warranties depart from contract's general commitment to establishing legal obligation purely at the pleasure of the contracting parties concerns the fact that something that might loosely be called reliance has a special place in the contract doctrines that govern warranties. Reliance enters the contract law of warranties, moreover, not

---

31. *Metropolitan Coal Co. v. Howard*, 155 F.2d 780, 784 (2d Cir. 1946).

as a measure of remedy but as a ground for obligation. The precise contours of the required reliance depart from the forms made familiar in tort. Certainly the reliance required to sustain a contract claim for breach of warranty is not the same as the reliance required to sustain a tort claim for misrepresentation. A plaintiff bringing the contract action need not show that it was reasonable for him respond to the warranty by taking actions whose prudence depended on the warranty's accuracy. Just what conception of reliance replaces this one remains, however, unstable and uncertain.

The main issues are illustrated by the U.C.C.'s insistence that in order to become part of the contract, a warranty must be part of "basis of bargain" (§ 2–313). This is a kind of reliance requirement, but it does not involve reliance in the conventional sense associated with tort. The plaintiff need not incur costs specifically on account of the truth of the representations that the warranty involves. Rather, the reliance may (and generally will) come in the form of opportunity costs—the alternative arrangements foregone in order to strike the bargain to which the warranty belongs. Moreover, the role of the warranty in supporting the bargain may be general rather than particular: it is enough that the warranty played a part in securing the plaintiff's overall agreement; there is no need to identify any individual concessions that the plaintiff made in exchange for the warranty.

Some courts insist that in order to succeed on a breach of warranty claim, a plaintiff must have relied on the *truth* of the warranty representation. *Hendricks* illustrates this view. The plaintiff there bought the stock of a firm pursuant to a purchase agreement in which the firm's prior owner warranted that the firm held good and marketable title to all properties that it owned. In fact, one of these "properties"—a leasehold on a warehouse—was subject to a mechanic's lien (arising out of litigation that the firm had been involved in prior to being sold to the plaintiff), which had been disclosed to the buyer (notwithstanding the warranty of clear title) in other documents associated with the stock purchase. When the lien frustrated the plaintiff's subsequent efforts to sell the warehouse lease, and the defendant refused to take the steps required to satisfy the lien, the plaintiff sued to enforce the warranty of clear title. A federal court applying Minnesota law gave summary judgment against the plaintiff, emphasizing that the plaintiff knew of the lien when he purchased the stock. Along the way, the court suggested that the stock purchase agreement is best interpreted to exclude the lien on the lease from the warranty of clear title. But gravamen of the opinion concerns the reliance requirement and the fact that the plaintiff, given his actual knowledge of the lien, could not have relied on the warranty's representations concerning clear title in respect of that particular encumbrance. Indeed, even the interpretive part of the opinion implicitly adopts this logic: the warranty of clear title is understood not to encompass the mechanic's lien precisely because the plaintiff, knowing of the lien, could not believe that title was clear in this respect. *Hendricks* thus takes a view of reliance that closely tracks tort law. To succeed on a breach of warranty claim, according to this view, a plaintiff must have reasonably proceeded on the basis of the belief that the world was in fact as it was warranted to be. Reliance on legal rights established by the warranty does not count. That is a direct analog to the role of Restated (Second) of Torts § 548.

That is not the only possible interpretation of a warranty, however. An alternative approach follows Hand, and understands warranties not as representing that any facts obtain but instead as creating obligations to provide promisees with whatever value they would enjoy *if* the facts that they name obtained. This alternative seems better to match the parties' practical interest in warranties than the approach taken in *Hendricks*. As Hand noted, "[t]o argue that the promisee is responsible for failing independently to confirm (the warranty), is utterly to misconceive its office."[32] A warranty is a guarantee-promise, after all, rather than a mere recitation of fact or belief. The promisee seeks it precisely in order not to have to investigate whether or not the facts that it announces obtain. The promisee seeks the warranty not to rely on the truth of the warranted representations but rather to rely on the promisor's obligation to vindicate them.

Ziff–Davis illustrates this approach to warranties and to the reliance-requirement that they involve. As in *Hendricks*, a buyer agreed to purchase certain businesses based on financial information about them reported by his seller and on his seller's warranty that the provided information was correct. In spite of receiving the warranty, and after signing the purchase agreement that contained it, the buyer conducted its own investigation of the financial condition of the businesses at issue, which revealed that the condition was, in material respects, worse than warranted. The buyer closed on the purchase nevertheless and subsequently sought to enforce the warranty (whose express terms held that its guarantee would "survive the closing, notwithstanding any investigation made by or on behalf of the [buyer]") against the seller.

The seller argued that the buyer could not enforce the warranty because, having conducted his own investigations and come to disbelieve the warranty representations, he could not establish the reliance that a breach of warranty claim requires. As the court noted, the buyer thus proposed that "the reliance which is a necessary element for a claim of breach of express warranty is essentially that required for a tort action based on fraud or misrepresentation—i.e., a belief in the truth of the representations made in the express warranty and a change of position in reliance on that belief." The buyer rejected this approach, casting its warranty claim as centrally contractual. For this reason, the buyer argued, the claim turned not on whether it relied on the truth of the warranted representations but rather on "whether it purchased the express warranties as bargained for contractual terms that were part of the purchase agreement," so that the warranties "were the equivalent of promises by [the seller] to indemnify [the buyer] if the assurance proved unfounded."

---

32.   *Metropolitan Coal Co. v. Howard*, 155 F.2d 780, 784 (2d Cir. 1946).

The Court of Appeal of New York took the buyer's view. "The critical question," the Court insisted, "is not whether the buyer believed in the truth of the warranted information but whether it believed it was purchasing the seller's promise as to its truth." This approach reflects, the Court observed, "the prevailing perception of an action for breach of express warranty as one that is no longer grounded in tort, but essentially in contract." The contrast to tort could hardly be starker. Tort law—recall again, the rule of Restatement § 548—expressly rejects the suggestion that reliance may be established on the basis of the law's willingness to enforce a defendant's representations rather than on the basis of a reasonable belief directly in the representations' truth. Contract law, by contrast, essentially involves just such bootstrapping, which, after all, is just another way of characterizing what happens when a buyer who disbelieves his seller's representation nevertheless "purchas[es] the seller's promise as to its truth."

The *Ziff-Davis* court's suggestion that warranties are just like any other contractual promises opens up doctrinal difficulties of its own, however. These difficulties are reflected, moreover, in the substance of the court's opinion, even if they are disguised by the opinion's self-confident tone. Thus, even as it insists that "[t]he express warranty is as much a part of the contract as any other term," and that "the right to be indemnified in damages for its breach does not depend on proof that the buyer believed that the assurances of fact made in the warranty would be fulfilled," the court feels it necessary to add that the buyer can enforce the warranty only "[o]nce the express warranty is shown to have been relied on as part of the contract." That is, *Ziff-Davis* insists (in line with U.C.C.) that warranty promises are contractually enforceable only where the warranties (in respect of their enforceability, of course, and not of their truth) were essential to the buyer's willingness to participate in the contractual exchanges to which they belong—only, that is, where the warranties are part of the basis of the contractual bargain.

Even in this weaker form, the reliance requirement remains a little odd, or at least unusual. A promisee can enforce other contractual promises, for example, concerning concessions on price or quantity, without showing that they belong to the basis of the bargain or that she would have walked away from the deal had these promises not been included in it. The consideration doctrine of course requires that promises have the general form of an exchange before the law will enforce them. But it is enough, for purposes of that doctrine, to show that each side's overall promise reciprocally induces the other's. There is no need to show that individual, particular terms are essential to the inducement. So why require such a showing with respect to warranties?

Part of the answer may be found by revisiting the distinction between "promises that" and "promises to". Warranty promises seem odd insofar as they are understood (by analogy to the representations that they contain and on which tort theories of warranties fixate) as "promises that": so understood, warranties seem to promise the impossible (to control the past, as Hand suggested). That is why contractual approaches interpret warranties as promising indemnification, and thus as "promises to". But while this interpretation cures the formal problem concerning impossibility, it does not remove all difficulties that warranty promises raise in this connection. Warranty promises—especially where they would promise the impossible if interpreted as "promises that"—invite promisee windfalls. (Other promises might offer windfalls also, but the problem is especially acute with respect to warranties.) That is, contractual warranties—especially where they represent a contractual performance as more valuable than it is or could possibly be—run the risk of promising a greater return to the promisee than she could realize under any available alternative bargain. Put slightly differently, warranties run the risk of creating contractual expectations that exceed any costs that their promisees incur in reliance on them, including the opportunity costs associated with rejecting their next-best alternatives in favor of the contracts that contain the warranties at issue.

This brings the analysis back to *Overstreet*, which was discussed extensively in Chapter 11 and is now relevant again. The *Overstreet* defendant inaccurately advertised that a vaccine would protect horses from a disease that causes mares to miscarry. The plaintiff, having read the advertisement, bought the vaccine and administered it to his horses. The vaccine did not protect against the disease, and the plaintiff's mares miscarried. The plaintiff subsequently sued, alleging breach of warranty and seeking to recover the value of the lost foals. It turned out that no alternative vaccine (nor any other alternative treatment) could have prevented the mares from contracting the disease or saved the foals. In light of this, the court (over a vigorous dissent) denied recovery for the value of the foals lost to the disease, on the grounds that because no other vaccine existed, and nothing else could have been done by the buyer to prevent the disease, the buyer's foals were not lost in reliance on the warranty.

The discussion of *Overstreet* in Chapter 11 blithely asserted that the express warranty of the vaccine's effectiveness (created by the defendant's advertisements) unquestionably formed part of the basis of the bargain, "since the plaintiff surely would not have purchased the vaccine unless he had believed that it would work and so clearly did rely on the warranty in making his purchase." Accordingly, the earlier analysis treated the opinion as introducing a separate requirement of reliance into the law, namely that the plaintiff must show that he was worse off than he would have been had the warranty never been made, presumably because he would (but for the warranty promise) have acquired effective immunity for his mares by some other means. The *Overstreet* plaintiff could not show this—as there was no alternative method for protecting against the disease or saving the foals—and therefore lost. Put differently, the warranty promised the plaintiff a windfall—a much better deal than any other available to him—so that his expectations in the warranty could not be recast in terms of the reliance associated with the opportunities lost by dealing with the defendant and thus foregoing nearly as good alternative deals. That is why *Overstreet* was deployed, in the earlier argument, to illustrate contract law's unsteady commitment to vindicating pure promissory expectations—expectations that cannot be recharacterized in terms of reliance.[33]

The discussion in this chapter opens a new window onto the earlier analysis. The central distinction between tort liability for misrepresentation and contract liability for breach of warranty, this chapter has argued, concerns whether the plaintiff has relied directly on the truth of the defendant's statements or has relied, indirectly, on the law's willingness to hold the defendant liable for their truth (in the sense of enforcing a promise to indemnify the plaintiff in case the representations are false). Where the benefits described by the representations may be secured through alternative and economically equivalent means, reliance on the truth of the representations and reliance on the promise to indemnify are in important respects economically equivalent: the only difference between defendants who make their representations come true and those who indemnify for the fact that the representations are not true concerns whether the defendants provide the value associated with the representations directly or indirectly.[34] (Applied to *Overstreet*, this suggestion says that if an equivalently priced but effective alternative vaccine had existed, then the only difference between the defendant's vindicating the claim of effectiveness directly and indemnifying the plaintiff for its falsehood would be whether the defendant prevented the foals from miscarrying through its own vaccine or by replacing it with the effective alternative.) But where the benefits described by the representations exceed those associated with other opportunities, then securing the truth of the representations directly creates an economic value that indemnifying for their falsehood does not. And a promisee who knows or should know that the representations are false but nevertheless makes a bargain based on them uses (one might even say exploits) this difference to establish a bargain that creates no economic gain but merely shifts resources from his promisor to himself.

---

33. *Overstreet* is not an outlier in taking this line. Consider, for example, *Rachlin v. Libby–Owens–Ford Glass Co.*, 96 F.2d 597, 599–600 (2d Cir. 1938), in which the Second Circuit declined to sustain a claim that alleged breach of a warranty that automobile safety glass would afford passengers complete protection against injury from sharp glass fragments in case of an accident. The court observed that:

> There was no proximate causal relation between the deceit and the injuries she sustained. To establish such a causal relation she would have had to show that reliance upon the defendant's misrepresentations prevented her from taking other and more efficacious measures for her safety, or was the inducing cause of her being in the car at the time of the accident. [I]n the case at bar there is nothing to suggest that, if there had been no advertisement by the defendant, [the plaintiff] would not have bought the car or taken the trip South. She meant to buy a new car and she would have taken it where she did whether or not its windshield was equipped with safety glass. Her danger was not increased by her reliance upon the defendant's representations as to the quality of the article she bought. Her injuries were only a remote result of the contemplated use of the defendant's glass; the proximate cause was the collision, and with that the defendant has no connection. Hence, her only loss due to reliance on the defendant's representations was the $10 paid for the extra equipment, and this was not the damage for which she sued.

34. One might say that the only difference between a "promise that" and a "promise to", in such cases, concerns who makes it the case that.

One might even say that a promisee, in such a case, cannot reasonably make the windfall-promise to indemnify into part of the basis for the bargain. Certainly, a promise of a windfall cannot be a necessary basis for the promisee's entering into the bargain: a rational party requires only that his bargain is incrementally better than his next-best alternative; not that it is a windfall. And on the other hand, the windfall should foreclose the promisor's participation: since a true bargain, among free trading partners, would never produce the pure transfer (in which no economic surplus is created) that a windfall involves. These thoughts support reading contract law's requirement that warranty promises must be part of the basis of the bargain before they will be enforced along the lines favored by the *Overstreet* majority, so that where the promises are not just false, but have no true economic equivalents, warranty liability will not arise.[35]

The benefit-of-the-bargain requirement, although it remains unusual, may thus be recast as a necessary or at least prudent response to the ease with which understanding warranties as promises to indemnify (as promises not that the warranted facts obtain but rather to secure the value of the warranted facts should they not obtain) exposes contract to creating legal obligations to vindicate economic windfalls. In this way, the benefit-of-the-bargain requirement protects contract against the pressures that vindicating pure promissory obligation might otherwise subject it to.

16.1.C.2 Easy to Create; Hard to Waive

The doctrines that govern warranties depart from contract's general commitment to establishing legal obligation purely at the pleasure of the contracting parties in a second way also. A series of rules make warranties unusually easy to create and unusually difficult to disclaim. Together, these rules make certain warranties quasi-mandatory, or at least strongly encouraged by the law. The rules thus intervene among the sources of contractual obligations to displace, or at least to interfere with, the intentions of the parties. The interference may be read off the face of the sections of the U.C.C. reproduced above. It is illustrated by the following case.

Ford Motor Co. v. Lemieux Lumber Co., Inc.

Court of Civil Appeals of Texas, 1967.
418 S.W.2d 909.

■ STEPHENSON, J. This is an appeal from an order overruling the plea of privilege of the defendant, Ford Motor Company. This is an action for breach of both an implied warranty in law and an express warranty in writing, that a Ford truck was suitable for the purpose for which it was sold. The parties will be referred to here as they were in the trial court.

---

35. This is not to say that the plaintiff who seeks to vindicate a windfall warranty is left without a remedy; only that he is left without a contractual remedy. He still paid out money in reliance on the warranty statement (on its truth, now, and not its enforceability), and he may recover this in tort (or even in restitution).

Plaintiff alleged that defendant, N. A. Walker, was an individual engaged in the sale of Ford automobiles and trucks in Liberty County, Texas, and resided in Liberty County, Texas. Plaintiff also alleged that defendant, Ford Motor Company, was a foreign corporation doing business in the State of Texas, with an agent for service in Harris County, Texas.

Defendant, Ford Motor Company, filed its plea of privilege asking that the case be transferred to Harris County, Texas. Plaintiff filed its controverting affidavit, relying upon subdivisions 4, 23, 27 and 29a of Article 1995, Vernon's Ann.Civ.St., to maintain venue in Liberty County, Texas. Hearing was before the court and judgment rendered overruling such plea of privilege. In its brief, plaintiff contends only that venue was sustainable under sections 4 and 27, and we conclude the trial court's ruling is correct on both of these grounds.

Section 4 provides in part that if two or more defendants reside in different counties, suit may be brought in any county where one of the defendants resides. N. A. Walker is one of the defendants, and the undisputed evidence shows that he was a resident of Liberty County, where this suit was brought. The evidence also shows: That plaintiff bought a new Ford pick-up truck with four wheel drive from defendant Walker in Cleveland, Texas. That defendant Walker was the authorized dealer for defendant, Ford Motor Company, at the time of such purchase, and obtained such product from defendant, Ford Motor Company. That plaintiff had a contract to cut fifteen million feet of timber from International Paper Company land located in the Devers big thicket or swamps. That defendant, Walker, knew the purpose for which plaintiff was buying the truck in question, and that it was intended to be used to operate in muddy, rough, wet terrain to haul fuel and so forth to the plaintiff's equipment in the woods. That the needs for this truck were discussed by defendant Walker with Jesse H. Williams, president of plaintiff corporation, who negotiated for and concluded the purchase of this truck. That defendant, Ford Motor Company, furnished defendant, Walker, brochures, depicting in pictures and words the products offered for sale, which were distributed by defendant, Walker. That Williams read one of these brochures before buying the truck, which showed pictures of them crossing streams and ditches, and climbing mountains. That plaintiff relied upon such brochure in making this purchase. This particular truck was a four-wheel drive pick-up and was needed to perform services an ordinary pick-up truck would not. That the truck in question immediately began to have trouble in that the rear end would strip out and the universal joint would burst, even though all of the requirements for proper use and maintenance were complied with. That the truck was carried back to defendant Walker each of the three or four times it occurred and attempts were made to repair and correct the problems, but no solution was found. That plaintiff suffered damages. The evidence supported an implied finding by the court that this truck was not suitable for the purpose for which it was sold.

Defendant, Ford Motor Company, contends that no cause of action was proved against it because there was no privity between it and plaintiff as it was not a party to the sales transaction between plaintiff and defendant Walker. The Supreme Court of Texas, in United States Pipe & Foundry Co. v. City of Waco, 130 Tex. 126, permitted recovery directly against the manufacturer who made representations as to what the product would do, even though there was no privity between such parties. We think it is clear in Texas today that privity is no longer required in an action based upon a breach of an express or implied warranty that a product is suitable for the purpose for which it is sold. *McKisson v. Sales Affiliates, Inc., Tex.*, 416 S.W.2d 787.

Defendant also contends that a brochure cannot be construed to be an express warranty, citing *Welch Veterinary Supply Co. v. Martin*, Tex.Civ. App., 313 S.W.2d 111. We do not agree with defendant that such case makes such a holding. We have concluded that a manufacturer should be held responsible for the advertising done by it regardless of the medium, whether it be by television, radio, billboard or brochures and other literature. We further conclude that such manufacturer should be held responsible for economics or commercial losses where the product is not suitable for the use for which it is advertised.

Affirmed.

Randy Knitwear v. American Cyanamid Co.

Court of Appeals of New York, 1962.
181 N.E.2d 399.

■ FULD, JUDGE. 'The assault upon the citadel of privity', Chief Judge Cardozo wrote in 1931, 'is proceeding in these days apace.' (*Ultramares Corp. v. Touche*, 255 N.Y. 170, 180) In these days, too, for the present appeal, here by leave of the Appellate Division on a certified question, calls upon us to decide whether, under the facts disclosed, privity of contract is essential to maintenance of an action against a manufacturer for breach of express warranty.

American Cyanamid Company is the manufacturer of chemical resins, marketed under the registered trade-mark 'Cyana', which are used by textile manufacturers and finishers to process fabrics in order to prevent them from shrinking. Apex Knitted Fabrics and Fairtex Mills are manufacturers of fabrics who were licensed or otherwise authorized by Cyanamid to treat their goods with 'Cyana' and to sell such goods under the 'Cyana' label and with the guaranty that they were 'Cyana' finished. Randy Knitwear, a manufacturer of children's knitted sportswear and play clothes, purchased large quantities of these 'Cyana' treated fabrics from Apex and Fairtex. After most of such fabrics had been made up into garments and sold by Randy to customers, it was claimed that ordinary washing caused them to shrink and to lose their shape. This action for breach of express warranty followed, each of the 3 parties being made the subject of a separate count. After serving its answer, Cyanamid, urging lack of privity of contract, moved for summary judgment dismissing the cause of action asserted against it, and it is solely with this cause of action that we are concerned.

Insofar as relevant, the complaint alleges that Cyanamid 'represented' and 'warranted' that the 'Cyana' finished fabrics sold by Fairtex and Apex to the plaintiff would not shrink or lose their shape when washed and that the plaintiff purchased the fabrics and agreed to pay the additional charge for the cost involved in rendering them shrink-proof 'in reliance upon' Cyanamid's representations. However, the complaint continues, the fabrics were not as represented since, when manufactured into garments and subjected to ordinary washing, they shrank and failed to hold their shape. The damages suffered are alleged to be over $208,000.

According to the complaint and the affidavits submitted in opposition to Cyanamid's motion, the representations relied upon by the plaintiff took the form of written statements expressed not only in numerous advertisements appearing in trade journals and in direct mail pieces to clothing manufacturers, but also in labels or garment tags furnished by Cyanamid. These labels bore the legend,

'A CYANA FINISH, This Fabric Treated for SHRINKAGE CONTROL, Will Not Shrink or Stretch Out of Fit CYANAMID',

and were issued to fabric manufacturers using the 'Cyana Finish' only after Cyanamid had tested samples of the fabrics and approved them. Cyanamid delivered a large number of these labels to Fairtex and Apex and they, with Cyanamid's knowledge and approval, passed them on to garment manufacturers, including the plaintiff, so that they might attach them to the clothing which they manufactured from the fabrics purchased.

As noted, Cyanamid moved for summary judgment dismissing the complaint against it on the ground that there was no privity of contract to support the plaintiff's action. The court at Special Term denied the motion and the Appellate Division unanimously affirmed the resulting order.

Thirty-nine years ago, in *Chysky v. Drake Bros. Co.*, 139 N.E. 576, this court decided that an action for breach of implied warranty could not succeed absent privity between plaintiff and defendant and, some time later, in *Turner v. Edison Storage Battery Co.*, 161 N.E. 423, we reached a similar conclusion with respect to express warranties, writing, 'There can be no warranty where there is no privity of contract' (p. 74, 161 N.E. p. 424). This traditional privity limitation on a seller's liability for damage resulting from breach of warranty has not, however, been adhered to with perfect logical consistency and, just a year ago, in *Greenberg v. Lorenz*, 9 N.Y.2d 195, we noted the definite shift away from the technical privity requirement and recognized that it should be dispensed with in a proper case in the interest of justice and reason. More specifically, we held in *Greenberg* that, in cases involving foodstuffs and other household goods, the implied warranties of fitness and merchantability run from the retailer to the members of the purchaser's household, regardless of privity of contract. We are now confronted with the further but related question whether the traditional privity limitation shall also be dispensed with in an action for breach of express warranty by a remote purchaser against a manufacturer who induced the purchase by representing the quality of the goods in public advertising and on labels which accompanied the goods.

It was in this precise type of case, where express representations were made by a manufacturer to induce reliance by remote purchasers, that 'the citadel of privity' was successfully breached in the State of Washington in 1932. (See *Baxter v. Ford Motor Co.*, 168 Wash. 456; same case after new trial, 179 Wash. 123, 35 P.2d 1090.) It was the holding in the Baxter case that the manufacturer was liable for breach of express warranty to one who purchased an automobile from a retailer since such purchaser had a right to rely on representations made by the manufacturer in its sales literature, even though there was no privity of contract between them. And in the 30 years which have passed since that decision, not only have the courts throughout the country shown a marked, and almost uniform, tendency to discard the privity limitation and hold the manufacturer strictly accountable for the truthfulness of representations made to the public and relied upon by the plaintiff in making his purchase.

The rationale underlying the decisions rejecting the privity requirement is easily understood in the light of present-day commercial practices. It may once have been true that the warranty which really induced the sale was normally an actual term of the contract of sale. Today, however, the significant warranty, the one which effectively induces the purchase, is frequently that given by the manufacturer through mass advertising and labeling to ultimate business users or to consumers with whom he has no direct contractual relationship.

The world of merchandising is, in brief, no longer a world of direct contract; it is, rather, a world of advertising and, when representations expressed and disseminated in the mass communications media and on labels (attached to the goods themselves) prove false and the user or consumer is damaged by reason of his reliance on those representations, it is difficult to justify the manufacturer's denial of liability on the sole ground of the absence of technical privity. Manufacturers make extensive use of newspapers, periodicals and other media to call attention, in glowing terms, to the qualities and virtues of their products, and this advertising is directed at the ultimate consumer or at some manufacturer or supplier who is not in privity with them. Equally sanguine representations on packages and labels frequently accompany the article throughout its journey to the ultimate consumer and, as intended, are relied upon by remote purchasers. Under these circumstances, it is highly unrealistic to limit a purchaser's protection to warranties made directly to him by his immediate seller. The protection he really needs is against the manufacturer whose published representations caused him to make the purchase.

The policy of protecting the public from injury, physical or pecuniary, resulting from misrepresentations outweighs allegiance to an old and outmoded technical rule of law which, if observed, might be productive of great injustice. The manufacturer places his product upon the market and, by advertising and labeling, it, represents its quality to the public in such a way as to induce reliance upon his representations. He unquestionably intends and expects that the product will be purchased and used in reliance upon his express assurance of its quality and, in fact, it is so purchased and used. Having invited and solicited the use, the manufacturer should not be permitted to avoid responsibility, when the expected use leads to injury and loss, by claiming that he made no contract directly with the user.

It is true that in many cases the manufacturer will ultimately be held accountable for the falsity of his representations, but only after an unduly wasteful process of litigation. Thus, if the consumer or ultimate business user sues and recovers, for breach of warranty, from his immediate seller and if the latter, in turn, sues and recovers against his supplier in recoupment of his damages and costs, eventually, after several separate actions by those in the chain of distribution, the manufacturer may finally be obliged 'to shoulder the responsibility which should have been his in the first instance.' (*Hamon v. Digliani*, 148 Conn. 710, 717; see *Kasler & Cohen v. Salvouski* (1928), 1 K.B. 78, where there was a series of 5 recoveries, the manufacturer ultimately paying the consumer's damages, plus a much larger sum covering the costs of the entire litigation.) As is manifest, and as Dean Prosser observes, this circuity of action is 'an expensive, time-consuming and wasteful process, and it may be interrupted by insolvency, lack of jurisdiction, disclaimers, or the statute of limitations'. (Prosser, The Assault upon the Citadel (Strict Liability to the Consumer), 69 Yale L.J. 1099, 1124.)

Indeed, and it points up the injustice of the rule, insistence upon the privity requirement may well leave the aggrieved party, whether he be ultimate business user or consumer, without a remedy in a number of situations. For instance, he would be remediless either where his immediate seller's representations as to quality were less extravagant or enthusiastic than those of the manufacturer or where as is asserted by Fairtex in this very case there has been an effective disclaimer of any and all warranties by the plaintiff's immediate seller. Turning to the case before us, even if the representations respecting 'Cyana' treated fabric were false, the plaintiff would be foreclosed of all remedy against Fairtex, if it were to succeed on its defense of disclaimer, and against Cyanamid because of a lack of privity.

Although we believe that it has already been made clear, it is to be particularly remarked that in the present case the plaintiff's reliance is not on newspaper advertisements alone. It places heavy emphasis on the fact that the defendant not only made representations (as to the nonshrinkable character of 'Cyana Finish' fabrics) in newspapers and periodicals, but also repeated them on its own labels and tags which accompanied the fabrics purchased by the plaintiff from Fairtex and Apex. There is little in reason or logic to support Cyanamid's submission that it should not be held liable to the plaintiff even though the representations prove false in fact and it is ultimately found that the plaintiff relied to its harm upon such representations in making its purchases.

We perceive no warrant for holding as the appellant urges that strict liability should not here be imposed because the defect involved, fabric shrinkage, is not likely to cause personal harm or injury. Although there is language in some of the opinions which appears to support Cyanamid's contention, most of the courts which have dispensed with the requirement of privity in this sort of case have not limited their decisions in this manner. And this makes sense. Since the basis of liability turns not upon the character of the product but upon the representation, there is no justification for a distinction on the basis of the type of injury suffered or the type of article or goods involved.

We are also agreed that the present case may not be distinguished, and liability denied, on the ground that the article sold by the appellant, resin, is different from that purchased by the plaintiff, fabric. To be sure, as Cyanamid urges, the failure to render the fabric shrink-proof may rest with Fairtex and Apex, but the short and simple answer is that Cyanamid actually and expressly represented that fabrics accompanied by the labels which it supplied were 'Cyana Finish' and would not shrink or lose their shape. Since it made such representations, Cyanamid may not disclaim responsibility for them. If the ultimate fault for the plaintiff's loss is actually that of Fairtex and Apex, Cyanamid's appropriate recourse is against them.

Nor may it be urged that section 93 of the Personal Property Law renders privity of contract necessary. The Legislature has there defined a warranty as an 'affirmation' (or 'promise') made by a seller, but the section nowhere states that liability for breach of express warranty extends only to the warranting seller's immediate buyer and cannot extend to a later buyer who made the purchase from an intermediate seller but in foreseeable and natural reliance on the original seller's affirmations. Indeed, we made the matter clear in *Greenberg v. Lorenz* when, after observing that the rule requiring a direct contractual relationship between the plaintiff and the defendant is of 'judicial making', we went on to say, 'our statutes say nothing at all about privity' (9 N.Y.2d 195, 200).

In concluding that the old court-made rule should be modified to dispense with the requirement of privity, we are doing nothing more or less than carrying out an historic and necessary function of the court to bring the law into harmony 'with modern-day needs and with concepts of justice and fair dealing.' (*Bing v. Thunig*, 2 N.Y.2d 656, 667).

The order appealed from should be affirmed, with costs, and the question certified answered in the negative.

■ FROESSEL, J., concurring.

We concur in result only. We agree with Judge FULD that defendant, American Cyanamid Company, may be held liable for its express representations (as to the nonshrinkable character of 'Cyana Finish' fabrics) in newspapers and periodicals where they have been repeated on its own labels and tags delivered by Cyanamid to fabric manufacturers such as Fairtex and Apex, to be passed on to garment manufacturers such as plaintiff, so that they might attach them to the clothing cut from the fabrics purchased, all allegedly with Cyanamid's knowledge and authorization.

We do not agree that the so-called 'old court-made rule' should be modified to dispense with the requirement of privity without limitation. We decide cases as they arise, and would affirm in this case under the facts here disclosed.

Vlases v. Montgomery Ward & Co., Inc.

United States Court of Appeals for the Third Circuit, 1967.
377 F.2d 846.

■ McLAUGHLIN, CIRCUIT JUDGE. This case revolves around the charge that defendant-appellant, Montgomery Ward, was liable for the breach of implied warranties in the sale of one day old chickens to the plaintiff-appellee, Paul Vlases. The latter came to this country from Greece when he was sixteen and until 1954 his primary occupation was that of a coal miner. He had always raised chickens but because of his job as a miner his flocks were small, ranging from between twenty-five to one hundred chicks. In 1958 plaintiff began the construction of a two story chicken coop large enough to house 4,000 chickens and a smaller side building where he could wash, grade and sell the eggs. Vlases worked alone on the coop, twelve hours a day, fifty-two weeks a year, until its completion in 1961. In November of 1961 plaintiff placed an order at defendant's outlet store in Brownsville, Pennsylvania for the purchase of 2,000 one day old chicks. The chickens selected by the plaintiff from Ward's catalogue were hybrid Leghorns and were noted for their excellent egg production. On December 21, 1961 plaintiff received the 2,200 chickens and placed them on the first floor of the coop which had been equipped with new brooders, feeders and within a short time, waterers. As a further hygienic precaution wire and sugar cane were placed on the ground so the chickens would not come in contact with the dirt floor. For the first six months Vlases slept in the coop in order to give the new chicks his undivided attention.

During the first few weeks after delivery the chickens appeared to be in good health but by the third week plaintiff noticed that their feathers were beginning to fall off. This condition was brought to the attention of Mr. Howard Hamilton who represented the Agway Corporation which was supplying the plaintiff with feed on credit. In February of 1962 Mr. Hamilton took five chickens to the Bureau of Animal Industry Diagnostic Laboratory where they were examined by Dr. Daniel P. Ehlers. The examination revealed signs of drug intoxication and hemorrhagic disease involving the weakening of blood vessels. Four chicks were brought to Dr. Ehlers in May of 1962 and were found to be suffering from fatigue. On the 14th of August 1962 Mr. Hamilton brought three chickens to the laboratory where Dr. Ehlers' report noted that two of the chicks were affected with visceral leukosis, one with ocular leukosis, one had bumble foot and one had been picked. Visceral and ocular leukosis are two types of avian leukosis complex or bird cancer which disease infected plaintiff's flock either killing the chicks or causing those remaining to be destroyed.

Plaintiff in this two count suit in assumpsit charged negligence and breach of warranty with jurisdiction resting on the diversity provisions of 28 U.S.C.A. 1332. After the second day of trial the negligence claim was dropped leaving the breach of warranty as the sole problem for the jury's consideration. A verdict was returned in favor of the plaintiff in the amount of $23,028.77. Montgomery Ward appeals from the resultant judgment.

I

Appellant takes the position that an action for breach of implied warranties will not lie for the sale of one day old chicks where there is no human skill, knowledge or foresight which would enable the producer or supplier to prevent the occurrence of this disease, to detect its presence or to care for the sickness if it was present. The jury was instructed by the court that recovery on behalf of the plaintiff required a finding that the chickens were afflicted with leukosis at the time defendant made delivery. The expert testimony for both sides indicated that there was no way of determining whether newly hatched chicks have leukosis and that there is no medication available to prevent the disease from occurring. Assuming the chickens were diseased upon their arrival the thrust of appellant's argument questions the sufficiency of the law to support a finding that Ward is liable under Pennsylvania law for the breach of implied warranties.

The two implied warranties before us are the implied warranty of merchantability, 12A P.S. 2–314, and the implied warranty of fitness for a particular purpose, 12A P.S. 2–315. Both of these are designed to protect the buyer of goods from bearing the burden of loss where merchandise, though not violating a promise expressly guaranteed, does not conform to the normal commercial standards or meeting the buyer's particular purpose, a condition upon which he had the right to rely.

Were it to be assumed that the sale of 2,000 chickens infected with avian leukosis transgressed the norm of acceptable goods under both warranties, appellant's position is that the action will not lie in a situation where the seller is unable to discover the defect or cure the damage if it could be ascertained. That theory does not eliminate the consequences imposed by the Code upon the seller of commercially inferior goods. It is without merit.

The fact that avian leukosis is nondetectable could be an important issue but only as bearing on the charge of negligence, which is no longer in this suit. The Pennsylvania decision in *Vandenberg & Sons, N.V. v. Siter*, 204 Pa. Super. 392 (1964), buttresses our conclusion in upholding the implied warranties. There latent defects in certain tulip and hyacinth Bulbs went undetected in the face of two inspections and the court, though aware that the imperfections could only be uncovered after growth, limited its concern to the question of whether the seller's express provision that notice of any breach be communicated within a certain time, was reasonable. The entire purpose behind the implied warranty sections of the Code is to hold the seller responsible when inferior goods are passed along to the unsuspecting buyer. What the Code requires is not evidence that the defects should or could have been uncovered by the seller but only that the goods upon delivery were not of a merchantable quality or fit for their particular purpose. If those requisite proofs are established the only exculpatory relief afforded by the Code is a showing that the implied warranties were modified or excluded by specific language under Section 2–316. Lack of skill or foresight on the part of the seller in discovering the product's flaw was never meant to bar liability. The gravamen here is not so much with what precautions were taken by the seller but rather with the quality of the goods contracted for by the buyer. Even a provision specifically disclaiming any warrant against avian leukosis would not necessarily call for the defendant's freedom from liability. Section 1–102(3) of the Code's General Provisions states that standards which are manifestly unreasonable may not be disclaimed and prevents the enforcement of unconscionable sales where, as in this instance, the goods exchanged are found to be totally worthless.

The judgment of the District Court will be affirmed.

Weisz v. Parke–Bernet Galleries, Inc.

Civil Court, City of New York, 1971.
325 N.Y.S.2d 576.

■ SANDLER, JUDGE. On May 16, 1962, Dr. Arthur Weisz attended an auction conducted by the Parke–Bernet Galleries, Inc., where he ultimately bought for the sum of $3,347.50 a painting listed in the auction catalogue as the work of Raoul Dufy. Some two years later, on May 13, 1964, David and Irene Schwartz bought for $9,360.00 at a Parke–Bernet auction a painting also listed in the catalogue as the work of Raoul Dufy.

Several years after the second auction, as a result of an investigation conducted by the New York County District Attorney's office, the plaintiffs received information that the paintings were in fact forgeries. When this was called to Parke–Bernet's attention, Parke–Bernet denied any legal responsibility, asserting among other things that the Conditions of Sale for both auctions included a disclaimer of warranty as to genuineness, authorship and the like.

Following a formal demand by the plaintiffs for return of the purchase price, these two lawsuits were commenced against Parke–Bernet and one Carroll Hogan, a former employee actively concerned with the two auctions. Juries having been waived, both cases were tried jointly.

In each case, several causes of action are set forth, all of them quite closely interrelated, and all ultimately turning on the identification by Parke–Bernet of the paintings as the work of Dufy.

In the first cause of action, which adequately presents the issues to be resolved, the catalogue listing 'Raoul Dufy' is asserted to constitute an express warranty, as that term was defined under the former Sales Act, in effect when the auctions took place. Former Personal Property Law, Sec. 93.

The most substantial of the defenses interposed by Parke–Bernet is that the Conditions of Sale for the auctions, appearing on a preliminary page of each catalogue, included a disclaimer of any warranty and that the plaintiffs are bound by its terms.

This issue embraces two separate questions, each of which merits careful examination.

First, did the plaintiffs in fact know of the disclaimer, and, if they did not, are they legally chargeable with such knowledge.

Second, if the answer to either part of the first question is yes, was the disclaimer effective, under all the circumstances of the auctions, to immunize Parke–Bernet from the legal consequences that would normally follow where a sale results from a representation of genuineness that is thereafter disclosed to be completely inaccurate.

Although the auctions were separated in time by two years, the catalogues were quite similar in all legally significant respects, and the basic auction procedure was the same.

The catalogues open with several introductory pages of no direct relevance to the lawsuits. There then follows a page headed 'Conditions of Sale', in large black print, under which some 15 numbered paragraphs appears, covering the side of one page and most of a second side. These provisions are in clear black print, somewhat smaller than the print used in the greater part of the catalogue.

Paragraph 2, on which Parke–Bernet relies, provides as follows:

'The Galleries has endeavored to catalogue and describe the property correctly, but all property is sold 'as is' and neither the Galleries nor its consignor warrants or represents, and they shall in no event be responsible for, the correctness of description, genuineness, authorship, provenience or condition of the property, and no statement contained in the catalogue or made orally at the sale or elsewhere shall be deemed to be such a warranty or representation, or an assumption of liability.'

The next page in each catalogue is headed 'List of Artists', and contains in alphabetical order, one under the other, a list of the artists with a catalogue number or numbers appearing on the same line with the named artist. The implicit affirmation that the listed artists are represented in the auction and that the catalogue numbers appearing after their names represent their work could scarcely be clearer.

The name Raoul Dufy is listed in each catalogue, together with several catalogue numbers.

After the pages on which the artists are listed, over 80 pages follow in each catalogue on which the catalogue numbers appear in numerical order with descriptive material about the artist and the work.

Turning in each catalogue to the catalogue numbers for the paintings involved in the lawsuits, there appears on the top of the page a conventional black-and-white catalogue reproduction of the painting, directly under it the catalogue number in brackets, and the name RAOUL DUFY in large black print followed in smaller print by the words 'French 1880—1953'.

On the next line the catalogue number is repeated together with the name of the painting, a description of it, and the words, 'Signed at lower right RAOUL DUFY.' Finally, there appears a note that a certificate by M. Andre Pacitti, will be given to the purchaser.

The procedure followed at both auctions was to announced at the beginning of the auction that it was subject to the conditions of sale, without repeating the announcement, and at no point alluding directly to the disclaimer.

As to the first auction, I am satisfied that Dr. Weisz did not in fact know of the Conditions of Sale and may not properly be charged with knowledge of its contents. I accept as entirely accurate his testimony that on his prior appearances at Parke–Bernet auctions he had not made any bids, and that on the occasion of his purchase he did not observe the Conditions of Sale and was not aware of its existence.

The test proposed for this kind of issue by Williston, quite consistent with the decided cases, is whether 'the person should as a reasonable man understand that it contains terms of the contract that he must read at his peril.' 1 Williston on Contracts Sec. 90D (1937).

The most obvious characteristic of the two Parke–Bernet auctions is that they attracted people on the basis of their interest in owning works of art, not on the basis of their legal experience or business sophistication. Surely it is unrealistic to assume that people who did at such auctions will ordinarily understand that a gallery catalogue overwhelmingly devoted to descriptions of works of art also includes on its preliminary pages conditions of sale. Even less reasonable does it seem to me to expect a bidder at such an auction to appreciate the possibility that the conditions of sale would include a disclaimer of liability for the accuracy of the basic information presented throughout the catalogue in unqualified form with every appearance of certainty and reliability.

For someone in Dr. Weisz's position to be bound by conditions of sale, of which he in fact knew nothing, considerably more was required of Parke–Bernet to call those Conditions of Sale to his attention than occurred here.

As to the Schwartz case, I am satisfied from the evidence that Mrs. Schwartz knew of the Conditions of Sale, and that both Schwartz plaintiffs are chargeable with that knowledge since they both participated in the purchase.

This factual conclusion leads to consideration of the extremely interesting question whether the language of disclaimer relied upon as a bar to the actions should be deemed effective for that purpose. No case has come to my attention that squarely presents the issue raised by the underlying realities of this case.

What is immediately apparent from any review of the evidence is that notwithstanding the language of disclaimer, Parke–Bernet expected that bidders at its auctions would rely upon the accuracy of its descriptions, and intended that they should. Parke–Bernet, as the evidence confirms, is an exceedingly well-known gallery, linked in the minds of people with the handling, exhibition and sale of valuable artistic works and invested with an aura of expertness and reliability. The very fact that Parke–Bernet was offering a work of art for sale would inspire confidence that it was genuine and that the listed artist in fact was the creator of the work.

The wording of the catalogue was clearly designed to emphasize the genuineness of the works to be offered. The list of artists followed by catalogue numbers, the black-and-white reproductions of the more important works, the simple listing of the name of the artist with the years of his birth and death could not have failed to impress upon the buyer that these facts could be relied on and that one could safely part with large sums of money in the confident knowledge that a genuine artistic work was being acquired.

Where one party in a contractual relationship occupies a position of superior knowledge and experience, and where that superior knowledge is relied upon and intended to be relied upon by the other, surely more is required for an effective disclaimer than appears here.

After reassuring the reader that Parke–Bernet endeavored to catalogue the works of art correctly, there follow highly technical and legalistic words of disclaimer in a situation in which plain and emphatic words are required. And this provision, in light of the critical importance to the buyer of a warning that he may not rely on the fact that a work attributed to an artist was in fact his creation, is in no way given the special prominence that it clearly requires.

The language used, the understated manner of its presentation, the failure to refer to it explicitly in the preliminary oral announcement at the auction all lead to the conclusion that Parke–Bernet did not expect the bidders to take the disclaimer too seriously or to be too concerned about it. I am convinced that the average reader of this provision would view it as some kind of technicality that should in no way derogate from the certainty that he was buying genuine artistic works, and that this was precisely the impression intended to be conveyed.

In denying legal effect to the disclaimer I am acting consistently with a whole body of law that reflects an increasing sensitivity to the requirements of fair dealing where there is a relationship between parties in which there is a basic inequality of knowledge, expertness or economic power.

Judgment may be entered for the plaintiff Weisz against Parke–Bernet in the sum of $3,347.50, and for the plaintiffs David and Irene Schwartz in the sum of $9,360.00, both judgments of course with appropriate interest and costs. The actions against Carroll Hogan are dismissed, and judgments may be entered in his behalf with costs.

Weisz v. Parke–Bernet Galeries Inc.

New York App. Term, 1974.
351 N.Y.S.2d 911.

■ Before QUINN, J.P., and LUPIANO and FINE, JJ.

■ PER CURIAM:

Plaintiffs' purchases by competitive bids, at a public auction were made in 1962 and 1964. At that time neither the statutory nor decisional law, applicable to such purchases, recognized the expressed opinion or judgment of the seller as giving rise to any implied warranty of authenticity of authorship. (See Memorandum of the State Dept. of Law (McKinney's 1968 Session Laws, vol. 2, pp. 2284—2285) recommending remedial legislation (now secs. 219 and 219—a of the General Business Law) to change the then existing law).

Additionally defendant's auction-sale, catalogue listing, describing and illustrating these paintings gave leading and prominent place, in its prefatory terms of sale, (explaining and regulating the conduct of the auction) to a clear, unequivocal disclaimer of any express or implied warranty or representation of genuineness of any paintings as products of the ascribed artist.

One of the factors necessarily entering into the competition among bidders at the public auction was the variable value of the paintings depending upon the degree of certainty with which they could be authenticated and established as the works of the ascribed artist. (See *Backus v. MacLaury*, 278 App.Div. 504, 507). Since no element of a wilful intent to deceive is remotely suggested in the circumstances here present the purchasers assumed the risk that in judging the paintings as readily-identifiable, original works of the named artist, and scaling their bids accordingly, they might be mistaken. (Restatement, Contracts, sec. 502, comment f., p. 964). They will not now be heard to complain that, in failing to act with the caution of one in circumstances abounding with signals of Caveat emptor, they made a bad bargain. The judgments are reversed with $30 costs and the complaints dismissed.

Restatement (Second) of Contracts

§ 166.   When A Misrepresentation As To A Writing Justifies Reformation

If a party's manifestation of assent is induced by the other party's fraudulent misrepresentation as to the contents or effect of a writing evidencing or embodying in whole or in part an agreement, the court at the request of the recipient may reform the writing to express the terms of the agreement as asserted,

(a) if the recipient was justified in relying on the misrepresentation, and

(b) except to the extent that rights of third parties such as good faith purchasers for value will be unfairly affected.

Comments & Illustrations

Comment a.   Scope. Reformation is more broadly available for fraudulent misrepresentation than for mistake. Compare § 155. Reformation for mistake is limited to the situation in which the parties, having already reached an agreement, later fail to express it correctly in a writing. That limitation, stated in § 155, applies to all cases where both parties are mistaken, including those where one of the mistaken parties has made a non-fraudulent misrepresentation as to the contents or effect of a writing. Where, however, only one party is mistaken and the other has fraudulently misrepresented the writing's contents, or effect, reformation may be granted even though there was no prior agreement. Compare Comment *a* to § 155. The writing must be one that evidences or embodies, at least in part, the agreement of the parties. Otherwise it will not ordinarily have sufficient legal significance for its reformation to be necessary, and the dispute can be resolved simply in accordance with the general rules applicable to offer and acceptance. The rule stated in this Section also applies to the case where only one party is mistaken and the other, although aware of the mistake, says nothing to correct it. In that case his non-disclosure is equivalent to an assertion that the writing is as the other understands it to be (§ 161(c)). (Where only one party is mistaken and the other is not aware of the mistake, the rule stated in § 153, on mistake of only one party, applies.) The misrepresentation must, of course, be certain enough to permit a court to know how the writing should be reformed. Reformation is not precluded by the mere fact that the party who seeks it failed to exercise reasonable care in reading the writing, but his reliance on the misrepresentation must be justified and the right to reformation is therefore subject to the rule on fault stated in § 172. This Section, like § 155, only states the circumstances in which a court "may" grant reformation, and, since the remedy is equitable, a court has the discretion to withhold it, even if it would otherwise be appropriate, on grounds traditionally considered by courts of equity in exercising their discretion. See Comment *d* to § 155.

Illustrations

1. A and B agree that A will buy a tract of land from B for $100,000 and will assume an existing mortgage of $50,000. In reducing the agreement to writing, A intentionally omits the provision for assumption and tells B that the writing correctly expresses their agreement. B does not notice the omission and is induced by A's fraudulent misrepresentation to sign the writing, which is an integrated agreement. At the request of B, the court

will reform the writing to add the provision for assumption. Compare Illustration 3 to § 164. See Illustration 1 to § 155.

2. A, seeking to induce B to make a contract to sell a tract of land to A for $100,000, makes a written offer to B and tells B that it includes a provision under which A assumes an existing mortgage. A knows that the writing does not contain such a provision. B does not notice the omission and is induced by A's fraudulent misrepresentation to sign the writing, which is an integrated agreement. At the request of B, the court will reform the writing to add the provision for assumption.

3. A, seeking to induce B to make a contract to sell a tract of land to A for $100,000, makes a written offer to B and tells B that the legal effect of a particular provision is that A assumes an existing mortgage. A, who is a lawyer, knows that this is not the legal effect of the provision. B does not realize that the legal effect of the provision is not as asserted and is induced by A's fraudulent misrepresentation to sign the writing, which is an integrated agreement. See § 170. At the request of B, the court will reform the writing to add the provision for assumption.

4. A, seeking to induce B to make a contract to sell a tract of land to A for $100,000, makes a written offer to B. A knows that B mistakenly thinks that the offer contains a provision under which A assumes an existing mortgage and that it does not contain such a provision, but does not disclose this to B for fear that B will not accept. B is induced by A's non-disclosure to sign the writing, which is an integrated agreement. A's non-disclosure is equivalent to an assertion that the writing contains such a provision (§ 161(e)) and amounts to a fraudulent misrepresentation. At the request of B, the court will reform the writing to add the provision for assumption. See Illustration 13 to § 161.

Comment b. Relation to other rules. The rule stated in this Section applies only to misrepresentations as to the contents or effect of a writing. If the misrepresentation relates to some other fact, the contract may be voidable under § 164, but reformation is not appropriate. See also § 163. The availability of reformation based on a fraudulent misrepresentation does not, however, preclude the alternative of avoidance, and the recipient has a choice of remedies. See Illustration 12 to § 161 and compare Illustration 3 to § 164 with Illustration 1 to the present Section. This is in contrast to the rule for mutual mistake. See Introductory Note to Chapter 6 and to Comment *d* to § 152. In some instances, however, the problem may be merely one of interpretation of the writing, so that neither reformation nor avoidance is appropriate. See § 20.

Illustration

5. A, seeking to induce B to make a contract to buy a tract of land at a price of $100,000, makes a written offer to B and tells B that the tract contains 100 acres. A knows that it contains only 90

acres. B is induced by A's fraudulent misrepresentation to sign the writing. The court will not, at the request of B, reform the writing because the mistake of the parties was not one as to the contents or effect of the writing. B's right to avoidance is governed by the rule stated in § 164(1). See Illustration 1 to § 164 and Illustration 5 to § 155.

Comment c.   Parol evidence rule and Statute of Frauds. The parol evidence rule does not preclude proof of a fraudulent misrepresentation to justify reformation. See § 214(d). Furthermore, if reformation of a writing is otherwise appropriate, it is not precluded by the fact that the contract is within the Statute of Frauds. See § 156.

Comment d.   Protection of innocent third parties. The right of reformation under the rule stated in this Section is subject to the rights of good faith purchasers for value and other third parties who have similarly relied on the finality of a consensual transaction in which they have acquired an interest in property. Such other third parties include those who have given value and come within the definition of "purchaser" in Uniform Commercial Code § 1–201(33), (32), notably mortgagees, pledgees and other holders of a security interest. Judgment creditors and trustees in bankruptcy are not included. This is the same exception as that under § 155 where third parties have intervened. See Comment *f* to § 155 and Illustrations 8 and 9 to that Section.

* * *

The plaintiff in *Lemieux Lumber* was a firm that had bought a new four-wheel-drive Ford pickup truck from a local Ford dealer. The plaintiff intended to use the truck in its logging business, in particular in connection with work cutting trees from a large, densely wooded, swampy tract of land. The plaintiff's president had discussed his firm's requirements—that the truck should be capable of operating in "muddy, rough, wet terrain to haul fuel and so forth"—with the dealer. In addition, the plaintiff had seen advertising brochures that Ford Motor Company had given its dealers, which depicted Ford trucks "crossing streams and ditches, and climbing mountains;" and the plaintiff had relied on the brochures when it decided to buy a Ford. Nevertheless, the plaintiff's new Ford was not up to the tasks put to it. Almost immediately, the truck's universal joint, which connects the engine to the drive shaft and thus is essential for transmitting power to the wheels, failed. The truck could not be repaired to render it suitable to the uses to which the plaintiff sought to put it. The plaintiff suffered damages, including to its business.

The *Lemieux Lumber* court did not pause long in concluding that Ford's sales brochures created an express warranty that Ford Trucks would perform as depicted in the photographs that the brochures contained. The court thought it sufficient, in this connection, to observe that "a manufacturer should be held responsible for the advertising done by it regardless of the medium." The court did not think it necessary to ask whether images of a truck in generically demanding settings contained sufficiently complete and precise information to sustain warranties that the truck could satisfy any specific demands placed on it. This is striking. The issue is not simply whether the setting in which the plaintiff sought to employ the truck was similar to, or at least not more demanding than, the settings in the brochure-photographs. That was a question of fact, presumably to be decided at trial. Rather, there exists a prior question whether an image or set of images can convey enough information, and an intent to assume the risk of that information's being false, to constitute a contractually binding guarantee of product quality at all.

Not all communications made during pre-contractual negotiations enter into contracts in this way. An advertisement depicting happy employees vouching for their firm does not, for example, establish a contractual obligation that the advertising firm must possess a satisfied workforce, much less an obligation that the firm must maintain any particular labor policies or conditions of employment. Similarly, a seller's "revelation" that she must meet a monthly sales quota or suffers some other pressure to close a deal does not commit her to the fact that the price given in conjunction with the "revelation" is actually advantageous. Each of these alternative scenarios conveys information to a buyer in the course of negotiations, but in neither case does the information become part of the contract. The reason why not is straightforward and goes to the role of intent in contract formation and, ultimately, to freedom of contract. These features of contract law generally prevent stray representations from becoming binding on parties who make them while negotiating.

But where the representations concern the quality of products—especially of products sold to consumers—the law proceeds differently. Warranties are unusually easy to fall into even without specifically intending to, by choosing them. A reasonable consumer reading Ford's sales brochures might perhaps infer that Ford believes that its trucks can work in rough terrain, or perhaps that Ford trucks can in fact do so. (Although even with respect to these matters, one might wonder how rough, and even whether the difficulties of rough terrain are too subtle and unquantifiable for images of a particular setting, or even of many settings, to provide information about other settings not depicted.) But it is a big leap from these beliefs to the (reasonable?) belief that Ford intends to assume *legal responsibility* for its trucks' capacities in this respect—guaranteeing that the trucks can so work and acquiring an obligation to indemnify if they cannot. That is precisely what *Lemieux Lumber* holds, however.[36] Nor is *Lemieux Lumber* alone in taking this approach. As the U.C.C. emphasizes, affirmations of fact relating to goods sold, descriptions of these goods, and samples all create express warranties as long as they are made part of the basis of a bargain, even though the sellers do not use the words "warrant"

---

36. The facts made *Lemieux Lumber* easy in at least one respect: the truck's failure to perform as warranted did not just involve the truck's failing to traverse rough roads or traversing such roads only slowly or insecurely; rather, the failure manifested itself in the fact that the truck broke while being driven in conditions like those depicted in the brochure. This made the failure unambiguous, so that once the warranty was established, its breach was clear.

or "guarantee" and—critically—*even though they do not have any specific intention to make a warranty.*

When it reaches such results, contract law, through the doctrines governing warranties, treats representations that have a certain substance differently from others, making certain types of representations concerning product quality unusually obligation-generative.[37] Again, Ford's brochures presumably included images and text that made any number of other representations, not related to the quality of its products: concerning the happiness of Ford production workers, for example, or the work, domestic, and social successes of those who own and drive Ford trucks. But there is no question at all that these representations do not become part of any sales contracts for Ford's cars and trucks. This is natural. Contract obligation, being chosen, generally arises only out of the specific intent of those who are obligated. Not everything said in and around contract negotiations reflects or conveys this specific intent. Warranties are the outlier, in this respect.

Lemieux Lumber, moreover, unambiguously casts the breach of warranty action in contractual terms. In particular, the court blithely countenances remedies that include recovery for "economic[] or commercial losses where the product is not suitable for the use for which it is advertised," without making any reference to the doctrines that limit recovery for purely economic losses (as opposed to physical harms and in particular personal injuries) in tort.[38]

Finally, *Lemieux Lumber* found a warranty in spite of the fact that Ford did not deal directly with consumers (having been prevented from doing so by state franchise laws), but rather sold its trucks through dealerships. The plaintiff therefore had no conventional contract with Ford—there was, as the courts says, "no privity between [the] parties."

Randy Knitwear takes up this feature of many warranty actions and explains the modern rule abandoning the traditional requirement of privity of contract. The defendant, in *Randy Knitwear*, manufactured a chemical resin that prevented shrinking when applied to fabrics. The plaintiff was a

---

37. *Lemieux Lumber* is not an outlier in this respect. Any number of opinions accept that advertising brochures or other product descriptions establish analogous warranties by similar means. For another example, see *Sylvestri v. Warner & Swasey Co., Inc.*, 398 F.2d 598 (2d Cir. 1968). An advertising brochure containing a picture of a backhoe being used to lift a length of pipe and stating that the backhoe's "hydraulic system provides powerful lift force for material handling, sewer pipe laying, etc." and referring to the backhoe's "extremely rigid foundation" was held to create an express warranty concerning the backhoe's stability that was breached when lifting a similarly heavy but differently attached rock caused the backhoe to tilt to one side and throw its operator to the ground. The examples, once again, may be multiplied.

38. This feature of the holding is not fully secure or universally followed. Note that *Randy Knitwear*, discussed below, expressly engages this theme, rejecting the argument that liability for breach of warranty should be limited to cases in which the breach causes "personal harm or injury." As the court says: "this makes sense. Since the basis of liability turns not upon the character of the product but upon the representation, there is no justification for a distinction on the basis of the type of injury suffered or the type of article or goods involved." It does make functionalist sense; but it blithely rejects any number of formal distinctions that had enjoyed long and influential careers in tort law.

manufacturer of children's clothing that had bought fabrics treated with the defendant's product, not from the defendant directly but from a third party that (under a license with the defendant) marketed its fabrics as having been treated with the defendant's product. The plaintiff alleged that garments made from the treated fabrics shrunk and lost their shapes after ordinary washing. It sued not just the third party but also the defendant, alleging breach of an express warranty guaranteeing non-shrink fabric.

The defendant, citing decades-old precedents that "[t]here can be no warranty where there is no privity of contract," sought summary judgment on the ground that the plaintiff's breach of warranty claim sounded in contract and that it and the plaintiff were not in privity. The Court of Appeals of New York rejected the argument and the precedents behind it. Although the court sought, in a footnote, to cast formal doubt on a warranty action's contractual pedigree (observing the action's relatively recent roots in tort) the gravamen of the opinion is steadfastly functionalist. Modern contractual practice, the court observed, simply does not fit the classical form. The combination of large-scale manufacture and mass-marketing has resulted in a situation in which manufacturers advertise directly to consumers—in the press and also, as the court observed, in labeling provided by manufacturers for retailers to pass on to consumers—but do not sell directly to them. These facts on the ground, the court observed, make it "highly unrealistic to limit a purchaser's protection to warranties made directly to him by his immediate seller," where "[t]he protection he really needs is against the manufacturer whose published representations caused him to make the purchase." Such unreality has consequences, moreover. The formal requirements of privity constitute "an old and out-moded technical rule of law which, if observed, might be productive of great injustice." In order that the law may be brought into harmony with "modern-day needs and with concepts of justice and fair dealing," and that the public might be protected "from injury, physical or pecuniary, resulting from misrepresentations," technical "allegiance" to legal form must be "outweigh[ed]" by the imperatives of function.

The functionalist arguments for abandoning the privity requirement in connection with warranty claims against manufacturers are indeed strong. Frankly, it is difficult to imagine how a modern consumer economy could function with the classical rules concerning privity in place. But the theme of this Part of the text does not concern function so much as form, and no amount of functionalist good sense, and no salutary consequences of employing such good sense, can change the fact that abandoning privity fundamentally changes the formal character of contractual obligation in this area. Where manufacturers do not sell directly to consumers, no amount of advertising can change the fact that warranty obligations between manufacturers and consumers are not intended directly into existence by the parties to them, in the manner of classical contract, but are instead involuntary—created by the operation of law imposed in connection with other voluntary acts (advertising, buying, and so on), in the manner of classical tort. At least in the consumer context, even express warranties are thus creatures not so much of the intentions of the parties as of the law.

The law further intervenes in warranty arrangements in consumer contracts through the doctrines concerning implied warranties. Two implied warranties are worth especial mention. First, merchant sellers generally sell their goods subject to an implied warranty of merchantability, as elaborated in U.C.C. § 2–314. This is a warranty that goods sold will be fit for the ordinary purposes for which they are used. Second, U.C.C. § 2–315 provides that sellers who know or have reason to know that their buyers intend to use a good sold in a particular way and are relying on their expertise with respect to the good's suitability, sell their goods subject to an implied warranty of fitness for this particular purpose. This rule creates additional implied warranties based on known asymmetries in information and skill between sellers and their buyers.

These implied warranties can sweep broadly indeed. *Vlases* illustrates just how broadly. The plaintiff in that case had purchased 2,200 one-day-old chickens from the defendant, for use in his new egg-farm. The chickens turned out to suffer from a type of bird cancer, which either killed them or required that they be destroyed. The plaintiff sued his seller for breach of warranty concerning the health and quality of the chickens.

The court held that the seller of the infected chickens breached the implied warranties of merchantability and fitness for a particular purpose, even though the disease was undetectable by the seller. The two implied warranties, the court claimed, "are designed to protect the buyer of goods from bearing the burden of loss where merchandise, though not violating a promise expressly guaranteed, does not conform to the normal commercial standards or meet[] the buyer's particular purpose, a condition upon which he had the right to rely." The court concluded, effectively without argument, that the presence in the birds of even an *undetectable* disease violated normal commercial standards, and that the buyer had a right to rely on the birds' being disease free, even though the seller *could not have known otherwise.* The holding thus assigned the risk of an unavoidable loss to the seller, at least as a default. It reached this conclusion, moreover, without any argument that it was reasonable for the seller to bear this risk and without any evidence that the parties had decided to allocate that risk in that way. More striking still, the court (because its holding sounded in breach of warranty) reached its conclusion as a matter of contract law. The law thus implied a promise to the seller without giving any reason for believing that the seller had intended to assume that obligation (the risk) that the promise involved.

Perhaps this is all functionally justified. Certainly the seller in *Vlases* was larger and more sophisticated than the buyer, and thus presumptively better placed to absorb the risk posed by the disease and also to conduct research that might render the disease detectable in the future.[39] But the

---

39. Courts have construed implied warranties more narrowly where such functionalist reasons recommend limiting liability. An example is *Coffer v. Standard Brands, Inc.*, 226 S.E.

emphasis at the moment is, once again, on form; and this emphasis focuses attention not on the outcome in *Vlases* but on the reasoning. Implied warranties, in the hands of opinions like *Vlases*, could hardly stray farther or more clearly from the contractual form's core commitment to voluntary obligation. Instead of arising at the pleasure of the parties, implied warranties seem to track courts' sense of commercial efficiency and fairness.

Perhaps this formal account moves too quickly. After all, even implied warranties function formally as default terms, and the defaults may be overcome. One way to disclaim implied warranties is through a conspicuous writing, for example one that employs (in a suitably apparent presentation) language that expressly denies the existence of any save express warranties, say by using phrases such as "with all faults," or "as is." Another is by providing a sample that contains defects that should be apparent on a reasonable examination. Finally, a commercial practice of selling goods without implied warranties—either in the relevant industry (through what the U.C.C. calls "usage of trade") or as between the parties in their past dealings ("course of dealing") or within their current exchange ("course of performance")—may also disclaim implied warranties. As the materials on contract construction and interpretation in the next chapter will explain, no contract can ever specify all its terms. Rather, every contract requires defaults, both in order to fill in gaps where the parties say nothing and to interpret contractual language that otherwise remains ambiguous or vague. Every contract, therefore, must get some of its content from something besides the intentions of the parties: and doing so does not abandon the idea of chosen obligation so much as provide the necessary backdrop against which choices might be made. Insofar as implied warranties merely change the backdrop, they perhaps do not depart from the formal structure of contract—from the idea that contractual obligation is directly intended into being—as the argument so far has suggested.

This would be plausible if warranties were easy to disclaim—if the defaults established by the law's tendency to convert representations concerning the quality of goods sold into express warranties and to imply warranties even where no representations are made were not sticky. But in fact, warranties are hard to disclaim. This is illustrated by the pair of *Weisz* opinions. The defendant art gallery there sold two paintings to separate buyers, in the sincere belief that they were by Raoul Dufy. The defendant's auction catalogue listed Dufy as the artist, but also contained, on a separate page, "conditions of sale" asserting that all the gallery's paintings were to be sold "as is," that the gallery would not be responsible for any state-

---

2d 534 (N.C. App. 1976). The plaintiff bought a tin of "shelled nuts," among whose contents was a nut still in its shell. The plaintiff bit into the shell and broke a tooth, and sued the defendant for, among other things, breach of the implied warranty of merchantability. The court found that the warranty was not breached, citing various regulations concerning agriculture and foodstuffs that permitted "shelled nuts" to contain some shells without being therefor considered adulterated. At the back of the court's mind was the thought that measures required to secure nuts free from all shells were not cost-justified, in particular because consumers could more cheaply avoid the harms posed by shells by taking care when eating. The contrast to *Vlases*, where the buyer was surely worse-placed than the seller to adjust to the possibility of the disease, is clear.

ments concerning authorship, and that no such statements should be deemed as creating warranties. The paintings turned out to be forgeries, and both buyers sued.

The case turned on whether the disclaimers in the "conditions of sale" page successfully disclaimed the warranties that would otherwise have been created by listing Dufy as the artist elsewhere in the catalogue. The trial court held that the disclaimers were not effective—that they were not sufficiently prominent or forceful to counteract the more prominent and confident assertions concerning Dufy's authorship elsewhere in the catalog, so that a reasonable buyer would not expect or internalize the disclaimers or their efforts to shift the risk of forgery from seller to buyer. That settled the matter with respect to one buyer, who had in fact remained innocent of the disclaimer. But the other buyer, even though not charged with legal knowledge of the disclaimer, had as it happened discovered the disclaimer. This raised the question whether the disclaimer might be effective as to that buyer, in light of the buyer's actual knowledge. The court held that the disclaimer was ineffective even with respect to the buyer who knew of it. The court reached this conclusion based partly on the disclaimer's technical language, which it thought insufficient to impress upon the average reader that the risk of forgery was being shifted solely to the seller's benefit and buyer's detriment. The court also emphasized the seller's expertise and its business model of trading on this expertise, in effect surmising that the value of art is so closely connected to authenticity and that beliefs concerning authenticity are so dependent on the authority of those who assert it, that the disclaimer was fundamentally incompatible with the broader structure of the transaction. An appellate court reversed, insisting that since there was not even a remote suggestion, that the seller intended to deceive, the buyers—at an auction, after all—assumed the risks associated with authorship and forgery.

A functionalist analysis of *Weisz* and cases like it would ask who in fact might better ferret out forgeries and bear the risk that they are not identified. The functionalist will also ask what default rule concerning risk allocation (and what level of stickiness in the default) will in fact put the burdens of identification and mistake on the party best equipped to bear them.

These are interesting questions, to be sure, especially given the sense (instinct in the *Weisz* court's answer to them) that the seller is better— much better; categorically better, almost—equipped to bear the costs and risks associated with forgery-identification than the buyer. But for the formalist, this style of argument, and especially the substance of the trial court's conclusions, raises a further interesting question. The gallery seller in *Weisz* sought, in effect, to benefit from its expertise while avoiding the risk that its expertise might be inadequate. The gallery sought, in other words, to capture the value associated with its capacity authoritatively to authenticate paintings without acquiring a duty to indemnify its buyers should it, in spite of being expert, make a mistake. The gallery thus wished its assertions of authenticity to be taken for their epistemic content only, without creating any obligations that they be accurate. This is far from an outlandish wish. Rather, it is what people hope for whenever they say things like "I believe that such-and-such" or "I intend to so-and-so" and yet also add, insistently, *"but I'm not promising."*[40]

The trial holding in *Weisz* suggests that an art gallery cannot achieve this result—or at least can achieve it only by issuing disclaimers so prominent and powerful that they undermine the epistemic authority of its pronouncements of authenticity. The logic of the appellate court, moreover, does not reject that suggestion generally, but merely claims that the particular circumstances of *Weisz* do not exhibit the asymmetry on which the trial courts conclusion relied. The instincts behind such reasoning suggest that similar limitations apply wherever contracting parties possess vastly different levels of expertise and the values of the goods in which they trade turn on authoritative expert pronouncements. One might say that this characterization precisely describes those and only those cases in which no rational party would ever accept or make a disclaimer of warranty—in which case the law, including in respect of its resistance to recognizing warranty disclaimers, imposes no practical constraints on contracting parties' rational efforts to pursue their interests. But it is unlikely that principles like those laid down in *Weisz* can be rendered as precise as this suggestion requires; and it is unlikely that the courts that are attracted to such principles will be as modest. Rather, the *Weisz* rationale suggests a judicial effort not simply to facilitate but rather to interfere in parties' contracting: to make it difficult or impossible for experts, when dealing with non-experts, to sell their expertise and at the same time disavow the risks that, in spite of being experts, they make mistakes. Assertions of expertise, it seems, attract warranty obligations quite apart from any intentions, in the experts, to indemnify. And this result, the formalist observes, retreats from contract's insistence that obligations must be chosen, in favor of tort-like forms of obligation that are, at root, involuntary.

Tort and contract thus especially converge in areas that concern, speaking very roughly, transactions involving consumers. It turns out that one cannot run a modern, mass production and mass consumption economy using exclusively the forms of obligation associated with classical contract. Tort law—in particular, in connection with the misrepresentation torts—has had things to say about the values needed to manage such an economy efficiently and fairly. But these torts have not quite colonized contract from without. Rather, contract has changed from within, to incorporate some of the lessons of tort. In order to function modestly well in such an economy, contract has had to retreat some from its classical form and embrace some

---

40. Note that such speakers might acquire certain forms of liability even where their disclaimers of promissory obligations, and its associated strict liability succeed. Such speakers may, for example, be obligated in fact to believe what they say that they believe—that is, not to lie. And they may even be obligated to have employed reasonable means (including, where they are expert, means consistent with their expertise) in forming their beliefs—that is, not to be epistemically negligent. These are, of course, just the obligations associated with the tort doctrines that govern fraud and negligent misrepresentation.

of the ideas that underlie the misrepresentation torts. This is perhaps most clearly seen in the substantive overlap between the contract rules concerning warranties and the tort doctrines concerning liability for certain (warranty-like) misrepresentations within a contract, encapsulated in § 552C of the Restatement (Second) of Torts and § 9 of the Restatement (Third) of Torts: Products Liability. In these areas, the misrepresentation torts are construed sufficiently capaciously that they begin to resemble a tort-substitute for contract. And freedom of contract is cabined in ways that reflect the values immanent in tort.

16.1.D   *AVOIDING* CONTRACTUAL OBLIGATION ON ACCOUNT OF MISREPRESENTATION

The materials up to this point have focused on the possibility that persons who make false statements might be held liable, on a quasi- or fully-contractual model, for the truth of what they say. This is the structurally deepest point of engagement between tort and contract, as it is the point at which tort threatens to swallow contract entire, and in the process fundamentally to recast the form of obligation to which this Text is devoted.

But misrepresentation figures in contract law in another way, which remains practically important even as it is much less structurally deep. A victim of misrepresentation may deploy the misrepresentation not as a sword—to establish an obligation to secure the state of affairs that would obtain were the representation true—but as a shield, to avoid contractual obligations that she would not have undertaken but for the misrepresentation. When employed in this way, arguments about misrepresentation seek not to vindicate a promise-like interest (in the truth of what was represented) but rather to restore the status quo ante (to recover losses incurred in reliance on what was said). If the main line of argument asks whether the law of misrepresentation might allow tort to swallow contract; this alternative possibility asks whether contract might recognize that perfectly ordinary torts supply a defense against contractual obligation, conventionally understood.

This possibility has already been raised in the materials—by *Weisz*. The tortification of contract model would render the seller in *Weisz* obligated to provide the buyer with the value of genuine Raoul Dufy paintings, even though his representations concerning authorship were not genuinely promissory, and indeed disclaimed by the transaction's expressly promissory language. The alternative model—misrepresentation as a tort-based defense against contractual obligation—would merely render the buyer's contractual obligations void (or voidable) on account of being induced through misrepresentations. And indeed, this is the relief that the buyers in *Weisz* in fact sought.

The materials below—which are self-explanatory—illustrate this use of misrepresentation. The main issues that they raise involve the scope of a mis-representer's duty to disclose and the scope of a mis-representation victim's duty to read (this figured already in *Weisz* also). That is, when may a bargainer profit from private information and when must she inform her counterparty, on pain of his retaining a right to avoid contracts that he has made in ignorance? And to what extend is a contracting party obligated to inform himself of the terms of his agreements, including when it is difficult or costly for him to do so?

Restatement (Second) of Contracts

§ 163   When a Misrepresentation Prevents Formation of a Contract

If a misrepresentation as to the character or essential terms of a proposed contract induces conduct that appears to be a manifestation of assent by one who neither knows nor has reasonable opportunity to know of the character or essential terms of the proposed contract, his conduct is not effective as a manifestation of assent.

Comments & Illustrations

Comment a.   Rationale. Under the general principle stated in § 19(2), a party's conduct is not effective as a manifestation of his assent unless he knows or has reason to know that the other party may infer from it that he assents. This Section involves an application of that principle where a misrepresentation goes to what is sometimes called the "factum" or the "execution" rather than merely the "inducement." If, because of a misrepresentation as to the character or essential terms of a proposed contract, a party does not know or have reasonable opportunity to know of its character or essential terms, then he neither knows nor has reason to know that the other party may infer from his conduct that he assents to that contract. In such a case there is no effective manifestation of assent and no contract at all. Compare § 174. This result only follows, however, if the misrepresentation relates to the very nature of the proposed contract itself and not merely to one of its nonessential terms. The party may believe that he is not assenting to any contract or that he is assenting to a contract entirely different from the proposed contract. The mere fact that a party is deceived as to the identity of the other party, as when a buyer of goods obtains credit by impersonating a person of means, does not bring the case within the present Section, unless it affects the very nature of the contract. See Uniform Commercial Code § 2–403(1)(a). It is immaterial under the rule stated in this Section whether the misrepresentation is made by a party to the transaction or by a third person. See Comment *e* to § 164.

Illustration

1. A, seeking to induce B to make a contract to sell him goods on credit, tells B that he is C, a well-known millionaire. B is induced by the statement to make the proposed contract with A. B's apparent manifestation of assent is effective. However, the contract is voidable by B under the rule stated in § 164(1). Contrast Illustrations 2 and 4.

Comment b.   Effect of fault. If the recipient had a reasonable opportunity to know the character or essential terms of the proposed contract, the rule stated in this Section does not apply, and his conduct is effective as a manifestation of assent. Compare § 172. The case then comes within § 164 on avoidance or § 166 on reformation. In deciding whether the recipient has had such an opportunity, less care will ordinarily be expected of him if he did not intend to assume a legal obligation at all than if he intended to assume a legal obligation, although one of a different nature.

Illustrations

2. A and B reach an understanding that they will execute a written contract containing terms on which they have agreed. It is properly prepared and is read by B, but A substitutes a writing containing essential terms that are different from those agreed upon and thereby induces B to sign it in the belief that it is the one he has read. B's apparent manifestation of assent is not effective.

3. A and B reach an understanding that they will execute a written contract containing terms on which they have agreed. A prepares a writing containing essential terms that are different from those agreed upon and induces B to sign it by telling him that it contains the terms agreed upon and that it is not necessary for him to read it. B's apparent manifestation of assent is effective if B had a reasonable opportunity to read the writing. However, the contract is voidable by B under the rule stated in § 164. See Illustration 3 to § 164. In the alternative, at the request of B, the court will decree that the writing be reformed to conform to their understanding under the rule stated in § 166. See Illustration 1 to § 166.

4. The facts being otherwise as stated in Illustration 3, B is blind and gets C to read the writing to him, but C, in collusion with A, reads it wrongly. B's apparent manifestation of assent is not effective.

Comment c. "Void" rather than voidable. It is sometimes loosely said that, where the rule stated in this Section applies, there is a "void contract" as distinguished from a voidable one. See Comment *a* to § 7. This distinction has important consequences. For example, the recipient of a misrepresentation may be held to have ratified the contract if it is voidable but not if it is "void." Furthermore, a good faith purchaser may acquire good title to property if he takes it from one who obtained voidable title by misrepresentation but not if he takes it from one who obtained "void title" by misrepresentation.

Restatement (Second) of Contracts

§ 164 When a Misrepresentation Makes a Contract Voidable

(1) If a party's manifestation of assent is induced by either a fraudulent or a material misrepresentation by the other party upon which the recipient is justified in relying, the contract is voidable by the recipient.

(2) If a party's manifestation of assent is induced by either a fraudulent or a material misrepresentation by one who is not a party to the transaction upon which the recipient is justified in relying, the contract is voidable by the recipient, unless the other party to the transaction in good faith and without reason to know of the misrepresentation either gives value or relies materially on the transaction.

Comments & Illustrations

Comment a. Requirements. A misrepresentation may make a contract voidable under the rule stated in this Section, even though it does not prevent the formation of a contract under the rule stated in the previous section. Three requirements must be met in addition to the requirement that there must have been a misrepresentation. First, the misrepresentation must have been either fraudulent or material. See Comment *b*. Second, the misrepresentation must have induced the recipient to make the contract. See Comment *c*. Third, the recipient must have been justified in relying on the misrepresentation. See Comment *d*. Even if the contract is voidable, exercise of the power of avoidance is subject to the limitations stated in Chapter 16 on remedies.

Comment b. Fraudulent and non-fraudulent misrepresentation. A representation need not be fraudulent in order to make a contract voidable under the rule stated in this Section. However, a non-fraudulent misrepresentation does not make the contract voidable unless it is material, while materiality is not essential in the case of a fraudulent misrepresentation. One who makes a non-fraudulent misrepresentation of a seemingly unimportant fact has no reason to suppose that his assertion will induce assent. But a fraudulent misrepresentation is directed to attaining that very end, and the maker cannot insist on his bargain if it is attained, however unexpectedly, as long as the additional requirements of inducement and justifiable reliance are met. See Illustration 1. Compare Restatement, Second, Torts § 538, which limits liability for fraudulent misrepresentation to cases in which the matter misrepresented is material.

Illustrations

1. A, seeking to induce B to make a contract to buy a tract of land at a price of $1,000 an acre, tells B that the tract contains 100 acres. A knows that it contains only 90 acres. B is induced by the statement to make the contract. Because the statement is a fraudulent misrepresentation (§ 162(1)), the contract is voidable by B, regardless of whether the misrepresentation is material.

2. The facts being otherwise as stated in Illustration 1, A is mistaken and does not know that the tract contains only 90 acres. Because the statement is not a fraudulent misrepresentation, the contract is voidable by B only if the misrepresentation is material (§ 162(2)).

3. A and B agree that A will buy a tract of land from B for $100,000 and will assume an existing mortgage of $50,000. In

reducing the agreement to writing, A intentionally omits the provision for assumption but tells B that the writing correctly expresses their agreement. B does not notice the omission and is induced by A's statement to sign the writing. The misrepresentation is both fraudulent and material, and the contract is voidable by B. Compare Illustration 1 to § 166 and see Illustration 10 to § 161.

Comment c.   Inducement. No legal effect flows from either a non-fraudulent or a fraudulent misrepresentation unless it induces action by the recipient, that is, unless he manifests his assent to the contract in reliance on it. Whether a misrepresentation is an inducement is a question of fact governed by the rule stated in § 167. In general, the recipient of a misrepresentation need not show that he has actually been harmed by relying on it in order to avoid the contract. But see § 165.

Comment d.   Justification. A misrepresentation, even if relied upon, has no legal effect unless the recipient's reliance on it is justified. The most significant and troublesome applications of this principle occur in connection with assertions of opinion (§§ 168, 169), assertions as to matters of law (§ 170), assertions of intention (§ 171), and fault (§ 172). In other situations the requirement of justification is usually met unless, for example, the fact to which the misrepresentation relates is of only peripheral importance to the transaction or is one as to which the maker's assertion would not be expected to be taken seriously.

Comment e.   Misrepresentation by a third party. The rule stated in Subsection (2) makes a contract voidable for a misrepresentation by a third party, subject to the general principle of law that if an innocent person has in good faith and without notice given value or changed his position in reliance on the contract, it is not voidable on that ground. This is the same principle that protects an innocent person who purchases goods or commercial paper in good faith, without notice and for value from one who has obtained them from the original owner by a misrepresentation. See Uniform Commercial Code §§ 2–403(1), 3–305. In the cases that fall within Subsection (2), however, the innocent person deals directly with the recipient of the misrepresentation, which is made by one not a party to their contract. The contract is not voidable by the recipient if the innocent person gives value or relies materially on the transaction before learning or acquiring reason to know of the misrepresentation. The term "value" has the same meaning here as it does under Uniform Commercial Code § 1–201(44), and therefore the consideration given by the innocent party is value for this purpose. The rule does not protect a person who is responsible under the law of agency for the maker's misrepresentation. See Restatement, Second, Agency § 259. Assignees and intended beneficiaries, who derive their rights from a contract that is voidable for misrepresentation, take subject to the right of avoidance under §§ 309, 336. The rule stated in Subsection (2) does not preclude avoidance for mistake under the rules stated in Chapter 6.

Illustrations

4. A, who is not C's agent, induces B by a fraudulent misrepresentation to make a contract with C to sell land to C. C promises to pay the agreed price, not knowing or having reason to know of the fraudulent misrepresentation. Since C's promise to pay is value, the contract is not voidable by B. The contract would be voidable by B if C learned or acquired reason to know of the fraudulent misrepresentation before promising to pay the price.

5. A, who is not C's agent, induces B by a fraudulent misrepresentation to sign a pledge by which B promises C, a charitable corporation, to contribute a sum of money. C does not know or have reason to know of the fraudulent representation. B's promise, although binding under § 90(2), is voidable by B. B's promise would not be voidable if C materially changed its position in reliance on B's promise before learning or acquiring reason to know of the fraudulent misrepresentation.

Restatement (Second) of Contracts

§ 168. Reliance On Assertions Of Opinion

(1) An assertion is one of opinion if it expresses only a belief, without certainty, as to the existence of a fact or expresses only a judgment as to quality, value, authenticity, or similar matters.

(2) If it is reasonable to do so, the recipient of an assertion of a person's opinion as to facts not disclosed and not otherwise known to the recipient may properly interpret it as an assertion

(a) that the facts known to that person are not incompatible with his opinion, or

(b) that he knows facts sufficient to justify him in forming it.

Comments & Illustrations

Comment a. Knowledge and opinion. A statement of opinion is also a statement of fact because it states that a person has a particular state of mind concerning the matter to which his opinion relates. But it also implies that he does not have such definite information, that he is not certain enough of what he says, to make an assertion of his own knowledge as to that matter. It implies at most that he knows of no facts incompatible with the belief or that he knows of facts that justify him in holding it. The difference is that between "This is true," and "I think this is true, but I am not sure." The important distinction is between assertions of knowledge and those of opinion, rather than assertions of fact and those of opinion. The person whose opinion is asserted is usually the maker of the assertion himself, but the opinion may also be that of a third person. See Comment *b* to § 169.

Comment b. Criteria. The fact that points of view may be expected to differ on the subject of a statement suggests that the statement is one of opinion. Statements of judgment as to quality, value, authenticity, or similar matters are common examples. For instance, the statement that an automobile is a "good" car relates to a matter on which views may be expected to differ. The maker of such a statement will normally be understood as expressing only his own judgment and not as making assertions concerning such matters as horsepower or riding qualities. But see Comment *d* and Illustration 3. The form of the statement is important but not controlling. A statement that is in form an assertion of the maker's knowledge may be made in circumstances that suggest that it expresses only a belief, that he is not free from doubt. This may be so, for example, when the recipient knows that the maker has no information concerning the fact asserted and therefore can be stating only his belief. The problem is one of interpretation of the language used.

Comment c. Statements of quantity, quality, value and price. A seller's statement of the quantity of land or goods is virtually never a statement of opinion, even though he does not suggest that it is based on a survey, weighing or other measurement. The words "more or less" do not change such a statement into one of opinion, and the recipient is justified in believing that the quantity is substantially as stated although the measurement expressed may not be exact. In contrast, a seller's general statement of quality is usually one of opinion. There are, however, instances in which the gradations of quality are so marked that goods are usually sold as of a specified grade and an assertion of grade is not one of opinion. A statement of value is, like one of quality, ordinarily a statement of opinion. However, a statement of the price at which something has been offered for sale or sold is not one of opinion.

Illustrations

1. A, seeking to induce B to make a contract to buy goods, tells B that he paid $10,000 for them. A knows that he paid only $8,000 for the goods. The statement is not one of opinion.

2. The facts being otherwise as stated in Illustration 1, A tells B only that the goods are worth $10,000. The statement is one of opinion.

Comment d. Implication of a statement of opinion. In some circumstances the recipient may reasonably understand a statement of opinion to be more than an assertion as to the maker's state of mind. Under the rule stated in Subsection (2), if the statement of opinion relates to facts not known to the recipient, he may be justified in inferring that there are facts that justify the opinion, or at least that there are no facts that are incompatible with it. In such a case, the statement of opinion becomes, in effect, an assertion as to those facts and may be relied on as such. The rule is, however, applied in the light of the realities of the market place. The propensity of sellers and buyers to exaggerate the advantages to the other party of the bargains they promise is well recognized, and to some extent their assertions of opinion must be discounted. Nevertheless, while some allowance must be made for seller's puffing and buyer's depreciation, the other party is entitled to assume that a statement of opinion is not so far removed from the truth as to be incompatible with the facts known to the maker. Where circumstances justify it, a statement of opinion may also be reasonably understood as carrying with it an assertion that the maker knows facts sufficient to justify him in forming it. However, the rule stated in Subsection (2) applies only when the facts to which the opinion relates are not disclosed and not otherwise known to the recipient. An assertion of opinion that does not fall within Subsection (2) is one of opinion only. As to the circumstances in which reliance on such an assertion is justified, see § 169.

Illustrations

3. A, seeking to induce B to make a contract to buy real property, tells B that the sewage system is "good." A knows that the sewage system is unworkable. B interprets A's statement of opinion as an assertion that the facts known to A are not incompatible with his opinion and is induced by this assertion to make the contract. B's interpretation is reasonable, the assertion is a fraudulent misrepresentation, and the contract is voidable by B.

4. The facts being otherwise as stated in Illustration 3, A knows that the sewage system is not very good but is workable. There is no misrepresentation because the facts known to A are not incompatible with his opinion, and the contract is not voidable by B.

5. A, seeking to induce B to make a contract to become A's partner in A's business, tells B that the business is "a moneymaker." A knows that the business has been unprofitable since its inception. B interprets A's statement of opinion as an assertion that the facts known to A are not incompatible with his opinion and is induced by this assertion to make the contract. B's interpretation is reasonable, the assertion is a fraudulent misrepresentation, and the contract is voidable by B.

6. A, who is knowledgeable in financial matters, seeking to induce B, who is also knowledgeable in such matters, to make a contract to buy A's shares of stock in C Corporation, tells B that within five years the shares will pay dividends that will amount to the purchase price of the stock. Neither A nor B has information about the finances of C, which is, in fact, hopelessly insolvent. B interprets A's statement of opinion as an assertion that A knows facts sufficient to justify him in forming that opinion and is induced by this assertion to make the contract. B's interpretation is reasonable, the assertion is a fraudulent misrepresentation, and the contract is voidable by B.

7. A, seeking to induce B to make a contract to buy land, tells B, "There is water under this land and if you dig a well anywhere on the land, you will strike it." A does not know

whether there is water under the land, and there is none. B knows that no water survey has been made and that A has no information concerning the presence or absence of subterranean water, but interprets A's statement of opinion as an assertion that A knows facts sufficient to justify him in forming that opinion and is induced by this assertion to make the contract. B's interpretation is not reasonable, and the contract is not voidable by B. See also § 169.

Restatement (Second) of Contracts

§ 169. When Reliance On An Assertion Of Opinion Is Not Justified

To the extent that an assertion is one of opinion only, the recipient is not justified in relying on it unless the recipient

(a) stands in such a relation of trust and confidence to the person whose opinion is asserted that the recipient is reasonable in relying on it, or

(b) reasonably believes that, as compared with himself, the person whose opinion is asserted has special skill, judgment or objectivity with respect to the subject matter, or

(c) is for some other special reason particularly susceptible to a misrepresentation of the type involved.

Comments & Illustrations

Comment a.   Scope: The rule stated in this Section applies only to the extent that an assertion amounts to nothing more than an assertion of opinion, whether that of the maker or a third person. As is stated in § 168(2), an assertion of opinion as to facts not known to the recipient may, in proper circumstances, reasonably be interpreted to include an assertion as to those facts themselves. If that assertion is false, it may be the basis of avoidance regardless of the rule stated in this Section. The rule stated here determines whether reliance is justified whenever the assertion of opinion does not carry with it an assertion as to facts under the rule stated in § 168(2).

Comment b.   Rationale. If the subject matter of the transaction is one on which the two parties have roughly equal skill and judgment, each must generally from his own opinions and neither is justified in relying on the other's. The law assumes that the ordinary person is reasonably competent to form his own opinions as to the advisability of entering into those transactions that form part of the ordinary routine of life. The mere fact that one of the parties is less astute than the other does not justify him in relying on the other's opinion. This is true even though one party knows that the other is somewhat more conversant with the value and quality of the subject matter, since expressions of opinion by the other party are generally to be discounted. It may be assumed, for example, that a seller will express a favorable opinion concerning what he has to sell. When he praises it in general terms, commonly known as "puffing" or "sales talk," without specific content or reference to facts, buyers are expected to understand that they are not entitled to rely. See Uniform Commercial Code § 2–313(2). A similar assumption applies to deprecating statements by buyers. See Comment *d* to § 168.

Comment c.   Confidential relationship. In some situations a relationship of trust and confidence between the parties justifies the reliance of one on the other's opinion. Where there is a true fiduciary relation, the more stringent requirements of § 173 apply. But even where a party is not, strictly speaking, a fiduciary, he may stand in a relation of trust and confidence to the recipient. Such a relation often arises, for example, between members of the same family. See Comment *f* to § 161. It may also arise where one party has taken steps to induce the other to believe that he can safely rely on the first party's judgment, as where he has gained the other's confidence by stressing their common membership in a religious denomination, fraternal order or social group, or the fact that they were born in the same locality. In addition, some types of contracts, such as marine insurance and joint adventure, are recognized as creating in themselves a confidential relation and hence as requiring the utmost good faith and full and fair disclosure. As to contracts of suretyship, see Restatement of Security § 124(1). As to undue influence, see § 177.

Illustration

1.   A, professing friendship, offers to advise B, an elderly widow inexperienced in business, concerning her investments. He does so for five years, giving her good advice and acquiring her trust and confidence. At the end of this time he advises her to buy his worthless shares of stock, telling her that in his opinion it is a "good investment." B is induced by A's statement to make the contract. B's reliance on A's statement is justified, and the contract is voidable by B.

Comment d.   Special skill, judgment or objectivity. Ordinarily the recipient is not justified in relying on the other party's assertion of opinion because the recipient has as good a basis for forming his own opinion and the other party's opinion must be discounted because of his self-interest. Clause (b) applies to situations where this is not the case because the recipient reasonably believes that the other party has special skill or judgment, relative to that of the recipient, with respect to the subject matter. In modern commercial life, situations often occur in which special training or experience are necessary to the formation of a sound judgment. Often, in such a case, the recipient will be able to base a claim to relief on one of the assertions as to facts that arise under the rule stated in § 168(2). This will not be so, however, if the facts are known to both parties. In that event, the recipient's reliance may be justified under the rule stated in Clause (b). Compare Uniform Commercial Code § 2–315.

Clause (b) also applies to instances in which the recipient reasonably believes that the person whose opinion is asserted has special objectivity with respect to the subject matter that would give his opinion particular weight. This includes situations in which one who is not a party to the transaction and has no other adversary interest misrepresents his opinion. See § 164(2). It also includes situations in which the maker has an adversary interest but conceals this from the recipient. In such cases, the recipient's reasonable although erroneous belief that the maker is disinterested may be sufficient to justify his reliance. Finally, it applies to situations where a party to the transaction misrepresents that an apparently disinterested person holds a particular opinion. Thus an assertion that a third person has paid or offered a particular price for something, in addition to being a misrepresentation as to the conduct of that person, implies that that person holds an appropriate opinion of its value, and a prospective purchaser may be justified in taking this into account in determining whether to buy. Whether a person's apparent disinterest gives him the special objectivity required to justify reliance on this implied assertion of opinion depends on the circumstances of the particular case, including any special skill or judgment that may accompany his disinterest.

Illustrations

2. A, the proprietor of a dance studio, seeking to induce B, a 60–year–old widow with no background in dancing, to make a contract for dance lessons, tells B that she has "dance potential" and would develop into a "beautiful dancer." A knows that B has little aptitude as a dancer. B is induced by A's statement of opinion to make the proposed contract. B's reliance on A's statement of opinion is justified, and the contract is voidable by B.

3. A, seeking to induce B to make a contract to buy land, tells B that C, a local businessman, shortly before his death offered him $50,000 for the land. A knows that C offered only $40,000 for the land. B infers from A's statement that in C's opinion the land was worth $50,000 and, believing that C had special objectivity, is induced by the statement to make the contract. B's reliance is justified, and the contract is voidable by B.

Comment e. Particularly susceptible recipient. If the recipient is for some special reason, other than those covered by Clause (b), particularly vulnerable to misrepresentation of the kind practiced on him, his reliance on it is justified under Clause (c). Examples of such reasons include lack of intelligence, illiteracy, and unusual credulity or gullibility. One whose misrepresentation of opinion induces reliance because of such a characteristic will not be heard to say that the reliance he sought to induce was not justified because his statement was one of opinion and therefore should have been mistrusted.

Illustration

4. A, seeking to induce B, who is particularly inexperienced and gullible, to make a contract to buy property, tells B that its

value is $35,000. A knows that it is practically worthless. B is induced by A's statement to make the contract. If B's reliance is justified because his inexperience and gullibility make him particularly susceptible to such a misrepresentation, the contract is voidable by B.

Restatement (Second) of Contracts

§ 170.   Reliance On Assertions As To Matters Of Law

If an assertion is one as to a matter of law, the same rules that apply in the case of other assertions determine whether the recipient is justified in relying on it.

Comments & Illustrations

Comment a.   Law as fact. A statement as to a matter of law is subject to the same rules as are other assertions. Such a statement may or may not be one of opinion. Thus, an assertion that a particular statute has been enacted or repealed or that a particular decision has been rendered by a court is generally not a statement of opinion. The rules that determine the consequences of a misrepresentation of such a matter of law are the same as those that determine the consequences of a similar misrepresentation of any other fact.

Illustration

1.   A, seeking to sell goods to B, tells B that the government authorities have not fixed a maximum price for such goods. A knows that the authorities have fixed a maximum price for the goods. The assertion is a fraudulent misrepresentation, and the contract is voidable by B.

Comment b.   Law as opinion. Many statements of law involve assertions as to what a court would determine to be the legal consequences of a dispute if it were litigated, and such a statement is one of opinion. Such a statement may, as may any other statement of opinion, carry with it the assertion that the facts known to the maker are not incompatible with his opinion, or that he does know facts that justify him in forming it. See § 168(2). However, a statement that is limited to the maker's opinion as to the legal consequences of a state of facts and does not amount to an assertion as to the facts themselves is an assertion of opinion only. This is particularly true if all of the facts are known to both parties or are assumed by both of them to exist. Such a statement may be relied on, but to no greater extent than any other statement of opinion only (§ 169). Thus, as between the two parties to a contract, the recipient is ordinarily expected to draw his own conclusions or to seek his own independent legal advice. On the other hand, if the maker of the representation purports to have special expertise in the law which the recipient does not have, reliance on the opinion may be justified (§ 167(b)). If a lawyer states his opinion of law to a layman, the layman is entitled to assume his professional honesty and may justifiably rely on his opinion even though the two have an adverse relation in negotiating a contract. Even if the maker is not a lawyer, he may purport to have special knowledge that will enable him to form a reliable opinion, as where a real estate broker or an insurance agent gives his opinion on a routine problem within his competence to a layman.

Illustration

2. A, seeking to induce B to make a contract to buy land from him tells B, "I have good title to this land." Unknown to A, the person from whom he purchased the land had no title to it. B interprets A's statement as an assertion that he knows of conveyances sufficient to vest good title in him and is induced to make the contract. Although A's statement is in the form of a legal conclusion, B's interpretation is reasonable, the assertion is a material misrepresentation, and the contract is voidable by B. See § 168(2).

Comment c.   Foreign law. The rule stated in this Section applies to statements of foreign as well as domestic law. Some courts have refused to recognize that statements of the law of a state or country where the recipient neither resides nor habitually does business are mere statements of opinion, even though they purport to cover only the legal consequences of facts known to both parties. This refusal may often be explained on the ground that, although the statement is of opinion only, the recipient's reliance is more likely to be justified because he is less able to draw his own conclusions as to foreign law. Nevertheless, he is not justified in relying on a statement of opinion as to foreign law absent one of the circumstances enumerated in § 169. If the maker resides or habitually does business in the foreign jurisdiction, he may be expected to have special expertise as to its law. See § 169(b).

16.1.E   SUMMARY

There are several misrepresentation torts, and their elements vary. Nevertheless, they share a basic structure: The misrepresentation torts announce fault-based standards of care;[41] they emphasize (and indeed generally require) that misrepresentations cause harm, generally in the form of reliance costs, in order to count as tortious;[42] and they adopt

---

41.   See, e.g., RESTATEMENT (SECOND) OF TORTS § 304 (Negligent Misrepresentation Affecting the Conduct of Others), § 310 (Conscious Misrepresentation Involving Risk of Physical Harm), § 311 (Negligent Misrepresentation Involving Risk of Physical Harm), § 552 (Information Negligently Supplied for the Guidance of Others), § 557A (Fraudulent Misrepresentations Causing Physical Harm), § 525 (Liability for Fraudulent Misrepresentation), § 526 (Conditions Under Which Misrepresentation Is Fraudulent (Scienter)), § 530 (Misrepresentation of Intention).

42.   See, e.g., RESTATEMENT (SECOND) OF TORTS § 544 (Statement of Intention) ("The recipient of a fraudulent misrepresentation of intention is justified in relying upon it if the existence of the intention is material and the recipient has reason to believe that it will be carried out"), § 538 (Materiality of Misrepresentation), § 525 (Liability for Fraudulent Misrepresentation) (including, among the requirements for such liability, "inducing another to act

backward-rather than forward-looking remedies that reject the goal of vindicating the expectations that tortious statements engender and instead aspire only to undo the harms that the misrepresentations cause, that is, to compensate for lost reliance.[43] So there remains an enormous difference between contract liability on the one hand and tort liability for various forms of misrepresentation on the other. Even taken all together, the misrepresentation torts do not span the space of contract obligation. And contract—even accepting the objective theory of intent and the role of reliance in its remedies—therefore cannot be recast or reduced to a special case of tort. In the context of a contract, representations are made enforceable on a theory of strict liability. If there is no contract, things are *very* different.

At the same time as the general distinction between contract and tort survives, however, the two bodies of law look less different, and in fact penetrate each other, in certain specific substantive areas. The most prominent of these concerns consumer sales contracts. The misrepresentation torts cast their nets broadly in this area, to abandon many of the core limitations (fault-based liability, focused principally on protecting reliance interests) that generally keep these torts apart from contract.[44] At the same time, contract law, in particular through the doctrines concerning warranties, recasts its rules for this substantive area in tort-like terms, making reliance more important for liability and limiting freedom of contract.[45]

The special case of consumer sales contracts thus does not so much remake contract and tort generally in each other's image as illustrate, for a specific area, what such a general restructuring of private law doctrine would look like.

16.2   PROMISSORY ESTOPPEL: AN INTERNAL THREAT TO CONTRACT

The previous section principally emphasized the doctrines through which tort law might colonize contract from without. Tort might colonize

---

or to refrain from action in reliance upon it"). Tort law's commitment to requiring reliance, and in particular its resistance to suggestions that might allow expectation-based liability to bleed into tort by recasting expectations in terms of reliance, is vividly emphasized by Restatement (Second) of Torts § 548 (Reliance On Action for Misrepresentation) ("The Maker of a fraudulent misrepresentation is not liable to one who does not rely upon its truth but upon the expectation that the maker will be held liable in damages for its falsity").

43. See, e.g., RESTATEMENT (SECOND) OF TORTS § 552B (Damages for Negligent Misrepresentation) ("the damages recoverable for a negligent misrepresentation do not include the benefit of the plaintiff's contract with the defendant").

Fraud damages represent an exception to this rule. See RESTATEMENT (SECOND) OF TORTS § 549 (Measure of Damages for Fraudulent Misrepresentation).

44. See, e.g., RESTATEMENT (SECOND) OF TORTS § 402B (Misrepresentation by Seller of Chattels to Consumer), § 552C (Misrepresentation in Sale, Rental or Exchange Transaction), RESTATEMENT (THIRD) OF TORTS: PRODUCTS LIABILITY § 9 (Liability of Commercial Product Seller or Distributor for Harm Caused by Misrepresentation).

45. See, e.g., U.C.C. §§ 2–313–2–316.

contract in this way by establishing forms of legal liability inside tort proper that cover all the ground ordinarily associated with contract, using legal and moral constructions that are simpler than promise. This would render orthodox contract merely epiphenomenal; one might even say that contract would, in this case, be nothing more than an opaque elaboration of the relevant torts. But while tort clearly contains doctrines—surrounding the misrepresentation torts—that threaten contract in this way, various limitations on the scope and content of these torts prevent tort law from making good on the threat, so that contract survives tort's colonizing ambitions. The specific substantive areas in which the two converge— warranties and products liability—emphasize how far apart the bodies of law remain more generally, and thus reinforce the distinctiveness of contract.

This section takes up a related but distinct internal threat that tort poses to contract. Tort-like notions, that is, might infect contract doctrine by introducing, at the core of contract, a path or paths to liability that sound, ultimately, not in the morality of promise but in the morality of harm. If such harm-based doctrines became established within contract, and further possessed sufficient scope to sustain liability in all the instances in which liability traditionally arose pursuant to offer, acceptance, and consideration, then this conventional path to contract liability might be abandoned. Contract would have retained its separate name, but not its distinctive content or structure. A Trojan Horse of this sort might, therefore, undermine contract just as surely and just as completely as the open assault by self-avowed tort doctrines described in the previous section.

This possibility arises most dramatically and importantly under § 90 of the Restatement of Contracts and the cases decided under it. The form of obligation described by § 90, commonly called promissory estoppel, announces a means of contract formation developed in the alternative to orthodox offer, acceptance, and consideration. Promissory estoppel, at least potentially, does not just make reliance the *measure* of contractual obligation and reasonableness the test of promissory intent; it also makes reasonable care that others are not misled by one's utterances concerning future conduct into the *ground* of contractual obligation. This is plain from the Restatement text.

Restatement (Second) of Contracts

§ 90   Promise Reasonably Inducing Action Or Forbearance

(1) A promise which the promisor should reasonably expect to induce action or forbearance on the part of the promisee or a third person and which does induce such action or forbearance is binding if injustice can be avoided only by enforcement of the promise. The remedy granted for breach may be limited as justice requires.

(2) A charitable subscription or a marriage settlement is binding under Subsection (1) without proof that the promise induced action or forbearance.

Comments & Illustrations

Comment a. Relation to other rules. Obligations and remedies based on reliance are not peculiar to the law of contracts. This Section is often referred to in terms of "promissory estoppel," a phrase suggesting an extension of the doctrine of estoppel. Estoppel prevents a person from showing the truth contrary to a representation of fact made by him after another has relied on the representation. See Restatement, Second, Agency § 8B; Restatement, Second, Torts §§ 872, 894. Reliance is also a significant feature of numerous rules in the law of negligence, deceit and restitution. See, e.g., Restatement, Second, Agency §§ 354, 378; Restatement, Second, Torts §§ 323, 537; Restatement of Restitution § 55. In some cases those rules and this Section overlap; in others they provide analogies useful in determining the extent to which enforcement is necessary to avoid injustice.

It is fairly arguable that the enforcement of informal contracts in the action of assumpsit rested historically on justifiable reliance on a promise. Certainly reliance is one of the main bases for enforcement of the half-completed exchange, and the probability of reliance lends support to the enforcement of the executory exchange. See Comments to §§ 72, 75. This Section thus states a basic principle which often renders inquiry unnecessary as to the precise scope of the policy of enforcing bargains. Sections 87–89 state particular applications of the same principle to promises ancillary to bargains, and it also applies in a wide variety of non-commercial situations. See, e.g., § 94.

Illustration

1. A, knowing that B is going to college, promises B that A will give him $5,000 on completion of his course. B goes to college, and borrows and spends more than $5,000 for college expenses. When he has nearly completed his course, A notifies him of an intention to revoke the promise. A's promise is binding and B is entitled to payment on completion of the course without regard to whether his performance was "bargained for" under § 71.

Comment b. Character of reliance protected. The principle of this Section is flexible. The promisor is affected only by reliance which he does or should foresee, and enforcement must be necessary to avoid injustice. Satisfaction of the latter requirement may depend on the reasonableness of the promisee's reliance, on its definite and substantial character in relation to the remedy sought, on the formality with which the promise is made, on the extent to which the evidentiary, cautionary, deterrent and channeling functions of form are met by the commercial setting or otherwise, and on the extent to which such other policies as the enforcement of bargains and the prevention of unjust enrichment are relevant. Compare Comment to § 72. The force of particular factors varies in different types of cases: thus reliance need not be of substantial character in charitable subscription cases, but must in cases of firm offers and guaranties. Compare Subsection (2) with §§ 87, 88.

Illustrations

2. A promises B not to foreclose, for a specified time, a mortgage which A holds on B's land. B thereafter makes improvements on the land. A's promise is binding and may be enforced by denial of foreclosure before the time has elapsed.

3. A sues B in a municipal court for damages for personal injuries caused by B's negligence. After the one year statute of limitations has run, B requests A to discontinue the action and start again in the superior court where the action can be consolidated with other actions against B arising out of the same accident. A does so. B's implied promise that no harm to A will result bars B from asserting the statute of limitations as a defense.

4. A has been employed by B for 40 years. B promises to pay A a pension of $200 per month when A retires. A retires and forbears to work elsewhere for several years while B pays the pension. B's promise is binding.

Comment c. Reliance by third persons. If a promise is made to one party for the benefit of another, it is often foreseeable that the beneficiary will rely on the promise. Enforcement of the promise in such cases rests on the same basis and depends on the same factors as in cases of reliance by the promisee. Justifiable reliance by third persons who are not beneficiaries is less likely, but may sometimes reinforce the claim of the promisee or beneficiary.

Illustrations

5. A holds a mortgage on B's land. To enable B to obtain a loan, A promises B in writing to release part of the land from the mortgage upon payment of a stated sum. As A contemplated, C lends money to B on a second mortgage, relying on A's promise. The promise is binding and may be enforced by C.

6. A executes and delivers a promissory note to B, a bank, to give B a false appearance of assets, deceive the banking authorities, and enable the bank to continue to operate. After several years B fails and is taken over by C, a representative of B's creditors. A's note is enforceable by C.

7. A and B, husband and wife, are tenants by the entirety of a tract of land. They make an oral promise to B's niece C to give her the tract. B, C and C's husband expend money in building a house on the tract and C and her husband take possession and live there for several years until B dies. The expenditures by B and by C's husband are treated like those by C in determining whether justice requires enforcement of the promise against A.

Comment d.   Partial enforcement. A promise binding under this section is a contract, and full-scale enforcement by normal remedies is often appropriate. But the same factors which bear on whether any relief should be granted also bear on the character and extent of the remedy. In particular, relief may sometimes be limited to restitution or to damages or specific relief measured by the extent of the promisee's reliance rather than by the terms of the promise. See §§ 84, 89; compare Restatement, Second, Torts § 549 on damages for fraud. Unless there is unjust enrichment of the promisor, damages should not put the promisee in a better position than performance of the promise would have put him. See §§ 344, 349. In the case of a promise to make a gift it would rarely be proper to award consequential damages which would place a greater burden on the promisor than performance would have imposed.

Illustrations

8.   A applies to B, a distributor of radios manufactured by C, for a "dealer franchise" to sell C's products. Such franchises are revocable at will. B erroneously informs A that C has accepted the application and will soon award the franchise, that A can proceed to employ salesmen and solicit orders, and that A will receive an initial delivery of at least 30 radios. A expends $1,150 in preparing to do business, but does not receive the franchise or any radios. B is liable to A for the $1,150 but not for the lost profit on 30 radios. Compare Restatement, Second, Agency § 329.

9.   The facts being otherwise as stated in Illustration 8, B gives A the erroneous information deliberately and with C's approval and requires A to buy the assets of a deceased former dealer and thus discharge C's "moral obligation" to the widow. C is liable to A not only for A's expenses but also for the lost profit on 30 radios.

10.   A, who owns and operates a bakery, desires to go into the grocery business. He approaches B, a franchisor of supermarkets. B states to A that for $18,000 B will establish A in a store. B also advises A to move to another town and buy a small grocery to gain experience. A does so. Later B advises A to sell the grocery, which A does, taking a capital loss and foregoing expected profits from the summer tourist trade. B also advises A to sell his bakery to raise capital for the supermarket franchise, saying "Everything is ready to go. Get your money together and we are set." A sells the bakery taking a capital loss on this sale as well. Still later, B tells A that considerably more than an $18,000 investment will be needed, and the negotiations between the parties collapse. At the point of collapse many details of the proposed agreement between the parties are unresolved. The assurances from B to A are promises on which B reasonably should have expected A to rely, and A is entitled to his actual losses on the sales of the bakery and grocery and for his moving and temporary living expenses. Since the proposed agreement was never made, however, A is not enti-

tled to lost profits from the sale of the grocery or to his expectation interest in the proposed franchise from B.

11. A is about to buy a house on a hill. Before buying he obtains a promise from B, who owns adjoining land, that B will not build on a particular portion of his lot, where a building would obstruct the view from the house. A then buys the house in reliance on the promise. B's promise is binding, but will be specifically enforced only so long as A and his successors do not permanently terminate the use of the view.

12. A promises to make a gift of a tract of land to B, his son-in-law. B takes possession and lives on the land for 17 years, making valuable improvements. A then dispossesses B, and specific performance is denied because the proof of the terms of the promise is not sufficiently clear and definite. B is entitled to a lien on the land for the value of the improvements, not exceeding their cost.

Comment e. Gratuitous promises to procure insurance. This Section is to be applied with caution to promises to procure insurance. The appropriate remedy for breach of such a promise makes the promisor an insurer, and thus may result in a liability which is very large in relation to the value of the promised service. Often the promise is properly to be construed merely as a promise to use reasonable efforts to procure the insurance, and reliance by the promisee may be unjustified or may be justified only for a short time. Or it may be doubtful whether he did in fact rely. Such difficulties may be removed if the proof of the promise and the reliance are clear, or if the promise is made with some formality, or if part performance or a commercial setting or a potential benefit to the promisor provide a substitute for formality.

Illustrations

13. A, a bank, lends money to B on the security of a mortgage on B's new home. The mortgage requires B to insure the property. At the closing of the transaction A promises to arrange for the required insurance, and in reliance on the promise B fails to insure. Six months later the property, still uninsured, is destroyed by fire. The promise is binding.

14. A sells an airplane to B, retaining title to secure payment of the price. After the closing A promises to keep the airplane covered by insurance until B can obtain insurance. B could obtain insurance in three days but makes no effort to do so, and the airplane is destroyed after six days. A is not subject to liability by virtue of the promise.

Comment f. Charitable subscriptions, marriage settlements, and other gifts. One of the functions of the doctrine of consideration is to deny enforcement to a promise to make a gift. Such a promise is ordinarily enforced by virtue of the promisee's reliance only if his conduct is foreseeable and reasonable and involves a definite and substantial change of position which would not have occurred if the promise had not been made. In some cases, however, other policies reinforce the promisee's claim. Thus the promisor might be unjustly enriched if he could reclaim the subject of the promised gift after the promisee has improved it.

Subsection (2) identifies two other classes of cases in which the promisee's claim is similarly reinforced. American courts have traditionally favored charitable subscriptions and marriage settlements, and have found consideration in many cases where the element of exchange was doubtful or nonexistent. Where recovery is rested on reliance in such cases, a probability of reliance is enough, and no effort is made to sort out mixed motives or to consider whether partial enforcement would be appropriate.

Illustrations

15.   A promises B $5000, knowing that B desires that sum for the purchase of a parcel of land. Induced thereby, B secures without any payment an option to buy the parcel. A then tells B that he withdraws his promise. A's promise is not binding.

16.   A orally promises to give her son B a tract of land to live on. As A intended, B gives up a homestead elsewhere, takes possession of the land, lives there for a year and makes substantial improvements. A's promise is binding.

17.   A orally promises to pay B, a university, $100,000 in five annual installments for the purposes of its fund-raising campaign then in progress. The promise is confirmed in writing by A's agent, and two annual installments are paid before A dies. The continuance of the fund-raising campaign by B is sufficient reliance to make the promise binding on A and his estate.

18.   A and B are engaged to be married. In anticipation of the marriage A and his father C enter into a formal written agreement by which C promises to leave certain property to A by will. A's subsequent marriage to B is sufficient reliance to make the promise binding on C and his estate.

* * *

The central question posed by this form of reliance-based obligation concerns whether § 90 merely compensates for technical failures in orthodox contract formation (especially concerning consideration) in certain cases, or instead (and much more dramatically) displaces offer and acceptance more generally and (despite its name) creates contractual obligation even without promise, so that contracts can come into the world unchosen.

If promissory estoppel has this more dramatic character, then § 90 makes contractual obligation no longer voluntary in the orthodox sense—of being simply a creature of the parties' intent, that is willed directly into existence. Instead, contractual duties established under promissory estoppel are like the duty not to be drunk that is established by getting behind the wheel of a car. They are particular workings out of a general, involuntary duty of care owed to others: worked out with respect to the risks posed by driving in the one case; and worked out with respect to the risks posed by declaring one's intentions and describing one's future conduct in the case of contract. This possibility led no less than Grant Gilmore to suppose that promissory estoppel (which he thought of, remember, as *anti-contract*) might entirely cannibalize the orthodox approach to contract formation, at least in practice.

The materials below address this possibility. They conclude that orthodox contract survives the threat introduced by promissory estoppel, because liability under § 90 remains more narrowly cabined than Gilmore feared that it would become. Cases that illustrate this result follow. Before engaging their details, consider the basic doctrine that they all elaborate.

16.2.A PROMISSORY ESTOPPEL MODESTLY CONSTRUED: A CURE FOR TECHNICAL DEFECTS IN CONTRACT FORMATION ON THE ORTHODOX MODEL

One unambiguous effect of promissory estoppel is to correct for circumstances in which a literal application of the orthodox doctrine governing contract formation casts contract's net too narrowly. It can happen that the parties to a promissory interaction intend for contract obligation to arise but, for one reason or another, introduce a technical defect into their efforts to establish a contract along orthodox lines, through offer, acceptance, and consideration. It may even be that, in such cases, failing to recognize and enforce a contract produces injustice, as measured by promissory values. Section 90's narrowest effect is to expand contract law, modestly, to encompass such cases. Promissory estoppel understood in this way is especially important for establishing contract obligation in the absence of consideration.[46]

Feinberg v. Pfeiffer Co.

St. Louis Court of Appeals, Missouri, 1959.
322 S.W.2d 163.

■ DOERNER, COMMISSIONER. This is a suit brought in the Circuit Court of the City of St. Louis by plaintiff, a former employee of the defendant corporation, on an alleged contract whereby defendant agreed to pay plaintiff the sum of $200 per month for life upon her retirement. A jury being waived, the case was tried by the court alone. Judgment below was for plaintiff for $5,100, the amount of the pension claimed to be due as of the date of the trial, together with interest thereon, and defendant duly appealed.

---

46. Promissory Estoppel is not the only such response to technical failures of consideration. Another familiar response appears in what is commonly called the Material Benefit Rule, set out in Restatement (Second) of Contracts § 86. This rule makes legally enforceable (even without any new consideration) promises made in recognition of past benefits received where enforcement is necessary to prevent injustice. The rule expressly excepts cases in which the past benefits were conferred as gifts and in which the value of the new promise is disproportionate to the past benefit.

The parties are in substantial agreement on the essential facts. Plaintiff began working for the defendant, a manufacturer of pharmaceuticals, in 1910, when she was but 17 years of age. By 1947 she had attained the position of bookkeeper, office manager, and assistant treasurer of the defendant, and owned 70 shares of its stock out of a total of 6,503 shares issued and outstanding. Twenty shares had been given to her by the defendant or its then president, she had purchased 20, and the remaining 30 she had acquired by a stock split or stock dividend. Over the years she received substantial dividends on the stock she owned, as did all of the other stockholders. Also, in addition to her salary, plaintiff from 1937 to 1949, inclusive, received each year a bonus varying in amount from $300 in the beginning to $2,000 in the later years.

On December 27, 1947, the annual meeting of the defendant's Board of Directors was held at the Company's offices in St. Louis, presided over by Max Lippman, its then president and largest individual stockholder. The other directors present were George L. Marcus, Sidney Harris, Sol Flammer, and Walter Weinstock, who, with Max Lippman, owned 5,007 of the 6,503 shares then issued and outstanding. At that meeting the Board of Directors adopted the following resolution, which, because it is the crux of the case, we quote in full:

'The Chairman thereupon pointed out that the Assistant Treasurer, Mrs. Anna Sacks Feinberg, has given the corporation many years of long and faithful service. Not only has she served the corporation devotedly, but with exceptional ability and skill. The President pointed out that although all of the officers and directors sincerely hoped and desired that Mrs. Feinberg would continue in her present position for as long as she felt able, nevertheless, in view of the length of service which she has contributed provision should be made to afford her retirement privileges and benefits which should become a firm obligation of the corporation to be available to her whenever she should see fit to retire from active duty, however many years in the future such retirement may become effective. It was, accordingly, proposed that Mrs. Feinberg's salary which is presently $350.00 per month, be increased to $400.00 per month, and that Mrs. Feinberg would be given the privilege of retiring from active duty at any time she may elect to see fit so to do upon a retirement pay of $200.00 per month for life, with the distinct understanding that the retirement plan is merely being adopted at the present time in order to afford Mrs. Feinberg security for the future and in the hope that her active services will continue with the corporation for many years to come. After due discussion and consideration, and upon motion duly made and seconded, it was—

'Resolved, that the salary of Anna Sacks Feinberg be increased from $350.00 to $400.00 per month and that she be afforded the privilege of retiring from active duty in the corporation at any time she may elect to see fit so to do upon retirement pay of $200.00 per month, for the remainder of her life.'

At the request of Mr. Lippman his sons-in-law, Messrs. Harris and Flammer, called upon the plaintiff at her apartment on the same day to advise her of the passage of the resolution. Plaintiff testified on cross-examination that she had no prior information that such a pension plan was contemplated, that it came as a surprise to her, and that she would have continued in her employment whether or not such a resolution had been adopted. It is clear from the evidence that there was no contract, oral or written, as to plaintiff's length of employment, and that she was free to quit, and the defendant to discharge her, at any time.

Plaintiff did continue to work for the defendant through June 30, 1949, on which date she retired. In accordance with the foregoing resolution, the defendant began paying her the sum of $200 on the first of each month. Mr. Lippman died on November 18, 1949, and was succeeded as president of the company by his widow. Because of an illness, she retired from that office and was succeeded in October, 1953, by her son-in-law, Sidney M. Harris. Mr. Harris testified that while Mrs. Lippman had been president she signed the monthly pension check paid plaintiff, but fussed about doing so, and considered the payments as gifts. After his election, he stated, a new accounting firm employed by the defendant questioned the validity of the payments to plaintiff on several occasions, and in the Spring of 1956, upon its recommendation, he consulted the Company's then attorney, Mr. Ralph Kalish. Harris testified that both Ernst and Ernst, the accounting firm, and Kalish told him there was no need of giving plaintiff the money. He also stated that he had concurred in the view that the payments to plaintiff were mere gratuities rather than amounts due under a contractual obligation, and that following his discussion with the Company's attorney plaintiff was sent a check for $100 on April 1, 1956. Plaintiff declined to accept the reduced amount, and this action followed.

We come, then, to the basic issue in the case. While otherwise defined in defendant's third and fourth assignments of error, it is thus succinctly stated in the argument in its brief: 'whether plaintiff has proved that she has a right to recover from defendant based upon a legally binding contractual obligation to pay her $200 per month for life.'

It is defendant's contention, in essence, that the resolution adopted by its Board of Directors was a mere promise to make a gift, and that no contract resulted either thereby, or when plaintiff retired, because there was no consideration given or paid by the plaintiff. It urges that a promise to make a gift is not binding unless supported by a legal consideration; that the only apparent consideration for the adoption of the foregoing resolution was the 'many years of long and faithful service' expressed therein; and that past services are not a valid consideration for a promise. Defendant argues further that there is nothing in the resolution which made its effectiveness conditional upon plaintiff's continued employment, that she was not under contract to work for any length of time but was free to quit whenever she wished, and that she had no contractual right to her position and could have been discharged at any time.

Plaintiff concedes that a promise based upon past services would be without consideration, but contends that there were two other elements which supplied the required element: First, the continuation by plaintiff in the employ of the defendant for the period from December 27, 1947, the date when the resolution was adopted, until the date of her retirement on June 30, 1949. And, second, her change of position, i. e., her retirement, and the abandonment by her of her opportunity to continue in gainful employment, made in reliance on defendant's promise to pay her $200 per month for life.

We must agree with the defendant that the evidence does not support the first of these contentions. There is no language in the resolution predicating plaintiff's right to a pension upon her continued employment. She was not required to work for the defendant for any period of time as a condition to gaining such retirement benefits. She was told that she could quit the day upon which the resolution was adopted, as she herself testified, and it is clear from her own testimony that she made no promise or agreement to continue in the employ of the defendant in return for its promise to pay her a pension. Hence there was lacking that mutuality of obligation which is essential to the validity of a contract.

But as to the second of these contentions we must agree with plaintiff.

Section 90 of the Restatement of the Law of Contracts states that: 'A promise which the promisor should reasonably expect to induce action or forbearance of a definite and substantial character on the part of the promisee and which does induce such action or forbearance is binding if injustice can be avoided only by enforcement of the promise.' This doctrine has been described as that of 'promissory estoppel,' as distinguished from that of equitable estoppel or estoppel in pais, the reason for the differentiation being stated as follows:

> 'It is generally true that one who has led another to act in reasonable reliance on his representations of fact cannot afterwards in litigation between the two deny the truth of the representations, and some courts have sought to apply this principle to the formation of contracts, where, relying on a gratuitous promise, the promisee has suffered detriment. It is to be noticed, however, that such a case does not come within the ordinary definition of estoppel. If there is any representation of an existing fact, it is only that the promisor at the time of making the promise intends to fulfill it. As to such intention there is usually no misrepresentation and if there is, it is not that which has injured the promisee. In other words, he relies on a promise and not on a misstatement of fact; and the term 'promissory' estoppel or something equivalent should be used to make the distinction.' Williston on Contracts, Rev. Ed., Sec. 139, Vol. 1.

In speaking of this doctrine, Judge Learned Hand said in Porter v. Commissioner of Internal Revenue, 2 Cir., 60 F.2d 673, 675, that 'promissory estoppel' is now a recognized species of consideration.'

Was there such an act on the part of plaintiff, in reliance upon the promise contained in the resolution, as will estop the defendant, and therefore create an enforceable contract under the doctrine of promissory estoppel? We think there was. One of the illustrations cited under Section 90 of the Restatement is: '2. A promises B to pay him an annuity during B's life. B thereupon resigns a profitable employment, as A expected that he might. B receives the annuity for some years, in the meantime becoming disqualified from again obtaining good employment. A's promise is binding.' This illustration is objected to by defendant as not being applicable to the case at hand. The reason advanced by it is that in the illustration B became 'disqualified' from obtaining other employment *before* A discontinued the payments, whereas in this case the plaintiff did not discover that she had cancer and thereby became unemployable until *after* the defendant had discontinued the payments of $200 per month. We think the distinction is immaterial. The only reason for the reference in the illustration to the disqualification of A is in connection with that part of Section 90 regarding the prevention of injustice. The injustice would occur regardless of when the disability occurred. Would defendant contend that the contract would be enforceable if the plaintiff's illness had been discovered on March 31, 1956, the day before it discontinued the payment of the $200 a month, but not if it occurred on April 2nd, the day after? Furthermore, there are more ways to become disqualified for work, or unemployable, than as the result of illness. At the time she retired plaintiff was 57 years of age. At the time the payments were discontinued she was over 63 years of age. It is a matter of common knowledge that it is virtually impossible for a woman of that age to find satisfactory employment, much less a position comparable to that which plaintiff enjoyed at the time of her retirement.

The Commissioner therefore recommends, for the reasons stated, that the judgment be affirmed.

Rickets v. Scothorn

Supreme Court of Nebraska, 1898.
77 N.W. 365.

■ SULLIVAN, J. In the district court of Lancaster county the plaintiff, Katie Scothorn, recovered judgment against the defendant, Andrew D. Ricketts, as executor of the last will and testament of John C. Ricketts, deceased. The action was based upon a promissory note, of which the following is a copy: "May the first, 1891. I promise to pay to Katie Scothorn on demand, $2,000, to be at 6 per cent. per annum. J. C. Ricketts." In the petition the plaintiff alleges that the consideration for the execution of the note was that she should surrender her employment as bookkeeper for Mayer Bros., and cease to work for a living. She also alleges that the note was given to induce her to abandon her occupation, and that, relying on it, and on the annual interest, as a means of support, she gave up the employment in which she was then engaged. These allegations of the petition are denied by the administrator. The material facts are undisputed. They are as follows: John C. Ricketts, the maker of the note, was the grandfather of the plaintiff. Early in May—presumably on the day the note bears date—he called on her at the store where she was working. What transpired between them is thus described by Mr. Flodene, one of the plaintiff's witnesses: "A. Well, the old gentleman came in there one morning about nine o'clock, probably a little before or a little after, but early in the morning, and he unbuttoned his vest, and took out a piece of paper in the shape of a note; that is the way it looked to me; and he says to Miss Scothorn, 'I have fixed out something that you have not got to work any more.' He says, none of my grandchildren work, and you don't have to. Q. Where was she? A. She took the piece of paper and kissed him, and kissed the old gentleman, and commenced to cry." It seems Miss Scothorn immediately notified her employer of her intention to quit work, and that she did soon after abandon her occupation. The mother of the plaintiff was a witness, and testified that she had a conversation with her father, Mr. Ricketts, shortly after the note was executed, in which he informed her that he had given the note to the plaintiff to enable her to quit work; that none of his grandchildren worked, and he did not think she ought to. For something more than a year the plaintiff was without an occupation, but in September, 1892, with the consent of her grandfather, and by his assistance, she secured a position as bookkeeper with Messrs. Funke & Ogden. On June 8, 1894, Mr. Ricketts died. He had paid one year's interest on the note, and a short time before his death expressed regret that he had not been able to pay the balance. In the summer or fall of 1892 he stated to his daughter, Mrs. Scothorn, that if he could sell his farm in Ohio he would pay the note out of the proceeds. He at no time repudiated the obligation. We quite agree with counsel for the defendant that upon this evidence there was nothing to submit to the jury, and that a verdict should have been directed peremptorily for one of the parties. The testimony of Flodene and Mrs. Scothorn, taken together, conclusively establishes the fact that the note was not given in consideration of the plaintiff pursuing, or agreeing to pursue, any particular line of conduct. There was no promise on the part of the plaintiff to do, or refrain from doing, anything. Her right to the money promised in the note was not made to depend upon an abandonment of her employment with Mayer Bros., and future abstention from like service. Mr. Ricketts made no condition, requirement, or request. He exacted no quid pro quo. He gave the note as a gratuity, and looked for nothing in return. So far as the evidence discloses, it was his purpose to place the plaintiff in a position of independence, where she could work or remain idle, as she might choose. The abandonment of Miss Scothorn of her position as bookkeeper was altogether voluntary. It was not an act done in fulfillment of any contract obligation assumed when she accepted the note. The instrument in suit, being given without any valuable consideration, was nothing more than a promise to make a gift in the future of the sum of money therein named. Ordinarily, such promises are not enforceable, even when put in the form of a promissory note. But it has often been held that an action on a note given to a church, college, or other like institution, upon the faith of which money has been expended or obligations incurred, could not be successfully defended on the ground of a want of consideration. In this class of cases the note in suit is nearly always spoken of as a gift or donation, but the decision is generally put on the ground that the expenditure of money or assumption of liability by the donee on the faith of the promise constitutes a valuable and sufficient consideration. It seems to us that the true reason is the preclusion of the defendant, under the doctrine of estoppel, to deny the consideration. Such seems to be the view of the matter taken by the supreme court of Iowa in the case of *Simpson Centenary College v. Tuttle*, 71 Iowa, 596, where Rothrock, J., speaking for the court, said: "Where a note, however, is based on a promise to give for the support of the objects referred to, it may still be open to this defense [want of consideration], unless it shall appear that the donee has, prior to any revocation, entered into engagements, or made expenditures based on such promise, so that he must suffer loss or injury if the note is not paid. This is based on the equitable principle that, after allowing the donee to incur obligations on the faith that the note would be paid, the donor would be estopped from pleading want of consideration." And in the case of *Reimensnyder v. Gans*, 110 Pa. St. 17, which was an action on a note given as a donation to a charitable object, the court said: "The fact is that, as we may see from the case of *Ryerss v. Trustees*, 33 Pa. St. 114, a contract of the kind here involved is enforceable rather by way of estoppel than on the ground of consideration in the original undertaking." It has been held that a note given in expectation of the payee performing certain services, but without any contract binding him to serve, will not support an action. *Hulse v. Hulse*, 84 E. C. L. 709. But when the payee changes his position to his disadvantage in reliance on the promise, a right of action does arise.

Under the circumstances of this case, is there an equitable estoppel which ought to preclude the defendant from alleging that the note in controversy is lacking in one of the essential elements of a valid contract? We think there is. An estoppel in pais is defined to be "a right arising from acts, admissions, or conduct which have induced a change of position in accordance with the real or apparent intention of the party against whom they are alleged." Mr. Pomeroy has formulated the following definition: "Equitable estoppel is the effect of the voluntary conduct of a party whereby he is absolutely precluded, both at law and in equity, from asserting rights which might, perhaps, have otherwise existed, either of property, of contract, or of remedy, as against another person who in good faith relied upon such conduct, and has been led thereby to change his position for the worse, and who on his part acquires some corresponding right, either of property, of contract, or of remedy." 2 Pom. Eq. Jur. 804. According to the undisputed proof, as shown by the record before us, the plaintiff was a working girl, holding a position in which she earned a salary of $10 per week, Her grandfather, desiring to put her in a position of independence, gave her the note, accompanying it with the remark that his other grandchildren did not work, and that she would not be obliged to work any longer. In effect, he suggested that she might abandon her employment, and rely in the future upon the bounty which he promised. He doubtless desired that she should give up her occupation, but, whether he did or not, it is entirely certain that he contemplated such action on her part as a reasonable and probable consequence of his gift. Having intentionally influenced the plaintiff to alter her position for the worse on the faith of the note being paid when due, it would be grossly inequitable to permit the maker, or his executor, to resist payment on the ground that the promise was given without consideration. The petition charges the elements of an equitable estoppel, and the evidence conclusively establishes them. If errors intervened at the trial, they could not have been prejudicial. A verdict for the defendant would be unwarranted. The judgment is right, and is affirmed.

* * *

Feinberg represents perhaps the quintessential case of promissory estoppel, at least in its modest expression. The plaintiff had worked for the defendant for many years. In appreciation of her loyal service, the defendant's board of directors resolved to increase her salary in future years worked and to award her an annual pension on her retirement, whenever she chose to take it. The plaintiff eventually retired and claimed and received her pension for some time. When the defendant's new management reduced the plaintiff's pension payments by half, she refused the smaller payments and sued to recover the promised pension.

Feinberg is an easy case for several reasons. The plaintiff clearly relied, and to her detriment, on the defendant's promise: in taking her pension, she forewent a greater salary. Moreover, there is a strong and intuitive sense that it would be unjust for the defendant to be relieved of the obligation to pay. Quite apart from rendering herself vulnerable by retiring, the plaintiff had conferred a great benefit on the defendant, over many years; so that the defendant's new board appears, to most observers, heartless. Furthermore, the promise at issue was made in a clearly commercial context (between an employer and employee, and for payments closely associated with salary). The parties might reasonably have expected legal entitlements to come into play in such circumstances, and courts enforcing such rights need not fear intruding in more cooperative forms of personal solidarity, or replacing good motives with bad.

Finally, and perhaps most importantly, the facts of *Feinberg* render the promise very nearly supported by consideration, and hence enforceable on a purely orthodox contract theory. A problem concerning consideration arose only because the plaintiff was employed at will—that is, on terms that allowed the defendant to fire her for any reason or no reason, at its sole discretion. This prevented the plaintiff from arguing that she had given up her right to retain her job and salary in exchange for the pension.[47]

---

47. Might the plaintiff have argued that there was a bargain nevertheless, because the promised pension induced her to give up the opportunity to quit and seek alternative employment, or perhaps even because it induced her to work harder and more loyally on the

Moreover, even given the plaintiff's at will status, there would have been good consideration under the older benefit/detriment test. By retiring, the plaintiff both conferred a benefit on the defendant (relief from the obligation to pay her wage) and accepted a detriment for herself (relinquishing her wage). So promissory estoppel functions, in *Feinberg*, as a means for mitigating the tendency of a strict adherence to the bargain theory of consideration to frustrate the promissory intentions of commercial parties and the harshness associated with such frustrations. The ambitions of § 90, understood in these terms, could hardly be more modest.

Rickets is not formally so different from *Feinberg*, although it applies a similar reliance-logic in very different substantive circumstances. The plaintiff in *Rickets* was the defendant's granddaughter.[48] She worked as a shop girl and was one day visited by the defendant at work and given a promissory note that contemplated substantial regular annual payments. The defendant declared that "none of my grandchildren work, and you don't have to." The plaintiff thereupon quit her job and remained out of work for a while. Eventually, and with the defendant's consent and assistance, she took a new job.[49] The defendant's estate later refused to honor the note, and the plaintiff sued.

Many of the structural features of *Feinberg* are reprised in *Rickets*. The plaintiff had clearly relied on the defendant's promise, so that the subsequent refusal to honor the promise again had the character of pulling the rug out from under an innocent and indeed reasonable promisee. (And while it is true that the plaintiff's reliance eventually ceased, it did so with the defendant's consent and indeed endorsement, which countermands any sense that the plaintiff's subsequent insistence on the promise was grasping or exploitative.) The promise was made in a context—concerning the monies required for the plaintiff's maintenance—that suggests serious intent and, moreover, an interest in the kind of reliability associated with legal enforcement. Finally, finding consideration would once again have been perfectly straightforward under the older benefit/detriment approach. The plaintiff conferred an unambiguous benefit on the defendant—saving him from the displeasure (and perhaps social embarrassment) of having a working granddaughter; and she assumed an unambiguous detriment herself—the loss of her wages. There was no consideration on the bargain model only because the defendant's promise failed to tie the payments under the note to these consequences; he gave her the promissory note

---

defendant's behalf? Perhaps, but note that accepting this argument would effectively end (at least in part) the at-will character of her employment. Although the defendant would retain the right to fire the plaintiff and cease paying her salary at will, it would now require good cause to avoid paying her pension. And it was uncontested that, even after the promises at issue in *Feinberg*, the plaintiff remained an at will employee.

The character of at will employment, and the legal and moral complexities of this regime, will be taken up in greater detail in Part III below.

48. In fact, of course, the defendant was not the grandfather himself but the grandfather's estate. The text elides this distinction to make the exposition go more smoothly.

49. The promissory note was for $2000, at 6% interest. It thus would have yielded $120 per year. The plaintiff's job, by contrast, had paid $500 a year. So it was not quite clear how the note might have sustained the plaintiff's leisure; and in fact, it seems not to have done.

unconditionally, and she only happened to cease work (and resume it only with his support). Once again, § 90's intervention to establish an enforceable contract under these circumstances makes only the most modest formal revisions to orthodox law, filling in a gap in the orthodox paths to contract that might be recognized as a gap even in terms of the promissory ideals that these orthodox paths aspire to capture. Whatever extravagance exists in *Rickets* concerns substance rather than form, and in particular the court's willingness to intervene in personal (and indeed familial) affairs. And in this respect, *Rickets* perhaps remains an outlier, as some of the materials concerning marriage taken up in Part III will suggest.

The modesty of this incarnation of § 90 has consequences, including in particular the consequence that plaintiffs whose circumstances do not approach the circumstances of orthodox contract quite so fully or closely tend to lose even when they characterize their claims in terms of promissory estoppel (modestly construed). As the focus at the moment remains on understanding the formal structure of the doctrine, especially in respect of contract's relation to tort, rather than on drawing lines that can decide close cases, examples that illustrate this modesty will receive only brief attention. Thus in once case, a plaintiff whose brother had died sought to enforce her sister-in-law's promise to give her a portion of the brother's estate.[50] In another case, a plaintiff who announced plans to retire sought to enforce his employer's promise—made subsequent to the retirement announcement—to pay a pension.[51] In each case, the plaintiffs had reasonable moral complaints: the first defendant had claimed a share of the decedent's estate that the decedent had wished his sister to have and had made her promise to redress this wrong; and the second defendant stopped paying the pension only after an intra-family fight among the defendant-employer's owners resulted in the takeover of the defendant by new management. Both claims nevertheless failed, among other reasons, because the plaintiffs could not show that they had in fact relied on the promises. In the absence of reliance—and reliance specifically on the defendant's promises—the unreasonableness or even injustice of the defendants' conduct was thought insufficient to sustain contractual obligation. In these cases also, then, § 90 proceeds modestly—where the defects of orthodox contract formation are not merely technical but go, rather, to the question whether promises were essential instruments of the wrongs that the cases involve, the modest interpretation of promissory estoppel refuses to impose tort-like norms concerning care and harm on parties. It prefers to leave even deserving plaintiffs unsatisfied.

Not every application of promissory estoppel is quite so modest, however. And some cases employ the doctrine to do more than remedy purely technical defects in orthodox contract formation. These cases flirt with employing § 90 to establish contractual obligation on a non-promissory model. That possibility should be familiar from materials discussed earlier in these pages.

---

50. *Haase v. Cardoza*, 331 P.2d 419 (Cal.App. 1958).

51. *Hayes v. Plantations Steel Co.*, 438 A.2d 1091 (R.I. 1982).

James Baird Co. v. Gimbel Bros., Inc.

United States Court of Appeals for the Second Circuit, 1933.
64 F.2d 344.

(Reprised from Chapter 15)

Drennan v. Star Paving Co.

Supreme Court of California, 1958.
333 P.2d 757.

(Reprised from Chapter 13)

* * *

Gimbel Bros. and *Drennan*, recall, both involved general contractors who had asked sub-contractors to make bids to complete various parts of the larger project and then used these bids in preparing their own bids for the whole project. After the generals' bids were accepted, but before the generals could accept the subs' bids, the subs discovered mistakes in their bids and sought to revoke them. The generals sued, arguing that promissory estoppel bound the subs to honor their bids.

Learned Hand, adopting a modest approach to promissory estoppel, decided *Gimble Bros.* in favor of the sub. Hand insisted, remember, that promissory estoppel requires a *promise*; so that a mere *offer*, falling short of a promise because not accepted, cannot sustain obligation under the principle. This line of argument worries that once the promissory roots of promissory estoppel are abandoned, so that the doctrine may be applied to cause less than a promise to give rise to contract obligation, there will be no stopping. If promissory estoppel sustains obligations based on offers, then it might do so based on other types of speech: statements of intention, predictions of future conduct, perhaps even assertions generally. In this case, contract's distinctiveness would truly become undone. A tort-like principle, based on reasonable reliance, would sustain contract-like obligation without promise's playing any distinguishing or disciplining role. Understood in this way § 90 truly becomes Gilmore's "anti-contract."

Drennan might seem to embrace just this radical refusal to insist that a promise must precede every contract, and hence to fall prey to Hand's worries. Traynor, after all, applies promissory estoppel to bind the sub while accepting that the sub made an offer only. But recall that features of both the facts in that case and of Traynor's opinion serve to limit the scope of the holding's departure from the promissory principles on which Hand had insisted.

Begin with the facts. The sub's offer was anything but innocent of its effects on the general. The sub wasn't simply or casually representing that it might do the job at a given price, just in case the general might be curious. Rather, the sub was intensely interested in what the general did with its offer, and in particular in whether the general used the sub's offer to make its own, because that was a critical first step to the general's giving the sub the job. The value to the sub of making its offer thus turned on the prospect that the general might rely on the offer in just this way. The sub made its offer, one might say, for the purpose of generating reliance by the general. To return to a distinction developed earlier, the sub's offer was very far removed from a mere invitation to bargain—from a mere representation of terms that might, in principle, interest the sub in pursuing a deal. These features of the sub's offer entail that, in spite of remaining formally an offer rather than a promise, the sub's offer resides in the precincts of promise: it embraces promissory obligation as the end to which it aspires. This feature of *Drennan's* facts might enable Traynor's holding to avoid the slippery slope towards establishing contract-like liability on a purely tort model, towards anti-contract.

The facts, moreover, informed Traynor's opinion. Traynor's approach to the case, remember, did not in the end abandon the specialness of promise. Rather, Traynor observed that it would assist the sub's offer in serving its reliance inducing purpose if the offer were irrevocable—that the general would be more inclined to make the investments required to use the sub's bid in preparing its own if it could rely on engaging the sub on the terms of the bid. Moreover, the usual mechanism for making such reliance reasonable—namely accepting the offer and thereby converting it into a promise—was not available in *Drennan's* circumstances, as the general would not want to bind itself to the sub before knowing whether it would win the contract for the larger project. Traynor therefore imagined that the general and sub might structure their relationship to resolve this impasse and, moreover, that the resolution might itself follow a promissory model. He thus implied a secondary offer, made by the sub to the general, not to revoke the primary offer until the general had had a reasonable opportunity to consider it. The secondary offer, moreover, was accepted by the general, when the general used the sub's bid in constructing its own. This converted the secondary offer into a promise. Traynor's holding—that the sub was bound to honor its bid—thus involved not one application of offerory estoppel but rather two applications of promissory estoppel. Traynor first applied promissory estoppel to the implied secondary promise, to generate the result that the sub might not revoke its primary offer. This allowed the general to accept that offer, converting it into a promise, to which promissory estoppel might be applied for the second time, now to bind the sub to perform according to the offer's terms.

So even though no obvious or express promise underwrites the reliance in *Drennan*, a non-obvious, implied promise does. Even *Drennan* thus remains, fundamentally, a modest application of promissory estoppel—one that hews narrowly to the principle's promissory basis. Tort might be howling at contract's door; but it has not been let in.

16.2.B   PROMISSORY ESTOPPEL BEYOND PROMISE: THE ORTHODOX MODEL AT RISK

Other cases applying § 90 have gone further. Perhaps they have even opened contract up to tort. The following materials illustrate this possibility. Their interpretation remains contested. But the best account of the law again declines to abandon the orthodox, promissory foundations of contract.

On the one hand, the facts of the cases might be read to sustain liability in tort, for fraud, even given the limitations on such liability discussed earlier and thus without any significant recourse to contract-like notions. On this interpretation, § 90 serves at most to cure technical defects in tort doctrine (much as the earlier modest application of § 90 serves to cure technical defects in orthodox contract law). It does not insert tort into the heart of contract to supplant orthodox promissory ideals. And on the other hand, where the facts leave tort and fraud farther in the distance, the precedents below become substantially weaker. Quite possibly, they are not followed at all. They therefore once again do not in the end supplant contract with tort.

Hoffman v. Red Owl Stores, Inc.

Supreme Court of Wisconsin, 1965.
133 N.W.2d 267.

Action for damages. The Circuit Court for Outagamie County, A. W. Parnell, J., entered judgment approving all portions of verdict except for damages as to one item and the defendants appealed and the plaintiffs cross-appealed. The Supreme Court, Currie, C. J., held that court concluded that injustice would result if plaintiffs were not granted damages because of failure of corporation to keep promises made concerning operation of franchise agency store by plaintiffs who had been induced to act to their detriment by those promises.

Order affirmed.

Action by Joseph Hoffman (hereinafter 'Hoffman') and wife, plaintiffs, against defendants Red Owl Stores, Inc. (hereinafter 'Red Owl') and Edward Lukowitz.

The complaint alleged that Lukowitz, as agent for Red Owl, represented to and agreed with plaintiffs that Red Owl would build a store building in Chilton and stock it with merchandise for Hoffman to operate in return for which plaintiffs were to put up and invest a total sum of $18,000; that in reliance upon the above mentioned agreement and representations plaintiffs sold their bakery building and business and their grocery store and business; also in reliance on the agreement and representations Hoffman purchased the building site in Chilton and rented a residence for himself and his family in Chilton; plaintiffs' actions in reliance on the representations and agreement disrupted their personal and business life; plaintiffs lost substantial amounts of income and expended large sums of money as expenses. Plaintiffs demanded recovery of damages for the breach of defendants' representations and agreements.

The action was tried to a court and jury. The facts hereafter stated are taken from the evidence adduced at the trial. Where there was a conflict in the evidence the version favorable to plaintiffs has been accepted since the verdict rendered was in favor of plaintiffs.

Hoffman assisted by his wife operated a bakery at Wautoma from 1956 until sale of the building late in 1961. The building was owned in joint tenancy by him and his wife. Red Owl is a Minnesota corporation having its home office at Hopkins, Minnesota. It owns and operates a number of grocery supermarket stores and also extends franchises to agency stores which are owned by individuals, partnerships and corporations. Lukowitz resides at Green Bay and since September, 1960, has been divisional manager for Red Owl in a territory comprising Upper Michigan and most of Wisconsin in charge of 84 stores. Prior to September, 1960, he was district manager having charge of approximately 20 stores.

In November, 1959, Hoffman was desirous of expanding his operations by establishing a grocery store and contacted a Red Owl representative by the name of Jansen, now deceased. Numerous conversations were had in 1960 with the idea of establishing a Red Owl franchise store in Wautoma. In September, 1960, Lukowitz succeeded Jansen as Red Owl's representative in the negotiations. Hoffman mentioned that $18,000 was all the capital he had available to invest and he was repeatedly assured that this would be sufficient to set him up in business as a Red Owl store. About Christmastime, 1960, Hoffman thought it would be a good idea if he bought a small grocery store in Wautoma and operated it in order that he gain experience in the grocery business prior to operating a Red Owl store in some larger community. On February 6, 1961, on the advice of Lukowitz and Sykes, who had succeeded Lukowitz as Red Owl's district manager, Hoffman bought the inventory and fixtures of a small grocery store in Wautoma and leased the building in which it was operated.

After three months of operating this Wautoma store, the Red Owl representatives came in and took inventory and checked the operations and found the store was operating at a profit. Lukowitz advised Hoffman to sell the store to his manager, and assured him that Red Owl would find a larger store from him elsewhere. Acting on this advice and assurance, Hoffman sold the fixtures and inventory to his manager on June 6, 1961. Hoffman was reluctant to sell at that time because it meant losing the summer tourist business, but he sold on the assurance that he would be operating in a new location by fall and that he must sell this store if he wanted a bigger one. Before selling, Hoffman told the Red Owl representatives that he had $18,000 for 'getting set up in business' and they assured him that there would be no problems in establishing him in a bigger operation. The makeup of the $18,000 was not discussed; it was understood plaintiff's father-in-law would furnish part of it. By June, 1961, the towns for the new grocery store had been narrowed down to two, Kewaunee and Chilton. In Kewaunee, Red Owl had an option on a building site. In Chilton, Red Owl had nothing under option, but it did select a site to which plaintiff obtained an option at Red Owl's suggestion. The option stipulated a purchase price of $6,000 with $1,000 to be paid on election to purchase and the balance to be paid within 30 days. On Lukowitz's assurance that everything was all set plaintiff paid $1,000 down on the lot on September 15th.

On September 27, 1961, plaintiff met at Chilton with Lukowitz and Mr. Reymund and Mr. Carlson from the home office who prepared a projected financial statement. Part of the funds plaintiffs were to supply as their investment in the venture were to be obtained by sale of their Wautoma bakery building.

On the basis of this meeting Lukowitz assured Hoffman: '[E]verything is ready to go. Get your money together and we are set.' Shortly after this meeting Lukowitz told plaintiffs that they would have to sell their bakery business and bakery building, and that their retaining this property was the only 'hitch' in the entire plan. On November 6, 1961, plaintiffs sold their bakery building for $10,000. Hoffman was to retain the bakery equipment as he contemplated using it to operate a bakery in connection with his Red Owl store. After sale of the bakery Hoffman obtained employment on the night shift at an Appleton bakery.

The record contains different exhibits which were prepared in September and October, some of which were projections of the fiscal operation of the business and others were proposed building and floor plans. Red Owl was to procure some third party to buy the Chilton lot from Hoffman, construct the building, and then lease it to Hoffman. No final plans were ever made, nor were bids let or a construction contract entered. Some time prior to November 20, 1961, certain of the terms of the lease under which the building was to be rented by Hoffman were understood between him and Lukowitz. The lease was to be for 10 years with a rental approximating $550 a month calculated on the basis of 1 percent per month on the building cost, plus 6 percent of the land cost divided on a monthly basis. At the end of the 10–year term he was to have an option to renew the lease for an additional 10–year period or to buy the property at cost on an installment basis. There was no discussion as to what the installments would be or with respect to repairs and maintenance.

On November 22nd or 23rd, Lukowitz and plaintiffs met in Minneapolis with Red Owl's credit manager to confer on Hoffman's financial standing and on financing the agency. Another projected financial statement was there drawn up entitled, 'Proposed Financing For An Agency Store.' This showed Hoffman contributing $24,100 of cash capital of which only $4,600 was to be cash possessed by plaintiffs. Eight thousand was to be procured as a loan from a Chilton bank secured by a mortgage on the bakery fixtures, $7,500 was to be obtained on a 5 percent loan from the father-in-law, and $4,000 was to be obtained by sale of the lot to the lessor at a profit.

A week or two after the Minneapolis meeting Lukowitz showed Hoffman a telegram from the home office to the effect that if plaintiff could get another $2,000 for promotional purposes the deal could go through for $26,000. Hoffman stated he would have to find out if he could get another $2,000. He met with his father-in-law, who agreed to put $13,000 into the business provided he could come into the business as a partner. Lukowitz told Hoffman the partnership arrangement 'sounds fine' and that Hoffman should not go into the partnership arrangement with the 'front office.' On January 16, 1962, the Red Owl credit manager teletyped Lukowitz that the father-in-law would have to sign an agreement that the $13,000 was either a gift or a loan subordinate to all general creditors and that he would prepare the agreement. On January 31, 1962, Lukowitz teletyped the home office that the father-in-law would sign one or other of the agreements. However, Hoffman testified that it was not until the final meeting some time between January 26th and February 2nd, 1962, that he was told that his father-in-law was expected to sign an agreement that the $13,000 he was advancing was to be an outright gift. No mention was then made by the Red Owl representatives of the alternative of the father-in-law signing a subordination agreement. At this meeting the Red Owl agents presented Hoffman with the following projected financial statement:

"Capital required in operation:

"Cash	$5,000.00	
"Merchandise	20,000.00	
"Bakery	18,000.00	
"Fixtures	17,500.00	
"Promotional Funds	1,500.00	
"TOTAL:		$62,000.00

"Source of funds:

"Red Owl 7–day terms	$5,000.00
"Red Owl Fixture contract (Term 5 years)	14,000.00
"Bank loans (Term 9 years Union State Bank	8,000.00
"of Chilton	
"(Secured by Bakery Equipment)	
"Other loans (Term No-pay) No interest	13,000.00
"Father-in-law	
"(Secured by None)	
"(Secured by Mortgage on	2,000.00

"Wautoma Bakery Bldg.)

"Resale of land   6,000.00

"Equity Capital: $5,000.00–Cash

"Amount owner has 17,500.00–Bakery Equip.

"to invest: 22,500.00

"TOTAL: $70,500.00"

Hoffman interpreted the above statement to require of plaintiffs a total of $34,000 cash made up of $13,000 gift from his father-in-law, $2,000 on mortgage, $8,000 on Chilton bank loan, $5,000 in cash from plaintiff, and $6,000 on the resale of the Chilton lot. Red Owl claims $18,000 is the total of the unborrowed or unencumbered cash, that is, $13,000 from the father-in-law and $5,000 cash from Hoffman himself. Hoffman informed Red Owl he could not go along with this proposal, and particularly objected to the requirement that his father-in-law sign an agreement that his $13,000 advancement was an absolute gift. This terminated the negotiations between the parties.

[The trial court found in Hoffman's favor on a theory of promissory estoppel and awarded substantial damages.]

Opinion

■ CURRIE, CHIEF JUSTICE.

The instant appeal and cross-appeal present these questions:

(1) Whether this court should recognize causes of action grounded on promissory estoppel as exemplified by sec. 90 of Restatement, 1 Contracts?

(2) Do the facts in this case make out a cause of action for promissory estoppel?

(3) Are the jury's findings with respect to damages sustained by the evidence?

Recognition of a Cause of Action Grounded on Promissory Estoppel.

Sec. 90 of Restatement, 1 Contracts, provides (at p. 110):

'A promise which the promisor should reasonably expect to induce action or forbearance of a definite and substantial character on the part of the promisee and which does induce such action of forbearance is binding if injustice can be avoided only by enforcement of the promise.'

The Wisconsin Annotations to Restatement, Contracts, prepared under the direction of the late Professor William H. Page and issued in 1933, stated (at p. 53, sec. 90):

'The Wisconsin cases do not seem to be in accord with this section of the Restatement. It is certain that no such proposition has ever been announced by the Wisconsin court and it is at least doubtful if it would be approved by the court.'

Since 1933, the closest approach this court has made to adopting the rule of the Restatement occurred in the recent case of *Lazarus v. American Motors Corp.* (1963), 123 N.W.2d 548, 553, wherein the court stated:

'We recognize that upon different facts it would be possible for a seller of steel to have altered his position so as to effectuate the equitable considerations inherent in sec. 90 of the Restatement.'

While it was not necessary to the disposition of the Lazarus Case to adopt the promissory estoppel rule of the Restatement, we are squarely faced in the instant case with that issue. Not only did the trial court frame the special verdict on the theory of sec. 90 of Restatement, 1 Contracts, but no other possible theory has been presented to or discovered by this court which would permit plaintiffs to recover. Of other remedies considered that of an action for fraud and deceit seemed to be the most comparable. An action at law for fraud, however, cannot be predicated on unfulfilled promises unless the promisor possessed the present intent not to perform. *Suskey v. Davidoff* (1958), 2 Wis.2d 503, 507, and cases cited. Here, there is no evidence that would support a finding that Lukowitz made any of the promises, upon which plaintiffs' complaint is predicated, in bad faith with any present intent that they would not be fulfilled by Red Owl.

Many courts of other jurisdictions have seen fit over the years to adopt the principle of promissory estoppel, and the tendency in that direction continues.

The Restatement avoids use of the term 'promissory estoppel,' and there has been criticism of it as an inaccurate term. See 1A Corbin, Contracts, p. 232, et seq., sec. 204. On the other hand, Williston advocated the use of this term or something equivalent. 1 Williston, Contracts (1st ed.), p. 308, sec. 139. Use of the word 'estoppel' to describe a doctrine upon which a party to a lawsuit may obtain affirmative relief offends the traditional concept that estoppel merely serves as a shield and cannot serve as a sword to create a cause of action. See *Utschig v. McClone* (1962), 16 Wis.2d 506, 509. 'Attractive nuisance' is also a much criticized term. See concurring opinion, *Flamingo v. City of Waukesha* (1952), 262 Wis. 219, 227. However, the latter term is still in almost universal use by the courts because of the lack of the better substitute. The same is also true of the wide use of the term 'promissory estoppel.' We have employed its use in this opinion not only because of its extensive use by other courts but also since a more accurate equivalent has not been devised.

Because we deem the doctrine of promissory estoppel, as stated in sec. 90 of Restatement, 1 Contracts, is one which supplies a needed tool which courts may employ in a proper case to prevent injustice, we endorse and adopt it.

Applicability of Doctrine to Facts of this Case.

The record here discloses a number of promises and assurances given to Hoffman by Lukowitz in behalf of Red Owl upon which plaintiffs relied and acted upon to their detriment.

Foremost were the promises that for the sum of $18,000 Red Owl would establish Hoffman in a store. After Hoffman had sold his grocery store and paid the $1,000 on the Chilton lot, the $18,000 figure was changed to $24,100. Then in November, 1961, Hoffman was assured that if the $24,100 figure were increased by $2,000 the deal would go through. Hoffman was induced to sell his grocery store fixtures and inventory in June, 1961, on the promise that he would be in his new store by fall. In November, plaintiffs sold their bakery building on the urging of defendants and on the assurance that this was the last step necessary to have the deal with Red Owl go through.

We determine that there was ample evidence to sustain the answers of the jury to the questions of the verdict with respect to the promissory representations made by Red Owl, Hoffman's reliance thereon in the exercise of ordinary care, and his fulfillment of the conditions required of him by the terms of the negotiations had with Red Owl.

There remains for consideration the question of law raised by defendants that agreement was never reached on essential factors necessary to establish a contract between Hoffman and Red Owl. Among these were the size, cost, design, and layout of the store building; and the terms of the lease with respect to rent, maintenance, renewal, and purchase options. This poses the question of whether the promise necessary to sustain a cause of action for promissory estoppel must embrace all essential details of a proposed transaction between promisor and promisee so as to be the equivalent of an offer that would result in a binding contract between the parties if the promisee were to accept the same.

Originally the doctrine of promissory estoppel was invoked as a substitute for consideration rendering a gratuitous promise enforceable as a contract. See Williston, Contracts (1st ed.), p. 307, sec. 139. In other words, the acts of reliance by the promisee to his detriment provided a substitute for consideration. If promissory estoppel were to be limited to only those situations where the promise giving rise to the cause of action must be so definite with respect to all details that a contract would result were the promise supported by consideration, then the defendants' instant promises to Hoffman would not meet this test. However, see. 90 of Restatement, 1 Contracts, does not impose the requirement that the promise giving rise to the cause of action must be so comprehensive in scope as to meet the requirements of an offer that would ripen into a contract if accepted by the promisee. Rather the conditions imposed are:

(1) Was the promise one which the promisor should reasonably expect to induce action or forbearance of a definite and substantial character on the part of the promisee?

(2) Did the promise induce such action or forbearance?

(3) Can injustice be avoided only by enforcement of the promise?

We deem it would be a mistake to regard an action grounded on promissory estoppel as the equivalent of a breach of contract action. As Dean Boyer points out, it is desirable that fluidity in the application of the concept be maintained. 98 University of Pennsylvania Law Review (1950), 459, at page 497. While the first two of the above listed three requirements of promissory estoppel present issues of fact which ordinarily will be resolved by a jury, the third requirement, that the remedy can only be invoked where necessary to avoid injustice, is one that involves a policy decision by the court. Such a policy decision necessarily embraces an element of discretion.

We conclude that injustice would result here if plaintiffs were not granted some relief because of the failure of defendants to keep their promises which induced plaintiffs to act to their detriment.

Coley v. Lang

Court of Civil Appeals of Alabama, 1976.
339 So.2d 70.

■ HOLMES, JUDGE. This is an appeal from the Circuit Court of Mobile County's action awarding damages to appellee-Lang for breach of agreement. The appellant-Coley appeals.

The record reveals the following: Lang sued Coley for specific performance. Lang's complaint alleged that Coley and Lang had entered into an agreement whereby Coley was to purchase the stock of Lang's corporation. The price was to be $60,000. The specific performance prayed for was the payment of $60,000. The complaint was later amended to include a claim for damages incurred by Lang in reliance on Coley's promise to buy the stock.

After a hearing Ore tenus the trial court entered a judgment for Lang in the amount of $7,500 'due to their (Lang's) reliance upon the representation of the agreement by respondent (Coley) that he would purchase the stock.' As noted earlier, Coley appeals from this judgment.

The issues as presented by appellant for this court's consideration are: (1) Did the 'letter agreement' entered into by the parties contractually bind the parties? (2) Can the award be supported on the basis of promissory estoppel or reliance on a promise?

Viewing the trial court's decree with the attendant presumption of correctness, our review of the testimony as shown by the transcript of the evidence reveals the following:

Coley, in late August of 1972, entered into discussions with Lang concerning the purchase of IAS Corporation. Lang owned the vast majority of the stock of IAS. Coley did not desire to purchase the assets of IAS, but only desired to purchase the name and good will of IAS. Coley's purpose in acquiring the corporation was to enable Coley to be in a favorable position to bid on government contracts.

During the negotiation, the parties contacted an attorney, who represented Coley, and the following document was drafted and signed by each party:

'September 1, 1972

'Mr. Robert J. Lang, President

International Aerospace Services, Inc.

Post Office Box 9516

Charleston, South Carolina 29410

'Dear Bob:

'This letter is to express the agreement which we have reached today.

'Subject to the approval of your Board of Directors and stockholders, you have agreed to sell to nominee to buy, all of the outstanding stock of every kind of International Aerospace Services, Inc. ('IAS'). The purchase price for the stock shall be the sum of Sixty Thousand Dollars ($60,000.00) payable as follows:

'$10,000 on the date of sale;

$8,000 on December 31, 1972;

$21,000 on December 31, 1973,

and $21,000 on December 31, 1974.

'The unpaid portion of the purchase price shall be represented by a promissory note executed by me, or guaranteed by me for execution by my nominee. Principal payments due on the note shall not bear interest to their stated maturity, but any past due payments shall bear interest at the rate of 10% per annum.

'It is our understanding that prior to the sale of the IAS stock to me you will cause IAS to transfer all of its assets and liabilities (other than its corporate name and the right to use that corporate name in foreign jurisdictions, and its corporate franchise) to a new corporation or partnership as you and the other present stockholders of IAS may determine. The new corporation or partnership, herein called IASCO, shall indemnify IAS against all liabilities of IAS which it has assumed. If IASCO fails to perform this indemnity and IAS is required to pay off liabilities assumed by IASCO, then I shall have the right to setoff any such payments against amounts due on the note representing the purchase price of the IAS stock. IAS will, of course, be responsible for any liabilities which it creates or incurs after you sell the stock to me. All work and contracts in progress of IAS shall be transferred to IASCO at the same time as the transfer of assets and liabilities.

'I recognize that you must consider the method to complete this transaction to the best advantage of you and the other shareholders of IAS. We agree together that on or before September 18, this letter agreement will be reduced to a definitive agreement binding upon all of the parties hereto and accomplishing the sale and purchase contemplated by this agreement.

'You agree that until we reach a definitive agreement I may request bid sets from the government and attend bidding conferences on behalf of an in the name of IAS.

'If the foregoing correctly reflects our agreement, please execute and return to me the enclosed copy of this letter.

'Yours very truly,

/s/ William H. Coley

'Agreed to and accepted.

/s/ R. L. Lang'

Both parties testified at great length regarding their understanding of the 'letter agreement.' Suffice it to say that Lang testified that the agreement was binding and only certain details remained to be done. Additionally, Lang testified that stockholder approval was obtained and further, that the corporation (Lang) had lost $30,000 as a result of the reliance on the 'letter agreement.' We should note that details of the loss are not spelled out with any degree of specificity.

Coley testified that the letter agreement was only a basic outline of points which had been agreed upon; that there remained many items that had to be worked out; and further, that time was of the essence.

Specifically, Coley testified that Lang had not sought approval of the IRS concerning a pension and profit sharing plan nor had certain details with the government been completed. And that because of this he (Coley) realized that the sale would not work out within the contemplated time frame. Coley, on September 18, 1972, notified Lang of this fact.

We note that Coley did attend certain bid conferences conducted by the U.S. Government and registered with the government as a representative of Lang's corporation. This action occurred after the 'letter agreement' had been executed.

The attorney who drafted the 'letter agreement' testified that he informed both parties that the document in question was not binding. Lang denied that the attorney so informed him.

I

We [agree with the trial court and] do not find as a matter of law that the 'letter agreement' is an agreement upon which specific performance can be based.

II

The [trial] court decreed complainants recover $7,500 as damages suffered 'due to their reliance upon the representation of the agreement by the Respondents.' The record viewed in the most favorable light for Mr. Lang does not support such a decree, irrespective of whether premised on a theory of equitable estoppel or promissory estoppel.

The purpose of the former doctrine is to prevent inconsistency and fraud resulting from injustice. *Fiscus v. Young*, 243 Ala. 39. "It rests at last for its vindication on the manifest idea that to allow such representation to be gainsaid would be fraud on him who had thus acted, believing it to be true." *Cosby v. Moore*, 259 Ala. 41, 47; *Leinkauff v. Munter*, 76 Ala. 194, 198. The record in this case shows no misrepresentation or deliberate conduct designed to consciously and unfairly mislead Mr. Lang. The most that can be said is that Mr. Coley and Mr. Lang conducted negotiations which both parties hoped would eventually result in consummation of a contract. That the negotiations proved unfruitful does not warrant application of equitable estoppel. For cases applying the doctrine see *Dunn v. Fletcher*, 266 Ala. 273; *Birmingham Trust and Savings Co. v. Strong*, 239 Ala. 118, wherein the facts markedly differ from those herein. As stated by the Alabama Supreme Court in *Messer v. City of Birmingham*, 243 Ala. 520, 524, 'A mere breach of Promise cannot constitute an estoppel en pais.' (Emphasis supplied.)

Neither do we deem promissory estoppel applicable. Restatement (First) of Contracts, s 90 (1932) states:

'A promise which the promisor should reasonably expect to induce action or forbearance of a definite and substantial character on the part of the promisee and which does induce such action or forbearance is binding if injustice can be avoided only by enforcement of the promise.' Accord *Bush v. Bush*, 278 Ala. 244, 245.

Assuming the existence of a promise on the part of Mr. Coley to purchase the name and stock of IAS, the record discloses no 'action or forbearance of a definite and substantial character' on the part of Mr. Lang. The total time during which Mr. Lang could have curtailed his profit generating activities due to his reliance on Mr. Coley's promise extended only from September 1, 1972, the date of the signing of the documents by the parties, to September 18, 1972, when the negotiations were terminated. Moreover, Mr. Lang could testify with certainty only that he missed opportunities to bid on two contracts during the period. There was no evidence showing the probability that IAS's bid would have been the lowest in either instance. Furthermore, Mr. Lang attended at least one pre-bid conference during the eighteen-day period; and, presumably, he could have attended others. The circumstances of this case do not constitute the 'substantial' forbearance or action in reliance contemplated by the Restatement.

It follows that the trial court misapplied the law to the facts in this case.

Disposition of other issues is rendered unnecessary by our resolution of this issue.

The case is due to be and is, accordingly, reversed.

* * *

The defendant in *Hoffman* was a prominent Midwestern grocery store chain (the opening sequence of the *Mary Tyler Moore Show* depicted the lead character in the meat department of a Red Owl store), and the plaintiff wanted to acquire and operate a franchise. He contacted the defendant expressing his desire and stating that he possessed roughly $20,000 of capital. Thus began a long, frustrating negotiation that ultimately failed, in which the defendant repeatedly and manipulatively changed its demands of the plaintiff.

The first steps seemed reasonable enough. The plaintiff and the defendant's agent jointly concluded that it would be a good idea for the plaintiff to buy and operate a smaller grocer, in order to obtain experience in the business. The plaintiff did so, and the defendant inspected the store and found it profitable. The defendant then advised the plaintiff to sell the smaller store just before the start of the lucrative summer season, saying that this was required if the plaintiff was to obtain a Red Owl franchise, and that if the plaintiff sold, he would have a Red Owl store by fall. After seeking and receiving assurances that his capital was sufficient for obtaining a franchise, the plaintiff reluctantly did sell. The plaintiff then commenced a series of concrete acts in reliance on receiving the store: making payments towards acquiring a store site, selling an existing bakery that had been his primary business, and moving his family. The defendant, however, repeatedly raised its capital requirements, until they came nearly to double the amounts initially discussed. The defendant further insisted that some of the additional capital, which was to come from the plaintiff's family members, be styled as a gift to the plaintiff, rather than as a loan. The plaintiff refused to provide capital in these quantities and on these terms, which ended negotiations between the parties. The plaintiff then sued.

There was no question that the negotiations had never concluded in the formation of a contract by the orthodox route of offer and acceptance: the parties had never reached agreement on the key terms of the contract towards which they were aiming. The crucial question in the case—both at trial and on appeal to the Supreme Court of Wisconsin—therefore concerned whether the defendant might be liable in contract nevertheless, on a theory of promissory estoppel. Certainly the defendant had, in a general way, promised the plaintiff a store if he did certain acts. The plaintiff, moreover did these acts in reliance on the promise, and his reliance was both reasonable (in the sense of being consistent with ordinary care in the face of the defendant's assurances) and of a definite and substantial character.[52] *Hoffman*, however, raised a further question about the context

---

52. *Hoffman* was adjudicated under the version of § 90 that appeared in the Restatement (First) of Contracts, which expressly required that in order to ground a claim for

of liability for promissory estoppel. Although the defendant had promised the plaintiff a franchise in general terms, it had remained vague about details. Certainly, the defendant's representations had never become complete or precise enough to fix all the particulars required to establish a contract by orthodox means: They had never reached the point at which they might constitute an *offer*, which the plaintiff might have converted into a completed contract simply by accepting. *Hoffman* thus concerns the next step on the slope away from contract that these materials have been considering. *Drennan's* departure from *Gimbel Bros.* signaled that courts might apply promissory estoppel even in the absence of a primary promise, to an offer only (although Traynor did insist on implying a secondary promise, and so cast *Drennan's* innovation in relatively modest terms). *Hoffman* raises the question whether promissory estoppel might be applied even without an offer. Might reasonable reliance on some other representation—say an invitation to bargain or the representations concerning current intentions or future prospects that such an invitation contains—be sufficient to sustain contract liability under § 90?

The *Hoffman* court appears to suggest that something less than an offer might suffice. The opinion expressly rejects a standard that would limit promissory estoppel to representations whose character is sufficiently definite and complete that they might, if subject to offer and acceptance, establish a contract by the orthodox route. (Note that the representation in *Drennan* was definite and complete in just this way.) In place of this rule, *Hoffman* announces a weaker requirement: that the representation be such that its maker should reasonably expect definite and substantial reliance from its recipient;[53] that the recipient does so rely; and that injustice may be avoided only by promissory enforcement of the representation. The representations in *Hoffman*, the court concluded, pass this test, and they thus sustained the plaintiff's § 90 reliance claim. The remedy for such a claim might but need not be full contractual expectation, depending on what is necessary to avoid injustice. In *Hoffman* itself, the appropriate remedy was modest.

Read naïvely, *Hoffman* is a radical—indeed a transformative—opinion. It seems to announce a form of legal liability for negligent misrepresentation that abandons the limits on such liability generally established by conventional tort law and that accepts, at least in principle, that the liability might take a contractual form. *Hoffman* seems to announce a general cause of action for what was earlier called *promissory negligence*, freed from the constraints that conventional tort law imposes on negligent misrepresentation. In particular, *Hoffman* casts the cause of action in a way that, at least where justice requires, will vindicate promissory expectations and not just lost reliance; and *Hoffman* abandons the conventional requirement that a defendant must have some antecedent duty of care with

---

promissory estoppel, a plaintiff's reliance must be of a "definite and substantial character." This language was dropped from the Restatement (Second).

53. The *Hoffman* court went so far as to suggest that even a third party (one to whom a representation is not addressed) might have a § 90 style claim if the maker of a representation actually or reasonably foresees reliance by that third party and justice requires enforcement.

respect to the interests that her misrepresentations invade. Liability under *Hoffman* thus appears to arise directly and free-standingly out of negligence in making representations; and it appears to extend to vindicating contractual interests in the truth of the representations. *Hoffman*, that is, appears to create a set of contract-like rights built solely on tort-like foundations and thus to abandon contract's structural commitment to promissory, which is to say chosen, obligation. This, to return once again to Gilmore's formulation, would truly be anti-contract.

This may not be the best way to read *Hoffman*, however. The facts of the case fell into a dramatic and quite particular pattern. The defendant could not just reasonably anticipate reliance on its representations, nor did it even just invite reliance. Rather, the defendant required reliance; at several points, it effectively (and in some cases expressly) made the plaintiff's reliance into a condition for moving forward in the negotiations towards completing a contract. Moreover, the required reliance inured substantially to the benefit of the defendant: the reliance gave the defendant valuable information about the plaintiff's attractiveness as a franchisee (information that was generated at the plaintiff's expense); and it weakened the plaintiff's bargaining position going forward (by eliminating alternatives to an eventual deal with the defendant and thus worsening the plaintiff's fallback position or disagreement point). Although the court observed that there was no evidence of fraud, one suspects that better lawyering might have produced some, or at least sustained a complaint for promissory fraud. And this suspicion gives rise to a very different reading of the opinion. Perhaps *Hoffman* is best understood not as establishing an alternative path to contract at all, but rather an alternative path to fraud, in tort. Other promissory estoppel cases, including even *Drennan*, may be understood as correctives that recognize contracts where the core elements of the orthodox promissory model all obtain, but purely technical defects prevent the model from applying. Similarly, *Hoffman* may be understood as a corrective that recognizes fraud where the core elements of the orthodox tort all obtain, but a purely technical defect prevents the tort from applying. On this reading, *Hoffman* poses no threat to the promissory foundations of contract at all.

There is good reason to read *Hoffman* in just this conservative fashion. Certainly the law generally has declined to follow the approach taken under the naïve and radical reading of *Hoffman*. *Coley* is in fact much more representative of the general state of play. There, the plaintiff and defendant entered into a letter agreement under which the defendant was to buy the stock of the plaintiff's corporation for a set sum. The letter expressly set a later date at which the parties would reduce their preliminary agreement to a definitive, binding contract. The defendant pulled out of the sale before that contract was established, and the plaintiff sued, seeking specific performance of the letter agreement and alleging a $30,000 loss in reliance on that agreement. Although the trial court awarded the plaintiff modest reliance damages, the appellate court reversed, refusing to apply either equitable or promissory estoppel against the defendant. The court offered distinct reasons for rejecting the plaintiff's claims under each doctrine. There could be no equitable estoppel, it said, because there was no evidence that the defendant sought consciously or unfairly to mislead the plaintiff, or indeed that it made any misrepresentation at all. There could be no promissory estoppel because *Coley* was adjudicated under the Restatement (First), whose version of promissory estoppel required "definite and substantial" reliance, which the plaintiff's equivocal testimony of failed opportunities, unbacked by evidence that they would have been consummated but for the defendant's promise, could not establish.

One suspects that the considerations concerning the *Coley* court's rejection of equitable estoppel also affected its attitude with respect to promissory estoppel (so that the change in language between the First and Second Restatements would not have altered the outcome of the case). Just as the *Hoffman* court reasoned as it did because it believed that it confronted a tortuously bad actor, so the *Coley* court reasoned as it did because it believed that it confronted an innocent mind-changer.

These suspicions involve a sociological sense for the fact patterns in the cases and a psychological sense for the sensibilities of the judges involved, to be sure. But they also have a structural element, which goes to the heart of the current inquiry into the relations between contract and tort. Even in *Hoffman*, even under the most naïve reading of the opinion, non-promissory representations can generate contractual obligations only insofar recognizing such obligations is required to avoid injustice. This makes it inevitable to ask just what the injustice wrought by the relevant representations might consist in. On the one hand, if the representations are promissory in substance—which is to say directly engender new entitlements in the manner of promises—in spite of being non-promissory in form, then the injustice might be identified by reference to the principles of promissory morality. In such circumstances, promissory estoppel serves as a cure for the defects associated with the formal technicalities through which contract law implements fundamentally promissory moral ideals. These are the circumstances associated with the modest § 90 cases, such as *Ricketts* and even *Drennan*. On the other hand, if the representations function as tools to invade previously and independently established entitlements, then the injustice might be identified by reference to the principles associated with the morality of harm. In such circumstances, promissory estoppel serves to cure defects associated with the technical rules through which tort doctrine elaborates the morality of harm. These are the circumstances associated with *Hoffman*, now read non-naïvely as proposing that § 90 might in some circumstances play a role similar to the law of fraud. Similar principles inform *Coley* also, which is different from *Hoffman* not so much on the law as on its facts.

On this structural argument there is no space in between contract and tort for § 90 to occupy. Either promissory estoppel is, at base, a form of promissory obligation and hence properly contractual (whatever the technicalities); or it is fundamentally harm-based, in which case the principles of equitable estoppel must inform and infect it. This appears to be how § 90 has been applied in the years following *Hoffman*, which is rarely followed, so that its rule is effectively narrowed to its facts. A recent substantial survey of appellate opinions concludes that where negotiating parties do not reach an agreement or make promises—where the gap between negotiations and a completed contract involves more than mere technicalities—"the case data thus show that, absent misrepresentation or deceit, there generally is no liability for inducing reliance investments during the negotiation process."[54]

One might say, then that contract and tort remain distinct because they must be distinct, if the law is to remain conceptually coherent.

---

54. Alan Schwartz and Robert Scott, *Precontractual Liability and Preliminary Agreements*, 120 HARV. L. REV. 661, 672 (2007).

CHAPTER 17

FIXING CONTRACTUAL MEANING

In between the formation of a contract and its performance (or judicial enforcement, through one or another remedy) lies the project of fixing the content of the obligations that the contract establishes. At the most abstract level, this is not a difficult or substantial task: if contracts are chosen obligations, the creatures directly of the intentions of the contracting parties, then the contents of these obligations should also be fixed according to the parties' intentions. But the concrete task of divining the parties' intentions is much more difficult.

Contract's abstract character as chosen obligation entails that fixing contractual meaning is a hermeneutic task—that is, one that looks to extract meaning from the contractual text that the parties create. It further entails that the interpretive methods to be employed should be in some broad sense intentionalist—that is, that interpreters should aim to recapture the plans of the contracting parties rather than, say, of third parties, or indeed the interpreters' own sense for what would be to the contracting parties' advantage. These general sensibilities leave many details open, however, and many general methodological decisions must be made in order to specify a practically implementable technique for fixing contractual meaning. These decisions have been, and to a certain degree remain, controversial. The materials below set out some of the ways in which they have been made. In keeping with the general themes of this Part of the text, they emphasize a historical shift across two different styles for fixing contractual meaning: a formalist style that dominated classical contract law, and a more functionalist style that came of age in the second half of the prior century. The functionalist approach to contractual meaning will prove subtle, however, so that some functionalists have recently gravitated back to certain of the doctrines historically associated with formalism, although of course for their own, entirely forward-looking reasons.

The hermeneutic character of the problem of fixing contractual meaning entails that the meaning-fixing project consists of two interconnected but nevertheless distinct tasks: contract *construction* and contract *interpretation*.

Contract construction is the task of identifying the contractual text through which the parties express and memorialize their contractual intent in the world—the text in which acceptance meets offer. This requires determining which writings, oral utterances, images, samples, etc. belong to the contractual text and which do not. Construction is not as simple or easy as it may seem to be. To be sure, some materials—a signed writing that purports to be the contract—are easily included in a contract's text. And

other materials—a single party's entirely private and internal notes, perhaps even on a subject matter unrelated to the contract—are easily excluded. But there also exists a substantial and treacherous middle ground. As
the materials below display, contracting parties typically write, say, depict,
and display many things, on their way to a contract, that they do not finally
intend to become part of the agreement that the end up striking. Indeed,
the parties' success at reaching an eventual agreement may turn, in part,
on their capacity to produce expressions of their thoughts and intentions
that do not end up in that agreement's text. So the problem of construction
is much more fine-grained, and consequently much more difficult, than
merely distinguishing between things that are related to the ultimate
contract and things that are not.

Contract interpretation begins from the constructed contractual text
and seeks to extract meaning from it. Interpretation is difficult partly for
familiar reasons relating to the inevitable imperfectness with which language reflects the ideas of its users, and in particular, the vaguenesses and
ambiguities that infect every text. A further difficulty, which especially
plagues contract interpretation, concerns the fact that contracting parties
often belong to linguistic sub-communities that are separate and distinct
from the broader linguistic community and from the linguistic sub-communities of the courts called on to interpret contracts. Commercial usage—
including of ordinarily recognizable terms such as weight, quantity, or
quality—often departs from ordinary usage, and usage in one trade may
depart from usage in others. Finally, contract interpretation may be rendered more difficult still by the fact that some of the parties' utterances,
made in the precincts of their contract, might inform the meaning of the
contractual text even if they do not themselves belong to it. Materials
excluded in contract construction may thus become relevant again for
contract interpretation.

Although contract construction and contract interpretation are clearly
distinct enterprises, they are also interconnected. It may seem that construction comes before interpretation, as the boundaries of a text must be
fixed before its meaning may be divined. But contractual texts often include
descriptions of their own boundaries, and thus instructions that aim to
guide contract construction. These instructions must themselves be interpreted, so that one cannot do contract construction without first doing
some contract interpretation. Of course, before one can interpret the parts
of the contractual text that control construction, one must identify them as
belonging to the text. This involves construction, which thus becomes again
prior to interpretation. The nesting may be continued ad infinitum. Still,
an account of fixing contractual meaning must begin somewhere. And the
one in these pages will begin with construction and then take up interpretation.

The materials below fill in this outline in greater doctrinal and
conceptual detail. As occurred in other chapters in this Part, they will
document shifting doctrinal styles concerning contract construction and
interpretation, as a highly formalist classical regime is displaced by more

functionalist approaches. The materials on construction and interpretation illustrate another point about doctrinal styles also—and indeed illustrate it especially well. This is the interaction among doctrines from different areas of contract law in respect of their styles. Formalist doctrine concerning contract formation will be necessarily paired with certain doctrines concerning construction and, especially, interpretation. Without this pairing, contract law will quite literally fall apart. This pattern is worth paying close attention to. Once again, the focus of Part II of these materials is not only and perhaps not even primarily to ask which style of doctrine is best. Rather, it is to understand how the different styles of doctrine work internally, and across doctrinal sub-headings.

17.1   CONTRACT CONSTRUCTION

Call a thing that conveys meaning a *text*. To understand a text's meaning, one must first establish its boundaries. This is not always easy: does the text of the Christian Bible include the Apocrypha? In spite of the name, this question generated a millennium-long, and to some degree ongoing, dispute. Establishing the boundaries of contractual texts is also difficult. Often, these boundaries are contested; contracting partners typically do and say many things on the way to their agreements, and it can matter intensely to them which of these things becomes incorporated into the agreements, as a part of their contractual texts. Fixing the boundaries of contractual texts determines the outcomes of many contract disputes. The process of identifying the boundaries of a contractual text is called contract *construction*.

Construction is difficult because there may be many sources of a contract's text. The most prominent source of a contractual text is the negotiation that led up to the contract. In many but not all instances, this negotiation will conclude by producing a writing, which memorializes the contractual agreement, in whole or in part.[1] The negotiation may also produce prior or contemporaneous oral agreements, which may or may not become part of the contract. Sometimes, including these oral agreements would add to or even vary the writing. In addition, a contract may draw on sources from outside the immediate negotiation between the parties. These include usage of trade in the industry to which the contract parties belong, prior dealings between the parties in connection with other contracts, and even the course of the parties' contractual performance.

These potential sources, because they may sometimes provide conflicting contract terms, must be marshaled to produce a single, more-or-less coherent, contractual text. The problem of combining writings with prior or contemporaneous oral agreements is especially pressing, because negotiations commonly include many way-stations towards a writing. Any effort to

---

1.   The writing may include, sometimes even explicitly by reference, non-verbal sources of text—for example, samples that provide sources for warranties in the spirit of the previous chapter.

construct the final agreement must decide what the relative role of these potential sources of contractual text should be.

Contract law provides guidance in the project of contract construction, most prominently through a doctrine called the *parol evidence rule*. The parol evidence rule addresses the balance between writings and prior or contemporaneous oral agreements as sources of contractual text. It expresses a preference for written contract text over other kinds, although (as the materials below illustrate) the strength and scope of that preference has long been and remains uncertain and contested. The parties themselves, through their negotiations and in the contracts that they make, might also seek to guide and control contract construction, principally by stating explicitly what are the boundaries of their contractual texts.

Contract construction is thus governed principally by two sets of rules. First, there are the default rules provided by the law. When the parties are silent concerning the boundaries of the contractual text, what is in the text and what is out? The core of these doctrines, once again, is the parol evidence rule. And second, the parties might themselves make choices concerning contract construction, for example by inserting *merger clauses* into their written contracts, which assert that the writings represent the entire agreement between them and thus to exclude other materials from the contractual text. These two rules interact with each other, insofar as the parol evidence rule functions as a sticky default, which reasserts itself in the face of half-hearted, unclear, or incomplete party commands concerning construction, and hence is difficult for the parties to vary. Nevertheless, it will be helpful to take up each doctrine in turn, noting the interactions as they come up.

17.1.A   THE PAROL EVIDENCE RULE

Begin by taking up the classical, or hard, parol evidence rule. This rule articulated a broad and insistent preference for writings over other sources of contractual text, and in particular over text rooted in oral agreements made prior to or contemporaneous with the writings.

Mitchell v. Lath

Court of Appeals of New York, 1928.
160 N.E. 646.

■ ANDREWS, J. In the fall of 1923 the Laths owned a farm. This they wished to sell. Across the road, on land belonging to Lieutenant Governor Lunn, they had an icehouse which they might remove. Mrs. Mitchill looked over the land with a view to its purchase. She found the icehouse objectionable. Thereupon 'the defendants orally promised and agreed, for and in consideration of the purchase of their farm by the plaintiff, to remove the said icehouse in the spring of 1924.' Relying upon this promise, she made a written contract to buy the property for $8,400, for cash and mortgage and containing various provisions usual in such papers. Later receiving a deed, she entered into possession, and has spent considerable sums in improving the property for use as a summer residence. The defendants have not fulfilled their promise as to the icehouse, and do not intend to do so. We are not dealing, however, with their moral delinquencies. The question before us is whether their oral agreement may be enforced in a court of equity.

This requires a discussion of the parol evidence rule—a rule of law which defines the limits of the contract to be construed. *Glackin v. Bennett*, 115 N. E. 490. It is more than a rule of evidence, and oral testimony, even if admitted, will not control the written contract, unless admitted without objection. It applies, however, to attempts to modify such a contract by parol. It does not affect a parol collateral contract distinct from and independent of the written agreement. It is, at times, troublesome to draw the line. Williston, in his work on Contracts (section 637) points out the difficulty. 'Two entirely distinct contracts,' he says, 'each for a separate consideration, may be made at the same time, and will be distinct legally. Where, however, one agreement is entered into wholly or partly in consideration of the simultaneous agreement to enter into another, the transactions are necessarily bound together. Then if one of the agreements is oral and the other in writing, the problem arises whether the bond is sufficiently close to prevent proof of the oral agreement.' That is the situation here. It is claimed that the defendants are called upon to do more than is required by their written contract in connection with the sale as to which it deals.

The principal may be clear, but it can be given effect by no mechanical rule. As so often happens it is a matter of degree, for, as Prof. Williston also says, where a contract contains several promises on each side it is not difficult to put any one of them in the form of a collateral agreement. If this were enough, written contracts might always be modified by parol. Not from, but substance, is the test.

In applying this test, the policy of our courts is to be considered. We have believed that the purpose behind the rule was a wise one, not easily to be abandoned. Notwithstanding injustice here and there, on the whole it works for good. Old precedents and principles are not to be lightly cast aside, unless it is certain that they are an obstruction under present conditions. New York has been less open to arguments that would modify this particular rule, than some jurisdictions elsewhere. Thus in *Eighmie v. Taylor*, 98 N. Y. 288, it was held that a parol warranty might not be shown, although no warranties were contained in the writing.

Under our decisions before such an oral agreement as the present is received to vary the written contract, at least three conditions must exist: (1) The agreement must in form be a collateral one; (2) it must not contradict express or implied provisions of the written contract; (3) it must be one that parties would not ordinarily be expected to embody in the writing, or, put in another way, an inspection of the written contract, read in the light of surrounding circumstances, must not indicate that the writing appears 'to contain the engagements of the parties, and to define the object and measure the extent of such engagement.' Or, again, it must not be so clearly connected with the principal transaction as to be part and parcel of it.

The respondent does not satisfy the third of these requirements. It may be, not the second. We have a written contract for the purchase and sale of land. The buyer is to pay $8,400 in the way described. She is also to pay her portion of any rents, interest on mortgages, insurance premiums, and water meter charges. She may have a survey made of the premises. On their part, the sellers are to give a full covenant deed of the premises as described, or as they may be described by the surveyor, if the survey is had, executed, and acknowledged at their own expense; they sell the personal property on the farm and represent they own it; they agree that all amounts paid them on the contract and the expense of examining the title shall be a lien on the property; they assume the risk of loss or damage by fire until the deed is delivered; and they agree to pay the broker his commissions. Are they to do more? Or is such a claim inconsistent with these precise provisions? It could not be shown that the plaintiff was to pay $500 additional. Is it also implied that the defendants are not to do anything unexpressed in the writing?

That we need not decide. At least, however, an inspection of this contract shows a full and complete agreement, setting forth in detail the obligations of each party. On reading it, one would conclude that the reciprocal obligations of the parties were fully detailed. Nor would his opinion alter if he knew the surrounding circumstances. The presence of the icehouse, even the knowledge that Mrs. Mitchell thought it objectionable, would not lead to the belief that a separate agreement existed with regard to it. Were such an agreement made it would seem most natural that the inquirer should find it in the contract. Collateral in form it is found to be, but it is closely related to the subject dealt with in the written agreement—so closely that we hold it may not be proved.

Where the line between the competent and the incompetent is narrow the citation of authorities is of slight use. Each represents the judgment of the court on the precise facts before it. How closely bound to the contract is the supposed collateral agreement is the decisive factor in each case.

It is argued that what we have said is not applicable to the case as presented. The collateral agreement was made with the plaintiff. The contract of sale was with her husband, and no assignment of it from him appears. Yet the deed was given to her. It is evident that here was a transaction in which she was the principal from beginning to end. We must treat the contract as if in form, as it was in fact, made by her.

Our conclusion is that the judgment of the Appellate Division and that of the Special Term should be reversed and the complaint dismissed, with costs in all courts.

■ LEHMAN, J., dissenting. I accept the general rule as formulated by Judge ANDREWS. I differ with him only as to its application to the facts shown in the record. The plaintiff contracted to purchase land from the defendants for an agreed price. A formal written agreement was made between the sellers and the plaintiff's husband. It is on its face a complete contract for the conveyance of the land. It describes the property to be conveyed. It sets forth the purchase price to be paid. All the conditions and terms of the conveyance to be made are clearly stated. I concede at the outset that parol evidence to show additional conditions and terms of the conveyance would be inadmissible. There is a conclusive presumption that the parties intended to integrate in that written contract every agreement relating to the nature or extent of the property to be conveyed, the contents of the deed to be delivered, the consideration to be paid as a condition precedent to the delivery of the deeds, and indeed all the rights of the parties in connection with the land. The conveyance of that land was the subject-matter of the written contract, and the contract completely covers that subject.

The parol agreement which the court below found the parties had made was collateral to, yet connected with, the agreement of purchase and sale. It has been found that the defendants induced the plaintiff to agree to purchase the land by a promise to remove an icehouse from land not covered by the agreement of purchase and sale. No independent consideration passed to the defendants for the parol promise. To that extent the written contract and the alleged oral contract are bound together. The same bond usually exists wherever attempt is made to prove a parol agreement which is collateral to a written agreement. Hence 'the problem arises whether the bond is sufficiently close to prevent proof of the oral agreement.' See Judge ANDREWS citation from Williston on Contracts, § 637.

Judge Andrews has formulated a standard to measure the closeness of the bond. Three conditions, at least, must exist before an oral agreement may be proven to increase the obligation imposed by the written agreement. I think we agree that the first condition that the agreement 'must in form be a collateral one' is met by the evidence. I concede that this condition is met in most cases where the courts have nevertheless excluded evidence of the collateral oral agreement. The difficulty here, as in most cases, arises in connection with the two other conditions.

The second condition is that the 'parol agreement must not contradict express or implied provisions of the written contract.' Judge Andrews voices doubt whether this condition is satisfied. The written contract has been carried out. The purchase price has been paid; conveyance has been made; title has passed in accordance with the terms of the written contract. The mutual obligations expressed in the written contract are left unchanged by the alleged oral contract. When performance was required of the written contract, the obligations of the parties were measured solely by its terms. By the oral agreement the plaintiff seeks to hold the defendants to other obligations to be performed by them thereafter upon land which was not conveyed to the plaintiff. The assertion of such further obligation is not inconsistent with the written contract, unless the written contract contains a provision, express or implied, that the defendants are not to do anything not expressed in the writing. Concededly there is no such express provision in the contract, and such a provision may be implied, if at all, only if the asserted additional obligation is 'so clearly connected with the principal transaction as to be part and parcel of it,' and is not 'one that the parties would not ordinarily be expected to embody in the writing.' The hypothesis so formulated for a conclusion that the asserted additional obligation is inconsistent with an implied term of the contract is that the alleged oral agreement does not comply with the third condition as formulated by Judge ANDREWS. In this case, therefore, the problem reduces itself to the one question whether or not the oral agreement meets the third condition.

I have conceded that upon inspection the contract is complete. 'It appears to contain the engagements of the parties, and to define the object and measure the extent of such engagement;' it constitutes the contract between them, and is presumed to contain the whole of that contract. *Eighmie v. Taylor*, 98 N. Y. 288. That engagement was on the one side to convey land; on the other to pay the price. The plaintiff asserts further agreement based on the same consideration to be performed by the defendants after the conveyance was complete, and directly affecting only other land. It is true, as Judge ANDREWS points out, that 'the presence of the icehouse, even the knowledge that Mrs. Mitchill though it objectionable, would not lead to the belief that a separate agreement existed with regard to it'; but the question we must decide is whether or not, *assuming* an agreement was made for the removal of an unsightly icehouse from one parcel of land as an inducement for the purchase of another parcel, the parties would ordinarily or naturally be expected to embody the agreement for the removal of the icehouse from one parcel in the written agreement to convey the other parcel. Exclusion of proof of the oral agreement on the ground that it varies the contract embodied in the writing may be based only upon a finding or presumption that the written contract was intended to cover the oral negotiations for the removal of the icehouse which lead up to the contract of purchase and sale. To determine what the writing was intended to cover, 'the document alone will not suffice. What it was intended to cover cannot be known till we know what there was to cover. The question being whether certain subjects of negotiation were intended to be covered, we must compare the writing and the negotiations before we can determine whether they were in fact covered.' Wigmore on Evidence (2d Ed.) § 2430.

The subject-matter of the written contract was the conveyance of land. The contract was so complete on its face that the conclusion is inevitable that the parties intended to embody in the writing all the negotiations covering at least the conveyance. The promise by the defendants to remove the icehouse from other land was not connected with their obligation to convey except that one agreement would not have been made unless the other was also made. The plaintiff's assertion of a parol agreement by the defendants to remove the icehouse was completely established by the great weight of evidence. It must prevail unless that agreement was part of the agreement to convey and the entire agreement was embodied in the writing.

The fact that in this case the parol agreement is established by the overwhelming weight of evidence is, of course, not a factor which may be considered in determining the competency or legal effect of the evidence. Hardship in the particular case would not justify the court in disregarding or emasculating the general rule. It merely accentuates the outlines of our problem. The assumption that the parol agreement was made is no longer obscured by any doubts. The problem, then, is clearly whether the parties are presumed to have intended to render that parol agreement legally ineffective and nonexistent by failure to embody it in the writing. Though we are driven to say that nothing in the written contract which fixed the terms and conditions of the stipulated conveyance suggests the existence of any further parol agreement, an inspection of the contract, though it is complete on its face in regard to the subject of the conveyance, does not, I think, show that it was intended to embody negotiations or agreements, if any, in regard to a matter so loosely bound to the conveyance as the removal of an icehouse from land not conveyed.

The rule of integration undoubtedly frequently prevents the assertion of fraudulent claims. Parties who take the precaution of embodying their oral agreements in a writing should be protected against the assertion that other terms of the same agreement were not integrated in the writing. The limits of the integration are determined by the writing, read in the light of the surrounding circumstances. A written contract, however complete, yet covers only a limited field. I do not think that in the written contract for the conveyance of land here under consideration we can find an intention to cover a field so broad as to include prior agreements, if any such were made, to do other acts on other property after the stipulated conveyance was made.

In each case where such a problem is presented, varying factors enter into its solution. Citation of authority in this or other jurisdictions is useless, at least without minute analysis of the facts. The analysis I have made of the decisions in this state leads me to the view that the decision of the courts below is in accordance with our own authorities and should be affirmed.

* * *

The plaintiff in *Mitchell* had bought a farm from the defendant. The purchase was completed by means of a written contract. In connection with the arrangement, the seller orally agreed to remove an ice-house across the way from the farm, in order to improve the view from the farmhouse. The written contract, however, made no mention of the icehouse or the oral promise. After the buyer took title to the farm pursuant to the written contract, the seller refused to remove the ice house. The buyer then sued to enforce the oral promise.

The *Mitchell* court adopts a two-stage approach to contract construction, which prefers writings at each stage.

First, the court commences construction by employing the *four corners test*: according to this approach, a writing, where one exists, provides the exclusive or at least dominant guidance to the sources of contractual text. So to determine whether a writing excludes other sources of contractual text—whether, as the law says, the writing is *integrated*—one should look not to other potential sources of text (for example, to prior or contemporaneous oral agreements), but rather to the writing itself. Where a writing appears complete on its face, the question whether or not the writing represents the entire agreement between the parties is to be answered by looking to the writing. Instructions concerning construction from outside the writing—for example, oral remarks at signing that the writing is partial only—are to be ignored.

The doctrine that a facially complete writing provides the dominant (and perhaps even exclusive) source of instruction concerning contract construction does not settle how construction should go, however, as it remains to interpret the writing's instructions concerning sources of contractual text. In principle, the doctrine that writings control construction might be compatible with practices of construction that readily allow prior or contemporaneous oral agreements into the contractual text: interpretive rules might instruct courts to interpret writings to be open to parol agreements.

The second stage of *Mitchell's* analysis rejects this possibility and adopts its polar opposite. *Mitchell* thus expands the preference for writings in contract construction to include not just the source of instruction concerning construction but also the source of contractual text itself. The majority and dissent in *Mitchell* agree that where a writing exists, a prior or contemporaneous oral agreement might be included in the contractual text only if three conditions are met: the oral agreement must be collateral in form; it may not contradict the express or implied terms of the writing; and it must be an agreement that the parties would not ordinarily expect to put into the writing. These conditions are sometimes referred to as the *collateral agreement* and *natural omission* doctrines. The majority concluded that the oral agreement to remove the ice house clearly violated the third of these requirements: that one *would* expect further burdens on the seller, clearly related to the sale of the property, to be included in the written sales contract. The oral agreement was thus neither collateral to the writing nor a natural omission, and it was therefore excluded from the contractual text.[2]

This analysis focuses on the first and third prongs of the doctrine set out in *Mitchell* and ignores the second—the principle that parol agreements will be excluded from the contractual text if they contradict the express or implied terms of a writing. This rule is commonly expressed by saying that

---

2. The dissenter agreed with the majority's statement of the law but would have applied the doctrine differently to the facts at hand. He believed that it was natural to omit the agreement to remove the ice-house from the writing, because it was not connected to the seller's legal obligation to convey title to the farm. Indeed, land conveyances are commonly performed by pre-printed form contracts, which do not necessarily contain space for memorializing such collateral agreements in writing. Finally, the seller did not even own the land on which the ice-house stood, further increasing the naturalness of excluding agreements in respect of it from a writing that created obligations to transfer title to land.

parol agreements may add to but may not vary a writing. But the line between adding to and varying is not always so clear. In particular, where that line falls turns on how writings are interpreted. This is vividly revealed by a stray remark that the *Mitchell* majority makes concerning the second prong of its test (a remark not required to decide the case because of the application of the test's third prong). The majority opinion observes that the oral agreement to remove the ice house did not merely add to but varied the writing. The oral agreement imposed an additional burden on the seller, and, the majority argued, the written contract might be interpreted to imply that it rehearsed the only burdens on the seller contemplated by the contract. In this way, the *Mitchell* majority would imply into every writing a *merger* clause, which says that "no other obligations between the parties with respect to this writing's subject matter exist." Under this approach, every addition to a writing is in fact a variance from it (as it departs from the writing's implied term that no additions exist). The collateral agreement and natural omission doctrines (which must, under this approach, be narrowly construed) fix the outer bounds of the implied merger clause: these doctrines merely acknowledge that parol agreements might become binding between the parties to a written agreement where the oral agreements concern a subject matter so far removed from the writing that their existence does not contradict the implied merger clause's denials.[3]

This interpretive approach to contracts—the idea a writing that appears complete on its face contains an implied merger clause and thus is presumed to be exclusive source of contractual text—is the most powerful and general doctrinal proposition in *Mitchell*. It reveals the strength of the classical or hard parol evidence rule's preference for writings in contract construction. Indeed, the rest of *Mitchell's* argument—concerning the collateral agreement and natural omissions doctrines—is really just a sideshow to this main event. But *Mitchell's* is not the only possible interpretive presumption concerning writings' commands with respect to contract construction. The dissenter in *Mitchell* begins to articulate an alternative approach, observing that the writing there did not claim to provide the exclusive source of obligations between the seller and buyer. As soon as this is conceded, and the general interpretive habit of implying strict merger clauses to silent writings is abandoned, parol agreements that provide additional terms no longer automatically vary writings. That opens up space for admitting the additional terms into the contractual text. And indeed, developments since *Mitchell* have taking this possibility to heart, substantially reducing the law's preference for sourcing contractual text in writings rather than parol agreements.

---

3. Note that the collateral agreement and natural omissions doctrines are almost literally the minimal concession that the legal preference for writings might make to prior or contemporaneous oral agreements. If these doctrines did not exist in any form, then parties who entered into a written contract with respect to some subject matter would be prevented, by the parol evidence rule, from having any prior or contemporaneous oral contracts with respect to any other subject.

Masterson v. Sine

Supreme Court of California, In Bank, 1968.
436 P.2d 561.

■ TRAYNOR, CHIEF JUSTICE. Dallas Masterson and his wife Rebecca owned a ranch as tenants in common. On February 25, 1958, they conveyed it to Medora and Lu Sine by a grant deed 'Reserving unto the Grantors herein an option to purchase the above described property on or before February 25, 1968' for the 'same consideration as being paid heretofore plus their depreciation value of any improvements Grantees may add to the property from and after two and a half years from this date.' Medora is Dallas' sister and Lu's wife. Since the conveyance Dallas has been adjudged bankrupt. His trustee in bankruptcy and Rebecca brought this declaratory relief action to establish their right to enforce the option.

The case was tried without a jury. Over defendants' objection the trial court admitted extrinsic evidence that by 'the same consideration as being paid heretofore' both the grantors and the grantees meant the sum of $50,000 and by 'depreciation value of any improvements' they meant the depreciation value of improvements to be computed by deducting from the total amount of any capital expenditures made by defendants grantees the amount of depreciation allowable to them under United States income tax regulations as of the time of the exercise of the option.

The court also determined that the parol evidence rule precluded admission of extrinsic evidence offered by defendants to show that the parties wanted the property kept in the Masterson family and that the option was therefore personal to the grantors and could not be exercised by the trustee in bankruptcy.

The court entered judgment for plaintiffs, declaring their right to exercise the option, specifying in some detail how it could be exercised, and reserving jurisdiction to supervise the manner of its exercise and to determine the amount that plaintiffs will be required to pay defendants for their capital expenditures if plaintiffs decide to exercise the option.

Defendants appeal.

When the parties to a written contract have agreed to it as an 'integration'—a complete and final embodiment of the terms of an agreement—parol evidence cannot be used to add to or vary its terms. When only part of the agreement is integrated, the same rule applies to that part, but parol evidence may be used to prove elements of the agreement not reduced to writing.

The crucial issue in determining whether there has been an integration is whether the parties intended their writing to serve as the exclusive embodiment of their agreement. The instrument itself may help to resolve that issue. It may state, for example, that 'there are no previous understandings or agreements not contained in the writing,' and thus express the parties' 'intention to nullify antecedent understandings or agreements.' (See 3 Corbin, Contracts (1960) s 578, p. 411.) Any such collateral agreement itself must be examined, however, to determine whether the parties intended the subjects of negotiation it deals with to be included in, excluded from, or otherwise affected by the writing. Circumstances at the time of the writing may also aid in the determination of such integration. (See 3 Corbin, Contracts (1960) ss 582–584; McCormick, Evidence (1954) s 216, p. 441.

California cases have stated that whether there was an integration is to be determined solely from the face of the instrument (e.g., *Thoroman v. David* (1926) 199 Cal. 386, 389–390), and that the question for the court is whether it 'appears to be a complete agreement.' (See *Ferguson v. Koch* (1928) 204 Cal. 342, 346.) Neither of these strict formulations of the rule, however, has been consistently applied. The requirement that the writing must appear incomplete on its face has been repudiated in many cases where parol evidence was admitted 'to prove the existence of a separate oral agreement as to any matter on which the document is silent and which is not inconsistent with its terms'—even though the instrument appeared to state a complete agreement. (E.g., *American Industrial Sales Corp. v. Airscope, Inc.* (1955) 44 Cal.2d 393, 397. Even under the rule that the writing alone is to be consulted, it was found necessary to examine the alleged collateral agreement before concluding that proof of it was precluded by the writing alone. (See 3 Corbin, Contracts (1960) s 582, pp. 444–446.) It is therefore evident that 'The conception of a writing as wholly and intrinsically self-determinative of the parties' intent to make it a sole memorial of one or seven or twenty-seven subjects of negotiation is an impossible one.' (9 Wigmore, Evidence (3d ed. 1940) s 2431, p. 103.) For example, a promissory note given by a debtor to his creditor may integrate all their present contractual rights and obligations, or it may be only a minor part of an underlying executory contract that would never be discovered by examining the face of the note.

In formulating the rule governing parol evidence, several policies must be accommodated. One policy is based on the assumption that written evidence is more accurate than human memory. This policy, however, can be adequately served by excluding parol evidence of agreements that directly contradict the writing. Another policy is based on the fear that fraud or unintentional invention by witnesses interested in the outcome of the litigation will mislead the finder of facts. McCormick has suggested that the party urging the spoken as against the written word is most often the economic underdog, threatened by severe hardship if the writing is enforced. In his view the parol evidence rule arose to allow the court to control the tendency of the jury to find through sympathy and without a dispassionate assessment of the probability of fraud or faulty memory that the parties made an oral agreement collateral to the written contract, or that preliminary tentative agreements were not abandoned when omitted from the writing. (See McCormick, Evidence (1954) s 210.) He recognizes, however, that if this theory were adopted in disregard of all other considerations, it would lead to the exclusion of testimony concerning oral agreements whenever there is a writing and thereby often defeat the true intent of the parties. See McCormick, op. cit. supra, s 216, p. 441.)

Evidence of oral collateral agreements should be excluded only when the fact finder is likely to be misled. The rule must therefore be based on the credibility of the evidence. One such standard, adopted by section 240(1)(b) of the Restatement of Contracts, permits proof of a collateral agreement if it 'is such an agreement as might naturally be made as a separate agreement by parties situated as were the parties to the written contract.' The draftsmen of the Uniform Commercial Code would exclude the evidence in still fewer instances: 'If the additional terms are such that, if agreed upon, they would Certainly have been included in the document in the view of the court, then evidence of their alleged making must be kept from the trier of fact.' (Com. 3, s 2—202, italics added.)

The option clause in the deed in the present case does not explicitly provide that it contains the complete agreement, and the deed is silent on the question of assignability. Moreover, the difficulty of accommodating the formalized structure of a deed to the insertion of collateral agreements makes it less likely that all the terms of such an agreement were included. The statement of the reservation of the option might well have been placed in the recorded deed solely to preserve the grantors' rights against any possible future purchasers and this function could well be served without any mention of the parties' agreement that the option was personal. There is nothing in the record to indicate that the parties to this family transaction, through experience in land transactions or otherwise, had any warning of the disadvantages of failing to put the whole agreement in the deed. This case is one, therefore, in which it can be said that a collateral agreement such as that alleged 'might naturally be made as a separate agreement.' A fortiori, the case is not one in which the parties 'would certainly' have included the collateral agreement in the deed.

It is contended, however, that an option agreement is ordinarily presumed to be assignable if it contains no provisions forbidding its transfer or indicating that its performance involves elements personal to the parties. The fact that there is a written memorandum, however, does not necessarily preclude parol evidence rebutting a term that the law would otherwise presume. In *American Industrial Sales Corp. v. Airscope, Inc.*, supra, 44 Cal.2d 393, 397–398, we held it proper to admit parol evidence of a contemporaneous collateral agreement as to the place of payment of a note, even though it contradicted the presumption that a note, silent as to the place of payment, is payable where the creditor resides. Of course a statute may preclude parol evidence to rebut a statutory presumption. Here, however, there is no such statute. In the absence of a controlling statute the parties may provide that a contract right or duty is nontransferable. Moreover, even when there is no explicit agreement—written or oral—that contractual duties shall be personal, courts will effectuate presumed intent to that effect if the circumstances indicate that performance by substituted person would be different from that contracted for.

In the present case defendants offered evidence that the parties agreed that the option was not assignable in order to keep the property in the Masterson family. The trial court erred in excluding that evidence.

The judgment is reversed.

■ BURKE, J., dissenting. I dissent. The majority opinion:

(1) Undermines the parol evidence rule as we have known it in this state since at least 1872 by declaring that parol evidence should have been admitted by the trial court to show that a written option, absolute and unrestricted in form, was intended to be limited and nonassignable;

(2) Renders suspect instruments of conveyance absolute on their face;

(3) Materially lessens the reliance which may be placed upon written instruments affecting the title to real estate; and

(4) Opens the door, albeit unintentionally to a new technique for the defrauding of creditors.

The opinion permits defendants to establish by parol testimony that their grant to their brother (and brother-in-law) of a written option, absolute in terms, was nevertheless agreed to be nonassignable by the grantee (now a bankrupt), and that therefore the right to exercise it did not pass, by operation of the bankruptcy laws, to the trustee for the benefit of the grantee's creditors.

And how was this to be shown? By the proffered testimony of the bankrupt optionee himself! Thereby one of his assets (the option to purchase defendants' California ranch) would be withheld from the trustee in bankruptcy and from the bankrupt's creditors. Understandably the trial court, as required by the parol evidence rule, did not allow the bankrupt by parol to so contradict the unqualified language of the written option.

The court properly admitted parol evidence to explain the intended meaning of the 'same consideration' and 'depreciation value' phrases of the written option to purchase defendants' land, as the intended meaning of those phrases was not clear. However, there was nothing ambiguous about the Granting language of the option and not the slightest suggestion in the document that the option was to be nonassignable. Thus, to permit such words of limitation to be added by parol is to contradict the absolute nature of the grant, and to directly violate the parol evidence rule.

Just as it is unnecessary to state in a deed to 'lot X' that the house located thereon goes with the land, it is likewise unnecessary to add to 'I grant an option to Jones' the words 'and his assigns' for the option to be assignable. As hereinafter emphasized in more detail, California statutes expressly declare that it is assignable, and only if I add language in writing showing my intent to withhold or restrict the right of assignment may the grant be so limited. Thus, to seek to restrict the grant by parol is to contradict the written document in violation of the parol evidence rule.

The majority opinion arrives at its holding via a series of false premises which are not supported either in the record of this case or in such California authorities as are offered.

The parol evidence rule is set forth in clear and definite language in the statutes of this state. (Civ.Code, s 1625; Code Civ.Proc., s 1856.) It 'is not a rule of evidence but is one of substantive law. The rule as applied to contracts is simply that as a matter of substantive law, a certain act, the act of embodying the complete terms of an agreement in a writing (the 'integration'), Becomes the contract of the parties.' (*Hale v. Bohannon* (1952) 38 Cal.2d 458, 465, 241 P.2d 4, 7(1, 2), quoting from *In re Estate of Gaines* (1940) 15 Cal.2d 255, 264–265) The rule is based upon the sound principle that the parties to a written instrument, after committing their agreement to or evidencing it by the writing, are not permitted to add to, vary or contradict the terms of the writing by parol evidence. As aptly expressed by the author of the present majority opinion, speaking for the court in *Parsons v. Bristol Development Co.* (1965) 62 Cal.2d 861, 865(2), and in *Coast Bank v. Minderhout* (1964) 61 Cal.2d 311, 315, such evidence is 'admissible to interpret the instrument, but not to give it a meaning to which it is not reasonably susceptible.' (Italics added.)

At the outset the majority in the present case reiterate that the rule against contradicting or varying the terms of a writing remains applicable when only part of the agreement is contained in the writing, and parol evidence is used to prove elements of the agreement not reduced to writing. But having restated this established rule, the majority opinion inexplicably proceeds to subvert it.

Each of the three cases cited by the majority holds that although parol evidence is admissible to prove the parts of the contract not put in writing, it is not admissible to vary or contradict the writing or prove collateral agreements which are inconsistent therewith. The meaning of this rule (and the application of it found in the cases) is that if the asserted unwritten elements of the agreement would contradict, add to, detract from, vary or be inconsistent with the written agreement, then such elements may not be shown by parol evidence.

The contract of sale and purchase of the ranch property here involved was carried out through a title company upon written escrow instructions executed by the respective parties after various preliminary negotiations. The deed to defendant grantees, in which the grantors expressly reserved an option to repurchase the property within a ten-year period and upon a specified consideration, was issued and delivered in consummation of the contract. In neither the written escrow instructions nor the deed containing the option is there any language even suggesting that the option was agreed or intended by the parties to be personal to the grantors, and so nonassignable. The trial judge, on at least three separate occasions, correctly sustained objections to efforts of defendant optionors to get into evidence the testimony of Dallas Masterson (the bankrupt holder of the option) that a part of the agreement of sale of the parties was that the option to repurchase the property was personal to him, and therefore unassignable for benefit of creditors. But the majority hold that that testimony should have been admitted, thereby permitting defendant optionors to limit, detract from and contradict the plain and unrestricted terms of the written option in clear violation of the parol evidence rule and to open the door to the perpetration of fraud.

Options are property, and are widely used in the sale and purchase of real and personal property. One of the basic incidents of property ownership is the right of the owner to sell or transfer it.

The right of an optionee to transfer his option to purchase property is accordingly one of the basic rights which accompanies the option unless limited under the language of the option itself. To allow an optionor to resort to parol evidence to support his assertion that the written option is not transferable is to authorize him to limit the option by attempting to restrict and reclaim rights with which he has already parted. A clearer violation of two substantive and basic rules of law—the parol evidence rule and the right of free transferability of property—would be difficult to conceive.

The majority opinion attempts to buttress its approach by asserting that 'California cases have stated that whether there was an integration is to be determined solely from the face of the instrument, and that the question for the court is whether it 'appears to be a complete agreement' but that 'neither of these strict formulations of the rule has been consistently applied.'

The majority's claim of inconsistent application of the parol evidence rule by the California courts fails to find support in the examples offered. First, the majority opinion asserts that 'The requirement that the writing must appear incomplete on its face has been repudiated in many cases where parol evidence was admitted 'to prove the existence of a separate oral agreement as to any matter on which the document is silent and which is not inconsistent with its terms'—even though the instrument appeared to state a complete agreement.' But an examination of the cases cited in support of the quoted statement discloses that on the contrary in every case which is pertinent here (with a single exception) the writing was obviously incomplete on its face. In the one exception (*Stockburger v. Dolan* (1939) 94 P.2d 33) it was held that lessors under a lease to drill for oil in an area zoned against such drilling should be permitted to show by parol that the lessee had contemporaneously agreed orally to seek a variance—an agreement which, as the opinion points out, Did not contradict the written contract. But what is additionally noteworthy in Stockburger, and controlling here, is the further holding that lessors Could not show by parol that lessee had orally agreed that a lease provision suspending payment of rental under certain circumstances would not apply during certain periods of time—as 'evidence to that effect would vary the terms of the contract in that particular.' (P. 317(5) of p. 35 of 94 P.2d.)

In further pursuit of what would appear to be nonexistent support for its assertions of inconsistency in California cases, the majority opinion next declares that 'Even under the rule that the writing alone is to be consulted, it was found necessary to examine the alleged collateral agreement before concluding that proof of it was precluded by the writing alone. (See 3 Corbin, Contracts (1960) s 582.)' Not only are No California cases cited by the majority in supposed support for the quoted declaration (offered by the majority as an example of inconsistent applications of the parol evidence rule by California courts), but 3 Corbin, Contracts, which the majority do cite, likewise refers to No California cases, and makes but scanty citation to any cases whatever. In any event, in what manner other than by 'examining' an alleged collateral agreement is it possible for a court to rule upon the admissibility of testimony or upon an offer of proof with respect to such agreement?

The majority opinion has thus demonstrably failed to substantiate its next utterance that 'The conception of a writing as wholly and intrinsically self-determinative of the parties' intent to make it a sole memorial of one or seven or twenty-seven subjects of negotiation is an impossible one,' citing 9 Wigmore, Evidence (3d ed. 1940) section 2431, page 103, whose Views on the subject were Rejected by this court as early as 1908 in *Germain Fruit Co. v. J. K. Armsby Co.*, 96 P. 319, which, indeed, is Also cited by the Majority in the present case. And the example given, that of a promissory note, is obviously specious. Rarely, if ever, does a promissory note given by a debtor to his creditor integrate All their agreements (that is not the purpose it serves); it may or it may not integrate All their present contractual rights and obligations; but relevant to the parol evidence rule, at least until the advent of the majority opinion in this case, alleged collateral agreements which would vary or contradict the terms and conditions of a promissory note may Not be shown by parol. (*Bank of America etc. Ass'n v. Pendergrass* (1935) 48 P.2d 659.)

Upon this structure of incorrect premises and unfounded assertions the majority opinion arrives at its climax: The pronouncement of 'several policies (to) be accommodated (i)n formulating the rule governing parol evidence.' Two of the 'policies' as declared by the majority are: Written evidence is more accurate than human memory; fraud or unintentional invention by interested witnesses may well occur.

I submit that these purported 'policies' are in reality two of the basic and obvious reasons for adoption by the legislature of the parol evidence rule as the policy in this state. Thus the speculation of the majority concerning the views of various writers on the subject and the advisability of following them in this state is not only superfluous but flies flatly in the face of established California law and policy. It serves only to introduce uncertainty and confusion in a field of substantive law which was codified and made certain in this state a century ago.

However, despite the law which until the advent of the present majority opinion has been firmly and clearly established in California and relied upon by attorneys and courts alike, that parol evidence may Not be employed to vary or contradict the terms of a written instrument, the majority now announce that such evidence 'should be excluded only when the fact finder is Likely to be misled,' and that 'The rule must therefore be based on the Credibility of the evidence.' But was it not, inter alia, to avoid misleading the fact finder, and to further the introduction of only the evidence which is most likely to be credible (the written document), that the Legislature adopted the parol evidence rule as a part of the substantive law of this state?

Next, in an effort to implement this newly promulgated 'credibility' test, the majority opinion offers a choice of two 'standards': one, a 'certainty' standard, quoted from the Uniform Commercial Code, and the other a 'natural' standard found in the Restatement of Contracts, and concludes that at least for purposes of the present case the 'natural' viewpoint should prevail.

This new rule, not hitherto recognized in California, provides that proof of a claimed collateral oral agreement is admissible if it is such an agreement as might naturally have been made a separate agreement by the parties under the particular circumstances. I submit that this approach opens the door to uncertainty and confusion. Who can know what its limits are? Certainly I do not. For example, in its application to this case who could be expected to divine as 'natural' a separate oral agreement between the parties that the assignment, absolute and unrestricted on its face, was intended by the parties to be limited to the Masterson family?

Or, assume that one gives to his relative a promissory note and that the payee of the note goes bankrupt. By operation of law the note becomes an asset of the bankruptcy. The trustee attempts to enforce it. Would the relatives be permitted to testify that by a separate oral agreement made at the time of the execution of the note it was understood that should the payee fail in his business the maker would be excused from payment of the note, or that, as here, it was intended that the benefits of the note would be Personal to the payee? I doubt that trial judges should be burdened with the task of conjuring whether it would have been 'natural under those circumstances for such a separate agreement to have been made by the parties. Yet, under the application of the proposed rule, this is the task the trial judge would have, and in essence the situation presented in the instant case is no different.

Under the application of the codes and the present case law, proof of the existence of such an agreement would not be permitted, 'natural' or 'unnatural.' But conceivably, as loose as the new rule is, one judge might deem it natural and another judge unnatural. And in each instance the ultimate decision would have to be made ('naturally') on a case-by-case basis by the appellate courts.

In an effort to provide justification for applying the newly pronounced 'natural' rule to the circumstances of the present case, the majority opinion next attempts to account for the silence of the writing in this case concerning assignability of the option, by asserting that 'the difficulty of accommodating the formalized structure of a deed to the insertion of collateral agreements makes it less likely that all the terms of such an agreement were included.' What difficulty would have been involved here, to add the words 'this option is nonassignable'? The asserted 'formalized structure of a deed' is no formidable barrier. The Legislature has set forth the requirements in simple language in section 1092 of the Civil Code. It is this: 'I, A B, grant to C D all that real property situated in (naming county), State of California described as follows: (describing it).' To this the grantor desiring to reserve an option to repurchase need only so state, as was done here. It is a matter of common knowledge that collateral agreements (such as the option clause here involved, or such as deed restrictions) are frequently included in deeds, without difficulty of any nature.

To support further speculation, that 'the reservation of the option might well have been placed in the recorded deed solely to preserve the grantors' rights against any possible future purchasers, and this function could well be served without any mention of the parties' agreement that the option was personal,' the majority assert that 'There is nothing in the record to indicate that the parties to this family transaction, through experience in land transactions or otherwise, had any warning of the disadvantages of failing to put the whole agreement in the deed.' The facts of this case, however, do not support such claim of naiveté. The grantor husband (the bankrupt businessman) testified that as none of the parties were attorneys 'we wanted to contact my attorney which we did. The wording in the option was obtained from (the attorney). I told him what my discussion was with the Sines (defendant grantees) and he wanted a little time to compose it. And, then this (the wording provided by the attorney) was taken to the title company at the time Mr. and Mrs. Sine and I went in to complete the transaction.' The witness was an experienced businessman who thus demonstrated awareness of the wisdom of seeking legal guidance and advice in this business transaction, and who did so. Wherein lies the naive family transaction postulated by the majority?

The majority opinion then proceeds on the fallacious assertion that the right to transfer or to assign an option, if it contains no provisions forbidding transfer or indicating that performance involves elements personal to the parties, is a mere disputable presumption, and in purported support cites cases Not one of which involves an option and in each of which the presumption which was invoked served to supply a missing but essential element of a complete agreement. As already emphasized hereinabove, the right of free transferability of property, including options, is one of the most fundamental tenets of substantive law, and the crucial distinction would appear self-evident between such a basic right on the one hand, and on the other hand the disputable evidentiary presumptions which the law has developed to supply terms lacking from a written instrument but essential to making it whole and complete. There is no such lack in the deed and the option reservation now at issue.

The statement of the majority opinion that in the absence of a controlling statute the parties may provide that a contract right or duty is non-transferable, is of course true. Equally true is the next assertion that 'even when there is no explicit agreement—written or oral—that contractual duties shall be personal, courts will effectuate a presumed intent to that effect if the circumstances indicate that performance by a substituted person would be different from that contracted for.' But to apply the law of contracts for the rendering of personal services to the reservation of an option in a deed of real estate calls for a misdirected use of the rule, particularly in an instrument containing not one word from which such 'a presumed intent to that effect' could be gleaned. Particularly is the holding objectionable when the result is to upset established statutory and case law in this state that 'circumstances' shown by parol may Not be employed to contradict, add to or detract from, the agreement of the parties as expressed by them in writing. And once again the quoted pronouncement of the majority concerning the showing of 'circumstances' by parol fails to find support in the cases they cite, which relate to a patent license agreement, held to be assignable absent terms indicating a contrary intent; a contract to sell grapes, also held assignable; a contract which included language showing the intent that it be nonassignable; a contract to buy land held to be assignable because approval of title by the buyer was held not to be a personal privilege attaching only to the assignor; and to contracts for personal services.

Neither personal skill nor personal qualities can be conjured as a requirement for the exercise of the option reserved in the deed here, regardless of how ardent may be the desire of the parties (the bankrupt husband-optionee and his sister), 'to keep the property in the family.' Particularly is this true when a contrary holding would permit the property to be acquired by plaintiff referee in bankruptcy for the benefit of the creditors of the bankrupt husband.

Comment hardly seems necessary on the convenience to a bankrupt of such a device to defeat his creditors. He need only produce parol testimony that any options (or other property, for that matter) which he holds are subject to an oral 'collateral agreement' with family members (or with friends) that the property is nontransferable 'in order to keep the property in the family' on in the friendly group. In the present case the value of the ranch which the bankrupt and his wife held an option to purchase has doubtless increased substantially during the years since they acquired the option. The initiation of this litigation by the trustee in bankruptcy to establish his right to enforce the option indicates his belief that there is substantial value to be gained for the creditors from this asset of the bankrupt. Yet the majority opinion permits defeat of the trustee and of the creditors through the device of an asserted collateral oral agreement that the option was 'personal' to the bankrupt and nonassignable 'in order to keep the property in the family'!

It also seems appropriate to inquire as to the rights of plaintiff wife in the option which she holds with her bankrupt husband. Is her interest therein also subject to being shown to be personal and not salable or assignable? And, what are her rights and those of her husband in the ranch land itself, if they exercise their option to purchase it? Will they be free to then sell the land? Or, if they prefer, may they hold it beyond the reach of creditors? Or can other members of 'the family' claim some sort of restriction on it in perpetuity, established by parol evidence?

And if defendants sell the land subject to the option, will the new owners be heard to assert that the option is 'personal' to the optionees, 'in order to keep the property in the Masterson family'? Or is that claim 'personal' to defendants only?

These are only a few of the confusions and inconsistencies which will arise to plague property owners and, incidentally, attorneys and title companies, who seek to counsel and protect them.

I would hold that the trial court ruled correctly on the proffered parol evidence, and would affirm the judgment.

* * *

Masterson illustrates the movement away from the classical, hard parol evidence rule. The plaintiff—and seller—in *Masterson* contracted to sell a ranch to the defendant—and buyer—to whom he was related. The sales contract reserved to the "grantor" (that is, the seller) an option to repurchase the farm before a fixed date, for the "same consideration" as the "purchase price" paid by the buyer plus the "depreciation value of any improvements" made by the buyer. The seller subsequently went bankrupt, and his trustee in bankruptcy sought to exercise the option to repurchase. The buyer refused to reconvey the farm. He claimed that the parties had wished the farm to remain in their family (recall that the buyer and seller were related) and had thus included, in the terms of the initial sale, a parol agreement that made option to repurchase personal to the seller. The alleged parol agreement, if part of the contractual text, would thus have precluded the seller's trustee in bankruptcy from exercising the option. The seller (through his trustee in bankruptcy) argued that the parol evidence rule excluded the agreement from the construction of the contract, so that the trustee might exercise the option to repurchase, forcing the buyer to reconvey the farm.

A trial court would have excluded the oral agreement making the repurchase option personal to the seller and thus would have permitted the seller's trustee in bankruptcy to repurchase the farm. The Supreme Court of California, per Justice Traynor (the same Justice who decided *Drennan*), disagreed. Traynor accepted that a fully integrated writing—a writing that effectively announced its own exclusivity and completeness—could be neither added to nor varied by prior or contemporaneous oral agreements. (Note that conceptually, it was necessary only to say that no writing may be varied by parol agreements and then to observe that where a writing is fully integrated, every so-called "addition" is in fact a variance.) Traynor emphasized, however, that this principle simply raises the question when a writing is fully integrated. Traynor characterized the classical parol evidence rule in terms that should be familiar from *Mitchell*: saying that according to this view, a writing is fully integrated unless it appears incomplete on its face. Traynor decisively rejected this approach, insisting instead that writings do not (at least generally, or ordinarily) integrate themselves. Rather, Traynor proposed, a court engaged in contract construct should look beyond the face of a writing, *including to parol evidence*, to determine whether or not that writing is fully integrated. Even a writing that is facially complete will not be integrated, under Traynor's approach, where prior or contemporaneous oral exchanges demonstrate that the writing was to be added to by parol agreements. In *Masterson*, the oral exchanges concerning the option to repurchase might, if credited appropriately by a fact finder at trial, demonstrate just this. Accordingly, the parol evidence rule did not exclude the oral agreement to make the repurchase option personal to the seller from the contract.

The classical, hard parol evidence rule looks to the text of a writing to determine the writing's integration. It reads the text, moreover, in a fashion that embodies two inclinations to favor writings. First, the procedure by which the classical parol evidence rule determines a writing's integration focuses almost exclusively on the writing itself. The classical approach applies a largely trans-contextual standard to determine whether or not writings are complete. In *Mitchell*, this standard is articulated in the language of naturalness. Traynor expressed it in terms of facial completeness. (To see that the two expressions capture the same sensibilities, observe that every writing is facially incomplete in respect of natural omissions to it.) On both accounts, a court applying the classical parol evidence rule will not look to the facts and circumstances in which a writing was produced (which inevitably include prior and contemporaneous oral remarks) in order to assess whether the writing has natural omissions or facial incompleteness; rather, the text of the writing itself will suffice. And second, the substantive tendencies of the classical parol evidence rule tend strongly to favor integration. The classical approach is skeptical of new contract terms. It tends to cast proposed parol agreements as standing in tension to writings, even where the tension requires implying terms in writings that are not express. Most obviously and most broadly, the classical approach tends to imply merger clauses into writings, which announce that there are no other agreements and thus convert every proposed parol addition into a variance. More narrowly, the classical approach tends to emphasize the way in which individual terms allocate contractual surplus and hence to treat proposed parol additions that might redistribute the surplus in question as variances away from these terms.[4]

Traynor's soft parol evidence rule rejects both features of the classical approach. First, and in respect of procedure, Traynor insisted that a court cannot determine whether or not a writing is integrated save by looking to all the facts and circumstances surrounding a writing, including to prior or contemporaneous oral representations that led to the writing. This

---

4. Note the implications of these observations for the interplay between the parol evidence rule and the distinction between parol agreements that vary and those that merely add to a writing. The oral agreement to make the option to repurchase personal to the seller reduced the option's value (by making it non-transferable) and thus effected a redistribution of contractual surplus from the seller to the buyer. (Precisely the redistribution that the buyer, as the facts in *Masterson* played out, took advantage of.) Proponents of the classical hard parol evidence rule would cite this fact in order to characterize making the option personal to the seller as varying the writing rather than just adding to it. (They would ask, perfectly sensibly, how an oral agreement that re-allocates surplus solely to the advantage of one party can be said to merely add to a writing with which it remains consistent.) This thought reprises and expands upon the logic articulated in an earlier note, according to which every addition is a variance, adding that the term that every addition varies is not just an implied merger clause but also an implied commitment to whatever surplus division a writing establishes. According to this logic, the only time a parol agreement truly merely adds to a writing is when it generates additional surplus, rather than reallocating surplus created by the writing's terms. Perhaps this idea—of the distinction between generating new surplus and reallocating existing surplus—returns to, and fleshes out, the collateral agreement doctrine (so that "collateral agreement" becomes just the name for agreements that generate new surplus).

amounts to rejecting the very ideas of facial completeness and natural omissions, at least insofar as these ideas have trans-contextual application (which they must do in order to serve their purpose, in the classical regime). According to Traynor, the relationship between a writing and the parol agreements surrounding it in the parties' overall contractual arrangements inevitably varies with the case—nothing is natural, and so no conclusions may be drawn from the face of a writing. Instead, one must look to all the facts and circumstances to learn the relative priority of writings among them. And second, in respect of substance, Traynor inclines, in performing this general investigation into facts and circumstances, to downplay the specialness or priority of writings. For Traynor, contract construction (put together with contract interpretation) is meant to promote contract's overall usefulness as a technique for implementing the intentions and plans of the contracting parties. Moreover, Traynor suspected that these intentions are often most accurately reflected in parol agreements, so that focusing too narrowly or preferentially on writings reduces rather than increases the usefulness of contract in this regard.

Observe the enormous gap between Traynor's methodological instincts and those of the classical approach. Traynor is relentlessly functionalist. The question for him is, always, what regime for contract construction best promotes the contract's usefulness for promoting the purposes—generally the commercial purposes—of the contracting parties. Traynor thus prefers writings over parol agreements only insofar as writings are well-suited to capturing party-intent or, alternatively, avoid the vagaries of memory and protect against the ex post manipulation of contractual text by interested parties. Because Traynor is colloquial and populist about language, he doubts whether writings are well-suited to capturing party intent. And because Traynor is not just a functionalist but a confident one, he believes that courts are well-able to mitigate the risks of parol agreements, and hence comes down in favor of including them in contract construction. Indeed, Traynor's commitments in these respects are so strong that he is willing to impose them even against California's statutory preference, pointed out by the dissenter, for requiring limitations of assignability to be in writing.[5]

The sensibilities behind the classical parol evidence rule, by contrast, are insistently formalist. The classical approach inclines towards treating

---

5. Note that one may stand with Traynor's functionalism about construction, insisting that the doctrines of construction should be chosen in order to make contracts as applied best serve the broader purposes of contracting parties, and yet believe that this alignment is best achieved by favoring writings and so reject Traynor's openness to parol agreements in practice.

The functionalist appeal of the softer approach to parol agreements taken in *Masterson* is connected to the fact that a hard exclusion of parol agreements requires all parties to incur the additional costs associated with reducing agreements to writing. Where they do not incur these costs, the rule precludes courts from giving effect to their true plans, even though the courts might, ex post, divine these plans from parol agreements at a lower cost than would have been involved in reducing them to writing ex ante. Moreover, a hard parol evidence rule can leave unsophisticated parties (who do not know of the preference for writings) without contract rights that they thought they had bargained for.

contract not as a tool for the commercial purposes of the parties but rather as a legal order, with its own internal logics. Principal among these logics is the idea that contracts constitute chosen obligation—that promises, and in particular the specific intent to be bound that promises involve—is essential for contract obligation. Writings are thus privileged in *Mitchell* not because doing so creates any immediate advantage for the efficiency or general usefulness of contractual practice but because they are categorically preferred. *Mitchell* formalism in contract construction, together with a parallel formalism in contract interpretation, is thus strongly promoted by the formalism associated with the subjective approach to contract formation that also dominated classical contract law. If forming a contract at all depends on the intent of the parties, as constructed through the classical doctrine's meeting of minds test, then allowing parol agreements to affect contract construction (or giving writings something other than their natural or facial meaning) makes it easy for a party to avoid contractual obligation entirely. It need only introduce evidence of prior or contemporaneous oral terms that suggests that the parties' minds never met, even with respect to the writing. It is thus tempting to say that under classical principles of contract formation, parol agreements *must* be excluded at contract construction, in order for any contracts reliably to be formed at all.[6] The modern approach to contract formation (with its emphasis on objective rather than subjective intent) avoids these risks of admitting parol agreements. By finding offers and acceptances wherever reasonable parties would perceive them, the modern approach dramatically reduced

---

This is not, however, the whole of the functionalist story, and a hard parol evidence rule also has a certain functionalist appeal. This appeal lies partly in the fact (made familiar from the earlier discussion of the distinction between firm offers and mere invitations to bargain) that this rule protects parties against ending up bound to things that they say in the course of negotiating towards an eventual agreement but ultimately abandon. (Note, moreover, that the parties can capture the gains from being bound (the gains that the earlier analysis observed render it appealing not just to issue invitations to bargain but also to make offers) simply by including the oral terms in their final writing.) A hard parol evidence rule also protects parties against the risk that unscrupulous counterparties will seek to vary contract terms to their advantage ex post, by inventing oral agreements that never in fact existed.

The dissenter in *Masterson* was impressed by thoughts such as these. The dissent thus worried that although the seller was formally opposed to the buyer in the lawsuit, the opposition all came from the seller's trustee in bankruptcy. The actual seller preferred the interests of the buyer over the interests of the creditors whose interests the trustee sought to promote. *Masterson* thus posed particularly large risks of unscrupulous ex post manipulation of evidence of parol agreements, or so the dissenter thought.

The discussion of interpretation below will explore other instances of the sensibility that prefers hard over soft doctrine, but for functionalist rather than formalist reasons.

6. Might this be a tendency only? Just as a functionalist might prefer a hard parol evidence rule *for functionalist reasons*, might a formalist prefer a softer approach *for formalist reasons*? Perhaps not. The problem is that formalism, by making the creation of contractual obligation depend too closely and narrowly on the subjective intentions of the contracting parties, runs the constant risk of failing in practice to recognize any contractual obligation at all. It has been one of the themes of this Part that in order to function even modestly well, formalism must strategically abandon its core commitments to the chosenness of contractual obligation through a series of presumptions about what parties' intend. The classical hard parol evidence rule is one of these presumptions. Even though it is commonly understood in terms of what it excludes from contract construction, the classical approach is perhaps more properly understood as a means of making contract construction possible for the formalist at all.

the capacity to avoid contractual obligation entirely by muddying the waters concerning subjective intent.

17.1.B   MERGER CLAUSES

The discussion of parol agreements has up to this point suffered a sense of unreality, in one important respect. It has repeatedly butted up against the fact that the parties to a contract might try to influence its construction, including especially in ways that countermand the friendliness to parol agreements embodied in Traynor's approach. They might draft a writing in a manner designed to convey a clear implication of completeness, either in general or with respect to certain issues and the terms that address them. Or, they might attempt to make their writing complete through express terms, by including in it a *merger clause*, which announces that the writing represents the entire agreement between them. Such a clause, it is sometimes said, *integrates* the agreement.

Both techniques are employed, against the backdrop of the modern soft parol evidence rule, in an attempt to opt back into the hard parol evidence rule associated with classical contract doctrine.[7] The two techniques raise different—really mirror-image—questions. Writings that strongly imply their completeness (at least with respect to certain questions) but do not include express merger clauses raise the question whether merger clauses are *necessary* for excluding parol agreements under the modern regime. Writings that contain express merger clauses raise the question whether such clauses are *sufficient* for excluding parol agreements from contract construction.

Begin by asking whether, and when, merger clauses are necessary for excluding parol agreements from the contractual text. The following materials take up this question.

Uniform Commercial Code

§ 2–202   Final Written Expression: Parol or Extrinsic Evidence

Terms with respect to which the confirmatory memoranda of the parties agree or which are otherwise set forth in a writing intended by the parties as a final expression of their agreement with respect to such terms as are included therein may not be contradicted by evidence of any prior agreement or of a contemporaneous oral agreement but may be explained or supplemented

---

7. Note that the reverse maneuver—opting out of the hard parol evidence rule and into a regime that welcomed parol agreements in contract construction—was not so easy under the classical regime. It might appear that parties might opt out of the hard parol evidence rule and force courts to combine written and oral agreements in contract construction simply by drafting highly incomplete writings, which required supplementation from parol agreements in order effectively to govern the parties' contractual relations. But classical contract law would not have looked kindly on such efforts. As the earlier materials on contract formation revealed, a classical court confronting such an incomplete writing might very well conclude that the parties had failed to reach a contract at all.

(a) by course of performance, course of dealing, or usage of trade (Section 1–303); and

(b) by evidence of consistent additional terms unless the court finds the writing to have been intended also as a complete and exclusive statement of the terms of the agreement.

Official Comment

Prior Uniform Statutory Provisions: None.

Purposes:

1. This section definitely rejects:

(a) Any assumption that because a writing has been worked out which is final on some matters, it is to be taken as including all the matters agreed upon;

(b) The premise that the language used has the meaning attributable to such language by rules of construction existing in the law rather than the meaning which arises out of the commercial context in which it was used; and

(c) The requirement that a condition precedent to the admissibility of the type of evidence specified in paragraph (a) is an original determination by the court that the language used is ambiguous.

2. Paragraph (a) makes admissible evidence of course of dealing, usage of trade and course of performance to explain or supplement the terms of any writing stating the agreement of the parties in order that the true understanding of the parties as to the agreement may be reached. Such writings are to be read on the assumption that the course of prior dealings between the parties and the usages of trade were taken for granted when the document was phrased. Unless carefully negated they have become an element of the meaning of the words used. Similarly, the course of actual performance by the parties is considered the best indication of what they intended the writing to mean.

3. Under paragraph (b) consistent additional terms, not reduced to writing, may be proved unless the court finds that the writing was intended by both parties as a complete and exclusive statement of all the terms. If the additional terms are such that, if agreed upon, they would certainly have been included in the document in the view of the court, then evidence of their alleged making must be kept from the trier of fact.

Restatement (Second) of Contracts

§ 212 Interpretation Of Integrated Agreement

(1) The interpretation of an integrated agreement is directed to the meaning of the terms of the writing or writings in the light of the circumstances, in accordance with the rules stated in this Chapter.

(2) A question of interpretation of an integrated agreement is to be determined by the trier of fact if it depends on the credibility of extrinsic evidence or on a choice among reasonable inferences to be drawn from extrinsic evidence. Otherwise a question of interpretation of an integrated agreement is to be determined as a question of law.

Comments & Illustrations

Comment a. "Objective" and "subjective" meaning. Interpretation of contracts deals with the meaning given to language and other conduct by the parties rather than with meanings established by law. But the relevant intention of a party is that manifested by him rather than any different undisclosed intention. In cases of misunderstanding, there may be a contract in accordance with the meaning of one party if the other knows or has reason to know of the misunderstanding and the first party does not. See §§ 200, 201. The meaning of one party may prevail as to one term and the meaning of the other as to another term; thus the contract as a whole may not be entirely in accordance with the understanding of either. When a party is thus held to a meaning of which he had reason to know, it is sometimes said that the "objective" meaning of his language or other conduct prevails over his "subjective" meaning. Even so, the operative meaning is found in the transaction and its context rather than in the law or in the usages of people other than the parties.

Illustrations

1. In an integrated agreement A promises to sell and B to buy described real estate. A intends to sell Blackacre; B intends to buy Whiteacre. The writing reasonably describes Greenacre, and neither party has any more reason than the other to know of the misdescription. There is no contract.

2. In an integrated agreement A agrees to sell and B to buy certain patent rights. A intends to sell only the rights under the British patent on a certain invention; B intends also to buy rights under American and French patents. If A has reason to know that B intends to buy the American rights, B has reason to know that A does not intend to sell the French rights, and the language used can be read to cover the British and American but not the French rights, that may be determined to be the proper interpretation.

Comment b. Plain meaning and extrinsic evidence. It is sometimes said that extrinsic evidence cannot change the plain meaning of a writing, but meaning can almost never be plain except in a context. Accordingly, the rule stated in Subsection (1) is not limited to cases where it is determined that the language used is ambiguous. Any determination of meaning or ambiguity should only be made in the light of the relevant evidence of the situation and relations of the parties, the subject matter of the transaction, preliminary negotiations and statements made therein, usages of trade, and the course of dealing between the parties. See §§ 202, 219–23. But after the transaction has been shown in all its length and breadth, the words of an integrated agreement remain the most important evidence of intention.

Standards of preference among reasonable meanings are stated in §§ 203, 206, 207.

Illustrations

3. A agrees orally with B, a stockbroker, that in transactions between them "abracadabra" shall mean X Company. A sends a signed written order to B to buy 100 shares "abracadabra," and B buys 100 shares of X Company. The parties are bound in accordance with the oral agreement.

4. A and B are engaged in buying and selling shares of stock from each other, and agree orally to conceal the nature of their dealings by using the word "sell" to mean "buy" and using the word "buy" to mean "sell." A sends a written offer to B to "sell" certain shares, and B accepts. The parties are bound in accordance with the oral agreement.

Comment c. Statements of intention. The rule of Subsection (1) permits reference to the negotiations of the parties, including statements of intention and even positive promises, so long as they are used to show the meaning of the writing. A contrary rule in the interpretation of wills is sometimes stated broadly enough to apply to the interpretation of contracts, but that rule is subject to exceptions and rests in part on the more rigorous formal requirements to which wills are subject. Statements of a contracting party subsequent to the adoption of an integration are admissible against him to show his understanding of the meaning asserted by the other party.

Illustrations

5. In an integrated agreement A promises B to insert B's "business card" in A's "advertising chart" for a price to be paid when the chart is "published." The quoted terms are to be read in the light of the circumstances known to the parties, including their oral statements as to their meaning.

6. In an integrated agreement A contracts to sell "my horse," and B contracts to buy it. A owns two horses. It may be shown by oral evidence, including statements of the parties, that both A and B meant the same horse.

Comment d. "Question of law." Analytically, what meaning is attached to a word or other symbol by one or more people is a question of fact. But general usage as to the meaning of words in the English language is commonly a proper subject for judicial notice without the aid of evidence extrinsic to the writing. Historically, moreover, partly perhaps because of the fact that jurors were often illiterate, questions of interpretation of written documents have been treated as questions of law in the sense that they are decided by the trial judge rather than by the jury. Likewise, since an appellate court is commonly in as good a position to decide such questions as the trial judge, they have been treated as questions of law for purposes of appellate review. Such treatment has the effect of limiting the power of the trier of fact to exercise a dispensing power in the guise of a finding of fact, and thus contributes to the stability and predictability of contractual relations. In cases of standardized contracts such as insurance policies, it also provides a method of assuring that like cases will be decided alike.

Comment e. Evaluation of extrinsic evidence. Even though an agreement is not integrated, or even though the meaning of an integrated agreement depends on extrinsic evidence, a question of interpretation is not left to the trier of fact where the evidence is so clear that no reasonable person would determine the issue in any way but one. But if the issue depends on evidence outside the writing, and the possible inferences are conflicting, the choice is for the trier of fact.

Hunt Foods v. Doliner

Supreme Court, Appellate Division, New York, 1966.
26 A.D.2d 41.

■ STEUER, J. In February 1965 plaintiff corporation undertook negotiations to acquire the assets of Eastern Can Company. The stock of the latter is owned by defendant George M. Doliner and his family to the extent of 73%. The balance is owned by independent interests. At a fairly early stage of the negotiations agreement was reached as to the price to be paid by plaintiff ($5,922,500 if in cash, or $5,730,000 in Hunt stock), but several important items, including the form of the acquisition, were not agreed upon. At this point it was found necessary to recess the negotiations for several weeks. The Hunt negotiators expressed concern over any adjournment and stated that they feared that Doliner would use their offer as a basis for soliciting a higher bid from a third party. To protect themselves they demanded an option to purchase the Doliner stock. Such an option was prepared and signed by George Doliner and the members of his family and at least one other person associated with him who were stockholders. It provides that Hunt has the option to buy all of the Doliner stock at $5.50 per share. The option is to be exercised by giving notice on or before June 1, 1965, and if notice is not given the option is void. If given, Hunt is to pay the price and the Doliners to deliver their stock within seven days thereafter. The agreement calls for Hunt to pay $1,000 for the option, which was paid. To this point there is substantial accord as to what took place.

Defendant claims that when his counsel called attention to the fact that the option was unconditional in its terms, he obtained an understanding that it was only to be used in the event that he solicited an outside offer; and that plaintiff insisted that unless the option was signed in unconditional form negotiations would terminate. Plaintiff contends there was no condition. Concededly, on resumption of negotiations the parties failed to reach agreement and the option was exercised. Defendants declined the tender and refused to deliver the stock.

Plaintiff moved for summary judgment for specific performance. We do not believe that summary judgment lies. Plaintiff's position is that the condition claimed could not be proved under the parol evidence rule and, eliminating that, there is no defense to the action.

The parol evidence rule, at least as that term refers to contracts of sale, is now contained in Section 2–202 of the Uniform Commercial Code, which reads:

> Terms with respect to which the confirmatory memoranda of the parties agree or which are otherwise set forth in a writing intended by the parties as a final expression of their agreement with respect to such terms as are included therein may not be contradicted by evidence of any prior agreement or of a contemporaneous oral agreement but may be explained or supplemented by evidence of consistent additional terms unless the court finds the writing to have been intended also as a complete and exclusive statement of the terms of the agreement.

The term (that the option was not to be exercised unless Doliner sought outside bids), admittedly discussed but whose operative effect is disputed, not being set out in the writing, is clearly 'additional' to what is in the writing. So the first question presented is whether that term is 'consistent' with the instrument. In a sense any oral provision which would prevent the ripening of the obligations of a writing is inconsistent with the writing. But that obviously is not the sense in which the word is used. To be inconsistent the term must contradict or negate a term of the writing. A term or condition which has a lesser effect is provable.

The Official Comment prepared by the drafters of the Code contains this statement:

> 'If the additional terms are such that, if agreed upon, they would certainly have been included in the document in the view of the court, then evidence of their alleged making must be kept from the trier of fact.' (McKinney's Uniform Commercial Code, Part 1, p. 158)

Special Term interpreted this language as not only calling for an adjudication by the court in all instances where proof of an 'additional oral term' is offered, but making that determination exclusively the function of the court. We believe the proffered evidence to be inadmissible only where the writing contradicts the existence of the claimed additional term The conversations in this case, some of which are not disputed, and the expectation of all the parties for further negotiations, suggest that the alleged oral condition precedent cannot be precluded as a matter of law or as factually impossible. It is not sufficient that the existence of the condition is implausible. It must be impossible.

The order should be reversed on the law and the motion for summary judgment denied with costs and disbursements to abide the event.

Order and judgment (one paper) unanimously reversed, on the law, with $50 costs and disbursements to abide the event, and plaintiff's motion for summary judgment denied. All concur.

* * *

U.C.C. § 2–202(b) allows parol agreements to enter into contract construction as long as the terms of the parol agreements are consistent with a writing and (which is really redundant) the writing is not fully integrated. This seems straightforwardly to announce a regime in which writings are presumptively partially but not fully integrated: terms inconsistent with a writing are difficult to include in a contractual text; whereas terms additional to but consistent with a writing are easy to include. But while these formulations appear straightforward in the abstract, they are anything but in concrete application. Efforts to decide actual cases almost immediately confront the question when a parol term is consistent with a writing and when it is inconsistent. If a written agreement recites a price of 8 and a seller seeks to construct the contract around a prior or contemporaneous oral agreement fixing the price at 10, then it seems intuitively plain that the proposed parol agreement would vary rather than merely add to the writing; that it would be inconsistent with the writing rather than consistent with it. But what if a party to a contract proposed to construct it to include a parol agreement that accomplishes a substantively equivalent redistribution of contractual surplus only by less crass, and more indirect, means? A regime that excludes as inconsistent any parol agreements that would reallocate contractual surplus (or even create new surplus but alter the parties' overall shares) in effect recreates the classical, hard parol evidence rule. Contrariwise, a regime that treats parol agreements as consistent regardless of their effects on surplus allocation and so long as they do not directly contradict express terms in effect eliminates every preference for writings in contract construction, and makes merger clauses necessary for excluding parol evidence (although even such clauses may yet fail to be sufficient).

Hunt Foods illustrates these considerations. The plaintiff and defendant contracted for the plaintiff to buy the assets of the defendant's firm. When they had bargained to agreement on the sale price but not on their contract's other terms, a recess from their negotiations became necessary. The plaintiff worried that the defendant would use its bid to extract a higher offer from another buyer and, as a means of protecting itself against this risk, demanded and received a written option to acquire the defendant's stock at a later date. (The option would discourage other buyers from acquiring the defendant's assets by rendering them vulnerable to expropriation should the plaintiff exercise its option, and it would cost the defendant little, as the option price was much higher than the value that the assetless firm would have if the asset sale to the plaintiff went through.) Negotiations between the parties subsequently broke down, and the plaintiff eventually sought to exercise its option to acquire the firm's stock. The defendant refused to sell, claiming that the parties had reached an oral agreement that the option gave the plaintiff a right to purchase the firm's stock only if the defendant had solicited other offers for the firm's assets, which he had not done. (The parol agreement would, in effect, have conditioned the option in a manner related to the purpose for which it was granted.) The plaintiff did not deny the defendant had sought no other buyers but sought to exclude the oral condition from the option's contractual text, citing the parol evidence rule.

Although *Hunt Foods* concerned a sale of securities rather than of goods, the governing article of the U.C.C. (Article 8) borrows its parol evidence rule from Article 2, so the case was adjudicated under U.C.C. § 2–202. The *Hunt Foods* court thus began by observing that U.C.C. § 2–202(b) allows parol agreements to provide terms additional to a writing so long as the additional terms are consistent with the writing (and the writing is not fully integrated). It then asked what *consistent* means. The court answered that a term is consistent as long as it is not inconsistent; and it interpreted this less-than-obviously helpful formulation to mean that a term is consistent as long as it does not *negate* or *contradict* a term in the writing. The court thus concluded that any lesser tension between a writing and a parol agreement is insufficient to exclude the parol agreement from the construction of the ultimate contract. Furthermore, the court, looking to the U.C.C.'s official comments, concluded that a parol term negates or contradicts a term from a writing only where the parol term, if it had been agreed to, would *certainly* have been included in the text of the writing. And finally, the court held that the only circumstance in which a parol term would certainly have been included in a writing is that in which the writing *contradicts the existence* of the additional term outside it. This logic of course entails that the parol agreement at issue in *Hunt Foods* might, if proved before a fact finder, be included in the construction of the overall contract. More generally, it entails—note the language about contradicting the existence of additional terms—that a merger clause is necessary for keeping parol agreements out of contract construction.

These entailments follow the logic of the language in *Hunt Foods*, but they cannot possibly settle how contract construction will go under the U.C.C. (or its analogs). To see why not, return to the earlier example, in which a writing recites a price of 8 and a seller seeks to include in the contract a parol agreement setting the price at 10. The writing in this case does not contradict the *existence* of the parol agreement; it is merely incompatible with the substance of that agreement. Even so, it is hard to imagine that the *Hunt Foods* court would allow the parol agreement into the construction of the contract in such a case. After all (and returning to the language of the U.C.C. itself), the proposed parol term does contradict the writing (even if the writing does not deny the existence of the term). But while this intuition is so strong to be virtually undeniable, it does not settle anything in general but merely reprises a familiar problem. The parol term proposed in *Hunt Foods* itself, which made the plaintiff's stock option conditional on the defendant's having sought other offers for his firm's assets, dramatically reduced the option's value—converting it, in effect, from a free-standing economic asset to a guarantor of the defendant's good faith in the asset-purchase negotiations. The difference in contractual surplus sharing associated with that change was likely as great, if not greater, than the difference associated with changing a price from 8 to 10. And so the parol condition at issue in the construction of the contract in *Hunt Foods* becomes difficult to distinguish from the parol agreement at issue in the case of the imagined price change. Neither parol term's existence is directly contradicted by the writing against which it is proposed. And both parol terms make material differences in the distribution of contractual surplus, solely to the advantage of the party seeking to include them. So neither the language of the *Hunt Foods* opinion nor the economic facts on the ground seem able to draw the distinction that the two cases clearly require.

The difference between the two cases lies not in the logical entailments of the writings that they involve nor in the economic stakes at issue but rather in the practical connection between the two proposed parol agreements and the overall aims and purposes of the contracts to which they might be added. The parol agreement raising a price from 8 to 10 does not have its existence contradicted by the writing, but it is at odds with the internal logic of the agreement or plan that the writing memorializes. Unless the circumstances are unusual indeed, it is hard to imagine that a buyer who insisted on a written price of 8 intended to accept paying 10. (And if the circumstances become sufficiently unusual—for example, that the writing is not designed to structure the relation between the buyer and seller but is instead drafted for the seller's regulators or tax or customs authorities, in an effort to understate the seller's income—then the case for admitting the parol agreement becomes stronger.[8]) But it is not hard to imagine that parties taking an unexpected adjournment in complex negotiation, and quickly drafting an agreement designed to protect their negotiations against manipulation, might omit from their writing a parol agreement restricting it to its purpose.

This is a practical distinction based on lived experience rather than a theoretical distinction based on logic; and it is not captured (indeed it is obscured) by the formulaic language of *Hunt Foods*. Perhaps for this reason, *Hunt Foods* is not always followed, at least linguistically. Other cases replace discussions of whether or not a writing *contradicts the existence* of parol agreements with discussions of whether or not the writing and the parol agreements are *in reasonable harmony*.[9] *Hunt Foods* is worth focusing on because it shows the logical high-water mark of the rejection of the classical, hard parol evidence rule, and so establishes the boundaries of the logical space in this area of doctrine.

The classical rule rendered writings *presumptively fully integrated*, so that even where there was no express merger clause, a merger clause would be implied and parol terms would be excluded unless they constituted, in effect, a separate agreement. Under the literal language of *Hunt Foods*, writings are *presumptively not integrated*, so that a merger clause is necessary for excluding even parol terms that materially redistribute contractual surplus, solely to the advantage of the party proposing to include them. An intermediate rule makes contracts *presumptively partially inte-*

---

8. Note of course that the illegality of the purposes in the imaged examples might complicate the construction or enforcement of the contracts in them.

9. A prominent example is *Snyder v. Herbert Greenbaum & Associates,* 380 A.2d 618 (Md. App. 1977).

grated, so that incompatible parol terms are excluded even without a merger clause while compatible terms are excluded only where there is one. Finally, the boundary between what is compatible and what is incompatible cannot be settled formulaically, either by language and logic (contradicting the existence) or by economic considerations (redistributing surplus). Instead, determining whether parol terms are compatible or not requires understanding the full facts and circumstances of the negotiations from which both the writings and the proposed parol terms arise. This is the only method that can conceivably determine whether or not a writing and a parol agreement are in reasonable harmony. And this simply returns the discussion to the central methodological insight of *Masterson*.

Merger clauses are thus not strictly speaking necessary for excluding all parol agreements from contract construction, even under the modern approach. But they are necessary for focusing the determination whether or not to include a parol agreement on the text of a writing and avoiding the full facts-and-circumstances inquiry made express in *Masterson* and employed implicitly in *Hunt Foods*.

Of course, the fact that merger clauses are necessary for integrating contracts does not mean that they are sufficient, either for excluding parol agreement from contract construction *tout court* or for ensuring that the decision whether or not to exclude will be focused on the text of a writing rather than on the broader circumstances in which that text arose. The materials below address these questions.

Connell v. Diamond T. Truck Company

Supreme Court of New Hampshire, 1936.
188 A. 463.

Assumpsit, to recover the purchase price paid for a truck. A trial by jury resulted in a verdict for the plaintiff.

On September 5, 1932, the plaintiff called at the defendant's garage for the purpose of purchasing a truck for use in his business as a highway patrolman. The defendant's general manager showed him the body of one and the chassis of another, both used, which seemed to the plaintiff suitable for his purpose, and he agreed to purchase them, paying therefor $245 and his old truck, provided the defendant would mount the selected body on the selected chassis. This the defendant agreed to do, and did, and on September 7 the plaintiff returned, paid the balance of the purchase price, left his old truck, and drove his purchase away. On the day following the plaintiff discovered that the truck which he had bought was not suitable for the work required of it, and he returned it to the defendant's place of business and demanded his money back. The defendant refused to comply with this demand, but, after some discussion, permitted the plaintiff to take his old truck back and leave the one which he had just bought.

At the trial the plaintiff was permitted to introduce testimony to the effect that upon either September 5, or September 7, the defendant's general manager agreed that the plaintiff might try out the new truck for a week, and, if it did not prove satisfactory, that he might return it and have his money back. The general manager denied that he made such an agreement.

The defendant produced at the trial a written contract of sale, signed by both parties, bearing at the head the date of September 6, and at the foot the date of September 7. The general manager above referred to testified that it was really signed on September 5. This contract was absolute and unconditional in form, and contained the following provision: "There are no promises, verbal understandings, or agreements of any kind, pertaining to this contract other than specified herein."

The defendant seasonably objected and excepted to the admission of the testimony concerning the parol agreement to rescind the contract of sale if the truck should later prove unsatisfactory, and excepted to the denial of its motions for a nonsuit and for a directed verdict. Its bill of exceptions was allowed by Young, J.

WOODBURY, J. The evidence is conflicting not only as to the date of the written contract of sale but also as to the date of the alleged oral agreement to rescind it. As a result of this conflict, it could be found that the oral agreement was made either after, contemporaneously with, or before, the written one. In the event of a finding that the oral agreement was made after the written contract, the parol evidence rule would not apply, because that rule operates to exclude evidence of only those parol agreements at variance with a written contract which were made contemporaneously with or prior to the integration of the agreement in writing. *Piper v. Meredith*, 83 N.H. 107, 112. It does not follow from this, however, that the plaintiff is entitled to recover on the alleged oral agreement as a subsequent independent contract. The reason for this is that the plaintiff gave or promised no valid consideration for the alleged promise of the defendant to rescind if the truck should prove inadequate. The most that he could be found to have given as consideration for the defendant's promise to rescind upon condition was his promise to continue to perform the contractual obligations which he had already assumed by signing the written contract of sale. This, with certain exceptions not here material, is not such consideration as will support a promise. *Eleftherion v. Great Falls Mfg. Company*, 146 A. 172, and cases cited.

On the other hand, if the other interpretation of the evidence is accepted, that is, if it is taken to establish that the oral agreement was made either contemporaneously with or prior to the writing, then the parol evidence rule does apply and the evidence of the oral agreement is inadmissible.

The plaintiff's contention that the oral promise related to a matter not covered by the written contract but supplementary to it, in other words, that it was a separate and separable undertaking not within the four corners of the writing, as was the situation in *Webber v. Loranger*, 79 N.H. 3, and *Steinfield v. Monadnock Mills*, 81 N.H. 152, is without merit. The scope of the written contract, how much of their undertaking they included therein, presents the question of whether or not they intended the writing to be a complete memorial of all their agreements upon the subject. Piper v. Meredith, supra. In the case at bar this question is susceptible of but one answer. The writing itself stipulates in specific terms that it embodies the complete agreement.

It follows that the plaintiff's evidence was inadmissible and that the defendant's motions should have been granted.

Judgment for the defendant.

Columbia Nitrogen v. Royster

United States Court of Appeals for the Fourth Circuit, 1971.
451 F.2d 3.

■ BUTZNER, J. Columbia Nitrogen Corp. appeals a judgment in the amount of $750,000 in favor of F. S. Royster Guano Co. for breach of a contract for the sale of phosphate to Columbia by Royster. Columbia defended on the grounds that the contract, construed in light of the usage of the trade and course of dealing, imposed no duty to accept at the quoted prices the minimum quantities stated in the contract. It also asserted an antitrust defense and counterclaim based on Royster's alleged reciprocal trade practices. The district court excluded the evidence about course of dealing and usage of the trade. It submitted the antitrust issues based on coercive reciprocity to the jury, but refused to submit the alternative theory of non-coercive reciprocity. The jury found for Royster on both the contract claim and the antitrust counterclaim. We hold that Columbia's proffered evidence was improperly excluded and Columbia is entitled to a new trial on the contractual issues. With respect to the antitrust issues, we affirm.

I.

Royster manufactures and markets mixed fertilizers, the principal components of which are nitrogen, phosphate and potash. Columbia is primarily a producer of nitrogen, although it manufactures some mixed fertilizer. For several years Royster had been a major purchaser of Columbia's products, but Columbia had never been a significant customer of Royster. In the fall of 1966, Royster constructed a facility which enabled it to produce more phosphate than it needed in its own operations. After extensive negotiations, the companies executed a contract for Royster's sale of a minimum of 31,000 tons of phosphate each year for three years to Columbia, with an option to extend the term. The contract stated the price per ton, subject to an escalation clause dependent on production costs.

Minimum Tonnage
Per Year

"Diammonium Phosphate 18–46–0	15,000
Granular Triple Superphosphate 0–46–0	15,000

Run-of-Pile Triple Superphosphate 0–46–0   1,000

Phosphate prices soon plunged precipitously. Unable to resell the phosphate at a competitive price, Columbia ordered only part of the scheduled tonnage. At Columbia's request, Royster lowered its price for diammonium phosphate on shipments for three months in 1967, but specified that subsequent shipments would be at the original contract price. Even with this concession, Royster's price was still substantially above the market. As a result, Columbia ordered less than a tenth of the phosphate Royster was to ship in the first contract year. When pressed by Royster, Columbia offered to take the phosphate at the current market price and resell it without brokerage fee. Royster, however, insisted on the contract price. When Columbia refused delivery, Royster sold the unaccepted phosphate for Columbia's account at a price substantially below the contract price.

II.

Columbia assigns error to the pretrial ruling of the district court excluding all evidence on usage of the trade and course of dealing between the parties. It offered the testimony of witnesses with long experience in the trade that because of uncertain crop and weather conditions, farming practices, and government agricultural programs, express price and quantity terms in contracts for materials in the mixed fertilizer industry are mere projections to be adjusted according to market forces.

Columbia also offered proof of its business dealings with Royster over the six-year period preceding the phosphate contract. Since Columbia had not been a significant purchaser of Royster's products, these dealings were almost exclusively nitrogen sales to Royster or exchanges of stock carried in inventory. The pattern which emerges, Columbia claimed, is one of repeated and substantial deviation from the stated amount or price, including four instances where Royster took none of the goods for which it had contracted. Columbia offered proof that the total variance amounted to more than $500,000 in reduced sales. This experience, a Columbia officer offered to testify, formed the basis of an understanding on which he depended in conducting negotiations with Royster.

The district court held that the evidence should be excluded. It ruled that "custom and usage or course of dealing are not admissible to contradict the express, plain, unambiguous language of a valid written contract, which by virtue of its detail negates the proposition that the contract is open to variances in its terms."

A number of Virginia cases have held that extrinsic evidence may not be received to explain or supplement a written contract unless the court finds the writing is ambiguous. *E.g., Mathieson Alkali Works v. Virginia Banner Coal Corp.*, 147 Va. 125 (1927). This rule, however, has been changed by the Uniform Commercial Code which Virginia has adopted. The Code expressly states that it "shall be liberally construed and applied to promote its underlying purposes and policies," which include "the continued expansion of commercial practices through custom, usage and agreement of the parties." Va.Code Ann. § 8.1–102 (1965). The importance of usage of trade and course of dealing between the parties is shown by § 8.2–202, which authorizes their use to explain or supplement a contract. The official comment states this section rejects the old rule that evidence of course of dealing or usage of trade can be introduced only when the contract is ambiguous. And the Virginia commentators, noting that "[t]his section reflects a more liberal approach to the introduction of parol evidence than has been followed in Virginia," express the opinion that *Mathieson, supra,* and similar Virginia cases no longer should be followed. Va. Code Ann. § 8.2–202, Va. Comment. We hold, therefore, that a finding of ambiguity is not necessary for the admission of extrinsic evidence about the usage of the trade and the parties' course of dealing.

We turn next to Royster's claim that Columbia's evidence was properly excluded because it was inconsistent with the express terms of their agreement. There can be no doubt that the Uniform Commercial Code restates the well established rule that evidence of usage of trade and course of dealing should be excluded whenever it cannot be reasonably construed as consistent with the terms of the contract. Royster argues that the evidence should be excluded as inconsistent because the contract contains detailed provisions regarding the base price, escalation, minimum tonnage, and delivery schedules. The argument is based on the premise that because a contract appears on its face to be complete, evidence of course of dealing and usage of trade should be excluded. We believe, however, that neither the language nor the policy of the Code supports such a broad exclusionary rule. Section 8.2–202 expressly allows evidence of course of dealing or usage of trade to explain or supplement terms intended by the parties as a final expression of their agreement. When this section is read in light of Va. Code Ann. § 8.1–205(4), it is clear that the test of admissibility is not whether the contract appears on its face to be complete in every detail, but whether the proffered evidence of course of dealing and trade usage reasonably can be construed as consistent with the express terms of the agreement.

The proffered testimony sought to establish that because of changing weather conditions, farming practices, and government agricultural programs, dealers adjusted prices, quantities, and delivery schedules to reflect declining market conditions. For the following reasons it is reasonable to construe this evidence as consistent with the express terms of the contract:

The contract does not expressly state that course of dealing and usage of trade cannot be used to explain or supplement the written contract.

The contract is silent about adjusting prices and quantities to reflect a declining market. It neither permits nor prohibits adjustment, and this neutrality provides a fitting occasion for recourse to usage of trade and prior dealing to supplement the contract and explain its terms.

Minimum tonnages and additional quantities are expressed in terms of "Products Supplied Under Contract." Significantly, they are not expressed as just "Products" or as "Products Purchased Under Contract." The description used by the parties is consistent with the proffered testimony.

Finally, the default clause of the contract refers only to the failure of the buyer to pay for delivered phosphate. During the contract negotiations, Columbia rejected a Royster proposal for liquidated damages of $10 for each ton Columbia declined to accept. On the other hand, Royster rejected a Columbia proposal for a clause that tied the price to the market by obligating Royster to conform its price to offers Columbia received from other phosphate producers. The parties, having rejected both proposals, failed to state any consequences of Columbia's refusal to take delivery—the kind of default Royster alleges in this case. Royster insists that we span this hiatus by applying the general law of contracts permitting recovery of damages upon the buyer's refusal to take delivery according to the written provisions of the contract. This solution is not what the Uniform Commercial Code prescribes. Before allowing damages, a court must first determine whether the buyer has in fact defaulted. It must do this by supplementing and explaining the agreement with evidence of trade usage and course of dealing that is consistent with the contract's express terms. Va.Code Ann. §§ 8.1–205(4), 8.2–202. Faithful adherence to this mandate reflects the reality of the marketplace and avoids the overly legalistic interpretations which the Code seeks to abolish.

Royster also contends that Columbia's proffered testimony was properly rejected because it dealt with mutual willingness of buyer and seller to adjust contract terms to the market. Columbia, Royster protests, seeks unilateral adjustment. This argument misses the point. What Columbia seeks to show is a practice of mutual adjustments so prevalent in the industry and in prior dealings between the parties that it formed a part of the agreement governing this transaction. It is not insisting on a unilateral right to modify the contract.

Nor can we accept Royster's contention that the testimony should be excluded under the contract clause:

"No verbal understanding will be recognized by either party hereto; this contract expresses all the terms and conditions of the agreement, shall be signed in duplicate, and shall not become operative until approved in writing by the Seller."

Course of dealing and trade usage are not synonymous with verbal understandings, terms and conditions. Section 8.2–202 draws a distinction between supplementing a written contract by consistent additional terms and supplementing it by course of dealing or usage of trade. Evidence of additional terms must be excluded when "the court finds the writing to have been intended also as a complete and exclusive statement of the terms of the agreement." Significantly, no similar limitation is placed on the introduction of evidence of course of dealing or usage of trade. Indeed the official comment notes that course of dealing and usage of trade, unless carefully negated, are admissible to supplement the terms of any writing, and that contracts are to be read on the assumption that these elements were taken for granted when the document was phrased. Since the Code assigns course of dealing and trade usage unique and important roles, they should not be conclusively rejected by reading them into stereotyped language that makes no specific reference to them. Indeed, the Code's official commentators urge that overly simplistic and overly legalistic interpretation of a contract should be shunned.

We conclude, therefore, that Columbia's evidence about course of dealing and usage of trade should have been admitted. Its exclusion requires that the judgment against Columbia must be set aside and the case retried.

Southern Concrete Services v. Mabelton Contractors, Inc.

United States District Court for the Northern District of Georgia, 1975.
407 F.Supp. 581.

■ EDENFIELD, C.J. This is a diversity action in which plaintiff seller seeks to recover lost profits and out-of-pocket expenses from defendant buyer for buyer's alleged breach of contract. The case is currently before the court on plaintiff's motion for a ruling on the admissibility of certain evidence.

In September 1972 the parties entered into a contract for the sale of concrete for use in the construction of the building foundation of a power plant near Carrollton, Georgia. The contract stipulated that plaintiff was to supply "approximately 70,000 cubic yards" of concrete from September 1, 1972 to June 15, 1973. The price to be paid for such concrete was $19.60 per cubic yard. The contract further stipulated that "No conditions which are not incorporated in this contract will be recognized." During the time period involved defendant ordered only 12,542 cubic yards of concrete, that being the total amount needed by the defendant for its construction work. The plaintiff has brought this action to recover the profits lost by defendant's alleged breach and the costs plaintiff incurred in purchasing and delivering over $20,000 in raw materials to the jobsite.

The defendant claims that the written contract must be interpreted both in light of the custom of the trade and in light of additional terms allegedly intended by the parties. Defendant contends that under such custom and additional terms, it was understood that the quantity stipulated in the contract was not mandatory upon either of the parties and that both quantity and price were understood to be subject to renegotiation. It is this evidence of custom in the trade and of additional conditions allegedly agreed to by the parties that defendant seeks to introduce at trial.

In support of its position, defendant relies upon Georgia Code Ann. s 109A–2–202 (U.C.C. s 2–202) which provides that a written contract may be explained or supplemented "by a course of dealing or usage of trade" and by evidence of "consistent additional terms." This section was meant to liberalize the common law parol evidence rule to allow evidence of agreements outside the contract, without a prerequisite finding that the contract was ambiguous. In addition, the section requires contracts to be interpreted in light of the commercial context in which they were written and not by the rules of legal construction. See Draftsmen's Comment to U.C.C. s 2–202, *Warren's Kiddie Shoppe, Inc. v. Casual Slacks, Inc.*, 120 Ga.App. 578 (1969).

The question then becomes what is meant by the term "explained or supplemented"; does defendant's evidence "explain" the contract or does it attempt to "contradict" it? The court will examine this question with regard to the trade usage issue first, and then deal with the "additional terms" question.

I.

In the official comment to U.C.C. s 2–202, the draftsmen emphasize that contracts are to be interpreted with the assumption that the usages of trade "were taken for granted when the document was phrased. Unless carefully negated they have become an element of the meaning of the words used," Comment No. 2. In *Columbia Nitrogen Corp. v. Royster Co.*, 451 F.2d 3 (4th Cir. 1971), the court was faced with a contract similar to the one in the instant case. The contract provided for the sale of at least 31,000 tons of phosphate each year for three years at a stated price, subject to an escalation clause dependent on production costs. The buyer bought less than one-tenth the minimum amount contracted for in the first year and the seller brought suit. The defendant offered to introduce evidence showing that contracts of the type involved were meant to be mere projections of price and quantity due to the rapid fluctuation in demand in the fertilizer industry. The defendant buyer also sought to introduce evidence of prior dealings between the parties in which the plaintiff, as buyer, often failed to purchase the entire amount contracted for from defendant. Since the contract was silent on the subject of adjusting prices and quantities to reflect a declining market, and since it did "not expressly state that course of dealing and usage of trade cannot be used to explain or supplement the written contract", the court allowed the evidence to be admitted. 451 F.2d at 9, 10.

There are, however, certain important differences between Royster and the case at hand. In Royster, the court noted that the contract default clause dealt only with the buyer's failure to pay for delivered phosphate, thus raising the possibility that the contract was not meant to require the buyer to accept the entire contract amount. In addition, the court was faced with a situation where the equities were strongly in favor of the defendant. In previous dealings between the parties, the defendant had apparently never insisted on purchase of the entire contract amount by plaintiff. Now that plaintiff was the seller it was insisting on strict compliance with the literal terms of the contract. The plaintiff also enjoyed the protection of an escalation clause in the contract which allowed it to raise prices to compensate for increased production costs, while plaintiff refused to allow the defendant to renegotiate for a lower price to reflect market conditions. Thus the court in Royster faced a situation in which one party may have been trying to take unfair advantage of a long-standing customer.

Such a situation is not present in this case, however, and this court has grave doubts about applying the reasoning of *Royster* to different fact situations. Here, no prior dealings are alleged by either party; the contract by its terms does not intimate that the buyer would only be liable for concrete actually delivered, and the contract does not contain provisions granting one party special repricing rights. Instead, the contract sets out fairly specific quantity, price, and time specifications. To allow such specific contracts to be challenged by extrinsic evidence might jeopardize the certainty of the contractual duties which parties have a right to rely on. Certainly customs of the trade should be relevant to the interpretation of certain terms of a contract, see Warren's Kiddie Shoppe, supra, and should be considered in determining what variation in specifications is considered acceptable, see *Modine Manufacturing Co. v. Northeast Ind. School District,* 503 S.W.2d 833 (Texas Ct. of Civ.App.1973) (where the court allowed a 6% deviation in cooling capacity of an air-conditioning system since such deviation was acceptable in the trade), but this court does not believe that section 2–202 was meant to invite a frontal assault on the essential terms of a clear and explicit contract.

The type of evidence which the *Royster* decision might allow and which the defendant here undoubtedly wishes to introduce would probably show that very few contracts specifying quantity and price in a particular industry have been strictly enforced. (See, e. g., *Royster*, supra, at 7–8, n. 3.) While in some industries it may be virtually impossible to predict future needs under a contract, in other industries, such contracts may not be strictly adhered to for entirely different reasons. Lawsuits are costly and they do not facilitate good business relations with customers. A party to a contract may very much prefer to work out a renegotiation of a contract rather than rest on its strict legal rights. Yet, the supplier or purchaser knows that he may resort to those enforceable contract rights if necessary. If the courts were to conclude that this reluctance to enforce legal rights resulted in an industry-wide waiver of such rights, then contracts would lose their utility as a means of assigning the risks of the market. The defendant here may be correct in its assertion that contracts for the sale of concrete are often subject to renegotiation, but that fact alone does not convince the court that the parties here did not contemplate placing on the buyer the risk of variation in quantity needs.

The court recognizes that all ambiguity as to the applicability of trade usage could be eliminated by a blanket condition that the express terms of the contract are in no way to be modified by custom, usage, or prior dealings. Indeed, the *Royster* court found the absence of such a clause to be a determinative factor in allowing in extrinsic evidence. This court, however, is reluctant to encourage the use of yet another standard boilerplate provision in commercial contracts. If such a clause is necessary to preserve the very essence of a contract, then the purposes of the Code will be quickly frustrated. Consideration of commercial custom is an important aid in the interpretation of the terms of a contract, but parties will have no choice but to foreclose the use of such an aid if the inevitable result of such consideration is to have explicit contracts negated by an evidentiary free-for-all.

Although the official comments suggest that parties which do not want trade usage to apply should so stipulate in the contract (Comment 2 to s 2–202), that provision could not have been meant to allow the full-scale attack on the contract suggested here. The more reasonable approach is to assume that specifications as to quantity and price are intended to be observed by the parties and that the unilateral right to make a major departure from such specifications must be expressly agreed to in the written contract. That way, the courts will still be free to apply custom and trade usage in interpreting terms of the contract without raising apprehension in the commercial world as to the continued reliability of those contracts. Such an approach is consistent with the underlying purposes of the Uniform Commercial Code, which dictates that the express terms of a contract and trade usage shall be construed as consistent with each other only when such construction is reasonable. A construction which negates the express terms of the contract by allowing unilateral abandonment of its specifications is patently unreasonable.

II.

The defendant also claims that section 2–202 allows the introduction of evidence of additional terms of the agreement between the parties. Those terms presumably called for price renegotiation and contained an understanding that the quantity quoted in the contract was intended only as an estimate. The court suspects, however, that the defendant is attempting to use section 2–202(b) as merely an alternative vehicle to get in evidence as to trade usage. The defendant does not specify in its brief the terms of the alleged extrinsic agreement and does not indicate whether it was oral or written, prior or contemporaneous. Rather, the defendant merely tags its 202(b) request on its trade usage claim as an apparent afterthought. But even if this court assumes that defendant will attempt to show additional terms of the contract, such evidence would be inadmissible. Section 2–202 requires that written contracts "not be contradicted" by evidence of agreements outside of the written contract, but that they may be explained or supplemented by evidence of "consistent additional terms" if the court finds the contract was not meant to be the complete statement of the agreement.

Whether or not the contract in issue was meant to be complete in itself, it is clear that the additional terms sought to be proved are not consistent with it. The type of evidence which may be admitted under subsection (b) deals with agreements covering matters not dealt with in the written contract. See, e. g., *Flamm v. Scherer*, 198 N.W.2d 702 (1972). To admit evidence of an agreement which would contradict the express terms of the contract would clearly eviscerate the purpose of s 2–202, *Bunge Corp. v. Recker*, 519 F.2d 449 (8th Cir. 1975), see also Comment 3 to s 2–202.

The court is aware that at least one court has favored a broader construction of s 2–202, holding that evidence of a contemporaneous oral agreement to provide up to 500 tons of steel was consistent with a written provision in the contract stipulating delivery of 500 tons. *Schiavone &*

Sons, Inc. v. Securalloy Co., Inc., 312 F.Supp. 801 (D.Conn.1970). That court explained:

> In making this determination, it must be borne in mind that to be inconsistent the terms must contradict or negate a term of the written agreement; and a term which has a lesser effect is deemed to be a consistent term." 312 F.Supp. 804.

This court respectfully disagrees with the above reasoning; for the buyer who wished to obtain all 500 tons, and who had to cover his requirements elsewhere, the term "up to 500" tons was clearly inconsistent with the contract. Similarly, a hypothetical agreement between the instant parties that quantity and price terms were to be mere estimates is inconsistent with the written contract.

Finally, the contract at issue specified that conditions not incorporated in the contract would not be recognized. In contrast, in *Schiavone*, supra, the court noted the absence of such a clause in finding the parol evidence admissible. The presence of such a clause here further convinces the court that the writing was intended to be the "complete and exclusive statement" of the terms of the agreement, Ga.Code Ann. s 109A–2–202(b).

The court therefore concludes that the evidence sought to be introduced by the defendant is inadmissible at trial.

* * *

The central question raised by merger clauses is whether, and to what extent, they are effective, and hence how much control the parties possess over the construction of their contracts. In other words, how sticky is the soft parol evidence rule associated with *Masterson* and *Hunt Foods*? Is it simply a default, which the parties may vary at will; or is it in fact a quasi-mandatory rule, which the parties must incur costs to vary—costs that will not always pay off?

The shallow logic of *Masterson* seems to favor making the softness of the parol evidence rule a default only. The rule in *Masterson* states, after all, that even as prior or contemporaneous oral agreements may add to writings, they may not vary writings. By stating that a writing contains the entire agreement between the parties, a merger clause entails that there exist no terms outside the writing. Accordingly, every resort to prior or contemporaneous oral agreements would not merely add to but vary the writing, specifically the merger clause (indeed merger clause would contradict the existence of such agreements). So doctrine set out in *Masterson* (and *Hunt Foods*), at least on its face, allows the parties to return to the hard parol evidence rule of the classical regime simply by writing that they wish to do so. The soft parol evidence rule seems a default rule only. But although some easy cases illustrate just this logic; harder cases show that the problem is in fact much more difficult than the shallow logic supposes.

Connell is an easy case, which illustrates how merger clauses work when their workings are uncomplicated. The plaintiff in that case bought a truck from the defendant, pursuant to a written sales contract. The writing stated that the sale was unconditional and that the written text constituted the entire agreement between the parties. The plaintiff nevertheless sought to return the truck, arguing that an oral agreement permitted the plaintiff one week to inspect the truck and determine whether or not to keep it. The defendant sought to exclude the parol grant of an inspection period, citing the merger clause and the parol evidence rule. The court sided straightforwardly with the defendant; the merger clause, the court observed, directly excluded (indeed contradicted the existence of) the parol promise from the contractual text. Moreover, the circumstances surrounding the written agreement (at least, as they are reported in the court's opinion) gave no reason to doubt the merger clause's sincerity or that the alleged oral agreement concerning the inspection time fell within the merger clause's scope.[10]

Royster by contrast, is a difficult case. It is a difficult case precisely because any number of facts and circumstances concerning the contract at issue there suggest that the merger clause that that contract contained might have a highly limited scope and be only dubiously sincere. The plaintiff and defendant, in *Royster*, entered into substantial negotiations for the plaintiff to sell the defendant phosphate. The negotiations culminated in a written sales contract, under which the defendant agreed to buy a minimum quantity of 31,000 tons of phosphate per year, for three years. The writing included a merger clause, which stated both that no "verbal" understandings between the parties would be recognized and that the writing expressed all the terms and conditions of the parties' agreement.[11] When phosphate prices fell precipitously over the period of the contract, and the defendant ordered substantially less than the minimum quantity, the plaintiff sued.

The defendant sought to introduce testimony concerning usage of trade generally in the phosphate industry and the prior course of dealing specifically between the parties that would reveal that express price and quantity terms in phosphate contracts are mere projections, to be adjusted in response to market fluctuations. The defendant contended that this evi-

---

10. The only complication in *Connell* concerned the timing of the writing and the oral agreement. There was a suggestion, in the case, that the oral agreement did not precede but rather followed the writing. No version of the parol evidence rule excludes oral agreements that come after a writing (such subsequent oral agreements are, after all, naturally—indeed necessarily—omitted from the prior written text).

This is just to say that oral agreements can effectively modify a written contract. But in order to do so, they must validly form contracts of their own. The oral term in *Connell*, if it really did come after the writing, could not establish such a contract, as it was not supported by consideration.

11. Note that the merger clause's use of the word "verbal" represented a drafting error, which rendered the clause literally false. The parties intended to refer to "oral" understandings rather than "verbal" ones. The writing itself, after all, is a verbal agreement, constructed out of words rather than (say) images or samples.

This observation is partly pedantry, to be sure (but be careful how you use words nevertheless). But it also emphasizes the need for contextualism in interpretation (see Section 17.2 below). A "plain meaning" reading of the clause would have it deny that any contract existed at all. Only the context reveals (and makes overwhelmingly clear) that this is not what the parties had in mind.

dence would reveal that the literal obligation to purchase the minimum quantity expired with the market fluctuation. The defendant cast this contention in two lights. On the one hand, the defendant argued, as a matter of contract interpretation, that usage of trade and course of dealing revealed that the minimum quantity clause meant something other than what a literal reading of its words would suggest. On the other hand, the defendant argued, as a matter of contract construction, that even if the best interpretation of the minimum quantity clause remained the literal one, the parties had a parol agreement, separate from the writing, according to which market conditions might entitle it to order less than this quantity. The defendant argued that this parol agreement, again based on course of dealing and usage of trade, properly belonged in the contractual text.

Notwithstanding the merger clause, the court was sympathetic to both the defendant's arguments. With respect to interpretation (of which more in the next section), the court observed that under modern doctrine, a finding that a writing is ambiguous on its face is not required in order for extrinsic evidence to be admissible as to the meaning of the written text. With respect to construction, the court asserted that under the U.C.C., a parol agreement may be included in the contractual text even where the text is complete (and indeed exclusive) on its face, as long only as the parol agreement (drawn, in this case, from usage of trade and course of dealing) may be reasonably construed as consistent with the writing, itself reasonably construed.

To begin with, the court thought that such reasonable consistency could be achieved in respect of the minimum quantity clause at issue in *Royster*. It read that clause as being quite weak, observing: that the clause did not expressly reject adjustments to price or quantity;[12] that the clause referred to "product supplied" rather than "product purchased," which opened up the possibility that it referred to the plaintiff's obligation to make an amount available to the defendant rather than to the defendant's obligation to buy an amount; and that the parties had considered but rejected a liquidated damages clause that would have charged the defendant for amounts by which its purchases fell below the minimum.

Moreover, the court also construed the merger clause weakly. That clause, the court observed, referred only to "verbal understandings," while courses of dealing and usages of trade are not "verbal" and indeed not necessarily "understandings" at all. Accordingly, the merger clause, by its own terms, excluded only discrete spoken promises, and not the patterns and practices on which the defendant relied. Furthermore, the court connected its preference for course of dealing and usage of trade in *Royster* to an analogous broader preference that it purported to identify in the U.C.C. The court observed that whereas U.C.C. § 2–202(b), which concerns additional terms of the type that the court called "verbal understandings,"

---

12.   One might think that the word *minimum* expressly means "zero downward adjustment," but the court seemed to treat a single word as less forceful or effective than this phrase.

rejects the inclusion of such additional terms where a contractual writing is fully integrated, no such integration condition is included in § 2–202(a) on course of dealing and usage of trade. Accordingly, the court reasoned, course of dealing and usage of trade may be kept out of a contractual text only by language that specifically names and excludes such parol terms. The merger clause at issue in *Royster*, the court concluded, not only failed to name course of dealing and usage of trade expressly and specifically, but it used language that implied that course of dealing and usage of trade fell outside the scope of its integration.

Royster thus gave the defendant an opportunity to prove up parol agreements that would permit downward departures from the minimum quantity requirements imposed by the written text. Whatever one thinks of the merits of the *Royster* court's analysis, this result clearly calls into question whether contracts might *ever* be fully integrated under the U.C.C. regime that the opinion describes and applies. This regime thus not only makes merger clauses necessary to produce any significant partial integration of a contractual writing; it also entails that merger clauses are never sufficient for full integration. To be sure, an adequately express and specific merger clause might reliably exclude a type of parol agreement, or perhaps just a particular token agreement, from the construction of a contract's text. Even *Royster* acknowledged that if the merger clause had referred expressly to course of dealing, say, or better yet to particular instances of course of dealing, then parol agreements based on these instances could not be included in the ultimate contract. But blanket exclusions of parol agreements are not possible under the regime announced by *Royster*. The various biases in favor of including parol agreements in a contract's text that this regime includes are simply too strong to be overcome by party stipulations in favor of an alternative regime, especially where the equities favor the outcomes that these biases would produce. Although *Royster's* approach to particular parol agreements remains a default rule only (which the parties may vary through sufficiently specific and explicit language), the general permissive approach to parol agreements—the broad inclination to eliminate the law's traditional preference for writings—takes on the character of a mandatory rule.

Southern Concrete takes issue precisely with the quasi-mandatory aspect of the inclusion of parol agreements under *Royster*. The plaintiff in *Southern Concrete* contracted to sell the defendant 70,000 cubic yards of concrete. The written agreement between the parties stated that "[n]o conditions which are not incorporated in this contract will be recognized." The defendant ordered only 12,500 cubic yards, and the plaintiff sued for damages arising out of the shortfall. The defendant, relying on U.C.C. § 2–202, argued that the writing might be "explained or supplemented" by usage of trade and by additional terms agreed to orally by the parties.

The *Southern Concrete* court distinguished *Royster*, and in terms that amounted to an attack on *Royster's* reasoning.[13] On the one hand, the

---

13. More narrowly, the *Southern Concrete* court also observed that the case before it presented no analog of the rejected liquidated damages clause in *Royster*, which gave the parol

Southern Concrete court declined to infer agreements from usage of trade. The court observed that if apparently mandatory terms in writings went regularly unenforced, this might be simply because of the high costs of enforcement in practice, rather than because they were regarded as less than binding in principle. This argument strikes at the heart of one of *Royster's* central points, namely that the distinction between oral agreements on the one hand and course of dealing and usage of trade on the other entails that the latter may be included in contract construction even where a merger clause expressly rules out the former. According to *Southern Concrete*, the very features of course of dealing and usage of trade that exempt these from the scope of merger clauses addressed to oral agreements also render them unlikely to constitute agreements capable of entering into a contractual text at all. And on the other hand, *Southern Concrete* rejected *Royster's* preference for explicitness and specificity in merger clauses. The court recognized that the plaintiff might have excluded the defendant's supplemental terms, even under the rule of *Royster*, by drafting an express merger provision excluding usage of trade, for example, or even excluding certain specific usages. But the court reasoned that such express merger clauses should not be encouraged. Doing so would simply lead to their pro-forma inclusion in pre-printed forms, as boilerplate. That practice would further clutter already over-long contracts and also raise any number of thorny issues concerning their enforceability (to be addressed in Chapter 20 below). It would also deprive contracting parties of the valuable opportunity to rely on usage of trade or course of dealing to flesh out their contracts and reduce the transactions costs of drafting.

Southern Concrete recognized that the U.C.C.'s regime concerning parol evidence is significantly softer and more inclusive than the classical rule and especially favors parol agreements based on course of dealing and usage of trade. But it refused to read the U.C.C. in a manner that allows a full "frontal assault on the essential terms of a clear and explicit [written] contract."

Both logic and common sense seem to suggest that whatever the equities of the particular dispute in *Royster*, the *Southern Concrete* court rightly refused to adopt *Royster's* approach as a general and expansive rule. The logic of contract—the idea that contracts should capture the intentions and plans of the contracting parties—strongly suggests that the U.C.C.'s inclusive approach to including parol agreements in contract construction must be meaningfully alterable by the parties. Parol agreements, after all, are prior to or contemporaneous with a writing; and parties who wish their writing to control their contract relation must retain the power to make their relation on these terms. A mandatory soft parol evidence rule—which refuses to give effect to merger clauses, so that contracts remain conclusively un-integrated—undermines contract law's basic commitment to respecting the intentions of the parties.

---

agreements admitted there a least a foothold in the written text. The court also observed that the equities favored inclusion of the parol agreement in *Royster* much more than in the case before it.

But *Royster* might also be read a little differently, and much more flatteringly. Merger clauses simply cannot exclude all parol agreements. To begin with, it is always possible that, as a matter of fact, an oral agreement more actually reflects the contracting parties' soberest intentions than their writing. (In a world of boilerplate form contracts, this is not just possible but often actual.) Furthermore, merger clauses cannot actually exclude all parol agreements. No writing can ever be complete, and no writing can practically come close to completeness. The costs of contract drafting entail that writings must always leave gaps that can, if the circumstances develop in a certain way, require filling-in before a contract may be effectively applied. This rule of incompleteness, moreover, applies not only to written contracts, but also to written contract law: the law's gap-fillers will also be necessarily sometimes incomplete. There is thus always the possibility that both an integrated writing and the background law will, even taken together, fail to provide a term required to operate a contract as circumstances develop. The way in which the missing term is filled-in may, moreover, influence the division of contractual surplus associated with the contract's other terms. As long as it is not an option simply to reject that a contract exists in such cases (and the deep structure of modern contract law and common sense both insist that this is indeed not an option), the missing terms must be supplied. And in such cases, prior and contemporaneous oral agreements are surely relevant to supplying the terms. Moreover, they remain relevant even in the face of general merger clauses.

This is just a roundabout way of observing that merger clauses cannot, in principle, be sufficient fully to integrate a contractual writing. That, at the most abstract level, is the general learning of *Royster*. And once the general point is accepted, deciding cases inevitably requires fixing the limits of such merger clauses as actual contracts contain, in light of the facts and circumstances in which these clauses were drafted. And this, again at the most abstract level, is the decision-making process that *Royster* adopts.

Finally, *Southern Concrete* does not reject these propositions, cast at such a high level of generality and abstraction. That is why the *Southern Concrete* court recognized that, as a general matter, the U.C.C. softens the classical parol evidence rule and opens up contract construction to parol agreements, even in the presence of merger clauses. That is also why the *Southern Concrete* court bothered to mention the equities of the case before it (such considerations would have been irrelevant had the case been decided under the classical regime).

Both opinions thus acknowledge (because *Royster* does not deny) that a merger clause can influence contract construction, making it more difficult to introduce parol agreements into a contractual text. And both opinions acknowledge (because *Southern Concrete* does not deny) that a merger clause cannot be self-authorizing, so that appropriate facts and circumstances will support including parol agreements in contact construction, including in the teeth of express written efforts to exclude them. Both opinions therefore leave courts room for maneuver, to balance writings and parol agreements in the way that leads to the most accurate contract construction possible. This free-play, and the judicial effort to identify and promote the plans of the contracting parties that it invites, is the ultimate hallmark of functionalist contract law. Functionalists might disagree about how courts should go about identifying the parties' plans. Some will think, with the *Royster* court, that while the parties are best able to balance the costs and benefits of merger clauses ex ante (which is why the rules of contract construction should not be mandatory), courts can do better ex post than the parties can do ex ante (which is why courts should remain free to side-step party instructions concerning contract construction where they think it best to do so). Others will think, with *Southern Concrete*, that courts' distance from the parties' negotiations and parties' capacities to manipulate the evidence that the courts see combine to make even ex post judicial discretion concerning construction less accurate than a mechanical following of the ex ante instructions given by the contracting parties themselves. Some might so worry about the manipulability of courts that they go even further than the *Southern Concrete* court was prepared to go and adopt something approaching the categorical preference for writings, even in the absence of merger clauses, associated with hard parol evidence rule. But they do so contingently, and for functionalist reasons (so that if courts became more accurate, they would change their minds), rather than in the categorical manner of the classical doctrine.

The *Royster* and *Southern Concrete* courts thus disagree less about logic than about experience: they agree on a functionalist rather than formalist approach to contract construction; and they disagree only about what substantive doctrines functionalism recommends.

17.2   CONTRACT INTERPRETATION

Even after the confines of a contractual text have been established, the text's meaning may remain unclear. This is because contractual texts, like all texts, must be interpreted. Among the grounds of the constant need for interpretation to mediate between text and meaning are these: language may be used figuratively rather than literally; it may be ambiguous; and it may be vague.[14]

---

14. Note that these three characterizations pick out conceptually distinct possibilities. Three example illustrate this point.

When Larkin says that human misery "deepens as a coastal shelf" he is writing figuratively, in the sense that he does not actually mean that misery exists in three-dimensional space. But he is not being ambiguous—there is no doubt that he is writing about the human condition or that he thinks us a miserable species indeed. Nor is he being vague—the misery he points to is as deep as deep can be.

The phrase "Let's give the job to Alvarez" is literal rather than figurative. If there are two Alvarezes in the candidate pool, then it is also ambiguous. But it is not vague.

Finally, the sentence "She is a fabulous lawyer" is again literal rather than figurative. It is not ambiguous: there is no doubt that it means to praise the person whom it describes. But it is vague: how good is fabulous; is fabulousness measured on an absolute or relative scale; if relative, what percentage of lawyers qualify?

Drawing meaning from a contractual text—even after that text has been fixed through appropriate contract construction—requires deciphering the literal implications of figurative language, resolving ambiguities, and drawing clear lines in the face of vagueness. These can all be difficult tasks in particular instances. The interpretive tasks also raise difficult questions of general method. Perhaps the most important of these methodological questions has already been flagged by some of the cases on contract construction. Several of the opinions in these cases observed that even if parol agreements remain excluded from a contractual text, they may still influence the contract's ultimate meaning, because they may affect the interpretation of the contract's written text. But ought parol agreements be accorded such interpretive weight? More generally, ought the interpretation of a contractual text (whether written or not) be focused principally or even exclusively on the four-corners of the text itself, or ought the context from which the text arose also be permitted to influence contract interpretation?

The following materials take up this question. They begin by setting out the classical (formalist) and modern (more functionalist) doctrinal styles of contract interpretation. Next, they take up theoretical arguments concerning the dispute between these approaches to interpretation, which sound in ideas about the general nature of language. Finally, they take up more practical arguments, which emphasize the role of contract interpretation in supporting the reliability and efficiency of contractual practice. One theme of the discussion will be that the practical arguments are both sounder and more weighty than the theoretical ones.

In re Soper's Estate

Supreme Court of Minnesota, 1935.
264 N.W. 427.

■ OLSON, J. Plaintiffs appeal from an order denying their motion for new trial after the cause had been heard and decision rendered for defendants. The facts are not in substantial conflict. But solution of the legal problems presented thereby is decidedly controversial, at least so counsel for the parties seem to think.

Ira Collins Soper, a native and resident of Kentucky, was the central figure in the drama now to be depicted. In October, 1911, he and plaintiff Adeline Johnson Westphal were united in marriage. She was a widow with three young daughters, the issue of her first marriage. She and her three daughters lived with him until August, 1921, when he suddenly disappeared, not to be heard of again by his wife during his remaining lifetime. Their family life is said to have been a happy one. But there were many occasions when Mrs. Soper undoubtedly had real difficulties with which to contend. Soper was inclined to go on periodic sprees. He had been on such a spree immediately prior to his last departure from plaintiff wife. His sister, who was visiting at that time with the Soper family, had upbraided him about this affair and so had the wife of one of his friends. The Sopers are said to be proud of their family name, and the good repute of its members was a matter not to be lightly treated. On at least two prior occasions he had made unannounced trips, once to Memphis and at another time to St. Louis, after having been on such drunken sprees. But at the time of the last-mentioned occasion he studiously and almost fiendishly made his disappearance take on the aspect of suicide. He wrote several suicide notes to his wife, one of them ending with this significant statement: 'If there is any hereafter may meet you again.' His car was found at the bank of a nearby canal and so were his hat and portions of his clothing. Pinned to his business card and left in his car was a note reading: 'This belongs to Mrs. Soper.'

The record abundantly supports the view that he did not intend to end his life but went through these performances for the sole purpose of deceiving his wife and to leave with her the impression that he had in fact committed suicide. He managed to leave Louisville, that being his home, without clue or trace. He first went to Canada and shortly thereafter came to Minneapolis. There he assumed the name of John W. Young. By that name, and that name only, he was known to his business and social acquaintances from the time he came to Minneapolis until his death in 1932, something like eleven years. In Minneapolis he became well acquainted and established both in a business and social way. He entered the fuel business and with one Karstens formed a corporation known as the Young Fuel Company. In 1922 he married a widow, Mary Christopher, a resident of Minneapolis, and they lived together as husband and wife and were so known until she died in 1925. In May, 1927, he married defendant Gertrude Whitby, another Minneapolis widow, with whom he had been acquainted and had kept company for some six or eight months prior to their marriage. They lived together as husband and wife from the time of this marriage until his death in 1932, when he actually did commit suicide. Gertrude in good faith believed him to be a widower, he having informed her and many others that his first wife died of pneumonia many years prior thereto.

Some time after Young's marriage to Gertrude, he and Karstens were interviewed by one Smith, an insurance agent, who devised a stock insurance plan whereby provision was to be made for the surviving partner of the fuel company to acquire the entire business in event of death of one of them, the surviving wife of such deceased partner to be compensated by life insurance to be taken out by each partner upon his life, premiums to be paid by the fuel company and charged as an item of operating expense. The purpose was to keep the corporate enterprise from becoming split up as to stock ownership in event of death of either owner. The capital of the fuel company was $10,000 represented by 400 shares of the par value of $25 each. The ownership of the stock was as follows: Karstens had 175 shares, Mrs. Karstens 25, Young 195, and Gertrude 5. Each owner, i. e., Karstens and Young, was to take out a policy of life insurance in the amount of $5,000 payable to First Minneapolis Trust Company, as trustee. The resulting agreement, designated 'escrow receipt,' after reciting the deposit of 200 shares by each depositor, provides:

'Upon the decease of either John W. Young or Ferdinand J. Karstens, the Trust Company shall proceed to collect the proceeds of the Insurance Policies upon the life of such deceased Depositor, and shall handle and dispose of such proceeds as follows:

'The Trust Company shall deliver the stock certificate of the deceased Depositor to the surviving Depositor and it shall deliver the proceeds of the insurance on the life of the deceased Depositor to the wife of the deceased Depositor if living, and if not living, then to the representative of his estate, and the stock certificates that were deposited by the Depositor who is then the surviving Depositor, together with the policies of insurance upon his life shall be delivered to such surviving Depositor.

'All of the stock deposited hereunder and all of the policies deposited hereunder or any part thereof may be withdrawn by said two Depositors on the joint receipt of both of them.'

The policies were duly issued and, with the stock certificates, appropriately indorsed, deposited with the trustee. The insurance premiums were paid by the fuel company. Shortly after Young's death the trustee collected the insurance money upon the policy issued upon his life and paid the proceeds over to defendant Gertrude as his surviving wife, and at the same time delivered to Mr. Karstens as the surviving partner decedent's 200 shares in the fuel company, together with the policy issued upon his life.

The trust officer who dealt with the parties was informed that the relationship between Young and Gertrude was that of husband and wife, likewise that of Karstens and his wife. No one except Young knew anything about the first wife. She was to all intents and purposes, as to all arrangements and engagements heretofore related, entirely out of the picture.

Several months elapsed after these matters had been properly closed by the parties, as they in good faith thought, when Mrs. Soper, the true wife of Young, put in her appearance. An administrator of the estate of the late Soper, alias Young, was appointed. He and Mrs. Soper brought this suit against defendants to recover the insurance money. The suit was brought upon the theory that this fund had been erroneously paid by the trustee to Gertrude.

Plaintiffs have assigned 40 errors and devote pages 18 to 50, inclusive, in their printed brief thereto. These are summarized, however, into more compact form thus: 'The essential issue, as it really presented itself at the trial, was this: granting that Mrs. Whitby was not the deceased's wife, could not be his wife, was not his heir, did not have and could not have any rights of inheritance, statutory or otherwise, did Soper, by some valid, clear, effective supervening instrument, valid as a will or as a present deed or conveyance inter vivos, shut off and determine, in her or in some one else's favor, the clear rights which his wife and heir would otherwise plainly have had? And further, if it first be found that he actually did execute a valid instrument which clearly and unmistakably has that effect, to deprive his wife of her rights, did he have the power to do that, without his wife's consent, under our law?'

It must be conceded that defendant Gertrude never was the legal wife of decedent. Although her innocence of wrongdoing is clearly established and her good faith in entering into her marriage relation with Young is amply sustained, the fact remains that she can take nothing under the laws of descent. Nor do we think the escrow agreement can be considered a testamentary disposition of the insurance money or of any other property included in that instrument. It was not so intended, and nothing therein contained can be so construed. Rather, so it seems to us, it takes the form of and functions as an insurance trust.

Even if it be conceded that this was not an insurance trust, the authorities generally seem to hold that such arrangements, even if not involving the trust aspect, are valid as inter vivos transactions because they are contractual in nature. Thus in *Coe v. Winchester* (Ariz.) 33 P.2d 286, it appears that two partners entered into a written agreement whereby each agreed that he would effect a policy of life insurance payable to his wife. On the death of either, the wife of the deceased was to get the insurance and the surviving partner was to take the deceased's interest in the partnership. Under Arizona law each partner's interest in the business is community property belonging equally to the partner and his wife. But as to such property the husband has complete right of disposal of the entire interest by any deal inter vivos, but cannot make a testamentary disposition of his wife's interest. One of the partners died. His wife claimed a one-fourth interest in the business upon the theory that the attempted disposition of the property was testamentary and therefore could not affect her community interest. The court came to the conclusion that the contract was not a testamentary disposition of property and that as such the entire one-half interest of the deceased partner had been validly transferred. In the last-cited case the court held an agreement between a stockholder and a corporation, of similar nature, import, and purpose to those partnership cases hereinbefore cited, to be mutually binding upon each and all the parties thereto from the date of its execution. It was held there that there was no testamentary disposition of the property.

We conclude that Gertrude neither did nor could take anything as the 'wife' of Young. As a matter of law, she never became such. But this conclusion does not solve our problem because she does not lay claim to the insurance merely as his lawful wife, but as the person intended to be the beneficiary under the escrow agreement as fully as if her name had been written into that contract instead of the word 'wife.' So the real question presented is whether under the escrow agreement designating the 'wife' of depositor Young as the beneficiary parol proof is admissible that Gertrude was so intended and not Mrs. Soper, the true wife. Plaintiffs claim that the written instrument is free from ambiguity, latent or otherwise, and that as such it was improper for the trial court to permit oral evidence to show who was intended thereby to be such beneficiary. They strenuously assert that the agreement is not subject to construction, that it is perfectly plain in its language, and that the only thing for the court to determine is whether Mrs. Soper was the lawful wife of the deceased husband, or if Gertrude was such.

From the facts and circumstances hereinbefore related, the conclusion seems inescapable that Gertrude was intended. She was the only one known or considered by the contracting parties. True, Young knew otherwise, but that he did not intend his real wife to take anything as beneficiary seems obvious. From the time he left Louisville and came to Minneapolis, and until some time after his death, no one amongst his business or social acquaintances knew anything of or concerning his true wife. Gertrude alone answered the descriptive designation of 'wife.' Public records disclosed her and her alone to be such. There was no one else.

The question of who is one's wife is at times, under circumstances similar to what we are here considering, a matter of grave concern and genuine dispute. There may be involved the question of divorce, whether the court had jurisdiction of the status or of the parties, and many other difficulties. In many cases fact questions arise ordinarily capable of proof only by means of the aid of oral testimony. The question of identification of the individual intended by the written instrument very often involves and requires oral proof. That is the situation here. The right to the money here involved is claimed by both Adeline Soper and Gertrude Young. In what manner may either establish relationship to the decedent as his 'wife' except by means of oral testimony? Ira Collins Soper and John W. Young, in the absence of proof contra, would likely lead an inquirer to the view that two different mean were involved. Adeline, to establish her relationship, was necessarily required to and did furnish proof, principally oral, that her husband, Ira Collins Soper, was in fact the same individual as John W. Young. Gertrude by similar means sought to establish her claim. Of course the proof was such as to require a finding sustaining Adeline's claim. No one questions that result. But until such proof was adduced, it is equally clear, both from public records in Hennepin county and general repute, that Gertrude had been duly married to John W. Young. All friends and acquaintances knew and recognized her as his wife. There was nothing in Minneapolis or in this state indicating otherwise. Were we to award the insurance fund to plaintiff Adeline, it is obvious that we would thereby be doing violence to the contract entered into by the decedent Young with his associate Mr. Karstens. That agreement points to no one else than Gertrude as Young's 'wife.' To hold otherwise is to give the word 'wife' 'a fixed symbol,' as 'something inherent and objective, not subjective and personal.' Dean Wigmore, in his excellent work on Evidence, 5 Wigmore, Evidence (2d Ed.) § 2462, p. 378, has this to say: 'The ordinary standard, or 'plain meaning,' is simply the meaning of the people who did not write the document. The fallacy consists in assuming that there is or ever can be some one real or absolute meaning. In truth, there can be only some person's meaning; and that person, whose meaning the law is seeking, is the writer of the document.' And, further, page 379: 'The truth is that whatever virtue and strength lies in the argument for the antique rule leads not to a fixed rule of law, but only to a general maxim of prudent discretion. In the felicitous alliteration of that great judge, Lord Justice Bowen, it is 'not so much a canon of construction as a counsel of caution.''

It is argued that in two other life insurance policies, issued by the same company upon the life of John W. Young, the beneficiary was named 'Gertrude Young, wife' of insured. These policies were issued respectively on October 6 and 26, 1925. Both policies were payable to 'the executors, administrators or assigns of the insured, or to the duly designated beneficiary.' On October 6, 1927, both policies were changed as to beneficiary so as to read as above stated, 'Gertrude Young, wife.' This does not tend to prove a different intention on the part of the insured than what he sought to accomplish when the escrow agreement was made. Rather, it points strongly to the conclusion reached by the trial court that Gertrude Young was the 'wife' whom he sought to protect. As to these policies, no issue is raised. They were not included in the escrow agreement. We are limited strictly to the policy deposited with the trust company wherein it was designated the beneficiary.

In the books are found numerous cases wherein similar situations have arisen. Several cases have come before this court wherein the particular question now being considered has arisen. Thus in *Re Swenson's Estate*, 55 Minn. 300, testator had made a will in 1884. He and his wife had no children, and they were then of such age that it could not be expected that they would have any. Under the statutes of descent then in force, his heirs would have been his next of kin, of whom there were then living a brother and two sisters. While testator was still living the statute was changed so that the sole heir would be his wife. However, the will gave certain property to his wife with the residue to 'my heirs at law, share and share alike.' There it was held that the next of kin took the residuary estate. The court said, 55 Minn. 300, 310: 'Nor is there an inflexible rule for determining the meaning of the words 'heirs at law,' or any other words found in a will. From an examination of the authorities it will be found that these particular words have been construed to mean children, adopted children, next of kin, heirs of a particular class or description, heirs presumptive, heirs apparent, heirs at the date of the will, heirs at the decease of the testator, or heirs at a later date even, the construction seeming to rest and to be predicated upon an ascertainment of the testator's intention from the words used, from the context of the instrument and *from the surrounding circumstances*.' (Italics ours.)

In *Anderson v. Brower*, 148 Minn. 44, the facts were that testator had by will made specific provision for his wife. He had also made provision for his son wherein, upon certain conditions arising, the son should not take and the property was to go to testator's 'legal heirs.' The son did not take because of the proviso, and the issue arose as to who were the legal heirs within the meaning of the will. The court said, 148 Minn. 44, 48: 'It is sometimes said that the intent of the testator is to be derived by a 'four-cornered' view of the will. Words used may or may not be given their technical meaning. They are to be given such meaning as gives effect to the real intent of the testator. Such words as heirs, or legal heirs, though their technical significance is not to be overlooked, may, to give effect to the testator's intent, be held to refer to others than those who are technically heirs and may exclude those who are technically heirs.' (Citing many cases.)

In *Wilmot v. Minneapolis Auto. Trade Ass'n*, 169 Minn. 140, 142, this court said: 'The duty of courts is to apply contracts to their subject-matter and so effect the purpose of the parties. Their interpretation is incidental. To accomplish the main object, resort may and frequently must be had to the circumstances under which the contract was made, and, if there be need for resort to extraneous aids to construction, it is immaterial whether such need arises from an uncertainty in the instrument itself, or that being clear, standing alone, it ceases to be so, and ambiguity arises when the contract is applied to its subject-matter. In either case construction must follow, and resort must be had to the aids furnished by extrinsic circumstances. The prohibition of the law is not against their being used for interpretation, but against making them the instruments of contradiction of an expressed contractual intent. The old distinction between patent and latent ambiguities, never more than 'an unprofitable subtlety' (Thayer, Preliminary Treatise on Evidence, 434), 'so far as contracts are concerned, may be wholly disregarded.' 2 Williston on Contracts, § 627.' To hold as plaintiffs would have us do, 169 Minn. 140, 143, 'would thwart the one purpose of construction, which is to ascertain the intention of the parties themselves. It would sacrifice rationalism to that 'primitive formalism which views the document as a self-contained and self-operative formula,' rather than an instrument the whole of which is in relation to extrinsic matter, and concerning which very frequently there can be no adequate understanding of purpose, without first an understanding of the extrinsic facts and things upon which the writing must have its only operation.'

After all, as we said in *City of Marshall v. Gregoire*, 193 Minn. 188, 198, 199: 'A. written contract is little more than a scrap of writing save as it operates with legal effect on matters extraneous to itself. Construction deals with the dynamic rather than the static phase of the instrument. The question is not just what words mean literally, but how they are intended to operate practically on the subject-matter. Thus, seemingly plain language becomes susceptible of construction, and frequently requires it, if ambiguity appears when attempt is made to operate the contract.' That is the situation here. The trust agreement has become 'susceptible of construction' because 'ambiguity appears when attempt is made to operate the contract.'

The order is affirmed.

■ I. M. OLSEN, JUSTICE, dissenting.

I am unable to agree that this court should make a new contract for the parties and so change either the policy or the trust agreement as to substitute a new beneficiary. A man can have only one wife. If, while married, a man fraudulently and in violation of law, goes through a marriage ceremony with another woman, she does not become his wife, however innocent such woman may be of any wrongdoing. She cannot inherit from the man who has wronged her or claim any benefits as his wife. Much is said in the opinion as to the wrong done to the innocent woman whom he purported to marry. Nothing is said about the wrong done to the lawful wife. To have her husband abandon her and then purport to marry another, and live in co-habitation with such other, was about as great a wrong as any man could inflict upon his wife. While there are some intimations that there may have been some unpleasant incidents in the Soper family life because of the husband's habits in using liquor to excess, there is nothing to show that the wife was in any way to blame.

The contract in this case designates the 'wife' as the one to whom the money was to be paid. I am unable to construe this word to mean any one else than the only wife of Soper then living.

Soper's suicide is readily explainable. He had committed two felonies in this state. One was bigamy and, assuming that the clerk of court did his duty, perjury was committed in obtaining a marriage license here. About two years before Soper's suicide, his brother had discovered that he was alive and in Minneapolis. There was constant danger of his situation becoming known and being investigated. He was an educated man, had been a teacher in a commercial school, and was a good business man. He was fully aware of what he had been doing.

As to the trust company's liability, there are other questions in the case which I do not discuss.

Pacific Gas and Electric Co. v. G.W. Thomas Drayage & Rigging Co.

Supreme Court of California, 1968.
442 P.2d 641.

■ TRAYNOR, C.J. Defendant appeals from a judgment for plaintiff in an action for damages for injury to property under an indemnity clause of a contract.

In 1960 defendant entered into a contract with plaintiff to furnish the labor and equipment necessary to remove and replace the upper metal cover of plaintiff's steam turbine. Defendant agreed to perform the work 'at (its) own risk and expense' and to 'indemnify' plaintiff 'against all loss, damage, expense and liability resulting from injury to property, arising out of or in any way connected with the performance of this contract.' Defendant also agreed to procure not less than $50,000 insurance to cover liability for injury to property. Plaintiff was to be an additional named insured, but the policy was to contain a cross-liability clause extending the coverage to plaintiff's property.

During the work the cover fell and injured the exposed rotor of the turbine. Plaintiff brought this action to recover $25,144.51, the amount it subsequently spent on repairs. During the trial it dismissed a count based on negligence and thereafter secured judgment on the theory that the indemnity provision covered injury to all property regardless of ownership.

Defendant offered to prove by admissions of plaintiff's agents, by defendant's conduct under similar contracts entered into with plaintiff, and by other proof that in the indemnity clause the parties meant to cover injury to property of third parties only and not to plaintiff's property. Although the trial court observed that the language used was 'the classic language for a third party indemnity provision' and that 'one could very easily conclude that its whole intendment is to indemnify third parties,' it nevertheless held that the 'plain language' of the agreement also required defendant to indemnify plaintiff for injuries to plaintiff's property. Having determined that the contract had a plain meaning, the court refused to admit any extrinsic evidence that would contradict its interpretation.

When a court interprets a contract on this basis, it determines the meaning of the instrument in accordance with the 'extrinsic evidence of the judge's own linguistic education and experience.' (3 Corbin on Contracts (1960 ed.) (1964 Supp. s 579, p. 225, fn. 56).) The exclusion of testimony that might contradict the linguistic background of the judge reflects a judicial belief in the possibility of perfect verbal expression. (9 Wigmore on Evidence (3d ed. 1940) s 2461, p. 187.) This belief is a remnant of a primitive faith in the inherent potency and inherent meaning of words.

The test of admissibility of extrinsic evidence to explain the meaning of a written instrument is not whether it appears to the court to be plain and unambiguous on its face, but whether the offered evidence is relevant to prove a meaning to which the language of the instrument is reasonably susceptible.

A rule that would limit the determination of the meaning of a written instrument to its four-corners merely because it seems to the court to be clear and unambiguous, would either deny the relevance of the intention of the parties or presuppose a degree of verbal precision and stability our language has not attained.

Some courts have expressed the opinion that contractual obligations are created by the mere use of certain words, whether or not there was any intention to incur such obligations. Under this view, contractual obligations flow, not from the intention of the parties but from the fact that they used certain magic words. Evidence of the parties' intention therefore becomes irrelevant.

In this state, however, the intention of the parties as expressed in the contract is the source of contractual rights and duties. A court must ascertain and give effect to this intention by determining what the parties meant by the words they used. Accordingly, the exclusion of relevant, extrinsic evidence to explain the meaning of a written instrument could be justified only if it were feasible to determine the meaning the parties gave to the words from the instrument alone.

If words had absolute and constant referents, it might be possible to discover contractual intention in the words themselves and in the manner in which they were arranged. Words, however, do not have absolute and constant referents. 'A word is a symbol of thought but has no arbitrary and fixed meaning like a symbol of algebra or chemistry.' (*Pearson v. State Social Welfare Board* (1960) 54 Cal.2d 184, 195.) The meaning of particular words or groups of words varies with the 'verbal context and surrounding circumstances and purposes in view of the linguistic education and experience of their users and their hearers or readers (not excluding judges). A word has no meaning apart from these factors; much less does it have an objective meaning, one true meaning.' (Corbin, The Interpretation of Words and the Parol Evidence Rule (1965) 50 Cornell L.Q. 161, 187.) Accordingly, the meaning of a writing 'can only be found by interpretation in the light of all the circumstances that reveal the sense in which the writer used the words. The exclusion of parol evidence regarding such circumstances merely because the words do not appear ambiguous to the reader can easily lead to the attribution to a written instrument of a meaning that was never intended. (Citations omitted.)' (*Universal Sales Corp. v. Cal. Press Mfg. Co.*, supra, 20 Cal.2d 751, 776 (concurring opinion)).

Although extrinsic evidence is not admissible to add to, detract from, or vary the terms of a written contract, these terms must first be determined before it can be decided whether or not extrinsic evidence is being offered for a prohibited purpose. The fact that the terms of an instrument appear clear to a judge does not preclude the possibility that the parties chose the language of the instrument to express different terms. That possibility is not limited to contracts whose terms have acquired a particular meaning by trade usage, but exists whenever the parties' understanding of the words used may have differed from the judge's understanding.

Accordingly, rational interpretation requires at least a preliminary consideration of all credible evidence offered to prove the intention of the parties. (Civ.Code, s 1647; Code Civ.Proc. s 1860; see also 9 Wigmore on Evidence, op. cit. supra, s 2470, fn. 11, p. 227.) Such evidence includes testimony as to the 'circumstances surrounding the making of the agreement including the object, nature and subject matter of the writing' so that the court can 'place itself in the same situation in which the parties found themselves at the time of contracting.' (*Universal Sales Corp. v. Cal. Press Mfg. Co.*, supra, 20 Cal.2d 751, 761) If the court decides, after considering this evidence, that the language of a contract, in the light of all the circumstances, is 'fairly susceptible of either one of the two interpretations contended for.' (*Balfour v. Fresno C. & I. Co.* (1895) 109 Cal. 221, 225; extrinsic evidence relevant to prove either of such meanings is admissible.

In the present case the court erroneously refused to consider extrinsic evidence offered to show that the indemnity clause in the contract was not intended to cover injuries to plaintiff's property. Although that evidence was not necessary to show that the indemnity clause was reasonably susceptible of the meaning contended for by defendant, it was nevertheless relevant and admissible on that issue. Moreover, since that clause was reasonably susceptible of that meaning, the offered evidence was also admissible to prove that the clause had that meaning and did not cover injuries to plaintiff's property. Accordingly, the judgment must be reversed.

Uniform Commercial Code

§ 1–303.   Course of Performance, Course of Dealing, and Usage of Trade

(a) A "course of performance" is a sequence of conduct between the parties to a particular transaction that exists if:

(1) the agreement of the parties with respect to the transaction involves repeated occasions for performance by a party; and

(2) the other party, with knowledge of the nature of the performance and opportunity for objection to it, accepts the performance or acquiesces in it without objection.

(b) A "course of dealing" is a sequence of conduct concerning previous transactions between the parties to a particular transaction that is fairly to be regarded as establishing a common basis of understanding for interpreting their expressions and other conduct.

(c) A "usage of trade" is any practice or method of dealing having such regularity of observance in a place, vocation, or trade as to justify an expectation that it will be observed with respect to the transaction in question. The existence and scope of such a usage must be proved as facts. If it is established that such a usage is embodied in a trade code or similar record, the interpretation of the record is a question of law.

(d) A course of performance or course of dealing between the parties or usage of trade in the vocation or trade in which they are engaged or of which they are or should be aware is relevant in ascertaining the meaning of the parties' agreement, may give particular meaning to specific terms of the agreement, and may supplement or qualify the terms of the agreement. A usage of trade applicable in the place in which part of the performance under the agreement is to occur may be so utilized as to that part of the performance.

(e) Except as otherwise provided in subsection (f), the express terms of an agreement and any applicable course of performance, course of dealing, or usage of trade must be construed whenever reasonable as consistent with each other. If such a construction is unreasonable:

(1) express terms prevail over course of performance, course of dealing, and usage of trade;

(2) course of performance prevails over course of dealing and usage of trade; and

(3) course of dealing prevails over usage of trade.

(f) Subject to Section 2–209, a course of performance is relevant to show a waiver or modification of any term inconsistent with the course of performance.

(g) Evidence of a relevant usage of trade offered by one party is not admissible unless that party has given the other party notice that the court finds sufficient to prevent unfair surprise to the other party.

Official Comments

Changes from former law: This section integrates the "course of performance" concept from Articles 2 and 2A into the principles of former Section 1–205, which deals with course of dealing and usage of trade. In so doing, the section slightly modifies the articulation of the course of performance rules to fit more comfortably with the approach and structure of former Section 1–205. There are also slight modifications to be more consistent with the definition of "agreement" in former Section 1–201(3). It should be noted that a course of performance that might otherwise establish a defense to the obligation of a party to a negotiable instrument is not available as a defense against a holder in due course who took the instrument without notice of that course of performance.

1. The Uniform Commercial Code rejects both the "lay-dictionary" and the "conveyancer's" reading of a commercial agreement. Instead the meaning of the agreement of the parties is to be determined by the language used by them and by their action, read and interpreted in the light of commercial practices and other surrounding circumstances. The measure and background for interpretation are set by the commercial context, which may explain and supplement even the language of a formal or final writing.

2. "Course of dealing," as defined in subsection (b), is restricted, literally, to a sequence of conduct between the parties previous to the agreement. A sequence of conduct after or under the agreement, however, is a "course of performance." "Course of dealing" may enter the agreement either by explicit provisions of the agreement or by tacit recognition.

3. The Uniform Commercial Code deals with "usage of trade" as a factor in reaching the commercial meaning of the agreement that the parties have made. The language used is to be interpreted as meaning what it may fairly be expected to mean to parties involved in the particular commercial transaction in a given locality or in a given vocation or trade. By adopting in this context the term "usage of trade," the Uniform Commercial Code expresses its intent to reject those cases which see evidence of "custom" as representing an effort to displace or negate "established rules of law." A distinction is to be drawn between mandatory rules of law such as the Statute of Frauds provisions of Article 2 on Sales whose very office is to control and restrict the actions of the parties, and which cannot be abrogated by agreement, or by a usage of trade, and those rules of law (such as those in Part 3 of Article 2 on Sales) which fill in points which the parties have not considered and in fact agreed upon. The latter rules hold "unless otherwise agreed" but yield to the contrary agreement of the parties. Part of the agreement of the parties to which such rules yield is to be sought for in the usages of trade which furnish the background and give particular meaning to the language used, and are the

framework of common understanding controlling any general rules of law which hold only when there is no such understanding.

4. A usage of trade under subsection (c) must have the "regularity of observance" specified. The ancient English tests for "custom" are abandoned in this connection. Therefore, it is not required that a usage of trade be "ancient or immemorial," "universal," or the like. Under the requirement of subsection (c) full recognition is thus available for new usages and for usages currently observed by the great majority of decent dealers, even though dissidents ready to cut corners do not agree. There is room also for proper recognition of usage agreed upon by merchants in trade codes.

5. The policies of the Uniform Commercial Code controlling explicit unconscionable contracts and clauses (Sections 1–304, 2–302) apply to implicit clauses that rest on usage of trade and carry forward the policy underlying the ancient requirement that a custom or usage must be "reasonable." However, the emphasis is shifted. The very fact of commercial acceptance makes out a *prima facie* case that the usage is reasonable, and the burden is no longer on the usage to establish itself as being reasonable. But the anciently established policing of usage by the courts is continued to the extent necessary to cope with the situation arising if an unconscionable or dishonest practice should become standard.

6. Subsection (d), giving the prescribed effect to usages of which the parties "are or should be aware," reinforces the provision of subsection (c) requiring not universality but only the described "regularity of observance" of the practice or method. This subsection also reinforces the point of subsection (c) that such usages may be either general to trade or particular to a special branch of trade.

7. Although the definition of "agreement" in Section 1–201 includes the elements of course of performance, course of dealing, and usage of trade, the fact that express reference is made in some sections to those elements is not to be construed as carrying a contrary intent or implication elsewhere. Compare Section 1–302(c).

8. In cases of a well established line of usage varying from the general rules of the Uniform Commercial Code where the precise amount of the variation has not been worked out into a single standard, the party relying on the usage is entitled, in any event, to the minimum variation demonstrated. The whole is not to be disregarded because no particular line of detail has been established. In case a dominant pattern has been fairly evidenced, the party relying on the usage is entitled under this section to go to the trier of fact on the question of whether such dominant pattern has been incorporated into the agreement.

9. Subsection (g) is intended to insure that this Act's liberal recognition of the needs of commerce in regard to usage of trade shall not be made into an instrument of abuse.

* * *

Soper's Estate sets out the strict textualism associated with the classical approach to contract interpretation (even if the majority does not finally apply that approach). Soper married his first wife and then faked his suicide and took on a new identity as Young. In his new life, as Young, he "married" a second "wife." He also founded a successful business and, together with his business partner, invested in a stock and insurance plan, which would, should they die, make payments to their respective "wives." Finally, Soper/Young actually committed suicide. The first wife subsequently learned of his later life and both she and his second "wife" sought to collect under the stock and insurance plan.

The case turned on who was Soper's *wife*, for purposes of the contract establishing the stock and insurance plan. There was no doubt that the first wife was Soper's only legal wife—his bigamy rendered the second marriage invalid. As the contract fixed its beneficiary by referring to Soper's *wife*, the four corners of the contractual text unambiguously singled out the first wife as the beneficiary. But extrinsic evidence, connected to Soper's life and circumstances at the time of drafting the contract, unambiguously suggested that Soper's intent was to benefit his second "wife." The case thus raised the question when a contractual text should be interpreted based on its four corners and when extrinsic evidence might be admitted in order to discern the text's meaning. The first approach to interpretation is commonly called *textualist* and the second *contextualist*.

As the majority opinion observed (and the dissenter insisted), the classical principles of contractual interpretation held that as long as a contractual text is not ambiguous on its face (so that no ambiguity appears from reading the four-corners of the contractual text), then the contract should be accorded the plain meaning of its text.[15] That is, where a contract is not *patently* ambiguous, interpretation must concentrate exclusively on the text itself, and extrinsic evidence may not be applied to discern the contract's meaning. The majority rejected this approach, concluding instead that extrinsic evidence might be admitted to interpret a text even where the text contains only *latent* ambiguities—that is, ambiguities that appear only when the text is applied to its subject matter, in an attempt to operate the contract. The majority thought that the text at issue in *Soper's Estate* contained just such latent but not patent ambiguities. Although the plain meaning of *wife* picked out Soper/Young's first wife; an effort to apply the text to the circumstances of his life when it was drafted revealed that Soper/Young had two *wives*. And extrinsic evidence might be employed to demonstrate that his intent was to benefit his second "wife."

Soper's Estate thus takes an initial step away from classical contract law's hard textualism. The latent ambiguity rule does not allow contract interpretation to turn to context in all cases, but only in those in which applying the plain text reveals an ambiguity that the four corners of the text concealed. But it is not clear that this initial step can produce a stable doctrine. On the one hand, a textualist might insist that the contract at

---

15. Note the connection to the four corners rule of contract construction asserted in *Mitchell*.

issue in *Soper's Estate* contains not even a latent ambiguity. After all, there was no doubt that only the first wife was Soper's legal wife—that is why these pages have referred to the second as his "wife," in scare-quotes. So an interpreter who retained her confidence in textual plain meaning might resist context in applying a text, as much as in the initial stage of engaging a text's four corners. The text of the contract in *Soper's Estate,* she would insist, points unambiguously to the first wife, even when applied; the second wife is no more in its sights than any other person or thing. On the other hand, the gravamen of the majority's argument in *Soper's Estate* applies just a powerfully within the four corners of the contract's text as without them. This is the idea—to which the argument here will return shortly—that *wife* is a shallowly conventional term: one which refers to both a formal legal and an informal social relationship. Once that is acknowledged, the contractual text in *Soper's Estate* becomes ambiguous even on its face.

Pacific Gas embraces considerations just like these in order to reject classical textualism in favor of an approach to contract interpretation that is fully and confidently contextual. The parties in *Pacific Gas* contracted for the defendant to replace the cover of the plaintiff's steam turbine. As part of this contract, the defendant agreed to "indemnify [the plaintiff] against all loss, damage, expense and liability resulting from injury to property connected with the performance of this contract." While the defendant was working, the turbine cover fell and damaged the plaintiff's turbine itself. This raised the question whether the *property* covered by the indemnification clause included the plaintiff's property or was limited to property owned by third persons.

A trial court held that the contractual text had a plain meaning, namely that the term *property*, unqualified, plainly drew no distinctions based on ownership. It therefore refused to consider the extrinsic evidence, offered by the defendant, that tended to show that the parties had intended the indemnification clause to cover only losses to third parties. The California Supreme Court (per Justice Traynor, of *Drennan* and *Masterson*) rejected this approach. For Traynor, the purpose of contract interpretation is to discern the intent of the contracting parties. In order most accurately to do so, Traynor believed, an interpreter must look to extrinsic evidence not only when a contract is patently or even latently ambiguous, but rather *whenever extrinsic evidence is relevant to prove a meaning to which the text is reasonably susceptible*. This approach entirely rejects the two-stage approach to contract interpretation that the classical approach embraced and even the *Soper's Estate* court sought to retain. According to that approach, an interpreter should begin with a text—either on its own terms or in application—and look to context only where the initial focus on the text generates an interpretive problem. According to Traynor's robust contextualism, an interpreter should always, right from the very start, read text and context together. That, Traynor believed, is the best way to give life to the intentions that the parties contract in order to realize.

Now that the distinctions between the textualist and contextualist approaches to contract interpretation have been drawn, the arguments made by proponents of the two approaches may be assessed. One such argument is principally historical, and explains why the classical approach to interpretation was so insistently textualist. The classical regime of contract formation, recall, insisted that offer and acceptance must match as mirror images and that contracts could be formed only through a meeting of the parties' minds. The strong preference for writings reflected in the classical regime's hard parol evidence rule helped to insure that the texts of offers and acceptances matched up in the required, mirror-image, fashion. Textualism concerning interpretation helped to insure that matched-up texts reflected met-up minds. Textualism thus served (in parallel to other doctrines considered earlier) as a kind of stipulation concerning subjective contractual intent that made contract formation, on the classical model, possible at all. The sensibilities associated with contextualist interpretation, by contrast, would have made it easy for regretful parties to act opportunistically *ex post* to avoid contractual obligation entirely. There is thus a sense in which the classical regime of contract formation simply *required* classical textualism concerning contract interpretation.

This is a powerful argument on its own terms. But its suppositions (concerning contract formation) no longer hold. So its principal interest is historical and reflective—it belongs to the effort to understand how doctrinal styles work and how various doctrines in a body of law must fit together into a coherent whole. Other arguments concerning the choice between textualism and contextualism have a greater presentist interest. The materials below engage these, now against the backdrop of the other doctrines of modern contract law.

Trident Center v. Connecticut General Life Ins. Co.

United States Court of Appeals for the Ninth Circuit, 1988.
847 F.2d 564.

■ KOZINSKI, J. The parties to this transaction are, by any standard, highly sophisticated business people: Plaintiff is a partnership consisting of an insurance company and two of Los Angeles' largest and most prestigious law firms; defendant is another insurance company. Dealing at arm's length and from positions of roughly equal bargaining strength, they negotiated a commercial loan amounting to more than $56 million. The contract documents are lengthy and detailed; they squarely address the precise issue that is the subject of this dispute; to all who read English, they appear to resolve the issue fully and conclusively.

Plaintiff nevertheless argues here, as it did below, that it is entitled to introduce extrinsic evidence that the contract means something other than what it says. This case therefore presents the question whether parties in California can ever draft a contract that is proof to parol evidence. Somewhat surprisingly, the answer is no.

Facts

The facts are rather simple. Sometime in 1983 Security First Life Insurance Company and the law firms of Mitchell, Silberberg & Knupp and Manatt, Phelps, Rothenberg & Tunney formed a limited partnership for the purpose of constructing an office building complex on Olympic Boulevard in West Los Angeles. The partnership, Trident Center, the plaintiff herein, sought and obtained financing for the project from defendant, Connecticut General Life Insurance Company. The loan documents provide for a loan of $56,500,000 at 12¼ percent interest for a term of 15 years, secured by a deed of trust on the project. The promissory note provides that "[m]aker shall not have the right to prepay the principal amount hereof in whole or in part" for the first 12 years. Note at 6. In years 13–15, the loan may be prepaid, subject to a sliding prepayment fee. The note also provides that in case of a default during years 1–12, Connecticut General has the option of accelerating the note and adding a 10 percent prepayment fee.

Everything was copacetic for a few years until interest rates began to drop. The 12¼ percent rate that had seemed reasonable in 1983 compared unfavorably with 1987 market rates and Trident started looking for ways of refinancing the loan to take advantage of the lower rates. Connecticut General was unwilling to oblige, insisting that the loan could not be prepaid for the first 12 years of its life, that is, until January 1996.

Trident then brought suit in state court seeking a declaration that it was entitled to prepay the loan now, subject only to a 10 percent prepayment fee. Connecticut General promptly removed to federal court and brought a motion to dismiss, claiming that the loan documents clearly and unambiguously precluded prepayment during the first 12 years. The district court agreed and dismissed Trident's complaint. The court also "*sua sponte,* sanction[ed] the plaintiff for the filing of a frivolous lawsuit." Order of Dismissal, No. CV 87–2712 JMI (Kx), at 3 (C.D. Cal. June 8, 1987). Trident appeals both aspects of the district court's ruling.

Discussion

I

Trident makes two arguments as to why the district court's ruling is wrong. First, it contends that the language of the contract is ambiguous and proffers a construction that it believes supports its position. Second, Trident argues that, under California law, even seemingly unambiguous contracts are subject to modification by parol or extrinsic evidence. Trident faults the district court for denying it the opportunity to present evidence that the contract language did not accurately reflect the parties' intentions.

A.   The Contract

As noted earlier, the promissory note provides that Trident "shall not have the right to prepay the principal amount hereof in whole or in part before January 1996." Note at 6. It is difficult to imagine language that more clearly or unambiguously expresses the idea that Trident may not unilaterally prepay the loan during its first 12 years. Trident, however, argues that there is an ambiguity because another clause of the note provides that "[i]n the event of a prepayment resulting from a default hereunder or the Deed of Trust prior to January 10, 1996 the prepayment fee will be ten percent (10%)." Note at 6–7. Trident interprets this clause as giving it the option of prepaying the loan if only it is willing to incur the prepayment fee.

We reject Trident's argument out of hand. In the first place, its proffered interpretation would result in a contradiction between two clauses of the contract; the default clause would swallow up the clause prohibiting Trident from prepaying during the first 12 years of the contract. The normal rule of construction, of course, is that courts must interpret contracts, if possible, so as to avoid internal conflict. *See* 4 S. Williston, *A Treatise on the Law of Contracts* § 618, at 714–15 (3d ed. 1961).

In any event, the clause on which Trident relies is not on its face reasonably susceptible to Trident's proffered interpretation. Whether to accelerate repayment of the loan in the event of default is entirely Connecticut General's decision. The contract makes this clear at several points. *See* Note at 4 ("in each such event [of default], the entire principal indebtedness, or so much thereof as may remain unpaid at the time, shall, *at the option of Holder,* become due and payable immediately" (emphasis added)); *id.* at 7 ("[i]n the event Holder exercises its *option to accelerate* the maturity hereof ..." (emphasis added)); Deed of Trust ¶ 2.01, at 25 ("in each such event [of default], Beneficiary *may* declare all sums secured hereby immediately due and payable ..." (emphasis added)). Even if Connecticut General decides to declare a default and accelerate, it "may rescind any notice of breach or default." *Id.* ¶ 2.02, at 26. Finally, Connecticut General has the option of doing nothing at all: "Beneficiary reserves the right at its sole option to waive noncompliance by Trustor with any of the conditions or covenants to be performed by Trustor hereunder." *Id.* ¶ 3.02, at 29.

Once again, it is difficult to imagine language that could more clearly assign to Connecticut General the exclusive right to decide whether to declare a default, whether and when to accelerate, and whether, having chosen to take advantage of any of its remedies, to rescind the process before its completion.

Trident nevertheless argues that it is entitled to precipitate a default and insist on acceleration by tendering the balance due on the note plus the 10 percent prepayment fee. The contract language, cited above, leaves no room for this construction. It is true, of course, that Trident is free to stop making payments, which may then cause Connecticut General to declare a default and accelerate. But that is not to say that Connecticut General would be required to so respond. The contract quite clearly gives Connecticut General other options: It may choose to waive the default, or to take advantage of some other remedy such as the right to collect "all the income, rents, royalties, revenue, issues, profits, and proceeds of the Property." Deed of Trust ¶ 1.18, at 22. By interpreting the contract as Trident suggests, we would ignore those provisions giving Connecticut

General, not Trident, the exclusive right to decide how, when and whether the contract will be terminated upon default during the first 12 years.

In effect, Trident is attempting to obtain judicial sterilization of its intended default. But defaults are messy things; they are supposed to be. Once the maker of a note secured by a deed of trust defaults, its credit rating may deteriorate; attempts at favorable refinancing may be thwarted by the need to meet the trustee's sale schedule; its cash flow may be impaired if the beneficiary takes advantage of the assignment of rents remedy; default provisions in its loan agreements with other lenders may be triggered. Fear of these repercussions is strong medicine that keeps debtors from shirking their obligations when interest rates go down and they become disenchanted with their loans. That Trident is willing to suffer the cost and delay of a lawsuit, rather than simply defaulting, shows far better than anything we might say that these provisions are having their intended effect. We decline Trident's invitation to truncate the lender's remedies and deprive Connecticut General of its bargained-for protection.

B. Extrinsic Evidence

Trident argues in the alternative that, even if the language of the contract appears to be unambiguous, the deal the parties actually struck is in fact quite different. It wishes to offer extrinsic evidence that the parties had agreed Trident could prepay at any time within the first 12 years by tendering the full amount plus a 10 percent prepayment fee. As discussed above, this is an interpretation to which the contract, as written, is not reasonably susceptible. Under traditional contract principles, extrinsic evidence is inadmissible to interpret, vary or add to the terms of an unambiguous integrated written instrument. *See* 4 S. Williston, *supra* p. 5, § 631, at 948–49; 2 B. Witkin, *California Evidence* § 981, at 926 (3d ed. 1986). Trident points out, however, that California does not follow the traditional rule. Two decades ago the California Supreme Court in *Pacific Gas & Electric Co. v. G.W. Thomas Drayage & Rigging Co.,* 69 Cal.2d 33 (1968), turned its back on the notion that a contract can ever have a plain meaning discernible by a court without resort to extrinsic evidence. The court reasoned that contractual obligations flow not from the words of the contract, but from the intention of the parties. "Accordingly," the court stated, "the exclusion of relevant, extrinsic, evidence to explain the meaning of a written instrument could be justified only if it were feasible to determine the meaning the parties gave to the words from the instrument alone." 69 Cal.2d at 38. This, the California Supreme Court concluded, is impossible: "If words had absolute and constant referents, it might be possible to discover contractual intention in the words themselves and in the manner in which they were arranged. Words, however, do not have absolute and constant referents." *Id.* In the same vein, the court noted that "[t]he exclusion of testimony that might contradict the linguistic background of the judge reflects a judicial belief in the possibility of perfect verbal expression. This belief is a remnant of a primitive faith in the inherent potency and inherent meaning of words." *Id.* at 37.

Under *Pacific Gas,* it matters not how clearly a contract is written, nor how completely it is integrated, nor how carefully it is negotiated, nor how squarely it addresses the issue before the court: the contract cannot be rendered impervious to attack by parol evidence. If one side is willing to claim that the parties intended one thing but the agreement provides for another, the court must consider extrinsic evidence of possible ambiguity. If that evidence raises the specter of ambiguity where there was none before, the contract language is displaced and the intention of the parties must be divined from self-serving testimony offered by partisan witnesses whose recollection is hazy from passage of time and colored by their conflicting interests. *See Delta Dynamics, Inc. v. Arioto,* 69 Cal.2d 525, 532 (Mosk, J., dissenting). We question whether this approach is more likely to divulge the original intention of the parties than reliance on the seemingly clear words they agreed upon at the time.

Pacific Gas casts a long shadow of uncertainty over all transactions negotiated and executed under the law of California. As this case illustrates, even when the transaction is very sizeable, even if it involves only sophisticated parties, even if it was negotiated with the aid of counsel, even if it results in contract language that is devoid of ambiguity, costly and protracted litigation cannot be avoided if one party has a strong enough motive for challenging the contract. While this rule creates much business for lawyers and an occasional windfall to some clients, it leads only to frustration and delay for most litigants and clogs already overburdened courts.

It also chips away at the foundation of our legal system. By giving credence to the idea that words are inadequate to express concepts, *Pacific Gas* undermines the basic principle that language provides a meaningful constraint on public and private conduct. If we are unwilling to say that parties, dealing face to face, can come up with language that binds them, how can we send anyone to jail for violating statutes consisting of mere words lacking "absolute and constant referents"? How can courts ever enforce decrees, not written in language understandable to all, but encoded in a dialect reflecting only the "linguistic background of the judge"? Can lower courts ever be faulted for failing to carry out the mandate of higher courts when "perfect verbal expression" is impossible? Are all attempts to develop the law in a reasoned and principled fashion doomed to failure as "remnant[s] of a primitive faith in the inherent potency and inherent meaning of words"?

Be that as it may. While we have our doubts about the wisdom of *Pacific Gas,* we have no difficulty understanding its meaning, even without extrinsic evidence to guide us. As we read the rule in California, we must reverse and remand to the district court in order to give plaintiff an opportunity to present extrinsic evidence as to the intention of the parties in drafting the contract. It may not be a wise rule we are applying, but it is a rule that binds us.

II

In imposing sanctions on plaintiff, the district court stated:

Pursuant to Fed.R.Civ.P. 11, the Court, *sua sponte,* sanctions the plaintiff for the filing of a frivolous lawsuit. The Court concludes that the language in the note and deed of trust is plain and clear. No reasonable person, much less firms of able attorneys, could possibly misunderstand this crystal-clear language. Therefore, this action was brought in bad faith.

Order of Dismissal at 3. Having reversed the district court on its substantive ruling, we must, of course, also reverse it as to the award of sanctions. While we share the district judge's impatience with this litigation, we would suggest that his irritation may have been misdirected. It is difficult to blame plaintiff and its lawyers for bringing this lawsuit. With this much money at stake, they would have been foolish not to pursue all remedies available to them under the applicable law. At fault, it seems to us, are not the parties and their lawyers but the legal system that encourages this kind of lawsuit. By holding that language has no objective meaning, and that contracts mean only what courts ultimately say they do, *Pacific Gas* invites precisely this type of lawsuit. With the benefit of 20 years of hindsight, the California Supreme Court may wish to revisit the issue. If it does so, we commend to it the facts of this case as a paradigmatic example of why the traditional rule, based on centuries of experience, reflects the far wiser approach.

Conclusion

The judgment of the district court is REVERSED. The case is REMANDED for reinstatement of the complaint and further proceedings in accordance with this opinion. The parties shall bear their own costs on appeal.

* * *

Judge Kozinski's opinion in *Trident Center* emphasizes a general, theoretical argument against contextualism and in favor of textualism. The plaintiff in *Trident Center* took out a loan from the defendant to finance an office tower. The note set out the interest rate and stated, further, that the borrower "shall not have the right to prepay the principal amount hereof in whole or in part" for the first twelve years of the loan period. Interest rates dropped dramatically, and the plaintiff sought to prepay the loan. When the defendant refused to accept the prepayment, the plaintiff sued and sought to introduce extrinsic evidence to support an interpretation of the contract according to which it had the right to prepay. The plaintiff argued that the intrinsic evidence was admissible both because the loan agreement was ambiguous on its face and because California law permits the resort to extrinsic evidence in the interpretation of even facially unambiguous contracts.

Judge Kozinksi sharply rejected the plaintiff's argument that the contract was ambiguous on its face, saying that the intratextual conflict by means of which the plaintiff sought to create ambiguity involved plain mis-readings of the contractual text. Kozinski unhappily accepted the plaintiff's second argument, concerning California contract law's thoroughgoing interpretive contextualism. Kozinski's unhappiness stemmed in part from the reasonable worry that interpretive contextualism allows parties who have come to regret their contractual commitments to impose long and costly litigation on their counterparties and to use the threat of this litigation to drive renegotiations. More on this practical observation in a moment. Kozinski's unhappiness also stemmed from a theoretical observation, namely that the contextualist's abandonment of plain meaning undermines the idea that words can be meaningful at all and so "chips away at the foundation of our legal system." Kozinski is not alone among textualists in pursuing this argument. The dissenter in *Soper's Estate* adopted a similar line, when he insisted that the law must control the meaning of the word *wife*.

The theoretical argument that language must—by its nature, or in order to convey meaning—be subjected to textualist interpretation is nonsense. At least with respect to the meanings of individual words, language is a convention: meanings are fixed by self-conscious usage. With respect to some words, the convention is both broad and deep, in the sense of being widely shared and also relatively impervious to conscious manipulation. With respect to others, it is narrow and shallow. As it happens, several of the words at issue in *Soper's Estate* reveal the narrowness and shallowness of linguistic convention. The most obvious examples are *Ira Soper* and *John Young*. The meaning of these words is fixed by the conscious choices of a small number of people (those who grant the names and those who use them). The proper names were not directly relevant to the case, but their narrowness and shallowness casts light on the relative narrowness and shallowness of another word that was crucial to the case—*wife*. The reason why Soper/Young's second "wife" was not his legal wife was narrowly and shallowly conventional—an immediate product of the bigamy laws of the relevant jurisdictions. If a legislature or court intervened to permit bigamy, or to change the means by which it was prohibited away from the rule that subsequent marriages are not recognized, then the second "wife" would have been a legal wife.

This thought at once reveals that, like *Ira Soper* and *John Young*, the word *wife* quite literally has no plain meaning. Its meaning is fixed by (relatively shallow) conventions. In *Soper's Estate*, there were two such conventions: the legal convention concerning bigamy just discussed; and the social convention associated with the circumstances in which Soper/Young lived when he remarried and wrote the contract whose interpretation was at issue. Accordingly, that contract (indeed every contract) cannot have a purely textual meaning. Every purportedly textualist interpretation merely smuggles into interpretation context that is hidden from view. In *Soper's Estate*, that context is provided by the regulation of marriage. But this context is no less contextual than the one associated with the usage of those who drafted the contract at issue. It is also, as it happens, farther removed from their intentions, although that is not the main point here.

The main point, rather, is that far from having its meaningfulness undermined by contextualism, language is given meaning by context. And as Traynor says, the interpretive method called textualism, far from avoiding context, merely privileges one context over others, and in particular the context of the judges over the context of the parties.

Moreover, the fact that the parties had established a linguistic context that departed from the context familiar to judges is not limited to eccentric cases like *Soper's Estate*. It is worth pausing a moment to consider an example that illustrates just how elaborately linguistic usage among those who contract in some area might depart from usage familiar to lawyers or judges. The example is not unusual; rather, the pattern that it reveals is widely repeated in other contexts also.

Contracts for the sale of softwood lumber name nominal dimensions that depart from the true dimensions of the lumber that is bought and sold (the softwood regime does not apply to hardwood lumber, which is differently described). A 2 by 4, in other words, is not actually 2 inches by 4 four inches but rather thinner and narrower—specifically $1\frac{1}{2}$ inches by $3\frac{1}{2}$ inches. The true or *dressed* dimensions of other boards depart similarly from their nominal dimensions, in complex and irregular ways, as the table reproduced below reveals.

Item	Thicknesses			Widths		
	Nominal	Minimum Dressed		Nominal	Minimum Dressed	
	Inch	mm	inch	Inch	mm	inch
Finish	3/8	8	5/16	2	38	1-1/2
	1/2	11	7/16	3	64	2-1/2
	5/8	14	9/16	4	89	3-1/2
	3/4	16	5/8	5	114	4-1/2
	1	19	3/4	6	140	5-1/2
	1-1/4	25	1	7	165	6-1/2
	1-1/2	32	1-1/4	8	184	7-1/4
	1-3/4	35	1-3/8	9	210	8-1/4
	2	38	1-1/2	10	235	9-1/4
	2-1/2	51	2	11	260	10-1/4
	3	64	2-1/2	12	286	11-1/4
	3-1/2	76	3	14	337	13-1/4
	4	89	3-1/2	16	387	15-1/4
Flooring ª	3/8	8	5/16	2	29	1-1/8
	1/2	11	7/16	3	54	2-1/8
	5/8	14	9/16	4	79	3-1/8
	1	19	3/4	5	105	4-1/8
	1-1/4	25	1	6	130	5-1/8
	1-1/2	32	1-1/4			
Ceiling ª	3/8	8	5/16	3	54	2-1/8
	1/2	11	7/16	4	79	3-1/8
	5/8	14	9/16	5	105	4-1/8
	3/4	17	11/16	6	130	5-1/8
Partition ª	1	18	23/32	3	54	2-1/8
				4	79	3-1/8
				5	105	4-1/8
				6	130	5-1/8
Stepping	1	19	3/4	8	184	7-1/4
	1-1/4	25	1	10	235	9-1/4
	1-1/2	32	1-1/4	12	286	11-1/4
	2	38	1-1/2			

Table 17.1

Dressed and Nominal Dimensions of Softwood
Lumber in the United States[16]

The table, and the actual measurements that it describes (together with certain quality requirements), is set by the American Lumber Standard Committee, which "in accordance with the *Procedures for the Development of Voluntary Product Standards* of the U.S. Department of Commerce and through a consensus process establishes sizes, green/dry relationships, inspection provisions, grade marking requirements and the policies and enforcement regulations for the accreditation program."[17] These national standards developed gradually out of regional variation over the course of the twentieth century.

---

16. Source: *Voluntary Product Standard PS 20–10*, American Softwood Lumber Standard June 2010. Available at www.alsc.org/greenbook% 20collection/ps20.pdf

17. *Summary*. American Standard Lumber Committee, Incorporated. Available at http://www.alsc.org/geninfo_summary_mod.htm.

Contracts for the sale of softwood lumber nevertheless typically name nominal rather than true dimensions. Typically, sophisticated contracts make reference, in their text (either directly or in supplemental materials), to Product Standard PS–20.[18] But many contracts fail to make such a reference. Certainly a consumer who buys a board at a lumber yard or do-it-yourself store never receives any explanation of the divergence between nominal and dressed dimensions; and although many of these sellers may possess form contracts that contain a reference to PS–20 somewhere in boilerplate, these forms do not always get into the contract between the seller and its customers. (Think of the last time you bought a 2 by 4: did you receive or sign any form?) Finally, relatively informal contracts between professionals might neglect to include any mention of the standard because the divergence between nominal and dressed dimensions is common knowledge among carpenters.

Notwithstanding this, no interpreter confronting a contract—especially between construction professionals—mentioning simply a "2 by 4" could plausibly say that the text's meaning requires the seller to deliver a board that is actually 2 inches by 4 inches. The divergence between nominal and dressed dimensions is too well established within the trade for meanings from without—no matter how "plain" they might seem to outsiders—to control lumber contracts. In fact, there are today virtually no contract disputes concerning the dimensions of softwood lumber (although there were in the past, before national standards were fixed). Nevertheless, the plain or ordinary meaning of "2 by 4" surely is 2 inches by 4 inches. Certainly this is the meaning that will appear plain to many judges or jury-members, who are not carpenters and do not know of the American Softwood Lumber Standard. And formally, the case of lumber dimensions is no different from *Soper's Estate*, or from any number of other cases. Once again, the battle over textualism and plain meaning is a battle over which context fixes meaning, not over whether or not meaning is contextual. It is a battle over the size and content of the evidentiary base for contract interpretation, not over whether or not some evidentiary base outside the four corners of the text is required.

Framing the problem in this way—and rejecting the theoretical case for textualism—does not settle whose context should fix meaning, however. One might, after all, accept that interpretation is always necessarily contextual and yet agree with the classical textualists that it is best, for practical reasons, if courts ignore the local context in which particular contracts are drafted and instead interpret contractual texts by reference to the broader conventions of commonplace linguistic usage. The practical, functionalist case for relatively narrow textualism proceeds in several steps.

The first step is to characterize the choice between textualism and contextualism in a manner that enables functionalist considerations to

---

18. A typical such recitation says: "Lumber Standards: Manufacture lumber to comply with PS 20 'American Softwood Lumber Standard' and with applicable grading rules of inspection agencies certified by American Lumber Standards Committee's (ALSC) Board of Review."

engage that choice. Contextualism admits a wider evidentiary base into contract interpretation than textualism: it invites interpreters to consider not just the text and the context normally familiar to them but also the local context of the contracting parties. Broadening the base in this way raises the costs of contract interpretation, as the additional evidence is costly to assess and to weigh. In order for contextualism to be plausible at all, it must therefore hold the promise of improving the quality of interpretation: for any fixed level of textual detail, contextualism must reduce the extent to which courts depart from the true intent of the contracting parties ex post; and by reducing inaccuracy ex post, enable the parties to include less detail and hence reduce drafting costs ex ante. Some functionalists (recall the second theme of Judge Kozinski's opinion in *Trident Center*) doubt whether contextualism can do even this—that is they fear that contextualism's principal effect on contract interpretation is to allow unscrupulous parties to make opportunistic and deceptive arguments ex post, which the honest will be unable effectively to counter. If that doubt is sound, then the case for contextualist interpretation falls at the first hurdle.

But even though the risks of opportunistic arguments are real, such arguments may be countered at trial (and are costly not only to those who must counter them but also to those who make them). Accordingly, most commentators (even those who in the end oppose contextualist contract interpretation) accept that contexualism enables courts more precisely to track party intentions. This acknowledgement inaugurates the second phase of the functionalist argument for textualist contract interpretation. That argument asks whether contextualism's increased accuracy is worth contextualism's costs. Textualists argue that it is not.

One important argument[19] why not observes that not all forms of inaccuracy in interpretation will trouble contracting parties equally. In particular, parties will distinguish between errors that are symmetrically distributed between being pro-plaintiff and pro-defendant and errors that are biased in one direction or another. Biased errors will of course greatly concern the parties whom they are biased against (and because this ex post concern will reduce the value that such parties place on contractual promises ex ante, they will also concern the parties that they nominally favor). But unbiased, or symmetrical, errors are another matter. Insofar as parties are repeat-players (and sophisticated parties to contract disputes typically are), they will not care much about such symmetrical errors. These will balance out on average, and save in cases where an error can cost the losing side its business (and so prevent it from reaping the benefits of subsequent opposite errors), repeat players can afford to wait for the averaging out to occur. Next, textualists argue that while there is good reason to suspect that textualist contract interpretation produces absolutely greater errors than contextualist interpretation, there is not good reason

---

19. This argument is most rigorously developed in Alan Schwartz & Robert E. Scott, *Contract Theory and the Limits of Contract Law*, 113 YALE L.J. 541 (2003); Alan Schwartz & Robert E. Scott, *Contract Interpretation Redux*, 119 YALE L.J. 926 (2008); Alan Schwartz & Joel Watson, *The Law and Economics of Costly Contracting*, 20 J. L. ECON. & ORG. 2 (2004).

to suspect that it produces more biased errors. Contextualism, that is, reduces the *variance* of a court's interpretation of contracts; but it does not change the *mean*. And insofar as repeat-player parties do not care about variance, or care about it only a little, they will be less willing to bear the increased costs of contextualism in order to secure its variance-reducing benefits.

Textualists have observed that drafting and interpretive practice reflects textualist theory. The common use of merger clauses evinces a desire to limit the sources of contractual text, and this suggests a parallel interest in limiting the evidentiary base for interpreting such text as is admitted into contract construction. Moreover, courts do not actually use context—and in particular course of dealing or usage of trade evidence of the sort mentioned by U.C.C. § 1–303—in order to render contract interpretation more accurate ex post and reduce drafting costs ex ante.[20] Although these sources of context are sometimes used for the narrow and specific purpose of giving meaning to industry terms of art (think of the 2 by 4), they are not generally used to fill in gaps in a sparse contractual text or provide contextual corrections to plain meaning that more closely track the actual intentions of contracting parties. Rather, contextualist evidence is more frequently used in the narrow circumstances associated with the battle of the forms. In addition, the ex post costs of the turn to context are high (which renovates the early textualist concern that context does not in fact improve accuracy): often, context is provided solely by interested witnesses (the parties to the dispute or their employees), and experts on trade usage are only rarely employed; furthermore, a significant use of contextualist evidence is to defeat motions for summary judgment and hence subject an adversary to the full expense of a trial. Finally, commercial contractors seem to vote with their feet in ways that confirm the textualist's skepticisms. Although a jurisdiction's law of contract interpretation typically establishes mandatory rules, or at least sticky defaults, different jurisdictions are differently contextualist. California, as the origins of the cases just rehearsed suggests, is at the contextualist end of the spectrum. New York, as it happens, takes a much more textualist approach. There is good reason to think that parties with a choice select out of California and into New York law on account of this difference.[21] And privately made law, in particular law created by private trade associations to govern arbitration under their auspices, again tends toward textualism.

This discussion of efforts by contracting parties to assert control over the methods by which their contracts will be interpreted immediately recalls analogous efforts to assert control over contract construction through merger clauses. The conventional view—both among courts and among commentators—is that the law should adopt a harder, more narrow-

---

20. The account of the actual functioning of contextualism is drawn from Lisa Bernstein. See, e.g., Lisa Bernstein, *The Questionable Empirical Basis of Article 2's Incorporation Strategy: A Preliminary Study*, 66 U.CHI.L.REV. 76 (1999).

21. See Alan Schwartz & Robert E. Scott, *Contract Interpretation Redux*, 119 YALE L.J. 926, 956 (2008).

ly cabined approach to fixing contractual meaning with respect to construction than with respect to interpretation. (Hence the commonplace that evidence of parol agreements must be excluded from the construction of the contractual text but may be revisited to generate contextualist interpretations of the written text's meaning.) But the discussion here suggests that the conventional view might get things backwards. Parties appear to have more control over contract construction than they do over contract interpretation: it is easier to draft an effective merger clause than to opt out of a jurisdiction's interpretive regime or to opt out of the jurisdiction altogether. If this is so, and if parties are better placed than courts to choose the doctrines that should govern their contractual relation, then perhaps it would be better for the law to adopt a soft parol evidence rule and readily admit parol agreements into the contractual text but then insist on textualist interpretation of the verbal, and especially of the written, components of the text that is so constructed.

PART THREE

FREEDOM OF CONTRACT AND ITS LIMITS (HEREIN OF LAW AND MORALS)

CHAPTER 18

INTRODUCTION

At several places in these materials, including most recently in the discussions of contract construction and interpretation, the question has arisen how much control the parties should have over their contracts. To what extent, that is, should the law respect the decisions of contracting parties and enforce whatever agreements they make; and to what extent should the law constrain parties' capacity to arrange their contractual affairs as they see fit? This Part of the text addresses these questions. It takes up the freedom of contract: its scope and grounds; and also its limits.

Before introducing the inquiry in slightly greater detail, two conceptual points should be made.

The first concerns the methods by which freedom of contract might be policed. There are several. Earlier materials have illustrated one: the discussion of the consideration doctrine and also the discussion of *Soper's Estate* illustrate that the law may constrain freedom of contract simply by declining to recognize and enforce certain promises. Freedom of contract constitutes a legal power—the power to create legally enforceable obligations by choosing them—and the law may constrain freedom by denying that power. Alternatively, the law might police freedom of contract by making certain promises, or at least attempts to render certain promises legally enforceable by establishing them as contracts, themselves illegal, subjecting those who make such promises or attempt to enter such contracts to civil or criminal sanction. The most obvious example of this approach concerns the law's regulation of agreements to commit crimes, which are themselves criminalized through the law of conspiracy.

The second conceptual preamble concerns the distinction between particular contracts and contract *law*. A legal regime that recognizes freedom of contract grants persons the power to make particular contracts of whatever substance they choose (as long as the substance falls within the scope of the freedom that the regime grants). Individual contracts are, however, something entirely different from contract law—namely the set of legal rules and practices (including those that establish freedom of contract) through which individual contracts are administered. Freedom of contract therefore does not entail freedom to make or change contract law. Insofar as the latter power exists, it exists as an instance of the general power to make law and is constituted and regulated as that power is constituted and regulated. The rules governing the exercise of these two powers—to make individual contracts and to make contract law—are formally and substantively distinct. For example, in our legal order the power to make particular contracts is regulated, roughly, by the rules governing offer, acceptance, and consideration; the power to make law, including contract law, is governed in our constitutional democracy by the rules that govern the choice of representatives and that govern chosen representatives' legislative activities as well as by the rules that govern the choice of common law judges and judges' making of new precedents.[1] The distinction between making contracts and making contract law has been taken up earlier in these materials—perhaps most clearly in connection with the law of remedies. Recall the remark, in *Groves*, that "the obligation of the contract does not inhere or subsist in the agreement itself . . . but in . . . the act of the law in binding the promisor to perform his promise. . . . A contract is not a law, nor does it make law. It is the agreement plus the law that makes the ordinary contract an enforceable obligation." It is important to bear in mind now because freedom of contract—the freedom to make particular contracts—does not entail freedom to control or even influence the rules of contract law. Moreover, these rules of law may (simply by their formal structure) have certain entailments that limit the range of individual contracts that parties can make. The fact that contract law provides remedies for breach (and indeed remedies that have a particular doctrinal structure), for example, limits the content of the agreements that persons can successfully have recognized as contracts: recall the remark from the Comment [1] to U.C.C. § 2–719 that "it is of the very essence of a sales contract that at least minimum adequate remedies be available." An attempt to establish a contract that permits breach with impunity must fail because the resulting agreement does not constitute a contract at all. The constraints associated with the conceptual point undoubtedly limit the legal powers that persons enjoy in connection with their contracting behaviors. But they are quite different from some of the constraints that will be discussed below. The freedom that they limit, one might say, is not freedom *of contract* at all.

Perhaps the most commonly observed ground of freedom of contract—both among legal scholars and in the general legal imagination—is instrumental. It is a bedrock principle of our economic and political order that there exist many realms of life in which individual persons are better placed than the state effectively and efficiently to administer their affairs. This principle especially applies to commercial life, and so a familiar refrain arises: commerce will run more smoothly and efficiently if the terms of trade are fixed by traders themselves than if they are imposed from above by some state bureaucrat.[2] Variants of this thought have repeatedly fig-

---

1. It is even possible that there might exist freedom of contract without any freedom to make or change contract law. Perhaps this is the state in which persons find themselves when they participate in a contractual regime as political outsiders, who are excluded from all influence over lawmaking, in a legal order that nevertheless permits outsiders to make contracts.

The analogous possibility arises in morals still more clearly than in law. Certainly the freedom to make particular morally binding promises can coexist with complete lack of freedom over the moral rules that govern promising. Indeed, this coexistence is probably the natural state of affairs, at least insofar as promissory morality is not based on convention or practice.

2. In addition, it is commonly said that freedom of contract improves not only commerce but politics. The sources of private commercial power that freedom of contract establishes and supports, it is thought, help to reign in public political power and prevent its abuse.

ured—both implicitly and explicitly—in the arguments presented in these pages. The argument that the expectation remedy may be understood as the specific enforcement of an implied promise to make an efficient transfer in lieu of trade constitutes a prominent example of the implicit appeal to instrumental grounds for freedom of contract.[3] The arguments in favor of enabling parties to control the construction of their contracts through the use of merger clauses constitute a prominent example of the express appeal to instrumental grounds for freedom of contract.

Morality of course recognizes instrumental considerations. Indeed, an important part of contract's moral appeal lies not in contract's intrinsic moral character but rather in its instrumental effectiveness in enabling contracting parties to pursue their antecedent, and independently valuable, ends. The instrumental analysis of contract law has been intently pursued through the economic arguments developed in Part I of these materials, however, so that it will be more profitable to devote this Part's discussion of morality to contract's non-instrumental value. Nevertheless, it is worthwhile to devote an additional page or so of this Introduction to the instrumental analysis of freedom of contract, in order to display the general close connection between freedom of contract and the instrumental benefits that contracting engenders. From an instrumental perspective, embodied in the economic approach to contract law, the realm of contract just *is* the realm in which efficiency is served by allowing people freely to fix the terms of their interactions.

This thought receives its clearest expression in the Coasean theory of the contract. This theory begins by drawing a basic distinction between two types of allocative mechanism. Resources may be allocated *vertically*, through hierarchical command and control; or, they may be allocated *horizontally*, through contracts among independent market actors.

Vertical allocation will be efficient insofar as it directs resources to their most valued uses. This requires that the person in charge of command and control identifies persons' productive capacities and consumption preferences and balances them optimally against each other. An omniscient social planner might costlessly achieve a perfectly efficient allocation by vertical methods, if she were benign. But every actual mechanism for command and control incurs costs and thus countenances allocative inefficiencies. *Administration*, which is what one might call the discipline of vertical allocation, seeks to reduce the costs of vertical allocation.

Horizontal allocation—by contracts, made in markets—improves allocative efficiency by facilitating mutually beneficial exchanges. This requires the many traders across whom allocations will arise to identify optimal trading partners and trades and to negotiate to fix the optimal terms of trade. In an ideal world—one without transactions costs—markets will also achieve efficient allocations. Market exchanges will cease only when all

---

3. Note that this example also illustrates the distinction between freedom of contract and freedom to control contract law. The argument of the example suggests that there is but one, mandatory remedy in contract law—namely specific performance. The freedom of the parties is limited to fixing the contents of the promises to which this mandatory remedy will be applied; the substance of the particular obligations that will be specifically enforced.

goods are held by those who, on the margin, value them most highly (so that no further exchanges can receive the assent of both sides). But every actual market mechanisms again incurs costs and thus also countenances allocative inefficiencies. *Contract theory* is understood, on the Coasean account, as the horizontal analog to administration—the discipline of horizontal allocation. It seeks to reduce the costs of market mechanisms.

The Coasean approach recommends that contract law should be adjusted, flexibly, according to contract theory's recommendations, so that it takes whatever shape best serves the efficiency of the horizontal market-mechanism for allocation. That is, the Coasean approach recommends that the scope of freedom of contract should be fixed so that it corresponds precisely with the realm of decision in which horizontal allocation is more efficient than vertical.[4] Freedom of contract, on this approach, is *identified* with contract's efficiency.

Finally, the Coasean theory employs these ideas to construct a general comparative account of vertical and horizontal allocative mechanisms. The comparison produces powerful arguments in favor of fixing the boundary between contract and administration in a fashion that gives substantial scope to freedom of contract.

Efficiency, the theory observes, will improve overall whenever the joint transactions costs associated with vertical and horizontal mechanisms are reduced. Accordingly, the Coasean theory argues that if the aim is to promote efficiency, the location of the boundary between vertical and horizontal allocative mechanisms—between administration and the contract—should be fixed according to the balance of the transactions costs associated with these two forms. Horizontal mechanisms will be preferred over vertical just where the costs associated with employing them to solve the allocative problem are lower than the costs associated with vertical mechanisms.

Precisely where the boundary between vertical and horizontal allocation is best drawn depends on facts about production and consumption (including about persons' capacities and preferences). It also depends on the state of administration and contract theory. Insofar as administration succeeds, the optimal boundary between vertical and horizontal allocative mechanisms will shift towards the vertical. Accordingly, better administration will (all else equal) increase the optimal size of vertically integrated allocative institutions—of firms—and reduce the allocative role of markets.[5]

---

4. It is worth pausing a moment to observe that Coase himself developed this line of argument in an analysis of the boundary between the market and the private firm. That is, the limits of freedom of contract are fixed not just by the state, through contract law, but also by private firms, whose employees' coordinate their conduct not through contracts but through command and control within the firm. Employees enter their firms through contracts, to be sure. And so the command and control of the firm's management is different from the command and control of the state in the sense that it is itself contracted for. But, as later materials on form contracts and on the employment relation will show, the arrangements through which employees enter the firm are not simple, ordinary contracts—especially with respect to the freedom of those entering them.

5. Such considerations figure commonly and prominently in administrative practice. Whenever merging firms cite management economies, they implicitly claim that their adminis-

Contrariwise, successes in contract theory will tip the balance of transactions costs in favor of horizontal over vertical coordination—in favor of markets over firms. Accordingly, better contract law will (all else equal) increase the scope of market orderings and reduce the optimal size of firms.[6]

But in spite of these contingencies, the Coasean approach can sustain general laws. The costs of vertical allocation—of balancing each of an organization's members' productive capacities and consumption preferences again every other's—necessarily grow more than proportionally with the size of the organizations within which vertical allocation occurs.[7] Accordingly, even with the best achievable administration in place, allocative efficiency will at some point counsel abandoning vertical coordination in favor of horizontal; preferring contractual exchange among independent parties over command and control within an integrated firm. There is thus an upper limit to efficient organization size. By the same token, the costs of horizontal allocation—of finding trading partners, negotiating terms, and implementing contracts—also grow, again more than proportionally, as the number of traders grows. Accordingly, even with the best achievable contract law in place, allocative efficiency will at some point counsel abandoning horizontal coordination in favor of vertical; preferring administration within an integrated firm over contractual exchange among independent parties. There is thus also a lower limit to efficient firm size. In this way, the Coasean theory answers the striking question: why is it that there are (and should be) many firms rather than none (with all allocation performed horizontally by contracts among individual natural persons) or one (with all allocation performed vertically by administration in a firm that subsumes all natural persons)?[8]

The Coasean theory of contract thus generates a powerful defense of freedom of contract. The theory casts markets as an important—indeed an

---

trative capacity renders vertical allocation concerning their people and resources transactions cheaper than horizontal. They claim that efficiency requires increasing the scope of administration and reducing the scope of the market.

6. This consideration is also familiar from practice. A common argument in favor of a hard parol evidence rule in contract construction and of textualism in contract interpretation, for example, asserts that these rules reduce the transactions costs of contract interpretation and construction, with the consequence that firms can more cheaply coordinate by contract and resist pressures to merge. The reduced size of firms and states is not, however, in itself either an intended or a desired effect of contract law's efficiency. For general discussions along these lines, see Robert Scott and Alan Schwartz, *Contract Theory and the Limits of Contract Law*, 113, Yale L. J. 541 (2003) and Oliver Williamson, *The Vertical Integration of Production: Market Failure Considerations* 61 Am. Econ. R. 112 (1971).

7. This account of the supra-linear increase in the costs of vertical allocation may also be derived from the opposite direction, from the optimizing behavior of the organizations through which vertical allocation occurs. Insofar as the organizations will continue to grow until the increase in the transactions costs of vertical allocation associated with a marginal increase in size exceeds the associated reduction in the transactions costs of horizontal allocation, they will not cease to grow before they have reached a size at which the costs of vertical allocation increase supra-linearly. The supra-linearity may therefore be inferred from the observed existence of more than one firm, which is to say, of firms that have ceased to grow and rely instead on market allocations by contracts made among them. Coase himself reasoned in roughly this way.

8. See Ronald Coase, *The Nature of the Firm*, 4 Economica 386 (1937).

essential—allocative technology. Markets harness the judgments and motivations of market-participants to produce efficient allocations. In many circumstances, and *necessarily* in at least some circumstances, markets allocate more accurately and nimbly—that is, at lower cost—than any vertical mechanism of administration could ever do. The decentralized, horizontal market mechanism established by freedom of contract functions as a problem-solving machine, which produces solutions that (at the efficient margin) no centralized planner, exercising vertical powers of command and control, could match. This is why there will necessarily be many firms at the optimum and hence also free market exchanges among them.

These instrumental considerations in favor of freedom of contract are powerful, and there is much to be gained from efforts to refine the general approach in the service of fixing contractual freedom's precise limits in particular areas. But non-instrumental arguments in favor of freedom of contract are also important; and, in keeping with the broader ambition to display a variety of approaches to contract law, this Part of the text will emphasize such non-instrumental arguments. The arguments try to answer the question: why is freedom of contract good intrinsically, for itself?

A prominent non-instrumental argument for freedom of contract emphasizes the connection between contractual capacity—that is, the freedom to make and have recognized such contractual promises as one chooses—and the dignity of those who possess it. "[H]olding people to their obligations," Charles Fried once wrote, "is a way of taking them seriously and thus of giving the concept of sincerity itself serious content."[9] He continued, at "a more abstract level," to argue "that respect for others as free and rational requires taking seriously their capacity to determine their own values."[10] To respect someone is to allow her to fix her obligations, according to the content that *she* gives them—through her "will binding itself"[11]—and not according to the costs that her doing so may impose on others. Promise and contract are commensurate to the dignity of persons—to their reasoned freedom—precisely in respect of reaching beyond the ordinary, fault-based morality of harm and thus standing apart from tort. This line of argument carries an echo of Nietzsche's remarks that "[t]o breed an animal *that is permitted to promise*—isn't this precisely the paradoxical task nature has set for itself with regard to man? isn't this the real problem *of* man?"[12] so that a person who possesses promissory capacity holds "his kick in readiness for the frail dogs who promise although they are not permitted to do so."[13] Certainly contractual capacity has been an important mark of legal status and dignity in our particular history: it was denied to slaves before abolition and to married women before the married

---

9. CHARLES FRIED, CONTRACT AS PROMISE 20 (1982).

10. *Id.*

11. *Id* at 19.

12. ON THE GENEALOGY OF MORALS Second Essay, Section 2 (trans. Maudemarie Clark and Alan J. Swensen 1998).

13. *Id.*

women's property acts; and it is denied to unemancipated minor children today.

The state undoubtedly possesses the legal power to grant citizens contractual capacity. And it is equally clearly wrong for the state to grant such capacity unequally to some persons and not others, especially where the discrimination serves a caste or apartheid social order. But the thoughts that the state possesses the power to embrace freedom of contract, and that it ought not discriminate in how it grants freedom of contract, do not yet sustain a general argument in favor of freedom of contract *tout court*. Perhaps the state (regardless of what it can do) *should* grant contractual capacity to no one, after all. And while there are good instrumental reasons in favor of freedom of contract (whose general structure is captured by the Coasean theory just rehearsed), the current focus is on the intrinsic good of freedom of contract. And, as Nietzche's suggestion that there is a paradox in promising reveals, deep complications almost at once confront the suggestion that the power to promise and the capacity to contract are intrinsically valuable for the dignity that they confer on those who possess them.

To observe that the capacity to promise imbues those who possess it with a dignity that creatures without this power lack is not yet to establish that persons *actually possess* the dignity required to sustain promissory capacity. The root of the doubt about our promissory capacity lies in the peculiar character of promissory obligation. Morality, it is commonly thought, condemns even what one might call the *bare wrong* of promise-breaking:[14] the breach of a promise where the promisee, perhaps because he has doubted his promisor all along, has not relied on nor even formed any expectation of performance. Contract, as earlier discussions concerning remedies and the distinction between contract and tort emphasize, possesses an analogous structure. Contracts whose breach would generate only bare wrongs may be uncommon in practice. (Promisees and promisors both find promises useful in large part because they make it reasonable to expect and to rely on the promised performance.) But such contracts remain important for the theory of promise—so important, in fact, that they represent the *pure form* of promise and contract.

Pure contracts are theoretically important, and troubling, because they are constructed so that the wrong of breaking them cannot be explained as an application of the general morality of harm. Promisees have not relied or formed expectations based on them, after all. Instead, the obligations associated with pure contracts arise (if they arise at all) directly out of intentions of the parties to them. Pure contractual obligations are directly willed into existence. But the normative power associated with pure contracts—the will's power to bind itself directly and unmediatedly, without invoking the ordinary morality of fault and harm—is odd indeed. It presents a profound philosophical puzzle.

---

14. The term comes from David Owens, *The Problem with Promising*, in HANOCH SHEINMAN, ed., PROMISES AND AGREEMENTS (2011).

One way of stating the puzzle focuses on the bareness of the alleged wrong in such cases. An obligation, including a contractual obligation, is a kind of reason. Reasons track values. Values depend on interests. But it is difficult to explain what interest might ground a contractual obligation whose breach is a bare wrong. The ordinary interests, associated with reliance or expectations, that might be in play have been excluded by the construction of the case. This is just an abstract and general way of stating the remedial problems that, Chapter 11 observed, arise when contracts are not backed by reliance.

A second account of the puzzle focuses on the origins of pure contractual obligation. Insofar as pure promises obligate apart from inducing reliance or expectations, promisors purport to establish a new obligation simply by communicating an intention to obligate themselves in just this way. It is easy to understand how obligations might arise in conjunction with intentional action: for example, a surgeon who intentionally commences an operation that she was entitled to decline to do thereby incurs obligations to perform it with diligence and care; similarly, a promisor who intentionally induces her promisee reasonably to rely on or to expect a promised performance thereby incurs obligations of fidelity in respect of her promisee's trust that the performance will be forthcoming. But in those cases, and in the myriad others like them, something else—the vulnerabilities that the intentional action has engendered—*grounds* whatever obligations arise. (Given the vulnerabilities, the obligation arises whether the obligor specifically intends it to or not.) The obligations alleged to arise in connection with pure contractual obligation, by contrast, are themselves directly chosen and would not exist were they not themselves chosen: they are, that is, literally *willed into existence*. And it is difficult to explain how the will might possess the normative power to create an obligation in this direct and unmediated way.[15] The difficulty so impressed Hume that he famously compared pure promissory obligation to the mystery of transubstantiation, because both involve intentions that, when communicated, purport directly to "change[] entirely the nature of an external object, and even of a human creature."[16]

The two accounts of the puzzle concerning pure contractual obligation are related, as Hume's remark emphasizes. The case of the pure contract is so constructed that the only resources available for answering the problem of the bare wrong are the intentions of the promisor and promisee. In order

---

15. The problem of normative power is not limited to promising. It arises, for example, in connection with command. Indeed the problem of normative power seems also to arise where obligation is not on the horizon. When a person who judges herself to have been wronged by another chooses, furthermore, to *blame* the wrongdoer, she purports, by blaming, to change his practical circumstances by giving him additional reasons to seek forgiveness. These reasons are probably not best understood as obligations (after all, the wrongdoer has obligations to redress his wrong quite apart from whether or not his victim blames him). But at least in the pure case of blame—the case in which blaming has no emotional or prudential concomitants—their ground is as mysterious as the ground associated with the obligations of promisee-keeping.

16. David Hume, *Of Morals, in* A Treatise of Human Nature Bk. III, Pt. 2, Ch. v, at 455, 524 (2d ed., Oxford Univ. Press 1978) (1888).

to obligate, these intentions must somehow directly affect the interests of the parties to pure contracts. And the theory of the pure contract must therefore face up to the concern that the will lacks the normative power to have such an effect. One might thus express the pair of puzzles together in the following fashion: intentions lack the capacity to clothe the bare wrong of breaching a pure contract in a philosophically respectable way. Put more dramatically, one worries that we are all, in respect of promising, Nietzsche's frail dogs. And if we are, then the argument for freedom of contract cannot find its ground in the reasons that the law has for respecting our innate promissory dignity; for we possess none.

The philosophical puzzle is worth raising for its own sake; it states, clearly and articulately and in general terms, a worry about contract as a free-standing legal form that has permeated these materials but so far received only implicit expression in connection with particular doctrinal problems. The puzzle is also worth examining because its general framing points the way to a solution. As the discussion of contract formation made plain, one thing that (especially reciprocal) promises unquestionably do is place the intentions of the parties to them into engagement with each other. Promisors and promises—especially in contracts established through offer, acceptance, and consideration—form intentions that make reference to each other's intentions: each agrees to obligate herself to the other if the other agrees to obligate himself to her. In the course of doing so, each party recognizes the other as possessing moral capacities equivalent to her own, and in particular the capacity to exercise authority over another person. Each party to a contract grants the other the moral and legal power to either release her from her obligation or insist that she honor it; that is, each party grants the other the moral and legal power to determine what she ought to do. Only persons—possessed of full legal capacity and the social and political status that goes with it—can possess and exercise such power. That is why legal systems, including our own, connect contractual capacity so intimately to broader practices of legal recognition and social membership; why it is a mark of emancipation—from slavery, from coverture, from childhood—to acquire the legal capacity to contract.

The intrinsic value of the recognition relation that contracts establish, and the good that is achieved when a legal order opens up this relation to citizens generally, allowing them to contract as they will, gives freedom of contract a non-instrumental grounding. The form of recognition at play in contract also distinguishes contract from its doctrinal neighbors.

On the one hand, contractual recognition is more particular and more demanding than the general recognition of others associated with the morality of harm and, in law, with tort. Tort law requires persons not to harm one another; and it thus requires them to take one another's interests reasonably into account. The structure of the relations among persons established by tort law is expressed by tort doctrine. And the ways in which it departs from the contract relation are well-summarized by the gap between the obligations created by the misrepresentation torts and those associated with contract proper. As Chapter 16 explained, the misrepresentation torts announce fault-based standards of care; they emphasize (and indeed generally require) that misrepresentations cause harm, generally in the form of reliance costs, in order to count as tortious; and they adopt backward- rather than forward-looking remedies that reject the goal of vindicating the expectations that tortious statements engender and instead aspire only to undo the harms that the misrepresentations cause, that is, to compensate for lost reliance.

On the other hand, contractual recognition is more generic and less demanding than the form of recognition associated with personal loyalty and intimacy in morality and, in law, with fiduciary duty. Fiduciary law again possesses a distinctive structure: Fiduciary law announces a standard of conduct that requires not just care but also loyalty;[17] it imposes on fiduciaries a duty not just to avoid harming or disappointing their principals but also to avoid benefiting themselves on account of actions taken on their principals' behalves;[18] and it adopts remedies that aspire to undo a disloyal fiduciary's gains by ordering that those gains be disgorged to the betrayed beneficiary.[19]

The contract relation falls between these two extremes, and contract law once again possesses a distinctive legal structure, which reflects this middle ground in-between the structures of tort law and fiduciary law. Contract law requires promisors not just to display due care for their promisees but rather strictly to honor their promises. It thus emphasizes the promisee's interest in avoiding not just harm but also disappointment, and his authority to require the promisor to honor her promise, even as the promise imposes duties that she does not owe to persons generally. At the same time, however, contract law constrains contract obligation to the terms of the contractual promise, and rejects any requirement that promisors display broader, altruistic fidelity to their promisees. Contract thus denies that promisees may insist that promisors be motivated altruistically

---

17. See, e.g., RESTATEMENT (THIRD) OF AGENCY § 8.01 (General Fiduciary Principle) ("An agent has a fiduciary duty to act loyally for the principal's benefit in all matters connected with the agency relationship"). A comment to the Restatement section adds that "the general fiduciary principle requires that the agent subordinate the agent's interests to those of the principal and place the principal's interests first as to matters connected with the agency relationship." RESTATEMENT (THIRD) OF AGENCY § 8.01 cmt. [b].

18. See, e.g., RESTATEMENT (THIRD) OF AGENCY § 8.02 (Material Benefit Arising Out Of Position) ("An agent has a duty not to acquire a material benefit from a third party in connection with transactions conducted or other actions taken on behalf of the principal or otherwise through the agent's use of the agent's position").

19. See, e.g., RESTATEMENT (THIRD) OF RESTITUTION AND UNJUST ENRICHMENT § 43(2) (Tentative Draft No. 4, 2005) (generally requiring that "[a] defaulting fiduciary ... will be required to disgorge all gains (including consequential gains) derived from the wrongful transaction"), RESTATEMENT (THIRD) OF AGENCY § 8.01 cmt. [d] ("The law of restitution and unjust enrichment also creates a basis for an agent's liability to a principal when the agent breaches a fiduciary duty, even though the principal cannot establish that the agent's breach caused loss to the principal. If through the breach the agent has realized a material benefit, the agent has a duty to account to the principal for the benefit, its value, or its proceeds. The agent is subject to liability to deliver the benefit, its proceeds, or its value to the principal"), Restatement (Third) of Agency § 8.02 cmt.[e] ("When an agent breaches the duty stated in this section, ... [t]he principal may recover any material benefit received by the agent through the agent's breach, the value of the benefit, or proceeds of the benefit retained by the agent").

to promote their interests or that they have any entitlements in respect of their promisors' enrichment in connection with the promised performance.

The structure of the contract relation—which pairs recognition of a special authority to demand compliance with the terms of the contractual agreement together with an on-going arm's length relation aside from this agreement—generally informs the non-instrumental analysis of freedom of contract and its limits. The doctrinal materials that dominate the remainder of this Part of the text should be read with the character of the contract relation in mind.[20]

The next chapter, on good faith, elaborates the basic moral norm of contract law. The duty of good faith in performance might initially seem to state a limit on freedom of contract; after all, it announces, quite exceptionally for modern contract law, a mandatory duty, which the parties cannot waive by agreement. But in fact, good faith in performance is best understood as doctrine's effort to capture the promisor's recognition of her promisee's authority to insist on the promise that lies at the heart of the contract relation; it is the necessary minimum required for the contract relation to endure. Good faith is thus not a limit on freedom of contract so much as the backstop that supports the authority of contractual obligations and so makes such freedom meaningful.

The two chapters after this take up areas of current contractual practice that place the contract relation under strain. One chapter addresses form contracts—more precisely, contracts of adhesion—in which the

---

20. It is worth pausing for a moment to draw out the contrast between the emphasis on the contract relation taken by the moral argument for contract's intrinsic value and the structure of the instrumental, economic argument for freedom of contract.

The deep structure of the economic account of efficient contracting becomes clearer when the pre-suppositions of the economic approach are made explicit, as Alan Schwartz and Robert Scott have admirably done in recent work. See Alan Schwartz & Robert E. Scott, *Contract Theory and the Limits of Contract Law*, 113 YALE L.J. 541 (2003). Schwartz and Scott argue that contract law for economic firms should be designed single-mindedly to maximize contractual surplus, that is, to serve efficiency. They argue that concerns of corrective justice should not inform contract law for firms. The firms' broad-ranging contractual engagements generally cause them to occupy both sides of contractual relationships, so that corrective-justice-inspired preferences for one side or the other (for buyers, say, or for licensees) will inevitably come out in the wash. Such preferences will therefore be rejected by the firms themselves, who will never benefit from corrective principles that shift surplus around in particular contracts at the cost of reducing the overall surplus that is available. And Schwartz and Scott add, with respect to distributive justice, that because the individual persons who own firms will (and should) diversify their holdings, even legal rules that did prefer firms on one side of business transactions would have no distributive effects across owners. The owners will own shares in both the firms that are benefited and those that are burdened by any particular legal rule and hence again look to the total value of their portfolios, indifferent to increases in the values of some of their holdings that come at the expense of decreases in the values of others.

Behind this approach lies a picture of commercial transactions among business firms in which the only morally freestanding principal is the representative owner of a fully diversified portfolio of shares in all the firms that engage in the transactions Schwartz and Scott take as their subject. The firms themselves are mere instrumentalities that interact with each other on behalf of this common owner, who has a perfectly balanced share in both sides of every transaction. Contract law, and the non-instrumental accounts of contract law developed in this Part, insist that contracts establish a relation between *two* distinct, independent parties. But the economic approach to contract, this analysis reveals, imagines that there is at bottom just one.

ideal of the contract relation comes up against the mechanics of modern mass-contracting. Although contracts of adhesion retain all the elements of the contract relation, they do not combine these elements in the way needed to make the contract relation, and the reciprocal recognition that the relation involves, come alive for those who inhabit it. The law's uncertain attitude towards contracts of adhesion—its tendency to subject these contracts to a kind of scrutiny that the background commitment to freedom of contract would generally reject—may be explained in terms of the deficiencies in the contract relation that contracts of adhesion establish. Another chapter addresses arbitration agreements, through which parties seek to employ the contract relation to supplant adjudication, understood as a form of dispute resolution. The chapter asks whether the contract relation can bear the strain that carrying adjudication's burdens places it under—whether freedom of contract should extend to using contract to supplant adjudication in this way. The question becomes especially pressing insofar as many arbitration agreements are adopted as parts of contracts of adhesion. These two chapters thus consider the manner and circumstances in which current contractual practice so attenuates the relation among contracting parties that its capacity to sustain contractual obligation is called into question, so that freedom of contract becomes possibly restricted as well.

The next two chapters reverse the focus and address circumstances in which contracts are embedded in prior relations between the parties that are so thick that it is unclear whether the thinner form of obligation associated with contract can survive within them. One chapter takes up employment; the other, marriage. In each case, contractual versions of the relation grew slowly out of thicker, status-like legal regimes. The chapters ask whether contract has effectively supplanted status in these areas; or whether instead constraints on freedom of contract (perhaps even related to the old status orders) continue to govern employment and marriage.

A final chapter takes up topics that are more conventionally associated with the limits of freedom of contract: illegality, mental incapacity, duress, undue influence, and unconscionability. The first topic considers cases in which freedom of contract is limited on substantive grounds. These can range from the viciousness or criminality of the plans that the contracts contemplate to concerns about improper commodification. The next several topics concern cases in which procedural considerations that might limit freedom of contract come into play. In spite of being conventionally emphasized, these subjects are not nearly as important, either to contract theory or contractual practice, as the topics presented in earlier chapters in this Part. The discussions of duress and especially unconscionability will also return, in some measure, to instrumental and in particular economic arguments about contract. They thus close out the text in a manner that circles back to some of the themes with which it began.

CHAPTER 19

GOOD FAITH

Duties of good faith in contract law may apply both within the contract relation and without it. The duty of good faith within the relation is called the duty of good faith in performance; the duty of good faith without the relation is called the duty of good faith in negotiations. The common law of contracts recognizes the former, but not the latter, although it is (as the discussions in Chapters 13 and 14 suggested) sometimes willing to recognize efforts by bargainers to impose duties to negotiate in good faith on themselves, by contract.[1] This chapter will therefore emphasize the duty of good faith in performance. At the end, it will briefly take up good faith in negotiations.

19.1 GOOD FAITH IN PERFORMANCE

The common law has, at least since eighteenth century,[2] imposed a duty of good faith in performance on every contract. The following materials state the black letter of the duty as it is expressed in doctrine today.

Restatement (Second) of Contracts

§ 205 Duty of Good Faith and Fair Dealing

Every contract imposes upon each party a duty of good faith and fair dealing in its performance and its enforcement.

Comments & Illustrations

Comment a. Meanings of "good faith." Good faith is defined in Uniform Commercial Code § 1–201(19) as "honesty in fact in the conduct or transaction concerned." "In the case of a merchant" Uniform Commercial Code § 2–103(1)(b) provides that good faith means "honesty in fact and the observance of reasonable commercial standards of fair dealing in the trade." The phrase "good faith" is used in a variety of contexts, and its meaning varies somewhat with the context. Good faith performance or enforcement of a contract emphasizes faithfulness to an agreed common

---

1. Civil Law does recognize a generalized duty of good faith in negotiations.

2. A seminal authority is Lord Mansfield's opinion in *Boone v. Eyre*, 1 H. Bl. 273, 126 Eng. Rep. 160 (K.B. 1777). An early case imposing this duty in an American jurisdiction is *Kirke La Shelle Co. v. Paul Armstrong Co.*, 188 N.E. 163, 167 (N.Y. 1933).

purpose and consistency with the justified expectations of the other party; it excludes a variety of types of conduct characterized as involving "bad faith" because they violate community standards of decency, fairness or reasonableness. The appropriate remedy for a breach of the duty of good faith also varies with the circumstances.

Comment b.   Good faith purchase. In many situations a good faith purchaser of property for value can acquire better rights in the property than his transferor had. See, e.g., § 342. In this context "good faith" focuses on the honesty of the purchaser, as distinguished from his care or negligence. Particularly in the law of negotiable instruments inquiry may be limited to "good faith" under what has been called "the rule of the pure heart and the empty head." When diligence or inquiry is a condition of the purchaser's right, it is said that good faith is not enough. This focus on honesty is appropriate to cases of good faith purchase; it is less so in cases of good faith performance.

Comment c.   Good faith in negotiation. This Section, like Uniform Commercial Code § 1–203, does not deal with good faith in the formation of a contract. Bad faith in negotiation, although not within the scope of this Section, may be subject to sanctions. Particular forms of bad faith in bargaining are the subjects of rules as to capacity to contract, mutual assent and consideration and of rules as to invalidating causes such as fraud and duress. See, for example, §§ 90 and 208. Moreover, remedies for bad faith in the absence of agreement are found in the law of torts or restitution. For examples of a statutory duty to bargain in good faith, see, e.g., National Labor Relations Act § 8(d) and the federal Truth in Lending Act. In cases of negotiation for modification of an existing contractual relationship, the rule stated in this Section may overlap with more specific rules requiring negotiation in good faith. See §§ 73, 89; Uniform Commercial Code § 2–209 and Comment.

Comment d.   Good faith performance. Subterfuges and evasions violate the obligation of good faith in performance even though the actor believes his conduct to be justified. But the obligation goes further: bad faith may be overt or may consist of inaction, and fair dealing may require more than honesty. A complete catalogue of types of bad faith is impossible, but the following types are among those which have been recognized in judicial decisions: evasion of the spirit of the bargain, lack of diligence and slacking off, willful rendering of imperfect performance, abuse of a power to specify terms, and interference with or failure to cooperate in the other party's performance.

Illustrations

   1.   A, an oil dealer, borrows $100,000 from B, a supplier, and agrees to buy all his requirements of certain oil products from B on stated terms until the debt is repaid. Before the debt is repaid, A makes a new arrangement with C, a competitor of B. Under the new arrangement A's business is conducted by a corporation formed and owned by A and C and managed by A, and the corporation buys all its oil products from C. The new arrangement

may be found to be a subterfuge or evasion and a breach of contract by A.

2.   A, owner of a shopping center, leases part of it to B, giving B the exclusive right to conduct a supermarket, the rent to be a percentage of B's gross receipts. During the term of the lease A acquires adjoining land, expands the shopping center, and leases part of the adjoining land to C for a competing supermarket. Unless such action was contemplated or is otherwise justified, there is a breach of contract by A.

3.   A Insurance Company insures B against legal liability for certain bodily injuries to third persons, with a limit of liability of $10,000 for an accident to any one person. The policy provides that A will defend any suit covered by it but may settle. C sues B on a claim covered by the policy and offers to settle for $9,500. A refuses to settle on the ground that the amount is excessive, and judgment is rendered against B for $20,000 after a trial defended by A. A then refuses to appeal, and offers to pay $10,000 only if B satisfies the judgment, impairing B's opportunity to negotiate for settlement. B prosecutes an appeal, reasonably expending $7,500, and obtains dismissal of the claim. A has failed to deal fairly and in good faith with B and is liable for B's appeal expense.

4.   A and B contract that A will perform certain demolition work for B and pay B a specified sum for materials salvaged, the contract not to "become effective until" certain insurance policies "are in full force and effect." A makes a good faith effort to obtain the insurance, but financial difficulty arising from injury to an employee of A on another job prevents A from obtaining them. A's duty to perform is discharged.

5.   B submits and A accepts a bid to supply approximately 4000 tons of trap rock for an airport at a unit price. The parties execute a standard form of "Invitation, Bid, and Acceptance (Short Form Contract)" supplied by A, including typed terms "to be delivered to project as required," "delivery to start immediately," "cancellation by A may be effected at any time." Good faith requires that A order and accept the rock within a reasonable time unless A has given B notice of intent to cancel.

6.   A contracts to perform services for B for such compensation "as you, in your sole judgment, may decide is reasonable." After A has performed the services, B refuses to make any determination of the value of the services. A is entitled to their value as determined by a court.

7.   A suffers a loss of property covered by an insurance policy issued by B, and submits to B notice and proof of loss. The notice and proof fail to comply with requirements of the policy as to form and detail. B does not point out the defects, but remains silent and evasive, telling A broadly to perfect his claim. The defects do not bar recovery on the policy.

Comment e.   Good faith in enforcement. The obligation of good faith and fair dealing extends to the assertion, settlement and litigation of contract claims and defenses. See, e.g., §§ 73, 89. The obligation is violated by dishonest conduct such as conjuring up a pretended dispute, asserting an interpretation contrary to one's own understanding, or falsification of facts. It also extends to dealing which is candid but unfair, such as taking advantage of the necessitous circumstances of the other party to extort a modification of a contract for the sale of goods without legitimate commercial reason. See Uniform Commercial Code § 2–209, Comment 2. Other types of violation have been recognized in judicial decisions: harassing demands for assurances of performance, rejection of performance for unstated reasons, willful failure to mitigate damages, and abuse of a power to determine compliance or to terminate the contract. For a statutory duty of good faith in termination, see the federal Automobile Dealer's Day in Court Act, 15 U.S.C. §§ 1221–25 (1976).

Illustrations

8. A contracts to sell and ship goods to B on credit. The contract provides that, if B's credit or financial responsibility becomes impaired or unsatisfactory to A, A may demand cash or security before making shipment and may cancel if the demand is not met. A may properly demand cash or security only if he honestly believes, with reason, that the prospect of payment is impaired.

9. A contracts to sell and ship goods to B. On arrival B rejects the goods on the erroneous ground that delivery was late. B is thereafter precluded from asserting other unstated grounds then known to him which A could have cured if stated seasonably.

Uniform Commercial Code

§ 1–201(b)(20)

"Good faith," except as otherwise provided in Article 5, means honesty in fact and the observance of reasonable commercial standards of fair dealing.

Official Comment

Source: Former Section 1–201.

20. "Good faith." Former Section 1–201(19) defined "good faith" simply as honesty in fact; the definition contained no element of commercial reasonableness. Initially, that definition applied throughout the Code with only one exception. Former Section 2–103(1)(b) provided that, in that Article, "'good faith' in the case of a merchant means honesty in fact and the observance of reasonable commercial standards of fair dealing in the trade." This alternative definition was limited in applicability, though, because it applied only to transactions within the scope of Article 2 and it applied only to merchants.

Over time, however, amendments to the Uniform Commercial Code brought the Article 2 merchant concept of good faith (subjective honesty and objective commercial reasonableness) into other Articles. First, Article 2A explicitly incorporated the Article 2 standard. See Section 2A-103(7). Then, other Articles broadened the applicability of that standard by adopting it for all parties rather than just for merchants. *See, e.g.,* Sections 3–103(a)(4), 4A-105(a)(6), 7–102(a)(6), 8–102(a)(10), and 9–102(a)(43). Finally, Articles 2 and 2A were amended so as to apply the standard to non-merchants as well as merchants. See Sections 2–103(1)(j), 2A-103(1)(m). All of these definitions are comprised of two elements-honesty in fact *and* the observance of reasonable commercial standards of fair dealing. Only revised Article 5 defines "good faith" solely in terms of subjective honesty, and only Article 6 (in the few states that have not chosen to delete the Article) is without a definition of good faith. (It should be noted that, while revised Article 6 did not define good faith, Comment 2 to revised Section 6–102 states that "this Article adopts the definition of 'good faith' in Article 1 in all cases, even when the buyer is a merchant.")

Thus, the definition of "good faith" in this section merely confirms what has been the case for a number of years as Articles of the UCC have been amended or revised-the obligation of "good faith," applicable in each Article, is to be interpreted in the context of all Articles except for Article 5 as including both the subjective element of honesty in fact and the objective element of the observance of reasonable commercial standards of fair dealing. As a result, both the subjective and objective elements are part of the standard of "good faith," whether that obligation is specifically referenced in another Article of the Code (other than Article 5) or is provided by this Article.

Of course, as noted in the statutory text, the definition of "good faith" in this section does not apply when the narrower definition of "good faith" in revised Article 5 is applicable.

As noted above, the definition of "good faith" in this section requires not only honesty in fact but also "observance of reasonable commercial standards of fair dealing." Although "fair dealing" is a broad term that must be defined in context, it is clear that it is concerned with the fairness of conduct rather than the care with which an act is performed. This is an entirely different concept than whether a party exercised ordinary care in conducting a transaction. Both concepts are to be determined in the light of reasonable commercial standards, but those standards in each case are directed to different aspects of commercial conduct. See e.g., Sections 3–103(a)(9) and 4–104(c) and Comment 4 to Section 3–103.

Uniform Commercial Code

§ 1–304.   Obligation of Good Faith

Every contract or duty within [the Uniform Commercial Code] imposes an obligation of good faith in its performance and enforcement.

Official Comment

Source: Former Section 1–203.

Changes from former law: Except for changing the form of reference to the Uniform Commercial Code, this section is identical to former Section 1–203.

1. This section sets forth a basic principle running throughout the Uniform Commercial Code. The principle is that in commercial transactions good faith is required in the performance and enforcement of all agreements or duties. While this duty is explicitly stated in some provisions of the Uniform Commercial Code, the applicability of the duty is broader than merely these situations and applies generally, as stated in this section, to the performance or enforcement of every contract or duty within this Act. It is further implemented by Section 1–303 on course of dealing, course of performance, and usage of trade. This section does not support an independent cause of action for failure to perform or enforce in good faith. Rather, this section means that a failure to perform or enforce, in good faith, a specific duty or obligation under the contract, constitutes a breach of that contract or makes unavailable, under the particular circumstances, a remedial right or power. This distinction makes it clear that the doctrine of good faith merely directs a court towards interpreting contracts within the commercial context in which they are created, performed, and enforced, and does not create a separate duty of fairness and reasonableness which can be independently breached.

2. "Performance and enforcement" of contracts and duties within the Uniform Commercial Code include the exercise of rights created by the Uniform Commercial Code.

* * *

The Uniform Commercial Code imposes a mandatory duty of good faith in performance on "every contract" within its scope. The Restatement (Second) of Contracts similarly says that "[e]very contract imposes upon each party a duty of good faith and fair dealing in its performance and its enforcement." Moreover, the two authorities begin to elaborate good faith in similar terms. The U.C.C. thus adds that "good faith" means "honesty in fact and the observance of reasonable commercial standards of fair dealing." The comments to the Restatement explain that good faith "excludes a variety of types of conduct characterized as involving 'bad faith' because they violate community standards of decency, fairness or reasonableness."[3] While the Restatement takes the position that a "complete catalogue of types of bad faith is impossible," it provides representative examples. These include: "evasion of the spirit of the bargain, lack of diligence and slacking off, willful rendering of imperfect performance, abuse of a power to specify terms, and interference with or failure to cooperate in the other party's performance."[4] The comments add that good faith:

---

3. RESTATEMENT (SECOND) OF CONTRACTS § 205 cmt. [a].

4. RESTATEMENT (SECOND) OF CONTRACTS § 205 cmt. [d].

is violated by dishonest conduct [in enforcing contract rights] such as conjuring up a pretended dispute, asserting an interpretation contrary to one's own understanding, or falsification of facts. [Good faith is also violated by] dealing which is candid but unfair, such as taking advantage of the necessitous circumstances of the other party to extort a modification of a contract for the sale of goods without a legitimate commercial reason. [Good faith is also violated by] harassing demands for assurances of performance, rejection of performance for unstated reasons, willful failure to mitigate damages, and abuse of a power to determine compliance or to terminate the contract.[5]

This duty of good faith in performance has been applied to regulate advantage-taking within the contract relation in any number of circumstances.

Thus good faith forbids parties from hiding behind indefinite contract terms, either by construing them in an excessively self-serving light or by claiming that the indefiniteness renders the contracts containing them void, *tout court*. Instead, where a contract leaves the particulars of performance to be specified by one of the parties, that party is constrained to make the specification in good faith,[6] which, as the comments to the UCC say, entails that "the range of permissible variation is limited by what is commercially reasonable."[7] In the context of sales contracts that measure quantity by the output of the seller or the requirements of the buyer, good faith requires that the quantity a party orders or delivers not be unreasonably disproportionate to the legitimate expectations of the counterparty.[8] Contracts for exclusive dealings in some class of goods similarly require parties to use their best or at least reasonable efforts to supply or promote the goods in question.[9]

A similar regime governs contracts in which terms essential to operating the contracts as circumstances have developed are not just left indefinite but are not included at all. Where the parties have failed to make adequate arrangements for some contingency ex ante, they must employ good faith in making arrangements ex post. For example, termination is governed by good faith,[10] at least where the contract does not establish any specific regime. A party seeking to terminate may not do so before the non-terminating party has had "reasonable notification,"[11] which is to say a "reasonable time to seek a substitute arrangement."[12] Similarly, the warranties concerning title that a seller provides her buyer are also governed

---

5.   RESTATEMENT (SECOND) OF CONTRACTS § 205 cmt. [e].

6.   U.C.C. § 2–311(1).

7.   U.C.C. § 2–311 cmt. 1.

8.   U.C.C. § 2–306(1).

9.   See U.C.C. § 2–306(2); *Wood v. Lucy, Lady Duff–Gordon*, 222 N.Y. 88 (1917).

10.   See U.C.C. § 2–309 cmt. 8.

11.   U.C.C. § 2–309 cmt. 5.

12.   U.C.C. § 2–309 cmt. 8.

by good faith. In particular, where a contract does not specify otherwise, a seller warrants that her title is good and its transfer is rightful, and that the buyer will not be unreasonably exposed to litigation based on third parties' colorable claims or interests in the goods.[13]

Finally, good faith applies to create effectively mandatory duties in circumstances in which the parties' contractual relations have broken down in ways such that no prior agreement could reliably govern conduct. The most common such circumstances involve a party's response to his counter-party's breach, and thus in particular concern the party's efforts to recover damages. The parties cannot contract ex ante for the case in which a promisor denies her contractual obligations entirely, because this denial would cover any agreement that they had made for such a case. The promisor's denial of the contract does not, however, disentangle the parties from each other's affairs. The disappointed promisee will continue to insist on her contractual rights and to take steps to vindicate these rights. Insofar as the steps that she takes might impose costs on her promisor, the law must regulate her conduct (as the parties' agreement cannot). A mandatory duty of good faith figures prominently in this regulation.

For example, although a seller whose buyer has breached may, in appropriate circumstances, avoid the burden and expense of proving up market damages and instead resell the goods and recover damages based on the contract-resale price difference,[14] the resale must be made in good faith.[15] Relatedly, although sellers whose buyers breach may recover consequential damages, their recovery is limited according to their duty to make a good faith effort to minimize (including by resale) the consequential damages suffered as a result of the breach.[16] Analogous duties of good faith apply to buyers with respect to cover when their sellers breach[17] and to buyers' duties to mitigate (including by purchasing cover) their consequential damages from breach.[18]

Nor are these the only circumstances in which good faith supplies mandatory terms to govern aspects of the contract relation that, for structural reasons, the parties' agreements cannot reach. Thus good faith requires a seller to disclose known material but hidden defects in goods sold.[19] The disclosure may be waived by a disclaimer that asserts that there may be hidden defects, but this of course puts the buyer on notice that goods may not be as they appear.

Similarly, although contracting parties generally can, "if they consciously desire, make their own bargain as they wish,"[20] good faith pre-

---

13. U.C.C. § 2–312(1) and cmt. 1.

14. U.C.C. § 2–706.

15. U.C.C. § 2–706(1).

16. See U.C.C. § 2–708 and cmt. 6.

17. See U.C.C. § 2–712(1) and cmt. 4

18. See U.C.C. § 2–715 and cmt. 2.

19. U.C.C. § 2–314 cmt. 4.

20. U.C.C. § 2–313 cmt. 6.

cludes a party from using one clause to undo a promise made in another, at least in circumstances in which honoring the undoing cannot be understood except as implementing the manipulative term of a bait and switch. This principle applies with especial force to preclude sellers' efforts to disclaim warranties that their selling methods are designed to convey the impression of having given. The comments to one of the U.C.C. sections on warranties thus observe that "a contract is normally a contract for a sale of something describable and described. A clause generally disclaiming 'all warranties, express or implied' cannot reduce the seller's obligation with respect to such description and therefore cannot be given literal effect."[21] Rather, "in determining what [the parties] have agreed upon good faith is a factor and consideration should be given to the fact that the probability is small that a real price is intended to be exchanged for a pseudo-obligation."[22]

In all these instances, good faith steps in to *require* contracting parties to respect each other's contractual intentions even where they, preferring manipulation, are disinclined to do so.

The duty of good faith thus polices advantage-taking within the contract relation. It seeks to prevent the respectful frame of the contract relation—the fact that the parties to this relation open themselves up to one another's intentions—from becoming itself an opportunity for manipulation or exploitation. The examples all share the general sentiment that it is bad faith for one party to use the fact of the contract to exploit the other going forward. Thus it said that good faith precludes a party from using its inevitable room to maneuver within the contract "to recapture opportunities forgone upon contracting."[23] Bad faith in performance, that is, "consists of an exercise of discretion in performance to recapture opportunities forgone at formation."[24]

Most importantly, a party cannot use the very fact that after negotiations had concluded in an agreement, his counterparty took steps (pursuant to that agreement) that rendered her more vulnerable than she was in the negotiations, now to re-negotiate aspects of the agreement on more favorable terms. In the words of a prominent early opinion, "In every contract there is an implied covenant that neither party shall do anything which will have the effect of destroying or injuring the right of the other party to receive the fruits of the contract, which means that in every contract there exists an implied covenant of good faith and fair dealing."[25]

---

21. U.C.C. § 2–313 cmt. 4.

22. U.C.C. § 2–313 cmt. 4. How is the consistent with the principle of U.C.C. § 2–316, which allows even quite general disclaimers of warranty ("sold as is," for example)?

23. Steven J. Burton, *Breach of Contract and the Common Law Duty to Perform in Good Faith*, 94 HARV. L. REV. 369, 373 (1980).

24. *Id.* at 387.

25. *Kirke La Shelle Co. v. Paul Armstrong Co.* 263 N.Y. 79, 87, 188 N.E. 163, 167 (1933). The case involved a silent-film era agreement to share "motion picture" rights to a play and the question whether rights to make a "talkie" based on the play were within the scope of the agreement. The court held that they were not. It has seemed to many that that this is a mistake on the facts. *See L.C. Page & Co. v. Fox Film Corp.*, 83 F.2d 196, 199 (2d Cir. 1936)

This formulation is revealing. It is tempting to think that the duty of good faith in performance *adds* to the content of contractual obligation—to this obligation's metes and bounds—concretely and in the context of particular contracts. To understand good faith in this way would be to be able to use the duty to decide (close) cases. But the connection between good faith and respecting a counterparty's right to the fruits of his contract suggests that the additional duty conception of good faith rests on a fundamental mistake. Good faith does not determine the *content* of contract obligation, and certainly not at the margins of performance (by adding an incremental duty or right to what the contract would have required in its absence). The Official Comment to U.C.C. § 1–304 makes this plain:

> This section does not support an independent cause of action for failure to perform or enforce in good faith. Rather, this section means that a failure to perform or enforce, in good faith, a specific duty or obligation under the contract, constitutes a breach of that contract or makes unavailable, under the particular circumstances, a medial right or power. This distinction makes it clear that the doctrine of good faith merely directs a court towards interpreting contracts within the commercial context in which they are created, performed, and enforced, and does not create a separate duty of fairness and reasonableness which can be independently breached.[26]

Rather than adding substance to the obligations established by a contract, good faith characterizes contract obligation's *form*: good faith supports the parties' contractual settlement, working to "effectuate the intentions of the parties, or to protect their reasonable expectations."[27]

This introduces a theme that will be elaborated in much greater and more careful detail below: Good faith is, fundamentally, an attitude of respect for the contract relation, and the measure of good faith is the contract itself. Good faith thus establishes the character of the contract relation. It involves a distinctively contractual form of recognition and respect. This form is thin and flexible but neither inconsequential nor slight; indeed, contractual solidarity, although it arises at arm's length, possess a value in which more intimate forms of recognition cannot share. Among other things, this form reconciles contractual solidarity with freedom of contract. Good faith, properly understood, identifies and elaborates this value. An understanding of good faith thus does not so much help to decide cases as to characterize what has been decided.

(words "motion picture" in pre-"talkie" contract held to include "talkies"). *See also Bartsch v. Metro–Goldwyn–Mayer, Inc.*, 391 F.2d 150 (2d Cir.), *cert. denied*, 393 U.S. 826 (1968).

26.   U.C.C. § 1–304 cmt. [1].

27.   Steven J. Burton, *Breach of Contract and the Common Law Duty to Perform in Good Faith*, 94 HARV. L. REV. 369, 371 (1980). For cases, see *Sessions, Inc. v. Morton*, 491 F.2d 854, 857 (9th Cir. 1974); *Ryder Truck Rental, Inc. v. Central Packing Co.*, 341 F.2d 321, 323–24 (10th Cir. 1965); *Perkins v. Standard Oil Co.*, 235 Or. 7, 15–17, 383 P.2d 107, 111–12 (1963) (*en banc*).

19.1.A   THE METES AND BOUNDS OF GOOD FAITH

Even the formal understanding of good faith can be useful in deciding cases, at least when this understanding is supplemented by the specific facts and circumstances in which particular contracts or classes of contracts arise. Rich, circumstance-specific information about the intentions and purposes of the parties and their contractual bargaining makes it possible confidently to identify ex post exploitation by one party of vulnerabilities the contractual settlement has imposed on the other.

This is vividly illustrated in connection with employment contracts. Thus is it bad faith for an employer to discharge a sales employee who is paid on commission after the employee has obtained an extraordinarily large order but before completion of all the formalities required to make the commission come due.[28] Similarly, it is bad faith for an employer to fire an employee just before the employee meets a performance quota that triggers a substantial bonus. In each case, the employee has expended effort that the employment contract contemplated and indeed was designed to induce and, by rendering this effort a sunk cost, eliminated her power to bargain for a share of the return to the effort. In refusing to pay the commission or the bonus, the employer has deprived the employee of the share of the return to her effort that the contract had allocated to her ex ante and exploited the employee's weakened bargaining position ex post. This is bad faith.[29]

---

28. See *Fortune v. National Cash Register*, 364 N.E.2d 1251, 1255 (Mass. 1977):

The contract at issue is a classic terminable at will employment contract. It is clear that the contract itself reserved to the parties an explicit power to terminate the contract without cause on written notice. It is also clear that under the express terms of the contract Fortune has received all the bonus commissions to which he is entitled. Thus, NCR claims that it did not breach the contract, and that it has no further liability to Fortune. According to a literal reading of the contract, NCR is correct.

However, Fortune argues that, in spite of the literal wording of the contract, he is entitled to a jury determination on NCR's motives in terminating his services under the contract and in finally discharging him. We agree. We hold that NCR's written contract contains an implied covenant of good faith and fair dealing, and a termination not made in good faith constitutes a breach of the contract.

We do not question the general principles that an employer is entitled to be motivated by and to serve its own legitimate business interests; that an employer must have wide latitude in deciding whom it will employ in the face of the uncertainties of the business world; and that an employer needs flexibility in the face of changing circumstances. We recognize the employer's need for a large amount of control over its work force. However, we believe that where, as here, commissions are to be paid for work performed by the employee, the employer's decision to terminate its at will employee should be made in good faith. NCR's right to make decisions in its own interest is not, in our view, unduly hampered by a requirement of adherence to this standard.

A more detailed discussion of employment at will appears in Chapter 22.

29. Other cases display a similar, and similarly clear, pattern, in different fact settings. Thus, it is bad faith for a buyer who has contracted to purchase a specific asset from a middleman subsequently to buy this asset directly from the middleman's supplier in order to save having to pay his profit. To do so would be to exploit the vulnerability to which the contract has exposed the middleman—the revelation of the asset to the buyer—in order to deprive the middleman of the very gain that the contract was designed to secure him. See, e.g.,

The application of good faith to insurance contracts provides another vivid, if somewhat more complex, example. These contracts typically impose two duties on insurers: first, a duty to pay damage awards or settlements secured against the insured by injured third persons in connection with covered events, up to some limit set by the policy; and, second, a duty to defend the insured against claims for such damages, which includes a duty to participate in settlement negotiations.

Usually, the joint duties to pay and to defend align the interests of the parties to an insurance contract. But where an insured facing a damages suit is offered a settlement for an amount at or near the policy limit, the insurance contract causes the interests of the insurer and the insured to diverge. The insured has a strong interest in accepting the settlement, as this ends the lawsuit on terms that protect her from personal liability. The insurer has an equally strong interest in rejecting the settlement, because the policy limit entails that it bears none of the risk that proceeding to trial will generate a larger adverse verdict. Finally, the insurance contract has rendered the parties strategically vulnerable to each other. The insurer has exposed itself to a litigation risk triggered by the party's conduct, and cannot simply walk away from the lawsuit; and the insured has exposed herself to the insurer's management of her defense, and cannot purchase new or more insurance.

Accordingly, it might be bad faith for the insured to exploit the insurer's position by insisting on accepting unreasonably large settlement offers, and refusing to cooperate in any further defense, on the ground that this costs her nothing and saves her the burden of the lawsuit. And, much more practically important, it might be bad faith for the insurer to reject reasonable settlement offers near the policy limit, on the ground that it bears none of the litigation risk associated with rejecting the offers.[30] An insurer who refuses reasonable settlement offers on these grounds exploits the insured's *ex post* vulnerability to deprive her of two of the benefits that the insurance contract was designed to confer on her: protection against personal liability for losses within the policy limit; and the assistance of her insurer in defending herself.

These are vivid examples and they cover practically important ground. But they are difficult to generalize into a trans-substantive statement of the content and limits of good faith that is capable of deciding cases. Too much of the argument turns on peculiar facts about employment and insurance contracts and the respective interests and vulnerabilities of the parties to them. Such considerations do not readily generalize.

Moreover, such general statements of the duty of good faith as the cases employ are conclusory, at least when approached as rules of decision. This is especially true of the proposition that good faith precludes a

---

Patterson v. Meyerhofer, 97 N.E. 472 (N.Y. 1912). Similarly, it can be bad faith for a financing-dependent buyer completely to fail to seek financing. See, e.g., *Fry v. George Elkins Co.*, 327 P.2d 905 (Cal. Ct. App. 1958); *Goldberg v. Charlie's Chevrolet, Inc.*, 672 S.W.2d 177 (Mo. Ct. App 1984).

30.   Here recall the discussions of *Communale* and *Crisci* in Chapter 8.

promisor's exploiting strategic vulnerabilities created by the contract against the reasonable expectations of her counterparty or to deprive the counterparty of benefits that the contract was designed to confer. This form of words simply cannot say just when advantage-taking crosses the line from legitimate self-interest to bad faith. Precisely how are the reasonable expectations of promisees to be identified? Just what benefits is the contract designed to confer?

Answers to these questions depend on the content of promisors' duties of good faith performance. But now the answers cannot be used to fix the duty. In the examples, rich context makes it possible to cut off the circle. But context does not generalize, and the circularity reasserts itself.

Something general can be said, of course. The inner and outer bounds of good faith may be fixed securely.

On the one hand, it is commonly and rightly observed, for example by Richard Posner, that "conduct that might not rise to the level of fraud may nonetheless violate the duty of good faith in dealing with one's contractual partners."[31] Good faith must require more of the parties than just that they abjure fraud, because good faith refers to rights established by a completed bargain rather than only to rights against being misused in bargaining.

On the other hand, it is equally familiar that good faith requires less than fiduciary loyalty and devotion.[32] A fiduciary, as it is sometimes said, is "required to treat his principal as if the principal were he."[33] In fact, a fiduciary must treat his principal more carefully still: there is any number of risks that a person might (even reasonably) take on his own account that he may not, acting as fiduciary, take on his principal's. Good faith, by contrast, does not require contracting parties to display substantive other-regard or altruism, preferring their partners' interests over their own, or even weighting the two interests equally, within their contracts. As Posner also observed, "[t]he contractual duty of good faith is thus not some newfangled bit of welfare-state paternalism or the sediment of an altruistic strain in contract law."[34] Similarly, "even after you have signed a contract, you are not obliged to become an altruist toward the other party."[35] Nor does good faith require contracting parties to adopt even an attitude of substantive impartiality between their contractual interests and the interests of their contracting partners. The duty of good faith in performance applies, after all, to every contract, including to contracts among sophisticated parties who deal at arm's length. The law does not seek, "in the

---

31. *Market St. Assocs. Ltd. P'ship v. Frey*, 941 F.2d 588, 594–95 (7th Cir. 1991).

32. But see *Parev Prods. Co. v. I. Rokeach & Sons, Inc.*, 124 F.2d 147 (2d Cir. 1941), which comes close to taking a fiduciary duty view, seeking "the really equitable solution" as opposed to "a limited rule of good faith.".

33. *Market St. Assocs. Ltd. P'ship v. Frey*, 941 F.2d 588, 593 (7th Cir. 1991).

34. *Id.* at 595.

35. *Id.* at 594.

name of good faith, to make every contract signatory his brother's keeper."[36]

The difficulties that trouble efforts to elaborate a conception of good faith capable of deciding cases all arise in between these extremes. The following case, which concerns the meaning of good faith in connection with a requirements contract, vividly illustrates how hard it is reliably to map the terrain of the middle ground in which good faith must operate.

Eastern Air Lines, Inc. v. Gulf Oil Corp.

United States District Court for the Southern District of Florida, 1975.
415 F. Supp. 429.

(Reprised from Chapter 15)

* * *

The facts in *Eastern Air Lines* were straightforward. A brief summary will recall them. Eastern had contracted with Gulf Oil Corporation for Gulf to supply Eastern's requirements of jet fuel over a several year period. The contract fixed the purchase price by reference to a price indicator called "West Texas Sour" reported in a trade publication called Platts Oilgram Service–Crude Oil Supplement. In the middle of the contract period, the 1973 OPEC oil embargo surprised world oil and fuel markets, causing prices to rise unexpectedly. However, and layering a second surprise on top of this first, the West Texas Sour price indicator did not reflect the hike in prices. (This was due to intricacies involving price controls implemented following the crisis.) The contract price therefore came to depart dramatically from the market price, and litigation ensued.

Gulf began by arguing, perhaps wishfully, that the language allowing Eastern to set its requirements was vague and indefinite and therefore rendered the contract invalid on the ground that it lacked mutuality of obligation. The court, unsurprisingly, was not impressed. It observed that the common law has come to accept the validity of requirements contracts, at least where a purchaser has a history of past use from which reasonable estimates of requirements might be made. Furthermore, the court argued, the Uniform Commercial Code takes just this line, rendering the obligations in a requirements contract definite by imposing on buyers a duty to set their requirements in good faith and, moreover, at levels not unreasonably disproportionate to stated estimates or prior usage.[37]

This of course merely shifted the field of dispute to focus on the precise metes and bounds of good faith. Eastern's airplanes had taken on more fuel at certain airports than required to reach their next destinations, in order to refuel less frequently and to avoid refueling at certain other airports entirely. This practice, known as fuel-freighting, had allowed Eastern to avoid the inefficiencies associated with frequent refueling and with refuel-

---

36. *Id.* at 593.

37. U.C.C. § 2–306(1).

ing at awkward locations. On the other hand, by increasing the flying weight of its airplanes, fuel-freighting had also increased Eastern's total fuel-consumption. By lowering Eastern's fuel prices (through the anomalous West Texas Sour indicator), the contract with Gulf had shifted the balance of these costs in a fashion that increased the amount of fuel-freighting that was optimal for Eastern. Gulf claimed that Eastern's fuel-freighting violated its obligation to set its requirements reasonably and in good faith.

These facts illustrate the immense difficulty involved in applying the idea that good faith requires protecting the reasonable contractual expectations of the parties in a way that can decide close cases.

As usual, the extremes of bad and good faith may be confidently identified. Thus it would have been clear bad faith, for example, for Eastern to use the contract to support fuel-arbitrage, buying at below market prices from Gulf and selling to its competitors at market prices. The contract, after all, unambiguously concerned Eastern's jet-fuel requirements as an *airline*, that is, for use in its airplanes, and not as a jet-fuel *dealer*. At the other extreme, it would have been clear good faith for Eastern to fuel and fly in precisely the patterns that it would have adopted, pursuant to the contract, had the contract and market prices not diverged.

But these extremes mark out an immense middle ground, and assessing the extremes leaves it unclear where in this middle ground the edge of good faith lies.

Would it have been bad faith for Eastern to increase its requirements in connection with acquiring a competitor, where the acquisition is motivated exclusively by Eastern's access to cheaper fuel? Presumably so, since such an acquisition (with its exclusive motivation) looks like fuel arbitrage by other means. But if this is so, then surely the same argument applies to render it bad faith for Eastern to add airplanes or even just flights to its operations, at least where the growth is driven by cheap fuel. (The airplanes and routes, after all, will be won—and sometimes even literally bought—from Eastern's competitors; and it cannot matter to Eastern's good faith whether its expansion occurs by buying the competitor's stock or by acquiring its business assets.) And now it is only a small, and seemingly inexorable, step to calling it bad faith for Eastern to increase its fuel requirements in any way (or indeed to fail to decrease them in any way) on account of its advantageous price. This conclusion, however, cannot be right, as one of the points of a requirements contract—one of the benefits that the contract is intended to confer on a buyer and hence something that it must be good faith for her to insist on—is surely to allow a buyer to improve its business position (and hence among other things to grow) on account of having a reliable supply of inputs. The examples slide seamlessly from clear bad faith, at odds with the contract's purposes, to clear good faith, which embraces these purposes. The thought that good faith protects the reasonable contractual expectations of the parties cannot insert a seam.[38]

The root-reason why the idea that good faith in performance "protects the reasonable contractual expectations of the parties against *ex post* advantage taking" cannot fix the boundaries of good faith in a fashion that can decide close cases is that good faith is required precisely because the contractual intentions of the parties, and hence also their reasonable expectations, are not complete or clear. This account of good faith, understood as a *rule of decision*, thus commits a circle: it supposes what it purports to decide, that is, how much the terms of the contract allow each side to exploit subsequent developments to its unilateral advantage. That, presumably, is why the U.C.C. insists that good faith does not add to a party's contractual obligations but merely supports such obligations as the contract independently establishes.

This is not to say that the content of good faith is indeterminate in every, or indeed in any, case. In *Eastern Airlines*, for example, the double-accident at the heart of the fact-pattern strongly suggests the right outcome of the case. Jet-fuel prices had changed not in response to ordinary shifts in supply and demand but rather in response to an unexpected oil shock, which threw markets into turmoil. And this turmoil, by prompting an unforeseeable (at least in its details) and haphazard regulatory response, caused the West–Texas Sour indicator chosen to fix the contract price to depart, again unforeseeably, from market-prices that it has been constructed to reflect. These facts strongly suggest, first, that even if the requirements contract was intended to generally stabilize Eastern's fuel costs, it was not intended to resist the particular source of instability at issue in the case. Moreover, and more powerfully, the facts suggest that the West–Texas Sour price indicator was inserted into the contract in an effort to ensure that contract-prices *tracked* market prices rather than *departed* from them. The gap between contract- and market-prices that actually arose thus did not reflect the intentions of the parties so much as a drafting error that caused the writing inaccurately to memorialize these intentions. So understood, the contract precluded Eastern from exploiting the divergence of the West–Texas Sour indicator from the true market price by increasing its requirements over what they would have been at market prices. Indeed, the contract might even have required Eastern to pay market prices, notwithstanding the price indicator's departure from them. It might, that is, be said that the proper interpretation of the contract term "West–Texas Sour"

---

38. Nor will it help to say, as some cases do, that the U.C.C. requires that quantities not be "unreasonably disproportionate" to expectations. Even if the demands of reasonableness depart from those of good faith in some way (whose point or purpose is difficult to imagine), they will be no easier to fix.

The view of the U.C.C. that emphasizes the distinction between "reasonable" and good faith may be found in *Orange and Rockland Utilities Inc. v. Amerada Hess Corp.*, 59 A.D.2d 110 (N.Y. 1977) ("[E]ven where one party acts with complete good faith, the section limits the other party's risk in accordance with the reasonable expectations of the parties."). A contrary view, which reads the requirements of "good faith" and "reasonableness" as interlocking, appears in *Empire Gas Corp. v. American Bakeries Co.*, 840 F.2d 1333 (7th Cir. 1988) ("The proviso [concerning reasonability] thus seems to have been designed to explicate the term 'good faith' rather than to establish an independent legal standard.").

was the market-price that this indicator was designed to reflect, so that imperfections in the indicator's design were not imported into the contract that referenced it.

One might *characterize* this conclusion by saying that the duty of good faith in performance prevented Eastern from exploiting the imperfections in the West–Texas Sour indicator to deprive Gulf of the orderly demand for its fuel, at market-prices, that the contract was designed to provide. But the general principle of good faith has not done any independent work in reaching this conclusion, which turns entirely on an independent inquiry into the intentions of the contracting parties and the particularistic meaning of contract terms.

Nor could good faith have done this work. If the boundaries of good faith are to be fixed by reference to the intentions and reasonable expectations of the contracting parties, then good faith cannot identify the *content* of these intentions and expectations (although it may importantly identify an *attitude* towards them). Instead, a non-conclusory account of good faith capable of usefully intervening to decide concrete cases must say, directly and without reference to other theory-laden terms, how contracting parties must balance self- and other-regard as they fill out and interpret their contractual arrangements.

19.1.B   GOOD FAITH AND CONTRACTUAL SOLIDARITY

Good faith requires contracting parties to vindicate reasonable contractual expectations but cannot be called on to fix the content of the expectations in whose terms it is defined. The measure of each party's good faith is the agreed purpose memorialized in the contract, which is to say the legitimate contractual expectation of the other.

Good faith is not a principle of substantive fairness in the face of new contingencies. The parties thus remain free to be self-interested within the contract—as self-interested as they were without it, subject only to honoring the terms of their agreement. Even as they may not use unanticipated contingencies to deprive the other party of a benefit that the contract allocated to them, the parties also need not sacrifice anything in the face of new contingencies that the contract does not require, nor need they assist the other parties in gaining from contingencies. This feature of good faith—that it does not establish intimacy or affection so much as articulate respect among parties who remain at arm's length—turns out to be essential to the character and intrinsic value of the contract relation, and thus also to freedom of contract.

The arms-length character of good faith is rendered concrete in doctrine, for example, in the expectation remedy and the associated practice of "efficient breach" discussed in Part One. The expectation remedy, recall, establishes a default that promisors insure their promisees against breach by guaranteeing the promisees' value of performance—through it, the law vindicates promisees' contractual expectations. At the same time, the remedy allows a promisor who confronts an opportunity to increase overall surplus by diverting the promised performance to a higher-valuing third party self-interestedly to appropriate the gains from dealing with the third party for herself. As long as she transfers to the promisee an amount equal to the expectation remedy, a promisor who commits such an "efficient breach" displays no bad faith. The transfer vindicates the promisees' reasonable contractual expectations. After all, the parties, bargaining in the shadow of the remedy, will have reduced the contract price (and increased the promisee's contractual expectations) in light of the promisor's right to retain the gains from the "efficient breach."[39] The parties' contractual intentions will have contemplated that the promisor retains such gains ex post, and she will have paid for them ex ante. Her payment will have been memorialized in a lower price term, which is to say that the promisor's entitlement to the gains from efficient breach is made express in the contract, or at least implied in fact rather than in law. (This approach to the expectation remedy thus sounds in the parties' actual rather than ideal agreement.) Indeed, given this arrangement, it would be bad faith for a promisee to insist on specific performance, as this would give the promisee a benefit that he did not pay for and deprive the promisor of one of the benefits that the contract expressly gave her.

The expectation remedy thus does not eliminate contractual sharing (including of the surplus generated by "efficient breach") but instead cabins contractual surplus-sharing according to the parties' agreement, ex ante. In this way, the expectation remedy embodies the attitude towards contractual obligation, and the structure of the contract relation, associated with good faith. It establishes a contrast to what the contract relation would be like were it governed by a regime of reciprocal fiduciary obligation between promisor and promisee. This fiduciary regime requires each party to display affirmative other-regard within the contract and to adjust its conduct not only to vindicate whatever expectations were fixed by the parties *ex ante* but also fairly to balance its and its counterparties' interests as these develop *ex post*. Such fiduciary arrangements are possible, and indeed are recognized in law. But they remain starkly and expressly different from the contract relation.

The contrast between contractual good faith—as illuminated through the expectation remedy—and fiduciary obligation is worth exploring. In particular, it illuminates the relationship between good faith in performance and freedom of contract—the fashion in which the duty of good faith serves as the core doctrinal expression of freedom of contract.

It is commonly said that the degree of other-regard required by contract is *less* than that required of fiduciaries. In one sense, the account just elaborated supports the commonplace view: if a beneficiary asks his fiduciary to walk a mile with him, she must, altruistically, walk with him twain; a contractual promisor, by contrast, may self-interestedly walk only the mile that she promised, and not an inch further.

---

39. The parties will generally prefer this, as the overall gains from trade (which the parties may divide however they can agree) will be greater under the expectation regime than under a property right regime.

But contractual good faith is not simply a lesser version of fiduciary other-regard—altruism light, as it were. Rather, contractual good faith involves a distinctive form of recognition of the other to whom it is owned—a form of recognition that fiduciary altruism forecloses, or at least impedes.

A fiduciary's obligation to take the initiative on her beneficiary's behalf is coupled with an entitlement to pursue the beneficiary's interests as the fiduciary sees them, including even where the beneficiary takes a different view. These are two sides of fiduciary intimacy's single coin, as altruism becomes quite literally a nonsense in the absence of a right, in the altruist, to promote the other's true interests rather than false ones. This thought is reflected in fiduciary law, through doctrines that limit the terms on which a beneficiary might engage a fiduciary. Broadly speaking, fiduciary arrangements must hold fiduciaries to standards of reasonable care on their beneficiaries' behalves and must give fiduciaries a right to pursue their independent judgments in their exercise of this care. Doctors must sometimes over-ride the choices of their patients, for example, and lawyers must over-ride the choices of their clients; at least, they must refuse to go along. Beneficiaries cannot impose their unreasonable preferences or beliefs on their fiduciaries.

By contrast, a contractual promisor's entitlement to good faith self-interest comes with an obligation to take her counterparty's intentions at face value. Both are, equally, expressions of the contractual arrangement—to go only the distance, and only along the path, that the contract to which she and her counterparty agreed specifies. The contractual promisor's freedom from any altruistic obligation thus also deprives her of any entitlement to promote her perspective over her promisee's. Just as fiduciary altruism carries with it paternalism and associated limits on the freedom of the beneficiary, so good faith self-interest (the fact that a promisor may, within the constraints of the contractual agreement, remain as self-interested within the contract as she was without it) carries with it anti-paternalism. Anti-paternalism is, in fact, just another facet of freedom of contract, as a promisee subjected to the mercies of her promisor's paternalism within the promise would be deprived of promise as a reliable mechanism for pursuing her own purposes (a deprivation that the promisor's altruism reduces not one whit).

Finally, returning to the connection between good faith and freedom of contract casts the recognition involved in every contract in a revealing light. Fiduciaries, because of their altruism and the paternalism that this carries with it, recognize their beneficiaries in terms of their peculiar, idiosyncratic needs and interests—one might say, as the particular persons whom they are. Contractual promisors, by contrast, proceeding anti-paternalistically and in good faith, recognize their promisees for their general intentional capacities to pursue whatever interests and needs they have—one might say, for their generic moral personalities.

In a nutshell, then, good faith allows contracting parties to remain as self-interested, and as much at arm's length, within the contract as they were without it, *except* that they must accept, as a side-constraint, that the best interpretation of what they agreed to in contracting binds them to limit their self-interest. And the distinctive balance of self-interest and other-regarding constraint articulated by good faith elaborates a particular form of interpersonal recognition and respect.

This chain of characterizations—from good faith to self-interest to anti-paternalism to freedom of contract to recognition of general personality—generates a striking conclusion, moreover. Contractual recognition (the basis of contractual solidarity) is not lesser but rather different from more intimate and altruistic forms of recognition. Indeed, the contract relation—precisely because good faith is thinner, more generic, and more abstract than particular, concrete altruism—opens up possibilities for solidarity at arm's length that intimates cannot achieve. Good faith thus underwrites a distinctive form of recognition in which contracting parties recognize one another's expressed intentions, at face value. When they do so, the parties to contracts recognize one another as sovereign wills, whose freedom and hence also choices must be respected. Fiduciary relations lack this variety of respect, not in spite but rather because of the other-regard that they involve.

19.1.C   GOOD FAITH AS A PEDESTRIAN IDEAL

The connection between good faith and freedom of contract—including through its emphasis that the boundaries of good faith in particular cases are determined by rather than determining the actual intentions and expectations of the parties—goes to the core of good faith and to its structural role in the contract relation. The duty of good faith in performance, once again, is *not a separate undertaking* of the parties to a contract but an *attitude towards whatever undertakings the parties have adopted*. To display good faith in contract performance is simply to recognize the authority of the contract, and hence the authority of one's counterparty to insist on performance according to the contract's terms.

The duty of good faith in contract performance is thus a private analog—as between the contracting parties—of the public duty to obey the law that arises among citizens generally. Good faith expresses a commitment to a particular normative (and indeed legal) relation. Honoring the duty involves internalizing the authority structures of that relation and implementing them in one's own practical life. This, incidentally, is why good faith, even as its content may be varied almost arbitrarily by the parties (to take on any substance consistent with there being a contract between them), remains a mandatory rule that cannot be waived. Good faith in performance just is the attitude of taking contractual obligation appropriately seriously. To reject good faith is, in effect, to deny the contractual obligation to which good faith attaches—a private law analog of the revolutionary's denial of the political obligation to which the duty to obey the law attaches. To make such a denial at the moment of contract formation, as would be involved in a waiver of good faith, is to forswear the intent to obligate. And that necessarily causes contractual obligation to fail from the get-go.

The analogy to the duty to obey the law reveals something important about good faith. The duty to obey the law is not simply a duty to act in accordance with justice or natural law, but rather attaches (defeasibly, of course) to *positive law*.[40] Similarly, the duty of good faith in performance is not simply a duty to coordinate optimally but rather attaches to the *positive contract*—to the contract that was actually agreed rather than to some ideal alternative. Good faith in performance is thus a pedestrian ideal, which takes as its lodestar the actual contract that the parties' intentions established rather than some contract that it would have been optimal for them to establish. Indeed, good faith underwrites a distinctive, intrinsically valuable relation among the parties, at all, *only* in respect of its connection to their actual, concrete intentions.

This is not a trivial or obvious point, and it is not always understood. It is tempting to idealize good faith by connecting it not to what the parties intended—to their actual joint plan—but to what they ought, rationally or ideally, to have agreed, or even just to what they would have agreed ex ante had they known then what they have discovered ex post. But overlooking the actual in favor of the ideal—rejecting *pedestrian* good faith (based on the parties actual agreement) in favor of a *utopian* alternative (that invokes the agreement that the parties ideally would have struck)—introduces confusions into discussions of good faith.

Natural justice has long tempted political thinkers towards skepticism concerning the authority of merely positive law. Similarly, the rational idealization of good faith has, at various times, attracted all manner of thinkers to resist the positive terms of actual contracts. In private law, the utopian approach to the contract relation is at the moment especially tempting to writers in the economic tradition (even as these typically resist the moralistic idealizations associated with the social contract tradition in politics).

Consider, in this light, the following well-known case, decided by Richard Posner.

Market St. Assocs. Ltd. P'ship v. Frey

United States Court of Appeals for the Seventh Circuit, 1991.
941 F.2d 588.

■ POSNER, CIRCUIT JUDGE.

---

40. The theory of civil disobedience elaborates the metes and bounds of the duty to obey the law. The critical feature of this theory is that the positive law must reach a threshold level of injustice before the duty to obey it is defeated on natural law grounds (else the positive law could have no authority to begin with, and anarchism would be true). An analogous result holds with respect to the duty of good faith in contract performance. Contract terms (the analog of the positive law) must reach a threshold level of wrongfulness (the analog of injustice) before the obligation to perform in good faith is defeated (else the contract would have no authority to begin with, and skepticism about contract would be true). This is just the legal analog to the observation, familiar from the morality of promising, that what it is for promises to generate obligation is that it does not count as a sufficient reason for breaking a promise that given how things have turned out to break it is best overall. See, e.g., Joseph Raz, *Promises and Obligations*, in LAW, MORALITY, AND SOCIETY, 210, 277–28 (Joseph Raz & P.M.S. Hacker, eds., 1977).

Market Street Associates Limited Partnership and its general partner appeal from a judgment for the defendants, General Electric Pension Trust and its trustees, entered upon cross-motions for summary judgment in a diversity suit that pivots on the doctrine of "good faith" performance of a contract. Cf. Robert Summers, " 'Good Faith' in General Contract Law and the Sales Provisions of the Uniform Commercial Code," 54 *Va.L.Rev.* 195, 232–43 (1968). Wisconsin law applies-common law rather than Uniform Commercial Code, because the contract is for land rather than for goods, UCC § 2–102; Wis.Stat. § 402.102, and because it is a lease rather than a sale and Wisconsin has not adopted UCC art. 2A, which governs leases.

We come at last to the contract dispute out of which the case arises. In 1968, J.C. Penney Company, the retail chain, entered into a sale and leaseback arrangement with General Electric Pension Trust in order to finance Penney's growth. Under the arrangement Penney sold properties to the pension trust which the trust then leased back to Penney for a term of 25 years. Paragraph 34 of the lease entitles the lessee to "request Lessor [the pension trust] to finance the costs and expenses of construction of additional Improvements upon the Premises," provided the amount of the costs and expenses is at least $250,000. Upon receiving the request, the pension trust "agrees to give reasonable consideration to providing the financing of such additional Improvements and Lessor and Lessee shall negotiate in good faith concerning the construction of such Improvements and the financing by Lessor of such costs and expenses." Paragraph 34 goes on to provide that, should the negotiations fail, the lessee shall be entitled to repurchase the property at a price roughly equal to the price at which Penney sold it to the pension trust in the first place, plus 6 percent a year for each year since the original purchase. So if the average annual appreciation in the property exceeded 6 percent, a breakdown in negotiations over the financing of improvements would entitle Penney to buy back the property for less than its market value (assuming it had sold the property to the pension trust in the first place at its then market value).

One of these leases was for a shopping center in Milwaukee. In 1987 Penney assigned this lease to Market Street Associates, which the following year received an inquiry from a drugstore chain that wanted to open a store in the shopping center, provided (as is customary) that Market Street Associates built the store for it. Whether Market Street Associates was pessimistic about obtaining financing from the pension trust, still the lessor of the shopping center, or for other reasons, it initially sought financing for the project from other sources. But they were unwilling to lend the necessary funds without a mortgage on the shopping center, which Market Street Associates could not give because it was not the owner but only the lessee. It decided therefore to try to buy the property back from the pension trust. Market Street Associates' general partner, Orenstein, tried to call David Erb of the pension trust, who was responsible for the property in question. Erb did not return his calls, so Orenstein wrote him, expressing an interest in buying the property and asking him to "review your file on this matter and call me so that we can discuss it further." At first, Erb did not reply. Eventually Orenstein did reach Erb, who promised to review the file and get back to him. A few days later an associate of Erb called Orenstein and indicated an interest in selling the property for $3 million, which Orenstein considered much too high.

That was in June of 1988. On July 28, Market Street Associates wrote a letter to the pension trust formally requesting funding for $2 million in improvements to the shopping center. The letter made no reference to paragraph 34 of the lease; indeed, it did not mention the lease. The letter asked Erb to call Orenstein to discuss the matter. Erb, in what was becoming a habit of unresponsiveness, did not call. On August 16, Orenstein sent a second letter-certified mail, return receipt requested-again requesting financing and this time referring to the lease, though not expressly to paragraph 34. The heart of the letter is the following two sentences: "The purpose of this letter is to ask again that you advise us immediately if you are willing to provide the financing pursuant to the lease. If you are willing, we propose to enter into negotiation to amend the ground lease appropriately." The very next day, Market Street Associates received from Erb a letter, dated August 10, turning down the original request for financing on the ground that it did not "meet our current investment criteria": the pension trust was not interested in making loans for less than $7 million. On August 22, Orenstein replied to Erb by letter, noting that his letter of August 10 and Erb's letter of August 16 had evidently crossed in the mails, expressing disappointment at the turn-down, and stating that Market Street Associates would seek financing elsewhere. That was the last contact between the parties until September 27, when Orenstein sent Erb a letter stating that Market Street Associates was exercising the option granted it by paragraph 34 to purchase the property upon the terms specified in that paragraph in the event that negotiations over financing broke down.

The pension trust refused to sell, and this suit to compel specific performance followed. Apparently the price computed by the formula in paragraph 34 is only $1 million. The market value must be higher, or Market Street Associates wouldn't be trying to coerce conveyance at the paragraph 34 price; whether it is as high as $3 million, however, the record does not reveal.

The district judge granted summary judgment for the pension trust on two grounds that he believed to be separate although closely related. The first was that, by failing in its correspondence with the pension trust to mention paragraph 34 of the lease, Market Street Associates had prevented the negotiations over financing that are a condition precedent to the lessee's exercise of the purchase option from taking place. Second, this same failure violated the duty of good faith, which the common law of Wisconsin, as of other states, reads into every contract. *Restatement (Second) of Contracts* § 205 (1981). In support of both grounds the judge emphasized a statement by Orenstein in his deposition that it had occurred to him that Erb mightn't know about paragraph 34, though this was unlikely (Orenstein testified) because Erb or someone else at the pension trust would probably check the file and discover the paragraph and realize that if the trust refused to negotiate over the request for financing, Market Street Associates, as Penney's assignee, would be entitled to walk off with the property for (perhaps) a song. The judge inferred that Market Street Associates didn't want financing from the pension trust-that it just wanted an opportunity to buy the property at a bargain price and hoped that the pension trust wouldn't realize the implications of turning down the request for financing. Market Street Associates should, the judge opined, have advised the pension trust that it was requesting financing pursuant to paragraph 34, so that the trust would understand the penalty for refusing to negotiate.

We begin our analysis by setting to one side two extreme contentions by the parties. The pension trust argues that the option to purchase created by paragraph 34 cannot be exercised until negotiations over financing break down; there were no negotiations; therefore they did not break down; therefore Market Street Associates had no right to exercise the option. This argument misreads the contract. Although the option to purchase is indeed contingent, paragraph 34 requires the pension trust, upon demand by the lessee for the financing of improvements worth at least $250,000, "to give reasonable consideration to providing the financing." The lessor who fails to give reasonable consideration and thereby prevents the negotiations from taking place is breaking the contract; and a contracting party cannot be allowed to use his own breach to gain an advantage by impairing the rights that the contract confers on the other party. Often, it is true, if one party breaks the contract, the other can walk away from it without liability, can in other words exercise self-help. *First National Bank v. Continental Illinois National Bank,* 933 F.2d 466, 469 (7th Cir.1991). But he is not required to follow that course. He can stand on his contract rights.

But what exactly are those rights in this case? The contract entitles the lessee to reasonable consideration of its request for financing, and only if negotiations over the request fail is the lessee entitled to purchase the property at the price computed in accordance with paragraph 34. It might seem, therefore, that the proper legal remedy for a lessor's breach that consists of failure to give the lessee's request for financing reasonable consideration would not be an order that the lessor sell the property to the lessee at the paragraph 34 price, but an order that the lessor bargain with the lessee in good faith. But we do not understand the pension trust to be arguing that Market Street Associates is seeking the wrong remedy. We understand it to be arguing that Market Street Associates has no possible remedy. That is an untenable position.

Market Street Associates argues, with equal unreason as it seems to us, that it could not have broken the contract because paragraph 34 contains no express requirement that in requesting financing the lessee mention the lease or paragraph 34 or otherwise alert the lessor to the consequences of his failing to give reasonable consideration to granting the request. There is indeed no such requirement (all that the contract requires is a demand). But no one says there is. The pension trust's argument, which the district judge bought, is that either as a matter of simple contract interpretation or under the compulsion of the doctrine of good faith, a provision requiring Market Street Associates to remind the pension trust of paragraph 34 should be read into the lease.

It seems to us that these are one ground rather than two. A court has to have a reason to interpolate a clause into a contract. The only reason that has been suggested here is that it is necessary to prevent Market Street Associates from reaping a reward for what the pension trust believes to have been Market Street's bad faith. So we must consider the meaning of the contract duty of "good faith." The Wisconsin cases are cryptic as to its meaning though emphatic about its existence, so we must cast our net wider. We do so mindful of Learned Hand's warning, that "such words as 'fraud,' 'good faith,' 'whim,' 'caprice,' 'arbitrary action,' and 'legal fraud' ... obscure the issue." *Thompson–Starrett Co. v. La Belle Iron Works*, 17 F.2d 536, 541 (2d Cir.1927). Indeed they do. The particular confusion to which the vaguely moralistic overtones of "good faith" give rise is the belief that every contract establishes a fiduciary relationship. A fiduciary is required to treat his principal as if the principal were he, and therefore he may not take advantage of the principal's incapacity, ignorance, inexperience, or even naïveté. If Market Street Associates were the fiduciary of General Electric Pension Trust, then (we may assume) it could not take advantage of Mr. Erb's apparent ignorance of paragraph 34, however exasperating Erb's failure to return Orenstein's phone calls was and however negligent Erb or his associates were in failing to read the lease before turning down Orenstein's request for financing.

But it is unlikely that Wisconsin wishes, in the name of good faith, to make every contract signatory his brother's keeper, especially when the brother is the immense and sophisticated General Electric Pension Trust, whose lofty indifference to small (= < \$7 million) transactions is the signifier of its grandeur. In fact the law contemplates that people frequently will take advantage of the ignorance of those with whom they contract, without thereby incurring liability. *Restatement, supra*, § 161, comment d. The duty of honesty, of good faith even expansively conceived, is not a duty of candor. You can make a binding contract to purchase something you know your seller undervalues. That of course is a question about formation, not performance, and the particular duty of good faith under examination here relates to the latter rather than to the former. But even after you have signed a contract, you are not obliged to become an altruist toward the other party and relax the terms if he gets into trouble in performing his side of the bargain. *Kham & Nate's Shoes No. 2, Inc. v. First Bank*, 908 F.2d 1351, 1357 (7th Cir.1990). Otherwise mere difficulty of performance would excuse a contracting party-which it does not.

But it is one thing to say that you can exploit your superior knowledge of the market-for if you cannot, you will not be able to recoup the investment you made in obtaining that knowledge-or that you are not required to spend money bailing out a contract partner who has gotten into trouble. It is another thing to say that you can take deliberate advantage of an oversight by your contract partner concerning his rights under the contract. Such taking advantage is not the exploitation of superior knowledge or the avoidance of unbargained-for expense; it is sharp dealing. Like theft, it has no social product, and also like theft it induces costly defensive expenditures, in the form of overelaborate disclaimers or investigations into the trustworthiness of a prospective contract partner, just as the prospect of theft induces expenditures on locks. See generally Steven J. Burton, "Breach of Contract and the Common Law Duty to Perform in Good Faith," 94 *Harv.L.Rev.* 369, 393 (1980).

The form of sharp dealing that we are discussing might or might not be actionable as fraud or deceit. That is a question of tort law and there the rule is that if the information is readily available to both parties the failure of one to disclose it to the other, even if done in the knowledge that the other party is acting on mistaken premises, is not actionable. *Kamuchey v. Trzesniewski*, 8 Wis.2d 94 (1959); *Southard v. Occidental Life Ins. Co.*, 36 Wis.2d 708 (1967); *Lenzi v. Morkin*, 103 Ill.2d 290 (1984); *Guyer v. Cities Service Oil Co.*, 440 F.Supp. 630 (E.D.Wis.1977); W. Page Keeton *et al.*, *Prosser and Keeton on the Law of Torts* § 106, at p. 737 (5th ed. 1984). All of these cases, however, with the debatable exception of *Guyer*, involve failure to disclose something in the negotiations leading up to the signing of the contract, rather than failure to disclose after the contract has been signed. (*Guyer* involved failure to disclose during the negotiations leading up to a renewal of the contract.) The distinction is important, as we explained in *Maksym v. Loesch*, 937 F.2d 1237, 1242 (7th Cir.1991). Before the contract is signed, the parties confront each other with a natural wariness. Neither expects the other to be particularly forthcoming, and therefore there is no deception when one is not. Afterwards the situation is different. The parties are now in a cooperative relationship the costs of which will be considerably reduced by a measure of trust. So each lowers his guard a bit, and now silence is more apt to be deceptive. Cf. *AM-PAT/Midwest, Inc. v. Illinois Tool Works Inc.*, 896 F.2d 1035, 1040–41 (7th Cir.1990).

Moreover, this is a contract case rather than a tort case, and conduct that might not rise to the level of fraud may nonetheless violate the duty of good faith in dealing with one's contractual partners and thereby give rise to a remedy under contract law. Burton, *supra*, at 372 n. 17. This duty is, as it were, halfway between a fiduciary duty (the duty of *utmost* good faith) and the duty merely to refrain from active fraud. Despite its moralistic overtones it is no more the injection of moral principles into contract law than the fiduciary concept itself is. It would be quixotic as well as presumptuous for judges to undertake through contract law to raise the ethical standards of the nation's business people. The concept of the duty of good faith like the concept of fiduciary duty is a stab at approximating the terms the parties would have negotiated had they foreseen the circumstances that have given rise to their dispute. The parties want to minimize the costs of performance. To the extent that a doctrine of good faith designed to do this by reducing defensive expenditures is a reasonable measure to this end, interpolating it into the contract advances the parties' joint goal.

It is true that an essential function of contracts is to allocate risk, and would be defeated if courts treated the materializing of a bargained-over, allocated risk as a misfortune the burden of which is required to be shared between the parties (as it might be within a family, for example) rather than borne entirely by the party to whom the risk had been allocated by mutual agreement. But contracts do not just allocate risk. They also (or some of them) set in motion a cooperative enterprise, which may to some extent place one party at the other's mercy. "The parties to a contract are embarked on a cooperative venture, and a minimum of cooperativeness in the event unforeseen problems arise at the performance stage is required even if not an explicit duty of the contract." *AMPAT/Midwest, Inc. v. Illinois Tool Works, Inc., supra,* 896 F.2d at 1041. The office of the doctrine of good faith is to forbid the kinds of opportunistic behavior that a mutually dependent, cooperative relationship might enable in the absence of rule. " 'Good faith' is a compact reference to an implied undertaking not to take opportunistic advantage in a way that could not have been contemplated at the time of drafting, and which therefore was not resolved explicitly by the parties." *Kham & Nate's Shoes No. 2, Inc. v. First Bank, supra,* 908 F.2d at 1357. The contractual duty of good faith is thus not some newfangled bit of welfare-state paternalism or (*pace* Duncan Kennedy, "Form and Substance in Private Law Adjudication," 89 *Harv.L.Rev.* 1685, 1721 (1976)) the sediment of an altruistic strain in contract law, and we are therefore not surprised to find the essentials of the modern doctrine well established in nineteenth-century cases, a few examples being *Bush v. Marshall,* 47 U.S. (6 How.) 284, 291 (1848); *Chicago, Rock Island & Pac. R.R. v. Howard,* 74 U.S. (7 Wall.) 392, 413 (1868); *Marsh v. Masterson,* 101 N.Y. 401, 410–11 (1886), and *Uhrig v. Williamsburg City Fire Ins. Co.,* 101 N.Y. 362 (1886).

The emphasis we are placing on post-contractual versus pre-contractual conduct helps explain the pattern that is observed when the duty of contractual good faith is considered in all its variety, encompassing not only good faith in the *performance* of a contract but also good faith in its *formation,* Summers, *supra,* at 220–32, and in its *enforcement. Harbor Ins. Co. v. Continental Bank Corp.,* 922 F.2d 357, 363 (7th Cir.1990). The formation or negotiation stage is pre-contractual, and here the duty is minimized. It is greater not only at the performance but also at the enforcement stage, which is also post-contractual. "A party who hokes up a phony defense to the performance of his contractual duties and then when that defense fails (at some expense to the other party) tries on another defense for size can properly be said to be acting in bad faith." *Id.;* see also *Larson v. Johnson,* 1 Ill.App.2d 36, 46 (1953). At the formation of the contract the parties are dealing in present realities; performance still lies in the future. As performance unfolds, circumstances change, often unforeseeably; the explicit terms of the contract become progressively less apt to the governance of the parties' relationship; and the role of implied conditions-and with it the scope and bite of the good-faith doctrine-grows.

We could of course do without the term "good faith," and maybe even without the doctrine. We could, as just suggested, speak instead of implied conditions necessitated by the unpredictability of the future at the time the contract was made. Farnsworth, "Good Faith Performance and Commercial Reasonableness under the Uniform Commercial Code," 30 *U.Chi.L.Rev.* 666, 670 (1963). Suppose a party has promised work to the promisee's "satisfaction." As Learned Hand explained, "he may refuse to look at the work, or to exercise any real judgment on it, in which case he has prevented performance and excused the condition." *Thompson–Starrett Co. v. La Belle Iron Works, supra,* 17 F.2d at 541. See also *Morin Building Products Co. v. Baystone Construction, Inc.,* 717 F.2d 413, 415 (7th Cir. 1983). That is, it was an implicit condition that the promisee examine the work to the extent necessary to determine whether it was satisfactory; otherwise the performing party would have been placing himself at the complete mercy of the promisee. The parties didn't write this condition into the contract either because they thought such behavior unlikely or failed to foresee it altogether. In just the same way-to switch to another familiar example of the operation of the duty of good faith-parties to a requirements contract surely do not intend that if the price of the product covered by the contract rises, the buyer shall be free to increase his "requirements" so that he can take advantage of the rise in the market price over the contract price to resell the product on the open market at a guaranteed profit. *Empire Gas Corp. v. American Bakeries Co.,* 840 F.2d 1333 (7th Cir.1988). If they fail to insert an express condition to this effect, the court will read it in, confident that the parties would have inserted the condition if they had known what the future held. Of similar character is the implied condition that an exclusive dealer will use his best efforts to promote the supplier's goods, since otherwise the exclusive feature of the dealership contract would place the supplier at the dealer's mercy. *Wood v. Duff–Gordon,* 222 N.Y. 88, 118 N.E. 214 (1917) (Cardozo, J.).

But whether we say that a contract shall be deemed to contain such implied conditions as are necessary to make sense of the contract, or that a contract obligates the parties to cooperate in its performance in "good faith" to the extent necessary to carry out the purposes of the contract, comes to much the same thing. They are different ways of formulating the overriding purpose of contract law, which is to give the parties what they would have stipulated for expressly if at the time of making the contract they had had complete knowledge of the future and the costs of negotiating and adding provisions to the contract had been zero.

The two formulations would have different meanings only if "good faith" were thought limited to "honesty in fact," an interpretation perhaps permitted but certainly not compelled by the Uniform Commercial Code, see Summers, *supra,* at 207–20—and anyway this is not a case governed by the UCC. We need not pursue this issue. The dispositive question in the present case is simply whether Market Street Associates tried to trick the pension trust and succeeded in doing so. If it did, this would be the type of opportunistic behavior in an ongoing contractual relationship that would violate the duty of good faith performance however the duty is formulated. There is much common sense in Judge Reynolds' conclusion that Market Street Associates did just that. The situation as he saw it was as follows.

Market Street Associates didn't want financing from the pension trust (initially it had looked elsewhere, remember), and when it learned it couldn't get the financing without owning the property, it decided to try to buy the property. But the pension trust set a stiff price, so Orenstein decided to trick the pension trust into selling at the bargain price fixed in paragraph 34 by requesting financing and hoping that the pension trust would turn the request down without noticing the paragraph. His preliminary dealings with the pension trust made this hope a realistic one by revealing a sluggish and hidebound bureaucracy unlikely to have retained in its brontosaurus's memory, or to be able at short notice to retrieve, the details of a small lease made twenty years earlier. So by requesting financing without mentioning the lease Market Street Associates might well precipitate a refusal before the pension trust woke up to paragraph 34. It is true that Orenstein's second letter requested financing "pursuant to the lease." But when the next day he received a reply to his first letter indicating that the pension trust was indeed oblivious to paragraph 34, his response was to send a lulling letter designed to convince the pension trust that the matter was closed and could be forgotten. The stage was set for his thunderbolt: the notification the next month that Market Street Associates was taking up the option in paragraph 34. Only then did the pension trust look up the lease and discover that it had been had.

The only problem with this recital is that it construes the facts as favorably to the pension trust as the record will permit, and that of course is not the right standard for summary judgment. The facts must be construed as favorably to the nonmoving party, to Market Street Associates, as the record permits (that Market Street Associates filed its own motion for summary judgment is irrelevant, as we have seen). When that is done, a different picture emerges. On Market Street Associates' construal of the record, $3 million was a grossly excessive price for the property, and while $1 million might be a bargain it would not confer so great a windfall as to warrant an inference that if the pension trust had known about paragraph 34 it never would have turned down Market Street Associates' request for financing cold. And in fact the pension trust may have known about paragraph 34, and either it didn't care or it believed that unless the request mentioned that paragraph the pension trust would incur no liability by turning it down. Market Street Associates may have assumed and have been entitled to assume that in reviewing a request for financing from one of its lessees the pension trust would take the time to read the lease to see whether it bore on the request. Market Street Associates did not desire financing from the pension trust initially-that is undeniable-yet when it discovered that it could not get financing elsewhere unless it had the title to the property it may have realized that it would have to negotiate with the pension trust over financing before it could hope to buy the property at the price specified in the lease.

On this interpretation of the facts there was no bad faith on the part of Market Street Associates. It acted honestly, reasonably, without ulterior motive, in the face of circumstances as they actually and reasonably appeared to it. The fault was the pension trust's incredible inattention, which misled Market Street Associates into believing that the pension trust had no interest in financing the improvements regardless of the purchase option. We do not usually excuse contracting parties from failing to read and understand the contents of their contract; and in the end what this case comes down to-or so at least it can be strongly argued-is that an immensely sophisticated enterprise simply failed to read the contract. On the other hand, such enterprises make mistakes just like the rest of us, and deliberately to take advantage of your contracting partner's mistake during the performance stage (for we are not talking about taking advantage of superior knowledge at the formation stage) is a breach of good faith. To be able to correct your contract partner's mistake at zero cost to yourself, and decide not to do so, is a species of opportunistic behavior that the parties would have expressly forbidden in the contract had they foreseen it. The immensely long term of the lease amplified the possibility of errors but did not license either party to take advantage of them.

The district judge jumped the gun in choosing between these alternative characterizations. The essential issue bearing on Market Street Associates' good faith was Orenstein's state of mind, a type of inquiry that ordinarily cannot be concluded on summary judgment, and could not be here. If Orenstein believed that Erb knew or would surely find out about paragraph 34, it was not dishonest or opportunistic to fail to flag that paragraph, or even to fail to mention the lease, in his correspondence and (rare) conversations with Erb, especially given the uninterest in dealing with Market Street Associates that Erb fairly radiated. To decide what Orenstein believed, a trial is necessary. As for the pension trust's intimation that a bench trial (for remember that this is an equity case, since the only relief sought by the plaintiff is specific performance) will add no illumination beyond what the summary judgment proceeding has done, this overlooks the fact that at trial the judge will for the first time have a chance to see the witnesses whose depositions he has read, to hear their testimony elaborated, and to assess their believability.

The judgment is reversed and the case is remanded for further proceedings consistent with this opinion.

* * *

The plaintiffs in *Frey*, in order to raise capital to finance the growth of their retail business, arranged to sell various retail properties to the defendants and to lease the premises back for a term of 25 years.[41] The contract contained two further provisions that became especially relevant in the dispute. The first provision entitled the plaintiffs to request the defendants to finance the construction of certain additional improvements to the properties and obligated the defendants to give "reasonable consideration" to providing the requested financing and to "negotiate in good faith" concerning the construction of the improvements and the provision of the financing for them. The second provision stated that, should the contemplated negotiations concerning improvements fail, the plaintiffs

---

41. This summary simplifies the parties somewhat.

would be entitled to repurchase the properties from the defendants, at a price equal to roughly the initial sales price, increased by 6% compounded annually over the period between the initial sale and the repurchase. As Posner observed, these clauses together entailed that if negotiations concerning improvements failed, and the properties had been sold at market value and had appreciated at greater than 6%, then the plaintiffs could buy them back from the defendants at a below-market price.

About 20 years into the lease, the plaintiffs wished to make improvements to one of the properties and sought third-party financing for the improvements. After failing to obtain such outside financing, the plaintiffs inquired of the defendants about repurchasing this property (with no reference to the contract or the option). The defendants responded with a price that the plaintiffs considered too high. Shortly thereafter, the plaintiffs twice requested that the defendants finance the improvements that they contemplated (making no mention of the contract in their first request, and mentioning the contract but not the relevant provisions in their second). The defendants summarily declined to provide financing (citing their "current investment criteria"). After another brief delay, the plaintiffs informed the defendants that, the negotiations concerning financing having broken down, they were exercising their option to repurchase, at the price specified by the formula in the original contract. This was the first time that the plaintiffs mentioned the price formula, the repurchase option, or even the specific contractual paragraph in which these provisions appeared. The defendants refused to sell, and the plaintiffs sued, seeking to compel specific performance of the repurchase clause.

A trial court granted summary judgment for the defendants. The court emphasized that the plaintiffs had acknowledged that although they had never informed the defendants of the repurchase option, they had contemplated the possibility that the defendant might not know of it. The trial court concluded, on this basis, that that the plaintiffs had not in fact wanted their financing request of the defendants to succeed but had instead merely hoped to trigger their option, without the defendants' knowledge, and hence to repurchase the property at a below-market price. According to the trial court, this conduct violated the common law duty of good faith in performance, which governed the contract, as it does every other.

Posner disagreed. The case's central question, as he sensibly observed, was whether (even in the absence of any express contractual language requiring the plaintiffs to notify the defendants of the connection between the financing and the repurchase option) the duty of good faith in performance required the plaintiffs to remind the defendants that a failure to reach agreement on financing would trigger their right to repurchase, at a possibly advantageous price. Posner concluded that it did not. The point of good faith, according to Posner, is to "minimize the costs of performance by [reasonably] reducing defensive expenditures [thus] advance[ing] the parties' joint goal." Or, as he alternatively expressed himself, "[t]he office of the doctrine of good faith is to forbid the kinds of opportunistic behavior that a mutually dependent, cooperative relationship might enable in the absence of [the] rule." According to Posner, these considerations would have rendered it bad faith had the plaintiff "tried to trick the [defendant] and succeeded in doing so." Taking "deliberate advantage of an oversight by [a] contract partner concerning his rights under the contract," Posner insisted, "like theft has no social product, and also like theft induces costly defensive expenditures, in the form of overelaborate disclaimers or investigations into the trustworthiness of a prospective contract partner." But good faith is not fiduciary other-regard, and the same considerations equally would have rendered it *not* bad faith if the plaintiffs had genuinely sought financing from the defendants, "without ulterior motive," including even if they knew of the repurchase option (but not that the defendants did not).

The plaintiffs' bad or good faith thus turned on whether or not they "believed that [the defendants] knew or would surely find out about" the repurchase option. That, Posner observed, was a question of fact, of a type with respect to which the uncontested evidence would not usually and did not in *Frey* compel reasonable belief. "The essential issue bearing on good faith was [the plaintiff's] state of mind," and "[t]o decide what [the plaintiff] believed, a trial [was] necessary." Accordingly, the district judge had "jumped the gun" in granting summary judgment.

Posner's conclusion is less interesting than the logic through which he reached it.[42] "The duty of good faith," he wrote, "is a stab at approximat-

---

42.   Partly that is because it is far from clear that Posner's logic in fact sustains his conclusion. Plausibly—indeed more than plausibly—the costs of performance would have been minimized by a duty not only not knowingly to exploit a counterparty's ignorance of the repurchase option but affirmatively to disclose the option.

To begin with, such a duty would reduce each party's costs of monitoring its contractual rights and obligations (the parties likely had many such obligations, so that these costs were not trivial) without imposing any new costs of its own. (Here it is important that the duty to disclose at issue is much less demanding, because it is much more narrowly cabined, than the general fiduciary obligation that Posner rightly rejects.)

Furthermore, and probably more importantly, Posner's formulation of the duty of good faith dramatically increases the cost of contract administration because it dramatically increases the uncertainty of contract adjudication *ex post*. Posner's standard makes bad faith a question of fact, and of a sort of fact that is virtually unresolvable at summary judgment. It thus entails that disputes about good faith will raise the specter of extremely expensive trials. And this, in fact, is just what occurred in *Frey*. As others have pointed out, see Todd D. Rakoff, *Good Faith in Contract Performance:* Market Street Associates Ltd. Partnership v. Frey, 120 HARV. L. REV. 1187, 1191–92 (2007), it is unlikely that the costs of performance are minimized by a standard that invites and almost requires such high-cost forms of dispute resolution concerning the adequacy of performance.

Accordingly, parties in possession of what Posner called "complete knowledge of the future" and "zero" transactions costs, would likely not bargain for the standard of good faith that Posner's opinion adopts. And although the opinion adopts the language of utopian good faith, it does not actually decide the case in utopian terms. Quite possibly, the decision in fact tracks the pedestrian standard of good faith that this text prefers: regardless of what was optimal, the self-respect of the parties, and hence also their commercial practice, included an ideal that rejected trickery (or the intentional exploitation of a counterparty's known forgetfulness concerning its contractual obligations) but did not require affirmatively reminding counterparties of the terms of an agreement. (The contract, after all, did not include an express duty to remind about the option, even though such a duty might have been drafted at little incremental cost and would not have been onerous on the plaintiff.)

ing the terms the parties would have negotiated had they foreseen the circumstances that have given rise to their dispute."[43] Good faith, on this approach, is thus just another "way[] of formulating the overriding purpose of contract law, which is to give the parties what they would have stipulated for expressly if at the time of making the contract they had had complete knowledge of the future and the costs of negotiating and adding provisions to the contract had been zero."[44] This is as clear a statement of the utopian approach as can be made: good faith, for Posner, is the doctrinal pathway for making the ideal actual.

That vision of good faith cannot be the right one, however. At least, it cannot be right without in effect eliminating contract as a distinctive legal category, which constructs a distinctive human relation.

To see why good faith cannot be understood in this utopian fashion, begin by observing that a gap inevitably exists between the ideal contract and the contract that the parties have actually made. In some cases, parties expressly adopt optimal terms. (Quantity terms set by sophisticated parties are likely optimal, for example.) In others there exist good reasons to suspect that silent parties have in fact struck the optimal agreement. (One such case, familiar from earlier discussion, concerns the expectation remedy, which may profitably be understood in terms of a legal presumption that otherwise silent parties have, through a contract's price term, adopted an efficient liquidated damages clause.) But in many cases, it will be clear (or even just on balance the best view) that the parties are interacting on terms that are not optimal. In some cases, parties who have established no contractual relation at all would be better off had they established one. In others, parties have made a contract but on terms whose departure from the optimum has been undeniably memorialized in the express terms of their agreement. In still other cases, the parties' intentions receive only implicit expression, in the interstices of their express agreement, but the best reconstruction of the parties' real contractual intentions again departs from the ideal, optimal contract.

This is not just contingently but necessarily so. Parties to contracts, needless to say, do not reason perfectly or costlessly in their contractual practices, and the costs that they face are reflected in the (inevitable!) gaps between agreements that the parties actually make and the ideal agreement. And in all cases in which the actual departs from the ideal—involving suboptimal failures to contract *tout court*, suboptimal express contract terms, and suboptimal implied in fact contract terms—good faith depends, at least partially, not on what would have been optimal for the parties to agree but rather on what they did agree.

Someone who tries to impute an efficient contract where there has been no agreement at all—providing an unrequested good or service,

In this case, Posner's standard quite possibly captures pedestrian good faith well, even if its consequences are not optimal, so that it falls short of utopia.

43. *Market St. Assocs. Ltd. P'ship v. Frey*, 941 F.2d 588, 595 (7th Cir. 1991).

44. *Id.* at 596.

including one that benefits the non-requester, on the ground that it would be efficient—cannot vindicate rights under the imaginary contract, regardless of its efficiency. There is no doctrine of "efficient conversion" and even persons who provide good value cannot recover the price of what they have provided, in *quantum meruit*, on the ground that those whom they have "served" would have been rational to engage them. Rather, they are cast as mere volunteers or, less generously still, officious intermeddlers.

Moreover, the mere fact that parties have agreed to *some* terms cannot be thought later to subject them ex post to untrammeled reconstruction of these terms in the service of what would have been best ex ante. To do so would introduce a stark and unjustified asymmetry into the law between how parties are treated before they contract and once they have contracted. Thus no one supposes that respect for contractual intentions, expressed in terms of good faith or in any other way, requires or indeed even permits remaking the parties' agreement against its express terms. And it is equivalently impermissible to remake a contract against the implications of the parties' actual agreement. Epistemic access to the parties' implied agreement is more limited than in the express case, of course; but once access has been had, the implied terms impose the actual over the ideal just as surely as the express. Mere assent to a contract does not leave a party obligated—through the doctrine of good faith—to whatever terms it would have been rational for her to adopt. Rather, the same reasons that prevent contracts from being imputed *tout court* also prevent them from being completed against the best reconstruction of the terms of the relation that the parties have established, imperfectly but in actual fact.

There is thus a large gap between the idea that good faith completes or even adapts the agreement of the parties to the circumstances as they have developed and the further thought that good faith is nothing but a shorthand for the terms that the parties would have struck had they (reasoning costlessly) addressed ex ante the scenario to which good faith is applied ex post. Good faith requires sharing on the pedestrian terms that the parties have struck, not the terms that they would have struck if they were utopianly different from what they are like. Good faith requires respecting the parties' deal, not perfecting (and thus remaking, which is to say, violating) it.

This recounting of the good faith's insistently pedestrian character is not just a pedantic emphasizing of the contingent and concrete against the universal and abstract, moreover. The distinction between pedestrian and utopian is essential to the character of good faith—really, to the character of the contract relation elaborated in terms of good faith.

A utopian standard of good faith, which looked to an ideal rather than to the parties' actual contract, would undermine rather than promote contractual values. Indeed, just as pedestrian good faith promotes freedom of contract and constitutes the contract relation as a site of recognition, so utopian good faith undermines both contractual freedom and recognition.

If persons really could reason perfectly and costlessly in the manner that utopian good faith imagines, they would have no need of, and hence would not (and could not rationally) resort to contract at all. Rather than ordering their affairs by private agreements, perfectly and costlessly rational parties would engage in ideal public social planning to arrange all their affairs maximally well (efficiently, let us say) for all time. For perfectly, costlessly rational parties, private law, including contract law, is otiose: the only contract that they require required is the social contract.

Moreover, treating imperfectly rational parties as if they were perfectly rational, by giving good faith in their contractual relations a utopian bent, undermines their actual contractual practices in the service of this contract-free ideal. That good faith retains its pedestrian character therefore turns out to be essential to both freedom of contract and contractual recognition among the imperfect, costly deliberators to whom contract law actually applies.

The connection between the pedestrian account of good faith and freedom of contract is easy to see. Pedestrian good faith protects the parties' actual contractual intentions against ex post exploitation, thereby allowing the parties to project their intentions into the future. By contrast, utopian good faith imposes on the parties a bargain that they did not make. That the parties would be better off under the ideal bargain than under their actual one does not by itself eliminate the imposition. Nor does the possibility that the parties would have chosen the ideal bargain had they perfected their deliberations. The fact that pedestrian and utopian good faith come apart entails that the parties did not perfect their intentions.[45] Utopian good faith thus necessarily encroaches on actual freedom in the sense associated with negative liberty in the name of ideal freedom, or positive liberty. (The economic focus on what the parties would have intended is just a reference to positive liberty dressed up in negative libertarian clothes.) That is the commonest apology of the paternalist.

The analogy between good faith towards the positive contract and the authority of the positive law is once again useful in this context. The thought that a utopian standard of good faith undermines individual freedom of contract is set into sharp relief by considering the more familiar thought that the utopian social contract—the idea that the state is constructed perfectly to instantiate ideal justice and that positive law can have no authority of its own—undermines collective political freedom, replacing democratic sovereignty with a tyranny of rights. This explains why good faith, in spite of being a mandatory rule, promotes rather than impedes freedom of contract. Good faith is of a piece with the contract law's

---

45. None of this is to deny that contracting parties might, *in some instances*, form the actual intention that gaps in their contractual understandings shall be filled using ideal terms. Indeed, the discussion of the expectation remedy that appears in the following paragraphs illustrates just such a case. But there will also arises cases in which the parties' actual intentions either expressly or by clear implication depart from the ideal. (The case discussed just following this note is such a one.) And a contract cannot arise simply out of a *general* intention in favor of optimal exchange, as this necessarily remains too abstract to resolve concrete questions. The analogy to the law is again helpful here. As a public order cannot be established simply by justice but requires positive law, so a contract cannot be established simply by ideal intentions but requires actual ones. Like utopian politics, so utopian contract is quite literally impossible—both practices are by their nature pedestrian.

negative-libertarian elements. Pedestrian good faith serves rather than limiting freedom of contract by insistently refusing to require the parties' agreement to adopt any particular terms, or even to make any particular division of contractual surplus, but only to respect whatever division they have agreed.

The same point—in favor of pedestrian and against utopian good faith—may also be made in terms not of freedom of contract but of contractual recognition and community. Utopian good faith, recall, reconstructs contracts according to ideal efficiency, that is, without reference to the actual intentions of the contracting parties. A party who applies utopian good faith to her own contractual performance can thus proceed without engaging her counterparty at all—she can reason in isolation rather than together with him. This is rendered vivid by imagining, once again, a world in which persons deliberate in the fashion that utopian good faith supposes. If persons could deliberate and coordinate ex ante in the perfect and costless style that utopian good faith attributes to them ex post, then all contracts would be unambiguously complete, so that it would be possible to perform and assess them purely mechanically, with no faith at all, either good or bad. Contracts would, literally, cease to involve a leap of faith. They would also cease to involve respect or recognition among the parties to them, or indeed to involve communication at all. The parties, being ideal and costless deliberators, would each know the other's intentions without needing to be told, just as ideal reasoners would all commonly know the entire truth without needing to communicate. This is why persons who deliberated in the perfect and costless fashion imagined by utopian good faith would not pursue individual engagements with one another at all. Creatures capable of planning perfectly do not need private, obligation-based coordination mechanisms to supplement public coordination. They can simply make their public arrangements perfect, and then optimally achieve all their purposes by living perfectly within them.

These observations merely emphasize in an extreme case a basic objection to utopian good faith quite generally. By drawing its content out of the thin air of reason and quite apart from any concrete intentions or contractual engagements, utopian good faith replaces contractual recognition and solidarity *among the parties* with each party's substantively identical but wholly separate relation to right reason. Parties who operate their contracts according to utopian good faith might, to borrow a form of words from Hume, be *in agreement*, but there is not *an agreement* among them. And without a contractual agreement to serve as a substrate to sustain it, there can be no contractual recognition, either.

The contractual duty of good faith in performance is thus necessarily a pedestrian ideal rather than a utopian one, whose content is fixed according to the actual intentions of the imperfect parties rather than the counterfactual intentions that the parties would have formed had they deliberated perfectly. Finally, this explains why good faith cannot add much to deciding close cases: although the duty of good faith in performance requires the parties to respect each other's reasonable contractual expectations, good faith cannot be called on to identify the reasonable expectations in terms of which it is defined. Whereas utopian good faith might usefully decide cases, by specifying the content of reasonable contractual expectations according to its own free-standing substantive principle, pedestrian good faith simply directs a court to contractual intentions whose content must be gleaned from elsewhere, using other means.

19.1.D   GOOD FAITH AT CONTRACT'S CORE

These reflections connect good faith, in its pedestrian elaboration, to contract law's commitment to formal equality, introduced in connection with the consideration doctrine. The thinness of good faith in perform-ance—the fact that good faith does not require altruism or even modest affirmative other-regard but rather is consistent with remaining as self-interested within the contract as without it—connects good faith to formal rather than substantive conceptions of equality. And the fact that good faith nevertheless requires promisors to recognize the authority of their contracts, and hence also of their counterparties to insist on contract rights, connects good faith to equality of status—namely to the shared status of possessing full and equal contractual capacity. Such a formal equality of status is likely the only conception of private equality compati-ble with freedom of contract in a dynamic open economy populated by non-ideal costly economic deliberators. (Similarly, the formal equality of demo-cratic citizenship is likely the only conception of public equality compatible with collective sovereignty in an open political community populated by imperfect moral deliberators and hence condemned to pluralist collective life subject to non-ideal positive law. Good faith is the measure of equal arm's length relations among free contractors in private just as the duty to obey democratic law is the measure of equal arm's length relations among free citizens in public.) Good faith in contractual performance thus con-nects the solidarity of the contract relation (solidarity within the contract, one might say) to the broader formal equality that lies at the bottom of the democratic, market-oriented societies in which contract typically flourishes. The doctrinal order and the economic structure thus converge.

The pedestrian account also returns the idea of good faith to its doctrinal beginnings. The discussion of good faith began by observing that it is a distinctively contractual notion, as opposed to an ideal from either tort on the one hand or fiduciary law on the other. This is what it means for good faith to be bounded below by fraud (which even tort law forbids) and from above by fidelity (which fiduciary law requires). Good faith applies not among strangers and is not owed to everyone (like tort duties) nor does it apply only among intimates (like fiduciary fidelity). Rather, it applies among persons who have forged a relationship with each other, structured around a shared understanding of a voluntary obligation, that they do not have with the general mass of humanity. Good faith applies only in respect of this obligation relation, and not in respect of other unrelated dealings and interests even among these persons. This, finally, is why good faith makes no independent contribution to the content of contract obligation. The measure of good faith is the shared project of the contract; apart from this shared project, the persons' relation continues to be characterized by arm's length dealing.

This is made express in the Restatement's admonition that "[g]ood faith performance or enforcement of a contract emphasizes faithfulness to an agreed common purpose and consistency with the justified expectations of the other party."[46] Good faith thus takes the shared perspective of the contract—the joint activity of the contract's performance—as its lodestar. It is an attitude that the parties display towards each other in virtue of, one might even say by, respecting their agreement.[47] Good faith requires the parties to take a certain attitude with respect to whatever terms, whatever division of surplus, they have adopted (to honor these terms, roughly). A promisor cannot, that is, abandon her contractual intentions, including the intention to adjust to unanticipated contingencies in a fashion that secures the success of the contractual collaboration's shared plan. To return to the language of Posner's opinion, and this time to agree with it, contracts:

> set in motion a cooperative enterprise, which may to some extent place one party at the other's mercy. The parties to a contract are embarked on a cooperative venture, and a minimum of coopera-tiveness in the event unforeseen problems arise at the perform-ance stage is required even if not an explicit duty of the contract. The office of the doctrine of good faith is to forbid the kinds of opportunistic behavior that a mutually dependent, cooperative relationship might enable in the absence of the rule.[48]

It is thus commonly acknowledged that good faith is essential for preventing the contract relation from becoming a locus of exploitation. In fact, good faith plays a more fundamental role still in contract obligation, although this role remains unacknowledged. Good faith does not just prevent exploitation; it is essential for contract to exist at all. For imperfect planners, who cannot plan clearly for every contingency but whose plans inevitably involve haziness and have gaps, good faith is required to make joint planning possible. Good faith in performance is the attitude that imperfect planners must adopt towards their plans in order for the plans to be joint plans at all. It is, quite literally, the matrix in which the joint perspective of contract is possible.[49]

---

46. RESTATEMENT (SECOND) OF CONTRACTS § 205 cmt. [a].

47. Note that the account here rejects the long-dominant (but perhaps now more generally retreating) view that good faith "has no general meaning or meanings of its own," Robert Summers, *'Good Faith' in General Contract Law and the Sales Provisions of the Uniform Commercial Code*, 54 VA. L. REV. 195, 196 (1968) but instead merely "serves to exclude many heterogeneous forms of bad faith." *Id.* Good faith does have a general content, which is set out in the main text.

48. *Market St. Assocs. Ltd. P'ship v. Frey*, 941 F.2d 588, 595 (7th Cir. 1991). (internal quotation marks and citation omitted).

49. It is not coincidence, then, that good faith was often used to overcome the require-ment of mutuality of obligation, *See, e.g., Imperial Ref. Co. v. Kanotex Ref. Co.*, 29 F.2d 193 (8th Cir. 1928). That requirement reflects the fact that contracts must be joint endeavors. Good faith is the measure of the *ongoing* jointness.

One is tempted to say, in light of all of this, that good faith is the very essence of contract. To make a contract with another *just is* to adopt attitudes of solidarity in favor of the joint project fixed by the contractual intentions. To make a contract *just is* to accept the duty of good faith in performance.

19.2   GOOD FAITH IN NEGOTIATIONS

The duty of good faith that the prior section analyzed applies only once a completed contract has been made—that is, to contract performance and enforcement. The law might, however, also impose a duty of good faith applied to the pre-contractual relation. This would be a duty of good faith in negotiations. Civil law recognizes just such a duty. The common law quite clearly does not. But while the common law rejects any mandatory duty of good faith in negotiations, and refuses even to impose this duty as a default rule, it does increasingly allow parties voluntarily to commit to bargaining in good faith. This section will therefore focus on how the law treats efforts by the parties to regulate their negotiations, with a special emphasis on the contracts through which parties seek to commit to bargaining in good faith.

19.2.A   THE NEGOTIATION RELATION

Before taking up the legal regime governing contracts to bargain in good faith, consider the negotiation relation more generally.

One might think that the reason why there is no duty of good faith in negotiations is that there cannot sensibly be—that the fundamental structure of the negotiation relation invites ruthless competition that makes good faith in negotiations a nonsense.

Negotiating is something done by free persons. So it makes sense to police negotiations through doctrines that protect the freedom of the parties, including most prominently through those concerning fraud and duress. Indeed, these doctrines establish backstops against bad behavior that must be respected in order for negotiations to be, properly speaking, negotiations at all. Without protections against fraud and duress, negotiations become shams created for the impositions of offers one side literally cannot reasonably understand, or cannot reasonably refuse. This is negotiation in the mafia sense only.

But beyond these narrowly cabined backstop principles, it might be thought, negotiation is essentially an agonistic enterprise: a practice in which each side seeks exclusively its own advantage. Sellers want high prices, buyers low ones, this view observes. And the battle over price, it emphasizes, is a zero sum game. On this competitive view of negotiations, the nature of the relation leaves no space for policing advantage taking through doctrines, such as good faith, that demand more than merely abjuring duress and fraud. A duty of good faith in negotiation on this view, would contradict the fundamental purpose and structure of bargaining. And so it would be, literally, a non-sense.

The purely competitive view of negotiations is mistaken, however. While negotiations undoubtedly do possess a competitive side (and certain components of negotiation may even involve zero-sum competition), this competition is embedded in a cooperative venture (in which the parties play a positive-sum game). Bargainers, that is, engage in a cooperative effort to create joint surplus before they compete to maximize their private shares. And often, cooperation dominates negotiations, both in the sense of taking up most of the parties' time and energy and in the sense of being the site at which the parties can do most to advance their interests. This does not require the law to impose a duty of good faith in negotiations. But it permits the law to do so—in the sense that it entails that extending good faith to the negotiation relation does not undermine the deep structure of that relation. The contemporary common law's trend towards recognizing party commitments to negotiate in good faith (and indeed also the civilian practice of adopting a general duty of good faith in negotiations) is therefore perfectly consistent with the internal structure of the economic practice that these regimes regulate.

To understand these points, begin by observing that in order to sustain an eventual deal, each side must believe that it will do better within the deal than without it.[50] Each side must believe that it will profit from the deal, moreover, even taking into account the opportunity cost of the other deals that it must forgo in order to do the deal in question. Furthermore, where there exists mistrust (which is usually, but not always) each side must also persuade the other that *it* will do better (including considering opportunity costs) within the deal than without it. For if it could not profit from a deal, then it would not be pursuing one; which possibility will trigger its counterparty's suspicion that the deal is other than it appears. Finally, the gains from dealing that both sides must expect in order to make the effort to strike a deal persuasive generally cannot come from a third party, since the third party will not (again, generally) allow herself to be expropriated. Instead, the gains must come from the special synergy of the negotiating partners—from the fact that the partners will each and thus also both do better together than they will separately; better within their deal than without it.[51]

In order for a negotiation to succeed, and indeed in order for the effort towards success to be worthwhile, the parties to the negotiation must thus persuade themselves and each other that there exists a unique gain to be

---

50. The discussion that follows owes an enormous debt to Arthur Leff's Swindling and Selling (1976). Leff's official ambition, in that book, was to show how closely the illicit swindle and the licit sale resemble each other. He sought, that is, "[t]ease out and display the rather elegant, basic, shared structure of swindling and selling." Id. at 5. The materials here will focus more on the structure and less on whether it is shared, although the eventual emphasis on good faith will of course seek in some measure to identify, in order to prohibit, the swindle.

51. Notice that this must be true even taking into account opportunity costs. For a deal to be worth doing, it must create unique surplus, not replicable elsewhere. Every true negotiation thus represents, in respect of this surplus, a bilateral monopoly.

had from striking a deal, a relation-specific value that neither of them can achieve elsewhere. To generate that surplus, and certainly to maximize it, the deal must be constructed in a particular way. And much of the point and effort of negotiation is directed at discovering just what terms will produce the maximum joint surplus: at planning the deal so that it is best overall. In order to do any deal, the parties must discover and communicate their own preferences and capacities and then arrange their efforts in the way that enables them each to generate value for the other. In this way, negotiation becomes not merely a mechanism for exchange, but a mechanism for production. Arthur Leff expressed this idea well when he observed that "[w]ithin any 'competitive' trading situation, then, there is almost always hidden a cooperative partnership: each party does try to maximize his utility at the expense of the other, but it is only *together* that they can increase the total utility in their joint system;" so that "[e]ven deals made between 'independent' factors at arm's length are still simultaneously competitive and cooperative."[52] Furthermore, the cooperation must, logically, precede the competition. The parties must persuade themselves that the surplus from their deal exists before it makes sense for them to begin their fight about how to divide it.

Of course, once the joint surplus is established to exist, a battle for private shares commences. Interestingly, this battle will involve each side's claiming that it can get nearly as good a return without the deal as within it, just what the joint-surplus-construction phase of the negotiation is structured to deny. Indeed, it may even involve each side's taking action to reduce the attractiveness of the other's outside options, so that the other side becomes more dependent on doing the deal, and hence willing to close the deal on harsher terms, which give it a smaller share of the deal's surplus. This pattern introduces a kind of internal tension into the natural attitudes and activities of bargainers, across the phases of their bargaining. They are initially inclined to pursue and invest in the creation of the shared surplus on whose existence (and recognition by their counterparties) reaching a deal depends; but they then become inclined to maximize their own shares, even if the behaviors that do so reduce the joint surplus, including in ways that cause the deals, ex post, to cease to recoup their counterparties' opportunity costs.

This pattern introduces a problem for parties seeking to reach a joint-surplus-maximizing, and hence mutually beneficial bargain.[53] The parties'

---

52. Arthur Leff, Swindling and Selling 14 (first quotation) and 15 (second quotation).

53. Leff worries about a separate problem, namely distinguishing between licit and illicit deals, or as he says between sales and swindles.

At the most abstract level, the distinction is easy to draw. The quintessential sale arises between a seller and a buyer who really are best placed to trade: so that the seller really does have lower costs in producing the traded good than her nearest competitor and the buyer really does value the good more highly than his nearest competitor; and there is a real, unique, relation specific gain to create and apportion through the sale. In the quintessential swindle, by contrast, the surplus from trade is imaginary—conjured up by the swindler, who intents then to take her "share" as a purely redistributive grab from the swindled party.

knowledge of how they will behave when they compete for surplus, and in particular that they will act to destroy joint surplus if this maximizes their private shares, can undermine their efforts to construct joint surplus to begin with.

This is just an abstract and general statement of a problem already discussed more concretely in connection with contract formation. An offeror may wish to induce her offeree to invest in determining whether or not the offered bargain will benefit him. But once the offeree has invested, this cost becomes sunk, and so the offeror will have an incentive to change her offer to capture surplus that she could not have captured before the cost was sunk (as doing so would have left the offeree with insufficient surplus to make the deal worth pursuing). The offeree will in turn refuse to invest in considering the offer, as he knows that once he has so invested, the offer will change in a way that prevents him from recouping the investment. And so a profitable bargain will fall apart, or rather never be struck.

The solution to this problem, as the chapter on offer and acceptance explained, is for the offeror to commit not to change the offer in response to the offeree's sunk investment. One way in which the law enables this commitment is built into the notion of offer itself: in contrast to a mere invitation to bargain, an offeree may unilaterally convert an offer into a contract on that offer's terms, simply by accepting. The offeree can use his power of acceptance to prevent the offeror from making the expropriating changes. Of course, the offeror may revoke prior to acceptance; and so the power of acceptance will not always be sufficient to solve the problem. Partly in recognition of this, the law also enables offerors to make a stronger commitment still—namely by making irrevocable offers.

These solutions assume, however, that the parties can get quite far in the cooperative enterprise of specifying the joint surplus maximizing deal before destructive competition sets in. In particular, it assumes that joint surplus is maximized by a negotiation in which one side fixes the terms of an ultimate deal, which the other then takes or leaves. But in fact, it will often happen that reaching jointly optimal terms requires investments by both parties at many stages along the way. (Parties might need to conduct research to determine the value of a particular deal that will have no value,

---

But quintessential sales are not so easy to come by, Leff argues. As he observes, it is in the nature of markets that "in almost any recognizable real-world business context, every competitive advantage sufficient to permit giving a bargain to another is likely to be either very small or highly ephemeral, and is most likely to be both." Id. at 125. Accordingly, actual sales tend to be only uncertainly distinguishable from swindles. They rely on insecure sources of relationship-specific surplus, ranging from product differentiation backed by intellectual property (relatively more secure) to seller-specific demand produced artificially through advertising (relatively less secure).

Moreover, Leff observes, there exists a large grey area between sales and swindles, in which trading surplus is manufactured through dubious sources of cost advantage. Some sellers allege that purchasing mistakes or impending bankruptcies in effect lower their opportunity costs. Other sellers, more dubious still, take steps to induce buyers to act in ways that will reduce the buyers' opportunity costs, be rendering other sellers relatively less attractive. Loss leaders that draw buyers into a seller's store, thus making it costlier for the buyers to deal with that seller's competitors, function in this way.

And so, in two short steps, a negotiation traverses the distance from a sale to a swindle.

or less value, in connection with their other business dealings; or they might have to reveal valuable secrets.) These investments will, once again, render those who make them vulnerable to exploitation, by converting their costs from costs of the contract to sunk costs, and hence preventing the party that makes them from recouping them in the competitive phase of bargaining.[54]

In such situations, a jointly optimal bargain might be made more likely, or be made possible at all, if the parties could commit before commencing their bargaining not to allow the competitive phase of their negotiations to encroach on the cooperative phase. More concretely, it would serve efficiency, and hence serve both parties' interests ex ante, if the parties could commit not to use vulnerabilities incurred during cooperative bargaining in order to extract a greater share of surplus in competitive bargaining. It would serve efficiency, in other words, if the parties could commit to bargaining in good faith.

Sun Printing & Publishing Ass'n v. Remington Paper & Power Co.

Court of Appeals of New York, 1923.
139 N.E. 470.

(Reprised from Chapter 14)

Teachers Insurance and Annuity Association of America v. Tribune Company

United States District Court for the Southern District of New York, 1987.
670 F. Supp. 491.

■ LEVAL, DISTRICT JUDGE.

---

54. A concrete example might help to illustrate the problem.

Imagine that a manufacturer seeks a retailer to sell its products. A potential retailer appears, and the parties begin negotiating. In order determine whether a distribution deal will be profitable for it (and also how to structure the deal in order to maximize the gains that it produces), the retailer must engage in expensive market research. So the retailer will know how and whether it wishes to deal with the manufacturer—how and whether a cooperative bargain is available—only after it has sunk significant research costs.

The trouble is, that once these costs have been sunk, the retailer will be in a weaker position with respect to competitive bargaining against the manufacturer. Once the costs have been sunk, they will no longer be counted (including by the retailer) against the gains from any deal: like all rational parties, the retailer will always bargain looking forward rather than backward. The parties' competitive bargaining will therefore allocate surplus against a balance of bargaining power in which the retailer's need to expend the research costs no longer allows it credibly to demand a commensurate share of surplus. It can happen that this vulnerability entails that the surplus that the retailer can command, having sunk the research costs, is smaller than these costs. In that case, the retailer, knowing how everything will end, will refuse to incur the research costs. And now the manufacturer will be deprived of a beneficial deal.

That gives the manufacturer an incentive to commit itself to not exploiting the vulnerabilities created by the retailer's incurring the research costs. One means for so committing itself, the materials below reveal, is to agree to bargain in good faith about consummating the distribution relationship if the retailer's research suggests that it will be worthwhile.

This action is brought by an institutional lender against a prospective borrower charging the borrower with breach of a commitment letter agreement for a 14–year $76 million loan yielding 15.25%. The exchange of letters constituting the commitment agreement stated that the borrower and lender had made a "binding agreement," to borrow and to lend on the agreed terms, subject to the preparation and execution of final documents satisfactory to both sides and the approval of the borrower's Board of Directors. Prior to the preparation of final agreements the borrower broke off negotiations, declining to negotiate further unless the lender agreed that the borrower's obligation to borrow would be contingent on its ability to report the loan on its financial statement by an off-balance-sheet offset. The lender contends the borrower's withdrawal was attributable to an intervening decline in interest rates which permitted the borrower to secure funds at a much lower cost than agreed in the commitment letter. The borrower contends that the change in interest rates had nothing to do with its refusal to go ahead and that the availability of offset accounting had always been understood to be a condition of the loan. It contends also that its acceptance of the commitment reserving right of approval to its Board of Directors left it free to decline to take down the loan if the loan did not serve its interest.

Facts

The borrower is Tribune Company, a Chicago communications enterprise which owned the New York Daily News. The lender is Teachers Insurance and Annuity Association of America, a large non-profit tax exempt organization that provides pension annuities and insurance programs to educational institutions. The contemplated loan was an element of a three-cornered arrangement for the sale by Tribune of the Daily News Building at 220 E. 42nd Street in New York.

For some time, Tribune had been contemplating the possibility of outright sale of the News. The Morgan Guaranty Trust Company of New York prepared a memorandum recommending to Tribune that it structure a deal in which the purchaser's payment would be deferred, and Tribune would borrow equivalent funds from a financial institution under terms that permitted Tribune the right to repay its borrowing by assigning the purchaser's installment note to the lending institution. (DX 1–4.) This device was designed to secure installment tax deferral of Tribune's gain, notwithstanding immediate realization of the full proceeds of the sale through the loan. And because its borrowing could be repaid by tender of the purchaser's note, Tribune's debt could be offset against its receivable and reported off-balance-sheet in the notes to its financial statement.

In the spring of 1982 Tribune dropped the plan to sell the News. Instead, it restructured the News subsidiary, which occasioned a nonrecurring tax loss of $75 million. To raise cash that was needed for a number of purposes including the operations of the News, Tribune decided to sell the News Building which would no longer be needed in the restructured operation.

Tribune entered into negotiations to sell the Building to LaSalle Partners, a Chicago real estate firm, with Tribune retaining an equity interest. It was important that the transaction be accomplished during the calendar year 1982 so that the loss realized from the restructuring of the News could be offset against taxable gain realized from the sale of the News Building. A suggestion was made to adapt to the sale of the Building the proposal which Morgan had made with respect to the contemplated sale of the *News*. A substantial portion of the purchase price would be deferred: LaSalle would deliver to Tribune a non-recourse long-term (35 year) purchase money mortgage note. (As the equity "kicker", this mortgage would give the mortgagee not only conventional interest payments but also a percentage of the operating profits of the building.) Tribune would "match-fund" the mortgage, *i.e.,* it would borrow from a third party in an amount approximately equal to the mortgage note. The loan agreement would give Tribune an unconditional right to satisfy its obligation to repay by putting to the lender the mortgage note which Tribune received for its sale of the building. To compensate the lender for the additional risk inherent in the possible put of the mortgage, Tribune would pay a premium above the market interest rate.

In this manner, Tribune would realize only so much gain as it could set off against its 1982 tax loss. The taxability of the remainder of its gain would be deferred by reason of the installment sale. At the same time, through the loan, Tribune would obtain immediate use of the full purchase price in cash. It would not be obliged to carry the borrowing as a liability on its balance sheet: by reason of its right to put its mortgage receivable to the lender in satisfaction of the debt, it could employ offset accounting, setting off the asset represented by the purchase money notes against the liability to the lending institution, eliminating both from its balance sheet, and describing them rather in the footnotes to the financial statements.

The use of offset accounting was important to Tribune. Up to this point, its common stock had been privately held. It was now contemplating a public offering and believed that the market for its shares would be adversely affected if it were required to carry so large a liability on its balance sheet.

In August, Tribune prepared an offering brochure to be shown to prospective lenders. This was a document of about 50 pages, describing the proposed mortgage and loan, together with financial information about Tribune and the Building. The brochure included two term sheets—one describing the proposed purchase money mortgage Tribune would receive upon the sale of the Building, the other giving the terms of its proposed match-fund borrowing.

Tribune's advisers believed that only a small number of institutions would have the means and flexibility to contemplate a loan of these specifications. Together with LaSalle, Tribune prepared a list of six institutions including Teachers. The other five promptly rejected the deal.

Gary Waterman of LaSalle called Martha Driver of Teachers to discuss the concept. Driver told him that Teachers would be interested in receiving a proposal from Tribune. On August 20 Scott Smith, the Vice President and Treasurer of Tribune, sent Driver the offering circular. (DX 5.) Smith's covering letter stated:

> Our objective is to "match fund" this PMM [purchase money mortgage] so that we can obtain cash equivalent to the PMM's value while maintaining the tax deferral and the upside potential associated with the cash flow participation feature. A second objective is to avoid showing both the PMM and match funding on our balance sheets since conceptually these real estate loans are not related to our basic businesses.

> According to our advisers, we can meet these objectives by adding a "put" or alternative payment option to the private place- ment.... [giving] Tribune Company the unconditional right, at any time, to assign the PMM to the private placement lender in full satisfaction of its obligations under the Notes.

The letter went on to state that "[t]he likelihood of the 'put' being exercised is very low because of the 'penalties' Tribune would incur through loss of the tax deferral and the value of the cash flow partic- ipation." Finally, Smith's letter stated, "While we are flexible on funds delivery, our objective is to have a *firm commitment* from a lender by September 15, 1982. Consequently, we need to move the due diligence and negotiation process along very quickly." (Emphasis supplied.)

In the next weeks discussions proceeded promptly between Teachers and Tribune, with Teachers' representatives making due diligence visits to Tribune. Teachers requested and Tribune agreed to an additional ¼% yield. Both sides agree that during these meetings Smith talked about Tribune's desire to use offset accounting. Driver testified that she told Smith Teach- ers could not make a commitment if the deal were conditioned on Tribune's ability to use a particular method of accounting. Smith denies that Driver made any such statement. Both agree that Smith spoke of Tribune's urgent need for a commitment by September 15. Driver told Smith that the commitment could not be issued before approval by Teachers' Finance Committee which would not meet until September 16. This brief delay was acceptable to Tribune.

The loan had attractive features for Teachers: It was satisfied with Tribune as a credit risk; it would receive a premium over market interest rates to compensate it for the additional risk of being paid by tender of a long-term mortgage rather than in cash; nonetheless, absent catastrophic changes, Tribune was unlikely to exercise the right to tender the mortgage, because by doing so it would give up the tax deferment as well as its participation in the profits of the building; furthermore, an independent appraisal delivered by Tribune to Teachers valued the building at $150 million or nearly double the amount of the loan, providing a comfortable cushion of protection in the mortgaged collateral.

On September 16th, Teachers Finance Committee met and approved the Tribune loan. Driver promptly called Smith, gave him the good news, and told him that Teachers would issue its commitment letter promptly. Tribune's Assistant Treasurer wrote to Driver, "We look forward to receiving your commitment letter next week...." (DX 46.) Driver promptly undertook the drafting of Teacher's commitment letter.

The letter, mailed on September 22, included a two page Summary of Proposed Terms drawn from the term sheet included in Tribune's Offering Circular and the ensuing conversations. Teacher's term sheet covered all the basic economic terms of a loan. Neither the term sheet nor the covering commitment letter made reference to offset accounting. The letter stated that the agreement was "contingent upon the preparation, execution and delivery of documents ... in form and substance satisfactory to TIAA and to TIAA's special counsel ...," and that the transaction documents would contain the "usual and customary" representations and warranties, closing conditions, other covenants, and events of default "as we and our special counsel may deem reasonably necessary to accomplish this transaction." It concluded by inviting Tribune to "evidence acceptance of the conditions of this letter by having it executed below by a duly authorized officer ...," and finally stated:

> Upon receipt by TIAA of an accepted counterpart of this letter, our agreement to purchase from you and your agreement to issue sell and deliver to us ... the captioned securities, shall become a binding agreement between us. (DX 13.)

When Tribune received this commitment letter, the "binding agreement" language caused serious concern to its lawyers. Tribune's outside counsel, Alfred Spada of the firm of Reuben & Proctor, advised Smith not to sign a letter containing "binding agreement" language. But, having been turned down by five other institutions, Smith did not want to risk losing Teacher's commitment. He made no comment orally or in writing to Teachers questioning the "binding agreement" language. He executed and returned the letter on behalf of Tribune Company adding the notation that it was subject to certain modifications outlined in his accompanying letter. In the accompanying letter Smith wrote,

> [O]ur acceptance and agreement is subject to approval by the Company's Board of Directors and the preparation and execution of legal documentation satisfactory to the Company. (DX 14.)

Smith's acceptance letter made no mention of offset accounting.

During October Tribune proceeded with negotiations on two fronts to conclude the sale of the News Building to LaSalle and the consummation of the loan from Teachers. Tribune's lawyers had advised that in order to assure the desired tax deferral these negotiations should be conducted separately and no direct negotiation should occur between Teachers and LaSalle. The document which pertained to both transactions was the purchase money mortgage, which would be given by LaSalle to Tribune to secure its deferred payment, and could eventually be put by Tribune to Teachers in satisfaction of its obligations under the loan. As the negotiations over the mortgage proceeded, Tribune found itself pulled between the conflicting interests of its counterparties. LaSalle, as purchaser of the building, wanted a mortgage that would allow little interference by the mortgagee in the operation of the building; such mortgages are characteristically given in purchase money transactions, and Tribune, as seller, was willing to agree to such loose terms. Teachers, on the other hand, as the possible eventual holder of the mortgage, was interested in terms characteristic of institutional mortgages that give the mortgagee substantial control over the mortgagor's operation of the building. LaSalle and Teachers each served on Tribune adamant objections to the other's position. Tribune ferried these objections from one set of negotiations to the other.

A second subject of controversy in the negotiations between Tribune and Teachers was conditions on Tribune's put of the mortgage. Teachers expressed concern over a variety of problems: First, it worried that the mortgage might already be in default when put to Teachers; it sought to include as a condition of exercise of the put that the mortgage not be in default. Second, because the purchase money mortgage gave the mortgagee an equity participation in the profits of the building, Teachers worried that its possession of such a mortgage might give it "unrelated business income" that would threaten its tax exempt status. It also worried that such a mortgage might not be a legal holding for it at the time of exercise of the put, fourteen years hence. Teachers sought terms that would make Tribune's right to put the mortgage conditional on these issues being resolved to Teachers' satisfaction at the time of exercise. Tribune insisted that its right to put the mortgage to Teachers must be unconditional. Tribune believed that without an unconditional right to tender the mortgage in full satisfaction of the loan, Tribune could not justify offset accounting.

Eventually, because of the urgent need to conclude the sale of the building during the tax loss year, Tribune decided to conclude its negotiations with LaSalle, deferring the issue of Teachers satisfaction. Tribune entered into final binding agreements with LaSalle for the sale of the News Building on November 5. (DX 22.) The agreement was substantially on the terms reflected in the offering circular that Tribune had delivered to Teachers in August.

Tribune's board was scheduled to meet on October 28th. Tribune's negotiators had advised Teachers that formal board approval would be obtained at that meeting. At this meeting, Tribune's board passed resolutions which approved the sale of the Building to LaSalle. With respect to the Teachers loan, the Minutes of the meeting state that the Chairman "requested that the Board authorize the Finance Committee to approve the terms of such borrowing should the loan become available to the Company;" and that, following discussion, resolutions were adopted "that the proper officers of the Company be and they hereby are authorized" to effect the borrowing "with all of the actual terms and conditions to be subject to the prior approval by resolution of the Finance Committee." (DX 19.)

During the month of November, Tribune's accountants Price Waterhouse became worried about the availability of offset accounting. Prior to the delivery of the commitment letter, on September 7, Price Waterhouse had given Tribune an opinion letter that an unconditional option to put the mortgage note to the lender in full satisfaction of Tribune's obligation to repay the borrowing "allows (but does not require)" Tribune to offset its mortgage note receivable against its note payable. (DX 7.) In the meantime, in mid-October, the Financial Accounting Standards Board (FASB) had issued an exposure draft dealing with the appropriateness of offsetting restricted assets against related debt. (DX 25.) The exposure draft underlined the problem that the conditions Teachers had been seeking to impose on Tribune's exercise on the put were incompatible with offset accounting. In addition, Price Waterhouse began to worry that if Tribune proceeded to offer securities to the public, as it was planning, the SEC in passing on Tribune's registration statement might ask Price Waterhouse for an opinion as to whether offset accounting was "preferable." Although Price Waterhouse believed an unconditional put option would make offset accounting "appropriate," it had doubts whether it could give the opinion that such an accounting was "preferable" and whether, without such an opinion, the SEC would permit the liability to be kept off the balance sheet.

Smith called Driver and expressed Tribune's concerns about the accounting issue. Meetings and discussions were held during November concerning Tribune's dissatisfaction with the conditions Teachers had demanded as to the put, the availability of offset accounting, and Teachers' problems with the terms of the mortgage.

In the meantime, interest rates had dropped rapidly, and were now substantially below the rates that prevailed when Teachers and Tribune had entered into the commitment. Driver became concerned that Tribune, which could now make a new deal to borrow at substantially cheaper rates, was seeking to back out of the transaction. Having heard nothing about the actions of Tribune Board at its meeting on October 28, she inquired of Smith whether Board approval had been voted. Smith answered to the effect that the Board had given "general approval" to the transaction.

Around December 2 Smith began to advance proposals varying the form of the transaction. He suggested delaying Tribune's take-down, paying Teachers a commitment fee in the meantime, and specifying that Tribune would not go ahead with the proposed loan if it did not receive assurance as to the availability of offset accounting. Teachers indicated flexibility as to delaying the take-down in return for a commitment fee, but not as to making the deal conditional on Tribune's accounting.

On December 6th Tribune closed with LaSalle on the sale of the building. The mortgage was executed. Teachers began to press Tribune to meet with it to put the loan documents into final form. Teachers dropped its demand for conditions on the exercise of the put that had been unacceptable to Tribune. It asked for Tribune's comments on the draft note which it had circulated on December 1. Driver asked Smith to schedule a meeting to iron out all open issues. But the drop in interest rates together with doubts as to the availability of offset accounting now made the deal much less attractive to Tribune. Smith responded that there was no point having a meeting unless Teachers were willing to make Tribune's obligation conditional on the availability of offset accounting. Driver told Smith that Tribune's satisfaction as to its accounting was not part of their deal. Teachers sent Tribune an unsolicited letter extending Teachers' commitment for another 30 days. Tribune exhibited no further interest in pursuing the transaction. Teachers then brought the suit.

Discussion

The primary contested issue is as to the nature of the obligations that arose out of the commitment letter agreement:

Tribune contends that although the commitment letter was an undertaking to negotiate, it did not obligate either side to enter into a loan contract that was adverse to its interest. Pointing out that the commitment letter agreement left many terms open, that both sides had reserved the right of approval of satisfactory documentation, and that Tribune had furthermore made its obligation conditioned on the approval of its Board of Directors, it argues that it had no binding commitment to the loan agreement, especially if it found the terms adverse to its interests.

Teachers argues that although the commitment letter did not constitute a concluded *loan agreement,* it was nonetheless a binding commitment which obligated both sides to negotiate in good faith toward a final contract conforming to the agreed terms; it thus committed both sides not to abandon the deal, nor to break it by a demand that was outside the scope of the agreement. Although Teachers recognizes that the letter agreement left many points unspecified, it argues that the open terms were of minor economic significance and were covered by the provision that "[t]he documents shall contain such representations and warranties, closing conditions, other covenants, events of default and remedies, requirements for delivery of financial statements, and other information and provisions *as are usual and customary in this type of transaction....*" (Emphasis supplied.) (DX 13.) It argues that these minor open terms did not render the contract illusory or unenforceable. Nor did they indicate an intention of the parties not to be bound when taken together with the express language of "binding agreement." Although it was of course possible for the deal to break without liability on either side by reason of inability of the parties to reach agreement on the open terms, Teachers argues that neither side was free to break the deal over conditions which were either inconsistent with the agreed terms or outside the scope of provisions that would be "usual and customary in this type of transaction." (DX 13.)

There has been much litigation over preliminary agreements. It is difficult to generalize about their legal effect. They cover a broad scope ranging in innumerable forms and variations from letters of intent which presuppose that no binding obligations will be placed upon any party until final contract documents have been signed, to firm binding commitments which, notwithstanding a need for a more detailed documentation of agreement, can bind the parties to adhere in good faith to the deal that has been agreed. As is commonly the case with contract disputes, prime significance attaches to the intentions of the parties and to their manifestations of intent. Labels such as "letter of intent" or "commitment letter" are not necessarily controlling although they may be helpful indicators of the parties' intentions. Notwithstanding the intention of the parties at the time, if the agreement is too fragmentary, in that it leaves open terms of too fundamental importance, it may be incapable of sustaining binding legal obligation. Furthermore, the conclusion that a preliminary agreement created binding obligations does not necessarily resolve disputes because it leaves open the further question of the nature, scope and extent of the binding obligations.

A primary concern for courts in such disputes is to avoid trapping parties in surprise contractual obligations that they never intended. Ordinarily in contract negotiation, enforceable legal rights do not arise until either the expression of mutual consent to be bound, or some equivalent event that marks acceptance of offer. Contractual liability, unlike tort liability, arises from consent to be bound (or in any event from the manifestation of consent). It is fundamental to contract law that mere participation in negotiations and discussions does not create binding obligation, even if agreement is reached on all disputed terms. More is needed than agreement on each detail, which is overall agreement (or offer and acceptance) to enter into the binding contract. Nor is this principle altered by the fact that negotiating parties may have entered into letters of intent or preliminary agreements if those were made with the understanding that neither side would be bound until final agreement was reached. The Court of Appeals in several recent cases has stressed the importance of recognizing the freedom of negotiating parties from binding obligations, notwithstanding their having entered into various forms of non-binding preliminary assent. Those decisions have underlined various indicia that can be helpful in making the determination whether a manifestation of preliminary assent amounted to a legally binding agreement.

Notwithstanding the importance of protecting negotiating parties from involuntary judicially imposed contract, it is equally important that courts enforce and preserve agreements that were intended as binding, despite a need for further documentation or further negotiation. It is, of course, the aim of contract law to gratify, not to defeat, expectations that arise out of intended contractual agreement, despite informality or the need for further proceedings between the parties.

Preliminary contracts with binding force can be of at least two distinct types. One occurs when the parties have reached complete agreement (including the agreement to be bound) on all the issues perceived to require negotiation. Such an agreement is preliminary only in form—only in the sense that the parties desire a more elaborate formalization of the agreement. The second stage is not necessary; it is merely considered desirable. As the Court of Appeals stated with respect to such preliminary agreements in *V'Soske v. Barwick*, 404 F.2d 495, 499 (2d Cir. 1969), "the mere fact that the parties contemplate memorializing their agreement in a formal document does not prevent their informal agreement from taking effect prior to that event.... Restatement (Second) of Contracts, § 26; 1 Corbin on Contracts § 30 (1950); 1 Williston on Contracts § 28 (3d ed. 1957)."

The second and different sort of preliminary binding agreement is one that expresses mutual commitment to a contract on agreed major terms, while recognizing the existence of open terms that remain to be negotiated. Although the existence of open terms generally suggests that binding agreement has not been reached, that is not necessarily so. For the parties can bind themselves to a concededly incomplete agreement in the sense that they accept a mutual commitment to negotiate together in good faith in an effort to reach final agreement within the scope that has been settled in the preliminary agreement. To differentiate this sort of preliminary agreement from the first, it might be referred to as a binding preliminary commitment. Its binding obligations are of a different order than those which arise out of the first type discussed above. The first type binds both sides to their ultimate contractual objective in recognition that that contract has been reached, despite the anticipation of further formalities. The second type—the binding preliminary commitment—does not commit the parties to their ultimate contractual objective but rather to the obligation to negotiate the open issues in good faith in an attempt to reach the alternate objective within the agreed framework. In the first type, a party may lawfully demand performance of the transaction even if no further steps have been taken following the making of the "preliminary" agreement. In the second type, he may not. What he may demand, however, is that his counterparty negotiate the open terms in good faith toward a final contract incorporating the agreed terms. This obligation does not guarantee that the final contract will be concluded if both parties comport with their obligation, as good faith differences in the negotiation of the open issues may prevent a reaching of final contract. It is also possible that the parties will lose interest as circumstances change and will mutually abandon the negotiation. The obligation does, however, bar a party from renouncing the deal, abandoning the negotiations, or insisting on conditions that do not conform to the preliminary agreement.

It may often be difficult for a court to determine whether a preliminary manifestation of assent should be found to be a binding commitment. The factors mentioned by the Court of Appeals in *Winston,* 777 F.2d 78, and *R.G. Group,* 751 F.2d 69, as relevant to a determination whether final contracts had been reached in preliminary form are also relevant to determination whether preliminary commitments are to be considered binding. But, for this different inquiry, the factors must be applied in a different way. For example, in *R.G. Group,* 751 F.2d at 76, the court identified the third factor as "whether there was literally nothing left to negotiate or settle, so that all that remained to be done was to sign what had already been fully agreed to." The existence of open terms is always a factor tending against the conclusion that the parties have reached a binding agreement. But open terms obviously have a somewhat different significance where, unlike *R.G. Group,* the nature of the contract alleged is that it commits the parties in good faith to negotiate the open terms. To consider the existence of open terms as fatal would be to rule, in effect, that preliminary binding commitments cannot be enforced. That is not the law.

In seeking to determine whether such a preliminary commitment should be considered binding, a court's task is, once again, to determine the intentions of the parties at the time of their entry into the understanding, as well as their manifestations to one another by which the understanding was reached. Courts must be particularly careful to avoid imposing liability where binding obligation was not intended. There is a strong presumption against finding binding obligation in agreements which include open terms, call for future approvals and expressly anticipate future preparation and execution of contract documents. Nonetheless, if that is what the parties intended, courts should not frustrate their achieving that objective or disappoint legitimately bargained contract expectations.

Giving legal recognition to preliminary binding commitments serves a valuable function in the marketplace, particularly for relatively standardized transactions like loans. It permits borrowers and lenders to make plans in reliance upon their preliminary agreements and present market conditions. Without such legal recognition, parties would be obliged to expend enormous sums negotiating every detail of final contract documentation before knowing whether they have an agreement, and if so, on what terms. At the same time, a party that does not wish to be bound at the time of the preliminary exchange of letters can very easily protect itself by not accepting language that indicates a "firm commitment" or "binding agreement."

Upon careful consideration of the circumstances and the express terms of this commitment letter, I conclude that it represented a binding preliminary commitment and obligated both sides to seek to conclude a final loan agreement upon the agreed terms by negotiating in good faith to resolve such additional terms as are customary in such agreements. I reject Tribune's contention that its reservation of the right of approval to its Board of Directors left it free to abandon the transaction.

Expression of Intent

The Court of Appeals' first and most important factor looks to the language of the preliminary agreement for indication whether the parties considered it binding or whether they intended not to be bound until the conclusion of final formalities. This factor strongly supports Teachers. The exchange of letters constituting the commitment was replete with the terminology of binding contract, for example:

> If the foregoing properly sets forth your understanding of this transaction, please evidence acceptance of the conditions of this letter by having it executed below by a duly authorized officer ... and by returning one executed counterpart....

> Upon receipt by [Teachers] of an accepted counterpart of this letter, our agreement to purchase from you and your agreement to

issue, sell and deliver to us ... the captioned securities, shall become a binding agreement between us.

In signing, Tribune used the words "Accepted and agreed to." Tribune's additional letter of acceptance began "Attached is an executed copy of the Commitment Letter ... for a $76 million loan." The intention to create mutually binding contractual obligations is stated with unmistakable clarity, in a manner not comfortably compatible with Tribune's contention that either side was free to walk away from the deal if it decided its interests were not served thereby.

Tribune argues that this language of binding agreement was effectively contradicted by its statement that "our acceptance and agreement is subject to approval by the Company's Board of Directors and the preparation and execution of legal documentation satisfactory to the Company," as well as by similar reservations in Teachers' letter.

Contracts of preliminary commitment characteristically contain language reserving rights of approval and establishing conditions such as the preparation and execution of documents satisfactory to the contracting party. Although such reservations, considered alone, undoubtedly tend to indicate an intention not to be finally bound, they do not necessarily require that conclusion. Such terms are not to be considered in isolation, but in the context of the overall agreement. Such terms are by no means incompatible with intention to be bound. Since the parties recognize that their deal will involve further documentation and further negotiation of open terms, such reservations make clear the right of a party, or of its Board, to insist on appropriate documentation and to negotiate for or demand protections which are customary for such transactions. In *Reprosystem,* 727 F.2d at 262, and *R.G. Group,* 751 F.2d at 75, the court reasoned that a term stating the agreement would be effective "when executed" could conclusively establish that no binding force was intended prior to execution. That reasoning is of diminished force, however, where the inquiry is not whether the parties had concluded their deal, but only whether they had entered into a binding preliminary commitment which required further steps. Here, the reservation of Board approval and the expressed "contingen[cy] upon the preparation, execution and delivery of documents" did not override and nullify the acknowledgement that a "binding agreement" had been made on the stated terms; those reservations merely recognized that various issues and documentation remained open which also would require negotiation and approval. If full consideration of the circumstances and the contract language indicates that there was a mutual intent to be bound to a preliminary commitment, the presence of such reservations does not free a party to walk away from its deal merely because it later decides that the deal is not in its interest.

The Context of the Negotiations

These conclusions are further reinforced by the particular facts of the negotiation. As Smith's proposal letter of August 20 advised Teachers, Tribune wanted "to have a firm commitment from a lender by September

15, 1982." If such a "firm commitment" meant nothing more than Tribune now contends it does, such a commitment would have been of little value, as the lender would have remained free to abandon the loan if it decided at anytime that the transaction did not suit its purposes, whether because of changed interest rates or for any reason: Tribune wanted a firm commitment because it felt it needed to be sure the transaction would be concluded by the end of the year.

This same thinking governed Tribune's conduct a month later when it received the Teachers' commitment letter. Tribune's lawyers, recognizing that the form of agreement committed Tribune to a "binding" obligation, warned about the consequences of signing it. Tribune, however, wanted Teachers' binding commitment to make the loan. Tribune had been turned down by the five other lenders it considered eligible, and it did not want to risk losing Teachers' commitment. Accordingly, Smith refrained from raising any question about the "binding agreement" language. If he intended by adding the reservation of approval of Tribune's Board of Directors to change the deal fundamentally by freeing Tribune from binding obligations without Teachers noticing the change, he did not accomplish this. Tribune remained committed, as Teachers did. That is to say each was obligated to seek in good faith to conclude a final agreement within the terms specified in the commitment letter, supplemented by such representations, warranties and other conditions as are customary in such transactions. Teachers would not have been free to walk away from the loan by reason of a subsequent decision that the transaction was not in Teachers' interest. Nor could Tribune.

Tribune further contends that, given the uncertainties implicit in the three-cornered deal, neither party could have considered the loan commitment as binding. The agreed terms required Tribune to pay a premium over the prevailing interest rates for the privilege of its option to put the mortgage to Teachers. If Tribune had failed to conclude its deal with LaSalle for the sale of the Building, there would have been no purchase money mortgage and no reason for paying an interest premium.

The argument is not frivolous, but nor is it compelling. If Tribune had failed to sell the News Building and Teachers had nonetheless sought to compel it to take down the loan, Tribune might have succeeded in arguing that the sale of the Building was a mutually agreed implicit condition of the enforceability of the loan agreement. Tribune's argument in those circumstances would have been supported by the references in the commitment letter to the purchase money mortgage resulting from the Building sale.

But, however that dispute would have been resolved had it arisen, it does not compel the conclusion that there was no binding obligation. The Building sale did not fall through. It was concluded on the anticipated terms. If the sale of the Building was an implicit condition of the borrowing, that condition was fulfilled.

Open Terms

Tribune contends that the commitment letter agreement included so many open terms that it could not be deemed a binding contract. It argues also that the numerous open terms indicate a lack of intention on either side to be bound. Neither contention is convincing. Tribune does cite reputable authority to the effect that, notwithstanding language of binding agreement, if a contract fails to include agreement on basic terms of prime importance, it can be considered a nullity. This principle, however, has no application to the present facts. The two page term sheet attached to the commitment letter covered the important economic terms of a loan. The fact that countless pages of relatively conventional minor clauses remained to be negotiated does not render the agreement unenforceable.

The contention is superficially appealing with respect to the mortgage. The commitment letter, although referring to Tribune's optional right to put a mortgage to Teachers in satisfaction of its obligations, did not specify any of the terms of such a mortgage. Absence of agreement on so important a specification as the basic terms of the mortgage would render this agreement illusory. There was, however, no absence of agreement on the basic terms of the mortgage. The references in the commitment letter to the mortgage were understood by both parties as references to the mortgage term sheet that Tribune had furnished to Teachers in its Offering Circular. [The commitment letter stated that the mortgage to be tendered by Tribune "shall preserve the economics proposed for the present Mortgagee (Tribune Company)."] That two-page term sheet described the important economic terms of the proposed LaSalle purchase money mortgage. Notwithstanding its silence as to countless pages of secondary conventional mortgage clauses which remained to be negotiated, it sufficiently specified the important terms to make the commitment letter agreement meaningful and enforceable.

Nor did the existence of open secondary terms compel the conclusion that the parties did not intend to be bound. In support of this argument, Tribune cites the implication of the Court of Appeals in *R.G. Group,* 751 F.2d at 76–77 and *Winston,* 777 F.2d at 80, 82, that the existence of any single open term requires the conclusion that a binding contract had not yet been reached. This takes the Court's observation out of context and distorts its meaning. If the issue is whether the parties have reached final agreement requiring only formal memorialization, the recognized existence of open terms may be a strong indication that they have not. If, on the other hand, as here, the question is whether a preliminary expression of commitment was intended to bind the parties to negotiate the open terms in good faith, the mere fact of the existence of open terms is, of course, far less persuasive. Although the existence of open terms may always be a factor that suggests intention not to be bound, it is by no means conclusive. Where the parties have manifested intention to make a binding agreement, the mere fact of open terms will not permit them to disavow it.

Partial Performance

The factor of partial performance slightly favors Teachers. The evidence shows that for Teachers, its "commitment" to lend involved a budgeting of the funds, albeit somewhat informal. Teachers was in the business of lending its funds. The amount it had available for placement in long-term loans was finite, if large. In its loan budgeting process, Teachers would informally allocate funds which had been so committed. Such allocation reduced the net amount considered available for commitments to new loans. In fact, Teachers advised Tribune that it had only $25 million remaining available to be advanced in 1982 and that the rest would be advanced in 1983.

Tribune argues that because there was no formal segregation, it was of no significance. This misses the point. However informally it was done, the allocation of the loan commitment effectively reserved the funds for the Tribune loan. It reduced the amount of Teachers' funds that it would consider available to competing borrowers. It meant that Teachers would forego opportunities to procure commitments from other borrowers when its own commitments exhausted its available funds.

In urgently seeking Teachers' "firm commitment" by September 15, Tribune well understood that the commitment would involve a partial performance on Teachers' part. By virtue of the commitment given in September, Tribune was assured that when the time came in December for concluding final documents and drawdown, it would not be told that Teachers had nothing left to lend. Tribune was negotiating to reserve those funds. Teachers acceded and issued the commitment. That constituted a partial performance.

A party's partial performance does not necessarily indicate a belief that the other side is bound. A party may make some partial performance merely to further the likelihood of consummation of a transaction it considers advantageous. This factor was not the subject of highly focused evidence. I have not attached great importance to it and mention it primarily because it is listed among the factors suggested by the Court of Appeals in *R.G. Group* and *Winston*. I conclude, however, that this factor favors the conclusion that both sides considered the commitment binding.

The Customary Form for Such Transactions

The fourth factor mentioned in *R.G. Group,* and *Winston,* is "whether the agreement at issue is the type of contract that is usually committed to writing." 777 F.2d at 80. *See also* 751 F.2d at 77. Of course, the agreement here, unlike those cases, was in writing, but that does not dispose of the issue. To give this factor a broader application, it would better be put in terms of whether in the relevant business community, it is customary to accord binding force to the type of informal or preliminary agreement at issue. The evidence on that question tends to favor Teachers.

Of course it is true, as Tribune argues, that $80 million loans involving mortgages are generally not concluded by means of a four-page letter. But that is not the issue. The question is rather whether the customary practices of the relevant financial community include according such binding force as Teachers here advocates to such preliminary commitment agreements. Teachers' expert evidence showed that it is within the recognized practices of the financial community to accept that preliminary commitments can be binding. Not all preliminary commitments are binding. Some are not. Some are binding on only one side: Where, for example, the borrower pays a commitment fee for the purpose of binding the lender, the agreement may be in the nature of an option to the borrower to decide by a specified date whether to go ahead with the transaction. In such cases the seller has been paid for its one-sided commitment. Some such preliminary agreements are properly seen as merely letters of intent which leave both sides free to abandon the transaction. The point is that the practices of the marketplace are not rigid or uniform. They encompass a considerable variety of transactions negotiated to suit the needs of the parties, including mutually binding preliminary commitments. Each transaction must be examined carefully to determine its characteristics.

Tribune has failed to show to the court's satisfaction that such binding commitments are outside the usages of the marketplace.

Action by Tribune's Board of Directors

The parties disagree as to whether the Teachers' loan was or was not approved by Tribune's Board of Directors. Tribune contends that the resolutions adopted by its Board on October 28th did not involve any approval whatsoever, but merely a delegation of responsibility to the Finance Committee to approve or disapprove the transaction. Teachers contends that the action of the Board did approve the loan in concept, while delegating to the Finance Committee the right and authority to pass on the particular loan documents. Teachers contends that its interpretation is reinforced by Smith's statement to Driver, when she inquired in late November, that the Board had given "general approval" to the transaction at the October 28 meeting (a statement Smith denies having made).

I need not rule on whether the resolutions adopted by the Board of Directors did or did not constitute approval of the transaction, because nothing turns on this. As noted above, although Tribune had reserved the right of approval of the final transaction to its Board of Directors, this did not mean Tribune could defeat its obligations under the binding agreement of commitment merely by having its Board do nothing. The commitment agreement called for conclusion of the transaction and a $25 million first drawdown before the end of the year. Even if I were to accept Tribune's contention that its Board took no action other than to delegate responsibility to the Finance Committee, that would not justify Tribune's backing out of its binding agreement to negotiate in good faith to reach a complete final contract.

Tribune's argument would construe the commitment letter agreement either as a free option to Tribune to decide over the next three months whether to hold Teachers to its commitment to make the loan, or alternatively as a nonbinding statement of mutual intention. Neither is consistent with either the written agreement or the conduct of the parties. Tribune had requested the "firm commitment" of Teachers to make the loan. Teachers' firm commitment was not given for free but in exchange for Tribune's similarly binding commitment. The reservations as to preparation and execution of documents and as to the satisfaction of Teachers' counsel and Tribune's Board permitted each side to negotiate the implementation of the agreement and to require the inclusion of customary terms in a form which it deemed necessary or appropriate to its protection. But those reservations did not authorize either side to escape its obligation simply by declining to negotiate or to give approval.

In any event, I conclude that Tribune's Board did give approval within the meaning of the agreement. The Minutes reflect that the proper officers were expressly authorized to arrange for the borrowing at a maximum interest rate of 15.25%, "with all of the actual terms and conditions to be subject to the prior approval by resolution of the Finance Committee...." The Resolution went on to say that the "authority granted by this resolution shall expire if not utilized prior to April 30, 1983." (DX 19.) This express authorization to "the proper officers ... to arrange for" the borrowing (which would expire if not acted on by April 30, 1983), surely went beyond a mere delegation to the Finance Committee of the Board's responsibility to approve or disapprove. The fact that the authorization was "subject to" Finance Committee approval recognized rather that there were terms and documents that remained to be negotiated, calling for Board level approval. It did not mean that the Board had done nothing but delegate. On consideration of the minutes and resolutions, as well as the testimony of Tribune officers and directors who were present at the meeting, I find, as Smith later told Driver, that the Board gave "general approval" to the transaction.

Tribune's October 6 letter reserving approval to Tribune's Board did not specify any particular form of Board approval, nor did it require that approval be of the final loan documents. Indeed, it distinguished between the requirements of "*approval* by the Company's Board of Directors" and "the preparation and execution of legal documentation *satisfactory to the Company.*" The general approval given was sufficient under the contract.

Tribune's Right to Condition the Loan on Offset Accounting

Tribune contends that its right to carry the loan off-balance-sheet by offset accounting was always deemed an essential condition of the deal. It points out that the Offering Circular which it delivered to Teachers, and the Price Waterhouse background memoranda, which also were delivered to Teachers during the early due diligence and discussion phase, all underlined offset accounting as an important Tribune concern. Nor does Teachers deny that in the early discussions, Smith spoke of Tribune's accounting and tax objectives. The witnesses disagree along predictable lines as to whether Driver told Smith that Teachers would not take the risk of Tribune's accounting treatment. The conflict need not be resolved. For regardless whether Driver orally refused to have Teachers assume the risk of Tribune's right to satisfactory accounting, the signed agreement did not provide for any such condition. The written agreement between the parties contains no basis whatever for the proposition that Tribune's obligation was conditioned on satisfactory assurance that it could report the loan off balance sheet. The fact that Tribune considered this significant is not disputed, but it is not determinative.

Both parties were aware of Tribune's objectives as to both the tax and accounting for the proposed deal. Tribune could, of course, have demanded as a condition of its commitment that it receive satisfactory assurances (in the form of opinion letters of counsel and auditors, or otherwise) as to both deferred taxation and offset accounting. It could have offered to pay a fee for Teachers' commitment on terms that would have left Tribune free to proceed with the loan or not, at its option. Alternatively, it could have negotiated for the option to prepay if the Internal Revenue Service or the SEC disallowed the desired tax or accounting consequences. The problem was that in September of 1982, Tribune believed that it needed an immediate "firm commitment" from Teachers to be sure of its ability to conclude the transaction as planned within 1982. Had Tribune made such demands, Teachers might well have turned down Tribune's proposal (as the five other institutions had done). Indeed, Tribune was so sensitive to its need for Teachers' firm commitment that when its counsel warned of the consequences of signing the commitment letter with its "binding agreement" language, Tribune disregarded this advice so as not to lose the lender's commitment. Neither the language of the agreement, nor the negotiations of the parties give any support to the contention that offset accounting was a condition of the agreement.

There was perhaps an additional reason why Tribune did not negotiate for offset accounting as a condition of the deal, being that in September and early October it did not have the doubts that it later developed as to the availability of offset accounting. It had received a prior opinion of Price Waterhouse to the effect that the unconditional put would make offset accounting appropriate. Only after the FASB's mid-October exposure draft did Price Waterhouse begin to emphasize doubts about offset accounting and about the position the SEC might take in the event Tribune offered public securities under an SEC registration statement.

Whether the reason was that Tribune was afraid to lose Teachers prompt firm commitment, or that Tribune had not yet worried, as it later did, about the availability of its accounting objective, or simply that Tribune was willing to take the risk to secure this important deal, the fact is that Tribune did not negotiate for and did not obtain its right to offset accounting as a condition of its bargain.

By December of 1982 Tribune faced a completely different set of factors. Interest rates had declined very substantially. The loan agreement that it negotiated with Teachers was no longer to its benefit since it could now borrow money at substantially cheaper cost. Price Waterhouse's newly expressed doubts about the availability of offset accounting gave it further reason to question whether the deal it had made was a good one. With the benefit of two months' hindsight, Tribune most likely would not have entered into the commitment agreement it made in early October. That was, however, the agreement it made.

Judgment is granted to the plaintiff

* * *

Sun Printing was discussed in detail in Chapter 14. It is relevant here principally for some stray remarks that Cardozo made at the end of his opinion. He wondered whether a bargainer, without forming the intention to be bound in general even when no specific agreement can be reached, might form the intention to limit the grounds on which it might refuse to be bound in the future. (One way in which to understand the negotiations concerning the price term in *Sun Printing* is as reflecting an intention, in the defendant, not to break off dealings with the plaintiff on the specific ground that the plaintiff refused to accept any price above the stated maximum.) Cardozo further wondered how the law might treat a promise by the defendant not to break off the relationship "by an arbitrary refusal to reach any agreement." Perhaps more demandingly, a party might agree not to refuse to make a contract on account of receiving a better offer from a third party, or even quite generally to bargain in good faith towards an eventual agreement.

Teachers Insurance illustrates the modern law of agreements to bargain in good faith. An exchange of letters between parties contemplating a loan agreement stated that the borrower and lender had made a "binding agreement" subject to preparing and executing final documents satisfactory to both sides and the approval of the borrower's board of directors. Interest rates declined, and the borrower broke off negotiations, insisting that the lender agree to allow it to report the loan on its financial statements by an off-balance-sheet offset. The borrower further claimed that this condition left it free to decline to borrow if the loan did not best serve its interests.[55]

The court observed that the commitment letter was clearly not a complete contract to borrow money—a complete loan agreement. But the court asked (in a modern reprise of Cardozo's question) whether the letter might nevertheless bind the parties to negotiate towards a loan agreement in good faith, so that they might not avoid coming to a contract for reasons outside the scope of their agreement. In answering, the court set out from the proposition that contract law requires an actual agreement before recognizing any obligation. As the court observed, "[i]t is fundamental to contract law that mere participation in negotiations and discussions does not create binding obligation, even if agreement is reached on all disputed terms. More is needed than agreement on each detail, which is overall agreement (or offer and acceptance) to enter into the binding contract."

---

55. Notice how much of the negotiation described in the opinion was about maximizing the parties' joint surplus. The whole deal was driven by finding a way to let the borrower get immediate access to the proceeds of an asset sale while delaying the tax recognition of these proceeds. The idea was that the loan would give the borrower the sales price up front and that the actual sale, now structured as an installment sale, would service the loan, and give the lender its return.

Notice also that the borrower's lawyer was worried about the "binding agreement" language in the letters.

Being *in* agreement, in other words, does not establish obligation. There must be *an* agreement between the parties.

Nevertheless, the court recognized that an agreement might be struck in advance of the final contract at which the parties' negotiations aim. Such a preliminary agreement might arise in two ways. First, and less controversially, the final contract might be struck in substance even though the parties have not yet collected it in one text (typically in one writing). This is not really a preliminary agreement in substance (it is final in substance) but only in form. Second, and more controversially, the parties might reach an agreement that expresses mutual commitment to the final agreement's main terms but recognizes that there remain open terms (on which there has been no agreement, of any form), and the parties may agree to bargain in good faith towards agreement on those terms.

Teachers Insurance holds that although there is a "strong presumption" against finding obligation in such circumstances, agreements to bargain in good faith can be binding. Where they bind, they "bar a party from renouncing the deal, abandoning the negotiations, or insisting on conditions that do not conform to the preliminary agreement." The reason why the law must recognize agreements to bargain in good faith is precisely the one just given: "Without such legal recognition, parties would be obliged to expend enormous sums negotiating every detail of the final contract documentation before knowing whether they have an agreement, and if so, on what terms."[56]

Finally, *Teachers Insurance* set out the criteria that govern whether or not agreements to bargain in good faith will be binding. The first concerns whether or not the parties express an intent (specifically) to be so bound. The second concerns whether or not the context of the parties negotiation make a firm commitment to bargain in good faith essential to making the continued pursuit of a final deal worthwhile to one or both of the parties. The third concerns how many and how critical terms have been left open, and in particular whether or not there are enough agreed-upon terms to make the duty to bargain in good faith meaningfully specifiable (to make it possible for courts reliably to distinguish between good and bad faith reasons for breaking off negotiations). Finally, the fourth concerns custom, specifically concerning how many and which terms must be closed out (agreed upon) before a binding agreement to bargain in good faith towards the others is reached. Through these conditions, *Teachers Insurance* applies general principles concerning contract formation, in the ordinary way, to the special case of agreements to bargain in good faith.

In other words, freedom of contract today encompasses the freedom to structure pre-contractual bargaining.[57]

---

56. Note that the court further observed that "a party that does not wish to be bound at the time of the preliminary exchange of letters can very easily protect itself by not accepting language that indicates a 'firm commitment' or 'binding agreement.' " How plausible is it that such disclaimers will be reliably effective, given the principles of contract interpretation explained earlier?

57. Note the difference between this approach and both the civilian adoption of a mandatory duty of good faith in negotiations and the approach of *Hoffman*.

Those approaches both begin from the proposition that the bargain relation, in itself, has enough moral and legal content to subject parties to it to liability, in contract, based on their bargaining representations. That is why such approaches threaten freedom of contract. Freedom of contract, after all, encompasses not just freedom *to* contract but freedom *from* contract. It makes contractual intentions not just sufficient but also necessary for contractual obligations. It insists that contractual obligations cannot be imposed but must be chosen.

Mandatory contractual duties of good faith in negotiations undermine the special place of choice in contract, by basing obligations on something other than the contractual intentions of the parties to them. That is why Gilmore worried that promissory estoppel, at least if employed on the model of *Hoffman*, is in effect anti-contract.

CHAPTER 20

CONTRACTS OF ADHESION

Most of the concrete contracts discussed so far in these pages have been negotiated agreements struck between parties that both possessed the capacity to propose and to alter their contracts' terms. This model—of the individually tailored, or *bespoke*, contract—has been implicit in the broader doctrinal argument also. The discussions of offer and acceptance, for example, have largely imagined parties who adjust reciprocally to one another as they negotiate towards their contract.

Most actual contracts, at least nowadays, are not made on this model, however. Rather, they arise as *contracts of adhesion*—that is, contracts consummated through standard forms drafted by one party (generally a repeat player) and offered to the other party (generally a less-frequent contractor) on a take-it-or-leave-it basis[1] without any opportunity for bargaining or negotiation.[2] It is impossible to say certainly or precisely what proportion of contracts today are contracts of adhesion. One prominent but admittedly speculative estimate put the proportion at over 99%.[3] And even if this exaggerates matters, contracts of adhesion surely represent a prominent face of contractual practice. Familiar examples include the contracts that govern mobile telephone and internet service, credit card and bank deposit agreements, and also the contracts that govern virtually all major retail purchases.

Contracts of adhesion, and the standardized forms through which they are paradigmatically consummated, have for over a century been a familiar source of unease for contract lawyers.[4] Suspicion of such contracts has an

---

1. This feature likely gave this class of contracts its name. The term "adhesion" was borrowed from French legal scholars who likely themselves borrowed from the law of treaties, and in particular the practice whereby a group of states negotiating a treaty leave the treaty open for adhesion by additional states, who must, however, take or leave its terms. See ARTHUR LINTON CORBIN, CORBIN ON CONTRACTS s. 1.4 (page 13) (rev. ed. 1993).

2. This definition is standard in its substance. Its language closely tracks Todd. D. Rakoff, *Contracts of Adhesion: An Essay in Reconstruction*, 96 HARV. L. REV. 1173, 1177 (1983).

3. See W. David Slawson, *Standard Form Contracts and Democratic Control Over the Lawmaking Power*, 84 HARV. L. REV. 529, 529 (1970). Slawson went on to say that "[t]he contracting still imagined by courts and law teachers as typical, in which both parties participate in choosing the language of their entire agreement, is no longer of much more than historical importance." Id. Whether or not this was true when Slawson wrote, it seems less true today, in an economic environment in which greater access to information and greater computing power have made it enormously cheaper to dicker for contract terms (think, in this connection, of eBay and Craigslist.)

4. An early discussion, which may have introduced the term "contract of adhesion" to U.S. lawyers, is Edwin Patterson, *The Delivery of a Life–Insurance Policy*, 33 HARV. L. REV. 198,

august history in the case-law. As early as 1873, the United States Supreme Court, considering a form contract made between a drover and the New York Central Railroad, observed that the drover, being "only one individual of a million," could not "afford to higgle or stand out,"[5] and, partly for this reason, struck down a contractual limitation on the Railroad's liability.[6]

Although they capture an intuitive unease, these remarks do not unpack the unease and they certainly do not justify it. The materials below begin to elaborate and assess the missing arguments. The first section takes up functionalist arguments claiming that contracts of adhesion allow term-makers unfairly to exploit term-takers and, relatedly, that they are inefficient. Although there is something in these arguments, the materials also reveal that the functionalist case against contracts of adhesion remains uncertain. The second section considers a lawyerly instinct—a craft sense, almost—that even when they are fair, efficient, and freely adopted, there is something doctrinally suspect about adhesive agreements. This is a formalist concern that contracts of adhesion somehow represent only degenerate cases of the legal category *contract*; and that the law should be commensurately suspicious of them. A third section looks for bespoke contracting hidden in the interstices of adhesive contracting as actually practiced.

20.1   A FUNCTIONALIST ANALYSIS OF CONTRACTS OF ADHESION

Contracts of adhesion exacerbate certain strategic imbalances between term-makers (who are generally sophisticated repeat players) and term-takers (who are generally less sophisticated and merely occasional contractors). This raises the functionalist concern that, through these imbalances, contracts of adhesion allow term-makers unfairly to exploit term-takers. The exploitation is both unfair and (at least often) inefficient. Finally, exploitative term-makers deprive term-takers of meaningful choice and thus render them in important respects unfree. In these ways, the functionalist can explain why contracts of adhesion lend themselves to certain vices. But the functionalist approach cannot so easily say whether these infirmities outweigh the (functional) benefits that adhesive contracts also, unquestionably, possess. Moreover, the vices associated with contracts of adhesion also arise elsewhere in contractual practice, and contract law already contains a set of doctrines—including fraud, duress, and unconscionability—designed to address them. The functionalist thus has a hard time explaining why contracts of adhesion merit special and independent atten-

---

222 (1919). Patterson used the term "adhesion" only once, and introduced it with the following footnote:

> This expressive term seems worthy of a place in our legal vocabulary. See René Demogue in Modern French Legal Philosophy, 472, 477. 2 M. Planiol, Traité Elémextaire de Droit Civil, § 972. A similar usage occurs in international law. See 1 Oppenheim, International Law, §§ 532, 533.

5.   *New York Central Railroad Company v. Lockwood*, 84 U.S. 357, 379 (1873).

6.   *Id.* at 384.

tion—why the law should regulate such contracts through a doctrine of their own—rather than simply being assessed, in the usual way, by the general doctrines designed to prevent exploitative contracting.

The bargaining inequalities that underlie functionalist attacks on contracts of adhesion find their roots in the transactions costs of drafting and understanding agreements, especially in their technical details. Because the repeat-players (typically firms) who draft forms can spread these costs out over many contracts (and because they may antecedently have expertise and education that anyway lowers these costs for them), they may craft forms to incorporate contract terms that favor their own interests. And because the one shot players (typically natural persons) who receive form contracts do so rarely, or at least only intermittently, they cannot afford the costs of negotiating for alternative terms that better promote their interests. In many cases, term takers cannot afford even the costs of reading and understanding all but a few of the terms (price, quantity) in the forms that they receive.

Repeat players can therefore use forms to increase their share of the contractual surplus, including perhaps even in exploitative ways. Moreover, these terms may be privately profitable for the repeat players even though they are inefficient—the increase in the share of contractual surplus that the terms allocate to the term-maker may outweigh the decrease that the terms impose on the overall size of the surplus to which this share is applied. Finally, because the transactions costs of reading and understanding complex forms are so high, term-takers cannot meaningfully consent to the arrangements that term-makers in effect impose by fiat. Simply put, contracts of adhesion allow term-makers to behave unfairly and inefficiently against term-takers, whom they render unfree. The following case famously captures the sensibility behind such functionalist arguments.

Henningsen v. Bloomfield Motors

Supreme Court of New Jersey, 1960.
161 A.2d 69.

■ FRANCIS, J.

Plaintiff Clause H. Henningsen purchased a Plymouth automobile, manufactured by defendant Chrysler Corporation, from defendant Bloomfield Motors, Inc. His wife, plaintiff Helen Henningsen, was injured while driving it and instituted suit against both defendants to recover damages on account of her injuries. Her husband joined in the action seeking compensation for his consequential losses. The complaint was predicated upon breach of express and implied warranties and upon negligence. At the trial the negligence counts were dismissed by the court and the cause was submitted to the jury for determination solely on the issues of implied warranty of merchantability. Verdicts were returned against both defendants and in favor of the plaintiffs. Defendants appealed and plaintiffs cross-appealed from the dismissal of their negligence claim. The matter was certified by this court prior to consideration in the Appellate Division.

The facts are not complicated, but a general outline of them is necessary to an understanding of the case.

On May 7, 1955 Mr. and Mrs. Henningsen visited the place of business of Bloomfield Motors, Inc., an authorized De Soto and Plymouth dealer, to look at a Plymouth. They wanted to buy a car and were considering a Ford or a Chevrolet as well as a Plymouth. They were shown a Plymouth which appealed to them and the purchase followed. The record indicates that Mr. Henningsen intended the car as a Mother's Day gift to his wife. He said the intention was communicated to the dealer. When the purchase order or contract was prepared and presented, the husband executed it alone. His wife did not join as a party.

The purchase order was a printed form of one page. On the front it contained blanks to be filled in with a description of the automobile to be sold, the various accessories to be included, and the details of the financing. The particular car selected was described as a 1955 Plymouth, Plaza '6', Club Sedan. The type used in the printed parts of the form became smaller in size, different in style, and less readable toward the bottom where the line for the purchaser's signature was placed. The smallest type on the page appears in the two paragraphs, one of two and one-quarter lines and the second of one and one-half lines, on which great stress is laid by the defense in the case. These two paragraphs are the least legible and the most difficult to read in the instrument, but they are most important in the evaluation of the rights of the contesting parties. They do not attract attention and there is nothing about the format which would draw the reader's eye to them. In fact, a studied and concentrated effort would have to be made to read them. De-emphasis seems the motive rather than emphasis. More particularly, most of the printing in the body of the order appears to be 12 point block type, and easy to read. In the short paragraphs under discussion, however, the type appears to be six point script and the print is solid, that is, the lines are very close together.

The two paragraphs are:

'The front and back of this Order comprise the entire agreement affecting this purchase and no other agreement or understanding of any nature concerning same has been made or entered into, or will be recognized. I hereby certify that no credit has been extended to me for the purchase of this motor vehicle except as appears in writing on the face of this agreement.

'I have read the matter printed on the back hereof and agree to it as a part of this order the same as if it were printed above my signature. I certify that I am 21 years of age, or older, and hereby acknowledge receipt of a copy of this order.'

On the right side of the form, immediately below these clauses and immediately above the signature line, and in 12 point block type, the following appears:

'CASH OR CERTIFIED CHECK ONLY ON DELIVERY.'

On the left side, just opposite and in the same style type as the two quoted clauses, but in eight point size, this statement is set out:

'This agreement shall not become binding upon the Dealer until approved by an officer of the company.'

The two latter statements are in the interest of the dealer and obviously an effort is made to draw attention to them.

The testimony of Claus Henningsen justifies the conclusion that he did not read the two fine print paragraphs referring to the back of the purchase contract. And it is uncontradicted that no one made any reference to them, or called them to his attention. With respect to the matter appearing on the back, it is likewise uncontradicted that he did not read it and that no one called it to his attention.

The reverse side of the contract contains 8 ½ inches of fine print. It is not as small, however, as the two critical paragraphs described above. The page is headed 'Conditions' and contains ten separate paragraphs consisting of 65 lines in all. The paragraphs do not have headnotes or margin notes denoting their particular subject, as in the case of the 'Owner Service Certificate' to be referred to later. In the seventh paragraph, about two-thirds of the way down the page, the warranty, which is the focal point of the case, is set forth. It is as follows:

'7. It is expressly agreed that there are no warranties, express or implied, Made by either the dealer or the manufacturer on the motor vehicle, chassis, of parts furnished hereunder except as follows.

"The manufacturer warrants each new motor vehicle (including original equipment placed thereon by the manufacturer except tires), chassis or parts manufactured by it to be free from defects in material or workmanship under normal use and service. Its obligation under this warranty being limited to making good at its factory any part or parts thereof which shall, within ninety (90) days after delivery of such vehicle To the original purchaser or before such vehicle has been driven 4,000 miles, whichever event shall first occur, be returned to it with transportation charges prepaid and which its examination shall disclose to its satisfaction to have been thus defective; This warranty being expressly in lieu of all other warranties expressed or implied, and all other obligations or liabilities on its part, and it neither assumes nor authorizes any other person to assume for it any other liability in connection with the sale of its vehicles.

After the contract had been executed, plaintiffs were told the car had to be serviced and that it would be ready in two days. According to the dealer's president, a number of cars were on hand at the time; they had come in from the factory about three or four weeks earlier and at least some of them, including the one selected by the Henningsens, were kept in the back of the shop display purposes. When sold, plaintiffs' vehicle was not 'a serviced car, ready to go.' The testimony shows that Chrysler Corporation sends from the factory to the dealer a 'New Car Preparation Service Guide' with each new automobile. The guide contains detailed instructions as to what has to be done to prepare the car for delivery. The dealer is told to 'Use this form as a guide to inspect and prepare this new Plymouth for delivery.' It specifies 66 separate items to be checked, tested, tightened or adjusted in the course of the servicing, but dismantling the vehicle or checking all of its internal parts is not prescribed. The guide also calls for delivery of the Owner Service Certificate with the car.

This certificate, which at least by inference is authorized by Chrysler, was in the car when released to Claus Henningsen on May 9, 1955. It was not made part of the purchase contract, nor was it shown to him prior to the consummation of that agreement. The only reference to it therein is that the dealer 'agrees to promptly perform and fulfill and terms and conditions of the owner service policy.' The Certificate contains a warranty entitled 'Automobile Manufacturers Association Uniform Warranty.' The provisions thereof are the same as those set forth on the reverse side of the purchase order, except that an additional paragraph is added by which the dealer extends that warranty to the purchaser in the same manner as if the word 'Dealer' appeared instead of the word 'Manufacturer.'

The new Plymouth was turned over to the Henningsens on May 9, 1955. No proof was adduced by the dealer to show precisely what was done in the way of mechanical or road testing beyond testimony that the manufacturer's instructions were probably followed.

Mr. Henningsen drove it from the dealer's place of business in Bloomfield to their home in Keansburg. On the trip nothing unusual appeared in the way in which it operated. Thereafter, it was used for short trips on paved streets about the town. It had no servicing and no mishaps of any kind before the event of May 19. That day, Mrs. Henningsen drove to Asbury Park. On the way down and in returning the car performed in normal fashion until the accident occurred. She was proceeding north on Route 36 in Highlands, New Jersey, at 20–22 miles per hour. The highway was paved and smooth, and contained two lanes for northbound travel. She was riding in the right-hand lane. Suddenly she heard a loud noise 'from the bottom, by the hood.' It 'felt as if something cracked.' The steering wheel spun in her hands; the car veered sharply to the right and crashed into a highway sign and a brick wall. No other vehicle was in any way involved. A bus operator driving in the left-hand lane testified that he observed plaintiffs' car approaching in normal fashion in the opposite direction; 'all of a sudden (it) veered at 90 degrees and right into this wall.' As a result of the impact, the front of the car was so badly damaged that it was impossible to determine if any of the parts of the steering wheel mechanism or workmanship or assembly were defective or improper prior to the accident. The condition was such that the collision insurance carrier, after inspection, declared the vehicle a total loss. It had 468 miles on the speedometer at the time.

The insurance carrier's inspector and appraiser of damaged cars, with 11 years of experience, advanced the opinion, based on the history and his examination, that something definitely went 'wrong from the steering wheel down to the front wheels' and that the untoward happening must have been due to mechanical defect or failure; 'something down there had to drop off or break loose to cause the car' to act in the manner described.

As has been indicated, the trial court felt that the proof was not sufficient to make out a Prima facie case as to the negligence of either the manufacturer or the dealer. The case was given to the jury, therefore, solely on the warranty theory, with results favorable to the plaintiffs against both defendants.

The Claim of Implied Warranty against the Manufacturer.

In the ordinary case of sale of goods by description an implied warranty of merchantability is an integral part of the transaction. R.S. 46:30–20, N.J.S.A. If the buyer, expressly or by implication, makes known to the seller the particular purpose for which the article is required and it appears that he has relied on the seller's skill or judgment, an implied warranty arises of reasonable fitness for that purpose. R.S. 46:30–21(1), N.J.S.A. The former type of warranty simply means that the thing sold is reasonably fit for the general purpose for which it is manufactured and sold. As Judge (later Justice) Cardozo remarked in Ryan, supra, the distinction between a warranty of fitness for a particular purpose and of merchantability in many instances is practically meaningless. In the particular case he was concerned with food for human consumption in a sealed container. Perhaps no more apt illustration of the notion can be thought of than the instance of the ordinary purchaser who informs the automobile dealer that he desires a car for the purpose of business and pleasure driving on the public highway.

Of course such sales, whether oral of written, may be accompanied by an express warranty. Under the broad terms of the Uniform Sale of Goods Law any affirmation of fact relating to the goods is an express warranty if the natural tendency of the statement is to induce the buyer to make the purchase. R.S. 46:30–18, N.J.S.A. And over the years since the almost universal adoption of the act, a growing awareness of the tremendous development of modern business methods has prompted the courts to administer that provision with a liberal hand. Vold, Law of Sales, s 86, p. 429 (2d ed. 1959). Solicitude toward the buyer plainly harmonizes with the intention of the Legislature. That fact is manifested further by the later section of the act which preserves and continues any permissible implied warranty, despite an express warranty, unless the two are inconsistent. R.S. 46:30–21(6), N.J.S.A.

The uniform act codified, extended and liberalized the common law of sales. The motivation in part was to ameliorate the harsh doctrine of Caveat emptor, and in some measure to impose a reciprocal obligation on the seller to beware. The transcendent value of the legislation, particularly with respect to implied warranties, rests in the fact that obligations on the part of the seller were imposed by operation of law, and did not depend for their existence upon express agreement of the parties. And of tremendous significance in a rapidly expanding commercial society was the recognition of the right to recover damages on account of personal injuries arising from a breach of warranty. The particular importance of this advance resides in the fact that under such circumstances strict liability is imposed upon the maker or seller of the product. Recovery of damages does not depend upon proof of negligence or knowledge of the defect.

As the Sales Act and its liberal interpretation by the courts threw this protective cloak about the buyer, the decisions in various jurisdictions revealed beyond doubt that many manufacturers took steps to avoid these ever increasing warranty obligations. Realizing that the act governed the relationship of buyer and seller, they undertook to withdraw from actual and direct contractual contact with the buyer. They ceased selling products to the consuming public through their own employees and making contracts of sale in their own names. Instead, a system of independent dealers was established; their products were sold to dealers who in turn dealt with the buying public, ostensibly solely in their own personal capacity as sellers. In the past in many instances, manufacturers were able to transfer to the dealers burdens imposed by the act and thus achieved a large measure of immunity for themselves. But, as will be noted in more detail hereafter, such marketing practices, coupled with the advent of large scale advertising by manufacturers to promote the purchase of these goods from dealers by members of the public, provided a basis upon which the existence of express or implied warranties was predicated, even though the manufacturer was not a party to the contract of sale.

The general observations that have been made are important largely for purposes of perspective. They are helpful in achieving a point from which to evaluate the situation now presented for solution. Primarily, they reveal a trend and a design in legislative and judicial thinking toward providing protection for the buyer. It must be noted, however, that the sections of the Sales Act, to which reference has been made, do not impose warranties in terms of unalterable absolutes. R.S. 46:30–3, N.J.S.A., provides in general terms that an applicable warranty may be negatived or varied by express agreement. As to disclaimers or limitations of the obligations that normally attend a sale, it seems sufficient at this juncture to say they are not favored, and that they are strictly construed against the seller.

With these considerations in mind, we come to a study of the express warranty on the reverse side of the purchase order signed by Claus Henningsen. At the outset we take notice that it was made only by the manufacturer and that by its terms it runs directly to Claus Henningsen. On the facts detailed above, it was to be extended to him by the dealer as the agent of Chrysler Corporation. The consideration for this warranty is the purchase of the manufacturer's product from the dealer by the ultimate buyer. *Studebaker Corp. v. Nail*, 82 Ga.App. 779 (1950).

Although the franchise agreement between the defendants recites that the relationship of principal and agent is not created, in particular transactions involving third persons the law will look at their conduct and not to their intent or their words as between themselves but to their factual relation. The normal pattern that the manufacturer-dealer relationship follows relegates the position of the dealer to the status of a way station along the car's route from maker to consumer. This is indicated by the language of the warranty. Obviously the parties knew and so intended that the dealer would not use the automobile for 90 days or drive it 4,000 miles. And the words 'original purchaser,' taken in their context, signify the purchasing member of the public. Moreover, the language of this warranty is that of the uniform warranty of the Automobile Manufacturers Association, of which Chrysler is a member. See Automotive Facts & Figures, 1958 Edition, published by Automotive Manufacturers Association, p. 69; Automotive News 1959 Almanac (Slocum Publishing Co., Inc., Detroit) p. 25. And it is the form appearing in the Plymouth Owner Service Certificate mentioned in the servicing instruction guide sent with the new car from the factory. The evidence is overwhelming that the dealer acted for Chrysler in including the warranty in the purchase contract.

The terms of the warranty are a sad commentary upon the automobile manufacturers' marketing practices. Warranties developed in the law in the interest of and to protect the ordinary consumer who cannot be expected to have the knowledge or capacity or even the opportunity to make adequate inspection of mechanical instrumentalities, like automobiles, and to decide for himself whether they are reasonably fit for the designed purpose. But the ingenuity of the Automobile Manufacturers Association, by means of its standardized form, has metamorphosed the warranty into a device to limit the maker's liability. To call it an 'equivocal' agreement, as the Minnesota Supreme Court did, is the least that can be said in criticism of it. *Federal Motor Truck Sales Corporation v. Shanus*, 190 Minn. 5 (1933).

The manufacturer agrees to replace defective parts for 90 days after the sale or until the car has been driven 4,000 miles, whichever is first to occur, If the part is sent to the factory, transportation charges prepaid, and if examination discloses to its satisfaction that the part is defective. It is difficult to imagine a greater burden on the consumer, or less satisfactory remedy. Aside from imposing on the buyer the trouble of removing and shipping the part, the maker has sought to retain the uncontrolled discretion to decide the issue of defectiveness. Some courts have removed much of the force of that reservation by declaring that the purchaser is not bound by the manufacturer's decision. *Mills v. Maxwell Motor Sales Corporation*, 105 Neb. 465.

Putting aside for the time being the problem of the efficacy of the disclaimer provisions contained in the express warranty, a question of first importance to be decided is whether an implied warranty of merchantability by Chrysler Corporation accompanied the sale of the automobile to Claus Henningsen.

Preliminarily, it may be said that the express warranty against defective parts and workmanship is not inconsistent with an implied warranty of merchantability. Such warranty cannot be excluded for that reason.

Chrysler points out that an implied warranty of merchantability is an incident of a contract of sale. It concedes, of course, the making of the original sale to Bloomfield Motors, Inc., but maintains that this transaction marked the terminal point of its contractual connection with the car. Then

Chrysler urges that since it was not a party to the sale by the dealer to Henningsen, there is no privity of contract between it and the plaintiffs, and the absence of this privity eliminates any such implied warranty.

There is no doubt that under early common-law concepts of contractual liability only those persons who were parties to the bargain could sue for a breach of it. In more recent times a noticeable disposition has appeared in a number of jurisdictions to break through the narrow barrier of privity when dealing with sales of goods in order to give realistic recognition to a universally accepted fact. The fact is that the dealer and the ordinary buyer do not, and are not expected to, buy goods, whether they be foodstuffs or automobiles, exclusively for their own consumption or use. Makers and manufacturers know this and advertise and market their products on that assumption; witness, the 'family' car, the baby foods, etc. The limitations of privity in contracts for the sale of goods developed their place in the law when marketing conditions were simple, when maker and buyer frequently met face to face on an equal bargaining plane and when many of the products were relatively uncomplicated and conducive to inspection by a buyer competent to evaluate their quality. With the advent of mass marketing, the manufacturer became remote from the purchaser, sales were accomplished through intermediaries, and the demand for the product was created by advertising media. In such an economy it became obvious that the consumer was the person being cultivated. Manifestly, the connotation of 'consumer' was broader than that of 'buyer.' He signified such a person who, in the reasonable contemplation of the parties to the sale, might be expected to use the product. Thus, where the commodities sold are such that if defectively manufactured they will be dangerous to life or limb, then society's interests can only be protected by eliminating the requirement of privity between the maker and his dealers and the reasonably expected ultimate consumer. In that way the burden of losses consequent upon use of defective articles is borne by those who are in a position to either control the danger or make an equitable distribution of the losses when they do occur. As Harper & James put it, 'The interest in consumer protection calls for warranties by the maker that Do run with the goods, to reach all who are likely to be hurt by the use of the unfit commodity for a purpose ordinarily to be expected.' 2 Harper & James, supra 1571, 1572; also see, 1535; Prosser, supra, 506–511.

Although only a minority of jurisdictions have thus far departed from the requirement of privity, the movement in that direction is most certainly gathering momentum. Liability to the ultimate consumer in the absence of direct contractual connection has been predicated upon a variety of theories. Some courts hold that the warranty runs with the article like a covenant running with land; others recognize a third-party beneficiary thesis; still others rest their decision on the ground that public policy requires recognition of a warranty made directly to the consumer.

Most of the cases where lack of privity has not been permitted to interfere with recovery have involved food and drugs. In fact, the rule as to such products has been characterized as an exception to the general doctrine. But more recently courts, sensing the inequity of such limitation, have moved into broader fields: home permanent wave set; soap detergent; inflammable cowboy suit (by clear implication); exploding bottle; defective emery wheel; defective wire rope; defective cinder blocks.

We see no rational doctrinal basis for differentiating between a fly in a bottle of beverage and a defective automobile. The unwholesome beverage may bring illness to one person, the defective car, with its great potentiality for harm to the driver, occupants, and others, demands even less adherence to the narrow barrier of privity. In *Mannsz v. Macwhyte Co.*, supra, Chief Judge Biggs, speaking for the Third Circuit Court of Appeals, said: 'We think it is clear that whether the approach to the problem be by way of warranty or under the doctrine of negligence, the requirement of privity between the injured party and the manufacturer of the article which has injured him has been obliterated from the Pennsylvania law. The abolition of the doctrine occurred first in the food cases, next in the beverage decisions and now it has been extended to those cases in which the article manufactured, not dangerous or even beneficial if properly made, injured a person because it was manufactured improperly.' 155 F.2d at pages 449–450.

Under modern conditions the ordinary layman, on responding to the importuning of colorful advertising, has neither the opportunity nor the capacity to inspect or to determine the fitness of an automobile for use; he must rely on the manufacturer who has control of its construction, and to some degree on the dealer who, to the limited extent called for by the manufacturer's instructions, inspects and services it before delivery. In such a marketing milieu his remedies and those of persons who properly claim through him should not depend 'upon the intricacies of the law of sales. The obligation of the manufacturer should not be based alone on privity of contract. It should rest, as was once said, upon 'the demands of social justice.'' *Mazetti v. Armour & Co.*, 75 Wash. 622 (Sup.Ct.1913). 'If privity of contract is required,' then, under the circumstances of modern merchandising, 'privity of contract exists in the consciousness and understanding of all right-thinking persons.' *Madouros v. Kansas City Coca–Cola Bottling Co.*, supra, 90 S.W.2d at page 450.

Accordingly, we hold that under modern marketing conditions, when a manufacturer puts a new automobile in the stream of trade and promotes its purchase by the public, an implied warranty that it is reasonably suitable for use as such accompanies it into the hands of the ultimate purchaser. Absence of agency between the manufacturer and the dealer who makes the ultimate sale is immaterial.

II.

The Effect of the Disclaimer and Limitation of Liability Clauses on the Implied Warranty of Merchantability.

Judicial notice may be taken of the fact that automobile manufacturers, including Chrysler Corporation, undertake large scale advertising programs over television, radio, in newspapers, magazines and all media of communication in order to persuade the public to buy their products. As has been observed above, a number of jurisdictions, conscious of modern marketing practices, have declared that when a manufacturer engages in advertising in order to bring his goods and their quality to the attention of the public and thus to create consumer demand, the representations made constitute an express warranty running directly to a buyer who purchases in reliance thereon. The fact that the sale is consummated with an independent dealer does not obviate that warranty.

In view of the cases in various jurisdictions suggesting the conclusion which we have now reached with respect to the implied warranty of merchantability, it becomes apparent that manufacturers who enter into promotional activities to stimulate consumer buying may incur warranty obligations of either or both the express or implied character. These developments in the law inevitably suggest the inference that the form of express warranty made part of the Henningsen purchase contract was devised for general use in the automobile industry as a possible means of avoiding the consequences of the growing judicial acceptance of the thesis that the described express or implied warranties run directly to the consumer.

In the light of these matters, what effect should be given to the express warranty in question which seeks to limit the manufacturer's liability to replacement of defective parts, and which disclaims all other warranties, express or implied? In assessing its significance we must keep in mind the general principle that, in the absence of fraud, one who does not choose to read a contract before signing it, cannot later relieve himself of its burdens. *Fivey v. Pennsylvania R.R. Co.*, 67 N.J.L. 627 (E. & A.1902). And in applying that principle, the basic tenet of freedom of competent parties to contract is a factor of importance. But in the framework of modern commercial life and business practices, such rules cannot be applied on a strict, doctrinal basis. The conflicting interests of the buyer and seller must be evaluated realistically and justly, giving due weight to the social policy evinced by the Uniform Sales Act, the progressive decisions of the courts engaged in administering it, the mass production methods of manufacture and distribution to the public, and the bargaining position occupied by the ordinary consumer in such an economy. This history of the law shows that legal doctrines, as first expounded, often prove to be inadequate under the impact of later experience. In such case, the need for justice has stimulated the necessary qualifications or adjustments.

In these times, an automobile is almost as much a servant of convenience for the ordinary person as a household utensil. For a multitude of other persons it is a necessity. Crowded highways and filled parking lots are a commonplace of our existence. There is no need to look any farther than the daily newspaper to be convinced that when an automobile is defective, it has great potentiality for harm.

No one spoke more graphically on this subject than Justice Cardozo in the landmark case of *MacPherson v. Buick Motor Co.*, 217 N.Y. 382 (Ct.App.1916):

'Beyond all question, the nature of an automobile gives warning of probable danger if its construction is defective. This automobile was designed to go 50 miles per hour. Unless its wheels were sound and strong, injury was almost certain. It was as much a thing of danger as a defective engine for a railroad. The dealer was indeed the one person of whom it might be said with some approach to certainty that by him the car would not be used. Precedents drawn from the days of travel by stagecoach do not fit the conditions of travel to-day. The principle that the danger must be imminent does not change, but the things subject to the principle do change. They are whatever the needs of life in a developing civilization require them to be.'

In the 44 years that have intervened since that utterance, the average car has been constructed for almost double the speed mentioned; 60 miles per hour is permitted on our parkways. The number of automobiles in use has multiplied many times and the hazard to the user and the public has increased proportionately. The Legislature has intervened in the public interest, not only to regulate the manner of operation on the highway but also to require periodic inspection of motor vehicles and to impose a duty on manufacturers to adopt certain safety devices and methods in their construction. R.S. 39:3–43 et seq., N.J.S.A. It is apparent that the public has an interest not only in the safe manufacture of automobiles, but also, as shown by the Sales Act, in protecting the rights and remedies of purchasers, so far as it can be accomplished consistently with our system of free enterprise. In a society such as ours, where the automobile is a common and necessary adjunct of daily life, and where its use is so fraught with danger to the driver, passengers and the public, the manufacturer is under a special obligation in connection with the construction, promotion and sale of his cars. Consequently, the courts must examine purchase agreements closely to see if consumer and public interests are treated fairly. What influence should these circumstances have on the restrictive effect of Chrysler's express warranty in the framework of the purchase contract? As we have said, warranties originated in the law to safeguard the buyer and not to limit the liability of the seller or manufacturer. It seems obvious in this instance that the motive was to avoid the warranty obligations which are normally incidental to such sales. The language gave little and withdrew much. In return for the delusive remedy of replacement of defective parts at the factory, the buyer is said to have accepted the exclusion of the maker's liability for personal injuries arising from the breach of the warranty, and to have agreed to the elimination of any other express or implied warranty. An instinctively felt sense of justice cries out against such a sharp bargain. But does the doctrine that a person is bound by his signed agreement, in the absence of fraud, stand in the way of any relief?

In the modern consideration of problems such as this, Corbin suggests that practically all judges are 'chancellors' and cannot fail to be influenced by any equitable doctrines that are available. And he opines that 'there is sufficient flexibility in the concepts of fraud, duress, misrepresentation and undue influence, not to mention differences in economic bargaining power' to enable the courts to avoid enforcement of unconscionable provisions in long printed standardized contracts. 1 Corbin on Contracts (1950) s 128, p. 188. Freedom of contract is not such an immutable doctrine as to admit of no qualification in the area in which we are concerned. As Chief Justice Hughes said in his dissent in *Morehead v. People of State of New York ex rel. Tipaldo*, 298 U.S. 587(1936):

'We have had frequent occasion to consider the limitations on liberty of contract. While it is highly important to preserve that liberty from arbitrary and capricious interference, it is also necessary to prevent its abuse, as otherwise it could be used to override all public interests and thus in the end destroy the very freedom of opportunity which it is designed to safeguard.'

That sentiment was echoed by Justice Frankfurter in his dissent in *United States v. Bethlehem Steel Corp.*, 315 U.S. 289 (1942):

'It is said that familiar principles would be outraged if Bethlehem were denied recovery on these contracts. But is there any principle which is more familiar or more firmly embedded in the history of Anglo–American law than the basic doctrine that the courts will not permit themselves to be used as instruments of inequity and injustice? Does any principle in our law have more universal application than the doctrine that courts will not enforce transactions in which the relative positions of the parties are such that one has unconscionably taken advantage of the necessities of the other?

'These principles are not foreign to the law of contracts. Fraud and physical duress are not the only grounds upon which courts refuse to enforce contracts. The law is not so primitive that it sanctions every injustice except brute force and downright fraud. More specifically, the courts generally refuse to lend themselves to the enforcement of a 'bargain' in which one party has unjustly taken advantage of the economic necessities of the other.'

The traditional contract is the result of free bargaining of parties who are brought together by the play of the market, and who meet each other on a footing of approximate economic equality. In such a society there is no danger that freedom of contract will be a threat to the social order as a whole. But in present-day commercial life the standardized mass contract has appeared. It is used primarily by enterprises with strong bargaining power and position. 'The weaker party, in need of the goods or services, is frequently not in a position to shop around for better terms, either because the author of the standard contract has a monopoly (natural or artificial) or because all competitors use the same clauses. His contractual intention is but a subjection more or less voluntary to terms dictated by the stronger party, terms whose consequences are often understood in a vague way, if at all.' Kessler, *Contracts of Adhesion–Some Thoughts About Freedom of Contract*,' 43 Colum.L.Rev. 629, 632 (1943). Such standardized contracts have been described as those in which one predominant party will dictate its law to an undetermined multiple rather than to an individual. They are said to resemble a law rather than a meeting of the minds. *Siegelman v. Cunard White Star*, 221 F.2d 189, 206 (2 Cir.1955).

Vold, in the recent revision of his Law of Sales (2d ed. 1959) at page 447, wrote of this type of contract and its effect upon the ordinary buyer:

'In recent times the marketing process has been getting more highly organized than ever before. Business units have been expanding on a scale never before known. The standardized contract with its broad disclaimer clauses is drawn by legal advisers of sellers widely organized in trade associations. It is encountered on every hand. Extreme inequality of bargaining between buyer and seller in this respect is now often conspicuous. Many buyers no longer have any real choice in the matter. They must often accept what they can get though accompanied by broad disclaimers. The terms of these disclaimers deprive them of all substantial protection with regard to the quality of the goods. In effect, this is by force of contract between very unequal parties. It throws the risk of defective articles on the most dependent party. He has the least individual power to avoid the presence of defects. He also has the least individual ability to bear their disastrous consequences.'

The warranty before us is a standardized form designed for mass use. It is imposed upon the automobile consumer. He takes it or leaves it, and he must take it to buy an automobile. No bargaining is engaged in with respect to it. In fact, the dealer through whom it comes to the buyer is without authority to alter it; his function is ministerial-simply to deliver it. The form warranty is not only standard with Chrysler but, as mentioned above, it is the uniform warranty of the Automobile Manufacturers Association. Members of the Association are: General Motors, Inc., Ford, Chrysler, Studebaker–Packard, American Motors, (Rambler), Willys Motors, Checker Motors Corp., and International Harvester Company. Automobile Facts and Figures (1958 Ed., Automobile Manufacturers Association) 69. Of these companies, the 'Big Three' (General Motors, Ford, and Chrysler) represented 93.5% of the passenger-car production for 1958 and the independents 6.5%. Standard & Poor (Industrial Surveys, Autos, Basic Analysis, June 25, 1959) 4109. And for the same year the 'Big Three' had 86.72% of the total passenger vehicle registrations. Automotive News, 1959 Almanac (Slocum Publishing Co., Inc.) p. 25.

The gross inequality of bargaining position occupied by the consumer in the automobile industry is thus apparent. There is no competition among the car makers in the area of the express warranty. Where can the buyer go to negotiate for better protection? Such control and limitation of his remedies are inimical to the public welfare and, at the very least, call for great care by the courts to avoid injustice through application of strict common-law principles of freedom of contract. Because there is no competition among the motor vehicle manufacturers with respect to the scope of protection guaranteed to the buyer, there is no incentive on their part to stimulate good will in that field of public relations. Thus, there is lacking a factor existing in more competitive fields, one which tends to guarantee the safe construction of the article sold. Since all competitors operate in the same way, the urge to be careful is not so pressing.

Although the courts, with few exceptions, have been most sensitive to problems presented by contracts resulting from gross disparity in buyer-seller bargaining positions, they have not articulated a general principle condemning, as opposed to public policy, the imposition on the buyer of a skeleton warranty as a means of limiting the responsibility of the manufacturer. They have endeavored thus far to avoid a drastic departure from age-old tenets of freedom of contract by adopting doctrines of strict construction, and notice and knowledgeable assent by the buyer to the attempted exculpation of the seller. Accordingly to be found in the cases are statements that disclaimers and the consequent limitation of liability will not be given effect if 'unfairly procured'; if not brought to the buyer's attention and he was not made understandingly aware of it; or if not clear and explicit.

The rigid scrutiny which the courts give to attempted limitations of warranties and of the liability that would normally flow from a transaction is not limited to the field of sales of goods. Clauses on baggage checks restricting the liability of common carriers for loss or damage in transit are not enforceable unless the limitation is fairly and honestly negotiated and understandingly entered into. If not called specifically to the patron's attention, it is not binding. It is not enough merely to show the form of a contract; it must appear also that the agreement was understandingly made. The same holds true in cases of such limitations on parcel check room tickets; and on storage warehouse receipts; on automobile parking lot or garage tickets or claim checks; as to exculpatory clauses in leases releasing a landlord of apartments in a multiple dwelling house from all liability for negligence where inequality of bargaining exists. And the validity of release clauses in orders signed by a depositor directing a bank to stop payment of his check, exonerating the bank from liability for negligent payment, has been seriously questioned on public policy grounds in this State, *Reinhardt v. Passaic–Clifton Nat. Bank*, 16 N.J.Super. 430, 436 (App.Div.1951). Elsewhere they have been declared void as opposed to public policy. *Speroff v. First–Cent. Trust Co.*, 149 Ohio St. 415 (Sup.Ct. 1948).

French v. Bekins Moving & Storage Co., supra (118 Colo. 424), is particularly significant in the present connection. There the patron signed a storage receipt which contained blanks in which were written the details of removal of the household articles, charges and other information. Toward the bottom, in 'smaller poorly printed five-point type' were eight lines authorizing the handling of the goods at a limited valuation. Plaintiff testified that she did not read the provision and no one informed her of it or of its implications. The Supreme Court of Colorado, in commenting upon the clause, said:

"While a warehouseman may not avoid his liability for negligence, he may nevertheless stipulate with the owner as to what the extent of the latter's recovery shall be, where the rate charged the owner is based upon an agreed valuation which is put upon the property. If the condition was to become a part of the contract, it was necessary that plaintiff's attention be called to it, and that she be advised that the rate to be charged was a reduced rate to be applied in consideration of her consent to the limitation of defendant's liability.'' 195 P.2d at page 971.

It is true that the rule governing the limitation of liability cases last referred to is generally applied in situations said to involve services of a public or semi-public nature. Typical, of course, are the public carrier or storage or parking lot cases. But in recent times the books have not been barren of instances of its application in private contract controversies. In the last named matter, which has been noted earlier, the court relied upon the public interest cases as authority. It said:

'Although these cases have to do with limitation on the liability of common carriers, their reasoning applies with equal force to the facts in the case at bar. When a party to a contract seeks to bind the other party with the unyielding thongs of a warrant of attorney-confession of judgment, a device not ordinarily expected by a homeowner in a simple agreement for alterations and repairs, the inclusion of such a self-abnegating provision must appear in the body of the contract and cannot be incorporated by casual reference with a designation not its own.' 97 A.2d at page 238.

Basically, the reason a contracting party offering services of a public or quasi-public nature has been held to the requirements of fair dealing, and, when it attempts to limit its liability, of securing the understanding consent of the patron or consumer, is because members of the public generally have no other means of fulfilling the specific need represented by the contract. Having in mind the situation in the automobile industry as detailed above, and particularly the fact that the limited warranty extended by the manufacturers is a uniform one, there would appear to be no just reason why the principles of all of the cases set forth should not chart the course to be taken here.

It is undisputed that the president of the dealer with whom Henningsen dealt did not specifically call attention to the warranty on the back of the purchase order. The form and the arrangement of its face, as described above, certainly would cause the minds of reasonable men to differ as to whether notice of a yielding of basic rights stemming from the relationship with the manufacturer was adequately given. The words 'warranty' or 'limited warranty' did not even appear in the fine print above the place for signature, and a jury might well find that the type of print itself was such as to promote lack of attention rather than sharp scrutiny. The inference from the facts is that Chrysler placed the method of communicating its warranty to the purchaser in the hands of the dealer. If either one or both of them wished to make certain that Henningsen became aware of that agreement and its purported implications, neither the form of the document nor the method of expressing the precise nature of the obligation intended to be assumed would have presented any difficulty.

But there is more than this. Assuming that a jury might find that the fine print referred to reasonably served the objective of directing a buyer's attention to the warranty on the reverse side, and, therefore, that he should be charged with awareness of its language, can it be said that an ordinary layman would realize what he was relinquishing in return for what he was being granted? Under the law, breach of warranty against defective parts or workmanship which caused personal injuries would entitle a buyer to damages even if due care were used in the manufacturing process. Because of the great potential for harm if the vehicle was defective, that right is the most important and fundamental one arising from the relationship. Difficulties so frequently encountered in establishing negligence in manufacture in the ordinary case make this manifest. Any ordinary layman of reasonable intelligence, looking at the phraseology, might well conclude that Chrysler was agreeing to replace defective parts and perhaps replace anything that went wrong because of defective workmanship during the first 90 days or 4,000 miles of operation, but that he would not be entitled to a new car. It is not unreasonable to believe that the entire scheme being conveyed was a proposed remedy for physical deficiencies in the car. In the context of this warranty, only the abandonment of all sense of justice would permit us to hold that, as a matter of law, the phrase 'its obligation under this warranty being limited to making good at its factory any part or parts thereof' signifies to an ordinary reasonable person that he is relinquishing any personal injury claim that might flow from the use of a defective automobile. Such claims are nowhere mentioned. The draftsmanship is reflective of the care and skill of the Automobile Manufacturers Association in undertaking to avoid warranty obligations without drawing too much attention to its effort in that regard. No one can doubt that if the will to do so were present, the ability to inform the buying public of the intention to disclaim liability for injury claims arising from breach of warranty would present no problem.

In this connection, attention is drawn to the Plymouth Owner Certificate mentioned earlier. Obviously, Chrysler is aware of it because the New Car Preparation Service Guide sent from the factory to the dealer directs that it be given to the purchaser. That certificate contains a paragraph called 'Explanation of Warranty.' Its entire tenor relates to replacement of defective parts. There is nothing about it to stimulate the idea that the intention of the warranty is to exclude personal injury claims.

The task of the judiciary is to administer the spirit as well as the letter of the law. On issues such as the present one, part of that burden is to protect the ordinary man against the loss of important rights through what, in effect, is the unilateral act of the manufacturer. The status of the automobile industry is unique. Manufacturers are few in number and strong in bargaining position. In the matter of warranties on the sale of their products, the Automotive Manufacturers Association has enabled them to present a united front. From the standpoint of the purchaser, there can be no arms length negotiating on the subject. Because his capacity for bargaining is so grossly unequal, the inexorable conclusion which follows is that he is not permitted to bargain at all. He must take or leave the automobile on the warranty terms dictated by the maker. He cannot turn to a competitor for better security.

Public policy is a term not easily defined. Its significance varies as the habits and needs of a people may vary. It is not static and the field of application is an ever increasing one. A contract, or a particular provision therein, valid in one era may be wholly opposed to the public policy of another. Courts keep in mind the principle that the best interests of society demand that persons should not be unnecessarily restricted in their freedom to contract. But they do not hesitate to declare void as against public policy contractual provisions which clearly tend to the injury of the public in some way. *Hodnick v. Fidelity Trust Co.*, 96 Ind.App. 342 (App.Ct.1932).

Public policy at a given time finds expression in the Constitution, the statutory law and in judicial decisions. In the area of sale of goods, the legislative will has imposed an implied warranty of merchantability as a general incident of sale of an automobile by description. The warranty does not depend upon the affirmative intention of the parties. It is a child of the law; it annexes itself to the contract because of the very nature of the transaction. *Minneapolis Steel & Machinery Co. v. Casey Land Agency*, 51 N.D. 832 (Sup.Ct.1924). The judicial process has recognized a right to recover damages for personal injuries arising from a breach of that warranty. The disclaimer of the implied warranty and exclusion of all obligations except those specifically assumed by the express warranty signify a studied effort to frustrate that protection. True, the Sales Act authorizes agreements between buyer and seller qualifying the warranty obligations. But quite obviously the Legislature contemplated lawful stipulations (which are determined by the circumstances of a particular case) arrived at freely by parties of relatively equal bargaining strength. The lawmakers did not authorize the automobile manufacturer to use its grossly disproportionate bargaining power to relieve itself from liability and to impose on the ordinary buyer, who in effect has no real freedom of choice, the grave danger of injury to himself and others that attends the sale of such a dangerous instrumentality as a defectively made automobile. In the framework of this case, illuminated as it is by the facts and the many decisions noted, we are of the opinion that Chrysler's attempted disclaimer of an implied warranty of merchantability and of the obligations arising there from is so inimical to the public good as to compel an adjudication of its invalidity.

III.

The Dealer's Implied Warranty.

The principles that have been expounded as to the obligation of the manufacturer apply with equal force to the separate express warranty of the dealer. This is so, irrespective of the absence of the relationship of principal and agent between these defendants, because the manufacturer and the Association establish the warranty policy for the industry. The bargaining position of the dealer is inextricably bound by practice to that of the maker and the purchaser must take or leave the automobile, accompanied and encumbered as it is by the uniform warranty.

Moreover, it must be remembered that the actual contract was between Bloomfield Motors, Inc., and Claus Henningsen, and that the description of the car sold was included in the purchase order. Therefore, R.S. 46:30–21(2), N.J.S.A., annexed an implied warranty of merchantability to the agreement. It remains operative unless the disclaimer and liability limitation clauses were competent to exclude it and the ordinary remedy for its breach. It has been said that this doctrine is harsh on retailers who generally have only a limited opportunity for inspection of the car. But, as Chief Judge Cardozo said in Ryan, supra:

'The burden may be heavy. It is one of the hazards of the business.'

'In such circumstances, the law casts the burden on the seller, who may vouch in the manufacturer, if the latter was to blame. The loss in its final incidence will be borne where it is placed by the initial wrong.' 175 N.E. at pages 106 and 107.

Re-examination of the purchase contract discloses an ambiguous situation with respect to the warranty position of the dealer. Section 7, on the reverse side thereof, says no warranties, express or implied, are made by the dealer or manufacturer except the express warranty of the manufacturer discussed above. However, the last paragraph of the section says that: 'The dealer also agrees to promptly perform and fulfill all terms and conditions of the owner service policy.' That policy, as noted above, sets forth the same manufacturer's warranty and then adds a stipulation substituting 'dealer' in the context wherever 'manufacturer' appears. Presumably the intention was to incorporate the policy into the sales contract by reference. Accepting that to be the dealer's intention, the binding character of the limitation on its liability to the buyer under the warranty is even less apparent than in the case of Chrysler. The uncontradicted proof shows that the policy was not shown or given to Henningsen prior to or at the time of execution of the sales agreement; it was delivered with the car. No one suggests that the clause limiting the dealer's liability to replacement of defective parts and excluding implied warranties as well as responsibility for personal injury claims was specifically brought to Henningsen's attention, or that any attempt was made to make him understand that he was yielding his right, and that of any third person claiming in his right, to recover for such injuries.

For the reasons set forth in Part I hereof, we conclude that the disclaimer of an implied warranty of merchantability by the dealer, as well as the attempted elimination of all obligations other than replacement of defective parts, are violative of public policy and are void.

The trial court submitted to the jury, on the same basis as in the claim against the manufacturer, the issue of whether the disclaimer provisions in the contract were fairly procured by the dealer. The dealer also contends that the language is susceptible of the conclusion that the jurors were told as a matter of law that an implied warranty of merchantability came into existence once the sale was made by him. As we have said, a reasonable purport of the instructions in context is that upon the evidence adduced at the trial a decision was to be made as to whether the disclaimer clauses were valid, and if it was found that they were not valid, then an implied warranty existed, breach of which would support plaintiffs' action. Submission of the case to the jury on that basis represented more favorable treatment than the dealer was entitled to receive. But assuming the contention to be correct that the only conclusion to be drawn from the court's statements is that the jury were told that an implied warranty of merchantability arose from the sale as a matter of law, and that they were to decide if the proof demonstrated a breach of it, such advice was correct for the public policy reasons already expressed. Under the circumstances, there is nothing in defendant Bloomfield Motors' criticism of the charge on that score which would warrant reversal of the judgment.

Under all of the circumstances outlined above, the judgments in favor of the plaintiffs and against the defendants are affirmed.

* * *

Ten days after the plaintiff in *Henningsen* bought a new Plymouth, the car's steering mechanism failed and the plaintiff crashed into a brick wall, destroying the car and seriously injuring herself. The plaintiff sued, and the defendant answered by asserting a contract clause, buried deep within the pre-printed form contract through which the car was sold, broadly disavowing both express and implied warranties in respect of the car. The *Henningsen* court refused to give the disclaimer effect. In reaching this conclusion, the court repeatedly emphasized the "gross inequality of bargaining position occupied by the consumer in the automobile industry." The court observed that the form was long, detailed, technically drafted, and hence difficult to read and understand; it observed that the structure of the sales context rendered the buyer literally incapable of bargaining to alter the disclaimer even if she did come to understand it; and it observed that the disclaimer "is not only standard with [Plymouth], but is the uniform warranty of the Automobile Manufacturer's Association," whose members almost entirely filled out the market for cars, rendering the plaintiff incapable of avoiding the disclaimer by taking her custom to another seller.

These observations were accurate, as far as they went. But it is far from clear that the features of form contracts that the *Henningsen* court observed in themselves render the contracts exploitative, inefficient, or coercive. The drawbacks of contracts of adhesion should not be overstated.

In particular, many of the same mechanisms that discipline mass-markets in other respects may also serve to discipline the crafting and promulgation of form contracts, including in ways that correct for the exploitation, inefficiency, and manipulation that such contracts might otherwise produce. Most notably, competition for contract terms among the drafters of forms will exert pressure to craft forms that maximize surplus and will drive down the share of surplus that the term-makers may keep for themselves. The modern auto industry illustrates this point, indeed with respect specifically to warranties: car companies today expressly and prominently compete in their warranties (think of Hyundai's advertisements trumpeting a "ten-year 100,000 mile" guarantee), offering much more generous terms than the law requires. At the very least, therefore, those who oppose contracts of adhesion along functionalist lines must explain why such competition for contract terms should be especially susceptible of market failures and therefore subject to special judicial oversight that is not applied to other elements of contracts, for example concerning the quality or variety of the physical attributes of goods sold.[7] Providing the required explanation is made more difficult by the fact that, under certain conditions, a relatively small proportion of sophisticated term-takers—who read and understand form contracts and thus accurately value their terms—can sustain market equilibria in which term-makers provide efficient and fair terms for all term-takers.[8]

Moreover, although *Henningsen* emphasizes the term-makers' monopoly power, monopolists have no special reason to draft sub-optimal contract terms. A monopolist, unlike a seller in a competitive market, can extract surplus from her customers. She therefore wishes to face as large an aggregate demand as she can, to maximize the surplus out of which she may extract her monopoly rents. Typically, the monopolist will do so by making her product as appealing to her customers as she can, including by making her contracts as appealing to term-takers as she can. None of this denies that the monopolist seeks to exploit her customers. But there is no simple, general reason to think that contracts of adhesion add to her exploitative powers or that their use indicates that exploitation is occurring.

Finally, and perhaps most importantly, functionalist approaches to contract (regardless of whether they proceed in terms of efficiency, fairness, or freedom) must also acknowledge that, insofar as they reduce various transactions costs, contracts of adhesion have an appealing side that directly counterbalances their demerits. To begin with, they are "a rational and economically efficient response to the rapidity of market transactions and the high cost of negotiations"[9] in a mass-consumption economy. Moreover, reduced direct transactions costs of contracting—reduced costs of fixing the terms of a bargain—do not exhaust the benefits offered by form contracts. Thus, as has long been familiar, form contracts also serve much more generally to "stabilize [firms'] market relationships and serve

---

7. Critics have indeed long offered such explanations, speculating that the inability or unwillingness of persons presented with form contracts (typically consumers) to read and understand the forms allows form-drafters to insert exploitative terms. See, e.g., W. David Slawson, *Standard Form Contracts and Democratic Control Over the Lawmaking Power*, 84 HARV. L. REV. 529, 531 (1970); Todd. D. Rakoff, *Contracts of Adhesion: An Essay in Reconstruction*, 96 HARV. L. REV. 1173, 1225–29 (1983). More recently, speculation has given way to systematic empirical study. See, e.g., Robert A. Hillman & Jeffrey J. Rachlinsky, *Standard Form Contracting in the Electronic Age*, 77 N.Y.U. L. REV. 429 (2002); Russell Korobkin, *Bounded Rationality, Standard Form Contracts, and Unconscionability*, 70 U. CHI. L. REV. 1203 (2003).

8. See Alan Schwartz and Louis L. Wilde, *Imperfect Information in Markets for Contract Terms: The Examples of Warranties and Security Interests*, 69 VA. L. REV. 1387 (1983).

9. ARTHUR LINTON CORBIN, CORBIN ON CONTRACTS s. 1.4 (page 14) (rev. ed. 1993). This has not been lost on a wide range of courts. *See, e.g., Lackey v. Green Tree Fin. Corp.*, 330 S.C. 388, 395–96 (Ct. App. 1998).

the needs of a hierarchical and internally segmented [firm] structure."[10] They are a technique of firm management: for example, form contracts facilitate coordination among a firm's several departments (sales, collection, customer service, and so on), and they help to control wayward agents who might otherwise bind a firm in undesirable ways.[11] And customers, all else equal, prefer to deal with well-managed than poorly managed firms, as good management reduces firms' costs and increases the quality of their outputs and thus increases the contractual surplus out of which customers take their shares.

These examples may be multiplied—so much so that it seems plausible that bespoke contracting is just as inefficient in a mass-market economy containing large and complex firms as bespoke manufacturing. Nor have functionalist courts remained innocent of that possibility, as the following opinion illustrates.

Northwestern Nat'l Ins. Co. v. Donovan

United States Court of Appeals for the Seventh Circuit, 1990.
916 F.2d 372.

■ POSNER, CIRCUIT JUDGE.

An insurance company appeals from the dismissal, for want of personal jurisdiction, of five diversity breach of contract suits that it brought in a federal district court in Wisconsin. The principal ground of appeal and the only one we need discuss is that the defendants consented, in a valid forum-selection clause contained in the contract on which the suits are based, to defend the suits in Wisconsin.

The parties agree that the validity of the clause is a matter of federal common law even though state law controls the substantive issues in the suits. There is a division between the circuits on the question, with the Ninth and Eleventh agreeing with the parties to this case that federal common law does indeed govern the question, while the Third believes that the validity of a forum selection clause is a matter of state law. The former position is supported by *Stewart Organization, Inc. v. Ricoh Corp.*, 487 U.S. 22 (1988), and perhaps the circuit split will not survive it. The specific question in *Stewart* was whether, if a party moves for a change of venue under 28 U.S.C. § 1404(a) to the forum designated in the parties' forum selection clause, the court in considering the motion should treat the issue of the clause's validity as one of federal law; the Court said "yes," over a strong dissent by Justice Scalia which argued on grounds independent of the existence of section 1404(a)—particularly the spur to forum shopping that is created when the choice of a federal court over a state court determines the validity of a forum selection clause and hence the venue of the suit—that state law should apply. Probably, therefore, the parties

---

10.   Todd. D. Rakoff, *Contracts of Adhesion: An Essay in Reconstruction*, 96 HARV. L. REV. 1173, 1220 (1983).

11.   These examples come from Rakoff supra note 10 at 1222–23.

before us are correct to concede that the issue of validity is one of federal law, though we need not decide this, since litigants are, within limits not exceeded here, permitted to designate what law shall control their case.

Validity and interpretation are separate issues, and it can be argued that as the rest of the contract in which a forum selection clause is found will be interpreted under the principles of interpretation followed by the state whose law governs the contract, so should that clause be. But this is another issue we need not decide; neither side invokes any interpretive principles founded on a particular state's law.

The defendants are well-to-do individuals (millionaires, in fact, though millionairehood is not what it used to be), Texans for the most part, who early in the last decade bought limited partnerships in one of two closely related tax-shelter enterprises that for simplicity we shall treat as one. In 1984 the enterprise decided it needed more money. The lender to whom it turned required it to secure its promissory notes by a financial obligation bond, issued by Northwestern National Insurance Company, the plaintiff in these cases. Northwestern in turn required the limited partners to agree to indemnify it should it be forced to make good on its bond to the lender. Each of the partners in the cases before us executed the indemnification agreement that Northwestern furnished it, and this is the agreement that contains the forum selection clause. The enterprise later defaulted and Northwestern had to pay off the notes, after which it sued the limited partners to enforce their agreement to indemnify it.

The agreement is a two-page printed form. The first page is dominated by a blank table that the indemnitor is to fill in with his financial statement. The second page, which is on the back of the first, consists of six paragraphs in a small but fully legible typeface. The first and longest paragraph sets forth the indemnitor's obligation to indemnify the insurance company upon the occurrence of stated conditions. The second paragraph, much shorter, sets forth several reservations of no relevance here designed to protect the company. The third and shortest paragraph is the one in issue. It states: "Venue, at the Company's option for litigation and/or arbitration, shall be in the County designated on the front page under the description of the Company's address." That county, we see if we turn back to the first page, is Milwaukee County. The fourth sixth paragraphs are also short: they are a severability clause, a clause binding heirs and other successors, and a clause fixing the date on which the indemnity is to become effective. At the bottom is a space for signatures by the indemnitor and by a notary.

The district judge refused to enforce the forum selection clause and went on to hold that there was no other basis for obtaining jurisdiction over these out-of-state defendants. "In this case the forum selection clause is not compelling ... The clause was not freely negotiated. It is buried in the fine print. It does not clearly state where the case should be litigated. It compels an individual with no contacts with Wisconsin to travel to Wisconsin to defend a case brought by a Wisconsin insurance company. I cannot find that it would be reasonable or just, on the basis of this forum selection clause, to say that [the defendants] waived [their] rights to object to the court's personal jurisdiction over [them]. Because no other basis for personal jurisdiction exists, this action is DISMISSED."

In holding that a forum selection clause should be enforced only if reasonable and just, the district court relied on the *Stewart* case. The question in *Stewart,* however, was not the validity of the forum selection clause, but the criteria for granting a motion for a change of venue under 28 U.S.C. § 1404(a). The question here is not the most convenient place for trying these suits; it is whether the defendants consented to being sued in Wisconsin and by doing so waived their right to object to the jurisdiction of the courts (including federal courts) in Wisconsin over them. This case is governed by *M/S Bremen v. Zapata Off–Shore Co.,* 407 U.S. 1 (1972), and *Heller Financial, Inc. v. Midwhey Powder Co.,* 883 F.2d 1286 (7th Cir. 1989), decisions in which the enforceability of a forum selection clause was the issue. Those decisions bury the outmoded judicial hostility to forum selection clauses. They make clear that since a defendant is deemed to waive (that is, he forfeits) objections to personal jurisdiction or venue simply by not making them in timely fashion, a potential defendant can waive such objections in advance of suit by signing a forum selection clause. Their approach is to treat a forum selection clause basically like any other contractual provision and hence to enforce it unless it is subject to any of the sorts of infirmity, such as fraud and mistake, that justify a court's refusing to enforce a contract, or unless it does not mean what it seems to mean—unless, in other words, properly interpreted it is not a forum selection clause at all.

The attentive reader will have noticed a hedge word in the previous paragraph—"basically." Neither *Bremen* nor *Heller* says outright that a forum selection clause is just like any other contract. *Bremen* for example, using the terminology echoed in Judge Evans' opinion in this case, says that the clause will be enforced unless it is "unreasonable and unjust," which may or may not coincide, at least as a matter of semantics, with "subject to a contractual infirmity," another formulation found in the opinion. 407 U.S. at 12–13, 92 S.Ct. at 1914–15. Why might a court be more suspicious of a forum selection clause contained in a contract than of the contract itself? There are two reasons, one bad, one good. The bad reason is that courts used to look askance at agreements to "oust" their jurisdiction. The best-known example is arbitration. Agreements to arbitrate were not enforceable, because they deprived the objecting party of his right to litigate the parties' dispute in court. No reason why that right should not be waivable was ever given, and the rule that it could not be went down the tubes long ago. Likewise in the bad old days, invoking a forum selection clause as a ground for dismissal of a suit brought in violation of the clause was considered an improper effort to "oust" the court's jurisdiction. *M/S Bremen v. Zapata Off–Shore Co., supra,* 407 U.S. at 9–12. Although the use of such a clause not to defeat but, as in this case, to defend a court's assumption of jurisdiction resulted in taking away another court's jurisdiction over the case, so formalistic was the concept of "ouster" that courts treated the use of such clauses to retain rather than to defeat jurisdiction far more leniently. Annot., 69 A.L.R.2d 1324 (1959). The analogy was to waiving objections to venue and personal jurisdiction, yet it could also have been used in the cases in which a forum selection clause was used to argue for dismissing a suit in a court barred by the clause, for in effect the party opposing dismissal was reneging on his agreement to waive objections to venue and personal jurisdiction in the court designated by the clause. All this nonsense was swept away by *Bremen.*

Yet there really is something special about forum selection clauses after all. They could interfere with the orderly allocation of judicial business and injure other third-party interests (that is, interests of persons other than the parties to the contract containing the clause) as well. Suppose, to take an extreme but illustrative example, that the state and federal courts in Alaska became immensely popular forums for litigating contract disputes and as a result thousands of contracts were signed designating Alaska as the forum in the event of suit. Not only would these clauses impose great burdens on the courts in Alaska; they would impose great burdens on witnesses who were not employees of the parties (the inconvenience to employees would have been taken into account when the clause was drafted). The burdens on the Alaska courts would include not only the obvious ones but also the difficulty of having always to be applying other states' laws, one of the considerations that has been thought to justify limiting parties' power to specify by contract the law to be applied to their dispute if one arises. Restatement (Second) of Conflict of Laws, *supra,* § 187(2)(a).

We are persuaded that the only good reason for treating a forum selection clause differently from any other contract (specifically, from the contract in which the clause appears) is the possibility of adverse effects on third parties. Where that possibility is slight, the clause should be treated like any other contract. What is more, if any inconvenience to third parties can be cured by a change of venue under section 1404(a), that is the route to follow, rather than striking down the clause. This approach enables a clean separation between issues of general contract validity and the third-party consequences which alone justify treating the validity of a forum selection clause differently from that of the contract that contains it.

We acknowledge a tension between our approach and that of the Ninth Circuit in *Shute v. Carnival Cruise Lines,* 897 F.2d 377, 388–89 (9th Cir.1990), cert. granted, 498 U.S. 807, 111 S.Ct. 39, 112 L.Ed.2d 16 (1990), which refused to enforce a forum selection clause contained in a form contract that had not been negotiated. The opinion bristles with hostility to non-negotiated form contracts, but the facts were special. A passenger was injured on a cruise ship and brought suit. The cruise line sought to dismiss the suit on the basis of a forum selection clause printed on the passenger's ticket. The ticket had not even been mailed to the passenger until after she bought it, and as a result she had had no knowledge of the clause until the transaction was complete. *Id.* at 389 n. 11. If ever there was a case for stretching the concept of fraud in the name of unconscionability, it was *Shute;* and perhaps no stretch was necessary.

Before considering the validity of the forum selection clause at bar, we must consider whether it really is a forum selection clause. The clause certainly is not as clear as it could be. It should just have said, "In the event of litigation or arbitration, the undersigned consents to suit, at Northwestern's option, in Milwaukee County." But this is what it must mean. There would be no point to a clause that placed venue in Milwaukee County at Northwestern's option but left the defendants free to object that they were outside the court's jurisdiction. On that reading, what did Northwestern gain by inserting the clause in the indemnity agreement?

So it is a forum selection clause, after all. Is it a valid one? Concretely, should Northwestern be prevented from enforcing the clause because it is "buried in the fine print" and was not "freely negotiated"?—for this is the only ground on which the defendants attack the validity of the clause, as distinct from trying to interpret it away. *Shute* illustrates the widespread judicial suspicion of the form contract—the dreaded "contract of adhesion," the contract that is offered by the authoring party on a take it or leave it basis rather than being negotiated between the parties. The suspicion has never crystallized, however, in a rule making such contracts unenforceable, on grounds of fraud or duress or unconscionability or mistake or what have you, or even presumptively unenforceable as urged by Professor Rakoff and others; the facts in *Shute,* as we saw, were special. Although the vagueness of the concept of unconscionability may seem to place contracts of adhesion under a cloud, they are generally upheld against attacks from that direction. "That the agreement was an adhesion contract—of pre-specified form and not actually negotiated—does not lead to the conclusion that it was unconscionable. . . . [M]ere non-negotiability or inequality in bargaining power do[es] not render an adhesion contract's terms unconscionable." *Harper Tax Services, Inc. v. Quick Tax Ltd.,* 686 F.Supp. 109, 112–13 (D.Md.1988). "The circumstances do indicate an adhesion contract, but mere inequality of bargaining power does not of itself make every term of the contract unconscionable. The questions are rather whether the parties had a reasonable opportunity to read and understand the term, and whether the term itself is unreasonable or oppressive." *Bastian v. Wausau Homes, Inc.,* 635 F.Supp. 201, 203–04 (N.D.Ill.1986).

Perhaps the correct inference to be drawn from these and other cases that might be cited is that "unconscionability" is little more than an umbrella term for fraud, duress, illegality, and violation of a fiduciary relationship—all of which are conventional grounds for invalidating a contract and have nothing special to do with form contracts. Ours is not a bazaar economy in which the terms of every transaction, or even of most transactions, are individually dickered; even when they are, standard clauses are commonly incorporated in the final contract, without separate negotiation of each of them. Form contracts, and standard clauses in individually negotiated contracts, enable enormous savings in transaction costs, and the abuses to which they occasionally give rise can be controlled without altering traditional doctrines, provided those doctrines are interpreted flexibly, realistically. If a clause really is buried in illegible "fine print"—or if as in *Shute* it plainly is neither intended nor likely to be read by the other party—this circumstance may support an inference of fraud, and fraud is a defense to a contract. There was no burial in fine print here. The print is small, but it is not fine; it is large enough that even the pale copies in the appendix on appeal can be read comfortably by the author of this opinion, with his heavily corrected middle-aged eyesight. As the shortest of only six paragraphs, occupying less than a full page of a two-page contract, the forum selection clause is possibly the most, and certainly not the least, conspicuous paragraph; yet the defendants do not suggest that any of the other paragraphs are unenforceable. The clause could of course be made even more conspicuous, but highlighted in this fashion it would throw the other clauses into shadow—inviting litigation over *their* validity.

Could this be a case in which the drafting party has taken advantage of special vulnerabilities known to him to afflict the other party, with the result that what would not be fraud in an ordinary case becomes fraud by virtue of those vulnerabilities? Restatement (Second) of Torts, § 545A, comment a (1977). If the draftsman told a blind man that the contract said thus and so, it would be no defense that the blind man had failed to read the contract. And perhaps most of us are blind when confronted by a parking receipt with disclaimers of liability on the back. There is nothing of that sort here. The defendants are wealthy tax-shelter investors. They knew that by signing the indemnity agreement they were incurring a potential liability to Northwestern. They also knew how great a liability. They had bought their interests in the limited partnership with promissory notes that the partnership wanted to put up as collateral for the loan that it needed. The indemnity agreement in effect empowered Northwestern to enforce the notes against the limited partners in the event that the partnership defaulted on the loan, as it did. Knowing as they did that the agreement imposed a potential liability in the face amount of their notes, it behooved the limited partners to read the agreement with care or show it to their lawyers. If they make a practice of signing contracts without reading them, they must bear the consequences.

Those consequences may seem harsh. The defendants claim that it will be a huge inconvenience for them to defend these suits in Wisconsin. Maybe so. But it is not a gratuitous imposition. For if it proves a huge inconvenience to them to have to trundle up to Milwaukee to attend the trials in these cases (if the cases ever go to trial, which of course most cases do not), it will prove an equally huge convenience to Northwestern to be able to defend these suits in home territory. We may assume, since the market in surety bonds is a competitive one, that the cost savings that accrue to Northwestern from contractual terms that facilitate the enforcement of one of its bonds will be passed on, in part anyway, to the purchaser of those bonds—the enterprise in which the defendants invested—in the form of a lower premium. If so, the defendants were compensated in advance for bearing the burden of which they now complain, and will reap a windfall if they are permitted to repudiate the forum selection clause.

The clause is enforceable. And this means that it is not to be circumvented by the grant of a motion for a change of venue, a motion that has been filed with but not as yet acted on by the district judge. We held in *Heller,* and we repeat, that the signing of a valid forum selection clause is a waiver of the right to move for a change of venue on the ground of inconvenience to the moving party. 883 F.2d at 1293. If there is inconvenience to some third party of which that third party may not even be aware, or to the judicial system itself, then either party to the suit is free to move for a change of venue. But one who has agreed to be sued in the forum selected by the plaintiff has thereby agreed not to seek to retract his agreement by asking for a change of venue on the basis of costs or inconvenience to himself; such an effort would violate the duty of good faith that modern law reads into contractual undertakings. A party can seek to rescind a forum selection clause, as the defendants have sought to do here, but if the attempt fails and the clause is held to be valid, then section 1404(a) may not be used to make an end run around it.

The judgments dismissing the suits are reversed and the cases are remanded for further proceedings consistent with this opinion.

Reversed and Remanded, With Directions.

* * *

The defendants in *Donovan* sought to avoid a forum selection clause contained in a loan agreement made with the plaintiffs. The specific circumstances of the case—concerning the loan and the forum selected—are less important for the current discussion than the fact that the loan agreement, and hence also the forum selection clause at issue, was consummated through a pre-printed form. (Forum selection clauses and their close cousins, arbitration agreements, will be taken up in the next chapter.) The *Donovan* court, per Judge Posner, regarded this as an opportunity to write more generally about the functionalist analysis of contracts of adhesion.

Posner notes that some prominent critics have proposed that the portions of contracts of adhesion that the term-taker cannot reasonably be expected to read and understand gain no legitimacy whatsoever on the basis of standard contract notions such as consent and therefore should be treated as "presumptively unenforceable,"[12] so that they become binding only insofar as they comply with standards in the "public interest."[13] But Posner, citing the various benefits of form contracting, rejects this blanket condemnation of contracts of adhesion. He prefers a more narrowly targeted effort to discourage certain sub-classes of these contracts. This approach, Posner suggests, follows from the structure of functionalist legal analysis, which drives steadily and perhaps even inexorably towards the conclusion that there is in fact no intrinsic or general objection to contracts of adhesion. Whatever objections there are in particular cases may be sub-

---

12. This was Todd Rakoff's view. See Todd. D. Rakoff, *Contracts of Adhesion: An Essay in Reconstruction*, 96 HARV. L. REV. 1173 (1983). He continues to stand by it today and the quoted language was written last year. See Todd D. Rakoff, *The Law and Sociology of Boilerplate* in Omri Ben–Shachar, ed., BOILERPLATE: THE FOUNDATIONS OF MARKET CONTRACTS 200, 200 (2007).

13. W. David Slawson, *Standard Form Contracts and Democratic Control Over the Lawmaking Power*, 84 HARV. L. REV. 529, 566 (1970).

sumed under other contract-law defenses for non-performance in circumstances that are identified, finally, on independent grounds.[14]

Functionalist considerations thus exert a steady pressure towards moderation in criticisms of contracts of adhesion. Contracts of adhesion do indeed impose costs that functionalists recognize. But the costs are often moderated by the very circumstances that give rise to form contracting. Moreover contracts of adhesion also offer compensating advantages, including several important ones that cause such contracts to tend to promote fairness, efficiency, and even freedom. The balance of these functionalist considerations almost certainly favors embracing the adhesion form in many contexts and may even favor embracing contracts of adhesion quite generally. Finally, insofar as the balance of costs and benefits favors embracing contracts of adhesion, that renders reasonable term-takers' general policy of assenting to such contracts even without reading or understanding particular forms. It therefore no longer seems natural (or even sensible) to say that these contracts make term-takers meaningfully unfree. Instead, they are a case in which term-takers—perhaps even knowingly—exploit mechanisms whose details they do not fully understand in a way that serves their general capacity to achieve their ends and hence increases their freedom.

On the functionalist approach, therefore, contracts of adhesion are merely *correlated* with contractual infirmities that must be identified without reference to the adhesion form, rather than *constitutive* of any distinctive infirmities in their own right. And the correlation may well turn out to be quite weak—so weak, indeed, that it would be a mistake to give the category *contracts of adhesion* any free-standing doctrinal status in the law.[15]

---

14. More specifically, Posner observed that "[i]f a clause really is buried in illegible 'fine print'—or if it plainly is neither intended nor likely to be read by the other party—this circumstance may support an inference of fraud, and fraud is a defense to a contract. There was no burial in fine print here. The print is small, but it is not fine; it is large enough that even the pale copies in the appendix on appeal can be read comfortably by the author of this opinion, with his heavily corrected middle-aged eyesight." *Northwestern Nat'l Ins. Co. v. Donovan*, 916 F. 2d 372, 377 (7th Cir. 1990). Other courts have adopted a similar approach. *See, e.g., Seus v. John Nuveen & Co. 146 F. 3d 175, 184 (3d Cir. 1998); Morris v. Snappy Cart Rental, Inc., 84 N.Y. 2d 21, 30 (1994); Aviall, Inc. v. Ryder Sys., 913 F. Supp. 826, 832 (S.D.N.Y. 1996)* ("A court may refuse to enforce an agreement only if the contract is the product of procedural unfairness and suffers from one of the enumerated substantive defects. If either feature is absent, the court will enforce the contract."). See also, Restatement (Second) of Contracts s. 211 cmt c. Thus Farnsworth notes that "[t]he mere fact that [a] contract is one of adhesion is not generally regarded as fatal". E. ALAN FARNSWORTH, CONTRACTS § 4.28, 585 (3d ed. 2004).

An alternative approach that similarly declines to make the contract of adhesion into its own doctrinal category or to support a general skepticism about such contracts requires disclosure of specific substantive terms (or classes of terms) or perhaps even prohibits certain terms entirely. This approach was taken by Arthur Leff in a series of articles. See Arthur Leff, *Unconscionability and the Code—The Emperor's New Clause*, 115 U. PA. L. REV. 485 (1967); Arthur Leff, *Contract as Thing*, 19 AM U. L REV. 13 (1970); Arthur Leff, *Unconscionability and the Crowd—Consumers and the Common Law Tradition*, 31 U. PITT. L. REV. 349 (1970).

15. Even when they are critical and seek to regulate or undo contracts of adhesion, functionalist critiques naturally suggest remedies—most notably, replacing adhesive terms with terms provided by law, in the public interest—that accept the initial retreat from

For a functionalist, this is all as it should be. A careful attention to the benefits as well as the costs of contracts of adhesion, especially if marshaled in the service of identifying legally administrable principles for deciding when the costs exceed the benefits, provides the foundation for sound functionalist legal analysis. And within the functionalist frame, nothing has gone wrong when this careful analysis reports back that the best approach is to deny the category *contract of adhesion* any independent role in analyzing the validity of form contracts.

20.2   CONTRACTS OF ADHESION AND THE CONTRACTUAL FORM

In pursuing this path, functionalist analyses lose touch with at least a part of the intuition that made contracts of adhesion a compelling topic to begin with. This was the lawyerly craft-sense that there is something amiss—misshapen, or degenerate—in even the most efficient and fair contract of adhesion. It seems, somehow, to distort or even to betray the contract *form*—to replace contract with some other mode of legal and economic organization. As the *Henningsen* court observed, contracts of adhesion "resemble a law rather than a meeting of the minds." Functionalist analyses cannot accommodate this intuition. Indeed, functionalist approaches become in a way complicit in and even expand the distortions that contracts of adhesion instigate. The functionalist accepts the law-like rather than contractual character of adhesive arrangements and asks only what type of vertical administration of form contracting is most desirable—

ordinary contracting and merely substitute one non-contractual order for another. As Randy Barnett has observed, this approach, if anything "moves an agreement much further from the consent of the parties and towards a regime in which the legal system supplies terms that others think best." Randy E. Barnett, *Consenting to Form Contracts*, 71 FORDHAM L. REV. 627, 734 (2002). And insofar as they come down in favor of contracts of adhesion, functionalist approaches embrace the retreat from contract proper, so that it has been observed that, for functionalists, it is by now a banality that, "on a theoretical level, boilerplate is a legal phenomenon different from contract." Omri Ben–Shachar, *Introduction* in Omri Ben–Shachar, ed., BOILERPLATE: THE FOUNDATIONS OF MARKET CONTRACTS ix, xiv (2007). Instead, contracts of adhesion have been variously analogized to statutes (See W. David Slawson, *Standard Form Contracts and Democratic Control of Lawmaking Power*, 84 HARV. L. REV. 529 (1971)), products (See Schwartz and Wilde, *Intervening in Markets on the Basis of Imperfect Information: A Legal and Economic Analysis*, 127 U. PA. L. REV. 630 (1979)), and even property (See Henry E. Smith, *Modularity in Contracts: Boilerplate and Information Flow* in Omri Ben–Shachar, ed., BOILERPLATE: THE FOUNDATIONS OF MARKET CONTRACTS 163–175 (2007)). Indeed, boilerplate's departure from the contract form is self-consciously celebrated in the interstices of functionalist analyses, for example in the thought that boilerplate's efficiency is a direct result of its abandoning the intensiveness of communication that characterizes contract-proper in favor of a more extensive form of expression. (See Henry E. Smith, *Modularity in Contracts: Boilerplate and Information Flow* in Omri Ben–Shachar, ed., BOILERPLATE: THE FOUNDATIONS OF MARKET CONTRACTS 163, 163 (2007).)

Contracts of adhesion thus leave the functionalist in a bind. If she rejects their legal validity, she is able to replace them only with legal orderings that—whatever their efficiency or fairness—are even farther removed from the ordinary modalities of contract than the adhesive arrangements that they replace. And if she accepts the legal validity of contracts of adhesion—as functionalists are increasingly inclined to do—she must be willing to enforce such agreements even though their form departs from the forms that characterize contract proper.

administration by term-makers disciplined by market-forces, or administration by legislatures subject to democratic accountability.

If there is something *per se* objectionable in the contract of adhesion, then this must be explained by formalist considerations—the considerations that suggest that contracts of adhesion are, in important respects, not contracts properly-so-called at all. The formalist analysis of contracts of adhesion seeks to render this intuition vivid and theoretically articulate and to explain why it matters. This project once again has its roots directly in the cases.

Steven v. The Fidelity and Casualty Company of New York

Supreme Court of California, 1962.
377 P.2d 284.

■ TOBRINER, JUSTICE.

We point out here why we have concluded that the provisions of an airplane trip insurance policy on the life of the beneficiary's husband did not plainly or clearly provide for non coverage, and why, in the absence of such provision, in this unusual case, the insurer is liable. Accordingly, we do not believe that the judgment for the insurer, rendered after trial without a jury, should stand.

On March 3, 1957, Mr. George A. Steven purchased at Los Angeles, California, a round-trip airplane ticket to Dayton, Ohio. As part of the return trip Mr. Steven's itinerary included a flight from Terre Haute, Indiana, to Chicago, Illinois. Mr. Steven simultaneously purchased for a premium of $2.50 a $62,500 life insurance policy which named his wife, appellant, as the beneficiary.

Mr. Steven bought the policy by means of a vending machine. The policy set out across the top the following specifications: "Do Not Purchase More Than a Total of $62,500 Principal Sum—Nor for Travel on Other Than Scheduled Air Carriers. This Policy Covers on One–Way Trip Only Unless Round Trip Ticket Is Purchased Before Departure." Below this printed statement a box form provided for the insertion on appropriate lines of the insured's name, the name and address of the beneficiary, the point of departure and destination, the extent of the trip as on a one-way or round-trip ticket, the date, the principal sum of insurance ($62,500), the amount of the premium ($2.50), and the insured's signature. The evidence does not clearly show whether at the time of purchase the aperture of the vending machine disclosed the entire top portion of the policy, including the printed warning as to amount and coverage for travel on "scheduled air carriers," or merely the form for the personal data and flight information to be furnished by the purchaser. After obtaining the policy, Mr. Steven, using the envelope provided by the machine, mailed it to his wife.

On March 6, 1957, on his return trip from Dayton, Mr. Steven, according to his original plan, stopped off at Terre Haute. He arrived there between 7 and 8 o'clock in the morning. His round-trip ticket scheduled him to take a Lake Central Airlines plane to Chicago at noon that day. At about that time the public address system at the airport announced that the Lake Central plane had been grounded in Indianapolis and that there would be some delay. After several further announcements of repeated delays, the scheduled Lake Central flight to Chicago was finally cancelled at 4:30 p.m.

The agent of Lake Central Airlines then attempted to arrange for Mr. Steven and three other men substitute means of transportation to Chicago. The agent phoned railroads, bus lines and even an automobile rental company. After concluding that he could not thereby arrange a connection with the scheduled Chicago flight to Los Angeles, the agent took Mr. Steven and the other three men to the office of the Turner Aviation Corporation (hereinafter designated Turner) at the Terre Haute airport and introduced them to the agent there in charge. The Lake Central agent indicated that a flight on a Turner plane provided the only means for Mr. Steven to make his scheduled connection with the Chicago plane, a connection which Mr. Steven particularly desired because an essential work project awaited him in Los Angeles the next morning. Turner agreed to fly the men to Chicago for $36 per person, or, if two more passengers could be obtained, for $21 a person. Two additional passengers were obtained and accordingly Mr. Steven and each of the other passengers paid Turner $21 for his ticket.

Mr. Steven boarded the Turner aircraft, a Piper Tri–Pacer airplane, which took off from the Terre Taute airfield at 5:55 p.m. Some time around 7 p.m. on March 6, 1957, near Grant Park, Illinois, the plane crashed. Mr. Steven suffered fatal injuries.

During March 1957 Turner operated out of Terre Haute under an air-taxi certificate issued either by the Civil Aeronautics Board or the Civil Aeronautics Administration. As of the date of the crash, Turner held no certificate of public convenience and necessity from the Civil Aeronautics Board, the governmental authority empowered to issue such certificates. Neither the State of Illinois nor the State of Indiana grants certificates of public convenience and necessity or other authorization to air carriers of any kind. During March 1957 Turner did not publish schedules and tariffs for regular passenger service between named cities within the boundaries of either Illinois or Indiana at regular and specified times. The plane trip on which the accident occurred was not a regular and scheduled flight of Turner.

The trial court found that the deceased at the time of the accident "was not riding as a passenger on an aircraft operated by a scheduled air carrier, as defined in [the] policy, and further that he was riding a charter plane from Terre Haute, Indiana, to Chicago, Illinois," and concluded that appellant could not recover on the policy.

Applying the principle that ambiguous clauses in insurance policies are to be interpreted against the insurer, we believe, for the reasons we shall set out, the provisions of the policy both as to coverage for a substituted flight and as to coverage for scheduled air carriers must be held to impose liability upon the insurer. We shall also explain why we have concluded that Mr. Steven's failure to exchange his ticket at Terre Haute does not absolve the insurer from such liability.

The special circumstances of this case establish a second reason for our conclusion that the insurer cannot successfully claim that the policy did not cover the substituted transportation. In this type of standardized contract, sold by a vending machine, the insured may reasonably expect coverage for the whole trip which he inserted in the policy, including reasonable substituted transportation necessitated by emergency. If the insurer did not propose such coverage, it should have plainly and clearly brought to the attention of the purchaser such limitation of liability.

We turn to the first point. We must determine whether, when Mr. Steven faced the necessity of arranging substituted transportation at Terre Haute, the policy afforded him clear notice of non coverage of such substituted transportation. We examine the question in the light of the purpose and intent of the parties in entering into the contract, Mr. Steven's knowledge and understanding as a reasonable layman, his normal expectation of the extent of coverage of the policy and the effect, if any, of the substitution of the transportation upon the risk undertaken by the insurer.

The purpose and intent of the insured in taking out the insurance was to obtain insurance protection for the trip. The insured could fairly believe that the policy would cover a reasonable emergency substitution necessitated by the exigencies of the situation. Since weather conditions and mechanical failure upon not infrequent occasions require such substitution, the insured would not ordinarily expect that his insurance would fail in the event of these foreseeable contingencies. Since his contract covered the *trip*, he would not contemplate a hiatus in coverage; he bargained for protection for the whole, not part of, the trip.

A reasonable person, having bought his ticket for a fixed itinerary, and thus having at the moment of purchase of the policy gained insurance protection for the whole trip, would normally expect that if a flight were interrupted by breakdown or other causes, his coverage would apply to substitute transportation for the same flight. If, for instance, the scheduled plane crash-landed, he would certainly assume that the policy covered the emergency relief plane whether or not it were a scheduled airliner. The same normal expectation would apply to the substitution of an alternate plane because the scheduled one had been grounded by mechanical failure.

The risk of injury on the substitute conveyance in many cases will be no greater than the risk on the scheduled flight; in all cases it will be less than if the scheduled airline attempts to fly the scheduled flight despite bad weather or mechanical difficulty. Thus, both in the terms of occurrence and magnitude of risk, substitute emergency transportation falls well within the obligation undertaken by the insurer.

The language of the policy does not specifically exclude the expected coverage for the substituted flight. Neither the insuring clause, the definitions of a scheduled air carrier nor section 3(b) *infra* negates, without ambiguity, protection for the emergency substitute flight.

The insuring clause alludes to a loss occurring "during the first one-way or round airline trip taken by the Insured after the purchase of this policy on Aircraft Operated by a Scheduled Air Carrier as defined below." and does not mention the subject of substitution of another carrier in the event of breakdown. Section 4, which defines "aircraft operated by a scheduled air carrier" differentiates between the scheduled and nonscheduled carriers but likewise does not describe the accorded coverage if an emergency causes the use of a nonscheduled carrier. These sections provide that the policy applies, as the heading in the box states, to the "round trip ticket purchased before departure." Mr. Steven complied with these requirements: he purchased the round trip ticket on the scheduled airliner, and, when initially ensconced upon his plane, enjoyed the protection of his policy.

The only allusion to substituted transportation in the policy, contained in clause 3(b), does not in and of itself exclude coverage for the Turner flight. This provision affirmatively extends coverage to injuries sustained "while riding in or on a land conveyance provided or arranged for, directly or indirectly, by such scheduled air carrier for the transportation of passengers necessitated by an interruption or temporary suspension of such scheduled air carrier's service." It thus makes clear that, at least in some cases, substitute emergency transportation will be included in the policy, and that, despite the narrowing of the insuring clause of the policy to "Aircraft Operated by a Scheduled Air Carrier," coverage may be extended to a nonscheduled non flying vehicle not operated by an air carrier.

The crucial issue resolves into whether the limitation of that extension to "land conveyances" sufficiently overcomes the normal expectation that coverage would extend *to any reasonable form of substitute conveyance*. The clause clearly does not specifically *exclude* substitute emergency aircraft; it does not mention non land conveyances at all. An inference of such non coverage could arise only with the aid of the rule of construction *expressio unius est exclusio alterius*; i.e., that mention of one matter implies the exclusion of all others.

We do not believe the application of the maxim can resolve the present case. The maxim serves as an aid to resolve the ambiguities of a contract. If we invoke the *expressio unius* approach, we must necessarily thereby recognize the ambiguity of the contract; in that event other legal techniques for the resolution of ambiguities, including the rule that they should be interpreted against the draftsman, also come into play. Thus *McNee v. Harold Hensgen & Associates* (1960) 178 Cal.App.2d 881, holds that if the applicability of a contract provision can be determined only by use of the maxim *expressio unius*, the contract is ambiguous, and extrinsic evidence is therefore admissible to prove the intent of the parties.

The rule of resolving ambiguities against the insurer does not serve as a mere tie-breaker; it rests upon fundamental considerations of policy. In view of the somewhat fictional nature of intent in standardized contracts, the considerations which support the rule that ambiguities in the policy are to be interpreted against the insurer are more compelling than those which prompt the application of the mechanical *expressio unius* maxim. We do not believe the maxim should serve to defeat the basic rule that the insurance contract should be interpreted against the draftsman.

In any event, the maxim of *expressio unius*, which is surely a legalistic concept, hardly enters into the thinking of the reasonable layman. As we have stated, we interpret an insurance contract in the light of that understanding. We could not logically conclude that when Mr. Steven, unversed in legal abstractions, boarded the Turner plane at Terre Haute, he invoked this maxim of interpretation.

The facts of this case buttress the above conclusion. Mr. Steven planned a round trip entirely on scheduled air carriers; he purchased his policy with the expectation that it would provide insurance against death or injury in such contingencies as might arise in the course of such a trip. In Terre Haute, Mr. Steven, upon learning that the Lake Central flight had been cancelled, exhausted all of the possibilities of obtaining substitute land transportation. He could complete his original itinerary only by the Turner flight. Indeed, the Lake Central agent suggested the Turner substitution, took him over to the Turner office and introduced him to the Turner agent. While the policy specified coverage for injuries suffered in a *land* conveyance provided by the scheduled carrier, it contains no statement whatsoever as to such substituted *air* conveyance. We do not see how such verbal vacuity can serve as clear and plain notice to the insured of noncoverage.

We therefore conclude that section 3(b) should not be interpreted to restrict coverage exclusively to land conveyances. The policy did not clearly notify Mr. Steven that in spite of his expectation, and in view of the intention of the parties in entering into the contract, the coverage did not extend to a substitute flight in the event of emergency. The provision for substitute transportation did not clearly overcome the normal expectation that coverage would extend to *any reasonable form of substitute conveyance.*

Turning to the second aspect of the policy which affects the substituted Turner flight, that is, the definition of scheduled air carrier, we find that it, too, created an ambiguity and failed to apprise Mr. Steven of the asserted noncoverage.

The definition, set out in the fourth provision of the policy, states: "The words 'Aircraft Operated by a Scheduled Air Carrier' as used in this policy, mean and are defined as follows: (1) aircraft of United States registry, operated on a *regular*, special or chartered flight by a *scheduled air carrier* holding a Certificate of Public Convenience and Necessity issued by the Civil Aeronautics Board and which in accordance therewith files, prints, maintains and publishes schedules and tariffs for regular passenger service between named cities at regular and specified times. Specifically *excluded* from the above definition of 'Aircraft Operated by a Scheduled Air Carrier' are any and all aircraft operated by scheduled *military airlines* and any and all aircraft operated by air carriers recognized, designated, licensed or determined by the governmental authority having jurisdiction over civil aviation as being *irregular or non-scheduled* air carriers." (Emphasis added.)

The regulations of the Civil Aeronautics Board do not divide airlines into scheduled and nonscheduled carriers but, instead, establish a number of classifications. One class consists of carriers holding board certificates of convenience and necessity; airlines of this class comply completely with the definition in the policy of "scheduled air carrier." On the other hand, the only classification which contains the designation "irregular or non-scheduled air carriers" is that of "large irregular carriers," which is defined in 14 Code of Federal Regulations section 291.1 as carriers flying planes of more than 12,500 lbs. weight without certificates of public convenience and necessity, and not flying regular routes.

Turner Aviation did not fall within either of the above classifications. Instead, it held a certificate as an air-taxi operator, defined in 14 Code of Federal Regulations section 298.3 as a carrier using planes of less than 12,500 lbs. weight and not having a certificate of public convenience and necessity. The definition of air-taxi carrier does not mention regularity of flights; with certain exceptions not here pertinent an air-taxi carrier may, without obtaining a certificate of public convenience and necessity, publish and maintain schedules for regular passenger service. Turner, however, did not publish schedules. No evidence was introduced to show whether Turner maintained regular service, although 14 Code of Federal Regulations section 298.21, which prohibits air-taxi operators from holding out to perform "regular" service in competition with scheduled helicopter service, appears to make maintenance of regular schedules the distinction between "regular" and "irregular" air-taxi service.

Since Turner did not file and publish regular schedules, nor possess a certificate of public convenience and necessity, Turner does not fall under the literal affirmative definition of scheduled air carrier in the policy. Neither does Turner qualify under the exclusionary language in the last sentence of clause 4; it was not a military airline and was not designated by government regulations as an irregular carrier. Thus the negative definition of the term in the exclusionary phrase may serve to *extend* coverage to all types of air transport except the two that were specifically excluded.

In summary, the air-taxi carrier constitutes a third category of aircraft under the federal regulations; the air-taxi is neither a scheduled carrier nor a nonscheduled carrier. So regarded, air-taxi carriers are neither included in, nor excluded from, the coverage of the policy; clause 4 creates an ambiguity. "The burden in such a case as this is on the defendant to establish that the words and expressions used not only are susceptible of the construction sought by defendant but that it is the *only* construction which may fairly be placed on them." (*Lachs v. Fidelity & Cas. Co.*, supra, 118 N.E.2d at p. 555; emphasis added.) This burden has not been met.

Nor does the claim of the beneficiary here founder upon the provisions of the policy which require an exchange of tickets. The insurer argues that Mr. Steven lost the protection of the policy because he purchased a ticket from Turner and travelled under that ticket at the time of the crash.

Respondent posits this position upon two policy provisions: (1) the requirement in the last three lines of the insuring clause "that at the time that the Insured sustains such injury he is traveling on a transportation ticket or pass covering the whole of said airline trip issued to him for transportation on an aircraft operated by a scheduled air carrier"; (2) the requirement in clause 2 that on substituted flights "the transportation ticket or pass issued to the Insured for said first airline trip has been exchanged for another ticket or pass issued for transportation on an aircraft operated by a scheduled air carrier on the substituted trip."

We doubt the applicability and effectiveness of these requirements. Neither refers to substitute transportation taken because of the cancellation of a scheduled flight. Clause 2 applies to "a change in itinerary." No change in itinerary occurred here; Mr. Steven took the substitute flight to complete the itinerary. The policy limitation, reasonably interpreted, refers to the situation in which a passenger freely chooses to change his original itinerary, not to the contingency in which he seeks to follow it, and in order to do so obtain alternate transportation because of flight cancellation.

Both clauses were considered in the cases of *Fidelity & Cas. Co. of New York v. Smith* (10th Cir. 1951) 189 F.2d 315, and *Rosen v. Fidelity & Cas. Co. of New York* (E.D. Pa. 1958) 162 F.Supp. 211. In these cases the courts noted that airlines did not customarily accept unused tickets on other lines or issue substitute tickets covering the whole of the trip. Indeed, in *Smith* the court found that it was impossible to exchange tickets. Both courts further noted that the risk would not be affected in the slightest degree by whether or not the passenger exchanged his ticket, cancelled it and used the proceeds to buy substituted transportation, or merely bought the substituted transportation with the expectation of obtaining a later refund. Both courts concluded that the provisions in question would not bar recovery.

Respondent argues that *Smith* and *Rosen* are distinguishable in that there the substituted flights were on scheduled carriers. But the rationale of those cases rests upon the fact that compliance with the ticket exchange requirement is difficult or impossible, and that compliance does not materially affect the insurer's risk. Compliance is no easier with a nonscheduled than a scheduled airline, and even if, as respondent contends, nonscheduled airlines entail a greater risk, surely that risk is not increased by the failure of the passenger to exchange his ticket. Whatever reason there may be to deny liability for injuries occurring on flights of nonscheduled carriers, it can bear no reasonable relation to the enforcement of a ticket exchange requirement for nonscheduled lines and not for scheduled lines.

Whether or not a passenger has exchanged his ticket does not remotely increase the risk borne by the company; furthermore, the exchange of tickets is unusual and at times impossible. Hence the enforcement of the requirement would convert a clause which seemingly extends coverage of the policy for substituted flights into one which denies coverage except in highly unusual situations. Since in the present case appellant asserts, and respondent does not deny, that compliance with the ticket exchange requirement would have been impossible, we conclude that this requirement in the circumstances of this case cannot fairly be enforced against appellant.

If the classic rules of interpretation lead to the conclusion that the policy afforded coverage here, we must point out additionally that they apply with special force in the circumstances of this case. We do not deal here with the orthodox insurance policy sold in the protective aura of the insurer's explanation and discussion of its terms. The vending machine emitted a complex stereotyped document, which, because of the short time elapsing before the start of Mr. Steven's flight, hardly afforded him an opportunity even to read the policy. The mass-made contract, sold by the machine under such conditions, symbolizes the kind of transaction that lends to the accepted rules a special gloss of interpretation. As we shall explain in more detail, the cases have held that in such contracts the expected coverage of the policy can only be defeated by a provision for limitation which has been plainly brought to the attention of the insured.

Nothing in the instant contract or transaction apprised the insured that the protection of the policy would not extend to the substituted emergency flight. The manner of sale of the policy negated any possibility of such notice. The inanimate machine told the purchaser nothing, and even if he had wanted to ask about the coverage in the event of emergency, the box could not have answered. While the testimony leaves us in some doubt as to whether Mr. Steven saw the words in the window of the machine stating "Nor for travel on other than Scheduled Air Carriers," we know that if he did see them, he could neither have read the definition of "scheduled air carrier" nor the clause concerning substitute emergency transportation on "land conveyances." These clauses lay hidden behind the mechanized face of the vendor. Even after Mr. Steven purchased the policy he would only have found such clauses among the many complexities of the instrument. They were inconspicuous clauses, and, as we have stated, they were unclear.

To assume that Mr. Steven read the provisions, or conceivably understood them, is to rest upon hypothesis rather than fact. The insurer *instructed* the purchaser to mail the policy to the beneficiary and provided envelopes for this purpose. Like most purchasers, Mr. Steven, before boarding the plane at the very commencement of the trip, did mail the policy to the beneficiary. The company provided no duplicate. Thus, when Mr. Steven found it necessary at Terre Haute to take the Turner flight he could not have consulted the policy to determine its applicability. Instead, even assuming that three days earlier he had read it carefully, he would have been compelled to rely upon his memory. The policy is about 2,000 words long. It is so tightly drawn that if Mr. Steven had forgotten a single word in clause 3(b) or a short phrase in clause 4 he might well have concluded that the policy covered the Turner trip.

Even upon the highly unrealistic assumption that Mr. Steven surmounted all of these obstacles, the policy still would not have notified him that he was not covered. The policy, in defining scheduled airlines, refers to an airline possessing certificates of public convenience and necessity and filing schedules. Later it attempts to exclude lines designated in government regulations as irregular or nonscheduled. These facts, important in determining whether the Turner flight were covered, obviously do not compose the facts a passenger typically knows. "[The] average man is [not] expected to carry the Civil Aeronautics Act or the Code of Federal Regulations when taking a plane." (*Lachs v. Fidelity & Cas. Co.*, supra, 118 N.E.2d at p. 558.) Neither can he generally be expected to inquire into the nature of the certification of the airline.

The company so arranged this transaction that Mr. Steven could not possibly read the policy before purchase and could not practically consult the policy after purchase. The language of the policy in itself was insufficient to afford the necessary notice of noncoverage. The facts of the case foreclose any contention of the company that it afforded Mr. Steven plain warning of noncoverage of the Turner flight. While the insurer has every right to sell insurance policies by methods of mechanization, and present-day economic conditions may well justify such distribution, the insurer cannot then rely upon esoteric provisions to limit coverage. If it deals with the public upon a mass basis, the notice of noncoverage of the policy, in a situation in which the public may reasonably expect coverage, must be conspicuous, plain and clear.

Finally, the one provision that deals with substitution of transportation in the event of emergency, section 3(b) of the policy, was not only hidden beneath the machine before purchase, and, subject after purchase, to obscurity and ambiguity, but literally applied, tended toward the harsh and unconscionable. The section states that coverage for "the transportation of passengers necessitated by an interruption or temporary suspension of such scheduled air carrier's service before arrival at destination" is limited to "riding in or on a *land conveyance* provided or arranged for, directly or indirectly, by such scheduled air carrier" (emphasis added). Yet innumerable flights traverse bodies of water; if a plane were forced down at such a point and the scheduled carrier arranged for conveyance by water, the language would not apply. Indeed, if the plane were forced down upon land or water and relief was afforded by a chartered nonscheduled carrier, which, of course, is a very likely contingency the language again would not apply. Does not such a provision approach a trap for the unwary purchasing public?

In standardized contracts, such as the instant one, which are made by parties of unequal bargaining strength, the California courts have long been disinclined to effectuate clauses of limitation of liability which are unclear, unexpected, inconspicuous or unconscionable. The attitude of the courts has been manifested in many areas of contract.

This approach has been applied to insurance contracts. Thus in *Raulet v. Northwestern Nat. Ins. Co.* (1910) 157 Cal. 213, the court upheld coverage of a fire insurance policy which "provided that the entire policy should be void 'if the subject of insurance be personal property and be or become encumbered with a chattel mortgage'" (p. 219), despite the fact that a chattel mortgage had been "given to secure the payment of rent." (P. 217.) Holding that the company had waived the provision, the court adopted the decision of the District Court of Appeal to the effect that "It must be presumed, ordinarily, that persons are familiar with the terms of written contracts to which they are parties, and in the absence of fraud they are justly bound by the provisions therein, but the rule should not be strictly applied to insurance policies. It is a matter almost of common knowledge that a very small percentage of policy-holders are actually cognizant of the provisions of their policies and many of them are ignorant of the names of the companies issuing the said policies. The policies are prepared by the experts of the companies, they are highly technical in their phraseology, they are complicated and voluminous—the one before us covering thirteen pages of the transcript—and in their numerous conditions and stipulations furnishing what sometimes may be veritable traps for the unwary." (P. 230.)

The court points out that the exclusionary clause was not brought to the attention of the insured and that it would be unjust to apply the unknown provision to him so that it voided his insurance. The California court quoted the Montana case of *Wright v. Fire Ins. Assn.* (1892) 12 Mont. 474, 485, "discussing a similar provision," (p. 231) to the effect that "*No mention was made that the company would not take a risk on mortgaged property.* It seems to us that it would be unjust to the insurer, as well as the assured, to put such a construction on the transaction." (Emphasis added.) The California court also states: "In *German Mut. Ins. Co. v. Niewedde,* 11 Ind.App. 624, it is held by the appellate court of Indiana that 'where application for insurance is orally made, and there are no questions asked concerning encumbrances and *the insured is unaware* that the existence of a mortgage was fatal to his insurance, the insurer will be deemed to have waived a provision for forfeiture by reason of existing encumbrances.' " (Emphasis added.) The court further quoted the Indiana court, "In quite a number of cases it has been adjudged that *the failure of the company to inquire about, or call any attention to, some particular fact,* operates to relieve the insured from a forfeiture which would follow his omission to disclose it." (Emphasis added.)

Other cases involving insurance contracts take the same approach to similar factual situations. In *Coniglio v. Connecticut Fire Ins. Co.* (1919) 180 Cal. 596, defendant fire insurance company contended "that the policy was vitiated because there was contained among the fixtures a certain computing scale of which the plaintiff was not the sole and unconditional owner, title being vested in the vendor." (P. 597.) The court held that despite the declaration of the policy "that the interest of the insured in the property was 'fee simple' there was no showing that [defendant] was or could be injured in the slightest degree by such alleged misrepresentation." (P. 599.)

The same general principle has been applied to the standardized bank passbook. Thus in *Los Angeles Inv. Co. v. Home Sav. Bank* (1919) 180 Cal. 601, the court did not enforce a condition printed in front of a commercial passbook that the depositor was concluded as to the genuineness of endorsements on cancelled checks unless he made an objection in writing within 10 days. The court said: "But it is evident that the statement comes in the category of 'traps for the unwary,' and before such statement can be given effect as a contract binding upon the depositor and changing in a substantial particular the relation which presumably he thought he was entering into, it must appear affirmatively that he consented and agreed to it either by being required to sign it or by having his attention particularly called to it." (P. 613.) Following *Home Sav. Bank* the later case of *Frankini v. Bank of America etc. Assn.* (1936) 12 Cal.App.2d 298, holds that the "burden was on the [bank] to establish" (p. 304) that the depositor accepted the waiver, noting that the "provision was not called to his attention" (p. 303) and that its rigid application "seems like a harsh rule" (p. 304).

The courts of this state have likewise applied the same test to exclusionary clauses in delivery sheets, warehouse receipts, and freight bills. Witkin states, "Where the contractual terms of a delivery sheet are not obvious, they may be denied enforcement." (Summary of California Law, p. 42.) In striking down a limitation of liability in a warehouse receipt to $25, the court pointed out in *Wilson v. Crown Transfer etc. Co.* (1927) 201 Cal. 701, 714 that the warehouse bore the duty "of bringing home to the respondents notice that the goods were accepted and held under such limited liability." *McQueen v. Tyler* (1943) 61 Cal.App.2d 263, notes that the carrier, relying upon such a provision in a freight bill "must show that the shipper accepted the contract 'with a knowledge of its terms.'" (P. 267.) In upholding findings that a disclaimer of liability in an invoice for defective paint did not bind the buyer, the court alluded to the "finely-printed statements as to disclaimer" and the fact that "the provisions are so located as to easily escape attention."

The approach of the California courts to the exculpatory or exclusionary clause of the standardized contract finds a reflection in cases of other states and in the writings of the commentators. Indeed, some legal authorities categorize the instant contract and comparable agreements under the term "contract of adhesion" to give it a more definite place in the law and to emphasize the need for the strict judicial scrutiny of its terms. The term refers to a standardized contract prepared entirely by one party to the transaction for the acceptance of the other; such a contract, due to the disparity in bargaining power between the draftsman and the second party, must be accepted or rejected by the second party on a "take it or leave it" basis, without opportunity for bargaining and under such conditions that the "adherer" cannot obtain the desired product or service save by acquiescing in the form agreement.

In an exhaustive analysis of such contracts the New Jersey Supreme Court in the recent case of *Henningsen v. Bloomfield Motors, Inc.* (1960) 32 N.J. 358, held void as against public policy an exculpatory provision of an express warranty that excluded claims against a dealer or manufacturer for personal injuries resulting from a defective car. The court stated the rationale of its ruling in these words: "The task of the judiciary is to administer the spirit as well as the letter of the law. On issues such as the present one, part of that burden is to protect the ordinary man against the loss of important rights through what, in effect, is the unilateral act of the manufacturer. From the standpoint of the purchaser, there can be no arms length negotiating on the subject. Because his capacity for bargaining is so grossly unequal, the inexorable conclusion which follows is that he is not permitted to bargain at all." (P. 94.) The court emphasizes the requirement for an *understanding* consent of the consumer to any limitation of liability. "Basically, the reason a contracting party offering services of a public or quasi-public nature has been held to the requirements of fair dealing, and, when it attempts to limit its liability, of securing the understanding consent of the patron or consumer, is because members of the public generally have no other means of fulfilling the specific need represented by the contract." (P. 92.)

The instant contract presents an even stronger case than *Henningsen* for the requirement that the exclusionary clause of the contract should not be enforced in the absence of plain and clear notification to the public. The disparity in bargaining power between the insured and the insurer here is so tremendous that the insurer had adopted a means of selling policies which makes bargaining totally impossible. The purchaser lacks any opportunity to clarify ambiguous terms or to discover inconspicuous or concealed ones. He must purchase the policy before he even knows its provisions.

Because of the special dangers inherent in the mechanized selling of air travel insurance, the New York Court of Appeals has insisted that the burden of giving clear notice of noncoverage rests with the insurer. In *Lachs* v. *Fidelity & Cas. Co. of New York* (1954) *supra*, 306 N.Y. 357, an "Airline Trip Insurance" vending machine stood near a ticket counter for sales of nonscheduled flights in the airport; a smaller placard limited coverage to "any scheduled airline"; the printed policy provided for coverage for "Civilian Scheduled Airlines." As in the instant case the insurer provided envelopes for the immediate mailing of the policy to the beneficiary. Unlike the passenger in the instant case the New York purchaser arranged for her trip to Miami on a nonscheduled flight, which subsequently crashed. The Court of Appeals held that the trial court properly denied the insurer's motion for summary judgment. The court points to the ambiguity of the term "Civilian Scheduled Airline" and to the ambiguity of the situation itself. It holds " . . . [The] burden in such a case as this is on the defendant to establish that the words and expressions used not only are susceptible of the construction sought by defendant but that it is the only construction which may fairly be placed on them. The defendant in its large illuminated lettering and in its application could have added proper, unambiguous words or a definition or could have avoided allowing its vending machine to be placed in front of the ticket counter 'utilized by all nonscheduled airlines operating out of the Newark Airport,' thus removing the ambiguity or equivocal character of the invitation to insure, of the application for insurance and the contract of insurance itself." (P. 559.)

We must view the instant claim in the composite of its special and unique circumstances. To equate the bargaining table, where each clause is the subject of debate, to an automatic vending machine, which issues a policy before it can even be read, is to ignore basic distinctions. The proposition that the precedents must be viewed in the light of the imperatives of the age of the machine has become almost axiomatic. Here the age of the machine is no mere abstraction; it presents itself in the shape of an instrument for the mass distribution of standard contracts. The exclusionary clause of that contract, upon which the insurance company relies, is an unexpected one. Its application in some circumstances would be unconscionable. It is placed in an inconspicuous position in the document. In view of all these characteristics its rigid application would cast an unexpected burden upon the traveling public and would prefer formality of phrase to the reality of the transaction.

The judgment is reversed, and the cause is remanded to the trial court with directions to enter judgment for the plaintiff.

* * *

In *Steven*, the Supreme Court of California took up a travel insurance contract, sold by airport-vending-machine, and invalidated a provision that purported to limit insurance coverage to losses sustained during travel specifically by scheduled air carrier. Notice the almost literary, highly metaphorical, character of the Court's objection to the contract. The Court distinguished between "the orthodox insurance policy sold in the protective aura of the insurer's explanation and discussion of its terms," and the "mass-made contract, sold by machine." The court insisted that

> [t]o equate the bargaining table, where each clause is the subject of debate, to an automatic vending machine, which issues a policy even before it can be read, is to ignore basic distinctions. The proposition that the precedents must be viewed in the light of the imperatives of the age of the machine has become almost axiomatic. Here the age of the machine is no mere abstraction; it presents itself in the shape of an instrument for the mass distribution of standard contracts.

The Court thus concluded that "rigid application [of the printed form] would cast an unexpected burden upon the traveling public and would prefer formality of phrase to the reality of the transaction."

The Court's language—especially about the "basic distinctions" between the bespoke and the adhesion contract—emphasizes the inherent power of the contract *form* and analyses contracts of adhesion by reference to their departure from this form. The language does not, however, explain itself: it does not say what the basic distinctions consist in or what the essential aspects of the contract form are. Completing such an argument requires excavating the basic structure and value of the contractual form—the inherent value of the relation of reciprocal adjustment associated with the bespoke agreement—and explaining how that form is threatened by boilerplate.

The required account sets out from the ideas about the nature of the contract relation with which this Part of the overall text began. Contract is a socially *integrative* practice. Every individual contract binds the contracting parties to each other, and the web of contracts that underwrites a modern market economy binds persons generally. Contract's integrative powers are, moreover, built into contract obligation's legal structure. Contracting parties, as Chapters 18 and 19 observed, engage each other not just on the terms of reasonable care that persons owe to one another generally but rather in the shared project characterized by the reciprocal performance that their agreements name: they commit not just to avoid harming each other but to vindicating their expectations in the performance; and they commit not just to make reasonable efforts to perform but actually to perform. The parties to contracts, moreover, each grant the other a normative power to demand this performance: they commit to performing in good faith and to accepting the authority of the contract as good faith requires; and, in doing so, they submit, reciprocally, to each other's authority. As the discussion of good faith observed, contracts "set in motion a cooperative enterprise,"[16] defined by the joint pursuit of what the Restatement calls the contracting parties' "agreed common purpose."[17] One might say, putting this all together, that the parties to a contract stand in a kind of *solidarity* with each other.[18]

This account of contractual solidarity resonates most clearly for contracts that are, first, established by individualized bargaining and, second, arise among parties who are already embedded in a solidaristic relationship. A long-term requirements contract between a lumber yard and a cabinet-maker, for example, and a collective bargaining agreement between a teacher's union and a school board illustrate the types of cases in which contracts most obviously establish solidarity among the parties to them. In these cases, and in other similar ones, the contracting parties have long histories together, are co-dependent (and perhaps even in a bi-lateral monopoly), and engage in detailed and intensive bargaining which aims both to maximize the surplus that their joint activities produce and to divide the surplus up between them. Such relational contracts do more than merely record or memorialize solidarity that exists on other grounds, to be sure; no matter how intense the pre-contractual relation, after all, the contracts in these cases nevertheless establish forms of obligation and authority, and thus a form of solidarity, that did not previously exist. But equally clearly, the solidarity associated with a relational contract receives substantial support from the pre-existing and on-going relations onto which it is grafted—something that the law recognizes in any number of ways, for example by giving informal course-of-dealing and course-of-performance

---

16. *Market St. Assocs. Ltd. P'ship v. Frey*, 941 F.2d 588, 595 (7th Cir. 1991) (internal quotation marks and citation omitted).

17. RESTATEMENT (SECOND) OF CONTRACTS § 205 cmt. a.

18. This account of contract is formalist rather than functionalist in that it proposes not that contracts *produce* social integration among the parties as a consequence but rather that they are *in themselves* integrative, in virtue of their form.

evidence a substantial influence over the interpretation of formal contracts in such cases.

The solidaristic character of individual contracts, and the socially integrative character of contract law more broadly, are not however confined to the narrow case of relational contracts, properly-so-called. Instead, even one-shot agreements, enacted between parties who have no prior experience or knowledge of each other and who deal at arm's length, establish a solidaristic relation among the participants. In particular, the obligations established by a one-shot contract are sandwiched between antecedent bargaining and subsequent performance practices that themselves involve reciprocal adjustment. The last chapter's discussions of the cooperative character of bargaining and of the analogy between good faith in performance and the duty to obey the law illustrated and fleshed out these forms of reciprocity. Bespoke contracts thus support the solidarity of the moment of contractual agreement—of the meeting of the minds—from both below and above.

Contractual solidarity is, of course, not the only kind of social integration that a legal order might support, nor even the only kind of integration that typically is supported by the legal orders in which contract thrives. For example, these legal orders typically (indeed perhaps even necessarily) also generate social integration, and sustain the solidarity of the persons who live under them, through political structures and in particular through the authority of government. The contrast between political and contractual solidarity almost at once generates an important insight into the character of contractual integration. Whereas political integration is *vertical*, the social integration associated with contract is essentially *horizontal*. Political integration, that is, functions through citizens' recognizing the authority of a sovereign who stands, asymmetrically, over them;[19] contract-based integration, by contrast, functions through contract-partners' recognizing each other's reciprocal authority.

Contractual integration is important, moreover—a big deal. Because it is a free-standing source of social integration, contractual solidarity can sustain social order even in the gaps left open by other integrative orders. Thus, even where the parties to a contract reach agreement against a background in which bargaining power is allocated unjustly, the contract that they agree to remains binding. The less powerful party, in such a case, has a political claim against the more powerful to rectify the underlying injustice and undo the bargaining advantage that it confers. But the more powerful party nevertheless retains its contractual entitlements against the less powerful, including even insofar as the terms of the contract merely reflect her unjust bargaining advantage. This is a direct consequence of freedom of contract, which requires, in order that it should mean anything at all, that the law recognizes and enforces not only ideal contracts (ideal because they are perfectly just or perfectly efficient) but rather the con-

---

19. Even in democracies, where sovereignty ultimately resides in the people, the authority-relations between citizen and sovereign are hierarchical rather than reciprocal. Each citizen is a part of the sovereign, to be sure, but no citizen has authority of the sovereign.

tracts that the parties have actually made (even where they are unjust and inefficient). Contractual solidarity is thus sufficiently powerful so that contracts can, one might say, launder injustice.

Contracts of adhesion abandon the horizontal character of bespoke contracts and degrade contractual solidarity. And in this way, the widespread dispersion of form contracting degrades the broader contractual order's capacity to support social order in free-standing ways, which remain independent of the vertical forms of social integration associated, for example, with politics and the state.

The parties to contracts of adhesion (unlike the parties to bespoke contracts) typically do not approach each other reciprocally through formally symmetric bargaining or adjust reciprocally during performance. Instead, the term-taker typically accepts a contract of adhesion without even communicating with anyone authorized to bargain on the term-maker's behalf; and the contract's performance, rather than requiring reciprocal adjustments, occurs according to pre-set schedules and routines adopted unilaterally by the term-maker. Contracts of adhesion replace horizontal solidarity with an essentially vertical relation, associated with the internal administrative structure and control of the term-maker. But this vertical relation lacks the participatory processes and controls that make vertical integration through democratic politics legitimate. This is the root of the trouble with contracts of adhesion. The details of the practice of form contracting—concerning both how contracts of adhesion are made and how they are administered—illustrate this general point.

Begin by comparing how bespoke and adhesive contracts are made. The processes that generate contracts of adhesion fail to trigger the relational morality of negotiations. Term-makers and term-takers do not participate in any processes of reciprocal adjustment in forming contracts of adhesion, or indeed engage each other at all. Instead, each party to such contracts acts purely unilaterally, and they make their contracts of adhesion not together, but severally.[20] In contracts of adhesion, there is no pre-contractual relationship at all—indeed, it is the nature of contracts of adhesion that there should be no such relationship. Good faith, and indeed bad faith, in the process of consummating a contract of adhesion is quite literally impossible.[21]

It is almost, although of course not precisely, as if contracts of adhesion lack offer and acceptance. Perhaps more helpfully put, contracts of adhe-

---

20. This is not to deny that term-makers, in particular, take into account the desires of term-takers when they draft contract terms. Of course they do, and they may even compete with other term-makers to draft attractive terms. But term-makers to not respond to individual term-takers or indeed enter into any pre-contractual relations with individual term-takers.

21. Note, moreover, that this analysis applies quite apart from whether or not term-takers read and understand the forms to which they agree. Although this question—of the duty to read, both concerning its scope and concerning the consequences of not reading—figures prominently in instrumental analyses of contracts of adhesion, it is not directly relevant to the approach taken here. Even when a term-taker reads and fully understands the forms that she (freely) signs, the process of contract formation continues to be defective in respect of the engagement between the parties.

sion involve offer and acceptance not concretely, through the interlocking and thus reciprocally adjusting intentions of actual contract partners, but in a purely abstract sense only. Term-makers' offers are not directed at term-takers (they neither engage term-takers nor are the products of a prior engagement with term-takers) but are in substance just general statements of terms on which the term-makers are willing to proceed. And term-takers' acceptances arise without any sense that that they have had a hand in creating the arrangement that they are accepting.

The purely abstract character of the offer and acceptance involved in contracts of adhesion is perhaps most vividly illustrated by the case in which such contracts arise between two term-makers, the scenario discussed previously in these pages under the heading the battle of the forms. In this case, the offer and acceptance quite literally fail to engage each other, and the parties proceed to performance even though they each openly deny, through their forms, that their efforts at contract formation have been successful. The parties, in this case, cannot meaningfully be said to have negotiated towards a contract at all, and if an exchange of performance nevertheless arises between them, it arises not as a form of reciprocal recognition or any other solidaristic engagement, but rather because the parties' independent pursuit of their purely private interests recommends the exchange. And this is anything but a model of solidarity, or a foundation for horizontal social integration.

Social psychology bears this out. Thus persons who enter contracts without integrative pre-contractual negotiations generally do not take their contractual commitments seriously in the fashion that contractual solidarity requires. Instead of conceiving of themselves as authors and hence owners of their contractual obligations, they experience these obligations as imposed from without, and even as alienating.

These are speculative claims, of course. But they are supported by introspection—do *you* recognize your counterparties in form contracts in anything like the same way in which you recognize your counterparties after dickering terms to reach a bespoke contract? The suggestion that contracts of adhesion integrate less effectively than bespoke contracts is also increasingly supported by social science, which has begun to investigate the sociology and social psychology of form-contracting. Thus in one recent experiment, subjects who were more actively engaged in the pre-consent phase of contract-making were more likely to perform their contracts than subjects who had made contracts of adhesion.[22] Moreover, appeals to morality generated performance more effectively when contracts were dickered than when they arose through adhesion.[23] Even if contracts of adhesion might in principle sustain social integration on the model of bespoke contracting, their lack of pre-contractual support prevents them from integrating in practice.

---

22.   Zev Eigen, *When and Why Individuals Obey Form–Adhesive Contracts: Experimental Evidence of Consent, Compliance, Promise, and Performance*, 41 J. LEGAL STUD. (forthcoming 2012).

23.   Id.

Next, compare how bespoke and form contracts are administered. Form contracts are deficient, from the perspective of contractual solidarity, not just in their formation but also in their performance. One might express the defect in this following way: whereas the formation of contracts of adhesion proceeds almost as if there were no offer and acceptance, the performance of these contracts proceeds almost as if there were no consideration.

The consideration doctrine functions to ensure that contracts are truly reciprocal, in the sense of involving a formal equality of recognition. Moreover, although equality of recognition remains formal only even in bespoke contracts—in the sense that the consideration doctrine imposes no substantive constraints on the fairness or equality of the division of contractual surplus—the performance of bespoke contracts gives concrete expression to the recognition that they involve. Over the course of performance of a bespoke contract, each party must in fact attend to the wishes and intentions of the other and make adjustments in light of these wishes and intentions. That is, the performance of a bespoke contract carries the attentiveness that each party displayed to the wishes and intentions of the other during pre-contractual negotiations forward into the performance of the contract, which involves a process of ongoing reciprocal adjustment and engagement between the parties. The fact that contracts are necessarily incomplete entails that the parties' performance obligations cannot be adequately specified in advance. Rather, the parties must fill in gaps in their contract's account of these obligations as their performance progresses. The consideration doctrine's requirement of a bargain-in-fact, when applied in the context of inevitable contractual incompleteness, insures that this inevitable gap-filling involves the patterns of reciprocal adjustment and recognition that make it, in itself, a solidaristic practice. This distinguishes bargains from gratuitous promises, which impose obligations on only one side and therefore require no reciprocal recognition in their performance, which for this reason does constitute any formally equal, solidaristic activity.

The lived experience of contracts of adhesion suggests that their administration suffers, with respect to ongoing social integration, a deficiency analogous to that involved in gratuitous contracts. The asymmetries between the parties to contracts of adhesion only begin in their formation and extend, importantly, to apply also to their administration. Term-makers reject any obligation to adjust their performance to the particular needs of individual term-takers but rather apply generalized, bureaucratic criteria to executing their contractual obligations. Even when a term-maker differentiates among its many contract partners, for example by adjusting delivery terms to suit their several schedules, it will not have had any commitment to adjusting its conduct to achieve a successful performance with any individual term-taker, and so it will not have engaged any term-taker individually. Instead, the term-maker will have adopted a set of policies and practices that, in general, on average, offer the broad class of term-takers options that are acceptable to them. If a particular term-taker successfully avails herself of one of these options then that is, with respect to the normative structure of her relation to her term-maker, happenstance only. It is not the result of any commitment, on the part of the term-maker, to recognizing her individual authority to demand adequate performance.

In both these respects, the legal orders established by form contracts are not structured by the individualized interactions between the parties to them but rather by the discipline of the market, in which exit replaces voice as the principal mechanism through which contractual performance is managed. (Of course, although lawsuits may be possible in principle, as a practical matter the most that a dissatisfied term-taker can do is to swallow her sunk costs and take her business elsewhere, and often, as in the insurance context, she cannot even do that.)

When market discipline is effective, this may produce efficient and indeed fair processes of contractual management; when market discipline is ineffective, it will produce exploitative and inefficient contracting. Functionalist analyses of contracts of adhesion focus on the balance between these cases.

But the formalist argument just developed reveals that the problem with contracts of adhesion extends even to circumstances in which markets do effectively discipline, and term-makers proceed fairly and efficiently, although still without individual responsiveness. Whereas the negotiations that produce bespoke contracts are themselves media for social integration, the processes through which contracts of adhesion are formed fail to constitute morally valuable, solidaristic relations among the parties who eventually agree to them. Similarly, whereas the performance of bespoke contracts is itself a reciprocal, solidaristic practice, contracts of adhesion are asymmetrically administered. Contracts of adhesion thus do not participate in the form of reciprocal recognition and social solidarity that ordinary contracts establish but rather represent a mechanism for alienated control. They do not establish a truly contractual relation among the parties to them; rather, if they sustain a contractual engagement at all, contracts of adhesion do so only on the model of two ships crashing in the night.

These reflections render articulate the craft sensibilities of lawyers and of courts—the conventional wisdom that contracts of adhesion are somehow an anomalous and perhaps even degraded species of contract. Whatever social coordination is achieved by contracts of adhesion is not horizontal at all but rather vertical. That is why one often hears lawyerly critics analogize contracts of adhesion to another vertical form of social organization—legislation. But if contracts of adhesion possess a legislative form, they adopt this form without the political (and certainly democratic) framework that gives ordinary legislation its legitimacy. Contracts of adhesion thus abandon both contract proper and legislation proper and hence tend towards alienation rather than solidarity.

20.3 DISPLACED BARGAINING

In spite of their formal failings, contracts of adhesion remain functionally necessary. The *Steven* court was not speaking casually when it referred to "the imperatives of the age of the machine." Rather, it meant what it said: modern contract law cannot adequately serve the functionalist needs of a modern mass economy save as mass contract law. This raises the question how—indeed, whether—the functionalist imperative in favor of contracts of adhesion might be squared with the formalist concern for contractual solidarity. Perhaps the practice of contracts of adhesion offers possibilities for recapturing the contract form even within them and thus redeeming boilerplate's legal validity? Perhaps it is possible to promote genuinely integrative (and contract-like) bargaining *within* an adhesive contract relation, once the contract has been consummated, including especially when the relation comes under stress because disputes arise concerning its adhesive terms—that is, when the merely abstract integration that the adhesive arrangement reflects proves inadequate to sustaining solidarity around an actual plan among the parties.

Consider in this connection the commonly asserted principle that an adhesive "contract or provision which does not fall within the reasonable expectations of the weaker or 'adhering' party will not be enforced against him."[24] The principle is often applied, especially in connection with retail sales contracts, where it inclines courts to refuse to respect terms in form contracts that violate the "reasonable expectations of consumers."[25] But what, concretely, does it require?

One view—the commonest one—gives reasonable expectations a substantive cast. The gravamen of this view is that adhering parties, and in particular consumers, may reasonably expect boilerplate terms to be efficient and fair; so that the "reasonable expectations of consumers" test converges with the principle, discussed earlier, that adhesive terms are "presumptively unenforceable"[26] and govern the contracts in which they appear only insofar as they comply with standards in the "public interest."[27] When it is understood in this way, the doctrine serves to make certain substantive contract terms (for example, terms that establish default warranties) quasi-mandatory.[28] The substantive approach to the rea-

---

24. *Armendariz v. Foundation Health Psychcare Services, Inc.*, 6 P.3d 669, 689 (Cal. 2000). This doctrinal strand finds its historical origins in the insurance context, see, e.g., *Kievit v. Loyal Protective Life*, 34 N.J. 475 (1961); Robert E. Keeton, *Insurance Law Rights at Variance with Policy Provisions*, 83 HARV. L. REV. 961 (1970); Kenneth S. Abraham, *Judge Made Law and Judge Made Insurance: Honoring the Reasonable Expectations of the Insured*, 67 VA. L. REV. 1151 (1981). Here see especially RESTATEMENT (SECOND) OF CONTRACTS § 211 cmt. f. (1981).

25. Recall the emphasis that the *Steven* court placed on the fact that enforcing the boilerplate limitation of coverage to scheduled flights "would cast an unexpected burden on the traveling public."

26. Todd D. Rakoff, *The Law and Sociology of Boilerplate* in Omri Ben–Shachar, ed., BOILERPLATE: THE FOUNDATIONS OF MARKET CONTRACTS 200, 200 (2007).

27. W. David Slawson, *Standard Form Contracts and Democratic Control Over the Lawmaking Power*, 84 HARV. L. REV. 529, 566 (1970).

28. They are not fully mandatory because the doctrine denies recognition only to boilerplate clauses that attack such terms; they may be varied by bespoke contracting. Of course, part of boilerplate's appeal lies in the fact that bespoke contracting is not economical in many circumstances—the game isn't worth the candle. So a principle that requires

sonable expectations test thus abandons the aspiration to retain freedom of contract even in the face of the imperatives of mass-contracting. It therefore also abandons the hope that contract might even now constitute a freestanding site of horizontal social solidarity. Rather, mass-contracting becomes merely one among many applications of the vertical solidarity associated with the political processes of the state, whose organs decide what consumers might reasonably expect and hence determine the content of the quasi-mandatory terms that reasonable expectations impose on boilerplate.

An alternative view, which the remainder of this section will explore in greater detail, emphasizes process rather than substance.

For most exchanges implemented through contracts of adhesion, the individually dickered or otherwise highly salient terms of the contracts—price, quantity, etc.—will be sufficient to consummate the transactions. In a typical consumer contract, the term-maker seller gets paid, the term-taker buyer receives goods that she regards as satisfactory, and this is the end of the matter. The boilerplate terms—for example, concerning warranties, consequential damages, and mechanisms for dispute resolution—simply never become relevant to the contractual relation, as it in fact develops. In these instances, the operative substance of contractual solidarity is established by terms that are consciously chosen and perhaps even dickered even by the term-taker.[29] The adhesive elements of the contract are epiphenomenal, and the contract as implemented is effectively bespoke.[30]

The boilerplate elements of contracts of adhesion typically come into play only where something goes wrong and one party becomes dissatisfied. Often in such cases, the dissatisfied party, especially where he is a term-taker or consumer, has no fixed substantive expectations about how his complaint will be resolved. Instead, he expects to commence a process that aims towards the resolution of his complaint. Term makers, for their part, join in this process and even encourage their term-takers' procedural expectations. The term-makers establish and advertise customer complaint departments, which by their natures specialize in dealing with those of the term-makers' contracts for which the salient or dickered terms were

---

warranty disclaimers to be individually dickered actually makes the warranties effectively undisclaimable.

29. It may appear that even the salient terms are not dickered—so that while retail consumers of course *know* prices, for example, they cannot bargain to change them. But this is not actually so clear. For many large consumer purchase, direct negotiation over salient terms is not only possible but actually common: think of the haggling over price associated with buying a car. (And notice, furthermore, that there is in this context virtually no haggling over the boilerplate terms.) Moreover, even where there is no direct negotiation over salient terms, there is often substantial and significant indirect negotiation. Retail sales involve substantial price discrimination, and consumers can do something like bargaining by shopping around. And the common practice of offering price guarantees ("We will not be undersold") converts shopping around into actual dickering.

30. Of course, the substance of the salient terms may itself be influenced by the hidden boilerplate: a seller is likely to offer a better price if she has insulated herself from consequential damages caused by defects in the goods that she sells.

insufficient to bring the contract-relation to a successful conclusion. This raises the question how to understand what goes on between customer complaints departments and the consumers whose complaints they engage. The best account of this engagement understands it as an instance of *negotiation*—now *bespoke*—between the firm and its customers.[31] In this way, contracts of adhesion conserve the resources that negotiation requires. Adhesive contracts' salient or dickered terms are cheaply arrived at and suffice to govern the overwhelming majority of the relations that these contracts establish. And rather than incurring the much greater transactions costs required to reach actual, bespoke agreement on the non-salient boilerplate terms ex ante in every instance, the contracts instead *displace bargaining* concerning these terms to renegotiation, ex post, where they can concentrate negotiating resources on the instances in which the terms become actually relevant.

The ex post negotiations associated with customer complaint resolution are both common and complicated. It is one of the banalities of the sociology of business relations that just as retailers commonly reject reasonable consumer complaints, so they also commonly acquiesce to complaining consumers' demands, including when doing so provides consumers with benefits that their sales contracts *deny*, often expressly in boilerplate.[32] The liberal return policies adopted by many retailers represent only the most obvious example of this practice. Others include policies that waive published change fees for airline ticket holders, relieve complaining credit card holders of fees triggered by occasional and accidental late payments, and even enable credit card holders to renegotiate repayment schedules (and even interest rates) on their debt and patients to negotiate ex post price reductions for medical care.[33]

The widespread practice of ex post renegotiations conducted in the shadow of boilerplate immediately raises the question how these renegotiations should be regulated. In particular to what extent should boilerplate that gives term-makers a strong position in the renegotiations be enforced by courts?

---

31. One must resist the urge to characterize in-firm complaint resolution on the model of adjudication—that is, as a process that takes the boilerplate terms to establish the parties' respective rights and seeks to determine what these terms require when they are applied to the facts that have developed. The firm's customer complaints department is itself a party in interest in the dispute rather than a neutral judge or arbitrator. Further, as the discussions that follow reveal, adjudication is simply not how customer complaints are in fact processed.

The next chapter, on arbitration, takes up private, contract-based efforts to resolve disputes about contractual rights. It argues that even some (although not all) arbitration is best understood on the model of negotiation rather than adjudication.

32. An early and prominent study that focused on contractual practice among business people is Stewart Macaulay, *Non–Contractual Relations in Business: A Preliminary Study*, 28 AMERICAN SOCIOLOGICAL REVIEW 1 (1963).

33. These examples come from Jason Scott Johnston, *Cooperative Negotiations in the Shadow of Boilerplate*, in Omri Ben–Shachar, ed., BOILERPLATE: THE FOUNDATION OF MARKET CONTRACTS 12, 14–16 (2007). See also Jason Scott Johnston, *The Return of Bargain: An Economic theory of How Standard–Form Contracts Enable Cooperative Negotiation Between Business and Consumer*, 104 MICH. L. REV. 857 (2006).

The sociological fact of renegotiation has recently been noticed by some contracts scholars, who have sought to incorporate it into functionalist analyses of contracts of adhesion.[34] These analyses emphasize that when consumer opportunism is difficult for courts to verify, firms may wish to retain broad discretion to deny certain benefits to consumers whom they regard as behaving opportunistically or in some other way in bad faith. On the other hand, insofar as firms have a reputational interest in appearing fair or even generous, they may wish to extend discretionary benefits to consumers whom they regard as proceeding in good faith or in some other way as desirable future customers. Accordingly, firms' customer relations (or complaints) departments may restore some of the benefits to consumers that contracts of adhesion remove.

Functionalist analyses disagree about what attitude courts should take to this feature of contracts of adhesion. Some argue that judicial intervention to give consumers a legally protected contractual interest in firms' generous practices—for example, by treating common practice as establishing an implicit promise that consumers will enjoy whatever benefits firms typically provide—would undermine the point of the firms' policy of granting benefits in excess of their written promises. It would place courts in the position of policing firm-discretion by reference to their own judgments of consumer good faith, judgments whose cost and unreliability led firms— efficiently—to seek to retain discretion to begin with.[35] Others argue that, at least where there exists strong evidence that a firm has adopted a practice of providing benefits in excess those specified by a written form, preventing firm opportunism requires that courts compel the firm grant "discretionary" benefits in at least some cases in which it wishes not to.[36]

The functionalist debate takes an all-or-nothing approach to boilerplate. One side would enforce boilerplate against complaining consumers whenever firms request it, so that whenever firms confer benefits on complaining consumers that boilerplate would permit the firms to withhold, they do so as a matter of unilateral grace. The other side would refuse to enforce boilerplate, at least against consumers who complain in good faith, and so would vindicate good faith consumer complaints as a matter of right. Both functionalist positions thus deny that the consumer complaints process represents a genuine negotiation: they treat the rights of the

---

34. See Lucian A. Bebchuck and Richard A. Posner, *One–Sided Contracts in Competitive Consumer Markets*, in Omri Ben–Shachar, ed., BOILERPLATE: THE FOUNDATION OF MARKET CONTRACTS 3–11 (2007) and Jason Scott Johnston, *Cooperative Negotiations in the Shadow of Boilerplate*, in Omri Ben–Shachar, ed., BOILERPLATE: THE FOUNDATION OF MARKET CONTRACTS 12, 14–16 (2007).

35. See Lucian A. Bebchuck and Richard A. Posner, *One–Sided Contracts in Competitive Consumer Markets*, in Omri Ben–Shachar, ed., BOILERPLATE: THE FOUNDATION OF MARKET CONTRACTS 3, 9–10 (2007).

36. Jason Scott Johnston, *Cooperative Negotiations in the Shadow of Boilerplate*, in Omri Ben–Shachar, ed., BOILERPLATE: THE FOUNDATION OF MARKET CONTRACTS 12, 25 (2007). Johnston acknowledges Bebchuck's and Posner's concern about the non-verifiability of consumer opportunism. See id. But he also worries, as Bebchuck and Posner seem not to, about firm opportunism, specifically that firms (especially when they are short-run players) may seek to "creat[e] a false appearance of pursuing a policy of forgiveness by mimicking the behavior of a firm that really does implement these strategies." Id. at 23.

parties as fixed by their contract, ex ante, and disagree only about how they are fixed, because they disagree about whether or not the firms' boilerplate reservations become part of the contract.

The formalist of analysis of contracts of adhesion—with its focus on contractual solidarity—opens up a quite different possibility. Courts might regulate contracts of adhesion in order to ensure that the consumer complaints process proceeds as a genuine, good-faith negotiation. Boilerplate that does not undermine this negotiating posture would be respected and enforced. But boilerplate clauses would not be permitted to give term-makers bargaining advantages ex post that they could not have acquired through bespoke negotiations ex ante. In particular, courts would refuse to allow boilerplate to enable retailers to exploit the fact that consumers, having begun to deal with the retailers with whom they have become dissatisfied, can no longer credibly threaten, ex post, to take their custom elsewhere. (Note the analogy between this approach and the duty of good faith in performance: both focus on cases in which one party uses strategic vulnerabilities associated with entering a contract relation to extract surplus ex post that would not have been given up in an ex ante negotiation.)

Courts taking this approach would seek to structure the ex post renegotiation so that it approximates, as nearly as possible, the negotiation that would have occurred ex ante, had the contracting parties possessed the negotiating resources to dicker over the contingency that has generated their dispute. Boilerplate would be enforced insofar as it promotes such renegotiations (for example, by protecting term-makers against the vulnerabilities to opportunistic consumers that the functionalist analysis just rehearsed emphasizes); it would be rejected insofar as it hinders them.

These ideas bring customer service departments out of the shadows and into the limelight of contract theory, studying their potential to function as sites of social solidarity—as analogs to the village market for bespoke contracts that are adapted to the needs of a mass-contracting age. They emphasize the essential role that law might play in eliminating the most alienating feature of adhesive consumer contracts: the experience (all-to-familiar) of consumers who complain to customer service departments that operate in bad faith, employing unresponsive bureaucratic administration to insist on boilerplate terms that could never have been reached by negotiation ex ante. The alienation arises not simply because the complaining consumers do not receive substantive satisfaction; it arises because they cannot manage to get *heard*. A legal regime that gave consumers contractual entitlements to complaints procedures structured as good faith negotiations might not cause all their complaints to be satisfactorily answered, but it would require them all to be engaged. At the same time, the displaced negotiation that this regime requires—and the return to individual tailoring that it involves—would avoid many of the inefficiencies of the more ordinary forms of negotiation that it displaces. Renegotiation occurs in only a subset of contracts—in which something has gone wrong—and arises against a richer informational backdrop than was reasonably available at earlier stages in the contracting process.

This approach would refashion consumer contracts of adhesion on the genuinely reciprocal model of the bespoke contract. In this way, boilerplate would become a support for contract's solidaristic form—an adaptation to the world of mass-contracting that concentrates contractual solidarity where it is most needed. The craft sense that drives judicial skepticism of contracts of adhesion would be vindicated.

CHAPTER 21

ARBITRATION AGREEMENTS

Although the parties to contracts compete for shares of contractual surplus, contract is also, as the materials up to this point have at various places illustrated, a site of social cooperation. At the most abstract level, contracting parties recognize each other's moral status and authority, and a legal order that grants a person contractual capacity recognizes her full moral personality. More concretely, much of bargaining emphasizes the effort to maximize the joint surplus available for contracting parties to divide; and contractual performance is governed by a duty of good faith that requires contracting parties to recognize that their agreements constitute an authoritative structure for regulating their engagements.

Both individual contracts and the broader economic and legal web of contractual practice thus establish a form of social solidarity, a system of dispute resolution, really, by which parties might achieve a legitimate settlement among their competing interests (and competing views about how best to serve these interests). Contract does not just implement an exogenous balance of advantage, so that the legitimacy of the allocations that contracts produce depends not on contracts but rather entirely on the legitimacy of the balance of advantage from which contractual bargaining begins. Instead, contract constitutes a free-standing form of legal legitimation. Even where parties bargain against a backdrop of undeserved and unjust advantage and disadvantage, they become bound by the contracts that they strike. Contract possesses the power to launder injustice.

Freedom of contract expands the sphere of influence of contractual dispute resolution. Our broader legal order's embrace of freedom of contract reflects a commitment to allowing any number of disputes that might be collectively resolved through the hierarchical political process to be resolved instead by the bilateral, horizontal agreements of the parties to them. Some other legal orders determine the relative shares of social surplus that will go to capital and to labor, for example, or to producers and consumers, by fixing legislatively determined wages and prices. By embracing freedom of contract, our legal order leaves these and other similar matters to be negotiated in the market.

Adjudication presents another party-driven mechanism for individualized dispute resolution. Adjudication arises where disputants cannot reach agreement on their own but instead present their disputes to a third party, commonly called a court, for decision. Although it is commonly supposed that courts merely identify the outcomes that truth and justice independently require, that is a mistake. Adjudication serves not just an epistemic but a moral function: adjudication authorizes or legitimates the resolutions of disputes that it recommends; and the procedures that adjudication employs are designed to support this form of legitimation.[1] This happens most obviously when common law courts make new (positive) law—so that the principles on which they decide a dispute had no prior legal authority or existence, and so could not possibly have been discovered but must have been made. And even where courts apply existing precedent, adjudication still performs the moral (and not just epistemic) function of shaping the disputants' claims into forms that the law recognizes and can manage, and shaping their reactions to a court's decision so that even the losers accept its authority.[2] In this way, adjudication establishes agreement about which resolution of a dispute to obey even in the fact of entrenched disagreement about which to adopt. Finally, just as our legal order embraces freedom of contract in order to give contractual dispute resolution a wide sphere of application, so our legal order embraces what might be called adversary license in order to give adjudication a similarly wide sphere of application. Adjudication embraces a system of legal rules that allow disputants to press colorable but losing claims by insulating them from the liability that the law would ordinarily impose for the harms that pressing these claims causes others.[3]

---

1. Adjudication pursues not truth and justice but rather legitimacy, which is to say convergence about which resolutions of disputes to obey in the face of entrenched disagreement about which resolutions to adopt. Adjudication, on this account, is designed to promote affective engagements among disputants about how general laws should be applied in particular cases, and in this way, it is designed to transform disputants' claims and sustain a sense of authorship even of decisions that the disputants initially opposed and continue to think mistaken even after adjudication's decision has been made.

2. It is common to think of adjudication as a *transparent* process, in the sense that it has "no effect on the values, goals, and desires of those who use the system." David M. Trubek, *The Handmaiden's Revenge: On Reading and Using the Newer Sociology of Civil Procedure,* 51 LAW & CONTEMP. PROBS., Autumn 1988, at 111, 115. "Transparent procedure," as Trubek says, "takes the litigants as they come to the court." *Id.* at 115. Procedure "does not add or subtract anything" to their dispute, so the procedure "should not make a difference in the [right] outcome of a dispute." *Id.* at 114. According to this approach, one can look backwards through a legal process, from its end to its beginning, and see the same claims asserted throughout, in undistorted form.

But as legal sociologists have long contended, the transparent view of adjudication is in fact mistaken, a vestige of a formalist jurisprudence that is now discredited. Instead, "[T]he relationship between objectives [in a dispute] and mechanisms [of dispute resolution] is reciprocal; not only do objectives influence the choice of mechanisms, but mechanisms chosen may alter objectives." *See* William L.F. Felstiner, Richard L. Abel & Austin Sarat, *The Emergence and Transformation of Disputes: Naming, Blaming, Claiming, ...,* 15 LAW & SOC'Y REV. 631, 642–43 (1980). Adjudication is not transparent but *transformative.* Where one person negligently injures another, for example, adjudication transforms the victim's anger (and its attendant desire for vengeance) into a tort claim for money damages (whose payment would ordinarily be thought literally to add insult to injury).

3. The rules that insulate adjudication from ordinary principles of liability for harming others appear throughout the American legal system. First, they are reflected in the often unnoticed but important fact that tort law declines to apply its ordinary regimes of liability, including most notably the law of negligence, to harms caused when one person asserts legal claims, including losing legal claims, against another. Second, the commitment to adversary adjudication is reflected in rules of procedure that allow litigants to present claims and arguments to courts as long only as their filings are not made for an improper purpose, are non frivolous, and the claims have or are likely to have evidentiary support. Third, the legal system's commitments to adversary adjudication include rules of professional conduct that obligate lawyers to assist their clients' adversary assertiveness.

Contract and adjudication thus both elaborate forms of legal and social solidarity that might each (within its proper sphere) achieve legitimacy on its own bottom. The structural similarities between contract and adjudication immediately suggest that a legal order might shift the boundary between these two modes of dispute resolution. Certain disputes might be given to one mechanism or the other, depending on choices made by both the parties to the disputes and the broader legal order. (To see this intuitively, one need only look to settlement, which literally uses contract to close a rift whose repair was initially assigned to adjudication.)

Arbitration agreements—clauses in contracts through which parties agree to submit certain matters concerning the contracts' performance to privately-created tribunal rather than to public courts—are the commonest, most important, and most prominent mechanism by which our legal order toggles between contract and adjudication. Just as contracts of adhesion stand at the nexus of contract and administration, so arbitration agreements stand at the nexus of contract and adjudication.

This makes it natural to ask how arbitration should be understood, to ask what arbitration's true nature is. Perhaps arbitration constitutes its own fully distinctive legal form, whose characteristic features may be elaborated in much the same way in which these pages describe the characteristic features of contract (and gesture towards the characteristic features of adjudication). In this case, arbitration's true nature would be to be fully and distinctively itself.

But it seems injudicious to embrace the theoretical agenda of producing such an elaboration too readily. Arbitration obviously does lie between adjudication and contract. Accordingly, a shrewd theorist should begin by considering whether arbitral solidarity might be understood by reference to these two more familiar forms. And in fact, it can be, although not in a uniform fashion. Arbitration is best understood as not one but *two* things. Some instances of arbitration—which might be called *third-party* arbitration or arbitration as *judging*—stand in for adjudication and must succeed or fail according to the standards that govern adjudication. Other instances of arbitration—which might be called *first-party* arbitration or arbitration as *gap-filling*—stand in for contract and must succeed or fail according to the standards that govern contract.

Enough of actual arbitral practice can be accommodated by such a bifurcated, reductive account, so that there is no need for any more fundamental theoretical innovation. At the same time, the logics of adjudication and contract remain distinct, and arbitration must conform to one logic or the other in order to sustain its legitimacy. Arbitration's enthusiasts and critics both tend to forget this and to conflate the two forms of arbitration. Arbitration's enthusiasts arbitrage the strengths of the third- and first-party models in order expand arbitration's authority in ways that neither model, taken alone, can sustain. Arbitration's critics arbitrage the limits of the third- and first-party models in order to limit arbitration's authority by saddling each model with the limitations of both. Neither effort at arbitrage is intellectually defensible.

21.1   THIRD-PARTY ARBITRATION

In some cases, arbitration does indeed stand in for court-provided processes of dispute resolution, including adjudication. This is third-party arbitration or arbitration as judging. Arbitration practiced on this model is a contractually created *substitute* for adjudication. According to this view, an agreement to arbitrate *transfers* disputes whose natural venue is a court to an arbitral tribunal, which *does the work of courts*. Arbitration, on this view, is a case of *displacing* adjudication with an alternative, party-chosen procedure that nevertheless retains adjudication's *judgment-rendering* function.

Classical courts cited this displacement as a ground for skepticism about arbitration, as the following case illustrates.

Nute v. Hamilton Mutual Insurance Co.

Supreme Judicial Court of Massachusetts, 1856.
72 Mass. 174.

■ SHAW, C. J. The defence to this action, on a policy entered into by a mutual fire insurance company, is, that by the terms of the policy the contract was that the suit should be brought at a proper court in the county of Essex, within four months after the determination by the directors that nothing was due to the plaintiff upon the loss claimed. By a comparison of dates, it appears that this suit was brought within four months; but it was brought in the county of Suffolk, and not in the county of Essex; and on that ground the court of common pleas held that the action could not be maintained. The correctness of that ruling is the sole question now presented to this court.

In cases recently determined, it has been held that a stipulation in a policy of insurance, or in a by-law constituting in legal effect a part of such policy, by way of condition to their liability, that no recovery shall be had unless a suit is commenced within a certain time limited, was a valid condition, and that, unless complied with, the plaintiffs were not entitled to recover. In this case it is strenuously insisted that a stipulation, that an action shall be brought in a particular county, where by law it may be brought, is strictly analogous, and ought to be enforced as a condition precedent by a court which, without such stipulation and condition, would clearly have jurisdiction of the subject matter and of the parties.

[T]he by-laws direct that the risks of the Hamilton Company shall be divided into four classes, to be called "the Farmers'," "the Citizens'," "the Merchants'" and the "Manufacturers' Insurance Company"; so that in effect this is the policy of the Hamilton Company, insuring the plaintiff's property in that class of risks called the Manufacturers' Insurance Company; and the name used in the policy does not designate a corporation, but a class of risks in the Hamilton Company. It seems to be an inconvenient and awkward arrangement, by which, in the form of their contracts, they renounce their own corporate name, usually the very test of corporate identity, and adopt what, on the face of it, would appear to be the name of another corporation. But when the plaintiff alleges that the Hamilton Company did thus make this contract by such name, that the policy annexed is their policy, regardless of the name; and the defendants, being served with process, come into court and admit it, and tender an issue; and the plaintiff takes issue with them on the question of breach and damages; no question is presented to this court on the subject. It follows conclusively that the policy being the act and contract of the Hamilton Company, the charter and by-laws of "the said company," referred to in the policy, are their charter and by-laws, and are those stated at length on the back of said policy.

It is the Hamilton Mutual Insurance Company, of which the plaintiff, by force of his application and by the acceptance of his policy, became a member, with the usual rights and powers of a corporator. By this fact, as well as by the definite reference in the policy itself, we think the plaintiff as well as the defendants were bound; and their rules are to be regarded, in construing the policy, as if they were embodied in it. The clause in the policy is, that the company do promise and agree to insure him against loss or damage by fire, "subject to the provisions, conditions and limitations of the charter and by-laws of said company."

The provision on which this defence depends is found in art. 22d of the by-laws. After providing that notice of loss shall be given, and that thereupon the directors shall proceed to determine whether any loss has occurred for which the company are liable, and if so, ascertain the amount, it provides that, if the assured do not acquiesce in such determination, as to the liability or the extent of it, and both parties do not agree to refer, as they may, "the assured may, within four months after such determination, but not after that time, bring an action at law against the company for the loss claimed, *which action shall be brought at a proper court in the county of Essex.*"

Here are no negative words, and, strictly speaking, no stipulation that the action shall not be brought elsewhere, unless they are implied by the term "shall be brought" in Essex. These words were not necessary to give the assured a remedy, because without them it is conceded that they would have a remedy at common law, as in all cases of breach of contract, for which no stipulation is necessary. In this respect, the case differs essentially from that of *Boynton v. Middlesex Mutual Fire Ins. Co.* 4 Met. 212. There it was provided by the act of incorporation, which has all the force and effect of a general law, that in case the directors should find the company liable and award a certain sum, and the assured should not acquiesce, but be dissatisfied with the amount, the action should be brought in the county of Middlesex. In such case, the action to be brought was in the nature of an appeal from the decision of the directors, as in a case of allowance or disallowance of a debt by commissioners of insolvency on the estates of deceased persons, or, under the insolvent laws, in the case of a claim against a living insolvent debtor; and the legislature might rightfully regulate the time and mode of entering and prosecuting such appeal; and, as the law gave a new and specific right in such case of dissatisfaction with the amount awarded, and pointed out a specific remedy, by a well known rule of law, the specific remedy must be pursued. But it was also held, in that case, that as the directors had determined that the company were not liable and had awarded nothing, it was not the specific case of the statute, and that the assured were remitted to their remedy at law, by action in either of the counties where, by the general law, it might be brought.

Upon the particular question here presented, the court are of opinion that there is an obvious distinction between a stipulation by contract as to the time when a right of action shall accrue and when it shall cease, on the one hand; and as to the forum before which, and the proceedings by which an action shall be commenced and prosecuted. The one is a condition annexed to the acquisition and continuance of a legal right, and depends on contract and the acts of the parties; the other is a stipulation concerning the remedy, which is created and regulated by law. Perhaps it would not be easy or practicable to draw a line of distinction, precise and accurate enough to govern all these classes of cases, because the cases run so nearly into each other; but we think the general distinction is obvious.

The time within which money shall be paid, land conveyed, a debt released, and the like, are all matters of contract, and depend on the will and act of the parties; but, in case of breach, the tribunal before which a remedy is to be sought, the means and processes by which it is to be conducted, affect the remedy, and are created and regulated by law. The stipulation, that a contracting party shall not be liable to pay money or perform any other collateral act, before a certain time, is a regulation of the right, too familiar to require illustration; a stipulation, that his obligation shall cease if payment or other performance is not demanded before a certain time, seems equally a matter affecting the right. A stipulation, that an action shall not be brought after a certain day or the happening of a certain event, although, in words, it may seem to be a contract respecting the remedy yet it is so in words only; in legal effect, it is a stipulation that a right shall cease and determine if not pursued in a particular way within a limited time, and then it is a fit subject for contract, affecting the right created by it.

But the remedy does not depend on contract, but upon law, generally the *lex fori*, regardless of the *lex loci contractus,* which regulates the construction and legal effect of the contract.

Suppose it were stipulated in an ordinary contract, that in case of breach no action shall be brought; or that the party in default shall be liable in equity only and not at law, or the reverse; that in any suit to be commenced no property shall be attached on mesne process or seized on execution for the satisfaction of a judgment, or that the party shall never be liable to arrest; that, in any suit to be brought on such contract, the party sued will confess judgment, or will waive a trial by jury, or consent that the report of an auditor appointed under the statute shall be final, and judgment be rendered upon it, or that the parties may be witnesses, or, as the law now stands, that the plaintiff will not offer himself as a witness; that, when sued on the contract, the defendant will not plead the statute of limitations, or a discharge in insolvency; and many others might be enumerated; is it not obvious, that, although in a certain sense these are rights or privileges which the party, in the proper time and place, may give or waive, yet a compliance with them cannot be annexed to the contract, cannot be taken notice of and enforced by the court or tribunal before which the remedy is sought, and cannot therefore be relied on by way of defence to the suit brought on the breach of such contract?

We do not mean to say that many of these are stipulations which it would be unlawful to make, or void in their creation, if made on good consideration, or that they do not become executory contracts upon which an action would lie, and upon which damages, if any were sustained, might be recovered. Still they would not be conditions annexed to the contract, to defeat it if not complied with, and so to be used by way of defence to an action upon it.

This seems to have been the distinction taken in the latest English case cited at the bar. *Livingston v. Ralli*, 5 El. & Bl. 132. The point decided there was, that, though an agreement to submit a difference arising on a contract to arbitration is not a good plea in bar to an action on such contract, the breach of it may be a good ground of action.

It is true that a covenant never to sue after the breach of a contract, though a stipulation respecting the remedy to be pursued, may be allowed as a bar to an action upon it; but this is upon the ground that a covenant never to sue is, in legal effect, equivalent to a release, and, to avoid circuity of action, may be pleaded by way of release. The distinction between that which is matter of contract and may be a proper subject of consideration, to be applied in expounding it, making it what it is, and to be applied to the construction of it, whenever and wherever it is to be enforced; and that which is matter of remedy regulated by law, the law of the place where the remedy is sought, is recognized and stated in an early case of our own. *Pearsall v. Dwight,* 2 Mass. 84.

Supposing then the rule to be well settled by principle and authority, that a stipulation is valid which provides that no action shall be brought unless commenced within a specified time, which appears to us to be equivalent to a condition in the contract, that all liability shall cease and determine unless the claim upon it is made by an action within the time limited, and attaches to the contract itself, still, in our opinion, there is not such an analogy between that and the stipulation as to the forum in which a suit shall be commenced, that the one can be taken as an authority for the other. Upon the grounds stated, we think the two cases stand upon very different reasons.

Supposing the words in the by-law, "which action shall be brought at a proper court in the county of Essex," be deemed equivalent to a negative provision, that no action shall be brought in any other county—of which we give no opinion—we are not aware of any authority bearing upon the question that such stipulation or condition can be regarded as a condition of the contract, or that a noncompliance with it will be a defence to the action before a court having jurisdiction of the subject matter and of the parties. In recurring to the full and elaborate written argument of the defendants' counsel, we find no authority upon this part of the case. In referring to the case of *Boynton v. Middlesex Mutual Fire Ins. Co.,* 4 Met. 212, which we have already alluded to, it is urged that the ground on which the court decided must have been the contract of the parties, and not the law of the land. But the court, in 4 Met. 215, [direct] that all acts of incorporation shall be deemed public acts. If so, they are the law of the land, controlling, and, as far as they go, repealing other public acts. Whether this ground was correct or not, it was that on which the court decided, and the case therefore is not an authority for giving a like effect to matters of mere contract.

In a certain sense, all persons are said to be parties and assent to the laws of the government to which they owe allegiance; such laws are binding on them, and enter into and make part of every agreement which such persons make. But we are speaking of the known and familiar distinction between contracts between parties *in pais,* which are binding on them because they have so agreed; and duties created by law, which are binding on the parties because they are law, and do not derive their force from contract. A party is barred by the statute of limitations, not because he has so agreed, but because such is the positive law, the *lex fori,* the aid of which he is seeking to obtain his rights. So of arrest of the person, sequestration of goods, levy on lands, and the like; the plaintiff does not derive his right to the use of these means from the agreement of the contractor, but from the positive law which gives him the remedy, and the means of obtaining satisfaction, incident thereto.

Most of the cases cited, both English and American, are conditions annexed to the contract; such as bringing the action within a certain time, procuring certificates of churchwardens, magistrates or others, practising no fraud, making seasonable and true representations of loss, and the like; as such, they are modifications of the contract, not of the remedy.

We place no great reliance upon considerations of public policy, though, as far as they go, we think they are opposed to the admission of such a defence. The rules to determine in what courts and counties actions may be brought are fixed, upon considerations of general convenience and expediency, by general law; to allow them to be changed by the agreement of parties would disturb the symmetry of the law, and interfere with such convenience. Such contracts might be induced by considerations tending to bring the administration of justice into disrepute; such as the greater or less intelligence and impartiality of judges, the greater or less integrity and capacity of juries, the influence, more or less, arising from the personal, social or political standing of parties in one or another county. It might happen that a mutual insurance company, in which every holder of a policy is a member, and of course interested, would embrace so large a part of the men of property and business in the county, that it would be difficult to find an impartial and intelligent jury. But as already remarked, these considerations are not of much weight. The greatest inconvenience would be in requiring courts and juries to apply different rules of law to different cases, in the conduct of suits, in matters relating merely to the remedy, according to the stipulations of parties in framing and diversifying their contracts in regard to remedies.

There being no authority upon which to determine the case it must be decided upon principle. The question is not without difficulty, but, upon the best consideration the court have been able to give it, they are of opinion that it is not a good defence to this action, that it was brought in the county of Suffolk and not in the county of Essex; and therefore that the exceptions must be sustained, the verdict set aside, and a new trial granted.

* * *

Chief Justice Lemuel Shaw of the Supreme Judicial Court of Massachusetts was sufficiently protective of the prerogative of courts that he asserted this prerogative against even forum selection clauses. Shaw worried, in *Nute*, that enforcing even forum selection clauses would allow "the rules [that] determine in what courts and counties actions may be brought," which are "fixed, upon considerations of general convenience and expediency, by general law," to be "changed by the agreement of the parties." The same concern applies, *a fortiori*, to arbitration agreements, which select a non-judicial forum. Shaw's concerns, moreover, invoked not just prudential considerations but conceptual and even formal ideas about the distinction between resolving disputes by contract and by adjudication. Thus, Shaw categorically distinguished between *establishing* contractual rights on the one hand, and *asserting* established rights on the other. He wrote that "the remedy," which stands, in Shaw's argument, for the entire apparatus of assessing and enforcing previously established contractual rights, "does not depend on [the] contract, but upon law, generally the *lex fori*, regardless of the *lex loci contractus*, which regulates the construction and legal effect of the contract." Shaw observed, in effect, that the grounds of adjudicatory authority are distinct from the grounds of contractual authority, and he concluded from this that the parties could not, by contract, displace adjudication.

There is, however, no deep or structural reason why third-party arbitration should be viewed with such skepticism. Adjudicative legitimacy is not formally limited to the institutions that we call courts. Nothing in the theory of adjudication invokes the thought that adjudication occurs in tribunals that are creatures of the wholesale political structures that otherwise govern the parties to a dispute—as the lower federal courts, for example, are arguably creatures of the political branches of the federal government. The authority of adjudication turns on the transformative and thus legitimating procedures that adjudication employs. Arbitration might employ procedures that are equivalently intensive to those associated with adjudication; and it may do so in the service of applying substantive law that, like the law applied in adjudication, is a creature of the tribunal rather than of the parties. Accordingly, the processes of third-party arbitration can possess, at least in principle, all of the transformative powers associated with the adjudicatory process: they may employ similar mechanisms in order to induce disputants to recast their claims in terms that allow the arbitral tribunal successfully to resolve them. In this way, third-party arbitration resolves conflict by creating a public perspective that exists independent of the disputants and then, in just the same manner as adjudication, by drawing the disputants into that perspective, apart from, and perhaps even against, their initial intentions. This is all just to say that third-party arbitration raises no special concerns about legitimacy (although it does of course raise all of the normal concerns). Third-party arbitration can in theory function, in all relevant respects, just as adjudication proper.

Moreover, especially in a common law system, history in this respect accords with theory. Thus, the judiciary's historical origins are at least partly independent of the executive and the legislature. This is reflected in the fact that even today it is familiar to hear courts, harkening back to these theoretical ideas and historical roots, refer to their "inherent authority."[4] Indeed, insofar as the best account of the authority of adjudication reflects and even valorizes this independence from the other branches of government, one might even say that courts are best understood as a special kind of third-party arbitral tribunal. Indeed, courts may not even be so clearly privileged in respect of legitimacy. Certainly it is the case in many instances of arbitration that the disputants' connections to the arbitral tribunals are no less morally respectable than the connections that ordinary disputants have to the courts before which they appear: the combination of consent to arbitration and truly voluntary membership in a commercial community whose norms affirm the authority of arbitration that binds sophisticated firms to the arbitrators before whom they appear is at least as morally solid as the notoriously unsettled political obligations that connect parties to courts based on the happenstance that they, often involuntarily and by accident of birth, find themselves within the courts' geographical jurisdictions.

Nor is the possibility that third-party arbitration might achieve legitimacy in just the fashion of adjudication merely a theorist's fancy. Forum selection clauses in effect transform one jurisdiction's courts into adjudication unbacked by the ordinary mechanisms of wholesale political authority—that is, into third-party arbitral tribunals—for the parties who invoke them.[5] Perhaps the best contemporary example of such court-based third-

---

4. *See, e.g., United States v. Nelson*, 277 F.3d 164, 208 (2d Cir. 2002) (claiming an "inherent supervisory authority" over the jury selection practices of a federal district court judge); *State v. Quitman County*, 807 So. 2d 401, 409–10 (Miss. 2001) (claiming an inherent authority to require the appointment of counsel for indigent defendants). State courts sometimes rely on their inherent authority to demand increased funding from state and local governments. *See* ROBERT W. TOBIN, CREATING THE JUDICIAL BRANCH: THE UNFINISHED REFORM 16–17 (2004).

5. American law has increasingly favored forum selection clauses. The National Conference of Commissioners on Uniform State Laws has approved a Model Act that gives some recognition to such clauses. *See* Willis L.M. Reese, *The Model Choice of Forum Act*, 17 AM. J. COMP. L. 292, 292 (1969). The American Law Institute has approved enforcing forum selection

party arbitration is the willingness of the courts of the United Kingdom to accept jurisdiction over contract disputes based solely on a forum selection clause, including even where neither the disputants nor the contract being adjudicated bears any other connection to the United Kingdom.[6]

Moreover, tribunals that are purely arbitral—those that never convene as ordinary courts but rather always operate entirely outside of the ordinary structures of government, while owing their authority only to their own procedures—might also achieve solidarity on the adjudicatory model. Indeed, as the Supreme Court has recognized, an agreement to arbitrate, on this model, "is in effect, a specialized kind of forum selection clause that posits not only the situs of the suit but also the procedure to be used in resolving the dispute."[7] Something like this probably occurs in international arbitration that is convened under the model adopted by the International Chamber of Commerce.[8] This form of third-party arbitration follows adjudication-like procedures involving the presentation of evidence, advocacy on both sides, a reasoned decision by a neutral arbitrator, and perhaps even the supervision of individual arbitrators' conduct and decisions by a higher body.[9]

---

clauses as long as they are not "unfair or unreasonable." *See* RESTATEMENT (SECOND) OF CONFLICT OF LAWS § 80 (1969). And the U.S. Supreme Court has held that forum selection clauses may be enforceable in connection with cases that reach federal courts under their admiralty jurisdiction. *See M/S Bremen v. Zapata Off–Shore Co.*, 407 U.S. 1 (1972). The Court has, over time and in conjunction with the lower federal courts, greatly expanded the class of cases in which forum selection clauses will be enforced. *See Carnival Cruise Lines, Inc. v. Shute*, 499 U.S. 585, 601 (1991) (Stevens, J., dissenting). Much of the law concerning the enforcement of forum selection clauses, including the law governing such clauses when they arise in federal courts under diversity jurisdiction, is of course state law. The doctrine here is mixed. *See* Paul D. Carrington & Paul H. Haagen, *Contract and Jurisdiction*, 1996 SUP. CT. REV. 331, 358–9 (1996).

6. *See, e.g.*, CIV. PROC. R. 1998, S.I. 1998/3231, Practice Direction 6B, r.6 (U.K.) (permitting English courts to assume jurisdiction over a contract dispute, even though the contracting parties do not trade or reside within the courts' ordinary jurisdiction and even though the contract was not made within the jurisdiction, as long as the contract "contains a term to the effect that the court shall have jurisdiction to determine any claim in respect of the contract"). Similarly, the 1968 Brussels Convention of the European Economic Community and the subsequent Commission Regulation No. 44/2001 provides that when one or more parties to a contract are domiciled in a state that belongs to the convention, then the parties may agree that the courts of *any* signatory state shall have exclusive jurisdiction to settle any dispute that might arise under the contract. *See, e.g.*, JOHN O'HARE & KEVIN BROWN, CIVIL LITIGATION 166, 169 (13th ed.).

7. Scherk v. Alberto–Culver Co., 417 U.S. 506, 519 (1974).

8. *See* INT'L CHAMBER OF COMMERCE, RULES OF ARBITRATION (1998), *available at* http://www. iccwbo.org/uploadedFiles/Court/Arbitration/other/rules_arb_english.pdf. It is sometimes suggested, with some support in the case law, that the U.S. Supreme Court is sensitive to the value of third-party commercial arbitration's employing processes that resemble adjudication and hence are adequate to the problem of adjudicatory solidarity. *See, e.g See* Paul D. Carrington & Paul H. Haagen, *Contract and Jurisdiction*, 1996 SUP. CT. REV. 331, 332–33 (1996) (commenting on *Vimar Seguros y Reaseguros, S.A. v. M/V Sky Reefer*, 515 U.S. 528 (1995), and *Mitsubishi Motors Corp. v. Soler Chrysler–Plymouth, Inc.*, 473 U.S. 614 (1985)). Some domestic arbitral organizations are also internalizing due process norms. Thus the Consumer Due Process Protocol, for example, calls for a "fundamentally-fair" arbitral process, meaning a process that requires notice, opportunities to be heard, and an independent decision maker. *See* American Arbitration Association, National Consumer Disputes Advisory Committee, Consumer Due Process Protocol, http://www.adr.org/sp.asp?id=22019.

9. Appellate review remains admittedly rare in even the most highly formalized arbitral proceedings.

Insofar as it follows these procedures, such arbitration achieves a court-like legitimacy, entirely independent of the political structures in which ordinary courts are embedded.[10] Indeed, it may even happen that third-party arbitration, precisely because it arises independent of the ordinary political process, can achieve adjudicatory solidarity more successfully than courts can do. An example is religious arbitration, which occurs when members of a religious subculture seek to resolve disputes in tribunals that are more sympathetic to their basic worldviews than the courts of the dominant culture are prepared to be.[11] It may be that the subculture suspects the substantive aims of the dominant courts, or it may be that certain features of the processes followed in those courts are alienating to members of the subculture. In some societies and for some bodies of law—for example for family law in Israel—such third-party arbitration has become a standard form of dispute resolution.[12] In all these cases, the success of third-party arbitral solidarity may be identified insofar as parties subject to such arbitration, even if they initially fought removal from the ordinary courts, accept the authority of the arbitral decisions.

At least where an arbitral tribunal adopts court-like procedures, third-party arbitration just *is* adjudication. And it is therefore competent, from the perspective of its legitimate authority, to reach all the questions that ordinary adjudication reaches, including, for example, to decide the scope of its own authority. If there is an objection to third-party arbitration, it must sound not in concerns about its procedural legitimacy but rather in concerns about substantive justice. The objection must argue, in other words, that third-party arbitration in practice produces outcomes that objective observers should disapprove, even if they come to seem legitimate to the parties who have gone through the arbitral process. That is a perfectly plausible style of argument; it proposes, for example, that the secular legal order should be skeptical of the attitudes of women who accept the decisions of religious family courts, or that a state's legal order should be skeptical when its citizens come to accept the decisions of arbitral tribunals (including of courts sitting as third-party arbitrators) outside their jurisdiction.

Perhaps such skepticism can give a state sufficient ground to refuse to enforce the judgments of arbitral tribunals. But an argument of this sort has two features that may not be ignored: first, the argument amounts to a

---

10. This list does not include the publication of decisions in a forum accessible by third parties. This practice, which is prominent in adjudication, may be essential to integrating a practice of retail dispute resolution into the other forms of open government, including most notably legislation. Insofar as it is essential, that is a strike against arbitration's overall appeal. For an argument that develops related ideas, see Judith Resnik, *Courts: In and Out of Sight, Site, and Cite*, 53 VILLANOVA L. REV. 771 (2008). But the lack of publication of arbitral decisions does not undercut arbitration's authority with respect to the disputants whose conflicts it decides.

11. *See generally* Michael A. Helfand, *Religious Arbitration and the New Multiculturalism: Negotiating Conflicting Legal Orders*, 86 N.Y.U. L. Rev. 1231 (2011).

12. *See, e.g.*, Marc Galanter & Jayanth Krishnan, *Personal Law and Human Rights in India and Israel*, 34 ISR. L. REV. 101, 127 (2000); Gabriela Shalley, *Israel, in* THE ELGAR ENCYCLOPEDIA OF COMPARATIVE LAW 348, 350 (Jan M. Smits ed., 2006).

paternalistic insult to the persons whose acceptance of arbitral legitimacy it disrespects as ideological; and second, the argument may be applied equally, indeed, formally equivalently, to the core cases of perfectly ordinary court-based adjudication, because adjudication's solidaristic powers do not necessarily track justice more closely than third-party arbitration's solidaristic powers.

Perhaps for these reasons, the law has for some time rejected Shaw's skepticism and favored third-party arbitration. Indeed, the law's openness to arbitration continues to increase. The Federal Arbitration Act enshrines the legislature's prudential choice to favor third-party arbitration in general. And any number of cases, decided against the backdrop of the statute, favor arbitration in particular instances. The materials below reproduce key sections of the statute and also an opinion, decided under the statute, whose language and conceptual structure represent a striking and almost complete about-face from the sensibilities that animated Chief Justice Shaw's approach in *Nute*.

The Federal Arbitration Act

9 U.S.C.A. Selected Sections

Section 1.   "Maritime transactions" and "commerce" defined; exceptions to operation of title

"Maritime transactions", as herein defined, means charter parties, bills of lading of water carriers, agreements relating to wharfage, supplies furnished vessels or repairs to vessels, collisions, or any other matters in foreign commerce which, if the subject of controversy, would be embraced within admiralty jurisdiction; "commerce", as herein defined, means commerce among the several States or with foreign nations, or in any Territory of the United States or in the District of Columbia, or between any such Territory and another, or between any such Territory and any State or foreign nation, or between the District of Columbia and any State or Territory or foreign nation, but nothing herein contained shall apply to contracts of employment of seamen, railroad employees, or any other class of workers engaged in foreign or interstate commerce.

Section 2.   Validity, irrevocability, and enforcement of agreements to arbitrate

A written provision in any maritime transaction or a contract evidencing a transaction involving commerce to settle by arbitration a controversy thereafter arising out of such contract or transaction, or the refusal to perform the whole or any part thereof, or an agreement in writing to submit to arbitration an existing controversy arising out of such a contract, transaction, or refusal, shall be valid, irrevocable, and enforceable, save upon such grounds as exist at law or in equity for the revocation of any contract.

Section 3. Stay of proceedings where issue therein referable to arbitration

If any suit or proceeding be brought in any of the courts of the United States upon any issue referable to arbitration under an agreement in writing for such arbitration, the court in which such suit is pending, upon being satisfied that the issue involved in such suit or proceeding is referable to arbitration under such an agreement, shall on application of one of the parties stay the trial of the action until such arbitration has been had in accordance with the terms of the agreement, providing the applicant for the stay is not in default in proceeding with such arbitration.

Section 4. Failure to arbitrate under agreement; petition to United States court having jurisdiction for order to compel arbitration; notice and service thereof; hearing and determination

A party aggrieved by the alleged failure, neglect, or refusal of another to arbitrate under a written agreement for arbitration may petition any United States district court which, save for such agreement, would have jurisdiction under Title 28, in a civil action or in admiralty of the subject matter of a suit arising out of the controversy between the parties, for an order directing that such arbitration proceed in the manner provided for in such agreement. Five days' notice in writing of such application shall be served upon the party in default. Service thereof shall be made in the manner provided by the Federal Rules of Civil Procedure. The court shall hear the parties, and upon being satisfied that the making of the agreement for arbitration or the failure to comply therewith is not in issue, the court shall make an order directing the parties to proceed to arbitration in accordance with the terms of the agreement. The hearing and proceedings, under such agreement, shall be within the district in which the petition for an order directing such arbitration is filed. If the making of the arbitration agreement or the failure, neglect, or refusal to perform the same be in issue, the court shall proceed summarily to the trial thereof. If no jury trial be demanded by the party alleged to be in default, or if the matter in dispute is within admiralty jurisdiction, the court shall hear and determine such issue. Where such an issue is raised, the party alleged to be in default may, except in cases of admiralty, on or before the return day of the notice of application, demand a jury trial of such issue, and upon such demand the court shall make an order referring the issue or issues to a jury in the manner provided by the Federal Rules of Civil Procedure, or may specially call a jury for that purpose. If the jury find that no agreement in writing for arbitration was made or that there is no default in proceeding there under, the proceeding shall be dismissed. If the jury find that an agreement for arbitration was made in writing and that there is a default in proceeding there under, the court shall make an order summarily directing the parties to proceed with the arbitration in accordance with the terms thereof.

Section 5. Appointment of arbitrators or umpire

If in the agreement provision be made for a method of naming or appointing an arbitrator or arbitrators or an umpire, such method shall be followed; but if no method be provided therein, or if a method be provided and any party thereto shall fail to avail himself of such method, or if for any other reason there shall be a lapse in the naming of an arbitrator or arbitrators or umpire, or in filling a vacancy, then upon the application of either party to the controversy the court shall designate and appoint an arbitrator or arbitrators or umpire, as the case may require, who shall act under the said agreement with the same force and effect as if he or they had been specifically named therein; and unless otherwise provided in the agreement the arbitration shall be by a single arbitrator.

Section 7. *Witnesses before arbitrators; fees; compelling attendance*

The arbitrators selected either as prescribed in this title or otherwise, or a majority of them, may summon in writing any person to attend before them or any of them as a witness and in a proper case to bring with him or them any book, record, document, or paper which may be deemed material as evidence in the case. The fees for such attendance shall be the same as the fees of witnesses before masters of the United States courts. Said summons shall issue in the name of the arbitrator or arbitrators and shall be signed by the arbitrators and shall be directed to the said person and shall be served in the same manner as subpoenas to appear and testify before the court; if any person or persons so summoned to testify shall refuse or neglect to obey said summons, upon petition the United States district court for the district in which such arbitrators are sitting may compel the attendance of such person or persons before said arbitrators, or punish said person or persons for contempt in the same manner provided by law for securing the attendance of witnesses or their punishment for neglect or refusal to attend in the courts of the United States.

Section 9. *Award of arbitrators; confirmation; jurisdiction; procedure*

If the parties in their agreement have agreed that a judgment of the court shall be entered upon the award made pursuant to the arbitration, and shall specify the court, then at any time within one year after the award is made any party to the arbitration may apply to the court so specified for an order confirming the award, and thereupon the court must grant such an order unless the award is vacated, modified, or corrected as prescribed in sections 10 and 11 of this title. If no court is specified in the agreement of the parties, then such application may be made to the United States court in and for the district within which such award was made. Notice of the application shall be served upon the adverse party, and thereupon the court shall have jurisdiction of such party as though he had appeared generally in the proceeding. If the adverse party is a resident of the district within which the award was made, such service shall be made upon the adverse party or his attorney as prescribed by law for service of notice of motion in an action in the same court. If the adverse party shall be a nonresident, then the notice of the application shall be served by the marshal of any district within which the adverse party may be found in like manner as other process of the court.

Section 10. *Same; vacation; grounds; rehearing*

(a) In any of the following cases the United States court in and for the district wherein the award was made may make an order vacating the award upon the application of any party to the arbitration—

(1) where the award was procured by corruption, fraud, or undue means;

(2) where there was evident partiality or corruption in the arbitrators, or either of them;

(3) where the arbitrators were guilty of misconduct in refusing to postpone the hearing, upon sufficient cause shown, or in refusing to hear evidence pertinent and material to the controversy; or of any other misbehavior by which the rights of any party have been prejudiced; or

(4) where the arbitrators exceeded their powers, or so imperfectly executed them that a mutual, final, and definite award upon the subject matter submitted was not made.

(b) If an award is vacated and the time within which the agreement required the award to be made has not expired, the court may, in its discretion, direct a rehearing by the arbitrators.

Section 11.   Same; modification or correction; grounds; order

In either of the following cases the United States court in and for the district wherein the award was made may make an order modifying or correcting the award upon the application of any party to the arbitration—

(a) Where there was an evident material miscalculation of figures or an evident material mistake in the description of any person, thing, or property referred to in the award.

(b) Where the arbitrators have awarded upon a matter not submitted to them, unless it is a matter not affecting the merits of the decision upon the matter submitted.

(c) Where the award is imperfect in matter of form not affecting the merits of the controversy.

The order may modify and correct the award, so as to effect the intent thereof and promote justice between the parties.

Section 16.   Appeals

(a) An appeal may be taken from—

(1) an order—

(A) refusing a stay of any action under section 3 of this title,

(B) denying a petition under section 4 of this title to order arbitration to proceed,

(C) denying an application under section 206 of this title to compel arbitration,

(D) confirming or denying confirmation of an award or partial award, or

(E) modifying, correcting, or vacating an award;

(2) an interlocutory order granting, continuing, or modifying an injunction against an arbitration that is subject to this title; or

(3) a final decision with respect to an arbitration that is subject to this title.

(b) Except as otherwise provided in section 1292(b) of title 28, an appeal may not be taken from an interlocutory order—

(1) granting a stay of any action under section 3 of this title;

(2) directing arbitration to proceed under section 4 of this title;

(3) compelling arbitration under section 206 of this title; or

(4) refusing to enjoin an arbitration that is subject to this title.

Section 201.   Enforcement of Convention

The Convention on the Recognition and Enforcement of Foreign Arbitral Awards of June 10, 1958, shall be enforced in United States courts in accordance with this chapter.

Section 202.   Agreement or award falling under the Convention

An arbitration agreement or arbitral award arising out of a legal relationship, whether contractual or not, which is considered as commercial, including a transaction, contract, or agreement described in section 2 of this title, falls under the Convention. An agreement or award arising out of such a relationship which is entirely between citizens of the United States shall be deemed not to fall under the Convention unless that relationship involves property located abroad, envisages performance or enforcement abroad, or has some other reasonable relation with one or more foreign states. For the purpose of this section a corporation is a citizen of the United States if it is incorporated or has its principal place of business in the United States.

Vimar Seguros y Reaseguros, S.A. v. M/V Sky Reefer

Supreme Court of the United States, 1995.
515 U.S. 528.

■ KENNEDY, J. This case requires us to interpret the Carriage of Goods by Sea Act (COGSA), 46 U.S.C.App. § 1300 *et seq.*, as it relates to a contract containing a clause requiring arbitration in a foreign country. The question is whether a foreign arbitration clause in a bill of lading is invalid under COGSA because it lessens liability in the sense that COGSA prohibits. Our holding that COGSA does not forbid selection of the foreign forum makes it unnecessary to resolve the further question whether the Federal Arbitration Act (FAA), 9 U.S.C. § 1 *et seq.* would override COGSA were it interpreted otherwise. In our view, the relevant provisions of COGSA and the FAA are in accord, not in conflict.

I

The contract at issue in this case is a standard form bill of lading to evidence the purchase of a shipload of Moroccan oranges and lemons. The purchaser was Bacchus Associates (Bacchus), a New York partnership that distributes fruit at wholesale throughout the Northeastern United States. Bacchus dealt with Galaxie Negoce, S.A. (Galaxie), a Moroccan fruit supplier. Bacchus contracted with Galaxie to purchase the shipload of fruit and chartered a ship to transport it from Morocco to Massachusetts. The ship was the M/V Sky Reefer, a refrigerated cargo ship owned by M.H. Maritima, S.A., a Panamanian company, and time-chartered to Nichiro Gyogyo Kaisha, Ltd., a Japanese company. Stevedores hired by Galaxie loaded and stowed the cargo. As is customary in these types of transactions, when it received the cargo from Galaxie, Nichiro as carrier issued a form bill of lading to Galaxie as shipper and consignee. Once the ship set sail from Morocco, Galaxie tendered the bill of lading to Bacchus according to the terms of a letter of credit posted in Galaxie's favor.

Among the rights and responsibilities set out in the bill of lading were arbitration and choice-of-law clauses. Clause 3, entitled "Governing Law and Arbitration," provided:

"(1) The contract evidenced by or contained in this Bill of Lading shall be governed by the Japanese law.

"(2) Any dispute arising from this Bill of Lading shall be referred to arbitration in Tokyo by the Tokyo Maritime Arbitration Commission (TOMAC) of The Japan Shipping Exchange, Inc., in accordance with the rules of TOMAC and any amendment thereto, and the award given by the arbitrators shall be final and binding on both parties."

When the vessel's hatches were opened for discharge in Massachusetts, Bacchus discovered that thousands of boxes of oranges had shifted in the cargo holds, resulting in over $1 million damage. Bacchus received $733,442.90 compensation from petitioner Vimar Seguros y Reaseguros (Vimar Seguros), Bacchus' marine cargo insurer that became subrogated *pro tanto* to Bacchus' rights. Petitioner and Bacchus then brought suit against Maritima *in personam* and M/V Sky Reefer *in rem* in the District Court for the District of Massachusetts under the bill of lading. These defendants, respondents here, moved to stay the action and compel arbitration in Tokyo under clause 3 of the bill of lading and § 3 of the FAA, which requires courts to stay proceedings and enforce arbitration agreements covered by the Act. Petitioner and Bacchus opposed the motion, arguing the arbitration clause was unenforceable under the FAA both because it was a contract of adhesion and because it violated COGSA § 3(8). The premise of the latter argument was that the inconvenience and costs of proceeding in Japan would "lesse[n] liability" as those terms are used in COGSA.

The District Court rejected the adhesion argument, observing that Congress defined the arbitration agreements enforceable under the FAA to include maritime bills of lading, 9 U.S.C. § 1, and that petitioner was a sophisticated party familiar with the negotiation of maritime shipping transactions. It also rejected the argument that requiring the parties to submit to arbitration would lessen respondents' liability under COGSA § 3(8). The court granted the motion to stay judicial proceedings and to compel arbitration; it retained jurisdiction pending arbitration; and at petitioner's request, it certified for interlocutory appeal under 28 U.S.C. § 1292(b) its ruling to compel arbitration, stating that the controlling question of law was "whether [COGSA § 3(8)] nullifies an arbitration clause contained in a bill of lading governed by COGSA."

The First Circuit affirmed the order to arbitrate. Although it expressed grave doubt whether a foreign arbitration clause lessened liability under COGSA § 3(8), the Court of Appeals assumed the clause was invalid under COGSA and resolved the conflict between the statutes in favor of the FAA, which it considered to be the later enacted and more specific statute. We granted certiorari to resolve a Circuit split on the enforceability of foreign arbitration clauses in maritime bills of lading. Compare the case below (enforcing foreign arbitration clause assuming *arguendo* it violated COGSA), with *State Establishment for Agricultural Product Trading v. M/V Wesermunde*, 838 F.2d 1576 (CA11) (declining to enforce foreign arbitration clause because that would violate COGSA), cert. denied, 488 U.S. 916 (1988). We now affirm.

II

The parties devote much of their argument to the question whether COGSA or the FAA has priority. "[W]hen two statutes are capable of co-existence," however, "it is the duty of the courts, absent a clearly expressed congressional intention to the contrary, to regard each as effective." *Morton v. Mancari*, 417 U.S. 535, 551 (1974). There is no conflict unless COGSA by its own terms nullifies a foreign arbitration clause, and we choose to address that issue rather than assume nullification *arguendo*, as the Court of Appeals did. We consider the two arguments made by petitioner. The first is that a foreign arbitration clause lessens COGSA liability by increasing the transaction costs of obtaining relief. The second is that there is a risk foreign arbitrators will not apply COGSA.

A

The leading case for invalidation of a foreign forum selection clause is the opinion of the Court of Appeals for the Second Circuit in *Indussa Corp. v. S.S. Ranborg*, 377 F.2d 200 (1967) (en banc). The court there found that COGSA invalidated a clause designating a foreign judicial forum because it "puts 'a high hurdle' in the way of enforcing liability, and thus is an effective means for carriers to secure settlements lower than if cargo [owners] could sue in a convenient forum." *Id.*, at 203 (citation omitted). The court observed "there could be no assurance that [the foreign court] would apply [COGSA] in the same way as would an American tribunal subject to the uniform control of the Supreme Court." *Id.*, at 203–204. Following *Indussa*, the Courts of Appeals without exception have invalidated foreign forum selection clauses under § 3(8). As foreign arbitration clauses are but a subset of foreign forum selection clauses in general, the *Indussa* holding has been extended to foreign arbitration clauses as well. The logic of that extension would be quite defensible, but we cannot endorse the reasoning or the conclusion of the *Indussa* rule itself.

The determinative provision in COGSA, examined with care, does not support the arguments advanced first in *Indussa* and now by petitioner. Section 3(8) of COGSA provides as follows:

> "Any clause, covenant, or agreement in a contract of carriage relieving the carrier or the ship from liability for loss or damage to or in connection with the goods, arising from negligence, fault, or failure in the duties and obligations provided in this section, or lessening such liability otherwise than as provided in this chapter, shall be null and void and of no effect." 46 U.S.C.App. § 1303(8).

The liability that may not be lessened is "liability for loss or damage arising from negligence, fault, or failure in the duties and obligations provided in this section." The statute thus addresses the lessening of the specific liability imposed by the Act, without addressing the separate question of the means and costs of enforcing that liability. The difference is that between explicit statutory guarantees and the procedure for enforcing them, between applicable liability principles and the forum in which they are to be vindicated.

The liability imposed on carriers under COGSA § 3 is defined by explicit standards of conduct, and it is designed to correct specific abuses by carriers. In the 19th century it was a prevalent practice for common carriers to insert clauses in bills of lading exempting themselves from liability for damage or loss, limiting the period in which plaintiffs had to present their notice of claim or bring suit, and capping any damages awards per package. Thus, § 3, entitled "Responsibilities and liabilities of carrier and ship," requires that the carrier "exercise due diligence to [m]ake the ship seaworthy" and "[p]roperly man, equip, and supply the ship" before and at the beginning of the voyage, § 3(1), "properly and carefully load, handle, stow, carry, keep, care for, and discharge the goods carried," § 3(2), and issue a bill of lading with specified contents, § 3(3). 46 U.S.C.App. §§ 1303(1), (2), and (3). Section 3(6) allows the cargo owner to provide notice of loss or damage within three days and to bring suit within one year. These are the substantive obligations and particular procedures that § 3(8) prohibits a carrier from altering to its advantage in a bill of lading. Nothing in this section, however, suggests that the statute prevents the parties from agreeing to enforce these obligations in a particular forum. By its terms, it establishes certain duties and obligations, separate and apart from the mechanisms for their enforcement.

Petitioner's contrary reading of § 3(8) is undermined by the Court's construction of a similar statutory provision in *Carnival Cruise Lines, Inc. v. Shute*, 499 U.S. 585 (1991). There a number of Washington residents argued that a Florida forum selection clause contained in a cruise ticket should not be enforced because the expense and inconvenience of litigation in Florida would "caus[e] plaintiffs unreasonable hardship in asserting their rights," *id.*, at 596, and therefore " 'lessen, weaken, or avoid the right of any claimant to a trial by court of competent jurisdiction on the question of liability for loss or injury, or the measure of damages therefor' " in violation of the Limitation of Vessel Owner's Liability Act, *id.*, at 595–596 (quoting 46 U.S.C.App. § 183c). We observed that the clause "does not purport to limit petitioner's liability for negligence," 499 U.S., at 596–597, and enforced the agreement over the dissent's argument, based in part on the *Indussa* line of cases, that the cost and inconvenience of traveling thousands of miles "lessens or weakens [plaintiffs'] ability to recover," 499 U.S., at 603 (Stevens, J., dissenting).

If the question whether a provision lessens liability were answered by reference to the costs and inconvenience to the cargo owner, there would be no principled basis for distinguishing national from foreign arbitration clauses. Even if it were reasonable to read § 3(8) to make a distinction based on travel time, airfare, and hotels bills, these factors are not susceptible of a simple and enforceable distinction between domestic and foreign forums. Requiring a Seattle cargo owner to arbitrate in New York likely imposes more costs and burdens than a foreign arbitration clause requiring it to arbitrate in Vancouver. It would be unwieldy and unsupported by the terms or policy of the statute to require courts to proceed case by case to tally the costs and burdens to particular plaintiffs in light of their means, the size of their claims, and the relative burden on the carrier.

Our reading of "lessening such liability" to exclude increases in the transaction costs of litigation also finds support in the goals of the Brussels Convention for the Unification of Certain Rules Relating to Bills of Lading, 51 Stat. 233 (1924) (Hague Rules), on which COGSA is modeled. Sixty-six countries, including the United States and Japan, are now parties to the Convention, and it appears that none has interpreted its enactment of § 3(8) of the Hague Rules to prohibit foreign forum selection clauses. The English courts long ago rejected the reasoning later adopted by the *Indussa* court. See *Maharani Woollen Mills Co. v. Anchor Line*, [1927] 29 Lloyd's List L. Rep. 169 (C.A.) (Scrutton, L.J.) ("[T]he liability of the carrier appears to me to remain exactly the same under the clause. The only difference is a question of procedure-where shall the law be enforced?—and I do not read any clause as to procedure as lessening liability"). And other countries that do not recognize foreign forum selection clauses rely on specific provisions to that effect in their domestic versions of the Hague Rules. In light of the fact that COGSA is the culmination of a multilateral effort "to establish uniform ocean bills of lading to govern the rights and liabilities of carriers and shippers inter se in international trade," *Robert C. Herd & Co. v. Krawill Machinery Corp.*, 359 U.S. 297, 301 (1959), we decline to interpret our version of the Hague Rules in a manner contrary to every other nation to have addressed this issue.

It would also be out of keeping with the objects of the Convention for the courts of this country to interpret COGSA to disparage the authority or competence of international forums for dispute resolution. Petitioner's skepticism over the ability of foreign arbitrators to apply COGSA or the

Hague Rules, and its reliance on this aspect of *Indussa Corp. v. S.S. Ranborg*, 377 F.2d 200 (CA2 1967), must give way to contemporary principles of international comity and commercial practice. As the Court observed in *The Bremen v. Zapata Off–Shore Co.*, 407 U.S. 1 (1972), when it enforced a foreign forum selection clause, the historical judicial resistance to foreign forum selection clauses "has little place in an era when businesses once essentially local now operate in world markets." *Id.*, at 12. "The expansion of American business and industry will hardly be encouraged," we explained, "if, notwithstanding solemn contracts, we insist on a parochial concept that all disputes must be resolved under our laws and in our courts." *Id.*, at 9. See *Mitsubishi Motors Corp. v. Soler Chrysler–Plymouth, Inc.*, 473 U.S. 614, 638 (1985) (if international arbitral institutions "are to take a central place in the international legal order, national courts will need to 'shake off the old judicial hostility to arbitration,' and also their customary and understandable unwillingness to cede jurisdiction of a claim arising under domestic law to a foreign or transnational tribunal") (citation omitted); *Scherk v. Alberto–Culver Co.*, 417 U.S., at 516 ("A parochial refusal by the courts of one country to enforce an international arbitration agreement" would frustrate "the orderliness and predictability essential to any international business transaction").

That the forum here is arbitration only heightens the irony of petitioner's argument, for the FAA is also based in part on an international convention, 9 U.S.C. § 201 *et seq.* (codifying the United Nations Convention on the Recognition and Enforcement of Foreign Arbitral Awards, June 10, 1958, [1970] 21 U.S.T. 2517, T.I.A.S. No. 6997), intended "to encourage the recognition and enforcement of commercial arbitration agreements in international contracts and to unify the standards by which agreements to arbitrate are observed and arbitral awards are enforced in the signatory countries," *Scherk*, supra, at 520, n. 15. The FAA requires enforcement of arbitration agreements in contracts that involve interstate commerce and in maritime transactions, including bills of lading, see 9 U.S.C. §§ 1, 2, 201, 202, where there is no independent basis in law or equity for revocation, cf. *Carnival Cruise Lines*, 499 U.S., at 595 ("[F]orum-selection clauses contained in form passage contracts are subject to judicial scrutiny for fundamental fairness"). If the United States is to be able to gain the benefits of international accords and have a role as a trusted partner in multilateral endeavors, its courts should be most cautious before interpreting its domestic legislation in such manner as to violate international agreements. That concern counsels against construing COGSA to nullify foreign arbitration clauses because of inconvenience to the plaintiff or insular distrust of the ability of foreign arbitrators to apply the law.

B

Petitioner's second argument against enforcement of the Japanese arbitration clause is that there is no guarantee foreign arbitrators will apply COGSA. This objection raises a concern of substance. The central guarantee of § 3(8) is that the terms of a bill of landing may not relieve the carrier of the obligations or diminish the legal duties specified by the Act.

The relevant question, therefore, is whether the substantive law to be applied will reduce the carrier's obligations to the cargo owner below what COGSA guarantees.

Petitioner argues that the arbitrators will follow the Japanese Hague Rules, which, petitioner contends, lessen respondents' liability in at least one significant respect. The Japanese version of the Hague Rules, it is said, provides the carrier with a defense based on the acts or omissions of the stevedores hired by the shipper, Galaxie, see Article 3(1) (carrier liable "when he or the persons employed by him" fail to take due care), while COGSA, according to petitioner, makes non delegable the carrier's obligation to "properly and carefully stow the goods carried," COGSA § 3(2), 46 U.S.C.App. § 1303(2). But see COGSA § 4(2)(i), 46 U.S.C.App. § 1304(2)(i) ("Neither the carrier nor the ship shall be responsible for loss or damage arising or resulting from ... [a]ct or omission of the shipper or owner of the goods, his agent or representative"); COGSA § 3(8), 46 U.S.C.App. § 1303(8) (agreement may not relieve or lessen liability "otherwise than as provided in this chapter").

Whatever the merits of petitioner's comparative reading of COGSA and its Japanese counterpart, its claim is premature. At this interlocutory stage it is not established what law the arbitrators will apply to petitioner's claims or that petitioner will receive diminished protection as a result. The arbitrators may conclude that COGSA applies of its own force or that Japanese law does not apply so that, under another clause of the bill of lading, COGSA controls. Respondents seek only to enforce the arbitration agreement. The District Court has retained jurisdiction over the case and "will have the opportunity at the award-enforcement stage to ensure that the legitimate interest in the enforcement of the ... laws has been addressed." *Mitsubishi Motors*, supra, 473 U.S., at 638; cf. 1 Restatement (Third) of Foreign Relations Law of the United States § 482(2)(d) (1986) ("A court in the United States need not recognize a judgment of the court of a foreign state if ... the judgment itself, is repugnant to the public policy of the United States"). Were there no subsequent opportunity for review and were we persuaded that "the choice-of-forum and choice-of-law clauses operated in tandem as a prospective waiver of a party's right to pursue statutory remedies, we would have little hesitation in condemning the agreement as against public policy." *Mitsubishi Motors*, supra, at 637, n. 19, n. 19. Under the circumstances of this case, however, the First Circuit was correct to reserve judgment on the choice-of-law question as it must be decided in the first instance by the arbitrator. As the District Court has retained jurisdiction, mere speculation that the foreign arbitrators might apply Japanese law which, depending on the proper construction of COGSA, might reduce respondents' legal obligations, does not in and of itself lessen liability under COGSA § 3(8).

Because we hold that foreign arbitration clauses in bills of lading are not invalid under COGSA in all circumstances, both the FAA and COGSA may be given full effect. The judgment of the Court of Appeals is affirmed, and the case is remanded for further proceedings consistent with this opinion.

It is so ordered.

■ JUSTICE BREYER took no part in the consideration or decision of this case.

■ [A concurrence by O'CONNOR, J. and a dissent by STEVENS, J. are omitted.]

* * *

Vimar Seguros is interesting for the way in which it adopts virtually all the formal distinctions drawn in *Nute* but employs the distinctions to almost precisely the opposite effect from the outcome reached in the earlier case. *Vimar Seguros* held that even if an arbitration clause in a bill of lading selects a foreign arbitral tribunal and increases the transactions costs faced by a U.S. shipper who is seeking to enforce contractual rights against a foreign carrier, this does not constitute a "lessening" of the carrier's liability of the sort that is prohibited by the Carriage of Goods at Sea Act. In reaching this conclusion, the Court insisted that the "duties and obligations" that are established by the Act are *"separate and apart* from the mechanisms for their enforcement," and that arbitration affects only the latter. This is, of course, precisely Shaw's formal distinction between creating rights and enforcing them, although the distinction is now employed in support of a substantive pro-arbitration agenda that is directly opposed to Shaw's.

21.2   FIRST-PARTY ARBITRATION

First-party arbitration functions very differently from third and possesses authority on the model not of adjudication but of contract. Indeed, a first-party arbitrator's decision, being an instance of contractual gap-filling, just *is* a term of the parties' contract.

To see how this model might work, return to *Eastern Airlines v. Gulf Oil Co.* from Chapter 19, and in particular the clause that set the price of Eastern's fuel by reference to the Crude Oil Supplement West Texas Sour price indicator. In a sense, this clause established the Platts Oilgram Service, the publisher of the Crude Oil Supplement, as an arbitrator authorized by the parties to settle post contractual disputes about price. But this would for any number of reasons be an odd way to characterize the Crude Oil Supplement's role in the contract. A better characterization calls the Crude Oil Supplement a gap-filler. That is, the parties in *Eastern Airlines* did not contract for their disputes about price to be resolved by the Crude Oil Supplement. Rather, they contracted directly for the West Texas Sour price indicator.

This account may be generalized: an agreement to submit to first-party arbitration is not in principle any different from a contract that leaves certain terms open but includes an account of the mechanism by which these gaps will be filled. Common mechanisms of this sort include formulas, references to market conditions, and commitments to bargain in good faith.

First-party arbitration may be understood as simply another such mechanism, as the alternative name "arbitration as gap-filling" emphasizes. First-party arbitration does not so much contractualize adjudication as replace adjudication and the adjudicatory process with contract *tout court*. First-party arbitration—the gap-filling conception reveals—is not a *process* for deciding the content of independent legal entitlements at all, but rather a part of the *substance* of the contracts that create it, a means of fixing the content of contractual rights.

Perhaps unsurprisingly, not just third-but also first-party arbitration receives prominent recognition in the case law.

United Steelworkers of America v. American Mfg. Co.

Supreme Court of the United States, 1960.
363 U.S. 564.

■ Opinion of the Court by DOUGLAS, J., announced by BRENNAN, J. This suit was brought by petitioner union in the District Court to compel arbitration of a "grievance" that petitioner, acting for one Sparks, a union member, had filed with the respondent, Sparks' employer. The employer defended on the ground (1) that Sparks is estopped from making his claim because he had a few days previously settled a workmen's compensation claim against the company on the basis that he was permanently partially disabled, (2) that Sparks is not physically able to do the work, and (3) that this type of dispute is not arbitrable under the collective bargaining agreement in question.

The agreement provided that during its term there would be "no strike," unless the employer refused to abide by a decision of the arbitrator. The agreement sets out a detailed grievance procedure with a provision for arbitration (regarded as the standard form) of all disputes between the parties "as to the meaning, interpretation and application of the provisions of this agreement."

The agreement reserves to the management power to suspend or discharge any employee "for cause." It also contains a provision that the employer will employ and promote employees on the principle of seniority "where ability and efficiency are equal." Sparks left his work due to an injury and while off work brought an action for compensation benefits. The case was settled, Sparks' physician expressing the opinion that the injury had made him 25% "permanently partially disabled." That was on September 9. Two weeks later the union filed a grievance which charged that Sparks was entitled to return to his job by virtue of the seniority provision of the collective bargaining agreement. Respondent refused to arbitrate and this action was brought. The District Court held that Sparks, having accepted the settlement on the basis of permanent partial disability, was estopped to claim any seniority or employment rights and granted the motion for summary judgment. The Court of Appeals affirmed, 264 F.2d 624, for different reasons. After reviewing the evidence it held that the grievance is "a frivolous, patently baseless one, not subject to arbitration under the collective bargaining agreement." *Id.*, at 628. The case is here on a writ of certiorari.

Section 203 (d) of the Labor Management Relations Act, 1947, 29 U. S. C. § 173 (d), states, "Final adjustment by a method agreed upon by the parties is hereby declared to be the desirable method for settlement of grievance disputes arising over the application or interpretation of an existing collective-bargaining agreement." That policy can be effectuated only if the means chosen by the parties for settlement of their differences under a collective bargaining agreement is given full play.

A state decision that held to the contrary announced a principle that could only have a crippling effect on grievance arbitration. The case was *International Assn. of Machinists v. Cutler–Hammer, Inc.*, 67 N.Y.S.2d 317 (1947), aff'd 74 N.E.2d 464 (NY Ct. of App. 1947). It held that "If the meaning of the provision of the contract sought to be arbitrated is beyond dispute, there cannot be anything to arbitrate and the contract cannot be said to provide for arbitration." 67 N.Y.S.2d, at 318. The lower courts in the instant case had a like preoccupation with ordinary contract law. The collective agreement requires arbitration of claims that courts might be unwilling to entertain. In the context of the plant or industry the grievance may assume proportions of which judges are ignorant. Yet, the agreement is to submit all grievances to arbitration, not merely those that a court may deem to be meritorious. There is no exception in the "no strike" clause and none therefore should be read into the grievance clause, since one is the quid pro quo for the other. The question is not whether in the mind of the court there is equity in the claim. Arbitration is a stabilizing influence only as it serves as a vehicle for handling any and all disputes that arise under the agreement.

The collective agreement calls for the submission of grievances in the categories which it describes, irrespective of whether a court may deem them to be meritorious. In our role of developing a meaningful body of law to govern the interpretation and enforcement of collective bargaining agreements, we think special heed should be given to the context in which collective bargaining agreements are negotiated and the purpose which they are intended to serve. The function of the court is very limited when the parties have agreed to submit all questions of contract interpretation to the arbitrator. It is confined to ascertaining whether the party seeking arbitration is making a claim which on its face is governed by the contract. Whether the moving party is right or wrong is a question of contract interpretation for the arbitrator. In these circumstances the moving party should not be deprived of the arbitrator's judgment, when it was his judgment and all that it connotes that was bargained for.

The courts, therefore, have no business weighing the merits of the grievance, considering whether there is equity in a particular claim, or determining whether there is particular language in the written instrument which will support the claim. The agreement is to submit all grievances to arbitration, not merely those which the court will deem meritorious. The processing of even frivolous claims may have therapeutic values of which those who are not a part of the plant environment may be quite unaware.[6]

The union claimed in this case that the company had violated a specific provision of the contract. The company took the position that it had not violated that clause. There was, therefore, a dispute between the parties as to "the meaning, interpretation and application" of the collective bargaining agreement. Arbitration should have been ordered. When the judiciary undertakes to determine the merits of a grievance under the guise of interpreting the grievance procedure of collective bargaining agreements, it usurps a function which under that regime is entrusted to the arbitration tribunal.

Reversed.

■ FRANKFURTER, J. concurs in the result.

WHITTAKER, J., believing that the District Court lacked jurisdiction to determine the merits of the claim which the parties had validly agreed to submit to the exclusive jurisdiction of a Board of Arbitrators (*Textile Workers v. Lincoln Mills*, 353 U.S. 448), concurs in the result of this opinion.

■ BLACK, J., took no part in the consideration or decision of this case.

■ BRENNAN, J., with whom HARLAN, J. joins, concurring.*

While I join the Court's opinions in [*Warrior, American,* and *Enterprise Wheel*], I add a word in [*Warrior* and *American*].

In each of these two cases the issue concerns the enforcement of but one promise—the promise to arbitrate in the context of an agreement dealing with a particular subject matter, the industrial relations between employers and employees. Other promises contained in the collective bargaining agreements are beside the point unless, by the very terms of the arbitration promise, they are made relevant to its interpretation. And I emphasize this, for the arbitration promise is itself a contract. The parties are free to make that promise as broad or as narrow as they wish, for there is no compulsion in law requiring them to include any such promises in

---

6. Cox, *Current Problems in the Law of Grievance Arbitration*, 30 ROCKY MT. L. REV. 247, 261 (1958), writes:

> The typical arbitration clause is written in words which cover, without limitation, all disputes concerning the interpretation or application of a collective bargaining agreement. Its words do not restrict its scope to meritorious disputes or two-sided disputes, still less are they limited to disputes which a judge will consider two-sided. Frivolous cases are often taken, and are expected to be taken, to arbitration. What one man considers frivolous another may find meritorious, and it is common knowledge in industrial relations circles that grievance arbitration often serves as a safety valve for troublesome complaints. Under these circumstances it seems proper to read the typical arbitration clause as a promise to arbitrate every claim, meritorious or frivolous, which the complainant bases upon the contract. The objection that equity will not order a party to do a useless act is outweighed by the cathartic value of arbitrating even a frivolous grievance and by the dangers of excessive judicial intervention.

* [This opinion applies also to *United Steelworkers of America v. Warrior & Gulf Navigation Co.* and *United Steelworkers of America v. Enterprise Wheel & Car Corp.*]

their agreement. The meaning of the arbitration promise is not to be found simply by reference to the dictionary definitions of the words the parties use, or by reference to the interpretation of commercial arbitration clauses. Words in a collective bargaining agreement, rightly viewed by the Court to be the charter instrument of a system of industrial self-government, like words in a statute, are to be understood only by reference to the background which gave rise to their inclusion. The Court therefore avoids the prescription of inflexible rules for the enforcement of arbitration promises. Guidance is given by identifying the various considerations which a court should take into account when construing a particular clause—considerations of the milieu in which the clause is negotiated and of the national labor policy. It is particularly underscored that the arbitral process in collective bargaining presupposes that the parties wanted the informed judgment of an arbitrator, precisely for the reason that judges cannot provide it. Therefore, a court asked to enforce a promise to arbitrate should ordinarily refrain from involving itself in the interpretation of the substantive provisions of the contract.

To be sure, since arbitration is a creature of contract, a court must always inquire, when a party seeks to invoke its aid to force a reluctant party to the arbitration table, whether the parties have agreed to arbitrate the particular dispute. In this sense, the question of whether a dispute is "arbitrable" is inescapably for the court.

On examining the arbitration clause, the court may conclude that it commits to arbitration any "dispute, difference, disagreement, or controversy of any nature or character." With that finding the court will have exhausted its function, except to order the reluctant party to arbitration. Similarly, although the arbitrator may be empowered only to interpret and apply the contract, the parties may have provided that any dispute as to whether a particular claim is within the arbitration clause is itself for the arbitrator. Again the court, without more, must send any dispute to the arbitrator, for the parties have agreed that the construction of the arbitration promise itself is for the arbitrator, and the reluctant party has breached his promise by refusing to submit the dispute to arbitration.

In *American*, the Court deals with a request to enforce the "standard" form of arbitration clause, one that provides for the arbitration of "any disputes, misunderstandings, differences or grievances arising between the parties as to the meaning, interpretation and application of this agreement." Since the arbitration clause itself is part of the agreement, it might be argued that a dispute as to the meaning of that clause is for the arbitrator. But the Court rejects this position, saying that the threshold question, the meaning of the arbitration clause itself, is for the judge unless the parties clearly state to the contrary. However, the Court finds that the meaning of that "standard" clause is simply that the parties have agreed to arbitrate any dispute which the moving party asserts to involve construction of the substantive provisions of the contract, because such a dispute necessarily does involve such a construction.

The issue in the *Warrior* case is essentially no different from that in *American*, that is, it is whether the company agreed to arbitrate a particular grievance. In contrast to *American*, however, the arbitration promise here excludes a particular area from arbitration—"matters which are strictly a function of management." Because the arbitration promise is different, the scope of the court's inquiry may be broader. Here, a court may be required to examine the substantive provisions of the contract to ascertain whether the parties have provided that contracting out shall be a "function of management." If a court may delve into the merits to the extent of inquiring whether the parties have expressly agreed whether or not contracting out was a "function of management," why was it error for the lower court here to evaluate the evidence of bargaining history for the same purpose? Neat logical distinctions do not provide the answer. The Court rightly concludes that appropriate regard for the national labor policy and the special factors relevant to the labor arbitral process, admonish that judicial inquiry into the merits of this grievance should be limited to the search for an explicit provision which brings the grievance under the cover of the exclusion clause since "the exclusion clause is vague and arbitration clause quite broad." The hazard of going further into the merits is amply demonstrated by what the courts below did. On the basis of inconclusive evidence, those courts found that Warrior was in no way limited by any implied covenants of good faith and fair dealing from contracting out as it pleased—which would necessarily mean that Warrior was free completely to destroy the collective bargaining agreement by contracting out all the work.

The very ambiguity of the *Warrior* exclusion clause suggests that the parties were generally more concerned with having an arbitrator render decisions as to the meaning of the contract than they were in restricting the arbitrator's jurisdiction. The case might of course be otherwise were the arbitration clause very narrow, or the exclusion clause quite specific, for the inference might then be permissible that the parties had manifested a greater interest in confining the arbitrator; the presumption of arbitrability would then not have the same force and the Court would be somewhat freer to examine into the merits.

The Court makes reference to an arbitration clause being the *quid pro quo* for a no-strike clause. I do not understand the Court to mean that the application of the principles announced today depends upon the presence of a no-strike clause in the agreement.

■ FRANKFURTER, J. joins these observations.

United Steelworkers of Am. v. Warrior & Gulf Navigation Co.

Supreme Court of the United States, 1960.
363 U.S. 574.

Opinion of the Court by DOUGLAS, J., announced by BRENNAN, J. Respondent transports steel and steel products by barge and maintains a terminal at Chickasaw, Alabama, where it performs maintenance and repair work on its barges. The employees at that terminal constitute a bargaining unit covered by a collective bargaining agreement negotiated by petitioner union. Respondent between 1956 and 1958 laid off some employees, reducing the bargaining unit from 42 to 23 men. This reduction was due in part to respondent contracting maintenance work, previously done by its employees, to other companies. The latter used respondent's supervisors to lay out the work and hired some of the laid-off employees of respondent (at reduced wages). Some were in fact assigned to work on respondent's barges. A number of employees signed a grievance which petitioner presented to respondent, the grievance reading:

> "We are hereby protesting the Company's actions, of arbitrarily and unreasonably contracting out work to other concerns, that could and previously has been performed by Company employees.

> "This practice becomes unreasonable, unjust and discriminatory in lieu [sic] of the fact that at present there are a number of employees that have been laid off for about 1 and 1/2 years or more for allegedly lack of work.

> "Confronted with these facts we charge that the Company is in violation of the contract by inducing a partial lock-out, of a number of the employees who would otherwise be working were it not for this unfair practice."

The collective agreement had both a "no strike" and a "no lockout" provision. It also had a grievance procedure which provided in relevant part as follows:

> "Issues which conflict with any Federal statute in its application as established by Court procedure or matters which are strictly a function of management shall not be subject to arbitration under this section.

> "Should differences arise between the Company and the Union or its members employed by the Company as to the meaning and application of the provisions of this Agreement, or should any local trouble of any kind arise, there shall be no suspension of work on account of such differences but an earnest effort shall be made to settle such differences immediately in the following manner:

> "A. For Maintenance Employees:

> > "First, between the aggrieved employees, and the Foreman involved;

> > "Second, between a member or members of the Grievance Committee designated by the Union, and the Foreman and Master Mechanic.

> > "Fifth, if agreement has not been reached the matter shall be referred to an impartial umpire for decision. The parties shall meet to decide on an umpire acceptable to both. If no agreement on selection of an umpire is reached, the parties shall

jointly petition the United States Conciliation Service for suggestion of a list of umpires from which selection will be made. The decision of the umpire shall be final."

Settlement of this grievance was not had and respondent refused arbitration. This suit was then commenced by the union to compel it.[1]

The District Court granted respondent's motion to dismiss the complaint. 168 F.Supp. 702. It held after hearing evidence, much of which went to the merits of the grievance, that the agreement did not "confide in an arbitrator the right to review the defendant's business judgment in contracting out work." *Id.*, at 705. It further held that "the contracting out of repair and maintenance work, as well as construction work, is strictly a function of management not limited in any respect by the labor agreement involved here." *Ibid.* The Court of Appeals affirmed by a divided vote, 269 F.2d 633, the majority holding that the collective agreement had withdrawn from the grievance procedure "matters which are strictly a function of management" and that contracting out fell in that exception. The case is here on a writ of certiorari.

We held in *Textile Workers v. Lincoln Mills*, 353 U.S. 448, that a grievance arbitration provision in a collective agreement could be enforced by reason of § 301 (a) of the Labor Management Relations Act and that the policy to be applied in enforcing this type of arbitration was that reflected in our national labor laws. *Id.*, at 456–457. The present federal policy is to promote industrial stabilization through the collective bargaining agreement. *Id.*, at 453–454. A major factor in achieving industrial peace is the inclusion of a provision for arbitration of grievances in the collective bargaining agreement.[4]

Thus the run of arbitration cases becomes irrelevant to our problem. There the choice is between the adjudication of cases or controversies in courts with established procedures or even special statutory safeguards on the one hand and the settlement of them in the more informal arbitration tribunal on the other. In the commercial case, arbitration is the substitute for litigation. Here arbitration is the substitute for industrial strife. Since arbitration of labor disputes has quite different functions from arbitration under an ordinary commercial agreement, the hostility evinced by courts toward arbitration of commercial agreements has no place here. For arbitration of labor disputes under collective bargaining agreements is part and parcel of the collective bargaining process itself.

---

1. Section 301 (a) of the Labor Management Relations Act, 1947, 61 Stat. 156, 29 U. S. C. § 185 (a), provides:

"Suits for violation of contracts between an employer and a labor organization representing employees in an industry affecting commerce as defined in this Act, or between any such labor organizations, may be brought in any district court of the United States having jurisdiction of the parties, without respect to the amount in controversy or without regard to the citizenship of the parties."

4. Complete effectuation of the federal policy is achieved when the agreement contains both an arbitration provision for all unresolved grievances and an absolute prohibition of strikes, the arbitration agreement being the "*quid pro quo*" for the agreement not to strike. *Textile Workers v. Lincoln Mills*, 353 U.S. 448, 455.

The collective bargaining agreement states the rights and duties of the parties. It is more than a contract; it is a generalized code to govern a myriad of cases which the draftsmen cannot wholly anticipate. The collective agreement covers the whole employment relationship. It calls into being a new common law—the common law of a particular industry or of a particular plant. As one observer has put it:[6]

> It is not unqualifiedly true that a collective-bargaining agreement is simply a document by which the union and employees have imposed upon management limited, express restrictions of its otherwise absolute right to manage the enterprise, so that an employee's claim must fail unless he can point to a specific contract provision upon which the claim is founded. There are too many people, too many problems, too many unforeseeable contingencies to make the words of the contract the exclusive source of rights and duties. One cannot reduce all the rules governing a community like an industrial plant to fifteen or even fifty pages. Within the sphere of collective bargaining, the institutional characteristics and the governmental nature of the collective-bargaining process demand a common law of the shop which implements and furnishes the context of the agreement. We must assume that intelligent negotiators acknowledged so plain a need unless they stated a contrary rule in plain words.

A collective bargaining agreement is an effort to erect a system of industrial self-government. When most parties enter into contractual relationship they do so voluntarily, in the sense that there is no real compulsion to deal with one another, as opposed to dealing with other parties. This is not true of the labor agreement. The choice is generally not between entering or refusing to enter into a relationship, for that in all probability preexists the negotiations. Rather it is between having that relationship governed by an agreed-upon rule of law or leaving each and every matter subject to a temporary resolution dependent solely upon the relative strength, at any given moment, of the contending forces. The mature labor agreement may attempt to regulate all aspects of the complicated relationship, from the most crucial to the most minute over an extended period of time. Because of the compulsion to reach agreement and the breadth of the matters covered, as well as the need for a fairly concise and readable instrument. Gaps may be left to be filled in by reference to the practices of the particular industry and of the various shops covered by the agreement. Many of the specific practices which underlie the agreement may be unknown, except in hazy form, even to the negotiators. Courts and arbitration in the context of most commercial contracts are resorted to because there has been a breakdown in the working relationship of the parties; such resort is the unwanted exception. But the grievance machinery under a collective bargaining agreement is at the very heart of the system of industrial self-government. Arbitration is the means of solving the unforeseeable by molding a system of private law for all the problems which may

---

6. Cox, *Reflections Upon Labor Arbitration*, 72 Harv. L. Rev. 1482, 1498–1499 (1959).

arise and to provide for their solution in a way which will generally accord with the variant needs and desires of the parties. The processing of disputes through the grievance machinery is actually a vehicle by which meaning and content are given to the collective bargaining agreement.

Apart from matters that the parties specifically exclude, all of the questions on which the parties disagree must therefore come within the scope of the grievance and arbitration provisions of the collective agreement. The grievance procedure is, in other words, a part of the continuous collective bargaining process. It, rather than a strike, is the terminal point of a disagreement.

The labor arbitrator performs functions which are not normal to the courts; the considerations which help him fashion judgments may indeed be foreign to the competence of courts.

Congress, however, has by § 301 of the Labor Management Relations Act, assigned the courts the duty of determining whether the reluctant party has breached his promise to arbitrate. For arbitration is a matter of contract and a party cannot be required to submit to arbitration any dispute which he has not agreed so to submit. Yet, to be consistent with congressional policy in favor of settlement of disputes by the parties through the machinery of arbitration, the judicial inquiry under § 301 must be strictly confined to the question whether the reluctant party did agree to arbitrate the grievance or did agree to give the arbitrator power to make the award he made. An order to arbitrate the particular grievance should not be denied unless it may be said with positive assurance that the arbitration clause is not susceptible of an interpretation that covers the asserted dispute. Doubts should be resolved in favor of coverage.

We do not agree with the lower courts that contracting-out grievances were necessarily excepted from the grievance procedure of this agreement. To be sure, the agreement provides that "matters which are strictly a function of management shall not be subject to arbitration." But it goes on to say that if "differences" arise or if "any local trouble of any kind" arises, the grievance procedure shall be applicable.

"Strictly a function of management" might be thought to refer to any practice of management in which, under particular circumstances prescribed by the agreement, it is permitted to indulge. But if courts, in order to determine arbitrability, were allowed to determine what is permitted and what is not, the arbitration clause would be swallowed up by the exception. Every grievance in a sense involves a claim that management has violated some provision of the agreement.

Accordingly, "strictly a function of management" must be interpreted as referring only to that over which the contract gives management complete control and unfettered discretion. Respondent claims that the contracting out of work falls within this category. Contracting out work is the basis of many grievances; and that type of claim is grist in the mills of the arbitrators. A specific collective bargaining agreement may exclude contracting out from the grievance procedure. Or a written collateral agreement may make clear that contracting out was not a matter for arbitration. In such a case a grievance based solely on contracting out would not be arbitrable. Here, however, there is no such provision. Nor is there any showing that the parties designed the phrase "strictly a function of management" to encompass any and all forms of contracting out. In the absence of any express provision excluding a particular grievance from arbitration, we think only the most forceful evidence of a purpose to exclude the claim from arbitration can prevail, particularly where, as here, the exclusion clause is vague and the arbitration clause quite broad. Since any attempt by a court to infer such a purpose necessarily comprehends the merits, the court should view with suspicion an attempt to persuade it to become entangled in the construction of the substantive provisions of a labor agreement, even through the back door of interpreting the arbitration clause, when the alternative is to utilize the services of an arbitrator.

The grievance alleged that the contracting out was a violation of the collective bargaining agreement. There was, therefore, a dispute "as to the meaning and application of the provisions of this Agreement" which the parties had agreed would be determined by arbitration.

The judiciary sits in these cases to bring into operation an arbitral process which substitutes a regime of peaceful settlement for the older regime of industrial conflict. Whether contracting out in the present case violated the agreement is the question. It is a question for the arbiter, not for the courts.

Reversed.

■ FRANKFURTER, J. concurs in the result.

■ BLACK, J. took no part in the consideration or decision of this case.

■ [A dissent by JUSTICE WHITTAKER is omitted.]

United Steelworkers of Am. v. Enterprise Wheel & Car Corp.

Supreme Court of the United States, 1960.
363 U.S. 593.

Opinion of the Court by DOUGLAS, J., announced by BRENNAN, J. Petitioner union and respondent during the period relevant here had a collective bargaining agreement which provided that any differences "as to the meaning and application" of the agreement should be submitted to arbitration and that the arbitrator's decision "shall be final and binding on the parties." Special provisions were included concerning the suspension and discharge of employees. The agreement stated:

"Should it be determined by the Company or by an arbitrator in accordance with the grievance procedure that the employee has been suspended unjustly or discharged in violation of the provisions of this Agreement, the Company shall reinstate the employee and pay full compensation at the employee's regular rate of pay for the time lost."

The agreement also provided:

"It is understood and agreed that neither party will institute civil suits or legal proceedings against the other for alleged violation of any of the provisions of this labor contract; instead all disputes will be settled in the manner outlined in this Article III—Adjustment of Grievances."

A group of employees left their jobs in protest against the discharge of one employee. A union official advised them at once to return to work. An official of respondent at their request gave them permission and then rescinded it. The next day they were told they did not have a job any more "until this thing was settled one way or the other."

A grievance was filed; and when respondent finally refused to arbitrate, this suit was brought for specific enforcement of the arbitration provisions of the agreement. The District Court ordered arbitration. The arbitrator found that the discharge of the men was not justified, though their conduct, he said, was improper. In his view the facts warranted at most a suspension of the men for 10 days each. After their discharge and before the arbitration award the collective bargaining agreement had expired. The union, however, continued to represent the workers at the plant. The arbitrator rejected the contention that expiration of the agreement barred reinstatement of the employees. He held that the provision of the agreement above quoted imposed an unconditional obligation on the employer. He awarded reinstatement with back pay, minus pay for a 10–day suspension and such sums as these employees received from other employment.

Respondent refused to comply with the award. Petitioner moved the District Court for enforcement. The District Court directed respondent to comply. 168 F.Supp. 308. The Court of Appeals, while agreeing that the District Court had jurisdiction to enforce an arbitration award under a collective bargaining agreement, held that the failure of the award to specify the amounts to be deducted from the back pay rendered the award unenforceable. That defect, it agreed, could be remedied by requiring the parties to complete the arbitration. It went on to hold, however, that an award for back pay subsequent to the date of termination of the collective bargaining agreement could not be enforced. It also held that the requirement for reinstatement of the discharged employees was likewise unenforceable because the collective bargaining agreement had expired. 269 F.2d 327. We granted certiorari.

The refusal of courts to review the merits of an arbitration award is the proper approach to arbitration under collective bargaining agreements. The federal policy of settling labor disputes by arbitration would be undermined if courts had the final say on the merits of the awards. As we stated in *United Steelworkers of America v. Warrior & Gulf Navigation Co.*, decided this day, the arbitrators under these collective agreements are indispensable agencies in a continuous collective bargaining process. They sit to settle disputes at the plant level—disputes that require for their solution knowledge of the custom and practices of a particular factory or of a particular industry as reflected in particular agreements.

When an arbitrator is commissioned to interpret and apply the collective bargaining agreement, he is to bring his informed judgment to bear in order to reach a fair solution of a problem. This is especially true when it comes to formulating remedies. There the need is for flexibility in meeting a wide variety of situations. The draftsmen may never have thought of what specific remedy should be awarded to meet a particular contingency. Nevertheless, an arbitrator is confined to interpretation and application of the collective bargaining agreement; he does not sit to dispense his own brand of industrial justice. He may of course look for guidance from many sources, yet his award is legitimate only so long as it draws its essence from the collective bargaining agreement. When the arbitrator's words manifest an infidelity to this obligation, courts have no choice but to refuse enforcement of the award.

The opinion of the arbitrator in this case, as it bears upon the award of back pay beyond the date of the agreement's expiration and reinstatement, is ambiguous. It may be read as based solely upon the arbitrator's view of the requirements of enacted legislation, which would mean that he exceeded the scope of the submission. Or it may be read as embodying a construction of the agreement itself, perhaps with the arbitrator looking to "the law" for help in determining the sense of the agreement. A mere ambiguity in the opinion accompanying an award, which permits the inference that the arbitrator may have exceeded his authority, is not a reason for refusing to enforce the award. Arbitrators have no obligation to the court to give their reasons for an award. To require opinions free of ambiguity may lead arbitrators to play it safe by writing no supporting opinions. This would be undesirable for a well-reasoned opinion tends to engender confidence in the integrity of the process and aids in clarifying the underlying agreement. Moreover, we see no reason to assume that this arbitrator has abused the trust the parties confided in him and has not stayed within the areas marked out for his consideration. It is not apparent that he went beyond the submission. The Court of Appeals' opinion refusing to enforce the reinstatement and partial back pay portions of the award was not based upon any finding that the arbitrator did not premise his award on his construction of the contract. It merely disagreed with the arbitrator's construction of it.

The collective bargaining agreement could have provided that if any of the employees were wrongfully discharged, the remedy would be reinstatement and back pay up to the date they were returned to work. Respondent's major argument seems to be that by applying correct principles of law to the interpretation of the collective bargaining agreement it can be determined that the agreement did not so provide, and that therefore the arbitrator's decision was not based upon the contract. The acceptance of this view would require courts, even under the standard arbitration clause, to review the merits of every construction of the contract. This plenary review by a court of the merits would make meaningless the provisions that the arbitrator's decision is final, for in reality it would almost never be final. This underlines the fundamental error which we have alluded to in *United Steelworkers of America v. American Manufacturing Co.*, decided this day. As we there emphasized, the question of interpretation of the collective bargaining agreement is a question for the arbitrator. It is the arbitrator's construction which was bargained for; and so far as the arbitrator's decision concerns construction of the contract, the courts have no business overruling him because their interpretation of the contract is different from his.

We agree with the Court of Appeals that the judgment of the District Court should be modified so that the amounts due the employees may be definitely determined by arbitration. In all other respects we think the judgment of the District Court should be affirmed. Accordingly, we reverse the judgment of the Court of Appeals, except for that modification, and remand the case to the District Court for proceedings in conformity with this opinion.

It is so ordered.

■ FRANKFURTER, J. concurs in the result.

■ BLACK, J. took no part in the consideration or decision of this case.

■ [A dissent by JUSTICE WHITTAKER is omitted.]

* * *

These three cases—collectively called the *Steelworkers' Trilogy*—held, among other things, that labor arbitrators possess gap-filling authority. In fact the Supreme Court expressly recognized the structural connection between arbitration and gap-filling. As the Court observed in *Enterprise Wheel & Car Corp.*, "The question of the interpretation of [a] collective bargaining agreement is a question for the arbitrator: *It is the arbitrator's construction which was bargained for*" (emphasis added). Indeed, the Court, in adopting this approach, re-characterized labor arbitration by drawing a distinction equivalent to the one just introduced, between third- and first-party arbitration. In *Warrior & Gulf Navigation Co.*, the Court observed that whereas "in the commercial case, arbitration is the substitute for litigation," in the context of labor relations, "arbitration is the substitute for industrial strife." But "industrial strife," of course, is just another name for bargaining; as the Court admitted when, in the same paragraph, it accepted that "arbitration of labor disputes under collective bargaining agreements is part and parcel of the collective bargaining process itself." Here the Court expressly followed academic commentary, quoting at length from Archibald Cox's *Reflections upon Labor Arbitration*.[13] Following a discussion of Cox's work, the Court noted that although a resort to arbitration in commercial contexts, like a resort to adjudication,

---

13. Archibald Cox, *Reflections upon Labor Arbitration*, 72 HARV. L. REV. 1482 (1958).

reflects "a breakdown in the working relationship of the parties," labor arbitration, by contrast, "is at the very heart of industrial self-government." On this view, the Court observed, arbitration is "a part of the continuous collective bargaining process. It, rather than a strike, is the terminal point of disagreement."[14]

To be sure, the Court never elaborated a general theory of arbitration as gap-filling and indeed included language in its opinions that might be read to reject this model. Thus, the *Steelworkers' Trilogy* Court embedded its analysis of arbitration as gap-filling in a model that departed from, and indeed expressly rejected, the contractual frame. First, the Court (in *American Manufacturing Company*) grounded its argument on the functionalist claim that arbitration can be "a stabilizing influence" on labor relations only if courts keep out of its way. This led the Court (in *Warrior & Gulf Navigation Co.*) to draw a sharp distinction between labor arbitration and the general "commercial" case, so that the "run of arbitration cases" became "irrelevant" to the problem before it, and presumably *vice versa*. Second, the Court's focus on the special character of labor relations caused it to reject the general conceptual point about arbitration and contract that its language otherwise invites. Thus, the Court (again in *Warrior and Gulf Navigation Co.*) said that a collective bargaining agreement "is more than a contract" and that "[i]t calls into being a new common law."

But these caveats reflect the Court's parochial concerns rather than general considerations arising out of the structures of contract, adjudication, and arbitration. Once again, as the existence of settlement reveals, there is no principled reason why contractual forms of solidarity cannot step in to resolve disputes ordinarily given over to adjudication. And first-party arbitration just is an instance of such a contractual resolution of otherwise adjudicable disputes: its only innovation is that, in first-party arbitration, the settlement contract (as it were) *precedes* the dispute.

This account of first-party arbitration helps to illuminate the otherwise mysterious and indeed misleading fact that so many clauses that establish arbitration on the first-party model appear in contracts of adhesion. It is common to hear critics of arbitration lament this fact, which they treat as an additional ground for skepticism concerning arbitration, including arbitration on the first-party model.[15] It is, these critics say, not just that arbitration is suspect in light of the gap between arbitral processes and adjudication proper; instead, arbitration is also suspect because agreements to arbitrate are not even proper agreements.[16]

---

14. Other commentators saw the same point. *See, e.g.*, Theodore J. St. Antoine, *Judicial Review of Labor Arbitration Awards: A Second Look at Enterprise Wheel and Its Progeny*, 75 MICH. L. REV. 1137, 1140 (1977).

15. *See, e.g.*, See Paul D. Carrington & Paul H. Haagen, *Contract and Jurisdiction*, 1996 SUP. CT. REV. 331, 334–35 (1996).

16. *See, e.g.*, Mark E. Budnitz, *Arbitration of Disputes Between Consumers and Financial Institutions: A Serious Threat to Consumer Protection*, 10 OHIO ST. J. ON DISP. RESOL. 267 (1995).

This lament, however, reflects a conceptual confusion. The adhesive character of the contracts in which agreements to first-party arbitration appear should not add to the general skepticism concerning arbitration as an *additional* ground for doubting the validity of these agreements. Rather, first-party, gap-filling arbitration just *is* a case of an adhesive contract term. A contract of adhesion fills in the gaps in the dickered terms with boilerplate that one or both parties (both, when the form is drafted by a third party) neither read nor understand and cannot in practice change. An agreement concerning first-party arbitration fills in the gaps in the dickered terms of the contract in which the agreement appears with the arbitrator's decisions, which, being rendered in the future, neither party knows. The outcome of the arbitration is therefore, from the perspective of the parties, just like another printed clause, save that it is post-printed rather than pre-printed. It is therefore natural rather than surprising or sinister that arbitration agreements appear in printed form contracts: the very same grounds that render the printed form appealing to the parties also render the first-party arbitration appealing. And there is thus no additional or recursive problem in the fact that agreements to arbitrate are themselves often adhesive.

That is not, however, to insulate first-party arbitration from every criticism or to argue that first-party arbitration need satisfy no standards in order to achieve legitimacy. Rather, the proper model for first-party arbitral processes is not adjudication at all but rather *bargaining*. That is, first-party arbitration is authoritative as long as it reflects the bargain-based solidarity that has been established by the contracts to which it belongs.

The proper standard for assessing first-party arbitration is therefore not due process or some analog (the standard for evaluating third-party arbitration) but rather the procedural standards that govern contracts, namely, fraud, duress, and procedural unconscionability in contract negotiations and good faith in contract performance. These are not toothless requirements. An agreement to first-party arbitration may, after all, be procured by coercion or deception, and it may, under a slightly less demanding standard, be unconscionable. Alternatively, first-party arbitration may be structurally designed by one party to deprive the other of the very benefits that the contract establishing the tribunal was designed to secure. This may occur, for example, because the arbitrator is simply in the pocket of the designing party. In such cases, the agreement to arbitrate is not freely procured, or it renders the contract to which it belongs illusory, in the sense that it fails effectively to secure any gains for one side and fails effectively to bind the other. These possibilities, and perhaps others— return, here, to the discussion of good faith in ex post bargaining developed in the materials on contracts of adhesion—provide the doctrinal (and indeed moral) materials that are needed to attack particular instances of first-party arbitration. But they neither underwrite blanket skepticism about contracts to arbitrate nor make arbitration in itself distinctively problematic. They therefore fundamentally recast the debate about arbitration.

Finally, the gap-filling account of first-party arbitration also helps to explain the otherwise peculiar fact that when a party attempts to avoid an agreement to arbitrate in order to press her claims in a court, courts typically decline even to hear the claims and instead insist that the party takes them to arbitration. Critics of arbitration have suggested that this approach to arbitration agreements amounts to ordering their specific performance, which mysteriously and unjustifiably departs from the law's general rule of vindicating contractual rights through the expectation remedy.[17] Indeed, traditional opposition in courts to compelling arbitration proceeded precisely on the ground that principles of federal equity precluded an arbitration agreement from being specifically enforced.[18] These critics of arbitration treat the arbitral agreement as addressing the question "To what process are the parties entitled in pursuing disputes concerning their contractual rights?" When courts refuse to hear claims consigned to arbitration, critics say, they are concluding both that the answer to this question is "arbitration" and that the court should specifically enforce this answer.

The gap-filling account reveals that this criticism reflects a doctrinal confusion. In gap-filling cases, the agreement to arbitrate is not, in fact, an agreement concerning process at all. It is, rather, an agreement concerning substance—the arbitrator fills in a substantive gap in the contract. (Note the contrast between such cases and third-party arbitration, as emphasized by both *Nute* and *Vimar Seguros*.) Therefore, when courts refuse to hear a claim consigned to arbitration, they are not specifically enforcing the arbitral agreement, any more than they would be issuing specific performance were they directly to apply a price-formula in a contract rather than deciding the price themselves.

Of course, if a first-party arbitrator reaches a decision about how a contractual gap should be filled, and a contracting party refuses to proffer the performance that this gap-filling describes, then the question of specific performance does squarely arise. The standard law of contract remedies should apply in such a case: the court should, as a general matter, give the disappointed party a money award sufficient to vindicate the value that she accords to the gap-filling that the arbitrator has produced. Insofar as most arbitral awards contemplate money payments, there will often be no practical difference between the expectation remedy and specific performance.

The theory that first-party arbitration is just gap-filling renders it unproblematic. Indeed, the theory renders arbitration less problematic than

---

17. *See, e.g.*, David H. Taylor & Sarah M. Cliffe, *Civil Procedure by Contract: A Convoluted Confluence of Private Contract and Public Procedure in Need of Congressional Control*, 35 U. Rich. L. Rev., 1085, 1132–34 (2002).

18. *See, e.g.*, *United States Asphalt Refining Co. v. Trinidad Lake Petro. Co.*, 222 Fed. 1006, 1011 (S.D.N.Y. 1915).

settlement, which unlike arbitration actually does replace adjudication as a method of evaluating independent substantive legal claims.

21.3 ARBITRATION'S ARBITRAGE

Third- and first-party arbitration are thus structurally different phenomena: a form of adjudication and a form of contract, respectively. Each form possesses, in virtue of its deep structure, characteristic strengths and weakness.

Third-party arbitration—arbitration as judging—is in fact a form of adjudication, which can enjoy a scope commensurate to the legitimating power that adjudication's procedural intensity confers, but whose legitimacy depends on actually replicating the procedural intensity that adjudication proper involves. Here, it is particularly striking that when the arbitration process has an appropriate form, arbitral authority does not depend on any ordinary political connection between the disputants and the arbitral institution before which they bring their dispute. By the same token, the authority of third-party arbitration vanishes insofar as it abandons adjudicative procedures.

First-party arbitration—arbitration as gap-filling—is in fact a form of contract, which constructs legitimacy out of the comparatively casual materials associated with bargain and exchange, but whose scope is commensurately narrower than the scope of arbitration as judging. Here it is particularly striking that the authority of first-party arbitration arises entirely independent of the quality of first-party arbitral procedures (recall the process by which the West Texas Sour indicator "arbitrated" prices in *Eastern Airlines*). Of course, the gap-filling account of first-party arbitration also immediately entails that there are natural limits to first-party arbitration's legitimacy. If arbitration achieves solidarity on the model of contract, then it must limit its scope to the sorts of disputes that contractual solidarity might successfully resolve. In particular, first-party arbitration, unlike third-party arbitration, cannot lay claim to *any* of the forms of authority associated with adjudication.

In spite of these deep differences, both third- and first-party arbitration are engaged through the same mechanism, namely the arbitration agreement, and this mechanism does not generally announce which kind of arbitration it creates. This makes tempting, natural even, to conflate the two phenomena, and indeed to arbitrage between them: to pick and chose from the features of both in order to praise or to criticize a generic form, arbitration *simpliciter*, which does not in fact exist.

The following materials illustrate the use of this arbitrage by arbitration's enthusiasts.

Mitsubishi Motors Corp. v. Soler Chrysler–Plymouth, Inc.

Supreme Court United States, 1985.
473 U.S. 614.

■ BLACKMUN, J. The principal question presented by these cases is the arbitrability, pursuant to the Federal Arbitration Act, 9 U. S. C. § 1 *et seq.*, and the Convention on the Recognition and Enforcement of Foreign Arbitral Awards (Convention), [1970] 21 U.S.T. 2517, T.I.A.S. No. 6997, of claims arising under the Sherman Act, 15 U. S. C. § 1 *et seq.*, and encompassed within a valid arbitration clause in an agreement embodying an international commercial transaction.

I

Petitioner-cross-respondent Motors Corporation (Mitsubishi) is a Japanese corporation which manufactures automobiles and has its principal place of business in Tokyo, Japan. Mitsubishi is the product of a joint venture between, on the one hand, Chrysler International, S.A. (CISA), a Swiss corporation registered in Geneva and wholly owned by Chrysler Corporation, and, on the other, Mitsubishi Heavy Industries, Inc., a Japanese corporation. The aim of the joint venture was the distribution through Chrysler dealers outside the continental United States of vehicles manufactured by Mitsubishi and bearing Chrysler and Mitsubishi trademarks. Respondent-cross-petitioner Soler Chrysler–Plymouth, Inc. Click for Enhanced Coverage Linking Searches (Soler), is a Puerto Rico corporation with its principal place of business in Pueblo Viejo, Guaynabo, Puerto Rico.

On October 31, 1979, Soler entered into a Distributor Agreement with CISA which provided for the sale by Soler of Mitsubishi-manufactured vehicles within a designated area, including metropolitan San Juan. App. 18. On the same date, CISA, Soler, and Mitsubishi entered into a Sales Procedure Agreement (Sales Agreement) which, referring to the Distributor Agreement, provided for the direct sale of Mitsubishi products to Soler and governed the terms and conditions of such sales. *Id.*, at 42. Paragraph VI of the Sales Agreement, labeled "Arbitration of Certain Matters," provides:

> "All disputes, controversies or differences which may arise between [Mitsubishi] and [Soler] out of or in relation to Articles I–B through V of this Agreement or for the breach thereof, shall be finally settled by arbitration in Japan in accordance with the rules and regulations of the Japan Commercial Arbitration Association."
> *Id.*, at 52–53.

Initially, Soler did a brisk business in Mitsubishi-manufactured vehicles. As a result of its strong performance, its minimum sales volume, specified by Mitsubishi and CISA, and agreed to by Soler, for the 1981 model year was substantially increased. *Id.*, at 179. In early 1981, however, the new-car market slackened. Soler ran into serious difficulties in meeting the expected sales volume, and by the spring of 1981 it felt itself compelled to request that Mitsubishi delay or cancel shipment of several orders.

About the same time, Soler attempted to arrange for the transshipment of a quantity of its vehicles for sale in the continental United States and Latin America. Mitsubishi and CISA, however, refused permission for any such diversion, citing a variety of reasons, and no vehicles were transshipped. Attempts to work out these difficulties failed. Mitsubishi eventually withheld shipment of 966 vehicles, apparently representing orders placed for May, June, and July 1981 production, responsibility for which Soler disclaimed in February 1982.

The following month, Mitsubishi brought an action against Soler in the United States District Court for the District of Puerto Rico under the Federal Arbitration Act and the Convention. Mitsubishi sought an order, pursuant to 9 U. S. C. §§ 4 and 201,[3] to compel arbitration in accord with para. VI of the Sales Agreement. Shortly after filing the complaint, Mitsubishi filed a request for arbitration before the Japan Commercial Arbitration Association.

Soler denied the allegations and counterclaimed against both Mitsubishi and CISA. It alleged numerous breaches by Mitsubishi of the Sales Agreement,[5] raised a pair of defamation claims, and asserted causes of action under the Sherman Act, 15 U. S. C. § 1 *et seq.*; the federal Automobile Dealers' Day in Court Act, 70 Stat. 1125, 15 U. S. C. § 1221 et seq.; the Puerto Rico competition statute, P.R. Laws Ann., Tit. 10, § 257 et seq. (1976); and the Puerto Rico Dealers' Contracts Act, P.R. Laws Ann., Tit. 10, § 278 et seq. (1976 and Supp. 1983). In the counterclaim premised on the Sherman Act, Soler alleged that Mitsubishi and CISA had conspired to divide markets in restraint of trade. To effectuate the plan, according to Soler, Mitsubishi had refused to permit Soler to resell to buyers in North, Central, or South America vehicles it had obligated itself to purchase from Mitsubishi; had refused to ship ordered vehicles or the parts, such as heaters and defoggers, that would be necessary to permit Soler to make its vehicles suitable for resale outside Puerto Rico; and had coercively attempted to replace Soler and its other Puerto Rico distributors with a wholly owned subsidiary which would serve as the exclusive Mitsubishi distributor in Puerto Rico.

---

3. Section 201 provides [in pertinent part]: "The Convention on the Recognition and Enforcement of Foreign Arbitral Awards of June 10, 1958, shall be enforced in United States courts in accordance with this chapter." Article II of the Convention, in turn, provides:

"1.   Each Contracting State shall recognize an agreement in writing under which the parties undertake to submit to arbitration all or any differences which have arisen or which may arise between them in respect of a defined legal relationship, whether contractual or not, concerning a subject matter capable of settlement by arbitration.

"3.   The court of a Contracting State, when seized of an action in a matter in respect of which the parties have made an agreement within the meaning of this article, shall, at the request of one of the parties, refer the parties to arbitration, unless it finds that the said agreement is null and void, inoperative or incapable of being performed." 21 U.S.T., at 2519.

Title 9 U. S. C. § 203 confers jurisdiction on the district courts of the United States over an action falling under the Convention.

5.   The alleged breaches included wrongful refusal to ship ordered vehicles and necessary parts, failure to make payment for warranty work and authorized rebates, and bad faith in establishing minimum-sales volumes.

After a hearing, the District Court ordered Mitsubishi and Soler to arbitrate each of the issues raised in the complaint and in all the counterclaims save two and a portion of a third. With regard to the federal antitrust issues, it recognized that the Courts of Appeals uniformly had held that the rights conferred by the antitrust laws were "of a character inappropriate for enforcement by arbitration." *Wilko v. Swan*, 201 F.2d 439, 444 (CA2 1953), rev'd, 346 U.S. 427 (1953). The District Court held, however, that the international character of the Mitsubishi–Soler undertaking required enforcement of the agreement to arbitrate even as to the antitrust claims. It relied on *Scherk v. Alberto–Culver Co.*, 417 U.S. 506, 515–520 (1974), in which this Court ordered arbitration, pursuant to a provision embodied in an international agreement, of a claim arising under the Securities Exchange Act of 1934 notwithstanding its assumption, *arguendo*, that *Wilko*, supra, which held non arbitrable claims arising under the Securities Act of 1933, also would bar arbitration of a 1934 Act claim arising in a domestic context.

The United States Court of Appeals for the First Circuit affirmed in part and reversed in part. 723 F.2d 155 (1983). It first rejected Soler's argument that Puerto Rico law precluded enforcement of an agreement obligating a local dealer to arbitrate controversies outside Puerto Rico. It also rejected Soler's suggestion that it could not have intended to arbitrate statutory claims not mentioned in the arbitration agreement. Assessing arbitrability "on an allegation-by-allegation basis," *id.*, at 159, the court then read the arbitration clause to encompass virtually all the claims arising under the various statutes, including all those arising under the Sherman Act.

Finally, after endorsing the doctrine of *American Safety*, precluding arbitration of antitrust claims, the Court of Appeals concluded that neither this Court's decision in *Scherk* nor the Convention required abandonment of that doctrine in the face of an international transaction. 723 F.2d, at 164–168. Accordingly, it reversed the judgment of the District Court insofar as it had ordered submission of "Soler's antitrust claims" to arbitration. Affirming the remainder of the judgment, the court directed the District Court to consider in the first instance how the parallel judicial and arbitral proceedings should go forward.

We granted certiorari primarily to consider whether an American court should enforce an agreement to resolve antitrust claims by arbitration when that agreement arises from an international transaction.

II

At the outset, we address the contention raised in Soler's cross-petition that the arbitration clause at issue may not be read to encompass the statutory counterclaims stated in its answer to the complaint. In making this argument, Soler does not question the Court of Appeals' application of para. VI of the Sales Agreement to the disputes involved here as a matter of standard contract interpretation. Instead, it argues that as a matter of law a court may not construe an arbitration agreement to encompass claims arising out of statutes designed to protect a class to which the party resisting arbitration belongs "unless [that party] has expressly agreed" to arbitrate those claims by which Soler presumably means that the arbitration clause must specifically mention the statute giving rise to the claims that a party to the clause seeks to arbitrate. Soler reasons that, because it falls within the class for whose benefit the federal and local antitrust laws and dealers' Acts were passed, but the arbitration clause at issue does not mention these statutes or statutes in general, the clause cannot be read to contemplate arbitration of these statutory claims.

We do not agree, for we find no warrant in the Arbitration Act for implying in every contract within its ken a presumption against arbitration of statutory claims. The Act's centerpiece provision makes a written agreement to arbitrate "in any maritime transaction or a contract evidencing a transaction involving commerce valid, irrevocable, and enforceable, save upon such grounds as exist at law or in equity for the revocation of any contract." 9 U. S. C. § 2. The "liberal federal policy favoring arbitration agreements," *Moses H. Cone Memorial Hospital v. Mercury Construction Corp.*, 460 U.S. 1, 24 (1983), manifested by this provision and the Act as a whole, is at bottom a policy guaranteeing the enforcement of private contractual arrangements: the Act simply "creates a body of federal substantive law establishing and regulating the duty to honor an agreement to arbitrate." *Id.*, at 25, n. 32.[14] As this Court recently observed, "[the] preeminent concern of Congress in passing the Act was to enforce private agreements into which parties had entered," a concern which "requires that we rigorously enforce agreements to arbitrate." *Dean Witter Reynolds Inc. v. Byrd*, 470 U.S. 213, 221 (1985).

Accordingly, the first task of a court asked to compel arbitration of a dispute is to determine whether the parties agreed to arbitrate that dispute. The court is to make this determination by applying the "federal substantive law of arbitrability, applicable to any arbitration agreement within the coverage of the Act." *Moses H. Cone Memorial Hospital*, 460 U.S., at 24. And that body of law counsels

> "that questions of arbitrability must be addressed with a healthy regard for the federal policy favoring arbitration. The Arbitration Act establishes that, as a matter of federal law, any doubts concerning the scope of arbitrable issues should be resolved in favor of arbitration, whether the problem at hand is the construction of the contract language itself or an allegation of waiver, delay, or a like defense to arbitrability." *Moses H. Cone Memorial Hospital*, 460 U.S., at 24–25.

Thus, as with any other contract, the parties' intentions control, but those intentions are generously construed as to issues of arbitrability.

There is no reason to depart from these guidelines where a party bound by an arbitration agreement raises claims founded on statutory

---

14. The Court previously has explained that the Act was designed to overcome an anachronistic judicial hostility to agreements to arbitrate, which American courts had borrowed from English common law.

rights. Some time ago this Court expressed "hope for [the Act's] usefulness both in controversies based on statutes or on standards otherwise created," *Wilko v. Swan*, 346 U.S. 427, 432 (1953) (footnote omitted), and we are well past the time when judicial suspicion of the desirability of arbitration and of the competence of arbitral tribunals inhibited the development of arbitration as an alternative means of dispute resolution. Just last Term in [*Southland Corp. v. Keating*, 465 U.S. 1 (1984)] where we held that § 2 of the Act declared a national policy applicable equally in state as well as federal courts, we construed an arbitration clause to encompass the disputes at issue without pausing at the source in a state statute of the rights asserted by the parties resisting arbitration. 465 U.S., at 15, and n. 7. Of course, courts should remain attuned to well-supported claims that the agreement to arbitrate resulted from the sort of fraud or overwhelming economic power that would provide grounds "for the revocation of any contract." 9 U. S. C. § 2. But, absent such compelling considerations, the Act itself provides no basis for disfavoring agreements to arbitrate statutory claims by skewing the otherwise hospitable inquiry into arbitrability.

That is not to say that all controversies implicating statutory rights are suitable for arbitration. There is no reason to distort the process of contract interpretation, however, in order to ferret out the inappropriate. Just as it is the congressional policy manifested in the Federal Arbitration Act that requires courts liberally to construe the scope of arbitration agreements covered by that Act, it is the congressional intention expressed in some other statute on which the courts must rely to identify any category of claims as to which agreements to arbitrate will be held unenforceable. For that reason, Soler's concern for statutorily protected classes provides no reason to color the lens through which the arbitration clause is read. By agreeing to arbitrate a statutory claim, a party does not forgo the substantive rights afforded by the statute; it only submits to their resolution in an arbitral, rather than a judicial, forum. It trades the procedures and opportunity for review of the courtroom for the simplicity, informality, and expedition of arbitration. We must assume that if Congress intended the substantive protection afforded by a given statute to include protection against waiver of the right to a judicial forum, that intention will be deducible from text or legislative history. Having made the bargain to arbitrate, the party should be held to it unless Congress itself has evinced an intention to preclude a waiver of judicial remedies for the statutory rights at issue. Nothing, in the meantime, prevents a party from excluding statutory claims from the scope of an agreement to arbitrate.

In sum, the Court of Appeals correctly conducted a two-step inquiry, first determining whether the parties' agreement to arbitrate reached the statutory issues, and then, upon finding it did, considering whether legal constraints external to the parties' agreement foreclosed the arbitration of those claims. We endorse its rejection of Soler's proposed rule of arbitration-clause construction.

III

We now turn to consider whether Soler's antitrust claims are non arbitrable even though it has agreed to arbitrate them. In holding that they are not, the Court of Appeals followed the decision of the Second Circuit in *American Safety Equipment Corp. v. J. P. Maguire & Co.*, 391 F.2d 821 (1968). Notwithstanding the absence of any explicit support for such an exception in either the Sherman Act or the Federal Arbitration Act, the Second Circuit there reasoned that "the pervasive public interest in enforcement of the antitrust laws, and the nature of the claims that arise in such cases, combine to make antitrust claims inappropriate for arbitration." *Id.*, at 827–828. We find it unnecessary to assess the legitimacy of the American Safety doctrine as applied to agreements to arbitrate arising from domestic transactions. As in *Scherk v. Alberto–Culver Co.*, 417 U.S. 506 (1974), we conclude that concerns of international comity, respect for the capacities of foreign and transnational tribunals, and sensitivity to the need of the international commercial system for predictability in the resolution of disputes require that we enforce the parties' agreement, even assuming that a contrary result would be forthcoming in a domestic context.

Even before *Scherk*, this Court had recognized the utility of forum-selection clauses in international transactions. In *The Bremen*, supra, an American oil company, seeking to evade a contractual choice of an English forum and, by implication, English law, filed a suit in admiralty in a United States District Court against the German corporation which had contracted to tow its rig to a location in the Adriatic Sea. Notwithstanding the possibility that the English court would enforce provisions in the towage contract exculpating the German party which an American court would refuse to enforce, this Court gave effect to the choice-of-forum clause. It observed:

> "The expansion of American business and industry will hardly be encouraged if, notwithstanding solemn contracts, we insist on a parochial concept that all disputes must be resolved under our laws and in our courts. We cannot have trade and commerce in world markets and international waters exclusively on our terms, governed by our laws, and resolved in our courts." 407 U.S., at 9.

Recognizing that "agreeing in advance on a forum acceptable to both parties is an indispensable element in international trade, commerce, and contracting," *id.*, at 13–14, the decision in The Bremen clearly eschewed a provincial solicitude for the jurisdiction of domestic forums.

Identical considerations governed the Court's decision in *Scherk*, which categorized "[an] agreement to arbitrate before a specified tribunal [as], in effect, a specialized kind of forum-selection clause that posits not only the situs of suit but also the procedure to be used in resolving the dispute." 417 U.S., at 519. In *Scherk*, the American company Alberto–Culver purchased several interrelated business enterprises, organized under the laws of Germany and Liechtenstein, as well as the rights held by those enterprises in certain trademarks, from a German citizen who at the time of trial resided in Switzerland. Although the contract of sale contained a clause providing for arbitration before the International Chamber of Commerce in Paris of "any controversy or claim [arising] out of this agreement or the breach thereof," Alberto–Culver subsequently brought suit against *Scherk* in a Federal District Court in Illinois, alleging that *Scherk* had violated § 10(b) of the Securities Exchange Act of 1934 by fraudulently misrepresenting the status of the trademarks as unencumbered. The District Court denied a motion to stay the proceedings before it and enjoined the parties from going forward before the arbitral tribunal in Paris. The Court of Appeals for the Seventh Circuit affirmed, relying on this Court's holding in *Wilko v. Swan*, 346 U.S. 427 (1953), that agreements to arbitrate disputes arising under the Securities Act of 1933 are non arbitrable. This Court reversed, enforcing the arbitration agreement even while assuming for purposes of the decision that the controversy would be non arbitrable under the holding of *Wilko* had it arisen out of a domestic transaction. Again, the Court emphasized:

> "A contractual provision specifying in advance the forum in which disputes shall be litigated and the law to be applied is an almost indispensable precondition to achievement of the orderliness and predictability essential to any international business transaction.

> "A parochial refusal by the courts of one country to enforce an international arbitration agreement would not only frustrate these purposes, but would invite unseemly and mutually destructive jockeying by the parties to secure tactical litigation advantages. [It would] damage the fabric of international commerce and trade, and imperil the willingness and ability of businessmen to enter into international commercial agreements." 417 U.S., at 516–517.

Accordingly, the Court held Alberto–Culver to its bargain, sending it to the international arbitral tribunal before which it had agreed to seek its remedies.

The Bremen and *Scherk* establish a strong presumption in favor of enforcement of freely negotiated contractual choice-of-forum provisions. Here, as in *Scherk*, that presumption is reinforced by the emphatic federal policy in favor of arbitral dispute resolution. And at least since this Nation's accession in 1970 to the Convention, see [1970] 21 U.S.T. 2517, T.I.A.S. 6997, and the implementation of the Convention in the same year by amendment of the Federal Arbitration Act, that federal policy applies with special force in the field of international commerce. Thus, we must weigh the concerns of *American Safety* against a strong belief in the efficacy of arbitral procedures for the resolution of international commercial disputes and an equal commitment to the enforcement of freely negotiated choice-of-forum clauses.

At the outset, we confess to some skepticism of certain aspects of the *American Safety* doctrine. As distilled by the First Circuit, 723 F.2d, at 162, the doctrine comprises four ingredients. First, private parties play a pivotal role in aiding governmental enforcement of the antitrust laws by means of the private action for treble damages. Second, "the strong possibility that contracts which generate antitrust disputes may be contracts of adhesion militates against automatic forum determination by contract." Third, antitrust issues, prone to complication, require sophisticated legal and economic analysis, and thus are "ill-adapted to strengths of the arbitral process, i.e., expedition, minimal requirements of written rationale, simplicity, resort to basic concepts of common sense and simple equity." Finally, just as "issues of war and peace are too important to be vested in the generals, decisions as to antitrust regulation of business are too important to be lodged in arbitrators chosen from the business community—particularly those from a foreign community that has had no experience with or exposure to our law and values." See *American Safety*, 391 F.2d, at 826–827.

Initially, we find the second concern unjustified. The mere appearance of an antitrust dispute does not alone warrant invalidation of the selected forum on the undemonstrated assumption that the arbitration clause is tainted. A party resisting arbitration of course may attack directly the validity of the agreement to arbitrate. Moreover, the party may attempt to make a showing that would warrant setting aside the forum-selection clause—that the agreement was "[affected] by fraud, undue influence, or overweening bargaining power"; that "enforcement would be unreasonable and unjust"; or that proceedings "in the contractual forum will be so gravely difficult and inconvenient that [the resisting party] will for all practical purposes be deprived of his day in court." *The Bremen*, 407 U.S., at 12, 15, 18. But absent such a showing—and none was attempted here—there is no basis for assuming the forum inadequate or its selection unfair.

Next, potential complexity should not suffice to ward off arbitration. We might well have some doubt that even the courts following *American Safety* subscribe fully to the view that antitrust matters are inherently insusceptible to resolution by arbitration, as these same courts have agreed that an undertaking to arbitrate antitrust claims entered into after the dispute arises is acceptable. And the vertical restraints which most frequently give birth to antitrust claims covered by an arbitration agreement will not often occasion the monstrous proceedings that have given antitrust litigation an image of intractability. In any event, adaptability and access to expertise are hallmarks of arbitration. The anticipated subject matter of the dispute may be taken into account when the arbitrators are appointed, and arbitral rules typically provide for the participation of experts either employed by the parties or appointed by the tribunal. Moreover, it is often a judgment that streamlined proceedings and expeditious results will best serve their needs that causes parties to agree to arbitrate their disputes; it is typically a desire to keep the effort and expense required to resolve a dispute within manageable bounds that prompts them mutually to forgo access to judicial remedies. In sum, the factor of potential complexity alone does not persuade us that an arbitral tribunal could not properly handle an antitrust matter.

For similar reasons, we also reject the proposition that an arbitration panel will pose too great a danger of innate hostility to the constraints on business conduct that antitrust law imposes. International arbitrators frequently are drawn from the legal as well as the business community; where the dispute has an important legal component, the parties and the arbitral body with whose assistance they have agreed to settle their dispute can be expected to select arbitrators accordingly. We decline to indulge the presumption that the parties and arbitral body conducting a proceeding will be unable or unwilling to retain competent, conscientious, and impartial arbitrators.

We are left, then, with the core of the *American Safety* doctrine—the fundamental importance to American democratic capitalism of the regime of the antitrust laws. Without doubt, the private cause of action plays a central role in enforcing this regime. As the Court of Appeals pointed out:

> " 'A claim under the antitrust laws is not merely a private matter. The Sherman Act is designed to promote the national interest in a competitive economy; thus, the plaintiff asserting his rights under the Act has been likened to a private attorney-general who protects the public's interest.' " 723 F.2d, at 168, quoting *American Safety*, 391 F.2d, at 826.

The treble-damages provision wielded by the private litigant is a chief tool in the antitrust enforcement scheme, posing a crucial deterrent to potential violators.

The importance of the private damages remedy, however, does not compel the conclusion that it may not be sought outside an American court. Notwithstanding its important incidental policing function, the treble-damages cause of action conferred on private parties by § 4 of the Clayton Act, 15 U. S. C. § 15, and pursued by Soler here by way of its third counterclaim, seeks primarily to enable an injured competitor to gain compensation for that injury.

> "Section 4 is in essence a remedial provision. It provides treble damages to '[any] person who shall be injured in his business or property by reason of anything forbidden in the antitrust laws.' Of course, treble damages also play an important role in penalizing wrongdoers and deterring wrongdoing, as we also have frequently observed. It nevertheless is true that the treble-damages provision, which makes awards available only to injured parties, and measures the awards by a multiple of the injury actually proved, is designed primarily as a remedy." *Brunswick Corp. v. Pueblo Bowl–O–Mat, Inc.*, 429 U.S. 477, 485–486 (1977).

After examining the respective legislative histories, the Court in Brunswick recognized that when first enacted in 1890 as § 7 of the Sherman Act, 26 Stat. 210, the treble-damages provision "was conceived of primarily as a remedy for '[the] people of the United States as individuals,' " 429 U.S., at 486, n. 10, quoting 21 Cong. Rec. 1767–1768 (1890) (remarks of Sen. George); when reenacted in 1914 as § 4 of the Clayton Act, 38 Stat. 731, it was still "conceived primarily as '[opening] the door of justice to every man, whenever he may be injured by those who violate the antitrust laws, and [giving] the injured party ample damages for the wrong suffered.' " 429 U.S., at 486, n. 10, quoting 51 Cong. Rec. 9073 (1914) (remarks of Rep. Webb). And, of course, the antitrust cause of action remains at all times under the control of the individual litigant: no citizen is under an obligation to bring an antitrust suit, see *Illinois Brick Co. v. Illinois*, 431 U.S. 720, 746 (1977), and the private antitrust plaintiff needs no executive or judicial approval before settling one. It follows that, at least where the international cast of a transaction would otherwise add an element of uncertainty to dispute resolution, the prospective litigant may provide in advance for a mutually agreeable procedure whereby he would seek his antitrust recovery as well as settle other controversies.

There is no reason to assume at the outset of the dispute that international arbitration will not provide an adequate mechanism. To be sure, the international arbitral tribunal owes no prior allegiance to the legal norms of particular states; hence, it has no direct obligation to vindicate their statutory dictates. The tribunal, however, is bound to effectuate the intentions of the parties. Where the parties have agreed that the arbitral body is to decide a defined set of claims which includes, as in these cases, those arising from the application of American antitrust law, the tribunal therefore should be bound to decide that dispute in accord with the national law giving rise to the claim. And so long as the prospective litigant effectively may vindicate its statutory cause of action in the arbitral forum, the statute will continue to serve both its remedial and deterrent function.

Having permitted the arbitration to go forward, the national courts of the United States will have the opportunity at the award-enforcement stage to ensure that the legitimate interest in the enforcement of the antitrust laws has been addressed. The Convention reserves to each signatory country the right to refuse enforcement of an award where the "recognition or enforcement of the award would be contrary to the public policy of that country." Art. V(2)(b), 21 U.S.T., at 2520; see *Scherk*, 417 U.S., at 519, n. 14. While the efficacy of the arbitral process requires that substantive review at the award-enforcement stage remain minimal, it would not require intrusive inquiry to ascertain that the tribunal took cognizance of the antitrust claims and actually decided them.

As international trade has expanded in recent decades, so too has the use of international arbitration to resolve disputes arising in the course of that trade. The controversies that international arbitral institutions are called upon to resolve have increased in diversity as well as in complexity. Yet the potential of these tribunals for efficient disposition of legal disagreements arising from commercial relations has not yet been tested. If they are to take a central place in the international legal order, national courts will need to "shake off the old judicial hostility to arbitration," *Kulukundis Shipping Co. v. Amtorg Trading Corp.*, 126 F.2d 978, 985 (CA2 1942), and also their customary and understandable unwillingness to cede jurisdiction of a claim arising under domestic law to a foreign or transnational tribunal. To this extent, at least, it will be necessary for national courts to subordinate domestic notions of arbitrability to the international policy favoring commercial arbitration.

Accordingly, we "require this representative of the American business community to honor its bargain," *Alberto–Culver Co. v. Scherk*, 484 F.2d

611, 620 (CA7 1973) (Stevens, J., dissenting), by holding this agreement to arbitrate "[enforceable] in accord with the explicit provisions of the Arbitration Act." *Scherk*, 417 U.S., at 520.

The judgment of the Court of Appeals is affirmed in part and reversed in part, and the cases are remanded for further proceedings consistent with this opinion.

It is so ordered.

■ POWELL, J. took no part in the decision of these cases.

■ [A dissent, authored by STEVENS, J., with whom BRENNAN, J. joins, and with whom MARSHALL, J. joins in part, is omitted.]

14 Penn Plaza LLC v. Pyett

Supreme Court of the United States, 2009.
556 U.S. 247.

■ THOMAS, J. The question presented by this case is whether a provision in a collective-bargaining agreement that clearly and unmistakably requires union members to arbitrate claims arising under the Age Discrimination in Employment Act of 1967 (ADEA), 81 Stat. 602, as amended, 29 U.S.C. § 621 et seq., is enforceable. The United States Court of Appeals for the Second Circuit held that this Court's decision in *Alexander v. Gardner–Denver Co.*, 415 U.S. 36 (1974), forbids enforcement of such arbitration provisions. We disagree and reverse the judgment of the Court of Appeals.

I

Respondents are members of the Service Employees International Union, Local 32BJ (Union). Under the National Labor Relations Act (NLRA), 49 Stat. 449, as amended, the Union is the exclusive bargaining representative of employees within the building-services industry in New York City, which includes building cleaners, porters, and doorpersons. See 29 U.S.C. § 159(a). In this role, the Union has exclusive authority to bargain on behalf of its members over their "rates of pay, wages, hours of employment, or other conditions of employment." *Ibid.* Since the 1930's, the Union has engaged in industry-wide collective bargaining with the Realty Advisory Board on Labor Relations, Inc. (RAB), a multiemployer bargaining association for the New York City real-estate industry. The agreement between the Union and the RAB is embodied in their Collective Bargaining Agreement for Contractors and Building Owners (CBA). The CBA requires union members to submit all claims of employment discrimination to binding arbitration under the CBA's grievance and dispute resolution procedures:

> "30. NO DISCRIMINATION. There shall be no discrimination against any present or future employee by reason of race, creed, color, age, disability, national origin, sex, union membership, or any characteristic protected by law, including, but not limited to, claims made pursuant to Title VII of the Civil Rights Act, the

Americans with Disabilities Act, the Age Discrimination in Employment Act, the New York State Human Rights Law, the New York City Human Rights Code, or any other similar laws, rules, or regulations. All such claims shall be subject to the grievance and arbitration procedure (Articles V and VI) as the sole and exclusive remedy for violations. Arbitrators shall apply appropriate law in rendering decisions based upon claims of discrimination." ...

Petitioner 14 Penn Plaza LLC is a member of the RAB. It owns and operates the New York City office building where, prior to August 2003, respondents worked as night lobby watchmen and in other similar capacities. Respondents were directly employed by petitioner Temco Service Industries, Inc. (Temco), a maintenance service and cleaning contractor. In August 2003, with the Union's consent, 14 Penn Plaza engaged Spartan Security, a unionized security services contractor and affiliate of Temco, to provide licensed security guards to staff the lobby and entrances of its building. Because this rendered respondents' lobby services unnecessary, Temco reassigned them to jobs as night porters and light duty cleaners in other locations in the building. Respondents contend that these reassignments led to a loss in income, caused them emotional distress, and were otherwise less desirable than their former positions.

At respondents' request, the Union filed grievances challenging the reassignments. The grievances alleged that petitioners: (1) violated the CBA's ban on workplace discrimination by reassigning respondents on account of their age; (2) violated seniority rules by failing to promote one of the respondents to a handyman position; and (3) failed to equitably rotate overtime. After failing to obtain relief on any of these claims through the grievance process, the Union requested arbitration under the CBA.

After the initial arbitration hearing, the Union withdrew the first set of respondents' grievances—the age-discrimination claims—from arbitration. Because it had consented to the contract for new security personnel at 14 Penn Plaza, the Union believed that it could not legitimately object to respondents' reassignments as discriminatory. But the Union continued to arbitrate the seniority and overtime claims, and, after several hearings, the claims were denied.

In May 2004, while the arbitration was ongoing but after the Union withdrew the age-discrimination claims, respondents filed a complaint with the Equal Employment Opportunity Commission (EEOC) alleging that petitioners had violated their rights under the ADEA. Approximately one month later, the EEOC issued a Dismissal and Notice of Rights, which explained that the agency's " 'review of the evidence fail[ed] to indicate that a violation ha[d] occurred,' " and notified each respondent of his right to sue. *Pyett v. Pa. Bldg. Co.*, 498 F.3d 88, 91 (CA2 2007).

Respondents thereafter filed suit against petitioners in the United States District Court for the Southern District of New York, alleging that their reassignment violated the ADEA and state and local laws prohibiting age discrimination. Petitioners filed a motion to compel arbitration of respondents' claims pursuant to §§ 3 and 4 of the Federal Arbitration Act

(FAA), 9 U.S.C. §§ 3, 4. The District Court denied the motion because under Second Circuit precedent, "even a clear and unmistakable union-negotiated waiver of a right to litigate certain federal and state statutory claims in a judicial forum is unenforceable." Respondents immediately appealed the ruling under § 16 of the FAA, which authorizes an interlocutory appeal of "an order refusing a stay of any action under section 3 of this title" or "denying a petition under section 4 of this title to order arbitration to proceed." 9 U.S.C. §§ 16(a)(1)(A)–(B).

The Court of Appeals affirmed. 498 F.3d 88. According to the Court of Appeals, it could not compel arbitration of the dispute because Gardner–Denver, which "remains good law," held "that a collective bargaining agreement could not waive covered workers' rights to a judicial forum for causes of action created by Congress." 498 F.3d at 92, 91, n. 3 (citing Gardner–Denver, 415 U.S., at 49–51). The Court of Appeals observed that the Gardner–Denver decision was in tension with this Court's more recent decision in Gilmer v. Interstate/Johnson Lane Corp., 500 U.S. 20 (1991), which "held that an individual employee who had agreed individually to waive his right to a federal forum could be compelled to arbitrate a federal age discrimination claim." 498 F.3d at 91, n. 3 (citing Gilmer, supra, at 33–35; emphasis in original). The Court of Appeals also noted that this Court previously declined to resolve this tension in Wright v. Universal Maritime Service Corp., 525 U.S. 70, 82 (1998), where the waiver at issue was not "clear and unmistakable." 498 F.3d at 91, n. 3.

The Court of Appeals attempted to reconcile Gardner–Denver and Gilmer by holding that arbitration provisions in a collective-bargaining agreement, "which purport to waive employees' rights to a federal forum with respect to statutory claims, are unenforceable." 498 F.3d at 93–94. As a result, an individual employee would be free to choose compulsory arbitration under Gilmer, but a labor union could not collectively bargain for arbitration on behalf of its members. We granted certiorari to address the issue left unresolved in Wright, which continues to divide the Courts of Appeals, and now reverse.

II

A

The NLRA governs federal labor-relations law. As permitted by that statute, respondents designated the Union as their "exclusive representativ[e] for the purposes of collective bargaining in respect to rates of pay, wages, hours of employment, or other conditions of employment." 29 U.S.C. § 159(a). As the employees' exclusive bargaining representative, the Union "enjoys broad authority in the negotiation and administration of [the] collective bargaining contract." Communications Workers v. Beck, 487 U.S. 735, 739 (1988) (internal quotation marks omitted). But this broad authority "is accompanied by a responsibility of equal scope, the responsibility and duty of fair representation." Humphrey v. Moore, 375 U.S. 335, 342 (1964). The employer has a corresponding duty under the NLRA to bargain in good faith "with the representatives of his employees" on wages, hours, and conditions of employment. 29 U.S.C. § 158(a)(5); see also § 158(d).

In this instance, the Union and the RAB, negotiating on behalf of 14 Penn Plaza, collectively bargained in good faith and agreed that employment-related discrimination claims, including claims brought under the ADEA, would be resolved in arbitration. This freely negotiated term between the Union and the RAB easily qualifies as a "conditio[n] of employment" that is subject to mandatory bargaining under § 159(a). [The] decision to fashion a collective bargaining agreement to require arbitration of employment-discrimination claims is no different from the many other decisions made by parties in designing grievance machinery.

Respondents, however, contend that the arbitration clause here is outside the permissible scope of the collective-bargaining process because it affects the "employees' individual, non-economic statutory rights." Brief for Respondents. We disagree. Parties generally favor arbitration precisely because of the economics of dispute resolution. As in any contractual negotiation, a union may agree to the inclusion of an arbitration provision in a collective-bargaining agreement in return for other concessions from the employer. Courts generally may not interfere in this bargained-for exchange. "Judicial nullification of contractual concessions is contrary to what the Court has recognized as one of the fundamental policies of the National Labor Relations Act—freedom of contract." *NLRB v. Magnavox Co.*, 415 U.S. 322, 328 (1974) (Stewart, J., concurring in part and dissenting in part) (internal quotation marks and brackets omitted).

As a result, the CBA's arbitration provision must be honored unless the ADEA itself removes this particular class of grievances from the NLRA's broad sweep. It does not. This Court has squarely held that ADEA does not preclude arbitration of claims brought under the statute.

In *Gilmer*, the Court explained that "[a]lthough all statutory claims may not be appropriate for arbitration, '[h]aving made the bargain to arbitrate, the party should be held to it unless Congress itself has evinced an intention to preclude a waiver of judicial remedies for the statutory rights at issue.'" *Id.*, at 26 (quoting *Mitsubishi Motors Corp.*, *supra*, at 628). And "[i]f Congress intended the substantive protection afforded by the ADEA to include protection against waiver of the right to a judicial forum, that intention will be deducible from text or legislative history." 500 U.S., at 29 (internal quotation marks and some brackets omitted). The Court determined that "nothing in the text of the ADEA or its legislative history explicitly precludes arbitration." *Id.*, at 26–27. The Court also concluded that arbitrating ADEA disputes would not undermine the statute's "remedial and deterrent function." *Id.*, at 28 (internal quotation marks omitted). In the end, the employee's "generalized attacks" on "the adequacy of arbitration procedures" were "insufficient to preclude arbitration of statutory claims," *id.*, at 30, because there was no evidence that "Congress, in enacting the ADEA, intended to preclude arbitration of claims under that Act," *id.*, at 35.

The *Gilmer* Court's interpretation of the ADEA fully applies in the collective-bargaining context. Nothing in the law suggests a distinction between the status of arbitration agreements signed by an individual employee and those agreed to by a union representative. This Court has required only that an agreement to arbitrate statutory antidiscrimination claims be "explicitly stated" in the collective-bargaining agreement. *Wright*, 525 U.S., at 80 (internal quotation marks omitted). The CBA under review here meets that obligation. Respondents incorrectly counter that an individual employee must personally "waive" a "[substantive] right" to proceed in court for a waiver to be "knowing and voluntary" under the ADEA. 29 U.S.C. § 626(f)(1). As explained below, however, the agreement to arbitrate ADEA claims is not the waiver of a "substantive right" as that term is employed in the ADEA. *Wright, supra,* at 80. Indeed, if the "right" referred to in § 626(f)(1) included the prospective waiver of the right to bring an ADEA claim in court, even a waiver signed by an individual employee would be invalid as the statute also prevents individuals from "waiv[ing] rights or claims that may arise after the date the waiver is executed." § 626(f)(1)(C).

Examination of the two federal statutes at issue in this case, therefore, yields a straightforward answer to the question presented: The NLRA provided the Union and the RAB with statutory authority to collectively bargain for arbitration of workplace discrimination claims, and Congress did not terminate that authority with respect to federal age-discrimination claims in the ADEA. Accordingly, there is no legal basis for the Court to strike down the arbitration clause in this CBA, which was freely negotiated by the Union and the RAB, and which clearly and unmistakably requires respondents to arbitrate the age-discrimination claims at issue in this appeal. Congress has chosen to allow arbitration of ADEA claims. The Judiciary must respect that choice.

B

The CBA's arbitration provision is also fully enforceable under the *Gardner–Denver* line of cases. Respondents interpret *Gardner–Denver* and its progeny to hold that "a union cannot waive an employee's right to a judicial forum under the federal antidiscrimination statutes" because "allowing the union to waive this right would substitute the union's interests for the employee's antidiscrimination rights." Brief for Respondents. The "combination of union control over the process and inherent conflict of interest with respect to discrimination claims," they argue, "provided the foundation for the Court's holding [in *Gardner–Denver*] that arbitration under a collective bargaining agreement could not preclude an individual employee's right to bring a lawsuit in court to vindicate a statutory discrimination claim." *Id.* We disagree.

1

The holding of *Gardner–Denver* is not as broad as respondents suggest. The employee in that case was covered by a collective-bargaining agreement that prohibited "discrimination against any employee on account of race, color, religion, sex, national origin, or ancestry" and that guaranteed that "[n]o employee will be discharged except for just cause." 415 U.S., at 39 (internal quotation marks omitted). The agreement also included a "multistep grievance procedure" that culminated in compulsory arbitration for any "differences aris[ing] between the Company and the Union as to the meaning and application of the provisions of this Agreement" and "any trouble aris[ing] in the plant." *Id.*, at 40–41 (internal quotation marks omitted).

The employee was discharged for allegedly producing too many defective parts while working for the respondent as a drill operator. He filed a grievance with his union claiming that he was " 'unjustly discharged' " in violation of the " 'just cause' " provision within the collective-bargaining agreement. *Id.*, at 39, 49. Then at the final pre-arbitration step of the grievance process, the employee added a claim that he was discharged because of his race. *Id.*, at 38–42.

The arbitrator ultimately ruled that the employee had been " 'discharged for just cause,' " but "made no reference to [the] claim of racial discrimination." *Id.*, at 42. After obtaining a right-to-sue letter from the EEOC, the employee filed a claim in Federal District Court, alleging racial discrimination in violation of Title VII of the Civil Rights Act of 1964. The District Court issued a decision, affirmed by the Court of Appeals, which granted summary judgment to the employer because it concluded that "the claim of racial discrimination had been submitted to the arbitrator and resolved adversely to [the employee]." *Id.*, at 43. In the District Court's view, "having voluntarily elected to pursue his grievance to final arbitration under the nondiscrimination clause of the collective-bargaining agreement," the employee was "bound by the arbitral decision" and precluded from suing his employer on any other grounds, such as a statutory claim under Title VII. *Ibid.*

This Court reversed the judgment on the narrow ground that the arbitration was not preclusive because the collective-bargaining agreement did not cover statutory claims. As a result, the lower courts erred in relying on the "doctrine of election of remedies" to bar the employee's Title VII claim. *Id.*, at 49. "That doctrine, which refers to situations where an individual pursues remedies that are legally or factually inconsistent" with each other, did not apply to the employee's dual pursuit of arbitration and a Title VII discrimination claim in district court. *Id.*, at 49. The employee's collective-bargaining agreement did not mandate arbitration of statutory antidiscrimination claims. *Id.*, at 49–50. "As the proctor of the bargain, the arbitrator's task is to effectuate the intent of the parties." *Id.*, at 53. Because the collective-bargaining agreement gave the arbitrator "authority to resolve only questions of contractual rights," his decision could not prevent the employee from bringing the Title VII claim in federal court "regardless of whether certain contractual rights are similar to, or duplicative of, the substantive rights secured by Title VII." *Id.*, at 53–54.

The Court also explained that the employee had not waived his right to pursue his Title VII claim in federal court by participating in an arbitration that was premised on the same underlying facts as the Title VII claim. See *id.*, at 52. Thus, whether the legal theory of preclusion advanced by the employer rested on "the doctrines of election of remedies" or was recast "as resting instead on the doctrine of equitable estoppel and on themes of res judicata and collateral estoppel," *id.*, at 49, n. 10 (internal quotation marks omitted), it could not prevail in light of the collective-bargaining agreement's failure to address arbitration of Title VII claims. See *id.*, at 46, n. 6 ("[W]e hold that the federal policy favoring arbitration does not establish that an arbitrator's resolution of a *contractual* claim is dispositive of a statutory claim under Title VII" (emphasis added)).

The Court's decisions following *Gardner–Denver* have not broadened its holding to make it applicable to the facts of this case. In *Barrentine v. Arkansas–Best Freight System, Inc.*, 450 U.S. 728 (1981), the Court considered "whether an employee may bring an action in federal district court, alleging a violation of the minimum wage provisions of the Fair Labor Standards Act, after having unsuccessfully submitted a wage claim based on the same underlying facts to a joint grievance committee pursuant to the provisions of his union's collective-bargaining agreement." *Id.*, at 729–730. The Court held that the unsuccessful arbitration did not preclude the federal lawsuit. Like the collective-bargaining agreement in *Gardner–Denver*, the arbitration provision under review in *Barrentine* did not expressly reference the statutory claim at issue. See 450 U.S., at 731, n. 5. The Court thus reiterated that an "arbitrator's power is both derived from, and limited by, the collective-bargaining agreement" and "[h]is task is limited to construing the meaning of the collective-bargaining agreement so as to effectuate the collective intent of the parties." *Id.*, at 744.

McDonald v. West Branch, 466 U.S. 284 (1984), was decided along similar lines. The question presented in that case was "whether a federal court may accord preclusive effect to an unappealed arbitration award in a case brought under [42 U.S.C. § 1983]." *Id.*, at 285. The Court declined to fashion such a rule, again explaining that "because an arbitrator's authority derives solely from the contract, *Barrentine, supra*, at 744, [101 S. Ct. 1437, 67 L. Ed. 2d 641], an arbitrator may not have the authority to enforce § 1983" when that provision is left unaddressed by the arbitration agreement. *Id.*, at 290. Accordingly, as in both *Gardner–Denver* and *Barrentine*, the Court's decision in *McDonald* hinged on the scope of the collective-bargaining agreement and the arbitrator's parallel mandate.

The facts underlying *Gardner–Denver*, *Barrentine*, and *McDonald* reveal the narrow scope of the legal rule arising from that trilogy of decisions. Summarizing those opinions in *Gilmer*, this Court made clear that the *Gardner–Denver* line of cases "did not involve the issue of the enforceability of an agreement to arbitrate statutory claims." 500 U.S., at 35. Those decisions instead "involved the quite different issue whether arbitration of contract-based claims precluded subsequent judicial resolution of statutory claims. Since the employees there had not agreed to arbitrate their statutory claims, and the labor arbitrators were not authorized to resolve such claims, the arbitration in those cases understandably was held not to preclude subsequent statutory actions." *Ibid. Gardner–Denver* and its progeny thus do not control the outcome where, as is the case here, the collective-bargaining agreement's arbitration provision expressly covers both statutory and contractual discrimination claims.

2

We recognize that apart from their narrow holdings, the *Gardner–Denver* line of cases included broad dicta that were highly critical of the use of arbitration for the vindication of statutory antidiscrimination rights. That skepticism, however, rested on a misconceived view of arbitration that this Court has since abandoned.

First, the Court in *Gardner–Denver* erroneously assumed that an agreement to submit statutory discrimination claims to arbitration was tantamount to a waiver of those rights. See 415 U.S., at 51 ("[T]here can be no prospective *waiver* of an employee's rights under Title VII" (emphasis added)). For this reason, the Court stated, "the rights conferred [by Title VII] can form no part of the collective-bargaining process since waiver of these rights would defeat the paramount congressional purpose behind Title VII." *Ibid*.

The Court was correct in concluding that federal antidiscrimination rights may not be prospectively waived, see 29 U.S.C. § 626(f)(1)(C), but it confused an agreement to arbitrate those statutory claims with a prospective waiver of the substantive right. The decision to resolve ADEA claims by way of arbitration instead of litigation does not waive the statutory right to be free from workplace age discrimination; it waives only the right to seek relief from a court in the first instance. See *Gilmer*, supra, at 26 (" '[B]y agreeing to arbitrate a statutory claim, a party does not forgo the substantive rights afforded by the statute; it only submits to their resolution in an arbitral, rather than a judicial, forum' " (quoting *Mitsubishi Motors Corp.*, 473 U.S., at 628)). This "Court has been quite specific in holding that arbitration agreements can be enforced under the FAA without contravening the policies of congressional enactments giving employees specific protection against discrimination prohibited by federal law." *Circuit City Stores, Inc.*, 532 U.S., at 123. The suggestion in *Gardner–Denver* that the decision to arbitrate statutory discrimination claims was tantamount to a substantive waiver of those rights, therefore, reveals a distorted understanding of the compromise made when an employee agrees to compulsory arbitration.

In this respect, *Gardner–Denver* is a direct descendant of the Court's decision in *Wilko v. Swan*, 346 U.S. 427 (1953), which held that an agreement to arbitrate claims under the Securities Act of 1933 was unenforceable. See *id.*, at 438. The Court subsequently overruled *Wilko* and, in so doing, characterized the decision as "pervaded by 'the old judicial hostility to arbitration.' " *Rodriguez de Quijas v. Shearson/American Express, Inc.*, 490 U.S. 477, 480 (1989). The Court added: "To the extent that *Wilko* rested on suspicion of arbitration as a method of weakening the protections afforded in the substantive law to would-be complainants, it has fallen far out of step with our current strong endorsement of the federal statutes favoring this method of resolving disputes." *Id.*, at 481. The timeworn "mistrust of the arbitral process" harbored by the Court in *Gardner–Denver* thus weighs against reliance on anything more than its core holding. *Shearson/American Express Inc. v. McMahon*, 482 U.S. 220, 231–232 (1987). Indeed, in light of the "radical change, over two decades, in the Court's receptivity to arbitration," *Wright*, 525 U.S., at 77, reliance on any judicial decision similarly littered with *Wilko*'s overt hostility to the enforcement of arbitration agreements would be ill advised.9

Second, *Gardner–Denver* mistakenly suggested that certain features of arbitration made it a forum "well suited to the resolution of contractual disputes," but "a comparatively inappropriate forum for the final resolution of rights created by Title VII." 415 U.S., at 56. According to the Court, the "factfinding process in arbitration" is "not equivalent to judicial factfinding" and the "informality of arbitral procedure makes arbitration a less appropriate forum for final resolution of Title VII issues than the federal courts." *Id.*, at 57, 58. The Court also questioned the competence of arbitrators to decide federal statutory claims. In the Court's view, "the resolution of statutory or constitutional issues is a primary responsibility of courts, and judicial construction has proved especially necessary with respect to Title VII, whose broad language frequently can be given meaning only by reference to public law concepts." *Gardner–Denver, supra*, at 57.

These misconceptions have been corrected. For example, the Court has "recognized that arbitral tribunals are readily capable of handling the factual and legal complexities of antitrust claims, notwithstanding the absence of judicial instruction and supervision" and that "there is no reason to assume at the outset that arbitrators will not follow the law." *McMahon, supra*, at 232; *Mitsubishi Motors Corp.*, 473 U.S., at 634 ("We decline to indulge the presumption that the parties and arbitral body conducting a proceeding will be unable or unwilling to retain competent, conscientious, and impartial arbitrators"). An arbitrator's capacity to resolve complex questions of fact and law extends with equal force to discrimination claims brought under the ADEA. Moreover, the recognition that arbitration procedures are more streamlined than federal litigation is not a basis for finding the forum somehow inadequate; the relative informality of arbitration is one of the chief reasons that parties select arbitration. Parties "trad[e] the procedures and opportunity for review of the courtroom for the simplicity, informality, and expedition of arbitration." *Id.*, at 628. In any event, "[i]t is unlikely that age discrimination claims require more extensive discovery than other claims that we have found to be arbitrable, such as Racketeer Influenced and Corrupt Organizations Act and antitrust claims." *Gilmer*, supra, at 31. At bottom, objections centered on the nature of arbitration do not offer a credible basis for discrediting the choice of that forum to resolve statutory antidiscrimination claims.[10]

---

10. Moreover, an arbitrator's decision as to whether a unionized employee has been discriminated against on the basis of age in violation of the ADEA remains subject to judicial review under the FAA. 9 U.S.C. § 10(a). "[A]lthough judicial scrutiny of arbitration awards necessarily is limited, such review is sufficient to ensure that arbitrators comply with the requirements of the statute." *Shearson/American Express Inc. v. McMahon*, 482 U.S. 220, 232 (1987).

Third, the Court in Gardner–Denver raised in a footnote a "further concern" regarding "the union's exclusive control over the manner and extent to which an individual grievance is presented." 415 U.S., at 58, n. 19. The Court suggested that in arbitration, as in the collective-bargaining process, a union may subordinate the interests of an individual employee to the collective interests of all employees in the bargaining unit. *Ibid.*

We cannot rely on this judicial policy concern as a source of authority for introducing a qualification into the ADEA that is not found in its text. Absent a constitutional barrier, "it is not for us to substitute our view of policy for the legislation which has been passed by Congress." *Fla. Dep't of Revenue v. Piccadilly Cafeterias, Inc.*, 554 U.S. 33, 52 (2008) (internal quotation marks omitted). Congress is fully equipped "to identify any category of claims as to which agreements to arbitrate will be held unenforceable." *Mitsubishi Motors Corp., supra*, at 627. Until Congress amends the ADEA to meet the conflict-of-interest concern identified in the *Gardner–Denver* dicta, and seized on by respondents here, there is "no reason to color the lens through which the arbitration clause is read" simply because of an alleged conflict of interest between a union and its members. *Mitsubishi Motors Corp., supra*, at 628. This is a "battl[e] that should be fought among the political branches and the industry. Those parties should not seek to amend the statute by appeal to the Judicial Branch." *Barnhart v. Sigmon Coal Co.*, 534 U.S. 438, 462 (2002).

The conflict-of-interest argument also proves too much. Labor unions certainly balance the economic interests of some employees against the needs of the larger work force as they negotiate collective-bargaining agreements and implement them on a daily basis. But this attribute of organized labor does not justify singling out an arbitration provision for disfavored treatment. This "principle of majority rule" to which respondents object is in fact the central premise of the NLRA. *Emporium Capwell Co. v. Western Addition Community Organization*, 420 U.S. 50, 62 (1975). "In establishing a regime of majority rule, Congress sought to secure to all members of the unit the benefits of their collective strength and bargaining power, in full awareness that the superior strength of some individuals or groups might be subordinated to the interest of the majority." *Ibid.* (footnote omitted). It was Congress' verdict that the benefits of organized labor outweigh the sacrifice of individual liberty that this system necessarily demands. Respondents' argument that they were deprived of the right to pursue their ADEA claims in federal court by a labor union with a conflict of interest is therefore unsustainable; it amounts to a collateral attack on the NLRA.

In any event, Congress has accounted for this conflict of interest in several ways. As indicated above, the NLRA has been interpreted to impose a "duty of fair representation" on labor unions, which a union breaches "when its conduct toward a member of the bargaining unit is arbitrary, discriminatory, or in bad faith." *Marquez v. Screen Actors*, 525 U.S. 33, 44 (1998). This duty extends to "challenges leveled not only at a union's contract administration and enforcement efforts but at its negotiation activities as well." *Beck*, 487 U.S., at 743 (citation omitted). Thus, a union is subject to liability under the NLRA if it illegally discriminates against older workers in either the formation or governance of the collective-bargaining agreement, such as by deciding not to pursue a grievance on behalf of one of its members for discriminatory reasons. Respondents in fact brought a fair representation suit against the Union based on its withdrawal of support for their age-discrimination claims. Given this avenue that Congress has made available to redress a union's violation of its duty to its members, it is particularly inappropriate to ask this Court to impose an artificial limitation on the collective-bargaining process.

In addition, a union is subject to liability under the ADEA if the union itself discriminates against its members on the basis of age. See 29 U.S.C. § 623(d). Union members may also file age-discrimination claims with the EEOC and the National Labor Relations Board, which may then seek judicial intervention under this Court's precedent. In sum, Congress has provided remedies for the situation where a labor union is less than vigorous in defense of its members' claims of discrimination under the ADEA.

III

Finally, respondents offer a series of arguments contending that the particular CBA at issue here does not clearly and unmistakably require them to arbitrate their ADEA claims. But respondents did not raise these contract-based arguments in the District Court or the Court of Appeals. To the contrary, respondents acknowledged on appeal that the CBA provision requiring arbitration of their federal antidiscrimination statutory claims "is sufficiently explicit" in precluding their federal lawsuit. In light of respondents' litigating position, both lower courts assumed that the CBA's arbitration clause clearly applied to respondents and proceeded to decide the question left unresolved in *Wright*. We granted review of the question presented on that understanding.

"Without cross-petitioning for certiorari, a prevailing party may, of course, 'defend its judgment on any ground properly raised below whether or not that ground was relied upon, rejected, or even considered by the District Court or the Court of Appeals.'" *Granfinanciera, S. A. v. Nordberg*, 492 U.S. 33, 38–39 (1989) (quoting *Washington v. Confederated Bands and Tribes of Yakima Nation*, 439 U.S. 463, 476, n. 20 (1979)). But this Court will affirm on grounds that have "'not been raised below "only in exceptional cases."'" *Nordberg, supra*, at 39 (quoting *Heckler v. Campbell*, 461 U.S. 458, 468–469, n. 12 (1983)). This is not an "exceptional case." As a result, we find that respondents' alternative arguments for affirmance have been forfeited. We will not resurrect them on respondents' behalf.

Respondents also argue that the CBA operates as a substantive waiver of their ADEA rights because it not only precludes a federal lawsuit, but also allows the Union to block arbitration of these claims. Petitioners contest this characterization of the CBA, and offer record evidence suggesting that the Union has allowed respondents to continue with the arbitration even though the Union has declined to participate. But not only does this question require resolution of contested factual allegations, it was not fully briefed to this or any court and is not fairly encompassed within the question presented, see this Court's Rule 14.1(a). Thus, although a substantive waiver of federally protected civil rights will not be upheld, we are not positioned to resolve in the first instance whether the CBA allows the Union to prevent respondents from "effectively vindicating" their "federal statutory rights in the arbitral forum," *Green Tree Financial Corp.–Ala. v. Randolph*, 531 U.S. 79, 90 (2000). Resolution of this question at this juncture would be particularly inappropriate in light of our hesitation to invalidate arbitration agreements on the basis of speculation. See *id.*, at 91.

IV

We hold that a collective-bargaining agreement that clearly and unmistakably requires union members to arbitrate ADEA claims is enforceable as a matter of federal law. The judgment of the Court of Appeals is reversed, and the case is remanded for further proceedings consistent with this opinion.

It is so ordered.

■ [Dissenting opinions authored by STEVENS, J., and by SOUTER J., joined by STEVENS, J., GINSBURG, J., and BREYER, J. are omitted.]

* * *

When arbitration's enthusiasts, including the federal courts, consider the scope of arbitral authority, they approach arbitration on the third-party model as an instance of judging. This enables arbitration's enthusiasts to exploit the analogy to adjudication in order to construct an expansive account of arbitral authority—so that an arbitrator's authority might extend well beyond the range of freedom of contract, for example, to deciding statutory claims and even (when courts affirm the arbitrability of arbitrability) to determining its own scope.

But enthusiasts treat arbitration on the first-party model when they ask on what procedural safeguards the authority of arbitration depends. This enables them to exploit background ideals concerning freedom of contract in order to construct a relaxed account of the procedural standards that govern arbitration, even though such relaxed procedures could not possibly sustain arbitration's authority on the third-party model that is invoked to justify arbitration's expansive scope.

Arbitration's defenders, including the Supreme Court, are thus trying to have it both ways. They model arbitration on adjudication in order to exploit the broad but demanding authority of third-party arbitration and hence to expand arbitration's scope beyond contract's. And they then emphasize arbitration's contractual roots in order to exploit the narrow but easy authority that first-party arbitration enjoys entirely apart from the procedures that it employs and hence to relax the law's scrutiny of the actual arbitral process.

This effort at arbitrage sometimes appears even on the face of arguments in favor of arbitration, and specifically in their immanent narrative structure. This is illustrated in the Supreme Court's opinion in *Mitsubishi Motors Corp. v. Soler Chrysler–Plymouth*, which held that antitrust claims arising under the Sherman Act[19] are arbitrable, and indeed generally rejected a presumption against the arbitrability of statutory claims.[20]

That opinion, which cites the *Steelworkers' Trilogy* and hence begins in the context of first-party arbitration, observes that in resolving questions of arbitrability, "as with any other contract, the parties' intentions control."[21] The opinion—seamlessly, without comment, and indeed in the very next sentence—applies the same observation to the arbitrability of statutory claims: "There is no reason," the Court says, "to depart from these guidelines when a party bound by an arbitration agreement raises claims founded on statutory rights." But in explaining itself further, the Court, without recognizing what it has done, gives just such a reason. As the opinion goes on to say,

> By agreeing to arbitrate a statutory claim, a party does not forgo the substantive rights afforded by the statute; it only submits to their resolution in an arbitral, rather than a judicial, forum. It trades the procedures and opportunities for review of the courtroom for the simplicity, informality, and expedition of arbitration.

This, of course, is decidedly *not* the first-party model of arbitration that drove the result in the *Steelworkers' Trilogy* or that makes arbitration's authority easily established, "as with any other contract," simply on the basis of "the parties' intentions." It is the third-party model, and it immediately raises the question how intensive an arbitral procedure must be in order legitimately to reject a statutory claim raised by a party who did *not* intend to waive it. The Court never seriously addresses this question, let alone answers it.

The mistake of *Mitsubishi Motors* has, moreover, become a commonplace of the Supreme Court's approach to arbitration. *14 Penn Plaza LLC v. Pyett*, illustrates how deeply the mistake has become entrenched. That case concerned the arbitrability of claims arising under the Age Discrimination in Employment Act of 1967 (ADEA),[22] where the claims were brought by union members whose collective bargaining agreement expressly contemplated submitting them to binding arbitration. The case therefore arose (like *Mitsubishis Motors*) in the context of first-party arbitration, and the majority opinion again began by discussing the NLRA's structures for collective bargaining and citing the *Steelworkers' Trilogy*.

The *Pyett* Court next acknowledged that the ADEA prohibits prospective waivers of substantive claims arising under it.[23] That is, the ADEA

---

19.   15 U.S.C. §§ 1–7 (2000).

20.   *Mitsubishi Motors Corp.*, 473 U.S. at 625.

21.   The opinion adds that, in light of the Federal Arbitration Act, "those intentions are generously construed as to issues of arbitrability."

22.   29 U.S.C. § 621 *et seq.*

23.   As the Court said, "if the "right" referred to in § 626(f)(1) [restricting prospective waivers of "substantive" rights under the ADEA] included the prospective waiver of the right

prohibits prospectively contracting out of such claims, including presumably where the contracts consist in first-party arbitration. But the Court concluded that this prohibition does not prevent the enforcement of agreements to arbitrate such rights, on the ground that "the agreement to arbitrate ADEA claims is not the waiver of a 'substantive right' as that term is employed in the ADEA." Instead, the Court (quoting *Mitsubishi Motors*) objected to "confus[ing] an agreement to arbitrate those statutory claims with a prospective waiver of the substantive right." Thus, the Court insisted, "The decision to resolve ADEA claims by way of arbitration instead of litigation does not waive the statutory right to be free from workplace age discrimination; it waives only the right to seek relief from a court in the first instance."

As in *Mitsubishi Motors*, these remarks decidedly reject the first-personal conception of arbitration for the third-personal one. But once again, they are not accompanied, in the *Pyett* opinion, by the kind of concern for the quality and intensity of the arbitral process on which the authority of third-party arbitration depends. In place of this concern about authority, the *Pyett* court blithely observes that "the recognition that arbitration procedures are more streamlined than federal litigation is not a basis for finding the forum somehow inadequate; the relative informality of arbitration is one of the chief reasons that parties select arbitration."[24] This is, of course, fair enough on the first-party model; it is entirely inadequate, however, where arbitration is conceived, on the third-party model, as a genuine substitute for adjudication. If arbitration is to stand in for adjudication, then it must possess the legitimacy of adjudication. And an ex ante preference for informality cannot underwrite that kind of legitimacy.

The arbitrage between first- and third-party arbitration that these and similar opinions employ cannot replace an argument in favor of arbitral authority under one model or the other. The question addressed by *Mitsubishi Motors* and *Pyett*—concerning the arbitrability of statutory claims—

---

to bring an ADEA claim in court, even a waiver signed by an individual employee would be invalid as the statute also prevents individuals from "waiv[ing] rights or claims that may arise after the date the waiver is executed. § 626(f)(1)(C)." The court similarly observed that "federal anti-discrimination rights may not be prospectively waived, see 29 U.S.C. § 626(f)(1)(C)."

24. To be fair, the Court also recited a conclusory defense of the quality of arbitral procedure:

"We recognize that the *Gardner–Denver* line of cases included broad dicta that was highly critical of the use of arbitration for the vindication of statutory antidiscrimination rights. That skepticism, however, rested on a misconceived view of arbitration that this Court has since abandoned. These misconceptions have been corrected. For example, the Court has recognized that arbitral tribunals are readily capable of handling the factual and legal complexities of antitrust claims, notwithstanding the absence of judicial instruction and supervision and that there is no reason to assume at the outset that arbitrators will not follow the law. We decline to indulge the presumption that the parties and arbitral body conducting a proceeding will be unable or unwilling to retain competent, conscientious, and impartial arbitrators. At bottom, objections centered on the nature of arbitration do not offer a credible basis for discrediting the choice of that forum to resolve statutory antidiscrimination claims" (internal quotation marks and citations omitted).

displays why it cannot. A first-party arbitrator, in contrast to her third-party counterpart, simply cannot have general authority to decide statutory claims.[25]

Insofar as arbitration is understood as gap-filling, its outcomes just *are* contract terms. Accordingly, a clear-eyed appreciation of the structure of first-party arbitration makes plain that *every* such arbitration of statutory rights amounts, conceptually, to a contractual *waiver* of these rights. As long as the first-party arbitrator *might* rule against the party who is claiming a statutory right, that party has, by agreeing to the arbitration, waived the right in whatever circumstances the arbitrator would so decide. Thus, although a first-party arbitrator might in some circumstances decide questions concerning statutory rights, she may not do so where the rights cannot be waived by contract. Again, the key question in such cases is whether the statutory right *itself* may be waived, and not, as the *Mitsubishi* and *Pyett* Courts supposed, whether "judicial remedies"[26] for the right may be waived. The observation made in *Mitsubishi Motors* and repeated in *Pyett* that the party has waived only the judicial process and not the substantive right is correct on the third-party model only, because it depends on the idea that the arbitrator possesses procedural authority apart from any party agreement to the substance of her decision. Hence, this observation invites (indeed demands) systematic investigation into the qualities of arbitral procedure on which the legitimacy of third-party arbitration depends. This investigation, however, is absent in the case law.

The ground of the incapacity of first-party arbitrators to decide non-waivable statutory claims is not that, because arbitrators are less careful or sympathetic to plaintiffs than courts, arbitration involves the plaintiff's capitulation to the defendant. Rather, the ground is that arbitration in these cases involves plaintiffs' and defendants' together thwarting the legislature.[27] The first-party arbitration of statutory claims therefore does not, as critics commonly suppose, reflect an encroachment of contract on adjudication; rather, it reflects an encroachment of contract on legislation, and, in particular, on the authority of the democratic process that produces legislation.[28]

---

25. Similarly, a first-party arbitrator, again in contrast to third-party arbitrators, cannot legitimately determine the scope of her own competence, that is, an arbitrator cannot arbitrate arbitrability. The argument for this conclusion proceeds analogously to the argument in the main text.

26. *Mitsubishi Motors Corp.*, 473 U.S. at 628; *Pyett*, 556 U.S. at 258. It is, of course, in the very nature of anti-trust law (which deals with limits on freedom of contracts in restraint of trade) that the rights it establishes may *not* be waived by contract.

27. Justice Souter's dissent, in *Pyett*, notes that the Congress intended that employees' rights to seek enforcement of anti-discrimination statutes in a judicial forum should survive arbitration clauses adopted as parts of collective bargaining agreements. But even the dissent presents this observation almost as an afterthought and fails to connect it to any structural analysis of arbitral authority.

28. The conflation between unproblematic but limited first-party arbitration and problematic but more expansive third-party arbitration is also illustrated by *Vimar Seguros*. The decision in that case turned, recall, on a strict and formal distinction between substantive rights and procedures for enforcing such rights. The Supreme Court held that the arbitration agreement did not violate the COGSA and was hence enforceable because it addressed only

Next, consider arbitration's critics, although more briefly because they have largely lost the argument in the courts.

These engage in a parallel but opposite conflation. Thus, they exploit the analogy to contract, treating arbitration on the first-party model, when they consider the scope of arbitral authority. This enables them to restrict an arbitrator's authority according to the narrow limits of contractual authority, so that, for example, it cannot extend to claims involving statutory rights in which the state has an interest that stands apart from the parties.

But the critics treat arbitration on the third-party model, as an instance of judging, when they ask what procedural safeguards arbitration must adopt in order to sustain its authority even within the relatively narrow scope in which it is permitted to act. This enables them to insist that arbitration must mimic adjudication's intensive procedures, even when it involves only contractual claims. Arbitration's critics are therefore also trying to have it both ways: they model arbitration on contract in order to restrict its scope, and they then emphasize arbitration's roots in adjudication in order to increase the law's scrutiny of the arbitral process even within this scope.

21.4   CONCLUSION

Arbitration—in both its third-party and first-party varieties—is here to stay. Third-party arbitration is here to stay because economic markets, and hence the contracts through which market exchanges proceed, are becoming increasingly untethered from the various political jurisdictions into which the earth has been carved up, and thus also from the various court systems associated with these jurisdictions. First-party arbitration is here to stay because complete contracts cannot ever be written, and contractual gap-filling in a mass-market economy increasingly requires the mass-production of contract terms through form contracts and hence also through arbitration understood on the model of the contractual form. In both of these respects, the scale of contemporary economic activity is coming to exceed the scale of political authority, which raises the very real question whether the forces that this economic activity is unleashing may be contained or at least controlled—whether, that is, social solidarity can survive where an economic order outstrips its political counterpart.

---

process and not substance. In employing this mode of argument, the Court implicitly adopted a third-party conception of arbitration. Under the first-party model, the distinction between process and substance breaks down, because the substantive entitlement *just is* whatever the arbitral process concludes. Accordingly, first-party arbitration of a claim like that at issue in *Vimar Seguros* is conceptually equivalent to a waiver of that claim, and hence forbidden by the COGSA. The Court's holding in *Vimar Seguros* employs a third-party model of arbitration and therefore turns on whether the arbitral tribunal at issue in that case—the Tokyo Maritime Arbitration Commission—employs procedures that can achieve free-standing authority under the adjudicatory model. The tribunal may do so, but the Court made no investigation of the question, and indeed never even considered it.

The law—and in particular courts—cannot, however, simply declare war on arbitration. Some accommodation must be and therefore of course has been made. But accommodation is not the same thing as capitulation. And courts have in recent years increasingly—and mistakenly—ceded their core competences to arbitrators. They have treated arbitrators as authoritative under the third-party model without insisting upon the intensive process values on which this model depends, and they have allowed arbitration understood on the first-party model to address questions beyond the scope of the authority that this model can sustain.

The truth about arbitration is more subtle, but also more hopeful. Arbitration properly occupies a prominent place in the broader legal pantheon. Moreover, when it is properly regulated (so that the intrinsic structures of third- and first-party arbitration are respected) arbitration presents no threat to adjudication and contract. Instead, arbitration reflects a natural evolution of these classical forms and so possesses the potential to help sustain the legal order to which they belong in the face of the challenges posed by a new age.

CHAPTER 22

THE EMPLOYMENT CONTRACT

Contracts of adhesion and arbitration agreements both raise questions concerning what might be called the thinner bound of the contract relation. The discussion of contracts of adhesion thus focused on whether the parties to form contracts, who contract without bargaining or even a meaningful opportunity for bargaining, stand in too distant, impersonal, or fleeting a relation for their agreements to sustain contractual solidarity or contractual obligation. And the discussion of arbitration agreements—especially in respect of the limited authority of first-party arbitration—focused on whether ex ante contractual solidarity is ever sufficient to stand in for the forms of dispute resolution provided by the ex post procedures associated with adjudication.

This chapter and the next raise questions concerning what might be called the thicker bound of the contract relation. They ask, that is, whether the purely chosen form of obligation associated with contract—in which the appropriate intentions of the parties are both necessary and sufficient for setting the terms of their legal relations—can survive inside of personal, intimate, and organically evolving relationships. Such thick relationships, after all, possess an internal normativity of their own: they can succeed or fail according to their own terms. And these internal norms are independent of and hence can develop apart from the thinner morality of promising. Moreover, the law recognizes the value of certain such relationships and gives legal expression to the norms that govern them. It is therefore possible that this legal recognition, which embraces unchosen obligations, might constrain or perhaps even eliminate the capacities of the parties to such thick relationships to govern their engagements through contract. This chapter explores that possibility in connection with the employment relation; and the next chapter takes up marriage.

22.1 CLASSICAL EMPLOYMENT AT WILL

The law of the modern employment contract developed out of the older law of master and servant. *Very* roughly, under the older law, being a servant was not a contractual but a status relationship; and this relationship, even as it gave masters certain prerogatives of command, also placed upon masters certain duties to provide for their servants. In line with these principles, the English common law presumed that an agreement for employment stating an annual salary created a one-year obligation, which the master/employer breached if he terminated the servant/employee without cause within the year.

Over the course of the 19th century, the status relationship of master and servant was replaced with the contractual relationship of employer and employee. This resulted in the development, in the U.S., of the doctrine of employment at will. The timing and micro-history of the shift have been disputed, with repeated revisionist ripples in the historical accounts. Thus the shift was first traced back to an 1877 treatise by HG Wood, which adopted the at-will rule.[1] Then this treatise was attacked on the ground that it cited only four cases in support of the rule, none of which actually adopted the rule.[2] The suggestion underlying the attack was that Wood invented the rule and that anti-employee courts viewed the invention as convenient (in other words that the rule was adopted without ever having to justify it as an innovation). But the most recent scholarship suggests that in fact by 1877 the at-will rule was commonly and widely adopted quite independent of Wood's treatise. Wood had made an ideologically innocent mistake in his choice of cases to cite.[3]

So the historical origins of employment at will remain a little obscure. But the doctrinal consequence of this development that is most important for present purposes is crystal clear. By the end of the development, employees were presumptively employed at will. This meant that they might be fired by their employers at any time, for no reason or even for a bad reason (as long as the reason does not fall foul of antidiscrimination law). The following case illustrates an application of employment at will at a time at which it had achieved the status of being the traditional legal rule.

Forrer v. Sears, Roebuck & Co.

Supreme Court of Wisconsin, 1967.
153 N.W.2d 587.

■ HEFFERNAN, JUSTICE.

---

1. H.G. WOOD, A TREATISE ON THE LAW OF MASTER AND SERVANT (1877).

2. *E.g.* J. Peter Shapiro, *Implied Contract Rights to Job Security,* 26 Stan. L. Rev. 335, 341 (1974) ("[Wood] cited only four American cases as authority for his approach to general hirings, none of which supported him").

3. The discussion here sets aside American slavery and its abolition, even though this was obviously the most morally and politically significant development in 19th century American law concerning work. The reason why is simple. American slavery, being chattel slavery, did not just construct the labor relation on a non-contractual model; rather, and much more chattel slavery, deprived slaves of legal personality quite generally. So the abolition of slavery did not just transform a relation among persons from status to contract. Rather, and antecedently, it transformed the legal status of those who had been slaves—from things to persons.

Slavery and abolition of course did interact in complicated ways with the rise of the modern American legal order governing the employment of free persons. But these interactions are not essential to understanding the conceptual structure of the modern employment contract.

The plaintiff, appellant in this court, brought an action, which he now denominates as one founded upon promissory estoppel, against the defendant and respondent, Sears Roebuck & Co. The defendant's demurrer to the complaint was sustained, and this appeal is from that order. The plaintiff bases his claim on the following facts.

It appears that he had worked for Sears for almost eighteen years, when, due to ill health, he left its employment in 1963 and commenced operating a farm near Stoughton, Wisconsin. The defendant's agents thereafter attempted to induce him to return to work. In November of 1964 he was persuaded to become the manager of the hardware department on a part-time basis. During December of 1964 the general manager of the Madison store promised him 'permanent employment'[1] as manager of the hardware division of the Madison store in consideration of giving up his farming operations and working full time for the defendant. It is alleged that thereupon the plaintiff sold his stock of hogs and cattle and rented the barn to a neighbor-all at a loss, placed his acreage in the United States Department of Agriculture feed-grain program, and on February 1, 1965, commenced working full time for the defendant. He alleges that thereafter, despite the understanding with Sears, he was discharged without cause on June 1, 1965. He claims damages in excess of $11,000.

The trial court sustained the defendant's demurrer, holding that no cause of action was stated.

In *Hoffman v. Red Owl Stores, Inc.* (1965), 26 Wis.2d 683 this court adopted the doctrine embodied in sec. 90 of Restatement, 1 Contracts, p. 110, which states:

'A promise which the promisor should reasonably expect to induce action or forbearance of a definite and substantial character on the part of the promisee and which does induce such action or forbearance is binding if injustice can be avoided only by enforcement of the promise.'

We stated in Hoffman that we chose to use the phrase, 'promissory estoppel' to describe this doctrine. It is promissory estoppel upon which the plaintiff, William E. Forrer, bases his action.

In Hoffman we stated that three questions must be answered affirmatively to support an action for promissory estoppel:

'(1) Was the promise one which the promisor should reasonably expect to induce action or forbearance of a definite and substantial character on the part of the promisee?

'(2) Did the promise induce such action or forbearance?

'(3) Can injustice be avoided only by enforcement of the promise?'
Hoffman v. Red Owl Stores, Inc., supra, p. 698, 133 N.W.2d p. 275.

---

1. Although the complaint used the phrase, 'continuing permanent employment for at least one year,' appellant's counsel conceded during oral argument that the phrase, 'for at least one year,' was not a factual statement of the representation made to the plaintiff by the respondent, but was rather counsel's legal conclusion interpreting the meaning of permanent employment. It is not contended that the modifier, 'continuing,' adds anything to the meaning of 'permanent.'

That all of these questions can be answered affirmatively is evident from the face of the complaint. Plaintiff alleged that he was promised full-time permanent employment in consideration of giving up his farming operations. He also alleges that he thereupon gave up his farming operations at great financial loss. It is apparent that the plaintiff alleges that his action was not only induced by the defendant's promise, but was the conduct that was specifically required as the condition of the defendant's promise. In light of all the circumstances, the sale of the livestock, the leasing of the barn, and putting the farm into the feed-grain program were all acts which the promisor should reasonably have expected that his promise would induce. We would not hesitate to apply the doctrine of promissory estoppel under these facts if justice required it. Justice, however, does not require the invocation of the doctrine, for the promise of the defendant was kept, and this court is not required, therefore, to enforce it.

The defendant's promise was that of 'permanent employment.' We conclude that the employment relationship that was established as the result of the defendant's inducements and the plaintiff's conduct is properly denominated as permanent employment. The plaintiff, in his brief, gives us the accepted and usual definition of what is meant by that term:

> 'the assumption will be that, even though the parties speak in terms of permanent employment, the parties have in mind merely the ordinary business contract for a continuing employment, terminable at the will of either party.' 56 C.J.S. Master and Servant s 8, p. 78.

We concur with plaintiff's conclusion in that respect.

Generally speaking, a contract for permanent employment, for life employment, or for other terms purporting permanent employment, where the employee furnishes no consideration additional to the services incident to the employment, amounts to an indefinite general hiring terminable at the will of either party, and a discharge without cause does not constitute a breach of such contract justifying week, or month. Annot. (1917), 11 A.L.R. A.L.R. 1432, (1941) 135 A.L.R. 646. The same is true where the contract of hiring specifies no term of duration but fixes compensation at a certain amount per day, week, or month. Annot. (1917), 11 A.L.R. 469, (1934) 100 A.L.R. 834. Although not absolute, the above stated rule appears to be in the nature of a strong presumption in favor of a contract terminable at will unless the terms of the contract or other circumstances clearly manifest the parties' intent to bind each other. The presumption is grounded on a policy that it would otherwise be unreasonable for a man to bind himself permanently to a position, thus eliminating the possibility of later improving that position. Moreover, a contract of permanent employment is by its very nature indefinite, and thus any effort to interpret the duration of the contract and assess the amount of damages becomes difficult. Wisconsin has aligned itself with the overwhelming majority of jurisdictions that have adopted the above stated principles.

We thus conclude that the most that was promised by Sears was employment terminable at will. This promise was carried out when the plaintiff was hired as the defendant's full-time manager. The defendant's obligation was discharged when its promise was kept, and, hence, the doctrine of promissory estoppel is not applicable.

The plaintiff in his oral argument stated that he chose to rely on promissory estoppel only, and specifically stated that he abandoned any claim based upon contract law. Nevertheless, it should be stated that conceivably the plaintiff could state a cause of action if it were affirmatively shown that he furnished 'additional consideration' in exchange for the defendant's promise of permanent employment.

Under circumstances where an employee has given consideration of benefit to the employer, additional to the services of employment, a contract for permanent employment is valid and enforceable and not against public policy and continues to operate as long as the employer remains in business and has work for the employee, and the employee is willing and able to do his work satisfactorily and does not give cause for his discharge. See Annot. (1941), 135 A.L.R. 646, 654. We do not deem that the detriment to the plaintiff herein in giving up his farming operations at a loss constituted such additional consideration. We conclude that a permanent employment contract is terminable at will unless there is additional consideration in the form of an economic or financial benefit to the employer. A mere detriment to the employee is not enough. See Annot. (1941), 135 A.L.R. 646, 660, in regard to release of a claim against an employer being held additional consideration. In *Wright v. C. S. Graves Land Co.* (1898), 100 Wis. 269, an employment contract was held not to be terminable at will when the employee had obligated himself to, and did, purchase land and furnish a horse for clearing of fields. The court pointed out that the plaintiff had bound himself for at least two years and, hence, the contract was not terminable at the will of the employer. In so doing, the court gave recognition to those acts of the plaintiff that resulted in a benefit to the employer, and not to those acts that were merely of a detriment to the employee.

We conclude, therefore, that the facts as set forth in the plaintiff's complaint fail to spell out a cause of action for the breach of a contract for permanent employment supported by additional consideration of benefit to the defendant-employer. The only benefit to the defendant was the plaintiff's rendering of services. There was nothing more.

We are therefore obliged to conclude that the permanent employment alleged was a relationship that could be terminated at will by either party. Hence, once the relationship was established, the promise, which plaintiff seeks to enforce by promissory estoppel, was fulfilled. This court need not enforce the promise. It has been carried out. Promissory estoppel is not applicable to this case. Nor is there evidence of additional consideration that would bind the employer to a period not terminable at his will. The demurrer must be sustained.

Order affirmed.

* * *

The plaintiff in *Forrer*, having worked for the defendant for 18 years, retired to farming. The defendant subsequently persuaded the plaintiff to return to his old job, by making an offer of "permanent employment." In order to accept this offer and return to work, the plaintiff divested himself of his farm, at a loss. Six months later, the defendant fired the plaintiff without cause. The plaintiff sued.

One strand of the opinion in *Forrer* concerned contract *interpretation*. Thus the court held that, as a general matter, where an employee enters into a contract for "permanent employment" or for "life employment" (and furnishes his employer with no additional consideration beyond doing the work of the job that he is hired to do), this creates *employment at will*. The employer may thus discharge the employee at any time, with or without cause. More specifically, the defendant in *Forrer* carried out all of its contractual obligations when it hired the plaintiff, and the subsequent firing (even though without cause) was not in any way a breach of the defendant's promise. The plaintiff's orthodox contractual claim thus failed.[4]

Forrer thus makes an essentially interpretive claim about the meaning of the phrases "permanent employment," "life employment," and the like. Note that for ordinary speakers of English, the interpretive move is surprising, to say the least. As a counterpoint, consider that university faculties commonly use the language "professor without term," a formulation that closely resembles "permanent" or "life" employment, to refer to an appointment with academic tenure: an arrangement that carries with it protections against discharge for all but the most serious causes. An ordinary speaker might not quite understand these terms as universities do, but she would gravitate towards a meaning in the same family. Certainly the plaintiff in *Forrer* seems to have done so and to have been surprised by his employer's rights.

Insofar as the basic principle of contract interpretation calls for understanding the contractual text either as the parties subjectively do or as a reasonable person in the position of the parties would do, the interpretation in *Forrer* seems surprising and even unwarranted. It seems so surprising, in fact, that one suspects that *Forrer* stands for more than just an interpretive approach to employment contracts that use certain forms of words.

---

4. Note that the plaintiff in *Forrer* also brought a reliance claim based on § 90 of the Restatement, and that the court rejected this claim also, and indeed for the same reason for which it rejected the orthodox contract claim. The court accepted that the plaintiff may well have relied to his detriment on the defendant's promise (for example, by selling his farm). But, the court observed, § 90 obligations will be enforced only as justice requires. And in *Forrer*, the court thought, there was no injustice. Put more precisely, although there may have been injustice in some grand sense—in that the plaintiff was harmed in a manner that he did not deserve, and indeed was treated shabbily by the defendant—there was no specifically *promissory* wrong. The defendant, when it initially hired the plaintiff, did everything that it had promised. This argument follows the general discussions of promissory estoppel presented earlier in these materials. Promissory estoppel may be used to enforce promises even where they fail for technical reasons to establish contracts. But promissory estoppel remains promissory and will not apply to vindicate moral considerations from outside the specific morality of promising.

The opinion buttresses this suspicion. Although *Forrer* states that the at will rule is "not absolute," it also articulates "a strong presumption in favor of a contract terminable at will." The opinion does not make the nature of the presumption entirely clear. It refers to the possibility that "the terms of the contract or other circumstances" might "clearly manifest the parties' intent to bind each other" to something other than employment at will. But one would think that the terms of the contract and surrounding circumstances in *Forrer* manifested just such a clear intent, and yet the court remained unmoved. Instead of emphasizing the general principle that contracts should track the intentions of the parties, whatever they are, the *Forrer* court seems to focus on specific substantive principles of law. The opinion suggests as much when it observes that the presumption in favor of the at-will regime is "grounded on a policy that it would otherwise be unreasonable for a man to bind himself permanently to a position, thus eliminating the possibility of later improving that position." The suggestion is driven home by the observation that a promise of permanent employment does *not* create mere employment at will if the employee furnishes his employer with additional consideration that is independent of his simply doing the work he is hired to do. The court seems to worry that a regime requiring employers to have good cause before firing employees might introduce a formal asymmetry into the employment contract, given that *employees* retain the right to quit without cause. That is why the court focuses exceptions to the at-will regime on "circumstances where an employee has given consideration of benefit to the employer, additional to the services of employment." Such additional consideration can (almost standing in for obligations limiting the employee's right to quit) match the employer's obligation to fire only for cause.

The most historically prominent example of such additional consideration was probably the abandonment of a tort claim against the employer, typically a claim relating to a workplace accident. Thus, even during the heyday of employment at will, any number of cases recognized that contracts might require employers to terminate employment only for cause where employees been promised lifetime employment in exchange for waiving their rights to hold their employers liable for workplace injuries. But this is just an example only, and (at least to the modern imagination) almost immediately raises the question why the additional consideration must take a form separate from the employee's work or work-effort. Why cannot an employee provide some portion of her work in exchange for her wage and then the remainder of her work in exchange for job security, perhaps implemented through a right to be fired only for cause? This possibility will turn out to be quite important to the analysis, taken up below, of the limits of freedom of contract in the employment context.

22.2 MODERN DEPARTURES FROM EMPLOYMENT AT WILL

Now consider, against the backdrop of the classical at-will regime, more recent departures from employment at will. Begin this consideration with *Wagenseller v. Scottsdale Memorial Hospital*. This is a panoramic opinion, which surveys a great deal of the ground in this area of law. The commentary following the opinion will be even slightly more panoramic than the opinion itself. It lays out the several theories on which the at will rule might be modified or abandoned.[5]

Wagenseller v. Scottsdale Memorial Hospital

Supreme Court of Arizona, 1985.
710 P.2d 1025.

■ Feldman, Justice.

Catherine Sue Wagenseller petitioned this court to review a decision of the court of appeals affirming in part the trial court's judgment in favor of Scottsdale Memorial Hospital and certain Hospital employees (defendants). The trial court had dismissed all causes of action on defendants' motion for summary judgment. The court of appeals affirmed in part and remanded, ruling that the only cause of action available to plaintiff was the claim against her supervisor, Kay Smith. *Wagenseller v. Scottsdale Memorial Hospital,* 148 Ariz. 242 (1984). We have jurisdiction pursuant to Ariz. Const. art. 6, § 5(3) and Rule 23(c), Ariz.R.Civ.App.P., 17A A.R.S. We granted review to consider the law of this state with regard to the employment-at-will doctrine. The issues we address are:

1. Is an employer's right to terminate an at-will employee limited by any rules which, if breached, give rise to a cause of action for wrongful termination?

2. If "public policy" or some other doctrine does form the basis for such an action, how is it determined?

3. Did the trial court err, in view of *Leikvold v. Valley View Community Hospital,* 141 Ariz. 544 (1984), when it determined as a matter of law that the terms of Scottsdale Memorial Hospital's personnel policy manual were not part of the employment contract?

---

5. In keeping with the broader themes of Part III, the main text will focus on moral structure of the employment relation and on the extent to which the purely chosen obligation associated with freedom of contract can survive within this structure. But that is of course not the only question that one might ask about employment at will. Another, and very common, question to ask concerns whether employment at will is worse or better for employees than a regime that requires cause for termination.

One view of this matter, noting that employers are more contractually sophisticated and experienced than employees and observing that employees must make themselves vulnerable by, in effect, investing a large portion of their wealth in their jobs, argues that courts should re-write employers' forms to protect employees against certain types of unfair, exploitative, and possibly even inefficient advantage-taking by employers. A representative statement of this position appears in Lawrence E. Blades, *Employment at Will v. Individual Freedom*, 67 Colum. L. Rev. 1404 (1967).

An opposed view notes that market competition for workers will anyway exert pressure on employers to treat employees efficiently and well and adds that legal interventions to give employees more than the market can sustain only allows them to hold-up their employers, with the end effect of reducing equilibrium employment levels. A representative statement of this position appears in Richard Epstein, *In Defense of the Contract at Will*, 51 U. Chi. L. Rev. 947 (1984).

4. Do employment contracts contain an implied covenant of "good faith and fair dealing," and, if so, what is the nature of the covenant?

5. What is the scope of a supervisor's privilege to interfere in the beneficial employment relationship between a supervised employee and the common employer?

FACTUAL BACKGROUND

Catherine Wagenseller began her employment at Scottsdale Memorial Hospital as a staff nurse in March 1975, having been personally recruited by the manager of the emergency department, Kay Smith. Wagenseller was an "at-will" employee—one hired without specific contractual term. Smith was her supervisor. In August 1978, Wagenseller was assigned to the position of ambulance charge nurse, and approximately one year later was promoted to the position of paramedic coordinator, a newly approved management position in the emergency department. Three months later, on November 1, 1979, Wagenseller was terminated.

Most of the events surrounding Wagenseller's work at the Hospital and her subsequent termination are not disputed, although the parties differ in their interpretation of the inferences to be drawn from and the significance of these events. For more than four years, Smith and Wagenseller maintained a friendly, professional, working relationship. In May 1979, they joined a group consisting largely of personnel from other hospitals for an eight-day camping and rafting trip down the Colorado River. According to Wagenseller, "an uncomfortable feeling" developed between her and Smith as the trip progressed—a feeling that Wagenseller ascribed to "the behavior that Kay Smith was displaying." Wagenseller states that this included public urination, defecation and bathing, heavy drinking, and "grouping up" with other rafters. Wagenseller did not participate in any of these activities. She also refused to join in the group's staging of a parody of the song "Moon River," which allegedly concluded with members of the group "mooning" the audience. Smith and others allegedly performed the "Moon River" skit twice at the Hospital following the group's return from the river, but Wagenseller declined to participate there as well.

Wagenseller contends that her refusal to engage in these activities caused her relationship with Smith to deteriorate and was the proximate cause of her termination. She claims that following the river trip Smith began harassing her, using abusive language and embarrassing her in the company of other staff. Other emergency department staff reported a similar marked change in Smith's behavior toward Wagenseller after the trip, although Smith denied it.

Up to the time of the river trip, Wagenseller had received consistently favorable job performance evaluations. Two months before the trip, Smith completed an annual evaluation report in which she rated Wagenseller's performance as "exceed[ing] results expected," the second highest of five possible ratings. In August and October 1979, Wagenseller met first with Smith and then with Smith's successor, Jeannie Steindorff, to discuss some problems regarding her duties as paramedic coordinator and her attitude toward the job. On November 1, 1979, following an exit interview at which Wagenseller was asked to resign and refused, she was terminated.

She appealed her dismissal in letters to her supervisor and to the Hospital administrative and personnel department, answering the Hospital's stated reasons for her termination, claiming violations of the disciplinary procedure contained in the Hospital's personnel policy manual, and requesting reinstatement and other remedies. When this appeal was denied, Wagenseller brought suit against the Hospital, its personnel administrators, and her supervisor, Kay Smith.

Wagenseller, an "at-will" employee, contends that she was fired for reasons which contravene public policy and without legitimate cause related to job performance. She claims that her termination was wrongful, and that damages are recoverable under both tort and contract theories. The Hospital argues that an "at-will" employee may be fired for cause, without cause, or for "bad" cause. We hold that in the absence of contractual provision such an employee may be fired for good cause or for no cause, but not for "bad" cause.

THE EMPLOYMENT–AT–WILL DOCTRINE

History

As early as 1562, the English common law presumed that an employment contract containing an annual salary provision or computation was for a one-year term. Murg & Scharman, *Employment at Will: Do the Exceptions Overwhelm the Rule?* 23 B.C.L.Rev. 329, 332 (1982). Originally designed for the protection of seasonal farm workers, the English rule expanded over the years to protect factory workers as well. Workers were well protected under this rule, for the one-year presumption was not easy to overcome. *Id.* English courts held an employer liable for breaching the employment contract if he terminated an employee at any time during the year without "reasonable cause to do so." 1 *W. Blackstone, Commentaries.* To uphold an employer's discharge of an employee without a showing of "good cause," the courts required a clear expression of a contrary intent as evidenced either on the face of the contract or by a clearly defined custom of the industry. Murg & Scharman, *supra,* at 332.

In the early nineteenth century, American courts borrowed the English rule. The legal rationale embodied in the rule was consistent with the nature of the predominant master-servant employment relationship at the time because it reflected the master's duty to make provision for the general well-being of his servants. *Id.* at 334 and n. 22. In addition, the master was under a duty to employ the servant for a term, either a specified or implied time of service, and could not terminate him strictly at will. Hermann & Sor, *Property Rights in One's Job: The Case for Limiting Employment-at-Will,* 24 Ariz.L.Rev. 763, 770 (1982). The late nineteenth century, however, brought the Industrial Revolution; with it came the decline of the master-servant relationship and the rise of the more impersonal employer-employee relationship. In apparent response to the economic changes sweeping the country, American courts abandoned the English rule and adopted the employment-at-will doctrine. Murg & Scharman, *supra,* at 334. This new doctrine gave the employer freedom to terminate an at-will employee for any reason, good or bad.

The at-will rule has been traced to an 1877 treatise by H.G. Wood, in which he wrote:

> With us the rule is inflexible, that a general or indefinite hiring is *prima facie* a hiring at will, and if the servant seeks to make it out a yearly hiring, the burden is upon him to establish it by proof. [I]t is an indefinite hiring and is determinable at the will of either party.

H.G. Wood, Law of Master and Servant § 134 at 273 (1877). As commentators and courts later would point out, none of the four cases cited by Wood actually supported the rule. *See Toussaint v. Blue Cross & Blue Shield,* 408 Mich. 579, 602 & nn. 13–14 (1980); Note, *Implied Contract Rights to Job Security,* 26 Stan.L.Rev. 335, 341–42 n. 54 (1974). Wood's rule also ran directly counter to another American treatise that stated the one-year presumption as the rule that some courts continued to follow. Note, *Protecting At Will Employees Against Wrongful Discharge: The Duty to Terminate Only in Good Faith,* 93 Harv.L.Rev. 1816, 1825 n. 51 (1980) (citing *C. Smith, Law of Master and Servant* 53–57 (1852)).

However unsound its foundation, Wood's at-will doctrine was adopted by the New York courts in *Martin v. New York Life Insurance Co.,* 148 N.Y. 117 (1895), and soon became the generally accepted American rule. In 1932, this court first adopted the rule for Arizona: "The general rule in regard to contracts for personal services, ... where no time limit is provided, is that they are terminable at pleasure by either party, or at most upon reasonable notice." *Dover Copper Mining Co. v. Doenges,* 40 Ariz. 349, 357 (1932). Thus, an employer was free to fire an employee hired for an indefinite term "for good cause, for no cause, or even for cause morally wrong, without being thereby guilty of legal wrong." Blades, *Employment at Will v. Individual Freedom: On Limiting the Abusive Exercise of Employer Power,* 67 Colum.L.Rev. 1404, 1405 (1967) (quoting *Payne v. Western & Allegheny Railroad Co.,* 81 Tenn. (13 Lea) 507, 519–20 (1884), *overruled on other grounds, Hutton v. Watters,* 132 Tenn. 527 (1915)).

Present–Day Status of the At–Will Rule

In recent years there has been apparent dissatisfaction with the absolutist formulation of the common law at-will rule. The Illinois Supreme Court is representative of courts that have acknowledged a need for a less mechanical application of the rule:

> With the rise of large corporations conducting specialized operations and employing relatively immobile workers who often have no other place to market their skills, recognition that the employer and employee do not stand on equal footing is realistic. In addition, unchecked employer power, like unchecked employee power, has been seen to present a distinct threat to the public policy carefully considered and adopted by society as a whole. As a result,

it is now recognized that a proper balance must be maintained among the employer's interest in operating a business efficiently and profitably, the employee's interest in earning a livelihood, and society's interest in seeing its public policies carried out.

Palmateer v. International Harvester Co., 85 Ill.2d 124, 129 (1981) (citation omitted). Today, courts in three-fifths of the states have recognized some form of a cause of action for wrongful discharge. Lopatka, *The Emerging Law of Wrongful Discharge—A Quadrennial Assessment of the Labor Law Issue of the 80s,* 40 Bus.Law. 1 (1984).

The trend has been to modify the at-will rule by creating exceptions to its operation. Three general exceptions have developed. The most widely accepted approach is the "public policy" exception, which permits recovery upon a finding that the employer's conduct undermined some important public policy. The second exception, based on contract, requires proof of an implied-in-fact promise of employment for a specific duration, as found in the circumstances surrounding the employment relationship, including assurances of job security in company personnel manuals or memoranda. Under the third approach, courts have found in the employment contract an implied-in-law covenant of "good faith and fair dealing" and have held employers liable in both contract and tort for breach of that covenant. Wagenseller raises all three doctrines.

THE PUBLIC POLICY EXCEPTION

The public policy exception to the at-will doctrine began with a narrow rule permitting employees to sue their employers when a statute expressly prohibited their discharge. *See Kouff v. Bethlehem–Alameda Shipyard,* 90 Cal.App.2d 322 (1949) (statute prohibiting discharge for serving as an election officer). This formulation was then expanded to include any discharge in violation of a statutory expression of public policy. *See Petermann v. Teamsters Local 396,* 174 Cal.App.2d 184 (1959) (discharge for refusal to commit perjury). Courts later allowed a cause of action for violation of public policy, even in the absence of a specific statutory prohibition. *See Nees v. Hocks,* 272 Or. 210 (1975) (discharge for being absent from work to serve on jury duty). The New Hampshire Supreme Court announced perhaps the most expansive rule when it held an employer liable for discharging an employee who refused to go out with her foreman. The court concluded that termination "motivated by bad faith or malice or based on retaliation is not [in] the best interest of the economic system or the public good and constitutes a breach of the employment contract." *Monge v. Beebe Rubber Co.,* 114 N.H. 130, 133 (1974). Although no other court has gone this far, a majority of the states have now either recognized a cause of action based on the public policy exception or have indicated their willingness to consider it, given appropriate facts. The key to an employee's claim in all of these cases is the proper definition of a public policy that has been violated by the employer's actions.

Before deciding whether to adopt the public policy exception, we first consider what kind of discharge would violate the rule. The majority of courts require, as a threshold showing, a "clear mandate" of public policy. *E.g., Parnar v. Americana Hotels,* 65 Hawaii 370, 652 P.2d 625, 631 (1982); *Geary v. United States Steel Corp.,* 456 Pa. 171, 184 (1974); *Thompson v. St. Regis Paper Co.,* 102 Wash.2d 219 (1984). The leading case recognizing a public policy exception to the at-will doctrine is *Palmateer v. International Harvester Co., supra,* which holds that an employee stated a cause of action for wrongful discharge when he claimed he was fired for supplying information to police investigating alleged criminal violations by a co-employee. Addressing the issue of what constitutes "clearly mandated public policy," the court stated:

> There is no precise definition of the term. In general, it can be said that public policy concerns what is right and just and what affects the citizens of the State collectively. It is to be found in the State's constitution and statutes and, when they are silent, in its judicial decisions. Although there is no precise line of demarcation dividing matters that are the subject of public policies from matters purely personal, a survey of cases in other States involving retaliatory discharges shows that a matter must strike at the heart of a citizen's social rights, duties, and responsibilities before the tort will be allowed.

85 Ill.2d at 130 (citation omitted).

Other courts have allowed a cause of action where an employee was fired for refusing to violate a specific statute. Similarly, courts have found terminations improper where to do otherwise would have impinged on the employee's exercise of statutory rights or duties.

It is difficult to justify this court's further adherence to a rule which permits an employer to fire someone for "cause morally wrong." So far as we can tell, no court faced with a termination that violated a "clear mandate of public policy" has refused to adopt the public policy exception. Certainly, a court would be hard-pressed to find a rationale to hold that an employer could with impunity fire an employee who refused to commit perjury. Why should the law imply an agreement which would give the employer such power? It may be argued, of course, that our economic system functions best if employers are given wide latitude in dealing with employees. We assume that it is in the public interest that employers continue to have that freedom. We also believe, however, that the interests of the economic system will be fully served if employers may fire for good cause or without cause. The interests of society as a whole will be promoted if employers are forbidden to fire for cause which is "morally wrong."

We therefore adopt the public policy exception to the at-will termination rule. We hold that an employer may fire for good cause or for no cause. He may not fire for bad cause—that which violates public policy. To the extent that it is contrary to the foregoing, we overrule *Dover Copper Mining Co. v. Doenges, supra.*

We turn then to the questions of where "public policy" may be found and how it may be recognized and articulated. As the expressions of our founders and those we have elected to our legislature, our state's constitution and statutes embody the public conscience of the people of this state. It is thus in furtherance of their interests to hold that an employer may not with impunity violate the dictates of public policy found in the provisions of our statutory and constitutional law.

We do not believe, however, that expressions of public policy are contained only in the statutory and constitutional law, nor do we believe that all statements made in either a statute or the constitution are expressions of public policy. Turning first to the identification of other sources, we note our agreement with the following:

> Public policy is usually defined by the political branches of government. Something "against public policy" is something that the Legislature has forbidden. But the Legislature is not the only source of such policy. In common-law jurisdictions the courts too have been sources of law, always subject to legislative correction, and with progressively less freedom as legislation occupies a given field. It is the courts, to give one example, that originated the whole doctrine that certain kinds of businesses—common carriers and innkeepers—must serve the public without discrimination or preference. In this sense, then, courts make law, and they have done so for years.

Lucas v. Brown & Root, 736 F.2d 1202, 1205 (8th Cir.1984). Other state courts have similarly recognized judicial decisions as a source of public policy. *E.g., Palmateer v. International Harvester Co.,* 85 Ill.2d at 130; *Pierce v. Ortho Pharmaceutical Corp.,* 84 N.J. 58, 72 (1980); *Thompson v. St. Regis Paper Co.,* 102 Wash.2d at 232–233. Thus, we believe that reliance on prior judicial decisions, as part of the body of applicable common law, is appropriate, although we agree with the Hawaii Supreme Court that "courts should proceed cautiously if called upon to declare public policy absent some prior legislative or judicial expression on the subject." *Parnar v. Americana Hotels,* 65 Hawaii at 380. Thus, we will look to the pronouncements of our founders, our legislature, and our courts to discern the public policy of this state.

All such pronouncements, however, will not provide the basis for a claim of wrongful discharge. Only those which have a singularly *public* purpose will have such force. Lord Truro set forth the classic formulation of the public policy doctrine nearly 150 years ago:

> Public policy is that principle of the law which holds that no subject can lawfully do that which has a tendency to be injurious to the public, or against the public good, which may be termed, as it sometimes has been, the policy of the law, or public policy in relation to the administration of the law.

Egerton v. Earl Brownlow, 4 H.L.Cas. 1, 196 (1853). Where the interest involved is merely private or proprietary, the exception does not apply. In *Pierce v. Ortho Pharmaceutical Corp., supra,* for instance, the court held that the plaintiff did not have a cause of action for wrongful discharge based on her refusal to do certain research, where she had failed to articulate a clear public policy that had been violated. Citing the personal nature of Dr. Pierce's opposition, the court stated:

> Chaos would result if a single doctor engaged in research were allowed to determine, according to his or her individual conscience, whether a project should continue. An employee does not have a right to continued employment when he or she refuses to conduct research simply because it would contravene his or her personal morals. An employee at will who refuses to work in answer to a call of conscience should recognize that other employees and their employer might heed a different call.

84 N.J. at 75 (citation omitted). Although an employee facing such a quandary may refuse to do the work believed to violate her moral philosophy, she may not also claim a right to continued employment. *Id.* The Oregon Supreme Court announced a similar limitation when it refused to recognize a cause of action for the discharge of an employee who claimed he was wrongfully terminated for exercising his statutory right as a stockholder to examine the books of his corporate employer. *Campbell v. Ford Industries,* 274 Or. 243 (1976). The court based its determination on its finding that the right claimed was "not one of public policy, but the private and proprietary interest of stockholders, as owners of the corporation." *Id.* at 249–50.

However, some legal principles, whether statutory or decisional, have a discernible, comprehensive public purpose. A state's criminal code provides clear examples of such statutes. Thus, courts in other jurisdictions have consistently recognized a cause of action for a discharge in violation of a criminal statute. In a seminal case involving the public policy exception, *Petermann v. International Brotherhood of Teamsters Local 396,* 174 Cal. App.2d 184 (1959), the California Court of Appeals upheld an employee's right to refuse to commit perjury, stating:

> The public policy of this state as reflected in the Penal Code ... would be seriously impaired if it were to be held that one could be discharged by reason of his refusal to commit perjury. To hold that one's continued employment could be made contingent upon his commission of a felonious act at the instance of his employer would be to encourage criminal conduct upon the part of both the employee and employer and would serve to contaminate the honest administration of public affairs. This is patently contrary to the public welfare.

Id. at 189.

Although we do not limit our recognition of the public policy exception to cases involving a violation of a criminal statute, we do believe that our duty will seldom be clearer than when such a violation is involved. We agree with the Illinois Supreme Court that "[t]here is no public policy more basic, nothing more implicit in the concept of ordered liberty, than the enforcement of a State's criminal code." *Palmateer v. International Harvester Co.*, 85 Ill.2d at 132 (citations omitted).

In the case before us, Wagenseller refused to participate in activities which arguably would have violated our indecent exposure statute, A.R.S. § 13–1402. She claims that she was fired because of this refusal. The statute provides:

> § 13–1402.   Indecent exposure; classifications
>
> A.   A person commits indecent exposure if he or she exposes his or her genitals or anus or she exposes the areola or nipple of her breast or breasts and another person is present, and the defendant is reckless about whether such other person, as a reasonable person, would be offended or alarmed by the act.
>
> B.   Indecent exposure is a class 1 misdemeanor. Indecent exposure to a person under the age of fifteen years is a class 6 felony.

While this statute may not embody a policy which "strikes at the heart of a citizen's social right, duties and responsibilities" (*Palmateer, supra*) as clearly and forcefully as a statute prohibiting perjury, we believe that it was enacted to preserve and protect the commonly recognized sense of public privacy and decency. The statute does, therefore, recognize bodily privacy as a "citizen's social right." We disagree with the court of appeals' conclusion that a minor violation of the statute would not violate public policy. (Slip op. at 6.) The nature of the act, and not its magnitude, is the issue. The legislature has already concluded that acts fitting the statutory description contravene the public policy of this state. We thus uphold this state's public policy by holding that termination for refusal to commit an act which might violate A.R.S. § 13–1402 may provide the basis of a claim for wrongful discharge. The relevant inquiry here is not whether the alleged "mooning" incidents were either felonies or misdemeanors or constituted purely technical violations of the statute, but whether they contravened the important public policy interests embodied in the law. The law enacted by the legislature establishes a clear policy that public exposure of one's anus or genitals is contrary to public standards of morality. We are compelled to conclude that termination of employment for refusal to participate in public exposure of one's buttocks is a termination contrary to the policy of this state, even if, for instance, the employer might have grounds to believe that all of the onlookers were voyeurs and would not be offended. In this situation, there might be no crime, but there would be a violation of public policy to compel the employee to do an act ordinarily proscribed by the law.

From a theoretical standpoint, we emphasize that the "public policy exception" which we adopt does not require the court to make a new contract for the parties. In an at-will situation, the parties have made no express agreement regarding the duration of employment or the grounds for discharge. The common law has presumed that in so doing the parties have intended to allow termination at any time, with or without good cause. It might be more properly argued that the law has recognized an implied covenant to that effect. Whether it be presumption or implied contractual covenant, we do not disturb it. We simply do not raise a presumption or imply a covenant that would require an employee to do that which public policy forbids or refrain from doing that which it commands.

Thus, in an at-will hiring we continue to recognize the presumption or to imply the covenant of termination at the pleasure of either party, whether with or without cause. Firing for bad cause—one against public policy articulated by constitutional, statutory, or decisional law—is not a right inherent in the at-will contract, or in any other contract, even if expressly provided. *See 1 A. Corbin, Contracts* § 7; *6A A. Corbin, Contracts* §§ 1373–75 (1962). Such a termination violates rights guaranteed to the employee by law and is tortious. *See Prosser & Keeton on Torts* § 92 at 655 (5th ed. 1984).

THE "PERSONNEL POLICY MANUAL" EXCEPTION

Although an employment contract for an indefinite term is presumed to be terminable at will, that presumption, like any other presumption, is rebuttable by contrary evidence. *See* Restatement (Second) of Agency § 442; *Leikvold v. Valley View Community Hospital,* 141 Ariz. 544, 547 (1984). Thus, in addition to relying on the public policy analysis to restrict the operation of the terminable-at-will rule, courts have turned to the employment contract itself, finding in it implied terms that limit the employer's right of discharge. Two types of implied contract terms have been recognized by the courts: implied-in-law terms and implied-in-fact terms. An implied-in-law term arises from a duty imposed by law where the contract itself is silent; it is imposed even though the parties may not have intended it, and it binds the parties to a legally enforceable duty, just as if they had so contracted explicitly. 1 *A. Corbin, Contracts* § 17, at 38 (1960). The covenant of good faith and fair dealing, discussed *post* at 1038–1041, is an implied-in-law contract term that has been recognized by a small number of courts in the employment-at-will context.

An implied-in-fact contract term, on the other hand, is one that is inferred from the statements or conduct of the parties. *Id.* It is not a promise defined by the law, but one made by the parties, though not expressly. Courts have found such terms in an employer's policy statements regarding such things as job security and employee disciplinary procedures, holding that by the conduct of the parties these statements may become part of the contract, supplementing the verbalized at-will agreement, and thus limiting the employer's absolute right to discharge an at-will employee. *Toussaint v. Blue Cross & Blue Shield of Michigan, supra; Pine River State Bank v. Mettille,* 333 N.W.2d 622 (Minn.1983). Arizona is among the jurisdictions that have recognized the implied-in-fact contract term as an exception to the at-will rule. In *Leikvold v. Valley View Community Hospital, supra,* this court held that a personnel manual can become part of an employment contract and remanded the cause for a jury determination as to whether the particular manual given to Leikvold had become part of her employment contract with Valley View. 141 Ariz. at 548.

The relevant facts in the case before us are not dissimilar to those in *Leikvold*. In October 1978, Scottsdale Memorial Hospital established a four-step disciplinary procedure to achieve the Hospital's stated policy of "provid[ing] fair and consistent discipline as required to assist with the improvement of employees' behavior or performance." Subject to 32 listed exceptions, prior to being terminated a Hospital employee must be given a verbal warning, a written performance warning, a letter of formal reprimand, and a notice of dismissal. The manual further qualifies the mandatory procedure by providing that the 32 exceptions "are not inclusive and are only guidelines." In appealing her dismissal, Wagenseller cited violations of this procedure, but the trial court ruled as a matter of law that the manual had not become part of the employment contract between Wagenseller and the Hospital. The court of appeals held that the Hospital's failure to follow the four-step disciplinary procedure did not violate Wagenseller's contract rights because she failed to prove her reliance on the procedure as a part of her employment contract. (Slip op. at 14.) We disagree with both of these rulings.

First, we need look only to *Leikvold* for the rule governing the determination of whether a particular statement by an employer becomes a part of an employment contract:

Whether any particular personnel manual modifies any particular employment-at-will relationship and becomes part of the particular employment contract is a *question of fact*. Evidence relevant to this factual decision includes the language used in the personnel manual as well as the employer's course of conduct and oral representations regarding it.

141 Ariz. at 548 (emphasis added). Thus, we held in *Leikvold* that entry of summary judgment was inappropriate "[b]ecause a material question—whether the policies manual was incorporated into and became part of the terms of the employment contract—remain[ed] in dispute." *Id.* The court may determine as a matter of law the proper construction of contract terms which are "clear and unambiguous." *Id.* Here, the court of appeals ruled, in effect, that the Hospital had adequately disclaimed any liability for failing to follow the procedure it had established. It found this disclaimer in the final item in the Hospital's list of exceptions to its disciplinary procedure: "20. These major and minor infractions are not inclusive and are only guidelines." The court concluded that the effect of this "clear" and "conspicuous" provision was "to create, by its terms, no rights at all." (Slip op. at 14.)

We do not believe this document, read in its entirety, has the clarity that the court of appeals attributed to its individual portions. One reading the document might well infer that the Hospital had established a procedure that would generally apply in disciplinary actions taken against employees. Although such a person would also note the long list of exceptions, he might not conclude from reading the list that an exception would apply in every case so as to swallow the general rule completely. We do not believe that the provision for unarticulated exceptions destroys the entire articulated general policy as a matter of law. Not only does such a result defy common sense, it runs afoul of our reasoning in *Leikvold,* where we addressed this problem directly:

> Employers are certainly free to issue no personnel manual at all or to issue a personnel manual that clearly and conspicuously tells their employees that the manual is not part of the employment contract and that their jobs are terminable at the will of the employer with or without reason. Such actions, either not issuing a personnel manual or issuing one with clear language of limitation, instill no reasonable expectations of job security and do not give employees any reason to rely on representations in the manual. However, if an employer does choose to issue a policy statement, in a manual or otherwise, and, by its language or by the employer's actions, encourages reliance thereon, the employer cannot be free to only selectively abide by it. Having announced a policy, the employer may not treat it as illusory.

141 Ariz. at 548.

We emphasize here that the rule set forth in *Leikvold* is merely a reiteration of employment law as it has existed for centuries, exemplified by the English common law one-year presumption (*see ante* at 1030) and the at-will employment doctrine itself. The right of discharge without cause is an implied contractual term which is said to exist in an at-will relationship when there are no factual indications to the contrary. The intent to create a different relationship, as well as the parameters of that relationship, are to be discerned from the totality of the parties' statements and actions regarding the employment relationship. *Leikvold,* 141 Ariz. at 548.

The general rule is that the determination whether in a particular case a promise should be implied in fact is a question of fact. Where reasonable minds may draw different conclusions or inferences from undisputed evidentiary facts, a question of fact is presented. *Dietz v. Waller,* 141 Ariz. 107, 110–111 (1984). "[T]he very essence of [the jury's] function is to select from among conflicting inferences and conclusions that which it considers most reasonable." *Apache Railway Co. v. Shumway,* 62 Ariz. 359, 378 (1945). We believe that reasonable persons could differ in the inferences and conclusions they would draw from the Hospital's published manual regarding disciplinary policy and procedure. Thus, there are questions of fact as to whether this policy and procedure became a part of Wagenseller's employment contract. *See Leikvold,* 141 Ariz. at 548. The trial court therefore erred in granting summary judgment on this issue.

The court of appeals' resolution of the reliance issue also was incorrect. A party may enforce a contractual provision without showing reliance. *Leikvold* does not require a plaintiff employee to show reliance in fact. The employee's reliance on an announced policy is only one of several factors that are relevant in determining whether a particular policy was intended by the parties to modify an at-will agreement. The employer's course of conduct and oral representations regarding the policy, as well as the words of the policy itself, also may provide evidence of such a modification. *Leikvold,* 141 Ariz. at 548.

THE "GOOD FAITH AND FAIR DEALING" EXCEPTION

We turn next to a consideration of implied-in-law contract terms which may limit an employer's right to discharge an at-will employee. Wagenseller claims that discharge without good cause breaches the implied-in-law covenant of good faith and fair dealing contained in every contract. In the context of this case, she argues that discharge without good cause violates the covenant of good faith and is, therefore, wrongful. The covenant requires that neither party do anything that will injure the right of the other to receive the benefits of their agreement. The duty not to act in bad faith or deal unfairly thus becomes a part of the contract, and, as with any other element of the contract, the remedy for its breach generally is on the contract itself. *Zancanaro v. Cross,* 85 Ariz. 394 (1959). In certain circumstances, breach of contract, including breach of the covenant of good faith and fair dealing, may provide the basis for a tort claim.

The question whether a duty to terminate only for good cause should be implied into all employment-at-will contracts has received much attention in the case law and other literature. Courts have generally rejected the invitation to imply such a duty in employment contracts, voicing the concern that to do so would place undue restrictions on management and would infringe the employer's "legitimate exercise of management discretion." *Pugh v. See's Candies,* 116 Cal.App.3d at 330. We think this concern is appropriate.

California has come closer than any other jurisdiction to implying a good cause duty in all employment-at-will contracts. The case most often cited for this rule is *Cleary v. American Airlines,* 111 Cal.App.3d 443 (1980). In *Cleary,* the plaintiff was discharged after eighteen years of employment with the defendant. He alleged that the discharge violated both an express policy of the company regarding employee grievances and the implied covenant of good faith and fair dealing. *Id.* at 448, 168 Cal.Rptr. at 725. The court agreed:

> Termination of employment without legal cause after such a period of time offends the implied-in-law covenant of good faith and fair dealing contained in all contracts, including employment contracts. As a result of this covenant, a duty arose on the part of the employer ... to do nothing which would deprive plaintiff, the employee, of the benefits of the employment bargain—benefits described in the complaint as having accrued during plaintiff's 18 years of employment.

Id. at 455. Thus, the court held that the employer could not discharge this employee without good cause, based on both the longevity of the employee's service and the express policy of the employer. *Id.* If the plaintiff could sustain his burden of proving that he had been terminated unjustly, the court held further that his cause of action would sound in tort as well as contract. *Id.*

Only one other court has allowed a tort recovery for breach of the implied covenant of good faith in an employment contract, and, in that case as well as in *Cleary*, the court relied in part upon the existence of an employee handbook on which plaintiff had relied. *Gates v. Life of Montana Insurance Co., supra.* Cf. *Moore v. Home Insurance Co.,* 601 F.2d 1072 (9th Cir.1979) (applying Arizona law, court held that the good faith duty did not limit employment discharges to those for which good cause could be shown).

Tort recovery for breach of the implied covenant of good faith and fair dealing is well established in actions brought on insurance contracts. Courts have been reluctant, however, to extend the tort action beyond the insurance setting. The rationale for permitting tort recovery in insurance contract disputes and not in disputes involving other contracts has been founded largely upon the existence of a "special relationship" between insurer and insured. *See Egan v. Mutual of Omaha Insurance Co.,* 24 Cal.3d 809 (1979). The California Court of Appeals recently found such a relationship present in the breach of an employment contract and held that the employee had stated a claim in tort for breach of the covenant of good faith and fair dealing. *Wallis v. Superior Court,* 160 Cal.App.3d at 1119–1122.

We find neither the logic of the California cases nor their factual circumstances compelling for recognition of so broad a rule in the case before us. Were we to adopt such a rule, we fear that we would tread perilously close to abolishing completely the at-will doctrine and establishing by judicial fiat the benefits which employees can and should get *only* through collective bargaining agreements or tenure provisions. Cf. *Fleming v. Pima County,* 141 Ariz. 149 (1984) (county employee protected by a merit system was permitted to bring a tort action for wrongful discharge). While we do not reject the propriety of such a rule, we are not persuaded that it should be the result of judicial decision.

In reaching this conclusion, however, we do not feel that we should treat employment contracts as a special type of agreement in which the law refuses to imply the covenant of good faith and fair dealing that it implies in all other contracts. As we noted above, the implied-in-law covenant of good faith and fair dealing protects the right of the parties to an agreement to receive the benefits of the agreement that they have entered into. The denial of a party's right to those benefits, whatever they are, will breach the duty of good faith implicit in the contract. Thus, the relevant inquiry always will focus on the contract itself, to determine what the parties did agree to. In the case of an employment-at-will contract, it may be said that the parties have agreed, for example, that the employee will do the work required by the employer and that the employer will provide the necessary working conditions and pay the employee for work done. What cannot be said is that one of the agreed benefits to the at-will employee is a guarantee of continued employment or tenure. The very nature of the at-will agreement precludes any claim for a prospective benefit. Either employer or employee may terminate the contract at any time.

We do, however, recognize an implied covenant of good faith and fair dealing in the employment-at-will contract, although that covenant does not create a duty for the employer to terminate the employee only for good cause. The covenant does not protect the employee from a "no cause" termination because tenure was never a benefit inherent in the at-will agreement. The covenant does protect an employee from a discharge based on an employer's desire to avoid the payment of benefits already earned by the employee, such as the sales commissions in *Fortune, supra,* but not the tenure required to earn the pension and retirement benefits in *Cleary, supra.* Thus, plaintiff here has a right to receive the benefits that were a part of her employment agreement with defendant Hospital. To the extent, however, that the benefits represent a claim for prospective employment, her claim must fail. The terminable-at-will contract between her and the Hospital made no promise of continued employment. To the contrary, it was, by its nature, subject to termination by either party at any time, subject only to the legal prohibition that she could not be fired for reasons which contravene public policy.

Thus, because we are concerned not to place undue restrictions on the employer's discretion in managing his workforce and because tenure is contrary to the bargain in an at-will contract, we reject the argument that a no cause termination breaches the implied covenant of good faith and fair dealing in an employment-at-will relationship.

SUMMARY AND CONCLUSIONS

The trial court granted summary judgment against Wagenseller on the count alleging the tort of wrongful discharge in violation of public policy. We adopt the "public policy" exception to the at-will termination rule and hold that the trial court erred in granting judgment against plaintiff on this theory. On remand plaintiff will be entitled to a jury trial if she can make a prima facie showing that her termination was caused by her refusal to perform some act contrary to public policy, or her performance of some act which, as a matter of public policy, she had a right to do. The obverse, however, is that mere dispute over an issue involving a question of public policy is not equivalent to establishing causation as a matter of law and will not automatically entitle plaintiff to judgment. In the face of conflicting evidence or inferences as to the actual reason for termination, the question of causation will be a question of fact.

The trial court granted summary judgment against Wagenseller on the count alleging breach of implied-in-fact provisions of the contract. We hold that this was error. On this record, there is a jury question as to whether the provisions of the employment manual were part of the contract of employment.

We affirm the grant of summary judgment on the count seeking recovery for breach of the implied covenant of good faith and fair dealing. We recognize that covenant as part of this and other contracts, but do not construe it to give either party to the contract rights—such as tenure—different from those for which they contracted.

We reverse the grant of summary judgment against Wagenseller on the count alleging tortious interference with a contractual relationship. On this record, there is a question of fact with respect to whether the discharge was tortious. Summary judgment was inappropriate.

For the foregoing reasons, we affirm in part and reverse in part. The decision of the court of appeals is vacated and the case remanded to the trial court for proceedings not inconsistent with this opinion.

■ GORDON, V.C.J., and HAYS and CAMERON, JJ., concur.

■ HOLOHAN, CHIEF JUSTICE, dissenting and specially concurring.

The Court of Appeals held in this case that the personnel manual was not, as a matter of law, part of the employment contract. I concur in that position because I find the analysis of the Court of Appeals more convincing than that advanced by the majority of this court. I, therefore, dissent from the opinion of the court on that issue.

On the remaining issues I concur in the result.

* * *

At the time of the events behind *Wagenseller*, the plaintiff, who had been hired as an at-will employee, had worked for the defendant-hospital as a staff nurse for four years, receiving systematically positive performance evaluations. The plaintiff, her supervisor, and other colleagues took a camping and river-rafting trip. During the expedition, the plaintiff's supervisor and others engaged in public urination, defecation, bathing, heavy drinking, and what the court (or perhaps the plaintiff) called "grouping up." The campers also create a performance skit that involved "mooning" the audience to the tune of Moon River, which they allegedly also performed on two occasions after returning to work. The plaintiff refused to engage in any of these activities, and her relations with her supervisor deteriorated. Five months later, the plaintiff was fired, without following the procedures concerning employee discipline and termination set forth in the defendant-hospital's personnel manual.

The plaintiff sued both the hospital and her supervisor for wrongful discharge. She claimed that she was fired without legitimate cause related to job performance and for reasons that contravened public policy. The plaintiff sought relief in both contract and tort.

The court used the case as an opportunity to review the development of the law of the employment contract. It began by observing that the modern trend is to modify the at-will doctrine and to recognize some form of cause of action for wrongful discharge. This doctrinal development, as the court noted, has proceeded through three theories. The first, which sounds in both contract and tort, establishes a public policy exception to the rule of employment at will, according to which an employee might succeed if she can show that her employer discharged her on grounds that violate an important public policy. The second, which sounds in contract only, recognizes that even where a person is hired as an at-will employee, the circumstances surrounding her employment—including in particular management practices both as set forth in employee manuals and as implemented—might establish implied-in-fact contractual promises that modify the at-will regime to establish constraints on discharge. The third, which sounds in contract and perhaps also in tort, recognizes that certain forms of wrongful discharge may violate the implied-in-law covenant of good faith and fair dealing that governs every contract.

The *public policy* exception to employment at will is the structurally simplest and also the least interesting, at least from the perspective of the broader theory of freedom of contract. This doctrine holds that even though employers may generally terminate at-will employees without respect to cause, they may not discharge employees for reasons that violate public policy. Formally, this doctrine generalizes the way in which anti-discrimination law limits employment at will. It renders contract law, at least in the employment area, generally subject to norms from outside contract, so that employers' contractual discretion becomes limited by these norms.

The central question raised by the public policy exception to employment at will asks what constitutes a public policy capable of supporting the exception. This question has two facets. First, what are the sources from which public policy may be divined, and how much discretion do courts possess in respect of finding public policy in these sources? And second, how public must an interest be in order appropriately to underwrite a public policy for purposes of the doctrine?

The *Wagenseller* court gave an expansive answer to the first question, suggesting that a court might find a relevant public policy in constitutional, statutory, or even decisional law, and even based on judges' own senses of what is *malum in se*. (For example, in respect of the facts of *Wagenseller*, in statutes prohibiting public nudity.) But other courts, and also state legislatures, have sought to limit the grounds of public policy in this area more narrowly.[6] They have, for example, sought to limit the sources of public policy to constitutional or statutory enactments. Or they have imposed requirements that claims of public policy must be based on specifically identifiable and narrowly tailored language, addressed directly to the practices that give rise to a termination. Such limitations retrench employers' prerogatives in respect of employment at will by preventing courts from doing equity when faced with sympathetic employees who have been discharged for non-specific but intuitively bad reasons.

The second question asks how public an interest must be to underwrite a public-policy-based claim of wrongful discharge. In particular, must the interests of society writ large be at stake in this policy, or might some narrower, more private interest also qualify? In other words, can an employee successfully claim that she was discharged in violation of public policy where she is fired for refusing to violate some norm that protects only private and not the public interest? Suppose, for example, that an

---

6. As it happens, the Arizona legislature responded to *Wagenseller* in just this way, enacting a statute that substantially limited the set of public policies that might underwrite an otherwise at-will employee's claim of wrongful discharge in violation of public policy. See ARIZ. REV. STAT. § 23–1501(3)(b)–(d).

employee is fired for informing her employer that her supervisor (who also works for the employer) is stealing, perhaps even from the employer itself. Would this firing, which shows immediate disregard for only the private interest of the victim of the theft, who may even be the employer itself, violate any truly public policy? Some courts have held that it would not.

The exceptions to employment at will based on *implied-in-fact* promises of job security and the *implied-in-law* covenant of good faith and fair dealing are substantially more complicated and substantially more interesting, structurally, for a broader understanding of freedom of contract. In particular, these doctrines—which allow contractual practice to establish obligations even in the teeth of express statements that this practice shall *not* create contractual rights—raise the question whether freedom of contract can resist the non-voluntary forms of obligation that inevitably arise alongside contract in long-lived, complex, adaptive, and evolving relations like the employment relation.

Employers, especially when they are large and have human resources departments, commonly adopt more-or-less formal rules and practices for managing their employees. (The hospital in *Wagenseller* was no exception to this rule.) These rules and practices may be announced orally, or even just informally through repeated use;[7] or they may be announced in writing and more formally, in particular by being promulgated through employee manuals. The rules typically state a set of expectations concerning employee behavior—honesty, punctuality, deference to supervisors, and so on. The rules may also state precise (and even exclusive) lists of substantive grounds for discharge. In addition, and importantly, the rules also emphasize procedure as well as or indeed in preference over substance. They announce that instead of firing capriciously, employers will follow fixed processes—often quite formal—in determining whether and when to fire their employees. A typical regime gives delinquent employees multiple warnings or "pink slips" prior to a firing (although perhaps not in cases of egregious employee misconduct). The procedure may even give employees some access to "appellate review" of decisions concerning misconduct made by their immediate supervisors, conducted either by human resource officers or by the supervisors' own bosses.

Employers establish these mechanisms for any number of reasons. Perhaps they wish to control lower level managers, whose interests, after all, will not always coincide with the interests of the employers for whom they, also, merely work. Perhaps the mechanisms improve information flow within hierarchical organizations, by providing a centralized and public repository of expectations concerning employee behavior—a kind of support system for corporate culture. Perhaps such policies induce employees to develop emotional attachments to each other and to their jobs, thereby rendering management more effective and workers more productive.

---

7. The statute of frauds does not invalidate oral promises of this sort, because even a long term employment contract may be completed within a year—the employee may die, for example, or the employer may fold.

Another reason for establishing orderly and fair procedures to regulate the discipline and discharge of formally at-will employees bears more detailed analysis, because of the way in which it interacts with the contract doctrines that modify employment at will. To understand this reason, begin by imagining a simplified model of the employment contract. Employers pay employees a wage to *work*. Work creates *products* for the employers, but costs the employees their *labor burdens*. Where employees do not work—where they *shirk*—they create no products but also bear no labor burdens. The contractual gain for the employers equals the value of the employees' work products minus the wages paid. The gain to employees equals the wages received minus the labor burdens borne.[8]

Employers would ideally like their employees to work and still to avoid paying wages. Contract law forbids this, however (which is just to say that refusing to pay wages constitutes a breach of the employment contract). Employers nevertheless prefer having employees who work and are paid over having no workers (the workers' products exceed their wages). Finally, the worst outcome, for employers, is to pay employees who shirk, thus losing wages and gaining no work products. The preferences of employees are the mirror image of this. Employees prefer to shirk while still getting paid rather than to work (contract law forbids this, making shirking a breach); but they prefer to work and be paid rather than not working while unemployed (their wages, that is, exceed their labor burdens);[9] and their worst outcome is to work without being paid.

Given these preferences, an equilibrium may arise in which employees work and employers pay. Sustaining the equilibrium requires that each side monitors the other's performance. The employees' monitoring activities are not interesting, in the current context (the employees know whether or not they've been paid almost automatically, which is to say at no cost). The employers' monitoring is extremely interesting, by contrast. Monitoring is effective because employees prefer paid work over unpaid unemployment. They thus wish to avoid being caught shirking and fired (for cause). But monitoring of employees is also expensive; and, for this reason, any actual employer's efforts to monitor employees will be imperfectly accurate: it will sometimes report that shirkers are working; and it will sometimes report that workers are shirking. Employers may improve the accuracy of their monitoring by investing more in monitoring.

Employees decide whether to work or to shirk against the backdrop of this wage and monitoring regime. In particular, a self-interested employee will decide whether to work or to shirk by comparing her expected return

---

8. The model is highly stylized. Employers and employees are not purely self-interested, of course. And working together may have intrinsic rewards for both. But the stylized model conveys a point that remains valid even in the face of these complications.

9. In fact, of course, a fired worker's unemployment would not be permanent, as she would eventually find another job. So a more precise account of workers' preferences focuses on the extent to which the workers prefer the wage and labor burden package offered by their current employers over what they might receive if they left their present employment and sought work from other employers instead. The argument will set this possibility aside, although only to ease exposition and without loss of generality.

from each strategy. The employee's return from working equals the difference between her wage and her labor burden multiplied by the probability that her employer will find her to be working given that she is working, minus her labor burden multiplied by the probability that, even though she is actually working, her employer will conclude that she is shirking and thus fire her. The employee's return from shirking equals her wage multiplied by the probability that, although she is actually shirking, her employer will conclude that she is working and thus pay her. (Where a shirking employee is caught shirking and fired, her return is zero.) The employee will thus work as long as the first return exceeds the second. Otherwise, she will shirk.

These observations reveal that an employer may encourage her employees to work through improved monitoring. On the one hand, she may expend more on monitoring that identifies shirkers—that avoids false negatives, in which shirkers escape detection and register as workers. By raising the chances of being caught and discharged for shirking, the employer decreases the return to shirking, and so encourages work. On the other hand, an employer may expend more on monitoring that identifies workers—that avoids false positives, in which workers are registered as shirkers. By reducing the chances that an employee who works will be falsely discharged for shirking, the employer increases the return to working, and so encourages work. Employers have reason to combine these various techniques, depending on the relative costs of identifying shirkers and identifying workers.[10]

This way of characterizing the employers' practices reveals that monitoring designed to prevent false attributions of shirking in effect increases the return to working; it is a kind of wage-substitute, which increases a worker's expected wage, especially where the worker is nominally an at-will employee and hence legally exposed to being fired capriciously in spite of working.[11] One prominent form of such monitoring involves establishing procedural protections against arbitrary discharge—that is, the very proce-

---

10. An employer may also encourage her employees to work by raising her workers' wages. As long as the probability that workers will be found to be working exceeds the probability that shirkers will be found to be working, higher wages increase the relative return of working over shirking, for every level of monitoring accuracy.

Economists have observed that the costs of monitoring can in fact be high enough so that it is cheaper for employers to encourage work by paying higher wages (and thus increasing the costs of being caught shirking) than by investing additional monitoring to identify shirkers (and thus increasing the chance of being caught shirking). When this balance of costs obtains, employers have reason to pay employees wages that exceed their marginal products. Economists call these *efficiency wages*. The fact that firms pay inflated wages implies that the natural rate of unemployment will be positive. See Janet L. Yellen, *Efficiency Wage Models of Unemployment*, 74 Am. Econ. Rev. 200 (1984).

The thought that efficiency wages generate structural unemployment is just a special case of a more general functionalist analysis of the consequences of worker benefits for employment more broadly. Thus it is often, and plausibly, said that legal regimes that constrain employers' powers to terminate employees reduce overall employment, by making employees more expensive (in expectation) to hire. See, e.g., Stephen Nickel, *Unemployment and Labor Market Rigidities: Europe versus North America*, 11 J. Econ. Perspectives 55 (1997).

11. Monitoring designed to prevent true workers from being falsely fired as shirkers functions, from the workers' perspective, as a kind of efficiency wage.

dures associated with the management practices just described. Protection against arbitrary termination thus constitutes a part of an employee's effective compensation, a part of the exchange occasioned by the employment agreement. (The employer finds the compensation worth paying and worth advertising to employees, once again, because it increases the benefits of working and so also the costs to employees of being caught shirking and fired for cause and therefore increases the incentives of even purely self-interested employees to work effortfully.)

Now, with these explanations for why employers establish procedures for terminating even at-will employees as a backdrop, return to employer practice and to contract law's doctrinal engagement with this practice. Even as employers establish internal rules and procedures to administer how they will in practice decide whom and when to fire, they seek to retain the full measure of the discretion associated with employment at will. Thus it is common to find that employee manuals, even as they announce orderly procedures for administering employee discipline, expressly disclaim that these procedures modify the employment contract and reserve for employers absolute discretion to depart from these procedures whenever they wish, and once again to fire at will. But orderly management procedures and the protections that these procedures provide against arbitrary terminations are valuable to employers in (large) part *because* they are valuable to employees. Regardless of the disclaimers, the procedures thus become, as a matter of fact, a part of the exchange between employers and employees. This raises the question whether the law should recognize this fact, and modify the employment relation accordingly, abandoning the at-will regime in favor of one that contractualizes employers' management procedures.

Courts, confronting this pattern of promise and practice, have been willing to treat sufficiently well-promulgated and regularly applied personnel management procedures as establishing an *implied-in-fact* contractual obligation in employers with respect to the procedures.[12] They have sometimes, although not in all jurisdictions or in all cases, reached this result even in the face of express disclaimers through which employers have sought to retain the at-will rule in law, regardless of their management practices.[13]

Most modestly, even courts that have allowed disclaimers to reserve for employers the right to disregard their own procedures have nevertheless recognized that disclaimers are "not controlling in every case"[14] and

---

12. Note that this is an orthodox contract theory rather than a theory that invokes promissory estoppel, perhaps under § 90 or the Restatement. The theory proposes (as a formal matter) that the employment manuals, etc., represent an offer that the employee accepts by continuing to do her job. This means that an employee may win on a claim that employer practices establish an implied-in-fact promise to limit arbitrary terminations *without* showing that she relied on these implied-in-fact promises.

13. It is practically important, in this connection, that whether or not such implied-in-fact promises exist is itself a question of fact. For this reason plaintiffs who allege a breach of implied-in-fact promises established by personnel manuals or management practices will generally be able to get past summary judgment, as long as they can raise factual questions about the manuals and practices that they allege give rise to the implied-in-fact terms.

14. *Guz v. Bechtel National, Inc.*, 24 Cal. 4th 317, 340 (Cal. 2000).

insisted that the disclaimers must be "clear and prominent" in order to be effective.[15] Indeed, such disclaimers are commonly construed "in accordance with the reasonable expectations of the employees,"[16] so that "[t]he burden is not on the employee to draw inferences from the handbook language."[17]

More aggressively, some courts have held that employers cannot ever unilaterally modify promises contained in employee manuals by introducing disclaimers into subsequent editions of the manuals. Instead, such modifications are effective only if they are accepted by employees who receive good consideration for their acceptances (where consideration requires a benefit beyond continued employment).[18] This approach allows employers to retain unfettered discretion to fire at the time of hiring an employee, but then creates a one-way ratchet effect, according to which protections once granted cannot easily be removed.

More aggressively still, some courts have even held that regular compliance with employer-announced disciplinary procedures constitutes a contract modification or course-of-performance evidence that the contractually binds employers to comply with these procedures quite generally, which no written reservation of the right to fire at will (not even backed by an integration clause) can undo.[19] This asymmetrical treatment is often directly related to differences in the formal circumstances surrounding the adoption of the procedures and the announcement of the disclaimers. Whereas the procedures that the manuals adopt are often embedded in reciprocal engagements between employers and employees—who certainly have direct experience of their ongoing administration and may even be consulted in their design—the reservations arise solely as contracts of adhesion, which employers one-sidedly include in their manuals (that is, on their forms).

---

15.   *Woolley v. Hoffmann–LaRoche, Inc.*, 491 A.2d 1257, 1258 (N.J. 1985).

16.   Id. at 1264. See also, Id. at 1266.

17.   *Nicosia v. Wakefern Food Corp.*, 643 A.2d 554, 560 (N.J. 1994) (quotation marks and citation omitted).

18.   A prominent example is *Demasse v. ITT Corporation*, 194 Ariz. 500 (1999). In *Demasse*, the Arizona Supreme Court (answering a certification from the Ninth Circuit) effectively reversed a federal district court's conclusion that disclaimers in effect at the time of an employee's termination govern her contract rights, regardless of their having been introduced only after she was hired. See *Chambers v. Valley National Bank*, 721 F. Supp 1128 (D. Ariz. 1988).

19.   This suggestion emphasizes that, as with all theories involving implied-in-fact contracts, assessing this theory involves taking a stand on fundamental ideas about contract interpretation, including the right readings of ambiguity and the effect of the parol evidence rule.

Some judges who are hostile to implied-in-fact contractual departures from employment at will connect this specific view to a more general objection to parol agreements in contract construction and contextualism in contract interpretation. An excellent example is Judge Kozinski's fervent dissent in *Kern v. Levolor Lorentzen, Inc.*, 899 F.2d 772 (9th Cir. 1990). Some legislatures have taken a similar view. An example is an Arizona statute that requires contractual terms that limit an employer's right to fire an employee to be accepted by both parties in writing. See Ariz. Rev. Stat. § 23–1501(2).

The logic of the employment agreement would support going further still, and some (although now far fewer) courts have taken another step. This is to treat arbitrary firings, when they violate internal employee management practices, as breaches of the *implied-in-law* covenant of good faith and fair dealing that governs every contract. This additional step is important principally because characterizing such firings as bad faith opens up the possibility that wrongfully terminated employees might be able to sue not just in contract but also in tort. This possibility matters because a cause of action in tort comes with tort remedies, including in particular damages for emotional distress and perhaps even punitive damages. This observation at once suggests that courts will by and large remain skeptical of arguments asserting bad-faith breaches of contracts that began by establishing employment at will. All the arguments against treating bad-faith breach of contract as in itself tortious—rehearsed already in Chapter 8—apply to the employment context.

But the internal structure of the claim concerning bad faith breach remains interesting and important, in spite of these reservations from without. The implied-in-law covenant of good faith and fair dealing functions, as Chapter 19 explained, to prevent one party from using the other party's strategic vulnerabilities (especially those incurred as a result of contracting) to expropriate gains that the contract allocated to the vulnerable party. As one commentator put it, "[b]ad faith performance occurs precisely when discretion is used to recapture opportunities forgone upon contracting."[20] There is no doubt that breaches of an employment contract may amount to bad faith under this standard. Typical examples of such bad-faith include firing sales people the day before they makes sales quotas that would entitle them to bonuses and firing executives the day before stock options vest. The following case illustrates this pattern.

Fortune v. National Cash Register Co.

Supreme Judicial Court of Massachusetts, 1977.
364 N.E.2d 1251.

■ ABRAMS, JUSTICE.

Orville E. Fortune (Fortune), a former salesman of The National Cash Register Company (NCR), brought a suit to recover certain commissions allegedly due as a result of a sale of cash registers to First National Stores Inc. (First National) in 1968. Counts 1 and 2 of Fortune's amended declaration claimed bonus payments under the parties' written contract of employment. The third count sought recovery in quantum meruit for the reasonable value of Fortune's services relating to the same sales transaction. Judgment on a jury verdict for Fortune was reversed by the Appeals Court, Fortune v. National Cash Register Co., 4 Mass.App.Ct. 386 (1976), and this court granted leave to obtain further appellate review. We affirm the judgment of the Superior Court. We hold, for the reasons stated herein,

---

20. Steven J. Burton, *Breach of Contract and the Common Law Duty to Perform in Good Faith*, 94 HARV. L. REV. 369, 373 (1980).

there was no error in submitting the issue of "bad faith" termination of an employment at will contract to the jury.

The issues before the court are raised by NCR's motion for directed verdicts. Accordingly, we summarize the evidence most favorable to the plaintiff. *H. P. Hood & Sons v. Ford Motor Co.*, 370 Mass. 69 (1976).

Fortune was employed by NCR under a written "salesman's contract" which was terminable at will, without cause, by either party on written notice. The contract provided that Fortune would receive a weekly salary in a fixed amount plus a bonus for sales made within the "territory" (i. e., customer accounts or stores) assigned to him for "coverage or supervision," whether the sale was made by him or someone else. The amount of the bonus was determined on the basis of "bonus credits," which were computed as a percentage of the price of products sold. Fortune would be paid a percentage of the applicable bonus credit as follows: (1) 75% if the territory was assigned to him at the date of the order, (2) 25% if the territory was assigned to him at the date of delivery and installation, or (3) 100% if the territory was assigned to him at both times. The contract further provided that the "bonus interest" would terminate if shipment of the order was not made within eighteen months from the date of the order unless (1) the territory was assigned to him for coverage at the date of delivery and installation, or (2) special engineering was required to fulfill the contract. In addition, NCR reserved the right to sell products in the salesman's territory without paying a bonus. However, this right could be exercised only on written notice.

In 1968, Fortune's territory included First National. This account had been part of his territory for the preceding six years; he had been successful in obtaining several orders from First National, including a million dollar order in 1963. Sometime in late 1967, or early 1968, NCR introduced a new model cash register, Class 5. Fortune corresponded with First National in an effort to sell the machine. He also helped to arrange for a demonstration of the Class 5 to executives of First National on October 4, 1968. NCR had a team of men also working on this sale.

On November 27, 1968, NCR's manager of chain and department stores, and the Boston branch manager, both part of NCR's team, wrote to First National regarding the Class 5. The letter covered a number of subjects, including price protection, trade-ins, and trade-in protection against obsolescence. While NCR normally offered price protection for only an eighteen-month term, apparently the size of the proposed order from First National caused NCR to extend its price protection terms for either a two-year or four-year period. On November 29, 1968, First National signed an order for 2,008 Class 5 machines to be delivered over a four-year period at a purchase price of approximately $5,000,000. Although Fortune did not participate in the negotiation of the terms of the order, his name appeared on the order form in the space entitled "salesman credited." The amount of the bonus credit as shown on the order was $92,079.99.

On January 6, 1969, the first working day of the new year, Fortune found an envelope on his desk at work. It contained a termination notice addressed to his home dated December 2, 1968. Shortly after receiving the notice, Fortune spoke to the Boston branch manager with whom he was friendly. The manager told him, "You are through," but, after considering some of the details necessary for the smooth operation of the First National order, told him to "stay on," and to "(k)eep on doing what you are doing right now." Fortune remained with the company in a position entitled "sales support." In this capacity, he coordinated and expedited delivery of the machines to First National under the November 29 order as well as servicing other accounts.

Commencing in May or June, Fortune began to receive some bonus commissions on the First National order. Having received only 75% of the applicable bonus due on the machines which had been delivered and installed, Fortune spoke with his manager about receiving the full amount of the commission. Fortune was told "to forget about it." Sixty-one years old at that time, and with a son in college, Fortune concluded that it "was a good idea to forget it for the time being."

NCR did pay a systems and installations person the remaining 25% of the bonus commissions due from the First National order although contrary to its usual policy of paying only salesmen a bonus. NCR, by its letter of November 27, 1968, had promised the services of a systems and installations person; the letter had claimed that the services of this person, Bernie Martin (Martin), would have a forecasted cost to NCR of over $45,000. As promised, NCR did transfer Martin to the First National account shortly after the order was placed.

Approximately eighteen months after receiving the termination notice, Fortune, who had worked for NCR for almost twenty-five years, was asked to retire. When he refused, he was fired in June of 1970. Fortune did not receive any bonus payments on machines which were delivered to First National after this date.

At the close of the plaintiff's case, the defendant moved for a directed verdict, arguing that there was no evidence of any breach of contract, and adding that the existence of a contract barred recovery under the quantum meruit count. Ruling that Fortune could recover if the termination and firing were in bad faith, the trial judge, without specifying on which count, submitted this issue to the jury. NCR then rested and, by agreement of counsel, the case was sent to the jury for special verdicts on two questions:

"1.   Did the Defendant act in bad faith when it decided to terminate the Plaintiff's contract as a salesman by letter dated December 2, 1968, delivered on January 6, 1969?

"2.   Did the Defendant act in bad faith when the Defendant let the Plaintiff go on June 5, 1970?"

The jury answered both questions affirmatively, and judgment entered in the sum of $45,649.62.

The central issue on appeal is whether this "bad faith" termination constituted a breach of the employment at will contract. Traditionally, an employment contract which is "at will" may be terminated by either side without reason. Although the employment at will rule has been almost uniformly criticised, see Blades, Employment at Will vs. Individual Freedom: On Limiting the Abusive Exercise of Employer Power, 67 Colum.L.Rev. 1404 (1967); Blumrosen, Workers' Rights Against Employers and Unions: Justice Francis A Judge for Our Season, 24 Rutgers L.Rev. 480 (1970), it has been widely followed.

The contract at issue is a classic terminable at will employment contract. It is clear that the contract itself reserved to the parties an explicit power to terminate the contract without cause on written notice. It is also clear that under the express terms of the contract Fortune has received all the bonus commissions to which he is entitled. Thus, NCR claims that it did not breach the contract, and that it has no further liability to Fortune. According to a literal reading of the contract, NCR is correct.

However, Fortune argues that, in spite of the literal wording of the contract, he is entitled to a jury determination on NCR's motives in terminating his services under the contract and in finally discharging him. We agree. We hold that NCR's written contract contains an implied covenant of good faith and fair dealing, and a termination not made in good faith constitutes a breach of the contract.

We do not question the general principles that an employer is entitled to be motivated by and to serve its own legitimate business interests; that an employer must have wide latitude in deciding whom it will employ in the face of the uncertainties of the business world; and that an employer needs flexibility in the face of changing circumstances. We recognize the employer's need for a large amount of control over its work force. However, we believe that where, as here, commissions are to be paid for work performed by the employee, the employer's decision to terminate its at will employee should be made in good faith. NCR's right to make decisions in its own interest is not, in our view, unduly hampered by a requirement of adherence to this standard.

On occasion some courts have avoided the rigidity of the "at will" rule by fashioning a remedy in tort. We believe, however, that in this case there is remedy on the express contract. In so holding we are merely recognizing the general requirement in this Commonwealth that parties to contracts and commercial transactions must act in good faith toward one another. Good faith and fair dealing between parties are pervasive requirements in our law; it can be said fairly, that parties to contracts or commercial transactions are bound by this standard. See G.L. c. 106, s 1–203 (good faith in contracts under Uniform Commercial Code); G.L. c. 93B, s 4(3)(c) (good faith in motor vehicle franchise termination).

A requirement of good faith has been assumed or implied in a variety of contract cases. The requirement of good faith was reaffirmed in *RLM Assocs. v. Carter Mfg. Corp.*, 356 Mass. 718 (1969). In that case the plaintiff (RLM), a manufacturer's representative of the defendant (Carter), was entitled to a commission on all of Carter's sales within a specified territory. Either party could terminate this arrangement on thirty days' notice.

Carter cancelled the agreement shortly before being awarded a contract discovered and brought to Carter's attention by RLM. Because "(t)he evidence permitted the conclusion that Carter's termination of the arrangement was in part based upon a desire to avoid paying a commission to RLM" (ibid.), we held that the question of bad faith was properly placed before the jury. The present case differs from RLM Assocs., in that Fortune was credited with the sale to First National but was fired immediately thereafter. NCR seeks to avoid the thrust of RLM Assocs. by arguing that bad faith is not an issue where it has been careful to protect a portion of Fortune's bonus commission under the contract. We disagree. The fact that the discharge was after a portion of the bonus vested still creates a question for the jury on the defendant's motive in terminating the employment.

Recent decisions in other jurisdictions lend support to the proposition that good faith is implied in contracts terminable at will. In a recent employment at will case, *Monge v. Beebe Rubber Co.*, 114 N.H. 130, 133 (1974), the plaintiff alleged that her oral contract of employment had been terminated because she refused to date her foreman. The New Hampshire Supreme Court held that "(i)n all employment contracts, whether at will or for a definite term, the employer's interest in running his business as he sees fit must be balanced against the interest of the employee in maintaining his employment, and the public's interest in maintaining a proper balance between the two. We hold that a termination by the employer of a contract of employment at will which is motivated by bad faith or malice constitutes a breach of the employment contract. Such a rule affords the employee a certain stability of employment and does not interfere with the employer's normal exercise of his right to discharge, which is necessary to permit him to operate his business efficiently and profitably."

We believe that the holding in the Monge case merely extends to employment contracts the rule that " 'in every contract there is an implied covenant that neither party shall do anything which will have the effect of destroying or injuring the right of the other party to receive the fruits of the contract, which means that in every contract there exists an implied covenant of good faith and fair dealing' (emphasis supplied). *Uproar Co. v. National Broadcasting Co.*, 81 F.2d 373, 377 (1st Cir.), cert. denied, 298 U.S. 670, 56 S.Ct. 835, quoting from *Kirke LaShelle Co. v. Paul Armstrong Co.*, 263 N.Y. 79, 87 (1933)."

In the instant case, we need not pronounce our adherence to so broad a policy nor need we speculate as to whether the good faith requirement is implicit in every contract for employment at will. It is clear, however, that, on the facts before us, a finding is warranted that a breach of the contract occurred. Where the principal seeks to deprive the agent of all compensation by terminating the contractual relationship when the agent is on the brink of successfully completing the sale, the principal has acted in bad faith and the ensuing transaction between the principal and the buyer is to be regarded as having been accomplished by the agent. Restatement (Second) of Agency s 454, and Comment a (1958). The same result obtains where the principal attempts to deprive the agent of any portion of a commission due the agent. Courts have often applied this rule to prevent overreaching by employers and the forfeiture by employees of benefits almost earned by the rendering of substantial services. In our view, the Appeals Court erroneously focused only on literal compliance with payment provisions of the contract and failed to consider the issue of bad faith termination. Restatement (Second) of Agency s 454, and Comment a (1958).

NCR argues that there was no evidence of bad faith in this case; therefore, the trial judge was required to direct a verdict in any event. We think that the evidence and the reasonable inferences to be drawn therefrom support a jury verdict that the termination of Fortune's twenty-five years of employment as a salesman with NCR the next business day after NCR obtained a $5,000,000 order from First National was motivated by a desire to pay Fortune as little of the bonus credit as it could. The fact that Fortune was willing to work under these circumstances does not constitute a waiver or estoppel; it only shows that NCR had him "at their mercy." *Commonwealth v. DeCotis*, 366 Mass. 234, 243 (1974).

NCR also contends that Fortune cannot complain of his firing in June, 1970, as his employment contract clearly indicated that bonus credits would be paid only for an eighteen-month period following the date of the order. As we have said, the jury could have found that Fortune was stripped of his "salesman" designation in order to disqualify him for the remaining 25% Of the commissions due on cash registers delivered prior to the date of his first termination. Similarly, the jury could have found that Fortune was fired so that NCR would avoid paying him any commissions on cash registers delivered after June, 1970.

Conversely, the jury could have found that Fortune was assigned by NCR to the First National account; that all he did in this case was arrange for a demonstration of the product; that he neither participated in obtaining the order nor did he assist NCR in closing the order; and that nevertheless NCR credited him with the sale. This, however, did not obligate the trial judge to direct a verdict. Where evidence is conflicting, the rule is clear: "If upon any reasonable view of the evidence there is found any combination of circumstances from which a rational inference may be drawn in favor of the plaintiff, then there was no error in the denial of the motion, even if there may be other and different circumstances disclosed in the evidence which, if accepted as true by the jury, would support a conclusion adverse to the plaintiff." *Howes v. Kelman*, 326 Mass. 696, 696–697 (1951).

We think that NCR's conduct in June, 1970 permitted the jury to find bad faith.

Judgment of the Superior Court affirmed.

* * *

The plaintiff, who had worked for the defendant as salesman for twenty-five years, was fired shortly after making a $5 million sale. A jury found that defendant acted to deprive plaintiff of his full commission and that this breached the implied in law covenant of good faith and fair dealing.

The crassness of the defendant's conduct makes *Fortune* an easy case. But the account of orderly management practices developed earlier in these pages—and in particular of the way in which these practices are valuable to employers because of their value to employees—reveals that *every* firing that violates personnel procedures shares the same formal structure as the firing in *Fortune*. The procedures represent a benefit to employees—they protect otherwise-at-will employees from arbitrary firings and thus from working rather than shirking (and so expending a labor burden) and being fired (and losing future wages) nevertheless. Moreover, employers intend the procedures to convey this benefit upon employees, because by doing so, they increase employees' incentives to work rather than to shirk and hence increase employers' expected products and profits. Orderly management practices are thus (no less than bonuses or stock options) *in themselves* benefits that employment arrangements are designed to provide employees, benefits of which the employees are deprived by terminations that depart from the procedures that these practices establish. Finally, arbitrarily terminated employees have already decided to work rather than shirk and have hence incurred a strategic vulnerability (their sunk work effort and labor burden) on the basis of the orderly management procedures and the protections against arbitrary termination that these procedures provide. An employer who encourages employee effort by promulgating orderly management procedures but then terminates employees arbitrarily and in violation of these very procedures thus "uses [discretion] to recapture opportunities forgone upon contracting." And that is quintessentially bad faith.

Perhaps unsurprisingly, this formal argument has not generally been embraced by courts. *Fortune* does not stand alone, to be sure. Courts, including in principle the *Wagenseller* court, have been willing to find bad faith breach where terminations are not just arbitrary and capricious but also outrageous or badly motivated, especially where the fired employees have worked for their employers for a long time and created a great deal of firm specific human capital. But courts have been reluctant to find breaches of the implied in law covenant of good faith in all but the most exceptional employment cases. This reaction is connected to the relationship between claims based on the theory of an implied-in-fact contract and claims based on the implied-in-law covenant of good faith. The latter claims do not add any substantive rights to the former. Good faith, after all, does not create independent contractual rights but rather merely states a general obligation to respect whatever rights contracts otherwise establish. The implied-in-law theory thus does not expand the scope of employers' contractual obligations but merely gives them a new characterization, which promises innovative and more substantial remedies.[21] But these tort-

---

21. This characterization reveals that the arguments against bad faith breach are not special to the employment context. In particular, the substance of employment at will does not underwrite any distinctive arguments against bad faith breach of employment contracts. This

like remedies are generally suspect in contract law, as Chapter 8 has explained in greater detail. The employment context has not proved capable of sustaining an exception to the general rule.

Finally, note that this abstract account of judicial skepticism concerning bad-faith firings white-washes some of the local history of judicial rejection of tort-like remedies for such firings. The story, especially as it played out in California, illustrates the relationship between courts and legislatures and certain generally important ideas concerning judicial review.

California's experiment in judicial recognition of a tort of bad-faith termination began in earnest in June of 1980, with a case called *Tameny v. Atlantic Richfield Co.*[22] The plaintiff was fired after 15 years of service because he refused to participate in an illegal price-fixing scheme. He sued, seeking recovery in tort as well as in contract. More specifically, the plaintiff claimed that the firing was tortious because it violated public policy (being in effect a part of a scheme to pursue illegal activities) and because it constituted a breach of the implied in law covenant of good faith and fair dealing. The Supreme Court of California adopted the plaintiff's first theory, and allowed the plaintiff to recover tort damages. Given this holding, the Court found no need to adjudicate the plaintiff's second theory, although it did issue dicta friendly to that theory.

Next, in October of 1980, a California Appellate Court held, in *Cleary v. American Airlines, Inc.*,[23] that where an employer terminates a sufficiently long-serving employee with sufficient disregard for its own policies concerning firing, the employee may state a claim for wrongful termination in violation of the implied in law covenant of good faith and fair dealing. The court further held that this claim sounds in both contract and tort. Subsequent cases in the early 1980's took a similar line.[24]

These developments triggered a backlash, which came to a head in December of 1988, in *Foley v. Interactive Data Corp.*[25] The plaintiff in *Foley* had informed the defendant, his employer, that his supervisor was under investigation by the FBI for embezzlement. The plaintiff alleged that the defendant had reacted by firing *him*. He sued, seeking relief in both contract and tort. The California Supreme Court used the case substantially to retrench the employment law of the state, significantly narrowing the claims that prior cases had begun to recognize. (*Foley* did continue to

---

is worth emphasizing, as some courts have mistakenly thought that legal recognition of a cause of action for bad faith firings is inconsistent with the very idea of employment at will. *See, e.g., Murphy v. American Home Products Corp.*, 58 N.Y. 2d 293, 448 N.E.2d 86 (1983). Once again, this view mistakes the structure of the argument and in particular the way in which the implied-in-law claim gives employees no substantive rights but merely piggy-backs on the implied-in-fact claim.

22.   27 Cal. 3d 167 (Cal. 1980).

23.   111 Cal. App. 3d 443 (Cal. App. 1980).

24.   See, e.g., *Pugh v. See's Candies*, 203 Cal. App. 3d 743 (Cal. App. 1988) and *Cancellier v. Federated Department Stores*, 672 F.2d 1312 (9th Cir. 1982).

25.   47 Cal. 3d 654 (Cal. 1988).

recognize that even where they were hired as employees at-will, discharged employees may recover in contract on the theory that their firings violated an implied in fact promise based on their employers' management practices and procedures.)

On the one hand, the Court held that while an employee may recover tort damages when his employer fires him for a reason that terminates public policy, public policy should in this connection be narrowly construed. In particular, a firing will trigger the doctrine only where the policy that it violates is substantial, fundamental, basic, and public. *Foley* further held that the protection of the employee's employer from internal thefts does not qualify under this standard. A subsequent case further narrowed the tort by holding that to trigger the doctrine, the violated public policy must be derived specifically from a statutory or constitutional provision.[26]

And on the other hand, the Court held that an employee may *not* recover in tort on the theory that his firing violates an implied-in-law covenant of good faith and fair dealing. The majority suggested that the earlier recognition of this cause of action turned on an unsupportable analogy to the insurance context, where such a cause of action is proper. The majority argued that relationship between employer and employee is not the same as the special relationship between insurer and insured. In particular, the employer does not have the same degree of control and superior expertise as an insurer; the employee's and employer's interests are not fundamentally at odds in the way in which the insurer's and insured's interests are at odds; and the purpose of the employment contract, unlike the purpose of the insurance contract, is not to protect the employee from catastrophic loss but rather to advance the employee's ordinary commercial interests.

Foley generated ringing and angry dissents. In part, the dissents rejected the substance of the majority's arguments. The dissenters thus insisted that the employment relationship is special, that employees are vulnerable strategically and do have a lot to lose, and that society has an interest in the good faith and dignified treatment of employees. The dissents also, and interestingly, emphasized legal process. They called the majority opinion a piece of untrammeled judicial activism and argued that the circumstances of the case rendered this activism particularly illegitimate, from the perspective of the broader political process and legal order.

The last point is worth dwelling on for a moment. Alexander Bickel and Guido Calabresi have developed a view of the interaction between courts and legislatures that recasts democracy to give courts a role in democratic self-government—as opposed to the more familiar role of policing rights that even democratic majorities may not infringe. The basic idea is that legislatures do not, for a variety of reasons (good and bad) capture the will of the people. These reasons turn on the idea that there is legislative inertia (i.e., a legislative bias for the status quo), which means that the failure to change a law—to abandon an old rule and adopt a new

---

26. *Gantt v. Sentry Ins.*, 1 Cal. 4th 1083 (Cal. 1992).

one—does not mean that the old rule has democratic support or legitimacy whereas the new one does not.[27]

This means that a proper role for courts is to act against legislatures to counteract legislative inertia and test whether one rule or another in fact enjoys the democratic support of the people. Courts should thus disfavor old legal rules, for example, or legal rules whose abandonment can be effectively blocked by some or other organized minority.

The majority's decision in *Foley* had the opposite democratic effect. The *Foley* majority acted to strike down a legal rule—the retreat from employment at will—that has the feature that its opponents (business interests) are much better organized and more powerful than its beneficiaries (*un*-organized labor). That cannot be a pro-democratic thing to do.

22.3 SUBSTANTIVE VERSUS PROCEDURAL RIGHTS IN THE EMPLOYMENT CONTRACT

The modifications to employment at will accomplished by contracts implied in fact from employers' management practices—in the face of initial hirings at will and even in the face of repeated re-affirmations of at-will status and disclaimers that practices departing from this status carry contractual intent—merit closer attention. Just what rights do these contracts give employees? In particular, do the implied in fact contracts give the employees *substantive* rights not to be fired save for cause? Or do they merely give employees rights not to be fired in violation of certain *procedures* (so that terminations that follow the appropriate procedures do not constitute breach, even if the procedures reach erroneous substantive judgments concerning employee misconduct)?

Some circumstances support the substantive account. In one case,[28] an employee manual listing forms of misconduct which it characterized as the exclusive grounds for discharge was incorporated into an employment contract, and an employee was found to have a breach of contract claim insofar as she was fired for reasons not on the list. In another,[29] an employee manual giving seniority protection from firing was held contractually to obligate an employer forced to reduce its workforce to lay off the most senior employees last.

The suggestion that the implied in fact doctrine operates to give formerly at-will employees substantive rights may seem natural, if employment contracts are categorized in terms of the dichotomy between employ-

---

27. See Harry Wellington and Alexander Bickel, *Legislative Purpose and the Judicial Process: The Lincoln Mills Case*, 71 HARV. L. REV. 1 (1957); GUIDO CALABRESI, A COMMON LAW FOR THE AGE OF STATUTES (1985).

28. See *Leikvold v. Valley View Hospital*, 141 Ariz. 544, 688 P.2d 170 (1984).

29. See *Ex Parte Amoco Fabrics and Fibers Co.*, 729 So.2d 336 (Ala. 1998). The court reached this result even though the employees were never actually given a copy of the handbook, but rather just told that the policy existed. The court also seems to have relied on the fact that the language was specific and the policy had previously been followed by Amoco.

ment at will and employment that may be terminated only for cause. But nothing in the structure of the doctrine requires this substantive interpretation of implied in fact employment contracts. As the discussion of first-party arbitration in Chapter 21 emphasized, there is no reason why contracting parties cannot bargain not for a substantive term but for a *term-fixing process*, where the process is not an epistemic mechanism for identifying an agreement's antecedently set contents but rather becomes, itself, constitutive of the parties' agreement. And as this chapter's earlier discussion of the rationales for the practices that underwrite the implied in fact contracts at issue emphasized, employees and employers might both have an interest in the procedures associated with good management practices and hence in contractualizing the procedures themselves, quite apart from the outcomes at which these procedures aim.

When approached on this model, the implied in fact contracts established through employee manuals and management practices transform at-will employees not into employees who may be fired only for cause but rather into employees who may be fired (with or without cause) only following the procedures that these manuals and practices establish. The difference matters to the work of courts confronting employees seeking to enforce their implied in fact contractual rights. On the substantive approach, courts function in effect as appellate review of internal employer decisions, conducting an independent inquiry into whether or not a terminated employee engaged in the misconduct alleged against her and also whether or not this misconduct constitutes good cause for the firing. On the procedural approach, courts should conduct only a much more limited inquiry, into whether or not the employer followed its own procedures.

There are good reasons to favor the procedural approach over the substantive. Functionalists might argue that the procedural approach strikes an optimal balance between the interests associated with employer flexibility (lower hiring costs and hence lower structural unemployment, for example) and protecting employees (avoiding exploitation and promoting employment stability and workplace dignity). Functionalists might also observe that the procedural approach substantially reduces the transactions costs associated with adjudication: courts are much better placed to assess whether or not an employer followed its own procedures in terminating an employee than they are to assess the accuracy of employers' substantive conclusions concerning whether or not the employee's conduct constituted good cause for the firing.

Formalists, for their part, can apply many of the ideas about good faith bargaining ex post developed in connection with contracts of adhesion to the context of the employment relation. For many employees, especially those who work for large employers, the at-will status is imposed through a form contract; and the management practices through which employers seek to avoid arbitrary or capricious firings therefore function as analogs of the customer complaint departments through which retailers seek to mitigate the harshness of the terms imposed in their contractual forms. Courts that require even employers who sought to avoid contractualizing their procedures to adhere to them thus impose a kind of good faith requirement on bespoke ex post reciprocal adjustments that are inevitably required to manage conflicts that arise in the shadow of mass-produced, unbargained-over ex ante employment contracts.

The legal doctrines that subject employers to implied-in-fact contractual duties to comply with previously announced personnel policies in effect re-insert individual, reciprocal adjustment—that is, socially integrative bargaining—into employment relations that began as contracts of adhesion. The bargaining is, to be sure, displaced. It is removed from contract formation and performance and appears, instead, in the parties' resolution of disputes concerning breach. It is therefore less transactions costly, because it arises only sometimes, and against a richer informational background than bespoke contracting on the standard model can provide.

Some (but by no means all) courts have indeed responded to the pattern of nominal employment at will combined with management practices that aspire to limit terminations to cases of cause in just the way that this analysis recommends. That is, these courts do *not* impose a *substantive* for-cause standard on the firing decisions of employers who promulgate personnel manuals to nominally at-will employees, but rather by require employers to follow their own *procedures* when they make firing decisions. Such courts vindicate the claims of employees who are fired in violation of their employers' established procedures. But they reject lawsuits by employees who were fired in accordance with their employers' personnel procedures but claim that their employers nevertheless lacked good cause for the firings, in effect because the employers were led by their procedures to draw factually inaccurate conclusions concerning the employees' conduct.

The following case illustrates this approach.

Cotran v. Rollins Hudig Hall International, Inc.

Supreme Court of California, 1998.
948 P.2d 412.

■ BROWN, JUSTICE.

When an employee hired under an *implied* agreement not to be dismissed except for "good cause" is fired for misconduct and challenges the termination in court, what is the role of the jury in deciding whether misconduct occurred? Does it decide whether the acts that led to the decision to terminate happened? Or is its role to decide whether the employer had reasonable grounds for *believing* they happened and otherwise acted fairly? The Courts of Appeal are divided over the question. The majority of California decisions suggest the jury's role is to decide whether the employer concluded misconduct occurred "fairly, honestly, and in good faith." That standard, or variations on it, appears to be the rule in most other jurisdictions as well. But at least one Court of Appeal opinion adopts a more expansive view. It holds the jury must decide whether the alleged misconduct occurred as a *matter of fact*, and places the burden of proving it on the employer.

We granted review to clarify the role of the jury in litigation alleging breach of an implied contract not to terminate employment except for good or just cause, and to resolve the conflict among the Courts of Appeal. The better reasoned view, we conclude, prescribes the jury's role as deciding whether the employer acted with " 'a fair and honest cause or reason, regulated by good faith.' " That language is from *Pugh v. See's Candies, Inc.* (1981) 116 Cal. App. 3d 311 (*Pugh I*), the font of implied-contract-based wrongful termination law in California. Recently, in *Scott v. Pacific Gas & Electric Co.* (1995) 11 Cal. 4th 454, 467(*Scott*), we elaborated on the content of good or just cause by enumerating what it is *not*: reasons that are " 'trivial, capricious, unrelated to business needs or goals, or pretextual.' " (Quoting *Wood v. Loyola Marymount University* (1990) 218 Cal. App. 3d 661.)

Today, we expressly adopt a governing standard that combines the formulations in both *Scott*, *supra*, 11 Cal. 4th at page 467, and *Pugh I*, *supra*, 116 Cal. App. 3d at page 330 (the *Scott–Pugh* standard), elaborating on its meaning and how it should be administered by trial judges to promote the policies underlying implied-contract-based wrongful discharge claims involving employee misconduct. And because the Court of Appeal relied on a substantially similar standard in overturning a jury verdict in favor of the plaintiff-employee in this case and ordering a new trial, we affirm its judgment as well. We disapprove *Wilkerson v. Wells Fargo Bank* (1989) 212 Cal. App. 3d 1217, the only published Court of Appeal decision adopting a broader view of the jury's function in this species of wrongful discharge litigation.

I.   *FACTS AND PROCEDURAL BACKGROUND; ROLLINS'S INVESTIGATION AND THE DECISION TO TERMINATE PLAINTIFF*

In 1987, Rollins Hudig Hall International, Inc. (Rollins), an insurance brokerage firm, approached plaintiff, then a vice-president of a competitor, with a proposal to head its new West Coast international office. Following a series of telephone conferences, meetings and exchanges of letters, plaintiff joined Rollins in January 1988 as senior vice-president and western regional international manager. He held that position until 1993 when he was fired.

The events leading to plaintiff's termination began in March 1993, when an employee in Rollins's international department reported to Deborah Redmond, the firm's director of human resources, that plaintiff was sexually harassing two other employees, Carrie Dolce and Shari Pickett. On March 24, Redmond called both women to her office. In separate interviews, she asked each if they had been harassed. Both said yes; each accused plaintiff as the harasser. Two days later, both women furnished statements to Redmond stating that plaintiff had exposed himself and masturbated in their presence more than once; both also accused plaintiff of making repeated obscene telephone calls to them at home. Redmond sent copies of these statements to Rollins's equal employment opportunity (EEO) office in Chicago. Rollins's president, Fred Feldman, also was given copies. He arranged for a meeting with plaintiff at Rollins's Chicago office, attended by Robert Hurvitz, the firm's head of EEO, and Susan Held, Rollins's manager for EEO compliance. At the meeting, Feldman reviewed the accusations made by Dolce and Pickett against plaintiff. He explained that an investigation would ensue and that its outcome would turn on credibility. After reading the Dolce and Pickett statements to plaintiff, Held explained how the investigation would proceed. Plaintiff said nothing during the meeting about having had consensual relations with either of his two accusers, and offered no explanation for the complaints.

Pending completion of the EEO investigation, Rollins suspended plaintiff. Over the next two weeks, Held interviewed 21 people who had worked with plaintiff, including 5 he had asked her to interview. Held concluded that both Dolce and Pickett, who reiterated the incidents described in their statements, appeared credible. Her investigation failed to turn up anyone else who accused plaintiff of harassing them while at Rollins. One Rollins account executive, Gail Morris, told Held that plaintiff had made obscene telephone calls to her when they both worked for another company, soon after a sexual relationship between the two had ended. Susan Randall, one of those plaintiff had asked to be interviewed and who had described plaintiff as a "perfect gentleman," later called Held to relate "a strange early morning phone call" from plaintiff which "was not for any business purpose." Randall "couldn't figure out what [plaintiff] wanted, yelled at him, told him to leave her alone, and never to call her in the middle of the night again." Held's investigation also confirmed that plaintiff had telephoned Dolce and Pickett at home. In April, both women signed sworn affidavits reciting in detail the charges made against plaintiff in their original statements.

On the basis of her investigation, her assessment of Dolce's and Pickett's credibility, and the fact that no one she interviewed had said it was "impossible" to believe plaintiff had committed the alleged sexual harassment, Held concluded it was more likely than not the harassment had occurred. She met with Feldman and Hurvitz to present her conclusions and gave Feldman copies of the affidavits of Dolce, Pickett, and Gail Morris. After reviewing Held's investigative report and the affidavits, Feldman fired plaintiff on April 23, 1993. This suit followed.

II.   *THE TRIAL*

A.   *Plaintiff's Case; the Defense*

At trial, plaintiff testified he met Dolce in December 1990 when she was employed temporarily at Rollins. After she left, Dolce telephoned plaintiff and suggested they meet socially. The two had lunch several times. Dolce asked plaintiff for a job as a temporary secretary in his department. Plaintiff agreed. Dolce began work at the end of February 1991, becoming a permanent employee in April. In May, plaintiff testified, he and Dolce began an intermittent affair that continued through February 1993. They had sex between six and ten times, including three times at a hotel room plaintiff had reserved for their lunch hour; he produced credit card receipts from the hotel for rooms rented during that period.

As for Pickett, plaintiff testified they had a brief affair from January to April 1992. Plaintiff's mother testified she saw Pickett at her son's house and leave with him a short time later. He was carrying bedding, she testified, and returned two hours later, explaining he had been to his unfurnished condominium nearby. This incident, plaintiff testified, was the first time he and Pickett had sex. Plaintiff's tae kwon do trainer testified he met Pickett at plaintiff's house in February 1992. According to plaintiff, he and Pickett had sex on several occasions before their relationship ended. He began a sexual relationship with his wife-to-be in June 1992. She moved in with him in July, and they were married in October. During this time, plaintiff continued his sexual liaison with Dolce, but not with Pickett. He had not disclosed these liaisons during the Chicago interview with Feldman because he was upset, "frightened," and felt "ambushed." Plaintiff presented additional evidence through several witnesses suggesting Dolce had been "flirtatious" in front of others, that both she and Pickett were angry because he had been "two-timing" them, and that Dolce's real motive was to force plaintiff to grant her a substantial raise in pay. Indeed, more than one of plaintiff's witnesses testified that on the same day plaintiff met in Chicago with Feldman and other Rollins executives to discuss the allegations against him, Dolce faxed him a proposal seeking a substantial pay increase.

Rollins called Dolce as a witness. She testified in detail about the masturbation incidents at the office and in plaintiff's car, and the obscene telephone calls described in her affidavit. In the fall of 1992, Dolce testified, she discovered plaintiff had been "doing exactly the same thing[s]" to Pickett. She never had sex with plaintiff, never went to his house, was never with him in a hotel room. Pickett testified to the similar incidents described in her affidavit; she denied ever having sex with plaintiff. Employees involved in Rollins's EEO investigation also testified. Rollins's president, Feldman, testified that in addition to the affidavits of Dolce and Pickett, he relied on Gail Morris's affidavit in deciding to discharge plaintiff. Over Rollins's objection, the trial court ruled Gail Morris's affidavit hearsay and inadmissible.

B. *The Jury Instructions and Verdict*

Rollins defended its decision to fire plaintiff on the ground that it had been reached honestly and in good faith, not that Rollins was required to prove the acts of sexual harassment occurred. Plaintiff objected to Rollins's defense theory, and the trial court rejected it as not available in a breach of contract action, the only one of plaintiff's claims to go to the jury. Boiled down, the trial judge remarked, the case was nothing more than "a contract dispute" and it was Rollins's burden to *prove* plaintiff committed the acts that led to his dismissal; "whether [Rollins] in good faith believed [plaintiff] did it is not at issue." THE TRIAL COURT TOLD THE JURY:

"What is at issue is whether the claimed acts took place. The issue for the jury to determine is whether the acts are in fact true. Those are issues that the jury has to determine." The trial court also read the jury BAJI No. 10.13, the standard instruction defining "good cause" in employment discharge litigation. It refused an instruction requested by Rollins directing the jury not to substitute its opinion for the employer's.

The jury returned a special verdict. Asked whether plaintiff "engaged in any of the behavior on which [Rollins] based its decision to terminate plaintiff's employment," it answered "no." It set the present cash value of plaintiff's lost compensation at $1.78 million. Rollins appealed from the judgment entered on the verdict. The Court of Appeal reversed. We granted review to clarify the standard juries apply in wrongful termination litigation to evaluate an employer's "good cause" defense based on employee misconduct. We decide, in other words, the question the jury answers when the discharged employee denies committing the acts that provoked the decision to terminate employment. The question of the jury's role in resolving the related but separate issue of whether the reasons assigned by an employer for termination are legally sufficient to constitute good cause is one we leave for another case.

III. *DISCUSSION*

A. *The Law*

We begin at the beginning. The Court of Appeal opinion in *Pugh I, supra,* 116 Cal. App. 3d 311, recognized that "[t]he terms 'just cause' and 'good cause,' connote 'a fair and honest cause or reason, regulated by good faith on the part of the party exercising the power.' " (*Id.* at p. 330, quoting *R. J. Cardinal Co. v. Ritchie* (1963) 218 Cal. App. 2d 124, 144.) "Care must be taken, however," the *Pugh I* opinion continued, "not to interfere with the legitimate exercise of managerial discretion. And where the employee occupies a sensitive managerial or confidential position, the employer must of necessity be allowed substantial scope for the exercise of subjective judgment." (116 Cal. App. 3d at p. 330, fn. omitted.)

In *Walker v. Blue Cross of California* (1992) 4 Cal. App. 4th 985, the court described "good cause" as "relative. Whether good cause exists is dependent upon the particular circumstances of each case. In deciding whether good cause exists, there must be a balance between the employer's interest in operating its business efficiently and profitably and the employee's interest in continued employment. Care must be exercised so as not to interfere with the employer's legitimate exercise of managerial discretion. While the scope of such discretion is substantial, it is not unrestricted." (*Id.* at p. 994.)

In its posttrial opinion in the *Pugh* litigation—*Pugh v. See's Candies, Inc.* (1988) 203 Cal. App. 3d 743 (*Pugh II*)—the Court of Appeal elaborated on the jurisprudential significance of employer discretion: "[A]n employer must have wide latitude in making independent, good faith judgments about high-ranking employees without the threat of a jury second-guessing its business judgment. Measuring the effective performance of such an employee involves the consideration of many intangible attributes such as personality, initiative, ability to function as part of the management team and to motivate subordinates, and the ability to conceptualize and effectuate management style and goals. *Although the jury must assess the legitimacy of the employer's decision to discharge, it should not be thrust into a managerial role.*" (*Id.* at p. 769, italics added.)

These statements are helpful in the sense that, by articulating legal policies immanent in the employment relationship, they point the way to the appropriate standard. They do not, however, answer directly the question before us—*what* does the trier of fact decide in evaluating a defense based on employee misconduct? Before the Court of Appeal opinion in this case, California law on the point was comparatively undeveloped. A lone published Court of Appeal decision, however—*Wilkerson v. Wells Fargo Bank*, *supra*, 212 Cal. App. 3d 1217 (*Wilkerson*)—had wrestled directly with the issue. In *Wilkerson*, the court held that in a wrongful termination suit by an employee terminable only for good cause, the employer must prove, as part of its defense burden, that the misconduct leading to dismissal actually occurred. That is, *Wilkerson* directs the jury to reexamine the facts on which the employer relied in terminating the employee and, if it finds them erroneous, to award damages.

"[I]n contract law," the court in *Wilkerson* reasoned, "the belief of the breaching party does not determine whether a breach of the contract occurred. Obviously, a defaulting borrower's good faith belief he or she has repaid a loan is not a defense to a lender's claim for payment. Similarly, an employer's subjective belief it possessed good cause does not dispose of a wrongfully discharged employee's claim for breach of contract. [A]n employer's belief is not a substitute for good cause. For that reason, the employer's broad latitude does not extend to being *factually* incorrect. If an employer claims the employee was discharged for specific misconduct, and the employee denies the charge, the question of *whether the misconduct occurred is one of fact for the jury.* (*Pugh v. See's Candies, Inc.*, *supra*, 203 Cal. App. 3d at p. 767.)" (212 Cal. App. 3d at p. 1230, second italics added.)

This quotation from *Wilkerson*, *supra*, 212 Cal. App. 3d at page 1230— asserting a proposition central to plaintiff's contention, that we should overturn the Court of Appeal's judgment—misreads the passage from *Pugh II*, *supra*, 203 Cal. App. 3d 743, 767, on which it relies. More importantly, it suggests a misunderstanding of the policies identified in our cases as supporting implied-contract-based wrongful termination claims. The first point—that *Wilkerson* misreads the passage from *Pugh II* on which it relied for the proposition that "the employer's broad latitude does not extend to being *factually* incorrect"—was convincingly made in Justice Miriam Vogel's opinion herein for the Court of Appeal. She pointed out that although *Wilkerson* had relied exclusively on *Pugh II*, that part of the *Pugh II* opinion actually cited as authority is a quotation from a Michigan case— *Toussaint v. Blue Cross & Blue Shield of Mich.* (1980) 408 Mich. 579 (*Toussaint*). "What this means," Justice Vogel concluded, "is that *Wilkerson* is based on *Toussaint*, not on *Pugh II*." We agree.

The decision of a sharply divided court, *Toussaint, supra,* 292 N.W.2d 880, is known and cited principally as Michigan's equivalent of California's *Pugh I, supra,* 116 Cal. App. 3d 311, that is, the case in which the Michigan Supreme Court adopted the rule that an implied-in-fact "good cause" term can limit the common law at-will employment rule. (*Toussaint, supra,* 292 N.W.2d at p. 885; cf. *Foley v. Interactive Data Corp., supra,* 47 Cal. 3d 654, 676.) The *Toussaint* majority went further, however, and took up the question of *who*—employer or trier of fact—decides whether the misconduct leading to the decision to terminate employment occurred. (*Toussaint, supra,* at pp. 895–896.) In concluding the issue of specific misconduct—"did the employee do what the employer said he did?"—was "one of fact for the jury," the *Toussaint* majority posits that a "promise to terminate employment for cause only would be illusory if the employer were permitted to be the sole judge and final arbiter of the propriety of the discharge. There must be some review of the employer's decision if the [good] cause contract is to be distinguished from the satisfaction contract." (*Toussaint, supra,* 292 N.W.2d at pp. 896, 895, fn. omitted.)

Unlike the majority in *Toussaint,* we do not believe permitting juries to decide the factual basis for allegations of employee misconduct is the only way to give meaning and substance to an employer's promise to terminate for "good cause," or that barring such factfinding leaves for-cause provisions toothless. Judicial review of decisions to terminate employees subject to such provisions for misconduct *is* vital; however, de novo jury review of the factual basis supporting the employer's decision is neither the only alternative to a "no review" standard, nor the one best adapted to adjust the competing interests of employer and employee.

Instead of adopting the de novo rule set forth in *Toussaint, supra,* 292 N.W.2d 880, and followed by the Court of Appeal in *Wilkerson, supra,* 212 Cal. App. 3d 1217, we adopt a different standard under which the jury assesses the factual basis for the decision to terminate employment. The standard crafted by a number of state high courts which have confronted the issue and rejected the *Toussaint* solution demonstrates that a middle ground—combining a balanced regard for the employee's interest in continuing employment with the employer's interest in efficient personnel decisions—exists. As we explain, these courts have arrived at a standard under which the jury's role is to assess the *objective reasonableness* of the employer's factual determination of misconduct.

In concluding it is the employer that decides whether acts of an employee amounting to just cause have occurred—and that the role of the jury is to assess, through the lens of an objective standard, the reasonableness of that decision under the circumstances known to the employer at the time it was made—these courts have relied for analytical support on the contract model of the employment relationship out of which contemporary limitations on the at-will doctrine arose. An Oregon decision, *Simpson v. Western Graphics Corp.* (1982) 293 Or. 96 (*Simpson*), typifies the reasoning of these cases.

In *Simpson, supra*, 643 P.2d 1276, three employees were fired for allegedly threatening a fellow worker. They denied making the threats and filed suit. The trial court found the employer had acted in good faith after a reasonable investigation, refused to make a finding whether the threats had *in fact* been made, and entered judgment for the employer. The Oregon Supreme Court granted review "to consider whether by agreeing to discharge employees only for 'just cause,' a private employer also relinquishes its right to determine whether facts constituting just cause exist." (*Id.* at p. 1278.) Analyzing the contractual origin of the employment relationship, the *Simpson* opinion concluded there was no basis to infer that "the employer *intended to surrender its power to determine whether facts constituting cause for termination exist. In the absence of any evidence of express or implied agreement whereby the employer contracted away its fact-finding prerogative, we shall not infer it.*" (*Id.* at p. 1279, italics added.)

The reasoning of *Simpson, supra*, 643 P.2d 1276, was relied on by the Nevada Supreme Court in *Southwest Gas v. Vargas* (1995) 111 Nev. 1064 [901 P.2d 693] (*Vargas*). There the plaintiff employee was fired for sexually harassing a coworker. After he prevailed at trial, the employer appealed. Addressing "the role of the trier of fact in determining whether an employer's stated reasons for terminating an employee with a long-term employment contract amount to good cause," (*id.* at p. 698) the Nevada Supreme Court rejected the argument that the jury reviews de novo the factual basis for the employer's decision and reversed the trial court's judgment. Citing *Simpson*, the *Vargas* opinion discusses some of the concerns raised by an instruction directing the jury to reexamine the factual accuracy supporting the employer's decision to terminate employment.

"[A]llowing a jury to trump the factual findings of an employer that an employee has engaged in misconduct rising to the level of 'good cause' for discharge, made in good faith and in pursuit of legitimate business objectives, is a highly undesirable prospect," the Nevada high court said. (*Vargas, supra*, 901 P.2d at p. 699.) "In effect, such a system would create the equivalent of a preeminent fact-finding board unconnected to the challenged employer, that would have the ultimate right to determine anew whether the employer's decision to terminate an employee was based upon an accurate finding of misconduct. This ex officio 'fact-finding board,' unattuned to the practical aspects of employee suitability over which it would exercise consummate power, and unexposed to the entrepreneurial risks that form a significant basis of every state's economy, would be empowered to impose substantial monetary consequences on employers whose employee termination decisions are found wanting." (*Ibid.*)

The opinion of the Washington Supreme Court in *Baldwin v. Sisters of Providence in Washington* (1989) 112 Wn.2d 127 [769 P.2d 298] (*Baldwin*), demonstrates how these courts have both adopted the contract model of just cause analysis and conjoined with it a requirement that the employer adhere to—and juries apply—an "objective" good faith standard in deciding whether just cause exists to terminate employment. *Baldwin* was a wrongful termination case involving a hospital employee with a "just cause" contract fired for sexually abusing a patient. The high court first applied traditional contract principles. Finding no contract basis for concluding the employer's fact-finding prerogative had been transferred elsewhere, either unilaterally or by agreement, it held that "an employer's agreement to restrict discharges to those supported by just cause should not be followed by a further judicial implication which takes the determination of just cause away from the employer." (*Id.* at p. 304.)

Although the *Baldwin* court thus endorsed the view that the power to decide whether acts amounting to misconduct had occurred continued to reside with the employer, it went on to apply a supplemental standard of "just cause." The court's opinion describes that standard as one which "checks the subjective good faith of the employer with an *objective* reasonable belief standard." (769 P.2d at p. 304, italics added.) " '[J]ust cause,' " the *Baldwin* opinion holds—echoing the formulation in *Pugh I, supra,* 116 Cal. App. 3d at page 330—is not only "a fair and honest cause or reason, regulated by good faith," but—presaging our subsequent formulation in *Scott, supra,* 11 Cal. 4th at page 467—is "one which is not for [an] arbitrary, capricious, or illegal reason and which is based on facts (1) supported by substantial evidence and (2) reasonably believed by the employer to be true." (769 P.2d at p. 304.)

In *Kestenbaum v. Pennzoil Co.* (1988) 108 N.M. 20, the New Mexico Supreme Court adopted a standard much like the majority rule exemplified by *Simpson, Vargas,* and *Baldwin.* The trial court had refused an instruction offered by the employer that it need only show a "good faith belief" that employee misconduct had occurred. (*Id.* at p. 287.) Although it rejected the *unqualified* "good faith belief" standard urged by the employer, the court framed a "middle position" between instructing that "an employer only is required to demonstrate a good faith *belief* that cause existed to terminate [and instructing] that the employer must prove good cause *in fact.*" (*Ibid.,* italics added.) According to the opinion in *Kestenbaum,* the jury had been properly instructed that the issue was whether the employer "had *reasonable grounds to believe* that sufficient cause existed to justify [the employee's] termination." (*Ibid.,* italics added.)

Because Pennzoil's proposed instruction suggested a jury "could find good cause from the employer's *subjective* good faith belief as opposed to an *objective* standard of reasonable belief," it would have been error to so instruct. (766 P.2d at p. 288, italics added.) On the other hand, the court said, "the jury could have absolved Pennzoil of liability under its implied contract provided [it] had *reasonable grounds to believe* that sufficient cause existed to justify his termination." (*Id.* at p. 287, italics added.)

In addition to the answer yielded by formal contract principles, pragmatic considerations support what the *Kestenbaum* opinion calls the "middle position." As several courts have pointed out, a standard permitting juries to reexamine the factual basis for the decision to terminate for misconduct—typically gathered under the exigencies of the workaday world and without benefit of the slow-moving machinery of a contested trial—

dampens an employer's willingness to act, intruding on the "wide latitude" the court in *Pugh II* recognized as a reasonable condition for the efficient conduct of business. (See, e.g., *Vargas, supra,* 901 P.2d at p. 699.) We believe the *Wilkerson–Toussaint* standard is too intrusive, that it tips unreasonably the balance between the conflicting interests of employer and employee that California courts have sought to sustain as a hallmark of the state's modern wrongful termination employment law. (See, e.g., *Pugh II, supra,* 203 Cal. App. 3d at p. 769; see also cases cited, *ante,* at p. 100.)

Equally significant is the jury's relative remoteness from the everyday reality of the workplace. The decision to terminate an employee for misconduct is one that not uncommonly implicates organizational judgment and may turn on intractable factual uncertainties, even where the grounds for dismissal are fact specific. If an employer is required to have in hand a signed confession or an eyewitness account of the alleged misconduct before it can act, the workplace will be transformed into an adjudicatory arena and effective decisionmaking will be thwarted. Although these features do not justify a rule permitting employees to be dismissed arbitrarily, they do mean that asking a civil jury to reexamine in all its factual detail the triggering cause of the decision to dismiss—including the retrospective accuracy of the employer's comprehension of that event—months or even years later, in a context distant from the imperatives of the workplace, is at odds with an axiom underlying the jurisprudence of wrongful termination. That axiom, clearly enunciated in *Pugh II, supra,* 203 Cal. App. 3d at page 769, is the need for a sensible latitude for managerial decisionmaking and its corollary, an optimum balance point between the employer's interest in organizational efficiency and the employee's interest in continuing employment.

Plaintiff argues that withdrawing from the jury the factual issue underlying the decision to terminate employment will destroy the protections afforded by the implied good cause contract term. It will permit the discharge decision to be based on subjective reasons, the argument runs, reasons that may be pretextual, and mask arbitrary and unlawful motives made practically unreviewable by a standardless "good faith" rule. But as we have tried to show, this argument is founded on a misunderstanding of the nature and effect of an *objective* good faith standard. The rule we endorse today, carefully framed as a jury instruction and honestly administered, will not only *not* have the effects plaintiff claims, but by balancing the interests of *both* parties, will ensure that "good cause" dismissals continue to be scrutinized by courts and juries under an objective standard, without infringing more than necessary on the freedom to make efficient business decisions. At least one state high court has reasoned that striking a fair balance between the interests of the parties to the employment contract through an objective just-cause standard will *promote* the continued use of such limitations on the at-will doctrine; imbalances, on the other hand, encourage employers to adopt defensive measures by "remov[ing] such [just-cause] provisions from their [employment] handbooks." (*Baldwin, supra,* 769 P.2d at p. 304.)

The proper inquiry for the jury, in other words, is not, "Did the employee *in fact* commit the act leading to dismissal?" It is, "Was the factual basis on which the employer concluded a dischargeable act had been committed reached honestly, after an appropriate investigation and for reasons that are not arbitrary or pretextual?" The jury conducts a factual inquiry in both cases, but the questions are not the same. In the first, the jury decides the ultimate truth of the employee's alleged misconduct. In the second, it focuses on the *employer's response* to allegations of misconduct. Thus, to follow the Nevada Supreme Court in *Vargas*, we "reaffirm our prior rulings that employers are obligated to act in good faith and upon a reasonable belief that good cause for terminating a for-cause employee exists." (901 P.2d at p. 700; see also *Pugh I*, *supra*, 116 Cal. App. 3d at p. 330 ["'[t]he term[] 'good cause'" "connote[s] 'a fair and honest cause or reason, regulated by good faith.' "].)

B. *The Governing Standard*

It was the precedents from other jurisdictions discussed above— *Simpson*, *Vargas*, *Baldwin*, and *Kestenbaum*—on which Justice Miriam Vogel based her opinion for the Court of Appeal, identifying a handful of considerations relevant to the jury's resolution of an employer's defense that an employee terminable only for good cause was properly dismissed for misconduct. We give operative meaning to the term "good cause" in the context of implied employment contracts by defining it, under the combined *Scott–Pugh* standard (*ante*, at p. 96), as fair and honest reasons, regulated by good faith on the part of the employer, that are not trivial, arbitrary or capricious, unrelated to business needs or goals, or pretextual. A reasoned conclusion, in short, supported by substantial evidence gathered through an adequate investigation that includes notice of the claimed misconduct and a chance for the employee to respond.

The law of wrongful discharge is largely a creature of the common law. Hence, it would be imprudent to specify in detail the essentials of an adequate investigation. It is better, we believe, to adhere to the common law's incremental, case-by-case jurisprudence, adjusting the standard as its sufficiency is tested in practice. Two descriptions, however—one from turn-of-the-century English common law, the other from an opinion of this court only a little over twenty years ago—provide a sense of what investigative fairness in this context contemplates. In *Board of Education v. Rice* (1911) App. Cas. 179, 182, Lord Halsbury, describing the duties of a school board in resolving a claim of salary discrimination, wrote: "I need not add that [the board] must act in good faith and fairly listen to both sides, for that is a duty lying upon every one who decides anything. But I do not think they are bound to treat such a question as though it were a trial. They can obtain information in any way they think best, always giving a fair opportunity to those who are parties in the controversy for correcting or contradicting any relevant statement prejudicial to their view."

Closer to home, Justice Tobriner wrote on behalf of a unanimous court in *Pinsker v. Pacific Coast Society of Orthodontists* (1974) 12 Cal. 3d 541, that "[t]he common law requirement of a fair procedure does not compel formal proceedings with all the embellishments of a court trial [citation], nor adherence to a single mode of process. It may be satisfied by any one of a variety of procedures which afford a fair opportunity for an applicant to present his position. [T]his court should not attempt to fix a rigid procedure that must invariably be observed." (*Id.* at p. 555; see also Friendly, *"Some Kind of Hearing"* (1975) 123 U. Pa. L.Rev. 1267, 1269–1270, fn. 10 ["The precise content of the common law 'fair procedure' requirement is far more flexible than that which the Supreme Court has found to be mandated by due process."].)

All of the elements of the governing standard are triable to the jury.

IV. *THE DISPOSITION*

Because it was error to instruct that Rollins could prevail only if the jury was satisfied sexual harassment actually occurred, the case must be retried. On retrial, the jury should be instructed, in accordance with the views we have expressed, that the question critical to defendants' liability is not whether plaintiff in fact sexually harassed other employees, but whether at the time the decision to terminate his employment was made, defendants, acting in good faith and following an investigation that was appropriate under the circumstances, had reasonable grounds for believing plaintiff had done so.

We also conclude that a handful of additional issues resolved by the Court of Appeal which plaintiff seeks to reargue here—the admissibility of the Gail Morris affidavit, whether the existence *vel non* of an implied good cause term in plaintiff's employment agreement was an issue that should have gone to the jury, and whether the trial court erred in not instructing on the statutory presumption of employment at will—do not warrant review by this court. Although we have not formally limited the scope of our review in this cause, that does not affect our power to consider "any or all" of the issues addressed by the Court of Appeal.

The judgment of the Court of Appeal is affirmed.

■ GEORGE, C. J., BAXTER, J., WERDEGAR, J., and CHIN, J., concurred.

* * *

In *Cotran*, an otherwise at-will employee, referencing personnel policies, sued his employer for firing him in response to purportedly erroneous allegations of sexual harassment. The Supreme Court of California limited judicial review of the employer's actions to "deciding whether the employer acted with a fair and honest cause or reason, regulated by good faith." Thus, the court held that that it was error to instruct the jury to find for the employee if it concluded that he had not, in fact, committed the harassment. In other words, it was error to instruct the jury to find for the employee unless he had in fact been fired for good cause. Instead, the fact-finder should determine only whether the employer had honored its own procedures in reaching its decision to discharge the employee. The High Court thus agreed with a lower court's argument that "[t]o require an employer to be 'right' about the facts on which it bases its decision to terminate an employee is to interfere with the 'wide latitude' an employer must have 'in making independent, good faith judgments about high-ranking employees without the threat of a jury second-guessing its business judgment.' "[30]

To be sure, the *Cotran* court (like many others in analogous cases) spoke in terms of an employer's "appropriate investigation" into the facts, leaving it open that appropriateness establishes a mandatory standard requiring, for example, "substantial evidence gathered through an adequate investigation that includes notice of the claimed misconduct and a chance for the employee to respond." In this case, the *Cotran* rule would have the same practical effect as a rule granting employees protection against all but good-cause firings.

But both the internal logic of the *Cotran* opinion and the immanent structure of contract law recommend a different approach, according to which the meaning of "appropriate" is itself fixed by the parties' contract, and in particular by the employers' personnel policies, so that a right in the procedure is really no more than a right in the procedure. Justice Mosk, concurring in *Cotran*, recognized this. He observed that the majority's "appropriate investigation" standard should be treated not as mandatory but as "the likely bargain struck by an employer and an employee in an implied contract not to terminate except for good cause." And he added that

> there is nothing, of course, in the majority's standard that precludes an employer and an employee from negotiating or impliedly forming a contract with a 'good cause' clause that defines the term more explicitly, in which case the jury's good cause determination would be shaped by this contractual definition. For example, the contract may spell out in greater detail the due process protections enjoyed by the employee. In short, the majority's definition of 'good cause' is a 'default' definition that applies only in the absence of more specific contractual provisions.

The difference between the substantive approach to implied in fact contracts that abandon employment at will—namely, that personnel manuals convert at-will employees into employees who may be discharged only for good cause—and the procedural approach—namely, that such manuals give employees rights only in the personnel procedures that they an-

---

30. Other courts have reached similar results. See, e.g., *Garvey v. Buhler*, 430 N.W. 2d 616 (Wis. App. 1988); *Simpson v. Western Graphics Corp.*, 643 P.2d 1276 (Ore. 1982); *Kestenbaum v. Pennzoil Co.*, 766 P.2d 280 (N.M. 1988); *Baldwin v. Sisters of Providence in Washington* 769 P.2d 298 (Wash. 1989); *Gaglidari v. Denny's Restaurants, Inc.*, 815 P.2d 1362 (Wash. 1991); *Southwest Gas v. Vargas*, 901 P.2d 693 (Nev. 1995).

At the same time, other jurisdictions have taken an opposed view, namely that personnel manuals announcing employee management procedures establish for-cause rights in previously at will employees, so that judicial review should extend to whether a fired employee actually did the thing that was the ground of his firing. See, e.g., Toussaint v. Blue Cross & Blue Shield of Michigan, 292 N.W.2d 880 (Mich. 1980); *Sanders v.Parker Drilling Co.*, 911 F.2d 191 (9th Cir. 1990).

nounce—reveals something extremely important about contractual solidarity in employment relations, and in particular about the ways in which the law might manage contracts in this area in order to support such solidarity.

The substantive view treats the right to be fired only for-cause as a matter of substantive justice and treats judicial intervention in the employment relation as an effort to intervene in the parties' negotiations on the side of justice. The personnel procedures that employee manuals announce become, on this view, merely a technology for ascertaining what justice requires in particular cases (whether or not a there was good cause for a particular firing). They function as substitutes for adjudication—perhaps on the model of contractually agreed third-party arbitration. And it therefore becomes natural to assess personnel procedures in terms of how closely they track the procedures that courts themselves would employ in making factual findings concerning good cause. As Lauren Edelman—focusing principally on internal grievance procedures concerning employment discrimination but expressly including procedures to assess whether an employee firing was for-cause—has observed, personnel procedures "appear rational because they *look like* the system of appeals available in the public legal process, a basic and well-institutionalized feature of a legitimate normative order."[31] Finally, it becomes natural to criticize courts that defer to decisions that employers have made following their procedures on the ground that this makes the employer a judge in his own case. As one dissenting California appellate court put the point, "the belief of the breaching party does not determine whether a breach of the contract occurred. Obviously, a defaulting borrower's good faith belief he or she has repaid a loan is not a defense to a lender's claim for payment. Similarly, an employer's subjective belief it possessed good cause does not dispose of a wrongfully discharged employee's claim for breach of contract."[32] The court therefore concluded, unsurprisingly given its starting point, that the employer's procedures were no substitute for independent fact-finding: "If an employer claims the employee was discharged for specific misconduct, and the employee denies the charge, the question of whether the misconduct occurred is one of fact for the jury."[33]

This would all be perfectly sensible if employees had an effectively noncontractual right (either a statutory right or a very hard to wave, quasi-mandatory, contractual right) to be fired only for cause. It also makes sense where an employment contract, instead of announcing procedures to regulate employee discipline and termination, establishes a substantive right to be fired only for cause. In these cases employers' personnel procedures could hardly be anything but a method for determining whether or not cause to fire exists and, like internal review procedures for employment

---

31. Lauren Edelman, Christopher Uggen, and Howard Erlanger, *The Endogeneity of Legal Regulation: Grievance Procedures and Rational Myth*, 105 Am. J. Soc. 406, 416 (1999). For the analogy between procedures concerning employment discrimination and those concerning employment at will see id., at 447–48.

32. *Wilkerson v. Wells Fargo Bank*, 212 Cal. App. 3d 1217, 1230 (1989).

33. Id.

discrimination, they could not possibly substitute adequately for third-party adjudication as a process for protecting what are, after all, substantive employee rights whose origins may even lie in law rather than just in a contractual bargain.

But matters look very different if the analysis begins from the position that there is no non-contractual right to be fired only for cause, that the grounds for firings are a matter for employers and employees to bargain over, and that employer personnel procedures should be understood as the product of such a bargain, and hence (where personnel manuals emphasize procedures only) as constitutive of employees' rights. On this view, the procedures do not function as substitutes for third-party adjudication—how could they, given that there is no procedure-independent right to adjudicate—but rather as extensions, and indeed intensifications, of pre-contractual bargaining between employers and employees. Nor should this characterization of personnel procedures be surprising. Employers resort to procedures, after all, rather than just announcing substantive grounds for discharge, at least in part because the precise contours of these substantive grounds are impossible to specify in advance of particular cases. And each particular case is, therefore, naturally at least in part a negotiation between the employer and the employee concerning whether or not the employee's conduct was acceptable.

Courts, moreover, view their engagements with employer personnel manuals in just this light—not as inserting third-party decision-making into the employment relation but rather as an effort to protect and indeed to promote bargaining, especially in the shadow of a probably adhesive initial employment contract. Indeed, courts requiring employers to honor the procedures announced in their personnel manuals have sometimes even expressly treated these manuals—although they were nominally imposed as adhesive forms by employers—as the result of bargaining between the employer and his employees.[34] The line of doctrine set out above may thus be understood as an effort to give legal recognition to bargaining that actually occurs in the employment relation even where an employer's adhesive forms seek to deny this bargaining any legal effect. The doctrine functions, in other words, to require employers to conform their management of the employment relation—at least in respect of its termination—to rules that have previously been made public between them and their employees following actual or even only hypothetical bargaining (recall that efforts to reserve a right to fire without process may be invalidated if they do not fall within the reasonable expectations of employees), and to the reciprocal adjustment that bargaining involves. The doctrine requires employers to give employees opportunities to be heard and to adjust their own conduct to what the employees say, that is, to treat the employees' points of

---

34. See, e.g., *Woolley v. Hoffmann–LaRoche, Inc.*, 491 A.2d 1257, 1264 (N.J. 1985) ("While the employer viewed a collective bargaining agreement as an intrusion on management prerogatives, it recognized in addition to the advantages of an employment manual to both sides, that unless this kind of company manual were given to the workforce, collective bargaining, and the agreements that result from collective bargaining, would more likely take place.") This led the *Woolley* court to treat the manual as the result of bargaining.

view as free-standing constraints on their administration of the employment relation. The doctrine thus re-constitutes a nominally adhesive arrangement as one that embraces—not everywhere but specifically at its greatest points of stress—the richer and more concrete forms of engagement and recognition associated with bespoke contracting, and in particular with the pre-contractual negotiations by which bespoke contracts are established.

Courts dealing with employer personnel manuals in this way thus hold insistently to a bargain-based model of social integration: it is not just that they assess the manuals' announcements concerning personnel procedures on the model of a bargain; they also, and critically, address the procedures themselves as negotiations, that is, as standing in for the socially integrative negotiations that the nominally adhesive form of the employee manuals seeks to deny legal recognition. Courts thus intervene, in this area, not to decide the negotiations' outcomes but rather to protect the negotiating process—that is, to require employers to apply their own procedures—so that they negotiate, as it were, in good faith.

This analysis will not satisfy those who wish to use employment law to adjust the relative power of capital and labor in the service of achieving substantial justice (perhaps returning to the model of employment discrimination law, which provides substantive protections against discrimination through imposing mandatory standards on all employers). Insofar as substantial justice requires that employees be discharged only for good cause, achieving substantial justice requires that employer personnel procedures make (at least reasonably) accurate determinations concerning cause and that courts defer to these procedures only insofar as they are reliable. When actual courts reject this approach in favor of one that understands the personnel procedures that employers provide as constitutive of employees' employment rights—not as substitutes for adjudication but rather as negotiations, which is to say as sites of contractual solidarity—injustice will occur. But that should come as no surprise. Contract does not aim at producing substantial justice. That is why freedom of contract is recognized even in spite of unjust starting points, so that contract operates as a free-standing source of social solidarity, which can lauder prior injustices. The dominant case-law recognizing implied-in-fact contracts in the employment context may be read as an effort to extend contracts' capacity to integrate in this way.

22.4   CONCLUSION

There is a great deal at stake—both practically and theoretically—in the doctrines and disputes that govern employment at will.

Some basic facts emphasize the practical importance of the doctrines discussed in this chapter. In developed societies, the single greatest source of wealth for most people is their human capital, and this is overwhelmingly invested in their jobs. Furthermore, many employees make firm specific investments in human capital—that is, they develop skills that make them more productive in their own firm than in other firms. This gives such employees a substantial interest in the specific jobs that they currently hold. Finally, the employment relation is complex at every point in time and constantly developing over time. This makes contracts governing employment unusually incomplete, so that even default rules of law will be sticky and hence retain a substantial impact over the actual governance of the employment relation. The legal doctrines that apply to the employment contract thus have a substantial impact on both aggregate wealth and on the distribution of wealth in modern economies.

Moreover, in spite of its importance, the law governing the employment contract is not well understood by most American workers. Surveys suggest that substantial supermajorities of workers who were hired as at will employees nevertheless believe that they may be fired only for cause.[35] It is not clear *why* American workers hold this belief. One possible explanation looks to management practices discussed earlier in these pages, under which even employers who seek to retain the legal right to fire employees at will nevertheless generally employ cause-based standards in making actual employment decisions. Another possible explanation concerns the enormous economic importance of work to workers and the natural sense, among citizens of democratic, rule-of-law societies, that institutions that control decisions concerning such important matters should be bound to make them rationally and fairly. (Recall the tenor of Edelman's sociology of human resources departments.) It is worth noting, in this connection, that non-American legal systems have generally incorporated these intuitions into the legal regulation of employment. In fact, the United States is the only major industrialized nation to have embraced employment at will.

Finally, and in contrast to much of contract law, the law of the employment relation has seen substantial doctrinal changes in recent years. *Forrer* was decided in 1967. By 2012, a study could report that 40 states and the District of Columbia recognized a tort cause of action for a firing in violation of public policy[36] (and 21 of these appear to allow punitive damages under that theory), 43 states recognized implied in fact contracts based on personnel manuals,[37] and 9 states recognized claims based on the

---

35. See, e.g., Forbes and Jones, *A Comparative, Attitudinal, and Analytical Study of At-Will Employees Without Cause*, 37 LABOR LAW JOURNAL 157 (1986) and Pauline Kim, *Norms, Learning, and the Law: Exploring the Influences on Workers' Legal Knowledge*, 1999 U ILL. L. REV. 447.

36. JOHN F. BUCKLEY, et. al. 2012 STATE BY STATE GUIDE TO HUMAN RESOURCES LAW (2012). § 5.03, Table 5–3. Note that in Arizona this is by statute. In the District of Columbia, the violation of public policy covers only employees' refusal to violate a statute. In Ohio, a "public policy claim [is] not available to employees under contract, such as collective bargaining agreement". In Texas, it "[a]pplies when employee is discharged for refusing to commit an illegal act and when employee is discharged primarily so that employer can avoid contributing to or paying benefits from a pension fund."

37. BUCKLEY, § 5.02, Table 5–1. States with indications of unusual treatment are Indiana, in which employees "may have to provide additional independent consideration"; Montana, where a 1987 law protecting at-will employees from "discharge without cause . . .

application of the implied in law covenant of good faith and fair dealing applied in the context of the employment relation. By contrast, the 1994 version of the same study reported almost identical results with respect to the first two causes of action but also reported that 17 states recognized claims based on the application of the implied in law covenant of good faith and fair dealing applied in the context of the employment relation.[38] The employment contract is thus an area in which great material interests are at stake, and the law is in flux, as employee rights expand but also contract.

The employment contract is theoretically important because it tests certain structural limits of freedom of contract. Contract is, as these materials have repeatedly emphasized, distinctive for being *chosen* obligation: contracts are creatures of the intentions of the contracting parties; they are directly willed into existence.

The employment relation is created, initially, in just this intentional way: employees and employers agree to be bound to work and to pay wages. But the employment relation also and necessarily has an ongoing and organically developing character. The precise duties of employees and employers cannot possibly be specified in advance but must instead be settled (negotiated?) as the joint project of creating the products of the firm progresses. Employers must, that is, be permitted to manage their employees, and employees must be permitted to work. Indeed, discretion within the employment relation is one of the reasons for the existence of the firm. As the Coasean theory of the firm explains, the firm boundary reflects the balance of transactions costs between coordinating conduct through discretionary management on the one hand and through arm's length contracting on the other. Where coordination through management is more efficient, decisions tend to be taken within the firm.

This suggests that obligations arise within the firm, and hence within the employment relation, on a non-contractual model. They arise, that is, not because they are directly intended into existence but rather involuntarily, in response to the imperatives of efficient managerial coordination. Indeed, as the discussion of implied in fact contracts in this chapter illustrates, obligations associated with employment may arise even in the face of intentions that they should not. These obligations—for example, obligations to follow established management practices before terminating even employees hired at will—may be called contractual, in the sense that they are governed by and enforced through contract law. But they are not in fact formally contractual at all, because they are imposed against rather than created by the intentions of those whom they obligate. The implied in

preempts all other causes of action arising from terminating at-will employees"; New York, where an implied contract based on personnel manuals is deemed to exist if the manual "express[es] [a] limitation on employer's right to terminate"; and, South Carolina, where a 2004 state law determines that "an employee handbook cannot create a contract of employment where there is a disclaimer meeting statutory requirements".

38. See 1 STEWART MACAULEY et.al., CONTRACTS: LAW IN ACTION 486–87 (1995) citing JOHN F. BUCKLEY, et. al. 1994 STATE BY STATE GUIDE TO HUMAN RESOURCES LAW (1994).

fact contracts described in these pages thus represent not an expression of but rather a limit on freedom of contract.

The nature of the limit is worth reflecting on and may be understood by contrasting the limits on employer discretion to terminate nominally at-will employees associated with implied in fact contracts on the one hand and with public policy on the other.

The doctrine that prohibits terminating even at will employees for grounds that violate public policy represents a straightforward limit on freedom of contract, imposed from without the contract relation, based on norms that apply, mandatorily, to all persons. The analogy to employment discrimination law once again illustrates this character of the public policy doctrine: just as employers are straightforwardly not free to discriminate, so they are straightforwardly not free to take other actions that would subvert the common good. There is no surprise in this. Like every other freedom, freedom of contract is not absolute.

The limits on freedom of contract associated with implied in fact promises established through management practice are quite different, and much subtler. These limits are not imposed on the employment relation from without. Rather, they are imposed on the contractual part of the employment relation by other aspects of the relation itself. The tendency of management practices to bind even employers who intend not to be bound reveals that when relationships become sufficiently complicated, intensive, and adaptive, they tend organically to develop their own, internal regulative ideals. These ideals cannot be captured or cabined by the intentions of the parties to the relationships, and certainly not by the *ex ante* intentions through which the relationships were initially commenced. The success of the relationship requires that these regulative ideals be respected, including even where the parties intend otherwise. And these relationships therefore quite literally cannot possibly be governed on a purely contractual model. Doctrines that allow management practices to create unintended obligations represent contract law's recognition that employment is such a relation, and that orthodox contract cannot be the exclusive source of its regulation.

Employment is not the only familiar relation to outstrip the possibilities of purely contractual regulation. The next chapter, on marriage, takes up a second instance of this pattern. Marriage is interesting both for its own sake and because the interactions between contractual and non-contractual norms in that arena take on a pattern very different from the pattern concerning employment described in this chapter.

CHAPTER 23

MARRIAGE

The law of marriage is nowadays in a state of flux, even more so than the law of the employment contract.

The most publically prominent questions facing this body of law concern who may marry whom—and in particular whether the marriage relation should be available exclusively to persons of opposite sex or also, and on equal terms, to persons of the same sex. This question invokes deep and important moral and political principles, concerning equality and civil rights and also the proper place of religious morality in a cosmopolitan legal order. It is therefore natural and indeed proper that same sex marriage should capture the public moral and political imagination.

But from the perspective of contract law and theory, the deepest questions raised by marriage are quite different and go to the formal structure that the marriage relation has, regardless of who may enter into it. These do not concern particular terms of the marriage relation (not even to what partners these terms make the relation available), but rather the general question how the relation is established and disbanded and how its terms are fixed. What role, that is, do the intentions of the parties play in marriage? Is marriage just an ordinary contract—purely a creature of the intentions of the marriage partners—and so created, disbanded, and modified by party intentions in the usual way? Or is marriage formally different, coming with its own distinctive and unchosen rules concerning entry, modification, and exit? Is marriage not a contract at all, but rather a status, whose character is set according to public politics and morality (which may either include or exclude same sex unions from marriage's scope) rather than private freedom?

As it happens, not just access to marriage but also the formal character of marriage for those who may enter it is also in flux today. The materials that follow take up marriage, and the legal developments surrounding it, from this formal—contract-theoretic—point of view.

23.1 THE LAW OF BARON AND FEME

As with employment, so also with marriage, it will help to understand today's legal order by beginning with a bit of simple (and simplified) history.

Blackstone called marriage a "civil contract,"[1] and he insisted that the parties must be "willing" and "able to contract" to enter into matrimony.[2]

For this reason, Blackstone observed, both youth and "want of consent of parents or guardians" could render a marriage void.[3]

Moreover, consent was not only necessary for establishing a marriage but also sufficient, or nearly so (at least for pairings that satisfied the criteria for a marital union—"one man and one woman" and so forth). Canon law, which also regulated marriage, recognized clandestine marriages based solely on the parties' consent until the Council of Trent. Even thereafter, the only requirements added to consent were that appropriate public announcements be made and that a priest officiate.[4] There did arise in England periodic efforts to limit the power to marry, especially among the young and wealthy (to prevent heirs and heiresses from marrying without parental permission). For example: statutes under Henry III provided penalties for heirs marrying without their guardian's consent;[5] a Parliamentary act of 1558 punished a husband of an heiress who married her without her father's consent with imprisonment or fines in the Star Chamber;[6] and the Marriage Act of 1753 allowed parents to void the clandestine marriages of children under 21 and required public marriage (in respect both of who officiated and of registering marriages).[7] The American colonies sometimes also sought to deny recognition to some consensual marriages. For example: Virginia sought to control the marriages of indentured servants by increasing their terms of service;[8] Massachusetts allowed parents to control courtship, even specifying legal remedies for defying parents (a fine)[9] and gave common law courts jurisdiction over marriage, which probably helped the state to refuse to recognize certain clandestine marriages;[10] and strict fornication laws more generally increased parents' control of their children's marriages, by preventing children from using premarital conception to force marriages to which the

---

1.   1 WILLIAM BLACKSTONE, COMMENTARIES *421.

2.   Id. at *422.

3.   Id. at *424–25.

4.   CAROLE SHAMMAS, A HISTORY OF HOUSEHOLD GOVERNMENT IN AMERICA 92 (2002).

5.   *See* Provisions of Merton, 1235–36, 20 Hen. 3, c. 6 (Eng.); Statute of Ireland Concerning Coparceners, 1236, 20 Hen. 3 (Eng.); Provisions by King & Council, 1259, 43 Hen. 3, c.17 (Eng.); Award at Kenilworth, 1236 & 1237, 51 & 52 Hen. 3, c. 15 (Eng.); Statute of Marlborough, 1267, 52 Hen. 3, c. 17 (Eng.). See also Eyre v. Countess of Shaftsbury, 2 P. Wms. 103, 24 Eng. Rep. 659, 661–63 (1722).

6.   *See* An Acte for the Punishement of suche as shall take awaye Maydens that bee Inheritoures, 1557–58,4 & 5 Phil. & M., c.8.

7.   An Act for the Better Preventing of Clandestine Marriage (Lord Harwicke's Marriage Act), 1753, 26 Geo. 2, c. 33 (Eng.).

8.   HOLLY BREWER, BY BIRTH OR CONSENT 311 (2005).

9.   For applicable text of the statute, see *id.* at 312.

10.   *Id.* at 313. For cases of fathers invoking these laws refer to Ruth H. Bloch, *Women and the Law of Courtship in Eighteenth–Century America*, in Bloch, GENDER AND MORALITY IN ANGLO-AMERICAN CULTURE, 1650–1800, at 78–101 (2003).

parents objected.[11]

But other forces opposed such restrictions and sought to sustain the sufficiency of party consent for marriage. The Anglican Church, for example, offered resistance to parental control of marriage in its early years.[12] In addition, there have long existed jurisdictions whose relatively lax laws attracted couples whose consent was treated as insufficient for marriage in their home jurisdictions. English couples who sought to avoid English restrictions on marriage (and in particular those associated with the 1753 Act), for example, ran away to Gretna Green across the Scottish border.[13] Finally, courts—responding to the enormous social costs of invalidating consensual marriages, especially where they had been consummated and produced children—might read statutes that purported to restrict consensual marriages narrowly. In one example, *The King v. The Inhabitants of Birmingham*, a court ruled that the then applicable Marriage Act, which made the consent of the father or guardian of any party under 21 years of age, "required for the marriage of such party," merely made it a duty for clergy not to proceed with a marriage where the absence of the father's consent was known but did not invalidate marriages performed without consent.[14]

Overall, then, the consent of the parties was substantially sufficient for marriages to arise under common law. Indeed, the periodic efforts to restrict consensual marriage were themselves likely responses to the enduring fact that parents and the state in practice lacked the control over their marriage that they wanted, or sought to have.

But although consent surely did play a critical, perhaps even an essential, role in entering marriage, it remains misleading to infer from this that marriage should be understood as a species of contract. Marriage under common law was, in important and indeed essential respects, not like any ordinary contract. It was, rather, a status. Three features of marriage under common law emphasize its character as status rather than contract.

First, and perhaps most obviously, exit from marriage was restricted in a way in which exit from contracts—that is, breach or rescission—was not. Certainly, the intention to exit (in one or even in both parties) was not sufficient to end a marriage. Blackstone thus observed that even adultery was not a ground for divorce in England, but rather for only separation from bed and board,[15] because if it were up to the parties, there would be too many divorces.[16] Divorce was also highly restricted in the United States, although what constituted a ground for divorce varied over time

---

11.   Shammas, *supra* note 4, at 89–90.

12.   Holly Brewer, By Birth or Consent 308 (2005).

13.   Shammas, *supra* note 4, at 93–95.

14.   *R. v. Birmingham*, 1828, 108 Eng. Rep. 954, 955 (Eng.).

15.   Separation from bed and board allowed married persons to live separately; but only a true divorce from the bonds of marriage allowed them to remarry.

16   1 William Blackstone, Commentaries *429.

and, at any given time, also from state to state.[17] Moreover, and from the point of view of the theory of marriage more importantly, marriages could not be dissolved simply by the concerted action of the parties seeking to end their relation, no matter what ground they gave. Rather, divorces had to be accomplished (or granted) by the competent legal authorities. (The formal point continues to apply today). In England, before 1857, this meant applying to Parliament for a private bill.[18] Practice in the United States was more varied, with some jurisdictions making the granting of divorces a legislative function and some making it a judicial function.[19] All this was so in spite of the fact that marriage, which of course involves highly personal services, is not the sort of agreement that contract law would ever specifically enforce, much less require to endure even in the face of the agreement (uncontested) among the parties that it should not.

Second, the substantive content of the marriage relation contained elements that ordinary contracts could not possibly establish. Marriage, that is, imposed changes on persons', and especially women's, legal status of a sort that contract could not ordinarily achieve. The legal powers associated with freedom of contract, that is, did not ordinarily extend to producing the legal effects associated with marriage.

Women at common law were categorized as either feme sole or feme covert (single or married). Feme sole possessed the legal capacities of persons, more or less. Feme covert, however, were treated very differently by the law. Under the institution of coverture, a marriage merged the husband and wife into a single legal person, and that person was the husband. This had immense effects on married women's legal capacities and in particular their capacities to contract. A prominent nineteenth century article summarized this legal regime thusly:

> At common law a wife's existence was gone,—merged into that of her husband,—and all her contracts were, not voidable, like those of infants, but absolutely void, at law and in equity. So strict was this rule, that a married woman's promise, during coverture, to pay an ante-nuptial debt did not affect the running of the statute of limitations; and her promise after her husband's death to pay a debt contracted during coverture was void as without consideration. When, however, the husband was an alien residing abroad, had abjured the realm, or was civilly dead, the wife had the capacities of an unmarried woman and could contract as if sole,

---

17. This created jurisdictional competition and divorce mills long before Mexico or Nevada assumed that role. For example, at the beginning of the 19th century, some states, such as New York, made adultery the sole ground for divorce. Others, including Vermont, allowed divorce more broadly, including for example on grounds of intolerable severity of treatment. Stricter states did not always recognize divorces obtained by their citizens who travelled to laxer ones. For a discussion of these matters, *see, e.g., Jackson v. Jackson*, 1 Johns 424 (N.Y.Sup. 1806).

18. LAWRENCE M. FRIEDMAN, A HISTORY OF AMERICAN LAW 142 (3d ed. 2005). Ecclesiastical authorities might grant married persons a separation from bed and board, but only the civil authorities could grant a true divorce from the bonds of marriage.

19. The question was even addressed by the United States Supreme Court. For an extensive discussion, see *Maynard v. Hill* 125 U.S. 190 (1888).

except, possibly, as far as the deeds of her realty were concerned. And equity has always recognized the separate existence of wives, and protected them in the enjoyment of property settled upon them for their sole and separate use,—called equitable separate property. As to her right to contract with respect to this property courts of equity in different States have enforced two rules: One, that she cannot bind it by her contracts unless the settlement expressly so empowers her. The other, and more common, rule was, that she was, in equity, with respect to this property, as *feme sole*, so far as her capacities were not limited by the settlement itself. These contracts, it must be remembered, gave no rights against herself, or against her general property, but only rights in equity against her equitable separate estate.[20]

Coverture was a sufficiently entrenched in the common law so as to trump general statutes concerning contracts that did not expressly refer to married women. Such statutes thus did not affect married women's contractual capacity or the validity of their contracts. In the 19th century, however, a series of specific statutes, conventionally called the Married Women's Property Acts—began to attack coverture and to restore married women's contractual capacity. Many of these statutes did not undo coverture generally or restore married women's contractual capacity completely and at a stroke. Rather, they gave married women contractual capacity in respect of certain classes of contracts, referring to certain classes of property. Under such statutes, "[a] married woman [was] not, with respect to her statutory separate property, a feme sole: she ha[d], by implication, the capacity to make such contracts, and no others, as [were] necessary to the exercise of the capacities, or the enjoyment of the rights, expressly given her by the statute."[21] Other statutes sought to cast themselves more broadly, staging a general assault on coverture. By "expressly enabling a married woman to contract as if unmarried," such statutes sought to allow married women to "make contracts generally entirely unaffected by her coverture."[22] These statutes especially faced resistance from courts, which often interpreted them to limit their effect, for example under the canon of construction that statutes in derogation of the common law (in this instance, the law of coverture) shall be narrowly construed.[23]

A particular question concerned whether such generalized Married Women's Property Acts permitted wives to make contracts directly with their husbands. This was no mere curiosity, moreover. Rather, the issue went directly to the core of the nature of the marriage relation, because contracts made between husbands and wives possessed the potential to remake the terms of that relation. The effect of the Acts on the recognition

---

20. David Steward, *Contracts of Married Women under Statutes*, 19 Am. L. Rev. 359, 361–63 (1885).

21. Id. at 367.

22. Id. at 371–72.

23. Here see, for example, Reva Siegel, *The Modernization of Marital Status Law: Adjudicating Wives' Rights to Earnings, 1860–1930*, Geo. L. J. 2127 (1994).

of contracts between husbands and wives thus caused considerable disagreement among nineteenth century courts and commentators. "On the one hand, it [was] said that the incapacity of the husband and wife to contract together is an incapacity of the husband as well as of the wife, and is not now removed when the incapacity of the wife alone is destroyed. On the other hand, it [was] assumed that legislatures intended to include contracts with husbands."[24] The controversy continues among historians today.[25] One thing is relatively clear, however, namely that even where contracts between husbands and wives were permitted, their substance was limited to matters outside the domestic sphere and certainly outside the marriage itself. A wife and her husband might perhaps be permitted to contract for her to work as a clerk in his jewelry store[26] (although their contract might also be ruled invalid). But a wife and her husband could not contract about the terms of their personal and domestic lives, for example, concerning housework, maintenance, and of course consortium.

Third, and most importantly, the formal character of the ongoing marriage relation was not contractual. That is, although marriage required consent and was assumed by contract, it was well understood that marriage was not itself a contractual relation.

A prominent treatise expressed this point in the following terms:

This contract of marriage differs from the marriage itself, as the agreement to build a house differs from the completed structure, or as the egg and the incubation differ from the bird produced. It has the properties of any other ordinary contract: as, for example, the parties must be capable of contracting; it must be founded on consideration, which, in the facts of most cases and in a certain sense of necessity, consists of mutual promises; the consideration must not involve what is immoral or against public policy; fraud or mistake, such as a concealed or undisclosed lack of chastity, will justify the breaking of the promise; the contract between an infant and an adult is binding on the adult but voidable by the infant; the 'act of God," occurring after the contract is made, whereby one becomes physically incapable of performing the functions of marriage, will justify its breach by either of the parties; an action of damages for a breach may be maintained; and this contract, like any other, ends when performance is fully done and accepted. Actual marriage, in any form which makes the parties in law husband and wife, is performance. Nothing short is. At marriage, therefore, the contract ceases.

24. David Steward, *Contracts of Married Women under Statutes*, 19 Am. L. Rev. 359, 372–73 (1885).

25. One source of uncertainty concerns how broadly the prohibition on intra-spousal contracts cast its net, and in particular whether it applied only (or principally) to contracts for the provision of domestic services or more generally to include even contracts for goods or services unrelated to the household. See Reva Siegel, *The Modernization of Marital Status Law: Adjudicating Wives' Rights to Earnings, 1860–1930*, 82 Geo. L. J. 2127 (1994).

26. See, e.g., *In re Davidson*, 233 F. 462 (D.C. Ala. 1916).

Actual marriage, moreover, replaced the contract of marriage with a relation that was profoundly non-contractual. The treatise thus continued that:

> Marriage, as distinguished from the agreement to marry and from the act of becoming married, is the civil status of one man and one woman united in law for life, for the discharge, to each other and the community, of the duties legally incumbent on those whose association is founded on the distinction of sex.

And it added that:

> The source of marriage is the law of nature, whence it has flowed into the municipal laws of every civilized country, and into the general law of nations. While the contract remains a mere agreement to marry, it is not essentially different from other executory civil contracts; it does not superinduce the status; and, on its violation an action may be maintained by the injured party to recover his damages of the other. But when it is executed in what the law accepts as a valid marriage, its nature as a contract is merged in the higher nature of the status. And though the new relation—that is, the status—retains some similitudes reminding us of its origin, the contract does in truth no longer exist, but the parties are governed by the law of husband and wife. In other words, the parties, when they agreed to marry, undertook only to assume the marital status; and, on its assumption, the agreement, being fully performed according to its terms, bound them no longer.

Thus, the analysis concludes:

> That marriage executed is not a contract we know, because the parties cannot mutually dissolve it, because the act of God incapacitating one to discharge its duties will not release the bond, because there is no accepted performance which will end it, because a minor of marriage age can no more recede from it than an adult, because it is not dissolved by a failure of the original consideration, because no suit for damages will lie for the nonfulfillment of its duties, because its duties are not derived from its terms but from the law, because legislation may annul it at pleasure, and because none of its other elements are those of contract, but all are of status.[27]

---

27. Joel Bishop, 1 Commentaries on the Law of Marriage and Divorce 1–4 (6th ed. 1881). Bishop expressly addressed the common habit (practiced even by Blackstone, see above) of calling marriage a contract in the following terms:

> Plain as [the status view of marriage] is, and incredible as it may seem that any thing contrary to it should be seriously entertained, marriage was generally in our books, prior to the present one, defined as a contract. But this definition, thus broadly stated, was so obviously inaccurate that it was commonly more or less qualified; and, by some, so much was excepted out of it as to leave little or nothing of the original. So that, if marriage was pronounced a contract, it was said also to be more than a contract, and to differ from all other contracts.

Id.

Nor was the treatise-writer alone in taking this view. The United States Supreme Court adopted a similar characterization of marriage (among other reasons, in order to explain why legislatively granted divorces did not constitute "Law[s] impairing the Obligation of Contracts" within the meaning of the prohibition of Article I § 10 of the United States Constitution). In the words of the Court:

> [W]hile marriage is often termed by text writings and in decisions of courts as a civil contract—generally to indicate that it must be founded upon the agreement of the parties, and does not require any religious ceremony for its solemnization—it is something more than a mere contract. The consent of the parties is of course essential to its existence, but when the contract to marry is executed by the marriage, a relation between the parties is created which they cannot change. Other contracts may be modified, restricted, or enlarged, or entirely released upon the consent of the parties. Not so with marriage. The relation once formed, the law steps in and holds the parties to various obligations and liabilities. It is an institution, in the maintenance of which in its purity the public is deeply interested, for it is the foundation of the family and of society, without which there would be neither civilization nor progress.[28]

These considerations led the Court to conclude, vividly, that "[w]hen formed, [the marriage] relation is no more a contract than 'fatherhood' or 'sonship' is a contract."[29]

---

28. *Maynard v. Hill*, 125 U.S. 190, 210–11 (1888). The Court also quoted various State high courts that adopted similar views, including:

> When the contracting parties have entered into the marriage state, they have not so much entered into a contract as into a new relation, the rights duties, and obligations of which rest not upon their agreement, but upon the general law of the State, statutory or common, which defines and prescribes those rights duties and obligations. They are of law, not of contract. It was of contract that the relation should be established, but, being established, the power of the parties as to its extent or duration is at an end. Their rights under it are determined by the will of the sovereign, as evidenced by law. They can neither be modified nor changed by any agreement of parties. It is a relation for life, and the parties cannot terminate it at any shorter period by virtue of any contract they may make. The reciprocal rights arising from this relation, so long as it continues, are such as the law determines from time to time, and none other. *Maynard*, 125 U.S. at 211 (quoting *Adams v. Palmer*, 41 Maine 481, 483 (1863)).

> *Marriage*, in the sense in which it is dealt with by a decree of divorce, is not a contract, but one of the domestic *relations*. In strictness, thought formed by contract, it signifies the *relation* of husband and wife, deriving both its rights and duties for a source higher than any contract of which the parties are capable, and as to these uncontrollable by any contract which they can make. When formed, this relation is no more a contract that 'fatherhood' or 'sonship' is a contract. *Maynard*, 125 U.S. at 212 (quoting (*Ditson v. Ditson*, 4 R.I. 87, 101 (1856)).

> At common law, marriage as a *status* has few elements of contract about it. For instance, no other contract merged the legal existence of the parties into one. Other distinctive elements will readily suggest themselves, which rob it of most of its characteristics as a contract, and leave it simply as a *status* or institution. As such, it is not so much the result of private agreement, as of public ordination. *Maynard*, 125 U.S. at 205 (quoting *Noel v. Ewing*, 9 Indiana 37, 49–50 (1857)).

29. *Maynard*, 125 U.S. at 212.

These formal or conceptual distinctions between contract and marriage had practical entailments. Most importantly, the fact that marriage was a status rather than a contract relation entailed that marriage's obligations could not be altered by the parties, as the following case illustrates.

Lewis v. Lewis

Court of Appeals of Kentucky, 1922.
245 S.W. 509.

■ SAMPSON, J. Some 30 years ago appellant, W. A. Lewis, and appellee, Sarah J. Lewis, were married in the state of Tennessee, but soon thereafter took up their residence in Warren County, Ky. To their union were born 11 children. W. A. Lewis owned and operated a general store at the ferry about seven miles from the city of Bowling Green in Warren County. After some of the children were almost grown appellant and appellee became estranged, and appellee, Sarah J. Lewis, brought an action in the Warren circuit court against her husband, W. A. Lewis, for a divorce from bed and board, alimony in the sum of $3,000, attorney fees, and maintenance during the pendency of the action. In her petition she alleged cruel and inhuman treatment on the part of W. A. Lewis. She set forth he was the owner of a farm worth about $10,000 or $12,000, containing 180 acres, and she herself owned a tract of 365 acres of land in Warren county of small value, and that she had no other property. The action was prepared by the taking of only a few depositions on each side, and submitted to the chancellor for decree. The wife was granted a divorce from bed and board according to her prayer, awarded $1,250 alimony and the custody and care of the 11 children. The defendant, W. A. Lewis, was required to pay the attorney fees of his wife's lawyers, and to pay certain unpaid installments of the maintenance theretofore ordered, and to pay the cost of the action. A general order of attachment which had been levied upon his land was sustained, and the wife given a lien upon the property for the payment of all these items. There was some evidence in the record showing that the lands which the wife claimed had been purchased and paid for by the husband out of his own estate and deeded to the wife as a result of their married relations. The wife in her petition claimed the land as her own, and averred she bought and paid for it. The answer of the husband denied this, and set forth the way and manner in which he bought and paid for the land. The judgment in the original suit made no reference whatever to the tract of 365 acres which the wife claimed.

It is the contention of counsel for appellee, Sarah J. Lewis, that inasmuch as the title to the tract of 365 acres was put in issue, evidence taken and heard, the judgment in favor of Sarah J. Lewis was a final determination in her favor, and this action is res judicata on the question determined in the first action. Counsel overlooks the fact that in the first action only a limited divorce was granted, and not one from the bonds of matrimony. By section 425, Civil Code, it is provided:

"Every judgment for a divorce from the bond of matrimony shall contain an order restoring any property not disposed of at the commencement of the action, which either party may have obtained, directly or indirectly, from or through the other, during marriage, in consideration or by reason thereof; and any property so obtained, without valuable consideration, shall be deemed to have been obtained by reason of marriage."

To much the same effect is section 2121, Kentucky Statutes, which provides that a divorce from bed and board alone may be granted even upon the same grounds for which a divorce may be granted. Said section of the Statutes provides:

"Upon final judgment of divorce from the bond of matrimony the parties shall be restored such property, not disposed of at the commencement of the action, as either obtained from or through the other before or during the marriage in consideration thereof."

Construing these sections, we have held that, where a divorce from bed and board only is granted, no order for the restoration of property obtained by reason of the marriage relation can rightfully be ordered. In discussing this question in the case of *Hoffman v. Hoffman*, 190 Ky. 17, we said:

"As part of the decree, the chancellor adjudged that the parties restore to each other all the property which either may have obtained directly or indirectly, from the other during the marriage, and in consideration or by reason thereof. This was error for the reason that the divorce was merely from bed and board, and it is only in cases of absolute divorce that such an order or restoration is authorized by the statute and Code." *Ratliff v. Ratliff*, 193 Ky. 708; *Lewis v. Lewis*, 194 Ky. 821.

It therefore appears that the chancellor who tried the case in 1915 and granted a limited divorce did not have jurisdiction to enter an order for the restoration of property between the litigants. While the court had jurisdiction of the parties and of the subject-matter, it would not, in a case where a limited divorce was granted, order one spouse to restore to the other property obtained by reason of or in consequence of the marriage relation, for this power is statutory only. It follows therefore that the question of who owned the tract of 365 acres claimed by Mrs. Sarah J. Lewis was not before the court in such way as to give the court jurisdiction, and the chancellor, no doubt realizing this, omitted to mention the said property in the judgment. Therefore the question is not res judicata. A judgment on the merits is conclusive between the parties in subsequent actions on the same cause, not only as to matters actually litigated, but as to all ground of recovery which might have been determined therein if the court had jurisdiction thereof; but if the court had no jurisdiction of the parties or of the subject-matter the rule of res judicata has no application.

At a later date, and after five years from the commencement of the divorce action by the wife, the husband brought a suit against her for absolute divorce on the ground of five-year separation. The wife made no defense whatever to the cause, and he was granted an absolute divorce from the wife. After the rendition of this judgment the husband instituted this action against the wife for the recovery of the tract of 365 acres of land, which he says he purchased with his own means and caused to be conveyed to her by reason of and in consideration of their marriage relation, and for no other consideration. In the new action the wife answered, and said she bought and paid for the tract of land in question, and, issue being joined and proof taken, both the wife and husband testified. The wife was asked:

"Q. Who did you buy it from [the land]? A. E. M. Harvey.

Q. Is he a relative of yours? A. Yes, sir; he is an uncle of mine.

Q. Who paid the purchase money on it? A. It was paid out of both of our work; I stayed in the store, and he went out part of the time.

Q. How many years ago did you and Mr. Lewis buy that land? A. It has been about 11 or 12 years ago.

Q. Who was the deed made to? A. Made to me."

Cross-examined:

"Q. Did you have any property when you married Mr. Lewis? A. Yes, sir; I didn't have much, but I had some property.

Q. What? A. Some little things my father gave me. I had a cow, chickens, bed, and quilts. That is all the property I had at the time I married. I had some featherbeds, pillows, and quilts.

Q. Did you ever work for wages or get anything for your work at any time? A. I worked in the store, but did not get any wages. I suppose my work was worth something, when I was attending to two little children and stayed in the store, too; it looks like it ought to be worth something.

Q. Did you work as one of the family, and help Mr. Lewis in the store, didn't you? A. Yes, sir; but a great deal of the time he was not in the store.

Q. The money for the farm was paid by Mr. Lewis? A. Paid by us out of what money we made by both of us out what we made in the store.

Q. Was it paid by yourself or by Mr. Lewis? A. It was paid out of our work in the store.

Q. I will ask you if you paid it personally? A. I know it was paid.

Q. Did you pay it personally? A. I helped to pay it—just the same as paid it.

Q. What person paid the money, yourself or Mr. Lewis? A. We were both there together, and it was paid mostly at the store, first by me and then by Mr. Lewis together.

Q. Was it paid out of the proceeds of the store? A. Some of it, part one way and part another. I could not tell how all of it was paid.

Q. Did you pay a copper cent on that farm? A. Yes, sir; I helped pay it.

Q. Did you pay it? A. Of course I worked and helped to pay it.

Q. To whom did you pay it? A. E. M. Harvey.

Q. Did you yourself pay Mr. Harvey? A. No, sir; I never paid it, but I seen it paid, and that was sufficient."

The wife further says she had no interest in the store whatever except as the wife of her husband, and that he did not contract or agree to pay her for her services in the store.

On the other hand, the husband very emphatically says he bought the land and paid for it with his own money, and that the wife had no interest whatever in the land. The title bond, which was executed when the trade was first made, shows the husband as the sole grantee of the land, and that he had paid at that time, March 22, 1905, $800 cash in hand, leaving a balance between $800 and $1,150, the total price yet unpaid. The title bond further shows that $200 was to be paid on the 1st day of the next July, and $150 to be paid on the 1st day of May, 1906, and a lien retained upon the land to secure the purchase money. It further recites that W. A. Lewis, the husband, "has this day executed and delivered to the said Harvey his two promissory notes as above mentioned, and to secure the prompt payment of said notes when due the said Lewis has sold and mortgaged all timber on said land except the poplar, and when the last note is paid the said Harvey agrees to make to the said Lewis a general warranty deed." This bond is signed by E. M. Harvey, the vendor. It therefore plainly appears that the wife had no interest whatever in the land, except as the spouse of her husband. She neither bought nor paid for it. After the final absolute divorce was granted, the husband was entitled, under section 425 of the Civil Code and section 2121, Kentucky Statutes, to a restoration of the said lands, and the chancellor erred to the great prejudice of appellant in holding otherwise.

At common law the husband and wife are under obligation to each other to perform certain duties. The husband to bring home the bacon, so to speak, and to furnish a home, while on the wife devolved the duty to keep said home in a habitable condition. Following this it has been held that an agreement by the husband to pay his wife for performing the ordinary household duties was not only without consideration, but against public policy. The rule was somewhat different with regard to service of a different nature, not domestic. It was not the duty of the wife, unless she desired to do so, to perform labor for the husband outside of her regular household duties, but it she did so she was not entitled to recover their value of her husband. There is no implied obligation on the part of the husband to pay the wife for such services as she renders outside of the ordinary household duties. 13 R. C. L. pp. 1089, 1090; 21 Cyc. pp. 1276, 1277.

Although Mrs. Lewis may have performed great services in the store of her husband, without a contract for remuneration she was not entitled to recover of him any part of the profits or other compensation, for the store belonged to the husband, and her assistance in the store was as a member of the family without pay or expectation of reward, save to aid the husband in making a living for the family, including their 11 children.

For the reasons indicated the judgment must be and is reversed for proceedings consistent with this opinion.

Judgment reversed.

* * *

The parties in *Lewis* had been married for thirty years and had had eleven children when they became estranged. The wife subsequently brought an action against the husband, alleging cruel and inhuman treatment and seeking divorce from bed and board and a maintenance. The wife received these, and five years later, the husband brought suit against her seeking an absolute divorce on the ground of the five year separation. The wife did not contest the divorce, and the divorce was granted.

The husband subsequently brought another suit against the wife, seeking to recover title to a tract of land that he claimed he had purchased with his own monies and had caused to be conveyed to her "by reason of and in consideration of their marriage relation, and for no other consideration." The wife answered that she had bought and paid for this tract of land. A trial was held to determine who had bought the land and hence who subsequently owned it.

The husband and wife had operated a store during their marriage, which had been owned formally by the husband. The wife testified at trial that she had worked in the store and had also kept the couple's joint household and cared for their children but had never received wages. She nevertheless observed that "I suppose my work was worth something" and that "it looks like it ought to be worth something." And the wife therefore sought to treat the profits from the store as hers as much as her husband's. She insisted that the land was paid for "by us out of what money we made by both of us out of what we made in the store" when "I stayed in the store, and he went out part of the time," so that "it was paid out of both our work," and "I helped to pay for it—just the same as paid it." As against this, the husband insisted that he had paid for the land entirely out of his own money, and various documents connected to the land purchase named only the husband as the payor. The court thus concluded that "the wife had no interest whatever in the land, except as the spouse of her husband. She neither bought nor paid for it."

The wife in *Lewis* argued, in effect, that her labor both in the home and in the business entitled her to a share of ownership in the proceeds that the couple acquired over the course of their marriage. More formally, she argued that she had provided her labor under an implied (in fact) contract that she should receive her fair share of the proceeds of their joint endeavors, or at least its fair value. The court rejected this argument emphatically.

With respect to the wife's domestic labor, the court held that no such contract could validly be made, period. Marriage was a status. Its terms imposed fixed duties on the parties to it: a duty on the husband to provide economically for the wife in their joint household; and a duty on the wife to perform the domestic services required to maintain the household. Being a status, marriage rejected efforts by the parties to contract around these terms. The court thus held that even an express "agreement by the husband to pay his wife for performing the ordinary household duties was not only without consideration, but against public policy."

Matters were a little more complicated with respect to the wife's labor in the store. Marriage did not impose on wives any duty to perform services for their husbands outside of the household, and so the wife had been free to refuse to work in the store. This, of course, did not settle the question how things might stand in case—as had happened in *Lewis*—the wife chose to work for the husband's benefit, outside of the house. The *Lewis* court concluded that "without a contract for remuneration [the wife] was not entitled to recover of [the husband] any part of the profits or other compensation, for the store belonged to the husband, and her assistance in the store was as a member of the family without pay or expectation of reward, save to aid the husband in making a living for the family, including their 11 children." The *Lewis* court, in other words, allowed that an *express* contract allocating the proceeds of non-domestic work between spouses might be valid, but it refused to *imply* such a contract where the parties had not contracted expressly.

The *Lewis* court's actual argument, in this connection, was conclusory, however. The court's assumption that the wife had worked "without a contract for remuneration" is warranted only with regard to express contracts. And the court's assertion that the wife had "worked without pay or expectation of reward" was at the very least gainsayed by the wife's testimony that she "suppose[d] [her] work was worth something" and had thought of the land as bought by her and her husband together. The *Lewis* court made no serious investigation into the actual (or reasonable) intentions of the husband and wife during the time when she worked in the store and provided no non-ideological reason for thinking that no implied agreement concerning her rights to the store's proceeds existed. Instead, the court simply assumed that the wife's work—including even her non-domestic work—was motivated by a domestic concern to support her husband and family. *Lewis* was not alone in making these assumptions, nor even an outlier. But unlike the refusal to acknowledge contracts in respect of domestic work, the assumptions concerning non-domestic work were not *required* by the status character of the marriage relation (nor by that relation's substance, once coverture had been abandoned and married women's contractual capacity restored). And some courts have been prepared to find implied-in-fact contracts concerning non-domestic labor and, on this basis, to give ex-spouses rights in jointly run business following divorces.[30]

Return, now, to efforts to employ contract to change the management of domestic life within a marriage. *Lewis* stated in no uncertain terms that such efforts could not succeed while the domestic life of the marriage was

---

30. *See, e.g., Dunn v. Dunn,* 609 So. 2d (Miss. 1992). Note also that, as a formal matter, community property regimes might be understood to imply such rights not in fact but in law.

ongoing. The following case addresses such efforts in connection with a domestic life's breakup.

Balfour v. Balfour

Court of Appeal (Civil Division), 1919.
2 KB 571.

■ APPEAL from a decision of SARGANT J., sitting as an additional judge of the King's Bench Division.

The plaintiff sued the defendant (her husband) for money which she claimed to be due in respect of an agreed allowance of £30 a month. The alleged agreement was entered into under the following circumstances. The parties were married in August, 1900. The husband, a civil engineer, had a post under the Government of Ceylon as Director of Irrigation, and after the marriage he and his wife went to Ceylon, and lived there together until the year 1915, except that in 1906 they paid a short visit to this country, and in 1908 the wife came to England in order to undergo an operation, after which she returned to Ceylon. In November, 1915, she came to this country with her husband, who was on leave. They remained in England until August, 1916, when the husband's leave was up and he had to return. The wife however on the doctor's advice remained in England. On August 8, 1916, the husband being about to sail, the alleged parol agreement sued upon was made. The plaintiff, as appeared from the judge's note, gave the following evidence of what took place: "In August, 1916, defendant's leave was up. I was suffering from rheumatic arthritis. The doctor advised my staying in England for some months, not to go out till November 4. On August 8 my husband sailed. He gave me a cheque from 8th to 31st for £24 and promised to give me £30 per month till I returned." Later on she said: "My husband and I wrote the figures together on August 8; £34 shown. Afterwards he said £30." In cross-examination she said that they had not agreed to live apart until subsequent differences arose between them, and that the agreement of August, 1916, was one which might be made by a couple in amity. Her husband in consultation with her assessed her needs, and said he would send £30 per month for her maintenance. She further said that she then understood that the defendant would be returning to England in a few months, but that he afterwards wrote to her suggesting that they had better remain apart. In March, 1918, she commenced proceedings for restitution of conjugal rights, and on July 30 she obtained a decree nisi. On December 16, 1918, she obtained an order for alimony.

Sargant J. held that the husband was under an obligation to support his wife, and the parties had contracted that the extent of that obligation should be defined in terms of so much a month. The consent of the wife to that arrangement was a sufficient consideration to constitute a contract which could be sued upon.

He accordingly gave judgment for the plaintiff.

The husband appealed.

■ WARRINGTON L.J.

(After stating the facts). Those being the facts we have to say whether there is a legal contract between the parties, in other words, whether what took place between them was in the domain of a contract or whether it was merely a domestic arrangement such as may be made every day between a husband and wife who are living together in friendly intercourse. It may be, and I do not for a moment say that it is not, possible for such a contract as is alleged in the present case to be made between husband and wife. The question is whether such a contract was made. That can only be determined either by proving that it was made in express terms, or that there is a necessary implication from the circumstances of the parties, and the transaction generally, that such a contract was made. It is quite plain that no such contract was made in express terms, and there was no bargain on the part of the wife at all. All that took place was this: The husband and wife met in a friendly way and discussed what would be necessary for her support while she was detained in England, the husband being in Ceylon, and they came to the conclusion that £30 a month would be about right, but there is no evidence of any express bargain by the wife that she would in all the circumstances treat that as in satisfaction of the obligation of the husband to maintain her. Can we find a contract from the position of the parties? It seems to me it is quite impossible. If we were to imply such a contract in this case we should be implying on the part of the wife that whatever happened and whatever might be the change of circumstances while the husband was away she should be content with this £30 a month, and bind herself by an obligation in law not to require him to pay anything more; and on the other hand we should be implying on the part of the husband a bargain to pay £30 a month for some indefinite period whatever might be his circumstances. Then again it seems to me that it would be impassible to make any such implication. The matter really reduces itself to an absurdity when one considers it, because if we were to hold that there was a contract in this case we should have to hold that with regard to all the more or less trivial concerns of life where a wife, at the request of her husband, makes a promise to him, that is a promise which can be enforced in law. All I can say is that there is no such contract here. These two people never intended to make a bargain which could be enforced in law. The husband expressed his intention to make this payment, and he promised to make it, and was bound in honour to continue it so long as he was in a position to do so. The wife on the other hand, so far as I can see, made no bargain at all. That is in my opinion sufficient to dispose of the case.

It is unnecessary to consider whether if the husband failed to make the payments the wife could pledge his credit or whether if he failed to make the payments she could have made some other arrangements. The only question we have to consider is whether the wife has made out a contract which she has set out to do. In my opinion she has not.

I think the judgment of Sargant J. cannot stand, the appeal ought to be allowed and judgment ought to be entered for the defendant.

■ DUKE L.J.

I agree. This is in some respects an important case, and as we differ from the judgment of the Court below I propose to state concisely my views and the grounds which have led me to the conclusion at which I have arrived. Substantially the question is whether the promise of the husband to the wife that while she is living absent from him he will make her a periodical allowance involves in law a consideration on the part of the wife sufficient to convert that promise into a binding agreement. In my opinion it does not. I do not dissent, as at present advised, from the proposition that the spouses in this case might have made an agreement which would have given the plaintiff a cause of action, and I am inclined to think that the promise of the wife in respect of her separate estate could have founded an action in contract within the principles of the Married Women's Property Act, 1882. But we have to see whether there is evidence of any such exchange of promises as would make the promise of the husband the basis of an agreement. It was strongly urged by Mr. Hawke that the promise being absolute in form ought to be construed as one of the mutual promises which make an agreement. It was said that a promise and an implied undertaking between strangers, such as the promise and implied undertaking alleged in this case would have founded an action on contract. That may be so, but it is impossible to disregard in this case what was the basis of the whole communications between the parties under which the alleged contract is said to have been formed. The basis of their communications was their relationship of husband and wife, a relationship which creates certain obligations, but not that which is here put in suit. There was a discussion between the parties while they were absent from one another, whether they should agree upon a separation. In the Court below the plaintiff conceded that down to the time of her suing in the Divorce Division there was no separation, and that the period of absence was a period of absence as between husband and wife living in amity. An agreement for separation when it is established does involve mutual considerations.

That was why in *Eastland v. Burchell* the agreement for separation was found by the learned judge to have been of decisive consequence. But in this case there was no separation agreement at all. The parties were husband and wife, and subject to all the conditions, in point of law, involved in that relationship. It is impossible to say that where the relationship of husband and wife exists, and promises are exchanged, they must be deemed to be promises of a contractual nature. In order to establish a contract there ought to be something more than mere mutual promises having regard to the domestic relations of the parties. It is required that the obligations arising out of that relationship shall be displaced before either of the parties can found a contract upon such promises. The formula which was stated in this case to support the claim of the lady was this: In consideration that you will agree to give me £30 a month I will agree to forego my right to pledge your credit. In the judgment of the majority of the Court of Common Pleas in *Jolly v. Rees*, which was affirmed in the decision of *Debenham v. Mellon*, Erle C.J. states this proposition: "But taking the law to be, that the power of the wife to charge her husband is in the capacity of his agent, it is a solecism in reasoning to say that she derives her authority from his will, and at the same time to say that the relation of wife creates the authority against his will, by a presumptio juris et de jure from marriage.'' What is said on the part of the wife in this case is that her arrangement with her husband that she should assent to that which was in his discretion to do or not to do was the consideration moving from her to her husband. The giving up of that which was not a right was not a consideration. The proposition that the mutual promises made in the ordinary domestic relationship of husband and wife of necessity give cause for action on a contract seems to me to go to the very root of the relationship, and to be a possible fruitful source of dissension and quarrelling. I cannot see that any benefit would result from it to either of the parties, but on the other hand it would lead to unlimited litigation in a relationship which should be obviously as far as possible protected from possibilities of that kind. I think, therefore, that in point of principle there is no foundation for the claim which is made here, and I am satisfied that there was no consideration moving from the wife to the husband or promise by the husband to the wife which was sufficient to sustain this action founded on contract. I think, therefore, that the appeal must be allowed.

■ ATKIN L.J.

The defence to this action on the alleged contract is that the defendant, the husband, entered into no contract with his wife, and for the determination of that it is necessary to remember that there are agreements between parties which do not result in contracts within the meaning of that term in our law. The ordinary example is where two parties agree to take a walk together, or where there is an offer and an acceptance of hospitality. Nobody would suggest in ordinary circumstances that those agreements result in what we know as a contract, and one of the most usual forms of agreement which does not constitute a contract appears to me to be the arrangements which are made between husband and wife. It is quite common, and it is the natural and inevitable result of the relationship of husband and wife, that the two spouses should make arrangements between themselves—agreements such as are in dispute in this action— agreements for allowances, by which the husband agrees that he will pay to his wife a certain sum of money, per week, or per month, or per year, to cover either her own expenses or the necessary expenses of the household and of the children of the marriage, and in which the wife promises either expressly or impliedly to apply the allowance for the purpose for which it is given. To my mind those agreements, or many of them, do not result in contracts at all, and they do not result in contracts even though there may be what as between other parties would constitute consideration for the agreement. The consideration, as we know, may consist either in some right, interest, profit or benefit accruing to one party, or some forbearance, detriment, loss or responsibility given, suffered or undertaken by the other. That is a well-known definition, and it constantly happens, I think, that such arrangements made between husband and wife are arrangements in which there are mutual promises, or in which there is consideration in form within the definition that I have mentioned. Nevertheless they are not contracts, and they are not contracts because the parties did not intend that they should be attended by legal consequences. To my mind it would be of the worst possible example to hold that agreements such as this resulted in legal obligations which could be enforced in the Courts. It would mean this, that when the husband makes his wife a promise to give her an allowance of 30s or £2 a week, whatever he can afford to give her, for the maintenance of the household and children, and she promises so to apply it, not only could she sue him for his failure in any week to supply the allowance, but he could sue her for non-performance of the obligation, express or implied, which she had undertaken upon her part. All I can say is that the small Courts of this country would have to be multiplied one hundredfold if these arrangements were held to result in legal obligations. They are not sued upon, not because the parties are reluctant to enforce their legal rights when the agreement is broken, but because the parties, in the inception of the arrangement, never intended that they should be sued upon. Agreements such as these are outside the realm of contracts altogether. The common law does not regulate the form of agreements between spouses. Their promises are not sealed with seals and sealing wax. The consideration that really obtains for them is that natural love and affection which counts for so little in these cold Courts. The terms may be repudiated, varied or renewed as performance proceeds or as disagreements develop, and the principles of the common law as to exoneration and discharge and accord and satisfaction are such as find no place in the domestic code. The parties themselves are advocates, judges, Courts, sheriff's officer and reporter. In respect of these promises each house is a domain into which the King's writ does not seek to run, and to which his officers do not seek to be admitted. The only question in this case is whether or not this promise was of such a class or not. For the reasons given by my brethren it appears to me to be plainly established that the promise here was not intended by either party to be attended by legal consequences. I think the onus was upon the plaintiff, and the plaintiff has not established any contract. The parties were living together, the wife intending to return. The suggestion is that the husband bound himself to pay £30 a month under all circumstances, and she bound herself to be satisfied with that sum under all circumstances, and, although she was in ill-health and alone in this country, that out of that sum she undertook to defray the whole of the medical expenses that might fall upon her, whatever might be the development of her illness, and in whatever expenses it might involve her. To my mind neither party contemplated such a result. I think that the parol evidence upon which the case turns does not establish a contract. I think that the letters do not evidence such a contract, or amplify the oral evidence which was given by the wife, which is not in dispute. For these reasons I think the judgment of the Court below was wrong and that this appeal should be allowed.

* * *

Mr. and Mrs. Balfour had been living in Ceylon (modern-day Sri Lanka), where he worked as an engineer, directing irrigation. They returned to England, intending to stay only temporarily, for the period of Mr. Balfour's professional leave. Mrs. Balfour suffered from arthritis while staying in England, and her doctor recommended that she remain there, rather than returning to Ceylon. Mr. Balfour thus returned to Ceylon on his own, but not before promising to pay Mrs. Balfour a maintenance of £30 a month until she joined him in Ceylon.[31] Subsequently, Mr. Balfour sent his wife a letter proposing to separate; in addition, he ceased sending the £30 per month. Mrs. Balfour sued, asserting that the agreement to pay her £30 per month constituted a contract and seeking to enforce it.

A trial court observed that marriage conferred on husbands a general duty to support their wives (as a counterpart to the wives' duty to tend to their husbands' domestic lives). When Mr. Balfour offered £30 per month and Mrs. Balfour accepted, this liquidated the general, open-ended obligation in favor of a particular and specific sum. The agreement was thus supported by good consideration on both sides: his £30 per month in exchange for her release from the general obligation of support that he would otherwise owe. The court thus concluded that the Balfours had executed a valid contract, and held in the wife's favor.

An appellate court reversed, citing a mix of reasons, of varying degrees of interest from the perspective of contract law and theory. Some of the judges worried that allowing promises exchanged between spouses to constitute enforceable contracts would, given the commonness of such promises and also of subsequent disputes concerning them, insert courts broadly and generally into domestic relations, undermining the internal norms governing such relations and overwhelming the court system. Other judges (echoing some of the sentiments of the contemporaneous but otherwise surely very different Kentucky judges who decided *Lewis*) flat refused to believe that the parties to such purely domestic promises intended to create legal relations or obligations.[32] Finally, the *Balfour* judges also revisited the status character of the marriage relation. As Duke, L.J., put the point:

> The parties were husband and wife, and subject to all the conditions, in point of law, involved in that relationship. It is impossible

---

31. £30 per month was a substantial sum at the time. Virginia Woolf, writing a decade later, would invoke £500 a year and a room of one's own to characterize security and independence.

32. Note that this general argument required different framings in English and American law. As Chapter 13's discussion of Restatement (Second) of Contracts § 21 emphasized, American law does not require parties to intend to create specifically legal obligations in order for their promises to become binding contracts. English contract law, as that discussion observed in a footnote, takes a different approach and does require intent to create legal relations.

The argument in *Balfour* could therefore directly assert that the parties did not have the required specifically legal intent. An argument against the backdrop that informed *Lewis,* by contrast, would need to proceed by a more circuitous and demanding route. It would have to claim that the parties did not intend to be *bound* distinctively to their agreement at all, but instead intended merely to lay out a provisional course for performing the duties established independently and antecedently by their marriage.

to say that where the relationship of husband and wife exists, and promises are exchanged, they must be deemed to be promises of a contractual nature. In order to establish a contract there ought to be something more than mere mutual promises having regard to the domestic relations of the parties. It is required that the obligations arising out of that relationship shall be displaced before either of the parties can found a contract upon such promises.

Put slightly more directly, and thus also tendentiously, the terms of a marriage relation, being creatures of the law rather than of the intentions of the parties to the relation, cannot be supplanted by the parties' mere intentions, and hence by their contracts. The status *marriage*, and its attendant obligations, endures.[33]

The common law of marriage thus departed from contract in both its substance and its form.

With respect to substance, the marriage relation changed the legal positions, and indeed the legal nature, of the marriage partners in ways in which contracts could not. Although wives did not marry into slavery in any social, economic, or moral sense, coverture did entail that wives broadly unpersoned themselves, with respect to law. Contract could not achieve so complete an erasure of legal personality.

With respect to form, the terms of marriage at common law (including those associated with coverture) were fixed not by the intentions of the parties but through the collective social and moral sense of the community. Moreover, the community sense of what marriage involved resisted party efforts to change it or even to add to it. The resistance was substantial even at the margins of the marriage relation, for example with respect to contracts that attempted to regulate the non-domestic relations of married persons or the fix the terms of separation and divorce. Marriage's resistance to party efforts to change its terms at its core—with respect to the domestic arrangements in ongoing marriages—was nearly absolute. Formally, then, marriage was less contract than status.

Marriage was often hailed—see the opinions in *Balfour*, for example—as an essentially private sphere, into which the collective (and in particular the state) did not and should not intervene. But these characterizations reveal that it was, formally and literally, anything but private. The hand of the collective, and in particular of the state, guided and manipulated marriage with overwhelming effect.

---

33. Lord Justice Duke briefly presented another argument, which is worth noting in the margin because it seems to reflect a confusion. He suggested that the agreement at issue in *Balfour* lacked consideration, so that even if contracts between spouses might sometimes be enforceable, the maintenance agreement was not.

More specifically, Duke asserted that a wife's general power to bind her husband, being the power of an agent to bind a principal, arises at his discretion rather than by her right. Accordingly, Mrs. Balfour could not have given good consideration for Mr. Balfour's promises, because "[t]he giving up of that which was not a right was not a consideration." This reasoning seems to turn on a legal incapacity of the wife, however, which was rejected when coverture was abandoned.

Moreover, the one respect in which marriage remained contract-like—that the status had to be assumed by choice—was also the site of substantial collective meddling in individual decision. To be sure, *at the moment of marrying*, the choice of the parties was (more or less) both necessary and sufficient for establishing a marriage, as the brief review earlier in this section suggested. But social and legal pressures powerfully structured the lead-in to the moment. The social pressures—concerning, for example, social control of (especially women's) sexuality—are familiar and do not need rehearsing here. The legal pressures are perhaps less familiar. But common law doctrines including breach of promise to marry, seduction, common law marriage, and dower all employed marriage as a mechanism for regulating the material lives of women and in effect encouraged women into marriage by connecting marriage and economic security.[34] Moreover, the state has long been (and continues to be) more willing to intervene expressly—including substantially through laws and state agencies that protect children and regulate parenting—in families that are not structured in the manner that marriage makes conventional than in families whose structure better fits marriage's norms.[35]

23.2 MARRIAGE TODAY

Does marriage remain a status relation today, or has it been contractualized?

Entry and exit have been *liberalized*, to be sure. Thus although the consent of the parties was *more or less* necessary and sufficient for a marriage even at common law, it is now *absolutely* necessary and sufficient. And although courts continue to be needed in order to grant divorces (so that even today, the parties cannot dissolve a marriage on literally their own), the advent of no fault divorce means that, with respect to the question whether a marriage will endure or not, the role of the courts has become largely ministerial. Courts continue (as some of the materials below will illustrate) actively to supervise the terms of divorce, but they cannot and do not try to prevent the fact of divorce. Thus a marriage today depends on the consent of the parties not only to arise but also to endure.

To liberalize is not necessarily to contractualize, however. And there are other senses in which the modern regime concerning entry to and exit from marriages remains non-contractual, and indeed is less contractual than the common law regime had been.

---

34. Here see, e.g., Ariela Dubler, *In the Shadow of Marriage: Single Women and the Legal Construction of the Family and the State*, 112 YALE L. J. 1641 (2003). Dubler observes that the law's preference for marriage continues today, for example through welfare policies that encourage marriage. Id. at 1713–14. An excellent more philosophical account of both the interference of the public in the structure of marriage and of the erasure of this interference in the dominant accounts of public law and power appears in Catherin MacKinnon, Toward a Feminist Theory of the State (1989).

35. Here see, e.g., Jill Elaine Hasday, *Parenthood Divided: A Legal History of the Bifurcated Law of Parental Relations*, 90 GEO. L. J. 299 (2001–2002).

With respect to entry, modern law has abandoned the cause of action for breach of promise to marry. So although the way into marriage remains contractual in the sense that each partner must intend to assume the rights and obligations associated with the marriage, the intent must occur contemporaneously with the creation of the marriage. The path to marriage can no longer involve a purely executory contract—that is, a contract that creates obligations for future performance. That is what the common law contract to marry did, and modern law has, once again, abandoned its breach as a cause of action.

Moreover, no fault divorce represents a mixed development with respect to the contractual character of exit from marriage. On the one hand, as just observed, no fault divorce increases married persons' freedom to determine the course of their marriages according to their intentions. As long as the law (through courts) imposed substantive limits on the grounds for divorce, parties who wished no longer to be married might be forced to maintain their marriage relations—something that the logic of (freedom of) contract would reject. On the other hand, no fault divorce moves marriage away from the contract model, in that it does away with the idea of the *breach* of a marriage relation and the associated idea that a breach requires a remedy. The identity of the party seeking to dissolve the marriage relation does not have consequences for the terms of the dissolution in the same way in which the identity of the party seeking to exit a contract has consequences for the winding up of the contract relation.

A separate, and more interesting, question concerns whether the marriage relation itself has been contractualized. Marriage at common law, recall, was contractual in neither its substance nor its form: it accomplished legal changes in married persons that no contract could; and its contours were shaped according to public policy and morality rather than according to the intentions of the marriage partners. How does marriage today stand in respect of these considerations? In particular, what is the formal character of marriage today? The substantive entailments of marriage are less dramatic today than they were at common law, to be sure: marriage today effects nothing like the erasure of legal personality associated with coverture. But even a more substantively modest relation may retain a status-like form. So it becomes important to ask: is the character of a marriage today a creature of the intentions of the parties, who may vary the terms of their marriages on the model of freedom of contract; or does even modern marriage depend on collective moral and political judgments, which continue to constitute marriage as a status?

The following materials begin to address this question in earnest. But before taking them up, it is worth making an aside in order to avoid a confusion. The rise of same-sex marriage does not constitute a transformation in the character of marriage, with respect to the distinction between status and contract. Rather, it merely changes, to expand, the set of pairings of persons that might avail themselves of marriage, however it is constituted. If marriage remains a status, then same-sex marriage changes the substantive rules of the status; and if marriage is a contract, then same-sex marriage removes an impediment to freedom of contract. These are morally and political important changes, but they are less important from the perspective of the formal structure of marriage and hence from the perspective of contract theory.

The legal materials through which same-sex marriage is being created generally recognize this distinction. For example, the most prominent judicial opinion concerning the right to same-sex marriage expressly recognizes marriage's status-like character:

> In a real sense, there are three partners to every civil marriage: two willing spouses and an approving State. While only the parties can mutually assent to marriage, the terms of the marriage—who may marry and what obligations, benefits, and liabilities attach to civil marriage—are set by the Commonwealth. Conversely, while only the parties can agree to end the marriage the Commonwealth defines the terms of exit.

Goodridge v. Department of Public Health, 798 N.E.2d 941 (Mass. 2003). The court thus framed the plaintiff's complaint in terms of a denial of access to a valuable status, observing that "Massachusetts, [by] denying marriage licenses to the plaintiffs was denying them access to civil marriage itself, with its appurtenant social and legal protections, benefits, and obligation." *Id.* at 950. Legislatures have framed the question in similar terms (including even where they have reached slightly different conclusions). The Hawai'i statute creating same-sex domestic partnerships, for example, explains that "[t]he purpose of this chapter is to extend certain rights and benefits which are presently available only to married couples to couples composed of two individuals who are legally prohibited from marrying under state law." Hawai'i Revised Statutes § 572C–1 (1997). These remarks recognize that same sex marriage and related legal developments expand access to marriage but do not change the marriage form.

Once again, liberalization of a status is not the same thing as its contractualization.

23.2.A   ANTE-NUPTIAL AGREEMENTS

The common law limited married persons' capacity to adjust their duties not just in marriage but also on the marriage's dissolution (recall *Balfour*). Modern marriage, by contrast, has been substantially contractualized in at least one respect: the parties to a marriage may today specify, in advance of becoming married, how their marriage partnership will be wound up in case of divorce. Parties achieve this control over their property at divorce through entering into ante-nuptial agreements.[36]

Where there is no ante-nuptial agreement, the law specifies the division of marital assets on divorce. In the United States, the legal regime

---

36. Note that these agreements govern only the financial relations between *spouses* on divorce. The arrangements between divorcing spouses and their shared children, including the obligation to pay *child support*, are another matter. These arrangements are not contractualized (nor, given that the children are minors) could they possibly be.

governing the division varies from State to State. Most States continue to follow the *common law* regime. Recall that at common law a husband acquired a duty to provide materially for his wife. This duty did not end at divorce, and husbands retained obligations to provide for their wives following divorce. Today, these obligations are no longer expressly gendered, but rather apply to the higher earner and in support of the lower earner. They require the higher wage earner to give the lower a fair and equitable portion of marital property. At the same time, the common law regime treats private title within the marriage as enduring through the divorce, as *Lewis* illustrated. A minority of States, mostly in the west and influenced by Mexican law, have adopted *community property* regimes of the form preferred by civil law. Under community property regimes, property acquired in a marriage (except for gifts and inheritances) is treated as jointly owned and divided, presumptively equally, on divorce. (Some community property states, including most notably California, mandate a 50/50 division by statute.) Community property is commonly thought to be more egalitarian than the common law regime, but it is no less a creature of the law. As with same-sex marriage, greater equality in the relation does not make for greater liberty in respect of fixing the relation's terms, and so it does not change marriage's status quality.

Ante-nuptial agreements are another matter. Insofar as such agreements are recognized by law, they allow the parties to a marriage to fix the terms of the marriage's breakup, as they see fit. Ante-nuptial agreements cause a marriage's dissolution to be governed not by the community's sense of morality or equity but rather by the intentions of the parties who made the marriage and its attendant agreements. Recognizing such agreements would truly import contract into marriage, at least with respect to certain aspects of the marriage relation. The following materials illustrate how far the law has gone in recognizing ante-nuptial agreements.

Crews v. Crews

Supreme Court of Connecticut, 2010.
989 A.2d 1060.

■ VERTEFEUILLE, J. In this certified appeal, the plaintiff, Melinda Crews, appeals from the judgment of the Appellate Court reversing in part the judgment of the trial court with regard to certain financial orders included in the dissolution of her marriage to the defendant, Stephen Crews. *Crews v. Crews,* 107 Conn.App. 279 (2008). On appeal to this court, the plaintiff first claims that the Appellate Court improperly applied a plenary standard of review to the trial court's conclusion that the antenuptial agreement between the parties was unenforceable. Rather, the plaintiff claims that the Appellate Court should have applied an abuse of discretion standard to review the trial court's judgment. The plaintiff further claims that even if the Appellate Court correctly employed a plenary standard, it improperly applied that standard to the facts of the present case. The defendant responds that the Appellate Court correctly applied plenary review in concluding that the parties' antenuptial agreement was enforceable. We agree with the defendant, and, accordingly, we affirm the judgment of the Appellate Court.

The Appellate Court majority opinion summarized the following relevant facts as found by the trial court: "The parties met at a corporate outing when they both were employed by the General Electric Corporation (General Electric). At the time, the defendant was the divorced father of three children. The plaintiff had not been married previously. The defendant holds a bachelor's degree; the plaintiff has bachelor's and master's degrees. The defendant was then residing in the future marital home, a house that he had purchased from his mother in an arm's-length transaction on December 31, 1986. The plaintiff owned a condominium unit in Bridgeport. At the time, each of the parties had bank accounts, pension plans and investments.

"The parties became engaged in January, 1988, and were married on June 25, 1988. About one year prior to their wedding, the defendant raised the subject of an antenuptial agreement. The defendant believed he had been 'burned' in his previous divorce and declared: 'No agreement; no wedding!' The plaintiff told the defendant that she was 'no fan [of an antenuptial agreement], but agreed with him in concept.' The defendant described the agreement as a precondition to the wedding itself and presented the plaintiff with a draft of the agreement on May 31, 1988. The parties signed the agreement on June 24, 1988, one day before they were married.

"Following their marriage, the parties resided in the marital home and had two children, a daughter born in May, 1989, and a learning disabled son born in May, 1992. Both parties were employed during their marriage, and initially each of them traveled extensively in connection with his or her employment. At the time of [the dissolution] trial, the defendant had been employed by General Electric for thirty-nine years, where he earned an annual base salary of $131,000 and regularly received annual bonuses. His annual net income was $98,540 at the time of dissolution. The [trial] court made no finding that the nature of the defendant's employment changed during the marriage from what it had been prior to the marriage. During the marriage, he also acquired General Electric stock and stock options, some of which was encumbered by margin loans. He also participated in two executive compensation plans in the 1990s.

"The plaintiff was fifty-three [years old] at the time of dissolution [in 2005]. From 1981 through 1986, she was a technical writer for General Electric, earning $50,000 per year. She left General Electric to join Practice Media and later the NYNEX Corporation. She worked steadily during the marriage, except for a three month maternity leave she took following the birth of each child. After the birth of the parties' children and an automobile accident, the plaintiff decided that corporate travel was too much for her in addition to her responsibilities at home. In 1993, she formed her own business known as M. Crews & Company, LLC, which she operated out of the marital home until just prior to trial. The value of the plaintiff's business then was about $96,000, and she had an annual net income of $69,056." Id., at 282–84.

The plaintiff filed her dissolution action in May, 2004. In her complaint, the plaintiff requested alimony, assignment of the marital home, an equitable division of marital assets and attorney's fees. In response, the defendant filed a cross complaint in which he sought enforcement of the antenuptial agreement, which he claimed established the appropriate financial determinations upon dissolution. The antenuptial agreement precluded the trial court from awarding the plaintiff alimony, a share in the marital home, a portion of the defendant's retirement and investment assets and attorney's fees.

Following a trial in June, 2005, the trial court rendered a judgment of dissolution, but refused to enforce the terms of the antenuptial agreement. The trial court determined that the antenuptial agreement was not governed by the provisions of the Connecticut Premarital Agreement Act (act), General Statutes § 46b–36a et seq., presumably because the act applies only to antenuptial agreements entered into on or after October 1, 1995; General Statutes § 46b–36a; and the parties had entered into their agreement on June 24, 1988. The trial court concluded, instead, that the antenuptial agreement was governed by the equitable rules established in *McHugh v. McHugh,* 181 Conn. 482 (1980).

The trial court concluded that enforcing the antenuptial agreement would be unjust under *McHugh.* It determined that a dramatic change in the parties' economic circumstances had occurred between the time that the agreement was executed and the time of the dissolution proceedings, which rendered enforcement of the ante-nuptial agreement inequitable. The trial court therefore ordered the defendant to make the following payments to the plaintiff: monthly alimony of $1000 until the death of either party, the plaintiff's remarriage, or August 31, 2010, whichever occurs first; $450,000 to compensate the plaintiff for her contribution to the appreciation in value of the marital home and for her share of the defendant's pension and investment accounts; and $25,000 for her attorney's fees.

The defendant appealed from the judgment of the trial court to the Appellate Court, claiming that the trial court, inter alia, improperly had failed to enforce the antenuptial agreement. *Crews v. Crews,* supra, 107 Conn.App. at 281. The Appellate Court majority, applying a plenary standard of review, concluded that the trial court incorrectly had applied the *McHugh* factors in determining that the antenuptial agreement was unenforceable and "reverse[d] that portion of the judgment requiring the defendant to pay the plaintiff time limited alimony, attorney's fees, a lump sum property settlement and a portion of his pension and investments." Id., at 299. In his dissent, Judge Gruendel concluded that the Appellate Court majority should have applied an abuse of discretion standard in its review of the trial court's judgment, and, further, that it should have affirmed that judgment. Id., at 317. This certified appeal followed. Additional facts and procedural history will be provided as necessary.

We begin our analysis with a brief overview of our common law governing antenuptial agreements. In *McHugh v. McHugh,* supra, 181 Conn. at 486, this court explicitly determined that "[a]n antenuptial agreement is a type of contract and must, therefore, comply with ordinary principles of contract law." The court specifically noted that "antenuptial agreements are to be construed according to the principles of construction applicable to contracts generally." Id., at 491. Although general contract principles apply to antenuptial agreements, this court additionally determined that "[t]he validity of an antenuptial contract depends upon the circumstances of the particular case." Id., at 485. This court then established the seminal, three-prong test governing the enforceability of antenuptial agreements in this state: "[a]ntenuptial agreements relating to the property of the parties, and more specifically, to the rights of the parties to that property upon the dissolution of the marriage, are generally enforceable where three conditions are satisfied: (1) the contract was validly entered into; (2) its terms do not violate statute or public policy; and (3) *the circumstances of the parties at the time the marriage is dissolved are not so beyond the contemplation of the parties at the time the contract was entered into as to cause its enforcement to work injustice.*" (Emphasis added.) Id., at 485–86.

On appeal, in both the Appellate Court and this court, the parties have not challenged the trial court's conclusion pursuant to *McHugh* that the parties validly entered into the agreement and that the terms of the agreement do not violate state or public policy. See *Crews v. Crews,* supra, 107 Conn.App. at 288 ("[t]he [trial] court further found that the agreement contains no provision that either shocks the conscience or violates public policy and that it was enforceable at the time of its execution"). Those two issues, therefore, are not in dispute and the present appeal turns on the third prong of the *McHugh* test.

I

The plaintiff first claims that the Appellate Court incorrectly applied plenary review to the trial court's decision that the antenuptial agreement between the parties was unenforceable. Specifically, the plaintiff contends that the Appellate Court should have reviewed the judgment of the trial court for abuse of discretion because the trial court based its decision on factual and equitable determinations that normally receive abuse of discretion review. The defendant responds that the Appellate Court properly applied plenary review because the trial court's decision was a legal determination governed by principles of contract law, and therefore is appropriately subjected to plenary review. We agree with the defendant.

The Appellate Court majority determined that plenary review was appropriate in this case due to the nature of the *McHugh* analysis. As the majority summarized: "[w]hen an appellant's claim alleges that the facts found by the court were insufficient to support its legal conclusions, we are presented with a mixed question of fact and law to which the plenary standard of review applies. Our task is to determine whether the court's conclusions are legally and logically correct and find support in the facts that appear in the record." (Citations omitted.) Id., at 289.

We begin our analysis with our own standard of review. Determining the appropriate standard of review is a question of law, and as a result, it is subject to plenary review. See, e.g., *Fish v. Fish,* 285 Conn. 24, 37 (2008) (trial court's determination of proper legal standard in any given case is question of law subject to plenary review); *Hartford Courant Co. v. Freedom of Information Commission,* 261 Conn. 86, 96–97 (2002) (same). We thus exercise plenary review of the Appellate Court's determination to apply a plenary standard of review of the trial court's decision in the present case.

As previously set forth herein, this appeal turns on the third *McHugh* prong, namely, whether the circumstances at the time of dissolution were so "beyond the contemplation" of the parties at the time the antenuptial agreement was signed that enforcement of the agreement would work an injustice. *McHugh v. McHugh,* supra, 181 Conn. at 485–86. This inquiry necessitates the determination of the parties' intent at the time they signed the agreement. "The intent of the parties as expressed in a contract is determined from the language used interpreted in the light of the situation of the parties and the circumstances connected with the transaction. [T]he intent of the parties is to be ascertained by a fair and reasonable construction of the written words and the language used must be accorded its common, natural, and ordinary meaning and usage where it can be sensibly applied to the subject matter of the contract. Where the language of the contract is clear and unambiguous, the contract is to be given effect according to its terms." (Internal quotation marks omitted.) *Connecticut Light & Power Co. v. Lighthouse Landings, Inc.,* 279 Conn. 90, 109–10 (2006). It is well established that "[w]here there is definitive contract language, *the determination of what the parties intended by their contractual commitments is a question of law.*" (Emphasis added.) Id., at 109,. It is axiomatic that a matter of law is entitled to plenary review on appeal. See, e.g., *Lopiano v. Lopiano,* 247 Conn. 356, 363 (1998) (matter of law subject to plenary review).

Moreover, "[s]o-called mixed questions of fact and law, which require the application of a legal standard to the historical-fact determinations, are not facts in this sense. [Such questions require] plenary review by this court unfettered by the clearly erroneous standard. When legal conclusions of the trial court are challenged on appeal, we must decide whether [those] conclusions are legally and logically correct and find support in the facts that appear in the record." (Citation omitted; internal quotation marks omitted.) *Friezo v. Friezo,* 281 Conn. 166, 181 (2007). In conducting an analysis pursuant to *McHugh,* a court must review the factual circumstances at the time the antenuptial agreement was signed and at the time the dissolution is ordered, both of which involve factual inquiries. A court also must ascertain the intent of the parties at the time the antenuptial agreement was signed, which, as set forth previously, is a legal conclusion. If the court finds that the circumstances at the time of dissolution are not so far beyond the contemplation of the parties at the time the antenuptial agreement was written, the antenuptial agreement is enforced as a matter of law. As a result, "[a] less deferential standard [of review] applies [because] the decision of the trial court is based not on an exercise of discretion but on a purported principle of law." (Internal quotation marks omitted.) *Loughlin v. Loughlin,* 280 Conn. 632, 641 (2006). It is settled that "[q]uestions of law and mixed questions of law and fact receive plenary review." *Duperry v. Solnit,* 261 Conn. 309, 318 (2002); see also *Winchester v. McCue,* 91 Conn.App. 721, 729 (applying plenary standard of review to *McHugh's* third prong).

Whether enforcement of an agreement would work an injustice is analogous to determining whether enforcement of an agreement would be unconscionable. It is well established that "[t]he question of unconscionability is a matter of law to be decided by the court based on all the facts and circumstances of the case. Thus, our review on appeal is unlimited by the clearly erroneous [or abuse of discretion] standard. This means that the ultimate determination of whether a transaction is unconscionable is a question of law, not a question of fact, and that the trial court's determination on that issue is subject to a plenary review on appeal." (Citations omitted; internal quotation marks omitted.) *Cheshire Mortgage Service, Inc. v. Montes,* 223 Conn. 80, 87–88 (1992). We therefore conclude that the Appellate Court majority properly applied a plenary standard of review to the trial court's ruling.

The plaintiff nevertheless contends that the abuse of discretion standard is normally employed to review family law matters. Although this is true, the abuse of discretion standard applies only to decisions based solely on factual determinations made by the trial court. See, e.g., *Simms v. Simms,* 283 Conn. 494, 502 (2007) (alimony orders subjected to abuse of discretion review); *Sablosky v. Sablosky,* 258 Conn. 713, 721 (2001) (contempt orders subjected to abuse of discretion review); *Madigan v. Madigan,* 224 Conn. 749, 758 (1993) (custody orders subjected to abuse of discretion review). When the trial court conducts a legal analysis or considers a mixed question of law and fact, plenary review is appropriate, even in the family law context. See, e.g., *Dutkiewicz v. Dutkiewicz,* 289 Conn. 362, 372 (2008) (claim that parenting order violated parent's right to decision-making authority subject to plenary review because it incorporated statutory interpretation); *Gershman v. Gershman,* 286 Conn. 341, 346 (2008) ("[a]lthough we generally apply the well settled abuse of discretion standard in domestic relations matters, our review in the present case is plenary because we address the question of what, as a matter of law, constitutes dissipation [of family assets] in the context of a marital dissolution proceeding"); *Montoya v. Montoya,* 280 Conn. 605, 612 (2006) (if antenuptial agreement is "unambiguous within its four corners," parties' intent is question of law necessitating plenary review). We therefore disagree with the plaintiff's contention that we should employ the abuse of discretion standard.

II

The plaintiff next claims that even if the Appellate Court properly employed a plenary standard of review, it improperly applied that standard to the facts of the present case. Specifically, the plaintiff contends that the trial court's conclusion that enforcement of the antenuptial agreement would result in an injustice is supported by the evidence in the record. The defendant responds that the Appellate Court correctly applied the plenary standard of review, and, further, that there is insufficient evidence in the record to demonstrate that the change in the circumstances between the parties at the time of dissolution was not contemplated. We agree with the defendant.

The following additional facts and procedural history are relevant to our analysis. The antenuptial agreement between the parties established their financial rights and responsibilities during the marriage, upon dissolution of the marriage, and upon the death of either party. During the marriage, each party was required to maintain continuous, gainful employment and to take all necessary measures to prevent voluntary or involuntary termination of his or her employment. The parties further agreed during the marriage to keep their respective property separate, whether owned prior to the marriage or acquired during the marriage. Each party also relinquished all rights, including all statutory rights and interests, in the other's probate estate.

The antenuptial agreement additionally provided that, in the event of dissolution, neither party would seek or accept any cash, property, alimony, attorney's fees or any other property from the other. In the event of divorce, the parties would be allowed to keep their separately owned property acquired either before or during the marriage, as well as their share of the marital property. The marital property would be divided in proportion to their respective contribution toward the purchase of that property. Other provisions related to child support and custody, including a provision that in the event of dissolution, child support would be determined on the basis of "the needs and best interest of the child and not as a function of the wealth of the noncustodial parent."

In its memorandum of decision, the trial court determined that the parties' financial circumstances had "changed dramatically" between the time they signed the agreement and the time of the dissolution, thus rendering the agreement unenforceable pursuant to the third prong of *McHugh*. The court reasoned that "the agreement was valid and enforceable at the time of its execution [but] that the evidence supports a finding that the economic circumstances of the parties have changed dramatically between the date of the agreement and the dissolution, in particular the economic circumstances of the [defendant], due in substantial part to the efforts of the [plaintiff], that given the length of the marriage, the birth of two children, and the substantial financial and nonfinancial contributions of the [plaintiff] from employment outside of the home to her parenting and homemaking efforts, it would be inequitable to enforce the terms of the prenuptial agreement of the parties."

The Appellate Court majority disagreed, concluding that "the [trial] court's finding that the changed circumstances were beyond the contemplation of the parties at the time they signed the agreement is not supported by the record." *Crews v. Crews,* supra, 107 Conn.App. at 292. Rather, the majority noted that "[t]he evidence demonstrates that the parties contemplated the possibility of a divorce proceeding and incorporated provisions in the agreement to cover such an eventuality and agreed on how to protect their respective assets. Furthermore, there is no evidence to suggest that the parties' financial circumstances at the time of [the] dissolution, relatively speaking, were anything other than what they contemplated when they signed the agreement." Id., at 293. As the Appellate Court elaborated, "[i]t is apparent that the [trial] court, in rendering its judgment, was moved by equitable considerations codified in our statutes. Those observations, however, have no bearing on whether the agreement should be enforced. In other words, whether the trial court or this court thinks the agreement was a good bargain for the plaintiff does not enter into the analysis of the issue." (Citations omitted.) Id., at 296–97. We agree.

We begin with our standard of review. As we concluded in part I of this opinion, the trial court's analysis under *McHugh* involved a mixed question of fact and law. These issues require "plenary review by this court unfettered by the clearly erroneous standard. When legal conclusions of the trial court are challenged on appeal, we must decide whether [those] conclusions are legally and logically correct and find support in the facts that appear in the record." (Citation omitted; internal quotation marks omitted.) *Friezo v. Friezo,* supra, 281 Conn. at 181. Moreover, "[w]e are mindful that [i]t is well settled that, in a certified appeal, the focus of our review is not on the actions of the trial court, but the actions of the Appellate Court. We do not hear the appeal de novo." (Internal quotation marks omitted.) *State v. Morelli,* 293 Conn. 147, 153 (2009).

We now turn to the text of the third prong of *McHugh,* which provides that "[a]ntenuptial agreements relating to the property of the parties, and more specifically, to the rights of the parties to that property upon the dissolution of the marriage, are generally enforceable [if] the circumstances of the parties at the time the marriage is dissolved *are not so beyond the contemplation* of the parties at the time the contract was entered into as to cause its enforcement to work injustice." (Emphasis added.) *McHugh v. McHugh,* supra, 181 Conn. at 485–86. Although we previously have not had occasion to elaborate on the requirements of the third prong of *McHugh,* we now clarify the appropriate analysis. To render unenforceable an otherwise valid ante-nuptial agreement, a court must determine: (1) the parties' intent and circumstances when they signed the antenuptial agreement; (2) the circumstances of the parties at the time of the dissolution of the marriage; (3) whether those circumstances are "so far beyond" the contemplation of the parties at the time of execution; and (4) if the circumstances are beyond the parties' initial contemplation, whether enforcement would cause an injustice.

The Appellate Court majority correctly determined that the trial court failed to make the requisite findings required by *McHugh* in concluding not to enforce the terms of the antenuptial agreement. As the Appellate Court noted, "[i]t is apparent that the [trial] court, in rendering its judgment, was moved by equitable considerations codified in our statutes. The agreement required the court to adjudicate a contract action in which the traditional notions of equity are not germane because there was an agreement and the evidence does not support a finding that there was a dramatic change in the parties' financial circumstances. In other words, whether the trial court or this court thinks the agreement was a good bargain for the plaintiff does not enter into the analysis.'' (Citations omitted.) *Crews v. Crews,* supra, 107 Conn.App. at 296–97. The Appellate Court thus clearly recognized that the trial court did not make the requisite findings on the parties' intent and whether that intent comported with their current circumstances, two critical elements of a proper analysis under *McHugh.*

It is additionally clear that the party seeking to challenge the enforceability of the antenuptial contract bears a heavy burden. In explaining the third prong in *McHugh,* this court offered the example that "where the economic status of [the] parties has *changed dramatically* between the date of the agreement and the dissolution, literal enforcement of the agreement may work injustice. Absent such *unusual circumstances,* however, antenuptial agreements freely and fairly entered into *will be honored and enforced by the courts as written.*" (Emphasis added.) *McHugh v. McHugh,* supra, 181 Conn. at 489, 436 A.2d 8. This heavy burden comports with the well settled general principle that "[c]ourts of law must allow parties to make their own contracts." *Connecticut Union of Telephone Workers v. Southern New England Telephone Co.,* 148 Conn. 192, 201 (1961). "It is established well beyond the need for citation that parties are free to contract for whatever terms on which they may agree." *Holly Hill Holdings v. Lowman,* 226 Conn. 748, 755 (1993). "Whether provident or improvident, an agreement moved on calculated considerations is entitled to the sanction of the law." *Collins v. Sears, Roebuck & Co.,* 164 Conn. 369, 375 (1973).

Although this court previously has not construed the third prong of *McHugh* in any significant manner, precedent from the Appellate Court supports our conclusion that proving uncontemplated, dramatically changed circumstances requires a significant showing. In *Winchester v. McCue,* supra, 91 Conn.App. at 729–31, the Appellate Court emphasized that *McHugh* requires an "extraordinary change in economic status" and noted "that the threshold for finding such a dramatic change is high." Id., at 730. In *Winchester,* the Appellate Court concluded that an alleged 430 percent increase in the value of the defendant husband's estate was *not* beyond the parties' comprehension when they drafted their antenuptial agreement. Id. The court reasoned "that it must have been contemplated by the parties that the defendant would continue working in the corporate arena and that, over the course of years, his income would increase as well as his retirement benefits and investments. *These circumstances do not constitute the type of dramatic or unusual circumstances contemplated by McHugh.*" (Emphasis added.) Id., at 731.

In the present case, it is clear that the Appellate Court majority properly recognized and applied the plaintiff's heightened burden. The court concluded that "[p]ursuant to *McHugh* and *Winchester,* which make it clear that the threshold for a finding of dramatic change in circumstances is high not only does the evidence not support the [trial] court's conclusion that there was a dramatic change in the financial circumstances of the parties between the time of their marriage and its dissolution but also [that court's determination] that the financial circumstances that existed at the time of dissolution were well within the contemplation of the parties when they signed the agreement, i.e., that is why the defendant wanted the plaintiff to sign the agreement." *Crews v. Crews,* supra, 107 Conn.App. at 298.

Moreover, the evidence supports the Appellate Court's conclusion that the circumstances at the time of dissolution were consistent with the parties' expectations and the intended purpose of the antenuptial agreement. Id. For instance, the antenuptial agreement had an express provision affirming the obligation of both parties to remain gainfully employed. In accordance with this obligation, the defendant maintained his employment during the length of the marriage. He therefore continued to receive his salary, bonuses and retirement and investment benefits, all of which continued to increase as he remained employed at General Electric and advanced his career. As the Appellate Court properly noted, "[t]he plaintiff has not argued that the appreciation of the defendant's assets was not in keeping with the economy's growth during the marriage." Id., at 294. The court specifically noted that, "[t]he plaintiff has not brought to our attention any evidence that the nature of the defendant's employment changed or that his salary and benefits changed in any fashion other than what one might expect for someone in his position." Id., at 295; see also *Winchester v. McCue,* supra, 91 Conn.App. at 731 (natural increase in assets and wealth from continued employment not uncontemplated change). Thus, the defendant's financial situation at the time of the dissolution was within the realm of the parties' contemplation at the time of execution of the antenuptial agreement.

Moreover, the Appellate Court correctly noted that "[b]y signing the [antenuptial] agreement, the plaintiff also recognized that the defendant desired to segregate all of his property from any interest she may have had in it"; *Crews v. Crews,* supra, 107 Conn.App. at 293; which included the marital residence. It was an express and intended consequence of the antenuptial agreement, and thus the parties' intent at the time of execution, that the defendant retain full ownership of the marital residence in the event the marriage was dissolved. The Appellate Court appropriately recognized that any increase in the defendant's equity as a result of his paying the mortgage on the marital home was a natural and probable result of his continued claim to the property. Id., at 294. The court correctly pointed out that "the plaintiff agreed to that financial arrangement [of the defendant paying the mortgage while the plaintiff paid daily expenses] knowing full well that the defendant owned the marital home and that the [antenuptial] agreement permitted him to retain it and the rest of his assets should a divorce occur." Id.

The evidence also clearly supports the Appellate Court's refusal to credit the trial court's emphasis on the plaintiff's employment and home-making efforts. As the Appellate Court summarized: "We also cannot agree [with the trial court's conclusion] that the plaintiff's efforts alone contributed to the increased value of the parties' finances. *Pursuant to the [antenuptial] agreement,* the plaintiff agreed to work throughout the marriage." (Emphasis added.) Id., at 296. The antenuptial agreement plainly requires both parties to maintain employment. It further contemplated the birth of children as evidenced by select provisions addressing the amount of maternity leave that the plaintiff would be allowed. Yet, despite its contemplation of the birth of children, the antenuptial agreement clearly intended and required that the plaintiff maintain her employment. It would be inappropriate, therefore, to give the plaintiff additional consideration for fulfilling her contractual obligation.

We conclude that the Appellate Court properly ordered the trial court to enforce the provisions for which the plaintiff contracted. The circumstances of the parties at the time of dissolution accurately reflected their initial intention as expressed in the agreement, namely, two working adults with separate financial arrangements and assets, each protected from claims by the other. As the antenuptial agreement provides, both the plaintiff and the defendant "[desire] to keep all of [his or her] property, now owned or hereafter acquired, free from any claim that [the other] might otherwise acquire by reason of the marriage, [or] any dissolution thereof." In the absence of a clear indication that the antenuptial agreement is unenforceable because it was not validly entered into, that it violated public policy, or that it would be unjust to enforce the agreement due to a significant and uncontemplated change in the parties' circumstances; *McHugh v. McHugh,* supra, 181 Conn. at 485–86; we are unable to rewrite the terms of the contract to which the parties themselves agreed. *Gibson v. Capano,* 241 Conn. 725, 732 (1997) ("[i]t is axiomatic that courts do not rewrite contracts for the parties").

The judgment of the Appellate Court is affirmed.

In this opinion the other justices concurred.

Uniform Premarital Agreement Act of 1983

PREFATORY NOTE

The number of marriages between persons previously married and the number of marriages between persons each of whom is intending to continue to pursue a career is steadily increasing. For these and other reasons, it is becoming more and more common for persons contemplating marriage to seek to resolve by agreement certain issues presented by the forthcoming marriage. However, despite a lengthy legal history for these premarital agreements, there is a substantial uncertainty as to the enforceability of all, or a portion, of the provisions of these agreements and a significant lack of uniformity of treatment of these agreements among the states. The problems caused by this uncertainty and nonuniformity are greatly exacerbated by the mobility of our population. Nevertheless, this uncertainty and nonuniformity seem reflective not so much of basic policy differences between the states but rather a result of spasmodic, reflexive response to varying factual circumstances at different times. Accordingly, uniform legislation conforming to modern social policy which provides both certainty and sufficient flexibility to accommodate different circumstances would appear to be both a significant improvement and a goal realistically capable of achievement.

This Act is intended to be relatively limited in scope. Section 1 defines a "premarital agreement" as "an agreement between prospective spouses made in contemplation of marriage and to be effective upon marriage." Section 2 requires that a premarital agreement be in writing and signed by both parties. Section 4 provides that a premarital agreement becomes effective upon the marriage of the parties. These sections establish significant parameters. That is, the Act does not deal with agreements between persons who live together but who do not contemplate marriage or who do not marry. Nor does the Act provide for postnuptial or separation agreements or with oral agreements.

On the other hand, agreements which are embraced by the act are permitted to deal with a wide variety of matters and Section 3 provides an illustrative list of those matters, including spousal support, which may properly be dealt with in a premarital agreement.

Section 6 is the key operative section of the Act and sets forth the conditions under which a premarital agreement is not enforceable. An agreement is not enforceable if the party against whom enforcement is sought proves that (a) he or she did not execute the agreement voluntarily or that (b) the agreement was unconscionable when it was executed and, before execution of the agreement, he or she (1) was not provided a fair and reasonable disclosure of the property or financial obligations of the other party, (2) did not voluntarily and expressly waive, in writing, any right to disclosure of the property or financial obligations of the other party beyond the disclosure provided, and (3) did not have, or reasonably could not have had, an adequate knowledge of the property and financial obligations of the other party.

Even if these conditions are not proven, if a provision of a premarital agreement modifies or eliminates spousal support, and that modification or elimination would cause a party to be eligible for support under a program of public assistance at the time of separation, marital dissolution, or death, a court is authorized to order the other party to provide support to the extent necessary to avoid that eligibility.

These sections form the heart of the Act; the remaining sections deal with more tangential issues. Section 5 prescribes the manner in which a premarital agreement may be amended or revoked; Section 7 provides for very limited enforcement where a marriage is subsequently determined to be void; and Section 8 tolls any statute of limitations applicable to an action asserting a claim for relief under a premarital agreement during the parties' marriage.

Uniform Premarital Agreement Act

SECTION 1. DEFINITIONS. As used in this Act:

(1) "Premarital agreement" means an agreement between prospective spouses made in contemplation of marriage and to be effective upon marriage.

(2) "Property" means an interest, present or future, legal or equitable, vested or contingent, in real or personal property, including income and earnings.

Comment

The definition of "premarital agreement" set forth in subsection (1) is limited to an agreement between prospective spouses made in contemplation of and to be effective upon marriage. Agreements between persons living together but not contemplating marriage (see *Marvin v. Marvin*, 18 Cal. 3d 660 (1976), judgment after trial modified, 122 Cal. App. 3d 871 (1981)) and postnuptial or separation agreements are outside the scope of this Act. Formal requirements are prescribed by Section 2. An illustrative list of matters which may be included in an agreement is set forth in Section 3.

Subsection (2) is designed to embrace all forms of property and interests therein. These may include rights in a professional license or practice, employee benefit plans, pension and retirement accounts, and so on. The reference to income or earnings includes both income from property and earnings from personal services.

SECTION 2. FORMALITIES. A premarital agreement must be in writing and signed by both parties. It is enforceable without consideration.

Comment

This section restates the common requirement that a premarital agreement be reduced to writing and signed by both parties (see Ariz. Rev. Stats. § 25–201; Ark. Stats. § 55–310; Cal. Civ. C. § 5134; 13 Dela. Code 1974 § 301; Idaho Code § 32–917; Ann. Laws Mass. ch. 209, § 25; Minn. Stats. Ann. § 519.11; Montana Rev. C. § 36–123; New Mex Stats. Ann. 1978 40–2–4; Ore. Rev. Stats. § 108.140; Vernon's Texas Codes Ann. § 5.44; Vermont Stats. Ann. Title 12, § 181). Many states also require other formalities, including notarization or an acknowledgement (see, e.g., Arizona, Arkansas, California, Idaho, Montana, New Mexico) but may then permit the formal statutory requirement to be avoided or satisfied subsequent to execution (see *In re Marriage of Cleveland*, 76 Cal. App. 3d 357 (1977) (premarital agreement never acknowledged but "proved" by sworn testimony of parties in dissolution proceeding)). This act dispenses with all formal requirements except a writing signed by both parties. Although the section is framed in the singular, the agreement may consist of one or more documents intended to be part of the agreement and executed as required by this section.

Section 2 also restates what appears to be the almost universal rule regarding the marriage as consideration for a premarital agreement (see, e.g., Ga. Code § 20–303; *Barnhill v. Barnhill*, 386 So. 2d 749 (Ala. Civ. App. 1980); *Estate of Gillilan v. Estate of Gillilan*, 406 N.E. 2d 981 (Ind. App. 1980); *Friedlander v. Friedlander*, 494 P.2d 208 (Wash. 1972); but cf. *Wilson v. Wilson*, 170 A. 2d 679, 685 (Me. 1961)). The primary importance of this rule has been to provide a degree of mutuality of benefits to support the enforceability of a premarital agreement. A marriage is a prerequisite for the effectiveness of a premarital agreement under this act (see Section 4). This requires that there be a ceremonial marriage. Even if this marriage is subsequently determined to have been void, Section 7 may provide limits of enforceability of an agreement entered into in contemplation of that marriage. Consideration as such is not required and the standards for enforceability are established by Sections 6 and 7. Nevertheless, this provision is retained here as a desirable, if not essential, restatement of the law. On the other hand, the fact that marriage is deemed to be consideration for the purpose of this act does not change the rules applicable in other areas of law (see, e.g., 26 U.S.C.A. § 2043 (release of certain marital rights not treated as consideration for federal estate tax), 2512; *Merrill v. Fahs*, 324 U.S. 308, rehearing denied 324 U.S. 888 (release of marital rights in premarital agreement not adequate and full consideration for purposes of federal gift tax).

Finally, a premarital agreement is a contract. As required for any other contract, the parties must have the capacity to contract in order to enter into a binding agreement. Those persons who lack the capacity to contract but who under other provisions of law are permitted to enter into a binding agreement may enter into a premarital agreement under those other provisions of law.

SECTION 3.   CONTENT.

(a) Parties to a premarital agreement may contract with respect to:

(1) the rights and obligations of each of the parties in any of the property of either or both of them whenever and wherever acquired or located;

(2) the right to buy, sell, use, transfer, exchange, abandon, lease, consume, expend, assign, create a security interest in, mortgage, encumber, dispose of, or otherwise manage and control property;

(3) the disposition of property upon separation, marital dissolution, death, or the occurrence or nonoccurrence of any other event;

(4) the modification or elimination of spousal support;

(5) the making of a will, trust, or other arrangement to carry out the provisions of the agreement;

(6) the ownership rights in and disposition of the death benefit from a life insurance policy;

(7) the choice of law governing the construction of the agreement; and

(8) any other matter, including their personal rights and obligations, not in violation of public policy or a statute imposing a criminal penalty.

(b) The right of a child to support may not be adversely affected by a premarital agreement.

Comment

Section 3 permits the parties to contract in a premarital agreement with respect to any matter listed and any other matter not in violation of public policy or any statute imposing a criminal penalty. The matters are intended to be illustrative, not exclusive. Paragraph (4) of subsection (a) specifically authorizes the parties to deal with spousal support obligations. There is a split in authority among the states as to whether an premarital agreement may control the issue of spousal support. Some few states do not permit a premarital agreement to control this issue (see, e.g., *In re Marriage of Winegard*, 278 N.W. 2d 505 (Iowa 1979); *Fricke v. Fricke*, 42 N.W. 2d 500 (Wis. 1950)). However, the better view and growing trend is to permit a premarital agreement to govern this matter if the agreement and the circumstances of its execution satisfy certain standards (see, e.g., *Newman v. Newman*, 653 P.2d 728 (Colo. Sup. Ct. 1982); *Parniawski v. Parniawski*, 359 A.2d 719 (Conn. 1976); *Volid v. Volid*, 286 N.E. 2d 42 (Ill. 1972); *Osborne v. Osborne*, 428 N.E. 2d 810 (Mass. 1981); *Hudson v. Hudson*, 350 P.2d 596 (Okla. 1960); *Unander v. Unander*, 506 P.2d 719 (Ore. 1973)) (see Sections 7 and 8).

Paragraph (8) of subsection (a) makes clear that the parties may also contract with respect to other matters, including personal rights and obligations, not in violation of public policy or a criminal statute. Hence, subject to this limitation, an agreement may provide for such matters as the choice of abode, the freedom to pursue career opportunities, the upbringing of children, and so on. However, subsection (b) of this section makes clear that an agreement may not adversely affect what would otherwise be the obligation of a party to a child.

SECTION 4.   EFFECT OF MARRIAGE. A premarital agreement becomes effective upon marriage.

Comment

This section establishes a marriage as a prerequisite for the effectiveness of a premarital agreement. As a consequence, the act does not provide for a situation where persons live together without marrying. In that situation, the parties must look to the other law of the jurisdiction (see *Marvin v. Marvin*, 18 Cal. 3d 660 (1976); judgment after trial modified, 122 Cal. App. 3d 871 (1981)).

SECTION 5.   AMENDMENT, REVOCATION. After marriage, a premarital agreement may be amended or revoked only by a written agreement signed by the parties. The amended agreement or the revocation is enforceable without consideration.

Comment

This section requires the same formalities of execution for an amendment or revocation of a premarital agreement as are required for its original execution (cf. *Estate of Gillilan v. Estate of Gillilan*, 406 N.E. 2d 981 (Ind. App. 1980) (agreement may be altered by subsequent agreement but not simply by inconsistent acts).

SECTION 6.   ENFORCEMENT.

(a) A premarital agreement is not enforceable if the party against whom enforcement is sought proves that:

(1) that party did not execute the agreement voluntarily; or

(2) the agreement was unconscionable when it was executed and, before execution of the agreement, that party:

(i) was not provided a fair and reasonable disclosure of the property or financial obligations of the other party;

(ii) did not voluntarily and expressly waive, in writing, any right to disclosure of the property or financial obligations of the other party beyond the disclosure provided; and

(iii) did not have, or reasonably could not have had, an adequate knowledge of the property or financial obligations of the other party.

(b) If a provision of a premarital agreement modifies or eliminates spousal support and that modification or elimination causes one party to the agreement to be eligible for support under a program of public assistance at the time of separation or marital dissolution, a court, notwithstanding the terms of the agreement, may require the other party to provide support to the extent necessary to avoid that eligibility.

(c) An issue of unconscionability of a premarital agreement shall be decided by the court as a matter of law.

Comment

This section sets forth the conditions which must be proven to avoid the enforcement of a premarital agreement. If prospective spouses enter into a premarital agreement and their subsequent marriage is determined to be void, the enforceability of the agreement is governed by Section 7.

The conditions stated under subsection (a) are comparable to concepts which are expressed in the statutory and decisional law of many jurisdictions. Enforcement based on disclosure and voluntary execution is perhaps most common (see, e.g., Ark. Stats. § 55–309; Minn. Stats. Ann. § 519.11; *In re Kaufmann's Estate*, 171 A. 2d 48 (Pa. 1961) (alternate holding)). However, knowledge or reason to know, together with voluntary execution, may also be sufficient (see, e.g., Tenn. Code Ann. § 36–606; *Barnhill v. Barnhill*, 386 So. 2d 749 (Ala. Civ. App. 1980); *Del Vecchio v. Del Vecchio*, 143 So. 2d 17 (Fla. 1962); *Coward and Coward*, 582 P. 2d 834 (Or. App.

1978); but see *Matter of Estate of Lebsock*, 618 P.2d 683 (Colo. App. 1980)) and so may a voluntary, knowing waiver (see *Hafner v. Hafner*, 295 N.W. 2d 567 (Minn. 1980)). In each of these situations, it should be underscored that execution must have been voluntary (see *Lutgert v. Lutgert*, 338 So. 2d 1111 (Fla. 1976); see also 13 Dela. Code 1974 § 301 (10 day waiting period)). Finally, a premarital agreement is enforceable if enforcement would not have been unconscionable at the time the agreement was executed (cf. *Hartz v. Hartz*, 234 A.2d 865 (Md. 1967) (premarital agreement upheld if no disclosure but agreement was fair and equitable under the circumstances)).

The test of "unconscionability" is drawn from Section 306 of the Uniform Marriage and Divorce Act (UMDA) (see *Ferry v. Ferry*, 586 S.W. 2d 782 (Mo. 1979); see also *Newman v. Newman*, 653 P.2d 728 (Colo. Sup. Ct. 1982) (maintenance provisions of premarital agreement tested for unconscionability at time of marriage termination)). The following discussion set forth in the Commissioner's Note to Section 306 of the UMDA is equally appropriate here:

"Subsection (b) undergirds the freedom allowed the parties by making clear that the terms of the agreement respecting maintenance and property disposition are binding upon the court unless those terms are found to be unconscionable. The standard of unconscionability is used in commercial law, where its meaning includes protection against onesidedness, oppression, or unfair surprise (see section 2–302, Uniform Commercial Code), and in contract law, Scott v. U.S., 12 Wall (U.S.) 443 (1870) ('contract unreasonable and unconscionable but not void for fraud'); Stiefler v. McCullough, 174 N.E. 823, 97 Ind.App. 123 (1931); Terre Haute Cooperage v. Branscome, 35 So.2d 537, 203 Miss. 493 (1948); Carter v. Boone County Trust Co., 92 S.W. 2d 647, 338 Mo. 629 (1936). It has been used in cases respecting divorce settlements or awards. Bell v. Bell, 371 P.2d 773, 150 Colo. 174 (1962) ('this division of property is manifestly unfair, inequitable and unconscionable'). Hence the act does not introduce a novel standard unknown to the law. In the context of negotiations between spouses as to the financial incidents of their marriage, the standard includes protection against overreaching, concealment of assets, and sharp dealing not consistent with the obligations of marital partners to deal fairly with each other.

"In order to determine whether the agreement is unconscionable, the court may look to the economic circumstances of the parties resulting from the agreement, and any other relevant evidence such as the conditions under which the agreement was made, including the knowledge of the other party. If the court finds the agreement not unconscionable, its terms respecting property division and maintenance may not be altered by the court at the hearing." (Commissioner's Note, Sec. 306, Uniform Marriage and Divorce Act.)

Nothing in Section 6 makes the absence of assistance of independent legal counsel a condition for the unenforceability of a premarital agreement. However, lack of that assistance may well be a factor in determining whether the conditions stated in Section 6 may have existed (see, e.g., *Del Vecchio v. Del Vecchio*, 143 So.2d 17 (Fla. 1962)).

Even if the conditions stated in subsection (a) are not proven, if a provision of a premarital agreement modifies or eliminates spousal support, subsection (b) authorizes a court to provide very limited relief to a party who would otherwise be eligible for public welfare (see, e.g., *Osborne v. Osborne*, 428 N.E. 2d 810 (Mass. 1981) (dictum); *Unander v. Unander*, 506 P.2d 719 (Ore. 1973) (dictum)).

No special provision is made for enforcement of provisions of a premarital agreement relating to personal rights and obligations. However, a premarital agreement is a contract and these provisions may be enforced to the extent that they are enforceable are under otherwise applicable law (see *Avitzur v. Avitzur*, 459 N.Y.S. 2d 572 (Ct. App.).

Section 6 is framed in a manner to require the party who alleges that a premarital agreement is not enforceable to bear the burden of proof as to that allegation. The statutory law conflicts on the issue of where the burden of proof lies (contrast Ark. Stats. § 55–313; 31 Minn. Stats. Ann. § 519.11 with Vernon's Texas Codes Ann. § 5.45). Similarly, some courts have placed the burden on the attacking spouse to prove the invalidity of the agreement. *Linker v. Linker*, 470 P.2d 921 (Colo. 1970); *Matter of Estate of Benker*, 296 N.W. 2d 167 (Mich. App. 1980); *In re Kauffmann's Estate*, 171 A.2d 48 (Pa. 1961). Some have placed the burden upon those relying upon the agreement to prove its validity. *Hartz v. Hartz*, 234 A.2d 865 (Md. 1967). Finally, several have adopted a middle ground by stating that a premarital agreement is presumptively valid but if a disproportionate disposition is made for the wife, the husband bears the burden of proof of showing adequate disclosure. (*Del Vecchio v. Del Vecchio*, 143 So.2d 17 (Fla. 1962); *Christians v. Christians*, 44 N.W.2d 431 (Iowa 1950); *In re Neis' Estate*, 225 P.2d 110 (Kans. 1950); *Truitt v. Truitt's Adm'r*, 162 S.W. 2d 31 (Ky. 1942); *In re Estate of Strickland*, 149 N.W. 2d 344 (Neb. 1967); *Kosik v. George*, 452 P.2d 560 (Or. 1969); *Friedlander v. Friedlander*, 494 P.2d 208 (Wash. 1972).

SECTION 7.   ENFORCEMENT: VOID MARRIAGE. If a marriage is determined to be void, an agreement that would otherwise have been a premarital agreement is enforceable only to the extent necessary to avoid an inequitable result.

Comment

Under this section a void marriage does not completely invalidate an premarital agreement but does substantially limit its enforceability. Where parties have married and lived together for a substantial period of time and one or both have relied on the existence of a premarital agreement, the failure to enforce the agreement may well be inequitable. This section, accordingly, provides the court discretion to enforce the agreement to the extent necessary to avoid the inequitable result (see Annot., 46 A.L.R. 3d 1403).

SECTION 8.   LIMITATION OF ACTIONS. Any statute of limitations applicable to an action asserting a claim for relief under a premarital agreement is tolled during the marriage of the parties to the agreement. However, equitable defenses limiting the time for enforcement, including laches and estoppel, are available to either party.

Comment

In order to avoid the potentially disruptive effect of compelling litigation between the spouses in order to escape the running of an applicable statute of limitations, Section 8 tolls any applicable statute during the marriage of the parties (contrast *Dykema v. Dykema*, 412 N.E. 2d 13 (Ill. App. 1980) (statute of limitations not tolled where fraud not adequately pleaded, hence premarital agreement enforced at death)). However, a party is not completely free to sit on his or her rights because the section does preserve certain equitable defenses.

SECTION 9.   APPLICATION AND CONSTRUCTION. This [Act] shall be applied and construed to effectuate its general purpose to make uniform the law with respect to the subject of this [Act] among states enacting it.

Comment

Section 9 is a standard provision in all Uniform Acts.

SECTION 10.   SHORT TITLE. This [Act] may be cited as the Uniform Premarital Agreement Act.

Comment

This is the customary "short title" clause, which may be placed in that order in the bill for enactment as the legislative practice of the state prescribes.

SECTION 11.   SEVERABILITY. If any provision of this [Act] or its application to any person or circumstance is held invalid, the invalidity does not affect other provisions or applications of this [Act] which can be given effect without the invalid provision or application, and to this end the provisions of this [Act] are severable.

Comment

Section 11 is a standard provision included in certain Uniform Acts.

Simeone v. Simeone

Supreme Court of Pennsylvania, 1990.
581 A.2d 162.

■ FLAHERTY, JUSTICE.

At issue in this appeal is the validity of a prenuptial agreement executed between the appellant, Catherine E. Walsh Simeone, and the appellee, Frederick A. Simeone. At the time of their marriage, in 1975, appellant was a twenty-three year old nurse and appellee was a thirty-nine year old neurosurgeon. Appellee had an income of approximately $90,000 per year, and appellant was unemployed. Appellee also had assets worth approximately $300,000. On the eve of the parties' wedding, appellee's attorney presented appellant with a prenuptial agreement to be signed. Appellant, without the benefit of counsel, signed the agreement. Appellee's attorney had not advised appellant regarding any legal rights that the agreement surrendered. The parties are in disagreement as to whether appellant knew in advance of that date that such an agreement would be presented for signature. Appellant denies having had such knowledge and claims to have signed under adverse circumstances, which, she contends, provide a basis for declaring it void.

The agreement limited appellant to support payments of $200 per week in the event of separation or divorce, subject to a maximum total payment of $25,000. The parties separated in 1982, and, in 1984, divorce proceedings were commenced. Between 1982 and 1984 appellee made payments which satisfied the $25,000 limit. In 1985, appellant filed a claim for alimony *pendente lite*. A master's report upheld the validity of the prenuptial agreement and denied this claim. Exceptions to the master's report were dismissed by the Court of Common Pleas of Philadelphia County. The Superior Court affirmed. *Simeone v. Simeone*, 380 Pa.Super. 37 (1988).

We granted allowance of appeal because uncertainty was expressed by the Superior Court regarding the meaning of our plurality decision in *Estate of Geyer*, 516 Pa. 492 (1987) (Opinion Announcing Judgment of the Court). The Superior Court viewed *Geyer* as permitting a prenuptial agreement to be upheld if it *either* made a reasonable provision for the spouse *or* was entered after a full and fair disclosure of the general financial positions of the parties and the statutory rights being relinquished. Appellant contends that this interpretation of *Geyer* is in error insofar as it requires disclosure of statutory rights *only* in cases where there has not been made a reasonable provision for the spouse. Inasmuch as the courts below held that the provision made for appellant was a reasonable one, appellant's efforts to overturn the agreement have focused upon an assertion that there was an inadequate disclosure of statutory rights. Appellant continues to assert, however, that the payments provided in the agreement were less than reasonable.

The statutory rights in question are those relating to alimony *pendente lite*. Other statutory rights, such as those pertaining to alimony and equitable distribution of marital property, did not exist in 1975. Those rights arose under the Divorce Code of 1980, and the Code expressly provides that marital agreements executed prior to its effective date are not affected thereby. 23 P.S. § 103. Certainly, at the time the present agreement was executed, no disclosure was required with respect to rights which were not then in existence. The present agreement did expressly state, however, that alimony *pendente lite* was being relinquished. It also recited that appellant "has been informed and understands" that, were it not for the agreement, appellant's obligation to pay alimony *pendente lite* "might, as a matter of law, exceed the amount provided." Hence, appellant's claim is not that the agreement failed to disclose the particular right affected, but rather that she was not adequately informed with respect to the nature of alimony *pendente lite.*

The plurality opinion in *Geyer* expressly applied and followed this Court's decision in *Hillegass Estate,* 431 Pa. 144 (1968), which held that a prenuptial agreement will be upheld if it *either* made a reasonable provision for the spouse *or* was entered after a full and fair disclosure of financial status. See *Geyer,* 516 Pa. at 502 n. 9. The concluding paragraph of the *Geyer* plurality opinion, however, injected a basis for uncertainty as to whether *Hillegass* was being strictly followed. It stated as follows:

> [A]ny agreement which seeks to change the duly enacted public policy of this Commonwealth must be based on nothing less than full and fair disclosure. Such disclosure must include both the general financial pictures of the parties involved, and evidence that the parties are aware of the statutory rights which they are relinquishing.

516 Pa. at 506 (emphasis added) (footnotes omitted).

The Superior Court attempted to reconcile this language with the earlier portion of *Geyer* which applied *Hillegass* and concluded that, viewed in context, this language meant that full and fair disclosure of financial positions and statutory rights was required *only* where the provisions made for a spouse were unreasonable. Because the Superior Court viewed the present agreement as having made an adequate provision for appellant, it held that the agreement was valid regardless of whether there had been a full disclosure of statutory rights being surrendered. The alternative, of course, would have been to require full and fair disclosure in *every* case, but such would plainly have been inconsistent with *Hillegass,* supra.

While the decision of the Superior Court reflects, perhaps, a reasonable interpretation of *Geyer,* we do not view this case as a vehicle to affirm that interpretation. Rather, there is need for a reexamination of the foundations upon which *Geyer* and earlier decisions rested, and a need for clarification of the standards by which the validity of prenuptial agreements will be judged.

There is no longer validity in the implicit presumption that supplied the basis for *Geyer* and similar earlier decisions. Such decisions rested upon a belief that spouses are of unequal status and that women are not knowledgeable enough to understand the nature of contracts that they enter. Society has advanced, however, to the point where women are no longer regarded as the "weaker" party in marriage, or in society generally. Indeed, the stereotype that women serve as homemakers while men work as breadwinners is no longer viable. Quite often today both spouses are income earners. Nor is there viability in the presumption that women are uninformed, uneducated, and readily subjected to unfair advantage in marital agreements. Indeed, women nowadays quite often have substantial education, financial awareness, income, and assets.

Accordingly, the law has advanced to recognize the equal status of men and women in our society. See, e.g., Pa. Const. art. 1, § 28 (constitutional prohibition of sex discrimination in laws of the Commonwealth). Paternalistic presumptions and protections that arose to shelter women from the inferiorities and incapacities which they were perceived as having in earlier times have, appropriately, been discarded. See *Geyer,* 516 Pa. at 509–14 (dissenting opinion of Mr. Chief Justice Nix setting forth detailed history of case law evidencing a shift away from the former paternalistic approach of protecting women towards a newer approach of equal treatment). It would be inconsistent, therefore, to perpetuate the standards governing prenuptial agreements that were described in *Geyer* and similar decisions, as these reflected a paternalistic approach that is now insupportable.

Further, *Geyer* and its predecessors embodied substantial departures from traditional rules of contract law, to the extent that they allowed consideration of the knowledge of the contracting parties and reasonableness of their bargain as factors governing whether to uphold an agreement. Traditional principles of contract law provide perfectly adequate remedies where contracts are procured through fraud, misrepresentation, or duress. Consideration of other factors, such as the knowledge of the parties and the reasonableness of their bargain, is inappropriate. See *Geyer,* 516 Pa. at 516–17 (Flaherty, J. dissenting). Prenuptial agreements are contracts, and, as such, should be evaluated under the same criteria as are applicable to other types of contracts. See *Geyer,* 516 Pa. at 508 ("These agreements are nothing more than contracts and should be treated as such." (Nix, C.J. dissenting)). Absent fraud, misrepresentation, or duress, spouses should be bound by the terms of their agreements.

Contracting parties are normally bound by their agreements, without regard to whether the terms thereof were read and fully understood and irrespective of whether the agreements embodied reasonable or good bargains. See *Standard Venetian Blind Co. v. American Empire Insurance Co.,* 503 Pa. 300, 305 (1983) (failure to read a contract does not warrant avoidance or nullification of its provisions). Based upon these principles, the terms of the present prenuptial agreement must be regarded as binding, without regard to whether the terms were fully understood by appellant. *Ignorantia non excusat.*

Accordingly, we find no merit in a contention raised by appellant that the agreement should be declared void on the ground that she did not consult with independent legal counsel. To impose a *per se* requirement that parties entering a prenuptial agreement must obtain independent legal counsel would be contrary to traditional principles of contract law, and would constitute a paternalistic and unwarranted interference with the parties' freedom to enter contracts.

Further, the reasonableness of a prenuptial bargain is not a proper subject for judicial review. *Geyer* and earlier decisions required that, at least where there had been an inadequate disclosure made by the parties, the bargain must have been reasonable at its inception. See *Geyer,* 516 Pa. at 503. Some have even suggested that prenuptial agreements should be examined with regard to whether their terms remain reasonable at the time of dissolution of the parties' marriage.

By invoking inquiries into reasonableness, however, the functioning and reliability of prenuptial agreements is severely undermined. Parties would not have entered such agreements, and, indeed, might not have entered their marriages, if they did not expect their agreements to be strictly enforced. If parties viewed an agreement as reasonable at the time of its inception, as evidenced by their having signed the agreement, they should be foreclosed from later trying to evade its terms by asserting that it was not in fact reasonable. Pertinently, the present agreement contained a clause reciting that "each of the parties considers this agreement fair, just and reasonable."

Further, everyone who enters a long-term agreement knows that circumstances can change during its term, so that what initially appeared desirable might prove to be an unfavorable bargain. Such are the risks that contracting parties routinely assume. Certainly, the possibilities of illness, birth of children, reliance upon a spouse, career change, financial gain or loss, and numerous other events that can occur in the course of a marriage cannot be regarded as unforeseeable. If parties choose not to address such matters in their prenuptial agreements, they must be regarded as having contracted to bear the risk of events that alter the value of their bargains.

We are reluctant to interfere with the power of persons contemplating marriage to agree upon, and to act in reliance upon, what *they* regard as an acceptable distribution scheme for their property. A court should not ignore the parties' expressed intent by proceeding to determine whether a prenuptial agreement was, in the court's view, reasonable at the time of its inception or the time of divorce. These are exactly the sorts of judicial determinations that such agreements are designed to avoid. Rare indeed is the agreement that is beyond possible challenge when reasonableness is placed at issue. Parties can routinely assert some lack of fairness relating to the inception of the agreement, thereby placing the validity of the agreement at risk. And if reasonableness at the time of divorce were to be taken into account an additional problem would arise. Virtually nonexistent is the marriage in which there has been absolutely no change in the circumstances of either spouse during the course of the marriage. Every change in circumstance, foreseeable or not, and substantial or not, might be asserted as a basis for finding that an agreement is no longer reasonable.

In discarding the approach of *Geyer* that permitted examination of the reasonableness of prenuptial agreements and allowed inquiries into whether parties had attained informed understandings of the rights they were surrendering, we do not depart from the longstanding principle that a full and fair disclosure of the financial positions of the parties is required. Absent this disclosure, a material misrepresentation in the inducement for entering a prenuptial agreement may be asserted. *Hillegass,* 431 Pa. at 152–53. Parties to these agreements do not quite deal at arm's length, but rather at the time the contract is entered into stand in a relation of mutual confidence and trust that calls for disclosure of their financial resources. *Id.*

at 149; *Gelb Estate,* 425 Pa. 117, 120 (1967). It is well settled that this disclosure need not be exact, so long as it is "full and fair." *Kaufmann Estate,* 404 Pa. 131, 136 n. 8 (1961). In essence therefore, the duty of disclosure under these circumstances is consistent with traditional principles of contract law.

If an agreement provides that full disclosure has been made, a presumption of full disclosure arises. If a spouse attempts to rebut this presumption through an assertion of fraud or misrepresentation then this presumption can be rebutted if it is proven by clear and convincing evidence. *Hillegass,* 431 Pa. at 152–53.

The present agreement recited that full disclosure had been made, and included a list of appellee's assets totalling approximately $300,000. Appellant contends that this list understated by roughly $183,000 the value of a classic car collection which appellee had included at a value of $200,000. The master, reviewing the parties' conflicting testimony regarding the value of the car collection, found that appellant failed to prove by clear and convincing evidence that the value of the collection had been understated. The courts below affirmed that finding. We have examined the record and find ample basis for concluding that the value of the car collection was fully disclosed. Appellee offered expert witnesses who testified to a value of approximately $200,000. Further, appellee's disclosure included numerous cars that appellee did not even own but which he merely hoped to inherit from his mother at some time in the future. Appellant's contention is plainly without merit.

Appellant's final contention is that the agreement was executed under conditions of duress in that it was presented to her at 5 p.m. on the eve of her wedding, a time when she could not seek counsel without the trauma, expense, and embarrassment of postponing the wedding. The master found this claim not credible. The courts below affirmed that finding, upon an ample evidentiary basis.

Although appellant testified that she did not discover until the eve of her wedding that there was going to be a prenuptial agreement, testimony from a number of other witnesses was to the contrary. Appellee testified that, although the final version of the agreement was indeed presented to appellant on the eve of the wedding, he had engaged in several discussions with appellant regarding the contents of the agreement during the six month period preceding that date. Another witness testified that appellant mentioned, approximately two or three weeks before the wedding, that she was going to enter a prenuptial agreement. Yet another witness confirmed that, during the months preceding the wedding, appellant participated in several discussions of prenuptial agreements. And the legal counsel who prepared the agreement for appellee testified that, prior to the eve of the wedding, changes were made in the agreement to increase the sums payable to appellant in the event of separation or divorce. He also stated that he was present when the agreement was signed and that appellant expressed absolutely no reluctance about signing. It should be noted, too, that during the months when the agreement was being discussed appellant had more than sufficient time to consult with independent legal counsel if she had so desired. See generally *Carrier v. William Penn Broadcasting Corp.,* 426 Pa. 427, 431 (1967) (concept of duress as applied to contracting parties). Under these circumstances, there was plainly no error in finding that appellant failed to prove duress.

Hence, the courts below properly held that the present agreement is valid and enforceable. Appellant is barred, therefore, from receiving alimony *pendente lite.*

Order affirmed.

■ Papadakos, J., files a concurring opinion.

■ McDermott files a dissenting opinion which is joined by Larsen, J.

■ Papadakos, Justice, concurring.

Although I continue to adhere to the principles enunciated in *Estate of Geyer,* 516 Pa. 492 (1987), I concur in the result because the facts fully support the existence of a valid and enforceable agreement between the parties and any suggestion of duress is totally negated by the facts. The full and fair disclosure, as well as the lack of unfairness and inequity, standards reiterated in *Geyer* are supported by the facts in this case so that I can concur in the result.

However, I cannot join the opinion authored by Mr. Justice Flaherty, because, it must be clear to all readers, it contains a number of unnecessary and unwarranted declarations regarding the "equality" of women. Mr. Justice Flaherty believes that, with the hard-fought victory of the Equal Rights Amendment in Pennsylvania, all vestiges of inequality between the sexes have been erased and women are now treated equally under the law. I fear my colleague does not live in the real world. If I did not know him better I would think that his statements smack of male chauvinism, an attitude that "you women asked for it, now live with it." If you want to know about equality of women, just ask them about comparable wages for comparable work. Just ask them about sexual harassment in the workplace. Just ask them about the sexual discrimination in the Executive Suites of big business. And the list of discrimination based on sex goes on and on.

I view prenuptial agreements as being in the nature of contracts of adhesion with one party generally having greater authority than the other who deals in a subservient role. I believe the law protects the subservient party, regardless of that party's sex, to insure equal protection and treatment under the law.

The present case does not involve the broader issues to which the gratuitous declarations in question are addressed, and it is injudicious to offer declarations in a case which does not involve those issues. Especially when those declarations are inconsistent with reality.

■ McDermott, Justice, dissenting.

I dissent. I would reverse and remand to the trial court for further consideration of the validity of the prenuptial agreement executed by the appellee, Dr. Frederick Simeone, and Catherine Simeone, on the eve of their wedding.

Let me begin by setting forth a common ground between my position in this matter and that of the majority. There can be no question that, in the law and in society, men and women must be accorded equal status. I am in full agreement with the majority's observation that "women nowadays quite often have substantial education, financial awareness, income, and assets." Majority Slip Op. at 6. However, the plurality decision I authored in *Estate of Geyer,* 516 Pa. 492 (1987), as well as the Dissenting Opinion I offer today, have little to do with the equality of the sexes, but everything to do with the solemnity of the matrimonial union. I am not willing to believe that our society views marriage as a mere contract for hire. On the contrary, our Legislature has set forth the public policy which must guide this Court: "The family is the basic unit of society and the protection of the family is of paramount public concern." *See* 23 P.S. § 102. In this Commonwealth, we have long declared our interest in the stability of marriage and in the stability of the family unit. Our courts must seek to protect, and not to undermine, those institutions and interests which are vital to our society.

The subject of the validity of pre-nuptial agreements is not a new issue for this Court. A pre-nuptial agreement is the reservation of ownership over land, money and any other property, acquired in the past, present or future, from the most unique of human bargains. A pre-nuptial agreement may also prove an intention to get the best out of a marriage without incurring any obligation to do more than be there so long as it suits a purpose. Certainly, a pre-nuptial agreement may serve many purposes consistent with love and affection in life. It may answer obligations incurred prior to present intentions, obligations to children, parents, relatives, friends and those not yet born. It may answer obligations owed for prior help and affection. It may serve to keep matters right and fair, for innumerable reasons arising antecedent to the marriage. Indeed, it may prove a fidelity in persons to prior obligations that makes their intended promises the more secure. Moreover, society has an interest in protecting the right of its citizens to contract, and in seeing the reduction, in the event of a dissolution of the marriage, of the necessity of lengthy, complicated, and costly litigation. Thus, while I acknowledge the longstanding rule of law that pre-nuptial agreements are presumptively valid and binding upon the parties, I am unwilling to go as far as the majority to protect the right to contract at the expense of the institution of marriage. Were a contract of marriage, the most intimate relationship between two people, not the surrender of freedom, an offering of self in love, sacrifice, hope for better or for worse, the begetting of children and the offer of effort, labor, precious time and care for the safety and prosperity of their union, then the majority would find me among them.

In my view, one seeking to avoid the operation of an executed prenuptial agreement must first establish, by clear and convincing evidence, that a full and fair disclosure of the worth of the intended spouse was not made at the time of the execution of the agreement. This Court has recognized that full and fair disclosure is needed because, at the time of the execution of a pre-nuptial agreement, the parties do not stand in the usual arm's length posture attendant to most other types of contractual undertakings, but "stand in a relation of mutual confidence and trust that calls for the highest degree of good faith." *See Gelb Estate,* 425 Pa. 117, 123 (1967). In addition to a full and fair disclosure of the general financial pictures of the parties, I would find a pre-nuptial agreement voidable where it is established that the parties were not aware, at the time of contracting, of existing statutory rights which they were relinquishing upon the signing of the agreement. *Estate of Geyer, supra.* It is here, with a finding of full and fair disclosure, that the majority would end its analysis of the validity of a pre-nuptial agreement. I would not. An analysis of the fairness and equity of a pre-nuptial agreement has long been an important part of the law of this state. *Hillegass Estate,* 431 Pa. 144 (1968). I am not willing to depart from this history, which would continue to serve our public policy.

At the time of dissolution of the marriage, a spouse should be able to avoid the operation of a pre-nuptial agreement upon clear and convincing proof that, despite the existence of full and fair disclosure at the time of the execution of the agreement, the agreement is nevertheless so inequitable and unfair that it should not be enforced in a court of this state. Although the spouse attempting to avoid the operation of the agreement will admittedly have a difficult burden given the standard of proof, and the fact of full and fair disclosure, we must not close our courts to relief where to enforce an agreement will result in unfairness and inequity. The majority holds to the view, without waiver, that parties, having contracted with full and fair disclosure, should be made to suffer the consequences of their bargains. In so holding, the majority has given no weight to the other side of the scales: the state's paramount interest in the preservation of marriage and the family relationship, and the protection of parties to a marriage who may be rendered wards of the state, unable to provide for their own reasonable needs. Our sister states have found such treatment too short a shrift for so fundamental a unit of society.

Thus, I believe that the door should remain open for a spouse to avoid the application of a pre-nuptial agreement where clear and convincing proof establishes that the result will be inequity and unfairness under the circumstances of the particular case and the public policy of this state. Some pre-nuptial agreements will be unfair and inequitable from their beginning. In *Hillegass Estate, supra.,* we recognized that reasonableness at the inception of the agreement necessarily depends upon the totality of all the facts and circumstances existing at the time of the execution of the agreement, including: (a) the financial situation of each spouse; (b) the age of the parties; (c) the number of children each has; (d) the intelligence of the parties; (e) the standard of living each spouse had before marriage and could reasonably expect to have during marriage. *Id.* at 150, 244 A.2d at 676. The plurality in *Estate of Geyer, supra.,* determined that the pre-nuptial agreement at issue there was so inequitable at its inception as to render it unenforceable against the wife upon her husband's death, given the fact that the wife, according to the agreement, was to receive, in essence, only the marital home which she could not possibly afford to keep or to maintain. "Appellant's plight was predictable, especially to decedent who, at the time of the antenuptial agreement, was aware of the costs of running his home. Nevertheless, no provision for the home's maintenance costs were included within the agreement. The net result of this was that the conveyance of the house to appellant was doomed to fail from the beginning. We can hardly say such a one-sided bargain represents reasonable provision under the *Hillegass* standard." *Id.* 516 Pa. at 504–505.

I would emphasize that there are circumstances at the inception of marriage that render a pre-nuptial agreement not only fair and equitable, but a knowing and acceptable reservation of ownership. Such are usually the circumstances surrounding a second marriage. One coming to a second marriage may reserve property created in a previous union, to satisfy what they think a proper and just disposition of that property should be, for children of that prior marriage, or other relations or obligations they feel it a duty to observe. Likewise, one of wealth or property entering a marriage need stake no more on its success than what is fair and reasonable independent of the value of their wealth. That is to say that one's previous wealth is not in itself a criterion of fairness. One is not required to give all they brought for an agreement to be reasonable. So too may one properly reserve things given them as heirlooms, or things of peculiar meaning expressly stated, so long as their value is not increased or preserved as a result of efforts or sacrifice by the union.

It is also apparent that, although a pre-nuptial agreement is quite valid when drafted, the passage of time accompanied by the intervening events of a marriage, may render the terms of the agreement completely unfair and inequitable. While parties to a pre-nuptial agreement may indeed foresee, generally, the events which may come to pass during their marriage, one spouse should not be made to suffer for failing to foresee all of the surrounding circumstances which may attend the dissolution of the marriage. Although it should not be the role of the courts to void pre-nuptial agreements merely because one spouse may receive a better result in an action under the Divorce Code to recover alimony or equitable distribution, it should be the role of the courts to guard against the enforcement of pre-nuptial agreements where such enforcement will bring about only inequity and hardship. It borders on cruelty to accept that after years of living together, yielding their separate opportunities in life to each other, that two individuals emerge the same as the day they began their marriage.

At the time of the dissolution of marriage, what are the circumstances which would serve to invalidate a pre-nuptial agreement? This is a question that should only be answered on a case-by-case basis. However, it is not unrealistic to imagine that in a given situation, one spouse, although trained in the workforce at the time of marriage, may, over many years, have become economically dependent upon the other spouse. In reliance upon the permanence of marriage and in order to provide a stable home for a family, a spouse may choose, even at the suggestion of the other spouse, not to work during the marriage. As a result, at the point of dissolution of the marriage, the spouse's employability has diminished to such an extent that to enforce the support provisions of the pre-nuptial agreement will cause the spouse to become a public charge, or will provide a standard of living far below that which was enjoyed before and during marriage. In such a situation, a court may properly decide to render void all or some of the provisions of the pre-nuptial agreement.

I can likewise conceive of a situation where, after a long marriage, the value of property may have increased through the direct efforts of the spouse who agreed not to claim it upon divorce or death. In such a situation, the court should be able to decide whether it is against the public policy of the state, and thus inequitable and unfair, for a spouse to be precluded from receiving that increase in the value of property which he or she had, at least in part, directly induced. I marvel at the majority's apparent willingness to enforce a pre-nuptial agreement in the interest of freedom to contract at any cost, even where unforeseen and untoward illness has rendered one spouse unable, despite his own best efforts, to provide reasonable support for himself. I would further recognize that a spouse should be given the opportunity to prove, through clear and convincing evidence, that the amount of time and energy necessary for that spouse to shelter and care for the children of the marriage has rendered the terms of a pre-nuptial agreement inequitable, and unjust and thus, avoidable.

The majority is concerned that parties will routinely challenge the validity of their pre-nuptial agreements. Given the paramount importance of marriage and family in our society, and the serious consequences that may accompany the dissolution of a marriage, we should not choose to close the doors of our courts merely to gain a measure of judicial economy. Further, although I would continue to allow parties to challenge the validity of pre-nuptial agreements, I would not alter the burden of proof which has been required to sustain such a challenge.

Turning to the facts of the present case, the Master and the trial court agreed that full and fair disclosure had been made as to the value of Dr. Simeone's antique cars. Thus, I agree with the majority that the appellant, Catherine Simeone, cannot seek to avoid the operation of the pre-nuptial agreement on the grounds that full and fair disclosure of financial status was lacking at the time the agreement was executed. However, at issue in the present appeal is the provision of the pre-nuptial agreement which bars appellant's claim for alimony *pendente lite*. In 1975, the following statutory provision was applicable:

> In the case of divorce from the bonds of matrimony or bed and board, the court may, upon petition, in proper cases, allow a spouse reasonable alimony pendente lite and reasonable counsel fees and expenses.

The Divorce Law, Act of May 2, 1929, P.L. 1237, § 46, as amended, June 27, 1974, P.L. 403, No. 139, § 1; 23 P.S. § 46. This statute was repealed in 1980 with the enactment of the new Divorce Code:

The court may, upon petition, in proper cases, allow a spouse reasonable alimony pendente lite, spousal support and reasonable counsel fees and expenses.

23 P.S. § 502.

I would remand this matter to provide the appellant with an opportunity to challenge the validity of the pre-nuptial agreement on two grounds. Although alimony *pendente lite* was mentioned in the pre-nuptial agreement, appellant should have an opportunity to establish that the mere recitation of this legal term did not advise her of the general nature of the statutory right she was relinquishing with the signing of the agreement. Appellant must establish this lack of full and fair disclosure of her statutory rights with clear and convincing evidence. Further, I would allow appellant the opportunity, with the same standard of proof, to challenge the validity of the pre-nuptial agreement's support provisions, relating to alimony *pendente lite* and alimony, for undue unfairness and inequity. I would express no opinion, however, on the appropriate final resolution of these issues. An appellate court should defer to the trial court in these determinations, and the trial court order should not be reversed absent an error of law or an abuse of discretion.

■ LARSEN, J., joins this dissenting opinion.

* * *

The materials are largely self-explanatory. But it is worth noting that they lie along a continuum with respect to the degree of contractualization of divorce that they allow.

Crews is the least comfortable with allowing the parties to a marriage to fix the terms of dissolution simply by intending to do so. While the *Crews* court does recognize ante-nuptial agreements, and recognizes them as a species of contract, it also insists on retaining an escape valve from contractual enforcement: "if the circumstances at the time of dissolution [of the marriage] were so beyond the contemplation of the parties at the time the antenuptial agreement was signed that enforcement would work an injustice," then the agreement shall not be enforced. In a sense, there is nothing distinctive here. Contract law generally recognizes a doctrine of changed circumstances, and the rule in *Crews* may be cast as simply a special case. But the application of the doctrine of course turns on what counts as a change. And the point of *Crews* is that although the facts in that case led the high court to think that there had not been any change— that the circumstances of the parties on divorce were consistent with their expectations in entering their antenuptial agreement—the path of that case through the courts, and the high court's own reasoning, indicate a greater sensitivity to the possibility of changed circumstances, and to the equitable consequences of such changes, in ante-nuptial agreements than in ordinary contracts. A regime like *Crews* contractualizes divorce, but limits parties' freedom to allocate risks on divorce in ways in which contractual risk allocation is not limited in other arenas. *Crews* invites courts to engage in a greater substantive review of the equities of ante-nuptial agreements than would be permissible for a more ordinary contract.[37]

The Uniform Premarital Agreement Act treats ante-nuptial agreement more nearly, but not quite fully, on the model of purely ordinary contracts. Most notably, the Act abjures the general equitable approach to changed circumstances embodied in *Crews* for a much more limited and narrowly specific approach. In particular, Section 6 (called the "key operative section of the Act" by the Prefatory Note), limits non-enforcement to cases in which an ante-nuptial agreement's modification or elimination of spousal support would so impoverish one of the divorcing spouses as to cause him or her "to be eligible for support under a program of public assistance at the time of separation or marital dissolution." This regime continues to limit ante-nuptial agreements according to criteria that would not apply to ordinary contracts: no business contract would be invalidated by a court on the ground that one party had assumed a risk which, on eventuating, left him impecunious. But this narrow standard is far from the broad equitable review contemplated in *Crews*.[38]

Finally, *Simeone* represents a more-or-less fully contractual approach. The case arose following the divorce of a neurosurgeon husband and his nurse wife. The opinion begins by reciting (almost aggressively) the various differences in bargaining positions between the parties to the ante-nuptial agreement at issue: in age and experience, wealth, access to advice from legal counsel, and time to consider the agreement and its terms. It then reports that the ante-nuptial agreement limited the husband's support payments to the wife to $200 per week, with a maximum total of $25,000, which is to say a trivial share of the marital property. In spite of these features, the court held the agreement enforceable and rejected the ex-wife's claim for alimony, asserted after the $25,000 limit had been reached. The court rejected the former wife's arguments that the ante-nuptial agreement should be invalidated because she had not had adequate opportunity to consult counsel, because the terms of the agreement were unreasonable, and because the parties' circumstances had changed too dramatically and unforeseeably over the course of their marriage. It insisted that "prenuptial agreements are contracts, and, a such, should be evaluated under the same criteria as are applicable to other types of contracts. Absent fraud, misrepresentation, or duress, spouses should be bound by the terms of their agreements." The court, applying these general principles, continued:

---

37. This is not the only respect in which the *Crews* regime departs from the principles that govern contracts more generally. *McHugh v. McHugh*, 436 A. 2d 8 (1980), which *Crews* cites, also imposed equitable rules governing the formation of ante-nuptial agreements. These rules impose procedural requirements—concerning the informedness of the parties and the equitable structure of their negotiations—on ante-nuptial agreements that are not imposed on contracts generally.

38. An articulate opinion interpreting and applying California's version of the Act, which has the added interest of involving a celebrity marriage, is *Bonds v. Bonds*, 5 P. 3d 815 (Cal. 2000).

Contracting parties are normally bound by their agreements, without regard to whether the terms thereof were read and fully understood and irrespective of whether the agreements embodied reasonable or good bargains. Based upon these principles, the terms of the present prenuptial agreement must be regarded as binding, without regard to whether the terms were fully understood by [the former wife]. Ignorantia non excusat.

The court based these principles on an assertion of women's education, financial, and legal equality and the insistence that, in the face of their newfound equality, any legal principles designed to protect wives against unfair ante-nuptial agreements are unacceptably paternalistic and unduly interfere with persons' ability to plan their lives. The court (as pointed out by an opinion concurring in the result but dissenting from the doctrinal innovations) made no serious empirical investigation into whether advances in gender equality generally had in fact eliminated inequalities in bargaining power concerning ante-nuptial agreements (nor did the court make any effort to gainsay the plain sense, based on the facts recited at the start of its opinion, that the ante-nuptial agreement at issue in *Simeone* was struck between highly unequal bargainers). Rather, the court's claims concerning bargaining and anti-paternalism were stipulative. This renders them highly unsatisfactory as claims about social reality or gender equality, of course. But, and this is the key point, the stipulative move is entirely appropriate for a wholly contractual approach to ante-nuptial agreements. Freedom of contract, as these materials have repeatedly emphasized, is *quite generally based on stipulative assumptions concerning bargaining power and responsibility, based on a purely formal conception of equality*. A contractual approach to ante-nuptial agreements simply imports these assumptions into the regulation of marriage and divorce. Along the way, it also insulates these agreements from broader social and moral concerns of the sort that motivated the dissenter to seek to insulate a particular conception of the marriage status from unconstrained modification by freedom of contract.

23.2.B CONTRACTUALIZING DOMESTIC RELATIONS

Lewis drew a distinction between contracts through which married spouses sought to regulate their non-domestic affairs (characteristically, the organization and work of a jointly operated business) and contracts that directly concerned the spouses' domestic lives. Whereas the former would not be implied (at least by the *Lewis* court) they might be recognized if express; the latter, by contrast could not be made even expressly, really in any way. At common law, the marriage status resisted every contractual effort to alter its terms. The following case drives the point home.

Miller v. Miller

Supreme Court of Iowa, 1887.
35 N.W. 464.

■ ADAMS, C. J.

The contract sued upon is in these words: "This agreement, made this fifth day of August, 1885, between the undersigned, husband and wife, in the interests of peace and for the best interests of each other and of their family, is signed in good faith by each party, with the promise each to the other and to their children that they will each honestly promise to help each other to observe and keep the same, which is as follows, to-wit: All past causes and subjects of dispute, disagreement, and complaint of whatever character or kind shall be absolutely ignored and buried, and no allusion thereto by word or talk to each other or any one else shall ever be made. Each party agrees to refrain from scolding, fault-finding, and anger in so far as relates to the future, and to use every means within their power to promote peace and harmony, and that each shall behave respectfully and fairly treat each other; that Mrs. Miller shall keep her home and family in a comfortable and reasonably good condition, and Mr. Miller shall provide for the necessary expenses of the family, and shall, in addition thereto, pay Mrs. Miller for her individual use $200 per year, payable $16 2/3 per month in advance, so long as Mrs. Miller shall faithfully observe the terms and conditions of their contract. They agree to live together as husband and wife and observe faithfully the marriage relation, and each to live virtuously with the other."

The petition demurred to is quite long. We cannot set it out. The defendant demurred upon the ground that it showed the contract to be without consideration and against public policy. His position is that the plaintiff merely agreed to do what by law she was bound to do. The majority think that the defendant's position must be sustained. The writer of this opinion is not able to concur in that view. The petition sets out several reasons and inducements for making the contract. Among other things, it avers, in substance, that the defendant, while improperly spending money upon other women, refused to furnish the plaintiff with necessary clothing, and she had been compelled to furnish it herself by her personal earnings. This the demurrer admits. It appears to the writer, then, that the plaintiff had the right to separate from the defendant, and go where she could best provide for her wants. This right she waived in consideration of the defendant's contract sued upon. The waiver of the right, it seems to the writer, constituted a consideration for the contract; but, as the majority think otherwise, the judgment must be affirmed,

■ SEEVERS, J., dissents from the majority, and concurs with the writer of the opinion.

* * *

The contractualization of the domestic relations need not proceed solely by means of contracts *arising within a formal marriage* (that aim to alter the domestic arrangements and obligations associated with that marriage). Marriage's character as a status relation that constructs and so regulates intimate domestic relations might also be threatened by contract from without: persons might avoid formal marriage entirely and seek, instead, to regulate their joint domestic lives directly, and purely privately, by contract. Such private contracts cannot achieve all the benefits of marriage: as the brief discussion of same-sex marriage pointed out, one important benefit of marriage is the public recognition, by the state, of a domestic partnership, and the bundle of rights and duties (for example, concerning inheritance, child-rearing, and medical decision-making) that such recognition entails. But private contracts might be able to achieve one important benefit of marriage—namely, the security that comes with state recognition of enforceable obligations of mutual support within a domestic partnership. This security assists domestic partners in making long-term investments on each other's behalves—for example, working to pay for a partner's education, or staying home from work to care for joint children— that would render them dangerously vulnerable if there were no guarantee that they might recoup a share of the returns should the relationship founder. Relatedly, enforceable obligations protect those who invest *ex ante* against exploitation *ex post*. Of course, to function in this way, contracts that regulate domestic life in lieu of marriage must actually be enforced. The following cases illustrate the uncertain patchwork of legal enforcement in this area.

Marvin v. Marvin

Supreme Court of California, 1976.
557 P.2d 106.

■ TOBRINER, J.

During the past 15 years, there has been a substantial increase in the number of couples living together without marrying. Such nonmarital relationships lead to legal controversy when one partner dies or the couple separates. Courts of Appeal, faced with the task of determining property rights in such cases, have arrived at conflicting positions: two cases (*In re Marriage of Cary* (1973) 34 Cal.App.3d 345; *Estate of Atherley* (1975) 44 Cal.App.3d 758 have held that the Family Law Act (Civ.Code, § 4000 et seq.) requires division of the property according to community property principles, and one decision (*Beckman v. Mayhew* (1975) 49 Cal.App.3d 529) has rejected that holding. We take this opportunity to resolve that controversy and to declare the principles which should govern distribution of property acquired in a nonmarital relationship.

We conclude: (1) The provisions of the Family Law Act do not govern the distribution of property acquired during a nonmarital relationship; such a relationship remains subject solely to judicial decision. (2) The courts should enforce express contracts between nonmarital partners except to the extent that the contract is explicitly founded on the consideration of meretricious sexual services. (3) In the absence of an express contract, the courts should inquire into the conduct of the parties to determine whether that conduct demonstrates an implied contract, agreement of partnership or joint venture, or some other tacit understanding between the parties. The courts may also employ the doctrine of quantum meruit, or equitable remedies such as constructive or resulting trust, when warranted by the facts of the case.

In the instant case plaintiff and defendant lived together for seven years without marrying; all property acquired during this period was taken in defendant's name. When plaintiff sued to enforce a contract under which she was entitled to half the property and to support payments, the trial court granted judgment on the pleadings for defendant, thus leaving him with all property accumulated by the couple during their relationship. Since the trial court denied plaintiff a trial on the merits of her claim, its decision conflicts with the principles stated above, and must be reversed.

1. *The factual setting of this appeal.*

(1) Since the trial court rendered judgment for defendant on the pleadings, we must accept the allegations of plaintiff's complaint as true, determining whether such allegations state, or can be amended to state, a cause of action. (See *Sullivan v. County of Los Angeles* (1974) 12 Cal.3d 710, 714–715, fn. 3; 4 Witkin, Cal.Procedure (2d ed. 1971) pp. 2817–2818.) We turn therefore to the specific allegations of the complaint.

Plaintiff avers that in October of 1964 she and defendant 'entered into an oral agreement' that while 'the parties lived together they would combine their efforts and earnings and would share equally any and all property accumulated as a result of their efforts whether individual or combined.' Furthermore, they agreed to 'hold themselves out to the general public as husband and wife' and that 'plaintiff would further render her services as a companion, homemaker, housekeeper and cook to defendant.'

Shortly thereafter plaintiff agreed to 'give up her lucrative career as an entertainer [and] singer' in order to 'devote her full time to defendant as a companion, homemaker, housekeeper and cook;' in return defendant agreed to 'provide for all of plaintiff's financial support and needs for the rest of her life.'

Plaintiff alleges that she lived with defendant from October of 1964 through May of 1970 and fulfilled her obligations under the agreement. During this period the parties as a result of their efforts and earnings acquired in defendant's name substantial real and personal property, including motion picture rights worth over $1 million. In May of 1970, however, defendant compelled plaintiff to leave his household. He continued to support plaintiff until November of 1971, but thereafter refused to provide further support.

On the basis of these allegations plaintiff asserts two causes of action. The first, for declaratory relief, asks the court to determine her contract and property rights; the second seeks to impose a constructive trust upon one half of the property acquired during the course of the relationship.

Defendant demurred unsuccessfully, and then answered the complaint. (2) Following extensive discovery and pretrial proceedings, the case came to trial. Defendant renewed his attack on the complaint by a motion to dismiss. Since the parties had stipulated that defendant's marriage to Betty Marvin did not terminate until the filing of a final decree of divorce in

January 1967, the trial court treated defendant's motion as one for judgment on the pleadings augmented by the stipulation.

After hearing argument the court granted defendant's motion and entered judgment for defendant. Plaintiff moved to set aside the judgment and asked leave to amend her complaint to allege that she and defendant reaffirmed their agreement after defendant's divorce was final. The trial court denied plaintiff's motion, and she appealed from the judgment.

2. *Plaintiff's complaint states a cause of action for breach of an express contract.*

In *Trutalli v. Meraviglia* (1932) 215 Cal. 698 we established the principle that nonmarital partners may lawfully contract concerning the ownership of property acquired during the relationship. We reaffirmed this principle in *Vallera v. Vallera* (1943) 21 Cal.2d 681, 685 [, stating that 'If a man and woman [who are not married] live together as husband and wife under an agreement to pool their earnings and share equally in their joint accumulations, equity will protect the interests of each in such property.'

In the case before us plaintiff, basing her cause of action in contract upon these precedents, maintains that the trial court erred in denying her a trial on the merits of her contention. Although that court did not specify the ground for its conclusion that plaintiff's contractual allegations stated no cause of action, defendant offers some four theories to sustain the ruling; we proceed to examine them.

Defendant first and principally relies on the contention that the alleged contract is so closely related to the supposed 'immoral' character of the relationship between plaintiff and himself that the enforcement of the contract would violate public policy. He points to cases asserting that a contract between nonmarital partners is unenforceable if it is 'involved in' an illicit relationship (see *Shaw v. Shaw* (1964) 227 Cal.App. 2d 159, 164 (dictum); *Garcia v. Venegas* (1951) 106 Cal.App.2d 364, 368 (dictum), or made in 'contemplation' of such a relationship (*Hill v. Estate of Westbrook* (1950) 95 Cal.App.2d 599, 602 see *Hill v. Estate of Westbrook* (1952) 39 Cal.2d 458, 460; *Barlow v. Collins* (1958) 166 Cal.App.2d 274, 277 (dictum); *Bridges v. Bridges* (1954) 125 Cal.App.2d 359, 362 (dictum)). A review of the numerous California decisions concerning contracts between nonmarital partners, however, reveals that the courts have not employed such broad and uncertain standards to strike down contracts. The decisions instead disclose a narrower and more precise standard: a contract between nonmarital partners is unenforceable only *to the extent* that it *explicitly* rests upon the immoral and illicit consideration of meretricious sexual services.

In the first case to address this issue, *Trutalli v. Meraviglia, supra,* 215 Cal. 698, the parties had lived together without marriage for 11 years and had raised two children. The man sued to quiet title to land he had purchased in his own name during this relationship; the woman defended by asserting an agreement to pool earnings and hold all property jointly. Rejecting the assertion of the illegality of the agreement, the court stated that 'The fact that the parties to this action at the time they agreed to invest their earnings in property to be held jointly between them were living together in an unlawful relation, did not disqualify them from entering into a lawful agreement with each other, so long as such immoral relation was not made *a consideration* of their agreement.' (Italics added.) (215 Cal. at pp. 701–702.)

In *Bridges v. Bridges, supra,* 125 Cal.App.2d 359, both parties were in the process of obtaining divorces from their erstwhile respective spouses. The two parties agreed to live together, to share equally in property acquired, and to marry when their divorces became final. The man worked as a salesman and used his savings to purchase properties. The woman kept house, cared for seven children, three from each former marriage and one from the nonmarital relationship, and helped construct improvements on the properties. When they separated, without marrying, the court awarded the woman one-half the value of the property. Rejecting the man's contention that the contract was illegal, the court stated that: 'Nowhere is it expressly testified to by anyone that there was anything in the agreement for the pooling of assets and the sharing of accumulations that contemplated meretricious relations as any part of the consideration or as any object of the agreement.' (125 Cal.App.2d at p. 363.)

Croslin v. Scott (1957) 154 Cal.App.2d 767 reiterates the rule established in *Trutalli* and *Bridges.* In *Croslin* the parties separated following a three-year nonmarital relationship. The woman then phoned the man, asked him to return to her, and suggested that he build them a house on a lot she owned. She agreed in return to place the property in joint ownership. The man built the house, and the parties lived there for several more years. When they separated, he sued to establish his interest in the property. Reversing a nonsuit, the Court of Appeal stated that 'The mere fact that parties agree to live together in meretricious relationship does not necessarily make an agreement for disposition of property between them invalid. It is only when the property agreement is made in connection with the other agreement, or the illicit relationship is made a consideration of the property agreement, that the latter becomes illegal.' (154 Cal.App.2d at p. 771.)

Numerous other cases have upheld enforcement of agreements between nonmarital partners in factual settings essentially indistinguishable from the present case.

Although the past decisions hover over the issue in the somewhat wispy form of the figures of a Chagall painting, we can abstract from those decisions a clear and simple rule. (4) The fact that a man and woman live together without marriage, and engage in a sexual relationship, does not in itself invalidate agreements between them relating to their earnings, property, or expenses. Neither is such an agreement invalid merely because the parties may have contemplated the creation or continuation of a nonmarital relationship when they entered into it. Agreements between nonmarital partners fail only to the extent that they rest upon a consideration of meretricious sexual services. Thus the rule asserted by defendant, that a contract fails if it is 'involved in' or made 'in contemplation' of a nonmarital relationship, cannot be reconciled with the decisions.

The tree cases cited by defendant which have *declined* to enforce contracts between nonmarital partners involved consideration that *was* expressly founded upon an illicit sexual services. In *Hill v. Estate of Westbrook, supra,* 95 Cal.App.2d 599, the woman promised to keep house for the man, to live with him as man and wife, and to bear his children; the man promised to provide for her in his will, but died without doing so. Reversing a judgment for the woman based on the reasonable value of her services, the Court of Appeal stated that 'the action is predicated upon a claim which seeks, among other things, the reasonable value of living with decedent in meretricious relationship and bearing him two children. The law does not award compensation for living with a man as a concubine and bearing him children. As the judgment is at least in part, for the value of the claimed services for which recovery cannot be had, it must be reversed.' (95 Cal.App.2d at p. 603.) Upon retrial, the trial court found that it could not sever the contract and place an independent value upon the legitimate services performed by claimant. We therefore affirmed a judgment for the estate. (*Hill v. Estate of Westbrook* (1952) 39 Cal.2d 458.)

In the only other cited decision refusing to enforce a contract, *Updeck v. Samuel* (1954) 123 Cal.App.2d 264, the contract 'was based on the consideration that the parties live together as husband and wife.' (123 Cal.App.2d at p. 267.) Viewing the contract as calling for adultery, the court held it illegal.

The decision in the *Hill* and *Updeck* cases thus demonstrate that a contract between nonmarital partners, even if expressly made in contemplation of a common living arrangement, is invalid only if sexual acts form an inseparable part of the consideration for the agreement. In sum, a court will not enforce a contract for the pooling of property and earnings if it is explicitly and inseparably based upon services as a paramour. The Court of Appeal opinion in *Hill,* however, indicates that even if sexual services are part of the contractual consideration, any *severable* portion of the contract supported by independent consideration will still be enforced.

The principle that a contract between nonmarital partners will be enforced unless expressly and inseparably based upon an illicit consideration of sexual services not only represents the distillation of the decisional law, but also offers a far more precise and workable standard than that advocated by defendant. Our recent decision in *In re Marriage of Dawley* (1976) 17 Cal.3d 342 [131 Cal.Rptr. 3] offers a close analogy. Rejecting the contention that an antenuptial agreement is invalid if the parties contemplated a marriage of short duration, we pointed out in *Dawley* that a standard based upon the subjective contemplation of the parties is uncertain and unworkable; such a test, we stated, "might invalidate virtually all antenuptial agreements on the ground that the parties contemplated dissolution, but it provides no principled basis for determining which antenuptial agreements offend public policy and which do not." (17 Cal.3d 342, 352.)

Similarly, in the present case a standard which inquires whether an agreement is "involved" in or "contemplates" a nonmarital relationship is vague and unworkable. Virtually all agreements between nonmarital partners can be said to be "involved" in some sense in the fact of their mutual sexual relationship, or to "contemplate" the existence of that relationship. Thus defendant's proposed standards, if taken literally, might invalidate all agreements between nonmarital partners, a result no one favors. Moreover, those standards offer no basis to distinguish between valid and invalid agreements. By looking not to such uncertain tests, but only to the consideration underlying the agreement, we provide the parties and the courts with a practical guide to determine when an agreement between nonmarital partners should be enforced.

(5) Defendant secondly relies upon the ground suggested by the trial court: that the 1964 contract violated public policy because it impaired the community property rights of Betty Marvin, defendant's lawful wife. Defendant points out that his earnings while living apart from his wife before rendition of the interlocutory decree were community property under 1964 statutory law (former Civ.Code, §§ 169, 169.2) and that defendant's agreement with plaintiff purported to transfer to her a half interest in that community property. But whether or not defendant's contract with plaintiff exceeded his authority as manager of the community property (see former Civ.Code, § 172), defendant's argument fails for the reason that an improper transfer of community property is not void *ab initio,* but merely voidable at the instance of the aggrieved spouse. See *Ballinger v. Ballinger* (1937) 9 Cal.2d 330, 334 [*Trimble v. Trimble* (1933) 219 Cal. 340].)

In the present case Betty Marvin, the aggrieved spouse, had the opportunity to assert her community property rights in the divorce action. (See *Babbitt v. Babbitt* (1955) 44 Cal.2d 289, 293.) The interlocutory and final decrees in that action fix and limit her interest. Enforcement of the contract between plaintiff and defendant against property awarded to defendant by the divorce decree will not impair any right of Betty's, and thus is not on that account violative of public policy.

(6) Defendant's third contention is noteworthy for the lack of authority advanced in its support. He contends that enforcement of the oral agreement between plaintiff and himself is barred by Civil Code section 5134, which provides that "All contracts for marriage settlements must be in writing." A marriage settlement, however, is an agreement in contemplation of marriage in which each party agrees to release or modify the property rights which would otherwise arise from the marriage. (See *Corker v. Corker* (1891) 87 Cal. 643, 648.) The contract at issue here does not conceivably fall within that definition, and thus is beyond the compass of section 5134.

(7) Defendant finally argues that enforcement of the contract is barred by Civil Code section 43.5, subdivision (d), which provides that "No cause of action arises for breach of promise of marriage." This rather strained contention proceeds from the premise that a promise of marriage impliedly includes a promise to support and to pool property acquired after marriage

(see *Boyd v. Boyd* (1964) 228 Cal.App.2d 374) to the conclusion that pooling and support agreements not part of or accompanied by promise of marriage are barred by the section. We conclude that section 43.5 is not reasonably susceptible to the interpretation advanced by defendant, a conclusion demonstrated by the fact that since section 43.5 was enacted in 1939, numerous cases have enforced pooling agreements between nonmarital partners, and in none did court or counsel refer to section 43.5.

(3b) In summary, we base our opinion on the principle that adults who voluntarily live together and engage in sexual relations are nonetheless as competent as any other persons to contract respecting their earnings and property rights. Of course, they cannot lawfully contract to pay for the performance of sexual services, for such a contract is, in essence, an agreement for prostitution and unlawful for that reason. But they may agree to pool their earnings and to hold all property acquired during the relationship in accord with the law governing community property; conversely they may agree that each partner's earnings and the property acquired from those earnings remains the separate property of the earning partner. So long as the agreement does not rest upon illicit meretricious consideration, the parties may order their economic affairs as they choose, and no policy precludes the courts from enforcing such agreements.

In the present instance, plaintiff alleges that the parties agreed to pool their earnings, that they contracted to share equally in all property acquired, and that defendant agreed to support plaintiff. The terms of the contract as alleged do not rest upon any unlawful consideration. We therefore conclude that the complaint furnishes a suitable basis upon which the trial court can render declaratory relief. (See 3 Witkin, Cal.Procedure (2d ed.) pp. 2335–2336.) The trial court consequently erred in granting defendant's motion for judgment on the pleadings.

3. Plaintiff's complaint can be amended to state a cause of action founded upon theories of implied contract or equitable relief.

As we have noted, both causes of action in plaintiff's complaint allege an express contract; neither assert any basis for relief independent from the contract. In *In re Marriage of Cary, supra,* 34 Cal.App.3d 345, however, the Court of Appeal held that, in view of the policy of the Family Law Act, property accumulated by nonmarital partners in an actual family relationship should be divided equally. Upon examining the *Cary* opinion, the parties to the present case realized that plaintiff's alleged relationship with defendant might arguably support a cause of action independent of any express contract between the parties. The parties have therefore briefed and discussed the issue of the property rights of a nonmarital partner in the absence of an express contract. Although our conclusion that plaintiff's complaint states a cause of action based on an express contract alone compels us to reverse the judgment for defendant, resolution of the *Cary* issue will serve both to guide the parties upon retrial and to resolve a conflict presently manifest in published Court of Appeal decisions.

Both plaintiff and defendant stand in broad agreement that the law should be fashioned to carry out the reasonable expectations of the parties. Plaintiff, however, presents the following contentions: that the decisions prior to *Cary* rest upon implicit and erroneous notions of punishing a party for his or her guilt in entering into a nonmarital relationship, that such decisions result in an inequitable distribution of property accumulated during the relationship, and that *Cary* correctly held that the enactment of the Family Law Act in 1970 overturned those prior decisions. Defendant in response maintains that the prior decisions merely applied common law principles of contract and property to persons who have deliberately elected to remain outside the bounds of the community property system. *Cary*, defendant contends, erred in holding that the Family Law Act vitiated the force of the prior precedents.

As we shall see from examination of the pre-*Cary* decisions, the truth lies somewhere between the positions of plaintiff and defendant. The classic opinion on this subject is *Vallera v. Vallera, supra*, 21 Cal.2d 681. Speaking for a four-member majority, Justice Traynor posed the question: "whether a woman living with a man as his wife but with no genuine belief that she is legally married to him acquires by reason of cohabitation alone the rights of a co-tenant in his earnings and accumulations during the period of their relationship." (21 Cal.2d at p. 684.) Citing *Flanagan v. Capital Nat. Bank* (1931) 213 Cal. 664, which held that a nonmarital "wife" could not claim that her husband's estate was community property, the majority answered that question "in the negative." (Pp. 684–685.) *Vallera* explains that "Equitable considerations arising from the reasonable expectation of the continuation of benefits attending the status of marriage entered into in good faith are not present in such a case." (P. 685.) In the absence of express contract, *Vallera* concluded, the woman is entitled to share in property jointly accumulated only "in the proportion that her funds contributed toward its acquisition." (P. 685.) Justice Curtis, dissenting, argued that the evidence showed an implied contract under which each party owned an equal interest in property acquired during the relationship.

The majority opinion in *Vallera* did not expressly bar recovery based upon an implied contract, nor preclude resort to equitable remedies. But *Vallera*'s broad assertion that equitable considerations "are not present" in the case of a nonmarital relationship (21 Cal.2d at p. 685) led the Courts of Appeal to interpret the language to preclude recovery based on such theories. (See *Lazzarevich v. Lazzarevich* (1948) 88 Cal.App.2d 708, 719; *Oakley v. Oakley* (1947) 82 Cal.App.2d 188, 191–192.)

Consequently, when the issue of the rights of a nonmarital partner reached this court in *Keene v. Keene* (1962) 57 Cal.2d 657, the claimant forwent reliance upon theories of contract implied in law or fact. Asserting that she had worked on her partner's ranch and that her labor had enhanced its value, she confined her cause of action to the claim that the court should impress a resulting trust on the property derived from the sale of the ranch. The court limited its opinion accordingly, rejecting her argument on the ground that the rendition of services gives rise to a resulting trust only when the services aid in acquisition of the property, not in its subsequent improvement, (57 Cal.2d at p. 668.) Justice Peters, dissenting, attacked the majority's distinction between the rendition of services and the contribution of funds or property; he maintained that both property and services furnished valuable consideration, and potentially afforded the ground for a resulting trust.

This failure of the courts to recognize an action by a nonmarital partner based upon implied contract, or to grant an equitable remedy, contrasts with the judicial treatment of the putative spouse. Prior to the enactment of the Family Law Act, no statute granted rights to a putative spouse. The courts accordingly fashioned a variety of remedies by judicial decision. Some cases permitted the putative spouse to recover half the property on a theory that the conduct of the parties implied an agreement of partnership or joint venture. (See *Estate of Vargas* (1974) 36 Cal.App.3d 714, 717–718; *Sousa v. Freitas* (1970) 10 Cal.App.3d 660, 666.) Others permitted the spouse to recover the reasonable value of rendered services, less the value of support received. (See *Sanguinetti v. Sanguinetti* (1937) 9 Cal.2d 95, 100–102.) Finally, decisions affirmed the power of a court to employ equitable principles to achieve a fair division of property acquired during putative marriage, (*Coats v. Coats* (1911) 160 Cal. 671, 677–678; *Caldwell v. Odisio* (1956) 142 Cal.App.2d 732, 735.)

Thus in summary, the cases prior to *Cary* exhibited a schizophrenic inconsistency. By enforcing an express contract between nonmarital partners unless it rested upon an unlawful consideration, the courts applied a common law principle as to contracts. Yet the courts disregarded the common law principle that holds that implied contracts can arise from the conduct of the parties. Refusing to enforce such contracts, the courts spoke of leaving the parties "in the position in which they had placed themselves" (*Oakley v. Oakley, supra,* 82 Cal.App.2d 188, 192), just as if they were guilty parties *in pari delicto.*

Justice Curtis noted this inconsistency in his dissenting opinion in *Vallera,* pointing out that "if an express agreement will be enforced, there is no legal or just reason why an implied agreement to share the property cannot be enforced."(21 Cal.2d 681, 686; see Bruch, *Property Rights of De Facto Spouses Including Thoughts on the Value of Homemakers' Services* (1976) 10 Family L.Q. 101, 117–121.) And in *Keene v. Keene, supra,* 57 Cal.2d 657, Justice Peters observed that if the man and woman "were not illegally living together it would be a plain business relationship and a contract would be implied," (Dis. opn. at p. 672.)

Still another inconsistency in the prior cases arises from their treatment of property accumulated through joint effort. To the extent that a partner had contributed *funds* or *property,* the cases held that the partner obtains a proportionate share in the acquisition, despite the lack of legal standing of the relationship. (*Vallera v. Vallera, supra,* 21 Cal.2d at p. 685; see *Weak v. Weak, supra,* 202 Cal.App.2d 632, 639.) Yet courts have refused to recognize just such an interest based upon the contribution of *services.* As Justice Curtis points out "Unless it can be argued that a woman's services as cook, housekeeper, and homemaker are valueless, it would seem logical that if, when she contributes money to the purchase of property, her interest will be protected, then when she contributes her services in the home, her interest in property accumulated should be protected." (*Vallera v. Vallera, supra,* 21 Cal.2d 681 686–687 (dis. opn.))

Thus as of 1973, the time of the filing of *In re Marriage of Cary, supra,* 34 Cal.App.3d 345, the cases apparently held that a nonmarital partner who rendered services in the absence of express contract could assert no right to property acquired during the relationship. The facts of *Cary* demonstrated the unfairness of that rule.

Janet and Paul Cary had lived together, unmarried, for more than eight years. They held themselves out to friends and family as husband and wife, reared four children, purchased a home and other property, obtained credit, filed joint income tax returns, and otherwise conducted themselves as though they were married. Paul worked outside the home, and Janet generally cared for the house and children.

In 1971 Paul petitioned for "nullity of the marriage." Following a hearing on that petition, the trial court awarded Janet half of the property acquired during the relationship, although all such property was traceable to Paul's earnings. The Court of Appeal affirmed the award.

Reviewing the prior decisions which had denied relief to the homemaking partner, the Court of Appeal reasoned that those decisions rested upon a policy of punishing persons guilty of cohabitation without marriage. The Family Law Act, the court observed, aimed to eliminate fault or guilt as a basis for dividing marital property. But once fault or guilt is excluded, the court reasoned, nothing distinguishes the property rights of a nonmarital "spouse" from those of a putative spouse. Since the latter is entitled to half the " 'quasi marital property' " (Civ.Code, § 4452), the Court of Appeal concluded that, giving effect to the policy of the Family Law Act, a nonmarital cohabitator should also be entitled to half the property accumulated during an "actual family relationship," (34 Cal.App.3d at p. 353.)

Cary met with a mixed reception in other appellate districts. In *Estate of Atherley, supra,* 44 Cal.App.3d 758, the Fourth District agreed with *Cary* that under the Family Law Act a nonmarital partner in an actual family relationship enjoys the same right to an equal division of property as a putative spouse. In *Beckman v. Mayhew, supra,* 49 Cal.App.3d 529, however, the Third District rejected *Cary* on the ground that the Family Law Act was not intended to change California law dealing with nonmarital relationships.

(9) If *Cary* is interpreted as holding that the Family Law Act requires an equal division of property accumulated in nonmarital "actual family relationships," then we agree with *Beckman v. Mayhew* that *Cary* distends the act. No language in the Family Law Act addresses the property rights of nonmarital partners, and nothing in the legislative history of the act suggests that the Legislature considered that subject. The delineation of the rights of nonmarital partners before 1970 had been fixed entirely by

judicial decision; we see no reason to believe that the Legislature, by enacting the Family Law Act, intended to change that state of affairs.

But although we reject the reasoning of *Cary* and *Atherley,* we share the perception of the *Cary* and *Atherley* courts that the application of former precedent in the factual setting of those cases would work an unfair distribution of the property accumulated by the couple. Justice Friedman in *Beckman v. Mayhew, supra,* 49 Cal.App.3d 529, 535, also questioned the continued viability of our decisions in *Vallera* and *Keene;* commentators have argued the need to reconsider those precedents. We should not, therefore, reject the authority of *Cary* and *Atherley* without also examining the deficiencies in the former law which led to those decisions.

The principal reason why the pre-*Cary* decisions result in a unfair distribution of property inheres in the court's refusal to permit a nonmarital partner to assert rights based upon accepted principles of implied contract or equity. We have examined the reasons advanced to justify this denial of relief, and find that none have merit.

First, we note that the cases denying relief do not rest their refusal upon any theory of "punishing" a "guilty" partner. Indeed, to the extent that denial of relief "punishes" one partner, it necessarily rewards the other by permitting him to retain a disproportionate amount of the property. Concepts of "guilt" thus cannot justify an unequal division of property between two equally "guilty" persons.

Other reasons advanced in the decisions fare no better. The principal argument seems to be that "[e]quitable considerations arising from the reasonable expectation of benefits attending the status of marriage are not present [in a nonmarital relationship]." (*Vallera v. Vallera, supra,* 21 Cal.2d at p. 685.) But, although parties to a nonmarital relationship obviously cannot have based any expectations upon the belief that they were married, other expectations and equitable considerations remain. The parties may well expect that property will be divided in accord with the parties' own tacit understanding and that in the absence of such understanding the courts will fairly apportion property accumulated through mutual effort. We need not treat nonmarital partners as putatively married persons in order to apply principles of implied contract, or extend equitable remedies; we need to treat them only as we do any other unmarried persons.

The remaining arguments advanced from time to time to deny remedies to the nonmarital partners are of less moment. There is no more reason to presume that services are contributed as a gift than to presume that funds are contributed as a gift; in any event the better approach is to presume, as Justice Peters suggested, "that the parties intend to deal fairly with each other." (*Keene v. Keene, supra,* 57 Cal.2d 657, 674 (dissenting opn.); see Bruch, *op. cit., supra,* 10 Family L.Q. 101, 113.)

The argument that granting remedies to the nonmarital partners would discourage marriage must fail; as *Cary* pointed out, "with equal or greater force the point might be that the pre–1970 rule was calculated to cause the income-producing partner to avoid marriage and thus retain the benefit of all of his or her accumulated earnings." (34 Cal.App.3d at p. 353.) Although we recognize the well-established public policy to foster and promote the institution of marriage (see *Deyoe v. Superior Court* (1903) 140 Cal. 476, 482), perpetuation of judicial rules which result in an inequitable distribution of property accumulated during a non marital relationship is neither a just nor an effective way of carrying out that policy.

In summary, we believe that the prevalence of nonmarital relationships in modern society and the social acceptance of them, marks this as a time when our courts should by no means apply the doctrine of the unlawfulness of the so-called meretricious relationship to the instant case. As we have explained, the nonenforceability of agreements expressly providing for meretricious conduct rested upon the fact that such conduct, as the word suggests, pertained to and encompassed prostitution. To equate the nonmarital relationship of today to such a subject matter is to do violence to an accepted and wholly different practice.

We are aware that many young couples live together without the solemnization of marriage, in order to make sure that they can successfully later undertake marriage. This trial period, preliminary to marriage, serves as some assurance that the marriage will not subsequently end in dissolution to the harm of both parties. We are aware, as we have stated, of the pervasiveness of nonmarital relationships in other situations.

The mores of the society have indeed changed so radically in regard to cohabitation that we cannot impose a standard based on alleged moral considerations that have apparently been so widely abandoned by so many. Lest we be misunderstood, however, we take this occasion to point out that the structure of society itself largely depends upon the institution of marriage, and nothing we have said in this opinion should be taken to derogate from that institution. The joining of the man and woman in marriage is at once the most socially productive and individually fulfilling relationship that one can enjoy in the course of a lifetime.

(8b) We conclude that the judicial barriers that may stand in the way of a policy based upon the fulfillment of the reasonable expectations of the parties to a nonmarital relationship should be removed. As we have explained, the courts now hold that express agreements will be enforced unless they rest on an unlawful meretricious consideration. We add that in the absence of an express agreement, the courts may look to a variety of other remedies in order to protect the parties' lawful expectations.

The courts may inquire into the conduct of the parties to determine whether that conduct demonstrates an implied contract or implied agreement of partnership or joint venture (see *Estate of Thornton* (1972) 81 Wn.2d 72), or some other tacit understanding between the parties. The courts may, when appropriate, employ principles of constructive trust (see *Omer v. Omer* (1974) 11 Wash.App. 386) or resulting trust (see *Hyman v. Hyman* (Tex.Civ.App. 1954) 275 S.W.2d 149). Finally, a nonmarital partner may recover in quantum meruit for the reasonable value of household services rendered less the reasonable value of support received if he can show that he rendered services with the expectation of monetary reward. (See *Hill v. Estate of Westbrook, supra,* 39 Cal.2d 458, 462.)

Since we have determined that plaintiff's complaint states a cause of action for breach of an express contract, and, as we have explained, can be amended to state a cause of action independent of allegations of express contract, we must conclude that the trial court erred in granting defendant a judgment on the pleadings.

The judgment is reversed and the cause remanded for further proceedings consistent with the views expressed herein.

■ WRIGHT, C.J., McCOMB, MOSK, SULLIVAN, and RICHARDSON, JJ., concurred.

■ CLARK, J., concurring and dissenting.

The majority opinion properly permit recovery on the basis of either express or implied in fact agreement between the parties. These being the issues presented, their resolution requires reversal of the judgment. Here, the opinion should stop.

This court should not attempt to determine all anticipated rights, duties and remedies within every meretricious relationship—particularly in vague terms. Rather, these complex issues should be determined as each arises in a concrete case.

The majority broadly indicate that a party to a meretricious relationship may recover on the basis of equitable principles and in quantum meruit. However, the majority fail to advise us of the circumstances permitting recovery, limitations on recovery, or whether their numerous remedies are cumulative or exclusive. Conceivably, under the majority opinion a party may recover half of the property acquired during the relationship on the basis of general equitable principles, recover a bonus based on specific equitable considerations, and recover a second bonus in quantum meruit.

The general sweep of the majority opinion raises but fails to answer several questions. First, because the Legislature specifically excluded some parties to a meretricious relationship from the equal division rule of Civil Code section 4452, is this court now free to create an equal division rule? Second, upon termination of the relationship, is it equitable to impose the economic obligations of lawful spouses on meretricious parties when the latter may have rejected matrimony to avoid such obligations? Third, does not application of equitable principles—necessitating examination of the conduct of the parties—violate the spirit of the Family law Act of 1969, designed to eliminate the bitterness and acrimony resulting from the former fault system in divorce? Fourth, will not application of equitable principles reimpose upon trial courts the unmanageable burden of arbitrating domestic disputes? Fifth, will not a quantum meruit system of compensation for services—discounted by benefits received—place meretricious spouses in a better position than lawful spouses? Sixth, if a quantum meruit system is to be allowed, does fairness not require inclusion of all services and all benefits regardless of how difficult the evaluation?

When the parties to a meretricious relationship show by express or implied in fact agreement they intend to create mutual obligations, the courts should enforce the agreement. However, in the absence of agreement, we should stop and consider the ramifications before creating economic obligations which may violate legislative intent, contravene the intention of the parties, and surely generate undue burdens on our trial courts.

By judicial overreach, the majority perform a nunc pro tunc marriage, dissolve it, and distribute its property on terms never contemplated by the parties, case law or the Legislature.

Morone v. Morone

Court of Appeals of New York, 1980.
413 N.E.2d 1154.

■ MEYER, JUDGE.

Presented by this appeal are the questions whether a contract as to earnings and assets may be implied in law from the relationship of an unmarried couple living together and whether an express contract of such a couple on those subjects is enforceable. Finding an implied contract such as was recognized in *Marvin v. Marvin*, 18 Cal.3d 660, to be conceptually so amorphous as practically to defy equitable enforcement, and inconsistent with the legislative policy enunciated in 1933 when common-law marriages were abolished in New York, we decline to follow the Marvin lead. Consistent with our decision in *Matter of Gorden*, 8 N.Y.2d 71, however, we conclude that the express contract of such a couple is enforceable. Accordingly, the order of the Appellate Division dismissing the complaint should be modified to dismiss only the first (implied contract) cause of action and as so modified should be affirmed, with costs to plaintiff.

On a motion to dismiss a complaint we accept the facts alleged as true and determine simply whether the facts alleged fit within any cognizable legal theory.

Plaintiff alleges that she and defendant have lived together and held themselves out to the community as husband and wife since 1952 and that defendant acknowledges that the two children born of the relationship are his. Her first cause of action alleges the existence of this long-continued relationship and that since its inception she has performed domestic duties and business services at the request of defendant with the expectation that she would receive full compensation for them, and that defendant has always accepted her services knowing that she expected compensation for them. Plaintiff suggests that defendant has recognized that their economic fortunes are united, for she alleges that they have filed joint tax returns "over the past several years." She seeks judgment in the amount of $250,000.

The second cause of action begins with the repetition and reallegation of all of the allegations of the first cause of action. Plaintiff then alleges that in 1952 she and the defendant entered into a partnership agreement by which they orally agreed that she would furnish domestic services and defendant was to have full charge of business transactions, that defendant "would support, maintain and provide for plaintiff in accordance with his earning capacity and that defendant further agreed on his part to take care of the plaintiff and do right by her," and that the net profits from the partnership were to be used for and applied to the equal benefit of plaintiff and defendant. Plaintiff avers that defendant commanded that she not obtain employment or he would leave her, and that since 1952 the defendant has collected large sums of money "from various companies and business dealings." Finally, plaintiff states that since December of 1975 defendant has dishonored the agreement, has failed to provide support or maintenance, and has refused her demands for an accounting. She asks that defendant be directed to account for moneys received by him during the partnership.

Special Term dismissed the complaint, concluding that no matter how liberally it was construed it sought recovery for "housewifely" duties within a marital-type arrangement for which no recovery could be had. The Appellate Division affirmed because the first cause of action did not assert an express agreement and the second cause of action, though asserting an express partnership agreement, was based upon the same arrangement which was alleged in the first cause of action and was therefore "contextually inadequate". The dissenting Justice was of the view that while the first cause of action was legally insufficient as premised upon an implied contract, the second, expressing as it does an explicit agreement, should have been sustained.

Development of legal rules governing unmarried couples has quickened in recent years with the relaxation of social customs (Douthwaite, Unmarried Couples and the Law, ch. 4, passim). It has not, however, been a development free of difficult problems: Is the length of time the relationship has continued a factor? Do the principles apply only to accumulated personal property or do they encompass earnings as well? If earnings are to be included how are the services of the homemaker to be valued? Should services which are generally regarded as amenities of cohabitation be included? Is there unfairness in compensating an unmarried renderer of domestic services but failing to accord the same rights to the legally married homemaker? Are the varying types of remedies allowed mutually exclusive or cumulative? (See, generally, Douthwaite, supra; and Clark, J., concurring and dissenting in Marvin v. Marvin, supra.)

New York courts have long accepted the concept that an express agreement between unmarried persons living together is as enforceable as though they were not living together (*Rhodes v. Stone*, 63 Hun. 624, opn in 17 N.Y.S. 561; *Vincent v. Moriarty*, 31 App.Div. 484, 52 N.Y.S. 519), provided only that illicit sexual relations were not "part of the consideration of the contract" (*Rhodes v. Stone*, supra, at 17 N.Y.S., p. 562, quoted in *Matter of Gorden*, 8 N.Y.2d 71, 75 supra). The theory of these cases is that while cohabitation without marriage does not give rise to the property and financial rights which normally attend the marital relation, neither does cohabitation disable the parties from making an agreement within the normal rules of contract law (*Matter of Gorden*, supra, at p. 75, 202 N.Y.S.2d 1; see Ann., 94 A.L.R.3d 552, 559).

Even an express contract presents problems of proof, however, as *Matter of Gorden* illustrates. There Ann Clark and Oliver Gorden moved from Brooklyn to West Fulton, in Schoharie County, where Gorden acquired a tavern in his own name. For seven years Clark and Gorden operated the tavern without other employees, she performing both the work required by her duties in the tavern and by their home life. They lived together and were known in the community as husband and wife until he died. Clark then filed a claim against the estate predicated upon an oral contract pursuant to which Gorden agreed to compensate her for the value of her services, to marry her, to grant her the same rights as she would have as his wife, and to make a will to compensate her. The Surrogate denied the claim because of the "meretricious" relationship. The Appellate Division, finding no proof that there was any relationship between the duties performed in the operation of the inn and the fact that the parties lived together, reversed and awarded claimant $9,000. We reversed, because the evidence was not of the clear and convincing character required to establish a claim against a decedent's estate, but expressly adopted the rationale of Rhodes v. Stone that the unmarried state of the couple did not bar an express contract between them. Ironically, part of the basis for holding the evidence less than clear and convincing was that "If she had been working as an employee instead of a de facto wife, she would not have labored from 8 o'clock in the morning until after midnight without demanding pay or without being paid" (8 N.Y.2d at p. 75).

While accepting *Gorden*'s concept that an unmarried couple living together are free to contract with each other in relation to personal services, including domestic or "housewifely" services, we reject the suggestion, implicit in the sentence quoted above, that there is any presumption that services of any type are more likely the result of a personal, rather than a contractual, bond, or that it is reasonable to infer simply because the compensation contracted for may not be payable in periodic installments that there was no such contract.

Changing social custom has increased greatly the number of persons living together without solemnized ceremony and consequently without benefit of the rules of law that govern property and financial matters between married couples. The difficulties attendant upon establishing property and financial rights between unmarried couples under available theories of law other than contract (see Douthwaite, loc. cit.) warrant application of *Gorden*'s recognition of express contract even though the services rendered be limited to those generally characterized as "housewifely" (*Matter of Adams*, 1 A.D.2d 259, 149 N.Y.S.2d 849; cf. *Dombrowski v. Somers*, 41 N.Y.2d 858). There is, moreover, no statutory requirement that such a contract as plaintiff here alleges be in writing (cf. General Obligations Law, s 5–701, subd. a, pars. 1, 3). The second cause of action is, therefore, sustained.

The first cause of action was, however, properly dismissed. Historically, we have required the explicit and structured understanding of an express contract and have declined to recognize a contract which is implied from the rendition and acceptance of services (*Rhodes v. Stone*, supra; *Vincent v. Moriarty*, 52 N.Y.S. 519, supra; see, also, *Matter of Adams*, supra). The major difficulty with implying a contract from the rendition of services for one another by persons living together is that it is not reasonable to infer an agreement to pay for the services rendered when the relationship of the parties makes it natural that the services were rendered gratuitously (*Matter of Adams*, supra, 1 A.D.2d at p. 262; *Robinson v. Munn*, 238 N.Y. 40, 43). As a matter of human experience personal services will frequently be rendered by two people living together because they value each other's company or because they find it a convenient or rewarding thing to do (see *Marvin v. Marvin*, 18 Cal.3d 660, 675–676, n. 11, supra). For courts to attempt through hindsight to sort out the intentions of the parties and affix jural significance to conduct carried out within an essentially private and generally noncontractual relationship runs too great a risk of error. Absent an express agreement, there is no frame of reference against which to compare the testimony presented and the character of the evidence that can be presented becomes more evanescent. There is, therefore, substantially greater risk of emotion-laden afterthought, not to mention fraud, in attempting to ascertain by implication what services, if any, were rendered gratuitously and what compensation, if any, the parties intended to be paid.

Similar considerations were involved in the Legislature's abolition by chapter 606 of the Laws of 1933 of common-law marriages in our State. Writing in support of that bill, Surrogate Foley informed Governor Lehman that it was the unanimous opinion of the members of the Commission to Investigate Defects in the Law of Estates that the concept of common-law marriage should be abolished because attempts to collect funds from decedents' estates were a fruitful source of litigation. Senate Minority Leader Fearon, who had introduced the bill, also informed the Governor that its purpose was to prevent fraudulent claims against estates and recommended its approval. The consensus was that while the doctrine of common-law marriage could work substantial justice in certain cases, there was no built-in method for distinguishing between valid and specious claims and, thus, that the doctrine served the State poorly.

The notion of an implied contract between an unmarried couple living together is, thus, contrary to both New York decisional law and the implication arising from our Legislature's abolition of common-law marriage. The same conclusion has been reached by a significant number of States other than our own which have refused to allow recovery in implied contract (see Ann., 94 A.L.R.3d 552, 559). Until the Legislature determines otherwise, therefore, we decline to recognize an action based upon an implied contract for personal services between unmarried persons living together.

For the foregoing reasons, the order of the Appellate Division should be modified in accordance with this opinion and, as so modified, should be affirmed, with costs to plaintiff.

■ JONES, JUDGE, dissenting.

I am in agreement with the majority that the first cause of action, seeking recovery of money damages predicated on an implied agreement between cohabiting persons not married to each other, fails to state a ground for relief under the law of this jurisdiction and that dismissal is appropriate. I would go further, however, and make similar disposition of the second cause of action, on the ground that the express agreement alleged is too vague and indefinite to be enforced.

The terms of the contract in the second cause of action are set forth in paragraph 15 of the complaint where it is alleged that "it was orally agreed and understood by and between the parties hereto that plaintiff would perform the work, services and labor of a domestic nature on her part as requested by the defendant, and that the defendant would support, maintain and provide for plaintiff in accordance with his earning capacity and that defendant further agreed on his part to take care of the plaintiff and do right by her". Thus, defendant's obligation is alleged first as one to support, maintain and provide for plaintiff in accordance with his earning capacity and, additionally, to take care of and do right by plaintiff. The latter segment of the purported undertaking is on its face patently indefinite and unenforceable; as we recently held in *Dombrowski v. Somers*, 41 N.Y.2d 858, 859, the words "to take care of" are "too vague to spell out a meaningful promise" nothing of substance is added by the words "to do right by plaintiff". The former segment imposing an apparent obligation to support, maintain and provide for in accordance with (defendant's) earning capacity is similarly nebulous and indeterminate. A reference of more substance is required than simply one to the provider's earning capacity to describe what it is to which the parties are agreeing. What is notably lacking is any statement of the standard of support and maintenance to be provided or of what relationship is to furnish the measure of the allegedly agreed-on life-style. Assuming a provider whose earning capacity places ample funds at his disposal, the level of support and maintenance he will provide for his wife and children will of course vary substantially from the level he will provide for a household retainer living within his residence. Is it the former style of maintenance or the latter or some other, such as might be extended to a favorite, impoverished aunt living outside the family establishment to which the defendant binds himself by the alleged agreement? By its terms the promise is indefinite and uncertain and it runs afoul of the basic premise of contract law viz., "It is a necessary requirement in the nature of things that an agreement in order to be binding must be sufficiently definite to enable a court to give it an exact meaning" (1 Williston, Contracts (3d ed), s 37).

The majority dismisses the problem of vagueness by reliance on the allegation included in the second pleaded cause of action that "the net profits from the agreement and partnership of the plaintiff and defendant were to be used for and applied to the equal benefit of plaintiff and defendant", apparently accepting this as a sufficiently definite statement of the obligation now sought to be enforced. But, rather than clarifying the ambiguity, this allegation only confounds the confusion. What are "net profits from the agreement and partnership" is wholly unelucidated and, when the agreement as described in paragraph 15 of the complaint is examined, the term seems strange indeed, for the compact is only that plaintiff will perform domestic services and defendant will support her to the undefined extent previously discussed. Although there is an allegation in paragraph 16 that defendant "was to have full charge of the business", no reference to any business appears elsewhere in the pleading and nowhere is it alleged that defendant bound himself to operate or carry on any profit-making activity. Surely it cannot be said that the domestic work for which plaintiff engaged would produce profits. How the "profits" not to mention the "net profits" from such an agreement are to be determined is a conundrum; as a consequence any provision for their application to the equal benefit of the parties is fatally vague and indefinite. Plaintiff invites our attention to no case in which courts have undertaken to enforce an agreement approaching the indefiniteness of that allegedly made by the parties to this litigation.

Because the second cause of action seeks recovery on the basis of an agreement the terms of which are too uncertain to admit of its enforcement, this action, like the first cause of action, should be dismissed.

■ COOKE, C. J., and GABRIELLI, WACHTLER and FUCHSBERG, JJ., concur with MEYER, J.

■ JONES, J., dissents in part and votes to affirm in a separate opinion in which JASEN, J., concurs.

Order modified, etc.

Hewitt v. Hewitt

Supreme Court of Illinois, 1979.
394 N.E.2d 1204.

■ UNDERWOOD, JUSTICE:

The issue in this case is whether plaintiff Victoria Hewitt, whose complaint alleges she lived with defendant Robert Hewitt from 1960 to 1975 in an unmarried, family-like relationship to which three children have been born, may recover from him "an equal share of the profits and properties accumulated by the parties" during that period.

Plaintiff initially filed a complaint for divorce, but at a hearing on defendant's motion to dismiss, admitted that no marriage ceremony had taken place and that the parties have never obtained a marriage license. In dismissing that complaint the trial court found that neither a ceremonial nor a common law marriage existed; that since defendant admitted the paternity of the minor children, plaintiff need not bring a separate action under the Paternity Act (Ill.Rev.Stat. 1975, ch. 1063/4, par. 51 Et seq.) to have the question of child support determined; and directed plaintiff to make her complaint more definite as to the nature of the property of which she was seeking division.

Plaintiff thereafter filed an amended complaint alleging the following bases for her claim: (1) that because defendant promised he would "share his life, his future, his earnings and his property" with her and all of defendant's property resulted from the parties' joint endeavors, plaintiff is entitled in equity to a one-half share; (2) that the conduct of the parties evinced an implied contract entitling plaintiff to one-half the property accumulated during their "family relationship"; (3) that because defendant fraudulently assured plaintiff she was his wife in order to secure her services, although he knew they were not legally married, defendant's property should be impressed with a trust for plaintiff's benefit; (4) that because plaintiff has relied to her detriment on defendant's promises and devoted her entire life to him, defendant has been unjustly enriched.

The factual background alleged or testified to is that in June 1960, when she and defendant were students at Grinnell College in Iowa, plaintiff became pregnant; that defendant thereafter told her that they were husband and wife and would live as such, no formal ceremony being necessary, and that he would "share his life, his future, his earnings and his property" with her; that the parties immediately announced to their respective parents that they were married and thereafter held themselves out as husband and wife; that in reliance on defendant's promises she devoted her efforts to his professional education and his establishment in the practice of pedodontia, obtaining financial assistance from her parents for this purpose; that she assisted defendant in his career with her own special skills and although she was given payroll checks for these services she placed them in a common fund; that defendant, who was without funds at the time of the marriage, as a result of her efforts now earns over $80,000 a year and has accumulated large amounts of property, owned either jointly with her or separately; that she has given him every assistance a wife and mother could give, including social activities designed to enhance his social and professional reputation.

The amended complaint was also dismissed, the trial court finding that Illinois law and public policy require such claims to be based on a valid marriage. The appellate court reversed, stating that because the parties had outwardly lived a conventional married life, plaintiff's conduct had not "so affronted public policy that she should be denied any and all relief" (62 Ill.App.3d 861, 869), and that plaintiff's complaint stated a cause of action on an express oral contract. We granted leave to appeal. Defendant apparently does not contest his obligation to support the children, and that question is not before us.

The appellate court, in reversing, gave considerable weight to the fact that the parties had held themselves out as husband and wife for over 15 years. The court noted that they lived "a most conventional, respectable and ordinary family life" (62 Ill.App.3d 861, 863) that did not openly flout accepted standards, the "single flaw" being the lack of a valid marriage.

Indeed the appellate court went so far as to say that the parties had "lived within the legitimate boundaries of a marriage and family relationship of a most conventional sort" (62 Ill.App.3d 861, 864), an assertion which that court cannot have intended to be taken literally. Nothing that the Illinois Marriage and Dissolution of Marriage Act (Ill.Rev.Stat.1977, ch. 40, par. 101 Et seq.) does not prohibit nonmarital cohabitation and that the Criminal Code of 1961 (Ill.Rev.Stat.1977, ch. 38, par. 11–8(a)) makes fornication an offense only if the behavior is open and notorious, the appellate court concluded that plaintiff should not be denied relief on public policy grounds.

In finding that plaintiff's complaint stated a cause of action on an express oral contract, the appellate court adopted the reasoning of the California Supreme Court in the widely publicized case of *Marvin v. Marvin* (1976), 18 Cal.3d 660, quoting extensively therefrom. In *Marvin*, Michelle Triola and defendant Lee Marvin lived together for 7 years pursuant to an alleged oral agreement that while "the parties lived together they would combine their efforts and earnings and would share equally any and all property accumulated as a result of their efforts whether individual or combined." (18 Cal.3d 660, 666.) In her complaint she alleged that, in reliance on this agreement, she gave up her career as a singer to devote herself full time to defendant as "companion, homemaker, housekeeper and cook." (18 Cal.3d 660, 666.) In resolving her claim for one-half the property accumulated in defendant's name during that period the California court held that "The courts should enforce express contracts between nonmarital partners except to the extent that the contract is explicitly founded on the consideration of meretricious sexual services" and that "In the absence of an express contract, the courts should inquire into the conduct of the parties to determine whether that conduct demonstrates an implied contract, agreement of partnership or joint venture, or some other tacit understanding between the parties. The courts may also employ the doctrine of quantum meruit, or equitable remedies such as constructive or resulting trusts, when warranted by the facts of the case." (18 Cal.3d 660, 665.) The court reached its conclusions because:

> "In summary, we believe that the prevalence of nonmarital relationships in modern society and the social acceptance of them, marks this as a time when our courts should by no means apply the doctrine of the unlawfulness of the so-called meretricious relationship to the instant case.

> The mores of the society have indeed changed so radically in regard to cohabitation that we cannot impose a standard based on alleged moral considerations that have apparently been so widely abandoned by so many." 18 Cal.3d 660, 683–84.

It is apparent that the *Marvin* court adopted a pure contract theory, under which, if the intent of the parties and the terms of their agreement are proved, the pseudo-conventional family relationship which impressed the appellate court here is irrelevant; recovery may be had unless the implicit sexual relationship is made the explicit consideration for the agreement. In contrast, the appellate court here, as we understand its opinion, would apply contract principles only in a setting where the relationship of the parties outwardly resembled that of a traditional family. It seems apparent that the plaintiff in *Marvin* would not have been entitled to recover in our appellate court because of the absence of that outwardly appearing conventional family relationship.

The issue of whether property rights accrue to unmarried cohabitants can not, however, be regarded realistically as merely a problem in the law of express contracts. Plaintiff argues that because her action is founded on an express contract, her recovery would in no way imply that unmarried cohabitants acquire property rights merely by cohabitation and subsequent separation. However, the *Marvin* court expressly recognized and the appellate court here seems to agree that if common law principles of express contract govern express agreements between unmarried cohabitants, common law principles of implied contract, equitable relief and constructive trust must govern the parties' relations in the absence of such an agreement. In all probability the latter case will be much the more common, since it is unlikely that most couples who live together will enter into express agreements regulating their property rights. (Bruch, Property Rights of De Facto Spouses, Including Thoughts on the Value of Homemakers' Services, 10 Fam.L.Q. 101, 102 (1976).) The increasing incidence of nonmarital cohabitation referred to in *Marvin* and the variety of legal remedies therein sanctioned seem certain to result in substantial amounts of litigation, in which, whatever the allegations regarding an oral contract, the proof will necessarily involve details of the parties' living arrangements.

Apart, however, from the appellate court's reliance upon *Marvin* to reach what appears to us to be a significantly different result, we believe there is a more fundamental problem. We are aware, of course, of the increasing judicial attention given the individual claims of unmarried cohabitants to jointly accumulated property, and the fact that the majority of courts considering the question have recognized an equitable or contractual basis for implementing the reasonable expectations of the parties unless sexual services were the explicit consideration. (See cases collected in Annot.,31 A.L.R.2d 1255 (1953) and A.L.R.2d Later Case Service supplementing vols. 25 to 31.) The issue of unmarried cohabitants' mutual property rights, however, as we earlier noted, cannot appropriately be characterized solely in terms of contract law, nor is it limited to considerations of equity or fairness as between the parties to such relationships. There are major public policy questions involved in determining whether, under what circumstances, and to what extent it is desirable to accord some type of legal status to claims arising from such relationships. Of substantially greater importance than the rights of the immediate parties is the impact of such recognition upon our society and the institution of marriage. Will the fact that legal rights closely resembling those arising from conventional marriages can be acquired by those who deliberately choose to enter into what have heretofore been commonly referred to as "illicit" or "meretricious" relationships encourage formation of such relationships and weaken marriage as the foundation of our family-based society? In the event of death shall the survivor have the status of a surviving spouse for purposes of inheritance, wrongful death actions, workmen's compensation, etc.? And still more importantly: what of the children born of such relationships? What are their support and inheritance rights and by what standards are custody questions resolved? What of the sociological and psychological effects upon them of that type of environment? Does not the recognition of legally enforceable property and custody rights emanating from nonmarital cohabitation in practical effect equate with the legalization of common law marriage at least in the circumstances of this case? And, in summary, have the increasing numbers of unmarried cohabitants and changing mores of our society (Bruch, Property Rights of De Facto Spouses Including Thoughts on the Value of Homemakers' Services, 10 Fam.L.Q. 101, 102–03 (1976); Nielson, In re Cary: A Judicial Recognition of Illicit Cohabitation, 25 Hastings L.J. 1226 (1974)) reached the point at which the general welfare of the citizens of this State is best served by a return to something resembling the judicially created common law marriage our legislature outlawed in 1905?

Illinois' public policy regarding agreements such as the one alleged here was implemented long ago in *Wallace v. Rappleye* (1882), 103 Ill. 229, 249, where this court said: "An agreement in consideration of future illicit cohabitation between the plaintiffs is void." This is the traditional rule, in force until recent years in all jurisdictions. (See, E. g., *Gauthier v. Laing* (1950), 96 N.H. 80; *Grant v. Butt* (1941), 198 S.C. 298.) Section 589 of the Restatement of Contracts (1932) states, "A bargain in whole or in part for or in consideration of illicit sexual intercourse or of a promise thereof is illegal." See also 6A Corbin, Contracts sec. 1476 (1962), and cases cited therein.

It is true, of course, that cohabitation by the parties may not prevent them from forming valid contracts about independent matters, for which it is said the sexual relations do not form part of the consideration. (Restatement of Contracts secs. 589, 597 (1932); 6A Corbin, Contracts sec. 1476 (1962).) Those courts which allow recovery generally have relied on this principle to reduce the scope of the rule of illegality. Thus, California courts long prior to *Marvin* held that an express agreement to pool earnings is supported by independent consideration and is not invalidated by cohabitation of the parties, the agreements being regarded as simultaneous but separate. (See, E. g., *Trutalli v. Meraviglia* (1932), 215 Cal. 698; see also Annot., 31 A.L.R.2d 1255 (1953), and cases cited therein.) More recently, several courts have reasoned that the rendition of housekeeping and homemaking services such as plaintiff alleges here could be regarded as the consideration for a separate contract between the parties, severable from the illegal contract founded on sexual relations. [O]n allegations similar to those in this case, the Minnesota Supreme Court adopted *Marvin* and the Oregon court expressly held that agreements in consideration of cohabitation were not void, stating:

> "We are not validating an agreement in which the only or primary consideration is sexual intercourse. The agreement here contem-

plated all the burdens and amenities of married life." 274 Or. 421, 427.

The real thrust of plaintiff's argument here is that we should abandon the rule of illegality because of certain changes in societal norms and attitudes. It is urged that social mores have changed radically in recent years, rendering this principle of law archaic. It is said that because there are so many unmarried cohabitants today the courts must confer a legal status on such relationships. This, of course, is the rationale underlying some of the decisions and commentaries. (See, e. g., *Marvin v. Marvin* (1976), 18 Cal.3d 660, 683; *Beal v. Beal* (1978), 282 Or. 115; Kay & Amyx, Marvin v. Marvin: Preserving the Options, 65 Cal.L.Rev. 937 (1977).) If this is to be the result, however, it would seem more candid to acknowledge the return of varying forms of common law marriage than to continue displaying the naiveté we believe involved in the assertion that there are involved in these relationships contracts separate and independent from the sexual activity, and the assumption that those contracts would have been entered into or would continue without that activity.

Even if we were to assume some modification of the rule of illegality is appropriate, we return to the fundamental question earlier alluded to: If resolution of this issue rests ultimately on grounds of public policy, by what body should that policy be determined? *Marvin*, viewing the issue as governed solely by contract law, found judicial policy-making appropriate. Its decision was facilitated by California precedent and that State's no-fault divorce law. In our view, however, the situation alleged here was not the kind of arm's length bargain envisioned by traditional contract principles, but an intimate arrangement of a fundamentally different kind. The issue, realistically, is whether it is appropriate for this court to grant a legal status to a private arrangement substituting for the institution of marriage sanctioned by the State. The question whether change is needed in the law governing the rights of parties in this delicate area of marriage-like relationships involves evaluations of sociological data and alternatives we believe best suited to the superior investigative and fact-finding facilities of the legislative branch in the exercise of its traditional authority to declare public policy in the domestic relations field. (*Strukoff v. Strukoff* (1979), 76 Ill.2d 53; *Siegall v. Solomon* (1960), 19 Ill.2d 145.) That belief is reinforced by the fact that judicial recognition of mutual property rights between unmarried cohabitants would, in our opinion, clearly violate the policy of our recently enacted Illinois Marriage and Dissolution of Marriage Act. Although the Act does not specifically address the subject of nonmarital cohabitation, we think the legislative policy quite evident from the statutory scheme.

The Act provides:

"This Act shall be liberally construed and applied to promote its underlying purposes, which are to:

(1) provide adequate procedures for the solemnization and registration of marriage;

(2) strengthen and preserve the integrity of marriage and safeguard family relationships." (Ill.Rev.Stat.1977, ch. 40, par. 102.)

We cannot confidently say that judicial recognition of property rights between unmarried cohabitants will not make that alternative to marriage more attractive by allowing the parties to engage in such relationships with greater security. As one commentator has noted, it may make this alternative especially attractive to persons who seek a property arrangement that the law does not permit to marital partners. (Comment, 90 Harv.L.Rev. 1708, 1713 (1977).) This court, for example, has held void agreements releasing husbands from their obligation to support their wives. In thus potentially enhancing the attractiveness of a private arrangement over marriage, we believe that the appellate court decision in this case contravenes the Act's policy of strengthening and preserving the integrity of marriage.

The Act also provides: "Common law marriages contracted in this State after June 30, 1905 are invalid." (Ill.Rev.Stat.1977, ch. 40, par. 214.) The doctrine of common law marriage was a judicially sanctioned alternative to formal marriage designed to apply to cases like the one before us. In Port v. Port (1873), 70 Ill. 484, this court reasoned that because the statute governing marriage did not "prohibit or declare void a marriage not solemnized in accordance with its provisions, a marriage without observing the statutory regulations, if made according to the common law, will still be a valid marriage." (70 Ill. 484, 486.) This court held that if the parties declared their present intent to take each other as husband and wife and thereafter did so a valid common law marriage existed. (*Cartwright v. McGown* (1887), 121 Ill. 388, 398.) Such marriages were legislatively abolished in 1905, presumably because of the problems earlier noted, and the above-quoted language expressly reaffirms that policy.

While the appellate court denied that its decision here served to rehabilitate the doctrine of common law marriage, we are not persuaded. Plaintiff's allegations disclose a relationship that clearly would have constituted a valid common law marriage in this State prior to 1905. The parties expressly manifested their present intent to be husband and wife; immediately thereafter they assumed the marital status; and for many years they consistently held themselves out to their relatives and the public at large as husband and wife. Revealingly, the appellate court relied on the fact that the parties were, to the public, husband and wife in determining that the parties living arrangement did not flout Illinois public policy. It is of course true, as plaintiff argues, that unlike a common law spouse she would not have full marital rights in that she could not, for example, claim her statutory one-third share of defendant's property on his death. The distinction appears unimpressive, however, if she can claim one-half of his property on a theory of express or implied contract.

Further, in enacting the Illinois Marriage and Dissolution of Marriage Act, our legislature considered and rejected the "no-fault" divorce concept that has been adopted in many other jurisdictions, including California. (See Uniform Marriage and Divorce Act secs. 302, 305.) Illinois appears to be one of three States retaining fault grounds for dissolution of marriage. (Ill.Rev.Stat.1977, ch. 40, par. 401; Comment, Hewitt v. Hewitt, Contract Cohabitation and Equitable Expectations Relief for Meretricious Spouses, 12 J. Mar. J. Prac. & Proc. 435, 452–53 (1979).) Certainly a significantly stronger promarriage policy is manifest in that action, which appears to us to reaffirm the traditional doctrine that marriage is a civil contract between three parties the husband, the wife and the State. (*Johnson v. Johnson* (1942), 381 Ill. 362; *VanKoten v. VanKoten* (1926), 323 Ill. 323.) The policy of the Act gives the State a strong continuing interest in the institution of marriage and prevents the marriage relation from becoming in effect a private contract terminable at will. This seems to us another indication that public policy disfavors private contractual alternatives to marriage.

Lastly, in enacting the Illinois Marriage and Dissolution of Marriage Act, the legislature adopted for the first time the civil law concept of the putative spouse. The Act provides that an unmarried person may acquire the rights of a legal spouse only if he goes through a marriage ceremony and cohabits with another in the good-faith belief that he is validly married. When he learns that the marriage is not valid his status as a putative spouse terminates; common law marriages are expressly excluded. (Ill.Rev.Stat.1977, ch. 40, par. 305.) The legislature thus extended legal recognition to a class of nonmarital relationships, but only to the extent of a party's good-faith belief in the existence of a valid marriage. Moreover, during the legislature's deliberations on the Act *Marvin* was decided and received wide publicity. (See Note, 12 J. Mar. J. Prac. & Proc. 435, 450 (1979).) These circumstances in our opinion constitute a recent and unmistakeable legislative judgment disfavoring the grant of mutual property rights to knowingly unmarried cohabitants. We have found no case in which recovery has been allowed in the face of a legislative declaration as recently and clearly enacted as ours. Even if we disagreed with the wisdom of that judgment, it is not for us to overturn or erode it. *Davis v. Commonwealth Edison Co.* (1975), 61 Ill.2d 494, 496–97.

Actually, however, the legislature judgment is in accord with the history of common law marriage in this country. "Despite its judicial acceptance in many states, the doctrine of common-law marriage is generally frowned on in this country, even in some of the states that have accepted it." (52 Am.Jur.2d 902 Marriage sec. 46 (1970).) Its origins, early history and problems are detailed in *In re Estate of Soeder* (1966), 7 Ohio App.2d 271 where that court noted that some 30 States did not authorize common law marriage. Judicial criticism has been widespread even in States recognizing the relationship. (See, E. g., *Baker v. Mitchell* (1941), 143 Pa.Super. 50, 54, "a fruitful source of perjury and fraud"; *Sorensen v. Sorensen* (1904), 68 Neb. 500.) "It tends to weaken the public estimate of the sanctity of the marriage relation. It puts in doubt the certainty of the rights of inheritance. It opens the door to false pretenses of marriage and the imposition on estates of supposititious heirs." 7 Ohio App.2d 271, 290.

In our judgment the fault in the appellate court holding in this case is that its practical effect is the reinstatement of common law marriage, as we earlier indicated, for there is no doubt that the alleged facts would, if proved, establish such a marriage under our pre–1905 law. (*Cartwright v. McGown* (1887), 121 Ill. 388.) The concern of both the *Marvin* court and the appellate court on this score is manifest from the circumstance that both courts found it necessary to emphasize marital values ("the structure of society itself largely depends upon the institution of marriage" (*Marvin v. Marvin* (1976), 18 Cal.3d 660, 684) and to deny any intent to "derogate from" (18 Cal.3d 660, 684) or "denigrate" (*Hewitt v. Hewitt* (1978), 62 Ill.App.3d 861, 868) that institution. Commentators have expressed greater concern: "(T)he effect of these cases is to reinstitute common-law marriage in California after it has been abolished by the legislature." (Clark, The New Marriage, Williamette L.J. 441, 449 (1976).) "(*Hewitt*) is, if not a direct resurrection of common-law marriage contract principles, at least a large step in that direction." Reiland, Hewitt v. Hewitt: Middle America, Marvin and Common–Law Marriage, 60 Chi.B.Rec. 84, 88–90 (1978).

We do not intend to suggest that plaintiff's claims are totally devoid of merit. Rather, we believe that our statement in *Mogged v. Mogged* (1973), 55 Ill.2d 221, 225, made in deciding whether to abolish a judicially created defense to divorce, is appropriate here:

"Whether or not the defense of recrimination should be abolished or modified in Illinois is a question involving complex public-policy considerations as to which compelling arguments may be made on both sides. For the reasons stated hereafter, we believe that these questions are appropriately within the province of the legislature, and that, if there is to be a change in the law of this State on this matter, it is for the legislature and not the courts to bring about that change."

We accordingly hold that plaintiff's claims are unenforceable for the reason that they contravene the public policy, implicit in the statutory scheme of the Illinois Marriage and Dissolution of Marriage Act, disfavoring the grant of mutually enforceable property rights to knowingly unmarried cohabitants. The judgment of the appellate court is reversed and the judgment of the circuit court of Champaign County is affirmed.

Appellate court reversed; circuit court affirmed.

Restatement (Second) of Contracts

§ 189 Promise in Restraint of Marriage

A promise is unenforceable on grounds of public policy if it is unreasonably in restraint of marriage.

Comments & Illustrations

Comment a. Rule of reason. Marriage is regarded by the common law as of concern to the state as well as to the individual, and the freedom of individuals to marry should not be impaired except for good reason. A promise in restraint of marriage is not necessarily unenforceable, but is subject to a rule of reason, analogous to that applicable to promises in restraint of trade. See § 186. Here, as there, the duration of the restraint and its extent, in terms of the narrowing of the likely area of choice, are important. In order for the restraint to be reasonable, it must serve some purpose other than that of merely discouraging marriage. The most common acceptable purpose is that of providing support until marriage. Courts are, therefore, relatively tolerant of restraints on marriages that condition a promise of support on the promisee's not marrying and thereby acquiring another provider. Particularly is this so when the restraint is imposed by one spouse on remarriage by the other spouse, since both the close family relationship and the limitation of the restraint to a subsequent marriage argue in favor of enforceability.

Illustrations

1.   A pays B, his twenty-one-year-old child, $100,000 in return for B's promise not to marry for ten years. B's promise is unreasonably in restraint of marriage and is unenforceable on grounds of public policy.

2.   A, a man of seventy years, promises B, his fifty-year-old unmarried niece, that if she will remain in his home as housekeeper and will not marry, he will leave her $50,000 in his will. B does so until A's death. A's promise is not unreasonably in restraint of marriage and its enforcement is not precluded on grounds of public policy.

3.   A and B, who are about to marry, make an antenuptial agreement in which A promises B that in case of A's death B shall receive a specified income from A's estate as long as B remains unmarried. A's promise is not unreasonably in restraint of marriage and its enforcement is not precluded on grounds of public policy.

Restatement (Second) of Contracts

§ 190   Promise Detrimental to Marital Relationship

(1) A promise by a person contemplating marriage or by a married person, other than as part of an enforceable separation agreement, is unenforceable on grounds of public policy if it would change some essential incident of the marital relationship in a way detrimental to the public interest in the marriage relationship. A separation agreement is unenforceable on grounds of public policy unless it is made after separation or in contemplation of an immediate separation and is fair in the circumstances.

(2) A promise that tends unreasonably to encourage divorce or separation is unenforceable on grounds of public policy.

Comments & Illustrations

Comment a.   Change in essential incident of marital relationship. Although marriage is sometimes loosely referred to as a "contract," the marital relationship has not been regarded by the common law as contractual in the usual sense. Many terms of the relationship are seen as largely fixed by the state and beyond the power of the parties to modify. Two reasons support this view. One is that there is a public interest in the relationship, and particularly in such matters as support and child custody, that makes it inappropriate to subject it to modification by the parties. Another is that the courts lack workable standards and are not an appropriate forum for the types of contract disputes that would arise if such promises were enforceable. The rule stated in Subsection (1) reflects this view by making a promise unenforceable if it changes an essential incident of marriage in a way detrimental to the public interest in the relationship. This rule, however, does not prevent persons contemplating marriage or married persons from making contracts between themselves for the disposition of property, since this is not ordinarily regarded as an essential incident of the marital relationship. Nor does it prevent their making contracts for services that are not an essential incident of the marital relationship within the rule stated here. But it does, for example, preclude them from changing in a way detrimental to the public interest in the relationship the duty imposed by law on one spouse to support the other. Whether a change in the duty of support is detrimental in this way will depend on the circumstances of each case. The presence of an unenforceable promise in an otherwise enforceable antenuptial or separation agreement does not, of course, necessarily entail the unenforceability of the entire agreement. See §§ 183, 184. The principles underlying this Section also apply to an agreement under which a third person as trustee is to hold sums in trust for the other spouse on separation. The rules stated in this Section apply only to the relations between the parties and do not govern the enforceability of promises relating to the duty of support owed to children. Even though enforcement of a promise is not precluded under the rule stated in Subsection (1), it may be precluded under the rule stated in Subsection (2).

Illustrations

1. A and B, who are about to marry, make an antenuptial agreement in which A promises to leave their home at any time on notice by B and to make no further claims against B, and B promises thereupon to pay A $100,000. The promises of A and B alter an essential incident of the marital relationship in a way detrimental to the public interest in that relationship and are unenforceable on grounds of public policy.

Comment b.   Separation agreements. The policy that limits the parties in modifying the marital relationship does not apply if that relationship has ended. The rule stated in Subsection (1) thus does not apply to a promise that is part of an enforceable separation agreement. A separation agreement, to be enforceable, must be made after the parties have separated or when they contemplate immediate separation, so that the marriage has, in effect, already disintegrated. It must also be fair in the circumstances, a matter as to which the court may exercise its continuing discretionary powers. Separation agreements commonly deal with such matters as support and are generally enforceable because the parties could usually accomplish the same result through a judicial separation. They are still subject to the rule stated in Subsection (2) if they tend unreasonably to encourage divorce.

Illustrations

2. A and B, who are married but have decided to separate, make a separation agreement that is fair in the circumstances, in which A promises to pay B a stated sum each month in return for B's promise to relinquish all other claims to support. Although the promises of A and B change an essential incident of the marital relationship, their enforcement is not for that reason precluded on grounds of public policy because they are part of a separation agreement. But see Subsection (2) and Comment *c*.

Comment c.   Tending to encourage divorce or separation. When persons contemplating marriage or married persons seek to determine by agreement their rights in the event of a divorce or separation, the rule stated in Subsection (2) comes into play, along with that stated in Subsection (1). See Illustration 2. Because of the public interest in the marriage relationship (see Comment *a*), a promise that undermines that relationship by tending unreasonably to encourage divorce or separation is unenforceable. Although the parties are free, if they choose, to terminate their relationship under the law providing for divorce or separation, a commitment that tends unreasonably in this direction will not be enforced. Whether a promise tends unreasonably to encourage divorce or separation in a particular case is a question of fact that depends on all the circumstances, including the state of disintegration of the marriage at the time the promise is made. A promise that merely disposes of property rights in the event of divorce or separation does not of itself tend unreasonably to encourage either.

Illustrations

3. A, who is married to B, promises to pay B $50,000 in return for B's promise to obtain a divorce. The promises of A and B tend unreasonably to encourage divorce and are unenforceable on grounds of public policy. The result does not depend on whether or not there are grounds for divorce or on whether or not B has performed.

4. A, who was married to B but has obtained a divorce that can possibly be set aside for fraud, promises to pay B $50,000 in return for B's promise not to attempt to have the divorce set aside. The promises of both A and B tend unreasonably to encourage divorce and are unenforceable on grounds of public policy. The result does not depend on whether or not B has performed.

5.   A and B, who are about to be married, make an antenuptial agreement in which A promises that in case of divorce, he will settle $1,000,000 on B. A court may decide that, in view of the large sum promised, A's promise tends unreasonably to encourage divorce and is unenforceable on grounds of public policy.

6.   A, who has begun divorce proceedings against B, promises B that if divorce is granted, alimony shall be fixed at a stated sum, in return for B's agreement to relinquish all other claims to alimony. A court may decide that in view of the disintegration of the marriage relationship, the promises of A and B do not tend unreasonably to encourage divorce and their enforcement is not precluded on grounds of public policy.

* * *

Hewitt is the most conservative of the three cases—in the sense of being most protective of marriage as the exclusive legal regime for governing domestic intimacy. It is therefore a good place to begin. The plaintiff and defendant in Hewitt dated in college, and the plaintiff became pregnant. The defendant told her that they were husband and wife and should live together as such, with no need for any formal marriage or wedding ceremony. The couple held themselves out as married, and the plaintiff devoted herself to supporting the defendant's career. By the time of the lawsuit, the defendant earned $80,000 per year and owned substantial property. After disputes arose in the parties' relationship, the plaintiff filed for divorce and learned (to her shock, presumably) that the parties were not married. She thereupon sued the defendant seeking a property settlement, stating that the defendant had said he would share his life and property with her and asserting theories of express and implied contract.

The *Hewitt* court recognized that the equities favored the plaintiff but nevertheless held in favor of the defendant. In part, the court cast its decision as an instance of judicial deference to legislative prerogative. Illinois, where *Hewitt* arose and was decided, had legislatively abandoned common law marriage; and the court worried that recognizing granting domestic partners contractual rights in the absence of marriage would, in effect, reinstate the abandoned regime. But the opinion's center of gravity concerned the status character of the marriage relation and value of regulating intimate domestic life according to public morality rather than at the pleasure of private intentions. The *Hewitt* court in effect refused to contractualize domestic relations, including even where the parties expressly intended to do so.[39]

---

39.   This emphasis explains why the court considered the plaintiff's case strengthened by the fact that the parties had held themselves out as married. One might have thought this a weakness in the plaintiff's case. For one thing, it increased the tension between the relation at issue and the legislative abandonment of common law marriage. For another, it rendered the parties' contract more nearly an effort to modify marriage per se, rather than simply to construct an alternative to it. But from the court's perspective, this feature of the case reduced their relation's threat to marriage generally by disguising it, so that the parties covertly nonmarital cohabitation avoided making any overt public challenge to marriage and the morality and mores that accompany it.

Morone seeks to occupy a middle ground. The parties in *Morone* had once again lived together holding themselves out as husband and wife, and the plaintiff had performed substantial domestic and business services for the defendant, but without any formal marriage. In *Morone*, however, both parties were aware of this fact. The plaintiff, moreover, alleged that she and the defendant had struck an implied-in-fact contract to share the burdens and benefits of their lives together. She also alleged that the parties had made (by an oral agreement struck when their joint domestic lives began) an express contract according to which the defendant "would support, maintain and provide for plaintiff in accordance with his earning capacity and that defendant further agreed on his part to take care of the plaintiff and do right by her, and that the net profits from the partnership were to be used for and applied to the equal benefit of plaintiff and defendant." The plaintiff's suit alleged that the defendant had ceased to honor these agreements.

The *Morone* court recognized that an express contract of the sort alleged by the plaintiff was valid and enforceable under New York law. As the court said, "while cohabitation without marriage does not give rise to the property and financial rights which normally attend the marital relation, neither does cohabitation disable the parties from making an agreement within the normal rules of contract law." Moreover, *Morone* rejected earlier New York opinions' presumptions against the existence of an express contract where the services at issue were traditionally "housewifely" or where, even though the services were of a sort ordinarily performed for wages, no wages were paid. Under the earlier precedents, the existence of an intimate relationship created an independent hurdle that even express efforts to contractualize the terms of exchange had to overcome. *Morone* eliminated that hurdle, and in principle treated express contracts between intimates just as contract law treats express contracts generally (provided only that illicit sexual relations were not "part of the consideration of the contract").

But *Morone* refused to apply ordinary contract logic more broadly, including even to claims of implied-in-fact contracts between domestic partners. The court at times cast this conclusion in evidentiary terms, proposing that the nature of intimate relationships makes it too difficult for courts to identify, ex post, when the parties expected services rendered by one to be compensated by the other and when they expected the services to be rendered gratuitously. But *Morone* never seriously pursues this evidentiary argument. In particular, it never seeks to balance the risks of the error that it worries the implied-in-fact doctrine *might* produce—finding an implied-in-fact contract where the parties did not intend one—against the error that its holding *guarantees*—failing to recognize implied-in-fact contracts that the parties did intend. The real gravamen of *Morone* is not evidentiary or epistemic but moral. The court insists that intimate domestic relations "make[] it natural that [services provided within them are] rendered gratuitously because [the partners] value each other's company or because they find it a convenient or rewarding thing to do." This is best read not as a claim about what is usual but rather as a claim about what it appropriate. The status character of marriage—the idea that intimate domestic relations should be organized according to social and moral norms rather than according to the intentions of the parties—thus continues to exercise substantial doctrinal influence, even in *Morone.*

Marvin comes closest to escaping the influence of status ideals and establishing a truly contractual regime governing intimate domestic arrangements. The plaintiff met the defendant (the actor Lee Marvin) and, abandoning her singing career, moved in with him. Although the parties never married, they lived a shared domestic life. After six years, the defendant left the plaintiff, whereupon the plaintiff sued, alleging that she and the defendant had made express and implied agreements to pool their efforts and earnings and to share equally in all property accumulated during their relationship.

A trial court granted the defendant judgment on the pleadings, but the California Supreme Court took a different view. The court observed that express contracts between non-married domestic partners are plainly enforceable except insofar as they are explicitly founded on consideration for meretricious sexual services. The court further argued that if the ordinary law of express contracts applies within domestic relations, then it would be inconsistent to decline also to apply the ordinary law of implied contracts. Accordingly, *Marvin* held that in the absence of an express contract courts assessing the obligations of non-married domestic partners should inquire into the conduct of the parties to see whether this conduct establishes an implied contract, partnership, joint venture, or other contractual relation.[40] (*Marvin* further held that courts might also apply quantum meruit or other equitable remedies, such as constructive trusts, in the domestic sphere, as warranted by cases as they arise.) *Marvin* thus effectively treats intimate domestic relations just as the law treats other forms of sharing or joint production—for example, businesses begun and jointly run by friends, either with or without an express agreement concerning cost- and profit-sharing. Under *Marvin* the status relation marriage is complemented, at least with respect to the duties and obligations that arise as between the domestic partners,[41] by a fully contractual legal regime.

Marvin does not stand alone in the contemporary legal order, but neither has it swept the field. Domestic relations in the United States remain less than fully contractualized even today. Two quite different reasons explain why this might be so.

First, and most obviously, the social, moral, and political ideals—concerning public control over sexuality and reproduction—that for centuries cast marriage as a status and sought to have this status dominate

---

40. The Supreme Court thus remanded the case for trial on the plaintiff's implied-in-fact contract theory. The plaintiff was unable to prove the implied-in-fact contract at trial and so in the end lost on the facts.

41. Remember that these are not the only accompaniments of marriage, which also establishes a series of rights and duties vis-à-vis third parties and the state of a character that private contracts cannot easily imitate (even if ordinary contract principles are given full effect).

intimate domestic arrangements retain a significant hold over current legal and political ideology. Indeed, there is some reason to think that these ideals—modified so that the substance of the marriage status is liberalized to render the status accessible to same-sex couples—have gained rather than lost ground in the years since *Marvin* was decided. Certainly the currently most prominent moral and legal movement concerning domestic life—the effort to get the law to recognize same-sex marriage—is better characterized as affirming marriage's specialness and status character than as the leading edge of an attack (in the style of the free love movements of earlier generations) on the marriage status, *tout court*. Both sides of the same-sex marriage debate, that is, seek to affirm that marriage is a status; they disagree only about the content of that status. Liberalization, once again, is not contractualization.

Second, and much less familiarly, the internal structure of contract poses a barrier to the contractualization of domestic relations. This reason against regulating domestic relations through contract is quite different from the first one—it concerns the intentions of the parties to domestic life rather than the morals of the broader community. Contract, as these pages have repeatedly emphasized, is characterized by a particular kind of sharing, which re-asserts itself repeatedly across doctrinal sub-areas. This style of sharing was characterized in one way in the discussion of the expectation remedy and the theory of efficient breach: contractual sharing, those discussions observed, permits promisors to exploit opportunities to promote their own interests within their contracts, as long only as they also vindicate their promisee's contractual expectations. It was characterized another way in the discussion of good faith: contract law, that discussion observed, requires the parties to contracts to respect the terms of their agreement, and prevents self-interested behavior within the contract only insofar as that behavior undermines the initial agreement, by seeking to claw back benefits forgone in it. Contractual sharing, in other words, is perfectly consistent with continued self-interest within a contract; and contractual sharing ex post is cabined according to the terms established by the contract ex ante.

The sharing that many intimate domestic arrangements aspire to is quite different in both respects. The parties to such arrangements, who love each other, do not foreswear their private interests entirely, of course. But each commits affirmatively to the other's interests, and to promoting the other's interests, even at some cost to his own. Moreover, and relatedly, the parties do not limit their sharing ex post according to terms fixed ex ante; rather, they commit to a generalized obligation to adjust, including in costly ways, to circumstances as they develop. Both these attitudes are captured, as it happens, in the traditional marriage vow—expressing a reciprocal commitment "for better or for worse." The sharing involved in non-marital domestic intimacy may not be quite as absolute as this, of course (and even marital sharing is never wholly absolute). But it nevertheless involves measures of other-regard that are at odds with the arm's length distance of contractual performance; and it involves flexible adjustments to circumstances that are at odds with contract law's focus on fixing behavior ex ante. Domestic intimacy is thus more like a fiduciary relation than like a contract. And the reason is not just that the collective wishes that the relation be so structured, on grounds of public morality. Rather, the parties themselves do not wish to be cabined by the contractual frame. Indeed, they cannot possibly fulfill their wishes (given what these wishes are) within that frame. One might even say that while many goods may be pursued purely intentionally (that is to say, may be specified ex ante and then pursued intentionally as specified), intimacy cannot be. Rather, to desire intimacy just is to desire a relation whose growth exceeds ones capacity to plan, or, put more colloquially, that takes on a life of its own.

These structural reflections suggest that marriage—and intimate domestic relations more generally—cannot succeed on a fully contractual model. The parties to such relations simply cannot achieve what they are after in the purely intentional manner of individualized contract. But that does not mean that marriage must remain a single status, either on the traditional model or even on the more liberal model being promoted by the proponents of same-sex marriage today. Perhaps, instead, there might arise a (potentially broad and varied) menu of non-contractual options for structuring domestic relations, among which persons might choose (even though they cannot create new alternatives bespoke, by contract).

This possibility suggests a new reading of the movement—fashioned in response to demands for same-sex marriage—in favor of what are variously called civil unions or domestic partnerships. Civil unions—which are generally statutory creatures designed to confer partners who enter them with many (although not always all) of the legal benefits of marriage without assuming the full cultural and social meanings of marriage proper—are commonly cast (by both proponents and opponents) as a stepping-stone to same sex marriage. They are perceived as a way for same-sex couples to gain the practical benefits of marriage without offending the moral or religious sensibilities of those who demand that marriage proper remain exclusively the union of one man and one woman. Two sample statutes creating civil unions (chosen not to be representative but for a particular purpose that will become plain in a moment) follow. They illustrate an alternative to the conventional view of civil unions, which casts civil unions as a stepping stone not to same sex marriage, but rather towards the partial contractualization of intimate life.

The Illinois Religious Freedom Protection and Civil Union Act

750 ILCS 75/1 et seq.

Sec. 1. Short title. This Act may be cited as the Illinois Religious Freedom Protection and Civil Union Act.

Sec. 5. Purposes; rules of construction. This Act shall be liberally construed and applied to promote its underlying purposes, which are to provide adequate procedures for the certification and registration of a civil union and provide persons entering into a civil union with the obligations, responsibilities, protections, and benefits afforded or recognized by the law of Illinois to spouses.

Sec. 10.   Definitions. As used in this Act:

"Certificate" means a document that certifies that the persons named on the certificate have established a civil union in this State in compliance with this Act.

"Civil union" means a legal relationship between 2 persons, of either the same or opposite sex, established pursuant to this Act.

"Department" means the Department of Public Health.

"Officiant" means the person authorized to certify a civil union in accordance with Section 40.

"Party to a civil union" means a person who has established a civil union pursuant to this Act. "Party to a civil union" means, and shall be included in, any definition or use of the terms "spouse", "family", "immediate family", "dependent", "next of kin", and other terms that denote the spousal relationship, as those terms are used throughout the law.

Sec. 15. Religious freedom. Nothing in this Act shall interfere with or regulate the religious practice of any religious body. Any religious body, Indian Nation or Tribe or Native Group is free to choose whether or not to solemnize or officiate a civil union.

Sec. 20. Protections, obligations, and responsibilities. A party to a civil union is entitled to the same legal obligations, responsibilities, protections, and benefits as are afforded or recognized by the law of Illinois to spouses, whether they derive from statute, administrative rule, policy, common law, or any other source of civil or criminal law.

Sec. 25. Prohibited civil unions. The following civil unions are prohibited:

> (1) a civil union entered into prior to both parties attaining 18 years of age;

> (2) a civil union entered into prior to the dissolution of a marriage or civil union or substantially similar legal relationship of one of the parties;

> (3) a civil union between an ancestor and a descendent or between siblings whether the relationship is by the half or the whole blood or by adoption;

> (4) a civil union between an aunt or uncle and a niece or nephew, whether the relationship is by the half or the whole blood or by adoption; and

> (5) a civil union between first cousins.

Sec. 30. Application, license, and certification.

(a) The Director of Public Health shall prescribe the form for an application, license, and certificate for a civil union.

(b) An application for a civil union shall include the following information:

(1) name, sex, occupation, address, social security number, date and place of birth of each party to the civil union;

(2) name and address of the parents or guardian of each party;

(3) whether the parties are related to each other and, if so, their relationship; and

(4) in the event either party was previously married or entered into a civil union or a substantially similar legal relationship, provide the name, date, place and the court in which the marriage or civil union or substantially similar legal relationship was dissolved or declared invalid or the date and place of death of the former spouse or of the party to the civil union or substantially similar legal relationship.

(c) When an application has been completed and signed by both parties, applicable fees have been paid, and both parties have appeared before the county clerk, the county clerk shall issue a license and a certificate of civil union upon being furnished satisfactory proof that the civil union is not prohibited.

(d) A license becomes effective in the county where it was issued one day after the date of issuance, and expires 60 days after it becomes effective.

(e) The certificate must be completed and returned to the county clerk that issued the license within 10 days of the civil union.

(f) A copy of the completed certificate from the county clerk or the return provided to the Department of Public Health by a county clerk shall be presumptive evidence of the civil union in all courts.

Sec. 35. Duties of the county clerk.

(a) Before issuing a civil union license to a person who resides and intends to continue to reside in another state, the county clerk shall satisfy himself or herself by requiring affidavits or otherwise that the person is not prohibited from entering into a civil union or substantially similar legal relationship by the laws of the jurisdiction where he or she resides.

(b) Upon receipt of the certificate, the county clerk shall notify the Department of Public Health within 45 days. The county clerk shall provide the Department of Public Health with a return on a form furnished by the Department of Public Health and shall substantially consist of the following items:

(1) a copy of the application signed and attested to by the applicants, except that in any county in which the information provided in a civil union application is entered into a computer, the county clerk may submit a computer copy of the information without the signatures and attestations of the applicants;

(2) the license number;

(3) a copy of the certificate; and

(4) the date and location of the civil union.

(c) Each month, the county clerk shall report to the Department of Public Health the total number of civil union applications, licenses, and certificates filed during the month.

(d) Any official issuing a license with knowledge that the parties are thus prohibited from entering into a civil union shall be guilty of a petty offense.

Sec. 40. Certification. A civil union may be certified: by a judge of a court of record; by a retired judge of a court of record, unless the retired judge was removed from office by the Judicial Inquiry Board, except that a retired judge shall not receive any compensation from the State, a county, or any unit of local government in return for the solemnization of a civil union and there shall be no effect upon any pension benefits conferred by the Judges Retirement System of Illinois; by a judge of the Court of Claims; by a county clerk in counties having 2,000,000 or more inhabitants; by a public official whose powers include solemnization of marriages; or in accordance with the prescriptions of any religious denomination, Indian Nation or Tribe or Native Group, provided that when such prescriptions require an officiant, the officiant be in good standing with his or her religious denomination, Indian Nation or Tribe or Native Group. The person performing a civil union shall complete the certificate and forward it to the county clerk within 10 days after a civil union.

Sec. 45. Dissolution; declaration of invalidity. Any person who enters into a civil union in Illinois consents to the jurisdiction of the courts of Illinois for the purpose of any action relating to a civil union even if one or both parties cease to reside in this State. A court shall enter a judgment of dissolution of a civil union if at the time the action is commenced it meets the grounds for dissolution set forth in Section 401 of the Illinois Marriage and Dissolution of Marriage Act. The provisions of Sections 401 through 413 of the Illinois Marriage and Dissolution of Marriage Act shall apply to a dissolution of a civil union. The provisions of Sections 301 through 306 of the Illinois Marriage and Dissolution of Marriage Act shall apply to the declaration of invalidity of a civil union.

Sec. 50. Application of the Civil Practice Law. The provisions of the Civil Practice Law shall apply to all proceedings under this Act, except as otherwise provided in this Act. A proceeding for dissolution of a civil union or declaration of invalidity of a civil union shall be entitled "In re the Civil Union of and". The initial pleading in all proceedings under this Act shall be denominated a petition. A responsive pleading shall be denominated a response. All other pleadings under this Act shall be denominated as provided in the Civil Practice Law.

Sec. 55. Venue. The proceedings shall be had in the county where the petitioner or respondent resides or where the parties' certificate of civil union was issued, except as otherwise provided herein, but process may be directed to any county in the State. Objection to venue is barred if not made within such time as the respondent's response is due. In no event shall venue be deemed jurisdictional.

Sec. 60. Reciprocity. A marriage between persons of the same sex, a civil union, or a substantially similar legal relationship other than common law marriage, legally entered into in another jurisdiction, shall be recognized in Illinois as a civil union.

Sec. 90. Severability. If any part of this Act or its application to any person or circumstance is adjudged invalid, the adjudication or application shall not affect the validity of this Act as a whole or of any other part.

(Source: P.A. 96–1513, eff. 6–1–11.)

The French Pacte Civil de Solidarité

Art. 515–1

A civil covenant of solidarity is a contract entered into by two natural persons of age, of different sexes or of a same sex, to organize their common life.

Art. 515–2

On pain of nullity, there may not be a civil covenant of solidarity:

1°   Between ascendants and descendants in direct line, between relatives by marriage in direct line and between collaterals until the third degree inclusive;

2°   Between two persons of whom one at least is bound by the bonds of marriage;

3°   Between two persons of whom one at least is already bound by a civil covenant of solidarity.

Art. 515–3

Two persons who enter into a civil covenant of solidarity shall make a joint declaration of it at the court office of the tribunal d'instance under the jurisdiction of which they fix their common residence.

On pain of dismissal, they shall file with the clerk the agreement concluded between them in duplicate original and add the documents of civil status which allow to establish the validity of the transaction with respect to Article 515–2, as well as a certificate of the court office of the tribunal d'instance of their places of birth or, in case of birth abroad, of the court office of the tribunal de grande instance of Paris, attesting that they are not already bound by a civil covenant of solidarity.

After the filing of the set of documents, the clerk shall enter that declaration into a register.

The clerk shall countersign and date the two originals of the agreement and give them back to each partner.

He shall have a mention of the declaration entered into a register held in the court office of the tribunal d'instance of the place of birth of each partner or, in case of birth abroad, in the court office of the tribunal de grande instance of Paris.

An entry in the register of the place of residence shall attribute an undisputable date to the civil covenant of solidarity and render it effective against third parties.

Any amendment to the covenant shall be the subject of a joint declaration entered at the court office that received the initial transaction, to which shall be added, on pain of dismissal and in duplicate original, the instrument amending the agreement. The formalities provided for in paragraph 4 shall apply.

Abroad, the entry of a joint declaration of a covenant binding two partners of whom one at least is of French nationality, the formalities provided for in paragraphs 2 and 4 and those required in case of an amendment of the covenant shall be the responsibility of French diplomatic and consular agents.

Art. 515–4

Partners bound by a civil covenant of solidarity shall provide mutual material and moral aid to each other. The terms of that aid shall be fixed by the covenant.

Partners shall be jointly and severally liable with regard to third parties for debts incurred by one of them for the needs of everyday life and for expenses relating to the common lodging.

Art. 515–5

Partners to a civil covenant of solidarity shall lay down, in the agreement referred to in Article 515–3, paragraph 2, whether they wish to submit to the system of undivided ownership the furniture they would acquire for value after the conclusion of the covenant. Failing which, that furniture shall be deemed undivided in halves. It shall be likewise where the date of acquisition of that property may not be established.

The other property of which partners become owners for value after the conclusion of the covenant shall be deemed undivided in halves where the instrument of acquisition or of subscription does not otherwise provide.

Art. 515–6

The provisions of Article 832 shall apply between partners to a civil covenant of solidarity in case of dissolution of it, save those relating to all or part of an agricultural holding, as well as to an undivided share or to partnership shares of that holding.

Art. 515–7

Where partners decide by mutual agreement to put an end to a civil covenant of solidarity, they shall file a joint written declaration with the court office of the tribunal d'instance under the jurisdiction of which one of them at least has his residence. The clerk shall enter that declaration into a register and shall ensure its preservation.

Where one of the partners decides to put an end to a civil covenant of solidarity, he or she shall serve notice of his or her decision on the other and shall send a copy of that notice to the court office of the tribunal d'instance which received the initial instrument.

Where one of the partners puts an end to a civil covenant of solidarity by marrying, he or she shall notify his or her decision to the other by service and shall send copies of the latter and of his or her record of birth on which mention of the marriage has been made, to the court office of the tribunal d'instance which received the initial instrument.

Where a civil covenant of solidarity comes to an end by the death of at least one of the partners, the survivor or any party concerned shall send a copy of the record of death to the court office of the tribunal d'instance which received the initial instrument.

A clerk who receives a declaration or instruments provided for in the preceding paragraphs shall enter or have entered mention of the end of the covenant into the margin of the initial instrument. He shall also have registration of that mention written into the margin of the register provided for in Article 515–3, paragraph 5.

Abroad, receiving, recording and preserving a declaration or instruments referred to in the first four paragraphs shall be the responsibility of French diplomatic or consular agents, who shall also undertake or have undertaken mentions provided for in the preceding paragraph.

A civil covenant of solidarity shall come to an end, according to the circumstances:

1. As soon as a mention is made in the margin of the initial instrument of the joint declaration provided for in the first paragraph;

2. Three months after service delivered under paragraph 2, provided that a copy of it was brought to the knowledge of the clerk of the court designated in that paragraph;

3. On the date of the marriage or of the death of one of the partners.

Partners shall undertake themselves the liquidation of the rights and obligations resulting on their behalf from the civil covenant of solidarity. Failing an agreement, the judge shall rule on the patrimonial consequences of the breach, without prejudice to damage possibly suffered.

* * *

Understood in the conventional way—as a kind of half-way house to marriage equality—domestic partnerships are deeply unsatisfying, particularly to those who insist that subordination and discrimination based on sexual orientation must be stamped out, and that aspirations towards equality cannot be satisfied with half-measures.

But the lasting legacy of domestic partnerships might turn out quite differently. In particular, civil unions open up the possibility, at least in principle, that partners might choose among a menu of legal options for regulating their intimate domestic lives. This possibility, moreover, is becoming practically real, at least in Illinois and in France (which is why these examples of civil union statutes are reproduced here).[42] The civil union regimes adopted in these jurisdictions make the new status available not only to same-sex couples, who remain excluded from marriage, but also to opposite-sex couples, who seek shared domestic lives but not marriages.

The Illinois law is, in respect of this menu account of civil unions, the less radical of the two, in that it seeks effectively to replicate marriage, save in name. The Act thus states that partners in a Civil Union shall be "entitled to the same legal obligations, responsibilities, protections, and benefits as are afforded or recognized by the law of Illinois to spouses." However, interactions between Illinois law and the legal orders of other jurisdictions give the Illinois Act the effect of creating a menu of options in spite of this aspiration. In particular, the Federal Defense of Marriage Act provides that for purposes of federal law, "the word 'marriage' means only a legal union between one man and one woman as husband and wife, and the word 'spouse' refers only to a person of the opposite sex who is a husband or a wife."[43] This opens up the possibility that partners who enter Illinois civil unions might be treated as married for purposes of state but not federal law. The benefit has been noticed, moreover: some partners have chosen to enter civil unions rather than marriages in order to preserve federal benefits (such as social security payments) associated with prior marriages, which would be lost on remarrying but not on entering a federally unrecognized civil union.[44]

The French Pacte Civil de Soidarité (Pacs) is more radical, in particular in that it makes the different legal consequences of marriage and civil union, which constituted a bug under the Illinois regime, into a feature. The Pacs regime was adopted in 1999 and has been modified and expanded since. A Pacs is available to two persons of either the same or opposite sex (but who may not be blood relations, or in existing marriages or Pacs). Parties enter a Pacs by registering the Pacs contract with an appropriate tribunal, which accepts the registration but does not monitor the terms of the arrangement. A Pacs may be terminated by the marriage of either party, by agreement of the parties (in which case it is terminated immedi-

---

42. These are not the only such jurisdictions. In the United States, Hawai'i, for example, has also made its newly created civil union status available to opposite sex couples. HRS § 572B, or 2011 Haw. Sess. Laws 1.

43. 1 USC 7 (1996).

44. This behavior has been reported in the press. See No to Nuptials, Slate, 3 January 2012. Available at: http://www.slate.com/articles/news_and_politics/jurisprudence/2012/01/are_states_that_experiment_with_opposite_sex_civil_unions_offering_a_way_to_opt_out_of_oppressive_ideas_about_marriage_.single.html.

ately), or by a unilateral repudiation communicated to an appropriate official (in which case it is terminated after a three month delay). A Pacs creates a property sharing regime. Pacs partners receive social security benefits as married partners would and growing survivor's rights and tax benefits. (Compare the rules set out above with the more modest initial regime, which gave succession rights only with respect to tenancies, conferred some tax advantages with respect to certain bequests on Pacs that endured for two years, and allowed partners whose Pacs had endured for three years to pay income tax as if married.) Finally, the distribution of property following the termination of a Pacs is determined by the contract that the parties write or, if they do not specify, by a court.[45] The Pacs thus creates a regime of domestic sharing that is substantial, and yet less complete than that created by marriage

Both Illinois Civil Unions and the French Pacs have been used by opposite-sex as well as same-sex couples. In Illinois, this use of the regime represents a side-show: in one survey of roughly 2000 Civil Unions consummated by the end of 2011, only about 150 were made by opposite sex couples.[46] In France, the situation is quite different. Although the French government has banned collecting data on Pacs, one reputable study estimates that of the roughly 350,000 people who had entered Pacs in 2004, 80–85% were in opposite-sex partnerships.[47] The French version of the civil union thus represents a serious and substantial alternative to marriage quite generally.

These examples do not yet constitute a broad trend. But they do suggest how a trend might develop. Contract cannot, on account of its structure or nature, regulate intimate domestic partnerships. These partnerships are built around an organic conception of the relations that they involve, in which sharing is not cabined by the intentions of the parties, ex ante, but rather evolves in response to events ex post. But the turn to contract reflects a dissatisfaction with the procrustean character of marriage, which has grown as society more generally has become increasingly free and diverse. And the formal desire for an organically shared life may be filled in through many different substantive regimes. A menu of options, of the sort initiated through civil unions, might thus simultaneously serve the interests of status and freedom. And civil unions might prove to be a half-way house not between discrimination against homosexuals and full marriage equality, but rather between status-based and fully-contractualized legal orders governing domestic life.

---

45. This summary follows Joëlle Godard, *Pacs Seven Years on: It is Moving Towards Marriage?*, 21 INT'L J. L. POL'Y & FAM. 310, 315–19 (2007) and Claude Martin and Irène Théry, *The Pacs and Marriage and Cohabitation in France*, 15 INT'L J. L. POL'Y & FAM. 135, 150–51 (2001).

46. The survey may be found at: http://www.cookcountyclerk.com/newsroom/newsfrom clerk/Documents/Opposite% 20Sex% 20Civil% 20Union% 20Report% 2012.19.11.pdf

A journalistic account of the results is available at: http://www.slate.com/articles/news_ and_politics/jurisprudence/2012/01/are_states_that_experiment_with_opposite_sex_civil_ unions_offering_a_way_to_opt_out_of_oppressive_ideas_about_marriage_.single.html

47. See Joëlle Godard, *Pacs Seven Years on: It is Moving Towards Marriage?*, 21 INT'L J. L. POL'Y & FAM. 310, 313 (2007).

CHAPTER 24

CONTRACT AND CONSTRAINT

The discussion of freedom of contract has so far, by and large, focused less on freedom in general and more on *contract*. That is, the parties to the contracts of adhesion, arbitration agreements, employment contracts, and marriages taken up in the previous chapters have in general acted freely and sought to deploy their free action in responsible and morally decent ways. The live question, in those areas, has been whether the free and decent activities of the parties are contractual, properly-so-called, and thus able to engage the moral and legal principles that underwrite distinctively contractual obligations. Does the form of commercial exchange associated with contracts of adhesion invoke or achieve distinctively contractual ideals; or, does the lack of bargaining and reciprocal adjustment render this some other, perhaps administrative or legislative, form of coordination? Is arbitration best understood as a kind of contractual gap-filling; or, which would make it formally very different, a kind of adjudication? And can the open-ended, organically developing relations associated with employment and marriage be constituted and regulated on the ex ante and arm's length model of contractual planning and sharing and still achieve their purposes; or, do these purposes require a very different, possibly status-based, approach to the relations? The text has focused on these questions because they cast the largest and most significant shadow over actual contractual practices and also because they pose the most profound difficulties for contract theory.

But freedom of contract has a second face also, which emphasizes not contract but *freedom*. This face may be viewed in two lights.

On the one hand, the question arises when contract law should respect persons' undoubtedly free choices to establish what, as a formal matter, are perfectly well-constructed contracts. As Chapter 18 observed, contract law confers on persons a normative power—the power to create legal obligations by intending them into existence. Our legal order's embrace of freedom of contract reflects a commitment to giving this normative power a broad, but of course also bounded, scope. And so it becomes natural to investigate the bounds that limit the normative power associated with contract. When should the law decline to recognize agreements that would ordinarily establish contracts, on the ground that the parties *should not* be free to make them? The materials below will consider two circumstances in which the law seeks to limit contractual freedom in this way: one concerning contracts to do things that are in themselves immoral or illegal; and one concerning contracts that threaten (roughly) to commodify goods or activities that, for moral or political reasons, our society seeks to insulate from market-forces in particular or, more generally, from exchange and alienation.

On the other hand, questions arise when the conduct of parties leading up to a contract suggests that, although their agreement appears to satisfy the contractual form, the parties in fact *were not* fully or meaningfully free in making it. Contract law must thus decide which constraints sufficiently deprive parties of meaningful freedom so as to undermine contractual obligations and which do not. This face of freedom of contract is very different from the others discussed so far. One prominent difference is that whereas the other doctrines discussed *limit* freedom of contract, doctrines that protect parties from being bound by contracts that they did not freely make *promote* freedom of contract, at least in the sense of making meaningful freedom essential to contract. One such doctrine has already been discussed: fraud interferes with its victims' deliberations in a way that might be said to deprive them of meaningful freedom of choice, and the doctrines that condemn fraud might therefore be cast as supporting freedom of contract. This chapter will take up additional doctrines that protect freedom of contract in a similar way, focusing on assaults against freedom whose centers of gravity concern not deception but coercion. The leading such doctrines are incapacity, duress, undue influence, and unconscionability.

24.1   LEGAL CONSTRAINTS ON CONTRACTUAL FREEDOM

Earlier portions of these materials have identified various ways in which the law imposes substantive limits on the contracts that persons might make. Penalty clauses, for example, are generally invalid;[1] as are certain contracts not to engage in economic competition.[2] These are just other ways of saying that freedom of contract does not extend to making contracts that impose super-compensatory remedies or restrain trade.[3]

Contracts to commit crimes are also generally invalid and may constitute crimes themselves, in particular, criminal conspiracies. This is unsurprising: a legal system that determines to render certain conduct punishable will naturally decline to lend its imprimatur and support to mechanisms

---

    1. Recall the discussions in Chapter 7.

    2. Recall the discussion of *Wolf* in Chapter 9, and observe that antitrust law adds further prohibitions (additional to those imposed by the common law) against covenants in restraint of trade.

    3. Note that a third previously discussed doctrine that limits the legal enforcement of promises—the consideration doctrine—has been left off this list. There is a reason: the consideration doctrine, at least the understanding most prominently pursued in these materials, is a doctrinal elaboration of the contractual form itself. Consideration is an essential element of an exchange's being a contract, properly-so-called, rather than a mark or filter that distinguishes some well-formed contracts from others. The consideration doctrine thus does not limit freedom of contract so much as focus the law's recognition of freedom on activities whose form is properly contractual. The discussion of consideration thus more nearly resembles the earlier discussions of contracts of adhesion, arbitration, employment, and marriage than the discussions pursued in this chapter.

for promoting this conduct. It is perhaps more surprising that simple substantive immorality may also render a contract invalid. Nevertheless, it may, as the following materials illustrate.

Restatement (Second) of Contracts

§ 178   When a Term is Unenforceable on Grounds of Public Policy

(1) A promise or other term of an agreement is unenforceable on grounds of public policy if legislation provides that it is unenforceable or the interest in its enforcement is clearly outweighed in the circumstances by a public policy against the enforcement of such terms.

(2) In weighing the interest in the enforcement of a term, account is taken of

(a) the parties' justified expectations,

(b) any forfeiture that would result if enforcement were denied, and

(c) any special public interest in the enforcement of the particular term.

(3) In weighing a public policy against enforcement of a term, account is taken of

(a) the strength of that policy as manifested by legislation or judicial decisions,

(b) the likelihood that a refusal to enforce the term will further that policy,

(c) the seriousness of any misconduct involved and the extent to which it was deliberate, and

(d) the directness of the connection between that misconduct and the term.

Comments & Illustrations

Comment a.   Legislation providing for unenforceability. Occasionally, on grounds of public policy, legislation provides that specified kinds of promises or other terms are unenforceable. Whether such legislation is valid and applicable to the particular term in dispute is beyond the scope of this Restatement. Assuming that it is, the court is bound to carry out the legislative mandate with respect to the enforceability of the term. But with respect to such other matters as the enforceability of the rest of the agreement (§§ 183, 184) and the possibility of restitution (Topic 5), a court will be guided by the same rules that apply to other terms unenforceable on grounds of public policy (see Illustration 1), absent contrary provision in the legislation itself (see Illustration 3). The term "legislation" is used here in the broadest sense to include any fixed text enacted by a body with authority to promulgate rules, including not only statutes, but constitutions and local ordinances, as well as administrative regulations issued pursuant to them. It also encompasses foreign laws to the extent that they are applicable under conflict of laws rules. See Restatement, Second, Conflict of Laws §§ 202, 203.

Illustrations

1. A promises to pay B $1,000 if the Buckets win their basketball game with the Hoops, and B promises to pay A $2,000 if the Hoops win. A state statute makes wagering a crime and provides that a promise such as A's or B's is "void." A's and B's promises are unenforceable on grounds of public policy. Any claims of A or B to restitution for money paid under the agreement are governed by the rules stated in Topic 5. See § 199(b) and Illustrations 4 and 5 to that section.

2. A and B make an agreement by which A agrees to sell and B to buy, at a fixed price per bushel, one thousand bushels of wheat from A at any time that A shall choose during the following month. The state statute that makes wagering a crime does not apply to such an agreement and it does not offend any judicially declared public policy. Enforcement of A's and B's promises is not precluded on grounds of public policy.

3. A borrows $10,000 from the B Bank, promising to repay it with interest at the rate of twelve per cent. A state statute that fixes the maximum legal rate of interest on such loans at ten per cent provides that a promise to pay a greater sum is "void" as usurious as to all the promised interest but not as to the principal. A's promise to pay the interest is unenforceable on grounds of public policy. The rule stated in § 184(2) does not make A's promise to pay interest enforceable up to ten per cent because the legislation provides otherwise. Compare Illustration 5 to § 184.

Comment b.   Balancing of interests. Only infrequently does legislation, on grounds of public policy, provide that a term is unenforceable. When a court reaches that conclusion, it usually does so on the basis of a public policy derived either from its own perception of the need to protect some aspect of the public welfare or from legislation that is relevant to that policy although it says nothing explicitly about unenforceability. See § 179. In some cases the contravention of public policy is so grave, as when an agreement involves a serious crime or tort, that unenforceability is plain. In other cases the contravention is so trivial as that it plainly does not preclude enforcement. In doubtful cases, however, a decision as to enforceability is reached only after a careful balancing, in the light of all the circumstances, of the interest in the enforcement of the particular promise against the policy against the enforcement of such terms. The most common factors in the balancing process are set out in Subsections (2) and (3). Enforcement will be denied only if the factors that argue against enforcement clearly outweigh the law's traditional interest in protecting the expectations of the parties, its abhorrence of any unjust enrichment, and any public interest in the enforcement of the particular term.

Comment c.   Strength of policy. The strength of the public policy involved is a critical factor in the balancing process. Even when the policy is one manifested by legislation, it may be too insubstantial to outweigh the interest in the enforcement of the term in question. See Illustrations 4 and 5. A court should be particularly alert to this possibility in the case of minor administrative regulations or local ordinances that may not be indicative of the general welfare. A disparity between a relatively modest criminal sanction provided by the legislature and a much larger forfeiture that will result if enforcement of the promise is refused may suggest that the policy is not substantial enough to justify the refusal. See Illustration 4.

Illustrations

4.   A and B make an agreement for the sale of goods for $10,000, in which A promises to deliver the goods in his own truck at a designated time and place. A municipal parking ordinance makes unloading of a truck at that time and place an offense punishable by a fine of up to $50. A delivers the goods to B as provided. Because the public policy manifested by the ordinance is not sufficiently substantial to outweigh the interest in the enforcement of B's promise, enforcement of his promise is not precluded on grounds of public policy.

5.   A promises to employ B and B promises to work for A, all work to be done on weekdays. The agreement is made on Sunday in violation of a statute that makes the doing of business on Sunday a misdemeanor. If the court decides that the public policy manifested by the statute is not sufficiently substantial to outweigh the interests in enforcement of A's and B's promises, it will hold that enforcement of their promises is not precluded on grounds of public policy.

Comment d.   Connection with term. The extent to which a refusal to enforce a promise or other term on grounds of public policy will further that policy depends not only on the strength of the policy but also on the relation of the term to that policy and to any misconduct involved. In most cases there is a promise that involves conduct offensive to the policy. The promise may be one to engage in such conduct. See Illustration 6. Or it may be one that tends to induce the other party to engage in such conduct. This tendency may result from the fact that the promise is made in return for the promisee's engaging in the conduct (see Illustration 7) or in return for the promisee's return promise to engage in the conduct (see Illustration 8). Or it may result from the fact that the duty to perform the promise is conditional on the promisee's engaging in the conduct (see Illustration 9). In such cases, it is the tendency itself that makes the promise unenforceable, even though the promise does not actually induce the conduct. There are other situations in which the conduct is not itself against public policy, but it is against public policy to promise to engage in such conduct or to attempt to induce it. It is sometimes objectionable to make a commitment to engage in conduct that is not in itself objectionable. This is the case, for example, for a promise to vote in a particular way. See Illustration 10. It is sometimes objectionable to attempt to induce conduct that is not in itself objectionable. This is the case, for example, for a promise made in consideration of the promisee's voting in a particular way. See Illustration 11. This list does not exhaust all of the possible relations between the conduct and the promise that may justify a decision that the promise is unenforceable. But as the relation between the conduct and the promise becomes tenuous, it becomes difficult to justify unenforceability unless serious misconduct is involved. A party will not be barred from enforcing a promise because of misconduct that is so remote or collateral that refusal to enforce the promise will not deter such conduct and enforcement will not amount to an inappropriate use of the judicial process. See Illustrations 15 and 16. However, a new promise to perform an earlier promise that was unenforceable on grounds of public policy is also unenforceable on those grounds unless the circumstances that made the first promise unenforceable no longer exist. The rules stated in §§ 183 and 184 involve special applications of these general principles concerning the relation between the conduct and the promise.

Illustrations

6.   A, the owner of a newspaper, promises B that he will publish a statement about C known by A and B to be false and defamatory if B pays him $10,000. B pays A $10,000. A's promise is one to commit a tort (§ 192) and is unenforceable on grounds of public policy.

7.   B promises to pay A, the owner of a newspaper, $10,000 if he will publish a statement about C known by A and B to be false and defamatory. A publishes the libel. B's promise is one tending to induce A to commit a tort (§ 192) and is unenforceable on grounds of public policy.

8.   A, the owner of a newspaper, promises B that he will publish a statement about C known by A and B to be false and defamatory if B will promise to pay him $10,000. B makes the promise. A's promise is one tending to induce A to commit a tort (§ 192). Both promises are unenforceable on grounds of public policy.

9.   B promises to convey a tract of land worth $11,000 to A, the owner of a newspaper, if A pays B $1,000, B's duty to be conditional on A's publishing a statement about C known by A and B to be false and defamatory. A pays B $1,000 and publishes the libel. B's promise is one tending to induce A to commit a tort (§ 192) and is unenforceable on grounds of public policy. Compare § 185.

10.   A pays B, a competitor, $10,000 for B's promise not to compete with A for a year. Although B's refraining from competition with A would not in itself be improper, B's promise not to compete with A unreasonably restrains B from competition (§ 186) and is unenforceable on grounds of public policy.

11. A promises to pay B, a competitor, $10,000 if he will refrain from competing with A for a year. Although B's refraining from competing with A would not in itself be improper, A's promise unreasonably tends to induce B to refrain from competition (§ 186) and is unenforceable on grounds of public policy.

12. A induces B to make an agreement to buy goods on credit from A by bribing B's purchasing agent. A delivers the goods to B. A's bribe tends to induce the agent to violate his fiduciary duty. B's promise to pay the price is unenforceable on grounds of public policy. See § 193.

13. A, who wants to induce B to buy goods from him, promises to pay C $1,000 if he will bribe B's purchasing agent to arrange the sale. C does so. C's bribe tends to induce the agent to violate his fiduciary duty. A's promise is unenforceable on grounds of public policy. See § 193.

14. A, who wants to induce B to buy goods from him, promises to pay C $1,000 if he arranges the sale. C arranges the sale by bribing B's purchasing agent. C's bribe tends to induce the agent to violate his fiduciary duty. A's promise is unenforceable on grounds of public policy. See § 193.

15. A and B make an agreement for exclusive dealing that is unenforceable because unreasonably in restraint of trade (§ 186). A sells and delivers goods pursuant to the unenforceable agreement to C, who promises to pay the price. Because the relation between C's promise to pay the price and the unreasonable restraint is too remote, enforcement of C's promise is not precluded on grounds of public policy.

16. A and B make a wagering agreement in violation of a statute that makes such agreements "void." When A loses, C pays B at A's request, and A promises C to pay him that amount. Because the relation between A's promise to pay C and the improper wager is too remote, enforcement of A's promise is not precluded on grounds of public policy.

Comment e. Other factors. A court will be reluctant to frustrate a party's legitimate expectations unless there is a corresponding benefit to be gained in deterring misconduct or avoiding an inappropriate use of the judicial process. See Illustration 17. The promisee's ignorance or inadvertence, even if it does not bring him within the rule stated in § 180, is one factor in determining the weight to be attached to his expectations. See Illustration 4 to § 181. To the extent, however, that he engaged in misconduct that was serious or deliberate, his claim to protection of his expectations fails. The interest in favor of enforcement becomes much stronger after the promisee has relied substantially on those expectations as by preparation or performance. The court will then take into account any enrichment of the promisor and any forfeiture by the promisee if he should lose his right to the agreed exchange after he has relied substantially on those expectations. See Comment *b* to § 227. The possibility of restitution may be significant in this connection. See Topic 5. In addition to the interest of the promisee, the court will also weigh any interest that the public or third parties may have in the enforcement of the term in question. Such an interest may be particularly evident where the policy involved is designed to protect third parties. See Illustrations 18 and 19.

Illustration

17.   A agrees to reimburse B for any legal expenses incurred if B will go on C's land in order to test a right of way that is disputed by A and C. B goes on C's land. Enforcement of A's promise is not precluded on grounds of public policy, even if it is later determined that B has committed a trespass. Compare § 192.

18.   A, a trustee under a will, makes an agreement with B in violation of A's fiduciary duty. If enforcement of A's and B's promises is desirable for the protection of the beneficiaries, it is not precluded on grounds of public policy. Compare § 193.

19.   A, B, and C, directors of a bank, make notes payable to the bank in order to deceive the bank examiner. They agree that the notes shall be returned and cancelled after they have served their purpose. Enforcement of the promises of A, B and C embodied in the notes is not precluded on grounds of public policy.

Comment f. Effect on rest of agreement. The rules stated in this Section determine only whether a particular promise or other term is unenforceable. The question of the effect of such a determination on the rest of the agreement is sometimes a complex one. If there is only one promise in the transaction and it is unenforceable, then the question will not arise. (As to the divisibility of such a promise, however, see §§ 184, 185). This is the case for offers that have been accepted by a performance rather than by a promise (§ 53), for promises enforceable because of reliance by the promisee (§ 90), and for promises under seal (§ 95). Furthermore, even when there is another promise, it too is often unenforceable under the rules stated in this Section. This is the case, for example, where one party's promise is unenforceable because the promised conduct offends public policy and the other party's return promise is unenforceable because it tends to induce that conduct. See Illustration 8. There are, however, situations in which only one party's promise is unenforceable while the other party's return promise is enforceable, as is the case where the promisee of the return promise belongs to the class sought to be protected by the policy in question. See Illustrations 3, 4 and 5 to § 179 and Illustration 5 to § 181. (That an unenforceable promise may be consideration for a return promise, see § 78.) Finally, there are circumstances in which the unenforceability of one part of an agreement does not entail the unenforceability of the rest of the agreement, and these are dealt with in §§ 183 and 184. As to the effect of public policy on conditions, see § 185.

Roddy–Eden v. Berle

Supreme Court, New York County, New York, 1951.
108 N.Y.S.2d 597.

■ EDER, J. Motion to dismiss complaint for legal insufficiency in failing to state facts sufficient to constitute a cause of action, and upon the further ground that the alleged agreement pleaded in the complaint is against public policy and hence unenforceable.

The action is to recover damages alleged to have been sustained by reason of breach of a contract entered into between the parties, dated October 31, 1950.

The complaint alleges plaintiff is the authoress of a certain novel originally entitled 'Sit Still My Soul', and presently entitled, 'The Kneeling God'.

Defendant, it is averred, at all times in concern, was and still is a famous comedian and theatrical performer with a vast public of admirers and fans, and has acquired great prominence in all fields of entertainment, including the legitimate stage, motion pictures, radio and television.

It is alleged by plaintiff that in February, 1950, defendant requested plaintiff to write a serious novel to be published under his name as sole author, in order to gain recognition in the literary field; that he advised plaintiff that if she agreed to write such novel, that the finished work would be published under defendant's name as the sole author thereof, 'thereby insuring the likelihood of a large sale' because of defendant's vast public of admirers and fans and because of his many public appearances before huge audiences, which afforded 'opportunities to exploit and sell said book' and thereby insure its success; that plaintiff and defendant agreed to divide equally all profits derived from the work; that plaintiff's share would be far greater than if the book were published under plaintiff's authorship.

The complaint alleges that plaintiff proceeded to write and complete the book; that she commenced in February 1950 and finished the work in July 1950, when she delivered to defendant a copy of her complete work. It is then alleged that on or about October 31, 1950, the parties entered into a written agreement, dated that day.

It is further alleged that defendant gave interviews to the press and issued statements announcing that he was the sole author of said book and that it was soon to be published.

That in breach and violation of the agreement defendant advised plaintiff that he would not permit her work to be published and had withdrawn it from the market; that plaintiff has performed all the terms and conditions of said contract on her part to be performed, and damages are sought to be recovered because of such breach.

In sum, therefore, plaintiff seeks to recover damages allegedly sustained by her by reason of defendant's refusal to permit a book written by plaintiff to be published under defendant's name as the sole author thereof.

Defendant contends, and the court is in accord therewith, that the alleged agreement upon which plaintiff's cause of action is predicated offends public policy and is unenforceable, in that it has for its purpose and object the practicing of a fraud and deception upon the public.

It is established by abundant authority that agreements which tend to or have for their purpose to defraud the public generally, even though they may not amount to a criminal conspiracy, are illegal and void. They are denounced as contravening public policy, a declaration of principle that no one can lawfully do that which has a tendency to be injurious to the public or against the public good. Public policy is the interest of others than the parties directly concerned in the contract.

By the allegations of the complaint there is, in my opinion, apodictically shown, a scheme concocted and devised by the parties to deliberately foist a fraud on the public in the manner described; in effect and ultimate result to extract from the public the cost of the book by means of deception practiced upon it.

To urge that such a scheme and such an agreement be upheld as valid and enforceable is to ignore multitudinous rulings to the converse.

Relative to the instant situation, it is appropriate to quote from the opinion in Skinner v. Oakes, 10 Mo.App. 45, 57: 'Thus, if an author were to assign to another the privilege of publishing books with his name upon their title-page, it cannot for a moment be supposed that any court would protect such a supposed right, even as against the original assignor. This point is absolutely clear, both upon principle and authority.'

The principle is applicable here.

It is not an instance of writing under a *nom de plume*. In such a case, regardless of the pen name employed by the writer, he is, in truth, the real author and is not exploiting the ability, talent and authorship of another, palming it off under the false pretense that it is his own. In the former instance, it is, however, the *true* and *real* author, but merely employing a pseudonym, which is permissible in the field of literature and recognized in law.

It is evident from the foregoing that the agreement in concern is void as against public policy.

What has been said, supra, expresses the policy of the law as it is conceived and enforced by and under decisional law. The same denouncement manifests itself in terms of positive law, see Sections 421 and 964, Penal Law, castigating fraudulent and deceptive practices upon the public.

But, assuming, arguendo, only the parties hereto were affected by the agreement under consideration, as pleaded in the complaint, it would, nonetheless, still be denied recognition by the courts, both at law and in equity.

No action can arise out of an immoral or unlawful consideration, and it is also a well established rule of law that where a contract has its genesis in fraud, deceit or violation of law, or violates accepted standards of right conduct, the contract is unenforceable and void. In other words, where the cause of action arises *ex turpi causa*, the courts deny relief.

In the situation disclosed by the complaint, the court is of opinion that the agreement pleaded and relied on by plaintiff is void and unenforceable as against public policy.

There is a further reason why the complaint should be dismissed, and it is that it is legally insufficient in that it does not state facts sufficient to constitute a cause of action.

The motion is granted and the complaint is dismissed. Settle order.

* * *

The dispute in *Roddy–Eden* concerned an agreement struck between Anita Roddy–Eden and Milton Berle, a famous comedian and entertainer, for her to write a serious novel to be published under his name (and for them to share the proceeds). Presumably the parties believed that she would write the better book, but that he was better placed to publish it and to sell copies. Roddy–Eden wrote the book, but Berle seems to have thought better of the plan and so refused to go ahead with publication. Roddy–Eden sued, seeking her share of the profits.

The case does not require much commentary, but three points are worth making.

The first concerns the court's second, subsidiary argument, in which it observes that even if the agreement were not invalid on grounds of immorality, it would nevertheless fail to constitute an enforceable contract. The writing, the court observed, merely required Roddy–Eden to allow Berle to publish the book as his own but did not require Berle actually to publish it. And the court, applying the parol evidence rule, held that writing excludes contrary prior or contemporaneous oral terms (for example, a term imposing any obligation to publish on Berle) from the construction of the contract.

This all goes by quickly (as dicta often does). It is too quick to be persuasive. On the one hand, there is no serious analysis of whether the publication obligation that Roddy–Eden seeks to include in the contractual text constitutes a variance from the writing or merely an addition to it and no serious engagement between that question and the parol evidence rule, as adopted in New York at the time. On the other hand, as the discussions in Part II repeatedly emphasized, oral agreements that are excluded from contract construction might nevertheless go to contract interpretation. And the general structure of the arrangement in *Roddy–Eden* surely makes it odd, at the very least, for Roddy–Eden to have written a book with Berle under *no* obligation to pursue its publication. Surely Cardozo's remark, from *Lucy, Lady Duff–Gordon*, about a writing "instinct with an obligation, imperfectly expressed" applies to *Roddy–Eden* as well. At the very least, it would take a sustained argument to show that this view does not apply.

Second, whatever the merits of the result in *Roddy–Eden*, the broad language in which the holding is couched cannot be taken too literally or too far. Although the court repeatedly writes as if Roddy–Eden and Berle had planned to "defraud the public," the claim concerning fraud should not be taken too literally, at least in the narrow legal sense of the term. Certainly the court makes no serious effort to establish the elements of fraud understood as a doctrinal category. Instead, the court focuses on the broader, and more obviously correct, thought that the parties sought to deceive the public, and in a manner that would have been, in some generic moral sense, wrongful. Thus the court asserts that it is "a well established rule of law that where a contract has its genesis in fraud, deceit or violation of law, or violates accepted standards of right conduct, the contract is unenforceable and void." This is a much broader principle than the one that invokes fraud proper, and it is surely broad enough to cover the facts of *Roddy–Eden*. But the court's bluster aside, it is less clearly a correct statement of the law. Indeed, it is unclear that it *could* be correct. Imagine a contract struck between a pair of adulterers and a (knowing) hotelier, for them to rent a room from her for their adulterous liaisons. Surely this contract "violates accepted standards of right conduct" both for the adulterers and for the hotelier, especially insofar as she specializes in profiting from such guests. But the contract is undoubtedly enforceable nevertheless. And the example may of course be multiplied. Only certain immoralities make the contracts that contemplate them void. And the question just which ones do so remains as difficult to answer after *Roddy–Eden* as it did before.

Third, the legal doctrine that contracts to promote immoral activities are void raises interesting questions concerning moral analogs. Do promises to commit immoral acts establish moral obligations, or are they also void (this time morally and not just legally)? This is a special case of the question whether or not there might be honor among thieves, as it were. Ordinary intuitions and philosophical theories differ with respect to its answer. Certainly it is not outlandish to think that where two thieves promise to share their loot and one takes it all for herself, the other may complain of being wronged by her (although this complaint of course does not give him any moral claim against the loot's original, and rightful, owner). Or, to take a still stronger case, it is natural to think that where a client hires a lawyer to help her to resist a legal obligation to do something that he has a clear moral obligation to do (for example, to raise the statute of limitations as a technical defense against a debt that he clearly morally owes), then the lawyer has a moral (and also, as it happens) a legal right to collect her fee. Immorality as between the parties to a promise and the outside the world may weigh against the promise's moral validity inside the parties' relation, but it does not generally undermine the promise.[4] Indeed,

---

4. Note that immorality *between* the parties to a promise, but apart from the promise, presents a different question. A promisee may wrong his promisor in a manner that undermines the promise generally, and hence also his promissory rights: the core such case is where the wrong involves a breach of a reciprocal promise. (Law, incidentally, recognizes this case through doctrines that cause a material breach by one contracting party to relieve the other of her performance obligations.) But not every wrong will have this character: one would not, for example, ordinarily think a promise to collect a roommate from the airport is voided by the fact that the roommate took one's coat without permission in order to keep warm on his trip.

such immorality is less likely to undermine promises than contracts. Contract, being a species of positive law, may be broadly adjusted to serve prudential or instrumental ends, including the end of making various forms of immoral conduct more difficult. But promise is a moral notion, and hence not so malleable.

Roddy–Eden and cases like it concern contracts whose content is *independently* immoral. But the law also refuses to enforce another class of contracts, which, speaking very roughly, concern conduct or goods that are not immoral in themselves but rather *become immoral when made the subject of contracts*. One instance in the class was introduced in the materials on marriage in Chapter 23: although commonplace morality does not condemn sexual relations among consenting adults, it does condemn exchanging sex for money or other goods; and the law correspondingly refuses to enforce what the cases call contracts founded on consideration for meretricious sexual services. Nor is this case all that unusual. Donating organs is morally commendable, but selling them morally dubious; and contracts to sell organs will not be enforced.[5] Voting has a similar moral

---

It is tempting to think that the line between these two types of cases may be fixed by promissory interpretation. According to this view (which simply generalizes the intuitions that guide the case of the broken reciprocal promise), whether or not a promisee's wrong eliminates a promisor's promissory obligation is determined by whether the promise is best read as making the obligation to perform contingent on the promisee's not committing the wrong in question.

5. See National Organ Transplant Act, 42 U.S.C. § 274e (2006). The relevant sections of the law in its current form are:

(a) Prohibition

It shall be unlawful for any person to knowingly acquire, receive, or otherwise transfer any human organ for valuable consideration for use in human transplantation if the transfer affects interstate commerce. The preceding sentence does not apply with respect to human organ paired donation.

(b) Penalties

Any person who violates subsection (a) of this section shall be fined not more than $50,000 or imprisoned not more than five years, or both.

(c) Definitions

For purposes of subsection (a) of this section:

(1) The term "human organ" means the human (including fetal) kidney, liver, heart, lung, pancreas, bone marrow, cornea, eye, bone, and skin or any subpart thereof and any other human organ (or any subpart thereof, including that derived from a fetus) specified by the Secretary of Health and Human Services by regulation.

(2) The term "valuable consideration" does not include the reasonable payments associated with the removal, transportation, implantation, processing, preservation, quality control, and storage of a human organ or the expenses of travel, housing, and lost wages incurred by the donor of a human organ in connection with the donation of the organ.

Note that a slightly different regime governs blood, which may be legally bought and sold. Most sales of blood involve blood banks

"All the centers that supply blood for transfusions—whether they're part of the American Red Cross or not—sell their products to cover operating expenses. Local hospitals work out contracts with regional suppliers or their local Red Cross facility. In general, they'll work with a single vendor, but they may shop around a bit to find the best prices. Regional suppliers provide about half the nation's blood supply, and

status; and contracts to sell votes are again void.[6]

This class of unenforceable contracts is not easy to define in general terms, not least because the precise source of immorality varies from case to case. Some goods—votes in democratic elections are a familiar example—cannot morally be *alienated* at all (not even given altruistically away), but must instead be used by those who initially possess them. Others—organs, for example—may morally be donated charitably but not *exchanged self-interestedly*. And still others—intimacy, for example, and especially sexual intimacy—may morally be exchanged but not exchanged for material goods and especially not in markets, for money, which is to say *commodified*.

The moral and legal principles at play in these several cases—inalienability, anti-interestedness, and anti-commodification—bear at most a family resemblance to one another. And particular cases must therefore inevitably be analyzed, both morally and legally, with a keen eye to their peculiar facts and circumstances.

Rather than trying to generalize, or even to survey the field of particulars, the materials that follow focus more narrowly on the limits of freedom of contract in one area in particular: the arrangements that might arise concerning assisted reproduction. The cases raise intrinsically interesting variations on commodification and related themes. In addition, technological developments, especially when combined with the increasingly advanced age at which (especially professional) couples in developed economies have their children, render the contractualization of assisted reproduction increasingly practically important.

---

the Red Cross kicks in 45 percent. Hospitals generate the remaining 5 percent through their own blood drives.

All blood suppliers are nonprofits, and the prices they charge follow the cost of production.''

Source: The Business of Blood, Slate (available at http://www.slate.com/articles/news_and_politics/explainer/2006/09/the_business_of_blood.html) As an aside, courts seem to treat contracts concerning blood as a sale of a service, so that the blood is incidental to the transfusion: "The supplying of blood by the hospital was entirely subordinate to its paramount function of furnishing trained personnel and specialized facilities in an endeavor to restore plaintiff's health. It was not for blood or iodine or bandages for which plaintiff bargained, but the wherewithal of the hospital staff and the availability of hospital facilities to provide whatever medical treatment was considered advisable." *Perlmutter v. Beth David Hosp.*, 308 N.Y. 100, 106, 123 N.E.2d 792, 795 (1954).

6. And indeed criminalized. See 18 U.S.C.A. § 597 Expenditures to Influence Voting:

Whoever makes or offers to make an expenditure to any person, either to vote or withhold his vote, or to vote for or against any candidate; and

Whoever solicits, accepts, or receives any such expenditure in consideration of his vote or the withholding of his vote—

Shall be fined under this title or imprisoned not more than one year, or both; and if the violation was willful, shall be fined under this title or imprisoned not more than two years, or both.

In re Baby M

Supreme Court of New Jersey, 1988.
537 A.2d 1227.

■ WILENTZ, C.J. In this matter the Court is asked to determine the validity of a contract that purports to provide a new way of bringing children into a family. For a fee of $10,000, a woman agrees to be artificially inseminated with the semen of another woman's husband; she is to conceive a child, carry it to term, and after its birth surrender it to the natural father and his wife. The intent of the contract is that the child's natural mother will thereafter be forever separated from her child. The wife is to adopt the child, and she and the natural father are to be regarded as its parents for all purposes. The contract providing for this is called a "surrogacy contract," the natural mother inappropriately called the "surrogate mother."

We invalidate the surrogacy contract because it conflicts with the law and public policy of this State. While we recognize the depth of the yearning of infertile couples to have their own children, we find the payment of money to a "surrogate" mother illegal, perhaps criminal, and potentially degrading to women. Although in this case we grant custody to the natural father, the evidence having clearly proved such custody to be in the best interests of the infant, we void both the termination of the surrogate mother's parental rights and the adoption of the child by the wife/stepparent. We thus restore the "surrogate" as the mother of the child. We remand the issue of the natural mother's visitation rights to the trial court, since that issue was not reached below and the record before us is not sufficient to permit us to decide it *de novo*.

We find no offense to our present laws where a woman voluntarily and without payment agrees to act as a "surrogate" mother, provided that she is not subject to a binding agreement to surrender her child. Moreover, our holding today does not preclude the Legislature from altering the current statutory scheme, within constitutional limits, so as to permit surrogacy contracts. Under current law, however, the surrogacy agreement before us is illegal and invalid.

I. FACTS

In February 1985, William Stern and Mary Beth Whitehead entered into a surrogacy contract. It recited that Stern's wife, Elizabeth, was infertile, that they wanted a child, and that Mrs. Whitehead was willing to provide that child as the mother with Mr. Stern as the father.

The contract provided that through artificial insemination using Mr. Stern's sperm, Mrs. Whitehead would become pregnant, carry the child to term, bear it, deliver it to the Sterns, and thereafter do whatever was necessary to terminate her maternal rights so that Mrs. Stern could thereafter adopt the child. Mrs. Whitehead's husband, Richard, was also a party to the contract; Mrs. Stern was not. Mr. Whitehead promised to do all acts necessary to rebut the presumption of paternity under the Parentage Act.

Although Mrs. Stern was not a party to the surrogacy agreement, the contract gave her sole custody of the child in the event of Mr. Stern's death. Mrs. Stern's status as a nonparty to the surrogate parenting agreement presumably was to avoid the application of the baby-selling statute to this arrangement.

Mr. Stern, on his part, agreed to attempt the artificial insemination and to pay Mrs. Whitehead $10,000 after the child's birth, on its delivery to him. In a separate contract, Mr. Stern agreed to pay $7,500 to the Infertility Center of New York ("ICNY"). The Center's advertising campaigns solicit surrogate mothers and encourage infertile couples to consider surrogacy. ICNY arranged for the surrogacy contract by bringing the parties together, explaining the process to them, furnishing the contractual form, and providing legal counsel.

The history of the parties' involvement in this arrangement suggests their good faith. William and Elizabeth Stern were married in July 1974, having met at the University of Michigan, where both were Ph.D. candidates. Due to financial considerations and Mrs. Stern's pursuit of a medical degree and residency, they decided to defer starting a family until 1981. Before then, however, Mrs. Stern learned that she might have multiple sclerosis and that the disease in some cases renders pregnancy a serious health risk. Her anxiety appears to have exceeded the actual risk, which current medical authorities assess as minimal. Nonetheless that anxiety was evidently quite real, Mrs. Stern fearing that pregnancy might precipitate blindness, paraplegia, or other forms of debilitation. Based on the perceived risk, the Sterns decided to forego having their own children. The decision had special significance for Mr. Stern. Most of his family had been destroyed in the Holocaust. As the family's only survivor, he very much wanted to continue his bloodline.

Initially the Sterns considered adoption, but were discouraged by the substantial delay apparently involved and by the potential problem they saw arising from their age and their differing religious backgrounds. They were most eager for some other means to start a family.

The paths of Mrs. Whitehead and the Sterns to surrogacy were similar. Both responded to advertising by ICNY. The Sterns' response, following their inquiries into adoption, was the result of their long-standing decision to have a child. Mrs. Whitehead's response apparently resulted from her sympathy with family members and others who could have no children (she stated that she wanted to give another couple the "gift of life"); she also wanted the $10,000 to help her family.

Both parties, undoubtedly because of their own self-interest, were less sensitive to the implications of the transaction than they might otherwise have been. Mrs. Whitehead, for instance, appears not to have been concerned about whether the Sterns would make good parents for her child; the Sterns, on their part, while conscious of the obvious possibility that surrendering the child might cause grief to Mrs. Whitehead, overcame their qualms because of their desire for a child. At any rate, both the Sterns and

Mrs. Whitehead were committed to the arrangement; both thought it right and constructive.

Mrs. Whitehead had reached her decision concerning surrogacy before the Sterns, and had actually been involved as a potential surrogate mother with another couple. After numerous unsuccessful artificial inseminations, that effort was abandoned. Thereafter, the Sterns learned of the Infertility Center, the possibilities of surrogacy, and of Mary Beth Whitehead. The two couples met to discuss the surrogacy arrangement and decided to go forward. On February 6, 1985, Mr. Stern and Mr. and Mrs. Whitehead executed the surrogate parenting agreement. After several artificial inseminations over a period of months, Mrs. Whitehead became pregnant. The pregnancy was uneventful and on March 27, 1986, Baby M was born.

Not wishing anyone at the hospital to be aware of the surrogacy arrangement, Mr. and Mrs. Whitehead appeared to all as the proud parents of a healthy female child. Her birth certificate indicated her name to be Sara Elizabeth Whitehead and her father to be Richard Whitehead. In accordance with Mrs. Whitehead's request, the Sterns visited the hospital unobtrusively to see the newborn child.

Mrs. Whitehead realized, almost from the moment of birth, that she could not part with this child. She had felt a bond with it even during pregnancy. Some indication of the attachment was conveyed to the Sterns at the hospital when they told Mrs. Whitehead what they were going to name the baby. She apparently broke into tears and indicated that she did not know if she could give up the child. She talked about how the baby looked like her other daughter, and made it clear that she was experiencing great difficulty with the decision.

Nonetheless, Mrs. Whitehead was, for the moment, true to her word. Despite powerful inclinations to the contrary, she turned her child over to the Sterns on March 30 at the Whiteheads' home.

The Sterns were thrilled with their new child. They had planned extensively for its arrival, far beyond the practical furnishing of a room for her. It was a time of joyful celebration-not just for them but for their friends as well. The Sterns looked forward to raising their daughter, whom they named Melissa. While aware by then that Mrs. Whitehead was undergoing an emotional crisis, they were as yet not cognizant of the depth of that crisis and its implications for their newly-enlarged family.

Later in the evening of March 30, Mrs. Whitehead became deeply disturbed, disconsolate, stricken with unbearable sadness. She had to have her child. She could not eat, sleep, or concentrate on anything other than her need for her baby. The next day she went to the Sterns' home and told them how much she was suffering.

The depth of Mrs. Whitehead's despair surprised and frightened the Sterns. She told them that she could not live without her baby, that she must have her, even if only for one week, that thereafter she would surrender her child. The Sterns, concerned that Mrs. Whitehead might indeed commit suicide, not wanting under any circumstances to risk that, and in any event believing that Mrs. Whitehead would keep her word, turned the child over to her. It was not until four months later, after a series of attempts to regain possession of the child, that Melissa was returned to the Sterns, having been forcibly removed from the home where she was then living with Mr. and Mrs. Whitehead, the home in Florida owned by Mary Beth Whitehead's parents.

The struggle over Baby M began when it became apparent that Mrs. Whitehead could not return the child to Mr. Stern. Due to Mrs. Whitehead's refusal to relinquish the baby, Mr. Stern filed a complaint seeking enforcement of the surrogacy contract. He alleged, accurately, that Mrs. Whitehead had not only refused to comply with the surrogacy contract but had threatened to flee from New Jersey with the child in order to avoid even the possibility of his obtaining custody. The court papers asserted that if Mrs. Whitehead were to be given notice of the application for an order requiring her to relinquish custody, she would, prior to the hearing, leave the state with the baby. And that is precisely what she did. After the order was entered, *ex parte,* the process server, aided by the police, in the presence of the Sterns, entered Mrs. Whitehead's home to execute the order. Mr. Whitehead fled with the child, who had been handed to him through a window while those who came to enforce the order were thrown off balance by a dispute over the child's current name.

The Whiteheads immediately fled to Florida with Baby M. They stayed initially with Mrs. Whitehead's parents, where one of Mrs. Whitehead's children had been living. For the next three months, the Whiteheads and Melissa lived at roughly twenty different hotels, motels, and homes in order to avoid apprehension. From time to time Mrs. Whitehead would call Mr. Stern to discuss the matter; the conversations, recorded by Mr. Stern on advice of counsel, show an escalating dispute about rights, morality, and power, accompanied by threats of Mrs. Whitehead to kill herself, to kill the child, and falsely to accuse Mr. Stern of sexually molesting Mrs. Whitehead's other daughter.

Eventually the Sterns discovered where the Whiteheads were staying, commenced supplementary proceedings in Florida, and obtained an order requiring the Whiteheads to turn over the child. Police in Florida enforced the order, forcibly removing the child from her grandparents' home. She was soon thereafter brought to New Jersey and turned over to the Sterns. The prior order of the court, issued *ex parte,* awarding custody of the child to the Sterns *pendente lite,* was reaffirmed by the trial court after consideration of the certified representations of the parties (both represented by counsel) concerning the unusual sequence of events that had unfolded. Pending final judgment, Mrs. Whitehead was awarded limited visitation with Baby M.

The Sterns' complaint, in addition to seeking possession and ultimately custody of the child, sought enforcement of the surrogacy contract. Pursuant to the contract, it asked that the child be permanently placed in their custody, that Mrs. Whitehead's parental rights be terminated, and that

Mrs. Stern be allowed to adopt the child, *i.e.,* that, for all purposes, Melissa become the Sterns' child.

The trial took thirty-two days over a period of more than two months. It included numerous interlocutory appeals and attempted interlocutory appeals. There were twenty-three witnesses to the facts recited above and fifteen expert witnesses, eleven testifying on the issue of custody and four on the subject of Mrs. Stern's multiple sclerosis; the bulk of the testimony was devoted to determining the parenting arrangement most compatible with the child's best interests. Soon after the conclusion of the trial, the trial court announced its opinion from the bench. It held that the surrogacy contract was valid; ordered that Mrs. Whitehead's parental rights be terminated and that sole custody of the child be granted to Mr. Stern; and, after hearing brief testimony from Mrs. Stern, immediately entered an order allowing the adoption of Melissa by Mrs. Stern, all in accordance with the surrogacy contract. Pending the outcome of the appeal, we granted a continuation of visitation to Mrs. Whitehead, although slightly more limited than the visitation allowed during the trial.

Although clearly expressing its view that the surrogacy contract was valid, the trial court devoted the major portion of its opinion to the question of the baby's best interests. The inconsistency is apparent. The surrogacy contract calls for the surrender of the child to the Sterns, permanent and sole custody in the Sterns, and termination of Mrs. Whitehead's parental rights, all without qualification, all regardless of any evaluation of the best interests of the child. As a matter of fact the contract recites (even before the child was conceived) that it is in the best interests of the child to be placed with Mr. Stern. In effect, the trial court awarded custody to Mr. Stern, the natural father, based on the same kind of evidence and analysis as might be expected had no surrogacy contract existed. Its rationalization, however, was that while the surrogacy contract was valid, specific performance would not be granted unless that remedy was in the best interests of the child. The factual issues confronted and decided by the trial court were the same as if Mr. Stern and Mrs. Whitehead had had the child out of wedlock, intended or unintended, and then disagreed about custody. The trial court's awareness of the irrelevance of the contract in the court's determination of custody is suggested by its remark that beyond the question of the child's best interests, "[a]ll other concerns raised by counsel constitute commentary." 217 *N.J.Super.* at 323, 525 *A.2d* 1128.

On the question of best interests—and we agree, but for different reasons, that custody was the critical issue—the court's analysis of the testimony was perceptive, demonstrating both its understanding of the case and its considerable experience in these matters. We agree substantially with both its analysis and conclusions on the matter of custody.

The court's review and analysis of the surrogacy contract, however, is not at all in accord with ours. The trial court concluded that the various statutes governing this matter, including those concerning adoption, termination of parental rights, and payment of money in connection with adoptions, do not apply to surrogacy contracts. It reasoned that because the Legislature did not have surrogacy contracts in mind when it passed those laws, those laws were therefore irrelevant. Thus, assuming it was writing on a clean slate, the trial court analyzed the interests involved and the power of the court to accommodate them. It then held that surrogacy contracts are valid and should be enforced, and furthermore that Mr. Stern's rights under the surrogacy contract were constitutionally protected.

Mrs. Whitehead appealed. This Court granted direct certification. The briefs of the parties on appeal were joined by numerous briefs filed by *amici* expressing various interests and views on surrogacy and on this case. We have found many of them helpful in resolving the issues before us.

Mrs. Whitehead contends that the surrogacy contract, for a variety of reasons, is invalid. She contends that it conflicts with public policy since it guarantees that the child will not have the nurturing of both natural parents-presumably New Jersey's goal for families. She further argues that it deprives the mother of her constitutional right to the companionship of her child, and that it conflicts with statutes concerning termination of parental rights and adoption. With the contract thus void, Mrs. Whitehead claims primary custody (with visitation rights in Mr. Stern) both on a best interests basis (stressing the "tender years" doctrine) as well as on the policy basis of discouraging surrogacy contracts. She maintains that even if custody would ordinarily go to Mr. Stern, here it should be awarded to Mrs. Whitehead to deter future surrogacy arrangements.

In a brief filed after oral argument, counsel for Mrs. Whitehead suggests that the standard for determining best interests where the infant resulted from a surrogacy contract is that the child should be placed with the mother absent a showing of unfitness. All parties agree that no expert testified that Mary Beth Whitehead was unfit as a mother; the trial court expressly found that she was *not* "unfit," that, on the contrary, "she is a good mother for and to her older children," 217 *N.J.Super.* at 397, 525 A.2d 1128; and no one now claims anything to the contrary.

One of the repeated themes put forth by Mrs. Whitehead is that the court's initial *ex parte* order granting custody to the Sterns during the trial was a substantial factor in the ultimate "best interests" determination. That initial order, claimed to be erroneous by Mrs. Whitehead, not only established Melissa as part of the Stern family, but brought enormous pressure on Mrs. Whitehead. The order brought the weight of the state behind the Sterns' attempt, ultimately successful, to gain possession of the child. The resulting pressure, Mrs. Whitehead contends, caused her to act in ways that were atypical of her ordinary behavior when not under stress, and to act in ways that were thought to be inimical to the child's best interests in that they demonstrated a failure of character, maturity, and consistency. She claims that any mother who truly loved her child might so respond and that it is doubly unfair to judge her on the basis of her reaction to an extreme situation rarely faced by any mother, where that situation was itself caused by an erroneous order of the court. Therefore, according to Mrs. Whitehead, the erroneous *ex parte* order precipitated a series of events that proved instrumental in the final result.

The Sterns claim that the surrogacy contract is valid and should be enforced, largely for the reasons given by the trial court. They claim a constitutional right of privacy, which includes the right of procreation, and the right of consenting adults to deal with matters of reproduction as they see fit. As for the child's best interests, their position is factual: given all of the circumstances, the child is better off in their custody with no residual parental rights reserved for Mrs. Whitehead.

Of considerable interest in this clash of views is the position of the child's guardian *ad litem,* wisely appointed by the court at the outset of the litigation. As the child's representative, her role in the litigation, as she viewed it, was solely to protect the child's best interests. She therefore took no position on the validity of the surrogacy contract, and instead devoted her energies to obtaining expert testimony uninfluenced by any interest other than the child's. We agree with the guardian's perception of her role in this litigation. She appropriately refrained from taking any position that might have appeared to compromise her role as the child's advocate. She first took the position, based on her experts' testimony, that the Sterns should have primary custody, and that while Mrs. Whitehead's parental rights should not be terminated, no visitation should be allowed for five years. As a result of subsequent developments, mentioned *infra,* her view has changed. She now recommends that no visitation be allowed at least until Baby M reaches maturity.

Although some of the experts' opinions touched on visitation, the major issue they addressed was whether custody should be reposed in the Sterns or in the Whiteheads. The trial court, consistent in this respect with its view that the surrogacy contract was valid, did not deal at all with the question of visitation. Having concluded that the best interests of the child called for custody in the Sterns, the trial court enforced the operative provisions of the surrogacy contract, terminated Mrs. Whitehead's parental rights, and granted an adoption to Mrs. Stern. Explicit in the ruling was the conclusion that the best interests determination removed whatever impediment might have existed in enforcing the surrogacy contract. This Court, therefore, is without guidance from the trial court on the visitation issue, an issue of considerable importance in any event, and especially important in view of our determination that the surrogacy contract is invalid.

II. INVALIDITY AND UNENFORCEABILITY OF SURROGACY CONTRACT

We have concluded that this surrogacy contract is invalid. Our conclusion has two bases: direct conflict with existing statutes and conflict with the public policies of this State, as expressed in its statutory and decisional law.

One of the surrogacy contract's basic purposes, to achieve the adoption of a child through private placement, though permitted in New Jersey "is very much disfavored." *Sees v. Baber,* 74 *N.J.* 201, 217, 377 A.2d 628 (1977). Its use of money for this purpose—and we have no doubt whatsoever that the money is being paid to obtain an adoption and not, as the Sterns argue, for the personal services of Mary Beth Whitehead—is illegal and perhaps criminal. *N.J.S.A.* 9:3–54. In addition to the inducement of money, there is the coercion of contract: the natural mother's irrevocable agreement, prior to birth, even prior to conception, to surrender the child to the adoptive couple. Such an agreement is totally unenforceable in private placement adoption. Even where the adoption is through an approved agency, the formal agreement to surrender occurs only *after* birth, and then, by regulation, only after the birth mother has been offered counseling. Integral to these invalid provisions of the surrogacy contract is the related agreement, equally invalid, on the part of the natural mother to cooperate with, and not to contest, proceedings to terminate her parental rights, as well as her contractual concession, in aid of the adoption, that the child's best interests would be served by awarding custody to the natural father and his wife-all of this before she has even conceived, and, in some cases, before she has the slightest idea of what the natural father and adoptive mother are like.

The foregoing provisions not only directly conflict with New Jersey statutes, but also offend long-established State policies. These critical terms, which are at the heart of the contract, are invalid and unenforceable; the conclusion therefore follows, without more, that the entire contract is unenforceable.

A. Conflict with Statutory Provisions

The surrogacy contract conflicts with: (1) laws prohibiting the use of money in connection with adoptions; (2) laws requiring proof of parental unfitness or abandonment before termination of parental rights is ordered or an adoption is granted; and (3) laws that make surrender of custody and consent to adoption revocable in private placement adoptions.

(1) Our law prohibits paying or accepting money in connection with any placement of a child for adoption. Violation is a high misdemeanor. Excepted are fees of an approved agency (which must be a non-profit entity) and certain expenses in connection with childbirth.

Considerable care was taken in this case to structure the surrogacy arrangement so as not to violate this prohibition. The arrangement was structured as follows: the adopting parent, Mrs. Stern, was not a party to the surrogacy contract; the money paid to Mrs. Whitehead was stated to be for her services-not for the adoption; the sole purpose of the contract was stated as being that "of giving a child to William Stern, its natural and biological father"; the money was purported to be "compensation for services and expenses and in no way a fee for termination of parental rights or a payment in exchange for consent to surrender a child for adoption"; the fee to the Infertility Center ($7,500) was stated to be for legal representation, advice, administrative work, and other "services." Nevertheless, it seems clear that the money was paid and accepted in connection with an adoption.

The Infertility Center's major role was first as a "finder" of the surrogate mother whose child was to be adopted, and second as the arranger of all proceedings that led to the adoption. Its role as adoption finder is demonstrated by the provision requiring Mr. Stern to pay another $7,500 if he uses Mary Beth Whitehead again as a surrogate, and by ICNY's agreement to "coordinate arrangements for the adoption of the child by the wife." The surrogacy agreement requires Mrs. Whitehead to surrender Baby M for the purposes of adoption. The agreement notes that Mr. *and Mrs.* Stern wanted to have a child, and provides that the child be "placed" with Mrs. Stern in the event Mr. Stern dies before the child is born. The payment of the $10,000 occurs only on surrender of custody of the child and "completion of the duties and obligations" of Mrs. Whitehead, including termination of her parental rights to facilitate adoption by Mrs. Stern. As for the contention that the Sterns are paying only for services and not for an adoption, we need note only that they would pay nothing in the event the child died before the fourth month of pregnancy, and only $1,000 if the child were stillborn, even though the "services" had been fully rendered. Additionally, one of Mrs. Whitehead's estimated costs, to be assumed by Mr. Stern, was an "Adoption Fee," presumably for Mrs. Whitehead's incidental costs in connection with the adoption.

Mr. Stern knew he was paying for the adoption of a child; Mrs. Whitehead knew she was accepting money so that a child might be adopted; the Infertility Center knew that it was being paid for assisting in the adoption of a child. The actions of all three worked to frustrate the goals of the statute. It strains credulity to claim that these arrangements, touted by those in the surrogacy business as an attractive alternative to the usual route leading to an adoption, really amount to something other than a private placement adoption for money.

The prohibition of our statute is strong. Violation constitutes a high misdemeanor, a third-degree crime, carrying a penalty of three to five years imprisonment. The evils inherent in baby-bartering are loathsome for a myriad of reasons. The child is sold without regard for whether the purchasers will be suitable parents. The natural mother does not receive the benefit of counseling and guidance to assist her in making a decision that may affect her for a lifetime. In fact, the monetary incentive to sell her child may, depending on her financial circumstances, make her decision less voluntary. Furthermore, the adoptive parents[5] may not be fully informed of the natural parents' medical history.

Baby-selling potentially results in the exploitation of all parties involved. Conversely, adoption statutes seek to further humanitarian goals, foremost among them the best interests of the child. The negative consequences of baby-buying are potentially present in the surrogacy context,

---

5. Of course, here there are no "adoptive parents," but rather the natural father and his wife, the only adoptive parent. As noted, however, many of the dangers of using money in connection with adoption may exist in surrogacy situations.

especially the potential for placing and adopting a child without regard to the interest of the child or the natural mother.

(2) The termination of Mrs. Whitehead's parental rights, called for by the surrogacy contract and actually ordered by the court, fails to comply with the stringent requirements of New Jersey law. Our law, recognizing the finality of any termination of parental rights, provides for such termination only where there has been a voluntary surrender of a child to an approved agency or to the Division of Youth and Family Services ("DYFS"), accompanied by a formal document acknowledging termination of parental rights, or where there has been a showing of parental abandonment or unfitness. A termination may ordinarily take one of three forms: an action by an approved agency, an action by DYFS, or an action in connection with a private placement adoption. The three are governed by separate statutes, but the standards for termination are substantially the same, except that whereas a written surrender is effective when made to an approved agency or to DYFS, there is no provision for it in the private placement context.

N.J.S.A. 9:2–18 to –20 governs an action by an approved agency to terminate parental rights. Such an action, whether or not in conjunction with a pending adoption, may proceed on proof of written surrender, *N.J.S.A.* 9:2–16,–17, "forsaken parental obligation," or other specific grounds such as death or insanity, *N.J.S.A.* 9:2–19. Where the parent has not executed a formal consent, termination requires a showing of "forsaken parental obligation," *i.e.,* "willful and continuous neglect or failure to perform the natural and regular obligations of care and support of a child." *N.J.S.A.* 9:2–13(d).

Where DYFS is the agency seeking termination, the requirements are similarly stringent, although at first glance they do not appear to be so. DYFS can, as can any approved agency, accept a formal voluntary surrender or writing having the effect of termination and giving DYFS the right to place the child for adoption. Absent such formal written surrender and consent, similar to that given to approved agencies, DYFS can terminate parental rights in an action for guardianship by proving that "the best interests of such child require that he be placed under proper guardianship." *N.J.S.A.* 30:4C–20. Despite this "best interests" language, however, this Court has recently held in *New Jersey Div. of Youth & Family Servs. v. A.W.,* 103 N.J. 591 (1986), that in order for DYFS to terminate parental rights it must prove, by clear and convincing evidence, that "[t]he child's health and development have been or will be seriously impaired by the parental relationship," *id.* at 604, that "[t]he parents are unable or unwilling to eliminate the harm and delaying permanent placement will add to the harm," *id.* at 605, that "[t]he court has considered alternatives to termination," *id.* at 608, and that "[t]he termination of parental rights will not do more harm than good," *id.* at 610. This interpretation of the statutory language requires a most substantial showing of harm to the child if the parental relationship were to continue, far exceeding anything that a "best interests" test connotes.

In order to terminate parental rights under the private placement adoption statute, there must be a finding of "intentional abandonment or a very substantial neglect of parental duties without a reasonable expectation of a reversal of that conduct in the future." *N.J.S.A.* 9:3–48c(1). This requirement is similar to that of the prior law and to that of the law providing for termination through actions by approved agencies.

In *Sees v. Baber,* 74 N.J. 201 (1977) we distinguished the requirements for terminating parental rights in a private placement adoption from those required in an approved agency adoption. We stated that in an unregulated private placement, "neither consent nor voluntary surrender is singled out as a statutory factor in terminating parental rights." *Id.* at 213. *Sees* established that without proof that parental obligations had been forsaken, there would be no termination in a private placement setting.

As the trial court recognized, without a valid termination there can be no adoption. This requirement applies to all adoptions, whether they be private placements or agency adoptions.

Our statutes, and the cases interpreting them, leave no doubt that where there has been no written surrender to an approved agency or to DYFS, termination of parental rights will not be granted in this state absent a very strong showing of abandonment or neglect. That showing is required in every context in which termination of parental rights is sought, be it an action by an approved agency, an action by DYFS, or a private placement adoption proceeding, even where the petitioning adoptive parent is, as here, a stepparent. While the statutes make certain procedural allowances when stepparents are involved, the substantive requirement for terminating the natural parents' rights is not relaxed one iota. It is clear that a "best interests" determination is never sufficient to terminate parental rights; the statutory criteria must be proved.

In this case a termination of parental rights was obtained not by proving the statutory prerequisites but by claiming the benefit of contractual provisions. From all that has been stated above, it is clear that a contractual agreement to abandon one's parental rights, or not to contest a termination action, will not be enforced in our courts. The Legislature would not have so carefully, so consistently, and so substantially restricted termination of parental rights if it had intended to allow termination to be achieved by one short sentence in a contract.

Since the termination was invalid, it follows, as noted above, that adoption of Melissa by Mrs. Stern could not properly be granted.

(3) The provision in the surrogacy contract stating that Mary Beth Whitehead agrees to "surrender custody and terminate all parental rights" contains no clause giving her a right to rescind. It is intended to be an irrevocable consent to surrender the child for adoption-in other words, an irrevocable commitment by Mrs. Whitehead to turn Baby M over to the Sterns and thereafter to allow termination of her parental rights. The trial court required a "best interests" showing as a condition to granting specific performance of the surrogacy contract. Having decided the "best

interests" issue in favor of the Sterns, that court's order included, among other things, specific performance of this agreement to surrender custody and terminate all parental rights.

Mrs. Whitehead, shortly after the child's birth, had attempted to revoke her consent and surrender by refusing, after the Sterns had allowed her to have the child "just for one week," to return Baby M to them. The trial court's award of specific performance therefore reflects its view that the consent to surrender the child was irrevocable. We accept the trial court's construction of the contract; indeed it appears quite clear that this was the parties' intent. Such a provision, however, making irrevocable the natural mother's consent to surrender custody of her child in a private placement adoption, clearly conflicts with New Jersey law.

Our analysis commences with the statute providing for surrender of custody to an approved agency and termination of parental rights on the suit of that agency. The two basic provisions of the statute are *N.J.S.A.* 9:2–14 and 9:2–16. The former provides explicitly that

> [e]xcept as otherwise provided by law or by order or judgment of a court of competent jurisdiction or by testamentary disposition, no surrender of the custody of a child shall be valid in this state unless made to an approved agency pursuant to the provisions of this act

There is no exception "provided by law," and it is not clear that there could be any "order or judgment of a court of competent jurisdiction" validating a surrender of custody as a basis for adoption when that surrender was not in conformance with the statute. Requirements for a voluntary surrender to an approved agency are set forth in *N.J.S.A.* 9:2–16. This section allows an approved agency to take a voluntary surrender of custody from the parent of a child but provides stringent requirements as a condition to its validity. The surrender must be in writing, must be in such form as is required for the recording of a deed, and, pursuant to *N.J.S.A.* 9:2–17, must

> be such as to declare that the person executing the same desires to relinquish the custody of the child, acknowledge the termination of parental rights as to such custody in favor of the approved agency, and acknowledge full understanding of the effect of such surrender as provided by this act.

If the foregoing requirements are met, the consent, the voluntary surrender of custody

> shall be valid whether or not the person giving same is a minor and shall be irrevocable except at the discretion of the approved agency taking such surrender or upon order or judgment of a court of competent jurisdiction, setting aside such surrender upon proof of fraud, duress, or misrepresentation. [*N.J.S.A.* 9:2–16.]

The importance of that irrevocability is that the surrender itself gives the agency the power to obtain termination of parental rights-in other words, permanent separation of the parent from the child, leading in the ordinary case to an adoption.

This statutory pattern, providing for a surrender in writing and for termination of parental rights by an approved agency, is generally followed in connection with adoption proceedings and proceedings by DYFS to obtain permanent custody of a child. Our adoption statute repeats the requirements necessary to accomplish an irrevocable surrender to an approved agency in both form and substance. *N.J.S.A.* 9:3–41a. It provides that the surrender "shall be valid and binding without regard to the age of the person executing the surrender," *ibid.*; and although the word "irrevocable" is not used, that seems clearly to be the intent of the provision. The statute speaks of such surrender as constituting "relinquishment of such person's parental rights in or guardianship or custody of the child *named therein* and consent by such person to adoption of the child." *Ibid.* (emphasis supplied). We emphasize "named therein," for we construe the statute to allow a surrender only after the birth of the child. The formal consent to surrender enables the approved agency to terminate parental rights.

Similarly, DYFS is empowered to "take voluntary surrenders and releases of custody and consents to adoption[s]" from parents, which surrenders, releases, or consents "when properly acknowledged shall be valid and binding irrespective of the age of the person giving the same, and shall be irrevocable except at the discretion of the Bureau of Childrens Services [currently DYFS] or upon order of a court of competent jurisdiction." *N.J.S.A.* 30:4C–23. Such consent to surrender of the custody of the child would presumably lead to an adoption placement by DYFS.

It is clear that the Legislature so carefully circumscribed all aspects of a consent to surrender custody-its form and substance, its manner of execution, and the agency or agencies to which it may be made-in order to provide the basis for irrevocability. It seems most unlikely that the Legislature intended that a consent not complying with these requirements would also be irrevocable, especially where, as here, that consent falls radically short of compliance. Not only do the form and substance of the consent in the surrogacy contract fail to meet statutory requirements, but the surrender of custody is made to a private party. It is not made, as the statute requires, either to an approved agency or to DYFS.

These strict prerequisites to irrevocability constitute a recognition of the most serious consequences that flow from such consents: termination of parental rights, the permanent separation of parent from child, and the ultimate adoption of the child. Because of those consequences, the Legislature severely limited the circumstances under which such consent would be irrevocable. The legislative goal is furthered by regulations requiring approved agencies, prior to accepting irrevocable consents, to provide advice and counseling to women, making it more likely that they fully understand and appreciate the consequences of their acts.

Contractual surrender of parental rights is not provided for in our statutes as now written. Indeed, in the Parentage Act, *N.J.S.A.* 9:17–38 to –59, there is a specific provision invalidating any agreement "between an alleged or presumed father and the mother of the child" to bar an action brought for the purpose of determining paternity "[r]egardless of [the contract's] terms." *N.J.S.A.* 9:17–45. Even a settlement agreement concerning parentage reached in a judicially-mandated consent conference is not valid unless the proposed settlement is approved beforehand by the court. There is no doubt that a contractual provision purporting to constitute an irrevocable agreement to surrender custody of a child for adoption is invalid.

In *Sees v. Baber, supra,* 74 N.J. 201, we noted that a natural mother's consent to surrender her child and to its subsequent adoption was no longer *required* by the statute in private placement adoptions. After tracing the statutory history from the time when such a consent had been an essential prerequisite to adoption, we concluded that such a consent was now neither necessary nor sufficient for the purpose of terminating parental rights. The consent to surrender custody in that case was in writing, had been executed prior to physical surrender of the infant, and had been explained to the mother by an attorney. The trial court found that the consent to surrender of custody in that private placement adoption was knowing, voluntary, and deliberate. The physical surrender of the child took place four days after its birth. Two days thereafter the natural mother changed her mind, and asked that the adoptive couple give her baby back to her. We held that she was entitled to the baby's return. The effect of our holding in that case necessarily encompassed our conclusion that "in an unsupervised private placement, since there is no statutory obligation to consent, there can be no legal barrier to its retraction."... The only possible relevance of consent in these matters, we noted, was that it *might* bear on whether there had been an abandonment of the child, or a forsaking of parental obligations. Otherwise, consent in a private placement adoption is not only revocable but, when revoked early enough, irrelevant.

The provision in the surrogacy contract whereby the mother irrevocably agrees to surrender custody of her child and to terminate her parental rights conflicts with the settled interpretation of New Jersey statutory law.[8] There is only one irrevocable consent, and that is the one explicitly provided for by statute: a consent to surrender of custody and a placement with an approved agency or with DYFS. The provision in the surrogacy contract, agreed to before conception, requiring the natural mother to surrender custody of the child without any right of revocation is one more indication of the essential nature of this transaction: the creation of a contractual system of termination and adoption designed to circumvent our statutes.

B. Public Policy Considerations

The surrogacy contract's invalidity, resulting from its direct conflict with the above statutory provisions, is further underlined when its goals

---

8. The surrogacy situation, of course, differs from the situation in *Sees,* in that here there is no "adoptive couple," but rather the natural father and the stepmother, who is the would-be adoptive mother. This difference, however, does not go to the basis of the *Sees* holding. In both cases, the determinative aspect is the vulnerability of the natural mother who decides to surrender her child in the absence of institutional safeguards.

and means are measured against New Jersey's public policy. The contract's basic premise, that the natural parents can decide in advance of birth which one is to have custody of the child, bears no relationship to the settled law that the child's best interests shall determine custody.

The fact that the trial court remedied that aspect of the contract through the "best interests" phase does not make the contractual provision any less offensive to the public policy of this State.

The surrogacy contract guarantees permanent separation of the child from one of its natural parents. Our policy, however, has long been that to the extent possible, children should remain with and be brought up by both of their natural parents. While not so stated in the present adoption law, this purpose remains part of the public policy of this State. This is not simply some theoretical ideal that in practice has no meaning. The impact of failure to follow that policy is nowhere better shown than in the results of this surrogacy contract. A child, instead of starting off its life with as much peace and security as possible, finds itself immediately in a tug-of-war between contending mother and father.[9]

The surrogacy contract violates the policy of this State that the rights of natural parents are equal concerning their child, the father's right no greater than the mother's. "The parent and child relationship extends equally to every child and to every parent, regardless of the marital status of the parents." *N.J.S.A.* 9:17–40. As the Assembly Judiciary Committee noted in its statement to the bill, this section establishes "the principle that regardless of the marital status of the parents, all children *and all parents* have equal rights with respect to each other." *Statement to Senate No. 888,* Assembly Judiciary, Law, Public Safety and Defense Committee (1983) (emphasis supplied). The whole purpose and effect of the surrogacy contract was to give the father the exclusive right to the child by destroying the rights of the mother.

The policies expressed in our comprehensive laws governing consent to the surrender of a child stand in stark contrast to the surrogacy contract and what it implies. Here there is no counseling, independent or otherwise, of the natural mother, no evaluation, no warning.

The only legal advice Mary Beth Whitehead received regarding the surrogacy contract was provided in connection with the contract that she previously entered into with another couple. Mrs. Whitehead's lawyer was referred to her by the Infertility Center, with which he had an agreement to act as counsel for surrogate candidates. His services consisted of spending one hour going through the contract with the Whiteheads, section by

---

9. And the impact on the natural parents, Mr. Stern and Mrs. Whitehead, is severe and dramatic. The depth of their conflict about Baby M, about custody, visitation, about the goodness or badness of each of them, comes through in their telephone conversations, in which each tried to persuade the other to give up the child. The potential adverse consequences of surrogacy are poignantly captured here-Mrs. Whitehead threatening to kill herself and the baby, Mr. Stern begging her not to, each blaming the other. The dashed hopes of the Sterns, the agony of Mrs. Whitehead, their suffering, their hatred-all were caused by the unraveling of this arrangement.

section, and answering their questions. Mrs. Whitehead received no further legal advice prior to signing the contract with the Sterns.

Mrs. Whitehead was examined and psychologically evaluated, but if it was for her benefit, the record does not disclose that fact. The Sterns regarded the evaluation as important, particularly in connection with the question of whether she would change her mind. Yet they never asked to see it, and were content with the assumption that the Infertility Center had made an evaluation and had concluded that there was no danger that the surrogate mother would change her mind. From Mrs. Whitehead's point of view, all that she learned from the evaluation was that "she had passed." It is apparent that the profit motive got the better of the Infertility Center. Although the evaluation was made, it was not put to any use, and understandably so, for the psychologist warned that Mrs. Whitehead demonstrated certain traits that might make surrender of the child difficult and that there should be further inquiry into this issue in connection with her surrogacy. To inquire further, however, might have jeopardized the Infertility Center's fee. The record indicates that neither Mrs. Whitehead nor the Sterns were ever told of this fact, a fact that might have ended their surrogacy arrangement.

Under the contract, the natural mother is irrevocably committed before she knows the strength of her bond with her child. She never makes a totally voluntary, informed decision, for quite clearly any decision prior to the baby's birth is, in the most important sense, uninformed, and any decision after that, compelled by a pre-existing contractual commitment, the threat of a lawsuit, and the inducement of a $10,000 payment, is less than totally voluntary. Her interests are of little concern to those who controlled this transaction.

Although the interest of the natural father and adoptive mother is certainly the predominant interest, realistically the *only* interest served, even they are left with less than what public policy requires. They know little about the natural mother, her genetic makeup, and her psychological and medical history. Moreover, not even a superficial attempt is made to determine their awareness of their responsibilities as parents.

Worst of all, however, is the contract's total disregard of the best interests of the child. There is not the slightest suggestion that any inquiry will be made at any time to determine the fitness of the Sterns as custodial parents, of Mrs. Stern as an adoptive parent, their superiority to Mrs. Whitehead, or the effect on the child of not living with her natural mother.

This is the sale of a child, or, at the very least, the sale of a mother's right to her child, the only mitigating factor being that one of the purchasers is the father. Almost every evil that prompted the prohibition on the payment of money in connection with adoptions exists here.

The differences between an adoption and a surrogacy contract should be noted, since it is asserted that the use of money in connection with surrogacy does not pose the risks found where money buys an adoption.

First, and perhaps most important, all parties concede that it is unlikely that surrogacy will survive without money. Despite the alleged selfless motivation of surrogate mothers, if there is no payment, there will be no surrogates, or very few. That conclusion contrasts with adoption; for obvious reasons, there remains a steady supply, albeit insufficient, despite the prohibitions against payment. The adoption itself, relieving the natural mother of the financial burden of supporting an infant, is in some sense the equivalent of payment.

Second, the use of money in adoptions does not *produce* the problem-conception occurs, and usually the birth itself, before illicit funds are offered. With surrogacy, the "problem," if one views it as such, consisting of the purchase of a woman's procreative capacity, at the risk of her life, is caused by and originates with the offer of money.

Third, with the law prohibiting the use of money in connection with adoptions, the built-in financial pressure of the unwanted pregnancy and the consequent support obligation do not lead the mother to the highest paying, ill-suited, adoptive parents. She is just as well-off surrendering the child to an approved agency. In surrogacy, the highest bidders will presumably become the adoptive parents regardless of suitability, so long as payment of money is permitted.

Fourth, the mother's consent to surrender her child in adoptions is revocable, even after surrender of the child, unless it be to an approved agency, where by regulation there are protections against an ill-advised surrender. In surrogacy, consent occurs so early that no amount of advice would satisfy the potential mother's need, yet the consent is irrevocable.

The main difference, that the unwanted pregnancy is unintended while the situation of the surrogate mother is voluntary and intended, is really not significant.

Initially, it produces stronger reactions of sympathy for the mother whose pregnancy was unwanted than for the surrogate mother, who "went into this with her eyes wide open." On reflection, however, it appears that the essential evil is the same, taking advantage of a woman's circumstances (the unwanted pregnancy or the need for money) in order to take away her child, the difference being one of degree.

In the scheme contemplated by the surrogacy contract in this case, a middle man, propelled by profit, promotes the sale. Whatever idealism may have motivated any of the participants, the profit motive predominates, permeates, and ultimately governs the transaction. The demand for children is great and the supply small. The availability of contraception, abortion, and the greater willingness of single mothers to bring up their children has led to a shortage of babies offered for adoption. The situation is ripe for the entry of the middleman who will bring some equilibrium into the market by increasing the supply through the use of money.

Intimated, but disputed, is the assertion that surrogacy will be used for the benefit of the rich at the expense of the poor. In response it is noted that the Sterns are not rich and the Whiteheads not poor. Nevertheless, it is clear to us that it is unlikely that surrogate mothers will be as proportionately numerous among those women in the top twenty percent income bracket as among those in the bottom twenty percent. Put differently, we doubt that infertile couples in the low-income bracket will find upper income surrogates.

In any event, even in this case one should not pretend that disparate wealth does not play a part simply because the contrast is not the dramatic "rich versus poor." At the time of trial, the Whiteheads' net assets were probably negative-Mrs. Whitehead's own sister was foreclosing on a second mortgage. Their income derived from Mr. Whitehead's labors. Mrs. Whitehead is a homemaker, having previously held part-time jobs. The Sterns are both professionals, she a medical doctor, he a biochemist. Their combined income when both were working was about $89,500 a year and their assets sufficient to pay for the surrogacy contract arrangements.

The point is made that Mrs. Whitehead *agreed* to the surrogacy arrangement, supposedly fully understanding the consequences. Putting aside the issue of how compelling her need for money may have been, and how significant her understanding of the consequences, we suggest that her consent is irrelevant. There are, in a civilized society, some things that money cannot buy. In America, we decided long ago that merely because conduct purchased by money was "voluntary" did not mean that it was good or beyond regulation and prohibition. *West Coast Hotel Co. v. Parrish,* 300 U.S. 379 (1937). Employers can no longer buy labor at the lowest price they can bargain for, even though that labor is "voluntary," 29 U.S.C. § 206 (1982), or buy women's labor for less money than paid to men for the same job, 29 U.S.C. § 206(d), or purchase the agreement of children to perform oppressive labor, 29 U.S.C. § 212, or purchase the agreement of workers to subject themselves to unsafe or unhealthful working conditions, 29 *U.S.C.* §§ 651 to 678. (Occupational Safety and Health Act of 1970). There are, in short, values that society deems more important than granting to wealth whatever it can buy, be it labor, love, or life. Whether this principle recommends prohibition of surrogacy, which presumably sometimes results in great satisfaction to all of the parties, is not for us to say. We note here only that, under existing law, the fact that Mrs. Whitehead "agreed" to the arrangement is not dispositive.

The long-term effects of surrogacy contracts are not known, but feared-the impact on the child who learns her life was bought, that she is the offspring of someone who gave birth to her only to obtain money; the impact on the natural mother as the full weight of her isolation is felt along with the full reality of the sale of her body and her child; the impact on the natural father and adoptive mother once they realize the consequences of their conduct. Literature in related areas suggests these are substantial considerations, although, given the newness of surrogacy, there is little information.

The surrogacy contract is based on, principles that are directly contrary to the objectives of our laws. It guarantees the separation of a child from its mother; it looks to adoption regardless of suitability; it totally ignores the child; it takes the child from the mother regardless of her wishes and her maternal fitness; and it does all of this, it accomplishes all of its goals, through the use of money.

Beyond that is the potential degradation of some women that may result from this arrangement. In many cases, of course, surrogacy may bring satisfaction, not only to the infertile couple, but to the surrogate mother herself. The fact, however, that many women may not perceive surrogacy negatively but rather see it as an opportunity does not diminish its potential for devastation to other women.

In sum, the harmful consequences of this surrogacy arrangement appear to us all too palpable. In New Jersey the surrogate mother's agreement to sell her child is void. Its irrevocability infects the entire contract, as does the money that purports to buy it.

III. TERMINATION

We have already noted that under our laws termination of parental rights cannot be based on contract, but may be granted only on proof of the statutory requirements. That conclusion was one of the bases for invalidating the surrogacy contract. Although excluding the contract as a basis for parental termination, we did not explicitly deal with the question of whether the statutory bases for termination existed. We do so here.

As noted before, if termination of Mrs. Whitehead's parental rights is justified, Mrs. Whitehead will have no further claim either to custody or to visitation, and adoption by Mrs. Stern may proceed pursuant to the private placement adoption statute. If termination is not justified, Mrs. Whitehead remains the legal mother, and even if not entitled to custody, she would ordinarily be expected to have some rights of visitation.

There is simply no basis to warrant termination of Mrs. Whitehead's parental rights. We therefore conclude that the natural mother is entitled to retain her rights as a mother.

IV. CONSTITUTIONAL ISSUES

Both parties argue that the Constitutions—state and federal—mandate approval of their basic claims. The source of their constitutional arguments is essentially the same: the right of privacy, the right to procreate, the right to the companionship of one's child, those rights flowing either directly from the fourteenth amendment or by its incorporation of the Bill of Rights, or from the ninth amendment, or through the penumbra surrounding all of the Bill of Rights. They are the rights of personal intimacy, of marriage, of sex, of family, of procreation. Whatever their source, it is clear that they are fundamental rights protected by both the federal and state Constitutions. The right asserted by the Sterns is the right of procreation; that asserted by Mary Beth Whitehead is the right to the companionship of her child. We find that the right of procreation does not extend as far as claimed by the Sterns. As for the right asserted by Mrs. Whitehead, since we uphold it on other grounds (*i.e.*, we have restored her as mother and recognized her right, limited by the child's best interests, to her companionship), we need not decide that constitutional issue, and for reasons set forth below, we should not.

The right to procreate, as protected by the Constitution, has been ruled on directly only once by the United States Supreme Court. Although *Griswold v. Connecticut*, 381 U.S. 479, is obviously of a similar class, strictly speaking it involves the right *not* to procreate. The right to procreate very simply is the right to have natural children, whether through sexual intercourse or artificial insemination. It is no more than that. Mr. Stern has not been deprived of that right. Through artificial insemination of Mrs. Whitehead, Baby M is his child. The custody, care, companionship, and nurturing that follow birth are not parts of the right to procreation; they are rights that may also be constitutionally protected, but that involve many considerations other than the right of procreation. To assert that Mr. Stern's right of procreation gives him the right to the custody of Baby M would be to assert that Mrs. Whitehead's right of procreation does *not* give her the right to the custody of Baby M; it would be to assert that the constitutional right of procreation includes within it a constitutionally protected contractual right to destroy someone else's right of procreation.

We conclude that the right of procreation is best understood and protected if confined to its essentials, and that when dealing with rights concerning the resulting child, different interests come into play. There is nothing in our culture or society that even begins to suggest a fundamental right on the part of the father to the custody of the child as part of his right to procreate when opposed by the claim of the mother to the same child. We therefore disagree with the trial court: there is no constitutional basis whatsoever requiring that Mr. Stern's claim to the custody of Baby M be sustained. Our conclusion may thus be understood as illustrating that a person's rights of privacy and self-determination are qualified by the effect on innocent third persons of the exercise of those rights.[13]

Mr. Stern also contends that he has been denied equal protection of the laws by the State's statute granting full parental rights to a husband in

---

13. As a general rule, a person should be accorded the right to make decisions affecting his or her own body, health, and life, unless that choice adversely affects others. Thus, the United States Supreme Court, while recognizing the right of women to control their own bodies, has rejected the view that the federal constitution vests a pregnant woman with an absolute right to terminate her pregnancy. Instead, the Court declared that the right was "not absolute" so that "at some point the state interests as to protection of health, medical standards, and prenatal life, become dominant." *Roe v. Wade*, 410 U.S. at 155. The balance struck in *Roe v. Wade* recognizes increasing rights in the fetus and correlative restrictions on the mother as the pregnancy progresses. Similarly, in the termination-of-treatment cases, courts generally have viewed a patient's right to terminate or refuse life-sustaining treatment as constrained by other considerations including the rights of innocent third parties, such as the patient's children. Consistent with that approach, this Court has directed a mother to submit to a life-saving blood transfusion to protect the interests of her unborn infant, even though the mother's religious scruples led her to oppose the transfusion.

In the present case, the parties' right to procreate by methods of their own choosing cannot be enforced without consideration of the state's interest in protecting the resulting child, just as the right to the companionship of one's child cannot be enforced without consideration of that crucial state interest.

relation to the child produced, with his consent, by the union of his wife with a sperm donor. The claim really is that of Mrs. Stern. It is that she is in precisely the same position as the husband in the statute: she is presumably infertile, as is the husband in the statute; her spouse by agreement with a third party procreates with the understanding that the child will be the couple's child. The alleged unequal protection is that the understanding is honored in the statute when the husband is the infertile party, but no similar understanding is honored when it is the wife who is infertile.

It is quite obvious that the situations are not parallel. A sperm donor simply cannot be equated with a surrogate mother. The State has more than a sufficient basis to distinguish the two situations-even if the only difference is between the time it takes to provide sperm for artificial insemination and the time invested in a nine-month pregnancy-so as to justify automatically divesting the sperm donor of his parental rights without automatically divesting a surrogate mother. Some basis for an equal protection argument might exist if Mary Beth Whitehead had contributed her egg to be implanted, fertilized or otherwise, in Mrs. Stern, resulting in the latter's pregnancy. That is not the case here, however.

Mrs. Whitehead, on the other hand, asserts a claim that falls within the scope of a recognized fundamental interest protected by the Constitution. As a mother, she claims the right to the companionship of her child. This is a fundamental interest, constitutionally protected. Furthermore, it was taken away from her by the action of the court below. Whether that action under these circumstances would constitute a constitutional deprivation, however, we need not and do not decide. By virtue of our decision Mrs. Whitehead's constitutional complaint-that her parental rights have been unconstitutionally terminated-is moot. We have decided that both the statutes and public policy of this state require that that termination be voided and that her parental rights be restored. It therefore becomes unnecessary to decide whether that same result would be required by virtue of the federal or state Constitutions. Refraining from deciding such constitutional issues avoids further complexities involving the full extent of a parent's right of companionship,[14] or questions involving the fourteenth amendment.

Having held the contract invalid and having found no other grounds for the termination of Mrs. Whitehead's parental rights, we find that nothing remains of her constitutional claim. It seems obvious to us that since custody and visitation encompass practically all of what we call "parental rights," a total denial of both would be the equivalent of termination of parental rights. That, however, as will be seen below, has not occurred here. We express no opinion on whether a prolonged suspen-

---

14. This fundamental right is not absolute. The parent-child biological relationship, by itself, does not create a protected interest in the absence of a demonstrated commitment to the responsibilities of parenthood; a natural parent who does not come forward and seek a role in the child's life has no constitutionally protected relationship. The right is not absolute in another sense, for it is also well settled that if the state's interest is sufficient the right may be regulated, restricted, and on occasion terminated.

sion of visitation would constitute a termination of parental rights, or whether, assuming it would, a showing of unfitness would be required.

V. CUSTODY

Having decided that the surrogacy contract is illegal and unenforceable, we now must decide the custody question without regard to the provisions of the surrogacy contract that would give Mr. Stern sole and permanent custody. (That does not mean that the existence of the contract and the circumstances under which it was entered may not be considered to the extent deemed relevant to the child's best interests.) With the surrogacy contract disposed of, the legal framework becomes a dispute between two couples over the custody of a child produced by the artificial insemination of one couple's wife by the other's husband. Under the Parentage Act the claims of the natural father and the natural mother are entitled to equal weight, *i.e.,* one is not preferred over the other solely because he or she is the father or the mother. The applicable rule given these circumstances is clear: the child's best interests determine custody.

We note again that the trial court's reasons for determining what were the child's best interests were somewhat different from ours. It concluded that the surrogacy contract was valid, but that it could not grant specific performance unless to do so was in the child's best interests. The approach was that of a Chancery judge, unwilling to give extraordinary remedies unless they well served the most important interests, in this case, the interests of the child. While substantively indistinguishable from our approach to the question of best interests, the purpose of the inquiry was not the usual purpose of determining custody, but of determining a contractual remedy.

We are not concerned at this point with the question of termination of parental rights, either those of Mrs. Whitehead or of Mr. Stern. As noted in various places in this opinion, such termination, in the absence of abandonment or a valid surrender, generally depends on a showing that the particular parent is unfit. The question of custody in this case, as in practically all cases, assumes the fitness of both parents, and no serious contention is made in this case that either is unfit. The issue here is which life would be *better* for Baby M, one with primary custody in the Whiteheads or one with primary custody in the Sterns.

The circumstances of this custody dispute are unusual and they have provoked some unusual contentions. The Whiteheads claim that even if the child's best interests would be served by our awarding custody to the Sterns, we should not do so, since that will encourage surrogacy contracts-contracts claimed by the Whiteheads, and we agree, to be violative of important legislatively-stated public policies. Their position is that in order that surrogacy contracts be deterred, custody should remain in the surrogate mother unless she is unfit, regardless of the best interests of the child. We disagree. Our declaration that this surrogacy contract is unenforceable and illegal is sufficient to deter similar agreements. We need not sacrifice the child's interests in order to make that point sharper.

The Whiteheads also contend that the award of custody to the Sterns *pendente lite* was erroneous and that the error should not be allowed to affect the final custody decision. As noted above, at the very commencement of this action the court issued an *ex parte* order requiring Mrs. Whitehead to turn over the baby to the Sterns; Mrs. Whitehead did not comply but rather took the child to Florida. Thereafter, a similar order was enforced by the Florida authorities resulting in the transfer of possession of Baby M to the Sterns. The Sterns retained custody of the child throughout the litigation. The Whiteheads' point, assuming the *pendente* award of custody *was* erroneous, is that most of the factors arguing for awarding permanent custody to the Sterns resulted from that initial *pendente lite* order. Some of Mrs. Whitehead's alleged character failings, as testified to by experts and concurred in by the trial court, were demonstrated by her actions brought on by the custody crisis. For instance, in order to demonstrate her impulsiveness, those experts stressed the Whiteheads' flight to Florida with Baby M; to show her willingness to use her children for her own aims, they noted the telephone threats to kill Baby M and to accuse Mr. Stern of sexual abuse of her daughter; in order to show Mrs. Whitehead's manipulativeness, they pointed to her threat to kill herself; and in order to show her unsettled family life, they noted the innumerable moves from one hotel or motel to another in Florida. Furthermore, the argument continues, one of the most important factors, whether mentioned or not, in favor of custody in the Sterns is their continuing custody during the litigation, now having lasted for one-and-a-half years. The Whiteheads' conclusion is that had the trial court not given initial custody to the Sterns during the litigation, Mrs. Whitehead not only would have demonstrated her perfectly acceptable personality-the general tenor of the opinion of experts was that her personality problems surfaced primarily in crises-but would also have been able to prove better her parental skills along with an even stronger bond than may now exist between her and Baby M. Had she not been limited to custody for four months, she could have proved all of these things much more persuasively through almost two years of custody.

The argument has considerable force. It is of course possible that the trial court was wrong in its initial award of custody. It is also possible that such error, if that is what it was, may have affected the outcome. We disagree with the premise, however, that in determining custody a court should decide what the child's best interests *would be* if some hypothetical state of facts had existed. Rather, we must look to what those best interests *are, today,* even if some of the facts may have resulted in part from legal error. The child's interests come first: we will not punish it for judicial errors, assuming any were made. The custody decision must be based on all circumstances, on everything that *actually* has occurred, on everything that is relevant to the child's best interests. Those circumstances include the trip to Florida, the telephone calls and threats, the substantial period of successful custody with the Sterns, and all other relevant circumstances. We will discuss the question of the correctness of the trial court's initial orders below, but for purposes of determining Baby M's best interests, the correctness of those initial orders has lost relevance.

There were eleven experts who testified concerning the child's best interests, either directly or in connection with matters related to that issue. Our reading of the record persuades us that the trial court's decision awarding custody to the Sterns (technically to Mr. Stern) should be affirmed since "its findings could reasonably have been reached on sufficient credible evidence present in the record." *Beck v. Beck,* 86 *N.J.* 480, 496, 432 A.2d 63 (1981) (quoting *State v. Johnson,* 42 *N.J.* 146, 161, 199 A.2d 809 (1964)). More than that, on this record we find little room for any different conclusion. The trial court's treatment of this issue is both comprehensive and, in most respects, perceptive. We agree substantially with its analysis with but few exceptions that, although important, do not change our ultimate views.

Our custody conclusion is based on strongly persuasive testimony contrasting both the family life of the Whiteheads and the Sterns and the personalities and characters of the individuals. The stability of the Whitehead family life was doubtful at the time of trial. Their finances were in serious trouble (foreclosure by Mrs. Whitehead's sister on a second mortgage was in process). Mr. Whitehead's employment, though relatively steady, was always at risk because of his alcoholism, a condition that he seems not to have been able to confront effectively. Mrs. Whitehead had not worked for quite some time, her last two employments having been part-time. One of the Whiteheads' positive attributes was their ability to bring up two children, and apparently well, even in so vulnerable a household. Yet substantial question was raised even about that aspect of their home life. The expert testimony contained criticism of Mrs. Whitehead's handling of her son's educational difficulties. Certain of the experts noted that Mrs. Whitehead perceived herself as omnipotent and omniscient concerning her children. She knew what they were thinking, what they wanted, and she spoke for them. As to Melissa, Mrs. Whitehead expressed the view that she alone knew what that child's cries and sounds meant. Her inconsistent stories about various things engendered grave doubts about her ability to explain honestly and sensitively to Baby M—and at the right time—the nature of her origin. Although faith in professional counseling is not a *sine qua non* of parenting, several experts believed that Mrs. Whitehead's contempt for professional help, especially professional psychological help, coincided with her feelings of omnipotence in a way that could be devastating to a child who most likely will need such help. In short, while love and affection there would be, Baby M's life with the Whiteheads promised to be too closely controlled by Mrs. Whitehead. The prospects for wholesome, independent psychological growth and development would be at serious risk.

The Sterns have no other children, but all indications are that their household and their personalities promise a much more likely foundation for Melissa to grow and thrive. There *is* a track record of sorts-during the one-and-a-half years of custody Baby M has done very well, and the relationship between both Mr. and Mrs. Stern and the baby has become very strong. The household is stable, and likely to remain so. Their finances are more than adequate, their circle of friends supportive, and their marriage happy. Most important, they are loving, giving, nurturing, and open-minded people. They have demonstrated the wish and ability to nurture and protect Melissa, yet at the same time to encourage her independence. Their lack of experience is more than made up for by a willingness to learn and to listen, a willingness that is enhanced by their professional training, especially Mrs. Stern's experience as a pediatrician. They are honest; they can recognize error, deal with it, and learn from it. They will try to determine rationally the best way to cope with problems in their relationship with Melissa. When the time comes to tell her about her origins, they will probably have found a means of doing so that accords with the best interests of Baby M. All in all, Melissa's future appears solid, happy, and promising with them.

Based on all of this we have concluded, independent of the trial court's identical conclusion, that Melissa's best interests call for custody in the Sterns. Our above-mentioned disagreements with the trial court do not, as we have noted, in any way diminish our concurrence with its conclusions. We feel, however, that those disagreements are important enough to be stated. They are disagreements about the evaluation of conduct. They also may provide some insight about the potential consequences of surrogacy.

It seems to us that given her predicament, Mrs. Whitehead was rather harshly judged-both by the trial court and by some of the experts. She was guilty of a breach of contract, and indeed, she did break a very important promise, but we think it is expecting something well beyond normal human capabilities to suggest that this mother should have parted with her newly born infant without a struggle. Other than survival, what stronger force is there? We do not know of, and cannot conceive of, any other case where a perfectly fit mother was expected to surrender her newly born infant, perhaps forever, and was then told she was a bad mother because she did not. We know of no authority suggesting that the moral quality of her act in those circumstances should be judged by referring to a contract made before she became pregnant. We do not countenance, and would never countenance, violating a court order as Mrs. Whitehead did, even a court order that is wrong; but her resistance to an order that she surrender her infant, possibly forever, merits a measure of understanding. We do not find it so clear that her efforts to keep her infant, when measured against the Sterns' efforts to take her away, make one, rather than the other, the wrongdoer. The Sterns suffered, but so did she. And if we go beyond suffering to an evaluation of the human stakes involved in the struggle, how much weight should be given to her nine months of pregnancy, the labor of childbirth, the risk to her life, compared to the payment of money, the anticipation of a child and the donation of sperm?

There has emerged a portrait of Mrs. Whitehead, exposing her children to the media, engaging in negotiations to sell a book, granting interviews that seemed helpful to her, whether hurtful to Baby M or not, that suggests a selfish, grasping woman ready to sacrifice the interests of Baby M and her other children for fame and wealth. That portrait is a half-truth, for while it may accurately reflect what ultimately occurred, its implication, that this is what Mary Beth Whitehead wanted, is totally inaccurate, at least insofar as the record before us is concerned. There is not one word in that record to support a claim that had she been allowed to continue her possession of her newly born infant, Mrs. Whitehead would have ever been heard of again; not one word in the record suggests that her change of mind and her subsequent fight for her child was motivated by anything other than love-whatever complex underlying psychological motivations may have existed.

We have a further concern regarding the trial court's emphasis on the Sterns' interest in Melissa's education as compared to the Whiteheads'. That this difference is a legitimate factor to be considered we have no doubt. But it should not be overlooked that a best-interests test is designed to create not a new member of the intelligentsia but rather a well-integrated person who might reasonably be expected to be happy with life. "Best interests" does not contain within it any idealized lifestyle; the question boils down to a judgment, consisting of many factors, about the likely future happiness of a human being. Stability, love, family happiness, tolerance, and, ultimately, support of independence-all rank much higher in predicting future happiness than the likelihood of a college education. We do not mean to suggest that the trial court would disagree. We simply want to dispel any possible misunderstanding on the issue.

Even allowing for these differences, the facts, the experts' opinions, and the trial court's analysis of both argue strongly in favor of custody in the Sterns. Mary Beth Whitehead's family life, into which Baby M would be placed, was anything but secure-the quality Melissa needs most. Furthermore, the evidence and expert opinion based on it reveal personality characteristics, mentioned above, that might threaten the child's best development. The Sterns promise a secure home, with an understanding relationship that allows nurturing and independent growth to develop together. Although there is no substitute for reading the entire record, including the review of every word of each experts' testimony and reports, a summary of their conclusions is revealing. Six experts testified for Mrs. Whitehead: one favored joint custody, clearly unwarranted in this case; one simply rebutted an opposing expert's claim that Mary Beth Whitehead had a recognized personality disorder; one testified to the adverse impact of separation on *Mrs. Whitehead;* one testified about the evils of adoption and, to him, the probable analogous evils of surrogacy; one spoke only on the question of whether Mrs. Whitehead's consent in the surrogacy agreement was "informed consent"; and one spelled out the strong bond between mother and child. None of them unequivocally stated, or even necessarily implied, an opinion that custody in the Whiteheads was in the best interests of Melissa-the ultimate issue. The Sterns' experts, both well qualified—as were the Whiteheads'—concluded that the best interests of Melissa required custody in Mr. Stern. Most convincingly, the three experts chosen by the court-appointed guardian *ad litem* of Baby M, each clearly free of all bias and interest, unanimously and persuasively recommended custody in the Sterns.

Some comment is required on the initial *ex parte* order awarding custody *pendente lite* to the Sterns (and the continuation of that order after a plenary hearing). The issue, although irrelevant to our disposition of this case, may recur; and when it does, it can be of crucial importance. When father and mother are separated and disagree, at birth, on custody, only in an extreme, truly rare, case should the child be taken from its mother *pendente lite, i.e.,* only in the most unusual case should the child be taken from its mother before the dispute is finally determined by the court on its merits. The probable bond between mother and child, and the child's need, not just the mother's, to strengthen that bond, along with the likelihood, in most cases, of a significantly lesser, if any, bond with the father-all counsel against temporary custody in the father. A substantial showing that the mother's continued custody would threaten the child's health or welfare would seem to be required.

In this case, the trial court, believing that the surrogacy contract might be valid, and faced with the probable flight from the jurisdiction by Mrs. Whitehead and the baby if *any* notice were served, ordered, *ex parte,* an immediate transfer of possession of the child, *i.e.,* it ordered that custody be transferred immediately to Mr. Stern, rather than order Mrs. Whitehead not to leave the State. We have ruled, however, that the surrogacy contract is unenforceable and illegal. It provides no basis for either an *ex parte,* a plenary, an interlocutory, or a final order requiring a mother to surrender custody to a father. Any application by the natural father in a surrogacy dispute for custody pending the outcome of the litigation will henceforth require proof of unfitness, of danger to the child, or the like, of so high a quality and persuasiveness as to make it unlikely that such application will succeed. Absent the required showing, all that a court should do is list the matter for argument on notice to the mother. Even her threats to flee should not suffice to warrant any other relief unless her unfitness is clearly shown. At most, it should result in an order enjoining such flight. The erroneous transfer of custody, as we view it, represents a greater risk to the child than removal to a foreign jurisdiction, unless parental unfitness is clearly proved. Furthermore, we deem it likely that, advised of the law and knowing that her custody cannot seriously be challenged at this stage of the litigation, surrogate mothers will obey any court order to remain in the jurisdiction.

VI.   VISITATION

The trial court's decision to terminate Mrs. Whitehead's parental rights precluded it from making any determination on visitation. Our reversal of the trial court's order, however, requires delineation of Mrs. Whitehead's rights to visitation. It is apparent to us that this factually sensitive issue, which was never addressed below, should not be determined *de novo* by this Court. We therefore remand the visitation issue to the trial court for an abbreviated hearing and determination.

CONCLUSION

This case affords some insight into a new reproductive arrangement: the artificial insemination of a surrogate mother. The unfortunate events that have unfolded illustrate that its unregulated use can bring suffering to all involved. Potential victims include the surrogate mother and her family, the natural father and his wife, and most importantly, the child. Although surrogacy has apparently provided positive results for some infertile couples, it can also, as this case demonstrates, cause suffering to participants, here essentially innocent and well-intended.

We have found that our present laws do not permit the surrogacy contract used in this case. Nowhere, however, do we find any legal prohibition against surrogacy when the surrogate mother volunteers, without any payment, to act as a surrogate and is given the right to change her mind and to assert her parental rights. Moreover, the Legislature remains free to deal with this most sensitive issue as it sees fit, subject only to constitutional constraints.

If the Legislature decides to address surrogacy, consideration of this case will highlight many of its potential harms. We do not underestimate the difficulties of legislating on this subject. In addition to the inevitable confrontation with the ethical and moral issues involved, there is the question of the wisdom and effectiveness of regulating a matter so private, yet of such public interest. Legislative consideration of surrogacy may also provide the opportunity to begin to focus on the overall implications of the new reproductive biotechnology-*in vitro* fertilization, preservation of sperm and eggs, embryo implantation and the like. The problem is how to enjoy the benefits of the technology-especially for infertile couples-while minimizing the risk of abuse. The problem can be addressed only when society decides what its values and objectives are in this troubling, yet promising, area.

The judgment is affirmed in part, reversed in part, and remanded for further proceedings consistent with this opinion.

Johnson v. Calvert

Supreme Court of California, 1993.
851 P.2d 776.

■ PANELLI, J. In this case we address several of the legal questions raised by recent advances in reproductive technology. When, pursuant to a surrogacy agreement, a zygote[1] formed of the gametes[2] of a husband and wife is implanted in the uterus of another woman, who carries the resulting fetus to term and gives birth to a child not genetically related to her, who is the child's "natural mother" under California law? Does a determination that the wife is the child's natural mother work a deprivation of the gestating woman's constitutional rights? And is such an agreement barred by any public policy of this state?

---

1. An organism produced by the union of two gametes.

2. A cell that participates in fertilization and development of a new organism, also known as a germ cell or sex cell.

We conclude that the husband and wife are the child's natural parents, and that this result does not offend the state or federal Constitution or public policy.

FACTS

Mark and Crispina Calvert are a married couple who desired to have a child. Crispina was forced to undergo a hysterectomy in 1984. Her ovaries remained capable of producing eggs, however, and the couple eventually considered surrogacy. In 1989 Anna Johnson heard about Crispina's plight from a coworker and offered to serve as a surrogate for the Calverts.

On January 15, 1990, Mark, Crispina, and Anna signed a contract providing that an embryo created by the sperm of Mark and the egg of Crispina would be implanted in Anna and the child born would be taken into Mark and Crispina's home "as their child." Anna agreed she would relinquish "all parental rights" to the child in favor of Mark and Crispina. In return, Mark and Crispina would pay Anna $10,000 in a series of installments, the last to be paid six weeks after the child's birth. Mark and Crispina were also to pay for a $200,000 life insurance policy on Anna's life.

The zygote was implanted on January 19, 1990. Less than a month later, an ultrasound test confirmed Anna was pregnant.

Unfortunately, relations deteriorated between the two sides. Mark learned that Anna had not disclosed she had suffered several stillbirths and miscarriages. Anna felt Mark and Crispina did not do enough to obtain the required insurance policy. She also felt abandoned during an onset of premature labor in June.

In July 1990, Anna sent Mark and Crispina a letter demanding the balance of the payments due her or else she would refuse to give up the child. The following month, Mark and Crispina responded with a lawsuit, seeking a declaration they were the legal parents of the unborn child. Anna filed her own action to be declared the mother of the child, and the two cases were eventually consolidated. The parties agreed to an independent guardian ad litem for the purposes of the suit.

The child was born on September 19, 1990, and blood samples were obtained from both Anna and the child for analysis. The blood test results excluded Anna as the genetic mother. The parties agreed to a court order providing that the child would remain with Mark and Crispina on a temporary basis with visits by Anna.

At trial in October 1990, the parties stipulated that Mark and Crispina were the child's genetic parents. After hearing evidence and arguments, the trial court ruled that Mark and Crispina were the child's "genetic, biological and natural" father and mother, that Anna had no "parental" rights to the child, and that the surrogacy contract was legal and enforceable against Anna's claims. The court also terminated the order allowing visitation. Anna appealed from the trial court's judgment. The Court of Appeal for the Fourth District, Division Three, affirmed. We granted review.

DISCUSSION

Determining Maternity Under the Uniform Parentage Act

The Uniform Parentage Act (the Act) was part of a package of legislation introduced in 1975 as Senate Bill No. 347. The legislation's purpose was to eliminate the legal distinction between legitimate and illegitimate children. The Act followed in the wake of certain United States Supreme Court decisions mandating equal treatment of legitimate and illegitimate children. A press release issued on October 2, 1975, described Senate Bill No. 347 this way: "The bill, as amended, would revise or repeal various laws which now provide for labeling children as legitimate or illegitimate and defining their legal rights and those of their parents accordingly. In place of these cruel and outmoded provisions, SB 347 would enact the Uniform Parentage Act which bases parent and child rights on the existence of a parent and child relationship rather than on the marital status of the parents."

The pertinent portion of Senate Bill No. 347, which passed with negligible opposition, became Part 7 of Division 4 of the California Civil Code.

Civil Code sections 7001 and 7002 replace the distinction between legitimate and illegitimate children with the concept of the "parent and child relationship." The "parent and child relationship" means "the legal relationship existing between a child and his natural or adoptive parents incident to which the law confers or imposes rights, privileges, duties, and obligations. It includes the mother and child relationship and the father and child relationship." (Civ.Code, § 7001.) "The parent and child relationship extends equally to every child and to every parent, regardless of the marital status of the parents." (Civ.Code, § 7002.) The "parent and child relationship" is thus a legal relationship encompassing two kinds of parents, "natural" and "adoptive."

Passage of the Act clearly was not motivated by the need to resolve surrogacy disputes, which were virtually unknown in 1975. Yet it facially applies to *any* parentage determination, including the rare case in which a child's maternity is in issue. We are invited to disregard the Act and decide this case according to other criteria, including constitutional precepts and our sense of the demands of public policy. We feel constrained, however, to decline the invitation. Not uncommonly, courts must construe statutes in factual settings not contemplated by the enacting legislature. We therefore proceed to analyze the parties' contentions within the Act's framework.

These contentions are readily summarized. Anna, of course, predicates her claim of maternity on the fact that she gave birth to the child. The Calverts contend that Crispina's genetic relationship to the child establishes that she is his mother. Counsel for the minor joins in that contention and argues, in addition, that several of the presumptions created by the Act dictate the same result. As will appear, we conclude that presentation of blood test evidence is one means of establishing maternity, as is proof of having given birth, but that the presumptions cited by minor's counsel do not apply to this case.

We turn to those few provisions of the Act directly addressing the determination of maternity. "Any interested party," presumably including a genetic mother, "may bring an action to determine the existence of a mother and child relationship." (Civ.Code, § 7015.) Civil Code section 7003 provides, in relevant part, that between a child and the natural mother a parent and child relationship "*may* be established by proof of her having given birth to the child, or under [the Act]." (Civ.Code, § 7003, subd. (1), emphasis added.) Apart from Civil Code section 7003, the Act sets forth no specific means by which a natural mother can establish a parent and child relationship. However, it declares that, insofar as practicable, provisions applicable to the father and child relationship apply in an action to determine the existence or nonexistence of a mother and child relationship. Thus, it is appropriate to examine those provisions as well.

A man can establish a father and child relationship by the means set forth in Civil Code section 7004. Paternity is presumed under that section if the man meets the conditions set forth in section 621 of the Evidence Code. The latter statute applies, by its terms, when determining the questioned paternity of a child born to a married woman, and contemplates reliance on evidence derived from blood testing. Alternatively, Civil Code section 7004 creates a presumption of paternity based on the man's conduct toward the child (e.g., receiving the child into his home and openly holding the child out as his natural child) or his marriage or attempted marriage to the child's natural mother under specified conditions.

In our view, the presumptions contained in Civil Code section 7004 do not apply here. They describe situations in which substantial evidence points to a particular man as the natural father of the child. In this case, there is no question as to who is claiming the mother and child relationship, and the factual basis of each woman's claim is obvious. Thus, there is no need to resort to an evidentiary presumption to ascertain the identity of the natural mother. Instead, we must make the purely legal determination as between the two claimants.

Significantly for this case, Evidence Code section 892 provides that blood testing may be ordered in an action when paternity is a relevant fact. When maternity is disputed, genetic evidence derived from blood testing is likewise admissible. The Evidence Code further provides that if the court finds the conclusions of all the experts, as disclosed by the evidence based on the blood tests, are that the alleged father is not the father of the child, the question of paternity is resolved accordingly. By parity of reasoning, blood testing may also be dispositive of the question of maternity. Further, there is a rebuttable presumption of paternity (hence, maternity as well) on the finding of a certain number of genetic markers.

Disregarding the presumptions of paternity that have no application to this case, then, we are left with the undisputed evidence that Anna, not Crispina, gave birth to the child and that Crispina, not Anna, is genetically related to him. Both women thus have adduced evidence of a mother and child relationship as contemplated by the Act. Yet for any child California law recognizes only one natural mother, despite advances in reproductive technology rendering a different outcome biologically possible.[8]

We see no clear legislative preference in Civil Code section 7003 as between blood testing evidence and proof of having given birth. "May" indicates that proof of having given birth is a permitted method of establishing a mother and child relationship, although perhaps not the exclusive one. The disjunctive "or" indicates that blood test evidence, as prescribed in the Act, constitutes an alternative to proof of having given birth. It may be that the language of the Act merely reflects "the ancient dictum *mater est quam [gestation] demonstrat* (by gestation the mother is demonstrated). This phrase, by its use of the word 'demonstrated,' has always reflected an ambiguity in the meaning of the presumption. It is arguable that, while gestation may demonstrate maternal status, it is not the sine qua non of motherhood. Rather, it is possible that the common law viewed genetic consanguinity as the basis for maternal rights. Under this latter interpretation, gestation simply would be irrefutable evidence of the more fundamental genetic relationship." (Hill, *What Does It Mean to Be a "Parent"? The Claims of Biology As the Basis for Parental Rights* (1991) 66 N.Y.U.L.Rev. 353, 370, fns. omitted.) This ambiguity, highlighted by the problems arising from the use of artificial reproductive techniques, is nowhere explicitly resolved in the Act.

Because two women each have presented acceptable proof of maternity, we do not believe this case can be decided without enquiring into the parties' intentions as manifested in the surrogacy agreement. Mark and Crispina are a couple who desired to have a child of their own genetic stock but are physically unable to do so without the help of reproductive technology. They affirmatively intended the birth of the child, and took the steps necessary to effect in vitro fertilization. But for their acted-on intention, the child would not exist. Anna agreed to facilitate the procreation of Mark's and Crispina's child. The parties' aim was to bring Mark's and Crispina's child into the world, not for Mark and Crispina to donate a zygote to Anna. Crispina from the outset intended to be the child's mother. Although the gestative function Anna performed was necessary to bring about the child's birth, it is safe to say that Anna would not have been given the opportunity to gestate or deliver the child had she, prior to implantation of the zygote, manifested her own intent to be the child's mother. No reason appears why Anna's later change of heart should vitiate the determination that Crispina is the child's natural mother.

We conclude that although the Act recognizes both genetic consanguinity and giving birth as means of establishing a mother and child relation-

---

8. We decline to accept the contention of amicus curiae the American Civil Liberties Union (ACLU) that we should find the child has two mothers. Even though rising divorce rates have made multiple parent arrangements common in our society, we see no compelling reason to recognize such a situation here. The Calverts are the genetic and intending parents of their son and have provided him, by all accounts, with a stable, intact, and nurturing home. To recognize parental rights in a third party with whom the Calvert family has had little contact since shortly after the child's birth would diminish Crispina's role as mother.

ship, when the two means do not coincide in one woman, she who intended to procreate the child—that is, she who intended to bring about the birth of a child that she intended to raise as her own—is the natural mother under California law.

Our conclusion finds support in the writings of several legal commentators. (See Hill, *What Does It Mean to Be a "Parent"? The Claims of Biology As the Basis for Parental Rights, supra,* 66 N.Y.U.L.Rev. 353; Shultz, *Reproductive Technology and Intent–Based Parenthood: An Opportunity for Gender Neutrality* (1990) Wis.L.Rev. 297 [Shultz]; Note, *Redefining Mother: A Legal Matrix for New Reproductive Technologies* (1986) 96 Yale L.J. 187, 197–202 [note].) Professor Hill, arguing that the genetic relationship per se should not be accorded priority in the determination of the parent-child relationship in the surrogacy context, notes that "while all of the players in the procreative arrangement are necessary in bringing a child into the world, *the child would not have been born but for the efforts of the intended parents.* [T]he intended parents are the first cause, or the prime movers, of the procreative relationship." (Hill, *op. cit. supra,* at p. 415, emphasis in original.)

Similarly, Professor Shultz observes that recent developments in the field of reproductive technology "dramatically extend affirmative intentionality. Steps can be taken to bring into being a child who would not otherwise have existed." (Shultz, *op. cit. supra,* p. 309.) "Within the context of artificial reproductive techniques," Professor Shultz argues, "intentions that are voluntarily chosen, deliberate, express and bargained-for ought presumptively to determine legal parenthood." (*Id.,* at p. 323, fn. omitted.)

Another commentator has cogently suggested, in connection with reproductive technology, that "[t]he mental concept of the child is a controlling factor of its creation, and the originators of that concept merit full credit as conceivers. The mental concept must be recognized as independently valuable; it creates expectations in the initiating parents of a child, and it creates expectations in society for adequate performance on the part of the initiators as parents of the child." (Note, *op. cit. supra,* 96 Yale L.J. at p. 196.)

Moreover, as Professor Shultz recognizes, the interests of children, particularly at the outset of their lives, are "[un]likely to run contrary to those of adults who choose to bring them into being." (Shultz, *op. cit. supra,* at p. 397.) Thus, "[h]onoring the plans and expectations of adults who will be responsible for a child's welfare is likely to correlate significantly with positive outcomes for parents and children alike." (*Ibid.*) Under Anna's interpretation of the Act, by contrast, a woman who agreed to gestate a fetus genetically related to the intending parents would, contrary to her expectations, be held to be the child's natural mother, with all the responsibilities that ruling would entail, if the intending mother declined to accept the child after its birth. In what we must hope will be the extremely rare situation in which neither the gestator nor the woman who provided the ovum for fertilization is willing to assume custody of the child after birth, a rule recognizing the intending parents as the child's legal, natural parents should best promote certainty and stability for the child.

In deciding the issue of maternity under the Act we have felt free to take into account the parties' intentions, as expressed in the surrogacy contract, because in our view the agreement is not, on its face, inconsistent with public policy.

Preliminarily, Mark and Crispina urge us to interpret the Legislature's 1992 passage of a bill that would have regulated surrogacy as an expression of this state's public policy despite the fact that Governor Wilson's veto prevented the bill from becoming law. Senate Bill No. 937 contained a finding that surrogate contracts are not against sound public and social policy. Had Senate Bill No. 937 become law, there would be no room for argument to the contrary. The veto, however, raises a question whether the legislative declaration truly expresses California's public policy.

In the Governor's veto message we find, not unequivocal agreement with the Legislature's public policy assessment, but rather reservations about the practice of surrogate parenting. "Surrogacy is a relatively recent phenomenon. The full moral and psychological dimensions of this practice are not yet clear. In fact, they are just beginning to emerge. Only two published court opinions in California have treated this nettlesome subject. Comprehensive regulation of this difficult moral issue is premature. To the extent surrogacy continues to be practical, it can be governed by the legal framework already established in the family law area." (Governor's veto message to Sen. on Sen. Bill No. 937 (Sept. 26, 1992) Sen. Daily File (1991–1992 Reg.Sess.) p. 68.) Given this less than ringing endorsement of surrogate parenting, we conclude that the passage of Senate Bill No. 937, in and of itself, does not establish that surrogacy contracts are consistent with public policy. (Of course, neither do we draw the opposite conclusion from the fact of the Governor's veto.)

Anna urges that surrogacy contracts violate several social policies. Relying on her contention that she is the child's legal, natural mother, she cites the public policy embodied in Penal Code section 273, prohibiting the payment for consent to adoption of a child. She argues further that the policies underlying the adoption laws of this state are violated by the surrogacy contract because it in effect constitutes a prebirth waiver of her parental rights.

We disagree. Gestational surrogacy differs in crucial respects from adoption and so is not subject to the adoption statutes. The parties voluntarily agreed to participate in in vitro fertilization and related medical procedures before the child was conceived; at the time when Anna entered into the contract, therefore, she was not vulnerable to financial inducements to part with her own expected offspring. As discussed above, Anna was not the genetic mother of the child. The payments to Anna under the contract were meant to compensate her for her services in gestating the fetus and undergoing labor, rather than for giving up "parental" rights to the child. Payments were due both during the pregnancy and after the child's birth. We are, accordingly, unpersuaded that the contract used in this case violates the public policies embodied in Penal Code section 273 and the adoption statutes. For the same reasons, we conclude these contracts do not implicate the policies underlying the statutes governing termination of parental rights.

It has been suggested that gestational surrogacy may run afoul of prohibitions on involuntary servitude. Involuntary servitude has been recognized in cases of criminal punishment for refusal to work. We see no potential for that evil in the contract at issue here, and extrinsic evidence of coercion or duress is utterly lacking. We note that although at one point the contract purports to give Mark and Crispina the sole right to determine whether to abort the pregnancy, at another point it acknowledges: "All parties understand that a pregnant woman has the absolute right to abort or not abort any fetus she is carrying. Any promise to the contrary is unenforceable." We therefore need not determine the validity of a surrogacy contract purporting to deprive the gestator of her freedom to terminate the pregnancy.

Finally, Anna and some commentators have expressed concern that surrogacy contracts tend to exploit or dehumanize women, especially women of lower economic status. Anna's objections center around the psychological harm she asserts may result from the gestator's relinquishing the child to whom she has given birth. Some have also cautioned that the practice of surrogacy may encourage society to view children as commodities, subject to trade at their parents' will.

We are all too aware that the proper forum for resolution of this issue is the Legislature, where empirical data, largely lacking from this record, can be studied and rules of general applicability developed. However, in light of our responsibility to decide this case, we have considered as best we can its possible consequences.

We are unpersuaded that gestational surrogacy arrangements are so likely to cause the untoward results Anna cites as to demand their invalidation on public policy grounds. Although common sense suggests that women of lesser means serve as surrogate mothers more often than do wealthy women, there has been no proof that surrogacy contracts exploit poor women to any greater degree than economic necessity in general exploits them by inducing them to accept lower-paid or otherwise undesirable employment. We are likewise unpersuaded by the claim that surrogacy will foster the attitude that children are mere commodities; no evidence is offered to support it. The limited data available seem to reflect an absence of significant adverse effects of surrogacy on all participants.

The argument that a woman cannot knowingly and intelligently agree to gestate and deliver a baby for intending parents carries overtones of the reasoning that for centuries prevented women from attaining equal economic rights and professional status under the law. To resurrect this view is both to foreclose a personal and economic choice on the part of the surrogate mother, and to deny intending parents what may be their only means of procreating a child of their own genetic stock. Certainly in the present case it cannot seriously be argued that Anna, a licensed vocational nurse who had done well in school and who had previously borne a child, lacked the intellectual wherewithal or life experience necessary to make an informed decision to enter into the surrogacy contract.

Constitutionality of the Determination That Anna Johnson Is Not the Natural Mother

Anna argues at length that her right to the continued companionship of the child is protected under the federal Constitution.

First, we note the constitutional rights that are *not* implicated here.

There is no issue of procedural due process: although Anna broadly contends that the procedures prescribed for adoptions should be followed in the situation of a gestational surrogate's relinquishment to the genetic parents of the child she has carried and delivered, she cites no specific deficiency in the notice or hearing this matter received.

Furthermore, neither Anna nor amicus curiae ACLU articulates a claim under the equal protection clause, and we are unable to discern in these facts the necessary predicate to its operation. This is because a woman who voluntarily agrees to gestate and deliver for a married couple a child who is their genetic offspring is situated differently from the wife who provides the ovum for fertilization, intending to mother the resulting child.

Anna relies mainly on theories of substantive due process, privacy, and procreative freedom, citing a number of decisions recognizing the fundamental liberty interest of natural parents in the custody and care of their children. Most of the cases Anna cites deal with the rights of unwed fathers in the face of attempts to terminate their parental relationship to their children. These cases do not support recognition of parental rights for a gestational surrogate. Although Anna quotes language stressing the primacy of a developed parent-child relationship in assessing unwed fathers' rights, certain language in the cases reinforces the importance of genetic parents' rights.

Anna's argument depends on a prior determination that she is indeed the child's mother. Since Crispina is the child's mother under California law because she, not Anna, provided the ovum for the in vitro fertilization procedure, intending to raise the child as her own, it follows that any constitutional interests Anna possesses in this situation are something less than those of a mother. As counsel for the minor points out, the issue in this case is not whether Anna's asserted rights as a natural mother were unconstitutionally violated, but rather whether the determination that she is not the legal natural mother at all is constitutional.

Anna relies principally on the decision of the United States Supreme Court in *Michael H. v. Gerald D.* (1989) 491 U.S. 110, to support her claim to a constitutionally protected liberty interest in the companionship of the child, based on her status as "birth mother." In that case, a plurality of the court held that a state may constitutionally deny a man parental rights with respect to a child he fathered during a liaison with the wife of another man, since it is the marital family that traditionally has been accorded a protected liberty interest, as reflected in the historic presumption of legitimacy of a child born into such a family. (491 U.S. at pp. 124–125 (plur. opn. by Scalia, J.).) The reasoning of the plurality in *Michael H.* does not assist Anna. Society has not traditionally protected the right of a woman who gestates and delivers a baby pursuant to an agreement with a couple who supply the zygote from which the baby develops and who intend to raise the child as their own; such arrangements are of too recent an origin to claim the protection of tradition. To the extent that tradition has a bearing on the present case, we believe it supports the claim of the couple who exercise their right to procreate in order to form a family of their own, albeit through novel medical procedures.

Moreover, if we were to conclude that Anna enjoys some sort of liberty interest in the companionship of the child, then the liberty interests of Mark and Crispina, the child's natural parents, in their procreative choices and their relationship with the child would perforce be infringed. Any parental rights Anna might successfully assert could come only at Crispina's expense. As we have seen, Anna has no parental rights to the child under California law, and she fails to persuade us that sufficiently strong policy reasons exist to accord her a protected liberty interest in the companionship of the child when such an interest would necessarily detract from or impair the parental bond enjoyed by Mark and Crispina.

Amicus curiae ACLU urges that Anna's right of privacy, embodied in the California Constitution, requires recognition and protection of her status as "birth mother." We cannot agree. Certainly it is true that our state Constitution has been construed to provide California citizens with privacy protections encompassing procreative decisionmaking—broader, indeed, than those recognized by the federal Constitution. However, amicus curiae fails to articulate persuasively how Anna's claim falls within even the broad parameters of the state right of privacy. Amicus curiae appears to assume that the choice to gestate and deliver a baby for its genetic parents pursuant to a surrogacy agreement is the equivalent, in constitutional weight, of the decision whether to bear a child of one's own. We disagree. A woman who enters into a gestational surrogacy arrangement is not exercising her own right to make procreative choices; she is agreeing to provide a necessary and profoundly important service without (by definition) any expectation that she will raise the resulting child as her own.

Drawing an analogy to artificial insemination, Anna argues that Mark and Crispina were mere genetic donors who are entitled to no constitutional protection. That characterization of the facts is, however, inaccurate. Mark and Crispina never intended to "donate" genetic material to anyone. Rather, they intended to procreate a child genetically related to them by the only available means. Civil Code section 7005, governing artificial insemination, has no application here.

Finally, Anna argues that the Act's failure to address novel reproductive techniques such as in vitro fertilization indicates legislative disapproval of such practices. Given that the Act was drafted long before such techniques were developed, we cannot agree. Moreover, we may not arrogate to ourselves the power to disapprove them. It is not the role of the judiciary to inhibit the use of reproductive technology when the Legislature has not seen fit to do so; any such effort would raise serious questions in light of the fundamental nature of the rights of procreation and privacy. Rather, our task has been to resolve the dispute before us, interpreting the Act's use of the term "natural mother" (Civ.Code, § 7003, subd. (1)) when the biological functions essential to bringing a child into the world have been allocated between two women.

DISPOSITION

The judgment of the Court of Appeal is affirmed.

A.Z. v. B.Z.

Supreme Judicial Court of Massachusetts, 2000.
696 N.E.2d 174.

■ Cowin, J. We transferred this case to this court on our own motion to consider for the first time the effect of a consent form between a married couple and an in vitro fertilization (IVF) clinic (clinic) concerning disposition of frozen preembryos.[1] B.Z., the former wife (wife) of A.Z. (husband), appeals from a judgment of the Probate and Family Court that included, inter alia,[2] a permanent injunction in favor of the husband, prohibiting the wife "from utilizing" the frozen preembryos held in cryopreservation[3] at the clinic. The probate judge bifurcated the issue concerning the disposition of the frozen preembryos from the then-pending divorce action.[4] The wife appeals only from the issuance of the permanent injunction. On February 8, 2000, we issued an order affirming the judgment of the Probate and Family Court. The order stated: "It is ordered that the permanent injunction entered on the docket on March 25, 1996 in Suffolk County Probate Court (Docket No. 95 D 1683 DV) be, and the same hereby is, affirmed. Opinion or opinions to follow." This opinion states the reasons for that order.

1. *Factual background.* We recite the relevant background facts as determined by the probate judge in his detailed findings of fact after a hearing concerning disposition of the preembryos at which both the hus-

---

1. We use the term "preembryo" to refer to the four-to-eight cell stage of a developing fertilized egg.

2. The issue arose in the context of a divorce proceeding.

3. Cryopreservation is the "[m]aintenance of the viability of excised tissues or organs at extremely low temperatures." Stedman's Medical Dictionary 375 (25th ed.1990).

4. The husband and wife separated in August, 1995, and later that month the husband filed for divorce. In September, 1995, the husband filed a motion for an ex parte temporary restraining order regarding a vial of frozen preembryos stored at the IVF clinic. The judge did not act on the motion, but ordered a hearing at which counsel for both the husband and the wife stipulated to a "standstill order." The judge then bifurcated the issue presented here from the pending divorce action, but stated that the disposition of the issue concerning the frozen preembryos would be a final determination incorporated into the final divorce judgment. The probate judge's order granting the husband a permanent injunction in this case was subsequently incorporated in the final divorce decree.

band and wife were separately represented by counsel. The probate judge's findings are supplemented by the record where necessary.

a. *History of the couple.* The husband and wife were married in 1977. For the first two years of their marriage they resided in Virginia, where they both served in the armed forces. While in Virginia, they encountered their first difficulties conceiving a child and underwent fertility testing. During their stay in Virginia the wife did become pregnant, but she suffered an ectopic pregnancy,[6] as a result of which she miscarried and her left fallopian tube was removed.

In 1980, the husband and wife moved to Maryland where they underwent additional fertility treatment. The treatment lasted one year and did not result in a pregnancy. In 1988, the wife was transferred to Massachusetts and the husband remained in Maryland to continue his schooling. After arriving in Massachusetts, the wife began IVF treatments at an IVF clinic here. At first the husband traveled from Maryland to participate in the treatments. In 1991, he moved to Massachusetts.

Given their medical history, the husband and wife were eligible for two types of fertility procedures: Gamete Inter–Fallopian Transfer (GIFT) and IVF. IVF involves injecting the woman with fertility drugs in order to stimulate production of eggs which can be surgically retrieved or harvested. After the eggs are removed, they are combined in a Petri dish with sperm produced by the man, on the same day as the egg removal, in an effort to fertilize the eggs. If fertilization between any of the eggs and sperm occurs, preembryos are formed that are held in a Petri dish for one or two days until a decision can be made as to which preembryos will be used immediately and which will be frozen and stored by the clinic for later use. Preembryos that are to be utilized immediately are not frozen.

GIFT involves the removal of eggs from the woman that are then transferred simultaneously with the sperm into the fallopian tube where fertilization occurs before the embryo implants in the uterus. The husband and wife initially chose the GIFT procedure because it has a higher success rate than IVF. The GIFT procedure was performed on November 6, 1988. Another ectopic pregnancy resulted and the wife's remaining fallopian tube was removed. Left with no alternatives, the husband and wife turned to the IVF procedure.

They underwent IVF treatment from 1988 through 1991. As a result of the 1991 treatment, the wife conceived and gave birth to twin daughters in 1992. During the 1991 IVF treatment, more preembryos were formed than were necessary for immediate implantation, and two vials of preembryos were frozen for possible future implantation. In the spring of 1995, before the couple separated, the wife desired more children and had one of the remaining vials of preembryos thawed and one preembryo was implanted. She did so without informing her husband. The husband learned of this when he received a notice from his insurance company regarding the

---

6. An ectopic pregnancy is one that occurs outside the uterus, the normal locus of pregnancy.

procedure. During this period relations between the husband and wife deteriorated. The wife sought and received a protective order against the husband. Ultimately, they separated and the husband filed for divorce.

At the time of the divorce, one vial containing four frozen preembryos remained in storage at the clinic. Using one or more of these preembryos, it is possible that the wife could conceive; the likelihood of conception depends, inter alia, on the condition of the preembryos which cannot be ascertained until the preembryos are thawed. The husband filed a motion to obtain a permanent injunction, prohibiting the wife from "using" the remaining vial of frozen preembryos.

b.   *The IVF clinic and the consent forms.* In order to participate in fertility treatment, including GIFT and IVF, the clinic required egg and sperm donors (donors) to sign certain consent forms for the relevant procedures. Each time before removal of the eggs from the wife, the clinic required the husband and wife in this case to sign a preprinted consent form concerning ultimate disposition of the frozen preembryos. The wife signed a number of forms on which the husband's signature was not required. The only forms that both the husband and the wife were required to sign were those entitled "Consent Form for Freezing (Cyropreservation) of Embryos" (consent form), one of which is the form at issue here.[8]

Each consent form explains the general nature of the IVF procedure and outlines the freezing process, including the financial cost and the potential benefits and risks of that process. The consent form also requires the donors to decide the disposition of the frozen preembryos on certain listed contingencies: "wife or donor" reaching normal menopause or age forty-five years; preembryos no longer being healthy; "one of us dying;" "[s]hould we become separated"; "[s]hould we both die." Under each contingency the consent form provides the following as options for disposition of the preembryos: "donated or destroyed-choose one or both." A blank line beneath these choices permits the donors to write in additional alternatives not listed as options on the form, and the form notifies the donors that they may do so. The consent form also informs the donors that they may change their minds as to any disposition, provided that both donors convey that fact in writing to the clinic.

The probate judge noted that the clinic's current GIFT and IVF handbook, which was in evidence, states that the consent forms were "good for one year." There was no evidence whether this one-year limitation was in effect between 1988 and 1991. If a one-year limitation existed at that time, there was no evidence whether the husband and wife were aware of it. We do not attach significance to the provision in the handbook.

c.   *The execution of the forms.* Every time before eggs were retrieved from the wife and combined with sperm from the husband, they each

---

8. The clinic required that a consent form be completed each time before the egg retrievals, regardless of whether any preembryos were ultimately produced and frozen. Once preembryos are produced and frozen, a new consent form does not need to be filled out by the husband and wife to authorize a thawing and transfer of frozen preembryos, unless they change their prior choices.

signed a consent form. The husband was present when the first form was completed by the wife in October, 1988. They both signed that consent form after it was finished. The form, as filled out by the wife, stated, inter alia, that if they "[s]hould become separated, [they] both agree[d] to have the embryo(s) return[ed] to [the] wife for implant." The husband and wife thereafter underwent six additional egg retrievals for freezing and signed six additional consent forms, one each in June, 1989, and February, 1989, two forms in December, 1989, and one each in August, 1990, and August, 1991. The August, 1991, consent form governs the vial of frozen preembryos now stored at the clinic.

Each time after signing the first consent form in October, 1988, the husband always signed a blank consent form. Sometimes a consent form was signed by the husband while he and his wife were traveling to the IVF clinic; other forms were signed before the two went to the IVF clinic. Each time, after the husband signed the form, the wife filled in the disposition and other information, and then signed the form herself. All the words she wrote in the later forms were substantially similar to the words she inserted in the first October, 1988, form. In each instance the wife specified in the option for "[s]hould we become separated," that the preembryos were to be returned to the wife for implantation.

2. *The Probate Court's decision.* The probate judge concluded that, while donors are generally free to agree as to the ultimate disposition of frozen preembryos, the agreement at issue was unenforceable because of "change in circumstances" occurring during the four years after the husband and wife signed the last, and governing, consent form in 1991: the birth of the twins as a result of the IVF procedure, the wife's obtaining a protective order against the husband, the husband's filing for a divorce, and the wife's then seeking "to thaw the preembryos for implantation in the hopes of having additional children." The probate judge concluded that "[n]o agreement should be enforced in equity when intervening events have changed the circumstances such that the agreement which was originally signed did not contemplate the actual situation now facing the parties." In the absence of a binding agreement, the judge determined that the "best solution" was to balance the wife's interest in procreation against the husband's interest in avoiding procreation. Based on his findings, the judge determined that the husband's interest in avoiding procreation outweighed the wife's interest in having additional children and granted the permanent injunction in favor of the husband.

3. *Legal background.* While IVF has been available for over two decades and has been the focus of much academic commentary, there is little law on the enforceability of agreements concerning the disposition of frozen preembryos. Only three States have enacted legislation addressing the issue.

Two State courts of last resort, the Supreme Court of Tennessee and the Court of Appeals of New York, have dealt with the enforceability of agreements between donors regarding the disposition of preembryos and have concluded that such agreements should ordinarily be enforced. The

Supreme Court of Tennessee, in *Davis v. Davis*, 842 S.W.2d 588 (Tenn. 1992), cert. denied sub nom. *Stowe v. Davis*, 507 U.S. 911 (1993), considered the issue in a dispute between a husband and his former wife after the two were divorced. The wife sought to donate the preembryos at issue to another couple for implantation. The court stated that agreements between donors regarding disposition of the preembryos "should be presumed valid and should be enforced." *Id.* at 597. In that case, because there was no agreement between the donors regarding disposition of the preembryos, the court balanced the equitable interests of the two parties and concluded that the husband's interest in avoiding parenthood outweighed the wife's interest in donating the preembryos to another couple for implantation. *Id.* at 603.

The Court of Appeals of New York, in *Kass v. Kass, supra,* agreed with the Tennessee court's view that courts should enforce agreements where potential parents provide for the disposition of frozen preembryos. *Id.* at 565. The issue arose in that case also in the context of a dispute between a husband and his former wife after divorce. The wife sought custody of the preembryos for implantation. According to the New York court, agreements "should generally be presumed valid and binding, and enforced in any dispute between [the donors]." *Id.,* citing *Davis v. Davis, supra* at 597. While recognizing that it is difficult for donors to anticipate the future of their relationship, the court concluded that such agreements minimize misunderstanding, maximize procreative liberty, and provide needed certainty to IVF programs. *Kass v. Kass, supra.* The court determined that the consent form signed by the donors with the IVF clinic unequivocally manifested the donors' mutual intent, and that this intent was further highlighted by the divorce instrument, which was consistent with the consent form and had been signed only months before suit was begun. Therefore the court enforced the agreement that provided that the frozen preembryos be donated to the IVF clinic.

4. *Legal analysis.* This is the first reported case involving the disposition of frozen preembryos in which a consent form signed between the donors on the one hand and the clinic on the other provided that, on the donors' separation, the preembryos were to be given to one of the donors for implantation. In view of the purpose of the form (drafted by and to give assistance to the clinic) and the circumstances of execution, we are dubious at best that it represents the intent of the husband and the wife regarding disposition of the preembryos in the case of a dispute between them. In any event, for several independent reasons, we conclude that the form should not be enforced in the circumstances of this case.

First, the consent form's primary purpose is to explain to the donors the benefits and risks of freezing, and to record the donors' desires for disposition of the frozen preembryos at the time the form is executed in order to provide the clinic with guidance if the donors (as a unit) no longer wish to use the frozen preembryos. The form does not state, and the record does not indicate, that the husband and wife intended the consent form to act as a binding agreement between them should they later disagree as to the disposition. Rather, it appears that it was intended only to define the donors' relationship as a unit with the clinic.

Second, the consent form does not contain a duration provision. The wife sought to enforce this particular form four years after it was signed by the husband in significantly changed circumstances and over the husband's objection. In the absence of any evidence that the donors agreed on the time period during which the consent form was to govern their conduct, we cannot assume that the donors intended the consent form to govern the disposition of the frozen preembryos four years after it was executed, especially in light of the fundamental change in their relationship (i.e., divorce).

Third, the form uses the term "[s]hould we become separated" in referring to the disposition of the frozen preembryos without defining "become separated." Because this dispute arose in the context of a divorce, we cannot conclude that the consent form was intended to govern in these circumstances. Separation and divorce have distinct legal meanings. Legal changes occur by operation of law when a couple divorces that do not occur when a couple separates. Because divorce legally ends a couple's marriage, we shall not assume, in the absence of any evidence to the contrary, that an agreement on this issue providing for separation was meant to govern in the event of a divorce.

The donors' conduct in connection with the execution of the consent forms also creates doubt whether the consent form at issue here represents the clear intentions of both donors. The probate judge found that, prior to the signing of the first consent form, the wife called the IVF clinic to inquire about the section of the form regarding disposition "upon separation": that section of the preprinted form that asked the donors to specify either "donated" or "destroyed" or "both." A clinic representative told her that "she could cross out any of the language on the form and fill in her own [language] to fit her wishes." Further, although the wife used language in each subsequent form similar to the language used in the first form that she and her husband signed together, the consent form at issue here was signed in blank by the husband, before the wife filled in the language indicating that she would use the preembryos for implantation on separation. We therefore cannot conclude that the consent form represents the true intention of the husband for the disposition of the preembryos.

Finally, the consent form is not a separation agreement that is binding on the couple in a divorce proceeding. The consent form does not contain provisions for custody, support, and maintenance, in the event that the wife conceives and gives birth to a child. In summary, the consent form is legally insufficient in several important respects and does not approach the minimum level of completeness needed to denominate it as an enforceable contract in a dispute between the husband and the wife.

With this said, we conclude that, even had the husband and the wife entered into an unambiguous agreement between themselves regarding the disposition of the frozen preembryos, we would not enforce an agreement that would compel one donor to become a parent against his or her will.[22] As a matter of public policy, we conclude that forced procreation is not an area amenable to judicial enforcement. It is well-established that courts will not enforce contracts that violate public policy. While courts are hesitant to invalidate contracts on these public policy grounds, the public interest in freedom of contract is sometimes outweighed by other public policy considerations; in those cases the contract will not be enforced. To determine public policy, we look to the expressions of the Legislature and to those of this court.

The Legislature has already determined by statute that individuals should not be bound by certain agreements binding them to enter or not enter into familial relationships. In G.L. c. 207, § 47A, the Legislature abolished the cause of action for the breach of a promise to marry. In G.L. c. 210, § 2, the Legislature provided that no mother may agree to surrender her child "sooner than the fourth calendar day after the date of birth of the child to be adopted" regardless of any prior agreement.

Similarly, this court has expressed its hesitancy to become involved in intimate questions inherent in the marriage relationship. *Doe v. Doe,* 314 N.E.2d 128 (Mass. 1974). "Except in cases involving divorce or separation, our law has not in general undertaken to resolve the many delicate questions inherent in the marriage relationship. We would not order either a husband or a wife to do what is necessary to conceive a child or to prevent conception, any more than we would order either party to do what is necessary to make the other happy." *Id.*

In our decisions, we have also indicated a reluctance to enforce prior agreements that bind individuals to future family relationships. In *R.R. v. M.H.,* 689 N.E.2d 790 (Mass. 1998), we held that a surrogacy agreement in which the surrogate mother agreed to give up the child on its birth is unenforceable unless the agreement contained, inter alia, a "reasonable" waiting period during which the mother could change her mind. *Id..* In *Capazzoli v. Holzwasser, supra,* we determined, as an expression of public policy, that a contract requiring an individual to abandon a marriage is unenforceable. And, in the same spirit, we stated in *Gleason v. Mann,* 45 N.E.2d 280 (Mass. 1942), that agreements providing for a general restraint against marriage are unenforceable.

We glean from these statutes and judicial decisions that prior agreements to enter into familial relationships (marriage or parenthood) should not be enforced against individuals who subsequently reconsider their decisions. This enhances the "freedom of personal choice in matters of marriage and family life." *Moore v. East Cleveland,* 431 U.S. 494, 499

---

22. That is the relief sought by the wife in this case. We express no view regarding whether an unambiguous agreement between two donors concerning the disposition of frozen preembryos could be enforced over the contemporaneous objection of one of the donors, when such agreement contemplated destruction or donation of the preembryos either for research or implantation in a surrogate.

We also recognize that agreements among donors and IVF clinics are essential to clinic operations. There is no impediment to the enforcement of such contracts by the clinics or by the donors against the clinics, consistent with the principles of this opinion.

(1977), quoting *Cleveland Bd. of Educ. v. LaFleur,* 414 U.S. 632, 639–640 (1974).

We derive from existing State laws and judicial precedent a public policy in this Commonwealth that individuals shall not be compelled to enter into intimate family relationships, and that the law shall not be used as a mechanism for forcing such relationships when they are not desired. This policy is grounded in the notion that respect for liberty and privacy requires that individuals be accorded the freedom to decide whether to enter into a family relationship. "There are 'personal rights of such delicate and intimate character that direct enforcement of them by any process of the court should never be attempted.' " *Doe v. Doe, supra* at 559, quoting *Kenyon v. Chicopee,* 70 N.E.2d 241 (Mass. 1946).

In this case, we are asked to decide whether the law of the Commonwealth may compel an individual to become a parent over his or her contemporaneous objection. The husband signed this consent form in 1991. Enforcing the form against him would require him to become a parent over his present objection to such an undertaking. We decline to do so.

Kass v. Kass

Court of Appeals of New York, 1998.
696 N.E.2d 174.

■ KAYE, C.J. Although *in vitro* fertilization (IVF) procedures are now more than two decades old and in wide use, this is the first such dispute to reach our Court. Specifically in issue is the disposition of five frozen, stored pre-embryos, or "pre-zygotes," created five years ago, during the parties' marriage, to assist them in having a child. Now divorced, appellant (Maureen Kass) wants the pre-zygotes implanted, claiming this is her only chance for genetic motherhood; respondent (Steven Kass) objects to the burdens of unwanted fatherhood, claiming that the parties agreed at the time they embarked on the effort that in the present circumstances the pre-zygotes would be donated to the IVF program for approved research purposes. Like the two-Justice plurality at the Appellate Division, we conclude that the parties' agreement providing for donation to the IVF program controls. The Appellate Division order should therefore be affirmed.

Facts

Appellant and respondent were married on July 4, 1988, and almost immediately began trying to conceive a child. While appellant believed that, owing to prenatal exposure to diethylstilbestrol (DES) she might have difficulty carrying a pregnancy to term, her condition in fact was more serious—she failed to become pregnant. In August 1989, the couple turned to John T. Mather Memorial Hospital in Port Jefferson, Long Island and, after unsuccessful efforts to conceive through artificial insemination, enrolled in the hospital's IVF program.

Typically, the IVF procedure begins with hormonal stimulation of a woman's ovaries to produce multiple eggs. The eggs are then removed by laparoscopy or ultrasound-directed needle aspiration and placed in a glass dish, where sperm are introduced. Once a sperm cell fertilizes the egg, this fusion—or pre-zygote—divides until it reaches the four- to eight-cell stage, after which several pre-zygotes are transferred to the woman's uterus by a cervical catheter. If the procedure succeeds, an embryo will attach itself to the uterine wall, differentiate and develop into a fetus. As an alternative to immediate implantation, pre-zygotes may be cryo-preserved indefinitely in liquid nitrogen for later use. Cryopreservation serves to reduce both medical and physical costs because eggs do not have to be retrieved with each attempted implantation, and delay may actually improve the chances of pregnancy. At the same time, the preservation of "extra" pre-zygotes—those not immediately implanted—allows for later disagreements, as occurred here.

Beginning in March 1990, appellant underwent the egg retrieval process five times and fertilized eggs were transferred to her nine times. She became pregnant twice—once in October 1991, ending in a miscarriage and again a few months later, when an ectopic pregnancy had to be surgically terminated.

Before the final procedure, for the first time involving cryopreservation, the couple on May 12, 1993 signed four consent forms provided by the hospital. Each form begins on a new page, with its own caption and "Patient Name." The first two forms, "GENERAL INFORMED CONSENT FORM NO. 1: IN VITRO FERTILIZATION AND EMBRYO TRANSFER" and "ADDENDUM NO. 1–1," consist of 12 single-spaced typewritten pages explaining the procedure, its risks and benefits, at several points indicating that, before egg retrieval could begin, it was necessary for the parties to make informed decisions regarding disposition of the fertilized eggs. ADDENDUM NO. 1–1 concludes as follows:

> "We understand that it is general IVF Program Policy, as medically determined by our IVF physician, to retrieve as many eggs as possible and to inseminate and transfer 4 of those mature eggs in this IVF cycle, unless our IVF physician determines otherwise. It is necessary that we decide [now] how excess eggs are to be handled by the IVF Program and how many embryos to transfer. *We are to indicate our choices by signing our initials where noted below.*

> "1. We consent to the retrieval of as many eggs as medically determined by our IVF physician. If more eggs are retrieved than can be transferred during this IVF cycle, we direct the IVF Program to take the following action (choose one):

> "(a) The excess eggs are to be inseminated and cryopreserved for possible use by us during a later IVF cycle. We understand that our choice of this option requires us to complete an additional Consent Form for Cryopreservation" (emphasis in original).

The "Additional Consent Form for Cryopreservation," a seven-page, single-spaced typewritten document, is also in two parts. The first, "INFORMED CONSENT FORM NO. 2: CRYOPRESERVATION OF HUMAN PRE–ZYGOTES," provides:

"III. *Disposition of Pre–Zygotes.*

"We understand that our frozen pre-zygotes will be stored for a maximum of 5 years. We have the principal responsibility to decide the disposition of our frozen pre-zygotes. Our frozen pre-zygotes will not be released from storage for any purpose without the written consent of *both* of us, consistent with the policies of the IVF Program and applicable law. In the event of divorce, we understand that legal ownership of any stored pre-zygotes must be determined in a property settlement and will be released as directed by order of a court of competent jurisdiction. Should we for any reason no longer wish to attempt to initiate a pregnancy, we understand that we may determine the disposition of our frozen pre-zygotes remaining in storage.

"The possibility of our death or any other unforeseen circumstances that may result in neither of us being able to determine the disposition of any stored frozen pre-zygotes requires that we now indicate our wishes. THESE IMPORTANT DECISIONS MUST BE DISCUSSED WITH OUR IVF PHYSICIAN AND OUR WISHES MUST BE STATED (BEFORE EGG RETRIEVAL) ON THE ATTACHED ADDENDUM NO. 2–1, STATEMENT OF DISPOSITION. THIS STATEMENT OF DISPOSITION MAY BE CHANGED ONLY BY OUR SIGNING ANOTHER STATEMENT OF DISPOSITION WHICH IS FILED WITH THE IVF PROGRAM" (emphasis in original).

The second part, titled "INFORMED CONSENT FORM NO. 2—ADDENDUM NO. 2–1: CRYOPRESERVATIONSTATEMENT OF DISPOSITION," states:

"We understand that it is IVF Program Policy to obtain our informed consent to the number of pre-zygotes which are to be cryopreserved and to the disposition of excess cryopreserved pre-zygotes. *We are to indicate our choices by signing our initials where noted below.*

"1. We consent to cryopreservation of all pre-zygotes which are not transferred during this IVF cycle for possible use by us in a future IVF cycle.

"2. In the event that we no longer wish to initiate a pregnancy or are unable to make a decision regarding the disposition of our stored, frozen pre-zygotes, we now indicate our desire for the disposition of our pre-zygotes and direct the IVF program to (choose one):

"(b) Our frozen pre-zygotes may be examined by the IVF Program for biological studies and be disposed of by the IVF Program for approved research investigation as determined by the IVF Program" (emphasis in original).

On May 20, 1993, doctors retrieved 16 eggs from appellant, resulting in nine pre-zygotes. Two days later, four were transferred to appellant's sister, who had volunteered to be a surrogate mother, and the remaining five were cryopreserved. The couple learned shortly thereafter that the results were negative and that appellant's sister was no longer willing to participate in the program. They then decided to dissolve their marriage. The total cost of their IVF efforts exceeded $75,000.

With divorce imminent, the parties themselves on June 7, 1993—barely three weeks after signing the consents—drew up and signed an "uncontested divorce" agreement, typed by appellant, including the following:

> "The disposition of the frozen 5 pre-zygotes at Mather Hospital is that they should be disposed of [in] the manner outlined in our consent form and that neither Maureen Kass[,] Steve Kass or anyone else will lay claim to custody of these pre-zygotes."

On June 28, 1993, appellant by letter informed the hospital and her IVF physician of her marital problems and expressed her opposition to destruction or release of the pre-zygotes.

One month later, appellant commenced the present matrimonial action, requesting sole custody of the pre-zygotes so that she could undergo another implantation procedure. Respondent opposed removal of the pre-zygotes and any further attempts by appellant to achieve pregnancy, and counterclaimed for specific performance of the parties' agreement to permit the IVF program to retain the pre-zygotes for research, as specified in ADDENDUM NO. 2–1. By stipulation dated December 17, 1993, the couple settled all issues in the matrimonial action except each party's claim with respect to the pre-zygotes, which was submitted to the court for determination. While this aspect of the case remained open, a divorce judgment was entered on May 16, 1994.

In connection with the continuing litigation over the pre-zygotes, by letter dated January 9, 1995 the parties agreed that the matter should be decided on the existing record.

Supreme Court granted appellant custody of the pre-zygotes and directed her to exercise her right to implant them within a medically reasonable time. The court reasoned that a female participant in the IVF procedure has exclusive decisional authority over the fertilized eggs created through that process, just as a pregnant woman has exclusive decisional authority over a nonviable fetus, and that appellant had not waived her right either in the May 12, 1993 consents or in the June 7, 1993 "uncontested divorce" agreement.

While a divided Appellate Division reversed that decision, all five Justices unanimously agreed on two fundamental propositions. First, they concluded that a woman's right to privacy and bodily integrity are not implicated before implantation occurs. Second, the court unanimously recognized that when parties to an IVF procedure have themselves determined the disposition of any unused fertilized eggs, their agreement should control.

The panel split, however, on the question whether the agreement at issue was sufficiently clear to control disposition of the pre-zygotes. According to the two-Justice plurality, the agreement unambiguously indicated the parties' desire to donate the pre-zygotes for research purposes if the couple could not reach a joint decision regarding disposition. The concurring Justice agreed to reverse but found the consent fatally ambiguous. In his view, but for the most exceptional circumstances, the objecting party should have a veto over a former spouse's proposed implantation, owing to the emotional and financial burdens of compelled parenthood. A fact-finding hearing would be authorized only when the party desiring parenthood could make a threshold showing of no other means of achieving genetic or adoptive parenthood, which was not shown on this stipulated record.

While agreeing with the concurrence that the informed consent document was ambiguous, the two-Justice dissent rejected a presumption in favor of either party and instead concluded that the fate of the pre-zygotes required a balancing of the parties' respective interests and burdens, as well as their personal backgrounds, psychological makeups, financial and physical circumstances. Factors would include appellant's independent ability to support the child and the sincerity of her emotional investment in this particular reproductive opportunity, as well as the burdens attendant upon a respondent's unwanted fatherhood and his motivations for objecting to parenthood. Finding that the record was insufficient to permit a fair balancing, and that the parties' January 9, 1995 stipulation that there would be no further submissions violated public policy because it precluded full review, the dissent would remit the case to the trial court for a full hearing.

We now affirm, agreeing with the plurality that the parties clearly expressed their intent that in the circumstances presented the pre-zygotes would be donated to the IVF program for research purposes.

Analysis

A. *The Legal Landscape Generally.* We begin analysis with a brief description of the broader legal context of this dispute. In the past two decades, thousands of children have been born through IVF, the best known of several methods of assisted reproduction. Additionally, tens of thousands of frozen embryos annually are routinely stored in liquid nitrogen canisters, some having been in that state for more than 10 years with no instructions for their use or disposal. As science races ahead, it leaves in its trail mind-numbing ethical and legal questions.

The law, whether statutory or decisional, has been evolving more slowly and cautiously. A handful of States—New York not among them—have adopted statutes touching on the disposition of stored embryos.

In the case law, only *Davis v Davis* (842 S.W.2d 588, 604 [Tenn 1992], *cert denied sub nom. Stowe v Davis,* 507 U.S. 911) attempts to lay out an analytical framework for disputes between a divorcing couple regarding the disposition of frozen embryos. Having declared that embryos are entitled to "special respect because of their potential for human life" (842 S.W.2d at 597, *supra*), *Davis* recognized the procreative autonomy of both gamete providers, which includes an interest in avoiding genetic parenthood as well as an interest in becoming a genetic parent. In the absence of any prior written agreement between the parties—which should be presumed valid, and implemented—according to *Davis,* courts must in every case balance these competing interests, each deserving of judicial respect. In *Davis* itself, that balance weighed in favor of the husband's interest in avoiding genetic parenthood, which was deemed more significant than the wife's desire to donate the embryos to a childless couple.

Although statutory and decisional law are sparse, abundant commentary offers a window on the issues ahead, particularly suggesting various approaches to the issue of disposition of pre-zygotes. Some commentators would vest control in one of the two gamete providers.

Yet a third approach is to regard the progenitors as holding a "bundle of rights" in relation to the pre-zygote that can be exercised through joint disposition agreements. The most recent view—a "default rule"—articulated in the report of the New York State Task Force on Life and the Law, is that, while gamete bank regulations should require specific instructions regarding disposition, no embryo should be implanted, destroyed or used in research over the objection of an individual with decision-making authority.

Proliferating cases regarding the disposition of embryos, as well as other assisted reproduction issues, will unquestionably spark further progression of the law. What is plain, however, is the need for clear, consistent principles to guide parties in protecting their interests and resolving their disputes, and the need for particular care in fashioning such principles as issues are better defined and appreciated. Against that backdrop we turn to the present appeal.

B. *The Appeal Before Us.* Like the Appellate Division, we conclude that disposition of these pre-zygotes does not implicate a woman's right of privacy or bodily integrity in the area of reproductive choice; nor are the pre-zygotes recognized as "persons" for constitutional purposes. The relevant inquiry thus becomes who has dispositional authority over them. Because that question is answered in this case by the parties' agreement, for purposes of resolving the present appeal we have no cause to decide whether the pre-zygotes are entitled to "special respect."[4]

Agreements between progenitors, or gamete donors, regarding disposition of their pre-zygotes should generally be presumed valid and binding, and enforced in any dispute between them. Indeed, parties should be

---

4. Parties' agreements may, of course, be unenforceable as violative of public policy. Significantly changed circumstances also may preclude contract enforcement. Here, however, appellant does not urge that the consents violate public policy, or that they are legally unenforceable by reason of significantly changed circumstances.

encouraged in advance, before embarking on IVF and cryopreservation, to think through possible contingencies and carefully specify their wishes in writing. Explicit agreements avoid costly litigation in business transactions. They are all the more necessary and desirable in personal matters of reproductive choice, where the intangible costs of any litigation are simply incalculable. Advance directives, subject to mutual change of mind that must be jointly expressed, both minimize misunderstandings and maximize procreative liberty by reserving to the progenitors the authority to make what is in the first instance a quintessentially personal, private decision. Written agreements also provide the certainty needed for effective operation of IVF programs.

While the value of arriving at explicit agreements is apparent, we also recognize the extraordinary difficulty such an exercise presents. All agreements looking to the future to some extent deal with the unknown. Here, however, the uncertainties inherent in the IVF process itself are vastly complicated by cryopreservation, which extends the viability of pre-zygotes indefinitely and allows time for minds, and circumstances, to change. Divorce; death, disappearance or incapacity of one or both partners; aging; the birth of other children are but a sampling of obvious changes in individual circumstances that might take place over time.

These factors make it particularly important that courts seek to honor the parties' expressions of choice, made before disputes erupt, with the parties' over-all direction always uppermost in the analysis. Knowing that advance agreements will be enforced underscores the seriousness and integrity of the consent process. Advance agreements as to disposition would have little purpose if they were enforceable only in the event the parties continued to agree. To the extent possible, it should be the progenitors—not the State and not the courts—who by their prior directive make this deeply personal life choice.

Here, the parties prior to cryopreservation of the pre-zygotes signed consents indicating their dispositional intent. While these documents were technically provided by the IVF program, neither party disputes that they are an expression of their own intent regarding disposition of their pre-zygotes. Nor do the parties contest the legality of those agreements, or that they were freely and knowingly made. The central issue is whether the consents clearly express the parties' intent regarding disposition of the pre-zygotes in the present circumstances. Appellant claims the consents are fraught with ambiguity in this respect; respondent urges they plainly mandate transfer to the IVF program.

The subject of this dispute may be novel but the common-law principles governing contract interpretation are not. Whether an agreement is ambiguous is a question of law for the courts. Ambiguity is determined by looking within the four corners of the document, not to outside sources. And in deciding whether an agreement is ambiguous courts

> "should examine the entire contract and consider the relation of the parties and the circumstances under which it was executed. Particular words should be considered, not as if isolated from the

context, but in the light of the obligation as a whole and the intention of the parties as manifested thereby. Form should not prevail over substance and a sensible meaning of words should be sought" (*Atwater & Co. v Panama R. R. Co.*, 246 N.Y. 519, 524).

Where the document makes clear the parties' over-all intention, courts examining isolated provisions " 'should then choose that construction which will carry out the plain purpose and object of the [agreement]' " (*Williams Press v. State of New York*, 37 N.Y.2d 434, 440, quoting *Empire Props. Corp. v. Manufacturers Trust Co.*, 288 N.Y. 242, 249). Applying those principles, we agree that the informed consents signed by the parties unequivocally manifest their mutual intention that in the present circumstances the pre-zygotes be donated for research to the IVF program.

The conclusion that emerges most strikingly from reviewing these consents as a whole is that appellant and respondent intended that disposition of the pre-zygotes was to be their joint decision. The consents manifest that what they above all did not want was a stranger taking that decision out of their hands. Even in unforeseen circumstances, even if they were unavailable, even if they were dead, the consents jointly specified the disposition that would be made. That sentiment explicitly appears again and again throughout the lengthy documents. Words of shared understanding—"we," "us" and "our"—permeate the pages. The overriding choice of these parties could not be plainer: "*We have the principal responsibility to decide the disposition of our frozen pre-zygotes. Our frozen pre-zygotes will not be released from storage for any purpose without the written consent of both of us, consistent with the policies of the IVF Program and applicable law*" (emphasis added).

That pervasive sentiment—both parties assuming "principal responsibility to decide the disposition of [their] frozen pre-zygotes"—is carried forward in ADDENDUM NO. 2–1:

"In the event that we are unable to make a decision regarding disposition of our stored, frozen pre-zygotes, we now indicate our desire for the disposition of our pre-zygotes and direct the IVF Program to

"Our frozen pre-zygotes may be examined by the IVF Program for biological studies and be disposed of by the IVF Program for approved research investigation as determined by the IVF Program."

Thus, only by joint decision of the parties would the pre-zygotes be used for implantation. And otherwise, by mutual consent they would be donated to the IVF program for research purposes.

The Appellate Division plurality identified, and correctly resolved, two claimed ambiguities in the consents. The first is the following sentence in INFORMED CONSENT NO. 2: "In the event of divorce, we understand that legal ownership of any stored pre-zygotes must be determined in a property settlement and will be released as directed by order of a court of competent jurisdiction." Appellant would instead read that sentence: "In the event of divorce, we understand that legal ownership of any stored pre-zygotes must be determined by a court of competent jurisdiction." That is not, however, what the sentence says. Appellant's construction ignores the direction that ownership of the pre-zygotes "must be determined in a property settlement"—words that also must be given meaning, words that connote the parties' anticipated agreement as to disposition. Indeed, appellant and respondent did actually reach a settlement stipulation, reserving only the issue of the pre-zygotes (the subject of their earlier consents).

Additionally, while extrinsic evidence cannot *create* an ambiguity in an agreement, the plurality properly looked to the "uncontested divorce" instrument, signed only weeks after the consents, to *resolve* any ambiguity in the cited sentence. Although that instrument never became operative, it reaffirmed the earlier understanding that neither party would alone lay claim to possession of the pre-zygotes.

Apart from construing the sentence in isolation, the plurality also read it in the context of the consents as a whole. Viewed in that light, we too conclude that the isolated sentence was not dispositional at all but rather was "clearly designed to insulate the hospital and the IVF program from liability in the event of a legal dispute over the pre-zygotes arising in the context of a divorce" (235 A.D.2d at 160). To construe the sentence as appellant suggests—surrendering all control over the pre-zygotes to the courts—is directly at odds with the intent of the parties plainly manifested throughout the consents that disposition be only by joint agreement.

For much the same reason, we agree with the plurality's conclusion that ADDENDUM NO. 2–1—the "STATEMENT OF DISPOSITION"—was not strictly limited to instances of "death or other unforseen circumstances." Those are contingencies that would be resolved by the ADDENDUM, but they are not the only ones. We reach this conclusion, again, from reviewing the provisions in isolation and then in the context of the consents as a whole. While we agree that the words "death or any other unforeseen circumstances" IN INFORMED CONSENT NO. 2 did not create a condition precedent, we also note that the present circumstances—including the parties' inability to reach the anticipated settlement—might well be seen as an "unforeseen" circumstance.

Moreover, viewing the ADDENDUM in isolation, there is no hint of the claimed condition in the document itself. The document is a free-standing form, separately captioned and separately signed by the parties. Finally, viewing the issue in the context of the consents as a whole, as the plurality noted, "the overly narrow interpretation advocated by [appellant] is refuted not only by the broad language of the dispositional provision itself, but by other provisions of the informed consent document as well" (235 A.D.2d at 159).

As they embarked on the IVF program, appellant and respondent—"husband" and "wife," signing as such—clearly contemplated the fulfillment of a life dream of having a child during their marriage. The consents they signed provided for other contingencies, most especially that in the present circumstances the pre-zygotes would be donated to the IVF program for approved research purposes. These parties having clearly manifested their intention, the law will honor it.

Accordingly, the order of the Appellate Division should be affirmed, with costs.

* * *

The four cases may be divided into two pairs, and the two courts in each pair reached roughly opposite outcomes.

In re Baby M and *Johnson* each involved contracts in which a couple that was unable to bear children itself contracted with a third party for that person to serve as a gestational surrogate, in exchange for a fee. The surrogate mother was to bear the child but then surrender it to her contractual counterparty (the couple, or one member thereof). The surrogate might (as in *In re Baby M*) provide genetic material to the child as well as gestational services; but the surrogate might also (as in *Johnson*) provide gestational services only. But in each case, the surrogate agreed to relinquish the child at birth, into the custody (both physical and legal) of the couple that had paid her to bear it. In each case, however, the surrogate became attached to the child over the course of the pregnancy and refused to hand over the baby at birth. The couple sued to establish its parental status and acquire custody over the child. In *In re Baby M*, the Supreme Court of New Jersey invalidated the contract as against public policy, making the surrogate the baby's legal mother and the male partner in the couple that had employed her the baby's legal father. The court ruled that custody should be determined according to the best interests of the child.[7] In *Johnson*, the Supreme Court of California adopted the opposite rule, holding that contracts establishing paid gestational surrogacy are valid and enforceable. The court reached this result by interpreting California's version of the Uniform Parentage Act. The court concluded that, under the Act, where both a gestational surrogate and a genetic mother claim parenthood over a baby, the woman "who intended to procreate the child—that is, she who intended to bring about the birth of a child that she intended to raise as her own—is the natural mother under California law." By this reasoning, the opinion imported contractual ideals deep into its holding: intent governs, it said.[8]

---

7. On the basis of this standard, custody was awarded to the father, with visitation rights for the mother. On reaching the age of majority, Baby M took legal steps to terminate the surrogate's maternity and make the female partner in the couple her legal mother. *In re Baby M* remains good law in New Jersey, and its holding invalidating contracts governing surrogate childbearing has recently been applied to purely gestational surrogacy (in which the surrogate provides none of the child's genetic material). See *A.G.R. v. D.R.H. & S.H.*, Docket #FD–09–001838–07 (N.J. Superior Ct., Hudson Cty, Dec. 23, 2009).

8. Some parts of *Johnson's* discussion of determining parentage under the California Act strike a curious tone. In substantial part, the Act addresses the epistemic question how most accurately to identify the person to whom a fixed concept *parent* (encompassing an overlapping set of biological, gestational, and conception-based relationships) applies. But the problem in *Johnson* is not epistemic at all, but rather goes to the question how to construct the concept *parent* in cases in which gestation, biology, and conception point in different directions.

A.Z. and *Kass* both involve contracts entered into by persons seeking to procreate together, but using *in vitro* fertilization, or IVF. The IVF process, for reasons of medical prudence and efficacy, involves creating and then freezing and storing more fertilized pre-embryos than are implanted in the gestational mother. In *A.Z.* and *Kass*, partners pursuing procreation through IFV drafted contracts that purported to govern the disposition of these excess frozen fertilized pre-embryos in the event that their relationships deteriorated and they divorced. In each case, the partners did divorce, and one of them—the former wife—sought subsequently to use the pre-embryos (which contained all the genetic material required to develop into a baby) to procreate outside of the (now ended) marriages. In *A.Z.*, the Supreme Judicial Court of Massachusetts declined to enforce a contract giving the wife the right to use the pre-embryos to procreate, holding that "we would not enforce an agreement that would compel one donor to become a parent against his or her will. As a matter of public policy, we conclude that forced procreation is not an area amenable to judicial enforcement." In *Kass*, the Court of Appeals of New York enforced a contract that denied the wife the use of the pre-embryos for procreation and called for the pre-embryos to be donated to medical research, holding that "the parties clearly expressed their intent that in the circumstances presented the pre zygotes would be donated to the IVF program for research purposes."

The two pairs of cases raise somewhat different issues, related to the differences in their underlying facts.

In re Baby M and *Johnson*—paid surrogacy cases—raise questions concerning anti-interestedness and anti-commodification. Paid surrogates use their gestational capacity to promote interests apart from those associated with procreation. They trade gestational services for other goods, including notably money.[9] This raises the question whether this capacity is appropriately used in this way. Money payments make the question especially troubling, for both instrumental and intrinsic reasons.

As an instrumental matter, paid surrogacy influences who bears children, in particular ways. Note that this poses two challenges to paid surrogacy.

First, and less obviously, it asks whether the burdens associated with child-bearing should be freely shifted according to *preferences*. There are certain preferences whose influence over conduct morality and law may wish to curtail. And allowing couples to shift the burdens of child-bearing to third parties dramatically increases the role preference plays in determining who bears children. This raises the question whether the increased role is proper. To be sure, egalitarian, rights-based legal orders have a commitment to allowing couples, and especially women, substantial freedom to determine whether and when to have children as they please: the

---

9. This need not always be so. A surrogate might offer her services out of charity, in order to help those who cannot otherwise do so produce genetic offspring, and request a fee only (or principally) to cover the risks and expenses of her pregnancy. Some of the concerns raised in the main text would not apply to such a case.

constitutionalization of the right to contraception guarantees that couples and especially women may adjust the number and timing of their pregnancies in part based on their assessments of the burdens of going through them. But surrogacy contracts, by out-sourcing the burden, give preference still wider influence: they allow those who prefer it to have genetic children without incurring the burdens of child-bearing. And it is not clear that the arguments that establish the right to contraception extend quite so confidently or conclusively to surrogacy or the out-sourcing that it involves. On the other hand, paid surrogacy arrangements promote the egalitarian aim of enabling women who can afford it to have genetic children on more nearly the same terms—free from the burdens of pregnancy and labor—that men already enjoy.

And second, and more obviously, introducing money into gestational choices causes preference to influence child-bearing against the backdrop of wealth, and hence also inequalities of wealth. It will come as no surprise that wealthy women do not generally choose to serve as paid gestational surrogates. This raises the question whether it is just for an activity that is as burdensome as child-bearing to be allocated (even if only in part) on the basis of wealth. The question is made more pressing by the thought, which is at least plausible, that the physical and emotional burdens associated with child-bearing cannot be simply erased or even directly compensated by money, even if a reasonable person would in certain circumstances choose to bear them in exchange for money. At the same time, these concerns must contend with the fact that paid surrogates choose to proceed, presumably because they believe that even given the burdens of child-bearing, the payments that they receive leave them better off, overall. Doctrines that invalidate paid surrogacy contracts based on concerns about inequality thus threaten to harm the very people by whose unequal positions they are motivated to begin with.[10]

The argument against commodifying child-bearing has a non-instrumental face also, associated with the particular form of valuation that occurs when a good or activity is exchanged not just based on preferences, but for money, and hence subject to market forces. Pricing a good embeds that good in a public shared frame of valuation, which obeys the rules of price theory. Pricing does not just give preference a role in allocating the good; it makes the good in principle exchangeable for every other good; and it makes the value of the good depend on the preferences not just of the parties to any given exchange but of all persons in the economy, who exert an influence on every exchange through the mechanism of market competition. Replacing non-market forms of valuing a good with a market price institutes a sea-change in the social meaning of that good. Such sea-changes have occurred in the past, perhaps most notably with the creation of wage-labor. But where the goods in question are socially important—as both ordinary labor and the labor of child-bearing surely are—the commodification changes social and moral life more broadly. Even if some measure of paid surrogacy were a good thing, this would leave wide open whether

---

10.   The discussion of unconscionability at the end of this chapter will investigate this possibility more systematically.

the general commodification of child-bearing would be good. And once the thin end of the pricing wedge is admitted into a social and legal order, it can prove difficult to keep the rest of the wedge out.[11]

In re Baby M and *Johnson* also worry about surrogacy contracts in ways that stand apart from the additional concerns raised specifically by paid surrogacy: the cases consider whether child-bearing is simply too important and emotionally powerful an activity for contracts made before conception to govern conduct after birth. These concerns take center stage in *A.Z.* and *Kass*—pre-embryo disposition cases—which ask whether, even where there is no question of commodification—the decision whether or not to become a genetic (and perhaps legal) parent may be alienated by contract.[12] The pre-embryo disposition cases worry that procreation is too emotionally powerful and morally significant an event for people to be able, either rationally or morally, to project their intentions across it. And they worry that the moral and legal burdens associated with parenthood are too great for one person to be permitted to impose them against the contemporaneous wishes of the person on whom they are imposed, or at least that they are so great as to overwhelm the moral and legal values associated with freedom of contract.[13] *A.Z.* clearly limits of freedom of contract in just this way. And *Kass* does not clearly affirm freedom to contract to become a parent, as the contract at issue in that case called for the pre-embryos to be destroyed rather than implanted for procreative purposes. This raises the question whether even the *Kass* court, for all its sympathetic discussion of freedom of contract, would actually enforce a contract to procreate.

24.2   LEGAL PROTECTIONS FOR CONTRACTUAL FREEDOM

The prior section dealt with doctrines by which the law restricts the contracts that free people might make—invalidating agreements based on

---

11.   This difficulty is illustrated by the decline of the professions—including in particular law and medicine—over the past two centuries. Professionalism involves, among other things, a resistance to the market-commodification of professionalized labor. It represents the hope that fees may be paid for work whose social and moral value remains insulated from market-prices. Lawyers and doctors have faced great and increasing difficulties in holding this ideological line and are, increasingly, becoming commodity laborers, like any others.

12.   Note as a threshold matter that contractually alienating the decision whether or not to become a parent is a particular way of giving the decision to another person. This is what distinguishes the pre-embryo disposition cases from the perfectly ordinary case in which a couple disagrees, following conception, about whether or not to carry the baby to term. In that case, morality and law require that the choice cannot be the man's, for the simple reason that the fetus is in the woman's body. The choice must thus be the woman's (insofar as abortion is a legally and even constitutionally protected right) or society's (insofar there is no right to abortion). But although one of these regimes may result in a man's losing a child he wishes to father and both may result in a man's fathering a child he does not wish to, the man does not, under either regime, alienate his choice concerning his reproduction. That is, he does not transfer his right to another, by intending to do so. Rather, he takes certain actions (sexual intercourse, resulting in conception) that make it the case that other moral considerations (relating to the woman's control over her body or the fetus's interest in its life) outweigh his interest in becoming or not becoming a parent.

13.   The values associated with abortion are another matter and are discussed in the previous note.

their substance even though they are fully contractual in form and were made by well-functioning and fully free parties. Those doctrines thus *limit* freedom of contract.

This section deals with doctrines that invalidate certain contracts in the service of *protecting and promoting* freedom of contract more broadly. These doctrines invalidate what would otherwise be perfectly good contracts—agreements that have a fully contractual form and whose substance triggers no especial moral or legal concern—on the ground that one of their parties was not adequately free in making them. The doctrines address a wide range of concerns. Only some of them are practically important, and the materials will focus commensurately on these.

24.2.A GENERAL CONTRACTUAL INCAPACITY

It may happen that a person fails, either for a moment or for a longer period, to possess contractual capacity quite generally. The laws of slavery and marriage illustrated this possibility in historical context. The materials below illustrate the possibility in the law today.

Restatement (Second) of Contracts

§ 12. Capacity to Contract

(1) No one can be bound by contract who has not legal capacity to incur at least voidable contractual duties. Capacity to contract may be partial and its existence in respect of a particular transaction may depend upon the nature of the transaction or upon other circumstances.

(2) A natural person who manifests assent to a transaction has full legal capacity to incur contractual duties thereby unless he is

(a) under guardianship, or

(b) an infant, or

(c) mentally ill or defective, or

(d) intoxicated.

Comments & Illustrations

Comment a. Total and partial incapacity. Capacity, as here used, means the legal power which a normal person would have under the same circumstances. See *Restatement, Second, Agency § 20; Restatement, Second, Trusts § 18.* Incapacity may be total, as in cases where extreme physical or mental disability prevents manifestation of assent to the transaction, or in cases of mental illness after a guardian has been appointed. Often, however, lack of capacity merely renders contracts voidable. See § 7. Incapacity sometimes relates only to particular types of transactions; on the other hand, persons whose capacity is limited in most circumstances may be bound by particular types of transactions. In cases of partial disability, the law of mistake or of misrepresentation, duress and undue influence may be relevant. See Chapters 6 and 7, particularly §§ 153, 157, 161(d), 163, 164, 167, 169(c) and 177, Comment *b* to § 172 and Comment *c* to § 175.

Comment b.   Types of incapacity. Historically, the principal categories of natural persons having no capacity or limited capacity to contract were married women, infants, and insane persons. Those formerly referred to as insane are included in the more modern phrase "mentally ill," and mentally defective persons are treated similarly. Statutes sometimes authorize the appointment of guardians for habitual drunkards, narcotics addicts, spendthrifts, aged persons or convicts as in cases of mental illness. Even without the appointment of a guardian, civil powers of convicts may be suspended in whole or in part during imprisonment; and American Indians are for some purposes treated as wards of the United States government. The contractual powers of convicts and Indians are beyond the scope of the Restatement of this Subject. As to convicts, see Model Penal Code § 306.5.

Comment c.   Inability to manifest assent. In order to incur a contractual duty, a party must make a promise, manifesting his intention; in most cases he must manifest assent to a bargain. See §§ 2, 17, 18. The conduct of a party is not effective as a manifestation of his assent unless he intends to engage in the conduct. See § 19. Hence if physical disability prevents a person from acting, or if mental disability is so extreme that he cannot form the necessary intent, there is no contract. Similarly, even if he intends to engage in the conduct, there is no contract if the other party knows or has reason to know that he does not intend the resulting appearance of assent. See § 20. In such cases it is proper to say that incapacity prevents the formation of a contract.

Comment d.   Married women. At common law a married woman had no capacity to incur contractual duties, although courts of equity recognized a limited power with respect to property conveyed to her separate use. Modern statutes in most States have given married women full power to contract, and they are therefore omitted from the list in subsection (2) of persons who may not have full capacity. In some States, however, capacity is still denied with respect to particular types of contracts, such as contracts between husband and wife, contracts of suretyship, contracts for the sale of real property, or contracts relating to the management of community property.

Comment e.   Artificial persons. The contractual powers of artificial persons such as corporations and governmental agencies are beyond the scope of the Restatement of this Subject. The tendency of modern legislation is to restrict the assertion of the defense of *ultra vires* by business corporations, and in effect to give them full capacity; what was once lack of capacity then resembles lack of authority as used in the law of agency. See Model Business Corporation Act § 6 (1961). Where partnerships or unincorporated associations have no power to contract as such, contracts made in their names bind the members instead. Compare *Restatement, Second, Agency § 20; Restatement, Second, Trusts §§ 97,* 98.

Comment f. Necessaries. Persons having no capacity or limited capacity to contract are often liable for necessaries furnished to them or to their wives or children. Though often treated as contractual, such liabilities are quasi-contractual: the liability is measured by the value of the necessaries rather than by the terms of the promise. The rules governing such liabilities are beyond the scope of the Restatement of this Subject. See *Restatement of Restitution §§ 62,* 112–17, 139.

Restatement (Second) of Contracts

§ 13. Persons Affected by Guardianship

A person has no capacity to incur contractual duties if his property is under guardianship by reason of an adjudication of mental illness or defect.

Comments & Illustrations

Comment a. Rationale. The reason for appointing a guardian of property is to preserve the property from being squandered or improvidently used. The guardianship proceedings are treated as giving public notice of the ward's incapacity and establish his status with respect to transactions during guardianship even though the other party to a particular transaction may have no knowledge or reason to know of the guardianship: the guardian is not required to give personal notice to all persons who may deal with the ward. The control of the ward's property is vested in the guardian, subject to court supervision; that control and supervision are not to be impaired or avoided by proof that the ward has regained his reason or has had a lucid interval, unless the guardianship is terminated or abandoned.

The rules governing contracts made by a guardian are beyond the scope of the Restatement of this Subject. A contract purporting not to bind the guardian personally but to bind the ward's estate raises problems much like those raised by a similar contract made by a trustee. *See Restatement, Second, Trusts §§ 262, 263, 271.* But the powers of guardians are usually defined by statute, and are ordinarily much narrower than those of trustees.

Comment b. Non-contractual obligations. Property under guardianship may be reached in some circumstances to redress the torts of the ward or to satisfy his quasi-contractual obligations. See *Restatement of Restitution § 139.* The guardian is not required, in order to defend the ward against contractual liability arising out of a transaction during guardianship, to restore the other party to his original position, since such a requirement might force the guardian to use other property to replace property dissipated by the ward. Compare *Restatement of Restitution § 62.* But the other party may be able to reclaim the consideration received by the ward if it can be found. In some cases, as where necessaries have been furnished, the other party, to avoid unjust enrichment, may recover the fair value of the consideration received by the ward. See Comment *f* to § 12.

Illustrations

1. A, under guardianship by reason of mental illness, buys an old car from B for $300, giving a promissory note for that amount. A subsequently abandons the car. A is not liable on the note. B may reclaim the car or, if the car is found to be a necessary, has a claim for having furnished it to A.

Comment c.   Types of guardianship. The rule of this Section had its origin in cases of insanity. It does not apply to cases where a person is committed or voluntarily admitted to an asylum or hospital without the appointment of a guardian, or where a guardian of the person only is appointed. In such cases the adjudication may have evidentiary value under § 15, but there may be a voidable contract notwithstanding mental illness or defect. Nor does the rule apply to infants: parents are natural guardians of the person but not the property of an infant, and the appointment of a guardian of the infant's property does not prevent the infant from affirming his contract when he becomes of age.

Unless a statute provides otherwise, the rule governing insane persons applies also to persons under guardianship by reason of mental illness or defect or as habitual drunkards, narcotics addicts, spendthrifts, aged persons or convicts. In some states it makes no difference that the guardian is known as a committee, conservator, or curator, or by some other title, but in others, conservatorship is a less drastic procedure not conclusive and sometimes not even probative on the issue of incompetency. Where a statute authorizes the appointment of a guardian on the voluntary application of the ward-to-be without any adjudication of disability, the ward may retain some capacity to contract, subject to subsequent judicial approval, either where the guardian consents or where the guardian's control of the property is not impaired.

Illustrations

2. Shortly after commitment to a hospital for the insane and while still confined, A conveys land to B, taking back a purchase-money mortgage. Subsequently C is appointed guardian of A's property. On A's behalf, C ratifies the conveyance and sues to enforce the mortgage by foreclosure. B has no defense: since A was not under guardianship, the conveyance and mortgage were voidable, not void. See § 15.

Comment d.   Termination of guardianship. When the reason for guardianship ceases, the guardianship should ordinarily be terminated by judicial decree. But when the ward recovers from mental illness, for example, the guardianship is sometimes abandoned without any formality. In such cases, if the guardian dies or is removed and no successor is appointed, the guardianship is no longer conclusive of contractual incapacity, and the same may be true in other cases if the ward resumes full control of his property without interference over a substantial period of time.

* * *

The two Restatement Sections just reproduced outline the general state of the law concerning contractual incapacity. The materials that follow elaborate this regime in modestly greater detail, with respect to three prominent cases of contractual incapacity.

Restatement (Second) of Contracts

§ 14.   Infants

Unless a statute provides otherwise, a natural person has the capacity to incur only voidable contractual duties until the beginning of the day before the person's eighteenth birthday.

Comments & Illustrations

Comment a.   Who are infants. The common law fixed the age of twenty-one as the age at which both men and women achieve full capacity to contract, and the rule that the critical moment is the beginning of the preceding day was established on the ground that the law disregards fractions of a day. In almost every State these rules have been changed by statute. It appears that 49 States have lowered the age of majority, either generally or for contract capacity, to less than twenty-one; usually, the age is eighteen. See the table in the Reporter's Note to this Comment. The birthday rather than the preceding day is the date of majority in some States; in some both men and women have full capacity upon marriage.

Comment b.   Obligations which are not voidable. Infants' contracts were at one time classified as void, voidable or valid, but the modern rule in the absence of statute is that they are voidable by the infant. See § 7. Compare Restatement, Second, Agency § 20. An infant may be bound by obligations imposed by law independently of contract, such as tort and quasi-contractual obligations. See Comment *f* to § 12, Restatement of Restitution § 139. In addition, certain contracts are held binding, ordinarily by statute, such as recognizances for appearance in court or contracts made with judicial approval. Modern statutes also sometimes deny the power of disaffirmance as to such transactions as withdrawal of bank deposits or payment of life insurance premiums.

Comment c.   Restoration of consideration. An infant need not take any action to disaffirm his contracts until he comes of age. If sued upon the contract, he may defend on the ground of infancy without returning the consideration received. His disaffirmance revests in the other party the title to any property received by the infant under the contract. If the consideration received by the infant has been dissipated by him, the other party is without remedy unless the infant ratifies the contract after coming of age or is under some non-contractual obligation. But some states, by statute or decision, have restricted the power of disaffirmance, either generally or under particular circumstances, by requiring restoration of the consideration received. Where the infant seeks to enforce the contract, the conditions of the other party's promise must be fulfilled. The problems arising when an infant seeks to disaffirm a conveyance or executed contract are beyond the scope of the Restatement of this Subject, whether the disaffirmance is attempted before or after he comes of age. As to what constitutes ratification, see § 85.

Keifer v. Fred Howe Motors, Inc.

Supreme Court of Wisconsin, 1968.
158 N.W.2d 288.

■ WILKIE, J. Three issues are presented on this appeal. They are:

1. Should an emancipated minor over the age of eighteen be legally responsible for his contracts?

2. Was the contract effectively disaffirmed?

3. Is the plaintiff liable in tort for misrepresentation?

Legal Responsibility of Emancipated Minor.

The law governing agreements made during infancy reaches back over many centuries. The general rule is that "the contract of a minor, other than for necessaries, is either void or voidable at his option." The only other exceptions to the rule permitting disaffirmance are statutory or involve contracts which deal with duties imposed by law such as a contract of marriage or an agreement to support an illegitimate child. The general rule is not affected by the minor's status as emancipated or unemancipated.

Appellant does not advance any argument that would put this case within one of the exceptions to the general rule, but rather urges that this court, as a matter of public policy, adopt a rule that an emancipated minor over eighteen years of age be made legally responsible for his contracts.

The underpinnings of the general rule allowing the minor to disaffirm his contracts were undoubtedly the protection of the minor. It was thought that the minor was immature in both mind and experience and that, therefore, he should be protected from his own bad judgments as well as from adults who would take advantage of him. The doctrine of the voidability of minors' contracts often seems commendable and just. If the beans that the young naive Jack purchased from the crafty old man in the fairy tale "Jack and the Bean Stalk" had been worthless rather than magical, it would have been only fair to allow Jack to disaffirm the bargain and reclaim his cow. However, in today's modern and sophisticated society the "infancy doctrine" seems to lose some of its gloss.

Paradoxically, we declare the infant mature enough to shoulder arms in the military, but not mature enough to vote; mature enough to marry and be responsible for his torts and crimes, but not mature enough to assume the burden of his own contractual indiscretions. In Wisconsin, the infant is deemed mature enough to use a dangerous instrumentality—a motor vehicle—at sixteen, but not mature enough to purchase it without protection until he is twenty-one.

No one really questions that a line as to age must be drawn somewhere below which a legally defined minor must be able to disaffirm his contracts for non-necessities. The law over the centuries has considered this age to be twenty-one. Legislatures in other states have lowered the age. We suggest that the appellant might better seek the change it proposes in the legislative halls rather than this court. A recent law review article in the Indiana Law Journal [41 Ind. L. J., 140] explores the problem of contractual disabilities of minors and points to three different legislative solutions leading to greater freedom to contract. The first approach is one gleaned from the statutes of California and New York, which would allow parties to submit a proposed contract to a court which would remove the infant's right of disaffirmance upon a finding that the particular contract is fair. This suggested approach appears to be extremely impractical in light of the expense and delay that would necessarily accompany the procedure. A second approach would be to establish a rebuttable presumption of incapacity to replace the strict rule. This alternative would be an open invitation to litigation. The third suggestion is a statutory procedure that would allow a minor to petition a court for the removal of disabilities. Under this procedure a minor would only have to go to court once, rather than once for each contract as in the first suggestion.

Undoubtedly, the infancy doctrine is an obstacle when a major purchase is involved. However, we believe that the reasons for allowing that obstacle to remain viable at this point outweigh those for casting it aside. Minors require some protection from the pitfalls of the marketplace. Reasonable minds will always differ on the extent of the protection that should be afforded. For this court to adopt a rule that the appellant suggests and remove the contractual disabilities from a minor simply because he becomes emancipated, which in most cases would be the result of marriage, would be to suggest that the married minor is somehow vested with more wisdom and maturity than his single counterpart. However, logic would not seem to dictate this result especially when today a youthful marriage is oftentimes indicative of a lack of wisdom and maturity.

Disaffirmance.

The appellant questions whether there has been an effective disaffirmance of the contract in this case.

Williston, while discussing how a minor may disaffirm a contract, states:

"Any act which clearly shows an intent to disaffirm a contract or sale is sufficient for the purpose. Thus a notice by the infant of his purpose to disaffirm a tender or even an offer to return the consideration or its proceeds to the vendor, is sufficient."

The testimony of Steven Kiefer and the letter from his attorney to the dealer clearly establish that there was an effective disaffirmance of the contract.

Misrepresentation.

Appellant's last argument is that the respondent should be held liable in tort for damages because he misrepresented his age. Appellant would use these damages as a set-off against the contract price sought to be reclaimed by respondent.

The 19th-century view was that a minor's lying about his age was inconsequential because a fraudulent representation of capacity was not the equivalent of actual capacity. This rule has been altered by time. There appear to be two possible methods that now can be employed to bind the defrauding minor: He may be estopped from denying his alleged majority, in which case the contract will be enforced or contract damages will be allowed; or he may be allowed to disaffirm his contract but be liable in tort for damages. Wisconsin follows the latter approach.

In *Wisconsin Loan & Finance Corp. v. Goodnough*, the defendant minor was a copartner in a business who had defaulted on a note given to the plaintiff in exchange for a loan. The defendant had secured the loan by fraudulently representing to the plaintiff that he was twenty-one years old. In adopting the tort theory and declining to adopt the estoppel theory, Mr. Chief Justice Rosenberry said:

"It is a matter of some importance, however, to determine whether an infant who secures benefits by misrepresenting his age to the person from whom he secured them is estopped to set up his infancy in order to defeat the contract or whether he becomes liable in an action for deceit for damages. In this case, if there is an estoppel which operates to prevent the defendant from repudiating the contract and he is liable upon it, the damages will be the full amount of the note plus interest and a reasonable attorney's fee. If he is held liable, on the other hand, in deceit, he will be liable only for the damages which the plaintiff sustained in this case, the amount of money the plaintiff parted with, which was $352 less the $25 repaid. There seems to be sound reason in the position of the English courts that to hold the contract enforceable by way of estoppel is to go contrary to the clearly declared policy of the law. But as was pointed out by the New Hampshire court, that objection lies no more for wrongs done by a minor by way of deceit than by way of slander or other torts. The contract is not enforced. He is held liable for deceit as he is for other torts such as slander, trover, and trespass.

"It is considered that the sounder rule is that which holds an infant under such circumstances liable in tort for damages."

Having established that there is a remedy against the defrauding minor, the question becomes whether the requisites for a tort action in misrepresentation are present in this case.

The trial produced conflicting testimony regarding whether Steven Kiefer had been asked his age or had replied that he was "twenty-one." Steven and his wife, Jacqueline, said "No," and Frank McHalsky, appellant's salesman, said "Yes." Confronted with this conflict, the question of credibility was for the trial court to decide, which it did by holding that Steven did not orally represent that he was "twenty-one." This finding is not contrary to the great weight and clear preponderance of the evidence and must be affirmed.

Even accepting the trial court's conclusion that Steven Kiefer had not orally represented his age to be over twenty-one, the appellant argues that there was still a misrepresentation. The "motor vehicle purchase contract" signed by Steven Kiefer contained the following language just above the purchaser's signature:

"I represent that I am 21 years of age or over and recognize that the dealer sells the above vehicle upon this representation."

Whether the inclusion of this sentence constitutes a misrepresentation depends on whether elements of the tort have been satisfied. They were not. In *First Nat. Bank in Oshkosh v. Scieszinski* [(25 Wis. 2d 569, 1964)] it is said:

"A party alleging fraud has the burden of proving it by clear and convincing evidence. The elements of fraud are well established:

" ' "To be actionable the false representation must consist, first of a statement of fact which is untrue; second, that it was made with intent to defraud and for the purpose of inducing the other party to act upon it; third, that he did in fact rely on it and was induced thereby to act, to his injury or damage." ' "

No evidence was adduced to show that the plaintiff had an intent to defraud the dealer. To the contrary, it is at least arguable that the majority of minors are, as the plaintiff here might well have been, unaware of the legal consequences of their acts.

Without the element of scienter being satisfied, the plaintiff is not susceptible to an action in misrepresentation. Furthermore, the reliance mentioned in *Scieszinski* must be, as Prosser points out, "justifiable reliance." We fail to see how the dealer could be justified in the mere reliance on the fact that the plaintiff signed a contract containing a sentence that said he was twenty-one or over. The trial court observed that the plaintiff was sufficiently immature looking to arouse suspicion. The appellant never took any affirmative steps to determine whether the plaintiff was in fact over twenty-one. It never asked to see a draft card, identification card, or the most logical indicium of age under the circumstances, a driver's license. Therefore, because there was no intent to deceive, and no justifiable reliance, the appellant's action for misrepresentation must fail.

Judgment affirmed.

Halbman v. Lemke

Supreme Court of Wisconsin, 1980.
298 N.W.2d 562.

■ CALLOW, J. On this review we must decide whether a minor who disaffirms a contract for the purchase of a vehicle which is not a necessity must make restitution to the vendor for damage sustained by the vehicle prior to the time the contract was disaffirmed. The court of appeals affirmed the judgment in part, reversed in part, and remanded the cause to the circuit court for Milwaukee County, the Honorable Robert J. Miech presiding.

I.

This matter was before the trial court upon stipulated facts. On or about July 13, 1973, James Halbman, Jr. (Halbman), a minor, entered into an agreement with Michael Lemke (Lemke) whereby Lemke agreed to sell Halbman a 1968 Oldsmobile for the sum of $1,250. Lemke was the manager of L & M Standard Station in Greenfield, Wisconsin, and Halbman was an employee at L & M. At the time the agreement was made Halbman paid Lemke $1,000 cash and took possession of the car. Arrangements were made for Halbman to pay $25 per week until the balance was paid, at which time title would be transferred. About five weeks after the purchase agreement, and after Halbman had paid a total of $1,100 of the purchase price, a connecting rod on the vehicle's engine broke. Lemke, while denying any obligation, offered to assist Halbman in installing a used engine in the vehicle if Halbman, at his expense, could secure one. Halbman declined the offer and in September took the vehicle to a garage where it was repaired at a cost of $637.40. Halbman did not pay the repair bill.

In October of 1973, Lemke endorsed the vehicle's title over to Halbman, although the full purchase price had not been paid by Halbman, in an effort to avoid any liability for the operation, maintenance, or use of the vehicle. On October 15, 1973, Halbman returned the title to Lemke by letter which disaffirmed the purchase contract and demanded the return of all money theretofore paid by Halbman. Lemke did not return the money paid by Halbman.

The repair bill remained unpaid, and the vehicle remained in the garage where the repairs had been made. In the spring of 1974, in satisfaction of a garageman's lien for the outstanding amount, the garage elected to remove the vehicle's engine and transmission and then towed the vehicle to the residence of James Halbman, Sr., the father of the plaintiff minor. Lemke was asked several times to remove the vehicle from the senior Halbman's home, but he declined to do so, claiming he was under no legal obligation to remove it. During the period when the vehicle was at the garage and then subsequently at the home of the plaintiff's father, it was subjected to vandalism, making it unsalvageable.

Halbman initiated this action seeking the return of the $1,100 he had paid toward the purchase of the vehicle, and Lemke counterclaimed for $150, the amount still owing on the contract. Based upon the uncontroverted facts, the trial court granted judgment in favor of Halbman, concluding that when a minor disaffirms a contract for the purchase of an item, he need only offer to return the property remaining in his hands without making restitution for any use or depreciation. In the order granting judgment, the trial court also allowed interest to the plaintiff dating from the disaffirmance of the contract. On postjudgment motions, the court amended its order for judgment to allow interest to the plaintiff from the date of the original order for judgment, July 26, 1978.

Lemke appealed to the court of appeals, and Halbman cross-appealed from the disallowance of prejudgment interest. The appellate court affirmed the trial court with respect to the question of restitution for depreciation, but reversed on the question of prejudgment interest, remanding the cause for reimposition of interest dating from the date of disaffirmance. The question of prejudgment interest is not before us on this review.

II.

The sole issue before us is whether a minor, having disaffirmed a contract for the purchase of an item which is not a necessity and having tendered the property back to the vendor, must make restitution to the vendor for damage to the property prior to the disaffirmance. Lemke argues that he should be entitled to recover for the damage to the vehicle up to the time of disaffirmance, which he claims equals the amount of the repair bill.

Neither party challenges the absolute right of a minor to disaffirm a contract for the purchase of items which are not necessities. That right, variously known as the doctrine of incapacity or the "infancy doctrine," is one of the oldest and most venerable of our common law traditions. Although the origins of the doctrine are somewhat obscure, it is generally recognized that its purpose is the protection of minors from foolishly squandering their wealth through improvident contracts with crafty adults who would take advantage of them in the marketplace. Kiefer v. Fred Howe Motors, Inc., 39 Wis. 2d 20, 24 (1968). Thus it is settled law in this state that a contract of a minor for items which are not necessities is void or voidable at the minor's option.

Once there has been a disaffirmance, however, as in this case between a minor vendee and an adult vendor, unresolved problems arise regarding the rights and responsibilities of the parties relative to the disposition of the consideration exchanged on the contract. As a general rule a minor who disaffirms a contract is entitled to recover all consideration he has conferred incident to the transaction. *Schoenung v. Gallet*, 206 Wis. 52 (1931). In return the minor is expected to restore as much of the consideration as, at the time of disaffirmance, remains in the minor's possession. The minor's right to disaffirm is not contingent upon the return of the property, however, as disaffirmance is permitted even where such return cannot be made.

The return of property remaining in the hands of the minor is not the issue presented here. In this case we have a situation where the property cannot be returned to the vendor in its entirety because it has been damaged and therefore diminished in value, and the vendor seeks to recover the depreciation. Although this court has been cognizant of this issue on previous occasions, we have not heretofore resolved it.

The law regarding the rights and responsibilities of the parties relative to the consideration exchanged on a disaffirmed contract is characterized by confusion, inconsistency, and a general lack of uniformity as jurisdictions attempt to reach a fair application of the infancy doctrine in today's marketplace. That both parties rely on this court's decision in *Olson v. Veum,* 197 Wis. 342 (1928), is symptomatic of the problem.

In *Olson* a minor, with his brother, an adult, purchased farm implements and materials, paying by signing notes payable at a future date. Prior to the maturity of the first note, the brothers ceased their joint farming business, and the minor abandoned his interest in the material purchased by leaving it with his brother. The vendor initiated an action against the minor to recover on the note, and the minor (who had by then reached majority) disaffirmed. The trial court ordered judgment for the plaintiff on the note, finding there had been insufficient disaffirmance to sustain the plea of infancy. This court reversed, holding that the contract of a minor for the purchase of items which are not necessities may be disaffirmed even when the minor cannot make restitution. Lemke calls our attention to the following language in that decision:

"To sustain the judgment below is to overlook the substantial distinction between a mere denial by an infant of contract liability where the other party is seeking to enforce it and those cases where he who was the minor not only disaffirms such contract but seeks the aid of the court to restore to him that with which he has parted at the making of the contract. In the one case he is using his infancy merely as a shield, in the other also as a sword." 197 Wis. at 344.

From this Lemke infers that when a minor, as a plaintiff, seeks to disaffirm a contract and recover his consideration, different rules should apply than if the minor is defending against an action on the contract by the other party. This theory is not without some support among scholars.

Additionally, Lemke advances the thesis in the dissenting opinion by court of appeals Judge Cannon, arguing that a disaffirming minor's obligation to make restitution turns upon his ability to do so. For this proposition, the following language in *Olson v. Veum, supra at 345*, is cited:

"The authorities are clear that when it is shown, as it is here, that the infant cannot make restitution, then his absolute right to disaffirm is not to be questioned."

In this case Lemke argues that the *Olson* language excuses the minor only when restitution is not possible. Here Lemke holds Halbman's $1,100, and accordingly there is no question as to Halbman's ability to make restitution.

Halbman argues in response that, while the "sword-shield" dichotomy may apply where the minor has misrepresented his age to induce the contract, that did not occur here and he may avoid the contract without making restitution notwithstanding his ability to do so.

The principal problem is the use of the word "restitution" in *Olson*. A minor, as we have stated, is under an enforceable duty to return to the vendor, upon disaffirmance, as much of the consideration as remains in his possession. When the contract is disaffirmed, title to that part of the purchased property which is retained by the minor revests in the vendor; it no longer belongs to the minor. The rationale for the rule is plain: a minor who disaffirms a purchase and recovers his purchase price should not also be permitted to profit by retaining the property purchased. The infancy doctrine is designed to protect the minor, sometimes at the expense of an innocent vendor, but it is not to be used to bilk merchants out of property as well as proceeds of the sale. Consequently, it is clear that, when the minor no longer possesses the property which was the subject matter of the contract, the rule requiring the return of property does not apply. The minor will not be required to give up what he does not have. We conclude that *Olson* does no more than set forth the foregoing rationale and that the word "restitution" as it is used in that opinion is limited to the return of the property to the vendor. We do not agree with Lemke and the court of appeals dissent that *Olson* requires a minor to make restitution for loss or damage to the property if he is capable of doing so.

Here Lemke seeks restitution of the value of the depreciation by virtue of the damage to the vehicle prior to disaffirmance. Such a recovery would require Halbman to return more than that remaining in his possession. It seeks compensatory value for that which he cannot return. Where there is misrepresentation by a minor or willful destruction of property, the vendor may be able to recover damages in tort. But absent these factors, as in the present case, we believe that to require a disaffirming minor to make restitution for diminished value is, in effect, to bind the minor to a part of the obligation which by law he is privileged to avoid.

The cases upon which the petitioner relies for the proposition that a disaffirming minor must make restitution for loss and depreciation serve to illustrate some of the ways other jurisdictions have approached this problem of balancing the needs of minors against the rights of innocent merchants. In *Barber v. Gross*, 74 S.D. 254 (1952), the South Dakota Supreme Court held that a minor could disaffirm a contract as a defense to an action by the merchant to enforce the contract but that the minor was obligated by a South Dakota statute, upon sufficient proof of loss by the plaintiff, to make restitution for depreciation. *Cain v. Coleman*, 396 S.W.2d 251 (Tex. Civ. App. 1965), involved a minor seeking to disaffirm a contract for the purchase of a used car where the dealer claimed the minor had misrepresented his age. In reversing summary judgment granted in favor of the minor, the court recognized the minor's obligation to make restitution for the depreciation of the vehicle. The Texas court has also ruled, in a case where there was no issue of misrepresentation, that upon disaffirmance and tender by a minor the vendor is obligated to take the property "as is." *Rutherford v. Hughes*, 228 S.W.2d 909, 912 (Tex. Civ. App. 1950). *Scalone v. Talley Motors, Inc.*, 158 N.Y.S.2d 615 (1957), and *Rose v. Sheehan Buick, Inc.*, 204 So.2d 903 (Fla. App. 1967), represent the proposition that a disaffirming minor must do equity in the form of restitution for loss or depreciation of the property returned. Because these cases would at some point force the minor to bear the cost of the very improvidence from which the infancy doctrine is supposed to protect him, we cannot follow them.

As we noted in *Kiefer*, modifications of the rules governing the capacity of infants to contract are best left to the legislature. Until such changes are forthcoming, however, we hold that, absent misrepresentation or tortious damage to the property, a minor who disaffirms a contract for the purchase of an item which is not a necessity may recover his purchase price without liability for use, depreciation, damage, or other diminution in value.

Recently the Illinois Court of Appeals came to the same conclusion. In *Weisbrook v. Clyde C. Netzley, Inc.*, 58 Ill. App.3d 862 (1978), a minor sought to disaffirm a contract for the purchase of a vehicle which developed engine trouble after its purchase. In the minor's action the dealer counterclaimed for restitution for use and depreciation. The court affirmed judgment for the minor and, with respect to the dealer's claim for restitution, stated:

"In the present case, of course, the minor plaintiff never misrepresented his age and, in fact, informed defendant that he was 17 years old. Nor did plaintiff represent to defendant that his father was to be the owner or have any interest in the automobile. There is no evidence in the present case that plaintiff at the time of entering the contract with defendant intended anything more than to enjoy his new automobile. He borrowed the total purchase price and paid it to defendant carrying out the transaction fully at the time of taking delivery of the vehicle. Plaintiff sought to disaffirm the contract and the return of the purchase price only when defendant declined to make repairs to it. In these circumstances we believe the weight of authority would permit the minor plaintiff to disaffirm the voidable contract and that defendant-vendor would not be entitled to recoup any damages which he believes he suffered as a result thereof." Id. at 1107. We believe this result is consistent with the purpose of the infancy doctrine.

The decision of the court of appeals is affirmed.

* * *

These materials are relatively straightforward.

They illustrate the general rule that the contracts of a minor are either void or voidable at the option of the minor. They also illustrate some possible and revealing exceptions to this rule. Thus, contracts for necessities might be excluded from the scope of the rule, for example. The purpose of the rule is to protect minors, after all; and a rule allowing a promisor to avoid her contractual obligations imposes burdens as well as protections, because it increases the difficulty of finding counterparties (at least for executory contracts). The law, sensitive to this fact, weights the benefits and burdens of contractual incapacity differently, depending on whether the contracts concern necessary or discretionary matters.[14]

Keifer, moreover, illustrates the interaction between contract and tort in this area. An infant might lack contractual capacity but nevertheless sue

---

14. The suggestion that incapacity on the ground of infancy might not apply to emancipated minors may be read to expand upon the principle concerning necessities.

and be sued in tort[15] (recall earlier suggestions that having contractual capacity indicates a higher legal status than merely being subject to tort law). The tort and contract regimes can clash, as when a minor fraudulently induces a person to enter into a contract. In such cases, as *Keifer* suggests, the minor might either be estopped from denying her majority in a contract suit or be held liable in tort for fraud (even though his contractual incapacity remains).[16]

Halbman, for its part, provides insight into the justification for permitting minors to avoid their contractual obligations. Such a rule might be based on the concern that minors are especially susceptible to being *exploited*, in the sense of accepting unfair divisions of surplus within their contracts. For example, a minor might be unusually likely to pay above market prices for poor quality cars. Alternatively, the rule might be based on the concern that minors are especially likely to make contracts that, even though they are internally fair, remain *imprudent*, in the sense that the do not promote the minor's true or substantial interests. For example, a minor might be unusually likely to buy sports cars that are frivolous or inappropriate given his needs, even when bought at fair (market) prices. *Halbman* suggests that at least part of the infancy doctrine reflects the second concern. It thus permits the minor buyer to recover the full purchase price of a car he bought, with no offset for depreciation to the car during his time of possession. Depreciation is almost by its nature the fair value of the use to which the minor has put the car, so to speak; certainly allowing the seller to offset the returned purchase price on account of depreciation would not allow her to exploit the minor buyer. The *Halbman* court declined to allow the offset nevertheless, and indeed declined on the express ground that granting the offset would force the minor to bear the costs of the very imprudence from which the infancy doctrine seeks to protect him. This states the protection-against-imprudence rather than the protection-against-exploitation rational for the infancy rule.

Mental illness and intoxication can constitute further sources of general contractual incapacity, as the following materials illustrate.

Restatement (Second) of Contracts

§ 15. Mental Illness or Defect

(1) A person incurs only voidable contractual duties by entering into a transaction if by reason of mental illness or defect

---

Emancipation decreased the likelihood that a minor might be under the care of others and increased the likelihood that he might have others under his care (note that emancipation before reaching the age of majority generally occurred on account of marriage). It thus increased the range of substantive areas for contracting that might involve necessities for him.

15. *See* Keeton, Dobbs, Keeton, and Owen, Prosser and Keeton on Torts § 134 (5th ed. 1984) (stating the "general rule" that "an infant has no [tort] immunity based solely on the fact of infancy" and describing exceptions).

16. For more, *see* Keeton, et. al. § 134 (reporting cases).

(a) he is unable to understand in a reasonable manner the nature and consequences of the transaction, or

(b) he is unable to act in a reasonable manner in relation to the transaction and the other party has reason to know of his condition.

(2) Where the contract is made on fair terms and the other party is without knowledge of the mental illness or defect, the power of avoidance under Subsection (1) terminates to the extent that the contract has been so performed in whole or in part or the circumstances have so changed that avoidance would be unjust. In such a case a court may grant relief as justice requires.

Comments & Illustrations

Comment a. Rationale. A contract made by a person who is mentally incompetent requires the reconciliation of two conflicting policies: the protection of justifiable expectations and of the security of transactions, and the protection of persons unable to protect themselves against imposition. Each policy has sometimes prevailed to a greater extent than is stated in this Section. At one extreme, it has been said that a lunatic has no capacity to contract because he has no mind; this view has given way to a better understanding of mental phenomena and to the doctrine that contractual obligation depends on manifestation of assent rather than on mental assent. See §§ 2, 19. At the other extreme, it has been asserted that mental incompetency has no effect on a contract unless other grounds of avoidance are present, such as fraud, undue influence, or gross inadequacy of consideration; it is now widely believed that such a rule gives inadequate protection to the incompetent and his family, particularly where the contract is entirely executory.

Comment b. The standard of competency. It is now recognized that there is a wide variety of types and degrees of mental incompetency. Among them are congenital deficiencies in intelligence, the mental deterioration of old age, the effects of brain damage caused by accident or organic disease, and mental illnesses evidenced by such symptoms as delusions, hallucinations, delirium, confusion and depression. Where no guardian has been appointed, there is full contractual capacity in any case unless the mental illness or defect has affected the particular transaction: a person may be able to understand almost nothing, or only simple or routine transactions, or he may be incompetent only with respect to a particular type of transaction. Even though understanding is complete, he may lack the ability to control his acts in the way that the normal individual can and does control them; in such cases the inability makes the contract voidable only if the other party has reason to know of his condition. Where a person has some understanding of a particular transaction which is affected by mental illness or defect, the controlling consideration is whether the transaction in its result is one which a reasonably competent person might have made.

Illustration

1. A, a school teacher, is a member of a retirement plan and has elected a lower monthly benefit in order to provide a benefit to her husband if she dies first. At age 60 she suffers a "nervous breakdown," takes a leave of absence, and is treated for cerebral arteriosclerosis. When the leave expires she applies for retirement, revokes her previous election, and elects a larger annuity with no death benefit. In view of her reduced life expectancy, the change is foolhardy, and there are no other circumstances to explain the change. She fully understands the plan, but by reason of mental illness is unable to make a decision based on the prospect of her dying before her husband. The officers of the plan have reason to know of her condition. Two months after the changed election she dies. The change of election is voidable.

Comment c. Proof of incompetency. Where there has been no previous adjudication of incompetency, the burden of proof is on the party asserting incompetency. Proof of irrational or unintelligent behavior is essential; almost any conduct of the person may be relevant, as may lay and expert opinions and prior and subsequent adjudications of incompetency. Age, bodily infirmity or disease, use of alcohol or drugs, and illiteracy may bolster other evidence of incompetency. Other facts have significance when there is mental illness or defect but some understanding: absence of independent advice, confidential or fiduciary relationship, undue influence, fraud, or secrecy; in such cases the critical fact often is departure from the normal pattern of similar transactions, and particularly inadequacy of consideration.

Comment d. Operative effect of incompetency. Where no guardian has been appointed, the effect on executory contracts of incompetency by reason of mental illness or defect is very much like that of infancy. Regardless of the other party's knowledge or good faith and regardless of the fairness of the terms, the incompetent person on regaining full capacity may affirm or disaffirm the contract, or the power to affirm or disaffirm may be exercised on his behalf by his guardian or after his death by his personal representative. There may, however, be related obligations imposed by law independently of contract which cannot be disaffirmed. See Comment *f* to § 12, Comment *b* to § 14. And if the other party did not know of the incompetency at the time of contracting he cannot be compelled to perform unless the contract is effectively affirmed.

Illustration

2. A, an incompetent not under guardianship, contracts to sell land to B, who does not know of the incompetency. A continues to be incompetent. On discovering the incompetency, B may refuse to perform until a guardian is appointed, and if none is appointed within a reasonable time may obtain a decree canceling the contract.

Comment e. Effect of performance. Where the contract has been performed in whole or in part, avoidance is permitted only on equitable terms. In the traditional action at law, the doing of equity by or on behalf of the incompetent was accomplished by a tender before suit, but in equity or under modern merged procedure it is provided for in the decree. Any benefits still retained by the incompetent must be restored or paid for, and restitution must be made for any necessaries furnished under the contract. See Comment *f* to § 12. If the other party knew of the incompetency at the time of contracting, or if he took unfair advantage of the incompetent, consideration not received by the incompetent or dissipated without benefit to him need not be restored.

Illustrations

3. A, an incompetent not under guardianship, contracts to buy land for a fair price from B, who does not know of the incompetency. Shortly after transfer of title to A and part payment by A, A dies. A's personal representative may recover A's part payment on reconveying the land to B.

4. The facts being otherwise as stated in Illustration 3, C, with knowledge of A's incompetency, renders legal services to A in the transaction; after learning of A's incompetency, B pays $500 to C pursuant to the contract. A's personal representative need not reimburse B for the payment.

Comment f. When avoidance is inequitable. If the contract is made on fair terms and the other party has no reason to know of the incompetency, performance in whole or in part may so change the situation that the parties cannot be restored to their previous positions or may otherwise render avoidance inequitable. The contract then ceases to be voidable. Where the other party, though acting in good faith, had reason to know of the incompetency at the time of contracting or performance, or where the equities can be partially adjusted by the decree, the court may grant or deny relief as the situation requires. Factors to be taken into account in such cases include not only benefits conferred and received on both sides but also the extent to which avoidance will benefit the incompetent and the extent to which others who will benefit from avoidance had opportunities to prevent the situation from arising.

Illustrations

5. A, an incompetent spouse not under guardianship, mortgages land on fair terms to B, a bank which has no knowledge or reason to know of the incompetency, for a loan of $2,000. At A's request the money is paid to the other spouse, C, who absconds with it. The contract is not voidable.

6. A, a congenital imbecile not under guardianship, has an interest in unimproved land which is contingent on his surviving his father B. A joins B and C, a cousin, in leasing the land on fair terms for 25 years to D, who has no reason to know of the incompetency. Subsequently A assigns his interest in the rent to C in return for C's agreement to support A for life, which C duly

performs. Five years later A joins B and C in an outright sale of the land to D. On B's death avoidance of the sale of A's interest may be equitable if D can be assured of repayment of the price and of retaining improvements made by him after the sale; avoidance of the lease would be inequitable.

7. A, an incompetent not under guardianship, lives on a homestead with his mother B and brother C. A also holds a mortgage on a second tract of land owned by C. To prevent foreclosure of a mortgage on the homestead, A, B and C join in borrowing money from D on a mortgage of both tracts on fair terms. D acts in good faith but has reason to know of A's incompetency. A dies, leaving B his sole heir. The mortgage to D is not voidable for the benefit of B.

Restatement (Second) of Contracts

§ 16. Intoxicated Persons

A person incurs only voidable contractual duties by entering into a transaction if the other party has reason to know that by reason of intoxication

(a) he is unable to understand in a reasonable manner the nature and consequences of the transaction, or

(b) he is unable to act in a reasonable manner in relation to the transaction.

Comments & Illustrations

Comment a. Rationale. Compulsive alcoholism may be a form of mental illness; and when a guardian is appointed for the property of a habitual drunkard, his transactions are treated like those of a person under guardianship by reason of mental illness. See §§ 13, 15. If drunkenness is so extreme as to prevent any manifestation of assent, there is no capacity to contract. See §§ 2, 12, 19. It would be possible to treat voluntary intoxication as a temporary mental disorder in all cases, but voluntary intoxication not accompanied by any other disability has been thought less excusable than mental illness. Compare Model Penal Code § 2.08 and Comment. Hence a contract made by an intoxicated person is enforceable by the other party even though entirely executory, unless the other person has reason to know that the intoxicated person lacks capacity. Elements of overreaching or other unfair advantage may be relevant on the issues of competency, of the other party's reason to know, and of the appropriate remedy. Compare Comments *c, e* and *f* to § 15. Use of drugs may raise similar problems.

Comment b. What contracts are voidable. The standard of competency in intoxication cases is the same as that in cases of mental illness. If the intoxication is so extreme as to prevent any manifestation of assent, there is no contract. Otherwise the other party is affected only by intoxication of which he has reason to know. A contract made by a person who is so drunk he does not know what he is doing is voidable if the other party has reason to know of the intoxication. Where there is some understanding of the transaction despite intoxication, avoidance depends on a showing that the other party induced the drunkenness or that the consideration was inadequate or that the transaction departed from the normal pattern of similar transactions; if the particular transaction in its result is one which a reasonably competent person might have made, it cannot be avoided even though entirely executory.

Illustrations

1.   A, while in a state of extreme intoxication, signs and mails a written offer on fair terms to B, who has no reason to know of the intoxication. B accepts the offer. A has no right to avoid the contract.

2.   A is ill and confined to his bed. B, knowing that the illness is incurable, plies A with intoxicating liquor for a week and then purports to treat him by rubbing him with oil. While intoxicated, A executes by mark a contract to sell land to B for a grossly inadequate consideration. Six days later A dies. A's heirs may avoid the contract.

3.   A has been drinking heavily. B, who has also been drinking, meets A, offers to buy A's farm for $50,000, a fair price, and offers A a drink which A accepts. In drunken exhilaration A, as a joke, writes out and signs a memorandum of agreement to sell, gets his wife to sign it, and delivers it to B, who understands the transaction as a serious one. A's intoxication is no defense to B's suit for specific performance.

Comment c.   Ratification and avoidance. Where a contract is voidable on the ground of intoxication, the rules as to ratification and avoidance are much the same as in cases of misrepresentation. See Chapter 7. On becoming sober, the intoxicated person must act promptly to disaffirm and must offer to restore consideration received. Such an offer may be excused, however, if the consideration has been dissipated during the period of drunkenness.

Illustration

4.   A buys a barber shop from B for $650. Shortly afterward, A, helplessly drunk and evidently not aware of what he is doing, sells the shop back to B for $200. On recovering his senses, A cannot remember the transaction and cannot find out what happened to the $200. On prompt disaffirmance, A may recover the shop without repaying the $200.

Faber v. Sweet Style Mfg. Corp.

Supreme Court of New York, 1963.
242 N.Y.S.2d 763.

■ MEYER, J. The relationship of psychiatry to the criminal law has been the subject of study and recommendation by the Temporary Commission on

Revision of the Penal Law and Criminal Code (Leg. Doc. [1963], No. 8, pp. 16–26). This court had reason to touch upon the relationship of psychiatry to matrimonial law in *Anonymous* v. *Anonymous* (37 Misc 2d 773). The instant case presents yet a third aspect of the same basic problem: that involving the law of contract.

Plaintiff herein seeks rescission of a contract for the purchase of vacant land in Long Beach on the ground that he was not at the time the contract was entered into of sufficient mental competence. Defendant counterclaims for specific performance.

The evidence demonstrates that from April until July, 1961, plaintiff was in the depressed phase of a manic-depressive psychosis and that from August until the end of October he was in the manic stage. Though under care of Dr. Levine, a psychiatrist, beginning June 8 for his depression, he cancelled his August 8 appointment and refused to see the doctor further. Previously frugal and cautious, he became more expansive beginning in August, began to drive at high speeds, to take his wife out to dinner, to be sexually more active and to discuss his prowess with others. In a short period of time, he purchased three expensive cars for himself, his son and his daughter, began to discuss converting his Long Beach bathhouse and garage property into a 12–story cooperative and put up a sign to that effect, and to discuss the purchase of land in Brentwood for the erection of houses. In September, against the advice of his lawyer, he contracted for land at White Lake in the Catskills costing $11,500 and gave a $500 deposit on acreage, the price of which was $41,000 and talked about erecting a 400–room hotel with marina and golf course on the land.

On September 16, 1961, he discussed with Mr. Kass, defendant's president, the purchase of the property involved in this litigation for the erection of a discount drugstore and merchandise mart. During the following week Kass advised plaintiff that defendant would sell. On the morning of Saturday, September 23, plaintiff and Kass met at the office of defendant's real estate broker. Kass asked $55,000, plaintiff offered $50,000; when the broker agreed to take $1,500 commission, Kass offered to sell for $51,500 and plaintiff accepted. It was agreed the parties would meet for contract that afternoon. Kass obtained the services of attorney Nathan Suskin who drew the contract prior to the 2:00 p.m. conference. Plaintiff returned to that conference with his lawyer (who is also his brother-in-law) who approved the contract as to form but asked plaintiff how he would finance it and also demanded that the contract include as a condition that a nearby vacant property would be occupied by Bohack. No mention was made of plaintiff's illness. When Suskin refused to consider such a condition, plaintiff's lawyer withdrew. The contract was signed in the absence of plaintiff's lawyer and the $5,150 deposit paid by check on plaintiff's checking account in a Rockaway bank.

On the following Monday morning, plaintiff transferred funds from his Long Beach bank account to cover the check. On the same day, he went to Jamaica and arranged with a title abstract company for the necessary search and policy, giving correct details concerning the property, price and his brother-in-law's address and phone number and asking that search be completed within one week. Between September 23 when the contract was signed and October 8 when plaintiff was sent to a mental institution, he persuaded Leonard Cohen, a former employee, to join in the building enterprise promising him a salary of $150 a week and a Lincoln Continental when the project was complete, caused a sign to be erected on the premises stating that "Faber Drug Company" and a "merchandise mart" were coming soon, hired an architect, initiated a mortgage application giving correct details as to price and property dimensions, hired laborers to begin digging (though title was not to close until Oct. 20), filed plans with city officials and when told by them that State Labor Department approval was required, insisted on driving to Albany with the architect and Leonard Cohen to obtain the necessary approval.

On September 25 plaintiff saw Dr. Levine as a result of *plaintiff's* complaint that his wife needed help, that she was stopping him from doing what he wanted to. He was seen again on September 26 and 28, October 2 and October 8, and hospitalized on October 8 after he had purchased a hunting gun. Dr. Levine, Dr. Sutton, who appeared for defendant, and the hospital all agree in a diagnosis of manic-depressive psychosis. Dr. Levine testified that on September 23 plaintiff was incapable of reasoned judgment; the hospital record shows that on October 9, Dr. Krinsky found plaintiff's knowledge good, his memory and comprehension fair, his insight lacking and his judgment defective. Dr. Sutton's opinion, based on the hospital record and testimony of plaintiff's wife and Dr. Levine, was that plaintiff was subject to mood swings, but that there was no abnormality in his thinking, that his judgment on September 23 was intact.

The contract of a mental incompetent is voidable at the election of the incompetent (*Blinn v. Schwarz*, 177 N. Y. 252) and if the other party can be restored to *status quo* rescission will be decreed upon a showing of incompetence without more (*Verstandig v. Schlaffer*, 296 N. Y. 62). If the *status quo* cannot be restored and the other party to the contract was ignorant of the incompetence and the transaction was fair and reasonable, rescission will, however, be denied notwithstanding incompetence (*Mutual Life Ins. Co. v. Hunt*, 79 N. Y. 541, 545). The burden of proving incompetence is upon the party alleging it, but once incompetence has been shown, the burden of proving lack of knowledge and fairness is upon the party asking that the transaction be enforced. In the instant case the contract concerns vacant land and is executory and though plaintiff caused some digging to be done on the premises, the proof shows that the land has been levelled again. Clearly, the *status quo* can be restored and plaintiff is, therefore, entitled to rescission if the condition described meets the legal test of incompetence.

The standards by which competence to contract is measured were, apparently, developed without relation to the effects of particular mental diseases or disorders and prior to recognition of manic-depressive psychosis as a distinct form of mental illness (*Matter of Martin*, 82 Misc. 574, 578). Primarily they are concerned with capacity to understand: (*Aldrich v.*

Bailey, 132 N. Y. 85, 87–88) "so deprived of his mental faculties as to be wholly, absolutely and completely unable to understand or comprehend the nature of the transaction"; (*Paine v. Aldrich*, 133 N. Y. 544, 546) "such mental capacity at the time of the execution of the deed that he could collect in his mind without prompting, all the elements of the transaction and retain them for a sufficient length of time to perceive their obvious relations to each other, and to form a rational judgment in regard to them"; (*Matter of Delinousha v. National Biscuit Co.*, 248 N. Y. 93, 95) "A contract may be avoided only if a party is so affected as to be unable to see things in their true relations and to form correct conclusions in regard thereto". If cognitive capacity is the sole criterion used, the manic must be held competent (*Lovell v. Keller*, 146 Misc. 100), for manic-depressive psychosis affects motivation rather than ability to understand.

The law does, however, recognize stages of incompetence other than total lack of understanding. Thus it will invalidate a transaction when a contracting party is suffering from delusions if there is "some such connection between the insane delusions and the making of the deed as will compel the inference that the insanity induced the grantor to perform an act, the purport and effect of which he could not understand, and which he would not have performed if thoroughly sane" (*Moritz v. Moritz*, 153 App. Div. 147, 152, affd. 211 N. Y. 580). Moreover, it holds that understanding of the physical nature and consequences of an act of suicide does not render the suicide voluntary within the meaning of a life insurance contract if the insured "acted under the control of an insane impulse caused by disease, and derangement of his intellect, which deprived him of the capacity of governing his own conduct in accordance with reason." (*Newton v. Mutual Benefit Life Ins. Co.*, 76 N. Y. 426, 429.) Finally, *Paine v. Aldrich* (supra) and the *Delinousha* case consider not only ability to understand but also capacity to form "a rational judgment" or "correct conclusions." Thus, capacity to understand is not, in fact, the sole criterion. Incompetence to contract also exists when a contract is entered into under the compulsion of a mental disease or disorder but for which the contract would not have been made.

Whether under the latter test a manic will be held incompetent to enter into a particular contract will depend upon an evaluation of (1) testimony of the claimed incompetent, (2) testimony of psychiatrists, and (3) the behavior of the claimed incompetent as detailed in the testimony of others (Green, Judicial Tests of Mental Incompetency, 6 Mo. L. R. 141), including whether by usual business standards the transaction is normal or fair (Green, Proof of Mental Incompetency and the Unexpressed Major Premise, 53 Yale L. J. 271, 299–305). Testimony of the claimed incompetent often is not available, and in any event is subject to the weakness of his mental disorder, on the one hand, and of his self-interest on the other. The psychiatrist in presenting his opinion is, in final analysis, evaluating factual information rather than medical data, and is working largely with the same evidence presented to the court by the other witnesses in the action (Leifer, Competence of the Psychiatrist to Assist In the Determination of Incompetency, 14 Syracuse L. R. 564). Moreover, in the great majority of cases psychiatrists of equal qualification and experience will reach diametrically opposed conclusions on the same behavioral evidence. The courts have, therefore, tended to give less weight to expert testimony than to objective behavioral evidence.

In the instant case, plaintiff did not testify at the trial but his examination before trial was read into the record. It shows that he understood the transaction in which he was engaged, but throws no light on his motivation. Plaintiff introduced no evidence concerning the rationality or fairness of the transaction (in the apparent belief that Merritt v. Merritt, 43 App. Div. 68, applied and that such proof, therefore, was not part of his case) so the court has no basis for comparison in that respect. Plaintiff's evidence concerning the location of the property and the nature of the business he proposed to carry on there fell short of establishing irrationality, nor can it be said that the making of an all cash contract was abnormal, even if the two earlier White Lake dealings are considered, in view of the testimony of plaintiff and his wife that the Long Beach bathhouse property was worth $200,000 and that it was free and clear. But the rapidity with which plaintiff moved to obtain an architect and plans, hire laborers, begin digging on the property, and his journey to Albany to obtain building approval, all prior to title closing, are abnormal acts. Viewing those acts in the context of his actions, detailed above, with respect to the White Lake properties, his plans with respect to the Brentwood property and the conversion of his bathhouse premises, and his complaint to Dr. Levine on September 25 that his wife was in need of help because she was trying to hold him back, the court is convinced that the contract in question was entered into under the compulsion of plaintiff's psychosis. That conclusion is contrary to the opinion expressed by Dr. Sutton, but the court concludes that Doctors Levine and Krinsky as treating physicians had the better basis for the opinions they expressed. In any event their opinions are but confirmatory of the conclusion reached by the court on the basis of the evidence above detailed.

Defendant argues, however, that the contract was ratified by the acts of plaintiff's attorney in forwarding a title objection sheet to defendant's attorney and in postponing the closing and by plaintiff himself. Ratification requires conscious action on the part of the party to be charged. Plaintiff was still in the mental hospital when the objection sheet was sent and the closing date postponed and these acts have not been shown to have been carried out with his knowledge or by his direction. As for his own action it was merely to answer, in reply to an inquiry from defendant's president as to when he was going to take title, that he did not know, it was up to his attorney. The contract with defendant had been signed on September 23, plaintiff had been sent to the hospital on October 8 and remained there until November 11, having a series of electroshock treatments while there, and the complaint in this action was verified November 20. The conversation with defendant's president could not have occurred until after November 11 and must have occurred several days prior to November 20. An answer as equivocal in nature and made under the circumstances as the one under consideration cannot in any fair sense be characterized as an exercise of plaintiff's right of election to "hold on to the bargain if it is good and let it go if it is bad" (*Blinn v. Schwarz*, 177 N. Y. 252, 263, *supra*).

Accordingly, defendant's motions at the end of plaintiff's case and of the whole case, on which decision was reserved, are now denied, and judgment will be entered declaring the contract rescinded and dismissing the counterclaim. The foregoing constitutes the decision of the court pursuant to section 440 of the Civil Practice Act.

Williamson v. Matthews

Supreme Court of Alabama, 1980.
379 So.2d 1245.

■ PER CURIAM. This is an appeal from an order denying appellant Williamson injunctive relief seeking to cancel a deed and to set aside a sale of property from Williamson to the Matthews. We reverse and remand.

The Matthews learned from members of their family that Williamson wanted to sell her home. Her mortgage was in default, and the mortgagee was threatening foreclosure. There was some evidence to the effect that Williamson wanted to get enough equity to help her finance a mobile home. When they went to Williamson's house to inquire about it, Williamson showed the Matthews through the house. Bobby Matthews asked Williamson how much she wanted for it. Williamson told the Matthews to come back the next day. It is at this point that the parties are in disagreement. The Matthews contend that Williamson offered to sell her equity for $1,700, and Williamson contends that she offered to sell her equity for $17,000, and that the Matthews agreed to pay off the mortgage. It is undisputed that on September 27, 1978, the parties went to attorney Arthur J. Cook's office to execute a contract for the sale of the property. The contract of sale stated the purchase price to be $1,800 ($100 increase reflecting an agreement between the parties concerning some of the furniture in the home) plus the unpaid balance of the mortgage. Attorney Cook testified that he read the terms of the sale to both parties.

The parties then met on October 10, 1978, at attorney Larry Keener's office to sign the deed and to close a loan from appellee Family Savings Federal Credit Union to the Matthews so that the Matthews could buy the property from Williamson. Appellee The Brooklyn Savings Bank was about to foreclose the mortgage on Williamson's property. Keener disbursed part of the loan proceeds to Williamson. Williamson signed the deed to the property.

This Court was advised at oral argument that further disbursement of funds has been held up pending final disposition of this appeal.

Immediately after the sale, Williamson became concerned that she had not received her full consideration and consulted an attorney.

Two days later, on October 12, 1978, Williamson filed a petition for injunctive relief alleging inadequate consideration and mental weakness. The trial court granted Williamson a temporary restraining order preventing the sale from being completed, but at a full hearing on the petition for injunctive relief, the court denied Williamson the relief she requested. Williamson moved for and was granted a rehearing and further testimony was taken on the issue of Williamson's alleged mental weakness. Following the rehearing, the court issued a final order, again denying Williamson injunctive relief. This appeal followed.

Williamson's contention of inadequacy of consideration is based upon evidence which she introduced at trial showing a property appraisal of $16,500. Using this figure and deducting the existing mortgage of approximately $6,500, Williamson's equity would amount to $10,000, $8,300 more than the $1,700 she was paid. Williamson contends that she was due $17,000 for her equity, which would result in the property being valued at $23,500 (adding the mortgage of $6,500). In other words, accepting Williamson's first contention, the Matthews should have paid her *$8,300 more*; accepting the second contention, Williamson should receive *$15,300 more*. There was also evidence that the credit union appraised the property for $19,500. This would reflect an equity of $13,000. Accepting this figure, she should have been paid *$11,300 more*. Thus, the claim of inadequacy of consideration (and it would seem to be well established) varied from *$8,300 to $15,300*.

Although it is a fundamental principle of law that inadequacy of consideration is not, by itself, a sufficient ground to set aside a contract for the sale of land, in *Judge v. Wilkins*, 19 Ala. 765, 772 (1851), over 128 years ago, this Court stated that:

> "Inadequacy of price *within itself*, and disconnected from all other facts, cannot be a ground for setting aside a contract, or affording relief against it. There must be something else besides the mere inadequacy of consideration or inequality in the bargain, to justify a court in granting relief by setting aside the contract. *What this something else besides the inadequacy* should be, perhaps no court ought to say, lest the wary and cunning, by employing other means than those named, should escape with their fraudulent gains. I, however, will venture to say, that it ought, in connection with the inadequacy of consideration, to superinduce the belief that there had been either a suppression of the truth, the suggestion of falsehood, abuse of confidence, a violation of duty arising out of some fiduciary relation between the parties, the exercise of undue influence, or the taking of an unjust and inequitable advantage of one whose peculiar situation at the time would be calculated to render him an easy prey to the cunning and the artful. But if no one of these appears, or if no fact is proved that will lead the mind to the conclusion, that the party against whom relief is sought has suppressed some fact that he ought to have disclosed, or that he has suggested some falsehood, or abused in some manner the confidence reposed in him, or that some fiduciary relation existed between the parties, or that the party complaining was under his influence, or at the time of the trade was in a condition, *from any*

cause, that would render him an easy victim to the unconscientious, then relief cannot be afforded; for inadequacy of consideration, *standing alone and unsupported by any thing else, can authorize no court, governed by the rules of the English law, to set aside a contract.*"19 Ala. at 772.

Even a total failure of consideration is an insufficient ground for the cancellation of an otherwise valid deed. *Ingram v. Horn*, 294 Ala. 353 (1975).

Although in the case at bar there is no proof of suppression of fact, presentation of falsehood, abuse of confidence, fiduciary relationship between the parties, overreaching, or undue influence, the Court in *Judge* did not limit "this something else" besides mere inadequacy of consideration to these factors alone.

Williamson contends that the "something else" in the case at bar is mental weakness, either due to some form of permanent mental incapacity or due to intoxication. Of course, the contracts of an insane person are absolutely void. *Walker v. Winn*, 142 Ala. 560 (1904). Williamson, however, is not contending that she was insane at the time of the contract, but rather is contending that she had a mental incapacity, which coupled with inadequacy of consideration requires the setting aside of the transaction.

Our rule in such a case is that a party cannot avoid, free from fraud or undue influence, a contract on the ground of mental incapacity, unless it be shown that the incapacity was of such a character that, at the time of execution, the person had no reasonable perception or understanding of the nature and terms of the contract. *Weaver v. Carothers*, 228 Ala. 157, 160 (1934).

Our rule regarding incapacity due to intoxication is much the same. The drunkenness of a party at the time of making a contract may render the contract voidable, but it does not render it void; and to render the contract voidable, it must be made to appear that the party was intoxicated to such a degree that he was, at the time of the contracting, incapable of exercising judgment, understanding the proposed engagement, and of knowing what he was about when he entered into the contract sought to be avoided. *Snead v. Scott*, 182 Ala. 97 (1913). Proof merely that the party was drunk on the day the sale was executed does not, per se, show that he was without contractual capacity; there must be some evidence of a resultant condition indicative of that extreme impairment of the faculties which amounts to contractual incapacity. *Snead v. Scott*, supra.

The burden was therefore cast on Williamson to show, by clear and convincing evidence, that she was incapable, at the time of execution, of executing the contract for sale and of executing the deed. *Snead v. Scott*, supra.

We hold that Williamson met this burden. The testimony elicited at trial by Williamson's attorney charted a history of aberrative behavior. A Mrs. Logan, Williamson's mother, provided lengthy testimony about her daughter's past aberrations. Additionally, Dr. Fredric Feist provided expert testimony regarding Williamson at the rehearing. He stated that she showed signs of an early organic brain syndrome due to her excessive drinking, that she had emotional problems, that he thought that some of her brain cells were destroyed, and that her ability to transact business had been impaired.

Indulging the usual presumption due the trial court, we nevertheless hold that, under the facts of this case, it appears to us that Williamson was not, at the time of execution, capable of fully and completely understanding the nature and terms of the contract and of the deed. *Cross v. Maxwell*, 263 Ala. 509 (1955). Williamson's contention that she was intoxicated supports this holding. Testimony was admitted from various witnesses to the effect that Williamson had a history of drinking, that she still had the problem at the time she executed the contract, and that she had in fact taken a couple of drinks before leaving for the meeting in attorney Arthur Cook's office. We do not hold that Williamson was so intoxicated as to render her incapable of contracting. However, numerous factors combine to warrant the conclusion that she was operating under diminished capacity. Testimony showed that Williamson's capacity to transact business was impaired, that she had a history of drinking, that she had been drinking the day she conducted negotiations, and that she had an apparent weakened will because she was pressured by the possibility of an impending foreclosure. Moreover, Williamson made complaint to an attorney only hours after the transaction. These factors are combined with a gross inadequacy of consideration.

No mitigating factors exist to the contrary. No right of any intervening third party is involved. Further disbursement of the loan proceeds has been frozen until final disposition of this appeal. No hardship is worked upon any party.

Although the evidence was presented before the trial court ore tenus, and in such a case where there is evidence to support the trial court's judgment, this Court will not ordinarily reverse that judgment unless there is a showing of plain and palpable error or manifest injustice [*Terry v. Buttram*, 368 So. 2d 859, 860 (Ala. 1979)], we consider that the record supports a finding in this case of such manifest injustice as to require a reversal of the judgment.

We recognize that two able and conscientious attorneys handled parts of the transaction. They are in no wise responsible for, nor were they aware of, the factors which prompt us to require a reversal of this case.

REVERSED AND REMANDED.

Uribe v. Olsen

Court of Appeals of Oregon, 1979.
601 P.2d 818.

■ Thornton, J. This is an appeal from a decree directing specific performance of two contracts to sell land. Defendant assigns as error the trial court's finding that one of the vendors, Mrs. Bonham, had the capacity to contract for the sale of her parcel. Defendant also assigns error to the decree of specific performance contending that the ten percent liquidated damages clause in the contracts was intended by the parties to be the exclusive remedy for breach.

The facts are as follows:

Ruby Bonham, aged 81 at the date of the contract, owned 80 acres of land near Grants Pass. Her daughter, defendant Pauline Olson (who appeals both in her personal capacity and as conservator of the estate of her mother) owned an adjacent 10 acre parcel. In early 1976, Mrs. Bonham decided to sell her property and, desiring a national listing, contacted Mr. Martin of United Farm Agency. She originally wanted to ask $80,000 for the property but was persuaded by Mr. Martin, based on his experience and the fact that he had listed a similar parcel for $55,000, to reduce the asking price to $60,000. Mr. Martin further advised her that she should consider any offer above $50,000.

In July, 1976, plaintiff became interested in the property. He visited it on July 31, 1976. Based on this inspection he offered $50,000 for the parcel, contingent on Mrs. Olson's agreeing to sell her adjacent property for which he offered $15,000. The following day, Mr. Martin discussed the offer with both women and they rejected the offer as too low. Following a discussion with Mrs. Olson's attorney, they made a counter offer to plaintiff of $52,500 and $20,000 for the two parcels respectively. This offer was accepted and Mr. Martin procured the signatures of each of them. He testified that before she signed the earnest money agreement on September 28, 1976, he had explained the details of the transaction to Mrs. Bonham in the presence of her sister. In December, 1976, Mrs. Olson decided that her mother was not competent at the time she signed the counter-offer and both refused to sign the final contracts.

Medical evidence of two doctors who treated Mrs. Bonham beginning in November, 1976, showed that she suffered from a heart blockage which caused seizures and blackouts and involutional psychosis resulting in depression. Both agreed that the condition would have been present prior to September, 1976, and could well have affected her mental processes.

Friends and relatives of Mrs. Bonham all testified to a gradual deterioration of her mental acuity over several years prior to the transaction in question. This deterioration manifested itself in a number of ways, including periods of disorientation and depression, occasional paranoia, an increase in eccentric habits and delusions concerning people long dead and imagined friendships with Barry Goldwater and Frank Sinatra.

On the other hand, plaintiff testified that while Mrs. Bonham appeared eccentric to him, he had no reason to question her capacity. When he visited the property, she showed him around and answered all his questions respecting the features of the property. Mr. Martin testified that she accurately answered all his questions when he prepared the listing agreement and appeared at all times to know that she was engaged in selling her property, apparently intending to move back to Tennessee, where she had grown up.

On September 28, 1976, when Mrs. Bonham signed the earnest money agreement, Mr. Martin testified he explained the details to her carefully, that she read the agreement and appeared to understand. Mrs. Bonham's sister, who was also present, testified that Mrs. Bonham just stared into space while Mr. Martin read the agreement to her and her only comment was, "I don't care what you do with this property. You can give it back to the Indians if you want to."

Mrs. Olson testified that she finally accepted that her mother was incompetent in October, 1976, and first discussed with her attorney the possibility of creating a conservatorship at that time. Based on this decision, she refused to sign the final contracts.

The test of contractual capacity is whether a person is able to understand the nature of his action and apprehend its consequences. *Coke v. Coke*, 242 Or 486, 489 (1966). This capacity is measured at the time of the execution of the contract, in this case, the earnest money agreement. *First Christian Church v. McReynolds*, 194 Or 68, 72 (1952). Even where there are substantial indications of mental incompetence, it is possible that a person may have "lucid intervals" during which he possesses the requisite capacity. *Pioneer Trust Co. v. Currin*, 210 Or 343, 347 (1957). Capacity includes the ability to reason and exercise judgment and, in essence, to bargain with the other party. *First Christian Church v. McReynolds, supra*, 194 Or at 72–73. Neither old age, illness nor extreme emotional distress is sufficient of itself to negate such capacity. *Id.*

In *Gindhart v. Skourtes*, 271 Or 115 (1975), the seller suffered from an arteriosclerotic condition which caused periods of confusion which he claimed reduced his mental competence. He suffered a stroke shortly after the sale. The evidence showed, however, that he had tried to sell the land for two years without success, rejected the buyers' first offer and subsequently reached a compromise price which defendant's experts testified was in line with other prices for land in the area. 271 Or at 119. The court found him competent.

In *Pioneer Trust Co. v. Currin, supra*, plaintiff's ward appeared disoriented and unresponsive and frequently talked to himself. He was committed to a mental hospital four months after selling the land in question. Nevertheless, he had lucid periods and defendant testified he had shown him around the place and answered all his questions in a normal fashion. The ward told defendant he was anxious to sell because he intended to leave the state soon and wanted cash. Defendant purchased the property for cash at a price below what probably could have been obtained. The court held the ward competent to enter into the contract.

While there is ample evidence to establish that Mrs. Bonham's mental state on September 28, 1976, had deteriorated substantially from what it once had been, this does not resolve the matter. We are persuaded, largely by the circumstances of the sale, that Mrs. Bonham was competent to sell her land. Mrs. Bonham had definite ideas about how the property should be listed and accurately supplied all the necessary information. The purchase price was negotiated over several months and the offer that was ultimately accepted was made by Mrs. Bonham and Mrs. Olson. Before obtaining her signature, Mr. Martin read the important features of the earnest money agreement to Mrs. Bonham and had her read the document, a point of considerable significance. *First Christian Church v. McReynolds, supra*, 194 Or at 83. Furthermore, Mrs. Olson and her attorney were constantly involved and no one, prior to November, 1976, suggested that Mrs. Bonham did not possess the requisite competence. In fact, defendant's primary dissatisfaction with the deal appears to be the price obtained, not the fact that the property was sold. In sum, the evidence indicates that Mrs. Bonham knew what she was doing and, though her reasons for selling may not have been altogether wise, she intended to sell and was cognizant of the consequences.

PROPRIETY OF THE REMEDY

Defendant contends that the liquidated damages clause in the earnest money agreements evinces the intent of the parties that it be the exclusive remedy in the event one party decided not to proceed with the sale.

The clause in question reads:

"It is agreed, if either seller or buyer fails to perform his part of this agreement, he shall forthwith pay to the other party hereto a sum equal to 10% of the agreed price of sale as consideration for the execution of this agreement by such other party."

The presence in a contract to sell real estate of a liquidated damages or forfeiture provision will not per se preclude specific performance. It must appear from the construction of the contract that the damages provision was intended by the parties to be the exclusive remedy for breach. *Potter Realty Co. v. Derby*, 75 Or 563, 571, 147 P 548 (1915). In *Potter*, the contract provided that in the event of breach by the buyer, installments made under the contract would be forfeited, and the "contract shall be null and void as to both parties hereto * * *." 75 Or at 566. The court held this remedy to be exclusive.

Defendant cites *Dillard Homes, Inc. v. Carroll*, 152 So 2d 738 (Fla App 1963). That case does not support defendant's position since the clause provided that the deposit of ten percent of the purchase price would be forfeited and "the parties hereto shall be relieved of all obligations under this instrument." 152 So 2d at 739. The authorities cited in that case support the proposition that the intent to preclude specific performance as a remedy must clearly appear.

The intent to eliminate specific performance as a remedy does not appear from the clause in the contracts at issue.

Affirmed.

* * *

The materials raise two sets of questions: first, what constitutes incompetence (on account of either mental illness or intoxication); and second, what protections does the law accord to incompetent persons (both with respect to allocating the burden of mental illness between those who are incompetent and innocent counterparties and with respect to whether incompetence undermines all contractual obligations or only unfair or unreasonable ones)? Consider each question in turn.

Common law tests of mental incapacity typically emphasized the understanding, and in particular the question whether or not a party alleging mental incapacity was *capable*,[17] at the time of contract formation, of understanding the terms and character of the contract that was formed. This approach, the *Faber* court proposed, gave little protection to parties like the plaintiff before it, whose mania did not really impair his capacity to understand the real estate deal that he contemplated so much as distort his motivations.[18] The *Faber* court, in line with the Restatement (Second), thus adopted a broader approach, according to which a contract might be voidable on grounds of mental incapacity where a party, even though he understands the transaction, cannot act in a reasonable manner in relation to it, because he lacks appropriate control over his will.

Uribe also addresses the question what counts as mental incapacity. The defendant in *Uribe* unquestionably suffered mental illness that threatened her contractual capacity, including on the understanding-based model: she suffered disorientation, paranoia, and delusions. But these symptoms were all intermittent, and the defendant continued (even in the face of her mental illness) to have lucid intervals. The *Uribe* court concluded that the defendant—who participated competently in negotiating an agreement whose terms and nature she understood when making it—contracted in the midst of such a lucid interval. Thus, although there may have been many times at which the defendant lacked the mental capacity to contract, she possessed adequate capacity at the time when she actually contracted and hence was bound by her agreement.

Uribe illustrates that, in spite of the innovations concerning deformations of the will reflected in the Restatement (Second) and *Faber*, the older idea that places inability to understand at the heart of incapacity retains a hold over the legal imagination. It is not just that the language of the opinion turns to the understanding-rather than the will-based formulation of the mental incapacity doctrine. Rather, and more significantly, the logic of the argument requires adopting the understanding-based view. It makes

---

17. Capacity to understand is the key here. A party cannot avoid a contractual obligation because she did not as a matter of fact understand the contract's terms (although she might have done had she considered them more carefully or sought explanation); and she certainly cannot avoid the obligation simply because she failed to read the contract in question.

18. Is this correct? The plaintiff in *Faber* plausibly did not experience a compulsion to do something that he regarded as self-destructive even as he did it. Rather, the plaintiff, on account of his mania, over-estimated the returns that his contract would generate and, in particular, underestimated the costs and risks associated with certain obstacles that the contract involved. The plaintiff seems, that is, to have lost his judgment rather than his will, and this is at least arguably closer to losing the capacity to understand than to suffering a compulsion.

sense to say that a person may recover her understanding during lucid intervals experienced in the middle of mental illness; but it makes much less sense to say that a person may recover her will. Understanding may be complete in and of a moment; but will requires planning across time.

Once it has been fixed what counts as mental incapacity, it remains to say what consequences follow from a determination that a person suffered mental incapacity when making a contract. In particular, how does the law balance an incapacitated party's interest in not being bound against the contractual interests of his counterparty, especially where the counterparty remained (reasonably) unaware that she was dealing with someone who lacked contractual capacity. The doctrine with respect to this question remains in flux, and it the materials here should not be treated as establishing what courts generally will do, but rather as identifying the considerations to which courts look in deciding what to do.

Three points in particular are worth making. First, a court is more likely to allow a party to avoid a contractual obligation on grounds of incapacity where the status quo ante can be restored than where it cannot be restored. (See, for example, *Faber*.) Put the other way around, one party's incapacity will sooner undermine his counterparty's expectation interest than her reliance interest. Second, a counterparty's reasonable failure to notice that she is dealing with someone who lacks contractual capacity is more likely to support enforcing a contract in spite of incapacity where the nature of the incapacity concerns the will than where it concerns the understanding. See, for example, Restatement (Second) of Contracts § 15(1)(b). This is another way in which the common law test of mental capacity retains its influence over the law today. And third, courts assessing efforts to avoid contractual obligations on grounds of incapacity remain sensitive to whether or not the contracts in question are fair and reasonable (although this raises the question, introduced in connection with infancy, whether the relevant standards concern non-exploitation or, more broadly, prudence and appropriateness). See, for example, Restatement (Second) of Contracts § 15(2). Overall, then, mental incapacity offers substantial protection against contractual obligations, but also (and strikingly) less protection than infancy (as those who deal with minors must, save in cases of fraud by the minors, bear the full costs of the protection against contractual obligation that the law affords minors).

24.2.B   Contract–Specific Protections

The doctrines just discussed address circumstances in which one party to a contract lacks contractual capacity *quite generally*, to make any contracts. But it may happen that a party who might freely and capably make any number of contracts, nevertheless is rendered unfree and incapable by the facts and circumstances under which she enters into a particular contract. The materials below take up several doctrines that address this possibility.

24.2.B.1   Duress

Duress is the narrowest doctrinal ground by which a party may void a particular contract on account of having been unfree in making it. Doctrine establishes a demanding test for duress—so demanding that actual cases of duress remain rare. Insofar as duress remains an interesting category, this is principally because the conceptual structure of duress reveals some difficulties concerning freedom of contract that reappear in other, and more practically important, doctrinal settings.

Restatement (Second) of Contracts

§ 174. When Duress By Physical Compulsion Prevents Formation Of A Contract

If conduct that appears to be a manifestation of assent by a party who does not intend to engage in that conduct is physically compelled by duress, the conduct is not effective as a manifestation of assent.

Comments & Illustrations

Comment a.   Rationale. Under the general principle stated in § 21(2), a party's conduct is not effective as a manifestation of his assent if he does not intend to engage in it. This Section involves an application of that principle to those relatively rare situations in which actual physical force has been used to compel a party to appear to assent to a contract. Compare § 163. The essence of this type of duress is that a party is compelled by physical force to do an act that he has no intention of doing. He is, it is sometimes said, "a mere mechanical instrument." The result is that there is no contract at all, or a "void contract" as distinguished from a voidable one. See Comment *a* to § 7. Cases, such as those involving hypnosis, in which conduct is compelled without physical force, are left to be governed by the general rule stated in § 19(2).

Illustration

   1. A presents to B, who is physically weaker than A, a written contract prepared for B's signature and demands that B sign it. B refuses. A grasps B's hand and compels B by physical force to write his name. B's signature is not effective as a manifestation of his assent, and there is no contract.

Comment b.   "Void" rather than voidable. The distinction between "void contract" and a voidable contract has important consequences. For example, a victim of duress may be held to have ratified the contract if it is voidable, but not if it is "void." Furthermore, a good faith purchaser may acquire good title to property if he takes it from one who obtained voidable title by duress but not if he takes it from one who obtained "void title" by duress. It is immaterial under the rule stated in this Section whether the duress is exercised by a party to the transaction or by a third person. See Comment *d* to § 175.

Restatement (Second) of Contracts

§ 175. When Duress By Threat Makes A Contract Voidable

(1) If a party's manifestation of assent is induced by an improper threat by the other party that leaves the victim no reasonable alternative, the contract is voidable by the victim.

(2) (2) If a party's manifestation of assent is induced by one who is not a party to the transaction, the contract is voidable by the victim unless the other party to the transaction in good faith and without reason to know of the duress either gives value or relies materially on the transaction.

Comments & Illustrations

Comment a. Improper threat. The essence of the type of duress dealt with in this Section is inducement by an improper threat. The threat may be expressed in words or it may be inferred from words or other conduct. Past events often import a threat. Thus, if one person strikes or imprisons another, the conduct may amount to duress because of the threat of further blows or continued imprisonment that is implied. Courts originally restricted duress to threats involving loss of life, mayhem or imprisonment, but these restrictions have been greatly relaxed and, in order to constitute duress, the threat need only be improper within the rule stated in § 176.

Comment b. No reasonable alternative. A threat, even if improper, does not amount to duress if the victim has a reasonable alternative to succumbing and fails to take advantage of it. It is sometimes said that the threat must arouse such fear as precludes a party from exercising free will and judgment or that it must be such as would induce assent on the part of a brave man or a man of ordinary firmness. The rule stated in this Section omits any such requirement because of its vagueness and impracticability. It is enough if the threat actually induces assent (see Comment *c*) on the part of one who has no reasonable alternative. The alternative may take the form of a legal remedy. For example, the threat of commencing an ordinary civil action to enforce a claim to money may be improper. See § 176(1)(c). However, it does not usually amount to duress because the victim can assert his rights in the threatened action, and this is ordinarily a reasonable alternative to succumbing to the threat, making the proposed contract, and then asserting his rights in a later civil action. See Illustration 1; cf. Restatement of Restitution § 71. This alternative may not, however, be reasonable if the threat involves, for instance, the seizure of property, the use of oppressive tactics, or the possibility of emotional consequences. See Illustration 2. The standard is a practical one under which account must be taken of the exigencies in which the victim finds himself, and the mere availability of a legal remedy is not controlling if it will not afford effective relief to one in the victim's circumstances. See Illustrations 3 and 4. The alternative to succumbing to the threat need not, however, involve a legal remedy at all. In the case of a threatened denial of needed goods or services, the availability on the market of similar goods or services may afford a reasonable means of avoiding the threat. Compare Illustrations 5 and 6. Since alternative sources of funds are ordinarily available, a refusal to pay money is not duress, absent a showing of peculiar necessity. See Illustration 7. Where the threat is one of minor vexation only, toleration of the inconvenience involved may be a reasonable alternative. Whether the victim has a reasonable alternative is a mixed question of law and fact, to be answered in clear cases by the court.

Illustrations

1. A makes an improper threat to commence civil proceedings against B unless B agrees to discharge a claim that B has against A. In order to avoid defending the threatened suit, B is induced to make the contract. Defense of the threatened suit is a reasonable alternative, the threat does not amount to duress, and the contract is not voidable by B.

2. A makes an improper threat to commence a civil action and to file a lis pendens against a tract of land owned by B, unless B agrees to discharge a claim that B has against A. Because B is about to make a contract with C for the sale of the land and C refuses to make the contract if the levy is made, B agrees to discharge the claim. B has no reasonable alternative, A's threat is duress, and the contract is voidable by B.

3. A, with whom B has left a machine for repairs, makes an improper threat to refuse to deliver the machine to B, although B has paid for the repairs, unless B agrees to make a contract to have additional repair work done. B can replevy the machine, but because he is in urgent need of it and delay would cause him heavy financial loss, he is induced by A's threat to make the contract. B has no reasonable alternative, A's threat amounts to duress, and the contract is voidable by B.

4. A, who has promised B to vacate leased premises in return for $10,000 in order to permit B to demolish the building and construct another, refuses to do so unless B agrees to purchase his worthless furniture for $5,000. B can resort to regular eviction proceedings, but because this will materially delay his construction schedule and cause him heavy financial loss, he is induced by A's threat to make the contract. B has no reasonable alternative, A's threat amounts to duress, and the contract is voidable by B.

5. A, who has contracted to sell goods to B, makes an improper threat to refuse to deliver the goods to B unless B modifies the contract to increase the price. B attempts to buy substitute goods elsewhere but is unable to do so. Being in urgent need of the goods, he makes the modification. See Uniform Commercial Code § 2–209(1). B has no reasonable alternative, A's threat amounts to duress, and the modification is voidable by B.

6. The facts being otherwise as stated in Illustration 5, B could buy substitute goods elsewhere but does not attempt to do so. The purchase of substitute goods and a claim for any damages is a reasonable alternative, the threat does not amount to duress, and the contract is not voidable by B.

7. A, who has contracted to pay for goods delivered by B, makes an improper threat to refuse to pay B unless B modifies the contract to reduce the price. B attempts to borrow money elsewhere but is unable to do so. Being in urgent need of cash to avoid foreclosure of a mortgage, he makes the modification. See Uniform Commercial Code § 2–209(1). B has no reasonable alternative, A's threat amounts to duress, and the modification is voidable by B.

Comment c.   Subjective test of inducement. In order to constitute duress, the improper threat must induce the making of the contract. The rule for causation in cases of misrepresentation stated in § 167 is also applied to analogous cases of duress. No special rule for causation in cases of duress is stated here because of the infrequency with which the problem arises. A party's manifestation of assent is induced by duress if the duress substantially contributes to his decision to manifest his assent. Compare § 167. The test is subjective and the question is, did the threat actually induce assent on the part of the person claiming to be the victim of duress. Threats that would suffice to induce assent by one person may not suffice to induce assent by another. All attendant circumstances must be considered, including such matters as the age, background and relationship of the parties. Persons of a weak or cowardly nature are the very ones that need protection; the courageous can usually protect themselves. Timid and inexperienced persons are particularly subject to threats, and it does not lie in the mouths of the unscrupulous to excuse their imposition on such persons on the ground of their victims' infirmities. However, here as under § 167 circumstantial evidence may be useful in determining whether a threat did in fact induce assent. For example, although it is not essential that a reasonable person would have believed that the maker of the threat had the ability to execute it, this may be relevant in determining whether the threat actually induced assent. Similarly, such factors as the availability of disinterested advice and the length of time that elapses between the making of the threat and the assent may also be relevant in determining whether the threat actually induced the assent.

Illustrations

8. A, seeking to induce B to make a contract to sell land to A, threatens to poison B unless B makes the contract. The threat would not be taken seriously by a reasonable person, but B is easily frightened and attaches importance to the threat in deciding to make the contract. The contract is voidable by B.

9. A seeks to induce B, A's wife, who has a history of severe emotional disturbances, to sign a separation agreement on unfavorable terms. B has no lawyer, while A does. A tells B that if she does not sign the agreement he will charge her with desertion, she

will never see her children again and she will get back none of her personal property, which is in A's possession. B signs the separation agreement. The agreement is voidable by B.

Comment d. Voidable. Duress by threat results in a contract voidable by the victim. It differs in this important respect from duress by physical compulsion, which results in there being no contract at all. See Comment *b* to § 174. The power of avoidance for duress is subject to limitations that are similar to those applicable to avoidance on other grounds, such as mistake and misrepresentation. These limitations are stated in §§ 378–84. The person making the threat may, of course, pursue any civil claim that he has against the victim independently of the contract induced by the threat. Furthermore, to the extent that such a claim is valid, the maker of the threat may be entitled to retain what he has actually received through performance of such a contract. These matters are not dealt with in this Section.

Comment e. Duress by a third person. If a party's assent has been induced by the duress of a third person, rather than that of the other party to the contract, the contract is nevertheless voidable by the victim. There is, however, an important exception if the other party has, in good faith and without reason to know of the duress, given value or changed his position materially in reliance on the transaction. "Value" includes a performance or a return promise that is consideration under the definition stated in § 71, so that the other party is protected if he has made the contract in good faith before learning of the duress. See Uniform Commercial Code § 1–201(44). The rule stated in this Section does not, however, protect a party to whom the duress is attributable under the law of agency. The rule is similar to that for misrepresentation (§ 163) and is analogous to the rule that protects against the original owner the good faith purchaser of property from another who obtained it by duress.

Illustrations

10. A, who is not C's agent, induces B by duress to contract with C to sell land to C. C, in good faith, promises B to pay the agreed price. The contract is not voidable by B.

11. The facts being otherwise as stated in Illustration 10, C learns of the duress before he promises to pay the agreed price. The contract is voidable by B.

Restatement (Second) of Contracts

§ 176. When A Threat Is Improper

(1) A threat is improper if

(a) what is threatened is a crime or a tort, or the threat itself would be a crime or a tort if it resulted in obtaining property,

(b) what is threatened is a criminal prosecution,

(c) what is threatened is the use of civil process and the threat is made in bad faith,or

(d) the threat is a breach of the duty of good faith and fair dealing under a contract with the recipient.

(2) A threat is improper if the resulting exchange is not on fair terms, and

(a) the threatened act would harm the recipient and would not significantly benefit the party making the threat,

(b) the effectiveness of the threat in inducing the manifestation of assent is significantly increased by prior unfair dealing by the party making the threat, or

(c) what is threatened is otherwise a use of power for illegitimate ends.

Comments & Illustrations

Comment a.   Rationale. An ordinary offer to make a contract commonly involves an implied threat by one party, the offeror, not to make the contract unless his terms are accepted by the other party, the offeree. Such threats are an accepted part of the bargaining process. A threat does not amount to duress unless it is so improper as to amount to an abuse of that process. Courts first recognized as improper threats of physical violence and later included wrongful seizure or detention of goods. Modern decisions have recognized as improper a much broader range of threats, notably those to cause economic harm. The rules stated in this Section recognize as improper both the older categories and their modern extensions under developing notions of "economic duress" or "business compulsion." The fairness of the resulting exchange is often a critical factor in cases involving threats. The categories within Subsection (1) involve threats that are either so shocking that the court will not inquire into the fairness of the resulting exchange (see Clauses (a) and (b)) or that in themselves necessarily involve some element of unfairness (see Clauses (c) and (d)). Those within Subsection (2) involve threats in which the impropriety consists of the threat in combination with resulting unfairness. Such a threat is not improper if it can be shown that the exchange is one on fair terms. Of course a threat may be improper for more than one reason. Any threat that comes within Subsection (1) as well as Subsection (2) is improper without an inquiry, under the rule stated in Subsection (2), into the fairness of the resulting exchange.

Comment b.   Crime or tort. A threat is improper if the threatened act is a crime or a tort, as in the traditional examples of threats of physical violence and of wrongful seizure or retention of goods. See Comment *a.* Where physical violence is threatened, it need not be to the recipient of the threat, nor even to a person related to him, if the threat in fact induces the recipient to manifest his assent. See Illustration 2. The threatened act need not involve harm to person or goods but may, for example, involve a tortious interference with another's contractual rights. Where the crime or tort is a minor one, however, the claim of duress may fail, even though the threat is improper, on the ground that the victim had a reasonable alternative (see Comment *b* to § 175) or that the threat was not an inducing cause (see Comment *c* to § 175). The threatened act need not be a crime or tort if the threat itself would have been one had it resulted in the obtaining of property. Therefore, in jurisdictions where a broad modern extortion statute has been enacted, many of the threats that come within Subsection (2) are elements of the crime of extortion and therefore also fall within Clause (1)(a). See Model Penal Code § 223.4. The fairness of the exchange is immaterial in such cases.

Illustrations

1. A is a good faith purchaser for value of a valuable painting stolen from B. When B demands the return of the painting, A threatens to poison B unless he releases all rights to the painting for $1,000. B, having no reasonable alternative, is induced by A's threat to sign the release, and A pays him $1,000. The threatened act is both a crime and a tort, and the release is voidable by B.

2. A threatens B that he will kill C, an employee of B, unless B makes a contract to sell A a tract of land that B owns. B, having no reasonable alternative, is induced by A's threat to make the contract. The threatened act is both a crime and a tort, and the contract is voidable by B.

3. A, a pawnbroker, has possession of a valuable heirloom pledged by B. B offers to redeem the pledge, but A threatens not to surrender it unless B signs a promissory note in compromise of another claim, the validity of which is in dispute. B, having no reasonable alternative, is induced by A's threat to sign the note. The threatened act is a tort, and the note is voidable by B.

Comment c.   Threat of prosecution. Under the rule stated in Clause (1)(b), a threat of criminal prosecution is improper as a means of inducing the recipient to make a contract. An explanation in good faith of the criminal consequences of another's conduct may not involve a threat. But if a threat is made, the fact that the one who makes it honestly believes that the recipient is guilty is not material. The threat involves a misuse, for personal gain, of power given for other legitimate ends. See Comment *f.* The threat may be to instigate prosecution against the recipient or some third person, who is commonly although not necessarily a relative of the recipient. The guilt or innocence of the person whose prosecution is threatened is immaterial in determining whether the threat is improper, although it may be easier to show that the threat actually induced assent in the case of guilt. A bargain to suppress prosecution may be unenforceable on grounds of public policy. See the Introductory Note to Chapter 8 on agreements against public policy.

Illustrations

4. A, who believes that B, his employee, has embezzled money from him, threatens B that a criminal complaint will be

filed and he will be prosecuted immediately unless he executes a promissory note for $5,000 in satisfaction of A's claim. B, having no reasonable alternative, is induced by A's threat to sign the note. The note is voidable by B. A may, however, have a claim against B for restitution of any money embezzled. See Comment *d* to § 175.

5. A is the payee of a valid $5,000 promissory note executed by B for the repayment of money embezzled by B. A makes a threat to C, a friend of B, that a criminal complaint will be filed and B will be prosecuted immediately unless C becomes a surety on the note in consideration of an extension of time for its payment. C is induced by A's threat to become a surety. The suretyship contract is voidable by C.

Comment d.   *Threat of civil process.* The policy in favor of free access to the judicial system militates against the characterization as improper of threats to commence civil process, even if the claim on which the process is based eventually proves to be without foundation. Nevertheless, if the threat is shown to have been made in bad faith, it is improper. Bad faith may be shown by proving that the person making the threat did not believe there was a reasonable basis for the threatened process, that he knew the threat would involve a misuse of the process or that he realized the demand he made was exorbitant. See Comment *f.* However, a threat to commence civil process, even if improper, may not amount to duress since defense of the threatened action is often a reasonable alternative. See Comment *b* to § 175.

Illustrations

6. A threatens to commence a civil action and file a lis pendens against a tract of land owned by B, unless B makes a contract to discharge a disputed claim that B has against A. A knows that the threatened action is without foundation. B, having no reasonable alternative, is induced by A's threat to make the contract. Since A does not believe that there is a reasonable basis for the threatened process, his threat is made in bad faith. A's threat is improper, and the contract is voidable by B. If, however, A believes that there is a reasonable basis for the threatened process and if the proposed contract is not exorbitant, the threat is not improper, and the contract is not voidable by B.

7. A, who has a valid claim for damages against B, threatens to attach a shipment of perishable goods unless B makes a contract to sell a machine to A. As A knows, other non-perishable goods are available for attachment. B, having no reasonable alternative, is induced by A's threat to make the contract. Since A knows that the threatened attachment would involve a misuse of that process to force a settlement rather than to preserve assets, his threat is made in bad faith. A's threat is improper and the contract is voidable by B.

Comment e. Breach of contract. A threat by a party to a contract not to perform his contractual duty is not, of itself, improper. Indeed, a modification induced by such a threat may be binding, even in the absence of consideration, if it is fair and equitable in view of unanticipated circumstances. See § 89. The mere fact that the modification induced by the threat fails to meet this test does not mean that the threat is necessarily improper. However, the threat is improper if it amounts to a breach of the duty of good faith and fair dealing imposed by the contract. See § 205. As under the Uniform Commercial Code, the "extortion of a 'modification' without legitimate commercial reason is ineffective as a violation of the duty of good faith. The test of 'good faith' between merchants or as against merchants includes 'observance of reasonable commercial standards of fair dealing in the trade' (Section 2–103), and may in some situations require an objectively demonstrable reason for seeking a modification. But such matters as a market shift which makes performance come to involve a loss may provide such a reason even though there is no such unforeseen difficulty as would make out a legal excuse from performance under Sections 2–615 and 2–616." Comment 2 to Uniform Commercial Code § 2–209. However, a threat of non-performance made for some purpose unrelated to the contract, such as to induce the recipient to make an entirely separate contract, is ordinarily improper. See Illustration 9. Furthermore, a threat may be a breach of the duty of good faith and fair dealing under the contract even though the threatened act is not itself a breach of the contract. See Illustrations 10 and 11. This is particularly likely to be the case if the threat is effective because of power not derived from the contract itself. See Comment *f.*

Illustrations

8. A contracts to excavate a cellar for B at a stated price. A unexpectedly encounters solid rock and threatens not to finish the excavation unless B modifies the contract to state a new price that is reasonable but is nine times the original price. B, having no reasonable alternative, is induced by A's threat to make the modification by a signed writing that is enforceable by statute without consideration. A's threat is not a breach of his duty of good faith and fair dealing, and the modification is not voidable by B. See Illustration 1 to § 89.

9. A contracts to excavate a cellar for B at a stated price. A begins the excavation and then threatens not to finish it unless B makes a separate contract to excavate the cellar of another building. B, having no reasonable alternative, is induced by A's threat to make the contract. A's threat is a breach of his duty of good faith and fair dealing, and the proposed contract is voidable by B. See Illustration 5 to § 175.

10. A contracts to sell part of a tract of land to B. B, solely to induce A to discharge him from his contract duty on favorable terms, threatens to resell the land to a purchaser whose industrial use will have an undesirable effect on A's remaining land, unless A

releases B in return for a stated sum. A, having no reasonable alternative, signs the release. B's threat is a breach of his duty of good faith and fair dealing, and the modification is voidable by A.

11.   A makes a threat to discharge B, his employee, unless B releases a claim that he has against A. The employment agreement is terminable at the will of either party, so that the discharge would not be a breach by A. B, having no reasonable alternative, releases the claim. A's threat is a breach of his duty of good faith and fair dealing, and the release is voidable by B.

Comment f.   Other improper threats. The proper limits of bargaining are difficult to define with precision. Hard bargaining between experienced adversaries of relatively equal power ought not to be discouraged. Parties are generally held to the resulting agreement, even though one has taken advantage of the other's adversity, as long as the contract has been dictated by general economic forces. See Illustration 14. Where, however, a party has been induced to make a contract by some power exercised by the other for illegitimate ends, the transaction is suspect. For example, absent statute, a threat of refusal to deal with another party is ordinarily not duress, but if other factors are present an agreement that results from such a threat may be called into question. Subsection (2) deals with threats that are improper if the resulting exchange is not on fair terms. Clause (a) is concerned with cases in which a party threatens to do an act that would not significantly benefit him but would harm the other party. If, on the recipient's refusal to contract, the maker of the threat were to do the threatened act, it would therefore be done maliciously and unconscionably, out of pure vindictiveness. A typical example is a threat to make public embarrassing information concerning the recipient unless he makes a proposed contract. See Illustration 12 and Model Penal Code § 223.4(g). Clause (b) is concerned with cases in which the party making the threat has by unfair dealing achieved an advantage over the recipient that makes his threat unusually effective. Typical examples involve manipulative conduct during the bargaining stage that leaves one person at the mercy of the other. See Illustration 13. Clause (c) is concerned with other cases in which the threatened act involves the use of power for illegitimate ends. Many of the situations encompassed by clauses (1)(b), (1)(c), (2)(a) and (2)(b) involve extreme applications of this general rule, but it is more broadly applicable to analogous cases. See Illustrations 15 and 16. If, in any of these cases, the threat comes within Subsection (1), as where the threatened act or the threat itself is criminal or tortious (Clause (1)(a)), it is improper without an inquiry into the fairness of the resulting exchange under Subsection 2. See Comment *a*.

Illustrations

12.   A makes a threat to B, his former employee, that he will try to prevent B's employment elsewhere unless B agrees to release a claim that he has against A. B, having no reasonable alternative, is thereby induced to make the contract. If the court concludes that the attempt to prevent B's employment elsewhere

would harm B and would not significantly benefit A, A's threat is improper and the contract is voidable by B.

13.   A, who has sold goods to B on several previous occasions, intentionally misleads B into thinking that he will supply the goods at the usual price and thereby causes B to delay in attempting to buy them elsewhere until it is too late to do so. A then threatens not to sell the goods to B unless he agrees to pay a price greatly in excess of that charged previously. B, being in urgent need of the goods, makes the contract. If the court concludes that the effectiveness of A's threat in inducing B to make the contract was significantly increased by A's prior unfair dealing, A's threat is improper and the contract is voidable by B.

14.   The facts being otherwise as stated in Illustration 13, A merely discovers that B is in great need of the goods and that they are in short supply but does not mislead B into thinking that he will supply them. A's threat is not improper, and the contract is not voidable by B.

15.   A operates a fur storage concession for customers of B's store. A becomes bankrupt and fails to pay C $1,000 for charges for storing furs of B's customers. C makes a threat to B not to deliver the furs to B's customers unless B makes a contract to pay C the $1,000 plus $2,000 that A owes C for storage of other furs. B, afraid of offending its customers and having no reasonable alternative, makes the contract. If the court concludes that C's threat to B is a use for illegitimate ends of its power as against B to retain the furs for the $1,000 owed for the storage of furs for B's customers, C's threat is improper and the contract is voidable by B.

16.   A, a municipal water company, seeking to induce B, a developer, to make a contract for the extension of water mains to his development at a price greatly in excess of that charged to those similarly situated, threatens to refuse to supply to B unless B makes the contract. B, having no reasonable alternative, makes the contract. Because the threat amounts to a use for illegitimate ends of A's power not to supply water, the contract is voidable by B.

Post v. Jones

Supreme Court of the United States, 1857.
60 U.S. 150.

■ MR. JUSTICE GRIER delivered the opinion of the court.

The libellants, owners of the ship Richmond and cargo, filed the libel in this case for an adjustment of salvage.

They allege, that the ship Richmond left the port of Cold Spring, Long Island, on a whaling voyage to the North and South Pacific Ocean, in July,

1846; that on the 2d of August, 1849, in successful prosecution of her voyage, and having nearly a full cargo, she was run upon some rocks on the coast of Behring's Straits, about a half mile from shore; that while so disabled, the whaling ships Elizabeth Frith and the Panama, being in the same neighborhood, and about to return home, but not having full cargoes, each took on board some seven or eight hundred barrels of oil and a large quantity of whalebone from the Richmond; that these vessels have arrived in the port of Sag Harbor, and their owners are proceeding to sell said oil, & c., without adjusting or demanding salvage, unjustly setting up a pretended sale of the Richmond and her cargo to them by her master.

The libellants pray to have possession delivered to them of the oil, & c., or its proceeds, if sold, subject to "salvage and freight."

The claimants, who are owners of the ships Frith and Panama, allege, in their answer, that the Richmond was wholly and irrevocably wrecked; that her officers and crew had abandoned her, and gone on a barren and uninhabited shore near by; that there were no inhabitants or persons on that part of the globe, from whom any relief could be obtained, or who would accept her cargo, or take charge thereof, for a salvage compensation; that the cargo of the Richmond, though valuable in a good market, was of little or no value where she lay; that the season during which it was practicable to remain was nigh its close; that the entire destruction of both vessel and cargo was inevitable, and the loss of the lives of the crew almost certain; that, under these circumstances, the master of the Richmond concluded to sell the vessel at auction, and so much of her cargo as was desired by the persons present, which was done on the following day, with the assent of the whole ship's company.

Respondents aver that this sale was a fair, honest, and valid sale of the property, made from necessity, in good faith, and for the best interests of all concerned, and that they are the rightful and bona fide owners of the portions of the cargo respectively purchased by them.

The District Court decreed in favor of claimants; on appeal to the Circuit Court, this decree was reversed; the sale was pronounced void, and the respondents treated as salvors only, and permitted to retain a moiety of the proceeds of the property as salvage.

The claimants have appealed to this court, and the questions proposed for our consideration are, 1st, whether, under the peculiar circumstances of this case, the sale should be treated as conferring a valid title; and, if not, 2d, whether the salvage allowed was sufficient.

1. In the examination of the first question, we shall not inquire whether there is any truth in the allegation that the master of the Richmond was in such a state of bodily and mental infirmity as to render him incapable of acting; or whether he was governed wholly by the undue influence and suggestions of his brother, the master of the Frith. For the decision of this point, it will not be found necessary to impute to him either weakness of intellect or want of good faith.

It cannot be doubted that a master has power to sell both vessel and cargo in certain cases of absolute necessity. This, though now the received doctrine of the modern English and American cases, has not been universally received as a principle of maritime law. The Consulado del Mare (art. 253) allows the master a power to sell, when a vessel becomes unseaworthy from age; while the laws of Oleron and Wisby, and the ancient French ordinances, deny such power to the master in any case. The reason given by Valin is, that such a permission, under any circumstances, would tend to encourage fraud. But, while the power is not denied, its exercise should be closely scrutinized by the court, lest it be abused. Without pretending to enumerate or classify the multitude of cases on this subject, or to state all the possible conditions under which this necessity may exist, we may say that it is applied to cases where the vessel is disabled, stranded, or sunk; where the master has no means and can raise no funds to repair her so as to prosecute his voyage; yet, where the spes recuperandi may have a value in the market, or the boats, the anchor, or the rigging, are or may be saved, and have a value in market; where the cargo, though damaged has a value, because it has a market, and it may be for the interest of all concerned that it be sold. All the cases assume the fact of a sale, in a civilized country, where men have money, where there is a market and competition. They have no application to wreck in a distant ocean, where the property is derelict, or about to become so, and the person who has it in his power to save the crew and salve the cargo prefers to drive a bargain with the master. The necessity in such a case may be imperative, because it is the price of safety, but it is not of that character which permits the master to exercise this power.

As many of the circumstances attending this case are peculiar and novel, it may not be improper to give a brief statement of them. The Richmond, after a ramble of three years on the Pacific, in pursuit of whales, had passed through the sea of Anadin, and was near Behring's Straits, in the Arctic ocean, on the 2d of August, 1849. She had nearly completed her cargo, and was about to return; but, during a thick fog, she was run upon rocks, within half a mile of the shore, and in a situation from which it was impossible to extricate her. The master and crew escaped in their boats to the shore, holding communication with the vessel, without much difficulty or danger. They could probably have transported the cargo to the beach, but this would have been unprofitable labor, as its condition would not have been improved. Though saved from the ocean, it would not have been safe. The coast was barren; the few inhabitants, savages and thieves. This ocean is navigable for only about two months in the year; during the remainder of the year it is sealed up with ice. The winter was expected to commence within fifteen or twenty days, at farthest. The nearest port of safety and general commercial intercourse was at the Sandwich Islands, five thousand miles distant. Their only hope of escape from this inhospitable region was by means of other whaling vessels, which were known to be cruising at no great distance, and who had been in company with the Richmond, and had pursued the same course.

On the 5th of August the fog cleared off, and the ship Elizabeth Frith was seen at a short distance. The officers of the Richmond immediately went on board, and the master informed the master of the Frith of the disaster which had befallen the Richmond. He requested him to take his crew on board, and said, "You need not whale any more; there is plenty of oil there, which you may take, and get away as soon as possible." On the following day they took on board the Frith about 300 barrels oil from the Richmond. On the 6th, the Panama and the Junior came near; they had not quite completed their cargoes; as there was more oil in the Richmond than they could all take, it was proposed that they also should complete their cargoes in the same way. Captain Tinkham, of the Junior, proposed to take part of the crew of the Richmond, and said he would take part of the oil, "provided it was put up and sold at auction." In pursuance of this suggestion, advertisements were posted on each of the three vessels, signed by or for the master of the Richmond. On the following day the forms of an auction sale were enacted; the master of the Frith bidding one dollar per barrel for as much as he needed, and the others seventy-five cents. The ship and tackle were sold for five dollars; no money was paid, and no account kept or bill of sale made out. Each vessel took enough to complete her cargo of oil and bone. The transfer was effected in a couple of days, with some trouble and labor, but little or no risk or danger, and the vessels immediately proceeded on their voyage, stopping as usual at the Sandwich Islands.

Now, it is evident, from this statement of the facts, that, although the Richmond was stranded near the shore upon which her crew and even her cargo might have been saved from the dangers of the sea, they were really in no better situation as to ultimate safety than if foundered or disabled in the midst of the Pacific ocean. The crew were glad to escape with their lives. The ship and cargo, though not actually derelict, must necessarily have been abandoned. The contrivance of an auction sale, under such circumstances, where the master of the Richmond was hopeless, helpless, and passive—where there was no market, no money, no competition— where one party had absolute power, and the other no choice but submission—where the vendor must take what is offered or get nothing—is a transaction which has no characteristic of a valid contract. It has been contended by the claimants that it would be a great hardship to treat this sale as a nullity, and thus compel them to assume the character of salvors, because they were not bound to save this property, especially at so great a distance from any port of safety, and in a place where they could have completed their cargo in a short time from their own catchings, and where salvage would be no compensation for the loss of this opportunity. The force of these arguments is fully appreciated, but we think they are not fully sustained by the facts of the case. Whales may have been plenty around their vessels on the 6th and 7th of August, but, judging of the future from the past, the anticipation of filling up their cargo in the few days of the season in which it would be safe to remain, was very uncertain, and barely probable. The whales were retreating towards the north pole, where they could not be pursued, and, though seen in numbers on one days, they would disappear on the next; and, even when seen in greatest numbers, their capture was uncertain. By this transaction, the vessels were enabled to proceed at once on their home voyage; and the certainty of a liberal salvage allowance for the property rescued with be ample compensation for the possible chance of greater profits, by refusing their assistance in saving their neighbor's property.

It has been contended, also, that the sale was justifiable and valid, because it was better for the interests of all concerned to accept what was offered, than suffer a total loss. But this argument proves too much, as it would justify every sale to a salvor. Courts of admiralty will enforce contracts made for salvage service and salvage compensation, where the salvor has not taken advantage of his power to make an unreasonable bargain; but they will not tolerate the doctrine that a salvor can take the advantage of his situation, and avail himself of the calamities of others to drive a bargain; nor will they permit the performance of a public duty to be turned into a traffic of profit. (See 1 Sumner, 210.) The general interests of commerce will be much better promoted by requiring the salvor to trust for compensation to the liberal recompense usually awarded by courts for such services are of opinion, therefore, that the claimants have not obtained a valid title to the property in dispute, but must be treated as salvors.

Order,

This cause came on to be heard on the transcript of the record from the Circuit Court of the United States for the southern district of New York, and was argued by counsel. On consideration whereof, it is now here ordered and decreed by this court, that the decree of the said Circuit Court in this cause be and the same is hereby reversed, and that this cause be and the same is hereby remanded to the said Circuit Court, with directions to have the amount due to each party adjusted, according to the principles stated in the opinion of this court, and that all the costs of said cause in this court, and in the Circuit and District Courts, be paid out of the fund in the said Circuit Court.

Austin Instruments, Inc. v. Loral Corp.

Court of Appeals of New York, 1971.
272 N.E.2d 533.

■ FULD, J. The defendant, Loral Corporation, seeks to recover payment for goods delivered under a contract which it had with plaintiff Austin Instrument, Inc., on the ground that the evidence establishes, as a matter of law, that it was forced to agree to an increase in price on the items in question under circumstances amounting to economic duress.

In July of 1965, Loral was awarded a $6,000,000 contract by the Navy for the production of radar sets. The contract contained a schedule of deliveries, a liquidated damages clause applying to late deliveries and a cancellation clause in case of default by Loral. The latter thereupon solicited bids for some 40 precision gear components needed to produce the radar sets, and awarded Austin a subcontract to supply 23 such parts. That party commenced delivery in early 1966.

In May, 1966, Loral was awarded a second Navy contract for the production of more radar sets and again went about soliciting bids. Austin bid on all 40 gear components but, on July 15, a representative from Loral informed Austin's president, Mr. Krauss, that his company would be awarded the subcontract only for those items on which it was low bidder. The Austin officer refused to accept an order for less than all 40 of the gear parts and on the next day he told Loral that Austin would cease deliveries of the parts due under the existing subcontract unless Loral consented to substantial increases in the prices provided for by that agreement—both retroactively for parts already delivered and prospectively on those not yet shipped—and placed with Austin the order for all 40 parts needed under Loral's second Navy contract. Shortly thereafter, Austin did, indeed, stop delivery. After contacting 10 manufacturers of precision gears and finding none who could produce the parts in time to meet its commitments to the Navy, Loral acceded to Austin's demands; in a letter dated July 22, Loral wrote to Austin that "We have feverishly surveyed other sources of supply and find that because of the prevailing military exigencies, were they to start from scratch as would have to be the case, they could not even remotely begin to deliver on time to meet the delivery requirements established by the Government. Accordingly, we are left with no choice or alternative but to meet your conditions."

Loral thereupon consented to the price increases insisted upon by Austin under the first subcontract and the latter was awarded a second subcontract making it the supplier of all 40 gear parts for Loral's second contract with the Navy. Although Austin was granted until September to resume deliveries, Loral did, in fact, receive parts in August and was able to produce the radar sets in time to meet its commitments to the Navy on both contracts. After Austin's last delivery under the second subcontract in July, 1967, Loral notified it of its intention to seek recovery of the price increases.

On September 15, 1967, Austin instituted this action against Loral to recover an amount in excess of $17,750 which was still due on the second subcontract. On the same day, Loral commenced an action against Austin claiming damages of some $22,250—the aggregate of the price increases under the first subcontract—on the ground of economic duress. The two actions were consolidated and, following a trial, Austin was awarded the sum it requested and Loral's complaint against Austin was dismissed on the ground that it was not shown that "it could not have obtained the items in question from other sources in time to meet its commitment to the Navy under the first contract." A closely divided Appellate Division affirmed (35 A D 2d 387). There was no material disagreement concerning the facts; as Justice Steuer stated in the course of his dissent below, "[the] facts are virtually undisputed, nor is there any serious question of law. The difficulty lies in the application of the law to these facts." (35 A D 2d 392.)

The applicable law is clear and, indeed, is not disputed by the parties. A contract is voidable on the ground of duress when it is established that the party making the claim was forced to agree to it by means of a wrongful threat precluding the exercise of his free will. The existence of economic duress or business compulsion is demonstrated by proof that "immediate possession of needful goods is threatened" (*Mercury Mach.* Importing Corp. v. City of New York, 3 N Y 2d 418, 425) or, more particularly, in cases such as the one before us, by proof that one party to a contract has threatened to breach the agreement by withholding goods unless the other party agrees to some further demand. However, a mere threat by one party to breach the contract by not delivering the required items, though wrongful, does not in itself constitute economic duress. It must also appear that the threatened party could not obtain the goods from another source of supply and that the ordinary remedy of an action for breach of contract would not be adequate.

We find without any support in the record the conclusion reached by the courts below that Loral failed to establish that it was the victim of economic duress. On the contrary, the evidence makes out a classic case, as a matter of law, of such duress.

It is manifest that Austin's threat—to stop deliveries unless the prices were increased—deprived Loral of its free will. As bearing on this, Loral's relationship with the Government is most significant. As mentioned above, its contract called for staggered monthly deliveries of the radar sets, with clauses calling for liquidated damages and possible cancellation on default. Because of its production schedule, Loral was, in July, 1966, concerned with meeting its delivery requirements in September, October and November, and it was for the sets to be delivered in those months that the withheld gears were needed. Loral had to plan ahead, and the substantial liquidated damages for which it would be liable, plus the threat of default, were genuine possibilities. Moreover, Loral did a substantial portion of its business with the Government, and it feared that a failure to deliver as agreed upon would jeopardize its chances for future contracts. These genuine concerns do not merit the label " 'self-imposed, undisclosed and subjective' " which the Appellate Division majority placed upon them. It was perfectly reasonable for Loral, or any other party similarly placed, to consider itself in an emergency, duress situation.

Austin, however, claims that the fact that Loral extended its time to resume deliveries until September negates its alleged dire need for the parts. A Loral official testified on this point that Austin's president told him he could deliver some parts in August and that the extension of deliveries was a formality. In any event, the parts necessary for production of the radar sets to be delivered in September were delivered to Loral on September 1, and the parts needed for the October schedule were delivered in late August and early September. Even so, Loral had to "work around the clock" to meet its commitments. Considering that the best offer Loral received from the other vendors it contacted was commencement of delivery sometime in October, which, as the record shows, would have made it late in its deliveries to the Navy in both September and October, Loral's claim that it had no choice but to accede to Austin's demands is conclusively demonstrated.

We find unconvincing Austin's contention that Loral, in order to meet its burden, should have contacted the Government and asked for an extension of its delivery dates so as to enable it to purchase the parts from another vendor. Aside from the consideration that Loral was anxious to perform well in the Government's eyes, it could not be sure when it would obtain enough parts from a substitute vendor to meet its commitments. The only promise which it received from the companies it contacted was for *commencement* of deliveries, not full supply, and, with vendor delay common in this field, it would have been nearly impossible to know the length of the extension it should request. It must be remembered that Loral was producing a needed item of military hardware. Moreover, there is authority for Loral's position that nonperformance by a subcontractor is not an excuse for default in the main contract. In light of all this, Loral's claim should not be held insufficiently supported because it did not request an extension from the Government.

Loral, as indicated above, also had the burden of demonstrating that it could not obtain the parts elsewhere within a reasonable time, and there can be no doubt that it met this burden. The 10 manufacturers whom Loral contacted comprised its entire list of "approved vendors" for precision gears, and none was able to commence delivery soon enough. As Loral was producing a highly sophisticated item of military machinery requiring parts made to the strictest engineering standards, it would be unreasonable to hold that Loral should have gone to other vendors, with whom it was either unfamiliar or dissatisfied, to procure the needed parts. As Justice Steuer noted in his dissent, Loral "contacted all the manufacturers whom it believed capable of making these parts" (35 A D 2d, at p. 393), and this was all the law requires.

It is hardly necessary to add that Loral's normal legal remedy of accepting Austin's breach of the contract and then suing for damages would have been inadequate under the circumstances, as Loral would still have had to obtain the gears elsewhere with all the concomitant consequences mentioned above. In other words, Loral actually had no choice, when the prices were raised by Austin, except to take the gears at the "coerced" prices and then sue to get the excess back.

Austin's final argument is that Loral, even if it did enter into the contract under duress, lost any rights it had to a refund of money by waiting until July, 1967, long after the termination date of the contract, to disaffirm it. It is true that one who would recover moneys allegedly paid under duress must act promptly to make his claim known. In this case, Loral delayed making its demand for a refund until three days after Austin's last delivery on the second subcontract. Loral's reason—for waiting until that time—is that it feared another stoppage of deliveries which would again put it in an untenable situation. Considering Austin's conduct in the past, this was perfectly reasonable, as the possibility of an application by Austin of further business compulsion still existed until all of the parts were delivered.

In sum, the record before us demonstrates that Loral agreed to the price increases in consequence of the economic duress employed by Austin. Accordingly, the matter should be remanded to the trial court for a computation of its damages.

The order appealed from should be modified, with costs, by reversing so much thereof as affirms the dismissal of defendant Loral Corporation's claim and, except as so modified, affirmed.

Alaska Packers Ass'n v. Domenico

Circuit Court of Appeals for the Ninth Circuit, 1902.
117 Fed. 99.

(Reprised from Chapter 15)

* * *

These materials raise questions along two dimensions. First, what degree of pressure is required before the pressure overcomes a party's freedom in a manner that constitutes duress and hence allows her to avoid contractual obligations incurred on account of the pressure. And second, when is the purpose or motivation behind pressure imposed on a contracting party improper in the fashion required to trigger the duress doctrine.

Begin by taking up the first question. Restatement (Second) § 174 addresses an easy instance in which a person's freedom may be overcome: this is what the comment to the Restatement section calls the "relatively rare situation[] in which actual physical force has been used to compel a party to appear to assent to a contract." In this case, the apparent assent is not only not free but not even *intentional*, and the contract is not only voidable by the compelled party, but void.

Further cases become much more difficult. In these cases, duress involves no physical compulsion, and the person subject to duress intends to act as she does. But the duress nevertheless deprives the person of meaningful freedom. In the words of the Restatement, it "leaves the victim no reasonable alternative" to making the contract that it imposes on her. And, as she has had no reasonable alternative, the law permits the victim of duress to void her contract (subject to restrictions whose general sense is captured in Restatement (Second) of Contracts § 175(2)). This language, of course, at once invites further questions, concerning just when a person actually has no reasonable alternative to agreeing to a contract.

Post presents a fairly straightforward example of such a case. The plaintiff's whaling ship had foundered with a cargo of whale oil aboard. Although the crew could have reached land, the nearest "coast was barren; the few inhabitants, savages and thieves." A safe harbor and the plaintiff's home port were both thousands of miles away. Several passing ships rescued the plaintiff's crew and cargo, but only after conducting an "auction" in which the cargo was "sold" to the rescuing ships. The sales prices fell far below the cargo's value and also below both its economic return to the rescuing ships (even including the lost opportunities they incurred by filling their holds with the plaintiff's cargo rather than their own catches) and the cargo's salvage allowance under maritime law. After the crew and cargo had been returned to the plaintiff's home port, the plaintiff sued, seeking to invalidate the sale and to treat the rescuers as salvors rather than purchasers. The *Post* court found in the plaintiff's favor, in spite of the fact that the defendants were under no duty to save the plaintiff's property. The facts of *Post* entailed that the plaintiff had literally no alternative means of selling its cargo save selling it to the defendants, on their terms. And simply allowing the cargo to be lost was also not reasonable. In this sense, *Post* is an easy case.[19]

But other cases are much harder. The reason why they are harder is simple: in all circumstances in which there is an optimal action, persons who know it have no reasonable alternatives to taking that action. In this sense, the "auction" in *Post* was no more coercive than an everyday sale, in which demand (low, or even high) contributes to fixing the price that a seller receives. Sellers facing few buyers receive lower prices than sellers facing many buyers, and they do so because they are constrained in how they might reasonably dispose of their goods. But such constraint does by itself not render them subject to duress, or unfree. Moreover, sellers facing many buyers, who receive extremely attractive offers, are similarly compelled by reason to accept the best ones. Indeed, the attractiveness of the offers makes the strength of the reasons for accepting all the more palpable. But it would be odd indeed, without a great deal more, to call such attractive offers coercive.[20] None of this shakes the strong intuitive sense that there was duress in *Post* as there is not in ordinary sales. It merely reveals that the language of the Restatement—concerning the absence of reasonable alternatives—does not explain or justify this sense but is, instead, conclusory.

---

19. *Post* is structurally very similar to any number of more commonplace forms of price-gouging: charging dramatically supra-normal prices for water or fuel during a hurricane (and attendant blackout) or for snow-plowing in the middle of a blizzard. Various states have enacted circumstance-specific anti-price-gouging statutes. See, e.g.,. N.Y. GEN. BUS. LAW § 396–r(1) (2008), and CONN. GEN. STAT. § 42–230 (2008). Some jurisdictions have adopted an open and general anti-price-gouging doctrine, which limits price hikes in response to emergencies or other unusual contingencies to a fixed multiple of normal prices. For example, in cases in which a state of emergency or a local emergency has been declared, CAL. PENAL CODE § 369 (2009) provides that "it is unlawful for a contractor to sell or offer to sell any repair or reconstruction services or any services used in emergency cleanup for a price of more than 10 percent above the price charged by that person for those services immediately prior to the proclamation of emergency" barring a proven increase in cost of goods or labor.

20. Coercive offers are possible. Intuitively, coercion on this model arises most clearly where an offer's attractiveness is set against a backdrop in which (for reasons that need have nothing to do with the conduct of the offeror) the offeree will do very badly on rejecting the offer. One might illustrate this possibility by returning to an earlier topic: an offer to pay an impoverished woman a genuinely attractive sum in order to serve as a gestational surrogate may be coercive, regardless of how high the sum is, if the woman's poverty is sufficiently bad and she has no other ways to acquire money.

The second question raised by the duress doctrine—concerning when a threat is improper (or, on some views, when an argument inducing action constitutes a *threat* properly-so-called)—is similarly difficult. *Austin Instruments* and *Alaska Packers* illustrate the difficulty. Both cases involved threats to breach existing contracts on whose performance the threats' victims had relied, made in order to extract new contracts with favorable terms. Courts considered the threats in both cases improper and relieved the threats' victims of the obligations that the contracts extracted under threat would otherwise have imposed. In *Austin Instruments*, the court openly held the contract voidable on grounds of duress. In *Alaska Packers*, the court held the contract void for want of consideration; even though, as the earlier discussion of that case revealed, the court's argument concerning consideration could not formally succeed, so that the gravamen of its holding must lie in duress. In both cases, it requires argument to explain the wrongfulness of the threats in question, and the required arguments are not obviously available. The facts of *Austin Instruments* illustrate the problem. On the one hand, it plainly is not improper to exploit a generic bargaining advantage in order to capture contractual surplus; and on the other hand, as the theory of efficient breach makes plain, it is equally plainly not improper to breach an existing contract in order to gain greater returns from other opportunities. And the party accused of duress in *Austin Instruments* merely combined these strategies: it threatened to breach an existing contract in pursuit of opportunities associated with the bargaining advantages that this very threat created. It is not obvious why two rights make a wrong.

The Restatement answers the question, but not in a way that dissolves the mystery. Thus whereas the common law doctrine of duress traditionally characterized the required impropriety of threats in a way that emphasized illegality (or its close-cousins), the Restatement (Second) of Contracts expands what counts as improper. Under the new approach, impropriety may include not just crimes and torts but also (under § 176(1)(d)) violations of the contractual duty of good faith and fair dealing and even (under § 176(2)) the general pursuit of illegitimate ends by means of imposing unfair exchanges. Of course, the Restatement formulations do not interpret themselves, and so it is not obvious how they might decide cases. In *Alaska Packers*,[21] the fishermen who made the threat induced a renegotiation of the terms of their employment that increased their wages, and this might be characterized as a bad faith effort to exploit their employers' (contractually induced) strategic vulnerability in order to recapture contractual surplus that their initial agreement had allocated to the employers. On the other hand, the fishermen claimed that their working conditions and work tools were worse than expected, so that the new contract might also be understood as a proper attempt to enforce rights given them by the old one. No mere language can settle which account is the correct one. And *Austin*

---

21. That case was of course decided under the older regime, and this might explain why duress did not play much of an explicit role in the opinion. Nevertheless, one might ask how the case would be decided if adjudicated as a case concerning duress, under the approach of the Restatement (Second).

Instruments presents a problem that is, if anything, more difficult still. In that case, the allegedly improper pressure, although made possible by the existence of a prior contract and reliance thereon, was used to extract surplus not from the existing contract but from a new one, which no party to the existing contract had any obligation to agree to on any terms. Any bad faith involved in the case thus most immediately concerned not the performance of the original contract but the negotiation of the new one. And there is, familiarly, no generalized duty of good faith in negotiations at common law. So however intuitively clear it might be, the impropriety in *Austin Instruments* remains in need of a theoretical explanation, something that neither the Restatement nor the court provides.

These observations simply play out, in application to particular contexts, general themes concerning that have long been familiar to lawyers and philosophers. An early and powerful American statement of the problem is Robert Hale's *Coercion and Distribution in a Supposedly Non–Coercive State*,[22] which pointed out that in spite of all the talk of individual liberty associated with free markets and freedom of contract, the legal orders that adopt these norms are replete with state-backed brute force.[23] Whether or not the force warrants the negative characterization *coercion* and all the consequences that follow depends on whether the force is employed in circumstances and towards ends that are judged unjust for independent reasons. And so the idea of coercion, characterized in terms of flat freedom and its opposite, and free of already moralized judgments, cannot settle any important disputes. A more recent engagement with the same theme is Robert Nozick's *Coercion*,[24] which emphasizes that in order to decide whether pressure amounts to a coercive threat, one must say whether the consequences that produce the pressure would leave its victim worse off than she would have been in the normal and expected course of events, where "normal and expected" straddles predicted and morally

---

22. 38 POLITICAL SCIENCE QUARTERLY (1923).

23. An older, European version of this argument also exists. It is the Marxist discussion of money fetishism, namely the claim that capitalist ideology concerning money disguises a relation of constraint as a thing.

The thing-ness of money is easy to perceive, especially from within the capitalist ideological frame. We pursue money, we own it, we even hold it in our hand.

To see that money is nevertheless really a relation of constraint, conduct the following thought experiment. Suppose that the state issued tickets which named goods and services: "one cashmere sweater," "one train trip from Boston to New York," and so on. Holders of tickets could use the things named on them; but if others tried, officers with guns would prevent them, and the state would punish them. There is no doubt that the tickets in the thought experiment are not things—they simply mark the permissions and prohibitions that the state imposes. But money is just an elaborate system of such tickets: a money bill is a disjunction of conjunctions granting permission for its holder to avail herself of all goods and services whose total price is equal to or lower than its face value.

Once one sees this, the thing-ness of money falls away. Money is revealed for what it really is—a system of marking permissions and prohibitions—which is to say constraints—imposed by the state. This discussion follows G. A. Cohen, *Back to Socialist Basics*, NEW LEFT REVIEW I/207 (September–October 1994).

24. Robert Nozick, *Coercion,* in PHILOSOPHY, SCIENCE, AND METHOD: ESSAYS IN HONOR OF ERNEST NAGEL, Sidney Morgenbesser, Patrick Suppes, and Morton White (eds.), New York: St. Martin's Press, 440–472 (1969).

required. Once again, cases of coercion cannot be adjudicated based on ideas of flat freedom and constraint, and without reference to antecedently justified principles of entitlement.

24.2.B.2   Undue Influence

Duress proper requires clear wrongfulness and overwhelming coercion. But in some circumstances, contracts might be have dubious validity even though the pressures used to extract them are less stark. This possibility arises especially where the victim of the pressure is vulnerable or stands antecedently in a special relationship to the party exerting the pressure. One doctrinal heading under which such cases are adjudicated is undue influence.

Restatement (Second) of Contracts

§ 177.   When Undue Influence Makes A Contract Voidable

(1) Undue influence is unfair persuasion of a party who is under the domination of the person exercising the persuasion or who by virtue of the relation between them is justified in assuming that that person will not act in a manner inconsistent with his welfare.

(2) If a party's manifestation of assent is induced by undue influence by the other party, the contract is voidable by the victim.

(3) If a party's manifestation of assent is induced by one who is not a party to the transaction, the contract is voidable by the victim unless the other party to the transaction in good faith and without reason to know of the undue influence either gives value or relies materially on the transaction.

Comments & Illustrations

Comment a.   Required domination or relation. The rule stated in this Section protects a person only if he is under the domination of another or is justified, by virtue of his relation with another in assuming that the other will not act inconsistently with his welfare. Relations that often fall within the rule include those of parent and child, husband and wife, clergyman and parishioner, and physician and patient. In each case it is a question of fact whether the relation is such as to give undue weight to the other's attempts at persuasion. The required relation may be found in situations other than those enumerated. However, the mere fact that a party is weak, infirm or aged does not of itself suffice, although it may be a factor in determining whether the required relation existed.

Comment b.   Unfair persuasion. Where the required domination or relation is present, the contract is voidable if it was induced by any unfair persuasion on the part of the stronger party. The law of undue influence therefore affords protection in situations where the rules on duress and misrepresentation give no relief. The degree of persuasion that is unfair depends on a variety of circumstances. The ultimate question is whether the result was produced by means that seriously impaired the free and competent exercise of judgment. Such factors as the unfairness of the resulting bargain, the unavailability of independent advice, and the susceptibility of the person persuaded are circumstances to be taken into account in determining whether there was unfair persuasion, but they are not in themselves controlling. Compare § 173.

Illustrations

1.   A, who is not experienced in business, has for years been accustomed to rely in business matters on the advice of his friend, B, who is experienced in business. B constantly urges A to make a contract to sell to C, B's confederate, a tract of land at a price that is well below its fair value. A is thereby induced to make the contract. Even though B's conduct does not amount to misrepresentation, it amounts to undue influence because A is justified in assuming that B will not act in a manner inconsistent with his welfare, and the contract is voidable.

2.   A, an elderly and illiterate man, lives with and depends for his support on B, his nephew. B tells A that he will no longer support him unless A makes a contract to sell B a tract of land. A is thereby induced to make the proposed contract. Even though B's conduct does not amount to duress, it amounts to undue influence because A is under the domination of B, and the contract is voidable by A.

Comment c.   Undue influence by a third person. If a party's assent has been induced by the undue influence of a third person rather than that of the other party to the contract, the contract is nevertheless voidable by the victim, unless the other party has in good faith either given value or changed his position materially in reliance on the transaction. The rule is similar to that for misrepresentation (see Comment *c* to § 164) and duress (see Comment *b* to § 175). Compare Illustration 1.

Vokes v. Arthur Murray, Inc.

District Court of Appeal of Florida, 1968.
212 So.2d 906.

■ PIERCE, JUDGE.

This is an appeal by Audrey E. Vokes, plaintiff below, from a final order dismissing with prejudice, for failure to state a cause of action, her fourth amended complaint, hereinafter referred to as plaintiff's complaint.

Defendant Arthur Murray, Inc., a corporation, authorizes the operation throughout the nation of dancing schools under the name of 'Arthur Murray School of Dancing' through local franchised operators, one of whom was defendant J. P. Davenport whose dancing establishment was in Clearwater.

Plaintiff Mrs. Audrey E. Vokes, a widow of 51 years and without family, had a yen to be 'an accomplished dancer' with the hopes of finding 'new interest in life'. So, on February 10, 1961, a dubious fate, with the assist of a motivated acquaintance, procured her to attend a 'dance party' at Davenport's 'School of Dancing' where she whiled away the pleasant hours, sometimes in a private room, absorbing his accomplished sales technique, during which her grace and poise were elaborated upon and her rosy future as 'an excellent dancer' was painted for her in vivid and glowing colors. As an incident to this interlude, he sold her eight 1/2–hour dance lessons to be utilized within one calendar month therefrom, for the sum of $14.50 cash in hand paid, obviously a baited 'comeon'.

Thus she embarked upon an almost endless pursuit of the terpsichorean art during which, over a period of less than sixteen months, she was sold fourteen 'dance courses' totalling in the aggregate 2302 hours of dancing lessons for a total cash outlay of $31,090.45, all at Davenport's dance emporium. All of these fourteen courses were evidenced by execution of a written 'Enrollment Agreement—Arthur Murray's School of Dancing' with the addendum in heavy black print, 'No one will be informed that you are taking dancing lessons. Your relations with us are held in strict confidence', setting forth the number of 'dancing lessons' and the 'lessons in rhythm sessions' currently sold to her from time to time, and always of course accompanied by payment of cash of the realm.

These dance lesson contracts and the monetary consideration therefor of over $31,000 were procured from her by means and methods of Davenport and his associates which went beyond the unsavory, yet legally permissible, perimeter of 'sales puffing' and intruded well into the forbidden area of undue influence, the suggestion of falsehood, the suppression of truth, and the free exercise of rational judgment, if what plaintiff alleged in her complaint was true. From the time of her first contact with the dancing school in February, 1961, she was influenced unwittingly by a constant and continuous barrage of flattery, false praise, excessive compliments, and panegyric encomiums, to such extent that it would be not only inequitable, but unconscionable, for a Court exercising inherent chancery power to allow such contracts to stand.

She was incessantly subjected to overreaching blandishment and cajolery. She was assured she had 'grace and poise'; that she was 'rapidly improving and developing in her dancing skill'; that the additional lessons would 'make her a beautiful dancer, capable of dancing with the most accomplished dancers'; that she was 'rapidly progressing in the development of her dancing skill and gracefulness', etc., etc. She was given 'dance aptitude tests' for the ostensible purpose of 'determining' the number of remaining hours instructions needed by her from time to time.

At one point she was sold 545 additional hours of dancing lessons to be entitled to award of the 'Bronze Medal' signifying that she had reached 'the Bronze Standard', a supposed designation of dance achievement by students of Arthur Murray, Inc.

Later she was sold an additional 926 hours in order to gain the 'Silver Medal', indicating she had reached 'the Silver Standard', at a cost of $12,501.35.

At one point, while she still had to her credit about 900 unused hours of instructions, she was induced to purchase an additional 24 hours of lessons to participate in a trip to Miami at her own expense, where she would be 'given the opportunity to dance with members of the Miami Studio'.

She was induced at another point to purchase an additional 123 hours of lessons in order to be not only eligible for the Miami trip but also to become 'a life member of the Arthur Murray Studio', carrying with it certain dubious emoluments, at a further cost of $1,752.30.

At another point, while she still had over 1,000 unused hours of instruction she was induced to buy 151 additional hours at a cost of $2,049.00 to be eligible for a 'Student Trip to Trinidad', at her own expense as she later learned.

Also, when she still had 1100 unused hours to her credit, she was prevailed upon to purchase an additional 347 hours at a cost of $4,235.74, to qualify her to receive a 'Gold Medal' for achievement, indicating she had advanced to 'the Gold Standard'.

On another occasion, while she still had over 1200 unused hours, she was induced to buy an additional 175 hours of instruction at a cost of $2,472.75 to be eligible 'to take a trip to Mexico'.

Finally, sandwiched in between other lesser sales promotions, she was influenced to buy an additional 481 hours of instruction at a cost of $6,523.81 in order to 'be classifies as a Gold Bar Member, the ultimate achievement of the dancing studio'.

All the foregoing sales promotions, illustrative of the entire fourteen separate contracts, were procured by defendant Davenport and Arthur Murray, Inc., by false representations to her that she was improving in her dancing ability, that she had excellent potential, that she was responding to instructions in dancing grace, and that they were developing her into a beautiful dancer, whereas in truth and in fact she did not develop in her dancing ability, she had no 'dance aptitude', and in fact had difficulty in 'hearing that musical beat'. The complaint alleged that such representations to her 'were in fact false and known by the defendant to be false and contrary to the plaintiff's true ability, the truth of plaintiff's ability being fully known to the defendants, but withheld from the plaintiff for the sole and specific intent to deceive and defraud the plaintiff and to induce her in the purchasing of additional hours of dance lessons'. It was averred that the lessons were sold to her 'in total disregard to the true physical, rhythm, and mental ability of the plaintiff'. In other words, while she first exulted that she was entering the 'spring of her life', she finally was awakened to the fact there was 'spring' neither in her life nor in her feet.

The complaint prayed that the Court decree the dance contracts to be null and void and to be cancelled, that an accounting be had, and judgment entered against, the defendants 'for that portion of the $31,090.45 not charged against specific hours of instruction given to the plaintiff'. The Court held the complaint not to state a cause of action and dismissed it with prejudice. We disagree and reverse.

The material allegations of the complaint must, of course, be accepted as true for the purpose of testing its legal sufficiency. Defendants contend that contracts can only be rescinded for fraud or misrepresentation when the alleged misrepresentation is as to a material fact, rather than an opinion, prediction or expectation, and that the statements and representations set forth at length in the complaint were in the category of 'trade puffing', within its legal orbit.

It is true that 'generally a misrepresentation, to be actionable, must be one of fact rather than of opinion'. But this rule has significant qualifications, applicable here. It does not apply where there is a fiduciary relationship between the parties, or where there has been some artifice or trick employed by the representor, or where the parties do not in general deal at 'arm's length' as we understand the phrase, or where the representee does not have equal opportunity to become apprised of the truth or falsity of the fact represented. As stated by Judge Allen of this Court in *Ramel v. Chasebrook Construction Company*, Fla.App.1961, 135 So.2d 876:

> 'A statement of a party having superior knowledge may be regarded as a statement of fact although it would be considered as opinion if the parties were dealing on equal terms.'

It could be reasonably supposed here that defendants had 'superior knowledge' as to whether plaintiff had 'dance potential' and as to whether she was noticeably improving in the art of terpsichore. And it would be a reasonable inference from the undenied averments of the complaint that the flowery eulogiums heaped upon her by defendants as a prelude to her contracting for 1944 additional hours of instruction in order to attain the rank of the Bronze Standard, thence to the bracket of the Silver Standard, thence to the class of the Gold Bar Standard, and finally to the crowning plateau of a Life Member of the Studio, proceeded as much or more from the urge to 'ring the cash register' as from any honest or realistic appraisal of her dancing prowess or a factual representation of her progress.

Even in contractual situations where a party to a transaction owes no duty to disclose facts within his knowledge or to answer inquiries respecting such facts, the law is if he undertakes to do so he must disclose the Whole truth. *Ramel v. Chasebrook Construction Company*, supra; *Beagle v. Bagwell*, Fla.App.1964, 169 So.2d 43. From the face of the complaint, it should have been reasonably apparent to defendants that her vast outlay of cash for the many hundreds of additional hours of instruction was not justified by her slow and awkward progress, which she would have been made well aware of if they had spoken the 'whole truth'.

In *Hirschman v. Hodges*, etc., 1910, 59 Fla. 517, 51 So. 550, it was said that—

'what is plainly injurious to good faith ought to be considered as a fraud sufficient to impeach a contract',

and that an improvident agreement may be avoided—

'because of surprise, or mistake, Want of freedom, undue influence, the suggestion of falsehood, or the suppression of truth'.

We repeat that where parties are dealing on a contractual basis at arm's length with no inequities or inherently unfair practices employed, the Courts will in general 'leave the parties where they find themselves'. But in the case sub judice, from the allegations of the unanswered complaint, we cannot say that enough of the accompanying ingredients, as mentioned in the foregoing authorities, were not present which otherwise would have barred the equitable arm of the Court to her. In our view, from the showing made in her complaint, plaintiff is entitled to her day in Court.

It accordingly follows that the order dismissing plaintiff's last amended complaint with prejudice should be and is reversed.

Reversed.

■ LILES, C.J., and MANN, J., concur.

* * *

As Restatement (Second) of Contracts § 177 makes plain, whereas a party may claim duress with respect to any other person (as long only as the circumstances establish requisitely powerful and wrongful coercion), claims of undue influence generally arise within ongoing relations of control and trust. These are the circumstances within which one person may ordinarily come under the domination of another or come justifiably to believe that the other is acting on her behalf. Many cases of undue influence in fact arise in the family setting, including in circumstances in which one family member influences another to contract unwisely with a third party.

Vokes illustrates that this is not the only setting in which undue influence may be exerted. It also illustrates a stark stylistic contrast between the doctrinal styles used to elaborate duress and undue influence. Whereas duress doctrine casts itself in formal terms—especially in respect of its insistence that a threat constitutes duress only if it leaves its victim with no reasonable alternatives to the coerced contract—the doctrine concerning undue influence is unabashedly functionalist and attuned to the all-things-considered equities of the circumstances in which it might be applied. Undue influence thus naturally and fluidly interacts with other doctrines through which contractual obligations might be avoided.

Vokes illustrates this also, and in particular with respect to the interaction between undue influence and misrepresentation. The defendant in *Vokes* taught the plaintiff dance, and in the course of doing so sold the plaintiff an absolutely extravagant quantity of dance lessons. The defendant sold the lessons, moreover, pursuant to a systematic policy of false flattery: it told the plaintiff that she had graces and talents that she in fact obviously lacked, and it established a scheme for measuring dancing achievement based not on actual skill, or even on application (hours of lessons taken), but (astonishingly) on hours of lessons paid for. In this way, the defendant sold the plaintiff over 2000 hours of dance lessons for over $30,000. The plaintiff eventually came to regret her purchases and sued to recover the payments that she had made for still unused lessons.

Misrepresentation figures prominently in the *Vokes* opinion, which concludes that the defendant engaged in more than mere puffery and instead made false statements of fact, in particular concerning the plaintiff's dancing talent and her progressing skill. But the opinion cannot plausibly succeed as an argument simply and a-contextually about misrepresentation. The purpose of amateur arts and theatricals is, after all, to flatter those who possess money but no talent. And even a less jaded view must accept that dance lessons are consumption in themselves rather than simply preparation for dances outside the class-studio and that self-confidence is an important component of dancing well. Both considerations make flattery and encouragement essential to the lessons' success and desired by dance students. Finally, many of the defendant's misrepresentations were so absurd (who could possibly believe in a scheme according to which merely *buying* dance lessons bestows awards for merit) that they could not be understood as statements of fact and so must serve some other purpose, for example encouragement.

Vokes therefore cannot be made sense of as a simple misrepresentation case.[25] And indeed, the opinion does not proceed in such simple terms. Instead, it emphasizes two further features of the facts before it. First, the plaintiff was vulnerable: a widow without a family, clearly lonely, and clearly seeking not just dance lessons but also companionship from the defendant. And second, the defendant not only had a greater knowledge of dance than the plaintiff but also engaged the plaintiff as teacher to student, and the teacher-student relation, even if not strictly fiduciary, involves a significant degree of confidence and trust. These features combined to enable to defendant to dominate the plaintiff and to justify the plaintiff's placing her trust in the defendant. In other words, they gave the defendant undue influence over the plaintiff, which the defendant's sales contracts improperly exploited.

24.2.B.3 Unconscionability

If undue influence is more functionalist and more openly attuned to the equities of a case than duress, unconscionability carries the inclination openly to seek to produce substantial justice further still. The materials

---

25. Perhaps the case might be made to turn simply on misrepresentation, although by a route that appears nowhere in the opinion. At least insofar as the defendant employed the selling methods described in *Vokes* generally, with respect to all of its customers, it might have sold more dance lessons than it could actually provide. That is, sufficiently many customers might have bought sufficiently many unused dance lessons so that the defendant lacked staff or studio time to teach them all. In this case, the defendant might be guilty of a misrepresentation entirely distinct from the one emphasized in the *Vokes* opinion, concerning not the plaintiff's talent but its own business model and plans. And that misrepresentation might allow the plaintiff to avoid the contract, even without more. Indeed, insofar as the defendant sold lessons that it *intended never to provide*, it might be guilty of promissory fraud.

reproduced below emphasize the functionalist character of the doctrine, and in particular the question whether or not unconscionability is well-suited to promoting the functionalist project—of protecting the vulnerable—in whose service the doctrine was developed.

Unconscionability has both a procedural and a substantive component: in order to be unconscionable, a contract must have been made in circumstances that deprived one party of meaningful choice, and its terms must unreasonably favor the other party. The two elements of unconscionability may, however, be satisfied on a sort of sliding scale: as procedural unconscionability increases, less substantive unconscionability is required to make the contract unconscionable overall; and vice versa. Thus, for example, § 2–719(3) of the U.C.C. states that "[l]imitation of consequential damages for injury to the person in the case of consumer goods is prima facie unconscionable but limitation of damages where the loss is commercial is not." In other words, contract terms that protect a retail seller from liability for personal injury caused by the goods it sells are so badly substantively unconscionable that no further inquiry into procedural unconscionability is required to sustain a conclusion of unconscionability, all-things-considered.

Cases collected in earlier chapters—for example, the cases in Chapter 20 on contracts of adhesion and, in particular, *Henningsen*—have introduced unconscionability, but always viewed through the lens of an additional doctrine. The materials below examine the doctrine on its own terms.

Uniform Commercial Code

§ 2–302   Unconscionable Contract or Clause.

(1) If the court as a matter of law finds the contract or any clause of the contract to have been unconscionable at the time it was made the court may refuse to enforce the contract, or it may enforce the remainder of the contract without the unconscionable clause, or it may so limit the application of any unconscionable clause as to avoid any unconscionable result.

(2) When it is claimed or appears to the court that the contract or any clause thereof may be unconscionable the parties shall be afforded a reasonable opportunity to present evidence as to its commercial setting, purpose and effect to aid the court in making the determination.

Official Comment:

Prior Uniform Statutory Provision: None.

Purposes:

1.   This section is intended to make it possible for the courts to police explicitly against the contracts or clauses which they find to be unconscionable. In the past such policing has been accomplished by adverse construction of language, by manipulation of the rules of offer and acceptance or by

determinations that the clause is contrary to public policy or to the dominant purpose of the contract. This section is intended to allow the court to pass directly on the unconscionability of the contract or particular clause therein and to make a conclusion of law as to its unconscionability. The basic test is whether, in the light of the general commercial background and the commercial needs of the particular trade or case, the clauses involved are so one-sided as to be unconscionable under the circumstances existing at the time of the making of the contract. Subsection (2) makes it clear that it is proper for the court to hear evidence upon these questions. The principle is one of the prevention of oppression and unfair surprise (Cf. Campbell Soup Co. v. Wentz, 172 F.2d 80, 3d Cir. 1948) and not of disturbance of allocation of risks because of superior bargaining power. The underlying basis of this section is illustrated by the results in cases such as the following:

Kansas City Wholesale Grocery Co. v. Weber Packing Corporation, 93 Utah 414, 73 P.2d 1272 (1937), where a clause limiting time for complaints was held inapplicable to latent defects in a shipment of catsup which could be discovered only by microscopic analysis; Hardy v. General Motors Acceptance Corporation, 38 Ga.App. 463, 144 S.E. 327 (1928), holding that a disclaimer of warranty clause applied only to express warranties, thus letting in a fair implied warranty; Andrews Bros. v. Singer & Co. (1934 CA) 1 K.B. 17, holding that where a car with substantial mileage was delivered instead of a "new" car, a disclaimer of warranties, including those "implied," left unaffected an "express obligation" on the description, even though the Sale of Goods Act called such an implied warranty; New Prague Flouring Mill Co. v. G. A. Spears, 194 Iowa 417, 189 N.W. 815 (1922), holding that a clause permitting the seller, upon the buyer's failure to supply shipping instructions, to cancel, ship, or allow delivery date to be indefinitely postponed 30 days at a time by the inaction, does not indefinitely postpone the date of measuring damages for the buyer's breach, to the seller's advantage; and Kansas Flour Mills Co. v. Dirks, 100 Kan. 376, 164 P. 273 (1917), where under a similar clause in a rising market the court permitted the buyer to measure his damages for non-delivery at the end of only one 30 day postponement; Green v. Arcos, Ltd. (1931 CA) 47 T.L.R. 336, where a blanket clause prohibiting rejection of shipments by the buyer was restricted to apply to shipments where discrepancies represented merely mercantile variations; Meyer v. Packard Cleveland Motor Co., 106 Ohio St. 328, 140 N.E. 118 (1922), in which the court held that a "waiver" of all agreements not specified did not preclude implied warranty of fitness of a rebuilt dump truck for ordinary use as a dump truck; Austin Co. v. J. H. Tillman Co., 104 Or. 541, 209 P. 131 (1922), where a clause limiting the buyer's remedy to return was held to be applicable only if the seller had delivered a machine needed for a construction job which reasonably met the contract description; Bekkevold v. Potts, 173 Minn. 87, 216 N.W. 790, 59 A.L.R. 1164 (1927), refusing to allow warranty of fitness for purpose imposed by law to be negated by clause excluding all warranties "made" by the seller; Robert A. Munroe & Co. v. Meyer (1930) 2 K.B. 312, holding that the warranty of description overrides a clause reading "with all faults and defects" where adulterated meat not up to the contract description was delivered.

2.   Under this section the court, in its discretion, may refuse to enforce the contract as a whole if it is permeated by the unconscionability, or it may strike any single clause or group of clauses which are so tainted or which are contrary to the essential purpose of the agreement, or it may simply limit unconscionable clauses so as to avoid unconscionable results.

3.   The present section is addressed to the court, and the decision is to be made by it. The commercial evidence referred to in subsection (2) is for the court's consideration, not the jury's. Only the agreement which results from the court's action on these matters is to be submitted to the general triers of the facts.

Williams v. Walker–Thomas Furniture Company I

District of Columbia Court of Appeals, 1964.
198 A.2d 914.

■ QUINN, CIRCUIT JUDGE. Appellant, a person of limited education separated from her husband, is maintaining herself and her seven children by means of public assistance. During the period 1957–1962 she had a continuous course of dealings with appellee from which she purchased many household articles on the installment plan. These included sheets, curtains, rugs, chairs, a chest of drawers, beds, mattresses, a washing machine, and a stereo set. In 1963 appellee filed a complaint in replevin for possession of all the items purchased by appellant, alleging that her payments were in default and that it retained title to the goods according to the sales contracts. By the writ of replevin appellee obtained a bed, chest of drawers, washing machine, and the stereo set. After hearing testimony and examining the contracts, the trial court entered judgment for appellee.

Appellant's principal contentions on appeal are (1) there was a lack of meeting of the minds, and (2) the contracts were against public policy.

Appellant signed fourteen contracts in all. They were approximately six inches in length and each contained a long paragraph in extremely fine print. One of the sentences in this paragraph provided that payments, after the first purchase, were to be prorated on all purchases then outstanding. Mathematically, this had the effect of keeping a balance due on all items until the time balance was completely eliminated. It meant that title to the first purchase, remained in appellee until the fourteenth purchase, made some five years later, was fully paid.

At trial appellant testified that she understood the agreements to mean that when payments on the running account were sufficient to balance the amount due on an individual item, the item became hers. She testified that most of the purchases were made at her home; that the contracts were signed in blank; that she did not read the instruments; and that she was not provided with a copy. She admitted, however, that she did not ask anyone to read or explain the contracts to her.

We have stated that 'one who refrains from reading a contract and in conscious ignorance of its terms voluntarily assents thereto will not be relieved from his bad bargain.' *Bob Wilson, Inc. v. Swann*, D.C.Mun.App., 168 A.2d 198, 199 (1961). 'One who signs a contract has a duty to read it and is obligated according to its terms.' *Hollywood Credit Clothing Co. v. Gibson*, D.C.App., 188 A.2d 348, 349 (1963). 'It is as much the duty of a person who cannot read the language in which a contract is written to have someone read it to him before he signs it, as it is the duty of one who can read to peruse it himself before signing it.' *Stern v. Moneyweight Scale Co.*, 42 App.D.C. 162, 165 (1914).

A careful review of the record shows that appellant's assent was not obtained 'by fraud or even misrepresentation falling short of fraud.' Hollywood Credit Clothing Co. v. Gibson, supra. This is not a case of mutual misunderstanding but a unilateral mistake. Under these circumstances, appellant's first contention is without merit.

Appellant's second argument presents a more serious question. The record reveals that prior to the last purchase appellant had reduced the balance in her account to $164. The last purchase, a stereo set, raised the balance due to $678. Significantly, at the time of this and the preceding purchases, appellee was aware of appellant's financial position. The reverse side of the stereo contract listed the name of appellant's social worker and her $218 monthly stipend from the government. Nevertheless, with full knowledge that appellant had to feed, clothe and support both herself and seven children on this amount, appellee sold her a $514 stereo set.

We cannot condemn too strongly appellee's conduct. It raises serious questions of sharp practice and irresponsible business dealings. A review of the legislation in the District of Columbia affecting retail sales and the pertinent decisions of the highest court in this jurisdiction disclose, however, no ground upon which this court can declare the contracts in question contrary to public policy. We note that were the Maryland Retail Installment Sales Act, Art. 83 §§ 128–153, or its equivalent, in force in the District of Columbia, we could grant appellant appropriate relief. We think Congress should consider corrective legislation to protect the public from such exploitive contracts as were utilized in the case at bar.

Affirmed.

Williams v. Walker–Thomas Furniture Co., Inc. II

United States Court of Appeals for the District of Columbia Circuit, 1965.
350 F.2d 445.

■ J. SKELLY WRIGHT, CIRCUIT JUDGE:

Appellee, Walker–Thomas Furniture Company, operates a retail furniture store in the District of Columbia. During the period from 1957 to 1962 each appellant in these cases purchased a number of household items from Walker–Thomas, for which payment was to be made in installments. The terms of each purchase were contained in a printed form contract which set forth the value of the purchased item and purported to lease the item to appellant for a stipulated monthly rent payment. The contract then provided, in substance, that title would remain in Walker–Thomas until the total of all the monthly payments made equaled the stated value of the item, at which time appellants could take title. In the event of a default in the payment of any monthly installment, Walker–Thomas could repossess the item.

The contract further provided that "the amount of each periodical installment payment to be made by [purchaser] to the Company under this present lease shall be inclusive of and not in addition to the amount of each installment payment to be made by [purchaser] under such prior leases, bills or accounts; *and all payments now and hereafter made by [purchaser] shall be credited pro rata on all outstanding leases, bills and accounts* due the Company by [purchaser] at the time each such payment is made." Emphasis added.) The effect of this rather obscure provision was to keep a balance due on every item purchased until the balance due on all items, whenever purchased, was liquidated. As a result, the debt incurred at the time of purchase of each item was secured by the right to repossess all the items previously purchased by the same purchaser, and each new item purchased automatically became subject to a security interest arising out of the previous dealings.

On May 12, 1962, appellant Thorne purchased an item described as a Daveno, three tables, and two lamps, having total stated value of $391.10. Shortly thereafter, he defaulted on his monthly payments and appellee sought to replevy all the items purchased since the first transaction in 1958. Similarly, on April 17, 1962, appellant Williams bought a stereo set of stated value of $514.95. She too defaulted shortly thereafter, and appellee sought to replevy all the items purchased since December, 1957. The Court of General Sessions granted judgment for appellee. The District of Columbia Court of Appeals affirmed, and we granted appellants' motion for leave to appeal to this court.

Appellants' principal contention, rejected by both the trial and the appellate courts below, is that these contracts, or at least some of them, are unconscionable and, hence, not enforceable. In its opinion in *Williams v. Walker–Thomas Furniture Company*, 198 A.2d 914, 916 (1964), the District of Columbia Court of Appeals explained its rejection of this contention as follows:

"Appellant's second argument presents a more serious question. The record reveals that prior to the last purchase appellant had reduced the balance in her account to $164. The last purchase, a stereo set, raised the balance due to $678. Significantly, at the time of this and the preceding purchases, appellee was aware of appellant's financial position. The reverse side of the stereo contract listed the name of appellant's social worker and her $218 monthly stipend from the government. Nevertheless, with full knowledge that appellant had to feed, clothe and support both herself and seven children on this amount, appellee sold her a $514 stereo set.

"We cannot condemn too strongly appellee's conduct. It raises serious questions of sharp practice and irresponsible business dealings. A review of the legislation in the District of Columbia affecting retail sales and the pertinent decisions of the highest court in this jurisdiction disclose, however, no ground upon which this court can declare the contracts in question contrary to public policy. We note that were the Maryland Retail Installment Sales Act, Art. 83 §§ 128–153, or its equivalent, in force in the District of Columbia, we could grant appellant appropriate relief. We think Congress should consider corrective legislation to protect the public from such exploitive contracts as were utilized in the case at bar."

We do not agree that the court lacked the power to refuse enforcement to contracts found to be unconscionable. In other jurisdictions, it has been held as a matter of common law that unconscionable contracts are not enforceable. While no decision of this court so holding has been found, the notion that an unconscionable bargain should not be given full enforcement is by no means novel. In *Scott v. United States*, 79 U.S. (12 Wall.) 443, 445 (1870), the Supreme Court stated:

"If a contract be unreasonable and unconscionable, but not void for fraud, a court of law will give to the party who sues for its breach damages, not according to its letter, but only such as he is equitably entitled to."

Since we have never adopted or rejected such a rule, the question here presented is actually one of first impression.

Congress has recently enacted the Uniform Commercial Code, which specifically provides that the court may refuse to enforce a contract which it finds to be unconscionable at the time it was made. 28 D.C.CODE § 2–302 (Supp. IV 1965). The enactment of this section, which occurred subsequent to the contracts here in suit, does not mean that the common law of the District of Columbia was otherwise at the time of enactment, nor does it preclude the court from adopting a similar rule in the exercise of its powers to develop the common law for the District of Columbia. In fact, in view of the absence of prior authority on the point, we consider the congressional adoption of § 2–302 persuasive authority for following the rationale of the cases from which the section is explicitly derived. Accordingly, we hold that where the element of unconscionability is present at the time a contract is made, the contract should not be enforced.

Unconscionability has generally been recognized to include an absence of meaningful choice on the part of one of the parties together with contract terms which are unreasonably favorable to the other party. Whether a meaningful choice is present in a particular case can only be determined by consideration of all the circumstances surrounding the transaction. In many cases the meaningfulness of the choice is negated by a gross inequality of bargaining power. The manner in which the contract was entered is also relevant to this consideration. Did each party to the contract, considering his obvious education or lack of it, have a reasonable opportunity to understand the terms of the contract, or were the important terms hidden in a maze of fine print and minimized by deceptive sales practices? Ordinarily, one who signs an agreement without full knowledge of its terms might be held to assume the risk that he has entered a one-sided bargain. But when a party of little bargaining power, and hence little real choice, signs a commercially unreasonable contract with little or no knowledge of its terms, it is hardly likely that his consent, or even an objective manifestation of his consent, was ever given to all the terms. In such a case the usual rule that the terms of the agreement are not to be questioned should be abandoned and the court should consider whether the terms of the contract are so unfair that enforcement should be withheld.

In determining reasonableness or fairness, the primary concern must be with the terms of the contract considered in light of the circumstances existing when the contract was made. The test is not simple, nor can it be mechanically applied. The terms are to be considered "in the light of the general commercial background and the commercial needs of the particular trade or case." Corbin suggests the test as being whether the terms are "so extreme as to appear unconscionable according to the mores and business practices of the time and place." 1 CORBIN, CONTRACTS § 128 (1963). We think this formulation correctly states the test to be applied in those cases where no meaningful choice was exercised upon entering the contract.

Because the trial court and the appellate court did not feel that enforcement could be refused, no findings were made on the possible unconscionability of the contracts in these cases. Since the record is not sufficient for our deciding the issue as a matter of law, the cases must be remanded to the trial court for further proceedings.

So ordered.

Jones v. Star Credit Corp.

Supreme Court of New York, 1969.
298 N.Y.S.2d 264.

■ WACHTLER, J. On August 31, 1965 the plaintiffs, who are welfare recipients, agreed to purchase a home freezer unit for $900 as the result of a visit from a salesman representing Your Shop At Home Service, Inc. With the addition of the time credit charges, credit life insurance, credit property insurance, and sales tax, the purchase price totaled $1,234.80. Thus far the plaintiffs have paid $619.88 toward their purchase. The defendant claims that with various added credit charges paid for an extension of time there is a balance of $819.81 still due from the plaintiffs. The uncontroverted proof at the trial established that the freezer unit, when purchased, had a maximum retail value of approximately $300. The question is whether this transaction and the resulting contract could be considered unconscionable within the meaning of section 2–302 of the Uniform Commercial Code which provides in part:

"(1) If the court as a matter of law finds the contract or any clause of the contract to have been unconscionable at the time it was made the court may refuse to enforce the contract, or it may enforce the remainder of the contract without the unconscionable clause, or it may so limit the application of any unconscionable clause as to avoid any unconscionable result.

"(2) When it is claimed or appears to the court that the contract or any clause thereof may be unconscionable the parties shall be afforded a reasonable opportunity to present evidence as to its commercial setting, purpose and effect to aid the court in making the determination." (L. 1962, ch. 553, eff. Sept. 27, 1964.)

There was a time when the shield of *caveat emptor* would protect the most unscrupulous in the marketplace—a time when the law, in granting parties unbridled latitude to make their own contracts, allowed exploitive and callous practices which shocked the conscience of both legislative bodies and the courts.

The effort to eliminate these practices has continued to pose a difficult problem. On the one hand it is necessary to recognize the importance of preserving the integrity of agreements and the fundamental right of parties to deal, trade, bargain, and contract. On the other hand there is the concern for the uneducated and often illiterate individual who is the victim of gross inequality of bargaining power, usually the poorest members of the community.

Concern for the protection of these consumers against overreaching by the small but hardy breed of merchants who would prey on them is not novel. The dangers of inequality of bargaining power were vaguely recognized in the early English common law when Lord Hardwicke wrote of a fraud, which "may be apparent from the intrinsic nature and subject of the bargain itself; such as no man in his senses and not under delusion would make". The English authorities on this subject were discussed in *Hume* v. *United States* (132 U.S. 406, 411 [1889]) where the United States Supreme Court characterized (p. 413) these as "cases in which one party took advantage of the other's ignorance of arithmetic to impose upon him, and the fraud was apparent from the face of the contracts."

The law is beginning to fight back against those who once took advantage of the poor and illiterate without risk of either exposure or interference. From the common-law doctrine of intrinsic fraud we have, over the years, developed common and statutory law which tells not only the buyer but also the seller to beware. This body of laws recognizes the importance of a free enterprise system but at the same time will provide the legal armor to protect and safeguard the prospective victim from the harshness of an unconscionable contract.

Section 2–302 of the Uniform Commercial Code enacts the moral sense of the community into the law of commercial transactions. It authorizes the court to find, as a matter of law, that a contract or a clause of a contract was "unconscionable at the time it was made", and upon so finding the court may refuse to enforce the contract, excise the objectionable clause or limit the application of the clause to avoid an unconscionable result. "The principle", states the Official Comment to this section, "is one of the prevention of oppression and unfair surprise''. It permits a court to accomplish directly what heretofore was often accomplished by construction of language, manipulations of fluid rules of contract law and determinations based upon a presumed public policy.

There is no reason to doubt, moreover, that this section is intended to encompass the price term of an agreement. In addition to the fact that it has already been so applied, the statutory language itself makes it clear that not only a clause of the contract, but the contract *in toto*, may be found unconscionable as a matter of law. Indeed, no other provision of an agreement more intimately touches upon the question of unconscionability than does the term regarding price.

Fraud, in the instant case, is not present; nor is it necessary under the statute. The question which presents itself is whether or not, under the circumstances of this case, the sale of a freezer unit having a retail value of $300 for $900 ($1,439.69 including credit charges and $18 sales tax) is unconscionable as a matter of law. The court believes it is.

Concededly, deciding the issue is substantially easier than explaining it. No doubt, the mathematical disparity between $300, which presumably includes a reasonable profit margin, and $900, which is exorbitant on its face, carries the greatest weight. Credit charges alone exceed by more than $100 the retail value of the freezer. These alone, may be sufficient to sustain the decision. Yet, a caveat is warranted lest we reduce the import of section 2–302 solely to a mathematical ratio formula. It may, at times, be that; yet it may also be much more. The very limited financial resources of the purchaser, known to the sellers at the time of the sale, is entitled to weight in the balance. Indeed, the value disparity itself leads inevitably to the felt conclusion that knowing advantage was taken of the plaintiffs. In addition, the meaningfulness of choice essential to the making of a contract can be negated by a gross inequality of bargaining power. (*Williams* v. *Walker–Thomas Furniture Co.*, 350 F. 2d 445.)

There is no question about the necessity and even the desirability of installment sales and the extension of credit. Indeed, there are many, including welfare recipients, who would be deprived of even the most basic conveniences without the use of these devices. Similarly, the retail merchant selling on installment or extending credit is expected to establish a pricing factor which will afford a degree of protection commensurate with the risk of selling to those who might be default prone. However, neither of these accepted premises can clothe the sale of this freezer with respectability.

Support for the court's conclusion will be found in a number of other cases already decided. In *American Home Improvement* v. *MacIver,* 105 N.H. 435 (1964) (the Supreme Court of New Hampshire held that a contract to install windows, a door and paint, for the price of $2,568.60, of which $809.60 constituted interest and carrying charges and $800 was a salesman's commission was unconscionable as a matter of law. In *Matter of State of New York* v. *ITM, Inc.* 52 Misc 2d 39 (1966), a deceptive and fraudulent scheme was involved, but standing alone, the court held that the sale of a vacuum cleaner, among other things, costing the defendant $140 and sold by it for $749 cash or $920.52 on time purchase was unconscionable as a matter of law. Finally, in *Frostifresh Corp.* v. *Reynoso*, 52 Misc 2d 26, revd. 54 Misc 2d 119 (1967); the sale of a refrigerator costing the seller $348 for $900 plus credit charges of $245.88 was unconscionable as a matter of law.

One final point remains. The defendant argues that the contract of June 15, 1966, upon which this suit is based, constitutes a financing agreement and not a sales contract. To support its position, it points to the typed words "Refinance of Freezer A/C #6766 and Food A/C #56788" on the agreement and to a letter signed by the plaintiffs requesting refinance of the same items. The request for "refinancing" is typed on the defendant's letterhead. The quoted refinance statement is typed on a form agreement entitled "Star Credit Corporation—Retail Instalment Contract". It is signed by the defendant as "seller" and by the purchasers as "buyer". Above the signature of the buyers, they acknowledge "receipt of an executed copy of this Retail Instalment Contract". The June 15, 1966 contract by defendant is on exactly the same form as the original contract of August 31, 1965. The original, too, is entitled "Star Credit Corporation—Retail Instalment Contract". It is signed, however, by "Your Shop At Home Service, Inc." Printed beneath the signatures is the legend "Duplicate for Star". In substance and effect, the agreement of June 25, 1966 constitutes a novation and replacement of the earlier agreement. It is, in all respects, as it reads, a "Retail Installment Contract".

Having already paid more than $600 toward the purchase of this $300 freezer unit, it is apparent that the defendant has already been amply compensated. In accordance with the statute, the application of the payment provision should be limited to amounts already paid by the plaintiffs and the contract be reformed and amended by changing the payments called for therein to equal the amount of payment actually so paid by the plaintiffs.

Patterson v. Walker–Thomas Furniture Co., Inc.

District of Columbia Court of Appeals, 1971.
277 A.2d 111.

■ KELLY. According to an agreed statement of proceedings and evidence the appellant, Mrs. Bernice Patterson, bought merchandise from appellee in three separate transactions during 1968. In January she bought an 18–inch Emerson portable television, with stand, for $295.95, signing an installment contract which obligated her to pay appellee $20 a month on account. In March she bought a five-piece dinette set for $119.95, increasing her monthly payments to $24. In July she purchased a set of wedding rings for $159.95 and the payments rose to $25 per month. The total price for all the goods, including sales tax, was $597.25. Mrs. Patterson defaulted in her payments after she had paid a total of $248.40 toward the agreed purchase price.

Appellant answered Walker–Thomas' action to recover the unpaid balance on the contracts by claiming, in pertinent part, that she had paid an amount in excess of the fair value of the goods received and that the goods themselves were so grossly overpriced as to render the contract terms unconscionable and the contracts unenforceable under the Uniform Commercial Code as enacted in the District of Columbia.

Objections to interrogatories addressed to appellee in an effort to establish her defense that the goods were in fact grossly overpriced were sustained, the court ruling in part that the information sought was outside the scope of discovery "because the defense of unconscionability based on price is not recognized in this jurisdiction". It ruled further "that certain information sought was readily obtainable to defendant by resort to the contracts admittedly in her possession and that certain of the interrogatories amounted to 'harassment of the business community'."

Appellant persisted in her efforts to present the defense of unconscionability by issuing a subpoena *duces tecum* for the production of appellee's records, and, alleging indigency, by moving for the appointment of a special master or expert witness to establish the value of the goods, the price Walker–Thomas paid for them, and their condition (whether new or secondhand) when she purchased them. The pretrial judge quashed the subpoena *duces tecum* on the ground that appellant was precluded from obtaining the same information by means of the subpoena that she had been denied through the use of interrogatories. The motion to appoint a special master or expert witness was also denied.

A trial judge subsequently held that the prior rulings of the motions judge and the pretrial judge established the law of the case. Inasmuch as appellant's then sole defense was that the goods were grossly overpriced and no proof on this issue was presented, the court entered judgment for appellee. We affirm.

Suggested guidelines for deciding whether or not a contract is unconscionable appear in *Williams v. Walker–Thomas Furniture Co.*, 350 F.2d 445 (1965), as follows:

> Unconscionability has generally been recognized to include an absence of meaningful choice on the part of one of the parties together with contract terms which are unreasonably favorable to the other party. Whether a meaningful choice is present in a particular case can only be determined by consideration of all the circumstances surrounding the transaction. In many cases the meaningfulness of the choice is negated by a gross inequality of bargaining power.

> In determining reasonableness or fairness, the primary concern must be with the terms of the contract considered in light of the circumstances existing when the contract was made. The test is not simple, nor can it be mechanically applied. The terms are to be considered "in the light of the general commercial background and the commercial needs of the particular trade or case." Corbin

suggests the test as being whether the terms are "so extreme as to appear unconscionable according to the mores and business practices of the time and place." We think this formulation correctly states the test to be applied in those cases where no meaningful choice was exercised upon entering the contract.

Later, citing *Williams* in another context, this court said that "two elements are required to exist to prove unconscionability; i.e., 'an absence of meaningful choice on the part of one of the parties together with contract terms which are *unreasonably favorable to the other party*.'" *Diamond Housing Corp. v. Robinson, D.C.App., 257 A.2d 492, 493 (1969).*

On the basis of these authorities we conclude that in a proper case gross overpricing may be raised in defense as an element of unconscionability. Under the test outlined in *Williams* price is necessarily an element to be examined when determining whether a contract is reasonable. The Corbin test mentioned in the opinion specifically deals with the "terms" of the contract and certainly the price one pays for an item is one of the more important terms of any contract. We emphasize, however, that price as an unreasonable contract term is only one of the elements which underpin proof of unconscionability. Specifically, therefore, in the instant case the reasonableness of the contracts is not to be gauged by an examination of the price stipulation alone or any other term of the contract without parallel consideration being given to whether or not appellant exercised a meaningful choice in entering into the contracts.

We conclude also that because excessive price-value may comprise one element of unconscionability, discovery techniques may be employed to garner information relevant to that issue for purposes of defense. By statute, upon a claim of unconscionability, the court determines as a matter of law whether a contract or any clause thereof is unconscionable *only* after the parties have been given a reasonable opportunity to present evidence as to its commercial setting, purpose and effect. Certainly, therefore, interrogatories may be used to develop evidence of the commercial setting, purpose and effect of a contract at the time it was made in order to assure an effective presentation of the defense at an evidentiary hearing.

In our judgment, however, appellant here was not erroneously precluded from developing evidence through the use of interrogatories by the ruling of the trial court. Having said that under proper circumstances excessive price may be a component of the defense of unconscionability and that discovery techniques may be used to develop that defense, we are nevertheless of the opinion that a sufficient factual predicate for the defense must be alleged before wholesale discovery is allowed. An unsupported conclusory allegation in the answer that a contract is unenforceable as unconscionable is not enough. Sufficient facts surrounding the "commercial setting, purpose and effect" of a contract at the time it was made should be alleged so that the court may form a judgment as to the existence of a valid claim of unconscionability and the extent to which discovery of evidence to support that claim should be allowed.

Admittedly, appellant neither alleged nor attempted to prove the existence of any fraud, duress or coercion when she entered into the instant contracts. Her verified complaint alleges only that the goods she purchased and still retains were grossly overpriced and that she has already paid appellee a sum in excess of their fair value. These are conclusions without factual support. It cannot be said that the goods were grossly overpriced merely from an examination of the prices which appear on the face of the contracts. No other term of the contract is alleged to be unconscionable, nor is an absence of meaningful choice claimed. We hold that the two elements of which unconscionability is comprised; namely, an absence of meaningful choice and contract terms unreasonably favorable to the other party, must be particularized in some detail before a merchant is required to divulge his pricing policies through interrogatories or through the production of records in court. An answer, such as the one here, asserting the affirmative defense of unconscionability only on the basis of a stated conclusion that the price is excessive is insufficient.

Accordingly, the judgment of the trial court is

Affirmed.

* * *

The doctrine itself and its progress through the cases are relatively straightforward. *Williams* involved a retailer who specialized in selling to the poor and who, by means of aggressive sales tactics, sold a series of household goods to a mother of seven "of limited education separated from her husband." The goods were all sold on seller-provided credit, subject to a cross-collateral clause included in the fine print of the sales contracts. According to this clause, each item sold functioned as collateral for the debts incurred on all items sold, and payments made on any of the purchases would be credited, pro-rata, to all outstanding debts. This arrangement maintained a balance due from the buyer on every item purchased until all items were fully paid off. It also gave the seller a priority over other creditors, with respect to the purchased items, in case the buyer defaulted on other debts also. Finally, the clause gave the seller the right to repossess the sold items in case of default, by self-help and in advance of judgment, that is, without the buyer's receiving judicial process. The buyer defaulted and the seller sought to replevin all the goods that the buyer had purchased, including children's toys, used sheets, and beds. The buyer responded by seeking to invalidate the cross-collateral clause, alleging not unconscionability but rather that there was no meeting of minds on the contracts and that the contracts were against public policy.

A trial court found that there was no evidence of fraud or misrepresentation and no mutual mistake. Instead, the only mistake that there might have been was a unilateral mistake by the buyer, brought on by the buyer's failure to read her contracts. The buyer's argument concerning meeting of minds thus failed. The trial court was more sympathetic to the buyer's claim concerning public policy. It observed that it could not "condemn too strongly the seller's conduct." But it added that, in contrast to other jurisdictions, the District of Columbia (where the sales occurred) had no statute granting relief in such cases and that the case law contained no resources that might serve as precedents for vindicating the buyer's claims. The court therefore called on the Congress to improve the law, but held for the seller.

The Court of Appeals for the District of Columbia Circuit, per Judge Skelly Wright,[26] reversed. The opinion set out from the broad proposition that where a contract is unconscionable and a party sues for its breach, a court will award damages not according to the letter of the contract but only as equity demands. The appellate court found this principle established not only by U.C.C. § 2–302 (recently enacted by Congress in its capacity as legislature for the District of Columbia, but too late to govern *Williams* directly) but more broadly in the common law. Moreover, the court found that the combination of the procedural defect established by the defendant's pressure sales tactics and the substantive harshness of the cross-collateral clause rendered the contract unconscionable.

Jones follows *Williams* and expands on it, in ways that represent perhaps the high-water market for unconscionability doctrine (at least in consumer sales contracts). The plaintiff in Jones, following a visit by the defendant's door-to-door salesperson, bought a home freezer for $900 plus taxes, insurance, and credit charges that brought the total purchase price up to $1,230. The maximum market price of the freezer (normal profit included) was $300. After having paid $620 under the contract, the buyer brought suit to avoid its obligation to pay the remaining balance of the contract price.

The *Jones* court found the contract unconscionable and held for the plaintiff. It did so in strikingly, indeed extravagantly, broad terms. On the one hand, the court held that unconscionability centrally encompasses the price term of a contract. Indeed, the court, quoting Lord Hardwicke went so far as to propose that fraud might be "apparent from the intrinsic nature and subject of the bargain itself; such as no man in his senses and not under delusion would make."[27] Jones thus effectively holds that substantive unconscionability, on its own, might establish a (rebuttable?) presumption of procedural unconscionability, and thus enable a party to avoid a contract. This is not far off from holding that the unconscionability doctrine establishes (at least for retail sales to consumers) the principle of a just price in American law. And on the other hand, *Jones* held that a court might, in appropriate circumstances, find a contract unconscionable *as a matter of law*, and so might refuse to enforce the contract (or part of it) without the need for fact-finding at trial. This is especially important in the consumer context. Cases tend to be idiosyncratically fact intensive (just how sophisticated was a buyer, what precise methods did the seller employ) and thus resistant to being combined as class actions, and the sums at

---

26. Skelly Wright was a liberal firebrand who had ordered the racial integration of Louisiana as a federal district judge and was, rumor had it, elevated to the Circuit Court in part so that the government would no longer have to protect him.

27. The court expressly noted, however, that fraud was not present in the case before it.

stake tend to be too small to warrant the time and expense of individual fact-finding. Moreover, even where cases are brought to trial, fact-based holdings of unconscionability do not, by their nature, establish precedents that control future sales conduct.

Patterson represents a substantial retreat from unconscionability, at least in the assertive form adopted by *Jones*. The facts in *Patterson* also involved a consumer purchase—of a dinette set and wedding rings—for an exorbitant price. After paying part of the contract price, the buyer defaulted and the seller tried to replevin the goods, whereupon the buyer answered that the purchase price so far exceeded the fair market value of the goods as to make the contract unconscionable under U.C.C. § 2–302.

The *Patterson* court acknowledged that in a proper case gross overpricing may be raised as an element of unconscionability, but it insisted that price (even grossly unreasonable) is only one of the elements of unconscionability. In particular, *Patterson* holds, unconscionability may not be found without an independent consideration of the whether or not the buyer exercised meaningful choice in entering into the contract. Moreover, *Patterson* restored the factual character of unconscionability and added that allegations of unconscionability must be pleaded with some particularity and detail before one making them may employ discovery to support the allegations at trial (for example, by forcing a merchant to divulge his pricing policies). *Patterson* thus insists that the two elements of unconscionability—substantive and procedural—are not just conceptually but also epistemically distinct, so that procedural unconscionability must be independently proven before the doctrine may be employed to avoid a contractual obligation. Moreover, *Patterson* raises the bar for pleading unconscionability (as the bar is raised for pleading fraud). Whereas *Jones* made it easier for buyers alleging unconscionability to win without trial, *Patterson* makes it easier for sellers defending against allegations of unconscionability to win without trial.

Procedural unconscionability protects freedom of contract in the same manner as the doctrines that control fraud, duress, and undue influence. Perhaps procedural unconscionability is warranted, in order to pick up fact patterns that involve genuine manipulation and hence draft people unfreely into contracts, but that the technical requirements of these other doctrines exclude. (It is, however, worth pointing out in this connection just how open-ended undue influence may be.) Substantive unconscionability is a different matter entirely, however. As its name directly suggests, substantive unconscionability limits the substance of contracts that the law will enforce. It thus restricts rather than protects freedom of contract. At least, substantive unconscionability has this effect insofar as it has any *independent* influence on the law: insofar, that is, as substantive unconscionability permits contracts to be attacked as unconscionable, all-things-considered, even though their procedural defects do not rise to whatever level protecting freedom of contract (as done through the other purely procedural doctrines) requires. In *Williams* and more clearly still in *Jones*, this effect was produced by limiting the capacity of buyers and sellers otherwise judged free to agree to sales contracts that fix credit or price terms in a manner deemed substantively unfair.

Substantive unconscionability thus raises the question whether contract law rules that require certain pro-consumer contract terms (or prohibit certain anti-consumer terms) in the end benefit the consumers that they are designed to protect? Procedural unconscionability raises the further question whether the conditions that the cases pick out as procedurally questionable (but that are not controlled for by other freedom-of-contract-protective doctrines) in fact reflect procedural circumstances that should concern the law?

Begin with the first question. As regards the substantive component of unconscionability, do rules that require certain pro-consumer contract terms (or prohibit certain anti-consumer terms) in the end benefit consumers? Examples of rules of this sort include, once again, a rule that disclaimers of liability for personal injury are invalid, a rule that cross-collateral clauses that allow creditors to retake goods without judicial process are invalid, and a rule invalidating contract prices set dramatically in excess of market prices. Answering this question requires returning, at the end of these materials, to the economic methods that dominated the materials at their beginning.[28]

Assume, to begin the analysis that follows, that consumer willingness to pay for a pro-consumer contract term—to fix ideas, imagine that this term is a *mandatory* warranty, say of merchantability—is a true measure of the benefits these terms confer on consumers. In other words, assume (1) that consumers accurately assess the money value to them of the warranty, (2) that this monetary valuation reflects the true benefit that the warranty confers on the consumers, and (3) that there are no externalities to the warranty (so that the value of the warranty to the consumers is its social value). With these assumptions in place, divide the analysis into two cases: first, the case in which consumers are all identical; and second, the case in which consumers' preferences and valuations vary.

Begin with the case in which all consumers value the warranty at exactly the same amount. Suppose that the cost to the seller of providing the warranty is some amount c, so that the addition of the warranty term to the contract causes the seller's supply curve to shift upward by c. (The seller's costs have gone up by c, so that for any quantity, the seller must receive a price that is higher by c in order to be willing to supply that quantity.) In figure 24.1, this is reflected by the shift from S1 to S2.

Now ask whether the consumers value the warranty by more than c or by less than c. In the first case, the demand curve shifts out from D1 to D2;

---

28. The discussion that follows is based on Richard Craswell, *Passing on the Costs of Legal Rules: Efficiency and Distribution in Buyer–Seller Relationships*, 43 STANFORD LAW REVIEW 361 (1991); Richard Markovits, *The Distributive Impact, Allocative Efficiency, and Overall Desirability of Ideal Housing Codes: Some Theoretical Clarifications*, 89 HARV. L. REV. 1815 (1976); Bruce Ackerman, *Regulating Slum Housing Markets on Behalf of the Poor*, 80 YALE L.J. 1093 (1971); and Richard Posner, *Wealth Redistribution by Liability Rules: The Case of Housing Code Enforcement*, ECONOMIC ANALYSIS OF LAW 470–474 (4th ed. 1992).

in the second case the demand curve shifts out to D2'. (The consumers' valuation has gone up in each case, so that consumers will be willing to pay more at every quantity.)

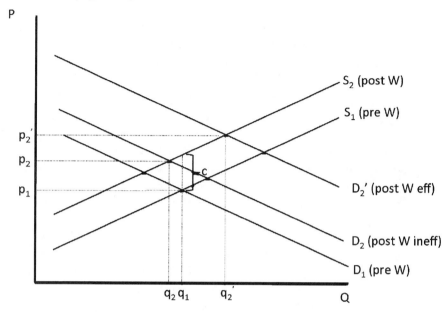

Figure 24.1

A Mandatory Warranty with Identical Consumers

Figure 24.1 thus illustrates several relationships.

First, with respect to the case in which the consumers value the warranty at less than c—the case involving D2—the new equilibrium price and quantity are P2 and Q2. Moreover, the mandatory warranty increases price and decreases quantity: P2 > P1 and Q2 < Q1.

The pro-consumer term is thus inefficient. The key to seeing why is that Q2 < Q1. That means that some consumers—those between Q2 and Q1—have ceased to make a contract (the sale without the warranty) that gave them some surplus. Furthermore, even the consumers who continue to make the contract with the mandatory warranty are worse off than they were without it. This follows from the assumption that all consumers value the warranty equally, so that if the marginal consumers value the warranty at less than the price increase, then the intramarginal consumers will do so as well. Even though they continue to buy the good with the warranty, their gains from the transaction have decreased. Finally, note that (P2–P1) < c. In other words, the seller has passed on less than 100% of the cost that the inefficient warranty imposes on him to his customers.

Second, consider the case in which the consumers value the warranty term at more than c—the case involving D2'. In this case, the new equilibrium price and quantity are P2' and Q2'.

The warranty is thus efficient. To see why, observe that Q2' > Q2, so that more consumers are buying and the new consumers create new consumer surplus. The old consumers, moreover, once again by assumption also value the term at more than they are paying for it. Finally, note that (P2'–P1) > c. In other words, the seller has passed on more than 100% of the cost of the efficient warranty to his customers.

This analysis sustains two fairly straightforward conclusions (at least under the assumptions set out earlier):

(1) A mandatory pro-consumer term benefits consumers only when it is efficient; only, that is, when consumers value the term by more than it costs sellers to provide. By and large, such terms will be provided by sellers in any event. This means that mandatory pro-consumer terms that actually alter seller behavior are generally bad for consumers.

(2) When sellers pass on more than 100% of the cost of a pro-consumer term, then this term benefits consumers; when sellers pass on less than 100% of the cost, then this term harms consumers. That is because a term that benefits consumers is one that they value at more than its cost, which means that the term increases the total surplus on the contract and gives sellers a chance to capture some of this increased surplus. And what it means for sellers to capture some of the surplus is—as an analytical matter—that they raise the price by more than it costs them to provide the term (that they pass on more than 100% of the cost of the term).

Now consider the case in which consumers do not all value the term identically. Assume, throughout the analysis, that the seller cannot price discriminate—in other words, that he cannot charge different consumers different prices. Next distinguish between two possibilities.[29] On the one hand, those consumers who are willing to pay the most for the underlying contract, the good sold, may also be willing to pay the most for the pro-consumer term, the mandatory warranty. In this case, most consumers might benefit from a warranty that will not be offered unless it is made mandatory; and such a warranty might be efficient. On the other hand, those consumers who are willing to pay the most for the good sold may be willing to pay the least for the warranty. In this case, most consumers might be harmed even by a warranty that sellers will voluntarily provide; and such a warranty might be inefficient. There might thus be a case for a mandatory rule prohibiting the warranty.

These results may again be depicted graphically, through variations on the previous figure.

---

29. The exists a third possibility, of course, namely that there is no correlation between the value consumers place on the underlying contract (the good purchased) and the value they place on the pro-consumer term in question (the warranty). In this case, the analysis of the homogenous consumer case roughly applies once again.

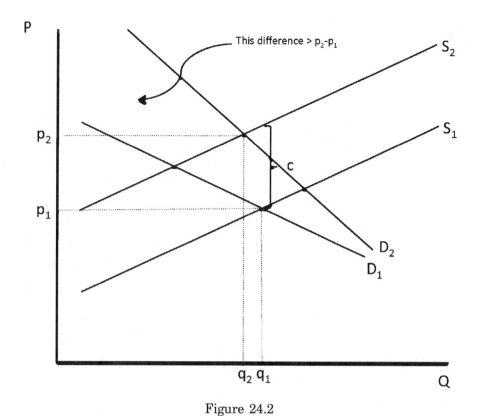

Figure 24.2

A Mandatory Warranty Valued Most Highly by the Consumers
Who Also Value the Warranted Good Most Highly

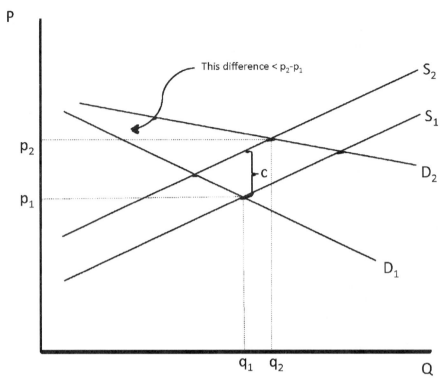

Figure 24.3

A Mandatory Warranty Valued Most Highly by the Consumers
Who Value the Warranted Good Least Highly

They key to understanding these graphs, and the effects that they illustrate, is to remember that where sellers cannot price discriminate, the effect of the warranty on the equilibrium price and quantity is determined by the behavior of the marginal consumers.

Thus in Figure 24.2, the intramarginal consumers (who value the good most highly) value the warranty by more than the marginal consumers, and this is depicted by the fact that D2 is more above D1 at the left of the graph than at the right. In this case, the effect of the mandatory warranty is, as before, to shift the supply curve up by c, from S1 to S2. Because this shift c is greater than the increase in demand (from D1 to D2)—at least, it is greater around the equilibrium quantity—the warranty will not be provided unless it is made mandatory, and a mandatory warranty will cause the new equilibrium quantity Q2 to fall before the old. But because of the skew in the jump from D1 to D2, it may be that *intramarginal* consumes value the warranty term at more than the price increase. Thus some consumers are benefited even though the warranty will not arise save by operation of law. Moreover, if the gains to the intramarginal consumers exceed the combined losses suffered by the marginal consumers and the seller, then the warranty may even be efficient.

Figure 24.3 represents the analogous result for the case in which the intramarginal consumers value the warranty by less than the marginal consumers, so that D2 is less above D1 at the left of the graph than at the right. In this case, the effect of the warranty is again to shift the supply curve up by c, from S1 to S2. But now the shift c is less than the increase in demand (from D1 to D2)—at least, it is less around the equilibrium quantity. And for this reason, the warranty will be provided unless it is forbidden by law and the new equilibrium quantity Q2 will be more than Q1. But because of the skew in the jump from D1 to D2, it may be that intramarginal consumers value the warranty at less than the price increase. Thus some consumers are hurt by the warranty. (These consumers stay in the market because, being intramarginal, they valued the good without the warranty at more than they had to pay for it, and this surplus was greater than the net cost that the mandatory warranty imposes on them (the difference between the amount by which they value the warranty and what they now have to pay for it).) Finally, if the losses to the intramarginal consumers exceed the combined gains realized by the marginal consumers and seller, then the warranty may be inefficient (even though it will be provided by the market). Accordingly, there may be an efficiency case for a mandatory rule forbidding the warranty.

The analysis is far from conclusive (for example, where consumers cannot accurately value mandatory contract terms, the analysis here does not apply), but it nevertheless underwrites skepticism about substantive unconscionability and related doctrines. Unless there are grounds for expecting consumers to misvalue contract terms *even where there are no procedural irregularities in establishing the contracts that include the terms*, most terms that consumers value more than it costs sellers to provide will be included in contracts. Thus in such cases, making the terms mandatory is unnecessary. Furthermore, when consumers are homogenous, then making mandatory a term that is not provided anyway (that consumers do not value at more than it costs to provide) will harm consumers. When consumers are not homogenous (and value the term in question differently) it may happen that consumers as a whole benefit even though marginal consumers value a term at less than it costs producers to provide. And that may constitute a reason for making the term mandatory. But this reasoning depends on uncertain assumptions about the relationship between the value consumers place on the underlying contract and the value they place on the term in question. And all the uncertainty should give pause to those who wish to benefit consumers—and in particular poor consumers—by adopting a robust principle of substantive unconscionability. Perhaps it is harder to benefit consumers in this way than unconscionability's early champions thought. And perhaps the difficulty provides a partial explanation of why unconscionability, and in particular substantive unconscionability, has had a limited career in contract law.

Of course, none of these arguments goes to procedural unconscionability. And so it remains worth asking whether the conditions that the cases pick out as procedurally unconscionable in fact reflect procedural circumstances that should concern the law?[30] Here one might identify two sources of procedural unconscionability that do not clearly warrant the application of the doctrine, and a third source that might do.

First, a contract may be thought procedurally unconscionable simply because of the poverty of the buyer. But it is difficult to vindicate this view without making strong—quite possibly unpalatably strong—assumptions about the correlation between poverty and analytic incapacity. As long as the poor are able to value contract terms accurately (as accurately as the rich can), poverty does not in itself establish procedural unconscionability.

Second, a contract may be thought procedurally unconscionable because of the market power of the seller, which may deprive buyers of any reasonable substitutes. But this argument must be tempered by the fact that a monopolist has an incentive to make his product, including his contract terms, maximally attractive to his potential buyers, since this is how he maximizes the demand from which he can extract monopoly rents. This means that the monopolist will be as likely as a competitive firm to offer contract terms that consumers want when it costs less to provide them than consumers are willing to pay. There may be good grounds (including grounds associated with consumer welfare) for breaking monopolies. But that does not entail that consumer welfare is advanced by allowing monopolies to persist, but subjecting monopolists to mandatory contract terms.

Third, and finally, procedural unconscionability may arise where there exist failures of consumer information. Such failures can be real and significant—just think of the difficulties that borrowers faced in understanding the terms of their mortgages during the (now burst) housing bubble. A doctrine of procedural unconscionability that responds to imperfect consumer information or information-processing may benefit consumers and be efficient. This makes the final argument concerning unconscionability turn on complicated and contested empirical questions concerning the rationality and information-processing capacity of consumers. Certainly there is no good reason for treating consumers as presumptively rational, without engaging in sustained empirical study. To the contrary, ordinary experience and the behaviors of retailers, including in the unconscionability cases rehearsed earlier, suggest that consumers suffer substantial imperfections in their information-processing and hence in their rationality. Thus Walker–Thomas Furniture, for example, employed aggressive door-to-door sales methods, privacy-invading and even threatening payment enforcement techniques, and sales pitches that revealed monthly payments and disguised total price. Indeed, the "easy credit" that Walker–Thomas offered involved high interest rates that were disguised by being built into the prices of goods sold on credit.

---

30. The discussion below follows Alan Schwartz, *A Reexamination of Nonsubstantive Unconscionability*, 63 VA.L.REV. 1053 (1977).

These procedural considerations are complicated, both conceptually and empirically.[31] Conceptually, it makes sense to distinguish between circumstances in which consumers face high costs in acquiring information and circumstances in which consumers cannot rationally process information that they possess.

Consumers may face materially imperfect information insofar as facts about product attributes or contract terms are difficult to acquire or so voluminous that they are difficult to read and know: foods possess both properties in respect of their nutritional content. A good policy response to this type of problem is to require sellers to provide consumers with the relevant facts, organized in a fashion that makes them easy to digest. Food labelling laws pursue this strategy.

Consumers may also face obstacles in rationally processing even such information as they do possess. The information may be easy to acquire and simply stated, but difficult to understand. The financial properties of interest rates and loan agreements may have this character. Alternatively, consumers may find it difficult, even as they understand the products and contracts that they buy, to integrate these into their lives in a prudent fashion. Failures of reasoning and will—ranging from addiction to cognitive biases such as misplaced optimism and hyperbolic discounting—can induce consumers to make unwise and inefficient choices even as, in a sense, they know precisely what they are doing. These circumstances are the hardest to cure by purely procedural means and so present the strongest case for substantive limits on freedom of contract.

---

31. The discussion that follows benefitted from an exchange with Alan Schwartz.

†